THE TORAH

Commentaries by

W. GUNTHER PLAUT

Genesis, Exodus, Numbers, Deuteronomy

BERNARD J. BAMBERGER ז"ל

Leviticus

Essays on Ancient Near Eastern Literature by

WILLIAM W. HALLO

THE TORAH

A
Modern
Commentary

Edited
by

W. Gunther Plaut

Union of American Hebrew Congregations

NEW YORK

LIBRARY OF CONGRESS CATALOGING IN PUBLICATION DATA

PLAUT, W. GUNTHER, 1912–

 [Torah] = The Torah.

 Includes original Hebrew text and the Jewish Publication
Society's English translation of the Pentateuch and of the traditional Haftarot.

 Bibliography: p.

 CONTENTS: Plaut, W. G. Commentaries on Genesis, Exodus, Numbers, Deuteronomy.—Bamberger, B. J. Leviticus.—
Hallo, W. W. Essays on ancient Near Eastern literature.

 I. Bible. O.T. Pentateuch—Commentaries.
I. Bamberger, Bernard Jacob, 1904–1980.   II. Hallo, William W.
Essays on ancient Near Eastern literature. 1981.   III. Bible. O.T.
Pentateuch. Hebrew. 1981.   IV. Bible. O.T. Pentateuch. Eng-
lish. Jewish Publication Society. 1981.   V. Jewish Publication
Society of America.   VI. Jews. Liturgy and ritual. Haftarot
(Reform, Plaut). English & Hebrew. 1981.   VII. Jews. Liturgy
and ritual. Reform rite, Plaut.   VIII. Title.

BS1225.3.P55   1981   222′.1077   80–26967
ISBN 0–8074–0055–6   AACR1
ISBN 0–8074–0165–X Hebrew open

MANUFACTURED IN THE UNITED STATES OF AMERICA

10 9 8 7 6

PUBLICATION OF THIS
SINGLE VOLUME OF

The Torah: A Modern Commentary

has been made possible
by a generous gift
from the late

MORTON ROBERT HIRSCHBERG

Publication of individual volumes of *The Torah: A Modern Commentary* has been made possible by the generosity of the Miriam Stern Fox Fund; Samuel H. Block; the Falk Foundation; Kivie Kaplan; Maurice Saltzman; the members of Holy Blossom Temple, Toronto; Rabbi Leon Fram; Florence P. Medwin; and Sophie Exstein.

The Union of American Hebrew Congregations expresses its deep and abiding appreciation to the primary commentator of the Torah, RABBI W. GUNTHER PLAUT, for the depth of his scholarly efforts and for his devotion and commitment during the duration of this extraordinary endeavor. Likewise, the Union acknowledges with gratitude the support of this project given by the Holy Blossom Temple, Toronto.

Preface

To the First Edition (5741/1981):

Sᴇᴠᴇɴᴛᴇᴇɴ ʏᴇᴀʀꜱ ʜᴀᴠᴇ passed since this commentary was first conceived. Its publication in complete form comes, alas, only after my co-worker in this enterprise, Rabbi Bernard J. Bamberger, has been taken to his eternal reward. He was a superior scholar, a teacher par excellence, a liberal to the core. His great Commentary on Leviticus (published separately before his death) stands, in more ways than one, at the center of this volume.

The two of us were joined in our enterprise by Professor William W. Hallo of Yale University whose knowledge of antiquity and whose sensitive comment on our work proved to be of singular importance. Throughout the commentary, we made abundant use of materials he supplied. In addition, his five essays which precede each of the Torah books open up to the reader the vast reaches of ancient Near Eastern literature.

Our work reflects a liberal point of view. This is at once obvious in the occasional divergencies of opinion that exist between the comments on Leviticus and those on the rest of the Pentateuch. These differences have been left standing side by side, without any attempt to reconcile them. We would like to think that, in the spirit of the traditional phrase, both opinions reflect the search after the living God.

In preparing our commentaries we have had the constant help and guidance of a number of erudite colleagues, chief amongst them Professors Alexander Guttmann and Matitiahu Tsevat of Hebrew Union College - Jewish Institute of Religion. Their great knowledge was always at our disposal; they were invariably gracious, whether their suggestions were adopted—as was most often the case—or whether they were modified or even rejected.

A larger board of advisors, chaired by Rabbi Robert I. Kahn, read the manuscript critically. Its members were Professors Sheldon H.

Blank, Julius Kravetz, Leonard S. Kravitz, Harry M. Orlinsky, and Stanley Gevirtz; as well as Rabbis Solomon B. Freehof, Roland B. Gittelsohn, Samuel E. Karff, Bernard H. Mehlman, Frederick C. Schwartz, and, last but not least, Mordecai M. Kaplan who assisted in the early stages and made available his own unpublished commentary on Genesis.

During the long years of preparation and composition we had occasion to have the unfailing support of two presidents of the Union of American Hebrew Congregations, Maurice N. Eisendrath ז״ל and Alexander M. Schindler, together with their associates, Rabbi Jack D. Spiro and Mr. Abraham Segal ז״ל. During these last few years, Rabbi Leonard A. Schoolman dealt with the administrative aspects of the commentary project and with persistence and energy helped it to final fruition. We also note with gratitude the assistance rendered to us by two directors of the Publications Department of the Union, Messrs. Ralph Davis and Stuart L. Benick, and their staff of editors and readers: Miss Myrna Pollak, Mesdames Louise Stern, Annette Abramson, Esther Fried Africk, and especially Josette Knight. We would indeed wish to acknowledge the invaluable assistance rendered to us by the staffs of two great libraries of the Hebrew Union College-Jewish Institute of Religion, in Cincinnati and in New York: their directors, Herbert C. Zafren, I. Edward Kiev ז״ל, and Phillip E. Miller, and their competent and helpful associates.

A Note on the Fourth Edition (5745/1985): My profound thanks to all who have called my attention to errors in earlier editions, and especially to Rabbi Israel C. Stein of Bridgeport, Connecticut, for his painstaking review and comments.

I know that Dr. Bamberger would join us in the fervent hope that this commentary may prove to be a means of advancing the study and understanding of this most precious of books, our Torah.

תודה לאל עליון
W. G. P.

Contents

GENESIS

x

EXODUS

Part I: Prologue

Part II: The Mission

LEVITICUS

NUMBERS

DEUTERONOMY

Part I: Prologue
First Discourse

Part II: Second Discourse

General Introduction to the Torah

W. GUNTHER PLAUT

The Book

Torah is the Hebrew term used for the Five Books of Moses or Pentateuch. Genesis is the first of these five books, and the Torah is the first part of the Bible. The term "Old Testament" is not used by Jews, since it implies a "new" testament. "Bible" as used in this book refers, therefore, to the Hebrew Bible and does not include the Christian Scriptures.

This commentary proceeds from the assumption that the Torah is a book which had its origin in the hearts and minds of the Jewish people.

Many people deny this basic assumption. They believe that the Torah is "the word of God," given (by direct inspiration or in some other way) by God to Moses. Some agree that the text in being transmitted from generation to generation may have been marred by certain scribal errors. But the book as a whole, they insist, is the word of God and not of man. This orthodox or fundamentalist viewpoint maintains, therefore, that if the text says that "God created" then this is a fact, for the word of God is by definition truth itself. It maintains further that the Torah, being given by God, must carry meaning in every word and that not even one letter can be superfluous. One may not understand everything, but that is a human shortcoming. If modern scientific knowledge appears to contradict the biblical word, then either our present-day science will prove to be in error or we do not understand the Bible properly. This was and is the position of Orthodox Judaism, fundamentalist Christianity, and of most commentaries of the past.

The commentator who differs with this approach and proceeds on the premise of human rather than divine authorship faces two initial questions: (1) Does God have anything to do with the Torah? (2) How is the book different from any other significant literature of the past?

1] DOES GOD HAVE ANYTHING TO DO WITH THE TORAH? While God is not the author of the Torah in the fundamentalist sense, the Torah is a book about humanity's understanding of and experience with God. This understanding has varied over the centuries as have human experiences. Since the Torah tradition was at first repeated by word of mouth, and only after many generations set down in writing, the final text testifies to divergent ideas about God and the people. These stand side by side in the book and tell us of our ancestors' changing and developing beliefs. In this sense, then, the book is not by God but by a people. While individual authors had a hand in its composition, the people of the Book made the Torah their own and impressed their character upon it.

Some would leave it at that and go no further; they would approach the Torah primarily as an antique document and say:

This is how the authors and their listeners saw the world. It is instructive to study their viewpoint and their faith.

This commentary goes further. We believe that it is possible to say: The Torah is ancient Israel's distinctive record of its search for God. It attempts to record the meeting of the human and the Divine, the great moments of encounter. Therefore, the text is often touched by the ineffable Presence. The Torah tradition testifies to a people of extraordinary spiritual sensitivity. God is not the author of the text, the people are; but God's voice may be heard through theirs if we listen with open minds.

Is this true for every verse and story? Not in our view. But it is often hard to know whether the voice that speaks has the ring of permanence or resounds to the apprehensions and misapprehensions of a particular age. Our own insights are not so secure that we can judge past ages with any easy sense of superiority. In the face of the unique tradition before us, modesty and caution are a necessary rule.

This does not mean, however, that we abdicate all judgment, treat legend as fact, or gloss over those texts which represent God in anthropomorphic terms. This commentary is neither an apology for, nor an endorsement of, every passage. It will present the modern readers with tools for understanding and leave the option to them. It is also well to know in advance that despite the enormous and imaginative scholarship—archeological, linguistic, anthropological, and other—which has been lavished on the Torah we still must often conclude that we do not know how to interpret a word, or passage, or do not understand the original context.

2] HOW IS THE TORAH DIFFERENT FROM ANY OTHER SIGNIFICANT LITERATURE OF THE PAST? For those of us who see in the Torah a people's search for and meeting with God the answer is self-evident. The search and the meeting provide a record which by its very nature has something to say about the essentials of human existence.

But even for those who see in the book only the human quest, with all its strengths and weaknesses, there ought to be something special about it. For over two and one-half millennia the Torah has been the keystone of Jewish life, the starting point of Christendom, and the background of Islam. As such it has played and continues to play a significant role in the world. Western people especially are what they are in part because of this book—because of what the Torah actually said or meant to say and because of what it was believed to have said and to have meant.

This distinction is important, for in reading the Torah one should keep in mind that what the authors said in their own time to their own contemporaries within their own intellectual framework is one thing and what later generations did with this text, what they contributed to it by commentary and homily is another. This long tradition of holding up the book like a prism, discovering through it and in it a vast spectrum of insights, makes the Torah unlike any other work. This is particularly true for the Jews. They cannot know their past or themselves without this book, for in it they will discover the framework of their own existence.

The Torah is important for yet another reason. This commentary proceeds from the assumption that in addition to the original meaning and the interpretations offered over the centuries the Torah has relevance for our time. Of course, not everything that was relevant yesterday speaks to us today, and passages which held little or minor meaning in the past now speak to us suddenly with an urgent voice. For instance, the story of Babel was for many years seen as a tale of human arrogance; today it speaks to us as a warning

about the dehumanizing effects of urban life.

The relevance of this story, as well as many other portions of the Torah, may be found in questions rather than answers; in fact, one of the contemporary "attractions" of the Torah is its open-endedness, which is to say, it raises issues without providing single answers that close the door to further inquiry. There is no doubt that tomorrow's generation will hear the words differently again and that the search for new answers will always continue. Our commentary attempts to reflect this open-ended quality of the Torah. It will often provide options, and it is our hope that many additional questions will be asked by the readers who will be motivated to search for their own answers.

But there are also a number of problems. Some of these arise needlessly, out of failure to read the text properly; others are due to the contrast between certain ancient and contemporary assumptions about our world and must be freely faced. The modern reader should clearly understand that biblical man thought and wrote in terms of his own time and not ours. For us, reading the Bible should be an attempt to understand it and not a cut-and-dried exercise in our own contemporary dogmatics. We must not come to the text with preconceptions but should try to let it speak to us in its own way. Only then will the door be open to meaningful reading.

Literalism

Contemporary readers are often put off because they have been exposed to a method of biblical interpretation which understands the text in a literal way. Thus, if Genesis says that God created woman out of the rib of man, or tells of a serpent speaking, or of ancient man living several hundred years, the literalist interprets the story to mean precisely what the words convey. This literal application reaches down to individual words and phrases.

Quite aside from the indisputable fact that the Torah text we use today is merely one available version (although the accepted one) and aside from the fact that most literalists not knowing the Hebrew original base their opinions on one particular translation (which is in itself a type of interpretation and therefore a secondary source),[1] the contemporary reader familiar with the history and nature of the text will have to remember that a literal understanding of the Torah may lead to grave misconceptions.

Even the ancient Jewish Sages, who believed that the Torah was a divinely authored book, did not take the text literally. They took it seriously, but they always looked behind the flat literal meaning. They realized that the Bible—in addition to everything else it was to them—abounded in subtle metaphors and allusions, that it used word plays and other literary devices, that it sometimes spoke satirically, and that its poetry could not be subjected to a simple approach. They agreed without embarrassment that one could disagree on what the Torah meant, and on this sound principle we ourselves should base our approach to the text.

Myth and Legend

The reader must further understand that the Torah contains a great variety of material: laws, narratives, history, folk tales, songs, proverbial sayings, poetry, and, especially in the early parts of Genesis, myths and legends. By myth we understand a tale involving human beings and divine powers, a tale which was meant and understood as having happened and which by its existence expressed, explained, or validated important aspects of existence. Thus the Eden myth

[1] See below, "Text and Translation."

explained the origin of death and validated, for Christian tradition, the concept of humanity's inherent sinfulness and need of salvation. Legends are sagas of the past amplified by folk memory, but they usually neither validate nor explain. Jacob's prowess at the well (Gen. 29:10) is of this category. As the Torah moves from the creation of the world toward the creation of the people of Israel, the mythic elements increasingly give way to legend and these in turn to history in the modern sense.[2]

In observing these distinctions the reader of the Bible should not, however, be misled into dismissing either myth or legend as "irrelevant" and accepting only history as "relevant." What usually passes for history is not an accurate scientific recording of events but an interpretation of such events—assuming even that one knows what the event "really" was. The best of modern historians is an interpreter, selective summarizer, commentator, and often philosopher who brings a point of view to the material. This is precisely what the Book of Genesis does. While its material included myths and legends, these in time became incorporated into the consciousness of the people. For what people believe their past to mean assumes a dynamism of its own; the experience itself becomes creative. Thus, while Abraham's vision of a

God who promised him the land of Canaan will not pass as historic "fact," its reality was accepted by generations of Abraham's descendants and, for them, validated their possession of the land.

One must not think that this kind of "mythicizing history" (as Buber called it[3]) is found only in ancient texts. Take for instance the selective way in which American tradition treats the lives of the old frontiersmen. They are presented primarily as enterprising pioneers, courageous people whose love of independence was indelibly stamped on the nation they helped to build. Such a picture is, of course, highly selective and slanted. It says little about the desire of the pioneers to get rich quickly or their need to move west after repeated failures in the east, and so on. But Americans have preferred to see their past in an idealized light, and their admiration of the value of personal independence and frontier virtues has itself shaped the psychology of the nation.

So it is with the Torah. It may be said to mirror the collective memory of our ancestors, and in the course of centuries this record became a source of truth for the Children of Israel. The reader will therefore do well to keep in mind that the Torah not only speaks of history but has made history by helping to shape human thought.

The origins of the Torah are one thing, its life through the centuries another, and its ability to speak to us today yet a third. This commentary is concerned with all three aspects separately and jointly.

How the Torah Came to Be Written

Doubts that the Torah was a book set down by one author, Moses, developed some centuries ago, but it was not until the nineteenth century that extensive investigations made the critical study of the biblical text a highly specialized discipline. The early critics

[2] One should also note that while there are myths in Genesis there is no mythology, i.e., there are no tales of the adventures of the gods (or God). The fragment in Gen. 6:1–4 is the only exception. Genesis is not concerned with the story of the divine realm but with the emergence of humanity; the drama is played out not on a supernatural stage but on earth and has a theme of rebellion, sin, and potential redemption.

[3] Martin Buber, *Moses* (Oxford: Oxford University Press, 1947), p. 17. Buber considers the emotion with which an event was experienced an important aspect of history, one which is often played down in the usual annalistic or "factual" treatment. See also Gerhard von Rad, *Genesis: A Commentary* (Philadelphia: Westminster Press, 1961), pp. 3 ff.

noted the differential use of the names of God in various parts of the Torah, the discrepancies of certain accounts and figures, and different literary styles. Later scholars further analyzed the text so that they could discern many authors and several editors, and they theorized about times and events when these sources and documents were created and finally combined into the Torah as we have it now.

The theory which continues to command general scholarly adherence is called the Documentary Hypothesis and is often referred to by two of its most prominent expositors, Karl Graf and Julius Wellhausen.[4] In substance it says that there are four major sources or documents (called J, E, P, and D), the combination of which during the fifth century B.C.E. resulted in the creation of a single book, the Torah, which was declared a sacred text by official canonization about the year 400.

J is the name given by biblical critics to the author who used the divine name יְהֹוָה (YHVH or YHWH) and probably lived in the Southern Kingdom some time after the death of Solomon; he was responsible for most of Genesis. E uses אֱלֹהִים (Elohim) and authored the binding of Isaac (Gen. 22) and other passages of Genesis, as well as much in Exodus and Numbers; he was most likely a northern contemporary of J.

D is the author of Deuteronomy, which is said to be the book found by King Josiah in 621 B.C.E. (II Kings 22; some also assign Gen. 14 to D).[5]

P is the author of the first chapter of Genesis, the Book of Leviticus, and other sections characterized by interest in genealogies and priesthood. When did the main body of the priestly writing originate? According to Dr. Bamberger:

"The nineteenth-century Bible critics considered P the latest part of the Torah, composed during or after the Babylonian exile (approximately 597 to 516 B.C.E.). It was intended as a sort of constitution for the Second Commonwealth when the Jews had no king and the High Priest was leader and spokesman of the nation. According to this theory, P was the framework into which J/E and D were fitted, in the fifth century B.C.E.

"This once widely accepted view has been challenged in various ways by many twentieth-century Bible scholars, amongst whom Yehezkel Kaufmann has been one of the boldest and most original.[6] He held that P is not the latest, but the earliest, of the sources incorporated in the Torah. It contains primitive elements, such as the rite of the scapegoat (Lev. 16:8–10, 20–22), which could not have originated after the period of the great prophets. Moreover, P often reflects conditions very different from those of the exile and its aftermath.

"The newer critics are in many ways persuasive but it is always easier to demolish old views than to construct viable new ones. The earlier critics proved conclusively that the Torah is not a unit and that it does not date as a whole from the time of Moses; but their reconstruction of early Israelite history was far from definitive. A host of difficulties has been marshalled against it in recent decades; but the newer attempts at synthesis, such as Kaufmann's, are also open to question."

It is the position of this commentary that P contains many old strands and traditions

---

[4] Since, even today, the Graf-Wellhausen school commands wide support, our commentary indicates from time to time the differentiation of sources suggested by the school. Some examples are provided in the analysis of the Flood story, Gen. 8, and the tale of Korah, Num. 16.

[5] A detailed analysis of how Deuteronomy came to be written will be found in the introduction to that book.

[6] *The Religion of Israel.* Abridged English translation by M. Greenberg (Chicago: University of Chicago Press, 1966).

(probably predating J and E) but also later additions when the document was put into final written form after the return from exile (see "Introducing Leviticus"). Altogether we would give 950 through 450 as the years during which the literary process and its redaction took place, that is, from the days of the divided kingdoms of Israel and Judah to their destruction and the time of exile and return.

Since Moses lived in the thirteenth century B.C.E. he had, in that view, nothing to do with the writing of the complete Torah. His name was attached to it as author at the time of the book's canonization. This whole analysis is vigorously disputed by those who attempt to show that Moses was indeed the author. They consider much or all higher literary criticism as erroneous and some of its foundations as infected by Christian bias.[7]

It has been suggested that the first four books of the Torah (Genesis, Exodus, Leviticus, Numbers) originally formed a four-part unit called Tetrateuch by modern scholars, while Deuteronomy, Joshua, Judges, Samuel, and Kings constituted another separate complex. Our commentary accepts this basic approach but with the understanding that, while Deuteronomy was put into its final

(or nearly final) form, at some time before the Tetrateuch assumed its *written* shape, the underlying traditions followed a different time sequence. We believe that the major sources from which the Tetrateuch was formed (J, E, P) were older than the Deuteronomist (D) tradition. That is to say: Deuteronomy as a *written* document preceded Genesis to Numbers; but the latter's narratives and laws are generally of earlier origin.

There are still other scholars who, while they accept the existence of different sources, would see the contribution of these sources to the final text in a different light. In this view the various strands of tradition were very old—some of them older than Moses while others are assignable to him—and were transmitted for many centuries by word of mouth. As the centuries wore on, all of these strands coalesced in popular telling, and in time, probably through the efforts of a literary genius of unknown name, they became a single story with many facets. Variants of the same story and even contradictions were left untouched because one did not tamper with sacred memories and also because the ancient era did not demand an either/or but could say that together both sides of the account represented the truth. If in one place it says that Israel spent 400 years in Egypt and in another that it was 430, the modern reader is tempted to ask: How many years was it really? The ancient reader was satisfied that both 400 and 430 meant a long, long time.

In general, our commentary favors the position just outlined, namely, that the Torah as we now know it is essentially the repository of centuries of traditions which became One Tradition and One Book. At what time it was set down as we have it now will likely remain a matter of conjecture; what is important is to both understand its background and at the same time treat the book as an integral unit. With Franz Rosenzweig we

---

[7] There are also those who, on the basis of critical studies, conclude that Moses' part in the creation of the Torah is commanding. For an advocacy of this view, see M. H. Segal, *The Pentateuch* (Jerusalem: Magnes Press, 1967); for a general critique, see Cassuto, *The Documentary Hypothesis* (Jerusalem: Magnes Press, 1961); for a specific critique, see Benno Jacob's massive commentaries on Genesis and Exodus.

"In general, it is probably true that much Jewish scholarship, even that which was not totally traditionalistic, was initially, and to a degree still remains, rather cool toward the standard results of German biblical scholarship, well aware of the subtle anti-Judaism, if not anti-Semitism, which by no means necessarily, but very often *de facto*, accompanies any depreciation of the Old Testament—and it is undeniable that such implications were often present in much of the classical 'critical' literature." (H. D. Hummel, *Encyclopaedia Judaica*, Vol. 4, col. 907.)

might call the final editor R, not because the initial reminds us of redactor, but of *Rabbenu*, our teacher. The finished book represents the teaching tradition of Israel, and as such it has had a dynamic life all of its own.

We therefore ask three questions: "What did the text mean originally?" "What has it come to mean?" and "What can it mean to us today?" Our commentary disagrees with traditional interpreters over divine origin and Mosaic authorship (that is to say, it finds higher criticism admissible), but it does agree with them on treating the text as it is, a unified whole, for it was approached this way by many generations and in this way it has made its impact on history. An antiquarian assessment will always be of historical interest and is reflected in this commentary, but to us the Bible is primarily the living textbook of the Jew and, with different emphasis, of the Christian.[8]

Text and Translation

Readers of the Bible are usually unaware that what they are reading is not "the" original version of the manuscript and that the translation they use is actually a kind of commentary on the Hebrew text which it means to render.

There is no original manuscript available which was written by any of the authors of the Bible. The oldest extant parchment scroll of the Torah dates from about 900 C.E., which is probably more than 1,300 years later than the likely time of its composition. Quite naturally, much happens to a text in the course of oral transmission and copying by hand, and one must not be astonished that a number of variants and versions arose. It is a great tribute to the care and devotion which were lavished on the text that the variants are relatively minor and the scribal corruptions rather few. Our commentary uses the Masoretic version. The Masoretes, so called because

they transmitted the *Masorah* (מָסוֹרָה) or textual traditions, were scholars who over the centuries attempted to ascertain and preserve the best text. One of these versions, produced in Tiberias in the tenth century C.E., found general acceptance and is the standard Hebrew text in synagogue use today.

Because the knowledge of classical Hebrew diminished or disappeared among many Jews after they returned from the Babylonian exile, the need for translations arose. In the course of centuries there appeared translations in Aramaic (Targum) which was the popular language of postexilic Jews, Greek (Septuagint), Latin (Vulgate), Syriac (Peshitta), Arabic, and in modern times in every written language of man. The important ancient translations often give us significant clues about the original from which they were translated, for there are differences between them. What is even more important is to recognize that every translator interprets the original text, for he renders it as he understands (or misunderstands) it.

This becomes particularly apparent when one follows modern translations. For instance, there are great differences between the famous and beloved English King James Version (published in 1611, and often called "Authorized," i.e., for the Church of England) and later renditions such as the American version, or the German Luther Bible and the translation by Rosenzweig and Buber. Many of these differences are stylistic since the language of translation has itself undergone vast changes; others are due to new insights into the philology of ancient days and the

---

[8] This holistic approach has lately received support from Christian scholars. Thus J. P. Fokkelman writes: "The birth of a text resembles that of a man: the umbilical cord, which connected the text with its time and the man or men who produced it, is severed once its existence has become a fact; the text is going to lead a life of its own. . . ." (*Narrative Art in Genesis*, Amsterdam: Van Gorcum, 1975, pp. 3 f.) See the survey by B. W. Anderson, *JBL*, 97, 1 (1978), 23ff.

political, social, and economic circumstances to which the text refers.

The translation of the Torah used is the New Jewish Version, published by the Jewish Publication Society (revised printing, 1967), with the kind permission of the publishers. This translation, in addition to its scholarly and linguistic merits,[9] has been made particularly valuable by the publication of the translators' *Notes on the New Translation of the Torah* (1969, referred to as JPS *Notes*) which explain in detail why certain translations were chosen and others rejected.

[9] The late Dr. B. J. Bamberger (who authored the Commentary on Leviticus in this volume) was a distinguished member of the Committee of Translators.

On Reading This Commentary

The commentary follows a particular pattern. Each book is divided into several major parts and a number of sections which exceed the number of traditional chapter divisions. While such an arrangement has no precise warrant in prior practice,[10] it has been introduced for convenience of study and for those synagogues which do not read the entire traditional weekly portion. Our units and their commentaries are more or less of similar length, except in Genesis, the early chapters and chapter 22 (because of the special importance of these sections), and in Numbers, chapters 22–24 (because they comprise a single theme). In attempting thus to divide the book both by reason of length and by subject matter, our arrangement frequently differs from the division into chapters which originated with medieval Christian scholarship.

In addition to the introductory essays, the Hebrew text and translation, each book is composed of the following parts:

1] THE TEXTUAL NOTES. These appear below and immediately following the text and are arranged by verse and number for easy reference to the text itself. The notes may be called "textual," i.e., they attempt to give the "plain meaning" (*peshat*) of words and sentences without going into deeper interpretations (which are reserved for the commentary proper). In the notes you will find explanations of terms, names, references to other biblical books, and notations on linguistic difficulties. It should be remembered that the notes comment not only on the English translation, and try to make it understandable, but also—and primarily—on the underlying Hebrew text. For instance, the Hebrew text uses word plays and assonances extensively, and these can rarely be translated into another language. The reader should also remember that the Torah tradition was originally transmitted by word of mouth so that many so-called etymological explanations of personal and place names may have served as popular memory devices. For instance, *Kayin* (Cain) is said to come from *kaniti* (I have gained) although linguistically there is no connection.

2] THE COMMENTARY. The brief essays which accompany each unit are largely interpretive:[11] they attempt to explain the intent of the Torah, how Jewish tradition saw these meanings, and how relevant they are today. The author has chosen and concentrated on a few themes in each section; he is aware that in so choosing he has omitted other themes which the reader might wish to have had included.

Just as the notes frequently offer alternative explanations, so does the commentary itself. Sometimes this is done because we really have at present no sure way of establishing one particular interpretation as *the* meaning; at other times the author feels that the Torah leaves us purposely with parallel or even contradictory ideas. If this seems unlikely to a modern reader who is used to a systematic and logical exposition of a subject, it must be remembered that the Torah is not a treatise, essay, or exposition, but poetry, prose, epic, and historic memory created in a prescientific age fundamentally different from ours. Where we are prone to say "either, or," the Bible may say "both" and let the

---

[10] It resembles to some degree the divisions of the old triennial cycle of Torah readings.
[11] In Leviticus, these essays precede the chapters in the form of extended introductions.

unresolved tension between the two stand without further comment. This sometimes lends the Torah a special quality of opaqueness which those who look for one and only one meaning are bound to miss.

3] THE GLEANINGS. Appended to all sections are gleanings from world literature which have a bearing on the text. Here especially will be found selections from that vast compendium of ancient Jewish lore and homily called Midrash,[12] and also some writings from Christian and Moslem sources as well as contemporary observations not included in the commentary proper. In Leviticus, because of its preponderance of legal materials, the gleanings are generally divided into legal (halachic) and nonlegal (haggadic) excerpts. (Where the source is not identified, the author himself is to be credited.) The gleanings are generally brief as they are intended to suggest something of the vast range of response elicited by the Torah. It is hoped that the reader will be moved to explore these areas further.

4] FOOTNOTES. Occasionally the text of commentary and gleanings is expanded by brief additions. These are indicated by superior notes in the text—such as [5]—and are printed at the bottom of the page.

5] THE REFERENCES. Notes, commentary, gleanings, and footnotes contain references only to the Bible (where no book is mentioned the reference is to the book in which it occurs). We follow the standard way of noting biblical passages; for instance, chapter 12, verse 3, is listed as 12:3.

All other sources may be found in the references, which for easier readability are grouped together at the end of the volume. These references—indicated by bracketed numbers such as [15]—are not meant primarily for scholars; hence they do not usually give alternative sources, divergent readings, and the like. They refer, wherever possible, to works which have appeared in English or English translation and to others only where no translation is available. (For abbreviations and principal bibliographical references, see backmatter.) The notation "See commentary on . . ." refers to passages in this volume.

6] HAFTAROT. The synagogue, and subsequently the church, established a tradition which provides that on each Sabbath and holy day a special portion be read from the Bible. At Jewish services, a section from the Torah, called *sidrah* or *parashah*, and an additional selection, called *haftarah* (meaning "conclusion"; originally signifying dismissal of the congregation; plural *haftarot*), are publicly read. Tradition has divided the Torah into 54 *sidrot*, the cycle of which begins on the Sabbath after Simchat Torah.

The *haftarot* (with a brief commentary) appear at the end of each book. The *haftarot* for special days are grouped together following the last *haftarah* for Deuteronomy. The Rabbis provided readings from the Earlier Prophets (Joshua, Judges, Samuel, and Kings), which are primarily historical in character, and the Later Prophets (fifteen in all, from Isaiah to Malachi), whose books form the bulk of our literary heritage. They are reprinted, with permission, from the New Jewish Version of *The Prophets* (Jewish Publication Society, copyright 1978). They follow the "Table of Scriptural Readings" suggested by the Central Conference of American Rabbis. The translation of the *haftarah* from the Book of Esther (which is read on Shabbat Zachor) is from *The Holy Scriptures According to the Masoretic Text* (Jewish Publication Society, copyright 1917).

[12] The total collection, spread over many sources will be written Midrash (with a capital M), while an individual homily will be written midrash (plural: *midrashim*).

Transliterations

When comment is made on a Hebrew word or phrase, the latter is usually rendered in Hebrew characters. Transliterations are utilized only where they are deemed of special help to the reader who is unfamiliar with Hebrew.

This commentary has adopted the simplified transliteration proposed by Prof. Werner Weinberg of Hebrew Union College - Jewish Institute of Religion and brought it into consonance with the usage of the Union of American Hebrew Congregations. Based on the Sephardic pronunciation, it makes no distinction between ס and שׂ, between ח and כ, ט and ת, nor between כּ and ק. צ is represented by tz; ב appears as v, and ח and כ as ch. It does not always take note of א or ע except when two vowels inside a word should be separated and could be mispronounced, in which case a hyphen or an apostrophe is introduced (as in רֹאִי, ro-i, or מוֹעֵד, mo'ed). The *dagesh* is omitted except where it is an aid to pronunciation (*shabbat* rather than *shabat*). Also omitted is the resting *sheva*; the moving *sheva* is shown as e when it represents a syllable (as in שְׁמַע, *shema*). Half

vowels are transliterated as full vowels (as in אֱמֶת, *emet*). Other vowels are rendered as follows:

ָ and ַ		as a
ֶ and ֵ		as e
ִ and ִי		as i
וֹ and ֹ		as o
וּ and ֻ		as u

The letter י is represented as y, except in ִי and יִ in which cases it is sometimes omitted.

There are a few Hebrew words which have become part of common usage, and therefore their usual spelling has been maintained. This is especially true for proper names, e.g., Ishmael rather than Yishmael. Also, the definite article *ha* (or *he*) has been separated from its noun by the introduction of a hyphen in order to facilitate the reading (*ha-yashar* rather than *hayashar*) except in some cases where by virtue of common usage the hyphen has been omitted.

The Torah and the Jewish People

BERNARD J. BAMBERGER

The Torah was always the possession of all Israel. It was addressed to the entire people, who were to learn its contents and teach them diligently to their children. A number of biblical passages, in particular Psalms 19 and 119, testify to the love which the Torah evoked and the widespread concern of the people with its teachings.

The Book of Nehemiah (chs. 8–10) reports a public reading of the Torah in Jerusalem, probably in the year 444 B.C.E. This reading was conducted by Ezra the Scribe, with the aid of assistants who were to make sure that all those present heard and understood what was read to them. A few days later, the entire people entered into a solemn undertaking to obey the Torah; and this agreement was ratified in writing by the leaders. From the traditional standpoint, this incident was a reaffirmation of the covenant at Sinai. But many modern scholars explain the event as marking the completion of the written Torah in substantially its present form and its adoption as the official "constitution" of the Jewish community.

The Torah and the Synagogue

We do not know exactly where, how, or when the synagogue came into existence; it must have been some time between 500 and 200 B.C.E. From the start, one of the principal activities of the synagogue was the public reading and exposition of the Torah. A portion was read every Sabbath. But there were farmers who lived in scattered communities, too far from a synagogue to travel to it on the Sabbath. That they might not be deprived of hearing the sacred word, a Torah passage was read in the synagogues each Monday and Thursday—the market days when the country-folk came to town to sell their produce. This custom survives to the present in the traditional synagogues.

The reading of the Torah portion in Hebrew was often followed by a translation, in Greek or Aramaic, for the benefit of those who did not understand the original. It is out of such translation or paraphrase, in all probability, that the sermon arose. This explains why the sermon was normally based on the Torah reading of the week.

From an early date, the instruction of children was associated with the synagogue. The effectiveness of its educational program, for young and old, was fully recognized by the enemies of Judaism. When the Syrian King Antiochus IV wished to break down Jewish solidarity and hasten the assimilation of Jews into Hellenistic society, he not only

forbade the practice of Jewish ritual but also prohibited the reading and teaching of the Torah, on pain of death. But the decrees could not be enforced.

Similarly, the Roman Emperor Hadrian, after he finally put down the Jewish revolt in 135 C.E., proscribed all those who persisted in teaching the Torah. It was then that the aged Rabbi Akiba defied the edict and suffered death by torture. The Torah, he declared in a famous parable, is Israel's natural element, as water is the natural element of the fish. In water the fish is exposed to many dangers, but out of water it is sure to perish at once (Berachot 61b).

The Oral Torah

Thus far we have used the word Torah with reference to the Five Books. But some kind of commentary was always needed. A sacred text, and especially one containing laws and commandments, must be interpreted and applied to the concrete situations of life. Those who proposed to make the Torah the rule of their life found many provisions which required more exact definition. The Torah, for example, forbids work on Sabbath; but what precisely constitutes work, and what activities are permissible? Again, the Torah speaks of divorce (Deut. 24:1 ff.) but does not make clear the grounds for divorce. And on many important subjects—the method of contracting a marriage, real estate law, the prayers in the synagogue, to name a few—the written Torah gives no guidance at all.

Such problems generated the concept of the oral Torah, in part explanation and elaboration of the written Torah, in part supplement to the latter. This oral Torah was not created consciously to meet the need of a certain time. Much of it was no doubt derived from established legal precedents and from popular custom and tradition. Once, however, the process of applying the law to new situations was undertaken in earnest, the material grew rapidly.

For a long time this was literally oral Torah; it was deemed improper to put down in writing what Moses had not written down at God's command. Only much later was it found necessary to compile this material in the Mishnah and other works of talmudic literature. But it was generally agreed that the entire body of oral Torah was also given to Moses at Sinai. It was to learn this vast corpus of teaching that Moses remained on the mountain forty days and nights.

The teachers of the oral Torah were chiefly laymen (that is, nonpriests) who are known to us as the Pharisees. From about the year 100 C.E. on, accredited teachers bore the title of rabbi. These teachers were opposed by a conservative party, made up mostly of priests, known as the Sadducees. They denied the validity of oral tradition and regarded the written text alone as authoritative. They interpreted the commandments in a strict literalist fashion. Perhaps it was this opposition which led the Pharisees to devise the method of midrash, in order to find some support in Scripture for their oral teachings. The Midrash uses a free, creative, and—let us admit—often far-fetched method of biblical interpretation. In expounding legal passages—what the Rabbis called halachah—the teachers were subject to some rules and restrictions in the use of midrash. But it was applied with virtually unlimited freedom to nonlegal materials, to the ethical, theological, and folkloristic subject matter known as aggadah or haggadah. Many beautiful examples of midrash are to be found in this commentary, especially in the sections headed "Gleanings." (It should be noted that the word "midrash" is used in three ways: to apply to a method in general, to a single instance of the method, and to literary works in which the method is employed.)

For most Jews, the written Torah was understood in accordance with the interpretation of the oral Torah, just as in modern law a written statute means what the courts interpret it to mean. The commandment "eye for eye, tooth for tooth" (Exod. 21:24) meant that one who injures another must pay money damages to his victim. "You shall not boil a kid in its mother's milk" (Exod. 23:19) was taken to prohibit the cooking or eating of any kind of meat with milk or milk products. Similarly, people did not always differentiate between biblical stories and their aggadic elaborations.

Though the growth of the oral Torah, later written down in the Talmud, obscured the plain sense of Scripture in many instances, it was a force for progress which enriched Judaism. Beginning in the eighth century C.E., a countertrend appeared in Persia and spread widely. The rebels against talmudic Judaism were called Karaites (Scripturalists). Returning to the Sadducean position, they proposed to live strictly by the simple word of the written Torah. But this program was not easy to carry out. The Karaites disputed bitterly among themselves as to the proper interpretation of many commandments. Moreover, many rabbinic modifications of scriptural law were both reasonable and humane, and to reject them meant turning the clock back—always a futile undertaking.

Christian and Moslem Views

The Christian apostle Paul, himself a Jew by birth, proposed in his writings a new view of the Torah. Its innumerable commandments, he held, constitute an overwhelming burden; no one can ever fulfill them properly. The "Law," in fact, was given by God to make us conscious of our sinfulness, that we may despair of attaining salvation by our own strivings. Now, Paul taught, salvation is available through faith in the crucified and risen Jesus; the "Law" has served its purpose, and, for Christian believers, it is abrogated (Romans 7:8; Galatians 2:15–3:14). This view has profoundly influenced Christian thought, though the churches rarely adopted Paul's teaching in its radical form and usually asserted the validity of the ethical laws of the Pentateuch (cf. Matthew 5:17–20; 19:18 f.).

In contrast to, and perhaps in reply to, the Pauline doctrine, Jewish teachers insisted on the continuing authority of the Torah and on its beneficent character. "The Holy One, blessed be He, desired to confer merit on Israel; that is why He gave them a voluminous Torah and many commandments" (Mishnah Makkot, end). Failure to obey the Torah fully does not result in damnation; rather it calls for repentance (return) and a fresh start.

Christian teachers through the centuries found in the Torah—and indeed the entire Hebrew Bible—many passages which they interpreted as prophecies of the career and the messianic (or divine) character of Jesus of Nazareth. In the past, Jewish spokesmen had to devote much time and effort to refuting these christological interpretations; today they have been discarded by competent Christian scholars.

Centuries later, Mohammed, founder of the third monotheistic religion, was to call the Jews also "the people of the Book" because their religion was founded on Scripture. He did not know the book at first hand, or even in translation, for he never learned to read, but in his contacts with Jews and Christians he acquired a sketchy knowledge of biblical narratives with their aggadic embellishments. To these stories he occasionally alludes in the Koran (some selections will be found in the Gleanings). The Koran, which records the revelations received by the prophet, holds a position in Islam similar to that of the Torah in Judaism. It is supple-

mented by a tradition analogous to the oral Torah.[1]

The Middle Ages

In its wanderings, Judaism encountered many new constellations of ideas. Sometimes these novelties were rejected by Jewish thinkers; but often they were accepted as compatible with Judaism. In such cases an effort was made to show that these ideas were already suggested in Scripture.

The first examplar using this method was Philo of Alexandria, who lived at the beginning of the Christian era. A devout Jew, Philo was deeply influenced by Plato and the Stoics; and so he was led to "discover" the ideas of the philosophers in the text of the Torah. For Philo, the biblical word veiled deeper meanings and had to be explained allegorically. (For instance, Sarah symbolizes divine wisdom, her handmaid Hagar typifies secular learning.) The Jewish philosophers of the Middle Ages also employed allegorical interpretations, though with more restraint. They used this method to deal with Bible passages which appeared to contradict reason or morality, especially those describing God in human terms. Such authors as Saadia, Maimonides, and Ibn Ezra frequently found sophisticated philosophic concepts in the biblical text.

Still more extreme were the methods of the mystics. "We possess an authentic tradition," wrote Rabbi Moses ben Nachman, "that the entire Torah consists of the names of God, in that the words may be redivided to yield a different sense, consisting of the names." In general, the Kabalists found cryptic meanings in the words and letters of Scripture, without any reference to the meaning of the text as a coherent whole. The Zohar, the chief work of the Kabalah, is a vast mystical midrash on the Torah; and many Kabalists, and later on Chasidim, wrote their mystical treatises in the form of commentaries on the Pentateuch.

Ultimately the view emerged that there are four ways to expound the Torah, each valid in its own area: the rabbinic midrash, the philosophical implication (*remez*), and the mystical arcanum (*sod*), in addition to the plain meaning (*peshat*).[2]

In the Middle Ages, in fact, Jews recovered an awareness of the literal meaning of Scripture. This trend away from midrash to a simpler exegesis may have been stimulated by the Karaite revolt. The first great exponent of the *peshat* was Rav Saadia Gaon, the outstanding critic of Karaism. He was followed by a distinguished school of grammarians and commentators in Moslem Spain, who developed a genuinely scientific approach to the Hebrew language and to textual studies. These scholars wrote chiefly in Arabic; their findings were made accessible to the Hebrew reading public by Abraham ibn Ezra, who hailed from northern (Christian) Spain, and the Provençal Hebraists Joseph and David Kimchi.

Meanwhile another school of biblical scholars appeared independently in northern France; they were more traditionalist, less systematic and philosophic than the Spaniards, but they displayed a keen sense for niceties of language and for the spirit of the Bible. The outstanding production of this school is the Torah commentary of Rashi (Rabbi Solomon Itzchaki of Troyes), the most popular commentary ever written in Hebrew. Its popularity was due both to the

---

[1] The Arabs regard themselves as descendants of Ishmael, Abraham's oldest son. Some of the Moslem teachers accused the Jews of misinterpreting (or even falsifying) the biblical text in order to give preference to their ancestor Isaac. Similar charges, that Jews have tampered with the Hebrew text of the Bible, were made by some early Christian teachers.

[2] A similar doctrine of the fourfold sense of Scripture was held by Christians.

clarity of Rashi's style and to the fact that he combined the exposition of the plain sense with a judicious selection of attractive *midrashim*, legal and nonlegal. His successors, however, concentrated more and more on the *peshat*.

The last of the great medieval expositors, Moses ben Nachman, despite his mystical tendencies, also offered original and independent comments on the plain sense. He and his predecessors had no difficulty with the fact that their simple exegesis sometimes contradicted biblical interpretations given in talmudic literature. In nonlegal matters there was no problem, since the aggadists gave many diverse explanations of the same verse. On halachic matters, these writers accepted the talmudic expositions for practical legal purposes but noted that, according to the rules of grammar, a given verse might be understood differently.

These medieval exegetes (and others we have not mentioned) made a permanently valuable contribution to the understanding of the biblical text. Though many other Hebrew commentaries on the Torah were written between the fourteenth and nineteenth centuries, they added little that was new. Only in the last two hundred years have new resources been available to broaden our understanding of Scripture; at the same time, new problems have arisen for the modern Bible reader.

The Torah Scroll

From an early date in the Christian era, manuscripts, including Hebrew manuscripts, were written in the form of books, consisting of a number of pages fastened together along one edge. We have many manuscripts of the Hebrew Bible of this sort; they are usually provided with vowel signs and with the punctuation indicating both sentence structure and the traditional chant. It is on such vocalized manuscripts that our printed Hebrew Bibles are based.

For ceremonial use in the synagogue, however, Jews have continued to employ Torah manuscripts in the more ancient scroll form. Each scroll is made up of numerous sheets of parchment, stitched together to make a continuous document, which is attached at either end to a wooden roller. The public reading of the Torah, to this day, is from such a scroll (*Sefer Torah*), containing only the consonantal text, without vowel points or punctuation, written on parchment with a vivid black ink. Tradition prescribes many details concerning the Sefer Torah—the beginning and end of paragraphs, the arrangement of certain poetic passages in broken instead of solid lines, the care of the scroll, the correction of mistakes, even the spiritual preparation of the scribe.

A synagogue usually possesses several scrolls. In ancient times they were kept in a chest (Hebrew *tevah* or *aron*), which was placed by the wall of the synagogue on the side nearest Jerusalem. In many early synagogues this "ark" stood in a niche, before which, in some cases, a curtain was hung. In modern synagogues the ark is usually a built-in recess, with a shelf for the scrolls; it is closed either by a curtain or by ornamental doors of wood or metal.

The removal of the scroll from the ark to the pulpit for reading and its return to the ark after the reading constitute a ceremony of considerable pomp, including the singing of processional melodies and demonstrations of respect and affection on the part of the congregants. When the ark is opened, and especially when the Sefer Torah is carried in procession, everyone stands.

The reverence and love evoked by the scroll is expressed in its outward adornments. Oriental Jews generally keep the scroll in a hinged metal or wooden case, often handsomely painted or carved, from which the

ends of the rollers project. The scroll remains in the case while it is open on the reading desk, and it may be rolled to a new passage without removing it from this receptacle. When it is closed, the upper rollers are often adorned with artistic metal finials (called *rimonim*, "pomegranates"). In most European and American congregations, however, the scroll, after being fastened with a band of some woven material, is covered with a robe of silk or velvet, through which the top rollers protrude. It may be decorated with a silver (or other metal) breastplate (*tas*) as well as with *rimonim*. Sometimes a single crown covers both wooden uprights. Eastern and Western Jews alike use a pointer (*yad*, literally, "hand"), most often of silver, with which the reader keeps his place in the scroll.

Some congregations, chiefly Sephardic, attach a silk or other woven strip to the outside of the parchment, which is rolled with the scroll to provide additional protection.

The Public Reading

It is customary to read from the scroll during every Sabbath and festival morning service, as well as on Monday and Thursday mornings. At the Saturday afternoon service (*minchah*), part of the following week's portion is read. There is no Torah reading on holy day afternoons, with the exception of the Day of Atonement and certain other fast days.

In the early centuries of the Christian era, the Jews of Palestine completed the reading of the entire Torah once in three years. We know, for the most part, how the text was divided into sections for this purpose; but scholars disagree as to when the triennial cycle began and ended—i.e., at what time in year 1 of the cycle the first chapter of Genesis was read.

Babylonian congregations, however, read through the entire Torah each year, and their custom ultimately became standard. It was the Babylonian Jews who created the festival of Simchat Torah, rejoicing over the Torah. On this day, all the scrolls of the congregation are carried around the synagogue in joyous procession; the closing chapter of Deuteronomy is read from one *sefer*, and then the first chapter of Genesis is read from another.

For the annual cycle, the Torah is divided into fifty-four sections, called *sidrot*. They are read consecutively, starting with the Sabbath following Simchat Torah. To complete the reading in a year, two sections must be read on certain Sabbaths, except when a leap year adds an additional month. Each *sidrah* is known by its first (or first distinctive) Hebrew word. For each holiday, a suitable selection is designated, apart from the weekly series. On holidays and certain special Sabbaths, an additional passage is read from a second scroll.

Each *sidrah* is divided into seven subsections. It is customary to "call up" seven worshipers to take part in reading the several subsections. (The number of participants varies on holidays, weekdays, etc.) Originally each person called up was expected to read a passage with the correct chant.

The participants who were insufficiently familiar with the text recited the benedictions and someone else read the portion for them. This was embarrassing to the unlearned; so it became customary long ago to assign the reading to one qualified person (the *ba-al keriah*), and those "called up," no matter how learned, recited only the benedictions.

In many traditional congregations, the lengthy period of the Torah reading became a disorderly part of the service. Those who had the honor of participating were expected to make contributions, which were duly acknowledged in the prayer (*Mi Sheberach*)

recited on behalf of the donor or the donor's dear ones. Others present might also have recited special prayers of thanks or petition. On important holidays, moreover, the honors were sold at auction before the Torah service was conducted.

In reaction against such practices, Reform synagogues abolished the entire system of honors and limited participation to the ministry and to the congregational officers on the pulpit. More recently, some temples have reintroduced participation from the membership, but eliminating the old abuses. In order to shorten the weekly reading, some of the early Reformers proposed a return to the triennial cycle; but the suggestion met with little favor. So Reform congregations follow the annual cycle, but instead they usually read only one subsection of each *sidrah*. The passage is most often read without the chant; and the reader frequently translates it into the vernacular after reading it, or even sentence by sentence.

In the interest of relevance and inspiration, Reform made a number of changes in the readings for the holy days. Recently, a few congregations have made changes also in the weekly reading, omitting *sidrot* which seem to have no message for our time (the opening sections of Leviticus, for example) and substituting selections from other parts of the Torah.

The Torah and the Modern Jew

The last three centuries have seen a great upheaval in the religious thinking of Western man, in general, and of the Jew, in particular. The development of natural science has undermined belief in the supernatural and miraculous and, thus, brought into question the authority of all sacred scriptures. Further, the champions of religion could no longer follow the method of Philo, who read into the Torah the ideas of Plato, or of Maimonides, who understood the same texts in terms of Aristotelian thought. We cannot claim to discover the findings of Darwin or Einstein in the Torah, for modern methods of Bible study preclude such an approach. Philological analysis and historical criticism make it impossible to "explain away" errors of fact and, to us, unacceptable theological apprehensions and moral injunctions. All of these must be understood in their own context and their own time. Furthermore, the rediscovery of the rich culture and literature of the ancient Near East revealed many similarities between biblical and non-Israelite writings, and even some cases in which the biblical authors borrowed from their pagan neighbors.

These new methods and discoveries have added enormously to our understanding of the biblical world. But they raise basic and difficult questions. Can the informed Jew of today regard the Torah as the word of God? And, if so, to what extent and in what sense? This question has been dealt with above, in our General Introduction to the Torah.

This commentary is an attempt to grapple with these questions. The readers are urged to base their judgments on a thoughtful reading of the Torah itself, with the aid of the comments in this volume. But a few suggestions are offered here.

1] We learn from the Torah how the Jewish people has understood its own character and destiny. For this reason it is indispensable for our own self-understanding. This would be true even if the whole Pentateuchal narrative were legendary. But modern scholarship has come more and more to the conclusion that beneath the legendary embellishments there is a solid core of historical memory, that Abraham and Moses really lived, and that the Egyptian bondage and the Exodus are undoubted facts.

2] Comparison reveals similarities between biblical writings and other old Near Eastern sources, but it also reveals striking dissimilarities. The resemblances are chiefly in concrete detail and in the use of words and phrases. In religious and ethical principles, the parallels are few. There is no other ancient writing which approaches the Torah in its lofty concept of a unique God, who is not subject to fate or destiny, has no female consort, and is concerned with the welfare of all humanity. The ethical teaching and social legislation of the Torah are unequalled in nobility and sensitivity by anything produced in Egypt or Babylonia.

3] The historical approach evokes our awe in another way. We see the vast distance between the more primitive elements of the Torah and its most sublime and advanced passages; and we marvel that such great progress occurred in a few centuries. At the same time, we no longer feel the need to rationalize or justify those things in the Torah which intellect forbids us to accept as true or conscience will not let us defend. No satisfactory explanation has ever been given in terms of climatic, geographical, economic, and political factors for the unique religio-ethical development in Israel. It is thus not unreasonable to discern revelation *within* the historical processes.

4] Though the Torah contains chapters that are, at most, of historical interest only, it also contains much that is relevant and vital today. If it sometimes expresses moral judgments we have discarded as unsatisfactory, it also challenges us with ideals we are far from having attained. Moreover, for us as for our ancestors, the line between written and oral Torah cannot be drawn oversharply. We too read the text in the light of the experiences and associations that have become attached to it. Every great classic suggests or reveals new insights to each succeeding generation. And the Torah is the classic of classics.

בראשית

GENESIS

Commentary by

W. GUNTHER PLAUT

Introducing Genesis

The Name

The name Genesis ("origin") goes back to the Greek translation, the Septuagint, while the usual Hebrew name is the same as the initial word in the book, בְּרֵאשִׁית (*bere-shit*). A few other titles were occasionally used such as *sefer beri-at ha-olam*, but they did not find wide acceptance.

Contents

Genesis tells a story which reaches from the creation of a world to the death of Joseph in Egypt. The first eleven chapters deal with universal history, the rest with the lives of Abraham, Isaac, Jacob, and their families. The total time elapsed from the beginning adds up to 1,946 (or 1,948) years.

The book is a tale of creations. In the beginning God is described as creating heaven and earth and all they contain. The crown of this creation is the human being who is to help God in perfecting His world. To achieve this, humanity is gifted with intellectual and moral freedom—a gift promptly used to disobey the injunction of the Creator. The consequence is exile from the innocence of Eden and the development of the human race.

But this development is a deep disappointment to the Creator who now destroys what He has fashioned and begins anew with Noah and his family. The result is no better: Humanity's new existence starts with alcoholic abuse and sexual perversion. Once more God is disappointed, and, because He had sworn not to eradicate humanity again,

He will work with it and within it in order to move it toward ultimate perfection. He chooses Abraham to begin this task by fathering a people who, in time, will become God's co-workers. The stories of the ancestors and their clan's descent into Egypt tell of the preparations which will lead to the creation of God's people, the Children of Israel, so called after Jacob-Israel, the last of the three Patriarchs. In Egypt, Israel will be created as a nation, and the Book of Exodus will then tell of this nation's formation: in slavery and liberation, at Sinai and in the wilderness.

Genesis then is the introduction to the Torah and to the rest of the Bible. In addition to its basic thrust it contains a number of subthemes which are interwoven into the major story. Among these are the basic unity of all mankind, its propensity for evil, human rebellion, and the covenant between God and Abraham's people. Last but not least, there is the supposition that all human beings derive from one common ancestor, which is to say that Genesis conceived of humanity as being of one kind, with no race or linguistic group superior to any other. In fact, in the table of nations (chapter 10), Israel plays a very subsidiary role. It will emerge only because God in His grace will choose it to perform a special function—but not because it possesses inherent characteristics as part of its national origins.

Some Literary Considerations

Genesis in its final form may be seen as a book of five parts. Part I is prologue, and

thereafter each part is introduced by the phrase, "These are the lines of" (*toledot*): the lines or genealogies of heaven, earth, and primeval man (Part II); of Terah, Abraham's father (Part III); of Isaac and of Jacob (Parts IV and V; see at 2:4).[1]

The book consists of two distinct literary entities: the first eleven chapters, which relate stories of creation and ancient mankind, and the chapters that follow which speak of Abraham and Sarah and their descendants. The two parts are quite distinct from each other, held together only by a brief genealogical bridge (Gen. 11:27–32). In the 39 later chapters there is, indeed, no mention of the first eleven, not even an allusion, which suggests that the two parts were originally quite separate and were later on joined into one book.

That is not to say that these two parts were the products of two entirely different traditions; they were not. Rather, the J, E, and P-sources (see above, General Introduction to the Torah) produced two sets of materials: one which dealt with pre-patriarchal traditions and were joined into one distinct "book" (now chapters 1–11), another which dealt with patriarchal traditions (now chapters 12–50). In time, a redactor joined the two parts into what is now the Book of Genesis.

Biblical scholars believe that one can still detect the origin of many stories. Thus, the style, the genealogical interest, and the moral stance of the priestly school (P) are seen in chs. 1; 2:1–4; 23; 36. Chapters 3–4:24 are traced to J; chapter 22 to E; and the Joseph cycle to the J/E tradition.

How old are these tales? Hallo's essay below suggests there are links and tracings in common Near Eastern traditions which go back a long time. It now appears that recent archeological finds at Ebla give the Abraham tales a contemporary reference point; but at least one scholar holds that the Abraham cycle is altogether a postexilic invention (fifth century C.E. or later).[2]

This commentary disagrees with the latter proposition and posits that the traditions underlying the patriarchal tales are very old and were put into written form at later times and eventually joined in a redactional process. In this process, as was pointed out, varying traditions were treated with great respect and were usually not adjusted in a way which would make one give way to the other. Thus, to give an example, one source had God state that the descent into Egypt would last 430 years (Exod. 12:40) and another that the time of servitude was 400 years (Gen. 15:13). Such manifest contradictions[3] were left standing side by side, because the ancient reader could say: Both traditions have come down to us and are therefore to be treated with reverence. The ancient reader did not feel compelled to say, as a modern reader would: These traditions can not both be true, one or both must be false. This capacity to accept diverse traditions is a distinguishing feature of the biblical redactors and their times.

Genesis calls God by many names, but there is one appellation that is uniquely His own, יְהוָֹה (YHVH or YHWH), which first appears in chapter 2. According to 4:26 it is a name of long standing, but how ancient was its use, what it betokened, or even how it was pronounced were and are matters of scholarly

---

[1] It has been suggested that certain Nuzi and Mari tablets provide a model for this generational approach and that, in fact, the book represented a kind of family archive.

[2] John van Seters, *Abraham in History and Tradition* (New Haven and London: Yale University Press, 1975).

[3] Orthodox commentators denied, of course, that any contradictions existed anywhere in the Torah and found ingenious ways of reconciling them. In the above cited case they said that 430 was reckoning time from the vision of Abraham and 400 from the birth of Isaac. See Luzzatto on Exod. 12:40 and also Talmud Meg. 9a.

controversy (on this, see commentaries to Gen. 2:4–24, Exod. 3:1–4:18 and 6:2–7:13). The name which describes the Creator in chapter 1 is אֱלֹהִים (Elohim), and throughout the Bible this is a term for gods in general and Israel's God in particular. It is a word with a plural ending (*im*). When it is used for pagan gods it commands a plural adjective or verb, but when denoting the One God the verb assumes the singular.[4] *Elohim* is an expanded form of *El*, a term current also in Canaanite religion. In Genesis, *El* appears always in connection with either another expanding term (*El Elyon*, "God on High"; *El Shaddai*, "God Almighty"), a place name (*El Beth-El*, "God of Beth-El"), or another identifying term (*El Avicha*, "God of Your Father"). Occasionally also, God is described by His relationship to humans (*Pachad Yitzchak*, "Fear of Isaac"; *Abir Ya'acov*, "Strength of Jacob"). Such multiplicity of terms is one way in which human language attempted to express the essentially inexpressible nature of the Divine.

The language of Genesis (and of Torah in general)—relying originally on being heard rather than being read—is distinguished by key words and by word plays which are meant to denote inner relationships or, sometimes, to serve as memory aids.[5]

Thus, the Jacob tale is distinguished by the repetition of the key root, רמה ("deceive"). It is a constant reminder that deceptions punctuated the turning points in Jacob's life: at his father's blessing, his dealings with Laban, the theft of the latter's household gods. Jacob deceives and is deceived in turn.

Word derivations may serve as memory devices or they may attempt to explain the name of a place or person: examples are Gen. 35:7 and 35:18. Word plays too play a role. For instance, in the Joseph story, the word יִשָּׂא is used to convey three meanings: to pardon, that is, to raise the chief butler to his former position; to lift off the head of the chief baker, that is, to kill him; and to single out or raise to prominence (Gen. 40:13, 19, 20).

A somewhat related aspect of textual presentation involves the use of numbers, which also reflects an ancient belief that numbers relate to the inner nature of the subject that is numbered. In the Book of Numbers we will come across two census takings approved by God (chapters 1 and 26), while in II Sam. 24 a census which did not have divine approval was said to have caused a severe plague. God is seen to be in charge of the secret of numbers; He literally is the one who "has our number"; and only He may dispose of its use. The lives of the Patriarchs are arranged in a numerical system: thus Abraham is 100 years old when Isaac is born, and he spends 100 years of his life in Canaan. He is 175 years old when he dies (7×5^2); Isaac reaches 180 years (5×6^2), and Jacob 147 (3×7^2). There were ten generations from Adam to Noah, and the same number from Noah to Terah, Abraham's father. Joseph spends the first 17 years of his life as his father Jacob's ward, and Jacob lives his 17 last years as Joseph's ward in Egypt. The number 7 plays a great role—possibly because there were then seven observed planets; 10 and 12 are important numbers and so is 40—likely to represent a generation. The priestly source (P) places particular emphasis on recording names and ages; its archival interests reflect the important role of Near Eastern record keeping.[6]

Finally, the reader should always keep in

---

[4] Examples are Exod. 20:3 and Gen. 1:1, respectively.
[5] On specific literary aspects of Torah texts see especially Zvi Adar, *The Biblical Narrative* (Jerusalem: World Zionist Organization, 1959); for sample studies of individual chapters, Erich Auerbach, *Mimesis* (Garden City, N.Y.: Doubleday, 1957) on Gen. 22; Robert Alter, *Commentary* (60, 6 [1975], 70 ff.) on Gen. 38; I. Avishur, *Beth Mikra*, 4 (1967), 613 ff.
[6] On the use of numbers in Genesis see especially Cassuto's commentary, *passim*.

mind that the text was composed in Hebrew and therefore partakes of the special thrust and meanings peculiar to the Hebrew tongue. No translation can ever fully capture the flavor of the original, and each translation is in itself a kind of interpretation. However skillfully created, however scholarly its renditions, it is but an image of the master text, clear at times and blurred at others. Our commentary seeks to illumine this divergence whenever possible, but in the end the full quality of the biblical text can be appreciated only in the Hebrew.

Science in Genesis

Ancient people considered the earth the center of the universe and natural law not as unalterable but as subservient to the will of God. This view is the basic principle underlying many stories, especially the opening chapters of the Book of Genesis which have become a formidable obstacle to the reading of the Bible. Why—it is asked—should we concern ourselves at all with stories of the six days of creation, with Adam and Eve, and the Garden of Eden? All these are unscientific, antiquated myths, and therefore appear to be irrelevant.

In answer, many defenders of the Bible agree that while the book has indeed little to tell about the scientific origins of the world and its inhabitants it does have a great deal to tell about God's relationship to His world and about human beings and their destiny. Since the Bible's scientific comprehension, they say, is limited to the world view of the ancients, just as ours is to that of our own time, it would be futile to look to the Bible for references to evolution or to suggest that "one day" in creation may correspond to millennia in scientific reckoning.

This view, while it appears to rescue the Bible from the worst problems of an outmoded literalism, nonetheless does not do the book full justice, for it approaches it with a facile sense of modern superiority. To be sure, our knowledge of science is vastly greater than that of the ancients. But that does not necessarily make our world view, based on such scientific insights, any more advanced.

It would be better, therefore, to come to the biblical text with full respect for its intellectual convictions and to understand that these are often expressed in metaphors and always in the vocabulary and framework of antiquity. The contemporary readers thus should restrain their inclination to do battle with or look for modern comparisons to ancient notions of creation. They should read the Bible for what it suggests about the nature of human history, the meaning of existence, and the presence of God.

With Stanley Gevirtz, one may approach the book in much the same manner as one approaches poetry:

"To the question of the 'truth' of Genesis the sensitive response can only be: It is, indeed, true; not in the sense in which a statement of a physical law is true, but few things that really matter to the poet ever are. It is true in the way that great poetry is always true: to the imagination of the human heart and the orderliness of the human mind. This God-and-Israel centered account discriminates, as every good historical narrative must, in its choice of events and presents us with history not, perhaps, as it was but as it ought to have been."[7]

---

[7] Unpublished. Quoted by permission of the author.

Genesis
and Ancient Near Eastern Literature

WILLIAM W. HALLO

The recovery of ancient Near Eastern literature has basically revolutionized our understanding of the Bible and of no book more so than Genesis. A glance at the authoritative volume, *Ancient Near Eastern Texts Relating to the Old Testament*,[1] will confirm this. Only Psalms and Proverbs outnumber Genesis in the parallels suggested by the various translators.[2] But the parallels to Proverbs all come from the well-nigh universal tradition of preceptual epigrams, most of them Egyptian. And when it is remembered that the five books of Psalms contain over 2,500 verses, compared to the 1,500 in Genesis, it will be seen that, proportionately, the first book of the Bible is most widely and most significantly paralleled in the literature of the ancient Near East.

Textual Comparison

The reasons behind these statistics are not difficult to find. Alone among the books of the Hebrew Bible, Genesis has the whole ancient Near East for its stage. Its first eleven chapters are set entirely in Babylonia, its last twelve in Egypt. The intervening 27 chapters occupy the geographical terrain between these two countries. They tell of repeated semi-nomadic movements back and forth throughout the entire broad stretch of Syria-Palestine including both sides of the Euphrates and Jordan rivers. The presence of ancient Near Eastern literary motifs in the tales of Genesis is thus no more startling than that of classical ones in Shakespeare's Greek and Roman dramas. Many of them are identified in this commentary, together with the similarities and differences between the biblical and other ancient Near Eastern treatments of common themes. It is not the purpose of this overview to anticipate them here one by one. Rather, we wish to sum up the evidence by analyzing the nature of the knowledge gained through the confrontation of Genesis and its ancient literary cognates.

To "prove" the accuracy or validity of one literary text by another is, of course, at once the most difficult and the most heatedly debated task of the critics. Many have wanted to employ the discoveries of archeology for this very purpose, many more for the opposite reason, and still others have despaired of resolving the issue. Unanimity is indeed impossible to achieve here, but at least we can

[1] Edited by James B. Pritchard (Princeton: Princeton University Press, 2nd ed., 1955). [Hereafter the work is referred to as Pritchard, *ANET*.]

[2] See the Index of Biblical References, *ibid.*, pp. 520–523.

hope to agree on what kind of questions we wish to prove. Put this way, it quickly becomes clear that we cannot gain greater confidence in the biblical version of the end of immortality simply because similar accounts have been found in the cuneiform sources (cf. chapters 2 and 3 below). Nor, on the contrary, are the rather variant Egyptian and Sumerian versions of creation needed to "disprove" that of Genesis. Whether Genesis accurately reports on these events is not the proper question. Rather we must ask: Does the text of Genesis, as we have it, accurately report what the ancient Israelites believed or asserted to have happened?

It is today generally assumed that an extended period of oral transmission introduced distortions into the traditions, that these distortions were aggravated by successive generations of scribes when the oral traditions were reduced to writing, and that their final canonization involved picking and choosing among the conflicting textual traditions on grounds other than that of their presumed antiquity or reliability.

On this premise, much modern criticism of Genesis has devoted itself to textual emendations and other attempts to recover a presumed original text. Such an "original text" is, however, unlikely ever to be found by the spade of the Palestinian archeologist, and all efforts to reconstruct it must therefore remain speculations not subject to scientific verification. Now the history of other ancient Near Eastern literatures has shown that, at least in a literate environment, textual transmission was indeed subject to occasional periods of substantial change and adaptation. To illustrate this point, we may cite the Mesopotamian versions of the story of the Flood. As a historical event and a chronological turning point, the concept of a great flood was an early and familiar fixture in cuneiform literature. The Sumerian King List[3] teaches that kingship came down (re-

spectively, came back) from heaven after the Flood and the idiom "before the Flood" (lām abūbi) signified pristine time. The earliest literary treatments of the theme are in Sumerian;[4] their hero is Ziusudra, ruler (or "son") of Shuruppak and last of the antediluvian dynasts. The first Akkadian flood story is associated with Atar-chasis whose epic is preserved in copies of the second and early first millennia B.C.E.[5] Finally, the flood story was incorporated into the eleventh tablet of the Akkadian Gilgamesh Epic, where its hero is Uta-napishtim, who is variously equated with both Ziusudra and Atar-chasis.[6] The Gilgamesh Epic in its final form cannot, as of now, be traced further back than circa 1100 B.C.E., and the extent to which it departed from its older Sumerian and Akkadian prototypes can be gauged even in translation. Certainly no Assyriologist would have ventured to reconstruct either of them from the late canonical version. Such an example inspires similar caution in current attempts to recover the original version or documents from which the canonical biblical text is presumed to have developed.

But, more than this, the recovery of the separate stages of many ancient Near Eastern compositions has revealed, by the side of a certain amount of editorial revision, a tenacious faithfulness to many received texts which is little short of astounding. Over widely scattered areas of cuneiform or hieroglyphic writing, and in periods separated by many centuries, certain canonical texts were copied verbatim and with an attention to textual detail not matched until the Alexandrian Greeks, or the Koranic specialists of the

[3] See the translation by A. L. Oppenheim, ibid., pp. 265–266.
[4] See the translations by S. N. Kramer, ibid., pp. 42–44 and in Expedition, 9, 4 (1967), pp. 12–18.
[5] Partial translation by E. A. Speiser in Pritchard, ANET, pp. 104–106.
[6] See the translation by Speiser, ibid., pp. 93–97.

Good Caliphs, or the Tiberian Masoretes who codified the Bible, counting, vocalizing, and accentuating its every letter. To cite just one example: The Sumerian myth of the warrior-god Ninurta probably was composed before the end of the third millennium; its first actual manuscripts date back to circa 1800 B.C.E., and it is known also in neo-Assyrian and neo-Babylonian copies beginning a thousand years later in which the Sumerian text is accompanied by an interlinear translation into Akkadian. Yet for all the time interval, the differences between the earlier and later Sumerian versions are little more than orthographic and dialectal. Such fidelity to a received text tradition has taught most biblical critics a new respect for the possibility of an equally reliable textual tradition underlying the Hebrew canon. It is little enough that we know of the technical details of textual creation and transmission in Israel before the time of the Dead Sea Scrolls.[7] Now we must at least reckon with the possibility that the process rated as much care as in the surrounding Near East before we venture to "improve" on the received text.

Thus ancient Near Eastern literary texts are seen to have met with different fates in the course of their millennial transmission; in some cases adaptation and reediting on a scale which defies prediction, in others extreme fidelity to the received text. Yet for all their differences, both examples impose the same conclusion for the biblical text: We cannot hope to achieve certainty in recovering a more authentic text than that codified by the Masoretes after the Arab conquest. Even with the discoveries at Qumran and else-where, we still have far fewer pre-Masoretic manuscripts than the Masoretes disposed of, and like them we lack a conclusive methodology for choosing between conflicting readings.[8]

Exegetic and Hermeneutic Parallels

But the history of ancient Near Eastern literature is relevant not only to the text of the Hebrew Bible but to its meaning. To return to the case of the Ninurta Epic, the Akkadian translations, added to the late versions, are, generally speaking, quite literal, but despite the best efforts of the late Assyrian and Babylonian scholars they are frequently faulty. They commit errors which modern philologists, with better knowledge of the original Sumerian, can often recognize as errors and sometimes correct. In other instances, they deliberately understand the Sumerian text in a new way not intended in the original. In still other cases, they obviously despaired of making any sense of the original and simply created de novo a meaning for the passage. All three of these tendencies can likewise be detected, albeit less clearly, in the absence of translations, i.e., in texts handed down from first to last in one and the same language. The conclusion to be drawn from all this is important for biblical criticism: The integrity of a textual tradition is no guarantee for the preservation, intact, of a continuous tradition of interpretation. On the contrary, the meaning assigned to a passage may change from age to age in part *in order to preserve* the integrity of the text. Here, then, we may use ancient Near Eastern literature to confirm a cardinal tenet of biblical criticism: Given the traditional text of a certain passage, we may hope to come closer to its original meaning than the traditional interpretations have done. In this attempt, specific ancient Near Eastern parallels are frequently of crucial help. Our examples here are taken from two levels.

[7] Cf. J. Philip Hyatt, "The Writing of an Old Testament Book," *Biblical Archaeologist Reader*, 1 (1961), pp. 22–31; reprinted from *Biblical Archaeologist*, 6 (1943), pp. 71–80.
[8] See F. M. Cross, Jr., "The Contribution of the Qumran Discoveries to the Study of the Biblical Text," *Israel Exploration Journal*, 16 (1966), pp. 81–95.

On the level of exegesis, or exposition of the text, the comparative approach may serve to illumine a word, form, or phrase which has proved a philological crux to all other approaches. Thus, for example, when Joseph is introduced to the Egyptians as Pharaoh's vizier, it is to the accompaniment of a shout "Abrek" (41:43) which has puzzled commentators ever since. Modern scholars have tended to see in it an Egyptian word meaning "Attention!" or a Coptic word meaning "incline." But the Greek translation prepared in Egypt by Jews who might have been expected to recognize such forms understood the word differently (as "herald"). Other ancient versions came up with Hebrew or even Latin etymologies which defy both literary and linguistic considerations. Such counsels of desperation led to discord among the tannaitic rabbis, as Rashi reports *ad loc.* But it is now known that Akkadian *abarakku* means "chief steward of a private or royal household" and that this title was widely attested wherever and whenever cuneiform was used, and beyond that as a loanword in Phoenician.[9] This almost certainly solves our textual problem. It also raises new questions.

Though now open to rational explanation without resort to emendations, popular etymology, or midrashic exegesis, the single word does not stand alone but in a context. Thus we move on to the level of hermeneutics, the interpretation and evaluation of the biblical context.

The presence of an Assyrian title (if this is conceded) in the midst of the Joseph stories raises significant questions about their date of composition and their source or sources of inspiration. Similarly the camels of the Ishmaelites (37:25) arouse suspicion, given the sporadic evidence, at best, for their use in Egypt before Ptolemaic times.[10] Again we must avoid extreme positions. These stories are not to be rejected because they are not verbatim transcripts of eyewitness accounts;

neither are they to be elevated above all criticism on the grounds of poetic (or theological) license. A sober appraisal must acknowledge the existence of different and even conflicting evidence within the stories themselves that bear on their possible place and date of origin. That they contain Egyptian elements is undeniable. There are proper names such as Potiphar with reasonable Egyptian etymologies; loanwords generally conceded to be Egyptian such as those for reed, magician, linen, and two different ones for signet ring; whole motifs paralleled in Egyptian literature such as the "Story of Two Brothers"[11] or the late tradition of seven lean years followed by years of plenty.[12]

But these elements bear some closer scrutiny. That an Israelite author should have some knowledge of Egyptian geographical and personal names is of no particular literary significance, given the near proximity and repeated contacts of the two cultures. As for the loanwords, they must be viewed in the perspective of biblical Hebrew as a whole. On the most conservative estimate, some forty Egyptian loanwords are attested with greater or lesser frequency in the Hebrew Bible.[13] Of these, only five occur in the Joseph stories. None of them is unique to these stories, and one cannot, therefore, describe them as inordinately full of authentic local diction. Finally, the thematic similarities cited are not of a kind to suggest that the Joseph stories are directly dependent on the Egyptian parallels or both on a common source. In sum, these stories are simply embellished

[9] Pritchard, *ANET*, p. 499 (3rd ed., p. 653) and note 1.
[10] Béatrix Midant-Reynes and Florence Braunstein-Silvestre, "Le chameau en Egypte," *Orientalia*, 46 (1977), pp. 337–362.
[11] See chs. 39–40, Gleanings, and the translation by J. A. Wilson, Pritchard, *ANET*, pp. 23–25.
[12] *Ibid.*, pp. 31–32.
[13] See T. O. Lambdin, *Journal of the American Oriental Society*, 73 (1953), pp. 145–155. [Hereafter this journal is referred to as *JAOS*.]

with Egyptian names, words, and literary motifs, all of which may have enjoyed a fairly wide currency. The presence of an intrusive Assyrianism or apparent anachronism in the story may or may not be a hint that the cycle of stories originated in an Assyrian setting, or in Egypt, or even in Israel, when these were under Assyrian rule. More important is the general conclusion to be derived from this example: Given sufficient familiarity with the literature, language, and proper names of an ancient Near Eastern culture such as Egypt, we can better evaluate the amount of influence it has exercised on a specific biblical composition. If in the case cited this amount is relatively negligible, that does not make the conclusion negative. Rather, it frees us to look for other sources, including native ones, of the biblical treatment.

Epigraphic Evidence

So far we have dealt, broadly speaking, with the text of Genesis and its context and with the considerable contribution of ancient Near Eastern literature to our evaluation of the one and interpretation of the other. But we need not confine our search to the biblical text or to the immediate parallels (and contrasts) from the cognate literatures. Rather, we may hope to gain a greater understanding of biblical people, places, and events than the text of Genesis explicitly vouchsafes us. True, we cannot expect to know more than the author or authors of Genesis knew, but we can sometimes hope to know more than he, or they, told. Here too ancient Near

Eastern literature comes to our aid, though the examples will be chosen from the Syro-Palestinian area which, lying between the high civilizations of Babylonia and Egypt, did not always match them in general literacy or specifically literary productivity. But we may take a broader view of written evidence and include in it not only strictly literary (so-called "canonical") writings but also historical (or "monumental") and economic ("archival") texts. Then this area too comes alive with a considerable corpus of inscriptions to fill in the interstices of Genesis.

Again we must put a reasonable limit on our expectations. The patriarchal narratives are no longer pure legend, like the tales of the antediluvians, and not yet the polished artifice of the "romance of Joseph." But neither are they to be understood as straightforward history. Therefore it is fruitless to look in the cuneiform or hieroglyphic inscriptions for references to the Patriarchs or in Gen. 12–36 for the names of ancient Near Eastern kings. Much effort has gone into both attempts, but even Gen. 14, potentially the most promising source in this regard, has resisted all such efforts. And small wonder, when it is remembered that the first identifiable foreign royal names reported as such in the Bible are Hiram of Tyre and Pharaoh Sheshonk of the Twenty-second Egyptian Dynasty, both dating to the tenth century B.C.E., while the first allusion to a Mesopotamian king[14] is the unnamed deliverer, probably Adad-nirari III of Assyria, who was a contemporary of Jehoahaz of Israel in the ninth century (II Kings 13:15). And, conversely, his predecessor "Jehu son of Omri" is the first Israelite king whose name (and portrait!) has turned up in the extra-biblical sources. No such individual connections can yet be provided for the second millennium, not even for its latter centuries. We should not therefore expect them for the patriarchal period, let alone its antecedents.

[14] An earlier ninth-century Assyrian king, Shalmaneser III, is recalled as Shalman in Hosea 10:14, according to M. C. Astour, *JAOS*, 91 (1971), pp. 383–389. And a still earlier one, Tiglat-pileser I (ca. 1100 B.C.E.), is alluded to in Psalm 83:9, according to Abraham Malamat in B. Mazar, ed., *World History of the Jewish People*, 3 (1971), p. 134.

What we do find, instead, are more general connections with the geography, history, and institutions of the third and second millennia as these are revealed one after another in the monuments and archives of the area. Two examples must suffice. The ongoing excavations at Ebla near Aleppo (Syria) have recovered, virtually intact, the archives and library of five successive kings who ruled a far-flung empire based on trade, diplomacy, and warfare during the second half of the third millennium before succumbing to the even greater ambitions of their rivals from Egypt and Mesopotamia. Thousands of large and well-preserved tablets have been found, employing the cuneiform script and Sumerian language of Mesopotamia but revealing at the same time a local Semitic dialect having affinities with both East Semitic (Akkadian) and Northwest Semitic (Amorite, Hebrew, etc.). Although only a handful of the texts have so far been published, they already show that, contrary to earlier estimates, Syria in pre-patriarchal times was a flourishing center of urban life whose greatest ruler, Ebrium (or Ebrum), bears a name intriguingly similar to Eber, longest-lived of the post-diluvians in the "line of Shem" (11:10), the "ancestor of all the descendants of Eber" (10:21).

For the first half of the second millennium, the history of the Middle Euphrates area has been thrown into wholly new and sharp relief by the discoveries at Mari. The palace of this ancient city has yielded an archive of over twenty thousand tablets which are particularly valuable for illuminating tribal structure, terminology, and genealogies. In the last connection, even the seemingly tedious family trees of Genesis assume a new significance. Some tribes and clans, for example, are linked to the Patriarchs by concubinage with an eponymous ancestress; it has been shown that these represent the splitting off of tribal segments and their migration, freely or otherwise, to the margins of the tribal terrain.[15] This is in effect stated, if obliquely, in the case of Abraham's "sons" by Hagar and Keturah (Gen. 25:6). But it is also implied where not actually stated, e.g., for the origin of Amalek (Gen. 36:12) on the strength of ample evidence for the process of tribal subdivision at Mari. The genealogies of Genesis, and their complements in Chronicles and elsewhere, have long been regarded, at best, as an artificial framework imposed on the text; at worst, they have been ignored altogether. But in the light of the cuneiform sources they may yet turn out to yield up, for those who can read between the lines, the most authentic remnants of early Israelite history.

It may be noted in passing that the reverse is also true, i.e., that ancient Near Eastern documents frequently defy understanding without help from the Bible. To return to Mari, its scribes wrote in Akkadian, the language of the settled East Semitic population of Babylonia. For tribal terminology, however, they had to turn to the West Semitic vocabulary of the nomadic and semi-nomadic Amorites. This language was much closer to biblical Hebrew, which therefore contributes fundamentally to the understanding of its tribal terminology. Many more examples could be cited to show that the comparative method thus works in both directions, but this is not the place to do so. Suffice it to say that, within its limitations, the method deserves an honored place in the canons of biblical criticism. The limitations of the comparative method have been well defined by W. A. Irwin thus: "The Bible itself is our first and altogether best source for the study of the Bible . . . the Bible itself with whatever

---

[15] Malamat, "The Settlement as Reflected in Tribal Genealogy," in H. H. Ben-Sasson, ed., *A History of the Jewish People* (Cambridge: Harvard University Press, 1976), pp. 38, 63–66.

we can make of it by all best known procedures is alone to tell us what the Bible is and what it means."[16] But surely the comparative method is one of the very best procedures for telling us what the Bible is and means, and what we make of Genesis today inevitably depends, in some measure, on the proper utilization of the literature of all of the ancient Near East.

[16] Presidential address to the Society of Biblical Literature, 1958; cf. *Journal of Biblical Literature*, 78 (1959), p. 3.

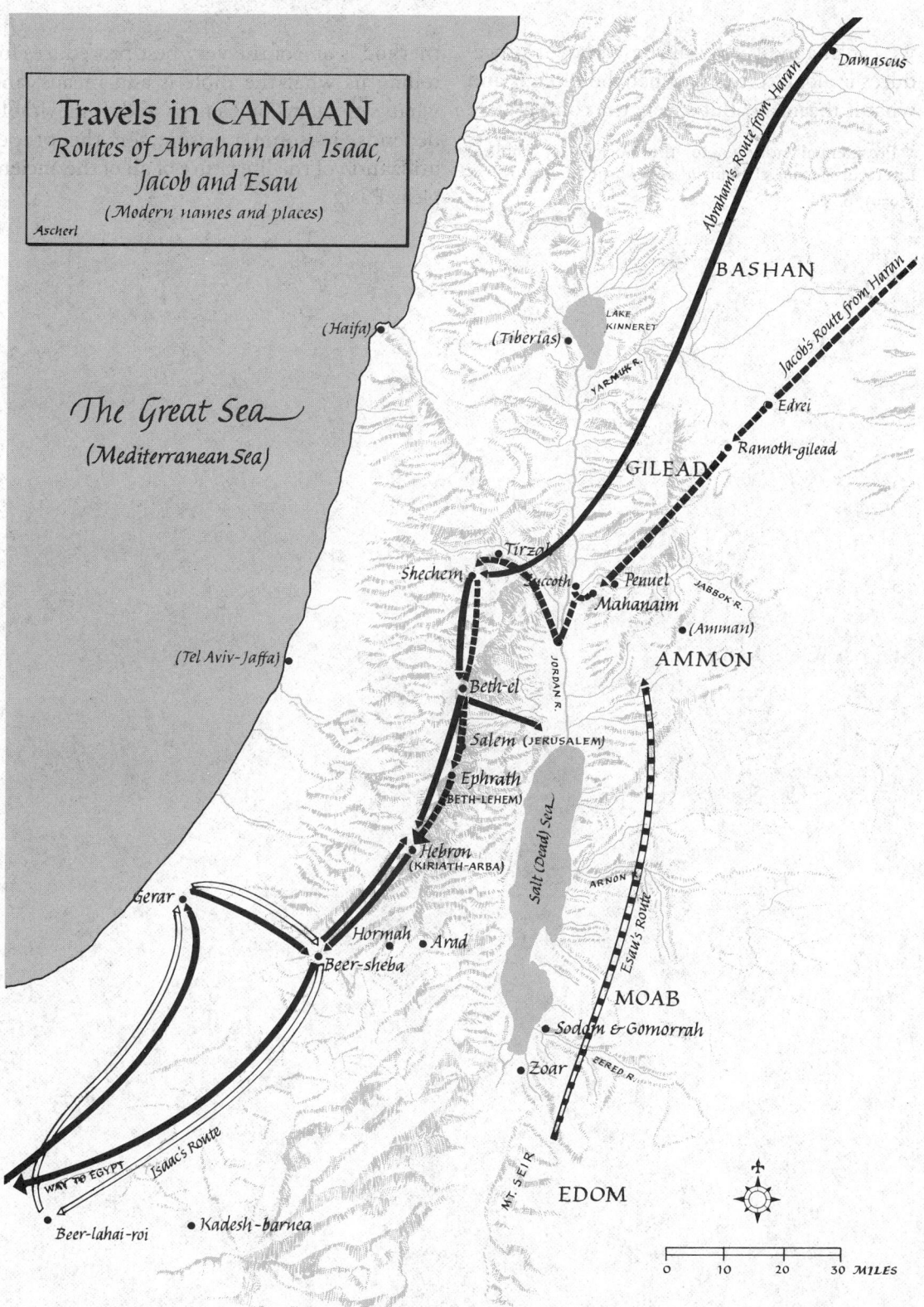

Travels in CANAAN
Routes of Abraham and Isaac, Jacob and Esau
(Modern names and places)

Ascherl

The Great Sea
(Mediterranean Sea)

Abraham's Route from Haran

Jacob's Route from Haran

Damascus

BASHAN

(Haifa)

(Tiberias)

LAKE KINNERET

YARMUK R.

GILEAD

Edrei

Ramoth-gilead

Tirzah

Shechem

Succoth

Penuel

Mahanaim

JABBOK R.

(Amman)

AMMON

(Tel Aviv-Jaffa)

JORDAN R.

Beth-el

Salem (JERUSALEM)

Ephrath
(BETH-LEHEM)

Hebron
(KIRIATH-ARBA)

Salt (Dead) Sea

ARNON

Esau's Route

Gerar

Hormah

Arad

Beer-sheba

MOAB

Sodom & Gomorrah

Zoar

ZERED R.

WAY TO EGYPT

Isaac's Route

Beer-lahai-roi

Kadesh-barnea

MT. SEIR

EDOM

0   10   20   30   MILES

14

PART I

Prologue

Creation

The Book of Genesis is a book of beginnings. Chapter 1 and the first three verses of chapter 2 serve as the poetic prologue, setting the stage for the universal drama that is about to commence. Once the scene is set, once order has been brought out of chaos, once heaven and earth, plants and animals have been created, the epic story of man himself can begin.

The prologue is cast in the form of a prose poem. It is written in terse, controlled phrases with rhythmic repetitions, the slow ascent of the cosmic drama culminating in the creation of man and the serene postscript describing the sanctification of the seventh day. In sparse, austere language it speaks of God, the world, and man in relationship to each other and reveals the basic and unalterable dependence of the world on the presence of God. The prologue tells, with the assurance of faith, of life's foundations, and it is in the light of this faith that it must be read and understood. (On the relationship of the Bible to ancient Near Eastern literature, see W. W. Hallo's essay.)

The Book of Genesis does not appear to tell of human growth and development in a way palatable to moderns, schooled in the principles of evolution. Indeed, Genesis as well as succeeding books freely mix devolution (descent from primal eminence) with evolution (ascent from a lower to a higher stage). Religion and moral insight are not generally presented in the Bible as a process of slow and painful moral growth; quite the contrary, religious genius appears repeatedly without traceable antecedents—as, for instance, in the case of Abraham. This, however, should not cause us to dismiss such stories as "improbable," for moral history is not like

physical history. Mutations in the realm of the spiritual seem to have occurred frequently in human experience, and the biblical record should in part be read as the record of such mutations. The very creation of the people of Israel, to which the Torah is devoted, bursts the rules of mechanical evolution.

(The first weekly portion, *Bereshit*, begins here.)

ה מֵעַל לָרָקִיעַ וַיְהִי־כֵן: וַיִּקְרָא אֱלֹהִים לָרָקִיעַ שָׁמָיִם
וַיְהִי־עֶרֶב וַיְהִי־בֹקֶר יוֹם שֵׁנִי: פ

ט וַיֹּאמֶר אֱלֹהִים יִקָּווּ הַמַּיִם מִתַּחַת הַשָּׁמַיִם אֶל־מָקוֹם
י אֶחָד וְתֵרָאֶה הַיַּבָּשָׁה וַיְהִי־כֵן: וַיִּקְרָא אֱלֹהִים לַיַּבָּשָׁה
אֶרֶץ וּלְמִקְוֵה הַמַּיִם קָרָא יַמִּים וַיַּרְא אֱלֹהִים
יא כִּי־טוֹב: וַיֹּאמֶר אֱלֹהִים תַּדְשֵׁא הָאָרֶץ דֶּשֶׁא עֵשֶׂב
מַזְרִיעַ זֶרַע עֵץ פְּרִי עֹשֶׂה פְּרִי לְמִינוֹ אֲשֶׁר זַרְעוֹ־בוֹ
יב עַל־הָאָרֶץ וַיְהִי־כֵן: וַתּוֹצֵא הָאָרֶץ דֶּשֶׁא עֵשֶׂב
מַזְרִיעַ זֶרַע לְמִינֵהוּ וְעֵץ עֹשֶׂה־פְּרִי אֲשֶׁר זַרְעוֹ־בוֹ
יג לְמִינֵהוּ וַיַּרְא אֱלֹהִים כִּי־טוֹב: וַיְהִי־עֶרֶב וַיְהִי־בֹקֶר
יוֹם שְׁלִישִׁי: פ

א בְּרֵאשִׁית בָּרָא אֱלֹהִים אֵת הַשָּׁמַיִם וְאֵת הָאָרֶץ:
ב וְהָאָרֶץ הָיְתָה תֹהוּ וָבֹהוּ וְחֹשֶׁךְ עַל־פְּנֵי תְהוֹם וְרוּחַ
ג אֱלֹהִים מְרַחֶפֶת עַל־פְּנֵי הַמָּיִם: וַיֹּאמֶר אֱלֹהִים יְהִי
ד אוֹר וַיְהִי־אוֹר: וַיַּרְא אֱלֹהִים אֶת־הָאוֹר כִּי־טוֹב
ה וַיַּבְדֵּל אֱלֹהִים בֵּין הָאוֹר וּבֵין הַחֹשֶׁךְ: וַיִּקְרָא
אֱלֹהִים לָאוֹר יוֹם וְלַחֹשֶׁךְ קָרָא לָיְלָה וַיְהִי־עֶרֶב
וַיְהִי־בֹקֶר יוֹם אֶחָד: פ

ו וַיֹּאמֶר אֱלֹהִים יְהִי רָקִיעַ בְּתוֹךְ הַמָּיִם וִיהִי מַבְדִּיל
ז בֵּין מַיִם לָמָיִם: וַיַּעַשׂ אֱלֹהִים אֶת־הָרָקִיעַ וַיַּבְדֵּל
בֵּין הַמַּיִם אֲשֶׁר מִתַּחַת לָרָקִיעַ וּבֵין הַמַּיִם אֲשֶׁר

* א ב' רבתי.

1] When God began to create the heaven and the earth—**2]** the earth being unformed and void, with darkness over the surface of the deep and a wind from God sweeping over the water—**3]** God said, "Let there be light"; and there was light. **4]** God saw that the light was good, and God separated the light from the darkness. **5]** God called the light Day, and the darkness He called Night. And there was evening and there was morning, a first day.

6] God said, "Let there be an expanse in the midst of the water, that it may separate water from water." **7]** God made the expanse, and it separated the water which was below the expanse from the water which was above the expanse. And it was so. **8]** God called the expanse Sky. And there was evening and there was morning, a second day.

9] God said, "Let the water below the sky be gathered into one area, that the dry land may appear." And it was so. **10]** God called the dry land Earth, and the gathering of waters He called Seas. And God saw that this was good. **11]** And God said, "Let the earth sprout vegetation: seed-bearing plants, fruit trees of every kind on earth that bear fruit with the seed in it." And it was so. **12]** The earth brought forth vegetation: seed-bearing plants of every kind, and trees of every kind bearing fruit with the seed in it. And God saw that this was good. **13]** And there was evening and there was morning, a third day.

1:1-2] *When God began to create . . . the earth being unformed and void.* Other translations render this, "In the beginning God created." Both translations are possible, but we cannot be sure that this difference is more than stylistic.
/ Our translation follows Rashi, who said that the text would have been written בָּרִאשׁוֹנָה if its *primary* purpose had been to teach the order in which creation took place. Later scholars used the translation "In the beginning" as proof that God created out of nothing (*ex nihilo*), but it is not likely that the biblical author was concerned with this problem [1]./
2] *The deep.* The Hebrew, תְּהוֹם (*tehom*), echoes the Mesopotamian creation story where it is told

that heaven and earth were formed from the carcass of the sea dragon, Tiamat.

A wind from God. רוּחַ (*ruach*) can mean both "wind" and "spirit" [2]. Wind, however, provides a closer parallel to Babylonian texts than the traditional translation, "spirit of God" [3].

The water. Here, as in other ancient traditions, it is given priority of existence.

3] *God said.* As though He were addressing the universe.

6] *An expanse.* רָקִיעַ (*rakia*) suggests a firm vault or dome over the earth. According to ancient belief, this vault, which held the stars, provided the boundary beyond which the Divine dwelt.

יד וַיֹּאמֶר אֱלֹהִים יְהִי מְאֹרֹת בִּרְקִיעַ הַשָּׁמַיִם לְהַבְדִּיל בֵּין הַיּוֹם וּבֵין הַלַּיְלָה וְהָיוּ לְאֹתֹת וּלְמוֹעֲדִים

טו וּלְיָמִים וְשָׁנִים: וְהָיוּ לִמְאוֹרֹת בִּרְקִיעַ הַשָּׁמַיִם לְהָאִיר

טז עַל-הָאָרֶץ וַיְהִי-כֵן: וַיַּעַשׂ אֱלֹהִים אֶת-שְׁנֵי הַמְּאֹרֹת הַגְּדֹלִים אֶת-הַמָּאוֹר הַגָּדֹל לְמֶמְשֶׁלֶת הַיּוֹם וְאֶת־ הַמָּאוֹר הַקָּטֹן לְמֶמְשֶׁלֶת הַלַּיְלָה וְאֵת הַכּוֹכָבִים:

יז וַיִּתֵּן אֹתָם אֱלֹהִים בִּרְקִיעַ הַשָּׁמָיִם לְהָאִיר עַל־

יח הָאָרֶץ: וְלִמְשֹׁל בַּיּוֹם וּבַלַּיְלָה וּלְהַבְדִּיל בֵּין הָאוֹר

יט וּבֵין הַחֹשֶׁךְ וַיַּרְא אֱלֹהִים כִּי-טוֹב: וַיְהִי-עֶרֶב וַיְהִי־ בֹקֶר יוֹם רְבִיעִי: פ

כ וַיֹּאמֶר אֱלֹהִים יִשְׁרְצוּ הַמַּיִם שֶׁרֶץ נֶפֶשׁ חַיָּה וְעוֹף

כא יְעוֹפֵף עַל-הָאָרֶץ עַל-פְּנֵי רְקִיעַ הַשָּׁמָיִם: וַיִּבְרָא

אֱלֹהִים אֶת-הַתַּנִּינִם הַגְּדֹלִים וְאֵת כָּל-נֶפֶשׁ הַחַיָּה הָרֹמֶשֶׂת אֲשֶׁר שָׁרְצוּ הַמַּיִם לְמִינֵהֶם וְאֵת כָּל-עוֹף

כב כָּנָף לְמִינֵהוּ וַיַּרְא אֱלֹהִים כִּי-טוֹב: וַיְבָרֶךְ אֹתָם אֱלֹהִים לֵאמֹר פְּרוּ וּרְבוּ וּמִלְאוּ אֶת-הַמַּיִם בַּיַּמִּים

כג וְהָעוֹף יִרֶב בָּאָרֶץ: וַיְהִי-עֶרֶב וַיְהִי-בֹקֶר יוֹם חֲמִישִׁי: פ

כד וַיֹּאמֶר אֱלֹהִים תּוֹצֵא הָאָרֶץ נֶפֶשׁ חַיָּה לְמִינָהּ בְּהֵמָה וָרֶמֶשׂ וְחַיְתוֹ-אֶרֶץ לְמִינָהּ וַיְהִי-כֵן: וַיַּעַשׂ אֱלֹהִים

כה אֶת-חַיַּת הָאָרֶץ לְמִינָהּ וְאֶת-הַבְּהֵמָה לְמִינָהּ וְאֵת כָּל-רֶמֶשׂ הָאֲדָמָה לְמִינֵהוּ וַיַּרְא אֱלֹהִים כִּי-טוֹב:

כו וַיֹּאמֶר אֱלֹהִים נַעֲשֶׂה אָדָם בְּצַלְמֵנוּ כִּדְמוּתֵנוּ וְיִרְדּוּ בִדְגַת הַיָּם וּבְעוֹף הַשָּׁמַיִם וּבַבְּהֵמָה וּבְכָל-הָאָרֶץ

14] God said, "Let there be lights in the expanse of the sky to separate day from night; they shall serve as signs for the set times—the days and the years; **15]** and they shall serve as lights in the expanse of the sky to shine upon the earth." And it was so. **16]** God made the two great lights, the greater light to dominate the day and the lesser light to dominate the night, and the stars. **17]** And God set them in the expanse of the sky to shine upon the earth, **18]** to dominate the day and the night, and to separate light from darkness. And God saw that this was good. **19]** And there was evening and there was morning, a fourth day.

20] God said, "Let the waters bring forth swarms of living creatures, and birds that fly above the earth across the expanse of the sky." **21]** God created the great sea monsters, and all the living creatures of every kind that creep, which the waters brought forth in swarms; and all the winged birds of every kind. And God saw that this was good. **22]** God blessed them, saying, "Be fertile and increase, fill the waters in the seas, and let the birds increase on the earth." **23]** And there was evening and there was morning, a fifth day.

24] God said, "Let the earth bring forth every kind of living creature: cattle, creeping things, and wild beasts of every kind." And it was so. **25]** God made wild beasts of every kind and cattle of every kind, and all kinds of creeping things of the earth. And God saw that this was good. **26]** And God said, "Let us make man in our image, after our likeness. They shall rule the fish of the sea, the birds of the sky, the cattle, the whole earth, and all the creeping

---

16] *Two great lights.* The sun and the moon are mentioned as part of creation but have none of the divine or semidivine status attributed to them in other ancient mythologies.

21] *The great sea monsters.* Elsewhere the Bible reflects popular legends about certain forces of the deep that battled with God. Here they are simply listed with the other animals.

/ The monsters are variously called Nahar, Yam, Leviathan, and Rahab. The latter especially recalls an ancient poetic tradition of a "lord of the sea" [4]./

26] *Let us make man.* Either a majestic plural or spoken to an angelic court [5].

/ Christian theology generally takes the phrase to indicate the triune nature of God./

כ וּבְכָל־הָרֶמֶשׂ הָרֹמֵשׂ עַל־הָאָרֶץ: וַיִּבְרָא אֱלֹהִים אֶת־
הָאָדָם בְּצַלְמוֹ בְּצֶלֶם אֱלֹהִים בָּרָא אֹתוֹ זָכָר וּנְקֵבָה
כח בָּרָא אֹתָם: וַיְבָרֶךְ אֹתָם אֱלֹהִים וַיֹּאמֶר לָהֶם אֱלֹהִים
פְּרוּ וּרְבוּ וּמִלְאוּ אֶת־הָאָרֶץ וְכִבְשֻׁהָ וּרְדוּ בִּדְגַת
הַיָּם וּבְעוֹף הַשָּׁמַיִם וּבְכָל־חַיָּה הָרֹמֶשֶׂת עַל־הָאָרֶץ:
כט וַיֹּאמֶר אֱלֹהִים הִנֵּה נָתַתִּי לָכֶם אֶת־כָּל־עֵשֶׂב זֹרֵעַ
זֶרַע אֲשֶׁר עַל־פְּנֵי כָל־הָאָרֶץ וְאֶת־כָּל־הָעֵץ אֲשֶׁר־
ל בּוֹ פְרִי־עֵץ זֹרֵעַ זָרַע לָכֶם יִהְיֶה לְאָכְלָה: וּלְכָל־
חַיַּת הָאָרֶץ וּלְכָל־עוֹף הַשָּׁמַיִם וּלְכֹל רוֹמֵשׂ עַל־

הָאָרֶץ אֲשֶׁר־בּוֹ נֶפֶשׁ חַיָּה אֶת־כָּל־יֶרֶק עֵשֶׂב לְאָכְלָה
לא וַיְהִי־כֵן: וַיַּרְא אֱלֹהִים אֶת־כָּל־אֲשֶׁר עָשָׂה וְהִנֵּה־
טוֹב מְאֹד וַיְהִי־עֶרֶב וַיְהִי־בֹקֶר יוֹם הַשִּׁשִּׁי: פ
ב וַיְכֻלּוּ הַשָּׁמַיִם וְהָאָרֶץ וְכָל־צְבָאָם: וַיְכַל אֱלֹהִים
בַּיּוֹם הַשְּׁבִיעִי מְלַאכְתּוֹ אֲשֶׁר עָשָׂה וַיִּשְׁבֹּת בַּיּוֹם
ג הַשְּׁבִיעִי מִכָּל־מְלַאכְתּוֹ אֲשֶׁר עָשָׂה: וַיְבָרֶךְ אֱלֹהִים
אֶת־יוֹם הַשְּׁבִיעִי וַיְקַדֵּשׁ אֹתוֹ כִּי בוֹ שָׁבַת מִכָּל־
מְלַאכְתּוֹ אֲשֶׁר־בָּרָא אֱלֹהִים לַעֲשׂוֹת: פ

things that creep on earth." **27]** And God created man in His image, in the image of God He created him; male and female He created them. **28]** God blessed them and God said to them, "Be fertile and increase, fill the earth and master it; and rule the fish of the sea, the birds of the sky, and all the living things that creep on earth."

29] God said, "See, I give you every seed-bearing plant that is upon all the earth, and every tree that has seed-bearing fruit; they shall be yours for food. **30]** And to all the animals on land, to all the birds of the sky, and to everything that creeps on earth, in which there is the breath of life, [I give] all the green plants for food." And it was so. **31]** And God saw all that He had made, and found it very good. And there was evening and there was morning, the sixth day.

1] The heaven and the earth were finished, and all their array. **2]** On the seventh day God finished the work which He had been doing, and He ceased on the seventh day from all the work which He had done. **3]** And God blessed the seventh day and declared it holy, because on it God ceased from all the work of creation which He had done.

28] *Be fertile and increase.* A blessing. Jewish tradition considers this to be the first of the Torah's 613 commandments.

/ The halachah derived therefrom establishes man's duty to marry and have children [6]. Extensive passages in the Talmud and the codes deal with the question whether this duty devolves only upon the man or also upon the woman. Preponderant opinion favored the male's sole responsibility (incurred at age eighteen, while all other commandments are obligatory at age thirteen)./

30] *Green plants for food.* According to the biblical scheme, men and beasts became carnivorous only after the Flood (Gen. 9:3). At first they had been vegetarians. According to Isaiah, in the messianic

age man and beast will return to this original state of harmony: beasts will become vegetarians once more; "the lion will eat straw like the ox" (11:7).

2:1] *Finished.* Heaven and earth "were finished," and God too "finished" His work. Both in Hebrew and in English, the word can have dual meanings. The same ambiguity is also echoed in the "Gilgamesh" epic.

2] *He ceased.* Or rested. שָׁבַת (*shavat*) is related to שַׁבָּת (*Shabbat*).
/ If creation ceased "on" the seventh day, was this not, at least in part, another day of creating? This question was much argued by the ancients [7]./

God in Genesis

Beginning with the first sentence of Genesis, it is apparent that the existence of God is taken for granted. Nowhere is it doubted or argued; neither, however, is the existence of other gods ever questioned. In this respect Genesis is radically different from the other books of the Torah and from the Prophets. Abraham, Isaac, and Jacob were distinguished in that they worshiped the One God and served Him alone, but the exclusive monotheism of later days was not theirs. They may have even believed that other gods were real. But only One had made a covenant with them and to Him they committed their lives and the future of their offspring [8].

This God appears in the pages of Genesis both as the Creator of the world and the Friend of the Patriarchs. In speaking of God, the book has no difficulty in moving from universal to personal proportions and concerns. Modern man is likely to experience some problems here, for his relationship to and concept of God is not usually as intimately personal and direct as that of biblical man. To the ancients, God was not an abstract force, principle, or process; rather, He was Father, Friend, King—all of which implied "person." Individuality was the highest expression of creation, and God the Creator could himself be spoken of only in such terms. It would not have occurred to the ancients to speak of God in any way other than the way one spoke of man (because man was created in God's image), and it was therefore most natural to think of God as speaking, seeing, regretting, and occasionally as walking or descending. The divinity and majesty of God were thereby not diminished. For instance, the expression, "God said to Abraham," was the natural and even best method of recording a vital experience.[1] Only much later did these human ascriptions of God (called anthropomorphisms) begin to create the kind of serious problems which are being experienced by the modern Bible reader.

However one interprets the nature of God—as person or as process, as individual reality or generalized principle—there are three basic ideas which the contemporary reader can share with biblical man and which are implicit in Genesis:

THAT GOD, as Father or Creative Force, provides all creation with purpose and that therefore to understand God means to understand one's own potential;

THAT GOD, as Lawgiver, validates the principles of justice and righteousness which must govern the affairs of men;

---

[1] "It was apparently easier in Old Testament faith to tolerate the danger of lessening God's greatness and 'absoluteness' by human description than to run the risk of giving up anything of God's personalness and His vital participation in everything earthly" [9].

Umberto Cassuto adds another consideration: "The Torah was not intended specifically for intellectuals but for the entire people, which is not concerned with philosophic or theological speculation. It uses ordinary language plainly and without sophistication and pays no heed to inferences that later readers who are accustomed to ways of thinking wholly alien to the Bible may draw from its works" [10].

Note also Herbert C. Brichto's important caution: "Nor may we summarily rule out the possibility, nor even the likelihood, that an ancient author may have formulated a message in such a way as to be addressed simultaneously to the most naive and most sophisticated of his generation, to be comprehended by each according to his level. That *Gulliver's Travels* is read by children as naive fantasy leads no one to exclude a deeper, more serious intent on the author's part. It is not the reputation of the biblical authors but our own understanding of them that suffers when we arbitrarily accord them less of a hearing than we grant Jonathan Swift" [11].

THAT GOD, as Redeemer, guarantees the ultimate goals of existence and enables man to find meaning in his life.

Added to these is a pervasive theme which above all has made the Bible, from Genesis through Chronicles, a Jewish book—that through Abraham and his descendants the realization of God's plan for humanity will be hastened and, in fact, be made possible altogether.

The Creation of Man

The Rabbis said that God, the Master Architect, worked with a master plan of creation before Him. This plan was the Torah, which provided that His world would exist not merely for the sake of existing but for a moral purpose bound up with the creation of man [12].

Man is placed on the stage of creation after all else has been formed; he is represented as the crown of God's labors. In anticipation, the text shifts into a slower gear; the words "God said" are not, as previously, directly followed by a creative act but by a further resolve, almost contemplative in nature: "Let us make man" [13].

The creature called man is formed in the image of God, in His likeness. These words reflect the Torah's abiding wonder over man's special stature in creation, over his unique intellectual capacity, which bears the imprint of the Creator. Marveling at man's powers, the Bible finds him to be "little less than divine" (Ps. 8:6).[2]

This likeness also describes man's moral potential. Man's *nature* is radically different from God's, but man is capable of approaching God's *actions*: His love, His mercy, His justice [15]. Man becomes truly human as he attempts to do godly deeds.[3]

Man's likeness to the Divine has a third and most important meaning: It stresses the essential holiness and, by implication, the dignity of all men, without any distinctions.

"Above all demarcations of races and nations, castes and classes, oppressors and servants, givers and recipients, above all delineations even of gifts and talents stands one certainty: Man. Whoever bears this image is created and called to be a revelation of human dignity" [17].

Six times the Bible says that God found His creation "good"; after man was created He found it "very good": Being is better than nothingness, order superior to chaos, and man's existence—with all its difficulties—a blessing. But creation is never called perfect; it will in fact be man's task to assist the Creator in perfecting His creation, to become His co-worker.

The Seventh Day

The Bible mentions the number seven more than 500 times. Some trace the concern with this number to the prominence of the sun, moon, and the five planets observed in antiquity; others to the fact that the lunar month falls roughly into four quarters of seven days each. Whatever the reason, it is the most prominent number in the Bible. In addition to the weekly cycle, the Pesach festival is governed by seven; so are the seven weeks' period between Pesach and Shavuot and the sabbatical year. There are some scholars who suggest that the entire Book of Genesis and even the Torah itself are elaborately and ingeniously constructed around this sacred number [18].

---

[2] In a midrash the angels at first mistook man for a divine person and sang hymns to him [14]. The word for "image" (*tzelem*) is related to the Akkadian *salmu*, which had the double meaning of image and statue and which applied specifically to divine statues in human guise. The biblical use is, of course, different.

[3] The Rabbis said: "As God is merciful, so be thou merciful; as He is just, so be thou just" [16].

When and how the seventh day became the holy day of Israel has never been ascertained. A Babylonian division of the lunar month into four seven-day periods and the designation of the day of the full moon as *shapattu* are possible links. Whatever the origins, in Genesis the day becomes the divine seal of creation. And while it is not yet called the Sabbath, its significance is unmistakable: It is built into the very structure of the universe; it is God's holy time; and Israel in ages to come will be called upon to make it the center of its existence, the mark of its covenant with God, "a memorial of the work of creation."[4]

Thus, in the biblical view, creation and history belong together. Creation is the foundation of a covenantal relationship between God and world and, in a specific and important sense, between God and Israel.[5]

[4] So in the Sabbath Kiddush. In the major Christian tradition, the seventh-day Sabbath was supplanted by a first-day Sabbath—"Lord's Day"—in memory of the Resurrection [19].

[5] Isaiah describes God's creation of Israel in the same terms that Genesis uses in describing the creation of the world (Isa. 43:1, 7, 15, 21; 44:2, 21, 24; 45:11).

GLEANINGS

Very Good

It says that God found His creation to be "very good," which implies a comparison. From this, it may be inferred that God had created and destroyed previous worlds.　　MIDRASH [20]

God would not have created the world if among all possible creations it had not been the best.
　　GOTTFRIED VON LEIBNITZ [21]

Of Every Kind

Of beasts it says that they were created "of every kind." Not so of man; there is only one human species.　　BENNO JACOB [22]

Let Us Make Man

As long as God is still creating, He does not in fact say "I," He says "We," an absolute, all-inclusive term which does not refer to an I outside the self but is the plural of all-encompassing majesty. It is an impersonal I, an I that does not face another Thou, that does not reveal anything but lives, like the metaphysical God of pre-creation, only in itself.　　FRANZ ROSENZWEIG [23]

In the Image

Beloved is man for he was created in the image of God. Still greater was God's love in that He gave to man the knowledge of his having been so created.　　ETHICS OF THE FATHERS [24]

Like None Other

A king of flesh and blood stamps his image on a coin, hence all coins look and are alike; but the King of Kings put the stamp of the first man on humanity, yet no man is like any other.
　　MISHNAH [25]

Created Single

Man was created single for the sake of peace among men, so that no one might say to his fellow: "My father was greater than yours."
　　MISHNAH [26]

Created Unique

Every man should know that since creation no other man ever was like him. Had there been such another, there would be no need for him to be. Each is called on to perfect his unique qualities. And it is his failure to heed this call which delays the Messiah.　　BAAL SHEM TOV [27]

Another Creation Story

[From an Akkadian epic dating probably to the early second millennium B.C.E.]

Then the lord [Marduk] paused to view her [Tiamat's] dead body,
That he might divide the monster and do artful works.
He split her like a shellfish into two parts:
Half of her he set up and ceiled it as a sky,
Pulled down the bar and posted guards.
He bade them to allow not her waters to escape,
He crossed the heavens and surveyed its regions. . . .
He constructed nations for the great gods,
Fixing their astral likenesses as constellations. . . .
In her [Tiamat's] belly he established the zenith.
The moon he caused to shine, the night to him entrusting.
[Marduk reveals his plan to create man]
Blood I will mass and cause bones to be.
I will establish a savage, "man" shall be his name.
Verily, savage man I will create.
He shall be charged with the service of the gods that they might be at ease!
　　FROM "ENUMA ELISH" [28]

Ancient Cosmology and Biblical Creation

Although the Bible takes for granted the contours of ancient cosmology, it has demythologized

the ancient understanding of existence. The Hebrew Bible contains no theogony, no myth which traces the creation to a primordial battle between divine powers, no ritual which enabled men to repeat the mythological drama and thereby ensure the supremacy of the national god. Mythological allusions have been torn out of their ancient context of polytheism and nature religion and have acquired a completely new meaning within the historical syntax of Israel's faith. The pagan language survives only as poetic speech for the adoration of the Lord of History.

BERNHARD W. ANDERSON [29]

The Sabbath and God's Freedom

[The first feature of God revealed by His rest on the seventh day is His freedom.]

A world-principle without this limit to its creative activity would not be free like God but would be tied to the infinite motion of its own development and evolution. In its unlimited creative activity it would not really belong to itself. It would not really be active but entangled in a process imposed upon it and subjected to its higher necessity. A being is free only when it can determine and limit its activity. God's creative activity has its limit in the rest from His works determined by Himself, i.e., the rest of the seventh day. His freedom revealed in this rest is a first criterion of the true deity of the Creator in the biblical saga.

KARL BARTH [30]

Dream of Perfection

The Sabbath is the dream of perfection, but it is only a dream. Only in its being both does it become the cornerstone of life, only as the festival of perfection does it become the constant renewal of creation. FRANZ ROSENZWEIG [31]

Uncompleted

The Lord created the world in a state of beginning. The universe is always in an uncompleted state, in the form of its beginning. It is not like a vessel at which the master works to finish it; it requires continuous labor and renewal by creative forces. Should these cease for only a second, the universe would return to primeval chaos.

SIMCHAH BUNAM OF PRZYSUCHA [32]

Fill the Earth and Master It (Gen. 1:28)

To claim that [this verse] provides "justification" for the exploitation of the environment, leading to the poisoning of the atmosphere, the pollution of our water, and the spoliation of natural resources is . . . a complete distortion of the truth. On the contrary, the Hebrew Bible and the Jewish interpreters *prohibit* such exploitation. Judaism goes much further and insists that man has an obligation not only to conserve the world of nature but to enhance it because man is the "co-partner of God in the work of creation." . . . All animal life and all growing and life-giving things have rights in the cosmos that man must consider, even as he strives to ensure his own survival. The war against the spoliation of nature and the pollution of the environment is therefore the command of the hour and the call of the ages.

ROBERT GORDIS [33]

Truth at Creation

A midrash begins as follows: Rabbi Shimon said: "In the hour when God was about to create Adam, the angels of service were divided. Some said, 'Let him not be created,' others, 'Let him be created, for he will do loving deeds.' But Truth said, 'Let him not be created, for he will be all falsity.' Righteousness said, 'Let him be created, for he will do righteous deeds.' Peace said, 'Let him not be created, for he will be full of strife.' What then did God do? He seized hold of Truth and cast her to the earth, as it is said [Dan. 8:12], 'Thou didst cast Truth to the ground.' "

That Truth alone is singled out for this treatment suggests the ominous possibility that all that might be said in favor of the creation of man is nothing but pious illusion; that Truth is so horrendous as to destroy everything for us unless we shun it, avoid it, evade it; that only after having cast Truth to the ground can God create man at all.

The midrash ends as follows: Then the angels of service said to God, "Lord of the universe, how canst Thou despise Thy seal? Let Truth arise from the earth, as it is said [Ps. 85:12], 'Truth springs from the earth.' "

Somehow it is possible for man to face Truth and yet to be. But do we know how?

EMIL L. FACKENHEIM [34]

25

PART II

Beginnings

THE LINES OF HEAVEN, EARTH,
AND PRIMEVAL MAN

Man in Eden

Chapter 2, verse 4, begins the tale of "earth and heaven" and particularly the epic of man. Language and tone change markedly: spare rhythms mark chapter 1; a familiar, personal, and frankly human manner when speaking of God marks what follows. He is referred to as Lord God, while before He was merely called God. The order of creation is changed, too: in chapter 1 the animals precede man, in chapter 2 the order is reversed; in chapter 1 humanity begins with male and female, in chapter 2 with male only. Where before man appeared in generic form, he now becomes concretely human: he speaks and feels. Because of these differences the two creation stories have been seen as stemming from two different traditions. The former is usually assigned to the P-source, the latter to the J-source, though this division is disputed by other scholars. In the combination of the two (that is, in the text as we now have it), chapter 1 may be seen as the *ideal* and chapter 2 as the *actual* state of creation. Thus, the derivative origin of woman in chapter 2 reflected her prevailing social condition, while ideally (as told in chapter 1) men and women were created equal.

ד אֵלֶּה תוֹלְדוֹת הַשָּׁמַיִם וְהָאָרֶץ בְּהִבָּרְאָם בְּיוֹם עֲשׂוֹת
ה יְהוָה אֱלֹהִים אֶרֶץ וְשָׁמָיִם: וְכֹל שִׂיחַ הַשָּׂדֶה טֶרֶם
יִהְיֶה בָאָרֶץ וְכָל־עֵשֶׂב הַשָּׂדֶה טֶרֶם יִצְמָח כִּי לֹא
הִמְטִיר יְהוָה אֱלֹהִים עַל־הָאָרֶץ וְאָדָם אַיִן לַעֲבֹד
ו אֶת־הָאֲדָמָה: וְאֵד יַעֲלֶה מִן־הָאָרֶץ וְהִשְׁקָה אֶת־כָּל־
פְּנֵי הָאֲדָמָה: וַיִּיצֶר יְהוָה אֱלֹהִים אֶת־הָאָדָם עָפָר
ז מִן־הָאֲדָמָה וַיִּפַּח בְּאַפָּיו נִשְׁמַת חַיִּים וַיְהִי הָאָדָם

ח לְנֶפֶשׁ חַיָּה: וַיִּטַּע יְהוָה אֱלֹהִים גַּן־בְּעֵדֶן מִקֶּדֶם
ט וַיָּשֶׂם שָׁם אֶת־הָאָדָם אֲשֶׁר יָצָר: וַיַּצְמַח יְהוָה אֱלֹהִים
מִן־הָאֲדָמָה כָּל־עֵץ נֶחְמָד לְמַרְאֶה וְטוֹב לְמַאֲכָל
י וְעֵץ הַחַיִּים בְּתוֹךְ הַגָּן וְעֵץ הַדַּעַת טוֹב וָרָע: וְנָהָר
יֹצֵא מֵעֵדֶן לְהַשְׁקוֹת אֶת־הַגָּן וּמִשָּׁם יִפָּרֵד וְהָיָה
יא לְאַרְבָּעָה רָאשִׁים: שֵׁם הָאֶחָד פִּישׁוֹן הוּא הַסֹּבֵב
יב אֵת כָּל־אֶרֶץ הַחֲוִילָה אֲשֶׁר־שָׁם הַזָּהָב: וּזֲהַב הָאָרֶץ

* ד ה זעירא.

4] Such is the story of heaven and earth when they were created. When the LORD God made earth and heaven—**5]** when no shrub of the field was yet on earth and no grasses of the field had yet sprouted, because the LORD God had not sent rain upon the earth and there was no man to till the soil, **6]** but a flow would well up from the ground and water the whole surface of the earth—**7]** the LORD God formed man from the dust of the earth. He blew into his nostrils the breath of life, and man became a living being.

8] The LORD God planted a garden in Eden, in the east, and placed there the man whom He had formed. **9]** And from the ground the LORD God caused to grow every tree that was pleasing to the sight and good for food, with the tree of life in the middle of the garden, and the tree of knowledge of good and bad.

10] A river issues from Eden to water the garden, and it then divides and becomes four branches. **11]** The name of the first is Pishon, the one that winds through the whole land of

2:4] *Such is the story.* אֵלֶּה תוֹלְדוֹת is elsewhere in Genesis rendered as "These are the lines of …" (i.e., the genealogy), making descent a keystone of biblical history. אֵלֶּה תוֹלְדוֹת serves as a heading for the major divisions of Genesis and, therefore, here too we should translate: "These are the lines of heaven and earth." In later chapters we hear of the lines of Adam, Noah, and the sons of Noah (of Shem in particular); and further, of Terah (Abraham's father), Isaac, and Jacob.

The Lord God. יְהוָה אֱלֹהִים is pronounced Adonai Elohim (see commentary to Gen. 2:4-24, "The Names of God").

7] *Man.* אָדָם (adam) is formed from the earth (אֲדָמָה, adamah). In modern terms, this is an assonance rather than correct etymology. Like-sounding words were thought to hint at a special association of concepts. An English equivalent might be: God fashioned an earthling from the earth.

Living being. A better translation than the older "living soul." The dichotomy between body and soul was of postbiblical origin [1].

8] *Eden.* A word derived ultimately from the Sumerian, where it referred originally to a specific locale noted at first for its fertility but which subsequently became barren. The word then came to have the meaning of the uncultivated steppe or hinterland generally. In the Greek translation, Paradise, an Iranian word meaning park, was used for Eden. In Jewish tradition, גַּן עֵדֶן (the Garden of Eden) came to stand for the after-death abode of the righteous; it was no longer thought of as a geographic location on earth.

10] *A river … four branches.* This concept occurs also in other cultures, notably in India and China [2].

הַהוּא טוֹב שָׁם הַבְּדֹלַח וְאֶבֶן הַשֹּׁהַם: וְשֵׁם הַנָּהָר

הַשֵּׁנִי גִּיחוֹן הוּא הַסּוֹבֵב אֵת כָּל־אֶרֶץ כּוּשׁ: וְשֵׁם־

הַנָּהָר הַשְּׁלִישִׁי חִדֶּקֶל הוּא הַהֹלֵךְ קִדְמַת אַשּׁוּר

וְהַנָּהָר הָרְבִיעִי הוּא פְרָת: וַיִּקַּח יְהוָה אֱלֹהִים אֶת־

הָאָדָם וַיַּנִּחֵהוּ בְגַן־עֵדֶן לְעָבְדָהּ וּלְשָׁמְרָהּ: וַיְצַו

יְהוָה אֱלֹהִים עַל־הָאָדָם לֵאמֹר מִכֹּל עֵץ־הַגָּן אָכֹל

תֹּאכֵל: וּמֵעֵץ הַדַּעַת טוֹב וָרָע לֹא תֹאכַל מִמֶּנּוּ כִּי

בְּיוֹם אֲכָלְךָ מִמֶּנּוּ מוֹת תָּמוּת: וַיֹּאמֶר יְהוָה אֱלֹהִים

לֹא־טוֹב הֱיוֹת הָאָדָם לְבַדּוֹ אֶעֱשֶׂה־לּוֹ עֵזֶר כְּנֶגְדּוֹ:

וַיִּצֶר יְהוָה אֱלֹהִים מִן־הָאֲדָמָה כָּל־חַיַּת הַשָּׂדֶה וְאֵת

כָּל־עוֹף הַשָּׁמַיִם וַיָּבֵא אֶל־הָאָדָם לִרְאוֹת מַה־יִּקְרָא־

לוֹ וְכֹל אֲשֶׁר יִקְרָא־לוֹ הָאָדָם נֶפֶשׁ חַיָּה הוּא שְׁמוֹ:

וַיִּקְרָא הָאָדָם שֵׁמוֹת לְכָל־הַבְּהֵמָה וּלְעוֹף הַשָּׁמַיִם

וּלְכֹל חַיַּת הַשָּׂדֶה וּלְאָדָם לֹא־מָצָא עֵזֶר כְּנֶגְדּוֹ:

וַיַּפֵּל יְהוָה אֱלֹהִים תַּרְדֵּמָה עַל־הָאָדָם וַיִּישָׁן וַיִּקַּח

אַחַת מִצַּלְעֹתָיו וַיִּסְגֹּר בָּשָׂר תַּחְתֶּנָּה: וַיִּבֶן יְהוָה

אֱלֹהִים אֶת־הַצֵּלָע אֲשֶׁר־לָקַח מִן־הָאָדָם לְאִשָּׁה

וַיְבִאֶהָ אֶל־הָאָדָם: וַיֹּאמֶר הָאָדָם זֹאת הַפַּעַם עֶצֶם

מֵעֲצָמַי וּבָשָׂר מִבְּשָׂרִי לְזֹאת יִקָּרֵא אִשָּׁה כִּי מֵאִישׁ

לֻקֳחָה־זֹּאת: עַל־כֵּן יַעֲזָב־אִישׁ אֶת־אָבִיו וְאֶת־אִמּוֹ

וְדָבַק בְּאִשְׁתּוֹ וְהָיוּ לְבָשָׂר אֶחָד:

Havilah, where the gold is. **12]** The gold of that land is good; bdellium is there, and lapis lazuli. **13]** The name of the second river is Gihon, the one that winds through the whole land of Cush. **14]** The name of the third river is Tigris, the one that flows east of Asshur. And the fourth river is the Euphrates.

15] The Lord God took the man and placed him in the garden of Eden, to till it and tend it. **16]** And the Lord God commanded the man, saying, "Of every tree of the garden you are free to eat; **17]** but as for the tree of knowledge of good and bad, you must not eat of it; for as soon as you eat of it, you shall die."

18] The Lord God said, "It is not good for man to be alone; I will make a fitting helper for him." **19]** And the Lord God formed out of the earth all the wild beasts and all the birds of the sky, and brought them to the man to see what he would call them; and whatever the man called each living creature, that would be its name. **20]** And the man gave names to all the cattle and to the birds of the sky and to all the wild beasts; but for Adam no fitting helper was found. **21]** So the Lord God cast a deep sleep upon the man; and, while he slept, He took one of his ribs and closed up the flesh at that spot. **22]** And the Lord God fashioned the rib that He had taken from the man into a woman; and He brought her to the man. **23]** Then the man said, "This one at last / Is bone of my bones / And flesh of my flesh. / This one shall be called Woman, / For from man was she taken." **24]** Hence a man leaves his father and mother and clings to his wife, so that they become one flesh.

12] *Lapis lazuli*. Others translate as "onyx"; the meaning of the Hebrew is uncertain.

13] *Cush*. Usually refers to Ethiopia or Midian, but here it is most probably the land of the Kassites, in Babylonia.

17] *Knowledge of good and bad*. Meaning "everything"; see at Deut. 29:18 for similar expressions. Others translate as "of good and evil."

As soon as you eat of it, you shall die. You shall become mortal.

21] *One of his ribs*. Some scholars suggest that this relates to a Sumerian story that knew of Nin-ti, meaning either "Lady of the Rib" or "Lady of Life" (hence the name Eve, Gen. 3:20) [3].

23] *Woman*. אִשָּׁה is here derived from אִישׁ (man).

24] *Clings to his wife*. This may be more than simply a statement of personal relationship; it may echo the custom of having the man become part of his wife's family and household (see note to Gen. 31:43).

Man and Woman

Biblical man was undoubtedly aware of the pervasive bisexual pattern of nature and knew that in this regard humanity was not different from the rest of creation. But the Torah gives this fact a special dimension by recognizing that man enters a fundamentally new state of life when he ceases to be alone. The words, "It is not good for man to be alone," speak about man's greatest need. The creation of woman becomes in effect the beginning of man's social history; man is able to fulfil his destiny completely only as a social being. Aloneness, in turn, is man's primary helplessness. Woman is more than man's female counterpart; like his rib, she is part of him, part of his structure, and without her he is essentially incomplete. The Talmud says: "He is called man only if he has a wife" [4].

However, the Bible does not see man and woman as equals. The Torah tradition is frankly male-oriented.

The Names of God

In the opening chapter of Genesis, the Creator is called "God" (Elohim), and now He is referred to as "Lord God" (Adonai Elohim). This difference has been noted since ancient days and has been the starting point for midrashic comment, as well as for modern biblical criticism, which has seen in the uses of different divine names important clues to the authorship of such passages.

Elohim (אֱלֹהִים, God or gods) is the generic term for divinity most frequently found in the Bible. It is used as a plural noun for gods of other nations and as a singular noun when applied to Israel's God. Elohim appears as an amplification of Eloah (אֱלֹהַּ), a poetic form that does not occur in Genesis, and of El (אֵל), which in Genesis occurs only in conjunction with other terms such as El Elyon (God Most High), El Bethel (God of Bethel), El Shaddai (usually rendered God Almighty), and as a part of proper names such as Israel.

Adonai (יְהֹוָה, Lord) is the unique, personal name of God and the name most frequently used in the Bible. The Torah gives the meaning of יהוה in Exod. 3:14, but that explanation is not clear. The original pronunciation was most likely Yahveh (יַהְוֶה), but since Jewish tradition permitted the name to be voiced only by the High Priest it became customary, after the destruction of the Second Temple, to substitute the word Adonai (meaning "my Lord") when reading יהוה.[1] The Masoretes who vocalized the Hebrew text (see above, General Introduction to the Torah) therefore took the vowels from the word Adonai (אֲדֹנָי) and put them with יהוה to remind the reader not to read Yahveh but Adonai. Hence, all vocalized texts of the Bible now read יְהֹוָה.[2] A Christian writer of the sixteenth century who was unaware of this substitution transcribed יְהֹוָה as he saw it, namely, as Jehovah, and this has since entered many Christian Bible translations. (See further at Exod. 6.)

Jewish tradition interprets the names Elohim and Adonai as explanations of the two sides of the nature of God, the former representing the quality of justice, the latter reflecting the quality of mercy. The Midrash says that the world was originally created by God as Elohim (Gen. 1), but that afterward He is called Adonai Elohim (Gen. 2) because He saw that without the added quality of mercy creation could not have endured.

---

[1] Orthodox Jews now go even further and use the substitutional "Adonai" only in prayer or actual Torah reading. Otherwise they substitute "Adoshem" for it and, in similar circumstances, say "Elokim" when speaking of God. They carry this respect for the sacredness of the divine name into translation as well and write "G-d" and "L-rd."

[2] However, when the combination אֲדֹנָי יהוה occurs, as in 15:2, the reading is Adonai Elohim and the vocalization is יְהֹוִה.

GLEANINGS

Another Beginning

When on high [*enuma 'elish*] the heavens had
    not been named,
Firm ground below had not been called by
    name,
Nought but primordial Apsu, their begetter,
And Mummu-Tiamat, she who bore them all,
Their waters commingling as a single body;
No reed but had been matted, no marsh land
    had appeared,
When no gods whatever had been brought into
    being,
Uncalled by name, their destinies undetermined,
Then it was that the gods were formed within
    them.   FROM "ENUMA ELISH" [5]

The Sumerian Paradise

[The Sumerian epic, "Enki and Ninhursag,"
is considerably older than "Enuma Elish." Note
also the images of lion, wolf, lamb, and kid living
peacefully in Dilmun. Well over a millennium
later, Isaiah used these images in his prophecy of
the end of time (11:6).]

The land Dilmun is clean, the land Dilmun is
    most bright.
In Dilmun the raven utters no cries,
The ittidu-bird utters not the cry of the
    ittidu-bird,
The lion kills not,
The wolf snatches not the lamb,
Unknown is the kid-devouring wild dog,
Unknown is the grain-devouring . . .,
The dove droops not the head,
The sick-eyed says not "I am sick-eyed,"
The sick-headed says not "I am sick-headed,"
Its old man says not "I am an old man."
           FROM "ENKI AND NINHURSAG" [6]

From the Dust

God took dust from the four corners of the
earth so that man might be at home everywhere.
                                      RASHI [7]

[According to Islamic legend, the dust was red,
white, and black—hence the skin colors of mankind. "At home" is represented by the possibility
of finding a suitable *permanent* home, i.e., a grave.
Every man can rest peacefully anywhere on earth.]

Solitude

In the process of naming the animals, Adam
realizes that he needs a helpmate (Gen. 2:20). How
are the two related? Man discovers his solitude
when he begins to give names, i.e., to use words,
and cannot say "man" to any other creature.

The Creation of Woman

God created woman while Adam slept so as
to prevent him from observing the divine power.
The deepest mysteries of divine creativity are
withheld from human gaze.   BENNO JACOB [8]

Undivided

Man and woman were originally undivided,
i.e., Adam was at first created bisexual, a herma-
phrodite.   MIDRASH [9]

The Original Adam

From our biblical text grew a considerable
body of ancient stories about the "Original Adam,"
Adam Harishon or *Adam Kadmon* (or *Kadmoni*) as
he was called. He was thought to have preceded
the biblical Adam and to have been a perfect man
who would return to the world at the time of
redemption. [10]

The Two Adams

The Adam of Genesis 1 was the idea of man,
and hence this ideal man never appeared on earth;
it was the Adam of Genesis 2, fashioned out of
material dust and immaterial spirit, who was the
ancestor of the race. Fashioned as he was of antithetical materials, he lived as all men live, under
the tension in which the material aspect of him

tugged in one direction, the immaterial aspect in the opposite.   PHILO [11]³

Mercy and Justice

    The quality of mercy is not strain'd,
It droppeth as the gentle rain from heaven
Upon the place beneath: it is twice bless'd;
It blesseth him that gives and him that takes:
'Tis mightiest in the mightiest; it becomes
The throned monarch better than his crown;
His sceptre shows the force of temporal power,
The attribute to awe and majesty,
Wherein doth sit the dread and fear of kings;
But mercy is above this sceptred sway,
It is enthroned in the hearts of kings,
It is an attribute to God himself,
And earthly power doth then show likest God's
When mercy seasons justice.
    WILLIAM SHAKESPEARE [12]

Blessing and Curse

    At the end of the first creation story stands a double blessing—of the first man and the first Shabbat; at the end of the second creation story stands a double curse—on the first man and the earth. Between both stands Sin. Natural man is established by a blessing; historical man by a curse. Both together form the dual nature and the dual fate of man.   MARTIN BUBER [13]

Man and Woman

    Sexuality was an aspect of beings created by YHVH and did not precede the existence of the earth or man. The animals were formed from earth as man had been, but the man rejected the animals as companions. In contrast to Enkidu in the Gilgamesh Epic, the lone man in Genesis rejected the animals, the animals did not reject the man. No woman came to seduce Adam from his wild beasts. Indeed, woman was created after the man rejected the animals and still yearned for a friend. Enkidu enjoyed the harlot, learned from her, but not even considered her as a companion. Rejected by the animals, Enkidu yearned for a friend, a man like himself. In startling contrast, Adam immediately and enthusiastically recognized the woman as his companion.
    ADRIEN J. BLEDSTEIN [14]

Man has no part in making woman. He exercises no control over her existence: He is neither participant nor spectator nor consultant at her birth. Like man, woman owes her life solely to God. To claim that the rib means inferiority or subordination is to assign the man qualities over the woman which are not in the narrative itself. Superiority, strength, aggressiveness, dominance, and power do not characterize man in Genesis 2. By contrast he is formed from dirt; his life hangs by a breath which he does not control; and he himself remains silent and passive while the Deity plans and interprets his existence.   PHYLLIS TRIBLE [15]

Good and Bad (or Evil)

    When God created man He created him with two impulses, the *yetzer ha-tov* and the *yetzer ha-ra*, both the good and evil inclination.⁴
    TALMUD [16]

When God had created man He found His work *tov me-od*, very good. Now *tov* stands for the inclination toward good and *me-od* for the opposite. But can the evil impulse be at all considered good? Yes, for were it not for this impulse no man would build a house, take a wife, or beget children.
    MIDRASH [17]

---

³ According to Philo (in Sandmel's words), "the original Adam (of Gen. 1:27) was a heavenly creation and unmixed with material things. He is the rational, preexistent soul. This soul becomes mixed with clay from the earth when God 'fashions' the earthy Adam of Gen. 2:7. There is joined to him Eve, sense-perception; but the serpent, pleasure, intrudes to divert man from lofty obligations into harmful ones. Man (mind) thereupon is quite different in his individual earthy state from what pure, generic mind was before it became mixed with body (in birth), and the mind intent on salvation must therefore free itself of the encumbrance of the body so as to regain its pristine immaterial purity."

⁴ This is derived from the spelling of וַיִּיצֶר ("formed" in 2:7), with a double י instead of one; hence each י was taken to stand for one יֵצֶר.

The Expulsion from Eden

The first two chapters of Genesis spoke of the origins of the world in its ideal condition. Now, it turns to growth, to man's actual condition, and to the problems he encounters in his humanness.

Here, once again, the underlying Near Eastern traditions that helped to shape the Eden story have been radically recast to express the specific biblical view of God and man: the transcendent Creator of all who forms man that he might freely do His will. In the Babylonian epic of "Gilgamesh" the hero loses his immortality not only through weakness but also through accident, for the serpent steals the life-giving plant. In another Near Eastern tradition, the tale of "Adapa," immortality is lost by deliberate misrepresentation. In the Bible, the loss of Eden is ultimately traceable to man's own volition and action. If man fails to live up to his potential, it is his and no one else's doing.

כה וַיִּהְיוּ שְׁנֵיהֶם עֲרוּמִּים הָאָדָם וְאִשְׁתּוֹ וְלֹא יִתְבֹּשָׁשׁוּ:
א וְהַנָּחָשׁ הָיָה עָרוּם מִכֹּל חַיַּת הַשָּׂדֶה אֲשֶׁר עָשָׂה
יְהֹוָה אֱלֹהִים וַיֹּאמֶר אֶל־הָאִשָּׁה אַף כִּי־אָמַר אֱלֹהִים
ב לֹא תֹאכְלוּ מִכֹּל עֵץ הַגָּן: וַתֹּאמֶר הָאִשָּׁה אֶל־הַנָּחָשׁ
ג מִפְּרִי עֵץ־הַגָּן נֹאכֵל: וּמִפְּרִי הָעֵץ אֲשֶׁר בְּתוֹךְ־הַגָּן
אָמַר אֱלֹהִים לֹא תֹאכְלוּ מִמֶּנּוּ וְלֹא תִגְּעוּ בּוֹ פֶּן
ד תְּמֻתוּן: וַיֹּאמֶר הַנָּחָשׁ אֶל־הָאִשָּׁה לֹא־מוֹת תְּמֻתוּן:
ה כִּי יֹדֵעַ אֱלֹהִים כִּי בְּיוֹם אֲכָלְכֶם מִמֶּנּוּ וְנִפְקְחוּ
ו עֵינֵיכֶם וִהְיִיתֶם כֵּאלֹהִים יֹדְעֵי טוֹב וָרָע: וַתֵּרֶא

הָאִשָּׁה כִּי טוֹב הָעֵץ לְמַאֲכָל וְכִי תַאֲוָה־הוּא לָעֵינַיִם
וְנֶחְמָד הָעֵץ לְהַשְׂכִּיל וַתִּקַּח מִפִּרְיוֹ וַתֹּאכַל וַתִּתֵּן
ז גַּם־לְאִישָׁהּ עִמָּהּ וַיֹּאכַל: וַתִּפָּקַחְנָה עֵינֵי שְׁנֵיהֶם וַיֵּדְעוּ
כִּי עֵירֻמִּם הֵם וַיִּתְפְּרוּ עֲלֵה תְאֵנָה וַיַּעֲשׂוּ לָהֶם
ח חֲגֹרֹת: וַיִּשְׁמְעוּ אֶת־קוֹל יְהֹוָה אֱלֹהִים מִתְהַלֵּךְ בַּגָּן
לְרוּחַ הַיּוֹם וַיִּתְחַבֵּא הָאָדָם וְאִשְׁתּוֹ מִפְּנֵי יְהֹוָה
ט אֱלֹהִים בְּתוֹךְ עֵץ הַגָּן: וַיִּקְרָא יְהֹוָה אֱלֹהִים אֶל־
י הָאָדָם וַיֹּאמֶר לוֹ אַיֶּכָּה: וַיֹּאמֶר אֶת־קֹלְךָ שָׁמַעְתִּי
יא בַּגָּן וָאִירָא כִּי־עֵירֹם אָנֹכִי וָאֵחָבֵא: וַיֹּאמֶר מִי הִגִּיד

25] The two of them were naked, the man and his wife, yet they felt no shame.

1] Now the serpent was the shrewdest of all the wild beasts that the LORD God had made. He said to the woman, "Did God really say: You shall not eat of any tree of the garden?" **2]** The woman replied to the serpent, "We may eat of the fruit of the other trees of the garden. **3]** It is only about fruit of the tree in the middle of the garden that God said: You shall not eat of it or touch it, lest you die." **4]** And the serpent said to the woman, "You are not going to die, **5]** but God knows that as soon as you eat of it your eyes will be opened and you will be like divine beings who know good and bad." **6]** When the woman saw that the tree was good for eating and a delight to the eyes, and that the tree was desirable as a source of wisdom, she took of its fruit and ate. She also gave some to her husband, and he ate. **7]** Then the eyes of both of them were opened and they perceived that they were naked; and they sewed together fig leaves and made themselves loincloths.

8] They heard the sound of the LORD God moving about in the garden at the breezy time of day; and the man and his wife hid from the LORD God among the trees of the garden. **9]** The LORD God called out to the man and said to him, "Where are you?" **10]** He replied, "I heard the sound of You in the garden, and I was afraid because I was naked, so I hid." **11]** Then He

2:25] *Naked.* עֲרוּמִּים, word play on עָרוּם (shrewd), in Gen. 3:1. The above printings of the text group verse 25 with chapter 3 because the sentence appears to introduce the subsequent story. The verse should, however, be considered a bridge, connecting one story to the other.

3:1] *The serpent.* The association of serpents with guile is an old one. In Mesopotamian, Hurrian, and Ugaritic myths serpents oppose the will of the gods; "snake" was already a derogatory term in an old Hittite document. A post-biblical book identifies the serpent of Eden with Satan and says: "Through Satan's envy death entered the world" [1]. Serpents play an important part in two incidents in Israel's history: Rods are turned into serpents by Moses and the Egyptian magicians (Exod. 4:3; 7:9–15), and serpents are agents of a

plague in the wilderness (Num. 21:6–9; cf. II Kings 18:4).

5] *Like divine beings.* אֱלֹהִים (*elohim*) usually means "God or gods" but at times also refers to celestial beings (as in Gen. 6:4) or to human judges and rulers (i.e., those who are "powerful") [2]. Another translation: "You will be like God in telling good from bad."

6] *Fruit.* Jewish tradition suggests wheat, grape, fig, or citron, all prominent Near Eastern products [3]. In Christian tradition, the fruit is generally thought to be an apple, both because it was a popular fruit in Europe and because the Latin translation of רַע (bad) is *malum* which also means apple. See further in Gleanings.

8] *Moving about.* God is pictured in human terms as inspecting His creation.

לְךָ כִּי עֵירֹם אַתָּה הֲמִן־הָעֵץ אֲשֶׁר צִוִּיתִיךָ לְבִלְתִּי
יא אֲכָל־מִמֶּנּוּ אָכָלְתָּ: וַיֹּאמֶר הָאָדָם הָאִשָּׁה אֲשֶׁר נָתַתָּה
יב עִמָּדִי הִוא נָתְנָה־לִּי מִן־הָעֵץ וָאֹכֵל: וַיֹּאמֶר יְהֹוָה
יג אֱלֹהִים לָאִשָּׁה מַה־זֹּאת עָשִׂית וַתֹּאמֶר הָאִשָּׁה הַנָּחָשׁ
יד הִשִּׁיאַנִי וָאֹכֵל: וַיֹּאמֶר יְהֹוָה אֱלֹהִים אֶל־הַנָּחָשׁ כִּי
עָשִׂיתָ זֹּאת אָרוּר אַתָּה מִכָּל־הַבְּהֵמָה וּמִכֹּל חַיַּת
הַשָּׂדֶה עַל־גְּחֹנְךָ תֵלֵךְ וְעָפָר תֹּאכַל כָּל־יְמֵי חַיֶּיךָ:
טו וְאֵיבָה אָשִׁית בֵּינְךָ וּבֵין הָאִשָּׁה וּבֵין זַרְעֲךָ וּבֵין
זַרְעָהּ הוּא יְשׁוּפְךָ רֹאשׁ וְאַתָּה תְּשׁוּפֶנּוּ עָקֵב: ס

טז אֶל־הָאִשָּׁה אָמַר הַרְבָּה אַרְבֶּה עִצְּבוֹנֵךְ וְהֵרֹנֵךְ בְּעֶצֶב
תֵּלְדִי בָנִים וְאֶל־אִישֵׁךְ תְּשׁוּקָתֵךְ וְהוּא יִמְשָׁל־בָּךְ: ס
יז וּלְאָדָם אָמַר כִּי שָׁמַעְתָּ לְקוֹל אִשְׁתֶּךָ וַתֹּאכַל מִן־
הָעֵץ אֲשֶׁר צִוִּיתִיךָ לֵאמֹר לֹא תֹאכַל מִמֶּנּוּ אֲרוּרָה
הָאֲדָמָה בַּעֲבוּרֶךָ בְּעִצָּבוֹן תֹּאכֲלֶנָּה כֹּל יְמֵי חַיֶּיךָ:
יח וְקוֹץ וְדַרְדַּר תַּצְמִיחַ לָךְ וְאָכַלְתָּ אֶת־עֵשֶׂב הַשָּׂדֶה:
יט בְּזֵעַת אַפֶּיךָ תֹּאכַל לֶחֶם עַד שׁוּבְךָ אֶל־הָאֲדָמָה כִּי
מִמֶּנָּה לֻקָּחְתָּ כִּי־עָפָר אַתָּה וְאֶל־עָפָר תָּשׁוּב:
כ וַיִּקְרָא הָאָדָם שֵׁם אִשְׁתּוֹ חַוָּה כִּי הִוא הָיְתָה אֵם

asked, "Who told you that you were naked? Did you eat of the tree from which I had forbidden you to eat?" **12]** The man said, "The woman You put at my side—she gave me of the tree, and I ate." **13]** And the LORD God said to the woman, "What is this you have done!" The woman replied "The serpent duped me, and I ate." **14]** Then the LORD God said to the serpent, "Because you did this, / More cursed shall you be / Than all cattle / And all the wild beasts: / On your belly shall you crawl / And dirt shall you eat / All the days of your life. / **15]** I will put enmity / Between you and the woman, / And between your offspring and hers; / They shall strike at your head, / And you shall strike at their heel." **16]** And to the woman He said, "I will make most severe / Your pangs in childbearing; / In pain shall you bear children. / Yet your urge shall be for your husband, / And he shall rule over you."

17] To Adam He said, "Because you did as your wife said and ate of the tree about which I commanded you, 'You shall not eat of it,' Cursed be the ground because of you; / By toil shall you eat of it / All the days of your life: / **18]** Thorns and thistles shall it sprout for you. / But your food shall be the grasses of the field; / **19]** By the sweat of your brow / Shall you get bread to eat, / Until you return to the ground— / For from it you were taken. / For dust you are, / And to dust you shall return."

20] The man named his wife Eve, because she was the mother of all the living. **21]** And the

14] *More cursed ... than all cattle.* Lower than cattle, which at least have legs to walk on.

16] *In pain shall you bear.* An explanation of birth pangs. Note also the expression "woman's curse" for menstruation.

17] *Cursed be the ground.* The earth was thought to share in man's guilt. "When man corrupts his way the land is corrupted" [4].

By toil shall you eat. Man's need to work appears to be part of God's curse. The Rabbis, however, interpreted God's dictum as a concession:

By work man is able to fend for and feed himself.

/ The Rabbis further interpreted that the task of providing human sustenance is God's greatest problem [5]./

20] *Eve.* חַוָּה (chavah); the text explains the name by connecting it with "living" (חַי, chai), but the true etymology of the name is obscure. This is probably a case of assonance. "Mother of all the living" may be an honorific title, like "Mother of all gods" in the "Atrahasis" epic.

כא כָּל־חָי: וַיַּעַשׂ יְהֹוָה אֱלֹהִים לְאָדָם וּלְאִשְׁתּוֹ כָּתְנוֹת
עוֹר וַיַּלְבִּשֵׁם: פ

כב וַיֹּאמֶר יְהֹוָה אֱלֹהִים הֵן הָאָדָם הָיָה כְּאַחַד מִמֶּנּוּ
לָדַעַת טוֹב וָרָע וְעַתָּה פֶּן־יִשְׁלַח יָדוֹ וְלָקַח גַּם מֵעֵץ
כג הַחַיִּים וְאָכַל וָחַי לְעֹלָם: וַיְשַׁלְּחֵהוּ יְהֹוָה אֱלֹהִים
מִגַּן־עֵדֶן לַעֲבֹד אֶת־הָאֲדָמָה אֲשֶׁר לֻקַּח מִשָּׁם:
כד וַיְגָרֶשׁ אֶת־הָאָדָם וַיַּשְׁכֵּן מִקֶּדֶם לְגַן־עֵדֶן אֶת־הַכְּרֻבִים
וְאֵת לַהַט הַחֶרֶב הַמִּתְהַפֶּכֶת לִשְׁמֹר אֶת־דֶּרֶךְ עֵץ־
הַחַיִּים: ס

LORD God made garments of skins for Adam and his wife, and clothed them.

22] And the LORD God said, "Now that the man has become like one of us, knowing good and bad, what if he should stretch out his hand and take also from the tree of life and eat, and live forever!" **23]** So the LORD God banished him from the garden of Eden, to till the soil from which he was taken. **24]** He drove the man out, and stationed east of the garden of Eden the cherubim and the fiery ever-turning sword, to guard the way to the tree of life.

24] *Cherubim.* Legendary winged beings who protect sacred places.
The flaming sword may represent bolts of lightning.

The Tree of Knowledge

Adam and Eve are depicted as living in an environment of ease, free from pain and worry. Man's only task is to till and tend the garden, as a steward of his Creator.[1] The tale of expulsion, of "Paradise Lost," which relates how man came to forfeit this condition, has been the subject of much theological speculation, which in turn has had a profound effect on the religious and psychological orientations of Western society.

At the center of the story, as in the middle of the garden, stands the Tree of Knowledge. The tree is unique to biblical tradition, and three major interpretations have been offered to explain it.

Ethical Interpretation. Eating from the Tree of Knowledge of good and bad (or "good and evil" as most older translations render it) provided man with moral discrimination and thereby made him capable of committing sin. Yielding to the serpent's temptation and eating the fruit were two parts of the same act; once it was done, the relationship of man to God was essentially changed. Man's expulsion from Eden meant that he could never return to his former state of ethical indifference; he had become a "choosing" creature. Two radically different theologies developed from this interpretation:

Christianity, building on certain, largely sectarian Jewish teachings,[2] taught that after Adam's transgression all men were inherently evil. In this interpretation the event has come to be known as "the fall of man," an expression absent from the Bible itself and from Jewish literature. "By one man, sin entered the world," says Paul in the Christian Scripture and again: "by the offense of one, judgment came upon all men to condemnation" [8]. An old New England primer put it simply: "In Adam's fall we sinned all." This was man's original sin, a fatal flaw, from which he could be redeemed only after Jesus came into the world as the Christ. Without faith in him as the redemptive savior men would live and die in their original sin. In the course of centuries the doctrine of man's inherent sinfulness led to a thoroughly pessimistic view of man and a heavy emphasis on the right kind of faith.[3]

The mainstream of Judaism refused to make the tale of Eden an important part of its world view and maintained that the only road to salvation was through godly deeds (*mitzvot*), rather than through belief in a savior, and that, while man tended to corruption (Gen. 6:5; 8:21), he was not basically a corrupt creature. Though he was constantly exposed to the evil impulse (יֵצֶר הָרַע), by carrying out God's commandments he could overcome or at least control it and thereby could develop his impulse for good (יֵצֶר טוֹב). The more closely he attended to *mitzvot*, the greater would be his protection from sin.

Intellectual Interpretation. In the Bible, the expression "good and bad" (טוֹב וָרַע) sometimes means "everything" (Deut. 1:39; II Sam.

---

[1] In Babylonian mythology, the task of raising food for the gods was the main reason for the creation of man [6].

[2] Especially, "O thou Adam, what hast thou done! For though it was thou that sinned, the fall was not thine alone, but ours also who are descendants" [7].

[3] God's judgment on Adam ("For dust you are and to dust you shall return") is spoken by the Catholic priest as he puts ashes on the worshiper's head on Ash Wednesday. The Mormons, however, say: "We believe that men will be punished for their own sins and not for Adam's transgressions" (Second Article of Faith). Original sin was also denied by the Pelagians (fifth century C.E.), who held that it was transmitted by bad example.

[4] Ethical interpretation: If Adam and Eve had no understanding of right and wrong, how could they be punished for their ignorance?

Intellectual interpretation: Man, having eaten of

19:35), as when we say, "I know its good and its bad features," meaning that I know everything about it that can be known [9]. The tale may therefore be understood to say that primal man ate of the Tree of Omniscience. Having tasted of it, man forever after will attempt to know everything; he will, in other words, play the part of God.

This intellectual overreaching is what the Greeks called *hubris*, self-exaltation. Man strives to be godlike, but God will not permit him to become "like one of us." When man persists in deifying his own powers, God will call him to account and exact a terrible punishment. Like Adam, man will have to leave his Eden, his desire for divine power turned back by the flaming sword at the gate of attainment [10].

Sexual Interpretation. The Eden story may also be read as the discovery not of man's ethical or intellectual knowledge but of his sexuality. This is suggested by the Hebrew word for "knowledge" (דַעַת), which has the meaning of experience, especially of sexual experience. Note that the story of the expulsion from Eden begins with a discovery of nakedness and sexual shame (Gen. 3:7). (Other ancient sources also stress the sexual theme, see Gleanings.)

Reading the Eden tale in this light we see a link between the Tree of (Sexual) Knowledge and the Tree of Life. The latter, whose fruit would have bestowed earthly immortality, is no longer accessible. Man must now perpetuate his species through procreation, in the same way as other creatures do. But being man, his sexuality has a special dimension; his process of passing from childhood to adulthood, from innocence to maturity, is shot through with love and pain. Each man repeats in his person the journey from Eden into the world. As a child he lives in a garden of innocence; when he discovers his sexual impulse and grows up, he must leave the garden forever.

Summary. All three interpretations do justice to the story, although there is some textual objection in each case.[4] Whatever intent went into the earliest strands of the story, the three major themes outlined above have been thoroughly interwoven so that the fabric of the text exhibits not one theme but all and each is discernible, depending on the light in which the text is viewed.

This becomes particularly evident when we ask the questions: How did the storyteller view the intention of God? What did he believe God wanted man to be? Thoroughly obedient or potentially defiant? A moral automaton or a free spirit? Did God want man to stay in Eden? And what was the punishment? Man was, in the end, "condemned" to be human.

These questions arise not only from the biblical text but also, in a wider sense, from the very creation of man. Man eats the tantalizing fruit, only to meet with disappointment and frustration. His is an act of

the Tree of Knowledge is said to have become like God. However, man does not in fact attain omniscience. Note also the question put to Maimonides, "It is a thing to be wondered at that man's punishment for his disobedience should consist in his being granted a perfection that he did not possess before, namely, the intellect." Maimonides' answer: "There is a difference between 'necessary' and 'apparent' truths. Before his sin Adam knew the former, afterwards the latter" [11].

Sexual interpretation: In Gen. 3:22, after the eating of the fruit, God says that man has now "become like one of us, knowing good and bad." If "knowing" here refers to sexuality, it would be in contrast to the biblical concept of a God who otherwise never bears a tinge of sexuality. For this reason the ancients suggested that Adam and Eve had marital relations *before* they ate of the fruit [12]. The biblical Eve can also be compared to the harlot in "Gilgamesh" as an agent of civilization [13].

disobedience and defiance, yet at the same time of growth and liberation. God appears to provide man with the possibility of remaining in Eden, but the very temptation of knowledge makes this impossible. God tempts man to be like Him, but, when man yields, God rejects the attempt decisively.

Thus the emergence of that contradictory creature called man is in itself a process of contradictions. Adam is free to defy God, at a price, and the theme of man's defiance runs through much of the Bible. For while man's freedom may be limited in all other respects, he must believe that toward God his freedom is without limits [14].

The Tree of Life

Questions of immortality were of central concern to many ancient peoples, and it was widely believed that eating or drinking a sacred substance might bestow eternal life. Egyptian mythology spoke of a sycamore from which the gods obtained their immortality, the Greeks told of ambrosia, and the Indians of soma. Gilgamesh was promised access to a life-giving sea plant, and the "Adapa" tale spoke of magical bread and water. Some Christian sacraments, though they have long been spiritualized, still reflect their origins in the tree-of-life motif. The Bible, however, while retaining the symbolism of a life-endowing tree, gives it a minor role (which explains why no prohibition is issued to Adam in this respect) and shifts its main attention to the Tree of Knowledge. The latter, whatever meaning assigned to its "knowledge," in effect became a Tree of Death, for eating of its fruit caused expulsion from Eden and the permanent inaccessibility of any magical fruit from the Tree of Life. By choosing "knowledge," man attained death. Immortality and knowledge are pictured as incompatible in the human sphere; man desires both but cannot have both.[5] Since man chose knowledge, mortality is now built into the very structure of human life, distinguishing creature from Creator.[6] By procreating, man can in part overcome death, but, like the rest of the creatures, he cannot "be like God."

---

[5] "Only ignorance holds life and human knowledge, death" [15]. The "Adapa" tale also deals with man being offered life but choosing death, a theme recurring in the Bible, which may be viewed as a guide to those who want to mitigate the effects of the choice [16].

[6] Midrash Tanchuma speculates that God created the Angel of Death before He created man, thus relating man's mortality not to human sin so much as to Providence itself and that, in fact, "death is good" [17]. The Talmud records a rabbinical debate which concludes that there is "death without sin" [18].

GLEANINGS

The Civilization of Savage Man

[Gilgamesh suggests that Enkidu, the savage man who dwells with beasts, be seduced by a woman and thereby be enticed away from his savage companions. Thus he would be civilized. Compare this passage to the sexual interpretation of the biblical Eden story.]

She treated him, the savage, to a woman's task,
As his love was drawn unto her.
For six days and seven nights Enkidu comes forth, mating with the lass.
After he had his fill of her charms,
He set his face toward his wild beasts.

On seeing him, Enkidu, the gazelles ran off,
The wild beasts of the steppe drew away from his body.
Enkidu had to slacken his pace—it was not as before;
But he now had wisdom, broader understanding . . .
The harlot says to him, to Enkidu:
"Thou art wise, Enkidu, art become like a god."

FROM "GILGAMESH" [19]

The Serpent Speaking

The serpent is the symbol of pleasure. It is said to have uttered a human voice, because pleasure employs innumerable champions and defenders who take care to advocate its interests and who dare to assert that it should exercise power over everything. PHILO [20]

Or Touch It (Gen. 3:3)

Eve said to the serpent that she was not even allowed to touch the fruit, although this was not part of the original prohibition. The Rabbis consider this (and any) embroidery of the truth to be the opening wedge of sin. [21]

They Perceived That They Were Naked (Gen. 3:7)

Man is the being who shudders at his own naturalness.

CARL FRIEDRICH VON WEIZSÄCKER [22]

Where Are You? (Gen. 3:9)

Did God not know where Adam was? He asked in order to open the way to repentance.

MIDRASH [23]

I Was Afraid Because I Was Naked (Gen. 3:10)

Not physical, but religious nakedness is meant. Adam was afraid because by his transgression he was stripped of the one commandment he had received. Man without a *mitzvah* is truly naked.

MIDRASH [24]

Paradise Lost

Of Man's First Disobedience, and the Fruit
Of that Forbidden Tree, whose mortal taste
Brought Death into the World, and all our woe,
With loss of *Eden* . . .
Sing, Heav'nly Muse . . .   JOHN MILTON [25]
[To Milton, as to much of the Christian tradition, the serpent was Satan incarnate.]

Freedom

Man has freedom, he can choose God or reject God, he can lead the world to perdition and to redemption. The creation of this being Man with such power of freedom means that God has made room for a co-determining power alongside of Himself. Man is the crossroad of the world.

HENRY SLONIMSKY [26]

The Eden of the World-to-Come

In Jewish and Christian traditions, Paradise or *Gan-Eden* also becomes a projection of the future. In the messianic era men will return to the harmony of Eden (see note to Gen. 2:8). This expecta-

tion is also applied to the afterlife of the righteous who will join the angels in singing the praises of God and in studying the holy books.

The traditional prayer book (*siddur*), in the memorial prayer (*El male rachamim*), asks God to accept the departed in Eden; the Reform prayer book has omitted the phrase.

A Controversy

For two years and a half the House of Shammai and the House of Hillel were arguing. The former said: "It would have been better if man had not been created." The latter said: "Better that he was created than that he had not been created." They concluded that it would have been better if man had not been created but, now that he has been created, let him examine his past deeds. Some say: "Let him consider his future actions."

TALMUD [27]

The Cherubim

According to tradition, they were angels of destruction, while those hovering over the ark [Exod. 25:22] were guardian angels. All had the faces of children. From this we may learn that if a child is trained properly he resembles the cherubim of the ark; if not, those of Eden.

MOSHE MORDECAI EPSTEIN [28]

Not against God

We can, objectively considered, speak of a "fall" of the soul of the primeval light man, only by overemphasizing the moral factor. The soul, certainly, has sinned against itself, frivolously sacrificing its original blissful and peaceful state—but not against God in the sense of offending any prohibition of His in its passional enterprise, for such a prohibition, at least according to the doctrine we have received, was not issued. True, pious tradition has handed down to us the command of God to the first man, not to eat of the tree of the "knowledge of good and evil"; but we must remember that we are here dealing with a secondary and already earthly event and with human beings who had with God's own creative aid been generated out of the knowledge of matter by the soul; if God really set this test, He undoubtedly knew beforehand how it would turn out, and the only obscurity lies in the question, why He did not refrain from issuing a prohibition which, being disobeyed, would simply add to the malicious joy of His angelic host, whose attitude towards man was already most unfavourable. But the expression "good and evil" is a recognized and admitted gloss upon the text, and what we are really dealing with is knowledge, which has as its consequence not the ability to distinguish between good and evil but rather death itself; so that we need scarcely doubt that the "prohibition" too is a well-meant but not very pertinent addition of the same kind.

THOMAS MANN [29]

The Fruit

The "fruit of the tree" from which Adam and Eve ate is not specified in the text. The Rabbis speculated that it was the fig (because it is subsequently mentioned, 3:7); or the grape (because its abuse leads one to forget his senses, 9:20 f.); or the *etrog* (because the word was seen as deriving from *ragag*, to desire); or wheat (because the Hebrew word for wheat, *chitah*, was seen as related to *chet*, sin); or that it was the carob, the Hebrew word suggesting destruction [30].

Sex and Death

Sex and death become known simultaneously. How are the two related? They constitute the opposing extremes of pleasure and agony. They are also the beginning and the end of life. . . . Consciousness of sex and time is associated in the tale with the fear of death which, according to modern psychology, is the basis of man's self-awareness and his need for self-expression in art and religion. Our present knowledge marks a time between approximately 40,000 and 80,000 years ago for the process conceptualized in this tale.

AVRAHAM RONEN [31]

Cain and Abel

Man's eviction from Eden and his consequent mortality imply a transfer of important powers from God to man. Both the creation and termination of life now rest with man—the former "with the help of the Lord" (Gen. 4:1), the latter in defiance of God (the killing of Abel). In the story of Cain and Abel, man's relationship to God is explored in a social setting. It is in the context of human relationships that choices between good and evil will henceforth have to be made. And it is in this context that the interplay between human and divine responsibility must be viewed.

The story of the brothers also introduces a secondary theme that will recur often in the Bible: the struggle between siblings. Time after time our sympathies are directed toward the younger one, and, even when like Abel he dies, it is a still younger sibling, Seth, who provides the link with the future.*

---

* Note the struggle between Jacob and Esau and between Joseph and his brothers. The first-born is often passed over: Ishmael, Reuben, Aaron, etc. This pattern may reflect a protest against the institution of primogeniture (see commentary to Gen. 25:19–34). The theme persists in later folklore.

נָפְלוּ פָנֶיךָ: הֲלוֹא אִם־תֵּיטִיב שְׂאֵת וְאִם לֹא תֵיטִיב ז

לַפֶּתַח חַטָּאת רֹבֵץ וְאֵלֶיךָ תְּשׁוּקָתוֹ וְאַתָּה תִּמְשָׁל־

בּוֹ: וַיֹּאמֶר קַיִן אֶל־הֶבֶל אָחִיו וַיְהִי בִּהְיוֹתָם בַּשָּׂדֶה ח

וַיָּקָם קַיִן אֶל־הֶבֶל אָחִיו וַיַּהַרְגֵהוּ: וַיֹּאמֶר יְהוָה אֶל־ ט

קַיִן אֵי הֶבֶל אָחִיךָ וַיֹּאמֶר לֹא יָדַעְתִּי הֲשֹׁמֵר אָחִי

אָנֹכִי: וַיֹּאמֶר מֶה עָשִׂיתָ קוֹל דְּמֵי אָחִיךָ צֹעֲקִים י

אֵלַי מִן־הָאֲדָמָה: וְעַתָּה אָרוּר אָתָּה מִן־הָאֲדָמָה יא

אֲשֶׁר פָּצְתָה אֶת־פִּיהָ לָקַחַת אֶת־דְּמֵי אָחִיךָ מִיָּדֶךָ:

וְהָאָדָם יָדַע אֶת־חַוָּה אִשְׁתּוֹ וַתַּהַר וַתֵּלֶד אֶת־קַיִן א

וַתֹּאמֶר קָנִיתִי אִישׁ אֶת־יְהוָה: וַתֹּסֶף לָלֶדֶת אֶת־ ב

אָחִיו אֶת־הָבֶל וַיְהִי־הֶבֶל רֹעֵה צֹאן וְקַיִן הָיָה עֹבֵד

אֲדָמָה: וַיְהִי מִקֵּץ יָמִים וַיָּבֵא קַיִן מִפְּרִי הָאֲדָמָה ג

מִנְחָה לַיהוָה: וְהֶבֶל הֵבִיא גַם־הוּא מִבְּכֹרוֹת צֹאנוֹ ד

וּמֵחֶלְבֵהֶן וַיִּשַׁע יְהוָה אֶל־הֶבֶל וְאֶל־מִנְחָתוֹ: וְאֶל־ ה

קַיִן וְאֶל־מִנְחָתוֹ לֹא שָׁעָה וַיִּחַר לְקַיִן מְאֹד וַיִּפְּלוּ

פָנָיו: וַיֹּאמֶר יְהוָה אֶל־קָיִן לָמָּה חָרָה לָךְ וְלָמָּה ו

1] Now the man knew his wife Eve, and she conceived and bore Cain, saying, "I have gained a male child with the help of the LORD." 2] She then bore his brother Abel. Abel became a keeper of sheep, and Cain became a tiller of the soil. 3] In the course of time, Cain brought an offering to the LORD from the fruit of the soil; 4] and Abel, for his part, brought the choicest of the firstlings of his flock. The LORD paid heed to Abel and his offering, 5] but to Cain and his offering He paid no heed. Cain was much distressed and his face fell. 6] And the LORD said to Cain, "Why are you distressed, / And why is your face fallen? / 7] Surely, if you do right, / There is uplift. / But if you do not do right / Sin couches at the door; / Its urge is toward you, / Yet you can be its master."

8] Cain said to his brother Abel...and when they were in the field, Cain set upon his brother Abel and killed him. 9] The LORD said to Cain, "Where is your brother Abel?" And he said, "I do not know. Am I my brother's keeper?" 10] Then He said, "What have you done? Hark, your brother's blood cries out to Me from the ground! 11] Therefore, you shall be more cursed than the ground, which opened its mouth to receive your brother's blood from

---

4:1] *Knew.* On the use of יָדַע (*yada*) in the sense of sexual experience, see commentary to Gen. 2:25–3:24, "Sexual Interpretation."

Cain. The name is explained in the text by a word play (קַיִן-קָנִיתִי, *kayin–kaniti*)—"I have gained [or made] a male child with the help of the Lord."

/Others: "I have bought a male offspring from the Lord," reflecting the idea that the first-born belongs to God and must be bought from Him (see Num. 3:46–47 and note the surviving ceremony of *pidyon ha-ben*, redemption of the first-born son). Some commentators see in Cain the ancestor of the Kenites, nomadic tribesmen in the Negev who earned their living as itinerant tinkers and smiths (*kenaya* in Aramaic, *kaynum* in Arabic). Thus the lowly status of the Kenites in later days would be explained by the curse put upon their progenitor [1]./

2] *Abel.* The name is not explained in the text. /The Hebrew הֶבֶל usually means "breath" or "puff"

or "vanity" as in Ps. 144:4: "Man is like a breath, his days are as a passing shadow," or as in Job 7:16: "My days are as a breath."/

4] *Choicest.* An idiomatic rendering of the Hebrew, literally, "the fat of" [2].

7] *There is uplift.* From your distress. Or, from the descent into evil. The meaning of the Hebrew is not clear, and any translation is merely an educated guess.

Sin couches at the door. Others translate as "sin is the demon at the door." Cain is free to choose good or evil.

/The suggestion is that רבץ is connected with the Akkadian word for demon [3]./

8] *Cain said to his brother Abel.* The text does not quote what was said. The Septuagint and Targum supply these words: "Come, let us go out into the field" [4].

/However, the omission of what Cain said may be a purposeful ellipsis [5]./

יב כִּי תַעֲבֹד אֶת־הָאֲדָמָה לֹא־תֹסֵף תֵּת־כֹּחָהּ לָךְ נָע
וָנָד תִּהְיֶה בָאָרֶץ: יג וַיֹּאמֶר קַיִן אֶל־יְהוָה גָּדוֹל עֲוֺנִי
מִנְּשֹׂא: יד הֵן גֵּרַשְׁתָּ אֹתִי הַיּוֹם מֵעַל פְּנֵי הָאֲדָמָה
וּמִפָּנֶיךָ אֶסָּתֵר וְהָיִיתִי נָע וָנָד בָּאָרֶץ וְהָיָה כָל־מֹצְאִי
יַהַרְגֵנִי: טו וַיֹּאמֶר לוֹ יְהוָה לָכֵן כָּל־הֹרֵג קַיִן שִׁבְעָתַיִם
יֻקָּם וַיָּשֶׂם יְהוָה לְקַיִן אוֹת לְבִלְתִּי הַכּוֹת־אֹתוֹ כָּל־
מֹצְאוֹ: טז וַיֵּצֵא קַיִן מִלִּפְנֵי יְהוָה וַיֵּשֶׁב בְּאֶרֶץ־נוֹד
קִדְמַת־עֵדֶן: יז וַיֵּדַע קַיִן אֶת־אִשְׁתּוֹ וַתַּהַר וַתֵּלֶד אֶת־
חֲנוֹךְ וַיְהִי בֹּנֶה עִיר וַיִּקְרָא שֵׁם הָעִיר כְּשֵׁם בְּנוֹ חֲנוֹךְ:

יח וַיִּוָּלֵד לַחֲנוֹךְ אֶת־עִירָד וְעִירָד יָלַד אֶת־מְחוּיָאֵל
וּמְחִיּיָאֵל יָלַד אֶת־מְתוּשָׁאֵל וּמְתוּשָׁאֵל יָלַד אֶת־לָמֶךְ:
יט וַיִּקַּח־לוֹ לֶמֶךְ שְׁתֵּי נָשִׁים שֵׁם הָאַחַת עָדָה וְשֵׁם
הַשֵּׁנִית צִלָּה: כ וַתֵּלֶד עָדָה אֶת־יָבָל הוּא הָיָה אֲבִי
יֹשֵׁב אֹהֶל וּמִקְנֶה: כא וְשֵׁם אָחִיו יוּבָל הוּא הָיָה אֲבִי כָּל־
תֹּפֵשׂ כִּנּוֹר וְעוּגָב: כב וְצִלָּה גַם־הִוא יָלְדָה אֶת־תּוּבַל
קַיִן לֹטֵשׁ כָּל־חֹרֵשׁ נְחֹשֶׁת וּבַרְזֶל וַאֲחוֹת תּוּבַל־קַיִן
נַעֲמָה: כג וַיֹּאמֶר לֶמֶךְ לְנָשָׁיו עָדָה וְצִלָּה שְׁמַעַן קוֹלִי
נְשֵׁי לֶמֶךְ הַאְזֵנָּה אִמְרָתִי כִּי אִישׁ הָרַגְתִּי לְפִצְעִי וְיֶלֶד

your hand.   12] If you till the soil, it shall no longer yield its strength to you. You shall become a ceaseless wanderer on earth.''

13] Cain said to the LORD, ''My punishment is too great to bear!   14] Since You have banished me this day from the soil, and I must avoid Your presence and become a restless wanderer on earth—anyone who meets me may kill me!''   15] The LORD said to him, ''I promise, if anyone kills Cain, sevenfold vengeance shall be taken on him.'' And the LORD put a mark on Cain, lest anyone who met him should kill him.   16] Cain left the presence of the LORD and settled in the land of Nod, east of Eden.

17] Cain knew his wife, and she conceived and bore Enoch. And he then founded a city, and named the city after his son Enoch.   18] To Enoch was born Irad, and Irad begot Mehujael, and Mehujael begot Methusael, and Methusael begot Lamech.   19] Lamech took to himself two wives: the name of the one was Adah, and the name of the other was Zillah.   20] Adah bore Jabal; he was the ancestor of those who dwell in tents and amidst herds.   21] And the name of his brother was Jubal; he was the ancestor of all who play the lyre and the pipe.   22] As for Zillah, she bore Tubal-cain, who forged all implements of copper and iron. And the sister of Tubal-cain was Naamah.

23] And Lamech said to his wives, ''Adah and Zillah, hear my voice; / O wives of Lamech, give ear to my speech. / I have slain a man for wounding me, / And a lad for bruising me. /

12] *A ceaseless wanderer.* The banished Cain did settle, but in the land of Nod, the land of "restlessness" (Gen. 4:16), for nowhere could he be at rest.

14] *You have banished me this day from the soil.* Which had sustained him as a farmer. Cain is punished by being exiled from his accustomed environment, from his occupation, and also from access to God. Human life, according to the Bible, is sacred; its wanton destruction is seen as a crime against God himself [6].

15] *I promise.* When God says לָכֵן (*lachen*, assuredly), it is a promise [7].

Sevenfold. Here meaning "many times."

A mark. Not a brand of rejection but a sign of protection against blood revenge.

לְקַיִן אוֹת/ is read by some scholars as: "And the Lord put Cain as a mark," i.e., Cain himself was the sign that warned men against murder. Medieval Christianity justified the Jewish badge as a "mark of Cain."/

23–24] It is not clear why the Bible recorded this fragment. Lamech's song is possibly meant to relate his invention of weapons to his vengefulness or brutal arrogance. His life span of 777 years (Gen. 5:31) is a sequence of the 7 and 77 of Gen. 4:24.

כד לְחַבְּרָתִי: כִּי שִׁבְעָתַיִם יֻקַּם־קָיִן וְלֶמֶךְ שִׁבְעִים   כו כִּי הֲרָגוֹ קָיִן: וּלְשֵׁת גַּם־הוּא יֻלַּד־בֵּן וַיִּקְרָא אֶת־שְׁמוֹ

כה וְשִׁבְעָה: וַיֵּדַע אָדָם עוֹד אֶת־אִשְׁתּוֹ וַתֵּלֶד בֵּן וַתִּקְרָא   אֱנוֹשׁ אָז הוּחַל לִקְרֹא בְּשֵׁם יְהוָה: ס

אֶת־שְׁמוֹ שֵׁת כִּי שָׁת־לִי אֱלֹהִים זֶרַע אַחֵר תַּחַת הָבֶל

24] If Cain is avenged sevenfold, / Then Lamech seventy-sevenfold."

25] Adam knew his wife again, and she bore a son and named him Seth, meaning, "God has provided me with another offspring in place of Abel," for Cain had killed him.   **26]** And to Seth, in turn, a son was born, and he named him Enosh. It was then that men began to invoke the LORD by name.

/ It has been suggested that verse 24 be understood: "If Cain is avenged two times seven, then Lamech seventy-seven." This is based on the sequence $2 \times 7 = 1^2 + 2^2 + 3^2$ and $77 = 4^2 + 5^2 + 6^2$, reflecting the pervasive number symbolism of Genesis [8]. See also at 5:23 and Gleanings to chapter 25./

25] *God has provided.* A word play, שֵׁת־שָׁת (Seth-provided).

26] *Enosh.* A poetic term for "man."

Began to invoke the Lord. Antediluvian man is pictured as being close to God and knowing Him by name [9].

Farmer and Shepherd

Much of Israel's early history is connected with shepherds, the nomadic life, and experiences encountered in traveling through desert lands. The Patriarchs were nomads or semi-nomads, and both Moses and David were shepherds. The nomad looked upon all settlers, urban as well as rural, with contempt: They were slaves to possession and therefore prone to corruption and idolatry.

Cain is a farmer, a settler, and Abel is a shepherd. One reading of the story suggests that the brothers represent man's two original cultures in tension.[1] It is interesting to note, however, that Cain is *condemned* to be a nomad. If the nomadic way of life is, indeed, superior, why this choice of punishment? Most probably, the farmer–shepherd theme contributed to the original story but was blurred in later generations. From time to time, the Bible returns to this theme, and especially when the city is portrayed as an object of distrust (see commentary to Gen. 11:1–26, "The City").

The Rejected Sacrifice

Both Cain and Abel bring sacrifices to God—only Abel's is accepted; the biblical writer offers no explanation for God's choice.

Some commentators maintain that the key to God's preference may be found in the intent of the two worshipers. While Cain brings merely "an offering," Abel brings "the choicest" of his flock. One performs outward motions, the other offers the service of his heart [10].

A better interpretation, however, is that God's rejection of Cain's offering is inexplicable in human terms. God acts in accordance with His own wisdom: "I will be gracious to whom I will be gracious" (Exod. 33:19). His reasons are unknown to man. The inexplicability of divine preferment marks Cain as an essentially tragic character; he reacts with blind violence to a rejection he cannot comprehend. "We are accustomed to think of him with revulsion: but the text of Genesis aims rather at evoking our sympathy for a man who atoned for his crime with homelessness and fear—a fate worse than death" [11].

Am I My Brother's Keeper?

Few phrases have been quoted more often than this bold counter-question that Cain flings back at God. But the meaning is far from clear. The following explanations have been suggested:

The question implies the answer, for by asking the question of God Cain acknowledges a higher moral authority. There is someone to whom man must answer for his deeds.

The theme is human responsibility. God, by the punishment He metes out, asserts that Cain was indeed his brother's keeper.

Cain's question is essentially defiant: "How would I know—or care?" Cain, the first product of the post-Eden world, is a man who defies God himself. "The idea of man's rebelliousness, by which Genesis explains the origins of the human condition, is a fundamental idea of biblical literature and of Israelite religion in general. One might call the Bible a chronicle of human rebellion" [12].

According to Rabbi Shimon bar Yochai, when God asked Cain "Where is your brother Abel?" Cain answered "Am *I* my brother's keeper? *You* are God. You have created man. It is Your task to watch him, not mine. If I ought not to have done what I did, You could have prevented me from doing it." Thus, Cain makes God responsible or at least co-responsible for his own actions.

Note that God does not reply. The question, "Am *I* my brother's keeper?" remains unanswered and has remained so despite the

---

[1] It also appears in Sumerian literature, but as a more friendly rivalry.

questions of succeeding generations. Why is God silent when men kill each other? Where does His power begin and where does it end? God asks man to account for his deeds. Man in turn asks God to account for His. Am I alone my brother's keeper? Are You not as well? If my brother's blood cries out against me, does it not cry out against You, too?[2]

This interpretation is appealing not only because it asks questions of great urgency today but also because it allows for a direct continuation of the Eden story. There, man's choice was essentially between life and death; now, in the post-Eden world, God offers man a new choice, the choice between good and evil. Cain chooses murder, the ultimate evil. And having granted man moral freedom, God, in a sense, shares in man's transgressions. But though man may ask where God was in the hour of violence, God's failure to answer does not reduce man's responsibility.

---

[2] Rabbi Shimon emphasizes this by pointing out that a slight shift in Gen. 4:10 (עלי instead of אלי) would make God, who now accuses Cain by stating, "Your brother's blood cries out *to* Me," say sorrowfully, "Your brother's blood cries out *against* Me." Rabbi Shimon, aware of the implications of his comment, says: "It is difficult to say such a thing [i.e., to read the text as it ought to be read] and the mouth cannot utter it [as it would imply the blaming of God]." He compared the God–Cain–Abel triangle to two gladiators fighting before a king. The ruler could stop the contest any minute, but he lets it proceed to the bitter, deadly end. Is he not, by his silence, involved in the killing [13]? Also note the talmudic saying: "Man does not lift a finger unless it is decreed from above" [14].

GLEANINGS

Cain Was Tested

The text says of sin that "its urge is toward you" [Gen. 4:7]. This implies that sin wants to be conquered by man; but if man fails to conquer it, sin returns to God and accuses man.

SAMSON RAPHAEL HIRSCH

[This interpretation suggests that Cain was tested by God and that the temptation was instituted for Cain's benefit. Such a theme is explicit in the stories of Abraham and Job.]

The Quarrel

Abel said: "My sacrifice was accepted because my good deeds exceeded yours." Cain answered: "There is no justice and there is no judge, there is no world-to-come and no reward or punishment for the righteous and wicked." About this the brothers quarreled. Cain set upon his brother Abel and killed him with a stone.

JONATHAN BEN UZZIEL [15]

Cain's Freedom

Say not: "God has led me astray," for He does not desire sin. No one is bidden to be godless, and to no one did He give permission to sin.

BEN SIRA [16]

Who is strong? He who masters his urge.

ETHICS OF THE FATHERS [17]

It is true that a man's temperament may make it easier to act in a certain way, but he is never thereby forced to do or not to do.

MAIMONIDES [18]

Your Brother's Blood

The Hebrew דְמֵי [Gen. 4:10] appears to read "bloods," as if it were collective: Abel's unborn descendants also cried out to God. MISHNAH [19]

From this we also learn that one man's life is equal to all of creation. MIDRASH [20]

Cain Built a City

To the ancient way of thinking, nothing seemed more natural than to represent a murderer and outlaw as the first builder of cities. The ancients did not think of a city as arising out of the exigencies of barter and trade. The complexity, the turmoil, and the degeneration which marked human life in the larger centers of population were to them proof that the city had sinister origins. Towns and cities were to them abnormal and the product of unnatural circumstances. The fact that nearly every town harbored refugees from justice or vengeance gave color to the belief that the corrupt character of town populations was due to the degenerate character of the founders.

MORDECAI M. KAPLAN [21]

To Conquer Death

One more war. The last. They always say that. Let us fight so as to fight no more. Let us kill so as to conquer death. Who knows, perhaps Cain himself aspired to be not just the first murderer in history but the last as well.

ELIE WIESEL [22]

The Rise of Civilization

The pessimistic interpretation of 4:17–22 [seeing the rise of civilization essentially as a turning from God] became prominent in the Occidental Christian tradition. It is, in fact, closer to the tale of Prometheus and the spirit of Greek mythology than to the Bible itself, which quite undramatically relates the acquisition of technical skills and intimates that it was God who enabled His creatures to accomplish such feats.

CLAUS WESTERMANN [23]

Primeval Man

In this section the Bible presents the second of its genealogical lines. The first was that of heaven and earth (Gen. 2:4), the second is the line of human progeny. The careful listing of names (which occurs twice) and the detailed accounts of legendary long lives find their parallels in other ancient Near Eastern traditions. These annotated genealogies bridge the gap between Adam and Noah, show the rise of civilization, and try to explain the present-day limitations of man's life expectancy.

יא וּשְׁמֹנֶה מֵאוֹת שָׁנָה וַיּוֹלֶד בָּנִים וּבָנוֹת: וַיִּהְיוּ כָּל־יְמֵי
אֱנוֹשׁ חָמֵשׁ שָׁנִים וּתְשַׁע מֵאוֹת שָׁנָה וַיָּמֹת: ס יב וַיְחִי
קֵינָן שִׁבְעִים שָׁנָה וַיּוֹלֶד אֶת־מַהֲלַלְאֵל: יג וַיְחִי קֵינָן
אַחֲרֵי הוֹלִידוֹ אֶת־מַהֲלַלְאֵל אַרְבָּעִים שָׁנָה וּשְׁמֹנֶה
מֵאוֹת שָׁנָה וַיּוֹלֶד בָּנִים וּבָנוֹת: יד וַיִּהְיוּ כָּל־יְמֵי קֵינָן עֶשֶׂר
שָׁנִים וּתְשַׁע מֵאוֹת שָׁנָה וַיָּמֹת: ס טו וַיְחִי מַהֲלַלְאֵל
חָמֵשׁ שָׁנִים וְשִׁשִּׁים שָׁנָה וַיּוֹלֶד אֶת־יָרֶד: טז וַיְחִי
מַהֲלַלְאֵל אַחֲרֵי הוֹלִידוֹ אֶת־יֶרֶד שְׁלֹשִׁים שָׁנָה וּשְׁמֹנֶה
מֵאוֹת שָׁנָה וַיּוֹלֶד בָּנִים וּבָנוֹת: יז וַיִּהְיוּ כָּל־יְמֵי מַהֲלַלְאֵל
חָמֵשׁ וְתִשְׁעִים שָׁנָה וּשְׁמֹנֶה מֵאוֹת שָׁנָה וַיָּמֹת: ס
יח וַיְחִי־יֶרֶד שְׁתַּיִם וְשִׁשִּׁים שָׁנָה וּמְאַת שָׁנָה וַיּוֹלֶד אֶת־
חֲנוֹךְ: יט וַיְחִי־יֶרֶד אַחֲרֵי הוֹלִידוֹ אֶת־חֲנוֹךְ שְׁמֹנֶה מֵאוֹת
שָׁנָה וַיּוֹלֶד בָּנִים וּבָנוֹת: כ וַיִּהְיוּ כָּל־יְמֵי־יֶרֶד שְׁתַּיִם
וְשִׁשִּׁים שָׁנָה וּתְשַׁע מֵאוֹת שָׁנָה וַיָּמֹת: ס כא וַיְחִי חֲנוֹךְ

א זֶה סֵפֶר תּוֹלְדֹת אָדָם בְּיוֹם בְּרֹא אֱלֹהִים אָדָם
ב בִּדְמוּת אֱלֹהִים עָשָׂה אֹתוֹ: זָכָר וּנְקֵבָה בְּרָאָם
וַיְבָרֶךְ אֹתָם וַיִּקְרָא אֶת־שְׁמָם אָדָם בְּיוֹם הִבָּרְאָם:
ג וַיְחִי אָדָם שְׁלֹשִׁים וּמְאַת שָׁנָה וַיּוֹלֶד בִּדְמוּתוֹ כְּצַלְמוֹ
ד וַיִּקְרָא אֶת־שְׁמוֹ שֵׁת: וַיִּהְיוּ יְמֵי־אָדָם אַחֲרֵי הוֹלִידוֹ
ה אֶת־שֵׁת שְׁמֹנֶה מֵאֹת שָׁנָה וַיּוֹלֶד בָּנִים וּבָנוֹת: וַיִּהְיוּ
כָּל־יְמֵי אָדָם אֲשֶׁר־חַי תְּשַׁע מֵאוֹת שָׁנָה וּשְׁלֹשִׁים שָׁנָה
ו וַיָּמֹת: ס וַיְחִי־שֵׁת חָמֵשׁ שָׁנִים וּמְאַת שָׁנָה וַיּוֹלֶד
ז אֶת־אֱנוֹשׁ: וַיְחִי־שֵׁת אַחֲרֵי הוֹלִידוֹ אֶת־אֱנוֹשׁ שֶׁבַע
ח שָׁנִים וּשְׁמֹנֶה מֵאוֹת שָׁנָה וַיּוֹלֶד בָּנִים וּבָנוֹת: וַיִּהְיוּ
כָּל־יְמֵי־שֵׁת שְׁתֵּים עֶשְׂרֵה שָׁנָה וּתְשַׁע מֵאוֹת שָׁנָה
וַיָּמֹת: ס
ט וַיְחִי אֱנוֹשׁ תִּשְׁעִים שָׁנָה וַיּוֹלֶד אֶת־קֵינָן: י וַיְחִי
אֱנוֹשׁ אַחֲרֵי הוֹלִידוֹ אֶת־קֵינָן חֲמֵשׁ עֶשְׂרֵה שָׁנָה

1] This is the record of Adam's line.—When God created man, He made him in the likeness of God; 2] male and female He created them. And when they were created, He blessed them and called them Man.—3] When Adam had lived 130 years, he begot a son in his likeness after his image, and he named him Seth. 4] After the birth of Seth, Adam lived 800 years and begot sons and daughters. 5] All the days that Adam lived came to 930 years; then he died.

6] When Seth had lived 105 years, he begot Enosh. 7] After the birth of Enosh, Seth lived 807 years and begot sons and daughters. 8] All the days of Seth came to 912 years; then he died.

9] When Enosh had lived 90 years, he begot Kenan. 10] After the birth of Kenan, Enosh lived 815 years and begot sons and daughters. 11] All the days of Enosh came to 905 years; then he died.

12] When Kenan had lived 70 years, he begot Mahalalel. 13] After the birth of Mahalalel, Kenan lived 840 years and begot sons and daughters. 14] All the days of Kenan came to 910 years; then he died.

15] When Mahalalel had lived 65 years, he begot Jared. 16] After the birth of Jared, Mahalalel lived 830 years and begot sons and daughters. 17] All the days of Mahalalel came to 895 years; then he died.

18] When Jared had lived 162 years, he begot Enoch. 19] After the birth of Enoch, Jared lived 800 years and begot sons and daughters. 20] All the days of Jared came to 962 years; then he died.

5:5] *Adam lived . . . 930 years.* We do not know whether these figures had any symbolic meaning or followed some particular scheme. In the Masoretic text the years of the antediluvians add up to 1656, in the Samaritan version to 1307, in the Septuagint to 2422.

51

חָמֵשׁ וְשִׁשִּׁים שָׁנָה וַיּוֹלֶד אֶת־מְתוּשָׁלַח: וַיִּתְהַלֵּךְ חֲנוֹךְ כב
אֶת־הָאֱלֹהִים אַחֲרֵי הוֹלִידוֹ אֶת־מְתוּשֶׁלַח שְׁלֹשׁ מֵאוֹת
שָׁנָה וַיּוֹלֶד בָּנִים וּבָנוֹת: וַיְהִי כָּל־יְמֵי חֲנוֹךְ חָמֵשׁ כג
וְשִׁשִּׁים שָׁנָה וּשְׁלֹשׁ מֵאוֹת שָׁנָה: וַיִּתְהַלֵּךְ חֲנוֹךְ אֶת־ כד
הָאֱלֹהִים וְאֵינֶנּוּ כִּי־לָקַח אֹתוֹ אֱלֹהִים: ס וַיְחִי כה
מְתוּשֶׁלַח שֶׁבַע וּשְׁמֹנִים שָׁנָה וּמְאַת שָׁנָה וַיּוֹלֶד אֶת־
לָמֶךְ: וַיְחִי מְתוּשֶׁלַח אַחֲרֵי הוֹלִידוֹ אֶת־לֶמֶךְ שְׁתַּיִם כו
וּשְׁמוֹנִים שָׁנָה וּשְׁבַע מֵאוֹת שָׁנָה וַיּוֹלֶד בָּנִים וּבָנוֹת:
וַיִּהְיוּ כָּל־יְמֵי מְתוּשֶׁלַח תֵּשַׁע וְשִׁשִּׁים שָׁנָה וּתְשַׁע כז
מֵאוֹת שָׁנָה וַיָּמֹת: ס

וַיְחִי־לֶמֶךְ שְׁתַּיִם וּשְׁמֹנִים שָׁנָה וּמְאַת שָׁנָה וַיּוֹלֶד כח
בֵּן: וַיִּקְרָא אֶת־שְׁמוֹ נֹחַ לֵאמֹר זֶה יְנַחֲמֵנוּ מִמַּעֲשֵׂנוּ כט
וּמֵעִצְּבוֹן יָדֵינוּ מִן־הָאֲדָמָה אֲשֶׁר אֵרְרָהּ יְהוָה:
וַיְחִי־לֶמֶךְ אַחֲרֵי הוֹלִידוֹ אֶת־נֹחַ חָמֵשׁ וְתִשְׁעִים ל
שָׁנָה וַחֲמֵשׁ מֵאֹת שָׁנָה וַיּוֹלֶד בָּנִים וּבָנוֹת: וַיִּהְיוּ לא
כָּל־יְמֵי־לֶמֶךְ שֶׁבַע וְשִׁבְעִים שָׁנָה וּשְׁבַע מֵאוֹת שָׁנָה
וַיָּמֹת: ס וַיְהִי־נֹחַ בֶּן־חֲמֵשׁ מֵאוֹת שָׁנָה וַיּוֹלֶד נֹחַ לב
אֶת־שֵׁם אֶת־חָם וְאֶת־יָפֶת:

וַיְהִי כִּי־הֵחֵל הָאָדָם לָרֹב עַל־פְּנֵי הָאֲדָמָה וּבָנוֹת א
יֻלְּדוּ לָהֶם: וַיִּרְאוּ בְנֵי־הָאֱלֹהִים אֶת־בְּנוֹת הָאָדָם כִּי ב

21] When Enoch had lived 65 years, he begot Methuselah.　22] After the birth of Methuselah, Enoch walked with God 300 years; and he begot sons and daughters.　23] All the days of Enoch came to 365 years.　24] Enoch walked with God; then he was no more, for God took him.

25] When Methuselah had lived 187 years, he begot Lamech.　26] After the birth of Lamech, Methuselah lived 782 years and begot sons and daughters.　27] All the days of Methuselah came to 969 years; then he died.

28] When Lamech had lived 182 years, he begot a son.　29] And he named him Noah, saying, "This one will provide us relief from our work and from the toil of our hands, out of the very soil which the LORD placed under a curse."　30] After the birth of Noah, Lamech lived 595 years and begot sons and daughters.　31] All the days of Lamech came to 777 years; then he died.

32] When Noah had lived 500 years, Noah begot Shem, Ham, and Japheth.

1] When men began to increase on earth and daughters were born to them,　2] the divine

23] *365 years.* A schematic number (unrelated to the days of the year): $10^2 + 11^2 + 12^2$. See at 4:24 and 50:22.

24] *Enoch walked with God.* Like Noah later on (Gen. 6:9), he was a righteous man.

God took him. Like Moses and Elijah, he died in a way befitting one of God's intimates. Many legends grew around Enoch, and the Book of Enoch (probably written in the first century C.E.) relates how he was shown the mysteries of heaven and the ushering in of the messianic era. Islamic legend identifies him with Idris ("the expounder of books") in the Koran.
/According to legend, Moses died by a kiss of God [1] and Elijah was taken to heaven on a fiery chariot (II Kings 2:11)./

29] *He named him Noah.* A word play on נֹחַ יְנַחֲמֵנוּ (Noah shall provide relief).

6:2] *Divine beings.* בְּנֵי הָאֱלֹהִים. Others translate as "the sons of God" [2]. Hurrian, Phoenician, and Greek myths told of Titans, supermen of great stature and strength, who were supposedly the offspring of unions between gods and men.
/One old understanding was that these were angels, perhaps fallen ones [3]. Another view is that the text in Gen. 6:2 records an angelic sin and that Ps. 82:1, 6, 7 are references to this incident [4]. Cassuto (*ad loc.*) denies this as does the view that "It is not so much survival of mythology as a reply to it. It is not a fragment: the biblical author disposes of a distasteful subject as quickly as he can" [5].

טבֹת הֵנָּה וַיִּקְחוּ לָהֶם נָשִׁים מִכֹּל אֲשֶׁר בָּחָרוּ:
ג וַיֹּאמֶר יְהֹוָה לֹא־יָדוֹן רוּחִי בָאָדָם לְעֹלָם בְּשַׁגַּם הוּא
ד בָשָׂר וְהָיוּ יָמָיו מֵאָה וְעֶשְׂרִים שָׁנָה: הַנְּפִלִים הָיוּ
בָאָרֶץ בַּיָּמִים הָהֵם וְגַם אַחֲרֵי־כֵן אֲשֶׁר יָבֹאוּ בְּנֵי
הָאֱלֹהִים אֶל־בְּנוֹת הָאָדָם וְיָלְדוּ לָהֶם הֵמָּה הַגִּבֹּרִים
אֲשֶׁר מֵעוֹלָם אַנְשֵׁי הַשֵּׁם: פ
ה וַיַּרְא יְהֹוָה כִּי רַבָּה רָעַת הָאָדָם בָּאָרֶץ וְכָל־יֵצֶר

י מַחְשְׁבֹת לִבּוֹ רַק רַע כָּל־הַיּוֹם: וַיִּנָּחֶם יְהֹוָה כִּי־עָשָׂה
ז אֶת־הָאָדָם בָּאָרֶץ וַיִּתְעַצֵּב אֶל־לִבּוֹ: וַיֹּאמֶר יְהֹוָה
אֶמְחֶה אֶת־הָאָדָם אֲשֶׁר־בָּרָאתִי מֵעַל פְּנֵי הָאֲדָמָה
מֵאָדָם עַד־בְּהֵמָה עַד־רֶמֶשׂ וְעַד־עוֹף הַשָּׁמָיִם כִּי
ח נִחַמְתִּי כִּי עֲשִׂיתִם: וְנֹחַ מָצָא חֵן בְּעֵינֵי יְהֹוָה:

Haftarah Bereshit, p. 320

beings saw how beautiful the daughters of men were and they took wives from among those that pleased them— **3]** The LORD said, "My breath shall not abide in man forever, since he too is flesh; let the days allowed him be one hundred and twenty years."— **4]** It was then, and later too, that the Nephilim appeared on earth—when the divine beings cohabited with the daughters of men, who bore them offspring. They were the heroes of old, the men of renown.

5] The LORD saw how great was man's wickedness on earth, and how every plan devised by his mind was nothing but evil all the time. **6]** And the LORD regretted that He had made man on earth, and His heart was saddened. **7]** The LORD said, "I will blot out from the earth the men whom I created—men together with beasts, creeping things, and birds of the sky; for I regret that I made them." **8]** But Noah found favor with the LORD.

Still another interpretation takes "divine beings" to refer to the descendants of Seth and takes "human daughters" to refer to the descendants of Cain [6]. The phrase has also been taken as recording inter-class marital unions: sons of the aristocracy married daughters of the common folk [7]./

3] *Shield.* The Hebrew meaning is uncertain.

One hundred and twenty years. Becomes the *ideal* life span (Moses will live 120 years), while the *expected* age of man is reduced to 70. "The days of our years are threescore years and ten" (Ps. 90:10). One hundred twenty is the multiple of $1 \times 2 \times 3 \times 4 \times 5$ and reflects the biblical predilection for number symbolism [8] (see commentary to Gen. 1:1–2:3, "The Seventh Day."
/According to some, one hundred twenty years represents a probationary period [9]./

4] *Nephilim.* A borrowed term or an archaism. Rashi, like most older sources, relates Nephilim to the word נָפַל (*nafal*, fall): They are "the fallen ones." The Septuagint translation is "giants."

/ When the spies whom Moses had sent returned, they reported that they had seen Nephilim in Canaan: "and we looked like grasshoppers to ourselves, and so we must have looked to them" (Num. 13:33). In another view, the "heroes of old," not the Nephilim, were the result of the superhuman marriages [10]./

5] *Plan devised by his mind.* This translation of לִבּוֹ (literally, "his heart") is idiomatic, since the heart was believed to be the seat of thought. The word יֵצֶר has been translated as "temperament" rather than "plan" [11].

6] *The Lord regretted.* The Hebrew root נחם can mean both "to change one's mind" and also "comfort," a word play referring to Gen. 5:29.

7] *Together with beasts.* Animals are included in the impending destruction because, according to the biblical view, they existed for the sake of man. According to Rashi, what use would there be for animals if man ceased to exist?

The Early Generations

The reader will look in vain for an explanation of how the world suddenly became filled with people, the men and women of whom Cain was apparently afraid and who would build cities. The ancients tried to solve this difficulty by suggesting that twin sisters were born to Cain, Abel, and later Seth, and that in this fashion the earth was populated.

There is, however, no need for the modern student of the Bible to follow this line of speculation. If the text is silent on the matter, it is probably because it is not the purpose of this chapter to present mankind's ongoing story as much as it is to present an explanation of man's spiritual state. Thus, the Bible should here be understood as speaking of prototypes, not of actual people.

A comparison between the names of Cain's and Seth's descendants reveals a startling similarity and some duplication:

Adam	1	Enosh
Cain	2	Kenan
Enoch	3	Mahalalel
Irad	4	Jared
Mehujael	5	Enoch
Methusael	6	Methuselah
Lamech	7	Lamech
Naamah	8	Noah

Adam and Enosh both mean "man." Other names in the two lists are like-sounding, and by exchanging the places of Enoch and Mehujael we arrive at a single basic list, which in the biblical tradition is presented in two variants. Mankind has one ancestor (Adam or Enosh) and one line of descent.[1] Noah appears when the seven generations of prehistoric man have run their course.

There are strong parallels between these biblical genealogies and the Babylonian lists of antediluvian kings and their counselors. In both cases they name "culture-heroes" responsible for basic contributions to civilization, including the first cities. In both cases they end with the protagonist of the Deluge story. The genealogical interest was characteristic of the Western Semites [13]. "To dedicated guardians of sacred traditions, unbroken lineage meant a secure link with the remotest past and hence also a firm basis from which to face the future. These were vital statistics in more ways than one" [14].

While the parallels between the biblical and Babylonian traditions are clearly visible, there are also significant differences. The Babylonians attached these traditions only to their king lists, but the Bible treats the antediluvians as ancestors of one another and ultimately of all mankind. The Bible eschews all mythological allusions in these lists; that is, it deals with men and not with semidivine kings. Even the longevity attributed to Seth's line must be compared with that of the Babylonians, who were reputed to live for thousands of years. In the Bible, a thousand years is regarded as a day of God (Ps. 90:4), and no one of the ancients in the biblical account reaches the millennial age.

The longevity of the antediluvians should, therefore, be seen in the context of such ancient traditions. To say that Methuselah's 969 years were meant as shorter units, such as months, merely subjects the Torah to artificial interpretation. The Bible presents the list of the primevals and their long lives as an intermediate stage in man's development. Adam possessed potential immortality; his immediate descendants had, by our standards, very long life spans; the Patriarchs,

---

[1] The inclusion of Seth and the change from Cain to Kenan was probably due to the understandable disinclination to have all men appear to be descended from a murderer. It may also be that for this reason the term תּוֹלְדוֹת (*toledot*) is denied the Cain line. Note the midrash that suggests Naamah was Noah's **wife** [12].

Joseph, Moses, and Joshua, all lived past the century mark; thereafter, however, men have only the "normal" life span. In the biblical view, man's longevity is limited severely at some stage between prehistory and history, and only in the messianic days will man again reach the high ages of old (Isa. 65:20).

The Divine Beings

The notation about the legendary "divine beings" and their giant offspring may be regarded as the one mythological fragment retained in Genesis. Why was it not excised? Possibly because it served as an introduction to the Flood story and as such appeared to say: Men became giants, achieved renown in their time, and were heroes by their own values. When God evaluated human development, He looked neither at man's size nor at his reputation but at his heart, and He found its devices evil. Hence, God resolved to make a new start with Noah.

GLEANINGS

Lamech

Marital problems, occasioned by the taking of two women, brought him mental distress, which explains the violent song attributed to him.

SAMUEL DAVID LUZZATTO [15]

Lamech's descendants were worthy of him: They developed great wealth and other doubtful accouterments of civilization; they refined the art of war and altogether encouraged man's belief in his own self-sufficiency. Lamech, the father of all of them, is thus represented as the very embodiment of human presumption.

MORDECAI M. KAPLAN [16]

The Most Important Verse in the Torah

Two second-century scholars, Rabbi Akiba and Ben Azzai, debated which was the most important principle in the Torah. Rabbi Akiba said: "Love your neighbor as yourself" [Lev. 19:18] is the greatest [for what is hateful to you do not do unto your neighbor]. Ben Azzai said: The greatest principle is Genesis 5:1: "This is the record of Adam's line. When God created man, He made him in the likeness of God." TALMUD [17]

Ben Azzai laid down a fundamental teaching of Judaism. For in the verse quoted, the scholar saw the basic declaration of human brotherhood: By tracing back the whole of the human race to one single ancestor, created by one God, the Bible taught that all men have *one* Creator—the heavenly Father—and *one* ancestor—the human father.

MENAHEM M. KASHER [18]

One Man

The same word, תּוֹלְדוֹת [lines], is used to describe the creation of the whole world [Gen. 2:4] and the creation of one man [Gen. 5:1]. This teaches that the life of one man is as dear in God's eyes as the whole universe. MIDRASH [19]

Men of Renown

Human corruption began at that time, and it began with the heroes of old, the men of renown (Gen. 6:4). Ever since, the debasement of society has started with "men of renown," that is, with those entrusted with responsibility and leadership. [20]

The Flood

Many diverse cultures tell stories about a great flood. It has been suggested that these recall an earth-wide catastrophe brought on either by a terrestrial eruption or by a celestial collision, which may have resulted in a rise in sea level sufficient to cover all continents. Recent scientific investigations have shown that, at some time near the transition between prehistory and history, flood waters from the Persian gulf may have covered the southern section of the Mesopotamian valley.

But the biblical account is far more than prehistoric memory or a variant of ancient folk legends; it is above all a story with a moral. Its themes are sin, righteousness, and man's second opportunity to live in accordance with, rather than opposed to, the will of God.

There is agreement between the biblical and other Near Eastern flood stories on many details—the ark, the raven, the dove—but there are fundamental differences in approach. In the Bible, it is human sin that causes the Flood; in the Babylonian-Akkadian epic of "Atrahasis," human boisterousness and noise disturb the sleep of the gods and cause them to react. In the Bible, Noah is saved so that he might begin the human voyage over again; in "Gilgamesh," the flood hero is elevated to immortal status and thereby is removed from human history. Most important: in the Torah, God institutes law as the counteragent of human wickedness, while in other Near Eastern traditions such a divine response is absent.

(A new weekly portion, *Noach*, begins here.)

פ פ פ פ

ט צֹהַר תַּעֲשֶׂה לַתֵּבָה וְאֶל־אַמָּה תְּכַלֶּנָּה מִלְמַעְלָה וּפֶתַח הַתֵּבָה בְּצִדָּהּ תָּשִׂים תַּחְתִּיִּם שְׁנִיִּם וּשְׁלִשִׁים תַּעֲשֶׂהָ: יז וַאֲנִי הִנְנִי מֵבִיא אֶת־הַמַּבּוּל מַיִם עַל־הָאָרֶץ לְשַׁחֵת כָּל־בָּשָׂר אֲשֶׁר־בּוֹ רוּחַ חַיִּים מִתַּחַת הַשָּׁמָיִם כֹּל אֲשֶׁר־בָּאָרֶץ יִגְוָע: יח וַהֲקִמֹתִי אֶת־בְּרִיתִי אִתָּךְ וּבָאתָ אֶל־הַתֵּבָה אַתָּה וּבָנֶיךָ וְאִשְׁתְּךָ וּנְשֵׁי־בָנֶיךָ אִתָּךְ: יט וּמִכָּל־הָחַי מִכָּל־בָּשָׂר שְׁנַיִם מִכֹּל תָּבִיא אֶל־הַתֵּבָה לְהַחֲיֹת אִתָּךְ זָכָר וּנְקֵבָה יִהְיוּ: כ מֵהָעוֹף לְמִינֵהוּ וּמִן־הַבְּהֵמָה לְמִינָהּ מִכֹּל רֶמֶשׂ הָאֲדָמָה לְמִינֵהוּ שְׁנַיִם מִכֹּל יָבֹאוּ אֵלֶיךָ לְהַחֲיוֹת: כא וְאַתָּה קַח־לְךָ מִכָּל־מַאֲכָל אֲשֶׁר יֵאָכֵל וְאָסַפְתָּ אֵלֶיךָ וְהָיָה לְךָ וְלָהֶם לְאָכְלָה: כב וַיַּעַשׂ נֹחַ כְּכֹל אֲשֶׁר צִוָּה אֹתוֹ אֱלֹהִים כֵּן עָשָׂה:

ט אֵלֶּה תּוֹלְדֹת נֹחַ נֹחַ אִישׁ צַדִּיק תָּמִים הָיָה בְּדֹרֹתָיו אֶת־הָאֱלֹהִים הִתְהַלֶּךְ־נֹחַ: י וַיּוֹלֶד נֹחַ שְׁלֹשָׁה בָנִים אֶת־שֵׁם אֶת־חָם וְאֶת־יָפֶת: יא וַתִּשָּׁחֵת הָאָרֶץ לִפְנֵי הָאֱלֹהִים וַתִּמָּלֵא הָאָרֶץ חָמָס: יב וַיַּרְא אֱלֹהִים אֶת־הָאָרֶץ וְהִנֵּה נִשְׁחָתָה כִּי־הִשְׁחִית כָּל־בָּשָׂר אֶת־דַּרְכּוֹ עַל־הָאָרֶץ: ס יג וַיֹּאמֶר אֱלֹהִים לְנֹחַ קֵץ כָּל־בָּשָׂר בָּא לְפָנַי כִּי־מָלְאָה הָאָרֶץ חָמָס מִפְּנֵיהֶם וְהִנְנִי מַשְׁחִיתָם אֶת־הָאָרֶץ: יד עֲשֵׂה לְךָ תֵּבַת עֲצֵי־גֹפֶר קִנִּים תַּעֲשֶׂה אֶת־הַתֵּבָה וְכָפַרְתָּ אֹתָהּ מִבַּיִת וּמִחוּץ בַּכֹּפֶר: טו וְזֶה אֲשֶׁר תַּעֲשֶׂה אֹתָהּ שְׁלֹשׁ מֵאוֹת אַמָּה אֹרֶךְ הַתֵּבָה חֲמִשִּׁים אַמָּה רָחְבָּהּ וּשְׁלֹשִׁים אַמָּה קוֹמָתָהּ:

9] This is the line of Noah.—Noah was a righteous man; he was blameless in his age; Noah walked with God.—10] Noah begot three sons: Shem, Ham, and Japheth.

11] The earth became corrupt before God; the earth was filled with lawlessness. 12] When God saw how corrupt the earth was, for all flesh had corrupted its ways on earth, 13] God said to Noah, "I have decided to put an end to all flesh, for the earth is filled with lawlessness because of them: I am about to destroy them with the earth. 14] Make yourself an ark of gopher wood; make it an ark with compartments, and cover it inside and out with pitch. 15] This is how you shall make it: the length of the ark shall be three hundred cubits, its width fifty cubits, and its height thirty cubits. 16] Make an opening for daylight in the ark, and terminate it within a cubit of the top. Put the entrance to the ark in its side; make it with bottom, second, and third decks.

17] "For My part, I am about to bring the Flood—waters upon the earth—to destroy all flesh under the sky in which there is breath of life; everything on earth shall perish. 18] But I will establish My covenant with you, and you shall enter the ark, with your sons, your wife, and your sons' wives. 19] And of all that lives, of all flesh, you shall take two of each into the ark to keep alive with you; they shall be male and female. 20] From birds of every kind, cattle of every kind, every kind of creeping thing on earth, two of each shall come to you to stay alive. 21] For your part, take of everything that is eaten and store it away, to serve as food for you and for them." 22] Noah did so; just as God commanded him, so he did.

6:11] *Lawlessness.* חָמָס. Others translate as "violence."

13] *Destroy them with the earth.* Others translate as "from the earth" [1].

14] *Gopher wood.* A species still unidentified.

15] *Cubit.* Figuring a cubit to be about eighteen inches, the ark's tonnage was over 40,000 tons, or as large as a good-sized modern passenger ship. To ancient man, such dimensions must have evoked a sense of great awe.

ט הָאֲדָמָה: שְׁנַיִם שְׁנַיִם בָּאוּ אֶל־נֹחַ אֶל־הַתֵּבָה זָכָר

י וּנְקֵבָה כַּאֲשֶׁר צִוָּה אֱלֹהִים אֶת־נֹחַ: וַיְהִי לְשִׁבְעַת

יא הַיָּמִים וּמֵי הַמַּבּוּל הָיוּ עַל־הָאָרֶץ: בִּשְׁנַת שֵׁשׁ־מֵאוֹת שָׁנָה לְחַיֵּי־נֹחַ בַּחֹדֶשׁ הַשֵּׁנִי בְּשִׁבְעָה־עָשָׂר יוֹם לַחֹדֶשׁ בַּיּוֹם הַזֶּה נִבְקְעוּ כָּל־מַעְיְנֹת תְּהוֹם רַבָּה וַאֲרֻבֹּת

יב הַשָּׁמַיִם נִפְתָּחוּ: וַיְהִי הַגֶּשֶׁם עַל־הָאָרֶץ אַרְבָּעִים יוֹם

יג וְאַרְבָּעִים לָיְלָה: בְּעֶצֶם הַיּוֹם הַזֶּה בָּא נֹחַ וְשֵׁם־וְחָם וָיֶפֶת בְּנֵי־נֹחַ וְאֵשֶׁת נֹחַ וּשְׁלֹשֶׁת נְשֵׁי־בָנָיו אִתָּם אֶל־

יד הַתֵּבָה: הֵמָּה וְכָל־הַחַיָּה לְמִינָהּ וְכָל־הַבְּהֵמָה לְמִינָהּ וְכָל־הָרֶמֶשׂ הָרֹמֵשׂ עַל־הָאָרֶץ לְמִינֵהוּ וְכָל־הָעוֹף

טו לְמִינֵהוּ כָּל־צִפּוֹר כָּל־כָּנָף: וַיָּבֹאוּ אֶל־נֹחַ אֶל־הַתֵּבָה

טז שְׁנַיִם שְׁנַיִם מִכָּל־הַבָּשָׂר אֲשֶׁר־בּוֹ רוּחַ חַיִּים: וְהַבָּאִים זָכָר וּנְקֵבָה מִכָּל־בָּשָׂר בָּאוּ כַּאֲשֶׁר צִוָּה אֹתוֹ אֱלֹהִים

א וַיֹּאמֶר יְהֹוָה לְנֹחַ בֹּא־אַתָּה וְכָל־בֵּיתְךָ אֶל־הַתֵּבָה

ב כִּי־אֹתְךָ רָאִיתִי צַדִּיק לְפָנַי בַּדּוֹר הַזֶּה: מִכֹּל הַבְּהֵמָה הַטְּהוֹרָה תִּקַּח־לְךָ שִׁבְעָה שִׁבְעָה אִישׁ וְאִשְׁתּוֹ וּמִן־הַבְּהֵמָה אֲשֶׁר לֹא טְהֹרָה הִוא שְׁנַיִם אִישׁ

ג וְאִשְׁתּוֹ: גַּם־מֵעוֹף הַשָּׁמַיִם שִׁבְעָה שִׁבְעָה זָכָר וּנְקֵבָה

ד לְחַיּוֹת זֶרַע עַל־פְּנֵי כָל־הָאָרֶץ: כִּי לְיָמִים עוֹד שִׁבְעָה אָנֹכִי מַמְטִיר עַל־הָאָרֶץ אַרְבָּעִים יוֹם וְאַרְבָּעִים לָיְלָה וּמָחִיתִי אֶת־כָּל־הַיְקוּם אֲשֶׁר עָשִׂיתִי

ה מֵעַל פְּנֵי הָאֲדָמָה: וַיַּעַשׂ נֹחַ כְּכֹל אֲשֶׁר־צִוָּהוּ יְהֹוָה:

ו וְנֹחַ בֶּן־שֵׁשׁ מֵאוֹת שָׁנָה וְהַמַּבּוּל הָיָה מַיִם עַל־הָאָרֶץ:

ז וַיָּבֹא נֹחַ וּבָנָיו וְאִשְׁתּוֹ וּנְשֵׁי־בָנָיו אִתּוֹ אֶל־הַתֵּבָה

ח מִפְּנֵי מֵי הַמַּבּוּל: מִן־הַבְּהֵמָה הַטְּהוֹרָה וּמִן־הַבְּהֵמָה אֲשֶׁר אֵינֶנָּה טְהֹרָה וּמִן־הָעוֹף וְכֹל אֲשֶׁר־רֹמֵשׂ עַל־

1] Then the LORD said to Noah, "Go into the ark, with all your household, for you alone have I found righteous before Me in this generation. **2]** Of every clean animal you shall take seven pairs, males and their mates, and of every animal which is not clean, two, a male and its mate; **3]** of the birds of the sky also, seven pairs, male and female, to keep seed alive upon all the earth. **4]** For in seven days' time I will make it rain upon the earth, forty days and forty nights, and I will blot out from the earth all existence that I created." **5]** And Noah did just as the LORD commanded him.

6] Noah was six hundred years old when the Flood came, waters upon the earth. **7]** Noah, with his sons, his wife, and his sons' wives, went into the ark because of the waters of the Flood. **8]** Of the clean animals, of the animals that are not clean, of the birds, and of everything that creeps on the ground, **9]** two of each, male and female, came to Noah into the ark, as God had commanded Noah. **10]** And on the seventh day the waters of the Flood came upon the earth.

11] In the six hundredth year of Noah's life, in the second month, on the seventeenth day of the month, on that day

All the fountains of the great deep burst apart,

And the flood-gates of the sky broke open.

(12] The rain fell on the earth forty days and forty nights.) **13]** That same day Noah and Noah's sons, Shem, Ham, and Japheth, went into the ark, with Noah's wife and the three wives of his sons—**14]** they and all beasts of every kind, all cattle of every kind, all creatures of every kind that creep on the earth, and all birds of every kind, every bird, every winged thing. **15]** They came to Noah into the ark, two each of all flesh in which there was breath of life. **16]** Thus they that entered comprised male and female of all flesh, as God had commanded him. And the LORD shut him in.

7:2] *Clean animal.* Fit, according to the laws of the Torah, for sacrifice. Rashi and others: "Clean" according to dietary laws; fit for eating.

11] *In the second month.* Probably of the fall, when the rainy season begins in the Near East.

יז וַיְהִי הַמַּבּוּל אַרְבָּעִים יוֹם עַל־הָאָרֶץ וַיִּרְבּוּ הַמַּיִם וַיִּשְׂאוּ אֶת־הַתֵּבָה וַתָּרָם מֵעַל הָאָרֶץ:
יח וַיִּגְבְּרוּ הַמַּיִם וַיִּרְבּוּ מְאֹד עַל־הָאָרֶץ וַתֵּלֶךְ הַתֵּבָה עַל־פְּנֵי הַמָּיִם:
יט וְהַמַּיִם גָּבְרוּ מְאֹד מְאֹד עַל־הָאָרֶץ וַיְכֻסּוּ כָּל־הֶהָרִים הַגְּבֹהִים אֲשֶׁר־תַּחַת כָּל־הַשָּׁמָיִם:
כ חֲמֵשׁ עֶשְׂרֵה אַמָּה מִלְמַעְלָה גָּבְרוּ הַמָּיִם וַיְכֻסּוּ הֶהָרִים:
כא וַיִּגְוַע כָּל־בָּשָׂר הָרֹמֵשׂ עַל־הָאָרֶץ בָּעוֹף וּבַבְּהֵמָה וּבַחַיָּה וּבְכָל־הַשֶּׁרֶץ הַשֹּׁרֵץ עַל־הָאָרֶץ וְכֹל הָאָדָם:
כב כֹּל אֲשֶׁר נִשְׁמַת־רוּחַ חַיִּים בְּאַפָּיו מִכֹּל אֲשֶׁר בֶּחָרָבָה מֵתוּ:
כג וַיִּמַח אֶת־כָּל־הַיְקוּם אֲשֶׁר עַל־פְּנֵי הָאֲדָמָה מֵאָדָם עַד־בְּהֵמָה עַד־רֶמֶשׂ וְעַד־עוֹף הַשָּׁמַיִם וַיִּמָּחוּ מִן־הָאָרֶץ וַיִּשָּׁאֶר
כד אַךְ־נֹחַ וַאֲשֶׁר אִתּוֹ בַּתֵּבָה: וַיִּגְבְּרוּ הַמַּיִם עַל־הָאָרֶץ חֲמִשִּׁים וּמְאַת יוֹם:
א וַיִּזְכֹּר אֱלֹהִים אֶת־נֹחַ וְאֵת כָּל־הַחַיָּה וְאֶת־כָּל־הַבְּהֵמָה אֲשֶׁר אִתּוֹ בַּתֵּבָה וַיַּעֲבֵר אֱלֹהִים רוּחַ עַל־הָאָרֶץ וַיָּשֹׁכּוּ הַמָּיִם:
ב וַיִּסָּכְרוּ מַעְיְנֹת תְּהוֹם וַאֲרֻבֹּת הַשָּׁמָיִם וַיִּכָּלֵא הַגֶּשֶׁם מִן־הַשָּׁמָיִם:
ג וַיָּשֻׁבוּ הַמַּיִם מֵעַל הָאָרֶץ הָלוֹךְ וָשׁוֹב וַיַּחְסְרוּ הַמַּיִם מִקְצֵה חֲמִשִּׁים
ד וּמְאַת יוֹם: וַתָּנַח הַתֵּבָה בַּחֹדֶשׁ הַשְּׁבִיעִי בְּשִׁבְעָה־עָשָׂר יוֹם לַחֹדֶשׁ עַל הָרֵי אֲרָרָט:
ה וְהַמַּיִם הָיוּ הָלוֹךְ וְחָסוֹר עַד הַחֹדֶשׁ הָעֲשִׂירִי בָּעֲשִׂירִי בְּאֶחָד לַחֹדֶשׁ

17] The Flood continued forty days on the earth, and the waters increased and raised the ark so that it rose above the earth. 18] The waters swelled and increased greatly upon the earth, and the ark drifted upon the waters. 19] When the waters had swelled much more upon the earth, all the highest mountains everywhere under the sky were covered. 20] Fifteen cubits higher did the waters swell, as the mountains were covered. 21] And all flesh that stirred on earth perished—birds, cattle, beasts, and all the things that swarmed upon the earth, and all mankind. 22] All in whose nostrils was the merest breath of life, all that was on dry land, died. 23] All existence on earth was blotted out—man, cattle, creeping things, and birds of the sky; they were blotted out from the earth. Only Noah was left, and those with him in the ark.

24] And when the waters had swelled on the earth one hundred and fifty days,

1] God remembered Noah and all the beasts and all the cattle that were with him in the ark, and God caused a wind to blow across the earth, and the waters subsided. 2] The fountains of the deep and the floodgates of the sky were stopped up, and the rain from the sky was held back; 3] the waters then receded steadily from the earth. At the end of one hundred and fifty days the waters diminished, 4] so that in the seventh month, on the seventeenth day of the month, the ark came to rest on the mountains of Ararat. 5] The waters went on diminishing until the tenth month; in the tenth month, on the first of the month, the tops of the mountains became visible.

8:4] *Ararat.* A district in Armenia, known in ancient history as Urartu.

/ Later traditions point to the Zagros mountains, east of the middle Tigris, as the resting place of Noah's and Utnapishtim's arks. Attempts to find remains of Noah's ark have proven fruitless and are likely to remain so. The Flood story is legend, not demonstrable history [2]./

יא הַתֵּבָה: וַתָּבֹא אֵלָיו הַיּוֹנָה לְעֵת עֶרֶב וְהִנֵּה עֲלֵה־זַיִת
טָרָף בְּפִיהָ וַיֵּדַע נֹחַ כִּי־קַלּוּ הַמַּיִם מֵעַל הָאָרֶץ:
יב וַיִּיָּחֶל עוֹד שִׁבְעַת יָמִים אֲחֵרִים וַיְשַׁלַּח אֶת־הַיּוֹנָה
וְלֹא־יָסְפָה שׁוּב־אֵלָיו עוֹד:
יג וַיְהִי בְּאַחַת וְשֵׁשׁ־מֵאוֹת שָׁנָה בָּרִאשׁוֹן בְּאֶחָד לַחֹדֶשׁ
חָרְבוּ הַמַּיִם מֵעַל הָאָרֶץ וַיָּסַר נֹחַ אֶת־מִכְסֵה הַתֵּבָה
וַיַּרְא וְהִנֵּה חָרְבוּ פְּנֵי הָאֲדָמָה: וּבַחֹדֶשׁ הַשֵּׁנִי
יד בְּשִׁבְעָה וְעֶשְׂרִים יוֹם לַחֹדֶשׁ יָבְשָׁה הָאָרֶץ: ס

ו נִרְאוּ רָאשֵׁי הֶהָרִים: וַיְהִי מִקֵּץ אַרְבָּעִים יוֹם וַיִּפְתַּח
ז נֹחַ אֶת־חַלּוֹן הַתֵּבָה אֲשֶׁר עָשָׂה: וַיְשַׁלַּח אֶת־הָעֹרֵב
וַיֵּצֵא יָצוֹא וָשׁוֹב עַד־יְבֹשֶׁת הַמַּיִם מֵעַל הָאָרֶץ:
ח וַיְשַׁלַּח אֶת־הַיּוֹנָה מֵאִתּוֹ לִרְאוֹת הֲקַלּוּ הַמַּיִם מֵעַל
ט פְּנֵי הָאֲדָמָה: וְלֹא־מָצְאָה הַיּוֹנָה מָנוֹחַ לְכַף־רַגְלָהּ
וַתָּשָׁב אֵלָיו אֶל־הַתֵּבָה כִּי־מַיִם עַל־פְּנֵי כָל־הָאָרֶץ
י וַיִּשְׁלַח יָדוֹ וַיִּקָּחֶהָ וַיָּבֵא אֹתָהּ אֵלָיו אֶל־הַתֵּבָה: וַיָּחֶל
עוֹד שִׁבְעַת יָמִים אֲחֵרִים וַיֹּסֶף שַׁלַּח אֶת־הַיּוֹנָה מִן

6] At the end of forty days, Noah opened the window of the ark that he had made **7]** and sent out the raven; it went to and fro until the waters had dried up from the earth. **8]** Then he sent out the dove to see whether the waters had decreased from the surface of the ground. **9]** But the dove could not find a resting place for its foot, and returned to him to the ark, for there was water over all the earth. So putting out his hand, he took it into the ark with him. **10]** He waited another seven days, and again sent out the dove from the ark. **11]** The dove came back to him toward evening, and there in its bill was a plucked-off olive leaf! Then Noah knew that the waters had decreased on the earth. **12]** He waited still another seven days and sent the dove forth; and it did not return to him any more.

13] In the six hundred and first year, in the first month, on the first of the month, the waters began to dry from the earth; and when Noah removed the covering of the ark, he saw that the surface of the ground was drying. **14]** And in the second month, on the twenty-seventh day of the month, the earth was dry.

7] *The raven.* Birds were often used by ancient mariners as compasses.
The Akkadian flood story also features a raven.

The Generation of the Flood

According to the Bible, Methuselah died just before the Flood,[1] and except for Noah the period of the antediluvians had run its course. Thus, the Flood closes the first era in man's post-Eden story. The Torah pictures this era as marked by devolution: The moral fibre of man deteriorated beyond hope of regeneration.

What was the monstrous evil that brought on God's judgment? The Bible does not specify it beyond calling it חָמָס (chamas, lawlessness). But lawlessness (or violence, as some render it) is the manifestation of a social disease and not its cause. The Midrash speculates that it was unbounded affluence that caused men to become depraved, that wealth afforded them the leisure to discover new thrills and to commit sexual aberrations. Hand in hand with material prosperity went an overbearing attitude toward God [4], whom people judged to be incapable of hearing prayer and of enforcing moral standards.[2]

In the Christian tradition, Noah and his generation prefigure the end of time: Only those who take refuge in faith will escape judgment [6]. Similarly, the water of baptism represents salvation brought through water to Noah and his family [7].

The Man Noah

The Bible says that God chose to save Noah and his family from the Flood because he was "blameless in his age." A discussion of this phrase is recorded in the Talmud:

Rabbi Jochanan said: "Noah was blameless only in *his* age, but in other ages he would not have been considered righteous." Resh Lakish said: "He was righteous *even* in his age; how much more so would he have been righteous in other ages." In Rabbi Jochanan's view, Noah stood out only because so much evil surrounded him, so that "in his age" is a dubious compliment; in Resh Lakish's opinion, Noah is rendered special homage, for nothing is more difficult than to be honest, peaceful, and loving when deceit, violence, and hatred are the accepted patterns of society [8].

It is not possible to say which reading was intended by the biblical author. But Resh Lakish's interpretation of Noah as a nonconformist who opposed the value system of his own time appears to speak more clearly across the centuries.[3]

Two Questions about God

How can natural events be understood as judgments of God? Biblical man saw the hand of God in the Flood, just as he saw it working in other natural phenomena. Thus, the Flood is said to have lasted 364 days, to indicate that the very cycle of nature was interrupted until heaven and earth returned to their spheres a year later. While there are those whose faith still permits them to see a warning in every bolt of lightning and a retribution of the Divine in every natural disaster, most modern men do not believe in a God who arranges natural forces for the sake of man. In their view, the relevance of the Noah story is confined to its emphasis on God's moral judgment.

---

[1] Traditional sources insist that it is no coincidence that God held off the Flood until the mourning period for Methuselah had passed [3].

[2] There was also a tradition that the chief sin of the generation of the Flood lay in their refusal to beget children. Even Noah originally refused to marry and have children—note that his first child was not born until he was 500 years old. For he too said: "Why should I bring offspring into a world which will likely be destroyed?" [5].

[3] Resh Lakish may have based his view on Ezek. 14:14, where Noah, Daniel, and Job are considered truly righteous.

In considering the story as a homily on the consequences of man's corruption, lawlessness, and violence, we can affirm that they do bring on the judgment of God. We may experience it in man's social and moral conditions, or in nature's physical realm (as in our pollution of the atmosphere and water, or our disturbance of the ecological balance) [9]. God guarantees life and its laws. An offense against these is an offense against Him and may occasion dire and unforeseen consequences.[4]

How are we to understand the phrase, "God remembered" (Gen. 8:1)? The expression וַיִּזְכֹּר (va-yizkor), referring to God, occurs frequently in the Bible and consistently reflects a belief in moral continuity. What happened yesterday is not forgotten. It is stored up in divine memory and has a bearing on God's judgment in the future. The remembering God thus makes justice possible, even as among men there can be no ethical presence without ethical memories.

Many prayers in Jewish and Christian traditions ask God to remember. The Jewish memorial prayer begins with the words יִזְכֹּר

אֱלֹהִים (yizkor Elohim, may God remember).

The Two Biblical Sources of the Flood Story

The Flood story presents a particularly striking example of the confluence of two traditions in the Torah. Occasionally—as in the first two chapters of Genesis and in the relation of the lines of Cain and Seth—the variant sources are fairly apparent. At other times, as here, the two traditions are so closely interwoven that at first glance they present a single strand.

The following excerpts will show how the two sources (generally assigned to the J and P traditions) may have told the basic story. The condensed J-version is seen in chapters 6:5–6; 7:1–4, 10, 12; 8:8–12; 8:20–22; the P-version in chapters 6:12–13; 6:14, 20; 7:11, 24; 8:3, 7; 8:13, 18–19; 9:1–17. Note, for instance, how J speaks of God's feelings while P merely reports the decree. Bible scholars disagree over details; for instance, the tale of the raven is often ascribed to J. There are also those who deny altogether that the text can be dissected in this way.

---

[4] The Sages paid special attention to the relationship of human sin to the destruction of the animals [10].

The Lord saw man's wickedness and He regretted that He had made him. The Lord's heart was saddened.

Then He said to Noah: "Go into the ark for you alone have I found righteous . . . take with you seven pairs of clean and one pair of unclean animals, and seven pairs of birds. I will send forty days and nights of rain."

After seven days the Flood came. Rain fell for forty days and nights. Noah sent out a dove, but the dove found no place to rest; he waited seven days, and the dove came back with an olive leaf. After another seven days the dove went out but did not return.

Noah left the ark. He built an altar and sacrificed of every clean animal and clean bird. The Lord in turn promised never to bring another flood.

God saw how corrupt man was and He said to Noah: "I have decided to put an end to all flesh.

Make yourself an ark. Take with you two of everything that lives, male and female, of birds, cattle, and creeping things."

In the six-hundredth year of Noah's life, in the second month, on the seventeenth day the rain began. The waters swelled for one hundred and fifty days. At the end of that time the waters diminished. Noah sent out a raven. It went to and fro until the waters had dried up.

In Noah's six hundred and first year, on the twenty-seventh day of the second month, he and his family left the ark. God then made a covenant with Noah and set His rainbow in the sky as a sign that He would not bring another flood.

GLEANINGS

Two Flood Story Parallels from the Ancient Near East
The land became wide, the people became
    numerous,
The land bellowed like wild oxen.
The god was disturbed by their uproar.
[Enlil] heard their clamor
[and] said to the great gods:
"Oppressive has become the clamor of mankind.
By their uproar they prevent sleep."
                FROM "ATRAHASIS" [11]

When the seventh day arrived
I sent forth and set free a dove.
The dove went forth but came back;
There was no resting place for it and she turned
    round.
Then I sent forth and set free a swallow.
The swallow went forth but came back;
There was no resting place for it and she turned
    round.
Then I sent forth and set free a raven.
The raven went forth and seeing the waters had
    diminished
He eats, circles, caws, but turns not round.
It ate, but returned not again.
                FROM "GILGAMESH" [12]

Three Parallels to Noah
[The theme of the Flood hero's relationship to
his contemporaries appears in the following three
separate sources, which were written over a period
spanning more than 2,000 years. The "Gilgamesh"
passage may also echo an older tradition of conflict between Enlil and Ea (Enki). The Koran
clearly follows the midrashic tradition.]
Man of Shuruppak, son of Ubartutu,
Tear down this house, build a ship!
Give up possessions, seek thou life.
Despise property and keep the soul alive!

Aboard the ship take thou the seed of all living
    things.
The ship that thou shalt build,
Her dimensions shall be to measure.
Equal shall be her width and her length.
Like the Apsu thou shalt ceil her.

I understood, and I said to Ea, my lord:
"Behold, my lord, what thou hast thus ordered,
I shall be honored to carry out.
But what shall I answer the city, the people and
    elders?"
Ea opened his mouth to speak,
Saying to me, his servant:
"Thou shalt then thus speak unto them:
'I have learned that Enlil is hostile to me,
So that I cannot reside in your city,
Nor set my foot in Enlil's territory.
To the Deep I will therefore go down,
To dwell with my lord Ea.'"
                FROM "GILGAMESH" [13]

Why did the Holy One, praised be He, command
Noah to make an ark? So that his fellow men might
see him at his labor and be moved to repent. Thus
thought God, but they paid no attention to Noah's
urgings.   MIDRASH [14]

We sent Noah to his people.
He said: "O my people,
Worship God! ye have
No other god but Him.
I fear for you the punishment
Of a dreadful day!"
The leaders of his people

Said: "Ah! we see thee
Evidently wandering (in mind)."
He said: "O my people!
No wandering is there

In my (mind): on the contrary
I am an apostle from
The Lord and cherisher
Of the worlds!

Do ye wonder that
There hath come to you
A message from your Lord,
Through a man of your own
People, to warn you,
So that ye may fear God
And haply receive His mercy?"

But they rejected him,
And We delivered him,
And those with him,
In the ark:
But We overwhelmed
In the Flood those
Who rejected Our signs.
They were indeed
A blind people!   KORAN [15]

Noah Lacked Compassion

Nowhere did Noah show a feeling of sadness and pathos that an entire generation was to be lost, and the world destroyed; that men had lost their way of life and surrendered to their own primeval drives and dark passions. At no time did a word of concern, of solicitude escape Noah's lips. It was as though he stood apart from the rest of the world. Nowhere was there an expression of tenderness, of regret that even though these men were wicked they would be lost—they, their wives, and their children. He did not leap forward with a request to God to spare those who, perhaps with the extension of greater mercy, might have been spared.

Noah was a righteous man; Noah deserves to be in the circle of the great. But there was a fatal flaw in Noah, and so he did not become the father of a new religion, a new faith, and a new community. He lacked compassion and, because he lacked compassion, he forfeited the far greater place in history that might have been accorded him.   MORRIS ADLER [16]

Noah and Abraham

Noah's fate is bound to "his generation," but Abraham's goes beyond his time, toward history. Abraham's faithfulness is God's hope—not because of what Abraham *is* "in his generation" but what he will *become*.   MARTIN BUBER [17]

65

After the Flood

With the Flood over, man begins once more to face the problems of existence. He is reassured that God will not again "destroy every living being" (Gen. 8:21) and that there is an immutable order that God himself will not abrogate. The rainbow is seen as God's signature to His promise, and the sons of Noah set out to people the world.

וַיְדַבֵּ֥ר אֱלֹהִ֖ים אֶל־נֹ֥חַ לֵאמֹֽר: טו

צֵ֖א מִן־הַתֵּבָ֑ה אַתָּ֕ה וְאִשְׁתְּךָ֛ וּבָנֶ֥יךָ וּנְשֵֽׁי־בָנֶ֖יךָ אִתָּֽךְ:   טז

כָּל־הַחַיָּ֣ה אֲשֶֽׁר־אִתְּךָ֗ מִכָּל־בָּשָׂ֞ר בָּע֧וֹף וּבַבְּהֵמָ֛ה   יז

וּבְכָל־הָרֶ֛מֶשׂ הָרֹמֵ֥שׂ עַל־הָאָ֖רֶץ הוצא [הַיְצֵ֣א] אִתָּ֑ךְ וְשָֽׁרְצ֣וּ

בָאָ֔רֶץ וּפָר֥וּ וְרָב֖וּ עַל־הָאָֽרֶץ: וַיֵּ֖צֵא־נֹ֑חַ וּבָנָ֛יו וְאִשְׁתּ֥וֹ   יח

וּנְשֵֽׁי־בָנָ֖יו אִתּֽוֹ: כָּל־הַֽחַיָּ֗ה כָּל־הָרֶ֙מֶשׂ֙ וְכָל־הָע֔וֹף כֹּ֖ל   יט

רוֹמֵ֣שׂ עַל־הָאָ֑רֶץ לְמִשְׁפְּחֹ֣תֵיהֶ֔ם יָצְא֖וּ מִן־הַתֵּבָֽה: וַיִּ֥בֶן   כ

נֹ֛חַ מִזְבֵּ֖חַ לַֽיהוָ֑ה וַיִּקַּ֞ח מִכֹּ֣ל ׀ הַבְּהֵמָ֣ה הַטְּהֹרָ֗ה וּמִכֹּל֙

הָע֣וֹף הַטָּהֹ֔ר וַיַּ֥עַל עֹלֹ֖ת בַּמִּזְבֵּֽחַ: וַיָּ֣רַח יְהוָה֮ אֶת־   כא

רֵ֣יחַ הַנִּיחֹחַ֒ וַיֹּ֨אמֶר יְהוָ֜ה אֶל־לִבּ֗וֹ לֹֽא־אֹ֠סִף לְקַלֵּ֨ל

ע֤וֹד אֶת־הָֽאֲדָמָה֙ בַּֽעֲב֣וּר הָֽאָדָ֔ם כִּ֠י יֵ֣צֶר לֵ֧ב הָֽאָדָ֛ם

* יח היצא קרי.

רַ֣ע מִנְּעֻרָ֑יו וְלֹֽא־אֹסִ֥ף ע֛וֹד לְהַכּ֥וֹת אֶת־כָּל־חַ֖י כַּֽאֲשֶׁ֥ר

עָשִֽׂיתִי: עֹ֖ד כָּל־יְמֵ֣י הָאָ֑רֶץ זֶ֡רַע וְ֠קָצִיר וְקֹ֨ר וָחֹ֜ם   כב

וְקַ֧יִץ וָחֹ֛רֶף וְי֥וֹם וָלַ֖יְלָה לֹ֥א יִשְׁבֹּֽתוּ:

וַיְבָ֣רֶךְ אֱלֹהִ֔ים אֶת־נֹ֖חַ וְאֶת־בָּנָ֑יו וַיֹּ֧אמֶר לָהֶ֛ם פְּר֥וּ   א

וּרְב֖וּ וּמִלְא֥וּ אֶת־הָאָֽרֶץ: וּמֽוֹרַֽאֲכֶ֤ם וְחִתְּכֶם֙ יִֽהְיֶ֔ה עַ֚ל   ב

כָּל־חַיַּ֣ת הָאָ֔רֶץ וְעַ֖ל כָּל־ע֣וֹף הַשָּׁמָ֑יִם בְּכֹל֩ אֲשֶׁ֨ר

תִּרְמֹ֧שׂ הָֽאֲדָמָ֛ה וּבְכָל־דְּגֵ֥י הַיָּ֖ם בְּיֶדְכֶ֥ם נִתָּֽנוּ: כָּל־   ג

רֶ֙מֶשׂ֙ אֲשֶׁ֣ר הוּא־חַ֔י לָכֶ֥ם יִֽהְיֶ֖ה לְאָכְלָ֑ה כְּיֶ֣רֶק עֵ֔שֶׂב

נָתַ֥תִּי לָכֶ֖ם אֶת־כֹּֽל: אַךְ־בָּשָׂ֕ר בְּנַפְשׁ֥וֹ דָמ֖וֹ לֹ֥א תֹאכֵֽלוּ:   ד

וְאַ֨ךְ אֶת־דִּמְכֶ֤ם לְנַפְשֹֽׁתֵיכֶם֙ אֶדְרֹ֔שׁ מִיַּ֥ד כָּל־חַיָּ֖ה   ה

אֶדְרְשֶׁ֑נּוּ וּמִיַּ֣ד הָֽאָדָ֗ם מִיַּד֙ אִ֣ישׁ אָחִ֔יו אֶדְרֹ֖שׁ אֶת־נֶ֥פֶשׁ

15] God spoke to Noah, saying, **16]** "Come out of the ark, together with your wife, your sons, and your sons' wives. **17]** Bring out with you every living thing of all flesh that is with you: birds, animals, and everything that creeps on earth; and let them swarm on the earth and be fertile and increase on earth." **18]** So Noah came out, together with his sons, his wife, and his sons' wives. **19]** Every animal, every creeping thing, and every bird, everything that stirs on earth came out of the ark by families.

20] Then Noah built an altar to the LORD and, taking of every clean animal and of every clean bird, he offered burnt offerings on the altar. **21]** The LORD smelled the pleasing odor, and the LORD said to Himself: "Never again will I doom the earth because of man, since the devisings of man's mind are evil from his youth; nor will I ever again destroy every living being, as I have done. **22]** So long as the earth endures, / Seedtime and harvest, / Cold and heat, / Summer and winter, / Day and night / Shall not cease."

1] God blessed Noah and his sons, and said to them, "Be fertile and increase, and fill the earth. **2]** The fear and the dread of you shall be upon all the beasts of the earth and upon all the birds of the sky—everything with which the earth is astir—and upon all the fish of the sea; they are given into your hand. **3]** Every creature that lives shall be yours to eat; as with the green grasses, I give you all these. **4]** You must not, however, eat flesh with its life-blood in it. **5]** But for your own life-blood I will require a reckoning: I will require it of every beast; of man, too, will I require a reckoning for human life, of every man for that of his fellow

---

8:21] *Smelled.* The Torah speaks of God in human terms. In its language, "smelling the pleasing odor" is equivalent to "accepting favorably" [1]. Compare this with a parallel incident in "Gilgamesh": "The gods smelled the savor, / The gods smelled the goodly savor, / The gods gathered like flies over the sacrificer" [2].

Evil from his youth. The Flood has not changed the nature of man.

9:3] *Yours to eat.* Adam was restricted to a vege-

tarian diet (Gen. 1:29); Noah and his descendants are permitted the flesh of animals.

4] *Life-blood in it.* The prohibition reflects the conviction that blood has a sacral character. For a full discussion, see commentary on Lev. 17.

5] *I will require it of every beast.* Animals, too, are held responsible for acts of violence against man: "When an ox gores a man or a woman to death, the ox shall be stoned" (Exod. 21:28) [3].

י הָאָדָם: שֹׁפֵךְ דַּם הָאָדָם בָּאָדָם דָּמוֹ יִשָּׁפֵךְ כִּי

ז בְּצֶלֶם אֱלֹהִים עָשָׂה אֶת־הָאָדָם: וְאַתֶּם פְּרוּ וּרְבוּ

שִׁרְצוּ בָאָרֶץ וּרְבוּ־בָהּ: ס וַיֹּאמֶר אֱלֹהִים אֶל־נֹחַ

ט וְאֶל־בָּנָיו אִתּוֹ לֵאמֹר: וַאֲנִי הִנְנִי מֵקִים אֶת־בְּרִיתִי

י אִתְּכֶם וְאֶת־זַרְעֲכֶם אַחֲרֵיכֶם: וְאֵת כָּל־נֶפֶשׁ הַחַיָּה

אֲשֶׁר אִתְּכֶם בָּעוֹף בַּבְּהֵמָה וּבְכָל־חַיַּת הָאָרֶץ אִתְּכֶם

יא מִכֹּל יֹצְאֵי הַתֵּבָה לְכֹל חַיַּת הָאָרֶץ: וַהֲקִמֹתִי אֶת־

בְּרִיתִי אִתְּכֶם וְלֹא־יִכָּרֵת כָּל־בָּשָׂר עוֹד מִמֵּי הַמַּבּוּל

יב וְלֹא־יִהְיֶה עוֹד מַבּוּל לְשַׁחֵת הָאָרֶץ: וַיֹּאמֶר אֱלֹהִים

זֹאת אוֹת־הַבְּרִית אֲשֶׁר־אֲנִי נֹתֵן בֵּינִי וּבֵינֵיכֶם וּבֵין

יג כָּל־נֶפֶשׁ חַיָּה אֲשֶׁר אִתְּכֶם לְדֹרֹת עוֹלָם: אֶת־קַשְׁתִּי

נָתַתִּי בֶּעָנָן וְהָיְתָה לְאוֹת בְּרִית בֵּינִי וּבֵין הָאָרֶץ:

יד וְהָיָה בְּעַנְנִי עָנָן עַל־הָאָרֶץ וְנִרְאֲתָה הַקֶּשֶׁת בֶּעָנָן:

טו וְזָכַרְתִּי אֶת־בְּרִיתִי אֲשֶׁר בֵּינִי וּבֵינֵיכֶם וּבֵין כָּל־נֶפֶשׁ

חַיָּה בְּכָל־בָּשָׂר וְלֹא־יִהְיֶה עוֹד הַמַּיִם לְמַבּוּל לְשַׁחֵת

טז כָּל־בָּשָׂר: וְהָיְתָה הַקֶּשֶׁת בֶּעָנָן וּרְאִיתִיהָ לִזְכֹּר בְּרִית

עוֹלָם בֵּין אֱלֹהִים וּבֵין כָּל־נֶפֶשׁ חַיָּה בְּכָל־בָּשָׂר אֲשֶׁר

יז עַל־הָאָרֶץ: וַיֹּאמֶר אֱלֹהִים אֶל־נֹחַ זֹאת אוֹת־הַבְּרִית

אֲשֶׁר הֲקִמֹתִי בֵּינִי וּבֵין כָּל־בָּשָׂר אֲשֶׁר עַל־הָאָרֶץ: פ

יח וַיִּהְיוּ בְנֵי־נֹחַ הַיֹּצְאִים מִן־הַתֵּבָה שֵׁם וְחָם וָיָפֶת וְחָם

יט הוּא אֲבִי כְנָעַן: שְׁלֹשָׁה אֵלֶּה בְּנֵי־נֹחַ וּמֵאֵלֶּה נָפְצָה

כ כָל־הָאָרֶץ: וַיָּחֶל נֹחַ אִישׁ הָאֲדָמָה וַיִּטַּע כָּרֶם: וַיֵּשְׁתְּ

כב מִן־הַיַּיִן וַיִּשְׁכָּר וַיִּתְגַּל בְּתוֹךְ אָהֳלֹה: וַיַּרְא חָם אֲבִי

כג כְנַעַן אֵת עֶרְוַת אָבִיו וַיַּגֵּד לִשְׁנֵי־אֶחָיו בַּחוּץ: וַיִּקַּח

man!   **6]** Whoever sheds the blood of man, / By man shall his blood be shed; / For in His image / Did God make man.   **7]** Be fertile, then, and increase; abound on the earth and increase on it."

8] And God said to Noah and to his sons with him,   **9]** "I now establish My covenant with you and your offspring to come,   **10]** and with every living thing that is with you—birds, cattle, and every wild beast as well—all that have come out of the ark, every living thing on earth.   **11]** I will maintain My covenant with you: never again shall all flesh be cut off by the waters of a flood, and never again shall there be a flood to destroy the earth."

12] God further said, "This is the sign that I set for the covenant between Me and you, and every living creature with you, for all ages to come.   **13]** I have set My bow in the clouds, and it shall serve as a sign of the covenant between Me and the earth.   **14]** When I bring clouds over the earth, and the bow appears in the clouds,   **15]** I will remember My covenant between Me and you and every living creature among all flesh, so that the waters shall never again become a flood to destroy all flesh.   **16]** When the bow is in the clouds, I will see it and remember the everlasting covenant between God and all living creatures, all flesh that is on earth.   **17]** That," God said to Noah, "shall be the sign of the covenant that I have established between Me and all flesh that is on earth."

18] The sons of Noah who came out of the ark were Shem, Ham, and Japheth—Ham being the father of Canaan.   **19]** These three were the sons of Noah, and from these the whole world branched out.

20] Noah, the tiller of the soil, was the first to plant a vineyard.   **21]** He drank of the wine and became drunk, and he uncovered himself within his tent.   **22]** Ham, the father of Canaan, saw his father's nakedness and told his two brothers outside.   **23]** But Shem and Japheth took a

---

9] *My covenant.* God now fulfills the promise made before the Flood (6:18). The term בְּרִית (berit) is often used with the verb כָּרַת (cut). "To cut a berit" is idiomatic for "to conclude a covenant." (See Gen. 15:10.)

18] *Shem.* Ancestor of all Semites.

Ham being the father of Canaan. As far as the Torah is concerned, this is Ham's primary importance.

20] *To plant a vineyard.* Wine growing is repre-

שֵׁם וָיֶפֶת אֶת־הַשִּׂמְלָה וַיָּשִׂימוּ עַל־שְׁכֶם שְׁנֵיהֶם וַיֵּלְכוּ
אֲחֹרַנִּית וַיְכַסּוּ אֵת עֶרְוַת אֲבִיהֶם וּפְנֵיהֶם אֲחֹרַנִּית
וְעֶרְוַת אֲבִיהֶם לֹא רָאוּ: וַיִּיקֶץ נֹחַ מִיֵּינוֹ וַיֵּדַע אֵת
אֲשֶׁר־עָשָׂה לוֹ בְּנוֹ הַקָּטָן: וַיֹּאמֶר אָרוּר כְּנָעַן עֶבֶד
עֲבָדִים יִהְיֶה לְאֶחָיו: וַיֹּאמֶר בָּרוּךְ יְהֹוָה אֱלֹהֵי שֵׁם

כב וַיְהִי כְנַעַן עֶבֶד לָמוֹ: יַפְתְּ אֱלֹהִים לְיֶפֶת וְיִשְׁכֹּן
כג בְּאָהֳלֵי־שֵׁם וִיהִי כְנַעַן עֶבֶד לָמוֹ: וַיְחִי־נֹחַ אַחַר
כט הַמַּבּוּל שְׁלֹשׁ מֵאוֹת שָׁנָה וַחֲמִשִּׁים שָׁנָה: וַיְהִי כָּל־
יְמֵי־נֹחַ תְּשַׁע מֵאוֹת שָׁנָה וַחֲמִשִּׁים שָׁנָה וַיָּמֹת: פ

cloth, placed it against both their backs and, walking backwards, they covered their father's nakedness; their faces were turned the other way, so that they did not see their father's nakedness. **24]** When Noah woke up from his wine and learned what his youngest son had done to him, **25]** he said, "Cursed be Canaan; / The lowest of slaves / Shall he be to his brothers." **26]** And he said, "Blessed be the LORD / The God of Shem; / Let Canaan be a slave to them. / **27]** May God enlarge Japheth, / And let him dwell in the tents of Shem; / And let Canaan be a slave to them."

28] Noah lived after the Flood 350 years. **29]** And all the days of Noah came to 950 years; then he died.

sented as an ancient practice.
/Compare the Greek stories of Deucalion and Dionysus and of "Gilgamesh" which tells of Utnapishtim giving wine to his ark-building workmen./

24] *His youngest son.* Ham is here called the youngest; elsewhere (Gen. 9:18; 10:1) he is listed as the middle brother. Critics see two separate traditions here. Older commentators took "youngest" to mean "unworthy," as in Gen. 32:11.

25] *The lowest of slaves.* The Hebrew idiom is "slave of slaves."

26] *Blessed be the Lord.* Noah blesses not Shem but Shem's God, for blessing a person's divine protector

represented or reinforced the blessing of the person himself (cf. I Sam. 25:32).

Canaan be a slave. Advocates of the black man's slavery used to base their beliefs on this text, but this passage deals with political subjection and has nothing whatsoever to do with race.

27] *May God enlarge Japheth.* A word play on יַפְתְּ־יֶפֶת. Japheth here most likely refers to the Philistines, while Shem refers to the Israelites. Genesis (unlike Judges and Samuel) envisions the Philistines and Israelites as living in harmony. The verse, therefore, probably means: "May God make room for the Philistines that they might dwell peacefully with Israel" [4].

The Rainbow

In ancient mythologies a rainbow represented instruments used by gods in battle. The bows would be hung in the sky as symbols of victory. In Babylonian tradition, for example, the god Marduk suspended his bow in the heavens after he had defeated Tiamat, the goddess of the deep waters. The Bible has retained aspects of such myths. The Hebrew word קֶשֶׁת (keshet) means both "bow of war" and "rainbow," but as usual the Torah has assimilated the material to convey a deeper meaning.

It believes that God is the proximate cause of all natural events and that manifestations of the natural order are invested with divine portent.[1] Thunder, earthquakes, and floods fall under this rubric as does the rainbow (see commentary to Gen. 6:9–8:14). The text sees the bow both as a sign of God's rulership over the natural order and as God's permanent signature to His promise. The rainbow is thought to remind God of this promise and to remind man of the grace and forbearance of his Creator.

The Crime of Ham

The punishment meted out to Ham seems harsh in the extreme, and this harshness suggests that the Bible was referring to a transgression far more serious than seeing one's father naked and in a drunken stupor. Uncovering a relative's nakedness was a biblical euphemism for sexual relations (see Lev. 18). The story of Ham and Noah should be read, therefore, as one of sexual perversion.

The brevity of the biblical story may be due to the expurgation of a more detailed version, but even in the condensed form the ancient Israelites doubtlessly understood its implication.[2] In the context of Genesis, the tale was a subtle assertion that the Hamites (Egyptians) and the Canaanites were the descendants of sexual deviates. The crime of Ham, therefore, belongs to the genre of polemics employed against Israel's nearest neighbors and dearest enemies.

It is worth noting that the Bible assigned a prominent place to the theme of sexuality in the stories of both the first antediluvians (Adam and Eve) and the first postdiluvians (Noah and his offspring). Further, the motif of sexual aberration linked to drunkenness occurs again in the story of Lot and his daughters—a story that ends by asserting that Moab and Ammon also were nations of indecent sexual background (Gen. 19:32–38).

The Noahide Laws

Even before the revelation at Sinai there were certain laws, according to the Rabbis, that were binding on all men. This view holds that while Jews are subject to the extensive provisions of the Torah all non-Jews must observe at least a number of fundamental precepts deemed essential for the maintenance of a decent society. These laws are called "Noahide"; they were believed to have been incumbent on the sons of Noah and therefore to have become obligatory for man-

---

[1] A number of commentators follow Saadia who interprets Gen. 9:13 to mean that while God had previously created the rainbow as part of the natural order He now invested it with meaning [5]. Ibn Ezra rejects this view.

[2] The Talmud records an argument on this matter between Rav and Samuel. One of them believed that Noah had been castrated, the other that he had been abused sexually [6]. The argument may appear far-fetched unless viewed in conjunction with an old Canaanite myth that told how the god El-Kronos had emasculated his father and with the Hurrian legend that told how Kumarbis severed the genitals of his father, the god Anu. In the Midrash [7] Ham is portrayed as laughing at his father, and so is Kumarbis who like Ham is cursed for his deed. Evidently these old mythic traditions were current millennia after they were first told, and we may assume that they were familiar to the biblical author.

kind, since from Noah's sons "the whole world branched out" (Gen. 9:19) [8].

In interpreting chapter 2, verse 16,[3] the Rabbis established six such basic laws: Man may not worship idols; he may not blaspheme God; he must establish courts of justice; he may not kill; he may not commit adultery; and he may not rob. A seventh law—that man may not eat flesh cut from a living animal—was added after the Flood (Gen. 9:4). Rabbinic lists vary [10], but the basic concept remains the same: every man can arrive at and must come to observe a minimum of religious and legal precepts.[4]

Consequently, Jewish tradition distinguished between three types of Gentiles: the *Nochri* (*Akkum*), who does not observe the Noahide laws; the *Ben Noah*, who does; and the *Ger Toshav*, who officially declares before a court that he will observe the seven precepts. The latter was then given the privilege of becoming a resident alien in the Holy Land. "Unlike Christianity, Judaism does not deny salvation to those outside of its fold, for, according to Jewish law, all non-Jews who observe the Noahide laws will participate in salvation and in the rewards of the world to come" [12].

But if most of these laws were already known to Adam, why were they named for Noah and not Adam? "The answer is that all law must be rooted in a covenant, and before Noah there was no covenant. There is a legal relationship implied in the fulfilment of ethical commandments" [13]. God's covenant with Noah established the framework in which it became possible to speak of law.

A Source of Jewish Law

Several biblical passages in this section became the reference points or proof texts for certain regulations of later Jewish law.

The prohibition against consuming blood was based on "You must not, however, eat flesh with its life-blood in it" (Gen. 9:4). While this was taken to refer primarily to a limb from a living animal (אֵבֶר מִן הַחַי), it also became a foundation for many Jewish dietary and slaughtering regulations [14].

The prohibition against self-injury and suicide was based on "for your own life-blood I will require a reckoning" (Gen. 9:5) [15]. Note that in biblical times suicide was rare (except under stress of battle; see I Sam. 31:4; I Kings 16:18). The only other incident recorded is the death of Ahithophel (II Sam. 17:23).

The limits of self-defense were discussed in reference to chapter 9, verse 6, which forbids bloodshed because God made man in His image. Since one man's blood is not redder (i.e., better) than another's, no man may take an innocent life even if this is the only way to save his own [16].

The prohibition against abortion was based on the same verse, but reading it in a different way: "Whoever sheds the blood of *man in man*" [17].

The duty to have children was derived from "Be fertile and increase" (Gen. 9:1, 7). When God first said that man should be fertile (Gen. 1:28), it was a blessing: here it is issued as a command, and several children must be fathered in order to fulfil it [18].

---

[3] The command (in Gen. 2:16) to Adam (i.e., to all men) is taken to imply that all men can have a concept of God and are therefore forbidden to blaspheme Him or to practice idolatry. "Commanded" is taken to presuppose law hence meaning that every society is bound to establish courts of law. In this homiletic fashion three other basic prohibitions are derived [9].

[4] The rabbinic tradition is reflected in Paul's teaching about Noahides. He requires of Gentiles that they abstain from the pollutions of idols, from eating blood and the meat of strange animals, and from fornication [11].

GLEANINGS

Carnivorous Man

God, surveying the survivors of the Flood, judges man to have remained what he always was, namely, "evil from his youth" (Gen. 8:21). Antediluvian man had been rapacious and violent, and postdiluvian man still is. The permission to eat flesh appears therefore as God's resigned adjustment to the human reality.

Noah's Drunkenness

God said to Noah: "You should have been warned by the example of Adam whose perdition came about through eating the fruit of the vine." It is taught that the tree from which the original Adam ate was the vine, for there is nothing which brings man as much misery as wine.

TALMUD [19]

The story of Noah's drunkenness expresses the healthy recoil of primitive Semitic morality from the licentious habits engendered by a civilization the salient feature of which was the enjoyment and abuse of wine. JOHN SKINNER [20]

The Waters of Noah

For this to Me is like the waters of Noah:
As I swore that the waters of Noah
Nevermore would flood the earth,
So I swear that I will not
Be angry with you or rebuke you.
For the mountains may move
And the hills be shaken,
But My loyalty shall never move from you,
Nor My covenant of friendship be shaken
—said the LORD, who takes you back in love.

ISAIAH 54:9–10

[Read as the prophetic portion (*Haftarah*) when the Noah story is the assigned weekly Torah reading (*sidrah*).]

A New Creation

In a number of ways Noah parallels Adam, for both are the progenitors of succeeding generations. Compare Gen. 1:27 and 9:6 (created in God's image); 1:28 and 9:1–2 (commanded to be fertile; given mastery over creation); 3:17 and 8:22 (Noah saved from the curse put upon Adam).

Humiliation

The Torah condemns shedding "the blood of man in man" (a literal reading of 9:6; see the halachic application above).

God will require the penalty also of him who publicly humiliates a fellow man, whose blood is "shed" when he is made to blush in shame.

CHAFETZ CHAYIM [21]

72

The Nations

Chapter 10 is an overview of the nations known to biblical tradition. It belongs to the last segment of the book in which the canvas is universal; thereafter, its focus contracts toward its major theme: the emergence of one family and the people who will descend from it. The table of nations is therefore more than a catalog of names; it is the background for the stories to follow.

א וְאֵ֣לֶּה תּוֹלְדֹ֣ת בְּנֵי־נֹ֔חַ שֵׁ֖ם חָ֣ם וָיָ֑פֶת וַיִּוָּלְד֥וּ לָהֶ֖ם
נִפְרְד֞וּ אִיֵּ֤י הַגּוֹיִם֙ בְּאַרְצֹתָ֔ם אִ֖ישׁ לִלְשֹׁנ֑וֹ לְמִשְׁפְּחֹתָ֖ם

ב בְּנֵ֥י יֶ֖פֶת גֹּ֣מֶר וּמָג֑וֹג וּמָדַ֣י וְיָוָ֔ן
בָּנִ֖ים אַחַ֣ר הַמַּבּ֑וּל׃ בְּגוֹיֵהֶֽם׃ וּבְנֵ֣י חָ֔ם כּ֥וּשׁ וּמִצְרַ֖יִם וּפ֥וּט וּכְנָֽעַן׃ וּבְנֵ֣י

ג וְתֻבַ֥ל וּמֶ֖שֶׁךְ וְתִירָֽס׃ וּבְנֵ֖י גֹּ֑מֶר אַשְׁכְּנַ֥ז וְרִיפַ֖ת וְתֹגַרְמָֽה׃
כ֔וּשׁ סְבָא֙ וַחֲוִילָ֔ה וְסַבְתָּ֥ה וְרַעְמָ֖ה וְסַבְתְּכָ֑א וּבְנֵ֣י

ד וּבְנֵ֥י יָוָ֖ן אֱלִישָׁ֣ה וְתַרְשִׁ֑ישׁ כִּתִּ֖ים וְדֹדָנִֽים׃ מֵאֵ֣לֶּה
רַעְמָ֖ה שְׁבָ֣א וּדְדָ֑ן׃ וְכ֖וּשׁ יָלַ֣ד אֶת־נִמְרֹ֑ד ה֣וּא הֵחֵ֔ל

1] These are the lines of Shem, Ham, and Japheth, the sons of Noah: sons were born to them after the Flood.

2] The descendants of Japheth: Gomer, Magog, Madai, Javan, Tubal, Meshech, and Tiras. 3] The descendants of Gomer: Ashkenaz, Riphath, and Togarmah. 4] The descendants of Javan: Elishah and Tarshish, the Kittim, and the Dodanim. 5] From these the maritime nations branched out. [These are the descendants of Japheth] by their lands—each with its language—their clans and their nations.

6] The descendants of Ham: Cush, Mizraim, Put, and Canaan. 7] The descendants of Cush: Seba, Havilah, Sabtah, Raamah, and Sabteca. The descendants of Raamah: Sheba and Dedan.

8] Cush also begot Nimrod, who was the first man of might on earth. 9] He was a mighty

---

10:2] *Gomer.* Probably the Cimmerians (from which today's Welsh derive their name Cymry).

Magog. The land of Gog (Ezek. 38:2; 39:6), in Armenia.

3] *Ashkenaz.* Probably the Scythians. In Medieval Hebrew this name was given to Germany, and Jews from Central and Eastern Europe were called Ashkenazim, in contrast to the Spanish and Oriental Jews, called Sephardim.

4] *Tarshish.* Best known as the place to which Jonah tried to flee. It is usually identified as Tartessos in Spain.

/However, since Spain seems to lie outside the geographic range mentioned in Gen. 10, this may refer to another place by the same name, perhaps Tarsus in Cilicia, Asia Minor. It is also possible that Tarshish was originally a generic word meaning refinery./

Dodanim. In I Chron. 1:7 and the Septuagint, the name given is *Rodanim*, possibly referring to people from Rhodes.

/Others have *Dordanim*, which would refer to Dardania, near Troy [1]./

5] *Descendants of Japheth.* The bracketed portion of the sentence was probably omitted through scribal error.

6] *Cush.* Either Ethiopia or Midian (north of the Gulf of Akaba).

/In other contexts the name may refer to the Kassites, a people who ruled Babylonia from the sixteenth to the twelfth centuries B.C.E. and then retreated to the highlands east of the Tigris. That Cush may refer to Midian is evidenced by Exod. 2:16, 21 ff. and Num. 12:1 [2] as well as by Egyptian execration texts which place Cush south of the Dead Sea./

Mizraim. Egypt.

Canaan. His listing as a descendant of Ham suggests an age in which Egypt's rule extended into Asia, Canaan, and beyond, before the invasions of the sea peoples (the Japhethites in the latter part of the second millennium B.C.E.) put an effective end to Egypt's Asiatic empire.

8] *Nimrod.* The brief reference to Nimrod is probably a fragment from a large epic, well known in its time, which likely dealt with Tukulti-Ninurta I, who ruled Assyria *ca.* 1244–1208 B.C.E. and who controlled both Babylonia and Assyria (as verse 10 suggests) [3].

וְאֶת־כַּסְלֻחִים אֲשֶׁר יָצְאוּ מִשָּׁם פְּלִשְׁתִּים וְאֶת־   לִהְיוֹת גִּבֹּר בָּאָרֶץ: הוּא־הָיָה גִבֹּר־צַיִד לִפְנֵי יְהוָה ט

כַּפְתֹּרִים: ס וּכְנַעַן יָלַד אֶת־צִידֹן בְּכֹרוֹ וְאֶת־חֵת: עַל־כֵּן יֵאָמַר כְּנִמְרֹד גִּבּוֹר צַיִד לִפְנֵי יְהוָה: וַתְּהִי י טו

וְאֶת־הַיְבוּסִי וְאֶת־הָאֱמֹרִי וְאֵת הַגִּרְגָּשִׁי: וְאֶת־הַחִוִּי   רֵאשִׁית מַמְלַכְתּוֹ בָּבֶל וְאֶרֶךְ וְאַכַּד וְכַלְנֵה בְּאֶרֶץ טז

וְאֶת־הָעַרְקִי וְאֶת־הַסִּינִי: וְאֶת־הָאַרְוָדִי וְאֶת־הַצְּמָרִי   שִׁנְעָר: מִן־הָאָרֶץ הַהִוא יָצָא אַשּׁוּר וַיִּבֶן אֶת־נִינְוֵה יא יז

וְאֶת־הַחֲמָתִי וְאַחַר נָפֹצוּ מִשְׁפְּחוֹת הַכְּנַעֲנִי: וַיְהִי   וְאֶת־רְחֹבֹת עִיר וְאֶת־כָּלַח: וְאֶת־רֶסֶן בֵּין נִינְוֵה וּבֵין יב יח

גְּבוּל הַכְּנַעֲנִי מִצִּידֹן בֹּאֲכָה גְרָרָה עַד־עַזָּה   כָּלַח הִוא הָעִיר הַגְּדֹלָה: וּמִצְרַיִם יָלַד אֶת־לוּדִים יג יט

בֹּאֲכָה סְדֹמָה וַעֲמֹרָה וְאַדְמָה וּצְבֹיִם* עַד־לָשַׁע: וְאֶת־עֲנָמִים וְאֶת־לְהָבִים וְאֶת־נַפְתֻּחִים: וְאֶת־פַּתְרֻסִים יד

* יָם וּצְבוֹיִם קרי.

hunter by the grace of the LORD; hence the saying, "Like Nimrod a mighty hunter by the grace of the LORD." **10]** The mainstays of his kingdom were Babylon, Erech, Accad, and Calneh in the land of Shinar. **11]** From that land Asshur went forth and built Nineveh, Rehoboth-ir, Calah, **12]** and Resen between Nineveh and Calah, that is the great city.

13] And Mizraim begot the Ludim, the Anamim, the Lehabim, the Naphtuhim, **14]** the Pathrusim, the Casluhim, and the Caphtorim, whence the Philistines came forth.

15] Canaan begot Sidon, his first-born, and Heth; **16]** and the Jebusites, the Amorites, the Girgashites, **17]** the Hivites, the Arkites, the Sinites, **18]** the Arvadites, the Zemarites, and the Hamathites. Afterward the clans of the Canaanites spread out, (**19]** The [original] Canaanite territory extended from Sidon as far as Gerar, near Gaza, and as far as Sodom,

---

9] *Hunter.* Hunting was practiced in ancient Israel (see Lev. 17:13) but apparently played only a small role in its largely agrarian and urban society.

/In later centuries Jews considered the hunt a cruel and therefore uncivilized sport. "He who hunts game with dogs as Gentiles do will not enjoy the life to come" [4]./

10] *And Calneh.* Probably a case of faulty vocalization of the text. The original Hebrew manuscript was written without vowels, which were added more than a thousand years later. By changing כַּלְנֵה (*kalneh*) to כֻּלָּנָה (*kulanah,* all of these), the sentence reads: "The mainstays of his kingdom were Babylon, Erech, Accad, all of these [being] in the land of Shinar" (see Gen. 42:36, where כֻּלָּנָה occurs) [5].

Shinar. Biblical name for the area of Babylonia, and especially for Sumer.

12] *Calah.* A Mesopotamian city founded by Shalmaneser I (*ca.* 1274–1245 B.C.E.), which has been thoroughly explored by archeologists. It was a "great city" in its day.

/It served as one of the great capital cities of the neo-Assyrian kings from 880–615 B.C.E. Today it is known as Nimrud./

13] *Begot.* To be understood as "was the ancestor of." Similarly, the expressions "father" and "son" often mean ancestor and descendant.

14] *And the Caphtorim.* In the Hebrew text these words come at the end of the sentence. The transposition in this translation is made because the Philistines came from Caphtor (see Amos 9:7). The Caphtorim are usually identified as Cretans. However, no archeological evidence has been found to make the identification certain.

15] *Sidon.* North of Acre.

Heth. A reference to the "Neo-Hittites," who established themselves in northern Syria after the overthrow of the old Hittite (Hatti) empire in Anatolia, about 1200 B.C.E. Biblical references to Hittites are generally to the Neo-Hittites, some of whom drifted into Canaan (see, e.g., 23:3). See also Deut. 7:1.

כ אֵ֣לֶּה בְנֵי־חָם֙ לְמִשְׁפְּחֹתָ֔ם לִלְשֹֽׁנֹתָ֖ם בְּאַרְצֹתָ֑ם   כּו שֶׁ֣לֶף וְאֶת־חֲצַרְמָ֔וֶת וְאֶת־יָֽרַח: וְאֶת־הֲדוֹרָ֥ם וְאֶת־אוּזָ֖ל
בְּגֽוֹיֵהֶֽם: ס   כח וְאֶת־דִּקְלָֽה: וְאֶת־עוֹבָ֥ל וְאֶת־אֲבִֽימָאֵ֖ל וְאֶת־שְׁבָֽא:
כא וּלְשֵׁ֥ם יֻלַּ֖ד גַּם־ה֑וּא אֲבִי֙ כָּל־בְּנֵי־עֵ֔בֶר אֲחִ֖י יֶ֥פֶת   כט וְאֶת־אוֹפִ֥ר וְאֶת־חֲוִילָ֖ה וְאֶת־יוֹבָ֑ב כָּל־אֵ֖לֶּה בְּנֵ֥י יָקְטָֽן:
הַגָּדֽוֹל: ל וַֽיְהִ֥י מֽוֹשָׁבָ֖ם מִמֵּשָׁ֑א בֹּֽאֲכָ֥ה סְפָ֖רָה הַ֥ר הַקֶּֽדֶם:
כב בְּנֵ֣י שֵׁ֔ם עֵילָ֣ם וְאַשּׁ֔וּר וְאַרְפַּכְשַׁ֖ד וְל֥וּד   לא אֵ֣לֶּה בְנֵי־שֵׁם֙ לְמִשְׁפְּחֹתָ֔ם לִלְשֹֽׁנֹתָ֖ם בְּאַרְצֹתָ֖ם לְגֽוֹיֵהֶֽם:
וַאֲרָֽם: לב אֵ֣לֶּה מִשְׁפְּחֹ֧ת בְּנֵי־נֹ֛חַ לְתֽוֹלְדֹתָ֖ם בְּגֽוֹיֵהֶ֑ם וּמֵאֵ֜לֶּה
כג וּבְנֵ֖י אֲרָ֑ם ע֥וּץ וְח֖וּל וְגֶ֥תֶר וָמַֽשׁ: וְאַרְפַּכְשַׁ֖ד   נִפְרְד֧וּ הַגּוֹיִ֛ם בָּאָ֖רֶץ אַחַ֥ר הַמַּבּֽוּל: פ
כד יָלַ֣ד אֶת־שָׁ֔לַח וְשֶׁ֖לַח יָלַ֥ד אֶת־עֵֽבֶר: וּלְעֵ֖בֶר יֻלַּ֣ד
שְׁנֵ֣י בָנִ֑ים שֵׁ֣ם הָֽאֶחָ֞ד פֶּ֗לֶג כִּ֤י בְיָמָיו֙ נִפְלְגָ֣ה הָאָ֔רֶץ
כה וְשֵׁ֥ם אָחִ֖יו יָקְטָֽן: וְיָקְטָ֣ן יָלַ֔ד אֶת־אַלְמוֹדָ֖ד וְאֶת־

Gomorrah, Admah, and Zeboiim, near Lasha.)   20] These are the descendants of Ham, according to their clans and languages, by their lands and nations.

21] Sons were also born to Shem, ancestor of all the descendants of Eber and older brother of Japheth.   22] The descendants of Shem: Elam, Asshur, Arpachshad, Lud, and Aram. 23] The descendants of Aram: Uz, Hul, Gether, and Mash.   24] Arpachshad begot Shelah, and Shelah begot Eber.   25] Two sons were born to Eber: the name of the first was Peleg, for in his days the earth was divided; and the name of his brother was Joktan.   26] Joktan begot Almodad, Sheleph, Hazarmaveth, Jerah,   27] Hadoram, Uzal, Diklah,   28] Obal, Abimael, Sheba,   29] Ophir, Havilah, and Jobab; all these were the descendants of Joktan.   30] Their settlements extended from Mesha as far as Sephar, the hill country to the east.   31] These are the descendants of Shem according to their clans and languages, by their lands, according to their nations.

32] These are the groupings of Noah's descendants, according to their origins, by their nations; and from these the nations branched out over the earth after the Flood.

21] *Eber.* See Gen. 11:16 and commentary to Gen. 14:1–24, "Abraham the Hebrew."

22] *Elam.* A country mentioned frequently in the literature of antiquity. Its capital city was Susa (Shushan, cf. Esther 1:2), located southeast of modern Luristan, in Iran.
/The Christian Scriptures note that Elamites along with Parthians and Medes were found in Jerusalem on Shavuot (Pentecost); Acts 2:9./
Arpachshad. Identified by some scholars as Ur-Casdim, the place of Abraham's origin.

Aram. Ancestor of the Arameans whose script and language (Aramaic) began to spread in the

Near East before 1,000 B.C.E. By the sixth century B.C.E., Aramaic was widely used in the area and after the Babylonian exile displaced Hebrew as the popular language in Palestine. Portions of the Books of Daniel and Ezra are in Aramaic, which is also the dominant language of the Talmud.

25] *In his days the earth was divided.* נִפְלְגָה is a word play on פֶּלֶג. The phrase means that during Peleg's lifetime the event described in Gen. 9:19 took place, i.e., the whole world branched out and became settled.

The Table of Nations

The geographic area covered by the biblical table reaches from the Caucasus mountains in the north to Ethiopia in the south, from the Aegean Sea in the west to the highlands of Iran in the east. Broadly speaking, Japheth refers to the peoples at the northern and western periphery of the Fertile Crescent, including the Medes, the Cypriots, the Scythians, and the Ionians. The offspring of Ham dwell about the Red Sea and include Ethiopians, Egyptians, and Canaanites. The descendants of Shem live in the heart of the Crescent itself and include Arabs, Arameans, and Assyrians.

This chapter represents the combination of two separate traditions. The older one (Gen. 10:8–19, 21, 22–30) is concerned primarily with tribes and clans; the more recent one stresses the term גוי (goy, nation) and is mainly a catalog of states and languages (as, for instance, in verses 5, 20, 31, 32). The table of nations is remarkable for its wide scope and may be considered a pioneering effort among the ethnographic inquiries of antiquity [6]. It is presented in a nonmythological way, unlike a comparable Babylonian list, which states that "when kingship came down from heaven the kingdom was in Eridu."

It is, however, important to see the biblical list as more than ethnographic information. It is an integral part of the story of God's promise to Noah; it portrays the peoples of the earth, related through this promise, as one common humanity. The implicit theme of the text is the unity of man within the framework of apparent diversity.

No reference to "race" or skin color can be detected in this list. This is not to say that the Bible is without prejudices or preferences (see commentary to Gen. 8:15–9:29, "The Noahide Laws"). Occasionally it reflects certain political animosities, and repeatedly it condemns various nations because of their immoral or idolatrous practices, but it is totally devoid of any notion of racial superiority. The dispassionate character of this chapter is indicative of the Bible's overall approach to the structure of humanity.

Israel is not listed in the catalog. In fact, the text underplays the origins of the people to whom, after all, the Bible is devoted. Israel's origins are (like the stories of Eden and Noah) located outside Israelite territory, and just as in its territory there was no original distinction so there was none in its early ancestry. Its origins were seen as no different from those of any other nation. Only through its covenantal relationship with God would Israel pursue a special destiny.

Although Shem was the oldest of Noah's sons, he is listed last in the table of nations. Most probably this was done because his genealogy commands the Bible's eventual focus and, after the brief interruption occasioned by the Tower of Babel story, the text turns (Gen. 11:10) to a detailed description of Shem's line, i.e., of Abraham's antecedents.

GLEANINGS

Nimrod

The name means "one who stirred up rebellion" (הִמְרִיד) so that people no longer trusted God but their own power. "Nimrod knew his Master but decided to rebel against Him."

TALMUD [7]

Nimrod was responsible for the building of the Tower of Babel; he wanted it to be his throne so that divine honors would be accorded him. He was king when the boy Abraham was brought before him. Nimrod worshiped fire while Abraham tried to convince him of the supremacy of God. Nimrod cast the boy into the fire but God saved him, thus demonstrating the supremacy of His power.

MIDRASH [8]

"He was a mighty hunter" means that he hunted men's souls; he ensnared them and incited them against God. The building of the Tower of Babel was the culmination of his activities.

RASHI [9]

Why is Nimrod's name linked to that of God in Gen. 10:9? Because he oppressed people in God's name.

He was the prototype of all tyrants who piously pretend that their crown is "by God's grace," and thus their power politics and hypocrisy are characterized by the expression, "like Nimrod, who pretends to hunt in God's name."

SAMSON RAPHAEL HIRSCH

But another tradition admired Nimrod for being "the first man of might on earth." As late as the Middle Ages Jewish fathers when blessing their sons would wish them "to be like Nimrod."

The Table of Nations

Israel cannot pass by the existence of nations without discovering a profound moral intent therein, for Israel is the poet of the spiritual life of mankind as other peoples are the poets of nature.

MORDECAI M. KAPLAN [10]

The differences among men emerge naturally, that is, as a consequence of the sinfulness of men, amply attested in the generations after the Flood by their decreasing longevity. Looking out at the triumphant, unbridled paganism which surrounded them simply verified the biblical judgment for the rabbis: nationhood is natural, but a natural expression of man's will to do evil.

EUGENE B. BOROWITZ [11]

Babel and after:
THE END OF PREHISTORY

The Tower of Babel story, interrupting the catalog of nations begun in chapter 10 and continued in chapter 11, verse 10, stands between the universal tableau of humanity and that specific list of families from which Terah, Abraham, and their line will spring.

The story attempts to answer two questions: Where did the variety of languages come from? How did man disperse and populate the world? These questions were not considered in chapter 10. By setting out to answer them, the Bible brings us a special tradition, one which must have existed independently from the table of nations. For the Babel story presents all mankind living undivided in one small area. This unity of language and living space ends because man's rebellious action once again brings down the judgment of God.

While there is a Sumerian story of the confounding of tongues, no parallel account has so far been found in Near Eastern records that would afford us the kind of comparison and contrast through which the biblical purpose of the Flood tale is seen in high relief.

Biblical scholars generally believe that the opening section of Genesis which concludes here was originally separate from the patriarchal cycles which follow. The joining of prehistory and history (in its wider sense) affords the biblical editors the opportunity to show the rise of Abraham and his descendants in the full context of God's plans for mankind.

אֶחָד וְשָׂפָה אַחַת לְכֻלָּם וְזֶה הַחִלָּם לַעֲשׂוֹת וְעַתָּה
ז לֹא־יִבָּצֵר מֵהֶם כֹּל אֲשֶׁר יָזְמוּ לַעֲשׂוֹת: הָבָה נֵרְדָה
וְנָבְלָה שָׁם שְׂפָתָם אֲשֶׁר לֹא יִשְׁמְעוּ אִישׁ שְׂפַת רֵעֵהוּ:
ח וַיָּפֶץ יְהוָה אֹתָם מִשָּׁם עַל־פְּנֵי כָל־הָאָרֶץ וַיַּחְדְּלוּ
ט לִבְנֹת הָעִיר: עַל־כֵּן קָרָא שְׁמָהּ בָּבֶל כִּי־שָׁם בָּלַל
יְהוָה שְׂפַת כָּל־הָאָרֶץ וּמִשָּׁם הֱפִיצָם יְהוָה עַל־פְּנֵי
כָל־הָאָרֶץ: פ

א וַיְהִי כָל־הָאָרֶץ שָׂפָה אֶחָת וּדְבָרִים אֲחָדִים: וַיְהִי
בְּנָסְעָם מִקֶּדֶם וַיִּמְצְאוּ בִקְעָה בְּאֶרֶץ שִׁנְעָר וַיֵּשְׁבוּ
ג שָׁם: וַיֹּאמְרוּ אִישׁ אֶל־רֵעֵהוּ הָבָה נִלְבְּנָה לְבֵנִים
וְנִשְׂרְפָה לִשְׂרֵפָה וַתְּהִי לָהֶם הַלְּבֵנָה לְאָבֶן וְהַחֵמָר
ד הָיָה לָהֶם לַחֹמֶר: וַיֹּאמְרוּ הָבָה נִבְנֶה־לָּנוּ עִיר
וּמִגְדָּל וְרֹאשׁוֹ בַשָּׁמַיִם וְנַעֲשֶׂה־לָּנוּ שֵׁם פֶּן־נָפוּץ עַל־
ה פְּנֵי כָל־הָאָרֶץ: וַיֵּרֶד יְהוָה לִרְאֹת אֶת־הָעִיר וְאֶת־
ו הַמִּגְדָּל אֲשֶׁר בָּנוּ בְּנֵי הָאָדָם: וַיֹּאמֶר יְהוָה הֵן עַם

1] All the earth had the same language and the same words. **2]** And as men migrated from the east, they came upon a valley in the land of Shinar and settled there. **3]** They said to one another, "Come, let us make bricks and burn them hard."—Brick served them as stone, and bitumen served them as mortar.—**4]** And they said, "Come, let us build us a city, and a tower with its top in the sky, to make a name for ourselves; else we shall be scattered all over the world." **5]** The LORD came down to look at the city and tower which man had built, **6]** and the LORD said, "If, as one people with one language for all, this is how they have begun to act, then nothing that they may propose to do will be out of their reach. **7]** Let us, then, go down and confound their speech there, so that they shall not understand one another's speech." **8]** Thus the LORD scattered them from there over the face of the whole earth; and they stopped building the city. **9]** That is why it was called Babel, because there the LORD confounded the speech of the whole earth; and from there the LORD scattered them over the face of the whole earth.

11:1] *The same words.* The expression parallels "the same language." (Chapter 10 speaks of לָשׁוֹן [tongue]; the author of the Babel story calls language שָׂפָה [lip].) Historically, the principal languages of Mesopotamia in the third millennium were Sumerian and Akkadian. The latter is a Semitic language related to Hebrew, though not as closely as are Amorite, Canaanite, and Aramaic. Today, the Semitic language most widely spoken in the area is Arabic.

2] *Men migrated from the east.* Where they had settled after the Flood.

Shinar. See note to Gen. 10:10.

3] *Bricks . . . stone, bitumen . . . mortar.* The Bible means to explain that in Babylon brick and bitumen were used instead of stone and mortar as in Israel. The entire story abounds in assonances and alliterations: לִבְנָה–לְאָבֶן, חֵמָר–חֹמֶר.
/In "Enuma Elish" we find this description of the building of a shrine to Marduk: "The first year they molded bricks. When the second year arrived they raised high the head of Esagila, the counterpart of Apsu" (Apsu was a poetic term for the abyss) [1]. Herodotus describes the construction of a Mesopotamian moat as follows: "As fast as they dug the moat, the soil which they got from the cutting was made into bricks, and when a sufficient number were completed they baked the brick in kilns. Then they set to building, using hot bitumen throughout for their cement" [2]./

5] *The Lord came down.* In order to judge man. The expression is also used in telling the story of Sodom and Gomorrah (Gen. 18:21).

7] *Let us.* See note to Gen. 1:26.

8] *They stopped building the city.* And, of course, the tower that was in it.

9] *Babel.* While Babylonian tradition explained the name as "Gate of God," the biblical author substituted a satirical play on words: Babylon is only confusion. An English parallel might be Babel-babble.

י אֵלֶּה תּוֹלְדֹת שֵׁם שֵׁם בֶּן־מְאַת שָׁנָה וַיּוֹלֶד אֶת־
יא אַרְפַּכְשָׁד שְׁנָתַיִם אַחַר הַמַּבּוּל׃ וַיְחִי־שֵׁם אַחֲרֵי
הוֹלִידוֹ אֶת־אַרְפַּכְשָׁד חֲמֵשׁ מֵאוֹת שָׁנָה וַיּוֹלֶד בָּנִים
יב וּבָנוֹת׃ ס וְאַרְפַּכְשַׁד חַי חָמֵשׁ וּשְׁלֹשִׁים שָׁנָה וַיּוֹלֶד
יג אֶת־שָׁלַח׃ וַיְחִי אַרְפַּכְשַׁד אַחֲרֵי הוֹלִידוֹ אֶת־שֶׁלַח
שָׁלֹשׁ שָׁנִים וְאַרְבַּע מֵאוֹת שָׁנָה וַיּוֹלֶד בָּנִים וּבָנוֹת׃ ס
יד טו וְשֶׁלַח חַי שְׁלֹשִׁים שָׁנָה וַיּוֹלֶד אֶת־עֵבֶר׃ וַיְחִי־שֶׁלַח
אַחֲרֵי הוֹלִידוֹ אֶת־עֵבֶר שָׁלֹשׁ שָׁנִים וְאַרְבַּע מֵאוֹת
טז שָׁנָה וַיּוֹלֶד בָּנִים וּבָנוֹת׃ ס וַיְחִי־עֵבֶר אַרְבַּע וּשְׁלֹשִׁים
יז שָׁנָה וַיּוֹלֶד אֶת־פָּלֶג׃ וַיְחִי־עֵבֶר אַחֲרֵי הוֹלִידוֹ אֶת־
פֶּלֶג שְׁלֹשִׁים שָׁנָה וְאַרְבַּע מֵאוֹת שָׁנָה וַיּוֹלֶד בָּנִים
יח וּבָנוֹת׃ ס וַיְחִי־פֶלֶג שְׁלֹשִׁים שָׁנָה וַיּוֹלֶד אֶת־רְעוּ׃
יט וַיְחִי־פֶלֶג אַחֲרֵי הוֹלִידוֹ אֶת־רְעוּ תֵּשַׁע שָׁנִים וּמָאתַיִם
שָׁנָה וַיּוֹלֶד בָּנִים וּבָנוֹת׃ ס
כ וַיְחִי רְעוּ שְׁתַּיִם וּשְׁלֹשִׁים שָׁנָה וַיּוֹלֶד אֶת־שְׂרוּג׃
כא וַיְחִי רְעוּ אַחֲרֵי הוֹלִידוֹ אֶת־שְׂרוּג שֶׁבַע שָׁנִים
וּמָאתַיִם שָׁנָה וַיּוֹלֶד בָּנִים וּבָנוֹת׃ ס
כב כג וַיְחִי שְׂרוּג שְׁלֹשִׁים שָׁנָה וַיּוֹלֶד אֶת־נָחוֹר׃ וַיְחִי שְׂרוּג

10] This is the line of Shem. Shem was 100 years old when he begot Arpachshad, two years after the Flood. **11]** After the birth of Arpachshad, Shem lived 500 years and begot sons and daughters.

12] When Arpachshad had lived 35 years, he begot Shelah. **13]** After the birth of Shelah, Arpachshad lived 403 years and begot sons and daughters.

14] When Shelah had lived 30 years, he begot Eber. **15]** After the birth of Eber, Shelah lived 403 years and begot sons and daughters.

16] When Eber had lived 34 years, he begot Peleg. **17]** After the birth of Peleg, Eber lived 430 years and begot sons and daughters.

18] When Peleg had lived 30 years, he begot Reu. **19]** After the birth of Reu, Peleg lived 209 years and begot sons and daughters.

20] When Reu had lived 32 years, he begot Serug. **21]** After the birth of Serug, Reu lived 207 years and begot sons and daughters.

22] When Serug had lived 30 years, he begot Nahor. **23]** After the birth of Nahor, Serug

10–26] With the exception of Shem, all ancestral names down to Terah appear to reflect the names of cities in upper Mesopotamia, a district later called Aram-Naharaim and Paddan-Aram [3]. Hence, the Israelites considered themselves to be Arameans in origin (Deut. 26:5).

Most of the pre-Patriarchs father their children at thirty years of age. Further, note the round numbers 100 and 500 and that 403, like 30, occurs twice. Whether the system is based on multiples of six and seven, or of seven, ten, twelve, and forty, is in doubt, but that an underlying scheme exists appears certain despite the fact that the ancient versions differ somewhat in their figures. The symbolism must once have been comprehensible but became less so as time went on.

/The numbers were later used to this end by the Seder Olam Rabba to arrive at 3760 B.C.E. as the year of creation. This date is not far from the archeologically suggested age for the emergence of civilization in Mesopotamia./

11] *After the birth of.* Literally, "after he begot."

16] *Eber.* Ancestors of the Hebrews (see commentary to Gen. 14:1–24, "Abraham the Hebrew").

אַחֲרֵי הוֹלִידוֹ אֶת־נָחוֹר מָאתַיִם שָׁנָה וַיּוֹלֶד בָּנִים כד וַיְחִי עֶשְׂרֵה שָׁנָה וּמְאַת שָׁנָה וַיּוֹלֶד בָּנִים וּבָנוֹת: ס וַיְחִי־
וּבָנוֹת: ס וַיְחִי נָחוֹר תֵּשַׁע וְעֶשְׂרִים שָׁנָה וַיּוֹלֶד אֶת־ תֶּרַח שִׁבְעִים שָׁנָה וַיּוֹלֶד אֶת־אַבְרָם אֶת־נָחוֹר וְאֶת־
תָּרַח: ס כה וַיְחִי נָחוֹר אַחֲרֵי הוֹלִידוֹ אֶת־תֶּרַח תֵּשַׁע־ הָרָן:

lived 200 years and begot sons and daughters.

24] When Nahor had lived 29 years, he begot Terah.   **25]** After the birth of Terah, Nahor lived 119 years and begot sons and daughters.

26] When Terah had lived seventy years, he begot Abram, Nahor, and Haran.

Conclusion of the Prologue

This chapter is a transition from universal prehistory to a story of more limited scope—that of Abraham and his people. The Bible sees humanity's early history as a series of rebellions against the will of God. The rebellion of the people of Babel prompts God to look for a new channel to man. To Abraham and his descendants He now entrusts the task of bringing blessings to all the nations of the earth (Gen. 12:3). The remainder of the Torah is devoted to the story of this particular people and to the road they must follow in order to fulfil their universal responsibility. The Babel tale of divine displeasure and the subsequent genealogical list thus constitute both the conclusion of the prologue and the introduction to the first act of the main biblical drama.

Historic Background

A tower-like structure called *zikurat*—literally, "that which has been raised high"—was a distinctive feature of all Babylonian temple complexes and may have served as the humanly constructed equivalent of the mythical holy mountain in Babylonian mythology. The *zikurat* called Etemenanki ("house of the foundation of heaven and earth") was reported to have consisted of seven stories receding in pyramid-like fashion toward a flat top and reaching a height of nearly 300 feet. Archeologists have uncovered the foundation of this *zikurat*, and its extent would seem to coincide with the reputed size of the Tower of Babel [4]. Scholars have also confirmed the special use of hardened brick for such an enterprise.

The biblical writer's contempt for the paganism of Babylon determined not only his interpretation of the catastrophe that befell the city and its tower but also the style of the story, with its obvious overtones of sarcasm, its repeated word plays, and its explanation of Babel as a place of confusion.

Interpretations

While we are told that God's judgment consisted of scattering the people of Babel and confounding their speech, their actual transgression is not specified. A city was built and in it a tower, and the builders hoped that its summit would reach high into the heavens. In viewing this activity, God said: "This is how they have begun to act" (Gen. 11:6). What the word "this" refers to is not explained. A number of interpretations have been offered:

Self-Aggrandizement. According to the great majority of commentators, the tower represents man's tendency to reach too high, his attempt to equal if not displace God. Just as Adam desired to be like God and in consequence was driven from Eden, so in Babel, too, men exhibited excessive arrogance. They prided themselves on their accomplishments—they invented brick, knew how to use bitumen, and proceeded to build a large city with a skyscraping tower. Like the generation of the Flood, they were given to self-exaltation. Having a common dwelling place and a unified language encouraged their designs. Once these elements were removed, their pretentious enterprise collapsed.

Rebellion. The sin of the generation of Babel consisted of their refusal to "fill the earth." They had been commanded to do so but still tried to defy the divine will. God's action, therefore, was not so much a punishment as a carrying out of His plan. Confounding the human language was merely an assurance that the Babel incident would not be repeated. Man proposed, but God disposed [5].

A certain pathos adheres to this interpretation of the story. It senses in the generation of Babel not arrogance but anxiety, not a desire to reach the heavens so much as the need to press together on earth. According to Benno Jacob, the tale is "a condemnation

of extreme centralization, the last consequence of which is one huge universal megalopolis which sees its final goal in bringing all men under One Tower" [6].[1]

The City. Related to the previous interpretation is one that sees the city as the center of the account and all else as secondary [8]. The tower is merely the embodiment of the city, and when the story closes it speaks only of the city. A brief notation reveals the whole purpose of the Babel story: "and they stopped building the city" (Gen. 11:8).

This understanding reflects most clearly a pervasive biblical motif. The city is the ultimate expression of man's presumption.

Babel was *the* city, and, to the anti-urban tradition of the Bible, its downfall appeared as a proper divine judgment. Babel referred of course to Babylon, but it also symbolized all empire building, corruption, arrogance, craving to erect monuments, desire for fame; it meant a turning away from what were considered the primary occupations of man—agriculture and the tending of flocks. Farmers and nomads "fill the earth," i.e., they live close to it and its creatures; city-dwellers flee from the earth. Babel was an alienation of man from the simple life, and it is no accident that the Bible next turns to Abraham, a semi-nomad, as the source of all future blessings.

[1] Still another interpretation sees the town not as a means of aggrandizement or rebellion but of supplication. In doing so, however, men came too close to God, as it were, and as in the Eden story He sees them as a threat to Himself [7].

GLEANINGS

Babel—A Problem in Communication

Men spoke one language and "the same words." The Hebrew could also be interpreted as "few words," which is to say that man had a small vocabulary. Since both the learned and the unlearned spoke "the same words," there was no philosophic or technical "jargon" to separate people from each other. IBN EZRA, MALBIM

Language promotes communication and understanding within the group, but it also accentuates the differences in traditions and beliefs between groups; it erects barriers between tribes, nations, regions, social classes. The Tower of Babel is an archetypal symbol of the process which turns the blessing into a curse and prevents man from reaching into heaven. According to Margaret Mead, among the two million aborigines in New Guinea, 750 different languages are spoken in 750 villages which are at permanent war with one another. ARTHUR KOESTLER [9]

Ancient Affluence

The Torah says that the people "settled" in Shinar. This expression implies a social criticism. The problem of the people of Babel was their mindless affluence. For whenever the Torah uses the term יָשַׁב [settled] it means that people are overly at ease. Rabbi Helbo said: "Wherever you find contented satisfaction, Satan is active." MIDRASH [10]

The Lord Came Down

If God himself did this, how much more so is this incumbent on a human judge who must personally examine the accused and gain the fullest comprehension of all details. MIDRASH [11]

God must draw near, not because He is nearsighted, but because He dwells at such tremendous heights and man's work is so small. God's movement must, therefore, be understood as a remarkable satirical contrast to man's behavior. OTTO PROCKSCH [12]

The Tower and Human Values

As the tower grew in height it took one year to get bricks from the base to the upper stories. Thus, bricks became more precious than human life. When a brick slipped and fell the people wept, but when a man fell and died no one paid attention. MIDRASH [13]

They drove forth multitudes of both men and women to make bricks; among whom, a woman making bricks was not allowed to be released in the hour of childbirth, but brought forth while she was making bricks, and carried her child in her apron, and continued to make bricks. BARUCH [14]

Why was the generation of the Flood destroyed while that of Babel was merely dispersed? The Babylonians said to one another: Come, let *us* build [Gen. 11:4]. They worked together, in peace and harmony. This distinguished them from the people of the Flood who committed violence against one another and were, therefore, destroyed. The generation of the Tower defied God openly, yet, because they practiced brotherhood toward each other, they were merely scattered. MIDRASH [15]

The City

With the city as its critical object the Babel story has a particularly contemporary ring. West-

ern urbanized man also struggles with his estrangement from God. He, too, reaches for and appears to achieve powers formerly ascribed to God. One may, therefore, find in the Babel tale a suggestion that ever greater urbanization, coupled with a concentration on technology and a reaching toward outer space as a step toward further conquests, leads man not to unity but to division. To put it in other terms: Will modern man drive God into deeper hiding and further dramatize His eclipse, or will his actions call forth, as they did in ancient days, a God who will "come down and look" and then confound man again?

The Blessing of Diversity

The real crime of the builders was that they tried to impose one religion on mankind. God prevented this and, by dispersing the peoples, kept alive a variety of idolatries. But He knew that out of this diversity would eventually come a recognition of the Supreme Ruler.   SFORNO

Not Sin But Exuberance

From that day to this, whenever men have become skilful architects at all, there has been a tendency in them to build high; not in any religious feeling but in mere exuberance of spirit and power—as they dance or sin—with a certain mingling of vanity—like the feeling in which a child builds a tower of cards.   JOHN RUSKIN [16]

Science

Babel is here, and now. Who speaks my language? —no one.
Science is so tall that no man sees its face:
This tower will not touch God.

The trick is this,—and it is a good trick worthy a divine
Chicanery: in our impious determination
To build this bean-stalk, Science; climb it; peep
On the ultimate Mystery; spy on God; learn all;
No man can both climb and see.

EDNA ST. VINCENT MILLAY [17]

One Language, Many Tongues

It is possible that the report of all the earth having one language [11:1] has a historic foundation. The co-existence of one lingua franca and many national tongues is attested at various stages of history. Greek, Latin, French, and English have at certain times served as the "one language" for many peoples, and such co-existence is reported also for the pre-Columbian Central America. The loss of a means of international communication must at all times be the prelude to international strife.   CYRUS H. GORDON [18]

A Fact of Existence (Ch. 10); a Consequence of Sinfulness (Ch. 11)

In chapter 10, particularity appears to be the natural consequence of the postdeluvian population explosion. Noah's children have children who in turn become "lands, families, tongues, and nations." It is obvious on this level that the biblical authors took these distinctions, and the importance men gave them, as a fact of existence. Even in the biblical messianic passages, the existence of separate nations is assumed.

But Genesis 11 gives us a somewhat different view. Here the division into languages and the scattering abroad come as a punishment for seeking to build a tower into heaven and to wrest a name. God divides men so that by their unity they will not be able to do whatever they propose to do.

The Rabbis had little difficulty in seeing a unity in the two approaches. The differences among men emerge naturally, that is, as a consequence of the sinfulness of men amply attested in the generations after the Flood by their decreasing longevity. Looking out at the triumphant, unbridled paganism which surrounded them simply verified the biblical judgment for the Rabbis: Nationhood is natural, but a natural expression of man's will to do evil.   EUGENE B. BOROWITZ [19]

PART III

———————————

The Line of Terah

ABRAHAM

The Book of Genesis now enters a new phase by moving from myth toward history. Abraham (although the Patriarch's name is Abram and that of his wife is Sarai until Gen. 15:5, 7, the later and more familiar names of Abraham and Sarah are used throughout this commentary) has been called the first major historical figure in the book; unlike Adam, Shem, or Noah, who were the symbols or legendary standard-bearers of primeval memories and traditions, he appears as an identifiable person at a certain time. We reach this conclusion because of the nature of his biography and because many details and references are corroborated by other sources—even though so far none has been found to mention Abraham by name. This is not surprising, for in his day he was not the great and commanding figure that he was to become in the light of later history. This absence of extra-biblical references makes it difficult to date Abraham precisely, a difficulty we encounter with biblical figures until Moses. Various elements in the patriarchal narratives seem to correspond to different periods; from the old Babylonian (nineteenth century B.C.E.) to the Hurrian (fifteenth century B.C.E.) to the Amarna age (fourteenth century B.C.E.). Our data are not precise enough for a definite decision in favor of any one school of thought [1]. (On the significance of the Ebla finds, see Hallo's essay above.)

We have a good deal of information about the political, social, and religious life of the Mesopotamian lands where the Abraham cycle had its beginnings. Documents and archeological evidence tell us that the culture of this area flowered during the second millennium B.C.E. Science, law, and social institutions were highly developed. We do not know the particular circumstances that caused Abraham's father, Terah, to leave Ur and to settle in Haran, nor do we know his occupation. Of Abraham we do know that he was a semi-nomad with cattle, and we may assume that this was his ancestors' way of life as well, since in ancient days the sons usually followed in the footsteps of their fathers. They were not Bedouin on camels, like the Midianites, but rather nomads with small cattle whose movements between the steppe and tilled areas were determined by the needs of their animals and by their relationships with the permanent population.

"A degree of settledness is not at all incompatible with their nomadic existence. Cities do attract them, but not to settle in them by force, which would at once compel them to give up their nomadic life as shepherds;

but they attract them rather because of their character as cultural centers—primarily therefore for reasons of commerce and connubium" [2].

Calling Abraham "historical" does not mean that everything the Book of Genesis says about him is history in the accepted sense of the word. Our text was written down many centuries after Abraham lived, and the intervening ages developed different traditions about him. There is a good deal of what may be called legendary embellishment, which, along with interpretive material, was added to the basic tradition in the course of time. Together these elements came to assume the form that we now have before us.

But it is not so important to fix Abraham's era or to determine which of the stories about Abraham are history and which are legendary. What is important is his role as the father of the nation.* While the authors of the Bible were concerned with history as the recounting of facts, it was the meaning of history that was their primary focus, the account of a spiritual message born of the continuing encounter between God and Abraham's descendants. The Torah does not purpose to teach antiquities as such but to give religious instruction.

---

* The Torah does not depict him as the founder of a new religion. On the contrary, as Yehezkel Kaufmann has shown, in Genesis primeval mankind from Adam on appears to have been monotheistic. Abraham was "a prince of God" who kept the faith in the one God pure and bequeathed it to his descendants, setting them aside from a world which became idolatrous. According to Kaufmann, this biblical view contrasts, however, with what we know of the history of religion. Monotheism in the narrower sense has its origins not with Abraham but with Moses. The latter is a fighter for יהוה, the former a man of unusual piety and moral principles (see also Gleanings, 11:27–12:9, "Abraham's Monotheism") [3]. A different view is held by Theophile J. Meek. He calls Abraham and Moses "monolatrous" and argues that not until the Hebrew prophets did monotheism arise [4].

The Call of Abraham

The opening passages of the Abraham story relate the genealogy of the Patriarch and then tell of the family's migration to Haran. This city—the name means "highway" or "crossroads"—was located in north-western Mesopotamia and played a large part in the patriarchal story. It was the crossing point of important highways and a center of the cult devoted to the moon-god Sin. A large collection of Hurrian records found in the town of Nuzi tells much about the area's life and law.

The Bible says that God spoke to Abraham at the "crossroads" of his life. This address of the Divine to one human being, the message and its portent form the starting point of Israel's history. For while Abraham's story must be read as the biography of an individual, he (and this applies to the other Patriarchs as well) is more than an individual. The Bible sees the Patriarch as the archetype who represents his descendants and their fate. He is the forefather, whose life hints at the later history of the people of Israel. This prefiguration begins when Abraham becomes a wanderer. Time and again his descendants will wander across the earth, along the highways of history.*

(A new weekly portion, *Lech-Lecha*, begins with 12:1.)

* כָּל מַה שֶׁאֵירַע לוֹ אֵירַע לְבָנָיו [1]. A variety of other classical sayings expresses the thought that the stories of the forefathers are signposts pointing to the history of their descendants [2]. There is disagreement over whether Abraham's knowledge of God may be considered the beginning of monotheism.

פ פ פ

כז וְאֵ֖לֶּה תּוֹלְדֹ֣ת תֶּ֑רַח תֶּ֚רַח הוֹלִ֣יד אֶת־אַבְרָ֔ם אֶת־

א וַיֹּ֤אמֶר יְהוָֹה֙ אֶל־אַבְרָ֔ם לֶךְ־לְךָ֛ מֵאַרְצְךָ֥ וּמִמּֽוֹלַדְתְּךָ֖

כח נָח֖וֹר וְאֶת־הָרָ֑ן וְהָרָ֖ן הוֹלִ֥יד אֶת־ל֑וֹט: וַיָּ֣מָת הָרָ֗ן עַל־

ב וּמִבֵּ֣ית אָבִ֑יךָ אֶל־הָאָ֖רֶץ אֲשֶׁ֣ר אַרְאֶ֑ךָּ: וְאֶֽעֶשְׂךָ֙ לְג֣וֹי

כט פְּנֵ֛י תֶּ֥רַח אָבִ֖יו בְּאֶ֣רֶץ מֽוֹלַדְתּ֑וֹ בְּא֖וּר כַּשְׂדִּֽים: וַיִּקַּ֨ח

ג גָּד֔וֹל וַאֲבָ֣רֶכְךָ֔ וַאֲגַדְּלָ֖ה שְׁמֶ֑ךָ וֶֽהְיֵ֖ה בְּרָכָֽה: וַאֲבָֽרֲכָה֙

אַבְרָ֧ם וְנָח֛וֹר לָהֶ֖ם נָשִׁ֑ים שֵׁ֣ם אֵֽשֶׁת־אַבְרָם֙ שָׂרָ֔י וְשֵׁ֤ם

מְבָ֣רֲכֶ֔יךָ וּמְקַלֶּלְךָ֖ אָאֹ֑ר וְנִבְרְכ֣וּ בְךָ֔ כֹּ֖ל מִשְׁפְּחֹ֥ת

אֵֽשֶׁת־נָחוֹר֙ מִלְכָּ֔ה בַּת־הָרָ֥ן אֲבִֽי־מִלְכָּ֖ה וַֽאֲבִ֥י יִסְכָּֽה:

ד הָֽאֲדָמָֽה: וַיֵּ֣לֶךְ אַבְרָ֗ם כַּֽאֲשֶׁ֨ר דִּבֶּ֤ר אֵלָיו֙ יְהוָֹ֔ה וַיֵּ֥לֶךְ

ל וַתְּהִ֥י שָׂרַ֖י עֲקָרָ֑ה אֵ֥ין לָ֖הּ וָלָֽד: וַיִּקַּ֨ח תֶּ֜רַח אֶת־

אִתּ֣וֹ ל֑וֹט וְאַבְרָ֗ם בֶּן־חָמֵ֨שׁ שָׁנִ֤ים וְשִׁבְעִים֙ שָׁנָ֔ה בְּצֵאת֖וֹ

לא אַבְרָ֣ם בְּנ֗וֹ וְאֶת־ל֤וֹט בֶּן־הָרָן֙ בֶּן־בְּנ֔וֹ וְאֵת֙ שָׂרַ֣י כַּלָּת֔וֹ

ה מֵֽחָרָֽן: וַיִּקַּ֣ח אַבְרָם֩ אֶת־שָׂרַ֨י אִשְׁתּ֜וֹ וְאֶת־ל֣וֹט בֶּן־

אֵ֖שֶׁת אַבְרָ֣ם בְּנ֑וֹ וַיֵּצְא֨וּ אִתָּ֜ם מֵא֣וּר כַּשְׂדִּ֗ים לָלֶ֨כֶת֙

אָחִ֗יו וְאֶת־כָּל־רְכוּשָׁם֙ אֲשֶׁ֣ר רָכָ֔שׁוּ וְאֶת־הַנֶּ֖פֶשׁ אֲשֶׁר־

לב אַ֣רְצָה כְּנַ֔עַן וַיָּבֹ֥אוּ עַד־חָרָ֖ן וַיֵּ֣שְׁבוּ שָׁ֑ם: וַיִּֽהְי֣וּ

עָשׂ֣וּ בְחָרָ֑ן וַיֵּֽצְא֗וּ לָלֶ֨כֶת֙ אַ֣רְצָה כְּנַ֔עַן וַיָּבֹ֖אוּ אַ֥רְצָה

יְמֵי־תֶ֗רַח חָמֵ֤שׁ שָׁנִים֙ וּמָאתַ֣יִם שָׁנָ֑ה וַיָּ֥מָת תֶּ֖רַח

בְּחָרָֽן:

Haftarah Noach, p. 326

27] Now this is the line of Terah: Terah begot Abram, Nahor, and Haran; and Haran begot Lot. 28] Haran died in the lifetime of his father Terah, in his native land, Ur of the Chaldeans. 29] Abram and Nahor took to themselves wives, the name of Abram's wife being Sarai and that of Nahor's wife Milcah, the daughter of Haran, the father of Milcah and Iscah. 30] Now Sarai was barren, she had no child.

31] Terah took his son Abram, his grandson Lot the son of Haran, and his daughter-in-law Sarai, the wife of his son Abram, and they set out together from Ur of the Chaldeans for the land of Canaan; but when they had come as far as Haran, they settled there. 32] The days of Terah came to 205 years; and Terah died in Haran.

1] The LORD said to Abram, "Go forth from your native land and from your father's house to the land that I will show you. 2] I will make of you a great nation, / And I will bless you; / I will make your name great, / And you shall be a blessing. / 3] I will bless those who bless you / And curse him that curses you; / And all the families of the earth / Shall bless themselves by you." 4] Abram went forth as the LORD had commanded him, and Lot went with him. Abram was seventy-five years old when he left Haran. 5] Abram took his wife Sarai and his brother's son Lot, and all the wealth that they had amassed, and the persons that they had acquired in Haran; and they set out for the land of Canaan. When they arrived in the land of

11:28] *Ur.* In southeastern Mesopotamia, near the mouth of the Euphrates at the Persian Gulf.
/ Or Ura in northern Syria, which is much closer to Haran [3]./

12:1] *Your native land.* However, according to a different tradition, Ur, not Haran, was Abraham's native place (Gen. 11:26–28).
/ Harmonizers therefore render "land of your kindred."/

2] *A great nation.* גּוֹי (goy, nation); used in the Bible to refer to the descendants of Abraham as well as to other peoples.

3] *Shall bless themselves.* When they utter a blessing they will invoke Abraham as a model [4] (cf. Gen. 48:20). Others interpret this: "In you all the families of the earth shall be blessed," i.e., "you will be the cause of their blessings."

מִקֶּדֶם לְבֵית־אֵל וַיֵּט אָהֳלֹה בֵּית־אֵל מִיָּם וְהָעַי   כְּנָעַן: וַיַּעֲבֹר אַבְרָם בָּאָרֶץ עַד מְקוֹם שְׁכֶם עַד

מִקֶּדֶם וַיִּבֶן־שָׁם מִזְבֵּחַ לַיהוָה וַיִּקְרָא בְּשֵׁם יְהוָה: אֵלוֹן מוֹרֶה וְהַכְּנַעֲנִי אָז בָּאָרֶץ: וַיֵּרָא יְהוָה אֶל־

פ   ט וַיִּסַּע אַבְרָם הָלוֹךְ וְנָסוֹעַ הַנֶּגְבָּה: אַבְרָם וַיֹּאמֶר לְזַרְעֲךָ אֶתֵּן אֶת־הָאָרֶץ הַזֹּאת וַיִּבֶן

שָׁם מִזְבֵּחַ לַיהוָה הַנִּרְאֶה אֵלָיו: וַיַּעְתֵּק מִשָּׁם הָהָרָה

Canaan,   6] Abram passed through the land as far as the site of Shechem, at the terebinth of Moreh. The Canaanites were then in the land.

7] The LORD appeared to Abram and said, "I will give this land to your offspring." And he built an altar there to the LORD who had appeared to him.   8] From there he moved on to the hill country east of Bethel and pitched his tent, with Bethel on the west and Ai on the east; and he built there an altar to the LORD and invoked the LORD by name.   9] Then Abram journeyed by stages toward the Negeb.

6]   *Shechem.* Near Nablus, north of Jerusalem.

The terebinth of Moreh. מוֹרֶה (*moreh*, teaching, informing), a large tree famed as a site of oracles. Trees played an important role in ancient religions (see Deut. 12:2; Isa. 1:29).

/Hence some render *elon moreh* as "oracle tree" [5]. The Septuagint mentions its height [6].   Note also the "terebinths of Mamre" in Gen. 18:1./

The Canaanites were then in the land. This passage has been a problem to those who believe that the Torah was written by Moses. For in his

age the Canaanites were indeed living in the land while the expression "then" (but not now) appears to deny it.

/Rashi substitutes "already" for "then" (אָז); Ibn Ezra hints that tradition here faces an insurmountable difficulty; and Spinoza pursues this further [7]./

7]   *I will give this land.* This promise is to be repeated again and again to Abraham and his descendants.

8]   *Bethel ... Ai.* Located north of Jerusalem, about a third of the way to Shechem.

9]   *Negeb.* Or Negev, the south land.

The Call

Did God in fact speak to Abraham and make the promise reported in this chapter? To biblical man and to believers today the matter was and is clear: God did speak, and His relationship to Abraham's children and to the land of Canaan was secured by His promise. Many interpreters, however, would understand God's challenge as something Abraham *believed* he had heard and that consequently he acted in accordance with this belief.

The issue here is, of course, not subject to objective verification. Those who cannot accept the possibility of God communicating directly with man will not be convinced by the biblical or any other report. But they will be able to agree that Abraham was indeed impelled by a voice he identified as the voice of God. We stand here face to face with "internal" history. Abraham acted on his comprehension of the Divine, and his descendants appropriated his experience and made it their own.

The Choice

Abraham is an old man when he is called by God. Why did God choose a man so advanced in age, and why him at all? The text is silent on this matter, but two divergent interpretations have been suggested.

The first maintains that God's reason is not humanly discernible. He arbitrarily cast His favor on Abraham, hence the Bible says nothing about Abraham's righteousness though it commented on Noah's. Abraham, through no merit of his own, is the vessel, the recipient of God's grace. This reasoning has been favored by Christian interpreters of the Bible, although it has had some Jewish supporters as well.[1]

The second interpretation says that Abraham, like Noah before him, deserved to be chosen. Just as Noah stood out as a uniquely righteous and moral man in his time, Abraham possessed and demonstrated qualities that caused God to single him out also. This approach, which has generally been favored by Jewish tradition, pictures Abraham from his earliest youth in search of God. To put it differently: Abraham found God because of an original intuition [9]. Thus, when God addressed the adult Abraham, He was in fact responding to Abraham's earlier dedication and searching; God reacted to the man's merits.

The Bible at times seems to support the former and at times the latter view. But both approaches together appear to offer the best answer: Man needs to be addressed by God, and God needs men who are capable of responding. It is a mutual relationship. The text begins with the divine urging, "Go forth!" It is couched as a demand but, like all divine demands, it implies a question: "Are you ready to do My will?" Abraham's "Yes" is therefore his human choice, as God's address to him is the divine choice. Both find each other ready; Abraham is open to God's desire and God opens the future to Abraham.

The Challenge

God's challenge to Abraham has a progressive sequence: "Go forth from your native land and from your father's house." This is more poetry than geographic information. It emphasizes the difficulties of the challenge Abraham is about to accept. It is difficult to leave one's land and to be an unprotected wanderer abroad; it is even more difficult to abjure all that is most dear in one's accus-

---

[1] "Scripture does not begin by reciting Abraham's merit in order to indicate that the choice was a divine mystery and by His will alone—a choice that would never be dissolved or denied. Israel will always remain the 'holy seed,' for though he sins Israel remains what he is" [8].

tomed house; it is most difficult of all to reject one's father's values and standards. The passage makes it clear that God's demand represents a severe trial of faith for Abraham, the first of several fundamental choices he will have to make in his life [10].

Blessing and Curse

Few biblical dicta have been more clearly reflected in history than the statement that those who bless Israel will be blessed and those who curse it will be cursed, or that those who are blessed bless Israel and those who are cursed curse Israel. The decline of a nation can often be clearly related to the way it has treated the Jew, and its prosperity stands in direct proportion to its sense of equity and human dignity. For if the Jew rests indeed at the fulcrum of spiritual history, his condition must be essential to the welfare of his environment. Enough historical evidence can be advanced—from the appearance of the Prophets to the events of the holocaust—to make a persuasive case for the archetypal significance of Jewish existence in the world, a significance that Jews themselves have considered central ever since patriarchal days.

To be sure, the world has but rarely given credence to this view. It has not usually seen the Jews as a "great nation," typifying man's highest and noblest aspirations. Christians and Moslems have exalted Abraham as their spiritual father and at the same time have denied validity to the religious quest of the Jews. The latter, however, have stoutly maintained, through ancient, medieval, and modern persecutions, that the blessing issued to Abraham has not been abrogated and that it is more important for the children of Abraham to be worthy of it than that others accord them recognition.

GLEANINGS

The Fathers

Not sole was I born, but entire genesis:
For to the fathers that begat me, this
Body is residence. Corpuscular,
They dwell in my veins, they eavesdrop at my
  ear,
They circle, as with Torahs, round my skull,
In exit and in entrance all day pull
The latches of my heart, descend, and rise—
And there look generations through my eyes.
ABRAHAM M. KLEIN [11]

Young Abraham

Young Abraham was an assistant to his father, a dealer in idols. After Abraham became convinced that there was only one true God, he tried to convince his father's customers of the folly of idolatry. Once a man came to buy and Abraham asked his age. On being told that he was fifty years old, the boy exclaimed: "Woe to him who at fifty would worship a one-day idol." The customer then departed in shame. Another story pictures Abraham as smashing the idols and facing the wrath of his father. "Who smashed the gods?" demanded Terah. "The chief god there," said Abraham. "You know perfectly well that clay idols don't move," said the father. "Why then do you adore them?" rejoined the boy.   MIDRASH [12]

A Comparison

In what way did God's choice of Abraham differ from the earlier choices of Adam and Noah? The blessing of Adam and the blessing of Noah were natural, bestowing natural gifts, promising fertility alone, whereas this third blessing [to Abraham] is dialogic, promising and demanding at the same time; promising the formation of a people and imposing the obligations of a people,

addressing the people in the person of its father and demanding in his person from it to "become a blessing," a blessing for the world of nations.

MARTIN BUBER [13]

A Gift

Man, until aware of God as a condition of his
    spiritual environment,
Would know no need of prayer.
Man, then, has not invented God, he has
    developed Faith,
To meet a God already there . . .
The Divine Gift, which empowers a man to
    believe,
Is marvellous and simple, like a gift of light . . .
Not to the sightless, but to men with eyes, who
    wander groping in the night.

EDNA ST. VINCENT MILLAY [14]

Go Forth—לֶךְ-לְךָ

Perhaps the Hebrew implies "Go by yourself." This is one journey which must be made alone. One must become a stranger in the world to view it clearly, a wanderer to find its resting point. Abraham is God's possession, not the world's. The aloneness of Abraham foreshadows that of all religious seekers and, above all, that of the people of Israel in their historic solitude.

BASED ON SAMSON RAPHAEL HIRSCH

Or the expression may be interpreted to mean, "Go *to* yourself," i.e., go to your roots, to find your potential.   CHASIDIC [15]

[Strictly speaking the Hebrew may not be translated this way. Nachmanides interprets it as "Get on with you" (similarly Hizkuni).]

Why did Abraham have to go forth to the world? At home he was like a flask of myrrh with a tight-fitting lid. Only when it is open can the fragrance be scattered to the winds.   MIDRASH [16]

An Allegorical Interpretation of "Go Forth"

Depart out of the earthly matter that encompasses you: escape, man, from the foul prison-house, your body, with all your might and main, and from the pleasures and lusts that act as its jailers.   PHILO. [17]

Abraham's Monotheism

The Bible itself attests indirectly to the fact that Israel's monotheism is postpatriarchal. Historical monotheism is associated always with certain phenomena which serve as its organic framework: apostolic prophecy, the battle with idolatry, and the name of YHWH. Patriarchal times know none of these. Genesis records divine manifestations and prophecies, but there is no trace of apostolic prophecy. No patriarch is charged with a prophetic mission; the first apostolic prophet is Moses. Nowhere in Genesis is there reference to a battle with idolatry. The divine covenants with the patriarchs promise personal protection and future material blessings. But they never involve a fight with idolatry, nor do the patriarchs ever appear as reproaching their contemporaries for idolatry. Indeed, there is no religious contrast between the patriarchs and their surroundings.

YEHEZKEL KAUFMANN [18]

A Blessing?

It is unlikely that the word gives the true meaning of that which happened to him in his vision and which corresponded to his temperament and to his experience of himself. For the word "blessing" carries with it an idea which but ill describes men of his sort: men, that is, of roving spirit and discomfortable mind, whose novel conception of the deity is destined to make its mark upon the future. The life of men with whom new histories begin can seldom or never be a sheer unclouded blessing; not this it is which their consciousness of self whispers in their ears. "And thou shalt be a destiny": such is the purer and more precise meaning of the promise, in whatever language it may have been spoken. THOMAS MANN [19]

Wanderings

Abraham emerges more clearly as a person. We meet him as a husband, as an uncle, and as a man who attempts to meet personal danger in what appears to be an ambiguous manner. This is an unadorned tale of the ancestor of a thoroughly human people who, like him, must respond to the claim of God, the claim of kin, and finally (as in the Sodom story) to the claim of all men. The land is promised again, this time in an extended fashion, which raises the question for the contemporary reader of how Abraham's descendants relate to the land.

י וַיְהִי רָעָב בָּאָרֶץ וַיֵּרֶד אַבְרָם מִצְרַיְמָה לָגוּר שָׁם

יא כִּי־כָבֵד הָרָעָב בָּאָרֶץ: וַיְהִי כַּאֲשֶׁר הִקְרִיב לָבוֹא מִצְרָיְמָה וַיֹּאמֶר אֶל־שָׂרַי אִשְׁתּוֹ הִנֵּה־נָא יָדַעְתִּי כִּי

יב אִשָּׁה יְפַת־מַרְאֶה אָתְּ: וְהָיָה כִּי־יִרְאוּ אֹתָךְ הַמִּצְרִים

יג וְאָמְרוּ אִשְׁתּוֹ זֹאת וְהָרְגוּ אֹתִי וְאֹתָךְ יְחַיּוּ: אִמְרִי־נָא אֲחֹתִי אָתְּ לְמַעַן יִיטַב־לִי בַעֲבוּרֵךְ וְחָיְתָה נַפְשִׁי

יד בִּגְלָלֵךְ: וַיְהִי כְּבוֹא אַבְרָם מִצְרָיְמָה וַיִּרְאוּ הַמִּצְרִים

טו אֶת־הָאִשָּׁה כִּי־יָפָה הִוא מְאֹד: וַיִּרְאוּ אֹתָהּ שָׂרֵי פַרְעֹה וַיְהַלְלוּ אֹתָהּ אֶל־פַּרְעֹה וַתֻּקַּח הָאִשָּׁה בֵּית

טז פַּרְעֹה: וּלְאַבְרָם הֵיטִיב בַּעֲבוּרָהּ וַיְהִי־לוֹ צֹאן וּבָקָר וַחֲמֹרִים וַעֲבָדִים וּשְׁפָחֹת וַאֲתֹנֹת וּגְמַלִּים:

יז וַיְנַגַּע יְהֹוָה אֶת־פַּרְעֹה נְגָעִים גְּדֹלִים וְאֶת־בֵּיתוֹ עַל־

יח דְּבַר שָׂרַי אֵשֶׁת אַבְרָם: וַיִּקְרָא פַרְעֹה לְאַבְרָם וַיֹּאמֶר מַה־זֹּאת עָשִׂיתָ לִּי לָמָּה לֹא־הִגַּדְתָּ לִּי כִּי אִשְׁתְּךָ הִוא:

יט לָמָה אָמַרְתָּ אֲחֹתִי הִוא וָאֶקַּח אֹתָהּ לִי לְאִשָּׁה וְעַתָּה

כ הִנֵּה אִשְׁתְּךָ קַח וָלֵךְ: וַיְצַו עָלָיו פַּרְעֹה אֲנָשִׁים וַיְשַׁלְּחוּ אֹתוֹ וְאֶת־אִשְׁתּוֹ וְאֶת־כָּל־אֲשֶׁר־לוֹ:

יג א וַיַּעַל אַבְרָם מִמִּצְרַיִם הוּא וְאִשְׁתּוֹ וְכָל־אֲשֶׁר־לוֹ וְלוֹט

ב עִמּוֹ הַנֶּגְבָּה: וְאַבְרָם כָּבֵד מְאֹד בַּמִּקְנֶה בַּכֶּסֶף

ג וּבַזָּהָב: וַיֵּלֶךְ לְמַסָּעָיו מִנֶּגֶב וְעַד־בֵּית־אֵל עַד־הַמָּקוֹם אֲשֶׁר־הָיָה שָׁם אָהֳלֹה בַּתְּחִלָּה בֵּין בֵּית־אֵל וּבֵין הָעָי:

ד אֶל־מְקוֹם הַמִּזְבֵּחַ אֲשֶׁר־עָשָׂה שָׁם בָּרִאשֹׁנָה וַיִּקְרָא

ה שָׁם אַבְרָם בְּשֵׁם יְהֹוָה: וְגַם־לְלוֹט הַהֹלֵךְ אֶת־אַבְרָם

ו הָיָה צֹאן־וּבָקָר וְאֹהָלִים: וְלֹא־נָשָׂא אֹתָם הָאָרֶץ

10] There was a famine in the land, and Abram went down to Egypt to sojourn there, for the famine was severe in the land. **11]** As he was about to enter Egypt, he said to his wife Sarai, "I know what a beautiful woman you are. **12]** If the Egyptians see you, and think, 'She is his wife,' they will kill me and let you live. **13]** Please say that you are my sister, that it may go well with me because of you, and that I may remain alive thanks to you."

14] When Abram entered Egypt, the Egyptians saw how very beautiful the woman was. **15]** Pharaoh's courtiers saw her and praised her to Pharaoh, and the woman was taken into Pharaoh's palace. **16]** And because of her, it went well with Abram; he acquired sheep, oxen, asses, male and female slaves, she-asses, and camels.

17] But the Lord afflicted Pharaoh and his household with mighty plagues on account of Sarai, the wife of Abram. **18]** Pharaoh sent for Abram and said, "What is this you have done to me! Why did you not tell me that she was your wife? **19]** Why did you say, 'She is my sister,' so I took her as my wife? Now, here is your wife; take her and begone!" **20]** And Pharaoh put men in charge of him, and they sent him off with his wife and all that he possessed.

1] From Egypt, Abram went up into the Negeb, with his wife and all that he possessed, together with Lot. **2]** Now Abram was very rich in cattle, silver, and gold. **3]** And he proceeded by stages from the Negeb as far as Bethel, to the place where his tent had been formerly, between Bethel and Ai, **4]** the site of the altar which he had built there at first; and there Abram invoked the Lord by name. **5]** Lot, who went with Abram, also had flocks and herds and tents, **6]** so that the land could not support them staying together; for their

---

12:10] *There was a famine in the land.* Canaan depended on rainfall, which was often insufficient, while Egypt, with its Nile waters, at times served as the bread basket of the area.

11] *A beautiful woman.* This story is told again with slight variations in chapter 20 and then a third time in chapter 26, where Isaac and Rebekah play the main roles. The tale here sees Sarah as young enough to attract the Egyptians, whereas in Gen. 12:4 we are told that Abraham was seventy-five years old, which would make Sarah (who was ten years younger, according to Gen. 17:17) sixty-five.

לָשֶׁבֶת יַחְדָּו כִּי־הָיָה רְכוּשָׁם רָב וְלֹא יָכְלוּ לָשֶׁבֶת
יָשַׁב בְּאֶרֶץ־כְּנָעַן וְלוֹט יָשַׁב בְּעָרֵי הַכִּכָּר וַיֶּאֱהַל
ז יַחְדָּו׃ וַיְהִי־רִיב בֵּין רֹעֵי מִקְנֵה־אַבְרָם וּבֵין רֹעֵי
יג עַד־סְדֹם׃ וְאַנְשֵׁי סְדֹם רָעִים וְחַטָּאִים לַיהוָה מְאֹד׃
ח מִקְנֵה־לוֹט וְהַכְּנַעֲנִי וְהַפְּרִזִּי אָז יֹשֵׁב בָּאָרֶץ׃ וַיֹּאמֶר
יד וַיהוָה אָמַר אֶל־אַבְרָם אַחֲרֵי הִפָּרֶד־לוֹט מֵעִמּוֹ שָׂא
אַבְרָם אֶל־לוֹט אַל־נָא תְהִי מְרִיבָה בֵּינִי וּבֵינֶךָ וּבֵין
נָא עֵינֶיךָ וּרְאֵה מִן־הַמָּקוֹם אֲשֶׁר־אַתָּה שָׁם צָפֹנָה
ט רֹעַי וּבֵין רֹעֶיךָ כִּי־אֲנָשִׁים אַחִים אֲנָחְנוּ׃ הֲלֹא כָל־
טו וָנֶגְבָּה וָקֵדְמָה וָיָמָּה׃ כִּי אֶת־כָּל־הָאָרֶץ אֲשֶׁר־אַתָּה
הָאָרֶץ לְפָנֶיךָ הִפָּרֶד נָא מֵעָלָי אִם־הַשְּׂמֹאל וְאֵימִנָה
טז רֹאֶה לְךָ אֶתְּנֶנָּה וּלְזַרְעֲךָ עַד־עוֹלָם׃ וְשַׂמְתִּי אֶת־
י וְאִם־הַיָּמִין וְאַשְׂמְאִילָה׃ וַיִּשָּׂא־לוֹט אֶת־עֵינָיו וַיַּרְא
זַרְעֲךָ כַּעֲפַר הָאָרֶץ אֲשֶׁר אִם־יוּכַל אִישׁ לִמְנוֹת
אֶת־כָּל־כִּכַּר הַיַּרְדֵּן כִּי כֻלָּהּ מַשְׁקֶה לִפְנֵי שַׁחֵת
יז אֶת־עֲפַר הָאָרֶץ גַּם־זַרְעֲךָ יִמָּנֶה׃ קוּם הִתְהַלֵּךְ
יְהוָה אֶת־סְדֹם וְאֶת־עֲמֹרָה כְּגַן־יְהוָה כְּאֶרֶץ מִצְרַיִם
יח בָּאָרֶץ לְאָרְכָּהּ וּלְרָחְבָּהּ כִּי לְךָ אֶתְּנֶנָּה׃ וַיֶּאֱהַל
יא בֹּאֲכָה צֹעַר׃ וַיִּבְחַר־לוֹ לוֹט אֵת כָּל־כִּכַּר הַיַּרְדֵּן
אַבְרָם וַיָּבֹא וַיֵּשֶׁב בְּאֵלֹנֵי מַמְרֵא אֲשֶׁר בְּחֶבְרוֹן וַיִּבֶן
יב וַיִּסַּע לוֹט מִקֶּדֶם וַיִּפָּרְדוּ אִישׁ מֵעַל אָחִיו׃ אַבְרָם
שָׁם מִזְבֵּחַ לַיהוָה׃ פ

possessions were so great that they could not remain together. **7]** And there was quarreling between the herdsmen of Abram's cattle and those of Lot's cattle.—The Canaanites and Perizzites were then dwelling in the land.—**8]** Abram said to Lot, "Let there be no strife between you and me, between my herdsmen and yours, for we are kinsmen. **9]** Is not the whole land before you? Let us separate: if you go north, I will go south; and if you go south, I will go north." **10]** Lot looked about him and saw how well watered was the whole plain of the Jordan, all of it—this was before the LORD had destroyed Sodom and Gomorrah—all the way to Zoar, like the garden of the LORD, like the land of Egypt. **11]** So Lot chose for himself the whole plain of the Jordan, and Lot journeyed eastward. Thus they parted from each other; **12]** Abram remained in the land of Canaan, while Lot settled in the cities of the Plain, pitching his tents near Sodom. **13]** Now the inhabitants of Sodom were very wicked sinners against the LORD.

14] And the LORD said to Abram, after Lot had parted from him, "Raise your eyes and look out from where you are, to the north and south, to the east and west, **15]** for I give all the land that you see to you and your offspring forever. **16]** I will make your offspring as the dust of the earth, so that if one can count the dust of the earth, then your offspring too can be counted. **17]** Up, walk about the land, through its length and its breadth, for I give it to you." **18]** And Abram moved his tent, and came to dwell at the terebinths of Mamre which are in Hebron; and he built an altar there to the LORD.

13:10] *Plain of the Jordan.* Recent explorations have shown that the area was once densely inhabited. It was probably one of the first settled sections of the country as well as one of its richest parts. "It remains today potentially what it was then indubitably, a garden of God" [1].

11] *Thus they parted.* Abraham stays in Canaan proper while Lot abandons it. One purpose of the story is to underscore that Moab and Ammon, Lot's descendants, have no right to the land which, in the passage immediately following, is once more promised to Abraham.

14] *Look out from where you are.* That is, from Bethel, from which there is a good view of the southern Jordan Valley.

18] *Hebron.* South of Jerusalem. Elsewhere Hebron is called Kiriath-arba (Gen. 23:2; 35:27). It became the Patriarchs' primary home in Canaan, as well as their burial place. According to Num. 13:22, Hebron was founded seven years before Zoan (or Avaris, in Egypt), i.e., in the eighteenth century B.C.E.

You Are My Sister

Abraham instructed his wife to tell the Egyptians that she was his sister. She was to say nothing of their marriage. This raises a number of historical as well as moral questions.

There is evidence that Sarah was indeed Abraham's sister. In the second version of the story we learn that although the two had different mothers they shared the same father (Gen. 20:12). It is possible that this latter notation reflects a stage of civilization in which descent was traced through the mother and marriages between offspring of the same father (but not the same mother) were permissible.[1] Hence, according to this assumption, when Abraham instructed Sarah to say she was his sister, he based his request on a real relationship.

Another explanation is based on the assumption that Abraham lived about 1500 B.C.E., when the word "sister" could have an additional, special meaning [3]. In American English today, "sister" can mean "nun." In English, French, German, and Hebrew, it can mean "nurse." In Abraham's time, "sister" was also a Hurrian legal term. Abraham and Sarah came from a Hurrian cultural background and it would have been natural for them to use Hurrian terminology. As documents from Nuzi show, a Hurrian could adopt his wife as his sister, thereby giving her special status, for she would be treated as a blood relative of her husband's family. It may be assumed that such adoptions took place in the upper stratum of society where inheritance and family bonds were important. Thus, in this interpretation Abraham instructed his wife to mention her privileged "sister" status, in order to provide assurance that both of them would be treated with respect. The Egyptians apparently understood Hurrian terminology and no harm befell the couple. It was in this fashion that the story was first told. Later on, however, as knowledge of Hurrian custom faded, Abraham's request seemed incomprehensible except as a lie and the story became transformed into one of deceit and divine intervention.

Whatever the early context, the biblical text shows us how Abraham's action caused Pharaoh, who did not know that Sarah was married, to take her into his house. Some commentators excuse Abraham's behavior by saying that his ruse was meant to bid for time, until the famine in Canaan would be ended and he could take his wife and leave Egypt [4]. Others frankly disapprove [5] and note that Abraham could not make reply to Pharaoh's reprimand since the latter's generosity had left the Patriarch in the rather embarrassing situation of having lied and having been rewarded for it.[2]

Abraham's behavior raises still another question. A man can be judged guilty when he has a choice—but what choices are open to a man who, like Abraham, believes he is faced with mortal danger? What could Abraham have done, given the knowledge

---

[1] This system of family relations is called metronymic, in contrast to patronymic which considers children born of the same father as members of the family. Traces of a metronymic society appear in various parts of the Bible, e.g., it is usually the mothers who name the children; descent is at times traced through mothers rather than fathers; a marriage between Amnon and Tamar is permissible even though they have the same father (II Sam. 13:13) [2].

[2] One view: The gifts were for teaching the Egyptians astronomy and mathematics [6]. Another view: "The narrator gloats over Abraham's astoundingly successful lie, which made a virtue out of necessity. He identifies himself joyfully with his forebears' sharp practice" [7]. And: "That is why they are so proudly conscious of the fact that their women are more beautiful than those living in the city . . . In moral considerations, too, they consider themselves superior: The city dwellers are weak and susceptible to feminine charm" [8].

of the prospects available to him? The text, as it does so often, merely states the problem, leaving it to the reader to ponder it further.

Jewish teaching has generally held that, even under duress, no man may intentionally kill or commit a sexual crime on an innocent person.[3] The application of this principle often poses agonizing questions that can be decided only within a given context. (The trials for war crimes after World War II essentially attempted to define the limits of a man's right to say, "I had no choice.") Since both Sarah and Pharaoh were put in jeopardy by Abraham, the proper judgment would seem to support Nachmanides' comment: "It was a sin."

The Promised Land

We can hardly overemphasize the importance of those biblical passages which, like Gen. 13:15, state that God gave Canaan to Abraham and his offspring forever. From these traditions and memories, amplified by centuries of sacred sentiment, grew a unique relationship between a people and a land. Some commentators deny the Abrahamic antiquity of the tradition and claim that it arose in later ages to give the military conquest of the land by Joshua an *ex post facto* religious legitimation. Even if this were so, it would emphasize that for Abraham's descendants military acquisition and physical possession—sufficient for all other nations' claims—were not the core of their relationship to the land. For them Canaan, Palestine, Zion, Israel, by whatever name it was known, was linked to the will and promise of God, and hence it was a Holy and Promised Land, as it was later to be called.

To someone who believes that God did indeed will the land to Abraham's people, the Jews' subsequent claim to it is beyond dispute. The claim has total force, encom-

passing legal and moral rights. But the matter should be left open as a question of faith, taking into account that for millennia Jews have *believed* that their relationship to the land had the sanction of God. Thus their claim obtained a spiritual basis nurtured in thousands of years of possession and loss, presence and absence, reality and memory. To be sure, the people survived without the land and the land without the people—but somehow God and Torah entered into this relationship and gave it a special stamp.

To the Jew, therefore, Zion has been more than a place of pilgrimage or a collection of ancestral sites. It has been both sacred dream and holy potential, the place where God's kingdom on earth would first emerge. The Jew has steadfastly believed that it is God's will that he possess the land and that he possess it in justice—for God casts out of this land those who defile it. The Amorites lost possession because of their sinfulness, and Israel itself was warned always to be heedful of this possibility (Gen. 15:16; Lev. 18:24; Deut. 9:5). Only a community of righteousness would match the dreams and prayers centered on this small strip of earth: "Zion shall be redeemed by justice, and those who return to her, by righteousness" (Isa. 1:27).

In the course of centuries, and especially in modern times, many Jews came to feel that God's role no longer needed to be considered in their relationship to the land. They were satisfied that history had forged an indissoluble bond between land and people and that as homeland and as the cultural and political center of Jewry it remained the focus of the age-old dreams. Thus, religion and history became intertwined for Zion's children: Believers and nonbelievers alike took the land to heart in their own way and made it the object of their hopes.

[3] A man came to Rabba and told him: "The governor of my town told me to kill a certain man, else I would be killed." Rabba said: "You must suffer death rather than commit murder. Who knows whether your blood is redder [i.e., more valuable] than his: perhaps the blood of the intended victim is redder than yours!" [9].

GLEANINGS

Sarah's Beauty

Of all the virgins and brides
That walk beneath the canopy,
None can compare with Sarah.

GENESIS APOCRYPHON [10]

When Abraham went with Sarah into Egypt,
The land was all illumined with her beauty.

HENRY WADSWORTH LONGFELLOW [11]

The Possibility of Adultery

Did not Abraham by his deception expose Sarah to adultery? Yes, but there was a possibility it might not occur, and in such a case his plan, executed under duress, was justified. Had adultery occurred, Abraham would have been held guilty.

MIDRASH [12]

The Scheme Which Failed

On this journey from Canaan to Egypt, Abraham first observed the beauty of Sarah. Chaste as he was, he had never before looked at her, but now, when they were wading through a stream, he saw the reflection of her beauty in the water like the brilliance of the sun. Wherefore he spoke to her thus, "The Egyptians are very sensual, and I will put thee in a casket that no harm befall me on account of thee." At the Egyptian boundary, the tax collectors asked him about the contents of the casket, and Abraham told them he had barley in it. "No," they said, "it contains wheat." "Very well," replied Abraham, "I am prepared to pay the tax on wheat." The officers then hazarded the guess, "It contains pepper!" Abraham agreed to pay the tax on pepper, and, when they charged him with concealing gold in the casket, he did not refuse to pay the tax on gold, and finally on precious stones. Seeing that he demurred to no charge,

however high, the tax collectors, made thoroughly suspicious, insisted upon his unfastening the casket and letting them examine the contents. When it was forced open, the whole of Egypt was resplendent with the beauty of Sarah.   MIDRASH [13]

In Arabic Literature

Sarah, the wife of Abraham, was, according to some accounts, the sister of Lot and the daughter of Aran, Abraham's paternal uncle. According to others, she was the daughter of the king of Haran, and her mother was daughter of Kutba, king of Babylon. Sarah was the most beautiful woman of her time and possessed a perfect figure. She resembled Eve, to whom God gave two-thirds of all beauty; indeed, she was so beautiful that Abraham transported her in a chest. When, on entering Egypt, Abraham was obliged to give a tithe of all his goods, he at first refused to open the chest in which Sarah was, and when he was finally forced to do so the official ran and told the king. Questioned by the latter regarding Sarah, Abraham replied that she was his sister, having instructed her to say the same. When, on that supposition, the king wished to marry her and reached out to take her, Sarah prayed God to wither his hand; and when the king promised not to touch her, she prayed God to restore it. Forgetful of his promise, the king reached toward her once more and his hand was again withered. This was repeated three times. Abraham was a witness of this interview, God causing the walls of the house to become transparent for the purpose. Finally the king restored Sarah to Abraham and loaded her with presents. He insisted on her choosing for herself one of his slave girls, and she selected Hagar for whom she had conceived a liking.

JEWISH ENCYCLOPEDIA [14]

The War of the Four against
the Five

The war of the four against the five appears as an intrusion in an otherwise smoothly flowing narrative. It is likely that this chapter comes from an Abrahamic tradition not otherwise represented in the Torah. Despite enormous research, both source and purpose of this story have remained an enigma [1]. Are we here face-to-face with a historic incident? Does the event have some special significance? We do not have enough knowledge to answer these questions.

We are told of certain kings who were bound for El-paran (near today's Eilat, in the Negev), possibly for the copper mines located there. The invaders had come from Mesopotamia, and after accomplishing their objective in the south they returned home, carrying Lot with them as a prisoner. Subsequently we meet Abraham in the unfamiliar role of warrior.

עַד אֵיל פָּארָן אֲשֶׁר עַל־הַמִּדְבָּר: וַיָּשֻׁבוּ וַיָּבֹאוּ אֶל־
עֵין מִשְׁפָּט הִוא קָדֵשׁ וַיַּכּוּ אֶת־כָּל־שְׂדֵה הָעֲמָלֵקִי
וְגַם אֶת־הָאֱמֹרִי הַיֹּשֵׁב בְּחַצְצֹן תָּמָר: וַיֵּצֵא מֶלֶךְ־
סְדֹם וּמֶלֶךְ עֲמֹרָה וּמֶלֶךְ אַדְמָה וּמֶלֶךְ צְבֹיִם וּמֶלֶךְ
בֶּלַע הִוא־צֹעַר וַיַּעַרְכוּ אִתָּם מִלְחָמָה בְּעֵמֶק הַשִּׂדִּים:
אֵת כְּדָרְלָעֹמֶר מֶלֶךְ עֵילָם וְתִדְעָל מֶלֶךְ גּוֹיִם
וְאַמְרָפֶל מֶלֶךְ שִׁנְעָר וְאַרְיוֹךְ מֶלֶךְ אֶלָּסָר אַרְבָּעָה
מְלָכִים אֶת־הַחֲמִשָּׁה: וְעֵמֶק הַשִּׂדִּים בֶּאֱרֹת בֶּאֱרֹת
חֵמָר וַיָּנֻסוּ מֶלֶךְ־סְדֹם וַעֲמֹרָה וַיִּפְּלוּ־שָׁמָּה וְהַנִּשְׁאָרִים

* ב צבוים קרי.
* ח צבוים קרי.

א וַיְהִי בִּימֵי אַמְרָפֶל מֶלֶךְ־שִׁנְעָר אַרְיוֹךְ מֶלֶךְ אֶלָּסָר
ב כְּדָרְלָעֹמֶר מֶלֶךְ עֵילָם וְתִדְעָל מֶלֶךְ גּוֹיִם: עָשׂוּ
מִלְחָמָה אֶת־בֶּרַע מֶלֶךְ סְדֹם וְאֶת־בִּרְשַׁע מֶלֶךְ עֲמֹרָה
שִׁנְאָב מֶלֶךְ אַדְמָה וְשֶׁמְאֵבֶר מֶלֶךְ צְבֹיִם וּמֶלֶךְ
ג בֶּלַע הִיא־צֹעַר: כָּל־אֵלֶּה חָבְרוּ אֶל־עֵמֶק הַשִּׂדִּים
ד הוּא יָם הַמֶּלַח: שְׁתֵּים עֶשְׂרֵה שָׁנָה עָבְדוּ אֶת־
ה כְּדָרְלָעֹמֶר וּשְׁלֹשׁ־עֶשְׂרֵה שָׁנָה מָרָדוּ: וּבְאַרְבַּע עֶשְׂרֵה
שָׁנָה בָּא כְדָרְלָעֹמֶר וְהַמְּלָכִים אֲשֶׁר אִתּוֹ וַיַּכּוּ אֶת־
רְפָאִים בְּעַשְׁתְּרֹת קַרְנַיִם וְאֶת־הַזּוּזִים בְּהָם וְאֵת
ו הָאֵימִים בְּשָׁוֵה קִרְיָתָיִם: וְאֶת־הַחֹרִי בְּהַרְרָם שֵׂעִיר

1] Now, when Amraphel king of Shinar, Arioch king of Ellasar, Chedorlaomer king of Elam, and Tidal king of Goiim **2]** made war on Bera king of Sodom, Birsha king of Gomorrah, Shinab king of Admah, Shemeber king of Zeboiim, and the king of Bela, which is Zoar, **3]** all the latter joined forces at the Valley of Siddim, now the Dead Sea. **4]** Twelve years they had served Chedorlaomer, and in the thirteenth year they rebelled. **5]** In the fourteenth year Chedorlaomer and the kings who were with him came and defeated the Rephaim at Ashteroth-karnaim, the Zuzim at Ham, the Emim at Shaveh-kiriathaim, **6]** and the Horites in their hill country of Seir as far as El-paran, which is by the wilderness. **7]** On their way back they came to En-mishpat, which is Kadesh, and subdued all the territory of the Amalekites, and also the Amorites who dwelt in Hazazon-tamar. **8]** Then the king of Sodom, the king of Gomorrah, the king of Admah, the king of Zeboiim, and the king of Bela, which is Zoar, went forth and engaged them in battle in the Valley of Siddim: **9]** Chedorlaomer king of Elam, Tidal king of Goiim, Amraphel king of Shinar, and Arioch king of Ellasar—four kings against those five.

10] Now the Valley of Siddim was dotted with bitumen pits; and the kings of Sodom and Gomorrah, in their flight, threw themselves into them, while the rest escaped to the hill

14:1] *Shinar*. A name for Babylonia (Gen. 10: 10).

/Some scholars suggest that Shinar must here refer to a location closer to Canaan [2]./

Arioch. This name is found in cuneiform sources, but Ellasar is not.

Elam. An eastern rival of Mesopotamia.

Tidal. A Hittite name.

Goiim. Literally, "nations," possibly used here to mean "foreigners," a term, like the Greek "barbarians," that came to have contemptuous overtones.

2] *Bera . . . Birsha*. Probably two unhistorical names that refer to the depravity of Sodom and Gomorrah (Gen. 18:16ff.). Bera could mean "with

evil," and the consonants of Birsha, "with wickedness" (בְּרֶשַׁע–בְּרַע).

/ The Ebla tablets were at first believed to mention the two cities, as well as Sodom and Zeboiim (verse 8), but these identifications are now considered unlikely [3]./

3] *Valley of Siddim, now the Dead Sea*. In Hebrew the "Salt Sea." The text recalls the time before the waters of the Dead Sea had submerged the valley at its southern end.

5] *Rephaim*. A mythical nation of giants.

7] *Hazazon-tamar*. Possibly another name for En-Gedi (see II Chron. 20:2) [4].

הָעָם: וַיֵּצֵא מֶלֶךְ־סְדֹם לִקְרָאתוֹ אַחֲרֵי שׁוּבוֹ מֵהַכּוֹת　יז
אֶת־כְּדָרְלָעֹמֶר וְאֶת־הַמְּלָכִים אֲשֶׁר אִתּוֹ אֶל־עֵמֶק
שָׁוֵה הוּא עֵמֶק הַמֶּלֶךְ: וּמַלְכִּי־צֶדֶק מֶלֶךְ שָׁלֵם　יח
הוֹצִיא לֶחֶם וָיָיִן וְהוּא כֹהֵן לְאֵל עֶלְיוֹן: וַיְבָרְכֵהוּ
וַיֹּאמַר בָּרוּךְ אַבְרָם לְאֵל עֶלְיוֹן קֹנֵה שָׁמַיִם וָאָרֶץ:　יט
וּבָרוּךְ אֵל עֶלְיוֹן אֲשֶׁר־מִגֵּן צָרֶיךָ בְּיָדֶךָ וַיִּתֶּן־לוֹ　כ
מַעֲשֵׂר מִכֹּל: וַיֹּאמֶר מֶלֶךְ־סְדֹם אֶל־אַבְרָם תֶּן־לִי　כא
הַנֶּפֶשׁ וְהָרְכֻשׁ קַח־לָךְ: וַיֹּאמֶר אַבְרָם אֶל־מֶלֶךְ סְדֹם
הֲרִמֹתִי יָדִי אֶל־יְהוָה אֵל עֶלְיוֹן קֹנֵה שָׁמַיִם וָאָרֶץ:　כב

הֵרָה נָסוּ: וַיִּקְחוּ אֶת־כָּל־רְכֻשׁ סְדֹם וַעֲמֹרָה וְאֶת־　יא
כָּל־אָכְלָם וַיֵּלֵכוּ: וַיִּקְחוּ אֶת־לוֹט וְאֶת־רְכֻשׁוֹ בֶּן־אֲחִי　יב
אַבְרָם וַיֵּלֵכוּ וְהוּא יֹשֵׁב בִּסְדֹם: וַיָּבֹא הַפָּלִיט וַיַּגֵּד　יג
לְאַבְרָם הָעִבְרִי וְהוּא שֹׁכֵן בְּאֵלֹנֵי מַמְרֵא הָאֱמֹרִי
אֲחִי אֶשְׁכֹּל וַאֲחִי עָנֵר וְהֵם בַּעֲלֵי בְרִית־אַבְרָם:
וַיִּשְׁמַע אַבְרָם כִּי נִשְׁבָּה אָחִיו וַיָּרֶק אֶת־חֲנִיכָיו יְלִידֵי　יד
בֵיתוֹ שְׁמֹנָה עָשָׂר וּשְׁלֹשׁ מֵאוֹת וַיִּרְדֹּף עַד־דָּן: וַיֵּחָלֵק　טו
עֲלֵיהֶם לַיְלָה הוּא וַעֲבָדָיו וַיַּכֵּם וַיִּרְדְּפֵם עַד־חוֹבָה
אֲשֶׁר מִשְּׂמֹאל לְדַמָּשֶׂק: וַיָּשֶׁב אֵת כָּל־הָרְכֻשׁ וְגַם　טז
אֶת־לוֹט אָחִיו וּרְכֻשׁוֹ הֵשִׁיב וְגַם אֶת־הַנָּשִׁים וְאֶת־

country. **11]** [The invaders] seized all the wealth of Sodom and Gomorrah and all their provisions, and went their way. **12]** They also took Lot, the son of Abram's brother, and his possessions, and departed; for he had settled in Sodom.

13] A fugitive brought the news to Abram the Hebrew, who was dwelling at the terebinths of Mamre the Amorite, kinsman of Eshkol and Aner, these being Abram's allies. **14]** When Abram heard that his kinsman had been taken captive, he mustered his retainers, born into his household, numbering three hundred and eighteen, and went in pursuit as far as Dan. **15]** At night, he and his servants deployed against them and defeated them; and he pursued them as far as Hobah, which is north of Damascus. **16]** He brought back all the possessions; he also brought back his kinsman Lot and his possessions, and the women and the rest of the people.

17] When he returned from defeating Chedorlaomer and the kings with him, the king of Sodom came out to meet him in the Valley of Shaveh, which is the Valley of the King. **18]** And Melchizedek, king of Salem, brought out bread and wine; he was a priest of God Most High. **19]** He blessed him, saying, "Blessed be Abram of God Most High, / Creator of heaven and earth. / **20]** And blessed be God Most High, / Who has delivered your foes into your hand." And [Abram] gave him a tenth of everything.

21] Then the king of Sodom said to Abram, "Give me the persons, and take the possessions for yourself." **22]** But Abram said to the king of Sodom, "I swear to the LORD, God Most

14] *Retainers.* Meaning of חֲנִיכָיו is uncertain.

Three hundred and eighteen. Probably a conventional number used for groups. The number is also part of the symbolism built around the number seven in the Book of Genesis. The prime numbers between 7 and 49 (7 × 7), when added together, total 318.

/ The number 318 is also found in a description of the retinue of a Mitanni princess [5]. It has further been noted that in the *Iliad* the number of men killed is

318. Another opinion is that the figure 318 is actual ancient memory: "To this very day there are old men in the tents of Arabia who can recite the history of their ancestors for forty generations, and, if in their recital they stray but a jot from the facts, others within hearing will immediately correct them, or supply forgotten details" [6]./

20] *A tenth of everything.* The tithe customarily given to the priests (see at Deut. 14:22).

22] *I swear.* Literally, "lift up my hand."

בראשית יד

כג אִם־מִחוּט וְעַד שְׂרוֹךְ־נַעַל וְאִם־אֶקַּח מִכָּל־אֲשֶׁר־לָךְ אֲשֶׁר אָכְלוּ הַנְּעָרִים וְחֵלֶק הָאֲנָשִׁים אֲשֶׁר הָלְכוּ אִתִּי
כד וְלֹא תֹאמַר אֲנִי הֶעֱשַׁרְתִּי אֶת־אַבְרָם: בִּלְעָדַי רַק עָנֵר אֶשְׁכֹּל וּמַמְרֵא הֵם יִקְחוּ חֶלְקָם: ס

High, Creator of heaven and earth: **23]** I will not take so much as a thread or a sandal strap of what is yours; you shall not say, 'It is I who made Abram rich.' **24]** For me, nothing but what my servants have used up; as for the share of the men who went with me—Aner, Eshkol, and Mamre—let them take their share."

23] *Will not take.* Abraham, true to nomadic tradition, does not wish to be beholden to anyone. Besides, as a trader, he need not rely on plunder as a source of income [7]. It is also possible that his bruskness signifies some contempt for the king of Sodom.

Abraham the Hebrew

For the first time since his introduction into the biblical text, Abraham is referred to —without preparation or explanation—as an *Ivri*, a Hebrew. The term is difficult to trace, but many scholars agree that it is in some way connected with the word "Habiru."[1]

During the nineteenth to fourteenth centuries B.C.E. a class of people known as Habiru lived in the Fertile Crescent. They may originally have come from Arabia [8] and may have been related by family ties; they became prominent in Mesopotamia and later spread out all the way to Egypt. The Habiru were a group with distinct occupations and appear to have specialized as mercenaries and administrators. Although at first they were nomads or semi-nomads, they later settled in the countries of their choice. They were, however, usually considered foreigners, which means that they succeeded in maintaining their group identity. Their status was often akin to that of modern civil servants, and when they were sufficiently numerous they would on occasion, by shifting their allegiance, influence a country's political fortunes. They were sometimes feared, and their cognomen was "wanderers who are also known as robbers." Thus, Habiru was not so much a gentilic term referring to a particular ethnic or linguistic group but rather a term of social or political significance [9].

What is the relationship between the Hebrews and these Habiru? Linguistically the words Habiru and *Ivri* appear to share a common root [10]. It is likely that in Egypt and elsewhere members of the Israelite tribes occupied positions similar to, or because of familial ties were identified with, the Habiru. The repeated application of this term by non-Israelites in time caused the Israelites themselves to use the cognomen Habiru,

which they pronounced *Ivri* (עִבְרִי; plural *Ivrim*, עִבְרִים). After the Habiru themselves had disappeared as an identifiable group, the name *Ivrim* was traced to the postdiluvian Eber (עֵבֶר, *Ever*), who was installed in the catalog of descent as the legendary ancestor or eponym (Gen. 11:16). Later folk etymology understood *Ever* to mean "the other side of"—presumably the Euphrates—thus linking the Israelites with Abraham who had come from Ur.

It is possible that for some time the term *Ivrim* was used only when the members of the Israelite tribes spoke of themselves to outsiders and when outsiders referred to them. Thus, Abraham is called *Ivri* vis-à-vis an outsider (Gen. 14:13) [11]; and Jonah says, "I am an *Ivri*," when asked his identity by gentile sailors (Jonah 1:9). Otherwise the people referred to themselves by their tribes (e.g., Judah, Ephraim) or by their more immediate common ancestor, Israel.

Melchizedek

The king of Salem, whose name may mean "The King Is Justice"[2] was the priest of *El Elyon* (Gen. 14:18), a deity mentioned in Phoenician records. *Elyon* later came to mean "Most High," and the expression *El Elyon* (God Most High) was also applied to the God of Abraham.

This identification led later tradition to classify Melchizedek with those righteous Gentiles who, like Job and Jethro, acknowledged the Lord of Abraham as their God. The Jews of Alexandria, who were interested in proselytizing the Gentiles, considered Melchizedek a monotheist whom Abraham admired and whose example other Gentiles followed. Thus, Melchizedek became a subject of speculation in Jewish and Christian traditions. Already in Psalms he is called the

[1] The word is also transcribed as hapiru or hap/biru. On the possibility of connecting *Ivri* with Ebrium, king of Ebla, see Hallo's essay.

[2] Or "King of Justice," or "The King Is Tzedek" (Tzedek being a divine name) [12].

prototype of the ideal king who will spring from the line of David:

The Lord has sworn and will not relent, "You are a priest forever, a rightful king by My decree" (Ps. 110:4).

The Christian Scriptures developed this tradition further and called Jesus the "high priest after the order of Melchizedek" [13]; the ancient king was also said to have resembled the Son of God [14] and to have been superior to Abraham. Melchizedek's merit is recalled in the daily Mass, and the entire communion tradition of bread and wine is traced back to this story.

The original importance accorded Melchizedek most likely arose from the fact that he was king of Salem and that Salem was identified with Jerusalem (Ps. 76:3) [15]. In this way tradition established a link between Abraham and the Holy City, for Abraham was thought to prefigure his people who in the centuries to come would pay their tithes to the Temple in the very spot where Abraham made his first covenant [16].

GLEANINGS

Three Hundred Eighteen Retainers

Abraham's victory over the kings was not due to the assistance of 318 men but of one single helper. For 318 is the numerical equivalent of the letters in Eliezer, the servant of Abraham. Having established that 318 means Eliezer, we further note that the word Eliezer itself means "God is my help"—which is to say that Abraham's helper was God, and that he defeated the kings with faith rather than force.   MIDRASH [17]

[The equivalency refers to an old method of biblical interpretation called *gematria*. Each letter of the Hebrew alphabet has a numerical value (א =1, ב =2, etc.); words of equal numerical value were compared and conclusions drawn on that basis. Thus the letters in Eliezer add up to 318: א = 1, ל = 30, י = 10, ע = 70, ז = 7, ר = 200. See further at Deut. 1:1–5, footnote 2.]

Abraham the Ivri

The word עִבְרִי [Ivri] is said to be derived from עֵבֶר [ever], on the other side of, or beyond. According to Rabbi Judah, the words "Abraham the *Ivri*" meant that the whole world stood on one side and he on the other, i.e., Abraham's faith ran counter to what all other men believed.   MIDRASH [18]

War

Why did Abraham get involved in the wars of those kings? Because his kinsman Lot was taken captive. Is there ever a war when Abraham does not hear the message, "Your brother is in trouble"?   MOSES AVIGDOR AMIEL [19]

The Language of Prayer

Melchizedek and Abraham use the same term, *El Elyon*, but they attach different meanings to it. Each refers to his own God—the pagan king to his pagan deity and Abraham to "God Most High." They worship together, each respecting the faith of the other. Thus, they set an example of ancient "interfaith worship": They use formulations, wholly acceptable to each other, and thereby make common prayer possible.

Abraham's God

There were no stories about God. That was indeed perhaps the most remarkable thing: the courage with which Abram represented and expressed God's essence from the first, without more ado, simply in that he said "God."

THOMAS MANN [20]

The Covenant between the Pieces;
the Birth of Ishmael

For a second time Abraham hears the divine promise that he will be the father of a great nation. The promise is made to him in a special and most solemn form—with darkness, smoking oven, and flaming torch.

A *berit*, or covenant, is made. Thereafter, God's promise seems to move toward its first stage of fulfilment: Abraham will at last have an offspring. But again there is a delay; the Patriarch finally fathers a son, yet not with Sarah. Chapter 16 heightens the dramatic tension by introducing Hagar and Ishmael as counterfoils to the main personages.

הַשָּׁמַיְמָה וּסְפֹר הַכּוֹכָבִים אִם־תּוּכַל לִסְפֹּר אֹתָם
וַיֹּאמֶר לוֹ כֹּה יִהְיֶה זַרְעֶךָ: וְהֶאֱמִן בַּיהֹוָה וַיַּחְשְׁבֶהָ
לּוֹ צְדָקָה: וַיֹּאמֶר אֵלָיו אֲנִי יְהֹוָה אֲשֶׁר הוֹצֵאתִיךָ
מֵאוּר כַּשְׂדִּים לָתֶת לְךָ אֶת־הָאָרֶץ הַזֹּאת לְרִשְׁתָּהּ:
וַיֹּאמַר אֲדֹנָי יֱהֹוִה בַּמָּה אֵדַע כִּי אִירָשֶׁנָּה: וַיֹּאמֶר
אֵלָיו קְחָה לִי עֶגְלָה מְשֻׁלֶּשֶׁת וְעֵז מְשֻׁלֶּשֶׁת וְאַיִל
מְשֻׁלָּשׁ וְתֹר וְגוֹזָל: וַיִּקַּח־לוֹ אֶת־כָּל־אֵלֶּה וַיְבַתֵּר אֹתָם
בַּתָּוֶךְ וַיִּתֵּן אִישׁ־בִּתְרוֹ לִקְרַאת רֵעֵהוּ וְאֶת־הַצִּפֹּר

א אַחַר הַדְּבָרִים הָאֵלֶּה הָיָה דְבַר־יְהֹוָה אֶל־אַבְרָם
בַּמַּחֲזֶה לֵאמֹר אַל־תִּירָא אַבְרָם אָנֹכִי מָגֵן לָךְ
ב שְׂכָרְךָ הַרְבֵּה מְאֹד: וַיֹּאמֶר אַבְרָם אֲדֹנָי יֱהֹוִה מַה־
תִּתֶּן־לִי וְאָנֹכִי הוֹלֵךְ עֲרִירִי וּבֶן־מֶשֶׁק בֵּיתִי הוּא
ג דַּמֶּשֶׂק אֱלִיעֶזֶר: וַיֹּאמֶר אַבְרָם הֵן לִי לֹא נָתַתָּה
ד זָרַע וְהִנֵּה בֶן־בֵּיתִי יוֹרֵשׁ אֹתִי: וְהִנֵּה דְבַר־יְהֹוָה
אֵלָיו לֵאמֹר לֹא יִירָשְׁךָ זֶה כִּי־אִם אֲשֶׁר יֵצֵא מִמֵּעֶיךָ
ה הוּא יִירָשֶׁךָ: וַיּוֹצֵא אֹתוֹ הַחוּצָה וַיֹּאמֶר הַבֶּט־נָא

1] Some time later, the word of the LORD came to Abram in a vision, saying, "Fear not, Abram, / I am a shield to you; / Your reward shall be very great." **2]** But Abram said, "O LORD God, what can You give me, seeing that I shall die childless, and the one in charge of my household is Dammesek Eliezer!" **3]** Abram said further, "Since You have granted me no offspring, my steward will be my heir." **4]** The word of the LORD came to him in reply, "That one shall not be your heir; none but your very own issue shall be your heir." **5]** He took him outside and said, "Look toward heaven and count the stars, if you are able to count them." And He added, "So shall your offspring be." **6]** And because he put his trust in the LORD, He reckoned it to his merit.

7] Then He said to him, "I am the LORD who brought you out from Ur of the Chaldeans to give you this land as a possession." **8]** And he said, "O LORD God, how shall I know that I am to possess it?" **9]** He answered, "Bring Me a three-year-old heifer, a three-year-old she-goat, a three-year-old ram, a turtledove, and a young bird." **10]** He brought Him all these and cut them in two, placing each half opposite the other; but he did not cut up the

15:1] *The word of the Lord came to.* The phrase is used frequently in Jeremiah and Ezekiel to introduce a prophetic vision. It occurs here, but nowhere else in the Torah.

I am a shield to you. Hence in Jewish tradition God is often referred to as "Shield of Abraham" (e.g., in the first of the eighteen benedictions in the prayer book).

2] *Dammesek Eliezer.* Most likely Abraham's servant, "the Damascan." Abraham may have adopted him as a son and, if Hurrian practice was applicable, he would be Abraham's beneficiary.

/ This was not so in later Jewish (rabbinic) law, in which technical adoption comparable to the Roman *adrogatio* did not exist, though it has a place in modern Israeli law. Albright believes that Abraham adopted Eliezer so that he would be able to obtain credit. The native-born Eliezer could own property, thus extending Abraham's credit base [1]./

6] *He reckoned it to his merit.* God rewards the faithful (repeated in Ps. 106:31). Paul, in the Christian Scripture, uses this verse to prove that merit depends on faith rather than law [2]; but James draws the opposite conclusion: Man is justified by works and not by faith only [3].

10] *And cut them.* The *berit* is concluded through a process of cutting, hence the Hebrew phrase, "to cut a covenant" (see note to Gen. 9:9). Smoke and flame are a frequent accompaniment of the divine presence.

הָיָה וְהִנֵּה תַנּוּר עָשָׁן וְלַפִּיד אֵשׁ אֲשֶׁר עָבַר בֵּין　　יא לֹא בָתָר: וַיֵּרֶד הָעַיִט עַל־הַפְּגָרִים וַיַּשֵּׁב אֹתָם

הַגְּזָרִים הָאֵלֶּה: בַּיּוֹם הַהוּא כָּרַת יְהוָה אֶת־אַבְרָם　　יב אַבְרָם: וַיְהִי הַשֶּׁמֶשׁ לָבוֹא וְתַרְדֵּמָה נָפְלָה עַל־

בְּרִית לֵאמֹר לְזַרְעֲךָ נָתַתִּי אֶת־הָאָרֶץ הַזֹּאת מִנְּהַר　　אַבְרָם וְהִנֵּה אֵימָה חֲשֵׁכָה גְדֹלָה נֹפֶלֶת עָלָיו:

מִצְרַיִם עַד־הַנָּהָר הַגָּדֹל נְהַר־פְּרָת: אֶת־הַקֵּינִי וְאֶת־　　יג וַיֹּאמֶר לְאַבְרָם יָדֹעַ תֵּדַע כִּי־גֵר יִהְיֶה זַרְעֲךָ בְּאֶרֶץ

הַקְּנִזִּי וְאֵת הַקַּדְמֹנִי: וְאֶת־הַחִתִּי וְאֶת־הַפְּרִזִּי וְאֶת־　　יד לֹא לָהֶם וַעֲבָדוּם וְעִנּוּ אֹתָם אַרְבַּע מֵאוֹת שָׁנָה: וְגַם

הָרְפָאִים: וְאֶת־הָאֱמֹרִי וְאֶת־הַכְּנַעֲנִי וְאֶת־הַגִּרְגָּשִׁי　　אֶת־הַגּוֹי אֲשֶׁר יַעֲבֹדוּ דָּן אָנֹכִי וְאַחֲרֵי־כֵן יֵצְאוּ

וְאֶת־הַיְבוּסִי: ס　　טו בִּרְכֻשׁ גָּדוֹל: וְאַתָּה תָּבוֹא אֶל־אֲבֹתֶיךָ בְּשָׁלוֹם תִּקָּבֵר

טז בְּשֵׂיבָה טוֹבָה: וְדוֹר רְבִיעִי יָשׁוּבוּ הֵנָּה כִּי לֹא־שָׁלֵם

א וְשָׂרַי אֵשֶׁת אַבְרָם לֹא יָלְדָה לוֹ וְלָהּ שִׁפְחָה מִצְרִית　　יז עֲוֹן הָאֱמֹרִי עַד־הֵנָּה: וַיְהִי הַשֶּׁמֶשׁ בָּאָה וַעֲלָטָה

ב וּשְׁמָהּ הָגָר: וַתֹּאמֶר שָׂרַי אֶל־אַבְרָם הִנֵּה־נָא עֲצָרַנִי

---

bird. **11]** Birds of prey came down upon the carcasses, and Abram drove them away. **12]** As the sun was about to set, a deep sleep fell upon Abram, and a great dark dread descended upon him. **13]** And He said to Abram, "Know well that your offspring shall be strangers in a land not theirs, and they shall be enslaved and oppressed four hundred years; **14]** but I will execute judgment on the nation they shall serve, and in the end they shall go free with great wealth. **15]** As for you, You shall go to your fathers in peace; / You shall be buried at a ripe old age. **16]** And they shall return here in the fourth generation, for the iniquity of the Amorites is not yet complete."

17] When the sun set and it was very dark, there appeared a smoking oven, and a flaming torch which passed between those pieces. **18]** On that day the LORD made a covenant with Abram, saying, "To your offspring I give this land, from the river of Egypt to the great river, the river Euphrates: **19]** the Kenites, the Kenizzites, the Kadmonites, **20]** the Hittites, the Perizzites, the Rephaim, **21]** the Amorites, the Canaanites, the Girgashites, and the Jebusites."

1] Sarai, Abram's wife, had borne him no children. She had an Egyptian maidservant whose

---

11] *Birds of prey.* Most likely forces that try to prevent the covenant from being concluded.

13] *Four hundred years.* In Exod. 12:40 the figure is 430. We have here an example of history presented in prophetic form: The sojourn in Egypt is envisioned as having been ordained in the time of Abraham.

16] *Fourth generation.* A round figure, meaning "much later."

The iniquity of the Amorites. Once it reaches its full measure, it will cause them to lose the land. This relationship of morality and possession is part of the Holy Land's special nature, which was to have a profound effect on the children of Israel (see commentary to Gen. 12:10–13:18, "The Promised Land").

18] *From the river of Egypt.* The boundaries of the Promised Land vary throughout the Torah (cf. Num. 34:1–12 and Deut. 1:7–8). Certainly, in these ancient conceptions, the borders were far greater than those of the State of Israel in 1948, or even after the Six Day War in 1967 [4].

19] *The Kenites.* Kenites and Kenizzites lived in the Negev; Kadmonites means "easterners" or "ancients." On Perizzites, see Gen. 13:7; on Rephaim, Gen. 14:5; Hittites, Amorites, Canaanites, Girgashites, and Jebusites are mentioned in chapter 10.

יְהוָה מִלֶּדֶת בֹּא־נָא אֶל־שִׁפְחָתִי אוּלַי אִבָּנֶה מִמֶּנָּה   שָׂרַי הִנֵּה שִׁפְחָתֵךְ בְּיָדֵךְ עֲשִׂי־לָהּ הַטּוֹב בְּעֵינָיִךְ

ג וַיִּשְׁמַע אַבְרָם לְקוֹל שָׂרָי: וַתִּקַּח שָׂרַי אֵשֶׁת־אַבְרָם   וַתְּעַנֶּהָ שָׂרַי וַתִּבְרַח מִפָּנֶיהָ: וַיִּמְצָאָהּ מַלְאַךְ יְהוָה

אֶת־הָגָר הַמִּצְרִית שִׁפְחָתָהּ מִקֵּץ עֶשֶׂר שָׁנִים לְשֶׁבֶת   עַל־עֵין הַמַּיִם בַּמִּדְבָּר עַל־הָעַיִן בְּדֶרֶךְ שׁוּר: וַיֹּאמַר

אַבְרָם בְּאֶרֶץ כְּנָעַן וַתִּתֵּן אֹתָהּ לְאַבְרָם אִישָׁהּ לוֹ   הָגָר שִׁפְחַת שָׂרַי אֵי־מִזֶּה בָאת וְאָנָה תֵלֵכִי וַתֹּאמֶר

ד לְאִשָּׁה: וַיָּבֹא אֶל־הָגָר וַתַּהַר וַתֵּרֶא כִּי הָרָתָה וַתֵּקַל   מִפְּנֵי שָׂרַי גְּבִרְתִּי אָנֹכִי בֹּרַחַת: וַיֹּאמֶר לָהּ מַלְאַךְ

ה גְּבִרְתָּהּ בְּעֵינֶיהָ: וַתֹּאמֶר שָׂרַי אֶל־אַבְרָם חֲמָסִי עָלֶיךָ   יְהוָה שׁוּבִי אֶל־גְּבִרְתֵּךְ וְהִתְעַנִּי תַּחַת יָדֶיהָ: וַיֹּאמֶר

אָנֹכִי נָתַתִּי שִׁפְחָתִי בְּחֵיקֶךָ וַתֵּרֶא כִּי הָרָתָה וָאֵקַל   לָהּ מַלְאַךְ יְהוָה הַרְבָּה אַרְבֶּה אֶת־זַרְעֵךְ וְלֹא

ו בְּעֵינֶיהָ יִשְׁפֹּט יְהוָה בֵּינִי וּבֵינֶיךָ: וַיֹּאמֶר אַבְרָם אֶל־   יִסָּפֵר מֵרֹב: וַיֹּאמֶר לָהּ מַלְאַךְ יְהוָה הִנָּךְ הָרָה

* ה נקוד על י' בתרא.

name was Hagar. **2]** And Sarai said to Abram, "Look, the LORD has kept me from bearing. Consort with my maid; perhaps I shall have a son through her." And Abram heeded Sarai's request. **3]** So Sarai, Abram's wife, took her maid, Hagar the Egyptian—after Abram had dwelt in the land of Canaan ten years—and gave her to her husband Abram as concubine. **4]** He cohabited with Hagar and she conceived; and when she saw that she had conceived, her mistress was lowered in her esteem. **5]** And Sarai said to Abram, "The wrong done me is your fault! I myself put my maid in your bosom; now that she sees that she is pregnant, I am lowered in her esteem. The LORD decide between you and me!" **6]** Abram said to Sarai, "Your maid is in your hands. Deal with her as you think right." Then Sarai treated her harshly, and she ran away from her.

7] An angel of the LORD found her by a spring of water in the wilderness, the spring on the road to Shur, **8]** and said, "Hagar, slave of Sarai, where have you come from, and where are you going?" And she said, "I am running away from my mistress Sarai."

9] And the angel of the LORD said to her, "Go back to your mistress, and submit to her harsh treatment." **10]** And the angel of the LORD said to her, "I will greatly increase your offspring, / And they shall be too many to count." **11]** The angel of the LORD said to her

16:2] *The Lord has kept me from bearing.* Childlessness is considered a mark of divine disfavor. The Bible relates several instances of barrenness, induced and then eliminated by God's will (e.g., Rachel, Hannah). This theme makes the late appearance of a first child (always a son) especially important.

/Compare the proverb: "One without a child is as dead and razed to the ground" [5]. See also Gen. 30:1./

    Have a son. Literally, "be built up," a word play on בֵּן (*ben*, son) and בָּנָה (*banah*, build up).

3] *Concubine.* The Hebrew word אִשָּׁה (*ishah*) is also the term used for wife. Hagar becomes

Abraham's אִשָּׁה, but she remains Sarah's servant. The Code of Hammurabi warns expressly that a slave girl elevated by her mistress should not and could not claim equality [6]. A Nuzi contract provided: "If Gillimninu bears children, Shennima shall not take another wife. But if Gillimninu fails to bear children, she shall get for him a slave girl as concubine. In that case, Gillimninu herself shall have authority over the offspring" [7].

6] *Sarai treated her harshly.* Since in her position Hagar could no longer be sold or expelled [8], Sarah abuses her maid, thereby causing her to leave of her own accord (cf. Deut. 21:14).

7] *Angel.* See commentary to Gen. 18:1–15, "Angels."

טו בֵּין־קָדֵשׁ וּבֵין בָּרֶד: וַתֵּלֶד הָגָר לְאַבְרָם בֵּן וַיִּקְרָא

טז אַבְרָם שֶׁם־בְּנוֹ אֲשֶׁר־יָלְדָה הָגָר יִשְׁמָעֵאל: וְאַבְרָם

בֶּן־שְׁמֹנִים שָׁנָה וְשֵׁשׁ שָׁנִים בְּלֶדֶת־הָגָר אֶת־יִשְׁמָעֵאל

ס   לְאַבְרָם:

וַיֵּלֵד בֵּן וְקָרָאת שְׁמוֹ יִשְׁמָעֵאל כִּי־שָׁמַע יְהוָה אֶל־ יא

עָנְיֵךְ: וְהוּא יִהְיֶה פֶּרֶא אָדָם יָדוֹ בַכֹּל וְיַד כֹּל בּוֹ יב

וְעַל־פְּנֵי כָל־אֶחָיו יִשְׁכֹּן: וַתִּקְרָא שֵׁם־יְהוָה הַדֹּבֵר יג

אֵלֶיהָ אַתָּה אֵל רֳאִי כִּי אָמְרָה הֲגַם הֲלֹם רָאִיתִי

אַחֲרֵי רֹאִי: עַל־כֵּן קָרָא לַבְּאֵר בְּאֵר לַחַי רֹאִי הִנֵּה יד

further, "Behold, you are with child / And shall bear a son; / You shall call him Ishmael, / For the LORD has paid heed to your suffering. / **12]** He shall be a wild ass of a man; / His hand against everyone, / And everyone's hand against him; / He shall dwell alongside of all his kinsmen." **13]** And she called the LORD who spoke to her, "You Are El-roi," by which she meant, "Have I not gone on seeing after He saw me!" **14]** Therefore the well was called Beer-lahai-roi; it is between Kadesh and Bered.— **15]** Hagar bore a son to Abram, and Abram gave the son that Hagar bore him the name Ishmael. **16]** Abram was eighty-six years old when Hagar bore Ishmael to Abram.

11] *Ishmael.* יִשְׁמָעֵאל means God heeds.

12] *A wild ass of a man.* A reference to the character of the Bedouin, who, like the wild ass of the desert, lives in highly mobile groups. On Ishmael as the ancestor of the Arabs, see Gleanings to Gen. 20:1–21:34, "Islam."

13] *El-roi.* Apparently, "God of my vision"; the

remainder of the Hebrew is obscure. / Various emendations have been offered to produce the sense: "I have lived after seeing God" [9]. /

14] *Beer-lahai-roi.* Meaning is uncertain, perhaps "the well of the Living One who sees me."

Between Kadesh and Bered. In the Negev.

The Reality of the Covenant

Did God really speak to Abraham and enter into a covenant or *berit* (בְּרִית) built on the verbal commitment reported by the text?

If we take the literal view (and Jewish as well as Christian tradition took it unequivocally), the nature of the compact cannot be in doubt. If, on the other hand, we read the story as the spiritual experience of one man who understood his God to address him in this unique fashion, the emphasis is shifted to a recounting of Abraham's internal vision. It is through him that God's promise is made known to us; it is through his eyes that the reality of the covenant must be viewed.

However we view the story, we are face to face with a remarkable human being who saw more in his environment than earth and sky, mountains and valleys: the story of a man who looked at the world as the proving ground for human opportunities, seeing all this in the context of mutual trust and obligation expressed in the concept of *berit*.

The *berit* thus adds a new dimension to human existence, a deepening of the call that he first heard in Haran, "Go forth!" These experiences of Abraham were the foundations on which his descendants built their house of faith and contributed their commitment to a covenant first envisioned in the dark of ancient Negev nights.

The Nature of the Covenant

"In a society in which the capriciousness[1] of the gods was taken for granted," writes Nahum Sarna, " 'the covenant between the pieces,' like the covenant with Noah, set religion on a bold, new, independent course" [10].

Both covenants have one outstanding feature in common: They obligate God but demand nothing of man. In contradistinction to many later references to *berit*—in which God's covenant with Israel is made dependent on the latter's continued faithfulness—the Bible here makes God's commitment unconditional. Not only has He created a physical universe with immutable laws, He has established conditions for an unchanging spiritual world as well. He is a faithful God—faithful in His natural as well as transnatural manifestations. And unlike the pagan deities whose universes were unpredictable and erratic, God shows himself, in the covenant between the pieces, to be an אֵל נֶאֱמָן (*El Ne-eman*)—a God who is both dependable and trustworthy. No such religious covenant is known outside of Israel.

The Ritual

What is the meaning of the ritual itself, which persisted into the time of Jeremiah (34:18)? It may have been a vestige of ancient blood magic that by Abraham's time had assumed legal importance amongst various nations. Thus, the Amorites finalized a pact by slaying an ass and cutting it into pieces [11]. It has been suggested that the current custom of cutting a ribbon to symbolize the opening of a bridge or a highway is a remnant of such ancient sentiments. The cutting ritual may have symbolized that the contracting parties were now the guarantors of wholeness. Abraham sees God himself passing through the pieces, thereby emphasizing that the divine promise is secure.

---

[1] The gods were capricious to the extent that they behaved like human beings, and it was human beings who by prayer, penance, and sacrifice could check this capriciousness.

GLEANINGS

The Friend of God

Who has a better religion than he who submits his whole self to God, who does what is good, and follows the way of Abraham, the true in faith? For God did take Abraham for a friend.

KORAN [12]

[Cf. Isa. 41:8. Islamic tradition derives the very word Moslem from the Abraham story: "This is the religion of your father Abraham. He called you *muslimin*" (those who surrender themselves to the will of God).]

Abraham Was Free to Disbelieve

[Gen. 15:6 says that after God had appeared to Abraham the latter evinced his trust in God, whereupon "He reckoned it to his merit."]

Scripture finds it necessary to make explicit what one should have thought to be obvious, that a divine revelation engendered faith in the first of the Patriarchs; and indeed deems it important to underscore this faith as being particularly meritorious!

Scripture is drawing our attention to the phenomena of revelation and faith and to the relation between them: Every revelation is a human experience; whatever its manner or form, its degree or content, it is a discrete event; it takes place in time—it has a beginning and an end. And after the event man is free—to remember or to forget, to formulate in words the impact of the event or the message—if any, to accept it or—yes—to question its reality. Was it a dream, a figment, a chimera, an illusion, a delusion, a hallucination?

HERBERT C. BRICHTO [13]

The Word of the Lord Came to Abram (Gen. 15:1)

Of course you can't imagine such a thing as that the word of God should ever come to you? Is that because you are worse, or better, than Abraham?—because you are a more, or less, civilized person than he? I leave you to answer that question for yourself;—only as I have told you often before, but cannot repeat too often, find out first what the word *is*.

JOHN RUSKIN [14]

The Covenant

In the language of the Bible the word *berit* became a characteristically religious word, one of those words in which the idea of great interrelatedness, the great unity of all, of mystery and ordered certainty seeks to express itself. The God-given order was to find expression in this term.... The Old Aramaic translation of the Bible translated *berit* as *kayama* [that which is established], indicating that which is above all change, above all that comes and goes.

LEO BAECK [15]

Barren Marriage in Jewish Law

In theory, when a man had lived with his wife for ten years and they had no children, even though it could not definitely be proven that she was barren, the court could force the man to divorce her. But this law fell into disuse.

Isserles, in the sixteenth century, wrote that in his day it was no longer customary for a court to force the divorce of a barren woman, even when her husband had not fulfilled the *mitzvah* of procreation. [16]

Hittite Parallel (from the text of a soldier's oath)

He places sinews and salt in their hands. He throws them on a pan and speaks as follows: "Just as these sinews split into fragments on the hearth, and just as the salt is scattered on the hearth—whoever breaks these oaths, shows disrespect to the king of the Hatti land, and turns his eyes in hostile fashion upon the Hatti land, let these oaths seize him! Let him split into fragments like the sinews, let him be scattered like the salt! Just as salt has no seed, even so let that man's name, seed, house, cattle, and sheep perish!" [17]

The Covenant of Circumcision

Heretofore God made no demands on Abraham in return for His promise. But a fundamental change in this one-sided obligation is about to take place. Henceforth Abraham—his name changed from Abram —and his descendants will bear the mark of the covenant on their flesh. Circumcision, so important to Jews and sometimes controversial in their history, makes Abraham and his descendants partners in the obligations of the covenant.

א וַיְהִי אַבְרָם בֶּן־תִּשְׁעִים שָׁנָה וְתֵשַׁע שָׁנִים וַיֵּרָא יְהֹוָה
אֶל־אַבְרָם וַיֹּאמֶר אֵלָיו אֲנִי־אֵל שַׁדַּי הִתְהַלֵּךְ לְפָנַי
ב וֶהְיֵה תָמִים: וְאֶתְּנָה בְרִיתִי בֵּינִי וּבֵינֶךָ וְאַרְבֶּה אוֹתְךָ
ג בִּמְאֹד מְאֹד: וַיִּפֹּל אַבְרָם עַל־פָּנָיו וַיְדַבֵּר אִתּוֹ
ד אֱלֹהִים לֵאמֹר: אֲנִי הִנֵּה בְרִיתִי אִתָּךְ וְהָיִיתָ לְאַב
ה הֲמוֹן גּוֹיִם: וְלֹא־יִקָּרֵא עוֹד אֶת־שִׁמְךָ אַבְרָם וְהָיָה
ו שִׁמְךָ אַבְרָהָם כִּי אַב־הֲמוֹן גּוֹיִם נְתַתִּיךָ: וְהִפְרֵתִי
אֹתְךָ בִּמְאֹד מְאֹד וּנְתַתִּיךָ לְגוֹיִם וּמְלָכִים מִמְּךָ יֵצֵאוּ:
ז וַהֲקִמֹתִי אֶת־בְּרִיתִי בֵּינִי וּבֵינֶךָ וּבֵין זַרְעֲךָ אַחֲרֶיךָ
לְדֹרֹתָם לִבְרִית עוֹלָם לִהְיוֹת לְךָ לֵאלֹהִים וּלְזַרְעֲךָ

ח אַחֲרֶיךָ: וְנָתַתִּי לְךָ וּלְזַרְעֲךָ אַחֲרֶיךָ אֵת אֶרֶץ מְגֻרֶיךָ
אֵת כָּל־אֶרֶץ כְּנַעַן לַאֲחֻזַּת עוֹלָם וְהָיִיתִי לָהֶם
ט לֵאלֹהִים: וַיֹּאמֶר אֱלֹהִים אֶל־אַבְרָהָם וְאַתָּה אֶת־
י בְּרִיתִי תִשְׁמֹר אַתָּה וְזַרְעֲךָ אַחֲרֶיךָ לְדֹרֹתָם: זֹאת
בְּרִיתִי אֲשֶׁר תִּשְׁמְרוּ בֵּינִי וּבֵינֵיכֶם וּבֵין זַרְעֲךָ אַחֲרֶיךָ
יא הִמּוֹל לָכֶם כָּל־זָכָר: וּנְמַלְתֶּם אֵת בְּשַׂר עָרְלַתְכֶם
יב וְהָיָה לְאוֹת בְּרִית בֵּינִי וּבֵינֵיכֶם: וּבֶן־שְׁמֹנַת יָמִים
יִמּוֹל לָכֶם כָּל־זָכָר לְדֹרֹתֵיכֶם יְלִיד בָּיִת וּמִקְנַת־
יג כֶּסֶף מִכֹּל בֶּן־נֵכָר אֲשֶׁר לֹא מִזַּרְעֲךָ הוּא: הִמּוֹל
יִמּוֹל יְלִיד בֵּיתְךָ וּמִקְנַת כַּסְפֶּךָ וְהָיְתָה בְרִיתִי

1] When Abram was ninety-nine years old, the LORD appeared to Abram and said to him, "I am El Shaddai. Walk in My ways and be blameless.   **2]** I will establish My covenant between Me and you, and I will make you exceedingly numerous."

3] Abram threw himself on his face, as God spoke to him further,   **4]** "As for Me, this is My covenant with you: You shall be the father of a multitude of nations.   **5]** And you shall no longer be called Abram, but your name shall be Abraham, for I make you the father of a multitude of nations.   **6]** I will make you exceedingly fertile, and make nations of you; and kings shall come forth from you.   **7]** I will maintain My covenant between Me and you, and your offspring to come, as an everlasting covenant throughout the ages, to be God to you and to your offspring to come.   **8]** I give the land you sojourn in to you and your offspring to come, all the land of Canaan, as an everlasting possession. I will be their God."

9] God further said to Abraham, "As for you, you and your offspring to come throughout the ages shall keep My covenant.   **10]** Such shall be the covenant between Me and you and your offspring to follow which you shall keep: every male among you shall be circumcised. **11]** You shall circumcise the flesh of your foreskin, and that shall be the sign of the covenant between Me and you.   **12]** And throughout the generations, every male among you shall be circumcised at the age of eight days. As for the homeborn slave and the one bought from an outsider who is not of your offspring,   **13]** they must be circumcised, homeborn and purchased

17:1]   *I am El Shaddai.* The meaning of "Shaddai" is in doubt. "God Almighty" is the most frequent translation.

/Some scholars derive the word *Shaddai* from the Akkadian for "mountain" or from the root "to send rain." Rashi explained the name homiletically: "I am He whose divinity is sufficient (שַׁדַּי) to all creation."/

Be blameless. Like Noah, for whom the same phrase was used (Gen. 6:9).

3]   *Abram threw himself on his face.* The common form of showing submission to gods, kings, and other important personages (cf. I Kings 18:7;

Ruth 2:10).

5]   *Abram.* This name is probably a contraction of *Abi-ram,* "my father is exalted." The additional syllable (*ha*) added by God to Abram's name is most likely an extension or enlargement of the original name [1], so that the biblical explanation of Abraham ("father of a multitude") is assonance rather than correct etymology.

10]   *Circumcised.* By removal of the foreskin of the penis (see Gleanings). Later in the Bible the term is applied figuratively to removing obstacles to understanding (Deut. 10:16; 30:6). Jer. 4:4 speaks of the "foreskin of the heart."

יד בִּבְשַׂרְכֶם לִבְרִית עוֹלָם: וְעָרֵל זָכָר אֲשֶׁר לֹא־יִמּוֹל אֶת־בְּשַׂר עָרְלָתוֹ וְנִכְרְתָה הַנֶּפֶשׁ הַהִוא מֵעַמֶּיהָ אֶת־בְּרִיתִי הֵפַר: ס

טו וַיֹּאמֶר אֱלֹהִים אֶל־אַבְרָהָם שָׂרַי אִשְׁתְּךָ לֹא־תִקְרָא אֶת־שְׁמָהּ שָׂרָי כִּי שָׂרָה שְׁמָהּ:

טז וּבֵרַכְתִּי אֹתָהּ וְגַם נָתַתִּי מִמֶּנָּה לְךָ בֵּן וּבֵרַכְתִּיהָ וְהָיְתָה לְגוֹיִם מַלְכֵי עַמִּים מִמֶּנָּה יִהְיוּ:

יז וַיִּפֹּל אַבְרָהָם עַל־פָּנָיו וַיִּצְחָק וַיֹּאמֶר בְּלִבּוֹ הַלְּבֶן מֵאָה־שָׁנָה יִוָּלֵד וְאִם־שָׂרָה הֲבַת־תִּשְׁעִים שָׁנָה תֵּלֵד:

יח וַיֹּאמֶר אַבְרָהָם אֶל־הָאֱלֹהִים לוּ יִשְׁמָעֵאל יִחְיֶה לְפָנֶיךָ:

יט וַיֹּאמֶר אֱלֹהִים אֲבָל שָׂרָה אִשְׁתְּךָ יֹלֶדֶת לְךָ בֵּן וְקָרָאתָ אֶת־שְׁמוֹ יִצְחָק וַהֲקִמֹתִי אֶת־בְּרִיתִי אִתּוֹ לִבְרִית עוֹלָם לְזַרְעוֹ אַחֲרָיו:

כ וּלְיִשְׁמָעֵאל שְׁמַעְתִּיךָ הִנֵּה בֵּרַכְתִּי אֹתוֹ וְהִפְרֵיתִי אֹתוֹ וְהִרְבֵּיתִי אֹתוֹ בִּמְאֹד

כא מְאֹד שְׁנֵים־עָשָׂר נְשִׂיאִם יוֹלִיד וּנְתַתִּיו לְגוֹי גָּדוֹל: וְאֶת־בְּרִיתִי אָקִים אֶת־יִצְחָק אֲשֶׁר תֵּלֵד לְךָ שָׂרָה

כב לַמּוֹעֵד הַזֶּה בַּשָּׁנָה הָאַחֶרֶת: וַיְכַל לְדַבֵּר אִתּוֹ וַיַּעַל אֱלֹהִים מֵעַל אַבְרָהָם:

כג וַיִּקַּח אַבְרָהָם אֶת־יִשְׁמָעֵאל בְּנוֹ וְאֵת כָּל־יְלִידֵי בֵיתוֹ וְאֵת כָּל־מִקְנַת כַּסְפּוֹ כָּל־זָכָר בְּאַנְשֵׁי בֵּית אַבְרָהָם וַיָּמָל אֶת־בְּשַׂר עָרְלָתָם

כד בְּעֶצֶם הַיּוֹם הַזֶּה כַּאֲשֶׁר דִּבֶּר אִתּוֹ אֱלֹהִים: וְאַבְרָהָם בֶּן־תִּשְׁעִים וָתֵשַׁע שָׁנָה בְּהִמֹּלוֹ בְּשַׂר עָרְלָתוֹ:

כה וְיִשְׁמָעֵאל בְּנוֹ בֶּן־שְׁלֹשׁ עֶשְׂרֵה שָׁנָה בְּהִמֹּלוֹ אֵת בְּשַׂר עָרְלָתוֹ:

כו בְּעֶצֶם הַיּוֹם הַזֶּה נִמּוֹל אַבְרָהָם וְיִשְׁמָעֵאל בְּנוֹ:

כז וְכָל־אַנְשֵׁי בֵיתוֹ יְלִיד בָּיִת וּמִקְנַת־כֶּסֶף מֵאֵת בֶּן־נֵכָר נִמֹּלוּ אִתּוֹ:

Haftarah Lech-Lecha, p. 330

alike. Thus shall My covenant be marked in your flesh as an everlasting pact. **14]** And if any male who is uncircumcised fails to circumcise the flesh of his foreskin, that person shall be cut off from his kin; he has broken My covenant."

15] And God said to Abraham, "As for your wife Sarai, you shall not call her Sarai, but her name shall be Sarah. **16]** I will bless her; indeed, I will give you a son by her. I will bless her so that she shall give rise to nations; rulers of peoples shall issue from her." **17]** Abraham threw himself on his face and laughed, as he said to himself, "Can a child be born to a man a hundred years old, or can Sarah bear a child at ninety?" **18]** And Abraham said to God, "Oh that Ishmael might live by Your favor!" **19]** God said, "Nevertheless, Sarah your wife shall bear you a son, and you shall name him Isaac; and I will maintain My covenant with him as an everlasting covenant for his offspring to come. **20]** As for Ishmael, I have heeded you. I hereby bless him. I will make him fertile and exceedingly numerous. He shall be the father of twelve chieftains, and I will make of him a great nation. **21]** But My covenant I will maintain with Isaac, whom Sarah shall bear to you at this season next year." **22]** And when He was done speaking with him, God was gone from Abraham.

23] Then Abraham took his son Ishmael, and all his homeborn slaves and all those he had bought, every male in Abraham's household, and he circumcised the flesh of their foreskins on that very day, as God had spoken to him. **24]** Abraham was ninety-nine years old when he circumcised the flesh of his foreskin, **25]** and his son Ishmael was thirteen years old when he was circumcised in the flesh of his foreskin. **26]** Thus Abraham and his son Ishmael were circumcised on that very day; **27]** and all his household, his homeborn slaves and those that had been bought from outsiders, were circumcised with him.

15] *Sarai.* This is probably an older linguistic form for Sarah, i.e., "princess."
/The Talmud records the opinion that Sarai's name change symbolized the end of her barrenness [2]./
18] *Oh that Ishmael might live by Your favor!* A

rejoinder either of humility [3] or of anxiety [4].

19] *Isaac.* From צחק (to laugh).

20] *I have heeded you.* שְׁמַעְתִּיךָ, a word play on יִשְׁמָעֵאל (Ishmael—God will heed).

Circumcision

Few, if any, Jewish practices are more significant than *berit milah*, the covenant of circumcision. While it does not make a child born to Jewish parents into a Jew, it confirms his special relationship to the God and the traditions of Israel. The Zohar considered the safeguarding of circumcision important to all mankind: "As long as Israel observes the custom of circumcision, heaven and earth will go on their appointed courses, but if Israel neglects the covenant, heaven and earth are disturbed" [5]. Neglecting to circumcise a child was, therefore, more than merely neglect of a rite; it was a rejection of God's sign and was subject to divine punishment, to being "cut off from the people," i.e., from the covenant. Indeed, throughout history, the continued observance of circumcision has been a mark of the Jewish will to survive, while its discontinuance has been a signal of assimilation.

Thus, during the reign of Antiochus IV (165 B.C.E), circumcision was prohibited by royal decree, but Jews observed the rite even at the risk of death. Some one hundred years later, political conditions had changed drastically and many upper-class Jews desirous of assimilation to the dominant Greco-Roman way of life began to neglect *berit milah*.[1] Two hundred years later, during the Hadrianic persecution (*ca.* 135 C.E.), the practice of this rite—as well as the teaching of Torah in general—was forbidden once again. Yet many Jews defied the edict and suffered death. During the Nazi reign of terror, circumcision was often the means by which the persecutors determined the Jewishness of their male victims; still the vast majority of Jewish parents continued to enter their children into the covenant. In present-day Soviet lands, on the other hand, the discouragement of all religious practices has caused the virtual disappearance of circumcision and, with it, widespread assimilation of the Jews.

In North America today, circumcision is encouraged by the medical profession as a hygienic measure and is accepted by most Gentiles. This generalized practice has made it essential that Jews should re-emphasize the religious aspects of the rite. Surgical circumcision alone is by no means the equivalent of *berit milah*. The act obtains its value not from the physical operation and its presumed medical benefits but from the idea and the history that underlie it, from the prayers that accompany it, and from the father's affirmation that his child will be brought up in the religion of his fathers. (In Christian tradition, baptism has taken the place of circumcision.)

An Ancient Practice

The antiquity of the rite of circumcision is attested by the biblical record itself. In the days of Moses and Joshua, when the Bronze Age was coming to an end, it was still a custom to use flint knives for the rite, that is to say, tools going back to the Stone Age (cf. Exod. 4:25; Josh. 5:2).

Circumcision has been practiced by many peoples besides the Jews. Jeremiah indicates that the Egyptians, Moabites, and Ammonites all underwent circumcision (9:24); among the nations bordering on Israel, only the Philistines did not practice it. In Mohammed's time (seventh century C.E.) it was apparently so generally observed by the peoples of the Middle East that the Koran no longer found it necessary to command it specifically [6].

Why was it so widespread? Although Herodotus ascribed it to hygienic reasons and Maimonides claimed that it reduced sexual activity to a manageable level [7],

---

[1] Often, in public athletic events, participants who were expected to compete in the nude submitted to an operation so that the sign of their Jewishness would be obliterated.

[2] In Arabic, too, the same term (*chatana*) means "to circumcise."

[3] "The commands were given to Israel to purify themselves" [9].

its ubiquity was doubtlessly due to the persistent popularity of ancient fertility rites. Originally, circumcision served as an initiation into puberty or into manhood prior to marriage. This is still reflected in the language of the Talmud [8], where the word חָתָן (chatan) means both a bridegroom and an infant fit for circumcision.[2]

The command to Abraham shifts the practice away from young adulthood to the eighth day after birth and thereby from sexual to spiritual significance.[3] Its purpose is now to be a "sign of the covenant." (Women received no such sign, because biblical tradition was male-oriented.) The rite of cutting, which is elsewhere associated with the *berit* (see Gen. 15:10), is here accorded special sanctity. Abraham circumcised is now a man fundamentally changed, in name and identity as well as in body. He is, as the Midrash puts it, a more nearly perfect human being.[4]

Identity and Name

Abram's name is changed to Abraham, and Sarai's to Sarah. Similar changes occur several times in the Bible: For instance, Jacob's name is changed to Israel, Hoshea's to Joshua, Mattaniah's to Zedekiah. In each case, the change of name symbolizes a change in the personality or status of the bearer. Thus, kings as well as popes take on new names when they accede to the throne, and so do some nuns on entering orders. A woman assumes the family name of her husband upon marriage. In the United States, some blacks have signified their strengthened sense of identity by the adoption of new names.[5]

Names express the predilections and traditions of a family and often say much about a civilization. For example, the medieval combination of Hebrew names with the Arabic word for son (*Ibn* Ezra, *Ibn* Chayim) expressed the joining of two cultural strands. The biblical names given to Christians in Puritan times expressed that age's commitment to religious tradition. The recent neglect of such names as Abraham and Sarah and the substitution of fashionable names among Jews suggest a lessening adherence to traditional values and an advance of assimilation.

In Europe, where familial traditions are still strong, a change of name (especially of a family name) is discouraged and made difficult. In North America, name changing is easy and widely practiced. Thus, names are increasingly losing their significance, especially in modern metropolitan societies. Many people already bear the same name; naming a Jewish child after a deceased relative is often done only in symbolic form by having the child's name start with the same initial. Some people change their first as well as their family names and become even less distinguishable in an environment that tends toward anonymity for the individual.

Naming a child at circumcision or in the synagogue can, therefore, be an important counteragent to the community's lack of tradition and the individual's sense of rootlessness. The giving of a Hebrew name, which may honor a member of the family or simply be a recognition of the child's membership in the covenant, can add a religious element to the important process of name-giving, which is nowadays primarily a matter of taste.

In Genesis, God is the supreme name-giver. The bestowal is, and must remain, a sacred act so that one's name may speak of identity, tradition, commitment, and membership in the Eternal People. "To honor a name" is not only to be true to one's self but also to that tradition for which the name stands.

[4] Why was Adam not born circumcised? Because everything God created needed perfecting [10] (see commentary to Gen. 1:1–2:3, "The Creation of Man").
[5] Related to this was the widespread Jewish custom of giving a desperately sick person a new name. It was believed that the heavenly decree of death was issued against the person as he was, his name being an integral part of his personality. With a new name he was therefore thought to have a better chance of recovery [11].

GLEANINGS

Laws of Circumcision

[Over the centuries, a great body of laws and customs about circumcision developed. A few excerpts follow.]

If the father knows how to perform the circumcision he should do it himself. Usually, however, the rite is performed by someone familiar with all required procedures and prayers, a professional circumciser (*mohel*).

Among liberal Jews, and in many smaller communities, a doctor often takes the place of the *mohel*, and the rabbi reads the accompanying prayers. [12]

Since the fulfilment of all precepts must be postponed in deference to human life, extreme care should be taken not to circumcise a sick infant. In such cases, circumcision may be performed at a later date than that prescribed by law, because the life of a human being, once sacrificed, can never be restored.

If a woman has lost two sons from the effects of circumcision (it having been proven that circumcision weakened their physical condition), her third son must not be circumcised until he is grown up and has a stronger constitution.

Circumcision is to be performed on the eighth day after birth and may take place on the Sabbath and festivals. If at all possible, it should be performed on the eighth day, not earlier and not later. [13]

After the circumcision the father of the child says this benediction: "Praised be Thou, O Lord, our God, King of the universe, who hast sanctified us with Thy commandments and hast bidden us to enter him into the covenant of Abraham, our father." Those present respond: "As he has been entered into the covenant, may he be introduced to the study of Torah, to the nuptial canopy, and to good deeds."

The custom of naming a child at the circumcision is of medieval origin, although traditional sentiment traces it back to Abraham who received a new name at the time of his circumcision. [14]

It is customary to make a feast on the day of the circumcision. [15]

Creation Uncompleted

A pagan sage asked Rabbi Judah: "If circumcision is so beloved of God, why was the mark of circumcision not given to Adam at his creation?" The rabbi replied: "Almost everything that was created during the six days of creation needs finishing—even man needs finishing."

MIDRASH [16]

The Messengers

A brief interlude tells how God once again assures Abraham and this time Sarah, too, of an offspring. The announcement is made by three "men," mysterious messengers of the Deity. The account sets forth an additional characteristic of Abraham—his hospitality.

(A new weekly portion, *Vayera*, begins here.)

פ פ פ

א וַיֵּרָא אֵלָיו יְהֹוָה בְּאֵלֹנֵי מַמְרֵא וְהוּא יֹשֵׁב פֶּתַח־
פַּת־לֶחֶם וְסַעֲדוּ לִבְּכֶם אַחַר תַּעֲבֹרוּ כִּי־עַל־כֵּן

ב הָאֹהֶל כְּחֹם הַיּוֹם: וַיִּשָּׂא עֵינָיו וַיַּרְא וְהִנֵּה שְׁלֹשָׁה
עֲבַרְתֶּם עַל־עַבְדְּכֶם וַיֹּאמְרוּ כֵּן תַּעֲשֶׂה כַּאֲשֶׁר

אֲנָשִׁים נִצָּבִים עָלָיו וַיַּרְא וַיָּרָץ לִקְרָאתָם מִפֶּתַח ג
דִּבַּרְתָּ: וַיְמַהֵר אַבְרָהָם הָאֹהֱלָה אֶל־שָׂרָה וַיֹּאמֶר

הָאֹהֶל וַיִּשְׁתַּחוּ אָרְצָה: וַיֹּאמַר אֲדֹנָי אִם־נָא מָצָאתִי ד
מַהֲרִי שְׁלֹשׁ סְאִים קֶמַח סֹלֶת לוּשִׁי וַעֲשִׂי עֻגוֹת:

חֵן בְּעֵינֶיךָ אַל־נָא תַעֲבֹר מֵעַל עַבְדֶּךָ: יֻקַּח־נָא ה
וְאֶל־הַבָּקָר רָץ אַבְרָהָם וַיִּקַּח בֶּן־בָּקָר רַךְ וָטוֹב

מְעַט־מַיִם וְרַחֲצוּ רַגְלֵיכֶם וְהִשָּׁעֲנוּ תַּחַת הָעֵץ: וְאֶקְחָה
וַיִּתֵּן אֶל־הַנַּעַר וַיְמַהֵר לַעֲשׂוֹת אֹתוֹ: וַיִּקַּח חֶמְאָה
וְחָלָב וּבֶן־הַבָּקָר אֲשֶׁר עָשָׂה וַיִּתֵּן לִפְנֵיהֶם וְהוּא־

1] The Lᴏʀᴅ appeared to him by the terebinths of Mamre; he was sitting at the entrance of the tent as the day grew hot. **2]** Looking up, he saw three men standing near him. As soon as he saw them, he ran from the entrance of the tent to greet them and, bowing to the ground, **3]** he said, "My lords, if it please you, do not go on past your servant. **4]** Let a little water be brought; bathe your feet and recline under the tree. **5]** And let me fetch a morsel of bread that you may refresh yourselves; then go on—seeing that you have come your servant's way." They replied, "Do as you have said."

6] Abraham hastened into the tent to Sarah, and said, "Quick, three measures of choice flour! Knead and make cakes!" **7]** Then Abraham ran to the herd, took a calf, tender and choice, and gave it to a servant-boy, who hastened to prepare it. **8]** He took curds and milk and the calf that had been prepared, and set these before them; and he waited on them under the tree as they ate.

18:1] *The Lord appeared.* The aim of this introduction is to make it clear that the visitors in the following story are an apparition of the Divine.

Terebinths of Mamre. Near Hebron, where Abraham had built an altar (Gen. 13:18).

2] *Three men standing near him.* Abraham did not see them coming and seems startled by their sudden appearance.

3] *My lords.* אֲדֹנָי (or, my Lord). The Hebrew sentences are couched alternately in the singular and plural, suggesting the fusion of two literary traditions. Maimonides understood the entire episode to have been a vision [1].
/Harmonizers suggest that the syntactical variance is due to Abraham's uncertainty over whether the messengers were mere men or represented God. There is a controversy whether אֲדֹנָי here is to be read as a sacred word. See also Gleanings./

5] *A morsel of bread.* The modest understatement of a gracious host who expects to serve much more. Says the Talmud: The pious promise little but perform much [2].

6] *Three measures.* סְאִים (singular, סְאָה), probably about twenty-eight cups, an overgenerous amount for three guests. However, it may have been customary on such occasions to include the important members of the household [3] or to supply provisions for the way [4].

8] *They ate.* Traditional interpreters experience great difficulties here. If the three are divine messengers, why do they eat? According to the Midrash, they merely appeared to eat [5]. According to Rashi, they pretended out of courtesy. The text is of course oblivious of later Jewish dietary laws which forbade serving milk and meat at the same meal [6].

ט   עֹמֵד עֲלֵיהֶם תַּחַת הָעֵץ וַיֹּאכֵלוּ: וַיֹּאמְרוּ אֵלָיו* אַיֵּה

שָׂרָה אִשְׁתֶּךָ וַיֹּאמֶר הִנֵּה בָאֹהֶל: י וַיֹּאמֶר שׁוֹב אָשׁוּב

אֵלֶיךָ כָּעֵת חַיָּה וְהִנֵּה־בֵן לְשָׂרָה אִשְׁתֶּךָ וְשָׂרָה

יא שֹׁמַעַת פֶּתַח הָאֹהֶל וְהוּא אַחֲרָיו: וְאַבְרָהָם וְשָׂרָה

זְקֵנִים בָּאִים בַּיָּמִים חָדַל לִהְיוֹת לְשָׂרָה אֹרַח כַּנָּשִׁים:

יב וַתִּצְחַק שָׂרָה בְּקִרְבָּהּ לֵאמֹר אַחֲרֵי בְלֹתִי הָיְתָה־לִּי

עֶדְנָה וַאדֹנִי זָקֵן: יג וַיֹּאמֶר יְהֹוָה אֶל־אַבְרָהָם לָמָּה זֶּה

צָחֲקָה שָׂרָה לֵאמֹר הַאַף אֻמְנָם אֵלֵד וַאֲנִי זָקַנְתִּי:

יד הֲיִפָּלֵא מֵיהֹוָה דָּבָר לַמּוֹעֵד אָשׁוּב אֵלֶיךָ כָּעֵת

חַיָּה וּלְשָׂרָה בֵן: טו וַתְּכַחֵשׁ שָׂרָה לֵאמֹר לֹא צָחַקְתִּי

כִּי יָרֵאָה וַיֹּאמֶר לֹא כִּי צָחָקְתְּ:

* ט נקוד על איו.

9] They said to him, "Where is your wife Sarah?" And he replied, "There, in the tent." **10]** Then one said, "I will return to you when life is due, and your wife Sarah shall have a son!" Sarah was listening at the entrance of the tent, which was behind him. **11]** Now Abraham and Sarah were old, advanced in years; Sarah had stopped having the periods of women. **12]** And Sarah laughed to herself, saying, "Now that I am withered, am I to have enjoyment—with my husband so old?" **13]** Then the LORD said to Abraham, "Why did Sarah laugh, saying, 'Shall I in truth bear a child, old as I am?' **14]** Is anything too wondrous for the LORD? I will return to you at the time that life is due, and Sarah shall have a son." **15]** Sarah lied saying, "I did not laugh," for she was frightened. But He replied, "You did laugh."

10] *When life is due.* After nine months (see II Kings 4:16–17, where Elisha uses the same expression [כָּעֵת חַיָּה] when promising a child to the Shunammite woman).

12] *Sarah laughed.* וַתִּצְחַק (va-titzchak). Sarah's be-havior explains the name Isaac, יִצְחָק (yitzchak) (see Gen. 21:6).

/ The Septuagint has: "Sarah laughed openly" (instead of "to herself")./

15] *She lied.* To Abraham when he confronted her.

Angels

The three "men" of whom the story speaks belong, according to the biblical setting, to a category of superior beings with special powers. They appear in a variety of forms, sometimes as men and sometimes in other shapes (such as cherubim). They can speak, stand, sit, walk, be clothed; they can have weapons, ride horses, descend from heaven on a ladder. Their function may be to worship God, to do His bidding (such as observing the activities of men, see Job 1:6–8), or, most frequently, to carry a divine message. Because of this latter function the name מַלְאָךְ (messenger) is often given to these beings. Its Greek translation is *angelos*, hence our English "angel."

As a group, angels were considered by tradition as a kind of nobility at God's court, singing His praises and acting at His counsel. As individuals, they were go-betweens. In this capacity they were thought to bring instruction, transmit revelation to prophets, announce the coming of events (here, Isaac's birth; in Genesis 19 the destruction of Sodom), and guard places (such as Eden or Bethel) or individuals (such as Hagar and Ishmael, Isaac and Jacob). However, they were not distinguished by name except for Gabriel and Michael (Dan. 9:21; 10:21). Angels were believed to have existed before the creation of the world (hinted at in Gen. 1:26) and to be generally benevolent to men.

Belief in angels was widespread in the ancient Near East. Mesopotamian and Hittite deities had their subordinate ministers, and Egyptian sources tell how the gods communicated with each other through couriers. In addition, the motif of hospitality to a divine being in disguise was well-known in ancient legend.[1] These ancient concepts formed the background out of which the biblical stories emerged. In post-biblical Judaism, as well as in Christianity and Islam, these concepts were developed into an elaborate structure of "angelology" [8].

In the biblical story, the "annunciation" by the angels is no more than an announcement of Isaac's forthcoming birth. There is no further hint of superhuman paternity as in similar myths of the Greeks. The announcement is supernatural, but not the conception. Isaac will not have the dual paternity of the Homeric heroes, who assume the office of their human fathers and derive their power from their divine fathers. Far from becoming a superman, Isaac will, in fact, be a rather undistinguished link in the patriarchal chain.[2]

---

[1] Note, e.g., the Greek story of Hyrieus and Tamagra who entertain three men not knowing that these men are gods. The couple is also recompensed by the gift of a son [7]. It has been noted that the biblical P-source does not speak of angels at all.

[2] However, it has been suggested that something of a much larger original "Isaac cycle" existed in which conception through divine agency played a much clearer role. The Bible reduced this and perhaps other aspects of some earlier Isaac saga; and normative Judaism divested itself of the consequences of the annunciation, which came to reecho in Christianity: "Jesus derives his human-office of Messianic King from Joseph, but his divine quality from his Divine Father. Moreover, the Church tradition that connects the sacrifice of Isaac with the sacrifice of Christ apparently rests on sound exegesis, for the sacrifice of Isaac would have meant not only the sacrifice of Abraham's son but of God's" [9].

GLEANINGS

The Mitzvah of Visiting the Sick

Why is the story of Abraham's circumcision [Gen. 17:10–14] followed by the visitation of God? He came to visit while Abraham was recuperating, to make clear the importance of the *mitzvah* of visiting the sick. TALMUD [10]

The Mitzvah of Hospitality

Why was Abraham sitting in the door of his tent? To watch for passing strangers whom he might invite into his abode. MIDRASH [11]

(A rabbinic saying was based on the reading of 18:3 as "My Lord." It suggested that Abraham was addressing God but that, when he saw three men approaching, he excused himself in order to show them hospitality. Hence:)

Greater than the reception of God is the practice of hospitality. TALMUD [12]

Abraham had his servant assist him in order to instruct him in the *mitzvah* of hospitality. The נַעַר [servant, literally, "lad"] was none other than his son Ishmael. MIDRASH [13]

Such instruction in the duty of hospitality to strangers may appear superfluous in the eyes of some parents and teachers today. They are in error. JOSEPH H. HERTZ

Once, however, Abraham's love of strangers clashed with his zeal for God. He invited a wayfarer to his home and, finding him praying to his idol, chased him away. God reprimanded Abraham severely: "I have borne with him these many years although he rebelled against Me, and you cannot bear with him one night?" Abraham realized his sin and did not rest until he had brought the stranger back. [14]

[Benjamin Franklin composed his "Parable against Persecution" on this theme.]

Three Men

The story opens by saying that *God* appeared to Abraham [Gen. 18:1], but when Abraham applies the vision to his own world he suddenly sees *three men* standing before him [Gen. 18:2]. Abraham is the religious man par excellence for he sees God in the human situation. FRANZ ROSENZWEIG [15]

For the Sake of Peace

Sarah laughed skeptically and said: "Am I to have enjoyment—with *my husband* so old?" [Gen. 18:12]; but God, repeating this to Abraham, reported her as saying: "... old as *I* am." He did this to safeguard Abraham's feelings and to preserve domestic peace. TALMUD [16]

Sodom and Gomorrah

No parallels in extra-biblical literature exist to the story of Sodom and Gomorrah. Yet the destruction of the cities is referred to so frequently in the Bible that only a historic cataclysm of startling proportions could have impressed itself so deeply on popular memory. The cities most likely stood near the south end of the present Dead Sea (where today's Sodom is situated). The district is filled with bitumen and salt formations (Gen. 14:10; 19:26; Deut. 29:22) and is part of a deep rift that reaches from Armenia to Central Africa and that runs north/south through the Aravah Valley. The rift is presumed to be the result of a catastrophic earthquake, which might have raised the level of the Dead Sea sufficiently to flood what was formerly the Valley of Siddim (Gen. 14:3) and to submerge the cities.*

The purpose of the biblical tale is not, however, to report natural events as such but to present these events in the light of religious insight. God destroyed the cities because the people were evil. The story therefore intertwines the natural and the supernatural, employing symbols and folklore, in order to teach the effects of moral depravity.

A remarkable confrontation introduces the drama. Apprised of the impending destruction of Sodom and Gomorrah, Abraham rises to argue God's justice and questions Him to His face. Abraham's pleading fails not

---

* The destruction encompassed apparently all the "cities of the Plain" (Gen. 13:12; 19:25), i.e., the cities mentioned in Gen. 14. Only Zoar was spared.

because his moral stance is faulty but because his premise is wrong: There are no righteous men in the cities.

With this story it becomes clear that Abraham's religion is more than a set of cultic practices. It deals with human beings and their problems and with Abraham's faith in a God of righteousness.

טז וַיָּקֻמוּ מִשָּׁם הָאֲנָשִׁים וַיַּשְׁקִפוּ עַל־פְּנֵי סְדֹם וְאַבְרָהָם הֹלֵךְ עִמָּם לְשַׁלְּחָם:
יז וַיהֹוָה אָמָר הַמְכַסֶּה אֲנִי מֵאַבְרָהָם אֲשֶׁר אֲנִי עֹשֶׂה:
יח וְאַבְרָהָם הָיוֹ יִהְיֶה לְגוֹי גָּדוֹל וְעָצוּם וְנִבְרְכוּ־בוֹ כֹּל
יט גּוֹיֵי הָאָרֶץ: כִּי יְדַעְתִּיו לְמַעַן אֲשֶׁר יְצַוֶּה אֶת־בָּנָיו וְאֶת־בֵּיתוֹ אַחֲרָיו וְשָׁמְרוּ דֶּרֶךְ יְהֹוָה לַעֲשׂוֹת צְדָקָה וּמִשְׁפָּט לְמַעַן הָבִיא יְהֹוָה עַל־אַבְרָהָם אֵת אֲשֶׁר־
כ דִּבֶּר עָלָיו: וַיֹּאמֶר יְהֹוָה זַעֲקַת סְדֹם וַעֲמֹרָה כִּי־
כא רָבָּה וְחַטָּאתָם כִּי כָבְדָה מְאֹד: אֵרֲדָה־נָּא וְאֶרְאֶה הַכְּצַעֲקָתָהּ הַבָּאָה אֵלַי עָשׂוּ כָּלָה וְאִם־לֹא אֵדָעָה:
כב וַיִּפְנוּ מִשָּׁם הָאֲנָשִׁים וַיֵּלְכוּ סְדֹמָה וְאַבְרָהָם עוֹדֶנּוּ

כג עֹמֵד לִפְנֵי יְהֹוָה: וַיִּגַּשׁ אַבְרָהָם וַיֹּאמַר הַאַף תִּסְפֶּה
כד צַדִּיק עִם־רָשָׁע: אוּלַי יֵשׁ חֲמִשִּׁים צַדִּיקִם בְּתוֹךְ הָעִיר הַאַף תִּסְפֶּה וְלֹא־תִשָּׂא לַמָּקוֹם לְמַעַן חֲמִשִּׁים
כה הַצַּדִּיקִם אֲשֶׁר בְּקִרְבָּהּ: חָלִלָה לְּךָ מֵעֲשֹׂת כַּדָּבָר הַזֶּה לְהָמִית צַדִּיק עִם־רָשָׁע וְהָיָה כַצַּדִּיק כָּרָשָׁע חָלִלָה לָּךְ הֲשֹׁפֵט כָּל־הָאָרֶץ לֹא יַעֲשֶׂה מִשְׁפָּט:
כו וַיֹּאמֶר יְהֹוָה אִם־אֶמְצָא בִסְדֹם חֲמִשִּׁים צַדִּיקִם בְּתוֹךְ
כז הָעִיר וְנָשָׂאתִי לְכָל־הַמָּקוֹם בַּעֲבוּרָם: וַיַּעַן אַבְרָהָם וַיֹּאמַר הִנֵּה־נָא הוֹאַלְתִּי לְדַבֵּר אֶל־אֲדֹנָי וְאָנֹכִי עָפָר
כח וָאֵפֶר: אוּלַי יַחְסְרוּן חֲמִשִּׁים הַצַּדִּיקִם חֲמִשָּׁה הֲתַשְׁחִית בַּחֲמִשָּׁה אֶת־כָּל־הָעִיר וַיֹּאמֶר לֹא אַשְׁחִית

16] The men set out from there and looked down toward Sodom, Abraham walking with them to see them off. 17] Now the LORD had said, "Shall I hide from Abraham what I am about to do, 18] since Abraham is to become a great and populous nation and all the nations of the earth are to bless themselves by him? 19] For I have singled him out, that he may instruct his children and his posterity to keep the way of the LORD by doing what is just and right, in order that the LORD may bring about for Abraham what He has promised him." 20] Then the LORD said, "The outrage of Sodom and Gomorrah is so great, and their sin so grave! 21] I will go down to see whether they have acted altogether according to the outcry that has come to Me; if not, I will take note."

22] The men went on from there to Sodom, while Abraham remained standing before the LORD. 23] Abraham came forward and said, "Will You sweep away the innocent along with the guilty? 24] What if there should be fifty innocent within the city; will You then wipe out the place and not forgive it for the sake of the innocent fifty who are in it? 25] Far be it from You to do such a thing, to bring death upon the innocent as well as the guilty, so that innocent and guilty fare alike. Far be it from You! Shall not the Judge of all the earth deal justly?" 26] And the LORD answered, "If I find within the city of Sodom fifty innocent ones, I will forgive the whole place for their sake." 27] Abraham spoke up, saying, "Here I venture to speak to my LORD, I who am but dust and ashes: 28] What if the fifty innocent should lack five? Will You destroy the whole city for want of the five?" And He answered, "I will not

18:17] *Shall I hide from Abraham what I am about to do?* God muses whether to share His thoughts with His chosen one. Perhaps He *wants* Abraham to argue the justice of the divine plan. Rashi writes: God has appointed Abraham as the "father of a multitude of nations" (Gen. 17:5), and hence the people of Sodom are his children, too. Should God not tell a father the fate of his children?
/Rashi's argument reflects the mishnaic discussion

about Hebrew prayers to be recited by converts. The proof text in the argument is in Gen. 17:5, because there Abraham is called the "father of a multitude of nations," and hence all converts to Judaism are called sons of Abraham [1]./

22] *Abraham remained standing before the Lord.* Abraham begins the dialogue but God finishes it. In this verse "the men" are clearly distinguished from God.

כט אִם־אָמָּצֵא שָׁם אַרְבָּעִים וַחֲמִשָּׁה: וַיֹּסֶף עוֹד לְדַבֵּר
אֵלָיו וַיֹּאמַר אוּלַי יִמָּצְאוּן שָׁם אַרְבָּעִים וַיֹּאמֶר לֹא
ל אֶעֱשֶׂה בַּעֲבוּר הָאַרְבָּעִים: וַיֹּאמֶר אַל־נָא יִחַר לַאדֹנָי
וַאֲדַבֵּרָה אוּלַי יִמָּצְאוּן שָׁם שְׁלֹשִׁים וַיֹּאמֶר לֹא אֶעֱשֶׂה
לא אִם־אָמָּצֵא שָׁם שְׁלֹשִׁים: וַיֹּאמֶר הִנֵּה־נָא הוֹאַלְתִּי
לְדַבֵּר אֶל־אֲדֹנָי אוּלַי יִמָּצְאוּן שָׁם עֶשְׂרִים וַיֹּאמֶר לֹא
לב אַשְׁחִית בַּעֲבוּר הָעֶשְׂרִים: וַיֹּאמֶר אַל־נָא יִחַר לַאדֹנָי
וַאֲדַבְּרָה אַךְ־הַפַּעַם אוּלַי יִמָּצְאוּן שָׁם עֲשָׂרָה וַיֹּאמֶר
לג לֹא אַשְׁחִית בַּעֲבוּר הָעֲשָׂרָה: וַיֵּלֶךְ יְהֹוָה כַּאֲשֶׁר
כִּלָּה לְדַבֵּר אֶל־אַבְרָהָם וְאַבְרָהָם שָׁב לִמְקֹמוֹ:

א וַיָּבֹאוּ שְׁנֵי הַמַּלְאָכִים סְדֹמָה בָּעֶרֶב וְלוֹט יֹשֵׁב
בְּשַׁעַר־סְדֹם וַיַּרְא־לוֹט וַיָּקָם לִקְרָאתָם וַיִּשְׁתַּחוּ אַפַּיִם
ב אָרְצָה: וַיֹּאמֶר הִנֶּה־נָּא אֲדֹנַי סוּרוּ נָא אֶל־בֵּית
עַבְדְּכֶם וְלִינוּ וְרַחֲצוּ רַגְלֵיכֶם וְהִשְׁכַּמְתֶּם וַהֲלַכְתֶּם
ג לְדַרְכְּכֶם וַיֹּאמְרוּ לֹא כִּי בָרְחוֹב נָלִין: וַיִּפְצַר־בָּם
מְאֹד וַיָּסֻרוּ אֵלָיו וַיָּבֹאוּ אֶל־בֵּיתוֹ וַיַּעַשׂ לָהֶם מִשְׁתֶּה
ד וּמַצּוֹת אָפָה וַיֹּאכֵלוּ: טֶרֶם יִשְׁכָּבוּ וְאַנְשֵׁי הָעִיר
אַנְשֵׁי סְדֹם נָסַבּוּ עַל־הַבַּיִת מִנַּעַר וְעַד־זָקֵן כָּל־הָעָם
ה מִקָּצֶה: וַיִּקְרְאוּ אֶל־לוֹט וַיֹּאמְרוּ לוֹ אַיֵּה הָאֲנָשִׁים
אֲשֶׁר־בָּאוּ אֵלֶיךָ הַלָּיְלָה הוֹצִיאֵם אֵלֵינוּ וְנֵדְעָה אֹתָם:

destroy if I find forty-five there." **29]** But he spoke to Him again, and said, "What if forty should be found there?" And He answered, "I will not do it, for the sake of the forty." **30]** And he said, "Let not the LORD be angry if I go on: What if thirty should be found there?" And He answered, "I will not do it if I find thirty there." **31]** And he said, "I venture again to speak to my LORD: What if twenty should be found there?" And He answered, "I will not destroy, for the sake of the twenty." **32]** And he said, "Let not the LORD be angry if I speak but this last time: What if ten should be found there?" And He answered, "I will not destroy, for the sake of the ten."

33] When the LORD had finished speaking to Abraham, He departed; and Abraham returned to his place.

1] The two angels arrived in Sodom in the evening, as Lot was sitting in the gate of Sodom. When Lot saw them, he rose to greet them and, bowing low with his face to the ground, **2]** he said, "Please, my lords, turn aside to your servant's house to spend the night, and bathe your feet; then you may be on your way early." But they said, "No, we will spend the night in the square." **3]** But he urged them strongly, so they turned his way and entered his house. He prepared a feast for them and baked unleavened bread, and they ate.

4] They had not yet lain down, when the townspeople, the men of Sodom, young and old— all the people to the last man—gathered about the house. **5]** And they shouted to Lot and said to him, "Where are the men who came to you tonight? Bring them out to us, that we may be

19:1] *The two angels.* Earlier, the Bible speaks of three men (Gen. 18:2), suggesting that there were two different sources for the story.

/ Rashi's explanation: The third messenger who had spoken with Abraham had left after completing his announcement that Sarah would have a child./

Arrived in Sodom in the evening. The distance from Hebron and Mamre to Sodom could not be covered in an afternoon's journey. However, since the messengers are thought of as supernatural

beings, this presents no problem to narrator or listener.

3] *Unleavened bread.* Which can be quickly baked.

4] *To the last man.* It is clear now that not a single righteous man dwelled in Sodom. (Lot was a sojourner, not a citizen.)

5] *That we may be intimate with them.* The Sodomites wanted the men for homosexual or other deviate practices (hence the term sodomy for unnatural sexual behavior).

פֹּה חָתָן וּבָנֶיךָ וּבְנֹתֶיךָ וְכֹל אֲשֶׁר־לְךָ בָּעִיר הוֹצֵא
מִן־הַמָּקוֹם: כִּי־מַשְׁחִתִים אֲנַחְנוּ אֶת־הַמָּקוֹם הַזֶּה כִּי־
גָדְלָה צַעֲקָתָם אֶת־פְּנֵי יְהֹוָה וַיְשַׁלְּחֵנוּ יְהֹוָה לְשַׁחֲתָהּ:
וַיֵּצֵא לוֹט וַיְדַבֵּר אֶל־חֲתָנָיו לֹקְחֵי בְנֹתָיו וַיֹּאמֶר
קוּמוּ צְּאוּ מִן־הַמָּקוֹם הַזֶּה כִּי־מַשְׁחִית יְהֹוָה אֶת־
הָעִיר וַיְהִי כִמְצַחֵק בְּעֵינֵי חֲתָנָיו: וּכְמוֹ הַשַּׁחַר
עָלָה וַיָּאִיצוּ הַמַּלְאָכִים בְּלוֹט לֵאמֹר קוּם קַח אֶת־
אִשְׁתְּךָ וְאֶת־שְׁתֵּי בְנֹתֶיךָ הַנִּמְצָאֹת פֶּן־תִּסָּפֶה בַּעֲוֺן
הָעִיר: וַיִּתְמַהְמָהּ וַיַּחֲזִיקוּ הָאֲנָשִׁים בְּיָדוֹ וּבְיַד־אִשְׁתּוֹ
וּבְיַד שְׁתֵּי בְנֹתָיו בְּחֶמְלַת יְהֹוָה עָלָיו וַיֹּצִאֻהוּ וַיַּנִּחֻהוּ
מִחוּץ לָעִיר: וַיְהִי כְהוֹצִיאָם אֹתָם הַחוּצָה וַיֹּאמֶר

י וַיֵּצֵא אֲלֵהֶם לוֹט הַפֶּתְחָה וְהַדֶּלֶת סָגַר אַחֲרָיו:
ח וַיֹּאמַר אַל־נָא אַחַי תָּרֵעוּ: הִנֵּה־נָא לִי שְׁתֵּי בָנוֹת
אֲשֶׁר לֹא־יָדְעוּ אִישׁ אוֹצִיאָה־נָּא אֶתְהֶן אֲלֵיכֶם וַעֲשׂוּ
לָהֶן כַּטּוֹב בְּעֵינֵיכֶם רַק לָאֲנָשִׁים הָאֵל אַל־תַּעֲשׂוּ
ט דָבָר כִּי־עַל־כֵּן בָּאוּ בְּצֵל קֹרָתִי: וַיֹּאמְרוּ גֶּשׁ־הָלְאָה
וַיֹּאמְרוּ הָאֶחָד בָּא־לָגוּר וַיִּשְׁפֹּט שָׁפוֹט עַתָּה נָרַע
לְךָ מֵהֶם וַיִּפְצְרוּ בָאִישׁ בְּלוֹט מְאֹד וַיִּגְּשׁוּ לִשְׁבֹּר
י הַדָּלֶת: וַיִּשְׁלְחוּ הָאֲנָשִׁים אֶת־יָדָם וַיָּבִיאוּ אֶת־לוֹט
יא אֲלֵיהֶם הַבָּיְתָה וְאֶת־הַדֶּלֶת סָגָרוּ: וְאֶת־הָאֲנָשִׁים אֲשֶׁר־
פֶּתַח הַבַּיִת הִכּוּ בַּסַּנְוֵרִים מִקָּטֹן וְעַד־גָּדוֹל וַיִּלְאוּ
יב לִמְצֹא הַפָּתַח: וַיֹּאמְרוּ הָאֲנָשִׁים אֶל־לוֹט עֹד מִי־לְךָ

intimate with them." 6] So Lot went out to them to the entrance, shut the door behind him. 7] and said, "I beg you, my friends, do not commit such a wrong. 8] Look, I have two daughters who have not known a man. Let me bring them out to you, and you may do to them as you please; but do not do anything to these men, since they have come under the shelter of my roof." 9] But they said, "Stand back! The fellow," they said, "came here as an alien, and already he acts the ruler! Now we will deal worse with you than with them." And they pressed hard against the person of Lot, and moved forward to break the door. 10] But the men stretched out their hands and pulled Lot into the house with them, and shut the door. 11] And the people who were at the entrance of the house, young and old, they struck with blinding light, so that they were helpless to find the entrance.

12] Then the men said to Lot, "Whom else have you here? Sons-in-law, your sons and daughters, or anyone else that you have in the city—bring them out of the place. 13] For we are about to destroy this place; because the outcry against them before the LORD has become so great that the LORD has sent us to destroy it." 14] So Lot went out and spoke to his sons-in-law, who had married his daughters, and said, "Up, get out of this place, for the LORD is about to destroy the city." But he seemed to his sons-in-law as one who jests.

15] As dawn broke, the angels urged Lot on, saying, "Up, take your wife and your two remaining daughters, lest you be swept away because of the iniquity of the city." 16] Still he delayed. So the men seized his hand, and the hands of his wife and his two daughters—in the LORD's mercy on him—and brought him out and left him outside the city. 17] When they had

8] *I have two daughters.* Lot's offer of his daughters to protect his guests may seem fantastically disproportionate. The implication in the text, however, is that Lot is a model host who will go to extreme lengths to honor the hospitality code.

9] *An alien, and already he acts the ruler!* The reaction of the native-born to the immigrant.

15] *Two remaining daughters.* The married daughters apparently chose to stay with their Sodomite husbands.

הִמָּלֵט עַל־נַפְשֶׁךָ אַל־תַּבִּיט אַחֲרֶיךָ וְאַל־תַּעֲמֹד בְּכָל־
הַכִּכָּר הָהָרָה הִמָּלֵט פֶּן־תִּסָּפֶה: וַיֹּאמֶר לוֹט אֲלֵהֶם
אַל־נָא אֲדֹנָי: הִנֵּה־נָא מָצָא עַבְדְּךָ חֵן בְּעֵינֶיךָ וַתַּגְדֵּל
חַסְדְּךָ אֲשֶׁר עָשִׂיתָ עִמָּדִי לְהַחֲיוֹת אֶת־נַפְשִׁי וְאָנֹכִי
לֹא אוּכַל לְהִמָּלֵט הָהָרָה פֶּן־תִּדְבָּקַנִי הָרָעָה וָמַתִּי:
הִנֵּה־נָא הָעִיר הַזֹּאת קְרֹבָה לָנוּס שָׁמָּה וְהִוא מִצְעָר
אִמָּלְטָה נָּא שָׁמָּה הֲלֹא מִצְעָר הִוא וּתְחִי נַפְשִׁי:
וַיֹּאמֶר אֵלָיו הִנֵּה נָשָׂאתִי פָנֶיךָ גַּם לַדָּבָר הַזֶּה לְבִלְתִּי
הָפְכִּי אֶת־הָעִיר אֲשֶׁר דִּבַּרְתָּ: מַהֵר הִמָּלֵט שָׁמָּה כִּי
לֹא אוּכַל לַעֲשׂוֹת דָּבָר עַד־בֹּאֲךָ שָׁמָּה עַל־כֵּן קָרָא

שֵׁם־הָעִיר צוֹעַר: הַשֶּׁמֶשׁ יָצָא עַל־הָאָרֶץ וְלוֹט בָּא
צֹעֲרָה: וַיהֹוָה הִמְטִיר עַל־סְדֹם וְעַל־עֲמֹרָה גָּפְרִית
וָאֵשׁ מֵאֵת יְהֹוָה מִן־הַשָּׁמָיִם: וַיַּהֲפֹךְ אֶת־הֶעָרִים הָאֵל
וְאֵת כָּל־הַכִּכָּר וְאֵת כָּל־יֹשְׁבֵי הֶעָרִים וְצֶמַח הָאֲדָמָה:
וַתַּבֵּט אִשְׁתּוֹ מֵאַחֲרָיו וַתְּהִי נְצִיב מֶלַח: וַיַּשְׁכֵּם
אַבְרָהָם בַּבֹּקֶר אֶל־הַמָּקוֹם אֲשֶׁר־עָמַד שָׁם אֶת־
פְּנֵי יְהֹוָה: וַיַּשְׁקֵף עַל־פְּנֵי סְדֹם וַעֲמֹרָה וְעַל־כָּל־פְּנֵי
אֶרֶץ הַכִּכָּר וַיַּרְא וְהִנֵּה עָלָה קִיטֹר הָאָרֶץ כְּקִיטֹר
הַכִּבְשָׁן: וַיְהִי בְּשַׁחֵת אֱלֹהִים אֶת־עָרֵי הַכִּכָּר וַיִּזְכֹּר
אֱלֹהִים אֶת־אַבְרָהָם וַיְשַׁלַּח אֶת־לוֹט מִתּוֹךְ הַהֲפֵכָה

brought them outside, one said, "Flee for your life! Do not look behind you, nor stop anywhere in the Plain; flee to the hills, lest you be swept away." **18]** But Lot said to them, "Oh no, my lord! **19]** You have been so gracious to your servant, and have already shown me so much kindness in order to save my life; but I cannot flee to the hills, lest disaster overtake me and I die. **20]** Look, that town there is near enough to flee to; it is such a little place! Let me flee there—it is such a little place—and let my life be saved." **21]** He replied, "Very well, I will grant you this favor too, and I will not annihilate the town of which you have spoken. **22]** Hurry, flee there, for I cannot do anything until you arrive there." Hence the town came to be called Zoar.

23] As the sun rose upon the earth and Lot entered Zoar, **24]** The LORD rained upon Sodom and Gomorrah sulfurous fire from the LORD out of heaven. **25]** He annihilated those cities and the entire Plain, and all the inhabitants of the cities and the vegetation of the ground. **26]** Lot's wife looked back, and she thereupon turned into a pillar of salt.

27] Next morning, Abraham hurried to the place where he had stood before the LORD, **28]** and, looking down toward Sodom and Gomorrah and all the land of the Plain, he saw the smoke of the land rising like the smoke of a kiln. **29]** Thus it was that, when God destroyed the cities of the Plain and annihilated the cities where Lot dwelt, God was mindful of Abraham and removed Lot from the midst of the upheaval.

17] *Do not look behind you.* Meaning either, "Do not waste a precious second," or "Do not look back in regret."

22] *Zoar.* Lot does not state why he prefers Zoar's safety and why, as soon as he reaches it, he finds it even more unbearable than a cave. The name Zoar is connected with the word מִצְעָר (*mitzar*, a little, insignificant thing) in Gen. 19:20.

24] *The Lord.* The repetition of the divine name in this sentence means to emphasize the supernatural origin of the catastrophe.

Sulfurous fire. Older translations: "Brimstone and fire," from which the proverbial "fire and brimstone."

26] *Pillar of salt.* To this day, salt-encrusted rock formations in the area suggest all manner of shapes. The legend has parallels in various mythologies, e.g., the Greek story of Orpheus and Eurydice.

/Ancient tradition thought it could fully identify the encrusted remains of Lot's wife [2]./

וַתֹּאמֶר הַבְּכִירָה אֶל־הַצְּעִירָה הֵן שָׁכַבְתִּי אֶמֶשׁ אֶת־　　ל בַּהֲפֹךְ אֶת־הֶעָרִים אֲשֶׁר־יָשַׁב בָּהֵן לוֹט: וַיַּעַל לוֹט
אָבִי נַשְׁקֶנּוּ יַיִן גַּם־הַלַּיְלָה וּבֹאִי שִׁכְבִי עִמּוֹ וּנְחַיֶּה　　מִצּוֹעַר וַיֵּשֶׁב בָּהָר וּשְׁתֵּי בְנֹתָיו עִמּוֹ כִּי יָרֵא לָשֶׁבֶת
לה מֵאָבִינוּ זָרַע: וַתַּשְׁקֶיןָ גַּם בַּלַּיְלָה הַהוּא אֶת־אֲבִיהֶן　　לא בְּצוֹעַר וַיֵּשֶׁב בַּמְּעָרָה הוּא וּשְׁתֵּי בְנֹתָיו: וַתֹּאמֶר
יַיִן וַתָּקָם הַצְּעִירָה וַתִּשְׁכַּב עִמּוֹ וְלֹא־יָדַע בְּשִׁכְבָהּ　　הַבְּכִירָה אֶל־הַצְּעִירָה אָבִינוּ זָקֵן וְאִישׁ אֵין בָּאָרֶץ
לו וּבְקֻמָהּ: וַתַּהֲרֶיןָ שְׁתֵּי בְנוֹת־לוֹט מֵאֲבִיהֶן: וַתֵּלֶד　　לב לָבוֹא עָלֵינוּ כְּדֶרֶךְ כָּל־הָאָרֶץ: לְכָה נַשְׁקֶה אֶת־
לז הַבְּכִירָה בֵּן וַתִּקְרָא שְׁמוֹ מוֹאָב הוּא אֲבִי־מוֹאָב　　לג אָבִינוּ יַיִן וְנִשְׁכְּבָה עִמּוֹ וּנְחַיֶּה מֵאָבִינוּ זָרַע: וַתַּשְׁקֶיןָ
עַד־הַיּוֹם: וְהַצְּעִירָה גַם־הִוא יָלְדָה בֵּן וַתִּקְרָא שְׁמוֹ　　אֶת־אֲבִיהֶן יַיִן בַּלַּיְלָה הוּא וַתָּבֹא הַבְּכִירָה וַתִּשְׁכַּב
לח בֶּן־עַמִּי הוּא אֲבִי בְנֵי־עַמּוֹן עַד־הַיּוֹם: ס　　לד אֶת־אָבִיהָ וְלֹא־יָדַע בְּשִׁכְבָהּ וּבְקוּמָהּ: וַיְהִי מִמָּחֳרָת

30] Lot went up from Zoar and settled in the hill country with his two daughters, for he was afraid to dwell in Zoar; and he and his two daughters lived in a cave. **31]** And the older one said to the younger, "Our father is old, and there is not a man on earth to consort with us in the way of all the world. **32]** Come, let us make our father drink wine, and let us lie with him, that we may maintain life through our father." **33]** That night they made their father drink wine, and the older one went in and lay with her father; he did not know when she lay down or when she rose. **34]** The next day the older one said to the younger, "See, I lay with Father last night; let us make him drink wine tonight also, and you go and lie with him, that we may maintain life through our father." **35]** That night also they made their father drink wine, and the younger one went and lay with him; he did not know when she lay down or when she rose.

36] Thus the two daughters of Lot came to be with child by their father. **37]** The older one bore a son and named him Moab; he is the father of the Moabites of today. **38]** And the younger also bore a son, and she called him Ben-ammi; he is the father of the Ammonites of today.

37] *Moab.* A word play on מֵאָב (*me-av,* from [my] father).

38] *Ben-ammi.* "Son of my [paternal] kindred." It is possible that this tale of sexual aberration arose to explain the names of Moab and Ammon.

Abraham's Argument with God

The dramatic confrontation between Abraham and God is told with the utmost simplicity; the cadences of repetitions vary as subtly as the repetitions of a symphonic theme.

Abraham does not doubt the existence of God's justice, he only asks its extent and limitations. The important thing is that he asks altogether and that God does not reject his question out of hand. The Bible thereby makes clear that man may, with impunity, question the behavior of God. Like Abraham, man need not surrender his own sense of justice; he remains free to accept or reject the divine judgment—although he will have to submit to it in the end. Man is not reduced to a moral automaton, his spiritual freedom is preserved.

It has been suggested that Abraham bargains with God, but in fact he does no more than plead. His pleas may be seen as attempts to penetrate the division separating the earthly and heavenly realms. In the end, Abraham has greater knowledge of the divine intention, but neither he nor the reader is given an intimation whether Abraham succeeded in changing God's mind, or whether—more likely—he merely learned what had been God's plan from the beginning. God's ways are ultimately "past finding out" (Job 9:10), but this does not prevent man from trying to bring them as much as possible within his own horizon of understanding.

And this horizon is not, in Abraham's case, limited by tribal considerations. His is a universal concept of justice. He is not concerned merely with Lot or his family but with people outside his tribe. He is a man for all men.

The Merit of the Few

Abraham does not plead merely for the innocent but for the sinners as well, through the merit of the few righteous. The story thereby introduces the concept of merit (זְכוּת), important in biblical and especially in post-biblical religion [3]. The concept stipulates that a handful of concerned, decent, and "righteous" men could have averted Sodom's calamity by their merit.

Yet the story also suggests that there are limits to the influence of even the best men. Unless they find a minimum of like-minded associates, they will be ineffective. Eventually, if they persist in living in such a society, they will perish with it. Thus, Abraham does not, in his pursuit of divine equity, go below the number ten. The Rabbis advised that if one could not find ten religiously minded people in a city one should move away. They also set ten as the minimal number (minyan) required for communal worship [4]. There comes a time when God, with all His mercy and justice, is "finished speaking" with man (Gen. 18:33) and when the punishment for unchecked evil will take its inevitable course and engulf all of society.

The Sins of Sodom and Gomorrah

The terms "outrage," "outcry," "destroy," are reminiscent of the story of the Flood, where we were told that the world was "filled with lawlessness." While here such a general definition is lacking, the similarity of expressions suggests that comparable moral conditions existed in both instances. We can infer from the story itself that Sodomites were inhospitable and that they were accustomed to some form or forms of sexual deviation. But while deviate sexual practice is strongly condemned in the Torah (Lev. 18), Jewish tradition stresses social rather than sexual aberrations as the reason for the cities' destruction.

Ezekiel, for instance, describes the sins of Sodom in social terms: "pride, fulness of bread, and careless ease was in her and in her daughters; neither did she strengthen the hand of the poor and needy. And they were haughty" (16:49–50). The tradition of Sodom's moral insensitivity, based on the way the

Sodomites treated strangers, highlighted, to biblical man, the community's essential depravity. To the ancients, hospitality included vastly more than good manners; it meant the treatment and acceptance of strangers and was a vital aspect of religion (Deut. 10:19). If Sodom had been a poor city, the sin of inhospitality might have been understandable and forgivable. But the city was rich, "like the garden of the Lord" (Gen. 13:10). The Midrash tells of the tradition that the streets were paved with gold and that the Sodomites flooded the approaches to their town so that strangers would be kept away and immigration effectively restricted [5].

Social evil, then, caused Sodom to perish. The Bible thus takes the old story of the physical destruction of the plain and turns it into a moral tale that carries its warning to all ages: Affluence without social concern is self-destructive; it hardens the conscience against repentance; it engenders cruelty and excess. The treatment accorded newcomers and strangers was then and may always be considered a touchstone of the community's moral condition.

Lot

Lot is in many ways the average man. He has streaks of greatness, moments of courage, but he is all too often subject to the attractions of comfort and pleasure. These in the end cause his downfall.

He appears in the text for the first time when he decides to leave the security of Haran to follow Abraham into an insecure future. Apparently he is a man of some conviction and initiative. But later, probably attracted by Sodom's affluence, he chooses that city as his home, despite its debased condition. Whatever other customs and habits of Sodom he adopts, he preserves his sense of hospitality and decency toward strangers. He risks his own and his family's safety in order to protect the men who are under his roof. This courage redeems much of his indecisiveness, faint-heartedness, and anxiety, which the remainder of the story reveals.

I Will Go Down to See (Gen. 18:21)

God wanted to give the cities time to repent. This, like the story of Babel, teaches that a judge must scrupulously examine a case before pronouncing judgment; and further, that just as God "went down" to see, so must man not judge his fellow man until he has come to see things from the other's viewpoint.   MIDRASH [6]

[This interpretation is also offered to counter the question: Did God not know whether Sodom was wicked?]

The Promethean

Abraham ranks among the biblical personages whose persuasive powers God had to acknowledge. Abraham would have surely snatched Sodom from destruction if only those few—ten, even—had been worthy of his prayer.   SHELDON H. BLANK [7]

The Sin

The sin of Sodom consisted not only in what its people did but in what they failed to do. Thus, no one raised his voice in protest when the crowd molested Lot's guests. Failure to protest is to participate in the sin of a community. [8]

Of Sodom it is written that it was well-watered everywhere [Gen. 13:10]; it possessed all the luxuries of the world, and its inhabitants were unwilling to share them with others. They punished anyone who offered food to a stranger; they even polled their fig trees lest birds would eat of them. R. Hiya said: "They deserved punishment both for their immorality and their uncharitableness. For whoever grudges assistance to the poor does not deserve to exist in this world, and he also forfeits the life of the world-to-come. Contrariwise, whoever is generous towards the poor deserves to exist in the world, and it is for his sake that the

world exists, and the fulness of life is reserved for him in the world-to-come."   MIDRASH, ZOHAR [9]

Because They Passed Wisdom By

Wisdom rescued a righteous man when the ungodly were perishing;
he escaped the fire that descended on the Five Cities.
Evidence of their wickedness still remains:
a continually smoking wasteland,
plants bearing fruit that does not ripen,
and a pillar of salt standing as a monument to an unbelieving soul.
For because they passed wisdom by,
they not only were hindered from recognizing the good,
but also left for mankind a reminder of their folly,
so that their failures could never go unnoticed.

   WISDOM OF SOLOMON [10]

The Site

From ancient times right down to the present day, popular imagination has been fascinated by the figure of Lot's thoughtless and inquisitive wife who, for disregarding God's command, was turned into a pillar of salt. As early as the time of the Second Temple, the pillar of salt was thought to be in the region of Mount Sodom. Thus Josephus writes: "I saw the pillar of salt on my travels, for it exists to this day."

Mount Sodom, at the southwestern corner of the Dead Sea, is remarkable for its sharp pinnacles, the lower parts of which consist of salt layers and the upper of salt and marl columns. One or another of these pinnacles which look like a human shape is regarded by popular tradition as the wife of Lot. However, as a result of climatic and geological factors the "pillars" are in a constant state of formation and disintegration. This has given rise to various legends about the transformation of Lot's wife.   VIEWS OF THE BIBLICAL WORLD [11]

Crises

After a repetition of the "sister" incident, the Bible finally tells of the long-awaited birth of Sarah's son. Two brief, almost anticlimactic verses tell us that the divine promise is now fulfilled and the spiritual continuity of Abraham guaranteed. But no sooner is the first stage reached than difficulties arise between the sons of Abraham. The text relates the harsh manner in which the rivalry is resolved.

Then follows a brief interlude dealing with another relationship, that of Abraham and Abimelech. This too finds its adjustment, leaving the reader with the impression that all is well in the household of the Patriarch. But the respite is short. This section may therefore be viewed as the introduction to the story of the Akedah, which follows.

א וַיִּסַּע מִשָּׁם אַבְרָהָם אַרְצָה הַנֶּגֶב וַיֵּשֶׁב בֵּין־קָדֵשׁ וּבֵין
שׁוּר וַיָּגָר בִּגְרָר: ב וַיֹּאמֶר אַבְרָהָם אֶל־שָׂרָה אִשְׁתּוֹ
אֲחֹתִי הִוא וַיִּשְׁלַח אֲבִימֶלֶךְ מֶלֶךְ גְּרָר וַיִּקַּח אֶת־
שָׂרָה: ג וַיָּבֹא אֱלֹהִים אֶל־אֲבִימֶלֶךְ בַּחֲלוֹם הַלָּיְלָה
וַיֹּאמֶר לוֹ הִנְּךָ מֵת עַל־הָאִשָּׁה אֲשֶׁר־לָקַחְתָּ וְהִוא
בְּעֻלַת בָּעַל: ד וַאֲבִימֶלֶךְ לֹא קָרַב אֵלֶיהָ וַיֹּאמַר
אֲדֹנָי הֲגוֹי גַּם־צַדִּיק תַּהֲרֹג: ה הֲלֹא הוּא אָמַר־לִי
אֲחֹתִי הִוא וְהִיא־גַם־הִוא אָמְרָה אָחִי הוּא בְּתָם־לְבָבִי
וּבְנִקְיֹן כַּפַּי עָשִׂיתִי זֹאת: ו וַיֹּאמֶר אֵלָיו הָאֱלֹהִים
בַּחֲלֹם גַּם אָנֹכִי יָדַעְתִּי כִּי בְתָם־לְבָבְךָ עָשִׂיתָ זֹּאת
וָאֶחְשֹׂךְ גַּם־אָנֹכִי אוֹתְךָ מֵחֲטוֹ־לִי עַל־כֵּן לֹא־נְתַתִּיךָ

ז לִנְגֹּעַ אֵלֶיהָ: וְעַתָּה הָשֵׁב אֵשֶׁת־הָאִישׁ כִּי־נָבִיא הוּא
וְיִתְפַּלֵּל בַּעַדְךָ וֶחְיֵה וְאִם־אֵינְךָ מֵשִׁיב דַּע כִּי־מוֹת
ח תָּמוּת אַתָּה וְכָל־אֲשֶׁר־לָךְ: וַיַּשְׁכֵּם אֲבִימֶלֶךְ בַּבֹּקֶר
וַיִּקְרָא לְכָל־עֲבָדָיו וַיְדַבֵּר אֶת־כָּל־הַדְּבָרִים הָאֵלֶּה
ט בְּאָזְנֵיהֶם וַיִּירְאוּ הָאֲנָשִׁים מְאֹד: וַיִּקְרָא אֲבִימֶלֶךְ
לְאַבְרָהָם וַיֹּאמֶר לוֹ מֶה־עָשִׂיתָ לָּנוּ וּמֶה־חָטָאתִי לָךְ
כִּי־הֵבֵאתָ עָלַי וְעַל־מַמְלַכְתִּי חֲטָאָה גְדֹלָה מַעֲשִׂים
י אֲשֶׁר לֹא־יֵעָשׂוּ עָשִׂיתָ עִמָּדִי: וַיֹּאמֶר אֲבִימֶלֶךְ אֶל־
יא אַבְרָהָם מָה רָאִיתָ כִּי עָשִׂיתָ אֶת־הַדָּבָר הַזֶּה: וַיֹּאמֶר
אַבְרָהָם כִּי אָמַרְתִּי רַק אֵין־יִרְאַת אֱלֹהִים בַּמָּקוֹם
יב הַזֶּה וַהֲרָגוּנִי עַל־דְּבַר אִשְׁתִּי: וְגַם־אָמְנָה אֲחֹתִי בַת־

1] Abraham journeyed from there to the region of the Negeb and settled between Kadesh and Shur. While he was sojourning in Gerar, 2] Abraham said of Sarah his wife, "She is my sister." So Abimelech king of Gerar had Sarah brought to him. 3] But God came to Abimelech in a dream by night and said to him, "You are to die because of the woman that you have taken, for she is a married woman." 4] Now Abimelech had not approached her. He said, "O Lord, will You slay people even though innocent? 5] He himself said to me, 'She is my sister!' And she also said, 'He is my brother.' When I did this, my heart was blameless and my hands were clean." 6] And God said to him in the dream, "I knew that you did this with a blameless heart, and so I kept you from sinning against Me. That was why I did not let you touch her. 7] Therefore, restore the man's wife—since he is a prophet, he will intercede for you—to save your life. If you fail to restore her, know that you shall die, you and all that are yours."

8] Early next morning, Abimelech called all his servants and told them all that had happened; and the men were greatly frightened. 9] Then Abimelech summoned Abraham and said to him, "What have you done to us? What wrong have I done you that you should bring so great a guilt upon me and my kingdom? You have done to me things that ought not to be done. 10] What, then," Abimelech demanded of Abraham, "was your purpose in doing this thing?" 11] "I thought," said Abraham, "surely there is no fear of God in this place, and they will kill me because of my wife. 12] And besides, she is in truth my sister, my father's

20:1] *Gerar.* Between Gaza and Beer-sheba. There are two other versions of the story (see chapters 12 and 26). Scholars assign authorship of this version to the E-school and authorship of the others to the J-school. Among the differences: Chapter 12 offers no excuse for Abraham's behavior; the excuse in this section is elaborate. J does not say what happened to Sarah in Pharaoh's court; E tells us she remained untouched. E is apologetic about Abraham and Sarah; J is not (for background, see Gen. 12:10–20).

7] *He is a prophet.* נָבִיא (*navi*), one who speaks up or announces God's will.

He will intercede for you. Objectively, you have wronged Abraham and Sarah, but Abraham will not press his claim and, on the contrary, will speak in your behalf.

12] *She is in truth my sister.* On the position and meaning of "sister" see commentary to Gen. 12:10–13:18 .

יח וַיֵּלֵדוּ: כִּי־עָצֹר עָצַר יְהוָה בְּעַד כָּל־רֶחֶם לְבֵית
אֲבִימֶלֶךְ עַל־דְּבַר שָׂרָה אֵשֶׁת אַבְרָהָם: ס

א וַיהוָה פָּקַד אֶת־שָׂרָה כַּאֲשֶׁר אָמָר וַיַּעַשׂ יְהוָה לְשָׂרָה
ב כַּאֲשֶׁר דִּבֵּר: וַתַּהַר וַתֵּלֶד שָׂרָה לְאַבְרָהָם בֵּן לִזְקֻנָיו
ג לַמּוֹעֵד אֲשֶׁר־דִּבֶּר אֹתוֹ אֱלֹהִים: וַיִּקְרָא אַבְרָהָם אֶת־
ד שֶׁם־בְּנוֹ הַנּוֹלַד־לוֹ אֲשֶׁר־יָלְדָה־לּוֹ שָׂרָה יִצְחָק: וַיָּמָל
אַבְרָהָם אֶת־יִצְחָק בְּנוֹ בֶּן־שְׁמֹנַת יָמִים כַּאֲשֶׁר צִוָּה
ה אֹתוֹ אֱלֹהִים: וְאַבְרָהָם בֶּן־מְאַת שָׁנָה בְּהִוָּלֶד לוֹ אֵת
ו יִצְחָק בְּנוֹ: וַתֹּאמֶר שָׂרָה צְחֹק עָשָׂה לִי אֱלֹהִים כָּל־
ז הַשֹּׁמֵעַ יִצְחַק־לִי: וַתֹּאמֶר מִי מִלֵּל לְאַבְרָהָם הֵינִיקָה

יג אָבִי הוּא אַךְ לֹא בַת־אִמִּי וַתְּהִי־לִי לְאִשָּׁה: וַיְהִי
כַּאֲשֶׁר הִתְעוּ אֹתִי אֱלֹהִים מִבֵּית אָבִי וָאֹמַר לָהּ זֶה
חַסְדֵּךְ אֲשֶׁר תַּעֲשִׂי עִמָּדִי אֶל כָּל־הַמָּקוֹם אֲשֶׁר נָבוֹא
יד שָׁמָּה אִמְרִי־לִי אָחִי הוּא: וַיִּקַּח אֲבִימֶלֶךְ צֹאן וּבָקָר
וַעֲבָדִים וּשְׁפָחֹת וַיִּתֵּן לְאַבְרָהָם וַיָּשֶׁב לוֹ אֵת שָׂרָה
טו אִשְׁתּוֹ: וַיֹּאמֶר אֲבִימֶלֶךְ הִנֵּה אַרְצִי לְפָנֶיךָ בַּטּוֹב
טז בְּעֵינֶיךָ שֵׁב: וּלְשָׂרָה אָמַר הִנֵּה נָתַתִּי אֶלֶף כֶּסֶף
לְאָחִיךְ הִנֵּה הוּא־לָךְ כְּסוּת עֵינַיִם לְכֹל אֲשֶׁר אִתָּךְ
יז וְאֵת כֹּל וְנֹכָחַת: וַיִּתְפַּלֵּל אַבְרָהָם אֶל־הָאֱלֹהִים
וַיִּרְפָּא אֱלֹהִים אֶת־אֲבִימֶלֶךְ וְאֶת־אִשְׁתּוֹ וְאַמְהֹתָיו

daughter though not my·mother's; and she became my wife. **13]** So when God made me wander from my father's house, I said to her, 'Let this be the kindness that you shall do me: whatever place we come to, say there of me: He is my brother.'"

14] Abimelech took sheep and oxen, and male and female slaves, and gave them to Abraham; and he restored his wife Sarah to him. **15]** And Abimelech said, "Here, my land is before you; settle wherever you please." **16]** And to Sarah he said, "I herewith give your brother a thousand pieces of silver; this will serve you as vindication before all who are with you, and you are cleared before everyone." **17]** Abraham then prayed to God, and God healed Abimelech and his wife and his slave girls, so that they bore children; **18]** for the LORD had closed fast every womb of the household of Abimelech because of Sarah, the wife of Abraham.

1] The LORD took note of Sarah as He had promised, and the LORD did for Sarah as He had spoken. **2]** Sarah conceived and bore a son to Abraham in his old age, at the set time of which God had spoken. **3]** Abraham gave his new-born son, whom Sarah had borne him, the name of Isaac. **4]** And when his son Isaac was eight days old, Abraham circumcised him, as God had commanded him. **5]** Now Abraham was a hundred years old when his son Isaac was born to him. **6]** Sarah said, "God has brought me laughter; everyone who hears will laugh with me." **7]** And she added, / "Who would have said to Abraham / That Sarah would suckle

13] *God*. The verb form attached to אֱלֹהִים (*elohim*) is here used in a rare plural construction. According to the Talmud [1], this is the only passage in the Abraham story where אֱלֹהִים is not holy, i.e., where it does not mean "God" (see commentary to Gen. 2:4–24, "The Names of God").

16] *As vindication*. Literally, "a covering of the eyes." The meaning of this is obscure but most probably it implies: In this fashion people cannot say I cast you out because I was tired of you [2].

17] *Abraham then prayed*. While he probably prayed previously, this is the first mention of prayer in the Torah. In early cuneiform sources, too, individual prayer is rarely mentioned and seems to have evolved rather slowly. /The development of personal prayer in Mesopotamia has been traced from the early letters to the deity to a fixed poetic form much like the individual laments of the biblical Psalter [3]./

ח בָנִים שָׂרָה כִּי־יָלַדְתִּי בֵן לִזְקֻנָיו: וַיִּגְדַּל הַיֶּלֶד וַיִּגָּמַל
וַיַּעַשׂ אַבְרָהָם מִשְׁתֶּה גָדוֹל בְּיוֹם הִגָּמֵל אֶת־יִצְחָק:
ט וַתֵּרֶא שָׂרָה אֶת־בֶּן־הָגָר הַמִּצְרִית אֲשֶׁר־יָלְדָה
י לְאַבְרָהָם מְצַחֵק: וַתֹּאמֶר לְאַבְרָהָם גָּרֵשׁ הָאָמָה
הַזֹּאת וְאֶת־בְּנָהּ כִּי לֹא יִירַשׁ בֶּן־הָאָמָה הַזֹּאת עִם־
יא בְּנִי עִם־יִצְחָק: וַיֵּרַע הַדָּבָר מְאֹד בְּעֵינֵי אַבְרָהָם עַל
יב אוֹדֹת בְּנוֹ: וַיֹּאמֶר אֱלֹהִים אֶל־אַבְרָהָם אַל־יֵרַע
בְּעֵינֶיךָ עַל־הַנַּעַר וְעַל־אֲמָתֶךָ כֹּל אֲשֶׁר תֹּאמַר אֵלֶיךָ

יג שָׂרָה שְׁמַע בְּקֹלָהּ כִּי בְיִצְחָק יִקָּרֵא לְךָ זָרַע: וְגַם
יד אֶת־בֶּן־הָאָמָה לְגוֹי אֲשִׂימֶנּוּ כִּי זַרְעֲךָ הוּא: וַיַּשְׁכֵּם
אַבְרָהָם בַּבֹּקֶר וַיִּקַּח־לֶחֶם וְחֵמַת מַיִם וַיִּתֵּן אֶל־הָגָר
שָׂם עַל־שִׁכְמָהּ וְאֶת־הַיֶּלֶד וַיְשַׁלְּחֶהָ וַתֵּלֶךְ וַתֵּתַע
טו בְּמִדְבַּר בְּאֵר שָׁבַע: וַיִּכְלוּ הַמַּיִם מִן־הַחֵמֶת וַתַּשְׁלֵךְ
טז אֶת־הַיֶּלֶד תַּחַת אַחַד הַשִּׂיחִם: וַתֵּלֶךְ וַתֵּשֶׁב לָהּ מִנֶּגֶד
הַרְחֵק כִּמְטַחֲוֵי קֶשֶׁת כִּי אָמְרָה אַל־אֶרְאֶה בְּמוֹת
יז הַיֶּלֶד וַתֵּשֶׁב מִנֶּגֶד וַתִּשָּׂא אֶת־קֹלָהּ וַתֵּבְךְּ: וַיִּשְׁמַע

children! / Yet I have borne a son in his old age." **8]** The child grew up and was weaned, and Abraham held a great feast on the day that Isaac was weaned.

9] Sarah saw the son, whom Hagar the Egyptian had borne to Abraham, playing. **10]** She said to Abraham, "Cast out that slavewoman and her son, for the son of that slave shall not share in the inheritance with my son Isaac." **11]** The matter distressed Abraham greatly, for it concerned a son of his. **12]** But God said to Abraham, "Do not be distressed over the boy or your slave; whatever Sarah tells you, do as she says, for it is through Isaac that offspring shall be continued for you. **13]** As for the son of the slave-woman, I will make a nation of him, too, for he is your seed." **14]** Early next morning Abraham took some bread and a skin of water, and gave them to Hagar. He placed them over her shoulder, together with the child, and sent her away. And she wandered about in the wildnerness of Beer-sheba. **15]** When the water was gone from the skin, she left the child under one of the bushes, **16]** and went and sat down at a distance, a bowshot away; for she thought, "Let me not look on as the child dies." And sitting thus afar, she burst into tears.

21:8] *A great feast.* Probably in connection with a weaning ceremony. According to the Talmud, children were weaned between eighteen and twenty-four months; the Book of Maccabees puts the age at three years; in some parts of the Orient weaning is delayed even further [4].

9] *Playing.* Some commentators have suggested that it was sexual play that brought forth Sarah's strong reaction [5]. There is nothing, however, to substantiate this. The use of מְצַחֵק (*metzachek*) is an allusion to יְצָחָק (*yitzchak*, i.e., Isaac). The word play seems to indicate that Sarah, seeing the children together, suddenly realizes their close affinity. It is then that she resolves to end the relationship by freeing Hagar and sending her away.

/ According to the laws of Lipit-Ishtar (25), which antedate Hammurabi by 150 years, the slave-girl and her son may become free but are not then entitled to an inheritance [6]./

12] *Shall be continued.* Literally, "called."

13] *A nation.* Some versions have "a great nation." Ishmael, too, will reflect Abraham's greatness. In both Jewish and Islamic traditions, many Arabs are considered Ishmael's descendants.

14] *Together with the child.* The Hebrew text is not clear. The Septuagint portrays Ishmael as a small child whom Hagar carries on her shoulder, even though according to Gen. 16:16 he is fourteen years older than Isaac.

Beer-sheba. See Gen. 21:31.

16] *A bowshot away.* Alluding to Ishmael's later profession as a bowman (Gen. 21:20).

אֱלֹהִים֙ אֶת־ק֣וֹל הַנַּ֔עַר וַיִּקְרָא֩ מַלְאַ֨ךְ אֱלֹהִ֤ים ׀ אֶל־ כֹּ֣ עִמָּדִ֔י וְעִם־הָאָ֖רֶץ אֲשֶׁר־גַּ֣רְתָּה בָּ֑הּ וַיֹּ֙אמֶר֙ אַבְרָהָ֔ם

הָגָ֜ר מִן־הַשָּׁמַ֗יִם וַיֹּ֤אמֶר לָהּ֙ מַה־לָּ֣ךְ הָגָ֔ר אַל־תִּ֣ירְאִ֔י כה אָנֹכִ֖י אִשָּׁבֵ֑עַ׃ וְהוֹכִ֤חַ אַבְרָהָם֙ אֶת־אֲבִימֶ֔לֶךְ עַל־

כִּֽי־שָׁמַ֧ע אֱלֹהִ֛ים אֶל־ק֥וֹל הַנַּ֖עַר בַּאֲשֶׁ֥ר הוּא־שָֽׁם׃ כו אֹד֣וֹת בְּאֵ֣ר הַמַּ֔יִם אֲשֶׁ֥ר גָּזְל֖וּ עַבְדֵ֥י אֲבִימֶֽלֶךְ׃ וַיֹּ֣אמֶר

יח ק֚וּמִי שְׂאִ֣י אֶת־הַנַּ֔עַר וְהַחֲזִ֥יקִי אֶת־יָדֵ֖ךְ בּ֑וֹ כִּֽי־לְ ג֥וֹי אֲבִימֶ֔לֶךְ לֹ֣א יָדַ֔עְתִּי מִ֥י עָשָׂ֖ה אֶת־הַדָּבָ֣ר הַזֶּ֑ה וְגַם־

יט גָּד֖וֹל אֲשִׂימֶֽנּוּ׃ וַיִּפְקַ֤ח אֱלֹהִים֙ אֶת־עֵינֶ֔יהָ וַתֵּ֖רֶא בְּאֵ֣ר אַתָּ֙ה לֹא־הִגַּ֣דְתָּ לִּ֔י וְגַ֧ם אָנֹכִ֛י לֹ֥א שָׁמַ֖עְתִּי בִּלְתִּ֥י

מָ֑יִם וַתֵּ֗לֶךְ וַתְּמַלֵּ֤א אֶת־הַחֵ֙מֶת֙ מַ֔יִם וַתַּ֖שְׁקְ אֶת־הַנָּֽעַר׃ כז הַיּֽוֹם׃ וַיִּקַּ֤ח אַבְרָהָם֙ צֹ֣אן וּבָקָ֔ר וַיִּתֵּ֖ן לַאֲבִימֶ֑לֶךְ

כ וַיְהִ֧י אֱלֹהִ֛ים אֶת־הַנַּ֖עַר וַיִּגְדָּ֑ל וַיֵּ֙שֶׁב֙ בַּמִּדְבָּ֔ר וַיְהִ֖י כח וַיִּכְרְת֥וּ שְׁנֵיהֶ֖ם בְּרִֽית׃ וַיַּצֵּ֣ב אַבְרָהָ֗ם אֶת־שֶׁ֛בַע כִּבְשֹׂ֥ת

כא רֹבֶ֥ה קַשָּֽׁת׃ וַיֵּ֖שֶׁב בְּמִדְבַּ֣ר פָּארָ֑ן וַתִּֽקַּֽח־ל֥וֹ אִמּ֛וֹ אִשָּׁ֖ה כט הַצֹּ֖אן לְבַדְּהֶֽן׃ וַיֹּ֥אמֶר אֲבִימֶ֖לֶךְ אֶל־אַבְרָהָ֑ם מָ֣ה

מֵאֶ֥רֶץ מִצְרָֽיִם׃ פ הֵ֗נָּה שֶׁ֤בַע כְּבָשֹׂת֙ הָאֵ֔לֶּה אֲשֶׁ֥ר הִצַּ֖בְתָּ לְבַדָּֽנָה׃

כב וַֽיְהִי֙ בָּעֵ֣ת הַהִ֔וא וַיֹּ֣אמֶר אֲבִימֶ֗לֶךְ וּפִיכֹל֙ שַׂר־צְבָא֔וֹ ל וַיֹּ֕אמֶר כִּ֚י אֶת־שֶׁ֣בַע כְּבָשֹׂ֔ת תִּקַּ֖ח מִיָּדִ֑י בַּעֲבוּר֙ תִּֽהְיֶה־

אֶל־אַבְרָהָ֖ם לֵאמֹ֑ר אֱלֹהִ֣ים עִמְּךָ֔ בְּכֹ֥ל אֲשֶׁר־אַתָּ֖ה לא לִּ֣י לְעֵדָ֔ה כִּ֥י חָפַ֖רְתִּי אֶת־הַבְּאֵ֥ר הַזֹּֽאת׃ עַל־כֵּ֗ן

כג עֹשֶֽׂה׃ וְעַתָּ֗ה הִשָּׁ֥בְעָה לִּ֤י בֵֽאלֹהִים֙ הֵ֔נָּה אִם־תִּשְׁקֹ֣ר לִ֔י קָרָ֛א לַמָּק֥וֹם הַה֖וּא בְּאֵ֣ר שָׁ֑בַע כִּ֛י שָׁ֥ם נִשְׁבְּע֖וּ שְׁנֵיהֶֽם׃

וּלְנִינִ֖י וּלְנֶכְדִּ֑י כַּחֶ֜סֶד אֲשֶׁר־עָשִׂ֤יתִי עִמְּךָ֙ תַּעֲשֶׂ֣ה

17] God heard the cry of the boy, and an angel of God called to Hagar from heaven and said to her, "What troubles you, Hagar? Fear not, for God has heeded the cry of the boy where he is. **18]** Come, lift up the boy and hold him by the hand, for I will make a great nation of him." **19]** Then God opened her eyes and she saw a well of water. She went and filled the skin with water, and let the boy drink. **20]** God was with the boy and he grew up; he dwelt in the wilderness and became a bowman. **21]** He lived in the wilderness of Paran; and his mother got a wife for him from the land of Egypt.

22] At that time Abimelech and Phicol, chief of his troops, said to Abraham, "God is with you in everything that you do. **23]** Therefore swear to me here by God that you will not deal falsely with me or with my kith and kin, but will deal with me and with the land in which you have sojourned as loyally as I have dealt with you." **24]** And Abraham said, "I swear it."

25] Then Abraham reproached Abimelech for the well of water which the servants of Abimelech had seized. **26]** But Abimelech said, "I do not know who did this; you did not tell me, nor have I heard of it until today." **27]** Abraham took sheep and oxen and gave them to Abimelech, and the two of them made a pact. **28]** Abraham then set seven ewes of the flock by themselves, **29]** and Abimelech said to Abraham, "What mean these seven ewes which you have set apart?" **30]** He replied, "You are to accept these seven ewes from me as proof that I dug this well." **31]** Hence that place was called Beer-sheba, for there the two of them

19] *Opened her eyes.* To see what she did not notice before. The Torah uses this expression in the figurative sense [7].

21] *His mother got a wife for him.* As was the custom. *Egypt.* Hagar's homeland.

22] *At that time.* Most probably at the weaning feast for Isaac.

25] *The well of water.* The incident has not been mentioned previously.

31] *Beer-sheba.* Well of seven, or well of oath. Abraham and Abimelech conclude a mutual non-aggression pact [8].

לב וַיִּכְרְתוּ בְרִית בִּבְאֵר שָׁבַע וַיָּקָם אֲבִימֶלֶךְ וּפִיכֹל   לד בִּבְאֵר שָׁבַע וַיִּקְרָא־שָׁם בְּשֵׁם יְהוָה אֵל עוֹלָם: וַיָּגָר

לג שַׂר־צְבָאוֹ וַיָּשֻׁבוּ אֶל־אֶרֶץ פְּלִשְׁתִּים: וַיִּטַּע אֶשֶׁל   אַבְרָהָם בְּאֶרֶץ פְּלִשְׁתִּים יָמִים רַבִּים: פ

swore an oath. **32]** When they had concluded the pact at Beer-sheba, Abimelech and Phicol, chief of his troops, departed and returned to the land of the Philistines. **33]** [Abraham] planted a tamarisk at Beer-sheba, and invoked there the name of the LORD, the Everlasting God. **34]** And Abraham resided in the land of the Philistines a long time.

33] *Planted a tamarisk.* Similar tree-planting ceremonies survive in later Jewish tradition. Later they are called "a planting of joy." At Betar they planted a cedar at the birth of a boy, a cypress when a girl was born. Later, the trees were used for the marriage canopy [9].

Everlasting God. אֵל עוֹלָם (*El Olam*), an unusual name, occurring in only one other verse in the Bible where God is called אֱלֹהֵי עוֹלָם (Isa. 40:28).

34] *A long time.* This appears inconsistent with the immediately preceding passage wherein Abraham dwells at Beer-sheba. Therefore, the verse should not be read as an end to the passage but should be detached and taken as a general postscript to the preceding chapters and as an introduction to what follows. In other words, during this time of his life, Abraham lived in the area later known as Philistia.

Human Feelings and Divine Purpose

Underlying this episode is the essential affinity between the Israelites and Ishmaelites; there can be no question over the writer's sympathy for his tribal cousin.

As in chapter 16, this sympathy is elicited for Hagar and her child, and again Abraham and Sarah are depicted as human and fallible. The aged Matriarch prevails upon her husband to relieve her of the presence of her maid. The Bible attempts no justification of Abraham or Sarah, nor certainly of God. In the story, His ultimate designs prevail; He directs the actions of men in His own mysterious way. What on a human plane appears as Sarah's harsh and overprotective behavior is on the divine level part of God's plan. Sarah's desires coincide with the idea of destiny; hence her actions find God's approval while Abraham's do not.

Here may be seen the deeper meaning of the story. Abraham's natural feelings of compassion for Hagar and Ishmael must yield to the divine scheme in which Isaac and his descendants will have a special place. The Bible portrays the human sentiments of the Patriarch in tension with the inexplicable divine choice, a tension between human love and divine will [10].

This is also the theme of the Akedah, of Isaac's sacrifice, which follows at once. There, too, Abraham's human love is pitted against the stern demands of God. Thus, the stories complement each other: Both deal with the mysterious purposes of the One who encompasses the whole world and is at the same time the Guiding Force of the people of Abraham and Isaac.

The Sages arranged that both stories be read on Rosh Hashanah. This remains the custom in Orthodox and Conservative synagogues, which assign chapter 21 to the first and chapter 22 to the second day. Reform synagogues, observing a single day of Rosh Hashanah, read only chapter 22.[1]

---

[1] Various reasons have been advanced for the choice of these Torah readings on Rosh Hashanah, e.g., that the opening sentence of Gen. 21, "The Lord took note . . .," fits with the holy day theme of remembrance (*zichronot*) and that Gen. 22 was chosen because a ram figures in the story, connecting it thereby with the practice of blowing the shofar on Rosh Hashanah. However, there may be a relationship between chapters 21 and 22: both may have been juxtaposed in the Torah as initiation rites for Ishmael and Isaac, similar to Greek traditions.

GLEANINGS

Elohim (Gen. 20:13)

Since the word is in the plural construction it cannot mean "God," but must mean "rulers." Abraham must therefore be understood to say: "Rulers made me go into exile because I was a God-seeker."   HAKETAV VE-HAKABBALAH

Abraham Prayed to God

R. Hama ben Hanina said: "This expression [prayed] occurs here for the first time in the Book of Genesis. When Abraham prayed, a knot was untied, i.e., the tangled relationship between man and God was straightened out and from now on men could pray."   MIDRASH [11]

Why was Abraham's prayer necessary? To emphasize that Abraham and his wife were totally vindicated.

The duty to pray was a punishment for Abraham, for he had to humble himself before God.
                BENNO JACOB

Christian Scriptures

Christian tradition utilizes the Ishmael–Isaac story as an allegory: As Ishmael is born in bondage but Isaac in freedom, so the first-born religion (Judaism) is in the bondage of law and the later (Christianity) free from it. [12]

Islam

In Moslem tradition, Hagar (Hadjar) went to Arabia after her quarrel with Sarah, and Abraham (Ibrahim), guided by God, followed her there. Ishmael (Ismail) and Abraham became founders of the Kaaba in Mecca, and both were buried in that city. Ismail is considered the ancestor of one of the three major Arabic groups. [13]

Also mention in the Book
The story of Ismail:
He was strictly true
To what he promised,
And he was an apostle
And a prophet.   KORAN [14]

Where He Is (Gen. 21:17)

God hears Ishmael's cry "where he is." God always hears and judges man on his present circumstances, not for where he was or will be.
                MIDRASH [15]

Sarah's Laughter

The entire beginning of the Jewish people is laughable, its history, its expectations, its hopes. God waited with the foundation of this people until its forefather had reached a "ridiculous" high age; therefore He began the realization of His promise only after all human hopes had come to an end. For a people was about to be created which was to stand with its whole existence in contrast to all historical experience. Therefore, until today, to those who in their shortsightedness deny God, this people must appear as the most ridiculous joke of all. The derisive laughter which has followed the Jew through history is the surest proof of the divine nature of its path. The Jew is not touched by this ridicule because from the beginning he has been prepared for it.
                SAMSON RAPHAEL HIRSCH

Abraham Planted a Tamarisk (Gen. 21:33)

The Hebrew for tamarisk is אֵשֶׁל [eshel] and its three letters signify the essentials of Abraham's hospitality: א for אֲכִילָה [food], שׁ for שְׁתִיָּה [drink], and ל for לְוָיָה [escort].   MIDRASH [16]

Beer-sheba stands at the edge of the desert. The

143

verse is the first notice of the transformation of the life of Abraham from that of the wandering nomad with his flocks to a settled agriculturist. Is it not possible that he planted those tamarisks for the same purpose as they are being planted today, as a windbreak against the sandstorms which blew in from the desert?　　　LOUIS I. RABINOWITZ [17]

[The comment implies Abraham planted an orchard which, unlike the low-growing grain of the Negev, needed a windbreak.]

Ishmael

Abraham, modest and unassuming as he was, was ready to do justice to Sarah and he conferred full power upon her to dispose of Hagar according to her pleasure. He added but one caution, "Having once made her a mistress, we cannot again reduce her to the state of a bondwoman." Unmindful of this warning, Sarah exacted the services of a slave from Hagar. Not alone this, she tormented her, and finally she cast an evil eye upon her, so that the unborn child dropped from her, and she ran away. On her flight she was met by several angels, and they bade her return, at the same time making known to her that she would bear a son who should be called Ishmael—one of the six men who have been given a name by God before their birth, the others being Isaac, Moses, Solomon, Josiah, and the Messiah.

Thirteen years after the birth of Ishmael the command was issued to Abraham that he put the sign of the covenant upon his body and upon the bodies of the male members of his household.

Abraham was reluctant at first to do the bidding of God, for he feared that the circumcision of his flesh would raise a barrier between himself and the rest of mankind. But God said unto him, "Let it suffice thee that I am thy God and thy Lord, as it sufficeth the world that I am its God and its Lord."　　　MIDRASH [18]

A Clash

Abraham finally submits, but to the divine command, not to Sarah's demand. God intervenes and orders Abraham to obey Sarah. Here we have another example of compliance with God's command in contradiction to a natural human feeling—and this case is to a certain extent a preparation for the great example of the binding of Isaac. Here Abraham is called upon to send out Ishmael into the desert, as he is afterwards called upon to sacrifice Isaac to God on one of the mountains. Superior to the "natural" human feeling there is the force of the divine command which is in accordance with God's will and the destiny of Israel. Abraham's natural feelings are here in contradiction to the idea of the destiny and the choice, and therefore they are rejected, while Sarah's natural feelings are in keeping with the idea of the destiny and therefore they are approved: "Whatever Sarah tells you, do as she says" (21:12). When there is a clash between the human principle of fatherhood and the principle of the choice of Israel, it is the second that is preferred, for it is the guiding force in Abraham's life and it joins up all the stories of Abraham into a meaningful cycle.

ZVI ADAR [19]

The Akedah

Few narrative sections of the Torah have been subjected to as much comment and study as the עֲקֵדָה (*akedah*, binding [of Isaac]). Jewish, Christian, and Moslem theologies have tried to fathom its intention. In his introduction to this chapter, Abarbanel called the story "worthier of study and investigation than any other section." Its subject matter ranges from the God who tests to the man who is tested, from the nature of faith to the demands it makes, and it considers many other questions as well. Says Von Rad: "One should renounce any attempt to discover one basic idea as *the* meaning of the whole. There are many levels of meaning."

The literary pattern of the section is reminiscent of the first passage of the Abraham story: A divine command is issued asking Abraham to set out toward an as yet unannounced place. The same unusual reflexive phrasing (see Gen. 12:1) contains the directive לֶךְ־לְךָ (*lech-lecha*, go forth). It is almost as though the external elements of the tale, while clear enough, hide deeper problems under the cover of simple words.

A small postscript follows the Akedah: a genealogical notation on the lines of Nahor. This serves as a bridge to the subsequent stories of Isaac and Rebekah.

וְהַנַּעַר נֵלְכָה עַד־כֹּה וְנִשְׁתַּחֲוֶה וְנָשׁוּבָה אֲלֵיכֶם:
ו וַיִּקַּח אַבְרָהָם אֶת־עֲצֵי הָעֹלָה וַיָּשֶׂם עַל־יִצְחָק בְּנוֹ
וַיִּקַּח בְּיָדוֹ אֶת־הָאֵשׁ וְאֶת־הַמַּאֲכֶלֶת וַיֵּלְכוּ שְׁנֵיהֶם
יַחְדָּו: וַיֹּאמֶר יִצְחָק אֶל־אַבְרָהָם אָבִיו וַיֹּאמֶר אָבִי
וַיֹּאמֶר הִנֶּנִּי בְנִי וַיֹּאמֶר הִנֵּה הָאֵשׁ וְהָעֵצִים וְאַיֵּה הַשֶּׂה
ח לְעֹלָה: וַיֹּאמֶר אַבְרָהָם אֱלֹהִים יִרְאֶה־לּוֹ הַשֶּׂה לְעֹלָה
ט בְּנִי וַיֵּלְכוּ שְׁנֵיהֶם יַחְדָּו: וַיָּבֹאוּ אֶל־הַמָּקוֹם אֲשֶׁר
אָמַר־לוֹ הָאֱלֹהִים וַיִּבֶן שָׁם אַבְרָהָם אֶת־הַמִּזְבֵּחַ
וַיַּעֲרֹךְ אֶת־הָעֵצִים וַיַּעֲקֹד אֶת־יִצְחָק בְּנוֹ וַיָּשֶׂם אֹתוֹ

א וַיְהִי אַחַר הַדְּבָרִים הָאֵלֶּה וְהָאֱלֹהִים נִסָּה אֶת־
ב אַבְרָהָם וַיֹּאמֶר אֵלָיו אַבְרָהָם וַיֹּאמֶר הִנֵּנִי: וַיֹּאמֶר
קַח־נָא אֶת־בִּנְךָ אֶת־יְחִידְךָ אֲשֶׁר־אָהַבְתָּ אֶת־יִצְחָק
וְלֶךְ־לְךָ אֶל־אֶרֶץ הַמֹּרִיָּה וְהַעֲלֵהוּ שָׁם לְעֹלָה עַל
ג אַחַד הֶהָרִים אֲשֶׁר אֹמַר אֵלֶיךָ: וַיַּשְׁכֵּם אַבְרָהָם
בַּבֹּקֶר וַיַּחֲבֹשׁ אֶת־חֲמֹרוֹ וַיִּקַּח אֶת־שְׁנֵי נְעָרָיו אִתּוֹ
וְאֵת יִצְחָק בְּנוֹ וַיְבַקַּע עֲצֵי עֹלָה וַיָּקָם וַיֵּלֶךְ אֶל־
ד הַמָּקוֹם אֲשֶׁר־אָמַר־לוֹ הָאֱלֹהִים: בַּיּוֹם הַשְּׁלִישִׁי וַיִּשָּׂא
ה אַבְרָהָם אֶת־עֵינָיו וַיַּרְא אֶת־הַמָּקוֹם מֵרָחֹק: וַיֹּאמֶר
אַבְרָהָם אֶל־נְעָרָיו שְׁבוּ־לָכֶם פֹּה עִם־הַחֲמוֹר וַאֲנִי

1] Some time afterward, God put Abraham to the test. He said to him, "Abraham," and he answered, "Here I am." **2]** And He said, "Take your son, your favored one, Isaac, whom you love, and go to the land of Moriah, and offer him there as a burnt offering on one of the heights which I will point out to you." **3]** So early next morning, Abraham saddled his ass and took with him two of his servants and his son Isaac. He split the wood for the burnt offering, and he set out for the place of which God had told him. **4]** On the third day Abraham looked up and saw the place from afar. **5]** Then Abraham said to his servants, "You stay here with the ass. The boy and I will go up there; we will worship and we will return to you."

6] Abraham took the wood for the burnt offering and put it on his son Isaac. He himself took the firestone and the knife; and the two walked off together. **7]** Then Isaac said to his father Abraham, "Father!" And he answered, "Yes, my son." And he said, "Here are the firestone and the wood; but where is the sheep for the burnt offering?" **8]** And Abraham said, "God will see to the sheep for His burnt offering, my son." And the two of them walked on together.

9] They arrived at the place of which God had told him. Abraham built an altar there; he laid out the wood; he bound his son Isaac; he laid him on the altar, on top of the wood.

22:1] *Some time afterward.* According to the Rabbis, Isaac was thirty-seven years old. However, the story should be read not in chronological order but rather as an unrelated unit; here Isaac is a mere boy.
/ The Rabbis took the death of Sarah (Gen. 23:1) to be immediately related to the Akedah (see Gleanings to Gen. 23:1–20, "Why Sarah Died"); therefore, with Sarah dying at 127 years of age, Isaac would be 37, having been born when his mother was 90 [1]./

2] *Moriah.* The original name is obscure and the actual location unknown. Subsequent biblical tradition, however, has suggested that it refers to the Temple mount in Jerusalem (II Chron. 3:1) [2]. It is believed that the city's famed Dome of the Rock is built over the rock on which Abraham bound his son.
/The Vulgate relates Moriah to מַרְאֶה (vision); the Septuagint to "high" or "lofty"—two word plays rather than etymologies./

9] Note the staccato phrases that heighten the tension. Abraham seems to move "like a sleep-walker" [3].

עַל־הַמִּזְבֵּחַ מִמַּעַל לָעֵצִים: וַיִּשְׁלַח אַבְרָהָם אֶת־ י

יָדוֹ וַיִּקַּח אֶת־הַמַּאֲכֶלֶת לִשְׁחֹט אֶת־בְּנוֹ: וַיִּקְרָא אֵלָיו יא

מַלְאַךְ יְהֹוָה מִן־הַשָּׁמַיִם וַיֹּאמֶר אַבְרָהָם אַבְרָהָם

וַיֹּאמֶר הִנֵּנִי: וַיֹּאמֶר אַל־תִּשְׁלַח יָדְךָ אֶל־הַנַּעַר וְאַל־ יב

תַּעַשׂ לוֹ מְאוּמָה כִּי עַתָּה יָדַעְתִּי כִּי־יְרֵא אֱלֹהִים

אַתָּה וְלֹא חָשַׂכְתָּ אֶת־בִּנְךָ אֶת־יְחִידְךָ מִמֶּנִּי: וַיִּשָּׂא יג

אַבְרָהָם אֶת־עֵינָיו וַיַּרְא וְהִנֵּה־אַיִל אַחַר נֶאֱחַז בַּסְּבַךְ

בְּקַרְנָיו וַיֵּלֶךְ אַבְרָהָם וַיִּקַּח אֶת־הָאַיִל וַיַּעֲלֵהוּ לְעֹלָה

תַּחַת בְּנוֹ: וַיִּקְרָא אַבְרָהָם שֵׁם־הַמָּקוֹם הַהוּא יְהֹוָה יד

יִרְאֶה אֲשֶׁר יֵאָמֵר הַיּוֹם בְּהַר יְהֹוָה יֵרָאֶה: וַיִּקְרָא טו

מַלְאַךְ יְהֹוָה אֶל־אַבְרָהָם שֵׁנִית מִן־הַשָּׁמַיִם: וַיֹּאמֶר טז

בִּי נִשְׁבַּעְתִּי נְאֻם־יְהֹוָה כִּי יַעַן אֲשֶׁר עָשִׂיתָ אֶת־הַדָּבָר

הַזֶּה וְלֹא חָשַׂכְתָּ אֶת־בִּנְךָ אֶת־יְחִידֶךָ: כִּי־בָרֵךְ יז

אֲבָרֶכְךָ וְהַרְבָּה אַרְבֶּה אֶת־זַרְעֲךָ כְּכוֹכְבֵי הַשָּׁמַיִם

וְכַחוֹל אֲשֶׁר עַל־שְׂפַת הַיָּם וְיִרַשׁ זַרְעֲךָ אֵת שַׁעַר

אֹיְבָיו: וְהִתְבָּרְכוּ בְזַרְעֲךָ כֹּל גּוֹיֵי הָאָרֶץ עֵקֶב יח

אֲשֶׁר שָׁמַעְתָּ בְּקֹלִי: וַיָּשָׁב אַבְרָהָם אֶל־נְעָרָיו וַיָּקֻמוּ יט

וַיֵּלְכוּ יַחְדָּו אֶל־בְּאֵר שָׁבַע וַיֵּשֶׁב אַבְרָהָם בִּבְאֵר

שָׁבַע: פ

וַיְהִי אַחֲרֵי הַדְּבָרִים הָאֵלֶּה וַיֻּגַּד לְאַבְרָהָם לֵאמֹר כ

10] And Abraham picked up the knife to slay his son. **11]** Then an angel of the LORD called to him from heaven: "Abraham! Abraham!" And he answered, "Here I am." **12]** And he said, "Do not raise your hand against the boy, or do anything to him. For now I know that you fear God, since you have not withheld your son, your favored one, from Me." **13]** When Abraham looked up, his eye fell upon a ram, caught in the thicket by its horns. So Abraham went and took the ram and offered it up as a burnt offering in place of his son. **14]** And Abraham named that site Adonai-yireh, whence the present saying, "On the mount of the LORD there is vision."

15] The angel of the LORD called to Abraham a second time from heaven, **16]** and said, "By Myself I swear, the LORD declares: because you have done this and have not withheld your son, your favored one, **17]** I will bestow My blessing upon you and make your descendants as numerous as the stars of heaven and the sands on the seashore; and your descendants shall seize the gates of their foes. **18]** All the nations of the earth shall bless themselves by your descendants, because you have obeyed My command." **19]** Abraham then returned to his servants, and they departed together for Beer-sheba; and Abraham stayed in Beer-sheba.

20] Some time later, Abraham was told, "Milcah too has borne children to your brother

---

13] *Ram.* The ram occupied an important place in ancient Israel's sacrificial cult (e.g., Lev. 5-15, 18; 19:21; Num. 5:8; 6:17). The image of a ram caught in the thicket was known in Ur of the Chaldees, where archeologists have found two Sumerian statues depicting the animal tied to a bush [4]. A similar substitutional offering is portrayed in Greek mythology [5].

The above translation is based, following ancient versions, on the reading אַיִל אֶחָד (a ram),

while the Masoretic text has אַחַר (after or afterward).

14] *Adonai-yireh.* "The Lord will see," an allusion to verse 8.

There is vision. Another assonance: *Adonai yera-eh.*

17] *Seize the gates of their foes.* Whereby they will possess the city.

20] *Milcah too.* Like Sarah. The names listed represent twelve tribes or princes. They parallel the

כד מִלְכָּה לְנָחוֹר אֲחִי אַבְרָהָם: וּפִילַגְשׁוֹ וּשְׁמָהּ רְאוּמָה
וַתֵּלֶד גַּם־הִוא אֶת־טֶבַח וְאֶת־גַּחַם וְאֶת־תַּחַשׁ וְאֶת־
מַעֲכָה:

כא הִנֵּה יָלְדָה מִלְכָּה גַם־הִוא בָּנִים לְנָחוֹר אָחִיךָ: אֶת־
עוּץ בְּכֹרוֹ וְאֶת־בּוּז אָחִיו וְאֶת־קְמוּאֵל אֲבִי אֲרָם:
כב וְאֶת־כֶּשֶׂד וְאֶת־חֲזוֹ וְאֶת־פִּלְדָּשׁ וְאֶת־יִדְלָף וְאֵת
כג בְּתוּאֵל: וּבְתוּאֵל יָלַד אֶת־רִבְקָה שְׁמֹנָה אֵלֶּה יָלְדָה

Haftarah Vayera, p. 334

Nahor: **21]** Uz the first-born, and Buz his brother, and Kemuel the father of Aram; **22]** and Chesed, Hazo, Pildash, Jidlaph and Bethuel"— **23]** Bethuel being the father of Rebekah. These eight Milcah bore to Nahor, Abraham's brother. **24]** And his concubine, whose name was Reumah, also bore children: Tebah, Gaham, Tahash, and Maacah.

twelve tribes of Israel and illustrate a duodecimal principle of tribal organization found also in extra-biblical sources.

/Others have suggested that these tribes were all Arameans [6]./

21] *Uz.* The name occurs several times in Genesis (10:23; 36:28). Job comes from "the land of Uz" (Job 1:1).

/Hence the talmudic tradition that Job lived in the days of Abraham [7]./

22] *Chesed.* Probably related to *Casdim*, Chaldeans.

24] *Concubine.* The institution of multiple marriage, with first-rank and second-rank wives, was widespread in the Fertile Crescent.

The Sacrifice

The practice of human sacrifice, which was well-known to the ancients and central to the cults of Israel's neighbors, stands as a backdrop to chapter 22.[1] In the framework of his time and experience, Abraham could have considered the command to sacrifice his son entirely legitimate. Otherwise he might have protested God's command with the kind of insistence he exhibited at Sodom and Gomorrah. God's demand must have struck Abraham as harsh and bitter but not as ungodly. It is therefore important to notice that in the beginning of the test the command is issued by Elohim—the generic term for God or gods—and the command is one that other elohim could and did make. But when the sacrifice is about to be performed it is Abraham's God, Adonai, who stays his hand. Elohim might ask him to proceed, but Adonai says "No." He, too, will ask extreme devotion, but it will never again take this form.

Abraham's religion not only rejects the sacrifice of a son by a father but rejects, as well, its use as a theological theme. This is in stark contrast to Eastern religions and to Christianity [9], in which a father's sacrificial gift of his son plays an important role.[2]

The Test

The text sets forth the main theme by saying that God puts Abraham to the test, but it does not state precisely what He is testing him for. Is it to test Abraham's faith that God will not go back on His promise, that somehow His design can be trusted? Or is it to test Abraham's unquestioning obedience, his faithfulness rather than his faith, his total submission to a mysterious divine will? Most likely both, for faith and faithfulness are dual aspects of biblical man's relation to God. Together they may be said to represent the quality of אֱמוּנָה (*emunah*, adherence without faltering, obedience with complete trust), which is as authentic a reflection of God's qualities as is humanly possible. For even God is obedient, not to man, to be sure, but to His own law and promise. Hence it is possible for the Bible to call God אֵל אֱמוּנָה (*El emunah*, a faithful God, in Deuteronomy 32:4). And in this sense we can speak of Abraham as אִישׁ אֱמוּנָה (*ish emunah*, a faithful man).

Abraham's act is represented as the ultimate sanctification of God in this world, the offering up of that which is dearest to him.[3] Such devotion is also shown by Hannah in Maccabean times ("She was in her spirit and courage equal to Abraham") [13] and by scores of generations to follow.

Yet the test, like Abraham's hand, remains suspended in air; like life, the test remains open-ended. When it is over, Abraham has proved himself for the moment. God sees what Abraham *is*, but what he *will be* remains hidden even from God himself. There will be new trials and challenges awaiting him in the future. In pursuing this thought, the Midrash reads the whole story of Abraham as a succession of ten severe tests [14].

Questions about the God of the Akedah

Why must God test man? Does He not know all things?

Maimonides answers that God tested (נִסָּה)

---

[1] Compare II Kings 3:27 where it is related that the king of Moab sacrificed his first-born. Sacrificing a child or passing him through fire belonged to the great abominations (see, e.g., Lev. 18:21; 20:2; Deut. 18:10), and the prophets inveighed against it (e.g.,

Mic. 6:7). There is some question whether Jephthah's daughter was indeed sacrificed (Judg. 11:29–40) and whether the custom ever did prevail in ancient Israel or what fire rites were involved [8].

[2] Note, however, the Greek tale of Phrixus in which

Abraham precisely because he knew that he would pass the test. Abraham's faith would shine like a beacon and be a sign (נֵס) to the nations. The emphasis is therefore not on Abraham's ordeal but on his strength [15].

A radically different explanation is offered by Franz Rosenzweig, who sees in the test a *temptation* by God. According to this view, God purposely conceals His true purpose; in fact, He must occasionally mislead man. If everything were clear, men would be automatons and those least free, most timid and fearful, would be the most "pious." But evidently God wants only the free to be His. He must make it difficult, nay impossible to understand His actions, so as to give man the opportunity truly to believe, that is, to ground his faith in trust and freedom. And so there remains nothing for God but to tempt man, even to deceive him [16].

Many will find it difficult to believe in a "misleading God," but if we believe at all in God we must believe in a deity who is free, just as we believe that man is free, free even to defy God's will or foreknowledge. There remains an unresolved contradiction between these freedoms, a contradiction inherent in God's relationship to man ever since the days of Eden.

What kind of a God is He? How can the compassionate God of the Bible be portrayed as asking for the sacrifice of a child?

One answer is that the test came at a time when human sacrifice was still an acceptable practice and that, therefore, in terms of its own age it was merely *the* extreme test (and after all, God did not exact the final price).

God thus may require of man in every age to give up that which he loves most. God often asks not the expected but the awesomely unexpected. Perhaps the final proof of faith and obedience rests indeed in attempting the impossible for the sake of God.

Another explanation re-interprets the text to say that it only *appeared* to Abraham that God asked him to sacrifice his child; such a request could not possibly square with the fundamental laws of morality. A midrash, therefore, suggests that Abraham misunderstood God altogether. It has God saying: "Did I tell you 'Slaughter him'? Did I not rather tell you 'Bring him up'? [A word play in Hebrew.] You brought him up on the altar, now take him down again!" [17]. In this view of the story the test both succeeds and fails. It succeeds in that it proves Abraham to be a man of faith and obedience, but it fails in that Abraham's understanding of God's nature remains deficient.

Father and Son

Even as God is the dominant Father and Abraham a trusting and obedient son, so in the purely human realm Abraham appears as the dominant father and Isaac as the archetype of the submissive son. Only once does Isaac speak and ask the fateful question; thereafter he is a mere object of the drama. Abraham, the prince and Patriarch, the honored and aged friend of God, overawes his timid son, whose will to independence may well have been crippled by doting and protective parents. He has no personality apart from his father. As one they walk together

human sacrifice is averted at the last moment because "Zeus, King of Heaven, loathes human sacrifices" [10].

[3] Compare the Christian Scriptures' appraisal of Abraham's faith and the theme of justification by

faith [11]. The Zohar emphasizes the quality of obedience that overcame Abraham's sense of compassion [12].

[4] One version suggests that, in fact, Isaac encouraged Abraham to proceed with the sacrifice [18].

to the sacrifice (Gen. 22:8), and silently Isaac submits to the dreadful act.[4]

The story may thus be read as a paradigm of a father-and-son relationship. In a way every parent seeks to dominate his child and is in danger of seeking to sacrifice him to his parental plans or hopes. In the biblical story, God is present and can therefore stay the father's hand.[5] In all too many repetitions of the scene God is absent and the knife falls. Thus is the Akedah repeated forever, with its test and its terror.

---

[5] There was, however, a remarkable tradition that insisted that Abraham completed the sacrifice and that afterward Isaac was miraculously revived. In part this arises out of the discussion on the question: "Why do people place ashes on their heads on the occasion of a public fast?" The answer is related to the "ashes of Isaac." According to this haggadah, Abraham slew his son, burnt his victim, and the ashes remain as a stored-up merit and atonement for Israel in all generations. For this reason Isaac's sacrifice is invoked in prayer, and Rabbi Ephraim ben Jacob of Bonn (twelfth century C.E.) composed a poem on the subject. This interpretation of the Akedah was given bitter relevance in medieval times when many Jewish parents killed their own children and then committed suicide to avoid forcible conversion, captivity, and torture [19].

GLEANINGS

Abraham Misunderstood

A God who asks man what the text appears to ask is not the true God but one whom man fashions in his own image. Man often believes that God wants him to sacrifice his children to an imagined demand. But then it is not God who is cruel but man; it is man who all too frequently is prepared to immolate his offspring to satisfy his own concept of duty and who will restrain his compassion before his own sense of righteousness. The history of humanity is replete with misdeeds committed in the name of religion.

AFTER A MIDRASH [20]

Go to the Land of Moriah

Two mountains were chosen by God: Mount Sinai upon which the Torah was given to Israel and Mount Moriah upon which Abraham bound his son Isaac and upon which the Temple was built. Now the matter makes one wonder: Why, indeed, was the Temple not built upon Mount Sinai which had been sanctified by the giving of the law? The answer is: The place on which a Jew bares his neck is sanctified by God more than any other place. Upon it the *Shechinah* appears and there, so to speak, the Torah is given again.

RABBI CHAIM OF TSANS [21]

Isaac Liberated

The text says that Abraham returned from Moriah but omits a mention of Isaac. Is it possible that Isaac did not come back with his father, that the trauma of near-death tore the taut strings that bound the son to the father? That Isaac now became a man who for the first time could let his father go and who would return later, at his own choosing and time? Isaac's nature is not radically changed in the Akedah, nor can his early childhood be denied its formative influence, but in the binding Isaac becomes an individual in his own right. If Abraham was tested and purified in agony, Isaac was liberated by it.

The Shofar

The shofar (usually made from a ram's horn) is nowadays blown on Rosh Hashanah and at the conclusion of Yom Kippur. It is also blown at morning services during the month preceding the new year; and it has been sounded on special occasions, such as the recapture of the Western or Wailing Wall by Israeli troops in 1967.

Said Rabbi Abbahu: "Why do we sound the horn of a ram? Because the Holy One, blessed be He, said: 'Blow Me a ram's horn that I may remember unto you the binding of Isaac the son of Abraham, and I shall account it unto you for a binding of yourselves before Me.'" TALMUD [22]

The shofar should be bent so that the children of Israel may bend their hearts toward their Father in Heaven. It is also best to blow the horn of a ram so that He may remember unto us the binding of Isaac. SHULCHAN ARUCH SHEL HA-RAV [23]

There are ten reasons for blowing the shofar.... The sixth is to remind us of the binding of Isaac who offered himself to Heaven. So ought we be ready at all times to offer our lives for the sanctification of His name. SAADIA [24]

Take Your Son

The Hebrew does not say merely קַח [take]. It says קַח-נָא [literally, "please take"]. This indicates that Abraham acted freely, and not from compulsion. It is also important to remember that the journey to Moriah took three days—time enough to arrive at a free decision. ALBO [25]

152

Note further that God says not merely "your son" but follows it by saying "your favored one," and then "Isaac." He issued the command gently, step by step, to a reluctant Abraham.   RASHI

A Prayer

Remember unto us, O Lord our God, the covenant and the lovingkindness and the oath which Thou didst swear on Mt. Moriah, and may the binding with which our father Abraham bound his son Isaac on the altar appear before Thee: how he overcame his compassion in order to perform Thy will with all his heart.

MACHZOR FOR ROSH HASHANAH [26]

The Service of Heaven

[In the Sephardic Rosh Hashanah ritual, between *Maftir* and shofar, a special hymn is sung that stresses the readiness of both Abraham and Isaac to do God's will. It also speculates about what Abraham said to Sarah before they left.]

Said he to Sarah: "Your darling Isaac is growing up,
But to serve the Heavens has he not yet learned.
I will go and teach him that he has a demanding God."
Said she: "Go, master, but go not far!"
Said he: "Rest your heart in God and trust in Him."   JUDAH SAMUEL ABBAS

Christian Interpretation

The Church Fathers saw in Akedah a prefiguration of the sacrifice of Jesus. This was based on the parallel drawn by Paul: As Abraham "did not withhold his son Isaac, so God did not withhold His own son [Jesus] but gave him up for us all."   ROMANS 8:32

The Moslem Story

And when he became a full-grown youth,
His father said to him, "My son, I have seen in a dream that I should sacrifice thee; therefore, consider what thou seest right."
He said, "My father, do what thou art bidden; of the patient, if God please, shalt thou find me."
And when they had surrendered them to the will of God, he laid him down upon his forehead.

We cried unto him, "O Abraham!
Now hast thou satisfied the vision." See how we recompense the righteous.
This was indeed a decisive test.
And we ransomed his son with a costly victim,
And we left this (salutation) for him among posterity, "Peace be on Abraham!"

KORAN [27]

A Second Time

"The angel of the Lord called to Abraham a second time" [Gen. 22:15]. Why this repetition? The reason is found in the concluding words, "because you have done this." These words place the Abrahamic promise in a totally different light. For, while hitherto the promise given to Abraham is mainly an expression of divine favor, it now comes for the first time as an acknowledgment of Abraham's worth. This is the point where divine effort meets with full response in the human being. It is toward this goal, first in Israel and then in all of mankind, that all divine efforts from the viewpoint of the Torah tend.

MORDECAI M. KAPLAN [28]

The Test

The sacrifice, though commanded, was not exacted. Abraham's hand was stayed before the fatal act was completed. This showed, once and for all, clearly and unmistakably, that, in contrast to what was imagined of the heathen deities worshiped by Israel's neighbors, the God of Israel did not demand human sacrifices of his worshipers. He demanded in reality only the surrender of Abraham's will. Abraham, by his obedience, demonstrated his readiness to part with what was dearest to him, and with something on which all his hopes for the future depended: Thus his character was "proved," the sincerity of his religion was established, and his devotion to God confirmed and strengthened. It was the supreme trial of his faith; and it triumphed. And so the narrative teaches two great lessons. On the one hand, it teaches the value set by God upon the surrender of self and obedience; on the other, it demonstrates, by a signal example, the moral superiority of Jehovah's religion above the religions of Israel's neighbors.   SAMUEL R. DRIVER [29]

Three Days

A journey is made, because God has designated the place where the sacrifice is to be performed; but we are told nothing about the journey except that it took three days, and even that we are told in a mysterious way: Abraham and his followers rose "early in the morning" and "went unto" the place of which God had told him; on the third day he lifted up his eyes and saw the place from afar. That gesture is the only gesture, is indeed the only occurrence during the whole journey, of which we are told; and though its motivation lies in the fact that the place is elevated, its uniqueness still heightens the impression that the journey took place through a vacuum; it is as if, while he traveled on, Abraham had looked neither to the right nor to the left, had suppressed any sign of life in his followers and himself save only their footfalls.

Thus the journey is like a silent progress through the indeterminate and the contingent, a holding of the breath, a process which has no present, which is inserted, like a blank duration, between what has passed and what lies ahead, and which yet is measured: three days! Three such days positively demand the symbolic interpretation which they later received.

ERICH AUERBACH [30]

Abraham Appals Me

Why then did Abraham do it? For God's sake and [in complete identity with this] for his own sake. He did it for God's sake because God required this proof of his faith; for his own sake he did it in order that he might furnish the proof. The unity of these two points of view is perfectly expressed by the word which has always been used to characterize this situation: It is a trial, a temptation. A temptation—but what does that mean? What ordinarily tempts a man is that which would keep him from doing his duty, but in this case the temptation is itself the ethical . . . which would keep him from doing God's will.

Therefore, though Abraham arouses my admiration, he at the same time appals me. . . . He who has explained this riddle has explained my life.

SÖREN KIERKEGAARD [31]

I Revere Abraham

I revere Abraham who lived the human paradox to the extreme and yet had faith that it was not fatal . . . Abraham waits for us, as the potential father of every Jew aspiring to be a good Jew: for he teaches us to live courageously the ethical under the moral law, in an existence which requires divine love superseding the ethical if it is to be healed of its tragic tensions. Hence we can confess with Kierkegaard: "No one is so great as Abraham! Who is capable of understanding him?"

EMIL L. FACKENHEIM [32]

A Psychological Interpretation

The Akedah motif is the biblical aspect of the psychology of family relationships. It is the biblical extension of the Oedipus Complex.

According to our interpretation of the Akedah motif the image of man's divine calling is introjected, in addition to the images of the parents. The introjected call of God contains an altruistic aim, and therefore love for this ego-ideal decreases narcissistic love and increases object-love. . . . The torturing inner struggle is overcome by the choice to follow the altruistic call. This is the turning point in the Akedah experience. It is accompanied by a modification of instincts. The life instinct and desire for action are promoted, and the death instinct and contentment with meditation only are relegated. Object-love is amplified to embrace all human beings and future generations. It becomes messianic love. ERIC WELLISCH [33]

The Mother's Weeping

The father lifted his eyes and a weeping
roams—wanders, endlessly, namelessly;
The son lifts his heart: the mother's weeping
flickers across heaven like a burning.

Generations climb and descend the pyre,
the slaughtered one is forgotten, the slaughterer,
  too—

but the mother's weeping lives forever.

HAYYIM ROBINSON [34]

The Death of Sarah

The recounting of the death of Sarah gives us an occasion for an assessment of the life and personality of the first Matriarch. The chapter itself is taken up with Abraham's acquisition of the cave of Machpelah for his wife's burial. The transaction is told in considerable detail because it is more than an act of deep sentiment on the part of a grieving husband.

(A new weekly portion, *Chaye Sarah*, begins here.)

פ פ פ

א וַיִּהְיוּ חַיֵּי שָׂרָה מֵאָה שָׁנָה וְעֶשְׂרִים שָׁנָה וְשֶׁבַע שָׁנִים
שְׁנֵי חַיֵּי שָׂרָה: וַתָּמָת שָׂרָה בְּקִרְיַת אַרְבַּע הִוא
חֶבְרוֹן בְּאֶרֶץ כְּנָעַן וַיָּבֹא אַבְרָהָם לִסְפֹּד לְשָׂרָה
וְלִבְכֹּתָהּ: וַיָּקָם אַבְרָהָם מֵעַל פְּנֵי מֵתוֹ וַיְדַבֵּר אֶל־
בְּנֵי־חֵת לֵאמֹר: גֵּר־וְתוֹשָׁב אָנֹכִי עִמָּכֶם תְּנוּ לִי אֲחֻזַּת־
קֶבֶר עִמָּכֶם וְאֶקְבְּרָה מֵתִי מִלְּפָנָי: וַיַּעֲנוּ בְנֵי־חֵת
אֶת־אַבְרָהָם לֵאמֹר לוֹ: שְׁמָעֵנוּ אֲדֹנִי נְשִׂיא אֱלֹהִים
אַתָּה בְּתוֹכֵנוּ בְּמִבְחַר קְבָרֵינוּ קְבֹר אֶת־מֵתֶךָ אִישׁ
מִמֶּנּוּ אֶת־קִבְרוֹ לֹא־יִכְלֶה מִמְּךָ מִקְּבֹר מֵתֶךָ: וַיָּקָם
אַבְרָהָם וַיִּשְׁתַּחוּ לְעַם־הָאָרֶץ לִבְנֵי־חֵת: וַיְדַבֵּר אִתָּם

לֵאמֹר אִם־יֵשׁ אֶת־נַפְשְׁכֶם לִקְבֹּר אֶת־מֵתִי מִלְּפָנַי
שְׁמָעוּנִי וּפִגְעוּ־לִי בְּעֶפְרוֹן בֶּן־צֹחַר: וְיִתֶּן־לִי אֶת־
מְעָרַת הַמַּכְפֵּלָה אֲשֶׁר־לוֹ אֲשֶׁר בִּקְצֵה שָׂדֵהוּ בְּכֶסֶף
מָלֵא יִתְּנֶנָּה לִי בְּתוֹכְכֶם לַאֲחֻזַּת־קָבֶר: וְעֶפְרוֹן יֹשֵׁב
בְּתוֹךְ בְּנֵי־חֵת וַיַּעַן עֶפְרוֹן הַחִתִּי אֶת־אַבְרָהָם בְּאָזְנֵי
בְנֵי־חֵת לְכֹל בָּאֵי שַׁעַר־עִירוֹ לֵאמֹר: לֹא־אֲדֹנִי שְׁמָעֵנִי
הַשָּׂדֶה נָתַתִּי לָךְ וְהַמְּעָרָה אֲשֶׁר־בּוֹ לְךָ נְתַתִּיהָ לְעֵינֵי
בְנֵי־עַמִּי נְתַתִּיהָ לָּךְ קְבֹר מֵתֶךָ: וַיִּשְׁתַּחוּ אַבְרָהָם
לִפְנֵי עַם־הָאָרֶץ: וַיְדַבֵּר אֶל־עֶפְרוֹן בְּאָזְנֵי עַם־הָאָרֶץ
לֵאמֹר אַךְ אִם־אַתָּה לוּ שְׁמָעֵנִי נָתַתִּי כֶּסֶף הַשָּׂדֶה
קַח מִמֶּנִּי וְאֶקְבְּרָה אֶת־מֵתִי שָׁמָּה: וַיַּעַן עֶפְרוֹן אֶת־

* ב כ' וְעֵרָא.

1] Sarah's lifetime—the span of Sarah's life—came to one hundred and twenty-seven years. 2] Sarah died in Kiriath-arba—now Hebron—in the land of Canaan; and Abraham proceeded to mourn for Sarah and to bewail her. 3] Then Abraham rose from beside his dead, and spoke to the Hittites, saying, 4] "I am a resident alien among you; sell me a burial site among you, that I may remove my dead for burial." 5] And the Hittites replied to Abraham, saying to him, 6] "Hear us, my lord; you are the elect of God among us. Bury your dead in the choicest of our burial places; none of us will withhold his burial place from you for burying your dead." 7] Thereupon Abraham bowed low to the people of the land, the Hittites, 8] and he said to them, "If it is your wish that I remove my dead for burial, you must agree to intercede for me with Ephron son of Zohar. 9] Let him sell me the cave of Machpelah which he owns, which is at the edge of his land. Let him sell it to me, at the full price, for a burial site in your midst."

10] Ephron was present among the Hittites; so Ephron the Hittite answered Abraham in the hearing of the Hittites, all who entered the gate of his town, saying, 11] "No, my lord, hear me: I give you the field and I give you the cave that is in it; I give it to you in the presence of my people. Bury your dead." 12] Then Abraham bowed low before the people of the land, 13] and spoke to Ephron in the hearing of the people of the land, saying, "If only you would hear me out! Let me pay the price of the land; accept it from me, that I may bury my dead

---

23:1] *One hundred and twenty-seven years.* A combination of the "ideal life span" (120) and the sacred number 7.

2] *Kiriath-arba—now Hebron.* See note at Gen. 13:18.
/Kiriath-arba may mean "City of Arba" (a non-Semitic name) or "City of Four" (the alternate "Hebron" might mean "group city")./
Mourn . . . bewail. A description both of sentiment and of a set ritual.

3] *The Hittites.* Southern migrants of the Syrian Neo-Hittites; see above at 10:15 [1].

4] *A resident alien.* Who lacks certain privileges that citizens have, in this case, the right to own land. The community must rule on any exceptions.

6] *Elect of God.* Or "mighty prince."

10] *All who entered the gate.* All his fellow townsmen.

בּוֹ וְכָל־הָעֵץ אֲשֶׁר בַּשָּׂדֶה אֲשֶׁר בְּכָל־גְּבֻלוֹ סָבִיב: יה אַבְרָהָם לֵאמֹר לוֹ: אֲדֹנִי שְׁמָעֵנִי אֶרֶץ אַרְבַּע מֵאֹת

יח לְאַבְרָהָם לְמִקְנָה לְעֵינֵי בְנֵי־חֵת בְּכֹל בָּאֵי שַׁעַר־   שֶׁקֶל־כֶּסֶף בֵּינִי וּבֵינְךָ מַה־הִוא וְאֶת־מֵתְךָ קְבֹר:

עִירוֹ: יט וְאַחֲרֵי־כֵן קָבַר אַבְרָהָם אֶת־שָׂרָה אִשְׁתּוֹ אֶל־   טז וַיִּשְׁמַע אַבְרָהָם אֶל־עֶפְרוֹן וַיִּשְׁקֹל אַבְרָהָם לְעֶפְרֹן

מְעָרַת שְׂדֵה הַמַּכְפֵּלָה עַל־פְּנֵי מַמְרֵא הִוא חֶבְרוֹן   אֶת־הַכֶּסֶף אֲשֶׁר דִּבֶּר בְּאָזְנֵי בְנֵי־חֵת אַרְבַּע מֵאוֹת

בְּאֶרֶץ כְּנָעַן: כ וַיָּקָם הַשָּׂדֶה וְהַמְּעָרָה אֲשֶׁר־בּוֹ   שֶׁקֶל כֶּסֶף עֹבֵר לַסֹּחֵר: יז וַיָּקָם שְׂדֵה עֶפְרוֹן אֲשֶׁר

לְאַבְרָהָם לַאֲחֻזַּת־קָבֶר מֵאֵת בְּנֵי־חֵת: ס   בַּמַּכְפֵּלָה אֲשֶׁר לִפְנֵי מַמְרֵא הַשָּׂדֶה וְהַמְּעָרָה אֲשֶׁר־

there." **14]** And Ephron replied to Abraham, saying to him, **15]** "My lord, do hear me! A piece of land worth four hundred shekels of silver—what is that between you and me? Go and bury your dead." **16]** Abraham accepted Ephron's terms. Abraham paid out to Ephron the money that he had named in the hearing of the Hittites—four hundred shekels of silver at the going merchants' rate.

17] So Ephron's land in Machpelah, near Mamre—the field with its cave and all the trees anywhere within the confines of that field— **18]** passed to Abraham as his possession, in the presence of the Hittites, of all who entered the gate of his town. **19]** And then Abraham buried his wife Sarah in the cave of the field of Machpelah, facing Mamre—now Hebron—in the land of Canaan. **20]** Thus the field with its cave passed from the Hittites to Abraham, as a burial site.

15] *Four hundred shekels.* A description not of generosities exchanged but of a typical business procedure that follows a pattern of introductory offers and refusals. Abraham wants no gift, he needs a purchase title like any citizen. Ephron takes full advantage of the situation and exacts what appears to be a very high price. While differences in time and monetary value make comparisons difficult, it might be noted that Omri (ninth century B.C.E.) paid 6,000 shekels (two talents) for the land on which Samaria was built (I Kings 16:24) and that a small plot like Machpelah could be had for 17 shekels *ca.* 600 B.C.E. (Jer. 32:9).

/The contractual arrangements between Abraham and Ephron follow a definite legal pattern known in the ancient Near East. Recent studies have suggested a relationship of Gen. 23 to the so-called "Dialogue Document" of neo-Babylonian times, attested first for the eighth century B.C.E. [2]./

16] *Merchants' rate.* For silver. There being no coinage, the silver was weighed. Shekel was a weight, hence there was a "shekel of silver" as well as a "shekel of gold."

19] *Machpelah.* Pilgrims of all three faiths visit the cave in Hebron as a holy site. The sarcophagi shown there, however, belong to a later age and may or may not stand over actual burial grounds [3]. There is a Moslem tradition that Joseph too was buried here and a Jewish tradition that Joseph's brothers found their resting place in Machpelah (see *Encyclopaedia Judaica*, Vol. 11, col. 673). According to Genesis all the Patriarchs and Matriarchs except for Rachel were buried here (Gen. 49:29–32; 50:13). No reference to Machpelah occurs in any other book of the Bible outside of Genesis.

Sarah

A midrash says that we hear of Sarah's death in connection with her lifetime (Gen. 23:1) because her years were truly filled with life and that this is one of the reasons why the Hebrew text expresses her life span of 127 years in an unusually extended fashion as 100 years and 20 years and 7 years [4].

The biblical text gives us relatively few facts about her life: She accompanied her husband to Haran and then on his fateful journey to Canaan; she was childless till her old age and then could not believe the prophecy of the divine messenger; she herself gave Hagar as a concubine to Abraham, only to expel her thereafter; and twice—in Egypt and Gerar—Sarah found that her beauty endangered Abraham and, therefore, agreed to dissemble their relationship. In the process, she incurred the grave peril of possibly becoming another man's mistress to save her husband's life.

What kind of woman was she? Above all, she was the wife of a pioneer. She left the ease of the city for the dangers of a semi-nomadic existence; she left her family to become, with her husband, a stranger in a strange land. She was a beautiful woman, jealous of her husband's love and zealous for her own position; she was a mother who, craving the best for her child, was cruel for his sake. Despite this, later generations considered her a paragon of beauty and piety (see Gen. 12:10–20 and Gleanings to Gen. 12:10–13:18). Her name means princess, and, though the information about her is scanty, we may conclude that the name properly describes the helpmate of the great Patriarch.

Machpelah

Why is the Bible so concerned with the acquisition of a grave site?

A close reading of the text reveals a profound anxiety behind Abraham's measured phrases. After all, he has no assurance that the Hittites will agree to his request. He might have to bury his wife somewhere by the roadside, in no man's land, just as Jacob was later forced to do. At this moment of his life, after the fearful trial at Moriah and bereaved of his beloved wife, Abraham seeks desperately for something physical, some place—even a grave site—to call his own. Yet again his hope is tried and he must ask others, strangers, to do what he cannot do for himself and what God can only promise—to obtain a mere piece of earth. The few moments of bargaining represent, therefore, another trial of the Patriarch. In the glimpse of this man bowing low before the Hittites, we see the friend of God torn once more between agony and hope.

Further, the burial place is a token. God promised Abraham and his descendants the land; Machpelah, then, is a visible sign of the future. A burial place for the dead is the only piece of land that Abraham, a nonresident, can hope to acquire. It represents a token title to the Promised Land and a symbol of possession when the people are far from the land—whether in Egyptian slavery or European exile.[1]

But why did Abraham, the faithful one, need Machpelah as a token? Simply because he was human; by his very humanity he represents the possibilities as well as the limits of faith. Men will live and die for ideals that they know will not be realized in their lifetime, yet they strive to see at least a portion, however small, accomplished. And just as Abraham represents the religious man, so does the Holy Land represent the possibilities and potentials of Jewish hope. Often a part has stood for the whole; often the acquisition of a single dunam of ground has been the promise of larger settlement in the future. Judaism has always been more than mere hope, or fulfilment postponed, and has always looked to some this-worldly expression of progress toward its long-range hopes.

---

[1] A midrash says: "Let no one claim that the land was stolen" [5]. The Talmud records a series of arguments over conflicting claims of the children of Isaac and of Ishmael [6].

GLEANINGS

Why Sarah Died

Abraham returned alone from Moriah, and Sarah, believing Isaac to have been sacrificed, died of grief.

MIDRASH [7]

Woman of Valor

Twenty-two biblical women are worthy of the term "woman of valor" [Prov. 31:10]. Among them, Sarah was the greatest, and therefore she is the only woman whose age is given in Scripture.

MIDRASH [8]

Abraham Mourned and Bewailed

One weeps for three days, mourns for seven, and, in some ways, for thirty.

TALMUD [9]

Humility

He who possesses these three traits is one of the disciples of our father Abraham: a generous eye, a meek spirit, and a humble soul. How do we know that Abraham possessed a meek spirit? While the children of Heth call him a prince, he refers to himself by saying: "I am a resident alien among you" [Gen. 23:4].

MIDRASH [10]

It further says: "Abraham bowed low before the people of the land" [Gen. 23:12]. The Hebrew literally says "before the עַם הָאָרֶץ" [am ha-aretz], which later came to mean "the common people." To do what Abraham did is the sign of the great man.

CHASIDIC [11]

By Purchase

Today, when Israel is again settled in its own land, Machpelah is of minor significance except, of course, for the sentiments of religious and historical respect it elicits. In ancient times, Machpelah represented title by purchase. Similarly in modern times, land in Israel was acquired by purchase only, until the wars of 1948 and 1967 unexpectedly altered the process.

Machpelah Today

The site of the cave is today generally identified with Kharam el Khalil in Hebron. A huge wall surrounds the area. Inside the compound, the Byzantines built a Christian church which was later converted into a mosque by the Moslems who gained possession of the city and the site. In time, both Jews and Christians were prohibited from praying inside the area, but Jews could approach it by ascending the first five (later, seven) steps. After 1967, when Israel conquered the city, all faiths were once more permitted to visit the tombs.

The actual cave which is below the site is presently inaccessible. Two small openings lead to it from inside the mosque. It is surmised that there are two or possibly three caverns below; their actual shape is not known.

ENCYCLOPAEDIA JUDAICA [12]

Rebekah at the Well

The story of Rebekah's betrothal is set in a society that was becoming increasingly patriarchal and that was also polygamous. However, the beginnings of monogamous alliances can already be found in Genesis. The phrase "Man leaves his father and mother and clings to his wife" (Gen. 2:24) strongly indicates this trend. Note that Isaac, unlike Abraham and Jacob, is monogamous [1].

A bride was obtained for a price (מֹהַר, *mohar*); although, as in Jacob's case, a bridegroom could on occasion substitute personal services for money. The marriage ceremony itself was minimal: The bride was veiled and brought to the bridegroom's tent.

With the idyllic narrative of Isaac's marriage to Rebekah, the Abraham cycle comes to a close. The focus shifts from the Patriarch to Rebekah, Matriarch-to-be of the next generation. Again, the reader is made aware of the ever-present theme of Genesis—behind all human arrangements stands God.

א וְאַבְרָהָם זָקֵן בָּא בַּיָּמִים וַיהוָה בֵּרַךְ אֶת־אַבְרָהָם

ב בַּכֹּל: וַיֹּאמֶר אַבְרָהָם אֶל־עַבְדּוֹ זְקַן בֵּיתוֹ הַמֹּשֵׁל

ג בְּכָל־אֲשֶׁר־לוֹ שִׂים־נָא יָדְךָ תַּחַת יְרֵכִי: וְאַשְׁבִּיעֲךָ
בַּיהוָה אֱלֹהֵי הַשָּׁמַיִם וֵאלֹהֵי הָאָרֶץ אֲשֶׁר לֹא־תִקַּח
אִשָּׁה לִבְנִי מִבְּנוֹת הַכְּנַעֲנִי אֲשֶׁר אָנֹכִי יוֹשֵׁב בְּקִרְבּוֹ:

ד כִּי אֶל־אַרְצִי וְאֶל־מוֹלַדְתִּי תֵּלֵךְ וְלָקַחְתָּ אִשָּׁה לִבְנִי

ה לְיִצְחָק: וַיֹּאמֶר אֵלָיו הָעֶבֶד אוּלַי לֹא־תֹאבֶה הָאִשָּׁה
לָלֶכֶת אַחֲרַי אֶל־הָאָרֶץ הַזֹּאת הֶהָשֵׁב אָשִׁיב אֶת־

ו בִּנְךָ אֶל־הָאָרֶץ אֲשֶׁר־יָצָאתָ מִשָּׁם: וַיֹּאמֶר אֵלָיו

ז אַבְרָהָם הִשָּׁמֶר לְךָ פֶּן־תָּשִׁיב אֶת־בְּנִי שָׁמָּה: יְהוָה
אֱלֹהֵי הַשָּׁמַיִם אֲשֶׁר לְקָחַנִי מִבֵּית אָבִי וּמֵאֶרֶץ
מוֹלַדְתִּי וַאֲשֶׁר דִּבֶּר־לִי וַאֲשֶׁר נִשְׁבַּע־לִי לֵאמֹר
לְזַרְעֲךָ אֶתֵּן אֶת־הָאָרֶץ הַזֹּאת הוּא יִשְׁלַח מַלְאָכוֹ

ח לְפָנֶיךָ וְלָקַחְתָּ אִשָּׁה לִבְנִי מִשָּׁם: וְאִם־לֹא תֹאבֶה
הָאִשָּׁה לָלֶכֶת אַחֲרֶיךָ וְנִקִּיתָ מִשְּׁבֻעָתִי זֹאת רַק אֶת־

ט בְּנִי לֹא תָשֵׁב שָׁמָּה: וַיָּשֶׂם הָעֶבֶד אֶת־יָדוֹ תַּחַת יֶרֶךְ

1] Abraham was now old, advanced in years, and the LORD had blessed Abraham in all things. **2]** And Abraham said to the senior servant of his household, who had charge of all that he owned, "Put your hand under my thigh **3]** and I will make you swear by the LORD, the God of heaven and the God of the earth, that you will not take a wife for my son from the daughters of the Canaanites among whom I dwell, **4]** but will go to the land of my birth and get a wife for my son Isaac." **5]** And the servant said to him, "What if the woman does not consent to follow me to this land, shall I then take your son back to the land from which you came?" **6]** Abraham answered him, "On no account must you take my son back there! **7]** The LORD, the God of heaven, who took me from my father's house and from my native land, who promised me on oath, saying, 'I will give this land to your offspring'—He will send His angel before you, and you will get a wife for my son from there. **8]** And if the woman does not consent to follow you, you shall then be clear of this oath to me; but do not take my son back there." **9]** So the servant put his hand under the thigh of his master Abraham and swore to him as bidden.

24:2] *The senior servant.* Possibly (though not definitely) the Eliezer of Gen. 15:2.

Under my thigh. See Gen. 47:29. The symbolic gesture may have implied a curse of sterility on the offender. (Sons are said to issue "from the thigh." See the Hebrew text of Exod. 1:5). Some suggest that this act involved touching the testicles [2]. Assyrians placed the hand on the breast; Greeks, on the knee; Arabs, under the armpit or on the belt. The custom of swearing while placing one's hand on some object persists in our time; in Jewish tradition certain oaths were made while holding *tefillin* or a scroll of the Torah. The servant is probably the executor of Abraham's will; hence he and not Isaac swears [3].

/Rashi compares the servant's procedure with oaths which require the holding of an object (חֵפֶץ שֶׁל

מִצְוָה). Ibn Ezra considers the act to be a symbol of submission; similarly Abarbanel who compares it to the servant holding the stirrup./

3] *Daughters of the Canaanites.* Abraham wants his son to remain a stranger in Canaan, hence he commands marriage within his own group. Here are the beginning strands of Judaism's strong feelings about mixed marriages—although the term cannot yet, of course, be applied for many centuries. What is at stake is religion and family tradition, not ethnic or racial "purity."

7] *My native land.* Or "land of my kindred" (see Gen. 12:1).

God . . . promised me on oath. That is, solemnly. Abraham's last words are about land and posterity.

9] *As bidden.* Literally, "about this matter."

אַבְרָהָם אֲדֹנָיו וַיִּשָּׁבַע לוֹ עַל־הַדָּבָר הַזֶּה: וַיִּקַּח י

הָעֶבֶד עֲשָׂרָה גְמַלִּים מִגְּמַלֵּי אֲדֹנָיו וַיֵּלֶךְ וְכָל־טוּב

אֲדֹנָיו בְּיָדוֹ וַיָּקָם וַיֵּלֶךְ אֶל־אֲרַם נַהֲרַיִם אֶל־עִיר

נָחוֹר: וַיַּבְרֵךְ הַגְּמַלִּים מִחוּץ לָעִיר אֶל־בְּאֵר הַמָּיִם יא

לְעֵת עֶרֶב לְעֵת צֵאת הַשֹּׁאֲבֹת: וַיֹּאמַר יְהוָֹה אֱלֹהֵי יב

אֲדֹנִי אַבְרָהָם הַקְרֵה־נָא לְפָנַי הַיּוֹם וַעֲשֵׂה־חֶסֶד עִם

אֲדֹנִי אַבְרָהָם: הִנֵּה אָנֹכִי נִצָּב עַל־עֵין הַמָּיִם וּבְנוֹת יג

אַנְשֵׁי הָעִיר יֹצְאֹת לִשְׁאֹב מָיִם: וְהָיָה הַנַּעֲרָ אֲשֶׁר יד

אֹמַר אֵלֶיהָ הַטִּי־נָא כַדֵּךְ וְאֶשְׁתֶּה וְאָמְרָה שְׁתֵה וְגַם־

גְּמַלֶּיךָ אַשְׁקֶה אֹתָהּ הֹכַחְתָּ לְעַבְדְּךָ לְיִצְחָק וּבָהּ

אֵדַע כִּי־עָשִׂיתָ חֶסֶד עִם־אֲדֹנִי: וַיְהִי־הוּא טֶרֶם כִּלָּה טו

לְדַבֵּר וְהִנֵּה רִבְקָה יֹצֵאת אֲשֶׁר יֻלְּדָה לִבְתוּאֵל

בֶּן־מִלְכָּה אֵשֶׁת נָחוֹר אֲחִי אַבְרָהָם וְכַדָּהּ עַל־שִׁכְמָהּ:

וְהַנַּעֲרָ טֹבַת מַרְאֶה מְאֹד בְּתוּלָה וְאִישׁ לֹא יְדָעָהּ טז

וַתֵּרֶד הָעַיְנָה וַתְּמַלֵּא כַדָּהּ וַתָּעַל: וַיָּרָץ הָעֶבֶד יז

לִקְרָאתָהּ וַיֹּאמֶר הַגְמִיאִינִי נָא מְעַט־מַיִם מִכַּדֵּךְ:

וַתֹּאמֶר שְׁתֵה אֲדֹנִי וַתְּמַהֵר וַתֹּרֶד כַּדָּהּ עַל־יָדָהּ יח

וַתַּשְׁקֵהוּ: וַתְּכַל לְהַשְׁקֹתוֹ וַתֹּאמֶר גַּם לִגְמַלֶּיךָ אֶשְׁאָב יט

עַד אִם־כִּלּוּ לִשְׁתֹּת: וַתְּמַהֵר וַתְּעַר כַּדָּהּ אֶל־הַשֹּׁקֶת כ

וַתָּרָץ עוֹד אֶל־הַבְּאֵר לִשְׁאֹב וַתִּשְׁאַב לְכָל־גְּמַלָּיו:

* יד הנערה קרי.   טז והנערה קרי.

10] Then the servant took ten of his master's camels and set out, taking with him all the bounty of his master; and he made his way to Aram-naharaim, to the city of Nahor. **11]** He made the camels kneel down by the well outside the city, at evening time, the time when women come out to draw water. **12]** And he said, "O LORD, God of my master Abraham, grant me good fortune this day, and deal graciously with my master Abraham: **13]** Here I stand by the spring as the daughters of the townsmen come out to draw water; **14]** let the maiden to whom I say, 'Please, lower your jar that I may drink,' and who replies, 'Drink, and I will also water your camels'—let her be the one whom You have decreed for Your servant Isaac. Thereby shall I know that You have dealt graciously with my master."

15] He had scarcely finished speaking, when Rebekah, who was born to Bethuel, the son of Milcah the wife of Abraham's brother Nahor, came out with her jar on her shoulder. **16]** The maiden was very beautiful, a virgin whom no man had known. She went down to the spring, filled her jar, and came up. **17]** The servant ran toward her and said, "Please, let me sip a little water from your jar." **18]** "Drink, my lord," she said, and she quickly lowered her jar upon her hand and let him drink. **19]** When she had let him drink his fill, she said, "I will also draw for your camels, until they finish drinking." **20]** Quickly emptying her jar into the trough, she ran back to the well to draw, and she drew for all his camels.

21] The man, meanwhile, stood gazing at her, silently wondering whether the LORD had

---

10] *Aram-naharaim.* Literally, "Aram-of-the-two-rivers." On Haran, see introduction to Gen. 11:27–12:9, "The Call of Abraham."

11] *By the well.* Jacob and Moses also wooed at a well (Gen. 29:9–11; Exod. 2:15–21).

12] The vocalizers of the Hebrew text put the musical sign *shalshelet* (chain) over וַיֹּאמַר. The *shalshelet* indicates a pause and occurs relatively seldom. Possibly its placement here was to indicate the hesitation of the servant.

כא וְהָאִישׁ מִשְׁתָּאֵה לָהּ מַחֲרִישׁ לָדַעַת הַהִצְלִיחַ יְהוָה
כב דַּרְכּוֹ אִם־לֹא: וַיְהִי כַּאֲשֶׁר כִּלּוּ הַגְּמַלִּים לִשְׁתּוֹת וַיִּקַּח הָאִישׁ נֶזֶם זָהָב בֶּקַע מִשְׁקָלוֹ וּשְׁנֵי צְמִידִים עַל־
כג יָדֶיהָ עֲשָׂרָה זָהָב מִשְׁקָלָם: וַיֹּאמֶר בַּת־מִי אַתְּ הַגִּידִי
כד נָא לִי הֲיֵשׁ בֵּית־אָבִיךְ מָקוֹם לָנוּ לָלִין: וַתֹּאמֶר אֵלָיו בַּת־בְּתוּאֵל אָנֹכִי בֶּן־מִלְכָּה אֲשֶׁר יָלְדָה לְנָחוֹר:
כה וַתֹּאמֶר אֵלָיו גַּם־תֶּבֶן גַּם־מִסְפּוֹא רַב עִמָּנוּ גַּם־מָקוֹם
כו לָלוּן: וַיִּקֹּד הָאִישׁ וַיִּשְׁתַּחוּ לַיהוָה: וַיֹּאמֶר בָּרוּךְ
כז יְהוָה אֱלֹהֵי אֲדֹנִי אַבְרָהָם אֲשֶׁר לֹא־עָזַב חַסְדּוֹ וַאֲמִתּוֹ מֵעִם אֲדֹנִי אָנֹכִי בַּדֶּרֶךְ נָחַנִי יְהוָה בֵּית אֲחֵי
כח אֲדֹנִי: וַתָּרָץ הַנַּעֲרָ וַתַּגֵּד לְבֵית אִמָּהּ כַּדְּבָרִים

* כח הנערה קרי.

כט הָאֵלֶּה: וּלְרִבְקָה אָח וּשְׁמוֹ לָבָן וַיָּרָץ לָבָן אֶל־הָאִישׁ
ל הַחוּצָה אֶל־הָעָיִן: וַיְהִי כִּרְאֹת אֶת־הַנֶּזֶם וְאֶת־הַצְּמִדִים עַל־יְדֵי אֲחֹתוֹ וּכְשָׁמְעוֹ אֶת־דִּבְרֵי רִבְקָה אֲחֹתוֹ לֵאמֹר כֹּה־דִבֶּר אֵלַי הָאִישׁ וַיָּבֹא אֶל־הָאִישׁ וְהִנֵּה עֹמֵד עַל־
לא הַגְּמַלִּים עַל־הָעָיִן: וַיֹּאמֶר בּוֹא בְּרוּךְ יְהוָה לָמָּה תַעֲמֹד בַּחוּץ וְאָנֹכִי פִּנִּיתִי הַבַּיִת וּמָקוֹם לַגְּמַלִּים:
לב וַיָּבֹא הָאִישׁ הַבַּיְתָה וַיְפַתַּח הַגְּמַלִּים וַיִּתֵּן תֶּבֶן וּמִסְפּוֹא לַגְּמַלִּים וּמַיִם לִרְחֹץ רַגְלָיו וְרַגְלֵי הָאֲנָשִׁים אֲשֶׁר
לג אִתּוֹ: וַיּוּשַׂם לְפָנָיו לֶאֱכֹל וַיֹּאמֶר לֹא אֹכַל עַד אִם־
לד דִּבַּרְתִּי דְּבָרָי וַיֹּאמֶר דַּבֵּר: וַיֹּאמַר עֶבֶד אַבְרָהָם
לה אָנֹכִי: וַיהוָה בֵּרַךְ אֶת־אֲדֹנִי מְאֹד וַיִּגְדָּל וַיִּתֶּן־לוֹ צֹאן

* לו וישם קרי.

made his errand successful or not. **22]** When the camels had finished drinking, the man took a gold nose-ring weighing a half-shekel, and two gold bands for her arms, ten shekels in weight. **23]** "Pray tell me," he said, "whose daughter are you? Is there room in your father's house for us to spend the night?" **24]** She replied, "I am the daughter of Bethuel the son of Milcah whom she bore to Nahor." **25]** And she went on, "There is plenty of straw and feed at home, and also room to spend the night." **26]** The man bowed low in homage to the LORD **27]** and said, "Blessed be the LORD, the God of my master Abraham, who has not withheld His steadfast kindness from my master. For I have been guided on my errand by the LORD, to the house of my master's kinsmen."

28] The maiden ran and told all this to her mother's household. **29]** Now Rebekah had a brother whose name was Laban. Laban ran out to the man at the spring— **30]** when he saw the nose-ring and the bands on his sister's arms, and when he heard his sister Rebekah say, "Thus the man spoke to me." He went up to the man, who was still standing beside the camels at the spring. **31]** "Come in, O blessed of the LORD," he said, "why do you remain outside, when I have made ready the house and a place for the camels?" **32]** So the man entered the house, and the camels were unloaded. The camels were given straw and feed, and water was brought to bathe his feet and the feet of the men with him. **33]** But when food was set before him, he said, "I will not eat until I have told my tale." He said, "Speak, then."

34] "I am Abraham's servant," he began. **35]** "The LORD has greatly blessed my master,

22] *Nose-ring.* A gift of special prominence that everyone would see (cf. the simile of God giving a nose-ring to Israel; Ezek. 16:12).

Weighing a half-shekel. בֶּקַע (beka), about 1/5 ounce (see Exod. 38:26).

25] *Straw.* תֶּבֶן (shredded straw), which in the East is mixed with feed (cf. verse 32).

34-41] Amidst the elaborate repetition (a device found also in other Near Eastern literature), we can observe subtle and finely worked out differences; for instance, Abraham's instructions are tactfully omitted here.

וּבָקָר֙ וָכֶ֔סֶף וְזָהָ֖ב וַעֲבָדִ֣ם וּשְׁפָחֹ֑ת וּגְמַלִּ֖ים וַחֲמֹרִֽים:

הָעַלְמָ֖ה הַיֹּצֵ֣את לִשְׁאֹ֑ב וְאָמַרְתִּ֥י אֵלֶ֖יהָ הַשְׁקִֽינִי־נָ֥א

לו וַתֵּ֡לֶד שָׂרָה֩ אֵ֨שֶׁת אֲדֹנִ֤י בֵן֙ לַֽאדֹנִ֔י אַחֲרֵ֖י זִקְנָתָ֑הּ

מד מְעַט־מַ֣יִם מִכַּדֵּ֑ךְ וְאָמְרָ֣ה אֵלַ֔י גַּם־אַתָּ֣ה שְׁתֵ֔ה וְגַ֥ם

לז וַיִּתֶּן־ל֖וֹ אֶת־כָּל־אֲשֶׁר־לֽוֹ: וַיַּשְׁבִּעֵ֥נִי אֲדֹנִ֖י לֵאמֹ֑ר לֹא־

לִגְמַלֶּ֖יךָ אֶשְׁאָ֑ב הִ֣וא הָֽאִשָּׁ֔ה אֲשֶׁר־הֹכִ֥יחַ יְהֹוָ֖ה לְבֶן־

תִקַּ֤ח אִשָּׁה֙ לִבְנִ֔י מִבְּנוֹת֙ הַֽכְּנַעֲנִ֔י אֲשֶׁ֥ר אָנֹכִ֖י יֹשֵׁ֥ב

מה אֲדֹנִֽי: אֲנִ֞י טֶ֣רֶם אֲכַלֶּ֣ה לְדַבֵּ֣ר אֶל־לִבִּ֗י וְהִנֵּ֨ה רִבְקָ֜ה

לח בְּאַרְצֽוֹ: אִם־לֹ֧א אֶל־בֵּית־אָבִ֛י תֵּלֵ֖ךְ וְאֶל־מִשְׁפַּחְתִּ֑י

יֹצֵ֗את וְכַדָּהּ֙ עַל־שִׁכְמָ֔הּ וַתֵּ֥רֶד הָעַ֖יְנָה וַתִּשְׁאָ֑ב וָאֹמַ֥ר

לט וְלָקַחְתָּ֥ אִשָּׁ֖ה לִבְנִֽי: וָאֹמַ֖ר אֶל־אֲדֹנִ֑י אֻלַ֛י לֹא־תֵלֵ֥ךְ

אֵלֶ֖יהָ הַשְׁקִ֣ינִי נָֽא: וַתְּמַהֵ֗ר וַתּ֤וֹרֶד כַּדָּהּ֙ מֵֽעָלֶ֔יהָ

מ הָאִשָּׁ֖ה אַחֲרָֽי: וַיֹּ֣אמֶר אֵלָ֑י יְהֹוָ֞ה אֲשֶׁר־הִתְהַלַּ֣כְתִּי

וַתֹּ֣אמֶר שְׁתֵ֔ה וְגַם־גְּמַלֶּ֖יךָ אַשְׁקֶ֑ה וָאֵ֕שְׁתְּ וְגַ֥ם הַגְּמַלִּ֖ים

לְפָנָ֗יו יִשְׁלַ֤ח מַלְאָכוֹ֙ אִתָּ֔ךְ וְהִצְלִ֣יחַ דַּרְכֶּ֑ךָ וְלָקַחְתָּ֣

מא הִשְׁקָֽתָה: וָאֶשְׁאַ֣ל אֹתָ֗הּ וָֽאֹמַר֙ בַּת־מִ֣י אַ֔תְּ וַתֹּ֗אמֶר

אִשָּׁ֤ה לִבְנִי֙ מִמִּשְׁפַּחְתִּ֔י וּמִבֵּ֖ית אָבִֽי: אָ֤ז תִּנָּקֶה֙ מֵאָ֣לָתִ֔י

בַּת־בְּתוּאֵל֙ בֶּן־נָח֔וֹר אֲשֶׁ֥ר יָֽלְדָה־לּ֖וֹ מִלְכָּ֑ה וָֽאָשִׂ֤ם

כִּ֥י תָב֖וֹא אֶל־מִשְׁפַּחְתִּ֑י וְאִם־לֹ֤א יִתְּנוּ֙ לָ֔ךְ וְהָיִ֥יתָ נָקִ֖י

מב מֵֽאָלָתִֽי: וָאָבֹ֥א הַיּ֖וֹם אֶל־הָעָ֑יִן וָֽאֹמַ֗ר יְהֹוָה֙ אֱלֹהֵ֣י

הַנֶּ֨זֶם֙ עַל־אַפָּ֔הּ וְהַצְּמִידִ֖ים עַל־יָדֶֽיהָ: וָאֶקֹּ֥ד וָאֶֽשְׁתַּחֲוֶ֖ה

אֲדֹנִ֣י אַבְרָהָ֔ם אִם־יֶשְׁךָ־נָּא֙ מַצְלִ֣יחַ דַּרְכִּ֔י אֲשֶׁ֥ר אָנֹכִ֖י

מג הֹלֵ֥ךְ עָלֶֽיהָ: הִנֵּ֛ה אָנֹכִ֥י נִצָּ֖ב עַל־עֵ֣ין הַמָּ֑יִם וְהָיָ֤ה

לַֽיהֹוָ֑ה וָאֲבָרֵ֗ךְ אֶת־יְהֹוָה֙ אֱלֹהֵי֙ אֲדֹנִ֣י אַבְרָהָ֔ם אֲשֶׁ֣ר

מט הִנְחַ֣נִי בְּדֶ֣רֶךְ אֱמֶ֔ת לָקַ֛חַת אֶת־בַּת־אֲחִ֥י אֲדֹנִ֖י לִבְנֽוֹ: וְעַתָּ֠ה אִם־יֶשְׁכֶ֨ם עֹשִׂ֥ים חֶ֛סֶד וֶֽאֱמֶ֖ת אֶת־אֲדֹנִ֑י הַגִּ֣ידוּ

and he has become rich: He has given him sheep and cattle, silver and gold, male and female slaves, camels and asses. **36]** And Sarah, my master's wife, bore my master a son in her old age, and he has given him everything he owns. **37]** Now my master made me swear, saying, 'You shall not get a wife for my son from the daughters of the Canaanites in whose land I dwell; **38]** but you shall go to my father's house, to my kindred, and get a wife for my son.' **39]** And I said to my master, 'What if the woman does not follow me?' **40]** He replied to me, 'The LORD, whose ways I have followed, will send His angel with you and make your errand successful; and you will get a wife for my son from my kindred, from my father's house. **41]** Thus only shall you be freed from my adjuration: if, when you come to my kindred, they refuse you—only then shall you be freed from my adjuration.'

42] "I came today to the spring, and I said: O LORD, God of my master Abraham, if You would indeed grant success to the errand on which I am engaged! **43]** As I stand by the spring of water, let the young woman who comes out to draw and to whom I say, 'Please, let me drink a little water from your jar,' **44]** and who answers, 'You may drink, and I will also draw for your camels'—let her be the wife whom the LORD has decreed for my master's son.' **45]** I had scarcely finished praying in my heart, when Rebekah came out with her jar on her shoulder, and went down the spring and drew. And I said to her, 'Please give me a drink.' **46]** She quickly lowered her jar and said, 'Drink, and I will also water your camels.' So I drank, and she also watered the camels. **47]** I inquired of her, 'Whose daughter are you?' And she said, 'The daughter of Bethuel son of Nahor, whom Milcah bore to him.' And I put the ring on her nose and the bands on her arms. **48]** Then I bowed low in homage to the LORD and blessed the LORD, the God of my master Abraham, who led me on the right way to get the daughter of my master's brother for his son. **49]** And now, if you mean to treat my master with true kindness,

לִי וְאִם־לֹא הַגִּידוּ לִי וְאֶפְנֶה עַל־יָמִין אוֹ עַל־שְׂמֹאל:

אֲלֵהֶם אַל־תְּאַחֲרוּ אֹתִי וַיהוָה הִצְלִיחַ דַּרְכִּי שַׁלְּחוּנִי
וְאֵלְכָה לַאדֹנִי: וַיֹּאמְרוּ נִקְרָא לַנַּעֲרָ וְנִשְׁאֲלָה אֶת־
פִּיהָ: וַיִּקְרְאוּ לְרִבְקָה וַיֹּאמְרוּ אֵלֶיהָ הֲתֵלְכִי עִם־
הָאִישׁ הַזֶּה וַתֹּאמֶר אֵלֵךְ: וַיְשַׁלְּחוּ אֶת־רִבְקָה אֲחֹתָם
וְאֶת־מֵנִקְתָּהּ וְאֶת־עֶבֶד אַבְרָהָם וְאֶת־אֲנָשָׁיו: וַיְבָרְכוּ
אֶת־רִבְקָה וַיֹּאמְרוּ לָהּ אֲחֹתֵנוּ אַתְּ הֲיִי לְאַלְפֵי רְבָבָה
וְיִירַשׁ זַרְעֵךְ אֵת שַׁעַר שֹׂנְאָיו: וַתָּקָם רִבְקָה וְנַעֲרֹתֶיהָ
וַתִּרְכַּבְנָה עַל־הַגְּמַלִּים וַתֵּלַכְנָה אַחֲרֵי הָאִישׁ וַיִּקַּח
הָעֶבֶד אֶת־רִבְקָה וַיֵּלַךְ: וְיִצְחָק בָּא מִבּוֹא בְּאֵר
לַחַי רֹאִי וְהוּא יוֹשֵׁב בְּאֶרֶץ הַנֶּגֶב: וַיֵּצֵא יִצְחָק

נ וַיַּעַן לָבָן וּבְתוּאֵל וַיֹּאמְרוּ מֵיהוָה יָצָא הַדָּבָר לֹא
נא נוּכַל דַּבֵּר אֵלֶיךָ רַע אוֹ־טוֹב: הִנֵּה־רִבְקָה לְפָנֶיךָ
קַח וָלֵךְ וּתְהִי אִשָּׁה לְבֶן־אֲדֹנֶיךָ כַּאֲשֶׁר דִּבֶּר יְהוָה:
נב וַיְהִי כַּאֲשֶׁר שָׁמַע עֶבֶד אַבְרָהָם אֶת־דִּבְרֵיהֶם וַיִּשְׁתַּחוּ
נג אַרְצָה לַיהוָה: וַיּוֹצֵא הָעֶבֶד כְּלֵי־כֶסֶף וּכְלֵי זָהָב
וּבְגָדִים וַיִּתֵּן לְרִבְקָה וּמִגְדָּנֹת נָתַן לְאָחִיהָ וּלְאִמָּהּ:
נד וַיֹּאכְלוּ וַיִּשְׁתּוּ הוּא וְהָאֲנָשִׁים אֲשֶׁר־עִמּוֹ וַיָּלִינוּ וַיָּקוּמוּ
נה בַבֹּקֶר וַיֹּאמֶר שַׁלְּחֻנִי לַאדֹנִי: וַיֹּאמֶר אָחִיהָ וְאִמָּהּ
נו תֵּשֵׁב הַנַּעֲרָ אִתָּנוּ יָמִים אוֹ עָשׂוֹר אַחַר תֵּלֵךְ: וַיֹּאמֶר

* נה הנערה קרי.　　נו לנערה קרי.

tell me; and if not, tell me also, that I may turn right or left."

50] Then Laban and Bethuel answered, "The matter was decreed by the LORD; we cannot speak to you bad or good. **51]** Here is Rebekah before you; take her and go, and let her be a wife to your master's son, as the LORD has spoken." **52]** When Abraham's servant heard their words, he bowed low to the ground before the LORD. **53]** The servant brought out objects of silver and gold, and garments, and gave them to Rebekah; and he gave presents to her brother and her mother. **54]** Then he and the men with him ate and drank, and they spent the night. When they arose next morning, he said, "Give me leave to go to my master." **55]** But her brother and her mother said, "Let the maiden remain with us some ten days; then you may go." **56]** He said to them, "Do not delay me, now that the LORD has made my errand successful. Give me leave that I may go to my master." **57]** And they said, "Let us call the girl and ask for her reply." **58]** They called Rebekah and said to her, "Will you go with this man?" And she said, "I will." **59]** So they sent off their sister Rebekah and her nurse along with Abraham's servant and his men. **60]** And they blessed Rebekah and said to her. "O sister! / May you grow into / Thousands of myriads; / May your offspring seize / The gates of their foes." **61]** Then Rebekah and her maids arose, mounted the camels, and followed the man. So the servant took Rebekah and went his way.

62] Isaac had just come back from the vicinity of Beer-lahai-roi, for he was settled in the

50] *Bethuel.* Some believe that the name was added later and that the story reads more easily if we assume that Laban acted as head of the family because Bethuel had already died. It is more likely, however, that this is a trace of an earlier societal pattern in which the "mother's household" (verse 28) played a sizable role (see commentary to Gen. 12:10–13:18, footnote 1).

53] *Presents.* Representing also the purchase price of the bride.

55] *Some ten days.* Literally, "days or ten." According to Rashi, the phrase means "a year or ten months" (the expression "days" is used in this way in Lev. 25:29). The Mishnah records: "An engaged virgin is to be granted twelve months to prepare herself" [4]. The servant would not have refused a delay of a mere ten days.

57] *Let us call the girl.* Note that Rebekah is asked to consent to the marriage, as was customary also in Nuzi.

לָשׂוּחַ בַּשָּׂדֶה לִפְנוֹת עָרֶב וַיִּשָּׂא עֵינָיו וַיַּרְא וְהִנֵּה   אֶת־זִמְרָן וְאֶת־יָקְשָׁן וְאֶת־מְדָן וְאֶת־מִדְיָן וְאֶת־יִשְׁבָּק
סד גְמַלִּים בָּאִים: וַתִּשָּׂא רִבְקָה אֶת־עֵינֶיהָ וַתֵּרֶא אֶת־   וְאֶת־שׁוּחַ: ג וְיָקְשָׁן יָלַד אֶת־שְׁבָא וְאֶת־דְּדָן וּבְנֵי דְדָן
סה יִצְחָק וַתִּפֹּל מֵעַל הַגָּמָל: וַתֹּאמֶר אֶל־הָעֶבֶד מִי־   ד הָיוּ אַשּׁוּרִם וּלְטוּשִׁם וּלְאֻמִּים: וּבְנֵי מִדְיָן עֵיפָה
הָאִישׁ הַלָּזֶה הַהֹלֵךְ בַּשָּׂדֶה לִקְרָאתֵנוּ וַיֹּאמֶר הָעֶבֶד   וָעֵפֶר וַחֲנֹךְ וַאֲבִידָע וְאֶלְדָּעָה כָּל־אֵלֶּה בְּנֵי קְטוּרָה:
סו הוּא אֲדֹנִי וַתִּקַּח הַצָּעִיף וַתִּתְכָּס: וַיְסַפֵּר הָעֶבֶד   ה וַיִּתֵּן אַבְרָהָם אֶת־כָּל־אֲשֶׁר־לוֹ לְיִצְחָק: ו וְלִבְנֵי
סז לְיִצְחָק אֵת כָּל־הַדְּבָרִים אֲשֶׁר עָשָׂה: וַיְבִאֶהָ יִצְחָק   הַפִּילַגְשִׁים אֲשֶׁר לְאַבְרָהָם נָתַן אַבְרָהָם מַתָּנֹת
הָאֹהֱלָה שָׂרָה אִמּוֹ וַיִּקַּח אֶת־רִבְקָה וַתְּהִי־לוֹ לְאִשָּׁה   וַיְשַׁלְּחֵם מֵעַל יִצְחָק בְּנוֹ בְּעוֹדֶנּוּ חַי קֵדְמָה אֶל־
וַיֶּאֱהָבֶהָ וַיִּנָּחֵם יִצְחָק אַחֲרֵי אִמּוֹ:   פ   ז אֶרֶץ קֶדֶם: וְאֵלֶּה יְמֵי שְׁנֵי־חַיֵּי אַבְרָהָם אֲשֶׁר־חָי
א וַיֹּסֶף אַבְרָהָם וַיִּקַּח אִשָּׁה וּשְׁמָהּ קְטוּרָה: וַתֵּלֶד לוֹ

region of the Negeb.   63] And Isaac went out walking in the field toward evening and, looking up, he saw camels approaching.   64] Raising her eyes, Rebekah saw Isaac. She alighted from the camel   65] and said to the servant, "Who is that man walking in the field toward us?" And the servant said, "That is my master." So she took her veil and covered herself.   66] The servant told Isaac all the things that he had done.   67] Isaac then brought her into the tent of his mother Sarah, and he took Rebekah as his wife. Isaac loved her, and thus found comfort after his mother's death.

1] Abraham took another wife, whose name was Keturah.   2] She bore him Zimran, Jokshan, Medan, Midian, Ishbak, and Shuah.   3] Jokshan begot Sheba and Dedan. The descendants of Dedan were the Asshurim, the Letushim, and the Leummim.   4] The descendants of Midian were Ephan, Epher, Enoch, Abida, and Eldaah. All these were descendants of Keturah.   5] Abraham willed all that he owned to Isaac;   6] but to Abraham's sons by concubines Abraham gave gifts while he was still living; and he sent them away from his son Isaac eastward, to the land of the East.

7] This was the total span of Abraham's life: one hundred and seventy-five years.   8] And

63] *Walking.* Or perhaps "meditating," which better fits the characterization of Isaac (see commentary to Gen. 26:1–35).

65] *She took her veil.* Veiling the bride was required of free women in Middle Assyrian law. A traditional Jewish marriage is even now preceded by the *bedecken* ceremony—the covering of the bride with a veil, while the groom utters the words from Gen. 24:60: "May you grow into/Thousands of myriads."

67] *Comfort after his mother's death.* A clue to Isaac's personality (see commentary to Gen. 26:1–35).

25:1–8] Clearly a postscript. Some commentators took this section to refer not to the time after Sarah's death but to an earlier phase in Abraham's life and identified Keturah with Hagar [5]. There is no textual evidence for this interpretation.

Medanites and Shebaites (Sabeans) were merchants in the Red Sea area as were the Midianites who dwelled farther to the north. Asshurim are not Assyrians but an Arab tribe. Others, like Hanoch (Enoch), are difficult to identify.

5–6] The notation about Abraham's will and the gifts to the other children serve to insure Isaac's title to the inheritance.

יג הַמִּצְרִית שִׁפְחַת שָׂרָה לְאַבְרָהָם: וְאֵלֶּה שְׁמוֹת בְּנֵי
יִשְׁמָעֵאל בִּשְׁמֹתָם לְתוֹלְדֹתָם בְּכֹר יִשְׁמָעֵאל נְבָיֹת
וְקֵדָר וְאַדְבְּאֵל וּמִבְשָׂם: וּמִשְׁמָע וְדוּמָה וּמַשָּׂא: חֲדַד
טו וְתֵימָא יְטוּר נָפִישׁ וָקֵדְמָה: אֵלֶּה הֵם בְּנֵי יִשְׁמָעֵאל
וְאֵלֶּה שְׁמֹתָם בְּחַצְרֵיהֶם וּבְטִירֹתָם שְׁנֵים־עָשָׂר נְשִׂיאִם
לְאֻמֹּתָם: וְאֵלֶּה שְׁנֵי חַיֵּי יִשְׁמָעֵאל מְאַת שָׁנָה וּשְׁלֹשִׁים
יז שָׁנָה וְשֶׁבַע שָׁנִים וַיִּגְוַע וַיָּמָת וַיֵּאָסֶף אֶל־עַמָּיו: וַיִּשְׁכְּנוּ
מֵחֲוִילָה עַד־שׁוּר אֲשֶׁר עַל־פְּנֵי מִצְרַיִם בֹּאֲכָה אַשּׁוּרָה
עַל־פְּנֵי כָל־אֶחָיו נָפָל:

Haftarah Chaye Sarah, p. 338

ח מְאַת שָׁנָה וְשִׁבְעִים שָׁנָה וְחָמֵשׁ שָׁנִים: וַיִּגְוַע וַיָּמָת
אַבְרָהָם בְּשֵׂיבָה טוֹבָה זָקֵן וְשָׂבֵעַ וַיֵּאָסֶף אֶל־עַמָּיו:
ט וַיִּקְבְּרוּ אֹתוֹ יִצְחָק וְיִשְׁמָעֵאל בָּנָיו אֶל־מְעָרַת
הַמַּכְפֵּלָה אֶל־שְׂדֵה עֶפְרֹן בֶּן־צֹחַר הַחִתִּי אֲשֶׁר עַל־
י פְּנֵי מַמְרֵא: הַשָּׂדֶה אֲשֶׁר־קָנָה אַבְרָהָם מֵאֵת בְּנֵי־חֵת
יא שָׁמָּה קֻבַּר אַבְרָהָם וְשָׂרָה אִשְׁתּוֹ: וַיְהִי אַחֲרֵי מוֹת
אַבְרָהָם וַיְבָרֶךְ אֱלֹהִים אֶת־יִצְחָק בְּנוֹ וַיֵּשֶׁב יִצְחָק
עִם־בְּאֵר לַחַי רֹאִי:
פ
יב וְאֵלֶּה תֹּלְדֹת יִשְׁמָעֵאל בֶּן־אַבְרָהָם אֲשֶׁר יָלְדָה הָגָר

Abraham breathed his last, dying at a good ripe age, old and contented; and he was gathered to his kin. **9]** His sons Isaac and Ishmael buried him in the cave of Machpelah, in the field of Ephron son of Zohar the Hittite, facing Mamre, **10]** the field that Abraham had bought from the Hittites; there Abraham was buried, and Sarah his wife. **11]** After the death of Abraham, God blessed his son Isaac. And Isaac settled near Beer-lahai-roi.

12] This is the line of Ishmael, Abraham's son, whom Hagar the Egyptian, Sarah's slave, bore to Abraham. **13]** These are the names of the sons of Ishmael, by their names, in the order of their birth: Nebaioth, the first-born of Ishmael, Kedar, Adbeel, Mibsam, **14]** Mishma, Dumah, Massa, **15]** Hadad, Tema, Jetur, Naphish, and Kedmah. **16]** These are the sons of Ishmael and these are their names by their villages and by their encampments: twelve chieftains of as many tribes.— **17]** These were the years of the life of Ishmael: one hundred and thirty-seven years; then he breathed his last and died, and was gathered to his kin.— **18]** They dwelt from Havilah, by Shur, which is close to Egypt, all the way to Asshur; they camped alongside all their kinsmen.

8] *Gathered to his kin.* An idiomatic expression for "he died."

9] *Isaac and Ishmael.* After Abraham's death, or possibly after Sarah's, the two brothers seem to live in harmony.

12-16] The list is a formal one, also featuring twelve tribes (see note to Gen. 22:20). Best known is Kedar, mentioned in prophetic writings (cf. Isa. 21:16; Jer. 2:10).

On Marriage

The story of Rebekah's betrothal reveals the biblical attitude toward the nature and content of marriage. The union between man and woman must be grounded in the finest qualities, and Rebekah exhibits them to perfection. Her behavior shows modesty and hospitality; she is kind to animals and respectful of her own family. It is for such attributes that the servant prays; a woman who possesses them is indeed "very beautiful."

The marriage was arranged although the two principals had not as yet met. Modern man who thinks of marriage primarily as the fulfilment of a romantic relationship will find it difficult to see significant values in arranged marriages. But, for biblical man, the ideal was not "first love, then marriage," as it is today, but the reverse, "first marriage, then love."

The older system rested on the assumption that two persons will have a proper foundation for marriage if their backgrounds are generally compatible and if they set themselves to establish a home in which each partner plays his expected role. The two will come to know each other through marriage, and it is hoped that in time love will follow. Such love grows from shared experience, from mutual respect, and from affection for offspring. This arrangement raised fewer expectations and, therefore, was less subject to breakdown. At its best, it was no less productive of deep and abiding love than modern marriages that are expected to begin with it and maintain it forever.

The acceptability of marital arrangements was strengthened by an ancient belief that marriages were literally "made in heaven." According to one midrash, arranging marriages has been one of God's important occupations since creation [6]. This midrash is not only a wry comment on the complexity of the problem but also implies that God is the ultimate guarantor of the union.[1] The relationship of man and wife is more than cohabitation and convenience, it is קִדּוּשִׁין (kiddushin, holiness), a sacred partnership. God directed the servant's way to Rebekah, whose qualities would match the great task to which Isaac was committed: to carry forward the divine promise to generations yet unborn. Thus, the story of Abraham, the friend of God, comes to its end with a vision of the future.

The Servant's Prayer

In chapter 24, verse 12, Abraham's servant prays for "good fortune" (הַקְרֵה, literally, bring something [good] to pass). This is the first prayer for divine guidance recorded in the Bible, and it comes from the heart and mouth of a nameless individual.

He asks for a sign, not a miracle; he uses neither magic nor divination and does not attempt to force the hand of God. To the storyteller, the fact that the ideal conditions stipulated in the servant's prayer were met precisely signifies that God guided not only the destiny of Isaac and Rebekah but also the prayer of the servant [8]. There is, in the framework of this story, no dividing line between the natural and the supernatural. Biblical man had a deep conviction about God's role in human affairs. God was thought to be approachable, as near as prayer itself, a guide and guardian who like a father looked after his children or like a master looked after his servants.

Abraham's messenger did what most modern men who pray still do: He looked for external manifestations of the Divine. Men who believe in God may differ on what prayer should be or how it is answered; they will disagree on whether the servant had a "right" to ask for a sign; but they themselves will frequently pray as did the servant and say simply, directly, and with hope: "Grant me good fortune."

[1] Another saying: "A heavenly voice goes forth and proclaims: so and so shall marry so and so" [7].

GLEANINGS

The Way of the Bible

The patriarchal stories, like the previous Genesis tales, frequently use numbers as symbols. Abraham lived for 175 years, Isaac 180, Jacob 147. These numbers form a series: 7×5^2 (175), 5×6^2 (180), 3×7^2 (147). [9]

The use of numerical symmetry is Scripture's way of conveying the conviction that the formative age in Israel's history was not a series of haphazard incidents but the fulfilment of God's grand design. . . . The patriarchal chronologies constitute paradigmatic rather than pragmatic history.

NAHUM SARNA [10]

Abraham Was Old

Until Abraham's time old people did not look their age; but Abraham asked God to match his looks to his age.

R. Aha said: "One may have the dignity of old age without its years, or length of days without the dignity of old age." Here, however, the dignity of old age was matched by length of days, and a long life was matched by the dignity of age.

MIDRASH [11]

Rebekah's Decision

She said "I will" (Gen. 24:58), meaning she would go of her own will even without her parents' consent. From this a halachah is derived that even if parents object to a child's moving to the land of Israel (as Rebekah was prepared to do) one need not listen to them. [12]

The Death of Abraham

While sitting under the oak of Mamre, Abraham perceived a flashing of light and a smell of sweet odor, and turning around he saw Death coming toward him in great glory and beauty. And Death said unto Abraham: "Think not, Abraham, that this beauty is mine or that I come thus to every man. Nay, but, if any one is righteous like thee, I thus take a crown and come to him; but, if he is a sinner, I come in great corruption and out of their sins I make a crown for my head, and I shake them with great fear so that they are dismayed." Abraham said to him, "And art thou, indeed, he that is called Death?" He answered and said, "I am the bitter name." But Abraham answered, "I will not go with thee." And Abraham said to Death, "Show us thy corruption." And Death revealed his corruption, showing two heads, the one had the face of a serpent, the other head was like a sword. All the servants of Abraham, looking at the fierce mien of Death, died, but Abraham prayed to the Lord, and He raised them up. As the looks of Death were not able to cause Abraham's soul to depart from him, God removed the soul of Abraham as in a dream, and the archangel Michael took it up into heaven. After great praise and glory had been given to the Lord by the angels who brought Abraham's soul, and after Abraham bowed down to worship, then came the voice of God, saying thus: "Take My friend Abraham into Paradise, where are the tabernacles of My righteous ones and the abodes of My saints Isaac and Jacob in his bosom, where there is no trouble, nor grief, nor sighing, but peace and rejoicing and life unending."

MIDRASH [13]

PART IV

The Line of Isaac

The Twins

With Abraham's death we might expect the Bible's attention to focus on Isaac. But it shifts immediately from him to his children, for Isaac serves primarily as the link between Abraham and Jacob.

The main theme continues: God watches over His chosen ones as they grow in understanding of the divine element in their lives.

(A new weekly portion, *Toledot*, begins here.)

פ פ פ

יט וְאֵ֣לֶּה תּוֹלְדֹ֥ת יִצְחָ֖ק בֶּן־אַבְרָהָ֑ם אַבְרָהָ֖ם הוֹלִ֥יד

כ אֶת־יִצְחָ֑ק וַיְהִ֤י יִצְחָק֙ בֶּן־אַרְבָּעִ֣ים שָׁנָ֔ה בְּקַחְתּ֣וֹ אֶת־

רִבְקָ֗ה בַּת־בְּתוּאֵל֙ הָֽאֲרַמִּ֔י מִפַּדַּ֖ן אֲרָ֑ם אֲח֛וֹת לָבָ֥ן

כא הָאֲרַמִּ֖י ל֥וֹ לְאִשָּֽׁה׃ וַיֶּעְתַּ֨ר יִצְחָ֤ק לַֽיהֹוָה֙ לְנֹ֣כַח אִשְׁתּ֔וֹ

כִּ֥י עֲקָרָ֖ה הִ֑וא וַיֵּעָ֤תֶר לוֹ֙ יְהֹוָ֔ה וַתַּ֖הַר רִבְקָ֥ה אִשְׁתּֽוֹ׃

כב וַיִּתְרֹֽצֲצ֤וּ הַבָּנִים֙ בְּקִרְבָּ֔הּ וַתֹּ֣אמֶר אִם־כֵּ֔ן לָ֥מָּה זֶּ֖ה

כג אָנֹ֑כִי וַתֵּ֖לֶךְ לִדְרֹ֥שׁ אֶת־יְהֹוָֽה׃ וַיֹּ֨אמֶר יְהֹוָ֜ה לָ֗הּ שְׁנֵ֤י

גֹיִים֙ בְּבִטְנֵ֔ךְ וּשְׁנֵ֣י לְאֻמִּ֔ים מִמֵּעַ֖יִךְ יִפָּרֵ֑דוּ וּלְאֹם֙

כד מִלְאֹ֣ם יֶֽאֱמָ֔ץ וְרַ֖ב יַעֲבֹ֥ד צָעִֽיר׃ וַיִּמְלְא֥וּ יָמֶ֖יהָ לָלֶ֑דֶת

כה וְהִנֵּ֥ה תוֹמִ֖ם בְּבִטְנָֽהּ׃ וַיֵּצֵ֤א הָרִאשׁוֹן֙ אַדְמוֹנִ֔י כֻּלּ֖וֹ

כו כְּאַדֶּ֣רֶת שֵׂעָ֑ר וַיִּקְרְא֥וּ שְׁמ֖וֹ עֵשָֽׂו׃ וְאַֽחֲרֵי־כֵ֞ן יָצָ֣א

אָחִ֗יו וְיָד֤וֹ אֹחֶ֙זֶת֙ בַּעֲקֵ֣ב עֵשָׂ֔ו וַיִּקְרָ֥א שְׁמ֖וֹ יַעֲקֹ֑ב

וְיִצְחָ֛ק בֶּן־שִׁשִּׁ֥ים שָׁנָ֖ה בְּלֶ֥דֶת אֹתָֽם׃ וַיִּגְדְּלוּ֙ הַנְּעָרִ֔ים

* כג גוים קרי. כד חסר.

19] This is the story of Isaac, son of Abraham. Abraham begot Isaac. 20] Isaac was forty years old when he took to wife Rebekah, daughter of Bethuel the Aramean of Paddan-aram, sister of Laban the Aramean. 21] Isaac pleaded with the LORD on behalf of his wife, because she was barren; and the LORD responded to his plea, and his wife Rebekah conceived. 22] But the children struggled in her womb, and she said, "If so, why do I exist?" She went to inquire of the LORD, 23] and the LORD answered her, "Two nations are in your womb,/ Two separate peoples shall issue from your body;/ One people shall be mightier than the other,/ And the older shall serve the younger." 24] When her time to give birth was at hand, there were twins in her womb. 25] The first one emerged red, like a hairy mantle all over; so they named him Esau. 26] Then his brother emerged, holding on to the heel of Esau; so they named him Jacob. Isaac was sixty years old when they were born.

25:19] *The story.* Or, "the line."

20] *Paddan-aram.* The area where Haran was located. The name came into use after the Arameans displaced the Hurrians.

21] *Barren.* For twenty years. Isaac was forty years old when he married and sixty when his children were born (Gen. 25:26). On the theme of barrenness, see Gen. 16:2. The Bible considers Rebekah's condition to be God's will.

22] *If so, why do I exist?* The intent of the Hebrew text is uncertain. Rebekah is probably asking, "What good is life if I have to suffer like this?"

She went to inquire. Rebekah consulted an oracle. The answer she is given explains her pain: She will give birth to twins who are at strife within her womb and who will be at odds with each other in years to come.

/ Rashi, like the Midrash: "She inquired at the teaching house of Shem."/

25] *Esau.* Possibly related to the Arabic *a'tha* (thick-haired); synonym of שֵׂעִיר (*se-ir*), a word play on שֵׂעָר (*se-ar*, hair). Esau resembles the uncivilized man of "Gilgamesh," Enkidu, who has shaggy hair and lives in open spaces [1].

Esau is later also known as Edom (Gen. 25:30). Esau, Seir, and Edom were probably geographical names originally, which in their application to the son of Isaac became largely interchangeable in the Bible.

26] *Jacob.* יַעֲקֹב, a word play on עָקֵב (*akev*, heel). The verb means to overreach (Jer. 9:3): Jacob tried to overreach his brother. Other names from the root are Akiba and Ukba. Modern scholars compare the name Jacob with Yakub-el (May El protect), a name found in numerous Syrian and Mesopotamian documents of the early second millennium B.C.E. [2].

/Note also A. Jeremias, who finds the ancient circle motif in Jacob's holding onto Esau's heel and compares it to the Eve-and-snake circle. Jacob in turn fears that Esau will try to crush him [3]./

וַיְהִי עֵשָׂו אִישׁ יֹדֵעַ צַיִד אִישׁ שָׂדֶה וְיַעֲקֹב אִישׁ תָּם כֹּז אֶת־בְּכֹרָתְךָ לִי: וַיֹּאמֶר עֵשָׂו הִנֵּה אָנֹכִי הוֹלֵךְ לָמוּת

כח יֹשֵׁב אֹהָלִים: וַיֶּאֱהַב יִצְחָק אֶת־עֵשָׂו כִּי־צַיִד בְּפִיו לֹב וְלָמָּה־זֶּה לִי בְּכֹרָה: וַיֹּאמֶר יַעֲקֹב הִשָּׁבְעָה לִּי כַּיּוֹם

כט וְרִבְקָה אֹהֶבֶת אֶת־יַעֲקֹב: וַיָּזֶד יַעֲקֹב נָזִיד וַיָּבֹא לד וַיִּשָּׁבַע לוֹ וַיִּמְכֹּר אֶת־בְּכֹרָתוֹ לְיַעֲקֹב: וְיַעֲקֹב נָתַן

ל עֵשָׂו מִן־הַשָּׂדֶה וְהוּא עָיֵף: וַיֹּאמֶר עֵשָׂו אֶל־יַעֲקֹב לְעֵשָׂו לֶחֶם וּנְזִיד עֲדָשִׁים וַיֹּאכַל וַיֵּשְׁתְּ וַיָּקָם וַיֵּלַךְ

הַלְעִיטֵנִי נָא מִן־הָאָדֹם הָאָדֹם הַזֶּה כִּי עָיֵף אָנֹכִי פ וַיִּבֶז עֵשָׂו אֶת־הַבְּכֹרָה:

לא עַל־כֵּן קָרָא־שְׁמוֹ אֱדוֹם: וַיֹּאמֶר יַעֲקֹב מִכְרָה כַיּוֹם

27] When the boys grew up, Esau became a skillful hunter, a man of the outdoors; but Jacob was a mild man, who stayed in camp. 28] Isaac favored Esau because he had a taste for game; but Rebekah favored Jacob. 29] Once when Jacob was cooking a stew, Esau came in from the open, famished. 30] And Esau said to Jacob, "Give me some of that red stuff to gulp down, for I am famished"—which is why he was named Edom. 31] Jacob said, "First sell me your birthright." 32] And Esau said, "I am at the point of death, so of what use is my birthright to me?" 33] But Jacob said, "Swear to me first." So he swore to him and sold his birthright to Jacob. 34] Jacob then gave Esau bread and lentil stew; and he ate and drank, and he rose and went away. Thus did Esau spurn the birthright.

27] *A mild man.* תָּם (tam) can also mean "simple" as in the Passover Haggadah in reference to the third son. Jacob, the mild indoor man, rather than Esau, the outdoor man and hunter, emerges as God's favorite.

/Compare also the stories of Parsifal and others that cast the physically inferior (or even the "perfect fool") in the role of hero. In Oriental tales the huntsman belongs to the lower (i.e., undesirable) world [4]./

28] *He had a taste for game.* Literally, "game was in his mouth." The literal reading may reflect the ancient custom of relatives pre-chewing food for children and old parents [5].

29] *Was cooking.* Among nomads and semi-nomads the males often prepared the food.

30] *Edom.* אֱדוֹם, word play on אָדַם (adom, red); others relate the word to *idam*, an Arabic dish [6]. Esau wants to "gulp down" the food and this depicts him as the uncouth, outdoor man.

The Birthright

In many cultures the first-born son has had preferred inheritance and status, succeeding his father as head of the family. In Canaan as in various Near Eastern countries, he received a double portion of inheritance and was given a seat of honor amongst his brothers (Gen. 43:33). In Judaism he had a special relation not only to his parents and siblings but also to God. He was considered quasi-holy, set aside as a possession of God (like the first fruit of herd and field), and this relationship was recognized in ceremonial ways (as in Exod. 13:12–15; 34:20; Num. 18:15; and the custom of *pidyon ha-ben*, redeeming the first-born on the thirtieth day of his life, which still survives in traditional Jewish practice). The people of Israel were called God's first-born (Exod. 4:22), which meant that they had a particular position in the divine scheme.

First-born status came through natural birth, although in early biblical days the right could be lost because of a misdeed as in Reuben's case (Gen. 49:3–4; I Chron. 5:1), cancelled through blessings as in Manasseh's case (Gen. 48:13–20), or sold as in Esau's case.[1] In later biblical times, depriving the first-born of his rights was expressly forbidden (Deut. 21:15–17).

While the natural order of birth was believed to have divine approval, God was not bound by it in an automatic relationship. He remains free to change His mind and to choose whom He needs in critical moments of history. This is the meaning of the recurrent theme of preferring the younger brother to the older. Many of Israel's great men came to their prominence because God took them out of their inferior natural position: Joseph, Ephraim, Moses, and David all were second- or late-born. While the sibling motif is not unique to biblical tradition—the Greeks have the story of Akrisios and Proitos, the Romans of Romulus and Remus—it is an important and even essential way of showing how divine guidance continually governs the history of Israel. For, though Jacob's acquisition of the birthright is given a legal basis,[2] the story is primarily one of spiritual blessings rather than legal advantages.

The Moral Problem

Buying and selling, indeed any change of birthright was no ordinary matter, yet here this important right is bartered away in what appears to be a shoddy manner. How could divine privilege come to a man such as Jacob who emerges from the story as somewhat less than admirable?

Some interpreters stress the folksy nature of the tale, saying that it is intended to make the listener or reader laugh at the way the stupid Esau stumbled into the trap laid by the clever Jacob. In those days, they say, Jacob's action was not subject to disapproval, so that the tale was one of gamesmanship without moral overtones [10].

Other commentators deny any presence of humor and, instead, see Jacob desperately striving to become the one who carries on the religious heritage of his fathers. Jewish tradition interpreted the fact that he "stayed in camp" to mean that he gave himself to learning and study and that through meditation came to a knowledge of God [11]. He believed himself to be more suited for the great task than Esau and, therefore, would not let this boorish and obviously indifferent brother stand in his way [12].

This latter theme is also pursued by others

---

[1] Nuzi records also deal with these relationships, and a document from northwest Syria permits the prenatal selection of the first-born [7].

[2] This was hermeneutically derived from כָּיוֹם in Gen. 25:33 [8]. The lentil stew was considered a token of the sale, not the true price [9].

who try to exculpate Jacob.[3] Esau was a hunter, they say, whose chief pleasure in life was killing and eating. "Esau's belly was his god; Esau's want lay in his fleshly appetite" [15]. He despised the birthright that he should have held sacred; to satisfy his appetite, he was willing to sacrifice eternity.

In this way the story is seen as a paradigm, i.e., as presenting a truth applicable to other men and other times. Esau stands for the run-of-the-mill man, Jacob for the exception. As Roger Williams wrote 300 years ago:

"What are all the contentions and wars of this world about, generally, but for greater dishes and bowls of porridge, of which, if we believe God's Spirit in Scripture, Esau and Jacob were types? Esau will part with the heavenly birthright for his supping, after his hunting, for god belly; and Jacob will part with porridge for an eternal inheritance" [16].

But although such explanations establish that Jacob was in fact more capable than his brother to carry the divine responsibility, they do not answer the question: Are the means Jacob employs to gain his ends morally justifiable? The answer must be no. On closer examination the Bible itself makes this judg-ment on Jacob. But the judgment is implicit, not explicit; it must be seen in the full context of Jacob's life, which develops into a tragedy.[4]

Where Abraham's life was struggle and triumph and Isaac's essentially one of quiescence and persistence, Jacob's is a long succession of trials and tragedies. What he touches often turns to ashes; from the moment he grasps his brother's heel at birth he desperately tries to fashion his fortune. Yet even as he succeeds, he fails. The doubtful exchange of food for birthright brings him a brother's enmity and still does not insure him his father's blessing. He deceives his father and will be deceived in turn by Laban; he will lose his beloved wife and his favorite son; and he will end his days in a strange land, a pensioner of his child. It is no wonder he will say in restrospect that his years were "few and evil" (Gen. 47:9) [18].

There is then a judgment; it lies in the tragic biography of a God-seeker who comprehends neither how to seek nor how to find. Much will happen before he becomes Israel. His failures and successes, his sufferings and joys, as well as his moral debilities and strengths, will foreshadow what will happen to the people who bear his name.

[3] A favorite explanation: Esau was wicked from the moment he was born and even before [13]. But one tradition at least suggests that, since the birthright was obtained by cunning, Jacob's descendants were destined to serve the descendants of Esau [14].

[4] See notes at Gen. 29:25, 26. Sarna, however, finds the Bible's disapproval to be quite explicit and remarkable as a moral stance at a time when what Jacob did was perfectly acceptable [17].

GLEANINGS

Heel and Hand

In allegorical language the present corrupt age is presented as Esau, the glorious age which is to follow at once is represented as Jacob: Jacob's hand held Esau's heel from the beginning. The "heel" of the first age is Esau; the "hand" of the second is Jacob. "The beginning of a man is his hand, and the end of a man is his heel. Between heel and hand seek for nothing else, Ezra!"

ESDRAS [19]

The Fateful Day

Esau sold his birthright on the day of Abraham's death; had the latter lived to see Esau despise his birthright, he could not have been said to have died in ripe old age. Jacob had prepared a mourner's meal. Why lentils? Because they are round, and mourning rolls from one person to another. Further, as lentils have no opening, so should one while mourning speak of no extraneous matters. From this also derives the custom of serving eggs at the beginning of a mourner's meal, for they roll and have no opening. RASHI

Esau's Failing

Esau was huntsman, nothing but huntsman, delivered up, heart and soul, body and spirit, to the ferocious pursuit of food when that stage of human subjection to nature had been left behind. He was a throwback, a case of arrested development. He despised his birthright as a civilized man, and how much more his birthright as the son of Isaac and the grandson of Abraham!

MAURICE SAMUEL [20]

A Psychological Interpretation

The submissive father encouraged in his son, Esau, what was repressed in him during his own childhood—the freedom of the hunter. The aggressive mother liked Jacob more, because she could not dominate the freer Esau as she dominated her husband and the younger twin. Each of the twins was only half-loved. Insufficiently loved by his feminine father, Jacob was filled with fear. Insufficiently loved by his masculine mother, Esau was filled with hate. It took the therapy of life's hardships before the twins matured enough to respect each other and be reconciled. The records of the families of the Bible are as up-to-date as modern texts in child rearing and much more fascinating because they are better written.

HENRY E. KAGAN [21]

The Life of Isaac

This one brief chapter relates the adult years of Isaac. The only other references to him concern his youth and his old age.

The episode in Gerar is an almost exact duplicate of Abraham's experience in the same city (Gen. 20). In both cases the Patriarch, in order to protect himself, states that his female companion is his "sister." Bible critics suggest that the duplication of these stories may be traced to two literary variants of one basic tradition, the first authored by E (in chapter 20), the second by J (in chapter 26). The basic differences in the tales are that in the J-version there is no divine intervention and no gifts are offered.

א וַיְהִי רָעָב בָּאָרֶץ מִלְּבַד הָרָעָב הָרִאשׁוֹן אֲשֶׁר הָיָה
בִּימֵי אַבְרָהָם וַיֵּלֶךְ יִצְחָק אֶל־אֲבִימֶלֶךְ מֶלֶךְ־
ב פְּלִשְׁתִּים גְּרָרָה: וַיֵּרָא אֵלָיו יְהֹוָה וַיֹּאמֶר אַל־תֵּרֵד
ג מִצְרָיְמָה שְׁכֹן בָּאָרֶץ אֲשֶׁר אֹמַר אֵלֶיךָ: גּוּר בָּאָרֶץ
הַזֹּאת וְאֶהְיֶה עִמְּךָ וַאֲבָרְכֶךָּ כִּי־לְךָ וּלְזַרְעֲךָ אֶתֵּן
אֶת־כָּל־הָאֲרָצֹת הָאֵל וַהֲקִמֹתִי אֶת־הַשְּׁבֻעָה אֲשֶׁר
ד נִשְׁבַּעְתִּי לְאַבְרָהָם אָבִיךָ: וְהִרְבֵּיתִי אֶת־זַרְעֲךָ
כְּכוֹכְבֵי הַשָּׁמַיִם וְנָתַתִּי לְזַרְעֲךָ אֵת כָּל־הָאֲרָצֹת
ה הָאֵל וְהִתְבָּרֲכוּ בְזַרְעֲךָ כֹּל גּוֹיֵי הָאָרֶץ: עֵקֶב אֲשֶׁר־
שָׁמַע אַבְרָהָם בְּקֹלִי וַיִּשְׁמֹר מִשְׁמַרְתִּי מִצְוֹתַי חֻקּוֹתַי
ו וְתוֹרֹתָי: וַיֵּשֶׁב יִצְחָק בִּגְרָר: וַיִּשְׁאֲלוּ אַנְשֵׁי הַמָּקוֹם

לְאִשְׁתּוֹ וַיֹּאמֶר אֲחֹתִי הִוא כִּי יָרֵא לֵאמֹר אִשְׁתִּי פֶּן־
יַהַרְגֻנִי אַנְשֵׁי הַמָּקוֹם עַל־רִבְקָה כִּי־טוֹבַת מַרְאֶה
ח הִוא: וַיְהִי כִּי אָרְכוּ־לוֹ שָׁם הַיָּמִים וַיַּשְׁקֵף אֲבִימֶלֶךְ
מֶלֶךְ פְּלִשְׁתִּים בְּעַד הַחַלּוֹן וַיַּרְא וְהִנֵּה יִצְחָק מְצַחֵק
ט אֵת רִבְקָה אִשְׁתּוֹ: וַיִּקְרָא אֲבִימֶלֶךְ לְיִצְחָק וַיֹּאמֶר
אַךְ הִנֵּה אִשְׁתְּךָ הִוא וְאֵיךְ אָמַרְתָּ אֲחֹתִי הִוא וַיֹּאמֶר
י אֵלָיו יִצְחָק כִּי אָמַרְתִּי פֶּן־אָמוּת עָלֶיהָ: וַיֹּאמֶר
אֲבִימֶלֶךְ מַה־זֹּאת עָשִׂיתָ לָּנוּ כִּמְעַט שָׁכַב אַחַד הָעָם
יא אֶת־אִשְׁתֶּךָ וְהֵבֵאתָ עָלֵינוּ אָשָׁם: וַיְצַו אֲבִימֶלֶךְ אֶת־
כָּל־הָעָם לֵאמֹר הַנֹּגֵעַ בָּאִישׁ הַזֶּה וּבְאִשְׁתּוֹ מוֹת יוּמָת:
יב וַיִּזְרַע יִצְחָק בָּאָרֶץ הַהִוא וַיִּמְצָא בַּשָּׁנָה הַהִוא מֵאָה

1] There was a famine in the land—aside from the previous famine that had occurred in the days of Abraham—and Isaac went to Abimelech, king of the Philistines, in Gerar. **2]** The LORD had appeared to him and said, "Do not go down to Egypt; stay in the land which I point out to you. **3]** Reside in this land, and I will be with you and bless you; I will give all these lands to you and to your offspring, fulfilling the oath that I swore to your father Abraham. **4]** I will make your descendants as numerous as the stars of heaven, and give to your descendants all these lands, so that all the nations of the earth shall bless themselves by your offspring— **5]** inasmuch as Abraham obeyed Me and kept my charge: My commandments, My laws, and My teachings."

6] So Isaac stayed in Gerar. **7]** When the men of the place asked him about his wife, he said, "She is my sister," for he was afraid to say "my wife," thinking, "The men of the place might kill me on account of Rebekah, for she is beautiful." **8]** When some time had passed, Abimelech king of the Philistines, looking out of the window, saw Isaac fondling his wife Rebekah. **9]** Abimelech sent for Isaac and said, "So she is your wife! Why then did you say: She is my sister?" Isaac said to him, "Because I thought I might lose my life on account of her." **10]** Abimelech said, "What have you done to us! One of the people might have lain with your wife, and you would have brought guilt upon us." **11]** Abimelech then charged all the people, saying, "Anyone who molests this man or his wife shall be put to death."

12] Isaac sowed in that land and reaped a hundredfold the same year. The LORD blessed

---

26:1] *Abimelech.* Apparently the same king who figured in the similar incident in the Abraham story (chapter 20). In both cases the king's chief officer is called Phicol.

King of the Philistines. An anachronism. Most scholars believe that the Philistines came to Canaan *ca.* 1200 B.C.E., much after Isaac's day, suggesting that the story comes from a later time when Philistines were prominent in the land and appeared to have been there for many centuries.

Gerar. See note at Gen. 20:1.

8] *Isaac fondling.* יִצְחָק מְצַחֵק, a word play similar to Gen. 21:9.

12] *A hundredfold.* Many times. Isaac does occasional farming and comes close to settling permanently.

יג שְׂעָרִים וַיְבָרֲכֵהוּ יְהֹוָה: וַיִּגְדַּל הָאִישׁ וַיֵּלֶךְ הָלוֹךְ
וְגָדֵל עַד כִּי־גָדַל מְאֹד: וַיְהִי־לוֹ מִקְנֵה־צֹאן וּמִקְנֵה
בָקָר וַעֲבֻדָּה רַבָּה וַיְקַנְאוּ אֹתוֹ פְּלִשְׁתִּים: וְכָל־
הַבְּאֵרֹת אֲשֶׁר חָפְרוּ עַבְדֵי אָבִיו בִּימֵי אַבְרָהָם אָבִיו
סִתְּמוּם פְּלִשְׁתִּים וַיְמַלְאוּם עָפָר: וַיֹּאמֶר אֲבִימֶלֶךְ
אֶל־יִצְחָק לֵךְ מֵעִמָּנוּ כִּי־עָצַמְתָּ מִמֶּנּוּ מְאֹד: וַיֵּלֶךְ
מִשָּׁם יִצְחָק וַיִּחַן בְּנַחַל־גְּרָר וַיֵּשֶׁב שָׁם: וַיָּשָׁב יִצְחָק
וַיַּחְפֹּר אֶת־בְּאֵרֹת הַמַּיִם אֲשֶׁר חָפְרוּ בִּימֵי אַבְרָהָם
אָבִיו וַיְסַתְּמוּם פְּלִשְׁתִּים אַחֲרֵי מוֹת אַבְרָהָם וַיִּקְרָא
לָהֶן שֵׁמוֹת כַּשֵּׁמֹת אֲשֶׁר־קָרָא לָהֶן אָבִיו: וַיַּחְפְּרוּ
עַבְדֵי־יִצְחָק בַּנָּחַל וַיִּמְצְאוּ־שָׁם בְּאֵר מַיִם חַיִּים:

כ וַיָּרִיבוּ רֹעֵי גְרָר עִם־רֹעֵי יִצְחָק לֵאמֹר לָנוּ הַמָּיִם
וַיִּקְרָא שֵׁם־הַבְּאֵר עֵשֶׂק כִּי הִתְעַשְּׂקוּ עִמּוֹ: וַיַּחְפְּרוּ
בְּאֵר אַחֶרֶת וַיָּרִיבוּ גַּם־עָלֶיהָ וַיִּקְרָא שְׁמָהּ שִׂטְנָה:
וַיַּעְתֵּק מִשָּׁם וַיַּחְפֹּר בְּאֵר אַחֶרֶת וְלֹא רָבוּ עָלֶיהָ
וַיִּקְרָא שְׁמָהּ רְחֹבוֹת וַיֹּאמֶר כִּי־עַתָּה הִרְחִיב יְהֹוָה
לָנוּ וּפָרִינוּ בָאָרֶץ: וַיַּעַל מִשָּׁם בְּאֵר שָׁבַע: וַיֵּרָא
אֵלָיו יְהֹוָה בַּלַּיְלָה הַהוּא וַיֹּאמֶר אָנֹכִי אֱלֹהֵי אַבְרָהָם
אָבִיךָ אַל־תִּירָא כִּי־אִתְּךָ אָנֹכִי וּבֵרַכְתִּיךָ וְהִרְבֵּיתִי
אֶת־זַרְעֲךָ בַּעֲבוּר אַבְרָהָם עַבְדִּי: וַיִּבֶן שָׁם מִזְבֵּחַ
וַיִּקְרָא בְּשֵׁם יְהֹוָה וַיֶּט־שָׁם אָהֳלוֹ וַיִּכְרוּ־שָׁם עַבְדֵי־
יִצְחָק בְּאֵר: וַאֲבִימֶלֶךְ הָלַךְ אֵלָיו מִגְּרָר וַאֲחֻזַּת

him, **13]** and the man grew richer and richer until he was very wealthy: **14]** he acquired flocks and herds, and a large household, so that the Philistines envied him. **15]** And the Philistines stopped up all the wells which his father's servants had dug in the days of his father Abraham, filling them with earth. **16]** And Abimelech said to Isaac, "Go away from us, for you have become far too big for us."

17] So Isaac departed from there and encamped in the wadi of Gerar, where he settled. **18]** Isaac dug anew the water wells which had been dug in the days of his father Abraham and which the Philistines had stopped up after Abraham's death; and he gave them the same names that his father had given them. **19]** But when Isaac's servants, digging in the wadi, found there a well of spring water, **20]** the herdsmen of Gerar quarreled with Isaac's hersdmen, saying, "This water is ours." He named that well Esek, because they contended with him. **21]** And when they dug another well, they disputed over that one also; so he named it Sitnah. **22]** He moved from there and dug yet another well, and they did not quarrel over it; so he called it Rehoboth, saying, "Now at last the LORD has granted us ample space to increase in the land."

23] From there he went up to Beer-sheba. **24]** That night the LORD appeared to him and said, "I am the God of your father Abraham. Fear not, for I am with you, and I will bless you and increase your offspring for the sake of My servant Abraham." **25]** So he built an altar there and invoked the LORD by name. Isaac pitched his tent there and his servants started digging a well. **26]** And Abimelech came to him from Gerar, with Ahuzzath his councilor

---

15] *Wells.* They belonged to the person who dug them. Stopping them up was a most serious invasion of property rights in an area where water was precious.

18] *The same names.* Meaning, "these wells have belonged to my family."

19] *Spring water.* Literally, "living water." This was later given a figurative meaning.

20] *Esek.* Contention.

21] *Sitnah.* Harassment.

22] *Rehoboth.* רְחֹבוֹת connected with רָחָב (ample, broad space). The location was some short distance southwest of Beer-sheba, not where today's Rehovot is found.

24] *For the sake of My servant Abraham.* On the principle of the merit of one's forebears, see commentary to Gen. 18:16–19:38.

כו מֵרֵעֵהוּ וּפִיכֹל שַׂר־צְבָאוֹ: וַיֹּאמֶר אֲלֵהֶם יִצְחָק מַדּוּעַ בָּאתֶם אֵלָי וְאַתֶּם שְׂנֵאתֶם אֹתִי וַתְּשַׁלְּחוּנִי מֵאִתְּכֶם:

כז וַיֹּאמְרוּ רָאוֹ רָאִינוּ כִּי־הָיָה יְהוָה עִמָּךְ וַנֹּאמֶר תְּהִי נָא אָלָה בֵּינוֹתֵינוּ בֵּינֵינוּ וּבֵינֶךָ וְנִכְרְתָה בְרִית עִמָּךְ:

כט אִם־תַּעֲשֵׂה עִמָּנוּ רָעָה כַּאֲשֶׁר לֹא נְגַעֲנוּךָ וְכַאֲשֶׁר עָשִׂינוּ עִמְּךָ רַק־טוֹב וַנְּשַׁלֵּחֲךָ בְּשָׁלוֹם אַתָּה עַתָּה בְּרוּךְ יְהוָה:

ל וַיַּעַשׂ לָהֶם מִשְׁתֶּה וַיֹּאכְלוּ וַיִּשְׁתּוּ:

לא וַיַּשְׁכִּימוּ בַבֹּקֶר וַיִּשָּׁבְעוּ אִישׁ לְאָחִיו וַיְשַׁלְּחֵם יִצְחָק

לב וַיֵּלְכוּ מֵאִתּוֹ בְּשָׁלוֹם: וַיְהִי בַּיּוֹם הַהוּא וַיָּבֹאוּ עַבְדֵי יִצְחָק וַיַּגִּדוּ לוֹ עַל־אֹדוֹת הַבְּאֵר אֲשֶׁר חָפָרוּ וַיֹּאמְרוּ

לג לוֹ מָצָאנוּ מָיִם: וַיִּקְרָא אֹתָהּ שִׁבְעָה עַל־כֵּן שֵׁם־

לד הָעִיר בְּאֵר שֶׁבַע עַד הַיּוֹם הַזֶּה: ס וַיְהִי עֵשָׂו בֶּן אַרְבָּעִים שָׁנָה וַיִּקַּח אִשָּׁה אֶת־יְהוּדִית בַּת־בְּאֵרִי

לה הַחִתִּי וְאֶת־בָּשְׂמַת בַּת־אֵילֹן הַחִתִּי: וַתִּהְיֶיןָ מֹרַת רוּחַ לְיִצְחָק וּלְרִבְקָה: ס

and Phicol chief of his troops. **27]** Isaac said to them, "Why have you come to me, seeing that you have been hostile to me and have driven me away from you?" **28]** And they said, "We now see plainly that the LORD has been with you, and we thought: Let there be a sworn treaty between our two parties, between you and us. Let us make a pact with you **29]** that you will not do us harm, just as we have not molested you but have always dealt kindly with you and sent you away in peace. From now on, be you blessed of the LORD!" **30]** Then he made them a feast, and they ate and drank.

31] Early in the morning, they exchanged oaths. Isaac then bade them farewell, and they departed from him in peace. **32]** That same day Isaac's servants came and told him about the well they had dug, and said to him, "We have found water!" **33]** He named it Shibah; therefore the name of the city is Beer-sheba to this day.

34] When Esau was forty years old, he took to wife Judith daughter of Beeri the Hittite, and Basemath daughter of Elon the Hittite; **35]** and they were a source of bitterness to Isaac and Rebekah.

29] *Be you blessed of the Lord.* By this solemn invocation Abimelech cancels the previous decree of expulsion [1].

33] *Shibah.* Beer-sheba is here connected with "oath," and elsewhere with the number seven.

34] *When Esau was forty years old.* The same age at which his father Isaac married. The number forty occurs so frequently in the Bible that it may have been a round number: e.g., the Flood

lasted forty days (Gen. 7:17); Moses spent forty days and nights on Mount Sinai (Exod. 34:28); Israel spent forty years in the desert (Josh. 5:6); and Elijah fasted forty days (I Kings 19:8).

Judith. This popular Jewish name of our day belonged originally to a Hittite woman. It appears nowhere else in the Bible but does recur in the Apocrypha, where it is the name of a book.

Hittite. See above at 10:15 and 23:3.

181

Isaac's Personality

Of the three Patriarchs, Isaac's personality is the least clearly defined. Much in his life is a repetition of Abraham's experience, and some critics have even suggested that Isaac never existed at all, that he was the creation of later legendary amplifications of the Abraham cycle. But it is rather unlikely for any people to invent a tradition with an ancestor of such obvious weaknesses. The biblical record makes Isaac a very real product of realistic circumstances.

He was the child of his parents' old age and was probably overprotected in his youth. Sarah was a woman of strong will, Abraham a man of deep conviction and great status who must have appeared as a towering giant to his son. It is not surprising that when Isaac was being offered as a sacrifice at Moriah he could not even raise his voice in protest. By coincidence (or, as the text seems to suggest, by divine design), the wife who was obtained for him turned out to be aggressive and resourceful, a "manager" [2]. The text is at pains to point out that Rebekah brought Isaac "comfort after his mother's death" (Gen. 24:67), which in contemporary terms may be said to indicate that he saw in Rebekah a mother substitute. Further, he repeated his father's experience with Abimelech, and the wells he dug were the old wells of Abraham.

Bad experiences seem to have followed him. He was nearly sacrificed by his father; he was caught in the crossfire of Sarah's and Hagar's jealousies; his children did not get along with each other; and in old age, when he was stricken with blindness, his wife and son conspired to deceive him, so that the one thing he truly owned, his paternal blessing, was bestowed equivocally on the son he did not prefer.

Still, Isaac had real strengths. He endured Mount Moriah, and the faith of Abraham became a vibrant force in his life. He remained in Palestine, even in times of hardship. He tried his hand at agriculture—a venture his father had not attempted—and became enormously successful at it. He was evidently a man of peace, and he gained the respect of a king who covenanted with him. We know little about his feelings, but we may assume that precisely because of suffering and difficulties, and because he was surrounded by strong and active people, Isaac became a reflective, perhaps even an introverted person (hinted at in Gen. 24:63).

Isaac thus represents an important stage in the patriarchal drama. After the revolutionary and often stormy experiences of his father, the son's life becomes the necessary halting place where new religious insights are absorbed and incorporated into patterns of thought and deed. Isaac is the bridge between Abraham and Jacob, the essential link in the chain of greatness.

GLEANINGS

Old Names

It is suggested that Abraham had named the wells with names which recalled religious experiences, like Adonai-yireh. Stopping these wells up was equivalent to eradicating evidences of Abraham's religion. That is why Isaac gave the wells the old names.   HAKETAV VE-HAKABBALAH

Too Big

Note what Abimelech says to Isaac: "You have become too big for us" (מִמֶּנּוּ). One should translate "through us," meaning: "You have become wealthy at our expense"—an old accusation against the Jew.   NEHAMA LEIBOWITZ [3]

Assimilation

Why did Isaac move away just when conditions were favorable for staying, i.e., after he concluded a covenant with Abimelech [Gen. 26:31]? When Isaac was being harassed, he was in no danger of adopting Philistinian ways, but when peace came he said to himself: "Who knows whether I can preserve my spiritual identity."

MORDECAI HACOHEN [4]

Isaac's Contribution

Nothing spectacular happened to Isaac. He made no particular contribution, no addition to the tradition he received from Abraham; he injected no idea, no startling insight. The tradition arising out of a great intellectual ferment seems, in the life of Isaac, to have reached a plateau.

What, then, did Isaac do? He preserved a tradition; he held on to it; he received it and he was loyal to it. In a world of constant change, in a world where new fashions are sought and new habits constantly arise, in a world that never stops for a moment in its fluctuations, Isaac is not simply a negative character. He is the son of Abraham and the father of Jacob. He kept the chain that was handed to him, and the tradition did not break with him. He remained loyal, and in all of his actions a tradition was preserved.

MORRIS ADLER [5]

Isaac Was Sacrificed

Was he not so in truth?
What there the child's eyes—wide with fear—
For once have seen, think you they can forget?
The hand—the father's hand—that shyly tender
Used to caress his fever-stricken face—
That arm which once embraced, clung so tightly
As though such nearness were not near enough—
That eye—whose look was longing, care and
  blessing—
And that whole countenance, that earliest
  childhood's home,
Whereto old age, long, weary and disheartened,
Still as to some enchanted island flies . . .
And now all this—hand, arm, eye,
  countenance—
Transformed into a madness filled with God,
Blind, deaf—forgetting his very self.
A single outcry only: "Kill!"
Whose faith was thus—in childhood—crushed
  by God—
In whom shall he then trust, where feel secure?

RICHARD BEER-HOFMANN [6]

Isaac Blesses His Sons

The Isaac story combines tragedy and play-acting as it reaches its climax in the tale of parental blessing. Such a blessing was accorded special significance, especially when it was given at life's end. The parent appeared to be in God's stead, and while he had no power to bind the Divinity he invoked his words were believed to reflect prophetic vision. In blessing his sons, Isaac assists God in revealing and confirming the future (see commentary to Gen. 47:28–48:22).

As the story unfolds, observe the strong note of sympathy for Esau and, once again, the absence of explicit moral judgment, which is characteristic of many Genesis narratives. It is in this section that Rebekah is clearly depicted as wife and mother.

ה וְעַתָּה בְנִי שְׁמַע בְּקֹלִי לַאֲשֶׁר אֲנִי מְצַוָּה אֹתָךְ: לֶךְ־
נָא אֶל־הַצֹּאן וְקַח־לִי מִשָּׁם שְׁנֵי גְּדָיֵי עִזִּים טֹבִים
וְאֶעֱשֶׂה אֹתָם מַטְעַמִּים לְאָבִיךָ כַּאֲשֶׁר אָהֵב: וְהֵבֵאתָ
לְאָבִיךָ וְאָכָל בַּעֲבֻר אֲשֶׁר יְבָרֶכְךָ לִפְנֵי מוֹתוֹ:
יא וַיֹּאמֶר יַעֲקֹב אֶל־רִבְקָה אִמּוֹ הֵן עֵשָׂו אָחִי אִישׁ שָׂעִר
יב וְאָנֹכִי אִישׁ חָלָק: אוּלַי יְמֻשֵּׁנִי אָבִי וְהָיִיתִי בְעֵינָיו
יג כִּמְתַעְתֵּעַ וְהֵבֵאתִי עָלַי קְלָלָה וְלֹא בְרָכָה: וַתֹּאמֶר
לוֹ אִמּוֹ עָלַי קִלְלָתְךָ בְּנִי אַךְ שְׁמַע בְּקֹלִי וְלֵךְ קַח־
יד לִי: וַיֵּלֶךְ וַיִּקַּח וַיָּבֵא לְאִמּוֹ וַתַּעַשׂ אִמּוֹ מַטְעַמִּים
טו כַּאֲשֶׁר אָהֵב אָבִיו: וַתִּקַּח רִבְקָה אֶת־בִּגְדֵי עֵשָׂו בְּנָהּ
הַגָּדֹל הַחֲמֻדֹת אֲשֶׁר אִתָּהּ בַּבָּיִת וַתַּלְבֵּשׁ אֶת־יַעֲקֹב

א וַיְהִי כִּי־זָקֵן יִצְחָק וַתִּכְהֶיןָ עֵינָיו מֵרְאֹת וַיִּקְרָא אֶת־
עֵשָׂו בְּנוֹ הַגָּדֹל וַיֹּאמֶר אֵלָיו בְּנִי וַיֹּאמֶר אֵלָיו הִנֵּנִי:
ב וַיֹּאמֶר הִנֵּה־נָא זָקַנְתִּי לֹא יָדַעְתִּי יוֹם מוֹתִי: וְעַתָּה
שָׂא־נָא כֵלֶיךָ תֶּלְיְךָ וְקַשְׁתֶּךָ וְצֵא הַשָּׂדֶה וְצוּדָה לִּי
ד צָיִד: וַעֲשֵׂה־לִי מַטְעַמִּים כַּאֲשֶׁר אָהַבְתִּי וְהָבִיאָה
לִּי וְאֹכֵלָה בַּעֲבוּר תְּבָרֶכְךָ נַפְשִׁי בְּטֶרֶם אָמוּת:
ה וְרִבְקָה שֹׁמַעַת בְּדַבֵּר יִצְחָק אֶל־עֵשָׂו בְּנוֹ וַיֵּלֶךְ עֵשָׂו
ו הַשָּׂדֶה לָצוּד צַיִד לְהָבִיא: וְרִבְקָה אָמְרָה אֶל־
יַעֲקֹב בְּנָהּ לֵאמֹר הִנֵּה שָׁמַעְתִּי אֶת־אָבִיךָ מְדַבֵּר
ז אֶל־עֵשָׂו אָחִיךָ לֵאמֹר: הָבִיאָה לִּי צַיִד וַעֲשֵׂה־לִי
מַטְעַמִּים וְאֹכֵלָה וַאֲבָרֶכְכָה לִפְנֵי יְהוָה לִפְנֵי מוֹתִי:

* נ ה' יתירה.

1] When Isaac was old and his eyes were too dim to see, he called his older son Esau and said to him, "My son." He answered, "Here I am." 2] And he said, "I am old now, and I do not know how soon I may die. 3] Take your gear, your quiver and bow, and go out into the open and hunt me some game. 4] Then prepare a dish for me such as I like, and bring it to me to eat, so that I may give you my innermost blessing before I die."

5] Rebekah had been listening as Isaac spoke to his son Esau. When Esau had gone out into the open to hunt game to bring home, 6] Rebekah said to her son Jacob, "I overheard your father speaking to your brother Esau, saying, 7] 'Bring me some game and prepare a dish for me to eat, that I may bless you, with the LORD's approval, before I die.' 8] Now, my son, listen carefully as I instruct you. 9] Go to the flock and fetch me two choice kids, and I will make of them a dish for your father, such as he likes. 10] Then take it to your father to eat, in order that he may bless you before he dies." 11] Jacob answered his mother Rebekah, "But my brother Esau is a hairy man and I am smooth-skinned. 12] If my father touches me, I shall appear to him as a trickster and bring upon myself a curse, not a blessing." 13] But his mother said to him, "Your curse, my son, be upon me! Just do as I say and go fetch them for me."

14] He got them and brought them to his mother, and his mother prepared a dish such as his father liked. 15] Rebekah then took the best clothes of her older son Esau, which were there in the house, and had her younger son Jacob put them on; 16] and she covered his hands and

---

27:2] *I am old now.* Nuzi records indicate that these words were a legal formula introducing a death-bed declaration and last will.

4] *My innermost blessing.* Indicating a blessing of special importance. Eating a meal was probably part of the ritual.

7] *With the Lord's approval.* Rebekah adds this to what Isaac has said in order to convince Jacob that the blessing will have divine sanction, thereby implying that once given it cannot be revoked [1] (see verse 33).

/According to some, Rebekah expected the blessing to have prophetic power [2]./

טז בָּנֶהּ הַקָּטָן: וְאֵת עֹרֹת גְּדָיֵי הָעִזִּים הִלְבִּישָׁה עַל־
יז יָדָיו וְעַל חֶלְקַת צַוָּארָיו: וַתִּתֵּן אֶת־הַמַּטְעַמִּים וְאֶת־
יח הַלֶּחֶם אֲשֶׁר עָשָׂתָה בְּיַד יַעֲקֹב בְּנָהּ: וַיָּבֹא אֶל־אָבִיו
יט וַיֹּאמֶר אָבִי וַיֹּאמֶר הִנֶּנִּי מִי אַתָּה בְּנִי: וַיֹּאמֶר יַעֲקֹב
אֶל־אָבִיו אָנֹכִי עֵשָׂו בְּכֹרֶךָ עָשִׂיתִי כַּאֲשֶׁר דִּבַּרְתָּ
אֵלָי קוּם־נָא שְׁבָה וְאָכְלָה מִצֵּידִי בַּעֲבוּר תְּבָרֲכַנִּי
כ נַפְשֶׁךָ: וַיֹּאמֶר יִצְחָק אֶל־בְּנוֹ מַה־זֶּה מִהַרְתָּ לִמְצֹא
כא בְּנִי וַיֹּאמֶר כִּי הִקְרָה יְהוָה אֱלֹהֶיךָ לְפָנָי: וַיֹּאמֶר
יִצְחָק אֶל־יַעֲקֹב גְּשָׁה־נָּא וַאֲמֻשְׁךָ בְּנִי הַאַתָּה זֶה בְּנִי
כב עֵשָׂו אִם־לֹא: וַיִּגַּשׁ יַעֲקֹב אֶל־יִצְחָק אָבִיו וַיְמֻשֵּׁהוּ
כג וַיֹּאמֶר הַקֹּל קוֹל יַעֲקֹב וְהַיָּדַיִם יְדֵי עֵשָׂו: וְלֹא הִכִּירוֹ
כד כִּי־הָיוּ יָדָיו כִּידֵי עֵשָׂו אָחִיו שְׂעִרֹת וַיְבָרֲכֵהוּ: וַיֹּאמֶר
כה אַתָּה זֶה בְּנִי עֵשָׂו וַיֹּאמֶר אָנִי: וַיֹּאמֶר הַגִּשָׁה לִּי

וְאָכְלָה מִצֵּיד בְּנִי לְמַעַן תְּבָרֶכְךָ נַפְשִׁי וַיַּגֶּשׁ־לוֹ וַיֹּאכַל
כו וַיָּבֵא לוֹ יַיִן וַיֵּשְׁתְּ: וַיֹּאמֶר אֵלָיו יִצְחָק אָבִיו גְּשָׁה־נָּא
כז וּשְׁקָה־לִּי בְּנִי: וַיִּגַּשׁ וַיִּשַּׁק־לוֹ וַיָּרַח אֶת־רֵיחַ בְּגָדָיו
וַיְבָרֲכֵהוּ וַיֹּאמֶר רְאֵה רֵיחַ בְּנִי כְּרֵיחַ שָׂדֶה אֲשֶׁר
כח בֵּרֲכוֹ יְהוָה: וְיִתֶּן־לְךָ הָאֱלֹהִים מִטַּל הַשָּׁמַיִם וּמִשְׁמַנֵּי
כט הָאָרֶץ וְרֹב דָּגָן וְתִירֹשׁ: יַעַבְדוּךָ עַמִּים וְיִשְׁתַּחֲו֖וּ לְךָ
לְאֻמִּים הֱוֵה גְבִיר לְאַחֶיךָ וְיִשְׁתַּחֲווּ לְךָ בְּנֵי אִמֶּךָ
ל אֹרֲרֶיךָ אָרוּר וּמְבָרֲכֶיךָ בָּרוּךְ: וַיְהִי כַּאֲשֶׁר כִּלָּה
יִצְחָק לְבָרֵךְ אֶת־יַעֲקֹב וַיְהִי אַךְ יָצֹא יָצָא יַעֲקֹב
לא מֵאֵת פְּנֵי יִצְחָק אָבִיו וְעֵשָׂו אָחִיו בָּא מִצֵּידוֹ: וַיַּעַשׂ
גַּם־הוּא מַטְעַמִּים וַיָּבֵא לְאָבִיו וַיֹּאמֶר לְאָבִיו יָקֻם
לב אָבִי וְיֹאכַל מִצֵּיד בְּנוֹ בַּעֲבוּר תְּבָרֲכַנִּי נַפְשֶׁךָ: וַיֹּאמֶר
לוֹ יִצְחָק אָבִיו מִי־אָתָּה וַיֹּאמֶר אֲנִי בִּנְךָ בְכֹרְךָ

* כט וישתחו קרי.

the hairless part of his neck with the skins of the kids. **17]** Then she put in the hands of her son Jacob the dish and the bread that she had prepared.

18] He went to his father and said, "Father." And he said, "Yes, which of my sons are you?" **19]** Jacob said to his father, "I am Esau, your first-born; I have done as you told me. Pray sit up and eat of my game, that you may give me your innermost blessing." **20]** Isaac said to his son, "How did you succeed so quickly, my son?" And he said, "Because the LORD your God granted me good fortune." **21]** Isaac said to Jacob, "Come closer that I may feel you, my son—whether you are really my son Esau or not." **22]** So Jacob drew close to his father Isaac, who felt him and wondered, "The voice is the voice of Jacob, yet the hands are the hands of Esau." **23]** He did not recognize him, because his hands were hairy like those of his brother Esau; and so he blessed him.

24] He asked, "Are you really my son Esau?" And when he said, "I am," **25]** he said, "Serve me and let me eat of my son's game that I may give you my innermost blessing." So he served him and he ate, and he brought him wine and he drank. **26]** Then his father Isaac said to him, "Come close and kiss me, my son"; **27]** and he went up and kissed him. And he smelled his clothes and he blessed him, saying, "Ah, the smell of my son is like the smell of the fields that the LORD has blessed. **28]** May God give you / Of the dew of heaven and the fat of the earth, / Abundance of new grain and wine. / **29]** Let peoples serve you, / And nations bow to you; / Be master over your brothers, / And let your mother's sons bow to you. / Cursed be they who curse you, / Blessed they who bless you."

30] No sooner had Jacob left the presence of his father Isaac—after Isaac had finished blessing Jacob—than his brother Esau came back from his hunt. **31]** He too prepared a dish and brought it to his father. And he said to his father, "Let my father sit up and eat of his son's game, so that you may give me your innermost blessing." **32]** His father Isaac said to him,

29] *Bow to you.* The younger one. This had been predicted by the birth oracle (Gen. 25:23).

לֹ עֵשָׂו: וַיֶּחֱרַד יִצְחָק חֲרָדָה גְּדֹלָה עַד־מְאֹד וַיֹּאמֶר
מִי־אֵפוֹא הוּא הַצָּד־צַיִד וַיָּבֵא לִי וָאֹכַל מִכֹּל בְּטֶרֶם

לֹד תָּבוֹא וָאֲבָרֲכֵהוּ גַּם־בָּרוּךְ יִהְיֶה: כִּשְׁמֹעַ עֵשָׂו אֶת־
דִּבְרֵי אָבִיו וַיִּצְעַק צְעָקָה גְּדֹלָה וּמָרָה עַד־מְאֹד

לֹה וַיֹּאמֶר לְאָבִיו בָּרֲכֵנִי גַם־אָנִי אָבִי: וַיֹּאמֶר בָּא אָחִיךָ

לֹו בְּמִרְמָה וַיִּקַּח בִּרְכָתֶךָ: וַיֹּאמֶר הֲכִי קָרָא שְׁמוֹ יַעֲקֹב
וַיַּעְקְבֵנִי זֶה פַעֲמַיִם אֶת־בְּכֹרָתִי לָקָח וְהִנֵּה עַתָּה

לֹז לָקַח בִּרְכָתִי וַיֹּאמֶר הֲלֹא־אָצַלְתָּ לִי בְּרָכָה: וַיַּעַן
יִצְחָק וַיֹּאמֶר לְעֵשָׂו הֵן גְּבִיר שַׂמְתִּיו לָךְ וְאֶת־כָּל־

אֶחָיו נָתַתִּי לוֹ לַעֲבָדִים וְדָגָן וְתִירֹשׁ סְמַכְתִּיו וּלְכָה
לֹח אֵפוֹא מָה אֶעֱשֶׂה בְּנִי: וַיֹּאמֶר עֵשָׂו אֶל־אָבִיו הַבְרָכָה
אַחַת הִוא־לְךָ אָבִי בָּרֲכֵנִי גַם־אָנִי אָבִי וַיִּשָּׂא עֵשָׂו
לֹט קֹלוֹ וַיֵּבְךְּ: וַיַּעַן יִצְחָק אָבִיו וַיֹּאמֶר אֵלָיו הִנֵּה מִשְׁמַנֵּי
מ הָאָרֶץ יִהְיֶה מוֹשָׁבֶךָ וּמִטַּל הַשָּׁמַיִם מֵעָל: וְעַל־חַרְבְּךָ
תִחְיֶה וְאֶת־אָחִיךָ תַּעֲבֹד וְהָיָה כַּאֲשֶׁר תָּרִיד וּפָרַקְתָּ
מא עֻלּוֹ מֵעַל צַוָּארֶךָ: וַיִּשְׂטֹם עֵשָׂו אֶת־יַעֲקֹב עַל־הַבְּרָכָה
אֲשֶׁר בֵּרֲכוֹ אָבִיו וַיֹּאמֶר עֵשָׂו בְּלִבּוֹ יִקְרְבוּ יְמֵי אֵבֶל
מב אָבִי וְאַהַרְגָה אֶת־יַעֲקֹב אָחִי: וַיֻּגַּד לְרִבְקָה אֶת־דִּבְרֵי

"Who are you?" And he said, "I am your son, Esau, your first-born!" **33]** Isaac was seized with very violent trembling. "Who was it then," he demanded, "that hunted game and brought it to me? Moreover, I ate of it before you came, and I blessed him; now he must remain blessed!" **34]** When Esau heard his father's words, he burst into wild and bitter sobbing, and said to his father, "Bless me too, Father!" **35]** But he answered, "Your brother came with guile and took away your blessing." **36]** [Esau] said, "Was he, then, named Jacob that he might supplant me these two times? First he took away my birthright and now he has taken away my blessing!" And he added, "Have you not reserved a blessing for me?" **37]** Isaac answered, saying to Esau, "But I have made him master over you: I have given him all his brothers for servants, and sustained him with grain and wine. What, then, can I still do for you, my son?" **38]** And Esau said to his father, "Have you but one blessing, Father? Bless me too, Father!" And Esau wept aloud. **39]** And his father Isaac answered, saying to him, "See, your abode shall enjoy the fat of the earth / And the dew of heaven above. / **40]** Yet by your sword you shall live, / And you shall serve your brother; / But when you grow restive, / You shall break his yoke from your neck."

41] Now Esau harbored a grudge against Jacob because of the blessing which his father had given him, and Esau said to himself, "Let but the mourning period of my father come, and I will kill my brother Jacob." **42]** When the words of her older son Esau were reported to

---

35] *Came with guile.* In retribution guile will in turn be visited on Jacob (see Gen. 29:25).

36] *Supplant me.* יַעְקְבֵנִי connected with יַעֲקֹב (Jacob); see Gen. 25:26. Esau is saying, "Just because he was named Jacob is no reason to take my rights away" [3]. A second word play is בְּכֹרָתִי־בִּרְכָתִי (my birthright—my blessing). Esau now implies that he was also cheated at the sale of the birthright.

38] *Bless me too, Father.* After these words the Septuagint adds a dramatic touch: "... and Isaac was silent."

39] *Enjoy the fat of the earth and.* The Hebrew is not clear. Others translate as "Be away from the fat of the earth and from," referring to the rocky soil of Edom.

40] *When you grow restive.* The meaning of the Hebrew text is unclear. B. Jacob translates: "When you grow rightly restive," meaning "when Israel becomes unjust." Best perhaps is Rashi's explanation: "When you shall suffer" [4]. Some hold that the blessing stems from later times, possibly Solomon's, when Edom broke loose from Israelite subjection.

עֵשָׂו בְּנָהּ הַגָּדֹל וַתִּשְׁלַח וַתִּקְרָא לְיַעֲקֹב בְּנָהּ הַקָּטָן
וַתֹּאמֶר אֵלָיו הִנֵּה עֵשָׂו אָחִיךָ מִתְנַחֵם לְךָ לְהָרְגֶךָ:
מג וְעַתָּה בְנִי שְׁמַע בְּקֹלִי וְקוּם בְּרַח־לְךָ אֶל־לָבָן אָחִי
מד חָרָנָה: וְיָשַׁבְתָּ עִמּוֹ יָמִים אֲחָדִים עַד אֲשֶׁר־תָּשׁוּב
מה חֲמַת אָחִיךָ: עַד־שׁוּב אַף־אָחִיךָ מִמְּךָ וְשָׁכַח אֵת
אֲשֶׁר־עָשִׂיתָ לּוֹ וְשָׁלַחְתִּי וּלְקַחְתִּיךָ מִשָּׁם לָמָה אֶשְׁכַּל
מו גַּם־שְׁנֵיכֶם יוֹם אֶחָד: וַתֹּאמֶר רִבְקָה אֶל־יִצְחָק קַצְתִּי
בְחַיַּי מִפְּנֵי בְּנוֹת חֵת אִם־לֹקֵחַ יַעֲקֹב אִשָּׁה מִבְּנוֹת־

חֵת כָּאֵלֶּה מִבְּנוֹת הָאָרֶץ לָמָּה לִּי חַיִּים:
א וַיִּקְרָא יִצְחָק אֶל־יַעֲקֹב וַיְבָרֶךְ אֹתוֹ וַיְצַוֵּהוּ וַיֹּאמֶר לוֹ
ב לֹא־תִקַּח אִשָּׁה מִבְּנוֹת כְּנָעַן: קוּם לֵךְ פַּדֶּנָה אֲרָם
בֵּיתָה בְתוּאֵל אֲבִי אִמֶּךָ וְקַח־לְךָ מִשָּׁם אִשָּׁה מִבְּנוֹת
ג לָבָן אֲחִי אִמֶּךָ: וְאֵל שַׁדַּי יְבָרֵךְ אֹתְךָ וְיַפְרְךָ וְיַרְבֶּךָ
ד וְהָיִיתָ לִקְהַל עַמִּים: וְיִתֶּן־לְךָ אֶת־בִּרְכַּת אַבְרָהָם
לְךָ וּלְזַרְעֲךָ אִתָּךְ לְרִשְׁתְּךָ אֶת־אֶרֶץ מְגֻרֶיךָ אֲשֶׁר־
ה נָתַן אֱלֹהִים לְאַבְרָהָם: וַיִּשְׁלַח יִצְחָק אֶת־יַעֲקֹב וַיֵּלֶךְ

* מו ק' זעירא.

Rebekah, she sent for her younger son Jacob and said to him, "Your brother Esau is consoling himself by planning to kill you. **43]** Now, my son, listen to me. Flee at once to Haran, to my brother Laban. **44]** Stay with him a while, until your brother's fury subsides— **45]** until your brother's anger against you subsides—and he forgets what you have done to him. Then I will fetch you from there. Let me not lose you both in one day!"

46] Rebekah said to Isaac, "I am disgusted with my life because of the Hittite women. If Jacob marries a Hittite woman like these, from among the native women, what good will life be to me?" **1]** So Isaac sent for Jacob and blessed him. He instructed him, saying, "You shall not take a wife from among the Canaanite women. **2]** Up, go to Paddan-aram, to the house of Bethuel, your mother's father, and take a wife there from among the daughters of Laban, your mother's brother. **3]** May El Shaddai bless you, make you fertile and numerous, so that you become an assembly of peoples. **4]** May He grant the blessing of Abraham to you and your offspring, that you may possess the land where you are sojourning, which God gave to Abraham."

5] Then Isaac sent Jacob off, and he went to Paddan-aram, to Laban the son of Bethuel the Aramean, the brother of Rebekah, mother of Jacob and Esau.

45] *Lose you both.* If Esau killed Jacob, he in turn would become a fugitive.

46] *Rebekah said to Isaac.* What follows was most likely adapted from another tradition (usually assigned to the P-school). Jacob is not rebuffed for his behavior nor is he sent away to escape Esau. The reason for his departure is escape from a bad marriage. Further, in this tradition, no deathbed declaration is involved since Isaac will live another eighty years.

/Rashbam explains the discrepancy by saying that Rebekah suggested a pretext to have Jacob sent away. See also the commentary below./

28:3] *Make you fertile.* Isaac has already bestowed on Jacob four other blessings: agricultural fertility, governmental sovereignty, and physical and spiritual salubrity. Only the final biblical category of blessings, military sovereignty, is withheld from Jacob. This is reserved for Esau, although given to him in an equivocal manner (Gen. 27:40) [5].

פַּדֶּנָה אֲרָם אֶל־לָבָן בֶּן־בְּתוּאֵל הָאֲרַמִּי אֲחִי רִבְקָה
אֵם יַעֲקֹב וְעֵשָׂו: וַיַּרְא עֵשָׂו כִּי־בֵרַךְ יִצְחָק אֶת־יַעֲקֹב
וְשִׁלַּח אֹתוֹ פַּדֶּנָה אֲרָם לָקַחַת־לוֹ מִשָּׁם אִשָּׁה בְּבָרֲכוֹ
אֹתוֹ וַיְצַו עָלָיו לֵאמֹר לֹא־תִקַּח אִשָּׁה מִבְּנוֹת
כְּנָעַן: וַיִּשְׁמַע יַעֲקֹב אֶל־אָבִיו וְאֶל־אִמּוֹ וַיֵּלֶךְ פַּדֶּנָה

ח אֲרָם: וַיַּרְא עֵשָׂו כִּי רָעוֹת בְּנוֹת כְּנָעַן בְּעֵינֵי יִצְחָק
ט אָבִיו: וַיֵּלֶךְ עֵשָׂו אֶל־יִשְׁמָעֵאל וַיִּקַּח אֶת־מָחֲלַת
בַּת־יִשְׁמָעֵאל בֶּן־אַבְרָהָם אֲחוֹת נְבָיוֹת עַל־נָשָׁיו לוֹ
לְאִשָּׁה:

Haftarah Toledot, p. 341

6] When Esau saw that Isaac had blessed Jacob and sent him off to Paddan-aram to take a wife from there, charging him, as he blessed him, "You shall not take a wife from among the Canaanite women," 7] and that Jacob had obeyed his father and mother and gone to Paddan-aram, 8] Esau realized that the Canaanite women displeased his father Isaac. 9] So Esau went to Ishmael and took to wife, in addition to the wives he had, Mahalath the daughter of Ishmael, sister of Nebaioth.

9] *Sister of Nebaioth*. Nebaioth is Ishmael's first-born (Gen. 25:13). Esau marries his first cousin.

The Deception

This story is bound to leave us with the same moral questions we asked at the sale of the birthright (Gen. 25:29–34). Again, Jacob does not come off very well. He practices outrageous deceit on a helpless father and a guileless brother, and he is rewarded for his deed. It has therefore been suggested that (as in the story of the birthright) the tale was originally told as a comedy: a goat cooked to taste like venison, the kid-skinned hands, the bumbling old father, the mother behind the door, and the inevitable dénouement. Such deception is said to have been an acceptable means of achieving God's purpose, because when these stories were first told morality and religion were presumably not yet clearly fixed or closely connected.[1]

But pathos rather than comedy is the story's main characteristic, and, moreover, Jacob's immorality does find its implicit judgment in the unfolding of his life, which turns into a prolonged tragedy (see commentary to Gen. 25:19–34, "The Moral Problem"). Jacob bears the burden of guilt all his lifetime and pays dearly for Esau's tears.[2] Ancient Jewish commentators even suggested that Jacob's entire heritage was weighted with this memory [9].

Ironically, Jacob and Rebekah involve themselves in moral turpitude in order to achieve what God would have brought to pass in any case. Here, too, lies the deeper issue of so many biblical stories: How free is man within the context of God's purposes? The Bible gives no explicit answer but implies that man is free to act morally or immorally. While what he does may not ultimately alter events, he is judged only on intent and deed, not on success or failure.

Was Isaac Really Deceived?

As we read the story with close attention to the personality of Isaac, we are led to conclude that throughout the episode he is subconsciously aware of Jacob's identity. However, since he is unable to admit this knowledge, he pretends to be deceived. Seen in this context, the tale contains a plot within a plot; Rebekah and Jacob lay elaborate plans for deceiving Isaac, while unknown to them Isaac looks for ways to deceive himself, in order that he might carry out God's design (though he does not really want to do it), namely, to bless his less-loved son [10].

Isaac is old, but not senile; his blessings are highly sophisticated. He has no doubts about Esau's identity; the latter's single word הִנֶּ֫נִּי (here I am) in chapter 27, verse 1 is enough to establish it, while Jacob's single word אָבִי (father) in verse 18 arouses doubt, so that no amount of play-acting, false skins, and goat-disguised-as-venison can really deceive Isaac. But he *wants* to be misled; in his heart he has long known that Esau cannot carry the burden of Abraham and that, instead, his quiet and complicated younger son must be chosen. Weak and indecisive man and father that he is, Isaac does not have the courage to face Esau with the truth. His own blindness and the ruse of Rebekah come literally as a godsend.[3] Consciously he cannot admit to knowing the identity of Jacob in verse 23; subconsciously he is relieved. So he proceeds and, as a start, gives a blessing of material goods to Jacob. Then comes the

---

[1] So Gunkel, who says tendentiously that "the hearers [of the story] are the happy heirs of the deceivers" [6]. The Church Fathers, like the Rabbis, excused the ruse. Jerome called it a laudable lie; others like Theodoret and Aquinas noted that Jacob, having acquired the birthright, was entitled to the blessing. Augustine saw Jacob as Jesus disguised: Jacob supplants Esau, as Jesus will assist the Gentiles to supplant the Jews; hence "it is not a deception but a divine mystery" [7].

[2] One view suggests that Esau's tears made Israel's exile bitter [8].

[3] Rashi says that Isaac grew dim-eyed so that Jacob might get the blessing.

hardest part, the pathetic confrontation with Esau—the father trembling and the son weeping bitterly. Only when this is past can Isaac call Jacob without anxiety and complete the blessing by invoking the memory of Abraham. Note that Isaac does not reprimand Jacob, for how can he who deceived himself be angry at deceit! In a sense, no one, not even Esau, is deceived, for he too knows that Jacob and not he is the chosen one [11].

Even in this reading of the story, however, the problem of Jacob's morality remains the same, for Jacob believes that he is deceiving his father and he acts on this belief.

Rebekah

The biblical text yields enough information about Rebekah to allow the reader to draw her personality in some detail. Her behavior at the well shows her basic qualities: She is utterly courteous, she is concerned for man and beast, she is modest, and she is deferential to her own family. She is also beautiful and appears self-assured and at ease with the stranger who meets her at the well. In other words, she is the perfect picture of a desirable and virtuous young woman.

She marries a man who sees in her a mother substitute (see commentary to Gen. 26:1–35) and who wants to be dominated. Indeed, she appears to manage both husband and household together [12]. Faced with a strong and independent son, Esau, she leaves him to his father, while she favors her younger son, who remains at home and gives promise of being as submissive as his father. She has little compunction in doing what she thinks ought to be done and, therefore, on the spur of the moment, invents a deception that she hopes will help her husband do the right thing.

Rebekah is what natural gifts and her marriage to Isaac have made her—clever, strong-willed, and clear-eyed, a mother who loves both of her children (Gen. 27:45) but loves them differently, a woman who finds herself in the chain of greatness and who attempts to shape a fate that she glimpses but perhaps cannot fully comprehend.

Rebekah is the most fully delineated of the four Matriarchs. Of Leah we learn little; we receive some insight into Rachel's personality; while Sarah's character is known to us primarily through the manner in which she deals with Hagar and Ishmael, although even these problematic incidents do not allow us a full view of her. Biblical stories deal usually with men, and only occasionally, as in the tales of Rebekah and Tamar, are a woman's intuition and ingenuity given a place of preeminence.

GLEANINGS

The Nature of Isaac's Blessings

Blessings like curses are ultimately prayers that God might translate them into reality, even as the Psalmist says: "Let them curse, but bless Thou" [109:28].

To be sure, there are scholars who see in Scripture, and especially in the blessing of Isaac, instances of magic, in that what has been said cannot be taken back. However, here too we have not magic but prayer, for it was not Isaac's intention to force God to do something against His will. The blessing cannot stand unless it represents God's will to begin with.   UMBERTO CASSUTO [13]

The Dilemma of Divine Choice

Apparently even God must select imperfect instruments to fulfil His purposes. He must choose between Jacob—a man who desires the birthright so deeply he will cheat to secure it—and Esau who so lightly esteems it that he forfeits the birthright for a bowl of lentils. Jacob's calculated cunning must be weighed against Esau's undisciplined craving for immediate self-gratification. Working with "human material" involved God in a difficult but inescapable choice, and God decides: It is better to care too much than too little.

SAMUEL E. KARFF [14]

He Knew

Think you he was so easily misled
That blindness made confusion possible
Between the son he thought he loved and
   him

Whom he must bless? . . . He blessed because
   he must,
Because God wrought in him. At such a
   time
Could our cheap trickery prevail? He knew.
This was the blessing of the chosen son,
Cross-purposed and reversing, it might seem,
The destiny of generations; strange
And repetitious are God's ways with man.

AMY K. BLANK [15]

God Uses Jacob

No, it *is* a deception which is reported by Scripture without being approved by it. The mystery is that of God's action who uses for His ends even human faults yet remains completely sovereign in His choice. He had preferred Jacob over Esau even before their birth.

ROLAND DE VAUX [16]

The Voice of Jacob

When Isaac said, "The voice is the voice of Jacob, yet the hands are the hands of Esau" [Gen. 27:22], he spoke prophetically. "The voice of Jacob" means learning and truth; "the hands of Esau" means force and violence. As long as the voice of Jacob is heard in the houses of prayer and learning, the hands of Esau will not prevail against him.   MIDRASH [17]

He Knew

The moment Isaac heard his son mention God's name (27:20) he knew it was Jacob, and not Esau.   MIDRASH [18]

Jacob's Dream

The narrative now comes to focus entirely on Jacob. He has his father's blessing and is on his way to his relatives in Haran. He will fall in love and be himself deceived. He will serve a master, yet his wages will be uncertain. While these stories of classical charm speak to us of human thoughts and deeds, it is God's master plan, revealed to Jacob in his first encounter with God, that determines their underlying theme.

(A new weekly portion, *Vayetze*, begins here.)

ס   ס   ס

יא וַיֵּצֵא יַעֲקֹב מִבְּאֵר שָׁבַע וַיֵּלֶךְ חָרָנָה: וַיִּפְגַּע בַּמָּקוֹם
וַיָּלֶן שָׁם כִּי־בָא הַשֶּׁמֶשׁ וַיִּקַּח מֵאַבְנֵי הַמָּקוֹם וַיָּשֶׂם
יב מְרַאֲשֹׁתָיו וַיִּשְׁכַּב בַּמָּקוֹם הַהוּא: וַיַּחֲלֹם וְהִנֵּה סֻלָּם
מֻצָּב אַרְצָה וְרֹאשׁוֹ מַגִּיעַ הַשָּׁמָיְמָה וְהִנֵּה מַלְאֲכֵי
יג אֱלֹהִים עֹלִים וְיֹרְדִים בּוֹ: וְהִנֵּה יְהוָה נִצָּב עָלָיו
וַיֹּאמַר אֲנִי יְהוָה אֱלֹהֵי אַבְרָהָם אָבִיךָ וֵאלֹהֵי יִצְחָק
הָאָרֶץ אֲשֶׁר אַתָּה שֹׁכֵב עָלֶיהָ לְךָ אֶתְּנֶנָּה וּלְזַרְעֶךָ:
יד וְהָיָה זַרְעֲךָ כַּעֲפַר הָאָרֶץ וּפָרַצְתָּ יָמָּה וָקֵדְמָה

וְצָפֹנָה וָנֶגְבָּה וְנִבְרְכוּ בְךָ כָּל־מִשְׁפְּחֹת הָאֲדָמָה
טו וּבְזַרְעֶךָ: וְהִנֵּה אָנֹכִי עִמָּךְ וּשְׁמַרְתִּיךָ בְּכֹל אֲשֶׁר־
תֵּלֵךְ וַהֲשִׁבֹתִיךָ אֶל־הָאֲדָמָה הַזֹּאת כִּי לֹא אֶעֱזָבְךָ
טז עַד אֲשֶׁר אִם־עָשִׂיתִי אֵת אֲשֶׁר־דִּבַּרְתִּי לָךְ: וַיִּיקַץ
יַעֲקֹב מִשְּׁנָתוֹ וַיֹּאמֶר אָכֵן יֵשׁ יְהוָה בַּמָּקוֹם הַזֶּה
יז וְאָנֹכִי לֹא יָדָעְתִּי: וַיִּירָא וַיֹּאמַר מַה־נּוֹרָא הַמָּקוֹם
הַזֶּה אֵין זֶה כִּי אִם־בֵּית אֱלֹהִים וְזֶה שַׁעַר הַשָּׁמָיִם:
יח וַיַּשְׁכֵּם יַעֲקֹב בַּבֹּקֶר וַיִּקַּח אֶת־הָאֶבֶן אֲשֶׁר־שָׂם
מְרַאֲשֹׁתָיו וַיָּשֶׂם אֹתָהּ מַצֵּבָה וַיִּצֹק שֶׁמֶן עַל־רֹאשָׁהּ:

10] Jacob left Beer-sheba, and set out for Haran.   11] He came upon a certain place and stopped there for the night, for the sun had set. Taking one of the stones of that place, he put it under his head and lay down in that place.   12] He had a dream; a stairway was set on the ground and its top reached to the sky, and angels of God were going up and down on it.   13] And the LORD was standing beside him and He said, "I am the LORD, the God of your father Abraham and the God of Isaac: the ground on which you are lying I will give to you and to your offspring.   14] Your descendants shall be as the dust of the earth; you shall spread out to the west and to the east, to the north and to the south. All the families of the earth shall bless themselves by you and your descendants.   15] Remember, I am with you: I will protect you wherever you go and will bring you back to this land. I will not leave you until I have done what I have promised you."

16] Jacob awoke from his sleep and said, "Surely the LORD is present in this place, and I did not know it!"   17] Shaken, he said, "How awesome is this place! This is none other than the abode of God, and that is the gateway to heaven."   18] Early in the morning, Jacob took the stone that he had put under his head and set it up as a pillar and poured oil on the top of

28:12] *A dream.* On the subject of dreams, see commentary to Gen. 39:1–40:23.

Stairway. Or "ramp," or "ladder." The סֻלָּם (*sulam*) of Jacob's dream reflects an ancient belief in a cosmic bond between heaven and earth [1].

13] *Beside him.* עָלָיו. Compare with Gen. 18:8. / This translation follows Luzzatto in that עָלָיו refers to Jacob, not to the stairway./

Your father Abraham. Abraham is mentioned here because of the earlier promise made to him.

17] *Shaken.* וַיִּירָא. "Awestruck" would better express the Hebrew word play with "awesome" (נוֹרָא).

Gateway to heaven. Similar to the "bond [or rope] of heaven and earth" in Babylonian texts.

18] *A pillar.* Many ancient peoples believed that gods lived in stones. It is therefore not surprising that Jacob also believed this at this stage of his life. Pillars such as the one mentioned here have been found at Gezer, Hazor, and other places. In later times the Torah forbade the use of stone markers (מַצֵּבוֹת) for worship purposes and ordered those of the pagans to be destroyed (Exod. 23:24; Lev. 26:1; Deut. 16:22). When Jacob returns from Haran he will revisit this place (Gen. 35:14).

כב אֶל־בֵּית אָבִי וְהָיָה יְהֹוָה לִי לֵאלֹהִים: וְהָאֶבֶן הַזֹּאת יט וַיִּקְרָא אֶת־שֵׁם־הַמָּקוֹם הַהוּא בֵּית־אֵל וְאוּלָם לוּז שֵׁם־

אֲשֶׁר־שַׂמְתִּי מַצֵּבָה יִהְיֶה בֵּית אֱלֹהִים וְכֹל אֲשֶׁר כ הָעִיר לָרִאשֹׁנָה: וַיִּדַּר יַעֲקֹב נֶדֶר לֵאמֹר אִם־יִהְיֶה

תִּתֶּן־לִי עַשֵּׂר אֲעַשְּׂרֶנּוּ לָךְ: אֱלֹהִים עִמָּדִי וּשְׁמָרַנִי בַּדֶּרֶךְ הַזֶּה אֲשֶׁר אָנֹכִי הוֹלֵךְ

כא וְנָתַן־לִי לֶחֶם לֶאֱכֹל וּבֶגֶד לִלְבֹּשׁ: וְשַׁבְתִּי בְשָׁלוֹם

it. **19]** He named that site Bethel; but previously the name of the city had been Luz.

20] Jacob then made a vow, saying, "If God remains with me, if He protects me on this journey that I am making, and gives me bread to eat and clothing to wear, **21]** and if I return safe to my father's house—the LORD shall be my God. **22]** And this stone, which I have set up as a pillar, shall be God's abode; and of all that You give me, I will set aside a tithe for You."

19] *Bethel*. House of God. Abraham built an altar there previously (Gen. 12:8; 13:3–4), and it will be here that Jacob's name will be changed to Israel (Gen. 35:10–15). Excavations have shown that Bethel was founded about 2000 B.C.E. To the Canaanites, it was a sanctuary city dedicated to the god El, and the association with Jacob gave it added importance [2]. It is more frequently mentioned in the Bible than any other town except Jerusalem. The Prophets later condemned the altars of Bethel (e.g., Hos. 10:15; Amos 3:14).

Trial and Trembling

On awakening from his dream, Jacob promises that if God will be His protector, he in turn will worship God, build a shrine for Him, and offer Him a tithe.[1] This formal promise or vow (נֶדֶר) is conditional, and, although other such vows are found in the Bible (e.g., Judg. 11:30–31; I Sam. 1:11), it appears at first sight rather unusual.[2] Jacob bargains with God: if God performs properly—and performs first—Jacob will accept Him as his God. Readers often find this a highly objectionable way of dealing with the Almighty, especially since Jacob is shown doubting God's word. One ancient commentator, R. Jonathan, so despaired of explaining Jacob's words that he concluded that the text must somehow be in disarray [4].

Indeed, Jacob at Bethel is not yet the man of faith who wrestles with the angel. He is only at the beginning of his quest. This is his first experience with trial. Understandably, in anxiety he cries that he will do anything if only someone will help. Jacob, to be sure, does not deliver a "proper" prayer. He prays realistically, from the heart. The vow is his human response to the covenant that God has offered him. It is the expression of his experience, not of his philosophy, and in similar ways men have always prayed and promised when in moments of crisis God appears as the only help.[3]

Jacob's first encounter with God produces fear and trembling. The forefather foreshadows the mystery of chosenness that will rest in his descendants: They too will dream of angels and wondrous things, but when they awake and face the realities of the world they too will tremble and find the service of God filled with terror.

---

[1] The sense of this passage would be seriously altered if Gen. 28:21–22 were read: "... and if I return safe to my father's house and the Lord shall be my God, then this stone, etc." The Hebrew permits this interpretation [3].

[2] The usual vow demonstrated devotion without condition, often involving abstinence and special sacrifice. The Torah devotes many passages to rules about vows. See Lev. 27; Num. 6.

[3] The Psalms show that vow and fulfilment are but a worshiper's way of moving from anxiety to thanksgiving: "I will pay Thee my vows, / That which my lips uttered / And my mouth promised when I was in trouble" (Ps. 66:13–14). Also see Pss. 22:26; 61:6; and 116:14, 18 [5].

GLEANINGS

The Dream

The stairway (סֻלָּם) was a symbol of Sinai (סִינַי). Both have the same numerical values (130). [6]

God showed Jacob the giving of the Torah and said: "If your descendants observe this Torah, they will ascend like these angels; if not, they will descend like them." MIDRASH [7]

This Place

The "place," observe: *any* place where God lets down the ladder. And how are you to know where that will be? Or how are you to determine where it may be, but by being ready for it always? JOHN RUSKIN [8]

Ha-Makom

In post-biblical usage הַמָּקוֹם (the place) was a name for God, so that (Gen. 28:11) "He came upon a certain place" could be read "He came upon God." Is God then a place? In a way, say the Rabbis, in that He encompasses the whole world: "God is the place of the world, but the world is not His place." [9]

The Gate of Heaven

Praying at any place is like standing at the very foot of God's throne of glory, for the gate of heaven is there and the door is open for prayer to be heard. MIDRASH [10]

I Did Not Know (Gen. 28:16)

When can man experience God's nearness? Only when he is suffused by "I don't know," when he himself knows that he does not know and does not pretend to have wisdom and insight. PANIM YAFOT [11]

Thy Holy Choice

Here—Lord—I lie, Jacob, whom Thou didst call—
Chosen by Thee—and yet . . . child of this earth!
Lord, what Thy will imposes soon or late—
I'll bear it not as yoke—but as a crown!
If Thou didst choose my blood to be a torch
Which flaming burns above the nations' ways,
Let none that from my blood come forth forget,
Ever forget, my God, Thy holy choice!
But if they should forget—in weariness
Drop on their way—let not their heart be faint—
RICHARD BEER-HOFMANN [12]

A Bursting Cloud

what angels, what memories
jacob dreamed that even though
man expelled himself from paradise
his hand would look upward
would see upward in god's grace
when he saw destiny
in the stretching skies beyond. . . .
and he looked up
to the mountains yon
and knew that god
had been accompanying his dream
and in waking will was now his own
and he bent to the stone
upon he slept
kissing it, seeing
the faces of his patriarchs
and for a moment
against the glitter of the sun
thought he saw adam's hand
against a bursting cloud.
DAVID WEISTUB [13]

197

Jacob in Haran

Jacob now tastes the fruit of deception and faces long service; he suffers and matures. This section deals with family life—with conception and birth, both human and animal. In the interplay of these biological forces, the Torah sees the working of God's plan.

In reading these accounts we should keep in mind that the Torah is interested less in describing the correct origin of names than it is in the background of the tribes, which these names represent. It answered questions for ancient Israel that in different form are asked by most groups: Who were our ancestors? How did we come to have our tribal and national structure?

א וַיִּשָּׂא יַעֲקֹב רַגְלָיו וַיֵּלֶךְ אַרְצָה בְנֵי־קֶדֶם: ב וַיַּרְא וְהִנֵּה בְאֵר בַּשָּׂדֶה וְהִנֵּה־שָׁם שְׁלֹשָׁה עֶדְרֵי־צֹאן רֹבְצִים עָלֶיהָ כִּי מִן־הַבְּאֵר הַהִוא יַשְׁקוּ הָעֲדָרִים וְהָאֶבֶן גְּדֹלָה עַל־פִּי הַבְּאֵר: ג וְנֶאֶסְפוּ־שָׁמָּה כָל־הָעֲדָרִים וְגָלֲלוּ אֶת־הָאֶבֶן מֵעַל פִּי הַבְּאֵר וְהִשְׁקוּ אֶת־הַצֹּאן וְהֵשִׁיבוּ אֶת־הָאֶבֶן עַל־פִּי הַבְּאֵר לִמְקֹמָהּ: ד וַיֹּאמֶר לָהֶם יַעֲקֹב אַחַי מֵאַיִן אַתֶּם וַיֹּאמְרוּ מֵחָרָן אֲנָחְנוּ: ה וַיֹּאמֶר לָהֶם הַיְדַעְתֶּם אֶת־לָבָן בֶּן־נָחוֹר וַיֹּאמְרוּ יָדָעְנוּ: ו וַיֹּאמֶר לָהֶם הֲשָׁלוֹם לוֹ וַיֹּאמְרוּ שָׁלוֹם וְהִנֵּה רָחֵל בִּתּוֹ בָּאָה עִם־הַצֹּאן: ז וַיֹּאמֶר הֵן עוֹד הַיּוֹם גָּדוֹל לֹא־עֵת הֵאָסֵף הַמִּקְנֶה הַשְׁקוּ הַצֹּאן וּלְכוּ רְעוּ:

ח וַיֹּאמְרוּ לֹא נוּכַל עַד אֲשֶׁר יֵאָסְפוּ כָּל־הָעֲדָרִים וְגָלֲלוּ אֶת־הָאֶבֶן מֵעַל פִּי הַבְּאֵר וְהִשְׁקִינוּ הַצֹּאן: ט עוֹדֶנּוּ מְדַבֵּר עִמָּם וְרָחֵל בָּאָה עִם־הַצֹּאן אֲשֶׁר לְאָבִיהָ כִּי רֹעָה הִוא: י וַיְהִי כַּאֲשֶׁר רָאָה יַעֲקֹב אֶת־רָחֵל בַּת־לָבָן אֲחִי אִמּוֹ וְאֶת־צֹאן לָבָן אֲחִי אִמּוֹ וַיִּגַּשׁ יַעֲקֹב וַיָּגֶל אֶת־הָאֶבֶן מֵעַל פִּי הַבְּאֵר וַיַּשְׁקְ אֶת־צֹאן לָבָן אֲחִי אִמּוֹ: יא וַיִּשַּׁק יַעֲקֹב לְרָחֵל וַיִּשָּׂא אֶת־קֹלוֹ וַיֵּבְךְּ: יב וַיַּגֵּד יַעֲקֹב לְרָחֵל כִּי אֲחִי אָבִיהָ הוּא וְכִי בֶן־רִבְקָה הוּא וַתָּרָץ וַתַּגֵּד לְאָבִיהָ: יג וַיְהִי כִשְׁמֹעַ לָבָן אֶת־שֵׁמַע יַעֲקֹב בֶּן־אֲחֹתוֹ וַיָּרָץ לִקְרָאתוֹ וַיְחַבֶּק־לוֹ וַיְנַשֶּׁק־לוֹ וַיְבִיאֵהוּ אֶל־בֵּיתוֹ וַיְסַפֵּר לְלָבָן אֵת

1] Jacob resumed his journey and came to the land of the Easterners. 2] There before his eyes was a well in the open. Three flocks of sheep were lying there beside it, for the flocks were watered from that well. The stone on the mouth of the well was large. 3] When all the flocks were gathered there, the stone would be rolled from the mouth of the well and the sheep watered; then the stone would be put back in its place on the mouth of the well.

4] Jacob said to them, "My friends, where are you from?" And they said, "We are from Haran." 5] He said to them, "Do you know Laban the son of Nahor?" And they said, "Yes, we do." 6] He continued, "Is he well?" They answered, "Yes, he is; and there is his daughter Rachel, coming with the flock." 7] He said, "It is still broad daylight, too early to round up the animals; water the flock and take them to pasture." 8] But they said, "We cannot, until all the flocks are rounded up; then the stone is rolled off the mouth of the well and we water the sheep."

9] While he was still speaking with them, Rachel came with her father's flock; for she was a shepherdess. 10] And when Jacob saw Rachel, the daughter of his uncle Laban, and the flock of his uncle Laban, Jacob went up and rolled the stone off the mouth of the well, and watered the flock of his uncle Laban. 11] Then Jacob kissed Rachel, and broke into tears. 12] Jacob told Rachel that he was her father's kinsman, that he was Rebekah's son; and she ran and told her father. 13] On hearing the news of his sister's son Jacob, Laban ran to greet him; he embraced him and kissed him, and took him into his house. He told Laban all that had

---

29:1] *Resumed his journey.* Literally, "lifted up his feet."

7] *Water the flock.* Jacob is the son of a rich man and is used to giving commands. Apparently he is listened to with respect even though he is a stranger.

10] *Uncle.* Literally, "his mother's brother."

Rolled the stone. Lifting and throwing heavy stones was an old way of proving prowess [1]. Jacob demonstrates his strength in order to impress the lovely girl.

11] *Kissed Rachel.* A formal greeting, here offered with deep emotion.

יד כָּל־הַדְּבָרִים הָאֵלֶּה: וַיֹּאמֶר לוֹ לָבָן אַךְ עַצְמִי
טו וּבְשָׂרִי אָתָּה וַיֵּשֶׁב עִמּוֹ חֹדֶשׁ יָמִים: וַיֹּאמֶר לָבָן
לְיַעֲקֹב הֲכִי־אָחִי אַתָּה וַעֲבַדְתַּנִי חִנָּם הַגִּידָה לִּי מַה־
טז מַּשְׂכֻּרְתֶּךָ: וּלְלָבָן שְׁתֵּי בָנוֹת שֵׁם הַגְּדֹלָה לֵאָה וְשֵׁם
יז הַקְּטַנָּה רָחֵל: וְעֵינֵי לֵאָה רַכּוֹת וְרָחֵל הָיְתָה יְפַת־
יח תֹּאַר וִיפַת מַרְאֶה: וַיֶּאֱהַב יַעֲקֹב אֶת־רָחֵל וַיֹּאמֶר
יט אֶעֱבָדְךָ שֶׁבַע שָׁנִים בְּרָחֵל בִּתְּךָ הַקְּטַנָּה: וַיֹּאמֶר
לָבָן טוֹב תִּתִּי אֹתָהּ לָךְ מִתִּתִּי אֹתָהּ לְאִישׁ אַחֵר
כ שְׁבָה עִמָּדִי: וַיַּעֲבֹד יַעֲקֹב בְּרָחֵל שֶׁבַע שָׁנִים

וַיִּהְיוּ בְעֵינָיו כְּיָמִים אֲחָדִים בְּאַהֲבָתוֹ אֹתָהּ:
כא וַיֹּאמֶר יַעֲקֹב אֶל־לָבָן הָבָה אֶת־אִשְׁתִּי כִּי מָלְאוּ יָמָי
כב וְאָבוֹאָה אֵלֶיהָ: וַיֶּאֱסֹף לָבָן אֶת־כָּל־אַנְשֵׁי הַמָּקוֹם וַיַּעַשׂ
כג מִשְׁתֶּה: וַיְהִי בָעֶרֶב וַיִּקַּח אֶת־לֵאָה בִתּוֹ וַיָּבֵא אֹתָהּ
כד אֵלָיו וַיָּבֹא אֵלֶיהָ: וַיִּתֵּן לָבָן לָהּ אֶת־זִלְפָּה שִׁפְחָתוֹ
כה לְלֵאָה בִתּוֹ שִׁפְחָה: וַיְהִי בַבֹּקֶר וְהִנֵּה־הִוא לֵאָה
וַיֹּאמֶר אֶל־לָבָן מַה־זֹּאת עָשִׂיתָ לִּי הֲלֹא בְרָחֵל
כו עָבַדְתִּי עִמָּךְ וְלָמָּה רִמִּיתָנִי: וַיֹּאמֶר לָבָן לֹא־יֵעָשֶׂה
כֵן בִּמְקוֹמֵנוּ לָתֵת הַצְּעִירָה לִפְנֵי הַבְּכִירָה: מַלֵּא

happened, 14] and Laban said to him, "You are truly my bone and flesh."

When he had stayed with him a month's time, 15] Laban said to Jacob, "Just because you are my kinsman, should you serve me for nothing? Tell me, what shall your wages be?" 16] Now Laban had two daughters; the name of the older one was Leah, and the name of the younger was Rachel. 17] Leah had weak eyes; Rachel was shapely and beautiful. 18] Jacob loved Rachel; so he answered, "I will serve you seven years for your younger daughter Rachel." 19] Laban said, "Better that I give her to you than that I should give her to an outsider. Stay with me." 20] So Jacob served seven years for Rachel and they seemed to him but a few days because of his love for her.

21] Then Jacob said to Laban, "Give me my wife, for my time is fulfilled, that I may consort with her." 22] And Laban gathered all the people of the place and made a feast. 23] When evening came, he took his daughter Leah and brought her to him; and he cohabited with her.— 24] Laban had given his maidservant Zilpah to his daughter Leah as her maid.— 25] When morning came, there was Leah! So he said to Laban, "What is this you have done to me? I was in your service for Rachel! Why did you deceive me?" 26] Laban said, "It is not the practice in our place to marry off the younger before the older. 27] Wait until the bridal week of this

17] *Weak eyes.* It seems preferable to translate this as "tender eyes" [2], for the contrast is not between ugliness and beauty but between two types of attraction.

18] *I will serve you seven years.* Jacob's offer of seven years is so extreme that Laban is bound to accept. Service or performance of some kind to obtain a wife is a recurring biblical motif (see Josh. 15:16; Judg. 1:12).

22] *A feast.* This was not only a testimony to the family's approval of the match, it also provided the opportunity to introduce the veiled bride into the marriage chamber; the subsequent marital relations would consummate the marriage. Once the feast was over, Leah would be considered married unless Jacob repudiated her. To prevent this, Laban asks Jacob to stay the week with her, before taking Rachel, too, as his wife. Laban's concern and cordiality last only one month [3].

24] *Maidservant.* According to Hurrian custom, high-status women received maidservants as part of their dowry.

25] *Deceive me.* Jacob uses the same Hebrew word (רִמִּיתָנִי) that Isaac used when he complained about being deceived (Gen. 27:35).

26] *The younger before the older.* Laban's remark makes it clear that Jacob has no right to complain, for he now receives retribution for having himself overtaken his older brother Esau [4].

שָׁבַע זֹאת וְנִתְּנָה לְךָ גַּם־אֶת־זֹאת בַּעֲבֹדָה אֲשֶׁר
תַּעֲבֹד עִמָּדִי עוֹד שֶׁבַע־שָׁנִים אֲחֵרוֹת: וַיַּעַשׂ יַעֲקֹב
כֵּן וַיְמַלֵּא שְׁבֻעַ זֹאת וַיִּתֶּן־לוֹ אֶת־רָחֵל בִּתּוֹ לוֹ לְאִשָּׁה:
וַיִּתֵּן לָבָן לְרָחֵל בִּתּוֹ אֶת־בִּלְהָה שִׁפְחָתוֹ לָהּ לְשִׁפְחָה:
וַיָּבֹא גַּם אֶל־רָחֵל וַיֶּאֱהַב גַּם־אֶת־רָחֵל מִלֵּאָה וַיַּעֲבֹד
עִמּוֹ עוֹד שֶׁבַע־שָׁנִים אֲחֵרוֹת: וַיַּרְא יְהוָה כִּי־שְׂנוּאָה
לֵאָה וַיִּפְתַּח אֶת־רַחְמָהּ וְרָחֵל עֲקָרָה: וַתַּהַר לֵאָה
וַתֵּלֶד בֵּן וַתִּקְרָא שְׁמוֹ רְאוּבֵן כִּי אָמְרָה כִּי־רָאָה
יְהוָה בְּעָנְיִי כִּי עַתָּה יֶאֱהָבַנִי אִישִׁי: וַתַּהַר עוֹד וַתֵּלֶד

בֵּן וַתֹּאמֶר כִּי־שָׁמַע יְהוָה כִּי־שְׂנוּאָה אָנֹכִי וַיִּתֶּן־לִי
גַּם־אֶת־זֶה וַתִּקְרָא שְׁמוֹ שִׁמְעוֹן: וַתַּהַר עוֹד וַתֵּלֶד בֵּן
וַתֹּאמֶר עַתָּה הַפַּעַם יִלָּוֶה אִישִׁי אֵלַי כִּי־יָלַדְתִּי לוֹ
שְׁלֹשָׁה בָנִים עַל־כֵּן קָרָא־שְׁמוֹ לֵוִי: וַתַּהַר עוֹד וַתֵּלֶד
בֵּן וַתֹּאמֶר הַפַּעַם אוֹדֶה אֶת־יְהוָה עַל־כֵּן קָרְאָה
שְׁמוֹ יְהוּדָה וַתַּעֲמֹד מִלֶּדֶת:

וַתֵּרֶא רָחֵל כִּי לֹא יָלְדָה לְיַעֲקֹב וַתְּקַנֵּא רָחֵל
בַּאֲחֹתָהּ וַתֹּאמֶר אֶל־יַעֲקֹב הָבָה־לִּי בָנִים וְאִם־אַיִן
מֵתָה אָנֹכִי: וַיִּחַר־אַף יַעֲקֹב בְּרָחֵל וַיֹּאמֶר הֲתַחַת

one is over and we will give you that one too, provided you serve me another seven years." **28]** Jacob did so: he waited out the bridal week of the one, and then he gave him his daughter Rachel as wife.— **29]** Laban had given his maidservant Bilhah to his daughter Rachel as her maid.— **30]** And Jacob cohabited with Rachel also; indeed, he loved Rachel more than Leah. And he served him another seven years.

31] The LORD saw that Leah was unloved and he opened her womb; but Rachel was barren. **32]** Leah conceived and bore a son, and named him Reuben; for she declared, "It means: 'The LORD has seen my affliction'; it also means: 'Now my husband will love me.'" **33]** She conceived again and bore a son, and declared, "This is because the LORD heard that I was unloved and has given me this one also"; so she named him Simeon. **34]** Again she conceived and bore a son and declared, "This time my husband will become attached to me, for I have borne him three sons." Therefore he was named Levi. **35]** She conceived again and bore a son, and declared, "This time I will praise the LORD." Therefore she named him Judah. Then she stopped bearing.

1] When Rachel saw that she had borne Jacob no children, she became envious of her sister; and Rachel said to Jacob, "Give me children, or I shall die." **2]** Jacob was incensed at Rachel,

28] *Gave him his daughter Rachel.* Marrying two sisters in this fashion was later forbidden (Lev. 18:18).

32] *Has seen.* רָאָה (ra-ah), connected with רְאוּ (re-u), which is the first part of Reuben.

Will love me. יֶאֱהָבַנִי (ye-ehevani) apparently meant as an assonance with בֵּן (ben), last part of Reuben. Note that it is the women who give the names (see commentary to Gen. 12:10–13:18).

33] *Heard.* שָׁמַע (shama), connected with שִׁמְעוֹן (shim-on). The real origin of the name is prob-

ably found in a word similar to the Arabic *sim'u* (wolf-hyena), a cognomen that would be descriptive of Simeon's violent nature. Examples of other personal names referring to animals are Rachel (ewe), Yael (mountain goat), Jonah (dove), Shaphan (rock-rabbit), Deborah (bee), and Hamor (donkey).

34] *Attached.* יִלָּוֶה, connected with לֵוִי.

35] *I will praise.* אוֹדֶה, connected with יְהוּדָה. Note Leah's pathetic hope that by giving him sons Jacob will come to love her.

ט נַפְתָּלִי: וַתֵּרֶא לֵאָה כִּי עָמְדָה מִלֶּדֶת וַתִּקַּח אֶת־
י זִלְפָּה שִׁפְחָתָהּ וַתִּתֵּן אֹתָהּ לְיַעֲקֹב לְאִשָּׁה: וַתֵּלֶד
יא זִלְפָּה שִׁפְחַת לֵאָה לְיַעֲקֹב בֵּן: וַתֹּאמֶר לֵאָה בְּגָד
יב וַתִּקְרָא אֶת־שְׁמוֹ גָּד: וַתֵּלֶד זִלְפָּה שִׁפְחַת לֵאָה בֵּן
יג שֵׁנִי לְיַעֲקֹב: וַתֹּאמֶר לֵאָה בְּאָשְׁרִי כִּי אִשְּׁרוּנִי בָּנוֹת
יד וַתִּקְרָא אֶת־שְׁמוֹ אָשֵׁר: וַיֵּלֶךְ רְאוּבֵן בִּימֵי קְצִיר־
חִטִּים וַיִּמְצָא דוּדָאִים בַּשָּׂדֶה וַיָּבֵא אֹתָם אֶל־לֵאָה
אִמּוֹ וַתֹּאמֶר רָחֵל אֶל־לֵאָה תְּנִי־נָא לִי מִדּוּדָאֵי
* יא בא גד קרי.

ג אֱלֹהִים אָנֹכִי אֲשֶׁר־מָנַע מִמֵּךְ פְּרִי־בָטֶן: וַתֹּאמֶר הִנֵּה
אֲמָתִי בִלְהָה בֹּא אֵלֶיהָ וְתֵלֵד עַל־בִּרְכַּי וְאִבָּנֶה גַם־
ד אָנֹכִי מִמֶּנָּה: וַתִּתֶּן־לוֹ אֶת־בִּלְהָה שִׁפְחָתָהּ לְאִשָּׁה
ה וַיָּבֹא אֵלֶיהָ יַעֲקֹב: וַתַּהַר בִּלְהָה וַתֵּלֶד לְיַעֲקֹב בֵּן:
ו וַתֹּאמֶר רָחֵל דָּנַנִּי אֱלֹהִים וְגַם שָׁמַע בְּקֹלִי וַיִּתֶּן־לִי
ז בֵּן עַל־כֵּן קָרְאָה שְׁמוֹ דָּן: וַתַּהַר עוֹד וַתֵּלֶד בִּלְהָה
ח שִׁפְחַת רָחֵל בֵּן שֵׁנִי לְיַעֲקֹב: וַתֹּאמֶר רָחֵל נַפְתּוּלֵי
אֱלֹהִים נִפְתַּלְתִּי עִם־אֲחֹתִי גַּם־יָכֹלְתִּי וַתִּקְרָא שְׁמוֹ

and said, "Can I take the place of God, who has denied you fruit of the womb?" **3]** She said, "Here is my maid Bilhah. Consort with her, that she may bear on my knees and that through her I too may have children." **4]** So she gave him her maid Bilhah as concubine, and Jacob cohabited with her. **5]** Bilhah conceived and bore Jacob a son. **6]** And Rachel said, "God has vindicated me; indeed, He has heeded my plea and given me a son." Therefore she named him Dan. **7]** Rachel's maid Bilhah conceived again and bore Jacob a second son. **8]** And Rachel said, "A fateful contest I waged with my sister; yes, and I have prevailed." So she named him Naphtali.

9] When Leah saw that she had stopped bearing, she took her maid Zilpah and gave her to Jacob as concubine. **10]** And when Leah's maid Zilpah bore Jacob a son, **11]** Leah said, "What luck!" So she named him Gad. **12]** When Leah's maid Zilpah bore Jacob a second son, **13]** Leah declared, "What fortune!" meaning, "Women will deem me fortunate." So she named him Asher.

14] Once, at the time of the wheat harvest, Reuben came upon some mandrakes in the field

30:3] *Here is my maid.* Sarah's dilemma is re-enacted (Gen. 16:2). Rachel performs the ancient custom of establishing the child's legitimacy or of adopting him by placing him on her knee. Henceforth she speaks of Bilhah's children as "mine."

/ This procedure is attested to in Babylonian, Hittite, Hurrian, and Greek laws./

6] *Vindicated me.* דָּנַנִּי is connected with דָּן (judged).

8] *A fateful contest I waged.* נַפְתּוּלֵי...נִפְתַּלְתִּי is connected with נַפְתָּלִי. Literally, "a contest of God," suggesting that an ordeal was involved.

11] *What luck.* The written text is בגד (bgd), while the understood text is בָּא גָד (ba gad), "luck has come," connected with Gad. This practice of reading the text differently from the written word constituted the Masoretes' way of providing an official reading which differed from the received manuscripts. In such cases the written text is referred to as כְּתִיב (ketiv), the official and pronounced word as קְרִי (kerey).

13] *What fortune.* בְּאָשְׁרִי is connected with אָשֵׁר. This translation is more exact than "happy."

14] *Mandrakes.* A plant whose potato-like bulbs sometimes look like faces. (The ancient belief in the mandrake as a sexual stimulant has persisted into modern times.) The potion fails for Rachel, while Leah, who does not use it, becomes pregnant. The intended meaning, then, is that only God can grant relief from barrenness.

טו בְּנֵךְ: וַתֹּאמֶר לָהּ הַמְעַט קַחְתֵּךְ אֶת־אִישִׁי וְלָקַחַת
גַּם אֶת־דּוּדָאֵי בְּנִי וַתֹּאמֶר רָחֵל לָכֵן יִשְׁכַּב עִמָּךְ
טז הַלַּיְלָה תַּחַת דּוּדָאֵי בְנֵךְ: וַיָּבֹא יַעֲקֹב מִן־הַשָּׂדֶה
בָּעֶרֶב וַתֵּצֵא לֵאָה לִקְרָאתוֹ וַתֹּאמֶר אֵלַי תָּבוֹא כִּי
שָׂכֹר שְׂכַרְתִּיךָ בְּדוּדָאֵי בְּנִי וַיִּשְׁכַּב עִמָּהּ בַּלַּיְלָה
יז הוּא: וַיִּשְׁמַע אֱלֹהִים אֶל־לֵאָה וַתַּהַר וַתֵּלֶד לְיַעֲקֹב
יח בֵּן חֲמִישִׁי: וַתֹּאמֶר לֵאָה נָתַן אֱלֹהִים שְׂכָרִי אֲשֶׁר־
יט נָתַתִּי שִׁפְחָתִי לְאִישִׁי וַתִּקְרָא שְׁמוֹ יִשָּׂשכָר: וַתַּהַר עוֹד
כ לֵאָה וַתֵּלֶד בֵּן־שִׁשִּׁי לְיַעֲקֹב: וַתֹּאמֶר לֵאָה זְבָדַנִי

אֱלֹהִים אֹתִי זֶבֶד טוֹב הַפַּעַם יִזְבְּלֵנִי אִישִׁי כִּי־יָלַדְתִּי
כא לוֹ שִׁשָּׁה בָנִים וַתִּקְרָא אֶת־שְׁמוֹ זְבֻלוּן: וְאַחַר יָלְדָה
כב בַּת וַתִּקְרָא אֶת־שְׁמָהּ דִּינָה: וַיִּזְכֹּר אֱלֹהִים אֶת־רָחֵל
כג וַיִּשְׁמַע אֵלֶיהָ אֱלֹהִים וַיִּפְתַּח אֶת־רַחְמָהּ: וַתַּהַר וַתֵּלֶד
כד בֵּן וַתֹּאמֶר אָסַף אֱלֹהִים אֶת־חֶרְפָּתִי: וַתִּקְרָא אֶת־
כה שְׁמוֹ יוֹסֵף לֵאמֹר יֹסֵף יְהֹוָה לִי בֵּן אַחֵר: וַיְהִי כַּאֲשֶׁר
יָלְדָה רָחֵל אֶת־יוֹסֵף וַיֹּאמֶר יַעֲקֹב אֶל־לָבָן שַׁלְּחֵנִי
כו וְאֵלְכָה אֶל־מְקוֹמִי וּלְאַרְצִי: תְּנָה אֶת־נָשַׁי וְאֶת־יְלָדַי
אֲשֶׁר עָבַדְתִּי אֹתְךָ בָּהֵן וְאֵלֵכָה כִּי אַתָּה יָדַעְתָּ אֶת־

and brought them to his mother Leah. Rachel said to Leah, "Please give me some of your son's mandrakes." **15]** But she said to her, "Was it not enough for you to take away my husband, that you would also take my son's mandrakes?" Rachel replied, "I promise, he shall lie with you tonight, in return for your son's mandrakes." **16]** When Jacob came home from the field in the evening, Leah went out to meet him and said, "You are to sleep with me, for I have hired you with my son's mandrakes." And he lay with her that night. **17]** God heeded Leah, and she conceived and bore him a fifth son. **18]** And Leah said, "God has given me my reward for having given my maid to my husband." So she named him Issachar. **19]** When Leah conceived again and bore Jacob a sixth son, **20]** Leah said, "God has given me a choice gift; this time my husband will exalt me, for I have borne him six sons." So she named him Zebulun. **21]** Lastly, she bore him a daughter, and named her Dinah.

22] Now God remembered Rachel; God heeded her and opened her womb. **23]** She conceived and bore a son, and said, "God has taken away my disgrace." **24]** So she named him Joseph, which is to say, "May the LORD add another son for me."

25] After Rachel had borne Joseph, Jacob said to Laban, "Give me leave to go back to my own homeland. **26]** Give me my wives and my children, for whom I have served you, that I

/Rashi translates "jasmine"; similarly B. Jacob, who denies that a potion was involved. Rather, Rachel wanted Leah's flowers to give to her husband. So also Luzzatto [5]./

18] *Issachar.* The text derives the name both from שָׂכֹר שְׂכַרְתִּיךָ (I have hired you) in Gen. 30:16 and from שְׂכָרִי (my reward).

20] *Zebulun.* Two derivations are offered: זֶבֶד (a choice gift) and יִזְבְּלֵנִי (will give me presents). The meaning of the second is uncertain. The two explanations appear to stem from separate traditions.

/Some scholars derive the name from the Akkadian

zubullu (bridegroom's gift), others link the name to the Ugaritic *zlb*, a divine epithet [6]./

22] *God remembered Rachel.* Stressing that He, not a potion, opened her womb.

24] *Joseph.* Again, two explanations are given for the name: אָסַף (has taken away) and יֹסֵף (may [He] add).

26] *Give me.* Jacob is Laban's son-in-law but also very much the servant who entreats his master for the wages due him.

כּי־תָבוֹא עַל־שְׂכָרִי לְפָנֶיךָ כֹּל אֲשֶׁר־אֵינֶנּוּ נָקֹד וְטָלוּא   כּ עָבַדְתִּי אֲשֶׁר עֲבַדְתִּיךָ: וַיֹּאמֶר אֵלָיו לָבָן אִם־נָא
בָּעִזִּים וְחוּם בַּכְּשָׂבִים גָּנוּב הוּא אִתִּי: וַיֹּאמֶר לָבָן   מָצָאתִי חֵן בְּעֵינֶיךָ נִחַשְׁתִּי וַיְבָרֲכֵנִי יְהוָה בִּגְלָלֶךָ:
לֹד הֵן לוּ יְהִי כִדְבָרֶךָ: וַיָּסַר בַּיּוֹם הַהוּא אֶת־הַתְּיָשִׁים   כּט וַיֹּאמֶר נָקְבָה שְׂכָרְךָ עָלַי וְאֶתֵּנָה: וַיֹּאמֶר אֵלָיו אַתָּה
הָעֲקֻדִּים וְהַטְּלֻאִים וְאֵת כָּל־הָעִזִּים הַנְּקֻדּוֹת וְהַטְּלֻאֹת   יָדַעְתָּ אֵת אֲשֶׁר עֲבַדְתִּיךָ וְאֵת אֲשֶׁר־הָיָה מִקְנְךָ אִתִּי:
כֹּל אֲשֶׁר־לָבָן בּוֹ וְכָל־חוּם בַּכְּשָׂבִים וַיִּתֵּן בְּיַד־בָּנָיו: ל כִּי מְעַט אֲשֶׁר־הָיָה לְךָ לְפָנַי וַיִּפְרֹץ לָרֹב וַיְבָרֶךְ
לו וַיָּשֶׂם דֶּרֶךְ שְׁלֹשֶׁת יָמִים בֵּינוֹ וּבֵין יַעֲקֹב וְיַעֲקֹב רֹעֶה   יְהוָה אֹתְךָ לְרַגְלִי וְעַתָּה מָתַי אֶעֱשֶׂה גַם־אָנֹכִי לְבֵיתִי:
אֶת־צֹאן לָבָן הַנּוֹתָרֹת: וַיִּקַּח־לוֹ יַעֲקֹב מַקַּל לִבְנֶה   לא וַיֹּאמֶר מָה אֶתֶּן־לָךְ וַיֹּאמֶר יַעֲקֹב לֹא־תִתֶּן־לִי מְאוּמָה
לַח וְלוּז וְעַרְמוֹן וַיְפַצֵּל בָּהֵן פְּצָלוֹת לְבָנוֹת מַחְשֹׂף   אִם־תַּעֲשֶׂה־לִּי הַדָּבָר הַזֶּה אָשׁוּבָה אֶרְעֶה צֹאנְךָ
הַלָּבָן אֲשֶׁר עַל־הַמַּקְלוֹת: וַיַּצֵּג אֶת־הַמַּקְלוֹת אֲשֶׁר   לב אֶעֱבֹר בְּכָל־צֹאנְךָ הַיּוֹם הָסֵר מִשָּׁם כָּל־שֶׂה
פִּצֵּל בָּרְהָטִים בְּשִׁקֲתוֹת הַמָּיִם אֲשֶׁר תָּבֹאןָ הַצֹּאן   נָקֹד וְטָלוּא וְכָל־שֶׂה־חוּם בַּכְּשָׂבִים וְטָלוּא וְנָקֹד
לט לִשְׁתּוֹת לְנֹכַח הַצֹּאן וַיֵּחַמְנָה בְּבֹאָן לִשְׁתּוֹת: וַיֶּחֱמוּ   בָּעִזִּים וְהָיָה שְׂכָרִי: וְעָנְתָה־בִּי צִדְקָתִי בְּיוֹם מָחָר

may go; for well you know what services I have rendered you." **27]** But Laban said to him, "If you will indulge me, I have learned by divination that the LORD has blessed me on your account." **28]** And he continued, "Name the wages due from me, and I will pay you." **29]** But he said, "You know well how I have served you and how your livestock has fared with me. **30]** For the little you had before I came has grown to much, since the LORD has blessed you wherever I turned. And now, when shall I make provision for my own household?" **31]** He said, "What shall I pay you?" And Jacob said, "Pay me nothing! If you will do this thing for me, I will again pasture and keep your flocks: **32]** let me pass through your whole flock today, removing from there every speckled and spotted animal—every dark-colored sheep and every spotted and speckled goat. Such shall be my wages. **33]** In the future when you go over my wages, let my honesty toward you testify for me: if there are among my goats any that are not speckled or spotted or any sheep that are not dark-colored, they got there by theft." **34]** And Laban said, "Very well, let it be as you say."

35] But that same day he removed the streaked and spotted he-goats and all the speckled and spotted she-goats—every one that had white on it—and all the dark-colored sheep, and left them in the charge of his sons. **36]** And he put a distance of three days' journey between himself and Jacob, while Jacob was pasturing the rest of Laban's flock.

37] Jacob then got fresh shoots of poplar, and of almond and plane, and peeled white stripes in them, laying bare the white of the shoots. **38]** The rods that he had peeled he set up in front of the goats in the troughs, the water receptacles, that the goats came to drink from. Their mating occurred when they came to drink, **39]** and since the goats mated by the rods, the

27] *Indulge me.* Literally, "if I have found favor in your eyes."

I have learned by divination. Laban apparently thought that many of his black sheep looked like goats, which was considered a good omen [7].

The Lord has blessed me. A deferential mention of Jacob's God by the wily Laban, who is polite to the extreme.

/However, other versions have אֱלֹהִים./

36] In the Samaritan version, the dream sequence related in Gen. 31:10–13 is inserted after this verse, which improves the sense of otherwise difficult passages.

39] *Goats.* Literally, "flocks" [8].

הַצֹּאן אֶל־הַמַּקְלוֹת וַתֵּלַדְןָ הַצֹּאן עֲקֻדִּים נְקֻדִּים מּ בָּרְחָטִים לְיַחְמֶנָּה בַּמַּקְלוֹת: וּבְהַעֲטִיף הַצֹּאן לֹא
וּטְלֻאִים: וְהַכְּשָׂבִים הִפְרִיד יַעֲקֹב וַיִּתֵּן פְּנֵי הַצֹּאן מּ יָשִׂים וְהָיָה הָעֲטֻפִים לְלָבָן וְהַקְּשֻׁרִים לְיַעֲקֹב: וַיִּפְרֹץ
אֶל־עָקֹד וְכָל־חוּם בְּצֹאן לָבָן וַיָּשֶׁת לוֹ עֲדָרִים לְבַדּוֹ הָאִישׁ מְאֹד מְאֹד וַיְהִי־לוֹ צֹאן רַבּוֹת וּשְׁפָחוֹת וַעֲבָדִים
מּ וְלֹא שָׁתָם עַל־צֹאן לָבָן: וְהָיָה בְּכָל־יַחֵם הַצֹּאן וּגְמַלִּים וַחֲמֹרִים:
הַמְקֻשָּׁרוֹת וְשָׂם יַעֲקֹב אֶת־הַמַּקְלוֹת לְעֵינֵי הַצֹּאן

goats brought forth streaked, speckled, and spotted young. **40]** But Jacob dealt separately with the sheep; he made these animals face the streaked or wholly dark-colored animals in Laban's flock. And so he produced special flocks for himself, which he did not put with Laban's flocks. **41]** Moreover, when the sturdier animals were mating, Jacob would place the rods in the troughs, in full view of the animals, so that they mated by the rods; **42]** but with the feebler animals he would not place them there. Thus the feeble ones went to Laban and the sturdy to Jacob. **43]** So the man grew exceedingly prosperous, and came to own large flocks, maidservants and menservants, camels and asses.

41] *Sturdier.* Or, "early-breeding."   42] *Feebler.* Or, "late-breeding."

The Tribal Ancestors

The births of Jacob's sons are described in great detail because the Torah depicts the twelve tribes of Israel as having originated from the twelve sons of Jacob. This genealogical conception of Israel's history is an important feature of the biblical tradition, for it traces the background not merely of kings but of the whole people. This conception is also reflected in the recurrent emphasis on descent, on the "lines" of the Patriarchs.

Some scholars have suggested that these ancestral figures were the projection of later generations, reflecting the time of the Judges, when the tribes were linked in a sacral confederation, or amphictyony. In this view of Israel's history, the tribes were related to the twelve calendar months, and each tribe made a monthly contribution to or participated in rites at the cultic center, as did the Mesopotamians and Greeks. Popular saga later transferred the story of the varying fortunes and characteristics of the tribes to the legendary ancestors and to one common forefather, Jacob-Israel. This reconstruction of Israel's history is, however, challenged by other scholars [9].

Whatever the precise nature of the process by which the biblical tradition was established, we may not overlook the fact that the Torah presents the ancestral figures as identifiable persons in their own age. The secret of the lasting vitality of these biblical tales is indeed to be found in this personalization, for the ancestors are now felt to be "not the reflection of Israelite fortunes in a specific period of time but as the poetic presentation of ever-recurring human fortunes and characteristics" [10].

Biology and Faith

The biblical account tells us the following: Sheep and goats were generally either white or dark, hence Jacob's offer to take only speckled animals meant that he was prepared to take merely a small portion of the flock. Laban agreed, but being suspicious of Jacob he wanted to make sure of his advantage and proceeded to cheat Jacob even of the few animals he had requested. Laban did not reckon with Jacob's plan to crossbreed white and dark animals by means of visual stimulation [11]. It was believed that the color of the offspring would be influenced by the color of the staves the animal had seen at mating time. Jacob ascribed his knowledge to divine inspiration, which helped him to overcome Laban's guile and to receive his just reward.

The section presents, therefore, more than an insight into ancient ideas of biology. Along with other biblical texts that deal with administrative, commercial, and legal matters, it connects everyday affairs with theology.[1] In this, the biblical accounts differ markedly from Babylonian texts. The vast number of sources that have been preserved in cuneiform rarely unite religious and historical-legal matters organically.

The final purpose of the story is to show Jacob's deepening faith in God's promise [12]. He comes to know God not only in His immediate manifestations but also in the long-range processes of nature. God is concerned with Jacob and the latter knows this concern, which here is expressed in a non-miraculous way: Jacob is favored in that he learns the secrets of nature and utilizes them in accordance with God's will.[2]

---

[1] This will be especially apparent in Leviticus.

[2] We may note that contemporary religious humanism would put the relation between God, man, and nature in a similar way: To know God means to use the laws of nature in the right way.

GLEANINGS

It Is Still Broad Daylight (Gen. 29:7)

How could a stranger like Jacob reprimand the shepherds? Learn from this that if one visits a strange place and sees a wrong being perpetrated it is his duty to prevent it. One must not say, "It is no business of mine."　MIDRASH [13]

Jacob Kissed Rachel

John Calvin thought that Moses, in saying that Rachel accepted a kiss from a stranger, must here have made an error in editing the Torah; for how could one believe that Rachel behaved otherwise than sixteenth-century morality demanded! [14]

It Is Not the Practice in Our Place (Gen. 29:26)

No one understood this better than Jacob, for he himself as the younger son had crossed the finishing line before his older brother. Thus the narrator shows how a serious nemesis is at work.　GERHARD VON RAD [15]

Laban

A masterful characterization: A selfish, greedy, exploiting, suspicious man of wealth, who never fails to observe good manners.　BENNO JACOB

Jacob the Shepherd

Before Jacob, Moses, David, Amos, or Ezekiel were made great, they were first tested as shepherds. Labor is beloved, for all the Prophets engaged in it.　MIDRASH [16]

Mandrakes

Because of the resemblance of its root to the human form, the mandrake is almost universally credited with magical powers. Dioscorides, the Greek physician, calls it "Circe's plant" (*kirkeion*), and among modern Arabs it is known as the "apple of the jinns" and is used in concocting philtres. Theophrastus says that it is an antidote against spells and enchantments, and Josephus records the popular belief that it expels demons. Indeed, it has been suggested that the drug named *moly* which Hermes supplied to Odysseus in order to counteract the magic potions brewed by Circe was really the mandrake.

The plant is used especially, as in our biblical narrative, as an aphrodisiac and as an antidote to barrenness. It is thus mentioned, for example, by the Greek comic dramatist Alexis (fourth century B.C.), and Aphrodite, the goddess of love, was sometimes styled, "Our Lady of the Mandrake." The Hebrew word rendered "mandrake" is indeed connected with a verbal root meaning "to love" and has its English counterpart in the popular term, "love-apple." In the Song of Songs (7:14), when the maiden invites her lover to enjoy her favors, she adds to her inducements the statement that she has stored up for him fragrant mandrakes. In Jewish folklore, the mandrake was long believed to relieve barrenness; while in Germany and some other parts of Europe it was customary to place mandrakes under a bridal bed.

THEODOR H. GASTER [17]

[The plants are still carried as aphrodisiacs in some pharmacies, although there is no medical evidence for their efficacy.]

Jacob's Departure from Haran

Jacob and his household leave Haran and Laban's sphere of influence. As the parting takes place, the last act of deception is perpetrated—but this time by neither Jacob nor Laban. This time both are being deceived. Laban is cheated of his household deities and Jacob, through his wife's theft, unknowingly exposes her to unforeseen danger. Thus, deception returns to visit its perpetrators.

At times the text appears disjointed. Critics distinguish two traditions—the J-school and the E-school (for example, in chapter 31 compare verses 1 with 2 and 46–50 with 51–54).

א וַיִּשְׁמַ֗ע אֶת־דִּבְרֵ֤י בְנֵֽי־לָבָן֙ לֵאמֹ֔ר לָקַ֣ח יַעֲקֹ֔ב אֵ֥ת כָּל־אֲשֶׁ֖ר לְאָבִ֑ינוּ וּמֵאֲשֶׁ֣ר לְאָבִ֔ינוּ עָשָׂ֕ה אֵ֥ת כָּל־הַכָּבֹ֖ד הַזֶּֽה׃ ב וַיַּ֥רְא יַעֲקֹ֖ב אֶת־פְּנֵ֣י לָבָ֑ן וְהִנֵּ֥ה אֵינֶ֛נּוּ עִמּ֖וֹ כִּתְמ֥וֹל שִׁלְשֽׁוֹם׃ ג וַיֹּ֤אמֶר יְהֹוָה֙ אֶֽל־יַעֲקֹ֔ב שׁ֛וּב אֶל־אֶ֥רֶץ אֲבוֹתֶ֖יךָ וּלְמוֹלַדְתֶּ֑ךָ וְאֶהְיֶ֖ה עִמָּֽךְ׃ ד וַיִּשְׁלַ֣ח יַעֲקֹ֔ב וַיִּקְרָ֖א לְרָחֵ֣ל וּלְלֵאָ֑ה הַשָּׂדֶ֖ה אֶל־צֹאנֽוֹ׃ ה וַיֹּ֣אמֶר לָהֶ֗ן רֹאֶ֤ה אָנֹכִי֙ אֶת־פְּנֵ֣י אֲבִיכֶ֔ן כִּֽי־אֵינֶ֥נּוּ אֵלַ֖י כִּתְמֹ֣ל שִׁלְשֹׁ֑ם וֵֽאלֹהֵ֣י אָבִ֔י הָיָ֖ה עִמָּדִֽי׃ ו וְאַתֵּ֖נָה יְדַעְתֶּ֑ן כִּ֚י בְּכָל־כֹּחִ֔י עָבַ֖דְתִּי אֶת־אֲבִיכֶֽן׃ ז וַאֲבִיכֶן֙ הֵ֣תֶל בִּ֔י וְהֶחֱלִ֥ף אֶת־מַשְׂכֻּרְתִּ֖י עֲשֶׂ֣רֶת מֹנִ֑ים וְלֹֽא־נְתָנ֣וֹ אֱלֹהִ֔ים לְהָרַ֖ע עִמָּדִֽי׃ ח אִם־כֹּ֣ה יֹאמַ֗ר נְקֻדִּים֙ יִהְיֶ֣ה שְׂכָרֶ֔ךָ וְיָלְד֥וּ כָל־הַצֹּ֖אן נְקֻדִּ֑ים וְאִם־כֹּ֣ה יֹאמַ֗ר עֲקֻדִּים֙

ט יִהְיֶ֣ה שְׂכָרֶ֔ךָ וְיָלְד֥וּ כָל־הַצֹּ֖אן עֲקֻדִּֽים׃ וַיַּצֵּ֧ל אֱלֹהִ֛ים אֶת־מִקְנֵ֥ה אֲבִיכֶ֖ם וַיִּתֶּן־לִֽי׃ י וַיְהִ֗י בְּעֵת֙ יַחֵ֣ם הַצֹּ֔אן וָאֶשָּׂ֥א עֵינַ֛י וָאֵ֖רֶא בַּחֲל֑וֹם וְהִנֵּ֤ה הָֽעַתֻּדִים֙ הָעֹלִ֣ים עַל־הַצֹּ֔אן עֲקֻדִּ֥ים נְקֻדִּ֖ים וּבְרֻדִּֽים׃ יא וַיֹּ֣אמֶר אֵלַ֞י מַלְאַ֧ךְ הָאֱלֹהִ֛ים בַּחֲל֖וֹם יַעֲקֹ֑ב וָאֹמַ֖ר הִנֵּֽנִי׃ יב וַיֹּ֗אמֶר שָׂא־נָ֨א עֵינֶ֤יךָ וּרְאֵה֙ כָּל־הָֽעַתֻּדִים֙ הָעֹלִ֣ים עַל־הַצֹּ֔אן עֲקֻדִּ֥ים נְקֻדִּ֖ים וּבְרֻדִּ֑ים כִּ֣י רָאִ֔יתִי אֵ֛ת כָּל־אֲשֶׁ֥ר לָבָ֖ן עֹ֥שֶׂה לָּֽךְ׃ יג אָנֹכִ֤י הָאֵל֙ בֵּֽית־אֵ֔ל אֲשֶׁ֨ר מָשַׁ֤חְתָּ שָּׁם֙ מַצֵּבָ֔ה אֲשֶׁ֨ר נָדַ֥רְתָּ לִּ֛י שָׁ֖ם נֶ֑דֶר עַתָּ֗ה ק֥וּם צֵ֤א מִן־הָאָ֣רֶץ הַזֹּ֔את וְשׁ֖וּב אֶל־אֶ֥רֶץ מוֹלַדְתֶּֽךָ׃ יד וַתַּ֤עַן רָחֵל֙ וְלֵאָ֔ה וַתֹּאמַ֖רְנָה ל֑וֹ הַע֥וֹד לָ֛נוּ חֵ֥לֶק וְנַחֲלָ֖ה בְּבֵ֥ית אָבִֽינוּ׃ טו הֲל֧וֹא נָכְרִיּ֛וֹת נֶחְשַׁ֥בְנוּ ל֖וֹ כִּ֣י מְכָרָ֑נוּ וַיֹּ֥אכַל

1] Now he heard the things that Laban's sons were saying: "Jacob has taken all that was our father's, and from that which was our father's he has built up all this wealth." **2]** Jacob also saw that Laban's manner toward him was not as it had been in the past. **3]** Then the LORD said to Jacob, "Return to the land of your fathers where you were born, and I will be with you." **4]** Jacob had Rachel and Leah called to the field, where his flock was, **5]** and said to them, "I see that your father's manner toward me is not as it has been in the past. But the God of my father has been with me. **6]** As you know, I have served your father with all my might; **7]** but your father has cheated me, changing my wages time and again. God, however, would not let him do me harm. **8]** If he said thus, 'The speckled shall be your wages,' then all the flocks would drop speckled young; and if he said thus, 'The streaked shall be your wages,' then all the flocks would drop streaked young. **9]** God has taken away your father's livestock and given it to me.

10] "Once, at the mating time of the flocks, I had a dream in which I saw that the he-goats mating with the flock were streaked, speckled, and mottled. **11]** And in the dream an angel of God said to me, 'Jacob!' 'Here,' I answered. **12]** And he said, 'Note well that all the he-goats which are mating with the flock are streaked, speckled, and mottled; for I have noted all that Laban has been doing to you. **13]** I am the God of Beth-el, where you anointed a pillar and where you made a vow to Me. Now, arise and leave this land and return to your native land.'"

14] Then Rachel and Leah answered him, saying, "Have we still a share in the inheritance of our father's house? **15]** Surely he regards us as outsiders, now that he has sold us and has used

31:4] *To the field.* To speak privately to them. Rachel is named first because she came first in Jacob's affection and because he had stayed on for her sake [1]. In the Book of Ruth (4:11) and in the Sabbath blessing of daughters, Rachel also precedes Leah.

7] *Time and again.* Literally, "ten times" [2] (see also Gen. 31:41).

10] *I had a dream.* Literally, "I raised my eyes and saw in a dream, behold."

13] *God of Bethel.* A reference to the events told in Gen. 28:10–15.

15] *Outsiders.* Or, foreigners. According to many ancient laws, foreigners did not have the same rights as other members of the family. Leah and Rachel believe that their father now considers

טו גַּם־אָכוֹל אֶת־כַּסְפֵּנוּ: כִּי כָל־הָעֹשֶׁר אֲשֶׁר הִצִּיל   אֶחָיו עִמּוֹ וַיִּרְדֹּף אַחֲרָיו דֶּרֶךְ שִׁבְעַת יָמִים וַיַּדְבֵּק
אֱלֹהִים מֵאָבִינוּ לָנוּ הוּא וּלְבָנֵינוּ וְעַתָּה כֹּל אֲשֶׁר   אֹתוֹ בְּהַר הַגִּלְעָד: וַיָּבֹא אֱלֹהִים אֶל־לָבָן הָאֲרַמִּי
יז אָמַר אֱלֹהִים אֵלֶיךָ עֲשֵׂה: וַיָּקָם יַעֲקֹב וַיִּשָּׂא אֶת־   בַּחֲלֹם הַלָּיְלָה וַיֹּאמֶר לוֹ הִשָּׁמֶר לְךָ פֶּן־תְּדַבֵּר
יח בָּנָיו וְאֶת־נָשָׁיו עַל־הַגְּמַלִּים: וַיִּנְהַג אֶת־כָּל־מִקְנֵהוּ   עִם־יַעֲקֹב מִטּוֹב עַד־רָע: וַיַּשֵּׂג לָבָן אֶת־יַעֲקֹב וְיַעֲקֹב
וְאֶת־כָּל־רְכֻשׁוֹ אֲשֶׁר רָכָשׁ מִקְנֵה קִנְיָנוֹ אֲשֶׁר רָכַשׁ   תָּקַע אֶת־אָהֳלוֹ בָּהָר וְלָבָן תָּקַע אֶת־אֶחָיו בְּהַר
יט בְּפַדַּן אֲרָם לָבוֹא אֶל־יִצְחָק אָבִיו אַרְצָה כְּנָעַן: וְלָבָן   הַגִּלְעָד: וַיֹּאמֶר לָבָן לְיַעֲקֹב מֶה עָשִׂיתָ וַתִּגְנֹב אֶת־
הָלַךְ לִגְזֹז אֶת־צֹאנוֹ וַתִּגְנֹב רָחֵל אֶת־הַתְּרָפִים אֲשֶׁר   לְבָבִי וַתְּנַהֵג אֶת־בְּנֹתַי כִּשְׁבֻיוֹת חָרֶב: לָמָּה נַחְבֵּאתָ
כ לְאָבִיהָ: וַיִּגְנֹב יַעֲקֹב אֶת־לֵב לָבָן הָאֲרַמִּי עַל־בְּלִי   לִבְרֹחַ וַתִּגְנֹב אֹתִי וְלֹא־הִגַּדְתָּ לִּי וָאֲשַׁלֵּחֲךָ בְּשִׂמְחָה
כא הִגִּיד לוֹ כִּי בֹרֵחַ הוּא: וַיִּבְרַח הוּא וְכָל־אֲשֶׁר־לוֹ   וּבְשִׁרִים בְּתֹף וּבְכִנּוֹר: וְלֹא נְטַשְׁתַּנִי לְנַשֵּׁק לְבָנַי
וַיָּקָם וַיַּעֲבֹר אֶת־הַנָּהָר וַיָּשֶׂם אֶת־פָּנָיו הַר הַגִּלְעָד: וְלִבְנֹתָי עַתָּה הִסְכַּלְתָּ עֲשׂוֹ: יֶשׁ־לְאֵל יָדִי לַעֲשׂוֹת
כב וַיֻּגַּד לְלָבָן בַּיּוֹם הַשְּׁלִישִׁי כִּי בָרַח יַעֲקֹב: וַיִּקַּח אֶת־   עִמָּכֶם רָע וֵאלֹהֵי אֲבִיכֶם אֶמֶשׁ אָמַר אֵלַי לֵאמֹר

up our purchase price. **16]** Truly, all the wealth that God has taken away from our father belongs to us and to our children. Now then, do just as God has told you."

17] Thereupon Jacob put his children and wives on camels; **18]** and he drove off all his livestock and all the wealth that he had amassed, the livestock in his possession that he had acquired in Paddan-aram, to go to his father Isaac in the land of Canaan.

19] Meanwhile Laban had gone to shear his sheep, and Rachel stole her father's household idols. **20]** Jacob kept Laban the Aramean in the dark, not telling him that he was fleeing, **21]** and fled with all that he had. Soon he was across the Euphrates and heading toward the hill country of Gilead.

22] On the third day, Laban was told that Jacob had fled. **23]** So he took his kinsmen with him and pursued him a distance of seven days, catching up with him in the hill country of Gilead. **24]** But God appeared to Laban the Aramean in a dream by night and said to him, "Beware of attempting anything with Jacob, good or bad."

25] Laban overtook Jacob. Jacob had pitched his tent on the Height, and Laban with his kinsmen encamped in the hill country of Gilead. **26]** And Laban said to Jacob, "What did you mean by keeping me in the dark and carrying off my daughters like captives of the sword? **27]** Why did you flee in secrecy and mislead me and not tell me? I would have sent you off with festive music, with timbrel and lyre. **28]** You did not even let me kiss my sons and daughters good-by! It was a foolish thing for you to do. **29]** I have it in my power to do you harm; but the God of your father said to me last night, 'Beware of attempting anything with Jacob, good

---

them foreigners because of their marriage to Jacob and that their dowry, set aside by their father, is "eaten up" or lost.

20] *Kept . . . in the dark.* Literally, "stole the mind of"; similarly Gen. 31:26.

21] *Euphrates.* הַנָּהָר. Literally, "the river."

24] *God appeared to Laban.* As He had, for in-

stance, appeared to Abimelech. Biblical tradition does not restrict divine communication to Abraham and his descendants.

Laban the Aramean. Laban spoke Aramaic (Gen. 31:47) and lived in Paddan-aram. The Patriarchs were also later referred to as Arameans because they had come from this area (see note at Gen. 25:20 and Deut. 26:5).

וַתָּשָׁב עֲלֵיהֶם וַיְמַשֵּׁשׁ לָבָן אֶת־כָּל־הָאֹהֶל וְלֹא מָצָא: לה וַתֹּאמֶר אֶל־אָבִיהָ אַל־יִחַר בְּעֵינֵי אֲדֹנִי כִּי לוֹא אוּכַל לָקוּם מִפָּנֶיךָ כִּי־דֶרֶךְ נָשִׁים לִי וַיְחַפֵּשׂ וְלֹא מָצָא אֶת־הַתְּרָפִים: לו וַיִּחַר לְיַעֲקֹב וַיָּרֶב בְּלָבָן וַיַּעַן יַעֲקֹב וַיֹּאמֶר לְלָבָן מַה־פִּשְׁעִי מַה חַטָּאתִי כִּי דָלַקְתָּ אַחֲרָי: לז כִּי־מִשַּׁשְׁתָּ אֶת־כָּל־כֵּלַי מַה־מָּצָאתָ מִכֹּל כְּלֵי־ בֵיתֶךָ שִׂים כֹּה נֶגֶד אַחַי וְאַחֶיךָ וְיוֹכִיחוּ בֵּין שְׁנֵינוּ: לח זֶה עֶשְׂרִים שָׁנָה אָנֹכִי עִמָּךְ רְחֵלֶיךָ וְעִזֶּיךָ לֹא שִׁכֵּלוּ וְאֵילֵי צֹאנְךָ לֹא אָכָלְתִּי: לט טְרֵפָה לֹא־הֵבֵאתִי אֵלֶיךָ

ל הִשָּׁמֶר לְךָ מְדַּבֵּר עִם־יַעֲקֹב מִטּוֹב עַד־רָע: וְעַתָּה הָלֹךְ הָלַכְתָּ כִּי־נִכְסֹף נִכְסַפְתָּה לְבֵית אָבִיךָ לָמָּה לא גָנַבְתָּ אֶת־אֱלֹהָי: וַיַּעַן יַעֲקֹב וַיֹּאמֶר לְלָבָן כִּי יָרֵאתִי לב כִּי אָמַרְתִּי פֶּן־תִּגְזֹל אֶת־בְּנוֹתֶיךָ מֵעִמִּי: עִם אֲשֶׁר תִּמְצָא אֶת־אֱלֹהֶיךָ לֹא יִחְיֶה נֶגֶד אַחֵינוּ הַכֶּר־לְךָ מָה עִמָּדִי וְקַח־לָךְ וְלֹא־יָדַע יַעֲקֹב כִּי רָחֵל גְּנָבָתַם: לג וַיָּבֹא לָבָן בְּאֹהֶל־יַעֲקֹב וּבְאֹהֶל לֵאָה וּבְאֹהֶל שְׁתֵּי הָאֲמָהֹת וְלֹא מָצָא וַיֵּצֵא מֵאֹהֶל לֵאָה וַיָּבֹא בְּאֹהֶל רָחֵל: לד וְרָחֵל לָקְחָה אֶת־הַתְּרָפִים וַתְּשִׂמֵם בְּכַר הַגָּמָל

or bad.' **30]** Very well, you had to leave because you were longing for your father's house; but why did you steal my gods?"

31] Jacob answered Laban, saying, "I was afraid because I thought you would take your daughters from me by force. **32]** But anyone with whom you find your gods shall not remain alive! In the presence of our kinsmen, point out what I have of yours and take it." Jacob, of course, did not know that Rachel had stolen them.

33] So Laban went into Jacob's tent and Leah's tent and the tents of the two maidservants; but he did not find them. Leaving Leah's tent, he entered Rachel's tent. **34]** Rachel, mean-while, had taken the idols and placed them in the camel cushion and sat on them; and Laban rummaged through the tent without finding them. **35]** For she said to her father, "Let not my lord take it amiss that I cannot rise before you, for the period of women is upon me." Thus he searched, but could not find the household idols.

36] Now Jacob became incensed and took up his grievance with Laban. Jacob spoke up and said to Laban, "What is my crime, what is my guilt that you should pursue me? **37]** You rummaged through all my things; what have you found of all your household objects? Set it here, before my kinsmen and yours, and let them decide between us two.

38] "These twenty years I have spent in your service, your ewes and she-goats never miscarried, nor did I feast on rams from your flock. **39]** That which was torn by beasts I

30] *Leave . . . longing.* The simple translation does not convey that in the Hebrew text each verb is provided with an added infinitive, providing special emphasis to Laban's words. A colloquial rendering might be: "So you wanted to leave—leave already! You longed for your father's house, all right! But why did you have to steal my gods?" In his discussion of biblical meanings, R. Ishmael (second century c.e.) cited this verse as proof that "the Torah speaks in the language of men" [3].

34] *Camel cushion.* The idea that a woman might sit on the *teraphim* during her menstrual period (*niddah*) subtly indicates the Torah's contempt for the idols. Biblical law prevented men from coming in contact with menstruating women [4].

/Hertz translates כַּר as "palanquin."/

37] *Household objects.* Jacob derisively calls Laban's *teraphim* "objects."

38] *These twenty years.* His long pent-up anger begins to emerge.

אָנֹכִי אֲחַטֶּנָּה מִיָּדִי תְּבַקְשֶׁנָּה גְּנֻבְתִי יוֹם וּגְנֻבְתִי לָיְלָה:

מ הָיִיתִי בַיּוֹם אֲכָלַנִי חֹרֶב וְקֶרַח בַּלָּיְלָה וַתִּדַּד שְׁנָתִי

מא מֵעֵינָי: זֶה־לִּי עֶשְׂרִים שָׁנָה בְּבֵיתֶךָ עֲבַדְתִּיךָ אַרְבַּע־

עֶשְׂרֵה שָׁנָה בִּשְׁתֵּי בְנֹתֶיךָ וְשֵׁשׁ שָׁנִים בְּצֹאנֶךָ וַתַּחֲלֵף

מב אֶת־מַשְׂכֻּרְתִּי עֲשֶׂרֶת מֹנִים: לוּלֵי אֱלֹהֵי אָבִי אֱלֹהֵי

אַבְרָהָם וּפַחַד יִצְחָק הָיָה לִי כִּי עַתָּה רֵיקָם שִׁלַּחְתָּנִי

אֶת־עָנְיִי וְאֶת־יְגִיעַ כַּפַּי רָאָה אֱלֹהִים וַיּוֹכַח אָמֶשׁ:

מג וַיַּעַן לָבָן וַיֹּאמֶר אֶל־יַעֲקֹב הַבָּנוֹת בְּנֹתַי וְהַבָּנִים בָּנַי

וְהַצֹּאן צֹאנִי וְכֹל אֲשֶׁר־אַתָּה רֹאֶה לִי־הוּא וְלִבְנֹתַי

מד מָה־אֶעֱשֶׂה לָאֵלֶּה הַיּוֹם אוֹ לִבְנֵיהֶן אֲשֶׁר יָלָדוּ: וְעַתָּה

לְכָה נִכְרְתָה בְרִית אֲנִי וָאָתָּה וְהָיָה לְעֵד בֵּינִי וּבֵינֶךָ:

מה וַיִּקַּח יַעֲקֹב אָבֶן וַיְרִימֶהָ מַצֵּבָה: וַיֹּאמֶר יַעֲקֹב

לְאֶחָיו לִקְטוּ אֲבָנִים וַיִּקְחוּ אֲבָנִים וַיַּעֲשׂוּ־גָל וַיֹּאכְלוּ

מו שָׁם עַל־הַגָּל: וַיִּקְרָא־לוֹ לָבָן יְגַר שָׂהֲדוּתָא וְיַעֲקֹב

קָרָא לוֹ גַּלְעֵד: וַיֹּאמֶר לָבָן הַגַּל הַזֶּה עֵד בֵּינִי וּבֵינֶךָ

מט הַיּוֹם עַל־כֵּן קָרָא־שְׁמוֹ גַּלְעֵד: וְהַמִּצְפָּה אֲשֶׁר אָמַר

never brought to you; I myself made good the loss; you exacted it of me, whether snatched by day or snatched by night.   40] Often, scorching heat ravaged me by day and frost by night; and sleep fled from my eyes.   41] Of the twenty years that I spent in your household, I served you fourteen years for your two daughters, and six years for your flocks, and you changed my wages time and again.   42] Had not the God of my father, the God of Abraham and the Fear of Isaac, been with me, you would have sent me away empty-handed. But God took notice of my plight and the toil of my hands, and He gave judgment last night."

43] Then Laban spoke up and said to Jacob, "The daughters are my daughters, the children are my children, and the flocks are my flocks; all that you see is mine. Yet what can I do now about my daughters or the children they have borne?   44] Come, then, let us make a pact, you and I, that there may be a witness between you and me."   45] Thereupon Jacob took a stone and set it up as a pillar.   46] And Jacob said to his kinsmen, "Gather stones." So they took stones and made a mound; and they partook of a meal there by the mound.   47] Laban named it Yegar-sahadutha, but Jacob named it Gal-ed.   48] And Laban declared, "This mound is a witness between you and me this day." That is why it was named Gal-ed;   49] And [it was

39] *I never brought.* The legal obligations of a shepherd were set forth in detail in the Code of Hammurabi. For instance: "If a visitation of God has occurred in a sheepfold or a lion has made a kill, the shepherd shall prove himself innocent in the presence of God, but the owner of the sheepfold shall receive from him the animal stricken in the fold" [5].   Jacob indicates that he has more than complied with the law (see Gleanings).

42] *Fear of Isaac.* פַּחַד יִצְחָק. Also in Gen. 31:53. The meaning is obscure. Isaiah, too, refers to God as "your fear" and "your dread" (8:13).

43] *The daughters are my daughters.* Laban places Jacob's marriages in a special Assyrian legal category, *erebu,* in which the husband lived with his

wife's family; if he left he could not take his wife or her belongings with him [6].

Yet what can I do. He gives in, knowing that his daughters want to leave.

47] *Yegar-sahadutha.* The only Aramaic words in the Torah, meaning "mound [or, stone-heap] of witness."

Gal-ed. A translation of Yegar-sahadutha into Hebrew. It reflects a popular etymology of the name Gilead, which occurs in Gen. 31:23.

48] *This mound.* Nothing was written down; the stones were symbols of the covenant.

49] *Watch.* יִצֶף (*yitzef*), associated with Mizpah. This is not a benediction but a warning: "Let God watch over us that we may not break our covenant" [7].

יד וַיִּשָּׁבַע יַעֲקֹב בְּפַחַד אָבִיו יִצְחָק: וַיִּזְבַּח זֶבַח בָּהָר וַיִּקְרָא לְאֶחָיו לֶאֱכָל־לָחֶם וַיֹּאכְלוּ לֶחֶם וַיָּלִינוּ בָּהָר:	ד יִצֶף יְהוָה בֵּינִי וּבֵינֶךָ כִּי נִסָּתֵר אִישׁ מֵרֵעֵהוּ: אִם־תְּעַנֶּה אֶת־בְּנֹתַי וְאִם־תִּקַּח נָשִׁים עַל־בְּנֹתַי אֵין אִישׁ
א וַיַּשְׁכֵּם לָבָן בַּבֹּקֶר וַיְנַשֵּׁק לְבָנָיו וְלִבְנוֹתָיו וַיְבָרֶךְ	נא עִמָּנוּ רְאֵה אֱלֹהִים עֵד בֵּינִי וּבֵינֶךָ: וַיֹּאמֶר לָבָן לְיַעֲקֹב הִנֵּה הַגַּל הַזֶּה וְהִנֵּה הַמַּצֵּבָה אֲשֶׁר יָרִיתִי
ב אֶתְהֶם וַיֵּלֶךְ וַיָּשָׁב לָבָן לִמְקֹמוֹ: וְיַעֲקֹב הָלַךְ לְדַרְכּוֹ	נב בֵּינִי וּבֵינֶךָ: עֵד הַגַּל הַזֶּה וְעֵדָה הַמַּצֵּבָה אִם־אָנִי לֹא־אֶעֱבֹר אֵלֶיךָ אֶת־הַגַּל הַזֶּה וְאִם־אַתָּה לֹא־תַעֲבֹר
ג וַיִּפְגְּעוּ־בוֹ מַלְאֲכֵי אֱלֹהִים: וַיֹּאמֶר יַעֲקֹב כַּאֲשֶׁר רָאָם מַחֲנֵה אֱלֹהִים זֶה וַיִּקְרָא שֵׁם־הַמָּקוֹם הַהוּא מַחֲנָיִם:	נג אֵלַי אֶת־הַגַּל הַזֶּה וְאֶת־הַמַּצֵּבָה הַזֹּאת לְרָעָה: אֱלֹהֵי אַבְרָהָם וֵאלֹהֵי נָחוֹר יִשְׁפְּטוּ בֵינֵינוּ אֱלֹהֵי אֲבִיהֶם

Haftarah Vayetze, p. 344

called] Mizpah, because he said, "May the LORD watch between you and me, when we are out of sight of each other. **50]** If you ill-treat my daughters or take other wives besides my daughters—though no one else be about, remember, God Himself will be witness between you and me."

51] And Laban said to Jacob, "Here is this mound and here the pillar which I have set up between you and me: **52]** this mound shall be witness and this pillar shall be witness that I am not to cross to you past this mound, and that you are not to cross to me past this mound and this pillar, with hostile intent. **53]** May the God of Abraham and the god of Nahor"—their ancestral deities—"judge between us." And Jacob swore by the Fear of his father Isaac. **54]** Jacob then offered up a sacrifice on the Height, and invited his kinsmen to partake of the meal. After the meal, they spent the night on the Height.

1] Early in the morning, Laban kissed his sons and daughters and bade them good-by; then Laban left on his journey homeward. **2]** Jacob went on his way, and angels of God encountered him. **3]** When he saw them, Jacob said, "This is God's camp." So he named that place Mahanaim.

53] *Their ancestral deities.* A parenthetical note. The Bible uses the word "elohim" generically, for Israel's Lord as well as pagan gods. In official Egyptian correspondence the writers bless Pharaoh in the name of his and their own gods.

54] *The Height.* The mount where the covenant was concluded.

32:1–3] The brevity of this account is puzzling; the three verses may have been part of a larger story now lost. They serve here as a postscript and conclusion to Jacob's wanderings. Angels met him when he first set out (Gen. 28:12) and meet him again here as if to signify that his exile for the past twenty years has always been guided by God.

3] *Mahanaim.* Connected with מַחֲנֶה (machaneh, camp, troup). The place is mentioned in later history (e.g., II Sam. 2:8).

Rachel's Theft

Rachel's theft of the household idols (*teraphim*), Laban's angry concern, and Jacob's extravagant denial all point to the great importance that ancient man attached to these objects. They were figurines, usually small and in the shape of men (see I Sam. 19:13, 16). Their use in Israel continued into the days of the Judges (17:5) and the Prophets (Hos. 3:4–5). Josephus reported that even in his day (first century C.E.) it was the custom "among all the people in that country to have objects of worship in their house and to take them along when going abroad" [8]. Rachel, therefore, may have felt it necessary to take household deities along on her journey and decided to appropriate her father's idols. By doing this, however, she left him without proper protection—hence his great anger [9].

Another interpretation gives legal rather than religious reasons for Rachel's action. Nuzi records indicate that *teraphim* were often symbols of property rights and family status. Their possession could indicate that certain privileges had been confirmed by transmitting the ownership of the *teraphim* (cf. the symbolism of the scepter or of keys to a house). Thus, Jacob's possession of the *teraphim* might prove that he was no longer Laban's servant and that he was, therefore, entitled to a part of the latter's estate. If Jacob had not in law attained this position, Rachel by her theft meant to assure it for him. Biblical tradition viewed Rachel as a resolute woman who did not hesitate to take the law—or what she believed to be the law—into her own hands [10]. She knew her husband's rights and she had ample reason to

doubt that Laban would voluntarily and formally transfer the images. That she might proceed in this fashion apparently never occurred to Jacob. He either did not know the intricacies of Hurrian law or he was not aware of his wife's capacity for action.[1]

We have already learned of Rachel's consideration and charm at the time of her first meeting with Jacob, of her agony over her long barrenness, her jealousy over her sister's good fortune, and of her attempt to utilize aphrodisiacs. We now see her to be an independent woman. With the rift between Laban and Jacob widening, she took the lead over her sister in siding with her husband instead of her father, and in the moment of parting it was she again who was stirred to decisive action. However, her impetuousness caused Jacob to make an extreme and tragic oath.

Here the theme of retribution may again be glimpsed. For while the Torah passes no explicit judgment on Rachel's behavior, its tragic consequences will all too soon become evident. The commentators who exculpate Rachel[2] are therefore wide of the mark. Jacob's oath that whoever may be found with the *teraphim* should not remain alive (Gen. 31:32) is exacted—not by Laban, as expected, but by God himself. Rachel dies in her next childbirth and is buried by the roadside (Gen. 35:16–20). She is the only Matriarch not interred in Machpelah, the grave site of the other Matriarchs and Patriarchs.[3] She died at a young age because she had been disloyal to her father, which to the ancients was a cardinal sin. Jacob by his rash oath unwittingly brought on his beloved's destruction, a plot found also in Greek tragedies.

---

[1] It is, of course, possible that if her marriage was of the *erebu* type (see note at Gen. 31:43) Laban and not she was in the right.

[2] She stole the idols to keep Laban from idolatry [11]. They were a means of divination and Rachel feared

Laban would discover her leaving [12].

[3] So, the Midrash on the Ten Commandments: Because she stole the *teraphim* she was not buried in Machpelah.

GLEANINGS

Jewish Law

Gen. 31:40 became an object lesson for defining the limitations of a paid watchman's responsibilities. Jewish law provides that a watchman engaged to guard property in the city must guard his charge constantly, while in the countryside he may be excused occasionally. Jacob's description of his own extreme attention to duty shows that he did more than the law required.   TALMUD [13]

Stealing the Heart

[Rachel appropriates (or steals) Laban's household gods while Jacob keeps Laban in the dark about his impending departure (literally, "he stole the heart of Laban," 31:20).]

The expression preserves an interesting piece of folklore. In ancient times the heart was considered, as it still is among primitive peoples, the seat not only of the emotions but also of the mental processes. Alike among the Hebrews and the Babylonians, for example, a common expression for "to think" was "to say in the heart." The heart was thus symbolic of the total self, and in moments, such as sleep or trance, when a man had temporarily lost consciousness, the heart was believed temporarily to have departed from him. It could even be enticed out of him by magic or by the action of demons. To "steal the heart" meant, therefore, more than to bemuse the emotions; it meant to gain complete control over a person's self-direction. In the Egyptian Pyramid Texts mention is made of a class of demons called "stealers of the heart" who were thought to divest the dead of consciousness.   THEODOR H. GASTER [14]

The Cairn

The custom of erecting cairns as witnesses is apparently not extinct in Syria even now. One of the most famous shrines of the country is that of Aaron on Mount Hor. The prophet's tomb on the mountain is visited by pilgrims, who pray the saint to intercede for the recovery of sick friends and pile up heaps of stones as witnesses (*meshhad*) of the vows they make on behalf of the sufferers.
   JAMES G. FRAZER [15]

Greek Parallel

To thee doth Troy commend her household gods;
Now take them as companions of thy fate.

   VERGIL [16]

Jacob Becomes Israel

Jacob's exile draws to a close. But he cannot go home without first settling accounts with his brother. Twenty years have elapsed since the frightened young man deceived Esau. Twenty years have changed him greatly, and they have changed Esau, too. The time has come to face the past and, in doing so, to secure the future. As Jacob prepares to meet Esau, he also meets his God. A "man" wrestles with him one night, and when morning breaks Jacob has become Israel. This story provides the background to the tale of reconciliation and raises important questions about the nature and meaning of the name "Israel."

(A new weekly portion, *Vayishlach*, begins here.)

פ פ פ

ד וַיִּשְׁלַח יַעֲקֹב מַלְאָכִים לְפָנָיו אֶל־עֵשָׂו אָחִיו אַרְצָה

ה שֵׂעִיר שְׂדֵה אֱדוֹם: וַיְצַו אֹתָם לֵאמֹר כֹּה תֹאמְרוּן
לַאדֹנִי לְעֵשָׂו כֹּה אָמַר עַבְדְּךָ יַעֲקֹב עִם־לָבָן גַּרְתִּי

ו וָאֵחַר עַד־עָתָּה: וַיְהִי־לִי שׁוֹר וַחֲמוֹר צֹאן וְעֶבֶד
וְשִׁפְחָה וָאֶשְׁלְחָה לְהַגִּיד לַאדֹנִי לִמְצֹא־חֵן בְּעֵינֶיךָ:

ז וַיָּשֻׁבוּ הַמַּלְאָכִים אֶל־יַעֲקֹב לֵאמֹר בָּאנוּ אֶל־אָחִיךָ
אֶל־עֵשָׂו וְגַם הֹלֵךְ לִקְרָאתְךָ וְאַרְבַּע־מֵאוֹת אִישׁ עִמּוֹ:

ח וַיִּירָא יַעֲקֹב מְאֹד וַיֵּצֶר לוֹ וַיַּחַץ אֶת־הָעָם אֲשֶׁר־
אִתּוֹ וְאֶת־הַצֹּאן וְאֶת־הַבָּקָר וְהַגְּמַלִּים לִשְׁנֵי מַחֲנוֹת:

ט וַיֹּאמֶר אִם־יָבוֹא עֵשָׂו אֶל־הַמַּחֲנֶה הָאַחַת וְהִכָּהוּ
וְהָיָה הַמַּחֲנֶה הַנִּשְׁאָר לִפְלֵיטָה:

י וַיֹּאמֶר יַעֲקֹב אֱלֹהֵי
אָבִי אַבְרָהָם וֵאלֹהֵי אָבִי יִצְחָק יְהוָה הָאֹמֵר אֵלַי

יא שׁוּב לְאַרְצְךָ וּלְמוֹלַדְתְּךָ וְאֵיטִיבָה עִמָּךְ: קָטֹנְתִּי
מִכֹּל הַחֲסָדִים וּמִכָּל־הָאֱמֶת אֲשֶׁר עָשִׂיתָ אֶת־עַבְדֶּךָ

יב כִּי בְמַקְלִי עָבַרְתִּי אֶת־הַיַּרְדֵּן הַזֶּה וְעַתָּה הָיִיתִי
לִשְׁנֵי מַחֲנוֹת: הַצִּילֵנִי נָא מִיַּד אָחִי מִיַּד עֵשָׂו כִּי־יָרֵא

יג אָנֹכִי אֹתוֹ פֶּן־יָבוֹא וְהִכַּנִי אֵם עַל־בָּנִים: וְאַתָּה אָמַרְתָּ
הֵיטֵב אֵיטִיב עִמָּךְ וְשַׂמְתִּי אֶת־זַרְעֲךָ כְּחוֹל הַיָּם

יד אֲשֶׁר לֹא־יִסָּפֵר מֵרֹב: וַיָּלֶן שָׁם בַּלַּיְלָה הַהוּא וַיִּקַּח
מִן־הַבָּא בְיָדוֹ מִנְחָה לְעֵשָׂו אָחִיו: עִזִּים מָאתַיִם

טו וּתְיָשִׁים עֶשְׂרִים רְחֵלִים מָאתַיִם וְאֵילִים עֶשְׂרִים:

טז גְּמַלִּים מֵינִיקוֹת וּבְנֵיהֶם שְׁלֹשִׁים פָּרוֹת אַרְבָּעִים

4] Jacob sent messengers ahead to his brother Esau in the land of Seir, the country of Edom, 5] and instructed them as follows, "Thus shall you say, 'To my lord Esau, thus says your servant Jacob: I stayed with Laban and remained until now; 6] I have acquired cattle, asses, sheep, and male and female slaves; and I send this message to my lord in the hope of gaining your favor.'" 7] The messengers returned to Jacob, saying, "We came to your brother Esau; he himself is coming to meet you, and there are four hundred men with him." 8] Jacob was greatly frightened; in his anxiety, he divided the people with him, and the flocks and herds and camels, into two camps, 9] thinking, "If Esau comes to the one camp and attacks it, the other camp may yet escape."

10] Then Jacob said, "O God of my father Abraham and God of my father Isaac, O LORD, who said to me, 'Return to your native land and I will deal bountifully with you'! 11] I am unworthy of all the kindness that You have so steadfastly shown Your servant: with my staff alone I crossed this Jordan, and now I have become two camps. 12] Deliver me, I pray, from the hand of my brother, from the hand of Esau; else, I fear, he may come and strike me down, mothers and children alike. 13] Yet You have said, 'I will deal bountifully with you and make your offspring as the sands of the sea, which are too numerous to count.'"

14] After spending the night there, he selected from what was at hand these presents for his brother Esau: 15] 200 she-goats and 20 he-goats; 200 ewes and 20 rams; 16] 30 milch camels

32:5] *Thus shall you say.* Jacob's instructions reflect a formula found in Sumerian and Akkadian letters.

/By punctuating the Hebrew text differently, we can read: "Thus shall you say to my Lord Esau, 'Thus says your servant Jacob'" [1]./

6] *In the hope.* Jacob does not pretend to make his gift out of pure love [2].

12] *Deliver me.* This is one of the few prayers recorded in the Torah.

14] *Presents for his brother.* The gifts are extremely generous. The numbers (like others of this type) probably had some symbolic significance that is no longer clear.

וּפָרִים עֶשְׂרָה אֲתֹנֹת עֶשְׂרִים וַעְיָרִם עֲשָׂרָה: וַיִּתֵּן ט

בְּיַד־עֲבָדָיו עֵדֶר עֵדֶר לְבַדּוֹ וַיֹּאמֶר אֶל־עֲבָדָיו

עִבְרוּ לְפָנַי וְרֶוַח תָּשִׂימוּ בֵּין עֵדֶר וּבֵין עֵדֶר: וַיְצַו יז

אֶת־הָרִאשׁוֹן לֵאמֹר כִּי יִפְגָּשְׁךָ עֵשָׂו אָחִי וּשְׁאֵלְךָ

לֵאמֹר לְמִי־אַתָּה וְאָנָה תֵלֵךְ וּלְמִי אֵלֶּה לְפָנֶיךָ:

וְאָמַרְתָּ לְעַבְדְּךָ לְיַעֲקֹב מִנְחָה הִוא שְׁלוּחָה לַאדֹנִי יט

לְעֵשָׂו וְהִנֵּה גַם־הוּא אַחֲרֵינוּ: וַיְצַו גַּם אֶת־הַשֵּׁנִי גַּם כ

אֶת־הַשְּׁלִישִׁי גַּם אֶת־כָּל־הַהֹלְכִים אַחֲרֵי הָעֲדָרִים

לֵאמֹר כַּדָּבָר הַזֶּה תְּדַבְּרוּן אֶל־עֵשָׂו בְּמֹצַאֲכֶם אֹתוֹ:

וַאֲמַרְתֶּם גַּם הִנֵּה עַבְדְּךָ יַעֲקֹב אַחֲרֵינוּ כִּי־אָמַר כא

אֲכַפְּרָה פָנָיו בַּמִּנְחָה הַהֹלֶכֶת לְפָנָי וְאַחֲרֵי־כֵן אֶרְאֶה

פָנָיו אוּלַי יִשָּׂא פָנָי: וַתַּעֲבֹר הַמִּנְחָה עַל־פָּנָיו וְהוּא כב

לָן בַּלַּיְלָה־הַהוּא בַּמַּחֲנֶה:

וַיָּקָם בַּלַּיְלָה הוּא וַיִּקַּח כג

אֶת־שְׁתֵּי נָשָׁיו וְאֶת־שְׁתֵּי שִׁפְחֹתָיו וְאֶת־אַחַד עָשָׂר

יְלָדָיו וַיַּעֲבֹר אֵת מַעֲבַר יַבֹּק: וַיִּקָּחֵם וַיַּעֲבִרֵם אֶת־ כד

הַנָּחַל וַיַּעֲבֵר אֶת־אֲשֶׁר־לוֹ: וַיִּוָּתֵר יַעֲקֹב לְבַדּוֹ וַיֵּאָבֵק כה

אִישׁ עִמּוֹ עַד עֲלוֹת הַשָּׁחַר: וַיַּרְא כִּי לֹא יָכֹל לוֹ כו

וַיִּגַּע בְּכַף־יְרֵכוֹ וַתֵּקַע כַּף־יֶרֶךְ יַעֲקֹב בְּהֵאָבְקוֹ עִמּוֹ:

וַיֹּאמֶר שַׁלְּחֵנִי כִּי עָלָה הַשָּׁחַר וַיֹּאמֶר לֹא אֲשַׁלֵּחֲךָ כז

כִּי אִם־בֵּרַכְתָּנִי: וַיֹּאמֶר אֵלָיו מַה־שְּׁמֶךָ וַיֹּאמֶר יַעֲקֹב: כח

וַיֹּאמֶר לֹא יַעֲקֹב יֵאָמֵר עוֹד שִׁמְךָ כִּי אִם־יִשְׂרָאֵל כט

כִּי־שָׂרִיתָ עִם־אֱלֹהִים וְעִם־אֲנָשִׁים וַתּוּכָל: וַיִּשְׁאַל ל

יַעֲקֹב וַיֹּאמֶר הַגִּידָה־נָּא שְׁמֶךָ וַיֹּאמֶר לָמָּה זֶּה תִּשְׁאַל

with their colts; 40 cows and 10 bulls; 20 she-asses and 10 he-asses. **17]** These he put in the charge of his servants, drove by drove, and he told his servants, "Go on ahead, and keep a distance between droves." **18]** He instructed the one in front as follows, "When my brother Esau meets you and asks you, 'Whose man are you? Where are you going? And whose [animals] are these ahead of you?' **19]** you shall answer, 'Your servant Jacob's; they are a gift sent to my lord Esau; and [Jacob] himself is right behind us.'" **20]** He gave similar instructions to the second one, and the third, and all the others who followed the droves, namely, "Thus and so shall you say to Esau when you reach him. **21]** And you shall add, 'And your servant Jacob himself is right behind us.'" For he reasoned, "If I propitiate him with presents in advance, and then face him, perhaps he will show me favor." **22]** And so the gift went on ahead, while he remained in camp that night.

23] That same night he arose, and taking his two wives, his two maidservants, and his eleven children, he crossed the ford of the Jabbok. **24]** After taking them across the stream, he sent across all his possessions. **25]** Jacob was left alone. And a man wrestled with him until the break of dawn. **26]** When he saw that he had not prevailed against him, he wrenched Jacob's hip at its socket, so that the socket of his hip was strained as he wrestled with him. **27]** Then he said, "Let me go, for dawn is breaking." But he answered, "I will not let you go, unless you bless me." **28]** Said the other, "What is your name?" He replied, "Jacob." **29]** Said he, "Your name shall no longer be Jacob, but Israel, for you have striven with beings divine and human, and have prevailed." **30]** Jacob asked, "Pray tell me your name." But he said, "You

23] *Eleven children.* That is, eleven sons. Benjamin was not yet born and Dinah was not included in the count (some commentators suggest that this narrative did not know of Dinah).

Jabbok. An eastern tributary of the Jordan, joining it about twenty-six miles north of the Dead Sea. Its steep banks make it a natural boundary: It divided the countries of Sihon and Og and,

later, north and south Gilead.

29] *Striven.* שָׂרִיתָ (sarita), connected with the first part of יִשְׂרָאֵל (Yisrael). But the word may at first have been יָשָׁר־אֵל (yashar-el, the one whom God makes straight), as opposed to ya-akov-el, the one whom God makes to limp [3].

Beings divine. Or, "God" (אֱלֹהִים), explaining the syllable אֵל (el) in יִשְׂרָאֵל (Yisrael).

שְׁבַע פְּעָמִים עַד־גִּשְׁתּוֹ עַד־אָחִיו: וַיָּרָץ עֵשָׂו לִקְרָאתוֹ
וַיְחַבְּקֵהוּ וַיִּפֹּל עַל־צַוָּארָו וַיִּשָּׁקֵהוּ וַיִּבְכּוּ: וַיִּשָּׂא אֶת־
עֵינָיו וַיַּרְא אֶת־הַנָּשִׁים וְאֶת־הַיְלָדִים וַיֹּאמֶר מִי־אֵלֶּה
לָּךְ וַיֹּאמַר הַיְלָדִים אֲשֶׁר־חָנַן אֱלֹהִים אֶת־עַבְדֶּךָ:
וַתִּגַּשְׁןָ הַשְּׁפָחוֹת הֵנָּה וְיַלְדֵיהֶן וַתִּשְׁתַּחֲוֶיןָ: וַתִּגַּשׁ גַּם־
לֵאָה וִילָדֶיהָ וַיִּשְׁתַּחֲווּ וְאַחַר נִגַּשׁ יוֹסֵף וְרָחֵל וַיִּשְׁתַּחֲווּ:
וַיֹּאמֶר מִי לְךָ כָּל־הַמַּחֲנֶה הַזֶּה אֲשֶׁר פָּגָשְׁתִּי וַיֹּאמֶר
לִמְצֹא־חֵן בְּעֵינֵי אֲדֹנִי: וַיֹּאמֶר עֵשָׂו יֶשׁ־לִי רָב אָחִי
יְהִי לְךָ אֲשֶׁר־לָךְ: וַיֹּאמֶר יַעֲקֹב אַל־נָא אִם־נָא מָצָאתִי
חֵן בְּעֵינֶיךָ וְלָקַחְתָּ מִנְחָתִי מִיָּדִי כִּי עַל־כֵּן רָאִיתִי
פָנֶיךָ כִּרְאֹת פְּנֵי אֱלֹהִים וַתִּרְצֵנִי: קַח־נָא אֶת־בִּרְכָתִי

ד צוארו קרי. נקוד על וישקהו.

לִשְׁמִי וַיְבָרֶךְ אֹתוֹ שָׁם: וַיִּקְרָא יַעֲקֹב שֵׁם הַמָּקוֹם
פְּנִיאֵל כִּי־רָאִיתִי אֱלֹהִים פָּנִים אֶל־פָּנִים וַתִּנָּצֵל
נַפְשִׁי: וַיִּזְרַח־לוֹ הַשֶּׁמֶשׁ כַּאֲשֶׁר עָבַר אֶת־פְּנוּאֵל וְהוּא
צֹלֵעַ עַל־יְרֵכוֹ: עַל־כֵּן לֹא־יֹאכְלוּ בְנֵי־יִשְׂרָאֵל אֶת־גִּיד
הַנָּשֶׁה אֲשֶׁר עַל־כַּף הַיָּרֵךְ עַד הַיּוֹם הַזֶּה כִּי נָגַע
בְּכַף־יֶרֶךְ יַעֲקֹב בְּגִיד הַנָּשֶׁה:
וַיִּשָּׂא יַעֲקֹב עֵינָיו וַיַּרְא וְהִנֵּה עֵשָׂו בָּא וְעִמּוֹ אַרְבַּע
מֵאוֹת אִישׁ וַיַּחַץ אֶת־הַיְלָדִים עַל־לֵאָה וְעַל־רָחֵל
וְעַל שְׁתֵּי הַשְּׁפָחוֹת: וַיָּשֶׂם אֶת־הַשְּׁפָחוֹת וְאֶת־יַלְדֵיהֶן
רִאשֹׁנָה וְאֶת־לֵאָה וִילָדֶיהָ אַחֲרֹנִים וְאֶת־רָחֵל וְאֶת־
יוֹסֵף אַחֲרֹנִים: וְהוּא עָבַר לִפְנֵיהֶם וַיִּשְׁתַּחוּ אַרְצָה

must not ask my name!" And he took leave of him there. **31]** So Jacob named the place Peniel, meaning, "I have seen a divine being face to face, yet my life has been preserved." **32]** The sun rose upon him as he passed Penuel, limping on his hip. **33]** That is why the children of Israel to this day do not eat the thigh muscle that is on the socket of the hip, since Jacob's hip socket was wrenched at the thigh muscle.

1] Looking up, Jacob saw Esau coming, accompanied by four hundred men. He divided the children among Leah, Rachel, and the two maids, **2]** putting the maids and their children first, Leah and her children next, and Rachel and Joseph last. **3]** He himself went on ahead and bowed low to the ground seven times until he was near his brother. **4]** Esau ran to greet him. He embraced him and, falling on his neck, he kissed him; and they wept. **5]** Looking about, he saw the women and the children. "Who," he asked, "are these with you?" He answered, "The children with whom God has favored your servant." **6]** Then the maids, with their children, came forward and bowed low; **7]** next Leah, with her children, came forward and bowed low; and lastly, Joseph and Rachel came forward and bowed low. **8]** And he asked, "What do you mean by all this company which I have met?" He answered, "To gain my lord's favor." **9]** Esau said, "I have enough, my brother; let what you have remain yours." **10]** But Jacob said, "No, I pray you; if you would do me this favor, accept from me this gift; for to see your face is like seeing the face of God, and you have received me favorably.

31] *Peniel.* Understood as "face of God." Compare: "We shall surely die for we have seen Elohim" (Judg. 13:22). A different tradition (Gen. 35:10, 15) places the changing of the name at Bethel. There it is done freely by God himself, and not on demand by a "man," as here.

32] *Penuel.* Another version of Peniel; referred to in Judg. 8:8, 17.

33] *Do not eat.* The abstinence was apparently so generally observed that it was not mentioned specifically in the dietary codes of the Torah

(Lev. 11; Deut. 14:3–21) [4].

33:2] *Rachel and Joseph last.* These two, as Jacob's favorites, come last.

3] *Bowed . . . seven times.* This custom is also mentioned in other ancient documents [5].

4] *Kissed him.* On the diacritical dots over the Hebrew word, see Gleanings.

9] *I have enough.* It was an old custom to preface an acceptance of a large gift by first making a refusal.

10] *Like seeing the face of God.* Extreme flattery

אֲשֶׁר הֵבֵאתִי לָךְ כִּי־חַנַּנִי אֱלֹהִים וְכִי יֶשׁ־לִי־כֹל

יא וַיִּפְצַר־בּוֹ וַיִּקָּח: וַיֹּאמֶר נִסְעָה וְנֵלֵכָה וְאֵלְכָה לְנֶגְדֶּךָ:

יב וַיֹּאמֶר אֵלָיו אֲדֹנִי יֹדֵעַ כִּי־הַיְלָדִים רַכִּים וְהַצֹּאן
וְהַבָּקָר עָלוֹת עָלָי וּדְפָקוּם יוֹם אֶחָד וָמֵתוּ כָּל־

יג הַצֹּאן: יַעֲבָר־נָא אֲדֹנִי לִפְנֵי עַבְדּוֹ וַאֲנִי אֶתְנָהֲלָה
לְאִטִּי לְרֶגֶל הַמְּלָאכָה אֲשֶׁר־לְפָנַי וּלְרֶגֶל הַיְלָדִים

טו עַד אֲשֶׁר־אָבֹא אֶל־אֲדֹנִי שֵׂעִירָה: וַיֹּאמֶר עֵשָׂו אַצִּיגָה־
נָּא עִמְּךָ מִן־הָעָם אֲשֶׁר אִתִּי וַיֹּאמֶר לָמָּה זֶּה אֶמְצָא־

טז חֵן בְּעֵינֵי אֲדֹנִי: וַיָּשָׁב בַּיּוֹם הַהוּא עֵשָׂו לְדַרְכּוֹ

יז שֵׂעִירָה: וְיַעֲקֹב נָסַע סֻכֹּתָה וַיִּבֶן לוֹ בָּיִת וּלְמִקְנֵהוּ
עָשָׂה סֻכֹּת עַל־כֵּן קָרָא שֵׁם־הַמָּקוֹם סֻכּוֹת: ס

11] Please accept my present which has been brought to you, for God has favored me and I have plenty." And when he urged him, he accepted.

12] And [Esau] said, "Let us start on our journey, and I will proceed at your pace." **13]** But he said to him, "My lord knows that the children are frail and that the flocks and herds, which are nursing, are a care to me; if they are driven hard a single day, all the flocks will die. **14]** Let my lord go on ahead of his servant, while I travel slowly, at the pace of the cattle before me and at the pace of the children, until I come to my lord in Seir."

15] Then Esau said, "Let me assign to you some of the men who are with me." But he said, "O no, my lord is too kind to me!" **16]** So Esau started back that day on his way to Seir. **17]** But Jacob journeyed on to Succoth, and built a house for himself and made stalls for his cattle; that is why the place was called Succoth.

and at the same time a reference to the danger of seeing the face of God.

/Rashi: Jacob thought that he had met Esau's angel at night./

14] *While I travel slowly.* Jacob wants reconciliation but not close association; he has no intention of going to his brother's home in Seir.

17] *Succoth.* Meaning "stalls," "huts," "booths." The place was slightly north of the Jabbok (see Josh. 13:27; Judg. 8:5) and is not to be confused with the Succoth of Exod. 12:37, an Egyptian town.

220

The Struggle

Since ancient days crossing a river has been symbolic of overcoming hazard and going forward to new experience (note such expressions as "crossing the Rubicon"). In this sense, Jacob passing over the Jabbok to meet Esau crosses the watershed of his life. Everything that has happened to him since he obtained both birthright and parental blessing by doubtful means has been tainted with his own guilt and his brother's enmity. Jacob can fully face his own past only as he seeks reconciliation with Esau, and this he can do only as he becomes a different man. When Jacob becomes Israel he can achieve reconciliation with his brother.

Rivers, it was believed, were infested by demons. We may therefore infer that Jacob first thought that the "man" who met him during the night was a river demon—the assonance between the words יַבֹּק (the river Jabbok) and וַיֵּאָבֵק (he struggled) is not accidental. The man's urgent request, "Let me go for dawn is breaking," fortifies Jacob's belief that he has met a demonic being who must not be seen and who therefore must depart before sunrise [6]. Until that moment arrives Jacob is still his old self, albeit struggling to emerge into a new moral consciousness. As long as he can assume that his adversary is a demonic force, the old Jacob stands rooted in his past; it is only as the light breaks that he realizes it was not Satan but God whom he resisted—and now he sees his own past and present struggle in a new light and asks his adversary for a blessing. The struggle may be seen as a reenactment of the Eden theme: God wants man to conform to His will, yet He also wants him to be free even to oppose and struggle with Him. Jacob becomes Israel only after he has wrestled with God. The Torah says that there was also physical evidence of the struggle. The formerly self-assured and successful Jacob is now diminished in appearance; no longer with proud purposeful strides but with a hesitant limp will he greet his brother.[1]

Some interpreters say that Jacob struggled with no one but himself, emerging from the fight purified in soul.[2] However, this complete internalization of the struggle does not reflect the biblical intent. The text tells of God's role in Jacob's renewal; Jacob becomes Israel only with God's help, hence God's name is embedded in the cognomen that the forefather now bears and that his descendants will bear after him. Its etymology appears to proclaim "May God rule." Like Abram and Sarai, like a new king ascending the throne, Jacob receives a name which testifies that he is ready to assume his inheritance and that he has founded his life on the pledge he made at Bethel.

The Reconciliation

Esau's readiness to make peace with his brother comes as a surprising climax to the carefully prepared encounter. Esau's retainer of 400 armed men allows us to suppose that he did not originally come with peaceful intentions, especially since his scouts must have informed him that Jacob was unarmed. Esau expected to meet the old Jacob, the hated sibling who had overtaken him with

---

[1] See also the incident involving Moses (Exod. 4:24–26) and the simile of God attacking Israel (Hos. 13:7–8). The effect on Jacob's thigh muscle may be related to Greek stories of injured sexual organs.

In popular stories, spirits were usually portrayed as leaving before sunrise [7].

[2] Some scholars see the struggle as having taken place in a dream [8]. "There are things which become so fixed in one's mind that they leave a physical effect" [9]. In the Koran the dietary restriction relating to the incident is said to have been Jacob's own decision [10].

cleverness and guile. He was prepared for violence.

But in the brothers' fateful meeting all is suddenly changed—and hardly because of the gifts that Jacob brings, for Esau is a wealthy man in his own right. The reconciliation occurs because it is Israel, not Jacob, whom Esau meets, and Jacob is a new man who asks forgiveness, if not in words then in manner, who limps toward him with repentant air and not deceitful arrogance. He is not a man to be put to the sword, he is a man who can be loved as a brother. The essentially simple and uncomplicated Esau, who himself has matured, senses this at once and runs to kiss his newly found brother. The two are now at peace and Jacob-Israel, who has no further need to flee from Esau's wrath, settles down and builds a house.

GLEANINGS

Still Smaller

The letter ט in קָטֹנְתִּי [I am unworthy] [Gen. 32:11] is in some manuscripts written smaller than the rest of the word. This shows that though a man humbles himself, as Jacob did in prayer, he is usually still smaller than he makes himself out to be. In the midst of "unworthy" there is often something unworthier yet. CHASIDIC [11]

Pious people think they are unworthy of God's gifts; while others think they are deserving of such gifts and even more. SEFAT EMET [12]

The Demonic

Modern rationalism until recently regarded all allusion to demons merely as a vestige of ancient superstition. Now, however, we realize that to a large extent the ancient belief in demons was a crude way of accounting for the unconscious and almost uncontrollable forces in human nature itself, and the Torah teaching that God wards off from Israel the danger of the demons acquires a new relevance. The latest outbreak of the demonic forces in the world that left Israel limping is very much in need of being countered by the faith that Israel will not only survive but come away from the tragic experience with renewed strength and blessing. That is to be the meaning of the establishment of the State of Israel.

MORDECAI M. KAPLAN [13]

He Did Not Know

While he struggled, Jacob did not know the nature of his opponent. Perhaps that is the way it had to be, for when a man struggles with a force beyond himself he can, at the moment, not be sure whether it is God or Satan who is his adversary, whether a divine or demonic force [14]. Both will engage him almost past endurance. The great agony of the soul is precisely that during the struggle we are in doubt and "the man" may get away before we know his name. Only afterwards, in the full light of day, may we know what we saw, whether it was God whom we met face to face. The mystery may never be completely unraveled; this is part of the ambiguity of man's meeting with God.

Two Kinds of Fear

It says that Jacob suffered both fright and anxiety [Gen. 32:8]. Fright—that he might be killed by Esau; anxiety—that he himself might be led to kill. RASHI [15]

He Kissed Him

The Hebrew vocalized text has dots over each letter of that expression [Gen. 33:4]. One tradition says that this means that Esau's kiss was not genuine, while another holds that it was because in the meeting Esau's latent love broke through.

RASHI [16]

Another tradition, which is roundly condemned by Ibn Ezra, states that Esau "bit" Jacob–a word play on נָשַׁק (kiss) and נָשַׁךְ (bite). [17]

Thigh Muscle

The halachah forbids the eating of that part of the thigh of large and small cattle which is served by the sciatic nerve. Birds are excluded from this prohibition. [18]

The process of cutting away the sinew, forbidden fat, and certain other parts is called porging (נִקּוּר), and because experts in porging were not always available many Jewish communities refrained from eating any part of an animal's hindquarter.

Prefiguration

The conquest of the Promised Land starts at the place where Jacob wrestled with the man (Num. 21:24). This is an added sign that the forefather prefigures his people: like him they will wrestle with a God who gets away from their grasp yet will leave them with a blessing.

Alone with Thee

Each one of us alone with God:
Behind the mask of face and deed
Each wrestles with an angel.

JESSIE SAMPTER [19]

O wrestlin' Jacob, Jacob day's a-breakin',
    I will not let thee go!
O wrestlin' Jacob, Jacob day's a-breakin',
    He will not let me go!
O, I hold my brudder wid a tremblin' hand;
    I would not let him go!
I hold my sister wid a tremblin' hand;
    I would not let her go!

SPIRITUAL [20]

Limping

By morning I was lame. Yet I did not let go until with the coming of the new day I had wrested the blessing of reassurance from my creator; then I rose up knowing that I had striven with God and with men and that I had prevailed. And I named the place Peniel because I knew that there I had truly seen *God face to face* and my life was preserved. And as the sun rose again upon me I went limping down to the ford thinking how unlike my youthful encounter with the God of my fathers on that journey out to Haran was this one. Then I had traveled in aweful wonder, now it was in painful and fearful perplexity. Then in the arrogant aspiration of my youth I had dreamed of a radiant ladder to distant divinity. Now in my maturer intention my God came down to me and I struggled with him as man with man. Then in my eager ignorant search for security I had bargained with him for his support. Now in my wrestling with him I tested my own powers. Both times I came away with renewed self-confidence, but then I had gone striding toward the bright beckoning future, now I was limping back to deal with the imperfect past.

I woke to the fact that a new day was come: the sun was rising; the rising wind tossed the night-stilled branches of the trees, adding its endless music to that of the irrevocable stream.

IRVING FINEMAN [21]

Psychological Interpretations

Jacob's struggle with the Adversary was a numinous confrontation with the Shadow, or the dark, selfish side of him. When the Adversary wanted to quit, Jacob said, "No. I will not let you go unless you bless me." What did Jacob mean by this? He meant, "I will not part from this experience unless I find a meaning to my suffering."

Suffering of itself does not heal. Only suffering that has a meaning, and is accepted willingly, has the power to heal, to transform an individual into a whole person; that is, someone who is undivided, who can come to terms with himself, and even with his enemies, as Jacob did with Esau and Laban.

Jung named this process of growth from one stage of awareness to another, *individuation*. Transformation, or real change of character, can take place in a person only when, through suffering, he engages in an active struggle with the Shadow, the dark side of himself.

ESTHER SPITZER [22]

The mysterious figure represents both elements of a conflict—the dangerous forces of the id and the strength of the superego. Therefore he is both man and angel at the same time. Even as within himself Jacob experiences the battle between different aspects of his personality, so the figure with whom he struggles is a mirror-like reflection of the self, with the forces of good and evil engaged in dramatic intrapsychic conflict. *Jacob was wrestling with his own projected image of himself.*

A further meaning of Jacob's uncanny guest may be to regard him as a symbol of Death. The situation fittingly calls for such a condensation. Death and a father image were certainly associated in Jacob's mind that night. To the unconscious, death is the punishment for aggression against the father.

DOROTHY F. ZELIGS [23]

The Rape of Dinah

This story of rape and cruel retribution puts Jacob's family in a different light. While the basic theme also occurs in other literatures (e.g., the tale of Helen of Troy), the biblical tale reflects a particular aspect of Israel's tribal history and fits into the overall pattern of the Jacob tragedy, with deception once again playing a central role.

An introduction of three verses (Gen. 33:18–20) forms the link between this section and the preceding. Jacob has now settled down and, since his children are seen as adults, much time has elapsed since he and Esau met at the river Jabbok.

בְּדִינָה בַּת־יַעֲקֹב וַיֶּאֱהַב אֶת־הַנַּעֲרָ וַיְדַבֵּר עַל־לֵב   וַיָּבֹא יַעֲקֹב שָׁלֵם עִיר שְׁכֶם אֲשֶׁר בְּאֶרֶץ כְּנַעַן בְּבֹאוֹ יח

ד הַנַּעֲרָ: וַיֹּאמֶר שְׁכֶם אֶל־חֲמוֹר אָבִיו לֵאמֹר קַח־לִי   מִפַּדַּן אֲרָם וַיִּחַן אֶת־פְּנֵי הָעִיר: וַיִּקֶן אֶת־חֶלְקַת יט

ה אֶת־הַיַּלְדָּה הַזֹּאת לְאִשָּׁה: וְיַעֲקֹב שָׁמַע כִּי טִמֵּא   הַשָּׂדֶה אֲשֶׁר נָטָה־שָׁם אָהֳלוֹ מִיַּד בְּנֵי־חֲמוֹר אֲבִי

אֶת־דִּינָה בִתּוֹ וּבָנָיו הָיוּ אֶת־מִקְנֵהוּ בַּשָּׂדֶה וְהֶחֱרִשׁ   שְׁכֶם בְּמֵאָה קְשִׂיטָה: וַיַּצֶּב־שָׁם מִזְבֵּחַ וַיִּקְרָא־לוֹ אֶל כ

ו יַעֲקֹב עַד־בֹּאָם: וַיֵּצֵא חֲמוֹר אֲבִי־שְׁכֶם אֶל־יַעֲקֹב   אֱלֹהֵי יִשְׂרָאֵל: ס

ז לְדַבֵּר אִתּוֹ: וּבְנֵי יַעֲקֹב בָּאוּ מִן־הַשָּׂדֶה כְּשָׁמְעָם   וַתֵּצֵא דִינָה בַּת־לֵאָה אֲשֶׁר יָלְדָה לְיַעֲקֹב לִרְאוֹת א

וַיִּתְעַצְּבוּ הָאֲנָשִׁים וַיִּחַר לָהֶם מְאֹד כִּי־נְבָלָה עָשָׂה   בִּבְנוֹת הָאָרֶץ: וַיַּרְא אֹתָהּ שְׁכֶם בֶּן־חֲמוֹר הַחִוִּי נְשִׂיא ב

ח בְיִשְׂרָאֵל לִשְׁכַּב אֶת־בַּת־יַעֲקֹב וְכֵן לֹא יֵעָשֶׂה: וַיְדַבֵּר   הָאָרֶץ וַיִּקַּח אֹתָהּ וַיִּשְׁכַּב אֹתָהּ וַיְעַנֶּהָ: וַתִּדְבַּק נַפְשׁוֹ ג

*נ הנערה קרי.   הנערה קרי.

18] Jacob arrived safe in the city of Shechem which is in the land of Canaan—having come thus from Paddan-aram—and he encamped before the city. **19]** The parcel of land where he pitched his tent he purchased from the children of Hamor, Shechem's father, for a hundred *kesitahs*. **20]** He set up an altar there, and called it El-elohe-yisrael.

1] Now Dinah, the daughter whom Leah had borne to Jacob, went out to visit the daughters of the land. **2]** Shechem son of Hamor the Hivite, chief of the country, saw her, and took her and lay with her by force. **3]** Being strongly drawn to Dinah daughter of Jacob, and in love with the maiden, he spoke to the maiden tenderly. **4]** So Shechem said to his father Hamor, "Get me this girl as a wife."

5] Jacob heard that he had defiled his daughter Dinah; but since his sons were in the field with his cattle, Jacob kept silent until they came home. **6]** Then Shechem's father Hamor came out to Jacob to speak to him. **7]** Meanwhile Jacob's sons, having heard the news, came in from the field. The men were distressed and very angry, because he had committed an outrage in Israel by lying with Jacob's daughter—a thing not to be done.

33:18] *Shechem.* An old Canaanite city, which had been visited previously by Abraham (Gen. 12:6). In later Israelite history it became an important religious and cultural center of the tribal confederacy (Josh. 24:1). Shechem, Hebrew for shoulder, is located in the area of today's Nablus, thirty-two miles north of Jerusalem, and is built on the slope of a large rise that is part of Mount Gerizim. Recent excavations show that the site was occupied as early as 4000 B.C.E.

19] *Shechem's father.* Shechem is also the name of the king's son, a major figure in the Dinah story.

A hundred kesitahs. Monetary unit of unknown value.
/In Job 42:11 the giving of a *kesitah* resembles the payment to a victor in Sumerian verbal disputations./

20] *El-elohe-yisrael. El*, God of Israel.

34:2] *Hivite.* The Septuagint has "Horite" (see note at Gen. 36:2).

By force. Literally, "lay with her and forced her." Such an offense brought guilt on the offender's whole community (Gen. 20:9; Deut. 24:4).
/According to the law of Deut. 22:28–29, if a man has violated a virgin, he has to marry her and is prohibited from ever divorcing her. In addition, her father is to receive compensation./

5] *In the field.* Most probably they did not return home every night.

7] *Outrage in Israel.* An idiomatic term (cf. Deut. 22:21; Jer. 29:23) that is an anachronism here, since Israel did not yet exist.

חֲמ֣וֹר אִתָּ֖ם לֵאמֹ֑ר שְׁכֶ֣ם בְּנִ֗י חָֽשְׁקָ֤ה נַפְשׁוֹ֙ בְּבִתְּכֶ֔ם
ט תְּנ֨וּ נָ֥א אֹתָ֛הּ ל֖וֹ לְאִשָּֽׁה: וְהִֽתְחַתְּנ֖וּ אֹתָ֑נוּ בְּנֹֽתֵיכֶם֙
י תִּתְּנוּ־לָ֔נוּ וְאֶת־בְּנֹתֵ֖ינוּ תִּקְח֥וּ לָכֶֽם: וְאִתָּ֖נוּ תֵּשֵׁ֑בוּ
וְהָאָ֨רֶץ֙ תִּֽהְיֶ֣ה לִפְנֵיכֶ֔ם שְׁבוּ֙ וּסְחָר֔וּהָ וְהֵֽאָחֲז֖וּ בָּֽהּ:
יא וַיֹּ֤אמֶר שְׁכֶם֙ אֶל־אָבִ֣יה וְאֶל־אַחֶ֔יהָ אֶמְצָא־חֵ֖ן בְּעֵֽינֵיכֶ֑ם
יב וַאֲשֶׁ֥ר תֹּאמְר֛וּ אֵלַ֖י אֶתֵּֽן: הַרְבּ֨וּ עָלַ֤י מְאֹד֙ מֹ֣הַר וּמַתָּ֔ן
וְאֶ֨תְּנָ֔ה כַּאֲשֶׁ֥ר תֹּאמְר֖וּ אֵלָ֑י וּתְנוּ־לִ֥י אֶת־הַֽנַּעֲרָ֖ לְאִשָּֽׁה:
יג וַיַּעֲנ֨וּ בְנֵֽי־יַעֲקֹ֜ב אֶת־שְׁכֶ֨ם וְאֶת־חֲמ֥וֹר אָבִ֛יו בְּמִרְמָ֖ה
יד וַיְדַבֵּ֑רוּ אֲשֶׁ֣ר טִמֵּ֔א אֵ֖ת דִּינָ֥ה אֲחֹתָֽם: וַיֹּאמְר֣וּ אֲלֵיהֶ֗ם
לֹ֤א נוּכַל֙ לַעֲשׂוֹת֙ הַדָּבָ֣ר הַזֶּ֔ה לָתֵת֙ אֶת־אֲחֹתֵ֔נוּ לְאִ֖ישׁ
טו אֲשֶׁר־ל֣וֹ עָרְלָ֑ה כִּֽי־חֶרְפָּ֥ה הִ֖וא לָֽנוּ: אַךְ־בְּזֹ֖את נֵא֣וֹת

טו לָכֶ֑ם אִ֚ם תִּהְי֣וּ כָמֹ֔נוּ לְהִמֹּ֥ל לָכֶ֖ם כָּל־זָכָֽר: וְנָתַ֤נּוּ
אֶת־בְּנֹתֵ֨ינוּ֙ לָכֶ֔ם וְאֶת־בְּנֹתֵיכֶ֖ם נִֽקַּח־לָ֑נוּ וְיָשַׁ֣בְנוּ אִתְּכֶ֔ם
יז וְהָיִ֖ינוּ לְעַ֥ם אֶחָֽד: וְאִם־לֹ֧א תִשְׁמְע֛וּ אֵלֵ֖ינוּ לְהִמּ֑וֹל
וְלָקַ֥חְנוּ אֶת־בִּתֵּ֖נוּ וְהָלָֽכְנוּ: וַיִּֽיטְב֥וּ דִבְרֵיהֶ֖ם בְּעֵינֵ֣י
יט חֲמ֑וֹר וּבְעֵינֵ֖י שְׁכֶ֥ם בֶּן־חֲמֽוֹר: וְלֹֽא־אֵחַ֤ר הַנַּ֨עַר֙ לַעֲשׂ֣וֹת
הַדָּבָ֔ר כִּ֥י חָפֵ֖ץ בְּבַֽת־יַעֲקֹ֑ב וְה֣וּא נִכְבָּ֔ד מִכֹּ֖ל בֵּ֥ית
כ אָבִֽיו: וַיָּבֹ֥א חֲמ֛וֹר וּשְׁכֶ֥ם בְּנ֖וֹ אֶל־שַׁ֣עַר עִירָ֑ם וַיְדַבְּר֛וּ
כא אֶל־אַנְשֵׁ֥י עִירָ֖ם לֵאמֹֽר: הָאֲנָשִׁ֨ים הָאֵ֜לֶּה שְֽׁלֵמִ֥ים הֵ֣ם
אִתָּ֗נוּ וְיֵשְׁב֤וּ בָאָ֨רֶץ֙ וְיִסְחֲר֣וּ אֹתָ֔הּ וְהָאָ֛רֶץ הִנֵּ֥ה רַֽחֲבַת־
יָדַ֖יִם לִפְנֵיהֶ֑ם אֶת־בְּנֹתָם֙ נִקַּֽח־לָ֣נוּ לְנָשִׁ֔ים וְאֶת־בְּנֹתֵ֖ינוּ
כב נִתֵּ֥ן לָהֶֽם: אַךְ־בְּ֠זֹאת יֵאֹ֨תוּ לָ֤נוּ הָאֲנָשִׁים֙ לָשֶׁ֣בֶת

* יב הנערה קרי

8] And Hamor spoke with them, saying, "My son Shechem longs for your daughter. Please give her to him in marriage. **9]** Intermarry with us: give your daughters to us, and take our daughters for yourselves. **10]** You will dwell among us, and the land will be open before you; settle, move about, and acquire holdings in it." **11]** Then Shechem said to her father and brothers, "Do me this favor, and I will pay whatever you tell me. **12]** Ask of me a bride price ever so high, as well as gifts, and I will pay what you tell me; only give me the maiden for a wife."

13] Jacob's sons answered Shechem and his father Hamor—speaking with guile because he had defiled their sister Dinah— **14]** and said to them, "We cannot do this thing, to give our sister to a man who is uncircumcised, for that is a disgrace among us. **15]** Only on this condition will we agree with you: that you will become like us in that every male among you is circumcised. **16]** Then we will give our daughters to you and take your daughters to ourselves; and we will dwell among you and become as one kindred. **17]** But if you will not listen to us and become circumcised, we will take our daughter and go."

18] Their words pleased Hamor and Hamor's son Shechem. **19]** And the youth lost no time in doing the thing, for he wanted Jacob's daughter. Now he was the most respected in his father's house. **20]** So Hamor and his son Shechem went to the public place of their town and spoke to their fellow townsmen, saying, **21]** "These people are our friends; let them settle in the land and move about in it, for the land is large enough for them; we will take their daughters to ourselves as wives and give our daughters to them. **22]** But only on this

---

10] *Move about.* The verb סָחַר (*sachar*) has a dual meaning, "to move about" and "to trade." It reflects ancient social conditions when to move about also meant a license to trade [1].

12] *Bride price.* Not "dowry" (money the bride brings to the groom), as מֹהַר is often translated.

13] *Jacob's sons.* Probably led by Simeon and Levi. The others may have assented by silence (see Gen. 34:25).

    Guile. מִרְמָה (*mirmah*), a key word in the Jacob story (see Gen. 27:35).

20] *Public place.* Literally, "gate."

227

אֹתָנוּ לִהְיוֹת לְעַם אֶחָד בְּהִמּוֹל לָנוּ כָּל־זָכָר כַּאֲשֶׁר
כג הֵם נִמֹּלִים: מִקְנֵהֶם וְקִנְיָנָם וְכָל־בְּהֶמְתָּם הֲלוֹא לָנוּ
כד הֵם אַךְ נֵאוֹתָה לָהֶם וְיֵשְׁבוּ אִתָּנוּ: וַיִּשְׁמְעוּ אֶל־חֲמוֹר
וְאֶל־שְׁכֶם בְּנוֹ כָּל־יֹצְאֵי שַׁעַר עִירוֹ וַיִּמֹּלוּ כָּל־זָכָר
כה כָּל־יֹצְאֵי שַׁעַר עִירוֹ: וַיְהִי בַיּוֹם הַשְּׁלִישִׁי בִּהְיוֹתָם
כֹּאֲבִים וַיִּקְחוּ שְׁנֵי־בְנֵי־יַעֲקֹב שִׁמְעוֹן וְלֵוִי אֲחֵי דִינָה
אִישׁ חַרְבּוֹ וַיָּבֹאוּ עַל־הָעִיר בֶּטַח וַיַּהַרְגוּ כָּל־זָכָר:
כו וְאֶת־חֲמוֹר וְאֶת־שְׁכֶם בְּנוֹ הָרְגוּ לְפִי־חָרֶב וַיִּקְחוּ אֶת־
כז דִּינָה מִבֵּית שְׁכֶם וַיֵּצֵאוּ: בְּנֵי יַעֲקֹב בָּאוּ עַל־הַחֲלָלִים

כח וַיָּבֹזּוּ הָעִיר אֲשֶׁר טִמְּאוּ אֲחוֹתָם: אֶת־צֹאנָם וְאֶת־
בְּקָרָם וְאֶת־חֲמֹרֵיהֶם וְאֵת אֲשֶׁר־בָּעִיר וְאֶת־אֲשֶׁר
כט בַּשָּׂדֶה לָקָחוּ: וְאֶת־כָּל־חֵילָם וְאֶת־כָּל־טַפָּם וְאֶת־
נְשֵׁיהֶם שָׁבוּ וַיָּבֹזּוּ וְאֵת כָּל־אֲשֶׁר בַּבָּיִת:
ל וַיֹּאמֶר יַעֲקֹב אֶל־שִׁמְעוֹן וְאֶל־לֵוִי עֲכַרְתֶּם אֹתִי
לְהַבְאִישֵׁנִי בְּיֹשֵׁב הָאָרֶץ בַּכְּנַעֲנִי וּבַפְּרִזִּי וַאֲנִי מְתֵי
מִסְפָּר וְנֶאֶסְפוּ עָלַי וְהִכּוּנִי וְנִשְׁמַדְתִּי אֲנִי וּבֵיתִי:
לא וַיֹּאמְרוּ הַכְזוֹנָה יַעֲשֶׂה אֶת־אֲחוֹתֵנוּ: פ

* לֹא ו' רבתי

condition will the men agree with us to dwell among us and be as one kindred: that all our males become circumcised as they are circumcised. 23] Their cattle and substance and all their beasts will be ours, if we only agree to their terms, so that they will settle among us." 24] All who went out of the gate of his town heeded Hamor and his son Shechem, and all males, all those who went out of the gate of his town were circumcised.

25] On the third day, when they were in pain, Simeon and Levi, two of Jacob's sons, brothers of Dinah, took each his sword, came upon the city unmolested, and slew all the males. 26] They put Hamor and his son Shechem to the sword, took Dinah out of Shechem's house, and went away. 27] The other sons of Jacob came upon the slain and plundered the town, because their sister had been defiled. 28] They seized their flocks and herds and asses, all that was inside the town and outside; 29] all their wealth, all their children, and their wives, all that was in the houses, they took as captives and booty.

30] Jacob said to Simeon and Levi, "You have brought trouble on me, making me odious among the inhabitants of the land, the Canaanites and Perizzites; my men are few in number, so that if they unite against me and attack me, I and my house will be destroyed." 31] But they answered, "Should our sister be treated like a whore?"

23] *If we only agree.* In his attempt to persuade his people, Shechem is careful to depict the advantages of attracting Jacob's family but passes over his own involvement with Dinah.

24] *All who went.* That is, all his fellow townsmen.

25] *Simeon and Levi.* Full brothers of Dinah. They probably had their personal retinue with them.

Unmolested. Referring to the brothers. Others translate "at ease" or "unawares," referring to the inhabitants [2].

27] *The other sons.* At the end of his life, Jacob will blame only Simeon and Levi for the slaughter of Shechem and his people (Gen. 49:5–7).

30] *You have brought trouble on me.* Or, "you have muddied what was clear," a reference to his reputation [3].

31] *Our sister.* Thereafter, nothing further is heard of Dinah.

/Tradition has her variously as the mother of Saul the Canaanite (cf. Gen. 46:10), as Job's second wife, or as the mother of Asenath [4]./

The Tragic Element

Obviously, the Bible does not retell this violent tale of rape and murder merely "because it happened." Many other incidents in the rich and varied lives of the Patriarchs were probably forgotten. Why not this one?

A partial answer lies in the fact that this incident would later serve to explain the landless status of Simeon and Levi. The Levites became hereditary temple servants without a territory of their own (Num. 18:20), while a portion of the tribe of Simeon seems to have intermingled with the tribe of Judah and also with the Canaanites. This may explain the startling difference between the census figures in Num. 1 (59,300) and Num. 26 (22,200) and the complete omission of Simeon in the blessing of Moses (Deut. 33). The story of the rape of Dinah may thus have helped to provide a moral explanation for certain geopolitical realities of later centuries.

The incident at Shechem must also be seen as another chapter in the Jacob tragedy. As a youth, Jacob had practiced deceit; now two of his sons dishonor themselves and him by deceiving the people of Shechem. Dinah, Simeon, and Levi are the first three children with whom Jacob has profound trouble; Judah, Reuben, and Joseph will follow in time. Jacob has become Israel but this fact has not erased the tragic element from his life. Quite the contrary, his perception and deep sensitivity have brought him a greater capacity for suffering. His children, who represent his future, will bring him untold agony. This long-range retribution visited on Jacob also underscores the Bible's condemnation of the hypocritical concern for religion with which Jacob's sons induced Shechem and his people to submit to circumcision. The story of Dinah exposes this pretense of faith in all its ugliness [5].

The Reprimand

Jacob's castigation of his sons is so weak that it is puzzling. He seems worried only that his own reputation will suffer. To be sure, he will speak more strongly on his deathbed (Gen. 49:5–7), but how is it possible that he would view the unwarranted killing of so many people merely as having brought trouble to himself?

Some critics say that there were two separate strands of the Dinah story. Jacob's response, they say, belonged to a tradition (attributed to J) that told of the slaying of only Hamor and Shechem, an act that could have appeared as justifiable retribution and that would elicit the reprimand now found in the text. The story of the killing of the city's inhabitants, they say, stems from another tradition (P), one which had no record of Jacob's reaction. But however persuasive this argument seems, we must approach the text as it is now. And it here portrays the biblical Jacob as a man who makes no moral judgment on his sons.

Jacob is silent because he has in fact nothing to say. He has already become the object of events and has entered the twilight of his life. He is still young enough to become a father once more, but he is already too old to be in sole command of his fate. The divine blessings that follow (in chapter 35) merely reiterate what has already been vouchsafed to him in the past, and Jacob returns to Bethel as if symbolically to revisit the earlier stages of his life. This is what men do when growing old. In Jacob's case, however, old age will betoken not serenity but further trials. It thus becomes painfully clear that "Israel" was merely a name, not a reward; a potential, not a fulfilment. Literally and figuratively, Jacob will limp through the remainder of his life.

GLEANINGS

Exculpation

Later tradition attempted to explain the guile and cruelty of the brothers: Why were the men of Shechem slain along with Hamor, the offending leader? Because they countenanced the crime or were incapable of restraining their leadership, either of which rendered them co-responsible. [6]

The Prayer of Judith

[In the Book of Judith, probably of the second century B.C.E., the deed of the brothers was seen as pious retribution.]

O Lord, God of my father Simeon, into whose hand You gave a sword to take vengeance on the strangers who loosened the girdle of a virgin to defile her. . . . [Your dear children] were moved with zeal for You and abhorred the pollution of their blood and called upon You for aid. O God, O my God, hear me also who am a widow.

JUDITH [7]

Dinah

How was Shechem attracted to the young girl? One tradition says that she went out to see the pagan revelries; another, that she pranced about bedecked with jewelry—and jewelry ought to be worn only inside the house. [8]

Goethe called her "this foolish Dinah who runs about in the land." [9]

The Deed

I am not one of those people who profess to be able to distinguish between good and bad warfare, who say that good fighters are those who observe certain humanitarian rules according to which warfare should be regulated. And combatants when they make excuses for their brutal or tricky reprisals by pointing to the cruelty or unscrupulousness of their opponents seem to me as absurd as were your brothers when they said it was because Shechem had "defiled" Dinah, their sister, that they did this. For war between men, no matter how it is waged, is abominable. . . .

. . . It was a brutal deed of my sons there in Shechem, and I, innocently thinking I was doing good, had been a party to its inception. Nor could I put a stop to it once it was under way; much as I abhorred what they were doing I could hardly make war on my own sons. But, when I looked upon the foul thing they had done after all my teaching, I thought how like it was to the behavior of a child who, left unwatched, will break the careful training of its mother and befoul itself.

IRVING FINEMAN [10]

Births and Deaths

These two chapters comprise the end of the Isaac cycle. The careful attention given to the lineages (תּוֹלְדוֹת) of the Patriarchs is an important characteristic of the Book of Genesis (see at 2:4). The "line of Esau," the older brother, precedes the "line of Jacob," just as the genealogy of Ishmael preceded that of his younger brother Isaac.

This section contains a number of difficult textual problems. Some of the names and circumstances referred to are no longer fully understandable.

א וַיֹּאמֶר אֱלֹהִים אֶל־יַעֲקֹב קוּם עֲלֵה בֵית־אֵל וְשֶׁב־
שָׁם וַעֲשֵׂה־שָׁם מִזְבֵּחַ לָאֵל הַנִּרְאֶה אֵלֶיךָ בְּבָרְחֲךָ
ב מִפְּנֵי עֵשָׂו אָחִיךָ: וַיֹּאמֶר יַעֲקֹב אֶל־בֵּיתוֹ וְאֶל כָּל־
אֲשֶׁר עִמּוֹ הָסִרוּ אֶת־אֱלֹהֵי הַנֵּכָר אֲשֶׁר בְּתֹכְכֶם
ג וְהִטַּהֲרוּ וְהַחֲלִיפוּ שִׂמְלֹתֵיכֶם: וְנָקוּמָה וְנַעֲלֶה בֵּית־
אֵל וְאֶעֱשֶׂה־שָּׁם מִזְבֵּחַ לָאֵל הָעֹנֶה אֹתִי בְּיוֹם צָרָתִי
ד וַיְהִי עִמָּדִי בַּדֶּרֶךְ אֲשֶׁר הָלָכְתִּי: וַיִּתְּנוּ אֶל־יַעֲקֹב אֵת
כָּל־אֱלֹהֵי הַנֵּכָר אֲשֶׁר בְּיָדָם וְאֶת־הַנְּזָמִים אֲשֶׁר

בְּאָזְנֵיהֶם וַיִּטְמֹן אֹתָם יַעֲקֹב תַּחַת הָאֵלָה אֲשֶׁר עִם־
ה שְׁכֶם: וַיִּסָּעוּ וַיְהִי חִתַּת אֱלֹהִים עַל־הֶעָרִים אֲשֶׁר
ו סְבִיבוֹתֵיהֶם וְלֹא רָדְפוּ אַחֲרֵי בְּנֵי יַעֲקֹב: וַיָּבֹא
יַעֲקֹב לוּזָה אֲשֶׁר בְּאֶרֶץ כְּנַעַן הִוא בֵּית־אֵל הוּא וְכָל־
ז הָעָם אֲשֶׁר־עִמּוֹ: וַיִּבֶן שָׁם מִזְבֵּחַ וַיִּקְרָא לַמָּקוֹם אֵל
בֵּית־אֵל כִּי שָׁם נִגְלוּ אֵלָיו הָאֱלֹהִים בְּבָרְחוֹ מִפְּנֵי
ח אָחִיו: וַתָּמָת דְּבֹרָה מֵינֶקֶת רִבְקָה וַתִּקָּבֵר מִתַּחַת
לְבֵית־אֵל תַּחַת הָאַלּוֹן וַיִּקְרָא שְׁמוֹ אַלּוֹן בָּכוּת: פ

1] God said to Jacob, "Arise, go up to Bethel and remain there; and build an altar there to the God who appeared to you when you were fleeing from your brother Esau." 2] So Jacob said to his household and to all who were with him, "Rid youselves of the alien god in your midst, purify yourselves, and change your clothes. 3] Come, let us go up to Bethel, and I will build an altar there to the God who answered me when I was in distress and who has been with me wherever I have gone." 4] They gave to Jacob all the alien gods that they had, and the rings that were in their ears, and Jacob buried them under the terebinth that was near Shechem. 5] As they set out, a terror from God fell on the cities round about, so that they did not pursue the sons of Jacob.

6] Thus Jacob came to Luz—that is, Bethel—in the land of Canaan, he and all the people who were with him. 7] There he built an altar and named the site El-bethel, for it was there that God had revealed Himself to him when he was fleeing from his brother.

8] Deborah, Rebekah's nurse, died, and was buried under the oak below Bethel; so it was named Allon-bacuth.

35:1] *Go up.* In the sense of pilgrimage, just as later one always "went up" to the Land of Israel. Jacob's journey to Bethel brings to a close the story of his exile.

2] *Alien gods.* Acquired either in Shechem or, through Rachel, in Haran. This is the only time in Genesis that foreign gods are contrasted with the God of the Patriarchs [1].

Purify yourselves. A ritual process that involved washing the body and clothes (cf. Exod. 19:10).

4] *Buried them.* Apparently there was an ancient taboo against destroying holy objects of any kind. Unlike Gideon, who used the golden earrings to fashion an object of idolatry (Judg. 8:24–27), Jacob does not allow the idols to become a snare [2].

/The Jewish practice of burying unusable Torah scrolls, phylacteries, and prayer books [3], or preserving them in a "Genizah," is based on the prohibition against destroying anything that has God's name written on it./

The terebinth. See note at Gen. 12:6.

5] *Terror from God.* Compare this to the story of the angels in Sodom (Gen. 19:11) for a similar case of divine intervention.

7] *El-bethel.* The God of Bethel. Since no reference is made to the fact that Jacob had already named the site Bethel (Gen. 28:19), some commentators suggest that the two passages arose from separate traditions [4].

8] *Deborah.* If she is the nurse mentioned in Gen. 24:59, she would have to be very old here.

Allon-bacuth. Understood as "the oak of weeping."

יַעֲקֹב מַצֵּבָ֗ה בַּמָּק֞וֹם אֲשֶׁר־דִּבֶּ֧ר אִתּ֛וֹ מַצֶּ֣בֶת אָ֑בֶן
וַיַּסֵּ֤ךְ עָלֶ֙יהָ֙ נֶ֔סֶךְ וַיִּצֹ֥ק עָלֶ֖יהָ שָֽׁמֶן: וַיִּקְרָ֧א יַעֲקֹ֛ב
אֶת־שֵׁ֣ם הַמָּק֗וֹם אֲשֶׁר֩ דִּבֶּ֨ר אִתּ֥וֹ שָׁ֛ם אֱלֹהִ֖ים בֵּֽית־אֵֽל:
וַיִּסְעוּ֙ מִבֵּ֣ית אֵ֔ל וַֽיְהִי־ע֥וֹד כִּבְרַת־הָאָ֖רֶץ לָב֣וֹא
אֶפְרָ֑תָה וַתֵּ֥לֶד רָחֵ֖ל וַתְּקַ֥שׁ בְּלִדְתָּֽהּ: וַיְהִ֥י בְהַקְשֹׁתָ֖הּ
בְּלִדְתָּ֑הּ וַתֹּ֨אמֶר לָ֤הּ הַמְיַלֶּ֙דֶת֙ אַל־תִּ֣ירְאִ֔י כִּֽי־גַם־זֶ֥ה
לָ֖ךְ בֵּֽן: וַיְהִ֞י בְּצֵ֤את נַפְשָׁהּ֙ כִּ֣י מֵ֔תָה וַתִּקְרָ֥א שְׁמ֖וֹ בֶּן־
אוֹנִ֑י וְאָבִ֖יו קָֽרָא־ל֥וֹ בִנְיָמִֽין: וַתָּ֖מָת רָחֵ֑ל וַתִּקָּבֵר֙

וַיֵּרָ֨א אֱלֹהִ֤ים אֶֽל־יַעֲקֹב֙ ע֔וֹד בְּבֹא֖וֹ מִפַּדַּ֣ן אֲרָ֑ם
וַיְבָ֖רֶךְ אֹתֽוֹ: וַיֹּֽאמֶר־ל֥וֹ אֱלֹהִ֖ים שִׁמְךָ֣ יַעֲקֹ֑ב לֹֽא־
יִקָּרֵא֩ שִׁמְךָ֨ ע֜וֹד יַעֲקֹ֗ב כִּ֤י אִם־יִשְׂרָאֵל֙ יִהְיֶ֣ה שְׁמֶ֔ךָ
וַיִּקְרָ֥א אֶת־שְׁמ֖וֹ יִשְׂרָאֵֽל: וַיֹּ֩אמֶר֩ ל֨וֹ אֱלֹהִ֜ים אֲנִ֣י אֵ֤ל
שַׁדַּי֙ פְּרֵ֣ה וּרְבֵ֔ה גּ֛וֹי וּקְהַ֥ל גּוֹיִ֖ם יִהְיֶ֣ה מִמֶּ֑ךָּ וּמְלָכִ֖ים
מֵחֲלָצֶ֥יךָ יֵצֵֽאוּ: וְאֶת־הָאָ֗רֶץ אֲשֶׁ֥ר נָתַ֛תִּי לְאַבְרָהָ֖ם
וּלְיִצְחָ֑ק לְךָ֣ אֶתְּנֶ֑נָּה וּֽלְזַרְעֲךָ֥ אַחֲרֶ֖יךָ אֶתֵּ֥ן אֶת־הָאָֽרֶץ:
וַיַּ֥עַל מֵֽעָלָ֖יו אֱלֹהִ֑ים בַּמָּק֖וֹם אֲשֶׁר־דִּבֶּ֥ר אִתּֽוֹ: וַיַּצֵּ֣ב

9] God appeared again to Jacob on his arrival from Paddan-aram, and He blessed him. 10] God said to him, "You whose name is Jacob, / You shall be called Jacob no more, / But Israel shall be your name." Thus He named him Israel.

11] And God said to him, "I am El Shaddai. / Be fertile and increase; / A nation, yea an assembly of nations, / Shall descend from you. / Kings shall issue from your loins. / 12] The land that I gave to Abraham and Isaac / I give to you; / And to your offspring to come / Will I give the land." 13] God parted from him at the spot where He had spoken to him; 14] and Jacob set up a pillar at the site where He had spoken to him, a pillar of stone, and he offered a libation on it and poured oil upon it. 15] Jacob gave the site, where God had spoken to him, the name of Bethel.

16] They set out from Bethel; but when they were still some distance short of Ephrath, Rachel was in childbirth, and she had hard labor. 17] When her labor was at its hardest, the midwife said to her, "Have no fear, for it is another boy for you." 18] But as she breathed

9–15] This tradition is not aware of Jacob's wrestling bout with the angel (see note at Gen. 32:31) nor of the site having been named El-bethel.
/ Traditional explanation: God confirms what His angel has done "in the heat of the contest" [5]./

10] *Jacob no more.* But in fact the appellation Jacob continues at once. Critics have attempted to distinguish between an "Israel tradition" and a "Jacob tradition." If these ever existed, they have been thoroughly interwoven, and the names have now become interchangeable.
/ B. Jacob has attempted, however, to show that each particular usage has a purpose. His analysis covers the forty-five times "Jacob" is used and the thirty-four times "Israel" is written from here to the end of Genesis. "Israel" is said to be used whenever the spiritual side of the Patriarch is emphasized, "Jacob" when material and physical aspects are involved [6]./
11] *El Shaddai.* The name of God as He appeared to Abraham (Gen. 17:1).

16] *Short of Ephrath.* Verse 19 identifies this as Bethlehem. Rachel's tomb may be seen not far from that city. However, according to I Sam. 10:2, the grave was farther north [7]. And one authority holds it was originally near the Jaffa-Jerusalem road at Kiryat Yearim [8].

18] *Ben-oni.* Understood as "son of my suffering [or, strength]."
Benjamin. That is, "son of the south." Others interpret the name as "son of the right hand," which was the favored side. Still others interpret Benjamin as "son of old age" (*ben-yamim*) [9]. Whatever the meaning, Jacob apparently did not want his son to live with the name *Ben-oni,* which recalled grief.
/ It is also possible that the names refer to Rachel's theft of the household gods and the oath Jacob had sworn (31:32). Ben-oni then would mean "son of my iniquity," and Ben-yamin "son of my oath" (as in Ps. 144:8) [10]./

כ בְּדֶרֶךְ אֶפְרָתָה הִוא בֵּית לָחֶם: וַיַּצֵּב יַעֲקֹב מַצֵּבָה

כא עַל־קְבֻרָתָהּ הִוא מַצֶּבֶת קְבֻרַת־רָחֵל עַד־הַיּוֹם: וַיִּסַּע

כב יִשְׂרָאֵל וַיֵּט אׇהֳלֹה מֵהָלְאָה לְמִגְדַּל־עֵדֶר: וַיְהִי בִּשְׁכֹּן
יִשְׂרָאֵל בָּאָרֶץ הַהִוא וַיֵּלֶךְ רְאוּבֵן וַיִּשְׁכַּב אֶת־בִּלְהָה
פִּילֶגֶשׁ אָבִיו וַיִּשְׁמַע יִשְׂרָאֵל ף

כג וַיִּהְיוּ בְנֵי־יַעֲקֹב שְׁנֵים עָשָׂר: בְּנֵי לֵאָה בְּכוֹר יַעֲקֹב

כד רְאוּבֵן וְשִׁמְעוֹן וְלֵוִי וִיהוּדָה וְיִשָּׂשכָר וּזְבֻלוּן: בְּנֵי

כה רָחֵל יוֹסֵף וּבִנְיָמִן: וּבְנֵי בִלְהָה שִׁפְחַת רָחֵל דָּן

כ וְנַפְתָּלִי: וּבְנֵי זִלְפָּה שִׁפְחַת לֵאָה גָּד וְאָשֵׁר אֵלֶּה בְּנֵי

כז יַעֲקֹב אֲשֶׁר יֻלַּד־לוֹ בְּפַדַּן אֲרָם: וַיָּבֹא יַעֲקֹב אֶל־
יִצְחָק אָבִיו מַמְרֵא קִרְיַת הָאַרְבַּע הִוא חֶבְרוֹן

כח אֲשֶׁר־גָּר־שָׁם אַבְרָהָם וְיִצְחָק: וַיִּהְיוּ יְמֵי יִצְחָק מְאַת

כט שָׁנָה וּשְׁמֹנִים שָׁנָה: וַיִּגְוַע יִצְחָק וַיָּמׇת וַיֵּאָסֶף אֶל־
עַמָּיו זָקֵן וּשְׂבַע יָמִים וַיִּקְבְּרוּ אֹתוֹ עֵשָׂו וְיַעֲקֹב
בָּנָיו: ף

לו וְאֵלֶּה תֹּלְדוֹת עֵשָׂו הוּא אֱדוֹם: עֵשָׂו לָקַח אֶת־נָשָׁיו

her last—for she was dying—she named him Ben-oni; but his father called him Benjamin. **19]** Thus Rachel died. She was buried on the road to Ephrath—now Bethlehem. **20]** Over her grave Jacob set up a pillar; it is the pillar at Rachel's grave to this day. **21]** Israel journeyed on, and pitched his tent beyond Migdal-eder.

22] While Israel stayed in that land, Reuben went and lay with Bilhah, his father's concubine; and Israel found out.

Now the sons of Jacob were twelve in number. **23]** The sons of Leah: Reuben—Jacob's first-born—Simeon, Levi, Judah, Issachar, and Zebulun. **24]** The sons of Rachel: Joseph and Benjamin. **25]** The sons of Bilhah, Rachel's maid: Dan and Naphtali. **26]** And the sons of Zilpah, Leah's maid: Gad and Asher. These are the sons of Jacob who were born to him in Paddan-aram.

27] And Jacob came to his father Isaac at Mamre, at Kiriath-arba—now Hebron—where Abraham and Isaac had sojourned. **28]** Isaac was a hundred and eighty years old **29]** when he breathed his last and died. He was gathered to his kin in ripe old age; and he was buried by his sons Esau and Jacob.

1] This is the line of Esau—that is, Edom.

2] Esau took his wives from among the Canaanite women—Adah daughter of Elon the

22] *Reuben . . . Bilhah.* This incident may hint at a revolt by the first-born against his father. (The revolt of Absalom against David takes the same form, II Sam. 16:20–22). Even though Jacob makes no immediate comment, the action will later on cost Reuben his birthright (Gen. 49:4). There is a blank space and double accentuation in the Hebrew text, suggesting that this verse presented some problem to the ancients; possibly the original story told of the incident in greater detail.

/The Mishnah says that this verse is to be read from the Torah in public but not to be translated. The

accentuation causes verses 22 and 23 to be read as one, so as to pass quickly over the passage [11]. The Talmud, however, explains Reuben's action away [12]./

28–29] Isaac's death is as quiet as his life. Most probably he died earlier [13] but the death notice is placed here to complete the patriarchal cycle before attention shifts to Joseph.

28] *One hundred and eighty years old.* On the relation of this age to the years of Abraham and Jacob, see Gleanings to 24:1 ff.

36:1] *Esau—that is, Edom.* Also called Seir. The land is southeast of the Dead Sea.

אֵ֣לֶּה שְׁמ֗וֹת בְּנֵֽי־עֵשָׂ֛ו אֱלִיפַ֖ז בֶּן־עָדָ֑ה אֵ֥שֶׁת עֵשָׂ֔ו
רְעוּאֵ֕ל בֶּן־בָּשְׂמַ֖ת אֵ֣שֶׁת עֵשָֽׂו׃ וַיִּֽהְי֖וּ בְּנֵ֣י אֱלִיפָ֑ז
תֵּימָ֣ן אוֹמָ֔ר צְפ֥וֹ וְגַעְתָּ֖ם וּקְנַֽז׃ וְתִמְנַ֣ע ׀ הָיְתָ֣ה פִילֶ֗גֶשׁ
לֶֽאֱלִיפַז֙ בֶּן־עֵשָׂ֔ו וַתֵּ֥לֶד לֶאֱלִיפַ֖ז אֶת־עֲמָלֵ֑ק אֵ֕לֶּה בְּנֵ֥י
עָדָ֖ה אֵ֥שֶׁת עֵשָֽׂו׃ וְאֵ֖לֶּה בְּנֵ֣י רְעוּאֵ֑ל נַ֥חַת וָזֶ֖רַח שַׁמָּ֣ה
וּמִזָּ֑ה אֵ֣לֶּה הָי֔וּ בְּנֵ֥י בָשְׂמַ֖ת אֵ֥שֶׁת עֵשָֽׂו׃ וְאֵ֣לֶּה הָי֗וּ בְּנֵ֣י
אָהֳלִֽיבָמָ֞ה בַּת־עֲנָ֛ה בַּת־צִבְע֖וֹן אֵ֣שֶׁת עֵשָׂ֑ו וַתֵּ֣לֶד
לְעֵשָׂ֔ו אֶת־יְע֥וּשׁ וְאֶת־יַעְלָ֖ם וְאֶת־קֹֽרַח׃ אֵ֖לֶּה אַלּוּפֵ֣י
בְנֵֽי־עֵשָׂ֑ו בְּנֵ֤י אֱלִיפַז֙ בְּכ֣וֹר עֵשָׂ֔ו אַלּ֤וּף תֵּימָן֙ אַלּ֣וּף
אוֹמָ֔ר אַלּ֥וּף צְפ֖וֹ אַלּ֣וּף קְנַֽז׃ אַלּ֤וּף קֹ֨רַח֙ אַלּ֣וּף
גַּעְתָּ֔ם אַלּ֖וּף עֲמָלֵ֑ק אֵ֣לֶּה אַלּוּפֵ֤י אֱלִיפַז֙ בְּאֶ֣רֶץ
אֱד֔וֹם אֵ֖לֶּה בְּנֵ֥י עָדָֽה׃ וְאֵ֗לֶּה בְּנֵ֤י רְעוּאֵל֙ בֶּן־עֵשָׂ֔ו

מִבְּנ֣וֹת כְּנָ֑עַן אֶת־עָדָ֗ה בַּת־אֵילוֹן֙ הַֽחִתִּ֔י וְאֶת־
אָהֳלִֽיבָמָה֙ בַּת־עֲנָ֔ה בַּת־צִבְע֖וֹן הַֽחִוִּֽי׃ וְאֶת־בָּ֣שְׂמַ֔ת
בַּת־יִשְׁמָעֵ֖אל אֲח֥וֹת נְבָיֽוֹת׃ וַתֵּ֧לֶד עָדָ֛ה לְעֵשָׂ֖ו אֶת־
אֱלִיפָ֑ז וּבָ֣שְׂמַ֔ת יָלְדָ֖ה אֶת־רְעוּאֵֽל׃ וְאָהֳלִֽיבָמָה֙ יָֽלְדָ֔ה
אֶת־יְע֥וּשׁ וְאֶת־יַעְלָ֖ם וְאֶת־קֹ֑רַח אֵ֗לֶּה בְּנֵ֤י עֵשָׂו֙ אֲשֶׁ֣ר
יֻלְּדוּ־ל֖וֹ בְּאֶ֥רֶץ כְּנָֽעַן׃ וַיִּקַּ֣ח עֵשָׂ֡ו אֶת־נָ֠שָׁיו וְאֶת־בָּנָ֣יו
וְאֶת־בְּנֹתָיו֮ וְאֶת־כָּל־נַפְשׁ֣וֹת בֵּיתוֹ֒ וְאֶת־מִקְנֵ֣הוּ וְאֶת־
כָּל־בְּהֶמְתּ֗וֹ וְאֵת֙ כָּל־קִנְיָנ֔וֹ אֲשֶׁ֥ר רָכַ֖שׁ בְּאֶ֣רֶץ כְּנָ֑עַן
וַיֵּ֣לֶךְ אֶל־אֶ֔רֶץ מִפְּנֵ֖י יַעֲקֹ֣ב אָחִֽיו׃ כִּֽי־הָיָ֧ה רְכוּשָׁ֛ם רָ֖ב
מִשֶּׁ֣בֶת יַחְדָּ֑ו וְלֹ֨א יָֽכְלָ֜ה אֶ֤רֶץ מְגֽוּרֵיהֶם֙ לָשֵׂ֣את אֹתָ֔ם
מִפְּנֵ֖י מִקְנֵיהֶֽם׃ וַיֵּ֤שֶׁב עֵשָׂו֙ בְּהַ֣ר שֵׂעִ֔יר עֵשָׂ֖ו ה֣וּא
אֱד֑וֹם׃ וְאֵ֣לֶּה תֹּלְד֧וֹת עֵשָׂ֛ו אֲבִ֥י אֱד֖וֹם בְּהַ֥ר שֵׂעִֽיר׃

Hittite, and Oholibamah daughter of Anah daughter of Zibeon the Hivite— 3] and also Basemath daughter of Ishmael and sister of Nebaioth. 4] Adah bore to Esau Eliphaz; Basemath bore Reuel; 5] and Oholibamah bore Jeush, Jalam, and Korah. Those were the sons of Esau, who were born to him in the land of Canaan.

6] Esau took his wives, his sons and daughters, and all the members of his household, his cattle and all his livestock, and all the property that he had acquired in the land of Canaan, and went to another land because of his brother Jacob. 7] For their possessions were too many for them to dwell together, and the land where they sojourned could not support them because of their livestock. 8] So Esau settled in the hill country of Seir—Esau being Edom.

9] This, then, is the line of Esau, the ancestor of the Edomites, in the hill country of Seir.

10] These are the names of Esau's sons: Eliphaz, the son of Esau's wife Adah; Reuel, the son of Esau's wife Basemath. 11] The sons of Eliphaz were Teman, Omar, Zepho, Gatam, and Kenaz. 12] Timna was a concubine of Esau's son Eliphaz; she bore Amalek to Eliphaz. Those were the descendants of Esau's wife Adah. 13] And these were the sons of Reuel: Nahath, Zerah, Shammah, and Mizzah. Those were the descendants of Esau's wife Basemath. 14] And these were the sons of Esau's wife Oholibamah, daughter of Anah daughter of Zibeon: she bore to Esau Jeush, Jalam, and Korah.

15] These are the clans of the children of Esau. The descendants of Esau's first-born Eliphaz: the clans Teman, Omar, Zepho, Kenaz, 16] Korah, Gatam, and Amalek; these are the clans of Eliphaz in the land of Edom. Those are the descendants of Adah. 17] And these are the

2] *Hivite.* Called Horite (חֹרִי) in Gen. 36:20, a Canaanite group of the same name as the Hori (Hurrians) in the north [14]. (Compare the dual use of "Cush" in the Bible, or "Indian" in our time.)

15] *Clans.* Better than "chiefs" of older translations [15].

אַלּוּף נַחַת אַלּוּף זֶרַח אַלּוּף שַׁמָּה אַלּוּף מִזָּה אֵלֶּה
אַלּוּפֵי רְעוּאֵל בְּאֶרֶץ אֱדוֹם אֵלֶּה בְּנֵי בָשְׂמַת אֵשֶׁת
יח עֵשָׂו: וְאֵלֶּה בְּנֵי אָהֳלִיבָמָה אֵשֶׁת עֵשָׂו אַלּוּף יְעוּשׁ
אַלּוּף יַעְלָם אַלּוּף קֹרַח אֵלֶּה אַלּוּפֵי אָהֳלִיבָמָה
יט בַּת־עֲנָה אֵשֶׁת עֵשָׂו: אֵלֶּה בְנֵי־עֵשָׂו וְאֵלֶּה אַלּוּפֵיהֶם
כ הוּא אֱדוֹם: ס אֵלֶּה בְנֵי־שֵׂעִיר הַחֹרִי יֹשְׁבֵי הָאָרֶץ
כא לוֹטָן וְשׁוֹבָל וְצִבְעוֹן וַעֲנָה: וְדִשׁוֹן וְאֵצֶר וְדִישָׁן
אֵלֶּה אַלּוּפֵי הַחֹרִי בְּנֵי שֵׂעִיר בְּאֶרֶץ אֱדוֹם:
כב וַיִּהְיוּ בְנֵי־לוֹטָן חֹרִי וְהֵימָם וַאֲחוֹת לוֹטָן תִּמְנָע:
כג וְאֵלֶּה בְּנֵי שׁוֹבָל עַלְוָן וּמָנַחַת וְעֵיבָל שְׁפוֹ וְאוֹנָם: וְאֵלֶּה

בְּנֵי־צִבְעוֹן וְאַיָּה וַעֲנָה הוּא עֲנָה אֲשֶׁר מָצָא אֶת־הַיֵּמִם
כה בַּמִּדְבָּר בִּרְעֹתוֹ אֶת־הַחֲמֹרִים לְצִבְעוֹן אָבִיו: וְאֵלֶּה
כו בְנֵי־עֲנָה דִּשֹׁן וְאָהֳלִיבָמָה בַּת־עֲנָה: וְאֵלֶּה בְּנֵי דִישָׁן
חֶמְדָּן וְאֶשְׁבָּן וְיִתְרָן וּכְרָן: אֵלֶּה בְּנֵי־אֵצֶר בִּלְהָן
כז־כח וְזַעֲוָן וַעֲקָן: אֵלֶּה בְנֵי־דִישָׁן עוּץ וַאֲרָן: אֵלֶּה אַלּוּפֵי
כט הַחֹרִי אַלּוּף לוֹטָן אַלּוּף שׁוֹבָל אַלּוּף צִבְעוֹן אַלּוּף
ל עֲנָה: אַלּוּף דִּשֹׁן אַלּוּף אֵצֶר אַלּוּף דִּישָׁן אֵלֶּה
אַלּוּפֵי הַחֹרִי לְאַלֻּפֵיהֶם בְּאֶרֶץ שֵׂעִיר: פ
לא וְאֵלֶּה הַמְּלָכִים אֲשֶׁר מָלְכוּ בְּאֶרֶץ אֱדוֹם לִפְנֵי
לב מְלָךְ־מֶלֶךְ לִבְנֵי יִשְׂרָאֵל: וַיִּמְלֹךְ בֶּאֱדוֹם בֶּלַע בֶּן

descendants of Esau's son Reuel: the clans Nahath, Zerah, Shammah, and Mizzah; these are the clans of Reuel in the land of Edom. Those are the descendants of Esau's wife Basemath. **18]** And these are the descendants of Esau's wife Oholibamah: the clans Jeush, Jalam, and Korah; these are the clans of Esau's wife Oholibamah, the daughter of Anah. **19]** Those were the sons of Esau—that is, Edom—and those are their clans.

20] These were the sons of Seir the Horite, who were settled in the land: Lotan, Shobal, Zibeon, Anah, **21]** Dishon, Ezer, and Dishan. Those are the clans of the Horites, the descendants of Seir, in the land of Edom.

22] The sons of Lotan were Hori and Hemam; and Lotan's sister was Timna. **23]** The sons of Shobal were these: Alvan, Manahath, Ebal, Shepho, and Onam. **24]** The sons of Zibeon were these: Aiah and Anah—that was the Anah who discovered the hot springs in the wilderness while pasturing the asses of his father Zibeon. **25]** The children of Anah were these: Dishon and Anah's daughter Oholibamah. **26]** The sons of Dishon were these: Hemdan, Eshban, Ithran, and Cheran. **27]** The sons of Ezer were these: Bilhan, Zaavan, and Akan. **28]** And the sons of Dishan were these: Uz and Aran.

29] These are the clans of the Horites: the clans Lotan, Shobal, Zibeon, Anah, **30]** Dishon, Ezer, and Dishan. Those are the clans of the Horites, clan by clan, in the land of Seir.

31] These are the kings who reigned in the land of Edom before any king reigned over the

24] *Aiah.* The Hebrew says "and Aiah."

Hot springs. The meaning of יֵמִם is uncertain. /This verse has given rise to much comment and speculation. Anah may be a word play on "female donkey": what Anah discovered was not "hot springs" but the crossbreeding of animals [16]./

26] *Dishon.* Spelled variously דִּישֹׁ (*Dishan*) and דִּישׁוֹן (*Dishon*). Compare Gen. 36:21, 25, 28; I Chron. 1:41.

31] *Before any king reigned over the Israelites.* The conclusion suggests itself that either this phrase or the entire section was added after the establishment of the Israelite monarchy. The verse was a stumbling block to traditional interpreters who had to maintain that "the king" was Moses or that Moses wrote this as a prophecy. However, as early as 1000 C.E., the Spanish commentator Isaac ben Yashush (Yitzchaki) wrote that this verse had been added in the ninth century B.C.E., in the reign of King Jehoshaphat. Ibn Ezra was careful to let his readers know of this view (apparently a way of venting his own doubts) but then added piously: "God forbid that he be right. His book deserves to be burnt."

לב בְּעוֹר וְשֵׁם עִירוֹ דִּנְהָבָה: וַיָּמָת בֶּלַע וַיִּמְלֹךְ תַּחְתָּיו

לד יוֹבָב בֶּן־זֶרַח מִבָּצְרָה: וַיָּמָת יוֹבָב וַיִּמְלֹךְ תַּחְתָּיו

לה חֻשָׁם מֵאֶרֶץ הַתֵּימָנִי: וַיָּמָת חֻשָׁם וַיִּמְלֹךְ תַּחְתָּיו הֲדַד בֶּן־בְּדַד הַמַּכֶּה אֶת־מִדְיָן בִּשְׂדֵה מוֹאָב וְשֵׁם עִירוֹ

לו עֲוִית: וַיָּמָת הֲדַד וַיִּמְלֹךְ תַּחְתָּיו שַׂמְלָה מִמַּשְׂרֵקָה:

לז וַיָּמָת שַׂמְלָה וַיִּמְלֹךְ תַּחְתָּיו שָׁאוּל מֵרְחֹבוֹת הַנָּהָר:

לח וַיָּמָת שָׁאוּל וַיִּמְלֹךְ תַּחְתָּיו בַּעַל חָנָן בֶּן־עַכְבּוֹר:

לט וַיָּמָת בַּעַל חָנָן בֶּן־עַכְבּוֹר וַיִּמְלֹךְ תַּחְתָּיו הֲדַר וְשֵׁם

עִירוֹ פָּעוּ וְשֵׁם אִשְׁתּוֹ מְהֵיטַבְאֵל בַּת־מַטְרֵד בַּת מֵי זָהָב:

מ וְאֵלֶּה שְׁמוֹת אַלּוּפֵי עֵשָׂו לְמִשְׁפְּחֹתָם לִמְקֹמֹתָם בִּשְׁמֹתָם אַלּוּף תִּמְנָע אַלּוּף עַלְוָה אַלּוּף יְתֵת: אַלּוּף

מב אָהֳלִיבָמָה אַלּוּף אֵלָה אַלּוּף פִּינֹן: אַלּוּף קְנַז אַלּוּף

מג תֵּימָן אַלּוּף מִבְצָר: אַלּוּף מַגְדִּיאֵל אַלּוּף עִירָם אֵלֶּה אַלּוּפֵי אֱדוֹם לְמֹשְׁבֹתָם בְּאֶרֶץ אֲחֻזָּתָם הוּא עֵשָׂו אֲבִי אֱדוֹם:

Haftarah Vayishlach, p. 349

Israelites. **32]** Bela son of Beor reigned in Edom, and the name of his city was Dinhabah. **33]** When Bela died, Jobab son of Zerah, from Bozrah, succeeded him as king. **34]** When Jobab died, Husham of the land of the Temanites succeeded him as king. **35]** When Husham died, Hadad son of Bedad, who defeated the Midianites in the country of Moab, succeeded him as king; the name of his city was Avith. **36]** When Hadad died, Samlah of Masrekah succeeded him as king. **37]** When Samlah died, Saul of Rehoboth-on-the-river succeeded him as king. **38]** When Saul died, Baal-hanan son of Achbor succeeded him as king. **39]** And when Baal-hanan son of Achbor died, Hadar succeeded him as king; the name of his city was Pau, and his wife's name was Mehetabel daughter of Matred daughter of Me-zahab.

40] These are the names of the clans of Esau, each with its families and locality, name by name: the clans Timna, Alvah, Jeteth, **41]** Oholibamah, Elah, Pinon, **42]** Kenaz, Teman, Mibzar, **43]** Magdiel, and Iram. Those are the clans of Edom—that is, of Esau, father of the Edomites—in their settlements in the land which they hold.

37] *Saul.* שָׁאוּל (Shaul). Note that the name of this Edomite will be the name of Israel's first king.

Rehoboth-on-the-river. The location is uncertain. It has no connection with today's Rehovot.

39] *Hadar.* Elsewhere called Hadad (I Chron. 1:50).

The Edomites

This section presents a number of difficulties. Scholars have not yet been successful in sorting out all the historical and geographical identities mentioned, especially since the Bible remains our only major source of knowledge in regard to the Edomites. Nothing remains of the language of Edom except proper names, and these suggest that the Edomites' tongue was similar to Hebrew [17]. There is no other written record of this people, and archeological discoveries have thus far been of no assistance. We have here an instance where traditions that were once meaningful to listener and reader and that carried nuances and references clear in their own time have become mere names and lists.

While this is not the first point at which the Bible discusses the Edomites, parts of this section appear to be based on traditions different from those recorded earlier. For instance, Basemath is here called the daughter of Ishmael (Gen. 36:3) but was earlier called the daughter of Elon (Gen. 26:34); Esau is married to Adah, daughter of Elon (Gen. 36:2), while earlier his wife is called Judith, daughter of Beeri (Gen. 26:34). Because of such inconsistencies and contradictions, the famous Bible scholar and critic Julius Wellhausen thought of chapter 36 as a show window for biblical criticism and said that either varying traditions stand here side by side or the whole system of biblical criticism must be pronounced invalid.[1]

The Character of Esau

Although the Bible relates many uncomplimentary incidents about Jacob, it records on the whole praiseworthy accounts of Esau. Nevertheless, Jacob-Israel became the chosen, Esau-Edom the rejected. Because of this, traditional interpreters felt compelled to whitewash Jacob's character and to blacken the name of Esau. After the Roman conquest of Judea (first century B.C.E.), "Edom" came to signify Rome, oppression, and evil. Not only was this a case of prejudicial stereotyping, it was also a misreading of the biblical intent. For Esau emerges from the text as a generally admirable man.

While he thought little of his birthright and contracted marriages displeasing to his parents, Esau was otherwise attentive to his father. One midrash even conceded that because he showed more respect to him than duty demanded he was mentioned first at the burial of his father (Gen. 35:29) [19]. Certainly his behavior at the reconciliation with Jacob was exemplary—he was generous and forgiving.

No wonder Isaac loved this outdoor man and skilful hunter who exuded strength. Yet precisely because Esau was the physical man, little concerned with things of the spirit, he could not be the inheritor of Abraham's and Isaac's blessings. Even before his birth (Gen. 25:23) it was foretold that God's mysterious choice would be Jacob, the complex and difficult man whose moral fibers needed building and strengthening, the man who ran from and toward fate, who would suffer deep pain and find the coveted blessing a source of bitter agony.

---

[1] Following ancient tradition, which saw in Esau the embodiment of evil, these passages have been called a "labyrinth of immoral connections," i.e., a somewhat veiled description of the presumed immorality of Edom [18].

GLEANINGS

Change Your Clothes (Gen. 35:2)

From this we learn that every Jew, when he goes to a place appointed for prayer, must be clean in body and clothes. IBN EZRA

Pillars

מַצֵּבוֹת served the ancients for worship and as tombstones, as in the case of Rachel. In talmudic times, when funds were collected to pay for burials, the surplus was applied to the purchase of a tombstone. However, R. Simeon ben Gamaliel, in order to prevent the erection of ostentatious markers, discouraged their use by teaching: "Tombstones are not erected for the righteous, since their teachings are their memorials." [20]

While the Patriarchs erected pillars for worship, this was later forbidden and gave way to altars at which cultic rites were to be performed. Why? Pillars were symbols of generalized faith; altars were symbols of faith plus *mitzvot*, i.e., Judaism. RAV KUK [21]

The Burden

Because he [Jacob] moves forever shadowed by
   deep questioning,
And you [Esau] rejoice, happy and safe and
   sated . . .
Because he does not shroud his God in distant
   heavens,
But wrestles with him daily, heart to heart!
Because you can but hunt, make offering,
   murder . . .

He bears the blessing—and the blessing's
   burden. RICHARD BEER-HOFMANN [22]

Edom and Israel

In rabbinical tradition Esau and Edom came to symbolize Rome, the colossal, temporal, material power, which sought to crush nations, which overran the earth with warfare and bloodshed, and found its highest pleasure in murderous gladiatorial combats. And Jacob continued to represent Israel, the spiritual people, the servant of the Lord, whose mission was to bind up the bleeding wounds of cruelty and oppression and to bring law and order, peace and brotherhood, and the knowledge of God unto all mankind.

JULIAN MORGENSTERN [23]

The Meeting

Rebecca's twin sons were at this time fifty-five years old: the sweet-smelling grass and the prickly plant, as they had been known in all the countryside between Hebron and Beersheba. But the sweet-smelling grass, the smooth man, Jacob, had never behaved very youthful; a tent-dweller, thoughtful and timid, he had shown himself even as a boy. And now he was a ripe man, with much experience, heavy with goods that had accrued unto him, preoccupied in spirit, bearing with dignity the weight of events. And on the other hand Esau, though like his brother grey-haired, seemed still to be as of yore, the same feckless insignificant child of nature.

THOMAS MANN [24]

PART V

The Line of Jacob

The last part of Genesis begins with the "line of Jacob" (37:2) for, with Isaac dead, Jacob is now, technically, the leading figure. In effect, however, the Patriarch at once fades into the background. His life provides the framework for the Joseph saga, which is distinguished from the preceding sections of Genesis in a number of ways: its length as a continuing account and the absence both of divine revelation (except in Gen. 46:2–4) and of specific references in the most important parts (neither Goshen nor Pharaoh is further identified) [1].

The effective impact of Joseph's biography is created by the device of what Aristotle called "dramatic reversal," which he considered essential to good drama [2] and which is often found in Greek writing. Fate thwarts the will of man by turning the effect of his actions to its own purposes rather than to his. Joseph is sold by his brothers so that they may be rid of the dreamer, yet the dreams come true, the slave becomes master, hatred turns to love, and the rejected one saves his brothers' lives. In sum, man cannot alter the overriding purposes of divine power.

The prominence of Joseph in these tales should not let us forget the continuing tragedy of Jacob. He who chased after the birthright and secured its blessings in deceitful fashion pays heavily for the privilege. His children will cause him anxieties and agonies, and he will end his life in exile, a pensioner of his son.

Young Joseph

The apparent calm of a wealthy shepherd's pastoral existence forms the setting of the opening chapter of the Joseph cycle, but parental preference, youthful conceit, and sibling envy will create a bitter drama. Dreams play an important role and hint at unusual developments. And once again there is a descent into Egypt. Abraham had gone there to escape a famine; Joseph makes the journey as a slave.

(A new weekly portion, *Vayeshev*, begins here.)

ה יָכְלוּ דַּבְּרוֹ לְשָׁלֹם: וַיַּחֲלֹם יוֹסֵף חֲלוֹם וַיַּגֵּד לְאֶחָיו
י וַיּוֹסִפוּ עוֹד שְׂנֹא אֹתוֹ: וַיֹּאמֶר אֲלֵיהֶם שִׁמְעוּ־נָא
הַחֲלוֹם הַזֶּה אֲשֶׁר חָלָמְתִּי: וְהִנֵּה אֲנַחְנוּ מְאַלְּמִים
אֲלֻמִּים בְּתוֹךְ הַשָּׂדֶה וְהִנֵּה קָמָה אֲלֻמָּתִי וְגַם־נִצָּבָה
וְהִנֵּה תְסֻבֶּינָה אֲלֻמֹּתֵיכֶם וַתִּשְׁתַּחֲוֶיןָ לַאֲלֻמָּתִי:
ח וַיֹּאמְרוּ לוֹ אֶחָיו הֲמָלֹךְ תִּמְלֹךְ עָלֵינוּ אִם־מָשׁוֹל
תִּמְשֹׁל בָּנוּ וַיּוֹסִפוּ עוֹד שְׂנֹא אֹתוֹ עַל־חֲלֹמֹתָיו וְעַל־
ט דְּבָרָיו: וַיַּחֲלֹם עוֹד חֲלוֹם אַחֵר וַיְסַפֵּר אֹתוֹ לְאֶחָיו

פ פ פ

א וַיֵּשֶׁב יַעֲקֹב בְּאֶרֶץ מְגוּרֵי אָבִיו בְּאֶרֶץ כְּנָעַן: אֵלֶּה
תֹּלְדוֹת יַעֲקֹב יוֹסֵף בֶּן־שְׁבַע־עֶשְׂרֵה שָׁנָה הָיָה רֹעֶה
אֶת־אֶחָיו בַּצֹּאן וְהוּא נַעַר אֶת־בְּנֵי בִלְהָה וְאֶת־בְּנֵי
זִלְפָּה נְשֵׁי אָבִיו וַיָּבֵא יוֹסֵף אֶת־דִּבָּתָם רָעָה אֶל־
ג אֲבִיהֶם: וְיִשְׂרָאֵל אָהַב אֶת־יוֹסֵף מִכָּל־בָּנָיו כִּי־בֶן־
ד זְקֻנִים הוּא לוֹ וְעָשָׂה לוֹ כְּתֹנֶת פַּסִּים: וַיִּרְאוּ אֶחָיו
כִּי־אֹתוֹ אָהַב אֲבִיהֶם מִכָּל־אֶחָיו וַיִּשְׂנְאוּ אֹתוֹ וְלֹא

1] Now Jacob was settled in the land where his father had resided, the land of Canaan. **2]** This, then, is the line of Jacob:

At seventeen years of age, Joseph tended the flocks with his brothers, as a helper to the sons of his father's wives Bilhah and Zilpah. And Joseph brought bad reports of them to their father. **3]** Now Israel loved Joseph best of all his sons, for he was the child of his old age; and he had made him an ornamented tunic. **4]** And when his brothers saw that their father loved him more than any of his brothers, they hated him so that they could not speak a friendly word to him.

5] Once Joseph had a dream which he told to his brothers; and they hated him even more. **6]** He said to them, "Hear this dream which I have dreamed: **7]** There we were binding sheaves in the field, when suddenly my sheaf stood up and remained upright; then your sheaves gathered around and bowed low to my sheaf." **8]** His brothers answered, "Do you mean to reign over us? Do you mean to rule over us?" And they hated him even more for his talk about his dreams.

9] He dreamed another dream and told it to his brothers, saying, "Look, I have had another

37:1–2] The first verse and half of the second form a literary bridge. They conclude the core of the Jacob story and provide an introduction to the Joseph cycle (see Gen. 2:4, which has a similar function in connecting the two creation stories).

2] *Joseph brought bad reports.* He was a talebearer. Traditional commentators attempt to whitewash Joseph's behavior by saying that he merely did his job and reported what he saw.

3] *Ornamented tunic.* The meaning is not clear. Others translate as "a coat of many colors," or "a robe with sleeves." In II Sam. 13:18, the same term signifies special distinction; perhaps it marked

those who did not have to work [1]. Jacob's affection for Joseph most likely sprang from his love for Rachel, whose first-born he was. Later, after Joseph's presumed death, Jacob's preference is transferred to Benjamin, Rachel's second son.

5] *Joseph had a dream.* Six dreams (two by Joseph, two by the prisoners, and two by Pharaoh) lend suspense to the story. While dreams are now studied as keys to hidden layers of personality, they were formerly thought to be prophetic. An Egyptian manual of the time gives instructions on how to interpret such premonitory dreams (see commentary to Gen. 39:1–40:23).

וַיֹּאמֶר הִנֵּה חָלַמְתִּי חֲלוֹם עוֹד וְהִנֵּה הַשֶּׁמֶשׁ וְהַיָּרֵחַ

וְאַחַד עָשָׂר כּוֹכָבִים מִשְׁתַּחֲוִים לִי: וַיְסַפֵּר אֶל־אָבִיו

וְאֶל־אֶחָיו וַיִּגְעַר־בּוֹ אָבִיו וַיֹּאמֶר לוֹ מָה הַחֲלוֹם הַזֶּה

אֲשֶׁר חָלָמְתָּ הֲבוֹא נָבוֹא אֲנִי וְאִמְּךָ וְאַחֶיךָ לְהִשְׁתַּחֲוֹת

לְךָ אָרְצָה: וַיְקַנְאוּ־בוֹ אֶחָיו וְאָבִיו שָׁמַר אֶת־הַדָּבָר:

וַיֵּלְכוּ אֶחָיו לִרְעוֹת אֶת־צֹאן אֲבִיהֶם בִּשְׁכֶם: וַיֹּאמֶר

יִשְׂרָאֵל אֶל־יוֹסֵף הֲלוֹא אַחֶיךָ רֹעִים בִּשְׁכֶם לְכָה

וְאֶשְׁלָחֲךָ אֲלֵיהֶם וַיֹּאמֶר לוֹ הִנֵּנִי: וַיֹּאמֶר לוֹ לֶךְ־נָא

רְאֵה אֶת־שְׁלוֹם אַחֶיךָ וְאֶת־שְׁלוֹם הַצֹּאן וַהֲשִׁבֵנִי

דָּבָר וַיִּשְׁלָחֵהוּ מֵעֵמֶק חֶבְרוֹן וַיָּבֹא שְׁכֶמָה: וַיִּמְצָאֵהוּ

אִישׁ וְהִנֵּה תֹעֶה בַּשָּׂדֶה וַיִּשְׁאָלֵהוּ הָאִישׁ לֵאמֹר מַה־

תְּבַקֵּשׁ: וַיֹּאמֶר אֶת־אַחַי אָנֹכִי מְבַקֵּשׁ הַגִּידָה־נָּא לִי

אֵיפֹה הֵם רֹעִים: וַיֹּאמֶר הָאִישׁ נָסְעוּ מִזֶּה כִּי שָׁמַעְתִּי

אֹמְרִים נֵלְכָה דֹּתָיְנָה וַיֵּלֶךְ יוֹסֵף אַחַר אֶחָיו וַיִּמְצָאֵם

בְּדֹתָן: וַיִּרְאוּ אֹתוֹ מֵרָחֹק וּבְטֶרֶם יִקְרַב אֲלֵיהֶם

וַיִּתְנַכְּלוּ אֹתוֹ לַהֲמִיתוֹ: וַיֹּאמְרוּ אִישׁ אֶל־אָחִיו הִנֵּה

בַּעַל הַחֲלֹמוֹת הַלָּזֶה בָּא: וְעַתָּה לְכוּ וְנַהַרְגֵהוּ

וְנַשְׁלִכֵהוּ בְּאַחַד הַבֹּרוֹת וְאָמַרְנוּ חַיָּה רָעָה אֲכָלָתְהוּ

וְנִרְאֶה מַה־יִּהְיוּ חֲלֹמֹתָיו: וַיִּשְׁמַע רְאוּבֵן וַיַּצִּלֵהוּ

מִיָּדָם וַיֹּאמֶר לֹא נַכֶּנּוּ נָפֶשׁ: וַיֹּאמֶר אֲלֵהֶם רְאוּבֵן

אַל־תִּשְׁפְּכוּ־דָם הַשְׁלִיכוּ אֹתוֹ אֶל־הַבּוֹר הַזֶּה אֲשֶׁר

בַּמִּדְבָּר וְיָד אַל־תִּשְׁלְחוּ־בוֹ לְמַעַן הַצִּיל אֹתוֹ מִיָּדָם

* יב נקוד על את.

dream: And this time, the sun, the moon, and eleven stars were bowing down to me." **10]** And when he told it to his father and brothers, his father berated him. "What," he said to him, "is this dream you have dreamed? Are we to come, I and your mother and your brothers, and bow low to you to the ground?" **11]** So his brothers were wrought up at him, and his father kept the matter in mind.

12] One time, when his brothers had gone to pasture their father's flock at Shechem, **13]** Israel said to Joseph, "Your brothers are pasturing at Shechem. Come, I will send you to them." He answered, "I am ready." **14]** And he said to him, "Go and see how your brothers are and how the flocks are faring, and bring me back word." So he sent him from the valley of Hebron.

When he reached Shechem, **15]** a man came upon him wandering in the fields. The man asked him, "What are you looking for?" **16]** He answered, "I am looking for my brothers. Could you tell me where they are pasturing?" **17]** The man said, "They have gone from here, for I heard them say: Let us go to Dothan." So Joseph followed his brothers and found them at Dothan.

18] They saw him from afar, and before he came close to them they conspired to kill him. **19]** They said to one another, "Here comes that dreamer! **20]** Come now, let us kill him and throw him into one of the pits; and we can say, 'A savage beast devoured him.' We shall see what comes of his dreams!" **21]** But when Reuben heard it, he tried to save him from them. He said, "Let us not take his life." **22]** And Reuben went on, "Shed no blood! Cast him into the pit out in the wilderness, but do not touch him yourselves"—intending to

11] *Kept the matter in mind.* Because he believed that as a dream it revealed the future.

14] *From the valley of Hebron.* Joseph will not return here, but hundreds of years later his remains will reach Shechem once again (Josh. 24:32). / The Talmud connects the passage with Gen. 15:13 and following, which predict enslavement in a foreign land and return to Canaan after 400 years [2]./

15] *A man.* His namelessness suggests a comparison with the nameless man who wrestled with Jacob.

17] *Dothan.* Today's Tell Dothan, north of Shechem. The city, excavated in 1953–1960, dates back to 3000 B.C.E.

כג לַהֲשִׁיבוֹ אֶל־אָבִיו: וַיְהִי כַּאֲשֶׁר־בָּא יוֹסֵף אֶל־אֶחָיו וַיַּפְשִׁיטוּ אֶת־יוֹסֵף אֶת־כֻּתָּנְתּוֹ אֶת־כְּתֹנֶת הַפַּסִּים אֲשֶׁר

כד עָלָיו: וַיִּקָּחֻהוּ וַיַּשְׁלִכוּ אֹתוֹ הַבֹּרָה וְהַבּוֹר רֵק אֵין בּוֹ

כה מָיִם: וַיֵּשְׁבוּ לֶאֱכָל־לֶחֶם וַיִּשְׂאוּ עֵינֵיהֶם וַיִּרְאוּ וְהִנֵּה אֹרְחַת יִשְׁמְעֵאלִים בָּאָה מִגִּלְעָד וּגְמַלֵּיהֶם נֹשְׂאִים

כו נְכֹאת וּצְרִי וָלֹט הוֹלְכִים לְהוֹרִיד מִצְרָיְמָה: וַיֹּאמֶר יְהוּדָה אֶל־אֶחָיו מַה־בֶּצַע כִּי נַהֲרֹג אֶת־אָחִינוּ וְכִסִּינוּ

כז אֶת־דָּמוֹ: לְכוּ וְנִמְכְּרֶנּוּ לַיִּשְׁמְעֵאלִים וְיָדֵנוּ אַל־תְּהִי־

כח בוֹ כִּי־אָחִינוּ בְשָׂרֵנוּ הוּא וַיִּשְׁמְעוּ אֶחָיו: וַיַּעַבְרוּ אֲנָשִׁים מִדְיָנִים סֹחֲרִים וַיִּמְשְׁכוּ וַיַּעֲלוּ אֶת־יוֹסֵף מִן־הַבּוֹר וַיִּמְכְּרוּ אֶת־יוֹסֵף לַיִּשְׁמְעֵאלִים בְּעֶשְׂרִים כָּסֶף

כט וַיָּבִיאוּ אֶת־יוֹסֵף מִצְרָיְמָה: וַיָּשָׁב רְאוּבֵן אֶל־הַבּוֹר

ל וְהִנֵּה אֵין־יוֹסֵף בַּבּוֹר וַיִּקְרַע אֶת־בְּגָדָיו: וַיָּשָׁב אֶל־

לא אֶחָיו וַיֹּאמַר הַיֶּלֶד אֵינֶנּוּ וַאֲנִי אָנָה אֲנִי־בָא: וַיִּקְחוּ אֶת־כְּתֹנֶת יוֹסֵף וַיִּשְׁחֲטוּ שְׂעִיר עִזִּים וַיִּטְבְּלוּ אֶת־

לב הַכֻּתֹּנֶת בַּדָּם: וַיְשַׁלְּחוּ אֶת־כְּתֹנֶת הַפַּסִּים וַיָּבִיאוּ אֶל־אֲבִיהֶם וַיֹּאמְרוּ זֹאת מָצָאנוּ הַכֶּר־נָא הַכְּתֹנֶת

לג בִּנְךָ הִוא אִם־לֹא: וַיַּכִּירָהּ וַיֹּאמֶר כְּתֹנֶת בְּנִי חַיָּה

לד רָעָה אֲכָלָתְהוּ טָרֹף טֹרַף יוֹסֵף: וַיִּקְרַע יַעֲקֹב שִׂמְלֹתָיו וַיָּשֶׂם שַׂק בְּמָתְנָיו וַיִּתְאַבֵּל עַל־בְּנוֹ יָמִים

לה רַבִּים: וַיָּקֻמוּ כָל־בָּנָיו וְכָל־בְּנֹתָיו לְנַחֲמוֹ וַיְמָאֵן לְהִתְנַחֵם וַיֹּאמֶר כִּי־אֵרֵד אֶל־בְּנִי אָבֵל שְׁאֹלָה וַיֵּבְךְּ

לו אֹתוֹ אָבִיו: וְהַמְּדָנִים מָכְרוּ אֹתוֹ אֶל־מִצְרַיִם לְפוֹטִיפַר סְרִיס פַּרְעֹה שַׂר הַטַּבָּחִים: פ

save him from them and restore him to his father. **23]** When Joseph came up to his brothers, they stripped Joseph of his tunic, the ornamented tunic that he was wearing, **24]** and took him and cast him into the pit. The pit was empty; there was no water in it.

25] Then they sat down to a meal. Looking up, they saw a caravan of Ishmaelites coming from Gilead, their camels bearing gum, balm, and ladanum to be taken to Egypt. **26]** Then Judah said to his brothers, "What do we gain by killing our brother and covering up his blood? **27]** Come, let us sell him to the Ishmaelites, but let us not do away with him ourselves. After all, he is our brother, our own flesh." His brothers agreed. **28]** When Midianite traders passed by, they pulled Joseph up out of the pit. They sold Joseph for twenty pieces of silver to the Ishmaelites, who brought Joseph to Egypt.

29] When Reuben returned to the pit and saw that Joseph was not in the pit, he rent his clothes. **30]** Returning to his brothers, he said, "The boy is gone! Now, what am I to do?" **31]** Then they took Joseph's tunic, slaughtered a kid, and dipped the tunic in the blood. **32]** They had the ornamented tunic taken to their father, and they said, "We found this. Please examine it; is it your son's tunic or not?" **33]** He recognized it, and said, "My son's tunic! A savage beast devoured him! Joseph was torn by a beast!" **34]** Jacob rent his clothes, put sackcloth on his loins, and observed mourning for his son many days. **35]** All his sons and daughters sought to comfort him; but he refused to be comforted, saying, "No, I will go down mourning to my son in Sheol." Thus his father bewailed him.

36] The Midianites, meanwhile, sold him in Egypt to Potiphar, a courtier of Pharaoh and his chief steward.

25] *Ishmaelites.* Later the traders are called Midianites (Gen. 37:28, 36; see commentary below).

Ladanum. Or labdanum, a resinous juice used in the manufacture of perfume.

26] *Covering up his blood.* The traces of the crime (cf. Gen. 4:10).

28] *Twenty pieces of silver.* The redemption price for a five- to twenty-year-old male (Lev. 27:5).

30] *Now, what am I to do?* As the oldest, Reuben feels himself responsible to his father.

35] *Sheol.* The place where dead spirits were believed to reside. It was not, like Hades, a frightening abode. The term Sheol occurs often in the Bible but is not further defined.

36] *Potiphar.* From the Egyptian *Pa-di-pa-re* (He whom Re [the sun god] has given) [3].

Pharaoh. Egyptian *per-aa* (great house).

Reuben and Judah

The charm and suspense of the Joseph story are appealing in any language and to any age. In the Hebrew, however, there are touches of literary artistry that escape the powers of the translator.

It is clear that originally two traditions existed: In one, Reuben is the protector and Joseph is sold to the Midianites (Gen. 37:18–24, 29–36); in the other, Judah protects his brother from being killed but also suggests his sale and Joseph is surrendered to the Ishmaelites (Gen. 37:25–27). In verse 28 the traditions are joined. This fusion is facilitated by the fact that by the time the text assumed its present form the terms "Ishmaelites" and "Midianites" were used as synonyms (cf. Judg. 8:24, 26). The term "Medanites" (as it occurs in the Hebrew of Gen. 37:36) was a third synonym that had the additional connotation of "quarrelsome people." All three expressions also signified "traders"—so that to the Hebrew ear the text was further filled with literary nuances [4].

We must also remember that the Reuben and Judah versions of the story had a strong political flavor in their day. Like the Tamar episode, which follows (Gen. 38), they cast a special light both on the tribal fathers and on the tribes themselves. Listeners of ancient days most likely compared the merits of the biblical Reuben and Judah with the latter day fates and fortunes of the Reuben and Judah tribes. Thus, these patriarchal stories spoke to them with special contemporary overtones not easily heard by later generations.

GLEANINGS

Nemesis

The beginning of the story of Joseph still stands under the shadow of Jacob–Israel's guilt, which had clung to the old man since his youth. Just as he had once deceived his father and robbed the brother whom his father had preferred, so Jacob is now in turn deceived by his sons who have sidetracked his favorite son. OTTO PROCKSCH

The Story in Moslem Tradition

In revealing to thee this Koran, one of the most beautiful of narratives will we narrate to thee, of which thou hast hitherto been regardless.

When Joseph said to his father, "O my father! verily I beheld eleven stars and the sun and the moon—beheld them make obeisance to me!"

He said, "O my son! tell not thy vision to thy brethren, lest they plot a plot against thee: for Satan is the manifest foe of man.

"It is thus that thy Lord shall choose thee and will teach thee the interpretation of dark sayings and will perfect His favours on thee and on the family of Jacob, as of old He perfected it on thy fathers Abraham and Isaac; verily thy Lord is Knowing, Wise!"

Now in Joseph and his brethren are signs for the enquirers;

When they said, "Surely better loved by our father than we, who are more in number, is Joseph and his brother; verily, our father hath clearly erred.

"Slay ye Joseph! or drive him to some other land, and on you alone shall your father's face be set! and after this, ye shall live as upright persons."

One of them said, "Slay not Joseph, but cast him down to the bottom of the well: if ye do so, some wayfarers will take him up."

They said, "O our father! why dost thou not entrust us with Joseph? indeed we mean him well.

"Send him with us to-morrow that he may enjoy himself and sport: we will surely keep him safely."

He said, "Verily, your taking him away will grieve me; and I fear lest while ye are heedless of him the wolf devour him."

They said, "Surely if the wolf devour him, and we so many, we must in that case be weak indeed."

And when they went away with him they agreed to place him at the bottom of the well. And we revealed to him, "Thou wilt yet tell them of this their deed, when they shall not know thee."

And they came at nightfall to their father weeping.

They said, "O our father! of a truth, we went to run races, and we left Joseph with our clothes, and the wolf devoured him: but thou wilt not believe us even though we speak the truth."

And they brought his shirt with false blood upon it. He said, "Nay, but yourselves have managed this affair. But patience is seemly: and the help of God is to be implored that I may bear what you tell me."

And wayfarers came and sent their drawer of water, and he let down his bucket. "Good news!" said he. "This is a youth!" And they kept his case secret, to make merchandise of him. But God knew what they did. KORAN [5]

Tamar

The story of Tamar is a complete unit that tells of various old traditions in meticulous detail. It is likely that we have here not only a personal vignette but also a tale of wider implications—Judah is represented as an individual, but he is also the ancestor of the Davidic line.[1]

This interlude interrupts the story of Joseph at a point of rising suspense. It covers many years and thus allows the Bible to take up the tale of Joseph again after the boy has grown into manhood.[2]

---

[1] Through his son Perez (Gen. 46:12; Ruth 4:18) [1]. Possibly the account of the rape of Tamar, David's daughter (II Sam. 13), is also to be read in the light of the Genesis story.
[2] It is not possible, however, to integrate the names and figures in this chapter with the Jacob-Joseph story. There, the grandsons of Tamar and Judah migrate to Egypt (Gen. 46:12), yet only twenty-two years have elapsed from the time of Joseph's sale to the time of the migration. Hence these traditions were originally independent of the Tamar tradition.

א וַיְהִי בָּעֵת הַהִוא וַיֵּרֶד יְהוּדָה מֵאֵת אֶחָיו וַיֵּט עַד־אִישׁ
ב עֲדֻלָּמִי וּשְׁמוֹ חִירָה: וַיַּרְא־שָׁם יְהוּדָה בַּת־אִישׁ כְּנַעֲנִי
ג וּשְׁמוֹ שׁוּעַ וַיִּקָּחֶהָ וַיָּבֹא אֵלֶיהָ: וַתַּהַר וַתֵּלֶד בֵּן
ד וַיִּקְרָא אֶת־שְׁמוֹ עֵר: וַתַּהַר עוֹד וַתֵּלֶד בֵּן וַתִּקְרָא
ה אֶת־שְׁמוֹ אוֹנָן: וַתֹּסֶף עוֹד וַתֵּלֶד בֵּן וַתִּקְרָא אֶת־שְׁמוֹ
ו שֵׁלָה וְהָיָה בִכְזִיב בְּלִדְתָּהּ אֹתוֹ: וַיִּקַּח יְהוּדָה אִשָּׁה
ז לְעֵר בְּכוֹרוֹ וּשְׁמָהּ תָּמָר: וַיְהִי עֵר בְּכוֹר יְהוּדָה רַע
ח בְּעֵינֵי יְהוָה וַיְמִתֵהוּ יְהוָה: וַיֹּאמֶר יְהוּדָה לְאוֹנָן בֹּא

ט אֶל־אֵשֶׁת אָחִיךָ וְיַבֵּם אֹתָהּ וְהָקֵם זֶרַע לְאָחִיךָ: וַיֵּדַע
אוֹנָן כִּי לֹא לוֹ יִהְיֶה הַזָּרַע וְהָיָה אִם־בָּא אֶל־אֵשֶׁת
י אָחִיו וְשִׁחֵת אַרְצָה לְבִלְתִּי נְתָן־זֶרַע לְאָחִיו: וַיֵּרַע
בְּעֵינֵי יְהוָה אֲשֶׁר עָשָׂה וַיָּמֶת גַּם־אֹתוֹ: וַיֹּאמֶר יְהוּדָה
יא לְתָמָר כַּלָּתוֹ שְׁבִי אַלְמָנָה בֵית־אָבִיךְ עַד־יִגְדַּל שֵׁלָה
בְנִי כִּי אָמַר פֶּן־יָמוּת גַּם־הוּא כְּאֶחָיו וַתֵּלֶךְ תָּמָר
יב וַתֵּשֶׁב בֵּית אָבִיהָ: וַיִּרְבּוּ הַיָּמִים וַתָּמָת בַּת־שׁוּעַ
אֵשֶׁת־יְהוּדָה וַיִּנָּחֶם יְהוּדָה וַיַּעַל עַל־גֹּזְזֵי צֹאנוֹ הוּא

1] About that time Judah left his brothers and camped near a certain Adullamite whose name was Hirah. 2] There Judah saw the daughter of a certain Canaanite whose name was Shua, and he married her and cohabited with her. 3] She conceived and bore a son, and he named him Er. 4] She conceived again and bore a son, and named him Onan. 5] Once again she bore a son, and named him Shelah; he was at Chezib when she bore him.

6] Judah got a wife for Er his first-born; her name was Tamar. 7] But Er, Judah's first-born, was displeasing to the LORD, and the LORD took his life. 8] Then Judah said to Onan, "Join with your brother's wife and do your duty by her as a brother-in-law, and provide offspring for your brother." 9] But Onan, knowing that the seed would not count as his, let it go to waste whenever he joined with his brother's wife, so as not to provide offspring for his brother. 10] What he did was displeasing to the LORD, and He took his life also. 11] Then Judah said to his daughter-in-law Tamar, "Stay as a widow in your father's house until my son Shelah grows up"—for he thought, "He too might die like his brothers." So Tamar went to live in her father's house. 12] A long time afterward, Shua's daughter, the wife of Judah, died. When his period of mourning was over, Judah went up to Timnah to his sheepshearers,

38:2] *Canaanite.* Some translate this as "trafficker" (as in Zech. 14:21) or "merchant" and thereby deny that intermarriage was involved [2].

5] *Chezib.* Possibly the same as Achzib (Josh. 15:44), a city southwest of Jerusalem.

6] *Tamar.* Palm tree.

8] *Do your duty.* A reference to levirate marriage (from the Latin *levir* [brother-in-law]). When a man died without male offspring his brother was obliged to marry the widow, and a son born of this union was considered the son of the dead man (see Deut. 25:5; Ruth, chapters 3 and 4; and Gleanings).

9] *Go to waste.* Literally, "spoil on the ground."

10] *What he did.* Namely, to have evaded his levirate duty. Later, all spilling of seed (called onanism), especially masturbation, was considered "displeasing to the Lord."

11] *For he thought.* Judah thought that if Tamar were removed from the house Shelah's duty to marry her might become less pressing as time passed. Judah may also have been influenced by the belief that one should not tempt fate three times.

/ In Jewish legal tradition, a woman whose first two husbands died was considered a poor candidate for a third marriage and should not be wedded again [3]./

12] *When his period of mourning was over.* Literally, "when he was comforted."

לָךְ וַתֹּאמֶר חֹתָמְךָ וּפְתִילֶךָ וּמַטְּךָ אֲשֶׁר בְּיָדֶךָ וַיִּתֶּן־
לָהּ וַיָּבֹא אֵלֶיהָ וַתַּהַר לוֹ: וַתָּקָם וַתֵּלֶךְ וַתָּסַר צְעִיפָהּ
מֵעָלֶיהָ וַתִּלְבַּשׁ בִּגְדֵי אַלְמְנוּתָהּ:

וַיִּשְׁלַח יְהוּדָה אֶת־גְּדִי הָעִזִּים בְּיַד רֵעֵהוּ הָעֲדֻלָּמִי
לָקַחַת הָעֵרָבוֹן מִיַּד הָאִשָּׁה וְלֹא מְצָאָהּ: וַיִּשְׁאַל אֶת־
אַנְשֵׁי מְקֹמָהּ לֵאמֹר אַיֵּה הַקְּדֵשָׁה הִוא בָעֵינַיִם עַל־
הַדָּרֶךְ וַיֹּאמְרוּ לֹא־הָיְתָה בָזֶה קְדֵשָׁה: וַיָּשָׁב אֶל־יְהוּדָה
וַיֹּאמֶר לֹא מְצָאתִיהָ וְגַם אַנְשֵׁי הַמָּקוֹם אָמְרוּ לֹא־הָיְתָה
בָזֶה קְדֵשָׁה: וַיֹּאמֶר יְהוּדָה תִּקַּח־לָהּ פֶּן נִהְיֶה לָבוּז הִנֵּה
שָׁלַחְתִּי הַגְּדִי הַזֶּה וְאַתָּה לֹא מְצָאתָהּ: וַיְהִי כְּמִשְׁלֹשׁ

וְחִירָה רֵעֵהוּ הָעֲדֻלָּמִי תִּמְנָתָה: וַיֻּגַּד לְתָמָר לֵאמֹר
הִנֵּה חָמִיךְ עֹלֶה תִמְנָתָה לָגֹז צֹאנוֹ: וַתָּסַר בִּגְדֵי
אַלְמְנוּתָהּ מֵעָלֶיהָ וַתְּכַס בַּצָּעִיף וַתִּתְעַלָּף וַתֵּשֶׁב
בְּפֶתַח עֵינַיִם אֲשֶׁר עַל־דֶּרֶךְ תִּמְנָתָה כִּי רָאֲתָה כִּי־
גָדַל שֵׁלָה וְהִוא לֹא־נִתְּנָה לוֹ לְאִשָּׁה: וַיִּרְאֶהָ יְהוּדָה
וַיַּחְשְׁבֶהָ לְזוֹנָה כִּי כִסְּתָה פָּנֶיהָ: וַיֵּט אֵלֶיהָ אֶל־
הַדֶּרֶךְ וַיֹּאמֶר הָבָה־נָּא אָבוֹא אֵלַיִךְ כִּי לֹא יָדַע כִּי
כַלָּתוֹ הִוא וַתֹּאמֶר מַה־תִּתֶּן־לִי כִּי תָבוֹא אֵלָי: וַיֹּאמֶר
אָנֹכִי אֲשַׁלַּח גְּדִי־עִזִּים מִן־הַצֹּאן וַתֹּאמֶר אִם־תִּתֵּן
עֵרָבוֹן עַד שָׁלְחֶךָ: וַיֹּאמֶר מָה הָעֵרָבוֹן אֲשֶׁר אֶתֶּן־

together with his friend Hirah the Adullamite. **13]** And Tamar was told, "Your father-in-law is coming up to Timnah for the sheepshearing." **14]** So she took off her widow's garb, covered her face with a veil and, wrapping herself up, sat down at the entrance to Enaim, which is on the road to Timnah; for she saw that Shelah was grown up, yet she had not been given to him as wife. **15]** When Judah saw her, he took her for a harlot; for she had covered her face. **16]** So he turned aside to her by the road and said, "Here, let me sleep with you"—for he did not know that she was his daughter-in-law. "What," she asked, "will you pay for sleeping with me?" **17]** He replied, "I will send a kid from my flock." But she said, "You must leave a pledge until you have sent it." **18]** And he said, "What pledge shall I give you?" She replied, "Your seal and cord, and the staff which you carry." So he gave them to her and slept with her, and she conceived by him. **19]** Then she went on her way. She took off her veil and again put on her widow's garb.

20] Judah sent the kid by his friend the Adullamite, to redeem the pledge from the woman; but he could not find her. **21]** He inquired of the people of that town, "Where is the cult prostitute, the one at Enaim, by the road?" But they said, "There has been no prostitute here." **22]** So he returned to Judah and said, "I could not find her; moreover, the townspeople said: There has been no prostitute here." **23]** Judah said, "Let her keep them, lest we become a laughingstock. I did send her this kid, but you did not find her."

13] *To Timnah for the sheepshearing.* And the festivities that were held on such occasions. The Timnah here referred to was located in the hill country south of Jerusalem (cf. Josh. 15:10). It was not the Timnah near the seacoast mentioned in the Samson story (Judg. 14:1).

14] *Enaim.* Probably the Enam of Josh. 15:34 "Entrance to Enaim" (literally, "opening of eyes") is a contrast to *kesut enayim* in 20:16 (literally, "closing of eyes"). There, Sarah was vindicated from hidden harlotry; here, Tamar's vindication follows an action openly performed [4].

18] *Seal.* It was usually of cylindrical shape, mounted on a pin, suspended by a cord, and worn by the owner as part of his public attire. Imprints of the seal were used as signatures, to represent the owner.

The staff. Often it was personalized and served as a symbol of transmission in sales proceedings.

21] *Cult prostitute.* Judah uses this term, rather than "harlot" (as in Gen. 38:15), to give the relationship a somewhat more acceptable status. Ritual prostitutes participated in fertility cults in many ancient countries [5].

23] *A laughingstock.* His relationship with a prostitute would become a matter for public discussion and mocking comment.

חֲדָשִׁים וַיֻּגַּד לִיהוּדָה לֵאמֹר זָנְתָה תָּמָר כַּלָּתֶךָ וְגַם כד וְלֹא־יָסַף עוֹד לְדַעְתָּהּ: וַיְהִי בְּעֵת לִדְתָּהּ וְהִנֵּה
הִנֵּה הָרָה לִזְנוּנִים וַיֹּאמֶר יְהוּדָה הוֹצִיאוּהָ וְתִשָּׂרֵף: תְאוֹמִים בְּבִטְנָהּ: וַיְהִי בְלִדְתָּהּ וַיִּתֶּן־יָד וַתִּקַּח כה
כה הִוא מוּצֵאת וְהִיא שָׁלְחָה אֶל־חָמִיהָ לֵאמֹר לְאִישׁ הַמְיַלֶּדֶת וַתִּקְשֹׁר עַל־יָדוֹ שָׁנִי לֵאמֹר זֶה יָצָא רִאשֹׁנָה:
אֲשֶׁר־אֵלֶּה לּוֹ אָנֹכִי הָרָה וַתֹּאמֶר הַכֶּר־נָא לְמִי וַיְהִי כְּמֵשִׁיב יָדוֹ וְהִנֵּה יָצָא אָחִיו וַתֹּאמֶר מַה־פָּרַצְתָּ כט
כו הַחֹתֶמֶת וְהַפְּתִילִים וְהַמַּטֶּה הָאֵלֶּה: וַיַּכֵּר יְהוּדָה עָלֶיךָ פָּרֶץ וַיִּקְרָא שְׁמוֹ פָּרֶץ: וְאַחַר יָצָא אָחִיו ל
וַיֹּאמֶר צָדְקָה מִמֶּנִּי כִּי־עַל־כֵּן לֹא־נְתַתִּיהָ לְשֵׁלָה בְנִי אֲשֶׁר עַל־יָדוֹ הַשָּׁנִי וַיִּקְרָא שְׁמוֹ זָרַח: ס

24] About three months later, Judah was told, "Your daughter-in-law Tamar has played the harlot; in fact she is with child by harlotry." "Bring her out," said Judah, "and let her be burned." 25] As she was being brought out, she sent this message to her father-in-law, "I am with child by the man to whom these belong." And she added, "Examine these: whose seal and cord and staff are these?" 26] Judah recognized them, and said, "She is more in the right than I, inasmuch as I did not give her to my son Shelah." And he was not intimate with her again.

27] When the time came for her to give birth, there were twins in her womb! 28] While she was in labor, one of them put out his hand, and the midwife tied a crimson thread on that hand, to signify: This one came out first. 29] But just then he drew back his hand, and out came his brother; and she said, "What a breach you have made for yourself!" So he was named Perez. 30] Afterwards his brother came out, on whose hand was the crimson thread; he was named Zerah.

24] *Let her be burned*. The laws of adultery included engaged people, and Tamar was considered engaged to Shelah. Judah, as head of the family, had judicial powers.

/ The Torah law in this case (Deut. 22:23–24) provides for stoning, not burning. Even as a ritual prostitute she was subject to punishment, for such a woman was not supposed to have children of her own [6]./

26] *Not intimate . . . again*. Although Tamar was

now considered Judah's wife, her previous relation to his sons made further intimacy undesirable.

28] *Crimson thread*. To make sure which was the first-born. The color was an allusion to harlotry: Red bands, like red lights in modern times, were the mark of prostitution (cf. Josh. 2:18) [7].

29] *Perez*. Breach.

30] *Zerah*. Brightness, perhaps alluding to the crimson thread [8].

Destiny

Why was the Tamar story included in the Jacob–Joseph cycle and why was it preserved with such careful attention to detail?

Perhaps the intriguing nature of the incident played a role, but the major reason does not lie in historical, literary, or dramatic factors. The chief figures are Tamar and Judah, and Judah is the ultimate preserver of the house of Israel. From the union of the tribal progenitor and his daughter-in-law, Perez is born, and from him will descend the person and the house of David. The Tamar tale thus became an important part of the David saga, just as the Book of Ruth did in later days. We are told that Ruth and Boaz would be forebears of the king and that Boaz traced his line to Perez, son of Tamar and Judah (Ruth 4:12–22).

Both accounts together emphasize that King David stemmed from a strange and non-indigenous line: Tamar and Ruth were not Israelites, both were widows, and both claimed a son by dint of the levirate tradition. David thus arises out of the most unlikely configurations. After tragedy had marred their lives, it appeared that Tamar and Ruth would remain childless, but God in His wisdom turned fate to His own design. The Judah–Tamar interlude is, therefore, not merely an old tribal tale but an important link in the main theme: to show the steady, though not always readily visible, guiding hand of God who never forgets His people and their destiny [9].

In this story, Tamar is His unlikely tool. She is a Canaanite, a daughter of the very people against whom Abraham had warned and whom the Children of Israel would later displace. Tamar is treated with respect; her desperate deed draws no condemnation from the Torah. What she did fulfilled the requirements of Hebrew law and, in addition, appeared to serve the higher purposes of God.

The tale of Judah is artfully interwoven into the Joseph story. In God's plan, primogeniture is clearly inapplicable, and the very language employed emphasizes that Judah's ultimate choice by God took place only after he (like Jacob) had passed through the cycle of the deceiver being deceived himself. Robert Alter has pointed to the key words *haker-na*, examine (verse 25), and *vayaker*, recognize (verse 26), the same words used in the deception of Jacob by his sons (37:32, 33). "The first use of the formula was for an act of deception; the second use is for an act of unmasking. Judah with Tamar after Judah with his brothers is an exemplary narrative instance of the deceiver deceived and, since he was the one who proposed selling Joseph into slavery instead of killing him, he can easily be thought of as the leader of the brothers in the deception practiced on their father. Now he becomes their surrogate in being subject to a bizarre but peculiarly fitting principle of retaliation, taken in by a piece of attire, as his father was, learning through his own obstreperous flesh that the divinely appointed process of election cannot be thwarted by human will or social convention. In the most artful of contrivances, the narrator shows him exposed through the symbols of his legal self given in pledge for a kid (*gedi izim*), as before Jacob had been tricked by the garment emblematic of his love for Joseph which had been dipped in the blood of a goat (*se-ir izim*). Finally, when we return (chapter 39) from Judah to the Joseph story, we move in pointed contrast from a tale of exposure through sexual incontinence to a tale of seeming defeat and ultimate triumph through sexual continence—Joseph and Potiphar's wife" [10].

GLEANINGS

The Burden of Leadership

It says that "about that time Judah left his brothers" [Gen. 38:1]. Why? It was in consequence of the sale of Joseph. The brothers suddenly appreciated the depth of their father's grief. Then they blamed Judah and said: "You suggested that we sell Joseph and we followed you. Had you suggested to set Joseph free we would have followed you also." That is when "Judah left his brothers."
MIDRASH [11]

The Levirate

In earlier ages, the duty of a man to marry the widow of his brother could probably not be evaded; such an obligatory union was called *yibum* in Jewish legal tradition. In later times, the brother could refuse *yibum* by making a public declaration to this effect through the ceremony of *chalitzah* (Deut. 25:5–10). Still later, *chalitzah* became mandatory and *yibum* was frowned upon, which is essentially the position of Jewish law today. In fact, the chief rabbinate of the State of Israel issued a decree (*takanah*) in 1950 prohibiting *yibum* and making *chalitzah* obligatory. The court may under certain circumstances compel the *levir* to grant *chalitzah*. [12]

Human Sin and Divine Guidance

The beginnings of the tribe of Judah were shaped by the remarkable interaction of human sin and divine guidance. How simple are the images of Israel's ancestors! They have almost more shadow than light. National ambition did not add to them or change them. No trace of an idealizing myth is noticeable. The nobleness of these figures consists in the fact that they conquer in the strength of the grace granted to them and, when defeated, they arise again and again. Their mistakes are the foils of their greatness for sacred history. By the yardstick of the Old Testament even Tamar, with all her going astray, is a saint because of her wisdom, her tenderness, her nobility.
FRANZ DELITZSCH [13]

Judah's Confession

Tamar threw the pledges before the feet of the judges, with the words: "By the man whose these are am I with child but, though I perish in the flames, I will not betray him. I hope in the Lord of the world that He will turn the heart of the man, so that he will make confession thereof." Then Judah rose up, and said: "With your permission, my brethren, and ye men of my father's house, I make it known that with what measure a man metes it shall be measured unto him, be it for good or for evil, but happy the man that acknowledgeth his sins. Because I took the coat of Joseph, and colored it with the blood of a kid, and then laid it at the feet of my father, saying, Know now whether it be thy son's coat or not, therefore must I now confess, before the court, unto whom belongeth this signet, this mantle, and this staff."
MIDRASH [14]

As for the insertion of 38 at exactly this point in the story (and not between 39 and 40, or 40 and 41), one can only protest (a) between chapters 37 and 39 there is a natural pause in the action and (b) certain coincidental features of chapter 38 bind it to chapters 37 and 39. Among the latter one may note the similarity between Judah in 38 and Jacob in 37: both are patriarchs, both are deceived, both are obliged to give legal recognition to a piece of evidence. Between Tamar and Potiphar's wife on the other hand there is a marked contrast; the former is an honorable woman faithful to the interests of her husband, while the latter is adulterous, malevolent, and contemptuous of her husband.
DONALD B. REDFORD [15]

Joseph in Egypt

"The Lord was with Joseph" (Gen. 39:2)—this is the key to the developing drama that now takes up the thread temporarily dropped because of the Tamar interlude. God's presence is constantly visible in the background, both when Joseph is tempted or in trouble and when he is successful: "Upon the Lord's word was he tried, until His word was fulfilled" (Ps. 105:19). God guides Joseph in his relationships and gives him the wisdom to interpret dreams. The divine power reaches to the men and the fate of Egypt, a theme that returns time and again in prophetic literature.

The traditions reflected in these chapters have an authentic ring. The descriptions are realistic, and the text contains numerous Egyptian loan words [1]. Still, all attempts to assign a precise historical setting to the Joseph cycle have failed. Neither the name of the Pharaoh whom Joseph served nor that of a Pharaoh in Exodus is given (Pharaoh is a title, not a name). Egyptian records show high officials with Semitic names such as Ben-Horen and Ben-Anath, but none with a name that would fit Joseph. The word יְאֹר (ye-or, river), which occurs in the Joseph tale to describe the Nile, appears in Egyptian use after the sixteenth century B.C.E., and cyclical seven-year famines are also mentioned—but without precise dating.

Some scholars believe that Jacob's migration to Egypt took place during the period of Hyksos rule, i.e., before the middle of the second millen-

nium B.C.E.[1] The Hyksos were probably an ethnically composite group who invaded Canaan and then Egypt,[2] where they succeeded in establishing themselves [3]. However, the data at our disposal are not sufficient to link them securely to the Jacob–Joseph stories or to suppose, as has been suggested, that Jacob's sons—described throughout as עִבְרִים (ivrim)[3]—were invited to settle in Egypt because their talents and experiences, already amply demonstrated by Joseph, would prove useful to the Hyksos [4].

[1] A more definite time assignment should be related to one's opinion about the date of the Abraham saga (see introduction to Part III, "The Line of Terah: Abraham").

[2] The capital was Avaris (or Tanis, the Hebrew Zoan). The Hyksos apparently spoke a Semitic tongue, possibly with Hurrian and Indo-European admixtures. One theory identifies the Hyksos as Amorites [2].

[3] On the term and its meaning as a group characteristic, see commentary to Gen. 14:1–24, "Abraham the Hebrew."

וַיְהִי יוֹסֵף יְפֵה־תֹאַר וִיפֵה מַרְאֶה: וַיְהִי אַחַר הַדְּבָרִים ז
הָאֵלֶּה וַתִּשָּׂא אֵשֶׁת־אֲדֹנָיו אֶת־עֵינֶיהָ אֶל־יוֹסֵף וַתֹּאמֶר
שִׁכְבָה עִמִּי: וַיְמָאֵן וַיֹּאמֶר אֶל־אֵשֶׁת אֲדֹנָיו הֵן אֲדֹנִי ח
לֹא־יָדַע אִתִּי מַה־בַּבָּיִת וְכֹל אֲשֶׁר־יֶשׁ־לוֹ נָתַן בְּיָדִי:
אֵינֶנּוּ גָדוֹל בַּבַּיִת הַזֶּה מִמֶּנִּי וְלֹא־חָשַׂךְ מִמֶּנִּי מְאוּמָה ט
כִּי אִם־אוֹתָךְ בַּאֲשֶׁר אַתְּ־אִשְׁתּוֹ וְאֵיךְ אֶעֱשֶׂה הָרָעָה
הַגְּדֹלָה הַזֹּאת וְחָטָאתִי לֵאלֹהִים: וַיְהִי כְּדַבְּרָהּ אֶל־ י
יוֹסֵף יוֹם יוֹם וְלֹא־שָׁמַע אֵלֶיהָ לִשְׁכַּב אֶצְלָהּ לִהְיוֹת
עִמָּהּ: וַיְהִי כְּהַיּוֹם הַזֶּה וַיָּבֹא הַבַּיְתָה לַעֲשׂוֹת מְלַאכְתּוֹ יא
וְאֵין אִישׁ מֵאַנְשֵׁי הַבַּיִת שָׁם בַּבָּיִת: וַתִּתְפְּשֵׂהוּ בְּבִגְדוֹ יב
לֵאמֹר שִׁכְבָה עִמִּי וַיַּעֲזֹב בִּגְדוֹ בְּיָדָהּ וַיָּנָס וַיֵּצֵא

וְיוֹסֵף הוּרַד מִצְרָיְמָה וַיִּקְנֵהוּ פּוֹטִיפַר סְרִיס פַּרְעֹה א
שַׂר הַטַּבָּחִים אִישׁ מִצְרִי מִיַּד הַיִּשְׁמְעֵאלִים אֲשֶׁר
הוֹרִדֻהוּ שָׁמָּה: וַיְהִי יְהוָה אֶת־יוֹסֵף וַיְהִי אִישׁ מַצְלִיחַ ב
וַיְהִי בְּבֵית אֲדֹנָיו הַמִּצְרִי: וַיַּרְא אֲדֹנָיו כִּי יְהוָה אִתּוֹ ג
וְכֹל אֲשֶׁר־הוּא עֹשֶׂה יְהוָה מַצְלִיחַ בְּיָדוֹ: וַיִּמְצָא ד
יוֹסֵף חֵן בְּעֵינָיו וַיְשָׁרֶת אֹתוֹ וַיַּפְקִדֵהוּ עַל־בֵּיתוֹ
וְכָל־יֶשׁ־לוֹ נָתַן בְּיָדוֹ: וַיְהִי מֵאָז הִפְקִיד אֹתוֹ בְּבֵיתוֹ ה
וְעַל כָּל־אֲשֶׁר יֶשׁ־לוֹ וַיְבָרֶךְ יְהוָה אֶת־בֵּית הַמִּצְרִי
בִּגְלַל יוֹסֵף וַיְהִי בִּרְכַּת יְהוָה בְּכָל־אֲשֶׁר יֶשׁ־לוֹ
בַּבַּיִת וּבַשָּׂדֶה: וַיַּעֲזֹב כָּל־אֲשֶׁר־לוֹ בְּיַד יוֹסֵף וְלֹא־ ו
יָדַע אִתּוֹ מְאוּמָה כִּי אִם־הַלֶּחֶם אֲשֶׁר־הוּא אוֹכֵל

1] When Joseph was taken down to Egypt, a certain Egyptian, Potiphar, a courtier of Pharaoh and his chief steward, bought him from the Ishmaelites who had brought him there. **2]** The LORD was with Joseph, and he was a successful man; and he stayed in the house of his Egyptian master. **3]** And when his master saw that the LORD was with him and that the LORD lent success to everything he undertook, **4]** he took a liking to Joseph. He made him his personal attendant and put him in charge of his household, placing in his hands all that he owned. **5]** And from the time that the Egyptian put him in charge of his household and of all that he owned, the LORD blessed his house for Joseph's sake, so that the blessing of the LORD was upon everything that he owned, in the house and outside. **6]** He left all that he had in Joseph's hands and, with him there, he paid attention to nothing save the food that he ate. Now Joseph was well built and handsome.

7] After a time, his master's wife cast her eyes upon Joseph and said, "Lie with me." **8]** But he refused. He said to his master's wife, "Look, with me here, my master gives no thought to anything in this house, and all that he owns he has placed in my hands. **9]** He wields no more authority in this house than I, and he has withheld nothing from me except yourself, since you are his wife. How then could I do this most wicked thing, and sin before God?" **10]** And much as she coaxed Joseph day after day, he did not yield to her request to lie beside her, to be with her.

11] One such day, he came into the house to do his work. None of the household being there inside, **12]** she caught hold of him by his coat and said, "Lie with me!" But he left his coat in

39:1] *Egyptian.* Also mentioned in verses 2 and 5. This triple emphasis suggests that Potiphar's background deserved special mention, possibly because an Egyptian civil servant among the ruling Hyksos was an oddity worth noting.

6] *Attention to nothing save the food.* As a Hebrew, Joseph could have nothing to do with food because of the dietary taboos observed by Egyptians (see Gen. 43:32 and comment there) [5].

7] *His master's wife.* Her name is not stated. Later tradition called her Zuleika [6]. The old Egyptian "Tale of Two Brothers" is based on the same plot of attempted seduction and subsequent false accusation; thereafter, however, the two stories diverge completely.

יג הַחוּצָה: וַיְהִי כִּרְאוֹתָהּ כִּי־עָזַב בִּגְדוֹ בְּיָדָהּ וַיָּנָס מְקוֹם אֲשֶׁר־אֲסוּרֵי הַמֶּלֶךְ אֲסוּרִים וַיְהִי־שָׁם בְּבֵית

יד הַחוּצָה: וַתִּקְרָא לְאַנְשֵׁי בֵיתָהּ וַתֹּאמֶר לָהֶם לֵאמֹר הַסֹּהַר: וַיְהִי יְהֹוָה אֶת־יוֹסֵף וַיֵּט אֵלָיו חָסֶד וַיִּתֵּן חִנּוֹ

רְאוּ הֵבִיא לָנוּ אִישׁ עִבְרִי לְצַחֶק בָּנוּ בָּא אֵלַי בְּעֵינֵי שַׂר בֵּית־הַסֹּהַר: וַיִּתֵּן שַׂר בֵּית־הַסֹּהַר בְּיַד־יוֹסֵף

טו לִשְׁכַּב עִמִּי וָאֶקְרָא בְּקוֹל גָּדוֹל: וַיְהִי כְשָׁמְעוֹ כִּי־ אֵת כָּל־הָאֲסִירִם אֲשֶׁר בְּבֵית הַסֹּהַר וְאֵת כָּל־אֲשֶׁר

הֲרִימֹתִי קוֹלִי וָאֶקְרָא וַיַּעֲזֹב בִּגְדוֹ אֶצְלִי וַיָּנָס וַיֵּצֵא עֹשִׂים שָׁם הוּא הָיָה עֹשֶׂה: אֵין שַׂר בֵּית־הַסֹּהַר רֹאֶה

טז הַחוּצָה: וַתַּנַּח בִּגְדוֹ אֶצְלָהּ עַד־בּוֹא אֲדֹנָיו אֶל־בֵּיתוֹ: אֶת־כָּל־מְאוּמָה בְּיָדוֹ בַּאֲשֶׁר יְהֹוָה אִתּוֹ וַאֲשֶׁר־הוּא

יז וַתְּדַבֵּר אֵלָיו כַּדְּבָרִים הָאֵלֶּה לֵאמֹר בָּא אֵלַי עֹשֶׂה יְהֹוָה מַצְלִיחַ: פ

יח הָעֶבֶד הָעִבְרִי אֲשֶׁר־הֵבֵאתָ לָּנוּ לְצַחֶק בִּי: וַיְהִי א וַיְהִי אַחַר הַדְּבָרִים הָאֵלֶּה חָטְאוּ מַשְׁקֵה מֶלֶךְ־

כַּהֲרִימִי קוֹלִי וָאֶקְרָא וַיַּעֲזֹב בִּגְדוֹ אֶצְלִי וַיָּנָס הַחוּצָה: ב מִצְרַיִם וְהָאֹפֶה לַאֲדֹנֵיהֶם לְמֶלֶךְ מִצְרָיִם: וַיִּקְצֹף

יט וַיְהִי כִשְׁמֹעַ אֲדֹנָיו אֶת־דִּבְרֵי אִשְׁתּוֹ אֲשֶׁר דִּבְּרָה פַּרְעֹה עַל שְׁנֵי סָרִיסָיו עַל שַׂר הַמַּשְׁקִים וְעַל שַׂר

אֵלָיו לֵאמֹר כַּדְּבָרִים הָאֵלֶּה עָשָׂה לִי עַבְדֶּךָ וַיִּחַר ג הָאוֹפִים: וַיִּתֵּן אֹתָם בְּמִשְׁמַר בֵּית שַׂר הַטַּבָּחִים אֶל־

כ אַפּוֹ: וַיִּקַּח אֲדֹנֵי יוֹסֵף אֹתוֹ וַיִּתְּנֵהוּ אֶל־בֵּית הַסֹּהַר ד בֵּית הַסֹּהַר מְקוֹם אֲשֶׁר יוֹסֵף אָסוּר שָׁם: וַיִּפְקֹד שַׂר

* כ אסירי קרי.

her hand and got away and fled outside. **13]** When she saw that he had left his coat in her hand and had fled outside, **14]** she called out to her servants and said to them, "Look, he had to bring us a Hebrew to dally with us! This one came to lie with me; but I screamed loud. **15]** And when he heard me screaming at the top of my voice, he left his coat with me and got away and fled outside." **16]** She kept his coat beside her, until his master came home. **17]** Then she told him the same story, saying, "The Hebrew slave whom you brought into our house came to me to dally with me; **18]** but when I screamed at the top of my voice, he left his coat with me and fled outside."

19] When his master heard the story that his wife told him, namely, "Thus and so your slave did to me," he was furious. **20]** So Joseph's master had him put in prison, where the king's prisoners were confined. But even while he was there in prison, **21]** the LORD was with Joseph: He extended kindness to him and disposed the chief jailer favorably toward him. **22]** The chief jailer put in Joseph's charge all the prisoners who were in that prison, and he was the one to carry out everything that was done there. **23]** The chief jailer did not supervise anything that was in Joseph's charge, because the LORD was with him, and whatever he did the LORD made successful.

1] Some time later, the cupbearer and the baker of the king of Egypt gave offense to their lord the king of Egypt. **2]** Pharaoh was angry with his two courtiers, the chief cupbearer and the chief baker, **3]** and put them in custody, in the house of the chief steward, in the same

14] *To dally with us.* The Hebrew לְצַחֶק (letzachek) has the additional meaning of "to mock."

20] *Prison.* סֹהַר (sohar), which appears in the Bible only in Genesis, was probably a special place where important prisoners were confined. Joseph was put in prison rather than punished in the usual way, by death; perhaps Potiphar was aware of his

wife's roving eyes and not at all sure of Joseph's guilt [7].

23] *In Joseph's charge.* Literally, "his charge."

40:2] *Cupbearer.* The royal taster, an important government official.

Chief baker. The Egyptians were renowned gourmets and knew fifty-seven varieties of bread and thirty-eight different kinds of cakes [8].

הַטַּבָּחִים אֶת־יוֹסֵף אִתָּם וַיְשָׁרֶת אֹתָם וַיִּהְיוּ יָמִים
בְּמִשְׁמָר: וַיַּחַלְמוּ חֲלוֹם שְׁנֵיהֶם אִישׁ חֲלֹמוֹ בְּלַיְלָה
אֶחָד אִישׁ כְּפִתְרוֹן חֲלֹמוֹ הַמַּשְׁקֶה וְהָאֹפֶה אֲשֶׁר
לְמֶלֶךְ מִצְרַיִם אֲשֶׁר אֲסוּרִים בְּבֵית הַסֹּהַר: וַיָּבֹא
אֲלֵיהֶם יוֹסֵף בַּבֹּקֶר וַיַּרְא אֹתָם וְהִנָּם זֹעֲפִים: וַיִּשְׁאַל
אֶת־סְרִיסֵי פַרְעֹה אֲשֶׁר אִתּוֹ בְּמִשְׁמַר בֵּית אֲדֹנָיו
לֵאמֹר מַדּוּעַ פְּנֵיכֶם רָעִים הַיּוֹם: וַיֹּאמְרוּ אֵלָיו
חֲלוֹם חָלַמְנוּ וּפֹתֵר אֵין אֹתוֹ וַיֹּאמֶר אֲלֵהֶם יוֹסֵף
הֲלוֹא לֵאלֹהִים פִּתְרֹנִים סַפְּרוּ־נָא לִי: וַיְסַפֵּר שַׂר־
הַמַּשְׁקִים אֶת־חֲלֹמוֹ לְיוֹסֵף וַיֹּאמֶר לוֹ בַּחֲלוֹמִי וְהִנֵּה־
גֶפֶן לְפָנָי: וּבַגֶּפֶן שְׁלֹשָׁה שָׂרִיגִם וְהִוא כְפֹרַחַת עָלְתָה

נִצָּהּ הִבְשִׁילוּ אַשְׁכְּלֹתֶיהָ עֲנָבִים: וְכוֹס פַּרְעֹה בְּיָדִי
וָאֶקַּח אֶת־הָעֲנָבִים וָאֶשְׂחַט אֹתָם אֶל־כּוֹס פַּרְעֹה
וָאֶתֵּן אֶת־הַכּוֹס עַל־כַּף פַּרְעֹה: וַיֹּאמֶר לוֹ יוֹסֵף זֶה
פִּתְרֹנוֹ שְׁלֹשֶׁת הַשָּׂרִגִים שְׁלֹשֶׁת יָמִים הֵם: בְּעוֹד
שְׁלֹשֶׁת יָמִים יִשָּׂא פַרְעֹה אֶת־רֹאשֶׁךָ וַהֲשִׁיבְךָ עַל־
כַּנֶּךָ וְנָתַתָּ כוֹס־פַּרְעֹה בְּיָדוֹ כַּמִּשְׁפָּט הָרִאשׁוֹן אֲשֶׁר
הָיִיתָ מַשְׁקֵהוּ: כִּי אִם־זְכַרְתַּנִי אִתְּךָ כַּאֲשֶׁר יִיטַב לָךְ
וְעָשִׂיתָ־נָּא עִמָּדִי חָסֶד וְהִזְכַּרְתַּנִי אֶל־פַּרְעֹה וְהוֹצֵאתַנִי
מִן־הַבַּיִת הַזֶּה: כִּי־גֻנֹּב גֻּנַּבְתִּי מֵאֶרֶץ הָעִבְרִים וְגַם־
פֹּה לֹא־עָשִׂיתִי מְאוּמָה כִּי־שָׂמוּ אֹתִי בַּבּוֹר: וַיַּרְא
שַׂר־הָאֹפִים כִּי טוֹב פָּתָר וַיֹּאמֶר אֶל־יוֹסֵף אַף־אֲנִי

prison house where Joseph was confined. **4]** The chief steward assigned Joseph to them, and he attended them.

When they had been in custody for some time, **5]** both of them—the cupbearer and the baker of the king of Egypt, who were confined in the prison—dreamed in the same night, each his own dream and each dream with its own meaning. **6]** When Joseph came to them in the morning, he saw that they were distraught. **7]** He asked Pharaoh's courtiers, who were with him in custody in his master's house, saying, "Why do you appear downcast today?" **8]** And they said to him, "We had dreams, and there is no one to interpret them." So Joseph said to them, "Surely God can interpret! Tell me [your dreams]."

9] Then the chief cupbearer told his dream to Joseph. He said to him, "In my dream, there was a vine in front of me. **10]** On the vine were three branches. It had barely budded, when out came its blossoms and its clusters ripened into grapes. **11]** Pharaoh's cup was in my hand, and I took the grapes, pressed them into Pharaoh's cup, and placed the cup in Pharaoh's hand." **12]** Joseph said to him, "This is its interpretation: The three branches are three days. **13]** In three days Pharaoh will pardon you and restore you to your post; you will place Pharaoh's cup in his hand, as was your custom formerly when you were his cupbearer. **14]** But think of me when all is well with you again, and do me the kindness of mentioning me to Pharaoh, so as to free me from this place. **15]** For in truth, I was kidnaped from the land of the Hebrews; nor have I done anything here that they should have put me in the dungeon."

16] When the chief baker saw how favorably he had interpreted, he said to Joseph, "In my

4] *Chief steward.* Potiphar, who had charge of the prison.

13] *Pardon you.* Literally, "lift up your head." A word play on יִשָּׂא. The same expression is used in verse 19 in a literal sense (to behead),

and in verse 20 in a third sense (to single out).

16] *Open-work baskets.* Others translate as "baskets with white bread" or "white baskets." Meaning of Hebrew is uncertain.

בַּיּוֹם הַשְּׁלִישִׁי יוֹם הֻלֶּדֶת אֶת־פַּרְעֹה וַיַּעַשׂ מִשְׁתֶּה
לְכָל־עֲבָדָיו וַיִּשָּׂא אֶת־רֹאשׁ שַׂר הַמַּשְׁקִים וְאֶת־רֹאשׁ
שַׂר הָאֹפִים בְּתוֹךְ עֲבָדָיו: וַיָּשֶׁב אֶת־שַׂר הַמַּשְׁקִים
עַל־מַשְׁקֵהוּ וַיִּתֵּן הַכּוֹס עַל־כַּף פַּרְעֹה: וְאֵת שַׂר
הָאֹפִים תָּלָה כַּאֲשֶׁר פָּתַר לָהֶם יוֹסֵף: וְלֹא־זָכַר שַׂר־
הַמַּשְׁקִים אֶת־יוֹסֵף וַיִּשְׁכָּחֵהוּ:

ט בַּחֲלוֹמִי וְהִנֵּה שְׁלֹשָׁה סַלֵּי חֹרִי עַל־רֹאשִׁי: וּבַסַּל
הָעֶלְיוֹן מִכֹּל מַאֲכַל פַּרְעֹה מַעֲשֵׂה אֹפֶה וְהָעוֹף
יח אֹכֵל אֹתָם מִן־הַסַּל מֵעַל רֹאשִׁי: וַיַּעַן יוֹסֵף וַיֹּאמֶר
יט זֶה פִּתְרֹנוֹ שְׁלֹשֶׁת הַסַּלִּים שְׁלֹשֶׁת יָמִים הֵם: בְּעוֹד
שְׁלֹשֶׁת יָמִים יִשָּׂא פַרְעֹה אֶת־רֹאשְׁךָ מֵעָלֶיךָ וְתָלָה
כ אוֹתְךָ עַל־עֵץ וְאָכַל הָעוֹף אֶת־בְּשָׂרְךָ מֵעָלֶיךָ: וַיְהִי

Haftarah Vayeshev, p. 352

dream, similarly, there were three openwork baskets on my head.   **17]** In the uppermost basket were all kinds of food for Pharaoh that a baker prepares; and the birds were eating it out of the basket above my head."   **18]** Joseph answered, "This is its interpretation: The three baskets are three days.   **19]** In three days Pharaoh will lift off your head and impale you upon a pole; and the birds will pick off your flesh."

20] On the third day—his birthday—Pharaoh made a banquet for all his officials, and he singled out his chief cupbearer and his chief baker from among his officials.   **21]** He restored the chief cupbearer to his cupbearing, and he placed the cup in Pharaoh's hand;   **22]** but the chief baker he impaled—just as Joseph had interpreted to them.

23] Yet the chief cupbearer did not think of Joseph; he forgot him.

19] *Lift off.* Literal meaning; see verse 13.   20] *Singled out.* A word play; see verse 13.

The Temptation

In his response to Potiphar's wife Joseph says that yielding to her invitation to commit adultery would be a "sin before God" (Gen. 39:9). In many other cultures adultery was merely a proprietary misdemeanor; a wife was considered property, and injury to a man's possessions drew punishment thought adequate to the act (Deut. 22:29) [9]. Joseph speaks in true accents of the Bible, which regards marriage as more than a relationship of civil law. Marital trust has divine sanction and is so fundamental to human relationships that Jewish tradition considers the command against adultery as one of the Noahide laws that every man is bound to observe [10].

Dreams

From ancient times, dreams have tantalized men with their secrets. Today dreams are used to explore the inner chambers of the dreamer's mind. In antiquity, however, dreams were thought to be signs from divine powers exposing their intent. While occasionally dreams contained a direct divine message (as in Gen. 15:13 when God appeared to Abraham in a dream), they usually were considered coded visions [11] to which a key was needed.[1]

Professional dream interpreters who claimed to possess the proper keys were prominent in Mesopotamia and especially in Egypt. An Egyptian manual of dreams (*ca.* 1300 B.C.E.) contains over 200 interpretations.[2] The ancient Israelites no doubt shared many of the prevailing ideas about dreams and considered them a legitimate source of divine guidance.[3] On the whole, however, the Bible says remarkably little on the subject of dream interpretation. Only Joseph and Daniel engage in it, and both give the credit unreservedly to God (see Dan. 2).

To be sure, there is a similarity between the superstitions of a dream book, which provides mechanical rules for divining the future, and the belief that God's will needs the interpretations of a qualified and pious man. Joseph and Daniel used no book; they used their imaginations, and both merely exposed to the eye that which was already ordained. Of course, this kind of activity could encourage fatalism and weaken one of the basic assumptions of the Bible, namely, that man has a share in shaping his fate. We may understand, therefore, the reticence of the Bible to give added room to the "science of dreams." Only because Joseph and Daniel were in the service of pagan powers and acted within a foreign mental and religious framework were their dream interpretations recorded with approbation.[4]

---

[1] But note the saying: "Man sees in his dreams only the stirrings of his own heart."

[2] Example: Seeing a large cat meant a large harvest. Dreams figured prominently in "Gilgamesh." There was also an Assyrian dream book [12].

[3] As were Urim, I Sam. 28:6.

[4] Note that Joseph does not interpret his own dreams; he merely relates them to his family. In post-biblical Judaism, however, dream interpretation played a significant role [13].

GLEANINGS

God Was with Joseph

Human friends can always be found when a man is successful, but in time of trouble they tend to forsake him. Not so God: He was with Joseph when he was a slave, when he was in prison, and also when he was viceroy. MIDRASH [14]

Bread and Wife

It says that Potiphar "paid attention to nothing save the food that he ate" [Gen. 39:6]. This is a hint at what is to follow; for לֶחֶם [food or bread] is here a synonym for "wife," as in: "Bread of falsehood is sweet to a man" [Prov. 20:17].

MIDRASH [15]

The Temptation

The musical note *shalshelet* over the word "he refused" was introduced in the text to indicate delay: The woman insisted again and again and Joseph refused again and again. MIDRASH [16]

Joseph did consider yielding, but the image of his father appeared to him, that is to say, he thought, "What would my father say?"

MIDRASH [17]

His Master's Wife

Why does it say expressly that Joseph refused "his master's wife"? Because as a servant, Joseph was obligated to obey her; still he chose to obey God's law instead. In the conflict between human duty and conscience he chose the latter.

NACHMANIDES

An Egyptian Parallel

[The "Story of Two Brothers" features an aggressive woman who lusts after her husband's younger brother.]

Then she stood up and took hold of him and said to him: "Come, let's spend an hour sleeping together! This will do you good, because I shall make fine clothes for you!" Then the lad became like a leopard with great rage at the wicked suggestion which she had made to him, and she was very, very much frightened. Then he argued with her, saying: "See here—you are like a mother to me, and your husband is like a father to me! Because—being older than I—he was the one who brought me up. What is this great crime which you have said to me? Don't say it to me again!"

But the wife of his elder brother was afraid because of the suggestion which she had made. Then she took fat and grease, and she became like one who had been criminally beaten, wanting to tell her husband: "It was your younger brother who did the beating!" So her husband said to her: "Who has been talking with you?" Then she said to him: "Not one person has been talking with me except your younger brother. He said to me: 'Come, let's spend an hour sleeping together! Put on your curls!' So he spoke to me. But I wouldn't listen to him: 'Aren't I your mother?—for your elder brother is like a father to you!' So I spoke to him. But he was afraid, and he beat me, so as not to let me tell you."

Then his elder brother became like a leopard, and he made his lance sharp, and stood behind the door of his stable to kill his younger brother when he came back in the evening to put his cattle in the stable. OLD EGYPTIAN FOLKTALE [18]

The Elevation of Joseph;
The Brothers' First Visit

The scene shifts to Pharaoh's court and to the dramatic elevation of the poor Hebrew boy to the vice-regal office of Egypt. As Joseph had predicted, seven years of plenty are followed by famine. Now the stage is set for the first meeting with his brothers. As they arrive in court, Joseph's adolescent dreams are realized, and in the stress and strain of reunion we can see the character of the dreamer clearly delineated.

Again, as the story progresses and reaches its midpoint, the reader is made aware that a grand design is being fulfilled.

(A new weekly portion, *Miketz*, begins here.)

פ פ פ

וַיִּשְׁלַח וַיִּקְרָא אֶת־כָּל־חַרְטֻמֵּי מִצְרַיִם וְאֶת־כָּל־   א וַיְהִי מִקֵּץ שְׁנָתַיִם יָמִים וּפַרְעֹה חֹלֵם וְהִנֵּה עֹמֵד עַל־

חֲכָמֶיהָ וַיְסַפֵּר פַּרְעֹה לָהֶם אֶת־חֲלֹמוֹ וְאֵין־פּוֹתֵר   ב הַיְאֹר: וְהִנֵּה מִן־הַיְאֹר עֹלֹת שֶׁבַע פָּרוֹת יְפוֹת מַרְאֶה

ט אוֹתָם לְפַרְעֹה: וַיְדַבֵּר שַׂר הַמַּשְׁקִים אֶת־פַּרְעֹה   ג וּבְרִיאֹת בָּשָׂר וַתִּרְעֶינָה בָּאָחוּ: וְהִנֵּה שֶׁבַע פָּרוֹת

י לֵאמֹר אֶת־חֲטָאַי אֲנִי מַזְכִּיר הַיּוֹם: פַּרְעֹה קָצַף עַל־   אֲחֵרוֹת עֹלוֹת אַחֲרֵיהֶן מִן־הַיְאֹר רָעוֹת מַרְאֶה וְדַקּוֹת

עֲבָדָיו וַיִּתֵּן אֹתִי בְּמִשְׁמַר בֵּית שַׂר הַטַּבָּחִים אֹתִי וְאֵת   בָּשָׂר וַתַּעֲמֹדְנָה אֵצֶל הַפָּרוֹת עַל־שְׂפַת הַיְאֹר:

יא שַׂר הָאֹפִים: וַנַּחַלְמָה חֲלוֹם בְּלַיְלָה אֶחָד אֲנִי וָהוּא   ד וַתֹּאכַלְנָה הַפָּרוֹת רָעוֹת הַמַּרְאֶה וְדַקֹּת הַבָּשָׂר אֵת

יב אִישׁ כְּפִתְרוֹן חֲלֹמוֹ חָלָמְנוּ: וְשָׁם אִתָּנוּ נַעַר עִבְרִי   שֶׁבַע הַפָּרוֹת יְפֹת הַמַּרְאֶה וְהַבְּרִיאֹת וַיִּיקַץ פַּרְעֹה:

עֶבֶד לְשַׂר הַטַּבָּחִים וַנְּסַפֶּר־לוֹ וַיִּפְתָּר־לָנוּ אֶת־   ה וַיִּישָׁן וַיַּחֲלֹם שֵׁנִית וְהִנֵּה שֶׁבַע שִׁבֳּלִים עֹלוֹת בְּקָנֶה

יג חֲלֹמֹתֵינוּ אִישׁ כַּחֲלֹמוֹ פָּתָר: וַיְהִי כַּאֲשֶׁר פָּתַר־לָנוּ   ו אֶחָד בְּרִיאוֹת וְטֹבוֹת: וְהִנֵּה שֶׁבַע שִׁבֳּלִים דַּקּוֹת

כֵּן הָיָה אֹתִי הֵשִׁיב עַל־כַּנִּי וְאֹתוֹ תָלָה: וַיִּשְׁלַח   ז וּשְׁדוּפֹת קָדִים צֹמְחוֹת אַחֲרֵיהֶן: וַתִּבְלַעְנָה הַשִּׁבֳּלִים

יד פַּרְעֹה וַיִּקְרָא אֶת־יוֹסֵף וַיְרִיצֻהוּ מִן־הַבּוֹר וַיְגַלַּח   הַדַּקּוֹת אֵת שֶׁבַע הַשִּׁבֳּלִים הַבְּרִיאוֹת וְהַמְּלֵאוֹת

וַיְחַלֵּף שִׂמְלֹתָיו וַיָּבֹא אֶל־פַּרְעֹה: וַיֹּאמֶר פַּרְעֹה אֶל־   ח וַיִּיקַץ פַּרְעֹה וְהִנֵּה חֲלוֹם: וַיְהִי בַבֹּקֶר וַתִּפָּעֶם רוּחוֹ

טו יוֹסֵף חֲלוֹם חָלַמְתִּי וּפֹתֵר אֵין אֹתוֹ וַאֲנִי שָׁמַעְתִּי

1] After two years' time, Pharaoh dreamed that he was standing by the Nile, 2] when out of the Nile there came up seven cows, handsome and sturdy, and they grazed in the reed grass. 3] But presently, seven other cows came up from the Nile close behind them, ugly and gaunt, and stood beside the cows on the bank of the Nile; 4] and the ugly gaunt cows ate up the seven handsome sturdy cows. And Pharaoh awoke.

5] He fell asleep and dreamed a second time: Seven ears of grain, solid and healthy, grew on a single stalk. 6] But close behind them sprouted seven ears, thin and scorched by the east wind. 7] And the thin ears swallowed up the seven solid and full ears. Then Pharaoh awoke: it was a dream!

8] Next morning, his spirit was agitated, and he sent for all the magicians of Egypt and all its wise men; and Pharaoh told them his dreams, but none could interpret them for Pharaoh.

9] The chief cupbearer then spoke up and said to Pharaoh, "I must make mention today of my offenses. 10] Once Pharaoh was angry with his servants, and placed me in custody in the house of the chief steward, together with the chief baker. 11] We had dreams the same night, he and I, each of us a dream with a meaning of its own. 12] A Hebrew youth was there with us, a servant of the chief steward; and when we told him our dreams, he interpreted them for us, telling each the meaning of his dream. 13] And as he interpreted for us, so it came to pass: I was restored to my post, and the other was impaled."

14] Thereupon Pharaoh sent for Joseph, and he was rushed from the dungeon. He had his hair cut and changed his clothes, and he appeared before Pharaoh. 15] And Pharaoh said to Joseph, "I have had a dream, but no one can intepret it. Now I have heard it said of you that for

---

41:9] *My offenses.* Those committed against Pharaoh and those committed against Joseph, by forgetting the promise he had made to him (Gen. 40:23).

טז עָלֶיךָ לֵאמֹר תִּשְׁמַע חֲלוֹם לִפְתֹּר אֹתוֹ: וַיַּעַן יוֹסֵף
אֶת־פַּרְעֹה לֵאמֹר בִּלְעָדָי אֱלֹהִים יַעֲנֶה אֶת־שְׁלוֹם

יז פַּרְעֹה: וַיְדַבֵּר פַּרְעֹה אֶל־יוֹסֵף בַּחֲלֹמִי הִנְנִי עֹמֵד

יח עַל־שְׂפַת הַיְאֹר: וְהִנֵּה מִן־הַיְאֹר עֹלֹת שֶׁבַע פָּרוֹת

יט בְּרִיאוֹת בָּשָׂר וִיפֹת תֹּאַר וַתִּרְעֶינָה בָּאָחוּ: וְהִנֵּה
שֶׁבַע־פָּרוֹת אֲחֵרוֹת עֹלוֹת אַחֲרֵיהֶן דַּלּוֹת וְרָעוֹת
תֹּאַר מְאֹד וְרַקּוֹת בָּשָׂר לֹא־רָאִיתִי כָהֵנָּה בְּכָל־אֶרֶץ

כ מִצְרַיִם לָרֹעַ: וַתֹּאכַלְנָה הַפָּרוֹת הָרַקּוֹת וְהָרָעוֹת אֵת

כא שֶׁבַע הַפָּרוֹת הָרִאשֹׁנוֹת הַבְּרִיאֹת: וַתָּבֹאנָה אֶל־
קִרְבֶּנָה וְלֹא נוֹדַע כִּי־בָאוּ אֶל־קִרְבֶּנָה וּמַרְאֵיהֶן רַע

כב כַּאֲשֶׁר בַּתְּחִלָּה וָאִיקָץ: וָאֵרֶא בַּחֲלֹמִי וְהִנֵּה שֶׁבַע

כג שִׁבֳּלִים עֹלֹת בְּקָנֶה אֶחָד מְלֵאֹת וְטֹבוֹת: וְהִנֵּה שֶׁבַע
שִׁבֳּלִים צְנֻמוֹת דַּקּוֹת שְׁדֻפוֹת קָדִים צֹמְחוֹת אַחֲרֵיהֶם:

כד וַתִּבְלַעְןָ הַשִּׁבֳּלִים הַדַּקֹּת אֵת שֶׁבַע הַשִּׁבֳּלִים הַטֹּבוֹת

כה וָאֹמַר אֶל־הַחַרְטֻמִּים וְאֵין מַגִּיד לִי: וַיֹּאמֶר יוֹסֵף
אֶל־פַּרְעֹה חֲלוֹם פַּרְעֹה אֶחָד הוּא אֵת אֲשֶׁר הָאֱלֹהִים

כו עֹשֶׂה הִגִּיד לְפַרְעֹה: שֶׁבַע פָּרֹת הַטֹּבֹת שֶׁבַע שָׁנִים
הֵנָּה וְשֶׁבַע הַשִּׁבֳּלִים הַטֹּבֹת שֶׁבַע שָׁנִים הֵנָּה חֲלוֹם

כז אֶחָד הוּא: וְשֶׁבַע הַפָּרוֹת הָרַקּוֹת וְהָרָעֹת הָעֹלֹת
אַחֲרֵיהֶן שֶׁבַע שָׁנִים הֵנָּה וְשֶׁבַע הַשִּׁבֳּלִים הָרֵקוֹת
שְׁדֻפוֹת הַקָּדִים יִהְיוּ שֶׁבַע שְׁנֵי רָעָב: הוּא הַדָּבָר

כח אֲשֶׁר דִּבַּרְתִּי אֶל־פַּרְעֹה אֲשֶׁר הָאֱלֹהִים עֹשֶׂה הֶרְאָה

כט אֶת־פַּרְעֹה: הִנֵּה שֶׁבַע שָׁנִים בָּאוֹת שָׂבָע גָּדוֹל בְּכָל־

ל אֶרֶץ מִצְרָיִם: וְקָמוּ שֶׁבַע שְׁנֵי רָעָב אַחֲרֵיהֶן וְנִשְׁכַּח
כָּל־הַשָּׂבָע בְּאֶרֶץ מִצְרַיִם וְכִלָּה הָרָעָב אֶת־הָאָרֶץ:

לא וְלֹא־יִוָּדַע הַשָּׂבָע בָּאָרֶץ מִפְּנֵי הָרָעָב הַהוּא אַחֲרֵי־

לב כֵן כִּי־כָבֵד הוּא מְאֹד: וְעַל הִשָּׁנוֹת הַחֲלוֹם אֶל־
פַּרְעֹה פַּעֲמָיִם כִּי־נָכוֹן הַדָּבָר מֵעִם הָאֱלֹהִים וּמְמַהֵר

you to hear a dream is to tell its meaning." 16] Joseph answered Pharaoh, saying, "Not I! God will see to Pharaoh's welfare."

17] Then Pharaoh said to Joseph, "In my dream, I was standing on the bank of the Nile, 18] when out of the Nile came up seven sturdy and well-formed cows and grazed in the reed grass. 19] Presently there followed them seven other cows, scrawny, ill-formed, and emaciated—never had I seen their likes for ugliness in all the land of Egypt! 20] And the seven lean and ugly cows ate up the first seven cows, the sturdy ones; 21] but when they had consumed them, one could not tell that they had consumed them, for they looked just as bad as before. And I awoke. 22] In my other dream, I saw seven ears of grain, full and healthy, growing on a single stalk; 23] but right behind them sprouted seven ears, shriveled, thin, and scorched by the east wind. 24] And the thin ears swallowed the seven healthy ears. I have told my magicians, but none has an explanation for me."

25] And Joseph said to Pharaoh, "Pharaoh's dreams are one and the same: God has told Pharaoh what He is about to do. 26] The seven healthy cows are seven years, and the seven healthy ears are seven years; it is the same dream. 27] The seven lean and ugly cows that followed are seven years, as are also the seven empty ears scorched by the east wind; they are seven years of famine. 28] It is just as I have told Pharaoh: God has revealed to Pharaoh what He is about to do. 29] Immediately ahead are seven years of great abundance in all the land of Egypt. 30] After them will come seven years of famine, and all the abundance in the land of Egypt will be forgotten. As the land is ravaged by famine, 31] no trace of the abundance will be left in the land because of the famine thereafter, for it will be very severe. 32] As for Pharaoh having had the same dream twice, it means that the matter has been determined by God, and that God will soon carry it out.

16] *Not I!* Joseph again gives honor to God and at the same time makes it clear that he is not a professional soothsayer (cf. Dan. 2:28).

לג　הָאֱלֹהִים לַעֲשׂוֹתוֹ: וְעַתָּה יֵרֶא פַרְעֹה אִישׁ נָבוֹן וְחָכָם
לד　וִישִׁיתֵהוּ עַל־אֶרֶץ מִצְרָיִם: יַעֲשֶׂה פַרְעֹה וְיַפְקֵד פְּקִדִים עַל־הָאָרֶץ וְחִמֵּשׁ אֶת־אֶרֶץ מִצְרַיִם בְּשֶׁבַע שְׁנֵי הַשָּׂבָע:
לה　וְיִקְבְּצוּ אֶת־כָּל־אֹכֶל הַשָּׁנִים הַטֹּבוֹת הַבָּאֹת הָאֵלֶּה וְיִצְבְּרוּ־בָר תַּחַת יַד־פַּרְעֹה אֹכֶל בֶּעָרִים וְשָׁמָרוּ:
לו　וְהָיָה הָאֹכֶל לְפִקָּדוֹן לָאָרֶץ לְשֶׁבַע שְׁנֵי הָרָעָב אֲשֶׁר תִּהְיֶיןָ בְּאֶרֶץ מִצְרָיִם וְלֹא־תִכָּרֵת הָאָרֶץ בָּרָעָב:
לז　וַיִּיטַב הַדָּבָר בְּעֵינֵי פַרְעֹה וּבְעֵינֵי כָּל־עֲבָדָיו:
לח　וַיֹּאמֶר פַּרְעֹה אֶל־עֲבָדָיו הֲנִמְצָא כָזֶה אִישׁ אֲשֶׁר רוּחַ אֱלֹהִים בּוֹ:
לט　וַיֹּאמֶר פַּרְעֹה אֶל־יוֹסֵף אַחֲרֵי

הוֹדִיעַ אֱלֹהִים אוֹתְךָ אֶת־כָּל־זֹאת אֵין־נָבוֹן וְחָכָם כָּמוֹךָ:
מ　אַתָּה תִּהְיֶה עַל־בֵּיתִי וְעַל־פִּיךָ יִשַּׁק כָּל־עַמִּי רַק הַכִּסֵּא אֶגְדַּל מִמֶּךָּ: וַיֹּאמֶר פַּרְעֹה אֶל־יוֹסֵף רְאֵה
מא　נָתַתִּי אֹתְךָ עַל כָּל־אֶרֶץ מִצְרָיִם: וַיָּסַר פַּרְעֹה אֶת־
מב　טַבַּעְתּוֹ מֵעַל יָדוֹ וַיִּתֵּן אֹתָהּ עַל־יַד יוֹסֵף וַיַּלְבֵּשׁ אֹתוֹ בִּגְדֵי־שֵׁשׁ וַיָּשֶׂם רְבִד הַזָּהָב עַל־צַוָּארוֹ: וַיַּרְכֵּב אֹתוֹ
מג　בְּמִרְכֶּבֶת הַמִּשְׁנֶה אֲשֶׁר־לוֹ וַיִּקְרְאוּ לְפָנָיו אַבְרֵךְ וְנָתוֹן אֹתוֹ עַל כָּל־אֶרֶץ מִצְרָיִם: וַיֹּאמֶר פַּרְעֹה אֶל־
מד　יוֹסֵף אֲנִי פַרְעֹה וּבִלְעָדֶיךָ לֹא־יָרִים אִישׁ אֶת־יָדוֹ וְאֶת־רַגְלוֹ בְּכָל־אֶרֶץ מִצְרָיִם: וַיִּקְרָא פַרְעֹה שֵׁם־
מה

33] "Accordingly, let Pharaoh find a man of discernment and wisdom, and set him over the land of Egypt. 34] And let Pharaoh take steps to appoint overseers over the land, and organize the land of Egypt in the seven years of plenty. 35] Let all the food of these good years that are coming be gathered, and let the grain be collected under Pharaoh's authority as food to be stored in the cities. 36] Let that food be a reserve for the land for the seven years of famine which will come upon the land of Egypt, so that the land may not perish in the famine."

37] The plan pleased Pharaoh and all his courtiers. 38] And Pharaoh said to his courtiers, "Could we find another like him, a man in whom is the spirit of God?" 39] So Pharaoh said to Joseph, "Since God has made all this known to you, there is none so discerning and wise as you. 40] You shall be in charge of my court, and by your command shall all my people be directed; only with respect to the throne shall I be superior to you." 41] Pharaoh further said to Joseph, "See, I put you in charge of all the land of Egypt." 42] And removing his signet ring from his hand, Pharaoh put it on Joseph's hand; and he had him dressed in robes of fine linen, and put a gold chain about his neck. 43] He had him ride in the chariot of his second-in-command, and they cried before him, "Abrek!" Thus he placed him over all the land of Egypt.

44] Pharaoh said to Joseph, "I am Pharaoh; yet without you, no one shall lift up hand or foot

34] *Organize*. Others translate as "take a fifth part of."

40] *Directed*. Others translate as "order themselves," or "pay homage." As vizier, Joseph had direct access to Pharaoh.

42] *Signet ring*. The vizier was called "Seal Bearer of the King." Impressing a document with the ring was equivalent to an authorized signature.

Gold chain. An ancient symbol of investiture

still in use today in British Commonwealth countries and elsewhere.

43] *Abrek*. Either an Egyptian word of unknown meaning or an Assyrian title.

/ The Akkadian word *abarakku* means "temple steward" or "steward of the royal household," which raises the question of how an Assyrian title came to be attached to the Joseph story. See W. W. Hallo's introductory essay./

מְאֹ֥ד עַד כִּי־חָדַ֖ל לִסְפֹּ֑ר כִּי־אֵ֥ין מִסְפָּֽר: וּלְיוֹסֵ֞ף	יוֹסֵ֜ף צָֽפְנַ֣ת פַּעְנֵ֗חַ וַיִּתֶּן־ל֣וֹ אֶת־אָֽסְנַ֗ת בַּת־פּ֥וֹטִי פֶ֛רַע
יֻלַּד֙ שְׁנֵ֣י בָנִ֔ים בְּטֶ֥רֶם תָּב֖וֹא שְׁנַ֣ת הָֽרָעָ֑ב אֲשֶׁ֤ר יָֽלְדָה־	כֹהֵ֥ן אֹ֖ן לְאִשָּׁ֑ה וַיֵּצֵ֥א יוֹסֵ֖ף עַל־אֶ֥רֶץ מִצְרָֽיִם: וְיוֹסֵף֙
לּוֹ֙ אָֽסְנַ֣ת בַּת־פּ֥וֹטִי פֶ֖רַע כֹּהֵ֥ן אֽוֹן: וַיִּקְרָ֧א יוֹסֵ֛ף אֶת־	בֶּן־שְׁלֹשִׁ֣ים שָׁנָ֔ה בְּעָמְד֕וֹ לִפְנֵ֖י פַּרְעֹ֣ה מֶֽלֶךְ־מִצְרָ֑יִם
שֵׁ֥ם הַבְּכ֖וֹר מְנַשֶּׁ֑ה כִּֽי־נַשַּׁ֤נִי אֱלֹהִים֙ אֶת־כָּל־עֲמָלִ֔י	וַיֵּצֵ֤א יוֹסֵף֙ מִלִּפְנֵ֣י פַרְעֹ֔ה וַֽיַּעֲבֹ֖ר בְּכָל־אֶ֥רֶץ מִצְרָֽיִם:
וְאֵ֖ת כָּל־בֵּ֣ית אָבִֽי: וְאֵ֛ת שֵׁ֥ם הַשֵּׁנִ֖י קָרָ֣א אֶפְרָ֑יִם כִּֽי־	וַתַּ֣עַשׂ הָאָ֔רֶץ בְּשֶׁ֖בַע שְׁנֵ֣י הַשָּׂבָ֑ע לִקְמָצִֽים: וַיִּקְבֹּ֞ץ
הִפְרַ֥נִי אֱלֹהִ֖ים בְּאֶ֥רֶץ עָנְיִֽי: וַתִּכְלֶ֕ינָה שֶׁ֖בַע שְׁנֵ֣י הַשָּׂבָ֑ע	אֶת־כָּל־אֹ֣כֶל ׀ שֶׁ֣בַע שָׁנִ֗ים אֲשֶׁ֤ר הָיוּ֙ בְּאֶ֣רֶץ מִצְרַ֔יִם
אֲשֶׁ֥ר הָיָ֖ה בְּאֶ֣רֶץ מִצְרָ֑יִם: וַתְּחִלֶּ֜ינָה שֶׁ֣בַע שְׁנֵ֤י הָֽרָעָב֙	וַיִּתֶּן־אֹ֖כֶל בֶּֽעָרִ֑ים אֹ֧כֶל שְׂדֵה־הָעִ֛יר אֲשֶׁ֥ר סְבִֽיבֹתֶ֖יהָ
לָב֔וֹא כַּֽאֲשֶׁ֖ר אָמַ֣ר יוֹסֵ֑ף וַיְהִ֤י רָעָב֙ בְּכָל־הָ֣אֲרָצ֔וֹת	נָתַ֥ן בְּתוֹכָֽהּ: וַיִּצְבֹּ֨ר יוֹסֵ֥ף בָּ֛ר כְּח֥וֹל הַיָּ֖ם הַרְבֵּ֣ה

in all the land of Egypt."   **45]** Pharaoh then gave Joseph the name Zaphenath-paneah; and he gave him for a wife Asenath daughter of Poti-phera, priest of On. Thus Joseph emerged in charge of the land of Egypt.—   **46]** Joseph was thirty years old when he entered the service of Pharaoh king of Egypt.—Leaving Pharaoh's presence, Joseph traveled through all the land of Egypt.

47] During the seven years of plenty, the land produced in abundance.   **48]** And he gathered all the grain of the seven years that the land of Egypt was enjoying, and stored the grain in the cities; he put in each city the grain of the fields around it.   **49]** So Joseph collected produce in very large quantity, like the sands of the sea, until he ceased to measure it, for it could not be measured.

50] Before the years of famine came, Joseph became the father of two sons, whom Asenath daughter of Poti-phera, priest of On, bore to him.   **51]** Joseph named the first-born Manasseh, meaning, "God has made me forget completely my hardship and my parental home." **52]** And the second he named Ephraim, meaning, "God has made me fertile in the land of my affliction."

53] The seven years of abundance that the land of Egypt enjoyed came to an end,   **54]** and the seven years of famine set in, just as Joseph had foretold. There was famine in all lands, but

---

45] *Zaphenath-paneah.* Egyptian for "God speaks; He lives" or "Creator of life." Joseph is no longer the "Hebrew youth" (Gen. 41:12); his new name signifies his acceptance into official society.
/ Targum: "He to whom hidden matters are revealed" [1]./
    Poti-phera. A fuller form of Potiphar, but here a different person, unless this passage represents a second tradition that remembers Joseph not as the steward of Potiphar but as his son-in-law.
    On. Later Heliopolis, the "Sun-city," near today's Cairo.
    In charge of the land. He probably bore the

title found in Egyptian records, "Chief of the Entire Land."

46] *Thirty years old.* His servitude thus lasted thirteen years. Apparently Joseph's youth was not a hindrance to his high appointment.

48] *The seven years.* Literally, "... that were in the land."

51] *God has made me forget.* נַשַּׁנִי, a word play on מְנַשֶּׁה. On the implications of this sentiment, see Gleanings.

52] *God has made me fertile.* הִפְרַנִי, a word play on אֶפְרָיִם.

וּבְכָל־אֶרֶץ מִצְרַיִם הָיָה לָחֶם: וַתִּרְעַב כָּל־אֶרֶץ נה
מִצְרַיִם וַיִּצְעַק הָעָם אֶל־פַּרְעֹה לַלָּחֶם וַיֹּאמֶר פַּרְעֹה
לְכָל־מִצְרַיִם לְכוּ אֶל־יוֹסֵף אֲשֶׁר־יֹאמַר לָכֶם תַּעֲשׂוּ:
וְהָרָעָב הָיָה עַל כָּל־פְּנֵי הָאָרֶץ וַיִּפְתַּח יוֹסֵף אֶת־כָּל־ נו
אֲשֶׁר בָּהֶם וַיִּשְׁבֹּר לְמִצְרַיִם וַיֶּחֱזַק הָרָעָב בְּאֶרֶץ
מִצְרָיִם: וְכָל־הָאָרֶץ בָּאוּ מִצְרַיְמָה לִשְׁבֹּר אֶל־יוֹסֵף נז
כִּי־חָזַק הָרָעָב בְּכָל־הָאָרֶץ:
וַיַּרְא יַעֲקֹב כִּי יֶשׁ־שֶׁבֶר בְּמִצְרָיִם וַיֹּאמֶר יַעֲקֹב א
לְבָנָיו לָמָּה תִּתְרָאוּ: וַיֹּאמֶר הִנֵּה שָׁמַעְתִּי כִּי יֶשׁ־שֶׁבֶר ב
בְּמִצְרָיִם רְדוּ־שָׁמָּה וְשִׁבְרוּ־לָנוּ מִשָּׁם וְנִחְיֶה וְלֹא
נָמוּת: וַיֵּרְדוּ אֲחֵי־יוֹסֵף עֲשָׂרָה לִשְׁבֹּר בָּר מִמִּצְרָיִם: ג
וְאֶת־בִּנְיָמִין אֲחִי יוֹסֵף לֹא־שָׁלַח יַעֲקֹב אֶת־אֶחָיו כִּי ד

אָמַר פֶּן־יִקְרָאֶנּוּ אָסוֹן: וַיָּבֹאוּ בְּנֵי יִשְׂרָאֵל לִשְׁבֹּר ה
בְּתוֹךְ הַבָּאִים כִּי־הָיָה הָרָעָב בְּאֶרֶץ כְּנָעַן: וְיוֹסֵף ו
הוּא הַשַּׁלִּיט עַל־הָאָרֶץ הוּא הַמַּשְׁבִּיר לְכָל־עַם
הָאָרֶץ וַיָּבֹאוּ אֲחֵי יוֹסֵף וַיִּשְׁתַּחֲווּ־לוֹ אַפַּיִם אָרְצָה:
וַיַּרְא יוֹסֵף אֶת־אֶחָיו וַיַּכִּרֵם וַיִּתְנַכֵּר אֲלֵיהֶם וַיְדַבֵּר ז
אִתָּם קָשׁוֹת וַיֹּאמֶר אֲלֵהֶם מֵאַיִן בָּאתֶם וַיֹּאמְרוּ
מֵאֶרֶץ כְּנַעַן לִשְׁבָּר־אֹכֶל: וַיַּכֵּר יוֹסֵף אֶת־אֶחָיו וְהֵם ח
לֹא הִכִּרֻהוּ: וַיִּזְכֹּר יוֹסֵף אֵת הַחֲלֹמוֹת אֲשֶׁר חָלַם ט
לָהֶם וַיֹּאמֶר אֲלֵהֶם מְרַגְּלִים אַתֶּם לִרְאוֹת אֶת־עֶרְוַת
הָאָרֶץ בָּאתֶם: וַיֹּאמְרוּ אֵלָיו לֹא אֲדֹנִי וַעֲבָדֶיךָ בָּאוּ י
לִשְׁבָּר־אֹכֶל: כֻּלָּנוּ בְּנֵי אִישׁ־אֶחָד נָחְנוּ כֵּנִים אֲנַחְנוּ יא
לֹא־הָיוּ עֲבָדֶיךָ מְרַגְּלִים: וַיֹּאמֶר אֲלֵהֶם לֹא כִּי־עֶרְוַת יב

throughout the land of Egypt there was bread. 55] And when all the land of Egypt felt the hunger, the people cried out to Pharaoh for bread; and Pharaoh said to all the Egyptians, "Go to Joseph; whatever he tells you, you shall do."— 56] Accordingly, when the famine became severe in the land of Egypt, Joseph laid open all that was within, and rationed out grain to the Egyptians. The famine, however, spread over the whole world. 57] So all the world came to Joseph in Egypt to procure rations, for the famine had become severe throughout the world.

1] When Jacob saw that there were food rations to be had in Egypt, he said to his sons, "Why do you keep looking at one another? 2] Now I hear," he went on, "that there are rations to be had in Egypt. Go down and procure rations for us there, that we may live and not die." 3] So ten of Joseph's brothers went down to get grain rations in Egypt; 4] for Jacob did not send Joseph's brother Benjamin with his brothers, since he feared that he might meet with disaster. 5] Thus the sons of Israel were among those who came to procure rations, for the famine extended to the land of Canaan.

6] Now Joseph was the vizier of the land; it was he who dispensed rations to all the people of the land. And Joseph's brothers came and bowed low to him, with their faces to the ground. 7] When Joseph saw his brothers, he recognized them; but he acted like a stranger toward them and spoke harshly to them. He asked them, "Where do you come from?" And they said, "From the land of Canaan, to procure food." 8] For though Joseph recognized his brothers, they did not recognize him. 9] Recalling the dreams that he had dreamed about them, Joseph said to them, "You are spies, you have come to see the land in its nakedness." 10] But they said to him, "No, my lord! Truly, your servants have come to procure food. 11] We are all of us sons of the same man; we are honest men; your servants have never been

---

57] *All the world.* Everyone from Canaan and perhaps even from Mesopotamia.

42:9] *Nakedness.* Joseph refers to Egypt's military exposure from the Sinai peninsula, where the country was most vulnerable. Garrisons transmitted daily reports detailing the entry and exit of all strangers.

הָאָרֶץ בָּאתֶם לִרְאוֹת: וַיֹּאמְרוּ שְׁנֵים עָשָׂר עֲבָדֶיךָ
אַחִים אֲנַחְנוּ בְּנֵי אִישׁ־אֶחָד בְּאֶרֶץ כְּנָעַן וְהִנֵּה הַקָּטֹן
אֶת־אָבִינוּ הַיּוֹם וְהָאֶחָד אֵינֶנּוּ: וַיֹּאמֶר אֲלֵהֶם יוֹסֵף
הוּא אֲשֶׁר דִּבַּרְתִּי אֲלֵכֶם לֵאמֹר מְרַגְּלִים אַתֶּם:
בְּזֹאת תִּבָּחֵנוּ חֵי פַרְעֹה אִם־תֵּצְאוּ מִזֶּה כִּי אִם־בְּבוֹא
אֲחִיכֶם הַקָּטֹן הֵנָּה: שִׁלְחוּ מִכֶּם אֶחָד וְיִקַּח אֶת־
אֲחִיכֶם וְאַתֶּם הֵאָסְרוּ וְיִבָּחֲנוּ דִּבְרֵיכֶם הַאֱמֶת אִתְּכֶם
וְאִם־לֹא חֵי פַרְעֹה כִּי מְרַגְּלִים אַתֶּם: וַיֶּאֱסֹף אֹתָם
אֶל־מִשְׁמָר שְׁלֹשֶׁת יָמִים: וַיֹּאמֶר אֲלֵהֶם יוֹסֵף בַּיּוֹם
הַשְּׁלִישִׁי זֹאת עֲשׂוּ וִחְיוּ אֶת־הָאֱלֹהִים אֲנִי יָרֵא: אִם־
כֵּנִים אַתֶּם אֲחִיכֶם אֶחָד יֵאָסֵר בְּבֵית מִשְׁמַרְכֶם
וְאַתֶּם לְכוּ הָבִיאוּ שֶׁבֶר רַעֲבוֹן בָּתֵּיכֶם: וְאֶת־אֲחִיכֶם

הַקָּטֹן תָּבִיאוּ אֵלַי וְיֵאָמְנוּ דִבְרֵיכֶם וְלֹא תָמוּתוּ
וַיַּעֲשׂוּ־כֵן: וַיֹּאמְרוּ אִישׁ אֶל־אָחִיו אֲבָל אֲשֵׁמִים אֲנַחְנוּ
עַל־אָחִינוּ אֲשֶׁר רָאִינוּ צָרַת נַפְשׁוֹ בְּהִתְחַנְנוֹ אֵלֵינוּ
וְלֹא שָׁמָעְנוּ עַל־כֵּן בָּאָה אֵלֵינוּ הַצָּרָה הַזֹּאת: וַיַּעַן
רְאוּבֵן אֹתָם לֵאמֹר הֲלוֹא אָמַרְתִּי אֲלֵיכֶם לֵאמֹר
אַל־תֶּחֶטְאוּ בַיֶּלֶד וְלֹא שְׁמַעְתֶּם וְגַם־דָּמוֹ הִנֵּה נִדְרָשׁ:
וְהֵם לֹא יָדְעוּ כִּי שֹׁמֵעַ יוֹסֵף כִּי הַמֵּלִיץ בֵּינֹתָם: וַיִּסֹּב
מֵעֲלֵיהֶם וַיֵּבְךְּ וַיָּשָׁב אֲלֵהֶם וַיְדַבֵּר אֲלֵהֶם וַיִּקַּח
מֵאִתָּם אֶת־שִׁמְעוֹן וַיֶּאֱסֹר אֹתוֹ לְעֵינֵיהֶם: וַיְצַו יוֹסֵף
וַיְמַלְאוּ אֶת־כְּלֵיהֶם בָּר וּלְהָשִׁיב כַּסְפֵּיהֶם אִישׁ אֶל־
שַׂקּוֹ וְלָתֵת לָהֶם צֵדָה לַדָּרֶךְ וַיַּעַשׂ לָהֶם כֵּן: וַיִּשְׂאוּ
אֶת־שִׁבְרָם עַל־חֲמֹרֵיהֶם וַיֵּלְכוּ מִשָּׁם: וַיִּפְתַּח הָאֶחָד

spies!" **12]** And he said to them, "No, you have come to see the land in its nakedness!" **13]** And they replied, "We your servants were twelve brothers, sons of a certain man in the land of Canaan; the youngest, however, is now with our father, and one is no more." **14]** But Joseph said to them, "It is just as I have told you: You are spies! **15]** By this you shall be put to the test: unless your youngest brother comes here, by Pharaoh, you shall not depart from this place! **16]** Let one of you go and bring your brother, while the rest of you remain confined, that your words may be put to the test whether there is truth in you. Else, by Pharaoh, you are nothing but spies!" **17]** And he confined them in the guardhouse for three days.

18] On the third day Joseph said to them, "Do this and you shall live, for I am a God-fearing man. **19]** If you are honest men, let one of your brothers be held in your place of detention, while the rest of you go and take home rations for your starving households; **20]** but you must bring me your youngest brother, that your words may be verified and that you may not die." And they did accordingly. **21]** They said to one another, "Alas, we are being punished on account of our brother, because we looked on at his anguish, yet paid no heed as he pleaded with us. That is why this distress has come upon us." **22]** Then Reuben spoke up and said to them, "Did I not tell you, 'Do no wrong to the boy'? But you paid no heed. Now comes the reckoning for his blood." **23]** They did not know that Joseph understood, for there was an interpreter between him and them. **24]** He turned away from them and wept. But he came back to them and spoke to them; and he took Simeon from among them and had him bound before their eyes. **25]** Then Joseph gave orders to fill their bags with grain, return each one's money to his sack and give them provisions for the journey; and this was done for them. **26]** So they loaded their asses with the rations and departed from there.

18] *On the third day.* Joseph changes his mind and comes up with a more workable scheme.

22] *Did I not tell you?* They assume that Joseph is dead and are now assailed by a sense of blood guilt (see Gen. 9:6).

269

אֶת־שַׂקּוֹ לָתֵת מִסְפּוֹא לַחֲמֹרוֹ בַּמָּלוֹן וַיַּרְא אֶת־

כח כַּסְפּוֹ וְהִנֵּה־הוּא בְּפִי אַמְתַּחְתּוֹ: וַיֹּאמֶר אֶל־אֶחָיו
הוּשַׁב כַּסְפִּי וְגַם הִנֵּה בְאַמְתַּחְתִּי וַיֵּצֵא לִבָּם וַיֶּחֶרְדוּ
אִישׁ אֶל־אָחִיו לֵאמֹר מַה־זֹּאת עָשָׂה אֱלֹהִים לָנוּ:

כט וַיָּבֹאוּ אֶל־יַעֲקֹב אֲבִיהֶם אַרְצָה כְּנָעַן וַיַּגִּידוּ לוֹ אֵת
ל כָּל־הַקֹּרֹת אֹתָם לֵאמֹר: דִּבֶּר הָאִישׁ אֲדֹנֵי הָאָרֶץ
לא אִתָּנוּ קָשׁוֹת וַיִּתֵּן אֹתָנוּ כִּמְרַגְּלִים אֶת־הָאָרֶץ: וַנֹּאמֶר
לב אֵלָיו כֵּנִים אֲנָחְנוּ לֹא הָיִינוּ מְרַגְּלִים: שְׁנֵים־עָשָׂר
אֲנַחְנוּ אַחִים בְּנֵי אָבִינוּ הָאֶחָד אֵינֶנּוּ וְהַקָּטֹן הַיּוֹם
לג אֶת־אָבִינוּ בְּאֶרֶץ כְּנָעַן: וַיֹּאמֶר אֵלֵינוּ הָאִישׁ אֲדֹנֵי
הָאָרֶץ בְּזֹאת אֵדַע כִּי כֵנִים אַתֶּם אֲחִיכֶם הָאֶחָד
לד הַנִּיחוּ אִתִּי וְאֶת־רַעֲבוֹן בָּתֵּיכֶם קְחוּ וָלֵכוּ: וְהָבִיאוּ

אֶת־אֲחִיכֶם הַקָּטֹן אֵלַי וְאֵדְעָה כִּי לֹא מְרַגְּלִים
אַתֶּם כִּי כֵנִים אַתֶּם אֶת־אֲחִיכֶם אֶתֵּן לָכֶם וְאֶת־
לה הָאָרֶץ תִּסְחָרוּ: וַיְהִי הֵם מְרִיקִים שַׂקֵּיהֶם וְהִנֵּה־אִישׁ
צְרוֹר־כַּסְפּוֹ בְּשַׂקּוֹ וַיִּרְאוּ אֶת־צְרֹרוֹת כַּסְפֵּיהֶם הֵמָּה
לו וַאֲבִיהֶם וַיִּירָאוּ: וַיֹּאמֶר אֲלֵהֶם יַעֲקֹב אֲבִיהֶם אֹתִי
שִׁכַּלְתֶּם יוֹסֵף אֵינֶנּוּ וְשִׁמְעוֹן אֵינֶנּוּ וְאֶת־בִּנְיָמִן תִּקָּחוּ
לז עָלַי הָיוּ כֻלָּנָה: וַיֹּאמֶר רְאוּבֵן אֶל־אָבִיו לֵאמֹר אֶת־
שְׁנֵי בָנַי תָּמִית אִם־לֹא אֲבִיאֶנּוּ אֵלֶיךָ תְּנָה אֹתוֹ עַל־
לח יָדִי וַאֲנִי אֲשִׁיבֶנּוּ אֵלֶיךָ: וַיֹּאמֶר לֹא־יֵרֵד בְּנִי עִמָּכֶם
כִּי־אָחִיו מֵת וְהוּא לְבַדּוֹ נִשְׁאָר וּקְרָאָהוּ אָסוֹן בַּדֶּרֶךְ
אֲשֶׁר תֵּלְכוּ־בָהּ וְהוֹרַדְתֶּם אֶת־שֵׂיבָתִי בְּיָגוֹן שְׁאוֹלָה:

27] As one of them was opening his sack to give feed to his ass at the night encampment, he saw his money right there at the mouth of his bag. **28]** And he said to his brothers, "My money has been returned! It is here in my bag!" Their hearts sank; and, trembling, they turned to one another, saying, "What is this that God has done to us?"

29] When they came to their father Jacob in the land of Canaan, they told him all that had befallen them, saying, **30]** "The man who is lord of the land spoke harshly to us and accused us of spying on the land. **31]** We said to him 'We are honest men; we have never been spies! **32]** There were twelve of us brothers, sons by the same father; but one is no more, and the youngest is now with our father in the land of Canaan.' **33]** But the man who is lord of the land said to us, 'By this I shall know that you are honest men: leave one of your brothers with me, and take something for your starving households and be off. **34]** And bring your youngest brother to me, that I may know that you are not spies but honest men. I will then restore your brother to you, and you shall be free to move about in the land.'"

35] As they were emptying their sacks, there, in each one's sack, was his money-bag! When they and their father saw their money-bags, they were dismayed. **36]** Their father Jacob said to them, "It is always me that you bereave: Joseph is no more and Simeon is no more, and now you would take away Benjamin. These things always happen to me!" **37]** Then Reuben said to his father, "You may kill my two sons if I do not bring him back to you. Put him in my care, and I will return him to you." **38]** But he said, "My son must not go down with you, for his brother is dead and he alone is left. If he meets with disaster on the journey you are taking, you will send my white head down to Sheol in grief."

37] *You may kill my two sons.* A hyperbole: "I swear I will bring him back."

A Man in Conflict

The attempts by older traditions to portray Joseph as a persistently noble character do injustice to the text and to its artistry.

Thirteen years as a slave, even though at times a privileged one, left their mark on the young man. He had been his father's favorite, a pampered youth, who told tales on his brothers and who overwhelmed his family with his ambitious dreams. But the trauma of near-death and his subsequent sale into slavery apparently brought on a profound change. Gone were the ornamented tunic and with it the easy arrogance. Bitterness over his lot, then a brief period of success followed by temptation and by imprisonment with long hours of solitude—all these combined to bring out Joseph's latent powers. The gifted son of Jacob developed a sense of humility, and with it his basic qualities of religious sentiment began to emerge.

Joseph was the first Hebrew who lived, so to speak, in Diaspora (גָּלוּת). He became thoroughly assimilated, adopted the customs of his environment, changed his name, wore Egyptian clothes, swore by Pharaoh's name (Gen. 42:15), and married an Egyptian wife.[1] In Potiphar's house and in prison he was still "the Hebrew"; as an Egyptian official, he became wholly Egyptian. He entered a new life of affluence and power, and the past seemed far away. He was moved to call his first-born Manasseh because "God has made me forget completely my hardship and my parental home" (Gen. 41:51).

The forgetting, of course, was only on the surface, in his everyday existence. His past would not and could not go away. He would have been more than human if he did not think how some day he would let his brothers know of his great position, put them to shame, and arouse their envy. But why did he not communicate with his father? Why did he not make inquiry through Pharaoh's subordinates in Canaan whether Jacob was still alive?

This failure hints at a severely strained relationship between son and father. Jacob doubtlessly loved Rachel's first-born son with a fierce and possessive love. He saw in Joseph (as he would later in Benjamin) a surrogate for Rachel, his dead wife. It is altogether possible that the ornamented tunic may have served to feminize young Joseph who, according to a midrash, curled his hair and painted his eyebrows [3]. The boy must have suffered deep agony in this intense relationship, and, when he was separated from his father, he must have found it easier to suppress the memory of Jacob than to face it with maturity.[2]

The turning point came with the sudden appearance of his brothers. At first, and understandably, Joseph thought of revenge, but, when he saw them from his new and elevated position, he glimpsed them—perhaps for the first time in his life—as human beings in need of help, as brothers. And now, inevitably, he had to think of his father.

Literary artistry here introduces a delay that heightens suspense and reflects Joseph's own inner conflict. He still wants revenge more than he wants love, and so he proceeds to imprison the most aggressive of his brothers and to subject his father to the severest trial: giving up his new Rachel-substitute, the beloved Benjamin. Only after this will the final act of the drama emerge. Only after this will Joseph have reached his full potential and be able to say, "I am Joseph" and "Is my father still well?" (Gen. 45:3).

---

[1] An apocryphal tale of Joseph and Asenath has been preserved in Greek, but not in Hebrew or Aramaic [2].

[2] Nachmanides calls Joseph's decision to keep his father ignorant of the situation a grave sin, while Abarbanel excuses it on grounds of political prudence.

GLEANINGS

The Dreams

Joseph interprets to Pharaoh not his dreams but his duties.

BENNO JACOB

Famine in Egypt

I was in distress on the Great Throne, and those who are in the palace were in heart's affliction from a very great evil, since the Nile had not come in my time for a space of seven years. Grain was scant, fruits were dried up, and everything which they eat was short. Every man robbed his companion. They moved without going ahead. The infant was wailing; the youth was waiting; the heart of the old men was in sorrow, their legs were bent, crouching on the ground, their arms were folded. The courtiers were in need. The temples were shut up; the sanctuaries held nothing but air. Everything was found empty.

A PHARAONIC RECORD [4]

Simeon

Joseph took his brother Simeon as a hostage, possibly because he was the one who had suggested that Joseph be killed. Thus punishment is exacted and the scales of justice begin to balance.

MIDRASH [5]

Double-Entendre

The word שֶׁבֶר (*shever*, rations) is used often in this story. Since the tale was probably first told by the tribe of Ephraim who pronounced "sh" as "s" [the Shibboleth-Sibboleth story, Judg. 12:6] they heard שֶׁבֶר (*shever*) as שֵׂבֶר (*sever*, i.e., hope). We have here an artistic double-entendre: Jacob means "food in Egypt," but the listener knows already that there is also "hope in Egypt." [6]

An Old Egyptian Proverb

A foreigner who drinks of the waters of the Nile forgets his native land.

Joseph

The nakedness of Joseph before Pharaoh
was the nakedness of an elm tree in winter.

Not like the pine, whose branches hold the snow
and bend and break in the cold, but like the elm
stood Joseph, stripped of his colored garments,
the ornaments of his youthful summer,
stripped of his pride as favorite son
and his pretensions to rule his brothers;
yet rooted in the teachings of his father,
as the elm tree is rooted in the deep earth
Joseph stood before the king of Egypt
as his father, Jacob, had stood before the
    Wrestler.

The nakedness of bare branches and deep roots
is the nakedness of the Jew before history.

RUTH BRIN [7]

The Second Visit

As the story of Joseph and his brothers advances to its climax, it becomes clear that Joseph is testing his brothers' feelings toward Benjamin and is working out his own new relationship to them.

In this section Judah rather than the first-born Reuben plays the commanding role. Critics have assigned this "Judah-strand" to the J-school and the "Reuben-strand" to the E-tradition. Another reason for supposing that we have varying traditions is that in this portion of the story Jacob seems to disregard the fate of the imprisoned Simeon. But the final text has woven the strands together so artfully that the flow of the tale and its emotional impact on the reader are not in the least diminished.

א וְהָרָעָב כָּבֵד בָּאָרֶץ: וַיְהִי כַּאֲשֶׁר כִּלּוּ לֶאֱכֹל אֶת־
הַשֶּׁבֶר אֲשֶׁר הֵבִיאוּ מִמִּצְרָיִם וַיֹּאמֶר אֲלֵיהֶם אֲבִיהֶם
ג שֻׁבוּ שִׁבְרוּ־לָנוּ מְעַט־אֹכֶל: וַיֹּאמֶר אֵלָיו יְהוּדָה
לֵאמֹר הָעֵד הֵעִד בָּנוּ הָאִישׁ לֵאמֹר לֹא־תִרְאוּ פָנַי
ד בִּלְתִּי אֲחִיכֶם אִתְּכֶם: אִם־יֶשְׁךָ מְשַׁלֵּחַ אֶת־אָחִינוּ
ה אִתָּנוּ נֵרְדָה וְנִשְׁבְּרָה לְךָ אֹכֶל: וְאִם־אֵינְךָ מְשַׁלֵּחַ
לֹא נֵרֵד כִּי־הָאִישׁ אָמַר אֵלֵינוּ לֹא־תִרְאוּ פָנַי
ו בִּלְתִּי אֲחִיכֶם אִתְּכֶם: וַיֹּאמֶר יִשְׂרָאֵל לָמָה הֲרֵעֹתֶם
ז לִי לְהַגִּיד לָאִישׁ הַעוֹד לָכֶם אָח: וַיֹּאמְרוּ שָׁאוֹל
שָׁאַל־הָאִישׁ לָנוּ וּלְמוֹלַדְתֵּנוּ לֵאמֹר הַעוֹד אֲבִיכֶם
חַי הֲיֵשׁ לָכֶם אָח וַנַּגֶּד־לוֹ עַל־פִּי הַדְּבָרִים
הָאֵלֶּה הֲיָדוֹעַ נֵדַע כִּי יֹאמַר הוֹרִידוּ אֶת־אֲחִיכֶם:
ח וַיֹּאמֶר יְהוּדָה אֶל־יִשְׂרָאֵל אָבִיו שִׁלְחָה הַנַּעַר אִתִּי
וְנָקוּמָה וְנֵלֵכָה וְנִחְיֶה וְלֹא נָמוּת גַּם־אֲנַחְנוּ גַם־אַתָּה גַּם־
ט טַפֵּנוּ: אָנֹכִי אֶעֶרְבֶנּוּ מִיָּדִי תְּבַקְשֶׁנּוּ אִם־לֹא הֲבִיאֹתִיו
י אֵלֶיךָ וְהִצַּגְתִּיו לְפָנֶיךָ וְחָטָאתִי לְךָ כָּל־הַיָּמִים: כִּי לוּלֵא
יא הִתְמַהְמָהְנוּ כִּי־עַתָּה שַׁבְנוּ זֶה פַעֲמָיִם: וַיֹּאמֶר אֲלֵהֶם
יִשְׂרָאֵל אֲבִיהֶם אִם־כֵּן אֵפוֹא זֹאת עֲשׂוּ קְחוּ מִזִּמְרַת
הָאָרֶץ בִּכְלֵיכֶם וְהוֹרִידוּ לָאִישׁ מִנְחָה מְעַט צֳרִי
יב וּמְעַט דְּבַשׁ נְכֹאת וָלֹט בָּטְנִים וּשְׁקֵדִים: וְכֶסֶף
מִשְׁנֶה קְחוּ בְיֶדְכֶם וְאֶת־הַכֶּסֶף הַמּוּשָׁב בְּפִי
יג אַמְתְּחֹתֵיכֶם תָּשִׁיבוּ בְיֶדְכֶם אוּלַי מִשְׁגֶּה הוּא: וְאֶת־

1] But the famine in the land was severe. **2]** And when they had eaten up the rations which they had brought from Egypt, their father said to them, "Go again and procure some food for us." **3]** But Judah said to him, "The man warned us, 'Do not let me see your faces unless your brother is with you.' **4]** If you will let our brother go with us, we will go down and procure food for you; **5]** but if you will not let him go, we will not go down, for the man said to us, 'Do not let me see your faces unless your brother is with you.'" **6]** And Israel said, "Why did you serve me so ill as to tell the man that you had another brother?" **7]** They replied, "But the man kept asking about us and our family, saying, 'Is your father still living? Have you another brother?' And we answered him accordingly. How were we to know that he would say, 'Bring your brother here'?"

8] Then Judah said to his father Israel, "Send the boy in my care, and let us be on our way, that we may live and not die—you and we and our children. **9]** I myself will be surety for him; you may hold me responsible: if I do not bring him back to you and set him before you, I shall stand guilty before you forever. **10]** For we could have been there and back twice if we had not dawdled."

11] Then their father Israel said to them, "If it must be so, do this: take some of the choice products of the land in your baggage, and carry them down as a gift for the man—some balm and some honey, gum, ladanum, pistachio nuts, and almonds. **12]** And take with you double the money, carrying back with you the money that was replaced in the mouths of your bags;

43:3] *Do not let me see your faces.* Reversing the literal Hebrew, "do not see my face."

9] *Surety.* A legal term denoting personal responsibility for someone else's performance.

10] *If we had not dawdled.* Because of Benjamin.

11] *Do this.* Once Jacob realizes the inevitable, he acts quickly and firmly.

12] *Double the money . . . perhaps it was a mistake.* These have similar sounds in Hebrew: מִשְׁגֶּה and מִשְׁנֶה (*mishgeh* and *mishneh*).

יד אֲחִיכֶם קָחוּ וְקוּמוּ שׁוּבוּ אֶל־הָאִישׁ: וְאֵל שַׁדַּי יִתֵּן
לָכֶם רַחֲמִים לִפְנֵי הָאִישׁ וְשִׁלַּח לָכֶם אֶת־אֲחִיכֶם
טו אַחֵר וְאֶת־בִּנְיָמִין וַאֲנִי כַּאֲשֶׁר שָׁכֹלְתִּי שָׁכָלְתִּי: וַיִּקְחוּ
הָאֲנָשִׁים אֶת־הַמִּנְחָה הַזֹּאת וּמִשְׁנֶה־כֶּסֶף לָקְחוּ בְיָדָם
וְאֶת־בִּנְיָמִן וַיָּקֻמוּ וַיֵּרְדוּ מִצְרַיִם וַיַּעַמְדוּ לִפְנֵי יוֹסֵף:
טז וַיַּרְא יוֹסֵף אִתָּם אֶת־בִּנְיָמִין וַיֹּאמֶר לַאֲשֶׁר עַל־בֵּיתוֹ
הָבֵא אֶת־הָאֲנָשִׁים הַבָּיְתָה וּטְבֹחַ טֶבַח וְהָכֵן כִּי אִתִּי
יז יֹאכְלוּ הָאֲנָשִׁים בַּצָּהֳרָיִם: וַיַּעַשׂ הָאִישׁ כַּאֲשֶׁר אָמַר
יח יוֹסֵף וַיָּבֵא הָאִישׁ אֶת־הָאֲנָשִׁים בֵּיתָה יוֹסֵף: וַיִּירְאוּ
הָאֲנָשִׁים כִּי הוּבְאוּ בֵּית יוֹסֵף וַיֹּאמְרוּ עַל־דְּבַר
הַכֶּסֶף הַשָּׁב בְּאַמְתְּחֹתֵינוּ בַּתְּחִלָּה אֲנַחְנוּ מוּבָאִים
לְהִתְגֹּלֵל עָלֵינוּ וּלְהִתְנַפֵּל עָלֵינוּ וְלָקַחַת אֹתָנוּ

יט לַעֲבָדִים וְאֶת־חֲמֹרֵינוּ: וַיִּגְּשׁוּ אֶל־הָאִישׁ אֲשֶׁר עַל־
כ בֵּית יוֹסֵף וַיְדַבְּרוּ אֵלָיו פֶּתַח הַבָּיִת: וַיֹּאמְרוּ בִּי
כא אֲדֹנִי יָרֹד יָרַדְנוּ בַּתְּחִלָּה לִשְׁבָּר־אֹכֶל: וַיְהִי כִּי־בָאנוּ
אֶל־הַמָּלוֹן וַנִּפְתְּחָה אֶת־אַמְתְּחֹתֵינוּ וְהִנֵּה כֶסֶף־אִישׁ
בְּפִי אַמְתַּחְתּוֹ כַּסְפֵּנוּ בְּמִשְׁקָלוֹ וַנָּשֶׁב אֹתוֹ בְּיָדֵנוּ:
כב וְכֶסֶף אַחֵר הוֹרַדְנוּ בְיָדֵנוּ לִשְׁבָּר־אֹכֶל לֹא יָדַעְנוּ
כג מִי־שָׂם כַּסְפֵּנוּ בְּאַמְתְּחֹתֵינוּ: וַיֹּאמֶר שָׁלוֹם לָכֶם אַל־
תִּירָאוּ אֱלֹהֵיכֶם וֵאלֹהֵי אֲבִיכֶם נָתַן לָכֶם מַטְמוֹן
בְּאַמְתְּחֹתֵיכֶם כַּסְפְּכֶם בָּא אֵלָי וַיּוֹצֵא אֲלֵהֶם אֶת־
כד שִׁמְעוֹן: וַיָּבֵא הָאִישׁ אֶת־הָאֲנָשִׁים בֵּיתָה יוֹסֵף וַיִּתֶּן־
מַיִם וַיִּרְחֲצוּ רַגְלֵיהֶם וַיִּתֵּן מִסְפּוֹא לַחֲמֹרֵיהֶם: וַיָּכִינוּ
כה אֶת־הַמִּנְחָה עַד־בּוֹא יוֹסֵף בַּצָּהֳרָיִם כִּי שָׁמְעוּ כִּי־שָׁם

perhaps it was a mistake. **13]** Take your brother too; and go back at once to the man. **14]** And may El Shaddai dispose the man to mercy toward you, that he may release to you your other brother, as well as Benjamin. As for me, if I am to be bereaved, I shall be bereaved."

15] So the men took that gift, and they took with them double the money, as well as Benjamin. They made their way down to Egypt, where they presented themselves to Joseph. **16]** When Joseph saw Benjamin with them, he said to his house steward, "Take the men into the house; slaughter and prepare an animal, for the men will dine with me at noon." **17]** The man did as Joseph said, and he brought the men into Joseph's house. **18]** But the men were frightened at being brought into Joseph's house. "It must be," they thought, "because of the money replaced in our bags the first time that we have been brought inside, as a pretext to attack us and seize us as slaves, with our pack animals." **19]** So they went up to Joseph's house steward and spoke to him at the entrance of the house. **20]** "If you please, my lord," they said, "we came down once before to procure food. **21]** But when we arrived at the night encampment and opened our bags, there was each one's money in the mouth of his bag, our money in full. So we have brought it back with us. **22]** And we have brought down with us other money to procure food. We do not know who put the money in our bags." **23]** He replied, "All is well with you; do not be afraid. Your God and the God of your father must have put treasure in your bags for you. I got your payment." And he brought out Simeon to them.

24] Then the man brought the men into Joseph's house; he gave them water to bathe their feet, and he provided feed for their asses. **25]** They laid out their gifts to await Joseph's arrival at noon, for they had heard they were to dine there.

13] *Your brother.* A subtle literary and psychological change of expression. Until then Jacob has said of Benjamin "my son" (Gen. 42:38); now he shifts the responsibility for the boy and says "your brother."

18] *With our pack animals.* Even though their personal liberty is at stake, the brothers are still concerned about their possessions—a timeless, universal trait [1].

21] *Money in full.* Literally, "by its weight."

כו יֹאכְלוּ לָחֶם: וַיָּבֹא יוֹסֵף הַבַּיְתָה וַיָּבִיאוּ לוֹ אֶת־
הַמִּנְחָה אֲשֶׁר־בְּיָדָם הַבָּיְתָה וַיִּשְׁתַּחֲווּ־לוֹ אָרְצָה:
כז וַיִּשְׁאַל לָהֶם לְשָׁלוֹם וַיֹּאמֶר הֲשָׁלוֹם אֲבִיכֶם הַזָּקֵן
כח אֲשֶׁר אֲמַרְתֶּם הַעוֹדֶנּוּ חָי: וַיֹּאמְרוּ שָׁלוֹם לְעַבְדְּךָ
כט לְאָבִינוּ עוֹדֶנּוּ חָי וַיִּקְּדוּ וַיִּשְׁתַּחֲווּ: וַיִּשָּׂא עֵינָיו וַיַּרְא
אֶת־בִּנְיָמִין אָחִיו בֶּן־אִמּוֹ וַיֹּאמֶר הֲזֶה אֲחִיכֶם הַקָּטֹן
ל אֲשֶׁר אֲמַרְתֶּם אֵלָי וַיֹּאמַר אֱלֹהִים יָחְנְךָ בְּנִי: וַיְמַהֵר
יוֹסֵף כִּי־נִכְמְרוּ רַחֲמָיו אֶל־אָחִיו וַיְבַקֵּשׁ לִבְכּוֹת
לא וַיָּבֹא הַחַדְרָה וַיֵּבְךְּ שָׁמָּה: וַיִּרְחַץ פָּנָיו וַיֵּצֵא וַיִּתְאַפַּק
לב וַיֹּאמֶר שִׂימוּ לָחֶם: וַיָּשִׂימוּ לוֹ לְבַדּוֹ וְלָהֶם לְבַדָּם
וְלַמִּצְרִים הָאֹכְלִים אִתּוֹ לְבַדָּם כִּי לֹא יוּכְלוּן

הַמִּצְרִים לֶאֱכֹל אֶת־הָעִבְרִים לֶחֶם כִּי־תוֹעֵבָה הִוא
לג לְמִצְרָיִם: וַיֵּשְׁבוּ לְפָנָיו הַבְּכֹר כִּבְכֹרָתוֹ וְהַצָּעִיר
לד כִּצְעִרָתוֹ וַיִּתְמְהוּ הָאֲנָשִׁים אִישׁ אֶל־רֵעֵהוּ: וַיִּשָּׂא
מַשְׂאֹת מֵאֵת פָּנָיו אֲלֵהֶם וַתֵּרֶב מַשְׂאַת בִּנְיָמִן מִמַּשְׂאֹת
כֻּלָּם חָמֵשׁ יָדוֹת וַיִּשְׁתּוּ וַיִּשְׁכְּרוּ עִמּוֹ:

א וַיְצַו אֶת־אֲשֶׁר עַל־בֵּיתוֹ לֵאמֹר מַלֵּא אֶת־אַמְתְּחֹת
הָאֲנָשִׁים אֹכֶל כַּאֲשֶׁר יוּכְלוּן שְׂאֵת וְשִׂים כֶּסֶף־אִישׁ
ב בְּפִי אַמְתַּחְתּוֹ: וְאֶת־גְּבִיעִי גְּבִיעַ הַכֶּסֶף תָּשִׂים בְּפִי
אַמְתַּחַת הַקָּטֹן וְאֵת כֶּסֶף שִׁבְרוֹ וַיַּעַשׂ כִּדְבַר יוֹסֵף
ג אֲשֶׁר דִּבֵּר: הַבֹּקֶר אוֹר וְהָאֲנָשִׁים שֻׁלְּחוּ הֵמָּה

* כח וישתחוו קרי.

26] When Joseph came home, they presented to him the gifts that they had brought with them into the house, bowing low before him to the ground. 27] He greeted them, and he said, "How is your aged father of whom you spoke? Is he still in good health?" 28] They replied, "It is well with your servant our father; he is still in good health." And they bowed and made obeisance.

29] Looking about, he saw his brother Benjamin, his mother's son, and asked, "Is this your youngest brother of whom you spoke to me?" And he went on, "May God be gracious to you, my boy." 30] With that, Joseph hurried out, for he was overcome with feeling toward his brother and was on the verge of tears; he went into a room and wept there. 31] Then he washed his face, reappeared, and—now in control of himself—gave the order, "Serve the meal." 32] They served him by himself, and them by themselves, and the Egyptians who ate with him by themselves; for the Egyptians could not dine with the Hebrews, since that would be abhorrent to the Egyptians. 33] As they were seated by his direction, from the oldest in the order of his seniority to the youngest in the order of his youth, the men looked at one another in astonishment. 34] Portions were served them from his table; but Benjamin's portion was several times that of anyone else. And they drank their fill with him.

1] Then he instructed his house steward as follows, "Fill the men's bags with food, as much as they can carry, and put each one's money in the mouth of his bag. 2] Put my silver goblet in the mouth of the bag of the youngest one, together with his money for the rations." And he did as Joseph told him.

3] With the first light of morning, the men were sent off with their pack animals. 4] They had just left the city and had not gone far, when Joseph said to his steward, "Up, go after the

30] *Overcome with feeling.* A pale translation of the Hebrew, which literally says "his innards were burning up."

32] *By himself.* Joseph ate alone, which apparently was befitting his rank [2].

Abhorrent to the Egyptians. The Egyptians disliked eating with strangers. Herodotus once noted that Egyptians despised the Greek habit of using

utensils while eating [3].

33] *In astonishment.* That Joseph had mysteriously seated them exactly in the order of their seniority.

34] *Several times.* Literally, "five times."

They drank their fill. Literally, "they drank and became drunk." This episode ends on a note of conviviality, in sharp contrast to what is to follow.

וְנֶחֱמָרִיהֶם: הֵם יָצְאֽוּ אֶת־הָעִיר לֹא הִרְחִיקוּ וְיוֹסֵף אִישׁ אַמְתַּחְתּֽוֹ: וַֽיְחַפֵּשׂ בַּגָּדוֹל הֵחֵל וּבַקָּטֹן כִּלָּה
אָמַר לַֽאֲשֶׁר עַל־בֵּיתוֹ קוּם רְדֹף אַחֲרֵי הָֽאֲנָשִׁים וַיִּמָּצֵא הַגָּבִיעַ בְּאַמְתַּחַת בִּנְיָמִֽן: וַיִּקְרְעוּ שִׂמְלֹתָם
וְהִשַּׂגְתָּם וְאָֽמַרְתָּ אֲלֵהֶם לָמָּה שִׁלַּמְתֶּם רָעָה תַּחַת וַֽיַּעֲמֹס אִישׁ עַל־חֲמֹרוֹ וַיָּשֻׁבוּ הָעִֽירָה: וַיָּבֹא יְהוּדָה
טוֹבָֽה: הֲלוֹא זֶה אֲשֶׁר יִשְׁתֶּה אֲדֹנִי בּוֹ וְהוּא נַחֵשׁ וְאֶחָיו בֵּיתָה יוֹסֵף וְהוּא עוֹדֶנּוּ שָׁם וַיִּפְּלוּ לְפָנָיו
יְנַחֵשׁ בּוֹ הֲרֵעֹתֶם אֲשֶׁר עֲשִׂיתֶֽם: וַֽיַּשִּׂגֵם וַיְדַבֵּר אֲלֵהֶם אָֽרְצָה: וַיֹּאמֶר לָהֶם יוֹסֵף מָֽה־הַמַּֽעֲשֶׂה הַזֶּה אֲשֶׁר
אֶת־הַדְּבָרִים הָאֵֽלֶּה: וַיֹּאמְרוּ אֵלָיו לָמָּה יְדַבֵּר אֲדֹנִי עֲשִׂיתֶם הֲלוֹא יְדַעְתֶּם כִּֽי־נַחֵשׁ יְנַחֵשׁ אִישׁ אֲשֶׁר
כַּדְּבָרִים הָאֵלֶּה חָלִילָה לַֽעֲבָדֶיךָ מֵֽעֲשׂוֹת כַּדָּבָר כָּמֹֽנִי: וַיֹּאמֶר יְהוּדָה מַה־נֹּאמַר לַֽאדֹנִי מַה־נְּדַבֵּר
הַזֶּֽה: הֵן כֶּסֶף אֲשֶׁר מָצָאנוּ בְּפִי אַמְתְּחֹתֵינוּ הֱשִׁיבֹנוּ וּמַה־נִּצְטַדָּק הָֽאֱלֹהִים מָצָא אֶת־עֲוֹן עֲבָדֶיךָ הִנֶּנּוּ
אֵלֶיךָ מֵאֶרֶץ כְּנָעַן וְאֵיךְ נִגְנֹב מִבֵּית אֲדֹנֶיךָ כֶּסֶף אוֹ עֲבָדִים לַֽאדֹנִי גַּם־אֲנַחְנוּ גַּם אֲשֶׁר־נִמְצָא הַגָּבִיעַ בְּיָדֽוֹ:
זָהָֽב: אֲשֶׁר יִמָּצֵא אִתּוֹ מֵֽעֲבָדֶיךָ וָמֵת וְגַם־אֲנַחְנוּ נִֽהְיֶה וַיֹּאמֶר חָלִילָה לִּי מֵֽעֲשׂוֹת זֹאת הָאִישׁ אֲשֶׁר נִמְצָא
לַֽאדֹנִי לַֽעֲבָדִֽים: וַיֹּאמֶר גַּם־עַתָּה כְדִבְרֵיכֶם כֶּן־הוּא הַגָּבִיעַ בְּיָדוֹ הוּא יִֽהְיֶה־לִּי עָבֶד וְאַתֶּם עֲלוּ לְשָׁלוֹם
אֲשֶׁר יִמָּצֵא אִתּוֹ יִֽהְיֶה־לִּי עָבֶד וְאַתֶּם תִּֽהְיוּ נְקִיִּֽם: אֶל־אֲבִיכֶֽם:
וַֽיְמַהֲרוּ וַיּוֹרִדוּ אִישׁ אֶת־אַמְתַּחְתּוֹ אָרְצָה וַֽיִּפְתְּחוּ

Haftarah Miketz, p. 355

men! And when you overtake them, say to them, 'Why did you repay good with evil? **5]** It is the very one from which my master drinks and which he uses for divination. It was a wicked thing for you to do!'"

6] He overtook them and spoke those words to them. **7]** And they said to him, "Why does my lord say such things? Far be it from your servants to do anything of the kind! **8]** Here we brought back to you from the land of Canaan the money that we found in the mouths of our bags. How then could we have stolen any silver or gold from your master's house! **9]** Whichever of your servants it is found with shall die; the rest of us, moreover, shall become slaves to my lord." **10]** He replied, "Although what you are proposing is right, only the one with whom it is found shall be my slave; but the rest of you shall go free."

11] So each one hastened to lower his bag to the ground, and each one opened his bag. **12]** He searched, beginning with the oldest and ending with the youngest; and the goblet turned up in Benjamin's bag. **13]** At this they rent their clothes. Each reloaded his pack animal, and they returned to the city.

14] When Judah and his brothers re-entered the house of Joseph, who was still there, they threw themselves on the ground before him. **15]** Joseph said to them, "What is this deed that you have done? Do you not know that a man like me practices divination?" **16]** Judah replied, "What can we say to my lord? How can we plead, how can we prove our innocence? God has uncovered the crime of your servants. Here we are, then, slaves of my lord, the rest of us as much as he in whose possession the goblet was found." **17]** But he replied, "Far be it from me to act thus! Only he in whose possession the goblet was found shall be my slave; the rest of you go back in peace to your father."

44:10] *My slave.* The servant speaks for Joseph.

16] *God has uncovered the crime.* They never directly admit Benjamin's guilt, but they accept the whole calamity as somehow being God's will because of the *real* crime, the sale of Joseph [4].

On Divination

Joseph is referred to as one who practices divination, that is to say, one who foretells events by certain external signs, sounds, or movements—here, by the surface motion of wine in a special cup. This practice, called hydromancy by the Greeks, was well known in the ancient Near East, as were numerous other forms of divination. The Bible itself mentions several: the shaking of arrows and the inspection of livers and various forms of astrological prognostication (Ezek. 21:26; Isa. 47:13; Jer. 10:2). Joseph's activity is described as *nachesh*, which may come from the Hebrew word for serpent (*nachash*), which in turn suggests that one of the early forms of divination was to prophesy from the hissing of a snake.

These and other forms of soothsaying came under severe attack from Torah law and the Prophets and were called "abhorrent practices." Deuteronomy warns: "Let no one be found among you who consigns his son or daughter to the fire, or who is an augur, a soothsayer, a diviner, a sorcerer, one who casts spells, or one who consults ghosts or familiar spirits, or who inquires of the dead" (18:10–11). The frequent repetition of these prohibitions bears witness to the continued popularity of such superstitions [5]. The Talmud enumerates a whole series of persistent (and condemned) divining practices:

"Who may be said to be practicing divination? Someone who draws conclusions from events such as these: a piece of food dropped out of his mouth by eating; a cane fell from his hand; a child called him from behind his back; a deer ran across his way; he saw a snake on his right or a fox on his left, and so forth" [6].

While the spread of modern science has reduced many forms of superstition, it has not succeeded in eliminating them entirely. At the root of such practices remains the human desire to know the future and the belief that this foreknowledge must somehow be available to men.

GLEANINGS

Jacob's Dilemma

You may learn from the story of Jacob that it is a man's worst trial to have his children ask him for food when he has nothing to give.

MIDRASH [7]

The Feast

The nagging anxiety which has befallen the brothers before the strange Egyptian prince is now replaced by an equally inexplicable sense of well-being. Meanwhile Joseph—still unknown to the brothers, yet so well-known to the reader—holds the key to the mystery and looks on with delight on the dearest of his guests whom God has led to him.

FRANZ DELITZSCH [8]

Go Back in Peace (Gen. 44:17)

Joseph really says "Go back *toward* peace" (לְשָׁלוֹם) rather than "in peace" (בְּשָׁלוֹם). For to say לְשָׁלוֹם always means to go forward to a peaceful life, while בְּשָׁלוֹם is associated with eternal peace, i.e., death (e.g., Gen. 15:15). [9]

Hence, Joseph's subtlety foretells the happy outcome.

[This is also the meaning of לְשָׁלוֹם in the Sabbath hymn שָׁלוֹם עֲלֵיכֶם.]

A Game

To Joseph had been granted, side by side with stupendous practical abilities, the unanalyzable and fatal gift of personal magnetism. He had that mysterious power to bewitch or to wound, which in contact with others gave him that advantage in the psychic field which a Samson has in the physical. The possession of either kind of strength is of course accompanied by the overwhelming need to make use of it.... He played with individuals. Individuals were to him material for psychic exercise, therefore material for dramatic exploitation and the enhancement of his personality. He was an actor who always had to "upstage" his fellow actors, and he expected them to like it.

MAURICE SAMUEL [10]

Joseph Reveals His Identity

The traditional weekly portion (*sidrah*) takes up the tale at its most dramatic point, Judah's superbly persuasive plea—"the most complete pattern of genuine natural eloquence," as Sir Walter Scott called it. The plea is followed by the long-postponed but finally inevitable climax, the self-disclosure of Joseph. However often we read these thirty-two verses, we are struck by the literary mastery of the text. "We know the outcome, yet we tremble—this is art at its highest" [1].

But more than art is involved. At first in the background and now emerging ever more clearly is the guiding hand of God. The human story has a link with divine purpose. Four times in succession Joseph avers that it was not he but God who brought these events to pass. The promise to Abraham will not be denied: "God has sent me ahead of you to insure your survival on earth, and to save your lives in an extraordinary deliverance" (Gen. 45:7). The tale here foreshadows slavery and exodus; what happens between Joseph and his brothers is therefore an introduction to the story of deliverance that will occupy the second book of the Torah.

The invitation to Jacob's family to settle in Egypt was not without parallel. A thirteenth-century-B.C.E. document records a similar event, probably under the Pharaoh Mernephtah and probably in the region of Goshen: Some Edomite Bedouin were permitted to settle in order "to keep them alive and to keep their cattle alive" [2].

(A new weekly portion, *Vayigash*, begins here.)

כּוֹ וַנֹּאמֶר לֹא נוּכַל לָרֶדֶת אִם־יֵשׁ אָחִינוּ הַקָּטֹן אִתָּנוּ
וְיָרַדְנוּ כִּי־לֹא נוּכַל לִרְאוֹת פְּנֵי הָאִישׁ וְאָחִינוּ
הַקָּטֹן אֵינֶנּוּ אִתָּנוּ: כּוֹ וַיֹּאמֶר עַבְדְּךָ אָבִי אֵלֵינוּ אַתֶּם
יְדַעְתֶּם כִּי שְׁנַיִם יָלְדָה־לִּי אִשְׁתִּי: וַיֵּצֵא הָאֶחָד מֵאִתִּי
וָאֹמַר אַךְ טָרֹף טֹרָף וְלֹא רְאִיתִיו עַד־הֵנָּה: וּלְקַחְתֶּם
גַּם־אֶת־זֶה מֵעִם פָּנַי וְקָרָהוּ אָסוֹן וְהוֹרַדְתֶּם אֶת־
שֵׂיבָתִי בְּרָעָה שְׁאֹלָה: וְעַתָּה כְּבֹאִי אֶל־עַבְדְּךָ אָבִי
וְהַנַּעַר אֵינֶנּוּ אִתָּנוּ וְנַפְשׁוֹ קְשׁוּרָה בְנַפְשׁוֹ: וְהָיָה
כִּרְאוֹתוֹ כִּי־אֵין הַנַּעַר וָמֵת וְהוֹרִידוּ עֲבָדֶיךָ אֶת־
שֵׂיבַת עַבְדְּךָ אָבִינוּ בְּיָגוֹן שְׁאֹלָה: כִּי עַבְדְּךָ עָרַב
אֶת־הַנַּעַר מֵעִם אָבִי לֵאמֹר אִם־לֹא אֲבִיאֶנּוּ אֵלֶיךָ
וְחָטָאתִי לְאָבִי כָּל־הַיָּמִים: וְעַתָּה יֵשֶׁב־נָא עַבְדְּךָ

ס ס ס

יֹח וַיִּגַּשׁ אֵלָיו יְהוּדָה וַיֹּאמֶר בִּי אֲדֹנִי יְדַבֶּר־נָא עַבְדְּךָ
דָבָר בְּאָזְנֵי אֲדֹנִי וְאַל־יִחַר אַפְּךָ בְּעַבְדֶּךָ כִּי כָמוֹךָ
כְּפַרְעֹה: יֹט אֲדֹנִי שָׁאַל אֶת־עֲבָדָיו לֵאמֹר הֲיֵשׁ־לָכֶם
כ אָב אוֹ־אָח: וַנֹּאמֶר אֶל־אֲדֹנִי יֶשׁ־לָנוּ אָב זָקֵן וְיֶלֶד
זְקֻנִים קָטָן וְאָחִיו מֵת וַיִּוָּתֵר הוּא לְבַדּוֹ לְאִמּוֹ וְאָבִיו
כֹּא אֲהֵבוֹ: וַתֹּאמֶר אֶל־עֲבָדֶיךָ הוֹרִדֻהוּ אֵלָי וְאָשִׂימָה
כֹּב עֵינִי עָלָיו: וַנֹּאמֶר אֶל־אֲדֹנִי לֹא־יוּכַל הַנַּעַר לַעֲזֹב
כֹּג אֶת־אָבִיו וְעָזַב אֶת־אָבִיו וָמֵת: וַתֹּאמֶר אֶל־עֲבָדֶיךָ
אִם־לֹא יֵרֵד אֲחִיכֶם הַקָּטֹן אִתְּכֶם לֹא תֹסִפוּן לִרְאוֹת
כֹּד פָּנָי: וַיְהִי כִּי עָלִינוּ אֶל־עַבְדְּךָ אָבִי וַנַּגֶּד־לוֹ אֵת
כֹּה דִּבְרֵי אֲדֹנִי: וַיֹּאמֶר אָבִינוּ שֻׁבוּ שִׁבְרוּ־לָנוּ מְעַט־אֹכֶל:

18] Then Judah went up to him and said, "Please, my lord, let your servant appeal to my lord, and do not be impatient with your servant, you who are the equal of Pharaoh. 19] My lord asked his servants, 'Have you a father or another brother?' 20] We told my lord, 'We have an old father, and there is a child of his old age, the youngest; his full brother is dead, so that he alone is left of his mother, and his father dotes on him.' 21] Then you said to your servants, 'Bring him down to me, that I may set eyes on him.' 22] We said to my lord, 'The boy cannot leave his father; if he were to leave him, his father would die.' 23] But you said to your servants, 'Unless your youngest brother comes down with you, do not let me see your faces.' 24] When we came back to your servant my father, we reported my lord's words to him.

25] "Later our father said, 'Go back and procure some food for us.' 26] We answered, 'We cannot go down; only if our youngest brother is with us can we go down, for we may not show our faces to the man unless our youngest brother is with us.' 27] Your servant my father said to us, 'As you know, my wife bore me two sons. 28] But one is gone from me, and I said: Alas, he was torn by a beast! And I have not seen him since. 29] If you take this one from me, too, and he meets with disaster, you will send my white head down to Sheol in grief.'

30] "Now, if I come to your servant my father and the boy is not with us—since his own life is so bound up with his— 31] when he sees that the boy is not with us, he will die, and your servants will send the white head of your servant our father down to Sheol in grief. 32] Now your servant has pledged himself for the boy to my father, saying, 'If I do not bring him back to you, I shall stand guilty before my father forever.' 33] Therefore, please let your servant

44:20] *Dead.* From their father's point of view.
26] *Show our faces to the man.* Literally, "see the man's face."

28] *Torn by a beast.* Joseph now learns what his

fate is said to have been. Judah's obvious and touching concern for Benjamin and Jacob prepares Joseph for his own disclosure.

ה וְעַתָּה אַל־תֵּעָצְבוּ וְאַל־יִחַר בְּעֵינֵיכֶם כִּי־מְכַרְתֶּם
ו אֹתִי הֵנָּה כִּי לְמִחְיָה שְׁלָחַנִי אֱלֹהִים לִפְנֵיכֶם: כִּי־זֶה
שְׁנָתַיִם הָרָעָב בְּקֶרֶב הָאָרֶץ וְעוֹד חָמֵשׁ שָׁנִים אֲשֶׁר
ז אֵין־חָרִישׁ וְקָצִיר: וַיִּשְׁלָחֵנִי אֱלֹהִים לִפְנֵיכֶם לָשׂוּם
לָכֶם שְׁאֵרִית בָּאָרֶץ וּלְהַחֲיוֹת לָכֶם לִפְלֵיטָה גְּדֹלָה:
ח וְעַתָּה לֹא־אַתֶּם שְׁלַחְתֶּם אֹתִי הֵנָּה כִּי הָאֱלֹהִים
וַיְשִׂימֵנִי לְאָב לְפַרְעֹה וּלְאָדוֹן לְכָל־בֵּיתוֹ וּמֹשֵׁל
ט בְּכָל־אֶרֶץ מִצְרָיִם: מַהֲרוּ וַעֲלוּ אֶל־אָבִי וַאֲמַרְתֶּם
אֵלָיו כֹּה אָמַר בִּנְךָ יוֹסֵף שָׂמַנִי אֱלֹהִים לְאָדוֹן
לְכָל־מִצְרָיִם רְדָה אֵלַי אַל־תַּעֲמֹד: וְיָשַׁבְתָּ בְאֶרֶץ־

לד תַּחַת הַנַּעַר עֶבֶד לַאדֹנִי וְהַנַּעַר יַעַל עִם־אֶחָיו: כִּי־
אֵיךְ אֶעֱלֶה אֶל־אָבִי וְהַנַּעַר אֵינֶנּוּ אִתִּי פֶּן אֶרְאֶה
בָרָע אֲשֶׁר יִמְצָא אֶת־אָבִי:
א וְלֹא־יָכֹל יוֹסֵף לְהִתְאַפֵּק לְכֹל הַנִּצָּבִים עָלָיו וַיִּקְרָא
הוֹצִיאוּ כָל־אִישׁ מֵעָלָי וְלֹא־עָמַד אִישׁ אִתּוֹ בְּהִתְוַדַּע
ב יוֹסֵף אֶל־אֶחָיו: וַיִּתֵּן אֶת־קֹלוֹ בִּבְכִי וַיִּשְׁמְעוּ מִצְרַיִם
ג וַיִּשְׁמַע בֵּית פַּרְעֹה: וַיֹּאמֶר יוֹסֵף אֶל־אֶחָיו אֲנִי יוֹסֵף
הַעוֹד אָבִי חָי וְלֹא־יָכְלוּ אֶחָיו לַעֲנוֹת אֹתוֹ כִּי נִבְהֲלוּ
ד מִפָּנָיו: וַיֹּאמֶר יוֹסֵף אֶל־אֶחָיו גְּשׁוּ־נָא אֵלַי וַיִּגָּשׁוּ
וַיֹּאמֶר אֲנִי יוֹסֵף אֲחִיכֶם אֲשֶׁר־מְכַרְתֶּם אֹתִי מִצְרָיְמָה:

remain as a slave to my lord instead of the boy, and let the boy go back with his brothers.
34] For how can I go back to my father unless the boy is with me? Let me not be witness to the
woe that would overtake my father!"

1] Joseph could no longer control himself before all his attendants, and he cried out, "Have
everyone withdraw from me!" So there was no one else about when Joseph made himself
known to his brothers.   **2]** His sobs were so loud that the Egyptians could hear, and so the
news reached Pharaoh's palace.

3] Joseph said to his brothers, "I am Joseph. Is my father still well?" But his brothers could
not answer him, so dumfounded were they on account of him.

4] Then Joseph said to his brothers, "Come forward to me." And when they came forward,
he said, "I am your brother Joseph, he whom you sold into Egypt.   **5]** Now, do not be
distressed or reproach yourselves because you sold me hither; it was to save life that God sent
me ahead of you.   **6]** It is now two years that there has been famine in the land, and there are
still five years to come in which there shall be no yield from tilling.   **7]** God has sent me ahead
of you to insure your survival on earth, and to save your lives in an extraordinary deliverance.
8] So, it was not you who sent me here, but God; and He has made me a father to Pharaoh, lord
of all his household, and ruler over the whole land of Egypt.

9] "Now, hurry back to my father and say to him: Thus says your son Joseph, 'God has made
me lord of all Egypt; come down to me without delay.   **10]** You will dwell in the region of
Goshen, where you will be near me—you and your children and your grandchildren, your

33] *Let the boy go back.* This offer marks Judah as a
man of exceptional character. He speaks for himself and also for his brothers; he speaks in accents
of love and not of sibling hatred.

45:1] *Have everyone withdraw.* The revelation will
be made in private; Joseph will not shame his
brothers [3].

3] *Is my father still well?* Or "Is he *really* alive?"
(see Gen. 43:27).

8] *Father to Pharaoh.* That is, vizier. This and the
two subsequent descriptions are translations of
official Egyptian titles. Joseph speaks to his brothers in his native tongue without the help of interpreters.

10] *Goshen.* The area of Wadi Tumilat, in the
eastern Nile delta, between today's Port Said and
Suez. It was a region, not a specific place in Egypt.

גֹּשֶׁן וְהָיִיתָ קָרוֹב אֵלַי אַתָּה וּבָנֶיךָ וּבְנֵי בָנֶיךָ וְצֹאנְךָ
בְּמִצְרַיִם וְאֵת כָּל־אֲשֶׁר רְאִיתֶם וּמִהַרְתֶּם וְהוֹרַדְתֶּם
יא וּבְקָרְךָ וְכָל־אֲשֶׁר־לָךְ: וְכִלְכַּלְתִּי אֹתְךָ שָׁם כִּי־עוֹד
אֶת־אָבִי הֵנָּה: וַיִּפֹּל עַל־צַוְּארֵי בִנְיָמִן־אָחִיו וַיֵּבְךְּ
חָמֵשׁ שָׁנִים רָעָב פֶּן־תִּוָּרֵשׁ אַתָּה וּבֵיתְךָ וְכָל־אֲשֶׁר־
טו וּבִנְיָמִן בָּכָה עַל־צַוָּארָיו: וַיְנַשֵּׁק לְכָל־אֶחָיו וַיֵּבְךְּ
לָךְ: וְהִנֵּה עֵינֵיכֶם רֹאוֹת וְעֵינֵי אָחִי בִנְיָמִין כִּי־פִי
עֲלֵהֶם וְאַחֲרֵי כֵן דִּבְּרוּ אֶחָיו אִתּוֹ:
יג הַמְדַבֵּר אֲלֵיכֶם: וְהִגַּדְתֶּם לְאָבִי אֶת־כָּל־כְּבוֹדִי

flocks and herds, and all that is yours.   11] There I will provide for you—for there are yet five years of famine to come—that you and your household and all that is yours may not suffer want.'   12] You can see for yourselves, and my brother Benjamin for himself, that it is indeed I who am speaking to you.   13] And you must tell my father everything about my high station in Egypt and all that you have seen; and bring my father here with all speed."

14] With that he embraced his brother Benjamin around the neck and wept, and Benjamin wept on his neck.   15] He kissed all his brothers and wept upon them; only then were his brothers able to talk to him.

12] *It is indeed I who am speaking.* Perhaps inferring that his use of Hebrew was additional
proof of his identity [4].   14] *Embraced.* Literally, "fell on."

283

A Test

The Midrash and many subsequent commentaries have dwelt on the theme of testing that underlies the story. Joseph first faces his brothers in bitterness and devises a cat-and-mouse game in order to have his revenge, but in the end, having worked out his own feelings toward his father and brothers, he is ready for reconciliation [5]. However, before this can take place, the brothers, too, must be ready, and Joseph wants to make certain that the new brotherly relationship will be mutual. Thus, the elaborate device of deception and delay that serves to heighten the suspense provides at the same time a sound motivational framework for the story. When the brothers' affection for each other and for their father becomes evident, when they hint that now they consider their sale of Joseph a crime, and when finally Judah offers himself as a slave to save Benjamin, the scales are balanced and Joseph can speak as the brother.[1] The test is over, for him as well as for them [7].

Yet more than human testing is at stake, more than revenge and repentance. The delays Joseph introduces strengthen not only his conviction about the changes in his brothers' attitude but also his conviction about God's incessant watchfulness over the seed of Abraham. Joseph believes that he is a tool of destiny, that as a child of his father he partakes of the heritage and the promise. When events single him out as a key factor in the covenant and everything begins to point to the validity of the promise, he becomes humble and thereby underscores his fitness as God's chosen servant. The heritage and its bearers had been in danger, but God has turned impending calamity into salvation. In Genesis this thread of rescue-and-deliverance becomes visible in the stories of Noah, Lot, Sarah, and Rebekah. Now, in the Joseph tale, the ground is laid for transferring the theme from the individual onto the nation.

---

[1] The expression וְעַתָּה in Gen. 45:5 is said always to refer to repentance [6].

Judah

The word וַיִּגַּשׁ [went up], which opens the section [Gen. 44:18], occurs as an introduction to three different kinds of action: to do battle [II Sam. 10:13], to conciliate [Josh. 14:6], to pray [I Kings 18:36]. The three are strangely related: Men are usually ready for any one of the three. So was Judah when he "went up."   MIDRASH [8]

וַיִּגַּשׁ יְהוּדָה can also be translated: "Then Judah drew near." To whom? To himself, for only when Judah became himself at his best was he able to speak as he did.   CHASIDIC [9]

At first Judah spoke softly and humbly, for he remembered his own crime against Joseph. But when punishment was to fall on the innocent Benjamin, Judah dropped all caution and spoke angrily and so loudly that his voice resounded throughout Egypt.   MIDRASH [10]

I Am Your Brother Joseph (Gen. 45:4)

These were the words with which, in October 1960, Pope John XXIII greeted a group of 130 Jewish leaders—Joseph being his baptismal name.

Jewish Survival

The story of the children of Israel had hardly begun, and already survival was the issue (Gen. 45:7). It was to remain the issue in Egypt and the desert, in Canaan and Palestine, Diaspora and return. This is the way Jewish history was shaped from its inception, and from Joseph's day down to modern times the children of Israel have looked into the abyss and, later, experienced the "extraordinary deliverance."

The Plea

[The following is the beginning of a long oration, hortatory in tone, put by Flavius Josephus into the mouth of Judah.]

But Judah who had persuaded their father to send the lad from him, being otherwise also a very bold and active man, determined to hazard himself for the preservation of his brother. "It is true," said he, "O governor, that we have been very wicked with regard to thee and, on that account, deserve punishment; even all of us may justly be punished, although the theft were not committed by all but only by one of us, and he the youngest also: but yet there remains some hope for us who otherwise must be under despair on his account, and this from thy goodness which promises us a deliverance out of our present danger. And now I beg thou wilt not look at us, or at that great crime we have been guilty of, but at thy own excellent nature and take advice of thine own virtue, instead of that wrath thou hast against us; which passion those that otherwise are of lower character indulge as they do their strength, and that not only on great but also on very trifling occasions. Overcome, Sir, that passion and be not subdued by it."

                   JOSEPHUS [11]

Jacob Goes to Egypt

After Joseph's emotion-filled disclosure the narrative resumes a leisurely pace. The text turns to the last act of the drama—Jacob's descent into Egypt, the reunion, and the deaths of Jacob and Joseph. The aged father learns that his son is still alive and elaborate preparations are made for the journey to Canaan. It is a moving scene described with the fewest of words.

The Egyptian sojourn begins with a vision, the last to be recounted in Genesis and in many ways one of the most important, for it speaks of God's part in exile and exodus.

טו וְהַקֹּל נִשְׁמַע בֵּית פַּרְעֹה לֵאמֹר בָּאוּ אֲחֵי יוֹסֵף וַיִּיטַב

טז לַדָּרֶךְ: לְכֻלָּם נָתַן לָאִישׁ חֲלִפוֹת שְׂמָלֹת וּלְבִנְיָמִן

בְּעֵינֵי פַרְעֹה וּבְעֵינֵי עֲבָדָיו: וַיֹּאמֶר פַּרְעֹה אֶל־יוֹסֵף

יז נָתַן שְׁלֹשׁ מֵאוֹת כֶּסֶף וְחָמֵשׁ חֲלִפֹת שְׂמָלֹת: וּלְאָבִיו

אֱמֹר אֶל־אַחֶיךָ זֹאת עֲשׂוּ טַעֲנוּ אֶת־בְּעִירְכֶם וּלְכוּ־

יח שָׁלַח כְּזֹאת עֲשָׂרָה חֲמֹרִים נֹשְׂאִים מִטּוּב מִצְרָיִם

בֹאוּ אַרְצָה כְּנָעַן: וּקְחוּ אֶת־אֲבִיכֶם וְאֶת־בָּתֵּיכֶם וּבֹאוּ

וְעֶשֶׂר אֲתֹנֹת נֹשְׂאֹת בָּר וָלֶחֶם וּמָזוֹן לְאָבִיו לַדָּרֶךְ:

אֵלָי וְאֶתְּנָה לָכֶם אֶת־טוּב אֶרֶץ מִצְרַיִם וְאִכְלוּ אֶת־

יט וַיְשַׁלַּח אֶת־אֶחָיו וַיֵּלֵכוּ וַיֹּאמֶר אֲלֵהֶם אַל־תִּרְגְּזוּ

חֵלֶב הָאָרֶץ: וְאַתָּה צֻוֵּיתָה זֹאת עֲשׂוּ קְחוּ־לָכֶם מֵאֶרֶץ

כ בַּדָּרֶךְ: וַיַּעֲלוּ מִמִּצְרָיִם וַיָּבֹאוּ אֶרֶץ כְּנַעַן אֶל־יַעֲקֹב

מִצְרַיִם עֲגָלוֹת לְטַפְּכֶם וְלִנְשֵׁיכֶם וּנְשָׂאתֶם אֶת־אֲבִיכֶם

כא אֲבִיהֶם: וַיַּגִּדוּ לוֹ לֵאמֹר עוֹד יוֹסֵף חַי וְכִי־הוּא

וּבָאתֶם: וְעֵינְכֶם אַל־תָּחֹס עַל־כְּלֵיכֶם כִּי־טוּב כָּל־

מֹשֵׁל בְּכָל־אֶרֶץ מִצְרָיִם וַיָּפָג לִבּוֹ כִּי לֹא־הֶאֱמִין

אֶרֶץ מִצְרַיִם לָכֶם הוּא: וַיַּעֲשׂוּ־כֵן בְּנֵי יִשְׂרָאֵל וַיִּתֵּן

לָהֶם: וַיְדַבְּרוּ אֵלָיו אֵת כָּל־דִּבְרֵי יוֹסֵף אֲשֶׁר דִּבֶּר

לָהֶם יוֹסֵף עֲגָלוֹת עַל־פִּי פַרְעֹה וַיִּתֵּן לָהֶם צֵדָה

אֲלֵהֶם וַיַּרְא אֶת־הָעֲגָלוֹת אֲשֶׁר־שָׁלַח יוֹסֵף לָשֵׂאת

16] The news reached Pharaoh's palace: "Joseph's brothers have come." Pharaoh and his courtiers were pleased. **17]** And Pharaoh said to Joseph, "Say to your brothers, 'Do as follows: load up your beasts and go at once to the land of Canaan. **18]** Take your father and your households and come to me; I will give you the best of the land of Egypt and you shall live off the fat of the land.' **19]** And you are bidden [to add], 'Do as follows: take from the land of Egypt wagons for your children and your wives, and bring your father here. **20]** And never mind your belongings, for the best of all the land of Egypt shall be yours.'"

21] The sons of Israel did so; Joseph gave them wagons as Pharaoh had commanded, and he supplied them with provisions for the journey. **22]** To each of them, moreover, he gave a change of clothing; but to Benjamin he gave three hundred pieces of silver and several changes of clothing. **23]** And to his father he sent the following: ten he-asses laden with the best things of Egypt, and ten she-asses laden with grain, bread, and provisions for his father on the journey. **24]** As he sent his brothers off on their way, he told them, "Do not be quarrelsome on the way."

25] They went up from Egypt and came to their father Jacob in the land of Canaan. **26]** And they told him, "Joseph is still alive; yes, he is ruler over the whole land of Egypt." His heart went numb, for he did not believe them. **27]** But when they recounted all that Joseph had said to them, and when he saw the wagons that Joseph had sent to transport him, the spirit

45:16] *Were pleased.* A simple statement showing how highly Joseph was esteemed. Yet some generations later his contribution was no longer remembered (Exod. 1:8).

17] *And Pharaoh said.* Pharaoh now officially confirms the invitation Joseph has already extended. It is to his advantage to have his vizier's family settle in Egypt; he will make Joseph a permanent resident [1].

19] [*To add*]. Septuagint and Vulgate supply these words, which do not appear in the Hebrew text.

22] *Three hundred.* Also used as a round number [2]. Should be understood as "a large sum."

Several. Literally, "five" (see Gen. 43:34).

24] *Do not be quarrelsome.* Joseph realizes his brothers will have to tell Jacob the full story of the sale. He cautions them not to blame one another [3].

/ Another interpretation: "Don't be afraid of robbers" (seeing you carry such wealth, for God will protect you) [4]./

27] *When they recounted.* The text is gently silent about what they said and also about the way in which they made a clean breast of their past sins [5].

כג אֹתוֹ וַתְּחִי רוּחַ יַעֲקֹב אֲבִיהֶם: וַיֹּאמֶר יִשְׂרָאֵל רַב
עוֹד־יוֹסֵף בְּנִי חָי אֵלְכָה וְאֶרְאֶנּוּ בְּטֶרֶם אָמוּת:

א וַיִּסַּע יִשְׂרָאֵל וְכָל־אֲשֶׁר־לוֹ וַיָּבֹא בְּאֵרָה שָּׁבַע וַיִּזְבַּח
זְבָחִים לֵאלֹהֵי אָבִיו יִצְחָק: וַיֹּאמֶר אֱלֹהִים לְיִשְׂרָאֵל

ב בְּמַרְאֹת הַלַּיְלָה וַיֹּאמֶר יַעֲקֹב יַעֲקֹב וַיֹּאמֶר הִנֵּנִי:

ג וַיֹּאמֶר אָנֹכִי הָאֵל אֱלֹהֵי אָבִיךָ אַל־תִּירָא מֵרְדָה

ד מִצְרַיְמָה כִּי־לְגוֹי גָּדוֹל אֲשִׂימְךָ שָׁם: אָנֹכִי אֵרֵד עִמְּךָ
מִצְרַיְמָה וְאָנֹכִי אַעַלְךָ גַם־עָלֹה וְיוֹסֵף יָשִׁית יָדוֹ

ה עַל־עֵינֶיךָ: וַיָּקָם יַעֲקֹב מִבְּאֵר שָׁבַע וַיִּשְׂאוּ בְנֵי־
יִשְׂרָאֵל אֶת־יַעֲקֹב אֲבִיהֶם וְאֶת־טַפָּם וְאֶת־נְשֵׁיהֶם

ו בָּעֲגָלוֹת אֲשֶׁר־שָׁלַח פַּרְעֹה לָשֵׂאת אֹתוֹ: וַיִּקְחוּ אֶת־
מִקְנֵיהֶם וְאֶת־רְכוּשָׁם אֲשֶׁר רָכְשׁוּ בְּאֶרֶץ כְּנַעַן וַיָּבֹאוּ

ז מִצְרַיְמָה יַעֲקֹב וְכָל־זַרְעוֹ אִתּוֹ: בָּנָיו וּבְנֵי בָנָיו אִתּוֹ
בְּנֹתָיו וּבְנוֹת בָּנָיו וְכָל־זַרְעוֹ הֵבִיא אִתּוֹ מִצְרָיְמָה: ס

ח וְאֵלֶּה שְׁמוֹת בְּנֵי־יִשְׂרָאֵל הַבָּאִים מִצְרַיְמָה יַעֲקֹב

ט וּבָנָיו בְּכֹר יַעֲקֹב רְאוּבֵן: וּבְנֵי רְאוּבֵן חֲנוֹךְ וּפַלּוּא
וְחֶצְרֹן וְכַרְמִי: וּבְנֵי שִׁמְעוֹן יְמוּאֵל וְיָמִין וְאֹהַד וְיָכִין

יא וְצֹחַר וְשָׁאוּל בֶּן־הַכְּנַעֲנִית: וּבְנֵי לֵוִי גֵּרְשׁוֹן קְהָת

יב וּמְרָרִי: וּבְנֵי יְהוּדָה עֵר וְאוֹנָן וְשֵׁלָה וָפֶרֶץ וָזָרַח
וַיָּמָת עֵר וְאוֹנָן בְּאֶרֶץ כְּנַעַן וַיִּהְיוּ בְנֵי־פֶרֶץ חֶצְרֹן

of their father Jacob revived.   28] "Enough!" said Israel. "My son Joseph is still alive! I must go and see him before I die."

1] So Israel set out with all that was his, and he came to Beer-sheba, where he offered sacrifices to the God of his father Isaac.   2] God called to Israel in a vision by night: "Jacob! Jacob!" He answered, "Here."   3] And He said, "I am God, the God of your father. Fear not to go down to Egypt, for I will make you there into a great nation.   4] I Myself will go down with you to Egypt, and I Myself will also bring you back; and Joseph's hand shall close your eyes."

5] So Jacob set out from Beer-sheba. The sons of Israel put their father Jacob and their children and their wives in the wagons which Pharaoh had sent to transport them;   6] and they took along their livestock and the wealth that they had amassed in the land of Canaan. Thus Jacob and all his offspring with him came to Egypt: 7] he brought with him to Egypt his sons and grandsons, his daughters and granddaughters—all his offspring.

8] These are the names of the Israelites, Jacob and his descendants, who came to Egypt. Jacob's first-born Reuben;   9] Reuben's sons: Enoch, Pallu, Hezron, and Carmi.   10] Simeon's sons: Jemuel, Jamin, Ohad, Jachin, Zohar, and Saul the son of a Canaanite woman.   11] Levi's sons: Gershon, Kohath, and Merari.   12] Judah's sons: Er, Onan, Shelah, Perez, and Zerah—but Er and Onan had died in the land of Canaan; and Perez's sons were Hezron and

---

46:1] *He came to Beer-sheba.* Probably from Hebron.

2] *Israel.* He is called Israel in his response though he remains Jacob. The fusion of past and present is complete [6] (see Gen. 35:10 and commentary to Gen. 32:4–33:17).

4] *Bring you back.* That is, your descendants.

Joseph's hand shall close your eyes. Jewish tradition [7] demands that the eyes of the deceased be closed, preferably, by a son.

/ Others render the biblical text figuratively: "He will take care of you" [8]./

8–27] The list of descendants is probably from another tradition; its insertion here creates some difficulties and discrepancies; e.g., that Perez and Benjamin are reported to have children, although they are too young to be fathers.

9] *Enoch.* The usual English rendering of חֲנוֹךְ.

10] *Jemuel.* Called Nemuel in Num. 26:12; I Chron. 4:24.

Saul. The usual English rendering of שָׁאוּל.

כ רָחֵל אֵשֶׁת יַעֲקֹב יוֹסֵף וּבִנְיָמִן: וַיִּוָּלֵד לְיוֹסֵף בְּאֶרֶץ
מִצְרַיִם אֲשֶׁר יָלְדָה־לּוֹ אָסְנַת בַּת־פּוֹטִי פֶרַע כֹּהֵן
כא אֹן אֶת־מְנַשֶּׁה וְאֶת־אֶפְרָיִם: וּבְנֵי בִנְיָמִן בֶּלַע וָבֶכֶר
וְאַשְׁבֵּל גֵּרָא וְנַעֲמָן אֵחִי וָרֹאשׁ מֻפִּים וְחֻפִּים וָאָרְדְּ:
כב אֵלֶּה בְּנֵי רָחֵל אֲשֶׁר יֻלַּד לְיַעֲקֹב כָּל־נֶפֶשׁ אַרְבָּעָה
כג עָשָׂר: וּבְנֵי־דָן חֻשִׁים: וּבְנֵי נַפְתָּלִי יַחְצְאֵל וְגוּנִי וְיֵצֶר
כד וְשִׁלֵּם: אֵלֶּה בְּנֵי בִלְהָה אֲשֶׁר־נָתַן לָבָן לְרָחֵל בִּתּוֹ
כה וַתֵּלֶד אֶת־אֵלֶּה לְיַעֲקֹב כָּל־נֶפֶשׁ שִׁבְעָה: כָּל־הַנֶּפֶשׁ

י וְחָמוּל: וּבְנֵי יִשָּׂשכָר תּוֹלָע וּפֻוָּה וְיוֹב וְשִׁמְרֹן:
יד וּבְנֵי זְבוּלֻן סֶרֶד וְאֵלוֹן וְיַחְלְאֵל: אֵלֶּה בְּנֵי לֵאָה אֲשֶׁר
יָלְדָה לְיַעֲקֹב בְּפַדַּן אֲרָם וְאֵת דִּינָה בִתּוֹ כָּל־נֶפֶשׁ
טו בָּנָיו וּבְנוֹתָיו שְׁלֹשִׁים וְשָׁלֹשׁ: וּבְנֵי גָד צִפְיוֹן וְחַגִּי שׁוּנִי
טז וְאֶצְבֹּן עֵרִי וַאֲרוֹדִי וְאַרְאֵלִי: וּבְנֵי אָשֵׁר יִמְנָה וְיִשְׁוָה
וְיִשְׁוִי וּבְרִיעָה וְשֶׂרַח אֲחֹתָם וּבְנֵי בְרִיעָה חֶבֶר
יז וּמַלְכִּיאֵל: אֵלֶּה בְּנֵי זִלְפָּה אֲשֶׁר־נָתַן לָבָן לְלֵאָה
יח בִּתּוֹ וַתֵּלֶד אֶת־אֵלֶּה לְיַעֲקֹב שֵׁשׁ עֶשְׂרֵה נָפֶשׁ: בְּנֵי

Hamul.   **13]** Issachar's sons: Tola, Puvah, Iob, and Shimron.   **14]** Zebulun's sons: Sered, Elon, and Jahleel.   **15]** Those were the sons whom Leah bore to Jacob in Paddan-aram, in addition to his daughter Dinah. Persons in all, male and female: 33.

16] Gad's sons: Ziphion, Haggi, Shuni, Ezbon, Eri, Arodi, and Areli.   **17]** Asher's sons: Imnah, Ishvah, Ishvi, and Beriah, and their sister Serah. Beriah's sons: Heber and Malchiel. **18]** These were the descendants of Zilpah, whom Laban had given to his daughter Leah. These she bore to Jacob—16 persons.

19] The sons of Jacob's wife Rachel were Joseph and Benjamin.   **20]** To Joseph were born in the land of Egypt Manasseh and Ephraim, whom Asenath daughter of Poti-phera priest of On bore to him.   **21]** Benjamin's sons: Bela, Becher, Ashbel, Gera, Naaman, Ehi, Rosh, Muppim, Huppim, and Ard.   **22]** These were the descendants of Rachel, who were born to Jacob—14 persons in all.

23] Dan's son: Hushim.   **24]** Naphtali's sons: Jahzeel, Guni, Jezer, and Shillem.   **25]** These were the descendants of Bilhah, whom Laban had given to his daughter Rachel. These she bore to Jacob—7 persons in all.

26] All the persons belonging to Jacob who came to Egypt—his own issue, aside from the

13] *Iob.* Called Jashub in Num. 26:24 and several ancient versions.

15] *Persons in all ... 33.* Including Jacob [9].

17] *Their sister Serah.* The insertion of her name in an all-male list gave rise to many midrashic speculations, especially that Serah was the one who first told Jacob of Joseph's survival [10].

19] *Jacob's wife Rachel.* The favorite one. Leah is simply called by name.

21] *Benjamin's sons.* Benjamin here has ten sons; in Num. 26:38–40, only five. The Septuagint gives him three and also grandchildren; further differences (suggesting different traditions) appear in I Chron. 8:1–5.

23] *Dan's son.* In Hebrew "sons," a formulaic plural [11].

26] *All the persons.* Here exclusive of Jacob, Joseph, and his two sons.

הַבָּאָה לְיַעֲקֹב מִצְרַיְמָה יֹצְאֵי יְרֵכוֹ מִלְבַד נְשֵׁי   יֻלַּד־לוֹ בְמִצְרַיִם נֶפֶשׁ שְׁנָיִם כָּל־הַנֶּפֶשׁ לְבֵית־יַעֲקֹב
כי בְנֵי־יַעֲקֹב כָּל־נֶפֶשׁ שִׁשִּׁים וָשֵׁשׁ: וּבְנֵי יוֹסֵף אֲשֶׁר־   הַבָּאָה מִצְרַיְמָה שִׁבְעִים: ס

wives of Jacob's sons—all these persons numbered 66.   **27]** And Joseph's sons who were born to him in Egypt were two in number. Thus the total of Jacob's household who came to Egypt was 70 persons.

27] *Total . . . 70 persons.* The entire family, here including Jacob and Joseph. The belabored method of counting represents an attempt to reconcile varying traditions [12]. It is also possible that "seventy" represented a round or "good" number as with Gideon's seventy sons (Judg. 8:30).

A Paradox

Quite obviously the biblical authors believed that God willed Jacob's descent into Egypt. They envisioned Him saying, "I Myself will go down with you to Egypt, and I Myself will also bring you back" (Gen. 46:4). Yet the Rabbis pictured Jacob pondering whether to remain in Canaan or to settle in Egypt. Had God not expressly forbidden Isaac to go there? And had Abraham not encountered grave dangers in Egypt? Should he, Jacob, now be the one to forsake the Promised Land? The Midrash says that he finally decided to leave because the decision was God's and not his [13].

The Torah appears to explain the foundations of Israel's existence through this interplay of divine plan and human decision. It shows God knowingly sending His children into Egypt and into subsequent oppression. Had not Abraham already been informed: "Know well that your offspring shall be strangers in a land not theirs, and they shall be enslaved and oppressed four hundred years" (Gen. 15:13).

The biblical authors offer no explanation why this should have been so. We may infer, however, that in their view God *had* to do what the human situation required; in Canaan the people of Israel could not or would not become what they were destined to be. In Canaan lurked the dangers of intermingling and absorption; in Goshen there would be isolation and segregation, both of which would provide fertile soil for the development of particular national characteristics [14]. If oppression, too, would be part of the experience, this would be the price the people-to-be would have to pay.

We meet here a paradox intrinsic in the biblical view of God's relation to Israel. He loves His people, yet they undergo deep suffering. God guards Israel, yet their freedom to act limits God's own domination of the future. Biblical man accepted this paradox as inevitable, for logic could not resolve the inaccessibility of God's ultimate nature (see commentary to Gen. 4:1–26).[1] Nowhere is this paradox of God's relationship to Israel better portrayed than in the old saying that God was exiled with His people and that as they wept He wept with them [16].[2]

---

[1] Note Rabbi Akiba's saying: "All is foreseen, yet freedom is given" [15].

[2] The Zohar compares God with Rachel in that both weep for their children [17]. Note also the rabbinic concept of "chastisements of divine love" (יִסּוּרִין שֶׁל אַהֲבָה) [18].

GLEANINGS

The News Reached Pharaoh's Palace (Gen. 45:16)

The word for news, קל [literally, "voice"], is written without the usual ו, that is, in a constricted fashion. For it is the voice that is small which is often heard more than any other. This also teaches us to pray silently, for God hears the prayer of the heart.　　　ZOHAR [19]

Pharaoh Was Pleased

Why? He was pleased to learn that Joseph after all had fine family connections.

　　　MIDRASH [20]

Full Circle

The gift of clothing and the preference shown to Benjamin are Joseph's subtle hint that the old quarrel over the ornamented tunic is shown to have been futile.　　　TOLEDOT YITZCHAK

Jacob Did Not Believe Them

When the brothers lied and told him Joseph was dead he believed them; when they spoke the truth and said that Joseph was alive he disbelieved them. This is the punishment of liars: even when they speak the truth they are not believed.

　　　MIDRASH [21]

Exile

Jacob's descent into Egypt was Israel's first Diaspora.　　　MIDRASH [22]

Jacob Hears the News

But when they arrived at home, and told their father their story about their brother, which was so apparently incredible and beyond all his hopes, he did not much believe them; for even though those who brought the account were trustworthy, still the greatness and extraordinary character of the circumstances which they reported did not allow him to believe them easily: but when the old man saw the vast preparation, and the supplies of all necessary things, at such a time, in such abundance, corresponding to the good fortune of his son which they were reporting to him, he praised God that he had made complete that part of his house which seemed to be deficient; but his joy immediately begat fear again in his soul, respecting his departure from his national laws and customs; for he knew that youth is by nature prone to fall and that in foreign nations there is great indulgence given to error and especially in the country of Egypt, a land in a state of utter blindness respecting the true God, in consequence of their making created and mortal things into gods.

Moreover, the addition of riches and glory is a snare to weak minds, and he also recollected that he had been left to himself, as no one had gone forth out of his father's house with him to keep him in the right way, but he had been left solitary and destitute of all good instructions and might therefore be supposed to be ready to change and adopt their foreign customs. Therefore, when that Being, who alone is able to behold the invisible soul, saw him in this frame of mind, he took pity on him and, appearing unto him by night while he was lying asleep, said unto him: "Fear nothing about your departure into Egypt; I myself will guide you on your way and will give you a safe and pleasant journey; and I will restore to you your long lamented son, who was once many years ago believed by you to have died but who is not only alive but is even governor of all that mighty country."　　　PHILO [23]

Jacob in Egypt

Jacob and Joseph meet at last. The Bible describes the fateful moment in very few words, leaving much to the reader's imagination. Next, Pharaoh is introduced to Joseph's family, and while here, too, the text understates the situation the recorded words are extremely revealing.

We learn about the effects of the famine and, so it seems to many, the morally puzzling aspects of Joseph's economic and political management. Israel now dwells in Goshen, and a new chapter in his people's history is about to begin.

וְאֶת־יְהוּדָה שָׁלַח
לְפָנָיו אֶל־יוֹסֵף לְהוֹרֹת לְפָנָיו גֹּשְׁנָה וַיָּבֹאוּ אַרְצָה
גֹּשֶׁן: וַיֶּאְסֹר יוֹסֵף מֶרְכַּבְתּוֹ וַיַּעַל לִקְרַאת־יִשְׂרָאֵל
אָבִיו גֹּשְׁנָה וַיֵּרָא אֵלָיו וַיִּפֹּל עַל־צַוָּארָיו וַיֵּבְךְּ עַל־
צַוָּארָיו עוֹד: וַיֹּאמֶר יִשְׂרָאֵל אֶל־יוֹסֵף אָמוּתָה הַפָּעַם
אַחֲרֵי רְאוֹתִי אֶת־פָּנֶיךָ כִּי עוֹדְךָ חָי: וַיֹּאמֶר יוֹסֵף
אֶל־אֶחָיו וְאֶל־בֵּית אָבִיו אֶעֱלֶה וְאַגִּידָה לְפַרְעֹה
וְאֹמְרָה אֵלָיו אַחַי וּבֵית־אָבִי אֲשֶׁר בְּאֶרֶץ־כְּנַעַן בָּאוּ
אֵלָי: וְהָאֲנָשִׁים רֹעֵי צֹאן כִּי־אַנְשֵׁי מִקְנֶה הָיוּ וְצֹאנָם
וּבְקָרָם וְכָל־אֲשֶׁר לָהֶם הֵבִיאוּ: וְהָיָה כִּי־יִקְרָא לָכֶם

פַּרְעֹה וְאָמַר מַה־מַּעֲשֵׂיכֶם: וַאֲמַרְתֶּם אַנְשֵׁי מִקְנֶה
הָיוּ עֲבָדֶיךָ מִנְּעוּרֵינוּ וְעַד־עַתָּה גַּם־אֲנַחְנוּ גַּם־אֲבֹתֵינוּ
בַּעֲבוּר תֵּשְׁבוּ בְּאֶרֶץ גֹּשֶׁן כִּי־תוֹעֲבַת מִצְרַיִם כָּל־
רֹעֵה צֹאן:
וַיָּבֹא יוֹסֵף וַיַּגֵּד לְפַרְעֹה וַיֹּאמֶר אָבִי וְאַחַי וְצֹאנָם
וּבְקָרָם וְכָל־אֲשֶׁר לָהֶם בָּאוּ מֵאֶרֶץ כְּנָעַן וְהִנָּם
בְּאֶרֶץ גֹּשֶׁן: וּמִקְצֵה אֶחָיו לָקַח חֲמִשָּׁה אֲנָשִׁים וַיַּצִּגֵם
לִפְנֵי פַרְעֹה: וַיֹּאמֶר פַּרְעֹה אֶל־אֶחָיו מַה־מַּעֲשֵׂיכֶם
וַיֹּאמְרוּ אֶל־פַּרְעֹה רֹעֵה צֹאן עֲבָדֶיךָ גַּם־אֲנַחְנוּ גַּם־
אֲבוֹתֵינוּ: וַיֹּאמְרוּ אֶל־פַּרְעֹה לָגוּר בָּאָרֶץ בָּאנוּ כִּי־

28] He had sent Judah ahead of him to Joseph, to point the way before him to Goshen. So when they came to the region of Goshen,   29] Joseph ordered his chariot and went to Goshen to meet his father Israel; he presented himself to him and, embracing him around the neck, he wept on his neck a good while.   30] Then Israel said to Joseph, "Now I can die, having seen for myself that you are still alive."

31] Then Joseph said to his brothers and to his father's household, "I will go up and tell the news to Pharaoh, and say to him, 'My brothers and my father's household, who were in the land of Canaan, have come to me.   32] The men are shepherds; they have always been breeders of livestock, and they have brought with them their flocks and herds and all that is theirs.'   33] So when Pharaoh summons you and asks, 'What is your occupation?'   34] you shall answer, 'Your servants have been breeders of livestock from the start until now, both we and our fathers'—so that you may stay in the region of Goshen. For all shepherds are abhorrent to Egyptians."

1] Then Joseph came and reported to Pharaoh, saying, "My father and my brothers, with their flocks and herds and all that is theirs, have come from the land of Canaan and are now in the region of Goshen."   2] And selecting a few of his brothers, he presented them to Pharaoh.   3] Pharaoh said to his brothers, "What is your occupation?" They answered Pharaoh, "We your servants are shepherds, as were also our fathers.   4] We have come," they

---

46:28] *Judah.* He is chosen by Jacob and now replaces Reuben as the leader. Simeon and Levi are likewise passed over. The reason will become clear in Jacob's blessing (Gen. 49:5–7).

29] *Ordered.* Literally, "hitched."

Presented himself. The Hebrew expression וַיֵּרָא (va-yera) is used in other biblical passages in reference to God in the sense of "He appeared." Here the text implies that Joseph suddenly stood before his father, as if in a vision.

/Some commentators feel that Jacob and not Joseph is the subject of the sentence [1]./

34] *Shepherds are abhorrent.* Egyptian sources do not support this statement.

/The attempt has been made to connect this reported attitude toward shepherds with the Egyptian's dislike for the Hyksos. This goes back to Manethos who understood the term Hyksos to mean "shepherd kings" [2]. In fact, it means "foreign rulers."/

47:2] *A few.* Literally, "five" (cf. Gen. 43:34; 45:22). The Bible does not say whom he picked; some interpreters say that he chose the weakest lest Pharaoh draft them for his army [3], others say he chose the strongest in order to make a good impression [4].

אֵין מִרְעֶה לַצֹּאן אֲשֶׁר לַעֲבָדֶיךָ כִּי־כָבֵד הָרָעָב
בְּאֶרֶץ כְּנָעַן וְעַתָּה יֵשְׁבוּ־נָא עֲבָדֶיךָ בְּאֶרֶץ גֹּשֶׁן:
ה וַיֹּאמֶר פַּרְעֹה אֶל־יוֹסֵף לֵאמֹר אָבִיךָ וְאַחֶיךָ בָּאוּ
אֵלֶיךָ: אֶרֶץ מִצְרַיִם לְפָנֶיךָ הִוא בְּמֵיטַב הָאָרֶץ
הוֹשֵׁב אֶת־אָבִיךָ וְאֶת־אַחֶיךָ יֵשְׁבוּ בְּאֶרֶץ גֹּשֶׁן וְאִם־
יָדַעְתָּ וְיֶשׁ־בָּם אַנְשֵׁי־חַיִל וְשַׂמְתָּם שָׂרֵי מִקְנֶה עַל־
אֲשֶׁר־לִי: וַיָּבֵא יוֹסֵף אֶת־יַעֲקֹב אָבִיו וַיַּעֲמִדֵהוּ לִפְנֵי
פַרְעֹה וַיְבָרֶךְ יַעֲקֹב אֶת־פַּרְעֹה: וַיֹּאמֶר פַּרְעֹה אֶל־
יַעֲקֹב כַּמָּה יְמֵי שְׁנֵי חַיֶּיךָ: וַיֹּאמֶר יַעֲקֹב אֶל־פַּרְעֹה
יְמֵי שְׁנֵי מְגוּרַי שְׁלֹשִׁים וּמְאַת שָׁנָה מְעַט וְרָעִים הָיוּ
יְמֵי שְׁנֵי חַיַּי וְלֹא הִשִּׂיגוּ אֶת־יְמֵי שְׁנֵי חַיֵּי אֲבֹתַי בִּימֵי

מְגוּרֵיהֶם: וַיְבָרֶךְ יַעֲקֹב אֶת־פַּרְעֹה וַיֵּצֵא מִלִּפְנֵי
פַרְעֹה: וַיּוֹשֵׁב יוֹסֵף אֶת־אָבִיו וְאֶת־אֶחָיו וַיִּתֵּן לָהֶם
אֲחֻזָּה בְּאֶרֶץ מִצְרַיִם בְּמֵיטַב הָאָרֶץ בְּאֶרֶץ רַעְמְסֵס
כַּאֲשֶׁר צִוָּה פַרְעֹה: וַיְכַלְכֵּל יוֹסֵף אֶת־אָבִיו וְאֶת־
אֶחָיו וְאֵת כָּל־בֵּית אָבִיו לֶחֶם לְפִי הַטָּף: וְלֶחֶם אֵין
בְּכָל־הָאָרֶץ כִּי־כָבֵד הָרָעָב מְאֹד וַתֵּלַהּ אֶרֶץ מִצְרַיִם
וְאֶרֶץ כְּנַעַן מִפְּנֵי הָרָעָב: וַיְלַקֵּט יוֹסֵף אֶת־כָּל־הַכֶּסֶף
הַנִּמְצָא בְאֶרֶץ־מִצְרַיִם וּבְאֶרֶץ כְּנַעַן בַּשֶּׁבֶר אֲשֶׁר־
הֵם שֹׁבְרִים וַיָּבֵא יוֹסֵף אֶת־הַכֶּסֶף בֵּיתָה פַרְעֹה:
וַיִּתֹּם הַכֶּסֶף מֵאֶרֶץ מִצְרַיִם וּמֵאֶרֶץ כְּנַעַן וַיָּבֹאוּ כָל־
מִצְרַיִם אֶל־יוֹסֵף לֵאמֹר הָבָה־לָּנוּ לֶחֶם וְלָמָּה נָמוּת

told Pharaoh, "to sojourn in this land, for there is no pasture for your servants' flocks, the famine being severe in the land of Canaan. Pray, then, let your servants stay in the region of Goshen." 5] Then Pharaoh said to Joseph, "As regards your father and your brothers who have come to you, 6] the land of Egypt is open before you: settle your father and your brothers in the best part of the land; let them stay in the region of Goshen. And if you know any capable men among them, put them in charge of my livestock."

7] Joseph then brought his father Jacob and presented him to Pharaoh; and Jacob greeted Pharaoh. 8] Pharaoh asked Jacob, "How many are the years of your life?" 9] And Jacob answered Pharaoh, "The years of my sojourn [on earth] are one hundred and thirty. Few and hard have been the years of my life, nor do they come up to the life-spans of my fathers during their sojourns." 10] Then Jacob bade Pharaoh farewell, and left Pharaoh's presence.

11] So Joseph settled his father and his brothers, giving them holdings in the choicest part of the land of Egypt, in the region of Rameses, as Pharaoh had commanded. 12] Joseph sustained his father, and his brothers, and all his father's household with bread, down to the little ones.

13] Now there was no bread in all the world, for the famine was very severe; both the land of Egypt and the land of Canaan languished because of the famine. 14] Joseph gathered in all the money that was to be found in the land of Egypt and in the land of Canaan, as payment for the rations that were being procured, and Joseph brought the money into Pharaoh's palace. 15] And when the money gave out in the land of Egypt and in the land of Canaan, all the Egyptians came to Joseph and said, "Give us bread, lest we die before your very eyes; for the

5] *Then Pharaoh said*. This and the following verse are possibly disarranged. The Septuagint reads differently from the Masoretic text.

9] *My sojourn [on earth]*. Literally, "wanderings." Jacob answers Pharaoh's quantitative question qualitatively as well and speaks of the essential tragedy and transitoriness of his years.

10] *Bade Pharaoh farewell*. Others translate as "he blessed." Both translations together render the Hebrew best. Compare this with the English "he bid Godspeed."

11] *Region of Rameses*. As Goshen later became known; named for Rameses II, who lived after Jacob.

טז　נֶגְדֶּ֑ךָ כִּ֣י אָפֵ֣ס כָּ֑סֶף: וַיֹּ֤אמֶר יוֹסֵף֙ הָב֣וּ מִקְנֵיכֶ֔ם
יז　וְאֶתְּנָ֤ה לָכֶם֙ בְּמִקְנֵיכֶ֔ם אִם־אָפֵ֖ס כָּֽסֶף: וַיָּבִ֣יאוּ אֶת־
מִקְנֵיהֶ֘ם אֶל־יוֹסֵף֒ וַיִּתֵּ֣ן לָהֶם֩ יוֹסֵ֨ף לֶ֜חֶם בַּסּוּסִ֗ים
וּבְמִקְנֵ֤ה הַצֹּאן֙ וּבְמִקְנֵ֣ה הַבָּקָ֔ר וּבַחֲמֹרִ֑ים וַיְנַהֲלֵ֤ם
יח　בַּלֶּ֙חֶם֙ בְּכָל־מִקְנֵהֶ֔ם בַּשָּׁנָ֖ה הַהִֽוא: וַתִּתֹּם֘ הַשָּׁנָ֣ה הַהִוא֒
וַיָּבֹ֨אוּ אֵלָ֜יו בַּשָּׁנָ֣ה הַשֵּׁנִ֗ית וַיֹּ֤אמְרוּ לוֹ֙ לֹֽא־נְכַחֵ֣ד
מֵֽאֲדֹנִ֔י כִּ֚י אִם־תַּ֣ם הַכֶּ֔סֶף וּמִקְנֵ֥ה הַבְּהֵמָ֖ה אֶל־אֲדֹנִ֑י
לֹ֤א נִשְׁאַר֙ לִפְנֵ֣י אֲדֹנִ֔י בִּלְתִּ֥י אִם־גְּוִיָּתֵ֖נוּ וְאַדְמָתֵֽנוּ:
יט　לָ֧מָּה נָמ֣וּת לְעֵינֶ֗יךָ גַּם־אֲנַ֙חְנוּ֙ גַּם־אַדְמָתֵ֔נוּ קְנֵֽה־אֹתָ֤נוּ
וְאֶת־אַדְמָתֵ֙נוּ֙ בַּלָּ֑חֶם וְנִֽהְיֶ֞ה אֲנַ֤חְנוּ וְאַדְמָתֵ֙נוּ֙ עֲבָדִ֣ים
לְפַרְעֹ֔ה וְתֶן־זֶ֗רַע וְנִֽחְיֶה֙ וְלֹ֣א נָמ֔וּת וְהָאֲדָמָ֖ה לֹ֥א תֵשָֽׁם:

כ　וַיִּ֨קֶן יוֹסֵ֜ף אֶת־כָּל־אַדְמַ֤ת מִצְרַ֙יִם֙ לְפַרְעֹ֔ה כִּֽי־
מָכְר֤וּ מִצְרַ֙יִם֙ אִ֣ישׁ שָׂדֵ֔הוּ כִּֽי־חָזַ֥ק עֲלֵהֶ֖ם הָרָעָ֑ב
כא　וַתְּהִ֥י הָאָ֖רֶץ לְפַרְעֹֽה: וְאֶ֨ת־הָעָ֔ם הֶעֱבִ֥יר אֹת֖וֹ לֶעָרִ֑ים
כב　מִקְצֵ֥ה גְבֽוּל־מִצְרַ֖יִם וְעַד־קָצֵֽהוּ: רַ֛ק אַדְמַ֥ת הַכֹּהֲנִ֖ים
לֹ֣א קָנָ֑ה כִּי֩ חֹ֨ק לַכֹּהֲנִ֜ים מֵאֵ֣ת פַּרְעֹ֗ה וְאָֽכְל֤וּ אֶת־
חֻקָּם֙ אֲשֶׁ֨ר נָתַ֤ן לָהֶם֙ פַּרְעֹ֔ה עַל־כֵּ֕ן לֹ֥א מָכְר֖וּ אֶת־
כג　אַדְמָתָֽם: וַיֹּ֤אמֶר יוֹסֵף֙ אֶל־הָעָ֔ם הֵן֩ קָנִ֨יתִי אֶתְכֶ֥ם
הַיּ֛וֹם וְאֶת־אַדְמַתְכֶ֖ם לְפַרְעֹ֑ה הֵֽא־לָכֶ֣ם זֶ֔רַע וּזְרַעְתֶּ֖ם
כד　אֶת־הָאֲדָמָֽה: וְהָיָה֙ בַּתְּבוּאֹ֔ת וּנְתַתֶּ֥ם חֲמִישִׁ֖ית לְפַרְעֹ֑ה
וְאַרְבַּ֣ע הַיָּדֹ֡ת יִהְיֶ֣ה לָכֶם֩ לְזֶ֨רַע הַשָּׂדֶ֧ה וּֽלְאָכְלְכֶ֛ם
כה　וְלַֽאֲשֶׁ֥ר בְּבָתֵּיכֶ֖ם וְלֶאֱכֹ֣ל לְטַפְּכֶֽם: וַיֹּ֣אמְרוּ הֶחֱיִתָ֔נוּ

money is gone!" **16]** And Joseph said, "Bring your livestock, and I will sell to you against your livestock, if the money is gone." **17]** So they brought their livestock to Joseph, and Joseph gave them bread in exchange for the horses, for the stocks of sheep and cattle, and the asses; thus he provided them with bread that year in exchange for all their livestock. **18]** And when that year was ended, they came to him the next year and said to him, "We cannot hide from my lord that, with all the money and animal stocks consigned to my lord, nothing is left at my lord's disposal save our persons and our farm land. **19]** Let us not perish before your eyes, both we and our land. Take us and our land in exchange for bread, and we with our land will be serfs to Pharaoh; provide the seed, that we may live and not die, and that the land may not become a waste."

20] So Joseph gained possession of all the farm land of Egypt for Pharaoh, every Egyptian having sold his field because the famine was too much for them; thus the land passed over to Pharaoh. **21]** And he removed the population town by town, from one end of Egypt's border to the other. **22]** Only the land of the priests he did not take over, for the priests had an allotment from Pharaoh, and they lived off the allotment which Pharaoh had made to them; therefore they did not sell their land.

23] Then Joseph said to the people, "Whereas I have this day acquired you and your land for Pharaoh, here is seed for you to sow the land. **24]** And when harvest comes, you shall give one-fifth to Pharaoh, and four-fifths shall be yours as seed for the fields and as food for you and those in your households, and as nourishment for your children." **25]** And they said, "You

17] *Brought their livestock.* Probably not in a literal sense, but by signing over ownership to Pharaoh.

21] *Town by town.* A wholesale removal of the population seems unlikely. הֶעֱבִיר … לֶעָרִים is obscure. By reading הֶעֱבִיד … לַעֲבָדִים, we get

the likely rendering, "He reduced them to servitude."

22] *An allotment.* In money or kind [5], so they did not have to sell their property. Landed clergy were found among many peoples, in contradistinction to the landless priesthood in Israel.

כז נִמְצָא־חֵן בְּעֵינֵי אֲדֹנִי וְהָיִינוּ עֲבָדִים לְפַרְעֹה: וַיֶּשֶׂם   כו לְפַרְעֹה: וַיֵּשֶׁב יִשְׂרָאֵל בְּאֶרֶץ מִצְרַיִם בְּאֶרֶץ גֹּשֶׁן
אֹתָהּ יוֹסֵף לְחֹק עַד־הַיּוֹם הַזֶּה עַל־אַדְמַת מִצְרַיִם   וַיֵּאָחֲזוּ בָהּ וַיִּפְרוּ וַיִּרְבּוּ מְאֹד:
לְפַרְעֹה לַחֹמֶשׁ רַק אַדְמַת הַכֹּהֲנִים לְבַדָּם לֹא הָיְתָה

Haftarah Vayigash, p. 357

have saved our lives! We are grateful to my lord, and we shall be serfs to Pharaoh." **26]** And Joseph made it into a land law in Egypt, which is still valid, that a fifth should be Pharaoh's; only the land of the priests did not become Pharaoh's.

27] Thus Israel settled in the country of Egypt, in the region of Goshen; they acquired holdings in it, and were fertile and increased greatly.

The Shepherds

Joseph carefully rehearses his brothers before they speak to Pharaoh and his court. It is obvious that he wants to make certain that his brothers mention their profession, even though "all shepherds are abhorrent to Egyptians" (Gen. 46:34). In essence, what Joseph wants his brothers to convey to Pharaoh is that they are ready to do unpopular labor and that like Joseph they are reliable and will be useful to the ruler. They can, therefore, be trusted with the sensitive border province of Goshen [6].

They subtly emphasize their point by hinting that the land itself is less important to them than who they are and the work they can do. They convey this by repeating the word אֶרֶץ (eretz, land) in three different senses in their carefully phrased statement (Gen. 47:4). Pharaoh understands the implications; he admits the newcomers and at once gives them important supervisory positions. When not long after Joseph's death the rulers (according to some, the Hyksos) were overthrown and a new kingdom was established, a Pharaoh ascended the throne "who did not know Joseph" (Exod. 1:8). He had no use for associates of the previous dynasty and therefore took no time in enslaving them in the very land of Goshen to which they had come to make their home. The experience of Joseph was to be repeated through many centuries of Jewish history: As long as the Jew was useful to the host country, he was tolerated and even elevated; but often when political circumstances changed, he was offered to the masses as a convenient scapegoat.

Later generations, no longer aware of the subtleties and political overtones of Joseph's advice to his brothers, praised him for displaying great character. Even though his family pursued a trade despised by the Egyptians, he was not, they said, ashamed of his kin and insisted that his father and brethren be presented to the Pharaoh precisely for what they were. Joseph, they claimed, was not one to dissemble his background [7].

Political Morality

Because of the careful and unemotional accounting of the disenfranchisement of the Egyptian people and the apparent approval of Joseph's role in it, this section has been made "a show piece of anti-Semitic polemic" [8]. Here is the Bible, it has been said, Jewry's sacred book, and look at the morality that, by its exaltation of Joseph, it obviously endorses [9].[1]

To reach a proper understanding of the text, we must approach it in its own context. Famine and depression endanger any regime, and it may be assumed that the rulers of that time, whether they were Hyksos or not, probably found a great deal of resistance to their policies among those likely to be their most severe critics: the aristocracy and local officials. The governmental loans of which the story speaks were probably made primarily to these groups. When the famine persisted and the rulers called in their pledges, they managed to ruin their chief debtors and antagonists. The Pharaoh did this with the help of a cadre of civil servants who, like Joseph and his clan, had been imported from abroad. The powerful priests were apparently not touched.

The economic and political changes initiated at that time were part of the country's complex economic and political development. "That they should be credited in this narrative to Joseph is part and parcel of his

[1] It has been pointed out that a rental payment of one-fifth to the king was, if anything, a *modest* percentage judged by ancient as well as later standards.

Under Syrian rule the Jews paid the king one-third of their seed and one-half of their fruits [10].

idealized historical image. Pharaonic Egypt followed its own due course regardless of ancient visitors or modern moralizers" [11].

To superimpose twentieth-century ideas of social and political morality on this story is, therefore, not helpful. Joseph served Pharaoh in his struggle with the Egyptian hierarchy. In so doing he saved the multitudes from starvation, and apparently this was worth any price to them—including a mortgage on their freedom. And it is altogether possible that they thought little of their freedom anyway. Jewish tradition sensed, long ago, that Joseph's actions might not have met with the same success had the Egyptians valued their liberty more highly. The Bible calls Egypt the "house of bondage" not only because Israel was enslaved there but also because its people accepted their own bondage as a normal condition of life.[2]

2 However, Joseph's participation in bringing about this condition left later generations with a sense of uneasiness, a trace of which may be found in the way the people of Egypt were treated in biblical literature. Egypt never became a pejorative term like Moab or Edom. One can even detect a vague sense of kinship with the people of Egypt, an affinity most notably expressed by Isaiah (19:25) who envisions God as saying, "Egypt, My people" [12].

GLEANINGS

He Sent Judah to Point the Way (Gen. 46:28)

But the other brothers knew the way! Some say that Judah was really sent לְהוֹרֹת [to teach], that is, to establish a school for the new arrivals. Our father Jacob teaches us that the first thing a Jew must consider in a new dwelling place is facilities for learning.   MIDRASH [13]

Jacob before Pharaoh

I stand before you, Pharaoh, yet I turn
Toward the past, the counting of my days.
Stretched out before my face I see my life,
I see the hungry hills, the well's dusty lips,
The long journeyings; and over-arching all,
Even from first to last of generations spanned,
The God who blessed my way . . .

The moonlight almost spent
Upon the river,
The stars spread far apart—
Jacob, the father, thought into the future:
"My hope is far removed."
The lissome Pharaoh thought:
"My hope is long fulfilled."
Deep silence fell
Upon the two old men who understood
Each other's separate earth and separate heaven.
    AMY K. BLANK [14]

Joseph the Statesman

Joseph was one of the earliest economic statesmen in history. Apparently he put the farmers on the relief rolls until the drought was over and then gave them back the use of their land in exchange for a very low rent . . . The cry "You cannot regiment nature," while true enough, is the cry of little men lost in primitive superstition. Joseph had a bigger vision than they. He didn't regiment nature but he prepared for the whims of nature.   HENRY A. WALLACE [15]

They Acquired Holdings (Gen. 47:27)

Although the brothers had come to Egypt as sojourners, they now became residents in a land not their own. Had they not acquired holdings and thereby become land-bound, they would not have become slaves.   KELI YEKAR

Joseph's Honesty

And the young man, Joseph, displayed such excessive good faith and honesty in all his dealings that, though the time and the circumstances of the time gave him innumerable opportunities of making money so that he might, in a short period, have become the richest man of that age or kingdom, he still so truly honoured genuine riches before illegitimate wealth, and the treasure which sees rather than that which is blind, that he stored up all the silver and gold which he collected as the price of the corn in the king's treasury, not appropriating a single drachm of it to his own use, but being satisfied with nothing beyond the gifts which the king bestowed on him voluntarily in acknowledgment of his services.   PHILO [16]

The Blessing of Ephraim and Manasseh

This section concentrates on the special blessings given to two of Jacob's grandsons. It is a subtle replay of the blessings given by Isaac: Jacob, too, cannot see, but unlike his father he gives his preferential blessing to the younger child consciously. As in his own case, the theme of the younger brother taking precedence over the older reappears.

In reading this highly emotional and poetically graceful account, we must remember that the ancients saw in Ephraim and Manasseh more than long-departed primal ancestors. For when these stories were told and retold in the days of settlement in Canaan, both narrator and listener must have related Jacob's blessing to the circumstances of their own day, when the tribe of Ephraim enjoyed numerical and economic superiority over Manasseh. We may be sure that many Israelites of that time believed the comparative strength of the two tribes within the tribal confederation to be directly related to Jacob's blessing.

(A new weekly portion, *Vayechi*, begins here.)

כח וַיְחִי יַעֲקֹב בְּאֶרֶץ מִצְרַיִם שְׁבַע עֶשְׂרֵה שָׁנָה וַיְהִי יְמֵי־
יַעֲקֹב שְׁנֵי חַיָּיו שֶׁבַע שָׁנִים וְאַרְבָּעִים וּמְאַת שָׁנָה:
כט וַיִּקְרְבוּ יְמֵי־יִשְׂרָאֵל לָמוּת וַיִּקְרָא לִבְנוֹ לְיוֹסֵף וַיֹּאמֶר
לוֹ אִם־נָא מָצָאתִי חֵן בְּעֵינֶיךָ שִׂים־נָא יָדְךָ תַּחַת
יְרֵכִי וְעָשִׂיתָ עִמָּדִי חֶסֶד וֶאֱמֶת אַל־נָא תִקְבְּרֵנִי
ל בְּמִצְרָיִם: וְשָׁכַבְתִּי עִם־אֲבֹתַי וּנְשָׂאתַנִי מִמִּצְרַיִם
וּקְבַרְתַּנִי בִּקְבֻרָתָם וַיֹּאמַר אָנֹכִי אֶעֱשֶׂה כִדְבָרֶךָ:
לא וַיֹּאמֶר הִשָּׁבְעָה לִי וַיִּשָּׁבַע לוֹ וַיִּשְׁתַּחוּ יִשְׂרָאֵל עַל־

פ   רֹאשׁ הַמִּטָּה:
א וַיְהִי אַחֲרֵי הַדְּבָרִים הָאֵלֶּה וַיֹּאמֶר לְיוֹסֵף הִנֵּה
אָבִיךָ חֹלֶה וַיִּקַּח אֶת־שְׁנֵי בָנָיו עִמּוֹ אֶת־מְנַשֶּׁה וְאֶת־
ב אֶפְרָיִם: וַיֻּגַּד לְיַעֲקֹב וַיֹּאמֶר הִנֵּה בִּנְךָ יוֹסֵף בָּא
אֵלֶיךָ וַיִּתְחַזֵּק יִשְׂרָאֵל וַיֵּשֶׁב עַל־הַמִּטָּה: וַיֹּאמֶר יַעֲקֹב
ג אֶל־יוֹסֵף אֵל שַׁדַּי נִרְאָה־אֵלַי בְּלוּז בְּאֶרֶץ כְּנָעַן
וַיְבָרֶךְ אֹתִי: וַיֹּאמֶר אֵלַי הִנְנִי מַפְרְךָ וְהִרְבִּיתִךָ
ד וּנְתַתִּיךָ לִקְהַל עַמִּים וְנָתַתִּי אֶת־הָאָרֶץ הַזֹּאת לְזַרְעֶךָ

28] Jacob lived seventeen years in the land of Egypt, so that the span of Jacob's life came to one hundred and forty-seven years. **29]** And when the time approached for Israel to die, he summoned his son Joseph and said to him, "Do me this favor, place your hand under my thigh as a pledge of your steadfast loyalty: please do not bury me in Egypt. **30]** When I lie down with my fathers, take me up from Egypt and bury me in their burial-place." He replied, "I will do as you have spoken." **31]** And he said, "Swear to me." And he swore to him. Then Israel bowed at the head of the bed.

1] Some time afterward, Joseph was told, "Your father is ill." So he took with him his two sons, Manasseh and Ephraim. **2]** When Jacob was told, "Your son Joseph has come to see you," Israel summoned his strength and sat up in bed.

3] And Jacob said to Joseph, "El Shaddai appeared to me at Luz in the land of Canaan, and He blessed me, **4]** and said to me, 'I will make you fertile and numerous, making of you a community of peoples; and I will give this land to your offspring to come for an everlasting

47:28] *Seventeen years.* The figure corresponds to the first seventeen years of Joseph's life, which Jacob had enjoyed with his son.

/ As Jacob sustained Joseph for seventeen years, so now Joseph sustains Jacob for the same length of time [1]./

One hundred and forty-seven. On the schematic nature of this figure (3×7^2), see Gleanings to Gen. 24:1–25:18, "The Way of the Bible."

29] *Under my thigh.* To stress the importance of the oath (see Gen. 24:2). Jacob knew that carrying a body to Canaan would be a matter of considerable difficulty (even today interment in another country is a complicated matter). Jacob also knew that such an act could conceivably cast some doubt

on Joseph's full identification with and loyalty to Egypt. By making his son take an oath, Jacob made it possible for Joseph to say to Pharaoh: "My father made me swear" (see Gen. 50:4–6) [2].

Steadfast loyalty. חֶסֶד וֶאֱמֶת (chesed ve-emet); today the name for a free burial society is often *chesed shel emet.*

30] *Burial-place.* Machpelah (see Gen. 23:17–20).

31] *Israel bowed.* A gesture of gratitude; but it is not clear whether he bowed to God [3] or to Joseph [4].

/"The *Shechinah* appears at the head of a sick person" [5]. The Septuagint appears to read מַטֶּה (staff) instead of מִטָּה (bed) [6]./

לֹא יוּכַל לִרְאוֹת וַיַּגֵּשׁ אֹתָם אֵלָיו וַיִּשַּׁק לָהֶם וַיְחַבֵּק   ה אַחֲרֶיךָ אַחַת עוֹלָם: וְעַתָּה שְׁנֵי־בָנֶיךָ הַנּוֹלָדִים לְךָ

יא לָהֶם: וַיֹּאמֶר יִשְׂרָאֵל אֶל־יוֹסֵף רְאֹה פָנֶיךָ לֹא   בְּאֶרֶץ מִצְרַיִם עַד־בֹּאִי אֵלֶיךָ מִצְרַיְמָה לִי־הֵם

פִלָּלְתִּי וְהִנֵּה הֶרְאָה אֹתִי אֱלֹהִים גַּם אֶת־זַרְעֶךָ:   ו אֶפְרַיִם וּמְנַשֶּׁה כִּרְאוּבֵן וְשִׁמְעוֹן יִהְיוּ־לִי: וּמוֹלַדְתְּךָ

יב וַיּוֹצֵא יוֹסֵף אֹתָם מֵעִם בִּרְכָּיו וַיִּשְׁתַּחוּ לְאַפָּיו אָרְצָה: אֲשֶׁר־הוֹלַדְתָּ אַחֲרֵיהֶם לְךָ יִהְיוּ עַל שֵׁם אֲחֵיהֶם

יג וַיִּקַּח יוֹסֵף אֶת־שְׁנֵיהֶם אֶת־אֶפְרַיִם בִּימִינוֹ מִשְּׂמֹאל   ז יִקָּרְאוּ בְּנַחֲלָתָם: וַאֲנִי בְּבֹאִי מִפַּדָּן מֵתָה עָלַי רָחֵל

יִשְׂרָאֵל וְאֶת־מְנַשֶּׁה בִשְׂמֹאלוֹ מִימִין יִשְׂרָאֵל וַיַּגֵּשׁ   בְּאֶרֶץ כְּנַעַן בַּדֶּרֶךְ בְּעוֹד כִּבְרַת־אֶרֶץ לָבֹא אֶפְרָתָה

יד אֵלָיו: וַיִּשְׁלַח יִשְׂרָאֵל אֶת־יְמִינוֹ וַיָּשֶׁת עַל־רֹאשׁ   ח וָאֶקְבְּרֶהָ שָּׁם בְּדֶרֶךְ אֶפְרָת הִוא בֵּית לָחֶם: וַיַּרְא

אֶפְרַיִם וְהוּא הַצָּעִיר וְאֶת־שְׂמֹאלוֹ עַל־רֹאשׁ מְנַשֶּׁה   ט יִשְׂרָאֵל אֶת־בְּנֵי יוֹסֵף וַיֹּאמֶר מִי־אֵלֶּה: וַיֹּאמֶר יוֹסֵף

טו שִׂכֵּל אֶת־יָדָיו כִּי מְנַשֶּׁה הַבְּכוֹר: וַיְבָרֶךְ אֶת־יוֹסֵף   אֶל־אָבִיו בָּנַי הֵם אֲשֶׁר־נָתַן־לִי אֱלֹהִים בָּזֶה וַיֹּאמַר

וַיֹּאמַר הָאֱלֹהִים אֲשֶׁר הִתְהַלְּכוּ אֲבֹתַי לְפָנָיו אַבְרָהָם   י קָחֶם־נָא אֵלַי וַאֲבָרֲכֵם: וְעֵינֵי יִשְׂרָאֵל כָּבְדוּ מִזֹּקֶן

possession.' **5]** Now, your two sons, who were born to you in the land of Egypt before I came to you in Egypt, shall be mine; Ephraim and Manasseh shall be mine no less than Reuben and Simeon. **6]** But progeny born to you after them shall be yours; they shall be recorded instead of their brothers in their inheritance. **7]** I [do this because], when I was returning from Paddan, Rachel died, to my sorrow, while I was journeying in the land of Canaan, when still some distance short of Ephrath; and I buried her there on the road to Ephrath"—now Bethlehem.

8] Noticing Joseph's sons, Israel asked, "Who are these?" **9]** And Joseph said to his father, "They are my sons, whom God has given me here." "Bring them up to me," he said, "that I may bless them." **10]** Now Israel's eyes were dim with age; he could not see. So [Joseph] brought them close to him, and he kissed them and embraced them. **11]** And Israel said to Joseph, "I never expected to see you again, and here God has let me see your children as well."

12] Joseph then removed them from his knees, and bowed low with his face to the ground. **13]** Joseph took the two of them, Ephraim with his right hand—to Israel's left—and Manasseh with his left hand—to Israel's right—and brought them close to him. **14]** But Israel stretched out his right hand and laid it on Ephraim's head, though he was the younger, and his left hand on Manasseh's head—thus crossing his hands—although Manasseh was the first-born. **15]** And he blessed Joseph, saying, "The God in whose ways my fathers Abraham and

48:5] *Shall be mine.* Jacob here adopts the two boys in a formal way, by placing them on his knees (verse 12). They now are like his own sons, hence Ephraim and Manasseh are reckoned among the tribes with Jacob's other sons.

6] *Instead.* Literally, "by the name."

7] *Paddan.* Short for Paddan-aram. The reason for this verse is much disputed [7]. It is perhaps an aside: "I am doing this for you, Rachel, since your early death prevented you from bearing more children."

9] *Bless them.* The expression could also mean, "place them on my knees," a gesture of adoption.

14] *Crossing his hands.* A subtle word play in Hebrew, for the same word can also mean to act wisely, and the like-sounding סָכַל means to act foolishly [8]. Later Torah law prohibited such preference of the younger son (Deut. 21:15–17).

וְיִצְחָק הָאֱלֹהִים הָרֹעֶה אֹתִי מֵעוֹדִי עַד־הַיּוֹם הַזֶּה:

טז הַמַּלְאָךְ הַגֹּאֵל אֹתִי מִכָּל־רָע יְבָרֵךְ אֶת־הַנְּעָרִים

וְיִקָּרֵא בָהֶם שְׁמִי וְשֵׁם אֲבֹתַי אַבְרָהָם וְיִצְחָק וְיִדְגּוּ

יז לָרֹב בְּקֶרֶב הָאָרֶץ: וַיַּרְא יוֹסֵף כִּי־יָשִׁית אָבִיו יַד־

יְמִינוֹ עַל־רֹאשׁ אֶפְרַיִם וַיֵּרַע בְּעֵינָיו וַיִּתְמֹךְ יַד־אָבִיו

לְהָסִיר אֹתָהּ מֵעַל רֹאשׁ־אֶפְרַיִם עַל־רֹאשׁ מְנַשֶּׁה:

יח וַיֹּאמֶר יוֹסֵף אֶל־אָבִיו לֹא־כֵן אָבִי כִּי־זֶה הַבְּכֹר

יט שִׂים יְמִינְךָ עַל־רֹאשׁוֹ: וַיְמָאֵן אָבִיו וַיֹּאמֶר יָדַעְתִּי

בְנִי יָדַעְתִּי גַם־הוּא יִהְיֶה־לְּעָם וְגַם־הוּא יִגְדָּל וְאוּלָם

אָחִיו הַקָּטֹן יִגְדַּל מִמֶּנּוּ וְזַרְעוֹ יִהְיֶה מְלֹא־הַגּוֹיִם:

כ וַיְבָרֲכֵם בַּיּוֹם הַהוּא לֵאמוֹר בְּךָ יְבָרֵךְ יִשְׂרָאֵל

לֵאמֹר יְשִׂמְךָ אֱלֹהִים כְּאֶפְרַיִם וְכִמְנַשֶּׁה וַיָּשֶׂם אֶת־

כא אֶפְרַיִם לִפְנֵי מְנַשֶּׁה: וַיֹּאמֶר יִשְׂרָאֵל אֶל־יוֹסֵף הִנֵּה

אָנֹכִי מֵת וְהָיָה אֱלֹהִים עִמָּכֶם וְהֵשִׁיב אֶתְכֶם אֶל־

כב אֶרֶץ אֲבֹתֵיכֶם: וַאֲנִי נָתַתִּי לְךָ שְׁכֶם אַחַד עַל־אַחֶיךָ

אֲשֶׁר לָקַחְתִּי מִיַּד הָאֱמֹרִי בְּחַרְבִּי וּבְקַשְׁתִּי: פ

Isaac walked, / The God who has been my shepherd from my birth to this day— / **16]** The Angel who has redeemed me from all harm— / Bless the lads. / In them may my name be recalled, / And the names of my fathers Abraham and Isaac, / And may they be teeming multitudes upon the earth."

17] When Joseph saw that his father was placing his right hand on Ephraim's head, he thought it wrong; so he took hold of his father's hand to move it from Ephraim's head to Manasseh's. **18]** "Not so, Father," Joseph said to his father, "for the other is the first-born; place your right hand on his head." **19]** But his father objected, saying, "I know, my son, I know. He too shall become a people, and he too shall be great. Yet his younger brother shall be greater than he, and his offspring shall be plentiful enough for nations." **20]** So he blessed them that day, saying, "By you shall Israel invoke blessings, saying: God make you like Ephraim and Manasseh." Thus he put Ephraim before Manasseh.

21] Then Israel said to Joseph, "I am about to die; but God will be with you and bring you back to the land of your fathers. **22]** And now, I give you one portion more than to your brothers, which I wrested from the Amorites with my sword and bow."

16] *The Angel.* In this moment, when past and future blend into one, Jacob recalls his dream at Bethel, when angels symbolized God's everlasting protection.

17] *He thought it wrong.* Knowing that deathbed blessings were irrevocable, Joseph tries to stop Jacob before he comes to the specific blessings for the two sons. In most cultures the right hand takes linguistic and emotional preference over the left, e.g., in English "right" also means just; while "left" has negative meanings (left-handed, gauche; the word sinister comes from the Latin word for "left").

20] *By you shall Israel invoke blessings.* Jacob here uses his other name to foreshadow the future. "The veil parts, the nation Israel appears before the breaking view of the old man" [9]. Jacob's words are the traditional formula with which a Jewish father blesses his sons on Sabbath eve.

22] *One portion.* שְׁכֶם (*shechem*); the meaning is uncertain. Some scholars maintain that this refers to the mountain slope of Shechem and that it is here deeded to Joseph as a burial place [10].

Wrested. In no other place has Jacob been portrayed as a military person. This notation is, therefore, either a remnant of another tradition [11] or "sword and bow" may be an idiom for "through my own labor," a reference to Jacob's purchase of property at Shechem with hard-earned money (Gen. 33:19) [12].

/ The Midrash says that prayer was Jacob's bow and sword [13]. Another view is that bow and sword were *mitzvot* and good deeds [14]./

The Blessing

Every blessing bestowed by man is at the core a prayer, since it asks God to help him accomplish what he by himself cannot. Yet the blessing is more than prayer, for it assigns a decisive role to the one who pronounces it. Placing his hands in the solemn act, the Patriarch sees himself as God's co-worker and as an essential link between the generations. Man cannot take God's place; but neither can God take the place of parents and grandparents in the shaping of the children's future.

Jacob's blessing has often served as a classic example of prayer: It begins with adoration, it proceeds to thanksgiving, and only then turns to the petition. Jacob speaks of the God of his fathers; this is his link with the past. God is his Lord because of tradition—but not only because of tradition. He is his God also through personal experience and relationship. This remains the basic nature of Jewish worship: God is approached as the God of history, especially Jewish history, but beyond that each generation has to rediscover for itself the God who was the God of the Fathers.[1]

Jacob sees his life spread before him. He is aware of the continued presence of God and acknowledges it with deep feeling. Past and future are now fused. He knows in this moment that his own complex life is crowned with hope, a hope that is represented by the God of his fathers and by the two boys at his side. His life is completed; the blessing of Abraham, which Isaac had bestowed on him, has now passed down to his children's children.

---

[1] This is the traditional interpretation given to the beginning of the Eighteen Benedictions: "Praised be Thou, O Lord, our God [i.e., of the present] and God of our Fathers [i.e., of the past], God of Abraham, God of Isaac, and God of Jacob [i.e., of each generation separately] . . . ."

GLEANINGS

Respect

Why does the *sidrah* start with verse 28 when it would have been more logical to start with verse 27? The reason is that in that case the previous *sidrah* would have concluded with Gen. 47:26 which speaks of the Egyptians surrendering their land to Pharaoh. Our congregations did not want to conclude that *sidrah* with the plight of the Egyptians.   RALBAG

Jacob Lived (Gen. 47:28)

Of how few men can we repeat a phrase like "Jacob *lived*"? When a man dies, a death notice appears in the press. In reality, it is a life notice; because but for it the world would never have known that the man had ever been alive. Only he who has been a force for human goodness can be said to have *lived*.   JOSEPH H. HERTZ

[The Romans also said *vixit* (he has lived) in reporting the death of a prominent man.]

Visiting the Sick

It is written that Joseph took his two sons to see Jacob when he heard that his father was ill. From this we learn the *mitzvah* of visiting the sick.   MIDRASH [15]

Deathbed Testament

The words of a dying man are as binding as a deed which is written and delivered.

TALMUD [16]

The End of Days

Why should Jacob have wanted to reveal the date of the end of days to his sons?

Because exile is easier to bear if one knows in advance when it will end. But God wanted Israel's exile to be difficult, and therefore He closed Jacob's vision from him so that the Children of Israel should not learn the date of their final redemption.

R. SIMCHAH BUNAM [17]

"And He Blessed Joseph" (Gen. 48:15)

The blessing that follows was actually addressed not to Joseph but only to Joseph's two sons. Why, then, does Scripture say that Jacob blessed Joseph?

In order to show that there is no greater blessing for a father than the wish that his children should take after him and become good people. Hence Jacob's blessing to Manasseh and Ephraim "The angel who has redeemed me from all evil, bless the lads and let my name be named in them and the name of my fathers, Abraham and Isaac" (verse 16) is the greatest blessing Joseph, their father, could possibly have received.

R. ISAIAH HOROWITZ [18]

Jacob's Testament

J acob's final words to his assembled sons are a combination of prayer, blessing, curse, warning, psychological assessment, parable, recollection, and hope.[1] They are presented in poetic form; and like much other poetry, ancient and modern, their meaning is not always readily accessible.

Traditional commentators have looked at the testament as a prophetic utterance pronounced by the dying forefather (see note to Gen. 49:1). It is more likely, however, that the testament is a collection of old tribal songs and memories, which were welded into a poem and then incorporated into the life story of Jacob. Historical references suggest that the chapter as it stands now was written during the period of the Judges, or some time before the year 1000 B.C.E., at a time when the tribes were already in Canaan, although not yet a nation, when differences were still keenly felt and old animosities were not yet forgotten.[2]

It was a time when the tribe of Levi fell far short of the position of priestly importance that the blessing of Moses (Deut. 33) assigned to it and when the tribe of Simeon (not named in Deuteronomy and later absorbed into the tribe of Judah) was still worthy of mention [3]. The reader might also compare this testament with the song of Deborah (Judg. 5), which comes from about the same general epoch, although it deals with a special military constellation rather than a general view of the tribal confederacy.

---

[1] For a full comparison with the blessing of Moses, see Deut. 33. The testament of Jacob may also be considered in the light of the recurrent patterns of blessings and curses in Genesis (1:28; 3:14; 9:12–17, 25; 12:1–3; 14:19; 24:60; 27:27, 39; 48:16, 20) [1].

[2] Some scholars believe that the twelve sons here represent the signs of the zodiac. Others say that they reveal traces of totemism, a social system based on belief in kinship with animals (or plants), for many of the tribes are here compared to animals [2].

ה שִׁמְעוֹן וְלֵוִי אַחִים כְּלֵי חָמָס מְכֵרֹתֵיהֶם: בְּסֹדָם אַל־   א וַיִּקְרָא יַעֲקֹב אֶל־בָּנָיו וַיֹּאמֶר הֵאָסְפוּ וְאַגִּידָה לָכֶם

תָּבֹא נַפְשִׁי בִּקְהָלָם אַל־תֵּחַד כְּבֹדִי כִּי בְאַפָּם הָרְגוּ   ב אֵת אֲשֶׁר־יִקְרָא אֶתְכֶם בְּאַחֲרִית הַיָּמִים: הֵקָּבְצוּ

אִישׁ וּבִרְצֹנָם עִקְּרוּ־שׁוֹר: אָרוּר אַפָּם כִּי עָז וְעֶבְרָתָם   ג וְשִׁמְעוּ בְּנֵי יַעֲקֹב וְשִׁמְעוּ אֶל־יִשְׂרָאֵל אֲבִיכֶם: רְאוּבֵן

כִּי קָשָׁתָה אֲחַלְּקֵם בְּיַעֲקֹב וַאֲפִיצֵם בְּיִשְׂרָאֵל: פ   בְּכֹרִי אַתָּה כֹּחִי וְרֵאשִׁית אוֹנִי יֶתֶר שְׂאֵת וְיֶתֶר עָז:

ח יְהוּדָה אַתָּה יוֹדוּךָ אַחֶיךָ יָדְךָ בְּעֹרֶף אֹיְבֶיךָ יִשְׁתַּחֲווּ   ד פַּחַז כַּמַּיִם אַל־תּוֹתַר כִּי עָלִיתָ מִשְׁכְּבֵי אָבִיךָ אָז

לְךָ בְּנֵי אָבִיךָ: גּוּר אַרְיֵה יְהוּדָה מִטֶּרֶף בְּנִי עָלִיתָ   חִלַּלְתָּ יְצוּעִי עָלָה: פ

1] And Jacob called his sons and said, "Come together that I may tell you what is to befall you in days to come.

2] Assemble and hearken, O sons of Jacob; / Hearken to Israel your father:

3] Reuben, you are my first-born, / My might and first fruit of my vigor, / Exceeding in rank / And exceeding in honor. / **4]** Unstable as water, you shall excel no longer; / For when you mounted your father's bed, / You brought disgrace—my couch he mounted!

5] Simeon and Levi are a pair; / Their weapons are tools of lawlessness. / **6]** Let not my person be included in their council, / Let not my being be counted in their assembly. / For when angry they slay men, / And when pleased they maim oxen. / **7]** Cursed be their anger so fierce, / And their wrath so relentless. / I will divide them in Jacob, / Scatter them in Israel.

8] You, O Judah, your brothers shall praise; / Your hand shall be on the nape of your foes; / Your father's sons shall bow low to you. / **9]** Judah is a lion's whelp; / On prey, my son, have you grown. / He crouches, lies down like a lion, / Like the king of beasts—who dare rouse

---

49:1] *In days to come.* Not a reference to messianic days as older translations ("In the end of days") suggest [4].

4] *Your father's bed.* Reuben had cohabited with Jacob's concubine (Gen. 35:22).

My couch he mounted! An aside to himself or to the assembled children to explain why Reuben will no longer enjoy the rights of the first-born [5].

/In the song of Deborah, Reuben is chastised for egotism and lack of cooperation; the blessing of Moses voices fear that the tribe may disappear altogether (Judg. 5:16 and Deut. 33:6, respectively), as in fact it did under the monarchy when Moab occupied the Trans-Jordanian territory of Reuben./

5] *A pair.* אַחִים (*achim*), literally, "brothers," here meaning "two of a kind" [6].

Weapons. The Hebrew is obscure [7].

6] *My being.* That is, "what I represent." Jacob had no part in their violence at Shechem and does not want his name connected with what the two sons might do in the future.

They maim oxen. Delighting in cruelty and senseless, wanton destruction.

/Radak, however, gives the verse a different sense by taking "ox" (שׁוֹר) as figurative for Hamor, son of Shechem. This would then refer to the Dinah incident and provide a parallel with the first half of the verse./

9] *Lion's whelp.* In Deut. 33:22, Dan is given this ascription.

י   כָּרַע רָבַץ כְּאַרְיֵה וּכְלָבִיא מִי יְקִימֶנּוּ: לֹא־יָסוּר
שֵׁבֶט מִיהוּדָה וּמְחֹקֵק מִבֵּין רַגְלָיו עַד כִּי־יָבֹא שִׁילֹה
יא   וְלוֹ יִקְּהַת עַמִּים: אֹסְרִי לַגֶּפֶן עִירֹה וְלַשֹּׂרֵקָה בְּנִי
יב   אֲתֹנוֹ כִּבֵּס בַּיַּיִן לְבֻשׁוֹ וּבְדַם־עֲנָבִים סוּתֹה: חַכְלִילִי
עֵינַיִם מִיָּיִן וּלְבֶן־שִׁנַּיִם מֵחָלָב: פ

יג   זְבוּלֻן לְחוֹף יַמִּים יִשְׁכֹּן וְהוּא לְחוֹף אֳנִיֹּת וְיַרְכָתוֹ
עַל־צִידֹן: פ
יד   יִשָּׂשכָר חֲמֹר גָּרֶם רֹבֵץ בֵּין הַמִּשְׁפְּתָיִם: וַיַּרְא מְנֻחָה
כִּי טוֹב וְאֶת־הָאָרֶץ כִּי נָעֵמָה וַיֵּט שִׁכְמוֹ לִסְבֹּל וַיְהִי
טו   לְמַס־עֹבֵד: ס דָּן יָדִין עַמּוֹ כְּאַחַד שִׁבְטֵי יִשְׂרָאֵל:

* יא עירו קרי.   סותו קרי.

---

him? / **10]** The scepter shall not depart from Judah, / Nor the ruler's staff from between his feet; / So that tribute shall come to him / And the homage of peoples be his.

11] He tethers his ass to a vine, / His ass's foal to a choice vine; / He washes his garment in wine, / His robe in blood of grapes. / **12]** His eyes are darker than wine; / His teeth are whiter than milk.

13] Zebulun shall dwell by the seashore; / He shall be a haven for ships, / And his flank shall rest on Sidon.

14] Issachar is a strong-boned ass, / Crouching among the sheepfolds. / **15]** When he saw how good was security, / And how pleasant was the country, / He bent his shoulder to the burden, / And became a toiling serf.

16] Dan shall govern his people, / As one of the tribes of Israel. / **17]** Dan shall be a

---

10] *Tribute shall come to him.* עַד כִּי־יָבֹא שִׁילֹה, literally, "until he comes to Shiloh," or "until Shiloh comes." The Hebrew is obscure; the above translation reads the text as if it were שַׁי לֹו (שַׁי meaning "tribute" and לֹה, an alternate form for לֹו, meaning "to him") [8].

Shiloh was an important religious center and pre-Jerusalem sanctuary located in the territory of Ephraim. One Jewish tradition, taking Jacob's blessing to be a prophecy for the end of time (see verse 1), interpreted "Shiloh" to mean the Messiah, a new David who would come out of the house of Judah [9]. Christianity expanded this interpretation into a direct reference to Jesus, especially since verse 11 alludes to the ruler riding an ass, as Jesus did when he entered Jerusalem [10]. If we abide by the Masoretic text it may be best to interpret: "Until Judah will come to worship at Shiloh," that is, "until the northern and southern kingdoms will be reunited."

12] *Darker than wine.* Or, "dark from wine."

Whiter than milk. Or, "white from milk." Judah is to have such abundance that he can even afford to wash his clothes in wine (we would say, bathe in champagne) and to tie his ass to a vine (ordinarily not done because the animal would consume it).

13] *By the seashore.* In this poem Zebulun's territory is seen situated on the coast, from today's Haifa northward into Lebanon, a picture contrary to all other (and probably later) attestation (cf. Josh. 19:10–16).

15] *Toiling serf.* A castigation of the tribe. At the time of the Judges it had apparently traded freedom for comfort and was subjected by the Canaanites.

16] *Dan shall govern.* A word play or possibly a reference to the Danite Samson and his rule [11]. In the early days of settlement Dan's territory was southeast of modern Tel Aviv but was later in northern Galilee; hence the expression, "From Dan to Beer-sheba."

יי יְהִי־דָן נָחָשׁ עֲלֵי־דֶרֶךְ שְׁפִיפֹן עֲלֵי־אֹרַח הַנֹּשֵׁךְ עִקְּבֵי־
סוּס וַיִּפֹּל רֹכְבוֹ אָחוֹר:

יח לִישׁוּעָתְךָ קִוִּיתִי יְהוָה: ס

יט גָּד גְּדוּד יְגוּדֶנּוּ וְהוּא יָגֻד עָקֵב: ס כ מֵאָשֵׁר שְׁמֵנָה
כא לַחְמוֹ וְהוּא יִתֵּן מַעֲדַנֵּי־מֶלֶךְ: ס נַפְתָּלִי אַיָּלָה
כב שְׁלֻחָה הַנֹּתֵן אִמְרֵי־שָׁפֶר: ס בֵּן פֹּרָת יוֹסֵף בֵּן
כג פֹּרָת עֲלֵי־עָיִן בָּנוֹת צָעֲדָה עֲלֵי־שׁוּר: וַיְמָרֲרֻהוּ וָרֹבּוּ
כד וַיִּשְׂטְמֻהוּ בַּעֲלֵי חִצִּים: וַתֵּשֶׁב בְּאֵיתָן קַשְׁתּוֹ וַיָּפֹזּוּ

וְזֹרעֵי יָדָיו מִידֵי אֲבִיר יַעֲקֹב מִשָּׁם רֹעֶה אֶבֶן יִשְׂרָאֵל:
כה מֵאֵל אָבִיךָ וְיַעְזְרֶךָּ וְאֵת שַׁדַּי וִיבָרֲכֶךָּ בִּרְכֹת שָׁמַיִם
מֵעָל בִּרְכֹת תְּהוֹם רֹבֶצֶת תָּחַת בִּרְכֹת שָׁדַיִם וָרָחַם:
כו בִּרְכֹת אָבִיךָ גָּבְרוּ עַל־בִּרְכֹת הוֹרַי עַד־תַּאֲוַת גִּבְעֹת
עוֹלָם תִּהְיֶיןָ לְרֹאשׁ יוֹסֵף וּלְקָדְקֹד נְזִיר אֶחָיו: פ
כז בִּנְיָמִין זְאֵב יִטְרָף בַּבֹּקֶר יֹאכַל עַד וְלָעֶרֶב יְחַלֵּק
שָׁלָל:

serpent by the road, / A viper by the path, / That bites the horse's heels / So that his rider is thrown backward.

18] I wait for Your deliverance, O LORD!

19] Gad shall be raided by raiders, / But he shall raid at their heels.

20] Asher's bread shall be rich, / And he shall yield royal dainties.

21] Naphtali is a hind let loose, / Which yields lovely fawns.

22] Joseph is a wild ass, / A wild ass by a spring / —Wild colts on a hillside. / **23]** Archers bitterly assailed him; / They shot at him and harried him. / **24]** Yet his bow stayed taut, / And his arms were made firm / By the hands of the Mighty One of Jacob— / There, the Shepherd, the Rock of Israel— / **25]** The God of your father who helps you, / And Shaddai who blesses you / With blessings of heaven above, / Blessings of the deep that couches below, / Blessings of the breast and womb. / **26]** The blessings of your father / Surpass the blessings of my ancestors, / To the utmost bounds of the eternal hills. / May they rest on the head of Joseph, / On the brow of the elect of his brothers.

27] Benjamin is a ravenous wolf; / In the morning he consumes the foe, / And in the evening he divides the spoil."

18] *I wait*. Another aside.
/ Many other explanations have been offered, e.g., "For your salvation [O Dan] I trust in the Lord" [12]. /

19] *Raided*. A quadruple word play in Hebrew on "Gad" and "raid," in praise of the tribe's bravery.

20] *Yield*. Produce and export to the neighboring Phoenicians.

21] *A hind let loose*. The simile expresses the feelings of exhilaration bred by the spaciousness of Upper Galilee [13].

22] *Joseph is a wild ass*. Others render as "Joseph is a fruitful bough, a fruitful bough by a spring, its branches run over a wall." The simile from the animal world is more in consonance with the rest of the poem [14].

24] *His bow stayed taut*. Making him able to withstand the onslaughts of other men's designs—those of his brothers, of Potiphar's wife, and presumably of enemies at court.
/ Some old commentators believe the expression to be a circumlocution for sexual temptation [15]. /
His arms. Or, "the sinews of his hands" [16].

26] *Surpass*. The first half of the verse is obscure. The blessing of Joseph has been interpreted as a political statement, referring to the positioning of the Joseph tribes [17].

27] *Ravenous wolf*. Benjamin's warlike temperament is here characterized. Two famous warriors, Ehud the Judge and Saul the King, were of this tribe.
Foe. Others translate as "booty."

The Vision of Jacob

If we look at Jacob's testament as a picture of the Israelites at the time of the Judges, as biblical scholars are generally wont to do, we recognize twelve tribes as different from each other as twelve sons could be. Their temperaments vary widely, from the war-loving Benjamin to the security-loving Issachar; from the morally unstable Reuben to the self-disciplined Joseph; from the violent natures of Simeon and Levi to the calm judgment of Judah. It is obvious that the tribes are still in a state of ferment, and it is equally remarkable that they seemingly have little cohesion. What unites them is not a sense of national purpose or identity; neither is in evidence. If anything binds them, it is their sense of common ancestry and the memory of an old covenant.

We would not do justice to the poem, however, were we to examine it only as a characterization of the twelve tribes at a certain point in later history. The poem also serves as a climax to the Book of Genesis and as an echo of its underlying purpose. Genesis follows one basic theme: God's guidance of His world and His special love of and promise to Abraham and his seed. Now the book comes to a close, and the next act in the great drama is about to open. The testament is to be seen as a bridge between the past and the future, and both are beheld through the eyes of Jacob.

Jacob's has not been a happy life and he cannot but reflect on his deep disappointments over his three oldest sons. Yet now, as death nears, a better future rises before his inner eye. This future is tied to Judah and Joseph, and these two he addresses directly (the others, with the exception of the first-born Reuben, are only spoken about).

Joseph has always had the deep affection of his father, whose grateful words pronounce praise and blessing and form a fitting summary of the life of his great son. The ultimate focus, however, is on Judah. It is through him that God's mysterious designs will be carried on. When the poem turns to Judah it turns resolutely to the future. It may not, in its enigmatic Shiloh passage, speak of the end of time, but it does reach into days to come. At whatever period these stanzas were composed, they looked forward in the sense of prophecy, and in the light of history the prophecy turned out to be remarkably accurate. It was Judah's tribe that survived destruction and deportation by the Babylonians (586 B.C.E.) and that provided continuity for the children of Israel. It was from Judah that the Jew took his name.

Thus Genesis concludes with a vision that looks to "the eternal hills" (Gen. 49:26). Perhaps the words that are now verse 18 and stand near the middle of the testament once formed the poem's concluding line and summary: "I wait for Your deliverance, O Lord!"

GLEANINGS

Joseph

Joseph is the ideal manifested, as the union of darkness and light, feeling and mind, the primitive and the civilized, wisdom and the happy heart—in short as the humanized mystery we call man.

THOMAS MANN [18]

The Man of Faith

[The Koran devotes an entire Sura to Joseph (Yusuf). It elaborates on the biblical tale and puts Mohammed's doctrines in his mouth.]

This is part of what my Lord has taught me; for I have abandoned the religion of those who do not believe in God and who deny the life-to-come. I follow the religion of my fathers Abraham, Isaac, and Jacob: We may not associate anything with God. . . . Judgment belongs to God alone. He has bidden you to worship none but Him. This is the right faith, but most men know it not.

KORAN [19]

The Blessing of Judah

Here we touch on one of those deep, sure insights which make the Jewish Bible incomparable among ancient writings and full of truth, which no modern conditions can outgrow. The great nation has for its hero the highest type of man. It was the instinct which felt this that made Israel unique . . . Israel has endured because of that inheritance.

WALTER R. BOWIE [20]

Joseph and Disraeli

He has been called the Disraeli of the ancient world. The comparison goes much further than is usually perceived, and if it has not yet been done someone should write two Plutarchian parallel lives of Victoria's prime minister and Pharaoh's vizier. There are many differences between the two men, but the similarities are astonishing. Both were brilliant, and brilliant alike in their ability to irritate and to charm. Both were "foreigners," though Disraeli was second-generation English-born. Both were democratic conservatives, concerned with the welfare of the masses as much as with the retention of the traditional authority.

MAURICE SAMUEL [21]

The Deaths of Jacob and Joseph

We now reach the end of the last division of Genesis and of the "line of Jacob." The finale of the book focuses on the death of Jacob, with the story of Joseph's death as a kind of epilogue. We obtain a brief insight into Egyptian burial customs, and the relationship of Joseph to his brothers receives its last test.

The main theme of Genesis emerges once more: God has guided the descendants of Abraham and has brought them to the land of Egypt. Thus, the conclusion of Genesis is an introduction to Exodus, where we read how God's guidance is manifested before the whole world as He leads His chosen ones from Egypt back to the Promised Land.

לֹ מִקְנֵה הַשָּׂדֶה וְהַמְּעָרָה אֲשֶׁר־בּוֹ מֵאֵת בְּנֵי־חֵת: וַיְכַל
יַעֲקֹב לְצַוֹּת אֶת־בָּנָיו וַיֶּאֱסֹף רַגְלָיו אֶל־הַמִּטָּה וַיִּגְוַע
וַיֵּאָסֶף אֶל־עַמָּיו:

א וַיִּפֹּל יוֹסֵף עַל־פְּנֵי אָבִיו וַיֵּבְךְּ עָלָיו וַיִּשַּׁק־לוֹ: וַיְצַו
ב יוֹסֵף אֶת־עֲבָדָיו אֶת־הָרֹפְאִים לַחֲנֹט אֶת־אָבִיו וַיַּחַנְטוּ
ג הָרֹפְאִים אֶת־יִשְׂרָאֵל: וַיִּמְלְאוּ־לוֹ אַרְבָּעִים יוֹם כִּי
כֵּן יִמְלְאוּ יְמֵי הַחֲנֻטִים וַיִּבְכּוּ אֹתוֹ מִצְרַיִם שִׁבְעִים
ד יוֹם: וַיַּעַבְרוּ יְמֵי בְכִיתוֹ וַיְדַבֵּר יוֹסֵף אֶל־בֵּית פַּרְעֹה
לֵאמֹר אִם־נָא מָצָאתִי חֵן בְּעֵינֵיכֶם דַּבְּרוּ־נָא בְּאָזְנֵי

כח כָּל־אֵלֶּה שִׁבְטֵי יִשְׂרָאֵל שְׁנֵים עָשָׂר וְזֹאת אֲשֶׁר־
דִּבֶּר לָהֶם אֲבִיהֶם וַיְבָרֶךְ אוֹתָם אִישׁ אֲשֶׁר כְּבִרְכָתוֹ
כט בֵּרַךְ אֹתָם: וַיְצַו אוֹתָם וַיֹּאמֶר אֲלֵהֶם אֲנִי נֶאֱסָף
אֶל־עַמִּי קִבְרוּ אֹתִי אֶל־אֲבֹתָי אֶל־הַמְּעָרָה אֲשֶׁר
ל בִּשְׂדֵה עֶפְרוֹן הַחִתִּי: בַּמְּעָרָה אֲשֶׁר בִּשְׂדֵה הַמַּכְפֵּלָה
אֲשֶׁר־עַל־פְּנֵי מַמְרֵא בְּאֶרֶץ כְּנָעַן אֲשֶׁר קָנָה אַבְרָהָם
לא אֶת־הַשָּׂדֶה מֵאֵת עֶפְרֹן הַחִתִּי לַאֲחֻזַּת־קָבֶר: שָׁמָּה
קָבְרוּ אֶת־אַבְרָהָם וְאֵת שָׂרָה אִשְׁתּוֹ שָׁמָּה קָבְרוּ אֶת־
יִצְחָק וְאֵת רִבְקָה אִשְׁתּוֹ וְשָׁמָּה קָבַרְתִּי אֶת־לֵאָה:

28] All these were the tribes of Israel, twelve in number, and this is what their father said to them as he bade them farewell, addressing to each a parting word appropriate to him.

29] Then he instructed them, saying to them, "I am about to be gathered to my kin. Bury me with my fathers in the cave which is in the field of Ephron the Hittite, **30]** the cave which is in the field of Machpelah, facing Mamre, in the land of Canaan, the field that Abraham bought from Ephron the Hittite for a burial site— **31]** there Abraham and his wife Sarah were buried; there Isaac and his wife Rebekah were buried; and there I buried Leah— **32]** the field and the cave in it, bought from the Hittites." **33]** When Jacob finished his instructions to his sons, he drew his feet into the bed and, breathing his last, he was gathered to his people.

1] Joseph flung himself upon his father's face and wept over him and kissed him. **2]** Then Joseph ordered the physicians in his service to embalm his father, and the physicians embalmed Israel. **3]** It required forty days, for such is the full period of embalming. The Egyptians bewailed him seventy days; **4]** and when the wailing period was over, Joseph spoke to Pharaoh's court, saying, "Do me this favor, and lay this appeal before Pharaoh: **5]** 'My father

49:28] *All these.* The verse serves as a conclusion to the testament and as an introduction to the final words of Genesis.

33] *Drew his feet... gathered to.* Hebrew assonances on the word Joseph (וַיֶּאֱסֹף ... וַיֵּאָסֶף).

50:2] *Embalm.* The purpose of embalming, widely practiced in Egypt, was to preserve the body for the eventual return of the soul. It involved removing the brain and filling the skull with spices; removing the entrails and cleaning the cavity with alcohol, then filling it with myrrh and similar substances; placing the whole body in a nitric solution for many days; washing and wrapping it, and finally sealing it with a rubber paste. There

were elaborate and quite costly mummifications as well as others more cursory and less expensive [1].

The physicians. Who specialized in embalming.

3] *Seventy days.* Almost as many as the seventy-two days of mourning customarily set aside for the Pharaoh. Jacob receives a quasi-royal treatment. The mourning period was characterized by official public observances.

4] *Pharaoh's court.* Joseph does not approach Pharaoh directly, perhaps because he had touched the corpse and was, therefore, considered unclean.

הַכְּנַעֲנִי אֶת־הָאֵבֶל בְּגֹרֶן הָאָטָד וַיֹּאמְרוּ אֵבֶל־כָּבֵד
זֶה לְמִצְרָיִם עַל־כֵּן קָרָא שְׁמָהּ אָבֵל מִצְרַיִם אֲשֶׁר
בְּעֵבֶר הַיַּרְדֵּן: וַיַּעֲשׂוּ בָנָיו לוֹ כֵּן כַּאֲשֶׁר צִוָּם: וַיִּשְׂאוּ
אֹתוֹ בָנָיו אַרְצָה כְּנַעַן וַיִּקְבְּרוּ אֹתוֹ בִּמְעָרַת שְׂדֵה
הַמַּכְפֵּלָה אֲשֶׁר קָנָה אַבְרָהָם אֶת־הַשָּׂדֶה לַאֲחֻזַּת־
קֶבֶר מֵאֵת עֶפְרֹן הַחִתִּי עַל־פְּנֵי מַמְרֵא: וַיָּשָׁב יוֹסֵף
מִצְרַיְמָה הוּא וְאֶחָיו וְכָל־הָעֹלִים אִתּוֹ לִקְבֹּר אֶת־
אָבִיו אַחֲרֵי קָבְרוֹ אֶת־אָבִיו: וַיִּרְאוּ אֲחֵי־יוֹסֵף כִּי־מֵת
אֲבִיהֶם וַיֹּאמְרוּ לוּ יִשְׂטְמֵנוּ יוֹסֵף וְהָשֵׁב יָשִׁיב לָנוּ אֵת
כָּל־הָרָעָה אֲשֶׁר גָּמַלְנוּ אֹתוֹ: וַיְצַוּוּ אֶל־יוֹסֵף לֵאמֹר
אָבִיךָ צִוָּה לִפְנֵי מוֹתוֹ לֵאמֹר: כֹּה־תֹאמְרוּ לְיוֹסֵף

ה   פַּרְעֹה לֵאמֹר: אָבִי הִשְׁבִּיעַנִי לֵאמֹר הִנֵּה אָנֹכִי
מֵת בְּקִבְרִי אֲשֶׁר כָּרִיתִי לִי בְּאֶרֶץ כְּנַעַן שָׁמָּה
תִּקְבְּרֵנִי וְעַתָּה אֶעֱלֶה־נָּא וְאֶקְבְּרָה אֶת־אָבִי וְאָשׁוּבָה:
ו   וַיֹּאמֶר פַּרְעֹה עֲלֵה וּקְבֹר אֶת־אָבִיךָ כַּאֲשֶׁר הִשְׁבִּיעֶךָ:
ז   וַיַּעַל יוֹסֵף לִקְבֹּר אֶת־אָבִיו וַיַּעֲלוּ אִתּוֹ כָּל־עַבְדֵי
פַרְעֹה זִקְנֵי בֵיתוֹ וְכֹל זִקְנֵי אֶרֶץ־מִצְרָיִם: וְכֹל בֵּית
ח   יוֹסֵף וְאֶחָיו וּבֵית אָבִיו רַק טַפָּם וְצֹאנָם וּבְקָרָם
ט   עָזְבוּ בְּאֶרֶץ גֹּשֶׁן: וַיַּעַל עִמּוֹ גַּם־רֶכֶב גַּם־פָּרָשִׁים וַיְהִי
י   הַמַּחֲנֶה כָּבֵד מְאֹד: וַיָּבֹאוּ עַד־גֹּרֶן הָאָטָד אֲשֶׁר
בְּעֵבֶר הַיַּרְדֵּן וַיִּסְפְּדוּ־שָׁם מִסְפֵּד גָּדוֹל וְכָבֵד מְאֹד
יא   וַיַּעַשׂ לְאָבִיו אֵבֶל שִׁבְעַת יָמִים: וַיַּרְא יוֹשֵׁב הָאָרֶץ

made me swear, saying, "I am about to die. Be sure to bury me in the grave which I made ready for myself in the land of Canaan." Now, therefore, let me go up and bury my father; then I shall return.'" **6]** And Pharaoh said, "Go up and bury your father, as he made you promise on oath."

7] So Joseph went up to bury his father; and with him went up all the officials of Pharaoh, the senior members of his court, and all of Egypt's dignitaries, **8]** together with all of Joseph's household, his brothers, and his father's household; only their children, their flocks, and their herds were left in the region of Goshen. **9]** Chariots, too, and horsemen went up with him; it was a very large troop.

10] When they came to Goren ha-Atad, which is beyond the Jordan, they held there a very great and solemn lamentation; and he observed a mourning period of seven days for his father. **11]** And when the Canaanite inhabitants of the land saw the mourning at Goren ha-Atad, they said, "This is a solemn mourning on the part of the Egyptians." That is why it was named Abel-mizraim, which is beyond the Jordan. **12]** Thus his sons did for him as he had instructed them. **13]** His sons carried him to the land of Canaan, and buried him in the cave of the field of Machpelah, the field near Mamre, which Abraham had bought for a burial site from Ephron the Hittite. **14]** After burying his father, Joseph returned to Egypt, he and his brothers and all who had gone up with him to bury his father.

15] When Joseph's brothers saw that their father was dead, they said, "What if Joseph still bears a grudge against us and pays us back for all the wrong that we did him!" **16]** So they sent this message to Joseph, "Before his death your father left this instruction: **17]** So shall

10] *Goren ha-Atad*. Others "the threshing floor of Atad."

Beyond the Jordan. East of the Jordan (see also verse 11). The procession took a circuitous route around the Dead Sea and approached Hebron from the north. Was the funeral an opportunity to impress as many people as possible? Or was it, in the context of the biblical scheme, a prefiguration of what would happen when the bones of Joseph would make the same journey, so that Jacob even in death showed his descendants the road to the Promised Land? [2].

Seven days. In Jewish tradition the basic time of mourning (*shivah*, seven).

/A talmudic passage derives the custom of *shivah* from this verse [3]./

11] *Abel-mizraim*. Interpreted as "the mourning of the Egyptians."

כג וָעֶ֣שֶׂר שָׁנִ֑ים וַיַּ֤רְא יוֹסֵף֙ לְאֶפְרַ֔יִם בְּנֵ֖י שִׁלֵּשִׁ֑ים גַּ֗ם
כד בְּנֵ֤י מָכִיר֙ בֶּן־מְנַשֶּׁ֔ה יֻלְּד֖וּ עַל־בִּרְכֵּ֥י יוֹסֵֽף: וַיֹּ֤אמֶר
יוֹסֵף֙ אֶל־אֶחָ֔יו אָנֹכִ֖י מֵ֑ת וֵֽאלֹהִ֞ים פָּקֹ֧ד יִפְקֹ֣ד אֶתְכֶ֗ם
וְהֶעֱלָ֤ה אֶתְכֶם֙ מִן־הָאָ֣רֶץ הַזֹּ֔את אֶל־הָאָ֕רֶץ אֲשֶׁ֥ר
כה נִשְׁבַּ֛ע לְאַבְרָהָ֥ם לְיִצְחָ֖ק וּֽלְיַעֲקֹֽב: וַיַּשְׁבַּ֣ע יוֹסֵ֔ף אֶת־
בְּנֵ֥י יִשְׂרָאֵ֖ל לֵאמֹ֑ר פָּקֹ֨ד יִפְקֹ֤ד אֱלֹהִים֙ אֶתְכֶ֔ם
כו וְהַֽעֲלִתֶ֥ם אֶת־עַצְמֹתַ֖י מִזֶּֽה: וַיָּ֣מָת יוֹסֵ֔ף בֶּן־מֵאָ֥ה וָעֶ֖שֶׂר
שָׁנִ֑ים וַיַּחַנְט֣וּ אֹת֔וֹ וַיִּ֥ישֶׂם בָּאָר֖וֹן בְּמִצְרָֽיִם:

Haftarah Vayechi, p. 359

אָ֣נָּ֡א שָׂ֣א נָ֠א פֶּ֣שַׁע אַחֶ֤יךָ וְחַטָּאתָם֙ כִּי־רָעָ֣ה גְמָל֔וּךָ
וְעַתָּ֕ה שָׂ֣א נָ֔א לְפֶ֖שַׁע עַבְדֵ֣י אֱלֹהֵ֣י אָבִ֑יךָ וַיֵּ֥בְךְּ יוֹסֵ֖ף
יח בְּדַבְּרָ֥ם אֵלָֽיו: וַיֵּֽלְכוּ֙ גַּם־אֶחָ֔יו וַיִּפְּל֖וּ לְפָנָ֑יו וַיֹּ֣אמְר֔וּ
יט הִנֶּ֥נּֽוּ לְךָ֖ לַעֲבָדִֽים: וַיֹּ֧אמֶר אֲלֵהֶ֛ם יוֹסֵ֖ף אַל־תִּירָ֑אוּ
כ כִּ֛י הֲתַ֥חַת אֱלֹהִ֖ים אָֽנִי: וְאַתֶּ֕ם חֲשַׁבְתֶּ֥ם עָלַ֖י רָעָ֑ה
אֱלֹהִים֙ חֲשָׁבָ֣הּ לְטֹבָ֔ה לְמַ֗עַן עֲשֹׂ֛ה כַּיּ֥וֹם הַזֶּ֖ה לְהַחֲיֹ֥ת
כא עַם־רָֽב: וְעַתָּה֙ אַל־תִּירָ֔אוּ אָנֹכִ֛י אֲכַלְכֵּ֥ל אֶתְכֶ֖ם
כב וְאֶֽת־טַפְּכֶ֑ם וַיְנַחֵ֣ם אוֹתָ֔ם וַיְדַבֵּ֖ר עַל־לִבָּֽם: וַיֵּ֤שֶׁב
יוֹסֵף֙ בְּמִצְרַ֔יִם ה֖וּא וּבֵ֣ית אָבִ֑יו וַיְחִ֣י יוֹסֵ֔ף מֵאָ֥ה

you say to Joseph, 'Forgive, I urge you, the offense and guilt of your brothers who treated you so harshly.' Therefore, please forgive the offense of the servants of the God of your father." And Joseph was in tears as they spoke to him.

18] His brothers went to him themselves, flung themselves before him, and said, "We are prepared to be your slaves. **19]** But Joseph said to them, "Have no fear! Am I a substitute for God? **20]** Besides, although you intended me harm, God intended it for good, so as to bring about the present result—the survival of many people. **21]** And so, fear not. I will sustain you and your children." Thus he reassured them, speaking kindly to them.

22] So Joseph and his father's household remained in Egypt. Joseph lived one hundred and ten years. **23]** Joseph lived to see children of the third generation of Ephraim; the children of Machir son of Manasseh were likewise born upon Joseph's knees. **24]** At length, Joseph said to his brothers, "I am about to die. God will surely take notice of you and bring you up from this land to the land which He promised on oath to Abraham, to Isaac, and to Jacob." **25]** So Joseph made the sons of Israel swear, saying, "When God has taken notice of you, you shall carry up my bones from here."

26] Joseph died at the age of one hundred and ten years; and he was embalmed and placed in a coffin in Egypt.

22] *One hundred and ten years.* Considered the ideal life span in Egypt.
/ Joshua, who will bring Joseph's bones back to Canaan, will also live 110 years [4]./
23] *Upon Joseph's knees.* Either to indicate Joseph's long life, which saw great-grandchildren, or the record of an adoption. Joseph may have adopted Machir as his son as Jacob adopted Ephraim and Manasseh. In the time of the Judges the clan of Machir became virtually equated with one-half of Manassesh and was renowned for its administrative abilities (Judg. 5:14), thus resembling Joseph.

24] *To Abraham, to Isaac, and to Jacob.* In this passage the Patriarchs are mentioned together for the first time.

25] *Carry my bones.* The promise will be fulfilled by Moses and Joshua (Exod. 13:19; Josh. 24:32).

26] *In Egypt.* The last word of Genesis is a bridge to Exodus, a reminder also that much of the book is set outside of Canaan, and that Israel's beginnings belonged to a nomadic or semi-nomadic past.

Measure of a Man

The last chapter of Genesis once again brings the character of Joseph into focus. In his devotion to his father and in his warm affection for his brothers, we see a full picture of this man who is "the true son, the true brother, the true servant . . . loyal and faithful, disinterested and sincere, modest and considerate" [5].[1] But while he is the obvious hero of the tale, the reader realizes that behind the man, behind the friend of Pharaoh and the guide of Egypt, stands God, the Friend of Abraham and the Guardian of Israel.

Joseph's greatness is in a large measure due to his own awareness that he is serving a higher destiny. Egypt has been good to him, it has given him everything a man could hope for. Still, to him it represents exile; his home is elsewhere. It is to a land not yet his that his bones will be taken; as his people wander, he will wander; as they find a home, he will find his home with them. Joseph is a man who in many ways represents the Jew-to-be, who remains a son of his father and of his people, who wants to return to his origins, and who even in death will not be separated from the fate of his descendants. A monument in Egypt is little to him when compared to the monument he will have erected in the hearts of his people; the survival about which he speaks is not his own so much as that of his heritage.

"Am I a substitute for God?" (Gen. 50:19) he asks and thereby shows himself the prototype of the religious man. He acknowledges his human limitations in the midst of affluence and power and, at the same time, acknowledges the ultimate power of God. This is true greatness fashioned out of suffering and hardship; it is great will and deep devotion fashioned out of ability and humility.

Thus ends the Book of Genesis. It opened with "When God began to create" and then turned to the story of the Fathers. It is a book that reaches from the creation of the world to the creation of the people of Israel. The Midrash says that God created the Torah even before He formed the world. Now, in Egyptian exile and slavery, a people will arise to whom He can entrust this precious gift.

---

[1] In assessing these qualities, one scholar finds Joseph the ideal of the Jewish "wisdom school" [6].

GLEANINGS

Hatred

The brethren of Joseph could never have done him so much good with their love and favor as they did with their malice and hatred.

THOMAS MORE [7]

A White Lie

The brothers told Joseph about Jacob's last instructions of which, however, nothing is recorded [Gen. 50:16, 17]. Said R. Ilaa: "A person may tell a white lie for the sake of peace." R. Simeon b. Gamaliel taught: "Great is peace, for even the tribal ancestors resorted to a fabrication in order to make peace between Joseph and themselves."

TALMUD [8]

Joseph's Kindness

The Rabbis taught: "He who shows himself merciful to his fellow men proves thereby that he is a descendant of Abraham, Isaac, and Jacob; and he who is cruel to his fellow man proves that he is no descendant of theirs."

MIDRASH [9]

Coffin and Ark

The word for both is אָרוֹן [aron, a word nowhere else in the Bible used for coffin]. Why? So that in their wanderings through the desert the children of Israel would carry with them both the aron of Joseph and the aron containing the Tablets of the Law, to show that in one aron was a man who fulfilled the commandments contained in the other. The Torah is indeed in the reach of man.

TALMUD [10]

Summation

And he lived a hundred and ten years and then died at a good old age, having enjoyed the greatest perfection of beauty, and wisdom, and eloquence of speech. The beauty of his person is testified to by the violent love with which he inflamed the wife of the eunuch; his wisdom by the evenness of his conduct in the indescribable variety of circumstances that attended the whole of his life, by which he wrought regularity among things that were irregular and harmony among things that were discordant. His eloquence of speech is displayed in his interpretation of the dreams, in his affability in ordinary conversation, and by the persuasion which followed his words; in consequence of which his subjects all obeyed him cheerfully and voluntarily rather than from any compulsion.

Of these hundred and ten years he spent seventeen, till the expiration of his boyhood, in his father's house; and thirteen he passed amid unforeseen events, being plotted against, and sold, and becoming a slave, and having false accusations brought against him, and being thrown into prison; and the remaining eighty years he spent in authority and in all manner of prosperity, being the most excellent manager and administrator, both of scarcity and plenty, and the most competent of all men to manage affairs under either complexion of circumstances.

PHILO [11]

318

הפטרות

HAFTAROT

בראשית

Isaiah

42 : 5 – 43 : 11

Chapters 40–66 of the Book of Isaiah are the work of an unknown author (often referred to as Deutero-Isaiah) who lived in Babylon during the days of the exile (sixth century B.C.E.). He preached unwavering trust in a God who would surely restore Israel to its homeland. Of all the prophets he is the most lyrical and his imagery the richest.

Addressing his people languishing in exile, Isaiah proclaims the absolute sovereignty of God. Even as He created heaven and earth (verse 5 which connects the haftarah with the Torah reading of Creation) so He is also master of history and will redeem Israel.

מב

5] כֹּה־אָמַ֞ר הָאֵ֣ל ׀ יְהֹוָ֗ה
בּוֹרֵ֤א הַשָּׁמַ֙יִם֙ וְנ֣וֹטֵיהֶ֔ם
רֹקַ֥ע הָאָ֖רֶץ וְצֶאֱצָאֶ֑יהָ
נֹתֵ֤ן נְשָׁמָה֙ לָעָ֣ם עָלֶ֔יהָ
וְר֖וּחַ לַהֹלְכִ֥ים בָּֽהּ׃

6] אֲנִ֧י יְהֹוָ֛ה קְרָאתִ֥יךָֽ בְצֶ֖דֶק
וְאַחְזֵ֣ק בְּיָדֶ֑ךָ
וְאֶצׇּרְךָ֙ וְאֶתֶּנְךָ֔
לִבְרִ֥ית עָ֖ם לְא֥וֹר גּוֹיִֽם׃

7] לִפְקֹ֖חַ עֵינַ֣יִם עִוְר֑וֹת
לְהוֹצִ֤יא מִמַּסְגֵּר֙ אַסִּ֔יר
מִבֵּ֥ית כֶּ֖לֶא יֹ֥שְׁבֵי חֹֽשֶׁךְ׃

8] אֲנִ֥י יְהֹוָ֖ה ה֣וּא שְׁמִ֑י
וּכְבוֹדִי֙ לְאַחֵ֣ר לֹֽא־אֶתֵּ֔ן
וּתְהִלָּתִ֖י לַפְּסִילִֽים׃

9] הָרִֽאשֹׁנ֖וֹת הִנֵּה־בָ֑אוּ
וַֽחֲדָשׁוֹת֙ אֲנִ֣י מַגִּ֔יד
בְּטֶ֥רֶם תִּצְמַ֖חְנָה אַשְׁמִ֥יע אֶתְכֶֽם׃

Chapter 42

5] Thus said God the LORD,
Who created the heavens and stretched them out,
Who spread out the earth and what it brings
   forth,
Who gave breath to the people upon it
And life to those who walk thereon:

6] I the LORD, in My grace, have summoned you,
And I have grasped you by the hand.
I created you, and appointed you
A b-covenant-people,-b c-a light of nations-c—

7] d-Opening eyes deprived of light,-d
Rescuing prisoners from confinement,
From the dungeon those who sit in darkness.

8] I am the LORD, that is My name;
I will not yield My glory to another,
Nor My renown to idols.

9] See, the things once predicted have come,
And now I foretell new things,
Announce to you ere they sprout up.

b-b *Lit. "covenant of a people"; meaning of Heb. uncertain*
c-c *See 49.6; "light": i.e., the agent of good fortune*
d-d *An idiom meaning "freeing the imprisoned"; cf. 61.1*

10] Sing to the LORD a new song,
His praise from the ends of the earth—
ᵉ˙You who sail the sea and you creatures in it,
You coastlands˙ᵉ and their inhabitants!

שִׁירוּ לַיהוָֹה שִׁיר חָדָשׁ [10
תְּהִלָּתוֹ מִקְצֵה הָאָרֶץ
יוֹרְדֵי הַיָּם וּמְלֹאוֹ
אִיִּים וְיֹשְׁבֵיהֶם:

11] Let the desert and its towns cry aloud,
The villages where Kedar dwells;
Let Sela's inhabitants shout,
Call out from the peaks of the mountains.

יִשְׂאוּ מִדְבָּר וְעָרָיו [11
חֲצֵרִים תֵּשֵׁב קֵדָר
יָרֹנּוּ יֹשְׁבֵי סֶלַע
מֵרֹאשׁ הָרִים יִצְוָחוּ:

12] Let them do honor to the LORD,
And tell His glory in the coastlands.

יָשִׂימוּ לַיהוָֹה כָּבוֹד [12
וּתְהִלָּתוֹ בָּאִיִּים יַגֵּידוּ:

13] The LORD goes forth like a warrior,
Like a fighter He whips up His rage.
He yeils, He roars aloud,
He charges upon His enemies.

יְהוָֹה כַּגִּבּוֹר יֵצֵא [13
כְּאִישׁ מִלְחָמוֹת יָעִיר קִנְאָה
יָרִיעַ אַף־יַצְרִיחַ
עַל־אֹיְבָיו יִתְגַּבָּר:

14] "I have kept silent ᶠ˙far too long,˙ᶠ
Kept still and restrained Myself;
Now I will scream like a woman in labor,
I will pant and I will gasp.

הֶחֱשֵׁיתִי מֵעוֹלָם [14
אַחֲרִישׁ אֶתְאַפָּק
כַּיּוֹלֵדָה אֶפְעֶה
אֶשֹּׁם וְאֶשְׁאַף יָחַד:

15] Hills and heights will I scorch,
Cause all their green to wither;
I will turn rivers into isles,ᵍ
And dry the marshes up.

אַחֲרִיב הָרִים וּגְבָעוֹת [15
וְכָל־עֶשְׂבָּם אוֹבִישׁ
וְשַׂמְתִּי נְהָרוֹת לָאִיִּים
וַאֲגַמִּים אוֹבִישׁ:

16] I will lead the blind
By a road they did not know,
And I will make them walk
By paths they never knew.
I will turn darkness before them to light,

וְהוֹלַכְתִּי עִוְרִים [16
בְּדֶרֶךְ לֹא יָדָעוּ
בִּנְתִיבוֹת לֹא־יָדְעוּ אַדְרִיכֵם
אָשִׂים מַחְשָׁךְ לִפְנֵיהֶם לָאוֹר

ᵉ˙ᵉ Emendation yields "Let the sea roar and its creatures, / The coastlands...." Cf.
  Ps. 98.7
ᶠ˙ᶠ Lit. "from of old"   ᵍ Emendation yields "desert"

Rough places into level ground.
These are the promises—
I will keep them without fail.

17] Driven back and utterly shamed
Shall be those who trust in an image,
Those who say to idols,
'You are our gods!' ''

18] Listen, you who are deaf;
You blind ones, look up and see!

19] Who is so blind as My servant,
So deaf as the messenger I send?
Who is so blind as the chosen[h] one,
So blind as the servant of the LORD?

20] Seeing many things, [i]he gives[i] no heed;
With ears open, he hears nothing.

21] [i]The LORD desires His [servant's] vindication,
That he may magnify and glorify [His] Teaching.

22] Yet it is a people plundered and despoiled:
All of them are trapped in holes,
Imprisoned in dungeons.
They are given over to plunder, with none to
     rescue them;
To despoilment, with none to say "Give back!"

23] If only you would listen to this,
Attend and give heed from now on!

ומְעַקַשִּׁים לְמִישׁוֹר

אֵלֶּה הַדְּבָרִים עֲשִׂיתָם

וְלֹא עֲזַבְתִּים:

17] נָסֹגוּ אָחוֹר יֵבֹשׁוּ בֹשֶׁת

הַבֹּטְחִים בַּפָּסֶל

הָאֹמְרִים לְמַסֵּכָה

אַתֶּם אֱלֹהֵינוּ:

18] הַחֵרְשִׁים שְׁמָעוּ

וְהַעִוְרִים הַבִּיטוּ לִרְאוֹת:

19] מִי עִוֵּר כִּי אִם־עַבְדִּי

וְחֵרֵשׁ כְּמַלְאָכִי אֶשְׁלָח

מִי עִוֵּר כִּמְשֻׁלָּם

וְעִוֵּר כְּעֶבֶד יְהוָה:

20] רָאוֹת רַבּוֹת וְלֹא תִשְׁמֹר

פָּקוֹחַ אָזְנַיִם וְלֹא יִשְׁמָע:

21] יְהוָה חָפֵץ לְמַעַן צִדְקוֹ

יַגְדִּיל תּוֹרָה וְיַאְדִּיר:

22] וְהוּא עַם־בָּזוּז וְשָׁסוּי

הָפֵחַ בַּחוּרִים כֻּלָּם

וּבְבָתֵּי כְלָאִים הָחְבָּאוּ

הָיוּ לָבַז וְאֵין מַצִּיל

מְשִׁסָּה וְאֵין־אֹמֵר הָשַׁב:

23] מִי בָכֶם יַאֲזִין זֹאת

יַקְשִׁב וְיִשְׁמַע לְאָחוֹר:

---

h Meaning of Heb. uncertain
i-i Heb. "you give"
i Meaning of verse uncertain; cf. 43.9-12

24] Who was it gave Jacob over to despoilment
And Israel to plunderers?
Surely, the LORD against whom they[k] sinned
In whose ways they would not walk
And whose Teaching they would not obey.

25] So He poured out wrath upon them,
His anger and the fury of war.
It blazed upon them all about, but they heeded
    not;
It burned among them, but they gave it no
    thought.

Chapter 43

1] But now thus said the LORD
Who created you, O Jacob,
Who formed you, O Israel:
Fear not, for I will redeem you;
I have singled you out by name,
You are Mine.

2] When you pass through water,
I will be with you;
Through streams,
They shall not overwhelm you.
When you walk through fire,
You shall not be scorched;
Through flame,
It shall not burn you.

3] For I the LORD am your God,
The Holy One of Israel, your Savior.
I give Egypt as a ransom for you,
Ethiopia and Saba in exchange for you.

[24] מִי־נָתַן לִמְשִׁסָּה יַעֲקֹב
וְיִשְׂרָאֵל לְבֹזְזִים
הֲלוֹא יְהֹוָה זוּ חָטָאנוּ לוֹ
וְלֹא־אָבוּ בִדְרָכָיו הָלוֹךְ
וְלֹא שָׁמְעוּ בְּתוֹרָתוֹ:

[25] וַיִּשְׁפֹּךְ עָלָיו חֵמָה
אַפּוֹ וֶעֱזוּז מִלְחָמָה
וַתְּלַהֲטֵהוּ מִסָּבִיב וְלֹא יָדָע
וַתִּבְעַר־בּוֹ וְלֹא־יָשִׂים עַל־לֵב:

מג

[1] וְעַתָּה כֹּה־אָמַר יְהֹוָה
בֹּרַאֲךָ יַעֲקֹב
וְיֹצֶרְךָ יִשְׂרָאֵל
אַל־תִּירָא כִּי גְאַלְתִּיךָ
קָרָאתִי בְשִׁמְךָ
לִי־אָתָּה:

[2] כִּי־תַעֲבֹר בַּמַּיִם
אִתְּךָ אָנִי
וּבַנְּהָרוֹת
לֹא יִשְׁטְפוּךָ
כִּי־תֵלֵךְ בְּמוֹ־אֵשׁ
לֹא תִכָּוֶה
וְלֶהָבָה
לֹא תִבְעַר־בָּךְ:

[3] כִּי אֲנִי יְהֹוָה אֱלֹהֶיךָ
קְדוֹשׁ יִשְׂרָאֵל מוֹשִׁיעֶךָ
נָתַתִּי כָפְרְךָ מִצְרַיִם
כּוּשׁ וּסְבָא תַּחְתֶּיךָ:

[k] Heb. "we"

4] Because you are precious to Me,
And honored, and I love you,
I give men in exchange for you
And peoples in your stead.

מֵאֲשֶׁר יָקַרְתָּ בְעֵינַי [4

נִכְבַּדְתָּ וַאֲנִי אֲהַבְתִּיךָ

וְאֶתֵּן אָדָם תַּחְתֶּיךָ

וּלְאֻמִּים תַּחַת נַפְשֶׁךָ:

5] Fear not, for I am with you:
I will bring your folk from the East,
Will gather you out of the West;

אַל־תִּירָא כִּי־אִתְּךָ אָנִי [5

מִמִּזְרָח אָבִיא זַרְעֶךָ

וּמִמַּעֲרָב אֲקַבְּצֶךָּ:

6] I will say to the North, "Give back!"
And to the South, "Do not withhold!
Bring My sons from afar,
And My daughters from the end of the earth—

אֹמַר לַצָּפוֹן תֵּנִי [6

וּלְתֵימָן אַל־תִּכְלָאִי

הָבִיאִי בָנַי מֵרָחוֹק

וּבְנוֹתַי מִקְצֵה הָאָרֶץ:

7] All who are linked to My name,
Whom I have created,
Formed, and made for My glory—

כֹּל הַנִּקְרָא בִשְׁמִי [7

וְלִכְבוֹדִי בְּרָאתִיו

יְצַרְתִּיו אַף־עֲשִׂיתִיו:

8] Setting free that people,
Blind though it has eyes
And deaf though it has ears."

הוֹצִיא עַם־ [8

עִוֵּר וְעֵינַיִם יֵשׁ

וְחֵרְשִׁים וְאָזְנַיִם לָמוֹ:

9] All the nations assemble as one,
The peoples gather.
Who among them declared this,
Foretold to us the things that have happened?
Let them produce their witnesses and be
    vindicated,
That men, hearing them, may say, "It is true!"[a]

כָּל־הַגּוֹיִם נִקְבְּצוּ יַחְדָּו [9

וְיֵאָסְפוּ לְאֻמִּים

מִי בָהֶם יַגִּיד זֹאת

וְרִאשֹׁנוֹת יַשְׁמִיעֻנוּ

יִתְּנוּ עֵדֵיהֶם וְיִצְדָּקוּ

וְיִשְׁמְעוּ וְיֹאמְרוּ אֱמֶת:

10] My witnesses are *you*
                    —declares the LORD—
My servant, whom I have chosen.
To the end that you[b] may take thought,
And believe in Me,

אַתֶּם עֵדַי [10

נְאֻם־יְהוָה

וְעַבְדִּי אֲשֶׁר בָּחָרְתִּי

לְמַעַן תֵּדְעוּ

וְתַאֲמִינוּ לִי

[a] I.e., that the other nations' gods are real
[b] Emendation yields "they"

324

And understand that I am He:
Before Me no god was formed,
And after Me none shall exist—

11] None but Me, the LORD.
Beside Me, none can grant triumph.

וְתָבִ֙ינוּ כִּי־אֲנִ֣י ה֔וּא
לְפָנַי֙ לֹא־נ֣וֹצַר אֵ֔ל
וְאַחֲרַ֖י לֹא־יִהְיֶֽה׃
11] אָנֹכִ֥י אָנֹכִ֖י יְהוָ֑ה
וְאֵ֥ין מִבַּלְעָדַ֖י מוֹשִֽׁיעַ׃

נח

Isaiah
54:1—55:5

Chapters 40–66 of the Book of Isaiah are the work of an unknown author (often referred to as Deutero-Isaiah) who lived in Babylon during the days of the exile (sixth century B.C.E.). He preached unwavering trust in a God who would surely restore Israel to its homeland. Of all the prophets he is the most lyrical and his imagery the richest.

Isaiah consoles his people whom he compares to a barren woman who desperately desires children that will assure her future. Even as God made a covenant with Noah (verse 11, the connection with the Torah reading) so will He maintain his covenant with Israel now languishing in exile.

נד

Chapter 54

1] Shout, O barren one,
You who bore no child!
Shout aloud for joy,
You who did not travail!
For the children of the wife forlorn
Shall outnumber those of the espoused
—said the LORD

א] רָנִּי עֲקָרָה
לֹא יָלָדָה
פִּצְחִי רִנָּה וְצַהֲלִי
לֹא־חָלָה
כִּי־רַבִּים בְּנֵי־שׁוֹמֵמָה
מִבְּנֵי בְעוּלָה
אָמַר יְהוָה:

2] Enlarge the site of your tent,
*Extend the size of your dwelling,*ᵃ
Do not stint!
Lengthen the ropes, and drive the pegs firm.

ב] הַרְחִיבִי מְקוֹם אָהֳלֵךְ
וִירִיעוֹת מִשְׁכְּנוֹתַיִךְ יַטּוּ
אַל־תַּחְשֹׂכִי
הַאֲרִיכִי מֵיתָרַיִךְ וִיתֵדֹתַיִךְ חַזֵּקִי:

3] For you shall spread out to the right and the
left;
Your offspring shall dispossess nationsᵇ
And shall people the desolate towns.

ג] כִּי־יָמִין וּשְׂמֹאול תִּפְרֹצִי
וְזַרְעֵךְ גּוֹיִם יִירָשׁ
וְעָרִים נְשַׁמּוֹת יוֹשִׁיבוּ:

4] Fear not, you shall not be shamed;
Do not cringe, you shall not be disgraced.
For you shall forget
The reproach of your youth,
And remember no more
The shame of your widowhood.

ד] אַל־תִּירְאִי כִּי־לֹא תֵבוֹשִׁי
וְאַל־תִּכָּלְמִי כִּי־לֹא תַחְפִּירִי
כִּי בֹשֶׁת עֲלוּמַיִךְ תִּשְׁכָּחִי
וְחֶרְפַּת אַלְמְנוּתַיִךְ לֹא תִזְכְּרִי־עוֹד:

מלא ו' v. 3.

ᵃ⁻ᵃ Lit. "Let the cloths of your dwelling extend"
ᵇ I.e., the foreigners who had occupied regions from which Israelites had been exiled;
cf. II Kings 17.24

5] For He who made you will espouse you—
His name is "Lord of Hosts";
The Holy One of Israel will redeem you,
Who is called "God of all the Earth."

6] The Lord has called you back
As a wife forlorn and forsaken.
Can one cast off the wife of his youth?
　　　　　　　　　　—said your God.

7] For a little while I forsook you,
But with vast love I will bring you back.

8] In slight anger, for a moment,
I hid My face from you;
But with kindness everlasting
I will take you back in love
　　　　　　　—said the Lord your Redeemer.

9] For this to Me is like the waters[c] of Noah:
As I swore that the waters of Noah
Nevermore would flood the earth,
So I swear that I will not
Be angry with you or rebuke you.

10] For the mountains may move
And the hills be shaken,
But my loyalty shall never move from you,
Nor My covenant of friendship be shaken
　　　—said the Lord, who takes you back in love.

11] Unhappy, storm-tossed one, uncomforted!
I will lay carbuncles[d] as your building stones
And make your foundations of sapphires.

כִּי בֹעֲלַיִךְ עֹשַׂיִךְ	5]
יְהוָה צְבָאוֹת שְׁמוֹ	
וְגֹאֲלֵךְ קְדוֹשׁ יִשְׂרָאֵל	
אֱלֹהֵי כָל־הָאָרֶץ יִקָּרֵא:	
כִּי־כְאִשָּׁה עֲזוּבָה	6]
וַעֲצוּבַת רוּחַ קְרָאָךְ יְהוָה	
וְאֵשֶׁת נְעוּרִים	
כִּי תִמָּאֵס	
אָמַר אֱלֹהָיִךְ:	
בְּרֶגַע קָטֹן עֲזַבְתִּיךְ	7]
וּבְרַחֲמִים גְּדוֹלִים אֲקַבְּצֵךְ:	
בְּשֶׁצֶף קֶצֶף הִסְתַּרְתִּי פָנַי רֶגַע מִמֵּךְ	8]
וּבְחֶסֶד עוֹלָם רִחַמְתִּיךְ	
אָמַר גֹּאֲלֵךְ יְהוָה:	
כִּי־מֵי נֹחַ זֹאת לִי	9]
אֲשֶׁר נִשְׁבַּעְתִּי מֵעֲבֹר מֵי־נֹחַ	
עוֹד עַל־הָאָרֶץ	
כֵּן נִשְׁבַּעְתִּי	
מִקְּצֹף עָלַיִךְ וּמִגְּעָר־בָּךְ:	
כִּי הֶהָרִים יָמוּשׁוּ	10]
וְהַגְּבָעוֹת תְּמוּטֶינָה	
וְחַסְדִּי מֵאִתֵּךְ לֹא־יָמוּשׁ	
וּבְרִית שְׁלוֹמִי לֹא תָמוּט	
אָמַר מְרַחֲמֵךְ יְהוָה:	
עֲנִיָּה סֹעֲרָה לֹא נֻחָמָה	11]
הִנֵּה אָנֹכִי מַרְבִּיץ בַּפּוּךְ אֲבָנַיִךְ	
וִיסַדְתִּיךְ בַּסַּפִּירִים:	

v. 9. נ״א כִּימֵי v. 10. עד כאן לספרדים

c Other Heb. mss. and the ancient versions read "days"
d Taking puch as a by-form of nofech; so already Rashi

12] I will make your battlements of rubies,
Your gates of precious stones,
The whole encircling wall of gems.

13] And all your children shall be disciples of the
LORD,
And great shall be the happiness of your children;

14] You shall be established through righteous-
ness.
You shall be safe from oppression,
And shall have no fear;
From ruin, and it shall not come near you.

15] ^eSurely no harm can be done
Without My consent:
Whoever would harm you
Shall fall because of you.

16] It is I who created the smith
To fan the charcoal fire
And produce the tools for his work;
So it is I who create
The instruments of havoc.

17] No weapon formed against you
Shall succeed,
And every tongue that contends with you at law
You shall defeat.
Such is the lot of the servants of the LORD,
Such their triumph through Me
—declares the LORD.

וְשַׂמְתִּי כַּדְכֹד שִׁמְשֹׁתַיִךְ [12]

וּשְׁעָרַיִךְ לְאַבְנֵי אֶקְדָּח

וְכָל־גְּבוּלֵךְ לְאַבְנֵי־חֵפֶץ:

וְכָל־בָּנַיִךְ לִמּוּדֵי יְהוָה [13]

וְרַב שְׁלוֹם בָּנָיִךְ:

בִּצְדָקָה תִּכּוֹנָנִי [14]

רַחֲקִי מֵעֹשֶׁק

כִּי־לֹא תִירָאִי

וּמִמְּחִתָּה כִּי לֹא־תִקְרַב אֵלָיִךְ:

הֵן גּוֹר יָגוּר [15]

אֶפֶס מֵאוֹתִי

מִי־גָר אִתָּךְ

עָלַיִךְ יִפּוֹל:

הִנֵּה אָנֹכִי בָּרָאתִי חָרָשׁ [16]

נֹפֵחַ בְּאֵשׁ פֶּחָם

וּמוֹצִיא כְלִי לְמַעֲשֵׂהוּ

וְאָנֹכִי בָּרָאתִי

מַשְׁחִית לְחַבֵּל:

כָּל־כְּלִי יוּצַר עָלַיִךְ [17]

לֹא יִצְלָח

וְכָל־לָשׁוֹן תָּקוּם־אִתָּךְ לַמִּשְׁפָּט

תַּרְשִׁיעִי

זֹאת נַחֲלַת עַבְדֵי יְהוָה

וְצִדְקָתָם מֵאִתִּי

נְאֻם־יְהוָה:

^e *Meaning of verse uncertain*

1] Ho, all who are thirsty,
Come for water,
Even if you have no money;
Come, buy food and eat:
Buy food without money,
Wine and milk without cost.

1] הוֹי כָּל־צָמֵא
לְכוּ לַמַּיִם
וַאֲשֶׁר אֵין־לוֹ כָּסֶף
לְכוּ שִׁבְרוּ וֶאֱכֹלוּ
וּלְכוּ שִׁבְרוּ בְּלוֹא־כֶסֶף
וּבְלוֹא מְחִיר יַיִן וְחָלָב:

2] Why do you spend money for what is not
        bread,
Your earnings for what does not satisfy?
Give heed to Me,
And you shall eat choice food
And enjoy the richest viands.

2] לָמָּה תִשְׁקְלוּ־כֶסֶף בְּלוֹא־לֶחֶם
וִיגִיעֲכֶם בְּלוֹא לְשָׂבְעָה
שִׁמְעוּ שָׁמוֹעַ אֵלַי
וְאִכְלוּ־טוֹב
וְתִתְעַנַּג בַּדֶּשֶׁן נַפְשְׁכֶם:

3] Incline your ear and come to Me;
Hearken, and you shall be revived.
And I will make with you an everlasting covenant,
The enduring loyalty promised to David.

3] הַטּוּ אָזְנְכֶם וּלְכוּ אֵלַי
שִׁמְעוּ וּתְחִי נַפְשְׁכֶם
וְאֶכְרְתָה לָכֶם בְּרִית עוֹלָם
חַסְדֵי דָוִד הַנֶּאֱמָנִים:

4] *ᵃ⁻As I made him a leaderᵇ of peoples,
A prince and commander of peoples,

4] הֵן עֵד לְאוּמִּים נְתַתִּיו
נָגִיד וּמְצַוֵּה לְאֻמִּים:

5] So you shall summon a nation you did not
        know,
And a nation that did not know you
Shall come running to you*ᵃ—
For the sake of the Lᴏʀᴅ your God,
The Holy One of Israel who has glorified you.

5] הֵן גּוֹי לֹא־תֵדַע תִּקְרָא
וְגוֹי לֹא־יְדָעוּךָ
אֵלֶיךָ יָרוּצוּ
לְמַעַן יְהוָה אֱלֹהֶיךָ
וְלִקְדוֹשׁ יִשְׂרָאֵל כִּי פֵאֲרָךְ:

ᵃ⁻ᵃ *Cf. II Sam. 22.44–45 //Ps. 18.44–45*
ᵇ *Cf. Targum; others "witness"*

Chapters 40–66 of the Book of Isaiah are the work of an unknown author (often referred to as Deutero-Isaiah) who lived in Babylon during the days of the exile (sixth century B.C.E.). He preached unwavering trust in a God who would surely restore Israel to its homeland. Of all the prophets he is the most lyrical and his imagery the richest.

In this haftarah, Isaiah attempts to still his people's cry of despair. God, he says, does neither slumber nor sleep; His love for Israel has never wearied. Even as He called Abraham from among the nations so will He call Israel from the uttermost ends of dispersion and redeem it in love. This imagery connects sidrah and haftarah.

לך-לך

Isaiah

40 : 27 — 41 : 16

Chapter 40

27] Why do you say, O Jacob,
Why declare, O Israel,
"My way is hid from the Lord,
My cause is ignored by my God"?

28] Do you not know?
Have you not heard?
The Lord is God from of old,
Creator of the earth from end to end,
He never grows faint or weary,
His wisdom cannot be fathomed.

29] He gives strength to the weary,
Fresh vigor to the spent.

30] Youths may grow faint and weary,
And young men stumble and fall;

31] But they who trust in the Lord shall renew
   their strength
As eagles grow new plumes:[^1]
They shall run and not grow weary,
They shall march and not grow faint.

מ

27] לָמָּה תֹאמַר יַעֲקֹב
וּתְדַבֵּר יִשְׂרָאֵל
נִסְתְּרָה דַרְכִּי מֵיהוָֹה
וּמֵאֱלֹהַי מִשְׁפָּטִי יַעֲבוֹר:

28] הֲלוֹא יָדַעְתָּ אִם־לֹא שָׁמַעְתָּ
אֱלֹהֵי עוֹלָם יְהֹוָה
בּוֹרֵא קְצוֹת הָאָרֶץ
לֹא יִיעַף וְלֹא יִיגָע
אֵין חֵקֶר לִתְבוּנָתוֹ:

29] נֹתֵן לַיָּעֵף כֹּחַ
וּלְאֵין אוֹנִים עָצְמָה יַרְבֶּה:

30] וְיִעֲפוּ נְעָרִים וְיִגָעוּ
וּבַחוּרִים כָּשׁוֹל יִכָּשֵׁלוּ:

31] וְקוֹיֵ יְהֹוָה יַחֲלִיפוּ כֹחַ
יַעֲלוּ אֵבֶר כַּנְּשָׁרִים
יָרוּצוּ וְלֹא יִיגָעוּ
יֵלְכוּ וְלֹא יִיעָפוּ:

[^1]: *Alluding to a popular belief that eagles regain their youth when they molt; cf. Ps. 103.5*

Chapter 41

1] Stand silent before Me, coastlands,
And let nations *-renew their strength.-*
Let them approach to state their case;
Let us come forward together for argument.

הַחֲרִישׁוּ אֵלַי אִיִּים

וּלְאֻמִּים יַחֲלִיפוּ כֹחַ

יִגְּשׁוּ אָז יְדַבֵּרוּ

יַחְדָּו לַמִּשְׁפָּט נִקְרָבָה:

2] Who has roused a victor*b* from the East,
Summoned him to His service?
Has delivered up nations to him,
And trodden sovereigns down?
Has rendered their*c* swords like dust,
Their*c* bows like wind-blown straw?

מִי הֵעִיר מִמִּזְרָח

צֶדֶק יִקְרָאֵהוּ לְרַגְלוֹ

יִתֵּן לְפָנָיו גּוֹיִם

וּמְלָכִים יַרְדְּ

יִתֵּן כֶּעָפָר חַרְבּוֹ

כְּקַשׁ נִדָּף קַשְׁתּוֹ:

3] He pursues them, he goes on unscathed;
No shackle*d* is placed on his feet.

יִרְדְּפֵם יַעֲבוֹר שָׁלוֹם

אֹרַח בְּרַגְלָיו לֹא יָבוֹא:

4] Who has wrought and achieved this?
He who announced the generations from the
   start—
I, the LORD, who was first
And will be with the last as well.

מִי־פָעַל וְעָשָׂה

קֹרֵא הַדֹּרוֹת מֵרֹאשׁ

אֲנִי יְהֹוָה רִאשׁוֹן

וְאֶת־אַחֲרֹנִים אֲנִי־הוּא:

5] The coastlands look on in fear,
The ends of earth tremble.
They draw near and come;

רָאוּ אִיִּים וְיִירָאוּ

קְצוֹת הָאָרֶץ יֶחֱרָדוּ

קָרְבוּ וַיֶּאֱתָיוּן:

6] Each one helps the other,
Saying to his fellow, "Take courage!"

אִישׁ אֶת־רֵעֵהוּ יַעְזֹרוּ

וּלְאָחִיו יֹאמַר חֲזָק:

7] The woodworker encourages the smith;
He who flattens with the hammer
[Encourages] him who pounds the anvil.
He says of the riveting, "It is good!"
And he fixes it with nails,
That it may not topple.

וַיְחַזֵּק חָרָשׁ אֶת־צֹרֵף

מַחֲלִיק פַּטִּישׁ אֶת־הוֹלֶם פָּעַם

אֹמֵר לַדֶּבֶק טוֹב הוּא

וַיְחַזְּקֵהוּ בְמַסְמְרִים לֹא יִמּוֹט:

---

a-a Connection of Heb. uncertain

b Lit. "victory"

c Heb. "his"

d Orach has this meaning in Old Aramaic

8] But you, Israel, My servant,
Jacob, whom I have chosen,
Seed of Abraham My friend—

וְאַתָּה יִשְׂרָאֵל עַבְדִּי [8

יַעֲקֹב אֲשֶׁר בְּחַרְתִּיךָ

זֶרַע אַבְרָהָם אֹהֲבִי:

9] You whom I drew from the ends of the earth
And called from its far corners,
To whom I said: You are My servant;
I chose you, I have not rejected you—

אֲשֶׁר הֶחֱזַקְתִּיךָ מִקְצוֹת הָאָרֶץ [9

וּמֵאֲצִילֶיהָ קְרָאתִיךָ

וָאֹמַר לְךָ עַבְדִּי־אַתָּה

בְּחַרְתִּיךָ וְלֹא מְאַסְתִּיךָ:

10] Fear not, for I am with you,
Be not frightened, for I am your God;
I strengthen you and I help you,
I uphold you with My victorious right hand.

אַל־תִּירָא כִּי־עִמְּךָ אָנִי [10

אַל־תִּשְׁתָּע כִּי־אֲנִי אֱלֹהֶיךָ

אִמַּצְתִּיךָ אַף־עֲזַרְתִּיךָ

אַף־תְּמַכְתִּיךָ בִּימִין צִדְקִי:

11] Shamed and chagrined shall be
All who contend with you;
They who strive with you
Shall become as naught and shall perish.

הֵן יֵבֹשׁוּ וְיִכָּלְמוּ [11

כֹּל הַנֶּחֱרִים בָּךְ

יִהְיוּ כְאַיִן וְיֹאבְדוּ

אַנְשֵׁי רִיבֶךָ:

12] You may seek, but shall not find
Those who struggle with you;
Less than nothing shall be
The men who battle against you.

תְּבַקְשֵׁם וְלֹא תִמְצָאֵם [12

אַנְשֵׁי מַצֻּתֶךָ

יִהְיוּ כְאַיִן וּכְאֶפֶס

אַנְשֵׁי מִלְחַמְתֶּךָ:

13] For I the LORD am your God,
Who grasped your right hand,
Who say to you: Have no fear;
I will be your help.

כִּי אֲנִי יְהוָה אֱלֹהֶיךָ [13

מַחֲזִיק יְמִינֶךָ

הָאֹמֵר לְךָ אַל־תִּירָא

אֲנִי עֲזַרְתִּיךָ:

14] Fear not, O worm Jacob,
O ͨ men of ͨ Israel:
I will help you
                    —declares the LORD—
I, your Redeemer, the Holy One of Israel.

אַל־תִּירְאִי תּוֹלַעַת יַעֲקֹב [14

מְתֵי יִשְׂרָאֵל

אֲנִי עֲזַרְתִּיךְ נְאֻם־יְהוָה

וְגֹאֲלֵךְ קְדוֹשׁ יִשְׂרָאֵל:

ͨ–ͨ *Emendation yields "maggot"*

15] I will make of you a threshing-board,
A new thresher, with many spikes;
You shall thresh mountains to dust,
And make hills like chaff.

16] You shall winnow them
And the wind shall carry them off;
The whirlwind shall scatter them.
But you shall rejoice in the LORD,
And glory in the Holy One of Israel.

[15] הִנֵּה שַׂמְתִּיךְ לְמוֹרַג חָרוּץ חָדָשׁ

בַּעַל פִּיפִיּוֹת

תָּדוּשׁ הָרִים וְתָדֹק

וּגְבָעוֹת כַּמֹּץ תָּשִׂים:

[16] תִּזְרֵם וְרוּחַ תִּשָּׂאֵם

וּסְעָרָה תָּפִיץ אוֹתָם

וְאַתָּה תָּגִיל בַּיהוָה

בִּקְדוֹשׁ יִשְׂרָאֵל תִּתְהַלָּל:

The Book of Kings is divided into two parts. It spans four centuries and reaches from the last days of David to the destruction of the Temple by the Babylonians in 586 (or 585) B.C.E. It approaches history from a theological point of view: the story of Israel and Judah must be seen as a judgment of God on the people and its rulers.

ויךא

Torah and haftarah speak of women who have no sons. Both Sarah and the Shunammite woman give birth after receiving a divine promise (delivered by three messengers and by the prophet Elisha, respectively). In both readings the son is thereafter saved from death. Elisha, disciple of Elijah, lived in the ninth century B.C.E.

Second Kings

4 : 1-37

Chapter 4

ד

1] A certain woman, the wife of one of the disciples of the prophets, cried out to Elisha: "Your servant my husband is dead, and you know how your servant revered the LORD. And now a creditor is coming to seize my two children as slaves."

1] וְאִשָּׁה אַחַת מִנְּשֵׁי בְנֵי־הַנְּבִיאִים צָעֲקָה אֶל־אֱלִישָׁע לֵאמֹר עַבְדְּךָ אִישִׁי מֵת וְאַתָּה יָדַעְתָּ כִּי עַבְדְּךָ הָיָה יָרֵא אֶת־יְהֹוָה וְהַנֹּשֶׁה בָּא לָקַחַת אֶת־שְׁנֵי יְלָדַי לוֹ לַעֲבָדִים:

2] Elisha said to her, "What can I do for you? Tell me, what have you in the house?" She replied, "Your maidservant has nothing at all in the house, except a jug of oil."

2] וַיֹּאמֶר אֵלֶיהָ אֱלִישָׁע מָה אֶעֱשֶׂה־לָּךְ הַגִּידִי לִי מַה־יֶּשׁ־לָךְ בַּבָּיִת וַתֹּאמֶר אֵין לְשִׁפְחָתְךָ

3] "Go," he said, "and borrow vessels outside, from all your neighbors, empty vessels, as many as you can.

כֹל בַּבַּיִת כִּי אִם־אָסוּךְ שָׁמֶן: 3] וַיֹּאמֶר לְכִי שַׁאֲלִי־לָךְ כֵּלִים מִן־הַחוּץ מֵאֵת כָּל־שְׁכֵנָיִךְ

4] Then go in and shut the door behind you and your children, and pour [oil] into all those vessels, removing each one as it is filled."

כֵּלִים רֵקִים אַל־תַּמְעִיטִי: 4] וּבָאת וְסָגַרְתְּ הַדֶּלֶת בַּעֲדֵךְ וּבְעַד־בָּנַיִךְ וְיָצַקְתְּ עַל כָּל־

5] She went away and shut the door behind her and her children. They kept bringing [vessels] to her and she kept pouring.

הַכֵּלִים הָאֵלֶּה וְהַמָּלֵא תַּסִּיעִי: 5] וַתֵּלֶךְ מֵאִתּוֹ וַתִּסְגֹּר הַדֶּלֶת בַּעֲדָהּ וּבְעַד בָּנֶיהָ

6] When the vessels were full, she said to her son, "Bring me another vessel." He answered her, "There are no more vessels"; and the oil stopped.

הֵם מַגִּישִׁים אֵלֶיהָ וְהִיא מוֹצָקֶת: 6] וַיְהִי כִּמְלֹאת הַכֵּלִים וַתֹּאמֶר אֶל־בְּנָהּ הַגִּישָׁה אֵלַי עוֹד כֶּלִי וַיֹּאמֶר אֵלֶיהָ אֵין עוֹד כֶּלִי וַיַּעֲמֹד

7] She came and told the man of God, and he said, "Go sell the oil and pay your debt, and you and your children can live on the rest."

הַשָּׁמֶן: 7] וַתָּבֹא וַתַּגֵּד לְאִישׁ הָאֱלֹהִים וַיֹּאמֶר לְכִי מִכְרִי אֶת־הַשֶּׁמֶן וְשַׁלְּמִי אֶת־נִשְׁיֵךְ וְאַתְּ וּבָנַיִךְ תִּחְיִי בַּנּוֹתָר:

8] One day Elisha visited Shunem. A wealthy woman lived there, and she urged him to have a

8] וַיְהִי הַיּוֹם וַיַּעֲבֹר אֱלִישָׁע אֶל־שׁוּנֵם וְשָׁם אִשָּׁה גְדוֹלָה וַתַּחֲזֶק־בּוֹ לֶאֱכָל־לָחֶם וַיְהִי מִדֵּי

meal; and whenever he passed by, he would stop there for a meal.

9] Once she said to her husband, "I am sure it is a holy man of God who comes this way regularly.

10] Let us make a small *enclosed upper chamber* and place a bed, a table, a chair, and a lampstand there for him, so that he can stop there whenever he comes to us."

11] One day he came there; he retired to the upper chamber and lay down there. 12] He said to his servant Gehazi, "Call that Shunammite woman." He called her, and she stood before him.

13] He said to him, "Tell her, 'You have gone to all this trouble for us. What can we do for you? Can we speak in your behalf to the king or to the army commander?'" She replied, "I live among my own people."

14] "What then can be done for her?" he asked. "The fact is," said Gehazi, "she has no son, and her husband is old." 15] "Call her," he said. He called her, and she stood in the doorway.

16] And Elisha said, "At this season next year, you will be embracing a son." She replied, "Please, my lord, man of God, do not delude your maidservant."

17] The woman conceived and bore a son at the same season the following year, as Elisha had assured her.

18] The child grew up. One day, he went out to his father among the reapers. 19] [Suddenly] he cried to his father, "Oh, my head, my head!" He said to a servant, "Carry him to his mother."
20] He picked him up and brought him to his mother. And the child sat on her lap until noon; and he died.

21] She took him up and laid him on the bed of the man of God, and left him and closed the door.

22] Then she called to her husband: "Please, send me one of the servants

9 וַתֹּאמֶר עָבְרוּ יָסֻר שָׁמָּה לֶאֱכָל־לָחֶם:
אֶל־אִישָׁהּ הִנֵּה־נָא יָדַעְתִּי כִּי אִישׁ אֱלֹהִים
קָדוֹשׁ הוּא עֹבֵר עָלֵינוּ תָּמִיד: 10 נַעֲשֶׂה־
נָּא עֲלִיַּת־קִיר קְטַנָּה וְנָשִׂים לוֹ שָׁם מִטָּה
וְשֻׁלְחָן וְכִסֵּא וּמְנוֹרָה וְהָיָה בְּבֹאוֹ אֵלֵינוּ יָסוּר
שָׁמָּה: 11 וַיְהִי הַיּוֹם וַיָּבֹא שָׁמָּה וַיָּסַר אֶל־
הָעֲלִיָּה וַיִּשְׁכַּב־שָׁמָּה: 12 וַיֹּאמֶר אֶל־גֵּחֲזִי
נַעֲרוֹ קְרָא לַשּׁוּנַמִּית הַזֹּאת וַיִּקְרָא־לָהּ וַתַּעֲמֹד
לְפָנָיו: 13 וַיֹּאמֶר לוֹ אֱמָר־נָא אֵלֶיהָ הִנֵּה
חָרַדְתְּ אֵלֵינוּ אֶת־כָּל־הַחֲרָדָה הַזֹּאת מֶה
לַעֲשׂוֹת לָךְ הֲיֵשׁ לְדַבֶּר־לָךְ אֶל־הַמֶּלֶךְ אוֹ
אֶל־שַׂר הַצָּבָא וַתֹּאמֶר בְּתוֹךְ עַמִּי אָנֹכִי יֹשָׁבֶת:
14 וַיֹּאמֶר וּמֶה לַעֲשׂוֹת לָהּ וַיֹּאמֶר גֵּיחֲזִי אֲבָל
בֵּן אֵין־לָהּ וְאִישָׁהּ זָקֵן: 15 וַיֹּאמֶר קְרָא־
לָהּ וַיִּקְרָא־לָהּ וַתַּעֲמֹד בַּפָּתַח: 16 וַיֹּאמֶר
לַמּוֹעֵד הַזֶּה כָּעֵת חַיָּה אַתְּ חֹבֶקֶת בֵּן וַתֹּאמֶר
אַל־אֲדֹנִי אִישׁ הָאֱלֹהִים אַל־תְּכַזֵּב בְּשִׁפְחָתֶךָ:

17 וַתַּהַר הָאִשָּׁה וַתֵּלֶד בֵּן לַמּוֹעֵד הַזֶּה
כָּעֵת חַיָּה אֲשֶׁר־דִּבֶּר אֵלֶיהָ אֱלִישָׁע:
18 וַיִּגְדַּל הַיָּלֶד וַיְהִי הַיּוֹם וַיֵּצֵא אֶל־אָבִיו
אֶל־הַקֹּצְרִים: 19 וַיֹּאמֶר אֶל־אָבִיו רֹאשִׁי
רֹאשִׁי וַיֹּאמֶר אֶל־הַנַּעַר שָׂאֵהוּ אֶל־אִמּוֹ:
20 וַיִּשָּׂאֵהוּ וַיְבִיאֵהוּ אֶל־אִמּוֹ וַיֵּשֶׁב עַל־בִּרְכֶּיהָ
עַד־הַצָּהֳרַיִם וַיָּמֹת: 21 וַתַּעַל וַתַּשְׁכִּבֵהוּ עַל־
מִטַּת אִישׁ הָאֱלֹהִים וַתִּסְגֹּר בַּעֲדוֹ וַתֵּצֵא:
22 וַתִּקְרָא אֶל־אִישָׁהּ וַתֹּאמֶר שִׁלְחָה נָא לִי
אֶחָד מִן־הַנְּעָרִים וְאַחַת הָאֲתֹנוֹת וְאָרוּצָה עַד־

− Or "upper wall-chamber"; lit. "an upper chamber of wall(s)"

335

and one of the she-asses, so I can hurry to the man of God and back."

23] But he said, "Why are you going to him today? It is neither new moon nor sabbath." She answered, b-"It's all right."-b

24] She had the ass saddled, and said to her servant, "Urge [the beast] on;c see that I don't slow down unless I tell you."

25] She went on until she came to the man of God on Mount Carmel. When the man of God saw her from afar, he said to his servant Gehazi, "There is that Shunammite woman.

26] Go, hurry toward her and ask her, 'How are you? How is your husband? How is the child?' " "We are well," she replied.

27] But when she came up to the man of God on the mountain, she clasped his feet. Gehazi stepped forward to push her away; but the man of God said, "Let her alone, for she is in bitter distress; and the Lord has hidden it from me and has not told me."

28] Then she said, "Did I ask my lord for a son? Didn't I say: 'Don't mislead me'?"

29] He said to Gehazi, d-"Tie up your skirts,-d take my staff in your hand, and go. If you meet anyone, do not greet him; and if anyone greets you, do not answer him. And place my staff on the face of the boy."

30] But the boy's mother said, "As the Lord lives and as you live, I will not leave you!" So he arose and followed her.

31] Gehazi had gone on before them and had placed the staff on the boy's face; but there was no sound or response. He turned back to meet him and told him, "The boy has not awakened."
32] Elisha came into the house, and there was the boy, laid out dead on his couch.

33] He went in,

אִישׁ הָאֱלֹהִים וְאָשׁוּבָה: 23] וַיֹּאמֶר מַדּוּעַ אַתְּ הֹלֶכֶת אֵלָיו הַיּוֹם לֹא־חֹדֶשׁ וְלֹא שַׁבָּת וַתֹּאמֶר שָׁלוֹם:

24] וַתַּחֲבֹשׁ הָאָתוֹן וַתֹּאמֶר אֶל־נַעֲרָהּ נְהַג וָלֵךְ אַל־תַּעֲצָר־לִי לִרְכֹּב כִּי אִם־אָמַרְתִּי לָךְ: 25] וַתֵּלֶךְ וַתָּבֹא אֶל־אִישׁ הָאֱלֹהִים אֶל־הַר הַכַּרְמֶל וַיְהִי כִּרְאוֹת אִישׁ־הָאֱלֹהִים אֹתָהּ מִנֶּגֶד וַיֹּאמֶר אֶל־גֵּיחֲזִי נַעֲרוֹ הִנֵּה הַשּׁוּנַמִּית הַלָּז: 26] עַתָּה רוּץ־נָא לִקְרָאתָהּ וֶאֱמָר־לָהּ הֲשָׁלוֹם לָךְ הֲשָׁלוֹם לְאִישֵׁךְ הֲשָׁלוֹם לַיָּלֶד וַתֹּאמֶר שָׁלוֹם: 27] וַתָּבֹא אֶל־אִישׁ הָאֱלֹהִים אֶל־הָהָר וַתַּחֲזֵק בְּרַגְלָיו וַיִּגַּשׁ גֵּיחֲזִי לְהָדְפָהּ וַיֹּאמֶר אִישׁ הָאֱלֹהִים הַרְפֵּה־לָהּ כִּי־נַפְשָׁהּ מָרָה־לָהּ וַיהוָה הֶעְלִים מִמֶּנִּי וְלֹא הִגִּיד לִי: 28] וַתֹּאמֶר הֲשָׁאַלְתִּי בֵן מֵאֵת אֲדֹנִי הֲלֹא אָמַרְתִּי לֹא תַשְׁלֶה אֹתִי:

29] וַיֹּאמֶר לְגֵיחֲזִי חֲגֹר מָתְנֶיךָ וְקַח מִשְׁעַנְתִּי בְיָדְךָ וָלֵךְ כִּי תִמְצָא־אִישׁ לֹא תְבָרְכֶנּוּ וְכִי־יְבָרֶכְךָ אִישׁ לֹא תַעֲנֶנּוּ וְשַׂמְתָּ מִשְׁעַנְתִּי עַל־פְּנֵי הַנָּעַר: 30] וַתֹּאמֶר אֵם הַנַּעַר חַי־יְהוָה וְחֵי־נַפְשְׁךָ אִם־אֶעֶזְבֶךָּ וַיָּקָם וַיֵּלֶךְ אַחֲרֶיהָ: 31] וְגֵחֲזִי עָבַר לִפְנֵיהֶם וַיָּשֶׂם אֶת־הַמִּשְׁעֶנֶת עַל־פְּנֵי הַנַּעַר וְאֵין קוֹל וְאֵין קָשֶׁב וַיָּשָׁב לִקְרָאתוֹ וַיַּגֶּד־לוֹ לֵאמֹר לֹא הֵקִיץ הַנָּעַר: 32] וַיָּבֹא אֱלִישָׁע הַבָּיְתָה וְהִנֵּה הַנַּעַר מֵת מֻשְׁכָּב עַל־מִטָּתוֹ: 33] וַיָּבֹא וַיִּסְגֹּר הַדֶּלֶת

v. 23. עד כאן לספרדים

b-b Heb. "Shalom"
c The servant runs behind the donkey and urges it on with a stick
d-d Lit. "Gird your loins"

336

shut the door behind the two of them, and prayed to the LORD.

34] Then he mounted [the bed] and placed himself over the child. He put his mouth on its mouth, his eyes on its eyes, and his hands on its hands, as he bent over it. And the body of the child became warm.

35] He stepped down, walked once up and down the room, then mounted and bent over him. Thereupon, the boy sneezed seven times, and the boy opened his eyes. 36] [Elisha] called Gehazi and said, "Call the Shunammite woman," and he called her. When she came to him, he said, "Pick up your son." 37] She came and fell at his feet and bowed low to the ground; then she picked up her son and left.

בַּעַד שְׁנֵיהֶם וַיִּתְפַּלֵּל אֶל־יְהוָה: 34] וַיַּעַל וַיִּשְׁכַּב עַל־הַיֶּלֶד וַיָּשֶׂם פִּיו עַל־פִּיו וְעֵינָיו עַל־עֵינָיו וְכַפָּיו עַל־כַּפָּיו וַיִּגְהַר עָלָיו וַיָּחָם בְּשַׂר הַיָּלֶד: 35] וַיָּשָׁב וַיֵּלֶךְ בַּבַּיִת אַחַת הֵנָּה וְאַחַת הֵנָּה וַיַּעַל וַיִּגְהַר עָלָיו וַיְזוֹרֵר הַנַּעַר עַד־שֶׁבַע פְּעָמִים וַיִּפְקַח הַנַּעַר אֶת־עֵינָיו: 36] וַיִּקְרָא אֶל־גֵּיחֲזִי וַיֹּאמֶר קְרָא אֶל־הַשֻּׁנַמִּית הַזֹּאת וַיִּקְרָאֶהָ וַתָּבֹא אֵלָיו וַיֹּאמֶר שְׂאִי בְנֵךְ: 37] וַתָּבֹא וַתִּפֹּל עַל־רַגְלָיו וַתִּשְׁתַּחוּ אָרְצָה וַתִּשָּׂא אֶת־בְּנָהּ וַתֵּצֵא:

The Book of Kings is divided into two parts. It spans four centuries and reaches from the last days of David to the destruction of the Temple by the Babylonians in 586 (or 585) B.C.E. It approaches history from a theological point of view: the story of Israel and Judah must be seen as a judgment of God on the people and its rulers.

The Torah deals with the last days of Abraham and the accession of Isaac to his father's spiritual estate. The haftarah tells us of David's impending death and how Solomon was chosen to succeed him. Though the son's election was fraught with uncertainty and danger, his rule will be crowned with God's blessing.

חיי שרה

First Kings

1 : 1–31

Chapter 1

א

1] King David was now old, advanced in years; and though they covered him with bed-clothes, he never felt warm.

2] His courtiers said to him, "Let a young virgin be sought for my lord the king, to wait upon Your Majesty and be his attendant;*a* and let her lie in your bosom, and my lord the king will be warm." 3] So they looked for a beautiful girl throughout the territory of Israel. They found Abishag the Shunammite and brought her to the king.

4] The girl was exceedingly beautiful. She became the king's attendant*a* and waited upon him; but the king was not intimate with her.

5] Now Adonijah son of Haggith *b*–went about boasting,–*b* "I will be king!" He provided himself with chariots and horses,*c* and an escort of fifty outrunners.

6] His father had never scolded him: "Why did you do that?" He was the one born after Absalom*d* and, like him, was very handsome.

7] He conferred with Joab son of Zeruiah and with the priest Abiathar, and they supported Adonijah;

8] but the priest Zadok, Benaiah son of Jehoiada, the prophet Nathan, Shimei and Rei, and David's own fighting men did not side with Adonijah.

א

1] וְהַמֶּ֤לֶךְ דָּוִד֙ זָקֵ֔ן בָּ֖א בַּיָּמִ֑ים וַיְכַסֻּ֙הוּ֙ בַּבְּגָדִ֔ים וְלֹ֥א יִחַ֖ם לֽוֹ: 2] וַיֹּ֧אמְרוּ ל֣וֹ עֲבָדָ֗יו יְבַקְשׁ֞וּ לַאדֹנִ֤י הַמֶּ֙לֶךְ֙ נַעֲרָ֣ה בְתוּלָ֔ה וְעָֽמְדָה֙ לִפְנֵ֣י הַמֶּ֔לֶךְ וּתְהִי־ל֖וֹ סֹכֶ֑נֶת וְשָׁכְבָ֣ה בְחֵיקֶ֔ךָ וְחַ֖ם לַאדֹנִ֥י הַמֶּֽלֶךְ: 3] וַיְבַקְשׁוּ֙ נַעֲרָ֣ה יָפָ֔ה בְּכֹ֖ל גְּב֣וּל יִשְׂרָאֵ֑ל וַיִּמְצְא֗וּ אֶת־אֲבִישַׁג֙ הַשּׁ֣וּנַמִּ֔ית וַיָּבִ֥אוּ אֹתָ֖הּ לַמֶּֽלֶךְ: 4] וְהַֽנַּעֲרָ֖ה יָפָ֣ה עַד־מְאֹ֑ד וַתְּהִ֙י לַמֶּ֤לֶךְ סֹכֶ֙נֶת֙ וַתְּשָׁ֣רְתֵ֔הוּ וְהַמֶּ֖לֶךְ לֹ֥א יְדָעָֽהּ:

5] וַאֲדֹנִיָּ֧ה בֶן־חַגִּ֛ית מִתְנַשֵּׂ֥א לֵאמֹ֖ר אֲנִ֣י אֶמְלֹ֑ךְ וַיַּ֣עַשׂ ל֗וֹ רֶ֚כֶב וּפָ֣רָשִׁ֔ים וַחֲמִשִּׁ֥ים אִ֖ישׁ רָצִ֥ים לְפָנָֽיו: 6] וְלֹֽא־עֲצָב֨וֹ אָבִ֤יו מִיָּמָיו֙ לֵאמֹ֔ר מַדּ֖וּעַ כָּ֣כָה עָשִׂ֑יתָ וְגַם־ה֤וּא טֽוֹב־תֹּ֙אַר֙ מְאֹ֔ד וְאֹת֥וֹ יָלְדָ֖ה אַחֲרֵ֥י אַבְשָׁלֽוֹם: 7] וַיִּהְי֣וּ דְבָרָ֔יו עִ֚ם יוֹאָ֣ב בֶּן־צְרוּיָ֔ה וְעִ֖ם אֶבְיָתָ֣ר הַכֹּהֵ֑ן וַֽיַּעְזְר֔וּ אַחֲרֵ֖י אֲדֹנִיָּֽה: 8] וְצָד֣וֹק הַ֠כֹּהֵן וּבְנָיָ֨הוּ בֶן־יְהוֹיָדָ֜ע וְנָתָ֣ן הַנָּבִ֗יא וְשִׁמְעִ֤י וְרֵעִי֙ וְהַגִּבּוֹרִ֔ים אֲשֶׁ֖ר לְדָוִ֑ד לֹ֥א הָי֖וּ

a Meaning of Heb. uncertain
b–b Or "presumed to think"
c Others "horsemen"; meaning of Heb. parash(im) not always certain
d Thus, Absalom having died, Adonijah was David's oldest living son

9] Adonijah made a sacrificial feast of sheep, oxen, and fatlings at the Zoheleth stone which is near En-rogel; he invited all his brother princes[e] and all the king's courtiers of the tribe of Judah;

10] but he did not invite the prophet Nathan, or Benaiah, or the fighting men, or his brother Solomon.

11] Then Nathan said to Bathsheba, Solomon's mother, "You must have heard that Adonijah son of Haggith has assumed the kingship without the knowledge of our lord David.

12] Now take my advice, so that you may save your life and the life of your son Solomon.

13] Go immediately to King David and say to him, 'Did not you, O lord king, swear to your maidservant: "Your son Solomon shall succeed me as king, and he shall sit upon my throne"? Then why has Adonijah become king?'

14] While you are still there talking with the king, I will come in after you and confirm your words."

15] So Bathsheba went to the king in his chamber.—The king was very old, and Abishag the Shunammite was waiting on the king.—

16] Bathsheba bowed low in homage to the king; and the king asked, "What troubles you?"

17] She answered him, "My lord, you yourself swore to your maidservant by the LORD your God: 'Your son Solomon shall succeed me as king, and he shall sit upon my throne.'

18] Yet now Adonijah has become king, and you,[f] my lord the king, know nothing about it.

19] He has prepared a sacrificial feast of a great many oxen, fatlings, and sheep, and he has invited all the king's sons and Abiathar the priest and Joab commander of the army; but he has not invited your servant Solomon.

20] And so the eyes of all Israel are upon

9 וַיִּזְבַּח אֲדֹנִיָּהוּ צֹאן וּבָקָר עִם־אֲדֹנִיָּהוּ:
וּמְרִיא עִם אֶבֶן הַזֹּחֶלֶת אֲשֶׁר־אֵצֶל עֵין רֹגֵל
וַיִּקְרָא אֶת־כָּל־אֶחָיו בְּנֵי הַמֶּלֶךְ וּלְכָל־אַנְשֵׁי
יְהוּדָה עַבְדֵי הַמֶּלֶךְ: 10 וְאֶת־נָתָן הַנָּבִיא
וּבְנָיָהוּ וְאֶת־הַגִּבּוֹרִים וְאֶת־שְׁלֹמֹה אָחִיו לֹא
קָרָא:

11 וַיֹּאמֶר נָתָן אֶל־בַּת־שֶׁבַע אֵם־שְׁלֹמֹה
לֵאמֹר הֲלוֹא שָׁמַעַתְּ כִּי מָלַךְ אֲדֹנִיָּהוּ בֶן־חַגִּית
וַאֲדֹנֵינוּ דָוִד לֹא יָדָע: 12 וְעַתָּה לְכִי
אִיעָצֵךְ נָא עֵצָה וּמַלְּטִי אֶת־נַפְשֵׁךְ וְאֶת־נֶפֶשׁ
בְּנֵךְ שְׁלֹמֹה: 13 לְכִי וּבֹאִי אֶל־הַמֶּלֶךְ דָּוִד
וְאָמַרְתְּ אֵלָיו הֲלֹא־אַתָּה אֲדֹנִי הַמֶּלֶךְ נִשְׁבַּעְתָּ
לַאֲמָתְךָ לֵאמֹר כִּי שְׁלֹמֹה בְנֵךְ יִמְלֹךְ אַחֲרַי
וְהוּא יֵשֵׁב עַל־כִּסְאִי וּמַדּוּעַ מָלַךְ אֲדֹנִיָּהוּ:
14 הִנֵּה עוֹדָךְ מְדַבֶּרֶת שָׁם עִם־הַמֶּלֶךְ וַאֲנִי
אָבוֹא אַחֲרַיִךְ וּמִלֵּאתִי אֶת־דְּבָרָיִךְ:

15 וַתָּבֹא בַת־שֶׁבַע אֶל־הַמֶּלֶךְ הַחַדְרָה
וְהַמֶּלֶךְ זָקֵן מְאֹד וַאֲבִישַׁג הַשּׁוּנַמִּית מְשָׁרַת
אֶת־הַמֶּלֶךְ: 16 וַתִּקֹּד בַּת־שֶׁבַע וַתִּשְׁתַּחוּ
לַמֶּלֶךְ וַיֹּאמֶר הַמֶּלֶךְ מַה־לָּךְ: 17 וַתֹּאמֶר
לוֹ אֲדֹנִי אַתָּה נִשְׁבַּעְתָּ בַּיהֹוָה אֱלֹהֶיךָ לַאֲמָתֶךָ
כִּי־שְׁלֹמֹה בְנֵךְ יִמְלֹךְ אַחֲרָי וְהוּא יֵשֵׁב עַל־
כִּסְאִי: 18 וְעַתָּה הִנֵּה אֲדֹנִיָּה מָלָךְ וְעַתָּה
אֲדֹנִי הַמֶּלֶךְ לֹא יָדָעְתָּ: 19 וַיִּזְבַּח שׁוֹר
וּמְרִיא־וְצֹאן לָרֹב וַיִּקְרָא לְכָל־בְּנֵי הַמֶּלֶךְ
וּלְאֶבְיָתָר הַכֹּהֵן וּלְיוֹאָב שַׂר הַצָּבָא וְלִשְׁלֹמֹה
עַבְדְּךָ לֹא קָרָא: 20 וְאַתָּה אֲדֹנִי הַמֶּלֶךְ

---

[e] Lit. "all his brothers, sons of the king"

[f] So many mss. and ancient versions; usual editions "now"

you, O lord king, to tell them who shall succeed my lord the king on the throne.

21] Otherwise, when my lord the king lies down with his fathers, my son Solomon and I will be regarded as traitors."

22] She was still talking to the king when the prophet Nathan arrived.

23] They announced to the king, "The prophet Nathan is here," and he entered the king's presence. Bowing low to the king with his face to the ground,

24] Nathan said, "O lord king, *you must have said,* 'Adonijah shall succeed me as king and he shall sit upon my throne.'

25] For he has gone down today and prepared a sacrificial feast of a great many oxen, fatlings, and sheep. He invited all the king's sons and the army officers and Abiathar the priest. At this very moment they are eating and drinking with him, and they are shouting, 'Long live King Adonijah!'

26] But he did not invite me your servant, or the priest Zadok, or Benaiah son of Jehoiada, or your servant Solomon.

27] Can this decision have come from my lord the king, without your telling your servant who is to succeed to the throne of my lord the king?"

28] King David's response was: "Summon Bathsheba!" She entered the king's presence and stood before the king.

29] And the king took an oath, saying, "As the LORD lives, who has rescued me from every trouble:

30] The oath I swore to you by the LORD, the God of Israel, that your son Solomon should succeed me as king and that he should sit upon my throne in my stead, I will fulfill this very day!"

31] Bathsheba bowed low in homage to the king with her face to the ground, and she said, "May my lord King David live forever!"

עֵינֵי כָל־יִשְׂרָאֵל עָלֶיךָ לְהַגִּיד לָהֶם מִי יֵשֵׁב עַל־כִּסֵּא אֲדֹנִי־הַמֶּלֶךְ אַחֲרָיו: 21] וְהָיָה כִּשְׁכַב אֲדֹנִי־הַמֶּלֶךְ עִם־אֲבֹתָיו וְהָיִיתִי אֲנִי וּבְנִי שְׁלֹמֹה חַטָּאִים:

22] וְהִנֵּה עוֹדֶנָּה מְדַבֶּרֶת עִם־הַמֶּלֶךְ וְנָתָן הַנָּבִיא בָּא: 23] וַיַּגִּידוּ לַמֶּלֶךְ לֵאמֹר הִנֵּה נָתָן הַנָּבִיא וַיָּבֹא לִפְנֵי הַמֶּלֶךְ וַיִּשְׁתַּחוּ לַמֶּלֶךְ עַל־אַפָּיו אָרְצָה: 24] וַיֹּאמֶר נָתָן אֲדֹנִי הַמֶּלֶךְ אַתָּה אָמַרְתָּ אֲדֹנִיָּהוּ יִמְלֹךְ אַחֲרָי וְהוּא יֵשֵׁב עַל־כִּסְאִי: 25] כִּי יָרַד הַיּוֹם וַיִּזְבַּח שׁוֹר וּמְרִיא־וְצֹאן לָרֹב וַיִּקְרָא לְכָל־בְּנֵי הַמֶּלֶךְ וּלְשָׂרֵי הַצָּבָא וּלְאֶבְיָתָר הַכֹּהֵן וְהִנָּם אֹכְלִים וְשֹׁתִים לְפָנָיו וַיֹּאמְרוּ יְחִי הַמֶּלֶךְ אֲדֹנִיָּהוּ: 26] וְלִי אֲנִי־עַבְדֶּךָ וּלְצָדֹק הַכֹּהֵן וְלִבְנָיָהוּ בֶן־יְהוֹיָדָע וְלִשְׁלֹמֹה עַבְדְּךָ לֹא קָרָא: 27] אִם מֵאֵת אֲדֹנִי הַמֶּלֶךְ נִהְיָה הַדָּבָר הַזֶּה וְלֹא הוֹדַעְתָּ אֶת־עַבְדְּךָ מִי יֵשֵׁב עַל־כִּסֵּא אֲדֹנִי־הַמֶּלֶךְ אַחֲרָיו:

28] וַיַּעַן הַמֶּלֶךְ דָּוִד וַיֹּאמֶר קִרְאוּ־לִי לְבַת־שָׁבַע וַתָּבֹא לִפְנֵי הַמֶּלֶךְ וַתַּעֲמֹד לִפְנֵי הַמֶּלֶךְ: 29] וַיִּשָּׁבַע הַמֶּלֶךְ וַיֹּאמַר חַי־יְהוָה אֲשֶׁר־פָּדָה אֶת־נַפְשִׁי מִכָּל־צָרָה: 30] כִּי כַּאֲשֶׁר נִשְׁבַּעְתִּי לָךְ בַּיהוָה אֱלֹהֵי יִשְׂרָאֵל לֵאמֹר כִּי־שְׁלֹמֹה בְנֵךְ יִמְלֹךְ אַחֲרַי וְהוּא יֵשֵׁב עַל־כִּסְאִי תַּחְתָּי כִּי כֵּן אֶעֱשֶׂה הַיּוֹם הַזֶּה: 31] וַתִּקֹּד בַּת־שֶׁבַע אַפַּיִם אֶרֶץ וַתִּשְׁתַּחוּ לַמֶּלֶךְ וַתֹּאמֶר יְחִי אֲדֹנִי הַמֶּלֶךְ דָּוִד לְעֹלָם:

⁻ Or (cf. Rashi, Ralbag, Radak) "have you said . . .?"

*Malachi is a descriptive term meaning "My messenger,"
and this name is attached to the last of the prophetic books.
While the identity of the prophet remains unknown, his
writings appear to be contemporary with Nehemiah who
rebuilt the Temple after the people's return from exile,
in the middle of the fifth century* B.C.E.

*In Malachi's time the people had lost faith in the efficacy
of the divine blessing, but he preaches confidence that
God's favor will be bestowed on Jacob and his offspring.
This reference to the forefather forms the link between
haftarah and sidrah.*

תּוֹלְדֹת

Malachi

1:1–2:7

א

Chapter 1

1] A pronouncement: The word of the Lord
to Israel through Malachi.

2] I have shown you love, said the Lord. But
you ask, "How have You shown us love?" After all
—declares the Lord—Esau is Jacob's brother; yet I
have accepted Jacob

3] and have rejected Esau.
I have made his hills a desolation, his territory
ᵃ⁻a home for beastsᵃ of the desert.

4] If Edom
thinks, "Though crushed, we can build the ruins
again," thus said the Lord of Hosts: They may
build, but I will tear down. And so they shall be
known as the region of wickedness, the people
damned forever of the Lord.

5] Your eyes shall
behold it, and you shall declare, "Great is the
Lord beyond the borders of Israel!"

6] A son should honor his father, and a slaveᵇ
his master. Now if I am a father, where is the
honor due Me? And if I am a master, where is the
reverence due Me?—said the Lord of Hosts to
you, O priests who scorn My name. But you ask,
"How have we scorned Your name?"

7] You of-
fer defiled food on My altar. But you ask, "How
have we defiled Youᶜ?" By saying, "The table of
the Lord can be treated with scorn."

8] When
you present a blind animal for sacrifice—it doesn't
matter! When you present a lame or sick one—it

מַשָּׂא דְבַר־יְהֹוָה אֶל־יִשְׂרָאֵל בְּיַד מַלְאָכִי׃ [1

אָהַבְתִּי אֶתְכֶם אָמַר יְהֹוָה וַאֲמַרְתֶּם בַּמָּה [2
אֲהַבְתָּנוּ הֲלוֹא־אָח עֵשָׂו לְיַעֲקֹב נְאֻם־יְהֹוָה
וָאֹהַב אֶת־יַעֲקֹב׃ [3 וְאֶת־עֵשָׂו שָׂנֵאתִי וָאָשִׂים
אֶת־הָרָיו שְׁמָמָה וְאֶת־נַחֲלָתוֹ לְתַנּוֹת מִדְבָּר׃
כִּי־תֹאמַר אֱדוֹם רֻשַּׁשְׁנוּ וְנָשׁוּב וְנִבְנֶה חֳרָבוֹת [4
כֹּה אָמַר יְהֹוָה צְבָאוֹת הֵמָּה יִבְנוּ וַאֲנִי אֶהֱרוֹס
וְקָרְאוּ לָהֶם גְּבוּל רִשְׁעָה וְהָעָם אֲשֶׁר־זָעַם
יְהֹוָה עַד־עוֹלָם׃ [5 וְעֵינֵיכֶם תִּרְאֶינָה וְאַתֶּם
תֹּאמְרוּ יִגְדַּל יְהֹוָה מֵעַל לִגְבוּל יִשְׂרָאֵל׃

בֵּן יְכַבֵּד אָב וְעֶבֶד אֲדֹנָיו וְאִם־אָב אָנִי [6
אַיֵּה כְבוֹדִי וְאִם־אֲדוֹנִים אָנִי אַיֵּה מוֹרָאִי אָמַר
יְהֹוָה צְבָאוֹת לָכֶם הַכֹּהֲנִים בּוֹזֵי שְׁמִי וַאֲמַרְתֶּם
בַּמֶּה בָזִינוּ אֶת־שְׁמֶךָ׃ [7 מַגִּישִׁים עַל־מִזְבְּחִי
לֶחֶם מְגֹאָל וַאֲמַרְתֶּם בַּמֶּה גֵאַלְנוּךָ בֶּאֱמָרְכֶם
שֻׁלְחַן יְהֹוָה נִבְזֶה הוּא׃ [8 וְכִי־תַגִּשׁוּן עִוֵּר
לִזְבֹּחַ אֵין רָע וְכִי תַגִּישׁוּ פִּסֵּחַ וְחֹלֶה אֵין רָע

ᵃ⁻ᵃ *Meaning of Heb. uncertain*
ᵇ *Septuagint and Targum add "should reverence"; cf. next part of verse*
ᶜ *Septuagint "it"*

doesn't matter! Just offer it to your governor: Will he accept you? Will he show you favor?—said the LORD of Hosts.

9] And now implore the favor of God! Will He be gracious to us? This is what you have done—will He accept any of you? The LORD of Hosts has said:

10] If only you would lock My doors, and not kindle fire on My altar to no purpose! I take no pleasure in you—said the LORD of Hosts—and I will accept no offering from you.

11] For from where the sun rises to where it sets, My name is honored among the nations, and everywhere incense and pure oblation are offered to My name; for My name is honored among the nations—said the LORD of Hosts.

12] But you profane it when you say, "The table of the LORD is defiled and the meat,[a] the food, can be treated with scorn."

13] You say, "Oh, what a bother!" And so you degrade[a] it—said the LORD of Hosts—and you bring the stolen, the lame, and the sick; and you offer such as an oblation. Will I accept it from you?—said the LORD.

14] A curse on the cheat who has an [unblemished] male in his flock, but for his vow sacrifices a blemished animal to the LORD! For I am a great King—said the LORD of Hosts—and My name is revered among the nations.

Chapter 2

1] And now, O priests, this charge is for you:
2] Unless you obey and unless you lay it to heart, and do honor to My name—said the LORD of Hosts—I will send a curse and turn your blessings into curses. (Indeed, I have turned them into curses, because you do not lay it to heart.)
3] I will [a-]put your seed under a ban,[-a] and I will strew dung upon your faces, the dung of your festal sacrifices, and you shall be carried out to its [heap].

הַקְרִיבֵהוּ נָא לְפֶחָתֶ֔ךָ הֲיִרְצְךָ֙ אוֹ הֲיִשָּׂ֣א פָנֶ֔יךָ אָמַ֖ר יְהֹוָ֥ה צְבָאֽוֹת׃ 9 וְעַתָּ֛ה חַלּוּ־נָ֥א פְנֵי־אֵ֖ל וִֽיחׇנֵּ֑נוּ מִיֶּדְכֶם֙ הָ֣יְתָה זֹּ֔את הֲיִשָּׂ֤א מִכֶּם֙ פָּנִ֔ים אָמַ֖ר יְהֹוָ֥ה צְבָאֽוֹת׃

10 מִ֤י גַם־בָּכֶם֙ וְיִסְגֹּ֣ר דְּלָתַ֔יִם וְלֹא־תָאִ֥ירוּ מִזְבְּחִ֖י חִנָּ֑ם אֵ֣ין־לִ֣י חֵ֗פֶץ בָּכֶ֗ם אָמַר֙ יְהֹוָ֣ה צְבָא֔וֹת וּמִנְחָ֖ה לֹֽא־אֶרְצֶ֥ה מִיֶּדְכֶֽם׃ 11 כִּ֣י מִמִּזְרַח־שֶׁ֜מֶשׁ וְעַד־מְבוֹא֗וֹ גָּד֤וֹל שְׁמִי֙ בַּגּוֹיִ֔ם וּבְכׇל־מָק֗וֹם מֻקְטָ֥ר מֻגָּ֛שׁ לִשְׁמִ֖י וּמִנְחָ֣ה טְהוֹרָ֑ה כִּֽי־גָד֤וֹל שְׁמִי֙ בַּגּוֹיִ֔ם אָמַ֖ר יְהֹוָ֥ה צְבָאֽוֹת׃ 12 וְאַתֶּ֖ם מְחַלְּלִ֣ים אוֹת֑וֹ בֶּאֱמׇרְכֶ֗ם שֻׁלְחַ֤ן אֲדֹנָי֙ מְגֹאָ֣ל ה֔וּא וְנִיב֖וֹ נִבְזֶ֥ה אׇכְלֽוֹ׃ 13 וַאֲמַרְתֶּם֩ הִנֵּ֨ה מַתְּלָאָ֜ה וְהִפַּחְתֶּ֣ם אוֹת֗וֹ אָמַר֙ יְהֹוָ֣ה צְבָא֔וֹת וַהֲבֵאתֶ֣ם גָּז֗וּל וְאֶת־הַפִּסֵּ֙חַ֙ וְאֶת־הַ֣חוֹלֶ֔ה וַהֲבֵאתֶ֖ם אֶת־הַמִּנְחָ֑ה הַאֶרְצֶ֥ה אוֹתָ֛הּ מִיֶּדְכֶ֖ם אָמַ֥ר יְהֹוָֽה׃

14 וְאָר֣וּר נוֹכֵ֗ל וְיֵ֤שׁ בְּעֶדְרוֹ֙ זָכָ֔ר וְנֹדֵ֕ר וְזֹבֵ֥חַ מׇשְׁחָ֖ת לַֽאדֹנָ֑י כִּי֩ מֶ֨לֶךְ גָּד֜וֹל אָ֗נִי אָמַר֙ יְהֹוָ֣ה צְבָא֔וֹת וּשְׁמִ֖י נוֹרָ֥א בַגּוֹיִֽם׃

ב

1 וְעַתָּ֗ה אֲלֵיכֶ֛ם הַמִּצְוָ֥ה הַזֹּ֖את הַכֹּהֲנִֽים׃ 2 אִם־לֹ֣א תִשְׁמְע֡וּ וְאִם־לֹא֩ תָשִׂ֨ימוּ עַל־לֵ֜ב לָתֵ֧ת כָּב֣וֹד לִשְׁמִ֗י אָמַר֙ יְהֹוָ֣ה צְבָא֔וֹת וְשִׁלַּחְתִּ֤י בָכֶם֙ אֶת־הַמְּאֵרָ֔ה וְאָרוֹתִ֖י אֶת־בִּרְכֽוֹתֵיכֶ֑ם וְגַם֙ אָר֣וֹתִ֔יהָ כִּ֥י אֵינְכֶ֖ם שָׂמִ֥ים עַל־לֵֽב׃ 3 הִנְנִ֨י גֹעֵ֤ר לָכֶם֙ אֶת־הַזֶּ֔רַע וְזֵרִ֣יתִי פֶ֗רֶשׁ עַל־פְּנֵיכֶ֔ם פֶּ֖רֶשׁ חַגֵּיכֶ֑ם וְנָשָׂ֥א אֶתְכֶ֖ם אֵלָֽיו׃

---

[a] Meaning of Heb. uncertain   [a-a] Meaning of Heb. uncertain

4] Know, then, that I have sent this charge to you so that My covenant with Levi may endure—said the Lord of Hosts.

5] I had with him a covenant of life and well-being, which I gave to him, and of reverence, which he showed Me. For he stood in awe of My name.

6] *b*Proper rulings were in his mouth,
And nothing perverse was on his lips;
He served Me with complete loyalty
And held the many back from iniquity.

7] *c*For the lips of a priest guard knowledge,
And men seek rulings from his mouth;*c*
For he is a messenger of the Lord of Hosts.

4] וִידַעְתֶּ֕ם כִּ֚י שִׁלַּ֣חְתִּי אֲלֵיכֶ֔ם אֵ֖ת הַמִּצְוָ֣ה הַזֹּ֑את לִהְי֤וֹת בְּרִיתִי֙ אֶת־לֵוִ֔י אָמַ֖ר יְהֹוָ֥ה צְבָאֽוֹת׃

5] בְּרִיתִ֣י ׀ הָיְתָ֣ה אִתּ֗וֹ הַֽחַיִּים֙ וְהַשָּׁל֔וֹם וָאֶתְּנֵֽם־ ל֥וֹ מוֹרָ֖א וַיִּֽירָאֵ֑נִי וּמִפְּנֵ֥י שְׁמִ֖י נִחַ֥ת הֽוּא׃

6] תּוֹרַ֤ת אֱמֶת֙ הָיְתָ֣ה בְּפִ֔יהוּ וְעַוְלָ֖ה לֹא־נִמְצָ֣א בִשְׂפָתָ֑יו בְּשָׁל֤וֹם וּבְמִישׁוֹר֙ הָלַ֣ךְ אִתִּ֔י וְרַבִּ֖ים הֵשִׁ֥יב מֵעָוֺֽן׃

7] כִּֽי־שִׂפְתֵ֤י כֹהֵן֙ יִשְׁמְרוּ־דַ֔עַת וְתוֹרָ֖ה יְבַקְשׁ֣וּ מִפִּ֑יהוּ כִּ֛י מַלְאַ֥ךְ יְהֹוָֽה־צְבָא֖וֹת הֽוּא׃

---

b See Hag. 2.10–13; cf. Lev. 10.8–11; Deut. 33.8, 10

c-c Or: *For the lips of a priest are observed;/Knowledge and ruling are sought from his mouth*

Hosea lived in the Northern Kingdom (Israel) in the eighth century B.C.E. *He frequently spoke of his people's relationship to God as that of a wife to a husband who had cast her out for her transgressions. But God still loved Israel, the prophet preached, and would take her back if she repented.*

Hosea recalls Jacob's sojourn in Aram (which forms the bulk of the sidrah) and his descendants' flirting with idolatry. But, though their sin is heavy, God will redeem them from the power of the netherworld. Verses 14:2–10 form the haftarah also for Shabbat Shuvah, the Sabbath of Return, between Rosh Hashanah and Yom Kippur.

Chapter 12

13] Then Jacob had to flee[l] to the land of Aram;
There Israel served for a wife,
For a wife he had to guard [sheep].

14] But when the LORD
Brought Israel up from Egypt,
It was through a prophet;[m]
Through a prophet[m] they were guarded.

15] [n]Ephraim gave bitter offense,
And his LORD cast his crimes upon him
And requited him for his mockery.

Chapter 13

1] When Ephraim spoke piety,
He was exalted in Israel;
But he incurred guilt through Baal,[a]
And so he died.

2] And now they go on sinning;
They have made them molten images,
Idols, by their skill, from their silver,

[l] *This is the punishment mentioned in 12.3*
[m] *I.e., not through an angel*
[n] *Meaning of 12.15–13.1 uncertain*
[a] *I.e., Baal-peor; cf. 9.10*

ויצא

Hosea
12 : 13 – 14 : 10

יב

13] וַיִּבְרַ֥ח יַעֲקֹ֖ב שְׂדֵ֣ה אֲרָ֑ם
וַיַּעֲבֹ֤ד יִשְׂרָאֵל֙ בְּאִשָּׁ֔ה
וּבְאִשָּׁ֖ה שָׁמָֽר:
14] וּבְנָבִ֕יא הֶעֱלָ֧ה יְהֹוָ֛ה
אֶת־יִשְׂרָאֵ֖ל מִמִּצְרָ֑יִם
וּבְנָבִ֖יא נִשְׁמָֽר:
15] הִכְעִ֥יס אֶפְרַ֖יִם תַּמְרוּרִ֑ים
וְדָמָיו֙ עָלָ֣יו יִטּ֔וֹשׁ
וְחֶ֨רְפָּת֔וֹ יָשִׁ֥יב ל֖וֹ אֲדֹנָֽיו:

יג

1] כְּדַבֵּ֤ר אֶפְרַ֨יִם֙ רְתֵ֔ת
נָשָׂ֥א ה֖וּא בְּיִשְׂרָאֵ֑ל
וַיֶּאְשַׁ֥ם בַּבַּ֖עַל וַיָּמֹֽת:
2] וְעַתָּ֣ה ׀ יוֹסִ֣פוּ לַחֲטֹ֗א
וַיַּעְשׂ֣וּ לָהֶם֩ מַסֵּכָ֨ה מִכַּסְפָּ֤ם
כִּתְבוּנָם֙ עֲצַבִּ֔ים

נ״א בתבונם v. 2.

Wholly the work of craftsmen.
ᵇ⁻Yet for these they appoint men to sacrifice;⁻ᵇ
They are wont to kiss calves!

3] Assuredly,
They shall be like morning clouds,
Like dew so early gone;
Like chaff whirled away from the threshing floor.
And like smoke from a lattice.

4] Only I the LORD have been your God
Ever since the land of Egypt;
You have never known a [true] God but Me,
You have never had a helper other than Me.

5] I looked after you in the desert,
In a thirsty land.

6] When they grazed, they were sated;
When they were sated, they grew haughty;
And so they forgot Me.

7] So I am become like a lion to them,
Like a leopard I lurk on the way;

8] Like a bear robbed of her young I attack them
And rip open the casing of their hearts;
ᶜ⁻I will devour them there like a lion,⁻ᶜ
The beasts of the field shall mangle them.

9] ᵇ⁻You are undone, O Israel!
You had no help but Me.⁻ᵇ

10] Where now is your king?
Let him save you!
Where are the chieftains in all your towns

מַעֲשֵׂה חָרָשִׁים כֻּלֹּה

לָהֶם הֵם אֹמְרִים

זֹבְחֵי אָדָם עֲגָלִים יִשָּׁקוּן:

3] לָכֵן יִהְיוּ כַּעֲנַן־בֹּקֶר

וְכַטַּל מַשְׁכִּים הֹלֵךְ

כְּמֹץ יְסֹעֵר מִגֹּרֶן

וּכְעָשָׁן מֵאֲרֻבָּה:

4] וְאָנֹכִי יְהוָה אֱלֹהֶיךָ

מֵאֶרֶץ מִצְרָיִם

וֵאלֹהִים זוּלָתִי לֹא תֵדָע

וּמוֹשִׁיעַ אַיִן בִּלְתִּי:

5] אֲנִי יְדַעְתִּיךָ בַּמִּדְבָּר

בְּאֶרֶץ תַּלְאֻבוֹת:

6] כְּמַרְעִיתָם וַיִּשְׂבָּעוּ

שָׂבְעוּ וַיָּרָם לִבָּם

עַל־כֵּן שְׁכֵחוּנִי:

7] וָאֱהִי לָהֶם כְּמוֹ־שָׁחַל

כְּנָמֵר עַל־דֶּרֶךְ אָשׁוּר:

8] אֶפְגְּשֵׁם כְּדֹב שַׁכּוּל

וְאֶקְרַע סְגוֹר לִבָּם

וְאֹכְלֵם שָׁם כְּלָבִיא

חַיַּת הַשָּׂדֶה תְּבַקְּעֵם:

9] שִׁחֶתְךָ יִשְׂרָאֵל

כִּי־בִי בְעֶזְרֶךָ:

10] אֱהִי מַלְכְּךָ אֵפוֹא

וְיוֹשִׁיעֲךָ בְּכָל־עָרֶיךָ

ᵇ⁻ᵇ *Meaning of Heb. uncertain*
ᶜ⁻ᶜ *Emendation yields "Their dogs shall devour them"; cf. Septuagint*

Whom you demanded:
"Give me a king and officers"?

11] I give you kings in My ire,
And take them away in My wrath.

12] Ephraim's guilt is bound up,
His sin is stored away.d

13] Pangs of childbirth assail him,
b-And the babe is not wise—
For this is no time to survive
At the birthstool of babes.-b

14] eFrom Sheol itself I will save them,
Redeem them from very Death.
Where, O Death, are your plagues?
Your pestilence where, O Sheol?
f-Revenge shall be far from My thoughts.-f

15] For though he flourish among reeds,
A blast, a wind of the LORD,
Shall come blowing up from the wilderness;
His fountain shall be parched,
His spring dried up.
That [wind] shall plunder treasures,
Every lovely object.

Chapter 14

1] Samaria must bear her guilt,
For she has defied her God.
They shall fall by the sword,

וּשְׁפָטֶיךָ אֲשֶׁר אָמַרְתָּ
תְּנָה־לִּי מֶלֶךְ וְשָׂרִים:

11] אֶתֶּן־לְךָ מֶלֶךְ בְּאַפִּי
וְאֶקַּח בְּעֶבְרָתִי:

12] צָרוּר עֲוֹן אֶפְרָיִם
צְפוּנָה חַטָּאתוֹ:

13] חֶבְלֵי יוֹלֵדָה יָבֹאוּ לוֹ
הוּא־בֵן לֹא חָכָם
כִּי־עֵת לֹא־יַעֲמֹד
בְּמִשְׁבַּר בָּנִים:

14] מִיַּד שְׁאוֹל אֶפְדֵּם
מִמָּוֶת אֶגְאָלֵם
אֱהִי דְבָרֶיךָ מָוֶת
אֱהִי קָטָבְךָ שְׁאוֹל
נֹחַם יִסָּתֵר מֵעֵינָי:

15] כִּי הוּא בֵּין אַחִים יַפְרִיא
יָבוֹא קָדִים רוּחַ יְהֹוָה
מִמִּדְבָּר עֹלֶה
וְיֵבוֹשׁ מְקוֹרוֹ וְיֶחֱרַב מַעְיָנוֹ
הוּא יִשְׁסֶה אוֹצַר כָּל־כְּלִי חֶמְדָּה:

יד

1] תֶּאְשַׁם שֹׁמְרוֹן
כִּי מָרְתָה בֵּאלֹהֶיהָ
בַּחֶרֶב יִפֹּלוּ

---

d I.e., for future retribution
b-b Meaning of Heb. uncertain
e This verse would read well before 14.5
f-f Lit. "Satisfaction (for this meaning of nchm see Deut. 32.36; Isa. 1.24) shall be
    hidden from My eyes"

Their infants shall be dashed to death,
And their women with child ripped open.

עֹלְלֵיהֶם יְרֻטָּשׁוּ
וְהָרִיּוֹתָיו יְבֻקָּעוּ׃

2] Return, O Israel, to the LORD your God,
For you have fallen because of your sin.

2 שׁוּבָה יִשְׂרָאֵל עַד יְהוָה אֱלֹהֶיךָ
כִּי כָשַׁלְתָּ בַּעֲוֹנֶךָ׃

3] Take words with you
And return to the LORD.
Say to Him:
ᵃ"Forgive all guilt
And accept what is good;
Instead of bulls we will pay
[The offering of] our lips."⁻ᵃ

3 קְחוּ עִמָּכֶם דְּבָרִים
וְשׁוּבוּ אֶל־יְהוָה
אִמְרוּ אֵלָיו כָּל־תִּשָּׂא עָוֹן
וְקַח־טוֹב
וּנְשַׁלְּמָה פָרִים שְׂפָתֵינוּ׃

4] Assyria shall not save us,
No more will we ride on steeds;ᵇ
Nor ever again will we call
Our handiwork our god,
Since in You alone orphans find pity!"

4 אַשּׁוּר לֹא יוֹשִׁיעֵנוּ
עַל־סוּס לֹא נִרְכָּב
וְלֹא־נֹאמַר עוֹד
אֱלֹהֵינוּ לְמַעֲשֵׂה יָדֵינוּ
אֲשֶׁר־בְּךָ יְרֻחַם יָתוֹם

5] I will heal their affliction,ᶜ
Generously will I take them back in love;
For my anger has turned away from them.ᵈ

5 אֶרְפָּא מְשׁוּבָתָם אֹהֲבֵם נְדָבָה
כִּי שָׁב אַפִּי מִמֶּנּוּ׃

6] I will be to Israel like dew;
He shall blossom like the lily,
He shall strike root like a ᵉLebanon tree.⁻ᵉ

6 אֶהְיֶה כַטַּל לְיִשְׂרָאֵל
יִפְרַח כַּשּׁוֹשַׁנָּה
וְיַךְ שָׁרָשָׁיו כַּלְּבָנוֹן׃

7] His boughs shall spread out far,
His beauty shall be like the olive tree's,
His fragrance like that of Lebanon.

7 יֵלְכוּ יֹנְקוֹתָיו
וִיהִי כַזַּיִת הוֹדוֹ
וְרֵיחַ לוֹ כַּלְּבָנוֹן׃

8] They who sit in his shade shall be revived:
They shall bring to life new grain,
They shall blossom like the vine;
His scent shall be like the wine of Lebanon.ᶠ

8 יָשֻׁבוּ יֹשְׁבֵי בְצִלּוֹ יְחַיּוּ דָגָן
וְיִפְרְחוּ כַגָּפֶן
זִכְרוֹ כְּיֵין לְבָנוֹן׃

ᵃ⁻ᵃ *Meaning of Heb. uncertain*
ᵇ *I.e., we will no longer depend on an alliance with Egypt; cf. II Kings 18.24 ||Isa. 36.9;*
  Isa. 30.16
ᶜ *For this meaning of* meshubah *see Jer. 2.19; 3.22*
ᵈ *Heb. "him"*   ᵉ⁻ᵉ *Emendation yields "poplar"*
ᶠ *Emendation yields "Helbon"; cf. Ezek. 27.18*

9] Ephraim [shall say]:
"What more have I to do with idols?
When I respond and look to Him,
I become like a verdant cypress."
⁻Your fruit is provided by Me.⁻

10] He who is wise will consider these words,
He who is prudent will take note of them.
For the paths of the LORD are smooth;
The righteous can walk on them,
While sinners stumble on them.

9 אֶפְרַ֕יִם מַה־לִּ֥י ע֖וֹד לָֽעֲצַבִּ֑ים
אֲנִ֥י עָנִ֖יתִי וַאֲשׁוּרֶ֑נּוּ
אֲנִ֣י כִּבְר֣וֹשׁ רַֽעֲנָ֔ן
מִמֶּ֖נִּי פֶּרְיְךָ֥ נִמְצָֽא׃

10 מִ֤י חָכָם֙ וְיָ֣בֵֽן אֵ֔לֶּה
נָב֖וֹן וְיֵֽדָעֵ֑ם
כִּֽי־יְשָׁרִ֞ים דַּרְכֵ֣י יְהֹוָ֗ה
וְצַדִּקִים֙ יֵ֣לְכוּ בָ֔ם
וּפֹשְׁעִ֖ים יִכָּ֥שְׁלוּ בָֽם׃

*Hosea lived in the Northern Kingdom (Israel) in the
eighth century B.C.E. He frequently spoke of his people's
relationship to God as that of a wife to a husband who
had cast her out for her transgressions. But God still
loved Israel, the prophet preached, and would take her
back if she repented.*

*Jacob's striving with the angel is recalled by Hosea (12:5),
a struggle which he sees as the forefather's attempt to return to God. Thus Israel too must return to Him and
wait continually for God's redeeming mercy.*

וישלח

Hosea

11:7–12:12

יא

Chapter 11

7] ⸢For My people persists
In its defection from Me;
When it is summoned upward,
It does not rise at all.⸣

8] How can I give you up, O Ephraim?
How surrender you, O Israel?
How can I make you like Admah,
Render you like Zeboiim?⁹
I have had a change of heart,
All My tenderness is stirred.

9] I will not act on My wrath,
Will not turn to destroy Ephraim.
For I am God, not man,
⸢The Holy One in your midst:
I will not come in fury.⸣

10] The LORD will roar like a lion,
And they shall march behind Him;
When He roars, His children shall come
Fluttering out of the west.

7] וְעַמִּי תְלוּאִים לִמְשׁוּבָתִי
וְאֶל־עַל יִקְרָאֻהוּ
יַחַד לֹא יְרוֹמֵם׃

8] אֵיךְ אֶתֶּנְךָ אֶפְרַיִם
אֲמַגֶּנְךָ יִשְׂרָאֵל
אֵיךְ אֶתֶּנְךָ כְאַדְמָה
אֲשִׂימְךָ כִּצְבֹאִים
נֶהְפַּךְ עָלַי לִבִּי
יַחַד נִכְמְרוּ נִחוּמָי׃

9] לֹא אֶעֱשֶׂה חֲרוֹן אַפִּי
לֹא אָשׁוּב לְשַׁחֵת אֶפְרָיִם
כִּי אֵל אָנֹכִי וְלֹא־אִישׁ
בְּקִרְבְּךָ קָדוֹשׁ
וְלֹא אָבוֹא בְּעִיר׃

10] אַחֲרֵי יְהוָה
יֵלְכוּ כְּאַרְיֵה יִשְׁאָג
כִּי־הוּא יִשְׁאַג
וְיֶחֶרְדוּ בָנִים מִיָּם׃

⸢⸣ Meaning of Heb. uncertain
⁹ *Admah and Zeboiim were destroyed with neighboring Sodom and Gomorrah; cf.*
Gen. 10.19; 14.2, 8; Deut. 29.22

נחה א' v. 8.

11] They shall flutter from Egypt like sparrows,
From the land of Assyria like doves;
And I will settle them in their homes
          —declares the Lord.

יֶחֶרְד֤וּ כְצִפּוֹר֙ מִמִּצְרַ֔יִם

וּכְיוֹנָ֖ה מֵאֶ֣רֶץ אַשּׁ֑וּר

וְהוֹשַׁבְתִּ֥ים עַל־בָּתֵּיהֶ֖ם [11

נְאֻם־יְהוָֽה׃

Chapter 12

יב

1] Ephraim surrounds Me with deceit,
The House of Israel with guile.[a]
[b-](But Judah stands firm with God
And is faithful to the Holy One.)[-b]

סְבָבֻ֤נִי בְכַ֙חַשׁ֙ אֶפְרַ֔יִם [1

וּבְמִרְמָ֖ה בֵּ֣ית יִשְׂרָאֵ֑ל

וִֽיהוּדָ֗ה עֹ֥ד רָ֛ד עִם־אֵ֖ל

וְעִם־קְדוֹשִׁ֥ים נֶאֱמָֽן׃

2] Ephraim tends the wind
And pursues the gale;
He is forever adding
Illusion to calamity.[c]
Now they make a covenant with Assyria,
Now oil is carried to Egypt.[d]

אֶפְרַ֜יִם רֹעֶ֥ה ר֙וּחַ֙ וְרֹדֵ֣ף קָדִ֔ים [2

כָּל־הַיּ֕וֹם כָּזָ֥ב וָשֹׁ֖ד יַרְבֶּ֑ה

וּבְרִית֙ עִם־אַשּׁ֣וּר יִכְרֹ֔תוּ

וְשֶׁ֖מֶן לְמִצְרַ֥יִם יוּבָֽל׃

3] The Lord once indicted Judah,[e]
And punished Jacob for his conduct,
Requited him for his deeds.

וְרִ֥יב לַיהוָ֖ה עִם־יְהוּדָ֑ה [3

וְלִפְקֹ֤ד עַֽל־יַעֲקֹב֙ כִּדְרָכָ֔יו

כְּמַעֲלָלָ֖יו יָשִׁ֥יב לֽוֹ׃

4] In the womb he tried to supplant his brother;
Grown to manhood, he strove with a divine being,[f]

בַּבֶּ֖טֶן עָקַ֣ב אֶת־אָחִ֑יו [4

וּבְאוֹנ֖וֹ שָׂרָ֥ה אֶת־אֱלֹהִֽים׃

5] He strove with an angel and prevailed—
The other had to weep and implore him.
At Bethel [Jacob] would meet him,
There to commune with him.[g]

וַיָּ֤שַׂר אֶל־מַלְאָךְ֙ וַיֻּכָ֔ל [5

בָּכָ֖ה וַיִּתְחַנֶּן־ל֑וֹ

בֵּֽית־אֵל֙ יִמְצָאֶ֔נּוּ

וְשָׁ֖ם יְדַבֵּ֥ר עִמָּֽנוּ׃

6] Yet the Lord, the God of Hosts,
Must be invoked as "Lord."[h]

וַֽיהוָ֖ה אֱלֹהֵ֣י הַצְּבָא֑וֹת יְהוָ֖ה זִכְרֽוֹ׃ [6

[a] I.e., the deceit and guile they practice on each other (below vv. 8–9) is constantly
  noted by the Lord
[b-b] Meaning of Heb. uncertain
[c] Septuagint reads "futility"
[d] I.e., they foolishly depend on alliances instead of on the Lord; cf. 5.13; 7.10–11
[e] Presumably the patriarch Judah. Emendation would yield "Israel"; cf. next note
[f] Cf. Gen. 25.26 and 32.29   [g] Heb. "us"
[h] I.e., one should not invoke any of the angelic hosts

7] You must return to your God!
Practice goodness and justice,
And constantly trust in your God.

8] A trader who uses false balances,
Who loves to overreach,

9] Ephraim thinks,
"Ah, I have become rich;
I have gotten power!
b-All my gains do not amount
To an offense which is real guilt."-b

10] I the LORD have been your God
Ever since the land of Egypt.
I will let you dwell in your tentsⁱ again
As in the days of old,ʲ

11] When I spoke to the prophets;
For I granted many visions,
b-And spoke parables through the prophets.

12] As for Gilead, it is worthless;
And to no purpose-b have they
Been sacrificing oxen in Gilgal:
The altars of these are also
Like stone heaps upon a plowed field.ᵏ

וְאַתָּה בֵּאלֹהֶיךָ תָשׁוּב [7

חֶסֶד וּמִשְׁפָּט שְׁמֹר

וְקַוֵּה אֶל־אֱלֹהֶיךָ תָּמִיד:

כְּנַעַן בְּיָדוֹ מֹאזְנֵי מִרְמָה [8

לַעֲשֹׁק אָהֵב:

וַיֹּאמֶר אֶפְרַיִם אַךְ עָשַׁרְתִּי [9

מָצָאתִי אוֹן לִי

כָּל־יְגִיעַי לֹא יִמְצְאוּ־לִי

עָוֹן אֲשֶׁר־חֵטְא:

וְאָנֹכִי יְהֹוָה אֱלֹהֶיךָ [10

מֵאֶרֶץ מִצְרָיִם

עֹד אוֹשִׁיבְךָ בָאֳהָלִים

כִּימֵי מוֹעֵד:

וְדִבַּרְתִּי עַל־הַנְּבִיאִים [11

וְאָנֹכִי חָזוֹן הִרְבֵּיתִי

וּבְיַד הַנְּבִיאִים אֲדַמֶּה:

אִם־גִּלְעָד אָוֶן [12

אַךְ־שָׁוְא הָיוּ

בַּגִּלְגָּל שְׁוָרִים זִבֵּחוּ

גַּם מִזְבְּחוֹתָם כְּגַלִּים

עַל תַּלְמֵי שָׂדָי:

ᵇ⁻ᵇ *Emendation yields "popular"*
ⁱ *I.e., securely; see II Kings 13.5*
ʲ *Lit. "fixed season"*
ᵏ *I.e., the cults of Gilead and Gilgal are as worthless as that of Bethel*

Amos was a Judean shepherd and tree farmer who lived in the eighth century B.C.E. and was the first of our literary prophets. His strong emphasis on social concerns made him a favorite of the Reform movement, which saw its own social impulse as a re-creation of Amos's spirit.

Amos castigates his contemporaries for their exploitation of the poor, for their ruthless pursuit of monetary gain. This denunciation provides a ready parallel to the sidrah which tells the story of Joseph who was sold by his brothers for twenty pieces of silver.

Amos

2:6—3:8

ב

Chapter 2

6] Thus said the LORD:
For three transgressions of Israel,
For four, I will not revoke it:
Because they have sold for silver
Those whose cause was just,
And the needy for a pair of sandals.

7 [Ah,] you *~who trample the heads of the poor
Into the dust of the ground,
And make the humble walk a twisted course!~*
Father and son go to the same girl,
And thereby profane My holy name.

8] They recline by every altar
On garments taken in pledge,
And drink in the House of their God
Wine bought with fines they imposed.

9] Yet I
Destroyed the Amorite before them,
Whose stature was like the cedar's
And who was stout as the oak,
Destroying his boughs above
And his trunk below!

[6] כֹּה אָמַר יְהֹוָה
עַל־שְׁלֹשָׁה פִּשְׁעֵי יִשְׂרָאֵל
וְעַל־אַרְבָּעָה לֹא אֲשִׁיבֶנּוּ
עַל־מִכְרָם בַּכֶּסֶף צַדִּיק
וְאֶבְיוֹן בַּעֲבוּר נַעֲלָיִם:

[7] הַשֹּׁאֲפִים עַל־עֲפַר־אֶרֶץ
בְּרֹאשׁ דַּלִּים
וְדֶרֶךְ עֲנָוִים יַטּוּ
וְאִישׁ וְאָבִיו יֵלְכוּ אֶל־הַנַּעֲרָה
לְמַעַן חַלֵּל אֶת־שֵׁם קָדְשִׁי:

[8] וְעַל־בְּגָדִים חֲבֻלִים יַטּוּ
אֵצֶל כָּל־מִזְבֵּחַ
וְיֵין עֲנוּשִׁים יִשְׁתּוּ בֵּית אֱלֹהֵיהֶם:

[9] וְאָנֹכִי הִשְׁמַדְתִּי
אֶת־הָאֱמֹרִי מִפְּנֵיהֶם
אֲשֶׁר כְּגֹבַהּ אֲרָזִים גָּבְהוֹ
וְחָסֹן הוּא כָּאַלּוֹנִים
וָאַשְׁמִיד פִּרְיוֹ מִמַּעַל
וְשָׁרָשָׁיו מִתָּחַת:

---

*~a Understanding sho'afim as equivalent to shafim. Emendation yields: "Who crush on the ground
|The heads of the poor, |And push off the road |The humble of the land"; cf. Job 24.4*

10] And I
Brought you up from the land of Egypt
And led you through the wilderness forty years,
To possess the land of the Amorite!

11] And I raised up prophets from among your
   sons
And nazirites from among your young men.
Is that not so, O people of Israel?
                              —says the LORD.

12] But you made the nazirites drink wine
And ordered the prophets not to prophesy.

13] b-Ah, I will slow your movements
As a wagon is slowed
When it is full of cut grain.-b

14] Flight shall fail the swift,
The strong shall find no strength,
And the warrior shall not save his life.

15] The bowman shall not hold his ground,
And the fleet-footed shall not escape,
Nor the horseman save his life.

16] Even the most stouthearted warrior
Shall run away unarmedc that day
                              —declares the LORD.

10 וְאָנֹכִ֞י הֶעֱלֵ֤יתִי אֶתְכֶם֙
מֵאֶ֣רֶץ מִצְרָ֔יִם
וָאוֹלֵ֨ךְ אֶתְכֶ֤ם בַּמִּדְבָּר֙
אַרְבָּעִ֣ים שָׁנָ֔ה
לָרֶ֖שֶׁת אֶת־אֶ֥רֶץ הָאֱמֹרִֽי׃

11 וָאָקִ֤ים מִבְּנֵיכֶם֙ לִנְבִיאִ֔ים
וּמִבַּחוּרֵיכֶ֖ם לִנְזִרִ֑ים
הַאַ֥ף אֵֽין־זֹ֛את בְּנֵ֥י יִשְׂרָאֵ֖ל
נְאֻם־יְהוָֽה׃

12 וַתַּשְׁק֥וּ אֶת־הַנְּזִרִ֖ים יָ֑יִן
וְעַל־הַנְּבִיאִים֙ צִוִּיתֶ֣ם לֵאמֹ֔ר
לֹ֖א תִּנָּבְאֽוּ׃

13 הִנֵּ֤ה אָנֹכִי֙ מֵעִ֣יק תַּחְתֵּיכֶ֔ם
כַּאֲשֶׁ֤ר תָּעִיק֙ הָעֲגָלָ֔ה
הַֽמְלֵאָ֥ה לָ֖הּ עָמִֽיר׃

14 וְאָבַ֤ד מָנוֹס֙ מִקָּ֔ל
וְחָזָ֖ק לֹא־יְאַמֵּ֣ץ כֹּח֑וֹ
וְגִבּ֖וֹר לֹא־יְמַלֵּ֥ט נַפְשֽׁוֹ׃

15 וְתֹפֵ֤שׂ הַקֶּ֙שֶׁת֙ לֹ֣א יַעֲמֹ֔ד
וְקַ֥ל בְּרַגְלָ֖יו לֹ֣א יְמַלֵּ֑ט
וְרֹכֵ֣ב הַסּ֔וּס לֹ֥א יְמַלֵּ֖ט נַפְשֽׁוֹ׃

16 וְאַמִּ֥יץ לִבּ֖וֹ בַּגִּבּוֹרִ֑ים
עָר֛וֹם יָנ֥וּס בַּיּוֹם־הַה֖וּא נְאֻם־יְהוָֽה׃

---

b-b Meaning of verse uncertain; alternatively: "I will slow your movements / As a
  threshing sledge (cf. Isa. 28.27–28) is slowed / When clogged by cut grain"
c Lit. "naked"

Chapter 3

1] Hear this word, O people of Israel,
That the LORD has spoken concerning you,
Concerning the whole family that I brought up
    from Egypt:

2] You alone have I singled out
Of all the families of the earth—
That is why I will call you to account
For all your iniquities.

3] Can two walk together
Without having met?

4] Does a lion roar in the forest
When he has no prey?
Does a great beast let out a cry from its den
Without having made a capture?

5] Does a bird drop on the ground—in a trap—
With no snare there?
Does a trap spring up from the ground
Unless it has caught something?

6] When a ram's horn is sounded in a town,
Do the people not take alarm?
Can misfortune come to a town
If the LORD has not caused it?

7] Indeed, my Lord GOD does nothing
Without having revealed His purpose
To His servants the prophets.

8] A lion has roared,
Who can but fear?
My Lord GOD has spoken,
Who can but prophesy?

1] שִׁמְעוּ אֶת־הַדָּבָר הַזֶּה
אֲשֶׁר דִּבֶּר יְהוָה עֲלֵיכֶם בְּנֵי יִשְׂרָאֵל
עַל כָּל־הַמִּשְׁפָּחָה אֲשֶׁר הֶעֱלֵיתִי מֵאֶרֶץ מִצְרַיִם
לֵאמֹר:

2] רַק אֶתְכֶם יָדַעְתִּי
מִכֹּל מִשְׁפְּחוֹת הָאֲדָמָה
עַל־כֵּן אֶפְקֹד עֲלֵיכֶם
אֵת כָּל־עֲוֹנֹתֵיכֶם:

3] הֲיֵלְכוּ שְׁנַיִם יַחְדָּו
בִּלְתִּי אִם־נוֹעָדוּ:

4] הֲיִשְׁאַג אַרְיֵה בַּיַּעַר וְטֶרֶף אֵין לוֹ
הֲיִתֵּן כְּפִיר קוֹלוֹ מִמְּעֹנָתוֹ
בִּלְתִּי אִם־לָכָד:

5] הֲתִפֹּל צִפּוֹר עַל־פַּח הָאָרֶץ
וּמוֹקֵשׁ אֵין לָהּ
הֲיַעֲלֶה־פַּח מִן־הָאֲדָמָה
וְלָכוֹד לֹא יִלְכּוֹד:

6] אִם־יִתָּקַע שׁוֹפָר בְּעִיר
וְעָם לֹא יֶחֱרָדוּ
אִם־תִּהְיֶה רָעָה בְּעִיר
וַיהוָה לֹא עָשָׂה:

7] כִּי לֹא יַעֲשֶׂה אֲדֹנָי יְהוָה דָּבָר
כִּי אִם־גָּלָה סוֹדוֹ
אֶל־עֲבָדָיו הַנְּבִיאִים:

8] אַרְיֵה שָׁאָג מִי לֹא יִירָא
אֲדֹנָי יְהוָה דִּבֶּר מִי לֹא יִנָּבֵא:

The Book of Kings is divided into two parts. It spans four centuries and reaches from the last days of David to the destruction of the Temple by the Babylonians in 586 (or 585) B.C.E. It approaches history from a theological point of view: the story of Israel and Judah must be seen as a judgment of God on the people and its rulers.

The haftarah begins by speaking of a dream King Solomon had, in which he had asked God for the gift of wisdom. The king is now portrayed as the wise judge who solves the difficult case of two women claiming the same child as their own. Solomon's wisdom recalls the wisdom of Joseph in the sidrah.

מקץ

First Kings

3:15—4:1

Chapter 3

15] Then Solomon awoke: it was a dream! He went to Jerusalem, stood before the Ark of the Covenant of the LORD, and sacrificed burnt offerings and presented offerings of well-being; and he made a banquet for all his courtiers.

16] Later two prostitutes came to the king and stood before him.

17] The first woman said, "Please, my lord! This woman and I live in the same house; and I gave birth to a child while she was in the house.

18] On the third day after I was delivered, this woman also gave birth to a child. We were alone; there was no one else with us in the house, just the two of us in the house. 19] During the night this woman's child died, because she lay on it.

20] She arose in the night and took my son from my side while your maidservant was asleep, and laid him in her bosom; and she laid her dead son in my bosom.

21] When I arose in the morning to nurse my son, there he was, dead; but when I looked at him closely in the morning, it was not the son I had borne."

22] The other woman spoke up, "No, the live one is my son, and the dead one is yours!" But the first insisted, "No, the dead boy is yours; mine is the live one!" And they went on arguing before the king.

23] The king said, "One says, 'This is my son, the live one, and the dead one is yours'; and the other says, 'No, the dead boy is yours, mine is the live one.'"

24] So the king gave the order, "Fetch

ג

15] וַיִּקַץ שְׁלֹמֹה וְהִנֵּה חֲלוֹם וַיָּבוֹא יְרוּשָׁלִַם וַיַּעֲמֹד לִפְנֵי אֲרוֹן בְּרִית־יְהוָֹה וַיַּעַל עֹלוֹת וַיַּעַשׂ שְׁלָמִים וַיַּעַשׂ מִשְׁתֶּה לְכָל־עֲבָדָיו:

16] אָז תָּבֹאנָה שְׁתַּיִם נָשִׁים זֹנוֹת אֶל־הַמֶּלֶךְ וַתַּעֲמֹדְנָה לְפָנָיו: 17] וַתֹּאמֶר הָאִשָּׁה הָאַחַת בִּי אֲדֹנִי אֲנִי וְהָאִשָּׁה הַזֹּאת יֹשְׁבֹת בְּבַיִת אֶחָד וָאֵלֵד עִמָּהּ בַּבָּיִת: 18] וַיְהִי בַּיּוֹם הַשְּׁלִישִׁי לְלִדְתִּי וַתֵּלֶד גַּם־הָאִשָּׁה הַזֹּאת וַאֲנַחְנוּ יַחְדָּו אֵין־זָר אִתָּנוּ בַּבַּיִת זוּלָתִי שְׁתַּיִם־אֲנַחְנוּ בַּבָּיִת: 19] וַיָּמָת בֶּן־הָאִשָּׁה הַזֹּאת לָיְלָה אֲשֶׁר שָׁכְבָה עָלָיו: 20] וַתָּקָם בְּתוֹךְ הַלַּיְלָה וַתִּקַּח אֶת־בְּנִי מֵאֶצְלִי וַאֲמָתְךָ יְשֵׁנָה וַתַּשְׁכִּיבֵהוּ בְּחֵיקָהּ וְאֶת־בְּנָהּ הַמֵּת הִשְׁכִּיבָה בְחֵיקִי: 21] וָאָקֻם בַּבֹּקֶר לְהֵינִיק אֶת־בְּנִי וְהִנֵּה־מֵת וָאֶתְבּוֹנֵן אֵלָיו בַּבֹּקֶר וְהִנֵּה לֹא־הָיָה בְנִי אֲשֶׁר יָלָדְתִּי:

22] וַתֹּאמֶר הָאִשָּׁה הָאַחֶרֶת לֹא כִי בְּנִי הַחַי וּבְנֵךְ הַמֵּת וְזֹאת אֹמֶרֶת לֹא כִי בְּנֵךְ הַמֵּת וּבְנִי הֶחָי וַתְּדַבֵּרְנָה לִפְנֵי הַמֶּלֶךְ:

23] וַיֹּאמֶר הַמֶּלֶךְ זֹאת אֹמֶרֶת זֶה־בְּנִי הַחַי וּבְנֵךְ הַמֵּת וְזֹאת אֹמֶרֶת לֹא כִי בְּנֵךְ הַמֵּת וּבְנִי הֶחָי: 24] וַיֹּאמֶר הַמֶּלֶךְ קְחוּ־לִי חָרֶב וַיָּבִאוּ

me a sword." A sword was brought before the king,

25] and the king said, "Cut the live child in two, and give half to one and half to the other."

26] But the woman whose son was the live one pleaded with the king, for she was overcome with compassion for her son. "Please, my lord," she cried, "give her the live child; only don't kill it!" The other insisted, "It shall be neither yours nor mine; cut it in two!"

27] Then the king spoke up. "Give the live child to her," he said, "and do not put it to death; she is its mother."

28] When all Israel heard the decision that the king had rendered, they stood in awe of the king; for they saw that he possessed divine wisdom to execute justice.

Chapter 4

1] King Solomon was now king over all Israel.

הַחֶ֖רֶב לִפְנֵ֥י הַמֶּֽלֶךְ׃ 25 וַיֹּ֣אמֶר הַמֶּלֶךְ֮ גִּזְר֣וּ אֶת־הַיֶּ֣לֶד הַחַ֜י לִשְׁנָ֗יִם וּתְנ֤וּ אֶֽת־הַחֲצִי֙ לְאַחַ֔ת וְאֶֽת־הַחֲצִ֖י לְאֶחָֽת׃

26 וַתֹּ֣אמֶר הָאִשָּׁה֩ אֲשֶׁר־בְּנָ֨הּ הַחַ֜י אֶל־הַמֶּ֗לֶךְ כִּֽי־נִכְמְר֣וּ רַחֲמֶיהָ֮ עַל־בְּנָהּ֒ וַתֹּ֣אמֶר בִּ֣י אֲדֹנִ֗י תְּנוּ־לָהּ֙ אֶת־הַיָּל֣וּד הַחַ֔י וְהָמֵ֖ת אַל־תְּמִיתֻ֑הוּ וְזֹ֣את אֹמֶ֗רֶת גַּם־לִ֥י גַם־לָ֛ךְ לֹ֥א יִהְיֶ֖ה גְּזֹֽרוּ׃ 27 וַיַּ֨עַן הַמֶּ֜לֶךְ וַיֹּ֗אמֶר תְּנוּ־לָהּ֙ אֶת־הַיָּל֣וּד הַחַ֔י וְהָמֵ֖ת לֹ֣א תְמִיתֻ֑הוּ הִ֖יא אִמּֽוֹ׃

28 וַיִּשְׁמְע֣וּ כָל־יִשְׂרָאֵ֗ל אֶת־הַמִּשְׁפָּט֙ אֲשֶׁ֣ר שָׁפַ֣ט הַמֶּ֔לֶךְ וַיִּֽרְא֖וּ מִפְּנֵ֣י הַמֶּ֑לֶךְ כִּ֣י רָא֔וּ כִּֽי־חָכְמַ֧ת אֱלֹהִ֛ים בְּקִרְבּ֖וֹ לַעֲשׂ֥וֹת מִשְׁפָּֽט׃

ד

1 וַֽיְהִי֙ הַמֶּ֣לֶךְ שְׁלֹמֹ֔ה מֶ֖לֶךְ עַל־כָּל־יִשְׂרָאֵֽל׃

*Ezekiel lived in Babylon during the days of the exile
(sixth century B.C.E.) and was a master of mystic dreams
and visions. Like Jeremiah and Deutero-Isaiah he fortified
his people's faith in God's forgiveness, but unlike them
he stressed the great need for structured ritual as a basis
for a religious revival.*

*The haftarah uses the simile of Judah and Joseph (who
in the sidrah are the chief protagonists) to foretell the return of all the tribes from their Babylonian exile. The
northern tribes had been devastated and driven out in
721 B.C.E., the southern tribes in 586 (or 585) B.C.E. God,
says Ezekiel, will return all of Israel to the Holy Land.*

ויגש

Ezekiel

37 : 15–28

לז

Chapter 37

15] The word of the Lord came to me:
16] And you, O mortal, take a stick and write on
it, "Of Judah and the Israelites associated with
him"; and take another stick and write on it, "Of
Joseph—the stick of Ephraim—and all the House
of Israel associated with him."

17] Bring them
close to each other, so that they become one stick,
joined together in your hand.

18] And when any
of your people ask you, "Won't you tell us what
these actions of yours mean?"

19] answer them,
"Thus said the Lord GOD: I am going to take the
stick of Joseph—which is in the hand of Ephraim—
and of the tribes of Israel associated with him,
and I will place the stick of Judah ᵃ⁻upon itᵃ and
make them into one stick; they shall be joined in
My hand."

20] You shall hold up before their
eyes the sticks which you have inscribed,

21] and
you shall declare to them: Thus said the Lord
GOD: I am going to take the Israelite people from
among the nations they have gone to, and gather
them from every quarter, and bring them to their
own land.

22] I will make them a single nation
in the land, on the hills of Israel, and one king
shall be king of them all. Never again shall they
be two nations, and never again shall they be divided into two kingdoms.

23] Nor shall they
ever again defile themselves by their fetishes and
their abhorrent things, and by their other trans-

[15] וַיְהִי דְבַר־יְהֹוָה אֵלַי לֵאמֹר: [16] וְאַתָּה
בֶן־אָדָם קַח־לְךָ עֵץ אֶחָד וּכְתֹב עָלָיו לִיהוּדָה
וְלִבְנֵי יִשְׂרָאֵל חֲבֵרָו וּלְקַח עֵץ אֶחָד וּכְתוֹב
עָלָיו לְיוֹסֵף עֵץ אֶפְרַיִם וְכָל־בֵּית יִשְׂרָאֵל
חֲבֵרָו: [17] וְקָרַב אֹתָם אֶחָד אֶל־אֶחָד לְךָ
לְעֵץ אֶחָד וְהָיוּ לַאֲחָדִים בְּיָדֶךָ: [18] וְכַאֲשֶׁר
יֹאמְרוּ אֵלֶיךָ בְּנֵי עַמְּךָ לֵאמֹר הֲלוֹא־תַגִּיד
לָנוּ מָה־אֵלֶּה לָּךְ: [19] דַּבֵּר אֲלֵהֶם כֹּה־
אָמַר אֲדֹנָי יֱהֹוִה הִנֵּה אֲנִי לֹקֵחַ אֶת־עֵץ יוֹסֵף
אֲשֶׁר בְּיַד־אֶפְרַיִם וְשִׁבְטֵי יִשְׂרָאֵל חֲבֵרָו וְנָתַתִּי
אוֹתָם עָלָיו אֶת־עֵץ יְהוּדָה וַעֲשִׂיתִם לְעֵץ אֶחָד
וְהָיוּ אֶחָד בְּיָדִי: [20] וְהָיוּ הָעֵצִים אֲשֶׁר
תִּכְתֹּב עֲלֵיהֶם בְּיָדְךָ לְעֵינֵיהֶם: [21] וְדַבֵּר
אֲלֵיהֶם כֹּה־אָמַר אֲדֹנָי יֱהֹוִה הִנֵּה אֲנִי לֹקֵחַ
אֶת־בְּנֵי יִשְׂרָאֵל מִבֵּין הַגּוֹיִם אֲשֶׁר הָלְכוּ־שָׁם
וְקִבַּצְתִּי אֹתָם מִסָּבִיב וְהֵבֵאתִי אוֹתָם אֶל־
אַדְמָתָם: [22] וְעָשִׂיתִי אֹתָם לְגוֹי אֶחָד בָּאָרֶץ
בְּהָרֵי יִשְׂרָאֵל וּמֶלֶךְ אֶחָד יִהְיֶה לְכֻלָּם לְמֶלֶךְ
וְלֹא יִהְיוּ־עוֹד לִשְׁנֵי גוֹיִם וְלֹא יֵחָצוּ עוֹד
לִשְׁתֵּי מַמְלָכוֹת עוֹד: [23] וְלֹא יִטַּמְּאוּ עוֹד
בְּגִלּוּלֵיהֶם וּבְשִׁקּוּצֵיהֶם וּבְכֹל פִּשְׁעֵיהֶם

ᵃ⁻ᵃ *Meaning of Heb. uncertain*

357

gressions. I will save them in all their settlements where they sinned, and I will cleanse them. Then they shall be My people, and I will be their God.

24] My servant David shall be king over them; there shall be one shepherd for all of them. They shall follow My rules and faithfully obey My laws. 25] Thus they shall remain in the land which I gave to My servant Jacob and in which your fathers dwelt; they and their children and their children's children shall dwell there forever, with My servant David as their prince for all time.

26] I will make a covenant of friendship with them—it shall be an everlasting covenant with them—I will establish[a] them and multiply them, and I will place My sanctuary among them forever. 27] My Presence[b] shall rest over them; I will be their God and they shall be My people.

28] And when My sanctuary abides among them forever, the nations shall know that I the LORD do sanctify Israel.

וְהוֹשַׁעְתִּ֣י אֹתָ֗ם מִכֹּ֤ל מוֹשְׁבֹֽתֵיהֶם֙ אֲשֶׁ֣ר חָטְא֣וּ בָהֶ֔ם וְטִֽהַרְתִּ֣י אוֹתָ֔ם וְהָֽיוּ־לִ֖י לְעָ֑ם וַֽאֲנִ֕י אֶהְיֶ֥ה לָהֶ֖ם לֵֽאלֹהִֽים:

24 וְעַבְדִּ֤י דָוִד֙ מֶ֣לֶךְ עֲלֵיהֶ֔ם וְרוֹעֶ֥ה אֶחָ֖ד יִֽהְיֶ֣ה לְכֻלָּ֑ם וּבְמִשְׁפָּטַ֣י יֵלֵ֔כוּ וְחֻקֹּתַ֥י יִשְׁמְר֖וּ וְעָשׂ֥וּ אוֹתָֽם: 25 וְיָשְׁב֣וּ עַל־הָאָ֗רֶץ אֲשֶׁ֤ר נָתַ֙תִּי֙ לְעַבְדִּ֣י לְיַֽעֲקֹ֔ב אֲשֶׁ֥ר יָֽשְׁבוּ־בָ֖הּ אֲבֽוֹתֵיכֶ֑ם וְיָֽשְׁב֣וּ עָלֶ֡יהָ הֵ֠מָּה וּבְנֵיהֶ֞ם וּבְנֵ֤י בְנֵיהֶם֙ עַד־עוֹלָ֔ם וְדָוִ֣ד עַבְדִּ֔י נָשִׂ֥יא לָהֶ֖ם לְעוֹלָֽם: 26 וְכָֽרַתִּ֤י לָהֶם֙ בְּרִ֣ית שָׁל֔וֹם בְּרִ֥ית עוֹלָ֖ם יִֽהְיֶ֣ה אוֹתָ֑ם וּנְתַתִּים֙ וְהִרְבֵּיתִ֣י אוֹתָ֔ם וְנָֽתַתִּ֧י אֶת־מִקְדָּשִׁ֛י בְּתוֹכָ֖ם לְעוֹלָֽם: 27 וְהָיָ֤ה מִשְׁכָּנִי֙ עֲלֵיהֶ֔ם וְהָיִ֥יתִי לָהֶ֖ם לֵֽאלֹהִ֑ים וְהֵ֖מָּה יִֽהְיוּ־לִ֥י לְעָֽם: 28 וְיָֽדְעוּ֙ הַגּוֹיִ֔ם כִּ֚י אֲנִ֣י יְהוָ֔ה מְקַדֵּ֖שׁ אֶת־יִשְׂרָאֵ֑ל בִּֽהְי֧וֹת מִקְדָּשִׁ֛י בְּתוֹכָ֖ם לְעוֹלָֽם:

---

[a] Meaning of Heb. uncertain
[b] Lit. "dwelling place"

The Book of Kings is divided into two parts. It spans four centuries and reaches from the last days of David to the destruction of the Temple by the Babylonians in 586 (or 585) B.C.E. It approaches history from a theological point of view: the story of Israel and Judah must be seen as a judgment of God on the people and its rulers.

Both sidrah and haftarah record the testaments of two leaders, Jacob and David. The contrast is, however, startling: Jacob's is a large vision, David's charge a practical and cruel piece of political advice. Note that the Bible does not hide this side of the dying poet-king.

First Kings

2 : 1–12

ב

Chapter 2

1] When David's life was drawing to a close, he instructed his son Solomon as follows:

2] "I am going the way of all the earth; be strong and show yourself a man.

3] Keep the charge of the LORD your God, walking in His ways and following His laws, His commandments, His rules, and His admonitions as recorded in the Teaching of Moses, in order that you may succeed in whatever you undertake and wherever you turn.

4] Then the LORD will fulfill the promise that He made concerning me: 'If your descendants are scrupulous in their conduct, and walk before Me faithfully, with all their heart and soul, *your line on the throne of Israel shall never end!'*

5] "Further, you know what Joab son of Zeruiah did to me, what he did to the two commanders of Israel's forces, Abner son of Ner and Amasa son of Jether: he killed them, shedding[b] blood of war in peacetime, staining the girdle of his loins and the sandals on his feet with blood of war.[c]

6] So act in accordance with your wisdom, and see that his white hair does not go down to Sheol in peace.

א] וַיִּקְרְבוּ יְמֵי־דָוִד לָמוּת וַיְצַו אֶת־שְׁלֹמֹה בְנוֹ לֵאמֹר: 2 אָנֹכִי הֹלֵךְ בְּדֶרֶךְ כָּל־הָאָרֶץ וְחָזַקְתָּ וְהָיִיתָ לְאִישׁ: 3 וְשָׁמַרְתָּ אֶת־מִשְׁמֶרֶת יְהֹוָה אֱלֹהֶיךָ לָלֶכֶת בִּדְרָכָיו לִשְׁמֹר חֻקֹּתָיו מִצְוֹתָיו וּמִשְׁפָּטָיו וְעֵדְוֺתָיו כַּכָּתוּב בְּתוֹרַת מֹשֶׁה לְמַעַן תַּשְׂכִּיל אֵת כָּל־אֲשֶׁר תַּעֲשֶׂה וְאֵת כָּל־אֲשֶׁר תִּפְנֶה שָׁם: 4 לְמַעַן יָקִים יְהֹוָה אֶת־דְּבָרוֹ אֲשֶׁר דִּבֶּר עָלַי לֵאמֹר אִם־יִשְׁמְרוּ בָנֶיךָ אֶת־דַּרְכָּם לָלֶכֶת לְפָנַי בֶּאֱמֶת בְּכָל־לְבָבָם וּבְכָל־נַפְשָׁם לֵאמֹר לֹא־יִכָּרֵת לְךָ אִישׁ מֵעַל כִּסֵּא יִשְׂרָאֵל:

5 וְגַם אַתָּה יָדַעְתָּ אֵת אֲשֶׁר־עָשָׂה לִי יוֹאָב בֶּן־צְרוּיָה אֲשֶׁר עָשָׂה לִשְׁנֵי־שָׂרֵי צִבְאוֹת יִשְׂרָאֵל לְאַבְנֵר בֶּן־נֵר וְלַעֲמָשָׂא בֶן־יֶתֶר וַיַּהַרְגֵם וַיָּשֶׂם דְּמֵי־מִלְחָמָה בְּשָׁלֹם וַיִּתֵּן דְּמֵי מִלְחָמָה בַּחֲגֹרָתוֹ אֲשֶׁר בְּמָתְנָיו וּבְנַעֲלוֹ אֲשֶׁר בְּרַגְלָיו: 6 וְעָשִׂיתָ כְּחָכְמָתֶךָ וְלֹא־תוֹרֵד שֵׂיבָתוֹ בְּשָׁלֹם שְׁאֹל:

---

a-a Lit. "there shall never cease to be a man of yours on the throne of Israel." Cf. II Sam. 7.12–16

b Meaning of Heb. uncertain

c I.e., Joab had thus brought bloodguilt on David's House; see II Sam. 3.27 and 20.10

7] "But deal graciously with the sons of Barzillai the Gileadite, for they befriended me when I fled from your brother Absalom; let them be among those that eat at your table.[d]

8] "You must also deal with Shimei son of Gera, the Benjaminite from Bahurim. He insulted me outrageously when I was on my way to Mahanaim; but he came down to meet me at the Jordan,[e] and I swore to him by the LORD: 'I will not put you to the sword.'

9] So do not let him go unpunished; for you are a wise man and you will know how to deal with him and send his gray hair down to Sheol in blood."

10] So David slept with his fathers, and he was buried in the City of David.

11] The length of David's reign over Israel was forty years: he reigned seven years in Hebron, and he reigned thirty-three years in Jerusalem.

12] And Solomon sat upon the throne of his father David, and his rule was firmly established.

7] וְלִבְנֵ֣י בַרְזִלַּ֤י הַגִּלְעָדִי֙ תַּֽעֲשֶׂה־חֶ֔סֶד וְהָי֖וּ בְּאֹכְלֵ֣י שֻׁלְחָנֶ֑ךָ כִּי־כֵ֞ן קָרְב֣וּ אֵלַ֗י בְּבָרְחִי֙ מִפְּנֵ֖י אַבְשָׁל֥וֹם אָחִֽיךָ׃

8] וְהִנֵּ֣ה עִ֠מְּךָ שִֽׁמְעִ֨י בֶן־גֵּרָ֥א בֶן־הַיְמִינִי֮ מִבַּֽחֻרִים֒ וְה֤וּא קִֽלְלַ֙נִי֙ קְלָלָ֣ה נִמְרֶ֔צֶת בְּי֖וֹם לֶכְתִּ֣י מַֽחֲנָ֑יִם וְהֽוּא־יָרַ֤ד לִקְרָאתִי֙ הַיַּרְדֵּ֔ן וָאֶשָּׁ֤בַֽע לוֹ֙ בַֽיהֹוָ֣ה לֵאמֹ֔ר אִם־אֲמִֽיתְךָ֖ בֶּחָֽרֶב׃

9] וְעַתָּה֙ אַל־תְּנַקֵּ֔הוּ כִּ֛י אִ֥ישׁ חָכָ֖ם אָ֑תָּה וְיָ֣דַעְתָּ֗ אֵ֚ת אֲשֶׁ֣ר תַּֽעֲשֶׂה־לּ֔וֹ וְהֽוֹרַדְתָּ֧ אֶת־שֵׂיבָת֛וֹ בְּדָ֖ם שְׁאֹֽול׃

10] וַיִּשְׁכַּ֥ב דָּוִ֖ד עִם־אֲבֹתָ֑יו וַיִּקָּבֵ֖ר בְּעִ֥יר דָּוִֽד׃

11] וְהַיָּמִ֗ים אֲשֶׁ֨ר מָלַ֤ךְ דָּוִד֙ עַל־יִשְׂרָאֵ֔ל אַרְבָּעִ֖ים שָׁנָ֑ה בְּחֶבְר֤וֹן מָלַךְ֙ שֶׁ֣בַע שָׁנִ֔ים וּבִירֽוּשָׁלַ֣͏ִם מָלַ֔ךְ שְׁלֹשִׁ֥ים וְשָׁלֹ֖שׁ שָׁנִֽים׃

12] וּשְׁלֹמֹ֗ה יָשַׁ֕ב עַל־כִּסֵּ֖א דָּוִ֣ד אָבִ֑יו וַתִּכֹּ֥ן מַלְכֻת֖וֹ מְאֹֽד׃

[d] I.e., for whose maintenance you provide; see II Sam. 19.32 ff.

[e] See II Sam. 16.5 ff.; 19.17 ff.

שמות

EXODUS

Commentary by

W. GUNTHER PLAUT

Introducing Exodus

Exodus is the book which speaks of the physical and spiritual birth of Israel as a nation. It contains the stories of enslavement and liberation, of revelation and wanderings, of belief and apostasy; it is the repository of fundamental laws and of the rules governing national worship. It has two settings, Egypt and the wilderness of Sinai, and its time frame is the latter part of the thirteenth century B.C.E.

A Continuation of Genesis

It is important to see the book as a continuation of Genesis, which we described earlier as a tale of beginnings and of God's disappointments (see "Introducing Genesis").

After many trials and disillusionments, God chooses a particular people whom in time to come He will make His allies and helpers. He selects Abraham and Sarah as the ancestors of this nation-to-be, and the rest of Genesis is the story of Abraham, Isaac, and Jacob and their families who will be the physical and spiritual forebears of the people Israel. During a severe famine Jacob and his children and grandchildren migrate to Egypt. They leave Canaan behind, the land which God had promised them as their permanent inheritance. Their fate will be now forged in a strange land, amidst a people who will turn from welcoming hosts into a nation of oppressors. It is at this point of change that the Book of Exodus begins. It will tell of the fashioning of Israel, the people of God's choice, the nation that God needs.

History and Faith

The tales of Genesis were a mixture of myth, legend, distant memory, and search for origins, bound together by the strands of a central theological concept. With Exodus, the Pentateuch enters the realm of history, albeit not history in the modern sense. The latter describes events which are rooted exclusively in the human realm; the former depicts the will of God as the hinge on which human events must turn. In that sense, Exodus is history grounded in faith. Thus, the escape of the Israelites from Egypt may be said to represent history in the accepted, contemporary meaning; that this was brought about by divine interference, and was so experienced by Israel, gives the tale of liberation an additional faith dimension.

The stories of enslavement and release are not attested by extrabiblical sources. There are scholars who therefore consider these memories to be pious constructions, folktales, and frameworks for the exaltation of Israel's God. But this is a minority view. Rather, it is generally agreed that no people would freely invent a history of slavery and that the events told in the first chapters of the book have a historical basis. The name Raamses (1:11) probably refers to Ramses II

who belonged to the Nineteenth Dynasty and reigned from 1304–1237. Either he or his son Merneptah was the pharaoh of the Exodus.

Who were the people enslaved in Egypt? They were Hebrews, possibly those who had come to Egypt from Canaan when the Hyksos ruled and were enslaved when the latter fell from power in the sixteenth century B.C.E. The Hebrews were apparently an aggregate of tribal and/or social groupings who traced their origins to a common ancestor, a legendary, "eponymous" father figure Jacob. Certain scholars believe that only a few tribes (those identified with Joseph and Benjamin, the "Rachel" tribes) were lodged in Egypt, while other Hebrew groupings (the "Leah" tribes) never left Canaan, and that all these tribes joined hands during the invasion. This highly speculative theory has not been taken into account in the preparation of this commentary. Rather, we have proceeded from the text as it now stands, and in this way—after its final redaction—it has been accepted by Israel and has exerted an enormous influence. Whether or not the events happened exactly as described is in the final instance less important than the way in which they were experienced and comprehended. Whether or not God "objectively" rescued Israel from Egypt is a question to which no historian can provide an answer. But Exodus, the repository of Israel's experience, says that He did, and on this basis history and faith together have shaped the minds and hearts of Israel.

Contents of Exodus

The book has an easily discernible structure: it begins with the story of enslavement and proceeds to the persons and events of the liberation. It then tells of the march to Sinai and of the climactic revelation. There-

after follows a body of laws which are to regulate Israel's society. A wilderness Tabernacle is projected and—after the people's apostasy has been forgiven—is eventually built. God now dwells permanently in Israel's midst.

1] THE PROLOGUE (Chapters 1 and 2). The children of Jacob-Israel, having settled in the Egyptian province of Goshen, have grown into a people of great size. They are enslaved by Pharaoh who did not know the service which Joseph had rendered and cry to God for relief. God prepares the future liberation by raising up Moses. The latter flees the country after he has slain an officer of the king.

2] THE MISSION (3:9–7:13). In the desert God reveals himself to Moses and sends him on his mission. Moses hesitates but, in the end, having been assured that God will aid him, returns to Egypt. There (with his brother Aaron) he inspires his own people with the vision of liberation and confronts Pharaoh with the demand to let Israel go. Pharaoh refuses; the Israelites waver between hope and despair.

3] CONFRONTATION (7:14–13:16). Through a series of punishments or plagues, the king's resolve is weakened and, when his own first-born is taken, he concedes defeat. The God of Israel subdues the god of Egypt. The drama reaches its climax during a fateful "night of watching," and forever after Israel is to retell the tale of redemption through the celebration of Passover. A nation is born.

4] THE ROAD TO SINAI (13:17–18:27). Instead of guiding the Children of Israel by the straight route to Canaan, God leads them by the Reed Sea (Sea of Reeds) where in miraculous fashion they are rescued from

the pursuing hosts of Pharaoh. They celebrate their salvation with a hymn of exaltation and gratitude and are now on their way to Sinai. Dissatisfaction sets in over food and water and the people begin to murmur against God and His human surrogates. Though their immediate needs are met, their rebellious spirit will thereafter surface time and again. They meet Amalek in battle and are victorious; the memory of this first struggle remains deeply imbedded in their minds. Jethro, Moses' father-in-law, arrives and gives Moses advice on the organization of the community.

5] REVELATION AND COMMANDMENT (19:1–20:18). At Mount Sinai, amidst awesome signs and manifestations, the Lord of Israel reveals himself to His people. The Ten Commandments are proclaimed and, since the people find themselves unable to stand further in the presence of the Divine, Moses becomes God's interpreter and the announcer of His will, Israel's first "prophet."

6] THE LAWS (20:19–24:18). Four chapters record a large number of diverse rules and regulations, most of them phrased as case law. Moses reads this "Book of the Covenant" to the people who proclaim: "All that the Lord has spoken we will faithfully do." The pact is formally entered into and both God and Israel are forever bound to each other.

7] SANCTUARY AND SERVICE (25:1–31:18). God now commands the building of the Tabernacle so that He might dwell in the people's midst. Bezalel and Oholiab are chosen to carry out the intricate and elaborate design which is set forth in great detail.

8] APOSTASY AND SECOND COVENANT (32:1–40:38). While Moses is on the mountain, the people grow restless. In their anxiety they press Aaron to build them a golden calf which might provide them with visible leadership. Moses returns and the rebels are punished. God is disillusioned with Israel and wants to make a fresh start with Moses and his family, but Moses dissuades Him and eventually God is reconciled and a new covenant concluded. The Tabernacle is now built and, almost exacly one year after the Exodus, it is set up (the dedication is reported in Numbers). The first and goal-setting phase of Israel's history is completed and, with it, the Book of Exodus.

Literary Aspects

The material contained in Exodus may be classified as consisting of biography, narrative, poetry, law, and archival records. A number of major and minor motifs are clearly discernible, some of which are paralleled in other biblical literature and in ancient Near Eastern texts.[1]

The three major motifs are:

The wilderness theme: a person or nation has to be isolated and refined by trial in the desolate desert.

The covenant theme: the divine or earthly suzerain and his vassal enter into a treaty which sets forth the obligations of both partners.

The exaltation theme: the deity is exalted in hymn and enthroned in a special structure.

Among the minor motifs are:

The deity overcomes the powers of the deep and commands the sea.

An infant who is to become ruler or savior is exposed to the elements and is wondrously rescued.

---

[1] Further on this subject and on the relation of Exodus to ancient Near Eastern literature, see Hallo's essay below.

The text of the book as we now have it is the result of a long literary development. In part it goes back to old traditions which were transmitted orally at first and then committed to writing.[2] That being the case, are there elements in Exodus which may be assigned to Moses and his time? Most likely some traditions went back to him and others may be even older. As the centuries wore on, new materials were added and old ones altered so that even within one segment we may now find diverse reflections. Thus, the first part of the Song at the Sea (ch. 15) is probably of presettlement origin while its second part contains references to postsettlement conditions.

The Book of Exodus is intimately connected with Genesis and Numbers, and after the composition of Leviticus the four were combined into one book,[3] and later on Deuteronomy was added to form the Torah

(or Pentateuch) as we have come to know it.

Name

"Exodus" is derived from the Greek *exodos* which is paralleled by an old Hebrew ascription סֵפֶר יְצִיאַת מִצְרַיִם ("The book of the departure from Egypt"). But the general Hebrew title is סֵפֶר שְׁמוֹת ("Book of names"), so called after the opening words of chapter 1: "These are the names. . . ."

[2] See our General Introduction to the Torah. The different sources can best be identified in some of the later chapters of Exodus; thus it is suggested that chs. 20–23 are from E; 25–31, 35–40 from P; 34:1–28 from J. The rest of the book derives from J/E, with isolated passages from other sources.

[3] This is, of course, merely an assumption, for no such book—referred to as Tetrateuch—has been preserved.

Exodus
and Ancient Near Eastern Literature

WILLIAM W. HALLO

The literary problems posed by the narratives in Exodus are rather different from those of Genesis. There we dealt with three distinct literary units, each woven together out of discrete documentary sources. The primeval history of man on earth (Gen. 1–11) reflected a mythological tradition shared with Mesopotamia and other parts of the ancient Near East. The patriarchal tales (Gen. 12–36) represented a legendary block of non-historical genre-pieces intended to convey the essence of a variety of local traditions associated with the shrines and other "sites and sights" of Syria and Palestine. The story of Joseph (Gen. 37–50) was an essential link between Patriarchs and Exodus enlarged into an elaborate novella with an ostensible Egyptian setting and background. None of the three units could be said to qualify as authentic historical record-keeping, though together they did enshrine the manner in which a later, united Israel chose to render account to itself of its own alleged past.[1]

The work which we know today as the Book of Exodus, on the other hand, must have laid some claims to being a chronicle of historical events, of history "as it really happened." The events recorded in Exodus were much closer in time to the time of the artist who gave us the finished book than were those of Genesis. Moreover they bear a much more crucial relation to the history of his own time, whatever precise date is assigned to that. A united Israel is hardly conceivable without the shared memory of the Exodus (or an exodus) preceding the conquest of Canaan. And the Exodus in turn presupposes the prior sojourn in Egypt and the subsequent wanderings in Sinai. Genesis moved in the realm of myth, legend, and novella— the formulation of what *may* have been, the almost random choice of one or more explanations for the present state of affairs in terms of their possible origins and of selected intervening stages, told by preference in the form of biographical details associated with paradigmatic individuals. We now leave that realm behind and move instead to what *must* have been: the necessary organization of group traditions into a meaningful sequence of events that can account for the group's present awareness of its collective destiny.

That being so, are we entitled, more than

[1] William W. Hallo in essay to Commentary on Genesis.

in Genesis, to look to the literature of the ancient Near East for confirmation of the claims to historical validity of Exodus? Hardly, for these claims are made strictly in the context of Israel's own formulations. Their neighbors had different preoccupations, and what was crucial to the Israelite historian was more likely than not outside or beneath the notice of any other people's chronicler. Surely the Egyptian contemporaries of the dramatic events at the Reed Sea and in Sinai are not apt to have recorded for posterity what at the time appeared as just one or two more episodes among countless others. Surely they would have had to be prophets to foresee their ultimate impact.

We can, however, look to the external sources for a general evaluation of the historical context in which the Bible places the events, and of the literary forms in which it transmitted them. That is to say, we can invoke the "contextual" approach, combining comparison and contrast to illuminate the conceptions that Israel shared with its general ancient Near Eastern setting, and to silhouette the memories that were uniquely hers.[2] To achieve this purpose, it helps to analyze the biblical book, not into the original documents which (by the documentary hypothesis or other critical estimates) went into its making, but into its major generic components. Reading the text as a single, finished work of literature, one tends to detect three such components—biography, history, and legislation. They characterize respectively the "mise-en-scène" of the book (Part I, which forms the Prologue, and Part II in this commentary), its narrative core (here Parts III and IV), and its development (here Parts V–VIII). All of them converge in its climactic centerpiece, the revelation at Sinai (chs. 18–20). They may serve as a thread in distinguishing the kinds of ancient Near Eastern literature—inevitably very diverse—respectively relevant for their elucidation.

The Biography of Moses and of His Kin

To turn from Genesis to Exodus is, then, to pass from legend to history. The gap is considerable, but the transition is facilitated by recourse in both books to biography: the biographies of the Patriarchs, the twelve sons of Jacob, and particularly Joseph at the end of Genesis, the biographies of Moses and his kin at the beginning of Exodus. The entire story of the Egyptian oppression, from the midwives who frustrated Pharaoh's intent to the enforced labor of the Israelites, is told in terms of its relationship to Miriam, Aaron, and Moses. The historicity of these three figures was an article of faith long before the close of the biblical period. References to them in pre-exilic prophecy (Mic. 6:4; Jer. 15:1), in the Deuteronomic history (Josh. 24:5; I Sam. 12:8), and in the Psalms (105:26, 106:16) show how deeply embedded was the belief in their crucial role in transforming the twelve tribes into one people. But precisely because of their part in the emergence of Israel's nationhood, later memory tended to invest them with legendary accretions which have the cumulative effect of discrediting their historicity in modern critical judgment. Thus it is important to identify the purely literary elements in their biographies, especially any so-called topos, that is a motif or theme cast in a recurrent literary form.

One such topos is the tale of Moses' birth. On the surface it resembles a familiar folkloristic motif: the exposure of the infant son by royal decree and his rescue and ultimate arrival at or return to the palace. Many secondary motifs are likewise shared by the

2 *Idem*, "Biblical History in Its Near Eastern Setting: The Contextual Approach," in *Scripture in Context: Essays on the Comparative Method*, ed. Carl D. Evans, William W. Hallo, and John B. White (Pittsburgh Theological Monograph Series, Vol. 34, 1980), pp. 1–26.

tale of Moses with particular versions of the theme as developed in other cultures. Among the most famous of these is the "Birth Legend of Sargon of Akkad" preserved in an Assyrian text cast in the form of a fictionalized autobiography. (See Gleanings to 2:1–25.) But while Sargon ruled in hoary antiquity, and legends began to accumulate about him at an early date, the motifs of exposure in a reed-basket and rescue by a person attached to the palace appear nowhere outside the "Birth Legend." And there is no indication that this goes further back than the late eighth century B.C.E., when it may have been composed to celebrate the triumphs of his namesake, Sargon II of Assyria (722–705 B.C.E.).[3]

Scores of comparable legends have been identified in other literatures, some of which can (unlike the Sargon legend) be shown to have originated before the first millennium B.C.E.[4] Such are, for example, the Hittite tales of "Brother Good and Brother Bad," "The Sun-God and the Cow," and "The City of Zalpa."[5] Others, while late, have at least a specifically Egyptian setting in common with the Moses legend, notably a version of the "Contending of Horus and Seth."[6] But none of them includes all the elements of the Moses birth legend, which evidently evolved in response to the felt need to explain both his name and his origins, or better: to explain them away, for there were surely more convincing etymologies available both in Egyptian and in Hebrew (see commentary to 2:10).[7]

Another topos crucial to the figure of Moses is his speech difficulty. It is remarked at least two and possibly three different times. Once Moses calls himself, literally, "heavy of mouth and heavy of tongue" (4:11; New Jewish Version: "slow of speech and slow of tongue") and twice "uncircumcised of lips" (6:12, 30; New Jewish Version: "of impeded speech"). Isaiah similarly protested that he was "unclean of lips" before he accepted his prophetic mission (Isa. 6:5; cf. also Jer. 1:4–10). The "heavy" speech organs are, perhaps, an artful counterpart to Pharaoh's "heart" (i.e., mind) which is repeatedly described as "heavy" (New Jewish Version: "hard") in the same (i.e., so-called "Yahwistic") version of the recital of the negotiations between the two, but the idiom itself is rooted in Near Eastern literature. In one of the earliest Sumerian epics, a central role is played by the messenger whose "mouth was too heavy" to repeat a message verbatim, leading by necessity to the invention of (letter-)writing. In later Akkadian literature, the "heavy mouth" became a recognized medical phenomenon and the beginning (hence: title) of an entire treatise on pathology.[8]

The marriage of Moses again involves familiar literary topoi, combined in unique

[3] James B. Pritchard, ed., *Ancient Near Eastern Texts* (Princeton: Princeton University Press, 3rd ed., 1969), p. 119. [Hereafter cited as Pritchard, *ANET*]; cf. Chaim Cohen, "The Legend of Sargon and the Birth of Moses," in *Journal of the Ancient Near Eastern Society of Columbia University*, 4 (1972), pp. 46–51.

[4] Theodor H. Gaster, *Myth, Legend and Custom in the Old Testament* (New York & Evanston: Harper & Row, 1969), pp. 224–230, 380–382; Brian C. Lewis, *The Sargon Legend* (American Schools of Oriental Research Dissertation Series, Vol. 4, 1980).

[5] *Ibid.*, pp. 156 f. Cf. Thomas L. Thompson and Dorothy Irvin, "The Joseph and Moses Narratives," in *Israelite and Judaean History*, ed. John H. Hayes and J. Maxwell Miller (Philadelphia: Westminster Press, 1977), ch. III, pp. 149–212, esp. pp. 155 and 192.

[6] *Ibid.*, p. 155. Cf. D. B. Redford, "The Literary Motif of the Exposed Child," *Numen*, 14 (1967), pp. 209–228, esp. pp. 221–224.

[7] I.e., "he who pulled his people out (of the water)." So interpreted, e.g., by Martin Buber, *Moses* (Oxford and London: East and West Library, 1946), p. 36. Cf. Isa. 63:11 f.

[8] Jeffrey H. Tigay, "Moses' Speech Difficulty," *Gratz College Annual*, 3 (1974), pp. 29–42; idem, "Heavy of Mouth and Heavy of Tongue: On Moses' Speech Difficulty," *Bulletin of the American Schools of Oriental Research*, 231(October, 1978), pp. 57–67. [Hereafter cited as *BASOR*.]

or novel ways. The initial encounter with Zipporah at the well, the insistent hospitality on the part of her family, and even her father's name here (Reuel; 2:15–20) are reminiscent of the wooing of Rebekah (Gen. 24) and to some extent of the first meeting of Jacob and Rachel (Gen. 29). But this idyllic beginning is combined with the less edifying events surrounding the return of the couple to Egypt (4:18–26), when Moses became "a bridegroom of (i.e., cleansed by) blood because of the circumcision." Circumcision serves as a puberty rite in Islam as well as in numerous pre-literate societies. That it was once a prerequisite for marital relations (like a first-fruit offering) is suggested by the biblical analogy of David's wooing Michal with the foreskins of two hundred slain Philistines (I Sam. 18:27), and by the Arabic cognate of the Hebrew term for "bridegroom" which derives from a verbal root meaning "to circumcise." (See commentary to 4:26.) And behind all these associations stands the Egyptian tale of the "Deliverance of Mankind from Destruction." Although it is not entirely certain that circumcision was widely practiced in Egypt,[9] we have in that tale a similar motif to Zipporah's touching Moses with the freshly-cut foreskin after God "sought to kill him": the assuaging of divine wrath by the application of human blood or its equivalent.[10]

Moses' persistent desire to encounter God is among the few biographical details in the later portions of the book. After the strange episode in which he is vouchsafed a view of God's "back" (33:23), Moses himself undergoes a physical transformation that terrifies the people. The skin of his face begins to become "radiant" (34:29 f.) or even to "grow horns" in the Latin translation of the passage and in Michelangelo's famous statue of Moses. Though the latter sense would normally call for a secondary verbal form derived from the simple noun for horn, there

is in fact a conceptual link between "radiant" and "horned." This is well illustrated in Sumerian and Akkadian prayers to the moon, conceived of as crescent-shaped like the horns of an ox and shining at the same time. The Sumerian epithet which literally means "growing horns" is sometimes translated into Akkadian by a word meaning "horned" and at other times by one meaning "radiant."[11] The "veil" with which Moses covers his face on this account (34:33–35) may also have a precedent in the idiom of Mesopotamian hymnography which uses a single term to describe the turban which surrounds the head of the High Priest, the "halo" around the divine statue, and the "corona" of cultivated land enveloping and sustaining the temple. (See also commentary to 34:33.)

The Emergence of Israel

When Moses assumes the divinely assigned leadership role, the focus of the narrative shifts from the development of an individual to the birth of a nation or, in literary terms, from the level of biography to that of history. Correspondingly, the significant literary unit grows from the isolated topos to the complex of motifs which together constitute an entire type of narrative within a given larger genre, and fruitful comparison must move from the level of what may be called "topology" to that of typology. The narrative portions of Exodus include the common experience of the Egyptian oppression, the dramatic escape from

[9] J. M. Sasson, "Circumcision in the Ancient Near East," *Journal of Biblical Literature*, 85 (1966), pp. 473–476.

[10] Pritchard, *ANET*, pp. 10 f.; cf. *ibid.*, p. 326 and Commentary on Genesis, ch. 17.

[11] For an earlier interpretation, see Julian Morgenstern, "Moses with the Shining Face," *Hebrew Union College Annual*, 2 (1925), pp. 1–27. [Hereafter cited as *HUCA*.]

Goshen and from the pursuing Egyptians, the first wanderings in Sinai, and the collective assent there to a code of laws—in short, all the constitutive elements of Israel's emergence into nationhood except for the conquest of the Promised Land. These events run like colored threads through all the rest of biblical literature, becoming paradigms and archetypes for the biblical conception of all of Israelite history.

At the same time, they recur in no other Near Eastern historiography. True, the general phenomenon of large-scale ethnic movements characterizes the late thirteenth century B.C.E. throughout the Eastern Mediterranean, and there are heroic echoes of these migrations in the epics of various peoples.[12] And Egyptian literature—in the form of model letters—attests, for the same period, to the concern for workmen and for straw to maintain the daily quota of brick production (cf. Exod. 5) and to the tight control exercised by Egypt over her eastern frontier, regulating the entry by tribes coming westward across the Sinai desert in the face of drought in Palestine (Edom), or sending military search parties eastward into Sinai in pursuit of individual runaway slaves.[13] But the specific events recorded by Exodus for Israel's history are not validated by independent testimony from any extrabiblical source. And no comparable events are claimed (or conceded) for any other people's history—unless it be by the Bible itself (cf. Amos 9:7). No other people preserved a record of its own enslavement, or of "despoiling" its oppressors by stealth, or of its grudging farewell to the "fleshpots of Egypt" (16:3; cf. Num. 16:13 where Egypt is even referred to as a "land flowing with milk and honey"), or finally of its collective entry into a social compact. The very uniqueness of these narratives in the literary sense argues in favor of their authenticity; at least they are not imitations of foreign models. By contrast, the interpretations put on them were conceptualized and formulated in terms shared with the surrounding world, as we shall see.

First a word about the oppression. In Exodus itself, it is dealt with in an extremely cursory manner. The "storage cities" of Pithom and Raamses are mentioned as the ostensible objects of the Israelites' forced labor (1:11); they provide a precious clue—possibly the sole clue—to the historical context of the oppression, since the cities with which they can best be identified were built in the Eastern Delta under the first kings of the Nineteenth (Ramesside) Dynasty in the thirteenth century B.C.E.[14] But the further details of the oppression, including Pharaoh's attempts to slay the male offspring and the increasing exactions of the foremen, are told in the context of Moses' biography (see above) and add little to the historical picture. It is in the legislative context, both inside and outside Exodus, that the oppression is most emphasized. The Decalogue insists "remember that you were a slave in the land of Egypt" (Deut. 5:15), and "for you were strangers in the land of Egypt" is a refrain in all the other law codes (22:20, 23:9; cf. Lev. 19:34, Deut. 10:19). The Bible elevates the theme of the oppression to a typological level, justifying thereby the legal protection to be accorded to the stranger living in Israel's midst or to the slave be he originally Israelite or stranger. Characteristically, the biblical legislation adds the stranger to the widow and orphan (e.g., 22:20 f.), the two categories of unprotected classes traditionally the object of (royal) solicitude in the ancient Near East. (See commentary to 21:37-23:9.) Thus the mem-

[12] Hallo in essay to Commentary on Numbers.
[13] Pritchard, ANET, pp. 258 f.
[14] E. P. Uphill, "Pithom and Raamses: Their Location and Significance," Journal of Near Eastern Studies, 27 (1968), pp. 291-316; 28 (1969), pp. 15-39.

ory of the oppression remains a living stimulus for a distinctive Israelite modification of an ancient Near Eastern concept of social justice.

If Exodus deals summarily with the oppression, it dwells elaborately on the negotiations to bring about the release. Moses and Aaron, assuming their first historical role, confront Pharaoh seven times and scourge Egypt with what were originally seven plagues (see Pss. 78 and 105 in Gleanings to Part III); they became ten plagues when two discrete sources were combined into the final artful redaction, the form familiar from the liturgy of the Passover Haggadah.[15] Whatever their precise number, nature, or order, however, the plagues are less a historical than a literary phenomenon (cf. already I Sam. 4:8). They are probably indebted to catalogues of calamities known from native Egyptian compositions, notably the "Admonitions of Ipuwer."[16] (See Gleanings to 7:14–9:12.) These are usually assigned to the First Intermediate Period (ca. 2100 B.C.E.), less often to the Second Intermediate Period (ca. 1600 B.C.E.), but in any event draw a classic picture of a chain of ecological disasters overtaking the usually stable Egyptian society: the sand dunes advance over the arable land, the peasant abandons his plot in despair, the birth rate declines and the death rate increases, corpses are abandoned to the Nile yet its waters, thus polluted, are drunk for want of better; law and order break down.[17] Such traditional evocations of Egyptian collapse can hardly be dissociated entirely from the stylized narrative of the ten plagues. It is somewhat less likely that it also owes something to the Akkadian omen literature, but that too is full of clichés descriptive of natural disasters.

The Exodus narrative climaxes in the slaying of the first-born, the dramatic crossing of the Reed Sea, and the rout of the pursuing Egyptians. A minor detail of the event may be preserved in a later allusion to the "mare in Pharaoh's chariotry" (Song of Songs 1:9), presumably let loose against him in order to stampede his stallions—a military stratagem which is already attested in an Egyptian inscription of the fifteenth century B.C.E.[18] But for the rest, the narrative itself is not demonstrably indebted to any extra-biblical model. On the contrary, it served as the model for subsequent deliverances down to our own day.[19] The memory of it was so effectively impressed on all subsequent generations (in line with injunctions like 12:27, 13:8 and 14) that it colored every subsequent crisis in the national experience. Every oppression was somehow regarded as another "Egypt," every liberation as a triumph over Pharaoh (cf., e.g., I Sam. 6:6). And the mold was secondarily imposed also on prior events, notably Creation which the account of Genesis turned into a divine triumph over the waters of chaos.

But if the narrative of the Exodus was uniquely Israelite, the interpretation put on it by the Bible was, on the contrary, couched in traditional Near Eastern terms. The Song at the Sea, in its short form as attributed to Miriam (15:21) as well as in the longer form attributed to Moses (15:1–18), is ancient tes-

[15] Moshe Greenberg, "The Redaction of the Plague Narrative in Exodus," in *Near Eastern Studies in Honor of William Foxwell Albright*, ed. Hans Goedicke (Baltimore and London: The Johns Hopkins Press, 1971), pp. 243–252.

[16] Pritchard, *ANET*, pp. 441–444.

[17] Barbara Bell, "The Dark Ages in Ancient History: I. The First Dark Age in Egypt," *American Journal of Archaeology*, 75 (1971), pp. 1–26; John van Seters, *The Hyksos: A New Investigation* (New Haven and London: Yale University Press, 1966), pp. 103–120.

[18] Pritchard, *ANET*, p. 241 (lines 27–29 and note 37); cf. p. 469 and note 9 and M. H. Pope, "A Mare in Pharaoh's Chariotry," *BASOR*, 200 (1970), pp. 56–61; idem, *The Anchor Bible: Song of Songs* (Garden City: Doubleday, 1977), pp. 336–341.

[19] Cf. "Exodus 1948" for the name of a ship that brought the remnants of European Jewry to Israel after World War II.

timony to this interpretation. Regarded by some scholars as one of the earliest surviving monuments of Hebrew literature, it proclaims, in effect, that Israel saw in its dramatic deliverance the hand (intervention) of its God, who thereby was exalted to a status equal or superior to the gods of other nations (15:11), entitled to His own sanctuary (15:13, 17), and acknowledged by His people as king for ever after (15:18). The connection between the historical triumph of the people and the enthronement or exaltation of its deity is explicit here, in later biblical passages, and in post-biblical liturgy (the Kedushah).

The same connection is present in the Ugaritic epic of Baal, which dates back to the fourteenth century B.C.E. at least and recounts how, after defeating Mot and Yam, the embodiments of death and sea, Baal is elevated to the head of the pantheon and installed in a palace built by the other gods.[20] The connection is even more explicit in the Babylonian "Epic of Creation." Here Marduk achieves the status of first among the gods by successfully defeating an older generation of deities led by Tiamat, symbol of the watery deep, a feat no other god dared to undertake. From the carcass of the slain monster he creates an orderly cosmos, but the text lays far more stress on the resulting acclamation of Marduk by all the other gods, and their undertaking to erect a temple for him. This "exaltation of Marduk" almost certainly has a historical background, not, as used to be thought, the rise of Babylon (Marduk's city) to prominence under Hammurabi in the eighteenth century B.C.E., nor yet the reunification of Babylonia under the Kassites in the fifteenth, but most probably the recovery of the cult statue of Marduk from Elamite captivity at the end of the twelfth.[21]

But the concept of divine exaltation was far older than this in Mesopotamia. As early as the twenty-third century B.C.E., the great Sargonic kings of Akkad forged the first Mesopotamian empire under the patronage of the goddess Inanna, and there is reason to believe that her elevation to the pinnacle of the Sumerian pantheon was celebrated in direct consequence of these political developments, and that other deities subsequently followed her example.[22] The theological interpretation put on the Exodus was thus of a piece with the entire "typology of exaltation" which had evolved over the centuries in the Near East: the deity of a dynasty, a city, or a people assumed his exalted place among all the gods as a consequence of the triumphs of his earthly protégés when these triumphs were attributed to him, i.e., when the protégés acknowledged their debt to him.[23]

Concomitant with this general typology of divine exaltation was the belief in divine presence, symbolized at the Reed Sea and in the desert by the pillar of cloud by day and of fire by night; after the departure from Mount Sinai, the divine presence was believed to reside in or sit (as if on a footstool) on the ark, which led the people in the battles of the conquest and eventually came to rest in the Temple of Solomon. Ancient Near Eastern armies similarly went into battle behind the symbols of their deities. This is abundantly clear from pictorial representations, notably the winged sun-disc with the portrait of the god Assur repeatedly depicted

[20] Pritchard, *ANET*, pp. 133 f.
[21] W. G. Lambert, "The Reign of Nebuchadnezzar I: A Turning Point in the History of Ancient Mesopotamian Religion," in *The Seed of Wisdom: Essays in Honor of T. J. Meek*, ed. W. S. McCullough (University of Toronto Press, 1964), pp. 3–13.
[22] W. W. Hallo and J. J. A. van Dijk, *The Exaltation of Inanna* (Yale Near Eastern Researches, Vol. 3, 1968), ch. 6: "The Typology of Divine Exaltation."
[23] T. W. Mann, *Divine Presence and Guidance in Israelite Traditions: The Typology of Exaltation* (Johns Hopkins Near Eastern Studies, Vol. 9, 1977).

in Assyrian reliefs, and corresponding standards carried in front of Assyrian armies or left by them in conquered cities as symbols of submission to the Assyrian god. At the same time, there may be a hint at a defiant distancing from the Near Eastern convention in the name Adonai-nissi, "the *Lord* is my banner" (17:15) by which the victory over Amalek was remembered.[24] (See commentary.)

The Covenant at Sinai

The consummate artist who was author or redactor of Exodus began with the genealogy of the sons of Jacob (1:1–7; cf. 6:14–26) and the biography of the children of Amram; he chronicled the climactic succession of events which led from oppression to freedom; and he will yet provide a legislative code to ensure that the new freedom be shared and respected for all future time. But now, in the middle of the book, he weaves together all these strands—biographical, historical, legislative—to create a true crescendo in the events at Mount Sinai.

The biographical element provides the prologue: Moses is reunited with his wife and children and with his Midianite father-in-law, here under the name of Jethro, whose timely counsel is willingly followed. The drama of the revelation ensues, first in oral form in the context of the theophany (ch. 19), then twice more in the form of the graven tablets (24:12–18 and 31:18). It fits into the typological pattern so far reconstructed, on the basis of Near Eastern parallels, on what may be called the "constitutional" level, in the sense both of a "constitutive" event in the continuing historical process of nation-building, and of a fundamental legislative enactment undergirding all more specific legislation. In both senses, the Decalogue seals the bargain struck at the Exodus: in return for God's military intervention on

their behalf, the Israelites obligate themselves to become His people (3:12, 6:7, etc.). Freed from enslavement to Pharaoh, Israel transfers its allegiance to its divine liberator, entering into a relationship with potential analogies to several Near Eastern models.

On one interpretation, the relationship created at Sinai was that between master and slave,[25] and indeed "worship" (of God) and "enslavement" (to man) are expressed by the same root (ᶜBD) in biblical Hebrew. The same ambiguity can be noted in other Semitic languages where, for example, Akkadian and Aramaic "fear, reverence" and Arabic "peasant" derive from a common root (PLḤ).[26] Another theory holds that the relationship created at Sinai was that between a king and his people, as documented at the beginning of the second millennium B.C.E. especially under the Amorite dynasts of Mesopotamia. These kings regularly proclaimed a release from debt slavery shortly after their coronation and sometimes coupled this proclamation with the promulgation of a code of laws "so that the strong might not oppress the weak," to quote the Laws of Hammurabi.[27] Since God was elevated to kingship over His people at the Reed Sea (above), the proclamation of the Decalogue and more especially the Covenant Code (21–24) could be the logical next step in line with Near Eastern precedent, albeit of an earlier age.[28]

The most widely held view of the matter today is that the covenant at Sinai casts God and Israel in the role of sovereign (suzerain)

[24] *Ibid.*, esp. ch. 3 and pp. 265 f., figs. 1–3.
[25] David Daube, *The Exodus Pattern in the Bible* (All Souls Studies, Vol. 2, 1963; London: Faber and Faber), esp. ch. V: "A Change of Master."
[26] Cf. the double sense of *cultus* as "work" (e.g., in "agriculture") and "worship."
[27] Pritchard, *ANET*, p. 164.
[28] Moshe Weinfeld, " 'Justice and Righteousness' in Ancient Israel against the Background of Social Reforms in the Ancient Near East" (Rencontre Assyriologique Internationale, 25).

and vassal. This is a relationship attested by the so-called suzerainty treaties which, like the Exodus, are dated precisely to the end of the Late Bronze Age. Such treaties are best known from examples preserved in the royal archives of the Hittite capital at Hattusha in Anatolia (modern Turkey), but were common throughout the Near East in the late fourteenth and thirteenth centuries B.C.E. Some points of comparison between the Decalogue and the suzerainty treaties may be noted, especially where they contrast with the contemporaneous parity treaties (i.e., treaties between kingdoms of equal rank) and with the vassal treaties of the first millennium B.C.E.[29]

The actual provisions of the suzerainty treaty are regularly preceded by a preamble including a historical prologue designed to justify the suzerainty relationship and to outlaw any future breach of it by the vassal. The body of the treaty provides for its public reading and for depositing it in the temple, and the conclusion invokes the gods of the vassal as witnesses and guarantors of his future obedience, on pain of dreadful curses subscribed to in formal oaths to the accompaniment of special sacrifices. Most of these elements recur in connection with the Decalogue. God's sovereignty is justified by His role in Israel's history in general (as this is detailed by "credal" synopses like Josh.

24:2–15[30]) and in the Exodus in particular. So in the first commandment, which is less commandment than prologue and, grammatically speaking, probably not even a separate sentence from the second commandment. The Decalogue is engraved in stone and deposited in the ark (and ultimately in the Temple), heaven and earth are called upon as witnesses (cf. Deut. 4:26, 30:19), and after suitable sacrifices the twelve tribes swear to "do and obey" all of the covenant (24:4–7). By contrast, the vassal treaties of the first millennium largely dispense with the legitimizing prologue, are far more apodictic (unconditional) in their provisions, and rely for their enforcement on more elaborate curses catalogued in lurid detail.[31] As for the contemporaneous parity treaties, they refer to the contracting parties as "brothers," in contrast to the "father-son" relationship which the vassal accords to his sovereign (cf. 4:22 f.).

What then of the Book of the Covenant (see commentary to 24:7) itself? It is a collection of "precedents" (New Jewish Version: "rules"; see 21:1, 24:3) of which a few are phrased apodictically (i.e., in the form of peremptory commands or prohibitions like the Decalogue), and a few more in participial form (notably 22:17–19). But the bulk is formulated as conditional sentences in the manner of the conditional or casuistic legislation known from the Near East in half a dozen major collections dating from the beginning of the Middle Bronze Age to the end of the Late Bronze Age (ca. 2100–1200 B.C.E.). It might thus be thought that the Book of the Covenant has adopted a form current in the time of the Exodus just as the Decalogue did. But the matter is not so simple, for in this case the comparison extends beyond form to content. Numerous specific provisions have precise counterparts in the cuneiform legislation. Where the comparison is with the famous Laws of Hammurabi,[32] one

[29] Pritchard, *ANET*, pp. 199–206, 529–541; cf. D. J. McCarthy, *Treaty and Covenant: A Study in Form in the Ancient Oriental Documents and in the Old Testament* (Analecta Biblica, Vol. 21, 1963; 2nd ed., 1978).

[30] Sometimes regarded as a "renewal of the treaty" at Sinai; cf. also I Sam. 12:6–12; Neh. 9; Pss. 78, 105 f., 135 f.

[31] Hallo in essay to Commentary on Deuteronomy.

[32] Pritchard, *ANET*, pp. 166–177; cf. especially paragraphs 1–4 (laws of procedure), 117 (distraint), 120 (deposit), 195–214 (personal injuries), 250–252 (the goring ox), and 266–267 (negligence). See commentary to chs. 21–23 for specific comparisons, with literature.

could perhaps appeal to the demonstrable and lasting fame of that corpus within Mesopotamia to account for the possibility that it was known also beyond Mesopotamia; where the comparison is with Hittite or Middle Assyrian laws,[33] one might be tempted to argue from their relatively late date to the feasibility of their being borrowed in Israel. But what are we to make of provisions shared with "codes" neither so famous nor so recent as these, like those of King Ur-Nammu of Ur, King Lipit-Ishtar of Isin, or of an as yet unidentified Old Babylonian king of Eshnunna beyond the Tigris (ca. 1800 B.C.E.)? The last, in particular, has revealed the existence of a provision for the case of an ox goring another ox which is not only absent from the corresponding legislation about the goring ox by Hammurabi, but so close in letter and spirit to Exod. 21:35 f. as to virtually rule out the chance that both traditions independently arrived at this truly Solomonic judgment.[34] (See commentary and Gleanings to 20:19–21:36.)

We are thus forced to conclude that the Book of the Covenant includes wise legal precedents from a period when knowledge of them could still have passed freely to both ends of the Fertile Crescent. The period of the Amorite migrations at the beginning of the second millennium B.C.E. comes to mind in this connection. This granted, the appearance of similarly formulated legislation in Deuteronomy (19–25) may be seen as an attempt to preserve more of the common Amorite heritage, with the portion in Exodus concentrating more on topics suggested by the context into which it was inserted. The period of the desert wanderings would, for example, justify the emphasis on family law, while of property law, only that relating to livestock would be called for. The recent experience of bondage would suggest the laws regulating slavery, and others of a general humanitarian cast. The connection of the legislation to the oppression is indeed drawn explicitly and repeatedly (see above) and differentiates the biblical case law from its Near Eastern cognates. A law such as that limiting the distraint of garments taken in pledge for loans (22:25 f.; cf. Deut. 24:10–13) is known nowhere else in the Near East but has an analogue in a Hebrew letter excavated south of Jaffa in 1960.[35] The real legislative concern of Exodus is with the Tabernacle, and this forms a fitting conclusion to the book.

The Tabernacle

The balance of the Book of Exodus is largely devoted to the Tabernacle and its personnel, first as divinely commanded (25–30) and then as executed (35–40).[36] The structure is explained as a portable sanctuary to serve during the period of wandering, or until a permanent house (cf. I Kings 8:12 f.) could be erected for the deity. So much attention to a temporary disposition seems hard to justify on simple considerations of narrative structure. And indeed critics have been quick to regard the material as a late, priestly interpolation intended to endow the later temple at Jerusalem with the antiquity and hence the authority implied by attaching it directly to the revelation at Sinai. But comparative literary considerations counsel a different assessment.

[33] Pritchard, *ANET*, pp. 180–197. See commentary to 22:17 f.
[34] J. J. Finkelstein, "The Goring Ox," *Temple Law Quarterly*, 46 (1973), pp. 169–290; B. S. Jackson, "The Goring Ox Again," *Journal of Juristic Papyrology*, 18 (1974), pp. 55–93, reprinted in *Essays in Jewish and Comparative Legal History* (Leiden, 1975), pp. 108–152.
[35] Joseph Naveh, "A Hebrew Letter from the Seventh Century B.C.," *Israel Exploration Journal*, 10 (1960), pp. 129–139; cf. Dennis Pardee, "The Judicial Plea from Meṣad Hashavyahu (Yavneh-Yam): A New Philological Study," *Maarav*, 1/1 (1978), pp. 33–66; see Pritchard, *ANET*, p. 568.
[36] For biblical and extra-biblical parallels to such "prescriptive" and "descriptive rituals" respectively,

We have already seen that the covenant at Sinai sealed the bargain struck at the Exodus: God became, in a legal sense, the new master of the slaves He had freed or, in a political sense, the sovereign of the vassal nation which He had forged. But in a literary and theological sense, one further debt remained to be paid: the time-honored Near Eastern typology of exaltation required that the newly enthroned king have a house of his own, erected for him by his subjects. The other gods carry out the work in the Ugaritic epic of Baal (see above) and in the Babylonian "Epic of Creation," where they build for Marduk the great temple Esagila, with the ziqqurrat (stepped tower) that may have become the model for the "Tower of Babel" (Gen. 11). In both of these compositions, and several others, the building of the victorious deity's house (i.e., his temple) is the climax of the epic. So far from being a subsidiary motif, it is the denouement toward which all the action moves, the visible symbol of the exalted status that the divine protagonist sought and achieved.

Thus the Tabernacle fills a traditional place in the literary structure of Exodus. Nevertheless, it again displays very distinctive elements that set it apart from its Near Eastern models, above all its connection with the Sabbath. In the sense of a consecrated day recurring with uninterrupted regularity

and free from ties to lunar phases or any other natural phenomena, the Sabbath is a uniquely Israelite innovation. No convincing parallels have been found for it in the surrounding Near East, while on the other hand its influence is manifest in many biblical contexts.[37] It is woven into the warp and woof of the Exodus, first as a memorial to the Egyptian oppression (cf. Deut. 5:15) and to the deliverance from it (cf. the liturgy); then as a feature of the desert wanderings in connection with the manna (16:22–31); finally in the fourth commandment where the six days of creation are invoked retroactively as a model for the solemn injunction to labor for six days (and cease on the seventh). And via creation, the Tabernacle too is tied to the sabbatical idea. The prescriptions for building the Tabernacle are revealed to Moses on the seventh day after he has spent six days on the mountain (24:16), and the description of the construction is concluded by Moses completing the work (40:33), beholding and blessing it (39:43), and hallowing it (40:9) in terms echoing almost verbatim God's consummation of creation (Gen. 1:31–2:3).[38] (See commentary to 38:21–40:38.) The laws of the Sabbath are, not surprisingly, the first ones that intrude into the long narrative of the Tabernacle (31:12–17; cf. commentary to 35:1–38:20).

In light of the comparable literary patterns, then, the Book of Exodus forms a coherent unit, moving ever upward, from slavery to freedom, from biography to history, from legal and political levels of meaning to esthetic and ethical planes, from the intercession of the man Moses to the abiding involvement of God.

see Hallo in essay to Commentary on Numbers.

[37] Hallo, "New Moons and Sabbaths: A Case-Study in the Contrastive Approach," *HUCA*, 48 (1977), pp. 1–18.

[38] Weinfeld, "Sabbath, Temple Building and the Enthronement of the Lord," *Beth Mikra*, 2 (1977), pp. 188–193 (Hebrew).

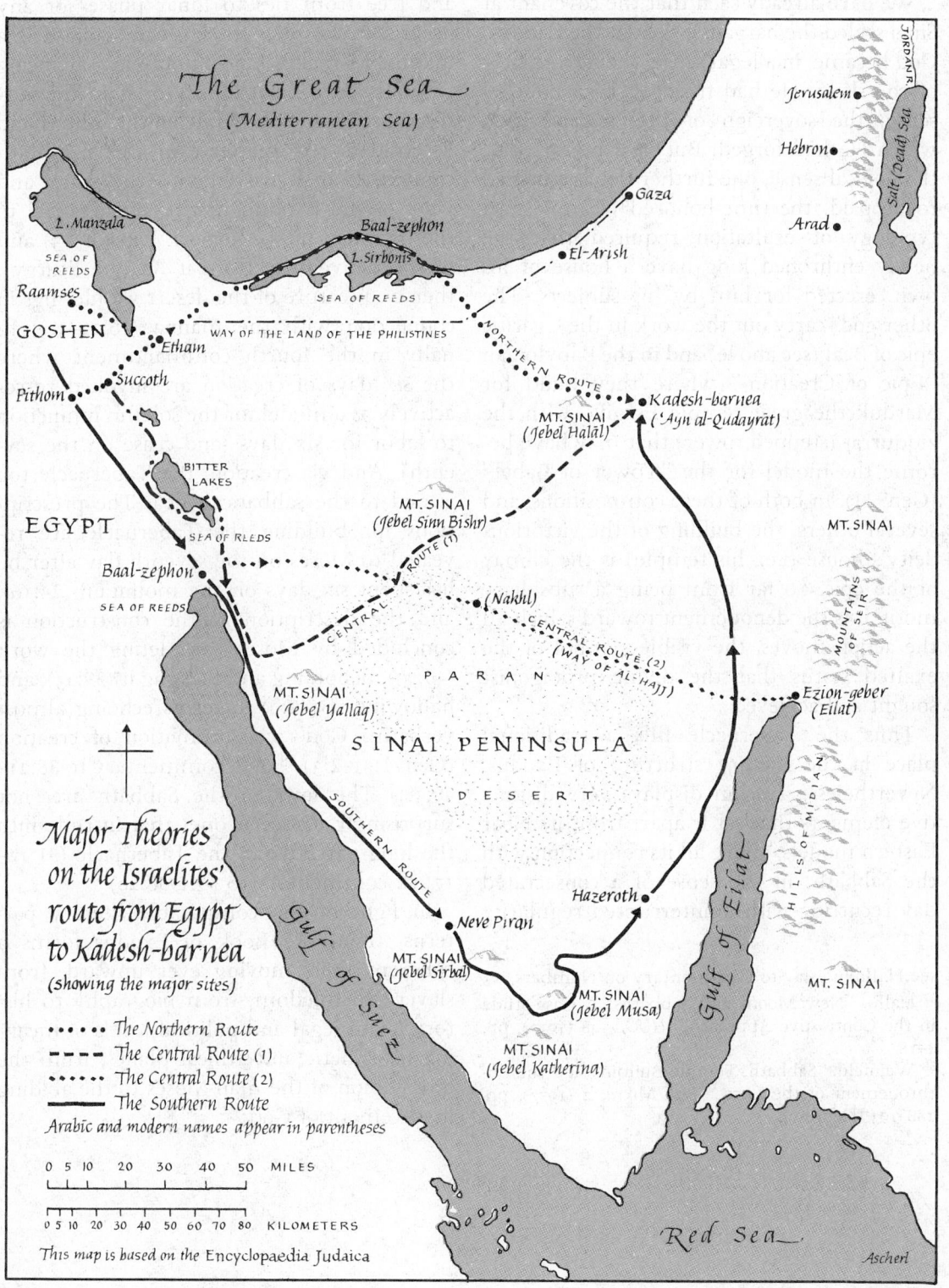

The Great Sea
(Mediterranean Sea)

L. Manzala

SEA OF REEDS

Raamses

GOSHEN

Pithom

Ethan

Succoth

WAY OF THE LAND OF THE PHILISTINES

Baal-zephon

L. Sirbonis

SEA OF REEDS

Gaza

El-Arish

NORTHERN ROUTE

MT. SINAI
(Jebel Halāl)

Kadesh-barnea
('Ayn al-Qudayrāt)

Jerusalem

Hebron

Arad

JORDAN R.

Salt (Dead) Sea

EGYPT

BITTER
LAKES

SEA OF REEDS

Baal-zephon

SEA OF REEDS

MT. SINAI
(Jebel Sinn Bishr)

CENTRAL ROUTE (1)

(Nakhl)

CENTRAL ROUTE (2)
(WAY OF AL-HAJJ)

MT. SINAI

MT. SINAI
(Jebel Yallaq)

P A R A N

Ezion-geber
(Eilat)

MOUNTAINS OF SEIR

S I N A I   P E N I N S U L A

D E S E R T

Hazeroth

Gulf of Suez

Gulf of Eilat

HILLS OF MIDIAN

SOUTHERN ROUTE

Neve Piran

MT. SINAI
(Jebel Sirbal)

MT. SINAI
(Jebel Musa)

MT. SINAI

Major Theories on the Israelites' route from Egypt to Kadesh-barnea
(showing the major sites)

MT. SINAI
(Jebel Katherina)

Red Sea

••••• The Northern Route
- - - - The Central Route (1)
•••••• The Central Route (2)
——— The Southern Route
Arabic and modern names appear in parentheses

0 5 10 20 30 40 50 MILES

0 5 10 20 30 40 50 60 70 80 KILOMETERS

This map is based on the Encyclopaedia Judaica

Ascherl

378

PART I

Prologue

The first two chapters of Exodus provide the background for the main story: Israel's rescue from Egypt. They tell of the people's enslavement in the land which in Joseph's time had welcomed them so hospitably. The prologue then proceeds to introduce the man who will help God in the task of deliverance. These chapters cover four generations and therefore tell their tale in the briefest form possible. After the conclusion of the prologue the tempo slows perceptibly, and the rest of the Book of Exodus covers events that took place in little more than a year's time.

Some see the prologue as a drama played through and with women: Israel's women are fertile; their fertility is Pharaoh's concern and target; and his plans are counteracted by the midwives, by Miriam and Jochebed, and by Pharaoh's daughter. Moses is saved by women at his birth, and before he sets out on his mission he will be saved by his wife Zipporah (4:24–26). The Midrash says: Israel was redeemed because of its righteous women [1].

Biblical critics have discerned two basic strands: one telling the story of Israel's enslavement in general, and another of the baby killings and the rescue of Moses by a member of Pharaoh's court. They have noted further that in the subsequent chapters the killings are not mentioned again (and instead the withholding of straw is pictured as the main aspect of Pharaoh's cruelty) nor is the fact of Moses' upbringing and experience at court ever alluded to [2]. In the text before us such originally separate traditions have been interwoven into a literary whole portraying the distress of God's people and the rise of its human savior who will be God's agent.

Finally, as so often in the Torah, certain key words point to deeper connections. James S. Ackerman has called attention to the use of the term *yarad*, which describes God's "descending" to earth, that is to say, His intervention in human affairs. He had promised Jacob that He would "descend" with him into Egypt (Gen. 46:4). However, not until many years of slavery have passed does God announce that He will indeed come down and rescue His people, even as later, at Sinai, He will come down to become Israel's partner in the covenant (Exod. 3:8 and 19:18–24) [3].

Israel in Egypt

The opening phrases of Exodus are a sequel to the end of Genesis. They recapitulate the names of Jacob's family who came to Egypt and then proceed to the story of Israel's enslavement in Egypt. The names appear in an order different from either the birth sequence (Gen. 29:31 ff.) or the blessing of Jacob (Gen. 49) but are the same as in the roster of Genesis 35:23–26. The text places Leah's children first, then lists Rachel's, and thereafter those of the two handmaidens, Bilhah and Zilpah. These differences are not necessarily due to varying traditions as has been claimed; rather, they may be stylistic in nature.

Similar questions have been raised regarding the flow of the story. Verses 13 and 14 appear to interrupt it and seem to belong with verses 1–7, suggesting two different sources, but this too may well be a matter of style. The New Jewish Version makes a paragraph after verse 12 to indicate that a new phase of the oppression tale begins with verse 13, while the Masoretic text gives no such indication.

(The first weekly portion, *Shemot*, begins here.)

ח וַיָּ֥קָם מֶֽלֶךְ־חָדָ֖שׁ עַל־מִצְרָ֑יִם אֲשֶׁ֥ר לֹֽא־יָדַ֖ע אֶת־   א וְאֵ֗לֶּה שְׁמוֹת֙ בְּנֵ֣י יִשְׂרָאֵ֔ל הַבָּאִ֖ים מִצְרָ֑יְמָה אֵ֣ת יַעֲקֹ֔ב

ט יוֹסֵ֑ף: וַיֹּ֖אמֶר אֶל־עַמּ֑וֹ הִנֵּ֗ה עַ֚ם בְּנֵ֣י יִשְׂרָאֵ֔ל רַ֥ב   ב אִ֥ישׁ וּבֵית֖וֹ בָּֽאוּ: רְאוּבֵ֣ן שִׁמְע֔וֹן לֵוִ֖י וִֽיהוּדָֽה: יִשָּׂשכָ֥ר

י וְעָצ֖וּם מִמֶּֽנּוּ: הָ֚בָה נִֽתְחַכְּמָ֣ה ל֑וֹ פֶּן־יִרְבֶּ֗ה וְהָיָ֞ה כִּֽי־   ד זְבוּלֻ֖ן וּבְנְיָמִֽן: דָּ֥ן וְנַפְתָּלִ֖י גָּ֥ד וְאָשֵֽׁר: וַֽיְהִ֗י כָּל־נֶ֛פֶשׁ

תִקְרֶ֤אנָה מִלְחָמָה֙ וְנוֹסַ֤ף גַּם־הוּא֙ עַל־שֹׂ֣נְאֵ֔ינוּ וְנִלְחַם־   ה יֹצְאֵ֥י יֶֽרֶךְ־יַעֲקֹ֖ב שִׁבְעִ֣ים נָ֑פֶשׁ וְיוֹסֵ֖ף הָיָ֥ה בְמִצְרָֽיִם:

יא בָּ֖נוּ וְעָלָ֣ה מִן־הָאָֽרֶץ: וַיָּשִׂ֤ימוּ עָלָיו֙ שָׂרֵ֣י מִסִּ֔ים לְמַ֖עַן   ו וַיָּ֤מָת יוֹסֵף֙ וְכָל־אֶחָ֔יו וְכֹ֖ל הַדּ֥וֹר הַהֽוּא: וּבְנֵ֣י יִשְׂרָאֵ֗ל

עַנֹּת֖וֹ בְּסִבְלֹתָ֑ם וַיִּ֜בֶן עָרֵ֤י מִסְכְּנוֹת֙ לְפַרְעֹ֔ה אֶת־   ז פָּר֧וּ וַֽיִּשְׁרְצ֛וּ וַיִּרְבּ֥וּ וַיַּֽעַצְמ֖וּ בִּמְאֹ֣ד מְאֹ֑ד וַתִּמָּלֵ֥א

יב פִּתֹ֖ם וְאֶת־רַֽעַמְסֵֽס: וְכַֽאֲשֶׁר֙ יְעַנּ֣וּ אֹת֔וֹ כֵּ֥ן יִרְבֶּ֖ה וְכֵ֥ן   הָאָ֖רֶץ אֹתָֽם: פ

1] These are the names of the sons of Israel who came to Egypt with Jacob, each coming with his household: 2] Reuben, Simeon, Levi, and Judah; 3] Issachar, Zebulun, and Benjamin; 4] Dan and Naphtali, Gad and Asher. 5] The total number of persons that were of Jacob's issue came to seventy, Joseph being already in Egypt. 6] Joseph died, and all his brothers, and all that generation. 7] But the Israelites were fertile and prolific; they multiplied and increased very greatly, so that the land was filled with them.

8] A new king arose over Egypt, who did not know Joseph. 9] And he said to his people, "Look, the Israelite people are much too numerous for us. 10] Let us deal shrewdly with them, so that they may not increase; otherwise in the event of war they may join our enemies in fighting against us and rise from the ground." 11] So they set taskmasters over them to oppress them with forced labor; and they built garrison cities for Pharaoh: Pithom and Raamses. 12] But the more they were oppressed, the more they increased and spread out, so that the [Egyptians] came to dread the Israelites.

1:5] *Seventy*. The figure was mentioned before in Gen. 46:27. See also Deut. 10:22. The seventy consisted of Jacob, his sixty-seven male offspring, and his two wives. In the Septuagint and in Christian Scriptures (Acts 7:14) the figure is seventy-five, apparently adding the son and grandson of Manasseh and the two sons and the grandson of Ephraim, all of whom were born and residing in Egypt [1].

7] *Multiplied*. The Hebrew word is related to "swarming creature" (Gen. 1:20), suggesting that the Israelites proliferated like animals. The Midrash speculates that they had sextuplets [2].

The land was filled with them. They spread beyond the region of Goshen, which was probably located in the northeastern part of the Nile Delta.

8] *Did not know Joseph*. Unaware of what he had done for the country. Or he did not want to know Joseph, for the latter had supported a dynasty now overthrown (see commentary on Gen. 46:28–47:27).

10] *Rise from the ground*. The Hebrew is not clear. The Talmud interprets: Pharaoh was worried that Israel would gain ascendancy over the country and displace the Egyptians [3].

11] *Forced labor*. A form of corvée.

Garrison cities. For provisions and war material.

Pithom and Raamses. The former on Egypt's eastern frontier, the latter probably the residential city Per-Ramses, named after Ramses II (1304–1237). However, some scholarly opinion holds that the mention of these cities was not based on any actual connection the Israelites had had with them but was a later addition designed to lend the stories an ancient flavor [4].

יי אֶת־הַיְלָדִים: וַיִּקְרָא מֶלֶךְ־מִצְרַיִם לַמְיַלְּדֹת וַיֹּאמֶר
לָהֶן מַדּוּעַ עֲשִׂיתֶן הַדָּבָר הַזֶּה וַתְּחַיֶּיןָ אֶת־הַיְלָדִים:
יט וַתֹּאמַרְןָ הַמְיַלְּדֹת אֶל־פַּרְעֹה כִּי לֹא כַנָּשִׁים הַמִּצְרִיֹּת
הָעִבְרִיֹּת כִּי־חָיוֹת הֵנָּה בְּטֶרֶם תָּבוֹא אֲלֵהֶן הַמְיַלֶּדֶת
כ וְיָלָדוּ: וַיֵּיטֶב אֱלֹהִים לַמְיַלְּדֹת וַיִּרֶב הָעָם וַיַּעַצְמוּ
כא מְאֹד: וַיְהִי כִּי־יָרְאוּ הַמְיַלְּדֹת אֶת־הָאֱלֹהִים וַיַּעַשׂ
כב לָהֶם בָּתִּים: וַיְצַו פַּרְעֹה לְכָל־עַמּוֹ לֵאמֹר כָּל־הַבֵּן
הַיִּלּוֹד הַיְאֹרָה תַּשְׁלִיכֻהוּ וְכָל־הַבַּת תְּחַיּוּן: פ

יג יִפְרֹץ וַיָּקֻצוּ מִפְּנֵי בְּנֵי יִשְׂרָאֵל: וַיַּעֲבִדוּ מִצְרַיִם אֶת־
יד בְּנֵי יִשְׂרָאֵל בְּפָרֶךְ: וַיְמָרְרוּ אֶת־חַיֵּיהֶם בַּעֲבֹדָה
קָשָׁה בְּחֹמֶר וּבִלְבֵנִים וּבְכָל־עֲבֹדָה בַּשָּׂדֶה אֵת כָּל־
טו עֲבֹדָתָם אֲשֶׁר־עָבְדוּ בָהֶם בְּפָרֶךְ: וַיֹּאמֶר מֶלֶךְ
מִצְרַיִם לַמְיַלְּדֹת הָעִבְרִיֹּת אֲשֶׁר שֵׁם הָאַחַת שִׁפְרָה
טז וְשֵׁם הַשֵּׁנִית פּוּעָה: וַיֹּאמֶר בְּיַלֶּדְכֶן אֶת־הָעִבְרִיּוֹת
וּרְאִיתֶן עַל־הָאָבְנָיִם אִם־בֵּן הוּא וַהֲמִתֶּן אֹתוֹ וְאִם־
יז בַּת הִוא וָחָיָה: וַתִּירֶאןָ הַמְיַלְּדֹת אֶת־הָאֱלֹהִים וְלֹא
עָשׂוּ כַּאֲשֶׁר דִּבֶּר אֲלֵיהֶן מֶלֶךְ מִצְרַיִם וַתְּחַיֶּיןָ

13] The Egyptians ruthlessly imposed upon the Israelites 14] the various labors that they made them perform. Ruthlessly they made life bitter for them with harsh labor at mortar and bricks and with all sorts of tasks in the field.

15] The king of Egypt spoke to the Hebrew midwives, one of whom was named Shiphrah and the other Puah, 16] saying, "When you deliver the Hebrew women, look at the birthstool: if it is a boy, kill him; if it is a girl, let her live."

17] The midwives, fearing God, did not do as the king of Egypt had told them; they let the boys live. 18] So the king of Egypt summoned the midwives and said to them, "Why have you done this thing, letting the boys live?" 19] The midwives said to Pharaoh, "Because the Hebrew women are not like the Egyptian women: they are vigorous. Before the midwife can come to them, they have given birth." 20] And God dealt well with the midwives; and the people multiplied and increased greatly. 21] And because the midwives feared God, He established households for them. 22] Then Pharaoh charged all his people, saying, "Every boy that is born you shall throw into the Nile, but let every girl live."

13] *Ruthlessly.* In cruel fashion. The same Hebrew term (בְּפָרֶךְ) is used in Lev. 25:43, 46, 53 which deal with the ethical dimensions of the laws of servitude.

15] *Hebrew midwives.* Their names are of northwest Semitic type, suggesting that they were Hebrews [5]. "Hebrew" is a term generally agreed to come from the name of a group called Habiru (or 'Apiru), people who had lost their status in the community to which they had originally belonged. They were not necessarily related except by common fate, and such may in part have been the case in their Egyptian slavery [6].

16] *Birthstool.* The brick or stone supports used during childbirth. Pharaoh's command to kill the boys aimed apparently at controlling any future insurrection, though it would also diminish his labor force.

21] *Households.* בָּתִּים. Possibly meaning "progeny," as in Ruth 4:12.

22] *All his people.* Thus making them partners to the crime.

Nile. It is called הַיְאֹר, literally, "the river"; another Hebrew term, הַנָּהָר, also literally meaning "the river," is typically used for the Euphrates. (See note at 23:31.)

The Absence of God

Although the theme of God's greatness, His guidance of and care for His people, is a major skein of Exodus, the opening chapter begins on what may be called a secular note. Here the story of oppression is told in a naturalistic way, and neither Israel's population increase nor the ensuing enslavement is expressly connected to the will of God. Were the people not aware of Him? Did they not cry to Him? The text merely says that their groaning "rose up before God" (2:23); quite clearly they did not address themselves directly to the God of their fathers. As if to emphasize this, the first mention of God concerns the godfearing midwives who saved the Israelite children. Not until Moses brought them His promise, not until he told them of the redeeming presence of יְהוָֹה, did the relationship begin—or resume—to which the Book of Exodus and most of subsequent Jewish history are devoted. The oppressed people doubtlessly knew of a God whom the ancestors worshiped, and they may have known His name, but they did not apparently deem Him capable of ending their distress.[1]

The reason that God let them be enslaved is not stated, neither does the Torah deal with the subject of God's absence from Israel's history for a period of four hundred years, suggesting by its silence that such was the mysterious plan of God. The writer does not explore it further; like the world before creation, it is part of the inexplicable. The human aspect of oppression is told but briefly; the divine aspect of redemption will be the elaborate subject of what follows. Exodus clearly puts its emphasis on the latter. The opening chapter sets the scene, not for a human struggle between Egypt and Israel, but for a confrontation between the divine ruler of Egypt and the divine protector and savior of Israel. His people may not know Him now; they will come to know Him as the drama of salvation unfolds.

Slavery in Egypt

In biblical tradition the enslavement of the Children of Israel in Egypt marks the nadir of their existence. When in time they were liberated and their oppressors punished at the Reed Sea, it appeared, however, that it was not the imposition of slavery as such that constituted the sin of the Egyptians but rather the merciless way in which it was imposed. Twice we are told that the oppression was ruthless; life was bitter for the Israelites; and the slaying of the Hebrew boys climaxed the Egyptians' cruelty, a crime which later Jewish tradition isolated as the chief sin of the oppressors.

One should not be surprised at this emphasis. For the practice of enslavement itself was the usual manner of dealing with a foreign element, and, furthermore, not only slaves but native born as well were impressed into forced labor (corvée) for the building of roads, temples, and other state edifices.[2]

---

[1] There was a tradition which tried to explain the divine silence and suggested that the very fact that the Children of Israel had forgotten God led to their continued enslavement. A midrash speculates that they were indeed a wicked people and deserved their enslavement [7]. But the biblical text gives no warrant for such assumption; in fact, most midrashim stress the unceasing faithfulness of Israel.

[2] However, as André Neher has pointed out, the Egyptians appear to have made distinctions between their own proletariat and the slaves in the levying of the corvée. Neher calls attention to the pictures of the times: "In their drawings there are spaces round the peasants and workmen who, in spite of their numbers, seem to retain a minimum of individuality. On the other hand the scenes depicting slavery and forced labor are brutal in their massiveness. Human beings are so closely packed and piled upon each other that they appear as a single whole yoked as such to its work, without any individuality at all" [8].

What the Torah emphasizes is that Pharaoh went to extremes and apparently became somehow afraid of the Hebrews. Subsequently his dealings with them assumed an irrational path; though he wanted the result of their labor, he made it at the same time difficult to obtain and even attempted to reduce his work force. This was probably not the first time that slaves received such treatment, and certainly not the last. In many ways the irrationality of Nazi oppression resembled this aspect of pharaonic ruthlessness, though in other regards it far exceeded it. (On the biblical attitude toward slavery, see commentary on 20:19–21:36, "Slavery in the Torah.")

GLEANINGS

These Are the Names

It says "names of the sons of Israel" (*shemot*), while formerly we were told of the "lines of Jacob" (*toledot*, as in Gen. 37:2). Why this distinction? Jacob represents the *toledot*, the natural man who engenders physical offspring or "lines." Israel is the spiritual man who cannot transmit his gifts by testament, whose sons have to mature and acquire their own *shemot* in order to merit and acquire the inheritance.   AFTER B. JACOB

Coming

One would expect the text to read (v. 1) that these were the names of those who *came*, i.e., in the past tense. [The Hebrew הַבָּאִים suggests that the present tense is used.] This shows us Israel's fate: they dwell in Diaspora lands for a long time, take root, build, and create, but they remain, in the eyes of their neighbors, sojourners—as if they had just been "coming."   AFTER HIZKUNI [9]

No Preference

The roster of the names of Jacob's sons appears here in an order different from other passages. This is to teach us that the sons of the handmaidens, Bilhah and Zilpah, were not inferior to their brothers.   MIDRASH [10]

Joseph Being Already in Egypt (Exod. 1:5)

Why is this stated, seeing that we know this already from Genesis? To let us know that though he was viceroy Joseph was still part of his family.   MIDRASH [11]

Another explanation: To let us know that though his official Egyptian name was Zaphenathpaneah he was still Joseph.   CHASIDIC [12]

With Words

The Egyptians oppressed the Israelites "ruthlessly" (בְּפָרֶךְ). Rabbi Eleazar said, Read this as if בְּפֶה־רַךְ "with smooth words": Pharaoh deceived them first with words and made them slaves before they realized their new status.   MIDRASH [13]

Collective Guilt

The Egyptians were silent when Pharaoh first proposed the oppression. Moreover, v. 11 says specifically that *they* (i.e., the Egyptians) were ruthless in setting taskmasters over Israel. The midwives, weak as they were, did not carry out Pharaoh's command, yet they avoided punishment. How much more easily could all the Egyptian people have avoided, or at least mitigated, Pharaoh's decrees.   LUZZATTO [14]

The Male Children

Astrologers had told Pharaoh that Israel's savior was about to be born. But they did not know whether he would be an Egyptian or a Hebrew, hence Pharaoh commanded "every boy" (v. 22) to be thrown into the Nile—"every boy," even Egyptians.   MIDRASH [15]

Strength

The Hebrew text of v. 9 may be understood to have Pharaoh say that the Israelite people *was*

(singular) very strong. When Israel is united (so that it may be spoken of in the singular) it is strong, and no nation can overcome it.   CHASIDIC [16]

Taskmasters to Oppress Them

They were appointed not for the sake of utility, to advance the work, but for the sake of oppression itself.   CHASIDIC [17]

Slavery in Egypt

Of the slaves, the Egyptian says: "They have no hearts," and here, as everywhere else in the Orient, the heart signifies the personality itself. This discovery, which is as positive as a law of physics, authorizes him to treat the serf like an inanimate object. The state and its prestige demand the systematic construction of colossal depots, fortresses, palaces, temples, cities, and tombs. The slaves provide the gratuitous and inexhaustible pool of labor for this immense task.

A. NEHER [18]

The Bitter Dish

This is the bread of our affliction, this
The symbol of the clay that built Ramses,
And that horseradish-root of bitterness,
And you, my brethren, yea,
You are the afflicted, the embittered, and
   the clay.   A. M. KLEIN [19]

Israel's Merit

The Israelites merited God's favor because they practiced chastity, avoided slander, retained a knowledge of Hebrew, and kept their own traditional names.   MIDRASH [20]

386

Moses

The story now turns to the birth and early fortunes of Moses, the man who will lead Israel out of the house of bondage. His life—like that of many great men— is surrounded by legends, but he always remains human and never takes on the mantle of a superman. However superior his mental and moral power, it always fades before the Power whose agent he is. "Not a single one of all these stories, in which Moses is the central figure, was really written about Moses. Great as was the veneration of the writers for this man to whom God had been pleased to reveal himself, in all these stories it is not Moses himself, Moses the man, but God who is the central figure. God's words and God's deeds, these are the things that the writers intend to set forth" [1].

Many aspects of Moses' life story find their parallels in Egyptian and other ancient folk memories, such as the tale of King Sargon of Akkad or of Romulus, the founder of Rome. Both these men were said to have been exposed as young children and marvelously saved from death; and other heroes were, like Moses, also cast into the water (see Gleanings) [2].

Moses' childhood and youth are treated in the briefest way; only ten verses are devoted to them. However, what the Bible omits, later Jewish as well as Moslem tradition replenished with loving elaboration (for some examples, see Gleanings). Verses 11–22 treat of Moses' adult years and give us our first insight into his character. Here too the biblical storyteller appears to hurry on. He clearly wants to reach the main theme: how Moses came to become God's agent in the drama of deliverance and how the rescue was effected.

387

א וַיֵּלֶךְ אִישׁ מִבֵּית לֵוִי וַיִּקַּח אֶת־בַּת־לֵוִי: וַתַּהַר הָאִשָּׁה

ב וַתֵּלֶד בֵּן וַתֵּרֶא אֹתוֹ כִּי־טוֹב הוּא וַתִּצְפְּנֵהוּ שְׁלֹשָׁה

ג יְרָחִים: וְלֹא־יָכְלָה עוֹד הַצְּפִינוֹ וַתִּקַּח־לוֹ תֵּבַת גֹּמֶא

וַתַּחְמְרָה בַחֵמָר וּבַזָּפֶת וַתָּשֶׂם בָּהּ אֶת־הַיֶּלֶד וַתָּשֶׂם

ד בַּסּוּף עַל־שְׂפַת הַיְאֹר: וַתֵּתַצַּב אֲחֹתוֹ מֵרָחֹק לְדֵעָה

ה מַה־יֵּעָשֶׂה לוֹ: וַתֵּרֶד בַּת־פַּרְעֹה לִרְחֹץ עַל־הַיְאֹר

וְנַעֲרֹתֶיהָ הֹלְכֹת עַל־יַד הַיְאֹר וַתֵּרֶא אֶת־הַתֵּבָה

ו בְּתוֹךְ הַסּוּף וַתִּשְׁלַח אֶת־אֲמָתָהּ וַתִּקָּחֶהָ: וַתִּפְתַּח

וַתִּרְאֵהוּ אֶת־הַיֶּלֶד וְהִנֵּה־נַעַר בֹּכֶה וַתַּחְמֹל עָלָיו

ז וַתֹּאמֶר מִיַּלְדֵי הָעִבְרִים זֶה: וַתֹּאמֶר אֲחֹתוֹ אֶל־בַּת־

פַּרְעֹה הַאֵלֵךְ וְקָרָאתִי לָךְ אִשָּׁה מֵינֶקֶת מִן הָעִבְרִיֹּת

ח וְתֵינִק לָךְ אֶת־הַיָּלֶד: וַתֹּאמֶר־לָהּ בַּת־פַּרְעֹה לֵכִי

ט וַתֵּלֶךְ הָעַלְמָה וַתִּקְרָא אֶת־אֵם הַיָּלֶד: וַתֹּאמֶר לָהּ

בַּת־פַּרְעֹה הֵילִיכִי אֶת־הַיֶּלֶד הַזֶּה וְהֵינִקִהוּ לִי וַאֲנִי

אֶתֵּן אֶת־שְׂכָרֵךְ וַתִּקַּח הָאִשָּׁה הַיֶּלֶד וַתְּנִיקֵהוּ: וַיִּגְדַּל

י הַיֶּלֶד וַתְּבִאֵהוּ לְבַת־פַּרְעֹה וַיְהִי־לָהּ לְבֵן וַתִּקְרָא

1] A certain man of the house of Levi went and married a Levite woman.   2] The woman conceived and bore a son; and when she saw how beautiful he was, she hid him for three months.   3] When she could hide him no longer, she got a wicker basket for him and calked it with bitumen and pitch. She put the child into it and placed it among the reeds by the bank of the Nile.   4] And his sister stationed herself at a distance, to learn what would befall him.

5] The daughter of Pharaoh came down to bathe in the Nile, while her maidens walked along the Nile. She spied the basket among the reeds and sent her slave girl to fetch it.   6] When she opened it, she saw that it was a child, a boy crying. She took pity on it and said, "This must be a Hebrew child."   7] Then his sister said to Pharaoh's daughter, "Shall I go and get you a Hebrew nurse to suckle the child for you?"   8] And Pharaoh's daughter answered, "Yes." So the girl went and called the child's mother.   9] And Pharaoh's daughter said to her, "Take this child and nurse it for me, and I will pay your wages." So the woman took the child and nursed it.   10] When the child grew up, she brought him to Pharaoh's daughter, who made him her son. She named him Moses, explaining, "I drew him out of the water."

2:1] *A certain man.* Identified in 6:20 as Amram; his wife was Jochebed, his aunt. Such marital relationship was later prohibited (Lev. 20:19).

2] *A son.* There is no mention here of the older Miriam and of Aaron who was three years his senior (7:7). The reason for this omission lies most likely in the focus of the story, similar to the story of Solomon's birth, which omits a mention of his three older brothers (cf. II Sam. 12:24 with 5:14 and I Chron. 3:5). Another possibility: Aaron and Moses had the same father but not the same mother, and Miriam was younger (see Num. 26:59 and below at verse 4).

3] *Wicker basket.* The Hebrew word תֵּבָה (*tevah*) occurs only in this tale and in the Flood story where it is used for "ark."

Reeds. Hebrew סוּף (*suf*), related to *suppatum* in Mari documents (ancient Mesopotamia). The appellation *yam suf* is therefore rendered "Sea of Reeds" or "Reed Sea" rather than the traditional "Red Sea"; see at 10:19.

4] *His sister.* Generally assumed to be Miriam. If, however, Miriam was younger than Moses, אֲחֹתוֹ could mean "his relative" [3].

6] *A Hebrew child.* Probably because of his clothing, and not because he was circumcised, for circumcision was most likely practiced by the Egyptians also.

10] *Moses.* מֹשֶׁה (Mosheh) is here associated with the word *mashah*, to draw out, which represents an assonance rather than correct etymology. The Rabbis overcame the linguistic problem ("drawn out" should be *mashuy*, while *mosheh* means "who draws out") by suggesting that he was given the name prophetically, in that Moses would draw out Israel from Egypt, or that Moses drew himself out, so to speak, because of his merits [4]. The word play is repeated by Isaiah (63:11).

יא שְׁמוֹ מֹשֶׁה וַתֹּאמֶר כִּי מִן־הַמַּיִם מְשִׁיתִהוּ: וַיְהִי בַּיָּמִים
הָהֵם וַיִּגְדַּל מֹשֶׁה וַיֵּצֵא אֶל־אֶחָיו וַיַּרְא בְּסִבְלֹתָם
יב וַיַּרְא אִישׁ מִצְרִי מַכֶּה אִישׁ־עִבְרִי מֵאֶחָיו: וַיִּפֶן כֹּה
וָכֹה וַיַּרְא כִּי אֵין אִישׁ וַיַּךְ אֶת־הַמִּצְרִי וַיִּטְמְנֵהוּ
יג בַּחוֹל: וַיֵּצֵא בַּיּוֹם הַשֵּׁנִי וְהִנֵּה שְׁנֵי־אֲנָשִׁים עִבְרִים
יד נִצִּים וַיֹּאמֶר לָרָשָׁע לָמָּה תַכֶּה רֵעֶךָ: וַיֹּאמֶר מִי
שָׂמְךָ לְאִישׁ שַׂר וְשֹׁפֵט עָלֵינוּ הַלְהָרְגֵנִי אַתָּה אֹמֵר

כַּאֲשֶׁר הָרַגְתָּ אֶת־הַמִּצְרִי וַיִּירָא מֹשֶׁה וַיֹּאמַר אָכֵן
טו נוֹדַע הַדָּבָר: וַיִּשְׁמַע פַּרְעֹה אֶת־הַדָּבָר הַזֶּה וַיְבַקֵּשׁ
לַהֲרֹג אֶת־מֹשֶׁה וַיִּבְרַח מֹשֶׁה מִפְּנֵי פַרְעֹה וַיֵּשֶׁב
טז בְּאֶרֶץ־מִדְיָן וַיֵּשֶׁב עַל־הַבְּאֵר: וּלְכֹהֵן מִדְיָן שֶׁבַע
בָּנוֹת וַתָּבֹאנָה וַתִּדְלֶנָה וַתְּמַלֶּאנָה אֶת־הָרְהָטִים
יז לְהַשְׁקוֹת צֹאן אֲבִיהֶן: וַיָּבֹאוּ הָרֹעִים וַיְגָרְשׁוּם וַיָּקָם
יח מֹשֶׁה וַיּוֹשִׁעָן וַיַּשְׁקְ אֶת־צֹאנָם: וַתָּבֹאנָה אֶל־רְעוּאֵל

11] Some time after that, when Moses had grown up, he went out to his kinsfolk and witnessed their toil. He saw an Egyptian beating a Hebrew, one of his kinsmen. **12]** He turned this way and that and, seeing no one about, he struck down the Egyptian and hid him in the sand. **13]** When he went out the next day, he found two Hebrews fighting; so he said to the offender, "Why do you strike your fellow?" **14]** He retorted, "Who made you chief and ruler over us? Do you mean to kill me as you killed the Egyptian?" Moses was frightened, and thought: Then the matter is known! **15]** When Pharaoh learned of the matter, he sought to kill Moses; but Moses fled from Pharaoh. He arrived in the land of Midian, and sat down beside a well.

16] Now the priest of Midian had seven daughters. They came to draw water, and filled their troughs to water their father's flock; **17]** but shepherds came and drove them off. Moses rose to their defense, and he watered their flock. **18]** When they returned to their father

More likely Moses was an Egyptian name, signifying "born of," as in Pharaoh Thutmosis, "born of Thut." Perhaps there was originally an Egyptian prefix to the name, which Pharaoh's daughter gave him, but this was later omitted in Jewish tradition and the Hebrew assonance was introduced. Egyptian sources also seem to know of an independent name Mose. A thirteenth-century B.C.E. papyrus speaks of "Amen-em-Opet, son of the steward Mose," and a stele of the same age notes a priest "Pa-ser, son of Mose" [5].

11] *Went out to his kinsfolk*. Either an objective statement, or indicating that his mother had taught him his true identity.

12] *Struck down*. The text does not reveal whether Moses killed the man deliberately or whether he beat him so severely that he died. The latter is suggested by the use of the same Hebrew word for "beat" and "struck" (מַכֶּה–וַיַּךְ) [6]. The Rabbis surmised that it was this manslaughter which

kept Moses from entering the Promised Land. (See Gleanings.)

14] *Who made you chief*. It was apparently known that Moses was of Hebrew origin.

15] *He arrived ... and [he] sat down*. The word וַיֵּשֶׁב is used both times, heightening the alliterative nature of the account.

Land of Midian. The location is not known. Some place it in the Sinai peninsula, but most scholars place it east of the Gulf of Akaba, in northwest Arabia. Eissfeldt suggests that "Midian" was a term covering a number of countries ruled but not necessarily settled by Midianites, so that Moses could be understood to have escaped Egyptian sovereignty into that of Midian [7]. The Midianites were considered kinfolk by the Israelites (Gen. 25:2), which was probably the reason that Moses went there [8]. Later on, enmity developed between Israel and Midian (Num. 31:1 ff.; Judg. 6:1 ff.).

Beside a well. A similar motif appears in the stories of Isaac and Jacob.

יט אֲבִיהֶן וַיֹּאמֶר מַדּוּעַ מִהַרְתֶּן בֹּא הַיּוֹם: וַתֹּאמַרְןָ
אִישׁ מִצְרִי הִצִּילָנוּ מִיַּד הָרֹעִים וְגַם־דָּלֹה דָלָה לָנוּ
כ וַיַּשְׁקְ אֶת־הַצֹּאן: וַיֹּאמֶר אֶל־בְּנֹתָיו וְאַיּוֹ לָמָּה זֶּה
כא עֲזַבְתֶּן אֶת־הָאִישׁ קִרְאֶן לוֹ וְיֹאכַל לָחֶם: וַיּוֹאֶל
מֹשֶׁה לָשֶׁבֶת אֶת־הָאִישׁ וַיִּתֵּן אֶת־צִפֹּרָה בִתּוֹ לְמֹשֶׁה:
כב וַתֵּלֶד בֵּן וַיִּקְרָא אֶת־שְׁמוֹ גֵּרְשֹׁם כִּי אָמַר גֵּר הָיִיתִי
בְּאֶרֶץ נָכְרִיָּה: פ

כג וַיְהִי בַיָּמִים הָרַבִּים הָהֵם וַיָּמָת מֶלֶךְ מִצְרַיִם וַיֵּאָנְחוּ
בְנֵי־יִשְׂרָאֵל מִן־הָעֲבֹדָה וַיִּזְעָקוּ וַתַּעַל שַׁוְעָתָם אֶל־
כד הָאֱלֹהִים מִן־הָעֲבֹדָה: וַיִּשְׁמַע אֱלֹהִים אֶת־נַאֲקָתָם
וַיִּזְכֹּר אֱלֹהִים אֶת־בְּרִיתוֹ אֶת־אַבְרָהָם אֶת־יִצְחָק
כה וְאֶת־יַעֲקֹב: וַיַּרְא אֱלֹהִים אֶת־בְּנֵי יִשְׂרָאֵל וַיֵּדַע
אֱלֹהִים: ס

Reuel, he said, "How is it that you have come back so soon today?"   **19]** They answered, "An Egyptian rescued us from the shepherds; he even drew water for us and watered the flock."

20] He said to his daughters, "Where is he then? Why did you leave the man? Ask him in to break bread."   **21]** Moses consented to stay with the man, and he gave Moses his daughter Zipporah as wife.   **22]** She bore a son whom he named Gershom, for he said, "I have been a stranger in a foreign land."

23] A long time after that, the king of Egypt died. The Israelites were groaning under the bondage and cried out; and their cry for help from the bondage rose up to God.   **24]** God heard their moaning, and God remembered His covenant with Abraham and Isaac and Jacob.   **25]** God looked upon the Israelites, and God took notice of them.

18] *Reuel.* In 3:1, 4:18, and ch. 18 he is called Jether and Jethro, and in Num. 10:29 we are told of "Hobab, son of Reuel, Moses' father-in-law." Tradition has attempted to harmonize these differences. Ibn Ezra, for instance, says that "father" in v. 18 really means "grandfather," and that Hobab is another name for Jethro. Critical scholarship considers the divergencies due to different traditions; thus, Jethro appears to be an older man with grown daughters, while Hobab is a potent wilderness guide (Num. 10:29–32). See further at 3:1 [9]. It is also possible that the text originally read "Hobab, son of Reuel."

22] *Gershom.* The biblical word play hides the real etymology: the name is derived from גֵּרשׁ, to drive out. Egypt was home for Moses, and Midian was "foreign land." His experience made him doubtlessly more understanding of his people's alien and oppressed status in Egypt [10].

23] *King of Egypt.* Probably Seti I, who ruled in the thirteenth century B.C.E.

Rose up to God. The text does not say "They cried to God," suggesting they had forgotten Him or did not know Him fully as the Redeemer (see commentary on chs. 1, 3, 6).

Literary Notes

The chapter is divided into three parts: the childhood and youth of Moses (verses 1–10), his adulthood (11–22), and a final literary bridge (23–25) which connects the Prologue with the story of redemption which starts in ch. 3 [11].

Childhood and adult years reveal parallel features. In each period a child receives a significant name (Moses, Gershom); the word *yeled* (child) occurs seven times in the first segment and the word *ish* (man) seven times in the second. The Hebrew features alliteration and repetition; in verses 24 and 25 the staccato succession, "God heard," "God remembered," "God looked," "God took notice," has been likened to the tolling of a bell [12].

The bell tolls of things to come. The vague, suggestive ending is perfectly suited to arouse our anticipation. Even though we may be thoroughly familiar with the tale of revelation we nonetheless feel reassured that God's concern for His people was present at all times.

The Character of Moses

"Moses," writes Elie Wiesel, "the most solitary and most powerful hero in biblical history. . . . After him, nothing else was the same again" [13].

However brief the notations on the birth and growth of Moses are, they give us an insight into the shaping of his character. He was brought up in the court of the Pharaoh, yet doubtlessly his humble origins were known to those around him. He himself knew his real parents, and the awareness of his double status must have weighed heavily on his mind. To be able to walk amongst the privileged while his kinfolk were serving as slaves must have put a severe emotional burden on him. This, added to the insecurity of his own position, made him into a person who was both introspective and sensitive to the thoughts and feelings of others. The foundations for religious receptivity were thus laid in his youth.

When he goes out into the world he sees injustice perpetrated and at once feels himself involved. His first pursuit of justice ends in tragedy: the young man becomes—even though most likely by accident—a killer. Once again he looks at the complex world around him, and once again he feels himself challenged to intervene for the sake of peace and equity. But those whom he would help reject his assistance. His position at court is now untenable, and the young slave-prince is suddenly a homeless refugee.

"But this experience does not teach him the worldly wisdom of caution. His passion for justice exiles him from his country; and as soon as he approaches another place of human habitation—even while he sits by the well outside the city, without a friend to offer him shelter—he hears the cry of outraged justice and immediately hastens to the rescue. This time the quarrel is not between Hebrews, but between people entirely unknown to him; but that makes no difference. The Prophet draws no distinction between man and man, only between right and wrong. He helps the weak women against the shepherds who trample on their rights" [14].

We may assume that in the long years he spent in exile, in Midian, Moses further deepened these characteristics. He became worthy to receive the call from God, and he was ready to hear and respond.

Moses' Beauty

Jochebed saw "how beautiful he was" (v. 2). The Hebrew *tov* usually means "good," referring to character. The mother knew that this was an extraordinary child, for when he was born the house was filled with light.　　　MIDRASH [15]

Literary Parallels

[An Egyptian text relating how the god Horus was saved from his persecutor Seth.]

Seth went searching for Horus, still a child, in his hiding place in Chemmis (the Nile Delta marshland), after his mother (Isis) had hidden him in a papyrus thicket. [The text goes on to say that the infant was in a reed boat.] [16]

[See also Hallo's introductory essay.]

[From an Akkadian legend]

Sargon, the mighty king, king of Agade, am I.
My mother was a high priestess, my father
　　I knew not.
The brother of my father loved the hills.
My city is Azupiranu, which is situated on
　　the banks of the Euphrates.
My priestly mother conceived me, in secret she
　　bore me.
She set me in a basket of rushes, with
　　bitumen she sealed my lid.
She cast me into the river which rose not
　　over me.
The river bore me up and carried me to Akki,
　　the drawer of water.
Akki, the drawer of water, lifted me out as
　　he dipped his ewer.
Akki, the drawer of water, took me as his
　　son and reared me. [17]

[From Greek mythology]

Telephus was born of a union between the god Heracles and Auge, daughter of King Aleus of Tegea. The enraged father put mother and son into a wooden chest and cast them into the sea. The chest floated to the land of King Teuthras who married Auge and raised Telephus as a prince. [18]

Water

The story of the hero retrieved in infancy from a river may perhaps reflect the primitive notion that charismatic men draw their special qualities from water, the primordial, uncontaminated element, which is the primal source of power and wisdom.　　　T. H. GASTER [19]

The Tevah

The word *tevah* (here translated as "basket," but in the Noah story as "ark") occurs only here and in the section of the Flood. By this verbal parallelism Scripture apparently intends to draw attention to the thematic analogy. In both instances one worthy of being saved and destined to bring salvation to others is to be rescued from death by drowning. In the earlier section the salvation of humanity is involved, here it is the salvation of the chosen people.　　　CASSUTO [20]

Moses Imperfect

Why is his name always spelled מֹשֶׁה and never מוֹשֶׁה (i.e., with a ו)? To indicate that a measure of wisdom was withheld from him.

MIDRASH [21]

The Coals

Moses used to play before Pharaoh and once took the king's crown off his head and placed it on his own. Pharaoh's advisers deemed this a bad omen and counseled to have the child killed, but Jethro advised a test: give the child a choice be-

tween a gold vessel and live coals. If he chooses the former he is clever and dangerous, but if the latter he is slow-witted and poses no threat to Pharaoh. The test was carried out and Moses (guided by an angel) took a hot coal and put it into his mouth, burning his tongue. Thus was his life saved and thus also did Moses become slow of speech and tongue. MIDRASH [22]

The Youth of Moses

(Jewish tradition was filled with tales of Moses' beauty, brilliance, piety, splendid education, and great wisdom. There were also tales of his successes as an Egyptian general.)

Being in a most eminent degree a practicer of abstinence and self-denial, and being above all men inclined to ridicule a life of effeminacy and luxury (for he desired to live for his soul alone, and not for his body), he exhibited the doctrines of philosophy in all his daily actions, saying precisely what he thought, and performing such actions only as were consistent with his words, so as to exhibit a perfect harmony between his language and his life, so that, as his words were, such also was his life, and, as his life was, such likewise was his language, like people who are playing together in tune on a musical instrument. PHILO [23]

Moses was far ahead of his years. His wisdom and education were such that they would have honored a much older person. His youthful charm was so great that people were fascinated with him and hated to part from him. JOSEPHUS [24]

Moses was learned in all the wisdom of the Egyptians and was mighty in words and deeds. CHRISTIAN SCRIPTURES [25]

The Violent Deed

The text does not moralize on Moses' act of violence. Nowhere is there an explicit evaluation that either praises or condemns it. Rather, a situation is painted with great realism and sensitivity, and the reader is left to ponder on the anomalies of the deed. Moses acts in order to right an injustice, not for his own sake, but for another's. He is motivated to react with violence out of love for his people which even jeopardizes his own life. B. S. CHILDS [26]

Moses "saw an Egyptian beating a Hebrew" (v. 11). Righteousness begins when one sees the yoke others bear. YALKUT ME'AM LO'EZ [27]

His birth was disorderly. Therefore he passionately loved order, the immutable, the bidden, and the forbidden. Early he killed in frenzy; therefore he knew better than the inexperienced that, though killing is delectable, having killed is detestable; he knew you should not kill. He was sensual, therefore he longed for the spiritual, the pure, and the holy—in a word, the invisible—for this alone seemed to him spiritual, holy, and pure. THOMAS MANN [28]

An Argument

When toward the end of his life Moses tried to stave off death, God said to him: "Did I tell you to slay the Egyptian?" Moses answered: "You slew all the first-born in Egypt." Then God silenced him by saying: "Can you liken yourself to Me? I cause death, but I also revive the dead."

Moses asked that at least his bones be buried in the Holy Land. God denied his wish, saying: "You did not acknowledge your nativity." (When the daughters of Jethro spoke of him as an Egyptian [2:19], he did not object.) MIDRASH [29]

Islamic Version

And when he had reached his age of strength and had become a man, we bestowed on him wisdom and knowledge; for thus do we reward the righteous.

And he entered a city at the time when its inhabitants would not observe him [i.e., at the noon hour when they were resting] and found therein two men fighting: the one, of his own people; the other, of his enemies. And he who was of his own people asked his help against him who was of his enemies. And Moses smote him with his fist and slew him. Said he [Moses], "This is a work of Satan; for he [the Israelite] is an enemy, a manifest misleader."

He said, "O my Lord, I have sinned to mine own hurt: forgive me." So God forgave him; for He is the Forgiving, the Merciful.

He said, "Lord, because thou hast showed me this grace, I will never again be the helper of the wicked."

And in the city at noon he was full of fear, casting furtive glances round him: and lo! the man whom he had helped the day before cried out to him again for help. Said Moses to him, "You are plainly a most depraved person."

And when he would have laid violent hands on him who was their common foe, he said to him, "O Moses, do you desire to slay me, as you slew a man yesterday? You desire only to become a tyrant in this land and desire not to become a peacemaker." KORAN [30]

Your People

Moses devoted himself with his whole soul to Israel and they were called "his," for in Exod. 32:7 God, speaking of Israel, says "your people." But were they not God's people? Yes, but because Moses went out to his brethren and identified with them Israel is forever identified with him. MIDRASH [31]

God Matched Moses

When he saw the burdens of his brothers, Moses, though a prince, assisted them like a common slave. God said: "You gave up all else to join yourself unto the Children of Israel in their sorrow, therefore I too will put all else aside in heaven and on earth and speak only with you." MIDRASH [32]

The Oppression

The Egyptians taunted the Israelites for observing the circumcision of their sons. They mocked the Hebrews for this, since the infants were to be put to death anyway. But the Hebrews answered, "We perform our duty; whatever you do later cannot affect our practice of our faith. As our ancestors were faithful to God's covenant, so shall we be." MIDRASH [33]

The Desert

In fleeing from Egypt Moses has broken with civilization. He is endeavoring to escape the machine which makes men into cogs and which at the time functioned with such immovable precision in Egypt. The desert calls him: it is a place of solitude, of silence, of forgetfulness; it is a sacred spot, a natural storehouse whose fruits, though scarce, satisfy your hunger; whose springs, though rare, quench your thirst. As Moses leads his flocks farther into the desert, his startled conscience finds peace. Soon he is surrounded by an atmosphere of renunciation, of asceticism, of poverty, and of a contented solitude. A. NEHER [34]

The Revolutionary

How Moses came to entertain his revolutionary ideas is no greater mystery than the revolutionary insights that come to all men of genius. The appearance of any great personality in history is unpredictable and his endowments are inexplicable. He leaps into his age unexpectedly, like lightning out of darkness, and his generation may grant him or deny him scope and opportunity. To be sure, he does not operate in a vacuum, but whatever truth he reveals wells up in his own soul with the force of an immediate and overpowering apprehension. Whatever he conceives of intellectually or experiences spiritually is a new act of creation and is his very own. It is not the product of evolution nor is it derived from his cultural environment, and it possesses timeless relevance.

A. H. SILVER [35]

God Took Notice (Exod. 2:25)

What did God know [that He had not known before]? When the Israelites had grown accustomed to their tasks, when the Hebrews began to labor without complaint, then God knew it was time that they be liberated. . . . As long as there was no prospect of freedom, God knew the Israelites would not awaken to the bitterness of bondage. First Moses had to teach the taste of freedom's hope, and only then did servitude taste bitter.

PASSOVER HAGGADAH [36]

PART II

The Mission

The Call

Moses experiences the wondrous and commanding Presence while tending the flock of his father-in-law in the desert. The shepherd theme occurs in other ancient Near Eastern literature* as well as in later biblical material, especially in the story of David: the chosen leader himself worthy of guiding his people even as he guides his animal flock. The Midrash further elaborated on this theme (see Gleanings).

Moses reacts to the vision first by claiming to be unworthy; then he professes ignorance of the Name; thereafter he posits the people's disbelief, his own lack of eloquence, and ends by asking that he be replaced. In each case of these rising objections God responds with patience, except when Moses requests that someone else be sent. God is angered—the first time in the Torah this emotion is ascribed to Him—and Moses, after receiving Aaron as a helpmate, acquiesces and returns to Jethro. The Prophet is now armed with three signs as well as with a foreknowledge of what will happen: Pharaoh will refuse to let Israel go until he is overcome "because of greater might."

The God who reveals himself to Moses is the God of the Fathers whose powers will be proven superior to those of the mighty Pharaoh. Though appearing in the forbidding mountain of the desert, He is not bound by its isolation; He is where His children are, and He will set them free. The wonder at the bush is the first of many signs He will give to

---

* Thus, Lipit-Ishtar is called a "wise shepherd"; and the opening section of Hammurabi's Code introduces the king as "Hammurabi, the shepherd, called by Enlil, am I" [1].

show that He is the master not only of men and their destinies but of nature as well.

The divine manifestation proclaiming God's readiness to redeem Israel begins with the revelation of God's name to Moses, who believes that only if he knows the Name can he authenticate the divine message before Israel. But it is in ambiguous terms that the information is communicated to him: He is Elohim, Ehyeh, and YHVH. The study of the latter two names has commanded an enormous amount of scholarly attention without, however, producing anything approaching a consensus. It has been suggested that verses 9–15 stem from a separate tradition, with אֱלֹהִים and שָׁלַח as key words, and that verses 1–8 and 16 ff. can be read consecutively with יְהוָֹה and עָלָה־הַצִּיל as key words [2]. However, the text confronts us as it is, and it is in this form that we shall discuss it.

א וּמֹשֶׁה הָיָה רֹעֶה אֶת־צֹאן יִתְרוֹ חֹתְנוֹ כֹּהֵן מִדְיָן
וַיִּנְהַג אֶת־הַצֹּאן אַחַר הַמִּדְבָּר וַיָּבֹא אֶל־הַר הָאֱלֹהִים
ב חֹרֵבָה: וַיֵּרָא מַלְאַךְ יְהֹוָה אֵלָיו בְּלַבַּת־אֵשׁ מִתּוֹךְ
הַסְּנֶה וַיַּרְא וְהִנֵּה הַסְּנֶה בֹּעֵר בָּאֵשׁ וְהַסְּנֶה אֵינֶנּוּ
ג אֻכָּל: וַיֹּאמֶר מֹשֶׁה אָסֻרָה־נָּא וְאֶרְאֶה אֶת־הַמַּרְאֶה
ד הַגָּדֹל הַזֶּה מַדּוּעַ לֹא־יִבְעַר הַסְּנֶה: וַיַּרְא יְהֹוָה כִּי

סָר לִרְאוֹת וַיִּקְרָא אֵלָיו אֱלֹהִים מִתּוֹךְ הַסְּנֶה וַיֹּאמֶר
ה מֹשֶׁה מֹשֶׁה וַיֹּאמֶר הִנֵּנִי: וַיֹּאמֶר אַל־תִּקְרַב הֲלֹם
שַׁל־נְעָלֶיךָ מֵעַל רַגְלֶיךָ כִּי הַמָּקוֹם אֲשֶׁר אַתָּה
ו עוֹמֵד עָלָיו אַדְמַת־קֹדֶשׁ הוּא: וַיֹּאמֶר אָנֹכִי אֱלֹהֵי
אָבִיךָ אֱלֹהֵי אַבְרָהָם אֱלֹהֵי יִצְחָק וֵאלֹהֵי יַעֲקֹב
וַיַּסְתֵּר מֹשֶׁה פָּנָיו כִּי יָרֵא מֵהַבִּיט אֶל־הָאֱלֹהִים:

1] Now Moses, tending the flock of his father-in-law Jethro, the priest of Midian, drove the flock into the wilderness, and came to Horeb, the mountain of God. **2]** An angel of the LORD appeared to him in a blazing fire out of a bush. He gazed, and there was a bush all aflame, yet the bush was not consumed. **3]** Moses said, "I must turn aside to look at this marvelous sight; why doesn't the bush burn up?" **4]** When the LORD saw that he had turned aside to look, God called to him out of the bush: "Moses! Moses!" He answered, "Here I am." **5]** And He said, "Do not come closer. Remove your sandals from your feet, for the place on which you stand is holy ground. **6]** I am," He said, "the God of your father, the God of Abraham, the God of Isaac, and the God of Jacob." And Moses hid his face, for he was afraid to look at God.

3:1] *Jethro.* In 2:18 he was called Reuel.

Horeb. Usually considered identical with Sinai. Critical scholars distinguish between a "Horeb" and a "Sinai" tradition (the former assigned to E and D, the latter to J and P), even as they distinguish between a "Jethro" and a "Reuel" tradition. For instance, the names of Horeb and Sinai may point to different mountains; one (Horeb) located in Midian and the other (Sinai) to be found somewhere in the Sinai peninsula. Hobab-Reuel, the Midianite priest, would fit with Horeb, while Jethro would be part of the Sinai story. In later ages these strands were interwoven into the text as we now have it [3].

Mountain of God. Its exact location is not known (see chs. 13 f.). Either the writer anticipates the experience that Moses will have here, or the mountain was already so known. (Some understand הַר הָאֱלֹהִים as "lordly mountain.")

2] *Angel.* A visible manifestation of God (see at Gen. 18).

In a blazing fire. An anticipation of the theophany at Mt. Sinai (19:18). Or, God appeared to Moses "*as* a blazing fire," a parallel to 6:3, [4]. וָאֵרָא . . . בְּאֵל שַׁדָּי.

Bush. סְנֶה (*seneh*) apparently related to the Arabic *sina*, a thorny shrub, *cassia obovata* (note also the plants called "senna" in English).

4] *Moses! Moses!* Call and answer resemble the experience of Abraham (Gen. 22:1).

5] *Remove your sandals.* Many explanations have been offered for the custom of removing one's footwear when entering a sacred place (practiced in various cultures, for instance, Moslem and Japanese): one enters the presence of divinity as clean as possible; one lowers his status in a gesture of self-abnegation; one unties all knots when coming before God. Joshua, too, when meeting a divine apparition, is bidden to remove his sandals, and the priests followed this custom when entering the Temple Mount [5].

6] *Your father.* Probably meant as a collective and indicating that God will protect Moses as He protected his ancestors. The repetition of the word "God" conveys a sense of divine constancy.

לְחָצִים אֹתָם: וְעַתָּה לְכָה וְאֶשְׁלָחֲךָ אֶל־פַּרְעֹה   וַיֹּאמֶר יְהוָה רָאֹה רָאִיתִי אֶת־עֳנִי עַמִּי אֲשֶׁר בְּמִצְרָיִם

וְהוֹצֵא אֶת־עַמִּי בְנֵי־יִשְׂרָאֵל מִמִּצְרָיִם: וַיֹּאמֶר מֹשֶׁה   וְאֶת־צַעֲקָתָם שָׁמַעְתִּי מִפְּנֵי נֹגְשָׂיו כִּי יָדַעְתִּי אֶת־

אֶל־הָאֱלֹהִים מִי אָנֹכִי כִּי אֵלֵךְ אֶל־פַּרְעֹה וְכִי אוֹצִיא   מַכְאֹבָיו: וָאֵרֵד לְהַצִּילוֹ מִיַּד מִצְרַיִם וּלְהַעֲלֹתוֹ

אֶת־בְּנֵי יִשְׂרָאֵל מִמִּצְרָיִם: וַיֹּאמֶר כִּי־אֶהְיֶה עִמָּךְ   מִן־הָאָרֶץ הַהִוא אֶל־אֶרֶץ טוֹבָה וּרְחָבָה אֶל־אֶרֶץ

וְזֶה־לְּךָ הָאוֹת כִּי אָנֹכִי שְׁלַחְתִּיךָ בְּהוֹצִיאֲךָ אֶת־   זָבַת חָלָב וּדְבָשׁ אֶל־מְקוֹם הַכְּנַעֲנִי וְהַחִתִּי וְהָאֱמֹרִי

הָעָם מִמִּצְרַיִם תַּעַבְדוּן אֶת־הָאֱלֹהִים עַל הָהָר הַזֶּה: וְהַפְּרִזִּי וְהַחִוִּי וְהַיְבוּסִי: וְעַתָּה הִנֵּה צַעֲקַת בְּנֵי־

וַיֹּאמֶר מֹשֶׁה אֶל־הָאֱלֹהִים הִנֵּה אָנֹכִי בָא אֶל־בְּנֵי   יִשְׂרָאֵל בָּאָה אֵלָי וְגַם־רָאִיתִי אֶת־הַלַּחַץ אֲשֶׁר מִצְרַיִם

7] And the LORD continued, "I have marked well the plight of My people in Egypt and have heeded their outcry because of their taskmasters; yes, I am mindful of their sufferings. **8]** I have come down to rescue them from the Egyptians and to bring them out of that land to a good and spacious land, a land flowing with milk and honey, the home of the Canaanites, the Hittites, the Amorites, the Perizzites, the Hivites, and the Jebusites. **9]** Now the cry of the Israelites has reached Me; moreover, I have seen how the Egyptians oppress them. **10]** Come, therefore, I will send you to Pharaoh, and you shall free My people, the Israelites, from Egypt."

11] But Moses said to God, "Who am I that I should go to Pharaoh and free the Israelites from Egypt?" **12]** And He said, "I will be with you, and it shall be your sign that it was I who sent you. And when you have freed the people from Egypt, you shall worship God at this mountain."

13] Moses said to God, "When I come to the Israelites and say to them 'The God of your fathers has sent me to you,' and they ask me, 'What is His name?' what shall I say to

---

7] *Marked . . . heeded . . . mindful.* The English does not convey the Hebrew progression which literally says "seen . . . heard . . . known."

8] *Milk and honey.* From here on frequently used to express the wealth of the land. Cattle and honey appear also in the Egyptian story of Sinuhe, describing the wealth of the land of Yaa [6].

The home of . . . . The six nations listed here are often described as inhabiting the land described as Canaan (in Gen. 15:19–21 additional nations are mentioned). "Canaanites" was a general descriptive term of various inhabitants, while "Amorites" was an ethnic term for certain west Semitic people in the land; the Hittites (to be distinguished from a large nation that was a major power in Anatolia, in the central area of today's Turkey) lived in the south, and the Jebusites, around Jerusalem (the city was originally known as Jebus). Little is known about the Hivites and Perizzites [7].

11] *Who am I . . . ?* The feeling of unworthiness is a hallmark of some prophets; see, for instance, Jeremiah's rejoinder to the divine call: "I am but

a youth" (Jer. 1:6). The Midrash speculates that God had tried for seven days to persuade Moses to accept the mission [8].

12] *It shall be your sign.* Namely, God's being with him [9].

13] *And they ask me.* Moses says "they," but most likely he himself wanted to learn it, believing that God could be approached only if one knew His name. For even as knowledge of another person's name provided access to and power over him, so was knowing the divine name the key to the Presence.

"The 'true' name of a person (said Buber) is the essence of the person, distilled from his real being, so that he is present in it once again. What is more, he is present in it in such a form that anybody who knows the true name and knows how to pronounce it in the correct way can gain control of him. The person himself is unapproachable, he offers resistance; but through the name he becomes approachable, the speaker has power over him" [10].

אֶרֶץ הַכְּנַעֲנִי וְהַחִתִּי וְהָאֱמֹרִי וְהַפְּרִזִּי וְהַחִוִּי וְהַיְבוּסִי

יִשְׂרָאֵל וְאָמַרְתָּ לָהֶם אֱלֹהֵי אֲבֹתֵיכֶם שְׁלָחַנִי אֲלֵיכֶם

אֶל־אֶרֶץ זָבַת חָלָב וּדְבָשׁ: וְשָׁמְעוּ לְקֹלֶךָ וּבָאתָ

יד וְאָמְרוּ־לִי מַה־שְּׁמוֹ מָה אֹמַר אֲלֵהֶם: וַיֹּאמֶר אֱלֹהִים

אַתָּה וְזִקְנֵי יִשְׂרָאֵל אֶל־מֶלֶךְ מִצְרַיִם וַאֲמַרְתֶּם אֵלָיו

אֶל־מֹשֶׁה אֶהְיֶה אֲשֶׁר אֶהְיֶה וַיֹּאמֶר כֹּה תֹאמַר לִבְנֵי

יְהֹוָה אֱלֹהֵי הָעִבְרִיִּים נִקְרָה עָלֵינוּ וְעַתָּה נֵלְכָה־נָּא

טו יִשְׂרָאֵל אֶהְיֶה שְׁלָחַנִי אֲלֵיכֶם: וַיֹּאמֶר עוֹד אֱלֹהִים

דֶּרֶךְ שְׁלֹשֶׁת יָמִים בַּמִּדְבָּר וְנִזְבְּחָה לַיהֹוָה אֱלֹהֵינוּ:

אֶל־מֹשֶׁה כֹּה תֹאמַר אֶל־בְּנֵי יִשְׂרָאֵל יְהֹוָה אֱלֹהֵי

יט וַאֲנִי יָדַעְתִּי כִּי לֹא־יִתֵּן אֶתְכֶם מֶלֶךְ מִצְרַיִם לַהֲלֹךְ

אֲבֹתֵיכֶם אֱלֹהֵי אַבְרָהָם אֱלֹהֵי יִצְחָק וֵאלֹהֵי יַעֲקֹב

כ וְלֹא בְּיָד חֲזָקָה: וְשָׁלַחְתִּי אֶת־יָדִי וְהִכֵּיתִי אֶת־מִצְרַיִם

שְׁלָחַנִי אֲלֵיכֶם זֶה־שְּׁמִי לְעֹלָם וְזֶה זִכְרִי לְדֹר דֹּר:

בְּכֹל נִפְלְאֹתַי אֲשֶׁר אֶעֱשֶׂה בְּקִרְבּוֹ וְאַחֲרֵי־כֵן יְשַׁלַּח

טז לֵךְ וְאָסַפְתָּ אֶת־זִקְנֵי יִשְׂרָאֵל וְאָמַרְתָּ אֲלֵהֶם יְהֹוָה

כא אֶתְכֶם: וְנָתַתִּי אֶת־חֵן הָעָם־הַזֶּה בְּעֵינֵי מִצְרַיִם וְהָיָה

אֱלֹהֵי אֲבֹתֵיכֶם נִרְאָה אֵלַי אֱלֹהֵי אַבְרָהָם יִצְחָק

כב כִּי תֵלֵכוּן לֹא תֵלְכוּ רֵיקָם: וְשָׁאֲלָה אִשָּׁה מִשְּׁכֶנְתָּהּ

וְיַעֲקֹב לֵאמֹר פָּקֹד פָּקַדְתִּי אֶתְכֶם וְאֶת־הֶעָשׂוּי לָכֶם

וּמִגָּרַת בֵּיתָהּ כְּלֵי־כֶסֶף וּכְלֵי זָהָב וּשְׂמָלֹת וְשַׂמְתֶּם

בְּמִצְרָיִם: וָאֹמַר אַעֲלֶה אֶתְכֶם מֵעֳנִי מִצְרַיִם אֶל־

them?" **14]** And God said to Moses, "Ehyeh-Asher-Ehyeh." He continued, "Thus shall you say to the Israelites, 'Ehyeh sent me to you.'" **15]** And God said further to Moses, "Thus shall you speak to the Israelites: The LORD, the God of your fathers, the God of Abraham, the God of Isaac, and the God of Jacob, has sent me to you:

> This shall be My name forever,
> This My appellation for all eternity.

16] "Go and assemble the elders of Israel and say to them: The LORD, the God of your fathers, the God of Abraham, Isaac, and Jacob, has appeared to me and said, 'I have taken note of you and of what is being done to you in Egypt,   **17]** and I have declared: I will take you out of the misery of Egypt to the land of the Canaanites, the Hittites, the Amorites, the Perizzites, the Hivites, and the Jebusites, to a land flowing with milk and honey.'   **18]** They will listen to you; then you shall go with the elders of Israel to the king of Egypt and you shall say to him, 'The LORD, the God of the Hebrews, manifested Himself to us. Now therefore, let us go a distance of three days into the wilderness to sacrifice to the LORD our God.'   **19]** Yet I know that the king of Egypt will let you go only because of a greater might.   **20]** So I will stretch out My hand and smite Egypt with various wonders which I will work upon them; after that he shall let you go.   **21]** And I will dispose the Egyptians favorably toward this people, so that when you go, you will not go away empty-handed.   **22]** Each woman shall borrow from her neighbor and the lodger in her house objects of silver and gold, and clothing, and you shall put these on your sons and daughters, thus stripping the Egyptians."

15] *Further.* Either then or at a later time. A midrash suggests a lapse of six days [11].

18] *Hebrews.* עִבְרִיִּים (ivriyim, the same as ivrim, singular ivri), a term used of Israelites primarily when they are dealing with non-Israelites; see at Gen. 14:13.

19] *Because of a greater might.* Which will be ex-

hibited by God. A more idiomatic translation would be "only if forced" [12].

21] *Empty-handed.* In the same manner as the law provides for the release of slaves; Deut. 15:13.

22] *Stripping the Egyptians.* See 12:35–36.

עַל־בְּנֵיכֶם וְעַל־בְּנֹתֵיכֶם וְנִצַּלְתֶּם אֶת־מִצְרָיִם:

א וַיַּעַן מֹשֶׁה וַיֹּאמֶר וְהֵן לֹא־יַאֲמִינוּ לִי וְלֹא יִשְׁמְעוּ

ב בְּקֹלִי כִּי יֹאמְרוּ לֹא־נִרְאָה אֵלֶיךָ יְהוָה: וַיֹּאמֶר אֵלָיו

ג יְהוָה מַזֶּה בְיָדֶךָ וַיֹּאמֶר מַטֶּה: וַיֹּאמֶר הַשְׁלִיכֵהוּ

אַרְצָה וַיַּשְׁלִכֵהוּ אַרְצָה וַיְהִי לְנָחָשׁ וַיָּנָס מֹשֶׁה מִפָּנָיו:

ד וַיֹּאמֶר יְהוָה אֶל־מֹשֶׁה שְׁלַח יָדְךָ וֶאֱחֹז בִּזְנָבוֹ וַיִּשְׁלַח

ה יָדוֹ וַיַּחֲזֶק בּוֹ וַיְהִי לְמַטֶּה בְּכַפּוֹ: לְמַעַן יַאֲמִינוּ כִּי־

נִרְאָה אֵלֶיךָ יְהוָה אֱלֹהֵי אֲבֹתָם אֱלֹהֵי אַבְרָהָם אֱלֹהֵי

ו יִצְחָק וֵאלֹהֵי יַעֲקֹב: וַיֹּאמֶר יְהוָה לוֹ עוֹד הָבֵא־נָא

יָדְךָ בְּחֵיקֶךָ וַיָּבֵא יָדוֹ בְּחֵיקוֹ וַיּוֹצִאָהּ וְהִנֵּה יָדוֹ

ז מְצֹרַעַת כַּשָּׁלֶג: וַיֹּאמֶר הָשֵׁב יָדְךָ אֶל־חֵיקֶךָ וַיָּשֶׁב

יָדוֹ אֶל־חֵיקוֹ וַיּוֹצִאָהּ מֵחֵיקוֹ וְהִנֵּה־שָׁבָה כִּבְשָׂרוֹ:

ח וְהָיָה אִם־לֹא יַאֲמִינוּ לָךְ וְלֹא יִשְׁמְעוּ לְקֹל הָאֹת

ט הָרִאשׁוֹן וְהֶאֱמִינוּ לְקֹל הָאֹת הָאַחֲרוֹן: וְהָיָה אִם־לֹא

יַאֲמִינוּ גַּם לִשְׁנֵי הָאֹתוֹת הָאֵלֶּה וְלֹא יִשְׁמְעוּן לְקֹלֶךָ

וְלָקַחְתָּ מִמֵּימֵי הַיְאֹר וְשָׁפַכְתָּ הַיַּבָּשָׁה וְהָיוּ הַמַּיִם

י אֲשֶׁר תִּקַּח מִן־הַיְאֹר וְהָיוּ לְדָם בַּיַּבָּשֶׁת: וַיֹּאמֶר

מֹשֶׁה אֶל־יְהוָה בִּי אֲדֹנָי לֹא אִישׁ דְּבָרִים אָנֹכִי גַּם

מִתְּמוֹל גַּם מִשִּׁלְשֹׁם גַּם מֵאָז דַּבֶּרְךָ אֶל־עַבְדֶּךָ כִּי

יא כְבַד־פֶּה וּכְבַד לָשׁוֹן אָנֹכִי: וַיֹּאמֶר יְהוָה אֵלָיו מִי

שָׂם פֶּה לָאָדָם אוֹ מִי־יָשׂוּם אִלֵּם אוֹ חֵרֵשׁ אוֹ פִקֵּחַ

יב אוֹ עִוֵּר הֲלֹא אָנֹכִי יְהוָה: וְעַתָּה לֵךְ וְאָנֹכִי אֶהְיֶה

1] But Moses spoke up and said, "What if they do not believe me and do not listen to me, but say: The LORD did not appear to you?" 2] The LORD said to him, "What is that in your hand?" And he replied, "A rod." 3] He said, "Cast it on the ground." He cast it on the ground and it became a snake; and Moses recoiled from it. 4] Then the LORD said to Moses, "Put out your hand and grasp it by the tail"—he put out his hand and seized it, and it became a rod in his hand— 5] "that they may believe that the LORD, the God of their fathers, the God of Abraham, the God of Isaac, and the God of Jacob, did appear to you."

6] The LORD said to him further, "Put your hand into your bosom." He put his hand into his bosom; and when he took it out, his hand was encrusted with snowy scales! 7] And He said, "Put your hand back into your bosom."—He put his hand back into his bosom; and when he took it out of his bosom, there it was again like the rest of his body.— 8] "And if they do not believe you or pay heed to the first sign, they will believe the second. 9] And if they are not convinced by both these signs and still do not heed you, take some water from the Nile and pour it on the dry ground, and it—the water that you take from the Nile—will turn to blood on the dry ground."

10] But Moses said to the LORD, "Please, O Lord, I have never been a man of words, either in times past or now that You have spoken to Your servant; I am slow of speech and slow of tongue." 11] And the LORD said to him, "Who gives man speech? Who makes him dumb or deaf, seeing or blind? Is it not I, the LORD? 12] Now go, and I will be with you as you speak

4:2] *Rod.* His shepherd's staff.

6] *Snowy scales.* Others, "leprosy"; see at Lev. 13:2–3. Moses is not reported to have performed this sign thereafter. Polemicists later on described Moses as a leper, to which Jewish midrashists responded with a description of his beauty [13].

10] *Slow of speech.* Literally, "heavy of mouth,"

not an orator [14]. Or, he had a speech defect [15]. God knows his shortcoming but chooses him nonetheless, even as he chose Jacob despite his moral immaturity. The speech difficulty of Moses is one of the motifs found also in ancient Near Eastern literature; see the introductory essay by W. W. Hallo.

11] *And the Lord said.* Reproving Moses.

יג עִם־פִּ֔יךָ וְהֽוֹרֵיתִ֖יךָ אֲשֶׁ֥ר תְּדַבֵּֽר: וַיֹּ֖אמֶר בִּ֣י אֲדֹנָ֑י
יד שְֽׁלַֽח־נָ֖א בְּיַד־תִּשְׁלָֽח: וַיִּֽחַר־אַ֨ף יְהֹוָ֜ה בְּמֹשֶׁ֗ה וַיֹּ֨אמֶר֙
הֲלֹ֨א אַהֲרֹ֤ן אָחִ֙יךָ֙ הַלֵּוִ֔י יָדַ֕עְתִּי כִּֽי־דַבֵּ֥ר יְדַבֵּ֖ר ה֑וּא
וְגַ֤ם הִנֵּה־הוּא֙ יֹצֵ֣א לִקְרָאתֶ֔ךָ וְרָאֲךָ֖ וְשָׂמַ֥ח בְּלִבּֽוֹ:
טו וְדִבַּרְתָּ֣ אֵלָ֔יו וְשַׂמְתָּ֥ אֶת־הַדְּבָרִ֖ים בְּפִ֑יו וְאָֽנֹכִ֗י אֶֽהְיֶ֤ה
עִם־פִּ֙יךָ֙ וְעִם־פִּ֔יהוּ וְהֽוֹרֵיתִ֣י אֶתְכֶ֔ם אֵ֖ת אֲשֶׁ֥ר תַּֽעֲשֽׂוּן:

טז וְדִבֶּר־ה֥וּא לְךָ֖ אֶל־הָעָ֑ם וְהָ֤יָה הוּא֙ יִֽהְיֶה־לְּךָ֣ לְפֶ֔ה
יז וְאַתָּ֖ה תִּֽהְיֶה־לּ֥וֹ לֵֽאלֹהִֽים: וְאֶת־הַמַּטֶּ֥ה הַזֶּ֖ה תִּקַּ֣ח
בְּיָדֶ֑ךָ אֲשֶׁ֥ר תַּֽעֲשֶׂה־בּ֖וֹ אֶת־הָֽאֹתֹֽת: פ
יח וַיֵּ֨לֶךְ מֹשֶׁ֜ה וַיָּ֣שָׁב ׀ אֶל־יֶ֣תֶר חֹֽתְנ֗וֹ וַיֹּ֤אמֶר לוֹ֙ אֵ֣לְכָה
נָּ֗א וְאָשׁ֙וּבָה֙ אֶל־אַחַ֣י אֲשֶׁר־בְּמִצְרַ֔יִם וְאֶרְאֶ֖ה
הַֽעוֹדָ֣ם חַיִּ֑ים וַיֹּ֧אמֶר יִתְר֛וֹ לְמֹשֶׁ֖ה לֵ֥ךְ לְשָׁלֽוֹם:

and will instruct you what to say." **13]** But he said, "Please, O Lord, make someone else Your agent." **14]** The LORD became angry with Moses, and He said, "There is your brother Aaron the Levite. He, I know, speaks readily. Even now he is setting out to meet you, and he will be happy to see you. **15]** You shall speak to him and put the words in his mouth—I will be with you and with him as you speak, and tell both of you what to do— **16]** and he shall speak for you to the people. Thus he shall serve as your spokesman, with you playing the role of God to him. **17]** And take with you this rod, with which you shall perform the signs."

18] Moses went back to his father-in-law Jether and said to him, "Let me go back to my kinsmen in Egypt and see how they are faring." And Jethro said to Moses, "Go in peace."

13] *Make someone else Your agent.* Literally, "send through whomever You will send," but not me.

14] *Aaron the Levite.* Here used like a title: Aaron probably already functioned as a priest.

16] *Playing the role of God to him.* Inspiring him; see at 7:1.

17] *This rod.* His shepherd's staff with which he had performed the sign.

18] *Jether.* Another form of Jethro. Moses had consented to stay with him (2:21) and therefore asks his permission to leave. He does not at this time reveal his mission.

Go in peace. According to the Talmud, the expression לֵךְ לְשָׁלוֹם (*lech le-shalom*) is to be used for one who goes and hopefully returns in peace, while לֵךְ בְּשָׁלוֹם (*lech be-shalom*) implies that he will (soon) die or is dead [16].

The Vision

The revelation of God at the bush is, in human terms, a vision seen by Moses. It was his, and his alone; he hears a voice which he knows to be the voice of God. That is the basis of the story, and the message he hears is its core. All attempts to externalize his experience are therefore of secondary interest. Some interpreters, for instance, would have Moses seeing certain crystals that formed on desert plants and, in the evening light, mistaking their glow for a mysterious fire that appeared to burn without consuming the bush. Such speculation leads nowhere; what is important is that Moses experiences the vision as a divine call. Those who deny that God can address man will not be convinced by any assertion to the contrary; whereas those who believe in a God who can be heard by man will likely find the account a realistic description of the encounter. The circumstances are marvelous and mysterious, and Moses is afraid.

The divine self-disclosure reveals a God who cares for man and is attracted to him; who takes account of his frailty, yet holds him in high regard. It is a relationship based on divine love, given freely and, at this juncture, outside a framework of reciprocal obligation.

Moses' Faith

The series of objections that Moses raises before he accepts the mission reveals a man who not only feels unworthy of the task but also has doubts about the efficacy of the mission itself. Although Moses has been categorically told that Israel would listen to his message (3:18), he demurs and says (4:1): "What if they do not believe me and do not listen to me?" In contrast to Abraham, who never questioned his being singled out by God and never sought to learn His essence by asking for His name, Moses is frankly doubtful; like a Jeremiah later on he resists the divine call and not long thereafter regrets that he ever agreed to go (5:22). Rashi therefore described Moses as one who had little faith, and the Talmud considered his response to God to have been a reason for not being allowed to enter the Promised Land [17].

But Rashi's assessment is too simple. Resistance of the prophet to the divine demand is a complex fabric woven of faith and doubt, anxiety and a sense of unworthiness. The Bible does not depict its heroes as cardboard saints who answer the divine challenge without question. (Abraham's apparent readiness to sacrifice his son is not necessarily an exception. He had evidently, by this time, reached a firm and unshakable faith.) Moses at the bush is at the beginning of his knowledge of God, and, while he is struck with awe and even fear, he remains also very much himself and preserves his right to refuse initially and then to doubt and question. He never loses this independence, even long after he becomes the intimate of his God.

The Signs

The Torah assumes that a prophet is capable of performing extraordinary signs, though signs alone do not confirm his authenticity, for even false prophets might perform them (see Deut. 13:2 ff.). It was an old and widespread tradition that heroes were capable of unusual feats. They could lift or throw objects of great weight, fight against several men,[1] kill dragons, stretch small provisions so that they could feed the multitude, or walk on water [18]. Similarly, rods or wands were believed to be instruments for bringing about wonderful results.

---

[1] Moses had already demonstrated such strength, 2:16–19. Jacob lifted a great stone, Gen. 29:2, 10.

Moses and Aaron use them, as does an angel of God (Judg. 6:21); in Greek mythology Athena transformed Odysseus with a rod, and Circe changed his companions into swine in like manner [19]. But though the Bible uses the symbol of the wand as a visible sign of authority, it never leaves the reader in doubt about the one and only source of the wonder, which is neither a magical rod nor the human agent who wields it; it is always God himself.

The signs appear to be meant first and foremost to convince Israel rather than Pharaoh. The latter need not believe, for he will in any case be coerced. But Israel's belief is essential for bringing salvation about, and even God cannot coerce such faith. Hence He himself cannot be certain and adds a third sign in case they refuse to heed. At the same time we cannot overlook the later story that Egypt's magicians could duplicate the signs, at least in part. Of what use were they then if their performance did not in fact guarantee the undoubted authenticity of Moses?

We must conclude that doing wonders of a kind was a ritual that Moses would be expected to perform, but which in itself was not the real proof of his mission. The Midrash therefore said that this proof came from what Moses *said*, not from what he *did*. The Israelites had a tradition that some day they would be redeemed, and Moses convinced them that the time had come. Not by accident does the text use the same words for God's readiness to act as it had for the promise of future redemption made by Joseph in his dying hour.[2]

The signs, then, were of secondary importance in convincing Israel and of no significance in convincing Pharaoh. Perhaps their primary impact was on Moses himself.

It is he who in a moment of great anxiety and upheaval needs some reassurance. The signs help him to gain confidence and to overcome his latest objection. They are a temporary device, of psychological import for him, and of ceremonial meaning to the people. In neither case are they of the essence.

The Divine Name Ehyeh

In this first theophany, the divine Presence is called by three names: "God" (Elohim, אֱלֹהִים), "Lord" (YHVH, יְהוָה), and a name not translated by our English text, "Ehyeh" (אֶהְיֶה). Of these, only the last name is new to Moses, the other two are familiar to him and are not explained: Elohim is the basic generic name for any god and hence also for the God of Abraham, Isaac, and Jacob (verse 6); and "Lord" or YHVH is God's own, personal name, known to him, but—as chapter 6 will show—not yet understood in its full meaning. Here it is merely restated that, whatever the additional and newly revealed name Ehyeh betokens, God's own name YHVH will not be affected, it will remain the same (verse 15) [21].

The name Elohim is known to the reader from the story of Creation on. It is an expansion or variant of the name El, which generally describes the godhead in Semitic languages (Ugaritic *El*; Babylonian *Ilu*; Arabic *Allah*). Prevailing scholarly opinion connects it with a root meaning "to be strong." In the Hebrew Bible, Elohim is used both for the God of Israel and generically for the gods of the nations, and, in the Torah, Elohim is the name preferred by the tradition called Elohist (or E; in contrast to J which prefers YHVH).[3]

YHVH ("Lord") is the distinguishing name by which the Israelites called their God. After the theophany related here, in chapter

---

[2] Even as Joseph had said פָּקֹד־יִפְקֹד ("He will most assuredly take note of you," Gen. 50:24), now God says פָּקֹד פָּקַדְתִּי ("I have most assuredly [or "indeed"] taken note," as Exod. 3:16 should be rendered) [20].

[3] See commentary to Genesis 2:4–24.

3, Moses will bring the message of salvation to Israel as well as to Egypt, and the result of this mission will necessitate a further revelation of God, who (in chapter 6) will give to the old name YHVH a new dimension. (Its proper pronunciation, its linguistic derivation, and its meaning will therefore be treated there.)

In the first meeting with God, Moses is satisfied that his knowledge of the divine Name, that is, his knowledge of God's nature, will be sufficient to arm him for the mission ahead, though we are not told how a knowledge of the Name, if it was unknown to the people, would validate Moses' claim [22]. But, in any case, upon his inquiry he is not given the clear answer he seeks; instead he is told that the Lord may, in addition to being and continuing to be YHVH, also be known as Ehyeh or Ehyeh-Asher-Ehyeh. This revelation only deepens the mystery, for the new name is not further explained. Still, Moses makes no additional inquiry, and we may therefore assume that the name was meaningful to him, or at least that he believed he understood its import. What then was it? Over the centuries a number of answers have been attempted, though none has won universal acceptance.

Ehyeh (אֶהְיֶה) is quite evidently the first person singular of the word "to be" (הָיָה). One problem is that the tense is not clear; it could mean "I am" or "I will be" (or "I shall be"). This uncertainty is multiplied in the name Ehyeh-Asher-Ehyeh, for the first Ehyeh might be one tense (for instance, "I am") and the second another (for instance, "I will be"), or they might both be the same tense ("I am who I am" or "I will be who I will be"). To add to the difficulty, Asher could mean either "who" or "what."

The majority of the commentators have understood both occurrences of Ehyeh to convey the future tense and to mean: "I will be what tomorrow demands," that is, God emphasizes that He is capable of responding to human need. This was the message, they say, Moses was to take back to the enslaved people and thereby assure them that the God whom they called YHVH was also "Ehyeh," who would be ready in the near future to redeem them [23]. A variant interpretation was offered by S. R. Hirsch who saw a philosophical meaning in Ehyeh-Asher-Ehyeh: "I will be what I *want* to be," that is, God stresses His own freedom to act as He wills, in contrast to earthly creatures who are never totally free. But is it likely that Moses could take such an opaque message to the people and satisfy their thirst for the knowledge that God was still their God?[4]

It appears therefore that the impact of this story lies elsewhere. The most important factor to be taken into consideration is that, though Moses is given the new name to take back to Israel, not a single instance is reported in the Torah where he is shown to have actually used it. From this we can conclude that the revelation was never meant for the people at all, nor did Moses really inquire for the sake of the people: *Moses had asked for*

---

[4] Some have considered Ehyeh as a variant of YHVH, which is linguistically possible, though not likely. If YHVH is a third person singular and Ehyeh a first person variation, one could understand God to say: "I am Ehyeh (first person) the same whom you know as YHVH (third person)." In this intimate conversation with Moses He therefore uses this very personal way of speaking of himself, while usually He speaks of himself as the people know Him, in the third person, "I am YHVH." But this theory has the evident weakness that it reveals nothing new to Moses, and, further, that Moses never uses the name thereafter, that in fact the only other two times Ehyeh occurs in the Bible it may or may not mean God's name, as it does here (see Judg. 6:16 and Hos. 1:9).

himself, and the answer he receives is also meant for him—for God understands what Moses wants, and the very vagueness of His answer is purposeful. When Moses asks, "What shall I say to *them?"* he is asking to satisfy his own needs and does so by pretending to ask for the sake of others. This view alone makes it possible to arrive at a satisfactory interpretation of God's mysterious self-revelation. Moses wants to know the nature of God by inquiring about the inner meaning of His name, but God will not be fully known and therefore evades a clear answer. His response is intentionally vague, for it is a response to Moses only, and not a name suitable for communication. "You ask to know My name," God says, "and I will tell you: I am what I am, I will be what I will be. And when you tell your people of this experience tell them it is the same YHVH they know about." God reveals himself to Moses as He does to no other human being (Deut. 34:10), but even to Moses He shows himself wrapped in mystery. It is an aspect of God's freedom to conceal His essence, and hence Ehyeh-Asher-Ehyeh must remain elusive. Therefore, it is well to keep the divine response in its original form and, as our English translation does, convey it, untranslated and inexplicable, as Ehyeh-Asher-Ehyeh. The Midrash conveys a similar interpretation: while God is called by many names, He is what He is by virtue of His deeds. That is to say, you cannot really know Him until you experience Him in your own life [24].

In the unfolding tale of redemption this knowledge—or, rather, limitation of knowledge—which Moses grasps will prove to be insufficient. After the message of deliverance is brought to Israel and to Pharaoh, the people in their increased suffering and the king in his increased stubbornness lack a comprehension of God's might. God himself will therefore reveal another aspect of His name YHVH, and we shall learn of it at the second revelation, in chapter 6.[5]

---

[5] It has been suggested that the spiritual development of Moses was based on a model, namely, the religious revolution of Amenophis IV (1367–1350 B.C.E.). This pharaoh abolished the cult of Amon and introduced Aten as the supreme deity in the plenopy of gods. Aten was represented by the sun disc and the king incorporated the god's name into his own, calling himself Akhenaten. But the insight of the Divine which Moses gains is radically different from Akhenaten's views, for Moses is a true monotheist. As a religious innovator he stands alone and like a meteor bursts upon the consciousness of Israel and humanity.

GLEANINGS

The Shepherd

The Psalmist (11:5) says that God tries the righteous. By what? By having them tend the flocks.

When Moses was tending the flock of Jethro in the desert, a little kid escaped and reached a shady place near a pool of water. Moses ran after the kid and, seeing it drink, said: "I did not know that you ran away because you were thirsty. You must be weary." And he carried the kid back to the flock. Whereupon God said: "Because you showed such mercy, you will tend my flock Israel."

MIDRASH [25]

The Bush

A pagan once asked a rabbi: "Why did God choose a bush from which to appear?" He answered: "Had He appeared in a carob tree or a sycamore, you would have asked the same question. However, it would be wrong to let you go without a reply, so I will tell you why it was a bush: to teach you that no place is devoid of God's presence, not even a lowly bush."   MIDRASH [26]

Allegories

The burning bush was a symbol of the oppressed people, and the burning fire was a symbol of the oppressors; and the circumstance of the burning bush not being consumed was an emblem of the fact that the people thus oppressed would not be destroyed by those who were attacking them.   PHILO [27]

One can put a hand into a thornbush without being hurt, but when he tries to pull it out he cannot. So it was with Israel in Egypt: they were welcome at first but afterward could not leave. So it has been with Israel many times in the Diaspora.

N. LEIBOWITZ, AFTER A MIDRASH [28]

Just as a thornbush is a fence to gardens, so Israel is a fence (i.e., a moral protection) to the world.

MIDRASH [29]

The bush resembles the heart. It too can burn without being consumed.   MIDRASH [30]

Moses Moses

The Masoretic text omits a divider between these two words, while in similar cases it provides it. Thus we find Abraham/Abraham, or Jacob/Jacob, and Samuel/Samuel (Gen. 22:11; 46:2; I Sam. 3:10). But here we find Moses Moses, to show how urgent God's call was.

MIDRASH [31]

The Sandals

Moses is bidden to remove both his sandals (the Hebrew is in the plural). Why both, whereas in another instance Joshua is commanded to remove only "a sandal" (singular, Josh. 5:15)? One shoe is the body, the other is the human soul. Hence, in commanding Joshua to remove his shoe, God meant to tell him: If you wish to understand the ways of God and reach the level at which you will be able to behold Me, you must first cast off the urges of the body that conceal the spirit within. But to Moses, whose perception was so great that he might penetrate the inner chambers, God commanded that he divest himself not only of his physical urges but, so to speak, of his spirit as well. (Therefore, he was to remove both sandals.) Only then would God reveal himself to Moses.

MALBIM

Only when one is barefoot can one feel the little stones underfoot. Moses was to lead his people in such a way that he could feel their smallest sorrows.   CHASIDIC [32]

Gematria

The bush (הַסְּנֶה) stands for 120, hinting at the years Moses would live.　　　　　MIDRASH [33]

[Traditional Jewish writings have since Greek times used the 22 letters of the alphabet to express numbers. Thus א stood for 1; ב for 2; ק for 100. *Gematria* (derived from the Greek word either for "geometry" or more probably for "script," *grammateia*) was a semioccult method for arriving at hidden relationships through the medium of adding the numerical values of the Hebrew letters. הַסְּנֶה (the bush) would add up to 120: ה—5; ס—60; נ—50; ה—5.]

God warned Moses: "Do not come closer (הֲלֹם=75) for you are a priest (כֹּהֵן=75), and like a priest you must remove your shoes."　　　　　CHASIDIC [34]

God's seal is truth (according to talmudic gematria, אֱמֶת=441). Hence he is Ehyeh–multiplied (אֶהְיֶה=21; 21 x 21 =441).　　　　　CHASIDIC [35]

Ehyeh stands for 21. So do the first letters of Abraham (א=1), Isaac (י=10), and Jacob (י=10).　　　　　MIDRASH [36]

The Name

And God said, "At first say unto them, 'I am that I am,' that, when they have learnt that there is a difference between Him that is and him that is not, they may be further taught that there is no name whatever that can properly be assigned to Me, who am the only being to whom existence belongs."　　　　　PHILO [37]

The Prophet

The legend of the bush is the first in which signs play a part; Moses is given signs to confirm his mission. The Egyptian technical wonder is fundamentally recast; Israel's prophet performs miracles by the word of God. Moses learns YHVH's name, but not for magical purposes. This is typical of the entire saga; Moses never acts as an independent magician. On the contrary, he is helpless until the word of God comes to him. Moses is the archetype of the wonder-working prophet.

Y. KAUFMANN [38]

Hidden

God says that YHVH shall be His name "forever" (3:15). The Hebrew word לְעֹלָם is written without the usual ו (לְעוֹלָם) to indicate that it should be understood as לְעַלֵּם (to hide): no man should pronounce the Name according to its letters. Hence we pronounce it Adonai.

MIDRASH [39]

Hebrews (Exod. 3:18)

The word is here spelled as nowhere else in the Torah עִבְרִיִּים, that is, the singular is not, as usual, absorbed in the plural (עִבְרִים). Moses was to indicate to Pharaoh that though the Israelites were one people they consisted of individuals.

S. R. HIRSCH

Moses Was Slow of Speech

It was so ordained in order that people might not say that it was his eloquence which convinced Israel.　　　　　RABBENU NISSIM [40]

Moses was to speak the truth, unvarnished and without compromise. Being slow of speech he could do this better than had he been eloquent, for the eloquent speaker easily reacts to the opinions of an audience and tends to incorporate *their* ideas so that he be better appreciated.

S. R. HIRSCH [41]

The Rod

The Hebrew word מַטֶּה (*mateh*) is related to נָטָה (*natah*, to bend), that is, to humility. Moses had already shown this quality when he had said, "Who am I?" Therefore, humility was the rod he was to take to the people.　　　　　CHASIDIC [42]

Moses Recoiled

Had he not sinned by his disbelief, he would not have recoiled and fled, for sin and not a serpent is apt to bring danger and death.

MIDRASH [43]

Moses' Hand

It became "diseased" because he had slandered Israel, suggesting they would not believe. [In this midrash, as elsewhere in traditional sources, Moses is taken to task for his failure to trust his people unconditionally.]　　　　　MIDRASH [44]

An Allegory

The Lord asked Moses: "What is that in your hand? What power have you in your hand to wield as the leader of Israel?" And Moses replied: "A rod," implying that he would lead Israel with the rod of stern discipline. But then the Lord explained to him that rigid discipline is not the right way. Such a method turns into an insidious serpent, as it were; the people resent it and eventually revolt against their leader. It was only when Moses "recoiled before it," when he abandoned the stern approach entirely and resolved to lead his people with humility alone, that the Lord said to him: "Put out your hand and take it by the tail. There will be times when it will become necessary for you to make use of the rod, when kindness must be reinforced with discipline for, without some discipline, no leadership can endure."

PARDES YOSEF [45]

Fire

The text says literally that the anger of the Lord was kindled *in* Moses (בְּמֹשֶׁה). This shows Moses as a true leader, for the divine wrath must also burn within him.　　CHASIDIC [46]

The Moslem Tradition

[The Koran retells the story of Moses in great detail, in different parts of the book. In doing so, it has absorbed various midrashic materials. The account quoted here greatly condenses the biblical text.]

Verily, I am thy Lord: therefore pull off thy
　　shoes: for thou art in the holy valley of Towa.
And I have chosen thee: hearken then to what
　　shall be revealed.
Verily, I am God: there is no God but Me:
therefore worship Me, and observe prayer for
　　a remembrance of Me.
Verily the hour is coming:—I all but manifest
　　it—
That every soul may be recompensed for its
　　labors.
Nor let him who believeth not therein and
　　followeth his lust, turn thee aside from this
　　truth, and thou perish.
Now, what is that in thy right hand, O Moses?
Said he, "It is my staff on which I lean, and with
　　which I beat down leaves for my sheep,
　　and I have other uses for it."
He said, "Cast it down, O Moses!"
So he cast it down, and lo! it became a serpent
　　that ran along.
He said, "Lay hold on it, and fear not: to its
　　former state will We restore it.
Now place thy right hand to thy arm-pit: it shall
　　come forth white, but unhurt;—another
　　sign!—
That We may shew thee the greatest of our
　　signs.
Go to Pharaoh, for he hath burst all bounds."
He said, "O my Lord! enlarge my breast for me,
And make my work easy for me,
And loose the knot of my tongue,
That they may understand my speech.
And give me a counselor from among my
　　family,
Aaron my brother;
By him gird up my loins,
And make him a colleague in my work,
That we may praise Thee oft and oft remember
　　Thee,
For Thou regardest us."

KORAN [47]

Return

Although the Masoretic text makes no division at this place, it appears that a new chapter in the redemption story begins here. Moses now sets out with his family to return to Egypt. A strange incident takes place. God suddenly attacks the family and His wrath is averted only when Zipporah circumcises the child. Moses then proceeds to Egypt; he meets Aaron who will be his new adjutant; they bring God's message to Israel and meet with grateful acceptance; finally, they go to Pharaoh but now encounter rejection and consequently harsher treatment of the slaves. The increased burdens lead to the first of Israel's murmurings against the new leaders, foreshadowing the troubled nature of Moses' relationship with his people.

יט וַיֹּאמֶר יְהוָה אֶל־מֹשֶׁה בְּמִדְיָן לֵךְ שֻׁב מִצְרָיִם כִּי־ הַמֹּפְתִים אֲשֶׁר־שַׂמְתִּי בְיָדֶךָ וַעֲשִׂיתָם לִפְנֵי פַרְעֹה
כ מֵתוּ כָּל־הָאֲנָשִׁים הַמְבַקְשִׁים אֶת־נַפְשֶׁךָ: וַיִּקַּח מֹשֶׁה וַאֲנִי אֲחַזֵּק אֶת־לִבּוֹ וְלֹא יְשַׁלַּח אֶת־הָעָם: וְאָמַרְתָּ
אֶת־אִשְׁתּוֹ וְאֶת־בָּנָיו וַיַּרְכִּבֵם עַל־הַחֲמֹר וַיָּשָׁב אַרְצָה אֶל־פַּרְעֹה כֹּה אָמַר יְהוָה בְּנִי בְכֹרִי יִשְׂרָאֵל: וָאֹמַר
כא מִצְרָיִם וַיִּקַּח מֹשֶׁה אֶת־מַטֵּה הָאֱלֹהִים בְּיָדוֹ: וַיֹּאמֶר אֵלֶיךָ שַׁלַּח אֶת־בְּנִי וְיַעַבְדֵנִי וַתְּמָאֵן לְשַׁלְּחוֹ הִנֵּה
יְהוָה אֶל־מֹשֶׁה בְּלֶכְתְּךָ לָשׁוּב מִצְרַיְמָה רְאֵה כָּל־ אָנֹכִי הֹרֵג אֶת־בִּנְךָ בְּכֹרֶךָ: וַיְהִי בַדֶּרֶךְ בַּמָּלוֹן

19] The LORD said to Moses in Midian, "Go back to Egypt, for all the men who sought to kill you are dead." **20]** So Moses took his wife and sons, mounted them on an ass, and went back to the land of Egypt; and Moses took the rod of God in his hand.

21] And the LORD said to Moses, "When you return to Egypt, see that you perform before Pharaoh all the marvels that I have put within your power. I, however, will stiffen his heart so that he will not let the people go. **22]** Then you shall say to Pharaoh, 'Thus says the LORD: Israel is My first-born son. **23]** I have said to you, "Let My son go, that he may worship Me," yet you refuse to let him go. Now I will slay your first-born son.'"

24] At a night encampment on the way, the LORD encountered him and sought to kill

4:19] *The Lord said.* This sentence and what follows appear not to fit with what preceded, hence Ibn Ezra suggests that the talmudic principle applies here, "There is no earlier and later in the Torah" (that is, narrative and chronological order do not necessarily coincide). Others have assumed that in verse 18 Moses announced his future intention, and in verse 19 the actual leaving is described.

All the men . . . are dead. Including, most likely, the Pharaoh. How much time Moses spent in Midian cannot be ascertained. The Torah says that he was eighty years old when he returned to Egypt and one hundred and twenty when he died (after forty years of Israel's wandering; Exod. 7:7; Deut. 34:7). Though tradition generally held him to be forty when he fled Egypt, one midrash speculated that Moses was very young at the time. This was based on interpreting 2:14 as reading: "Who made you a *man* already [seeing you are only a child]?" [1].

20] *Sons.* So far, we have heard only of Gershom (2:22) and not until later (18:4) are we told of Eliezer, the second son.

Mounted them on an ass. This literary image is evoked repeatedly in ancient literature for departures of crucial impact; in the Torah, compare, for instance, Abraham's departure for Moriah to sacrifice his son (Gen. 22:3); in Christian Scriptures, Jesus' entrance into Jerusalem [2].

21] *Perform before Pharaoh.* This is the first intimation that the signs are not meant exclusively for Israel.

22] *Israel is My first-born son.* In the scheme of spiritual inheritance. The violation of God's first-born will be punished through the death of Egypt's first-born (verse 23).

23] *I will slay.* Telescoping what follows [3].

24] *Sought.* Or perhaps "threatened" [4].

To kill him. It is possible that God's intent was seen in a serious illness which befell the victim [5]. The text is not clear whether it was Moses who was threatened or whether it was his son [6]. (See commentary below.)

411

כה וַיִּפְגְּשֵׁהוּ יְהֹוָה וַיְבַקֵּשׁ הֲמִיתוֹ: וַתִּקַּח צִפֹּרָה צֹר
וַתִּכְרֹת אֶת־עָרְלַת בְּנָהּ וַתַּגַּע לְרַגְלָיו וַתֹּאמֶר כִּי
כו חֲתַן־דָּמִים אַתָּה לִי: וַיִּרֶף מִמֶּנּוּ אָז אָמְרָה חֲתַן
דָּמִים לַמּוּלֹת: פ

כז וַיֹּאמֶר יְהֹוָה אֶל־אַהֲרֹן לֵךְ לִקְרַאת מֹשֶׁה הַמִּדְבָּרָה
כח וַיֵּלֶךְ וַיִּפְגְּשֵׁהוּ בְּהַר הָאֱלֹהִים וַיִּשַּׁק־לוֹ: וַיַּגֵּד מֹשֶׁה
לְאַהֲרֹן אֵת כָּל־דִּבְרֵי יְהֹוָה אֲשֶׁר שְׁלָחוֹ וְאֵת כָּל־
כט הָאֹתֹת אֲשֶׁר צִוָּהוּ: וַיֵּלֶךְ מֹשֶׁה וְאַהֲרֹן וַיַּאַסְפוּ אֶת־

ל כָּל־זִקְנֵי בְּנֵי יִשְׂרָאֵל: וַיְדַבֵּר אַהֲרֹן אֵת כָּל־הַדְּבָרִים
אֲשֶׁר־דִּבֶּר יְהֹוָה אֶל־מֹשֶׁה וַיַּעַשׂ הָאֹתֹת לְעֵינֵי הָעָם:
לא וַיַּאֲמֵן הָעָם וַיִּשְׁמְעוּ כִּי־פָקַד יְהֹוָה אֶת־בְּנֵי יִשְׂרָאֵל
וְכִי רָאָה אֶת־עָנְיָם וַיִּקְּדוּ וַיִּשְׁתַּחֲווּ:

א וְאַחַר בָּאוּ מֹשֶׁה וְאַהֲרֹן וַיֹּאמְרוּ אֶל־פַּרְעֹה כֹּה־
אָמַר יְהֹוָה אֱלֹהֵי יִשְׂרָאֵל שַׁלַּח אֶת־עַמִּי וְיָחֹגּוּ לִי
ב בַּמִּדְבָּר: וַיֹּאמֶר פַּרְעֹה מִי יְהֹוָה אֲשֶׁר אֶשְׁמַע בְּקֹלוֹ
לְשַׁלַּח אֶת־יִשְׂרָאֵל לֹא יָדַעְתִּי אֶת־יְהֹוָה וְגַם אֶת־

him. 25] So Zipporah took a flint and cut off her son's foreskin, and touched his legs with it, saying, "You are truly a bridegroom of blood to me!" 26] And when He let him alone, she added, "A bridegroom of blood because of the circumcision."

27] The LORD said to Aaron, "Go to meet Moses in the wilderness." He went and met him at the mountain of God, and he kissed him. 28] Moses told Aaron about all the things that the LORD had committed to him and all the signs about which He had instructed him. 29] Then Moses and Aaron went and assembled all the elders of the Israelites. 30] Aaron repeated all the words that the LORD had spoken to Moses, and he performed the signs in the sight of the people, 31] and the people were convinced. When they heard that the LORD had taken note of the Israelites and that He had seen their plight, they bowed low in homage.

1] Afterward Moses and Aaron went and said to Pharaoh, "Thus says the LORD, the God of Israel: Let My people go that they may celebrate a festival for Me in the wilderness." 2] But Pharaoh said, "Who is the LORD that I should heed Him and let Israel go? I do not know the

25] *Flint.* In Moses' and Joshua's time (Josh. 5:2, 3) the ceremony may still have been performed with ancient, pre–Bronze Age instruments.

His legs. The text leaves us uncertain whether Moses' or the son's are meant [7]. Furthermore, "legs" may be a euphemism for genitals.

26] *Bridegroom of blood.* The word חָתָן (*chatan*) is related to the Arabic *chatana*, a circumciser, suggesting that there was a connection between marriage and circumcision. H. Junker has shown that in the Arabic realm circumcision was a prerequisite for marriage (hence the etymological bond). The rite resembled the bringing of first fruits and represented an offering of blood which cleansed and atoned [8]. Moses' family apparently turned back after this incident (18:2).

27] *The Lord said to Aaron.* The text registers no reaction by Aaron to this direct, and apparently first, divine address.

At the mountain of God. Where Moses had received his original revelation (3:1). This account suggests that the mountain lay between Midian and Egypt.

30] *He performed.* Surprisingly Aaron, rather than Moses, performs the signs [9].

5:1] *Said to Pharaoh.* The text says nothing about the way two members of a slave nation might come to speak to the king, for it is apparently interested only in the developing confrontation and the unfolding of the events foretold at the burning bush.

A festival for Me. Moses and Aaron appear to allude to an observance known to the Israelites. This first request made of Pharaoh is relatively modest, as if to test him.

2] *Who is the Lord . . .?* The main theme of the confrontation is stated at the outset: While Pharaoh asserts that no power is superior to his, subsequent events will show this to be a blasphemous presumption.

ה יִשְׂרָאֵל לֹא אֲשַׁלֵּחַ: וַיֹּאמְרוּ אֱלֹהֵי הָעִבְרִים נִקְרָא
עָלֵינוּ נֵלְכָה נָּא דֶּרֶךְ שְׁלֹשֶׁת יָמִים בַּמִּדְבָּר וְנִזְבְּחָה
ד לַיהוָה אֱלֹהֵינוּ פֶּן־יִפְגָּעֵנוּ בַּדֶּבֶר אוֹ בֶחָרֶב: וַיֹּאמֶר
אֲלֵהֶם מֶלֶךְ מִצְרַיִם לָמָּה מֹשֶׁה וְאַהֲרֹן תַּפְרִיעוּ
ה אֶת־הָעָם מִמַּעֲשָׂיו לְכוּ לְסִבְלֹתֵיכֶם: וַיֹּאמֶר פַּרְעֹה
הֵן־רַבִּים עַתָּה עַם הָאָרֶץ וְהִשְׁבַּתֶּם אֹתָם מִסִּבְלֹתָם:
ו וַיְצַו פַּרְעֹה בַּיּוֹם הַהוּא אֶת־הַנֹּגְשִׂים בָּעָם וְאֶת־
ז שֹׁטְרָיו לֵאמֹר: לֹא תֹאסִפוּן לָתֵת תֶּבֶן לָעָם לִלְבֹּן
הַלְּבֵנִים כִּתְמוֹל שִׁלְשֹׁם הֵם יֵלְכוּ וְקֹשְׁשׁוּ לָהֶם תֶּבֶן:
ח וְאֶת־מַתְכֹּנֶת הַלְּבֵנִים אֲשֶׁר הֵם עֹשִׂים תְּמוֹל שִׁלְשֹׁם
תָּשִׂימוּ עֲלֵיהֶם לֹא תִגְרְעוּ מִמֶּנּוּ כִּי־נִרְפִּים הֵם עַל־כֵּן

ט הֵם צֹעֲקִים לֵאמֹר נֵלְכָה נִזְבְּחָה לֵאלֹהֵינוּ: תִּכְבַּד
הָעֲבֹדָה עַל־הָאֲנָשִׁים וְיַעֲשׂוּ־בָהּ וְאַל־יִשְׁעוּ בְּדִבְרֵי־
י שָׁקֶר: וַיֵּצְאוּ נֹגְשֵׂי הָעָם וְשֹׁטְרָיו וַיֹּאמְרוּ אֶל־הָעָם
יא לֵאמֹר כֹּה אָמַר פַּרְעֹה אֵינֶנִּי נֹתֵן לָכֶם תֶּבֶן: אַתֶּם
לְכוּ קְחוּ לָכֶם תֶּבֶן מֵאֲשֶׁר תִּמְצָאוּ כִּי אֵין נִגְרָע
יב מֵעֲבֹדַתְכֶם דָּבָר: וַיָּפֶץ הָעָם בְּכָל־אֶרֶץ מִצְרָיִם
יג לְקֹשֵׁשׁ קַשׁ לַתֶּבֶן: וְהַנֹּגְשִׂים אָצִים לֵאמֹר כַּלּוּ
מַעֲשֵׂיכֶם דְּבַר־יוֹם בְּיוֹמוֹ כַּאֲשֶׁר בִּהְיוֹת הַתֶּבֶן:
יד וַיֻּכּוּ שֹׁטְרֵי בְּנֵי יִשְׂרָאֵל אֲשֶׁר־שָׂמוּ עֲלֵהֶם נֹגְשֵׂי פַּרְעֹה
לֵאמֹר מַדּוּעַ לֹא כִלִּיתֶם חָקְכֶם לִלְבֹּן כִּתְמוֹל
טו שִׁלְשֹׁם גַּם־תְּמוֹל גַּם־הַיּוֹם: וַיָּבֹאוּ שֹׁטְרֵי בְּנֵי יִשְׂרָאֵל

LORD, nor will I let Israel go." **3]** They answered, "The God of the Hebrews has manifested Himself to us. Let us go, we pray, a distance of three days into the wilderness to sacrifice to the LORD our God, lest He strike us with pestilence or sword." **4]** But the king of Egypt said to them, "Moses and Aaron, why do you distract the people from their tasks? Get to your labors!" **5]** And Pharaoh continued, "The people of the land are already so numerous, and you would have them cease from their labors!"

6] That same day Pharaoh charged the taskmasters and foremen of the people, saying, **7]** "You shall no longer provide the people with straw for making bricks as heretofore; let them go and gather straw for themselves. **8]** But impose upon them the same quota of bricks as they have been making heretofore; do not reduce it, for they are shirkers; that is why they cry, 'Let us go and sacrifice to our God!' **9]** Let heavier work be laid upon the men; let them keep at it and not pay attention to deceitful promises."

10] So the taskmasters and foremen of the people went out and said to the people, "Thus says Pharaoh: I will not give you any straw. **11]** You must go and get the straw yourselves wherever you can find it; but there shall be no decrease whatever in your work." **12]** Then the people scattered throughout the land of Egypt to gather stubble for straw. **13]** And the taskmasters pressed them, saying, "You must complete the same work assignment each day as when you had straw." **14]** And the foremen of the Israelites, whom Pharaoh's taskmasters had set over them, were beaten. "Why," they were asked, "did you not complete the prescribed amount of bricks, either yesterday or today, as you did before?"

3] *Lest He strike us.* Nonperformance of a religious duty was believed to provoke divine wrath.

5] *So numerous.* The loss of their labor would be staggering.

7] *Bricks.* They were larger than those commonly manufactured nowadays (about 15 x 7 x 4 1/2 in., or 37.5 x 17.5 x 11.25 cm) and were made of mud from the Nile mixed with chopped straw or reeds and dried in the sun. A painting from an Egyptian tomb at Thebes, of the fifteenth century B.C.E., shows laborers making bricks [10].

14] *Foremen of the Israelites.* That is, Israelites who were to control their own people. (Such practices were also in vogue with the Nazis, who frequently appointed Jewish police in their labor and concentration camps.)

וַיִּצְעֲקוּ אֶל־פַּרְעֹה לֵאמֹר לָמָּה תַעֲשֶׂה כֹה לַעֲבָדֶיךָ: אֲשֶׁר הִבְאַשְׁתֶּם אֶת־רֵיחֵנוּ בְּעֵינֵי פַרְעֹה וּבְעֵינֵי עֲבָדָיו

טז תֶּבֶן אֵין נִתָּן לַעֲבָדֶיךָ וּלְבֵנִים אֹמְרִים לָנוּ עֲשׂוּ וְהִנֵּה לָתֶת־חֶרֶב בְּיָדָם לְהָרְגֵנוּ: וַיָּשָׁב מֹשֶׁה אֶל־יְהֹוָה

עֲבָדֶיךָ מֻכִּים וְחָטָאת עַמֶּךָ: וַיֹּאמֶר נִרְפִּים אַתֶּם וַיֹּאמַר אֲדֹנָי לָמָה הֲרֵעֹתָה לָעָם הַזֶּה לָמָּה זֶּה

נִרְפִּים עַל־כֵּן אַתֶּם אֹמְרִים נֵלְכָה נִזְבְּחָה לַיהֹוָה: שְׁלַחְתָּנִי: וּמֵאָז בָּאתִי אֶל־פַּרְעֹה לְדַבֵּר בִּשְׁמֶךָ הֵרַע

יח וְעַתָּה לְכוּ עִבְדוּ וְתֶבֶן לֹא־יִנָּתֵן לָכֶם וְתֹכֶן לְבֵנִים לָעָם הַזֶּה וְהַצֵּל לֹא־הִצַּלְתָּ אֶת־עַמֶּךָ:

יט תִּתֵּנוּ: וַיִּרְאוּ שֹׁטְרֵי בְנֵי־יִשְׂרָאֵל אֹתָם בְּרָע לֵאמֹר וַיֹּאמֶר יְהֹוָה אֶל־מֹשֶׁה עַתָּה תִרְאֶה אֲשֶׁר אֶעֱשֶׂה

כ לֹא־תִגְרְעוּ מִלִּבְנֵיכֶם דְּבַר־יוֹם בְּיוֹמוֹ: וַיִּפְגְּעוּ אֶת־ לְפַרְעֹה כִּי בְיָד חֲזָקָה יְשַׁלְּחֵם וּבְיָד חֲזָקָה יְגָרְשֵׁם

מֹשֶׁה וְאֶת־אַהֲרֹן נִצָּבִים לִקְרָאתָם בְּצֵאתָם מֵאֵת מֵאַרְצוֹ:

כא פַּרְעֹה: וַיֹּאמְרוּ אֲלֵהֶם יֵרֶא יְהֹוָה עֲלֵיכֶם וְיִשְׁפֹּט

Haftarah Shemot, p. 692

15] Then the Israelite foremen came to Pharaoh and cried: "Why do you deal thus with your servants? 16] No straw is issued to your servants, yet they demand of us: Make bricks! Thus your servants are being beaten, when the fault is with your own people." 17] He replied, "You are shirkers, shirkers! That is why you say, 'Let us go and sacrifice to the LORD.' 18] Be off now to your work! No straw shall be issued to you, but you must produce your quota of bricks!"

19] Now the foremen of the Israelites found themselves in trouble because of the order, "You must not reduce your daily quantity of bricks." 20] As they left Pharaoh's presence, they came upon Moses and Aaron standing in their path, 21] and they said to them, "May the LORD look upon you and punish you for making us loathsome to Pharaoh and his courtiers— putting a sword in their hands to slay us." 22] Then Moses returned to the LORD and said, "O Lord, why did You bring harm upon this people? Why did You send me? 23] Ever since I came to Pharaoh to speak in Your name, he has dealt worse with this people; and still You have not delivered Your people."

1] Then the LORD said to Moses, "You shall soon see what I will do to Pharaoh: he shall let them go because of a greater might; indeed, because of a greater might he shall drive them from his land."

6:1] *Because of a greater might.* Better, "only if forced" (see at 3:19).

The Bridegroom of Blood

There can be little doubt that the cryptic telling of this incident represents a contraction of an originally fuller tale. The abbreviation was probably due to the anthropomorphic nature of the story, which resembles the attack a divine agent made on Jacob (Gen. 32:25 ff.), but lacks the earlier tale's figurative overtones [11]. In both cases the demonic aspect is prominent: both Jacob and Moses are on their way home; as in similar ancient tales both heroes, on their return, have to master some challenge; and both have to overcome an onslaught by mysterious powers that block their way.[1] But beyond this, while in the tale of Jacob "the man" who wrestles with him is an ambiguous figure, the tale of Moses is itself highly ambiguous and open to various explanations. The major problem arises from the lack of identifiable subjects: we cannot be sure who was attacked (Moses or his son, and, if the latter, which one); who was the assailant (God or an unnamed messenger as in the Jacob story); and to whose legs the foreskin was touched (Moses' or the child's).

Nor can we be certain that it was the son's circumcision that was at stake. It has been suggested that Moses himself had never been subjected to the rite and that his son's circumcision was here substituted for his own. This may be hinted at in the Torah, for when describing the speech defect of Moses it calls him twice a man of "uncircumcised lips" (6:12, 30); thus the expression "bridegroom of blood" may refer to Moses. This explanation is made quite plausible by the etymological relationship, in Arabic, of circumcision and bridegroom (see 4:26). If indeed Moses had never been circumcised, then the passage might be understood as follows: At a night encampment on the way, the Lord encountered Moses and made him deathly ill (4:24). So Zipporah took a flint and cut off her son's foreskin and touched Moses' genitals with it, saying [to Moses], "You are now truly for me a bridegroom [cleansed by the blood of this substitute circumcision]" (4:25). And when Moses recovered she said: "Bridegroom of blood at circumcision" (4:26) [13]. The biblical story may thus be related to the tale of David wooing Michal, King Saul's daughter, with the offering of two hundred Philistine foreskins (I Sam. 18:20 ff.).[2]

The majority of commentators have held, however, that Moses' omission to have his child circumcised was the reason for the attack and that God, through a messenger, was the one who threatened to punish him [17]. Moses, so it is argued, had lived

---

[1] Buber writes: "We know from the life of the founders of religions . . . that there is such an 'event of the night'; the sudden collapse of the newly won certainty, the 'deadly factual' moment when the demon working with apparently unbounded authority appears in the world where God had been in control but a moment before. . . . The account of the manner in which YHVH meets Moses as a demon . . . is the unmistakable language of a tradition which also points to the obscure yet perceptible threshold of experience" [12].

[2] In a somewhat different vein Theodor Reik views the incident as the continuation of Moses' initiation, which had begun at the burning bush—a highly speculative theory, especially when seen as an aspect of the whole psychoanalytic interpretation of the Exodus [14]. An entirely different solution is proposed by Julian Morgenstern, who construes the ceremony as one by which Zipporah leaves her clan and joins that of Moses [15]. According to Beer, it was Zipporah who here introduces circumcision as a magic rite, after overpowering the demon who battled for the *jus primae noctis*. According to this theory, the incident was originally a wedding night tale and forms "one of the oldest and rawest stories" [16]. In such a setting the blood of the male bridegroom may be seen to match that of the woman's hymen.

under Midianite law—hence the child was called *her* son—and circumcision of young children may not have been the custom in that land.[3] For this reason also, says the Midrash, Moses called his first-born *Gershom* ("I was a stranger there") and his second son, who was presumably born outside Midian and therefore circumcised properly, *Eliezer* ("My God is help") [18]. All in all, this incident is said to highlight the overriding importance of the sacred rite which is greater than that of any man, even a Moses [19].

The most likely meaning of the story, however, is to be found elsewhere and can, in fact, be deduced from the context. Immediately preceding is the statement that Israel is God's first-born son and that, because Pharaoh will refuse to grant him freedom to worship, his own first-born will be taken. Moses now is on his way to deliver this dictum, and on this bridge between message and confrontation his own first-born is brought into the orbit of God's claim. Gershom, like all Israel's first-born later on, is God's own, and his blood averts the angel of death even as the blood on the doorposts will later avert calamity from the first-born of Israel. We have here, then, a tale which, though all too brief in its present form, is filled with the symbolism of the first-born, from Pharaoh to Israel to Moses—all leading to the climactic and dark events of the night of reckoning in Egypt.[4]

Pharaoh's Hardened Heart

Beginning with 4:21 the Torah tells us ten times that God intends to harden or stiffen Pharaoh's heart, which is to say, to make his intellect resistant to change. (In biblical times the heart was believed to be the seat of the intellect and the reins the seat of the emotions.)[5] Already in ancient days this divine plan puzzled readers of the Bible, for, if God made Pharaoh resistant to repentance, why punish him and wherein lay his guilt? The Midrash asked: "Does this not afford an opening to heretics?" [21].

Since it is a fundamental assumption of the Bible that man has a choice between good and evil, it seemed necessary to adduce special reasons that would justify this apparent breach of principle. These explanations, with some variations, say that Pharaoh had already sinned severely—by killing the infants—and therefore deserved his punishment and that when a man continues to act wickedly he will reach a point of no return. This is the way God has arranged man's moral structure, and in that sense He may be said to stiffen the human heart. Moral depravity may become irreversible, and that was the way it was with Pharaoh. God merely informs Moses of what He knows is bound to happen.

But it cannot be denied that the straightforward text, with its ten-fold repetition, makes the will of God pivotal to the story, and that therefore all explanations attempt-

---

[3] This is not, however, certain. To be sure, circumcised phalli have been found throughout the Near East, but they have not been traced to Midian. On the other hand, Midianites are never called "uncircumcised ones," as are the Philistines.

[4] The connection between the Passover sacrifice and the first-born is stated in Exod. 13:15; to this day, Jewish first-born sons of traditional families observe the day before Passover as a fast day, and the concept that all of Israel's first-born belong to God (Num. 3:13) survives in the rite of *pidyon ha-ben* [20].

[5] The same theme occurs also in other biblical passages: Deut. 2:30; Josh. 11:20; I Sam. 6:6. The Torah uses three roots קשה, חזק, כבד for harden or stiffen.

ing to "absolve" God will remain forced. Their failure to solve the problem of free will in the story lies in the simple fact that, when the Torah told of God's intent to harden Pharaoh's heart, its focus was not on the problem of free will but on its main intent: to praise the absolute power and unsurpassable glory of God. This above all else is the main theme of the Book of Exodus. Moses might appear like a god to Pharaoh, but he merely represents the real God. Of course, the Bible does not deny man his moral choices, but all history stands ultimately under God's will and all men can move only within the framework of His design. The Exodus from Egypt was the hinge of Israel's fate, and in the end God alone brought it to turn.[6]

The story as we find it is therefore not concerned with theological contradictions and niceties. As in so many other places, the Torah is capable of letting divergent points of view stand next to each other without finding it necessary to reconcile them.[7] The focus of the story is God's redemptive power, and the image presented tells of His assurance that whatever obstacles Moses and Israel may find in their way—especially a cruel Pharaoh who will not relent—God has already taken them into account and will in fact make them occasions for showing His glory before men. This is subtly but clearly underscored by one of the Torah's favorite means for such a purpose, the use of a key word that conveys a double meaning. For one of the words meaning "to stiffen" is כבד, and this word means also "to honor." In the final act of salvation, at the Reed Sea, God will *stiffen* Pharaoh's and Egypt's heart and thereby assert His authority and gain Him *honor* and glory (Exod. 14:4, 17). This was recognized long ago by a midrash: "God said to Pharaoh, 'You sinner! With the same word with which you prove yourself recalcitrant I will glorify Myself' " [23]. Free will is never at issue, for to deny man his ability to make moral decisions would be wholly at variance with all biblical thought. The linking of Pharaoh's and Israel's free volition should be enough to assuage one's doubts. "The Israelites would not listen to me," says Moses; "how then should Pharaoh heed me?" (6:12).

Within limits, all men are free, and so is God, but His freedom prevails over man's. He had promised freedom from bondage, and the fulfillment of His promise involved the lives, the thoughts, and the actions of men and nations.

---

[6] A related, though somewhat different, point of view is presented by M. Tsevat. He holds that ascribing Pharaoh's recalcitrance to God was another way of saying that it was inexplicable on grounds of normal human thought [22].

[7] See General Introduction to the Torah, "How the Torah Came to Be Written."

GLEANINGS

The Encounter on the Way

The incident is to be understood figuratively in part. Moses' concentration on God had weakened "on the way" (i.e., as time went on), and the encounter brought him back to his task.   MALBIM

Neglect

So great is the command to circumcise that Moses, who neglected it for a single hour, courted death, and all his other merits availed him nothing.   MIDRASH [24]

Lest He Strike Us (Exod. 5:3)

They did not say, "Lest He strike *you* (Pharaoh) with pestilence." Even in their adversary position Moses and Aaron showed respect to the ruler.   MIDRASH [25]

The Unbeliever

The run-of-the-mill atheist usually forsakes his disbelief when adversity strikes him; then he turns to God for help. But Pharaoh was a true unbeliever; he held out to the end saying, "Who is the Lord?"   CHASIDIC [26]

Two Questions

In his distress, Moses asks two questions of God (5:22): "Why did You bring harm upon this people?" and "Why did You select me?" To the second question he received an answer: his mission was part of the salvational scheme, but no reply was ever given to the first, that is, why Israel was tried by suffering. There is never an answer to this, for the ways of God are never fully disclosed.   CHASIDIC [27]

According to an old manuscript, there is, however, an explanation: the harm that comes to Israel is really meant for God. Whenever Israel is seen to represent the will of God it will most likely be subject to persecution by nations who wish to oppose Him. One of the explanations for the virulence of nazism runs along these lines. The extermination of Jews was subconsciously an attempt to "exterminate" the God of the Jews. [28]

Salvation

The Sages say that redemption will not come until all men despair of it. So here: all Israel despaired except Moses. But when even he said to God, "Still you have not delivered Your people" (5:23), God responded: "You shall soon see" (6:1).   J. PATZNOWSKI [29]

The Islamic Version

[The following excerpts are particularly clear examples of how in Islam's Holy Writ the biblical stories have been retold in "midrashic" fashion. In the first selection Moses requires Aaron for fear of being treated as an impostor, and in the second Moses admits that he erred in slaying the Egyptian.]

He (Moses) said, "Oh, my Lord! truly I have slain one of them, therefore I fear lest they slay me.

My brother Aaron is clearer of speech than I. Send him, therefore, with me as a help, and to make good my cause, for I fear lest they treat me as an impostor. . . ."

He (Pharaoh) said, "Did we not rear these among us when a child? And hast thou not passed years of thy life among us?

And yet what a deed is that which thou hast done! Thou art one of the ungrateful."

He said, "I did it indeed, and I was one of those who erred: And I fled from you because I feared you; but my Lord hath given me wisdom and hath made me one of His Apostles. . . ."

KORAN [30]

418

The Second Revelation

Before proceeding with the tale of redemption the text introduces a
brief review of what has happened until now. It then goes on to firm
up the position of Moses and Aaron by giving us their genealogy; thereafter the leaders return to Pharaoh, with Aaron performing the rod-and-
serpent sign. God's name YHVH is once more revealed, but as one that
was not known to the Patriarchs; but when Moses brings this insight to
his brethren they do not listen to him. He enters another demurrer to his
role of leadership and bases it again on his impeded speech which, he
claims, cannot overcome Pharaoh's resistance (and not Israel's, as before).
Finally, the stiffening of Pharaoh's heart is given a specific reason: it is to
provide God with an occasion to multiply His signs and marvels.

The revelation of the name YHVH stands at the core of this section
and indeed, if we understand it properly, presents us with an important
insight into the development of the God concept. Chapter 6 tells us about
the unique God of Israel and may be seen to describe the beginnings
of monotheism. It also provides the divine motivation for the later onset
of the plagues. Both this chapter and chapter 3 deal with aspects of God's
name and nature and are most likely variant traditions of the same theme.

(A new weekly portion, *Va'era*, begins here. The final verses, 7:8–13,
are a bridge to the story of the plagues.)

ס ס ס   ח מִצְרָיִם: וְהֵבֵאתִי אֶתְכֶם אֶל־הָאָרֶץ אֲשֶׁר נָשָׂאתִי אֶת־

ב וַיְדַבֵּר אֱלֹהִים אֶל־מֹשֶׁה וַיֹּאמֶר אֵלָיו אֲנִי יְהוָה: יָדִי לָתֵת אֹתָהּ לְאַבְרָהָם לְיִצְחָק וּלְיַעֲקֹב וְנָתַתִּי

ג וָאֵרָא אֶל־אַבְרָהָם אֶל־יִצְחָק וְאֶל־יַעֲקֹב בְּאֵל שַׁדָּי   אֹתָהּ לָכֶם מוֹרָשָׁה אֲנִי יְהוָה: ט וַיְדַבֵּר מֹשֶׁה כֵּן אֶל־

ד וּשְׁמִי יְהוָה לֹא נוֹדַעְתִּי לָהֶם: וְגַם הֲקִמֹתִי אֶת־בְּרִיתִי   בְּנֵי יִשְׂרָאֵל וְלֹא שָׁמְעוּ אֶל־מֹשֶׁה מִקֹּצֶר רוּחַ וּמֵעֲבֹדָה

אִתָּם לָתֵת לָהֶם אֶת־אֶרֶץ כְּנָעַן אֵת אֶרֶץ מְגֻרֵיהֶם   קָשָׁה: פ

ה אֲשֶׁר־גָּרוּ בָהּ: וְגַם אֲנִי שָׁמַעְתִּי אֶת־נַאֲקַת בְּנֵי יִשְׂרָאֵל   י וַיְדַבֵּר יְהוָה אֶל־מֹשֶׁה לֵּאמֹר: בֹּא דַבֵּר אֶל־פַּרְעֹה

ו אֲשֶׁר מִצְרַיִם מַעֲבִדִים אֹתָם וָאֶזְכֹּר אֶת־בְּרִיתִי: לָכֵן   יב מֶלֶךְ מִצְרָיִם וִישַׁלַּח אֶת־בְּנֵי־יִשְׂרָאֵל מֵאַרְצוֹ: וַיְדַבֵּר

אֱמֹר לִבְנֵי־יִשְׂרָאֵל אֲנִי יְהוָה וְהוֹצֵאתִי אֶתְכֶם מִתַּחַת   מֹשֶׁה לִפְנֵי יְהוָה לֵאמֹר הֵן בְּנֵי־יִשְׂרָאֵל לֹא־שָׁמְעוּ

סִבְלֹת מִצְרַיִם וְהִצַּלְתִּי אֶתְכֶם מֵעֲבֹדָתָם וְגָאַלְתִּי   אֵלַי וְאֵיךְ יִשְׁמָעֵנִי פַרְעֹה וַאֲנִי עֲרַל שְׂפָתָיִם: פ

ז אֶתְכֶם בִּזְרוֹעַ נְטוּיָה וּבִשְׁפָטִים גְּדֹלִים: וְלָקַחְתִּי   יג וַיְדַבֵּר יְהוָה אֶל־מֹשֶׁה וְאֶל־אַהֲרֹן וַיְצַוֵּם אֶל־בְּנֵי

אֶתְכֶם לִי לְעָם וְהָיִיתִי לָכֶם לֵאלֹהִים וִידַעְתֶּם כִּי   יִשְׂרָאֵל וְאֶל־פַּרְעֹה מֶלֶךְ מִצְרָיִם לְהוֹצִיא אֶת־בְּנֵי־

אֲנִי יְהוָה אֱלֹהֵיכֶם הַמּוֹצִיא אֶתְכֶם מִתַּחַת סִבְלוֹת   יד יִשְׂרָאֵל מֵאֶרֶץ מִצְרָיִם: ס אֵלֶּה רָאשֵׁי בֵית־אֲבֹתָם

2] God spoke to Moses and said to him, "I am the LORD. **3]** I appeared to Abraham, Isaac, and Jacob as El Shaddai, but I did not make Myself known to them by My name יהוה. **4]** I also established My covenant with them, to give them the land of Canaan, the land in which they lived as sojourners. **5]** I have now heard the moaning of the Israelites because the Egyptians are holding them in bondage, and I have remembered My covenant. **6]** Say, therefore, to the Israelite people: I am the LORD. I will free you from the burdens of the Egyptians and deliver you from their bondage. I will redeem you with an outstretched arm and through extraordinary chastisements. **7]** And I will take you to be My people, and I will be your God. And you shall know that I, the LORD, am your God who freed you from the labors of the Egyptians. **8]** I will bring you into the land which I swore to give to Abraham, Isaac, and Jacob, and I will give it to you for a possession, I the LORD." **9]** But when Moses told this to the Israelites, they would not listen to Moses, their spirits crushed by cruel bondage.

10] The LORD spoke to Moses, saying, **11]** "Go and tell Pharaoh king of Egypt to let the Israelites depart from his land." **12]** But Moses appealed to the LORD, saying, "The Israelites would not listen to me; how then should Pharaoh heed me, a man of impeded speech!"

13] So the LORD spoke to both Moses and Aaron in regard to the Israelites and Pharaoh king of Egypt, instructing them to deliver the Israelites from the land of Egypt.

14] The following are the heads of their respective clans.

6:3] *El Shaddai.* See, for instance, Gen. 17:1, where God says to Abraham: "I am El Shaddai." The name is frequently understood to mean "God Almighty," but the real meaning is in doubt. Some believe it to mean "Mountain God," linking it to the Akkadian *sâdû*, "mountain."

My name יהוה. Pronounced Adonai in Jewish worship; see commentary to this chapter.

9] *They would not listen.* This differs from what was reported in 4:31.

12] *Impeded speech.* Literally, "uncircumcised lips."

14] *The following.* Compare Gen. 46:8.

בְּנֵי רְאוּבֵן בְּכֹר יִשְׂרָאֵל חֲנוֹךְ וּפַלּוּא חֶצְרֹן וְכַרְמִי

טו אֵלֶּה מִשְׁפְּחֹת רְאוּבֵן: וּבְנֵי שִׁמְעוֹן יְמוּאֵל וְיָמִין וְאֹהַד
וְיָכִין וְצֹחַר וְשָׁאוּל בֶּן־הַכְּנַעֲנִית אֵלֶּה מִשְׁפְּחֹת שִׁמְעוֹן:

טז וְאֵלֶּה שְׁמוֹת בְּנֵי־לֵוִי לְתֹלְדֹתָם גֵּרְשׁוֹן וּקְהָת וּמְרָרִי

יז וּשְׁנֵי חַיֵּי לֵוִי שֶׁבַע וּשְׁלֹשִׁים וּמְאַת שָׁנָה: בְּנֵי גֵרְשׁוֹן

יח לִבְנִי וְשִׁמְעִי לְמִשְׁפְּחֹתָם: וּבְנֵי קְהָת עַמְרָם וְיִצְהָר
וְחֶבְרוֹן וְעֻזִּיאֵל וּשְׁנֵי חַיֵּי קְהָת שָׁלֹשׁ וּשְׁלֹשִׁים וּמְאַת

יט שָׁנָה: וּבְנֵי מְרָרִי מַחְלִי וּמוּשִׁי אֵלֶּה מִשְׁפְּחֹת הַלֵּוִי

כ לְתֹלְדֹתָם: וַיִּקַּח עַמְרָם אֶת־יוֹכֶבֶד דֹּדָתוֹ לוֹ לְאִשָּׁה

וַתֵּלֶד לוֹ אֶת־אַהֲרֹן וְאֶת־מֹשֶׁה וּשְׁנֵי חַיֵּי עַמְרָם שֶׁבַע

כא וּשְׁלֹשִׁים וּמְאַת שָׁנָה: וּבְנֵי יִצְהָר קֹרַח וָנֶפֶג וְזִכְרִי:

כב וּבְנֵי עֻזִּיאֵל מִישָׁאֵל וְאֶלְצָפָן וְסִתְרִי: וַיִּקַּח אַהֲרֹן
אֶת־אֱלִישֶׁבַע בַּת־עַמִּינָדָב אֲחוֹת נַחְשׁוֹן לוֹ לְאִשָּׁה
וַתֵּלֶד לוֹ אֶת־נָדָב וְאֶת־אֲבִיהוּא אֶת־אֶלְעָזָר וְאֶת־

כד אִיתָמָר: וּבְנֵי קֹרַח אַסִּיר וְאֶלְקָנָה וַאֲבִיאָסָף אֵלֶּה

כה מִשְׁפְּחֹת הַקָּרְחִי: וְאֶלְעָזָר בֶּן־אַהֲרֹן לָקַח־לוֹ מִבְּנוֹת
פוּטִיאֵל לוֹ לְאִשָּׁה וַתֵּלֶד לוֹ אֶת־פִּינְחָס אֵלֶּה רָאשֵׁי

כו אֲבוֹת הַלְוִיִּם לְמִשְׁפְּחֹתָם: הוּא אַהֲרֹן וּמֹשֶׁה אֲשֶׁר

The sons of Reuben, Israel's first-born: Enoch and Pallu, Hezron and Carmi; those are the families of Reuben. **15]** The sons of Simeon: Jemuel, Jamin, Ohad, Jachin, Zohar, and Saul the son of a Canaanite woman; those are the families of Simeon. **16]** These are the names of Levi's sons by their lineage: Gershon, Kohath, and Merari; and the span of Levi's life was 137 years. **17]** The sons of Gershon: Libni and Shimei, by their families. **18]** The sons of Kohath: Amram, Izhar, Hebron, and Uzziel; and the span of Kohath's life was 133 years. **19]** The sons of Merari: Mahli and Mushi. These are the families of the Levites by their lineage.

20] Amram took to wife his father's sister Jochebed, and she bore him Aaron and Moses; and the span of Amram's life was 137 years. **21]** The sons of Izhar: Korah, Nepheg, and Zichri. **22]** The sons of Uzziel: Mishael, Elzaphan, and Sithri. **23]** Aaron took to wife Elisheba, daughter of Amminadab and sister of Nahshon, and she bore him Nadab and Abihu, Eleazar and Ithamar. **24]** The sons of Korah: Assir, Elkanah, and Abiasaph. Those are the families of the Korahites. **25]** And Aaron's son Eleazar took to wife one of Putiel's daughters, and she bore him Phinehas. Those are the heads of the fathers' houses of the Levites by their families.

Enoch. Or, Hanoch; see Gen. 46:9.

20] *His father's sister.* The early origin of this family tradition is underscored by the fact that later Torah law prohibits such marriages (Lev. 18:12). The Septuagint has "cousin."

Aaron and Moses. Only male names are recorded here, while various other versions mention Miriam also.

137 years. An addition of all figures does not amount to the 400 years anticipated in Gen. 15:13 or the 430 of Exod. 12:40. Nor do the three generations (from Levi to Kohath, to Amram, to Aaron and Moses) conform to the ten generations from Joseph to Joshua (Moses' younger contemporary; see I Chron. 7:22–27). It has therefore been suggested that the number of years, like the genealogies supposed to correspond to them, was an artificial construction [1].

22] *Sons of Uzziel.* Who was Kohath's fourth son (verse 18). Hebron is not mentioned again, apparently because he had no offspring.

23] *Nadab and Abihu.* They will later die suddenly (Lev. 10:1–2).

Eleazar. After his brothers' death he will become Aaron's successor (Num. 20:26).

25] *One of Putiel's daughters.* No information is given about Putiel; only his lineage is preserved.

Phinehas. He later becomes the symbol of those who are zealous for God, and the everlasting priesthood is vouchsafed to him and his descendants (Num. 25:1–13).

אָמַר יְהֹוָה לָהֶם הוֹצִיאוּ אֶת־בְּנֵי יִשְׂרָאֵל מֵאֶרֶץ
מִצְרַיִם עַל־צִבְאֹתָם: הֵם הַמְדַבְּרִים אֶל־פַּרְעֹה כּג
מֶלֶךְ־מִצְרַיִם לְהוֹצִיא אֶת־בְּנֵי־יִשְׂרָאֵל מִמִּצְרָיִם הוּא
מֹשֶׁה וְאַהֲרֹן: וַיְהִי בְּיוֹם דִּבֶּר יְהֹוָה אֶל־מֹשֶׁה בְּאֶרֶץ כּח
מִצְרָיִם: ס וַיְדַבֵּר יְהֹוָה אֶל־מֹשֶׁה לֵּאמֹר אֲנִי יְהֹוָה כּט
דַּבֵּר אֶל־פַּרְעֹה מֶלֶךְ מִצְרַיִם אֵת כָּל־אֲשֶׁר אֲנִי
דֹּבֵר אֵלֶיךָ: וַיֹּאמֶר מֹשֶׁה לִפְנֵי יְהֹוָה הֵן אֲנִי עֲרַל ל
שְׂפָתָיִם וְאֵיךְ יִשְׁמַע אֵלַי פַּרְעֹה: פ
וַיֹּאמֶר יְהֹוָה אֶל־מֹשֶׁה רְאֵה נְתַתִּיךָ אֱלֹהִים לְפַרְעֹה א
וְאַהֲרֹן אָחִיךָ יִהְיֶה נְבִיאֶךָ: אַתָּה תְדַבֵּר אֵת כָּל־ ב
אֲשֶׁר אֲצַוֶּךָּ וְאַהֲרֹן אָחִיךָ יְדַבֵּר אֶל־פַּרְעֹה וְשִׁלַּח

אֶת־בְּנֵי־יִשְׂרָאֵל מֵאַרְצוֹ: וַאֲנִי אַקְשֶׁה אֶת־לֵב פַּרְעֹה ג
וְהִרְבֵּיתִי אֶת־אֹתֹתַי וְאֶת־מוֹפְתַי בְּאֶרֶץ מִצְרָיִם: וְלֹא־ ד
יִשְׁמַע אֲלֵכֶם פַּרְעֹה וְנָתַתִּי אֶת־יָדִי בְּמִצְרָיִם וְהוֹצֵאתִי
אֶת־צִבְאֹתַי אֶת־עַמִּי בְנֵי־יִשְׂרָאֵל מֵאֶרֶץ מִצְרַיִם
בִּשְׁפָטִים גְּדֹלִים: וְיָדְעוּ מִצְרַיִם כִּי־אֲנִי יְהֹוָה בִּנְטֹתִי ה
אֶת־יָדִי עַל־מִצְרָיִם וְהוֹצֵאתִי אֶת־בְּנֵי־יִשְׂרָאֵל מִתּוֹכָם:
וַיַּעַשׂ מֹשֶׁה וְאַהֲרֹן כַּאֲשֶׁר צִוָּה יְהֹוָה אֹתָם כֵּן עָשׂוּ: ו
וּמֹשֶׁה בֶּן־שְׁמֹנִים שָׁנָה וְאַהֲרֹן בֶּן־שָׁלֹשׁ וּשְׁמֹנִים שָׁנָה ז
בְּדַבְּרָם אֶל־פַּרְעֹה: פ
וַיֹּאמֶר יְהֹוָה אֶל־מֹשֶׁה וְאֶל־אַהֲרֹן לֵאמֹר: כִּי יְדַבֵּר ח
אֲלֵכֶם פַּרְעֹה לֵאמֹר תְּנוּ לָכֶם מוֹפֵת וְאָמַרְתָּ אֶל־ ט

26] It is the same Aaron and Moses to whom the LORD said, "Bring forth the Israelites from the land of Egypt, troop by troop." 27] It was they who spoke to Pharaoh king of Egypt to free the Israelites from the Egyptians; these are the same Moses and Aaron. 28] For when the LORD spoke to Moses in the land of Egypt 29] and the LORD said to Moses, "I am the LORD; speak to Pharaoh king of Egypt all that I will tell you," 30] Moses appealed to the LORD, saying, "See, I am of impeded speech; how then should Pharaoh heed me!"

1] The LORD replied to Moses, "See, I place you in the role of God to Pharaoh, with your brother Aaron as your prophet. 2] You shall repeat all that I command you, and your brother Aaron shall speak to Pharaoh to let the Israelites depart from his land. 3] But I will harden Pharaoh's heart, that I may multiply My signs and marvels in the land of Egypt. 4] When Pharaoh does not heed you, I will lay My hand upon Egypt and deliver My ranks, My people the Israelites, from the land of Egypt with extraordinary chastisements. 5] And the Egyptians shall know that I am the LORD, when I stretch out My hand over Egypt and bring out the Israelites from their midst." 6] This Moses and Aaron did; as the LORD commanded them, so they did. 7] Moses was eighty years old and Aaron eighty-three, when they made their demand on Pharaoh.

8] The LORD said to Moses and Aaron, 9] "When Pharaoh speaks to you and says,

29] *And the Lord.* The Masoretic text has a division before this sentence, but already Rashi connected verses 28 and 29.

7:1] *Role of God to Pharaoh.* Who considered himself divine.

4] *My ranks.* Better, "My army," God's shock troops. This concept has entered into the name "Salvation Army."

7] *Eighty years old.* This concludes the accreditation passages. The Torah is not bothered by Moses' high age. Since he was a much younger man when he fled Egypt and thus a whole lifetime remained unrecorded, Jewish tradition filled the gap with many tales of his dazzling mental and military feats.

אַהֲרֹן קַח אֶת־מַטְּךָ וְהַשְׁלֵךְ לִפְנֵי־פַרְעֹה יְהִי לְתַנִּין: לַחֲכָמִים וְלַמְכַשְּׁפִים וַיַּעֲשׂוּ גַם־הֵם חַרְטֻמֵּי מִצְרַיִם
י וַיָּבֹא מֹשֶׁה וְאַהֲרֹן אֶל־פַּרְעֹה וַיַּעֲשׂוּ כֵן כַּאֲשֶׁר יֹא בְּלַהֲטֵיהֶם כֵּן: וַיַּשְׁלִיכוּ אִישׁ מַטֵּהוּ וַיִּהְיוּ
צִוָּה יְהוָה וַיַּשְׁלֵךְ אַהֲרֹן אֶת־מַטֵּהוּ לִפְנֵי פַרְעֹה יֹג לְתַנִּינִם וַיִּבְלַע מַטֵּה־אַהֲרֹן אֶת־מַטֹּתָם: וַיֶּחֱזַק
יֹא וְלִפְנֵי עֲבָדָיו וַיְהִי לְתַנִּין: וַיִּקְרָא גַּם־פַּרְעֹה לֵב פַּרְעֹה וְלֹא שָׁמַע אֲלֵהֶם כַּאֲשֶׁר דִּבֶּר יְהוָה: ס

'Produce your marvel,' you shall say to Aaron, 'Take your rod and cast it down before Pharaoh.' It shall turn into a serpent." **10]** So Moses and Aaron came before Pharaoh and did just as the LORD had commanded: Aaron cast down his rod in the presence of Pharaoh and his courtiers, and it turned into a serpent. **11]** Then Pharaoh, for his part, summoned the wise men and the sorcerers; and the Egyptian magicians, in turn, did the same with their spells: **12]** each cast down his rod, and they turned into serpents. But Aaron's rod swallowed their rods. **13]** Yet Pharaoh's heart stiffened and he did not heed them, as the LORD had said.

9] *Serpent.* It was called נָחָשׁ (*nachash*, 4:3) but is now called תַּנִּין (*tanin*) and should perhaps be translated here as "crocodile," an animal well fitted to the Egyptian environment and to the satirical overtones of this story [2].

Egyptian magicians. Jonathan ben Uzziel gives them the names Yannes and Yambres. Magic flourished in ancient Egypt.

My Name יהוה

For the second time in the story of Moses, the divine name is revealed. At the burning bush the revelation had been made to Moses for his own sake, though it was invested with purposeful ambiguity. For while he learned that "Ehyeh" sent him, the knowledge thus received also deepened the mystery (see above, ch. 3). Now once more God states His identity, and this time both for the sake of the people and as an accreditation for Moses. For the latter's intimate understanding of the Deity would tend to make him more trustworthy and at the same time more confident that his leadership would be sustained. This appeared necessary for, while in the beginning the Israelites had believed in Moses and his God, they were now dubious about the promised redemption, and Pharaoh was not listening in any case.

The introduction to the revelation begins in a formulaic way, "I am the Lord." Such a solemn declaration occurs often in other Near Eastern texts [3] as well as in Torah passages. Notably among the latter are the repeated declarations in the Holiness Code (Lev., ch. 19), where major ethical injunctions are given emphasis by the formula, as for instance in "Love your neighbor as yourself: I am the Lord." A related formula is "I the Lord have spoken," which in Num. 14:35 is meant as added assurance that what God has promised will be brought to pass. Another formula reads "Thus says the Lord," which Ezekiel 20:5–6 employs in a manner similar to Exodus 6:6–8; in both cases the solemn emphasis is given to seven promises of God.

But when we come to the revelation which has been introduced so solemnly we are met with an immediate difficulty: we are told that it is יהוה (YHVH) who guarantees the ancient covenant He had made with the forefathers, although they had not known Him by this name. This statement contradicts the frequent occurrence of the name YHVH in Genesis, where the story of the Patriarchs is told. According to Genesis, the forefathers had known the Name. Biblical scholars have attempted to solve this contradiction in various ways.

Many hold that chapter 6 belongs to the P-tradition in which the Patriarchs knew God only as Elohim or El Shaddai. Now this God reveals himself to Moses as YHVH. The passages in Genesis where YHVH is used in connection with the Patriarchs are assigned to the J-tradition, and this tradition also is responsible for the passages in chapter 3 which refer to YHVH as the name God will forever have as His own. In chapter 6 the P-school too connects YHVH with Moses in order to establish the legitimacy of the priestly hierarchy: Moses will be "God to Pharaoh," while Aaron, emerging with a more important stature than before, will be His prophet. Finally, the partial genealogy climaxes with Levi and goes no farther, thereby underscoring that the important role which that tribe assumed in later history was traceable to ancient origins.[1]

While this explanation overcomes the apparent contradictions, it does not deal with the text as it now is. For we may assume that these problems were as clear to the redactor of the Torah as they are to us, and we must ask how he perceived the content of the revelation as arising from the story as he transmitted it to us. As elsewhere in the Torah, we shall attempt to deal with the question from that perspective.

Moses and the people had since patriarchal days known the name YHVH as God's name,

---

[1] One premodern commentator attempted an equally radical explanation. Rabbi Joshua is quoted by Ibn Ezra as saying that all occurrences of YHVH in Genesis were anachronistic additions made by Moses himself.

but in the centuries since then this knowledge had hardly been more than a customary appellation. At the first revelation, at the bush, Moses is charged with his mission but—despite being provided with access to the divine name Ehyeh—he does not come radically closer to the essence of the God he seeks to know. Now, however, after his first trials and failures, Moses confronts the Deity again, and this time God reveals His name more fully, which is to say that Moses glimpses the Divine more clearly than before. This approach was already favored by traditional interpreters like Ibn Ezra who said that the ancestors knew God (and His name) only in a limited way and that Moses now comes to understand the Divine to have yet another dimension. What is this new insight Moses acquires?

The Patriarchs from Abraham on conceived of God as endowed with qualities that set Him aside from all other gods. But His distinctiveness was essentially one of degree, not of essence. For the Patriarchs the existence of other gods presented no problem; their own God, known to them as YHVH or Elohim (or El Shaddai or El Elyon), commanded their total devotion. Moses, however, begins to see God in a new light: He is faithful, merciful, and compassionate; He remembers His people and—this is most important—He will redeem them because He will be shown to be superior to all the powers in heaven and on earth. Beside Him, as the second commandment will state specifically, there is none else, and any adoration of other gods will therefore be an idolatrous enterprise, useless for the nations and illegitimate for Israel.

This is the new insight that comes to Moses and which in the course of his career he will deepen, until at the end of his life he will fully develop and teach the fundamentals of monotheism. The people do not grasp the message at first; in fact, it will take them many centuries to assimilate it fully.

Moses then appears here not only as the political leader of his people; he now emerges also as a religious innovator, and as such he will make his indelible impact on mankind. The Patriarchs had glimpses of God's essence, but only now, through Moses, does it come into full view.[2]

In this sense it may be said that this section, which is given to the accreditation of the leadership of Moses and Aaron, submits, so to speak, God's credentials as well. They are contained in His name, in the four sacred letters that are the seal and pledge of redemption.

Linguistic Excursus on the Name יְהֹוָה

A large literature exists which deals with the proper pronunciation of the Name as well as its etymology, and much of this is of a highly technical nature. The following represents a brief summary:

VOCALIZATION. How the Name was originally vocalized is no longer certain. Its pronunciation was in time restricted to the Temple service, then to the High Priest intoning it on the Day of Atonement, and after the destruction of the Temple it received a substitute pronunciation both for the reading of Scripture and for its use at prayer.

The Masoretes who vocalized the Hebrew text took the vowels from the word Adonai (אֲדֹנָי) and put them with יהוה to remind the reader not to pronounce the Name but to substitute Adonai. Hence, all vocalized texts of the Bible now read יְהֹוָה. A Christian writer of the sixteenth century who was unaware of this substitution transcribed the word as he saw it, namely as Jehovah, and this error

---

[2] This view was first set forth by Yehezkel Kaufmann and has since been adopted by increasing numbers of scholars [4].

has since entered many Christian Bible translations [5].

Orthodox Jews use a further substitution and employ even the term Adonai only in prayer or actual Torah reading. Otherwise they say "Adoshem" or "Hashem" for it and, in similar circumstances, they say "Elokim" when speaking of God and "Kel" for El. They carry this respect for the sacredness of the divine Name into translation as well and write "G-d" and "L-rd."

Overwhelming scholarly opinion holds that יהוה was in Moses' time pronounced יְהֹוֶה (Yahveh).[3] There is also a shorter form of the Name, Yah (יָה), which may represent the original from which Yahveh was expanded or may, contrariwise, be a contraction of the longer ascription. Yah occurs sometimes alone (as in 15:2; 17:16), but more usually in conjunction with proper names like Elijah (*Eliyah* in Hebrew) and in the doxology, Halleluyah ("Praise the Lord").

ETYMOLOGY. The most widely accepted explanation of YHVH connects the Name with the word הָיָה (*hayah*, to be), a causative form of which could be Yahveh, "He who causes to be" [6]. Another form could be Yahuah, meaning "He who indeed will (show himself to) be" [7], or "He who proves himself" [8].

A different theory denies the connection of YHVH with the word *hayah*, and also that it was ever pronounced Yahveh. Rather, so this theory holds, the name was read Yahuh, this being a version of Yehu, a form which occurs several times independently in the Bible (as יֵהוּא) and frequently as a prefix or suffix to proper names [9]. According to Buber, Yahu was a kind of "primitive sound," an exclamation denoting awe, recognition, and affirmation: "Oh He!" or "Yah He!" or "Yah Is!" or "Yah Exists!"[4] Still another suggestion relates YHVH to Yahwi, which was a component of several Amorite names like Yahwi-Ila, Yahwi-Addu, Yahwi-Dagan, perhaps meaning "Ila (or Addu or Dagan) is present" [10].

A quite different approach to the problem sees YHVH as having developed from a cultic name connected with El, perhaps "El du Yahwi"—"El who creates"—and that in time Yahwi split off from El, ousting the latter from preeminence. Then, again, Yahu —as an earlier form of YHVH—might be of non-Semitic origin altogether, perhaps related to such names as Ju-piter [11].

In sum, it must be stated that our data are presently not sufficient to render a definitive judgment on these theories.

[3] This is often also transliterated Yahweh or Jahweh; the latter is the German scholarly tradition whence derives the notation "J" for the school that used the name יהוה predominantly.

[4] The Buber-Rosenzweig translation renders יהוה on this basis as ER, taking the original meaning to be

"Er ist da," i.e., "He is present (with you)." Yehu was the name of an Israelite king and several other biblical personages; the prefix יה occurs in such names as Yehonathan or Yehoshua; the suffix as in Eliyahu or Yirmiyahu. The expansion of a name by adding the letter ה may also be seen in the name Abram, which became Abraham (Gen. 17:5).

GLEANINGS

Moses' Concern

Abraham, Isaac, and Jacob never asked for God's name. They were satisfied with what was revealed to them, for only they and their families were involved in the relationship. But Moses was concerned with all of Israel, and hence he needed to know the nature of God.

M. HACOHEN [12]

Moses had evoked God's anger (5:22, 23) and the divine attribute of justice[5] was about to attack him. But then God reflected that Moses spoke of Israel's suffering and therefore dealt with him according to His quality of mercy. Note also that the text reads, "Elohim *spoke*" (i.e., harshly), but at once proceeds to meliorate into "and *said*" (i.e., gently).

MIDRASH [13]

It Was Time

Why had the time come now to free Israel from bondage? Because God felt that they were becoming accustomed to their burdens.

CHASIDIC [14]

Five Ways

God phrases His promise in five different ways. He says (6:6–8) that He would "free," "deliver," "redeem," "take," and "bring" Israel into the land He had sworn to the Patriarchs. The Talmud and the Haggadah connect the first four terms with the four cups drunk at the Passover Seder [15]. But why not a fifth cup to represent the promise that God would "bring" Israel into the land? A talmudic controversy dealt with this question and it has become a Jewish custom to have a fifth cup at the table but not to drink of it.

AFTER THE GAON OF VILNA [16]

[It is left there for Elijah to decide whether the fifth cup was indeed necessary—it being a tradition that Elijah will reappear and decide controversial issues.]

Moses Pleads

In his remonstration with God, Moses protests that Israel would not listen to him because he was of defective speech. He blamed his own inadequacy in order to protect Israel.

SEFAT EMET [17]

Marital Advice

In 6:23 we are told that Elisheba, Aaron's wife, was the daughter of Amminadab and the sister of Nahshon. Later, in Num. 1:7, we are informed again that Amminadab was Nahshon's father, hence it would not have been necessary to stress here that Nahshon and Elisheba were brother and sister. This is to teach us that he who marries should carefully investigate his bride's family and especially her brother.

MIDRASH [18]

It Began with Moses

The legends of Moses in Egypt do not tell explicitly of his battle with Israelite paganism, but the testimony to this battle is implicit in these stories throughout. The revelation of the name YHVH opens the battle with paganism and establishes the contrast between Israel and Egypt. It is the beginning of the monotheistic revolution in Israel.

---

[5] In midrashic tradition, "Elohim" represents God's justice and "YHVH" His mercy. Exodus 6:2 begins by saying, "Elohim spoke to Moses," and then proceeds to say, "I am YHVH."

When was the battle against the pagan folk religion joined, out of which a monotheistic people emerged? The Torah literature testifies that this battle took place, not only before the time of the literary prophets, but even before the formation of the Torah literature itself. That no story of a battle with paganism is recorded before the age of Moses suggests a *terminus a quo*. Only with Moses does the contrast between the faith of YHVH and paganism appear. The struggle with paganism began with Moses.　　　　Y. KAUFMANN [19]

PART III

Confrontation and Exodus

The confrontation between Pharaoh and the agents of God now begins in earnest. God's claim to possess Israel and wrest it from the hands of Egypt will be realized through a series of devastating events—not unlike the misfortunes of the Philistines who had possession of God's holy ark and were forced to release it [1].

To accomplish His design God sends His messenger Moses, who here emerges fully as the prophet who informs the ruler of God's will, a will dramatically demonstrated by natural signs, ten "plagues" as they have come to be called. Their progression does not follow a clearly visible pattern. One may, for instance, see them as 4–4–1–1—two groups of four plagues (the first four were nuisances; the second group, serious attacks on persons and property) and two final ones: a ninth plague of terror and the tenth, of destroying the first-born and leading to Israel's liberation. Or one may see the wonders as five groups of two: plagues one and two deal with the Nile; in plagues three and four lice and insects resemble each other, as do pestilence and boils in five and six; hail and locusts in seven and eight are directed toward crops; and in the final plagues darkness and death have a relationship.

Or one might see the wonders in three groups of three, plus one—a division popular in Jewish tradition and perpetuated in the mnemotechnical device that groups the first letters of the plagues: דצ״ך עד״ש באח״ב. In the beginning of each of the cycles Moses meets Pharaoh in the open; in each second plague Moses addresses himself to Pharaoh with a warning; and each third plague proceeds without warning [2]. This is the way this commentary has subdivided them. The first unit will deal with two sets of three plagues and the subsequent one with the last group of three, plus the final plague.

Scholars have sought in vain for a historical kernel to these tales. Some have attempted to fit them into the context of the Egyptian natural environment. But such procedure leads nowhere. "The reality that the tale intends to convey is not past historical but present affective: the experience of events as they were taken in first by eye witnesses, then through the consciousness of the generations who perennially relived and reflected on them as the basis of their own living faith" [3].

When all is told, it is in every way a wondrous story. The wonder lay not so much in the rise and fall of Pharaoh's will to resist as in the final liberation of the enslaved people. This above all was remembered

430

by ensuing generations who retold the tale in loving detail, adding wonder on wonder. They celebrated no festival more enthusiastically than the Passover Seder, which rehearses the Exodus and the birth of the Jewish people. It is not surprising, therefore, that the small storybook used at the Seder, the Haggadah, which is to a large extent a summation of midrashim, has seen more illustrated editions than any other book in the Jewish library.

The story of the plagues has no true parallel in ancient Near Eastern literature. There are some Egyptian materials, however, which antedate the likely time of the Exodus and which relate a series of natural disasters [4]. It is conceivable that these sources played a part in forming the biblical tradition, but one cannot presently say more than that.

Critical scholarship has attempted to separate the major literary strands in the biblical story (J, E, P) [5]. Thus, some have seen an interweaving of J (found in plagues 1, 2, 4, 5, 7–10), E (found in 1, 7–10), and P (1–3, 6, 10): they have found the J-source to report God's direct intervention at the behest of Moses, the E-source to have the response mediated by the use of the rod, and P to emphasize the role of Aaron. There is, however, no widespread consensus on such a division. Moreover, the number of plagues too appears to have differed in various old traditions. Thus, Psalms 78 and 105 recount the plagues but do not recount all of them, and their arrangements differ (see Gleanings below).

The Bible does not state how much time elapsed from the first to the last plague; tradition suggested that it was one year, enough time to accommodate the shift in both Pharaoh's and the Egyptians' opinion regarding the release of Israel.

GLEANINGS

Songs from the Psalms

He turned their rivers into blood;
 He made their waters undrinkable.
He inflicted upon them swarms of insects
  to devour them,
 frogs to destroy them.
He gave their crops over to grubs,
 their produce to locusts.
He killed their vines with hail,
 their sycamores with frost.
He gave their beasts over to hail,
 their cattle to lightning bolts.
He inflicted His burning anger upon them,
 wrath, indignation, trouble,
 a band of deadly messengers.
He cleared a path for His anger;
 He did not stop short of slaying them,
 but gave them over to pestilence.
He struck every first-born in Egypt,
 the first fruits of their vigor
  in the tents of Ham.

PSALM 78:44–51

Then Israel came to Egypt;
 Jacob dwelt in the land of Ham.
He made His people very fruitful,
 more numerous than their foes.
He changed their heart to hate His people,
 to plot against His servants.
He sent His servant Moses,
 and Aaron, whom He had chosen.
They performed His signs among them,
 His wonders, against the land of
  Ham.
He sent darkness; it was very dark;
 did they not defy His word?
He turned their waters into blood
 and killed their fish.

Their land teemed with frogs,
 even the rooms of their king.
Swarms of insects came at His command,
 lice throughout their country.
He gave them hail for rain,
 and flaming fire in their land.
He struck their vines and fig trees,
 broke down the trees of their country.
Locusts came at His command,
 grasshoppers without numbers.
They devoured every green thing in the land;
 they consumed the produce of the soil.
He struck down every first-born in the land,
 the first fruit of their vigor.
He led Israel out with silver and gold;
 none among their tribes faltered.
Egypt rejoiced when they left,
 for dread of Israel had fallen upon them.

PSALM 105:23–38

From the Passover Haggadah

We were slaves to Pharaoh in Egypt, and the Lord freed us from Egypt with a mighty hand. Had not the Holy One, praised be He, delivered our people from Egypt, then we, our children, and our children's children would still be enslaved.

Therefore, even if all of us were wise, all of us people of understanding, all of us learned in Torah, it would still be our obligation to tell the story of the Exodus from Egypt.

Black Decalogue

Compute the plagues; your little finger dip
In spittle of the grape, and at each pest
Shake off the drop with the vindictive zest:
Thus first: the Nile—a gash; then frogs that skip
Upon the princess' coverlet; the rip

432

Made by dark nails that seek the itching guest;
The plague of murrained carcasses; the pest;
Full boils that stud the Ethiop, leg to lip.
The guerdon of hot hail, the fists of God;
The swarm of locusts nibbling Egypt clean;

Thick darkness oozing from out Moses' rod;
And first-born slain, the mighty and the mean;
Compute these plagues that fell on Egypt's sod,
Then add: In Goshen these were never seen.

A. M. KLEIN [6]

433

The First Six Plagues

The first six signs bring blood, frogs, lice, insects, pestilence, and inflammation. The plague of blood finds Pharaoh unconcerned, but thereafter he is touched and becomes involved in the action that surges back and forth. The first three plagues are still a contest with Egypt's magicians, which ends with a recognition on their part that their art is defeated by "the finger of God."

The progression of the tales may be seen as a rising tide, designed both to punish and to instruct. "One can read the list of the plagues like a tragic history of the troubles of life. Starting with general unpleasantness, like the lack of good water and the stink of dead fish; followed by unpleasant company, hopping and croaking around everywhere; then stinging flocks of minor irritations, lice and flies; till in full earnest comes real sickness of man and beast, boils and blains and murrain; followed by storm, lightning and hail; and real enemies in battalions, locusts, the first inventors of the scorched earth policy; then terror in darkness, and death" [1].

יט לִשְׁתּוֹת מַיִם מִן־הַיְאֹר: ס וַיֹּאמֶר יְהוָֹה אֶל־מֹשֶׁה
אֱמֹר אֶל־אַהֲרֹן קַח מַטְּךָ וּנְטֵה־יָדְךָ עַל־מֵימֵי מִצְרַיִם
עַל־נַהֲרֹתָם עַל־יְאֹרֵיהֶם וְעַל־אַגְמֵיהֶם וְעַל כָּל־מִקְוֵה
מֵימֵיהֶם וְיִהְיוּ־דָם וְהָיָה דָם בְּכָל־אֶרֶץ מִצְרַיִם
כ וּבָעֵצִים וּבָאֲבָנִים: וַיַּעֲשׂוּ־כֵן מֹשֶׁה וְאַהֲרֹן כַּאֲשֶׁר
צִוָּה יְהוָֹה וַיָּרֶם בַּמַּטֶּה וַיַּךְ אֶת־הַמַּיִם אֲשֶׁר בַּיְאֹר
לְעֵינֵי פַרְעֹה וּלְעֵינֵי עֲבָדָיו וַיֵּהָפְכוּ כָּל־הַמַּיִם אֲשֶׁר־
כא בַּיְאֹר לְדָם: וְהַדָּגָה אֲשֶׁר־בַּיְאֹר מֵתָה וַיִּבְאַשׁ הַיְאֹר
וְלֹא־יָכְלוּ מִצְרַיִם לִשְׁתּוֹת מַיִם מִן־הַיְאֹר וַיְהִי הַדָּם

יד וַיֹּאמֶר יְהוָֹה אֶל־מֹשֶׁה כָּבֵד לֵב פַּרְעֹה מֵאֵן לְשַׁלַּח
טו הָעָם: לֵךְ אֶל־פַּרְעֹה בַּבֹּקֶר הִנֵּה יֹצֵא הַמַּיְמָה
וְנִצַּבְתָּ לִקְרָאתוֹ עַל־שְׂפַת הַיְאֹר וְהַמַּטֶּה אֲשֶׁר־נֶהְפַּךְ
טז לְנָחָשׁ תִּקַּח בְּיָדֶךָ: וְאָמַרְתָּ אֵלָיו יְהוָֹה אֱלֹהֵי
הָעִבְרִים שְׁלָחַנִי אֵלֶיךָ לֵאמֹר שַׁלַּח אֶת־עַמִּי וְיַעַבְדֻנִי
יז בַּמִּדְבָּר וְהִנֵּה לֹא־שָׁמַעְתָּ עַד־כֹּה: כֹּה אָמַר יְהוָֹה
בְּזֹאת תֵּדַע כִּי אֲנִי יְהוָֹה הִנֵּה אָנֹכִי מַכֶּה בַּמַּטֶּה
אֲשֶׁר־בְּיָדִי עַל־הַמַּיִם אֲשֶׁר בַּיְאֹר וְנֶהֶפְכוּ לְדָם:
יח וְהַדָּגָה אֲשֶׁר־בַּיְאֹר תָּמוּת וּבָאַשׁ הַיְאֹר וְנִלְאוּ מִצְרַיִם

14] And the LORD said to Moses, "Pharaoh is stubborn; he refuses to let the people go. 15] Go to Pharaoh in the morning, as he is coming out to the water, and station yourself before him at the edge of the Nile, taking with you the rod that turned into a snake. 16] And say to him, 'The LORD, the God of the Hebrews, sent me to you to say, "Let My people go that they may worship Me in the wilderness." But you have paid no heed until now. 17] Thus says the LORD, "By this you shall know that I am the LORD." See, I shall strike the water in the Nile with the rod that is in my hand, and it will be turned into blood; 18] and the fish in the Nile will die. The Nile will stink so that the Egyptians will find it impossible to drink the water of the Nile.' "

19] And the LORD said to Moses, "Say to Aaron: Take your rod and hold out your arm over the waters of Egypt—its rivers, its canals, its ponds, all its bodies of water—that they may turn to blood; there shall be blood throughout the land of Egypt, even in vessels of wood and stone." 20] Moses and Aaron did just as the LORD commanded: he lifted up the rod and struck the water in the Nile in the sight of Pharaoh and his courtiers, and all the water in the Nile was turned into blood 21] and the fish in the Nile died. The Nile stank so that the Egyptians could not drink water from the Nile; and there was blood throughout the land of Egypt.

7:15] *Coming out to the water.* Such visits were apparently regular (see 8:16). Ibn Ezra (twelfth century C.E.) reported that this royal practice persisted in his own day and that the king thus performed the important task of checking the daily water level of the Nile. S. R. Driver suggests a ritual encounter with the Nile which was seen as a personal deity.

19] *Say to Aaron: Take your rod.* Even though in verse 17 it was Moses who was to strike the water

with his rod. Two different traditions appear to be involved. Harmonizers suggest that Moses and Aaron used the same rod.

Vessels of wood and stone. An anachronistic reference. Such vessels were not common in ancient Egypt. Cassuto therefore supposes that this is an ironic reference to idols of wood and stone.

20] *He lifted up the rod.* It is not stated whether it was Moses or Aaron. The rod was a signal that God would begin the foretold event.

כב בְּכָל־אֶרֶץ מִצְרָיִם: וַיַּעֲשׂוּ־כֵן חַרְטֻמֵּי מִצְרַיִם בְּלָטֵיהֶם וַיֶּחֱזַק לֵב־פַּרְעֹה וְלֹא־שָׁמַע אֲלֵהֶם כַּאֲשֶׁר

כג דִּבֶּר יְהוָה: וַיִּפֶן פַּרְעֹה וַיָּבֹא אֶל־בֵּיתוֹ וְלֹא־שָׁת

כד לִבּוֹ גַּם־לָזֹאת: וַיַּחְפְּרוּ כָל־מִצְרַיִם סְבִיבֹת הַיְאֹר מַיִם לִשְׁתּוֹת כִּי לֹא יָכְלוּ לִשְׁתֹּת מִמֵּימֵי הַיְאֹר:

כה וַיִּמָּלֵא שִׁבְעַת יָמִים אַחֲרֵי הַכּוֹת־יְהוָה אֶת־הַיְאֹר: פ

כו וַיֹּאמֶר יְהוָה אֶל־מֹשֶׁה בֹּא אֶל־פַּרְעֹה וְאָמַרְתָּ אֵלָיו

כז כֹּה אָמַר יְהוָה שַׁלַּח אֶת־עַמִּי וְיַעַבְדֻנִי: וְאִם־מָאֵן אַתָּה לְשַׁלֵּחַ הִנֵּה אָנֹכִי נֹגֵף אֶת־כָּל־גְּבוּלְךָ

כח בַּצְפַרְדְּעִים: וְשָׁרַץ הַיְאֹר צְפַרְדְּעִים וְעָלוּ וּבָאוּ בְּבֵיתֶךָ וּבַחֲדַר מִשְׁכָּבְךָ וְעַל־מִטָּתֶךָ וּבְבֵית עֲבָדֶיךָ

כט וּבְעַמֶּךָ וּבְתַנּוּרֶיךָ וּבְמִשְׁאֲרוֹתֶיךָ: וּבְכָה וּבְעַמְּךָ וּבְכָל־עֲבָדֶיךָ יַעֲלוּ הַצְפַרְדְּעִים:

א וַיֹּאמֶר יְהוָה אֶל־מֹשֶׁה אֱמֹר אֶל־אַהֲרֹן נְטֵה אֶת־יָדְךָ בְּמַטֶּךָ עַל־הַנְּהָרֹת עַל־הַיְאֹרִים וְעַל־הָאֲגַמִּים וְהַעַל

ב אֶת־הַצְפַרְדְּעִים עַל־אֶרֶץ מִצְרָיִם: וַיֵּט אַהֲרֹן אֶת־יָדוֹ עַל מֵימֵי מִצְרָיִם וַתַּעַל הַצְפַרְדֵּעַ וַתְּכַס אֶת־אֶרֶץ

ג מִצְרָיִם: וַיַּעֲשׂוּ־כֵן הַחַרְטֻמִּים בְּלָטֵיהֶם וַיַּעֲלוּ אֶת־

22] But when the Egyptian magicians did the same with their spells, Pharaoh's heart stiffened and he did not heed them—as the LORD had spoken. 23] Pharaoh turned and went into his palace, paying no regard even to this. 24] And all the Egyptians had to dig round about the Nile for drinking water, because they could not drink the water of the Nile.

25] When seven days had passed after the LORD struck the Nile, 26] the LORD said to Moses, "Go to Pharaoh and say to him, 'Thus says the LORD: Let My people go that they may worship Me. 27] If your refuse to let them go, then I will plague your whole country with frogs. 28] The Nile shall swarm with frogs, and they shall come up and enter your palace, your bedchamber and your bed, the houses of your courtiers and your people, and your ovens and your kneading bowls. 29] The frogs shall come up on you and on your people and on all your courtiers.'"

1] And the LORD said to Moses, "Say to Aaron: Hold out your arm with the rod over the rivers, the canals, and the ponds, and bring up the frogs on the land of Egypt." 2] Aaron held out his arm over the waters of Egypt, and the frogs came up and covered the land of Egypt. 3] But the magicians did the same with their spells, and brought frogs upon the land of Egypt.

22] *The Egyptian magicians did the same.* The text expresses no surprise that the sign which God gave to Moses to demonstrate the divine power could be readily duplicated. It is therefore clear from the outset that the real battle is not between Moses and the magicians, or between one set of signs and their imitations, but between God and Pharaoh. The latter's will is the battleground, and he will be made to yield though his resolve to the contrary is hard and persistent. The Torah also pays no attention to the obvious question: Where did the magicians obtain water for their demonstration? The focus is solely on the recalcitrance of Pharaoh.

23] *Paying no regard.* It did not affect him, and,

besides, he perceived it as merely a matter of magic.

24] *Dig round about.* For surface water. This is at variance with verse 19, suggesting two traditions.

25] *Seven days.* A number denoting completeness. The Masoretic text makes a division after this verse. So do the King James Version and other translations, which begin chapter 8 here, giving to that chapter five additional verses [2].

28] *Enter your palace.* This time you too will be affected.

8:1] *Frogs.* In Egyptian mythology they were considered to have life-giving powers. Thus the plague is designed to exalt the might of God.

הַצְפַרְדְּעִים מִן־הַבָּתִּים מִן־הַחֲצֵרֹת וּמִן־הַשָּׂדֹת׃   הַצְפַרְדְּעִים עַל־אֶרֶץ מִצְרָיִם׃ וַיִּקְרָא פַרְעֹה לְמֹשֶׁה ד

יא וַיִּצְבְּרוּ אֹתָם חֳמָרִם חֳמָרִם וַתִּבְאַשׁ הָאָרֶץ׃ וַיַּרְא   וּלְאַהֲרֹן וַיֹּאמֶר הַעְתִּירוּ אֶל־יְהוָה וְיָסֵר הַצְפַרְדְּעִים

פַרְעֹה כִּי הָיְתָה הָרְוָחָה וְהַכְבֵּד אֶת־לִבּוֹ וְלֹא שָׁמַע   מִמֶּנִּי וּמֵעַמִּי וַאֲשַׁלְּחָה אֶת־הָעָם וְיִזְבְּחוּ לַיהוָה׃ וַיֹּאמֶר ה

יב אֲלֵהֶם כַּאֲשֶׁר דִּבֶּר יְהוָה׃ ס וַיֹּאמֶר יְהוָה אֶל־   מֹשֶׁה לְפַרְעֹה הִתְפָּאֵר עָלַי לְמָתַי אַעְתִּיר לְךָ

מֹשֶׁה אֱמֹר אֶל־אַהֲרֹן נְטֵה אֶת־מַטְּךָ וְהַךְ אֶת־עֲפַר   וְלַעֲבָדֶיךָ וּלְעַמְּךָ לְהַכְרִית הַצְפַרְדְּעִים מִמְּךָ

יג הָאָרֶץ וְהָיָה לְכִנִּם בְּכָל־אֶרֶץ מִצְרָיִם׃ וַיַּעֲשׂוּ־כֵן   וּמִבָּתֶּיךָ רַק בַּיְאֹר תִּשָּׁאַרְנָה׃ וַיֹּאמֶר לְמָחָר וַיֹּאמֶר י

וַיֵּט אַהֲרֹן אֶת־יָדוֹ בְמַטֵּהוּ וַיַּךְ אֶת־עֲפַר הָאָרֶץ   כִּדְבָרְךָ לְמַעַן תֵּדַע כִּי־אֵין כַּיהוָה אֱלֹהֵינוּ׃ וְסָרוּ ז

וַתְּהִי הַכִּנָּם בָּאָדָם וּבַבְּהֵמָה כָּל־עֲפַר הָאָרֶץ הָיָה   הַצְפַרְדְּעִים מִמְּךָ וּמִבָּתֶּיךָ וּמֵעֲבָדֶיךָ וּמֵעַמֶּךָ רַק

יד כִנִּים בְּכָל־אֶרֶץ מִצְרָיִם׃ וַיַּעֲשׂוּ־כֵן הַחַרְטֻמִּים   בַּיְאֹר תִּשָּׁאַרְנָה׃ וַיֵּצֵא מֹשֶׁה וְאַהֲרֹן מֵעִם פַּרְעֹה ח

בְּלָטֵיהֶם לְהוֹצִיא אֶת־הַכִּנִּים וְלֹא יָכֹלוּ וַתְּהִי הַכִּנָּם   וַיִּצְעַק מֹשֶׁה אֶל־יְהוָה עַל־דְּבַר הַצְפַרְדְּעִים אֲשֶׁר־

טו בָּאָדָם וּבַבְּהֵמָה׃ וַיֹּאמְרוּ הַחַרְטֻמִּם אֶל־פַּרְעֹה   שָׂם לְפַרְעֹה׃ וַיַּעַשׂ יְהוָה כִּדְבַר מֹשֶׁה וַיָּמֻתוּ ט

4] Then Pharaoh summoned Moses and Aaron and said, "Plead with the LORD to remove the frogs from me and my people, and I will let the people go to sacrifice to the LORD." **5]** And Moses said to Pharaoh, "You may have this triumph over me: for what time shall I plead in behalf of you and your courtiers and your people, that the frogs be cut off from you and your houses, to remain only in the Nile?" **6]** "For tomorrow," he replied. And [Moses] said, "As you say—that you may know that there is none like the LORD our God; **7]** the frogs shall retreat from you and your courtiers and your people; they shall remain only in the Nile." **8]** Then Moses and Aaron left Pharaoh's presence, and Moses cried out to the LORD in the matter of the frogs which He had inflicted upon Pharaoh. **9]** And the LORD did as Moses asked; the frogs died out in the houses, the courtyards, and the fields. **10]** And they piled them up in heaps, till the land stank. **11]** But when Pharaoh saw that there was relief, he became stubborn and would not heed them, as the LORD had spoken.

12] Then the LORD said to Moses, "Say to Aaron: Hold out your rod and strike the dust of the earth, and it shall turn to lice throughout the land of Egypt." **13]** And they did so. Aaron held out his arm with the rod and struck the dust of the earth, and vermin came upon man and beast; all the dust of the earth turned to lice throughout the land of Egypt. **14]** The magicians did the like with their spells to produce lice, but they could not. The vermin remained upon

4] *Plead with the Lord.* The magicians could increase but not decrease the nuisance.

5] *This triumph.* Moses taunts Pharaoh and challenges him to test God (compare Elijah's taunt, I Kings 18:24 ff.).

12] *Lice.* Others, "sandflies," "gnats," "mosquitoes." According to Philo, they were small insects which pierced the skin and caused a severe itch [3].

14] *But they could not.* For the first time the magicians are routed and now warn Pharaoh that a superior power is at work.

אֶצְבַּע אֱלֹהִים הִוא וַיֶּחֱזַק לֵב־פַּרְעֹה וְלֹא־שָׁמַע
אֲלֵהֶם כַּאֲשֶׁר דִּבֶּר יְהֹוָה: ס וַיֹּאמֶר יְהֹוָה אֶל־
מֹשֶׁה הַשְׁכֵּם בַּבֹּקֶר וְהִתְיַצֵּב לִפְנֵי פַרְעֹה הִנֵּה יוֹצֵא
הַמָּיְמָה וְאָמַרְתָּ אֵלָיו כֹּה אָמַר יְהֹוָה שַׁלַּח עַמִּי
וְיַעַבְדֻנִי: כִּי אִם־אֵינְךָ מְשַׁלֵּחַ אֶת־עַמִּי הִנְנִי מַשְׁלִיחַ
בְּךָ וּבַעֲבָדֶיךָ וּבְעַמְּךָ וּבְבָתֶּיךָ אֶת־הֶעָרֹב וּמָלְאוּ
בָּתֵּי מִצְרַיִם אֶת־הֶעָרֹב וְגַם הָאֲדָמָה אֲשֶׁר־הֵם עָלֶיהָ:
וְהִפְלֵיתִי בַיּוֹם הַהוּא אֶת־אֶרֶץ גֹּשֶׁן אֲשֶׁר עַמִּי עֹמֵד
עָלֶיהָ לְבִלְתִּי הֱיוֹת־שָׁם עָרֹב לְמַעַן תֵּדַע כִּי אֲנִי

יְהֹוָה בְּקֶרֶב הָאָרֶץ: וְשַׂמְתִּי פְדֻת בֵּין עַמִּי וּבֵין עַמֶּךָ
לְמָחָר יִהְיֶה הָאֹת הַזֶּה: וַיַּעַשׂ יְהֹוָה כֵּן וַיָּבֹא עָרֹב
כָּבֵד בֵּיתָה פַרְעֹה וּבֵית עֲבָדָיו וּבְכָל־אֶרֶץ מִצְרַיִם
תִּשָּׁחֵת הָאָרֶץ מִפְּנֵי הֶעָרֹב: וַיִּקְרָא פַרְעֹה אֶל־מֹשֶׁה
וּלְאַהֲרֹן וַיֹּאמֶר לְכוּ זִבְחוּ לֵאלֹהֵיכֶם בָּאָרֶץ:
וַיֹּאמֶר מֹשֶׁה לֹא נָכוֹן לַעֲשׂוֹת כֵּן כִּי תּוֹעֲבַת מִצְרַיִם
נִזְבַּח לַיהֹוָה אֱלֹהֵינוּ הֵן נִזְבַּח אֶת־תּוֹעֲבַת מִצְרַיִם
לְעֵינֵיהֶם וְלֹא יִסְקְלֻנוּ: דֶּרֶךְ שְׁלֹשֶׁת יָמִים נֵלֵךְ
בַּמִּדְבָּר וְזָבַחְנוּ לַיהֹוָה אֱלֹהֵינוּ כַּאֲשֶׁר יֹאמַר אֵלֵינוּ:

man and beast; **15]** and the magicians said to Pharaoh, "This is the finger of God!" But Pharaoh's heart stiffened and he would not heed them, as the LORD had spoken.

16] And the LORD said to Moses, "Early in the morning present yourself to Pharaoh, as he is coming out to the water, and say to him, 'Thus says the LORD: Let My people go that they may worship Me. **17]** For if you do not let My people go, I will let loose swarms of insects against you and your courtiers and your people and your houses; the houses of the Egyptians, and the very ground they stand on, shall be filled with swarms of insects. **18]** But on that day I will set apart the region of Goshen, where My people dwell, so that no swarms of insects shall be there, that you may know that I the LORD am in the midst of the land. **19]** And I will make a distinction between My people and your people. Tomorrow this sign shall come to pass.'" **20]** And the LORD did so. Heavy swarms of insects invaded Pharaoh's palace and the houses of his courtiers; throughout the country of Egypt the land was ruined because of the swarms of insects.

21] Then Pharaoh summoned Moses and Aaron and said, "Go and sacrifice to your God within the land." **22]** But Moses replied, "It would not be right to do this, for what we sacrifice to the LORD our God is untouchable to the Egyptians. If we sacrifice that which is untouchable to the Egyptians before their very eyes, will they not stone us! **23]** So we must go a distance of three days into the wilderness and sacrifice to the LORD our God as He may

15] *Finger of God.* Meaning the work of His hands (so used also in Ps. 8:4). In Egyptian literature a plague is called "the hand of God"; among the Babylonians this expression was the name of a sickness. In Christian Scriptures, Jesus says: "By the finger of God I cast out demons" [4].

16] *Coming out to the water.* See at 7:15.

17] *Swarms of insects.* The meaning of עָרֹב is uncertain. Others, "wild beasts."

18] *Set apart.* God's might is demonstrated both by the sign and by the special treatment accorded to Israel.

Goshen. East of the Nile, near the delta; see Gen. 45:10.

19] *Distinction.* The exact meaning of פְּדֻת is uncertain.

22] *Untouchable to the Egyptians.* Sacred to them. Or the Egyptians were accustomed to offer vegetables, poultry, and pieces of meat, but not generally whole animals [5]. The passage suggests that the Israelites did not bring any sacrifices while in Egypt.

ג בָּם: הִנֵּה יַד־יְהֹוָה הוֹיָה בְּמִקְנְךָ אֲשֶׁר בַּשָּׂדֶה בַּסּוּסִים
בַּחֲמֹרִים בַּגְּמַלִּים בַּבָּקָר וּבַצֹּאן דֶּבֶר כָּבֵד מְאֹד:
ד וְהִפְלָה יְהֹוָה בֵּין מִקְנֵה יִשְׂרָאֵל וּבֵין מִקְנֵה מִצְרָיִם
ה וְלֹא יָמוּת מִכָּל־לִבְנֵי יִשְׂרָאֵל דָּבָר: וַיָּשֶׂם יְהֹוָה
מוֹעֵד לֵאמֹר מָחָר יַעֲשֶׂה יְהֹוָה הַדָּבָר הַזֶּה בָּאָרֶץ:
ו וַיַּעַשׂ יְהֹוָה אֶת־הַדָּבָר הַזֶּה מִמָּחֳרָת וַיָּמָת כֹּל מִקְנֵה
ז מִצְרָיִם וּמִמִּקְנֵה בְנֵי־יִשְׂרָאֵל לֹא־מֵת אֶחָד: וַיִּשְׁלַח
פַּרְעֹה וְהִנֵּה לֹא־מֵת מִמִּקְנֵה יִשְׂרָאֵל עַד־אֶחָד וַיִּכְבַּד
לֵב פַּרְעֹה וְלֹא שִׁלַּח אֶת־הָעָם:
          פ

ח וַיֹּאמֶר יְהֹוָה אֶל־מֹשֶׁה וְאֶל־אַהֲרֹן קְחוּ לָכֶם מְלֹא
חָפְנֵיכֶם פִּיחַ כִּבְשָׁן וּזְרָקוֹ מֹשֶׁה הַשָּׁמַיְמָה לְעֵינֵי
ט פַּרְעֹה: וְהָיָה לְאָבָק עַל כָּל־אֶרֶץ מִצְרָיִם וְהָיָה
עַל־הָאָדָם וְעַל־הַבְּהֵמָה לִשְׁחִין פֹּרֵחַ אֲבַעְבֻּעֹת בְּכָל־

כד וַיֹּאמֶר פַּרְעֹה אָנֹכִי אֲשַׁלַּח אֶתְכֶם וּזְבַחְתֶּם לַיהֹוָה
אֱלֹהֵיכֶם בַּמִּדְבָּר רַק הַרְחֵק לֹא־תַרְחִיקוּ לָלֶכֶת
כה הַעְתִּירוּ בַּעֲדִי: וַיֹּאמֶר מֹשֶׁה הִנֵּה אָנֹכִי יוֹצֵא מֵעִמָּךְ
וְהַעְתַּרְתִּי אֶל־יְהֹוָה וְסָר הֶעָרֹב מִפַּרְעֹה מֵעֲבָדָיו
וּמֵעַמּוֹ מָחָר רַק אַל־יֹסֵף פַּרְעֹה הָתֵל לְבִלְתִּי שַׁלַּח
כו אֶת־הָעָם לִזְבֹּחַ לַיהֹוָה: וַיֵּצֵא מֹשֶׁה מֵעִם פַּרְעֹה
כז וַיֶּעְתַּר אֶל־יְהֹוָה: וַיַּעַשׂ יְהֹוָה כִּדְבַר מֹשֶׁה וַיָּסַר הֶעָרֹב
כח מִפַּרְעֹה מֵעֲבָדָיו וּמֵעַמּוֹ לֹא נִשְׁאַר אֶחָד: וַיַּכְבֵּד
פַּרְעֹה אֶת־לִבּוֹ גַּם בַּפַּעַם הַזֹּאת וְלֹא שִׁלַּח אֶת־
הָעָם:
          פ

א וַיֹּאמֶר יְהֹוָה אֶל־מֹשֶׁה בֹּא אֶל־פַּרְעֹה וְדִבַּרְתָּ אֵלָיו
כֹּה־אָמַר יְהֹוָה אֱלֹהֵי הָעִבְרִים שַׁלַּח אֶת־עַמִּי
ב וְיַעַבְדֻנִי: כִּי אִם־מָאֵן אַתָּה לְשַׁלֵּחַ וְעוֹדְךָ מַחֲזִיק

command us."   **24]** Pharaoh said, "I will let you go to sacrifice to the LORD your God in the wilderness; but do not go very far. Plead, then, for me."   **25]** And Moses said, "When I leave your presence, I will plead with the LORD that the swarms of insects depart tomorrow from Pharaoh and his courtiers and his people; but let not Pharaoh again act deceitfully, not letting the people go to sacrifice to the LORD."

26] So Moses left Pharaoh's presence and pleaded with the LORD.   **27]** And the LORD did as Moses asked: He removed the swarms of insects from Pharaoh, from his courtiers, and from his people; not one remained.   **28]** But Pharaoh became stubborn this time also, and would not let the people go.

1] The LORD said to Moses, "Go to Pharaoh and say to him, 'Thus says the LORD, the God of the Hebrews: Let My people go to worship Me.   **2]** For if you refuse to let them go, and continue to hold them,   **3]** then the hand of the LORD will strike your livestock in the fields— the horses, the asses, the camels, the cattle, and the sheep—with a very severe pestilence. **4]** But the LORD will make a distinction between the livestock of Israel and the livestock of the Egyptians, so that nothing shall die of all that belongs to the Israelites.   **5]** The LORD has fixed the time: tomorrow the LORD will do this thing in the land.'"   **6]** And the LORD did so the next day: all the livestock of the Egyptians died, but of the livestock of the Israelites not a beast died.   **7]** When Pharaoh inquired, he found that not a head of the livestock of Israel had died; yet Pharaoh remained stubborn, and he would not let the people go.

8] Then the LORD said to Moses and Aaron, "Each of you take handfuls of soot from the kiln, and let Moses throw it toward the sky in the sight of Pharaoh.   **9]** It shall become a fine dust all over the land of Egypt, and cause an inflammation breaking out in boils on man and beast

9:1] *Let My people go to worship Me.* Freedom for Israel is not described as desirable in itself, but as an opportunity to serve God.

3] *The hand of the Lord will strike.* The whole

hand, and not just a finger, that is, the punishment will be much more severe.

6] *All the livestock.* In view of verse 10 this must be taken as a hyperbole.

לִפְנֵ֣י מֹשֶׁ֔ה מִפְּנֵ֥י הַשְּׁחִ֖ין כִּֽי־הָיָ֣ה הַשְּׁחִ֔ין בַּֽחַרְטֻמִּ֖ם   אֶ֣רֶץ מִצְרָ֑יִם: וַיִּקְח֞וּ אֶת־פִּ֣יחַ הַכִּבְשָׁ֗ן וַיַּֽעַמְדוּ֙ לִפְנֵ֣י

וּבְכָל־מִצְרָֽיִם: וַיְחַזֵּ֤ק יְהוָה֙ אֶת־לֵ֣ב פַּרְעֹ֔ה וְלֹ֥א   פַרְעֹ֔ה וַיִּזְרֹ֥ק אֹת֛וֹ מֹשֶׁ֖ה הַשָּׁמָ֑יְמָה וַיְהִי֙ שְׁחִ֣ין אֲבַעְבֻּעֹ֔ת

שָׁמַ֖ע אֲלֵהֶ֑ם כַּֽאֲשֶׁ֛ר דִּבֶּ֥ר יְהוָ֖ה אֶל־מֹשֶֽׁה: ס   פֹּרֵ֕חַ בָּֽאָדָ֖ם וּבַבְּהֵמָֽה: וְלֹֽא־יָֽכְל֣וּ הַֽחַרְטֻמִּ֗ים לַֽעֲמֹ֛ד

throughout the land of Egypt." **10]** So they took soot of the kiln and appeared before Pharaoh; Moses threw it toward the sky, and it caused an inflammation breaking out in boils on man and beast. **11]** The magicians were unable to confront Moses because of the inflammation, for the inflammation afflicted the magicians as well as all the other Egyptians. **12]** But the LORD stiffened the heart of Pharaoh, and he would not heed them, just as the LORD had told Moses.

11] *Magicians.* Mentioned here because the plague had a magical appearance.

12] *Stiffened the heart.* For the first time in the narrative of the plagues, God himself is said to have intervened in this way.

The Plagues—Natural or Supernatural?

The straightforward meaning of the biblical text appears to be that God brought extraordinary events to pass which were designed to have an impact on Israel's fate. In doing so He interfered with the ordinary, familiar processes of nature. This intervention is usually described as "miracle" and has for many Bible readers become a formidable obstacle to reading the text with full appreciation. The story of the plagues uses primarily two expressions for the extraordinary acts of God: אוֹת (*ot*, "sign") and מוֹפֵת (*mofet*, "marvel").[1] Their use implies divine action as well as the concept that nature is not an impersonal structure governed by rigid laws, but an arrangement that is flexible and subject to personal forces. In that sense, the terms "natural" and "supernatural" do not fit the biblical outlook, which conceived both divine and demonic powers built into observable reality. Most moderns would take the opposite view: the stories are unacceptable as fact and must be deemed legendary and unhistorical [6]. A similar position was already taken by Spinoza: the universe itself is a miracle but its laws are inexorable [7].

Ancient and medieval scholars were also much concerned with the problems raised by biblical wonders. Already in Deut. 13:2–4 we are warned not to trust the performance of extraordinary signs as evidence of prophetic authenticity. In consequence, there was a tendency in Jewish life to discount or play down such evidences. In a famous story recorded in the Talmud, God himself brought about miracles in order to support Rabbi Eliezer ben Hyrcanos in a dispute: He uprooted a tree, made a river flow backward, inclined a wall, and even issued an audible judgment in the matter. But the majority of the Rabbis refused to be swayed and proclaimed that they had been given the Torah (which rules that the majority decides the law, precluding God's interference) and were not about to surrender their privilege. The legend then concludes by having God express His pleasure over this act of human independence even though He had suffered a "defeat" in the process [8].

But while postbiblical miracles could thus be discounted, biblical marvels could not be disposed of in this way. They were accepted as having happened in the manner described in the text. The solution that the Rabbis adopted and which was later reinforced by Maimonides was to assume that all so-called miracles recorded in the Bible only *appeared* as contemporaneous divine interventions. In fact, they had already been built into the process of creation. The crossing of the Reed Sea, the descent of manna, and so forth were precreated as it were and merely happened in a "natural" way when their time came [9].

Others tried to circumvent the problem by stating that a miracle was or is an event that cannot (yet) be explained. Thomas

---

[1] The Torah does not have a term which corresponds to "miracle" in the sense which later rabbinic and Christian literature gave it. The events were "signs and wonders," meaning manifestations and omens of divine concern and potential participation (in fact, in Deut. 34:11 *mofet* is rendered as portent). The problem of supernatural suspension of the natural order was not as such experienced by biblical man, who did not know the concept of miracle in its modern sense.

In addition to *ot* and *mofet*, additional terms are employed in the Torah and the rest of the Bible, especially פֶּלֶא (*pele*) and נִפְלָאוֹת (*nifla-ot*), meaning extraordinary, wondrous happenings. The plagues are in our story also referred to as מִשְׁפָּטִים (*mishpatim*, "judgments" or "punishments"), but this is a term alluding more to the reason for than to the nature of the divine acts. Only in postbiblical days did the term נֵס (*nes*) become the most popular word for miracle.

Aquinas took this view and said that men often call "miracle" what may not really be one, since they do not ever fully know the workings of nature [10]. The rigidity of natural laws itself was altogether questioned by Augustine who suggested that nature might be considered as including what God does, a position similar to the rabbinic teaching about precreation [11].

All these approaches to the text proceed from the assumption that the plagues occurred as recorded, and they attempt to explain the extraordinary nature of the events. But these efforts are wide of the mark, for they consider the story literally rather than for what it really is: essentially interpretive and legendary. The release of the Israelites from slavery was unprecedented, and the only explanation possible, repeated a thousand times in folk recital and eventually set down in writing, was to give the credit to God. The release and its attending events were experienced as signs and wonders by the people who saw themselves in a special relationship to Him. His presence transfigured history, and the eventual release from bondage became an aspect of salvation in both the material sense and the spiritual sense. Israel experienced the events in what Heschel called a state of "radical amazement" [12].

Whether there were any natural happenings which in their unusual nature gave rise to these sentiments and instilled anxiety in the hearts of the Egyptians is hard to say. There was possibly or even likely a historical kernel that became, in the biblical tradition, transposed into the moral-religious realm. Thus it has been claimed that the bloodiness of the Nile was caused by special deposits which the river picked up from the mountains (hence the name "Red Nile" for one branch); that frogs accompanied a large-scale inundation; and that lice or gnats as well as insects recurrently infested the area [13]. But such natural events would have had to be of extraordinary magnitude to classify as wonders, and, in any case, it is not possible to treat the biblical story as a historical account. It was an attempt to explain the inexplicable and it did so on a religious basis. Israel's redemption was the ultimate marvel, and it was caused by God. To bring it about, nature itself was harnessed, the drama of the plagues was unfolded, and the ground was laid for an experience that forever after was etched into the hearts of the people and their descendants. The mysterious power of God brought the redemption about, and His chosen ones knew this as certainty. The story of the plagues was the legendary framework of the tradition that dealt at its core with oppression and freedom, faith and resistance to faith, opposition to the will of God and His final, glorious victory.

GLEANINGS

Growth of a Legend

If we compare, for instance, the narrative of the Ten Plagues with the narrative of the Revolt of Absalom, we shall feel the difference. The one is nature itself, with all the flexibility and easy sequence that we associate with nature. The other is constructed upon a scheme which is so symmetrical that we cannot help seeing that it is really artificial. I do not mean artificial in the sense that the writer, with no materials before him, sat down consciously and deliberately to invent them in the form they now have; but I mean that, as the story passed from mouth to mouth, it gradually and almost imperceptibly assumed its present shape.

W. SANDAY [14]

Radical Amazement

It is not from experience but from our inability to experience what is given to our mind that certainty of the realness of God is derived. It is not the order of being but the transcendent in the contingency of all order, the allusions to transcendence in all acts and all things that challenge our deepest understanding.

Our certainty is the result of wonder and radical amazement, of awe before the mystery and meaning of the totality of life beyond our rational discerning. Faith is the response to the mystery, shot through with meaning; the response to a challenge which no one can for ever ignore. "The heaven" is a challenge. When you "lift up your eyes on high," you are faced with the question. Faith is an act of man who, transcending himself, responds to Him who transcends the world.

A. J. HESCHEL [15]

The real miracle means that in the astonishing experience of the event the current system of cause and effect becomes, as it were, transparent and permits a glimpse of the sphere in which a sole power, not restricted by any other, is at work. To live with the miracle means to recognize this power on every given occasion as the effecting one. That is the religion of Moses, the man who experienced the futility of magic, who learned to recognize the demonic as one of the forms by which the Divine functions, and who saw how all the gods of Egypt vanished at the blows of the One; and that is religion generally, as far as it is reality.

M. BUBER [16]

The Stiffened Heart

When God saw that Pharaoh did not yield after five plagues, He resolved to harden his heart in order to exact full punishment from him.

MIDRASH [17]

Blood

Changing water into blood was easy for the magicians. For that is a well-known practice, to drown mankind in rivers of blood.

CHASIDIC [18]

Frogs

Our forebears in Egypt had no home, no private chamber, no sleep, no bread. And now these shy frogs promenade through all the rooms of the Egyptians and show them what it means not to enjoy one's house, bed, and board without being constantly molested.

S. R. HIRSCH [19]

The Wicked

When Moses' prayer was answered, Pharaoh changed his mind. That is the way of the wicked: when in trouble they cry to God; when they have respite they return to their evil ways.

MIDRASH [20]

Into the Wilderness

Pharaoh offered Israel the opportunity to

443

bring their sacrifices in Egypt rather than in the wilderness (8:21). He did not comprehend that first Israel had to remove itself from that corruption of which Egypt was the symbol. Before man can pray he must "go into the wilderness," there to repent. Then only will he be ready to bring his offering to God.   CHASIDIC [21]

A Song

When Israel was in Egypt land,
Let My people go,
Oppressed so hard they could not stand,
Let My people go.
Go down, Moses,
'Way down in Egypt land,
Tell ole Pharaoh to let My people go.

"Thus spoke the Lord," bold Moses said:
Let My people go.
If not I'll smite your first-born dead,
Let My people go.
Go down, Moses,
'Way down in Egypt land,
Tell ole Pharaoh to let My people go.
O let My people go.

                    AMERICAN SPIRITUAL

Egyptian Parallel

["The Admonitions of Ipuwer" is the record of an otherwise unknown social and political critic who describes the anarchy reigning in Egypt. The manuscript is from the general era of Moses, but the original belongs to a time before 2000 B.C.E. The following is excerpted and simplified from a longer text.]

The Nile is in flood, but no one plows for himself, because every man says: "We do not know what may happen throughout the land!"

Many dead are buried in the river. The stream is a tomb, and the embalming–place has really become the stream.

The river is blood. If one drinks of it, one rejects it as human and thirsts for water.

The desert is spread throughout the land. The homes are destroyed. Barbarians from outside have come to Egypt.

Such is our water! Such is our welfare! What can we do about it? Going to ruin!

Laughter has disappeared and is no longer made. It is wailing that pervades the land, mixed with lamentation [22].

The Last Four Plagues

As indicated above, the literary structure of the story of the plagues provides for three sets of three punishments and the climactic death of the first-born. The section before us will recount the plagues of hail and thunder, of locusts, and of darkness; and these are followed by the announcement of the final blow. The story then pauses in order to introduce the Passover theme and thereafter returns to tell of the actual occurrence of the tenth plague and the subsequent liberation. The earlier pattern is repeated: the first two plagues are introduced by warnings; the third (i.e., plague 9) occurs without announcement. There is a steady rise in the severity of the marvels.

The story now offers greater detail than we were given with the earlier events and it enlarges their scope. The seventh plague is provided with an elaborate opening, setting the stage for the impressive demonstration of God's power. For it now becomes ever clearer that the plagues are above all "signs" that an obdurate Pharaoh needs to experience before at last he accepts the reality of God's superior might. The plagues are demonstrations that יְהוָה is uniquely powerful; He is not just another god protecting his own, He is master of all men and all nature. The signs are there for the world to see, and they are for Israel the basis of a new understanding of the Lord whose name Moses has communicated to them after the second revelation (chapter 6).

The plague of locusts stresses the educative element it contains in teaching Israel's generations about God's might; the plague of darkness

445

produces Pharaoh's first concession, which is, however, rejected by Moses. The announcement of the final blow (11:4–8) should follow directly after chapter 10 and may once have stood there.

(A new weekly portion, *Bo*, begins with 10:1.)

כא אֶת־עֲבָדָיו וְאֶת־מִקְנֵהוּ אֶל־הַבָּתִּים: וַאֲשֶׁר לֹא־שָׂם
לִבּוֹ אֶל־דְּבַר יְהוָה וַיַּעֲזֹב אֶת־עֲבָדָיו וְאֶת־מִקְנֵהוּ
בַּשָּׂדֶה: פ

כב וַיֹּאמֶר יְהוָה אֶל־מֹשֶׁה נְטֵה אֶת־יָדְךָ עַל־הַשָּׁמַיִם
וִיהִי בָרָד בְּכָל־אֶרֶץ מִצְרָיִם עַל־הָאָדָם וְעַל־הַבְּהֵמָה
וְעַל כָּל־עֵשֶׂב הַשָּׂדֶה בְּאֶרֶץ מִצְרָיִם: כג וַיֵּט מֹשֶׁה אֶת־
מַטֵּהוּ עַל־הַשָּׁמַיִם וַיהוָה נָתַן קֹלֹת וּבָרָד וַתִּהֲלַךְ־אֵשׁ
אָרְצָה וַיַּמְטֵר יְהוָה בָּרָד עַל־אֶרֶץ מִצְרָיִם: כד וַיְהִי
בָרָד וְאֵשׁ מִתְלַקַּחַת בְּתוֹךְ הַבָּרָד כָּבֵד מְאֹד אֲשֶׁר
לֹא־הָיָה כָמֹהוּ בְּכָל־אֶרֶץ מִצְרַיִם מֵאָז הָיְתָה לְגוֹי:
כה וַיַּךְ הַבָּרָד בְּכָל־אֶרֶץ מִצְרַיִם אֵת כָּל־אֲשֶׁר בַּשָּׂדֶה
מֵאָדָם וְעַד־בְּהֵמָה וְאֵת כָּל־עֵשֶׂב הַשָּׂדֶה הִכָּה הַבָּרָד
וְאֶת־כָּל־עֵץ הַשָּׂדֶה שִׁבֵּר: כו רַק בְּאֶרֶץ גֹּשֶׁן אֲשֶׁר־שָׁם
בְּנֵי יִשְׂרָאֵל לֹא הָיָה בָּרָד: וַיִּשְׁלַח פַּרְעֹה וַיִּקְרָא

יג וַיֹּאמֶר יְהוָה אֶל־מֹשֶׁה הַשְׁכֵּם בַּבֹּקֶר וְהִתְיַצֵּב לִפְנֵי
פַרְעֹה וְאָמַרְתָּ אֵלָיו כֹּה־אָמַר יְהוָה אֱלֹהֵי הָעִבְרִים
שַׁלַּח אֶת־עַמִּי וְיַעַבְדֻנִי: יד כִּי בַּפַּעַם הַזֹּאת אֲנִי שֹׁלֵחַ
אֶת־כָּל־מַגֵּפֹתַי אֶל־לִבְּךָ וּבַעֲבָדֶיךָ וּבְעַמֶּךָ בַּעֲבוּר
תֵּדַע כִּי אֵין כָּמֹנִי בְּכָל־הָאָרֶץ: טו כִּי עַתָּה שָׁלַחְתִּי אֶת־
יָדִי וָאַךְ אוֹתְךָ וְאֶת־עַמְּךָ בַּדָּבֶר וַתִּכָּחֵד מִן־הָאָרֶץ:
טז וְאוּלָם בַּעֲבוּר זֹאת הֶעֱמַדְתִּיךָ בַּעֲבוּר הַרְאֹתְךָ אֶת־
כֹּחִי וּלְמַעַן סַפֵּר שְׁמִי בְּכָל־הָאָרֶץ: יז עוֹדְךָ מִסְתּוֹלֵל
בְּעַמִּי לְבִלְתִּי שַׁלְּחָם: יח הִנְנִי מַמְטִיר כָּעֵת מָחָר בָּרָד
כָּבֵד מְאֹד אֲשֶׁר לֹא־הָיָה כָמֹהוּ בְּמִצְרַיִם לְמִן־הַיּוֹם
הִוָּסְדָה וְעַד־עָתָּה: יט וְעַתָּה שְׁלַח הָעֵז אֶת־מִקְנְךָ וְאֵת
כָּל־אֲשֶׁר לְךָ בַּשָּׂדֶה כָּל־הָאָדָם וְהַבְּהֵמָה אֲשֶׁר־
יִמָּצֵא בַשָּׂדֶה וְלֹא יֵאָסֵף הַבַּיְתָה וְיָרַד עֲלֵהֶם הַבָּרָד
וָמֵתוּ: כ הַיָּרֵא אֶת־דְּבַר יְהוָה מֵעַבְדֵי פַּרְעֹה הֵנִיס

13] The LORD said to Moses, "Early in the morning station yourself before Pharaoh and say to him, 'Thus says the LORD, the God of the Hebrews: Let My people go to worship Me. **14]** For this time I will send all My plagues upon your person, and your courtiers, and your people, in order that you may know that there is none like Me in all the world. **15]** I could have stretched forth My hand and stricken you and your people with pestilence, and you would have been effaced from the earth. **16]** Nevertheless I have spared you for this purpose: in order to show you My power, and in order that My fame may resound throughout the world. **17]** Yet you continue to thwart My people, and do not let them go! **18]** This time tomorrow I will rain down a very heavy hail, such as has not been in Egypt from the day it was founded until now. **19]** Therefore, order your livestock and everything you have in the open brought under shelter; every man and beast that is found outside, not having been brought indoors, shall perish when the hail comes down upon them!'" **20]** Those among Pharaoh's courtiers who feared the LORD's word brought their slaves and livestock indoors to safety; **21]** but those who paid no regard to the word of the LORD left their slaves and livestock in the open.

22] The LORD said to Moses, "Hold out your arm toward the sky that hail may fall on all the land of Egypt, upon man and beast and all the grasses of the field in the land of Egypt." **23]** So Moses held out his rod toward the sky, and the LORD sent thunder and hail, and fire streamed down to the ground, as the LORD rained down hail upon the land of Egypt. **24]** The hail was very heavy—fire flashing in the midst of the hail—such as had not fallen on the land of Egypt since it had become a nation. **25]** Throughout the land of Egypt the hail struck down all that were in the open, both man and beast; the hail also struck down all the grasses of the field and shattered all the trees of the field. **26]** Only in the region of Goshen, where the Israelites were, there was no hail.

9:17] *Thwart.* Others, "exalt yourself over."

לְמֹשֶׁה וּלְאַהֲרֹן וַיֹּאמֶר אֲלֵהֶם חָטָאתִי הַפָּעַם יְהֹוָה

כח הַצַּדִּיק וַאֲנִי וְעַמִּי הָרְשָׁעִים: הַעְתִּירוּ אֶל־יְהֹוָה וְרַב
מִהְיֹת קֹלֹת אֱלֹהִים וּבָרָד וַאֲשַׁלְּחָה אֶתְכֶם וְלֹא

כט תֹסִפוּן לַעֲמֹד: וַיֹּאמֶר אֵלָיו מֹשֶׁה כְּצֵאתִי אֶת־הָעִיר
אֶפְרֹשׂ אֶת־כַּפַּי אֶל־יְהֹוָה הַקֹּלוֹת יֶחְדָּלוּן וְהַבָּרָד

ל לֹא יִהְיֶה־עוֹד לְמַעַן תֵּדַע כִּי לַיהֹוָה הָאָרֶץ: וְאַתָּה
וַעֲבָדֶיךָ יָדַעְתִּי כִּי טֶרֶם תִּירְאוּן מִפְּנֵי יְהֹוָה אֱלֹהִים:

לא וְהַפִּשְׁתָּה וְהַשְּׂעֹרָה נֻכָּתָה כִּי הַשְּׂעֹרָה אָבִיב וְהַפִּשְׁתָּה

לב גִּבְעֹל: וְהַחִטָּה וְהַכֻּסֶּמֶת לֹא נֻכּוּ כִּי אֲפִילֹת הֵנָּה:

לג וַיֵּצֵא מֹשֶׁה מֵעִם פַּרְעֹה אֶת־הָעִיר וַיִּפְרֹשׂ כַּפָּיו אֶל־
יְהֹוָה וַיַּחְדְּלוּ הַקֹּלוֹת וְהַבָּרָד וּמָטָר לֹא־נִתַּךְ אָרְצָה:

לד וַיַּרְא פַּרְעֹה כִּי־חָדַל הַמָּטָר וְהַבָּרָד וְהַקֹּלֹת וַיֹּסֶף

לה לַחֲטֹא וַיַּכְבֵּד לִבּוֹ הוּא וַעֲבָדָיו: וַיֶּחֱזַק לֵב פַּרְעֹה
וְלֹא שִׁלַּח אֶת־בְּנֵי יִשְׂרָאֵל כַּאֲשֶׁר דִּבֶּר יְהֹוָה בְּיַד־
מֹשֶׁה:

Haftarah Va'era, p. 696

פ פ פ

א וַיֹּאמֶר יְהֹוָה אֶל־מֹשֶׁה בֹּא אֶל־פַּרְעֹה כִּי־אֲנִי הִכְבַּדְתִּי
אֶת־לִבּוֹ וְאֶת־לֵב עֲבָדָיו לְמַעַן שִׁתִי אֹתֹתַי אֵלֶּה

ב בְּקִרְבּוֹ: וּלְמַעַן תְּסַפֵּר בְּאָזְנֵי בִנְךָ וּבֶן־בִּנְךָ אֵת
אֲשֶׁר הִתְעַלַּלְתִּי בְּמִצְרַיִם וְאֶת־אֹתֹתַי אֲשֶׁר־שַׂמְתִּי

27] Thereupon Pharaoh sent for Moses and Aaron and said to them, "I stand guilty this time. The LORD is in the right, and I and my people are in the wrong. **28]** Plead with the LORD that there may be an end of God's thunder and of hail. I will let you go; you need stay no longer." **29]** Moses said to him, "As I go out of the city, I shall spread out my hands to the LORD; the thunder will cease and the hail will fall no more, so that you may know that the earth is the LORD's. **30]** But I know that you and your courtiers do not yet fear the LORD God."— **31]** Now the flax and barley were ruined, for the barley was in the ear and the flax was in bud; **32]** but the wheat and the emmer were not hurt, for they ripen late.— **33]** Leaving Pharaoh, Moses went outside the city and spread out his hands to the LORD: the thunder and hail ceased, and no rain came pouring down upon the earth. **34]** But when Pharaoh saw that the rain and the hail and the thunder had ceased, he reverted to his guilty ways, as did his courtiers. **35]** So Pharaoh's heart stiffened and he would not let the Israelites go, just as the LORD had foretold through Moses.

1] Then the LORD said to Moses, "Go to Pharaoh. For I have hardened his heart and the hearts of his courtiers, in order that I may display these My signs among them, **2]** and that you may recount in the hearing of your sons and of your sons' sons how I made a mockery of the Egyptians and how I displayed My signs among them—in order that you may know that I am

27] *This time.* Now I have to admit my guilt.
   Right . . . wrong. In the forensic rather than the ethical sense [1].

29] *Spread out my hands.* In the traditional gesture of prayer.

30] *Lord God.* Moses here uses this combination purposely to counteract the apparent distinction that Pharaoh had made between the Lord and God (verse 28) [2].

31] *Barley . . . in the ear.* The harvest time in Egypt is February–March.

32] *Emmer.* A kind of wheat. Others understand "spelt," found in bread loaves in Egyptian tombs.

10:1] *Go.* בֹּא (*bo*); better, "enter." The word gives its name to the weekly portion that starts here. The last stage of the confrontation begins and Pharaoh "enters" into negotiation [3].

לָנוּ לְמוֹקֵשׁ שַׁלַּח אֶת־הָאֲנָשִׁים וְיַעַבְדוּ אֶת־יְהֹוָה
אֱלֹהֵיהֶם הֲטֶרֶם תֵּדַע כִּי אָבְדָה מִצְרָיִם: וַיּוּשַׁב
אֶת־מֹשֶׁה וְאֶת־אַהֲרֹן אֶל־פַּרְעֹה וַיֹּאמֶר אֲלֵהֶם לְכוּ
עִבְדוּ אֶת־יְהֹוָה אֱלֹהֵיכֶם מִי וָמִי הַהֹלְכִים: וַיֹּאמֶר
מֹשֶׁה בִּנְעָרֵינוּ וּבִזְקֵנֵינוּ נֵלֵךְ בְּבָנֵינוּ וּבִבְנוֹתֵנוּ בְּצֹאנֵנוּ
וּבִבְקָרֵנוּ נֵלֵךְ כִּי חַג־יְהֹוָה לָנוּ: וַיֹּאמֶר אֲלֵהֶם יְהִי
כֵן יְהֹוָה עִמָּכֶם כַּאֲשֶׁר אֲשַׁלַּח אֶתְכֶם וְאֶת־טַפְּכֶם
רְאוּ כִּי רָעָה נֶגֶד פְּנֵיכֶם: לֹא כֵן לְכוּ נָא הַגְּבָרִים
וְעִבְדוּ אֶת־יְהֹוָה כִּי אֹתָהּ אַתֶּם מְבַקְשִׁים וַיְגָרֶשׁ אֹתָם
מֵאֵת פְּנֵי פַרְעֹה: ס וַיֹּאמֶר יְהֹוָה אֶל־מֹשֶׁה נְטֵה
יָדְךָ עַל־אֶרֶץ מִצְרַיִם בָּאַרְבֶּה וְיַעַל עַל־אֶרֶץ מִצְרָיִם

ג בָּם וִידַעְתֶּם כִּי־אֲנִי יְהֹוָה: וַיָּבֹא מֹשֶׁה וְאַהֲרֹן אֶל־
פַּרְעֹה וַיֹּאמְרוּ אֵלָיו כֹּה־אָמַר יְהֹוָה אֱלֹהֵי הָעִבְרִים
ד עַד־מָתַי מֵאַנְתָּ לֵעָנֹת מִפָּנָי שַׁלַּח עַמִּי וְיַעַבְדֻנִי: כִּי
אִם־מָאֵן אַתָּה לְשַׁלֵּחַ אֶת־עַמִּי הִנְנִי מֵבִיא מָחָר
ה אַרְבֶּה בִּגְבֻלֶךָ: וְכִסָּה אֶת־עֵין הָאָרֶץ וְלֹא יוּכַל
לִרְאֹת אֶת־הָאָרֶץ וְאָכַל אֶת־יֶתֶר הַפְּלֵטָה הַנִּשְׁאֶרֶת
לָכֶם מִן־הַבָּרָד וְאָכַל אֶת־כָּל־הָעֵץ הַצֹּמֵחַ לָכֶם
ו מִן־הַשָּׂדֶה: וּמָלְאוּ בָתֶּיךָ וּבָתֵּי כָל־עֲבָדֶיךָ וּבָתֵּי כָל־
מִצְרַיִם אֲשֶׁר לֹא־רָאוּ אֲבֹתֶיךָ וַאֲבוֹת אֲבֹתֶיךָ מִיּוֹם
הֱיוֹתָם עַל־הָאֲדָמָה עַד הַיּוֹם הַזֶּה וַיִּפֶן וַיֵּצֵא מֵעִם
ז פַּרְעֹה: וַיֹּאמְרוּ עַבְדֵי פַרְעֹה אֵלָיו עַד־מָתַי יִהְיֶה זֶה

the LORD.'' **3]** So Moses and Aaron went to Pharaoh and said to him, "Thus says the LORD, the God of the Hebrews, 'How long will you refuse to humble yourself before Me? Let My people go that they may worship Me. **4]** For if you refuse to let My people go, tomorrow I will bring locusts on your territory. **5]** They shall cover the surface of the land, so that no one will be able to see the land. They shall devour the surviving remnant that was left to you after the hail; and they shall eat away all your trees that grow in the field. **6]** Moreover, they shall fill your palaces and the houses of all your courtiers and of all the Egyptians—something that neither your fathers nor your fathers' fathers have seen from the day they appeared on earth to this day.'" With that he turned and left Pharaoh's presence.

7] Pharaoh's courtiers said to him, "How long shall this one be a snare to us? Let the men go to worship the LORD their God! Are you not yet aware that Egypt is lost?" **8]** So Moses and Aaron were brought back to Pharaoh and he said to them, "Go, worship the LORD your God! Who are the ones to go?" **9]** Moses replied, "We will all go, young and old: we will go with our sons and daughters, our flocks and herds; for we must observe the LORD's festival." **10]** But he said to them, "The LORD be with you the same as I mean to let your children go with you! Clearly, you are bent on mischief. **11]** No! You menfolk go and worship the LORD, since that is what you want." And they were expelled from Pharaoh's presence.

12] Then the LORD said to Moses, "Hold out your arm over the land of Egypt for the locusts,

5] *Able to see.* The plague of locusts is a forerunner of and parallel to the plague of darkness; see also verse 15.

Surviving remnant. The wheat and emmer.

8] *Who are the ones to go?* Among the males. In Egypt, only men participated in worship (see also verse 11), but Moses expressly includes the women.

10] *The Lord be with you.* Spoken in irony. Let Him be with you as much as I will let you go, namely, not at all.

Mischief. By your insistence on the whole people going you make clear that more than mere worship is intended.

וְיֹאכַל֙ אֶת־כָּל־עֵ֣שֶׂב הָאָ֔רֶץ אֵ֛ת כָּל־אֲשֶׁ֥ר הִשְׁאִ֖יר וְהַעְתִּ֙ירוּ֙ לַיהוָֹ֣ה אֱלֹֽהֵיכֶ֔ם וְיָסֵר֙ מֵֽעָלַ֔י רַ֖ק אֶת־הַמָּ֥וֶת
הַבָּרָ֑ד וַיֵּ֨ט מֹשֶׁ֜ה אֶת־מַטֵּ֗הוּ עַל־אֶ֣רֶץ מִצְרַ֔יִם וַֽיהוָֹ֗ה הַזֶּֽה: וַיֵּצֵ֖א מֵעִ֣ם פַּרְעֹ֑ה וַיֶּעְתַּ֖ר אֶל־יְהוָֹֽה: וַיַּהֲפֹ֣ךְ
נִהַ֣ג ר֤וּחַ קָדִים֙ בָּאָ֔רֶץ כָּל־הַיּ֥וֹם הַה֖וּא וְכָל־הַלָּ֑יְלָה יְהוָֹ֜ה רֽוּחַ־יָם֙ חָזָ֣ק מְאֹ֔ד וַיִּשָּׂא֙ אֶת־הָ֣אַרְבֶּ֔ה וַיִּתְקָעֵ֖הוּ
הַבֹּ֣קֶר הָיָ֔ה וְר֙וּחַ֙ הַקָּדִ֔ים נָשָׂ֖א אֶת־הָֽאַרְבֶּֽה: וַיַּ֣עַל יָ֣מָּה סּ֑וּף לֹ֤א נִשְׁאַר֙ אַרְבֶּ֣ה אֶחָ֔ד בְּכֹ֖ל גְּב֥וּל מִצְרָֽיִם:
הָֽאַרְבֶּ֗ה עַ֚ל כָּל־אֶ֣רֶץ מִצְרַ֔יִם וַיָּ֕נַח בְּכֹ֖ל גְּב֣וּל וַיְחַזֵּ֤ק יְהוָֹה֙ אֶת־לֵ֣ב פַּרְעֹ֔ה וְלֹ֥א שִׁלַּ֖ח אֶת־בְּנֵ֥י
מִצְרָ֑יִם כָּבֵ֣ד מְאֹ֔ד לְ֠פָנָיו לֹא־הָ֨יָה כֵ֤ן אַרְבֶּה֙ כָּמֹ֔הוּ יִשְׂרָאֵֽל: פ

וְאַחֲרָ֖יו לֹ֣א יִֽהְיֶה־כֵּ֑ן: וַיְכַ֣ס אֶת־עֵ֣ין כָּל־הָאָ֘רֶץ֮ וַתֶּחְשַׁ֣ךְ וַיֹּ֨אמֶר יְהוָֹ֜ה אֶל־מֹשֶׁ֗ה נְטֵ֤ה יָֽדְךָ֙ עַל־הַשָּׁמַ֔יִם וִ֥יהִי
הָאָרֶץ֒ וַיֹּ֜אכַל אֶת־כָּל־עֵ֣שֶׂב הָאָ֗רֶץ וְאֵת֙ כָּל־פְּרִ֣י חֹ֖שֶׁךְ עַל־אֶ֣רֶץ מִצְרָ֑יִם וְיָמֵ֖שׁ חֹֽשֶׁךְ: וַיֵּ֥ט מֹשֶׁ֛ה אֶת־יָד֖וֹ
הָעֵ֔ץ אֲשֶׁ֥ר הוֹתִ֖יר הַבָּרָ֑ד וְלֹא־נוֹתַ֨ר כָּל־יֶ֧רֶק בָּעֵ֛ץ עַל־הַשָּׁמָ֑יִם וַיְהִ֧י חֹֽשֶׁךְ־אֲפֵלָ֛ה בְּכָל־אֶ֥רֶץ מִצְרַ֖יִם
וּבְעֵ֥שֶׂב הַשָּׂדֶ֖ה בְּכָל־אֶ֥רֶץ מִצְרָֽיִם: וַיְמַהֵ֣ר פַּרְעֹ֔ה שְׁלֹ֥שֶׁת יָמִֽים: לֹֽא־רָא֞וּ אִ֣ישׁ אֶת־אָחִ֗יו וְלֹא־קָ֛מוּ אִ֥ישׁ
לִקְרֹ֖א לְמֹשֶׁ֣ה וּֽלְאַהֲרֹ֑ן וַיֹּ֣אמֶר חָטָ֗אתִי לַיהוָֹ֛ה מִתַּחְתָּ֖יו שְׁלֹ֣שֶׁת יָמִ֑ים וּֽלְכָל־בְּנֵ֧י יִשְׂרָאֵ֛ל הָ֥יָה א֖וֹר
אֱלֹֽהֵיכֶ֖ם וְלָכֶֽם: וְעַתָּ֗ה שָׂ֣א נָ֤א חַטָּאתִי֙ אַ֣ךְ הַפַּ֔עַם בְּמֽוֹשְׁבֹתָֽם: וַיִּקְרָ֨א פַרְעֹ֜ה אֶל־מֹשֶׁ֗ה וַיֹּ֙אמֶר֙ לְכ֣וּ

that they may come upon the land of Egypt and eat up all the grasses in the land, whatever the hail has left." **13]** So Moses held out his rod over the land of Egypt, and the LORD drove an east wind over the land all that day and all night; and when morning came, the east wind had brought the locusts. **14]** Locusts invaded all the land of Egypt and settled within all the territory of Egypt in a thick mass; never before had there been so many, nor will there ever be so many again. **15]** They hid all the land from view, and the land was darkened; and they ate up all the grasses of the field and all the fruit of the trees which the hail had left, so that nothing green was left, of tree or grass of the field, in all the land of Egypt.

16] Pharaoh hurriedly summoned Moses and Aaron and said, "I stand guilty before the LORD your God and before you. **17]** Forgive my offense just this once, and plead with the LORD your God that He but remove this death from me." **18]** So he left Pharaoh's presence and pleaded with the LORD. **19]** The LORD caused a shift to a very strong west wind, which lifted the locusts and hurled them into the Sea of Reeds; not a single locust remained in all the territory of Egypt. **20]** But the LORD stiffened Pharaoh's heart, and he would not let the Israelites go.

21] Then the LORD said to Moses, "Hold out your arm toward the sky that there may be darkness upon the land of Egypt, a darkness that can be touched." **22]** Moses held out his arm toward the sky and thick darkness descended upon all the land of Egypt for three days. **23]** People could not see one another, and for three days no one could get up from where he was; but all the Israelites enjoyed light in their dwellings.

13] *East wind.* Similar to a sirocco. Such a wind will also divide the Reed Sea (14:21) and supply Israel with quails (Num. 11:31).

19] *West wind.* Literally, a "wind from the sea," spoken from a Palestinian perspective.

Sea of Reeds. Or, Reed Sea. Traditionally, but erroneously, rendered as "Red Sea." For its location see commentary to 13:17–14:31, "The Route."

22] *Darkness.* How it was brought on is not stated; it is left to the imagination of the hearer whether it was through a sandstorm of sun-darkening proportions or in some other way.

עִבְדוּ אֶת־יְהוָֹה רַק צֹאנְכֶם וּבְקַרְכֶם יֻצָּג גַּם־טַפְּכֶם
יֵלֵךְ עִמָּכֶם: וַיֹּאמֶר מֹשֶׁה גַּם־אַתָּה תִּתֵּן בְּיָדֵנוּ זְבָחִים
וְעֹלֹת וְעָשִׂינוּ לַיהוָֹה אֱלֹהֵינוּ: וְגַם־מִקְנֵנוּ יֵלֵךְ עִמָּנוּ
לֹא תִשָּׁאֵר פַּרְסָה כִּי מִמֶּנּוּ נִקַּח לַעֲבֹד אֶת־יְהוָֹה
אֱלֹהֵינוּ וַאֲנַחְנוּ לֹא־נֵדַע מַה־נַּעֲבֹד אֶת־יְהוָֹה עַד־בֹּאֵנוּ
שָׁמָּה: וַיְחַזֵּק יְהוָֹה אֶת־לֵב פַּרְעֹה וְלֹא אָבָה לְשַׁלְּחָם:
וַיֹּאמֶר־לוֹ פַרְעֹה לֵךְ מֵעָלָי הִשָּׁמֶר לְךָ אַל־תֹּסֶף
רְאוֹת פָּנַי כִּי בְּיוֹם רְאֹתְךָ פָנַי תָּמוּת: וַיֹּאמֶר מֹשֶׁה
כֵּן דִּבַּרְתָּ לֹא־אֹסִף עוֹד רְאוֹת פָּנֶיךָ:
פ

וַיֹּאמֶר יְהוָֹה אֶל־מֹשֶׁה עוֹד נֶגַע אֶחָד אָבִיא עַל־
פַּרְעֹה וְעַל־מִצְרַיִם אַחֲרֵי־כֵן יְשַׁלַּח אֶתְכֶם מִזֶּה
כְּשַׁלְּחוֹ כָּלָה גָּרֵשׁ יְגָרֵשׁ אֶתְכֶם מִזֶּה: דַּבֶּר־נָא בְּאָזְנֵי
הָעָם וְיִשְׁאֲלוּ אִישׁ מֵאֵת רֵעֵהוּ וְאִשָּׁה מֵאֵת רְעוּתָהּ
כְּלֵי־כֶסֶף וּכְלֵי זָהָב: וַיִּתֵּן יְהוָֹה אֶת־חֵן הָעָם בְּעֵינֵי
מִצְרָיִם גַּם הָאִישׁ מֹשֶׁה גָּדוֹל מְאֹד בְּאֶרֶץ מִצְרַיִם
בְּעֵינֵי עַבְדֵי־פַרְעֹה וּבְעֵינֵי הָעָם: ס וַיֹּאמֶר מֹשֶׁה
כֹּה אָמַר יְהוָֹה כַּחֲצֹת הַלַּיְלָה אֲנִי יוֹצֵא בְּתוֹךְ
מִצְרָיִם: וּמֵת כָּל־בְּכוֹר בְּאֶרֶץ מִצְרַיִם מִבְּכוֹר פַּרְעֹה

24] Pharaoh then summoned Moses and said, "Go, worship the LORD! Only your flocks and your herds shall be left behind; even your children may go with you." 25] But Moses said, "You yourself must provide us with sacrifices and burnt offerings to offer up to the LORD our God; 26] our own livestock, too, shall go along with us—not a hoof shall remain behind: for we must select from it for the worship of the LORD our God; and we shall not know with what we are to worship the LORD until we arrive there." 27] But the LORD stiffened Pharaoh's heart and he would not consent to let them go. 28] Pharaoh said to him, "Be gone from me! Take care not to see me again, for the moment you look upon my face you shall die." 29] And Moses replied, "You have spoken rightly. I shall not see your face again!"

1] And the LORD said to Moses, "I will bring but one more plague upon Pharaoh and upon Egypt; after that he shall let you go from here; indeed, when he lets you go, he will drive you out of here one and all. 2] Tell the people to borrow, each man from his neighbor and each woman from hers, objects of silver and gold." 3] The LORD disposed the Egyptians favorably toward the people. Moreover, Moses himself was much esteemed in the land of Egypt, among Pharaoh's courtiers and among the people.

4] Moses said, "Thus says the LORD: Toward midnight I will go forth among the Egyptians, 5] and every first-born in the land of Egypt shall die, from the first-born of Pharaoh who sits

25] *But Moses said.* Once again he widens his demands so that the final confrontation may take place.

You yourself must provide us. As was required by the laws treating of provisions for released slaves; cf. Deut. 15:13. A similar pattern may be seen in the Laban-Jacob separation [4].

11:2] *Borrow.* שָׁאַל (sha-al) means also "ask," "demand." The latter is obviously meant, for return of the items was hardly intended. (Compare the English expression "borrow a match." A re-turn of the borrowed item is here in fact impossible.) The Book of Jubilees (48:18) is more direct: Israel plundered the Egyptians to make up for centuries of slavery [5].

From his neighbor. This suggests that the Israelites lived very near the Egyptians.

3] *Moses himself was much esteemed.* One of the two personal assessments of Moses in the Torah; the other describes him as humble or meek (Num. 12:3). Both times the expression is used: הָאִישׁ מֹשֶׁה, literally, "the man Moses."

הַיֹּשֵׁב עַל־כִּסְאוֹ עַד בְּכוֹר הַשִּׁפְחָה אֲשֶׁר אַחַר
הָרֵחָיִם וְכֹל בְּכוֹר בְּהֵמָה: וְהָיְתָה צְעָקָה גְדֹלָה
בְּכָל־אֶרֶץ מִצְרָיִם אֲשֶׁר כָּמֹהוּ לֹא נִהְיָתָה וְכָמֹהוּ
לֹא תֹסִף: וּלְכֹל בְּנֵי יִשְׂרָאֵל לֹא יֶחֱרַץ־כֶּלֶב לְשֹׁנוֹ
לְמֵאִישׁ וְעַד־בְּהֵמָה לְמַעַן תֵּדְעוּן אֲשֶׁר יַפְלֶה יְהֹוָה
בֵּין מִצְרַיִם וּבֵין יִשְׂרָאֵל: וְיָרְדוּ כָל־עֲבָדֶיךָ אֵלֶּה
אֵלַי וְהִשְׁתַּחֲווּ־לִי לֵאמֹר צֵא אַתָּה וְכָל־הָעָם אֲשֶׁר־

בְּרַגְלֶיךָ וְאַחֲרֵי־כֵן אֵצֵא וַיֵּצֵא מֵעִם־פַּרְעֹה בָּחֳרִי־
אָף: ס וַיֹּאמֶר יְהֹוָה אֶל־מֹשֶׁה לֹא־יִשְׁמַע אֲלֵיכֶם
פַּרְעֹה לְמַעַן רְבוֹת מוֹפְתַי בְּאֶרֶץ מִצְרָיִם: וּמֹשֶׁה
וְאַהֲרֹן עָשׂוּ אֶת־כָּל־הַמֹּפְתִים הָאֵלֶּה לִפְנֵי פַרְעֹה
וַיְחַזֵּק יְהֹוָה אֶת־לֵב פַּרְעֹה וְלֹא־שִׁלַּח אֶת־בְּנֵי־יִשְׂרָאֵל
מֵאַרְצוֹ: ס

on his throne to the first-born of the slave girl who is behind the millstones; and all the first-born of the cattle. 6] And there shall be a loud cry in all the land of Egypt, such as has never been or will ever be again; 7] but not a dog shall snarl at any of the Israelites, at man or beast—in order that you may know that the LORD makes a distinction between Egypt and Israel. 8] Then all these courtiers of yours shall come down to me and bow low to me, saying, 'Depart, you and all the people who follow you!' After that I will depart." And he left Pharaoh's presence in hot anger.

9] Now the LORD had said to Moses, "Pharaoh will not heed you, in order that My marvels may be multiplied in the land of Egypt." 10] Moses and Aaron had performed all these marvels before Pharaoh, but the LORD had stiffened the heart of Pharaoh so that he would not let the Israelites go from his land.

5] *First-born of the slave girl.* Even though both mother and child were innocent. The Torah does not treat this as a moral problem but rather as a realistic situation: everyone in the country, including the lowliest inhabitants, suffered from the misdeeds of the ruler.

8] *In hot anger.* Literally, "with flaring nostrils," a vivid description of the final confrontation.

9] *My marvels may be multiplied.* Summing up the ultimate purpose of the plagues: to publish God's might.

The Pharaonic View

This commentary proceeds from the position that even though the plagues and many details of the life of Moses cannot be classified as "external" (i.e., verifiable) history, the story of the Exodus has a historical kernel. This core consists primarily of the fact that Israel (or some portion of the people)[1] sojourned in Egypt, suffered servitude there, and, after a series of events that were later embellished in folk memory and then given form as tale and literature, left the land toward a new destiny. We do not know whether it was a fictional or real pharaoh who was Moses' antagonist. In the latter case[2] what kind of man might such a pharaoh have been who was confronted by Moses and Aaron?

We may take it for granted that at first he viewed the political and economic consequences of Israel's quest with contempt. Serfs had no rights in Egypt and their masters were not about to give them any.[3] This of course was not merely an Egyptian or Pharaonic attitude; it was universal and not bound to time. In fact, one may wonder how the biblical storyteller envisaged a meeting of the slave leaders with the king. However, the unlikelihood of any face-to-face negotiations was apparently of no interest to the text, which concentrated on the religious rather than other implications of the confrontation. Moses and Aaron appear primarily as *religious* leaders before Pharaoh. The latter must be seen in this exchange both as the man who held the key to Israel's freedom and as the godlike leader of his own people, who stood in the context of his own traditions, beliefs, and practices.

We discussed earlier the possible relationship of the religious revolution of Amenophis IV (Akhenaten) and the religious development of Moses.[4] In the age in which our story is set, this revolution had been reversed and the cult of Amon had been restored. Even in Akhenaten's time no strict monotheism had prevailed. The cult of Aten, the sun disc, was heavily favored, but Ptah, Ra, and Osiris continued to be worshiped, and the king himself continued to be regarded as divine. The pharaoh whom Moses opposed was most likely rooted firmly in the traditional polytheism of Egypt. The king was both god and chief priest who, though he recognized other deities as having influence in particular spheres, was himself used to reigning supreme and brooking no opposition from supermundane forces. Biblical tradition understood this Pharaonic view perfectly and therefore made the struggle between the god-king and Israel's God the center of the drama. However, in this conflict Pharaoh is depicted not so much as the wicked antagonist of the Lord but as a human being whose cruelty, stubbornness, and changes of heart, as well as whose reliance on the potency of magic, conform to a pattern of which he was as much victim as master. The hardening of his heart was providential because it was part of a larger design; he was who he was and God demonstrated His own superior powers against him, for the sake of both Egypt and Israel and for the generations of the future as well. Pharaoh's and God's authorities are shown to be unequal; and, though Pharaoh in the course of the plagues begins to understand a hitherto never encountered divine force and even accommodates himself to it to some degree, he is in the end incapable of surrender. His response

---

[1] See "Introducing Exodus."
[2] Many scholars suggest that Ramses II (about 1304–1237) fits this role.

[3] André Neher describes their lot as infinitely worse than that of the downtrodden Egyptian proletariat [6].
[4] See commentary to 3:1–4:18, footnote 5.

varies: he shows disdain, anxiety, and shrewdness; he even confesses to error—but cannot yield to God even under the imminent threat of fatal disaster. Only when his own son is dead does he give in, defeated both as pharaoh and as father.

All this had been foreordained by God and foretold by Moses. Yet within this framework of inevitability the Pharaoh remains an intelligible human being, acting as one would expect a man of his tradition and position to act. Later Jewish tradition depicted him as unusually evil, but this post-view does not conform with the biblical tale itself which recounts the release of Israel as a drama of cosmic proportions occurring at the same time in the framework of expectable human behavior. "Events unfold under the providence of God, yet their unfolding is always according to the motives of the human actors through whom God's will is done without their realizing it. . . . God had determined that Pharaoh should act as he did, indeed He saw to it; but Pharaoh conducted himself throughout conformably with his own motives and his own godless view of his status. God made it so, but Pharaoh had only to be himself to do God's will" [7].

GLEANINGS

Egyptian Oracle

How is this land? The sun disc is covered over. It will not shine so that people may see. No one can live when the clouds cover over the sun. Then everybody is deaf (i.e., stunned) for lack of it.

FROM THE PROPHECY OF NEFER-TUM
(early 2nd millennium B.C.E.) [8]

Darkness

Generally, darkness is merely the absence of light and can be dispelled by lighting a fire. But this darkness was so thick it could be touched. It was a darkness of a deeper nature.　　SFORNO

The darkness was so dense that people could not see one another. That is the worst of all darknesses: when people are unable to "see" their neighbors, that is, note their distress and help them.

CHASIDIC [9]

When a man does not see others or want to see them, there is darkness in the world.

KETAV SOFER [10]

The Best Teachers

In 10:2 the Israelites are instructed to teach their offspring about God's saving power. It does not, however, go on to say "that *they* (the offspring) may know that I am the Lord." Rather, it says "that *you* may know"—*you*, that is, the parents. The reason is that your teaching will have effect only if you yourselves remember that the Lord is God.　　CHASIDIC [11]

We Will All Go, Young and Old (Exod. 10:9)

Why did Moses mention the young before the old? The young needed to go more urgently, for they were endangered by assimilation; the old were more secure in their tradition and their rescue therefore less urgent.　　KETAV SOFER [12]

A child is orphaned if he has no parents, a people if it has no youth.　　CHASIDIC [13]

The Plagues

And then, one spring, a sandstorm of hitherto unknown fury bursts out. The air is black for days on end. The sun becomes invisible. The darkness can be felt. All and sundry are paralyzed and lose their senses. In the middle of all this, however, while a pestilence, a children's epidemic, begins to rage and do its work, the voice of the mighty man

454

sounds through the streets of the Royal City, unaffected by the driving masses of sand. The signs have persuaded his people. Massed around him, their hope is stronger than the darkness; they see light. And then, after three days of the furious storm, the first-born son of the young king perishes in the night. Disconsolate in his innermost chamber, bowed over the little corpse, no longer a god but the very man that he is, he suddenly sees the hated one standing before him; and, "Go forth!" he cries. M. BUBER [14]

Numerical Scheme

In several paragraphs of this section we have already observed a numerical schematism that finds expression in the mention of the name of a plague seven times (swarms of flies, locusts) or fourteen times (hail). The tendency toward numerical patterns based on the number seven and on the sexagesimal system is observable throughout the section. In the first cycle, the names of the plagues occur 21 times—3 times 7 (blood 5 times, frogs 11, gnats 5)—and with the paragraph pertaining to the crocodile (3 times), 24—2 times 12; in the second cycle, 12 times (swarms of flies 7, pest 1, boils 4); in the third cycle, 24 (hail 14, locusts 7,

darkness 3); in all, 60 times. All this can hardly be fortuitous. CASSUTO [15]

Men with a Mission

The admission wrung from the sorcerers of Egypt is only one of several; for, a number of biblical narratives make the point that Israel's God is God, as all must recognize. . . .

Whether by the performance of miracles or by the execution of justice and the doing of acts of salvation, Israel's God supplied the evidence which obtained from His own people and from others the acknowledgment that He is God. Whether He acted to clear His name of reproach or to impress with His saving power, He acted in order that all might know that He is God. Whether the prophetic authors burdened their God, as Ezekiel did, with the need to act himself on His own behalf and for the sake of His name, casting off all suspicion of weakness or inconstancy, or whether, as did the Second Isaiah, they assigned to their people the double burden, to avoid all such conduct as would discredit their God, and to witness as prophets, possessed of a momentous truth, to His divinity, they had a common property: they were men with a mission. S. H. BLANK [16]

455

Passover and Deliverance

The story is interrupted in the middle of the last plague to tell of Passover (*Pesach*) as a preparation for deliverance. The focus shifts from Pharaoh and Egypt to the Israelites and to the commandments given them. These are in part of temporary character, applying to the specific situation of the impending Exodus.[1] The liberation takes place in consequence of the accumulated terror brought on by the plagues and especially the death of the first-born. Suddenly Pharaoh goes beyond the expected; he not only permits the Children of Israel to leave, he drives them out in the middle of the night. The chapter is filled with repetitions, whence critics conclude that various sources contributed to the text.[2]

Though the Passover sacrifice is commanded as a prophylactic rite in connection with the impending Exodus, the occasion is to be remembered as the Feast of Unleavened Bread (*matzah*, plural *matzot*, verse 17). This double nomenclature can be explained best by supposing that the Passover and Feast of Matzot rituals were originally two separate observances which were combined sometime between the events of the Exodus and the redaction of the text. The detailed cultic provisions of the chapter hardly fit a people in revolutionary circumstances and may therefore be seen either to build on already existing practices or to be a later retrojection (see commentary below). The Book of Deuteronomy (15:19–16:8) adds a third

---

[1] Tradition deduces this from the words "in the land of Egypt" in verse 1.

[2] Thus, 11:9–12:20 are assigned to P; the following verses to J and D (the presumed redactor of Deuteronomy) [1].

element: it integrates the dedication of Israel's first-born (Exod. 13:3–5) into the observance by linking the Passover sacrifice to the first-born. The historic sequence of these three elements cannot be traced with certainty, but one fact is sure: the experience of the Exodus profoundly affected these observances and, whatever they were originally, made them into a memorial to the deliverance.

Jews rehearse the story of the Exodus each year at the Passover Seder and through the observance of the week-long festival;[3] Christians have developed Passover into the Easter celebration.[4]

[3] It is celebrated for seven days in Israel; in the Diaspora for eight days by Orthodox and Conservative Jews; and by Reform Jews for seven. The Exodus is also considered a foundation of the Sabbath observance (so the Sabbath Kiddush).

[4] In many languages Easter is still called by its Hebrew derivation: Pascua, Paask, Pâques, etc.

א וַיֹּאמֶר יְהֹוָה אֶל־מֹשֶׁה וְאֶל־אַהֲרֹן בְּאֶרֶץ מִצְרַיִם

ב לֵאמֹר: הַחֹדֶשׁ הַזֶּה לָכֶם רֹאשׁ חֳדָשִׁים רִאשׁוֹן הוּא

ג לָכֶם לְחָדְשֵׁי הַשָּׁנָה: דַּבְּרוּ אֶל־כָּל־עֲדַת יִשְׂרָאֵל לֵאמֹר בֶּעָשֹׂר לַחֹדֶשׁ הַזֶּה וְיִקְחוּ לָהֶם אִישׁ שֶׂה

ד לְבֵית־אָבֹת שֶׂה לַבָּיִת: וְאִם־יִמְעַט הַבַּיִת מִהְיוֹת מִשֶּׂה וְלָקַח הוּא וּשְׁכֵנוֹ הַקָּרֹב אֶל־בֵּיתוֹ בְּמִכְסַת

ה נְפָשֹׁת אִישׁ לְפִי אָכְלוֹ תָּכֹסּוּ עַל־הַשֶּׂה: שֶׂה תָמִים

זָכָר בֶּן־שָׁנָה יִהְיֶה לָכֶם מִן־הַכְּבָשִׂים וּמִן־הָעִזִּים

ו תִּקָּחוּ: וְהָיָה לָכֶם לְמִשְׁמֶרֶת עַד אַרְבָּעָה עָשָׂר יוֹם לַחֹדֶשׁ הַזֶּה וְשָׁחֲטוּ אֹתוֹ כֹּל קְהַל עֲדַת־יִשְׂרָאֵל בֵּין

ז הָעַרְבָּיִם: וְלָקְחוּ מִן־הַדָּם וְנָתְנוּ עַל־שְׁתֵּי הַמְּזוּזֹת וְעַל־הַמַּשְׁקוֹף עַל הַבָּתִּים אֲשֶׁר־יֹאכְלוּ אֹתוֹ בָּהֶם:

ח וְאָכְלוּ אֶת־הַבָּשָׂר בַּלַּיְלָה הַזֶּה צְלִי־אֵשׁ וּמַצּוֹת עַל־

ט מְרֹרִים יֹאכְלֻהוּ: אַל־תֹּאכְלוּ מִמֶּנּוּ נָא וּבָשֵׁל מְבֻשָּׁל

1] The LORD said to Moses and Aaron in the land of Egypt: 2] This month shall mark for you the beginning of the months; it shall be the first of the months of the year for you. 3] Speak to the whole community of Israel and say that on the tenth of this month each of them shall take a lamb to a family, a lamb to a household. 4] But if the household is too small for a lamb, then let him share one with the neighbor closest to his household in the number of persons: you shall apportion the lamb according to what each person should eat. 5] Your lamb shall be without blemish, a yearling male; you may take it from the sheep or from the goats. 6] You shall keep watch over it until the fourteenth day of this month; and all the aggregate community of the Israelites shall slaughter it at twilight. 7] They shall take some of the blood and put it on the two doorposts and the lintel of the houses in which they are to eat it. 8] They shall eat the flesh that same night; they shall eat it roasted over the fire, with unleavened bread and with bitter herbs. 9] Do not eat any of it raw, or cooked in any way

---

12:2] *This month.* חֹדֶשׁ (*chodesh*) means the new (Hebrew *chadash*) month and also, by extension, the whole month. The spring month was *Chodesh ha-Aviv* (as in Exod. 13:4; Deut. 16:1), hence Aviv came to mean spring (as in Tel Aviv, "Mound of Spring," Ezek. 3:15). When the Jews took over the Babylonian calendar they renamed the month Nisan (Neh. 2:1, from an Akkadian word probably meaning "first fruits"). This has remained its name. It is counted as the first month, although the beginning of the seventh month marks the start of the religious new year, Rosh Hashanah. According to Driver and others, the observance of the New Year in the seventh month is a leftover from an older custom. It has been claimed that in the days of the divided monarchy both systems were in use [2].

3] *Tenth of this month.* The reason for distinguishing the tenth is not clear. Both Yom Kippur and the proclamation of the jubilee were fixed for the tenth day; in Islam, the tenth day of the twelfth month is singled out for observance, as is the first day of the tenth month.

Lamb. Or, "kid"; either goat or sheep were acceptable (verse 5). The kid became the zodiacal sign for Nisan.

4] *Too small.* Rashi explains: If there are too few to consume a whole animal.

5] *Without blemish.* Fit for sacrifice. The whole people are to act as priests.

6] *Twilight.* Before it became completely dark. According to rabbinic tradition בֵּין הָעַרְבַּיִם was expanded to mean here the hours between noon and nightfall [3].

7] *Lintel.* The horizontal bar connecting the door posts.

8] *With unleavened bread.* Introduced here without an explanation, which is not forthcoming until verse 34, and then ex post facto.

Bitter herbs. To symbolize the people's bitter experience. Or, it may have been a custom in Egypt to eat bitter herbs with certain meals, possibly to ward off demons [4].

בַּמָּיִם כִּי אִם־צְלִי־אֵשׁ רֹאשׁוֹ עַל־כְּרָעָיו וְעַל־קִרְבּוֹ: י וְלֹא־תוֹתִירוּ מִמֶּנּוּ עַד־בֹּקֶר וְהַנֹּתָר מִמֶּנּוּ עַד־בֹּקֶר בָּאֵשׁ תִּשְׂרֹפוּ: יא וְכָכָה תֹּאכְלוּ אֹתוֹ מָתְנֵיכֶם חֲגֻרִים נַעֲלֵיכֶם בְּרַגְלֵיכֶם וּמַקֶּלְכֶם בְּיֶדְכֶם וַאֲכַלְתֶּם אֹתוֹ בְּחִפָּזוֹן פֶּסַח הוּא לַיהוָה: יב וְעָבַרְתִּי בְאֶרֶץ־מִצְרַיִם בַּלַּיְלָה הַזֶּה וְהִכֵּיתִי כָל־בְּכוֹר בְּאֶרֶץ מִצְרַיִם מֵאָדָם וְעַד־בְּהֵמָה וּבְכָל־אֱלֹהֵי מִצְרַיִם אֶעֱשֶׂה שְׁפָטִים אֲנִי

יג יְהוָה: וְהָיָה הַדָּם לָכֶם לְאֹת עַל הַבָּתִּים אֲשֶׁר אַתֶּם שָׁם וְרָאִיתִי אֶת־הַדָּם וּפָסַחְתִּי עֲלֵכֶם וְלֹא־יִהְיֶה יד בָכֶם נֶגֶף לְמַשְׁחִית בְּהַכֹּתִי בְּאֶרֶץ מִצְרָיִם: וְהָיָה הַיּוֹם הַזֶּה לָכֶם לְזִכָּרוֹן וְחַגֹּתֶם אֹתוֹ חַג לַיהוָה טו לְדֹרֹתֵיכֶם חֻקַּת עוֹלָם תְּחָגֻּהוּ: שִׁבְעַת יָמִים מַצּוֹת תֹּאכֵלוּ אַךְ בַּיּוֹם הָרִאשׁוֹן תַּשְׁבִּיתוּ שְּׂאֹר מִבָּתֵּיכֶם כִּי כָּל־אֹכֵל חָמֵץ וְנִכְרְתָה הַנֶּפֶשׁ הַהִוא מִיִּשְׂרָאֵל

with water, but roasted—head, legs, and entrails—over the fire. **10]** You shall not leave any of it over until morning; if any of it is left until morning, you shall burn it.

11] This is how you shall eat it: your loins girded, your sandals on your feet, and your staff in your hand; and you shall eat it hurriedly: it is a passover offering to the LORD. **12]** For that night I will go through the land of Egypt and strike down every first-born in the land of Egypt, both man and beast; and I will mete out punishments to all the gods of Egypt, I the LORD. **13]** And the blood on the houses in which you dwell shall be a sign for you: when I see the blood I will pass over you, so that no plague will destroy you when I strike the land of Egypt.

14] This day shall be to you one of remembrance: you shall celebrate it as a festival to the LORD throughout the ages; you shall celebrate it as an institution for all time. **15]** Seven days you shall eat unleavened bread; on the very first day you shall remove leaven from your houses, for whoever eats leavened bread from the first day to the seventh day, that person shall be cut off from Israel.

9] *Raw.* Considered a less civilized form of eating. The word does not occur in this sense elsewhere in the Bible; its meaning is assured by the context as well as an Arabic parallel.

11] *Passover.* פֶּסַח (*Pesach*) is in verse 27 connected with "pass over"—hence the English rendition of the term; but the original meaning of the word is not clear. Apparently the word was already known to the Israelites, so that verse 27 (referring to the Angel of Death "passing over") is a word play on a term meaning something else. One explanation is that it meant "to protect" [5]; another, that it was a technical term for a type of cultic dance (compare I Kings 18:26) [6].

12] *Punishments.* Destroy the gods to show their ineffectuality.

13] *When I see the blood.* As a sign of your faith and obedience.

14] *One of remembrance.* In future generations.

15] *Seven days.* In Deut. 16:8, six days. Tradition explains the discrepancy as follows: On the first day the eating of matzah is obligatory, on the other six days only the abstinence from leaven. (Of course, if bread is consumed during these days it would have to be matzah) [7].

Unleavened bread. Jewish tradition prescribes that for its baking only wheat, barley, spelt, rye, or oats are permitted, for they can also be leavened. Other species like millet, rice, poppyseed, sesame, or legumes are not to be used in the preparation of matzah, for they decay but do not leaven [8].

Leaven. The reason for its removal is not given.

Cut off. The exact meaning of this penalty (*karet*) is not clear. It may have been exile, or ostracism, or execution, but more probably meant premature death and, like the expression "bearing one's guilt" (חֵטְא or נָשָׂא עָוֹן), signified that God himself would punish the offender by cutting short his life at fifty or sixty years of age (see also Exod. 31:14; Num. 19:20) [9].

מִיּוֹם הָרִאשֹׁן עַד־יוֹם הַשְּׁבִעִי: וּבַיּוֹם הָרִאשׁוֹן מִקְרָא־ ט״ו
קֹדֶשׁ וּבַיּוֹם הַשְּׁבִיעִי מִקְרָא־קֹדֶשׁ יִהְיֶה לָכֶם כָּל־
מְלָאכָה לֹא־יֵעָשֶׂה בָהֶם אַךְ אֲשֶׁר יֵאָכֵל לְכָל־נֶפֶשׁ
הוּא לְבַדּוֹ יֵעָשֶׂה לָכֶם: וּשְׁמַרְתֶּם אֶת־הַמַּצּוֹת כִּי ט״ז
בְּעֶצֶם הַיּוֹם הַזֶּה הוֹצֵאתִי אֶת־צִבְאוֹתֵיכֶם מֵאֶרֶץ
מִצְרָיִם וּשְׁמַרְתֶּם אֶת־הַיּוֹם הַזֶּה לְדֹרֹתֵיכֶם חֻקַּת
עוֹלָם: בָּרִאשֹׁן בְּאַרְבָּעָה עָשָׂר יוֹם לַחֹדֶשׁ בָּעֶרֶב ט״ז
תֹּאכְלוּ מַצֹּת עַד יוֹם הָאֶחָד וְעֶשְׂרִים לַחֹדֶשׁ בָּעָרֶב:
שִׁבְעַת יָמִים שְׂאֹר לֹא יִמָּצֵא בְּבָתֵּיכֶם כִּי כָּל־אֹכֵל ט״ז

מַחְמֶצֶת וְנִכְרְתָה הַנֶּפֶשׁ הַהִוא מֵעֲדַת יִשְׂרָאֵל בַּגֵּר
וּבְאֶזְרַח הָאָרֶץ: כָּל־מַחְמֶצֶת לֹא תֹאכֵלוּ בְּכֹל כ׳
מוֹשְׁבֹתֵיכֶם תֹּאכְלוּ מַצּוֹת:
פ
וַיִּקְרָא מֹשֶׁה לְכָל־זִקְנֵי יִשְׂרָאֵל וַיֹּאמֶר אֲלֵהֶם מִשְׁכוּ כ״א
וּקְחוּ לָכֶם צֹאן לְמִשְׁפְּחֹתֵיכֶם וְשַׁחֲטוּ הַפָּסַח:
וּלְקַחְתֶּם אֲגֻדַּת אֵזוֹב וּטְבַלְתֶּם בַּדָּם אֲשֶׁר־בַּסַּף כ״ב
וְהִגַּעְתֶּם אֶל־הַמַּשְׁקוֹף וְאֶל־שְׁתֵּי הַמְּזוּזֹת מִן־הַדָּם
אֲשֶׁר בַּסָּף וְאַתֶּם לֹא תֵצְאוּ אִישׁ מִפֶּתַח־בֵּיתוֹ עַד־
בֹּקֶר: וְעָבַר יְהוָֹה לִנְגֹּף אֶת־מִצְרַיִם וְרָאָה אֶת־הַדָּם כ״ג

16] On the first day you shall hold a sacred convocation, and on the seventh day a sacred convocation; no work at all shall be done on them; only what every person is to eat, that alone may be prepared for you. **17]** You shall observe the [Feast of] Unleavened Bread, for on this very day I brought your ranks out of the land of Egypt; you shall observe this day throughout the ages as an institution for all time. **18]** In the first month, from the fourteenth day of the month at evening, you shall eat unleavened bread until the twenty-first day of the month at evening. **19]** No leaven shall be found in your houses for seven days. For whoever eats what is leavened, that person shall be cut off from the assembly of Israel, whether he is a stranger or a citizen of the country. **20]** You shall eat nothing leavened; in all your settlements you shall eat unleavened bread.

21] Moses then summoned all the elders of Israel and said to them, "Go, pick out lambs for your families, and slaughter the passover offering. **22]** Take a bunch of hyssop, dip it in the blood that is in the basin, and apply some of the blood that is in the basin to the lintel and to the two doorposts. None of you shall go outside the door of his house until morning. **23]** For

16] *No work at all.* This expression is also used for the other festivals, while for Shabbat and Yom Kippur the prohibiting term is "not any work," (see 20:10). Tradition considered the latter as more rigorous. For instance, the making of a fire for cooking or smoking is permitted on Passover but not on Shabbat or Yom Kippur.

May be prepared. What can be eaten on the holy day may be cooked and prepared on that day; and then only, according to some rabbis, if such labor could not be done beforehand [10].

18] *At evening.* The eve of the fifteenth of Nisan.

19] *Stranger.* He is enjoined to abstain from and

to remove the leaven, but he is not permitted to participate in the sacrifice unless circumcised (verse 48).

Citizen. A term for one who was born or accepted into the tribe.

21] *Moses then summoned.* According to some scholars, the J-account of the Exodus begins here [11].

Slaughter the passover offering. The practice appeared to be already known.

22] *Hyssop.* Better, "marjoram"; hyssop (*hyssopus officinalis*) was not found in Egypt.

עַל־הַמַּשְׁקוֹף וְעַל שְׁתֵּי הַמְּזוּזֹת וּפָסַח יְהוָה עַל־
הַפֶּתַח וְלֹא יִתֵּן הַמַּשְׁחִית לָבֹא אֶל־בָּתֵּיכֶם לִנְגֹּף:
כד וּשְׁמַרְתֶּם אֶת־הַדָּבָר הַזֶּה לְחָק־לְךָ וּלְבָנֶיךָ עַד־
עוֹלָם: כה וְהָיָה כִּי־תָבֹאוּ אֶל־הָאָרֶץ אֲשֶׁר יִתֵּן יְהוָה
לָכֶם כַּאֲשֶׁר דִּבֵּר וּשְׁמַרְתֶּם אֶת־הָעֲבֹדָה הַזֹּאת:
כו וְהָיָה כִּי־יֹאמְרוּ אֲלֵיכֶם בְּנֵיכֶם מָה הָעֲבֹדָה הַזֹּאת
לָכֶם: כז וַאֲמַרְתֶּם זֶבַח־פֶּסַח הוּא לַיהוָה אֲשֶׁר פָּסַח
עַל־בָּתֵּי בְנֵי־יִשְׂרָאֵל בְּמִצְרַיִם בְּנָגְפּוֹ אֶת־מִצְרַיִם וְאֶת־
כח בָּתֵּינוּ הִצִּיל וַיִּקֹּד הָעָם וַיִּשְׁתַּחֲווּ: וַיֵּלְכוּ וַיַּעֲשׂוּ בְּנֵי

יִשְׂרָאֵל כַּאֲשֶׁר צִוָּה יְהוָה אֶת־מֹשֶׁה וְאַהֲרֹן כֵּן עָשׂוּ: ס
כט וַיְהִי בַּחֲצִי הַלַּיְלָה וַיהוָה הִכָּה כָל־בְּכוֹר בְּאֶרֶץ
מִצְרַיִם מִבְּכֹר פַּרְעֹה הַיֹּשֵׁב עַל־כִּסְאוֹ עַד בְּכוֹר
הַשְּׁבִי אֲשֶׁר בְּבֵית הַבּוֹר וְכֹל בְּכוֹר בְּהֵמָה: ל וַיָּקָם
פַּרְעֹה לַיְלָה הוּא וְכָל־עֲבָדָיו וְכָל־מִצְרַיִם וַתְּהִי
צְעָקָה גְדֹלָה בְּמִצְרָיִם כִּי־אֵין בַּיִת אֲשֶׁר אֵין־שָׁם מֵת:
לא וַיִּקְרָא לְמֹשֶׁה וּלְאַהֲרֹן לַיְלָה וַיֹּאמֶר קוּמוּ צְּאוּ
מִתּוֹךְ עַמִּי גַּם־אַתֶּם גַּם־בְּנֵי יִשְׂרָאֵל וּלְכוּ עִבְדוּ אֶת־
לב יְהוָה כְּדַבֶּרְכֶם: גַּם־צֹאנְכֶם גַּם־בְּקַרְכֶם קְחוּ כַּאֲשֶׁר

when the LORD goes through to smite the Egyptians, He will see the blood on the lintel and the two doorposts, and the LORD will pass over the door and not let the Destroyer enter and smite your home.

24] You shall observe this as an institution for all time, for you and for your descendants. 25] And when you enter the land which the LORD will give you, as He has promised, you shall observe this rite. 26] And when your children ask you, 'What do you mean by this rite?' 27] you shall say, 'It is the passover sacrifice to the LORD, because He passed over the houses of the Israelites in Egypt when He smote the Egyptians, but saved our houses.'"

The people then bowed low in homage. 28] And the Israelites went and did so; just as the LORD had commanded Moses and Aaron, so they did.

29] In the middle of the night the LORD struck down all the first-born in the land of Egypt, from the first-born of Pharaoh who sat on the throne to the first-born of the captive who was in the dungeon, and all the first-born of the cattle. 30] And Pharaoh arose in the night, with all his courtiers and all the Egyptians—because there was a loud cry in Egypt; for there was no house where there was not someone dead. 31] He summoned Moses and Aaron in the night and said, "Up, depart from among my people, you and the Israelites with you! Go, worship the LORD as you said! 32] Take also your flocks and your herds, as you said, and begone! And may you bring a blessing upon me also!"

23] *Pass over*. A word play between "pass over" (פֶּסַח) and the name of the festival (פֶּסַח); see above at verse 11. Some see also a play on the word "door" (פֶּתַח).

Destroyer. Death personified. He was later called "Angel of Death."

26] *And when your children ask*. In the Haggadah this question is put in the mouth of the wicked son.

29] *In the middle of the night*. In the Haggadah,

these words form the refrain for a poem recited near the end of the Seder.

30] *There was no house*. Tradition went to great lengths to explain how every Egyptian household was affected [12].

32] *Upon me also*. Pharaoh now acknowledges that God has dominion over him. The first meeting of a pharaoh with Jacob, upon his arrival in Egypt, brought words of blessing, and so does the last—with Moses, upon this departure from Egypt.

לה וַיִּסְעוּ בְנֵי־יִשְׂרָאֵל מֵרַעְמְסֵס סֻכֹּתָה כְּשֵׁשׁ־מֵאוֹת אֶלֶף
 רַגְלִי הַגְּבָרִים לְבַד מִטָּף: וְגַם־עֵרֶב רַב עָלָה אִתָּם
לט וְצֹאן וּבָקָר מִקְנֶה כָּבֵד מְאֹד: וַיֹּאפוּ אֶת־הַבָּצֵק
 אֲשֶׁר הוֹצִיאוּ מִמִּצְרַיִם עֻגֹת מַצּוֹת כִּי לֹא חָמֵץ כִּי־
 גֹרְשׁוּ מִמִּצְרַיִם וְלֹא יָכְלוּ לְהִתְמַהְמֵהַּ וְגַם־צֵדָה לֹא־
מ עָשׂוּ לָהֶם: וּמוֹשַׁב בְּנֵי יִשְׂרָאֵל אֲשֶׁר יָשְׁבוּ בְּמִצְרָיִם
מא שְׁלֹשִׁים שָׁנָה וְאַרְבַּע מֵאוֹת שָׁנָה: וַיְהִי מִקֵּץ שְׁלֹשִׁים

לג דִּבַּרְתֶּם וָלֵכוּ וּבֵרַכְתֶּם גַּם־אֹתִי: וַתֶּחֱזַק מִצְרַיִם עַל־
 הָעָם לְמַהֵר לְשַׁלְּחָם מִן־הָאָרֶץ כִּי אָמְרוּ כֻּלָּנוּ
לד מֵתִים: וַיִּשָּׂא הָעָם אֶת־בְּצֵקוֹ טֶרֶם יֶחְמָץ מִשְׁאֲרֹתָם
לה צְרֻרֹת בְּשִׂמְלֹתָם עַל־שִׁכְמָם: וּבְנֵי־יִשְׂרָאֵל עָשׂוּ כִּדְבַר
 מֹשֶׁה וַיִּשְׁאֲלוּ מִמִּצְרַיִם כְּלֵי־כֶסֶף וּכְלֵי זָהָב וּשְׂמָלֹת:
לו וַיהֹוָה נָתַן אֶת־חֵן הָעָם בְּעֵינֵי מִצְרַיִם וַיַּשְׁאִלוּם
 וַיְנַצְּלוּ אֶת־מִצְרָיִם: פ

33] The Egyptians urged the people on, to make them leave in haste, for they said, "We shall all be dead." **34]** So the people took their dough before it was leavened, their kneading bowls wrapped in their cloaks upon their shoulders. **35]** The Israelites had done Moses' bidding and borrowed from the Egyptians objects of silver and gold, and clothing. **36]** And the LORD had disposed the Egyptians favorably toward the people, and they let them have their request; thus they stripped the Egyptians.

37] The Israelites journeyed from Raamses to Succoth, about six hundred thousand men on foot, aside from children. **38]** Moreover, a mixed multitude went up with them, and very much livestock, both flocks and herds. **39]** And they baked unleavened cakes of the dough that they had taken out of Egypt, for it was not leavened, since they had been driven out of Egypt and could not delay; nor had they prepared any provisions for themselves.

40] The length of time that the Israelites lived in Egypt was four hundred and thirty

34] *So the people.* Who were caught unprepared, having apparently expected the Exodus at a later time.

36] *Stripped.* Israel was seen to have been in the legal position of the slave wife who upon being expelled from the house was owed compensation [13]. (Note also the demands for restitution made by the black revolutionary movement in the United States.)

37] *Succoth.* Apparently a Hebraization of the Egyptian TKW, the ruins of which were found near Pithom.

Six hundred thousand men. Together with women and children this would amount to an unmanageably large multitude. Still, the figure is a firm part of Torah tradition and must be taken seriously. Therefore "600 *alef*" cannot mean "600 thousand" but means "600 contingents," a contingent being about nine or ten men. Altogether

there were somewhat fewer than 6,000 men [14].

38] *Mixed multitude.* עֵרֶב רַב (erev rav), similar to the אֲסַפְסֻף (asafsuf) of Num. 11:4. These were people from the bottom of Egypt's social strata who took the opportunity to escape from their fate [15].

40] *Four hundred and thirty years.* The figure is problematic, for in Gen. 15:13 the number 400 is given. Further, the forecast in Gen. 15:16 was that the fourth generation would leave Egypt (and indeed Exod. 6:13-30 lists four generations from Jacob to Moses), but I Chron. 7:20-27 lists ten generations from Jacob to Joshua; see comment at 6:20.

Tradition dealt with these figures in various ways. For instance, the 400 years were said to count from the decree (Gen. 15:13) to the liberation, but the actual sojourn in Egypt lasted only

שָׁנָה וְאַרְבַּע מֵאוֹת שָׁנָה וַיְהִי בְּעֶצֶם הַיּוֹם הַזֶּה יָצְאוּ   לַיהוָה לְהוֹצִיאָם מֵאֶרֶץ מִצְרַיִם הוּא־הַלַּיְלָה הַזֶּה

מב כָּל־צִבְאוֹת יְהוָה מֵאֶרֶץ מִצְרָיִם: לֵיל שִׁמֻּרִים הוּא   לַיהוָה שִׁמֻּרִים לְכָל־בְּנֵי יִשְׂרָאֵל לְדֹרֹתָם: פ

years;   **41]** at the end of the four hundred and thirtieth year, to the very day, all the ranks of the LORD departed from the land of Egypt.   **42]** That was for the LORD a night of vigil to bring them out of the land of Egypt; that same night is the LORD's, one of vigil for all the children of Israel throughout the ages.

210 years [16]. Or the extra thirty years were believed to have been added on because Israel neglected circumcision in Egypt [17]. Albright has suggested that the stele of Ramses II honoring the 400th anniversary of Tanis (or Zoan, built about 1700 B.C.E.) may be connected with the figure 400 or 430 in the Exodus story, which would bring the event to 1300–1270 [18]. Tur-Sinai has offered still another theory, basing himself on reading שְׁלֹשִׁים as שִׁלֵּשִׁים, which he understands as "three generations" [19].

42] *Night of vigil.* For God as well as for His people.

The Historical Passover

The festival that in Jewish history has become known as Passover (or Pesach) received its character and importance through the Exodus which made a preexisting festival into the celebration of deliverance. More precisely, there were probably three, and certainly two, separate observances which the Torah tradition combined into one great feast and which subsequent generations endowed with unique distinction.

The two major traditions that contributed to the Passover which we now know were the Passover sacrifice and the Feast of Matzot; while the dedication of the first-born was likely also a separate observance that became absorbed into the festival as it developed over the centuries. This process of confluence, completed by the time the Mishnah was written down (end of second or beginning of third century C.E.), had occurred some centuries before. In the time of the first war with the Romans (first century C.E.), the historian Flavius Josephus called the festival "Feast of Matzot," to which he adds, "which is called Passover"—possibly implying that the latter name was a popular, but not exact, ascription [20]. In time, this popular name, deriving from the sacrificial rite, came to cover all aspects of the festival.

a. The Feast of Matzot was an agricultural festival that celebrated the beginning of the grain harvest when an offering of the first fruits was made and unleavened bread eaten. There are parallels to such practices in other cultures; for instance, there was an observance in Rome when the high priest was enjoined from eating leavened food, and there are some parallels in Mesopotamia and Greece—but in no instance can a relationship be established.[1] The festival started on the 15th of Nisan[2] and was apparently known to the Israelites in Egypt, though it was not celebrated during the years of captivity. This is most likely the basis of Moses' original request of Pharaoh, to let the people go into the wilderness for three days (Exod. 5:1; 10:9).

b. The Passover sacrifice was observed on the 14th of Nisan, at eventide (Lev. 23:5), and was a thanksgiving rite of nomadic or semi-nomadic background. In time the propinquity of the two dates obscured and then eliminated the distinction so that matzot came to be eaten in conjunction with the sacrifice. At first the sacrifice was brought privately by each family, but later on Jerusalem became the center of the celebration. When the Temple was destroyed all sacrifice ceased eventually [22]; only the Samaritans (a sectarian group) continued to bring the offering in their own habitat. To this day they slaughter a lamb at sunset, read Exodus chapter 12, and eat the Passover meal after midnight together with matzot and bitter herbs, while wine and charoset (a paste made of apples, cinnamon, and nuts) are not used by them [23]. In Jewish tradition the Passover sacrifice became a memorial to freedom, but it is difficult to establish just when the coalescence of the feasts of Matzot and Passover was brought about[3] [25].

c. The dedication of the first-born to God is mentioned frequently in the Torah, for God was thought to have a claim on the first fruits of the womb as well as the field.

[1] According to Eichrodt, the Feast of Matzot originated with the (northern) agricultural tribes; hence references to this festival are found in the E-tradition, while the Passover sacrifice originated with the (southern) pastoral cultures and is found in J [21].
[2] The Feast of Tabernacles (Sukot) also starts on the 15th day (of the month of Tishri).
[3] Hyatt believes Passover to stem from pre-Mosaic times; that the Feast of Matzot was taken over from the Canaanites after the Israelite settlement; and that the two celebrations were joined in the days of the Judges [24].

Even as there is until this day a separate observance of redemption (*pidyon ha-ben*) [26], so there was probably an ancient rite that celebrated the arrival of a first son. The Exodus experience established the tradition that Israel as a people was God's first-born and that, by the sacrifice of Egypt's first-born in the night of vigil, He obligated His chosen ones forever. Thus the concept of a spiritual and national primogeniture was combined with the festivals of Matzot and the Passover sacrifice and welded into one tradition.[4] According to one theory, this joining took place under King Josiah (7th century B.C.E.) during the reform described in II Kings 23:21–23; but according to others this time saw merely a revival rather than the creation of the combined festival [27].

The foregoing attempts to describe the Passover of later tradition as having evolved over a number of centuries rather than as having been instituted by God (and Moses) at the time of the Exodus. This is, of course, a conjecture and cannot be considered (nor is it) an indisputable fact. This analysis does not deny, in fact it emphasizes strongly, the impact of the Exodus experience on the original festivals. Precisely because the memory of the event was overwhelmingly strong, and because a deep sense of awe and gratitude underlay the observance, it became in time one great festival, the people's most cherished national celebration, surrounded by elaborate practices of symbolic importance, and begun with a family Seder to the accompaniment of the text of the Haggadah, Israel's most cherished storybook until this day.

(A discussion of the Passover in Jewish tradition will be found in our commentary on Deuteronomy, at chapter 16.)

Passover in the Christian Tradition

Most Western languages still call the remembrances surrounding the death of Jesus "Passover" (English is among the few referring to it as "Easter"; see introduction to this chapter). Christian Scriptures set the end of Jesus' life into the time of a Passover observance in Jerusalem. He comes to the city to celebrate the festival and his execution is said to have taken place on the holy day itself. His last supper was possibly a Seder observance, which is perpetuated in the appurtenances of the communion ceremony, with its wine and matzah-like wafer.[5]

This connection suggests itself from the passages in Matthew 26:17–30: the meal was held at night and inside the gates of Jerusalem as required for a Passover repast by Jewish tradition; wine was served; the psalms of praise (Hallel) were said; and the event was enlivened by interpretation [29]. There are, however, other aspects that do not fit the Seder: in John 18:26 and 19:14 the judgment took place on the eve of Passover, which would disqualify the earlier meal as a Passover Seder. Also, bitter herbs are not mentioned and neither is the eating of a lamb; the former omission may be without significance, but the latter is more difficult to comprehend, particularly in view of the important symbolic value accorded to the lamb by Christian tradition. For, according to John 1:29, Jesus, by dying on Passover, was the lamb "who takes away the sin of the world." The Latin Church Fathers identified

---

[4] Opposed to this theme is, however, another one that runs through the Bible, namely, that God at times overlooks the first-born and chooses a younger sibling (like Jacob, Joseph, Moses, David).

[5] A discussion of the historical background of the death of Jesus as reported in the Gospels is outside the scope of this commentary. A large body of literature is available to guide the reader to an evaluation of this material, and especially also to set the events as reported in Christian Scriptures into the context of Jewish law and practice of that time [28].

the "lamb" as the Paschal offering, although in Jewish tradition the sacrifice was not connected with sin (which suggests that the reference to the lamb was based on Isaiah 53:7–12, where the suffering servant of the Lord is described as bearing the guilt of the many) [30].

Scholars are divided over the question whether the record suggests that Jesus saw himself as the Passover lamb, but later Christian interpretation so viewed him; and, even as in Judaism leaven must be removed from the house at this season, so is this the time for a Christian to remove the "old leaven" from one's life, namely, the habituation to evil: "Have you never heard the saying, 'A little leaven leavens all the dough'? The old leaven of corruption is working among you. Purge it out and then you will

be bread of a new baking. . . . So we who observe the festival must not eat the old leaven, the leaven of corruption and wickedness, but only the unleavened bread which is sincerity and truth" (I Corinthians 5:6–8).

The most obvious continuing link between the Christian Passover-Easter and its Jewish source is its dating. Unlike most Christian festivals it is regulated in part by the revolution of the moon, as are and were all Jewish holy days. The 15th of Nisan, which is the first day of Pesach, coincides with the moon's fullness; Easter was finally fixed on the first Sunday after the first full moon after the spring equinox. This arrangement offered a compromise between those Christians who wanted to preserve the link with Judaism and those who did not [31].

GLEANINGS

This Month

It says (verse 2): "This month shall mark *for you*. . . ." Before this, God had reserved the right to fix the months; now He surrendered it to the Children of Israel.   MIDRASH [32]

Another explanation: Heretofore, time was at the mercy of Israel's masters; now it was at its own command.   SFORNO

No Distinction

It says (verse 22) that during the night of vigil no one was to leave his house. This teaches that once the destroyer (death) would be let loose there would be no distinction between the righteous and the wicked.   RASHI

Hyssop

It is a lowly plant and, precisely because of this, God singled it out as essential for the performance of important tasks: for Passover, for the purification of the leper, and for burning the red heifer.   MIDRASH [33]

The First-born of the Captive

Jewish tradition attempted to justify their inclusion in the punishment by suggesting that they had rejoiced over Pharaoh's repressive decrees.
MIDRASH [34]

Sun and Moon

Israel orders its calendar by the moon, for it is used to living in the night of history.
SEFAT EMET [35]

[The calendar is based on the revolutions of the moon, but adjusted to the solar season in a nineteen-year cycle.]

On Their Shoulders

Why did the Israelites, though they had cattle, carry their kneading bowls on their own shoulders (verse 34)? Because they cherished their religious duties.   MIDRASH [36]

The Meaning of Passover

Since the night of the Exodus it has become a history feast, and indeed *the* history feast par excellence of the world; not a feast of pious remembrance, but of the ever-current contemporaneousness of that which once befell. Every celebrating generation becomes united with the first generation and with all those that have followed.   M. BUBER [37]

Addenda to the Passover Observance

The Passover story has two addenda: one dealing with the eating of the sacrifice and the other relating the Exodus to the first-born. Both addenda appear to speak from a context of settled conditions rather than wilderness wandering and read like postscripts or summations that were appended to the main story at a later time. The second of these is especially important in that it provides the rationale for the principle that the first-born are God's possession, a regulation that applied to animals as well and found its counterpart in God's claim on the first fruits of produce.

There is no evidence that human sacrifice was ever legitimate in Israel* and that the redemption of the first-born was a substitutional offering to compensate God for the loss of human sacrifice. It is likely that such a link existed in prehistoric times and that an awesome, mysterious relationship between the first-born and the Creator was felt to have continued. The Exodus experience deepened this bond and made the redemption of the first-born into a permanent rite of gratitude rather than substitution. The legislation is supplemented in other Torah passages: Exod. 22:28–29; Num. 3:11–13, 40–41; and Deut. 15:19–20.

---

* See the author's Commentary on Genesis, chapter 22.

מג וַיֹּאמֶר יְהוָה אֶל־מֹשֶׁה וְאַהֲרֹן זֹאת חֻקַּת הַפָּסַח
מד כָּל־בֶּן־נֵכָר לֹא־יֹאכַל בּוֹ: וְכָל־עֶבֶד אִישׁ מִקְנַת־
מה כֶּסֶף וּמַלְתָּה אֹתוֹ אָז יֹאכַל בּוֹ: תּוֹשָׁב וְשָׂכִיר לֹא־
מו יֹאכַל בּוֹ: בְּבַיִת אֶחָד יֵאָכֵל לֹא־תוֹצִיא מִן־הַבַּיִת
מז מִן־הַבָּשָׂר חוּצָה וְעֶצֶם לֹא תִשְׁבְּרוּ־בוֹ: כָּל־עֲדַת
מח יִשְׂרָאֵל יַעֲשׂוּ אֹתוֹ: וְכִי־יָגוּר אִתְּךָ גֵּר וְעָשָׂה פֶסַח
לַיהוָה הִמּוֹל לוֹ כָל־זָכָר וְאָז יִקְרַב לַעֲשֹׂתוֹ וְהָיָה
מט כְּאֶזְרַח הָאָרֶץ וְכָל־עָרֵל לֹא־יֹאכַל בּוֹ: תּוֹרָה אַחַת
נ יִהְיֶה לָאֶזְרָח וְלַגֵּר הַגָּר בְּתוֹכְכֶם: וַיַּעֲשׂוּ כָּל־בְּנֵי
יִשְׂרָאֵל כַּאֲשֶׁר צִוָּה יְהוָה אֶת־מֹשֶׁה וְאֶת־אַהֲרֹן כֵּן

א עָשׂוּ: ס וַיְהִי בְּעֶצֶם הַיּוֹם הַזֶּה הוֹצִיא יְהוָה אֶת־
בְּנֵי יִשְׂרָאֵל מֵאֶרֶץ מִצְרַיִם עַל־צִבְאֹתָם: פ
א וַיְדַבֵּר יְהוָה אֶל־מֹשֶׁה לֵּאמֹר: קַדֶּשׁ־לִי כָל־בְּכוֹר
ב פֶּטֶר כָּל־רֶחֶם בִּבְנֵי יִשְׂרָאֵל בָּאָדָם וּבַבְּהֵמָה לִי
ג הוּא: וַיֹּאמֶר מֹשֶׁה אֶל־הָעָם זָכוֹר אֶת־הַיּוֹם הַזֶּה
אֲשֶׁר יְצָאתֶם מִמִּצְרַיִם מִבֵּית עֲבָדִים כִּי בְּחֹזֶק יָד
ד הוֹצִיא יְהוָה אֶתְכֶם מִזֶּה וְלֹא יֵאָכֵל חָמֵץ: הַיּוֹם
ה אַתֶּם יֹצְאִים בְּחֹדֶשׁ הָאָבִיב: וְהָיָה כִי־יְבִיאֲךָ
יְהוָה אֶל־אֶרֶץ הַכְּנַעֲנִי וְהַחִתִּי וְהָאֱמֹרִי וְהַחִוִּי
וְהַיְבוּסִי אֲשֶׁר נִשְׁבַּע לַאֲבֹתֶיךָ לָתֶת לָךְ אֶרֶץ זָבַת

43] The LORD said to Moses and Aaron: This is the law of the passover offering: No foreigner shall eat of it. **44]** But any slave a man has bought may eat of it once he has been circumcised. **45]** A resident hireling shall not eat of it. **46]** It shall be eaten in one house: you shall not take any of the flesh outside the house; nor shall you break a bone of it. **47]** The whole assembly of Israel shall offer it. **48]** If a stranger who dwells with you would offer the passover to the LORD, all his males must be circumcised; then he shall be admitted to offer it; he shall then be as a citizen of the country. But no uncircumcised person may eat of it. **49]** There shall be one law for the citizen and for the stranger who dwells among you.

50] And all the Israelites did so; as the LORD had commanded Moses and Aaron, so they did.

51] That very day the LORD freed the Israelites from the land of Egypt, troop by troop.

1] The LORD spoke further to Moses, saying, **2]** "Consecrate to Me every first-born; man and beast, the first issue of every womb among the Israelites is Mine."

3] And Moses said to the people,

"Remember this day, on which you went free from Egypt, the house of bondage, how the LORD freed you from it with a mighty hand: no leavened bread shall be eaten. **4]** You go free on this day, in the month of Abib. **5]** So, when the LORD has brought you into the land of the Canaanites, the Hittites, the Amorites, the Hivites, and the Jebusites, which He swore to your

---

12:43] *This is the law.* Tradition was divided over whether these laws were meant for the Exodus only or for all generations [1].

Foreigner. A temporary resident. Targum Onkelos, however, renders "an apostate Israelite."

45] *Resident hireling.* It is not clear who was meant; possibly a foreign-born laborer who had become a permanent resident [2].

46] *Nor . . . break a bone.* Both Num. 9:12 and Christian Scriptures make reference to this [3].

49] *One law.* This applies to the Passover regula-

tion and only if the stranger joins himself to Israel. The general principle is stated in Lev. 19:34.

51] *That very day.* The sentence forms a literary bridge between chapters 12 and 13.

13:4] *In the month of Abib.* When the grain ripens (see Lev. 2:14); Abib, or Aviv, was the spring month later called Nisan; see at Exod. 12:2.

5] *Land of the Canaanites.* In 3:8, the list contains five of the Canaanite nations, of whom there were a good many more. In other passages, "seven" is the usual round number given to describe them.

חָלָ֖ב וּדְבָ֑שׁ וְעָבַדְתָּ֛ אֶת־הָעֲבֹדָ֥ה הַזֹּ֖את בַּחֹ֥דֶשׁ הַזֶּֽה׃

י שִׁבְעַ֥ת יָמִ֖ים תֹּאכַ֣ל מַצֹּ֑ת וּבַיּוֹם֙ הַשְּׁבִיעִ֔י חַ֖ג לַיהֹוָֽה׃

מַצּוֹת֙ יֵֽאָכֵ֔ל אֵ֖ת שִׁבְעַ֣ת הַיָּמִ֑ים וְלֹֽא־יֵרָאֶ֨ה לְךָ֜ חָמֵ֗ץ

וְלֹֽא־יֵרָאֶ֥ה לְךָ֛ שְׂאֹ֖ר בְּכׇל־גְּבֻלֶֽךָ׃ וְהִגַּדְתָּ֣ לְבִנְךָ֗ בַּיּ֥וֹם

הַה֛וּא לֵאמֹ֑ר בַּעֲב֣וּר זֶ֗ה עָשָׂ֤ה יְהֹוָה֙ לִ֔י בְּצֵאתִ֖י

מִמִּצְרָֽיִם׃ וְהָיָה֩ לְךָ֨ לְא֜וֹת עַל־יָֽדְךָ֗ וּלְזִכָּרוֹן֙ בֵּ֣ין

עֵינֶ֔יךָ לְמַ֗עַן תִּהְיֶ֛ה תּוֹרַ֥ת יְהֹוָ֖ה בְּפִ֑יךָ כִּ֚י בְּיָ֣ד

חֲזָקָ֔ה הוֹצִֽאֲךָ֥ יְהֹוָ֖ה מִמִּצְרָֽיִם׃ וְשָׁמַרְתָּ֛ אֶת־הַחֻקָּ֥ה

הַזֹּ֖את לְמוֹעֲדָ֑הּ מִיָּמִ֖ים יָמִֽימָה׃ פ

יא וְהָיָ֞ה כִּֽי־יְבִֽאֲךָ֤ יְהֹוָה֙ אֶל־אֶ֣רֶץ הַֽכְּנַעֲנִ֔י כַּאֲשֶׁ֛ר נִשְׁבַּ֥ע

יב לְךָ֖ וְלַֽאֲבֹתֶ֑יךָ וּנְתָנָ֖הּ לָֽךְ׃ וְהַעֲבַרְתָּ֥ כׇל־פֶּֽטֶר־רֶ֖חֶם

לַֽיהֹוָ֑ה וְכׇל־פֶּ֣טֶר ׀ שֶׁ֣גֶר בְּהֵמָ֗ה אֲשֶׁ֨ר יִהְיֶ֥ה לְךָ֛ הַזְּכָרִ֖ים

יג לַיהֹוָֽה׃ וְכׇל־פֶּ֤טֶר חֲמֹר֙ תִּפְדֶּ֣ה בְשֶׂ֔ה וְאִם־לֹ֥א תִפְדֶּ֖ה

יד וַעֲרַפְתּ֑וֹ וְכֹ֨ל בְּכ֥וֹר אָדָ֛ם בְּבָנֶ֖יךָ תִּפְדֶּֽה׃ וְהָיָ֞ה כִּֽי־

יִשְׁאָלְךָ֥ בִנְךָ֛ מָחָ֖ר לֵאמֹ֣ר מַה־זֹּ֑את וְאָמַרְתָּ֣ אֵלָ֔יו

בְּחֹ֣זֶק יָ֗ד הוֹצִיאָ֧נוּ יְהֹוָ֛ה מִמִּצְרַ֖יִם מִבֵּ֥ית עֲבָדִֽים׃

טו וַיְהִ֗י כִּֽי־הִקְשָׁ֣ה פַרְעֹה֮ לְשַׁלְּחֵנוּ֒ וַיַּהֲרֹ֨ג יְהֹוָ֤ה כׇּל־בְּכוֹר֙

בְּאֶ֣רֶץ מִצְרַ֔יִם מִבְּכֹ֥ר אָדָ֖ם וְעַד־בְּכ֣וֹר בְּהֵמָ֑ה עַל־

fathers to give you, a land flowing with milk and honey, you shall observe in this month the following practice:

6] "Seven days you shall eat unleavened bread, and on the seventh day there shall be a festival of the LORD. **7]** Throughout the seven days unleavened bread shall be eaten; no leavened bread shall be found with you, and no leaven shall be found in all your territory. **8]** And you shall explain to your son on that day, 'It is because of what the LORD did for me when I went free from Egypt.'

9] "And this shall serve you as a sign on your hand and as a reminder on your forehead—in order that the teachings of the LORD may be in your mouth—that with a mighty hand the LORD freed you from Egypt. **10]** You shall keep this institution at its set time from year to year.

11] "And when the LORD has brought you into the land of the Canaanites, as He swore to you and to your fathers, and has given it to you, **12]** you shall set apart for the LORD every first issue of the womb: every male firstling that your cattle drop shall be the LORD's. **13]** But every firstling ass you shall redeem with a sheep; if you do not redeem it, you must break its neck. And you must redeem every first-born male among your children. **14]** And when, in time to come, your son asks you, saying, 'What does this mean?' you shall say to him, 'It was with a mighty hand that the LORD brought us out from Egypt, the house of bondage. **15]** When Pharaoh stubbornly refused to let us go, the LORD slew every first-born in the land

8] *You shall explain.* In the Passover Haggadah this verse is taken to establish the obligation to tell the Exodus story to a small child who is too young to ask.

9] *Sign on your hand.* Explained by tradition to mean the wearing of *tefillin* (phylacteries) on arm and hand.

On your forehead. Literally, "between your eyes." The traditional basis for the wearing of tefillin on the head.

13] *Every firstling ass.* It had to be redeemed with sheep, perhaps because the ass was ritually unclean [4].

You must break its neck. No economic advantage may accrue from the animal if it was not redeemed.

כֵּן אֲנִי זֹבֵחַ לַיהוָֹה כָּל־פֶּטֶר רֶחֶם הַזְּכָרִים וְכָל־ ^{טו} בְּכוֹר בָּנַי אֶפְדֶּה: וְהָיָה לְאוֹת עַל־יָדְכָה וּלְטוֹטָפֹת בֵּין עֵינֶיךָ כִּי בְּחֹזֶק יָד הוֹצִיאָנוּ יְהוָֹה מִמִּצְרָיִם:

Haftarah Bo, p. 700

of Egypt, the first-born of both man and beast. Therefore I sacrifice to the LORD every first male issue of the womb, but redeem every first-born among my sons.'

16] "And so it shall be as a sign upon your hand and as a symbol on your forehead that with a mighty hand the LORD freed us from Egypt."

14] *Your son.* In the Haggadah, the simple son.
16] *Symbol.* Or, "frontlet." Translated as tefillin by the Targum, the Hebrew טוֹטָפֹת (*totafot*) may originally have described an ornament for women as shown on Nimrud ivories [5]. Like an ornament, the *totafot* were displayed prominently.

Tefillin

Tefillin is the postbiblical Hebrew term for two small boxes containing Torah passages written on pieces of parchment, with leather bands attached to the boxes in such a way that one may be worn on the forehead, between the eyes, and the other tied to the arm. Tefillin (from תְּפִלָּה, *tefillah*, prayer) is the name of a small tractate in the Talmud that assembles the relevant prescriptions of tradition [6].

The Torah demands four times that words of the law be put as signs on the hand and as frontlets (or symbols) between the eyes (or on the forehead).[1] Just what the Torah itself had in mind when these admonitions were set down can no longer be ascertained. They may have implied a demonstrative display similar to that of the mezuzah (with which they are linked in Deut. 6:8–9) or they may have been meant figuratively, as was maintained as late as in the Middle Ages by the Rashbam (Rabbi Samuel ben Meir, in his commentary on the Torah). These commandments, he writes, "shall be for you a reminder *as if* they were written on your hand. They are to be taken [figuratively] just as in 'Set me as a seal upon your heart'" (Song of Songs 8:6). At any rate, the custom of writing down some representative laws which could then be worn goes back to ancient days and may be connected with ideas that the wearing would have some prophylactic effect similar to that of amulets, or perhaps would show the wearer's membership in a sacred community. The Rabbis still had a tradition, however, that made it clear that some regulations pertaining to the tefillin were a post-Torah development, and

they held that such rules went back only to the *soferim* (scribes), that is, to the early teachers of the Oral Law, but no farther[2] [7].

Christian Scriptures allude to tefillin in a critical way, calling them "phylacteries" (i.e., prophylactic amulets) and attacking the Pharisees for their demonstrative usage of them [8]. The Rabbis themselves did in fact stress that public display of tefillin was one way in which one testified to God's lordship and glory, for He himself could be imagined as wearing them [9]. Tefillin were therefore worn by some Jews every time they ventured into the public domain, and occasionally women too wore them. But in time the practice was restricted to certain hours and occasions: they were to be worn at day and not by night; and they were to be put on during morning prayers, after the donning of the talit. On Sabbaths and holy days and on the morning of Tishah b'Av their wearing was omitted.

The tefillin contain the four paragraphs from the Torah that refer to them, and these passages are written in the order of their biblical occurrence.[3] Along with the other positive mitzvot the wearing of tefillin became obligatory for a Jewish boy upon his reaching the age of Bar Mitzvah, and traditional Judaism has stressed the great spiritual importance of carrying out the commandment. Says Maimonides: "The sanctity of tefillin is very great. So long as the tefillin are on the head and arm of a man, he is modest and God-fearing . . . and will devote his thoughts to truth and righteousness" [10].

Reform Jews, tending to stress internal commitment over adherence to external forms, have generally abandoned the practice

---

[1] Exod. 13:9, 16; Deut. 6:8 and 11:18. In the first passage they are described as a reminder (*zikaron*), in the others as symbols or frontlets (*totafot*).

[2] Thus, the Samaritans did not wear tefillin.

[3] Exod. 13:1–10; 13:11–16; Deut. 6:4–9; 11:13–20. This

practice follows Rashi, who in this matter was opposed by his grandson, Rabbenu Tam, who reversed the two Deuteronomic passages. Tefillin found at the Dead Sea indicate that this difference went back to early days.

of wearing tefillin, although the Reform movement as such has never taken an official stand on the matter. Its position may be said to be, however, an endorsement of Rashbam's point of view, that the biblical prescription was meant in a figurative way only.

Literary Analysis

There are some obvious differences between the Passover prescriptions of 13:6–8 and of 12:15 ff. In chapter 13 only the last day is stressed as the festival day, while chapter 12 prescribes observance of both the first and the seventh days. In chapter 13 a special symbol is provided to reinforce the memory of the Exodus. In both chapters the people are instructed to explain the festival to their children: in chapter 13 with regard to leaven and in chapter 12 with regard to the Passover sacrifice, but the two passages seem to have no relation to each other. Chapter 13 speaks of "the month of Abib," chapter 12 of "the first month."

Jewish tradition reconciled the major contradictions and problems in the following way: Both the first and last days are to be celebrated as holy days and no leavened bread may be eaten during the entire time of celebration; however, the eating of matzah is *commanded* only on the first day. That is to say, while it is customary to eat matzah throughout Passover it is obligatory only on the opening day, whereas the negative command—not to partake of leaven—applies beyond the first day [11]. As to the instructions to be issued to one's children, tradition stresses that in 12:26 and 13:8 two different subjects are involved, and, as the Haggadah

points out, two different types of sons are meant: In 13:8 the Jew is commanded to interpret the Exodus even if the child does not ask any questions because it is too small; in 12:26 the "wicked son" is addressed, that is, one who says, "What do *you* mean by this rite?" He says "you" and not "we," and by asking in this way excludes himself from his people.

Others explain the differences by basing themselves on the critical method: they posit the existence of separate sources. They also point out an internal literary problem in chapter 13 itself: the Hebrew varies between plural and singular cases. They see in chapter 12 the Passover story as told by the P-source, which is concluded at the end of the chapter. Chapter 13, on the other hand, is believed by some to be of an earlier time (J-source) and by others of a later, Deuteronomistic tradition [12], or possibly a combination of both.

It is not possible to draw definitive conclusions from the material on hand, but it should be remembered that variants were not necessarily considered antithetical and mutually exclusive of each other, and were not adjudged on an either-or basis. Biblical man was able to assimilate various versions and traditions as equally "true," and in that way they were handed down to later generations [13]. The importance of the Exodus and of Passover was underscored by the meticulous preservation of all details that tradition had prescribed, and these in turn became the foundation for the elaborate laws and customs of the Passover celebrations of subsequent ages.

GLEANINGS

Laws of Tefillin

The boxes must be square, black, and, like the straps, be made of the skin of clean animals. Black ink must be used for the writing.

The box worn on the arm contains the four scriptural passages in one scroll; the one for the head, in four separate scrolls.

According to the *Shulchan Aruch*, the boxes had no prescribed size [14], but some rabbis hold that it is desirable for them to be no smaller than the width of two fingers [15].

In putting on the tefillin, one starts with those for the hand. The box is placed on the inner side of the left arm, opposite the heart. The straps are wound seven times around the arm and brought to the hand there to form the letter *shin*.

Women are exempt and precluded from laying tefillin [though this was not the case in talmudic days]; a mourner is exempt on the first day of *shivah* as is a bridegroom on his wedding day (so according to some rabbis, Karo among them; Isserles disagrees) [16].

Tefillin are not worn on Sabbaths and holy days, for these are in themselves "signs" unto God; hence tefillin, which are also "signs," are unnecessary on these days.

In ancient days tefillin were worn throughout the day; nowadays their use is confined to morning prayers (except on Tishah b'Av, when they are worn at afternoon prayers) [17].

Remember (Exod. 13:3)

The command to remember was directed not merely to the generation of the Exodus but to all generations. Hence the verses from Numbers 15:40-41 ("Thus shall you be reminded...") are recited twice a day, at morning and evening prayers. Only in the days of the Messiah will this be no longer necessary [18].

Given

The expression that God swore to the forefathers "to give" the Promised Land to their descendants (13:5) emphasizes that it will be a gift, not an inherited right.　　　RASHI [19]

Fulfilling the Command

Rabbi Aba Arika (Rab), the disciple of Rabbi Judah the Prince, was never seen to walk four cubits without a scroll of the Torah, without fringes on his garments, and without wearing tefillin.　　　MAIMONIDES [20]

Passover and Kol Nidre

(A stranger may not celebrate the Passover sacrifice, verse 43. "Stranger" is rendered by the Targum as "apostate," that is, the sinner par excellence. This rendition makes possible a comparison between the eve of Passover and the eve of Atonement when, in the Kol Nidre prayer, the congregation is expressly allowed to include sinners. Why the difference?) If sinners come to weep and atone with us (on Yom Kippur), they are welcome; but when they join us only to rejoice and eat with us (on Passover), they are not.　　　MIDRASH [21]

PART IV

The Road to Sinai

If the Exodus is the hinge of Israel's fate, Sinai is the place which gives it meaning. It now becomes clear that liberation from Egypt, for all the seminal importance it will occupy in Israel's memory, does not stand by itself: it is to make the *liberated* people ready to become God's *covenanted* people. For other nations, freedom is a value of and in itself; for Israel, it is the foundation of its spiritual life, and its full meaning cannot be disclosed until the road to Sinai is completed.

But even this road is not a simple one. The Egyptians pursue and slavery threatens once again to overtake Israel, and once again God must descend into the realm of human history. At the Reed Sea the people experience His might and after the rescue celebrate their salvation and His victory in the Song at the Sea which in Jewish tradition has become Shirah (Song).

Now the people can resume their trek to Sinai, only to find that new foes lurk by the wayside: internal dissent as well as external danger. Sinai looms in the distance, but no easy road leads to it. Nothing comes easy to Israel, neither before the revelation nor after it.

Rescue at the Sea

The route of the Exodus is chosen by God, not by Moses, and is anything but a direct road to Canaan. The text is, however, silent on whether this was originally God's intent. There is a sudden change of direction, and this time another motive for God's decision is given. Israel's first trial as a free people now occurs: the Egyptians conclude that letting the slaves go had been a mistake and they set to recapture them, but the pursuit ends in the pursuers' own destruction in the waters of the Reed Sea. The indelible impression that this event made on Israel is recorded in the concluding verse of this section: "And when Israel saw the wondrous power which the Lord had wielded against the Egyptians, the people feared the Lord: they had faith in the Lord and in His servant Moses." The rescue at the sea bears the seal of God's providence.

In the Hebrew original, the opening phrases (13:17–22) are distinguished by a rhythm which lends the text an epic quality. Some scholars suggest that this section was part of the J/E-tradition, while 14:1–4 are assigned to P. Thus, in J/E the division of the sea is seen to be accomplished by an east wind, in P through the agency of Moses' rod [1].

(A new weekly portion begins with this section. It takes its name, *Beshalach,* from the second word of the first sentence.)

ס   ס   ס

יז וַיְהִי בְּשַׁלַּח פַּרְעֹה אֶת־הָעָם וְלֹא־נָחָם אֱלֹהִים דֶּרֶךְ פָּקֹד יִפְקֹד אֱלֹהִים אֶתְכֶם וְהַעֲלִיתֶם אֶת־עַצְמֹתַי
אֶרֶץ פְּלִשְׁתִּים כִּי קָרוֹב הוּא כִּי אָמַר אֱלֹהִים פֶּן כ מִזֶּה אִתְּכֶם: וַיִּסְעוּ מִסֻּכֹּת וַיַּחֲנוּ בְאֵתָם בִּקְצֵה
יִנָּחֵם הָעָם בִּרְאֹתָם מִלְחָמָה וְשָׁבוּ מִצְרָיְמָה: וַיַּסֵּב כא הַמִּדְבָּר: וַיהוָה הֹלֵךְ לִפְנֵיהֶם יוֹמָם בְּעַמּוּד עָנָן
אֱלֹהִים אֶת־הָעָם דֶּרֶךְ הַמִּדְבָּר יַם־סוּף וַחֲמֻשִׁים עָלוּ לַנְחֹתָם הַדֶּרֶךְ וְלַיְלָה בְּעַמּוּד אֵשׁ לְהָאִיר לָהֶם
יט בְנֵי־יִשְׂרָאֵל מֵאֶרֶץ מִצְרָיִם: וַיִּקַּח מֹשֶׁה אֶת־עַצְמוֹת כב לָלֶכֶת יוֹמָם וָלָיְלָה: לֹא־יָמִישׁ עַמּוּד הֶעָנָן יוֹמָם
יוֹסֵף עִמּוֹ כִּי הַשְׁבֵּעַ הִשְׁבִּיעַ אֶת־בְּנֵי יִשְׂרָאֵל לֵאמֹר וְעַמּוּד הָאֵשׁ לָיְלָה לִפְנֵי הָעָם: פ

17] Now when Pharaoh let the people go, God did not lead them by way of the land of the Philistines, although it was nearer; for God said, "The people may have a change of heart when they see war, and return to Egypt." **18]** So God led the people round-about, by way of the wilderness at the Sea of Reeds.

Now the Israelites went up armed out of the land of Egypt. **19]** And Moses took with him the bones of Joseph, who had exacted an oath from the children of Israel, saying, "God will be sure to take notice of you: then you shall carry up my bones from here with you."

20] They set out from Succoth and encamped at Etham, at the edge of the wilderness. **21]** The LORD went before them in a pillar of cloud by day, to guide them along the way, and in a pillar of fire by night, to give them light, that they might travel day and night. **22]** The pillar of cloud by day and the pillar of fire by night did not depart from before the people.

13:17] *Land of the Philistines.* Generally believed to be an anachronism, written from a later perspective, since the Philistines appear to have reached Canaan only after the Israelites had settled. The direct route would have led along the coast toward today's El-Arish and then to Gaza (see map).

Although it was nearer. It would have taken some ten to eleven days of unhindered travel. The divine precaution was clearly necessary, as was later shown (see Num. 14:4).

Change of heart. The Hebrew is a play on words with the earlier "lead them": נָחָם–יִנָּחֵם. Targum Jonathan's addendum, that God did not want them to see the bones of two hundred thousand Ephraimites who had left Egypt at a previous time and had died near the sea road, reflects an old tradition: the Children of Israel were not intact when they left Egypt (see also comment on verse 18).

18] *Sea of Reeds.* An exact translation of the Hebrew. The older translation "Red Sea" is merely an interpretation of where the Israelites might have crossed over but is not a proper rendition of the text.

Armed. The meaning of חֲמֻשִׁים is not certain. The rendering is based on Targum Onkelos. Rashi follows this but also gives an alternate explanation: חֲמֻשִׁים means that one-fifth went out, four-fifths having died during the plague of darkness. The theme that only a portion of the people left Egypt is found repeatedly in the Midrash, where traditions are recorded which said that only 1/50 or 1/500 went out [2]. It is also possible that, if חֲמֻשִׁים is related to חָמֵשׁ (five) or חֲמִשִּׁים (fifty), it may indicate "troops of five," or "troops of fifty," respectively, that is to say, Israel went out of Egypt like an organized army.

19] *Bones of Joseph.* As he had pledged them to do, Gen. 50:24–25.

20] *Succoth...Etham.* Succoth was mentioned previously (12:37), and there is a good tradition about its location (see map); but there is none concerning Etham.

21] *Travel day and night.* During the cool months they would travel by day; during the hot season, by night.

וְאֶת־עַמּוֹ לָקַח עִמּוֹ: וַיִּקַּח שֵׁשׁ־מֵאוֹת רֶכֶב בָּחוּר ז
וְכֹל רֶכֶב מִצְרַיִם וְשָׁלִשִׁם עַל־כֻּלּוֹ: וַיְחַזֵּק יְהֹוָה אֶת־ ח
לֵב פַּרְעֹה מֶלֶךְ מִצְרַיִם וַיִּרְדֹּף אַחֲרֵי בְּנֵי יִשְׂרָאֵל
וּבְנֵי יִשְׂרָאֵל יֹצְאִים בְּיָד רָמָה: וַיִּרְדְּפוּ מִצְרַיִם ט
אַחֲרֵיהֶם וַיַּשִּׂיגוּ אוֹתָם חֹנִים עַל־הַיָּם כָּל־סוּס רֶכֶב
פַּרְעֹה וּפָרָשָׁיו וְחֵילוֹ עַל־פִּי הַחִירֹת לִפְנֵי בַּעַל
צְפֹן: וּפַרְעֹה הִקְרִיב וַיִּשְׂאוּ בְנֵי־יִשְׂרָאֵל אֶת־עֵינֵיהֶם י
וְהִנֵּה מִצְרַיִם נֹסֵעַ אַחֲרֵיהֶם וַיִּירְאוּ מְאֹד וַיִּצְעֲקוּ
בְנֵי־יִשְׂרָאֵל אֶל־יְהֹוָה: וַיֹּאמְרוּ אֶל־מֹשֶׁה הֲמִבְּלִי אֵין יא

וַיְדַבֵּר יְהֹוָה אֶל־מֹשֶׁה לֵּאמֹר: דַּבֵּר אֶל־בְּנֵי יִשְׂרָאֵל א
וְיָשֻׁבוּ וְיַחֲנוּ לִפְנֵי פִּי הַחִירֹת בֵּין מִגְדֹּל וּבֵין הַיָּם ב
לִפְנֵי בַּעַל צְפֹן נִכְחוֹ תַחֲנוּ עַל־הַיָּם: וְאָמַר פַּרְעֹה ג
לִבְנֵי יִשְׂרָאֵל נְבֻכִים הֵם בָּאָרֶץ סָגַר עֲלֵיהֶם הַמִּדְבָּר:
וְחִזַּקְתִּי אֶת־לֵב־פַּרְעֹה וְרָדַף אַחֲרֵיהֶם וְאִכָּבְדָה ד
בְּפַרְעֹה וּבְכָל־חֵילוֹ וְיָדְעוּ מִצְרַיִם כִּי־אֲנִי יְהֹוָה
וַיַּעֲשׂוּ־כֵן: וַיֻּגַּד לְמֶלֶךְ מִצְרַיִם כִּי בָרַח הָעָם וַיֵּהָפֵךְ ה
לְבַב פַּרְעֹה וַעֲבָדָיו אֶל־הָעָם וַיֹּאמְרוּ מַה־זֹּאת עָשִׂינוּ
כִּי־שִׁלַּחְנוּ אֶת־יִשְׂרָאֵל מֵעָבְדֵנוּ: וַיֶּאְסֹר אֶת־רִכְבּוֹ ו

1] The LORD said to Moses: **2]** Tell the Israelites to turn back and encamp before Pi-hahiroth, between Migdol and the sea, before Baal-zephon; you shall encamp facing it, by the sea. **3]** Pharaoh will say of the Israelites, "They are astray in the land; the wilderness has closed in on them." **4]** Then I will stiffen Pharaoh's heart and he will pursue them, that I may assert My authority against Pharaoh and all his host; and the Egyptians shall know that I am the LORD.

And they did so.

5] When the king of Egypt was told that the people had fled, Pharaoh and his courtiers had a change of heart about the people and said, "What is this we have done, releasing Israel from our service?" **6]** He ordered his chariot and took his men with him; **7]** he took six hundred of his picked chariots, and the rest of the chariots of Egypt, with officers in all of them. **8]** The LORD stiffened the heart of Pharaoh, king of Egypt, and he gave chase to the Israelites. As the Israelites were departing boldly, **9]** the Egyptians gave chase to them, and all the chariot horses of Pharaoh, his horsemen, and his warriors overtook them encamped by the sea, near Pi-hahiroth, before Baal-zephon.

10] As Pharaoh drew near, the Israelites caught sight of the Egyptians advancing upon them. Greatly frightened, the Israelites cried out to the LORD. **11]** And they said to Moses, "Was it

14:2] *Pi-hahiroth.* Its location cannot be identified with certainty and can be suggested only in relation to one of the possible routes of the Exodus (see commentary below). This applies also to the other places mentioned.

4] *Assert My authority.* A better translation would read "be glorified" (see commentary on 4:19–6:1). This appears to be the reason for the change in direction given by God.

5] *Fled.* Permanently. It now becomes obvious to Pharaoh that Israel did not leave on a temporary journey for the purpose of worship as originally foreseen.

6] *Chariot.* Egyptian chariots were drawn by stallions hitched in pairs [3].

7] *Officers.* The Hebrew שָׁלִשִׁים (*shalishim*) is related to שָׁלֹשׁ (*shalosh*, three) and means most likely "men of the third (or special) rank" [4]. Examples of such officers were the third men on Egyptian chariots.

8] *Stiffened.* This is the last time the expression occurs in relation to Pharaoh himself. God will finally stiffen the hearts of the Egyptians also (verse 17), which will lead to their destruction.

Boldly. Literally, "with upraised hand," an idiom reflecting defiance. In modern days also an upraised clenched fist has taken on this significance.

קְבָרִים בְּמִצְרַיִם לְקַחְתָּנוּ לָמוּת בַּמִּדְבָּר מַה־זֹּאת עַל־הַיָּם וּבְקָעֵהוּ וְיָבֹאוּ בְנֵי־יִשְׂרָאֵל בְּתוֹךְ הַיָּם

עָשִׂיתָ לָּנוּ לְהוֹצִיאָנוּ מִמִּצְרָיִם: הֲלֹא־זֶה הַדָּבָר אֲשֶׁר ‏יב‏ בַּיַּבָּשָׁה: וַאֲנִי הִנְנִי מְחַזֵּק אֶת־לֵב מִצְרַיִם וְיָבֹאוּ

דִּבַּרְנוּ אֵלֶיךָ בְמִצְרַיִם לֵאמֹר חֲדַל מִמֶּנּוּ וְנַעַבְדָה אַחֲרֵיהֶם וְאִכָּבְדָה בְּפַרְעֹה וּבְכָל־חֵילוֹ בְּרִכְבּוֹ

אֶת־מִצְרָיִם כִּי טוֹב לָנוּ עֲבֹד אֶת־מִצְרַיִם מִמֻּתֵנוּ ‏יח‏ וּבְפָרָשָׁיו: וְיָדְעוּ מִצְרַיִם כִּי־אֲנִי יְהוָה בְּהִכָּבְדִי

בַּמִּדְבָּר: וַיֹּאמֶר מֹשֶׁה אֶל־הָעָם אַל־תִּירָאוּ הִתְיַצְּבוּ ‏יט‏ בְּפַרְעֹה בְּרִכְבּוֹ וּבְפָרָשָׁיו: וַיִּסַּע מַלְאַךְ הָאֱלֹהִים

וּרְאוּ אֶת־יְשׁוּעַת יְהוָה אֲשֶׁר־יַעֲשֶׂה לָכֶם הַיּוֹם כִּי הַהֹלֵךְ לִפְנֵי מַחֲנֵה יִשְׂרָאֵל וַיֵּלֶךְ מֵאַחֲרֵיהֶם וַיִּסַּע

אֲשֶׁר רְאִיתֶם אֶת־מִצְרַיִם הַיּוֹם לֹא תֹסִפוּ לִרְאֹתָם ‏כ‏ עַמּוּד הֶעָנָן מִפְּנֵיהֶם וַיַּעֲמֹד מֵאַחֲרֵיהֶם: וַיָּבֹא בֵּין

עוֹד עַד־עוֹלָם: יְהוָה יִלָּחֵם לָכֶם וְאַתֶּם תַּחֲרִשׁוּן: פ מַחֲנֵה מִצְרַיִם וּבֵין מַחֲנֵה יִשְׂרָאֵל וַיְהִי הֶעָנָן וְהַחֹשֶׁךְ

וַיֹּאמֶר יְהוָה אֶל־מֹשֶׁה מַה־תִּצְעַק אֵלָי דַּבֵּר אֶל־בְּנֵי וַיָּאֶר* אֶת־הַלָּיְלָה וְלֹא־קָרַב זֶה אֶל־זֶה כָּל־הַלָּיְלָה:

יִשְׂרָאֵל וְיִסָּעוּ: וְאַתָּה הָרֵם אֶת־מַטְּךָ וּנְטֵה אֶת־יָדְךָ ‏כא‏ וַיֵּט מֹשֶׁה אֶת־יָדוֹ עַל־הַיָּם וַיּוֹלֶךְ יְהוָה אֶת־הַיָּם בְּרוּחַ

*‏ יג סבירין כאשר.

for want of graves in Egypt that you brought us to die in the wilderness? What have you done to us, taking us out of Egypt?   **12]** Is this not the very thing we told you in Egypt, saying, 'Let us be, and we will serve the Egyptians, for it is better for us to serve the Egyptians than to die in the wilderness'?"   **13]** But Moses said to the people, "Have no fear! Stand by, and witness the deliverance which the LORD will work for you today; for the Egyptians whom you see today you will never see again.   **14]** The LORD will battle for you; you hold your peace!"

15] Then the LORD said to Moses, "Why do you cry out to Me? Tell the Israelites to go forward.   **16]** And you lift up your rod and hold out your arm over the sea and split it, so that the Israelites may march into the sea on dry ground.   **17]** And I will stiffen the hearts of the Egyptians so that they go in after them; and I will assert My authority against Pharaoh and all his warriors, his chariots and his horsemen.   **18]** Let the Egyptians know that I am LORD, when I assert My authority against Pharaoh, his chariots, and his horsemen."

19] The angel of God, who had been going ahead of the Israelite army, now moved and followed behind them; and the pillar of cloud shifted from in front of them and took up a place behind them,   **20]** and it came between the army of the Egyptians and the army of Israel. Thus there was the cloud with the darkness, and it cast a spell upon the night, so that the one could not come near the other all through the night.

21] Then Moses held out his arm over the sea and the LORD drove back the sea with a strong

12] *We told you.* Not mentioned before, but fitting in with the situation. Moses had previously met some resistance, now he faces his first serious murmuring.

15] *Why do you cry.* This too has not been mentioned, but obviously the story does not tell every detail. In his first confrontation with incipient rebellion Moses must have prayed for help [5].

Go forward. Toward the sea. The Israelites were to show their faith in God's saving power by marching farther toward the waters.

19] *The angel.* We have hitherto heard of a cloud and a pillar of fire (13:22); now the story introduces an angel to describe further the miraculous intervention of God. It is not clear what the function of the cloud is in this case since it too moves from the front to the rear. Perhaps two sources are here discernible. See footnote 1.

20] *Cast a spell.* Assuming וַיָּאֶר to come from אָרַר, curse.

קָדִים עַזָּה כָּל־הַלַּיְלָה וַיָּשֶׂם אֶת־הַיָּם לֶחָרָבָה וַיִּבָּקְעוּ
כב הַמָּיִם: וַיָּבֹאוּ בְנֵי־יִשְׂרָאֵל בְּתוֹךְ הַיָּם בַּיַּבָּשָׁה וְהַמַּיִם
כג לָהֶם חוֹמָה מִימִינָם וּמִשְּׂמֹאלָם: וַיִּרְדְּפוּ מִצְרַיִם
וַיָּבֹאוּ אַחֲרֵיהֶם כֹּל סוּס פַּרְעֹה רִכְבּוֹ וּפָרָשָׁיו אֶל־
כד תּוֹךְ הַיָּם: וַיְהִי בְּאַשְׁמֹרֶת הַבֹּקֶר וַיַּשְׁקֵף יְהוָה אֶל־
מַחֲנֵה מִצְרַיִם בְּעַמּוּד אֵשׁ וְעָנָן וַיָּהָם אֵת מַחֲנֵה
כה מִצְרָיִם: וַיָּסַר אֵת אֹפַן מַרְכְּבֹתָיו וַיְנַהֲגֵהוּ בִּכְבֵדֻת
וַיֹּאמֶר מִצְרַיִם אָנוּסָה מִפְּנֵי יִשְׂרָאֵל כִּי יְהוָה נִלְחָם
לָהֶם בְּמִצְרָיִם: פ
כו וַיֹּאמֶר יְהוָה אֶל־מֹשֶׁה נְטֵה אֶת־יָדְךָ עַל־הַיָּם וְיָשֻׁבוּ
כז הַמַּיִם עַל־מִצְרַיִם עַל־רִכְבּוֹ וְעַל־פָּרָשָׁיו: וַיֵּט מֹשֶׁה

אֶת־יָדוֹ עַל־הַיָּם וַיָּשָׁב הַיָּם לִפְנוֹת בֹּקֶר לְאֵיתָנוֹ
וּמִצְרַיִם נָסִים לִקְרָאתוֹ וַיְנַעֵר יְהוָה אֶת־מִצְרַיִם בְּתוֹךְ
כח הַיָּם: וַיָּשֻׁבוּ הַמַּיִם וַיְכַסּוּ אֶת־הָרֶכֶב וְאֶת־הַפָּרָשִׁים
לְכֹל חֵיל פַּרְעֹה הַבָּאִים אַחֲרֵיהֶם בַּיָּם לֹא־נִשְׁאַר
כט בָּהֶם עַד־אֶחָד: וּבְנֵי יִשְׂרָאֵל הָלְכוּ בַיַּבָּשָׁה בְּתוֹךְ
הַיָּם וְהַמַּיִם לָהֶם חֹמָה מִימִינָם וּמִשְּׂמֹאלָם:
ל וַיּוֹשַׁע יְהוָה בַּיּוֹם הַהוּא אֶת־יִשְׂרָאֵל מִיַּד מִצְרָיִם
לא וַיַּרְא יִשְׂרָאֵל אֶת־מִצְרַיִם מֵת עַל־שְׂפַת הַיָּם: וַיַּרְא
יִשְׂרָאֵל אֶת־הַיָּד הַגְּדֹלָה אֲשֶׁר עָשָׂה יְהוָה בְּמִצְרַיִם
וַיִּירְאוּ הָעָם אֶת־יְהוָה וַיַּאֲמִינוּ בַּיהוָה וּבְמֹשֶׁה
עַבְדּוֹ: פ

east wind all that night, and turned the sea into dry ground. The waters were split, **22]** and the Israelites went into the sea on dry ground, the waters forming a wall for them on their right and on their left. **23]** The Egyptians came in pursuit after them into the sea, all of Pharaoh's horses, chariots, and horsemen. **24]** At the morning watch, the LORD looked down upon the Egyptian army from a pillar of fire and cloud, and threw the Egyptian army into panic. **25]** He locked the wheels of their chariots so that they moved forward with difficulty. And the Egyptians said, "Let us flee from the Israelites, for the LORD is fighting for them against Egypt."

26] Then the LORD said to Moses, "Hold out your arm over the sea, that the waters may come back upon the Egyptians and upon their chariots and upon their horsemen." **27]** Moses held out his arm over the sea, and at daybreak the sea returned to its normal state, and the Egyptians fled at its approach. But the LORD hurled the Egyptians into the sea. **28]** The waters turned back and covered the chariots and the horsemen—Pharaoh's entire army that had followed after them into the sea; not one of them remained. **29]** But the Israelites marched through the sea on dry ground, the waters forming a wall for them on their right and on their left.

30] Thus the LORD delivered Israel that day from the Egyptians. Israel saw the Egyptians dead on the shore of the sea. **31]** And when Israel saw the wondrous power which the LORD had wielded against the Egyptians, the people feared the LORD: they had faith in the LORD and in His servant Moses.

22] *A wall.* In the recollection of the people, the crossing was truly miraculous. Some take this, however, as a poetic or hyperbolic expression [6].

24] *Morning watch.* The last of the three periods or "watches" into which the night was divided.

The Lord looked down. In this way the text means to stress the direct involvement of God.

25] *He locked the wheels.* A speculative translation that follows the Septuagint and other versions, understanding וַיָּסַר as if וַיֶּאְסֹר.

29] *But the Israelites.* A summation of the miracle. According to the Rabbis the last of the Egyptians entered the sea as the last of the Israelites left it [7].

31] *His servant Moses.* Moses is the original "servant of the Lord" (*eved Adonai;* Deut. 34:5; Josh. 1:13, 15), but in rabbinic times he was no longer so called because Christianity had appropriated the term for its savior [8].

The Pillar of Cloud and of Fire

The protective presence of God was seen in a pillar of cloud by day and in a pillar of fire by night. Exodus 13:21 explains their purpose by saying that the former was to guide the people and the latter was to light the way for travel by night. In the story of the rescue (14:19, 20) the cloud had the function of obscuring the vision of the Egyptians and was closely associated or identical with an angel of God who shifted his position accordingly. In other passages the cloud covered the Tabernacle and its lifting was the signal for breaking camp.[1]

Various attempts have been made to find a natural basis for the cloud. It has been called an "accurate description of a volcano" [9], and a parallel has been drawn to the eruption of Mount Pelé in Martinique in 1902. "The town of St. Pierre was destroyed not by lava but by a cloud spewed out by the volcano which was filled with mud, ashes, and stones, and poisonous sulphuric gases shot through by a thousand flames. An earthquake occurred at the same time which influenced the level of the ocean" [10]. Other explanations derived the cloud from a brazier or torch (which was supposed to have been carried at the head of the fighting units) or from other sources.[2] It was for the Israelites what an ensign was for ancient Near Eastern armies.

Whether or not such experiences formed the background of the biblical stories is a matter of conjecture. Clearly, however, the cloud—especially in its fiery appearance—was an aspect of a tradition in which the presence of God was experienced to the accompaniment of flames. Abraham is granted the vision of the covenant in such a way (Gen. 15:17); Moses hears God's voice in the burning bush (Exod. 3:2); and the grand revelation at Sinai occurs with thunder and lightning as well as a dense cloud (Exod. 19:16). Fire is the concretized symbol of man's awe, and the descending mist of a cloud a tactile encounter with heavenly forces. The cloud came to be viewed as God's messenger, and popular memory enshrined it as another manifestation of divine protection and guidance.[3]

Rescue at the Sea

The marvelous rescue of the Israelites from the pursuing Egyptians forms the conclusion of the tale of liberation, with the song of victory (ch. 15) its poetic summation. It is told straightforwardly, without pathos or sentimental embellishment, and this very simplicity reinforces the deep impression the story has made on the people of Israel, for it has left ample room for imagination. "The hurrying feet of a liberated people, the outstretched rod of the great leader, the banked-up seas at either side, the prints of dragging chariot wheels, the enemy corpses floating on the returning flood—no wind and weather can fully efface the image of these events from the sands of human history" [13].

---

[1] The cloud is in such cases not called a pillar: Exod. 40:34–38; Num. 9:15–23; 10:11–12, 34; 14:14. Still other passages portray the cloud not as a regular escort but as an occasional appearance at the tent: Exod. 33:9–10; Num. 11:25; 12:5. Critics assign these divergencies to different sources.

[2] According to Luzzatto, braziers were carried by the Persians. He adds, however, that God did miraculously what other nations were doing naturally [11].

[3] An entirely different interpretation of the cloud is given by G. E. Mendenhall. He calls it the "mask of YHVH," an apparition designed to hide the Presence of God from view. Thus it is God himself who moves with the Israelites, though the people see only the cloud. *Mal-ach* and *anan* were interchangeable at first but developed different nuances and meanings later on [12].

Interpreters and historians have often sought to find a natural basis for what the story clearly presents as God's intrusion into the events; they have looked for the proper locale where a reedy sea could be forded; where tides drive the waters back and forth; or where sudden east winds create natural upheavals that a grateful people saw as acts of God. Critics have pointed out that in one tradition (assigned to P) the sea is divided; in another (assigned to J) it was fear that caused the Egyptian withdrawal; in still another (assigned to E) it was the cloud [14]. Josephus compared the rescue to a divine interference in the military fortunes of Alexander the Great who was thereby enabled to overcome the Persians, and similar stories were told amongst other nations [15].

But when all is said, no examination of presumed natural causes should overshadow the central fact: Israel experienced the event as divinely determined, a miracle in the true sense. It was God who brought about the Egyptians' downfall; He may have used wind and water, cloud and darkness as His agents, but it was His will that Israel be saved, and saved it was. According to Buber, a discussion of the possibility of miracles, which has so long divided the faithful believer from critic and doubter, is therefore beside the point when one comes to assess the manner in which the rescue affected Israel's conception of God. "It is irrelevant whether 'much' or 'little,' unusual things or usual, tremendous or trifling events happened; what is vital is only that what happened was experienced, while it happened, as the act of God. The people saw in whatever it was they saw 'the wondrous power which the Lord had wielded' and 'they had faith in the Lord.' From the biblical viewpoint history always contains the element of wonder."[4] The Torah views God's power as operative both in the creation of the people and in the creation of the world; in both instances the forces of the deep recede before Him (Isa. 51:10 ff.), and thus the saving of Israel stands in direct relation to Creation as the ultimate marvel.

The Route

The exact route that the Israelites took upon leaving Egypt cannot be ascertained from the text. Only one thing appears certain: they did not go "by way of the land of the Philistines, although it was nearer" (13:17). This would have been along the Mediterranean from today's Kantara to El-Arish to Gaza. The Torah gives as the reason for the changed route God's concern over Israel's possible faintheartedness. Indeed, we know from an inscription of Pharaoh Seti I (about 1300 B.C.E.) that the sea road was dotted with Egyptian military posts, which doubtlessly would have involved the Israelites in immediate warfare—something for which they were not prepared. So they traveled in a different direction, crossing the Reed Sea somewhere, thence went through the Sinai peninsula to Mount Sinai, and eventually reached Kadesh (or Kadesh-barnea) in the northeastern part of the peninsula. This area became their center for a generation; for it took thirty-eight years to reach the borders of Moab prior to the entry into Canaan (Num. 33; Deut. 2:14). The problem is that while we are given many place names for

[4] Buber further says: "What is decisive with respect to the inner history of Mankind, however, is that the Children of Israel understood this as an act of their God, as a 'miracle'; which does not mean that they interpreted it as a miracle but that they experienced it as such, that as such they perceived it. This perception at the fateful hour, which is assuredly to be attributed largely to the personal influence of Moses, had a decisive influence on the coming into being of what is called 'Israel' in the history of the spirit; on the development of the element 'Israel' in the religious history of humanity" [16].

the route, their locations are in dispute, for the exact locale of neither the rescue at the sea nor of Mount Sinai itself is known. Three major theories have been proposed in this regard:

The Northern Route. Israel went along the Mediterranean, the Reed Sea being one of the large lagoons along the coast, near Port Said. From there they went southeast to Mount Sinai which was located west of Kadesh and was probably the same as to-day's Jebel Halal.

The Central Route. There are two theories: One holds that from Goshen the Israelites went eastward, toward the Bitter Lakes (at the southern end of today's Suez Canal, north of the town of Suez), where the Reed Sea is supposed to have been; from there they reached Mount Sinai, which is Jebel Sinn Bishr, about thirty miles southeast of

Suez. Other scholars, while they subscribe to the theory of a central route, believe that Israel crossed the Sinai peninsula all the way to Eilat and found Mount Sinai to the east of it, in the land of Midian (in today's southern Jordan or northern Saudia Arabia).[5]

The Southern Route. Israel went south at once, the Reed Sea being the northern part of the Gulf of Suez. From there the route went to the southern part of the peninsula and thence eastward. Mount Sinai is to be identified with Jebel Musa (i.e., Mountain of Moses), Jebel Katherina, or Jebel Sirbal. They then turned north toward Kadesh, possibly via Eilat.

Most scholars lean toward the theory of a central route, but, pending the discovery of new evidence, the exact route as envisaged by the text will remain in the realm of conjecture [17].

---

[5] This is based on Exod. 3:1; 4:27, which speak of the mountain of God as being in Midian, where Moses was a shepherd. It must be remembered, however, that the term "Midian" may not refer to an area with fixed boundaries; see at 2:15.

GLEANINGS

The Bones of Joseph

Why does it say that it was Moses who carried out the bones of Joseph (13:19)? To proclaim his piety; for while Israel looked for booty he occupied himself with loyal duty.   MIDRASH [18]

About Prayer

God's reaction to Israel's distress at the pursuit of the Egyptians is reported cryptically in 14:15. Rabbi Eliezer ruminated as follows: The Holy One said to Moses: "Moses, your children are in distress, the sea is barring the way while the enemy is pursuing, and you stand there and recite long prayers!" Thus Rabbi Eliezer used to say: There is a time to shorten and a time to lengthen

prayers. (He cited Num. 12:13 and Deut. 9:18 as examples of the shortest and longest prayers, respectively, found in the Torah.)

Another explanation, God said to Moses: "There is no need for you to pray. I have already heard Israel's prayer." Another explanation: "I know their prayers before they utter them." Hence: "Tell the Israelites to go forward."

MIDRASH [19]

Up to Their Nostrils

Why does it say (14:22): "And the Israelites went into the sea on dry ground"? To teach us that only after they had gone "into the sea" up to their very nostrils did the waters divide and expose "dry ground."   MIDRASH [20]

The Lesser Miracle

Splitting the sea was less of a miracle than the Exodus from Egypt. The first of the Ten Commandments mentions only the Exodus. Thus it is said that the rescue from Egypt is equal to all the miracles and deeds that God performed for Israel. MIDRASH [21]

Now When

Whenever it says וַיְהִי (now when) it is to indicate a tribulation. But here (13:17) the phrase is used at Israel's liberation. The trouble was that at the time of deliverance Israel had already lost faith and no longer desired to depart. Therefore it is said: "When *Pharaoh* let the people go." In fact, he drove them out.

R. ZADOK HACOHEN [22]

Armed

We are told that the Israelites went "armed" out of Egypt (13:18). What were their arms? The bones of Joseph they took with them, for the merit of the righteous is a shield.

TORAT MOSHEH [23]

The Essence of Joseph

It says that Moses took the עַצְמוֹת יוֹסֵף (atzmot Yosef, the bones of Joseph) with him. One may punctuate עַצְמוּת יוֹסֵף (atzmut Yosef, the essence of Joseph). This, rather than the bones, assisted Israel on their way.

TORAT HAMOREH [24]

Age-old Experience

What happened to Israel in Egypt and at the sea has happened many times since. Israel is oppressed and blamed for all ills of the land. "Get out of our country," we are told. But when we are ready to leave we are told: "Why do you want to leave?" and obstacles like those in Egypt are put in our way. PARDES YOSEF [25]

It Takes a Pharaoh

It says "Pharaoh drew near" (14:10). This means he drew Israel near to repentance. Alas, it takes a pharaoh to do this for us. CHASIDIC [26]

Slave Mentality

One must wonder why six hundred thousand men did not stand up to fight the Egyptians. The answer: Israel had from their youth learned to fear Egypt. They had not as yet learned to stand up to their masters. IBN EZRA

Miracles

The created world admits of no alteration of the natural law. God's miracles must be seen as if the world at that moment was in a state of original creation, and no alteration was involved.

KEDUSHAT LEVI [27]

[This argument resembles the rabbinic statement that many so-called miracles were built into the structure of the universe [28]. Thus it was suggested that God, foreseeing the events at the sea, had already arranged for its parting when He created it. See also Rosenzweig's statement which follows.]

Nothing in the miracle of revelation is novel, nothing is the intervention of sorcery in created creation, but rather it is wholly sign, wholly the process of making visible and audible the providence which had originally been concealed in the speechless night of creation, wholly—revelation! Thus revelation is at all times new only because it is primordially old. It makes the primeval creation over into an ever newly created present, because that primeval creation itself is nothing less than the sealed prophecy that God "renews day by day the work of creation." The human word is a symbol; with every moment it is newly created in the mouth of the speaker, but only because it is from the beginning and because it already bears in its womb every speaker who will one day effect the miracle of renewing it. But the divine word is more than symbol: it is revelation only because it is at the same time the word of creation. "God said, Let there be light"—and what is the light of God? It is the soul of man.

F. ROSENZWEIG [29]

Woe!

[The *sidrah* begins with the word וַיְהִי (13:17). The first two letters read וַי (vay), that is, "Woe!"]

485

Pharaoh said "Woe!" because the Israelites, his best workers, had left;

Moses said it, because, when God led the people by a circuitous route, he knew they would misuse their freedom;

Israel said it, because they now had to look after themselves;

God said it, because He knew Israel's weakness.

M. HACOHEN [30]

Franklin's Suggestion

Benjamin Franklin suggested a picture of Israel's liberation for the reverse of the official seal of the United States. However, Congress adopted only Franklin's proposed motto, *E Pluribus Unum*, and the "Eye of Providence." Ironically, it substituted a pyramid for the sea (see the current US one-dollar bill) [31].

Rescue, Then Faith

A woman came to the Belzer Rebbe entreating his help through prayer. He asked whether she had sufficient faith. Said she: "In the Torah it is written that God first rescued Israel and that then they believed" (14:30, 31). CHASIDIC [32]

Pharaoh Survived

All the Egyptians who entered the sea perished, except Pharaoh himself who was condemned to keep guard at the portals of hell. But others say he was the last to die, condemned to witness the destruction of his army.

MIDRASH [33]

Compassion

God does not rejoice at the death of sinners. On seeing the destruction of the Egyptians the angels wanted to break forth in song. But God silenced them saying: "The work of My hands is drowning in the sea, and you desire to sing songs!" TALMUD [34]

Though we descend from those redeemed from
   brutal Egypt,
And have ourselves rejoiced to see oppressors
   overcome,
Yet our triumph is diminished
By the slaughter of the foe,
As the wine within the cup is lessened
When we pour ten drops for the plagues upon
   Egypt. PASSOVER HAGGADAH [35]

[Referring to the Seder custom to spill ten drops of wine—one drop for each plague as it is mentioned.]

Shirah—The Song at the Sea

The victory song that Moses and Israel sang after their salvation is called שִׁירַת הַיָּם (*Shirat ha-Yam*, "Song at the Sea") or *Shirah* (Song). The Sabbath on which it is read in the order of weekly synagogal pericopes is called Shabbat Shirah, the Sabbath of the Song. At its reading the congregation stands in special respect, a custom which has developed with regard to only one other Torah reading, that of the Ten Commandments. The overwhelming sense of gratitude that the Children of Israel felt at the sea still reverberates in the hearts of their descendants.

The song is followed by another which is ascribed to Miriam. Much shorter, it appears to some as a summation of the *Shirah*, to others as an older form from which the longer poem developed. This theory presupposes that certain words and allusions in the *Shirah* stem from a time later than the rescue at the sea or that perhaps the poem was a recasting of an enthronement song, part of an annual ceremony in which the kingship of God was reaffirmed.

Moses, who is credited with the *Shirah*, is also listed as the author of two other poems: Deut. 32 (which is specifically called *Shirah*, Deut. 31:22; 30) and Psalm 90. The Blessing of Moses (Deut. 33) may also be classed in the poetic category. This combination of political leadership and poetry reappears most prominently in King David, who in popular affection was second only to Moses himself.

א אָז יָשִׁיר־מֹשֶׁה וּבְנֵי יִשְׂרָאֵל אֶת־הַשִּׁירָה הַזֹּאת לַיהֹוָה
וַיֹּאמְרוּ לֵאמֹר   אָשִׁירָה לַיהֹוָה כִּי־גָאֹה גָּאָה   סוּס
ב וְרֹכְבוֹ רָמָה בַיָּם: עָזִּי וְזִמְרָת יָהּ וַיְהִי־לִי
לִישׁוּעָה   זֶה אֵלִי וְאַנְוֵהוּ   אֱלֹהֵי
ג אָבִי וַאֲרֹמְמֶנְהוּ:   יְהֹוָה אִישׁ מִלְחָמָה יְהֹוָה
ד שְׁמוֹ:   מַרְכְּבֹת פַּרְעֹה וְחֵילוֹ יָרָה בַיָּם   וּמִבְחַר
ה שָׁלִשָׁיו טֻבְּעוּ בְיַם־סוּף: תְּהֹמֹת יְכַסְיֻמוּ יָרְדוּ בִמְצוֹלֹת

ו יְמִינְךָ   יְמִינְךָ יְהֹוָה נֶאְדָּרִי בַּכֹּחַ   כְּמוֹ־אָבֶן:
וּבְרֹב גְּאוֹנְךָ תַּהֲרֹס   יְהֹוָה תִּרְעַץ אוֹיֵב:
ז קָמֶיךָ   תְּשַׁלַּח חֲרֹנְךָ יֹאכְלֵמוֹ כַּקַּשׁ:   וּבְרוּחַ
אַפֶּיךָ נֶעֶרְמוּ מַיִם   נִצְּבוּ כְמוֹ־נֵד
ח נֹזְלִים   קָפְאוּ תְהֹמֹת בְּלֶב־יָם: אָמַר
ט אוֹיֵב אֶרְדֹּף אַשִּׂיג   אֲחַלֵּק שָׁלָל תִּמְלָאֵמוֹ
י נַפְשִׁי   אָרִיק חַרְבִּי תּוֹרִישֵׁמוֹ יָדִי: נָשַׁפְתָּ

1] Then Moses and the Israelites sang this song to the LORD. They said:
I will sing to the LORD, for He has triumphed gloriously; / Horse and driver He has hurled into the sea. / **2]** The LORD is my strength and might; / He is become my salvation. / This is my God and I will enshrine Him; / The God of my father, and I will exalt Him. / **3]** The LORD, the Warrior— / LORD is His name! **4]** Pharaoh's chariots and his army / He has cast into the sea; / And the pick of his officers / Are drowned in the Sea of Reeds. / **5]** The deeps covered them; / They went down into the depths like a stone. / **6]** Your right hand, O LORD glorious in power, / Your right hand, O LORD, shatters the foe! / **7]** In Your great triumph You break Your opponents; / You send forth Your fury, it consumes them like straw. / **8]** At the blast of Your nostrils the waters piled up, / The floods stood straight like a wall; / The deeps froze in the heart of the sea. / **9]** The foe said, / "I will pursue, I will overtake, I will divide the spoil; / My desire shall have its fill of them. / I will bare my sword— / My hand shall

15:2] *The Lord.* יָהּ (Yah), a form of the divine Name, either shortened from יְהֹוָה or its original form (see chs. 3 and 6). Yah occurs again in a poetic passage in Exod. 17:16 and is found frequently in Isaiah, once (perhaps) in the Song of Songs, and especially in Psalms, where it often forms the suffix in Halleluyah ("Praise Yah"). It alternates with Yahu as a part of personal names as in Yirmeyah/Yirmeyahu (Jeremiah). The first half of verse 2 is quoted in Isaiah 12:2 and Psalm 118:14.

Might. Others, "song." Rashi renders: "The strength and vengeance of the Lord have become my salvation." He takes עָזִּי to be a variant of עֹז and not a word with a possessive suffix, and he derives זִמְרָת from זָמַר, cut off.

Enshrine. Others, "glorify," "exalt."

3] *The Warrior.* Older translations: "The Lord is a man of war." The concept is natural to biblical thought: God is Israel's protector and, if need be, will fight for it.

4] *Sea of Reeds.* On the translation, see note at 13:18; on the likely location, see commentary to 13:17–14:31, "The Route."

5] *Deeps.* תְּהֹמֹת (tehomot), plural of תְּהוֹם (tehom) in the Creation story (Gen. 1:2). The word is a link in connecting the story of creating God's world with that of creating God's people (see following commentary).

8] *Blast of Your nostrils.* The poet pictures God as having blown the east wind of which verse 10 speaks.

9] *The foe said.* In a prose telling of the story one might expect this sentence to come first in the sequence of events told, but in a poem moving forward and backward in time it adds sparkle and interest. However, the Sages were bothered by this seeming "misplacement" and pointed to the principle that literary and chronological order do not necessarily coincide in the Torah [1].

עַד־   בְּגֹדֶל זְרוֹעֲךָ יִדְּמוּ כָּאָבֶן   וָפַחַד   צָלְלוּ כַּעוֹפֶרֶת בְּמַיִם   בְּרוּחֲךָ כִּסָּמוֹ יָם
יַעֲבֹר עַמְּךָ יְהֹוָה עַד־יַעֲבֹר עַם־זוּ   מִי כָמֹכָה בָּאֵלִם יְהֹוָה מִי   אַדִּירִים: יא
מָכוֹן   תְּבִאֵמוֹ וְתִטָּעֵמוֹ בְּהַר נַחֲלָתְךָ   קָנִיתָ: יז   כָּמֹכָה נֶאְדָּר בַּקֹּדֶשׁ נוֹרָא תְהִלֹּת עֹשֵׂה־
כּוֹנְנוּ   מִקְּדָשׁ אֲדֹנָי   לְשִׁבְתְּךָ פָּעַלְתָּ יְהֹוָה   פֶלֶא: יב   נָטִיתָ יְמִינְךָ תִּבְלָעֵמוֹ אָרֶץ: נָחִיתָ יג
כִּי   יָדֶיךָ: יח   יְהֹוָה יִמְלֹךְ לְעֹלָם וָעֶד: בְחַסְדְּךָ עַם־זוּ גָּאָלְתָּ נֵהַלְתָּ בְעָזְּךָ אֶל־נְוֵה
בָא סוּס פַּרְעֹה בְּרִכְבּוֹ וּבְפָרָשָׁיו בַּיָּם וַיָּשֶׁב יְהֹוָה   שָׁמְעוּ עַמִּים יִרְגָּזוּן חִיל   קָדְשֶׁךָ: יד
עֲלֵהֶם אֶת־מֵי הַיָּם וּבְנֵי יִשְׂרָאֵל הָלְכוּ בַיַּבָּשָׁה   אָז נִבְהֲלוּ אַלּוּפֵי   אָז אָחַז יֹשְׁבֵי פְלָשֶׁת: טו
בְּתוֹךְ הַיָּם: פ   נָמֹגוּ   אֱדוֹם אֵילֵי מוֹאָב יֹאחֲזֵמוֹ רָעַד
תִּפֹּל עֲלֵיהֶם אֵימָתָה: כֹּל יֹשְׁבֵי כְנָעַן טז

subdue them." / **10]** You made Your wind blow, the sea covered them; / They sank like lead in the majestic waters.

11] Who is like You, O LORD, among the celestials; / Who is like You, majestic in holiness, / Awesome in splendor, working wonders! / **12]** You put out Your right hand, / The earth swallowed them. / **13]** In Your love You lead the people You redeemed; / In Your strength You guide them to Your holy abode. / **14]** The peoples hear, they tremble; / Agony grips the dwellers in Philistia. / **15]** Now are the clans of Edom dismayed; / The tribes of Moab— trembling grips them; / All the dwellers in Canaan are aghast. / **16]** Terror and dread descend upon them; / Through the might of Your arm they are still as stone— / Till Your people cross over, O LORD, / Till Your people cross whom You have ransomed.

17] You will bring them and plant them in Your own mountain, / The place You made to dwell in, O LORD, / The sanctuary, O LORD, which Your hands established. / **18]** The LORD will reign for ever and ever!

19] For the horses of Pharaoh, with his chariots and horsemen, went into the sea; and the LORD turned back on them the waters of the sea; but the Israelites marched on dry ground in the midst of the sea.

11] *Celestials.* Or, "mighty." The verse has entered the daily Jewish liturgy. The *New Union Prayer Book* (*Gates of Prayer*) translates it "Who is like You among the gods men worship."

13] *Holy abode.* Wherever that may be. The poet's expression is nonspecific.

14] *Philistia.* Tradition had it that at an earlier time there had been a battle between the Philistines and the tribe of Ephraim, a part of which was said to have escaped from Egypt before the rest of the people and had met with disaster (see above, at 13:17). The Philistines made their entrance into the Middle East at about this time.

18] *The Lord will reign.* This verse, which ends the song, has also been taken into the liturgy.

19] *For.* Rashi renders "When . . ." and treats the first part of the verse as an opening clause to the second half.

^כ וַתִּקַּח מִרְיָם הַנְּבִיאָה אֲחוֹת אַהֲרֹן אֶת־הַתֹּף בְּיָדָהּ   לָהֶם מִרְיָם שִׁירוּ לַיהוָה כִּי־גָאֹה גָּאָה סוּס וְרֹכְבוֹ
^{כא} וַתֵּצֶאןָ כָל־הַנָּשִׁים אַחֲרֶיהָ בְּתֻפִּים וּבִמְחֹלֹת: וַתַּעַן   רָמָה בַיָּם: ס

20] Then Miriam the prophetess, Aaron's sister, took a timbrel in her hand, and all the women went out after her in dance with timbrels. 21] And Miriam chanted for them, "Sing to the LORD, for He has triumphed gloriously; / Horse and driver He has hurled into the sea."

20] *Miriam the prophetess.* Deborah (Judg. 4:4), Huldah (II Kings 22:14), and Noadiah (Neh. 6:14) are the only other biblical women to be given this accolade. In Num. 12:2 Miriam explains her prophetic role by saying that God has spoken through her.

Aaron's sister. One would have expected "Moses' sister," for the song just ended was sung by him—and now his sister leads the women. The tradition that preserved Miriam's song may have had a separate source in which Aaron and Miriam were closely linked with each other, a bond at which Numbers 12 hints, where Aaron and Miriam conspire against Moses. Rashi suggests: She is called Aaron's sister because she was a prophetess even before Moses' birth.

Timbrel. A hand drum.

21] *For them.* לָהֶם (*lahem*), the masculine form, but sometimes used for women too.

The Poem

"The ode of triumph," wrote Driver, "is one of the finest products of Hebrew poetry, remarkable for poetic fire and spirit, picturesque description, vivid imagery, quick movement, effective parallelism, and bright sonorous diction" [2]. This judgment was of course delivered on the Hebrew original, and no translation can fully render its special flavor, its rare poetic forms, its alliterations and assonances. Thus, for instance, instead of the usual endings *am* and *em*, the poet uses *amo* and *emo*, which impart to the song an additional euphonic effect. The internal rhythm of the strophes is also hard to reproduce in translation: they alternate between couplets, triplets, and quatrains and end in a single line (verse 18) which comes as a sudden and glorious climax, the final bars in a great poetic symphony.[1]

The Hebrew text as transmitted by the Masoretes is presented as a continuous whole, although one may discern the content to fall into three parts: verses 2–5, 6–10, 11–18. The poem moves from an exaltation of God's saving power to a vivid description of the miracle itself, and in the final, more contemplative part returns to adoration and future expectation.

Was the song indeed composed by Moses or does it belong to a later age and was then retrospectively ascribed to the ancient leader? Many scholars hold this latter view, although they disagree over the likely age of composition, their estimates varying from the time of Solomon (tenth century B.C.E.) to postexilic days (sixth or fifth centuries B.C.E.). Major reasons for believing the song to be post-Mosaic are these: the poet appears to speak from settled conditions rather than from the immediacy of terror and salvation; he contemplates the reactions of Israel's neighbors and enemies in a Canaanite setting; he uses the term "holy abode" (verse 13) as an apparent reference to Jerusalem;[2] and, finally, he uses a number of words that do not again occur in the Torah but are found in the later Prophets and Psalms [4].

While these arguments are weighty, they are not conclusive. The language and nature of the poetry argue for an ancient origin of the poem. Support for this supposition has further come from an unexpected extrabiblical source. A Ugaritic song has been found that exhibits some similarities to the Song at the Sea and which comes from the time of Moses. This suggests that this genre of poetry is indeed of ancient origins. It is a recasting of an old theme: the power of the Divine to command the forces of the deep, a theme reflected also in the opening verses of Genesis. God's power encompassed the creation of the world out of chaos, and it now manifests itself again in similar fashion to bring forth the people He has fashioned.[3] Moses' song is therefore most likely in substance his own, speaking in accents of his own age and out of the overwhelming marvel of the salvation he and his people had witnessed. But whether early or late, the poem conveys a sense of sweeping power, exaltation, and gratitude, and it has had a profound

---

[1] The rendition by Daiches comes closest to the original; see Gleanings.

[2] The Midrash [3] also thought that Jerusalem was meant and saw it as a prophecy by Moses, a conclusion supported by Nachmanides. Ibn Ezra took "holy abode" to refer to Mount Sinai, while others believe it to mean a tent shrine, and hence quite in keeping with desert conditions.

[3] It might be noted that the whole typology of divine exaltation is part of ancient Near Eastern literature. According to Frank M. Cross, the language of theophany of early Israel was primarily language drawn from Canaanite theophany. The splitting of the sea—absent from *Shirah*—must have been a later addition [5]. (For further historiographic parallels see W. W. Hallo's introductory essay.)

impact on Israel. It has been incorporated into the daily liturgy and has truly become the song of the people.

The Women Danced

In ancient Israel, as in other cultures, dancing was a normal aspect of worship. At the Reed Sea only the women are reported to have danced, but neither then nor later was this expression of emotion confined to women only. King David showed the depth of his joy through dancing when the Ark of the Covenant was brought to Jerusalem (II Sam. 6:14 ff.).

There are, in fact, no fewer than eleven Hebrew words denoting dance, suggesting that ritual choreography was extensive and highly sophisticated. There were dances to express communal joy, and various biblical passages picture such dancing as the opposite of mourning: there is "a time to mourn and a time to dance," says Koheleth [6]. There were victory dances [7], petitional dances [8], dances to celebrate the harvest with gratitude [9], and of course dances were indigenous to wooing and wedding [10]. It may be supposed that specific motions were customary or prescribed for these various occasions, with movements of choral and other participating groups having symbolic meaning. After the destruction of the Temple by the Romans in 70 C.E., however, music was banned from the synagogue and, with it, dancing too no longer fitted the popular mood: the time for mourning had come. There were but few exceptions, the most notable being the dancing that celebrated the sanctification of the new moon: "The worshiper must look steadily at the moon . . . and must perform three dances in front of the moon" [11].

In the course of time both music and dance returned to Jewish life, though for centuries only the wedding house was their abode. From the eighteenth century on, with the rise of Chasidism, these old modes of celebration spread again to other areas of Jewish living and eventually to the prayer service itself. To this day the joy of Chasidim on Simchat Torah, when they dance with the scrolls of Torah, is proverbial. Other Jewish groups have been slow to take up their example, but the eventual full readmission of ritual dancing to the synagogue can be safely predicted. The dance of the women at the Reed Sea will then be experienced once more as a natural and even necessary expression of religious joy, a complement to the Shirah: the two belonged together and complemented each other in a grand and memorable celebration of God's glory.

GLEANINGS

The Psalmist's Vision

The waters saw You, O God,
    the waters saw You and were convulsed;
    the very deep quaked as well.
Clouds streamed water;
    the heavens rumbled;
    Your arrows flew about;
    Your thunder rumbled like wheels;
    lightning lit up the world;
    the earth quaked and trembled.
Your way was through the sea,
    Your path, through the mighty waters;
    Your tracks could not be seen.
You led Your people like a flock
    in the care of Moses and Aaron.

Psalm 77:17–21

[See also Psalms 78 and 114; also Habakkuk 3, predominantly an ode to the Lord as Master of the sea.]

Recitation

Moses composed the hymn and taught it to Israel. Everyone chanted responsively, "I will sing unto the Lord."

IBN EZRA [12]

Writing

The Talmud prescribes that the song be written in the Torah scroll in a certain way: "Short brick over long brick, long brick over short brick" [13]. This is explained by Maimonides as follows: "The song has to be written in thirty lines. The first line is regular. The following lines alternate: one line is broken by one space in the middle, another is broken by two spaces, thus containing three units. Thus the lines alternate between two spaces and two written units" [14].

Poetry

Poetry prefers to express itself in unusual and unused words of ancient and remote origins, for their lack of currency, of wear and tear, adds to their tonic effect and charming appeal.

LUZZATTO [15]

Resurrection

The introduction to the song, according to rabbinic Hebrew, says: "Then Moses *will sing*" (אָז יָשִׁיר, future tense), not "Then Moses *sang*" (אָז שָׁר, past tense). [In biblical Hebrew, however, the word אָז can operate as a vav-consecutive.] R. Judah the Prince derived from this a hint for the resurrection of the dead: Moses not only sang then but will sing in the future as well.

MIDRASH [16]

Only Israel

God had saved men before, yet none had sung words of praise: not Abraham when saved from the fiery furnace (of which the Midrash speaks); nor Isaac when saved from the knife; nor Jacob when saved from the angel, from Esau, or the men of Shechem. But as soon as Israel was saved they uttered their song. And God responded: "I have been waiting for them."

MIDRASH [17]

This Is My God and I Will Glorify (or "Enshrine") Him (Exod. 15:2)

R. Ishmael said: "Is it possible for flesh and blood to add glory to the Creator? It means: I shall be beautiful before Him in observing the commandments. I shall prepare a beautiful sukah, beautiful tzitzit and tefillin." Abba Shaul explained that "glorify Him" means one should attempt to

be like God. Just as He is gracious and merciful, so man ought to be gracious and merciful.

MIDRASH [18]

The Lord, the Warrior, the Lord [יְהֹוָה] *Is His Name* (Exod. 15:3)

Even in war, God is יְהֹוָה, that is, He appears in His merciful quality.   RASHI

[See Gleanings (footnote 5) to Genesis 6:2–7:13.]

Redemption Then and Now
Ah, take her [that is, Israel] as of yore
And cast her forth no more;
Let sunlight crown her day
And shadows flee away.
    Then a new song
    Sang Thy redeemed throng.
For Thy beloved throng
Still come to Thee with song. . . .

J. HALEVI [19]

A Chasid's Argument
When R. Mendel of Kotsk was thirteen years old, his father (who was opposed to Chasidism) rebuked him for forsaking the old ways. Mendel then quoted verse 2 of the song: " 'This is my God'—I will have to find Him first for myself to enshrine Him, and only then is He 'the God of my father.' "

[R. Mendel here restates a classical interpretation of the first of the Eighteen Benedictions, which says "Blessed are You, O Lord, our God and God of our Fathers, God of Abraham, God of Isaac, God of Jacob. . . ." He is not only the God of tradition ("our Fathers"), He must also become the God of each individual ("God of Abraham").]

He also used to say "I will enshrine Him" means "I will make a dwelling for Him within me" [20].

From a Ugaritic Hymn
[The enemies of Baal are Prince Yam and Judge Nahar, that is, Sea and River.]
I tell thee, O Prince Baal,
I declare, O Rider of the Clouds,
Now thine enemy, O Baal,

Now thine enemy wilt thou smite,
Now wilt thou cut off thine adversary.

Thou'lt take thine eternal kingdom,
Thine everlasting dominion.

Baal would rend, would smash Yam,
Would annihilate Judge Nahar [21].

A Modern Rendition (Exod. 15:7–12)
[The author calls it "a paraphrase rather than a literal translation."]
Mighty in majesty thou hast mangled thine
    enemies,
Discharging thine anger thou hast consumed
    them like chaff.
In the rush of thy rage raised were the waters
Far down in the depths they were drawn to a
    heap.
Confident the foeman for conquest and
    capture,
Boastful in talking bold in his blood-lust.
Thou didst blow with thy blast they were
    borne to the bottom,
Plummeting low they were lodged in the
    seabed.
Who like our Lord hath such might among
    leaders,
What other hero so holy and high?
Praise him for his power the performer of
    wonders.
Thy hand is thrust outward the earth hath
    engulfed them.

D. DAICHES [22]

The Work Remains
"Then sang Moses. . . ." In this hour of happiness his heart overflows with emotion and pours itself out in song. He does not know that he is still at the beginning of his journey; he does not know that the real task, the most difficult task, has still to be commenced. Pharaoh is gone, but his work remains; the master has ceased to be master, but the slaves have not ceased to be slaves. A people trained for generations in the house of bondage cannot cast off in an instant the effects of that training and become truly free, even when the chains have been struck off.

AHAD HA-AM [23]

In the Wilderness

Secure now from Egyptian pursuit and finally free in the physical sense, the Israelites set out on their journey. From now on, until at last they will enter the Promised Land, the desert will be the locale of their story. Here the people will receive the law; here they will proclaim their faith and be present at God's self-disclosure; and here they will fall away to fashion the golden calf. The desert is Israel's proving ground, it is the place where God acquires a people.

There is another theme: that of rebellion. A shortage of drinkable water exacerbates a tendency toward grumbling about their fate, and it becomes clear that the Israelites are not as yet spiritually free, able to cope as a liberated people with the vagaries and challenges of life. The "murmuring motif" too will from here on be a constant aspect of their wilderness wanderings. The immediate targets of their dissatisfaction will usually be Moses and Aaron, but the sense of rebellion against the lordship of God, who stands behind His chosen leaders, is always present.

At Marah, the well of bitterness, Israel is given its first set of divine ordinances, although which ones they were is not specified. Shur, Elim, and Sin are also not clearly identifiable; all we know is that these stopping places in their wandering were east of Egypt, somewhere in the Sinai peninsula.

The shortage of water is followed by a pending scarcity of food. God intervenes; heaven-sent manna and quails supply the needs of the people. The section before us deals primarily with manna and mentions quails

only incidentally. At a later point, however, quails will be the center of interest when they are sent again to relieve the Israelites' boredom with manna (Num. 11:4 ff.). The contrast between the passages is striking: in Exodus both manna and quails appear to still the people's hunger, while in Numbers hunger is not an issue but satiety is. Biblical critics have therefore suggested different traditions to underlie these tales, P in Exodus, and a combination of other sources in Numbers [1].

The account mixes realistic experiences with supernatural incursions: God causes bitter water to become sweet, He provides food for the multitudes, and He spoils it for the Sabbath-breakers. This divine role is at the heart of the story for, while the appearance of manna and quail can be explained on a natural basis, the real impact of biblical intent lies somewhere else: to rehearse the theme of the world's creation in the tale of Israel, God's newly created people. Manna and Sabbath mirror the early story of humanity and universe.

כב וַיַּסַּע מֹשֶׁה אֶת־יִשְׂרָאֵל מִיַּם־סוּף וַיֵּצְאוּ אֶל־מִדְבַּר־
שׁוּר וַיֵּלְכוּ שְׁלֹשֶׁת־יָמִים בַּמִּדְבָּר וְלֹא־מָצְאוּ מָיִם:
כג וַיָּבֹאוּ מָרָתָה וְלֹא יָכְלוּ לִשְׁתֹּת מַיִם מִמָּרָה כִּי
מָרִים הֵם עַל־כֵּן קָרָא־שְׁמָהּ מָרָה: וַיִּלֹּנוּ הָעָם
כה עַל־מֹשֶׁה לֵּאמֹר מַה־נִּשְׁתֶּה: וַיִּצְעַק אֶל־יְהוָה וַיּוֹרֵהוּ
יְהוָה עֵץ וַיַּשְׁלֵךְ אֶל־הַמַּיִם וַיִּמְתְּקוּ הַמָּיִם שָׁם שָׂם

כו לוֹ חֹק וּמִשְׁפָּט וְשָׁם נִסָּהוּ: וַיֹּאמֶר אִם־שָׁמוֹעַ תִּשְׁמַע
לְקוֹל יְהוָה אֱלֹהֶיךָ וְהַיָּשָׁר בְּעֵינָיו תַּעֲשֶׂה וְהַאֲזַנְתָּ
לְמִצְוֹתָיו וְשָׁמַרְתָּ כָּל־חֻקָּיו כָּל־הַמַּחֲלָה אֲשֶׁר־שַׂמְתִּי
בְמִצְרַיִם לֹא־אָשִׂים עָלֶיךָ כִּי אֲנִי יְהוָה רֹפְאֶךָ: ס
כז וַיָּבֹאוּ אֵילִמָה וְשָׁם שְׁתֵּים עֶשְׂרֵה עֵינֹת מַיִם וְשִׁבְעִים
תְּמָרִים וַיַּחֲנוּ־שָׁם עַל־הַמָּיִם:

22] Then Moses caused Israel to set out from the Sea of Reeds. They went on into the wilderness of Shur; they traveled three days in the wilderness and found no water. **23]** They came to Marah, but they could not drink the water of Marah because it was bitter; that is why it was named Marah. **24]** And the people grumbled against Moses, saying, "What shall we drink?" **25]** So he cried out to the LORD, and the LORD showed him a piece of wood; he threw it into the water and the water became sweet.

There He made for them a fixed rule, and there He put them to the test. **26]** He said, "If you will heed the LORD your God diligently, doing what is upright in His sight, giving ear to His commandments and keeping all His laws, then I will not bring upon you any of the diseases that I brought upon the Egyptians, for I the LORD am your healer."

27] And they came to Elim, where there were twelve springs of water and seventy palm trees; and they encamped there beside the water.

15:22] *Shur.* Called Etham in Num. 33:8; the name of an area east of Egypt.

23] *Marah.* Meaning, "bitter."

25] *Piece of wood.* It has been suggested that there are scientific bases for this and similar procedures, which are known amongst people in various continents. For instance, the wood of the oak contains tannin, which neutralizes albuminous matter, coagulates it, and makes it sink to the bottom [2]. The biblical text limits the divine participation in this case to showing Moses a way to sweeten the water, without suggesting—as in the subsequent case of manna—that the process itself was miraculous.

For them. The Hebrew is in the singular and could refer to Moses; both in the preceding and in verse 27 the text is in the plural, so that the change

may be intentional. The passage is in any case cryptic, as if something was missing. The test is not specified; it is possibly a reference to 17:1–7.

Fixed rule. The usual translation of *chok umishpat* is "statute and ordinance." The Rabbis understood *mishpatim* to be laws that would have validity even without a written Torah, such as laws against adultery or robbery; while *chukim* are other Torah laws, such as those dealing with the prohibition of pork for food or wearing garments made of wool and flax [3]. The German rendition *Recht und Satzung* conveys this distinction better than the English.

26] *Your healer.* Probably referring to the waters that God helped to sweeten, i.e., heal them from their bitterness.

27] *Elim.* "Terebinths." The location is unknown.

א וַיִּסְעוּ מֵאֵילִם וַיָּבֹאוּ כָּל־עֲדַת בְּנֵי־יִשְׂרָאֵל אֶל־מִדְבַּר־
סִין אֲשֶׁר בֵּין־אֵילִם וּבֵין סִינָי בַּחֲמִשָּׁה עָשָׂר יוֹם
ב לַחֹדֶשׁ הַשֵּׁנִי לְצֵאתָם מֵאֶרֶץ מִצְרָיִם: וַיִּלּוֹנוּ כָּל־
עֲדַת בְּנֵי־יִשְׂרָאֵל עַל־מֹשֶׁה וְעַל־אַהֲרֹן בַּמִּדְבָּר:
ג וַיֹּאמְרוּ אֲלֵהֶם בְּנֵי יִשְׂרָאֵל מִי־יִתֵּן מוּתֵנוּ בְיַד־יְהוָה
בְּאֶרֶץ מִצְרַיִם בְּשִׁבְתֵּנוּ עַל־סִיר הַבָּשָׂר בְּאָכְלֵנוּ
לֶחֶם לָשֹׂבַע כִּי־הוֹצֵאתֶם אֹתָנוּ אֶל־הַמִּדְבָּר הַזֶּה
ד לְהָמִית אֶת־כָּל־הַקָּהָל הַזֶּה בָּרָעָב: ס וַיֹּאמֶר יְהוָה
אֶל־מֹשֶׁה הִנְנִי מַמְטִיר לָכֶם לֶחֶם מִן־הַשָּׁמַיִם וְיָצָא
הָעָם וְלָקְטוּ דְּבַר־יוֹם בְּיוֹמוֹ לְמַעַן אֲנַסֶּנּוּ הֲיֵלֵךְ

ה בְּתוֹרָתִי אִם־לֹא: וְהָיָה בַּיּוֹם הַשִּׁשִּׁי וְהֵכִינוּ אֵת אֲשֶׁר־
יָבִיאוּ וְהָיָה מִשְׁנֶה עַל אֲשֶׁר־יִלְקְטוּ יוֹם יוֹם: וַיֹּאמֶר
מֹשֶׁה וְאַהֲרֹן אֶל־כָּל־בְּנֵי יִשְׂרָאֵל עֶרֶב וִידַעְתֶּם כִּי
יְהוָה הוֹצִיא אֶתְכֶם מֵאֶרֶץ מִצְרָיִם: וּבֹקֶר וּרְאִיתֶם
אֶת־כְּבוֹד יְהוָה בְּשָׁמְעוֹ אֶת־תְּלֻנֹּתֵיכֶם עַל־יְהוָה וְנַחְנוּ
מָה כִּי תַלִּינוּ עָלֵינוּ: וַיֹּאמֶר מֹשֶׁה בְּתֵת יְהוָה לָכֶם
בָּעֶרֶב בָּשָׂר לֶאֱכֹל וְלֶחֶם בַּבֹּקֶר לִשְׂבֹּעַ בִּשְׁמֹעַ
יְהוָה אֶת־תְּלֻנֹּתֵיכֶם אֲשֶׁר־אַתֶּם מַלִּינִם עָלָיו וְנַחְנוּ מָה
לֹא־עָלֵינוּ תְלֻנֹּתֵיכֶם כִּי עַל־יְהוָה: וַיֹּאמֶר מֹשֶׁה אֶל־
אַהֲרֹן אֱמֹר אֶל־כָּל־עֲדַת בְּנֵי יִשְׂרָאֵל קִרְבוּ לִפְנֵי

ז תלונו קרי.　　　　　　　　　　　　　　　　ב וילונו קרי.

1] Setting out from Elim, the whole Israelite community came to the wilderness of Sin, which is between Elim and Sinai, on the fifteenth day of the second month after their departure from the land of Egypt. **2]** In the wilderness, the whole Israelite community grumbled against Moses and Aaron. **3]** The Israelites said to them, "If only we had died by the hand of the LORD in the land of Egypt, when we sat by the fleshpots, when we ate our fill of bread! For you have brought us out into this wilderness to starve this whole congregation to death!"

4] And the LORD said to Moses, "I will rain down bread for you from the sky, and the people shall go out and gather each day that day's portion—that I may thus test them, to see whether they will follow My instructions or not. **5]** But on the sixth day, when they prepare what they have brought in, it shall prove to be double the amount they gather each day." **6]** So Moses and Aaron said to all the Israelites, "By evening you shall know it was the LORD who brought you out from the land of Egypt; **7]** and in the morning you shall behold the Presence of the LORD, because He has heard your grumblings against the LORD. For who are we that you should grumble against us? **8]** Since it is the LORD," Moses continued, "who will give you flesh to eat in the evening and bread in the morning to the full, because the LORD has heard the grumblings you utter against Him, what is our part? Your grumbling is not against us, but against the LORD!"

9] Then Moses said to Aaron, "Say to the whole Israelite community: Advance toward the

---

16:1] *Sin.* Somewhere in the middle of the Sinai peninsula. Sin and Sinai are probably related. In Num. 33:11–12 Rephidim is located between Sin and Sinai. The wilderness of Sin is not to be confused with that of Zin (צִן).

Fifteenth day of the second month. One month after the Exodus, when the provisions the people had taken were beginning to run low.

2] *The whole Israelite community.* In 15:24 the word "whole" did not appear because only a portion of the people grumbled at Marah [4].

Now food is at issue and everyone is concerned, for, while a water shortage can be relieved at a convenient oasis, a food shortage cannot.

3] *Fleshpots.* In Num. 11:5 the Israelites will remember that in Egypt they ate delectable vegetables but not that they ate meat.

Bread. In Egypt, the baking of bread was a fine art; it is reported that there were 57 different kinds of bread. (See at Gen. 40:2.)

7] *Presence.* Others, "glory."

יְהוָה כִּי שָׁמַע אֶת תְּלֻנֹּתֵיכֶם: וַיְהִי כְּדַבֵּר אַהֲרֹן אֶל־
כָּל־עֲדַת בְּנֵי־יִשְׂרָאֵל וַיִּפְנוּ אֶל־הַמִּדְבָּר וְהִנֵּה כְּבוֹד
יְהוָה נִרְאָה בֶּעָנָן: פ

יא וַיְדַבֵּר יְהוָה אֶל־מֹשֶׁה לֵּאמֹר: שָׁמַעְתִּי אֶת־תְּלוּנֹּת
בְּנֵי יִשְׂרָאֵל דַּבֵּר אֲלֵהֶם לֵאמֹר בֵּין הָעַרְבַּיִם תֹּאכְלוּ
בָשָׂר וּבַבֹּקֶר תִּשְׂבְּעוּ־לָחֶם וִידַעְתֶּם כִּי אֲנִי יְהוָה
אֱלֹהֵיכֶם: וַיְהִי בָעֶרֶב וַתַּעַל הַשְּׂלָו וַתְּכַס אֶת־הַמַּחֲנֶה
וּבַבֹּקֶר הָיְתָה שִׁכְבַת הַטַּל סָבִיב לַמַּחֲנֶה: וַתַּעַל
שִׁכְבַת הַטָּל וְהִנֵּה עַל־פְּנֵי הַמִּדְבָּר דַּק מְחֻסְפָּס דַּק

ט כַּכְּפֹר עַל־הָאָרֶץ: וַיִּרְאוּ בְנֵי־יִשְׂרָאֵל וַיֹּאמְרוּ אִישׁ
אֶל־אָחִיו מָן הוּא כִּי לֹא יָדְעוּ מַה־הוּא וַיֹּאמֶר מֹשֶׁה
אֲלֵהֶם הוּא הַלֶּחֶם אֲשֶׁר נָתַן יְהוָה לָכֶם לְאָכְלָה:
טז זֶה הַדָּבָר אֲשֶׁר צִוָּה יְהוָה לִקְטוּ מִמֶּנּוּ אִישׁ לְפִי
אָכְלוֹ עֹמֶר לַגֻּלְגֹּלֶת מִסְפַּר נַפְשֹׁתֵיכֶם אִישׁ לַאֲשֶׁר
בְּאָהֳלוֹ תִּקָּחוּ: וַיַּעֲשׂוּ־כֵן בְּנֵי יִשְׂרָאֵל וַיִּלְקְטוּ הַמַּרְבֶּה
יח וְהַמַּמְעִיט: וַיָּמֹדּוּ בָעֹמֶר וְלֹא הֶעְדִּיף הַמַּרְבֶּה
וְהַמַּמְעִיט לֹא הֶחְסִיר אִישׁ לְפִי־אָכְלוֹ לָקָטוּ: וַיֹּאמֶר
כ מֹשֶׁה אֲלֵהֶם אִישׁ אַל־יוֹתֵר מִמֶּנּוּ עַד־בֹּקֶר: וְלֹא־

LORD, for He has heard your grumbling." **10]** And as Aaron spoke to the whole Israelite community, they turned toward the wilderness, and there, in a cloud, appeared the Presence of the LORD.

11] The LORD spoke to Moses: **12]** I have heard the grumbling of the Israelites. Speak to them and say: By evening you shall eat flesh, and in the morning you shall have your fill of bread; and you shall know that I the LORD am your God.

13] In the evening quail appeared and covered the camp; in the morning there was a fall of dew about the camp. **14]** When the fall of dew lifted, there, over the surface of the wilderness, lay a fine and flaky substance, as fine as frost on the ground. **15]** When the Israelites saw it, they said to one another, "What is it?"—for they did not know what it was. And Moses said to them, "That is the bread which the LORD has given you to eat. **16]** This is what the LORD has commanded: Gather as much of it as each of you requires to eat, an *omer* to a person for as many of you as there are; each of you shall fetch for those in his tent."

17] The Israelites did so, some gathering much, some little. **18]** But when they measured it by the *omer*, he who had gathered much had no excess, and he who had gathered little had no deficiency: they had gathered as much as they needed to eat. **19]** And Moses said to them, "Let no one leave any of it over until morning." **20]** But they paid no attention to Moses;

9] *Then Moses said.* Verses 9–12 would fit better after verse 5.

13] *Quail.* Which migrate north in the spring.

Fall of dew. Conceiving of dew not as a condensation on the ground but as coming from heaven.

15] *What is it?* מָן הוּא (*man hu*), a popular etymology assuming that מָן could mean "what"—for which there is, however, no precedent in Hebrew. The real origin of מָן is not known. The English manna comes from the Septuagint's rendition of Num. 11:6–7.

Bread. Or, "food"—utilized like bread as a substitute for grain, according to Num. 11:8.

16] *Omer.* Explained in verse 36 as one-tenth of an ephah, or about 6½ pints. According to Lev. 23:9 ff. the first omer (there understood as "sheaf") of the harvest was to be brought to the Temple "on the day after the Sabbath." The Rabbis ruled that such an offering would be made on the second day of Pesach and should be of barley [5]. With this offering the time of counting forty-nine days until Shavuot begins, and the whole period is therefore known as *sefirat ha-omer* (omer counting time).

18] *But when they measured.* They found they had gathered exactly one omer [6].

שִׁמְעוּ אֶל־מֹשֶׁה וַיּוֹתִרוּ אֲנָשִׁים מִמֶּנּוּ עַד־בֹּקֶר וַיָּרֻם כא

תּוֹלָעִים וַיִּבְאַשׁ וַיִּקְצֹף עֲלֵהֶם מֹשֶׁה: וַיִּלְקְטוּ אֹתוֹ

בַּבֹּקֶר בַּבֹּקֶר אִישׁ כְּפִי אָכְלוֹ וְחַם הַשֶּׁמֶשׁ וְנָמָס: וַיְהִי כב

בַּיּוֹם הַשִּׁשִּׁי לָקְטוּ לֶחֶם מִשְׁנֶה שְׁנֵי הָעֹמֶר לָאֶחָד

וַיָּבֹאוּ כָּל־נְשִׂיאֵי הָעֵדָה וַיַּגִּידוּ לְמֹשֶׁה: וַיֹּאמֶר אֲלֵהֶם כג

הוּא אֲשֶׁר דִּבֶּר יְהֹוָה שַׁבָּתוֹן שַׁבַּת־קֹדֶשׁ לַיהֹוָה מָחָר

אֵת אֲשֶׁר־תֹּאפוּ אֵפוּ וְאֵת אֲשֶׁר־תְּבַשְּׁלוּ בַּשֵּׁלוּ וְאֵת

כָּל־הָעֹדֵף הַנִּיחוּ לָכֶם לְמִשְׁמֶרֶת עַד־הַבֹּקֶר: וַיַּנִּיחוּ כד

אֹתוֹ עַד־הַבֹּקֶר כַּאֲשֶׁר צִוָּה מֹשֶׁה וְלֹא הִבְאִישׁ וְרִמָּה

לֹא־הָיְתָה בּוֹ: וַיֹּאמֶר מֹשֶׁה אִכְלֻהוּ הַיּוֹם כִּי־שַׁבָּת כה

הַיּוֹם לַיהֹוָה הַיּוֹם לֹא תִמְצָאֻהוּ בַּשָּׂדֶה: שֵׁשֶׁת יָמִים כו

תִּלְקְטֻהוּ וּבַיּוֹם הַשְּׁבִיעִי שַׁבָּת לֹא יִהְיֶה־בּוֹ: וַיְהִי כז

בַּיּוֹם הַשְּׁבִיעִי יָצְאוּ מִן־הָעָם לִלְקֹט וְלֹא מָצָאוּ: ס

וַיֹּאמֶר יְהֹוָה אֶל־מֹשֶׁה עַד־אָנָה מֵאַנְתֶּם לִשְׁמֹר מִצְוֹתַי כח

וְתוֹרֹתָי: רְאוּ כִּי־יְהֹוָה נָתַן לָכֶם הַשַּׁבָּת עַל־כֵּן הוּא כט

נֹתֵן לָכֶם בַּיּוֹם הַשִּׁשִּׁי לֶחֶם יוֹמָיִם שְׁבוּ אִישׁ תַּחְתָּיו

אַל־יֵצֵא אִישׁ מִמְּקֹמוֹ בַּיּוֹם הַשְּׁבִיעִי: וַיִּשְׁבְּתוּ הָעָם ל

בַּיּוֹם הַשְּׁבִיעִי: וַיִּקְרְאוּ בֵית־יִשְׂרָאֵל אֶת־שְׁמוֹ מָן וְהוּא לא

some of them left of it until morning, and it became infested with maggots and stank. And Moses was angry with them.

21] So they gathered it every morning, each as much as he needed to eat; for when the sun grew hot, it would melt. 22] On the sixth day they gathered double the amount of food, two *omers* for each; and when all the chieftains of the assembly came and told Moses, 23] he said to them, "This is what the LORD meant: Tomorrow is a day of rest, a holy sabbath of the LORD. Bake what you would bake and boil what you would boil; and all that is left put aside to be kept until morning." 24] So they put it aside until morning, as Moses had ordered; and it did not turn foul, and there were no maggots in it. 25] Then Moses said, "Eat it today, for today is a sabbath of the LORD; you will not find it today on the plain. 26] Six days you shall gather it; on the seventh day, the sabbath, there will be none."

27] Yet some of the people went out on the seventh day to gather, but they found nothing. 28] And the LORD said to Moses, "How long will you men refuse to obey My commandments and My teachings? 29] Mark that the LORD has given you the sabbath; therefore He gives you two days' food on the sixth day. Let everyone remain where he is: let no man leave his place on the seventh day." 30] So the people remained inactive on the seventh day.

31] The house of Israel named it manna; it was like coriander seed, white, and it tasted like

20] *No attention.* Not having faith that God's bounty would be renewed daily.

22] *They gathered double.* Without at first realizing why. Moses proceeds to explain God's will.

23] *Sabbath.* Tradition dates its introduction from this time, but it would seem that it was already known to the people. Moses utilizes the occasion to explain how the Sabbath is to be observed in relation to the manna. But see below, verse 30.

24] *They put it aside.* A portion of what they had gathered.

28] *Refuse to obey.* Though no mention of previous transgression has been made. Perhaps this verse stood originally at a later place.

30] *Inactive.* Or, "they rested," the same word as used in the Creation story (Gen. 2:2). The first Sabbath observance by Israel is here described as if the holy day had previously been unknown to Israel.

לד כַּאֲשֶׁר צִוָּה יְהֹוָה אֶל־מֹשֶׁה וַיַּנִּיחֵהוּ   כִּזְרַע גַּד לָבָן וְטַעְמוֹ כְּצַפִּיחִת בִּדְבָשׁ: וַיֹּאמֶר מֹשֶׁה
אַהֲרֹן לִפְנֵי הָעֵדֻת לְמִשְׁמָרֶת: וּבְנֵי יִשְׂרָאֵל אָכְלוּ   זֶה הַדָּבָר אֲשֶׁר צִוָּה יְהֹוָה מְלֹא הָעֹמֶר מִמֶּנּוּ לְמִשְׁמֶרֶת
אֶת־הַמָּן אַרְבָּעִים שָׁנָה עַד־בֹּאָם אֶל־אֶרֶץ נוֹשָׁבֶת   לְדֹרֹתֵיכֶם לְמַעַן יִרְאוּ אֶת־הַלֶּחֶם אֲשֶׁר הֶאֱכַלְתִּי
לו אֶת־הַמָּן אָכְלוּ עַד־בֹּאָם אֶל־קְצֵה אֶרֶץ כְּנָעַן: וְהָעֹמֶר   אֶתְכֶם בַּמִּדְבָּר בְּהוֹצִיאִי אֶתְכֶם מֵאֶרֶץ מִצְרָיִם:
עֲשִׂרִית הָאֵפָה הוּא: פ   לג וַיֹּאמֶר מֹשֶׁה אֶל־אַהֲרֹן קַח צִנְצֶנֶת אַחַת וְתֶן־שָׁמָּה
                                           מְלֹא־הָעֹמֶר מָן וְהַנַּח אֹתוֹ לִפְנֵי יְהֹוָה לְמִשְׁמָרֶת

wafers in honey.   **32]** Moses said, "This is what the LORD has commanded: let one *omer* of it be kept throughout the ages, in order that they may see the bread that I fed you in the wilderness when I brought you out from the land of Egypt."   **33]** And Moses said to Aaron, "Take a jar, put one *omer* of manna in it, and place it before the LORD, to be kept throughout the ages."   **34]** As the LORD had commanded Moses, Aaron placed it before the Pact, to be kept.   **35]** And the Israelites ate manna forty years, until they came to a settled land; they ate the manna until they came to the border of the land of Canaan.   **36]** The *omer* is a tenth of an *ephah*.

31] *Coriander.* An herbaceous plant bearing aromatic seedlike fruit which grows wild in the Sinai and which is used as a spice in bread and other foods. Num. 11:8 describes the plant differently and compares it to bdellium, a waxlike gum or resin. Ibn Ezra suggests that manna in its raw state resembled coriander and, in its boiled state, bdellium.

Wafers. The meaning of the Hebrew is uncertain. In Num. 11:8 the taste is said to be like "rich cream."

34] *The Pact.* הָעֵדֻת (*ha-edut*), a synonym for *berit*, covenant, of which the Tablets of the Ten Commandments will be the visible symbol (compare 32:15) [7].

35] *Until they came.* According to Josh. 5:12 the manna ceased at Passover time, at Gilgal, when they entered the Promised Land.

The Manna

It has long been known that the wondrous food that Israel ate in the desert for forty years and which they called manna has a natural model. "I found in Wadi Sheikh (in western Sinai) many tamarisks," writes Burckhardt. "It is the only part of the peninsula where this tree grows in profusion, and from it manna is obtained. It is called manna by the Bedouin and corresponds to the description given in Scripture. In June the substance falls to ground in little drops and is gathered up before sunrise for afterward it liquifies again once the sun shines on it. The Arabs preserve the manna in leather gourds and thus save it, like honey, for the future. Manna is found only when there is much rain; at other times there is none. It has a dirty yellow color, a pleasant taste, a bit spicy, but otherwise sweet like honey. The amount gathered even in the best of years is not great and amounts to no more than five to six hundred pounds. The Bedouin view it as the first delicacy which the land yields. The harvest is usually in June and lasts for six weeks" [8].

The substance referred to was in the past believed to be an exudation of the tamarisk itself but is now known to originate in an excretion of two scale-insects that live in symbiosis with the tamarisk. "A chemical analysis of these excretions has revealed that they contain a mixture of three basic sugars with pectin. The plant saps on which these insects feed are rich in carbohydrates but extremely poor in nitrogen. In order to acquire a minimum amount of nitrogen for their metabolism, they must consume great quantities of sap. The excess passes from them in honeydew excretions which in the dry air of the desert quickly change into drops of sticky solids" [9].

There is, then, a general resemblance of the biblical manna to what is still found under natural circumstances; this resemblance extends to appearance, color, and taste, and the need to gather it early in the morning and its subsequent melting in the warm sun. There are, at the same time, important differences: the manna we know from experience is relatively sparse and could not become a significant food for large numbers of people; it is dependent on certain weather conditions and is not found regularly; it is not subject to quick putrefaction; and of course it is found on Sabbaths as well as on other days. These differences are decisive. The Bible sees the manna not as a natural phenomenon; rather, it transforms natural occurrences into acts of God, willed by Him in support of Israel. Manna is thus, in the biblical view, literally *lechem shamayim*, the bread of heaven (Ps. 105:40), a gift of God. It is to remind Israel of God's unceasing care, but more than that: it places the creation of the people in direct relationship to the creation of the world itself.

Man in Eden was given his bread without having to toil for it.[1] Driven forth from paradise he had to earn his sustenance forever after by the sweat of his brow—forever, except for the forty years it took to make Israel, the new People of God, ready to enter its own post-Eden world. The giving of the manna continues the story of matzah, the bread of affliction, with an emphasis on what may be called the bread of Creation. The Wisdom of Solomon touches on this theme:

---

[1] The Eden story (Gen. 2 and 3) does not actually say so, but it seems to be implied in that man is punished to toil after being driven out of the garden. Toil thus appears as a new element.

"... You gave Your people the food of angels,
And without their toil supplied them with bread ready to eat."[2]

God interrupts the natural order to establish once more the ideal relationship between himself and man, the original and pure relationship between master and servant, in which the former takes total care of the latter [11]. He feeds a portion of His people as He had fed Adam and Eve and continues to do so until the process of this people's creation has been completed. Therefore, the institution of the Sabbath as a human day of rest is the natural complement to the Creation story. There, God rested on the seventh day, and now the people of His creation will also rest. The introduction of the Sabbath regulation is not just a *convenient* opportunity to acquaint Israel with its fundamental and central religious institution, it is the *necessary* outflow of the Creation theme. The Sabbath of Creation will henceforth be reflected and perpetuated in Israel's Sabbath observance. The "grain of heaven, the bread of the mighty" are limited gifts, but not the Sabbath, which will be His seal and sign forever.[3]

2 Wisdom 16:20. There are parallels to this theme in other traditions, in the same way that there are parallels to the biblical Creation and Eden tales. Thus the Greeks knew of nectar and ambrosia as divine nourishment, and the Scandinavian Edda speaks of a heavenly "honeyfall" [10].

3 Psalm 78:24–25. See there also (verses 17–31) for a poetic rendering of the manna-and-quail story. For the meaning of "rest" in Jewish law, see below, commentary on 20:8–11.

GLEANINGS

Bitterness

It says "they could not drink the water because it was bitter" (15:23). Bitterness was not the actual condition of the water; rather, the Israelites felt bitter and, therefore, whatever they tasted was bitter to them.   ITTURE TORAH [12]

The Test

We learn that God put Israel to the test by giving them manna (16:4). How so? Being free from worry over bread they were now tempted to disregard God's laws.   CHASIDIC [13]

From One to Many

The words "heed ... diligently" (15:26) are expressed in Hebrew by an idiomatic coupling of two verb forms, the infinitive absolute and a future tense of the same word, שָׁמֹעַ תִּשְׁמַע, literally, "if heed, you will heed." [On the grammatical form, see Gleanings to 19:1–25.] From this the Sages derived the meaning that heeding one commandment will lead to heeding many commandments, even as forgetting one commandment will lead to forgetting many commandments.   MIDRASH [14]

Flesh and Bread

Israel was promised bread to the full, but not flesh (verse 8). Their cry for bread was reasonable, but not for meat, for one can do without it.
                    RASHI

For Every Taste

It was one of the miracles that manna tasted

503

different to everyone. Whatever a man liked he found in the manna.　　　　　　　　MIDRASH [15]

A Wider Meaning

In 16:26 the word "sabbath" appears redundant, since it already says "on the seventh day." The word "sabbath" is therefore to be understood to have a wider meaning and to include Yom Kippur and the holy days.

MIDRASH [16]

Study

Only those who eat manna (that is, who have enough to eat) can truly study Torah.

MIDRASH [17]

Precreated

Manna was one of the ten wonders that God created when He fashioned the world. He brought it into being on the eve of the first Sabbath, at twilight.　　　　　　　　　MISHNAH [18]

The Sabbath

Rabbi Levi said: If Israel would truly keep the Sabbath for one single day the Messiah would come, for keeping the Sabbath is equivalent to keeping all the commandments.　　MIDRASH [19]

[Rabbi Levi may have used this interpretation to indicate his belief that the likelihood of the Messiah's coming was as small as that of Israel's keeping the commandments.]

Contradiction

If what was gathered of the manna amounted in any case to one omer, why should everyone be urged to collect "as much of it as each of you requires to eat" (16:16)? A little amount would have sufficed. This is to teach us that we must do what is necessary and not rely on miracles.

BACHYA [20]

Like Snow

Until Moses instructed them, the Israelites thought at first that the manna was snow. The substance still descends in that area in our day.

JOSEPHUS [21]

God's Way

The manna was not something that would be stored up and dispensed gradually, since God is accustomed always to give His gifts afresh.

PHILO [22]

God sent manna to teach Israel that "man does not live by bread alone."　　　　B. S. CHILDS [23]

Foes and Friends

Israel now proceeds from the wilderness of Sin to Mount Horeb, and another outbreak of rebellious feeling against Moses is reported. Thereafter, the people are confronted with their first military engagement. Under the leadership of Joshua, Israel defeats Amalek, although it is not military prowess but God's will that achieves victory. Ancient Near Eastern armies went into battle behind standards symbolizing their gods, hence the picture of Moses, his hands upraised and supported by Aaron and Hur, presents a symbolic standard which is to remind the people that God is fighting for them. (Appropriately, the altar built to commemorate the victory was called Adonai-nissi, "The Lord is my banner.") This event is accorded special historic significance, for Moses is bidden to record the conflict in a document and to note that henceforth Amalek is to be considered Israel's—and God's—implacable enemy.

Moses' father-in-law arrives, bringing Zipporah and her two sons with him. He observes Moses in his function as a judge and advises him how to establish a hierarchy of courts, an advice that Moses heeds. (Another story of Moses' sharing of responsibility will be found in Num. 11.)

The text exhibits a number of repetitions. Verses 1 and 2 are restated in verse 3: two names are given for the locale where the rebellion took place (verse 7), and that story itself could be a variant or shorter version of Numbers 20:1 ff. Biblical critics see these duplications as the results of different sources. Such variations occur also in the traditions concerning Moses' father-in-law, a subject that will be treated in greater detail in the commentary to this chapter.

(A new weekly portion, *Yitro*, begins with 18:1.)

ה וַיֹּאמֶר יְהוָה אֶל־מֹשֶׁה עֲבֹר לִפְנֵי הָעָם וְקַח אִתְּךָ
מִזִּקְנֵי יִשְׂרָאֵל וּמַטְּךָ אֲשֶׁר הִכִּיתָ בּוֹ אֶת־הַיְאֹר
ו קַח בְּיָדְךָ וְהָלָכְתָּ: הִנְנִי עֹמֵד לְפָנֶיךָ שָּׁם עַל־הַצּוּר
בְּחֹרֵב וְהִכִּיתָ בַצּוּר וְיָצְאוּ מִמֶּנּוּ מַיִם וְשָׁתָה הָעָם
ז וַיַּעַשׂ כֵּן מֹשֶׁה לְעֵינֵי זִקְנֵי יִשְׂרָאֵל: וַיִּקְרָא שֵׁם
הַמָּקוֹם מַסָּה וּמְרִיבָה עַל־רִיב בְּנֵי יִשְׂרָאֵל וְעַל נַסֹּתָם
אֶת־יְהוָה לֵאמֹר הֲיֵשׁ יְהוָה בְּקִרְבֵּנוּ אִם־אָיִן: פ
ח וַיָּבֹא עֲמָלֵק וַיִּלָּחֶם עִם־יִשְׂרָאֵל בִּרְפִידִם: וַיֹּאמֶר

א וַיִּסְעוּ כָּל־עֲדַת בְּנֵי־יִשְׂרָאֵל מִמִּדְבַּר־סִין לְמַסְעֵיהֶם
עַל־פִּי יְהוָה וַיַּחֲנוּ בִּרְפִידִים וְאֵין מַיִם לִשְׁתֹּת הָעָם:
ב וַיָּרֶב הָעָם עִם־מֹשֶׁה וַיֹּאמְרוּ תְּנוּ־לָנוּ מַיִם וְנִשְׁתֶּה
וַיֹּאמֶר לָהֶם מֹשֶׁה מַה־תְּרִיבוּן עִמָּדִי מַה־תְּנַסּוּן אֶת־
ג יְהוָה: וַיִּצְמָא שָׁם הָעָם לַמַּיִם וַיִּלֶּן הָעָם עַל־מֹשֶׁה
וַיֹּאמֶר לָמָּה זֶּה הֶעֱלִיתָנוּ מִמִּצְרַיִם לְהָמִית אֹתִי
ד וְאֶת־בָּנַי וְאֶת־מִקְנַי בַּצָּמָא: וַיִּצְעַק מֹשֶׁה אֶל־יְהוָה
לֵאמֹר מָה אֶעֱשֶׂה לָעָם הַזֶּה עוֹד מְעַט וּסְקָלֻנִי:

1] From the wilderness of Sin the whole Israelite community continued by stages as the LORD would command. They encamped at Rephidim, and there was no water for the people to drink.   2] The people quarreled with Moses. "Give us water to drink," they said; and Moses replied to them, "Why do you quarrel with me? Why do you try the LORD?"   3] But the people thirsted there for water; and the people grumbled against Moses and said, "Why did you bring us up from Egypt, to kill us and our children and livestock with thirst?"   4] Moses cried out to the LORD, saying, "What shall I do with this people? Before long they will be stoning me!"   5] Then the LORD said to Moses, "Pass before the people; take with you some of the elders of Israel, and take along the rod with which you struck the Nile, and set out.   6] I will be standing there before you on the rock at Horeb. Strike the rock and water will issue from it, and the people will drink." And Moses did so in the sight of the elders of Israel.   7] The place was named Massah and Meribah, because the Israelites quarreled and because they tried the LORD, saying, "Is the LORD present among us or not?"

8] Amalek came and fought with Israel at Rephidim.   9] Moses said to Joshua, "Pick some

17:1] *Rephidim.* Most likely not the place in the northern Sinai bearing that name today (called in Arabic "Bir Gafgafa"), but farther east and south. The exact location depends on the route the Israelites took.

2] *Try the Lord.* Test His patience.

3] *Why did you bring us . . .?* The text says literally "bring me": the people grumbled as one.

6] *I will be standing there.* The Hebrew idiom means "I will be present."

On the rock. The image of the rock as God's place denotes both loftiness and permanence. God himself is called "Rock" ("My Rock and my Redeemer," "Rock of my salvation").

At Horeb. On the relationship of Horeb and Sinai and their supposed identity see the textual note for 3:1. The beginning of chapter 19 states

that Israel was journeying to and arriving at Sinai, in which case the Horeb of this verse must mean an area rather than a single mountain—unless, as tradition suggests, chapter 17 should be placed later in the book, when Israel was already at Sinai-Horeb.

7] *Massah.* "Trial," from the root נסה.

Meribah. "Quarrel," from the root ריב. Another instance (or variant account) of water being brought forth from the rock at Meribah is described in Num. 20:1 ff. The names Massah and Meribah are here represented as arising out of the incidents described, but it is also possible that the stories were told to explain the etymology of the place names.

Is the Lord present. God, not Moses, is the real target of the unrest.

מֹשֶׁה אֶל־יְהוֹשֻׁעַ בְּחַר־לָנוּ אֲנָשִׁים וְצֵא הִלָּחֵם בַּעֲמָלֵק
מָחָר אָנֹכִי נִצָּב עַל־רֹאשׁ הַגִּבְעָה וּמַטֵּה הָאֱלֹהִים
בְּיָדִי: וַיַּעַשׂ יְהוֹשֻׁעַ כַּאֲשֶׁר אָמַר־לוֹ מֹשֶׁה לְהִלָּחֵם
בַּעֲמָלֵק וּמֹשֶׁה אַהֲרֹן וְחוּר עָלוּ רֹאשׁ הַגִּבְעָה:
וְהָיָה כַּאֲשֶׁר יָרִים מֹשֶׁה יָדוֹ וְגָבַר יִשְׂרָאֵל וְכַאֲשֶׁר
יָנִיחַ יָדוֹ וְגָבַר עֲמָלֵק: וִידֵי מֹשֶׁה כְּבֵדִים וַיִּקְחוּ־
אֶבֶן וַיָּשִׂימוּ תַחְתָּיו וַיֵּשֶׁב עָלֶיהָ וְאַהֲרֹן וְחוּר תָּמְכוּ
בְיָדָיו מִזֶּה אֶחָד וּמִזֶּה אֶחָד וַיְהִי יָדָיו אֱמוּנָה עַד־

בֹּא הַשָּׁמֶשׁ: וַיַּחֲלֹשׁ יְהוֹשֻׁעַ אֶת־עֲמָלֵק וְאֶת־עַמּוֹ לְפִי־
חָרֶב: פ
וַיֹּאמֶר יְהוָה אֶל־מֹשֶׁה כְּתֹב זֹאת זִכָּרוֹן בַּסֵּפֶר
וְשִׂים בְּאָזְנֵי יְהוֹשֻׁעַ כִּי־מָחֹה אֶמְחֶה אֶת־זֵכֶר עֲמָלֵק
מִתַּחַת הַשָּׁמָיִם: וַיִּבֶן מֹשֶׁה מִזְבֵּחַ וַיִּקְרָא שְׁמוֹ יְהוָה
נִסִּי: וַיֹּאמֶר כִּי־יָד עַל־כֵּס יָהּ מִלְחָמָה לַיהוָה
בַּעֲמָלֵק מִדֹּר דֹּר:

Haftarah Beshalach, p. 703

men for us, and go out and do battle with Amalek. Tomorrow I will station myself on the top of the hill, with the rod of God in my hand." **10]** Joshua did as Moses told him and fought with Amalek, while Moses, Aaron, and Hur went up to the top of the hill. **11]** Then, whenever Moses held up his hand, Israel prevailed; but whenever he let down his hand, Amalek prevailed. **12]** But Moses' hands grew heavy; so they took a stone and put it under him and he sat on it, while Aaron and Hur, one on each side, supported his hands; thus his hands remained steady until the sun set. **13]** And Joshua overwhelmed the people of Amalek with the sword.

14] Then the LORD said to Moses, "Inscribe this in a document as a reminder, and read it aloud to Joshua: I will utterly blot out the memory of Amalek from under heaven!" **15]** And Moses built an altar and named it Adonai-nissi. **16]** He said, "It means, 'Hand upon the throne of the LORD!' The LORD will be at war with Amalek throughout the ages."

9] *Joshua.* He was the son of Nun, from the tribe of Ephraim. Though this is his first mention in the Torah, his background is not stated at this time, for when this story was told he was already well known to the hearers. Another passage (Num. 13:16) tells us that Moses changed his name from Hosea to Joshua, probably after Israel had reached Kadesh, which suggests that the name of Moses' future successor may have been the subject of varying traditions. Joshua served both as military leader of the people and as Moses' attendant.

Rod of God. Perhaps to give confidence to the people, recalling the plagues and the passage through the sea.

11] *Held up his hand.* In prayer, or as a symbolic gesture. Rashbam believed that Moses held the rod aloft like a flag and that as long as the soldiers could see it they were spurred on. According to Beer, the horizontally outstretched hands formed, together with the body of Moses, a sort of cross which—like the mark of Cain (Gen. 4:15) or the

shape of the old letter *tav*—represented a figure of excellence [1].

12] *Hur.* Apparently an important personage, not mentioned before. According to one tradition he was Miriam's husband, according to another, her son (Caleb being her husband) [2].

13] *People of Amalek.* Literally, "Amalek and his people."

14] *In a document.* Its nature is not specified. Perhaps the reference is to the book of the *Wars of the Lord* (referred to in Num. 21:14) which has been lost. Or it might be to the Torah itself.

15] *Adonai-nissi.* "The Lord is my banner" or "my sign." See at verse 7.

16] *Hand upon the throne.* Or, reading נס for כס, "hand upon the Lord's banner," providing a parallel to verse 15: Moses' hands, uplifted in battle, became a sign for God to sustain Israel [3].

Throughout the ages. Jewish tradition took "Amalek" to represent figuratively Israel's foes in every age.

ם פ פ

הַר הָאֱלֹהִים: וַיֹּאמֶר אֶל־מֹשֶׁה אֲנִי חֹתֶנְךָ יִתְרוֹ   א וַיִּשְׁמַע יִתְרוֹ כֹהֵן מִדְיָן חֹתֵן מֹשֶׁה אֵת כָּל־אֲשֶׁר

בָּא אֵלֶיךָ וְאִשְׁתְּךָ וּשְׁנֵי בָנֶיהָ עִמָּהּ: וַיֵּצֵא מֹשֶׁה   עָשָׂה אֱלֹהִים לְמֹשֶׁה וּלְיִשְׂרָאֵל עַמּוֹ כִּי־הוֹצִיא יְהוָה

לִקְרַאת חֹתְנוֹ וַיִּשְׁתַּחוּ וַיִּשַּׁק־לוֹ וַיִּשְׁאֲלוּ אִישׁ־לְרֵעֵהוּ   ב אֶת־יִשְׂרָאֵל מִמִּצְרָיִם: וַיִּקַּח יִתְרוֹ חֹתֵן מֹשֶׁה אֶת־

לְשָׁלוֹם וַיָּבֹאוּ הָאֹהֱלָה: וַיְסַפֵּר מֹשֶׁה לְחֹתְנוֹ אֵת   ג צִפֹּרָה אֵשֶׁת מֹשֶׁה אַחַר שִׁלּוּחֶיהָ: וְאֵת שְׁנֵי בָנֶיהָ

כָּל־אֲשֶׁר עָשָׂה יְהוָה לְפַרְעֹה וּלְמִצְרַיִם עַל אוֹדֹת   אֲשֶׁר שֵׁם הָאֶחָד גֵּרְשֹׁם כִּי אָמַר גֵּר הָיִיתִי בְּאֶרֶץ

יִשְׂרָאֵל אֵת כָּל־הַתְּלָאָה אֲשֶׁר מְצָאָתַם בַּדֶּרֶךְ וַיַּצִּלֵם   ד נָכְרִיָּה: וְשֵׁם הָאֶחָד אֱלִיעֶזֶר כִּי־אֱלֹהֵי אָבִי בְּעֶזְרִי

יְהוָה: וַיִּחַדְּ יִתְרוֹ עַל כָּל־הַטּוֹבָה אֲשֶׁר־עָשָׂה יְהוָה   ה וַיַּצִּלֵנִי מֵחֶרֶב פַּרְעֹה: וַיָּבֹא יִתְרוֹ חֹתֵן מֹשֶׁה וּבָנָיו

לְיִשְׂרָאֵל אֲשֶׁר הִצִּילוֹ מִיַּד מִצְרָיִם: וַיֹּאמֶר יִתְרוֹ   וְאִשְׁתּוֹ אֶל־מֹשֶׁה אֶל־הַמִּדְבָּר אֲשֶׁר־הוּא חֹנֶה שָׁם

בָּרוּךְ יְהוָה אֲשֶׁר הִצִּיל אֶתְכֶם מִיַּד מִצְרַיִם וּמִיַּד

1] Jethro priest of Midian, Moses' father-in-law, heard all that God had done for Moses and for Israel His people, how the LORD had brought Israel out from Egypt. **2]** So Jethro, Moses' father-in-law, took Zipporah, Moses' wife, after she had been sent home, **3]** and her two sons—of whom one was named Gershom, that is to say, "I have been a stranger in a foreign land"; **4]** and the other was named Eliezer, meaning, "The God of my father was my help, and He delivered me from the sword of Pharaoh." **5]** Jethro, Moses' father-in-law, brought Moses' sons and wife to him in the wilderness, where he was encamped at the mountain of God. **6]** He sent word to Moses, "I, your father-in-law Jethro, am coming to you, with your wife and her two sons." **7]** Moses went out to meet his father-in-law; he bowed low and kissed him; each asked after the other's welfare, and they went into the tent.

8] Moses then recounted to his father-in-law everything that the LORD had done to Pharaoh and to the Egyptians for Israel's sake, all the hardships that had befallen them on the way, and how the LORD had delivered them. **9]** And Jethro rejoiced over all the kindness that the LORD had shown Israel when He delivered them from the Egyptians. **10]** "Blessed be the LORD," Jethro said, "who delivered you from the Egyptians and from Pharaoh, and who delivered the people from under the hand of the Egyptians. **11]** Now I know that the LORD is greater than

---

18:1] *Jethro.* A new weekly portion (*sidrah*), named *Yitro*, starts with this verse. It is noteworthy that the Decalogue is included in this *sidrah*, named after a Midianite priest.

2] *Moses' father-in-law.* The apposition is used in this chapter with such frequency that it appears like a title: Jethro was known by his famous son-in-law [4].

After she had been sent home. This notation harmonizes the passages to follow with 4:20 and

24–26 which seemed to suggest that Zipporah accompanied Moses to Egypt.

3] *Gershom.* As if גֵּר שָׁם (*ger sham*), "a stranger there."

4] *Eliezer.* Literally, "My God is help," the only mention in Torah of Moses' second son. Since only one son is listed in chapter 2, it has been suggested that the story there stems from the J-source and here from the E-source.

טז מֹשֶׁה לְחֹתְנוֹ כִּי־יָבֹא אֵלַי הָעָם לִדְרֹשׁ אֱלֹהִים: כִּי־
יִהְיֶה לָהֶם דָּבָר בָּא אֵלַי וְשָׁפַטְתִּי בֵּין אִישׁ וּבֵין
רֵעֵהוּ וְהוֹדַעְתִּי אֶת־חֻקֵּי הָאֱלֹהִים וְאֶת־תּוֹרֹתָיו:
יז וַיֹּאמֶר חֹתֵן מֹשֶׁה אֵלָיו לֹא־טוֹב הַדָּבָר אֲשֶׁר אַתָּה
יח עֹשֶׂה: נָבֹל תִּבֹּל גַּם־אַתָּה גַּם־הָעָם הַזֶּה אֲשֶׁר עִמָּךְ
יט כִּי־כָבֵד מִמְּךָ הַדָּבָר לֹא־תוּכַל עֲשֹׂהוּ לְבַדֶּךָ: עַתָּה
שְׁמַע בְּקֹלִי אִיעָצְךָ וִיהִי אֱלֹהִים עִמָּךְ הֱיֵה אַתָּה
לָעָם מוּל הָאֱלֹהִים וְהֵבֵאתָ אַתָּה אֶת־הַדְּבָרִים אֶל־
כ הָאֱלֹהִים: וְהִזְהַרְתָּה אֶתְהֶם אֶת־הַחֻקִּים וְאֶת־הַתּוֹרֹת
וְהוֹדַעְתָּ לָהֶם אֶת־הַדֶּרֶךְ יֵלְכוּ בָהּ וְאֶת־הַמַּעֲשֶׂה

פַּרְעֹה אֲשֶׁר הִצִּיל אֶת־הָעָם מִתַּחַת יַד־מִצְרָיִם:
יא עַתָּה יָדַעְתִּי כִּי־גָדוֹל יְהֹוָה מִכָּל־הָאֱלֹהִים כִּי בַדָּבָר
יב אֲשֶׁר זָדוּ עֲלֵיהֶם: וַיִּקַּח יִתְרוֹ חֹתֵן מֹשֶׁה עֹלָה
וּזְבָחִים לֵאלֹהִים וַיָּבֹא אַהֲרֹן וְכֹל זִקְנֵי יִשְׂרָאֵל
יג לֶאֱכָל־לֶחֶם עִם־חֹתֵן מֹשֶׁה לִפְנֵי הָאֱלֹהִים: וַיְהִי
מִמָּחֳרָת וַיֵּשֶׁב מֹשֶׁה לִשְׁפֹּט אֶת־הָעָם וַיַּעֲמֹד הָעָם
יד עַל־מֹשֶׁה מִן־הַבֹּקֶר עַד־הָעָרֶב: וַיַּרְא חֹתֵן מֹשֶׁה
אֵת כָּל־אֲשֶׁר־הוּא עֹשֶׂה לָעָם וַיֹּאמֶר מָה־הַדָּבָר
הַזֶּה אֲשֶׁר אַתָּה עֹשֶׂה לָעָם מַדּוּעַ אַתָּה יוֹשֵׁב לְבַדֶּךָ
טו וְכָל־הָעָם נִצָּב עָלֶיךָ מִן־בֹּקֶר עַד־עָרֶב: וַיֹּאמֶר

all gods, yes, by the result of their very schemes against [the people]." **12]** And Jethro, Moses' father-in-law, brought a burnt offering and sacrifices for God; and Aaron came with all the elders of Israel to partake of the meal before God with Moses' father-in-law.

13] Next day, Moses sat as magistrate among the people, while the people stood about Moses from morning until evening. **14]** But when Moses' father-in-law saw how much he had to do for the people, he said, "What is this thing that you are doing to the people? Why do you act alone, while all the people stand about you from morning until evening?" **15]** Moses replied to his father-in-law, "It is because the people come to me to inquire of God. **16]** When they have a dispute, it comes before me, and I decide between a man and his neighbor, and I make known the laws and teachings of God."

17] But Moses' father-in-law said to him, "The thing you are doing is not right; **18]** you will surely wear yourself out, and these people as well. For the task is too heavy for you; you cannot do it alone. **19]** Now listen to me. I will give you counsel, and God be with you! You represent the people before God: you bring the disputes before God, **20]** and enjoin upon them the laws and the teachings, and make known to them the way they are to go and the

---

11] *Yes.* . . . The remainder of the sentence is obscure. Possibly some words are missing [5].

12] *Brought a burnt offering.* Although the sacrificial cult had not yet been instituted. Ibn Ezra therefore believed that this chapter belongs after the Sinai revelation.

To partake. According to some scholars, sharing the meal was an essential aspect of the sacrificial communion with the Divine.

14] *Act.* Literally, "sit."

15] *Inquire of God.* In an oracular fashion, possibly by the use of divine lots like Urim and Thummim (see below at 28:30).

16] *I make known.* Either interpreting rules already known or divulging new ones.

Laws. On the term חֻקִּים see commentaries at 15:25 and 21:1.

Teachings. תּוֹרֹת (torot), the plural of תּוֹרָה (torah), here used in a judicial sense. In the Pentateuch, *torah* has the meaning of moral, legal, and ritual "teaching," or of "law" in general; also of the Pentateuch itself in particular. In later ages *torah* designated the whole teaching and legal tradition of Israel. The term is derived from the root ירה, to point, direct, though this is disputed.

כא אֲשֶׁ֣ר יַעֲשֽׂוּן: וְאַתָּ֣ה תֶחֱזֶ֣ה מִכָּל־הָעָ֡ם אַנְשֵׁי־חַ֩יִל֩ יִרְאֵ֨י
אֱלֹהִ֜ים אַנְשֵׁ֥י אֱמֶ֛ת שֹׂנְאֵ֥י בָ֖צַע וְשַׂמְתָּ֣ עֲלֵהֶ֗ם שָׂרֵ֤י
כב אֲלָפִים֙ שָׂרֵ֣י מֵא֔וֹת שָׂרֵ֥י חֲמִשִּׁ֖ים וְשָׂרֵ֥י עֲשָׂרֹֽת: וְשָׁפְט֣וּ
אֶת־הָעָם֮ בְּכָל־עֵת֒ וְהָיָ֞ה כָּל־הַדָּבָ֤ר הַגָּדֹל֙ יָבִ֣יאוּ
אֵלֶ֔יךָ וְכָל־הַדָּבָ֥ר הַקָּטֹ֖ן יִשְׁפְּטוּ־הֵ֑ם וְהָקֵל֙ מֵֽעָלֶ֔יךָ
כג וְנָשְׂא֖וּ אִתָּֽךְ: אִ֣ם אֶת־הַדָּבָ֤ר הַזֶּה֙ תַּעֲשֶׂ֔ה וְצִוְּךָ֣ אֱלֹהִ֔ים
וְיָכָלְתָּ֖ עֲמֹ֑ד וְגַם֙ כָּל־הָעָ֣ם הַזֶּ֔ה עַל־מְקֹמ֖וֹ יָבֹ֥א

כד בְּשָׁלֽוֹם: וַיִּשְׁמַ֥ע מֹשֶׁ֖ה לְק֣וֹל חֹתְנ֑וֹ וַיַּ֕עַשׂ כֹּ֖ל אֲשֶׁ֥ר
כה אָמָֽר: וַיִּבְחַ֨ר מֹשֶׁ֤ה אַנְשֵׁי־חַ֙יִל֙ מִכָּל־יִשְׂרָאֵ֔ל וַיִּתֵּ֥ן
אֹתָ֛ם רָאשִׁ֖ים עַל־הָעָ֑ם שָׂרֵ֤י אֲלָפִים֙ שָׂרֵ֣י מֵא֔וֹת
כו שָׂרֵ֥י חֲמִשִּׁ֖ים וְשָׂרֵ֣י עֲשָׂרֹֽת: וְשָׁפְט֥וּ אֶת־הָעָ֖ם בְּכָל־
עֵ֑ת אֶת־הַדָּבָ֤ר הַקָּשֶׁה֙ יְבִיא֣וּן אֶל־מֹשֶׁ֔ה וְכָל־הַדָּבָ֥ר
כז הַקָּטֹ֖ן יִשְׁפּוּט֥וּ הֵֽם: וַיְשַׁלַּ֥ח מֹשֶׁ֖ה אֶת־חֹתְנ֑וֹ וַיֵּ֥לֶךְ ל֖וֹ
אֶל־אַרְצֽוֹ:
פ

practices they are to follow. **21]** You shall also seek out from among all the people capable men who fear God, trustworthy men who spurn ill-gotten gain. Set these over them as chiefs of thousands, hundreds, fifties, and tens, and **22]** let them judge the people at all times. Have them bring every major dispute to you, but let them decide every minor dispute themselves. Make it easier for yourself, and let them share the burden with you. **23]** If you do this—and God so commands you—you will be able to bear up; and all these people too will go home unwearied."

24] Moses heeded his father-in-law and did just as he had said. **25]** Moses chose capable men out of all Israel, and appointed them heads over the people—chiefs of thousands, hundreds, fifties, and tens; **26]** and they judged the people at all times: the difficult matters they would bring to Moses, and all the minor matters they would decide themselves. **27]** Then Moses bade his father-in-law farewell, and he went his way to his own land.

21] *Set these over them.* Jethro suggests a hierarchy of judges similar to the organization of an army. The arrangement appears cumbersome and may have applied to families rather than individuals.

27] *His own land.* Midian, probably east of the Gulf of Akaba (see at 2:15).

The Memory of Amalek

In the Torah as well as the rest of the Bible, the people of Amalek occupy a unique position: they were among Israel's enemies, but alone among these their enmity will last in perpetuity. It will by divine fiat be irreconcilable, and only the disappearance of the Amalekites will satisfy God's anger. He himself will erase their traces and Israel is summoned to be the executioner of His will. This extraordinary judgment suggests that the battle between Israel and Amalek described in Exodus 17 and referred to in Deuteronomy 25 had some crucial significance and that later conflicts between these two peoples further deepened the antagonism.

Amalek was the name of a nomadic tribe or group of tribes located in the Sinai peninsula and the southern Negev. No literary sources outside the Bible relating to them have so far been found; from time to time the Amalekites have been identified with certain other population groups recorded in Near Eastern records, but the evidence brought for such identification cannot be said to be sufficient. The Amalekites were in existence already in Abraham's time (Gen. 14:7) and were called "a leading nation" in Balaam's prophecies (Num. 24:20).[1] In the biblical tradition they were considered descendants of Edom (Esau, Gen. 36:12) and were said to range "from Havilah to Shur," which meant from Arabia to Egypt—a territory similar to that of the Ishmaelites (I Sam. 15:7; Gen. 25:18). They are never mentioned as having been on friendly terms with Israel and are noted only in terms of warfare. They revenged their first defeat in a subsequent encounter;[2] they were crushed about 1000 B.C.E. by King Saul (I Sam. 15:5 ff.) and again by King David (I Sam. 27:8 ff.) and disappeared from historical view after their destruction by King Hezekiah about three hundred years later (I Chron. 4:39–43).

The origin of this traditional enmity and of the biblical insistence—twice repeated—on characterizing the conflict as a holy war is not clear. Deuteronomy 25 recalls that Amalek attacked Israel from the rear and overtook the weakest of the train, thus giving the account overtones of moral indignation. But this alone would not explain the deep-seated antipathy to Amalek that is pictured as originating with God himself. Nor would the prolonged struggle for Kadesh as a contested center of both Israel and Amalek appear to be more than a contributing reason. Possibly the fact that the Amalekites were the first foes Israel met after its liberation stamped them in the people's mind as the archenemy, the prototype of all whom they would and did meet subsequently. This sentiment is reflected in an old midrash: Moses was to write the judgment on Amalek in a document to let all men know that those who harm Israel will in the end come themselves to harm [6]. Israel's bitterest persecutors were dubbed Amalek; Haman himself is recorded to have been a descendant of Agag, king of Amalek (Esther 3:1), and the portion that commands to remember the misdeeds of Amalek (Deut. 25:17–19) is read as a special addition on the Sabbath before Purim, which is therefore called *Shabbat Zachor*.

In the person of this Agag, the nature of the holy war comes into full focus. King Saul is told to exterminate the Amalekites once and for all, root and branch, but he fails to do so, and especially does he save Agag. This failure causes the prophet Samuel to pronounce the ultimate judgment on Saul: because he failed in his holy duty he will be

---

[1] Some translate רֵאשִׁית גּוֹיִם as "first of the nations." [2] The defeat being ascribed to the will of God who wanted to punish Israel (Num. 14:44–45).

dispossessed of his kingdom. Samuel then proceeds to kill the Amalekite king who had wrought great destruction in Israel (I Sam. 15, read as the Haftarah on *Shabbat Zachor*). The episode starkly illumines the depth of the prophet's feeling that everything belonging to Amalek was banned for Israel and therefore proscribed by God himself. Martin Buber, reflecting the difficulty that modern man has with this concept of divine will, said simply that, with respect to Agag, Samuel misread the intent of God [7]. Indeed, we no longer can make the identification which to biblical man was basic: Israel's wars were, with a few exceptions, considered the wars of the Lord.[3] God was involved in Israel's fate; their victories were His, their enemies were His also.

The ancients attempted to draw lessons from Amalek's position as God's adversary. Its people, they said, were dedicated to Israel's destruction and tried to inveigle others to join them in this attempt. In a struggle for its own survival, Israel would be foolish to be lenient [8]. Or: Amalek's attack encouraged others, and all subsequent attempts to crush Israel stem from the example of Amalek. The phrase "Remember Amalek" (Deut. 25:17) was to remind Israel not only of the Amalekites' misdeeds but also of its own capacity to transgress God's commandments. For whenever Israel says, "Is the Lord present among us or not?" (17:7) and doubts its relationship with Him, this will at once be followed by "Amalek came" (verse 8) and by another bitter struggle for existence [9].

Jethro

The Torah depicts Moses' father-in-law as a man of religious commitment, hospitality, and wisdom. It was he who provided the refugee from Egypt with shelter and gave him his daughter Zipporah as a wife (2:16 ff.); he rejoiced in Israel's good fortune and was sympathetic to Moses' belief. In fact he declared יְהֹוָה to be greater than all the gods, which may indicate that he accepted יְהֹוָה as his God, and, when he sacrificed to Him, he resembled Melchizedek in his doing obeisance to Abram's God (Gen. 14:19); he gave Moses sage advice on how to administer justice and, in a later reference (Num. 10:29 ff., speaking of Hobab), he was asked by Moses to join Israel permanently in the conquest and settlement of Canaan. Though he refused the invitation, he departed to his own land as the staunch and admiring friend of Israel that he had been since he first entered into family relations with Moses.

The name of this man, however, is not always the same. He is called Reuel, Jether, Jethro, and Hobab. Jether seems to be a scribal variant of Jethro, and in Num. 10:29 Hobab is called Reuel's son (suggesting that the passage in Exod. 2:18 might have read "Hobab, son of Reuel"). This still leaves us with a father-in-law who is called both Jethro and Hobab. Since the Torah gives us no indication that two different men are meant, we are left with either the rabbinical explanation that Hobab is a different name for Jethro or the critical analysis that sees two different traditions joined in the text. The Hobab tradition links Moses to the Kenites (Judg. 4:11) and is ascribed to the J-source; the Jethro tradition links Moses to the Midianites and is ascribed to the E-source.

The latter theory commends itself as the more likely. It should not be surprising that various traditions grew up about this man from far away who suddenly appeared on the scene, who enjoyed the great admiration of Moses, and who apparently had a significant influence on his son-in-law. Some scholars

---

[3] An ancient book called *Wars of the Lord* is mentioned in the Bible, but it is no longer extant.

have concluded that in fact Moses acquired from Hobab the knowledge of יְהֹוָה, who was said to be the Kenite divinity. This "Kenite hypothesis"—although it does not command enough support as the explanation of the origins of Israel's religion (see chs. 3 and 6)—properly highlights the close relationship between the people of Israel and the people of Midian, of whom the Kenites were a subgroup. This relationship deteri-

orated in subsequent centuries, but in Moses' time it provided a remarkable contrast to the enmity of Amalek. Perhaps this contrast is the reason that the story of the battle with Amalek is followed by a chapter dealing with the friendship of the priest of Midian [10].

In the Druze religion, Jethro (called Shu'ayb) plays a significant role, being considered one of those who were incarnations of the "Universal Mind."

GLEANINGS

God's Presence

God said, "I will be standing there before you on the rock" (17:6). This implies: "In every place where a man leaves his footprint, there I too will stand."   MIDRASH [11]

This thought found its expression also in the legend that the rock that yielded water followed Israel miraculously throughout their wanderings in the desert [12].

Doubt

The attack by Amalek follows directly on the grumbling at Massah and Meribah. Israel said, "Is the Lord present among us or not?" (17:7), and immediately after this doubt "Amalek came" (17:8). The letters of "Amalek" (עמלק) and "doubt" (ספק) have the same numerical value of 240.   M. Y. EGER [13]

For Us

Moses says, "Pick some men for us" (17:9)—"us," not "me"—treating his junior as an equal. From this we learn that a teacher should hold a pupil as dear as himself.   MIDRASH [14]

The Source of Victory

Could the hands of Moses bring victory or defeat? Rather, when the Israelites directed their thoughts on high and kept their hearts subject to

their Father in Heaven, they prevailed; otherwise, they suffered defeat.   MISHNAH [15]

The Hands

Of Moses it is said that his hands were "steady" (17:12), literally they were אֱמוּנָה, faith. There is a faith which is only in the heart, and that is not enough. It must pervade the whole body, as with Moses whose hands "were faith."

R. NACHMAN OF BRATZLAV [16]

The reason that Moses' hands were heavy was due to sin: He had relegated the task of fighting Amalek to Joshua, rather than performing the mitzvah himself.   RASHI [17]

Allegory

And just as the two armies were about to engage in battle, a most marvelous miracle took place with respect to his hands; for they became by turns lighter and heavier. Then, whenever they were lighter, so that he could hold them up on high, the alliance between God and his people was strengthened, and waxed mighty, and became more glorious. But whenever his hands sank down the enemy prevailed, God showing thus by a figure that the earth and all the extremities of it were the appropriate inheritance of the one party and the most sacred air the inheritance of the other. And, as the heaven is in every respect

513

supreme to and superior over the earth, so also shall the nation which has heaven for its inheritance be superior to its enemies. PHILO [18]

The Throne of the Lord (Exod. 17:16)

The Hebrew words כֵּס יָה are both incomplete, the full reading would be כִּסֵּא יְהוָה. God swore that as long as Amalek exists, God's name and His throne cannot be whole. RASHI

Outsider

It took a Jethro, a non-Israelite, to come and say, "Blessed be the Lord" (18:10). (The inference is that it often takes others to turn us to God.)

MIDRASH [19]

True Judges

Jethro advises Moses to choose "capable men who fear God" (18:21)—who fear God, and not men. IBN EZRA

Amalek

The ancient Amalek has appeared and reappeared in Jewish history in many forms and guises: he wore the signet ring of the king as Haman; the royal crown as Antiochus; the general's uniform as Titus; the emperor's toga as Hadrian; the priestly robe as Torquemada; the cossack's boots as Chmielnitzki; or the brown shirt as Hitler. All of them had in common their hatred of Jews and Judaism, and they all failed in their objective to crush the faith and the people of God. W. G. P.

PART V

Revelation and Commandment

With deliverance accomplished the people now find themselves encamped before the holy mountain. While the Exodus from Egypt marked the birth of Israel as a *physical* nation, the experience at Sinai, which will now take place, provides the *spiritual* raison d'être of the nation. At Sinai, God reveals himself to the whole people; here He concludes His covenant with them; and here He promulgates the laws that are to govern Israel's existence. Revelation, Covenant, and Law are the three pillars upon which the structure of the people's history is reared. Without them, Israel would have been a nation like other nations; with them, it became a focal point of human destiny.

Revelation, the self-disclosure of God, is neither new in the biblical story as told up until now nor unknown in the annals of other religions. The Sinaitic revelation is singular in that it takes place before a whole people, who then act upon what they have seen and heard. No other people with a historical memory has set down such an experience for subsequent generations to read and relive, and no other people has apprehended the reasons for its existence in similar terms. "All that the Lord has spoken we will do!" (19:8) was a commitment which later generations understood to have bound them as well. It was a covenant, not merely for those who had witnessed its conclusion, "but both with those who are standing here with us this day before the Lord our God and with those who are not with us here this day," that is, with our descendants yet unknown (Deut. 29:14).

The revelation at Sinai differs markedly from private or personal meetings with the Divine in that it can be more closely related to history, in the sense in which modern man understands this term. Private revelation is not verifiable in the ordinary way, but public revelation is of a different kind. It is the Bible's claim that the theophany, the divine manifestation, was experienced by all the people. To those who deny the possibility of God's incursion into history in such a manner (and, of course, to those who deny God's existence altogether) such a claim has no historical validity. To them it was at best a religious interpretation of natural events —such as volcanic eruptions or some other, perhaps cosmic, occurrence. Or it may be considered by later generations as a retrojection of events as they imagined them to have happened, and who by this reconstruction gave a "historical" foundation to their religion. In the end, the matter comes down to what one believes rather than what one can prove to have

516

taken place. The foundations of Judaism as we have come to know them rest firmly on the tradition that the Lord of history revealed himself to one particular people and that in consequence of this revelation, and the compact which climaxed it, the people of Israel saw itself forever in the grasp of divine obligation. The law that became Israel's framework of life was seen as the tangible guideline for serving God's purposes. The content of this law and the extent to which it had indeed divine origin or sanction was and is often in doubt—various groupings within con-temporary Jewry as well as Christians and Moslems differ with each other in this respect—but the reality of the relationship of God to the governance of Israel remains a pivotal element of belief. Whether or not the events described in chapter 19 happened in exactly that fashion is of secondary significance; of primary importance is that "Sinai" in the sense of God revealing himself to Israel became the fundamental experience of the people, similar to their knowledge that the deliverance from Egypt was also the work of God. Thus, a new dimension is added to history: a whole people who walk through history as any other "natural" people have added the quality of a "supernatural" people to their wondrous existence. They live forever after on two planes that are yet one and the same, exposed to men and nations with their demands and exposed to God with His.

GLEANINGS

The Revelation

Just as Genesis is an explosive denial of the randomness of the physical universe, so the revelation at Sinai is a repudiation of the meaninglessness of history.   M. SAMUEL [1]

The One Revelation of the Absolute

Another characteristic evident in the Ten Commandments is the unity of the revelation. The revelation derives from God, the One, and thus includes all. The one spirit from which all spirit emanates, the eternal "I am," to which all belongs, speaks. Dualism, just as the worship of many gods, is rejected here and with it its tearing apart of worlds, its separating of the creative from the created, which caused so many cultures, particularly in antiquity, to die. Rather, there is a oneness and a wholeness to the cosmos, and therefore the world of goodness and light cannot be finally separated from the world of evil and darkness. As part of the cosmos it is entitled to receive possibility, sense, and a vocation. For everything is created by God, one revelation is in all—as the old story of Creation says: "God saw that it was good"; or, as a later, mystic imagery poetically states, some spark of the Divine is in all that lives. Creation means the great possibility.

   LEO BAECK [2]

Angels

When the angels protested that the Torah was entrusted to humans rather than to them, God said: "Were you, then, in Egyptian slavery?"

   TALMUD [3]

All Was Still

When God gave the Torah no bird sang, no fowl flew, no ox lowed, the sea ceased to roar, and all creatures were silent. The entire world was hushed into stillness and the Voice spoke forth: "I, the Lord...."

   MIDRASH [4]

What the People Heard

Each Israelite heard what was in his power to hear.   MIDRASH [5]

The Ungraspable

It lasted an eternity, it lasted an instant. It was an incident in human history not to be measured with the limited apprehension of man, but belonging to the province of the Eternal and the infinite of Divinity. And therefore it is impossible to speak of the duration of the exalted episode. Only when the voice of God ceased from speaking did the world fall back into its framework of time and space; and only then did Israel experience the fullness of fear. It was a peculiar dread of the ungraspable. They did not know where they were, whether on the earth or still hovering in space with God, held by an invisible power to the flying mountain.   S. ASCH [6]

Sinai

When Thou didst descend upon Sinai's
   mountain,
  It trembled and shook 'neath Thy mighty
   hand,
And the rocks were moved by Thy power and
   splendor:
  How then can my spirit before Thee stand
On the day when darkness o'erspread the
   heavens
  And the sun was hidden at Thy command?
The angels of God, for Thy great name's
   worship,
  Are ranged before Thee, a shining band,
And the children of men are awaiting ever
  Thy mercies unnumbered as grains of sand;

The Law they received from the mouth of Thy
    glory
  They learn and consider and understand.
O accept Thou their song and rejoice in their
    gladness
  Who proclaim Thy glory in every land.

J. HALEVI [7]

The Living and the Dead
  We received the Torah on Sinai
  and in Lublin we gave it back.
  Dead men don't praise God,
  the Torah was given to the living. . . .

And just as we all stood together
at the giving of the Torah,
so did we all die together in Lublin.
From all sides the souls came flocking,
The souls of those who had lived out their lives,
    of those
who had died young,
of those who were tortured, tested in every fire,
of those who were not yet born,
and of all the dead Jews from great-grandfather
    Abraham down,

they all came to Lublin for the great slaughter.
All those who stood at Mount Sinai
and received the Torah
took these holy deaths upon themselves.
"We want to perish with our whole people,
we want to be dead again,"
the ancient souls cried out.
Mama Sara, Mother Rachel,
Miriam and Deborah the prophetess
went down singing prayers and songs,
and even Moses, who so much didn't want to die
when his time came,
now died again.
And his brother, Aaron,
and King David
and the Rambam, the Vilna Gaon,
and Mahram and Maharshal,
the Seer and Abraham Eiger.
And with every holy soul
that perished in torture
hundreds of souls
of Jews long dead died with them. . . .

J. GLATSTEIN [8]

At Sinai

The Children of Israel arrive at Sinai and its surrounding area, called "the wilderness of Sinai." Everything that transpires from the beginning of chapter 19 through the rest of Exodus, all of Leviticus and Numbers up through 10:10 will be connected with this area: the theophany, the laws and priestly rules, the great rebellion with the building of the golden calf, and the planning and construction of the Tabernacle. Sinai is the locus for much of the Torah.

It must therefore appear passing strange that Jewish tradition has not preserved a firm tradition about the location of the sacred mountain. The Midrash lavished much attention on the question of why Mount Sinai was chosen above all other mountains, but beyond stating that it was not very high does not identify its location any further, and no other evidence is available to us to determine it conclusively.

The three theories that have been offered concerning Sinai and the route that led to it have been discussed in the commentary to Exod. 13:17–14:31. It may in fact be well to leave the question in abeyance altogether, for it is possible that the failure of Jewish tradition to preserve the knowledge of the locale had its deeper reason. The Torah states expressly (Deut. 34:6) that the place of Moses' grave remains unknown, presumably in order that it would not become a place of pilgrimage and the person of the lawgiver the object of adulation or even adoration. Similarly, had the locale of the holy mountain been firmly known in later centuries, Jerusalem and its Temple could never have become the center of Jewish life,

for they would have been inferior in holiness to the sacred mountain. Sinai thus became, either by design or happenstance, a concept rather than a place, its universal importance heightened by the vagueness of its site, its timelessness unfettered by an identifiable place.

The theophany described in chapter 19 contains some of the best known images of the Torah: protection of Israel is likened to being carried "on eagles' wings"; the people are distinguished as the Lord's "treasured possession"; and they are bidden to be "a kingdom of priests and a holy nation." The revelation is told in exalted, rhythmic language, denoting high tension, anticipation of events never before witnessed, "a dramatic picture, the details of which are not to be pressed" [1]. In the telling and retelling several old traditions were likely merged, which accounts for the occasional lack of sequence in the ascents and descents of Moses [2]. Withal, the story—in all its brevity—achieves its major goal: to convey to some degree the awesomeness of that moment when the Lord of the universe showed His glory to Israel and when He made His covenant with them, changing their history and the history of all men as well.

"The words were uttered not for one people alone, and not for one age, but for all peoples and for all generations until the end of time. And the Ten Commandments were a renewal of the act of creation; inasmuch as man and all else that lives issued from the first act of creation, so the continuation of life depends on the second act of creation, the giving of the law. And just as the first act of creation made a division between chaos and order, so the second act of creation made a division between good and evil, between right and wrong. From this day forth there would be a center of reference, a line of conduct, a standard whereby to measure good and evil in all the corners of the earth, for all men and for all generations until the coming of the great day of God" [3].

בַּחֹדֶשׁ הַשְּׁלִישִׁי לְצֵאת בְּנֵי־יִשְׂרָאֵל מֵאֶרֶץ מִצְרָיִם א
בַּיּוֹם הַזֶּה בָּאוּ מִדְבַּר סִינָי: וַיִּסְעוּ מֵרְפִידִים וַיָּבֹאוּ ב
מִדְבַּר סִינַי וַיַּחֲנוּ בַּמִּדְבָּר וַיִּחַן־שָׁם יִשְׂרָאֵל נֶגֶד הָהָר:
וּמֹשֶׁה עָלָה אֶל־הָאֱלֹהִים וַיִּקְרָא אֵלָיו יְהוָֹה מִן־הָהָר ג
לֵאמֹר כֹּה תֹאמַר לְבֵית יַעֲקֹב וְתַגֵּיד לִבְנֵי יִשְׂרָאֵל:
אַתֶּם רְאִיתֶם אֲשֶׁר עָשִׂיתִי לְמִצְרָיִם וָאֶשָּׂא אֶתְכֶם ד
עַל־כַּנְפֵי נְשָׁרִים וָאָבִא אֶתְכֶם אֵלָי: וְעַתָּה אִם־שָׁמוֹעַ ה

תִּשְׁמְעוּ בְּקֹלִי וּשְׁמַרְתֶּם אֶת־בְּרִיתִי וִהְיִיתֶם לִי סְגֻלָּה
מִכָּל־הָעַמִּים כִּי־לִי כָּל־הָאָרֶץ: וְאַתֶּם תִּהְיוּ־לִי ו
מַמְלֶכֶת כֹּהֲנִים וְגוֹי קָדוֹשׁ אֵלֶּה הַדְּבָרִים אֲשֶׁר
תְּדַבֵּר אֶל־בְּנֵי יִשְׂרָאֵל: וַיָּבֹא מֹשֶׁה וַיִּקְרָא לְזִקְנֵי ז
הָעָם וַיָּשֶׂם לִפְנֵיהֶם אֵת כָּל־הַדְּבָרִים הָאֵלֶּה אֲשֶׁר
צִוָּהוּ יְהוָֹה: וַיַּעֲנוּ כָל־הָעָם יַחְדָּו וַיֹּאמְרוּ כֹּל אֲשֶׁר־ ח
דִּבֶּר יְהוָֹה נַעֲשֶׂה וַיָּשֶׁב מֹשֶׁה אֶת־דִּבְרֵי הָעָם אֶל־

1] On the third new moon after the Israelites had gone forth from the land of Egypt, on that very day, they entered the wilderness of Sinai.   2] Having journeyed from Rephidim, they entered the wilderness of Sinai and encamped in the wilderness. Israel encamped there in front of the mountain,   3] and Moses went up to God. The LORD called to him from the mountain, saying, "Thus shall you say to the house of Jacob and declare to the children of Israel: 4] 'You have seen what I did to the Egyptians, how I bore you on eagles' wings and brought you to Me.   5] Now then, if you will obey Me faithfully and keep My covenant, you shall be My treasured possession among all the peoples. Indeed, all the earth is Mine,   6] but you shall be to Me a kingdom of priests and a holy nation.' These are the words that you shall speak to the children of Israel."

7] Moses came and summoned the elders of the people and put before them all the words that the LORD had commanded him.   8] All the people answered as one, saying, "All that the LORD has spoken we will do!" And Moses brought back the people's words to the LORD.

19:1] *On the third new moon.* The month of Sivan.

3] *Moses went up to God.* The image conveyed is that God has descended to or dwells in the lofty, inaccessible heights of this "mountain of God" (3:1).

Thus shall you say. As in 3:14–15, this is a solemn introduction to an important message. What follows is the core of Israel's relationship to God.

House of Jacob. בֵּית יַעֲקֹב (*Bet Ya-acov*), the first time this poetic synonym for Israel is used in the Bible. The Rabbis identified "House of Jacob" with the women and "Children of Israel" with the men [4].

4] *On eagles' wings.* Swiftly and securely. The image was dramatically concretized when in 1949 the Jews of Yemen, in southern Arabia, were transported en masse to Israel. Many believed their journey "on eagles' wings" to be a literal fulfillment of the biblical statement.

5] *Keep My covenant.* Which will be concluded

later, 24:3–8; or this refers to the covenant that God concluded with the Patriarchs, 6:4–8 [5].

Treasured possession. The King James Bible translated "peculiar treasure," a meaning based on the Latin *peculium* (private property), which in turn is derived from *pecus* (cattle), the original form of wealth. This linguistic connection reflects the probable relationship of the Hebrew *segullah* to the Akkadian *sugullu*, which has the double meaning of cattle and wealth [6].

6] *A kingdom of priests.* Ministering to the rest of humanity. This represented a unique idea: all the people and not merely a selected segment would have a special religious task.

A holy nation. גּוֹי קָדוֹשׁ (*goy kadosh*). Holiness requires a degree of separation, apartness. The word *goy* is a generic term here, and not referring to Gentiles, as in later parlance.

7] *Put before them.* To accept or reject.

8] *Moses brought back.* So far there has been no direct communication between God and Israel. Moses prepares the people for the theophany.

ט יְהוָֽה: וַיֹּ֨אמֶר יְהוָ֜ה אֶל־מֹשֶׁ֗ה הִנֵּ֨ה אָנֹכִ֜י בָּ֣א אֵלֶ֙יךָ֙ בְּעַ֣ב הֶֽעָנָ֔ן בַּעֲב֞וּר יִשְׁמַ֤ע הָעָם֙ בְּדַבְּרִ֣י עִמָּ֔ךְ וְגַם־בְּךָ֖ יַאֲמִ֣ינוּ לְעוֹלָ֑ם וַיַּגֵּ֥ד מֹשֶׁ֛ה אֶת־דִּבְרֵ֥י הָעָ֖ם אֶל־יְהוָֽה:

י וַיֹּ֨אמֶר יְהוָ֤ה אֶל־מֹשֶׁה֙ לֵ֣ךְ אֶל־הָעָ֔ם וְקִדַּשְׁתָּ֥ם הַיּ֖וֹם וּמָחָ֑ר וְכִבְּס֖וּ שִׂמְלֹתָֽם:

יא וְהָי֥וּ נְכֹנִ֖ים לַיּ֣וֹם הַשְּׁלִישִׁ֑י כִּ֣י בַּיּ֣וֹם הַשְּׁלִשִׁ֗י יֵרֵ֧ד יְהוָ֛ה לְעֵינֵ֥י כָל־הָעָ֖ם עַל־הַ֥ר סִינָֽי:

יב וְהִגְבַּלְתָּ֤ אֶת־הָעָם֙ סָבִ֣יב לֵאמֹ֔ר הִשָּׁמְר֥וּ לָכֶ֛ם עֲל֥וֹת בָּהָ֖ר וּנְגֹ֣עַ בְּקָצֵ֑הוּ כָּל־הַנֹּגֵ֥עַ בָּהָ֖ר מ֥וֹת יוּמָֽת:

יג לֹא־תִגַּ֨ע בּ֜וֹ יָ֗ד כִּֽי־סָק֤וֹל יִסָּקֵל֙ אֽוֹ־יָרֹ֣ה יִיָּרֶ֔ה אִם־

בְּהֵמָ֥ה אִם־אִ֖ישׁ לֹ֣א יִחְיֶ֑ה בִּמְשֹׁךְ֙ הַיֹּבֵ֔ל הֵ֖מָּה יַעֲל֥וּ בָהָֽר:

יד וַיֵּ֧רֶד מֹשֶׁ֛ה מִן־הָהָ֖ר אֶל־הָעָ֑ם וַיְקַדֵּשׁ֙ אֶת־הָעָ֔ם וַֽיְכַבְּס֖וּ שִׂמְלֹתָֽם:

טו וַיֹּ֙אמֶר֙ אֶל־הָעָ֔ם הֱי֥וּ נְכֹנִ֖ים לִשְׁלֹ֣שֶׁת יָמִ֑ים אַֽל־תִּגְּשׁ֖וּ אֶל־אִשָּֽׁה:

טז וַיְהִי֩ בַיּ֨וֹם הַשְּׁלִישִׁ֜י בִּֽהְיֹ֣ת הַבֹּ֗קֶר וַיְהִי֩ קֹלֹ֨ת וּבְרָקִ֜ים וְעָנָ֤ן כָּבֵד֙ עַל־הָהָ֔ר וְקֹ֥ל שֹׁפָ֖ר חָזָ֣ק מְאֹ֑ד וַיֶּחֱרַ֥ד כָּל־הָעָ֖ם אֲשֶׁ֥ר בַּֽמַּחֲנֶֽה:

יז וַיּוֹצֵ֨א מֹשֶׁ֧ה אֶת־הָעָ֛ם לִקְרַ֥את הָֽאֱלֹהִ֖ים מִן־הַֽמַּחֲנֶ֑ה וַיִּֽתְיַצְּב֖וּ בְּתַחְתִּ֥ית הָהָֽר:

יח וְהַ֤ר סִינַי֙ עָשַׁ֣ן כֻּלּ֔וֹ מִ֠פְּנֵי אֲשֶׁ֨ר יָרַ֥ד עָלָ֛יו יְהוָ֖ה בָּאֵ֑שׁ וַיַּ֤עַל עֲשָׁנוֹ֙ כְּעֶ֣שֶׁן הַכִּבְשָׁ֔ן

9] And the LORD said to Moses, "I will come to you in a thick cloud, in order that the people may hear when I speak with you and so trust you ever after." Then Moses reported the people's words to the LORD, 10] and the LORD said to Moses, "Go to the people and warn them to stay pure today and tomorrow. Let them wash their clothes. 11] Let them be ready for the third day; for on the third day the LORD will come down, in the sight of all the people, on Mount Sinai. 12] You shall set bounds for the people round about, saying, 'Beware of going up the mountain or touching the border of it. Whoever touches the mountain shall be put to death: 13] no hand shall touch him, but he shall be either stoned or shot; beast or man, he shall not live.' When the ram's horn sounds a long blast, they may go up on the mountain."

14] Moses came down from the mountain to the people and warned the people to stay pure, and they washed their clothes. 15] And he said to the people, "Be ready for the third day: do not go near a woman."

16] On the third day, as morning dawned, there was thunder, and lightning, and a dense cloud upon the mountain, and a very loud blast of the horn; and all the people who were in the camp trembled. 17] Moses led the people out of the camp toward God, and they took their places at the foot of the mountain.

18] Now Mount Sinai was all in smoke, for the LORD had come down upon it in fire; the smoke rose like the smoke of a kiln, and the whole mountain trembled violently. 19] The

---

9] *Then Moses reported*. The sequence of Moses' coming and going is not in order.

10] *To stay pure*. Literally, "sanctify them." Verses 14 and 15 define this as requiring ablutions and sexual abstinency.

13] *No hand shall touch him*. For he has himself become taboo, literally untouchable. Hence the death penalty is to be carried out from a distance, with stones or arrows. Some versions (as, for instance, King James) understand, "No hand shall touch *it*," that is, the mountain.

Ram's horn. יֹבֵל (yovel). The blast of a horn was also to mark the year of release (Lev. 25:8 ff.): hence that year was called *yovel* (jubilee).

Sounds a long blast. The Hebrew is uncertain.

15] *Do not go near a woman*. Intercourse was considered to cause ritual defilement, both partners needing ablution (Lev. 15:18).

16] *Horn*. Here called *shofar*, probably a synonym for *yovel* (verse 13).

18] *The whole mountain trembled*. The Septuagint and some manuscripts have "the whole *people* trembled."

כג יִתְקַדְּשׁוּ פֶּן־יִפְרֹץ בָּהֶם יְהוָה: וַיֹּאמֶר מֹשֶׁה אֶל־
יְהוָה לֹא־יוּכַל הָעָם לַעֲלֹת אֶל־הַר סִינָי כִּי־אַתָּה
כד הַעֵדֹתָה בָּנוּ לֵאמֹר הַגְבֵּל אֶת־הָהָר וְקִדַּשְׁתּוֹ: וַיֹּאמֶר
אֵלָיו יְהוָה לֶךְ־רֵד וְעָלִיתָ אַתָּה וְאַהֲרֹן עִמָּךְ וְהַכֹּהֲנִים
וְהָעָם אַל־יֶהֶרְסוּ לַעֲלֹת אֶל־יְהוָה פֶּן־יִפְרָץ־בָּם:
כה וַיֵּרֶד מֹשֶׁה אֶל־הָעָם וַיֹּאמֶר אֲלֵהֶם: ס

יט וַיֶּחֱרַד כָּל־הָהָר מְאֹד: וַיְהִי קוֹל הַשֹּׁפָר הוֹלֵךְ וְחָזֵק
כ מְאֹד מֹשֶׁה יְדַבֵּר וְהָאֱלֹהִים יַעֲנֶנּוּ בְקוֹל: וַיֵּרֶד
יְהוָה עַל־הַר סִינַי אֶל־רֹאשׁ הָהָר וַיִּקְרָא יְהוָה
כא לְמֹשֶׁה אֶל־רֹאשׁ הָהָר וַיַּעַל מֹשֶׁה: וַיֹּאמֶר יְהוָה
אֶל־מֹשֶׁה רֵד הָעֵד בָּעָם פֶּן־יֶהֶרְסוּ אֶל־יְהוָה לִרְאוֹת
כב וְנָפַל מִמֶּנּוּ רָב: וְגַם הַכֹּהֲנִים הַנִּגָּשִׁים אֶל־יְהוָה

blare of the horn grew louder and louder. As Moses spoke, God answered him in thunder.
20] The LORD came down upon Mount Sinai, on the top of the mountain, and the LORD called
Moses to the top of the mountain and Moses went up.　21] The LORD said to Moses, "Go
down, warn the people not to break through to the LORD to gaze, lest many of them
perish.　22] The priests also, who come near the LORD, must purify themselves, lest the LORD
break out against them."　23] But Moses said to the LORD, "The people cannot come up to
Mount Sinai, for You warned us saying, 'Set bounds about the mountain and sanctify it.'"
24] So the LORD said to him, "Go down, and come back together with Aaron; but let not the
priests or the people break through to come up to the LORD, lest He break out against
them."　25] And Moses went down to the people and spoke to them.

22] *The priests also.* While their usual task is to
"come near" to God (קָרְבָּן, sacrifice, has this basic
meaning), they must in this instance stay with
the people.

24] *So the Lord said.* Insisting that Moses repeat
the warning.

25] *And spoke to them.* The word לֵאמֹר is usually
followed by what is said, but occasionally this is
omitted, as here and in Gen. 4:8 .

The Covenant

Compacts or covenants between equal individuals have since the dawn of legal history been the foundation of civil law in general and commercial law in particular. When concluded between equal nations they have become the substance of international relations. Covenants between unequals are rarer but they too are attested in history. Such covenants, concluded between kings and their inferiors, especially victors and vanquished, are found in ancient Near Eastern records.

Among these, the Hittite vassal treaties between sovereign and subject-king (dating from the middle of the second millennium B.C.E.) appear to offer the closest parallel to the covenant God as sovereign concludes with Israel. Such covenants were usually of a tripartite construction: they began with a preamble and a historical prologue (listing blessings bestowed by the sovereign); then followed stipulations (including the promise by the protected not to enter into treaty with anyone but the protector); then a public reading, listing of witnesses, and sanctions (like curses and blessings). Many of these elements may be found in the covenant now to be concluded between God and Israel:[1] "I am the Lord your God" (preamble), "who brought you out..." (benefits bestowed); "You shall have no other gods" (exclusive protectorate), plus the other conditions listed as commandments; the public rehearsal of the covenant (24:3 ff.), and blessings and curses (23:20 ff.). The introduction to the covenant (19:3–6) lays the general foundation and describes the ultimate result of Israel's faithful adherence to its terms. The similarity of these forms to those of ancient Near Eastern models is striking.

One may therefore assume that the theophany and its sequel were seen by the people in a setting with which they were familiar: the divine King covenanting with those whom He promises to protect [7]. (See Gleanings for example of a Hittite treaty.)

If the framework of the compact was not new, neither were all its contents. The Code of Hammurabi and the legal system of Egypt contained prescriptions that dealt with the protection of persons and property rights and the basic organization of society. What then was new? What set this covenant apart from all others in human history, making it the foundation of Jewish existence and much of Christian, Moslem, and modern Western civilization?

It was, in Kaufmann's words, "in the very giving. For the first time morality was represented as a prophetic revelation, an expression of the supreme moral will of God" [8]. Furthermore, God revealed His will at this moment not to a selected prophet alone, or to a privileged class of priests, but to the whole people, and they in turn became together answerable for the terms of the covenant. They gave assent to the Torah they heard, and thus they made God's law their own. In this way the covenant at Sinai became the permanent incursion of God into the lives of a nation that pledged its faith to Him. The Children of Israel did it then and, despite lapses of commitment and practice, have continued to acknowledge the binding nature of the compact. Their experience profoundly influenced other nations and cultures across the centuries, but none of them felt the force of Sinai in the same way or with the same consequences.

For to Israel the Presence and the Word implied specific commands, laws that shaped

---

1 "Covenant" is here used to cover the text in Exod. 19:1–24:18, i.e., the preparation (chapter 19), the Decalogue and its postlude (20:1–18), and the section specifically called the "Book of the Covenant" (21:19–24:18).

its society then and thereafter. In biblical and postbiblical history, revelation meant divine command and covenant the existence of law. Sinai meant that Israel knew both the existence of the living God and at the same time that special demands were made by Him of His people. They knew, for they had become recipients of God's grace and its witnesses to history. The covenant that the King of Kings had concluded with them had its roots in His mysterious will, and not in Israel's merit. It was proclaimed in history's Great Moment, and in the Jewish conception this moment has not yet passed completely. Each generation, says tradition, should consider as if it itself were standing at Sinai, still hearing the thunder and the horn and the Voice proclaiming "I am the Lord."

The Chosen People

"You shall be My treasured possession among all the peoples" (19:5). This promise of special election or chosenness has been a core factor of Jewish life for thousands of years. In times of stress it was a source of hope and reassurance, and Jewish survival might not have been possible without the conviction that Israel was indeed God's beloved, destined for high purpose and spiritual glory [9]. From this, some have drawn the conclusion that in fact the concept of the Chosen People was essentially a survival mechanism, and that the biblical phrase—whatever it meant in its day—became the foundation for self-exaltation, religious conceit, and a false sense of superiority on the part of Jews, as well as a cause for contempt and even hatred on the part of non-Jews. Consequently, so it is held, in an age which decries inequality of every kind, the doctrine of special election has no further place and

should forthwith be disavowed. It had its role, but no longer; it was productive, but has become counterproductive. Jews and Gentiles both view it with suspicion [10].

Even in this negative evaluation the doctrine of election appears as a factor of surpassing importance. In the theophany as well as in the prophetic books of the Bible it provides the framework of God's relationship with the Children of Israel. He has singled them out, but He also makes special demands on them. They will have to conform to a standard set for no other people, and their failure to reach it will have dire consequences. Israel, of course, entered the compact of their own free will; they chose God even as He chose them. They were not the only ones given this opportunity, says the Midrash. The chance to accept the Torah was offered to every nation, and it was for this reason also that the Torah was given in the desert, in a public place accessible to all. Only Israel said: "All that the Lord has spoken we will do."[2]

To be sure, Israel's free will was not entirely free. When meeting God one is no longer in the realm of unlimited choice; the encounter leaves man with demands that can be rejected only at his peril. This is the meaning of the midrashic tale which pictures Israel at Sinai and God holding up the mountain above the people. "If you accept my Torah," He says, "well and good; but, if not, I will place the mountain over you like a kettle, and here shall be your grave" [11]. In one way or another, then, Israel has dwelt under the obligation of election. How much of this was the result of later interpretation and reinforcement is hard to say, but the overwhelming experience of Sinai gives strength to the belief that here the sense of being God's particular possession was first expe-

---

[2] See Gleanings, "Offered to Others."

rienced by all the people. They may each have heard the message differently [12]—some in accents of physical abundance and others of spiritual opportunity—but the uniqueness of God's care for and love of Israel suffused the vision. Israel was to be a holy people, set apart for this service. This would entail great happiness as well as deep suffering, hope as well as despair. The privilege conferred on Israel was the privilege of dwelling in the court of the Almighty, always ready for every task, prepared to do His bidding. In the biblical text, therefore, the revelation is followed by laws, from the exalted rules of the Decalogue to ordinary regulations governing diverse matters. In the conceptual world of the Torah (as well as post-Torah Judaism) God is served not so much with principles and pronouncements of faith as with mitzvot, deeds with which to approach the ineffable Presence as the God who hears prayers and who protects His people.

GLEANINGS

Hittite Vassal Treaty

[Excerpts from the final portion, containing blessings and curses, of the treaty between Suppiluliumas and Mattiwaza.]

If you, Mattiwaza, the prince, and you the sons of the Hurri country do not fulfill the words of this treaty, may the gods, the lords of the oath, blot you out, you Mattiwaza and you the Hurri men together with your country, your wives, and all that you have. May they draw you like malt from its hull. . . . May the soil of your country be a hardened quagmire so that you break in, but never get across. May you, Mattiwaza, and you, the Hurrians, be hateful to the thousand gods; may they pursue you.

If on the other hand you, Mattiwaza, the prince, and you, the Hurrians, fulfill this treaty and this oath, may these gods protect you, Mattiwaza, together with your wife, the daughter of the Hatti land, her children, and her children's children, and also you, the Hurrians, together with your wives, your children, and your children's children and together with your country. May the Mitanni country return to the place which it occupied before, may it thrive and expand. May you, Mattiwaza, your sons, and your sons' sons, descended from the daughter of the Great King of the Hatti land, and you, the Hurrians, exercise kingship forever. May the throne of your father persist, may the Mitanni country persist [13].

The Poet's Voice

Then the Lord thundered from heaven,
The Most High gave forth His voice—
Hail and fiery coals.
He let fly His shafts and scattered them:
He discharged lightning and routed them.

PSALM 18:14–15

Peace

All verbs at the start of the chapter (verses 1 and 2) are in the plural except the last: "Israel encamped there (וַיִּחַן) in front of the mountain." This shows that now they were of one heart and mind and had peace amongst them. God delayed giving the Torah until then.   MIDRASH [14]

Women First

Why did God mention the "House of Jacob" (that is, in the rabbinic interpretation, the women; see above at verse 3) before the "Children of Israel" (the men)? Because women are prompter in fulfilling the commandments. Another explanation: Because they will teach the children.

MIDRASH [15]

[That is, either by teaching them or by taking them to school.]

A Figure of Speech

According to Rabbi Jose (second century C.E.), the Shechinah never descended and Moses never ascended on high. "The heavens are the heavens of God, but the earth has He given to the children of men" (Ps. 115:16).   TALMUD [16]

[R. Jose maintained an opinion unpopular in his day, namely, that the biblical account is to be taken figuratively rather than literally. "Moses ascended" is to be understood as "Moses was raised high," that is, he was exalted by God above other men.]

But Once

God says (19:5): "If you will obey Me faithfully . . . you shall be My treasured possession." The Hebrew, taken literally, conveys: "If to obey, you will obey. . . ." This implies: If you will

528

hearken but once you will continue to hearken. All beginnings are hard. RASHI [17]

[In the Bible, the linking of an infinitive absolute to the regularly conjugated form of verb (שָׁמוֹעַ תִּשְׁמְעוּ) is a common idiomatic device to produce emphasis. The older JPS translation had "listen to My voice indeed."]

Israel's Distinction

God said to Israel: Your distinction will not lie in doing the kinds of things other nations do, in a natural way; your accomplishments will be brought about through mitzvot and prayer.

Others will look at your election and wonder why you deserved it. They should know that your choice as God's treasure is conditional and depends on your being a kingdom of priests. YALKUT ME'AM LO'EZ [18]

God's love for Israel, like its election, is unfathomable. Human rationality is not applicable to it. CHASIDIC [19]

Fire

God came down on Mt. Sinai "in fire" (verse 18). This teaches that the Torah is fire. If one draws too near one gets burned; if one stays too far away one gets cold. MIDRASH [20]

Sinai's Choice

The mountains quarreled with each other, each wanting the Shechinah to rest on it. Each extolled its own height and distinction. God said: My presence will rest on Sinai, the smallest and most insignificant of all. In this, Sinai resembled the humility of Moses who did not want to accept the mantle of leadership. MIDRASH [21]

Offered to Others

When other nations were asked to accept the Torah they declined after learning that its commands contradicted their national practices. But Israel accepted the Torah even before it had heard its full demands and said "We will do and listen" —they promised to carry out God's will before they had learned its demands. MIDRASH [22]

[Taking 24:7 (נַעֲשֶׂה וְנִשְׁמָע) literally, in sequence.]

Bondsmen

Even so, God hesitated to give the Torah to Israel and asked for bondsmen who would guarantee its observance. Israel offered the Patriarchs and the Prophets and, some say, heaven and earth. But God deemed all of these pledges insufficient. The Israelites then offered their children, including the unborn, and God agreed. MIDRASH [23]

In a Public Place

Why was the Torah not given in the land of Israel? In order that the nations of the world should not have an excuse and say: "Because it was given in Israel's land, therefore we did not accept it." Another reason: To avoid causing dissension among the tribes. Else one might have said: "In my territory the Torah was given." And another might have said: "In my territory the Torah was given." Therefore, the Torah was given in the desert, publicly and openly, in a place belonging to no one. MIDRASH [24]

Tomorrow

Israel was to "stay pure today and tomorrow" (verse 10). "Today" was easy—at Sinai (or with us, at prayer); but "tomorrow" was and is hard—when going out into the every day. There is the test. M. HACOHEN [25]

Coming Down

"Moses came down" (verse 14), for the leader must descend and sanctify himself alongside the people. M. HACOHEN [26]

Down and Up

It says "Go down and come back" (verse 24). In one's approach to God there is no straight way of going up: it is always ascent and descent and ascent. Hence, authentic repentance—"down" and then "up"—is greater than constant piety. CHASIDIC [27]

Everything

All authentic interpretations of Jewish tradition in ages to come were implied in the original revelation at Sinai. MIDRASH [28]

The Whole People

No one can by himself observe all the commandments, for some are addressed to priests, others to women, to owners of fields and houses, and so forth. Only all of Israel together can do God's will completely, hence "all the people answered as one" (verse 8).

THE GAON OF VILNA [29]

Mattan Torah

The word revelation is not traditionally Jewish. The Hebrew term is *mattan Torah*, the gift of Torah. This gift hides no mystery. In the blessing over the Torah it says "Who has given us the Torah" and God is called "Giver of the Torah" in the liturgical formulation. No reference to mystery, no unveiling (revelation). God gives the Torah as He gives all else: life and bread and also death.

H. COHEN [30]

The Thick Silence

Only in moments when we are able to share in the spirit of awe that fills the world are we able to understand what happened to Israel at Sinai. Revelation means that the thick silence which fills the endless distance between God and the human mind was pierced, and man was told that God is concerned with the affairs of man; that not only does man need God, God is also in need of man. It is such knowledge that makes the soul of Israel immune to despair.

A. J. HESCHEL [31]

All the People

One word is spoken emphatically here. Ever since, in contemplation and in will, it has had special emphasis: "the people," "all the people." That is the fundamental principle. The people received this revelation here. Not just chosen ones within it, but the people as a whole, as one individuality, was placed into obligation, into responsibility, into unified existence. There are no representatives here, no one who could assume the task for others. This people's appearance was immediate and complete, then and always.

LEO BAECK [32]

Sinai Today

A Jew, by the very condition of his Jewishness, pays the continuing price of Sinai. If Jewishness remains his fate, Judaism remains the framework of his native spiritual existence and God his partner. And therefore, as long as the people as a continuing organism in history keep alive the consciousness of Sinai, each Jew can find his roots. The *berit* was his father's, but it is his also. Each generation should regard itself as standing at Sinai, says the Passover ritual. This is no empty phrase; it is a challenge thrust before the doubting as well as the believing: "You are what you are. Accept yourself, fulfill your destiny by making the eternal potential the actuality of your life. You are a Jew. Therefore, live as one in depth and meaning as well as in name!"

W. G. P. [33]

The Word Eternal

And then the lightning and the unbridled
    storms
Upon the mount crouched in obedience to the
    will
That moves in silence. He stood close upon
The margin of my soul, and I outstretched
To that dim verge of spirit where
A man meets God speechless with him held
    speech.
Swift as the leap and pointing of a flame
He graved his word in fire within my mind,
The word eternal—though transient his stay
As shadow of a leaf upon a leaf.

A. K. BLANK [34]

O hear dat lumberin' thunder
A-roll f'om door to door,
A-callin' de people home to God,
Dey'll git home bime-by.

O see dat forked lightnin'
A-jump f'om cloud to cloud,
A-pickin' up God's chillun,
Dey'll git home bime-by.

AMERICAN SPIRITUAL

The Decalogue—
General Introduction; The First
Three Commandments

I

We have reached the climax of the Book of Exodus, the crowning moment, when God reveals himself to Israel. "Now all is still. There is no further mention of thunder, or lightning, or the sound of the horn, or of anything similar. All the forces of nature remain tranquil, and everything bespeaks the divine glory. And out of the amazing stillness that prevailed after the fearful storm are heard the words of the Lord who speaks to His people and makes known to them the fundamentals of His Torah" [1]. These fundamentals—which still need the particulars of specific legislation to make them applicable to everyday life—are commonly called the Ten Commandments or Decalogue. In several Torah passages the Hebrew term עֲשֶׂרֶת הַדְּבָרִים (*aseret ha-devarim*), literally, "a decade of words," is used.[1] The word "decalogue" was first applied by a Greek Church Father, Clement of Alexandria, about 200 C.E.

While in prevailing Jewish and Christian traditions the Decalogue is always identified with Exod. 20:1–14 (or its parallel in Deut. 5), there have been dissident opinions which hold that the words inscribed on the tablets were not those of this chapter but were from another "Decalogue," and most likely the ritual prescriptions of Exod. 34:14–26. This assumption was first put forward by a fifth-century writer, then vigorously pursued by the youthful J. W. von Goethe and later taken up by J. Wellhausen

---

[1] Exod. 34:28; Deut. 4:13; 10:4. On the translation of דְּבָרִים as either "words" or "commandments," see commentary to verse 1.

531

and the school of biblical criticism known by his name [2]. The theory had certain aspects to recommend it: the section in Exod. 34 has an introduction that sets it into a covenantal framework (verses 10–13); it has a conclusion in which Moses is bidden to write the commandments down, and it reports that he did in fact write them on tablets (verses 27 and 28); and, further, these passages contain a terse set of rules dealing with idolatry, mixed marriage, Passover, first-born and first fruits, the Sabbath, other festivals, and prohibitions of offering blood and boiling a kid in its mother's milk. But the theory has great drawbacks.

First, it was usually tied to the premise that the "ritual" covenant here pronounced—because it was "mere ritual"—must have antedated the "ethical" rules that dominate the traditionally acknowledged Decalogue. This assumption—that Judaism proceeded from "lower" or ritual rules to "higher" or ethical rules and that therefore the covenant of Exod. 34 must have preceded that of Exod. 20—was part and parcel of certain nineteenth-century beliefs about history. Such notions find limited support nowadays when it is recognized that great spiritual and intellectual advances do not necessarily follow a developmental line that rises from primitive beginnings through various stages to higher levels.[2] Rather, so it is now believed, such leaps occur because they may represent true mutations (to speak in evolutionary terms) or because they signify the unpredictable meeting between God and man (to speak in terms of religion). The choice of Abraham and the meeting of Moses and God—and indeed of Israel and God—arose because the partners were ready for each other. The results were spiritual breakthroughs without precedent or traceable preparation.

Second, the whole weight of postbiblical tradition which identifies the Decalogue as the ten words contained in Exod. 20 (and repeated substantially in Deut. 5) must be decisive. These soaring phrases have been called "the universal alphabet of religion for all mankind" [3], and they alone are the truly fitting climax of the theophany and the majestic introduction of the code to follow. They must be the words that the

---

[2] In fact, the whole notion of what is primitive is an aspect of contemporary taste rather than historical scholarship, even as is the labeling of ritual rules as more primitive than ethical norms. Furthermore, a separation of ritual (or cultic) and ethical laws is foreign to the spirit of the Torah, which fuses them even as it does positive and negative commandments.

tablets contained and they have retained their place of eminence long after the stones were destroyed [4].

II

Biblical scholars have also wondered whether the Ten Words as we have them now are perhaps an enlargement of an original, simpler formulation which did not know of the retributions and rewards of verses 5 and 6, or the reasons given in verses 7 and 11,[3] or the reward promised in verse 12, or the expansion of verse 14 after the words "your neighbor's house." This is a strong possibility, but it would not affect the antiquity of the basic commandments or prove that the Ten Words were post-Mosaic. The person of Moses remains inextricably connected with the theophany and its climactic proclamation.[4]

Nonetheless, the dictum by Ibn Ezra that the chapter presents many difficult questions is well founded. There is the matter of the two different versions of the commandments in Exod. 20 and Deut. 5.[5] In so vital a matter as the formulation of the divine revelation one would expect—in view of the careful manner in which tradition transmitted all sacred texts —that the Ten Words above all would be preserved precisely. Quite evidently, then, there was no single sure text on which our forebears could base themselves because several traditions had developed, probably because they were expansions of earlier formulations. In an old document,

[3] If the earliest form of the Sabbath commandment confined itself to the injunction itself, the fact that Exod. 20:11 gives creation as the reason for observance and Deut. 5:15 provides a socio-historic explanation would not affect the identity of the two versions in their basic forms.

[4] H. H. Rowley writes: "An ethical Decalogue is in harmony with the whole character of the bond between Israel and God which Moses mediated. YHVH had chosen Israel and delivered her from Egypt; Israel in response committed herself in loyalty and obedience to Him. That is the essence of Israel's covenant with God. It rested on her recognition of what God had done and on her gratitude to Him for His mercy. . . . There was thus an ethical strand in the very establishment of the religion of Israel through Moses since gratitude is essentially an ethical emotion. . . . It is therefore wholly consonant with the conditions of the time that the fundamental demands of the religion established through Moses should be couched in ethical terms, and far more likely that in such a moment and through such a man this great advance should be made than that it should just happen somehow by itself at some unknown time and in some unknown way" [5].

[5] The rabbinic explanation was that the two versions were uttered simultaneously, in a fashion transcending human understanding [6]. The differences between the texts will be analyzed in detail in our commentary on Deuteronomy.

the so-called Nash papyrus, which seems to have been written in the second or first century B.C.E., the text is identical with neither the Exodus nor the Deuteronomy version, as we have it; for instance, it lists the prohibition of adultery before that of murder.

Further, the division of the commandments themselves is not certain. There are altogether thirteen sentences in the accepted Jewish versions (seventeen in the Christian)[6] but we cannot conclude from the text itself what comprises the first commandment, what the second, and so forth. For while there are thirteen mitzvot to be found in the text, their allocation to ten commandments can be done in various ways. It is not surprising, therefore, that there are different traditions in this respect. The prevailing Jewish division is as follows [7]:

1st commandment: "I am the Lord . . ." (verse 2); this may be considered a preamble, implying the duty to believe in God;[7]

2nd commandment: "You shall have no other gods beside Me.
You shall not make for yourself a sculptured image . . ." (verses 3–6);

3rd commandment: "You shall not swear falsely . . ." (verse 7);

4th commandment: "Remember the sabbath day . . ." (verses 8–11);

5th commandment: "Honor your father and your mother" (verse 12);

6th commandment: "You shall not murder" (verse 13);

7th commandment: "You shall not commit adultery" (verse 13);

8th commandment: "You shall not steal" (verse 13);

9th commandment: "You shall not bear false witness . . ." (verse 13);

10th commandment: "You shall not covet . . ." (verse 14).

However, such ancient writers as Philo and Josephus, as well as the new JPS translation, the Greek Church Fathers, and most Protestant churches (except the Lutherans), consider the first commandment to be: "I am the Lord your God. . . . You shall have no other gods before Me" (verses 2 and 3).

---

[6] In most Jewish versions the commandments regarding murder, adultery, theft, and false witness all are part of verse 13, while in Christian versions they are numbered 13–16.

[7] It is, of course, also possible to understand verse 2 as a preamble only, in the manner of ancient Near Eastern monumental (or royal) inscriptions which usually begin with the introduction of the king in the first person singular (cf. Gen. 15:7). This would make verse 3

That is to say, God's existence, and His relation to Israel, and the prohibition of worshiping other gods are seen as belonging together, while the prohibition of idolatry forms the second commandment.

Another division, going back to Augustine, is used in the Roman Catholic and Lutheran churches. This follows the written text of Torah scrolls and combines verses 2 to 6 into one commandment, that is, it includes the prohibition of idolatry in the first of the commandments. And further, as in Torah scrolls, it divides the last phrase (verse 14 in Jewish, verse 17 in Christian versions) into two parts:

9th commandment: "You shall not covet your neighbor's house";
10th commandment: "You shall not covet your neighbor's wife. . . ."

III

There are further problems. In the first and second commandments God speaks of himself in the first person and thereafter in the third. However, consistency is not at all a hallmark of ancient writing. Biblical style does not conform to rules which later on were thought to be necessary. It is equally possible to say that in the beginning of the Decalogue God establishes himself as the Source of Being and thereafter reverts to a more "objective" language. Still, it was perhaps this stylistic shift or some of the other problems we noted that moved some talmudic scholars to suggest that only the first two commandments—in which God speaks in the first person—were heard by Israel directly from Him and that the others were mediated by Moses [8]. This view was taken up and expounded by the Christian Scriptures which in various places consider the entire Decalogue mediated [9]. These uncertainties caused Franz Rosenzweig to say that in the end one who wishes to believe in the reality of the theophany and yet wants to take account of all literary and historical difficulties will have to conclude: All that the people themselves experienced immediately and not through mediation was *God's overwhelming Presence*, which caused them to accept Him as the demanding force in their lives. The words themselves came to them through Moses and in time were given

the first commandment and require a division in order to arrive at ten commandments.
either after verse 3 or in the middle of verse 14

variant expressions—hence the uncertainties about order and division, or the differential formulation in Deuteronomy.[8] Such a view conforms with the general approach of this commentary regarding the nature of the Torah as a document that is both of God and of man.[9]

IV

The Ten Commandments are rooted in the covenant relationship. "This relationship is understood to have been initiated by a saving God who has demonstrated His graciousness and His authority in the deliverance of His people from Egyptian slavery. Obedience to the fundamental covenant law is thus an obedience born of gratitude and praise, not servile submission to an arbitrary or capricious Deity" [11]. The first four commandments regarding God the Redeemer, the One God, the use of God's name, and the observance of the Sabbath as God's day deal with man's relation to the Divine; the other six deal with the fundamentals of human society. They are presented as apodictic (that is, unconditionally applicable rules for human behavior),[10] and for Israel they represent, so to speak, the constitutional preamble to its code of laws which will follow in subsequent chapters. It is important to stress this function of the Decalogue, because it was never meant to stand alone as a complete repository of rules for life. It is a basic summation and must not be considered a substitute for detailed laws and ordinances. In memorable phrases it tersely states a set of principles that are not hedged in by cultic requirements or case law. Its impact on Western civilization has been incalculable and, in the history of law, without compare. Even in the jeweled crown of the Torah it shines with unmatched brilliance.

Yet there is more than language and content. G. E. Mendenhall em-

[8] According to Rosenzweig they apprehended directly that God "came down"; but "He spoke" or "I the Lord" came to them through Moses. A similar view was held by the chasidic teacher Mendel of Rymanov. He suggested that Israel at Sinai heard only the letter Alef, i.e., the first letter of the opening word of the Decalogue. According to Maimonides, Israel heard only inarticulate words which Moses had to interpret [10].

[9] See General Introduction to the Torah.

[10] In contrast to casuistic rules that are phrased conditionally, as if in response to precedent. For instance: "If you take your neighbor's garment in pledge, you must return it to him before the sun sets" (Exod. 22:25).

536

phasizes a third element and ascribes to it great importance in securing for the Decalogue its unique place in human history:

"There is nothing in the Decalogue that constitutes any new or profound philosophical insight into ethics or law. It is not in the content, but in functional relationships, that the Decalogue constitutes a revolutionary movement in human history. A covenant is not necessary to establish unity among a kin-bound group, particularly in Near Eastern history. On the other hand, a kinship-bound group is not likely to change the entire ideological basis of its religion, particularly when the 'new God' has already been proclaimed to be the 'god of your fathers.' What happened at Sinai was the formation of a new unity where none had existed before, a 'peace of God' among a mixed multitude and tribally affiliated families who had in common only the deliverance from an intolerable political monopoly of force. Perhaps for the first time in history, a real elevation to a new and unfamiliar ground in the formation of a community took place—a formation based on common obligations rather than common interests, on ethic rather than on covetousness" [12].

The tablets with the Ten Words inscribed on them were placed by Moses in the Ark of the Covenant (Deut. 10:5). These were the tablets that were substituted for the original ones broken during the incident of the golden calf (Exod. 32:19). (In Jewish tradition the first five commandments were believed to have been inscribed on one tablet, and the remaining five on the other.[11] This division recommended itself because the first five speak of God and the last five do not mention His name. The fifth commandment, dealing with honor due to parents, was seen as a fitting conclusion to the first section, for the parents are in fact assisting God in the creation and education of their children [13].) The final fate of the tablets (as of the ark) is not known. They were no longer in the Second Temple, and Jewish legend has it that King Josiah had hidden them to save them from desecration by the enemy, or that Jeremiah had secreted them on Mount Nebo [14].

A depiction of what the tablets might have looked like is found in most synagogues, usually above the ark which contains the scrolls. This depiction of rectangular tablets with rounded tops resembles both the

---

[11] In Roman Catholic depictions (in accordance with the Catholic division of the commandments), three are on one tablet and seven on the other.

shape of typical old Jewish tombstones and monumental steles and boundary markers in the ancient Near East [15]. The text of the Decalogue is read during the weekly portions *Yitro* (of which Exod. 20 forms the conclusion) and *Va-etchanan* (which contains Deut. 5), and also on the festival of Shavuot which is celebrated on the 6th of Sivan, the day which in tradition marks the proclamation of the Torah. In ancient times its reading was part of a regular, perhaps annual, ritual of renewing the covenant (Deut. 31:10) and may have constituted its climax.[12] Jewish congregations rise when they listen to the Ten Words, a mark of special respect accorded only to one other biblical passage—the Song at the Sea (Exod. 15). The latter celebrates the physical salvation of Israel, the Decalogue its abiding spiritual foundation [17].

---

[12] In the days of the Second Temple the reading of the Decalogue was included in the daily ritual of the Temple but prohibited as a regular part of daily worship outside the Temple, to counteract the contention of certain sectarians that only the Ten Words were divinely revealed [16]. To this day, the Decalogue is not part of the statutory daily liturgy.

א וַיְדַבֵּר אֱלֹהִים אֵת כָּל־הַדְּבָרִים הָאֵלֶּה לֵאמֹר: ס
ב אָנֹכִי יְהוָה אֱלֹהֶיךָ אֲשֶׁר הוֹצֵאתִיךָ מֵאֶרֶץ מִצְרַיִם
ג מִבֵּית עֲבָדִים: לֹא־יִהְיֶה לְךָ אֱלֹהִים אֲחֵרִים עַל־
ד פָּנָי: לֹא־תַעֲשֶׂה לְךָ פֶסֶל וְכָל־תְּמוּנָה אֲשֶׁר בַּשָּׁמַיִם
מִמַּעַל וַאֲשֶׁר בָּאָרֶץ מִתַּחַת וַאֲשֶׁר בַּמַּיִם מִתַּחַת
ה לָאָרֶץ: לֹא־תִשְׁתַּחֲוֶה לָהֶם וְלֹא תָעָבְדֵם כִּי אָנֹכִי

1] God spoke all these words, saying:

2] I the LORD am your God who brought you out of the land of Egypt, the house of bondage: **3]** You shall have no other gods beside Me.

4] You shall not make for yourself a sculptured image, or any likeness of what is in the heavens above, or on the earth below, or in the waters under the earth. **5]** You shall not bow down to them or serve them. For I the LORD your God am an impassioned God, visiting the

20:1] *Words.* דְּבָרִים (*devarim*), an expression that is broader than "commandments" (מִשְׁפָּטִים, חֻקִּים, מִצְוֺת). The number ten is applied to these words in Exod. 34:28, Deut. 4:13 and 10:4, and the term עֲשֶׂרֶת הַדְּבָרִים occurs as late as the second century C.E. [18]. The current Hebrew expression for Ten Words or Ten Commandments, עֲשֶׂרֶת הַדִּבְּרוֹת, is first found in the Talmud [19].

2] *1.* אָנֹכִי (*anochi*) has the same meaning as the more frequent אֲנִי (*ani*). It occurs especially in several stories of revelation: with Abraham (Gen. 15:1), Isaac (Gen. 26:24), Jacob (Gen. 31:13), Moses (Exod. 3:6). אָנֹכִי is the Hebrew version of a first person pronoun common to both Semitic and Hamitic languages (Akkadian *anaku*, Ugaritic *'ank*, Egyptian *'ink*). The Rabbis intuitively took it to be of possible Egyptian derivation, speculating that God addressed them to begin with in a language they knew well [20].

I the Lord. Other versions, "I am the Lord." The introductory phrase resembles ancient Near Eastern preambles; for instance: "Hammurabi, the shepherd, called by Enlil, am I"; or "I am Mesha, son of Chemosh . . . King of Moab, the Dibonite" [21].

Your God. In Hebrew, the singular "your" (*ton* in French; *dein* in German). Even though the whole people are addressed, the syntactical focus appears to be on each individual.

Who brought you. God's claim on Israel is as its Redeemer, not as Creator. The freedom He has brought the people is the necessary foundation for the covenant.

3] *No other gods.* The second commandment, establishing the singularity of YHVH, although the addition "beside Me" appears to weaken the main statement (see footnote 3 to commentary). In Genesis, other gods are not prohibited, leading to the supposition that monotheism's beginnings are to be connected with Moses [22]. Ibn Ezra warns that this commandment must not be transgressed even in one's thought.

4] *Sculptured image.* With the intent to adore it as a real or surrogate god. There is no prohibition here of the plastic arts as such, else verse 5 would be unnecessary. However, the strict attention given to the commandment by Jews precluded the type of religious art developed by the Christian church and for a long time restricted other forms of sculpture.

In the heavens above. Meaning anything, anywhere. The division into heaven, earth, and water focuses on the chief targets of the prohibition: heavenly bodies, animals, and fish—all of which were worshiped among ancient nations.

5] *Bow down . . . serve.* A biblical idiom for religious practice.

Impassioned God. Denoting passion rather than possessiveness and suggested by Luzzatto, who

יְהֹוָה אֱלֹהֶיךָ אֵל קַנָּא פֹּקֵד עֲוֹן אָבֹת עַל־בָּנִים

י עַל־שִׁלֵּשִׁים וְעַל־רִבֵּעִים לְשֹׂנְאָי: וְעֹשֶׂה חֶסֶד לַאֲלָפִים

ז לְאֹהֲבַי וּלְשֹׁמְרֵי מִצְוֹתָי: ס לֹא תִשָּׂא אֶת־שֵׁם־

יְהֹוָה אֱלֹהֶיךָ לַשָּׁוְא כִּי לֹא יְנַקֶּה יְהֹוָה אֵת אֲשֶׁר־
יִשָּׂא אֶת־שְׁמוֹ לַשָּׁוְא: פ

guilt of the fathers upon the children, upon the third and upon the fourth generations of those who reject Me,   **6]** but showing kindness to the thousandth generation of those who love Me and keep My commandments.

7] You shall not swear falsely by the name of the LORD your God; for the LORD will not clear one who swears falsely by His name.

related it to a word meaning "to be red." An English parallel would be "seeing red." Others, "jealous God."

Visiting the guilt. Punishing the offender. פֹּקֵד also means "remembering," which is the necessary basis for ethical consequences; see Gen. 21:1, Exod. 4:31.

Third and fourth generations. Idiomatic for "a long time."

6] *Thousandth generation.* Forever; a contrast to the mere third or fourth generation of verse 5, a "hyperbole for the sake of emphasis" [23].

Who love Me. The only time in the first four

books of the Torah where the love of God is stressed. In Deuteronomy love of God is an important aspect of man's duties.

7] *Swear falsely.* The third commandment. The meaning of the Hebrew is in doubt; others render "take in vain" or "abuse"—forbidding magical, profane, or even casual use of the divine Name. Proponents of this interpretation point out that the ninth commandment, which deals with false witness, implies the prohibition of swearing falsely [24].

Clear. Excuse, leave unpunished, as in Prov. 6:29.

The First Commandment (verse 2)

As noted above, in prevailing Jewish tradition verse 2 alone comprises the first of the Ten Words, while in other traditions it goes with verse 3 or with verses 3–6 to form the opening commandment. Verse 2 lays down the foundation of what follows, it is preamble, yet more than preamble: God is, and He is the One who gave Israel its existence as a nation. He brought it into history, for His own purposes—for Israel is to achieve through service to Him what the whole of mankind, even after the Flood, proved incapable of doing. Israel was redeemed by God so that it might redeem humanity.

The first commandment establishes at once that Israel's is a historical religion, anchored in the people's experience and validated by their free acceptance of the divine will. It is a religion directed to the individual—note the singular אֱלֹהֶיךָ[1]—as part of a people in history. The reference to Egypt is thus not a geographic but a spiritual notation: having traversed the road from slavery to freedom Israel can now fulfill its destiny, and it is the duty of each individual Israelite to do his share. The first commandment is in fact a confessional credo: Israel acknowledging that God delivered it from Egypt [25].

For not only humanity depends on Israel, God—in a manner of speaking— does also. A midrash expresses this thought in memo-rable fashion. It interprets the first commandment to imply: "I am the Lord (if I am) your God," that is, I can be Myself only if you acknowledge Me. In midrashic language [26]: If you do My will I am YHVH, the Merciful One, but if not I will be Elohim, the dispenser of stern justice.[2] Israel is dependent on God, and God depends on Israel to bring His redemptive plans to fruition. Thus seen, the first of the Words is both preamble and charter, the cornerstone of Israel's covenant and mankind's salvation.

The Second Commandment (verses 3–6)

Targum Jonathan, one of the Aramaic translations of the Torah, expands on this commandment by saying that these words came forth like storms, lightning, and flames. The first Word established the duty to acknowledge God, the second demands recognition of His singularity and forbids His presentation in any forms of sculptured image. The commandment is not argumentative: it does not refute polytheism but simply indicates that the gods of others are not for Israel. The commandment by itself takes no stand on whether or not such other deities actually exist, its subject matter is the faith of Israel.[3] In a world filled with myriads of deities which were worshiped by men, the stark and simple truth of God's lordship over Israel is here proclaimed and its acknowledgment demanded—nothing more, but also

---

[1] Perhaps even in the sense of "your own (personal) God." In the ancient Near East people often had their own private deities, who were considered their divine progenitors—these in addition to and distinct from the pantheon of official, "communal" gods. In the Bible, YHVH appears both as God of the world *and* as the God of the individual, his "own," as it were.

[2] See commentary on Gen. 2 for the interpretation of יְהֹוָה as God in His aspect of mercy and אֱלֹהִים in His aspect of justice.

[3] Some have therefore called this relationship henotheism (belief in one single god amongst many others), in contrast to monotheism (belief in one universal god beside whom there are no others). Monotheism, they hold, is a later development. But an evolutionary line from polytheism to henotheism to monotheism is not observable in Israel's history, which itself is a spiritual mutant. The Midrash avoids the problem by interpreting "You shall have none of those (whom others call) gods before Me" [27].

nothing less. Whatever other nations may do or believe, for Israel there is no compromise and, although it took some centuries to root this belief firmly amongst the people, it became in time the cornerstone of their spiritual existence and engaged their unshakable adherence under even the most trying conditions.

The prohibition of sculptured images for purposes of adoration stresses the incorporeality of God. "You saw no shape when the Lord your God spoke to you at Horeb out of the fire," Deuteronomy 4:15 reminds the people. The worship of images is proscribed in the most urgent and vivid terms: nothing, but absolutely nothing, is permitted that might lead to idolatry. This is no prohibition of the plastic arts as such but only of their misuse. This meant, however, that, in ages when the arts served primarily the goals of religion, sculpture and painting found no fertile soil amongst the Jewish people.[4] Instead, Judaism directed its creative powers toward the inner life, the vision of the soul rather than the eye, the invisible rather than the visible, the intangible rather than the sensual. Prayer became life's great dimension, while the visual arts were denied their place of eminence.

The rigor of the commandment[5] was emphasized through a large promise of both reward and punishment by a God who is described as "impassioned." Critics of the Torah have made much of contrasting a purportedly unrelenting, monstrously stern, and jealous God with one who is filled with mercy, kindness, and forebearance. Such a contrast—used frequently to show the "primitive" nature of the Jewish faith—does gross injustice to both the nature of monotheism and the range of the biblical view. To the Torah, belief in God by the people He chose as His servants is a condition of life itself. To have met Him at Sinai was awesome and fraught with incalculable consequences. Not tolerance is here at stake but Israel's spiritual existence. Further, the very same Book of Exodus tells the questing Moses that the Lord is "compassionate and gracious, slow to anger, rich in steadfast kindness" (34:6); and, in the commandment itself, love by far outlasts the judgment of evil: a thousand generations for the former are compared to three or four for the latter. The text expresses the principle of retribution in terms of ancient society, with its close familial patterns, where children were indeed part of their parents' ambience, where deeds or misdeeds of one member of the family involved the whole family. The commandment should therefore not be understood as providing for individual retribution; nor does it address itself to questions of criminal law. In that regard the Torah sets forth a different rule: "Parents shall not be put to death for children, nor children be put to death for parents" (Deut.

---

[4] Nor, on the whole, amongst the Moslems, who applied this prohibition with great severity. The Christian church declared at the Second Council of Nicea (787 C.E., acting against those who wanted to apply the commandment rigidly, the so-called "Iconoclasts") that the commandment applied to Israel only and permitted plastic and other arts.

[5] The rigorous phrasing of the prohibition stands in sharp contrast to the actual practice that prevailed in Israel for many hundreds of years after Moses [28]. Idols were abundant; hence the repeated exhortations of the Prophets. Even in desert days there was already the fiery serpent that Moses himself erected (Num. 21:8–9), and, though its original purpose may have been to remind the Israelites of God's healing power, the serpent became in time an object of adoration and was ordered destroyed. It may be noted that, despite widespread iconic practices in ancient Israel, no sculptured image has ever been found which can with certainty be said to represent the God of Israel himself, although Wisdom of Solomon 14:21 suggests that such did exist [29].

24:16; see also Ezek. 18:20). Furthermore, it should be noted that the threat of God's wrath, vivid and uncompromising though it is, pales ultimately before the promise of His abiding love. The second commandment ends on a note of hope: a faithful Israel will inherit a glorious future in the presence of a faithful God.

The Third Commandment (verse 7)

The second of the Words dealt with the misuse of images, the third turns to the misuse of God's name—a transition from the visual to the verbal. Both image and name are aspects of identity, and man must take care lest he infringe on the sanctity of God in any manner.[6] As noted before, the commandment intends most likely more than a prohibition of false oaths; its wider scope forbids man in every respect to use God's name wrongly or in vain. According to Ibn Ezra, this prohibition is more important than those that follow. For murder, adultery, and theft are circumscribed by opportunity and fear, but misuse of God's name, once it becomes a habit, will proliferate "and in the end one's every assertion will be preceded by using the Name." The result is a devaluation of awe and respect, and in time the holiness of God has no further meaning. Society is deeply affected by such deterioration, as was already reported by Philo who in his second-century C.E. Alexandria deplored that people held the prohibition to swear in small regard [31].

On the whole, however, Jewish tradition treated the prohibition with utmost regard. It frowned on all secular or self-serving use of the Name, in conversation, writing, and also in judicial proceedings. An oath was to be avoided at all costs, for God's name was too holy to be pronounced in matters affecting nothing more than one's own material welfare [32]. Every parchment or paper, religious or secular, on which the name of God had been inscribed was preserved and, when no longer in use, "hidden away" in storage (hence the name "Genizah," from *ganaz*, to hide) or formally buried in holy ground.

After the destruction of the Second Temple the sacred word יְהֹוָה was changed into variants like יי, ה', ד' or was given the substitute reading Adonai (my Lord), or Elohim (God), but even this only in prayerful usage; to this day Orthodox Jews will say "Adoshem" ("name of Ado-," leaving Adonai incompleted) or "Elokim" and write G–d and L–rd instead of the full words. This practice, though it is not followed by other Jews or by Christians, highlights the fact that the commandment does more than forbid profanity and sacrilegious oath-taking; it covers as well irresponsible, loose exclamations as "dear God," "good Lord," "by God," and the like. Whether the commandment forbids false swearing by God's name, or prohibits all wrong or vain usage, the basic intent remains: to safeguard His name from erosion and to maintain the sense of His holiness among His children.

---

6 Von Rad puts it somewhat differently. He takes the commandment to say a thorough and complete NO to "that desire that lies so deep in the heart of man, the desire to infringe the liberty of God" [30].

The Scope of the Decalogue

The precepts of the Decalogue contain the very intention of the lawgiver who is God . . . they admit of no dispensation.

T. AQUINAS (13th century) [33]

No work or anything can be good and pleasing to God, however great and costly in the eyes of the world, unless it is in keeping with the Ten Commandments.

M. LUTHER (16th century) [34]

It contains such wealth and loftiness of doctrine that it will never be fully conceived and exhausted.

P. MELANCHTHON (16th century) [35]

The Ten Words are for all peoples; and they will be, during all the centuries, the commandments of God.   E. RENAN (19th century) [36]

All the prophets received their prophecies from Sinai.   MIDRASH [37]

Alef-Bet

God created the world with ב, the second letter of the Hebrew alphabet (the opening word of the Torah בְּרֵאשִׁית begins with it). When the first letter, א, complained, God consoled it saying, "I will start the Decalogue with you (אָנֹכִי). For I am One and you are 'one.'"   MIDRASH [38]

Numbers for Mystics

The first seven words of the first Hebrew verse in Exodus, chapter 20, as well as those in Genesis, chapter 1, add up to twenty-eight letters and so do the words of the Aramaic response in the Kaddish prayer. He who says these words with devotion is as one who participates in the miracles of Creation and Sinai.

AFTER M. HACOHEN [39]

613 Mitzvot

(According to Jewish tradition, the Torah contains 613 commandments altogether, consisting of 248 positive and 365 negative rules. How the commandments are to be counted to arrive at a total of 613 is, however, a matter of controversy. An old tradition is the following.)

The letters of Torah (תורה) amount to 611 [ת = 400; ו = 6; ר = 200; ה = 5]. These 611 were transmitted by Moses ("Moses charged us with the Teaching," Deut. 33:4). The other two are "I the Lord . . ." and "You shall have no other gods . . . ," and they were given directly to the people by God.   TALMUD [40]

My God—and the God of the Philosophers

The so-called "belief in the existence of God," as ancient and modern theological philosophers like to express the idea of "the first commandment," is miles away from what this fundamental verse of Jewish thought and Jewish existence demands from Jewish thought and Jewish life. Not the fact that there is a God, also not that there is only one God, but that this One, unique, true God, is to be my God, that He created and formed me, placed me where I am, and goes on creating and forming me, keeps me, watches over me, leads and guides me; not that my connection with Him should be through ten thousand intermediaries as a chance product of a universe that He brought into being aeons ago, but that every present breath that I draw and every coming moment of my existence is to be a direct gift of His Almightiness and Love, and that I have to live every present and future second of my life solely in His service—in a word, not the knowledge of the existence of God, but the acknowledgment

of God, as my God, as the exclusive One in whose hands is the disposal of all my fate, and as the exclusive One guide of all my acts, it is only with this, only with the acceptance of this Truth, that I can lay the foundation of a Jewish life. To the demand, "I the Lord (am to be) your God," there is but one corresponding reply, "You *are* my God!"

S. R. HIRSCH

Every Slight Pretence

And hast thou sworn on every slight pretence,
Till perjuries are common like bad pence,
While thousands, careless of the damning sin,
Kiss the book's outside, who ne'er look'd within.

W. COWPER [41]

God's Unity in Islam

Say: He is God alone:
God the eternal!
He begetteth not, and He is not begotten;
And there is none like unto Him.

KORAN [42]

An Argument

A philosopher asked Rabbi Gamliel: "Why does God legislate against idols instead of simply destroying them?" Said R. Gamliel: "Men worship the sun, moon, stars, planets, and so forth, and even human beings. Shall He annihilate them all?"

MIDRASH [43]

Visiting Iniquity

Why does God punish sons for the sin of their fathers, as the third commandment states? This applies only to those sons who themselves are wicked like their fathers.

MIDRASH [44]

Mitzvot as Idols

The Rebbe of Kotsk said: The prohibition against idolatry includes the prohibition against making idols out of the mitzvot. We should never imagine that the chief purpose of a mitzvah is its outer form (i.e., the doing), rather it is the inward meaning (i.e., the devotion with which it is done).

CHASIDIC [45]

545

The Decalogue—
The Sabbath Day

The fourth commandment is the only one in the Decalogue to deal with a cultic practice. In the life of the Jewish people the Sabbath came to occupy a place of extraordinary importance, even as it deeply affected the social history of man through its influence on Christianity and Islam.

"Religious worship and religious instruction—the renewal of man's spiritual life in God—form an essential part of Sabbath observance. We, therefore, sanctify the Sabbath by a special Sabbath liturgy, by statutory lessons from the Torah and the Prophets, and by attention to discourse and instruction by religious teachers. The Sabbath has thus proved the great educator in Israel in the highest education of all, namely, the laws governing human conduct. The effect of these Sabbath prayers and synagogue homilies upon the Jewish people has been incalculable. Leopold Zunz... has shown that almost the whole of Israel's inner history since the close of Bible times can be traced in following the development of these Sabbath discourses on the Torah. Sabbath worship is still the chief bond which unites Jews into a *religious* brotherhood" [1].

יא כִּי שֵׁשֶׁת־יָמִים עָשָׂה יְהוָה אֶת־הַשָּׁמַיִם וְאֶת־הָאָרֶץ   ח זָכוֹר אֶת־יוֹם הַשַּׁבָּת לְקַדְּשׁוֹ: שֵׁשֶׁת יָמִים תַּעֲבֹד
אֶת־הַיָּם וְאֶת־כָּל־אֲשֶׁר־בָּם וַיָּנַח בַּיּוֹם הַשְּׁבִיעִי   י וְעָשִׂיתָ כָּל־מְלַאכְתֶּךָ: וְיוֹם הַשְּׁבִיעִי שַׁבָּת לַיהוָה
עַל־כֵּן בֵּרַךְ יְהוָה אֶת־יוֹם הַשַּׁבָּת וַיְקַדְּשֵׁהוּ: ס   אֱלֹהֶיךָ לֹא־תַעֲשֶׂה כָל־מְלָאכָה אַתָּה וּבִנְךָ־וּבִתֶּךָ
עַבְדְּךָ וַאֲמָתְךָ וּבְהֶמְתֶּךָ וְגֵרְךָ אֲשֶׁר בִּשְׁעָרֶיךָ:

8] Remember the sabbath day and keep it holy.   **9]** Six days you shall labor and do all your work,   **10]** but the seventh day is a sabbath of the LORD your God: you shall not do any work—you, your son or daughter, your male or female slave, or your cattle, or the stranger who is within your settlements.   **11]** For in six days the LORD made heaven and earth and sea, and all that is in them, and He rested on the seventh day; therefore the LORD blessed the sabbath day and hallowed it.

20:8] *Remember.* The Sabbath is understood to be already known to and practiced by the people. Tradition dates the institution of its observance from the first appearance of the manna (Exod. 16:30) but emphasizes that the idea of the Sabbath was built into creation itself (Gen. 2:1–3). On the historical background see commentary below.

In the parallel commandment in Deut. 5:12 the opening word is "Observe" (שָׁמוֹר) rather than "Remember" (זָכוֹר). Both terms are, in Hebrew, couched in the infinitive absolute, enhancing the formal character of the command and thereby giving it added importance. This formalism was known also to Egyptian ritualistic pronouncements and is paralleled in modern languages including contemporary Hebrew (*Ne pas fumer; Nicht rauchen;* נָא לֹא לְעַשֵׁן).

Sabbath day. Shabbat is connected with שָׁבַת (*shavat*, ceased, rested) in Gen. 2:2, 3.

Keep it holy. To set it apart. In Jewish tradition the expression לְקַדְּשׁוֹ implies the duty to sanctify it with a benediction [2].

9] *You shall labor.* The Rabbis interpreted this as a positive command: by labor mankind would emulate God's creative process in both work and rest [3].

Not do any work. Jewish tradition defined this in detail, developing a catalog of thirty-nine main types of prohibited labor [4]. They include the main agricultural and domestic activities that qualify as work, and from these categories later halachic rules were developed.

10] *Cattle.* It was not to be used on the Sabbath to substitute for human labor. Animals here receive the benefit of a legal enactment.

Settlements. Literally, "gates." All people without exception are covered by the command, as in the Passover regulation regarding the prohibition of eating leaven (Exod. 12:19).

11] *For in six days.* In Deut. 5:14–15 a different reason for Sabbath rest is given (see below).

Origins

In Babylonia the seventh, fourteenth, twenty-first, and twenty-eighth days of certain months, and also the nineteenth day (counting seven × seven days from the first of the preceding month) were considered "evil days" on which officials were not supposed to exercise their functions. It has therefore been suggested that these days were designated *shapattu* and formed the model for the biblical Sabbath. However, the connection between *shapattu* and the unlucky days is not definitely established, and there is too wide a gulf between such days and the Sabbath to consider the latter dependent on the former. More likely, both institutions derived from a common ancient model observing a lunisolar calendar and later developed in different directions. The most important distinction of the Sabbath is, however, its independence from both lunar and solar cycles: it occurs inexorably, and the festivals in the ritual calendar are so arranged that they take cognizance of the Sabbath, and not vice versa.[1]

Still others see a relationship between Sabbath and a day dedicated to the planet Saturn (note the English *Saturn*day), but there is no warrant in the Bible to consider the institution as an outgrowth of an antidote to such idolatrous practices. Similarly, the suggestion that originally the observance of the new moon festival (חֹדֶשׁ), which the Bible frequently mentions together with the Sabbath,[2] was connected with the celebration of the latter is no more than a surmise [5].

In fact, we do not really know how and when the Sabbath developed into the central institution of Judaism and why it alone of all cultic observances merited inclusion in the Decalogue. According to the Torah, it was instituted in the desert, while many modern scholars believe that it took form only later on when Israel came in contact with the agricultural calendar of Canaan, and that only after many centuries it grew into a day of rest. If, however, one maintains the high antiquity of and the Mosaic connection with the Decalogue, then one must conclude that the day was indeed known to Israel in its pre-Canaanite history and that in very early times it received special distinction as a recurrent occasion for sanctifying God. This is the testimony of the Torah, and, barring convincing evidence to the contrary, it will be best to leave it there.

The Sabbath is Israel's most original contribution to world law. It illustrates a genial marriage of social and cultic legislation, for it enjoins rest from labor in a cultic framework. Other ancient societies had rest days, some of them of fixed number and frequency, but none at unvarying, religiously demanded intervals. Instead of depending on royal generosity (which could be abrogated), the Decalogue gives the Sabbath divine sanction in perpetuity and makes its observance both an unchanging obligation and inalienable privilege[3] [6].

The Sabbath in the Bible

The Sabbath is often referred to in the

---

[1] Thus, the calendar is expanded or contracted annually, so that the Day of Atonement (although it always falls on the tenth day of Tishri) will never fall on a Friday or Sunday, that is, immediately before or after the Sabbath. Tishah b'Av, a day of mourning, is never to be observed on a Sabbath. This inexorable recurrence of the Sabbath has also produced strong Jewish resistance to a world calendar that would shift the Sabbath from year to year.

[2] See, e.g., Amos 8:5; Isa. 1:13; 66:23.

[3] Important also, though often overlooked, is the further positive injunction to labor for the other six days (see also Gleanings, "You Shall Labor"). Whether this has relevance in the light of debates over the four- or five-day work week is a question that cannot be treated here.

Torah and the other biblical books. In the Decalogue in Deuteronomy 5:12–15, the reason given for the observance is of a social nature, and Creation, mentioned in Exodus, is not at all referred to. The likelihood is that these reasons were provided after the Sabbath was already being observed. It was a proclamation of God as the Lord of Time, and the Sabbath was celebrated as a שַׁבָּת לַיהוָה (Shabbat Ladonai), a Sabbath for the sake of the Master of the Universe. It recurred every seven days, regardless of heavenly cycles, and thereby exalted the lordship of God over time and nature. "Every seventh day," writes M. Tsevat, "the Israelite is to renounce dominion over time, thereby re-nounce autonomy and recognize God's dominion over time and thus over himself. Keeping the Sabbath is acceptance of the sovereignty of God."[4]

Among important biblical references to the Sabbath the following may be noted (these references do not in any way indicate their relation to the historical development of the institution):

Gen. 2:2–3: God rests on the seventh day, which, however, is not here called *Shabbat*;

Exod. 31:13, 16; Ezek. 20:12: The Sabbath is a sign of the covenant;

Exod. 16:4–36: Manna was not to be gathered on this day;

Exod. 16:29: People should not move about unduly;[5]

Exod. 34:21: No labor is to be performed, to give both humans and animals an oppor-tunity for rest;

Exod. 35:3: No fire is to be kindled on the Sabbath;

Num. 28:9–10: Special sacrifices are to be offered;

Neh. 13:15–22: Commercial activities are incompatible with the Sabbath;

Exod. 31:14; Num. 15:32–36: The penalty for desecration is death and "cutting off" from the people.

Isa. 58:13–14: Israel will be exalted when it observes the true spirit of the Sabbath:

If you refrain from trampling the Sabbath,
From pursuing your affairs on My holy day;
If you call the Sabbath "delight,"
The Lord's holy day "honored." . . .
I will set you astride the heights of the earth,
And let you enjoy the heritage of your father Jacob. . . .

Isa. 66:23: In the end of time, all men shall observe new moons and Sabbaths.

Such passages hint at varied emphases which the observance of the day received at various times before it assumed its form as a day of complete rest, joy, prayer, and study and was embellished by popular love and practice and secured by traditional law.

In Later Days

"More than Israel has guarded the Shabbat, the Shabbat has guarded Israel"— this saying well describes the unique position the Sabbath assumed in Jewish history [9]. Its observance stretches from dusk on Friday to sundown on Saturday and is marked by family observance, synagogue attendance, and total rest. Its mood is both serene and joyous (mourning practices cease on this day as does fasting, except on Yom Kippur) [10]; it is the time for recollecting God's goodness and acknowledging His sovereignty; it pro-vides for social balm, intellectual expansion, and a shutting out of the day's cares. It is

---

[4] Tsevat reaches this conclusion after an inquiry into the meaning of the biblical Sabbath. He also empha-sizes the close connection of the weekly Sabbath with the jubilee year [7].

[5] Interpreted in Jewish law to be within a limit of two thousand cubits or medium steps from the outer buildings of the city. Within the city there is no restriction [8].

spiritually and physically restorative, the crown of the week's labors. While rules for its observances were marked out in the most careful detail in Mishnah and Talmud, its purpose was not, as was charged on occasion, to make it a day of painful restrictions. Several mitzvot, such as the duties of circumcision or of saving life, were considered to have precedence over ordinary Shabbat laws. In the general decline of modern religious observance the Shabbat too has suffered. The old practices have been widely eroded, and the need for earning a livelihood has caused many Jews to set aside the prohibition of work. Though for Christians the emphasis is somewhat different, they too are faced with serious problems of Sabbath observance. Vigorous efforts have been made in both religious communities to restore the pristine spirit of the day and to apply it to the needs of contemporary man [11].

The Sabbath in Christianity, Roman Antiquity, and Islam

Early Christians observed the biblical Sabbath. In time, however, when the influence of the Ebionite Christians (who had close links with Judaism) waned, the observance was gradually shifted to Sunday, called "the Lord's Day" in memory of the story of resurrection (Revelations 1:10), and the fourth commandment was declared abrogated along with the biblical law of circumcision. Sunday was made the official day of Christian worship in 321 C.E. and did not at first carry the demand for rest attached to the biblical and postbiblical Shabbat. Only much later, in medieval Catholicism and British-American Puritanism, did Sabbath rest become a major part of Sunday observance, but with the difference, especially among the Puritans, that the restrictive aspects of observance were not balanced by the innate joy of the Jewish Shabbat and instead tended toward the creation of a pleasureless day buttressed by "blue" laws. Some Christian groups, notably the Seventh Day Adventists and various Baptist sects, continue to observe the seventh day as their Sabbath.

Outside the Jewish-Christian realm, the world of Greek and Roman antiquity generally viewed Shabbat with suspicion and even antipathy. The historian Tacitus (born about 55 C.E.) found most Jewish customs "sinister and shameful" and thought that Shabbat was dedicated to the adoration of Saturn [12]; Seneca (died 65 C.E.) attacked the Jews as superstitious and wrote: "To spend every seventh day without doing anything means to lose a seventh part of life, besides suffering loss in pressing matters from such idleness" [13]. Plutarch (Tacitus's contemporary) reported that the conquest of Jerusalem took place on the Sabbath and that the Jews, "mired in their sordid habits," did not defend themselves but remained "caught in their superstitions as in a net."[6] Yet at the same time Josephus reported, "There is not one city, Greek or barbarian, nor a single nation to which our custom of abstaining from work on the seventh day has not spread" [15].

The Sabbath in Islam is called yom al-jum'ah, "day of assembly," and is observed on Fridays. Its observance most likely preceded Mohammed, and his rejection of the seventh day is traced by some scholars to Parsi influence which made that day an unlucky day. Friday was the day on which Creation was finished and when the prophet

---

[6] It is uncertain to which event Plutarch refers [14], perhaps to the incident reported in I Macc. 2:32–38, which did not, however, involve the capture of Jerusalem. The policy of pacific sufferance on the Sabbath was changed by Mattathias (verses 39–41). Since that time, in the second century B.C.E., self-defense on the seventh day was not only permitted but deemed obligatory.

made his first entry into Mecca. The Jews, in their observance of the seventh day, were considered to have chosen an inferior day but, having chosen it, must faithfully adhere to it [16]. Friday is not a day of strict rest, but attendance at the midday worship in the mosque is obligatory: "When you are summoned to prayer on the Day of the Assembly, hasten to the commemoration of God and quit your traffic. If you know it, this will be best for you. And, when the prayer is ended, then disperse yourselves and go in quest of the bounties of God; and, that it may be well with you, remember God often" [17].

GLEANINGS

Remember and Observe

(In Exod. 20 the text says "Remember the Sabbath," זָכוֹר; in Deut. 5, "Observe the Sabbath," שָׁמוֹר.)

Remember it before it comes, and observe it after it is gone.

The two words were, in a miraculous way, pronounced together by God.   MIDRASH [18]

"Observe" and "Remember"—one single sound did He who is one and single cause us to hear.

SOLOMON HALEVI ALKABETS
From the Shabbat hymn "Lecha Dodi"

To remember the Sabbath is to remember that God created the world.   IBN EZRA

The Shabbat and Man

The Sabbath is given to you, but you are not servants of the Sabbath. [This is echoed in Christian Scriptures (Mark 2:27): "The Sabbath was made for man, and not man for the Sabbath."]

We should disregard one Sabbath for the sake of saving the life of a person, so that he may observe many Sabbaths.

Shabbat outweighs all the mitzvot.

MIDRASH [19]

Shabbat at Creation

After the whole world had been completed according to the perfect nature of the number of six, God hallowed the day following, the seventh, praising it, and calling it holy. For that day is the festival, not of one city or country, but of all the earth; a day which alone it is right to call the day of festival for all people, and the birthday of the world.   PHILO [20]

Shabbat complained at Creation that everyone had been created with a mate, except Shabbat. God said: "I will give you Israel as your mate."

MIDRASH [21]

Testimony

Three testify for each other: Israel, Shabbat, and the Holy One, blessed be He. They testify to each other's uniqueness: God's in the world; Israel's among the nations; Shabbat's in time.

MIDRASH [22]

One Shabbat

God said to Israel: "If you observe one Shabbat I will account it to you as if you had observed all the mitzvot in the Torah; and if you desecrate one Shabbat I will reckon it to you as if you had desecrated all the mitzvot."

If Israel would keep but one Shabbat properly the Messiah would come.   MIDRASH [23]

Foretaste

God said: "If you observe My commandments I will give you My most precious gift." Israel asked: "What will that be?" God said: "The future world."

Said Israel: "But will there be no reward in this

world?" God said: "Shabbat will be a foretaste, for it is one-sixtieth of the world-to-come."

MIDRASH [24]

You Shall Labor

This is a positive commandment. Great is labor, for God's presence does not rest upon Israel until they perform labor, as it says: "Let them make Me a sanctuary that I may dwell among them" (Exod. 25:8). MIDRASH [25]

The Imitation of God

The commandment, in effect, says: Always imitate God; let that one period of seven days in which God created the world be to you a complete example of the way in which you are to obey the law and an all-sufficient model for your actions.

Moreover, the seventh day is also an example from which you may learn the propriety of studying philosophy; as on that day, it is said, God beheld the works which He had made, so that you also may yourself contemplate the works of nature, and all the separate circumstances which contribute towards happiness. PHILO [26]

Holiness in Time

The meaning of the Sabbath is to celebrate time rather than space. Six days a week we live under the tyranny of things of space; on the Sabbath we try to become attuned to holiness in time. It is a day on which we are called upon to share in what is eternal in time, to turn from the results of creation to the mystery of creation, from the world of creation to the creation of the world.

A. J. HESCHEL [27]

Not Idle Time

The Sabbath does not mean a mere not working, nor an empty idleness. It connotes something positive. It has guided the soul unto its mystery, so that it is not a day that just interrupts, but a day that renews, speaks through it, of something eternal. It is the expression of a direction for life and not just an instituted day of rest. If it were only that, or if it became that, its essence would be taken from it. It would then be only a hollow shell. LEO BAECK [28]

Useless

I view the Sabbath . . . as a "useless" day. We must once again understand that doing nothing, being silent and open to the world, letting things happen inside, can be as important as, and sometimes more important than, what we commonly call the useful. Let there be some special time during the week when we do for the sake of doing; when we love the trivial and, in fact, simply love; when we do for others rather than ourselves and thus provide a counterbalance for the weight of endless competition that burdens our every day. W. G. P. [29]

The Decalogue—The Fifth to Tenth Commandments; Postscript

We turn now to a consideration of the fifth to tenth commandments and to the postscript that follows the Decalogue, which tells again of the fear the people experience in the presence of the revelation. Moses reassures them he will from here on mediate between God and them, and they will no longer be addressed directly by the divine voice.

According to Jewish tradition, the opening five commandments were inscribed on the first tablet, the last five on the second. The latter concern man's relationship with his fellow men, the former are based on the encounter between God and humanity.* The respect for God promulgated on the first tablet is complemented by the respect for man permeating the second.

* Tradition considers honor to one's parents as an aspect of the honor due to God (see Gleanings).

Exodus 20   Yitro

לֹא תַחְמֹד אֵשֶׁת רֵעֶךָ וְעַבְדּוֹ וַאֲמָתוֹ וְשׁוֹרוֹ וַחֲמֹרוֹ   יב כַּבֵּד אֶת־אָבִיךָ וְאֶת־אִמֶּךָ לְמַעַן יַאֲרִכוּן יָמֶיךָ עַל

וְכֹל אֲשֶׁר לְרֵעֶךָ: פ   יג הָאֲדָמָה אֲשֶׁר־יְהֹוָה אֱלֹהֶיךָ נֹתֵן לָךְ: ס לֹא

וְכָל־הָעָם רֹאִים אֶת־הַקּוֹלֹת וְאֶת־הַלַּפִּידִים וְאֵת   תִרְצָח: ס לֹא תִנְאָף: ס לֹא תִגְנֹב: ס לֹא־

קוֹל הַשֹּׁפָר וְאֶת־הָהָר עָשֵׁן וַיַּרְא הָעָם וַיָּנֻעוּ   יד תַעֲנֶה בְרֵעֲךָ עֵד שָׁקֶר: ס לֹא תַחְמֹד בֵּית רֵעֶךָ ס

12] Honor your father and your mother, that you may long endure on the land which the LORD your God is giving you.

13] You shall not murder. / You shall not commit adultery. / You shall not steal. / You shall not bear false witness against your neighbor.

14] You shall not covet your neighbor's house: you shall not covet your neighbor's wife, or his male or female slave, or his ox or his ass, or anything that is your neighbor's.

15] All the people witnessed the thunder and lightning, the blare of the horn and the mountain smoking; and when the people saw it, they fell back and stood at a distance.

20:12] *Honor your father and your mother.* In Lev. 19:3 where the command is to "revere" (or "fear") one's parents, the mother is mentioned before the father. There, too, the command is linked closely to the observance of the Sabbath.

Long endure. Deut. 5:16 adds "and fare well."

Is giving you. Is in the process of giving you.

13] *Murder.* The King James Version and other older translations had "kill." However, the usual words for killing (הרג or המית) are not used here, rather it is רצח, which generally refers to un-authorized homicide [1], perhaps one that called forth blood vengeance. In time רצח came to be associated with killing out of hatred and malice. The penalty for murder is given in Exod. 21:12. See further at Deut. 5:17.

Adultery. Intercourse of a man with a married or betrothed woman, not with an unmarried or unbetrothed woman or a harlot (see Deut. 22:23–28). The prohibition was later widened by both rabbinic and Christian traditions. Adultery is only twice more noted in the Torah (Lev. 20:10 and Deut. 5:17), but often in the rest of the Bible. In the Nash papyrus and other old sources [2] this commandment precedes that concerning murder. The penalty is given in Lev. 20:10; Deut. 22:22.

Steal. Men or things. See also Lev. 19:11. The penalty is stated in Exod. 21:16; 22:1–3.

Bear false witness. Testify falsely. In Deut. 5:17 שָׁוְא instead of שֶׁקֶר is used, but this does not appear to imply any difference. The penalty is stated in Deut. 19:16–21.

Your neighbor. Idiomatic for "anyone." In the Torah, רֵעַ sometimes means an Israelite and some-times any person who dwells nearby. Clearly, the context of the Decalogue demands that the word be understood in its wider sense.

14] *Covet.* Desire improperly, with the hope to dispossess one's neighbor. "The most inward of the commandments, it is directed against one's greedy impulses" [3]. In Deut. 5:18, an addi-tional word for covet is used: תִתְאַוֶּה, crave; but this difference too is stylistic only.

Neighbor's house. Standing for household, for which wife, slaves, and so on are examples. (In Deut. 5:18 "field" is added.) "House" is a general term which encompasses "tent" and is therefore not anachronistic in a desert setting [4]. The original commandment may have ended with ". . . your neighbor's house," the rest being a later expansion.

15–18] Some traditional commentators consid-ered these verses to be out of place here, since

נַסּוֹת אֶתְכֶם בָּא הָאֱלֹהִים וּבַעֲבוּר תִּהְיֶה יִרְאָתוֹ עַל־פְּנֵיכֶם לְבִלְתִּי תֶּחֱטָאוּ: וַיַּעֲמֹד הָעָם מֵרָחֹק וּמֹשֶׁה נִגַּשׁ אֶל־הָעֲרָפֶל אֲשֶׁר־שָׁם הָאֱלֹהִים: ס

טו וַיַּעַמְדוּ מֵרָחֹק: וַיֹּאמְרוּ אֶל־מֹשֶׁה דַּבֶּר־אַתָּה עִמָּנוּ וְנִשְׁמָעָה וְאַל־יְדַבֵּר עִמָּנוּ אֱלֹהִים פֶּן־נָמוּת: יו וַיֹּאמֶר מֹשֶׁה אֶל־הָעָם אַל־תִּירָאוּ כִּי לְבַעֲבוּר

16] "You speak to us," they said to Moses, "and we will obey; but let not God speak to us, lest we die." **17]** Moses answered the people, "Be not afraid; for God has come only in order to test you, and in order that the fear of Him may be ever with you, so that you do not go astray." **18]** So the people remained at a distance, while Moses approached the thick cloud where God was.

they appear to refer to the time before, not after, the giving of the Decalogue [5].

Deut. 5:19 ff. is more detailed. There it says that God spoke only these words "and no more"; that He inscribed them on two tablets and gave them to Moses; that Israel came to Moses and made the request that he be their intermediary out of fear that they would be consumed by divine fire; that God heard their plea and lauded its intent; and that the people were bidden to return to their tents while Moses stayed with God to receive the Torah—which is defined as "the laws and the rules," which Moses would receive and impart to the people.

15] *Fell back.* Others, "trembled." The verb נוע is used in the Bible in both meanings [6].

16] *You speak to us.* In the future.

17] *Test you.* Moses appears to suggest that God wanted to see the people's reaction to the divine appearance. Luzzatto compares this to an initiation rite that tests the candidate's fitness and notes that such tests were already known in Egypt [7].

18] *While Moses approached.* Once again.

Where God was. From where the Voice appeared to come.

The Fifth Commandment (verse 12)

Jewish tradition has underscored the importance of one's duty to honor father and mother by listing it among the commandments on the first tablet. It is thus seen as concluding the catalog of man's basic obligations to God. Parents are God's representatives and partners in the rearing of their children, and children who fail to respect this special position are offending against God as well. Even as the penalty of death is prescribed for blasphemy (Lev. 24:15, 16), so it is also for striking, cursing—some say even insulting![1]—one's parents (Exod. 21:15, 17; Lev. 20:9) [8]. No difference is made between father and mother. The order of naming one before the other is of no consequence, as Lev. 19:3 makes amply clear, where the mother is named first [9]. In the Code of Hammurabi the striking of a father is made an offense, but the mother is not mentioned [10].

The fifth commandment is the only one which has a promise attached to it: those who will observe it will have long life—considered the mark of blessing—and, according to the Deuteronomic version, fare well in general.[2] This assumes that not only the command but the promise as well is directed to the individual. But this is by no means clear from the text, which can be understood to make the honoring of parents a prerequisite for the nation to remain in the Holy Land.

The commandment then would mean: The Holy Land will not tolerate you if you will fail to honor your parents, for in such a case harmonious social life by biblical standards would be impossible. Jewish tradition made these principles into pillars of its ethical structure, and in time the "Jewish way" of treating one's parents was considered a model to be emulated by others [12].

The inclusion of this commandment in the Decalogue may suggest that the treatment of parents left much to be desired, in which case the offer of a reward imparted a special urgency to the mitzvah.[3] On the other hand, no law was deemed necessary here or elsewhere in the Torah to ensure parental love for children. Apparently, the custom of exposing unwanted offspring to the elements (practised, for instance, in ancient Rome) seems to have presented no problem to Israelite society.

An extensive elaboration of the fifth commandment was provided by Sirach 3:1–16 (second century, B.C.E.). His book, though it did not gain access to the biblical canon, was popular and probably widely quoted.

> Listen to me, your father, O children,
>   and act accordingly, that you
>   may be kept in safety.
> For the Lord honored the father above
>   the children,
>   and he confirmed the right of
>   the mother over her sons.
> Whoever honors his father atones for sins,
>   and whoever glorifies his mother
>   is like one who lays up treasure.

---

[1] This is the translation of יְקַלֵּל in the New Jewish Version, Lev. 20:9.

[2] It has also been suggested that long life may mean the promise of being remembered by one's children [11], or that by having children one has acquired an extension to life.

[3] The saying in Psalm 71:9, "Do not cast me off in old age" lends strong emphasis to this. See also Prov. 20:20; 30:11, 17; and the comment by Jesus in Matthew 15:4–6. The Bible was not alone in urging honor to parents (for a Ugaritic example, see Gleanings). It is also possible, as Mendenhall has suggested, that the appearance of the commandment in the Decalogue indicated a change in social organization [13].

Whoever honors his father will be
  gladdened by his own children,
  and when he prays he will be heard.
Whoever glorifies his father will have long
    life,
  and whoever obeys the Lord will refresh
    his mother;
  he will serve his parents as his masters.
Honor your father by word and deed
  that a blessing from him may come upon
    you.
For a father's blessing strengthens the
    root,
  but a mother's curse uproots the young
    plant.
Do not glorify yourself by dishonoring your
    father,
  for your father's dishonor is no glory to
    you.
For a man's glory comes from honoring his
    father,
  and it is a disgrace for children not to
    respect their mother.
O son, help your father in his old age,
  and do not grieve him as long as he
    lives;
Even if he is lacking in understanding, show
    forbearance;
  in all your strength do not despise
    him.
For kindness to a father will not be
    forgotten,
  and against your sins it will be credited
    to you;
In the day of your affliction it will be
    remembered in your favor;
  as frost in fair weather, your sins will
    melt away.
Whoever forsakes his father is like a
    blasphemer,
  and whoever angers his mother is cursed
    by the Lord.

The Sixth to Tenth Commandments
(verses 13–14)

"You shall not murder"

The Rabbis gave this commandment great emphasis by stipulating that it was obligatory for all men [14].

As indicated above, only unauthorized homicide is meant by the text, and the older translation "You shall not kill" was too general and did not represent the more specific meaning of תִּרְצָח. Hence the claims of pacifists, who would see this command as a prohibition of all killing including that legitimized by the state during warfare, cannot be sustained. The same is true for the abolition of capital punishment. Laudable as these objectives are, they find no warrant in the text itself, which has been used to legitimize other prohibitions as well. Thus, the Church Father Augustine held that the commandment forbade not only the taking of other peoples' lives but of one's own as well, and many countries to this day make suicide a criminal offense. Jewish tradition, while it too frowned on suicide, deriving the prohibition from Gen. 9:5, did not include it in the catalogue of punishable crimes [15]. Although according to the Torah murder was punishable by death, the Rabbis proceeded nonetheless to make a judicial conviction, which would render the penalty mandatory, more and more difficult. Thus in the second century C.E. capital punishment was decried by most Sages [16], and it has been abolished in modern Israel.[4]

"You shall not commit adultery"

The command is directed to both the man and the woman, and both are to be executed when found guilty (Lev. 20:10). Purity of family life is another pillar of society as envisaged by the Bible. In time it

---

[4] There are narrow exceptions, such as for Holocaust murders.

became a distinguishing aspect of Israel's social structure, complementing the honor rendered to parents and the sense of responsibility felt for all members of the family.

In biblical days men were permitted to marry more than one wife, and concubinage—the acquisition of lesser-status wives—was also practiced. Jacob had two full-status wives and two concubines, and Solomon was said to have married a thousand, that is to say, very many women (I Kings 11:3). Nowhere in the Torah or the rest of the Bible is monogamy established as a rule or even a desirable principle, although in the course of time polygamy became the exception rather than the rule. Jews who lived among Moslems (who themselves were permitted multiple marriages) frequently continued to practice polygamy into the present age, while the majority who lived in Christian lands adopted the custom of their environment and practiced monogamy. This latter practice was given legal status by an enactment of Rabbenu Gershom (about 1000 C.E., in Germany). While the decree expired technically in the (Jewish) year 5000, that is, 1240 in the civil reckoning, it was generally considered as continuing in force in all countries where monogamy was the rule.[5] In modern Israel monogamy is established in law, but an exception may be made by special permission of the Chief Rabbinate, and immigrants who came with several wives from lands where polygamy was permitted have been allowed to maintain such status.

"You shall not steal"

The commandment appears to cover both property and people—kidnaping being already an ancient practice for which Exod. 21:16 specifically provides the penalty of death. (However, the Rabbis interpreted the commandment to refer to persons and Lev. 19:11 to property only [18].) Quite clearly, the right to private property is protected by the Torah, and no earthly ruler could deprive the owner of his property against his will. This principle is demonstrated with particular force in the story of Naboth's vineyard, which was desired by the king but which he could not legally acquire over the proprietor's objection (I Kings 21). Real property was meant to be kept in the family's and tribe's permanent possession, and if it was alienated by sale it would return to the original owners in the jubilee year (Lev. 25:10). We do not know how successfully this ideal was ever implemented, and it appears that, in any case, the law became inoperative after the Babylonian exile (586 B.C.E.).

"You shall not bear false witness"

The prohibition covers not only the act of witnessing but goes further: It addresses itself to the character of a person. The Hebrew text does not speak of false testimony (עֵדוּת) but of a false testifier (עֵד) [19]. The liar infects both himself and the social fabric, and, when he practices his deceit in court, the damage is doubly destructive. "Everything in the world was created by God," says a midrash, "except the art of lying" [20].

"You shall not covet"

The commandment, directed as it is to the heart, is primarily a warning that greed unchecked will likely lead to actual transgression. The intent of the command became an issue in the Christian church. Was inward desire to be reckoned as a sin (for which forgiveness needed to be asked) even if it did not lead to any outward act? Pope Pius V, in a rare act of official interpretation by the Church of a biblical text, ruled in 1567 that it was not. Only overt action was to be considered sinful, but not the mere desire.

---

[5] This tradition, reflected in the *Shulchan Aruch* [17], may however be a later development

GLEANINGS

On the Fifth Commandment

The commandment to honor father and mother is greater than all the other nine commandments.

If you honor your parents, your children will honor you.　　　　　SAADIA [21]

The fourth and fifth commandments belong together. They constitute the two great institutions of Jewish life.

The Hebrew כַּבֵּד אֶת (rather than merely כַּבֵּד) suggests that the honor is to be extended to stepparents, and even to an older brother who stands *in loco parentis*.

Three are partners in man's creation: God, a father, and a mother.　　　MIDRASH [22]

There is no earthly prosecution for transgressing a law for the observance of which a reward is promised in the Torah (as is done in this commandment). The enforcement is left to Heaven.
　　　　　　　　　　　　　MIDRASH [23]

There comes a generation which curses a father
And withholds blessings even from a mother.
　　　　　　　　　　　　PROVERBS 30:11

In Leviticus 19:3 the mother is mentioned before the father: "You shall revere (literally "fear") your mother and your father." Children generally *fear* a father more, hence the mother is listed first. In the fifth commandment the order is reversed, for children tend to *honor* mothers more than fathers. Where something is incomplete, Scripture attempts to right it.　　　MIDRASH [24]

A pagan, Dama ben Natina, was visited by emissaries of the Temple to buy a precious stone needed for the priestly breastplate. He refused to sell because the key to the jewel box was under the pillow upon which his father was sleeping at the time, and he did not want to waken him for commercial reasons. When later the opportunity to sell arose again and his profit chanced to increase, he sold it for the price he would have initially charged. He did not want to profit from honoring his father.　　　MIDRASH [25]

A Ugaritic Admonition (on the duties of a son)

Surely there's a son for him like his brethren's,
　　And a scion like unto his kindred's!
He gives oblation to the gods to eat,
　　Oblation to drink to the holy ones.
Wilt thou not bless him, O Bull El, my father,
　　Beatify him, O Creator of Creatures?
So shall there be a son in his house,
　　A scion in the midst of his palace:
Who sets up the stelae of his ancestral spirits,
　　In the holy place the protectors of his clan;
Who frees his spirit from the earth,
　　From the dust guards his footsteps;
Who smothers the life-force of his detractor,
　　Drives off who attacks his abode;
Who takes him by the hand when he's drunk,
　　Carries him when he's sated with wine . . .
Who plasters his roof when it leaks,
　　Washes his clothes when they're soiled [26].

The Second Tablet

The commandments on this tablet are briefer, issued in absolute terms, without object or complement, without definitions or qualifications, without particulars or conditions, like the enunciation of fundamental abstract and eternal principles which transcend any condition or circumstance, detailed definition or restriction.
　　　　　　　　　　　　　CASSUTO

The words on the second tablet were written

opposite those on the first: the shedder of blood (sixth) relates to one who diminishes the divine image (first); the adulterer (seventh) resembles the idolator (second): both break the covenant with God; the thief (eighth) will in the end swear falsely (third); the false witness par excellence (ninth) is he who profanes the Sabbath (fourth) and thus appear to testify that God's creative process did not culminate in the Sabbath; and he who covets (tenth) will in the end beget children who despise their parents (fifth). These were the words of R. Chananyah ben Gamliel, but others say that all Ten Words were written on each of the two tablets. MIDRASH [27]

Adultery

For on account of a harlot a man is brought to
    a loaf of bread,
But the adulteress hunteth for the precious life.
Can a man take fire in his bosom,
And his clothes not be burned?
Or can one walk upon hot coals,
And his feet not be scorched?
So he that goeth in to his neighbor's wife:
Whosoever toucheth her shall not go un-
    punished.
Men do not despise a thief, if he steal
To satisfy his soul when he is hungry;
But if he be found, he must restore sevenfold,
He must give all the substance of his house.
He that committeth adultery with a woman
    lacketh understanding;
He doeth it that would destroy his own soul.
Wounds and dishonor shall he get,
And his reproach shall not be wiped away.
For jealousy is the rage of a man,
And he will not spare in the day of vengeance.
He will not regard any ransom;
Neither will he rest content, though thou givest
    many gifts. PROVERBS 6:26–35

The Eighth Commandment

This prohibition belongs to those laws which men know even without the divine command.
YALKUT ME'AM LO'EZ

Theft includes deceit, for the latter is like stealing another's mind. It is forbidden to deceive anyone, whether Jew or non-Jew. TALMUD [28]

The Tenth Commandment

Who is strong? He who controls his desires.
ETHICS OF THE FATHERS [29]

They Saw

The people "witnessed" the thunder and ... the blare of the horn (verse 15). It says literally that they "saw" them. They saw what could be heard and heard what could be seen, because of the inner awareness granted them at that time.
MALBIM [30]

The voice of men is calculated to be heard; but that of God to be really and truly seen. Why? Because all that God says are not words, but actions which the eyes perceive before the ears do.
PHILO [31]

Mediation

When Israel heard the words "You shall have no other gods ..." the evil impulse left them. But when they said to Moses "You speak to us" it returned and will not leave again until messianic times. MIDRASH [32]

Another midrash phrases the same theme—that asking Moses to be their mediator was an irreparable error on Israel's side—as follows: Israel had been granted the gifts of learning and remembering, but the latter was now taken from them [33].

Having proven themselves incapable of hearing the Torah from God directly, Israel was now obligated to follow Moses unquestioningly.
S. R. HIRSCH

PART VI

Laws

The chapters now under consideration give the appearance of a self-contained code of laws. After a brief prelude this collection presents civil and criminal law, turns to cultic provisions, and ends with a description of how the covenant was concluded (chapter 24).[1] Because of this last portion the whole section is often referred to as the "Book of the Covenant" (*Sefer ha-Berit*) and it is so called in 24:7 [1]. Many scholars have concluded that this code was originally a separate book which was later joined with and incorporated into the story of "Revelation and Commandment" which forms the section immediately preceding. However, there is wide divergence of opinion as to the age of this code and the place of its origin [2].

Much depends on how one views the relationship of the code to the laws of the ancient Near East, of which we now have extensive knowledge. There can be no question that a number of these laws were familiar to Israelite society, either by way of patriarchal traditions which had been formed in the Mesopotamian past, or indirectly through the practices of nations with whom the Israelites came into intimate contact (especially the Canaanites after the conquest of the land). The codes that have the greatest number of similarities with the Torah are the laws of the kingdoms of Eshnunna and of Babylon, both composed in Akkadian in the "Old Babylonian" period, the former by an unidentified king, the latter by the famous Hammurabi.[2] However, we do not know nor may we ever know the full extent of these relationships, and neither do we know the role that Moses had in shaping the Torah laws, and especially those which have a particular religious cast. In subsequent Jewish tradition the whole code consisting of *devarim* ("words") and *mishpatim* ("rules" or "laws" or "ordinances") became the core of the Jewish legal system or Halachah.

The code deals with the following subjects:

20:19–22:16: worship preamble, serfs, capital and noncapital offenses, property;

[1] Some scholars hold that 34:14–26 belonged to this code.

[2] However, the laws of Eshnunna had long disappeared in Israelite days, and those of Hammurabi reflect a more stratified and urban society than do the Israelite laws. Extant ancient Near Eastern codes are the following

(the dates are approximations and not fully agreed upon by all scholars):

Laws of Ur-Nammu, Sumerian, about 2100 B.C.E.

Laws of Lipit-Ishtar, Sumerian, about 1930 B.C.E.

Laws of Eshnunna, Akkadian, about 1900–1800 B.C.E.

22:17–23:9:	moral and religious duties, justice;
23:10–19:	cultic calendar;
23:20–33:	exhortation;
24:1–18:	ratification of the code.

The laws do not appear to be arranged according to any system we would use,[3] except that certain passages are related by mnemotechnical connections, that is, in order to aid one's memory in the recital of these laws. This was important in an age when the knowledge of writing was not widespread. Furthermore, as has been pointed out repeatedly, what appears as "disarray" to moderns was acceptable "order" to the ancients, who did not have our penchant for systematic treatment. Besides, there was an overriding need to repeat a sacred tradition exactly as it was received. We thus find a mixture of apodictic rules, phrased in absolute formulation, and case law beginning with such conditional words as "When a fire is started . . ." or "If a man seduces. . . ." The format should not let us conclude that case law was less important than apodictic law; both appear to have had the same force and demanded the same degree of adherence. Finally, in studying the code one should always keep in mind that it derived its authority not from Moses but was traced to God's will. That means that Israel considered it to be at heart a religious document and thus essentially different from the legal systems of the age. In the words of Abba Hillel Silver, the laws "did not rest on custom but on divine authority. They were dogma and were based on revelation. There are man-made laws and there are traditional habits and usages of community life which are hardened into law. Both are responsive to the changing needs of man, and, when they are just and long-established, they come to be regarded as divinely sanctioned. But the ideals and the ultimate moral standards are conceived as having been revealed to man. They are given to him by his Creator. They do not change. They do not ratify long-established tribal customs and time-honored practices. They proclaim that which *should* be done now and for all future time" [5].

Laws of Hammurabi, Akkadian, about 1750 B.C.E.

Laws of the Hittites, about 1400–1300 B.C.E.

Laws of the Assyrians, about 1100 B.C.E. [3].

[3] However, if one combines the laws in Exodus with those in Deuteronomy [4], a general similarity to the arrangement of the laws in the Code of Hammurabi may be observed.

Laws on Worship, Serfdom, Injuries

The section before us falls into three parts:

1. A preamble that treats of the way God is to be worshiped: in simplicity and with full regard for modesty. By implication, no priests are required for the offering of sacrifices; rather, the text addresses itself to the whole people (20:19 to the end of the chapter).

2. Rules on slavery or serfdom. The Torah treats the institution as an established fact of civilization and looks to its melioration rather than its abolition (21:1–11). These laws begin the code itself by rehearsing the typology of the Exodus, i.e., the release from human serfdom and the entrance into service of God.

3. Laws dealing with various cases of injury (21:12 to the end of the chapter). In this section it is especially clear that the Torah aimed primarily at a humanization of existing practices. For instance, Hebrew serfs could regain their freedom, and the death penalty was (with one exception) reserved for offenses against life but ruled out for offenses against property—a basic premise underlying the legislation.

(A new weekly portion, *Mishpatim*, begins with 21:1.)

* In many versions, 20:22; hence subsequent verse numbers need to be adjusted accordingly. The commentary below lists these numbers in brackets.

הַמָּקוֹם אֲשֶׁר אַזְכִּיר אֶת־שְׁמִי אָבוֹא אֵלֶיךָ וּבֵרַכְתִּיךָ: כב וְאִם־מִזְבַּח אֲבָנִים תַּעֲשֶׂה־לִּי לֹא־תִבְנֶה אֶתְהֶן גָּזִית כֹּי כִּי חַרְבְּךָ הֵנַפְתָּ עָלֶיהָ וַתְּחַלְלֶהָ: וְלֹא־תַעֲלֶה בְמַעֲלֹת עַל־מִזְבְּחִי אֲשֶׁר לֹא־תִגָּלֶה עֶרְוָתְךָ עָלָיו:

Haftarah Yitro, p. 710

יט וַיֹּאמֶר יְהֹוָה אֶל־מֹשֶׁה כֹּה תֹאמַר אֶל־בְּנֵי יִשְׂרָאֵל: כ אַתֶּם רְאִיתֶם כִּי מִן־הַשָּׁמַיִם דִּבַּרְתִּי עִמָּכֶם: לֹא תַעֲשׂוּן אִתִּי אֱלֹהֵי כֶסֶף וֵאלֹהֵי זָהָב לֹא תַעֲשׂוּ לָכֶם: כא מִזְבַּח אֲדָמָה תַּעֲשֶׂה־לִּי וְזָבַחְתָּ עָלָיו אֶת־עֹלֹתֶיךָ וְאֶת־שְׁלָמֶיךָ אֶת־צֹאנְךָ וְאֶת־בְּקָרֶךָ בְּכָל־

19] The LORD said to Moses:

Thus shall you say to the Israelites: You yourselves saw that I spoke to you from the very heavens: **20]** With Me, therefore, you shall not make any gods of silver, nor shall you make for yourselves any gods of gold. **21]** Make for Me an altar of earth and sacrifice on it your burnt offerings and your sacrifices of well-being, your sheep and your oxen; in every place where I cause My name to be mentioned I will come to you and bless you. **22]** And if you make for Me an altar of stones, do not build it of hewn stones; for by wielding your tool upon them you have profaned them. **23]** Do not ascend My altar by steps, that your nakedness may not be exposed upon it.

20:19] [22] *The very heavens.* The translation attempts to convey the implied emphasis of the Hebrew. It does not negate what has been previously stated, namely, that God spoke from Mount Sinai or from a cloud.

20] [23] *With Me.* The text, as divided by the Masoretes (with a pausal sign under אִתִּי), is difficult to understand, for it seems to read "You shall not make with Me," without an object being given; while the second part of the sentence is clear and self-contained. The translation appears to put the pause after כֶסֶף (silver), thus giving a better reading by paralleling gold and silver [1]. The word אִתִּי could also be understood in an instrumental sense: You shall not make them "by means of Me," perhaps prohibiting the use of divine fire known in Kenite practice [2].

21] [24] *Altar.* Sacrificial altars for worship purposes were taken for granted.

Burnt offerings. Others, "holocausts." The term עֹלֹת (*olot;* singular *olah*) describes the offering of whole animals (Lev. 1:9).

Sacrifices of well-being. שְׁלָמִים (*shelamim*), also rendered "peace offerings." These were brought on festive occasions (see at Lev. chapter 3). It appears that the nature of the *shelamim* changed as time passed [3].

In every place. In the context this seems to mean that God reassures the people that He will continue to be present even after they will have left Sinai [4]. Rashi and other traditional commentators emphasize that God promises to be present in the place where He himself will cause His name to be mentioned, that is, in the sanctuary. Some versions punctuate the verse differently, moving the semicolon from after "oxen" to after "mentioned," thereby giving the text a different meaning.

22] [25] *Profaned them.* Reflecting the old idea that the numen or "soul" of the stone would thereby be driven out [5]. Rashbam interprets the verse as a prohibition of fancy, deluxe creations.

23] [26] *Nakedness.* Revealed by the short Egyptian skirt. For this reason, breeches were prescribed for priests (28:42).

אֲדֹנָיו אֶל־הָאֱלֹהִים וְהִגִּישׁוֹ אֶל־הַדֶּלֶת אוֹ אֶל־הַמְּזוּזָה

וְרָצַע אֲדֹנָיו אֶת־אָזְנוֹ בַּמַּרְצֵעַ וַעֲבָדוֹ לְעֹלָם: ס

וְכִי־יִמְכֹּר אִישׁ אֶת־בִּתּוֹ לְאָמָה לֹא תֵצֵא כְּצֵאת

הָעֲבָדִים: אִם־רָעָה בְּעֵינֵי אֲדֹנֶיהָ אֲשֶׁר־לֹא יְעָדָהּ

וְהֶפְדָּהּ לְעַם נָכְרִי לֹא־יִמְשֹׁל לְמָכְרָהּ בְּבִגְדוֹ־בָהּ:

אַחֶרֶת יִקַּח־לוֹ שְׁאֵרָהּ כְּסוּתָהּ וְעֹנָתָהּ לֹא יִגְרָע:

וְאִם־לִבְנוֹ יִיעָדֶנָּה כְּמִשְׁפַּט הַבָּנוֹת יַעֲשֶׂה־לָּהּ: אִם־

* ח' לו קרי.

פ פ פ

וְאֵלֶּה הַמִּשְׁפָּטִים אֲשֶׁר תָּשִׂים לִפְנֵיהֶם: כִּי תִקְנֶה א ב

עֶבֶד עִבְרִי שֵׁשׁ שָׁנִים יַעֲבֹד וּבַשְּׁבִעִת יֵצֵא לַחָפְשִׁי

חִנָּם: אִם־בְּגַפּוֹ יָבֹא בְּגַפּוֹ יֵצֵא אִם־בַּעַל אִשָּׁה הוּא ג

וְיָצְאָה אִשְׁתּוֹ עִמּוֹ: אִם־אֲדֹנָיו יִתֶּן־לוֹ אִשָּׁה וְיָלְדָה־ ד

לּוֹ בָנִים אוֹ בָנוֹת הָאִשָּׁה וִילָדֶיהָ תִּהְיֶה לַאדֹנֶיהָ

וְהוּא יֵצֵא בְגַפּוֹ: וְאִם־אָמֹר יֹאמַר הָעֶבֶד אָהַבְתִּי ה

אֶת־אֲדֹנִי אֶת־אִשְׁתִּי וְאֶת־בָּנָי לֹא אֵצֵא חָפְשִׁי: וְהִגִּישׁוֹ ו

1] These are the rules that you shall set before them:
2] When you acquire a Hebrew slave, he shall serve six years; in the seventh year he shall go free, without payment.   **3]** If he came single, he shall leave single; if he had a wife, his wife shall leave with him.   **4]** If his master gave him a wife, and she has borne him children, the wife and her children shall belong to the master, and he shall leave alone.   **5]** But if the slave declares, "I love my master, and my wife and children: I do not wish to go free,"   **6]** his master shall take him before God. He shall be brought to the door or the doorpost, and his master shall pierce his ear with an awl; and he shall then remain his slave for life.

7] When a man sells his daughter as a slave, she shall not be freed as male slaves are.   **8]** If she proves to be displeasing to her master, who designated her for himself, he must let her be redeemed; he shall not have the right to sell her to outsiders, since he broke faith with her.   **9]** And if he designated her for his son, he shall deal with her as is the practice with free maidens.   **10]** If he marries another, he must not withhold from this one her food, her

---

21:1] *Rules.* מִשְׁפָּטִים (*mishpatim*), others, "ordinances." The root of the Hebrew word means "to judge"; thus מִשְׁפָּטִים has a distinct legal connotation. In later interpretation the term covered all Torah laws except those that could not be comprehended by human reason and were to be obeyed because God had ordained them. (These were called *chukim.*) Another view considers *mishpatim* to refer to conditional or casuistic law and *chukim* to apodictic legislation.

2] *Hebrew slave.* עֶבֶד עִבְרִי (*eved ivri*). On the term *ivri,* see Commentary to Genesis, chapter 14. The law is extended further in Lev. 25:2 ff.

6] *Before God.* A solemn declaration before witnesses was necessary to make the slave's status permanent [6].

Door. Of the master's house (some say, of the sanctuary), to signify the perpetual attachment of

the slave who was now drawn also into the cultic community of the house [7].

For life. The Rabbis interpreted לְעֹלָם (literally, "forever") to be imprecisely meant, signifying "a long time"—until the jubilee year, when, according to Lev. 25:2 ff., the slave would be released [8].

7] *When a man sells his daughter.* Which was probably a frequent practice among the poor. The law for daughters did not provide for their release after six years; instead, it regulated their status in accordance with their sexual relation to the master or his son. Examples of female slaves elevated to marital status are Hagar and Keturah, Abraham's concubines; Bilhah and Zilpah, Jacob's concubines.

9] *Free maidens.* Probably, to be maintained like free maidens.

10] *If he marries another.* If the master marries a second concubine he must treat the first one ("this one") fairly.

יא וְאִם־שְׁלָשׁ־אֵלֶּה לֹא יַעֲשֶׂה לָהּ וְיָצְאָה חִנָּם אֵין

כָּסֶף: ס מַכֵּה אִישׁ וָמֵת מוֹת יוּמָת: וַאֲשֶׁר לֹא

צָדָה וְהָאֱלֹהִים אִנָּה לְיָדוֹ וְשַׂמְתִּי לְךָ מָקוֹם אֲשֶׁר

יד יָנוּס שָׁמָּה: ס וְכִי־יָזִד אִישׁ עַל־רֵעֵהוּ לְהָרְגוֹ

טו בְּעָרְמָה מֵעִם מִזְבְּחִי תִּקָּחֶנּוּ לָמוּת: ס וּמַכֵּה אָבִיו

וְאִמּוֹ מוֹת יוּמָת: ס וְגֹנֵב אִישׁ וּמְכָרוֹ וְנִמְצָא בְיָדוֹ

יז מוֹת יוּמָת: ס וּמְקַלֵּל אָבִיו וְאִמּוֹ מוֹת יוּמָת: ס

וְכִי־יְרִיבֻן אֲנָשִׁים וְהִכָּה־אִישׁ אֶת־רֵעֵהוּ בְּאֶבֶן אוֹ

clothing, or her conjugal rights.   **11]** If he fails her in these three ways, she shall go free, without payment.

12] He who fatally strikes a man shall be put to death.   **13]** If he did not do it by design, but it came about by an act of God, I will assign you a place to which he can flee.

14] When a man schemes against another and kills him treacherously, you shall take him from My very altar to be put to death.

15] He who strikes his father or his mother shall be put to death.

16] He who kidnaps a man—whether he has sold him or is still holding him—shall be put to death.

17] He who insults his father or his mother shall be put to death.

18] When men quarrel and one strikes the other with stone or fist, and he does not die but

Conjugal rights. Others, "ointment" [9]. The word עֹנָה occurs only here.

12-17] Capital offenses. Death is the punishment for killing (unless done unintentionally), kidnaping, and offending one's parents.

12] *Put to death.* In traditional exegesis the Hebrew יוּמָת denotes execution by human judges and מוֹת יוּמָת by divine act [10].

13] *Act of God.* Something over which he had no control.

A place to which he can flee. To escape the blood avenger. See commentary to Num. 35:9–34; Deut. 19:1–13 [11].

14] *From My very altar.* Which served as asylum in many ancient and medieval cultures. Adonijah found safety from Solomon by grasping the horns of the altar (I Kings 1:50 ff.) [12]. Horned altars have recently been discovered [13].

15] *Strikes.* Even without killing the parent. The Code of Hammurabi provided a penalty only when the father was offended (cutting off the hand), and none when the mother was struck [14].

16] *A man.* Any man—but Septuagint, Targum, and Mishnah restricted it to kidnaping an Israelite [15].

17] *Insults.* Other versions, "reviles," "repudiates," "dishonors" [16]. The Rabbis who understood it as "curses" stipulated that the legal offense was committed only when the Tetragrammaton (יהוה) was pronounced during the curse [17]. They thereby made the conviction of the wayward son unlikely, even as they did in their treatment of Deut. 21:18–21.

18] *Stone.* An example of any potential or actual weapon.

יט בְּאֶגְרֹף וְלֹא יָמוּת וְנָפַל לְמִשְׁכָּב: אִם־יָקוּם וְהִתְהַלֵּךְ
בַּחוּץ עַל־מִשְׁעַנְתּוֹ וְנִקָּה הַמַּכֶּה רַק שִׁבְתּוֹ יִתֵּן
כ וְרַפֹּא יְרַפֵּא: ס וְכִי־יַכֶּה אִישׁ אֶת־עַבְדּוֹ אוֹ אֶת־
כא אֲמָתוֹ בַּשֵּׁבֶט וּמֵת תַּחַת יָדוֹ נָקֹם יִנָּקֵם: אַךְ אִם־יוֹם
כב אוֹ יוֹמַיִם יַעֲמֹד לֹא יֻקַּם כִּי כַסְפּוֹ הוּא: ס וְכִי־
יִנָּצוּ אֲנָשִׁים וְנָגְפוּ אִשָּׁה הָרָה וְיָצְאוּ יְלָדֶיהָ וְלֹא
יִהְיֶה אָסוֹן עָנוֹשׁ יֵעָנֵשׁ כַּאֲשֶׁר יָשִׁית עָלָיו בַּעַל

כג הָאִשָּׁה וְנָתַן בִּפְלִלִים: וְאִם־אָסוֹן יִהְיֶה וְנָתַתָּה נֶפֶשׁ
כד תַּחַת נָפֶשׁ: עַיִן תַּחַת עַיִן שֵׁן תַּחַת שֵׁן יָד תַּחַת יָד
כה רֶגֶל תַּחַת רָגֶל: כְּוִיָּה תַּחַת כְּוִיָּה פֶּצַע תַּחַת פָּצַע
כו חַבּוּרָה תַּחַת חַבּוּרָה: ס וְכִי־יַכֶּה אִישׁ אֶת־עֵין
עַבְדּוֹ אוֹ־אֶת־עֵין אֲמָתוֹ וְשִׁחֲתָהּ לַחָפְשִׁי יְשַׁלְּחֶנּוּ
כז תַּחַת עֵינוֹ: וְאִם־שֵׁן עַבְדּוֹ אוֹ־שֵׁן אֲמָתוֹ יַפִּיל לַחָפְשִׁי
יְשַׁלְּחֶנּוּ תַּחַת שִׁנּוֹ:   פ

has to take to his bed— **19]** if he then gets up and walks outdoors upon his staff, the assailant shall go unpunished, except that he must pay for his idleness and his cure.

20] When a man strikes his slave, male or female, with a rod, and he dies there and then, he must be avenged. **21]** But if he survives a day or two, he is not to be avenged, since he is the other's property.

22] When men fight, and one of them pushes a pregnant woman and a miscarriage results, but no other damage ensues, the one responsible shall be fined according as the woman's husband may exact from him, the payment to be based on reckoning. **23]** But if other damage ensues, the penalty shall be life for life, **24]** eye for eye, tooth for tooth, hand for hand, foot for foot, **25]** burn for burn, wound for wound, bruise for bruise.

26] When a man strikes the eye of his slave, male or female, and destroys it, he shall let him go free on account of his eye. **27]** If he knocks out the tooth of his slave, male or female, he shall let him go free on account of his tooth.

19] *Upon his staff.* Testifying to his convalescence.
His cure. Medical costs. So also in the Code of Hammurabi [18].

20] *There and then.* Literally, "under his hand." He must be avenged although it was his master who had killed him (this differed from Roman practice) [19].

21] *He is the other's property.* He has human rights, but not those of a free man.

22] *On reckoning.* Others, "as the judges determine." The meaning of the Hebrew בִּפְלִלִים is uncertain. Speiser suggests it means "by calculating" the degree of the woman's pregnancy (such a calculation being known in Hittite law) [20]. The verse figured prominently in the halachic discussion of abortion.

23-25] *The law of retribution.* Usually called lex talionis (but see commentary following). Though stated only as applying to a specific case, it means to convey a general principle.

26 ff.] From here on, neglect cases are treated. Negligence is a legal concept which, in its biblical examples, had a long and complex history in ancient Near Eastern law. It is likely that the biblical provisions reflect conceptions that were developed from a common archetypical law.

26] *Eye of his slave.* While the slave did not exact "talion," his humanity was emphasized and, in fact, he fared better than if talion were to apply. This law differed substantially from Babylonian and Hittite provisions. There, compensation was stipulated only if someone else's, not one's own, slave was hurt; in the latter case no penalty was asked of the master [21].

כח וְכִי־יִגַּח שׁוֹר אֶת־אִישׁ אוֹ אֶת־אִשָּׁה וָמֵת סָקוֹל יִסָּקֵל

כט הַשּׁוֹר וְלֹא יֵאָכֵל אֶת־בְּשָׂרוֹ וּבַעַל הַשּׁוֹר נָקִי: וְאִם שׁוֹר נַגָּח הוּא מִתְּמֹל שִׁלְשֹׁם וְהוּעַד בִּבְעָלָיו וְלֹא יִשְׁמְרֶנּוּ וְהֵמִית אִישׁ אוֹ אִשָּׁה הַשּׁוֹר יִסָּקֵל וְגַם־

ל בְּעָלָיו יוּמָת: אִם־כֹּפֶר יוּשַׁת עָלָיו וְנָתַן פִּדְיֹן נַפְשׁוֹ

לא כְּכֹל אֲשֶׁר־יוּשַׁת עָלָיו: אוֹ־בֵן יִגָּח אוֹ־בַת יִגָּח כַּמִּשְׁפָּט

לב הַזֶּה יֵעָשֶׂה לּוֹ: אִם־עֶבֶד יִגַּח הַשּׁוֹר אוֹ אָמָה כֶּסֶף

לג שְׁלֹשִׁים שְׁקָלִים יִתֵּן לַאדֹנָיו וְהַשּׁוֹר יִסָּקֵל: ס וְכִי־

יִפְתַּח אִישׁ בּוֹר אוֹ כִּי־יִכְרֶה אִישׁ בֹּר וְלֹא יְכַסֶּנּוּ

לד וְנָפַל־שָׁמָּה שּׁוֹר אוֹ חֲמוֹר: בַּעַל הַבּוֹר יְשַׁלֵּם כֶּסֶף

לה יָשִׁיב לִבְעָלָיו וְהַמֵּת יִהְיֶה־לּוֹ: ס וְכִי־יִגֹּף שׁוֹר־אִישׁ אֶת־שׁוֹר רֵעֵהוּ וָמֵת וּמָכְרוּ אֶת־הַשּׁוֹר הַחַי וְחָצוּ

לו אֶת־כַּסְפּוֹ וְגַם אֶת־הַמֵּת יֶחֱצוּן: אוֹ נוֹדַע כִּי שׁוֹר נַגָּח הוּא מִתְּמוֹל שִׁלְשֹׁם וְלֹא יִשְׁמְרֶנּוּ בְּעָלָיו שַׁלֵּם יְשַׁלֵּם שׁוֹר תַּחַת הַשּׁוֹר וְהַמֵּת יִהְיֶה־לּוֹ: ס

28] When an ox gores a man or a woman to death, the ox shall be stoned and its flesh shall not be eaten, but the owner of the ox is not to be punished. **29]** If, however, that ox has been in the habit of goring, and its owner, though warned, has failed to guard it, and it kills a man or a woman—the ox shall be stoned and its owner, too, shall be put to death. **30]** If ransom is laid upon him, he must pay whatever is laid upon him to redeem his life. **31]** So, too, if it gores a minor, male or female, [the owner] shall be dealt with according to the same rule. **32]** But if the ox gores a slave, male or female, he shall pay thirty shekels of silver to the master, and the ox shall be stoned.

33] When a man opens a pit, or digs a pit and does not cover it, and an ox or an ass falls into it, **34]** the one responsible for the pit must make restitution; he shall pay the price to the owner, but shall keep the dead animal.

35] When a man's ox injures his neighbor's ox and it dies, they shall sell the live ox and divide its price; they shall also divide the dead animal. **36]** If, however, it is known that the ox was in the habit of goring, and its owner has failed to guard it, he must restore ox for ox, but shall keep the dead animal.

28] *The ox shall be stoned.* Similar to modern provisions for killing a rabid dog [22]. (Further on this, see commentary.)

Its flesh shall not be eaten. Either because the animal was deemed defiled, or because the owner was to derive no benefit from it.

29] *In the habit of goring.* At least three times, according to the Rabbis [23].

30] *Ransom.* Permissible in this case, though otherwise one could not ransom for killing.

32] *Thirty shekels.* Probably representing the value of a slave. A free man's value was fifty shekels, a woman's was thirty (Lev. 27:2–4). Joseph was sold for twenty shekels (Gen. 37:28).

Slavery in the Torah

Slavery was known throughout antiquity, as far back as the fourth millennium. The Torah deals with it as a fact of life, one, however, which involved a basic contradiction: a slave was in many ways treated as a chattel, a "thing," yet he was also a human being. The Torah did not resolve this contradiction and therefore did not portray slavery as something inherently evil but may be said to have viewed it as an institution that needed humanizing. This became practical because on the whole the ancient Near East was populated by small freeholders who treated a serf generally as a member of the family. He was a domestic servant rather than an indentured slave as in Roman or early American society [24]. In contrast to other contemporary or even later cultures, the Torah insisted on stressing the humanity of the serf, a person endowed with rights and entitled to dignity. Even the female serf who, being weighted down with the usual disabilities visited on women, still emerged as a person with clear-cut legal privileges.[1] While Aristotle took pains to defend slavery, the first-century C.E. Jewish philosopher and Bible commentator Philo rejected it, and so did some Jewish brotherhoods whose members refused to keep slaves.

In point of fact, the Bible does not have a specific word for the totally unfree person, a word which would correspond to the Latin *nerva* or *mancipium* or to the English slave. Its term is עֶבֶד (*eved*), which can mean anything from chattel slave to household hand, or—in the spiritualized form *eved Adonai*—"servant of God."[2] It was also used as an expression of modesty or submission; thus

עַבְדְּכֶם in Gen. 19:2 is comparable to "your obedient servant," a polite expression without legal significance.

Boaz Cohen, following the Talmud, has distinguished between two basic types of serfs in ancient Hebrew society [26]: the *eved* who was a slave in the common sense, a chattel who belonged body and soul to his master, and the *eved ivri* of Exod. 21:2–6 whom Cohen called "bondman," a person whose service was temporary and who retained his human rights. The former acquired his permanent status in various ways: by birth to indentured parents, by parental or by self-sale, by insolvency, or—most commonly—by being taken prisoner in warfare. The *eved ivri* was likely a person who paid off a debt by serving his master. In this sense Jacob became Laban's *eved ivri* and remained in his service until he had paid with his labor for Leah and Rachel. If *eved ivri* meant a man from an Israelite tribe (rather than a person belonging to a particular class of civil servants) then it is clear that the Torah aimed at wiping out slavery from the Israelite people and considered such bondage, if voluntarily perpetuated, an affront to the dignity of God's people.

It should further be noted that an escaped slave was not to be returned to his master (Deut. 23:16)—another clear indication that the Torah's acceptance of slavery showed ultimate reservations about the institution as such. Nonetheless, it never completely disappeared from ancient Jewry, and the Rabbis saw no way to abolish it entirely. They did, however, encourage the redemption of any Jewish slave (who had been impressed by capture in war, or by kidnaping,

---

[1] See also Commentary on Leviticus, chapter 25, "Slavery."

[2] Isa. 53 is understood by Jews to refer to the Jewish people and by most Christians to refer to their savior [25]. Note also that in later Jewish parlance the word עֲבוֹדָה (service) came to denote religious service or prayer. Similar semantic relationships are observable elsewhere, e.g., in Latin where *cultus* means both work and worship, or in Aramaic *pulchana.*

or by oppressive authority), wherever he might be found. Contributions to פִּדְיוֹן שְׁבוּיִים (pidyon shevuyim, ransom of prisoners) became a prime and all too often necessary adjunct of Jewish life in talmudic and medieval days, and the Psalmist exalts God as the one "who sets the prisoners free" (146:7). A people who had been servants in Egypt could never quite forget what it meant to be unfree; hence the repeated reminder "For you were servants in the land of Egypt." Job's comment on the human stature of the *eved* best sums up the Bible's viewpoint:

> Did not He that made me in the womb
> make him also?
>
> And did not One fashion us in the womb?
> (Job 31:15)

An Eye for an Eye

Few passages in the Torah have been so thoroughly misunderstood as the one which states that injuries to life and limb are to be met with punishments that reflect the seriousness of the crime. The many negative judgments pronounced on the Bible by latter-day critics, stressing the Torah's alleged "primitive" nature as encapsuled in these laws, are more a reflection on the judges than on the text and its real intent. For the rule "An eye for an eye"—which *appears* to lay down the principle of literal retribution (or "talion")[3]—was not at all formulated for such a purpose. To be sure, during the Middle Ages cruelly retributive legal practices, which were presumed to reflect these biblical injunctions, were introduced in many European countries. But in fact no case of physical talion is recorded in the Bible,[4] nor was such talion the intention of the biblical law, as has now been shown clearly from a study of older Near Eastern law codes.

The oldest of these exhibit a common feature in their treatment of offenses such as homicide and adultery: they considered them private injuries, to be dealt with privately, and the law fixed the amount of compensation which the injured party could demand [28]. The state itself did not punish crimes except when the welfare of the total community appeared to be at stake, as in cases of blasphemy or treason. Otherwise there was no "criminal law" in our sense, where the public itself exacts punishments for many offenses arising out of relationships between individuals. Thus, an injury inflicted on a person is today considered a *criminal act* which may land the offender in jail (because such an act is deemed injurious to the public weal), but the injured individual must seek monetary restitution in a *civil suit*. The earliest laws knew of no state interest in the injury, and only later was the public sphere enlarged, as in the Code of Hammurabi and in the Torah.[5] Now the state itself was entitled to exact the retribution, and this right was expressed in the principle of talion, and this in turn was transformed into compensation scaled to the degree of the injury: the value of an eye for the loss of an eye; the value of a limb for its loss, and so forth[6] [30]. Only intentional homicide was expressly exempted: it could not be

---

[3] That is, retaliation authorized by law, in which the punishment corresponds in kind and degree to the injury.

[4] While Deut. 25:11-12 does direct mutilation for one special crime, there is no record that the penalty was ever exacted. The mutilation of Adonibezek was an act of battlefield revenge and not a legal penalty (Judg. 1:6-7) [27].

[5] A similar development occurred in medieval England. Until 1100 C.E. adultery was subject to laws of compensation, as was wounding; later on, the wronged husband was permitted to slay the adulterers.

[6] The Rabbis pointed out that, inasmuch as the law seeks equity, its literal enforcement would frequently lead to gross inequity. For instance, they said, taking

compensated in money, and the offender had to give literally his life for the life he had taken (Num. 35:31). This may also be the meaning of the Hebrew formula *mot yumat*: "He shall [surely] be put to death" (Exod. 21:12; Lev. 24:17). But even in such cases there were the mitigating rules of asylum (see Commentary on Num., ch. 35).

The Rabbis' contention that financial compensation, and not literal, physical talion, was the intent of the law was therefore essentially correct [31]. The Torah law represented here an important stage in the development and extension of the sphere of criminal law and thereby had the important function of limiting private revenge, especially family or tribal feuds. Further, the Torah treats injuries to rich and poor, male and female, completely alike, except in some instances (as in the case of a slave, where the status of the victim plays a role), so that Philo could call these biblical laws "the interpreter and teacher of equality" [32]. This principle was clearly established in the covenant God made with Noah (in the case of homicide):

Whoever sheds the blood of man,
By man shall his blood be shed;
For in His image
Did God make man.   (Gen. 9:6)

In sum, the Torah law set down in this chapter of Exodus does not direct physical retribution, it speaks of monetary compensation, except in the case of intentional homicide. It thereby parallels the Code of Hammurabi to a significant degree, but it also diverges from it in two important respects: the Torah bases itself on the law of human equality and it eschews the provisions for mutilation which the Babylonian code contains (laws 194–197; see Gleanings). Later misunderstandings of the biblical intent have all too frequently overlaid these facts, which can now be securely deduced from our newly gained knowledge of ancient law.[7]

The Ox That Gores

Exodus 21:28 ff. presents us with an instance of case law that is found in both the laws of Eshnunna and of Hammurabi (see Gleanings). The close similarities between the three formulations are unquestionably far larger than the observable differences, so that the question of the relationship between these three codices is here especially acute.

Of the three, the biblical formulation of responsibility is the most complete, in that it posits a greater variety of possibilities than do the others. On the basis of this it would be possible to conclude, either that the Bible was the recipient of the other two traditions and added its own particular stamp, or that all three formulations derived from some common general model which is no longer known. The latter theory appears more likely if one takes into consideration other points of contact between ancient Near Eastern laws.

The major difference observable in the

___

the eye of a one-eyed assailant would not be just retribution but excessive punishment. Or, how was one to guard against the fatal effect of talion upon the offender? Were he to die he would give life for an eye or a hand, and the objective of the law would be thwarted [29]. Jewish law therefore made detailed stipulations for monetary compensation, much as modern insurance contracts are wont to do.

[7] Such misreadings of the biblical text were reinforced by the sayings of Jesus (Matthew 5:38–39) which were understood to be directed to a presumed Torah law of talion. Most likely, however, they dealt with the general idea that no recourse should be sought for any wrongs done, not even in the form of compensation.

biblical law is the disposition of the offending animal. The ox becomes taboo following the incident and, after being destroyed, is not allowed for food. This provision caused Frazer to suggest that we have here a remnant of the ancient principle of blood revenge exacted even against a beast. However, no similar provision exists in the older laws of Eshnunna and Hammurabi, which makes it more likely that the taboo of the oxen's flesh is part of the general biblical caution only to eat what has actually been slaughtered, while the destruction of the ox itself represented simply the removal of a dangerous animal. To be sure, the stoning of the ox appears to have the overtones of legal punishment, like the deodand of medieval English law [33], but the text goes no further than this and certainly does not enter the arena of animal trials, familiar from Plato's *Laws* down to the practices of eighteenth-century France [34].

GLEANINGS

Steps

The Torah cautions those who sacrifice not to expose themselves as they go up to the altar, and later tradition suggested that this was best observed if one took small steps. The principle applies also to the legal passages that follow: judges too are cautioned to take small steps rather than large ones, to arrive at judgments.

MIDRASH [35]

The prohibition of altar steps rests on the idea that the sexual sphere is part of a dark mysterious realm, a realm that played an elevated role in many cults in the ancient East. For this very reason, however, it was impossible for it to be associated with the sphere of the holy in Israel.

M. NOTH [36]

The Holy Name

It says (20:21), "In every place where I cause My name to be mentioned"—that can only mean the Temple. Hence, outside the Temple, God's holy name (יְהֹוָה) is not pronounced at all.

MIDRASH [37]

Altar and Sword

Why would the sword (i.e., an iron tool) profane the stones of the altar? The altar was made to lengthen man's life and the sword to shorten it. Hence it would be wrong to lift up that which is designed to curtail man's life against that which is designed to prolong it.

MISHNAH [38]

Many Laws

Concerning the large number of ordinances, God said: "I have given you many laws, but also much reward."

MIDRASH [39]

Before Them

It says that "these are rules you are to set before them" (21:1)—*them*, that is, before the Israelites and not others. Hence arose the practice among contending Jews to bring law suits before Jewish arbitration courts rather than before gentile judges.

RASHI [40]

Before *them* could also mean "before the rules," that is to say, these are rules which you are to observe to begin with, and then you should go on to observe what is not specified, to go even beyond what is just and right. This is why the Rabbis said that Jerusalem was destroyed because the judges merely executed justice without going beyond it.   M. HACOHEN [41]

The Ear

Why is the man who insists on remaining a slave pierced through the ear? Because it had heard that Israel was God's servant (Lev. 25:55), and one who prefers an earthly master shall have that very same ear pierced.   RASHI

What do ear and door have in common? They both can be opened and shut at will. I. CARO [42]

Treatment of Slaves

Jewish law attempted to alleviate the lot of the slave. The attitude of the Sages is summarized by Maimonides in the following way: "It is allowed to work the slave hard, but, while this is the law, ethics and prudence suggest that a master should be just and merciful, not impose too heavy a burden on his slave and not press him too hard, and he should give him of all (his own) food and drink. . . . Slaves may not be maltreated or offended: the law destined them for service, not for humiliation" [43].

A Second Wife

From verse 10 the Rabbis infer the rule that a man should not take another wife unless he can afford to treat her properly.   SFORNO

Ancient Near Eastern Parallels

(Only a few representative examples will be quoted below.)

"Talion"
(From the Code of Hammurabi)

194: When a seignior gave his son to a nurse and that son has died in the care of the nurse, if the nurse has then made a contract for another son without the knowledge of his father and mother,

they shall prove it against her and they shall cut off her breast because she made a contract for another son without the knowledge of his father and mother.

195: If a son has struck his father, they shall cut off his hand.

196: If a seignior has destroyed the eye of a member of the aristocracy, they shall destroy his eye.

197: If he has broken another seignior's bone, they shall break his bone.

198: If he has destroyed the eye of a commoner or broken the bone of a commoner, he shall pay one mina of silver.

199: If he has destroyed the eye of a seignior's slave or broken the bone of a seignior's slave, he shall pay one-half his value.

200: If a seignior has knocked out a tooth of a seignior of his own rank, they shall knock out his tooth.

201: If he has knocked out a commoner's tooth, he shall pay one-third mina of silver.

209: If a seignior struck another seignior's daughter and has caused her to have a miscarriage, he shall pay ten shekels of silver for her fetus.

210: If that woman has died, they shall put his daughter to death.

211: If by a blow he has caused a commoner's daughter to have a miscarriage, he shall pay five shekels of silver.

212: If that woman has died, he shall pay one-half mina of silver.

213: If he struck a seignior's female slave and has caused her to have a miscarriage, he shall pay two shekels of silver.

214: If that female slave has died, he shall pay one-third mina of silver [44].

(From the Hittite Laws)

1: If anyone kills a man or woman in a quarrel, he has to make amends for him/her. He shall give

four persons, man or woman, and pledge his estate as security.

2: If anyone kills a male or a female slave in a quarrel, he has to make amends for him/her. He shall give two persons, man or woman, and pledge his estate as security [45].

"The Ox That Gores"
(From the Laws of Eshnunna)

53: If an ox gores another ox and causes its death, both ox owners shall divide (among themselves) the price of the live ox and also the equivalent of the dead ox.

54: If an ox is known to gore habitually and the authorities have brought the fact to the knowledge of its owner, but he does not have his ox dehorned, and it gores a man and causes his death, then the owner of the ox shall pay two-thirds of a mina of silver.

55: If it gores a slave and causes his death, he shall pay 15 shekels of silver [46].

(From the Code of Hammurabi)

250: If an ox, when it was walking along the street, gored a seignior to death, that case is not subject to claim.

251: If a seignior's ox was a gorer and his city council made it known to him that it was a gorer, but he did not plaid its horns (or) tie up his ox, and that ox gored to death a member of the aristocracy, he shall give one-half mina of silver.

252: If it was a seignior's slave, he shall give one-third mina of silver [47].

Egypt and America

Pharaoh's country was cursed with plagues, and his hosts were lost in the Red Sea, for striving to retain a captive people who had already served them more than 400 years. May like disasters never befall us. ABRAHAM LINCOLN [48]

Laws on Property and Moral Behavior

The first sixteen verses of chapter 22 deal with property and comprise laws on theft, the destruction of property, and disputes over and guardianship of material things. To this category is added the compensation for loss of virginity—the maiden daughter being in the care of her father, and defloration therefore an injury to the father and the family.

Then, from verse 17 [18] on, follows a variety of interpersonal rules with a distinct moral import. They cover sorcery, pederasty, idolatry, the treatment of strangers, widows, and orphans, taking of interest, the first-born, flesh unfit to eat, false rumors, righteous judgment, and treatment of the enemy. Some of these are grouped together by subject, others—like laws dealing with the stranger (22:20 [21] and 23:9)—are not. Certain mnemotechnical connections are evident; thus the rule about the responsibility for an ox that gores is followed by laws about stealing an ox, about other forms of theft, and then by laws on burglary. (On modern and ancient needs for systematizing, see Introduction to Part VI.)**

* In many versions 21:37 is made the first sentence of ch. 22, so that our 22:1 becomes 22:2 in these versions. The latter numbering is listed in brackets.

** Even though form criticism is firmly established in biblical scholarship, the caution with which G. E. Mendenhall approaches it appears relevant here: "One must always ask whether a hypothetical literary 'form' which the literary critic extracts from the written materials was really a distinct functional 'form' to ancient man or whether it is accepted merely because it happens to correspond to some structured concept or pattern of thought to which modern scholars are at least temporarily sensitized" [1].

לה כִּי־תֵצֵא אֵשׁ וּמָצְאָה קֹצִים וְנֶאֱכַל גָּדִישׁ אוֹ הַקָּמָה
אוֹ הַשָּׂדֶה שַׁלֵּם יְשַׁלֵּם הַמַּבְעִר אֶת־הַבְּעֵרָה: ס

לו כִּי־יִתֵּן אִישׁ אֶל־רֵעֵהוּ כֶּסֶף אוֹ־כֵלִים לִשְׁמֹר וְגֻנַּב
מִבֵּית הָאִישׁ אִם־יִמָּצֵא הַגַּנָּב יְשַׁלֵּם שְׁנָיִם: אִם־לֹא
יִמָּצֵא הַגַּנָּב וְנִקְרַב בַּעַל־הַבַּיִת אֶל־הָאֱלֹהִים אִם־
לֹא שָׁלַח יָדוֹ בִּמְלֶאכֶת רֵעֵהוּ: עַל־כָּל־דְּבַר־פֶּשַׁע
עַל־שׁוֹר עַל־חֲמוֹר עַל־שֶׂה עַל־שַׂלְמָה עַל־כָּל־
אֲבֵדָה אֲשֶׁר יֹאמַר כִּי־הוּא זֶה עַד הָאֱלֹהִים יָבֹא

לז כִּי יִגְנֹב־אִישׁ שׁוֹר אוֹ־שֶׂה וּטְבָחוֹ אוֹ מְכָרוֹ חֲמִשָּׁה
בָקָר יְשַׁלֵּם תַּחַת הַשּׁוֹר וְאַרְבַּע־צֹאן תַּחַת הַשֶּׂה:

כא אִם־בַּמַּחְתֶּרֶת יִמָּצֵא הַגַּנָּב וְהֻכָּה וָמֵת אֵין לוֹ דָּמִים:
כב אִם־זָרְחָה הַשֶּׁמֶשׁ עָלָיו דָּמִים לוֹ שַׁלֵּם יְשַׁלֵּם אִם־
כג אֵין לוֹ וְנִמְכַּר בִּגְנֵבָתוֹ: אִם־הִמָּצֵא תִמָּצֵא בְיָדוֹ
הַגְּנֵבָה מִשּׁוֹר עַד־חֲמוֹר עַד־שֶׂה חַיִּים שְׁנַיִם יְשַׁלֵּם: ס
כד כִּי יַבְעֶר־אִישׁ שָׂדֶה אוֹ־כֶרֶם וְשִׁלַּח אֶת־בְּעִירֹה וּבִעֵר
בִּשְׂדֵה אַחֵר מֵיטַב שָׂדֵהוּ וּמֵיטַב כַּרְמוֹ יְשַׁלֵּם: ס

ד בעירו קרי.

37] When a man steals an ox or a sheep, and slaughters it or sells it, he shall pay five oxen for the ox, and four sheep for the sheep.— 1] If the thief is seized while tunneling, and he is beaten to death, there is no bloodguilt in his case. 2] If the sun has risen on him, there is bloodguilt in that case.—He must make restitution; if he lacks the means, he shall be sold for his theft. 3] But if what he stole—whether ox or ass or sheep—is found alive in his possession, he shall pay double.

4] When a man lets his livestock loose to graze in another's land, and so allows a field or vineyard to be grazed bare, he must make restitution for the impairment of that field or vineyard.

5] When a fire is started and spreads to thorns, so that stacked, standing, or growing grain is consumed, he who started the fire must make restitution.

6] When a man gives money or goods to another for safekeeping, and they are stolen from the man's house—if the thief is caught, he shall pay double; 7] if the thief is not caught, the owner of the house shall depose before God that he has not laid hands on his neighbor's property. 8] In all charges of misappropriation—pertaining to an ox, an ass, a sheep, a garment, or any other loss, whereof one party alleges, "This is it"—the case of both parties shall come before God: he whom God declares guilty shall pay double to the other.

21:37] [22:1] *And slaughters it.* Double restitution is to be paid if the animal is still found alive (22:3 [22:4]). Multiple restitution as a penalty was found in Hammurabi's code (where, however, death was provided in case the penalty could not be paid) [2] and exists in modern tax laws. Double restitution was also stipulated in many Babylonian contracts [3].

22:1] [2] *While tunneling.* Under a wall, for the purpose of housebreaking. The New English Bible renders idiomatically: "If a burglar is caught in the act."

No bloodguilt. For in such a case the heightened anxiety of the owner is understandable and his extreme reaction legitimate. A similar law was part of Greek tradition [4].

2] [3] *If the sun has risen.* When the burglar's intent not to kill can be recognized, the owner is liable for manslaughter if nonetheless he kills the intruder [5].

He. The thief of the preceding verse 21:37 [22:1] [6].

5] [6] *Growing grain.* The translation is uncertain.

6] [7] *Safekeeping.* If the owner says merely, "Keep an eye on it," but does not pay for the safekeeping, no liability is incurred in case the object is lost or stolen [7].

7] [8] *Before God.* Suggesting that an oath was to be taken in such a case (compare 21:6) [8]. The rest of the verse is difficult.

דְּבַר־שְׁנֵיהֶם אֲשֶׁר יַרְשִׁיעֻן אֱלֹהִים יְשַׁלֵּם שְׁנַיִם
לְרֵעֵהוּ: ס   ט כִּי־יִתֵּן אִישׁ אֶל־רֵעֵהוּ חֲמוֹר אוֹ־שׁוֹר
אוֹ־שֶׂה וְכָל־בְּהֵמָה לִשְׁמֹר וּמֵת אוֹ־נִשְׁבַּר אוֹ־נִשְׁבָּה
אֵין רֹאֶה: י שְׁבֻעַת יְהֹוָה תִּהְיֶה בֵּין שְׁנֵיהֶם אִם־לֹא
שָׁלַח יָדוֹ בִּמְלֶאכֶת רֵעֵהוּ וְלָקַח בְּעָלָיו וְלֹא יְשַׁלֵּם:
יא וְאִם־גָּנֹב יִגָּנֵב מֵעִמּוֹ יְשַׁלֵּם לִבְעָלָיו: אִם־טָרֹף יִטָּרֵף
יְבִאֵהוּ עֵד הַטְּרֵפָה לֹא יְשַׁלֵּם: פ

יג וְכִי־יִשְׁאַל אִישׁ מֵעִם רֵעֵהוּ וְנִשְׁבַּר אוֹ־מֵת בְּעָלָיו
אֵין־עִמּוֹ שַׁלֵּם יְשַׁלֵּם: אִם־בְּעָלָיו עִמּוֹ לֹא יְשַׁלֵּם
אִם־שָׂכִיר הוּא בָּא בִּשְׂכָרוֹ: ס   טו וְכִי־יְפַתֶּה אִישׁ
בְּתוּלָה אֲשֶׁר לֹא־אֹרָשָׂה וְשָׁכַב עִמָּהּ מָהֹר יִמְהָרֶנָּה
לּוֹ לְאִשָּׁה: אִם־מָאֵן יְמָאֵן אָבִיהָ לְתִתָּהּ לוֹ כֶּסֶף
יִשְׁקֹל כְּמֹהַר הַבְּתוּלֹת: ס   יז מְכַשֵּׁפָה לֹא תְחַיֶּה:
יח כָּל־שֹׁכֵב עִם־בְּהֵמָה מוֹת יוּמָת: ס   יט זֹבֵחַ לָאֱלֹהִים

9] When a man gives to another an ass, an ox, a sheep or any other animal to guard, and it dies or is injured or is carried off, with no witness about,   **10]** an oath before the LORD shall decide between the two of them that the one has not laid hands on the property of the other; the owner must acquiesce, and no restitution shall be made.   **11]** But if [the animal] was stolen from him, he shall make restitution to its owner.   **12]** If it was torn by beasts, he shall bring it as evidence; he need not replace what has been torn by beasts.

13] When a man borrows [an animal] from another and it dies or is injured, its owner not being with it, he must make restitution.   **14]** If its owner was with it, no restitution need be made; but if it was hired, he is entitled to the hire.

15] If a man seduces a virgin for whom the bride price has not been paid, and lies with her, he must make her his wife by payment of a bride price.   **16]** If her father refuses to give her to him, he must still weigh out silver in accordance with the bride price for virgins.

17] You shall not tolerate a sorceress.

18] Whoever lies with a beast shall be put to death.

9] [10] *To guard.* As a hired agent, for pay. Different from the provision for mere safekeeping in our verse 6 [9].

10] [11] *An oath before the Lord shall decide.* The sacredness of the oath was emphasized by using the Name יְהֹוָה.

12] [13] *Torn by beasts.* Which is hard to prevent [10].

What has been torn. This is the original meaning of *terefah*, which in later Jewish tradition came to signify all non-kosher meat. See also at our verse 30.

13] [14] *Its owner not being with it.* In such a case the borrower himself had to exercise proper care.

15] [16] *A virgin.* On the meaning of בְּתוּלָה (*betulah*), see commentary, "Virgins." The stated rule applies to an unbetrothed virgin; if she was

betrothed and another man slept with her, it was a case of adultery or rape (Deut. 22:23 ff.). Middle Assyrian law had provisions similar to those in Exod. 22 and Deut. 22 [11].

17] [18] ff.   Here begin moral rules, phrased in an imperative style, different from the preceding case law formulations.

Tolerate a sorceress. Others interpret לֹא תְחַיֶּה as "You shall not let her live" [12]. The female example ("sorceress") was used probably because the practitioner was most likely a woman (compare the English "witchcraft"). No particular type of sorcery is noted; the regulation appears to aim at local practices. (See further at Deut. 18:10.) Other Near Eastern laws also opposed sorcery [13].

18] [19] *Lies with a beast.* Bestiality was punished by death of the human (Deut. 27:21) and also of

כה לוֹ כְּנֹשֶׁה לֹא־תְשִׂימוּן עָלָיו נֶשֶׁךְ: אִם־חָבֹל תַּחְבֹּל
כו שַׂלְמַת רֵעֶךָ עַד־בֹּא הַשֶּׁמֶשׁ תְּשִׁיבֶנּוּ לוֹ: כִּי הִוא
כְסוּתֹה לְֿבַדָּהּ הִוא שִׂמְלָתוֹ לְעֹרוֹ בַּמֶּה יִשְׁכָּב
וְהָיָה כִּי־יִצְעַק אֵלַי וְשָׁמַעְתִּי כִּי־חַנּוּן אָנִי: ס
כז אֱלֹהִים לֹא תְקַלֵּל וְנָשִׂיא בְעַמְּךָ לֹא תָאֹר: מְלֵאָתְךָ
כח וְדִמְעֲךָ לֹא תְאַחֵר בְּכוֹר בָּנֶיךָ תִּתֶּן־לִי: כֵּן־תַּעֲשֶׂה

כ יֶחֱרָם בִּלְתִּי לַיהֹוָה לְבַדּוֹ: וְגֵר לֹא־תוֹנֶה וְלֹא
כא תִלְחָצֶנּוּ כִּי־גֵרִים הֱיִיתֶם בְּאֶרֶץ מִצְרָיִם: כָּל־אַלְמָנָה
כב וְיָתוֹם לֹא תְעַנּוּן: אִם־עַנֵּה תְעַנֶּה אֹתוֹ כִּי אִם־צָעֹק
כג יִצְעַק אֵלַי שָׁמֹעַ אֶשְׁמַע צַעֲקָתוֹ: וְחָרָה אַפִּי וְהָרַגְתִּי
אֶתְכֶם בֶּחָרֶב וְהָיוּ נְשֵׁיכֶם אַלְמָנוֹת וּבְנֵיכֶם יְתֹמִים: פ
כד אִם־כֶּסֶף תַּלְוֶה אֶת־עַמִּי אֶת־הֶעָנִי עִמָּךְ לֹא־תִהְיֶה

*כו כסותו קרי.

19] Whoever sacrifices to a god other than the LORD alone shall be proscribed.

20] You shall not wrong a stranger or oppress him, for you were strangers in the land of Egypt.

21] You shall not ill-treat any widow or orphan. 22] If you do mistreat them, I will heed their outcry as soon as they cry out to Me, 23] and My anger shall blaze forth and I will put you to the sword, and your own wives shall become widows and your children orphans.

24] If you lend money to My people, to the poor who is in your power, do not act toward him as a creditor: exact no interest from him. 25] If you take your neighbor's garment in pledge, you must return it to him before the sun sets; 26] it is his only clothing, the sole covering for his skin. In what else shall he sleep? Therefore, if he cries out to Me, I will pay heed, for I am compassionate.

27] You shall not revile God, nor put a curse upon a chieftain among your people.

28] You shall not put off the skimming of the first yield of your vats. You shall give Me the first-born among your sons. 29] You shall do the same with your cattle and your flocks: seven

the animal (Lev. 20:15 f.). Hittite laws treated bestiality with a cow or pig differently from that committed with a horse or mule [14].

19] [20] *Proscribed*. See at Lev. 27:29.

23] [24] *I will put you to the sword*. An idiom meaning "I will kill you."

24] [25] *If you lend money*. For details see at Deut. 24:6, 10–13. Throughout the ancient Near East taking interest on loans was permitted, with certain restrictions. For instance, in Old Babylonian law the legal maximum was 20 per cent for money and 33 1/3 per cent for grain [15]. In every period one can find examples of lending with interest, sometimes at exorbitant rates. In the nonurban context of the Torah all interest-taking was discouraged, so that the freeholder might not become indebted and indentured.

25] [26] *Garment in pledge*. The poor owned often little else; they would use their garments as clothing by day and as a cover at night (still to be observed in some countries like India and Nigeria). Consideration for the feelings of the debtor is further detailed in Deut. 24:6, 10–13.

27] [28] *God*. The suggestion by Josephus that אֱלֹהִים here signifies "gods"—because Jews should respect the gods of the pagans [16]—is contrary to the spirit of the Bible, which insists that pagan gods are worthless.

Chieftain. Or, "ruler." Compare Prov. 24:21. Putting a curse on a ruler is like lèse majesté in modern days. The law implies that undermining the stability of society is comparable to blasphemy. Noth suggests that we have here a rule reflecting an old Israelite confederacy, where each tribe had a chieftain or ruler (*nasi*).

28–30] [29–31] Laws promoting holiness through the consecration of food.

לְשֹׁרְךָ לְצֹאנֶךָ שִׁבְעַת יָמִים יִהְיֶה עִם־אִמּוֹ בַּיּוֹם   עַל־רֹב לִנְטֹת אַחֲרֵי רַבִּים לְהַטֹּת: וְדָל לֹא תֶהְדַּר
הַשְּׁמִינִי תִּתְּנוֹ־לִי: וְאַנְשֵׁי־קֹדֶשׁ תִּהְיוּן לִי וּבָשָׂר בַּשָּׂדֶה   בְּרִיבוֹ: ס   כִּי תִפְגַּע שׁוֹר אֹיִבְךָ אוֹ חֲמֹרוֹ תֹּעֶה
טְרֵפָה לֹא תֹאכֵלוּ לַכֶּלֶב תַּשְׁלִכוּן אֹתוֹ: ס   הָשֵׁב תְּשִׁיבֶנּוּ לוֹ: ס   כִּי־תִרְאֶה חֲמוֹר שֹׂנַאֲךָ רֹבֵץ
לֹא תִשָּׂא שֵׁמַע שָׁוְא אַל־תָּשֶׁת יָדְךָ עִם־רָשָׁע לִהְיֹת   תַּחַת מַשָּׂאוֹ וְחָדַלְתָּ מֵעֲזֹב לוֹ עָזֹב תַּעֲזֹב עִמּוֹ: ס
עֵד חָמָס: לֹא־תִהְיֶה אַחֲרֵי־רַבִּים לְרָעֹת וְלֹא־תַעֲנֶה   לֹא תַטֶּה מִשְׁפַּט אֶבְיֹנְךָ בְּרִיבוֹ: מִדְּבַר־שֶׁקֶר

---

days it shall remain with its mother; on the eighth day you shall give it to Me.

30] You shall be men holy to Me: you must not eat flesh torn by beasts in the field; you shall cast it to the dogs.

1] You must not carry false rumors; you shall not join hands with the guilty to act as a malicious witness: **2]** You shall neither side with the mighty to do wrong—you shall not give perverse testimony in a dispute so as to pervert it in favor of the mighty—   **3]** nor shall you show deference to a poor man in his dispute.

4] When you encounter your enemy's ox or ass wandering, you must take it back to him.

5] When you see the ass of your enemy lying under its burden and would refrain from raising it, you must nevertheless raise it with him.

6] You shall not subvert the rights of your needy in their disputes.   **7]** Keep far from a false charge; do not bring death on the innocent and the righteous, for I will not acquit the

---

28] [29] *Skimming of the first yield.* The exact meaning is uncertain. It is clear, however, that only after the first crop of the produce has been dedicated to God and/or the sanctuary may the rest be eaten. The same applies to animals and, in a figurative sense, to human beings. See above at 13:1 and at Num. 3:11 ff.

29] [30] *Seven days it shall remain.* That is, the first-born animal. In Lev. 22:27 this is expressed as a general principle. One explanation is that until the animal becomes eight days old its viability is not established [17];   another, that leaving the newborn with its mother for seven days has regard to the latter's feelings, similar to the rule not to boil a kid in its mother's milk (23:19) [18].

30] [31] *Men holy.* אַנְשֵׁי קֹדֶשׁ (*anshe kodesh*) means persons constantly aware of their relationship to God. Holiness is understood to be not only a moral outlook but a total life style. (For a discussion of holiness, see at Leviticus 19.)

Flesh torn by beasts. According to Hyatt, this is an old taboo, based on the belief that the wild

animal transferred its evil power to the torn animal. A similar prohibition is found in Deut. 14:21, where such a carcass is known as נְבֵלָה (*nevelah*). Later Jewish tradition provided that specific rules of ritual slaughtering had to be followed in order to make meat *kasher*.

23:1–9] Further moral rules. Verses 1–3 are similar to Lev. 19:15–18.

2] *With the mighty.* Others, "multitude." The Hebrew is difficult, and many interpretations have been offered. Rashi represents the prevailing traditional understanding: Do not follow a majority blindly if your conscience demands otherwise. Similarly Ibn Ezra, who warns against trusting a majority without question.

5] *Raising.* The meaning is doubtful; compare Deut. 22:4. Rashi interprets as if תַּעֲזֹב read תַּעֲזֹר. So also New English Bible: "Give him a hand." Cassuto sees here a word play: the first תַּעֲזֹב means forsake; the second, arrange [19].

תִּרְחָק וְנָקִי וְצַדִּיק אַל־תַּהֲרֹג כִּי לֹא־אַצְדִּיק רָשָׁע: ‏‏ט דִּבְרֵי צַדִּיקִים: וְגֵר לֹא תִלְחָץ וְאַתֶּם יְדַעְתֶּם
ח וְשֹׁחַד לֹא תִקָּח כִּי הַשֹּׁחַד יְעַוֵּר פִּקְחִים וִיסַלֵּף אֶת־נֶפֶשׁ הַגֵּר כִּי־גֵרִים הֱיִיתֶם בְּאֶרֶץ מִצְרָיִם:

wrongdoer. **8]** Do not take bribes, for bribes blind the clear-sighted and upset the pleas of the just.

9] You shall not oppress a stranger, for you know the feelings of the stranger, having yourselves been strangers in the land of Egypt.

8] *Clear-sighted.* Literally, "eyes of the wise." Compare Deut. 16:19.

9] *Oppress a stranger.* Taking up the theme of 22:20. Meant here in a special, judicial sense.

Protection of the Weak

Widows and orphans were prototypes of the native-born with whom fate had dealt harshly and who were likely to need particular protection in order to survive. Both appear in the same combination in Near Eastern languages and laws, so that in this respect the Torah legislation was not in itself new [20]. (For examples of other law codes, see Gleanings.) What was new, and unique to the Torah, was the addition of the stranger to the list of the protected. All Israel had suffered the fate of strangers in Egypt, and thereafter "stranger, widow, and orphan" together became the touchstone of biblical justice. In addition, their protection was raised to a divinely supported principle, with God himself made its guarantor. He is the One to whom the weak may appeal, and He will assist them in their plight, for His very nature is suffused with love and concern for them. The traditional prayer book speaks of God as the One who lifts up the downtrodden and helps the poor, and the Psalmist prays (86:1):

Incline Your ear, O Lord, answer me,
For I am poor and needy.

In modern times the principle of society's responsibility for the weak has been both expanded (by social legislation) and called into basic question (by Nietzschean and Nazi philosophies, or by the application of triage to the starving). The Torah and subsequent Jewish tradition are insistent on the scrupulous observance of the principle, and Jews considered themselves above all as merciful children of a merciful God.

The stranger (גֵר, ger) is mentioned thirty-three times in the Torah, and the rest of the Bible further supports the need for treating him kindly. *Ger* was the term applied to the resident non-Israelite who could no longer count on the protection of his erstwhile tribe or society.[1] This was not so with the נָכְרִי (nochri) or זָר (zar), foreigners whose abode in Israel was temporary and who had not abandoned their own protective background [21]. The *ger* was to be given every consideration, and care must be taken that not only his rights but his feelings as well were safeguarded. He must never be shamed, much like a debtor with whom the laws immediately following deal. The Midrash used the text's caution about the stranger for an extensive exploration of the subject [22]. Again and again the Israelites were reminded that they themselves had been strangers in Egypt. Even as God had then heard the cry of the oppressed, so would He hear the cry of the weak at any time. This was also a potent reminder that Israel remained dependent on God. Compassion is part of His nature and must therefore be carefully nurtured by His children in their own lives [23].

Dealing with the Enemy

Although Christian Scriptures say "You have learned that they were told: 'Love your neighbor and hate your enemy'" [24], no such injunction exists in the Torah or the whole Hebrew Bible. While there is no general rule that one ought to *love* one's enemy—a principle well nigh impossible to be translated into actual life—the Torah cites practical cases in which enmity between people is to have its limits. The enemy here alluded to is not a national but a personal adversary, someone toward whom one has ill feelings, perhaps because of an ongoing lawsuit. Especially when an animal is involved, such personal animosity must be

[1] Later Jewish tradition distinguished further between the *ger toshav*, the resident stranger, i.e., a non-Jewish resident of Palestine, who observed the seven Noahide laws, and the *ger tzedek*, who had become a full proselyte.

suspended, for animals too are the object of God's concern even as they are also the underpinning of an agricultural society. Out of such practices, rather than broad principles, did the Torah attempt to lead people to behave more generously and decently toward each other [25].

Capital Punishment

Prescribing capital punishment for a variety of offenses was part and parcel of the legislative system of the Torah, as it has been of most nations, ancient and modern. The reasons seem to have been mainly twofold: such punishment was believed to be a deterrent, but, more importantly, the perpetrator was deemed to be a serious detriment to the community because he had offended against God (or the gods). Consequently he had to be physically removed, and capital punishment was the common method of bringing it about. Such removal could also take the form of exile or imprisonment, but the former seems not to have been a custom in Israel,[2] and prisons were relatively rare and incapable of handling significant numbers of criminals.

In the Torah, the death penalty was prescribed for murder, adultery, blasphemy, false evidence in capital cases, false prophecy (that is, prophecy not inspired by God), actual idolatry, unnatural and incestuous sexual acts, insubordination to the authorities, licentious behavior of a priest's daughter, deceiving one's husband about chastity prior to marriage, raping a betrothed woman, insulting or striking one's parents, rebelling against their authority, profaning the Sabbath publicly, augury, witchcraft and related crimes.

Three major modes of execution are speci-

fied in the Torah: stoning, burning, and hanging, but the Rabbis specified that the last was to take place only after death had been brought on by another means (by stoning), and they further added the penalties of decapitation and strangulation, while they considered כָּרֵת (karet, or cutting off) to be a penalty reserved to Heaven itself. In later centuries the death penalty was virtually abandoned by the Rabbis, some of whom—while they could not abrogate the specific instructions of the Torah—made testimony in capital cases so difficult that no one could be convicted and sentenced to die [26]. Modern Israel has also no capital punishment except for participation in genocidal activities and under conditions of warfare [27].

Virgins

Virgins are by popular definition those girls who have not as yet had sexual intercourse. In the Bible, too, the term betulah (used in this chapter) is usually descriptive of the girl's sexual condition but it sometimes also refers to her age, denoting a matured, nubile girl (which is the way Akkadian and Ugaritic texts use the cognate word).

The concern with female sexual purity reflects the ancient preoccupation with women's procreative fitness. It was a family's duty to protect a daughter's virginity, and, when it was violated, the father (representing the family) was entitled to a certain compensation (mohar). In such a case he could, with the daughter's consent, either demand of the offender that he marry the girl or he could choose to refuse him marriage.[3] The monetary compensation due in this instance, as well as inferences drawn from various biblical stories, have led some scholars to suggest that the mohar was in effect the purchase

---

[2] However, one theory suggests that the penalty of karet, "cutting a person off," meant exile.

[3] However, if the daughter was a minor her consent

was not needed, though the Rabbis in general objected to marrying off a minor [28].

price one had to pay to obtain a virginal bride from the family. But, as the story of Jacob and Rebekah indicates (Gen. 24), the bride was not just a chattel that could be disposed of at will by the father. Her status was complex, composed of personal rights as well as filial obligations, and hence a simple description of her as "chattel" who could be bought does not do her situation justice. Later Jewish tradition developed the moral and legal aspects of virginity and betrothal in considerable detail [29].

GLEANINGS

Seven Kinds of Theft

These are the seven kinds of theft and their penalties:

1. Deceit ("stealing someone's mind") in a moral sense: no legal penalty provided;
2. Stealing things forbidden to be used: no restitution required, for one ought not to have these things in the first place;
3. Stealing certain things, like documents: simple restitution;
4. Stealing other things, like garments: double restitution;
5. Stealing a lamb: fourfold restitution at times;
6. Stealing an ox: fivefold restitution at times;
7. Stealing a human being (kidnaping): death penalty.

Saving Life

(22:1 permits taking the life of a thief in case there is doubt over his intent.)

From this you may learn about the importance of saving life. Since the shedding of blood—which defiles the land and causes the Shechinah to leave—is permitted to resolve a doubt, how much more so the saving of life to overcome doubt.

TALMUD [30]

[The allusion is to the Sabbath, which may be violated if there is a question of possible danger to life.]

Master and Servant

The Torah distinguishes between the thief who comes at night and the robber who comes by day, the former paying twofold but the latter only paying simple restitution. The reason is that the robber is afraid of neither God nor man, for he can be seen by both; while the thief is afraid only of man, for God can see him anyway. The thief honors the servant (man) more than the master (God).

MIDRASH [31]

Elijah

22:7 provides: "If the thief is not caught, (the owner) shall depose . . ." in which case the matter remains essentially unresolved. In Hebrew the first five words are אִם לֹא יִמָּצֵא הַגַּנָּב וְנִקְרַב. The first letters of these words form the acrostic אליהו (Elijah). There are some cases which will not be resolved until the coming of Elijah [the forerunner of the Messiah].

BAAL HA-TURIM [32]

Oaths

22:10 is one of the few occasions where the Torah explicitly prescribes that an oath be taken. It is to be done "before the Lord," that is, by using the sacred Name. From this we learn that the Name is to be used every time an oath is taken.

MIDRASH [33]

[In talmudic and later times an oath was taken in certain instances while wearing phylacteries and/or holding a scroll of the Torah.]

Interest

A rich man who gives to charity and lends his money without interest is considered as one who observes all commandments.　　MIDRASH [34]

Poverty

The text speaks of "the poor who is in your power" (22:24). There is nothing in the world more grievous than poverty. All sufferings are on one side of the ledger, and poverty on the other.　　MIDRASH [35]

My People

It says: "If you lend money to My people" (22:24). The emphasis is on the word *My*. God says: Do not worry about a guarantee for, when all Israelites are respectful of each other's needs, I the Lord am the prime guarantor of all My people.　　R. DAVID TAMAR [36]

It was asked: Can anyone lend money to "My people," that is, to all? The verse therefore refers to matters which affect all the people, like lending funds to Eretz Yisrael.　　M. HACOHEN [37]

Men Holy (Exod. 22:30)

Your holiness shall consist of being truly human, not angelic. God has plenty of angels.　　CHASIDIC [38]

(Of the laws here enumerated, this command alone is couched in the plural.) Whenever the duty or ideal of holiness is spoken of in the Torah, the plural is invariably used, because mortal man can attain to holiness when cooperating with others in the service of a great cause or ideal, as a member of a community, society, or "kingdom." Of God alone we can say, the Holy One.

　　M. LAZARUS [39]

Strangers

From the verse, "You shall not wrong (or vex) a stranger for you (yourselves) were strangers" (23:9), R. Nathan deduced another rule: Do not reproach your fellow man with the fault which you yourselves have.

Beloved are strangers, for in so many places Scripture compares them to the Israelites.

　　MIDRASH [40]

The Weak

(The warning in 22:21 not to mistreat widows and orphans is written emphatically עַנֵּה תְעַנֶּה, as if to say "in any wise whatsoever." The following tale is based on this understanding.)

When R. Simeon and R. Ishmael were led forth to their execution (because they had taught Torah in defiance of Hadrian's decree), R. Simeon said: "My heart fails me, for I do not know why I am to be killed (and God punishes me thusly)." R. Ishmael said to him: "Did it never happen that someone came to you and you let him wait until you had finished your drink or tied your sandals or put on your coat? The Torah says 'If you afflict in any wise,' whether small or large." R. Simeon replied: "Master, you have comforted me (that is, you have explained why God punishes me)."　　MIDRASH [41]

The Way

A man ought to be especially heedful of his behavior toward widows and orphans, for their souls are exceedingly depressed and their spirits low. Even if they are wealthy, even if they are the widow and orphan of a king, we are specifically enjoined concerning them.

How are we to conduct ourselves toward them? One may not speak to them otherwise than tenderly. One must show them unvarying courtesy; not hurt them physically with hard toil, nor wound their feelings with hard speech. One must take greater care of their property than of one's own. Whoever irritates them, provokes them to anger, pains them, tyrannizes over them, or causes them loss of money is guilty of a transgression, and all the more so if one beats them or curses them. . . .

The above only applies to cases where a person afflicts them for his own ends. But if a teacher punishes orphan children in order to teach them Torah or a trade, or lead them in the right way—this is permissible. And yet he should not treat them like others, but make a distinction in their favor. He should guide them gently, with the utmost tenderness and courtesy, as it is said, "For the Lord will plead their cause" (Prov. 22:23).

　　MAIMONIDES [42]

(*Relating to Exod.* 22:8)

The Priest Pa-ser appealed: "As for this field, it belongs to Pai. . . ." But the god remained still. Then he appealed to the god with the words: "It belongs to the Priest Pa-ser, son of Mose." Then the god nodded very much.

EGYPTIAN INSCRIPTION [43]

[Mose was a common name or part of a name in Egypt meaning "born of"; hence the likelihood that the biblical name Moses was derived from Egyptian and not from the Hebrew models. See commentary at Exod. 2:10.]

(*Relating to* 22:9)

If a seignior deposited property of his for safe-keeping and at the place where he made the deposit his property has disappeared along with the property of the owner of the house, either through breaking in or through scaling the wall,

the owner of the house, who was so careless that he let whatever was given to him for safekeeping get lost, shall make it good and make restitution to the owner of the goods, while the owner of the house shall make a thorough search for his lost property and take it from its thief.

CODE OF HAMMURABI [44]

(*Relating to* 23:2)

[The king had the stele inscribed with the laws of his code] "so that the strong might not oppress the weak, that justice might be dealt the orphan and the widow."

EPILOGUE TO THE CODE OF HAMMURABI [45]

(*Relating to* 22:21)

[The king saw to it that the orphan did not fall prey to the powerful] "and the man of one shekel did not fall prey to the man of one mina" [50 shekels].

LAWS OF UR-NAMMU [46]

Laws on Cultic Ordinances;
Affirmation of the Covenant

The Covenant Code now turns to cultic laws: to the sabbatical year; a repetition of the Sabbath injunction; the first mention of the "three festivals"; rules of sacrificial offerings and for boiling a kid in its mother's milk, the first of three times this law is stated in the Torah. This concludes the legal part of the code.

Then follows a foreshadowing of Israel's further advances in which it will be guided by an angel, and thereafter the people give their formal assent to the record (or book) of the covenant. They do it twice (24:3 and 7), once before the law is written down and once afterward. Moses, Aaron, two of the latter's sons, and seventy elders then ascend the mountain and are granted the privilege of "seeing the God of Israel"—the only time such a vision is recorded in the Torah. Moses spends forty days and nights on the mountain above where he is to receive stone tablets with the teachings and commandments inscribed on them. This concludes the Covenant Code, although some scholars believe that the original code ended with 23:19, the last of the noncultic laws [1].

There are difficulties in sequence (for instance, Moses ascends the mountain while already there) and in style, which have led critics to see three different traditions represented here. It has also been suggested that the story of writing down the covenant stood at first in another place and was connected with 34:28, or that the section 34:14–26 once was part of the code [2].

587

יד   אֲחֵרִים֙ לֹ֣א תַזְכִּ֔ירוּ לֹ֥א יִשָּׁמַ֖ע עַל־פִּֽיךָ: שָׁלֹ֣שׁ רְגָלִ֔ים

טו   תָּחֹ֥ג לִ֖י בַּשָּׁנָֽה: אֶת־חַ֣ג הַמַּצּוֹת֘ תִּשְׁמֹר֒ שִׁבְעַ֣ת יָמִים֩

תֹּאכַ֨ל מַצּ֜וֹת כַּֽאֲשֶׁ֣ר צִוִּיתִ֗ךָ לְמוֹעֵד֙ חֹ֣דֶשׁ הָֽאָבִ֔יב

טז   כִּי־ב֖וֹ יָצָ֣אתָ מִמִּצְרָ֑יִם וְלֹֽא־יֵרָא֥וּ פָנַ֖י רֵיקָֽם: וְחַ֣ג

הַקָּצִיר֙ בִּכּוּרֵ֣י מַֽעֲשֶׂ֔יךָ אֲשֶׁ֥ר תִּזְרַ֖ע בַּשָּׂדֶ֑ה וְחַ֤ג הָֽאָסִף֙

בְּצֵ֣את הַשָּׁנָ֔ה בְּאָסְפְּךָ֥ אֶֽת־מַֽעֲשֶׂ֖יךָ מִן־הַשָּׂדֶֽה: שָׁלֹ֥שׁ

י   וְשֵׁ֥שׁ שָׁנִ֖ים תִּזְרַ֣ע אֶת־אַרְצֶ֑ךָ וְאָֽסַפְתָּ֖ אֶת־תְּבֽוּאָתָֽהּ:

יא   וְהַשְּׁבִיעִ֣ת תִּשְׁמְטֶ֣נָּה וּנְטַשְׁתָּ֗הּ וְאָֽכְלוּ֙ אֶבְיֹנֵ֣י עַמֶּ֔ךָ

וְיִתְרָ֕ם תֹּאכַ֖ל חַיַּ֣ת הַשָּׂדֶ֑ה כֵּֽן־תַּֽעֲשֶׂ֥ה לְכַרְמְךָ֖ לְזֵיתֶֽךָ:

יב   שֵׁ֤שֶׁת יָמִים֙ תַּֽעֲשֶׂ֣ה מַֽעֲשֶׂ֔יךָ וּבַיּ֥וֹם הַשְּׁבִיעִ֖י תִּשְׁבֹּ֑ת

לְמַ֣עַן יָנ֗וּחַ שֽׁוֹרְךָ֙ וַֽחֲמֹרֶ֔ךָ וְיִנָּפֵ֥שׁ בֶּן־אֲמָֽתְךָ֖ וְהַגֵּֽר:

יג   וּבְכֹ֛ל אֲשֶׁר־אָמַ֥רְתִּי אֲלֵיכֶ֖ם תִּשָּׁמֵ֑רוּ וְשֵׁ֨ם אֱלֹהִ֤ים

10] Six years you shall sow your land and gather in its yield; **11]** but in the seventh you shall let it rest and lie fallow. Let the needy among your people eat of it, and what they leave let the wild beasts eat. You shall do the same with your vineyards and your olive groves.

12] Six days you shall do your work, but on the seventh day you shall cease from labor, in order that your ox and your ass may rest, and that your bondman and the stranger may be refreshed.

13] Be on guard concerning all that I have told you. Make no mention of the names of other gods; they shall not be heard on your lips.

14] Three times a year you shall hold a festival for Me: **15]** You shall observe the Feast of Unleavened Bread—eating unleavened bread for seven days as I have commanded you—at the set time in the month of Abib, for in it you went forth from Egypt; and none shall appear before Me empty-handed; **16]** and the Feast of the Harvest, of the first fruits of your work, of what you sow in the field; and the Feast of Ingathering at the end of the year, when you gather in

---

23:11] *Let it rest.* Whence the noun שְׁמִטָּה (*shemitah*), release. The *shemitah* year (so called in Deut. 15) is here given a social foundation, while in Lev. 25:1–7 (where the institution is fully discussed) the reason stated is that the *land* might benefit by such rest.

12] *In order that your ox and your ass may rest.* This expands the reasons given in Exod. 20:11 and anticipates Deut. 5:14.

14] *Three times.* שָׁלֹשׁ רְגָלִים (*shalosh regalim*), by which name Passover, Shavuot, and Sukot came to be known. On these three festivals Israelites were bidden to make a pilgrimage (generally undertaken on foot) to the sanctuary (verse 17) [3]. (רְגָלִים is a plural of רֶגֶל, a word usually meaning foot. In postbiblical as in modern Hebrew, "three times" would be expressed by שָׁלֹשׁ פְּעָמִים, using the biblical word for "beat" or "step." In both cases, a linguistic development from the foot's

beat, or footstep, to "times" is observable.) Since similar agricultural festivals seem to have been observed in ancient Canaan, this cultic calendar may have derived from there, for it clearly has no desert roots.

16] *Feast of the Harvest.* The festival occurs in May/June and became known as the "Festival of the First Fruits" (*Chag ha-Bikkurim*). Later on, it was identified with the "Festival of the Giving of the Torah" and Shavuot (Feast of Weeks). It is observed on the sixth day of Sivan, seven weeks after Passover. See at 34:22 and Lev. 23.

Feast of Ingathering. This became the Sukot festival (Tabernacles), beginning with the fifteenth of Tishri (September/October).

End of the year. Interpreted as "end of the harvest year," but it is also possible that "end of the calendar year" was meant. Some scholars believe that the feast included ceremonies of renewing the covenant.

פְּעָמִים בַּשָּׁנָה יֵרָאֶה כָּל־זְכוּרְךָ אֶל־פְּנֵי הָאָדֹן יְהֹוָה: כג

יח לֹא־תִזְבַּח עַל־חָמֵץ דַּם־זִבְחִי וְלֹא־יָלִין חֵלֶב־חַגִּי

עַד־בֹּקֶר: יט רֵאשִׁית בִּכּוּרֵי אַדְמָתְךָ תָּבִיא בֵּית יְהֹוָה

אֱלֹהֶיךָ לֹא־תְבַשֵּׁל גְּדִי בַּחֲלֵב אִמּוֹ: פ

כ הִנֵּה אָנֹכִי שֹׁלֵחַ מַלְאָךְ לְפָנֶיךָ לִשְׁמָרְךָ בַּדָּרֶךְ

כא וְלַהֲבִיאֲךָ אֶל־הַמָּקוֹם אֲשֶׁר הֲכִנֹתִי: הִשָּׁמֶר מִפָּנָיו

וּשְׁמַע בְּקֹלוֹ אַל־תַּמֵּר בּוֹ כִּי לֹא יִשָּׂא לְפִשְׁעֲכֶם

כב כִּי שְׁמִי בְּקִרְבּוֹ: כִּי אִם־שָׁמֹעַ תִּשְׁמַע בְּקֹלוֹ וְעָשִׂיתָ

כֹּל אֲשֶׁר אֲדַבֵּר וְאָיַבְתִּי אֶת־אֹיְבֶיךָ וְצַרְתִּי אֶת־

כו צֹרְרֶיךָ: כִּי־יֵלֵךְ מַלְאָכִי לְפָנֶיךָ וֶהֱבִיאֲךָ אֶל־הָאֱמֹרִי

וְהַחִתִּי וְהַפְּרִזִּי וְהַכְּנַעֲנִי הַחִוִּי וְהַיְבוּסִי וְהִכְחַדְתִּיו:

כד לֹא־תִשְׁתַּחֲוֶה לֵאלֹהֵיהֶם וְלֹא תָעָבְדֵם וְלֹא תַעֲשֶׂה

כְּמַעֲשֵׂיהֶם כִּי הָרֵס תְּהָרְסֵם וְשַׁבֵּר תְּשַׁבֵּר מַצֵּבֹתֵיהֶם:

כה וַעֲבַדְתֶּם אֵת יְהֹוָה אֱלֹהֵיכֶם וּבֵרַךְ אֶת־לַחְמְךָ וְאֶת־

כו מֵימֶיךָ וַהֲסִרֹתִי מַחֲלָה מִקִּרְבֶּךָ: ס לֹא תִהְיֶה

מְשַׁכֵּלָה וַעֲקָרָה בְּאַרְצֶךָ אֶת־מִסְפַּר יָמֶיךָ אֲמַלֵּא:

כז אֶת־אֵימָתִי אֲשַׁלַּח לְפָנֶיךָ וְהַמֹּתִי אֶת־כָּל־הָעָם אֲשֶׁר

כח תָּבֹא בָּהֶם וְנָתַתִּי אֶת־כָּל־אֹיְבֶיךָ אֵלֶיךָ עֹרֶף: וְשָׁלַחְתִּי

the results of your work from the field. **17]** Three times a year all your males shall appear before the Sovereign, the LORD.

18] You shall not offer the blood of My sacrifice with anything leavened; and the fat of My festal offering shall not be left lying until morning.

19] The choice first fruits of your soil you shall bring to the house of the LORD your God. You shall not boil a kid in its mother's milk.

20] I am sending an angel before you to guard you on the way and to bring you to the place which I have made ready. **21]** Pay heed to him and obey him. Do not defy him, for he will not pardon your offenses, since My Name is in him; **22]** but if you obey him and do all that I say, I will be an enemy to your enemies and a foe to your foes.

23] When My angel goes before you and brings you to the Amorites, the Hittites, the Perizzites, the Canaanites, the Hivites, and the Jebusites, and I annihilate them, **24]** you shall not bow down to their gods in worship or follow their practices, but shall tear them down and smash their pillars to bits. **25]** You shall serve the LORD your God, and He will bless your bread and your water. And I will remove sickness from your midst. **26]** No woman in your land shall miscarry or be barren. I will let you enjoy the full count of your days.

27] I will send forth My terror before you, and I will throw into panic all the people among whom you come, and I will make all your enemies turn tail before you. **28]** I will send a

---

17] *Appear before the Sovereign.* Visit the local (or later, the national) sanctuary.

18] *Anything leavened.* This rule is independent of the matzah prescription for Passover. The halachah applied this rule literally and strictly [4]. The identification of leaven as an agent of potential corruption is homiletical.

20] *An angel.* The distinction between the angel and God's own Presence is blurred.

21] *Pay heed to him.* How is not stated.

My name is in him. He will be My personal manifestation. On retribution in the Torah, see Bamberger's commentary on Lev. 26:1–46, "The Problem of Retribution."

23] *Amorites . . . Jebusites.* The six nations referred to before, in Exod. 3:8.

27] *Tail.* Literally, "back" or "neck."

אֶת־הַצְּרְעָה לְפָנֶיךָ וְגֵרְשָׁה אֶת־הַחִוִּי אֶת־הַכְּנַעֲנִי   אֹתְךָ לִי כִּי תַעֲבֹד אֶת־אֱלֹהֵיהֶם כִּי־יִהְיֶה לְךָ

כט וְאֶת־הַחִתִּי מִלְּפָנֶיךָ: לֹא אֲגָרְשֶׁנּוּ מִפָּנֶיךָ בְּשָׁנָה אֶחָת   פ   לְמוֹקֵשׁ:

פֶּן־תִּהְיֶה הָאָרֶץ שְׁמָמָה וְרַבָּה עָלֶיךָ חַיַּת הַשָּׂדֶה: א וְאֶל־מֹשֶׁה אָמַר עֲלֵה אֶל־יְהוָה אַתָּה וְאַהֲרֹן נָדָב

ל מְעַט מְעַט אֲגָרְשֶׁנּוּ מִפָּנֶיךָ עַד אֲשֶׁר תִּפְרֶה וְנָחַלְתָּ   וַאֲבִיהוּא וְשִׁבְעִים מִזִּקְנֵי יִשְׂרָאֵל וְהִשְׁתַּחֲוִיתֶם מֵרָחֹק:

לא אֶת־הָאָרֶץ: וְשַׁתִּי אֶת־גְּבֻלְךָ מִיַּם־סוּף וְעַד־יָם   ב וְנִגַּשׁ מֹשֶׁה לְבַדּוֹ אֶל־יְהוָה וְהֵם לֹא יִגָּשׁוּ וְהָעָם

פְּלִשְׁתִּים וּמִמִּדְבָּר עַד־הַנָּהָר כִּי אֶתֵּן בְּיֶדְכֶם אֵת   לֹא יַעֲלוּ עִמּוֹ: וַיָּבֹא מֹשֶׁה וַיְסַפֵּר לָעָם אֵת כָּל־

לב יֹשְׁבֵי הָאָרֶץ וְגֵרַשְׁתָּמוֹ מִפָּנֶיךָ: לֹא־תִכְרֹת לָהֶם   דִּבְרֵי יְהוָה וְאֵת כָּל־הַמִּשְׁפָּטִים וַיַּעַן כָּל־הָעָם קוֹל

לג וְלֵאלֹהֵיהֶם בְּרִית: לֹא יֵשְׁבוּ בְּאַרְצְךָ פֶּן־יַחֲטִיאוּ   אֶחָד וַיֹּאמְרוּ כָּל־הַדְּבָרִים אֲשֶׁר־דִּבֶּר יְהוָה נַעֲשֶׂה:

plague ahead of you, and it shall drive out before you the Hivites, the Canaanites, and the Hittites. **29]** I will not drive them out before you in a single year, lest the land become desolate and the wild beasts multiply to your hurt. **30]** I will drive them out before you little by little, until you have increased and possess the land. **31]** I will set your borders from the Sea of Reeds to the Sea of Philistia, and from the wilderness to the Euphrates; for I will deliver the inhabitants of the land into your power, and you will drive them out before you. **32]** You shall make no covenant with them and their gods. **33]** They shall not remain in your land, lest they cause you to sin against Me; for you will serve their gods— and it will prove a snare to you.

1] Then He said to Moses, "Come up to the LORD, with Aaron, Nadab and Abihu, and seventy elders of Israel, and bow low from afar. **2]** But only Moses shall come near the LORD. The others shall not come near; and the people shall not come up with him at all."

3] Moses went and repeated to the people all the commands of the LORD and all the rules; and all the people answered with one voice, saying, "All the things that the LORD has

---

28] *Plague.* Others, "hornets" [5].

31] *Sea of Reeds.* Here the Gulf of Akaba appears to be meant, perhaps its whole western coastline.

Sea of Philistia. The eastern coast of the Mediterranean where the Philistines dwelt.

From the wilderness to the Euphrates. From the Sinai and the Negev to Mesopotamia. The Euphrates is called הַנָּהָר, "the river" (compare הַיְאֹר, also meaning "the river," but referring to the Nile; see note at 1:22.) This is one of the passages describing the extent of the future Promised Land. Each stage of conquest (by Moses, Joshua, and the Judges) produced a corresponding "map" of the land of Canaan and of Israel. The people's ancient aspiration to have sole possession

of the land was apparently abandoned at the time of the Judges [6]. See further in commentary on Num. 34:1–12.

Drive them out. וְגֵרַשְׁתָּמוֹ is a poetic or antique form of וְגֵרַשְׁתָּם.

33] *They shall not remain.* However, they did remain at first and Israel intermingled with them after the occupation, causing these peoples' gradual disappearance through assimilation.

24:1] *Then He said.* From here on the sequence is not clear. Rashi suggests that these events took place before the giving of the Decalogue [7].

Nadab and Abihu. Aaron's sons (6:23) will suffer disaster later on (Lev. 10:1 ff.).

3] *With one voice.* Unanimously.

ה וַיֹּאמְר֗וּ כֹּ֛ל אֲשֶׁר־דִּבֶּ֥ר יְהוָ֖ה נַעֲשֶׂ֣ה וְנִשְׁמָ֑ע׃ וַיִּקַּ֣ח
מֹשֶׁה֮ אֶת־הַדָּם֒ וַיִּזְרֹ֣ק עַל־הָעָ֔ם וַיֹּ֕אמֶר הִנֵּ֤ה דַֽם־
הַבְּרִית֙ אֲשֶׁ֨ר כָּרַ֤ת יְהוָה֙ עִמָּכֶ֔ם עַ֖ל כָּל־הַדְּבָרִ֥ים
ט הָאֵֽלֶּה׃ וַיַּ֥עַל מֹשֶׁ֖ה וְאַהֲרֹ֑ן נָדָב֙ וַאֲבִיה֔וּא וְשִׁבְעִ֖ים
מִזִּקְנֵ֣י יִשְׂרָאֵֽל׃ וַיִּרְא֕וּ אֵ֖ת אֱלֹהֵ֣י יִשְׂרָאֵ֑ל וְתַ֣חַת
רַגְלָ֗יו כְּמַעֲשֵׂה֙ לִבְנַ֣ת הַסַּפִּ֔יר וּכְעֶ֥צֶם הַשָּׁמַ֖יִם לָטֹֽהַר׃

ד וַיִּכְתֹּ֣ב מֹשֶׁ֗ה אֵ֚ת כָּל־דִּבְרֵ֣י יְהוָ֔ה וַיַּשְׁכֵּ֣ם בַּבֹּ֔קֶר
וַיִּ֥בֶן מִזְבֵּ֖חַ תַּ֣חַת הָהָ֑ר וּשְׁתֵּ֤ים עֶשְׂרֵה֙ מַצֵּבָ֔ה לִשְׁנֵ֖ים
ה עָשָׂ֖ר שִׁבְטֵ֥י יִשְׂרָאֵֽל׃ וַיִּשְׁלַ֗ח אֶֽת־נַעֲרֵי֙ בְּנֵ֣י יִשְׂרָאֵ֔ל
וַיַּֽעֲל֖וּ עֹלֹ֑ת וַיִּזְבְּח֞וּ זְבָחִ֧ים שְׁלָמִ֛ים לַיהוָ֖ה פָּרִֽים׃
ו וַיִּקַּ֤ח מֹשֶׁה֙ חֲצִ֣י הַדָּ֔ם וַיָּ֖שֶׂם בָּאַגָּנֹ֑ת וַחֲצִ֣י הַדָּ֔ם זָרַ֖ק
ז עַל־הַמִּזְבֵּֽחַ׃ וַיִּקַּח֙ סֵ֣פֶר הַבְּרִ֔ית וַיִּקְרָ֖א בְּאָזְנֵ֣י הָעָ֑ם

commanded we will do!"   **4]** Moses then wrote down all the commands of the LORD.

Early in the morning, he set up an altar at the foot of the mountain, with twelve pillars for the twelve tribes of Israel.   **5]** He designated some young men among the Israelites, and they offered burnt offerings and sacrificed bulls as offerings of well-being to the LORD.   **6]** Moses took one part of the blood and put it in basins, and the other part of the blood he dashed against the altar.   **7]** Then he took the record of the covenant and read it aloud to the people. And they said "All that the LORD has spoken we will faithfully do!"   **8]** Moses took the blood and dashed it on the people and said, "This is the blood of the covenant which the LORD now makes with you concerning all these commands."

9] Then Moses and Aaron, Nadab and Abihu, and seventy elders of Israel ascended; **10]** and they saw the God of Israel: under His feet there was the likeness of a pavement of

4]   *Wrote down.* The first mention of committing the teachings to writing. The document will be called *sefer ha-berit* (verse 7).

Twelve pillars. As witnesses; compare Gen. 31:45 ff.

6]   *He dashed [the blood] against the altar.* Thereby symbolically committing God himself to this covenant sealed by blood. Moses then dashes it on the people (verse 8), committing them in the same manner. Blood represented the essence of life.

7]   *Record of the covenant.* Its extent is not speci-fied—perhaps it encompassed merely the Deca-logue or it included the entire preceding "Code of the Covenant" (beginning in chapter 21). Cassuto suggests that here Moses may have written down nothing more than the people's promise to observe the laws he had communicated to them,

and that they at once confirmed again that they would faithfully do (literally "do and obey").

9–11]   The vision recorded in these three verses departs in many ways from other biblical appre-hensions of the Divine: God is not hidden; there is neither cloud nor smoke; Moses is in no wise distinguished from those who accompany him; and, further, the setting appears bereft of the covenantal framework. Most likely, therefore, we have here a separate tradition [8].

10]   *They saw.* They saw as much of the Divine Presence as it was possible for a human being to behold and remain alive. Such limitations are clearly set forth in 33:20. The early translations attempt to make this unmistakable. The Septua-gint renders "saw the place"; the Targumim, "saw the glory of God." Ezekiel (1:26) beheld God in a similar way.

יא וְאֶל־אֲצִילֵי בְּנֵי יִשְׂרָאֵל לֹא שָׁלַח יָדוֹ וַיֶּחֱזוּ אֶת־
יב הָאֱלֹהִים וַיֹּאכְלוּ וַיִּשְׁתּוּ: ס וַיֹּאמֶר יְהֹוָה אֶל־מֹשֶׁה
עֲלֵה אֵלַי הָהָרָה וֶהְיֵה־שָׁם וְאֶתְּנָה לְךָ אֶת־לֻחֹת
הָאֶבֶן וְהַתּוֹרָה וְהַמִּצְוָה אֲשֶׁר כָּתַבְתִּי לְהוֹרֹתָם:
יג וַיָּקָם מֹשֶׁה וִיהוֹשֻׁעַ מְשָׁרְתוֹ וַיַּעַל מֹשֶׁה אֶל־הַר
יד הָאֱלֹהִים: וְאֶל־הַזְּקֵנִים אָמַר שְׁבוּ־לָנוּ בָזֶה עַד אֲשֶׁר־
נָשׁוּב אֲלֵיכֶם וְהִנֵּה אַהֲרֹן וְחוּר עִמָּכֶם מִי־בַעַל

טו דְּבָרִים יִגַּשׁ אֲלֵהֶם: וַיַּעַל מֹשֶׁה אֶל־הָהָר וַיְכַס
טז הֶעָנָן אֶת־הָהָר: וַיִּשְׁכֹּן כְּבוֹד־יְהֹוָה עַל־הַר סִינַי
וַיְכַסֵּהוּ הֶעָנָן שֵׁשֶׁת יָמִים וַיִּקְרָא אֶל־מֹשֶׁה בַּיּוֹם
יז הַשְּׁבִיעִי מִתּוֹךְ הֶעָנָן: וּמַרְאֵה כְּבוֹד יְהֹוָה כְּאֵשׁ
אֹכֶלֶת בְּרֹאשׁ הָהָר לְעֵינֵי בְּנֵי יִשְׂרָאֵל: וַיָּבֹא מֹשֶׁה
יח בְּתוֹךְ הֶעָנָן וַיַּעַל אֶל־הָהָר וַיְהִי מֹשֶׁה בָּהָר אַרְבָּעִים
יוֹם וְאַרְבָּעִים לָיְלָה:

Haftarah Mishpatim, p. 714

sapphire, like the very sky for purity. **11]** Yet He did not raise His hand against the leaders of the Israelites; they beheld God, and they ate and drank.

12] The LORD said to Moses, "Come up to Me on the mountain and wait there, and I will give you the stone tablets with the teachings and commandments which I have inscribed to instruct them." **13]** So Moses and his attendant Joshua arose, and Moses ascended the mountain of God. **14]** To the elders he had said, "Wait here for us until we return to you. You have Aaron and Hur with you; let anyone who has a legal matter approach them."

15] When Moses had ascended the mountain, the cloud covered the mountain. **16]** The Presence of the LORD abode on Mount Sinai, and the cloud hid it for six days. On the seventh day He called to Moses from the midst of the cloud. **17]** Now the Presence of the LORD appeared in the sight of the Israelites as a consuming fire on the top of the mountain. **18]** Moses went inside the cloud and ascended the mountain; and Moses remained on the mountain forty days and forty nights.

11] *Leaders.* Others, "nobles."

They beheld. The Hebrew verb חָזָה is usually employed in connection with visions.

They ate and drank. A confirming, covenantal meal. See Exod. 18:12 and Gen. 31:46, 54 for sealing a covenant amongst humans by sharing a meal. The custom survives today in toasts drunk to an agreement [9].

12] *I will give you the stone tablets.* Which, when transmitted to him (31:18), Moses will shatter at the incident of the golden calf. Verses 12–14 appear to be from a different tradition: the preceding written covenant and Moses' presence on the mountain are not taken into consideration; Joshua and Hur are suddenly introduced into the account while Nadab and Abihu are absent. Critics also distinguish between various expressions used for the tablets and assign different sources to their use: Stone Tablets (E), Tablets of the Pact (P), and Tablets of the Covenant (D); see General Introduction to the Torah, "How the Torah Came to Be Written."

Teachings and commandments. הַתּוֹרָה וְהַמִּצְוָה (ha-Torah veha-mitzvah). The expression seems too large for the Decalogue, hence Rashi explains that God's inscription on the tablets comprised all 613 mitzvot of tradition. הַתּוֹרָה וְהַמִּצְוָה was taken by the nineteenth-century scholar Meir Lev ben Yechiel Michael (Malbim) as the title of his popular Torah commentary.

14] *Approach them.* In my forthcoming absence from the camp.

15] *When Moses had ascended.* This passage would fit better before the Book of the Covenant.

Israel's Society (as reflected in the Book of the Covenant)

"The economic, social, judicial, religious, and ethical aspects which the Book of the Covenant presupposes and regulates do not reflect a nomadic or even seminomadic society, but a people who have passed the beginning stages of settled civilization and have achieved some degree of well-being. They have not, however, acquired as yet those luxuries destructive of public and private life which were denounced by the great ethical teachers Amos and Hosea in Israel, and Isaiah and Micah in Judah in the eighth century (B.C.E.)" [10]. This suggests that many of the laws belong to the time of Israel's settlement in Canaan. At the same time the foundations of the code most likely go back into Israel's desert past.

The family is the basis of society. The father is at the head; offense to parents is a capital crime. Children are considered their fathers' quasi property. When the father-protector is removed, widows and orphans are the moral responsibility of the community. This community is called עַם (*am*), which also harbors the resident alien גֵּר (*ger*) and the nonresident stranger נָכְרִי (*nochri*). Tribes are not mentioned in the code.

There are rich and poor and a developed system of justice. The poor are protected by law and moral injunction, and if they are reduced to selling themselves into bondage they are automatically freed after six years. This limited bondage appears to exist for members of the *am* only, while a *nochri* may be held in actual slavery, but the line is blurred, and in any case the institution of bondage/slavery appears to play a minor role only.

The society knows of shepherds and farmers, judges and priests, but of no special class of merchants or soldiers. Money in the form of silver weights is in use, but domestic animals—especially bovines and sheep—are the mainstay of wealth. Camels and horses are not mentioned; their use may have been confined to the few.

The legal system resembles patterns and rules known in the ancient Near East in many respects but frequently humanizes them significantly. An ethical urgency underlies the law: the weak must be protected, be they Israelites or strangers, and even aid to an enemy may be required.

Religious practices reflect both earlier and later traditions. Altars made of earth are still known and God appears to be worshiped under the open sky, but the cultic calendar refers to agricultural conditions. The only worship permitted is that of Israel's God, unadulterated by any form of idolatry, which is prohibited upon pain of death. The Sabbath is the core of all observances; then, as it did later, it guaranteed the continuity of the cult and was to be observed by all people in their private and public life. Altogether, the law is not the king's law as in Babylon, or the Pharaoh's as in Egypt; it is God's and belongs to the whole people who have pledged themselves to observe it faithfully.

"You Shall Not Boil a Kid in Its Mother's Milk"

Many explanations have been offered for this thrice-repeated injunction.[1] They have ranged from the magical to the symbolic, from the educational to the moral and theological.

Thus, Frazer compared the law with

---

[1] Exod. 23:19, and repeated in Exod. 34:26 and Deut. 14:21 in identical words. This underlines the importance given to it, and critics note that the three occurrences place the command in three of the four major sources, E, J, and D.

African customs that prohibited certain mixtures and intermingling of various kinds and suggested that the purpose here was magical and prophylactic: to preserve the milk-giving capacity of the cow [11]. But in the case of the Torah law no mixture is involved (mother and kid are of the same kind), and, further, such prophylaxis would be out of keeping with the biblical spirit and most certainly would not deserve a triple emphasis. Nor is it convincing to hold that the law must be seen in the light of the Torah's repeated rejection of intermingling various kinds of seed, or of making a garment of linen and wool, or of working an ass and an ox together, all of which carry out the principle already stated in the first chapter of Genesis that all things are created "according to their kind," that is, each was assigned a particular place in the world [12]. In the law before us, it is precisely the same and not different kinds which are not to be mixed. Still other commentators have sought the purpose in the moral realm: the law was to tame man's cruel instincts and serve as yet another means of sanctifying his life [13].

Long ago Maimonides, judging the law in its context, suspected that what was at stake here was another attempt to discourage idolatry [14]. His analysis appears to have been given support by a Ugaritic text that describes a prevailing Canaanite sacrificial rite. The text, which is defective, has been read to say: "On the fire seven times the young men boil a kid in milk, a lamb in butter."[2] Boiling a kid in this way might therefore have been considered part of the "abominations" of the nations against which Israel was warned so often and so insistently. Such a practice had possibly wide currency, for many centuries later it was still a magical procedure to sprinkle milk boiled in such fashion on trees, fields, and orchards in order to assure their fertility [16].

Whether or not later generations were still aware of the original intent of the law (whatever it was), they came to consider it the fundamental proof text for the dietary halachah that forbade the mixing of any milk with meat and, thus, provided an observance certainly never contemplated when the injunction was first formulated. (Reform Jews have generally disregarded this halachah.)

---

[2] In English rendition the fragment might be reconstructed thus: "Over a fire, young men seven times c(ook a ki)d in milk a . . . in curd." It should be noted, however, that the reconstruction has the biblical text in mind, which weakens the above-stated argument [15].

GLEANINGS

No Other Gods

The Torah forbids the "mention of the names of other gods" (23:13). This warns us also against quoting heretical books or drawing conclusions about the Torah from extrabiblical works.

ZOHAR [17]

(Although R. Akiba forbade even the book of Ben Sirach or Ecclesiasticus [18], nonreligious works like Homer's were not proscribed; they were considered like letters, of which it was said that reading them neither benefited nor harmed the reader.) You may not swear by another's deity or even pronounce its name by the way, as in saying "Wait for me at the place of such-and-such an idol."

MIDRASH [19]

All the People

They all answered "with one voice" (24:3). The great and humble were all alike before God.

MIDRASH [20]

We Will Do! (Exod. 24:3)

(They said this without having as yet heard the whole law.) The Israelites made their action precede their hearing, for if one hears, but does not intend to do, it would be better had he not been created. Hence we are taught that he who learns in order to do is given the chance to learn, teach, *and* do.

(A similar sense is derived from 24:7, the literal translation of נַעֲשֶׂה וְנִשְׁמָע being: "We will [first] do and [then] listen.")

Moses said to Israel: "How can you let your doing precede your listening? Does not the deed usually arise from learning what to do?" They answered him: "We will do whatever we will hear from God." They thus took it upon themselves to observe the Torah even before they had heard it.

From this also derives the saying: "He whose works exceed his wisdom, his wisdom will endure."

MIDRASH [21]

When the Israelites declared their willingness to perform the mitzvot before hearing them, six hundred thousand ministering angels came and bestowed on each Israelite two crowns, one for the promise to perform (נַעֲשֶׂה) and one for the promise to hear (נִשְׁמָע).

TALMUD [22]

Males Only

The obligation to visit the sanctuary three times a year is laid upon males only (Exod. 23:17). This is one of the verses from which the Sages derived the rule that positive commandments which must be performed at a certain time are obligatory only for males [23].

You Shall Not Boil (Exod. 23:19)

Why is the commandment stated three times in the Torah? To correspond to three covenants the Holy One, blessed be He, made with Israel: one at Sinai, one in the plains of Moab (Deut. 28:69), and one at Mt. Gerizim and Mt. Ebal (Deut. 27:8).

Another interpretation: To prohibit also the eating of the mixture, its cooking, and deriving any benefit from it.

MIDRASH [24]

Some halachic rules: Although the law speaks only of goats ("a kid"), it was applied first to any four-legged animal fit for eating, and later to fowl as well, as regards mixing milk and meat.

Although the law speaks only of "its [own] mother's milk," it was applied to all milk.

Although the law speaks only of boiling, it was applied to mixing meat and milk for eating, and later even to eating dairy food after a meat dish without waiting a certain length of time. Special

and elaborate rules obtain for keeping eating utensils used for milk products strictly apart from those used for meat dishes [25].

[See further at Leviticus, chapter 11, Appendix.]

Youth

Why is it expressly stated that Moses "designated some *young* men" (Exod. 24:5)? Unless the young were willing to serve, there would have been little point to Israel's acceptance of the covenant. Only after the young proved themselves did Moses proceed.   CHASIDIC [26]

A Feast

After the leaders had seen the glory of God they ate and drank (Exod. 24:11). From this the Sages derived the custom to make a feast whenever a unit of Torah study has been completed (upon which mitzvah the Shechinah is believed to rest).
                                          NACHMANIDES

A Story

During the time Moses stayed on the mountain he observed that God in preparing the Torah was placing ornaments and crowns on the letters.

[Torah scrolls are written with specially ornamented letters.] He asked the reason. God answered: "Some day there will be a man, Akiba ben Joseph, who will pile a mountain of laws upon each of these letters." Thereupon Moses begged to be shown that man. God then transported him forward in time [into the second century C.E., when Rabbi Akiba taught in Palestine] and seated him in the back of the room, in the eighteenth rank. Moses was unable to follow the discussion, which grieved him greatly. But when he heard a disciple ask R. Akiba: "Master, whence do you know this ruling?" and the teacher replied: "This is the halachah already given to Moses on Mt. Sinai," Moses was content. When he was restored to Sinai he asked God: "Why give the Torah through me when you will have a man like Akiba?" God replied: "Be silent; such is My will."   TALMUD

The story has a disturbing sequel. It goes on to have Moses ask God: "Show me Akiba's reward." God then showed him how Akiba was martyred. Said Moses: "This is Your Torah, and such is Your reward?" God answered again: "Be silent, this is My will" [27].

PART VII

Sanctuary and Service

The next six chapters deal with the Tabernacle that Israel is bidden to build at this time, and with the service which will take place within.[1] A number of reasons have been advanced why the construction of the sanctuary is now introduced, following directly the theophany and the Covenant Code. To begin with, ancient Near Eastern typologies of exultation demanded that the deity be enthroned in a house of its own. To some this has appeared as an anticlimax, but to Franz Rosenzweig the building of the Tabernacle was in fact the high point, even the goal and pinnacle of the Pentateuch: in Egyptian slavery Israel made buildings for the pharaohs, now they were privileged to expend their labor for God's sake. This more than anything else concretized their freedom. For even as God "made" the world so Israel now "makes" the sanctuary in a new act of creation, and the same words used in the opening chapters of Genesis characterize the creation of the Tabernacle [1]. (See commentary on 38:21–40:38.)

Cassuto finds the reason elsewhere: "In order to understand the significance and purpose of the Tabernacle, we must realize that the Children of Israel, after they had been privileged to witness the revelation of God on Mount Sinai, were about to journey from there and thus draw away from the site of the theophany. So long as they were encamped in the place, they were conscious of God's nearness; but, once they set out on their journey, it seemed to them as though the link had been broken, unless there were in their midst a tangible symbol of God's presence among them. It was the function of the Tabernacle (literally, 'Dwelling') to serve as such a symbol" [2].

Most scholars consider the account at least in part as fictitious, a retrojection from later days, when the Temple was already built and when this Torah section was introduced to give the sanctuary and its priestly attendants a legitimacy stemming from desert days [3]. Von Rad, who believes the Tent to be old and the Tabernacle to be largely a later invention, states the reason differently: the priestly writer (P, to whom critics

---

[1] While critical analysis would often demand a distinction between Tabernacle and Tent, we will use both terms (as the Torah text in its present form seems to do most of the time) as if they were interchangeable. For a distinction between Tabernacle (capital T) and tabernacle (lower case letter), see at 26:1. It should also be noted that the Tent of Meeting may at some time have served social and political, and not merely cultic, purposes; see W. W. Hallo's essay in Numbers, under "The Genealogical Framework."

assign all or much of this section) wanted to reestablish God's absolute transcendency for which purpose the Tabernacle, filled with symbolic furniture, was an ideal vehicle [4]. Many scholars hold that a good many of the materials prescribed for the Tabernacle were available only in a settled, and not in a nomadic, environment. But this too has been disputed. For instance, H. M. Orlinsky says unequivocally:

"There can be little doubt that these institutions are the product of a nomadic or seminomadic society, even if later priestly writers embellished the original account considerably. Acacia wood—cedar, cyprus, or olive was later used in Canaan—ramskins, lambskins, cloth of goat's hair, and the like are all manifestations of nomadic existence. Again, while little is really known about many aspects of life among the nomads in antiquity, e.g., the religious—they left virtually no records—we do know that among some nomadic, pre-Mohammedan Arabs portable shrines (sacred tents) were employed" [5].

This appears as the most likely reflection of the history of the Tabernacle, for Israel did possess an ark which accompanied it during the conquest of the land, and one may feel certain that it was housed in a special portable tent, and portability is in fact a major feature of the Tabernacle as described in the text. Thus what follows is essentially an old tradition stemming from desert days describing the beginnings of Israel's centralized cult, to which were added details that reflected later conditions.[2] On the other hand, some cultic practices even antedated the Tabernacle, such as the observance of the Sabbath or the use of sacrifices and altars.

The furnishings of the Tabernacle, from ark and curtains to altar and candlestick, are described in great detail as part of the vision that Moses has on the mountain. He also learns in the smallest detail of the priestly garments and of the consecration procedures for Tabernacle and priests. The artisans specially chosen to carry out the instructions, Bezalel and Oholiab, are given their divine appointments, and a postscript once more emphasizing Sabbath observance ends the section.

[2] To be sure, the total Tabernacle as now described in the text was doubtlessly too heavy to be carried. Still, the major emphasis on poles, rings, tenons, and the like, and especially regarding the ark, never leave the element of possibility out of sight. The ark was first placed at a shrine in Gilgal and had seven resting places—amongst them Shiloh—before it entered Jerusalem. According to tradition, the Shiloh sanctuary was built of stones with curtains covering them [6].

There are literary problems. The main construction concerns the Tabernacle (*Mishkan*), but there is also the Tent (*Ohel*), called sometimes Tent of Meeting, sometimes Tent of Witness, sometimes Tent of Testimony, and it is not always clear what the different names signify. Nor do their locations remain the same: sometimes we find them inside and sometimes outside the camp, especially if all the Torah passages where they occur are taken into consideration [7]. Critics have distinguished between two tents where Moses would encounter God: in one (assigned to the E-tradition) the tent stood outside the camp and was attended by Joshua (see, for instance, Exod. 33:7, 11); it was apparently a relatively simple structure, simply furnished. Moses entered it to speak with the Deity, and a pillar of cloud descended and stood at the Tent's entrance and from there God spoke; in the other version (assigned to P) the Tent was inside the camp and was attended by Aaron and his sons as well as by levitical assistants; and the cloud, always present when the camp was at rest, was not the locus from which God spoke; rather, His voice came from between the cherubim. The very existence of two traditions—sometimes agreeing, sometimes differing—suggests that in part they go back a long way into Israel's past and are not likely complete retrojections or idealized reconstructions of a later age. The variances also make it nearly impossible to form an entirely clear picture of Tabernacle and Tent. This difficulty is further enlarged by some doubts over how exactly the instructions were meant.[3]

A Physical Overview

The Tabernacle (*Mishkan*, "Dwelling") or Tent (*Ohel*) is a structure roughly forty-five feet (about fifteen meters or thirty cubits) long and thirty-six feet (about twelve meters) high and fifteen feet (about five meters) wide, at the rear of which is the inner tabernacle, fifteen by fifteen by fifteen feet (five x five x five meters) in which stood the ark. This chamber (called Holy of Holies) is curtained off from the rest of the structure. In front of this is a holy area, with table, bread, lampstand, and altar. Curtained off from this is the enclosed forecourt. The Tabernacle is thus accessible on the basis of graded sanctity, and the materials em-

[3] See commentary following. An ambitious attempt to recreate the Tabernacle visually has been made by Moshe Levine who bases himself on Jewish oral tradition [8].

ployed are similarly graded. Its most precious components are made of gold, the least sacred, of copper. There are three degrees of workmanship, according to their sacredness: the degrees are called *choshev*, *rokem*, and *oreg*.[4] A mixture of wool and linen is prescribed for some of the materials but forbidden for private use.[5]

Tabernacle or Tent [9]

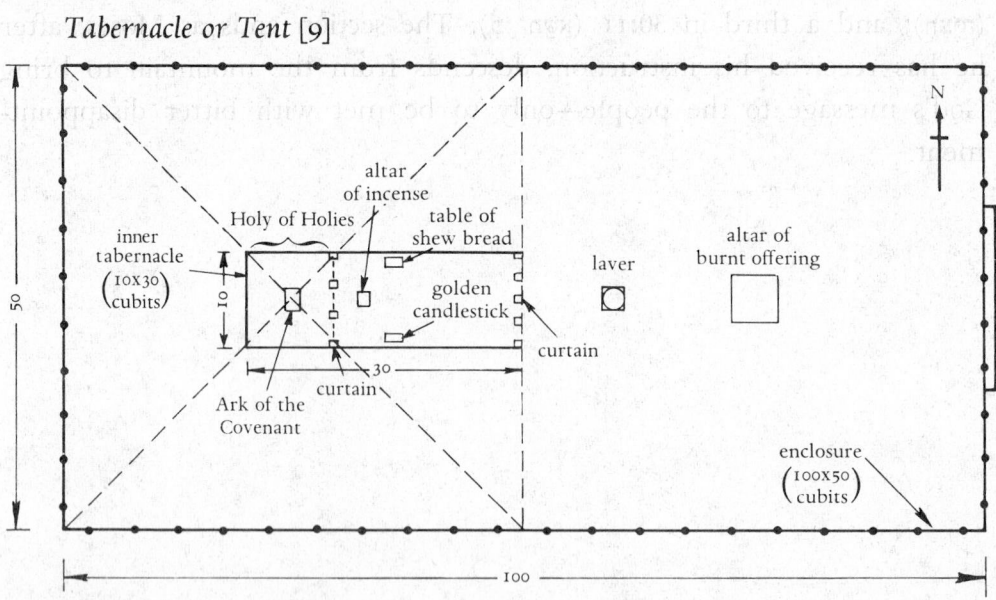

Most sacred is the Holy of Holies with its ark and cherubim; from there on, as indicated, the holiness decreases until one reaches the entrance of the Tent. This gradation is also emphasized by the type of person who may enter the various precincts: Moses could enter the Holy of Holies at all times, whereas Aaron was admitted only under special circumstances (Lev. 16:2 ff.); from there on outward, the priests, the Levites, and the people at large were admitted to assigned precincts. The priests themselves were clothed in garments of varying importance: the High Priest alone wore *ephod*, *choshen*, and *tzitz* (or *nezer*, the diadem). There were, finally, gradations of color: blue was reserved for the most sacred, then followed purple, and finally crimson. Holiness was the key word, for the Tabernacle represented the presence of God in Israel's midst. When in his

[4] While the different degrees of sacredness are evident, we are not sure what these terms mean exactly. They are probably varieties of weaving and embroidery.
[5] See Deut. 22:11.

vision Moses saw the *Mishkan*, he saw it, so to speak, as a reflection of God himself.

The whole subject received the most careful and loving attention from the Jewish Sages. A special treatise exists which is called "On the Erection of the Tabernacle" [10].

A new weekly *sidrah* starts at chapter 25 (תְּרוּמָה); another in 27:20 (תְּצַוֶּה); and a third in 30:11 (כִּי תִשָּׂא). The section ends as Moses, after he has received his instruction, descends from the mountain to bring God's message to the people—only to be met with bitter disappointment.

Ark, Lampstand, Tent, and Altar

The ark (which will contain the Tablets of Stone) is the most important item in the furnishings of the Tabernacle and is here listed first, although when the instructions are carried out the Tabernacle is constructed first (Exod. 36:8 ff.).

The details recorded in the text are not always clear, and even the dimensions are somewhat uncertain, for there were several types of measurement called cubit. The cherubim and the lampstand are described with great care, but even they cannot be securely visualized. The section describes also the altar of which the later Temple altar was an enlarged replica [1], and the Tabernacle itself is characterized by appurtenances that assure its quick assembly for the purpose of moving about.

At least one other ancient Near Eastern text also knew of the kind of vision here reported: Ningirsu showing Gudea in a dream the likeness of a sanctuary he was to build.* Still other sources speak of a divine throne and footstool (comparable to the ark and cherubim, see commentary), a lamp, chest, table, and a bed (necessary for the god to rest upon). As in other parts of the Torah such parallels attest to the contiguity of cultures and do not in any wise detract from the special nature of the Torah tradition.

(A new weekly portion, *Terumah*, begins here.)

* See Gleanings to Exod. 35:1 ff.

אֲנִי מַרְאֶה אוֹתְךָ אֵת תַּבְנִית הַמִּשְׁכָּן וְאֵת תַּבְנִית

פ פ פ

א וַיְדַבֵּר יְהוָה אֶל־מֹשֶׁה לֵּאמֹר: דַּבֵּר אֶל־בְּנֵי יִשְׂרָאֵל

כָּל־כֵּלָיו וְכֵן תַּעֲשׂוּ: ס וְעָשׂוּ אֲרוֹן עֲצֵי שִׁטִּים

וְיִקְחוּ־לִי תְּרוּמָה מֵאֵת כָּל־אִישׁ אֲשֶׁר יִדְּבֶנּוּ לִבּוֹ

אַמָּתַיִם וָחֵצִי אָרְכּוֹ וְאַמָּה וָחֵצִי רָחְבּוֹ וְאַמָּה וָחֵצִי

ג תִּקְחוּ אֶת־תְּרוּמָתִי: וְזֹאת הַתְּרוּמָה אֲשֶׁר תִּקְחוּ מֵאִתָּם

יא קֹמָתוֹ: וְצִפִּיתָ אֹתוֹ זָהָב טָהוֹר מִבַּיִת וּמִחוּץ תְּצַפֶּנּוּ

ד זָהָב וָכֶסֶף וּנְחֹשֶׁת: וּתְכֵלֶת וְאַרְגָּמָן וְתוֹלַעַת שָׁנִי

וְעָשִׂיתָ עָלָיו זֵר זָהָב סָבִיב: וְיָצַקְתָּ לּוֹ אַרְבַּע

ה וְשֵׁשׁ וְעִזִּים: וְעֹרֹת אֵילִם מְאָדָּמִים וְעֹרֹת תְּחָשִׁים

טַבְּעֹת זָהָב וְנָתַתָּה עַל אַרְבַּע פַּעֲמֹתָיו וּשְׁתֵּי טַבָּעֹת

ו וַעֲצֵי שִׁטִּים: שֶׁמֶן לַמָּאֹר בְּשָׂמִים לְשֶׁמֶן הַמִּשְׁחָה

עַל־צַלְעוֹ הָאֶחָת וּשְׁתֵּי טַבָּעֹת עַל־צַלְעוֹ הַשֵּׁנִית:

ז וְלִקְטֹרֶת הַסַּמִּים: אַבְנֵי־שֹׁהַם וְאַבְנֵי מִלֻּאִים לָאֵפֹד

יג וְעָשִׂיתָ בַדֵּי עֲצֵי שִׁטִּים וְצִפִּיתָ אֹתָם זָהָב: וְהֵבֵאתָ

ח וְלַחֹשֶׁן: וְעָשׂוּ לִי מִקְדָּשׁ וְשָׁכַנְתִּי בְּתוֹכָם: כְּכֹל אֲשֶׁר

אֶת־הַבַּדִּים בַּטַּבָּעֹת עַל צַלְעֹת הָאָרֹן לָשֵׂאת אֶת־

1] The Lord spoke to Moses, saying: 2] Tell the Israelite people to bring Me gifts; you shall accept gifts for Me from every person whose heart so moves him. 3] And these are the gifts that you shall accept from them: gold, silver, and copper; 4] blue, purple, and crimson yarns, fine linen, goats' hair; 5] tanned ram skins, dolphin skins, and acacia wood; 6] oil for lighting, spices for the anointing oil and for the aromatic incense; 7] lapis lazuli and other stones for setting, for the ephod and for the breastpiece. 8] And let them make Me a sanctuary that I may dwell among them. 9] Exactly as I show you—the pattern of the Tabernacle and the pattern of all its furnishings—so shall you make it.

10] They shall make an ark of acacia wood, two and a half cubits long, a cubit and a half wide, and a cubit and a half high. 11] Overlay it with pure gold—overlay it inside and out—and make upon it a gold molding round about. 12] Cast four gold rings for it, to be attached to its four feet, two rings on one of its side walls and two on the other. 13] Make poles of

---

25:2] *Gifts.* תְּרוּמָה (*terumah*, which gives the weekly Torah portion its name) is treated as a collective noun.

3] *Copper.* As in Gen. 4:22. Others, "brass" or "bronze."

4] *Blue.* The dye was derived from a Mediterranean shellfish, which became very rare later on.

Purple. Made by adding certain chemicals to the blue.

Crimson. תּוֹלַעַת (*tola'at*), also the name of a worm of the species *coccidae*, from which the dye was obtained [2].

5] *Tanned.* Others, "dyed red." The women will do the weaving (Exod. 35:25).

Dolphin skins. The translation represents "a reasonable guess" [3]. Dolphin and dugong (believed by some to be the meaning of תְּחָשִׁים) occur in the Red Sea and have a hardy skin from which Bedouin make shoes.

6] *Oil.* Probably olive oil is meant [4].

7] *Lapis lazuli.* A deep blue stone. But others translate "onyx."

Ephod. A shoulder garment, probably sleeveless; its most important part was the pouch which held the Urim and Thummim, devices used for oracular purposes (see 28:31–35) [5].

8] *Sanctuary.* מִקְדָּשׁ (*mikdash*). The Temple in Jerusalem was later referred to as *bet ha-mikdash* (house of the sanctuary).

10] *Ark.* A box or chest. The ark in the synagogue containing the Torah scrolls is called *aron ha-kodesh* (ark of holiness) and is a direct descendant of the ark that contained the tablets.

Cubits. Similar to a Ugaritic and Akkadian measure. It represented the length of the forearm down to the tip of the middle finger. There were two types of cubits in Israel, one about 17 1/2 inches (about 44 1/2 cm), the other about 20 1/2 inches (about 52 cm).

כא פְּנֵי הַכְּרֻבִים: וְנָתַתָּ אֶת־הַכַּפֹּרֶת עַל־הָאָרֹן מִלְמָעְלָה   טו הָאָרֹן בָּהֶם: בְּטַבְּעֹת הָאָרֹן יִהְיוּ הַבַּדִּים לֹא יָסֻרוּ
כב וְאֶל־הָאָרֹן תִּתֵּן אֶת־הָעֵדֻת אֲשֶׁר אֶתֵּן אֵלֶיךָ: וְנוֹעַדְתִּי   טז מִמֶּנּוּ: וְנָתַתָּ אֶל־הָאָרֹן אֵת הָעֵדֻת אֲשֶׁר אֶתֵּן אֵלֶיךָ:
לְךָ שָׁם וְדִבַּרְתִּי אִתְּךָ מֵעַל הַכַּפֹּרֶת מִבֵּין שְׁנֵי   יז וְעָשִׂיתָ כַפֹּרֶת זָהָב טָהוֹר אַמָּתַיִם וָחֵצִי אָרְכָּהּ
הַכְּרֻבִים אֲשֶׁר עַל־אֲרוֹן הָעֵדֻת אֵת כָּל־אֲשֶׁר אֲצַוֶּה   יח וְאַמָּה וָחֵצִי רָחְבָּהּ: וְעָשִׂיתָ שְׁנַיִם כְּרֻבִים זָהָב מִקְשָׁה
אוֹתְךָ אֶל־בְּנֵי יִשְׂרָאֵל: פ   יט תַּעֲשֶׂה אֹתָם מִשְּׁנֵי קְצוֹת הַכַּפֹּרֶת: וַעֲשֵׂה כְּרוּב
כג וְעָשִׂיתָ שֻׁלְחָן עֲצֵי שִׁטִּים אַמָּתַיִם אָרְכּוֹ וְאַמָּה רָחְבּוֹ   אֶחָד מִקָּצָה מִזֶּה וּכְרוּב־אֶחָד מִקָּצָה מִזֶּה מִן־
כד וְאַמָּה וָחֵצִי קֹמָתוֹ: וְצִפִּיתָ אֹתוֹ זָהָב טָהוֹר וְעָשִׂיתָ   כ הַכַּפֹּרֶת תַּעֲשׂוּ אֶת־הַכְּרֻבִים עַל־שְׁנֵי קְצוֹתָיו: וְהָיוּ
כה לּוֹ זֵר זָהָב סָבִיב: וְעָשִׂיתָ לּוֹ מִסְגֶּרֶת טֹפַח סָבִיב   הַכְּרֻבִים פֹּרְשֵׂי כְנָפַיִם לְמַעְלָה סֹכְכִים בְּכַנְפֵיהֶם
כו וְעָשִׂיתָ זֵר־זָהָב לְמִסְגַּרְתּוֹ סָבִיב: וְעָשִׂיתָ לּוֹ אַרְבַּע   עַל־הַכַּפֹּרֶת וּפְנֵיהֶם אִישׁ אֶל־אָחִיו אֶל־הַכַּפֹּרֶת יִהְיוּ

---

acacia wood and overlay them with gold; **14]** then insert the poles into the rings on the side walls of the ark, for carrying the ark. **15]** The poles shall remain in the rings of the ark: they shall not be removed from it. **16]** And deposit in the ark [the tablets of] the Pact which I will give you.

17] You shall make a cover of pure gold, two and a half cubits long and a cubit and a half wide. **18]** Make two cherubim of gold—make them of hammered work—at the two ends of the cover. **19]** Make one cherub at one end and the other cherub at the other end; of one piece with the cover shall you make the cherubim at its two ends. **20]** The cherubim shall have their wings spread out above, shielding the cover with their wings. They shall confront each other, the faces of the cherubim being turned toward the cover. **21]** Place the cover on top of the ark, after depositing inside the ark the Pact which I will give you. **22]** There I will meet with you, and I will impart to you—from above the cover, from between the two cherubim that are on top of the ark of the Pact—all that I will command you concerning the Israelite people.

23] You shall make a table of acacia wood, two cubits long, one cubit wide, and a cubit and a half high. **24]** Overlay it with pure gold, and make a gold molding around it. **25]** Make a rim of a hand's breadth around it, and make a gold molding for its rim round about. **26]** Make

---

15] *Shall not be removed.* Shall always be ready to be carried.

16] *[The tablets of] the Pact.* The bracketed words seem to be implied: Moses placed into the ark the tablets that constituted the עֵדֻת (*edut*), literally the witness or testimony.

18] *Two cherubim.* The Hebrew כְּרֻבִים is not translated because the figures did not represent the likeness of any known creature. See commentary.

19] *Of one piece.* With the cover.

20] *Turned toward the cover.* Their eyes were cast down.

22] *There.* As you stand before the ark. Rashi attempts to solve the apparent contradiction with Lev. 1:1 (God speaking to Moses from the Tent of Meeting) by suggesting that, as soon as Moses entered the Tent, God spoke to him from above the cover (see Num. 7:89).

From above the cover. Which is My footstool. The unseen God will speak to His subjects as if He were sitting on His throne.

גְּבִעִים מְשֻׁקָּדִים בַּקָּנֶה הָאֶחָד כַּפְתֹּר וָפֶרַח כֵּן   טַבַּעֹת זָהָב וְנָתַתָּ אֶת־הַטַּבָּעֹת עַל אַרְבַּע הַפֵּאֹת

לד לְשֵׁשֶׁת הַקָּנִים הַיֹּצְאִים מִן־הַמְּנֹרָה: וּבַמְּנֹרָה אַרְבָּעָה   כג אֲשֶׁר לְאַרְבַּע רַגְלָיו: לְעֻמַּת הַמִּסְגֶּרֶת תִּהְיֶןָ הַטַּבָּעֹת

לה גְּבִעִים מְשֻׁקָּדִים כַּפְתֹּרֶיהָ וּפְרָחֶיהָ: וְכַפְתֹּר תַּחַת   כד לְבָתִּים לְבַדִּים לָשֵׂאת אֶת־הַשֻּׁלְחָן: וְעָשִׂיתָ אֶת־

שְׁנֵי הַקָּנִים מִמֶּנָּה וְכַפְתֹּר תַּחַת שְׁנֵי הַקָּנִים מִמֶּנָּה   הַבַּדִּים עֲצֵי שִׁטִּים וְצִפִּיתָ אֹתָם זָהָב וְנִשָּׂא־בָם

וְכַפְתֹּר תַּחַת־שְׁנֵי הַקָּנִים מִמֶּנָּה לְשֵׁשֶׁת הַקָּנִים הַיֹּצְאִים   כט אֶת־הַשֻּׁלְחָן: וְעָשִׂיתָ קְּעָרֹתָיו וְכַפֹּתָיו וּקְשׂוֹתָיו

לו מִן־הַמְּנֹרָה: כַּפְתֹּרֵיהֶם וּקְנֹתָם מִמֶּנָּה יִהְיוּ כֻּלָּהּ מִקְשָׁה   וּמְנַקִּיֹּתָיו אֲשֶׁר יֻסַּךְ בָּהֵן זָהָב טָהוֹר תַּעֲשֶׂה אֹתָם:

לז אַחַת זָהָב טָהוֹר: וְעָשִׂיתָ אֶת־נֵרֹתֶיהָ שִׁבְעָה וְהֶעֱלָה   ל וְנָתַתָּ עַל־הַשֻּׁלְחָן לֶחֶם פָּנִים לְפָנַי תָּמִיד: פ

לח אֶת־נֵרֹתֶיהָ וְהֵאִיר עַל־עֵבֶר פָּנֶיהָ: וּמַלְקָחֶיהָ   לא וְעָשִׂיתָ מְנֹרַת זָהָב טָהוֹר מִקְשָׁה תֵּיעָשֶׂה הַמְּנוֹרָה

לט וּמַחְתֹּתֶיהָ זָהָב טָהוֹר: כִּכָּר זָהָב טָהוֹר יַעֲשֶׂה אֹתָהּ   יְרֵכָהּ וְקָנָהּ גְּבִיעֶיהָ כַּפְתֹּרֶיהָ וּפְרָחֶיהָ מִמֶּנָּה יִהְיוּ:

מ אֵת כָּל־הַכֵּלִים הָאֵלֶּה: וּרְאֵה וַעֲשֵׂה בְּתַבְנִיתָם   לב וְשִׁשָּׁה קָנִים יֹצְאִים מִצִּדֶּיהָ שְׁלֹשָׁה קְנֵי מְנֹרָה מִצִּדָּהּ

אֲשֶׁר־אַתָּה מָרְאֶה בָּהָר: ס   לג הָאֶחָד וּשְׁלֹשָׁה קְנֵי מְנֹרָה מִצִּדָּהּ הַשֵּׁנִי: שְׁלֹשָׁה

גְבִעִים מְשֻׁקָּדִים בַּקָּנֶה הָאֶחָד כַּפְתֹּר וָפֶרַח וּשְׁלֹשָׁה

---

four gold rings for it, and attach the rings to the four corners at its four legs. **27]** The rings shall be next to the rim, as holders for poles to carry the table. **28]** Make the poles of acacia wood, and overlay them with gold; by these the table shall be carried. **29]** Make its bowls, ladles, jars, and jugs with which to offer libations; make them of pure gold. **30]** And on the table you shall set the bread of display, to be before Me always.

31] You shall make a lampstand of pure gold; the lampstand shall be made of hammered work; its base and its shaft, its cups, calyxes, and petals shall be of one piece. **32]** Six branches shall issue from its sides: three branches from one side of the lampstand and three branches from the other side of the lampstand. **33]** On one branch there shall be three cups shaped like almond-blossoms, each with calyx and petals, and on the next branch there shall be three cups shaped like almond-blossoms, each with calyx and petals; so for all six branches issuing from the lampstand. **34]** And on the lampstand itself there shall be four cups shaped like almond-blossoms, each with calyx and petals: **35]** a calyx, of one piece with it, under a pair of branches; and a calyx, of one piece with it, under the second pair of branches; and a calyx, of one piece with it, under the last pair of branches; so for all six branches issuing from the lampstand. **36]** Their calyxes and their stems shall be of one piece with it, the whole of it a single hammered piece of pure gold. **37]** Make its seven lamps—the lamps shall be so mounted as to give the light on its front side— **38]** and its tongs and fire pans of pure gold. **39]** It shall be made, with all these furnishings, out of a talent of pure gold. **40]** Note well, and follow the patterns for them that are being shown you on the mountain.

29] *Bowls.* The exact meaning of the ceramic pieces is not certain.

30] *Bread of display.* Or, shew bread. See commentary.

31] *Lampstand.* מְנוֹרָה (*menorah*). Others, "candlestick," but candles were not known in antiquity. See commentary.

Calyxes. Others, "knops," "capitals." The outer parts of the flower.

39] *A talent of pure gold.* כִּכָּר (*kikkar*), the largest weight mentioned in the Bible. Its name, related to the Ugaritic *KKR*, indicates that it was round-shaped. Estimates vary from 13.7 to 68.4 kilos (about 30 to 150 pounds) depending on how many shekels are assigned to a kikkar.

וְעָשִׂ֙יתָ֙ יְרִיעֹ֣ת עִזִּ֔ים לְאֹ֖הֶל עַל־הַמִּשְׁכָּ֑ן עַשְׁתֵּֽי־עֶשְׂרֵ֥ה
יְרִיעֹ֖ת תַּעֲשֶׂ֥ה אֹתָֽם: אֹ֣רֶךְ ׀ הַיְרִיעָ֣ה הָֽאַחַ֗ת שְׁלֹשִׁים֙
בָּֽאַמָּ֔ה וְרֹ֙חַב֙ אַרְבַּ֣ע בָּֽאַמָּ֔ה הַיְרִיעָ֖ה הָאֶחָ֑ת מִדָּ֣ה
אַחַ֔ת לְעַשְׁתֵּ֥י עֶשְׂרֵ֖ה יְרִיעֹֽת: וְחִבַּרְתָּ֞ אֶת־חֲמֵ֤שׁ הַיְרִיעֹת֙
לְבָ֔ד וְאֶת־שֵׁ֥שׁ הַיְרִיעֹ֖ת לְבָ֑ד וְכָפַלְתָּ֙ אֶת־הַיְרִיעָ֣ה
הַשִּׁשִּׁ֔ית אֶל־מ֖וּל פְּנֵ֥י הָאֹֽהֶל: וְעָשִׂ֜יתָ חֲמִשִּׁ֣ים לֻֽלָאֹ֗ת
עַ֣ל שְׂפַ֤ת הַיְרִיעָה֙ הָֽאֶחָ֔ת הַקִּֽיצֹנָ֖ה בַּחֹבָ֑רֶת וַֽחֲמִשִּׁ֣ים
לֻֽלָאֹ֗ת עַ֚ל שְׂפַ֣ת הַיְרִיעָ֔ה הַֽחֹבֶ֖רֶת הַשֵּׁנִֽית: וְעָשִׂ֛יתָ
קַרְסֵ֥י נְחֹ֖שֶׁת חֲמִשִּׁ֑ים וְהֵֽבֵאתָ֤ אֶת־הַקְּרָסִים֙ בַּלֻּ֣לָאֹ֔ת
וְחִבַּרְתָּ֥ אֶת־הָאֹ֖הֶל וְהָיָ֥ה אֶחָֽד: וְסֶ֙רַח֙ הָֽעֹדֵ֔ף בִּֽירִיעֹ֖ת
הָאֹ֑הֶל חֲצִ֤י הַיְרִיעָה֙ הָֽעֹדֶ֔פֶת תִּסְרַ֕ח עַ֖ל אֲחֹרֵ֥י
הַמִּשְׁכָּֽן: וְהָֽאַמָּ֨ה מִזֶּ֜ה וְהָֽאַמָּ֤ה מִזֶּה֙ בָּֽעֹדֵ֔ף בְּאֹ֖רֶךְ
יְרִיעֹ֣ת הָאֹ֑הֶל יִֽהְיֶ֙ה סָר֧וּחַ עַל־צִדֵּ֛י הַמִּשְׁכָּ֖ן מִזֶּ֥ה

וְאֶת־הַמִּשְׁכָּ֥ן תַּעֲשֶׂ֖ה עֶ֣שֶׂר יְרִיעֹ֑ת שֵׁ֣שׁ מָשְׁזָ֗ר וּתְכֵ֤לֶת
וְאַרְגָּמָן֙ וְתֹלַ֣עַת שָׁנִ֔י כְּרֻבִ֛ים מַעֲשֵׂ֥ה חֹשֵׁ֖ב תַּעֲשֶׂ֥ה
אֹתָֽם: אֹ֣רֶךְ ׀ הַיְרִיעָ֣ה הָֽאַחַ֗ת שְׁמֹנֶ֤ה וְעֶשְׂרִים֙ בָּֽאַמָּ֔ה
וְרֹ֙חַב֙ אַרְבַּ֣ע בָּֽאַמָּ֔ה הַיְרִיעָ֖ה הָאֶחָ֑ת מִדָּ֥ה אַחַ֖ת
לְכָל־הַיְרִיעֹֽת: חֲמֵ֣שׁ הַיְרִיעֹ֗ת תִּֽהְיֶ֙ןָ֙ חֹֽבְרֹ֔ת אִשָּׁ֖ה
אֶל־אֲחֹתָ֑הּ וְחָמֵ֤שׁ יְרִיעֹת֙ חֹֽבְרֹ֔ת אִשָּׁ֖ה אֶל־אֲחֹתָֽהּ:
וְעָשִׂ֜יתָ לֻֽלְאֹ֣ת תְּכֵ֗לֶת עַ֣ל שְׂפַ֤ת הַיְרִיעָה֙ הָֽאֶחָ֔ת
מִקָּצָ֖ה בַּֽחֹבָ֑רֶת וְכֵ֤ן תַּֽעֲשֶׂה֙ בִּשְׂפַ֣ת הַיְרִיעָ֔ה הַקִּ֣יצֹונָ֔ה
בַּמַּחְבֶּ֖רֶת הַשֵּׁנִֽית: חֲמִשִּׁ֣ים לֻֽלָאֹ֗ת תַּֽעֲשֶׂה֙ בַּיְרִיעָ֣ה
הָֽאֶחָ֔ת וַֽחֲמִשִּׁ֣ים לֻֽלָאֹ֗ת תַּֽעֲשֶׂה֙ בִּקְצֵ֣ה הַיְרִיעָ֔ה אֲשֶׁ֖ר
בַּמַּחְבֶּ֖רֶת הַשֵּׁנִ֑ית מַקְבִּילֹת֙ הַלֻּ֣לָאֹ֔ת אִשָּׁ֖ה אֶל־אֲחֹתָֽהּ:
וְעָשִׂ֕יתָ חֲמִשִּׁ֖ים קַרְסֵ֣י זָהָ֑ב וְחִבַּרְתָּ֙ אֶת־הַיְרִיעֹ֜ת
אִשָּׁ֤ה אֶל־אֲחֹתָהּ֙ בַּקְּרָסִ֔ים וְהָיָ֥ה הַמִּשְׁכָּ֖ן אֶחָֽד:

1] As for the tabernacle, make it of ten strips of cloth; make these of fine twisted linen, of blue, purple, and crimson yarns, with a design of cherubim worked into them. **2]** The length of each cloth shall be twenty-eight cubits, and the width of each cloth shall be four cubits, all the cloths to have the same measurements. **3]** Five of the cloths shall be joined to one another, and the other five cloths shall be joined to one another. **4]** Make loops of blue wool on the edge of the outermost cloth of the one set; and do likewise on the edge of the outermost cloth of the other set: **5]** make fifty loops on the one cloth, and fifty loops on the edge of the end cloth of the other set, the loops to be opposite one another. **6]** And make fifty gold clasps, and couple the cloths to one another with the clasps, so that the tabernacle becomes one whole.

7] You shall then make cloths of goats' hair for a tent over the tabernacle; make the cloths eleven in number. **8]** The length of each cloth shall be thirty cubits, and the width of each cloth shall be four cubits, the eleven cloths to have the same measurements. **9]** Join five of the cloths by themselves, and the other six cloths by themselves; and fold over the sixth cloth at the front of the tent. **10]** Make fifty loops on the edge of the outermost cloth of the one set, and fifty loops on the edge of the cloth of the other set. **11]** Make fifty copper clasps, and fit the clasps into the loops, and couple the tent together so that it becomes one whole. **12]** As for the overlapping excess of the cloths of the tent, the extra half-cloth shall overlap the back of the tabernacle, **13]** while the extra cubit at either end of each length of tent cloth shall hang

---

26:1] *The tabernacle.* The word is spelled with lower case letters whenever it represents, as here, a smaller structure within the larger Tabernacle. The lower five strips belonged to this tabernacle and the ark stood beneath them [6].

Twisted linen. According to the Rabbis, every strand consisted of four threads (three woollen and one linen, a combination of materials called *sha-atnez* which, for reasons not understood, is pro-

hibited by the Torah for private use, Deut. 22:11). Further, since the Hebrew word for linen (שֵׁשׁ) also means six, this was interpreted to mean that each thread was wound twenty-four (six × four) times [7].

Design of cherubim. The translation is not sure [8].

7] *For a tent.* For a roof.

כא וְאַרְבָּעִים אַדְנֵיהֶם כֶּסֶף שְׁנֵי אֲדָנִים תַּחַת הַקֶּרֶשׁ
כב הָאֶחָד וּשְׁנֵי אֲדָנִים תַּחַת הַקֶּרֶשׁ הָאֶחָד: וּלְיַרְכְּתֵי
כג הַמִּשְׁכָּן יָמָּה תַּעֲשֶׂה שִׁשָּׁה קְרָשִׁים: וּשְׁנֵי קְרָשִׁים
כד תַּעֲשֶׂה לִמְקֻצְעֹת הַמִּשְׁכָּן בַּיַּרְכָתָיִם: וְיִהְיוּ תֹאֲמִם
מִלְּמַטָּה וְיַחְדָּו יִהְיוּ תַמִּים עַל-רֹאשׁוֹ אֶל-הַטַּבַּעַת
הָאֶחָת כֵּן יִהְיֶה לִשְׁנֵיהֶם לִשְׁנֵי הַמִּקְצֹעֹת יִהְיוּ:
כה וְהָיוּ שְׁמֹנָה קְרָשִׁים וְאַדְנֵיהֶם כֶּסֶף שִׁשָּׁה עָשָׂר אֲדָנִים
שְׁנֵי אֲדָנִים תַּחַת הַקֶּרֶשׁ הָאֶחָד וּשְׁנֵי אֲדָנִים תַּחַת
כו הַקֶּרֶשׁ הָאֶחָד: וְעָשִׂיתָ בְרִיחִם עֲצֵי שִׁטִּים חֲמִשָּׁה
כז לְקַרְשֵׁי צֶלַע-הַמִּשְׁכָּן הָאֶחָד: וַחֲמִשָּׁה בְרִיחִם לְקַרְשֵׁי
צֶלַע-הַמִּשְׁכָּן הַשֵּׁנִית וַחֲמִשָּׁה בְרִיחִם לְקַרְשֵׁי צֶלַע

יד וּמִזֶּה לְכִסֹּתוֹ: וְעָשִׂיתָ מִכְסֶה לָאֹהֶל עֹרֹת אֵילִם
מְאָדָּמִים וּמִכְסֵה עֹרֹת תְּחָשִׁים מִלְמָעְלָה: פ
טו וְעָשִׂיתָ אֶת-הַקְּרָשִׁים לַמִּשְׁכָּן עֲצֵי שִׁטִּים עֹמְדִים:
טז עֶשֶׂר אַמּוֹת אֹרֶךְ הַקָּרֶשׁ וְאַמָּה וַחֲצִי הָאַמָּה רֹחַב
יז הַקֶּרֶשׁ הָאֶחָד: שְׁתֵּי יָדוֹת לַקֶּרֶשׁ הָאֶחָד מְשֻׁלָּבֹת
אִשָּׁה אֶל-אֲחֹתָהּ כֵּן תַּעֲשֶׂה לְכֹל קַרְשֵׁי הַמִּשְׁכָּן:
יח וְעָשִׂיתָ אֶת-הַקְּרָשִׁים לַמִּשְׁכָּן עֶשְׂרִים קֶרֶשׁ לִפְאַת
יט נֶגְבָּה תֵימָנָה: וְאַרְבָּעִים אַדְנֵי-כֶסֶף תַּעֲשֶׂה תַּחַת
עֶשְׂרִים הַקֶּרֶשׁ שְׁנֵי אֲדָנִים תַּחַת-הַקֶּרֶשׁ הָאֶחָד לִשְׁתֵּי
יְדֹתָיו וּשְׁנֵי אֲדָנִים תַּחַת-הַקֶּרֶשׁ הָאֶחָד לִשְׁתֵּי יְדֹתָיו:
כ וּלְצֶלַע הַמִּשְׁכָּן הַשֵּׁנִית לִפְאַת צָפוֹן עֶשְׂרִים קָרֶשׁ:

down to the bottom of the two sides of the Tabernacle and cover it.   **14]** And make for the tent a covering of tanned ram skins, and a covering of dolphin skins above.

15] You shall make the planks for the Tabernacle of acacia wood, upright.   **16]** The length of each plank shall be ten cubits and the width of each plank a cubit and a half.   **17]** Each plank shall have two tenons, parallel to each other; do the same with all the planks of the Tabernacle.   **18]** Of the planks of the Tabernacle, make twenty planks on the south side: **19]** making forty silver sockets under the twenty planks, two sockets under the one plank for its two tenons and two sockets under each following plank for its two tenons;   **20]** and for the other side wall of the Tabernacle, on the north side, twenty planks,   **21]** with their forty silver sockets, two sockets under the one plank and two sockets under each following plank. **22]** And for the rear of the Tabernacle, to the west, make six planks;   **23]** and make two planks for the corners of the Tabernacle at the rear.   **24]** They shall match at the bottom, and terminate alike at the top inside one ring; thus shall it be with both of them: they shall form the two corners.   **25]** Thus there shall be eight planks with their sockets of silver: sixteen sockets, two sockets under the first plank, and two sockets under each of the other planks.

26] You shall make bars of acacia wood: five for the planks of the one side wall of the Tabernacle,   **27]** five bars for the planks of the other side wall of the Tabernacle, and five bars

17] *Parallel.* The meaning of the Hebrew is uncertain.

18] *South side.* נֶגְבָּה תֵּמָנָה (*negbah temanah*), two words meaning the same. The latter word, connected with יָמִין (*yamin*, right), indicates the south, which is on the right when one faces east. (In biblical times Teman meant the southern part

of Edom; today it signifies Yemen.) See also at Gen. 35:18, where Rachel's son is called Ben-Yamin (Benjamin) by Jacob.

19] *Tenons.* Projections for insertion into the sockets [9].

24] *They shall match.* The Hebrew is uncertain.

כז הַמִּשְׁכָּן לַיַּרְכָתַיִם יָמָּה: וְהַבְּרִיחַ הַתִּיכֹן בְּתוֹךְ
הַקְּרָשִׁים מַבְרִחַ מִן־הַקָּצֶה אֶל־הַקָּצֶה: וְאֶת־הַקְּרָשִׁים
תְּצַפֶּה זָהָב וְאֶת־טַבְּעֹתֵיהֶם תַּעֲשֶׂה זָהָב בָּתִּים
לַבְּרִיחִם וְצִפִּיתָ אֶת־הַבְּרִיחִם זָהָב: וַהֲקֵמֹתָ אֶת־
הַמִּשְׁכָּן כְּמִשְׁפָּטוֹ אֲשֶׁר הָרְאֵיתָ בָּהָר: ס וְעָשִׂיתָ
פָרֹכֶת תְּכֵלֶת וְאַרְגָּמָן וְתוֹלַעַת שָׁנִי וְשֵׁשׁ מָשְׁזָר
מַעֲשֵׂה חֹשֵׁב יַעֲשֶׂה אֹתָהּ כְּרֻבִים: וְנָתַתָּה אֹתָהּ עַל־
אַרְבָּעָה עַמּוּדֵי שִׁטִּים מְצֻפִּים זָהָב וָוֵיהֶם זָהָב
עַל־אַרְבָּעָה אַדְנֵי־כָסֶף: וְנָתַתָּה אֶת־הַפָּרֹכֶת תַּחַת
הַקְּרָסִים וְהֵבֵאתָ שָׁמָּה מִבֵּית לַפָּרֹכֶת אֵת אֲרוֹן
הָעֵדוּת וְהִבְדִּילָה הַפָּרֹכֶת לָכֶם בֵּין הַקֹּדֶשׁ וּבֵין
קֹדֶשׁ הַקֳּדָשִׁים: וְנָתַתָּ אֶת־הַכַּפֹּרֶת עַל אֲרוֹן הָעֵדֻת

בְּקֹדֶשׁ הַקֳּדָשִׁים: וְשַׂמְתָּ אֶת־הַשֻּׁלְחָן מִחוּץ לַפָּרֹכֶת
וְאֶת־הַמְּנֹרָה נֹכַח הַשֻּׁלְחָן עַל צֶלַע הַמִּשְׁכָּן תֵּימָנָה
וְהַשֻּׁלְחָן תִּתֵּן עַל־צֶלַע צָפוֹן: וְעָשִׂיתָ מָסָךְ לְפֶתַח
הָאֹהֶל תְּכֵלֶת וְאַרְגָּמָן וְתוֹלַעַת שָׁנִי וְשֵׁשׁ מָשְׁזָר
מַעֲשֵׂה רֹקֵם: וְעָשִׂיתָ לַמָּסָךְ חֲמִשָּׁה עַמּוּדֵי שִׁטִּים
וְצִפִּיתָ אֹתָם זָהָב וָוֵיהֶם זָהָב וְיָצַקְתָּ לָהֶם חֲמִשָּׁה
אַדְנֵי נְחֹשֶׁת: ס

וְעָשִׂיתָ אֶת־הַמִּזְבֵּחַ עֲצֵי שִׁטִּים חָמֵשׁ אַמּוֹת אֹרֶךְ
וְחָמֵשׁ אַמּוֹת רֹחַב רָבוּעַ יִהְיֶה הַמִּזְבֵּחַ וְשָׁלֹשׁ אַמּוֹת
קֹמָתוֹ: וְעָשִׂיתָ קַרְנֹתָיו עַל אַרְבַּע פִּנֹּתָיו מִמֶּנּוּ תִּהְיֶיןָ
קַרְנֹתָיו וְצִפִּיתָ אֹתוֹ נְחֹשֶׁת: וְעָשִׂיתָ סִּירֹתָיו לְדַשְּׁנוֹ

for the planks of the wall of the Tabernacle at the rear to the west. **28]** The center bar halfway up the planks shall run from end to end. **29]** Overlay the planks with gold, and make their rings of gold, as holders for the bars; and overlay the bars with gold. **30]** Then set up the Tabernacle according to the manner of it that you were shown on the mountain.

31] You shall make a curtain of blue, purple, and crimson yarns, and fine twisted linen; it shall have a design of cherubim worked into it. **32]** Hang it upon four posts of acacia wood overlaid with gold and having hooks of gold, [set] in four sockets of silver. **33]** Hang the curtain under the clasps, and carry the Ark of the Pact there, behind the curtain, so that the curtain shall serve you as a partition between the Holy and the Holy of Holies. **34]** Place the cover upon the Ark of the Pact in the Holy of Holies. **35]** Place the table outside the curtain, and the lampstand by the south wall of the Tabernacle opposite the table, which is to be placed by the north wall.

36] You shall make a screen for the entrance of the Tent, of blue, purple, and crimson yarns, and fine twisted linen, done in embroidery. **37]** Make five posts of acacia wood for the screen and overlay them with gold—their hooks being of gold—and cast for them five sockets of copper.

1] You shall make the altar of acacia wood, five cubits long and five cubits wide—the altar is to be square—and three cubits high. **2]** Make its horns on the four corners, the horns to be of one piece with it; and overlay it with copper. **3]** Make the pails for removing its ashes, as

31] *Curtain.* פָּרֹכֶת (*parochet*). Others, "veil." *Parochet* is still the name given to the curtain covering the synagogue ark.

33] *Between the Holy.* The area in front of the curtain.

And the Holy of Holies. A superlative, meaning "the most holy." It designates the area behind the curtain, where the ark was.

36] *A screen.* To hide the inside from view.

37] *Posts.* Others, "nails."

27:2] *Horns.* These protrusions are clearly shown on an altar excavated at Tel Beer-Sheba which conforms in the measurement of its height precisely to the three cubits prescribed in verse 1.

עֶשְׂרִים נְחֹשֶׁת וָוֵי הָעַמֻּדִים וַחֲשֻׁקֵיהֶם כָּסֶף:
יא וְכֵן לִפְאַת צָפוֹן בָּאֹרֶךְ קְלָעִים מֵאָה אֹרֶךְ וְעַמְדָו
עֶשְׂרִים וְאַדְנֵיהֶם עֶשְׂרִים נְחֹשֶׁת וָוֵי הָעַמֻּדִים
וַחֲשֻׁקֵיהֶם כָּסֶף: יב וְרֹחַב הֶחָצֵר לִפְאַת־יָם קְלָעִים
חֲמִשִּׁים אַמָּה עַמֻּדֵיהֶם עֲשָׂרָה וְאַדְנֵיהֶם עֲשָׂרָה:
יג וְרֹחַב הֶחָצֵר לִפְאַת קֵדְמָה מִזְרָחָה חֲמִשִּׁים אַמָּה:
יד וַחֲמֵשׁ עֶשְׂרֵה אַמָּה קְלָעִים לַכָּתֵף עַמֻּדֵיהֶם שְׁלֹשָׁה
וְאַדְנֵיהֶם שְׁלֹשָׁה: טו וְלַכָּתֵף הַשֵּׁנִית חֲמֵשׁ עֶשְׂרֵה קְלָעִים
עַמֻּדֵיהֶם שְׁלֹשָׁה וְאַדְנֵיהֶם שְׁלֹשָׁה: טז וּלְשַׁעַר הֶחָצֵר
מָסָךְ עֶשְׂרִים אַמָּה תְּכֵלֶת וְאַרְגָּמָן וְתוֹלַעַת שָׁנִי

וְיָעָיו וּמִזְרְקֹתָיו וּמִזְלְגֹתָיו וּמַחְתֹּתָיו לְכָל־כֵּלָיו תַּעֲשֶׂה
ד נְחֹשֶׁת: וְעָשִׂיתָ לּוֹ מִכְבָּר מַעֲשֵׂה רֶשֶׁת נְחֹשֶׁת וְעָשִׂיתָ
עַל־הָרֶשֶׁת אַרְבַּע טַבְּעֹת נְחֹשֶׁת עַל אַרְבַּע קְצוֹתָיו:
ה וְנָתַתָּה אֹתָהּ תַּחַת כַּרְכֹּב הַמִּזְבֵּחַ מִלְּמָטָּה וְהָיְתָה
ו הָרֶשֶׁת עַד חֲצִי הַמִּזְבֵּחַ: וְעָשִׂיתָ בַדִּים לַמִּזְבֵּחַ
ז בַּדֵּי עֲצֵי שִׁטִּים וְצִפִּיתָ אֹתָם נְחֹשֶׁת: וְהוּבָא אֶת־
בַּדָּיו בַּטַּבָּעֹת וְהָיוּ הַבַּדִּים עַל־שְׁתֵּי צַלְעֹת הַמִּזְבֵּחַ
ח בִּשְׂאֵת אֹתוֹ: נְבוּב לֻחֹת תַּעֲשֶׂה אֹתוֹ כַּאֲשֶׁר הֶרְאָה
ט אֹתְךָ בָּהָר כֵּן יַעֲשׂוּ: ס וְעָשִׂיתָ אֵת חֲצַר הַמִּשְׁכָּן
לִפְאַת נֶגֶב־תֵּימָנָה קְלָעִים לֶחָצֵר שֵׁשׁ מָשְׁזָר מֵאָה
י בָּאַמָּה אֹרֶךְ לַפֵּאָה הָאֶחָת: וְעַמֻּדָיו עֶשְׂרִים וְאַדְנֵיהֶם

* יא וְעַמֻּדָיו קרי.

---

well as its scrapers, basins, flesh hooks, and fire pans—make all its utensils of copper. 4] Make for it a grating of meshwork in copper; and on the mesh make four copper rings at its four corners. 5] Set the mesh below, under the ledge of the altar, so that it extends to the middle of the altar. 6] And make poles for the altar, poles of acacia wood, and overlay them with copper. 7] The poles shall be inserted into the rings, so that the poles remain on the two sides of the altar when it is carried. 8] Make it hollow, of boards. As you were shown on the mountain, so shall they be made.

9] You shall make the enclosure of the Tabernacle:

On the south side, a hundred cubits of hangings of fine twisted linen for the length of the enclosure on that side— 10] with its twenty posts and their twenty sockets of copper, the hooks and bands of the posts to be of silver.

11] Again a hundred cubits of hangings for its length along the north side—with its twenty posts and their twenty sockets of copper, the hooks and bands of the posts to be of silver.

12] For the width of the enclosure, on the west side, fifty cubits of hangings, with their ten posts and their ten sockets.

13] For the width of the enclosure on the front, or east side, fifty cubits: 14] fifteen cubits of hangings on the one flank, with their three posts and their three sockets; 15] fifteen cubits of hangings on the other flank, with their three posts and their three sockets; 16] and for the

---

It is likely that these protrusions were symbols of strength, like the horns of a bull [10]. The word *keren* is also used figuratively in the Bible. (Today, as formerly, it often denotes a fund, as in Keren Kayemet [11].) Holding on to the horns provided temporary protection to a refugee from justice.

8] *Hollow, of boards*. The obvious question arises: If indeed the word means "hollow" (which is not certain), how would such a wooden altar resist the sacrificial fires? Cassuto has suggested that the wooden frame made transportation easier and when set up would be filled with earth, to satisfy the command in 20:21 [12].

בָּאַמָּה וְרֹחַב חֲמִשִּׁים בַּחֲמִשִּׁים וְקֹמָה חָמֵשׁ אַמּוֹת   וְשֵׁשׁ מָשְׁזָר מַעֲשֵׂה רֹקֵם עַמֻּדֵיהֶם אַרְבָּעָה וְאַדְנֵיהֶם

יח שֵׁשׁ מָשְׁזָר וְאַדְנֵיהֶם נְחֹשֶׁת: לְכֹל כְּלֵי הַמִּשְׁכָּן בְּכֹל   אַרְבָּעָה: כָּל־עַמּוּדֵי הֶחָצֵר סָבִיב מְחֻשָּׁקִים כֶּסֶף

עֲבֹדָתוֹ וְכָל־יְתֵדֹתָיו וְכָל־יִתְדֹת הֶחָצֵר נְחֹשֶׁת: יט וָוֵיהֶם כָּסֶף וְאַדְנֵיהֶם נְחֹשֶׁת: אֹרֶךְ הֶחָצֵר מֵאָה

Haftarah Terumah, p. 717

gate of the enclosure, a screen of twenty cubits, of blue, purple, and crimson yarns, and fine twisted linen, done in embroidery, with their four posts and their four sockets.

17] All the posts round the enclosure shall be banded with silver and their hooks shall be of silver; their sockets shall be of copper.

18] The length of the enclosure shall be a hundred cubits, and the width fifty throughout; and the height five cubits—[with hangings] of fine twisted linen. The sockets shall be of copper: 19] all the utensils of the Tabernacle, for all its service, as well as all its pegs and all the pegs of the court, shall be of copper.

19] *All the utensils of the Tabernacle ... shall be of copper.* Since inside everything was made of gold, the outer enclosure must here be meant. Others interpret "utensils" to refer to the implements needed for the work, such as hammers, anvils, and saws [13].

The Cherubim

The text does not describe the two intended figures in detail; it merely states that they have wings and faces, and it does so in a manner which suggests that cherubim were well fixed in the reader's imagination. Most likely they were conceived as having the body of an animal, such as a bull or lion, and the head of a human.[1] Figures like cherubim (*karibu* in Akkadian) were established in ancient Mesopotamian folklore as creatures that mediated between man and his god, bringing prayers before the deity and guarding holy places. The Egyptian sphinx seems to be of a similar order as the cherub; it had the body of a lion and a human face. In the Torah cherubim are said to guard the ark and the Garden of Eden from unauthorized intruders (Gen. 3:24). In Ezekiel's famous vision (Ezek. 1:5 ff.; 10:1 ff.) they were creatures with four faces, of man, lion, ox, and eagle, similar to the four winds upon which God was poetically said to ride:

> Mounted on a cherub, He flew,
> Gliding on the wings of the wind.
>
> (Ps. 18:11)[2]

The cherubim and the ark cover (*kapporet*) were of one piece, and the latter was described by Ezekiel as well as in I Chron. 28:18 as God's chariot (*merkavah*). Above this chariot Ezekiel saw the likeness of the divine throne and doubtlessly he meant by this that he saw the cherubim. So also elsewhere in the Bible are they conceived as His throne: "The Lord of Hosts is enthroned on the cherubim" (I Sam. 4:4). This then seems to have been their function on the cover of the ark: to symbolize both the empty throne of the unseen God, with the *kapporet* as His footstool, and at the same time their guardianship of the ark. Like human beings the cherubim look downward, averting their eyes from the Divine Presence, perhaps, as in Isaiah's vision of the seraphim (6:2), shielding them with their wings.[3]

The question how images of this kind could have had a place in an otherwise strictly imageless cult has often been asked and has not been satisfactorily answered. Apparently the cherubim belonged to an old mythological tradition that could not be dislodged, and by hiding them away in a place totally inaccessible to the people at large the danger of their adoration was minimized, and indeed the Bible makes no mention of such adoration ever having become a problem.[4] One must therefore simply conclude that the cherubim were permitted or perhaps merely tolerated images, while all others were prohibited [15]. With the destruction of the First Temple they disappeared and were not reconstructed when the Second Temple was built. Thereafter, Jewish law rejected even a hint of imagery that could conceivably lead to idol worship, inside or outside sacred settings.

Table and Bread

Already the medieval commentator Isaac Abarbanel raised the question of the likely pagan origin of these sacred appurtenances. The idea was widespread in the ancient Near East that the gods needed

---

[1] So usually in the Aggadic tradition [14].

[2] God is also depicted as riding upon the clouds (Ps. 68:5), similar to the Canaanite Baal who is depicted as a rider of clouds.

[3] Moses, at the burning bush, hides his face from the vision (Exod. 3:6).

[4] This was not so with the copper serpent that Moses fashioned during a plague and which had to be destroyed in the time of King Hezekiah because people paid it homage. For a discussion of the difference between cherubim and golden calf, see commentary on 32:1–33:6.

food, which therefore had to be sacrificed to them at regular intervals. Here, too, the prescriptions of the text are most likely remnants of old practices, but the Torah also makes sure that these origins are well covered. Table and bread are removed from the Holy of Holies; the table vessels remain empty, and the bread is consumed by the priests themselves as part of the sacrificial rite (Lev. 24:9, see commentary there). Abarbanel's suggestion that the Israelites were still in need of such symbols seems to be the best explanation for the Torah's retention of the custom.

The use of the two loaves of bread (*chalot*) at the inauguration of Sabbaths and holy days is not based on the shew bread but on tradition arising from the double portion of manna which was gathered on the sixth day in preparation for the Sabbath [16].

The Lampstand (*Menorah*)

Scholars assumed for a long time that the description of the lampstand belonged to a time as late as the fifth or fourth century

B.C.E., but, since Assyrian seals were found in Cappadocia showing a seven-branched candelabrum, the antiquity of the menorah has once again become likely. Further, the depiction, though detailed, is far from clear, which may suggest that the Torah text as set down dealt with an old oral tradition rather than a known candelabrum.[5]

The height of the candelabrum is not stated; the Talmud had a tradition that it was eighteen handbreaths (about fifty-two inches or 132 cm) tall [19]. It burned from evening until morning (Lev. 24:3) and was referred to as the נֵר תָּמִיד (*ner tamid*), the regular light, because of the fixed routine that attended its lighting. In the Second Temple a different procedure prevailed. There, three lights were never allowed to go out, while the others were kindled at night [20]. The Solomonic Temple had ten lampstands, the Second Temple only a single one,[6] and it was this which was taken by the Romans and represented on the Arch of Titus.

---

[5] Nogah Hareuveni calls attention to the fact that the biblical description "is couched almost completely in botanical terms: branches, calyxes, petals, and cups. Ancient Jewish sources, like the Babylonian Talmud, hint at a direct relationship between the menorah and a specific plant. In fact, there is a plant native to the Land of Israel that bears an uncanny resemblance to the menorah, even though it is not always seven-branched. It is a type of sage (*salvia*) called *moriah* in Hebrew. Varieties of this plant grow all over the world, but some of the species found growing wild in Israel very obviously resemble the menorah" [17]. Whether or not the *moriah* was the original model of the menorah, it is most likely that the cultic object was a form of sacred tree, presented in stylized form. The subject has been explored in detail by Carol L. Meyers [18].

[6] For Solomon's Temple see I Kings 7:49; for the postexilic Temple, I Macc. 1:21; 4:49.

GLEANINGS

A Willing Heart

All contributions to the Tabernacle were voluntary except the half shekel, which was required of all. Contributions in kind were left to generosity, money was not.

IBN EZRA (on 25:3)

God said: "Take Me gifts" (which is the literal understanding of verse 2). For when Israel acquires Torah and Tabernacle it acquires Me too. Hence, "Take Me...."

MIDRASH [21]

Verse 2 of chapter 25 is the heart and substance of the Torah: *tzedakah* and good deeds.

CHASIDIC [22]

Taking and Giving

The two are placed side by side ("*take* Me *gifts*," verse 2). This should remind a giver how it feels to accept a gift.

MUSAR LITERATURE [23]

Another explanation: This demonstrated the difference between a fool and a wise man. When giving to charity the former thinks it is he who gives, the latter knows that even in giving he receives.

CHASIDIC [24]

Instructions

All instructions regarding the furnishings are commanded in the singular (וְעָשִׂיתָ), but the making of the ark is commanded in the plural (וְעָשׂוּ, verse 10). The furnishings are for the service which is carried out by the priests, but the ark is like the Torah it contains: it belongs to all. Thus also a popular saying: "A bastard who is learned in Torah outranks a High Priest who is ignorant."

MOSES BEN CHAYIM ALSHECH [25]

In Each Heart

It says (25:8), "Let them make Me a sanctuary that I may dwell among (or within) them"—in *them*, the people, not in *it*, the sanctuary. Each person is to build Him a Tabernacle in his own heart for God to dwell in.

MALBIM

All gold and silver belong to God, but the willingness of the heart is ours to give.

TORAT MOSHEH [26]

Symbolism

The three divisions of the Tabernacle correspond to the world's three realms: the first two to earth and sea which belong to humanity; the third to the heavens which are God's alone.

There were twelve loaves of bread, corresponding to the twelve months; seven lamps, corresponding to the sun, moon, and the five planets [then known]; and the four materials in the curtain to the four elements.

JOSEPHUS [27]

The materials were made of things grown from the earth; the purple color is like that of water; the blue resembles the sky; and scarlet is like fire. Together, materials and colors represent the four elements.

PHILO [28]

There were two cherubim, one corresponding to God's quality of mercy (יְהֹוָה), the other to that of justice (אֱלֹהִים).

MIDRASH [29]

[On these two qualities of mercy and justice, see commentary to Genesis 2:4–24, "The Names of God."]

Fractions

The Tabernacle's measurements are given in fractions (see, for instance, Exod. 25:10). Scholars should remember that in learning too there are always fractions still to be added.

NATHAN BEN SIMEON HA-KOHEN ADLER [30]

Cherubim

They stood ten spans above the ark cover whence God spoke. This is another hint that God never quite descended to earth, even as man— including Moses and Elijah—never quite ascended to heaven.   TALMUD [31]

Inside and Outside

The ark was covered with gold "inside and out" (25:11). From this you learn that a wise man whose inside does not match his outside is not genuinely wise.   TALMUD [32]

Close

The table with its bread and the ark stood close together, for where there is no bread there is no Torah, and vice versa.

CHASIDIC [33]

Boards

The name for the board used in the construction of the Tabernacle is קֶרֶשׁ (keresh). The word is an anagram of שֶׁקֶר (sheker), falsehood. Whoever or whatever can alter falsehood is worthy of being part of the sanctuary.   N. ELIMELECH [34]

The Altar

The Rabbis explained the symbolism of the altar by making each letter of the Hebrew name for altar (מִזְבֵּחַ) the initial of a word, thus: מְחִילָה "forgiveness"—the altar was the channel whereby the Israelite could seek reconciliation with God from Whom he had become estranged by sin; זְכוּת "merit"—gratitude, humility, contrition found an outlet on the altar, and, by the exercise of these virtues, life was ennobled and "merit" acquired; בְּרָכָה "blessing"—by being true to the teachings that centered round the altar, man earns the divine blessings and himself becomes a blessing to his fellowmen; חַיִּים "life"—the altar points the way of the life everlasting, to the things that abide for evermore, truth, righteousness, holiness.   J. H. HERTZ [35]

The Four Directions

In the west, the Ark of the Law stood with its cherubim-cover; in the north, the table with the shew bread; in the south, the lamp with its lights; the east was turned toward the people, on that side was the entrance, and there, one behind the other in two different places, stood the altars which invited the people to happy self-sacrificing giving themselves up to the divine Torah awaiting them in the west. We believe that we are not in error if we take the west side to represent the Torah and the presence of God that it, and it alone, brings about; the north side, the material life; the south, the spiritual; and the east, the concrete nation, the people of Israel invited to self-sacrificing dedication to God and His Torah.

S. R. HIRSCH [36]

Copper

(The sidrah ends by stating that all the utensils were to be made of copper, Exod. 27:19.) Copper was an atonement for the people's stiff-neckedness as Isaiah said (48:4): "Your neck is like an iron sinew, and your forehead like copper."

RASHI [37]

The Pledge

The reason then why the Tabernacle was called Mishkan is because the Holy One, blessed be He, said to Moses: "Tell Israel to grant Me a mashkon (pledge) so that if they sin it shall be forfeited by them."   MIDRASH [38]

The Regular ("Perpetual") Light; Priests and Their Vestments

A new *sidrah* (תְּצַוֶּה) begins here. It opens with instructions for kindling the regular light (*ner tamid*), more commonly known as "perpetual" or "eternal" light. The brief paragraph which describes it forms a bridge between a discussion of the sacred appurtenances in the sanctuary and the people who will use them.

Aaron and his family are introduced as "priests." The term is not further defined, though the hereditary nature of this "priestly" office appears to be taken for granted. One may therefore assume that either the institution was already well known in its day (the Egyptians and Midianites had priests) or that the story is a later retrojection, told in a time and for an audience which had long become accustomed to priests and their service.* While most likely the text contains numerous embellishments and enlargements stemming from later generations, we have little reason to doubt that it also reports many traditions going back to Israel's earliest days.

The priestly vestments—and especially those of the High Priest—are described in great detail: breastpiece, ephod, robe, tunic, headdress, and sash. Inside the breastpiece rested the Urim and Thummim, oracular

---

* Scholars have assigned this section largely to the P-source. They point out that the priestly vestments as described are idealized rather than realistic and that they are highly complex and extravagant, hardly befitting a desert environment.

devices on which much speculation has centered; and the headpiece had a frontlet with an inscription of expiatory properties [1].

The vestments here described are the direct antecedents of those now in use in the Roman Catholic and Greek Orthodox churches, whose priests —and especially whose bishops—wear similar robes while officiating. In the synagogue, the Torah scroll exhibits some of these features: it is generally dressed in an embroidered mantle and sash and crowned by pomegranates and bells.

ס ט ס

כ וְאַתָּה תְּצַוֶּה אֶת־בְּנֵי יִשְׂרָאֵל וְיִקְחוּ אֵלֶיךָ שֶׁמֶן זַיִת
כא זָךְ כָּתִית לַמָּאוֹר לְהַעֲלֹת נֵר תָּמִיד: בְּאֹהֶל מוֹעֵד
מִחוּץ לַפָּרֹכֶת אֲשֶׁר עַל־הָעֵדֻת יַעֲרֹךְ אֹתוֹ אַהֲרֹן
וּבָנָיו מֵעֶרֶב עַד־בֹּקֶר לִפְנֵי יְהוָה חֻקַּת עוֹלָם לְדֹרֹתָם
מֵאֵת בְּנֵי יִשְׂרָאֵל: ס

א וְאַתָּה הַקְרֵב אֵלֶיךָ אֶת־אַהֲרֹן אָחִיךָ וְאֶת־בָּנָיו אִתּוֹ
מִתּוֹךְ בְּנֵי יִשְׂרָאֵל לְכַהֲנוֹ־לִי אַהֲרֹן נָדָב וַאֲבִיהוּא
ב אֶלְעָזָר וְאִיתָמָר בְּנֵי אַהֲרֹן: וְעָשִׂיתָ בִגְדֵי־קֹדֶשׁ לְאַהֲרֹן
ג אָחִיךָ לְכָבוֹד וּלְתִפְאָרֶת: וְאַתָּה תְּדַבֵּר אֶל־כָּל־

חַכְמֵי־לֵב אֲשֶׁר מִלֵּאתִיו רוּחַ חָכְמָה וְעָשׂוּ אֶת־
ד בִּגְדֵי אַהֲרֹן לְקַדְּשׁוֹ לְכַהֲנוֹ־לִי: וְאֵלֶּה הַבְּגָדִים אֲשֶׁר
יַעֲשׂוּ חֹשֶׁן וְאֵפוֹד וּמְעִיל וּכְתֹנֶת תַּשְׁבֵּץ מִצְנֶפֶת
וְאַבְנֵט וְעָשׂוּ בִגְדֵי־קֹדֶשׁ לְאַהֲרֹן אָחִיךָ וּלְבָנָיו לְכַהֲנוֹ־
ה לִי: וְהֵם יִקְחוּ אֶת־הַזָּהָב וְאֶת־הַתְּכֵלֶת וְאֶת־הָאַרְגָּמָן
וְאֶת־תּוֹלַעַת הַשָּׁנִי וְאֶת־הַשֵּׁשׁ: פ
ו וְעָשׂוּ אֶת־הָאֵפֹד זָהָב תְּכֵלֶת וְאַרְגָּמָן תּוֹלַעַת שָׁנִי
וְשֵׁשׁ מָשְׁזָר מַעֲשֵׂה חֹשֵׁב: שְׁתֵּי כְתֵפֹת חֹבְרֹת יִהְיֶה־לּוֹ
ז אֶל־שְׁנֵי קְצוֹתָיו וְחֻבָּר: וְחֵשֶׁב אֲפֻדָּתוֹ אֲשֶׁר עָלָיו
ח כְּמַעֲשֵׂהוּ מִמֶּנּוּ יִהְיֶה זָהָב תְּכֵלֶת וְאַרְגָּמָן וְתוֹלַעַת

20] You shall further instruct the Israelites to bring you clear oil of beaten olives for lighting, for kindling lamps regularly. **21]** Aaron and his sons shall set them up in the Tent of Meeting, outside the curtain which is over the Pact, [to burn] from evening to morning before the LORD. It shall be a due from the Israelites for all time, throughout the ages.

1] You shall bring forward your brother Aaron, with his sons, from among the Israelites, to serve Me as priests: Aaron, Nadab and Abihu, Eleazar and Ithamar, the sons of Aaron. **2]** Make sacral vestments for your brother Aaron, for dignity and adornment. **3]** Next you shall instruct all who are skillful, whom I have endowed with the gift of skill, to make Aaron's vestments, for consecrating him to serve Me as priest. **4]** These are the vestments they are to make: a breastpiece, an ephod, a robe, a fringed tunic, a headdress, and a sash. They shall make those sacral vestments for your brother Aaron and his sons, for priestly service to Me; **5]** they, therefore, shall receive the gold, the blue, purple, and crimson yarns, and the fine linen.

6] They shall make the ephod of gold, of blue, purple, and crimson yarns, and of fine twisted linen, worked into designs. **7]** It shall have two shoulder-pieces attached; they shall be attached at its two ends. **8]** And the decorated band that is upon it shall be made like it, of

27:20] *Kindling lamps regularly.* The lights were to be kindled on the lampstand previously described. The translation of נֵר תָּמִיד as "perpetual light" or "eternal light" is grammatically inaccurate and is also contradicted by verse 21. (The so-called נֵר תָּמִיד of the synagogue is of much later origin. See commentary below.)

28:3] *Skillful . . . gift of skill.* An idiomatic translation of חָכְמָה (chochmah), literally, "wisdom."

4] *Fringed tunic.* Others, "checkered." A basic garment over which robe and ephod were worn.

6] *Ephod.* The word is not explained further, probably because the ephod was a familiar item. It was a kind of pinafore composed of two pieces of linen joined at the shoulder by straps. Noth believes it to have originally been a loin cloth, expressly prescribed to contrast with cultic nakedness in other nations [2]. In later centuries the ephod apparently became something carried by hand, perhaps the wrapping for the Urim and Thummim; see I Sam. 23:6 and 9.

שָׁנִי וְשֵׁשׁ מָשְׁזָר: וְלָקַחְתָּ אֶת־שְׁתֵּי אַבְנֵי־שֹׁהַם וּפִתַּחְתָּ
עֲלֵיהֶם שְׁמוֹת בְּנֵי יִשְׂרָאֵל: שִׁשָּׁה מִשְּׁמֹתָם עַל הָאֶבֶן
הָאֶחָת וְאֶת־שְׁמוֹת הַשִּׁשָּׁה הַנּוֹתָרִים עַל־הָאֶבֶן הַשֵּׁנִית
כְּתוֹלְדֹתָם: מַעֲשֵׂה חָרַשׁ אֶבֶן פִּתּוּחֵי חֹתָם תְּפַתַּח
אֶת־שְׁתֵּי הָאֲבָנִים עַל־שְׁמֹת בְּנֵי יִשְׂרָאֵל מְסַבֹּת
מִשְׁבְּצוֹת זָהָב תַּעֲשֶׂה אֹתָם: וְשַׂמְתָּ אֶת־שְׁתֵּי הָאֲבָנִים
עַל כִּתְפֹת הָאֵפֹד אַבְנֵי זִכָּרֹן לִבְנֵי יִשְׂרָאֵל וְנָשָׂא
אַהֲרֹן אֶת־שְׁמוֹתָם לִפְנֵי יְהוָה עַל־שְׁתֵּי כְתֵפָיו

לְזִכָּרֹן: ס וְעָשִׂיתָ מִשְׁבְּצֹת זָהָב: וּשְׁתֵּי שַׁרְשְׁרֹת
זָהָב טָהוֹר מִגְבָּלֹת תַּעֲשֶׂה אֹתָם מַעֲשֵׂה עֲבֹת וְנָתַתָּה
אֶת־שַׁרְשְׁרֹת הָעֲבֹתֹת עַל־הַמִּשְׁבְּצֹת: ס וְעָשִׂיתָ
חֹשֶׁן מִשְׁפָּט מַעֲשֵׂה חֹשֵׁב כְּמַעֲשֵׂה אֵפֹד תַּעֲשֶׂנּוּ
זָהָב תְּכֵלֶת וְאַרְגָּמָן וְתוֹלַעַת שָׁנִי וְשֵׁשׁ מָשְׁזָר תַּעֲשֶׂה
אֹתוֹ: רָבוּעַ יִהְיֶה כָּפוּל זֶרֶת אָרְכּוֹ וְזֶרֶת רָחְבּוֹ:
וּמִלֵּאתָ בוֹ מִלֻּאַת אֶבֶן אַרְבָּעָה טוּרִים אָבֶן טוּר
אֹדֶם פִּטְדָה וּבָרֶקֶת הַטּוּר הָאֶחָד: וְהַטּוּר הַשֵּׁנִי

one piece with it: of gold, of blue, purple, and crimson yarns, and of fine twisted linen.
9] Then take two lazuli stones and engrave on them the names of the sons of Israel: **10]** six of their names on the one stone, and the names of the remaining six on the other stone, in the order of their birth. **11]** On the two stones you shall make seal engravings—the work of a lapidary—of the names of the sons of Israel. Having bordered them with frames of gold, **12]** attach the two stones to the shoulder-pieces of the ephod, as stones for remembrance of the Israelite people, whose names Aaron shall carry upon his two shoulder-pieces for remembrance before the LORD.

13] Then make frames of gold **14]** and two chains of pure gold; braid these like corded work, and fasten the corded chains to the frames.

15] You shall make a breastpiece of decision, worked into a design; make it in the style of the ephod: make it of gold, of blue, purple, and crimson yarns, and of fine twisted linen. **16]** It shall be square and doubled, a span in length and a span in width. **17]** Set in it mounted stones, in four rows of stones. The first row shall be a row of carnelian, chrysolite, and emerald;

9] *Lazuli stones.* See at Exod. 25:7.

10] *Six of their names on the one stone.* According to Rashi: Reuben, Simeon, Levi, Judah, Dan, Naphtali. The other stone contained: Gad, Asher, Issachar, Zebulon, Joseph, and Benjamin, which would make twenty-five Hebrew letters on each stone [3].

13] *Frames of gold.* Others, "filigree settings" [4], "rosettes" [5].

15] *Breastpiece of decision.* Or, "judgment," חֹשֶׁן מִשְׁפָּט (*choshen mishpat*), so called because of the Urim and Thummim it contained. A breastpiece of a similar nature was found in a tomb of the king of Byblos (or Gebal, in Phoenicia). The piece is called *choshen ha-mishpat* in verse 30, which name

was given to the fourth parts of both *Tur* and *Shulchan Aruch* (major works on Jewish law; see at verse 17). The breastpiece was attached to the ephod (verse 25).

16] *Square and doubled.* To form a pouch. One scholar has explored this text as an example of quasi-architectural design expressed through the intricate use of certain letters and words [6].

Span in length. From the thumb to the little finger, when the hand is spread. In English custom it became nine inches (22.5 cm).

17] *Four rows.* אַרְבָּעָה טוּרִים (*arba'ah turim*), the name given to Jacob ben Asher's famous halachic work (fourteenth century C.E.), which became model for Joseph Karo's *Shulchan Aruch* (sixteenth century).

יט נֹפֶךְ סַפִּיר וְיָהֲלֹם: וְהַטּוּר הַשְּׁלִישִׁי לֶשֶׁם שְׁבוֹ
כ וְאַחְלָמָה: וְהַטּוּר הָרְבִיעִי תַּרְשִׁישׁ וְשֹׁהַם וְיָשְׁפֵה
כא מְשֻׁבָּצִים זָהָב יִהְיוּ בְּמִלּוּאֹתָם: וְהָאֲבָנִים תִּהְיֶיןָ עַל־
שְׁמֹת בְּנֵי־יִשְׂרָאֵל שְׁתֵּים עֶשְׂרֵה עַל־שְׁמֹתָם פִּתּוּחֵי
כב חוֹתָם אִישׁ עַל־שְׁמוֹ תִּהְיֶיןָ לִשְׁנֵי עָשָׂר שָׁבֶט: וְעָשִׂיתָ
עַל־הַחֹשֶׁן שַׁרְשֹׁת גַּבְלֻת מַעֲשֵׂה עֲבֹת זָהָב טָהוֹר:
כג וְעָשִׂיתָ עַל־הַחֹשֶׁן שְׁתֵּי טַבְּעוֹת זָהָב וְנָתַתָּ אֶת־שְׁתֵּי
כד הַטַּבָּעוֹת עַל־שְׁנֵי קְצוֹת הַחֹשֶׁן: וְנָתַתָּה אֶת־שְׁתֵּי עֲבֹתֹת
כה הַזָּהָב עַל־שְׁתֵּי הַטַּבָּעֹת אֶל־קְצוֹת הַחֹשֶׁן: וְאֵת שְׁתֵּי
קְצוֹת שְׁתֵּי הָעֲבֹתֹת תִּתֵּן עַל־שְׁתֵּי הַמִּשְׁבְּצוֹת וְנָתַתָּה
כו עַל־כִּתְפוֹת הָאֵפֹד אֶל־מוּל פָּנָיו: וְעָשִׂיתָ שְׁתֵּי טַבְּעוֹת
זָהָב וְשַׂמְתָּ אֹתָם עַל־שְׁנֵי קְצוֹת הַחֹשֶׁן עַל־שְׂפָתוֹ

כז אֲשֶׁר אֶל־עֵבֶר הָאֵפוֹד בָּיְתָה: וְעָשִׂיתָ שְׁתֵּי טַבְּעוֹת
זָהָב וְנָתַתָּה אֹתָם עַל־שְׁתֵּי כִתְפוֹת הָאֵפוֹד מִלְמַטָּה
מִמּוּל פָּנָיו לְעֻמַּת מַחְבַּרְתּוֹ מִמַּעַל לְחֵשֶׁב הָאֵפוֹד:
כח וְיִרְכְּסוּ אֶת־הַחֹשֶׁן מִטַּבְּעֹתָו אֶל־טַבְּעֹת הָאֵפוֹד
בִּפְתִיל תְּכֵלֶת לִהְיוֹת עַל־חֵשֶׁב הָאֵפוֹד וְלֹא־יִזַּח
כט הַחֹשֶׁן מֵעַל הָאֵפוֹד: וְנָשָׂא אַהֲרֹן אֶת־שְׁמוֹת בְּנֵי־
יִשְׂרָאֵל בְּחֹשֶׁן הַמִּשְׁפָּט עַל־לִבּוֹ בְּבֹאוֹ אֶל־הַקֹּדֶשׁ
ל לְזִכָּרֹן לִפְנֵי־יְהוָה תָּמִיד: וְנָתַתָּ אֶל־חֹשֶׁן הַמִּשְׁפָּט
אֶת־הָאוּרִים וְאֶת־הַתֻּמִּים וְהָיוּ עַל־לֵב אַהֲרֹן בְּבֹאוֹ
לִפְנֵי יְהוָה וְנָשָׂא אַהֲרֹן אֶת־מִשְׁפַּט בְּנֵי־יִשְׂרָאֵל עַל־
לא לִבּוֹ לִפְנֵי יְהוָה תָּמִיד: ס וְעָשִׂיתָ אֶת־מְעִיל
לב הָאֵפוֹד כְּלִיל תְּכֵלֶת: וְהָיָה פִי־רֹאשׁוֹ בְּתוֹכוֹ שָׂפָה

* כח מִטַּבְּעֹתָיו קרי

18] the second row: a turquoise, a sapphire, and an amethyst;　19] the third row: a jacinth, an agate, and a crystal;　20] and the fourth row: a beryl, a lapis lazuli, and a jasper. They shall be framed with gold in their mountings.　21] The stones shall correspond [in number] to the names of the sons of Israel: twelve, corresponding to their names. They shall be engraved like seals, each with its name, for the twelve tribes.

22] On the breastpiece make braided chains of corded work in pure gold.　23] Make two rings of gold on the breastpiece, and fasten the two rings at the two ends of the breastpiece, 24] attaching the two golden cords to the two rings at the ends of the breastpiece.　25] Then fasten the two ends of the cords to the two frames, which you shall attach to the shoulder-pieces of the ephod, at the front.　26] Make two rings of gold and attach them to the two ends of the breastpiece, at its inner edge, which faces the ephod.　27] And make two other rings of gold and fasten them on the front of the ephod, low on the two shoulder-pieces, close to its seam above the decorated band.　28] The breastpiece shall be held in place by a cord of blue from its rings to the rings of the ephod, so that the breastpiece rests on the decorated band and does not come loose from the ephod.　29] Aaron shall carry the names of the sons of Israel on the breastpiece of decision over his heart, when he enters the sanctuary, for remembrance before the LORD at all times.　30] Inside the breastpiece of decision you shall place the Urim and Thummim, so that they are over Aaron's heart when he comes before the LORD. Thus Aaron shall carry the instrument of decision for the Israelites over his heart before the LORD at all times.

31] You shall make the robe of the ephod of pure blue.　32] The opening for the head shall

31] *Robe of the ephod.* That is, the robe over which the ephod was worn.

32] *Coat of mail.* The exact meaning of תַּחְרָא is not clear. It was evidently something of unusual strength, a reinforced edge.

לב יִהְיֶה לְפִיו סָבִיב מַעֲשֵׂה אֹרֵג כְּפִי תַחְרָא יִהְיֶה־לּוֹ
לֹא יִקָּרֵעַ: וְעָשִׂיתָ עַל־שׁוּלָיו רִמֹּנֵי תְּכֵלֶת וְאַרְגָּמָן
וְתוֹלַעַת שָׁנִי עַל־שׁוּלָיו סָבִיב וּפַעֲמֹנֵי זָהָב בְּתוֹכָם
לד סָבִיב: פַּעֲמֹן זָהָב וְרִמּוֹן פַּעֲמֹן זָהָב וְרִמּוֹן עַל־
לה שׁוּלֵי הַמְּעִיל סָבִיב: וְהָיָה עַל־אַהֲרֹן לְשָׁרֵת וְנִשְׁמַע
קוֹלוֹ בְּבֹאוֹ אֶל־הַקֹּדֶשׁ לִפְנֵי יְהוָה וּבְצֵאתוֹ וְלֹא
לו יָמוּת: ס וְעָשִׂיתָ צִּיץ זָהָב טָהוֹר וּפִתַּחְתָּ עָלָיו

לז פִּתּוּחֵי חֹתָם קֹדֶשׁ לַיהוָה: וְשַׂמְתָּ אֹתוֹ עַל־פְּתִיל
תְּכֵלֶת וְהָיָה עַל־הַמִּצְנָפֶת אֶל־מוּל פְּנֵי־הַמִּצְנֶפֶת
לח יִהְיֶה: וְהָיָה עַל־מֵצַח אַהֲרֹן וְנָשָׂא אַהֲרֹן אֶת־עֲוֹן
הַקֳּדָשִׁים אֲשֶׁר יַקְדִּישׁוּ בְּנֵי יִשְׂרָאֵל לְכָל־מַתְּנֹת
קָדְשֵׁיהֶם וְהָיָה עַל־מִצְחוֹ תָּמִיד לְרָצוֹן לָהֶם לִפְנֵי
לט יְהוָה: וְשִׁבַּצְתָּ הַכְּתֹנֶת שֵׁשׁ וְעָשִׂיתָ מִצְנֶפֶת שֵׁשׁ וְאַבְנֵט
תַּעֲשֶׂה מַעֲשֵׂה רֹקֵם: וְלִבְנֵי אַהֲרֹן תַּעֲשֶׂה כֻתֳּנֹת

be in the middle of it; the opening shall have a binding of woven work round about—it shall be like the opening of a coat of mail—so that it does not tear. **33]** On its hem make pomegranates of blue, purple, and crimson yarns, all around the hem, with bells of gold between them all around: **34]** a golden bell and a pomegranate, a golden bell and a pomegranate, all around the hem of the robe. **35]** Aaron shall wear it while officiating, so that the sound of it is heard when he comes into the sanctuary before the LORD and when he goes out—that he may not die.

36] You shall make a frontlet of pure gold and engrave on it the seal inscription: "Holy to the LORD." **37]** Suspend it on a cord of blue, so that it may remain on the headdress; it shall remain on the front of the headdress. **38]** It shall be on Aaron's forehead, that Aaron may take away any sin arising from the holy things that the Israelites consecrate, from any of their sacred donations; it shall be on his forehead at all times, to win acceptance for them before the LORD.

39] You shall make the fringed tunic of fine linen. / You shall make the headdress of fine linen. / You shall make the sash of embroidered work.

33] *Pomegranates*. Popular decorative figures in the ancient Near East [7].

34] *Golden bell*. To announce Aaron's entrance and alert the people. According to J. G. Frazer, bells of this type were widely used in Europe, Asia, and Africa, mostly to ward off evil spirits [8]. This old belief might explain what follows: wearing the bells would keep Aaron from dying.

36] *Frontlet*. צִיץ (*tzitz*). Others, "flower." It was a form of golden plate worn on the forehead (verse 38) and tied by a blue cord to the headdress. The *tzitz* was similar to the *nezer* (often translated diadem) of the king (II Sam. 1:10) and linked to it as *tzitz-nezer* in Exod. 39:30 and Lev. 8:9. In Exod. 29:6 *nezer* appears to be another term for

tzitz. (The nonpriestly Jew also wears a form of *tzitz* when he dons the phylacteries, one set of which is worn as a frontlet.) *Tzitz* is connected with *tzitzit* (fringe or tassel) in that the latter also means a bunch of hair (a "lock," so Ezek. 8:3). The *tzitz* may have been considered to have life-giving or apotropaic purposes [9].

37] *Suspend it*. Tradition dealt extensively with the difficulties of the arrangement [10].

38] *To win acceptance*. The real reason for the prescription: Aaron's precise observance will win acceptance for Israel before God by creating a framework of holiness. The latter has substance not only in faith and deed but also in form, which would be marred by casual dress and behavior.

מ עָרְוָה מִמָּתְנַיִם וְעַד־יְרֵכַיִם יִהְיוּ: וְהָיוּ עַל־אַהֲרֹן וְעַל־בָּנָיו בְּבֹאָם אֶל־אֹהֶל מוֹעֵד אוֹ בְגִשְׁתָּם אֶל־הַמִּזְבֵּחַ לְשָׁרֵת בַּקֹּדֶשׁ וְלֹא־יִשְׂאוּ עָוֺן וָמֵתוּ חֻקַּת עוֹלָם לוֹ וּלְזַרְעוֹ אַחֲרָיו: ס

וְעָשִׂיתָ לָהֶם אַבְנֵטִים וּמִגְבָּעוֹת תַּעֲשֶׂה לָהֶם לְכָבוֹד מא וּלְתִפְאָרֶת: וְהִלְבַּשְׁתָּ אֹתָם אֶת־אַהֲרֹן אָחִיךָ וְאֶת־בָּנָיו אִתּוֹ וּמָשַׁחְתָּ אֹתָם וּמִלֵּאתָ אֶת־יָדָם וְקִדַּשְׁתָּ מב אֹתָם וְכִהֲנוּ־לִי: וַעֲשֵׂה לָהֶם מִכְנְסֵי־בָד לְכַסּוֹת בְּשַׂר

40] And for Aaron's sons also you shall make tunics, and make sashes for them, and make turbans for them, for dignity and adornment.   **41]** Put these on your brother Aaron and on his sons as well; anoint them, and ordain them and consecrate them to serve Me as priests.

42] You shall also make for them linen breeches to cover their nakedness; they shall extend from the hips to the thighs.   **43]** They shall be worn by Aaron and his sons when they enter the Tent of Meeting or when they approach the altar to officiate in the sanctuary, so that they do not incur punishment and die. It shall be a law for all time for him and for his offspring to come.

40] *And for Aaron's sons.* The only time their anointing is treated in the Torah, which otherwise focuses on the High Priest. (See further at Lev. 8:13.)

Turbans. Different from Aaron's headdress, evidently of a less impressive shape.

41] *Anoint them.* A common procedure in antiquity to induct priests or kings into office. Anointing oil was a symbol of well-being, and for the well-to-do (especially in later Rome) its daily use was a part of the good life. Pouring the oil on the head of the chosen in a special ceremony became the sign for his having been favored by or set apart for the deity.

In Israel, olive oil was the chief base of oint-ments; in Babylonia, they also used sesame oil and animal fats; in Egypt, almond oil and animal fats.

Ordain them. Literally, "fill their hands." The candidate was given a tool for or symbol of his office. (In modern days too a mayor receives the chain, a king the scepter, a parliamentary speaker the mace.) In Akkadian also, the expression "to fill into the hand" meant "to appoint."

Consecrate them. "Anoint," "ordain," "consecrate" form a rising trilogy of near synonyms.

42] *Linen breeches.* They were apparently not regular apparel for men, so that the priests' modesty was in this way especially protected when they officiated at the altar (see at 20:26).

The Regular Light

The prescription to maintain the lights regularly (27:20–21) is repeated almost verbatim in Lev. 24:2–3,[1] however, there, an additional verse makes it quite clear that the kindling of the lights does not refer to anything separate but to the lampstand itself: "He shall set up the lamps on the pure lampstand before the LORD (to burn) regularly." The light was in time called נֵר מַעֲרָבִי (ner maʿaravi), the western light, because it lit up the Holy of Holies, which was west of it, and, since usually three lamps (and at least one) were kept burning constantly in the Second Temple to assure regularity of upkeep and maintenance,[2] such a light came to be known as נֵר תָּמִיד (ner tamid) or perpetual light. When the Temple was destroyed and the menorah deported to Rome as war booty, a separate light was lit in the synagogues (the "small sanctuaries" [13]) to maintain as far as possible the intent of the Torah command. Originally this light too was set opposite the ark, that is, on the western wall, but eventually was moved to the vicinity of the ark itself, into a niche by its side, and later as a suspended lamp above it. This is where the ner tamid is most often placed today. It has come to symbolize God's presence in Israel, a spiritual light emanating as if from the Temple of old.

For a long time oil lamps were used for the ner tamid, to be in time replaced by electric bulbs in most synagogues. However, there has lately been a return to the original method of kindling, with designated members of the congregation assuming the responsibility for the light's maintenance as it had been the case with the priests of old.[3]

Urim and Thummim

The biblical evidence about the nature of the oracular devices called Urim and Thummim is neither clear nor consistent. They are introduced into the Torah text as items which were well known and needed no explanation. Yet the instances when their actual use is recorded are rare. In the Torah not a single such instance is related, because Moses, having direct access to God, was in no need of such devices. However, his successor, Joshua, was specifically ordered, should the occasion require it in the future, to make inquiry through the priest Eleazar by way of the Urim; it was by such decision that the people would or would not go to war (Num. 27:21). In this instance Urim stood for both devices and in other cases the ephod, to which they were attached through the breastpiece, was considered as an oracle-box. Thus David, fleeing from Saul, asked the priest Abiathar to bring his ephod and then made two inquiries: "Will Saul come down?" and "Will the men of Keilah surrender?" Both times the answer was affirmative; in fact, there is no biblical record of a specific negative response. Apparently in such a case, if divine silence ensued, it was interpreted as "No" (I Sam. 14:36–37; 28:6).

The most dramatic example of the use of oracles is recorded in I Sam. 14:40 ff. Saul had put a curse on anyone who would eat during the battle, but Jonathan, not knowing of the curse, had tasted honey. In a public inquiry, Saul asked—apparently through Urim and Thummim[4]—for the guilty party and the lot pointed to Jonathan (who was subsequently saved by the people).

---

[1] Except that in Leviticus the direct imperative צַו is used; in Exodus תְּצַוֶּה [11].

[2] It was considered a sign of ill omen if the lights went out. The Talmud reports that exactly forty years before the Temple's destruction (70 C.E.) the lights went out [12].

[3] The perpetual light in Roman Catholic churches is also a direct development of the old Tabernacle lamp.

[4] I Sam. 14:41, according to the Masoretic text, reads

Neither in this passage nor anywhere else do we find a description of the devices. They may have been stones (with inscriptions "Yes" and "No" or perhaps a blank) which were employed like dice. In time they fell into disuse, the same fate accorded to the other oracular practice mentioned in the Torah, the testing waters for the woman suspected of adultery (Num. 5:11–31). Priests and judges were taking the place of these devices, and in the first century C.E. Josephus reported that the Urim and Thummim had not been used for two hundred years [15]. They may have disappeared even earlier, perhaps at the time of the Babylonian exile, and appear to have been briefly reinstated by Ezra and Nehemiah (Ezra 2:63; Neh. 7:65). At any rate, they belonged to the pre-Torah customs of the people which the Torah tolerated but underplayed and which in time were abandoned.

The names Urim and Thummim are of uncertain origin. An old and popular theory derived אוּרִים from אוֹר (light) and תֻּמִּים from תָּמִים (just, right). The Septuagint calls the lots "brightness and perfection," and the Vulgate, "teaching and truth."[5]

תָּמִים (tamim), "just," but the context as well as the Septuagint suggests that one should read תֻּמִּים (tummim) [14].

[5] אוּרִים has also been connected with אָרוֹן, which could explain I Kings 2:26 to mean that Abiathar had "carried the Urim" before David. It may be noted that the words Urim and Thummim (in Hebrew) are part of the seal of Yale University and that an Israeli kibbutz bears the name, Urim.

GLEANINGS

Moses Not Mentioned

In this whole weekly portion (תְּצַוֶּה) the name of Moses is not mentioned at all. The reason was that God knew that the day of Moses' future death would be Adar 7, the time תְּצַוֶּה is usually read at services. (It was, so to speak, God's anticipatory mourning.)

THE GAON OF VILNA [16]

Israel, like the Olive

Why does Jeremiah (11:16) call Israel a "verdant olive tree, fair, with choice fruit"? Because, like the olive, Israel is beaten and ground up.

Another explanation: Other liquids commingle, but oil refuses to do so and remains separate, like Israel.

MIDRASH [17]

Light for God and Man

When Israel lights the menorah it gives light, as it were, to God himself—even as He gives light to Israel.

They also said: As the oil gives light, so did the Temple give light to the whole world, as the Prophet says: "And nations shall walk by your light" (Isa. 60:3).

Those who study Torah give light wherever they are.

MIDRASH [18]

The Ner Tamid (Regular Light)

Why does Proverbs 6:23 say: "For the commandment (mitzvah) is a light"? Because just as a light is not diminished when a flame is kindled from it, so he who does a mitzvah (here meaning "gives charity") is not thereby diminished in his possessions.

MIDRASH [19]

Every Jew must light the ner tamid in his own heart, and not only in Tabernacle or Tent, that

is, in synagogue or school. He must light it "outside the curtain" (Exod. 27:21): in street and market place, in profane activities, in all matters relating him to his fellow human beings.

An allegory: נֵר can be seen to be the acrostic of נֶפֶשׁ רוּחַ, a soul with spirit. (This is the lamp we must light regularly.) ITTURE TORAH [20]

The Breastplate

The first stone, which was a carnelian, had not only the name of Reuben inscribed upon it, but also the names of Abraham, Isaac, and Jacob, so that they too might be represented when the High Priest represented all of Israel.

Further, by including the names of the Patriarchs all the letters of the alphabet were included on the breastplate, all, that is, save the letter ט. Hence the words שִׁבְטֵי יְשׁוּרוּן (shivte Yeshurun, tribes of Jeshurun, i.e., Israel) were also added (which contain the ט). TALMUD [21]

The Golden Bell

(According to Frazer, as in the poem from Milton here quoted, bells had a prophylactic function, and hence the High Priest was to have a bell attached to his garments so that when he entered the sanctuary he would not die, 28:35; see above, at 28:34.)

> . . . the bellman's drowsy charm
> To bless the doors from nightly harm.
> JOHN MILTON [22]

About Urim and Thummim

One inquired about them only in the case of a (nonobligatory) "war of discretion" (מִלְחֶמֶת רְשׁוּת).

How were they consulted? The High Priest would face the ark and the questioner stood behind him. If he prayed from the heart the holy spirit would envelop the priest at once. He would look into the ephod and do so with prophetic insight, seeing the letters on the Urim and Thummim facing him with "Yes" or "No." And thus he would answer. People would not ask two questions at once, but one after the other.
MIDRASH [23]

Investiture

Following the prescription of the priestly vestments in the previous chapter the text now turns to the ceremonies for their use in sacred office (hence called in English "investiture").[1] The contents will strike the modern reader as strange: they consist largely of detailed instructions for the sacrifice of a bull and a ram, with their blood dashed about and put on the priest's ear, thumb, and toe. The ordination proceedings further provide for special kinds of sacrifices called wave, heave, and sin offerings, and for the consecration of the altar itself through a sin offering. In reading of these ancient rules it is well to keep in mind the purpose and meaning of sacrifice to biblical man, as well as his keen feeling that blood was the very seat and essence of life. These laws do not ask for our approval; they address themselves to the framework of their own time which saw in such offerings the means of creating a sacred context for the faith community.[2]

It is consistent with the Torah's literary style to connect the investiture and its sacrifices with a further group of sacrificial laws, even though these do not at all deal with ordination. We are told about the daily sacrifices of two lambs along with "meal offerings," which consist of flour, oil, and wine. These offerings are expressly instituted as perpetual practices, which

---

[1] The ceremonies, however, were usually referred to as "ordination."

[2] The nature of biblical sacrifice is discussed in detail in Leviticus, chapters 1–8, and, with a somewhat different viewpoint, in the introduction to Numbers, chapters 28–30. The carrying out of the instructions prescribed is recorded in Leviticus, chapter 8.

has led many to believe that the text is here attempting to provide a historical basis for the daily sacrifices of later Temple times.

We further read of the incense altar, which is to be used when the lamps are tended in the morning and when they are kindled at night. This altar is to be reconsecrated once a year.

The subject matter then shifts to the projection of a census and the provision that enrollment in the lists requires a one-half shekel contribution from every male aged twenty years and older. Then come prescriptions for the construction of a wash basin that will assist the priest in maintaining ritual cleanliness; these are followed by rules that return to the subject of ordination: the mixing of the anointing oil for both the priests and the utensils, and of the incense. The particular mixtures are commanded for public but forbidden for private use.

With all the instructions now complete, two skilled craftsmen, Bezalel and his assistant Oholiab, are chosen to carry out the complex work. The section ends with the statement that God "finished speaking" with Moses and that He gave him "the two Tablets of the Pact, stone tablets inscribed with the finger of God."

(A new weekly portion, *Ki Tisa*, begins with 30:11.)

וְזֶ֣ה הַדָּבָ֞ר אֲשֶֽׁר־תַּעֲשֶׂ֤ה לָהֶם֙ לְקַדֵּ֥שׁ אֹתָ֖ם לְכַהֵ֣ן לִ֑י א
לְקַ֡ח פַּ֣ר אֶחָ֧ד בֶּן־בָּקָ֛ר וְאֵילִ֥ם שְׁנַ֖יִם תְּמִימִֽם: וְלֶ֣חֶם ב
מַצּ֗וֹת וְחַלֹּ֤ת מַצֹּת֙ בְּלוּלֹ֣ת בַּשֶּׁ֔מֶן וּרְקִיקֵ֥י מַצּ֖וֹת
מְשֻׁחִ֣ים בַּשָּׁ֑מֶן סֹ֥לֶת חִטִּ֖ים תַּעֲשֶׂ֥ה אֹתָֽם: וְנָתַתָּ֣ אוֹתָם֩ ג
עַל־סַ֨ל אֶחָ֜ד וְהִקְרַבְתָּ֥ אֹתָ֛ם בַּסָּ֑ל וְאֶ֨ת־הַפָּ֔ר וְאֵ֖ת
שְׁנֵ֥י הָאֵילִֽם: וְאֶֽת־אַהֲרֹ֤ן וְאֶת־בָּנָיו֙ תַּקְרִ֔יב אֶל־פֶּ֖תַח ד
אֹ֣הֶל מוֹעֵ֑ד וְרָחַצְתָּ֥ אֹתָ֖ם בַּמָּֽיִם: וְלָקַחְתָּ֣ אֶת־הַבְּגָדִ֗ים ה
וְהִלְבַּשְׁתָּ֤ אֶֽת־אַהֲרֹן֙ אֶת־הַכֻּתֹּ֔נֶת וְאֵת֙ מְעִ֣יל הָֽאֵפֹ֔ד
וְאֶת־הָ֣אֵפֹ֔ד וְאֶת־הַחֹ֑שֶׁן וְאָפַדְתָּ֣ ל֔וֹ בְּחֵ֖שֶׁב הָאֵפֹֽד:
וְשַׂמְתָּ֥ הַמִּצְנֶ֖פֶת עַל־רֹאשׁ֑וֹ וְנָתַתָּ֛ אֶת־נֵ֥זֶר הַקֹּ֖דֶשׁ עַל־ ו

הַמִּצְנָֽפֶת: וְלָקַחְתָּ֣ אֶת־שֶׁ֤מֶן הַמִּשְׁחָה֙ וְיָצַקְתָּ֖ עַל־ ז
רֹאשׁ֑וֹ וּמָשַׁחְתָּ֖ אֹתֽוֹ: וְאֶת־בָּנָ֖יו תַּקְרִ֑יב וְהִלְבַּשְׁתָּ֖ם ח
כֻּתֳּנֹֽת: וְחָגַרְתָּ֩ אֹתָ֨ם אַבְנֵ֜ט אַהֲרֹ֣ן וּבָנָ֗יו וְחָבַשְׁתָּ֤ לָהֶם֙ ט
מִגְבָּעֹ֔ת וְהָיְתָ֥ה לָהֶ֛ם כְּהֻנָּ֖ה לְחֻקַּ֣ת עוֹלָ֑ם וּמִלֵּאתָ֥
יַד־אַהֲרֹ֖ן וְיַד־בָּנָֽיו: וְהִקְרַבְתָּ֙ אֶת־הַפָּ֔ר לִפְנֵ֖י אֹ֣הֶל י
מוֹעֵ֑ד וְסָמַ֨ךְ אַהֲרֹ֤ן וּבָנָיו֙ אֶת־יְדֵיהֶ֔ם עַל־רֹ֖אשׁ הַפָּֽר:
וְשָׁחַטְתָּ֥ אֶת־הַפָּ֖ר לִפְנֵ֣י יְהוָ֑ה פֶּ֖תַח אֹ֥הֶל מוֹעֵֽד: יא
וְלָקַחְתָּ֙ מִדַּ֣ם הַפָּ֔ר וְנָתַתָּ֛ה עַל־קַרְנֹ֥ת הַמִּזְבֵּ֖חַ יב
בְּאֶצְבָּעֶ֑ךָ וְאֶת־כָּל־הַדָּ֣ם תִּשְׁפֹּ֔ךְ אֶל־יְס֖וֹד הַמִּזְבֵּֽחַ:
וְלָקַחְתָּ֗ אֶֽת־כָּל־הַחֵלֶב֮ הַֽמְכַסֶּ֣ה אֶת־הַקֶּ֒רֶב֒ וְאֵ֗ת יג

1] This is what you shall do to them in consecrating them to serve Me as priests: Take a young bull of the herd and two rams without blemish;   **2]** also unleavened bread, unleavened cakes with oil mixed in, and unleavened wafers spread with oil—make these of choice wheat flour.   **3]** Place these in one basket and present them in the basket, along with the bull and the two rams.   **4]** Lead Aaron and his sons up to the entrance of the Tent of Meeting, and wash them with water.   **5]** Then take the vestments, and clothe Aaron with the tunic, the robe of the ephod, the ephod, and the breastpiece, and gird him with the decorated band of the ephod.   **6]** Put the headdress on his head, and place the holy diadem upon the headdress. **7]** Take the anointing oil and pour it on his head and anoint him.   **8]** Then bring his sons forward; clothe them with tunics   **9]** and wind turbans upon them. And gird both Aaron and his sons with sashes. And so they shall have priesthood as their right for all time.

You shall then ordain Aaron and his sons.   **10]** Lead the bull up to the front of the Tent of Meeting, and let Aaron and his sons lay their hands upon the head of the bull.   **11]** Slaughter the bull before the LORD, at the entrance of the Tent of Meeting,   **12]** and take some of the bull's blood and put it on the horns of the altar with your finger; then pour out the rest of the blood at the base of the altar.   **13]** Take all the fat that covers the entrails, the protuberance on the liver, and the two kidneys with the fat on them, and turn them into smoke upon the

29:6] *Holy diadem.* נֵזֶר הַקֹּדֶשׁ (*nezer ha-kodesh*), apparently synonymous with צִיץ (*tzitz*, frontlet); see Exod. 30:30 and above, at 28:36.

7] *And anoint him.* That is, Aaron; other priests were not so anointed. Moses acts as the priest from whom the original ordination proceeds.

9] *For all time.* An addition meant to underline the exclusive right of Aaron's line.
    Ordain. Literally, "fill the hand" (see at Exod. 28:41 and commentary, "Ordination").

The sacrifice connected with the ordination was apparently both for past sins and as a prophylactic for the future.

10] *Lay their hands upon the head of the bull.* Thus transferring their sin, similar to the ceremony of the scapegoat (Lev. 16:8, 10, 26). The word for rabbinic ordination, *semichah*, derives from סָמַךְ (*samach*), to lay on (hands).

13] *Protuberance on the liver.* In the Mishnah called "finger" of the liver [1]. (See commentary on Lev. 3:4.)

הַיֹּתֶרֶת עַל־הַכָּבֵד וְאֵת שְׁתֵּי הַכְּלָיֹת וְאֶת־הַחֵלֶב
יד אֲשֶׁר עֲלֵיהֶן וְהִקְטַרְתָּ הַמִּזְבֵּחָה: וְאֶת־בְּשַׂר הַפָּר
וְאֶת־עֹרוֹ וְאֶת־פִּרְשׁוֹ תִּשְׂרֹף בָּאֵשׁ מִחוּץ לַמַּחֲנֶה
חַטָּאת הוּא: וְאֶת־הָאַיִל הָאֶחָד תִּקָּח וְסָמְכוּ אַהֲרֹן
טו וּבָנָיו אֶת־יְדֵיהֶם עַל־רֹאשׁ הָאָיִל: וְשָׁחַטְתָּ אֶת־הָאַיִל
טז וְלָקַחְתָּ אֶת־דָּמוֹ וְזָרַקְתָּ עַל־הַמִּזְבֵּחַ סָבִיב: וְאֶת־
יז הָאַיִל תְּנַתֵּחַ לִנְתָחָיו וְרָחַצְתָּ קִרְבּוֹ וּכְרָעָיו וְנָתַתָּ
עַל־נְתָחָיו וְעַל־רֹאשׁוֹ: וְהִקְטַרְתָּ אֶת־כָּל־הָאַיִל
יח הַמִּזְבֵּחָה עֹלָה הוּא לַיהוָה רֵיחַ נִיחוֹחַ אִשֶּׁה לַיהוָה
יט הוּא: וְלָקַחְתָּ אֵת הָאַיִל הַשֵּׁנִי וְסָמַךְ אַהֲרֹן וּבָנָיו
כ אֶת־יְדֵיהֶם עַל־רֹאשׁ הָאָיִל: וְשָׁחַטְתָּ אֶת־הָאַיִל
וְלָקַחְתָּ מִדָּמוֹ וְנָתַתָּה עַל־תְּנוּךְ אֹזֶן אַהֲרֹן וְעַל־
תְּנוּךְ אֹזֶן בָּנָיו הַיְמָנִית וְעַל־בֹּהֶן יָדָם הַיְמָנִית וְעַל־

בֹּהֶן רַגְלָם הַיְמָנִית וְזָרַקְתָּ אֶת־הַדָּם עַל־הַמִּזְבֵּחַ
כא סָבִיב: וְלָקַחְתָּ מִן־הַדָּם אֲשֶׁר עַל־הַמִּזְבֵּחַ וּמִשֶּׁמֶן
הַמִּשְׁחָה וְהִזֵּיתָ עַל־אַהֲרֹן וְעַל־בְּגָדָיו וְעַל־בָּנָיו וְעַל־
בִּגְדֵי בָנָיו אִתּוֹ וְקָדַשׁ הוּא וּבְגָדָיו וּבָנָיו וּבִגְדֵי בָנָיו
כב אִתּוֹ: וְלָקַחְתָּ מִן־הָאַיִל הַחֵלֶב וְהָאַלְיָה וְאֶת־הַחֵלֶב
הַמְכַסֶּה אֶת־הַקֶּרֶב וְאֵת יֹתֶרֶת הַכָּבֵד וְאֵת שְׁתֵּי
הַכְּלָיֹת וְאֶת־הַחֵלֶב אֲשֶׁר עֲלֵיהֶן וְאֵת שׁוֹק הַיָּמִין
כג כִּי אֵיל מִלֻּאִים הוּא: וְכִכַּר לֶחֶם אַחַת וְחַלַּת לֶחֶם
שֶׁמֶן אַחַת וְרָקִיק אֶחָד מִסַּל הַמַּצּוֹת אֲשֶׁר לִפְנֵי
כד יְהוָה: וְשַׂמְתָּ הַכֹּל עַל כַּפֵּי אַהֲרֹן וְעַל כַּפֵּי בָנָיו
וְהֵנַפְתָּ אֹתָם תְּנוּפָה לִפְנֵי יְהוָה: וְלָקַחְתָּ אֹתָם מִיָּדָם
כה וְהִקְטַרְתָּ הַמִּזְבֵּחָה עַל־הָעֹלָה לְרֵיחַ נִיחוֹחַ לִפְנֵי
כו יְהוָה אִשֶּׁה הוּא לַיהוָה: וְלָקַחְתָּ אֶת־הֶחָזֶה מֵאֵיל

altar. **14]** The rest of the flesh of the bull, its hide, and its dung shall be put to the fire outside the camp; it is a sin offering.

15] Next take the one ram, and let Aaron and his sons lay their hands upon the ram's head. **16]** Slaughter the ram, and take its blood and dash it against all sides of the altar. **17]** Cut up the ram into sections, wash its entrails and legs, and put them with its quarters and its head. **18]** Turn all of the ram into smoke upon the altar. It is a burnt offering to the LORD, a pleasing odor, an offering by fire to the LORD.

19] Then take the other ram, and let Aaron and his sons lay their hands upon the ram's head. **20]** Slaughter the ram, and take some of its blood and put it on the ridge of Aaron's right ear and on the ridges of his sons' right ears, and on the thumbs of their right hands, and on the big toes of their right feet; and dash the rest of the blood against every side of the altar round about. **21]** Take some of the blood that is on the altar and some of the anointing oil and sprinkle upon Aaron and his vestments, and also upon his sons and his sons' vestments. Thus shall he and his vestments be holy, as well as his sons and his sons' vestments.

22] You shall take from the ram the fat parts—the broad tail, the fat that covers the entrails, the protuberance on the liver, the two kidneys with the fat on them—and the right thigh; for this is a ram of ordination. **23]** Add one flat loaf of bread, one cake of oil bread, and one wafer, from the basket of unleavened bread that is before the LORD. **24]** Place all these on the palms of Aaron and his sons, and offer them as a wave offering before the LORD. **25]** Take them from their hands and turn them into smoke upon the altar with the burnt offering, as a pleasing odor before the LORD; it is an offering by fire to the LORD.

20] *Ridge.* Others, "lobe."
24] *Wave offering.* A popular rendering; the Hebrew does not specify the motion. A better translation would be "by lifting [the sacrifice] high" or "by presenting [it] as a special gift" (see further Gleanings and at Lev. 7:30 and Num. 8:11).

הַמִּלֻּאִים אֲשֶׁר לְאַהֲרֹן וְהֵנַפְתָּ אֹתוֹ תְּנוּפָה לִפְנֵי

יְהוָה וְהָיָה לְךָ לְמָנָה: וְקִדַּשְׁתָּ אֵת חֲזֵה הַתְּנוּפָה

וְאֵת שׁוֹק הַתְּרוּמָה אֲשֶׁר הוּנַף וַאֲשֶׁר הוּרָם מֵאֵיל

הַמִּלֻּאִים מֵאֲשֶׁר לְאַהֲרֹן וּמֵאֲשֶׁר לְבָנָיו: וְהָיָה לְאַהֲרֹן

וּלְבָנָיו לְחָק־עוֹלָם מֵאֵת בְּנֵי יִשְׂרָאֵל כִּי תְרוּמָה

הוּא וּתְרוּמָה יִהְיֶה מֵאֵת בְּנֵי־יִשְׂרָאֵל מִזִּבְחֵי שַׁלְמֵיהֶם

תְּרוּמָתָם לַיהוָה: וּבִגְדֵי הַקֹּדֶשׁ אֲשֶׁר לְאַהֲרֹן יִהְיוּ

לְבָנָיו אַחֲרָיו לְמָשְׁחָה בָהֶם וּלְמַלֵּא־בָם אֶת־יָדָם:

שִׁבְעַת יָמִים יִלְבָּשָׁם הַכֹּהֵן תַּחְתָּיו מִבָּנָיו אֲשֶׁר יָבֹא

אֶל־אֹהֶל מוֹעֵד לְשָׁרֵת בַּקֹּדֶשׁ: וְאֵת אֵיל הַמִּלֻּאִים

לב תִּקַּח וּבִשַּׁלְתָּ אֶת־בְּשָׂרוֹ בְּמָקֹם קָדֹשׁ: וְאָכַל אַהֲרֹן

וּבָנָיו אֶת־בְּשַׂר הָאַיִל וְאֶת־הַלֶּחֶם אֲשֶׁר בַּסָּל פֶּתַח

לג אֹהֶל מוֹעֵד: וְאָכְלוּ אֹתָם אֲשֶׁר כֻּפַּר בָּהֶם לְמַלֵּא

אֶת־יָדָם לְקַדֵּשׁ אֹתָם וְזָר לֹא־יֹאכַל כִּי־קֹדֶשׁ הֵם:

לד וְאִם־יִוָּתֵר מִבְּשַׂר הַמִּלֻּאִים וּמִן־הַלֶּחֶם עַד־הַבֹּקֶר

וְשָׂרַפְתָּ אֶת־הַנּוֹתָר בָּאֵשׁ לֹא יֵאָכֵל כִּי־קֹדֶשׁ הוּא:

לה וְעָשִׂיתָ לְאַהֲרֹן וּלְבָנָיו כָּכָה כְּכֹל אֲשֶׁר־צִוִּיתִי אֹתָכָה

שִׁבְעַת יָמִים תְּמַלֵּא יָדָם: וּפַר חַטָּאת תַּעֲשֶׂה לַיּוֹם

עַל־הַכִּפֻּרִים וְחִטֵּאתָ עַל־הַמִּזְבֵּחַ בְּכַפֶּרְךָ עָלָיו

וּמָשַׁחְתָּ אֹתוֹ לְקַדְּשׁוֹ: שִׁבְעַת יָמִים תְּכַפֵּר עַל־

26] Then take the breast of Aaron's ram of ordination and offer it as a wave offering before the LORD; it shall be your portion. 27] You shall consecrate the breast that was offered as a wave offering and the thigh that was offered as a heave offering from the ram of ordination—from that which was Aaron's and from that which was his sons'— 28] and those parts shall be a due for all time from the Israelites to Aaron and his descendants. For they are a gift; and so shall they be a gift from the Israelites, their gift to the LORD out of their sacrifices of well-being.

29] The sacral vestments of Aaron shall pass on to his sons after him, for them to be anointed and ordained in. 30] He among his sons who becomes priest in his stead, who enters the Tent of Meeting to officiate within the sanctuary, shall wear them seven days.

31] You shall take the ram of ordination and boil its flesh in the sacred precinct; 32] and Aaron and his sons shall eat the flesh of the ram, and the bread that is in the basket, at the entrance of the Tent of Meeting. 33] These things shall be eaten only by those for whom expiation was made with them when they were ordained and consecrated; they may not be eaten by a layman, for they are holy. 34] And if any of the flesh of ordination, or any of the bread, is left until morning, you shall put what is left to the fire; it shall not be eaten, for it is holy.

35] Thus you shall do to Aaron and his sons, just as I have commanded you. You shall ordain them through seven days, 36] and each day you shall prepare a bull as a sin offering for expiation; you shall purge the altar by performing purification upon it, and you shall anoint it

---

28] *And those parts.* This interrupts the context with a larger injunction applying to future generations.

30] *Who becomes priest in his stead.* But, according to tradition, only if he is worthy [2].

33] *Layman.* זָר (*zar*), literally, "an outsider" (to the priestly caste), as both Targumim translate. (See also Num. 1:51 and 3:10.)

35] *Ordain them through seven days.* Apparently the procedure was repeated seven times.

36] *For expiation.* עַל־הַכִּפֻּרִים (*al ha-kippurim*). Or, "for atonement," in the sense of reconciliation or at-one-ment with God (the early English meaning of the word) [3]. This is one of the instances where atonement is made for a material object which, like a human being, was believed to be taintable by sin. (For a discussion of Yom Kippur, the Day of Atonement, see Commentary on Leviticus, chapter 16.)

הַמִּזְבֵּחַ וְקִדַּשְׁתָּ אֹתוֹ וְהָיָה הַמִּזְבֵּחַ קֹדֶשׁ קָדָשִׁים
לח כָּל־הַנֹּגֵעַ בַּמִּזְבֵּחַ יִקְדָּשׁ: ס וְזֶה אֲשֶׁר תַּעֲשֶׂה עַל־
לט הַמִּזְבֵּחַ כְּבָשִׂים בְּנֵי־שָׁנָה שְׁנַיִם לַיּוֹם תָּמִיד: אֶת־
הַכֶּבֶשׂ הָאֶחָד תַּעֲשֶׂה בַבֹּקֶר וְאֵת הַכֶּבֶשׂ הַשֵּׁנִי
מ תַּעֲשֶׂה בֵּין הָעַרְבָּיִם: וְעִשָּׂרֹן סֹלֶת בָּלוּל בְּשֶׁמֶן
כָּתִית רֶבַע הַהִין וְנֵסֶךְ רְבִיעִת הַהִין יַיִן לַכֶּבֶשׂ
מא הָאֶחָד: וְאֵת הַכֶּבֶשׂ הַשֵּׁנִי תַּעֲשֶׂה בֵּין הָעַרְבָּיִם
כְּמִנְחַת הַבֹּקֶר וּכְנִסְכָּהּ תַּעֲשֶׂה־לָּהּ לְרֵיחַ נִיחֹחַ אִשֶּׁה
מב לַיהֹוָה: עֹלַת תָּמִיד לְדֹרֹתֵיכֶם פֶּתַח אֹהֶל־מוֹעֵד
לִפְנֵי יְהֹוָה אֲשֶׁר אִוָּעֵד לָכֶם שָׁמָּה לְדַבֵּר אֵלֶיךָ
מג שָׁם: וְנֹעַדְתִּי שָׁמָּה לִבְנֵי יִשְׂרָאֵל וְנִקְדַּשׁ בִּכְבֹדִי:
מד וְקִדַּשְׁתִּי אֶת־אֹהֶל מוֹעֵד וְאֶת־הַמִּזְבֵּחַ וְאֶת־אַהֲרֹן

מה וְאֶת־בָּנָיו אֲקַדֵּשׁ לְכַהֵן לִי: וְשָׁכַנְתִּי בְּתוֹךְ בְּנֵי יִשְׂרָאֵל
מו וְהָיִיתִי לָהֶם לֵאלֹהִים: וְיָדְעוּ כִּי אֲנִי יְהֹוָה אֱלֹהֵיהֶם
אֲשֶׁר הוֹצֵאתִי אֹתָם מֵאֶרֶץ מִצְרַיִם לְשָׁכְנִי בְתוֹכָם
אֲנִי יְהֹוָה אֱלֹהֵיהֶם: פ

א וְעָשִׂיתָ מִזְבֵּחַ מִקְטַר קְטֹרֶת עֲצֵי שִׁטִּים תַּעֲשֶׂה
ב אֹתוֹ: אַמָּה אָרְכּוֹ וְאַמָּה רָחְבּוֹ רָבוּעַ יִהְיֶה וְאַמָּתַיִם
ג קֹמָתוֹ מִמֶּנּוּ קַרְנֹתָיו: וְצִפִּיתָ אֹתוֹ זָהָב טָהוֹר אֶת־
גַּגּוֹ וְאֶת־קִירֹתָיו סָבִיב וְאֶת־קַרְנֹתָיו וְעָשִׂיתָ לּוֹ זֵר
ד זָהָב סָבִיב: וּשְׁתֵּי טַבְּעֹת זָהָב תַּעֲשֶׂה־לּוֹ מִתַּחַת לְזֵרוֹ
עַל שְׁתֵּי צַלְעֹתָיו תַּעֲשֶׂה עַל־שְׁנֵי צִדָּיו וְהָיָה לְבָתִּים
ה לְבַדִּים לָשֵׂאת אֹתוֹ בָּהֵמָּה: וְעָשִׂיתָ אֶת־הַבַּדִּים עֲצֵי
שִׁטִּים וְצִפִּיתָ אֹתָם זָהָב: וְנָתַתָּה אֹתוֹ לִפְנֵי הַפָּרֹכֶת

to consecrate it.　**37]** Seven days you shall perform purification for the altar to consecrate it, and the altar shall become most holy; whatever touches the altar shall become consecrated.

38] Now this is what you shall offer upon the altar: two yearling lambs each day, regularly. **39]** You shall offer the one lamb in the morning, and you shall offer the other lamb at twilight. **40]** There shall be a tenth of a measure of choice flour with a quarter of a *hin* of beaten oil mixed in, and a libation of a quarter *hin* of wine for one lamb; **41]** and you shall offer the other lamb at twilight, repeating with it the meal offering of the morning with its libation—an offering by fire for a pleasing odor to the LORD, **42]** a regular burnt offering throughout the generations, at the entrance of the Tent of Meeting before the LORD.

For there I will meet with you, and there I will speak with you, **43]** and there I will meet with the Israelites, and it shall be sanctified by My Presence. **44]** I will sanctify the Tent of Meeting and the altar, and I will consecrate Aaron and his sons to serve Me as priests. **45]** I will abide among the Israelites, and I will be their God. **46]** And they shall know that I the LORD am their God, who brought them out from the land of Egypt that I might abide among them, I the LORD their God.

1] You shall make an altar for burning incense; make it of acacia wood. **2]** It shall be a cubit long and a cubit wide—it shall be square—and two cubits high, its horns of one piece with it. **3]** Overlay it with pure gold: its top, its sides round about, and its horns; and make a gold molding for it round about. **4]** And make two gold rings for it under its molding; make them on its two side walls, on opposite sides. They shall serve as holders for poles with which to carry it. **5]** Make the poles of acacia wood, and overlay them with gold.

37] *Whatever touches . . . shall become consecrated.* Become part of the Tabernacle and subject to its rules. Ibn Ezra understands: "*Whoever* touches. . . ."

38] *Regularly.* תָּמִיד (*tamid*). A treatise in the Talmud, called Tamid, is devoted to the daily sacrifice.

43] *It shall be sanctified.* That is, the entrance.

By My Presence. Targum Jonathan, apparently using Lev. 10:3 as a parallel, understands ". . . sanctified by those who sanctify Me" (as if בִּמְכַבְּדַי instead of בִּכְבֹדִי) [4].

46] *That I might abide among them.* This is the purpose of Israel's existence in general and of the Tabernacle in particular.

אֲשֶׁר עַל־אָרֹן הָעֵדֻת לִפְנֵי הַכַּפֹּרֶת אֲשֶׁר עַל־הָעֵדֻת

ז אֲשֶׁר אִוָּעֵד לְךָ שָׁמָּה: וְהִקְטִיר עָלָיו אַהֲרֹן קְטֹרֶת
סַמִּים בַּבֹּקֶר בַּבֹּקֶר בְּהֵיטִיבוֹ אֶת־הַנֵּרֹת יַקְטִירֶנָּה:

ח וּבְהַעֲלֹת אַהֲרֹן אֶת־הַנֵּרֹת בֵּין הָעַרְבַּיִם יַקְטִירֶנָּה

ט קְטֹרֶת תָּמִיד לִפְנֵי יְהוָה לְדֹרֹתֵיכֶם: לֹא־תַעֲלוּ עָלָיו
קְטֹרֶת זָרָה וְעֹלָה וּמִנְחָה וְנֵסֶךְ לֹא תִסְּכוּ עָלָיו:

י וְכִפֶּר אַהֲרֹן עַל־קַרְנֹתָיו אַחַת בַּשָּׁנָה מִדַּם חַטַּאת
הַכִּפֻּרִים אַחַת בַּשָּׁנָה יְכַפֵּר עָלָיו לְדֹרֹתֵיכֶם
קֹדֶשׁ־קָדָשִׁים הוּא לַיהוָה:

Haftarah Tetzaveh, p. 719

פ   פ   פ

יב וַיְדַבֵּר יְהוָה אֶל־מֹשֶׁה לֵּאמֹר: כִּי תִשָּׂא אֶת־רֹאשׁ

בְּנֵי־יִשְׂרָאֵל לִפְקֻדֵיהֶם וְנָתְנוּ אִישׁ כֹּפֶר נַפְשׁוֹ לַיהוָה

יג בִּפְקֹד אֹתָם וְלֹא־יִהְיֶה בָהֶם נֶגֶף בִּפְקֹד אֹתָם: זֶה
יִתְּנוּ כָּל־הָעֹבֵר עַל־הַפְּקֻדִים מַחֲצִית הַשֶּׁקֶל בְּשֶׁקֶל
הַקֹּדֶשׁ עֶשְׂרִים גֵּרָה הַשֶּׁקֶל מַחֲצִית הַשֶּׁקֶל תְּרוּמָה

יד לַיהוָה: כֹּל הָעֹבֵר עַל־הַפְּקֻדִים מִבֶּן עֶשְׂרִים שָׁנָה
וָמָעְלָה יִתֵּן תְּרוּמַת יְהוָה: הֶעָשִׁיר לֹא־יַרְבֶּה וְהַדַּל
לֹא יַמְעִיט מִמַּחֲצִית הַשֶּׁקֶל לָתֵת אֶת־תְּרוּמַת יְהוָה

טז לְכַפֵּר עַל־נַפְשֹׁתֵיכֶם: וְלָקַחְתָּ אֶת־כֶּסֶף הַכִּפֻּרִים
מֵאֵת בְּנֵי יִשְׂרָאֵל וְנָתַתָּ אֹתוֹ עַל־עֲבֹדַת אֹהֶל מוֹעֵד
וְהָיָה לִבְנֵי יִשְׂרָאֵל לְזִכָּרוֹן לִפְנֵי יְהוָה לְכַפֵּר עַל־
נַפְשֹׁתֵיכֶם: פ

יז וַיְדַבֵּר יְהוָה אֶל־מֹשֶׁה לֵּאמֹר: וְעָשִׂיתָ כִּיּוֹר נְחֹשֶׁת

6] Place it in front of the curtain that is over the Ark of the Pact—in front of the cover that is over the Pact—where I will meet with you.   **7]** On it Aaron shall burn aromatic incense: he shall burn it every morning when he tends the lamps,   **8]** and Aaron shall burn it at twilight when he lights the lamps—a regular incense offering before the LORD throughout the ages. **9]** You shall not offer alien incense on it, or a burnt offering or a meal offering; neither shall you pour a libation on it.   **10]** Once a year Aaron shall perform purification upon its horns with blood of the sin offering of purification; purification shall be performed upon it once a year throughout the ages. It is most holy to the LORD.

11] The LORD spoke to Moses, saying: **12]** When you take a census of the Israelite people according to their enrollment, each shall pay the LORD a ransom for himself on being enrolled, that no plague may come upon them through their being enrolled.   **13]** This is what every one who is entered in the records shall pay: a half-shekel by the sanctuary weight—twenty *gerahs* to the shekel—a half-shekel as an offering to the LORD.   **14]** Every one who is entered in the records, from the age of twenty years up, shall give the LORD's offering: **15]** the rich shall not pay more and the poor shall not pay less than half a shekel when giving the LORD's offering as expiation for your persons.   **16]** You shall take the expiation money from the Israelites and assign it to the service of the Tent of Meeting; it shall serve the Israelites as a reminder before the LORD, as expiation for your persons.

17] The LORD spoke to Moses, saying: **18]** Make a laver of copper and a stand of copper

30:10] *Once a year.* See commentary on Lev. 16:15-19.

12] *A census.* Counting was considered a privilege belonging to God, and humans conducting a census without divine approval thereby placed themselves in dire danger (see Commentary on Numbers, chapter 1).

14] *From the age of twenty years up.* The military age. In Mari records, too, the census counted only men of military age. Twenty was also the age

which divided the generation who had left Egypt and would die in the desert from those who would be permitted to enter Canaan.

16] *Expiation money.* According to tradition, this was a regular tax raised in addition to the one-half shekel for the census, which was a onetime levy. From the threefold demands for contributions (verses 13, 14, 15) the Rabbis decreed three offerings altogether, two compulsory and one voluntary [5].

שֶׁמֶן מִשְׁחַת־קֹדֶשׁ יִהְיֶה: וּמָשַׁחְתָּ֥ בּוֹ אֶת־אֹהֶל מוֹעֵד כו

וְאֵ֖ת אֲרוֹן הָעֵדֻת: וְאֶת־הַשֻּׁלְחָן וְאֶת־כָּל־כֵּלָיו וְאֶת־ כז

הַמְּנֹרָ֖ה וְאֶת־כֵּלֶיהָ וְאֵ֖ת מִזְבַּ֥ח הַקְּטֹרֶת: וְאֶת־מִזְבַּ֤ח כח

הָעֹלָ֖ה וְאֶת־כָּל־כֵּלָ֑יו וְאֶת־הַכִּיֹּ֖ר וְאֶת־כַּנּ֑וֹ: וְקִדַּשְׁתָּ֣ כט

אֹתָ֔ם וְהָי֖וּ קֹ֣דֶשׁ קָֽדָשִׁ֑ים כָּל־הַנֹּגֵ֥עַ בָּהֶ֖ם יִקְדָּֽשׁ:

וְאֶֽת־אַהֲרֹ֥ן וְאֶת־בָּנָ֖יו תִּמְשָׁ֑ח וְקִדַּשְׁתָּ֥ אֹתָ֖ם לְכַהֵ֥ן לִֽי: ל

וְאֶל־בְּנֵ֥י יִשְׂרָאֵ֖ל תְּדַבֵּ֣ר לֵאמֹ֑ר שֶׁ֠מֶן מִשְׁחַת־קֹ֨דֶשׁ לא

יִהְיֶ֥ה זֶ֛ה לִ֖י לְדֹרֹתֵיכֶֽם: עַל־בְּשַׂ֤ר אָדָם֙ לֹ֣א יִיסָ֔ךְ לב

וּבְמַ֨תְכֻּנְתּ֔וֹ לֹ֥א תַעֲשׂ֖וּ כָּמֹ֑הוּ קֹ֣דֶשׁ ה֔וּא קֹ֖דֶשׁ יִהְיֶ֥ה

לָכֶֽם: אִ֣ישׁ אֲשֶׁ֤ר יִרְקַח֙ כָּמֹ֔הוּ וַאֲשֶׁ֛ר יִתֵּ֥ן מִמֶּ֖נּוּ עַל־ לג

וְכַנּ֣וֹ נְחֹ֔שֶׁת לְרָחְצָ֑ה וְנָתַתָּ֣ אֹת֗וֹ בֵּֽין־אֹ֤הֶל מוֹעֵד֙ וּבֵ֣ין יח

הַמִּזְבֵּ֔חַ וְנָתַתָּ֥ שָׁ֖מָּה מָֽיִם: וְרָחֲצ֛וּ אַהֲרֹ֥ן וּבָנָ֖יו מִמֶּ֑נּוּ יט

אֶת־יְדֵיהֶ֖ם וְאֶת־רַגְלֵיהֶֽם: בְּבֹאָ֞ם אֶל־אֹ֤הֶל מוֹעֵד֙ כ

יִרְחֲצוּ־מַ֖יִם וְלֹ֣א יָמֻ֑תוּ א֣וֹ בְגִשְׁתָּ֤ם אֶל־הַמִּזְבֵּ֨חַ֙ לְשָׁרֵ֔ת

לְהַקְטִ֥יר אִשֶּׁ֖ה לַֽיהוָֽה: וְרָחֲצ֛וּ יְדֵיהֶ֥ם וְרַגְלֵיהֶ֖ם וְלֹ֣א כא

יָמֻ֑תוּ וְהָיְתָ֨ה לָהֶ֤ם חָק־עוֹלָם֙ ל֣וֹ וּלְזַרְע֖וֹ לְדֹרֹתָֽם: פ

וַיְדַבֵּ֥ר יְהוָ֖ה אֶל־מֹשֶׁ֥ה לֵּאמֹֽר: וְאַתָּ֣ה קַח־לְךָ֮ בְּשָׂמִ֣ים כב

רֹ֠אשׁ מָר־דְּרוֹר֙ חֲמֵ֣שׁ מֵא֔וֹת וְקִנְּמָן־בֶּ֥שֶׂם מַחֲצִית֖וֹ כג

חֲמִשִּׁ֣ים וּמָאתָ֑יִם וּקְנֵה־בֹ֖שֶׂם חֲמִשִּׁ֥ים וּמָאתָֽיִם: וְקִדָּ֕ה כד

חֲמֵ֥שׁ מֵא֖וֹת בְּשֶׁ֣קֶל הַקֹּ֑דֶשׁ וְשֶׁ֥מֶן זַ֖יִת הִֽין: וְעָשִׂ֣יתָ כה

אֹת֗וֹ שֶׁ֚מֶן מִשְׁחַת־קֹ֔דֶשׁ רֹ֥קַח מִרְקַ֖חַת מַעֲשֵׂ֣ה רֹקֵ֑חַ

for it, for washing; and place it between the Tent of Meeting and the altar. Put water in it, **19]** and let Aaron and his sons wash their hands and feet [in water drawn] from it. **20]** When they enter the Tent of Meeting they shall wash with water, that they may not die; or when they approach the altar to serve, to turn into smoke an offering by fire to the LORD, **21]** they shall wash their hands and feet, that they may not die. It shall be a law for all time for them—for him and his offspring—throughout the ages.

22] The LORD spoke to Moses, saying: **23]** Next take choice spices: five hundred weight of solidified myrrh, half as much—two hundred and fifty—of fragrant cinnamon, two hundred and fifty of aromatic cane, **24]** five hundred—by the sanctuary weight—of cassia, and a *hin* of olive oil. **25]** Make of this a sacred anointing oil, a compound of ingredients expertly blended, to serve as sacred anointing oil. **26]** With it anoint the Tent of Meeting, the Ark of the Pact, **27]** the table and all its utensils, the lampstand and all its fittings, the altar of incense, **28]** the altar of burnt offering and all its utensils, and the laver and its stand. **29]** Thus you shall consecrate them so that they may be most holy; whatever touches them shall be consecrated. **30]** You shall also anoint Aaron and his sons, consecrating them to serve Me as priests.

31] And speak to the Israelite people, as follows: This shall be an anointing oil sacred to Me throughout the ages. **32]** It must not be rubbed on any person's body, and you must not make anything like it in the same proportions; it is sacred, to be held sacred by you. **33]** Whoever

18] *Laver of copper.* For priestly ablutions. Like the incense altar, it had not been mentioned amongst the appurtenances of the Tabernacle described in chapters 25–27. In later centuries Solomon's Temple had an elaborate "molten sea," a basin placed on twelve sculptured oxen that faced in four directions (I Kings 7:23–29).

23] *Choice spices.* For the sacred oil. It appears that ancient tradition is here related.

Solidified myrrh. Others, "flowing" or "liquid" myrrh. Myrrh (מֹר, *mor*) is an aromatic resinous exudation from a spiny shrub, genus *commiphora*. The Hebrew word is related to מַר, bitter; the same word, basically, was used in Akkadian and Greek.

24] *Cassia.* A variety of cinnamon bark.

Hin of olive oil. The exact measure of a *hin* is not known. One suggestion is that it represented 3.6 liters (about 7 pints) [6].

לד זָר וְנִכְרַת מֵעַמָּיו: ס וַיֹּאמֶר יְהוָה אֶל־מֹשֶׁה קַח־
לְךָ סַמִּים נָטָף וּשְׁחֵלֶת וְחֶלְבְּנָה סַמִּים וּלְבֹנָה זַכָּה
לה בַּד בְּבַד יִהְיֶה: וְעָשִׂיתָ אֹתָהּ קְטֹרֶת רֹקַח מַעֲשֵׂה
לו רוֹקֵחַ מְמֻלָּח טָהוֹר קֹדֶשׁ: וְשָׁחַקְתָּ מִמֶּנָּה הָדֵק
וְנָתַתָּה מִמֶּנָּה לִפְנֵי הָעֵדֻת בְּאֹהֶל מוֹעֵד אֲשֶׁר אִוָּעֵד
לז לְךָ שָׁמָּה קֹדֶשׁ קָדָשִׁים תִּהְיֶה לָכֶם: וְהַקְּטֹרֶת
אֲשֶׁר תַּעֲשֶׂה בְּמַתְכֻּנְתָּהּ לֹא תַעֲשׂוּ לָכֶם קֹדֶשׁ תִּהְיֶה
לח לְךָ לַיהוָה: אִישׁ אֲשֶׁר־יַעֲשֶׂה כָמוֹהָ לְהָרִיחַ בָּהּ

וְנִכְרַת מֵעַמָּיו: ס
צא וַיְדַבֵּר יְהוָה אֶל־מֹשֶׁה לֵּאמֹר: רְאֵה קָרָאתִי בְשֵׁם
בְצַלְאֵל בֶּן־אוּרִי בֶן־חוּר לְמַטֵּה יְהוּדָה: וָאֲמַלֵּא
אֹתוֹ רוּחַ אֱלֹהִים בְּחָכְמָה וּבִתְבוּנָה וּבְדַעַת וּבְכָל־
מְלָאכָה: לַחְשֹׁב מַחֲשָׁבֹת לַעֲשׂוֹת בַּזָּהָב וּבַכֶּסֶף
וּבַנְּחֹשֶׁת: וּבַחֲרֹשֶׁת אֶבֶן לְמַלֹּאת וּבַחֲרֹשֶׁת עֵץ לַעֲשׂוֹת
בְּכָל־מְלָאכָה: וַאֲנִי הִנֵּה נָתַתִּי אִתּוֹ אֵת אָהֳלִיאָב
בֶּן־אֲחִיסָמָךְ לְמַטֵּה־דָן וּבְלֵב כָּל־חֲכַם־לֵב נָתַתִּי

compounds its like, or puts any of it on a layman, shall be cut off from his kin.

34] And the LORD said to Moses: Take the herbs stacte, onycha, and galbanum—these herbs together with pure frankincense; let there be an equal part of each. **35]** Make them into incense, a compound expertly blended, refined, pure, sacred. **36]** Beat some of it into powder, and put some before the Pact in the Tent of Meeting, where I will meet with you; it shall be most holy to you. **37]** But when you make this incense, you must not make any in the same proportions for yourselves; it shall be held by you sacred to the LORD. **38]** Whoever makes any like it, to smell of it, shall be cut off from his kin.

1] The LORD spoke to Moses, saying: **2]** See, I have singled out by name Bezalel, son of Uri son of Hur, of the tribe of Judah. **3]** I have endowed him with a divine spirit of skill, ability, and knowledge in every kind of craft: **4]** to make designs for work in gold, silver, and copper, **5]** to cut stones for setting and to carve wood—to work in every kind of craft. **6]** Moreover, I have assigned to him Oholiab son of Ahisamach, of the tribe of Dan; and I have

33] *Cut off from his kin.* This punishment (כָּרֵת, *karet*) is often mentioned in the Torah, but what it meant is nowhere specified. That it was the Hebrew parallel of the Greek ostracism or exile is possible; however, there is no single incident in the vast array of biblical stories and histories that specifically describes such forced exile. Jewish tradition therefore concluded that *karet* was a punishment reserved to God who would apply it in His own way and time: by letting the offender die before his time, or die without offspring, or in some other fashion. Altogether, *karet* is provided for thirty-six offenses, ranging from the omission of circumcision to sexual offenses to passing a child through the fire, that is, idolatry of a specific nature [7].

34] *Stacte.* A sweet spice. According to Cassuto, a balsam dripping from resinous trees, similar to myrrh (*styrax officinalis*).

Onycha. An aromatic substance otherwise unidentified. According to some, it was derived from a mollusc [8].

Galbanum. A gum resin, genus *ferula*, of strong, somewhat unpleasant odor. Used in medical practice.

Frankincense. Another aromatic gum resin, genus *boswellia*. It is white in appearance, hence the Hebrew name לְבֹנָה, derived from לָבָן, white.

31:2] *Bezalel, son of Uri son of Hur.* According to I Chr. 2:18–20, Bezalel belonged to the family of Caleb, who, along with Joshua, was exempted from the decree that the generation of Egypt must die in the desert (Num. 14:24).

3] *Divine spirit.* Their extraordinary craftsmanship was considered a divine gift. (See above, at Exod. 31:3) [9].

חָכְמָה וְעָשׂוּ אֵת כָּל־אֲשֶׁר צִוִּיתִךָ: אֵת אֹהֶל מוֹעֵד ז

וְאֶת־הָאָרֹן לָעֵדֻת וְאֶת־הַכַּפֹּרֶת אֲשֶׁר עָלָיו וְאֵת כָּל־

כְּלֵי הָאֹהֶל: וְאֶת־הַשֻּׁלְחָן וְאֶת־כֵּלָיו וְאֶת־הַמְּנֹרָה ח

הַטְּהֹרָה וְאֶת־כָּל־כֵּלֶיהָ וְאֵת מִזְבַּח הַקְּטֹרֶת: וְאֶת־ ט

מִזְבַּח הָעֹלָה וְאֶת־כָּל־כֵּלָיו וְאֶת־הַכִּיּוֹר וְאֶת־כַּנּוֹ:

וְאֵת בִּגְדֵי הַשְּׂרָד וְאֶת־בִּגְדֵי הַקֹּדֶשׁ לְאַהֲרֹן הַכֹּהֵן י

וְאֶת־בִּגְדֵי בָנָיו לְכַהֵן: וְאֵת שֶׁמֶן הַמִּשְׁחָה וְאֶת־ יא

קְטֹרֶת הַסַּמִּים לַקֹּדֶשׁ כְּכֹל אֲשֶׁר־צִוִּיתִךָ יַעֲשׂוּ: פ

וַיֹּאמֶר יְהוָה אֶל־מֹשֶׁה לֵּאמֹר: וְאַתָּה דַּבֵּר אֶל־בְּנֵי יב

יִשְׂרָאֵל לֵאמֹר אַךְ אֶת־שַׁבְּתֹתַי תִּשְׁמֹרוּ כִּי אוֹת

הִוא בֵּינִי וּבֵינֵיכֶם לְדֹרֹתֵיכֶם לָדַעַת כִּי אֲנִי יְהוָה

מְקַדִּשְׁכֶם: וּשְׁמַרְתֶּם אֶת־הַשַּׁבָּת כִּי קֹדֶשׁ הִוא לָכֶם יד

מְחַלְלֶיהָ מוֹת יוּמָת כִּי כָּל־הָעֹשֶׂה בָהּ מְלָאכָה

וְנִכְרְתָה הַנֶּפֶשׁ הַהִוא מִקֶּרֶב עַמֶּיהָ: שֵׁשֶׁת יָמִים טו

יֵעָשֶׂה מְלָאכָה וּבַיּוֹם הַשְּׁבִיעִי שַׁבַּת שַׁבָּתוֹן קֹדֶשׁ

לַיהוָה כָּל־הָעֹשֶׂה מְלָאכָה בְּיוֹם הַשַּׁבָּת מוֹת יוּמָת:

וְשָׁמְרוּ בְנֵי־יִשְׂרָאֵל אֶת־הַשַּׁבָּת לַעֲשׂוֹת אֶת־הַשַּׁבָּת טז

לְדֹרֹתָם בְּרִית עוֹלָם: בֵּינִי וּבֵין בְּנֵי יִשְׂרָאֵל אוֹת יז

הִוא לְעֹלָם כִּי־שֵׁשֶׁת יָמִים עָשָׂה יְהוָה אֶת־הַשָּׁמַיִם

וְאֶת־הָאָרֶץ וּבַיּוֹם הַשְּׁבִיעִי שָׁבַת וַיִּנָּפַשׁ: ס וַיִּתֵּן יח

אֶל־מֹשֶׁה כְּכַלֹּתוֹ לְדַבֵּר אִתּוֹ בְּהַר סִינַי שְׁנֵי לֻחֹת

הָעֵדֻת לֻחֹת אֶבֶן כְּתֻבִים בְּאֶצְבַּע אֱלֹהִים:

also granted skill to all who are skillful, that they may make everything that I have commanded you: 7] the Tent of Meeting, the Ark for the Pact and the cover upon it, and all the furnishings of the Tent; 8] the table and its utensils, the pure lampstand and all its fittings, and the altar of incense; 9] the altar of burnt offering and all its utensils, and the laver and its stand; 10] the service vestments, the sacral vestments of Aaron the priest and the vestments of his sons, for their service as priests; 11] as well as the anointing oil and the aromatic incense for the sanctuary. Just as I have commanded you, they shall do.

12] And the LORD spoke to Moses, saying: 13] Speak to the Israelite people and say: Nevertheless, you must keep My sabbaths, for this is a sign between Me and you throughout the ages, that you may know that I the LORD have consecrated you. 14] You shall keep the sabbath, for it is holy for you. He who profanes it shall be put to death: whoever does work on it, that person shall be cut off from among his kin. 15] Six days may work be done, but on the seventh day there shall be a sabbath of complete rest, holy to the LORD; whoever does work on the sabbath day shall be put to death. 16] The Israelite people shall keep the sabbath, observing the sabbath throughout the ages as a covenant for all time: 17] it shall be a sign for all time between Me and the people of Israel. For in six days the LORD made heaven and earth, and on the seventh day He ceased from work and was refreshed.

18] When He finished speaking with him on Mount Sinai, He gave Moses the two tablets of the Pact, stone tablets inscribed with the finger of God.

8] *Pure lampstand.* Lampstand of pure gold.

10] *Service vestments* [10]. Others, "plaited," "stitched" vestments.

13] *Nevertheless.* A translation which follows later Jewish understanding: You may think that the construction of the Tabernacle sets aside the Sabbath laws, but it does not [11]. However, the word אַךְ is here better translated as "above all" or "mark especially" (as in the festive calendar, Lev. 23:27, 39; see commentary thereon).

15] *Sabbath of complete rest.* שַׁבַּת שַׁבָּתוֹן (*shabbat shabbaton*). The Day of Atonement too is so called (Lev. 23:32), as is the sabbatical year (Lev. 25:4).

16] *Shall keep the sabbath.* Verses 16 and 17 (known as וְשָׁמְרוּ, *Veshameru*) have become part of the Sabbath liturgy and also precede the Sabbath morning *Kiddush*. In traditional synagogues worshipers rise for the recitation of these verses.

18] *Inscribed with the finger of God.* Idiomatic for "the work of God." (See at Exod. 8:15.)

Incense

Incense was probably used originally for prophylactic purposes (warding off demonic powers) and also as an aid in purifying the air. Its use in a sacred setting was (and in many religions still is) considered an important rite. "A sweet savor" before God became an idiom for "acceptable to Him," making the olfactory sense part of the relationship between human and Divine [12]. Of all the senses it is probably the one that has the strongest faculty of evoking past experience. In Jewish practice smelling the fragrance of spices has survived only in the ceremony of *havdalah*, which separates the departing Sabbath from the weekday experience. A spice box is passed around for everyone to smell and remember the sweet savor of the *besamim* as a symbol of the fragrance of the day of rest.

An entirely different function has been ascribed to the incense by G. E. Mendenhall [13]. He suggests that it was its main function to hide the presence of God in a cloud of mystery. For Lev. 16:2 states that God appears "in a cloud over the cover [of the ark]," and verse 13 further elaborates: "He shall put the incense on the fire before the Lord, so that the cloud from the incense screens the cover . . . lest he die." The incense was to represent, in post-desert days, the pillar of cloud in which God had descended upon the Tent and which (using Mendenhall's term) had been His "mask." In this view, incense was to the Israelite a means of assuring that God could not be seen, and its other properties were strictly secondary interpretations of later ages [14].

The altar for burning incense (Exod. 30:27) was not mentioned in the original vision of the Tabernacle.[1] It appears to be the "golden altar" of Solomon's Temple (I Kings 7:48) and was found in the Second Temple also (I Macc. 1:21). In contrast, the altar mentioned in Exod. 27:1 ff. was made of wood and copper. Whether or not several small altars found in Megiddo were for incense burning has not been definitely established.

Ordination

Ordination or installation into the service of God and Tabernacle rendered the priest "holy" (קָדוֹשׁ, *kadosh*) in the original sense of the word: he was now a man set apart. Special ceremonies were provided to symbolize his entrance into the new sacred status.

The two terms, used synonymously for these rituals, were "to fill his hands" (with either the sacrifice or with a symbol of office) and "to support," whereby a consecrating officiant (here, Moses) would put his hands on Aaron and transfer priestly powers to him in this act of "supporting" him. In this way probably Moses transmitted part of his power to the seventy elders (Num. 11:16, 17, 24, 25, although the technical term is not used there) and "leaned" on Joshua when he installed him as his successor (סָמַךְ, *samach*, Num. 27:22, 23; Deut. 34:9).[2] It was his example above all that determined the terminology and nature of ordination in ages after. (See further in Gleanings.)

The Shekel

The shekel was a weight (שָׁקַל means "to weigh"), a similar word being used in other ancient Semitic languages. It was usually made of stone; metal weights and coins came only later in the history of money. The Bible knows of seven weights: the kikkar

---

[1] It is therefore often considered a late addition to the text, though proof for this is not conclusive [15].
[2] The same term סָמַךְ is used in the Torah also for transferring sin from worshiper to sacrificial animal.

The other term מִלּוּאִים has taken on an entirely different meaning in contemporary Hebrew: reserve (military) duty.

(talent), mina, shekel, beka, gerah, pim, and kesitah (the last and smallest one, of uncertain quantity). Exod. 38:25–26 shows that the 603,550 men over twenty, who were recorded as having contributed one-half shekel of silver each, totaled their tax at 100 talents and 1,775 shekels, which figures the talent at 3,000 shekels.[3] In our section the Bible further gives the shekel as consisting of 20 gerahs, a weight also known in Babylonia. The "sanctuary weight," which 30:13 mentions expressly, was probably the lighter of two shekels in use, or about 11 grams.

Traditional commentators felt that in terms of their own age the plain Torah text posed a serious moral and social problem: if rich and poor were to pay one-half shekel each, the burden on the well-to-do was small, but heavy on the less fortunate, and doubtless there must have been those who could not afford any contribution at all. The answer most frequently provided was that the phrase (Exod. 30:15), "the rich shall not pay more," meant: they shall not legally have to pay more but should make it up by generosity; and the second part, "the poor shall not pay less," meant: if they can afford it [17]. This ingenious construction is, however, misplaced. The Torah addressed itself to a fairly simple, as yet nonurbanized, society in which the extremes of great wealth and abject poverty had not yet taken hold. It aimed to state the principle of equality before God and fixed a relatively small sum to demonstrate it in practice.

(For more on the use of the shekel, see Gleanings, "The Shekel in Later Ages.")

---

[3] Taking *alafim* to mean "thousands," though in the usual statistic it meant "contingents," averaging nine to ten men; see at 12:37. The mathematics are here clearly based on the understanding that more than six hundred *thousand* (אֶלֶף) men were enrolled, the original meaning of אֶלֶף having been forgotten when this set of figures was computed. (On the likely *actual* number of Israelites see Commentary on Numbers, chapter 1.) [16]

GLEANINGS

On the History of Ordination

According to the opening phrase of *Ethics of the Fathers*, the transmission of authority went in time to the men of the Great Sanhedrin and then to a series of recognized leaders, and from them to a new class of teachers called Rabbis. (The High Priesthood ceased after 70 C.E., and no ordination was required to belong to the priestly caste, membership in which was hereditary.) The rabbinic ordination needed originally the presence of three elders, one of whom himself had ordination; in later ages only a recognized authority, like the Patriarch or the head of the court, would perform the סְמִיכָה (*semichah*), as it came to be called. But this type of ordination, which reached back into ancient days, ceased some time after the persecutions of the second century C.E. and, though several attempts both in medieval and modern times were made to reestablish it, has never been resumed officially.

Today's permission to rabbis to render decisions (*torat hora-ah*) resembles *semichah* except that it does not confer on rabbis the authority enjoyed by members of the old Sanhedrin, which included the right to reshape Jewish law significantly. The matter of spiritual succession has played a great part also in the controversies dividing the Roman Catholic church from other Christian denominations [18].

Ear, Hand, and Foot

(The ordination procedure involved putting blood on the priest's earlobe, thumb, and toe, Exod. 29:20.) This signifies that the perfect man must be pure in every word and action as a whole, for it is the hearing that judges his words, the hands that are the symbols of action, and the foot that symbolizes the way a person walks through life. PHILO [19]

The Wave Offering

The worshiper who brought it stood before the altar and waved the sacrifice in ritual motion in all directions of the compass as well as up and down, both to show that God's domain was everywhere and to ward off evil portents. RASHI

Concurrence

God informs Moses of His choice of Bezalel before He proceeds to appoint him. He says: "*See*, I have singled out . . ." (31:1). When Moses repeats this to the people, he uses the same approach and he too says: "*See*, the Lord has singled out . . ." (35:30). From this we learn that one must ask the community before appointing an official.

TALMUD [20]

Everyone Is to Know

It says (31:13) that the Sabbath "is a sign between Me and you . . . that you may know that I the Lord have consecrated you." "You"—that means all the world. RASHI

Traditional interpreters were puzzled by Rashi's comment since it clearly contradicts the Midrash [21], which states expressly that the Sabbath was to be a sign between God and Israel, but not others. They therefore harmonized as follows: "You" in the sense of "all the world" applies only to the phrase "that you may know": every nation is to know that you are My special people [22].

638

Signs

Rabbi Akiba taught that phylacteries, inasmuch as they are to remind a Jew of his special relation to God, need not be worn on the Sabbath because that day is in itself a "sign" and reminder.

TALMUD [23]

Expiation

Why was the sum chosen for expiation fixed at one-half shekel (30:15)? Because Joseph had been sold into Egypt by his brothers for twenty dinars, that is, five shekels. There being ten brothers, this amounted to a profit of one-half shekel for each.

Another explanation: It was expiation for the sin of the golden calf.

(Though this sin is told later, in chapter 32, the comment is based on the talmudic principle that the Torah is not always arranged in chronological order.)   YALKUT ME'AM LO'EZ [24]

The Shekel in Later Ages

In the days of the monarchy, the shekel tax had become a permanent institution, and its proceeds together with other freewill offerings were used to maintain and repair the Temple (II Kings 12:15–17; 22:3–7).

Since the shekel tax was due on the first of Nisan, the Rabbis ordained that this section (30:11–16) be read as an added Torah portion about a month before: on the Sabbath before the new moon of Adar or on the new moon itself if it fell on the Sabbath. Because of this added reading the Sabbath has become known as שַׁבַּת שְׁקָלִים (Shabbat Shekalim).   MISHNAH [25]

[There is also a talmudic treatise called Shekalim. Christian Scriptures [26] note that Peter paid the tax for both himself and his master.]

It became a custom at Purim time to contribute one-half of the current major coin (in North America, one-half dollar) to the poor, in honor of the festival.

The Jews outside Palestine were as zealous in their contribution of this Temple tax as the inhabitants of Judea. Anti-Semites, in consequence, even raised the cry that the Jews "were sending too much money out of the country." One of the Roman provincial governors who seized these offerings was defended by Cicero in an anti-Jewish speech. After the destruction of the Temple, the Jews of the empire were compelled to pay this contribution to the temple of Jupiter at Rome. When this iniquitous tax was eventually abolished, the contribution from the Jews in the Diaspora was used for the support of the rabbinical academies in Palestine.   J. H. HERTZ [27]

The Zionist movement at its first congress (1897) revived the shekel as a common expression of support for Eretz Yisrael. The number of shekel holders became an indication of the strength of political Zionism: there were 165,000 in 1907; 2,160,000 in 1946.

Nothing

During his forty days and nights on Mount Sinai, Moses learned much but kept forgetting what he learned. Said he in despair: "I know nothing!" Therefore God gave him the Torah as a gift.

Could Moses indeed have learned the whole Torah of which it is said that it is "longer than the earth and broader than the sea" (Job 11:9)? No, therefore God taught him only the principles (and hence gave him the tablets).   MIDRASH [28]

The Tablets

The word for tablets (31:18) is not written לֻחוֹת but לֻחֹת (as if לֻחַת, formal singular). The two tablets were like one: they were equal in size.   MIDRASH [29]

The duties toward God, written on one tablet, are equal to the duties toward man, written on the other.   S. R. HIRSCH

[More on the tablets, see Gleanings to 32:1–33:6.]

PART VIII

Apostasy and Second Covenant

Moses, descending from the mountain, finds the people dancing around the idol of a golden calf they have fashioned. The incident, which looms so large in the later recollections of Israel, is placed between the vision of the Tabernacle and the report of its construction. This occasioned much comment in Jewish tradition, one opinion defending this literary arrangement as an actual sequence, the other—notably put forth by Rashi—holding that the apostasy happened a good deal prior to Moses' vision and that his descent from the mountain and his shattering of the tablets occurred before he had received the instructions for the Tabernacle. As indicated earlier, Rashi could hold this view by applying the talmudic dictum that the events in the Torah are not necessarily told in chronological sequence. In our discussion we will, however, treat the text as we have it, although from a critical point of view much is to be said for Rashi's approach. We will discuss the entire subject of the Tabernacle as a unit, seeing it as the cooperative venture of God and Israel in restoring the latter to God's grace.[1]

With Israel's sin the terms of the original covenant are broken; the fragments of the tablets are a dramatic demonstration of this bitter reality. But Moses rejects the offer of God to substitute a new people for the old, stiffnecked Israel and instead wins His forgiveness for them. The human leader is here at his greatest, and as a reward he is given the privilege of understanding God's nature, in as full a revelation of His attributes as will be granted to man.

The Book of Exodus ends with the elaborate description of the Tabernacle's construction, which includes the readying of the priests for the sacred service. Once again the Torah exhibits repetition as a well-loved literary device, and once again the modern reader must be cautioned not to approach these chapters with his own stylistic prejudices. Repetition of words and terms, let alone whole sets of details, is nowadays considered

[1] Principal among Rashi's opponents was Nachmanides, who proposed this sequence: Moses ascended Mount Sinai on the sixth of Sivan and received the Decalogue on that day; he descended on the fortieth day after having received the instructions for the Tabernacle (on the 17th of Tamuz) to find the people committing idolatry; the next day he ascended again to plead their cause; stayed forty days more and received forgiveness and the command to hew out the second tablets; he descended on the 29th of Av to do so; reascended the next day (the new moon of Elul) and stayed another forty days; descended on the Day of Atonement (10th of Tishri) and instructed the people [1].

tedious or unimaginative, while the man of the ancient Near East, who was primarily a listener to and not a reader of traditional material, found repetition a welcome way of supporting his familiarity with the text. In an age of relatively few written records it was his added assurance that the tradition was transmitted as faithfully as possible.[2]

In Israel's history the progression of the people's grasp of the Divine leads from the theophany at Sinai to the apostasy with the calf; and from the cherubim and ark as God's throne and footstool (for which parallels in Mesopotamian iconography exist) to the eventual concept of Jerusalem as His abode. This vision is vividly expressed by Jeremiah (3:16–17): "... in those days, declares the Lord, men shall no longer speak of the Ark of the Covenant of the Lord, nor shall it come to mind. They shall not mention it, or miss it, or make another. At that time they shall call Jerusalem the throne of the Lord. ..."

But that time is still in the far-off future as the newly liberated people struggle to understand their God and, as it were, God struggles to understand His people.

---

[2] It should be noted that repetition occurs in ancient Near Eastern texts in epic literature and certain poetic genres. The biblical chapters under consideration are largely of the archival type, and their meticulous method of accounting *appeared* like epic and poetic repetition and was equally familiar as a literary pattern [2].

The Golden Calf

For the first time since the events at the Reed Sea were described, the Torah now tells a story of human dimensions, a story of anxiety and restlessness over the absence of visible leadership, of incomprehension over the true meaning of the theophany, and of a calf fashioned for worship. Moses' mysterious connection with the unseen God must have been a source of constant discussion and doubt among the people. "And now, to cap it all, the man has vanished completely. He said that he is going aloft to the God up there, when we need the God down here just where we are; but he has not come back, and it must be supposed that that God of his made away with him, since something or other between them was clearly not as it should have been. What are we to do now? We have to take matters into our own hands. An image has to be made, and then the power of the God will enter the image and there will be proper guidance" [1].

Later Jewish tradition blamed the "mixed multitude" which had left Egypt along with Israel for instigating the apostasy [2], but the Torah itself gives no warrant for this. The same tradition also excused Aaron, suggesting that he had attempted to thwart or at least delay the making of the calf. Again, the text itself leads to other conclusions about the man who was to serve as High Priest in the Tabernacle. Some scholars believe that the whole story comes from a time when Aaron's descendants participated in illegal cults [3].

About Moses, too, a question arises: How could he, yielding to his

anger, destroy the precious tablets, the greatest gift mankind had ever received? Yet this same man Moses defended his people against the destroying God and also was stern in punishing his opponents with the sword.

The incident left deep scars on the memory of Israel. Nothing would be quite the same thereafter, and a midrash says that all ills which have befallen the people since that time are in part traceable to the sin with the golden calf [4].

אַהֲרֹן וַיִּבֶן מִזְבֵּחַ לְפָנָיו וַיִּקְרָא אַהֲרֹן וַיֹּאמַר חַג

לַיהוָה מָחָר: וַיַּשְׁכִּימוּ מִמָּחֳרָת וַיַּעֲלוּ עֹלֹת וַיַּגִּשׁוּ

שְׁלָמִים וַיֵּשֶׁב הָעָם לֶאֱכֹל וְשָׁתוֹ וַיָּקֻמוּ לְצַחֵק: פ

וַיְדַבֵּר יְהוָה אֶל־מֹשֶׁה לֶךְ־רֵד כִּי שִׁחֵת עַמְּךָ אֲשֶׁר

הֶעֱלֵיתָ מֵאֶרֶץ מִצְרָיִם: סָרוּ מַהֵר מִן־הַדֶּרֶךְ אֲשֶׁר

צִוִּיתִם עָשׂוּ לָהֶם עֵגֶל מַסֵּכָה וַיִּשְׁתַּחֲווּ־לוֹ וַיִּזְבְּחוּ־לוֹ

וַיֹּאמְרוּ אֵלֶּה אֱלֹהֶיךָ יִשְׂרָאֵל אֲשֶׁר הֶעֱלוּךָ מֵאֶרֶץ

מִצְרָיִם: וַיֹּאמֶר יְהוָה אֶל־מֹשֶׁה רָאִיתִי אֶת־הָעָם הַזֶּה

וְהִנֵּה עַם־קְשֵׁה־עֹרֶף הוּא: וְעַתָּה הַנִּיחָה לִּי וְיִחַר־

וַיִּרְא הָעָם כִּי־בֹשֵׁשׁ מֹשֶׁה לָרֶדֶת מִן־הָהָר וַיִּקָּהֵל

הָעָם עַל־אַהֲרֹן וַיֹּאמְרוּ אֵלָיו קוּם עֲשֵׂה־לָנוּ אֱלֹהִים

אֲשֶׁר יֵלְכוּ לְפָנֵינוּ כִּי־זֶה מֹשֶׁה הָאִישׁ אֲשֶׁר הֶעֱלָנוּ

מֵאֶרֶץ מִצְרַיִם לֹא יָדַעְנוּ מֶה־הָיָה לוֹ: וַיֹּאמֶר אֲלֵהֶם

אַהֲרֹן פָּרְקוּ נִזְמֵי הַזָּהָב אֲשֶׁר בְּאָזְנֵי נְשֵׁיכֶם בְּנֵיכֶם

וּבְנֹתֵיכֶם וְהָבִיאוּ אֵלָי: וַיִּתְפָּרְקוּ כָּל־הָעָם אֶת־נִזְמֵי

הַזָּהָב אֲשֶׁר בְּאָזְנֵיהֶם וַיָּבִיאוּ אֶל־אַהֲרֹן: וַיִּקַּח מִיָּדָם

וַיָּצַר אֹתוֹ בַּחֶרֶט וַיַּעֲשֵׂהוּ עֵגֶל מַסֵּכָה וַיֹּאמְרוּ אֵלֶּה

אֱלֹהֶיךָ יִשְׂרָאֵל אֲשֶׁר הֶעֱלוּךָ מֵאֶרֶץ מִצְרָיִם: וַיַּרְא

1] When the people saw that Moses was so long in coming down from the mountain, the people gathered against Aaron and said to him, "Come, make us a god who shall go before us, for that man Moses, who brought us from the land of Egypt—we do not know what has happened to him." **2]** Aaron said to them, "Take off the gold rings that are on the ears of your wives, your sons, and your daughters, and bring them to me." **3]** And all the people took off the gold rings that were in their ears and brought them to Aaron. **4]** This he took from them and cast in a mold and made it into a molten calf. And they exclaimed, "This is your god, O Israel, who brought you out of the land of Egypt!" **5]** When Aaron saw this, he built an altar before it; and Aaron announced: "Tomorrow shall be a festival of the LORD!" **6]** Early next day, the people offered up burnt offerings and brought sacrifices of well-being; they sat down to eat and drink, and then rose to dance.

7] The LORD spoke to Moses, "Hurry down, for your people, whom you brought out of the land of Egypt, have acted basely. **8]** They have been quick to turn aside from the way that I enjoined upon them. They have made themselves a molten calf and bowed low to it and sacrificed to it, saying: 'This is your god, O Israel, who brought you out of the land of Egypt!'"

9] The LORD further said to Moses, "I see that this is a stiffnecked people. **10]** Now, let Me be, that My anger may blaze forth against them and that I may destroy them, and make of

---

32:1] *Against Aaron.* The second in command.

That man Moses. To the speaker he is still somewhat enigmatic.

4] *Cast in a mold.* Likely a wooden framework overlaid with gold. A better translation, however, may be "tied it in a bag," as in II Kings 5:23 [5].

Calf. עֵגֶל (egel), a young bull. Compare Ps. 106:19–20 where שׁוֹר (shor, ox) and עֵגֶל are parallel in the poetic retelling of the episode.

This is your god. This translation runs counter to the literal Hebrew which reads, "These are your gods, O Israel, who have brought you. . . ." The translation as a singular is used here because only one calf was made. (See the fuller discussion below. One may also note the singular in Neh.

9:18.) "Your" god rather than "our" god suggested to the Rabbis that the speakers were the non-Israelite "riffraff" [6].

5] *Tomorrow.* Tradition saw this postponement as a delaying tactic, Aaron hoping that Moses would return by then.

6] *Rose to dance.* לְצַחֵק; the translation follows Luzzatto, possibly a euphemism for sexual orgies. (See commentary on Genesis 21:9.)

7] *Your people.* In His anger God says "your" rather than "My" people. A midrash has Moses reply: "Why mine? They are Yours!" [7]

10] *Now, let Me be.* As if inviting Moses to assuage God's anger.

אֲשֶׁר דִּבֶּר לַעֲשׂוֹת לְעַמּוֹ: פ

יא אַפִּי בָהֶם וַאֲכַלֵּם וְאֶעֱשֶׂה אוֹתְךָ לְגוֹי גָּדוֹל: וַיְחַל

טו וַיִּפֶן וַיֵּרֶד מֹשֶׁה מִן־הָהָר וּשְׁנֵי לֻחֹת הָעֵדֻת בְּיָדוֹ

מֹשֶׁה אֶת־פְּנֵי יְהוָה אֱלֹהָיו וַיֹּאמֶר לָמָה יְהוָה יֶחֱרֶה

לֻחֹת כְּתֻבִים מִשְּׁנֵי עֶבְרֵיהֶם מִזֶּה וּמִזֶּה הֵם כְּתֻבִים:

אַפְּךָ בְּעַמֶּךָ אֲשֶׁר הוֹצֵאתָ מֵאֶרֶץ מִצְרַיִם בְּכֹחַ

טז וְהַלֻּחֹת מַעֲשֵׂה אֱלֹהִים הֵמָּה וְהַמִּכְתָּב מִכְתַּב אֱלֹהִים

גָּדוֹל וּבְיָד חֲזָקָה: לָמָּה יֹאמְרוּ מִצְרַיִם לֵאמֹר בְּרָעָה

יז הוּא חָרוּת עַל־הַלֻּחֹת: וַיִּשְׁמַע יְהוֹשֻׁעַ אֶת־קוֹל הָעָם

הוֹצִיאָם לַהֲרֹג אֹתָם בֶּהָרִים וּלְכַלֹּתָם מֵעַל פְּנֵי

בְּרֵעֹה וַיֹּאמֶר אֶל־מֹשֶׁה קוֹל מִלְחָמָה בַּמַּחֲנֶה: וַיֹּאמֶר

הָאֲדָמָה שׁוּב מֵחֲרוֹן אַפֶּךָ וְהִנָּחֵם עַל־הָרָעָה לְעַמֶּךָ:

יח אֵין קוֹל עֲנוֹת גְּבוּרָה וְאֵין קוֹל עֲנוֹת חֲלוּשָׁה קוֹל

יג זְכֹר לְאַבְרָהָם לְיִצְחָק וּלְיִשְׂרָאֵל עֲבָדֶיךָ אֲשֶׁר

עַנּוֹת אָנֹכִי שֹׁמֵעַ: וַיְהִי כַּאֲשֶׁר קָרַב אֶל־הַמַּחֲנֶה וַיַּרְא

נִשְׁבַּעְתָּ לָהֶם בָּךְ וַתְּדַבֵּר אֲלֵהֶם אַרְבֶּה אֶת־זַרְעֲכֶם

יט אֶת־הָעֵגֶל וּמְחֹלֹת וַיִּחַר־אַף מֹשֶׁה וַיַּשְׁלֵךְ מִיָּדָו אֶת־

כְּכוֹכְבֵי הַשָּׁמָיִם וְכָל־הָאָרֶץ הַזֹּאת אֲשֶׁר אָמַרְתִּי

כ הַלֻּחֹת וַיְשַׁבֵּר אֹתָם תַּחַת הָהָר: וַיִּקַּח אֶת־הָעֵגֶל

יד אֶתֵּן לְזַרְעֲכֶם וְנָחֲלוּ לְעֹלָם: וַיִּנָּחֶם יְהוָה עַל־הָרָעָה

you a great nation." **11]** But Moses implored the LORD his God, saying, "Let not Your anger, O Lord, blaze forth against Your people, whom You delivered from the land of Egypt with great power and with a mighty hand. **12]** Let not the Egyptians say, 'It was with evil intent that He delivered them, only to kill them off in the mountains and annihilate them from the face of the earth.' Turn from Your blazing anger, and renounce the plan to punish Your people. **13]** Remember Your servants, Abraham, Isaac, and Jacob, how You swore to them by Your Self and said to them: I will make your offspring as numerous as the stars of heaven, and I will give to your offspring this whole land of which I spoke, to possess forever." **14]** And the LORD renounced the punishment He had planned to bring upon His people.

15] Thereupon Moses turned and went down from the mountain bearing the two tablets of the Pact, tablets inscribed on both their surfaces: they were inscribed on the one side and on the other. **16]** The tablets were God's work, and the writing was God's writing, incised upon the tablets. **17]** When Joshua heard the sound of the people in its boisterousness, he said to Moses, "There is a cry of war in the camp." **18]** But he answered, / "It is not the sound of the tune of triumph. / Or the sound of the tune of defeat; / It is the sound of song that I hear!"

19] As soon as Moses came near the camp and saw the calf and the dancing, he became enraged; and he hurled the tablets from his hands and shattered them at the foot of the mountain. **20]** He took the calf that they had made and burned it; he ground it to powder and strewed it upon the water and so made the Israelites drink it.

11] *Moses implored.* He offers two considerations: one, what would Egypt say? (concern for God's reputation) and, two, he reminds God of the covenant He made. Verses 11–14 form part of the traditional Torah reading for the afternoon of Tishah b'Av (along with Exod. 34:1–10). Since the words of Moses saved his people in ancient times, they were considered especially suited for the urgent petitions of later generations.

13] *Remember Your servants.* And their merits.

17] *When Joshua heard.* He had been waiting somewhere on the mountin slope.

Its boisterousness. בְּרֵעֹה (be-re-oh), a word play with בְּרָעָה (be-ra-ah) in verse 12.

18] *Sound of song.* Another word play, עֲנוֹת–עַנּוֹת.

19] *Dancing.* See Gleanings.

20] *Burned it.* Melted it down.

Made the Israelites drink it. An immediate psychological punishment (compare the English idiom: "swallowing one's words"). Mixing the ashes with water turned the mixture into a kind of bitter water like that given the suspected unfaithful wife (Num. 5:26) [8].

לַיהוָֹה וַיֵּאָסְפוּ אֵלָיו כָּל־בְּנֵי לֵוִי: וַיֹּאמֶר לָהֶם

כֹּה־אָמַר יְהוָֹה אֱלֹהֵי יִשְׂרָאֵל שִׂימוּ אִישׁ־חַרְבּוֹ עַל־

יְרֵכוֹ עִבְרוּ וָשׁוּבוּ מִשַּׁעַר לָשַׁעַר בַּמַּחֲנֶה וְהִרְגוּ

אִישׁ־אֶת־אָחִיו וְאִישׁ אֶת־רֵעֵהוּ וְאִישׁ אֶת־קְרֹבוֹ:

וַיַּעֲשׂוּ בְנֵי־לֵוִי כִּדְבַר מֹשֶׁה וַיִּפֹּל מִן־הָעָם בַּיּוֹם הַהוּא

כִּשְׁלֹשֶׁת אַלְפֵי אִישׁ: וַיֹּאמֶר מֹשֶׁה מִלְאוּ יֶדְכֶם הַיּוֹם

לַיהוָֹה כִּי אִישׁ בִּבְנוֹ וּבְאָחִיו וְלָתֵת עֲלֵיכֶם הַיּוֹם

בְּרָכָה: וַיְהִי מִמָּחֳרָת וַיֹּאמֶר מֹשֶׁה אֶל־הָעָם אַתֶּם

חֲטָאתֶם חֲטָאָה גְדֹלָה וְעַתָּה אֶעֱלֶה אֶל־יְהוָֹה אוּלַי

אֲכַפְּרָה בְּעַד חַטַּאתְכֶם: וַיָּשָׁב מֹשֶׁה אֶל־יְהוָֹה וַיֹּאמַר

אָנָּא חָטָא הָעָם הַזֶּה חֲטָאָה גְדֹלָה וַיַּעֲשׂוּ לָהֶם

אֲשֶׁר עָשׂוּ וַיִּשְׂרֹף בָּאֵשׁ וַיִּטְחַן עַד אֲשֶׁר־דָּק וַיִּזֶר

עַל־פְּנֵי הַמַּיִם וַיַּשְׁקְ אֶת־בְּנֵי יִשְׂרָאֵל: וַיֹּאמֶר מֹשֶׁה

אֶל־אַהֲרֹן מֶה־עָשָׂה לְךָ הָעָם הַזֶּה כִּי־הֵבֵאתָ עָלָיו

חֲטָאָה גְדֹלָה: וַיֹּאמֶר אַהֲרֹן אַל־יִחַר אַף אֲדֹנִי

אַתָּה יָדַעְתָּ אֶת־הָעָם כִּי בְרָע הוּא: וַיֹּאמְרוּ לִי

עֲשֵׂה־לָנוּ אֱלֹהִים אֲשֶׁר יֵלְכוּ לְפָנֵינוּ כִּי־זֶה מֹשֶׁה

הָאִישׁ אֲשֶׁר הֶעֱלָנוּ מֵאֶרֶץ מִצְרַיִם לֹא יָדַעְנוּ מֶה־

הָיָה לוֹ: וָאֹמַר לָהֶם לְמִי זָהָב הִתְפָּרָקוּ וַיִּתְּנוּ־לִי

וָאַשְׁלִכֵהוּ בָאֵשׁ וַיֵּצֵא הָעֵגֶל הַזֶּה: וַיַּרְא מֹשֶׁה אֶת־

הָעָם כִּי פָרֻעַ הוּא כִּי־פְרָעֹה אַהֲרֹן לְשִׁמְצָה

בְּקָמֵיהֶם: וַיַּעֲמֹד מֹשֶׁה בְּשַׁעַר הַמַּחֲנֶה וַיֹּאמֶר מִי

21] Moses said to Aaron, "What did this people do to you that you have brought such great sin upon them?" 22] Aaron said, "Let not my lord be enraged. You know that this people is bent on evil. 23] They said to me, 'Make us a god to lead us; for that man Moses, who brought us from the land of Egypt—we cannot tell what has happened to him.' 24] So I said to them. 'Whoever has gold, take it off!' They gave it to me and I hurled it into the fire and out came this calf!"

25] Moses saw that the people were out of control—since Aaron had let them get out of control—so that they were a menace to any who might oppose them. 26] Moses stood up in the gate of the camp and said, "Whoever is for the LORD, come here!" And all the Levites rallied to him. 27] He said to them, "Thus says the LORD, the God of Israel: Each of you put sword on thigh, go back and forth from gate to gate throughout the camp, and slay brother, neighbor, and kin." 28] The Levites did as Moses had bidden; and some three thousand of the people fell that day. 29] And Moses said, "Dedicate yourselves to the LORD this day—for each of you has been against son and brother—that He may bestow a blessing upon you today."

30] The next day Moses said to the people, "You have been guilty of a great sin. Yet I will now go up to the LORD; perhaps I may win forgiveness for your sin." 31] Moses went back to the LORD and said, "Alas, this people is guilty of a great sin in making for themselves a god of

24] *Out came this calf.* Aaron's excuse: It just happened, I had little to do with it.

25] *A menace.* Others, "an object of derision."

27] *Slay brother, neighbor, and kin.* This suggests that there was a split among the Levites. Moses authorized a battlefield execution. Rashi justified it on the basis of Exod. 22:19; Nachmanides's

explanation suggests that there were too many offenders to be brought to justice in the courts.

29] *Dedicate yourselves.* Literally, "fill your hands." The meaning is that killing—even in a righteous cause—impairs man's relationship to God and requires rectification (compare Num. 31:19, 20).

לֵאלֹהֵי זָהָב: וְעַתָּה אִם־תִּשָּׂא חַטָּאתָם וְאִם־אַיִן מְחֵנִי לב   לְאַבְרָהָם לְיִצְחָק וּלְיַעֲקֹב לֵאמֹר לְזַרְעֲךָ אֶתְּנֶנָּה:

נָא מִסִּפְרְךָ אֲשֶׁר כָּתָבְתָּ: וַיֹּאמֶר יְהוָה אֶל־מֹשֶׁה מִי לג   וְשָׁלַחְתִּי לְפָנֶיךָ מַלְאָךְ וְגֵרַשְׁתִּי אֶת־הַכְּנַעֲנִי הָאֱמֹרִי

אֲשֶׁר חָטָא־לִי אֶמְחֶנּוּ מִסִּפְרִי: וְעַתָּה לֵךְ נְחֵה אֶת־ לד   וְהַחִתִּי וְהַפְּרִזִּי הַחִוִּי וְהַיְבוּסִי: אֶל־אֶרֶץ זָבַת חָלָב

הָעָם אֶל אֲשֶׁר־דִּבַּרְתִּי לָךְ הִנֵּה מַלְאָכִי יֵלֵךְ לְפָנֶיךָ   וּדְבָשׁ כִּי לֹא אֶעֱלֶה בְּקִרְבְּךָ כִּי עַם־קְשֵׁה־עֹרֶף

וּבְיוֹם פָּקְדִי וּפָקַדְתִּי עֲלֵהֶם חַטָּאתָם: וַיִּגֹּף יְהוָה לה   אַתָּה פֶּן־אֲכֶלְךָ בַּדָּרֶךְ: וַיִּשְׁמַע הָעָם אֶת־הַדָּבָר

אֶת־הָעָם עַל אֲשֶׁר עָשׂוּ אֶת־הָעֵגֶל אֲשֶׁר עָשָׂה   הָרָע הַזֶּה וַיִּתְאַבָּלוּ וְלֹא־שָׁתוּ אִישׁ עֶדְיוֹ עָלָיו: ד

אַהֲרֹן: ס   וַיֹּאמֶר יְהוָה אֶל־מֹשֶׁה אֱמֹר אֶל־בְּנֵי־יִשְׂרָאֵל אַתֶּם ה

וַיְדַבֵּר יְהוָה אֶל־מֹשֶׁה לֵךְ עֲלֵה מִזֶּה אַתָּה וְהָעָם א   עַם־קְשֵׁה־עֹרֶף רֶגַע אֶחָד אֶעֱלֶה בְקִרְבְּךָ וְכִלִּיתִיךָ

אֲשֶׁר הֶעֱלִיתָ מֵאֶרֶץ מִצְרַיִם אֶל־הָאָרֶץ אֲשֶׁר נִשְׁבַּעְתִּי   וְעַתָּה הוֹרֵד עֶדְיְךָ מֵעָלֶיךָ וְאֵדְעָה מָה אֶעֱשֶׂה־

לָךְ: וַיִּתְנַצְּלוּ בְנֵי־יִשְׂרָאֵל אֶת־עֶדְיָם מֵהַר חוֹרֵב: ו

gold. **32]** Now, if You will forgive their sin [well and good]; but if not, erase me from the record which You have written!" **33]** But the LORD said to Moses, "He who has sinned against Me, him only will I erase from My record. **34]** Go now, lead the people where I told you. See, My angel shall go before you. But when I make an accounting, I will bring them to account for their sins."

35] Then the LORD sent a plague upon the people, for what they did with the calf that Aaron made.

1] Then the LORD said to Moses, "Set out from here, you and the people that you have brought up from the land of Egypt, to the land of which I swore to Abraham, Isaac, and Jacob, saying, 'To your offspring will I give it'— **2]** I will send an angel before you, and I will drive out the Canaanites, the Amorites, the Hittites, the Perizzites, the Hivites, and the Jebusites— **3]** a land flowing with milk and honey. But I will not go in your midst, since you are a stiffnecked people, lest I destroy you on the way."

4] When the people heard this harsh word, they went into mourning, and none put on his finery.

5] The LORD said to Moses, "Say to the Israelite people, 'You are a stiffnecked people. If I were to go in your midst for one moment, I would destroy you. Now, then, leave off your finery, and I will consider what to do to you.'" **6]** So the Israelites remained stripped of their finery from Mount Horeb on.

34] *I will bring them to account.* This will come to pass after the incident with the spies (Num. 14:20–24).

35] *For what they did.* The second part of the verse is uncertain.

33:3] *I will not go in your midst.* A highly an-

thropomorphic passage: God will remove himself as if He did not trust His own temper, having been so sorely tried by His people. An angel will take His place.

6] *Mount Horeb.* On its identity with Sinai, see at Exod. 3:1.

The Calf—History

Historical and theological considerations have made the incident of the golden calf one of the subjects in the Torah to which traditional comment and modern scholarship have given a great deal of attention [9]. The major historical questions revolve around the relation of the story to the introduction of two golden calves into the sanctuary by Jeroboam; and the theological questions, around Israel's precipitous return to idolatry as well as the basic difference between fashioning the cherubim for the ark as holy objects and of the calf as a forbidden one.

The Book of Kings (I Kings 12:28–33) reports that Jeroboam I, the first king of Israel after the division following Solomon's death (tenth century B.C.E.), introduced the calf or bull worship into his country. It was his method of detaching his people from their allegiance to the Temple in Jerusalem, which was located in Judah. He made two golden bulls and set one up at Beth-el and the other at Dan and said, in the same words used in Exod. 32:4 and 8: "These are your gods, O Israel, who brought you out of the land of Egypt." There being two bulls, the use of the plural is natural with Jeroboam here; while in Exodus, with only one idol, the use of the plural is clearly out of place.[1] The suggestion has therefore been made that the Jeroboam tale is the primary one and the Exodus story of later origin—told to legitimize the Levites and to devalue the Beth-el and Dan sanctuaries and perhaps all northern religious practices [10]. Others dispute this and hold that arguments weightier than a stylistic plural must be considered; especially that Jeroboam could not have succeeded had there not been since olden days a strong propensity among the people to consider the bull worship with some favor. If that was the case, as seems likely in the light of the popularity of the bull cult in the area,[2] the story told in Exodus reflects the memory of ancient sentiments and practices.

The Calf—Theology

Two questions have been raised about the golden calf: How could the people revert so quickly to idolatry (and did they in fact consider the calf as a substitute for God)? What relationship, if any, existed between the golden cherubim and the golden calf?

A closer look reveals that idolatry in the strict sense was not involved [12]. The people were leaderless since Moses had left them, and his prolonged absence created great anxiety amongst them. He had been their visible contact with the invisible God, and it was such a contact they craved as reassurance that they were not forsaken. Bulls were thought of as divine pedestals, and it was such a pedestal—later legitimized by the cherubim on the ark—that the people constructed [13]. Any idea that the Israelites really believed that the gold from their earrings could fashion a god at will rests on a misunderstanding of ancient beliefs, which were considerably more sophisticated than later generations—and often the Bible itself—gave them credit for. The bull was the new link with God and was meant to replace "that man Moses" who, so to speak, had been His footstool.

If, then, the people had fashioned a part of the divine throne as they imagined it, why was the incident weighted with such condemnation when shortly thereafter a new footstool would not only be authorized but

---

[1] The Hebrew אֱלֹהֶיךָ may be singular or plural, but the verb הֶעֱלוּךָ is a plural. About translating the phrase nonetheless as a singular, see at 32:4.

[2] The storm god Hadad is represented as standing on a bull [11]; and the Canaanite god El is frequently called "Bull El." Fertility and strength were identified with the bull.

obligatory? The parallel between the gold contributed in both cases must be striking, and therefore the judgment of Albright seems well founded, that *conceptually* there was "no essential difference between the invisible enthroned on the cherubim or as standing on a bull" [14]. Already the medieval poet-philosopher Judah Halevi took this view. He said that the only difference between cherubim and calf was that *one form had been permitted and the other one had not* [15]. It was a breach of trust, but not a rejection of God, nor a return to idolatry. Consequently the punishment (except that meted out to the ringleaders) was not of a permanent nature, and the divine plan to have Israel erect a sanctuary in its midst would go forward as soon as Moses had assuaged God's anger.

The Role of Aaron

An unprejudiced reading of the text shows Aaron as a collaborator in the building of the golden calf and even in arranging the festivities swirling around it. We are told that Aaron failed to restrain the people, that he allowed them to get out of control (32:25), and the excuses he offered were those of an ineffective leader who proclaimed that he could do no more than he had done. A later passage in the Torah (Deut. 9:20) delivers the devastating judgment that God was angry enough to have killed Aaron, but that He refrained because of Moses' intercession. The derogation of Aaron which the text appears to exhibit has been taken to support a theory that sees here a reflection of the struggle between two priestly houses: Aaron was the prototype of the (later) "Aaronide" priesthood in Beth-el and Jerusalem, and Moses the patron of the "Mushite" (i.e., Mosaic) priesthood at Shiloh and Dan, as well as Arad and Kadesh-Naphtali. In this view, the part Aaron played in the story of the golden calf was portrayed as semi-pagan and was a severe judgment on the families claiming priestly supremacy in his name [16]. (See also Gleanings.)

However, later tradition generally tried to exculpate Aaron and picture him as a victim of the people.[3] Aaron, it was held, had tried delaying tactics until Moses would return; the whole process of gathering gold and of saying "tomorrow" (32:5) was meant to retard the idolatrous impulses of the people. Satan was involved; magicians produced an illusion that showed Moses dead; and his nephew Hur, who had attempted to oppose the popular hysteria, was killed by the enraged mob. Aaron could act no differently than he did, for he hated confrontations and was above all a man of peace who did not want to reproach his people. God knew his intent in any case and, as for God, He himself was in part responsible for what Israel did: Had He not been the one who had exposed His people to the experience of idolatry when He brought them down to Egypt? Had He not seen to it that they received gold in compensation for the years of slavery [18]? (For an evaluation of Aaron, see Commentary on Numbers, chapter 12.)

---

[3] An exception is the midrash which tells that Aaron was punished later, through the death of his two sons, Nadab and Abihu [17].

GLEANINGS

The Sin

(The real sin lay not in the making of the calf but in what Israel thought and said when Moses failed to return.) Israel said: God redeemed only himself but not us; He is concerned with himself but not with us.　　MIDRASH [19]

The Delay

Moses "was so long in coming down" (32:1). The Hebrew בֹּשֵׁשׁ (boshesh) is to be understood as בָּא שֵׁשׁ (ba shesh): "the sixth (hour of the day) had come." It was the fortieth day and Moses had said he would return by the sixth hour. But he had excluded the day of his ascent and the people miscalculated because of this. When he failed to return at the promised time they thought him dead.　　MIDRASH [20]

The Contrast

While Aaron wants to express the idea of God by an understandable image, Moses demands unconditional surrender to an almighty invisible deity. Aaron is convinced that the people will not believe in a god they cannot see. It is the clash between the ideal that the crowd needs to worship and the pure idea of deity—the collision between corporeality and spirituality. When Moses rebukes Aaron because he has sullied the purity of the faith, Aaron points out that the tablets Moses is carrying are also corporeal corruptions of total purity. In sudden despair Moses smashes the tablets, whereupon Aaron rebukes him because the tablets could have helped Israel's faith.　　A. SCHÖNBERG [21]

The Women

"All the people took off the gold rings that were in their ears" (32:3). In Hebrew "their" is in the masculine gender, indicating that the women did not cooperate. They preserved their piety.　　MIDRASH [22]

The Tablets

They were inscribed miraculously in a way that they were equally legible on both sides. They were 6 x 6 handbreaths in size, and, between the words of the Decalogue, all the other laws of the Torah were inscribed. The tablets shed a light on Moses' face giving it a permanent radiance.　　MIDRASH [23]

The words were "incised" on the tablets (32:16: חָרוּת, charut). One should read חֵרוּת (cherut), meaning "freedom." The tablets' words spelled freedom for Israel if it would obey them.　　TALMUD AND MIDRASH [24]

Thus man must know that he is tempted from time to time for the sake of his freedom. He must learn to believe in his freedom. He must believe that his freedom, limited though it may be everywhere else, is limitless vis-à-vis God. The very commandments of God, "graven on stone tablets," must be for him, as in an untranslatable rabbinic play on words, "freedom on tablets." Everything, it says in the same source, everything is in God's hands except for one thing: the fear of God. And how can this freedom show itself more audaciously than in the certainty of being able to tempt God? In prayer, then, the possibilities of temptation really do converge from both sides, from God's side as well as man's. Prayer is strung between these two possibilities; while fearing God's temptation, it nevertheless knows itself capable of itself tempting God.　　F. ROSENZWEIG [25]

How Moses Broke the Tablets

Moses, as he approached the camp, saw the writing vanish from the tablets, the letters flying back to God. At once the stones became too heavy and they slipped from his hands.

The majority opinion held, however, that he broke them willingly (see Deut. 9:17). This was one of the three things he did on his own initiative. [The other two: he stayed an extra day on the mountain; he abstained from intercourse with his wife, deeming this necessary for his prophetic function.] Despite this, God thanked Moses for breaking the tablets.   TALMUD [26]

[But in another passage, He rebuked him and fined him by having him hew out new tablets by himself] [27].

Moses broke the tablets out of his love for Israel, for as long as they did not know the Torah they would be judged less harshly. God consoled him, saying: The second tablets will contain much more material, Halachah, Midrash, and Aggadah.
          MIDRASH [28]

Unbroken Tablets

The word unto the prophet spoken
Was writ on tablets yet unbroken
The word by seers and sibyls told,
On graves of oak or fanes of gold,
Still floats upon the morning wind,
Still whispers to the willing mind.
          R. W. EMERSON [29]

Descent

Down sank the great sun, and in golden, glim-
    mering vapors
Veiled the light of his face, like the Prophet
    descending from Sinai.
          H. W. LONGFELLOW [30]

Alone

How weary is the downward path alone!
All the lost glories on the height, the flame,
The thunder of the Voice, the grey-seamed
    stone—
Seared in his fire, responsive to his name,
Stone near the heart of God—these on the mount
Still flame and thunder and forever burn.

From them with shuttered eyes and brain I turn
Uncertain steps into the folding cloud.
Deeper and deeper in the blind mist go
My lagging feet; the night with slow
Obliteration wraps its shroud.
          A. K. BLANK [31]

Step by Step

Sinai
down from your peak
Moses bore the opened sky
on his forehead
cooling step by step
until they who waited in the shadow
were able to bear, trembling,
What shone beneath the veil—

Is there still an heir
to the succession of them that trembled?
Oh, may he glow
in the crowd of them that do not remember,
of the petrified!
          N. SACHS [32]

Consequence

In repentance, the Israelites "went into mourning and none put on his finery" (33:4). "Finery" meant the phylacteries; hence it is a rule that mourners during *shivah* (the first seven days after internment) do not don phylacteries when they pray.   MIDRASH [33]

In Christian tradition the story of Israel dancing around the golden calf became a reason to prohibit dancing on public and private occasions. While the Roman Catholic church of the Middle Ages often made exceptions for national occasions and weddings, regnant Protestant, and especially Puritan, custom for centuries opposed any such activity on biblical grounds [34].

Reversed

How could God reverse a punishment already pronounced? He had to ask Moses to help Him annul His own vow.   MIDRASH [35]

Golden Calf in Polemics

Josephus (first century C.E.), afraid that pagan anti-Semites would exploit the story, omits it

653

entirely and instead has the people rejoice at Moses' descent and the latter displaying the tablets [36].

Christian medieval polemics denounced the Jews for the act, holding that because of it the covenant was never consummated; drinking the waters mixed with the ashes of the calf had permanently imbued them with the execration of the devil who had played a part in the incident [37].

The Role of the Brothers

Why Aaron is shown as having played such a prominent part in the golden calf episode is not clear. It has been suggested by those who believe that the primary golden calf story is the one concerning Jeroboam in I Kings that worship of YHVH by means of a bull image in the time of the monarchy was believed to have been originally sanctioned by Aaron, and that the Exodus story is a deliberate attempt to discredit Aaron in order to stamp out the use of the bull. But this seems a rather extravagant hypothesis. What emerges in the text of Exodus as we have it is the difference between Moses, meek yet stern and absolute in his ethical and ritual demands, and the compromising character of Aaron, who did not share Moses' lonely visions and did not possess his brother's absolute sense of mission. The historical reality behind the stories of Aaron remains shadowy, but in the golden calf episode the real emphasis is on the character of Moses and of the God whose character and demands he mediates to the people. Moses is revealed as the noncompromiser, as opposed to Aaron, but also, and perhaps more significantly, as intercessor.

D. DAICHES [38]

Aaron saw the people "bent on evil"; Moses defended them before God's hot anger. Aaron exonerated himself from all active involvement; Moses put his own life on the line for Israel's sake. Aaron was too weak to restrain the people; Moses was strong enough to restrain even God.

B. S. CHILDS [39]

The Story in the Koran

And Moses returned to his people, angered, sorrowful.

He said, "O my people, did not your Lord promise you a good promise? Was the time of my absence long to you, or desired ye that wrath from your Lord should light upon you, that ye failed in your promise to me?"

They said, "Not of our own accord have we failed in the promise to thee, but we were made to bring loads of the people's trinkets, and we threw them into the fire"—and Samiri likewise cast them in and brought forth to them a corporeal lowing calf; and they said, "This is your God and the God of Moses, whom he hath forgotten."

What! Saw they not that it returned them no answer and could neither hurt nor help them?

And Aaron had before said to them, "O my people! By this calf are ye only proved—surely your Lord is the God of Mercy: follow me therefore and obey my bidding."

KORAN [40]

Measure for Measure

Moses pleads with God: "Now, if you will forgive their sin (well and good), but, if not, erase me from the record which you have written" (32:32). Moses has destroyed, "erased," the covenant by breaking the tablets. He understands that his own "erasure" would be a just consequence of the principle "measure for measure." This is why the Midrash has him say to God:

"They sinned, and I sinned in that I broke the tablets. If you forgive them, forgive me too. If you do not forgive them, do not forgive me, but erase me from the book you have written" [41].

The Zohar appropriately declares that there was none who protected his generation like Moses, for he was the faithful shepherd.

N. M. WALDMAN [42]

A New Covenant; the Nature of God

The command has been given to lead the people away from Sinai (32:34 and 33:1). But, with the covenant broken, how can Israel go forward with confidence? Moses therefore pleads with God to lead His own people and the plea is accepted. Moses goes further: since he himself has also been beset by doubt and anxiety, he asks the ultimate reassurance, namely, to behold the Divine Presence. Though he is not granted this privilege he is given an insight into the nature of God whose attributes are revealed to him.

Now the covenant is renewed. The terms are only partially the same as in the Decalogue. Idolatry is again forbidden; thereafter the terms diverge and turn to cultic matters: matzot; dedication of the first-born; Sabbaths and festivals; the incompatibility of leaven and sacrifice; first fruits; and for the second time the prohibition of boiling a kid in its mother's milk. Again Moses spends forty days and nights on the mountain, and again he writes down the law. The section ends with the focus on Moses himself. His face shines with a reflection of the divine glory, and he must cover it with a veil, for ordinary people cannot look on it. Moses has been favored in unique fashion and his position has become even more exalted; in fact, his status is now so high that it has been described as semi-divine [1]. But this description does not do justice to the Torah, for when all is said and done Moses remains human and, as the years wear on, it is his humanity that the Torah stresses, not his superhumanity.

There are literary problems. For instance, a "Tent of Meeting" is

suddenly mentioned which is located outside the camp. This Tent might be seen as a temporary device: until a complete reconciliation with God would be effected His Presence could not appear in the midst of the people. More likely, the introduction of the Tent of Meeting as well as other aspects of the section suggest that we confront traditions diverging substantially from earlier portions of Exodus. Thus, except for one reference to the new tablets (34:1), the tale of the golden calf seems to be unknown, and there is even a hint that the Decalogue of chapter 20 was not part of the tradition now unfolded. Consequently, many scholars have theorized that the covenant terms of chapter 34 formed another Decalogue, and possibly the older one, especially since the title "Ten Commandments" is used for the first time here (34:28), and not in relation to the Decalogue of chapter 20. Morgenstern called it "the oldest document in the Hexateuch." "It is here," avers Noth, "that we have the fundamental action of the covenant" [2]. (For a further discussion, see above, introduction to Exod. 20:1–7.)*

* The section poses other questions which medieval commentators considered in detail, especially regarding the somewhat different account in Deut. 9. There is a debate on this matter between Ibn Ezra and Nachmanides [3].

אֶל־מֹשֶׁה פָּנִים אֶל־פָּנִים כַּאֲשֶׁר יְדַבֵּר אִישׁ אֶל־רֵעֵהוּ
וְשָׁב אֶל־הַמַּחֲנֶה וּמְשָׁרְתוֹ יְהוֹשֻׁעַ בִּן־נוּן נַעַר לֹא
יָמִישׁ מִתּוֹךְ הָאֹהֶל: פ

יב וַיֹּאמֶר מֹשֶׁה אֶל־יְהוָֹה רְאֵה אַתָּה אֹמֵר אֵלַי הַעַל
אֶת־הָעָם הַזֶּה וְאַתָּה לֹא הוֹדַעְתַּנִי אֵת אֲשֶׁר־תִּשְׁלַח
עִמִּי וְאַתָּה אָמַרְתָּ יְדַעְתִּיךָ בְשֵׁם וְגַם־מָצָאתָ חֵן
בְּעֵינָי: יג וְעַתָּה אִם־נָא מָצָאתִי חֵן בְּעֵינֶיךָ הוֹדִעֵנִי
נָא אֶת־דְּרָכֶךָ וְאֵדָעֲךָ לְמַעַן אֶמְצָא־חֵן בְּעֵינֶיךָ וּרְאֵה
כִּי עַמְּךָ הַגּוֹי הַזֶּה: יד וַיֹּאמַר פָּנַי יֵלֵכוּ וַהֲנִחֹתִי לָךְ:

ז וּמֹשֶׁה יִקַּח אֶת־הָאֹהֶל וְנָטָה־לוֹ מִחוּץ לַמַּחֲנֶה הַרְחֵק
מִן־הַמַּחֲנֶה וְקָרָא לוֹ אֹהֶל מוֹעֵד וְהָיָה כָּל־מְבַקֵּשׁ
יְהוָֹה יֵצֵא אֶל־אֹהֶל מוֹעֵד אֲשֶׁר מִחוּץ לַמַּחֲנֶה:
ח וְהָיָה כְּצֵאת מֹשֶׁה אֶל־הָאֹהֶל יָקוּמוּ כָּל־הָעָם וְנִצְּבוּ
אִישׁ פֶּתַח אָהֳלוֹ וְהִבִּיטוּ אַחֲרֵי מֹשֶׁה עַד־בֹּאוֹ
הָאֹהֱלָה: ט וְהָיָה כְּבֹא מֹשֶׁה הָאֹהֱלָה יֵרֵד עַמּוּד
הֶעָנָן וְעָמַד פֶּתַח הָאֹהֶל וְדִבֶּר עִם־מֹשֶׁה: י וְרָאָה
כָל־הָעָם אֶת־עַמּוּד הֶעָנָן עֹמֵד פֶּתַח הָאֹהֶל וְקָם
כָּל־הָעָם וְהִשְׁתַּחֲווּ אִישׁ פֶּתַח אָהֳלוֹ: יא וְדִבֶּר יְהוָֹה

7] Now Moses would take the Tent and pitch it outside the camp, at some distance from the camp. It was called the Tent of Meeting, and whoever sought the LORD would go out to the Tent of Meeting that was outside the camp. **8]** Whenever Moses went out to the Tent, all the people would rise and stand, each at the entrance of his tent, and gaze after Moses until he had entered the Tent. **9]** And when Moses entered the Tent, the pillar of cloud would descend and stand at the entrance of the Tent, while He spoke with Moses. **10]** When all the people saw the pillar of cloud poised at the entrance of the Tent, all the people would rise and bow low, each at the entrance of his tent. **11]** The LORD would speak to Moses face to face, as one man speaks to another. And he would then return to the camp; but his attendant, Joshua son of Nun, a youth, would not stir out of the Tent.

12] Moses said to the LORD, "See, You say to me, 'Lead this people forward,' but You have not made known to me whom You will send with me. Further, You have said, 'I have singled you out by name, and you have, indeed, gained My favor.' **13]** Now, if I have truly gained Your favor, pray let me know Your ways, that I may know You and continue in Your favor. Consider, too, that this nation is Your people." **14]** And He said, "I will go in the lead and

33:7] *The Tent.* This has not been mentioned before, and critics assign this to the E-source which did not know of the P-tradition regarding the Tabernacle, described in chapters 25–27, 35–40. (See commentary below on 38:21–40:38.) However, the difficulty is greatly reduced if הָאֹהֶל is translated not as *the* Tent, but "a tent" (which is grammatically admissible). With the New English Bible one can read: "Moses used to take a tent and pitch it outside the camp." Tradition considers the tent as having been Moses' own dwelling and that he withdrew from the camp because God himself had done so.

Tent of Meeting. אֹהֶל מוֹעֵד (*Ohel Mo-ed*), so called because God and Moses would meet there. **11]** *Face to face.* Not through the medium of dreams or visions; see Num. 12:6.

Joshua. He attends to the Tent, while the Tabernacle required priestly servants.

12] *See, You say to me.* Taking up the command of 33:1.

You have not made known to me. Moses speaks as if he had not been promised that an angel would accompany the people (33:2). The presence of different traditions is here most obvious. This is also emphasized by what follows.

Further, You have said. Though this was not recorded before.

14] *I will go in the lead.* Literally, "My face will go. . . ." Idiomatic for "My Presence" [4]. According to Rashi, who follows the Targum, this implies that God had changed His mind about the angel.

כב וְהָיָה בַּעֲבֹר כְּבֹדִי וְשַׂמְתִּיךָ בְּנִקְרַת הַצּוּר וְשַׂכֹּתִי

כג כַפִּי עָלֶיךָ עַד־עָבְרִי: וַהֲסִרֹתִי אֶת־כַּפִּי וְרָאִיתָ אֶת־

פ אֲחֹרָי וּפָנַי לֹא יֵרָאוּ:

א וַיֹּאמֶר יְהוָה אֶל־מֹשֶׁה פְּסָל־לְךָ שְׁנֵי־לֻחֹת אֲבָנִים

כָּרִאשֹׁנִים וְכָתַבְתִּי עַל־הַלֻּחֹת אֶת־הַדְּבָרִים אֲשֶׁר

ב הָיוּ עַל־הַלֻּחֹת הָרִאשֹׁנִים אֲשֶׁר שִׁבַּרְתָּ: וֶהְיֵה נָכוֹן

לַבֹּקֶר וְעָלִיתָ בַבֹּקֶר אֶל־הַר סִינַי וְנִצַּבְתָּ לִי שָׁם

ג עַל־רֹאשׁ הָהָר: וְאִישׁ לֹא־יַעֲלֶה עִמָּךְ וְגַם־אִישׁ אַל־

יֵרָא בְּכָל־הָהָר גַּם־הַצֹּאן וְהַבָּקָר אַל־יִרְעוּ אֶל־מוּל

ד הָהָר הַהוּא: וַיִּפְסֹל שְׁנֵי לֻחֹת אֲבָנִים כָּרִאשֹׁנִים וַיַּשְׁכֵּם

מֹשֶׁה בַבֹּקֶר וַיַּעַל אֶל־הַר סִינַי כַּאֲשֶׁר צִוָּה יְהוָה

טו וַיֹּאמֶר אֵלָיו אִם־אֵין פָּנֶיךָ הֹלְכִים אַל־תַּעֲלֵנוּ מִזֶּה:

טז וּבַמֶּה יִוָּדַע אֵפוֹא כִּי־מָצָאתִי חֵן בְּעֵינֶיךָ אֲנִי וְעַמֶּךָ

הֲלוֹא בְּלֶכְתְּךָ עִמָּנוּ וְנִפְלִינוּ אֲנִי וְעַמְּךָ מִכָּל־הָעָם

פ אֲשֶׁר עַל־פְּנֵי הָאֲדָמָה:

יז וַיֹּאמֶר יְהוָה אֶל־מֹשֶׁה גַּם אֶת־הַדָּבָר הַזֶּה אֲשֶׁר

דִּבַּרְתָּ אֶעֱשֶׂה כִּי־מָצָאתָ חֵן בְּעֵינַי וָאֵדָעֲךָ בְּשֵׁם:

יח וַיֹּאמַר הַרְאֵנִי נָא אֶת־כְּבֹדֶךָ: וַיֹּאמֶר אֲנִי אַעֲבִיר

כָּל־טוּבִי עַל־פָּנֶיךָ וְקָרָאתִי בְשֵׁם יְהוָה לְפָנֶיךָ וְחַנֹּתִי

יט אֶת־אֲשֶׁר אָחֹן וְרִחַמְתִּי אֶת־אֲשֶׁר אֲרַחֵם: וַיֹּאמֶר

כ לֹא תוּכַל לִרְאֹת אֶת־פָּנָי כִּי לֹא־יִרְאַנִי הָאָדָם

כא וָחָי: וַיֹּאמֶר יְהוָה הִנֵּה מָקוֹם אִתִּי וְנִצַּבְתָּ עַל־הַצּוּר:

will lighten your burden." **15]** And he said to Him, "Unless You go in the lead, do not make us leave this place. **16]** For how shall it be known that Your people have gained Your favor unless You go with us, so that we may be distinguished, Your people and I, from every people on the face of the earth?"

17] And the LORD said to Moses, "I will also do this thing that you have asked; for you have truly gained My favor and I have singled you out by name." **18]** He said, "Oh, let me behold Your Presence!" **19]** And He answered, "I will make all My goodness pass before you, and I will proclaim before you the name LORD, and the grace that I grant and the compassion that I show. **20]** But," He said, "you cannot see My face, for man may not see Me and live." **21]** And the LORD said, "See, there is a place near Me. Station yourself on the rock **22]** and, as My Presence passes by, I will put you in a cleft of the rock and shield you with My hand until I have passed by. **23]** Then I will take My hand away and you will see My back; but My face must not be seen."

1] The LORD said to Moses: "Carve two tablets of stone like the first, and I will inscribe upon the tablets the words that were on the first tablets, which you shattered. **2]** Be ready by morning, and in the morning come up to Mount Sinai and present yourself there to Me, on the top of the mountain. **3]** No one else shall come up with you, and no one else shall be seen anywhere on the mountain; neither shall the flocks and the herds graze at the foot of this mountain."

4] So Moses carved two tablets of stone, like the first, and early in the morning he went up on Mount Sinai, as the LORD had commanded him, taking the two stone tablets with him.

15] *Unless You go.* An affirmation of God's new promise: "Indeed, if you were not to go . . ." [5]. Still, Moses is not satisfied and wants a further personal assurance.

17] *I will also do this thing.* God yields, yet Moses dares to go even further (compare the dialogue of Abraham and God, Gen. 18:23 ff.).

19] *All My goodness.* I will reveal to you My essential nature.

The name Lord. יְהוָה. See at 3:15.

34:4] *He went up on Mount Sinai.* Where he will stay forty days and nights (verse 28). The setting of the first covenant is repeated.

עַמְּךָ אֶעֱשֶׂה נִפְלָאֹת אֲשֶׁר לֹא־נִבְרְאוּ בְכָל־הָאָרֶץ
וּבְכָל־הַגּוֹיִם וְרָאָה כָל־הָעָם אֲשֶׁר־אַתָּה בְקִרְבּוֹ
אֶת־מַעֲשֵׂה יְהֹוָה כִּי־נוֹרָא הוּא אֲשֶׁר אֲנִי עֹשֶׂה עִמָּךְ:
יא שְׁמָר־לְךָ אֵת אֲשֶׁר אָנֹכִי מְצַוְּךָ הַיּוֹם הִנְנִי גֹרֵשׁ
מִפָּנֶיךָ אֶת־הָאֱמֹרִי וְהַכְּנַעֲנִי וְהַחִתִּי וְהַפְּרִזִּי וְהַחִוִּי
וְהַיְבוּסִי: יב הִשָּׁמֶר לְךָ פֶּן־תִּכְרֹת בְּרִית לְיוֹשֵׁב הָאָרֶץ
אֲשֶׁר אַתָּה בָּא עָלֶיהָ פֶּן־יִהְיֶה לְמוֹקֵשׁ בְּקִרְבֶּךָ: יג כִּי
אֶת־מִזְבְּחֹתָם תִּתֹּצוּן וְאֶת־מַצֵּבֹתָם תְּשַׁבֵּרוּן וְאֶת־
אֲשֵׁרָיו תִּכְרֹתוּן: יד כִּי לֹא תִשְׁתַּחֲוֶה לְאֵל אַחֵר כִּי
יְהֹוָה קַנָּא שְׁמוֹ אֵל קַנָּא הוּא: טו פֶּן־תִּכְרֹת בְּרִית

ה אֹתוֹ וַיִּקַּח בְּיָדוֹ שְׁנֵי לֻחֹת אֲבָנִים: וַיֵּרֶד יְהֹוָה בֶּעָנָן
ו וַיִּתְיַצֵּב עִמּוֹ שָׁם וַיִּקְרָא בְשֵׁם יְהֹוָה: וַיַּעֲבֹר יְהֹוָה
עַל־פָּנָיו וַיִּקְרָא יְהֹוָה יְהֹוָה אֵל רַחוּם וְחַנּוּן אֶרֶךְ
ז אַפַּיִם וְרַב־חֶסֶד וֶאֱמֶת: נֹצֵר חֶסֶד לָאֲלָפִים נֹשֵׂא עָו‍ֹן
וָפֶשַׁע וְחַטָּאָה וְנַקֵּה לֹא יְנַקֶּה פֹּקֵד עֲו‍ֹן אָבוֹת עַל־
בָּנִים וְעַל־בְּנֵי בָנִים עַל־שִׁלֵּשִׁים וְעַל־רִבֵּעִים:
ח וַיְמַהֵר מֹשֶׁה וַיִּקֹּד אַרְצָה וַיִּשְׁתָּחוּ: ט וַיֹּאמֶר אִם־נָא
מָצָאתִי חֵן בְּעֵינֶיךָ אֲדֹנָי יֵלֶךְ־נָא אֲדֹנָי בְּקִרְבֵּנוּ
כִּי עַם־קְשֵׁה־עֹרֶף הוּא וְסָלַחְתָּ לַעֲו‍ֹנֵנוּ וּלְחַטָּאתֵנוּ
י וּנְחַלְתָּנוּ: וַיֹּאמֶר הִנֵּה אָנֹכִי כֹּרֵת בְּרִית נֶגֶד כָּל־

5] The LORD came down in a cloud; He stood with him there, and proclaimed the name LORD. 6] The LORD passed before him and proclaimed: "The LORD! the LORD! a God compassionate and gracious, slow to anger, abounding in kindness and faithfulness, 7] extending kindness to the thousandth generation, forgiving iniquity, transgression, and sin; yet He does not remit all punishment, but visits the iniquity of fathers upon children and children's children, upon the third and fourth generations."

8] Moses hastened to bow low to the ground in homage, 9] and said, "If I have gained Your favor, O Lord, pray let the Lord go in our midst, even though this is a stiffnecked people. Pardon our iniquity and our sin, and take us for Your own!"

10] He said: I hereby make a covenant. Before all your people I will work such wonders as have not been wrought on all the earth or in any nation; and all the people who are with you shall see how awesome are the LORD's deeds which I will perform for you. 11] Mark well what I command you this day. I will drive out before you the Amorites, the Canaanites, the Hittites, the Perizzites, the Hivites, and the Jebusites. 12] Beware of making a covenant with the inhabitants of the land against which you are advancing, lest they be a snare in your midst. 13] No, you must tear down their altars, smash their pillars, and cut down their sacred posts; 14] for you must not worship any other god, because the LORD, whose name is Impassioned, is an impassioned God. 15] You must not make a covenant with the inhabitants

6] *And proclaimed: "The Lord! the Lord!..."* This translation follows the Masoretic punctuation. Others read, "And the Lord proclaimed: The Lord. . . ." The phrase has entered the Jewish liturgy for the holy days.

7] *Extending kindness.* נֹצֵר (*notzer*). The נ is written large in traditional manuscripts; the reason is not clear. (On this, see Gleanings.)

9] *If I have gained Your favor.* Moses makes no further requests but returns to the beginning and asks for a full pardon for Israel which will result in a new covenant.

10] *Have not been wrought.* Literally, "created";

this is the terminology of creation, as if the people are to be fashioned anew.

11] *I will drive out.* Repetition of the warning about too close an association with the inhabitants. Compare 23:23–24.

13] *Sacred posts.* Such *asherim* stood near Canaanite altars and were perhaps symbols of sacred trees. The singular *asherah* was the name of the Canaanite goddess of fertility.

14] *Any other god.* לְאֵל אַחֵר (*le-el acher*). The ר is written large so as to distinguish the word from אֶחָד (*echad*, "one") and so as not to read: "You must not worship *one* God."

יָצָאתָ מִמִּצְרָיִם: כָּל־פֶּטֶר רֶחֶם לִי וְכָל־מִקְנְךָ תִּזָּכָר יּ
פֶּטֶר שׁוֹר וָשֶׂה: וּפֶטֶר חֲמוֹר תִּפְדֶּה בְשֶׂה וְאִם־לֹא כ
תִפְדֶּה וַעֲרַפְתּוֹ כֹּל בְּכוֹר בָּנֶיךָ תִּפְדֶּה וְלֹא־יֵרָאוּ
פָנַי רֵיקָם: שֵׁשֶׁת יָמִים תַּעֲבֹד וּבַיּוֹם הַשְּׁבִיעִי תִּשְׁבֹּת כא
בֶּחָרִישׁ וּבַקָּצִיר תִּשְׁבֹּת: וְחַג שָׁבֻעֹת תַּעֲשֶׂה לְךָ כב
בִּכּוּרֵי קְצִיר חִטִּים וְחַג הָאָסִיף תְּקוּפַת הַשָּׁנָה:

לְיוֹשֵׁב הָאָרֶץ וְזָנוּ אַחֲרֵי אֱלֹהֵיהֶם וְזָבְחוּ לֵאלֹהֵיהֶם
וְקָרָא לְךָ וְאָכַלְתָּ מִזִּבְחוֹ: וְלָקַחְתָּ מִבְּנֹתָיו לְבָנֶיךָ יּ
וְזָנוּ בְנֹתָיו אַחֲרֵי אֱלֹהֵיהֶן וְהִזְנוּ אֶת־בָּנֶיךָ אַחֲרֵי
אֱלֹהֵיהֶן: אֱלֹהֵי מַסֵּכָה לֹא תַעֲשֶׂה־לָּךְ: אֶת־חַג יז
הַמַּצּוֹת תִּשְׁמֹר שִׁבְעַת יָמִים תֹּאכַל מַצּוֹת אֲשֶׁר
צִוִּיתִךָ לְמוֹעֵד חֹדֶשׁ הָאָבִיב כִּי בְּחֹדֶשׁ הָאָבִיב

of the land, for they will lust after their gods and sacrifice to their gods and invite you, and you will eat of their sacrifices.   16] And when you take wives from among their daughters for your sons, their daughters will lust after their gods and will cause your sons to lust after their gods.

17] You shall not make molten gods for yourselves.

18] You shall observe the Feast of Unleavened Bread—eating unleavened bread for seven days, as I have commanded you—at the set time of the month of Abib, for in the month of Abib you went forth from Egypt.

19] Every first issue of the womb is Mine, from all your livestock that drop a male as firstling, whether cattle or sheep.   20] But the firstling of an ass you shall redeem with a sheep; if you do not redeem it, you must break its neck. And you must redeem every first-born among your sons.

None shall appear before Me empty-handed.

21] Six days you shall work, but on the seventh day you shall cease from labor; you shall cease from labor even at plowing time and harvest time.

22] You shall observe the Feast of Weeks, of the first fruits of the wheat harvest; and the

16] *And when you take wives.* Abraham had been concerned about the potentially baneful influence of a pagan wife on his son Isaac (Gen. 24:3–4), and Isaac similarly worried about Jacob (Gen. 28:1–2). The warning was often disregarded in subsequent history, so that in the fifth century B.C.E. Ezra instituted a forcible divorce of such mixed marriages (Ezra, chapters 9 and 10). During the long period of Jewish isolation in medieval ghettos the command was generally heeded, while in times of political and social emancipation it was not.

18] *Feast of Unleavened Bread.* On its relation to Passover see at chapter 12.

Month of Abib. See at 13:4.

19] *Every first issue.* This is mentioned here in

connection with the Exodus from Egypt when the first-born played a special role.

21] *Even at plowing time.* The Rabbis debated the intent of this seemingly redundant injunction [6].

22] *Feast of Weeks.* חַג שָׁבֻעֹת (*Chag Shavuot*), see at 23:16 and also Deut. 16:9–12. Shavuot is also called "Festival of the First Fruits" and was later identified as the "Festival of the Giving of the Torah" (tradition says it was given on the sixth day of Sivan). See Commentary on Leviticus, chapter 23.

Feast of Ingathering. Identified with Sukot, see at 23:16 and Commentary on Leviticus, chapter 23. The agricultural nature of these festivals has led a number of scholars to suggest that such celebrations belonged to an earlier tradition [7].

כז וַיֹּאמֶר יְהֹוָה אֶל־מֹשֶׁה כְּתָב־לְךָ אֶת־הַדְּבָרִים
הָאֵלֶּה כִּי עַל־פִּי הַדְּבָרִים הָאֵלֶּה כָּרַתִּי אִתְּךָ
בְּרִית וְאֶת־יִשְׂרָאֵל: כח וַיְהִי־שָׁם עִם־יְהֹוָה אַרְבָּעִים
יוֹם וְאַרְבָּעִים לַיְלָה לֶחֶם לֹא אָכַל וּמַיִם לֹא
שָׁתָה וַיִּכְתֹּב עַל־הַלֻּחֹת אֵת דִּבְרֵי הַבְּרִית עֲשֶׂרֶת
הַדְּבָרִים: כט וַיְהִי בְּרֶדֶת מֹשֶׁה מֵהַר סִינַי וּשְׁנֵי לֻחֹת
הָעֵדֻת בְּיַד־מֹשֶׁה בְּרִדְתּוֹ מִן־הָהָר וּמֹשֶׁה לֹא־יָדַע
ל כִּי קָרַן עוֹר פָּנָיו בְּדַבְּרוֹ אִתּוֹ: וַיַּרְא אַהֲרֹן וְכָל־

כג שָׁלֹשׁ פְּעָמִים בַּשָּׁנָה יֵרָאֶה כָּל־זְכוּרְךָ אֶת־פְּנֵי הָאָדֹן
כד יְהֹוָה אֱלֹהֵי יִשְׂרָאֵל: כִּי־אוֹרִישׁ גּוֹיִם מִפָּנֶיךָ
וְהִרְחַבְתִּי אֶת־גְּבֻלֶךָ וְלֹא־יַחְמֹד אִישׁ אֶת־אַרְצְךָ
בַּעֲלֹתְךָ לֵרָאוֹת אֶת־פְּנֵי יְהֹוָה אֱלֹהֶיךָ שָׁלֹשׁ פְּעָמִים
כה בַּשָּׁנָה: לֹא־תִשְׁחַט עַל־חָמֵץ דַּם־זִבְחִי וְלֹא־יָלִין
כו לַבֹּקֶר זֶבַח חַג הַפָּסַח: רֵאשִׁית בִּכּוּרֵי אַדְמָתְךָ
תָּבִיא בֵּית יְהֹוָה אֱלֹהֶיךָ לֹא־תְבַשֵּׁל גְּדִי בַּחֲלֵב
אִמּוֹ: פ

Feast of Ingathering at the turn of the year. **23]** Three times a year all your males shall appear before the Sovereign LORD, the God of Israel. **24]** I will drive out nations from your path and enlarge your territory; no one will covet your land when you go up to appear before the LORD your God three times a year.

25] You shall not offer the blood of My sacrifice with anything leavened; and the sacrifice of the Feast of Passover shall not be left lying until morning.

26] The choice first fruits of your soil you shall bring to the house of the LORD your God. You shall not boil a kid in its mother's milk.

27] And the LORD said to Moses: Write down these commandments, for in accordance with these commandments I make a covenant with you and with Israel.

28] And he was there with the LORD forty days and forty nights; he ate no bread and drank no water; and he wrote down on the tablets the terms of the covenant, the Ten Commandments.

29] So Moses came down from Mount Sinai. And as Moses came down from the mountain bearing the two tablets of the Pact, Moses was not aware that the skin of his face was radiant, since he had spoken with Him. **30]** Aaron and all the Israelites saw that the skin of Moses'

25] *Feast of Passover.* As if different from the Feast of Matzot.

26] *You shall not boil.* Discussed at 23:19.

28] *He ate no bread.* Moses' supernatural experience is emphasized.

And he wrote down. The Hebrew could refer either to God or to Moses as the subject [8].

The Ten Commandments. It is possible to say with some traditional commentators that God had spoken only the first two directly and that now the remainder was being communicated.

29] *Was radiant.* This is the proper way of rendering קָרַן (*karan*). Although the verb is related to the word קֶרֶן (*keren*, "horn"), its figurative meaning is well attested in Akkadian prayers. Hence the Latin translation—that Moses' face "was horned" (*cornuta esset*), an image that the famous sculpture by Michelangelo impressed on many minds—was erroneous. In Christian tradition the incident is referred to as "the transfiguration of Moses" [9].

לד וַיִּתֵּן עַל־פָּנָיו מַסְוֶה: וּבְבֹא מֹשֶׁה לִפְנֵי יְהֹוָה לְדַבֵּר
אִתּוֹ יָסִיר אֶת־הַמַּסְוֶה עַד־צֵאתוֹ וְיָצָא וְדִבֶּר אֶל־
לה בְּנֵי יִשְׂרָאֵל אֵת אֲשֶׁר יְצֻוֶּה: וְרָאוּ בְנֵי־יִשְׂרָאֵל
אֶת־פְּנֵי מֹשֶׁה כִּי קָרַן עוֹר פְּנֵי מֹשֶׁה וְהֵשִׁיב מֹשֶׁה
אֶת־הַמַּסְוֶה עַל־פָּנָיו עַד־בֹּאוֹ לְדַבֵּר אִתּוֹ:

בְּנֵי יִשְׂרָאֵל אֶת־מֹשֶׁה וְהִנֵּה קָרַן עוֹר פָּנָיו וַיִּירְאוּ
לא מִגֶּשֶׁת אֵלָיו: וַיִּקְרָא אֲלֵהֶם מֹשֶׁה וַיָּשֻׁבוּ אֵלָיו אַהֲרֹן
לב וְכָל־הַנְּשִׂאִים בָּעֵדָה וַיְדַבֵּר מֹשֶׁה אֲלֵהֶם: וְאַחֲרֵי־
כֵן נִגְּשׁוּ כָּל־בְּנֵי יִשְׂרָאֵל וַיְצַוֵּם אֵת כָּל־אֲשֶׁר דִּבֶּר
לג יְהֹוָה אִתּוֹ בְּהַר סִינָי: וַיְכַל מֹשֶׁה מִדַּבֵּר אִתָּם:

Haftarah Ki Tisa, p. 722

face was radiant; and they shrank from coming near him.   31] But Moses called to them, and Aaron and all the chieftains in the assembly returned to him, and Moses spoke to them. 32] Afterwards all the Israelites came near, and he instructed them concerning all that the LORD had imparted to him on Mount Sinai.   33] And when Moses had finished speaking with them, he put a veil over his face.

34] Whenever Moses went in before the LORD to speak with Him, he would leave the veil off until he came out; and when he came out and told the Israelites what he had been commanded,   35] the Israelites would see how radiant the skin of Moses' face was. Moses would then put the veil back over his face until he went in to speak with Him.

33] *A veil.* The Hebrew word occurs only in this story. It is possible that the veil was derived from the mask of Egyptian (and possibly also Mesopotamian) priests, whereby they assumed the "face" of the deity. But here the sense is clearly that the divine glory is dangerous to behold even when merely reflected; and, while in the ancient Near East a mask was sometimes worn by the priest when communicating the divine message to the people, here the reverse is true: Moses removes the veil when speaking in God's name [10].

The Nature of God

A few passages in chapters 33 and 34 set forth the Torah's view of God's nature. In direct or indirect fashion He had previously been shown as creator, father of the Patriarchs, Israel's protector, ruler of history, unique, without form, jealous of other gods, issuing reward and retribution, lawgiver, guardian of the weak, and guarantor of justice. Once again Moses asks God to disclose His nature as well as the fullness of His name, for the ambiguous *Ehyeh-Asher-Ehyeh* which had been communicated to him (3:14) had left him without the precise insight he had desired. But the answer Moses receives now is essentially the same and is again purposefully opaque: "I will be gracious to whom I will be gracious." It is a circular, self-defining statement, and Moses must at last understand that this is the limit of human knowledge.[1] Similarly, Moses' request to see God's "face" receives the answer that only His "back" can be seen, that is, His deeds and actions that reveal His existence and nature.

Jewish tradition has distinguished thirteen attributes of God, listed in 34:6–7 as follows:

1 and 2. יְהֹוָה יְהֹוָה. "The Lord, the Lord." The traditional interpretation of the divine Name is that it discloses God's attribute of mercy (in contradistinction to *Elohim*, which discloses His attribute of justice).[2] The repetition of the attribute of mercy was taken to mean that God is merciful both before and after man has sinned and repented; it is man who changes, not God [11].

3. אֵל (*El*). "God," meaning His rulership, His being the Almighty, comparable to "God Most High" (אֵל עֶלְיוֹן).

4. רַחוּם (*Rachum*). "Compassionate," sympathetic to suffering. (It may be noted that this quality is linguistically a "female principle," the word being of the same root as רֶחֶם, the mother's womb.)

5. חַנּוּן (*Chanun*). "Gracious," in His helpful concern.

6. אֶרֶךְ אַפַּיִם (*Erech apayim*). "Slow to anger," giving human beings an opportunity to repent.

7. רַב חֶסֶד (*Rav chesed*). "Abounding in kindness," beyond man's deserts.

8. אֱמֶת (*Emet*). "Truth," which in His case is here and elsewhere preceded by kindness [12].

9. נֹצֵר חֶסֶד לָאֲלָפִים (*Notzer chesed la-alafim*). "Extending kindness to the thousandth generation," remembering human merit.

10, 11, and 12. נֹשֵׂא עָוֹן וָפֶשַׁע וְחַטָּאָה (*No-se avon vafesha ve-chata-ah*). "Forgiving iniquity, transgression, and sin," God is indulgent with man's evil disposition (*avon*), his rebelliousness (*pesha*), and his guilt (*chata-ah*).

13. וְנַקֵּה לֹא יְנַקֶּה (*Ve-nakeh lo yenakeh*). "Yet He does not remit all punishment." There are limits to His mercy.[3]

These attributes became a matter of intense discussion among Jewish scholars from the days of Philo on. They attempted to elicit from them comprehensive principles that would give man an insight into God's true being. Thus Abraham ibn Daud deducted seven positive attributes: God's unity, truth, existence, omniscience, will, omnipotence,

---

[1] Cassuto sees this self-defining principle also in the opening words of 34:6 and interprets it as "The Lord, He is the Lord." Further examples of this *idem per idem* Hebrew construction are found in Exod. 4:13; 16:23; I Sam. 23:13. Also see the quotation in Christian Scriptures, Romans 9:15–16, where the interpretation is: Mercy does not depend on man's effort but on God's will.

[2] See commentary on Genesis 2:4–24, "The Names of God."

[3] See the discussion of this aspect at 20:5. There is also an understanding that נַקֵּה refers to the repentant and לֹא יְנַקֶּה to the unrepentant sinners [13].

and being; and Maimonides claimed that they only showed that God was ultimately unknowable. We cannot know Him in His "positive" attributes, that is, we cannot really know what and how He is; the thirteen attributes, he said, interpret His actions, not His being. At best we can only know what He is not, that is, His "negative" attributes. In modern times, Hermann Cohen took up the old argument once again and condensed the thirteen attributes into two: love and justice. In their various expressions in Exodus 34 and elsewhere they are meant as examples of what men ought to do in pursuit of a godly life [14].

The Jewish liturgy, too, contains formulations of God's nature; best known among them are *Adon Olam* and *Yigdal* (based on Maimonides's understanding of the thirteen principles).

GLEANINGS

Moses' Argument
(God dealt with Israel as a king who had taken a wife. One day he noticed her in intimate conversation with a servant; enraged, he turned her out of his house. Later he was entreated on her behalf because she had once been a servant herself, hence her intimacy with servants. He relented and ordered a new marriage contract to be drawn.)

Thus did Moses argue with God: Do you not remember that Israel learned idolatry in the land of idolaters, and who put them there but You! God then made a new covenant with Israel and gave Moses the second tablets.   MIDRASH [15]

Authority
When the Israelites accepted the Decalogue God thought that the acceptance might be due to their habit of accepting authority, as they had done in their days of slavery. But after the incident with the golden calf He knew that their original acceptance had been an act of free will and was therefore more inclined to forgive them.
CHASIDIC [16]

The Faithful Shepherd
Noah did not intercede with God for his fellow men when he was apprised of their impending doom, whereas Abraham did, and repeatedly, in behalf of Sodom. But Moses exceeded even Abraham, for he did not budge until God had pardoned Israel. There was none who equaled Moses in his people's defense; he was indeed the faithful shepherd.   ZOHAR [17]

The Servant
Moses is called the "servant of the Lord" (Deut. 34:5), and he is also the servant referred to in Isaiah (53:5): "He was wounded because of our sins, crushed by our iniquities, he bore the chastisement that made us whole, and by his bruises were we healed." For Moses offered his own life to God in behalf of Israel (Exod. 32:32).
NACHMANIDES [18]

[Christianity interpreted the passage in Isaiah to refer to Jesus, whereas Jewish interpreters usually considered Israel itself to be the "servant of the Lord."]

Kindness and Truth (34:6)
Lovingkindness precedes truth, both here and generally throughout Scripture, as if to say, "Speak the truth by all means, but be quite sure that you speak the truth *in love*."
J. H. HERTZ [19]

Four Times
A person sins once, twice, three times and is forgiven, as it says (Exod. 34:7), "forgiving iniquity, transgression, and sin"—three times, but thereafter God no longer remits punishment.
TOSEFTA [20]

The Enlarged נ

Why is the נ in נֹצֵר, "extending [kindness]," written large in Exod. 34:7, in the Masoretic text? Perhaps to prevent it from being read עֹצֵר, "withholding [kindness]." This is similar to verse 14, where the ר in אַחֵר is also written large (see note at 33:14).

W. G. P.

Moses with the Shining Face

The exalted status of Moses and his shining face is a tradition that stood under the influence of Assyro-Babylonian religion and especially certain solar elements thereof, which came to conceive of God as a divine radiant being, emitting dazzling brilliance, just like the great gods of the Assyrian pantheon, and particularly Shamash, the sun god.

J. MORGENSTERN [21]

(Note also that we too say of a person that his "face shines," when he appears to be aglow from an inner radiance.)

The glow on Moses' face was granted him as an extra sign to show that he was still God's agent.

This also helped to repair the crisis in leadership which had developed in Moses' absence.

H. H. COHEN [22]

In the two most famous artistic renditions of Moses, Rembrandt (Berlin Museum) shows him with a radiant countenance, holding tablets of black stone, engraved with gold letters; and Michelangelo (Church of Saint Peter in Chains, Rome) with horns protruding from his forehead.

Tablets and People

What the mob was really like, to what degree it was the rawest of raw material and flesh and blood, lacking the most elementary conception of purity and holiness, how Moses had to begin at the beginning and teach them beginnings, that is to be deduced from the simple precepts with which he started to work and chisel and blast. Not to their comfort, certainly, for the stone does not take sides with the master but against him; to the stone the first stroke struck to form it appears as a most unnatural action.

THOMAS MANN [23]

The Building of the Tabernacle

At last the order is given to construct the Tabernacle. This important chapter in Israel's desert story begins with the words וַיַּקְהֵל מֹשֶׁה (*vayakhel Mosheh*, "Moses then convoked"). The *sidrah* which begins here is called *vayakhel*. The opening word is thematic in that it heralds the conclusion of the cycle that started with the same word (though in a different form) וַיִּקָּהֵל in 32:1. There too the people assembled, but for the purpose of rebellion against the desires of God. The incident with the golden calf followed, Moses assuaged God's anger, and the covenant was renewed. Now, with a וַיַּקְהֵל which has the approval of God, His forgiving grace is demonstrated and the people are given an opportunity to show by their generosity and active participation that they deserve the divine mercy. They pass the test splendidly, and Bezalel begins to fashion the sanctuary that will assure the people that God's Presence will abide amongst them. Fittingly a midrash expresses this closing of the circle by saying that "Bezalel came and healed the wound" [1].

Again the Sabbath is the bridge connecting the building of the Tabernacle with its deeper purpose; just as its observance was commanded at the end of the original instructions (31:12–17) so it now precedes their execution (35:1–3).

The actual order of building does not follow the sequence of the earlier instructions. The ark, as the most important feature of the Tabernacle, had then stood first; now the Tabernacle itself leads the sequence of construction. This order does not reflect practical necessity (presumably,

the Tabernacle had to be made first before the ark could be placed in it[1]) but rather represents a subtle literary device called "chiastic": the order of events is inverted to conform to the sequence A-B, B-A: ark-Tabernacle, Tabernacle-ark [2].

The details of the construction follow the earlier prescriptions almost exactly. Some scholars have therefore concluded that this duplication represents a late addition to the text [3], but a study of both biblical and cognate texts reveals the opposite: such repetition was an integral part of the narrative style of the ancient Near East as it was an aspect of archival documentation. In the Torah the most elaborate other example is found in the story of Abraham's servant who prays for and then finds the perfect mate for Isaac (Genesis, chapter 24). In Ugaritic literature we have the tale of King Keret receiving and then executing instructions from El, and both sets are told in nearly the same words (see Gleanings).[2]

---

[1] In fact, though the Tabernacle was *made* first, it was *erected* last.

[2] A notable divergence exists, however, in the Septuagint, where chapters 35 and following have terms substantially different from those employed in chapters 25–31. It is probable that this difference is due to a late editor of the Greek text [4].

ס ס ס

וְלִקְטֹרֶת הַסַּמִּים: וְאַבְנֵי־שֹׁהַם וְאַבְנֵי מִלֻּאִים לָאֵפוֹד

ט

א וַיַּקְהֵל מֹשֶׁה אֶת־כָּל־עֲדַת בְּנֵי יִשְׂרָאֵל וַיֹּאמֶר

וְלַחֹשֶׁן: וְכָל־חֲכַם־לֵב בָּכֶם יָבֹאוּ וְיַעֲשׂוּ אֵת כָּל־

י

אֲלֵהֶם אֵלֶּה הַדְּבָרִים אֲשֶׁר־צִוָּה יְהוָה לַעֲשֹׂת אֹתָם:

אֲשֶׁר צִוָּה יְהוָה: אֶת־הַמִּשְׁכָּן אֶת־אָהֳלוֹ וְאֶת־מִכְסֵהוּ

יא

ב שֵׁשֶׁת יָמִים תֵּעָשֶׂה מְלָאכָה וּבַיּוֹם הַשְּׁבִיעִי יִהְיֶה

אֶת־קְרָסָיו וְאֶת־קְרָשָׁיו אֶת־בְּרִיחָו אֶת־עַמֻּדָיו

לָכֶם קֹדֶשׁ שַׁבַּת שַׁבָּתוֹן לַיהוָה כָּל־הָעֹשֶׂה בוֹ

וְאֶת־אֲדָנָיו: אֶת־הָאָרֹן וְאֶת־בַּדָּיו אֶת־הַכַּפֹּרֶת וְאֵת

יב

ג מְלָאכָה יוּמָת: לֹא־תְבַעֲרוּ אֵשׁ בְּכֹל מֹשְׁבֹתֵיכֶם

פָּרֹכֶת הַמָּסָךְ: אֶת־הַשֻּׁלְחָן וְאֶת־בַּדָּיו וְאֶת־כָּל־כֵּלָיו

יג

בְּיוֹם הַשַּׁבָּת: פ

וְאֵת לֶחֶם הַפָּנִים: וְאֶת־מְנֹרַת הַמָּאוֹר וְאֶת־כֵּלֶיהָ

יד

ד וַיֹּאמֶר מֹשֶׁה אֶל־כָּל־עֲדַת בְּנֵי־יִשְׂרָאֵל לֵאמֹר

וְאֶת־נֵרֹתֶיהָ וְאֵת שֶׁמֶן הַמָּאוֹר: וְאֶת־מִזְבַּח הַקְּטֹרֶת

טו

ה זֶה הַדָּבָר אֲשֶׁר־צִוָּה יְהוָה לֵאמֹר: קְחוּ מֵאִתְּכֶם

וְאֶת־בַּדָּיו וְאֵת שֶׁמֶן הַמִּשְׁחָה וְאֵת קְטֹרֶת הַסַּמִּים

תְּרוּמָה לַיהוָה כֹּל נְדִיב לִבּוֹ יְבִיאֶהָ אֵת תְּרוּמַת

וְאֶת־מָסַךְ הַפֶּתַח לְפֶתַח הַמִּשְׁכָּן: אֵת מִזְבַּח הָעֹלָה

טז

ו יְהוָה זָהָב וָכֶסֶף וּנְחֹשֶׁת: וּתְכֵלֶת וְאַרְגָּמָן וְתוֹלַעַת

וְאֶת־מִכְבַּר הַנְּחֹשֶׁת אֲשֶׁר־לוֹ אֶת־בַּדָּיו וְאֶת־כָּל־כֵּלָיו

ז שָׁנִי וְשֵׁשׁ וְעִזִּים: וְעֹרֹת אֵילִם מְאָדָּמִים וְעֹרֹת תְּחָשִׁים

אֶת־הַכִּיֹּר וְאֶת־כַּנּוֹ: אֵת קַלְעֵי הֶחָצֵר אֶת־עַמֻּדָיו

יז

ח וַעֲצֵי שִׁטִּים: וְשֶׁמֶן לַמָּאוֹר וּבְשָׂמִים לְשֶׁמֶן הַמִּשְׁחָה

וְאֶת־אֲדָנֶיהָ וְאֵת מָסַךְ שַׁעַר הֶחָצֵר: אֶת־יִתְדֹת

יח

יא בריחיו קרי

1] Moses then convoked the whole Israelite community and said to them:
These are the things that the LORD has commanded you to do: **2]** On six days work may be done, but on the seventh day you shall have a sabbath of complete rest, holy to the LORD; whoever does any work on it shall be put to death. **3]** You shall kindle no fire throughout your settlements on the sabbath day.

4] Moses said further to the whole community of Israelites:
This is what the LORD has commanded: **5]** Take from among you gifts to the LORD, everyone whose heart so moves him shall bring them—gifts for the LORD: gold, silver, and copper; **6]** blue, purple, and crimson yarns, fine linen, and goats' hair; **7]** tanned ram skins, dolphin skins, and acacia wood; **8]** oil for lighting; spices for the anointing oil and for the aromatic incense; **9]** lapis lazuli and other stones for setting, for the ephod and the breast-piece.

10] And let all among you who are skilled come and make all that the LORD has commanded: **11]** the Tabernacle, its tent and its covering, its clasps and its planks, its bars, its posts, and its sockets; **12]** the ark and its poles, the cover, and the curtain for the screen; **13]** the table, and its poles and all its utensils; and the bread of display; **14]** the lampstand for lighting, its furnishings and its lamps, and the oil for lighting; **15]** the altar of incense and its poles; the anointing oil and the aromatic incense; and the entrance screen for the entrance of the Tabernacle; **16]** the altar of burnt offering, its copper grating, its poles and all its furnishings; the laver and its stand; **17]** the hangings of the enclosure, its posts and its sockets, and the screen for the gate of the court; **18]** the pegs for the Tabernacle, the pegs for the enclosure,

---

35:3] *Throughout your settlements.* And not only during the building of the Tabernacle, to which the injunction primarily relates. A violation of the law is recorded in Num. 15:32 ff.

17] *Its posts and its sockets.* The Hebrew אֲדָנֶיהָ exhibits a change of gender from עַמֻּדָיו, which is an occasional stylistic device in the Bible; compare I Kings 19:11: רוּחַ גְּדוֹלָה וְחָזָק (instead of וַחֲזָקָה).

וַיָּבִיאוּ מַטֹּה אֶת־הַתְּכֵלֶת וְאֶת־הָאַרְגָּמָן אֶת־תּוֹלַעַת
הַשָּׁנִי וְאֶת־הַשֵּׁשׁ: וְכָל־הַנָּשִׁים אֲשֶׁר נָשָׂא לִבָּן אֹתָנָה
בְּחָכְמָה טָווּ אֶת־הָעִזִּים: וְהַנְּשִׂאִם הֵבִיאוּ אֵת אַבְנֵי
הַשֹּׁהַם וְאֵת אַבְנֵי הַמִּלֻּאִים לָאֵפוֹד וְלַחֹשֶׁן: וְאֶת־
הַבֹּשֶׂם וְאֶת־הַשָּׁמֶן לְמָאוֹר וּלְשֶׁמֶן הַמִּשְׁחָה וְלִקְטֹרֶת
הַסַּמִּים: כָּל־אִישׁ וְאִשָּׁה אֲשֶׁר נָדַב לִבָּם אֹתָם לְהָבִיא
לְכָל־הַמְּלָאכָה אֲשֶׁר צִוָּה יְהֹוָה לַעֲשׂוֹת בְּיַד־מֹשֶׁה
הֵבִיאוּ בְנֵי־יִשְׂרָאֵל נְדָבָה לַיהֹוָה: פ

ל וַיֹּאמֶר מֹשֶׁה אֶל־בְּנֵי יִשְׂרָאֵל רְאוּ קָרָא יְהֹוָה בְּשֵׁם
לא בְּצַלְאֵל בֶּן־אוּרִי בֶן־חוּר לְמַטֵּה יְהוּדָה: וַיְמַלֵּא
אֹתוֹ רוּחַ אֱלֹהִים בְּחָכְמָה בִּתְבוּנָה וּבְדַעַת וּבְכָל־
לב מְלָאכָה: וְלַחְשֹׁב מַחֲשָׁבֹת לַעֲשׂוֹת בַּזָּהָב וּבַכֶּסֶף
לג וּבַנְּחֹשֶׁת: וּבַחֲרֹשֶׁת אֶבֶן לְמַלֹּאת וּבַחֲרֹשֶׁת עֵץ

יט הַמִּשְׁכָּן וְאֶת־יְתֵדֹת הֶחָצֵר וְאֶת־מֵיתְרֵיהֶם: אֶת־בִּגְדֵי
הַשְּׂרָד לְשָׁרֵת בַּקֹּדֶשׁ אֶת־בִּגְדֵי הַקֹּדֶשׁ לְאַהֲרֹן
כ הַכֹּהֵן וְאֶת־בִּגְדֵי בָנָיו לְכַהֵן: וַיֵּצְאוּ כָּל־עֲדַת בְּנֵי
כא יִשְׂרָאֵל מִלִּפְנֵי מֹשֶׁה: וַיָּבֹאוּ כָּל־אִישׁ אֲשֶׁר־נְשָׂאוֹ לִבּוֹ
וְכֹל אֲשֶׁר נָדְבָה רוּחוֹ אֹתוֹ הֵבִיאוּ אֶת־תְּרוּמַת
יְהֹוָה לִמְלֶאכֶת אֹהֶל מוֹעֵד וּלְכָל־עֲבֹדָתוֹ וּלְבִגְדֵי
כב הַקֹּדֶשׁ: וַיָּבֹאוּ הָאֲנָשִׁים עַל־הַנָּשִׁים כֹּל נְדִיב לֵב
הֵבִיאוּ חָח וָנֶזֶם וְטַבַּעַת וְכוּמָז כָּל־כְּלִי זָהָב וְכָל־
כג אִישׁ אֲשֶׁר הֵנִיף תְּנוּפַת זָהָב לַיהֹוָה: וְכָל־אִישׁ
אֲשֶׁר־נִמְצָא אִתּוֹ תְּכֵלֶת וְאַרְגָּמָן וְתוֹלַעַת שָׁנִי וְשֵׁשׁ
וְעִזִּים וְעֹרֹת אֵילִם מְאָדָּמִים וְעֹרֹת תְּחָשִׁים הֵבִיאוּ:
כד כָּל־מֵרִים תְּרוּמַת כֶּסֶף וּנְחֹשֶׁת הֵבִיאוּ אֵת תְּרוּמַת
יְהֹוָה וְכֹל אֲשֶׁר נִמְצָא אִתּוֹ עֲצֵי שִׁטִּים לְכָל־מְלֶאכֶת
כה הָעֲבֹדָה הֵבִיאוּ: וְכָל־אִשָּׁה חַכְמַת־לֵב בְּיָדֶיהָ טָווּ

and their cords;   **19]** the service vestments for officiating in the sanctuary, the sacral vestments of Aaron the priest and the vestments of his sons for priestly service.

20] So the whole community of the Israelites left Moses' presence.   **21]** And everyone who excelled in ability and everyone whose spirit moved him came, bringing to the LORD his offering for the work of the Tent of Meeting and for all its service and for the sacral vestments.   **22]** Men and women, all whose hearts moved them, all who would make a wave-offering of gold to the LORD, came bringing brooches, earrings, rings, and pendants—gold objects of all kinds.   **23]** And everyone who had in his possession blue, purple, and crimson yarns, fine linen, goats' hair, tanned ram skins, and dolphin skins, brought them;   **24]** everyone who would make gifts of silver or copper brought them as gifts for the LORD; and everyone who had in his possession acacia wood for any work of the service, brought that.   **25]** And all the skilled women spun with their own hands, and brought what they had spun, in blue, purple, and crimson yarns, and in fine linen.   **26]** And all the women who excelled in that skill spun the goats' hair.   **27]** And the chieftains brought lapis lazuli and other stones for setting, for the ephod and for the breastpiece;   **28]** and spices and oil for lighting, for the anointing oil, and for the aromatic incense.   **29]** Thus the Israelites, all the men and women whose hearts moved them to bring anything for the work that the LORD, through Moses, had commanded to be done, brought it as a freewill offering to the LORD.

30] And Moses said to the Israelites: See, the LORD has singled out by name Bezalel, son of Uri son of Hur, of the tribe of Judah.   **31]** He has endowed him with a divine spirit of skill, ability, and knowledge in every kind of craft   **32]** and has inspired him to make designs for work in gold, silver, and copper,   **33]** to cut stones for setting and to carve wood—to work in

---

22] *Wave-offering of gold.* Meaning here "bring it with outstretched hands."

Brooches. Others, "nose rings."

Rings. טַבַּעַת (taba-at). The same term is used in the Jewish wedding vow.

Pendants. The meaning of the Hebrew is not certain.

כָּל־הַחֲכָמִים הָעֹשִׂים אֵת כָּל־מְלֶאכֶת הַקֹּדֶשׁ אִישׁ־ לַעֲשׂוֹת בְּכָל־מְלֶאכֶת מַחֲשָׁבֶת: וּלְהוֹרֹת נָתַן בְּלִבּוֹ: ל

אִישׁ מִמְּלַאכְתּוֹ אֲשֶׁר־הֵמָּה עֹשִׂים: וַיֹּאמְרוּ אֶל־מֹשֶׁה לה הוּא וְאָהֳלִיאָב בֶּן־אֲחִיסָמָךְ לְמַטֵּה־דָן: מִלֵּא אֹתָם לה

לֵאמֹר מַרְבִּים הָעָם לְהָבִיא מִדֵּי הָעֲבֹדָה לַמְּלָאכָה חָכְמַת־לֵב לַעֲשׂוֹת כָּל־מְלֶאכֶת חָרָשׁ וְחֹשֵׁב וְרֹקֵם

אֲשֶׁר־צִוָּה יְהוָֹה לַעֲשֹׂת אֹתָהּ: וַיְצַו מֹשֶׁה וַיַּעֲבִירוּ בַּתְּכֵלֶת וּבָאַרְגָּמָן בְּתוֹלַעַת הַשָּׁנִי וּבַשֵּׁשׁ וְאֹרֵג עֹשֵׂי

קוֹל בַּמַּחֲנֶה לֵאמֹר אִישׁ וְאִשָּׁה אַל־יַעֲשׂוּ־עוֹד מְלָאכָה כָּל־מְלָאכָה וְחֹשְׁבֵי מַחֲשָׁבֹת:

לִתְרוּמַת הַקֹּדֶשׁ וַיִּכָּלֵא הָעָם מֵהָבִיא: וְהַמְּלָאכָה וְעָשָׂה בְצַלְאֵל וְאָהֳלִיאָב וְכֹל אִישׁ חֲכַם־לֵב אֲשֶׁר א

הָיְתָה דַיָּם לְכָל־הַמְּלָאכָה לַעֲשׂוֹת אֹתָהּ וְהוֹתֵר: ס נָתַן יְהוָֹה חָכְמָה וּתְבוּנָה בָּהֵמָּה לָדַעַת לַעֲשֹׂת אֶת־

וַיַּעֲשׂוּ כָל־חֲכַם־לֵב בְּעֹשֵׂי הַמְּלָאכָה אֶת־הַמִּשְׁכָּן עֶשֶׂר ח כָּל־מְלֶאכֶת עֲבֹדַת הַקֹּדֶשׁ לְכֹל אֲשֶׁר־צִוָּה יְהוָֹה:

יְרִיעֹת שֵׁשׁ מָשְׁזָר וּתְכֵלֶת וְאַרְגָּמָן וְתֹלַעַת שָׁנִי וַיִּקְרָא מֹשֶׁה אֶל־בְּצַלְאֵל וְאֶל־אָהֳלִיאָב וְאֶל כָּל־ ב

כְּרֻבִים מַעֲשֵׂה חֹשֵׁב עָשָׂה אֹתָם: אֹרֶךְ הַיְרִיעָה ט אִישׁ חֲכַם־לֵב אֲשֶׁר נָתַן יְהוָֹה חָכְמָה בְּלִבּוֹ כֹּל

הָאַחַת שְׁמֹנֶה וְעֶשְׂרִים בָּאַמָּה וְרֹחַב אַרְבַּע בָּאַמָּה אֲשֶׁר נְשָׂאוֹ לִבּוֹ לְקָרְבָה אֶל־הַמְּלָאכָה לַעֲשֹׂת אֹתָהּ:

הַיְרִיעָה הָאֶחָת מִדָּה אַחַת לְכָל־הַיְרִיעֹת: וַיְחַבֵּר י וַיִּקְחוּ מִלִּפְנֵי מֹשֶׁה אֵת כָּל־הַתְּרוּמָה אֲשֶׁר הֵבִיאוּ ג

אֶת־חֲמֵשׁ הַיְרִיעֹת אַחַת אֶל־אֶחָת וְחָמֵשׁ יְרִיעֹת חִבַּר בְּנֵי יִשְׂרָאֵל לִמְלֶאכֶת עֲבֹדַת הַקֹּדֶשׁ לַעֲשֹׂת אֹתָהּ

וְהֵם הֵבִיאוּ אֵלָיו עוֹד נְדָבָה בַּבֹּקֶר בַּבֹּקֶר: וַיָּבֹאוּ ד

every kind of designer's craft—   34] and to give directions. He and Oholiab son of Ahisamach of the tribe of Dan   35] have been endowed with the skill to do any work—of the carver, the designer, the embroiderer in blue, purple, crimson yarns, and in fine linen, and of the weaver—as workers in all crafts and as makers of designs.   1] Let, then, Bezalel and Oholiab and all the skilled persons whom the LORD has endowed with skill and ability to perform expertly all the tasks connected with the service of the sanctuary, carry out all that the LORD has commanded.

2] Moses then called Bezalel and Oholiab, and every skilled person whom the LORD had endowed with skill, everyone who excelled in ability, to undertake the task and carry it out.   3] They took over from Moses all the gifts that the Israelites had brought, to carry out the tasks connected with the service of the sanctuary. But when these continued to bring freewill offerings morning after morning,   4] all the artisans who were engaged in the tasks of the sanctuary came, each from the task upon which he was engaged,   5] and said to Moses, "The people are bringing more than is needed for the tasks entailed in the work that the LORD has commanded to be done."   6] Moses thereupon had this proclamation made throughout the camp: "Let no man or woman make further effort toward gifts for the sanctuary!" So the people stopped bringing: 7] their efforts had been more than enough for all the tasks to be done.

8] Then all the skilled among those engaged in the work made the tabernacle of ten strips of cloth, which they made of fine twisted linen, blue, purple, and crimson yarns; into these they worked a design of cherubim.   9] The length of each cloth was twenty-eight cubits, and the width of each cloth was four cubits, all cloths having the same measurements.   10] They joined five of the cloths to one another, and they joined the other five cloths to one

36:1] This verse belongs to the preceding. When the division into chapters was made, the word וְעָשָׂה was probably taken to be in the past tense and assigned to the next chapter. It is, however, command (future).

יא אַחַת אֶל־אֶחָת: וַיַּעַשׂ לֻלְאֹת תְּכֵלֶת עַל שְׂפַת
הַיְרִיעָה הָאֶחָת מִקָּצָה בַּמַּחְבָּרֶת כֵּן עָשָׂה בִּשְׂפַת
יב הַיְרִיעָה הַקִּיצוֹנָה בַּמַּחְבֶּרֶת הַשֵּׁנִית: חֲמִשִּׁים לֻלָאֹת
עָשָׂה בַּיְרִיעָה הָאֶחָת וַחֲמִשִּׁים לֻלָאֹת עָשָׂה בִּקְצֵה
הַיְרִיעָה אֲשֶׁר בַּמַּחְבֶּרֶת הַשֵּׁנִית מַקְבִּילֹת הַלֻּלָאֹת
יג אַחַת אֶל־אֶחָת: וַיַּעַשׂ חֲמִשִּׁים קַרְסֵי זָהָב וַיְחַבֵּר אֶת־
הַיְרִיעֹת אַחַת אֶל־אַחַת בַּקְּרָסִים וַיְהִי הַמִּשְׁכָּן אֶחָד: פ
יד וַיַּעַשׂ יְרִיעֹת עִזִּים לְאֹהֶל עַל־הַמִּשְׁכָּן עַשְׁתֵּי־עֶשְׂרֵה
טו יְרִיעֹת עָשָׂה אֹתָם: אֹרֶךְ הַיְרִיעָה הָאֶחָת שְׁלֹשִׁים
בָּאַמָּה וְאַרְבַּע אַמּוֹת רֹחַב הַיְרִיעָה הָאֶחָת מִדָּה
טז אַחַת לְעַשְׁתֵּי עֶשְׂרֵה יְרִיעֹת: וַיְחַבֵּר אֶת־חֲמֵשׁ
יז הַיְרִיעֹת לְבָד וְאֶת־שֵׁשׁ הַיְרִיעֹת לְבָד: וַיַּעַשׂ לֻלָאֹת
חֲמִשִּׁים עַל שְׂפַת הַיְרִיעָה הַקִּיצֹנָה בַּמַּחְבָּרֶת
וַחֲמִשִּׁים לֻלָאֹת עָשָׂה עַל־שְׂפַת הַיְרִיעָה הַחֹבָרֶת

יח הַשֵּׁנִית: וַיַּעַשׂ קַרְסֵי נְחֹשֶׁת חֲמִשִּׁים לְחַבֵּר אֶת־הָאֹהֶל
יט לִהְיֹת אֶחָד: וַיַּעַשׂ מִכְסֶה לָאֹהֶל עֹרֹת אֵילִם
כ מְאָדָּמִים וּמִכְסֵה עֹרֹת תְּחָשִׁים מִלְמָעְלָה: ס וַיַּעַשׂ
אֶת־הַקְּרָשִׁים לַמִּשְׁכָּן עֲצֵי שִׁטִּים עֹמְדִים: עֶשֶׂר אַמֹּת
כא אֹרֶךְ הַקֶּרֶשׁ וְאַמָּה וַחֲצִי הָאַמָּה רֹחַב הַקֶּרֶשׁ הָאֶחָד:
כב שְׁתֵּי יָדֹת לַקֶּרֶשׁ הָאֶחָד מְשֻׁלָּבֹת אַחַת אֶל־אֶחָת כֵּן
עָשָׂה לְכֹל קַרְשֵׁי הַמִּשְׁכָּן: וַיַּעַשׂ אֶת־הַקְּרָשִׁים לַמִּשְׁכָּן
כג עֶשְׂרִים קְרָשִׁים לִפְאַת נֶגֶב תֵּימָנָה: וְאַרְבָּעִים אַדְנֵי־
כד כֶסֶף עָשָׂה תַּחַת עֶשְׂרִים הַקְּרָשִׁים שְׁנֵי אֲדָנִים
תַּחַת־הַקֶּרֶשׁ הָאֶחָד לִשְׁתֵּי יְדֹתָיו וּשְׁנֵי אֲדָנִים תַּחַת־
כה הַקֶּרֶשׁ הָאֶחָד לִשְׁתֵּי יְדֹתָיו: וּלְצֶלַע הַמִּשְׁכָּן הַשֵּׁנִית
כו לִפְאַת צָפוֹן עָשָׂה עֶשְׂרִים קְרָשִׁים: וְאַרְבָּעִים אַדְנֵיהֶם
כֶּסֶף שְׁנֵי אֲדָנִים תַּחַת הַקֶּרֶשׁ הָאֶחָד וּשְׁנֵי אֲדָנִים
כז תַּחַת הַקֶּרֶשׁ הָאֶחָד: וּלְיַרְכְּתֵי הַמִּשְׁכָּן יָמָּה עָשָׂה

another.   **11]** They made loops of blue wool on the edge of the outermost cloth of the one set, and did the same on the edge of the outermost cloth of the other set: **12]** they made fifty loops on the one cloth, and they made fifty loops on the edge of the end cloth of the other set, the loops being opposite one another.   **13]** And they made fifty gold clasps and coupled the units to one another with the clasps, so that the tabernacle became one whole.

14] They made cloths of goats' hair for a tent over the tabernacle; they made the cloths eleven in number.   **15]** The length of each cloth was thirty cubits, and the width of each cloth was four cubits, the eleven cloths having the same measurements.   **16]** They joined five of the cloths by themselves, and the other six cloths by themselves.   **17]** They made fifty loops on the edge of the outermost cloth of the one set, and they made fifty loops on the edge of the end cloth of the other set.   **18]** They made fifty copper clasps to couple the tent together so that it might become one whole.   **19]** And they made a covering of tanned ram skins for the tent, and a covering of dolphin skins above.

20] They made the planks for the Tabernacle of acacia wood, upright.   **21]** The length of each plank was ten cubits, the width of each plank a cubit and a half.   **22]** Each plank had two tenons, parallel to each other; they did the same with all the planks of the Tabernacle.   **23]** Of the planks of the Tabernacle, they made twenty planks for the south side,   **24]** making forty silver sockets under the twenty planks, two sockets under one plank for its two tenons and two sockets under each following plank for its two tenons;   **25]** and for the other side wall of the Tabernacle, the north side, twenty planks;   **26]** with their forty silver sockets, two sockets under one plank and two sockets under each following plank.   **27]** And for the rear of the

20] *The planks.* See 26:15 ff.

כח שִׁשָּׁה קְרָשִׁים: וּשְׁנֵי קְרָשִׁים עָשָׂה לִמְקֻצְעֹת הַמִּשְׁכָּן
כט בַּיַּרְכָתָיִם: וְהָיוּ תוֹאֲמִם מִלְּמַטָּה וְיַחְדָּו יִהְיוּ תַמִּים
אֶל־רֹאשׁוֹ אֶל־הַטַּבַּעַת הָאֶחָת כֵּן עָשָׂה לִשְׁנֵיהֶם
ל לִשְׁנֵי הַמִּקְצֹעֹת: וְהָיוּ שְׁמֹנָה קְרָשִׁים וְאַדְנֵיהֶם כֶּסֶף
שִׁשָּׁה עָשָׂר אֲדָנִים שְׁנֵי אֲדָנִים שְׁנֵי אֲדָנִים תַּחַת
לא הַקֶּרֶשׁ הָאֶחָד: וַיַּעַשׂ בְּרִיחֵי עֲצֵי שִׁטִּים חֲמִשָּׁה
לב לְקַרְשֵׁי צֶלַע־הַמִּשְׁכָּן הָאֶחָת: וַחֲמִשָּׁה בְרִיחִם לְקַרְשֵׁי
צֶלַע־הַמִּשְׁכָּן הַשֵּׁנִית וַחֲמִשָּׁה בְרִיחִם לְקַרְשֵׁי הַמִּשְׁכָּן
לג לַיַּרְכָתַיִם יָמָּה: וַיַּעַשׂ אֶת־הַבְּרִיחַ הַתִּיכֹן לִבְרֹחַ
לד בְּתוֹךְ הַקְּרָשִׁים מִן־הַקָּצֶה אֶל־הַקָּצֶה: וְאֶת־הַקְּרָשִׁים
צִפָּה זָהָב וְאֶת־טַבְּעֹתָם עָשָׂה זָהָב בָּתִּים לַבְּרִיחִם
לה וַיְצַף אֶת־הַבְּרִיחִם זָהָב: וַיַּעַשׂ אֶת־הַפָּרֹכֶת תְּכֵלֶת
וְאַרְגָּמָן וְתוֹלַעַת שָׁנִי וְשֵׁשׁ מָשְׁזָר מַעֲשֵׂה חֹשֵׁב עָשָׂה
לו אֹתָהּ כְּרֻבִים: וַיַּעַשׂ לָהּ אַרְבָּעָה עַמּוּדֵי שִׁטִּים

וַיְצַפֵּם זָהָב וָוֵיהֶם זָהָב וַיִּצֹק לָהֶם אַרְבָּעָה אַדְנֵי־
לז כָסֶף: וַיַּעַשׂ מָסָךְ לְפֶתַח הָאֹהֶל תְּכֵלֶת וְאַרְגָּמָן
לח וְתוֹלַעַת שָׁנִי וְשֵׁשׁ מָשְׁזָר מַעֲשֵׂה רֹקֵם: וְאֶת־עַמּוּדָיו
חֲמִשָּׁה וְאֶת־וָוֵיהֶם וְצִפָּה רָאשֵׁיהֶם וַחֲשֻׁקֵיהֶם זָהָב
וְאַדְנֵיהֶם חֲמִשָּׁה נְחֹשֶׁת:
א וַיַּעַשׂ בְּצַלְאֵל אֶת־הָאָרֹן עֲצֵי שִׁטִּים אַמָּתַיִם וָחֵצִי
ב אָרְכּוֹ וְאַמָּה וָחֵצִי רָחְבּוֹ וְאַמָּה וָחֵצִי קֹמָתוֹ: וַיְצַפֵּהוּ
זָהָב טָהוֹר מִבַּיִת וּמִחוּץ וַיַּעַשׂ לוֹ זֵר זָהָב סָבִיב:
ג וַיִּצֹק לוֹ אַרְבַּע טַבְּעֹת זָהָב עַל אַרְבַּע פַּעֲמֹתָיו
וּשְׁתֵּי טַבָּעֹת עַל־צַלְעוֹ הָאֶחָת וּשְׁתֵּי טַבָּעֹת עַל־
ד צַלְעוֹ הַשֵּׁנִית: וַיַּעַשׂ בַּדֵּי עֲצֵי שִׁטִּים וַיְצַף אֹתָם
ה זָהָב: וַיָּבֵא אֶת־הַבַּדִּים בַּטַּבָּעֹת עַל צַלְעֹת הָאָרֹן
לָשֵׂאת אֶת־הָאָרֹן: וַיַּעַשׂ כַּפֹּרֶת זָהָב טָהוֹר אַמָּתַיִם
ו וָחֵצִי אָרְכָּהּ וְאַמָּה וָחֵצִי רָחְבָּהּ: וַיַּעַשׂ שְׁנֵי כְרֻבִים

Tabernacle, to the west, they made six planks; 28] and they made two planks for the corners of the Tabernacle at the rear. 29] They matched at the bottom, but terminated as one at the top into one ring; they did so with both of them at the two corners. 30] Thus there were eight planks with their sockets of silver: sixteen sockets, two under each plank.

31] They made bars of acacia wood, five for the planks of the one side wall of the Tabernacle, 32] five bars for the planks of the other side wall of the Tabernacle, and five bars for the planks of the wall of the Tabernacle at the rear, to the west; 33] they made the center bar to run, halfway up the planks, from end to end. 34] They overlaid the planks with gold, and made their rings of gold, as holders for the bars; and they overlaid the bars with gold.

35] They made the curtain of blue, purple, and crimson yarns, and fine twisted linen, working into it a design of cherubim. 36] They made for it four posts of acacia wood and overlaid them with gold, with their hooks of gold; and they cast for them four silver sockets.

37] They made the screen for the entrance of the Tent, of blue, purple, and crimson yarns, and fine twisted linen, done in embroidery; 38] and five posts for it with their hooks. They overlaid their tops and their bands with gold; but the five sockets were of copper.

1] Bezalel made the ark of acacia wood, two and a half cubits long, a cubit and a half wide, and a cubit and a half high. 2] He overlaid it with pure gold, inside and out; and he made a gold molding for it round about. 3] He cast four gold rings for it, for its four feet: two rings on one of its side walls and two rings on the other. 4] He made poles of acacia wood, overlaid them with gold, 5] and inserted the poles into the rings on the side walls of the ark for carrying the ark.

6] He made a cover of pure gold, two and a half cubits long and a cubit and a half wide.

35] *The curtain.* See 26:31 for curtain and screen.
37:1] *Bezalel made.* His connection with the mak-

ing of the ark is emphasized [5]. For the ark see 25:10 ff.

זָהָב מִקְשָׁה עָשָׂה אֹתָם מִשְּׁנֵי קְצוֹת הַכַּפֹּרֶת:
אֶת־הַכֵּלִים אֲשֶׁר עַל־הַשֻּׁלְחָן אֶת־קְעָרֹתָיו וְאֶת־כַּפֹּתָיו

ח כְּרוּב־אֶחָד מִקָּצָה מִזֶּה וּכְרוּב־אֶחָד מִקָּצָה מִזֶּה מִן־
וְאֵת מְנַקִּיֹּתָיו וְאֶת־הַקְּשָׂוֹת אֲשֶׁר יֻסַּךְ בָּהֵן זָהָב

ט הַכַּפֹּרֶת עָשָׂה אֶת־הַכְּרֻבִים מִשְּׁנֵי קְצוֹתָו: וַיִּהְיוּ
טָהוֹר: פ

הַכְּרֻבִים פֹּרְשֵׂי כְנָפַיִם לְמַעְלָה סֹכְכִים בְּכַנְפֵיהֶם
יז וַיַּעַשׂ אֶת־הַמְּנֹרָה זָהָב טָהוֹר מִקְשָׁה עָשָׂה אֶת־הַמְּנֹרָה

עַל־הַכַּפֹּרֶת וּפְנֵיהֶם אִישׁ אֶל־אָחִיו אֶל־הַכַּפֹּרֶת הָיוּ
יְרֵכָהּ וְקָנָהּ גְּבִיעֶיהָ כַּפְתֹּרֶיהָ וּפְרָחֶיהָ מִמֶּנָּה הָיוּ:

פְּנֵי הַכְּרֻבִים: פ
יח וְשִׁשָּׁה קָנִים יֹצְאִים מִצִּדֶּיהָ שְׁלֹשָׁה קְנֵי מְנֹרָה מִצִּדָּהּ

י וַיַּעַשׂ אֶת־הַשֻּׁלְחָן עֲצֵי שִׁטִּים אַמָּתַיִם אָרְכּוֹ וְאַמָּה
הָאֶחָד וּשְׁלֹשָׁה קְנֵי מְנֹרָה מִצִּדָּהּ הַשֵּׁנִי: שְׁלֹשָׁה

יא רָחְבּוֹ וְאַמָּה וָחֵצִי קֹמָתוֹ: וַיְצַף אֹתוֹ זָהָב טָהוֹר וַיַּעַשׂ
יט גְבִעִים מְשֻׁקָּדִים בַּקָּנֶה הָאֶחָד כַּפְתֹּר וָפֶרַח וּשְׁלֹשָׁה

יב לוֹ זֵר זָהָב סָבִיב: וַיַּעַשׂ לוֹ מִסְגֶּרֶת טֹפַח סָבִיב וַיַּעַשׂ
גְבִעִים מְשֻׁקָּדִים בְּקָנֶה אֶחָד כַּפְתֹּר וָפָרַח כֵּן לְשֵׁשֶׁת

יג זֵר־זָהָב לְמִסְגַּרְתּוֹ סָבִיב: וַיִּצֹק לוֹ אַרְבַּע טַבְּעֹת
כ הַקָּנִים הַיֹּצְאִים מִן־הַמְּנֹרָה: וּבַמְּנֹרָה אַרְבָּעָה גְבִעִים

זָהָב וַיִּתֵּן אֶת־הַטַּבָּעֹת עַל אַרְבַּע הַפֵּאֹת אֲשֶׁר
מְשֻׁקָּדִים כַּפְתֹּרֶיהָ וּפְרָחֶיהָ: וְכַפְתֹּר תַּחַת שְׁנֵי הַקָּנִים

יד לְאַרְבַּע רַגְלָיו: לְעֻמַּת הַמִּסְגֶּרֶת הָיוּ הַטַּבָּעֹת בָּתִּים
כא מִמֶּנָּה וְכַפְתֹּר תַּחַת שְׁנֵי הַקָּנִים מִמֶּנָּה וְכַפְתֹּר תַּחַת־

טו לַבַּדִּים לָשֵׂאת אֶת־הַשֻּׁלְחָן: וַיַּעַשׂ אֶת־הַבַּדִּים עֲצֵי
שְׁנֵי הַקָּנִים מִמֶּנָּה לְשֵׁשֶׁת הַקָּנִים הַיֹּצְאִים מִמֶּנָּה:

טז שִׁטִּים וַיְצַף אֹתָם זָהָב לָשֵׂאת אֶת־הַשֻּׁלְחָן: וַיַּעַשׂ
כב כַּפְתֹּרֵיהֶם וּקְנֹתָם מִמֶּנָּה הָיוּ כֻּלָּהּ מִקְשָׁה אַחַת

ᵃ ח קצותיו קרי:

7] He made two cherubim of gold; he made them of hammered work, at the two ends of the cover: **8]** one cherub at one end and the other cherub at the other end; he made the cherubim of one piece with the cover, at its two ends. **9]** The cherubim had their wings spread out above, shielding the cover with their wings. They faced each other; the faces of the cherubim were turned toward the cover.

10] He made the table of acacia wood, two cubits long, one cubit wide, and a cubit and a half high; **11]** he overlaid it with pure gold and made a gold molding around it. **12]** He made a rim of a hand's breadth around it and made a gold molding for its rim round about. **13]** He cast four gold rings for it and attached the rings to the four corners at its four legs. **14]** The rings were next to the rim, as holders for the poles to carry the table. **15]** He made the poles of acacia wood for carrying the table, and overlaid them with gold. **16]** The utensils that were to be upon the table—its bowls, ladles, jugs, and jars with which to offer libations—he made of pure gold.

17] He made the lampstand of pure gold. He made the lampstand—its base and its shaft—of hammered work; its cups, calyxes, and petals were of one piece with it. **18]** Six branches issued from its sides: three branches from one side of the lampstand, and three branches from the other side of the lampstand. **19]** There were three cups shaped like almond-blossoms, each with calyx and petals, on one branch; and there were three cups shaped like almond-blossoms, each with calyx and petals, on the next branch; so for all six branches issuing from the lampstand. **20]** On the lampstand itself there were four cups shaped like almond-blossoms, each with calyx and petals: **21]** a calyx, of one piece with it, under a pair of branches; and a calyx, of one piece with it, under the second pair of branches; and a calyx, of one piece with it, under the last pair of branches; so for all six branches issuing from it. **22]** Their calyxes and their stems were of one piece with it, the whole of it a single

10] *The table.* See 25:23 ff.   **17]** *The lampstand.* See 25:31 ff.

כג זָהָב טָהוֹר: וַיַּעַשׂ אֶת־נֵרֹתֶיהָ שִׁבְעָה וּמַלְקָחֶיהָ

כד וּמַחְתֹּתֶיהָ זָהָב טָהוֹר: כִּכָּר זָהָב טָהוֹר עָשָׂה אֹתָהּ

וְאֵת כָּל־כֵּלֶיהָ:   פ

כה וַיַּעַשׂ אֶת־מִזְבַּח הַקְּטֹרֶת עֲצֵי שִׁטִּים אַמָּה אָרְכּוֹ

וְאַמָּה רָחְבּוֹ רָבוּעַ וְאַמָּתַיִם קֹמָתוֹ מִמֶּנּוּ הָיוּ קַרְנֹתָיו:

כו וַיְצַף אֹתוֹ זָהָב טָהוֹר אֶת־גַּגּוֹ וְאֶת־קִירֹתָיו סָבִיב

כז וְאֶת־קַרְנֹתָיו וַיַּעַשׂ לוֹ זֵר זָהָב סָבִיב: וּשְׁתֵּי טַבְּעֹת

זָהָב עָשָׂה־לוֹ מִתַּחַת לְזֵרוֹ עַל שְׁתֵּי צַלְעֹתָיו עַל

שְׁנֵי צִדָּיו לְבָתִּים לְבַדִּים לָשֵׂאת אֹתוֹ בָּהֶם:

כח וַיַּעַשׂ אֶת־הַבַּדִּים עֲצֵי שִׁטִּים וַיְצַף אֹתָם זָהָב: כט וַיַּעַשׂ

אֶת־שֶׁמֶן הַמִּשְׁחָה קֹדֶשׁ וְאֶת־קְטֹרֶת הַסַּמִּים טָהוֹר

מַעֲשֵׂה רֹקֵחַ:   ס

א וַיַּעַשׂ אֶת־מִזְבַּח הָעֹלָה עֲצֵי שִׁטִּים חָמֵשׁ אַמּוֹת

אָרְכּוֹ וְחָמֵשׁ אַמּוֹת רָחְבּוֹ רָבוּעַ וְשָׁלֹשׁ אַמּוֹת קֹמָתוֹ:

ב וַיַּעַשׂ קַרְנֹתָיו עַל אַרְבַּע פִּנֹּתָיו מִמֶּנּוּ הָיוּ קַרְנֹתָיו

ג וַיְצַף אֹתוֹ נְחֹשֶׁת: וַיַּעַשׂ אֶת־כָּל־כְּלֵי הַמִּזְבֵּחַ אֶת־

הַסִּירֹת וְאֶת־הַיָּעִים וְאֶת־הַמִּזְרָקֹת אֶת־הַמִּזְלָגֹת וְאֶת־

ד הַמַּחְתֹּת כָּל־כֵּלָיו עָשָׂה נְחֹשֶׁת: וַיַּעַשׂ לַמִּזְבֵּחַ מִכְבָּר

מַעֲשֵׂה רֶשֶׁת נְחֹשֶׁת תַּחַת כַּרְכֻּבּוֹ מִלְמַטָּה עַד־חֶצְיוֹ:

ה וַיִּצֹק אַרְבַּע טַבָּעֹת בְּאַרְבַּע הַקְּצָוֹת לְמִכְבַּר

ו הַנְּחֹשֶׁת בָּתִּים לַבַּדִּים: וַיַּעַשׂ אֶת־הַבַּדִּים עֲצֵי שִׁטִּים

ז וַיְצַף אֹתָם נְחֹשֶׁת: וַיָּבֵא אֶת־הַבַּדִּים בַּטַּבָּעֹת עַל

צַלְעֹת הַמִּזְבֵּחַ לָשֵׂאת אֹתוֹ בָּהֶם נְבוּב לֻחֹת עָשָׂה

ח אֹתוֹ:   ס   וַיַּעַשׂ אֵת הַכִּיּוֹר נְחֹשֶׁת וְאֵת כַּנּוֹ נְחֹשֶׁת

hammered piece of pure gold.   **23]** He made its seven lamps, its tongs, and its fire pans, of pure gold.   **24]** He made it and all its furnishings out of a talent of pure gold.

25] He made the incense altar of acacia wood, a cubit long and a cubit wide—square—and two cubits high; its horns were of one piece with it.   **26]** He overlaid it with pure gold: its top, its sides round about, and its horns; and he made a gold molding for it round about.   **27]** He made two gold rings for it under its molding, on its two walls—on opposite sides—as holders for the poles with which to carry it.   **28]** He made the poles of acacia wood, and overlaid them with gold.   **29]** He prepared the sacred anointing oil and the pure aromatic incense, expertly blended.

1] He made the altar for burnt offering of acacia wood, five cubits long and five cubits wide—square—and three cubits high.   **2]** He made horns for it on its four corners, the horns being of one piece with it; and he overlaid it with copper.   **3]** He made all the utensils of the altar—the pails, the scrapers, the basins, the flesh hooks, and the fire pans; he made all these utensils of copper.   **4]** He made for the altar a grating of meshwork in copper, extending below, under its ledge, to its middle.   **5]** He cast four rings, at the four corners of the copper grating, as holders for the poles.   **6]** He made the poles of acacia wood and overlaid them with copper;   **7]** and he inserted the poles into the rings on the side walls of the altar, to carry it by them. He made it hollow, of boards.

8] He made the laver of copper and its stand of copper, from the mirrors of the women who

---

25] *The incense altar.* See 30:1 ff. This is omitted in the Septuagint.

38:1] *The altar for burnt offering.* See 27:1 ff.

8] *The laver.* See 30:17 ff.

From the mirrors of the women. The introduction of this information is obscure, especially the words "who performed tasks." The Hebrew does not actually use the term "women" explicitly; the translation is derived from the feminine forms מַרְאֹת הַצֹּבְאֹת, which some render as "women arrayed" (for a sacred task). In I Sam. 2:22 it is reported that the priest Eli's sons acquired a bad reputation by sleeping with women "who performed tasks."

The task of these women is illumined by an ancient Near Eastern brick inscription of Tepti-

בְּמַרְאֹת֙ הַצֹּ֣בְאֹ֔ת אֲשֶׁ֣ר צָֽבְא֔וּ פֶּ֖תַח אֹ֥הֶל מוֹעֵֽד: ס

הֶֽחָצֵ֞ר קְלָעִ֣ים חֲמֵ֣שׁ עֶשְׂרֵ֥ה אַמָּ֛ה עַמֻּֽדֵיהֶ֖ם שְׁלֹשָׁ֑ה

ט וַיַּ֖עַשׂ אֶת־הֶֽחָצֵ֑ר לִפְאַ֣ת ׀ נֶ֣גֶב תֵּימָ֗נָה קַלְעֵ֤י הֶֽחָצֵר֙

וְאַדְנֵיהֶ֖ם שְׁלֹשָׁ֑ה כָּל־קַלְעֵ֧י הֶֽחָצֵ֛ר סָבִ֖יב שֵׁ֥שׁ מָשְׁזָֽר:

שֵׁ֣שׁ מָשְׁזָ֔ר מֵאָ֖ה בָּֽאַמָּֽה: עַמּֽוּדֵיהֶ֣ם עֶשְׂרִ֔ים וְאַדְנֵיהֶ֖ם

יח וְהָֽאֲדָנִ֣ים לָֽעַמֻּדִים֮ נְחֹשֶׁת֒ וָוֵ֨י הָֽעַמּוּדִ֜ים וַֽחֲשֻֽׁקֵיהֶ֣ם

יא עֶשְׂרִ֖ים נְחֹ֑שֶׁת וָוֵ֧י הָֽעַמּוּדִ֛ים וַֽחֲשֻֽׁקֵיהֶ֖ם כָּ֑סֶף וְלִפְאַ֤ת

כֶּ֗סֶף וְצִפּ֤וּי רָֽאשֵׁיהֶם֙ כֶּ֔סֶף וְהֵם֙ מְחֻשָּׁקִ֣ים כֶּ֔סֶף

צָפוֹן֙ מֵאָ֣ה בָֽאַמָּ֔ה עַמּֽוּדֵיהֶ֣ם עֶשְׂרִ֔ים וְאַדְנֵיהֶ֛ם

יח כֹּ֖ל עַמֻּדֵ֥י הֶֽחָצֵֽר: וּמָסַ֞ךְ שַׁ֤עַר הֶֽחָצֵר֙ מַֽעֲשֵׂ֣ה

עֶשְׂרִ֖ים נְחֹ֑שֶׁת וָוֵ֧י הָֽעַמּוּדִ֛ים וַֽחֲשֻֽׁקֵיהֶ֖ם כָּֽסֶף:

רֹקֵ֔ם תְּכֵ֧לֶת וְאַרְגָּמָ֛ן וְתוֹלַ֥עַת שָׁנִ֖י וְשֵׁ֣שׁ מָשְׁזָ֑ר

יב וְלִפְאַת־יָם֙ קְלָעִים֙ חֲמִשִּׁ֣ים בָּֽאַמָּ֔ה עַמּֽוּדֵיהֶ֣ם

וְעֶשְׂרִ֤ים אַמָּה֙ אֹ֔רֶךְ וְקוֹמָ֤ה בְרֹ֨חַב֙ חָמֵ֣שׁ אַמּ֔וֹת

עֲשָׂרָ֔ה וְאַדְנֵיהֶ֖ם עֲשָׂרָ֑ה וָוֵ֥י הָֽעַמֻּדִ֖ים וַֽחֲשֻֽׁקֵיהֶ֖ם

לְעֻמַּ֖ת קַלְעֵ֣י הֶֽחָצֵ֑ר: וְעַמֻּֽדֵיהֶ֣ם אַרְבָּעָ֔ה וְאַדְנֵיהֶ֖ם

כָּֽסֶף: יג וְלִפְאַ֛ת קֵ֥דְמָה מִזְרָ֖חָה חֲמִשִּׁ֥ים אַמָּֽה: יד קְלָעִ֞ים

אַרְבָּעָה֙ נְחֹ֔שֶׁת וָֽוֵיהֶ֣ם כֶּ֔סֶף וְצִפּ֧וּי רָֽאשֵׁיהֶ֛ם וַֽחֲשֻֽׁקֵיהֶ֖ם

חֲמֵֽשׁ־עֶשְׂרֵ֥ה אַמָּ֖ה אֶל־הַכָּתֵ֑ף עַמּֽוּדֵיהֶ֣ם שְׁלֹשָׁ֔ה

כָּֽסֶף: כ וְכָל־הַיְתֵדֹ֞ת לַמִּשְׁכָּ֧ן וְלֶֽחָצֵ֛ר סָבִ֖יב נְחֹֽשֶׁת:

וְאַדְנֵיהֶ֖ם שְׁלֹשָֽׁה: טו וְלַכָּתֵ֣ף הַשֵּׁנִ֗ית מִזֶּ֤ה וּמִזֶּה֙ לְשַׁ֣עַר

Haftarah Vayakhel, p. 726

performed tasks at the entrance of the Tent of Meeting.

9] He made the enclosure:

On the south side, a hundred cubits of hangings of fine twisted linen for the enclosure— **10]** with their twenty posts and their twenty sockets of copper, the hooks and bands of the posts being silver.

11] On the north side, a hundred cubits—with their twenty posts and their twenty sockets of copper, the hooks and bands of the posts being silver.

12] On the west side, fifty cubits of hangings—with their ten posts and their ten sockets, the hooks and bands of the posts being silver.

13] And on the front side, to the east, fifty cubits: **14]** fifteen cubits of hangings on the one flank, with their three posts and their three sockets, **15]** and fifteen cubits of hangings on the other flank—on each side of the gate of the enclosure—with their three posts and their three sockets.

16] All the hangings around the enclosure were of fine twisted linen. **17]** The sockets for the posts were of copper, the hooks and bands of the posts were of silver, the overlay of their tops was of silver; all the posts of the enclosure were banded with silver.— **18]** The screen of the gate of the enclosure, done in embroidery, was of blue, purple, and crimson yarns, and fine twisted linen. It was twenty cubits long. Its height—or width—was five cubits, like that of the hangings of the enclosure. **19]** The posts were four; their four sockets were of copper, their hooks of silver; and the overlay of their tops was of silver, as were also their bands.— **20]** All the pegs of the Tabernacle and of the enclosure round about were of copper.

ahar of Susa. It tells of four women as guards at the sanctuary, whose task it also was to pray at the foot of certain statues [6].

Mirrors were probably made of burnished copper and were fairly precious; hence they represented an extra offering.

9] *The enclosure.* This repeats in substance 27:9 ff.

Kindle No Fire on the Sabbath

Fire, says one aggadah, was created by God on the second day; and another, that after the first Sabbath the Creator gave Adam the knowledge to rub two stones together and thereby to ignite a spark [7]. These stories of God's connection with fire reflect man's primal marvel over the existence and potency of fire, a sentiment that was universal and was reflected in mythologies the world over. Fire was generally considered a phenomenon of divine origin and dimension.

The tradition that God was often beheld in fiery manifestations can therefore not be surprising. Abraham saw Him in a vision of smoking oven and flaming torch; Moses beheld Him at the burning bush; and to Israel He appeared at Sinai with the mountain aflame, or in a pillar of fire [8]. The Tabernacle featured the perpetual fire as a symbol of this mysterious relationship. Divine fire could be destructive also, as in the stories of the catastrophe enveloping Sodom, the company of Korah, and the sons of Aaron; and God's wrath was compared to fire [9].

The reasons for the biblical prohibition of kindling a fire on the Sabbath are not clear. It is doubtful that it was done to prevent onerous labor, for the rubbing of sticks together for the making of fire (which was one of the methods in use)[1] could hardly classify as labor in the way the word was then understood. Perhaps it related to the connection which the Divine Presence was believed to have had with fire, and on Sabbaths and festive days God was honored with fire in the Tabernacle and, later, in the Temple. We may therefore have here an early attempt to centralize worship to some degree; and thus one can understand, as the Rabbis did

also, the prohibition of such fire to apply only "throughout your [private] settlements," but not to the sanctuary proper [10].

The prohibition is differently explained by those who accept the "Kenite hypothesis" (which suggests that Moses' religion had a special relation to an itinerant tribe of smiths called Kenites). Fire was prominently used in their work, and therefore a prohibition to work on the Sabbath would have been highlighted by a special notation not to kindle a fire on that day [11].

In the subsequent development of Jewish law the use of fire that had been kindled before the Sabbath was allowed to a limited degree on the Sabbath day (so the Pharisees, in contrast to the Sadducees and, later, the Karaites who interpreted the law more strictly); and cooking was permitted on holy days when they did not fall on the Sabbath [12]. In modern times, smoking (prohibited on the Sabbath but allowed on fesitvals) often became a visible distinction between traditional Jews and others who, like Reform Jews, no longer felt such Sabbath laws to be applicable. Contemporary halachah rules that lighting by means of electricity is included in the intent of the biblical prohibition.

Bezalel—On Art in Judaism

The meticulous and loving attention that the Torah gives to the construction of the Tabernacle is probably a combination of ancient traditions and later projections. Both accord the practical arts an honored place, which is emphasized by the names of the chief artist and his assistant, Bezalel (meaning "in the shadow of God") and Oholiab (meaning "father's tent"), for their work was considered to be inspired. The account pro-

---

[1] The person who was punished for gathering sticks on the Sabbath probably gathered them in order to make fire, Num. 15:32 f.; see also I Kings 17:12.

vides an image of a nation in pursuit of artistic excellence, although in desert days Israel's creativity in this respect could probably not express itself [13].

To be sure, the models for such creativity were readily at hand, for the nations nearby developed the arts to a significant degree. This was true especially for the Egyptians and Mesopotamians whose paintings, sculptures, and handicrafts had reached a high level of artistry. The Israelites doubtless did learn much from them, and therefore the weaving and sculpturing skills required for the appurtenances of the sanctuary were likely to be found in their own midst. The fact that Solomon went to the Phoenicians for his top artist in the building of the Temple did not necessarily demean the skill of the Israelites, any more than today the importation of an architect or sculptor for a special task would be a general judgment on homegrown talent. Still, despite their own capacities and their continued contacts with the arts of other nations, especially the Greeks later on, the Israelites never made the fine arts their own field of particular competence. The prohibition against the religious representation of figures in the second commandment probably acted as a considerable brake. For a long time religious worship was the major artistic focus for many other cultures, and bereft of this major focus Israelite art was severely circumscribed. As time went on, the negative reaction to an idolatrous and then to the Christian environment further restricted all representational creativity, and in the Middle Ages great poverty and severe isolation served as additional restraining factors. Although at times vigorous attempts had been made to encourage the visual arts and adapt them to the Jewish milieu—numerous examples from the Greek period show the extent of these attempts[2]— it was not until modern times, when the opportunities for artistic creativity became once more available, that Jews participated fully in these ancient endeavors. To this day, however, there is continued resistance to all representational art forms among traditional Jews.

In sum, the oft-heard belief that the Jewish people leaned toward the auditive rather than the visual faculty has some foundation in history. It was founded not on innate capacity but on a combination of religious, social, and economic circumstances. Its result was an emphasis on the inner world, an exaltation of ethics over esthetics, which for many centuries was a hallmark of Jewish existence but which is now in the process of attenuation. In a way, the development has come full circle in modern Israel with its strong championship of all arts; and it is worthy of note that the major art school in the land bears the name of the man who was first identified with artistic creativity, Bezalel.

---

[2] We have extant floor pictures from various synagogues (like the famous Dura-Europos example), bas-reliefs from sarcophagi, etc., and in later eras Haggadot and Megillot were allowed to be illustrated.

Gutmann writes of the biblical and Hellenistic-Roman period: "A rigidly and uniformly anti-iconic attitude on the part of the Jews remains as much a myth as the procrustean bed" [14].

Labor

The word מְלָאכָה (*melachah*, work or labor) embodies what is totally forbidden on the Sabbath. Now the Torah uses this term most frequently in relation to three topics: creation, the prohibition of Sabbath work, and the construction of the Tabernacle. They are all distinguished by the creative element in work. Human intelligence and creative capacity reflect the godly part of man.

B. S. JACOBSON [15]

[In Jewish law, therefore, all "creative" activity is proscribed on the Sabbath, even as on it God rested from creating the world.]

Kindle No Fire on the Sabbath

(The prohibition is issued in relation to the building of the sanctuary, and therefore first and foremost applicable to it.)

Though you are engaged in work dedicated to divine purposes, be on guard not to perform any work on the Sabbath.   IBN EZRA [16]

The prohibition highlights man's acknowledgment that his ability to master matter (represented by fire) is lent to him by God and is to be used only in His service.   S. R. HIRSCH [17]

The rule applies figuratively as well. Do not add "fire" to your talk on the Sabbath, by adding to dissent, gossip, and negative criticism.

CHASIDIC [18]

Forgiveness and Affection

The building of the Tabernacle was commanded in order to show not only Israel but all the world that God had forgiven His people for the sin of the golden calf.   MIDRASH [19]

The Tabernacle was built, not because God needed it, but to show His affection for Israel.

MIDRASH [20]

Bezalel Son of Uri Son of Hur

Why is Hur, the third generation, mentioned (35:30)? Because at the incident with the golden calf he defended the purity of worship and was killed by the mob. Hence this memorial.

MIDRASH [21]

Art and Artists

The artist is not a special kind of man, but every man is a special kind of artist.

J. E. PARK [22]

All these rely upon their hands,
  and each is skilful in his own work.
Without them a city cannot be established,
  and men can neither sojourn nor live there.
Yet they are not sought out for the council of
    the people,
  nor do they attain eminence in the public
    assembly.
They do not sit in the judge's seat,
  nor do they understand the sentence of
    judgment.
They cannot expound discipline or judg-
    ment,
  and they are not found using proverbs.
But they keep stable the fabric of the world,
  and their prayer is in the practice of their
    trade.

SIRACH [23]

Eye and Ear

Moses banished painting and sculpture, with all their high repute and artistry, because their craft belies the nature of truth and works deception and illusion through the eyes to souls that are ready to be seduced.   PHILO [24]

[Philo overstates the intent of the Torah in order to make his case, which in part was a defense of a general absence of Jews from the arts of his day.]

To the Jews belonged the splendors and raptures of the word.   B. BERENSON [25]

Mirrors

The use of mirrors in the Tabernacle showed that the physical, sensual side of man is not excluded from the sphere to be sanctified by the Tabernacle; in fact it is the first and most essential object of sanctification.   S. R. HIRSCH [26]

Moses at first refused to accept a gift which appealed to the evil impulse (that is, vanity), but God insisted because in Egypt the women had sustained their men with food and drink and had persuaded them to have children.   RASHI

From Ancient Near Eastern Literature

Gudea Instructed by His God

(An early Sumerian inscription shows Gudea of Lagash as receiving divine instructions for building a temple in Girsu.)

After the god Ninzagga had given him a pertinent order, they brought copper for Gudea, the temple-builder; they brought great willow-logs, ebony-logs, together with abba-logs to the ensi, the temple-builder. Gudea, the en-priest of Ningirsu, made a path into the Cedar Mountain which nobody had entered before [27].

Repetition as a Literary Device

The Ugaritic "Legend of King Keret" (excerpted below) shows in Tablet II the instructions and in Tablets IV/V how the instructions were carried out.

Tablet II

March a day and a second;
  A third, a fourth day;
  A fifth, a sixth day—
Lo! at the sun on the seventh:

Thou arrivest at Udum the Great,
  Even at Udum the Grand.
—Now do thou attack the villages,
  Harass the towns.
Sweep from the fields the wood-cutting wives,
  From the threshing floors the straw-picking
    ones;
Sweep from the spring the women that draw,
  From the fountain those that fill.
Tarry a day and a second;
  A third, a fourth day;
  A fifth, a sixth day.
Thine arrows shoot not into the city,
  Nor thy hand-stones flung headlong.
And behold, at the sun on the seventh,
  King Pabel will sleep
Till the noise of the neighing of his stallion,
  Till the sound of the braying of his he-ass,
Until the lowing of the plow ox,
  Until the howling of the watchdog.

Tablets IV/V

He marches a day and a second;
  A third, a fourth day.
Then at the sun on the fourth,
  He arrives at Udum the Great,
  Even Udum the Grand.
He did attack the villages,
  Harassed the towns.
He swept from the fields the wood-cutting
    wives,
  And from the threshing floors the straw-
    picking ones.
He swept from the spring the women that drew,
  And from the fountain those that filled.
He tarried a day and a second;
  A third, a fourth day;
  A fifth, a sixth day.
And behold, at the sun on the seventh,
  King Pabel slept
Till the noise of the neighing of his stallion,
  Till the sound of the braying of his he-ass,
Until the lowing of the plow ox,
  Until the howling of the watchdog [28].

The Erection of the Tabernacle

The last section of the book, פְּקוּדֵי ("records"), begins with a statistical summary of the materials used for the Tabernacle (38:21–31). Then follows the account of producing the priestly vestments, containing a faithful repetition of earlier chapters (39:1–31). When everything is made, Moses blesses the people and proceeds to set up the Tabernacle. The text uses the expression "Tabernacle of the Tent of Meeting," which raises questions about its relationship to the Tent of Meeting of which we were previously told that it was set up outside the camp (33:7).

The priests and parts of the Tabernacle are then anointed, and in the first month of the second year, just about a year after the Exodus, the Tabernacle is erected and at once God signifies His approval of the enterprise. He manifests His forgiveness by having His cloud descend on the Tent. This Tent is manifestly different from the one mentioned in 33:7, for Moses cannot enter it when the cloud rests on it.* The cloud also serves as a signal to the people when to break camp and when to remain, and thus God's visible presence will lead His children by day and by night in all their journeys.

On this note the Book of Exodus ends. Leviticus, which follows, consists almost entirely of laws (save for the brief tale of the deaths of Nadab and Abihu). The desert narrative is taken up again in the Book of Numbers, which in this respect is a direct sequel to Exodus. The erection of the Tabernacle was placed in the first month of the second year, and Numbers will begin with the taking of a census in the second month.

---

* Tradition reconciles this difficulty by comparing the Tent to Mount Sinai:
Moses could not approach the Presence until he was called [1].

כה שֶׁקֶל בְּשֶׁקֶל הַקֹּדֶשׁ: וְכֶסֶף פְּקוּדֵי הָעֵדָה מְאַת
כִּכָּר וְאֶלֶף וּשְׁבַע מֵאוֹת וַחֲמִשָּׁה וְשִׁבְעִים שֶׁקֶל
כו בְּשֶׁקֶל הַקֹּדֶשׁ: בֶּקַע לַגֻּלְגֹּלֶת מַחֲצִית הַשֶּׁקֶל בְּשֶׁקֶל
הַקֹּדֶשׁ לְכֹל הָעֹבֵר עַל־הַפְּקֻדִים מִבֶּן עֶשְׂרִים שָׁנָה
וָמַעְלָה לְשֵׁשׁ־מֵאוֹת אֶלֶף וּשְׁלֹשֶׁת אֲלָפִים וַחֲמֵשׁ
כז מֵאוֹת וַחֲמִשִּׁים: וַיְהִי מְאַת כִּכַּר הַכֶּסֶף לָצֶקֶת אֵת
אַדְנֵי הַקֹּדֶשׁ וְאֵת אַדְנֵי הַפָּרֹכֶת מְאַת אֲדָנִים לִמְאַת
כח הַכִּכָּר כִּכָּר לָאָדֶן: וְאֶת־הָאֶלֶף וּשְׁבַע הַמֵּאוֹת
וַחֲמִשָּׁה וְשִׁבְעִים עָשָׂה וָוִים לָעַמּוּדִים וְצִפָּה רָאשֵׁיהֶם

ס ס ס
כא אֵלֶּה פְקוּדֵי הַמִּשְׁכָּן מִשְׁכַּן הָעֵדֻת אֲשֶׁר פֻּקַּד עַל־
פִּי מֹשֶׁה עֲבֹדַת הַלְוִיִּם בְּיַד אִיתָמָר בֶּן־אַהֲרֹן הַכֹּהֵן:
כב וּבְצַלְאֵל בֶּן־אוּרִי בֶן־חוּר לְמַטֵּה יְהוּדָה עָשָׂה אֵת
כג כָּל־אֲשֶׁר־צִוָּה יְהוָה אֶת־מֹשֶׁה: וְאִתּוֹ אָהֳלִיאָב בֶּן־
אֲחִיסָמָךְ לְמַטֵּה־דָן חָרָשׁ וְחֹשֵׁב וְרֹקֵם בַּתְּכֵלֶת
כד וּבָאַרְגָּמָן וּבְתוֹלַעַת הַשָּׁנִי וּבַשֵּׁשׁ: ס כָּל־הַזָּהָב
הֶעָשׂוּי לַמְּלָאכָה בְּכֹל מְלֶאכֶת הַקֹּדֶשׁ וַיְהִי זְהַב
הַתְּנוּפָה תֵּשַׁע וְעֶשְׂרִים כִּכָּר וּשְׁבַע מֵאוֹת וּשְׁלֹשִׁים

21] These are the records of the Tabernacle, the Tabernacle of the Pact, which were drawn up at Moses' bidding—the work of the Levites under the direction of Ithamar son of Aaron the priest. **22]** Now Bezalel, son of Uri son of Hur, of the tribe of Judah, had made all that the LORD had commanded Moses; **23]** at his side was Oholiab son of Ahisamach, of the tribe of Dan, carver and designer, and embroiderer in blue, purple, and crimson yarns, and in fine linen.

24] All the gold that was used for the work, in all the work of the sanctuary—the wave offering of gold—came to 29 talents and 730 shekels by the sanctuary weight. **25]** The silver of those of the community who were recorded came to 100 talents and 1,775 shekels by the sanctuary weight: **26]** a half-shekel a head, half a shekel by the sanctuary weight, for each one who was entered in the records, from the age of twenty years up, 603,550 men. **27]** The 100 talents of silver were for casting the sockets of the sanctuary and the sockets for the curtain, 100 sockets to the 100 talents, a talent a socket. **28]** And of the 1,775 shekels he made hooks for the posts, overlay for their tops, and bands around them.

29] The copper from the wave offering came to 70 talents and 2,400 shekels. **30]** Of it he

---

38:21] *Under the direction of Ithamar.* His role had not been indicated so far. His name adds importance to the overall responsibility of the Aaronides for the Tabernacle.

23] *Oholiab.* His specialties—carpentry and embroidery—are now listed.

24] *29 talents.* Figuring the talent at 3,000 shekels, this equaled 87,000 shekels.

730 shekels. For a total of 87,730. The final three digits also appear in the census, which counted 601,730 people (Num. 26:51). These combinations were probably part of a numerical scheme to which we lack the key [2].

26] *Half-shekel.* Called *beka* in Hebrew.

603,550. See 29:1–31:18, "The Shekel." The number reappears in Num. 1:46 (see commentary there for an analysis). The census recorded in Numbers was taken a month after the one listed in Exodus. Some see two separate censuses or consider the figure in verse 26 as having emerged from the contributions rather than from a separate census. In either case, the number of children born would then have to equal the number of those who died during the month, in order to account for the identical results. It is not possible to resolve this problem on the basis of contemporary accounting standards. Rather, the repetition of the figure should be viewed as a literary device and not as a mathematical statement.

כט וְחֻשַּׁק אֹתָם: וּנְחֹשֶׁת הַתְּנוּפָה שִׁבְעִים כִּכָּר וְאַלְפַּיִם
ל וְאַרְבַּע־מֵאוֹת שָׁקֶל: וַיַּעַשׂ בָּהּ אֶת־אַדְנֵי פֶּתַח אֹהֶל
מוֹעֵד וְאֵת מִזְבַּח הַנְּחֹשֶׁת וְאֶת־מִכְבַּר הַנְּחֹשֶׁת אֲשֶׁר־
לא לוֹ וְאֵת כָּל־כְּלֵי הַמִּזְבֵּחַ: וְאֶת־אַדְנֵי הֶחָצֵר סָבִיב
וְאֶת־אַדְנֵי שַׁעַר הֶחָצֵר וְאֵת כָּל־יִתְדֹת הַמִּשְׁכָּן וְאֶת־
כָּל־יִתְדֹת הֶחָצֵר סָבִיב:

א וּמִן־הַתְּכֵלֶת וְהָאַרְגָּמָן וְתוֹלַעַת הַשָּׁנִי עָשׂוּ בִגְדֵי־שְׂרָד
לְשָׁרֵת בַּקֹּדֶשׁ וַיַּעֲשׂוּ אֶת־בִּגְדֵי הַקֹּדֶשׁ אֲשֶׁר לְאַהֲרֹן
כַּאֲשֶׁר צִוָּה יְהוָה אֶת־מֹשֶׁה: פ

ב וַיַּעַשׂ אֶת־הָאֵפֹד זָהָב תְּכֵלֶת וְאַרְגָּמָן וְתוֹלַעַת
ג שָׁנִי וְשֵׁשׁ מָשְׁזָר: וַיְרַקְּעוּ אֶת־פַּחֵי הַזָּהָב וְקִצֵּץ
פְּתִילִם לַעֲשׂוֹת בְּתוֹךְ הַתְּכֵלֶת וּבְתוֹךְ הָאַרְגָּמָן
וּבְתוֹךְ תּוֹלַעַת הַשָּׁנִי וּבְתוֹךְ הַשֵּׁשׁ מַעֲשֵׂה חֹשֵׁב:

ד כְּתֵפֹת עָשׂוּ־לוֹ חֹבְרֹת עַל־שְׁנֵי *קְצוֹותָו חֻבָּר:
ה וְחֵשֶׁב אֲפֻדָּתוֹ אֲשֶׁר עָלָיו מִמֶּנּוּ הוּא כְּמַעֲשֵׂהוּ זָהָב
תְּכֵלֶת וְאַרְגָּמָן וְתוֹלַעַת שָׁנִי וְשֵׁשׁ מָשְׁזָר כַּאֲשֶׁר צִוָּה
ו יְהוָה אֶת־מֹשֶׁה: ס וַיַּעֲשׂוּ אֶת־אַבְנֵי הַשֹּׁהַם מֻסַבֹּת
מִשְׁבְּצֹת זָהָב מְפֻתָּחֹת פִּתּוּחֵי חוֹתָם עַל־שְׁמוֹת בְּנֵי
ז יִשְׂרָאֵל: וַיָּשֶׂם אֹתָם עַל כִּתְפֹת הָאֵפֹד אַבְנֵי זִכָּרֹן
לִבְנֵי יִשְׂרָאֵל כַּאֲשֶׁר צִוָּה יְהוָה אֶת־מֹשֶׁה: פ
ח וַיַּעַשׂ אֶת־הַחֹשֶׁן מַעֲשֵׂה חֹשֵׁב כְּמַעֲשֵׂה אֵפֹד זָהָב
ט תְּכֵלֶת וְאַרְגָּמָן וְתוֹלַעַת שָׁנִי וְשֵׁשׁ מָשְׁזָר: רָבוּעַ
הָיָה כָּפוּל עָשׂוּ אֶת־הַחֹשֶׁן זֶרֶת אָרְכּוֹ וְזֶרֶת רָחְבּוֹ
י כָּפוּל: וַיְמַלְאוּ־בוֹ אַרְבָּעָה טוּרֵי אָבֶן טוּר אֹדֶם
יא פִּטְדָה וּבָרֶקֶת הַטּוּר הָאֶחָד: וְהַטּוּר הַשֵּׁנִי נֹפֶךְ
יב סַפִּיר וְיָהֲלֹם: וְהַטּוּר הַשְּׁלִישִׁי לֶשֶׁם שְׁבוֹ וְאַחְלָמָה:

* ד קצותו קרי

made the sockets for the entrance of the Tent of Meeting; the copper altar and its copper grating and all the utensils of the altar; 31] the sockets of the enclosure round about and the sockets of the gate of the enclosure; and all the pegs of the Tabernacle and all the pegs of the enclosure round about.

1] Of the blue, purple, and crimson yarns they also made the service vestments for officiating in the sanctuary; they made Aaron's sacral vestments—as the LORD had commanded Moses.

2] The ephod was made of gold, blue, purple, and crimson yarns, and fine twisted linen. 3] They hammered out sheets of gold and cut threads to be worked into designs among the blue, the purple, and the crimson yarns, and the fine linen. 4] They made for it attaching shoulder-pieces; they were attached at its two ends. 5] The decorated band that was upon it was made like it, of one piece with it; of gold, blue, purple, and crimson yarns, and fine twisted linen—as the LORD had commanded Moses.

6] They bordered the lazuli stones with frames of gold, engraved with seal engravings of the names of the sons of Israel. 7] They were set on the shoulder-pieces of the ephod, as stones of remembrance for the Israelites—as the LORD had commanded Moses.

8] The breastpiece was made in the style of the ephod: of gold, blue, purple, and crimson yarns, and fine twisted linen. 9] It was square; they made the breastpiece doubled—a span in length and a span in width, doubled. 10] They set in it four rows of stones. The first row was a row of carnelian, chrysolite, and emerald; 11] the second row: a turquoise, a sapphire, and an amethyst; 12] the third row: a jacinth, an agate, and a crystal; 13] and the fourth row: a

39:2–31] The making of the vestments parallels the instructions of 28:6 ff.

2] *The ephod was made.* The English passive tense attempts to render the impersonal active of the Hebrew which literally reads "he (i.e., someone) made."

מִטַּבְּעֹתָיו֙ אֶל־טַבְּעֹ֣ת הָאֵפֹ֔ד בִּפְתִ֣יל תְּכֵ֔לֶת לִֽהְיֹת֙
עַל־חֵ֣שֶׁב הָאֵפֹ֔ד וְלֹֽא־יִזַּ֣ח הַחֹ֔שֶׁן מֵעַ֖ל הָאֵפֹ֑ד כַּאֲשֶׁ֛ר
צִוָּ֥ה יְהֹוָ֖ה אֶת־מֹשֶֽׁה: פ

כב וַיַּ֛עַשׂ אֶת־מְעִ֥יל הָאֵפֹ֖ד מַעֲשֵׂ֣ה אֹרֵ֑ג כְּלִ֖יל תְּכֵֽלֶת:

כג וּֽפִי־הַמְּעִ֥יל בְּתוֹכ֖וֹ כְּפִ֣י תַחְרָ֑א שָׂפָ֥ה לְפִ֛יו סָבִ֖יב

כד לֹ֥א יִקָּרֵֽעַ: וַֽיַּעֲשׂוּ֙ עַל־שׁוּלֵ֣י הַמְּעִ֔יל רִמּוֹנֵ֖י תְּכֵ֥לֶת

כה וְאַרְגָּמָ֛ן וְתוֹלַ֥עַת שָׁנִ֖י מׇשְׁזָֽר: וַיַּעֲשׂ֥וּ פַעֲמֹנֵ֖י זָהָ֣ב

טָה֑וֹר וַיִּתְּנ֨וּ אֶת־הַפַּֽעֲמֹנִ֜ים בְּת֣וֹךְ הָרִמֹּנִ֗ים עַל־שׁוּלֵ֤י

כו הַמְּעִיל֙ סָבִ֔יב בְּת֖וֹךְ הָרִמֹּנִֽים: פַּעֲמֹ֤ן וְרִמֹּן֙ פַּֽעֲמֹ֤ן

וְרִמֹּן֙ עַל־שׁוּלֵ֣י הַמְּעִ֔יל סָבִ֖יב לְשָׁרֵ֑ת כַּאֲשֶׁ֛ר צִוָּ֥ה

כז יְהֹוָ֖ה אֶת־מֹשֶֽׁה: ס וַֽיַּעֲשׂ֧וּ אֶת־הַכׇּתְנֹ֛ת שֵׁ֖שׁ מַעֲשֵׂ֥ה

כח אֹרֵ֑ג לְאַהֲרֹ֖ן וּלְבָנָֽיו: וְאֵת֙ הַמִּצְנֶ֣פֶת שֵׁ֔שׁ וְאֶת־פַּאֲרֵ֥י

הַמִּגְבָּעֹ֖ת שֵׁ֑שׁ וְאֶת־מִכְנְסֵ֥י הַבָּ֖ד שֵׁ֥שׁ מׇשְׁזָֽר: וְאֶת־

כט הָ֤אַבְנֵט֙ שֵׁ֣שׁ מׇשְׁזָ֔ר וּתְכֵ֥לֶת וְאַרְגָּמָ֖ן וְתוֹלַ֣עַת שָׁנִ֖י

יג וְהַטּ֣וּר הָֽרְבִיעִ֔י תַּרְשִׁ֥ישׁ שֹׁ֖הַם וְיָשְׁפֵ֑ה מֽוּסַבֹּ֥ת מִשְׁבְּצֹ֛ת

יד זָהָ֖ב בְּמִלֻּאֹתָֽם: וְ֠הָאֲבָנִ֠ים עַל־שְׁמֹ֨ת בְּנֵֽי־יִשְׂרָאֵ֥ל הֵ֛נָּה

שְׁתֵּ֥ים עֶשְׂרֵ֖ה עַל־שְׁמֹתָ֑ם פִּתּוּחֵ֤י חֹתָם֙ אִ֣ישׁ עַל־שְׁמ֔וֹ

טו לִשְׁנֵ֥ים עָשָׂ֖ר שָֽׁבֶט: וַיַּעֲשׂ֧וּ עַל־הַחֹ֛שֶׁן שַׁרְשְׁרֹ֥ת גַּבְלֻ֖ת

טז מַעֲשֵׂ֣ה עֲבֹ֑ת זָהָ֖ב טָהֽוֹר: וַֽיַּעֲשׂ֗וּ שְׁתֵּי֙ מִשְׁבְּצֹ֣ת זָהָ֔ב

וּשְׁתֵּ֖י טַבְּעֹ֣ת זָהָ֑ב וַֽיִּתְּנ֗וּ אֶת־שְׁתֵּי֙ הַטַּבָּעֹ֔ת עַל־שְׁנֵ֖י

יז קְצ֥וֹת הַחֹֽשֶׁן: וַֽיִּתְּנ֗וּ שְׁתֵּי֙ הָעֲבֹתֹ֣ת הַזָּהָ֔ב עַל־שְׁתֵּ֖י

יח הַטַּבָּעֹ֑ת עַל־קְצ֖וֹת הַחֹֽשֶׁן: וְאֵ֨ת שְׁתֵּ֤י קְצוֹת֙ שְׁתֵּ֣י

הָֽעֲבֹתֹ֔ת נָתְנ֖וּ עַל־שְׁתֵּ֣י הַֽמִּשְׁבְּצֹ֑ת וַֽיִּתְּנֻ֛ם עַל־כִּתְפֹ֥ת

יט הָאֵפֹ֖ד אֶל־מ֥וּל פָּנָֽיו: וַֽיַּעֲשׂ֗וּ שְׁתֵּי֙ טַבְּעֹ֣ת זָהָ֔ב וַיָּשִׂ֕ימוּ

עַל־שְׁנֵ֖י קְצ֣וֹת הַחֹ֑שֶׁן עַל־שְׂפָת֕וֹ אֲשֶׁ֖ר אֶל־עֵ֥בֶר

כ הָאֵפֹ֖ד בָּֽיְתָה: וַֽיַּעֲשׂוּ֮ שְׁתֵּ֣י טַבְּעֹ֣ת זָהָב֒ וַֽיִּתְּנֻ֗ם עַל־

שְׁתֵּ֨י כִתְפֹ֤ת הָאֵפֹד֙ מִלְּמַ֔טָּה מִמּ֣וּל פָּנָ֔יו לְעֻמַּ֖ת

כא מֶחְבַּרְתּ֑וֹ מִמַּ֕עַל לְחֵ֖שֶׁב הָאֵפֹֽד: וַיִּרְכְּס֣וּ אֶת־הַחֹ֗שֶׁן

---

beryl, a lapis lazuli, and a jasper. They were encircled in their mountings with frames of gold. **14]** The stones corresponded [in number] to the names of the sons of Israel: twelve, corresponding to their names; engraved like seals, each with its name, for the twelve tribes.

15] On the breastpiece they made braided chains of corded work in pure gold. **16]** They made two frames of gold and two rings of gold, and fastened the two rings at the two ends of the breastpiece, **17]** attaching the two golden cords to the two rings at the ends of the breastpiece. **18]** They then fastened the two ends of the cords to the two frames, attaching them to the shoulder-pieces of the ephod, at the front. **19]** They made two rings of gold and attached them to the two ends of the breastpiece, at its inner edge, which faced the ephod. **20]** They made two other rings of gold and fastened them on the front of the ephod, low on the two shoulder-pieces, close to its seam above the decorated band. **21]** The breastpiece was held in place by a cord of blue from its rings to the rings of the ephod, so that the breastpiece rested on the decorated band and did not come loose from the ephod—as the LORD had commanded Moses.

22] The robe for the ephod was made of woven work, of pure blue. **23]** The opening of the robe, in the middle of it, was like the opening of a coat of mail, with a binding around the opening, so that it would not tear. **24]** On the hem of the robe they made pomegranates of blue, purple, and crimson yarns, twisted. **25]** They also made bells of pure gold, and attached the bells between the pomegranates, all around the hem of the robe, between the pomegranates: **26]** a bell and a pomegranate, a bell and a pomegranate, all around the hem of the robe for officiating in—as the LORD had commanded Moses.

27] They made the tunics of fine linen, of woven work, for Aaron and his sons; **28]** and the headdress of fine linen, and the decorated turbans of fine linen, and the linen breeches of fine twisted linen; **29]** and sashes of fine twisted linen, blue, purple, and crimson yarns, done in

לח הַמַּעֲרָכָה וְאֶת־כָּל־כֵּלֶיהָ וְאֵת שֶׁמֶן הַמָּאוֹר: וְאֵת
מִזְבַּח הַזָּהָב וְאֵת שֶׁמֶן הַמִּשְׁחָה וְאֵת קְטֹרֶת הַסַּמִּים
לט וְאֵת מָסַךְ פֶּתַח הָאֹהֶל: אֵת מִזְבַּח הַנְּחֹשֶׁת וְאֶת־מִכְבַּר
הַנְּחֹשֶׁת אֲשֶׁר־לוֹ אֶת־בַּדָּיו וְאֶת־כָּל־כֵּלָיו אֶת־הַכִּיֹּר
מ וְאֶת־כַּנּוֹ: אֵת קַלְעֵי הֶחָצֵר אֶת־עַמֻּדֶיהָ וְאֶת־אֲדָנֶיהָ
וְאֶת־הַמָּסָךְ לְשַׁעַר הֶחָצֵר אֶת־מֵיתָרָיו וִיתֵדֹתֶיהָ וְאֵת
מא כָּל־כְּלֵי עֲבֹדַת הַמִּשְׁכָּן לְאֹהֶל מוֹעֵד: אֶת־בִּגְדֵי
הַשְּׂרָד לְשָׁרֵת בַּקֹּדֶשׁ אֶת־בִּגְדֵי הַקֹּדֶשׁ לְאַהֲרֹן הַכֹּהֵן
מב וְאֶת־בִּגְדֵי בָנָיו לְכַהֵן: כְּכֹל אֲשֶׁר־צִוָּה יְהוָה אֶת־
מג מֹשֶׁה כֵּן עָשׂוּ בְּנֵי יִשְׂרָאֵל אֵת כָּל־הָעֲבֹדָה: וַיַּרְא
מֹשֶׁה אֶת־כָּל־הַמְּלָאכָה וְהִנֵּה עָשׂוּ אֹתָהּ כַּאֲשֶׁר צִוָּה
יְהוָה כֵּן עָשׂוּ וַיְבָרֶךְ אֹתָם מֹשֶׁה: פ

ל מַעֲשֵׂה רֹקֵם כַּאֲשֶׁר צִוָּה יְהוָה אֶת־מֹשֶׁה: ס וַיַּעֲשׂוּ
אֶת־צִיץ נֵזֶר־הַקֹּדֶשׁ זָהָב טָהוֹר וַיִּכְתְּבוּ עָלָיו מִכְתַּב
לא פִּתּוּחֵי חוֹתָם קֹדֶשׁ לַיהוָה: וַיִּתְּנוּ עָלָיו פְּתִיל
תְּכֵלֶת לָתֵת עַל־הַמִּצְנֶפֶת מִלְמָעְלָה כַּאֲשֶׁר צִוָּה
לב יְהוָה אֶת־מֹשֶׁה: ס וַתֵּכֶל כָּל־עֲבֹדַת מִשְׁכַּן אֹהֶל
מוֹעֵד וַיַּעֲשׂוּ בְּנֵי יִשְׂרָאֵל כְּכֹל אֲשֶׁר צִוָּה יְהוָה
אֶת־מֹשֶׁה כֵּן עָשׂוּ: פ
לג וַיָּבִיאוּ אֶת־הַמִּשְׁכָּן אֶל־מֹשֶׁה אֶת־הָאֹהֶל וְאֶת־כָּל־
לד כֵּלָיו קְרָסָיו קְרָשָׁיו בְּרִיחָו וְעַמֻּדָיו וַאֲדָנָיו: וְאֶת־
מִכְסֵה עוֹרֹת הָאֵילִם הַמְאָדָּמִים וְאֶת־מִכְסֵה עֹרֹת
לה הַתְּחָשִׁים וְאֵת פָּרֹכֶת הַמָּסָךְ: אֶת־אֲרוֹן הָעֵדֻת וְאֶת־
לו בַּדָּיו וְאֵת הַכַּפֹּרֶת: אֶת־הַשֻּׁלְחָן אֶת־כָּל־כֵּלָיו וְאֵת
לז לֶחֶם הַפָּנִים: אֶת־הַמְּנֹרָה הַטְּהֹרָה אֶת־נֵרֹתֶיהָ נֵרֹת

embroidery—as the LORD had commanded Moses.

30] They made the frontlet for the holy diadem of pure gold, and incised upon it the seal inscription: "Holy to the LORD." **31]** They attached to it a cord of blue to fix it upon the headdress above—as the LORD had commanded Moses.

32] Thus was completed all the work of the Tabernacle of the Tent of Meeting. The Israelites did so; just as the LORD had commanded Moses, so they did.

33] Then they brought the Tabernacle to Moses, with the tent and all its furnishings: its clasps, its planks, its poles, its posts, and its sockets; **34]** the covering of tanned ram skins, the covering of dolphin skins, and the curtain for the screen; **35]** the Ark of the Pact and its poles, and the cover; **36]** the table and all its utensils, and the bread of display; **37]** the pure lampstand, its lamps—lamps in due order—and all its fittings, and the oil for lighting; **38]** the altar of gold, the oil for anointing, the aromatic incense, and the screen for the entrance of the Tent; **39]** the copper altar with its copper grating, its poles and all its utensils, and the laver and its stand; **40]** the hangings of the enclosure, its posts and its sockets, the screen for the gate of the enclosure, its cords and its pegs—all the furnishings for the service of the Tabernacle, the Tent of Meeting; **41]** the service vestments for officiating in the sanctuary, the sacral vestments of Aaron the priest, and the vestments of his sons for priestly service. **42]** Just as the LORD had commanded Moses, so the Israelites had done all the work. **43]** And when Moses saw that they had performed all the tasks—as the LORD had commanded, so they had done—Moses blessed them.

30] *Holy diadem.* Previously referred to more modestly as "frontlet" (28:36).

Incised. Literally, "wrote," but incising or engraving is meant (28:36).

33] *Then they brought.* From here to the end of the chapter a summary is provided which repeats 35:10 ff.

אַ וַיְדַבֵּ֥ר יְהוָ֖ה אֶל־מֹשֶׁ֥ה לֵּאמֹֽר: בְּיֹום־הַחֹ֥דֶשׁ הָרִאשֹׁ֖ון

ב בְּאֶחָ֣ד לַחֹ֑דֶשׁ תָּקִ֕ים אֶת־מִשְׁכַּ֖ן אֹ֣הֶל מֹועֵֽד: וְשַׂמְתָּ֣

שָׁ֗ם אֵ֚ת אֲרֹ֣ון הָעֵד֔וּת וְסַכֹּתָ֥ עַל־הָאָרֹ֖ן אֶת־הַפָּרֹֽכֶת:

ג וְהֵבֵאתָ֙ אֶת־הַשֻּׁלְחָ֔ן וְעָרַכְתָּ֖ אֶת־עֶרְכֹּ֑ו וְהֵבֵאתָ֙ אֶת־

ד הַמְּנֹרָ֔ה וְהַעֲלֵיתָ֖ אֶת־נֵרֹתֶֽיהָ: וְנָתַתָּ֞ה אֶת־מִזְבַּ֤ח הַזָּהָב֙

לִקְטֹ֔רֶת לִפְנֵ֖י אֲרֹ֣ון הָעֵדֻ֑ת וְשַׂמְתָּ֛ אֶת־מָסַ֥ךְ הַפֶּ֖תַח

ה לַמִּשְׁכָּֽן: וְנָ֣תַתָּ֔ה אֵ֖ת מִזְבַּ֣ח הָעֹלָ֑ה לִפְנֵ֕י פֶּ֖תַח מִשְׁכַּ֥ן

ו אֹֽהֶל־מֹועֵֽד: וְנָֽתַתָּ֙ אֶת־הַכִּיֹּ֔ר בֵּֽין־אֹ֥הֶל מֹועֵ֖ד וּבֵ֣ין

ז הַמִּזְבֵּ֑חַ וְנָתַתָּ֥ שָׁ֖ם מָֽיִם: וְשַׂמְתָּ֥ אֶת־הֶחָצֵ֖ר סָבִ֑יב

ח וְנָ֣תַתָּ֔ אֶת־מָסַ֖ךְ שַׁ֥עַר הֶחָצֵֽר: וְלָקַחְתָּ֙ אֶת־שֶׁ֣מֶן הַמִּשְׁחָ֔ה

ט וּמָשַׁחְתָּ֥ אֶת־הַמִּשְׁכָּ֖ן וְאֶת־כָּל־אֲשֶׁר־בֹּ֑ו וְקִדַּשְׁתָּ֥ אֹתֹ֛ו

וְאֶת־כָּל־כֵּלָ֖יו וְהָ֥יָה קֹֽדֶשׁ: וּמָשַׁחְתָּ֛ אֶת־מִזְבַּ֥ח הָעֹלָ֖ה

י וְאֶת־כָּל־כֵּלָ֑יו וְקִדַּשְׁתָּ֙ אֶת־הַמִּזְבֵּ֔חַ וְהָיָ֥ה הַמִּזְבֵּ֖חַ קֹ֥דֶשׁ

יא קָֽדָשִׁ֑ים: וּמָשַׁחְתָּ֥ אֶת־הַכִּיֹּ֖ר וְאֶת־כַּנֹּ֑ו וְקִדַּשְׁתָּ֖ אֹתֹֽו:

יב וְהִקְרַבְתָּ֤ אֶֽת־אַהֲרֹן֙ וְאֶת־בָּנָ֔יו אֶל־פֶּ֖תַח אֹ֣הֶל מֹועֵ֑ד

יג וְרָחַצְתָּ֥ אֹתָ֖ם בַּמָּֽיִם: וְהִלְבַּשְׁתָּ֙ אֶֽת־אַהֲרֹ֔ן אֵ֖ת בִּגְדֵ֥י

1] And the LORD spoke to Moses, saying: **2]** On the first day of the first month you shall set up the Tabernacle of the Tent of Meeting. **3]** Place there the Ark of the Pact, and screen off the ark with the curtain. **4]** Bring in the table and lay out its due setting; bring in the lampstand and light its lamps; **5]** and place the gold altar of incense before the Ark of the Pact. Then put up the screen for the entrance of the Tabernacle.

6] You shall place the altar of burnt offering before the entrance of the Tabernacle of the Tent of Meeting. **7]** Place the laver between the Tent of Meeting and the altar, and put water in it. **8]** Set up the enclosure round about, and put in place the screen for the gate of the enclosure.

9] You shall take the anointing oil and anoint the Tabernacle and all that is in it to consecrate it and all its furnishings, so that it shall be holy. **10]** Then anoint the altar of burnt offering and all its utensils to consecrate the altar, so that the altar shall be most holy. **11]** And anoint the laver and its stand to consecrate it.

12] You shall bring Aaron and his sons forward to the entrance of the Tent of Meeting and wash them with the water. **13]** Put the sacral vestments on Aaron, and anoint him and

---

40:2] *On the first day.* Of the spring month, Abib (called Nisan, after the introduction of Baby–lonian names for the months, sometime after the Exile), two weeks short of the anniversary of the Exodus. This chapter too is characterized by prescriptive-descriptive repetition: first the divine injunction is given, then it is shown to have been carried out faithfully.

Set up. The various parts are now inte–grated and described in the context of the whole structure.

Tabernacle of the Tent of Meeting. מִשְׁכַּן אֹהֶל מֹועֵד (*Mishkan Ohel Mo-ed*), combining terms here–tofore used separately. See commentary below.

3] *Screen off the ark with the curtain.* פָּרֹכֶת (*parochet*). Several versions have "cover the ark with the ark cover" (כַּפֹּרֶת, *kaporet*). Such inter–change of letters occurred occasionally despite the great care exercised in copying manuscripts. It is not possible to say which is the original version.

9] *Anoint the Tabernacle.* This will be retold in greater detail in Num. 7:1 ff.

12] *You shall bring Aaron.* The consecration of the priests will consist of washing, clothing, and anointing them. The earlier expression "ordain" (literally, "fill their hands," 28:41) is not used here. The process will be retold in detail in Lev. 8:6 ff.

יד הַקֹּדֶשׁ וּמָשַׁחְתָּ אֹתוֹ וְקִדַּשְׁתָּ אֹתוֹ וְכִהֵן לִי: וְאֶת־
טו בָּנָיו תַּקְרִיב וְהִלְבַּשְׁתָּ אֹתָם כֻּתֳּנֹת: וּמָשַׁחְתָּ אֹתָם
כַּאֲשֶׁר מָשַׁחְתָּ אֶת־אֲבִיהֶם וְכִהֲנוּ לִי וְהָיְתָה לִהְיֹת
טז לָהֶם מָשְׁחָתָם לִכְהֻנַּת עוֹלָם לְדֹרֹתָם: וַיַּעַשׂ מֹשֶׁה
כְּכֹל אֲשֶׁר צִוָּה יְהוָה אֹתוֹ כֵּן עָשָׂה: ס וַיְהִי
יז בַּחֹדֶשׁ הָרִאשׁוֹן בַּשָּׁנָה הַשֵּׁנִית בְּאֶחָד לַחֹדֶשׁ הוּקַם
יח הַמִּשְׁכָּן: וַיָּקֶם מֹשֶׁה אֶת־הַמִּשְׁכָּן וַיִּתֵּן אֶת־אֲדָנָיו וַיָּשֶׂם
אֶת־קְרָשָׁיו וַיִּתֵּן אֶת־בְּרִיחָיו וַיָּקֶם אֶת־עַמּוּדָיו:
יט וַיִּפְרֹשׂ אֶת־הָאֹהֶל עַל־הַמִּשְׁכָּן וַיָּשֶׂם אֶת־מִכְסֵה הָאֹהֶל
עָלָיו מִלְמָעְלָה כַּאֲשֶׁר צִוָּה יְהוָה אֶת־מֹשֶׁה: ס
כ וַיִּקַּח וַיִּתֵּן אֶת־הָעֵדֻת אֶל־הָאָרֹן וַיָּשֶׂם אֶת־הַבַּדִּים
עַל־הָאָרֹן וַיִּתֵּן אֶת־הַכַּפֹּרֶת עַל־הָאָרֹן מִלְמָעְלָה:

כא וַיָּבֵא אֶת־הָאָרֹן אֶל־הַמִּשְׁכָּן וַיָּשֶׂם אֵת פָּרֹכֶת הַמָּסָךְ
וַיָּסֶךְ עַל אֲרוֹן הָעֵדוּת כַּאֲשֶׁר צִוָּה יְהוָה אֶת־מֹשֶׁה: ס
כב וַיִּתֵּן אֶת־הַשֻּׁלְחָן בְּאֹהֶל מוֹעֵד עַל יֶרֶךְ הַמִּשְׁכָּן
צָפֹנָה מִחוּץ לַפָּרֹכֶת: וַיַּעֲרֹךְ עָלָיו עֵרֶךְ לֶחֶם
כד לִפְנֵי יְהוָה כַּאֲשֶׁר צִוָּה יְהוָה אֶת־מֹשֶׁה: ס וַיָּשֶׂם
אֶת־הַמְּנֹרָה בְּאֹהֶל מוֹעֵד נֹכַח הַשֻּׁלְחָן עַל יֶרֶךְ
כה הַמִּשְׁכָּן נֶגְבָּה: וַיַּעַל הַנֵּרֹת לִפְנֵי יְהוָה כַּאֲשֶׁר צִוָּה
יְהוָה אֶת־מֹשֶׁה: ס כו וַיָּשֶׂם אֶת־מִזְבַּח הַזָּהָב בְּאֹהֶל
מוֹעֵד לִפְנֵי הַפָּרֹכֶת: וַיַּקְטֵר עָלָיו קְטֹרֶת סַמִּים
כח כַּאֲשֶׁר צִוָּה יְהוָה אֶת־מֹשֶׁה: ס וַיָּשֶׂם אֶת־מָסַךְ
הַפֶּתַח לַמִּשְׁכָּן: כט וְאֵת מִזְבַּח הָעֹלָה שָׂם פֶּתַח מִשְׁכַּן
אֹהֶל־מוֹעֵד וַיַּעַל עָלָיו אֶת־הָעֹלָה וְאֶת־הַמִּנְחָה:

consecrate him, that he may serve Me as priest.   14] Then bring his sons forward, put tunics on them,   15] and anoint them as you have anointed their father, that they may serve Me as priests. This their anointing shall serve them for everlasting priesthood throughout the ages.

16] This Moses did; just as the LORD had commanded him, so he did.

17] In the first month of the second year, on the first of the month, the Tabernacle was set up. 18] Moses set up the Tabernacle, placing its sockets, setting up its planks, inserting its bars, and erecting its posts. 19] He spread the tent over the Tabernacle, placing the covering of the tent on top of it—just as the LORD had commanded Moses.

20] He took the Pact and placed it in the ark; he fixed the poles to the ark, placed the cover on top of the ark, 21] and brought the ark inside the Tabernacle. Then he put up the curtain for screening, and screened off the Ark of the Pact—just as the LORD had commanded Moses.

22] He placed the table in the Tent of Meeting, outside the curtain, on the north side of the Tabernacle. 23] Upon it he laid out the setting of bread before the LORD—as the LORD had commanded Moses. 24] He placed the lampstand in the Tent of Meeting opposite the table, on the south side of the Tabernacle. 25] And he lit the lamps before the LORD—as the LORD had commanded Moses. 26] He placed the altar of gold in the Tent of Meeting, before the curtain. 27] On it he burned aromatic incense—as the LORD had commanded Moses.

28] Then he put up the screen for the entrance of the Tabernacle. 29] At the entrance of

15] *Everlasting priesthood.* Considered by many scholars as the crucial statement of the P-tradition: it confirms the exclusive right of the Aaronides to administer the sanctuary.

18] *Moses set up.* The final realization of his vision belongs to him.

19] *Tent over the Tabernacle.* In this context "tent" means "tent cover" or "top" (and not Tent of Meeting as in verse 2). The whole Tabernacle was tented.

לה הַמִּשְׁכָּן: וְלֹא־יָכֹל מֹשֶׁה לָבוֹא אֶל־אֹהֶל מוֹעֵד כִּי־
שָׁכַן עָלָיו הֶעָנָן וּכְבוֹד יְהוָה מָלֵא אֶת־הַמִּשְׁכָּן:
לו וּבְהֵעָלוֹת הֶעָנָן מֵעַל הַמִּשְׁכָּן יִסְעוּ בְּנֵי יִשְׂרָאֵל
לז בְּכֹל מַסְעֵיהֶם: וְאִם־לֹא יֵעָלֶה הֶעָנָן וְלֹא יִסְעוּ עַד־
לח יוֹם הֵעָלֹתוֹ: כִּי עֲנַן יְהוָה עַל־הַמִּשְׁכָּן יוֹמָם וְאֵשׁ
תִּהְיֶה לַיְלָה בּוֹ לְעֵינֵי כָל־בֵּית־יִשְׂרָאֵל בְּכָל־
מַסְעֵיהֶם:

Haftarah Pekude, p. 728

ל כַּאֲשֶׁר צִוָּה יְהוָה אֶת־מֹשֶׁה: ס וַיָּשֶׂם אֶת־הַכִּיֹּר
בֵּין־אֹהֶל מוֹעֵד וּבֵין הַמִּזְבֵּחַ וַיִּתֵּן שָׁמָּה מַיִם לְרָחְצָה:
לא וְרָחֲצוּ מִמֶּנּוּ מֹשֶׁה וְאַהֲרֹן וּבָנָיו אֶת־יְדֵיהֶם וְאֶת־
לב רַגְלֵיהֶם: בְּבֹאָם אֶל־אֹהֶל מוֹעֵד וּבְקָרְבָתָם אֶל־
הַמִּזְבֵּחַ יִרְחָצוּ כַּאֲשֶׁר צִוָּה יְהוָה אֶת־מֹשֶׁה: ס
לג וַיָּקֶם אֶת־הֶחָצֵר סָבִיב לַמִּשְׁכָּן וְלַמִּזְבֵּחַ וַיִּתֵּן אֶת־
מָסַךְ שַׁעַר הֶחָצֵר וַיְכַל מֹשֶׁה אֶת־הַמְּלָאכָה: פ
לד וַיְכַס הֶעָנָן אֶת־אֹהֶל מוֹעֵד וּכְבוֹד יְהוָה מָלֵא אֶת־

the Tabernacle of the Tent of Meeting he placed the altar of burnt offering. On it he offered up the burnt offering and the meal offering—as the LORD had commanded Moses. **30]** He placed the laver between the Tent of Meeting and the altar, and put water in it for washing. **31]** From it Moses and Aaron and his sons would wash their hands and feet; **32]** they washed when they entered the Tent of Meeting and when they approached the altar—as the LORD had commanded Moses. **33]** And he set up the enclosure around the Tabernacle and the altar, and put up the screen for the gate of the enclosure.

When Moses had finished the work, **34]** the cloud covered the Tent of Meeting, and the Presence of the LORD filled the Tabernacle. **35]** Moses could not enter the Tent of Meeting, because the cloud had settled upon it and the Presence of the LORD filled the Tabernacle. **36]** When the cloud lifted from the Tabernacle, the Israelites would set out, on their various journeys; **37]** but if the cloud did not lift, they would not set out until such time as it did lift. **38]** For over the Tabernacle a cloud of the LORD rested by day, and fire would appear in it by night, in the view of all the house of Israel throughout their journeys.

34] *The Presence of the Lord filled the Tabernacle.* Fulfilling the promise of 25:8: "Let them make Me a sanctuary that I may dwell among them." The promise was fulfilled again when Solomon erected the Temple in Jerusalem: "And it came to pass, when the priests came out of the holy place [after setting it up], that the cloud filled the house of the Lord, so that the priests could not

abide to minister because of the cloud; for the glory of the Lord filled the house of the Lord" (I Kings 8:10–11; the parallels between the accounts in Exodus and Kings are frequent).

36] *When the cloud lifted.* This is repeated in detail in Num. 9:15 ff.

The Tabernacle—Its Form

The shape of the sanctuary as well as the literary problems inherent in its description and its various alternate names were discussed earlier (introduction to Part VI). They may be summarized as follows:

The shape of the structure, as it is presented in these chapters, may be ascertained with reasonable accuracy, but its historicity cannot. We doubtlessly have before us a mixture of tradition and imagination, of ancient memories and records as well as later retrojections. There were probably two basic traditions, one using the term "Tabernacle" (*Mishkan*), the other speaking of a "Tent" (*Ohel*). The Wellhausen school considered the *Ohel* tradition the older and the *Mishkan* passages as retrojections of the P-stratum and therefore as largely unhistorical. Another theory assigned ark and *Mishkan* to a northern and the *Ohel Mo-ed* to a southern source and held that David, by putting the ark into the *Ohel* (II Sam. 6:17), united the tribes and traditions and that thereafter the term *Mishkan Ohel Mo-ed* was coined (Exod. 40:2, see also Num. 9:15). Traditional commentators suggested that the *Ohel Mo-ed* outside the camp was Moses' dwelling, and that in any case it was used only temporarily until the *Mishkan* was set up. No complete resolution of these problems has so far been possible, especially since there is also the possibility that *Mishkan* and *Ohel* were in fact literary equivalents.

A Tent was erected in Shiloh and later destroyed (see Psalm 78:60); it was also called "house" (*bayit*) or "temple" (*hechal*[1]) and was finally housed in Jerusalem. Only from then on do we have what may be considered a firmly traceable historic tradition, and even then uncertainty prevails over the ultimate fate of the most important part of the sanctuary, namely, the Ark with the Tablets.

The Tabernacle—Its Meaning

The Tabernacle was the place where God could be served tangibly by the community. It concretized the basic cult, transferring the Divine Presence from an immovable Sinai to a movable structure that accompanied the people on all their journeys. The sanctuary was part of God's all-encompassing as well as contracting structure of holiness: it proceeded from Him to His creation and from there to Israel, and within the people from the Tabernacle and its court to the inner tent and the Holy of Holies. Here now was His throne [3]. The erection of the Tabernacle was thus traceable to the creation of the world itself. Even as God "made" the world, so Moses and his helpers "made" the Tabernacle (the key word עָשָׂה being used prominently in both instances), and even as God's work was "finished" so was Moses' (וַתֵּכֶל–וַיְכַלּוּ), and both contemplated and "saw" all the work that they had made (וַיַּרְא) [4].

This climax of divine exaltation appears as a motif in the Babylonian creation story, Enuma Elish (where Essagila is constructed for Marduk) and in Ugaritic epics [5]. There, however, other gods or semi-divine humans build the temple, while in Exodus it is the people who construct the Tabernacle.

The erection of the shrine was the symbolic conclusion of the Exodus tale. The latter had begun with the "absent" God during the years of enslavement and now ends with the "present" God who will lead His people to the Promised Land.

---

[1] I Sam. 1:7 and 9. The word derives most likely from the Sumerian *e-gal*, palace, literally, "large house." The seat of the Israeli Chief Rabbinate is called "Hechal Shelomoh," that is, Solomon's House.

GLEANINGS

Testimony

The Tabernacle testified to the whole world that God had forgiven Israel for the sin of the golden calf. Hence the Torah speaks of "the Tabernacle of the Testimony" (or Pact, עֵדֻת, 38:21).   MIDRASH [6]

Gold

The gold Israel contributed for the sanctuary was a means of reconciliation for the golden calf.

God said: "When you made the calf you provoked Me with אֵלֶּה ("*these are* your gods," 32:4 [so translated by many, but in our translation it is rendered "*this is* your god"]), but now that you have built the Tabernacle I have become reconciled with the same אֵלֶּה ("*these are* the records of the Tabernacle," 38:21).   MIDRASH [7]

38:24 says: "All the gold (that) was used for the work. . . ." Gold was put into this world so that it might be used for good and holy purposes.

TIFERET JONATHAN [8]

Records

Our Sages taught that in communal finances one should never give the responsibility to fewer than two or even three persons—yet Moses was given sole charge of all contributions [9]. But as soon as the Tabernacle was finished Moses, out of his own choice, had an audit made; hence "These are the accounts (or "records") of the Tabernacle" (38:21).   MIDRASH [10]

Broken Spirit

Why does the Torah emphasize that one-half rather than a full shekel per head was required (38:26 mentions it twice)? Note that שֶׁקֶל has the same numerical value as נֶפֶשׁ (soul). [Both have the value of 430: שׁ=300, ק=100, ל=30, together 430. נ=50, פ=80, שׁ=300, together 430.] God wants half a shekel because He wants half a soul: a broken spirit, not an arrogant one.

CHASIDIC [11]

One Whole

Here (in the Tabernacle) we have another symbol of unity, for while the Tabernacle was made up of many parts yet it says (26:6), "so that the Tabernacle becomes one whole." [The Hebrew says הַמִּשְׁכָּן אֶחָד, paralleling יְהֹוָה אֶחָד (Deut. 6:4).] Now just as the human body possesses many organs, higher and lower, some being internal and not visible, while others are external and visible, and yet they all form one body, so also was it with the Tabernacle: all its individual parts were formed in the pattern of that above, and when they were all properly fitted together "the Tabernacle was one." Of the commandments of the Torah the same is true: they are each and all members and limbs in the mystery above, and, when they all unite as one whole, they all ascend into the one mystery. The mystery of the Tabernacle, which thus consists of members and limbs all ascending into the mystery of the Heavenly Man, is after the pattern of the commandments of the Torah, which are all also in the mystery of Man, both Male and Female, which, when united, form one mystery of Man.   ZOHAR [12]

Paradigm for a Harassed People

The last words of Exodus, "on all their journeys," include Israel's resting places and sojourns as well, as Rashi says. This means that, even when Israel finds itself at times in quiet places which betoken sojourns, know that this is temporary and that we face new journeys and flights.   ITTURE TORAH [13]

Exile Completed

Exodus is the book of the first exile, which was decreed already in Gen. 15:13, where also Israel's redemption from exile was foretold. But the exile was not over until the Tabernacle was erected and God's presence dwelt amongst the people.   NACHMANIDES [14]

[According to tradition, four exiles were decreed for Israel, of which Egypt was the first.]

הפטרות

HAFTAROT

שמות

Isaiah

27 : 6 - 28 : 13; 29 : 22-23

Isaiah is the foremost name among the prophets. A member of the royal household in Jerusalem, he preached for some forty years in the latter part of the eighth century B.C.E., warning king and people to trust God rather than the might of their armies. Though Isaiah's name is attached to the whole book, chapters 40 to 66 stem from an unknown later prophet of exilic times.

The sidrah relates how the people are prepared for the deliverance vouchsafed by God. The haftarah too foretells that Israel, after many tribulations, will see the Lord's saving power and "hallow the Holy One of Jacob." What is required of Israel is to be open to God's will and walk the road of mitzvot slowly but persistently (28:10).

Chapter 27

כז

6] [In days] to come Jacob shall strike root,
Israel shall sprout and blossom,
And the face of the world
Shall be covered with fruit.

6] הַבָּאִים יַשְׁרֵשׁ יַעֲקֹב
יָצִיץ וּפָרַח יִשְׂרָאֵל
וּמָלְאוּ פְנֵי־תֵבֵל
תְּנוּבָה:

7] Was he beaten as his beater has been?
Did he suffer such slaughter as his slayers?

7] הַכְּמַכַּת מַכֵּהוּ הִכָּהוּ
אִם־כְּהֶרֶג הֲרֻגָיו הֹרָג:

8] ʲAssailing themʲ with fury unchained,
His pitiless blast bore them off
On a day of gale.

8] בְּסַאסְּאָה בְּשַׁלְחָהּ תְּרִיבֶנָּה
הָגָה בְּרוּחוֹ הַקָּשָׁה
בְּיוֹם קָדִים:

9] ᵍAssuredly, by this alone
Shall Jacob's sin be purged away;
This is the only price
For removing his guilt:
That he make all the altar-stones
Like shattered blocks of chalk—
With no sacred post left standing,
Nor any incense altar.

9] לָכֵן בְּזֹאת
יְכֻפַּר עֲוֺן־יַעֲקֹב
וְזֶה כָּל־פְּרִי
הָסִר חַטָּאתוֹ
בְּשׂוּמוֹ כָּל־אַבְנֵי מִזְבֵּחַ
כְּאַבְנֵי־גִר מְנֻפָּצוֹת
לֹא־יָקֻמוּ אֲשֵׁרִים וְחַמָּנִים:

10] Thus fortified cities lie desolate,
Homesteads deserted, forsaken like a wilderness;

10] כִּי עִיר בְּצוּרָה בָּדָד
נָוֶה מְשֻׁלָּח וְנֶעֱזָב כַּמִּדְבָּר

ʲ-ʲ *Lit. "Striving with her"; meaning of verse uncertain*

ᵍ *This verse would read well before v. 6; the thought of vv. 7–8, dealing with the punishment of Israel's enemies, is continued in vv. 10–11*

There calves graze, there they lie down
h-And consume its boughs.

שָׁם יִרְעֶה עֵגֶל וְשָׁם יִרְבָּץ

וְכִלָּה סְעִפֶיהָ:

11] When its crown is withered, they break;-h
Women come and make fires with them.
For they are a people without understanding;
That is why
Their Maker will show them no mercy,
Their Creator will deny them grace.

11] בִּיבֹשׁ קְצִירָהּ תִּשָּׁבַרְנָה

נָשִׁים בָּאוֹת מְאִירוֹת אוֹתָהּ

כִּי לֹא עַם־בִּינוֹת הוּא

עַל־כֵּן

לֹא־יְרַחֲמֶנּוּ עֹשֵׂהוּ

וְיֹצְרוֹ לֹא יְחֻנֶּנּוּ:

12] And in that day, the LORD will beat out
[the peoples like grain] from the channel of the
Euphrates to the Wadi of Egypt; and you shall be
picked up one by one, O children of Israel!

12] וְהָיָה בַּיּוֹם הַהוּא יַחְבֹּט יְהֹוָה מִשִּׁבֹּלֶת
הַנָּהָר עַד־נַחַל מִצְרָיִם וְאַתֶּם תְּלֻקְּטוּ לְאַחַד
אֶחָד בְּנֵי יִשְׂרָאֵל:

13] And in that day, a great ram's horn shall
be sounded; and the strayed who are in the land
of Assyria and the expelled who are in the land of
Egypt shall come and worship the LORD on the
holy mount, in Jerusalem.

13] וְהָיָה בַּיּוֹם הַהוּא יִתָּקַע בְּשׁוֹפָר גָּדוֹל
וּבָאוּ הָאֹבְדִים בְּאֶרֶץ אַשּׁוּר וְהַנִּדָּחִים בְּאֶרֶץ
מִצְרָיִם וְהִשְׁתַּחֲווּ לַיהֹוָה בְּהַר הַקֹּדֶשׁ
בִּירוּשָׁלָ͏ִם:

Chapter 28

כח

1] Ah, the proud crowns of the drunkards of
      Ephraim,
Whose glorious beauty is but wilted flowers
On the heads of men bloated^a with rich food,
Who are overcome by wine!

1] הוֹי עֲטֶרֶת גֵּאוּת שִׁכֹּרֵי אֶפְרַיִם

וְצִיץ נֹבֵל צְבִי תִפְאַרְתּוֹ

אֲשֶׁר עַל־רֹאשׁ גֵּיא־שְׁמָנִים

הֲלוּמֵי יָיִן:

2] Lo, my LORD has something strong and mighty,
Like a storm of hail,
A shower of pestilence.
Something like a storm of massive, torrential rain^b
Shall be hurled with force to the ground.

2] הִנֵּה חָזָק וְאַמִּץ לַאדֹנָי

כְּזֶרֶם בָּרָד

שַׂעַר קָטֶב

כְּזֶרֶם מַיִם כַּבִּירִים שֹׁטְפִים

הִנִּיחַ לָאָרֶץ בְּיָד:

h-h Meaning of Heb. uncertain. Emendation yields "Or like a terebinth whose boughs/
    Break when its crown is withered"

^a Ge is contracted from ge-e; cf. Ibn Ezra
^b Lit. "water"

3] Trampled underfoot shall be
The proud crowns of the drunkards of Ephraim,

4] The wilted flowers—
On the heads of men bloated[a] with rich food—
That are his glorious beauty.
They shall be like an early fig
Before the fruit harvest;
Whoever sees it devours it
While it is still [c]in his hand.[c]

5] In that day, the LORD of Hosts shall become a crown of beauty and a diadem of glory for the remnant of His people,
6] and a spirit of judgment for him who sits in judgment and of valor for those who repel attacks at the gate.

7] But these are also muddled by wine
And dazed by liquor:
Priest and prophet
Are muddled by liquor;
They are confused by wine,
They are dazed by liquor;
They are muddled in their visions,
They stumble in judgment.

8] Yea, all tables are covered
With vomit and filth,
So that no space is left.

9] [d]"To whom would he give instruction?
To whom expound a message?

בְּרַגְלַיִם תֵּרָמַסְנָה [3
עֲטֶרֶת גֵּאוּת שִׁכֹּרֵי אֶפְרָיִם:

וְהָיְתָה צִיצַת נֹבֵל [4
צְבִי תִפְאַרְתּוֹ
אֲשֶׁר עַל־רֹאשׁ גֵּיא שְׁמָנִים
כְּבִכּוּרָהּ
בְּטֶרֶם קַיִץ
אֲשֶׁר יִרְאֶה הָרֹאֶה אוֹתָהּ
בְּעוֹדָהּ בְּכַפּוֹ יִבְלָעֶנָּה:

בַּיּוֹם הַהוּא יִהְיֶה יְהֹוָה צְבָאוֹת לַעֲטֶרֶת [5
צְבִי וְלִצְפִירַת תִּפְאָרָה לִשְׁאָר עַמּוֹ: 6] וּלְרוּחַ
מִשְׁפָּט לַיּוֹשֵׁב עַל־הַמִּשְׁפָּט וְלִגְבוּרָה מְשִׁיבֵי
מִלְחָמָה שָׁעְרָה:

וְגַם־אֵלֶּה בַּיַּיִן שָׁגוּ [7
וּבַשֵּׁכָר תָּעוּ
כֹּהֵן וְנָבִיא
שָׁגוּ בַשֵּׁכָר
נִבְלְעוּ מִן־הַיַּיִן
תָּעוּ מִן־הַשֵּׁכָר
שָׁגוּ בָרֹאֶה
פָּקוּ פְּלִילִיָּה:

כִּי כָּל־שֻׁלְחָנוֹת מָלְאוּ [8
קִיא צֹאָה
בְּלִי מָקוֹם:

אֶת־מִי יוֹרֶה דֵעָה [9
וְאֶת־מִי יָבִין שְׁמוּעָה

---

[a] Ge is contracted from ge-e; cf. Ibn Ezra
[c-c] Emendation yields "on the bough"
[d] This is the drunkards' reaction to Isaiah's reproof

694

To those newly weaned from milk,
Just taken away from the breast?

10] That same mutter upon mutter,
Murmur upon murmur,
Now here, now there!"

11] Truly, as one who speaks to that people in a stammering jargon and an alien tongue
12] is he who declares to them, "This is the resting place, let the weary rest;ᵉ this is the place of repose." They refuse to listen.

13] To them the word of the Lᴏʀᴅ is:
"Mutter upon mutter,
Murmur upon murmur,
Now here, now there."
And so they will march,ᶠ
But they shall fall backward,
And be injured and snared and captured.

גְּמוּלֵי מֵחָלָב

עַתִּיקֵי מִשָּׁדָיִם:

10 כִּי צַו לָצָו צַו לָצָו

קַו לָקָו קַו לָקָו

זְעֵיר שָׁם וּזְעֵיר שָׁם:

11 כִּי בְּלַעֲגֵי שָׂפָה וּבְלָשׁוֹן אַחֶרֶת יְדַבֵּר

אֶל־הָעָם הַזֶּה: 12 אֲשֶׁר אָמַר אֲלֵיהֶם זֹאת

הַמְּנוּחָה הָנִיחוּ לֶעָיֵף וְזֹאת הַמַּרְגֵּעָה וְלֹא

אָבוּא שְׁמוֹעַ: 13 וְהָיָה לָהֶם דְּבַר־יְהֹוָה

צַו לָצָו צַו לָצָו

קַו לָקָו קַו לָקָו

זְעֵיר שָׁם וּזְעֵיר שָׁם

לְמַעַן יֵלְכוּ

וְכָשְׁלוּ אָחוֹר

וְנִשְׁבָּרוּ וְנוֹקְשׁוּ וְנִלְכָּדוּ:

Chapter 29

22] Assuredly, thus said the Lᴏʀᴅ to the House of Jacob, ᵍwho redeemed Abraham:ᵍ
No more shall Jacob be shamed,
No longer his face grow pale.

23] For when he—that is, his children—behold what My hands have wrought in his midst, they will hallow My name.
Men will hallow the Holy One of Jacob
And stand in awe of the God of Israel.

כט

22 לָכֵן כֹּה־אָמַר יְהֹוָה אֶל־בֵּית יַעֲקֹב

אֲשֶׁר פָּדָה אֶת־אַבְרָהָם

לֹא־עַתָּה יֵבוֹשׁ יַעֲקֹב

וְלֹא עַתָּה פָּנָיו יֶחֱוָרוּ:

23 כִּי בִרְאֹתוֹ יְלָדָיו מַעֲשֵׂה יָדַי בְּקִרְבּוֹ

יַקְדִּישׁוּ שְׁמִי

וְהִקְדִּישׁוּ אֶת־קְדוֹשׁ יַעֲקֹב

וְאֶת־אֱלֹהֵי יִשְׂרָאֵל יַעֲרִיצוּ:

ᵉ I.e., do not embark on any political adventure at this time

ᶠ I.e., embark on the political adventure

ᵍ⁻ᵍ Emendation yields "whose fathers He redeemed"

וארא

Ezekiel
28 : 25 - 29 : 21

Ezekiel lived in Babylon during the days of the exile (sixth century B.C.E.) and was a master of mystic dreams and visions. Like Jeremiah and Deutero-Isaiah he fortified his people's faith in God's forgiveness, but unlike them he stressed the great need for structured ritual as a basis for a religious revival.

Ezekiel comforts his listeners with a message of divine retribution: even as God once humbled Egypt (as described in the Torah portion) so will He dispose of it again and establish His glory.

Chapter 28

כח

25] Thus said the Lord GOD: When I have gathered the House of Israel from the peoples among which they have been dispersed, and have shown Myself holy through them in the sight of the nations, they shall settle on their own soil, which I gave to My servant Jacob,

26] and they shall dwell on it in security. They shall build houses and plant vineyards, and shall dwell on it in security, when I have meted out punishment to all those about them who despise them. And they shall know that I the LORD am their God.

[25] כֹּה־אָמַר֮ אֲדֹנָ֣י יֱהֹוִה֒ בְּקַבְּצִ֣י אֶת־בֵּ֣ית יִשְׂרָאֵ֗ל מִן־הָֽעַמִּים֙ אֲשֶׁ֣ר נָפֹ֣צוּ בָ֔ם וְנִקְדַּ֥שְׁתִּי בָ֖ם לְעֵינֵ֣י הַגּוֹיִ֑ם וְיָֽשְׁבוּ֙ עַל־אַדְמָתָ֔ם אֲשֶׁ֥ר נָתַ֖תִּי לְעַבְדִּ֥י לְיַעֲקֹֽב: 26] וְיָֽשְׁב֣וּ עָלֶ֘יהָ֮ לָבֶ֒טַח֒ וּבָנ֤וּ בָתִּים֙ וְנָֽטְע֣וּ כְרָמִ֔ים וְיָֽשְׁב֖וּ לָבֶ֑טַח בַּֽעֲשׂוֹתִ֣י שְׁפָטִ֗ים בְּכֹ֨ל הַשָּׁאטִ֤ים אֹתָם֙ מִסְּבִ֣יבוֹתָ֔ם וְיָֽדְע֕וּ כִּ֛י אֲנִ֥י יְהֹוָ֖ה אֱלֹֽהֵיהֶֽם:

Chapter 29

כט

1] In the tenth year, on the twelfth day of the tenth month, the word of the LORD came to me: 2] O mortal, turn your face against Pharaoh king of Egypt, and prophesy against him and against all Egypt.

3] Speak these words:

Thus said the Lord GOD:
I am going to deal with you, O Pharaoh king of Egypt,
Mighty monster, sprawling in your[a] channels,
Who said,

[1] בַּשָּׁנָה֙ הָֽעֲשִׂירִ֔ית בָּֽעֲשִׂרִ֖י בִּשְׁנֵ֣ים עָשָׂ֣ר לַחֹ֑דֶשׁ הָיָ֥ה דְבַר־יְהֹוָ֖ה אֵלַ֥י לֵאמֹֽר: 2] בֶּן־אָדָ֕ם שִׂ֥ים פָּנֶ֖יךָ עַל־פַּרְעֹ֣ה מֶ֣לֶךְ מִצְרָ֑יִם וְהִנָּבֵ֣א עָלָ֔יו וְעַל־מִצְרַ֖יִם כֻּלָּֽהּ: 3] דַּבֵּ֣ר וְאָֽמַרְתָּ֡

כֹּֽה־אָמַ֣ר ׀ אֲדֹנָ֣י יֱהֹוִ֗ה

הִנְנִ֤י עָלֶ֨יךָ֙ פַּרְעֹ֣ה מֶֽלֶךְ־מִצְרַ֔יִם

הַתַּנִּים֙ הַגָּד֔וֹל הָֽרֹבֵ֖ץ בְּת֣וֹךְ יְאֹרָ֑יו

אֲשֶׁ֥ר אָמַ֖ר

---

[a] Lit. "its"

ile is my own;
nade it for myself.

לִי יְאֹרִי
וַאֲנִי עֲשִׂיתִנִי:

4] I will put hooks in your jaws,
And make the fish of your channels
Cling to your scales;
I will haul you up from your channels,
With all the fish of your channels.
Clinging to your scales.

4 וְנָתַתִּי חַחִים בִּלְחָיֶיךָ
וְהִדְבַּקְתִּי דְגַת־יְאֹרֶיךָ
בְּקַשְׂקְשֹׂתֶיךָ
וְהַעֲלִיתִיךָ מִתּוֹךְ יְאֹרֶיךָ
וְאֵת כָּל־דְּגַת יְאֹרֶיךָ
בְּקַשְׂקְשֹׂתֶיךָ תִּדְבָּק:

5] And I will fling you into the desert,
With all the fish of your channels.
You shall be left lying in the open,
Ungathered and unburied:
I have given you as food
To the beasts of the earth
And the birds of the sky.

5 וּנְטַשְׁתִּיךָ הַמִּדְבָּרָה
אוֹתְךָ וְאֵת כָּל־דְּגַת יְאֹרֶיךָ
עַל־פְּנֵי הַשָּׂדֶה תִּפּוֹל
לֹא תֵאָסֵף וְלֹא תִקָּבֵץ
לְחַיַּת הָאָרֶץ
וּלְעוֹף הַשָּׁמַיִם
נְתַתִּיךָ לְאָכְלָה:

6] Then all the inhabitants of Egypt shall know
That I am the LORD.
Because you[b] were a staff of reed
To the House of Israel:

6 וְיָדְעוּ כָּל־יֹשְׁבֵי מִצְרַיִם
כִּי אֲנִי יְהֹוָה
יַעַן הֱיוֹתָם מִשְׁעֶנֶת קָנֶה
לְבֵית יִשְׂרָאֵל:

7] When they grasped you with the hand, you
would splinter,
And wound all their shoulders,[c]
And when they leaned on you, you would break,
And make all their loins unsteady.[d]

7 בְּתָפְשָׂם בְּךָ בכפך תֵּרוֹץ
וּבָקַעְתָּ לָהֶם כָּל־כָּתֵף
וּבְהִשָּׁעֲנָם עָלֶיךָ תִּשָּׁבֵר
וְהַעֲמַדְתָּ לָהֶם כָּל־מָתְנָיִם:

8] Assuredly, thus said the Lord GOD: Lo, I
will bring a sword against you, and will cut off
man and beast from you,

8 לָכֵן כֹּה אָמַר אֲדֹנָי יְהֹוִה הִנְנִי מֵבִיא
עָלַיִךְ חָרֶב וְהִכְרַתִּי מִמֵּךְ אָדָם וּבְהֵמָה:

9] so that the land of
Egypt shall fall into desolation and ruin. And they
shall know that I am the LORD—because he
boasted, "The Nile is mine, and I made it."

9 וְהָיְתָה אֶרֶץ־מִצְרַיִם לִשְׁמָמָה וְחָרְבָּה וְיָדְעוּ
כִּי־אֲנִי יְהֹוָה יַעַן אָמַר יְאֹר לִי וַאֲנִי עָשִׂיתִי:

---

[b] Lit. "they"   [c] Septuagint and Syriac read "palms"; cf. II Kings 18.21; Isa. 36.6
[d] Taking amad as a by-form of ma-ad; cf. Syriac translation

10] Assuredly, I am going to deal with you and your channels, and I will reduce the land of Egypt to utter ruin and desolation, ᵉfrom Migdol to Syene, all the way to the border of Nubia.ᵉ 11] No foot of man shall traverse it, and no foot of beast shall traverse it; and it shall remain uninhabited for forty years.

12] For forty years I will make the land of Egypt the most desolate of desolate lands, and its cities shall be the most desolate of ruined cities. And I will scatter the Egyptians among the nations and disperse them throughout the countries.

13] Further, thus said the Lord GOD: After a period of forty years I will gather the Egyptians from the peoples among whom they were dispersed. 14] I will restore the fortunes of the Egyptians and bring them back to the land of their origin, the land of Pathros,ᶠ and there they shall be a lowly kingdom.

15] It shall be the lowliest of all the kingdoms, and shall not lord it over the nations again. I will reduce the Egyptians,ᵍ so that they shall have no dominion over the nations. 16] Never again shall they be the trust of the House of Israel, recalling its guilt in having turned to them. And they shall know that I am the Lord GOD.

17] In the twenty-seventh year, on the first day of the first month, the word of the LORD came to me:

18] O mortal, King Nebuchadrezzar of Babylon has made his army expend vast labor on Tyre; every head is rubbed bald and every shoulder scraped. But he and his army have had no return for the labor he expended on Tyre.

19] Assuredly, thus said the Lord GOD: I will give the land of Egypt to Nebuchadrezzar, king of Babylon.

10] לָכֵן הִנְנִי אֵלֶיךָ וְאֶל־יְאֹרֶיךָ וְנָתַתִּי אֶת־אֶרֶץ מִצְרַיִם לְחׇרְבוֹת חֹרֶב שְׁמָמָה מִמִּגְדֹּל סְוֵנֵה וְעַד־גְּבוּל כּוּשׁ: 11] לֹא תַעֲבׇר־בָּהּ רֶגֶל אָדָם וְרֶגֶל בְּהֵמָה לֹא תַעֲבׇר־בָּהּ וְלֹא תֵשֵׁב אַרְבָּעִים שָׁנָה: 12] וְנָתַתִּי אֶת־אֶרֶץ מִצְרַיִם שְׁמָמָה בְּתוֹךְ אֲרָצוֹת נְשַׁמּוֹת וְעָרֶיהָ בְּתוֹךְ עָרִים מׇחֳרָבוֹת תִּהְיֶיןָ שְׁמָמָה אַרְבָּעִים שָׁנָה וַהֲפִצֹתִי אֶת־מִצְרַיִם בַּגּוֹיִם וְזֵרִיתִים בָּאֲרָצוֹת:

13] כִּי כֹּה אָמַר אֲדֹנָי יְהֹוִה מִקֵּץ אַרְבָּעִים שָׁנָה אֲקַבֵּץ אֶת־מִצְרַיִם מִן־הָעַמִּים אֲשֶׁר־נָפֹצוּ שָׁמָּה: 14] וְשַׁבְתִּי אֶת־שְׁבוּת מִצְרַיִם וַהֲשִׁבֹתִי אֹתָם אֶרֶץ פַּתְרוֹס עַל־אֶרֶץ מְכוּרָתָם וְהָיוּ שָׁם מַמְלָכָה שְׁפָלָה: 15] מִן־הַמַּמְלָכוֹת תִּהְיֶה שְׁפָלָה וְלֹא־תִתְנַשֵּׂא עוֹד עַל־הַגּוֹיִם וְהִמְעַטְתִּים לְבִלְתִּי רְדוֹת בַּגּוֹיִם: 16] וְלֹא יִהְיֶה־עוֹד לְבֵית יִשְׂרָאֵל לְמִבְטָח מַזְכִּיר עָוֺן בִּפְנוֹתָם אַחֲרֵיהֶם וְיָדְעוּ כִּי אֲנִי אֲדֹנָי יְהֹוִה:

17] וַיְהִי בְּעֶשְׂרִים וָשֶׁבַע שָׁנָה בָּרִאשׁוֹן בְּאֶחָד לַחֹדֶשׁ הָיָה דְבַר־יְהֹוָה אֵלַי לֵאמֹר: 18] בֶּן־אָדָם נְבוּכַדְרֶאצַּר מֶלֶךְ־בָּבֶל הֶעֱבִיד אֶת־חֵילוֹ עֲבֹדָה גְדוֹלָה אֶל־צֹר כׇּל־רֹאשׁ מֻקְרָח וְכׇל־כָּתֵף מְרוּטָה וְשָׂכָר לֹא־הָיָה לוֹ וּלְחֵילוֹ מִצֹּר עַל־הָעֲבֹדָה אֲשֶׁר־עָבַד עָלֶיהָ: 19] לָכֵן כֹּה אָמַר אֲדֹנָי יְהֹוִה הִנְנִי נֹתֵן לִנְבוּכַדְרֶאצַּר מֶלֶךְ־בָּבֶל אֶת־אֶרֶץ מִצְרַיִם

ᵉ⁻ᵉ I.e., the length of Egypt, from north to south. Syene is modern Aswan
ᶠ I.e., southern Egypt
ᵍ Heb. "them"

He shall carry off her wealth and take her spoil and seize her booty; and she shall be the recompense of his army.

20] As the wage for which he labored, for what they did for Me, I give him the land of Egypt—declares the Lord GOD.

21] On that day I will [h]endow the House of Israel with strength, and you shall be vindicated[h] among them. And they shall know that I am the LORD.

וְנָשָׂא הֲמֹנָהּ וְשָׁלַל שְׁלָלָהּ וּבָזַז בִּזָּהּ וְהָיְתָה שָׂכָר לְחֵילוֹ: 20] פְּעֻלָּתוֹ אֲשֶׁר־עָבַד בָּהּ נָתַתִּי לוֹ אֶת־אֶרֶץ מִצְרָיִם אֲשֶׁר עָשׂוּ לִי נְאֻם אֲדֹנָי יֱהֹוִה:

21] בַּיּוֹם הַהוּא אַצְמִיחַ קֶרֶן לְבֵית יִשְׂרָאֵל וּלְךָ אֶתֵּן פִּתְחוֹן־פֶּה בְּתוֹכָם וְיָדְעוּ כִּי־אֲנִי יֱהֹוָה:

[h-h] Lit. "cause a horn to sprout for the House of Israel, and I will grant you opening of the mouth"

Jeremiah was the most inward of the prophets. In his agonized visions he foresaw Jerusalem's destruction and was jailed for his preachments. When the Babylonians destroyed the city in 586 (or 585) B.C.E., he became one of the exiles and died in Egypt.

Jeremiah here preaches against Egypt, a power whom God will overcome as He did in the days of Moses. Egypt will learn again that her might will be crushed by the will of God.

Jeremiah

46 : 13–28

Chapter 46

מו

13] The word which the LORD spoke to the prophet Jeremiah about the coming of King Nebuchadrezzar of Babylon to attack the land of Egypt:

[13 הַדָּבָר אֲשֶׁר דִּבֶּר יְהֹוָה אֶל־יִרְמְיָהוּ הַנָּבִיא לָבוֹא נְבוּכַדְרֶאצַּר מֶלֶךְ בָּבֶל לְהַכּוֹת אֶת־אֶרֶץ מִצְרָיִם:

14] Declare in Egypt, proclaim in Migdol,
Proclaim in Noph and Tahpanhes!
Say: Take your posts and stand ready,
For the sword has devoured all around you!

[14 הַגִּידוּ בְמִצְרַיִם וְהַשְׁמִיעוּ בְמִגְדּוֹל וְהַשְׁמִיעוּ בְנֹף וּבְתַחְפַּנְחֵס אִמְרוּ הִתְיַצֵּב וְהָכֵן לָךְ כִּי־אָכְלָה חֶרֶב סְבִיבֶיךָ:

15] Why are your stalwarts swept away?
They did not stand firm,
For the LORD thrust them down;

[15 מַדּוּעַ נִסְחַף אַבִּירֶיךָ לֹא עָמַד כִּי יְהֹוָה הֲדָפוֹ:

16] He made many stumble,
They fell over one another.
They said:
"Up! let us return to our people,
To the land of our birth,
Because of the deadly[b] sword."

[16 הִרְבָּה כּוֹשֵׁל גַּם־נָפַל אִישׁ אֶל־רֵעֵהוּ וַיֹּאמְרוּ קוּמָה וְנָשֻׁבָה אֶל־עַמֵּנוּ וְאֶל־אֶרֶץ מוֹלַדְתֵּנוּ מִפְּנֵי חֶרֶב הַיּוֹנָה:

17] There they called Pharaoh king of Egypt:
[b]"Braggart who let the hour go by."[b]

[17 קָרְאוּ שָׁם פַּרְעֹה מֶלֶךְ־מִצְרַיִם שָׁאוֹן הֶעֱבִיר הַמּוֹעֵד:

---

[b] *Meaning of Heb. uncertain*

[b-b] *Meaning of Heb. uncertain*

18] As I live—declares the King,
Whose name is LORD of Hosts—
ᵇ⁻As surely as Tabor is among the mountains
And Carmel is by the sea,
So shall this come to pass.⁻ᵇ

חַי־אָנִי נְאֻם־הַמֶּלֶךְ [18
יְהוָה צְבָאוֹת שְׁמוֹ
כִּי כְּתָבוֹר בֶּהָרִים
וּכְכַרְמֶל בַּיָּם
יָבוֹא:

19] Equip yourself for exile,
Fair Egypt, you who dwell secure!
For Noph shall become a waste,
Desolate, without inhabitants.

כְּלֵי גוֹלָה עֲשִׂי לָךְ [19
יוֹשֶׁבֶת בַּת־מִצְרָיִם
כִּי־נֹף לְשַׁמָּה תִהְיֶה
וְנִצְּתָה מֵאֵין יוֹשֵׁב:

20] Egypt is a handsome heifer—
A gadflyᶜ from the north ᵈ⁻is coming, coming!⁻ᵈ

עֶגְלָה יְפֵה־פִיָּה מִצְרָיִם [20
קֶרֶץ מִצָּפוֹן בָּא בָא:

21] The mercenaries, too, in her midst
Are like stall-fed calves;
They too shall turn tail,
Flee as one, and make no stand.
Their day of disaster is upon them,
The hour of their doom.

גַּם־שְׂכִרֶיהָ בְקִרְבָּהּ [21
כְּעֶגְלֵי מַרְבֵּק
כִּי־גַם־הֵמָּה הִפְנוּ
נָסוּ יַחְדָּיו לֹא עָמָדוּ
כִּי יוֹם אֵידָם בָּא עֲלֵיהֶם
עֵת פְּקֻדָּתָם:

22] ᵇ⁻She shall rustle away like a snake⁻ᵇ
As they come marching in force;
They shall come against her with axes,
Like hewers of wood.

קוֹלָהּ כַּנָּחָשׁ יֵלֵךְ [22
כִּי־בְחַיִל יֵלֵכוּ
וּבְקַרְדֻּמּוֹת בָּאוּ לָהּ
כְּחֹטְבֵי עֵצִים:

23] They shall cut down her forest
—declares the LORD—
Though it cannot be measured;
For they are more numerous than locusts,
And cannot be counted.

כָּרְתוּ יַעְרָהּ [23
נְאֻם־יְהוָה
כִּי לֹא יֵחָקֵר
כִּי רַבּוּ מֵאַרְבֶּה
וְאֵין לָהֶם מִסְפָּר:

24] Fair Egypt shall be shamed,
Handed over to the people of the north.

הֹבִישָׁה בַּת־מִצְרָיִם [24
נִתְּנָה בְּיַד עַם־צָפוֹן:

ᵇ⁻ᵇ *Meaning of Heb. uncertain*   ᶜ *Or "butcher"; meaning of Heb. uncertain*
ᵈ⁻ᵈ *Many mss. read "will come upon her"*

25] The Lord of Hosts, the God of Israel, has said: I will inflict punishment on Amon[e] of No and on Pharaoh—on Egypt, her gods, and her kings—on Pharaoh and all who rely on him. 26] I will deliver them into the hands of those who seek to kill them, into the hands of King Nebuchadrezzar of Babylon and into the hands of his subjects. But afterward she shall be inhabited again as in former days, declares the Lord.

27] But you,
Have no fear, My servant Jacob,
Be not dismayed, O Israel!
I will deliver you from far away,
Your folk from their land of captivity;
And Jacob again shall have calm
And quiet, with none to trouble him.

28] But you, have no fear,
My servant Jacob

    —declares the Lord—

For I am with you.
I will make an end of all the nations
Among which I have banished you,
But I will not make an end of you!
I will not leave you unpunished,
But I will chastise you in measure.

25] אָמַר יְהֹוָה צְבָאוֹת אֱלֹהֵי יִשְׂרָאֵל הִנְנִי
פוֹקֵד אֶל־אָמוֹן מִנֹּא וְעַל־פַּרְעֹה וְעַל־מִצְרַיִם
וְעַל־אֱלֹהֶיהָ וְעַל־מְלָכֶיהָ וְעַל־פַּרְעֹה וְעַל
הַבֹּטְחִים בּוֹ: 26 וּנְתַתִּים בְּיַד מְבַקְשֵׁי נַפְשָׁם
וּבְיַד נְבוּכַדְרֶאצַּר מֶלֶךְ־בָּבֶל וּבְיַד עֲבָדָיו
וְאַחֲרֵי־כֵן תִּשְׁכֹּן כִּימֵי־קֶדֶם נְאֻם־יְהֹוָה:

27] וְאַתָּה
אַל־תִּירָא עַבְדִּי יַעֲקֹב
וְאַל־תֵּחַת יִשְׂרָאֵל
כִּי הִנְנִי מוֹשִׁעֲךָ מֵרָחוֹק
וְאֶת־זַרְעֲךָ מֵאֶרֶץ שִׁבְיָם
וְשָׁב יַעֲקֹב וְשָׁקַט
וְשַׁאֲנַן וְאֵין מַחֲרִיד:

28] אַתָּה אַל־תִּירָא
עַבְדִּי יַעֲקֹב
נְאֻם־יְהֹוָה
כִּי אִתְּךָ אָנִי
כִּי אֶעֱשֶׂה כָלָה בְּכָל־הַגּוֹיִם
אֲשֶׁר הִדַּחְתִּיךָ שָׁמָּה
וְאֹתְךָ לֹא־אֶעֱשֶׂה כָלָה
וְיִסַּרְתִּיךָ לַמִּשְׁפָּט
וְנַקֵּה לֹא אֲנַקֶּךָּ:

---

[e] *Tutelary deity of the city No (Thebes); cf. Nah. 3.8*

בשלח

After Joshua's initial conquest of Canaan a number of leaders ("Judges") guided the troubled and often disunited tribes during the twelfth and eleventh centuries B.C.E. Their military and personal adventures are recounted in the 21 chapters which portray the protracted difficulties Israel encountered in its attempt to make the Promised Land its own.

In the sidrah, Israel's "Song at the Sea" celebrates God's victory over Egypt; in the haftarah, the "Song of Deborah" reflects a similar mood some hundred years later. It reflects the internal divisions of Israel's tribes who had to fight bitter battles to maintain both their tribal cohesion and their common security.

Judges

4:4–5:31

ד

Chapter 4

4] Deborah, wife of Lappidoth, was a prophetess; she led Israel at that time.

5] She used to sit under the Palm of Deborah, between Ramah and Bethel in the hill country of Ephraim, and the Israelites would come to her for decisions.

6] She summoned Barak son of Abinoam, of Kedesh in Naphtali, and said to him, "The LORD, the God of Israel, has commanded: Go, march up to Mount Tabor, and take with you ten thousand men of Naphtali and Zebulun.

7] And I will draw Sisera, Jabin's army commander, with his chariots and his troops, toward you up to the Wadi Kishon; and I will deliver him into your hands."

8] But Barak said to her, "If you will go with me, I will go; if not, I will not go."

9] "Very well, I will go with you," she answered. "However, there will be no glory for you in the course you are taking, for then the LORD will deliver Sisera into the hands of a woman." So Deborah went with Barak to Kedesh.

10] Barak then mustered Zebulun and Naphtali at Kedesh; ten

4 וּדְבוֹרָה֙ אִשָּׁ֣ה נְבִיאָ֔ה אֵ֖שֶׁת לַפִּיד֑וֹת הִ֛יא שֹׁפְטָ֥ה אֶת־יִשְׂרָאֵ֖ל בָּעֵ֥ת הַהִֽיא: 5 וְ֠הִיא יוֹשֶׁ֨בֶת תַּֽחַת־תֹּ֜מֶר דְּבוֹרָ֗ה בֵּ֤ין הָֽרָמָה֙ וּבֵ֣ין בֵּֽית־אֵ֔ל בְּהַ֖ר אֶפְרָ֑יִם וַיַּֽעֲל֥וּ אֵלֶ֛יהָ בְּנֵ֥י יִשְׂרָאֵ֖ל לַמִּשְׁפָּֽט: 6 וַתִּשְׁלַ֗ח וַתִּקְרָא֙ לְבָרָ֣ק בֶּן־אֲבִינֹ֔עַם מִקֶּ֖דֶשׁ נַפְתָּלִ֑י וַתֹּ֨אמֶר אֵלָ֜יו הֲלֹ֥א צִוָּ֣ה יְהֹוָ֣ה אֱלֹהֵֽי־יִשְׂרָאֵ֗ל לֵ֤ךְ וּמָֽשַׁכְתָּ֙ בְּהַ֣ר תָּב֔וֹר וְלָֽקַחְתָּ֣ עִמְּךָ֗ עֲשֶׂ֤רֶת אֲלָפִים֙ אִ֔ישׁ מִבְּנֵ֥י נַפְתָּלִ֖י וּמִבְּנֵ֥י זְבֻלֽוּן: 7 וּמָֽשַׁכְתִּ֨י אֵלֶ֜יךָ אֶל־נַ֣חַל קִישׁ֗וֹן אֶת־סִֽיסְרָא֙ שַׂר־צְבָ֣א יָבִ֔ין וְאֶת־רִכְבּ֖וֹ וְאֶת־הֲמוֹנ֑וֹ וּנְתַתִּ֖יהוּ בְּיָדֶֽךָ: 8 וַיֹּ֤אמֶר אֵלֶ֨יהָ֙ בָּרָ֔ק אִם־תֵּֽלְכִ֥י עִמִּ֖י וְהָלָ֑כְתִּי וְאִם־לֹ֥א תֵֽלְכִ֛י עִמִּ֖י לֹ֥א אֵלֵֽךְ: 9 וַתֹּ֜אמֶר הָלֹ֧ךְ אֵלֵ֣ךְ עִמָּ֗ךְ אֶ֚פֶס כִּי֩ לֹ֨א תִֽהְיֶ֜ה תִּֽפְאַרְתְּךָ֗ עַל־הַדֶּ֨רֶךְ֙ אֲשֶׁ֣ר אַתָּ֣ה הוֹלֵ֔ךְ כִּ֣י בְֽיַד־אִשָּׁ֔ה יִמְכֹּ֥ר יְהֹוָ֖ה אֶת־סִֽיסְרָ֑א וַתָּ֧קׇם דְּבוֹרָ֛ה וַתֵּ֥לֶךְ עִם־בָּרָ֖ק קֶֽדְשָׁה: 10 וַיַּזְעֵ֨ק בָּרָ֜ק אֶת־זְבוּלֻ֤ן וְאֶת־נַפְתָּלִי֙ קֶ֔דְשָׁה

thousand men marched up *a*after him;*a* and Deborah also went up with him.

11] Now Heber the Kenite had separated *b*from the other Kenites,*b* descendants of Hobab, father-in-law of Moses, and had pitched his tent at Elon-bezaananim, which is near Kedesh.

12] Sisera was informed that Barak son of Abinoam had gone up to Mount Tabor.
13] So Sisera ordered all his chariots—nine hundred iron chariots—and all the troops he had to move from Harosheth-goiim to the Wadi Kishon.

14] Then Deborah said to Barak, "Up! This is the day on which the LORD will deliver Sisera into your hands: the LORD is marching before you." Barak charged down Mount Tabor, followed by the ten thousand men,

15] and the LORD threw Sisera and all his chariots and army into a panic *c*before the onslaught of Barak.*c* Sisera leaped from his chariot and fled on foot

16] as Barak pursued the chariots and the soldiers as far as Harosheth-goiim. All of Sisera's soldiers fell by the sword; not a man was left.

17] Sisera, meanwhile, had fled on foot to the tent of Jael, wife of Heber the Kenite; for there was friendship between King Jabin of Hazor and the family of Heber the Kenite.
18] Jael came out to greet Sisera and said to him, "Come in, my lord, come in here, do not be afraid." So he entered her tent, and she covered him with a blanket.

19] He said to her, "Please let me have some water; I am thirsty." She opened a skin of milk and gave him some to drink; and she covered him again.
20] He said to her, "Stand at the entrance

וַיַּעַל בְּרַגְלָיו עֲשֶׂרֶת אַלְפֵי אִישׁ וַתַּעַל עִמּוֹ דְּבוֹרָה:

11] וְחֶבֶר הַקֵּינִי נִפְרָד מִקַּיִן מִבְּנֵי חֹבָב חֹתֵן מֹשֶׁה וַיֵּט אָהֳלוֹ עַד־אֵלוֹן בְּצַעֲנַנִּים אֲשֶׁר אֶת־קֶדֶשׁ:

12] וַיַּגִּדוּ לְסִיסְרָא כִּי עָלָה בָּרָק בֶּן־אֲבִינֹעַם הַר־תָּבוֹר: 13] וַיַּזְעֵק סִיסְרָא אֶת־כָּל־רִכְבּוֹ תְּשַׁע מֵאוֹת רֶכֶב בַּרְזֶל וְאֶת־כָּל־הָעָם אֲשֶׁר אִתּוֹ מֵחֲרֹשֶׁת הַגּוֹיִם אֶל־נַחַל קִישׁוֹן: 14] וַתֹּאמֶר דְּבֹרָה אֶל־בָּרָק קוּם כִּי זֶה הַיּוֹם אֲשֶׁר נָתַן יְהוָה אֶת־סִיסְרָא בְּיָדֶךָ הֲלֹא יְהוָה יָצָא לְפָנֶיךָ וַיֵּרֶד בָּרָק מֵהַר תָּבוֹר וַעֲשֶׂרֶת אֲלָפִים אִישׁ אַחֲרָיו: 15] וַיָּהָם יְהוָה אֶת־סִיסְרָא וְאֶת־כָּל־הָרֶכֶב וְאֶת־כָּל־הַמַּחֲנֶה לְפִי־חֶרֶב לִפְנֵי בָרָק וַיֵּרֶד סִיסְרָא מֵעַל הַמֶּרְכָּבָה וַיָּנָס בְּרַגְלָיו: 16] וּבָרָק רָדַף אַחֲרֵי הָרֶכֶב וְאַחֲרֵי הַמַּחֲנֶה עַד חֲרֹשֶׁת הַגּוֹיִם וַיִּפֹּל כָּל־מַחֲנֵה סִיסְרָא לְפִי־חֶרֶב לֹא נִשְׁאַר עַד־אֶחָד: 17] וְסִיסְרָא נָס בְּרַגְלָיו אֶל־אֹהֶל יָעֵל אֵשֶׁת חֶבֶר הַקֵּינִי כִּי שָׁלוֹם בֵּין יָבִין מֶלֶךְ־חָצוֹר וּבֵין בֵּית חֶבֶר הַקֵּינִי: 18] וַתֵּצֵא יָעֵל לִקְרַאת סִיסְרָא וַתֹּאמֶר אֵלָיו סוּרָה אֲדֹנִי סוּרָה אֵלַי אַל־תִּירָא וַיָּסַר אֵלֶיהָ הָאֹהֱלָה וַתְּכַסֵּהוּ בַּשְּׂמִיכָה: 19] וַיֹּאמֶר אֵלֶיהָ הַשְׁקִינִי־נָא מְעַט־מַיִם כִּי צָמֵאתִי וַתִּפְתַּח אֶת־נֹאוד הֶחָלָב וַתַּשְׁקֵהוּ וַתְּכַסֵּהוּ: 20] וַיֹּאמֶר

a-a Lit. "at his feet"
b-b Lit. "from Cain"; cf. 1.16
c-c Lit. "at the edge of the sword before Barak"

of the tent. If anybody comes and asks you if there is anybody here, say 'No.'"

21] Then Jael wife of Heber took a tent pin and grasped the mallet. When he was fast asleep from exhaustion, she approached him stealthily and drove the pin through his temple till it went down to the ground. Thus he died.

22] Now Barak appeared in pursuit of Sisera. Jael went out to greet him and said, "Come, I will show you the man you are looking for." He went inside with her, and there Sisera was lying dead, with the pin in his temple.

23] On that day God subdued King Jabin of Hazor before the Israelites.
24] The hand of the Israelites bore harder and harder on King Jabin of Canaan, until they destroyed King Jabin of Canaan.

Chapter 5

1] On that day Deborah and Barak son of Abinoam sang:

2] *When *b*locks go untrimmed*-b* in Israel,
When people dedicate themselves—
Bless the LORD!

3] Hear, O kings! Give ear, O potentates!
I will sing, will sing to the LORD,
Will hymn the LORD, the God of Israel.

4] O LORD, when You came forth from Seir,
Advanced from the country of Edom,
The earth trembled;

אֵלֶיהָ עָמַד פֶּתַח הָאֹהֶל וְהָיָה אִם־אִישׁ יָבֹא
וּשְׁאֵלֵךְ וְאָמַר הֲיֵשׁ־פֹּה אִישׁ וְאָמַרְתְּ אָיִן:

21] וַתִּקַּח יָעֵל אֵשֶׁת־חֶבֶר אֶת־יְתַד הָאֹהֶל
וַתָּשֶׂם אֶת־הַמַּקֶּבֶת בְּיָדָהּ וַתָּבוֹא אֵלָיו בַּלָּאט
וַתִּתְקַע אֶת־הַיָּתֵד בְּרַקָּתוֹ וַתִּצְנַח בָּאָרֶץ
וְהוּא־נִרְדָּם וַיָּעַף וַיָּמֹת:

22] וְהִנֵּה בָרָק רֹדֵף אֶת־סִיסְרָא וַתֵּצֵא
יָעֵל לִקְרָאתוֹ וַתֹּאמֶר לוֹ לֵךְ וְאַרְאֶךָּ אֶת־
הָאִישׁ אֲשֶׁר־אַתָּה מְבַקֵּשׁ וַיָּבֹא אֵלֶיהָ וְהִנֵּה
סִיסְרָא נֹפֵל מֵת וְהַיָּתֵד בְּרַקָּתוֹ:

23] וַיַּכְנַע אֱלֹהִים בַּיּוֹם הַהוּא אֵת יָבִין
מֶלֶךְ־כְּנָעַן לִפְנֵי בְּנֵי יִשְׂרָאֵל: 24] וַתֵּלֶךְ יַד
בְּנֵי־יִשְׂרָאֵל הָלוֹךְ וְקָשָׁה עַל יָבִין מֶלֶךְ־כְּנָעַן
עַד אֲשֶׁר הִכְרִיתוּ אֵת יָבִין מֶלֶךְ־כְּנָעַן:

ה

1] וַתָּשַׁר דְּבוֹרָה וּבָרָק בֶּן־אֲבִינֹעַם בַּיּוֹם
הַהוּא לֵאמֹר:

2] בִּפְרֹעַ פְּרָעוֹת בְּיִשְׂרָאֵל
בְּהִתְנַדֵּב עָם
בָּרְכוּ יְהוָה:

3] שִׁמְעוּ מְלָכִים הַאֲזִינוּ רֹזְנִים
אָנֹכִי לַיהוָה אָנֹכִי אָשִׁירָה
אֲזַמֵּר לַיהוָה אֱלֹהֵי יִשְׂרָאֵל:

4] יְהוָה בְּצֵאתְךָ מִשֵּׂעִיר
בְּצַעְדְּךָ מִשְּׂדֵה אֱדוֹם
אֶרֶץ רָעָשָׁה

---

*a In many parts of this poem the meaning is uncertain
*b-b Apparently an expression of dedication; cf. Num. 6.5

The heavens dripped,
Yea, the clouds dripped water,

גַּם־שָׁמַיִם נָטָפוּ

גַּם־עָבִים נָטְפוּ מָיִם:

5] The mountains quaked[c]—
Before the Lord, Him of Sinai.
Before the Lord, God of Israel.

5] הָרִים נָזְלוּ

מִפְּנֵי יְהֹוָה זֶה סִינַי

מִפְּנֵי יְהֹוָה אֱלֹהֵי יִשְׂרָאֵל:

6] In the days of Shamgar [d]son of Anath,[d]
In the days of Jael, caravans[e] ceased,
And wayfarers went
By roundabout paths.

6] בִּימֵי שַׁמְגַּר בֶּן־עֲנָת

בִּימֵי יָעֵל חָדְלוּ אֳרָחוֹת

וְהֹלְכֵי נְתִיבוֹת יֵלְכוּ

אֳרָחוֹת עֲקַלְקַלּוֹת:

7] Deliverance ceased,
Ceased in Israel.
Till you[f] arose, O Deborah,
Arose, O mother, in Israel!

7] חָדְלוּ פְרָזוֹן

בְּיִשְׂרָאֵל חָדֵלּוּ

עַד שַׁקַּמְתִּי דְּבוֹרָה

שַׁקַּמְתִּי אֵם בְּיִשְׂרָאֵל:

8] When they chose new gods,
[g]Was there a fighter then in the gates?[g]
No shield or spear was seen
Among forty thousand in Israel!

8] יִבְחַר אֱלֹהִים חֲדָשִׁים

אָז לָחֶם שְׁעָרִים

מָגֵן אִם־יֵרָאֶה וָרֹמַח

בְּאַרְבָּעִים אֶלֶף בְּיִשְׂרָאֵל:

9] My heart is with Israel's leaders,
With the dedicated of the people—
Bless the Lord!

9] לִבִּי לְחוֹקְקֵי יִשְׂרָאֵל

הַמִּתְנַדְּבִים בָּעָם

בָּרְכוּ יְהֹוָה:

10] You riders on tawny she-asses,
You who sit on saddle rugs,
And you wayfarers, declare it!

10] רֹכְבֵי אֲתֹנוֹת צְחֹרוֹת

יֹשְׁבֵי עַל־מִדִּין

וְהֹלְכֵי עַל־דֶּרֶךְ שִׂיחוּ:

11] Louder than the [h]sound of archers,[h]
There among the watering places

11] מִקּוֹל מְחַצְצִים

בֵּין מַשְׁאַבִּים

[c] Taking nazelu *as a by-form of* nazolu; *cf.* Targum
[d-d] Or "the Bet-anathite"
[e] Or "roads"
[f] Heb. kamti, *archaic second person singular feminine*
[g-g] Meaning of Heb. uncertain; others "then was war in the gates"
[h-h] Or "thunder peals"; meaning of Heb. uncertain

Let them chant the gracious acts of the LORD,
His gracious deliverance of Israel.
Then did the people of the LORD
March down to the gates!

12] Awake, awake, O Deborah!
Awake, awake, strike up the chant!
Arise, O Barak;
Take your captives, O son of Abinoam!

13] Then was the remnant made victor over the
        mighty,
The LORD's people[i] won my victory over the war-
        riors.
14] From Ephraim came they whose roots are in
        Amalek;
After you, your kin Benjamin;
From Machir came down leaders,
From Zebulun such as hold the marshal's staff.

15] And Issachar's chiefs were with Deborah;
As Barak, so was Issachar—
Rushing after him into the valley.
Among the clans of Reuben
Were great decisions of heart.

16] Why then did you stay among the sheepfolds
And listen as they pipe for the flocks?
Among the clans of Reuben
Were great searchings of heart!

17] Gilead tarried beyond the Jordan;
And Dan—why did he linger [i]by the ships?[i]
Asher remained at the seacoast
And tarried at his landings.

שָׁם יְתַנּוּ צִדְקוֹת יְהֹוָה

צִדְקֹת פִּרְזוֹנוֹ בְּיִשְׂרָאֵל

אָז יָרְדוּ לַשְּׁעָרִים

עַם־יְהֹוָה:

12] עוּרִי עוּרִי דְּבוֹרָה

עוּרִי עוּרִי דַּבְּרִי־שִׁיר

קוּם בָּרָק

וּשְׁבֵה שֶׁבְיְךָ בֶּן־אֲבִינֹעַם:

13] אָז יְרַד שָׂרִיד לְאַדִּירִים עָם

יְהֹוָה יְרַד־לִי בַּגִּבּוֹרִים:

14] מִנִּי אֶפְרַיִם שָׁרְשָׁם בַּעֲמָלֵק

אַחֲרֶיךָ בִנְיָמִין בַּעֲמָמֶיךָ

מִנִּי מָכִיר יָרְדוּ מְחֹקְקִים

וּמִזְּבוּלֻן מֹשְׁכִים בְּשֵׁבֶט סֹפֵר:

15] וְשָׂרַי בְּיִשָּׂשכָר עִם־דְּבֹרָה

וְיִשָּׂשכָר כֵּן בָּרָק

בָּעֵמֶק שֻׁלַּח בְּרַגְלָיו

בִּפְלַגּוֹת רְאוּבֵן

גְּדֹלִים חִקְקֵי־לֵב:

16] לָמָּה יָשַׁבְתָּ בֵּין הַמִּשְׁפְּתַיִם

לִשְׁמֹעַ שְׁרִקוֹת עֲדָרִים

לִפְלַגּוֹת רְאוּבֵן

גְּדוֹלִים חִקְרֵי־לֵב:

17] גִּלְעָד בְּעֵבֶר הַיַּרְדֵּן שָׁכֵן

וְדָן לָמָּה יָגוּר אֳנִיּוֹת

אָשֵׁר יָשַׁב לְחוֹף יַמִּים

וְעַל מִפְרָצָיו יִשְׁכּוֹן:

---

[i] Reading am (with patach) Adonai; so many Heb. mss.
[i-i] Or "at Oniot," a presumed designation of Dan's region

18] Zebulun is a people ^kthat mocked at death,^{-k}
Naphtali—on the open heights.

19] Then the kings came, they fought:
The kings of Canaan fought
At Taanach, by Megiddo's waters—
They got no spoil of silver.

20] The stars fought from heaven,
From their courses they fought against Sisera.

21] The torrent Kishon swept them^l away,
The raging torrent, the torrent Kishon.
March on, my soul, with courage!

22] Then the horses' hoofs pounded
^mAs headlong galloped the steeds.^{-m}

23] "Curse Meroz!" said the angel of the LORD.
"Bitterly curse its inhabitants,
Because they came not to the aid of the LORD,
To the aid of the LORD amongⁿ the warriors."

24] Most blessed of women be Jael,
Wife of Heber the Kenite,
Most blessed of women in tents.

25] He asked for water, she offered milk;
In a princely bowl she brought him curds.

26] Her [left] hand reached for the tent pin,
Her right for the workmen's hammer.
She struck Sisera, crushed his head,
Smashed and pierced his temple.

18] וּזְבֻלוּן עַם חֵרֵף נַפְשׁוֹ לָמוּת
וְנַפְתָּלִי עַל מְרוֹמֵי שָׂדֶה:

19] בָּאוּ מְלָכִים נִלְחָמוּ
אָז נִלְחֲמוּ מַלְכֵי כְנַעַן
בְּתַעְנַךְ עַל־מֵי מְגִדּוֹ
בֶּצַע כֶּסֶף לֹא לָקָחוּ:

20] מִן־שָׁמַיִם נִלְחָמוּ הַכּוֹכָבִים
מִמְּסִלּוֹתָם נִלְחֲמוּ עִם סִיסְרָא:

21] נַחַל קִישׁוֹן גְּרָפָם
נַחַל קְדוּמִים נַחַל קִישׁוֹן
תִּדְרְכִי נַפְשִׁי עֹז:

22] אָז הָלְמוּ עִקְּבֵי־סוּס
מִדַּהֲרוֹת דַּהֲרוֹת אַבִּירָיו:

23] אוֹרוּ מֵרוֹז אָמַר מַלְאַךְ יְהֹוָה
אֹרוּ אָרוֹר יֹשְׁבֶיהָ
כִּי לֹא־בָאוּ לְעֶזְרַת יְהֹוָה
לְעֶזְרַת יְהֹוָה בַּגִּבּוֹרִים:

24] תְּבֹרַךְ מִנָּשִׁים יָעֵל
אֵשֶׁת חֶבֶר הַקֵּינִי
מִנָּשִׁים בָּאֹהֶל תְּבֹרָךְ:

25] מַיִם שָׁאַל חָלָב נָתָנָה
בְּסֵפֶל אַדִּירִים הִקְרִיבָה חֶמְאָה:

26] יָדָהּ לַיָּתֵד תִּשְׁלַחְנָה
וִימִינָהּ לְהַלְמוּת עֲמֵלִים
וְהָלְמָה סִיסְרָא מָחֲקָה רֹאשׁוֹ
וּמָחֲצָה וְחָלְפָה רַקָּתוֹ:

^{k-k} Lit. "belittled its life to die"
^l I.e., the kings of Canaan (v. 19)
^{m-m} Lit. "From the gallopings, the gallopings of his steeds"
ⁿ Or "against"

27] At her feet he sank, lay outstretched,
At her feet he sank, lay still;
Where he sank, there he lay—destroyed.

28] Through the window peered Sisera's mother,
Behind the lattice she whined:°
"Why is his chariot so long in coming?
Why so late the clatter of his wheels?"

29] The wisest of her ladies give answer;
She, too, replies to herself:

30] "They must be dividing the spoil they have
found:
A damsel or two for each man,
Spoil of dyed cloths for Sisera,
Spoil of embroidered cloths,
A couple of embroidered cloths
Round every neck as spoil."

31] So may all Your enemies perish, O LORD!
But may His friends be as the sun rising in might!
And the land was tranquil forty years.

בֵּין רַגְלֶיהָ כָּרַע נָפַל שָׁכָב [27
בֵּין רַגְלֶיהָ כָּרַע נָפָל
בַּאֲשֶׁר כָּרַע שָׁם נָפַל שָׁדוּד:

בְּעַד הַחַלּוֹן נִשְׁקְפָה [28
וַתְּיַבֵּב אֵם סִיסְרָא בְּעַד הָאֶשְׁנָב
מַדּוּעַ בֹּשֵׁשׁ רִכְבּוֹ לָבוֹא
מַדּוּעַ אֶחֱרוּ פַּעֲמֵי מַרְכְּבוֹתָיו:

חַכְמוֹת שָׂרוֹתֶיהָ תַּעֲנֶינָּה [29
אַף־הִיא תָּשִׁיב אֲמָרֶיהָ לָהּ:

הֲלֹא יִמְצְאוּ יְחַלְּקוּ שָׁלָל [30
רַחַם רַחֲמָתַיִם לְרֹאשׁ גֶּבֶר
שְׁלַל צְבָעִים לְסִיסְרָא
שְׁלַל צְבָעִים רִקְמָה
צֶבַע רִקְמָתַיִם
לְצַוְּארֵי שָׁלָל:

כֵּן יֹאבְדוּ כָל־אוֹיְבֶיךָ יְהוָה [31
וְאֹהֲבָיו כְּצֵאת הַשֶּׁמֶשׁ בִּגְבֻרָתוֹ
וַתִּשְׁקֹט הָאָרֶץ אַרְבָּעִים שָׁנָה:

° Or "gazed"; meaning of Heb. uncertain

Isaiah is the foremost name among the prophets. A member of the royal household in Jerusalem, he preached for some forty years in the latter part of the eighth century B.C.E., warning king and people to trust God rather than the might of their armies. Though Isaiah's name is attached to the whole book, chapters 40 to 66 stem from an unknown later prophet of exilic times.

The revelation at Sinai recounted in the sidrah finds its parallel in the personal revelation which Isaiah experiences and which culminates in the adoration of the seraphim: "Holy, Holy, Holy! The Lord of Hosts!" Jewish congregations take up the angels' song during the Kedushah, the holiness proclamation, at morning and afternoon services.

יתרו

Isaiah

6 : 1-7 : 6; 9 : 5-6

ו

Chapter 6

1] In the year that King Uzziah died, I beheld my LORD seated on a high and lofty throne; and the skirts of His robe filled the Temple.

2] Seraphs stood in attendance on Him. Each of them had six wings: with two he covered his face, with two he covered his legs, and with two he would fly.

3] And one would call to the other,
"Holy, holy, holy!
The LORD of Hosts!
His presence fills all the earth!"

4] The doorposts[a] would shake at the sound of the one who called, and the House kept filling with smoke.

5] I cried,
"Woe is me; I am lost!
For I am a man [b]of unclean lips[b]
And I live among a people
Of unclean lips;
Yet my own eyes have beheld
The King LORD of Hosts."

6] Then one of the seraphs flew over to me

[1] בִּשְׁנַת־מוֹת הַמֶּלֶךְ עֻזִּיָּהוּ וָאֶרְאֶה אֶת־אֲדֹנָי יֹשֵׁב עַל־כִּסֵּא רָם וְנִשָּׂא וְשׁוּלָיו מְלֵאִים אֶת־הַהֵיכָל: [2] שְׂרָפִים עֹמְדִים מִמַּעַל לוֹ שֵׁשׁ כְּנָפַיִם שֵׁשׁ כְּנָפַיִם לְאֶחָד בִּשְׁתַּיִם יְכַסֶּה פָנָיו וּבִשְׁתַּיִם יְכַסֶּה רַגְלָיו וּבִשְׁתַּיִם יְעוֹפֵף: [3] וְקָרָא זֶה אֶל־זֶה וְאָמַר

קָדוֹשׁ קָדוֹשׁ קָדוֹשׁ

יְהֹוָה צְבָאוֹת

מְלֹא כָל־הָאָרֶץ כְּבוֹדוֹ:

[4] וַיָּנֻעוּ אַמּוֹת הַסִּפִּים מִקּוֹל הַקּוֹרֵא וְהַבַּיִת

יִמָּלֵא עָשָׁן: [5] וָאֹמַר

אוֹי־לִי כִי־נִדְמֵיתִי

כִּי אִישׁ טְמֵא־שְׂפָתַיִם אָנֹכִי

וּבְתוֹךְ עַם־טְמֵא שְׂפָתַיִם

אָנֹכִי יֹשֵׁב

כִּי אֶת־הַמֶּלֶךְ יְהֹוָה צְבָאוֹת

רָאוּ עֵינָי:

[6] וַיָּעָף אֵלַי אֶחָד מִן־הַשְּׂרָפִים וּבְיָדוֹ

---

[a] *Meaning of Heb. uncertain*
[b-b] *I.e., speaking impiety; cf. 9.16, and contrast "pure of speech (lit. 'lip')" in Zeph. 3.9*

with a live coal, which he had taken from the altar with a pair of tongs.

7] He touched it to my lips and declared,
"Now that this has touched your lips,
Your guilt shall depart
And your sin be purged away."

8] Then I heard the voice of my Lord saying, "Whom shall I send? Who will go for us?" And I said, "Here am I; send me."

9] And He said,
"Go, say to that people:
'Hear, indeed, but do not understand;
See, indeed, but do not grasp.'

10] "Dull that people's mind,
Stop its ears,
And seal its eyes—
Lest, seeing with its eyes
And hearing with its ears,
It also grasp with its mind,
And repent and save[c] itself."

11] I asked, "How long, my Lord?" And He replied:
"Til towns lie waste without inhabitants
And houses without people,
And the ground lies waste and desolate—

12] "For the Lord will banish the population—
And deserted sites are many
In the midst of the land.

13] "But while a tenth part yet remains in it, it shall repent. It shall be ravaged like the terebinth and the oak, of which stumps are left even when they are felled: its stump shall be a holy seed."

c Lit. "heal"

רִצְפָּה בְּמֶלְקָחַיִם לָקַח מֵעַל הַמִּזְבֵּחַ: 7] וַיַּגַּע

עַל־פִּי וַיֹּאמֶר

הִנֵּה נָגַע זֶה עַל־שְׂפָתֶיךָ

וְסָר עֲוֺנֶךָ

וְחַטָּאתְךָ תְּכֻפָּר:

8] וָאֶשְׁמַע אֶת־קוֹל אֲדֹנָי אֹמֵר אֶת־מִי אֶשְׁלַח

וּמִי יֵלֶךְ־לָנוּ וָאֹמַר הִנְנִי שְׁלָחֵנִי: 9] וַיֹּאמֶר

לֵךְ וְאָמַרְתָּ לָעָם הַזֶּה

שִׁמְעוּ שָׁמוֹעַ וְאַל־תָּבִינוּ

וּרְאוּ רָאוֹ וְאַל־תֵּדָעוּ:

10] הַשְׁמֵן לֵב־הָעָם הַזֶּה

וְאָזְנָיו הַכְבֵּד

וְעֵינָיו הָשַׁע

פֶּן־יִרְאֶה בְעֵינָיו

וּבְאָזְנָיו יִשְׁמָע

וּלְבָבוֹ יָבִין

וָשָׁב וְרָפָא לוֹ:

11] וָאֹמַר עַד־מָתַי אֲדֹנָי וַיֹּאמֶר

עַד אֲשֶׁר אִם־שָׁאוּ עָרִים מֵאֵין יוֹשֵׁב

וּבָתִּים מֵאֵין אָדָם

וְהָאֲדָמָה תִּשָּׁאֶה שְׁמָמָה:

12] וְרִחַק יְהֹוָה אֶת־הָאָדָם

וְרַבָּה הָעֲזוּבָה

בְּקֶרֶב הָאָרֶץ:

13] וְעוֹד בָּהּ עֲשִׂרִיָּה וְשָׁבָה וְהָיְתָה לְבָעֵר

כָּאֵלָה וְכָאַלּוֹן אֲשֶׁר בְּשַׁלֶּכֶת מַצֶּבֶת בָּם

זֶרַע קֹדֶשׁ מַצַּבְתָּהּ:

Chapter 7

1] In the reign of Ahaz son of Jotham son of Uzziah, king of Judah, King Rezin of Aram and King Pekah son of Remaliah of Israel marched upon Jerusalem to attack it; but they were not able to attack it.

2] Now, when it was reported to the House of David that Aram had allied itself with Ephraim, their hearts and the hearts of their people trembled as trees of the forest sway before a wind. 3] But the LORD said to Isaiah, "Go out with your son Shear-jashub[a] to meet Ahaz at the end of the conduit of the Upper Pool, by the road of the Fuller's Field.

4] And say to him: Be firm and be calm. Do not be afraid and do not lose heart on account of those two smoking stubs of firebrands, on account of the raging of Rezin and his Arameans and the son of Remaliah.[b]

5] Because the Arameans—with Ephraim and the son of Remaliah—have plotted against you, saying, 6] 'We will march against Judah and invade and conquer it, and we will set up as king in it the son of Tabeel.'[b]

Chapter 9

5] For a child has been born to us,
A son has been given us.
And authority has settled on his shoulders.
He has been named
"The Mighty God is planning grace;[d]
The Eternal Father, a peaceable ruler"—

ז

1] וַיְהִי בִּימֵי אָחָז בֶּן־יוֹתָם בֶּן־עֻזִּיָּהוּ מֶלֶךְ יְהוּדָה עָלָה רְצִין מֶלֶךְ־אֲרָם וּפֶקַח בֶּן־רְמַלְיָהוּ מֶלֶךְ־יִשְׂרָאֵל יְרוּשָׁלַ͏ִם לַמִּלְחָמָה עָלֶיהָ וְלֹא יָכֹל לְהִלָּחֵם עָלֶיהָ:

2] וַיֻּגַּד לְבֵית דָּוִד לֵאמֹר נָחָה אֲרָם עַל־אֶפְרָיִם וַיָּנַע לְבָבוֹ וּלְבַב עַמּוֹ כְּנוֹעַ עֲצֵי־יַעַר מִפְּנֵי־רוּחַ: 3] וַיֹּאמֶר יְהֹוָה אֶל־יְשַׁעְיָהוּ צֵא־נָא לִקְרַאת אָחָז אַתָּה וּשְׁאָר יָשׁוּב בְּנֶךָ אֶל־קְצֵה תְּעָלַת הַבְּרֵכָה הָעֶלְיוֹנָה אֶל־מְסִלַּת שְׂדֵה כוֹבֵס: 4] וְאָמַרְתָּ אֵלָיו הִשָּׁמֵר וְהַשְׁקֵט אַל־תִּירָא וּלְבָבְךָ אַל־יֵרַךְ מִשְּׁנֵי זַנְבוֹת הָאוּדִים הָעֲשֵׁנִים הָאֵלֶּה בׇּחֳרִי־אַף רְצִין וַאֲרָם וּבֶן־רְמַלְיָהוּ: 5] יַעַן כִּי־יָעַץ עָלֶיךָ אֲרָם רָעָה אֶפְרַיִם וּבֶן־רְמַלְיָהוּ לֵאמֹר: 6] נַעֲלֶה בִיהוּדָה וּנְקִיצֶנָּה וְנַבְקִעֶנָּה אֵלֵינוּ וְנַמְלִיךְ מֶלֶךְ בְּתוֹכָהּ אֵת בֶּן־טָבְאַל:

ט

5] כִּי־יֶלֶד יֻלַּד־לָנוּ
בֵּן נִתַּן־לָנוּ
וַתְּהִי הַמִּשְׂרָה עַל־שִׁכְמוֹ
וַיִּקְרָא שְׁמוֹ
פֶּלֶא יוֹעֵץ אֵל גִּבּוֹר
אֲבִי־עַד שַׂר־שָׁלוֹם:

---

[a] Meaning "(only) a remnant will turn back," i.e., repent; cf. 6.13; 10.21
[b] To refer to a person only as "the son of—" is slighting

[d] As in 25.1

6] In token of abundant authority
And of peace without limit
Upon David's throne and kingdom,
That it may be firmly established
In justice and in equity
Now and evermore.
The zeal of the LORD of Hosts
Shall bring this to pass.

לְמַרְבֵּה הַמִּשְׂרָה
וּלְשָׁלוֹם אֵין־קֵץ
עַל־כִּסֵּא דָוִד וְעַל־מַמְלַכְתּוֹ
לְהָכִין אֹתָהּ וּלְסַעֲדָהּ
בְּמִשְׁפָּט וּבִצְדָקָה
מֵעַתָּה וְעַד־עוֹלָם
קִנְאַת יְהוָה צְבָאוֹת
תַּעֲשֶׂה־זֹּאת:

Jeremiah was the most inward of the prophets. In his agonized visions he foresaw Jerusalem's destruction and was jailed for his preachments. When the Babylonians destroyed the city in 586 (or 585) B.C.E., he became one of the exiles and died in Egypt.

The Torah portion opens with rules about the release of a slave; the haftarah recounts how in Jeremiah's days the ruling classes had gone back on their promise to liberate their indentured servants. Jeremiah foretells God's judgment on this collective sin, for He cares for the servant no less than He cares for the master.

Jeremiah

34 : 8-22; 33 : 25-26

לד

Chapter 34

8] The word which came to Jeremiah from the LORD after King Zedekiah had made a covenant with all the people in Jerusalem to proclaim a release^c among them—

9] that everyone should set free his Hebrew slaves, both male and female, and that no one should keep his fellow Judean enslaved.

10] Everyone, officials and people, who had entered into the covenant agreed to set their male and female slaves free and not keep them enslaved any longer; they complied and let them go.

11] But afterward they turned about and brought back the men and women they had set free, and forced them into slavery again.

12] Then it was that the word of the LORD came to Jeremiah from the LORD:

13] Thus said the LORD, the God of Israel: I made a covenant with your fathers when I brought them out of the land of Egypt, the house of bondage, saying:

14] "In the seventh year^d each of you must let go any fellow Hebrew^e who may be sold^{-e} to you; when he has served you six years,

8 הַדָּבָר אֲשֶׁר־הָיָה אֶל־יִרְמְיָהוּ מֵאֵת יְהֹוָה אַחֲרֵי כְּרֹת הַמֶּלֶךְ צִדְקִיָּהוּ בְּרִית אֶת־כָּל־ הָעָם אֲשֶׁר בִּירוּשָׁלַם לִקְרֹא לָהֶם דְּרוֹר: 9 לְשַׁלַּח אִישׁ אֶת־עַבְדּוֹ וְאִישׁ אֶת־שִׁפְחָתוֹ הָעִבְרִי וְהָעִבְרִיָּה חָפְשִׁים לְבִלְתִּי עֲבָד־בָּם בִּיהוּדִי אָחִיהוּ אִישׁ: 10 וַיִּשְׁמְעוּ כָל־הַשָּׂרִים וְכָל־הָעָם אֲשֶׁר־ בָּאוּ בַבְּרִית לְשַׁלַּח אִישׁ אֶת־עַבְדּוֹ וְאִישׁ אֶת־ שִׁפְחָתוֹ חָפְשִׁים לְבִלְתִּי עֲבָד־בָּם עוֹד וַיִּשְׁמְעוּ וַיְשַׁלֵּחוּ: 11 וַיָּשׁוּבוּ אַחֲרֵי־כֵן וַיָּשִׁבוּ אֶת־ הָעֲבָדִים וְאֶת־הַשְּׁפָחוֹת אֲשֶׁר שִׁלְּחוּ חָפְשִׁים וַיִּכְבְּשׁוּם לַעֲבָדִים וְלִשְׁפָחוֹת: 12 וַיְהִי דְבַר־ יְהֹוָה אֶל־יִרְמְיָהוּ מֵאֵת יְהֹוָה לֵאמֹר: 13 כֹּה־אָמַר יְהֹוָה אֱלֹהֵי יִשְׂרָאֵל אָנֹכִי כָּרַתִּי בְרִית אֶת־אֲבוֹתֵיכֶם בְּיוֹם הוֹצִאִי אוֹתָם מֵאֶרֶץ מִצְרַיִם מִבֵּית עֲבָדִים לֵאמֹר: 14 מִקֵּץ שֶׁבַע שָׁנִים תְּשַׁלְּחוּ אִישׁ אֶת־אָחִיו הָעִבְרִי אֲשֶׁר־יִמָּכֵר לְךָ וַעֲבָדְךָ שֵׁשׁ שָׁנִים וְשִׁלַּחְתּוֹ

---

^c Others "liberty"
^d I.e., of servitude. Lit. "After a period of seven years"; cf. Deut. 14.28 and 15.1
^{e-e} Or "who sells himself"

714

you must set him free." But your fathers would not obey Me or give ear.

15] Lately you turned about and did what is proper in My sight, and each of you proclaimed a release to his countrymen; and you made a covenant accordingly before Me in the House which bears My name.

16] But now you have turned back and have profaned My name; each of you has brought back the men and women whom you had given their freedom, and forced them to be your slaves again.

17] Assuredly, thus said the LORD: You would not obey Me and proclaim a release, each to his kinsman and countryman. Lo! I proclaim your release—declares the LORD—to the sword, to pestilence, and to famine; and I will make you a horror to all the kingdoms of the earth.

18] I will make the men who violated My covenant, who did not fulfill the terms of the covenant which they made before Me, [like] the calf which they cut in two so as to pass between the halves:ʲ

19] the officers of Judah and Jerusalem, the officials, the priests, and all the people of the land who passed between the halves of the calf,

20] shall be handed over to their enemies, to those who seek to kill them. Their carcasses shall become food for the birds of the sky and the beasts of the earth. 21] I will hand over King Zedekiah of Judah and his officers to their enemies, who seek to kill them—to the army of the king of Babylon which has withdrawn from you.

22] I hereby give the command—declares the LORD—by which I will bring them back against this city. They shall attack it and capture it, and burn it down. I will make the towns of Judah a desolation, without inhabitant.

חָפְשִׁי מֵעִמָּךְ וְלֹא־שָׁמְעוּ אֲבוֹתֵיכֶם אֵלַי וְלֹא הִטּוּ אֶת־אָזְנָם: 15] וַתָּשֻׁבוּ אַתֶּם הַיּוֹם וַתַּעֲשׂוּ אֶת־הַיָּשָׁר בְּעֵינַי לִקְרֹא דְרוֹר אִישׁ לְרֵעֵהוּ וַתִּכְרְתוּ בְרִית לְפָנַי בַּבַּיִת אֲשֶׁר־נִקְרָא שְׁמִי עָלָיו: 16] וַתָּשֻׁבוּ וַתְּחַלְּלוּ אֶת־שְׁמִי וַתָּשִׁבוּ אִישׁ אֶת־עַבְדּוֹ וְאִישׁ אֶת־שִׁפְחָתוֹ אֲשֶׁר־שִׁלַּחְתֶּם חָפְשִׁים לְנַפְשָׁם וַתִּכְבְּשׁוּ אֹתָם לִהְיוֹת לָכֶם לַעֲבָדִים וְלִשְׁפָחוֹת:

17] לָכֵן כֹּה־אָמַר יְהוָה אַתֶּם לֹא־שְׁמַעְתֶּם אֵלַי לִקְרֹא דְרוֹר אִישׁ לְאָחִיו וְאִישׁ לְרֵעֵהוּ הִנְנִי קֹרֵא לָכֶם דְּרוֹר נְאֻם־יְהוָה אֶל־הַחֶרֶב אֶל־הַדֶּבֶר וְאֶל־הָרָעָב וְנָתַתִּי אֶתְכֶם לְזַעֲוָה לְכֹל מַמְלְכוֹת הָאָרֶץ: 18] וְנָתַתִּי אֶת־הָאֲנָשִׁים הָעֹבְרִים אֶת־בְּרִתִי אֲשֶׁר לֹא־הֵקִימוּ אֶת־דִּבְרֵי הַבְּרִית אֲשֶׁר כָּרְתוּ לְפָנָי הָעֵגֶל אֲשֶׁר כָּרְתוּ לִשְׁנַיִם וַיַּעַבְרוּ בֵּין בְּתָרָיו: 19] שָׂרֵי יְהוּדָה וְשָׂרֵי יְרוּשָׁלַ͏ִם הַסָּרִסִים וְהַכֹּהֲנִים וְכֹל עַם הָאָרֶץ הָעֹבְרִים בֵּין בִּתְרֵי הָעֵגֶל: 20] וְנָתַתִּי אוֹתָם בְּיַד אֹיְבֵיהֶם וּבְיַד מְבַקְשֵׁי נַפְשָׁם וְהָיְתָה נִבְלָתָם לְמַאֲכָל לְעוֹף הַשָּׁמַיִם וּלְבֶהֱמַת הָאָרֶץ: 21] וְאֶת־צִדְקִיָּהוּ מֶלֶךְ־יְהוּדָה וְאֶת־שָׂרָיו אֶתֵּן בְּיַד אֹיְבֵיהֶם וּבְיַד מְבַקְשֵׁי נַפְשָׁם וּבְיַד חֵיל מֶלֶךְ בָּבֶל הָעֹלִים מֵעֲלֵיכֶם: 22] הִנְנִי מְצַוֶּה נְאֻם־יְהוָה וַהֲשִׁבֹתִים אֶל־הָעִיר הַזֹּאת וְנִלְחֲמוּ עָלֶיהָ וּלְכָדוּהָ וּשְׂרָפֻהָ בָאֵשׁ וְאֶת־עָרֵי יְהוּדָה אֶתֵּן שְׁמָמָה מֵאֵין יֹשֵׁב:

ʲ Cf. Gen. 15.9–10, 17–21

Chapter 33

25] Thus said the Lord: As surely as I have established My covenant with day and night—the laws of heaven and earth—

26] so I will never reject the offspring of Jacob and My servant David; I will never fail to take from his offspring rulers for the descendants of Abraham, Isaac, and Jacob. Indeed, I will restore their fortunes and take them back in love.

25] כֹּה אָמַר יְהֹוָה אִם־לֹא בְרִיתִי יוֹמָם וָלָיְלָה חֻקּוֹת שָׁמַיִם וָאָרֶץ לֹא־שָׂמְתִּי: 26] גַּם־זֶרַע יַעֲקוֹב וְדָוִד עַבְדִּי אֶמְאַס מִקַּחַת מִזַּרְעוֹ מֹשְׁלִים אֶל־זֶרַע אַבְרָהָם יִשְׂחָק וְיַעֲקֹב כִּי־אָשִׁיב אֶת־שְׁבוּתָם וְרִחַמְתִּים:

The Book of Kings is divided into two parts. It spans four centuries and reaches from the last days of David to the destruction of the Temple by the Babylonians in 586 (or 585) B.C.E. It approaches history from a theological point of view: the story of Israel and Judah must be seen as a judgment of God on the people and its rulers.

The sidrah describes the levy which Moses raised for building the Tabernacle in the desert; the haftarah tells of King Solomon conscripting 30,000 men for the construction of the Temple in Jerusalem, in the tenth century B.C.E. The temporary abode was at last to become permanent and the king spared no cost to make the Temple a magnificent structure.

Chapter 5

26] The Lord had given Solomon wisdom, as He had promised him. There was friendship between Hiram and Solomon, and the two of them made a treaty.

27] King Solomon imposed forced labor on all Israel; the levy came to 30,000 men.

28] He sent them to the Lebanon in shifts of 10,000 a month: they would spend one month in the Lebanon and two months at home. Adoniram was in charge of the forced labor. 29] Solomon also had 70,000 porters and 80,000 quarriers in the hills,

30] apart from Solomon's 3,300 officials who were in charge of the work and supervised the gangs doing the work.

31] The king ordered huge blocks of choice stone to be quarried, so that the foundations of the house might be laid with hewn stones. 32] Solomon's masons, Hiram's masons, and the men of Gebal shaped them. Thus the timber and the stones for building the house were made ready.

Chapter 6

1] In the four hundred and eightieth year after the Israelites left the land of Egypt, in the month of Ziv—that is, the second month—in the fourth year of his reign over Israel, Solomon began to build the House of the Lord.

HAFTARAH Terumah

תרומה

First Kings

5 : 26 - 6 : 13

ה

26] וַיהֹוָה נָתַן חָכְמָה לִשְׁלֹמֹה כַּאֲשֶׁר דִּבֶּר־לוֹ וַיְהִי שָׁלֹם בֵּין חִירָם וּבֵין שְׁלֹמֹה וַיִּכְרְתוּ בְּרִית שְׁנֵיהֶם:

27] וַיַּעַל הַמֶּלֶךְ שְׁלֹמֹה מַס מִכָּל־יִשְׂרָאֵל וַיְהִי הַמַּס שְׁלֹשִׁים אֶלֶף אִישׁ:

28] וַיִּשְׁלָחֵם לְבָנוֹנָה עֲשֶׂרֶת אֲלָפִים בַּחֹדֶשׁ חֲלִיפוֹת חֹדֶשׁ יִהְיוּ בַלְּבָנוֹן שְׁנַיִם חֳדָשִׁים בְּבֵיתוֹ וַאֲדֹנִירָם עַל־הַמַּס: 29] וַיְהִי לִשְׁלֹמֹה שִׁבְעִים אֶלֶף נֹשֵׂא סַבָּל וּשְׁמֹנִים אֶלֶף חֹצֵב בָּהָר: 30] לְבַד מִשָּׂרֵי הַנִּצָּבִים לִשְׁלֹמֹה אֲשֶׁר עַל־הַמְּלָאכָה שְׁלֹשֶׁת אֲלָפִים וּשְׁלֹשׁ מֵאוֹת הָרֹדִים בָּעָם הָעֹשִׂים בַּמְּלָאכָה:

31] וַיְצַו הַמֶּלֶךְ וַיַּסִּעוּ אֲבָנִים גְּדֹלוֹת אֲבָנִים יְקָרוֹת לְיַסֵּד הַבָּיִת אַבְנֵי גָזִית: 32] וַיִּפְסְלוּ בֹּנֵי שְׁלֹמֹה וּבֹנֵי חִירוֹם וְהַגִּבְלִים וַיָּכִינוּ הָעֵצִים וְהָאֲבָנִים לִבְנוֹת הַבָּיִת:

ו

1] וַיְהִי בִשְׁמוֹנִים שָׁנָה וְאַרְבַּע מֵאוֹת שָׁנָה לְצֵאת בְּנֵי־יִשְׂרָאֵל מֵאֶרֶץ־מִצְרַיִם בַּשָּׁנָה הָרְבִיעִית בְּחֹדֶשׁ זִו הוּא הַחֹדֶשׁ הַשֵּׁנִי לִמְלֹךְ שְׁלֹמֹה עַל־יִשְׂרָאֵל וַיִּבֶן הַבַּיִת לַיהֹוָה:

2] The House which King Solomon built for the LORD was 60 cubits long, 20 cubits wide, and 30 cubits high.

3] The portico in front of the Great Hall of the House was 20 cubits long—along the width of the House—and 10 cubits deep to the front of the House.

4] ªHe made windows for the House, recessed and latticed.

5] Against the outside wall of the House—the outside walls of the House enclosing the Great Hall and the Shrineᵇ—he built a storied structure; and he made side chambers all around.

6] The lowest story was five cubits wide, the middle one six cubits wide, and the third seven cubits wide; for he had provided recesses around the outside of the House so as not to penetrate the walls of the House.

7] When the House was built, only finished stones cut at the quarry were used, so that no hammer or ax or any iron tool was heard in the House while it was being built.

8] The entrance to the middleᶜ [story of] the side chambers was on the right side of the House; and winding stairs led up to the middle chambers, and from the middle chambers to the third story. 9] When he finished building the House, ᵈhe paneled the House with beams and planks of cedar.⁻ᵈ

10] He built the storied structure against the entire House—each story five cubits high, so that it encased the House with timbers of cedar.

11] Then the word of the LORD came to Solomon,

12] "With regard to this House you are building—if you follow My laws and observe My rules and faithfully keep My commandments, I will fulfill for you the promise that I gave to your father David:

13] I will abide among the children of Israel, and I will never forsake My people Israel."

ª Meaning of parts of vv. 4–6 uncertain
ᵇ I.e., the inner sanctuary, designated in v. 16 and elsewhere as the "Holy of Holies"
ᶜ Septuagint and Targum read "lowest"   ᵈ⁻ᵈ Meaning of Heb. uncertain

2] וְהַבַּ֗יִת אֲשֶׁ֨ר בָּנָ֜ה הַמֶּ֤לֶךְ שְׁלֹמֹה֙ לַֽיהוָ֔ה שִׁשִּֽׁים־אַמָּ֤ה אָרְכּוֹ֙ וְעֶשְׂרִ֣ים רָחְבּ֔וֹ וּשְׁלֹשִׁ֥ים אַמָּ֖ה קוֹמָתֽוֹ: 3] וְהָאוּלָ֗ם עַל־פְּנֵי֙ הֵיכַ֣ל הַבַּ֔יִת עֶשְׂרִ֤ים אַמָּה֙ אָרְכּ֔וֹ עַל־פְּנֵ֖י רֹ֣חַב הַבָּ֑יִת עֶ֧שֶׂר בָּאַמָּ֛ה רָחְבּ֖וֹ עַל־פְּנֵ֥י הַבָּֽיִת: 4] וַיַּ֣עַשׂ לַבָּ֔יִת חַלּוֹנֵ֖י שְׁקֻפִ֥ים אֲטֻמִֽים: 5] וַיִּ֜בֶן עַל־קִ֤יר הַבַּ֨יִת֙ יָצִ֣יעַ סָבִ֔יב אֶת־קִיר֤וֹת הַבַּ֨יִת֙ סָבִ֔יב לַהֵיכָ֖ל וְלַדְּבִ֑יר וַיַּ֥עַשׂ צְלָע֖וֹת סָבִֽיב: 6] הַיָּצִ֨יעַ הַתַּחְתֹּנָ֜ה חָמֵ֧שׁ בָּאַמָּ֣ה רָחְבָּ֗הּ וְהַתִּֽיכֹנָה֙ שֵׁ֤שׁ בָּֽאַמָּה֙ רָחְבָּ֔הּ וְהַשְּׁלִ֣ישִׁ֔ית שֶׁ֥בַע בָּאַמָּ֖ה רָחְבָּ֑הּ כִּ֡י מִגְרָע֞וֹת נָתַ֤ן לַבַּ֨יִת֙ סָבִ֣יב ח֔וּצָה לְבִלְתִּ֖י אֲחֹ֥ז בְּקִֽירוֹת־הַבָּֽיִת: 7] וְהַבַּ֨יִת֙ בְּהִבָּ֣נֹת֔וֹ אֶֽבֶן־שְׁלֵמָ֥ה מַסָּ֖ע נִבְנָ֑ה וּמַקָּב֤וֹת וְהַגַּרְזֶן֙ כָּל־כְּלִ֣י בַרְזֶ֔ל לֹֽא־נִשְׁמַ֥ע בַּבַּ֖יִת בְּהִבָּֽנֹתֽוֹ: 8] פֶּ֗תַח הַצֵּלָע֙ הַתִּ֣יכֹנָ֔ה אֶל־כֶּ֥תֶף הַבַּ֖יִת הַיְמָנִ֑ית וּבְלוּלִּ֗ים יַֽעֲלוּ֙ עַל־הַתִּ֣יכֹנָ֔ה וּמִן־הַתִּֽיכֹנָ֖ה אֶל־הַשְּׁלִשִֽׁים: 9] וַיִּ֥בֶן אֶת־הַבַּ֖יִת וַיְכַלֵּ֑הוּ וַיִּסְפֹּ֤ן אֶת־הַבַּ֨יִת֙ גֵּבִ֔ים וּשְׂדֵרֹ֖ת בָּאֲרָזִֽים: 10] וַיִּ֤בֶן אֶת־הַיָּצִ֨יעַ֙ עַל־כָּל־הַבַּ֔יִת חָמֵ֥שׁ אַמּ֖וֹת קֽוֹמָת֑וֹ וַיֶּֽאֱחֹ֥ז אֶת־הַבַּ֖יִת בַּעֲצֵ֥י אֲרָזִֽים: 11] וַֽיְהִי֙ דְּבַר־יְהוָ֔ה אֶל־שְׁלֹמֹ֖ה לֵאמֹֽר: 12] הַבַּ֨יִת הַזֶּ֜ה אֲשֶׁר־אַתָּ֣ה בֹנֶ֗ה אִם־תֵּלֵ֤ךְ בְּחֻקֹּתַי֙ וְאֶת־מִשְׁפָּטַ֣י תַּֽעֲשֶׂ֔ה וְשָׁמַרְתָּ֥ אֶת־כָּל־מִצְוֹתַ֖י לָלֶ֣כֶת בָּהֶ֑ם וַהֲקִמֹתִ֤י אֶת־דְּבָרִי֙ אִתָּ֔ךְ אֲשֶׁ֥ר דִּבַּ֖רְתִּי אֶל־דָּוִ֥ד אָבִֽיךָ: 13] וְשָׁ֣כַנְתִּ֔י בְּת֖וֹךְ בְּנֵ֣י יִשְׂרָאֵ֑ל וְלֹ֥א אֶֽעֱזֹ֖ב אֶת־עַמִּ֥י יִשְׂרָאֵֽל:

Ezekiel lived in Babylon during the days of the exile (sixth century B.C.E.) and was a master of mystic dreams and visions. Like Jeremiah and Deutero-Isaiah he fortified his people's faith in God's forgiveness, but unlike them he stressed the great need for structured ritual as a basis for a religious revival.

The sidrah concludes with a prescription for the building of an incense altar in the desert Tabernacle; the haftarah presents Ezekiel's vision of an altar in the reconstituted Temple in Jerusalem. The sacrificial worship, presided over by the priest, was to Ezekiel an assurance that Israel would have continuous access to God.

תצוה

Ezekiel

43 : 10–27

Chapter 43

10] [Now] you, O mortal, describe the Temple to the House of Israel,*e* and let them measure its design. But let them be ashamed of their iniquities:

11] When they are ashamed of all they have done, make known to them the plan of the Temple and its layout, its exits and entrances—its entire plan, and all the laws and instructions pertaining to its entire plan. Write it down before their eyes, that they may faithfully follow its entire plan and all its laws.

12] Such are the instructions for the Temple on top of the mountain: the entire area of its enclosure shall be most holy. Thus far the instructions for the Temple.

13] *f*And these are the dimensions of the altar, in cubits where each is a cubit and a handbreadth. The trench*g* shall be a cubit deep and a cubit wide, with a rim one span high around its edge. And the height*h* shall be as follows:

14] From the trench in the ground to the lower ledge, which shall be a cubit wide: 2 cubits; from the *i*lower ledge to the upper*-i* ledge, which shall likewise be a cubit wide: 4 cubits;

מג

10] אַתָּה בֶן־אָדָם הַגֵּד אֶת־בֵּית־יִשְׂרָאֵל אֶת־הַבַּיִת וְיִכָּלְמוּ מֵעֲוֺנוֹתֵיהֶם וּמָדְדוּ אֶת־תָּכְנִית: 11] וְאִם־נִכְלְמוּ מִכֹּל אֲשֶׁר־עָשׂוּ צוּרַת הַבַּיִת וּתְכוּנָתוֹ וּמוֹצָאָיו וּמוֹבָאָיו וְכָל־צוּרֹתָיו וְאֵת כָּל־חֻקֹּתָיו וְכָל־צוּרֹתָיו וְכָל־תּוֹרֹתָיו הוֹדַע אוֹתָם וּכְתֹב לְעֵינֵיהֶם וְיִשְׁמְרוּ אֶת־כָּל־צוּרָתוֹ וְאֶת־כָּל־חֻקֹּתָיו וְעָשׂוּ אוֹתָם: 12] זֹאת תּוֹרַת הַבָּיִת עַל־רֹאשׁ הָהָר כָּל־גְּבֻלוֹ סָבִיב סָבִיב קֹדֶשׁ קָדָשִׁים הִנֵּה־זֹאת תּוֹרַת הַבָּיִת: 13] וְאֵלֶּה מִדּוֹת הַמִּזְבֵּחַ בָּאַמּוֹת אַמָּה אַמָּה וָטֹפַח וְחֵיק הָאַמָּה וְאַמָּה־רֹחַב וּגְבוּלָהּ אֶל־שְׂפָתָהּ סָבִיב זֶרֶת הָאֶחָד וְזֶה גַּב הַמִּזְבֵּחַ: 14] וּמֵחֵיק הָאָרֶץ עַד־הָעֲזָרָה הַתַּחְתּוֹנָה שְׁתַּיִם אַמּוֹת וְרֹחַב אַמָּה אֶחָת וּמֵהָעֲזָרָה הַקְּטַנָּה עַד־הָעֲזָרָה הַגְּדוֹלָה אַרְבַּע אַמּוֹת וְרֹחַב הָאַמָּה:

e In accordance with the three preceding chapters; cf. 40.4
f Some of the terms and details in vv. 13–17 are obscure
g Lit. "bosom"
h Lit. "bulge"
i-i Lit. "lesser ledge to the greater"

15] and the height of the altar hearth shall be 4 cubits, with 4 horns projecting upward from the hearth: 4 cubits. 16] Now the hearth shall be 12 cubits long and 12 broad, square, with 4 equal sides. 17] Hence, the [upper] base[i] shall be 14 cubits broad, with 4 equal sides. The surrounding rim shall be half a cubit [high],[k] and the surrounding trench shall measure one cubit. And the ramp[l] shall face east.

18] Then he[b] said to me: O mortal, thus said the Lord GOD: These are the directions for the altar on the day it is erected, so that burnt offerings may be offered up on it and blood dashed against it.

19] You shall give to the levitical priests who are of the stock of Zadok, and so eligible to minister to Me—declares the LORD GOD—a young bull of the herd for a sin offering. 20] You shall take some of its blood and apply it to [m-]the four horns [of the altar],[-m] to the four corners of the base, and to the surrounding rim; thus you shall purge it and perform purification upon it. 21] Then you shall take the bull of sin offering and burn it in the [n-]designated area[-n] of the Temple, outside the Sanctuary.

22] On the following day, you shall offer a goat without blemish as a sin offering; and the altar shall be purged [with it] just as it was purged with the bull. 23] When you have completed the ritual of purging, you shall offer a bull of the herd without blemish and a ram of the flock without blemish. 24] Offer them to the LORD; let the priests throw salt on them and offer them up as a burnt offering to the LORD.

15] וְהָהַרְאֵל אַרְבַּע אַמּוֹת וּמֵהָאֲרִאֵל וּלְמַעְלָה הַקְּרָנוֹת אַרְבַּע: 16] וְהָאֲרִאֵל שְׁתֵּים עֶשְׂרֵה אֹרֶךְ בִּשְׁתֵּים עֶשְׂרֵה רֹחַב רָבוּעַ אֶל אַרְבַּעַת רְבָעָיו: 17] וְהָעֲזָרָה אַרְבַּע עֶשְׂרֵה אֹרֶךְ בְּאַרְבַּע עֶשְׂרֵה רֹחַב אֶל־אַרְבַּעַת רְבָעֶיהָ וְהַגְּבוּל סָבִיב אוֹתָהּ חֲצִי הָאַמָּה וְהַחֵיק־לָהּ אַמָּה סָבִיב וּמַעֲלֹתֵהוּ פְּנוֹת קָדִים:

18] וַיֹּאמֶר אֵלַי בֶּן־אָדָם כֹּה אָמַר אֲדֹנָי יְהוִֹה אֵלֶּה חֻקּוֹת הַמִּזְבֵּחַ בְּיוֹם הֵעָשׂוֹתוֹ לְהַעֲלוֹת עָלָיו עוֹלָה וְלִזְרֹק עָלָיו דָּם: 19] וְנָתַתָּה אֶל־הַכֹּהֲנִים הַלְוִיִּם אֲשֶׁר הֵם מִזֶּרַע צָדוֹק הַקְּרֹבִים אֵלַי נְאֻם אֲדֹנָי יְהוִֹה לְשָׁרְתֵנִי פַּר בֶּן־בָּקָר לְחַטָּאת: 20] וְלָקַחְתָּ מִדָּמוֹ וְנָתַתָּה עַל־אַרְבַּע קַרְנֹתָיו וְאֶל־אַרְבַּע פִּנּוֹת הָעֲזָרָה וְאֶל־הַגְּבוּל סָבִיב וְחִטֵּאתָ אוֹתוֹ וְכִפַּרְתָּהוּ: 21] וְלָקַחְתָּ אֵת הַפָּר הַחַטָּאת וּשְׂרָפוֹ בְּמִפְקַד הַבַּיִת מִחוּץ לַמִּקְדָּשׁ:

22] וּבַיּוֹם הַשֵּׁנִי תַּקְרִיב שְׂעִיר־עִזִּים תָּמִים לְחַטָּאת וְחִטְּאוּ אֶת־הַמִּזְבֵּחַ כַּאֲשֶׁר חִטְּאוּ בַּפָּר: 23] בְּכַלּוֹתְךָ מֵחַטֵּא תַּקְרִיב פַּר בֶּן־בָּקָר תָּמִים וְאַיִל מִן־הַצֹּאן תָּמִים: 24] וְהִקְרַבְתָּם לִפְנֵי יְהוָה וְהִשְׁלִיכוּ הַכֹּהֲנִים עֲלֵיהֶם מֶלַח

[i] Heb. azarah, which in v. 14 means "ledge." The altar consists of 3 blocks; each smaller than the one below it

[k] Half a cubit is identical with the one span of v. 13

[l] Leading up to the altar; cf. Exod. 20.23

[b] I.e., the guide of 40.3 ff.

[m-m] Heb. "its four horns"

[n-n] Meaning of Heb. uncertain. Emendation yields "burning place"; cf. Lev. 6.2; Isa. 33.14; Ps. 102.4 (for the word); and Lev. 4.12; 6.4 (for the place)

25] Every day, for seven days, you shall present a goat of sin offering, as well as a bull of the herd and a ram of the flock; you⁰ shall present unblemished ones. 26] Seven days they shall purge the altar and cleanse it; ᵖ‾thus shall it be consecrated.‾ᵖ

27] And when these days are over, then from the eighth day onward the priests shall offer your burnt offerings and your offerings of well-being on the altar; and I will extend My favor to you—declares the Lord GOD.

וְהֶעֱלוּ אוֹתָם עֹלָה לַיהוָה: 25] שִׁבְעַת יָמִים תַּעֲשֶׂה שְׂעִיר־חַטָּאת לַיּוֹם וּפַר בֶּן־בָּקָר וְאַיִל מִן־הַצֹּאן תְּמִימִם יַעֲשׂוּ: 26] שִׁבְעַת יָמִים יְכַפְּרוּ אֶת־הַמִּזְבֵּחַ וְטִהֲרוּ אֹתוֹ וּמִלְאוּ יָדָיו: 27] וִיכַלּוּ אֶת־הַיָּמִים וְהָיָה בַיּוֹם הַשְּׁמִינִי וָהָלְאָה יַעֲשׂוּ הַכֹּהֲנִים עַל־הַמִּזְבֵּחַ אֶת־עוֹלוֹתֵיכֶם וְאֶת־שַׁלְמֵיכֶם וְרָצִאתִי אֶתְכֶם נְאֻם אֲדֹנָי יֱהֹוִה:

The Book of Kings is divided into two parts. It spans four centuries and reaches from the last days of David to the destruction of the Temple by the Babylonians in 586 (or 585) B.C.E. It approaches history from a theological point of view: the story of Israel and Judah must be seen as a judgment of God on the people and its rulers.

In the sidrah, Moses confronts his people after the sin with the golden calf; in the haftarah, Elijah confronts the purveyors of idol worship in the ninth century B.C.E. Elijah's courage and defense of ordinary folk against predatory authority made him the legendary hero of popular tradition.

First Kings

18:1-39

Chapter 18

1] Much later, in the third year,ᵃ the word of the LORD came to Elijah: "Go, appear before Ahab; then I will send rain upon the earth."

2] Thereupon Elijah set out to appear before Ahab.

The famine was severe in Samaria. 3] Ahab had summoned Obadiah, the steward of the palace. (Obadiah revered the LORD greatly.

4] When Jezebel was killing off the prophets of the LORD, Obadiah had taken a hundred prophets and hidden them, fifty to a cave, and provided them with food and drink.)

5] And Ahab had said to Obadiah, "Go through the land, to all the springs of water and to all the wadis. Perhaps we shall find some grass to keep horses and mules alive, so that we are not left without beasts."

6] They divided the country between them to explore it, Ahab going alone in one direction and Obadiah going alone in another direction.

7] Obadiah was on the road, when Elijah suddenly confronted him. [Obadiah] recognized him and flung himself on his face, saying, "Is that you, my lord Elijah?"

יח

1] וַיְהִי יָמִים רַבִּים וּדְבַר־יְהֹוָה הָיָה אֶל־אֵלִיָּהוּ בַּשָּׁנָה הַשְּׁלִישִׁית לֵאמֹר לֵךְ הֵרָאֵה אֶל־אַחְאָב וְאֶתְּנָה מָטָר עַל־פְּנֵי הָאֲדָמָה: 2] וַיֵּלֶךְ אֵלִיָּהוּ לְהֵרָאוֹת אֶל־אַחְאָב וְהָרָעָב חָזָק בְּשֹׁמְרוֹן: 3] וַיִּקְרָא אַחְאָב אֶל־עֹבַדְיָהוּ אֲשֶׁר עַל־הַבָּיִת וְעֹבַדְיָהוּ הָיָה יָרֵא אֶת־יְהֹוָה מְאֹד: 4] וַיְהִי בְּהַכְרִית אִיזֶבֶל אֵת נְבִיאֵי יְהֹוָה וַיִּקַּח עֹבַדְיָהוּ מֵאָה נְבִאִים וַיַּחְבִּיאֵם חֲמִשִּׁים אִישׁ בַּמְּעָרָה וְכִלְכְּלָם לֶחֶם וָמָיִם: 5] וַיֹּאמֶר אַחְאָב אֶל־עֹבַדְיָהוּ לֵךְ בָּאָרֶץ אֶל־כָּל־מַעְיְנֵי הַמַּיִם וְאֶל כָּל־הַנְּחָלִים אוּלַי נִמְצָא חָצִיר וּנְחַיֶּה סוּס וָפֶרֶד וְלוֹא נַכְרִית מֵהַבְּהֵמָה: 6] וַיְחַלְּקוּ לָהֶם אֶת־הָאָרֶץ לַעֲבָר־בָּהּ אַחְאָב הָלַךְ בְּדֶרֶךְ אֶחָד לְבַדּוֹ וְעֹבַדְיָהוּ הָלַךְ בְּדֶרֶךְ־אֶחָד לְבַדּוֹ: 7] וַיְהִי עֹבַדְיָהוּ בַּדֶּרֶךְ וְהִנֵּה אֵלִיָּהוּ לִקְרָאתוֹ וַיַּכִּרֵהוּ וַיִּפֹּל עַל־פָּנָיו וַיֹּאמֶר הַאַתָּה זֶה אֲדֹנִי אֵלִיָּהוּ:

ᵃ *I.e., of the drought; see 17.1*

722

8] "Yes, it is I," he answered. "Go tell your lord: Elijah is here!"

9] But he said, "What wrong have I done, that you should hand your servant over to Ahab to be killed? 10] As the Lord your God lives, there is no nation or kingdom to which my lord has not sent to look for you; and when they said, 'He is not here,' he made that kingdom or nation swear that you could not be found.

11] And now you say, 'Go tell your lord: Elijah is here!' 12] When I leave you, the spirit of the Lord will carry you off I don't know where; and when I come and tell Ahab and he does not find you, he will kill me. Yet your servant has revered the Lord from my youth.

13] My lord has surely been told what I did when Jezebel was killing the prophets of the Lord, how I hid a hundred of the prophets of the Lord, fifty men to a cave, and provided them with food and drink.

14] And now you say, 'Go tell your lord: Elijah is here.' Why, he will kill me!"

15] Elijah replied, "As the Lord of Hosts lives, whom I serve, I will appear before him this very day."

16] Obadiah went to find Ahab, and informed him; and Ahab went to meet Elijah. 17] When Ahab caught sight of Elijah, Ahab said to him, "Is that you, you troubler of Israel?"

18] He retorted, "It is not I who have brought trouble on Israel, but you and your father's House, by forsaking the commandments of the Lord and going after the Baalim.

19] Now summon all Israel to join me at Mount Carmel, together with the four hundred and fifty prophets of Baal and the four hundred prophets of Asherah, *b-who eat at Jezebel's table."-b*

b-b I.e. who are maintained by Jezebel

8 וַיֹּ֣אמֶר ל֔וֹ אָ֖נִי לֵ֑ךְ אֱמֹ֥ר לַֽאדֹנֶ֖יךָ הִנֵּ֥ה אֵלִיָּֽהוּ: 9 וַיֹּ֖אמֶר מֶ֣ה חָטָ֑אתִי כִּֽי־אַתָּ֞ה נֹתֵ֧ן אֶֽת־עַבְדְּךָ֛ בְּיַד־אַחְאָ֖ב לַהֲמִיתֵֽנִי: 10 חַ֣י יְהֹוָ֣ה אֱלֹהֶ֗יךָ אִם־יֶשׁ־גּ֤וֹי וּמַמְלָכָה֙ אֲשֶׁ֣ר לֹֽא־שָׁלַ֣ח אֲדֹנִ֥י שָׁם֙ לְבַקֶּשְׁךָ֔ וְאָמְר֖וּ אָ֑יִן וְהִשְׁבִּ֤יעַ אֶת־הַמַּמְלָכָה֙ וְאֶת־הַגּ֔וֹי כִּ֖י לֹ֥א יִמְצָאֶֽכָּה: 11 וְעַתָּ֖ה אַתָּ֣ה אֹמֵ֑ר לֵ֛ךְ אֱמֹ֥ר לַֽאדֹנֶ֖יךָ הִנֵּ֥ה אֵלִיָּֽהוּ: 12 וְהָיָ֞ה אֲנִ֣י ׀ אֵלֵ֣ךְ מֵֽאִתָּ֗ךְ וְר֣וּחַ יְהֹוָ֤ה ׀ יִֽשָּׂאֲךָ֙ עַ֤ל אֲשֶׁר֙ לֹֽא־אֵדָ֔ע וּבָ֨אתִי לְהַגִּ֤יד לְאַחְאָב֙ וְלֹ֣א יִמְצָאֲךָ֔ וַהֲרָגָ֑נִי וְעַבְדְּךָ֛ יָרֵ֥א אֶת־יְהֹוָ֖ה מִנְּעֻרָֽי: 13 הֲלֹֽא־הֻגַּ֣ד לַֽאדֹנִ֔י אֵ֥ת אֲשֶׁר־עָשִׂ֖יתִי בַּֽהֲרֹ֣ג אִיזֶ֑בֶל אֵ֖ת נְבִיאֵ֣י יְהֹוָ֑ה וָֽאַחְבִּא֩ מִנְּבִיאֵ֨י יְהֹוָ֜ה מֵ֣אָה אִ֗ישׁ חֲמִשִּׁ֨ים חֲמִשִּׁ֥ים אִישׁ֙ בַּמְּעָרָ֔ה וָֽאֲכַלְכְּלֵ֖ם לֶ֥חֶם וָמָֽיִם: 14 וְעַתָּ֖ה אַתָּ֣ה אֹמֵ֔ר לֵ֛ךְ אֱמֹ֥ר לַֽאדֹנֶ֖יךָ הִנֵּ֥ה אֵלִיָּ֑הוּ וַהֲרָגָֽנִי:

15 וַיֹּ֨אמֶר֙ אֵֽלִיָּ֔הוּ חַ֚י יְהֹוָ֣ה צְבָא֔וֹת אֲשֶׁ֥ר עָמַ֖דְתִּי לְפָנָ֑יו כִּ֥י הַיּ֖וֹם אֵרָאֶ֥ה אֵלָֽיו:

16 וַיֵּ֧לֶךְ עֹבַדְיָ֛הוּ לִקְרַ֥את אַחְאָ֖ב וַיַּגֶּד־ל֑וֹ וַיֵּ֥לֶךְ אַחְאָ֖ב לִקְרַ֥את אֵלִיָּֽהוּ: 17 וַיְהִ֛י כִּרְא֥וֹת אַחְאָ֖ב אֶת־אֵלִיָּ֑הוּ וַיֹּ֤אמֶר אַחְאָב֙ אֵלָ֔יו הַאַתָּ֥ה זֶ֖ה עֹכֵ֥ר יִשְׂרָאֵֽל: 18 וַיֹּ֗אמֶר לֹ֤א עָכַ֙רְתִּי֙ אֶת־יִשְׂרָאֵ֔ל כִּ֥י אִם־אַתָּ֖ה וּבֵ֣ית אָבִ֑יךָ בַּֽעֲזׇבְכֶם֙ אֶת־מִצְוֺ֣ת יְהֹוָ֔ה וַתֵּ֖לֶךְ אַֽחֲרֵ֥י הַבְּעָלִֽים: 19 וְעַתָּ֗ה שְׁלַ֨ח קְבֹ֥ץ אֵלַ֛י אֶֽת־כָּל־יִשְׂרָאֵ֖ל אֶל־הַ֣ר הַכַּרְמֶ֑ל וְאֶת־נְבִיאֵ֤י הַבַּ֙עַל֙ אַרְבַּ֤ע מֵאוֹת֙ וַֽחֲמִשִּׁ֔ים וּנְבִיאֵ֤י הָֽאֲשֵׁרָה֙ אַרְבַּ֣ע מֵא֔וֹת אֹֽכְלֵ֖י שֻׁלְחַ֥ן אִיזָֽבֶל:

20] Ahab sent orders to all the Israelites and gathered the prophets at Mount Carmel. 21] Elijah approached all the people and said, "How long will you keep hopping e-between two opinions?-e If the LORD is God, follow Him; and if Baal, follow him!" But the people answered him not a word.

22] Then Elijah said to the people, "I am the only prophet of the LORD left, while the prophets of Baal are four hundred and fifty men.

23] Let two young bulls be given to us. Let them choose one bull, cut it up, and lay it on the wood, but let them not apply fire; I will prepare the other bull, and lay it on the wood, and will not apply fire.

24] You will then invoke your god by name, and I will invoke the LORD by name; and d-and let us agree:-d the god who responds with fire, that one is God." And all the people answered, "Very good!"

25] Elijah said to the prophets of Baal, "Choose one bull, and prepare it first, for you are the majority; invoke your god by name, but apply no fire."

26] They took the bull that was given them; they prepared it, and invoked Baal by name from morning until noon, shouting, "O Baal, answer us!" But there was no sound, and none who responded; so they performed a hopping dance about the altar that had been set up.

27] When noon came, Elijah mocked them, saying, "Shout louder! After all he is a god. e-But he may be in conversation, he may be detained, or he may be on a journey,-e or perhaps he is asleep and will wake up."

28] So they shouted louder, and gashed themselves with knives and spears, according to their practice, until the blood streamed over them. 29] When noon passed,

20] וַיִּשְׁלַ֥ח אַחְאָ֖ב בְּכָל־בְּנֵ֣י יִשְׂרָאֵ֑ל וַיִּקְבֹּ֥ץ אֶת־הַנְּבִיאִ֖ים אֶל־הַ֥ר הַכַּרְמֶֽל׃ 21] וַיִּגַּ֨שׁ אֵלִיָּ֜הוּ אֶל־כָּל־הָעָ֗ם וַיֹּ֙אמֶר֙ עַד־מָתַ֞י אַתֶּ֣ם פֹּסְחִים֮ עַל־שְׁתֵּ֣י הַסְּעִפִּים֒ אִם־יְהוָ֤ה הָֽאֱלֹהִים֙ לְכ֣וּ אַחֲרָ֔יו וְאִם־הַבַּ֖עַל לְכ֣וּ אַחֲרָ֑יו וְלֹֽא־עָנ֥וּ הָעָ֛ם אֹת֖וֹ דָּבָֽר׃ 22] וַיֹּ֤אמֶר אֵלִיָּ֙הוּ֙ אֶל־הָעָ֔ם אֲנִ֞י נוֹתַ֧רְתִּי נָבִ֛יא לַיהוָ֖ה לְבַדִּ֑י וּנְבִיאֵ֣י הַבַּ֔עַל אַרְבַּע־מֵא֥וֹת וַחֲמִשִּׁ֖ים אִֽישׁ׃ 23] וְיִתְּנוּ־ לָ֜נוּ שְׁנַ֣יִם פָּרִ֗ים וְיִבְחֲר֣וּ לָהֶם֩ הַפָּ֨ר הָאֶחָ֜ד וִֽינַתְּחֻ֗הוּ וְיָשִׂ֙ימוּ֙ עַל־הָ֣עֵצִ֔ים וְאֵ֖שׁ לֹ֣א יָשִׂ֑ימוּ וַאֲנִ֞י אֶעֱשֶׂ֣ה ׀ אֶת־הַפָּ֣ר הָאֶחָ֗ד וְנָֽתַתִּי֙ עַל־הָ֣עֵצִ֔ים וְאֵ֖שׁ לֹ֥א אָשִֽׂים׃ 24] וּקְרָאתֶ֞ם בְּשֵׁ֣ם אֱלֹֽהֵיכֶ֗ם וַֽאֲנִי֙ אֶקְרָ֣א בְשֵׁם־יְהוָ֔ה וְהָיָ֧ה הָאֱלֹהִ֛ים אֲשֶׁר־ יַעֲנֶ֥ה בָאֵ֖שׁ ה֣וּא הָאֱלֹהִ֑ים וַיַּ֧עַן כָּל־הָעָ֛ם וַיֹּאמְר֖וּ ט֥וֹב הַדָּבָֽר׃ 25] וַיֹּ֨אמֶר אֵלִיָּ֜הוּ לִנְבִיאֵ֣י הַבַּ֗עַל בַּחֲר֨וּ לָכֶ֜ם הַפָּ֤ר הָֽאֶחָד֙ וַעֲשׂ֣וּ רִֽאשֹׁנָ֔ה כִּ֥י אַתֶּ֖ם הָרַבִּ֑ים וְקִרְאוּ֙ בְּשֵׁ֣ם אֱלֹֽהֵיכֶ֔ם וְאֵ֖שׁ לֹ֥א תָשִֽׂימוּ׃ 26] וַ֠יִּקְחוּ אֶת־הַפָּ֨ר אֲשֶׁר־נָתַ֣ן לָהֶם֮ וַֽיַּעֲשׂוּ֒ וַיִּקְרְא֣וּ בְשֵׁם־הַ֠בַּעַל מֵהַבֹּ֨קֶר וְעַד־הַצָּהֳרַ֤יִם לֵאמֹר֙ הַבַּ֣עַל עֲנֵ֔נוּ וְאֵ֥ין ק֖וֹל וְאֵ֣ין עֹנֶ֑ה וַֽיְפַסְּח֔וּ עַל־הַמִּזְבֵּ֖חַ אֲשֶׁ֥ר עָשָֽׂה׃ 27] וַיְהִ֣י בַֽצָּהֳרַ֗יִם וַיְהַתֵּ֤ל בָּהֶם֙ אֵלִיָּ֔הוּ וַיֹּ֙אמֶר֙ קִרְא֣וּ בְקוֹל־גָּד֔וֹל כִּֽי־אֱלֹהִ֣ים ה֔וּא כִּ֣י שִׂ֧יחַ וְכִֽי־שִׂ֛יג ל֖וֹ וְכִי־דֶ֣רֶךְ ל֑וֹ אוּלַ֛י יָשֵׁ֥ן ה֖וּא וְיִקָֽץ׃ 28] וַֽיִּקְרְאוּ֙ בְּק֣וֹל גָּד֔וֹל וַיִּתְגֹּֽדְד֗וּ כְּמִשְׁפָּטָ֛ם בַּחֲרָב֖וֹת וּבָֽרְמָחִ֑ים עַד־שְׁפָךְ־דָּ֖ם עֲלֵיהֶֽם׃ 29] וַֽיְהִי֙ כַּעֲבֹ֣ר

---

they *f*‑kept raving‑*f* until the hour of presenting the meal offering. Still there was no sound, and none who responded or heeded.

30] Then Elijah said to all the people, "Come closer to me"; and all the people came closer to him. Elijah*g* repaired the damaged altar of the LORD.

31] He took twelve stones, corresponding to the number of the tribes of the sons of Jacob—to whom the word of the LORD came, saying, "Israel shall be your name"*h*—

32] and with the stones he built an altar in the name of the LORD. Around the altar he made a trench large enough for two seahs of seed.*i*

33] He laid out the wood, and he cut up the bull and laid it on the wood.

34] And he said, "Fill four jars with water and pour it over the burnt offering and the wood." Then he said, "Do it a second time"; and they did it a second time. "Do it a third time," he said; and they did it a third time. 35] The water ran down around the altar, and even the trench was filled with water.

36] When it was time to present the meal offering, the prophet Elijah came forward and said, "O LORD, God of Abraham, Isaac, and Israel! Let it be known today that You are God in Israel and that I am Your servant, and that I have done all these things at Your bidding.

37] Answer me, O LORD, answer me, that this people may know that You, O LORD, are God; *e*‑for You have turned their hearts backward."‑*e*

38] Then fire from the LORD descended and consumed the burnt offering, the wood, the stones, and the earth; and it licked up the water that was in the trench.

39] When they saw this, all the people flung themselves on their faces and cried out, "The LORD alone is God: The LORD alone is God!"

הַצׇּהֳרַיִם וַיִּֽתְנַבְּאוּ עַד לַעֲלוֹת הַמִּנְחָה וְאֵֽין־קוֹל וְאֵֽין־עֹנֶה וְאֵין קָֽשֶׁב:

30 וַיֹּ֨אמֶר אֵלִיָּ֤הוּ לְכׇל־הָעָם֙ גְּשׁ֣וּ אֵלַ֔י וַיִּגְּשׁ֥וּ כׇל־הָעָ֖ם אֵלָ֑יו וַיְרַפֵּ֛א אֶת־מִזְבַּ֥ח יְהֹוָ֖ה הֶהָרֽוּס: 31 וַיִּקַּ֣ח אֵלִיָּ֗הוּ שְׁתֵּ֤ים עֶשְׂרֵה֙ אֲבָנִ֔ים כְּמִסְפַּ֖ר שִׁבְטֵ֣י בְנֵֽי־יַעֲקֹ֑ב אֲשֶׁר֩ הָיָ֨ה דְבַר־יְהֹוָ֤ה אֵלָיו֙ לֵאמֹ֔ר יִשְׂרָאֵ֖ל יִהְיֶ֥ה שְׁמֶֽךָ: 32 וַיִּבְנֶ֧ה אֶת־הָאֲבָנִ֛ים מִזְבֵּ֖חַ בְּשֵׁ֣ם יְהֹוָ֑ה וַיַּ֣עַשׂ תְּעָלָ֗ה כְּבֵית֙ סָאתַ֣יִם זֶ֔רַע סָבִ֖יב לַמִּזְבֵּֽחַ: 33 וַֽיַּעֲרֹ֖ךְ אֶת־הָֽעֵצִ֑ים וַיְנַתַּח֙ אֶת־הַפָּ֔ר וַיָּ֖שֶׂם עַל־הָעֵצִֽים: 34 וַיֹּ֗אמֶר מִלְא֨וּ אַרְבָּעָ֤ה כַדִּים֙ מַ֔יִם וְיִֽצְק֥וּ עַל־הָעֹלָ֖ה וְעַל־הָעֵצִ֑ים וַיֹּ֤אמֶר שְׁנוּ֙ וַיִּשְׁנ֔וּ וַיֹּ֥אמֶר שַׁלֵּ֖שׁוּ וַיְשַׁלֵּֽשׁוּ: 35 וַיֵּלְכ֣וּ הַמַּ֔יִם סָבִ֖יב לַמִּזְבֵּ֑חַ וְגַ֥ם אֶת־הַתְּעָלָ֖ה מִלֵּא־מָֽיִם:

36 וַיְהִ֣י ׀ בַּעֲל֣וֹת הַמִּנְחָ֗ה וַיִּגַּ֞שׁ אֵלִיָּ֣הוּ הַנָּבִיא֮ וַיֹּאמַר֒ יְהֹוָ֗ה אֱלֹהֵי֙ אַבְרָהָם֙ יִצְחָ֣ק וְיִשְׂרָאֵ֔ל הַיּ֣וֹם יִוָּדַ֗ע כִּֽי־אַתָּ֧ה אֱלֹהִ֛ים בְּיִשְׂרָאֵ֖ל וַאֲנִ֣י עַבְדֶּ֑ךָ וּבִדְבָרְךָ֣ עָשִׂ֔יתִי אֵ֥ת כׇּל־הַדְּבָרִ֖ים הָאֵֽלֶּה: 37 עֲנֵ֤נִי יְהֹוָה֙ עֲנֵ֔נִי וְיֵ֣דְע֔וּ הָעָ֥ם הַזֶּ֖ה כִּֽי־אַתָּ֥ה יְהֹוָ֖ה הָאֱלֹהִ֑ים וְאַתָּ֛ה הֲסִבֹּ֥תָ אֶת־לִבָּ֖ם אֲחֹרַנִּֽית:

38 וַתִּפֹּ֣ל אֵשׁ־יְהֹוָ֗ה וַתֹּ֤אכַל אֶת־הָֽעֹלָה֙ וְאֶת־הָ֣עֵצִ֔ים וְאֶת־הָאֲבָנִ֖ים וְאֶת־הֶעָפָ֑ר וְאֶת־הַמַּ֥יִם אֲשֶׁר־בַּתְּעָלָ֖ה לִחֵֽכָה: 39 וַיַּרְא֙ כׇּל־הָעָ֔ם וַֽיִּפְּל֖וּ עַל־פְּנֵיהֶ֑ם וַיֹּ֣אמְר֔וּ יְהֹוָה֙ ה֣וּא הָאֱלֹהִ֔ים יְהֹוָ֖ה ה֥וּא הָאֱלֹהִֽים:

f‑f Others "prophesied"; see Num. 11.25–26
g The name is moved up from v. 31 for clarity   *h* See Gen. 35.10
i I.e., of an area which would require two seahs of seed if sown. Cf. Lev. 27.16; Isa. 5.10
e‑e Meaning of Heb. uncertain

ויקהל

The Book of Kings is divided into two parts. It spans four centuries and reaches from the last days of David to the destruction of the Temple by the Babylonians in 586 (or 585) B.C.E. It approaches history from a theological point of view: the story of Israel and Judah must be seen as a judgment of God on the people and its rulers.

In the sidrah, Moses now proceeds with the actual building of the Tabernacle; the haftarah tells of Solomon erecting the Temple. Both accounts have the form of archival records, a prominent literary genre of antiquity.

First Kings

7 : 40–50

ז

Chapter 7

40] Hiram also made the lavers, the scrapers, and the sprinkling bowls.

So Hiram finished all the work that he had been doing for King Solomon on the House of the LORD:

41] the two columns, the two globes of the capitals upon the columns; and the two pieces of network to cover the two globes of the capitals upon the columns;

42] the 400 pomegranates for the two pieces of network, two rows of pomegranates for each network, to cover the two globes of the capitals upon the columns;

43] the ten stands and the ten lavers upon the stands; 44] the one tank with the twelve oxen underneath the tank;

45] the pails, the scrapers, and the sprinkling bowls. All those vessels in the House of the LORD which Hiram made for King Solomon were of burnished bronze.

46] The king had them cast [n]in earthen molds,[n] in the plain of the Jordan between Succoth and Zarethan.

47] Solomon left all the vessels [unweighed] because of their very great quantity; the weight of the bronze was not reckoned.

[n-n] Lit. "in the thick of the earth"

40] וַיַּעַשׂ חִירוֹם אֶת־הַכִּיֹּרוֹת וְאֶת־הַיָּעִים וְאֶת־הַמִּזְרָקוֹת וַיְכַל חִירָם לַעֲשׂוֹת אֶת־כָּל־הַמְּלָאכָה אֲשֶׁר עָשָׂה לַמֶּלֶךְ שְׁלֹמֹה בֵּית יְהוָה: 41] עַמֻּדִים שְׁנַיִם וְגֻלֹּת הַכֹּתָרֹת אֲשֶׁר־עַל־רֹאשׁ הָעַמּוּדִים שְׁתָּיִם וְהַשְּׂבָכוֹת שְׁתַּיִם לְכַסּוֹת אֶת־שְׁתֵּי גֻּלֹּת הַכֹּתָרֹת אֲשֶׁר־עַל־רֹאשׁ הָעַמּוּדִים: 42] וְאֶת־הָרִמֹּנִים אַרְבַּע מֵאוֹת לִשְׁתֵּי הַשְּׂבָכוֹת שְׁנֵי־טוּרִים רִמֹּנִים לַשְּׂבָכָה הָאֶחָת לְכַסּוֹת אֶת־שְׁתֵּי גֻּלֹּת הַכֹּתָרֹת אֲשֶׁר עַל־פְּנֵי הָעַמּוּדִים: 43] וְאֶת־הַמְּכֹנוֹת עָשֶׂר וְאֶת־הַכִּיֹרֹת עֲשָׂרָה עַל־הַמְּכֹנוֹת: 44] וְאֶת־הַיָּם הָאֶחָד וְאֶת־הַבָּקָר שְׁנֵים־עָשָׂר תַּחַת הַיָּם: 45] וְאֶת־הַסִּירוֹת וְאֶת־הַיָּעִים וְאֶת־הַמִּזְרָקוֹת וְאֵת כָּל־הַכֵּלִים הָאֵלֶּה אֲשֶׁר עָשָׂה חִירָם לַמֶּלֶךְ שְׁלֹמֹה בֵּית יְהוָה נְחֹשֶׁת מְמֹרָט: 46] בְּכִכַּר הַיַּרְדֵּן יְצָקָם הַמֶּלֶךְ בְּמַעֲבֵה הָאֲדָמָה בֵּין סֻכּוֹת וּבֵין צָרְתָן: 47] וַיַּנַּח שְׁלֹמֹה אֶת־כָּל־הַכֵּלִים מֵרֹב מְאֹד מְאֹד לֹא נֶחְקַר מִשְׁקַל הַנְּחֹשֶׁת:

726

48] And Solomon made all the furnishings that were in the House of the LORD: the altar, of gold; the table for the bread of display, of gold;

49] the lampstands—five on the right side and five on the left—in front of the Shrine, of solid gold; and the petals, lamps, and tongs, of gold;

50] the basins, snuffers, sprinkling bowls, ladles, and fire pans, of solid gold; and the hinge sockets for the doors of the innermost part of the House, the Holy of Holies, and for the doors of the Great Hall of the House, of gold.

48 וַיַּעַשׂ שְׁלֹמֹה אֵת כָּל־הַכֵּלִים אֲשֶׁר בֵּית יְהֹוָה אֵת מִזְבַּח הַזָּהָב וְאֶת־הַשֻּׁלְחָן אֲשֶׁר עָלָיו לֶחֶם הַפָּנִים זָהָב: 49 וְאֶת־הַמְּנֹרוֹת חָמֵשׁ מִיָּמִין וְחָמֵשׁ מִשְּׂמֹאול לִפְנֵי הַדְּבִיר זָהָב סָגוּר וְהַפֶּרַח וְהַנֵּרֹת וְהַמֶּלְקַחַיִם זָהָב: 50 וְהַסִּפּוֹת וְהַמְזַמְּרוֹת וְהַמִּזְרָקוֹת וְהַכַּפּוֹת וְהַמַּחְתּוֹת זָהָב סָגוּר וְהַפֹּתוֹת לְדַלְתוֹת הַבַּיִת הַפְּנִימִי לְקֹדֶשׁ הַקֳּדָשִׁים לְדַלְתֵי הַבַּיִת לַהֵיכָל זָהָב:

First Kings

7 : 51 - 8 : 21

Chapter 7

51] When all the work that King Solomon had done in the House of the LORD was completed, Solomon brought in the sacred donations of his father David—the silver, the gold, and the vessels—and deposited them in the treasury of the House of the LORD.

Chapter 8

1] Then Solomon convoked the elders of Israel—all the heads of the tribes and the ancestral chieftains of the Israelites—before King Solomon in Jerusalem, to bring up the Ark of the Covenant of the LORD from the City of David, that is, Zion.

2] All the men of Israel gathered before King Solomon at the Feast,ᵃ in the month of Ethanim—that is, the seventh month.

3] When all the elders of Israel had come, the priests lifted the Ark

4] and carried up the Ark of the LORD. Then the priests and the Levites brought the Tent of Meeting and all the holy vessels that were in the Tent.

5] Meanwhile, King Solomon and the whole community of Israel, who were assem-

ᵃ *I.e., of Booths. Cf. Lev. 23.34*

ז

51] וַתִּשְׁלַם כָּל־הַמְּלָאכָה אֲשֶׁר עָשָׂה הַמֶּלֶךְ שְׁלֹמֹה בֵּית יְהֹוָה וַיָּבֵא שְׁלֹמֹה אֶת־קָדְשֵׁי דָּוִד אָבִיו אֶת־הַכֶּסֶף וְאֶת־הַזָּהָב וְאֶת־הַכֵּלִים נָתַן בְּאֹצְרוֹת בֵּית יְהֹוָה:

ח

1] אָז יַקְהֵל שְׁלֹמֹה אֶת־זִקְנֵי יִשְׂרָאֵל אֶת־כָּל־רָאשֵׁי הַמַּטּוֹת נְשִׂיאֵי הָאָבוֹת לִבְנֵי יִשְׂרָאֵל אֶל־הַמֶּלֶךְ שְׁלֹמֹה יְרוּשָׁלָםִ לְהַעֲלוֹת אֶת־אֲרוֹן בְּרִית־יְהֹוָה מֵעִיר דָּוִד הִיא צִיּוֹן:

2] וַיִּקָּהֲלוּ אֶל־הַמֶּלֶךְ שְׁלֹמֹה כָּל־אִישׁ יִשְׂרָאֵל בְּיֶרַח הָאֵתָנִים בֶּחָג הוּא הַחֹדֶשׁ הַשְּׁבִיעִי: 3] וַיָּבֹאוּ כֹּל זִקְנֵי יִשְׂרָאֵל וַיִּשְׂאוּ הַכֹּהֲנִים אֶת־הָאָרוֹן: 4] וַיַּעֲלוּ אֶת־אֲרוֹן יְהֹוָה וְאֶת־אֹהֶל מוֹעֵד וְאֶת־כָּל־כְּלֵי הַקֹּדֶשׁ אֲשֶׁר בָּאֹהֶל וַיַּעֲלוּ אֹתָם הַכֹּהֲנִים וְהַלְוִיִּם: 5] וְהַמֶּלֶךְ שְׁלֹמֹה וְכָל־עֲדַת יִשְׂרָאֵל הַנּוֹעָדִים

The Book of Kings is divided into two parts. It spans four centuries and reaches from the last days of David to the destruction of the Temple by the Babylonians in 586 (or 585) B.C.E. It approaches history from a theological point of view: the story of Israel and Judah must be seen as a judgment of God on the people and its rulers.

The Torah recounts the completion of the Tabernacle; the haftarah the completion of the Temple and Solomon's opening address. The ark which Moses carried in the desert has now been installed in the new, permanent sanctuary. The ark symbolizes God's presence amongst His people.

bled with him before the Ark, were sacrificing sheep and oxen in such abundance that they could not be numbered or counted.

6] The priests brought the Ark of the LORD's Covenant to its place underneath the wings of the cherubim, in the Shrine of the House, in the Holy of Holies;

7] for the cherubim had their wings spread out over the place of the Ark, so that the cherubim shielded the Ark and its poles from above.

8] The poles projected so that the ends of the poles were visible in the Sanctuary in front of the Shrine, but they could not be seen outside; and there they remain to this day. 9] There was nothing inside the Ark but the two tablets of stone which Moses placed there at Horeb, when the LORD made [a covenant] with the Israelites after their departure from the land of Egypt.

10] When the priests came out of the Sanctuary—for the cloud had filled the House of the LORD

11] and the priests were not able to remain and perform the service because of the cloud, for the Presence of the LORD filled the House of the LORD—

12] then Solomon declared:
"The LORD has chosen
To abide in a thick cloud:

13] I have now built for You
A stately House,
A place where You
May dwell forever."

14] Then, with the whole congregation of Israel standing, the king faced about and blessed the whole congregation of Israel.

15] He said:
"Praised be the LORD, the God of Israel, *b*who has fulfilled with deeds the promise He made*b* to my father David. For He said,

16] 'Ever since I brought My people Israel out of Egypt, I have not chosen a city among all the tribes of Israel for

עָלָיו אִתּוֹ לִפְנֵי הָאָרוֹן מְזַבְּחִים צֹאן וּבָקָר אֲשֶׁר לֹא־יִסָּפְרוּ וְלֹא יִמָּנוּ מֵרֹב:

6 וַיָּבִאוּ הַכֹּהֲנִים אֶת־אֲרוֹן בְּרִית־יְהוָה אֶל־מְקוֹמוֹ אֶל־דְּבִיר הַבַּיִת אֶל־קֹדֶשׁ הַקֳּדָשִׁים אֶל־תַּחַת כַּנְפֵי הַכְּרוּבִים: 7 כִּי הַכְּרוּבִים פֹּרְשִׂים כְּנָפַיִם אֶל־מְקוֹם הָאָרוֹן וַיָּסֹכּוּ הַכְּרֻבִים עַל־הָאָרוֹן וְעַל־בַּדָּיו מִלְמָעְלָה:

8 וַיַּאֲרִכוּ הַבַּדִּים וַיֵּרָאוּ רָאשֵׁי הַבַּדִּים מִן־הַקֹּדֶשׁ עַל־פְּנֵי הַדְּבִיר וְלֹא יֵרָאוּ הַחוּצָה וַיִּהְיוּ שָׁם עַד הַיּוֹם הַזֶּה: 9 אֵין בָּאָרוֹן רַק שְׁנֵי לֻחוֹת הָאֲבָנִים אֲשֶׁר הִנִּחַ שָׁם מֹשֶׁה בְּחֹרֵב אֲשֶׁר כָּרַת יְהוָה עִם־בְּנֵי יִשְׂרָאֵל בְּצֵאתָם מֵאֶרֶץ מִצְרָיִם:

10 וַיְהִי בְּצֵאת הַכֹּהֲנִים מִן־הַקֹּדֶשׁ וְהֶעָנָן מָלֵא אֶת־בֵּית יְהוָה: 11 וְלֹא־יָכְלוּ הַכֹּהֲנִים לַעֲמֹד לְשָׁרֵת מִפְּנֵי הֶעָנָן כִּי־מָלֵא כְבוֹד־יְהוָה אֶת־בֵּית יְהוָה: 12 אָז אָמַר שְׁלֹמֹה

יְהוָה אָמַר
לִשְׁכֹּן בָּעֲרָפֶל:

13 בָּנֹה בָנִיתִי
בֵּית זְבֻל לָךְ
מָכוֹן לְשִׁבְתְּךָ עוֹלָמִים:

14 וַיַּסֵּב הַמֶּלֶךְ אֶת־פָּנָיו וַיְבָרֶךְ אֵת כָּל־קְהַל יִשְׂרָאֵל וְכָל־קְהַל יִשְׂרָאֵל עֹמֵד: 15 וַיֹּאמֶר בָּרוּךְ יְהוָה אֱלֹהֵי יִשְׂרָאֵל אֲשֶׁר דִּבֶּר בְּפִיו אֵת דָּוִד אָבִי וּבְיָדוֹ מִלֵּא לֵאמֹר: 16 מִן־הַיּוֹם אֲשֶׁר הוֹצֵאתִי אֶת־עַמִּי אֶת־יִשְׂרָאֵל מִמִּצְרַיִם לֹא־בָחַרְתִּי בְעִיר מִכֹּל שִׁבְטֵי

---

b-b Lit. "who spoke with His own mouth . . . and has fulfilled with His own hand"

building a House where My name might abide; but I have chosen David to rule My people Israel.'

17] "Now my father David had intended to build a House for the name of the Lord, the God of Israel.

18] But the Lord said to my father David, 'As regards your intention to build a House for My name, you did right to have that intention.

19] However, you shall not build the House yourself; instead, your son, the issue of your loins, shall build the House for My name.'

20] "And the Lord has fulfilled the promise that He made: I have succeeded* my father David and have ascended the throne of Israel, as the Lord promised. I have built the House for the name of the Lord, the God of Israel;

21] and I have set a place there for the Ark, containing the covenant which the Lord made with our fathers when He brought them out from the land of Egypt."

יִשְׂרָאֵל לִבְנוֹת בַּיִת לִהְיוֹת שְׁמִי שָׁם וָאֶבְחַר בְּדָוִד לִהְיוֹת עַל־עַמִּי יִשְׂרָאֵל:

17] וַיְהִי עִם־לְבַב דָּוִד אָבִי לִבְנוֹת בַּיִת לְשֵׁם יְהוָה אֱלֹהֵי יִשְׂרָאֵל: 18] וַיֹּאמֶר יְהוָה אֶל־דָּוִד אָבִי יַעַן אֲשֶׁר הָיָה עִם־לְבָבְךָ לִבְנוֹת בַּיִת לִשְׁמִי הֱטִיבֹתָ כִּי הָיָה עִם־לְבָבֶךָ: 19] רַק אַתָּה לֹא תִבְנֶה הַבָּיִת כִּי אִם־בִּנְךָ הַיֹּצֵא מֵחֲלָצֶיךָ הוּא־יִבְנֶה הַבַּיִת לִשְׁמִי: 20] וַיָּקֶם יְהוָה אֶת־דְּבָרוֹ אֲשֶׁר דִּבֵּר וָאָקֻם תַּחַת דָּוִד אָבִי וָאֵשֵׁב עַל־כִּסֵּא יִשְׂרָאֵל כַּאֲשֶׁר דִּבֶּר יְהוָה וָאֶבְנֶה הַבַּיִת לְשֵׁם יְהוָה אֱלֹהֵי יִשְׂרָאֵל: 21] וָאָשִׂם שָׁם מָקוֹם לָאָרוֹן אֲשֶׁר־ שָׁם בְּרִית יְהוָה אֲשֶׁר כָּרַת עִם־אֲבֹתֵינוּ בְּהוֹצִיאוֹ אֹתָם מֵאֶרֶץ מִצְרָיִם:

---

c Lit. *"risen in place of"*

LEVITICUS

Commentary by

BERNARD J. BAMBERGER

Introducing Leviticus

The Character of the Book and the Commentary

The third book of the Torah, Leviticus, contains some of the loftiest passages found in the Bible. It is in this book that we read, "Love your neighbor as yourself" and "Proclaim liberty throughout the land."

But much of the book is devoted to matters completely remote from our present-day life—directions for sacrifice and rules of ritual defilement and purification. Nearly all these laws ceased to function when the Temple was destroyed in 70 C.E. They have no relevance to the conduct of even the most strictly Orthodox Jew, and they are omitted from such standard codes as the *Shulchan Aruch*. Orthodox belief, indeed, holds that this is only a temporary interruption: When the Messiah comes, the Temple will be rebuilt and the sacrificial cult resumed. Prayers for this restoration are included in the Orthodox prayer book. But most modern Jews—not only those committed to Reform Judaism—regard these sacrificial practices as completely out of date; they do not expect or want them to be revived.

The philosopher Philo (who lived in Alexandria at the beginning of the Christian era) found all sorts of spiritual meanings in the sacrificial cult; explaining the laws symbolically and allegorically, he honestly believed he had penetrated to their deepest and truest intent. This method is not possible for us. Our only honest approach is the historical approach, understanding the material in the light of the time when it was composed, against the background of ancient Near Eastern culture.

Such an enterprise is not entirely unprofitable even for the general reader. It reveals a dramatic development in concepts of religion and morality within the Bible itself. In this one book of Leviticus, there are a few passages where the word *kadosh* (usually rendered "holy") has the force of "taboo," and there are others where it designates the highest level of ethical and spiritual aspiration.

We shall find, moreover, that, while the ritual procedures here described resembled in some ways those of other ancient peoples, they also display significant differences. The distinctive outlook of developing Judaism made itself felt even in an area resistant to change—that of custom and ceremony administered by a hereditary, and therefore generally conservative, priesthood.

Most important, perhaps, is the fact that these materials were made accessible to all the people. Other Near Eastern nations had myths and legends that occasionally remind us of the stories of the Pentateuch. They also had bodies of civil and criminal law, such as the Code of Hammurabi which was inscribed on a monument set up in a public place. But their ritual and liturgical texts were generally kept in temples for the ex-

clusive use of the priests. Only in the Torah do we find stories, laws, and rituals combined into an inclusive document available to everyone.

The Book of Deuteronomy commands that parents shall teach its contents diligently to their children and provides that the entire book shall be read publicly every seven years. But even Deuteronomy left priestly matters entirely in the hands of the priests. It does not describe the procedures of sacrifice, and it refers the people to the priests for guidance regarding "leprosy" (Deut. 24:8). It was therefore something of a revolution when the priestly laws were included in a work designed for the entire population. These laws were not to be professional secrets any longer. A number of sections begin, "Speak to the priests, the sons of Aaron," or "Speak to Aaron and his sons," but others—among them the very first section on sacrifice—begin, "Speak to the Israelite people." The concept of a complete Torah, which all may study who have the will to do so, expresses a new democratic spirit.

In addition, the seemingly unpromising ritual sections have at times called forth by the talmudic rabbis comments that are worth noting for their beauty and profound insight.

There are other subjects treated in Leviticus that are still operative in the lives of many Jews. The dietary laws are a notable instance. Even those Jews who do not observe *kashrut* should know something of the character and spirit of the rules of food, which have often been misunderstood and misrepresented by well-meaning but uninformed amateurs.

Still other sections deal with topics that are of concern to all committed Jews. Examples are the chapters on permitted and forbidden sex relations and the detailed account of holy days and festivals. Our treatment of such passages will assume that we have much to learn from the Torah, even though we do not accept its authority blindly and without question. And in the great Law of Holiness and the section on the jubilee year we shall find ourselves challenged by the noblest and most exacting of ethical and religious ideals.

Our presentation will often refer to the origins and the primary intent of ancient observances. The reader, however, should bear in mind that a custom may continue long after its original meaning has been discarded and forgotten. We should not assume, for example, that the generations of Jews who brought sacrifices to the Temple, or the writers who compiled the sacrificial laws in Leviticus, still believed that God is literally in need of food.

Nor is the value of a living custom necessarily impaired because it originated in superstition. A simple instance (not related to the Book of Leviticus) will make this plain. Rites of burial and mourning are incredibly ancient; they were originally intended to protect the survivors from the spirits of the dead. The latter were deemed to be resentful at being deprived of the comforts and associations they had enjoyed in life. To keep the departed ones from returning and injuring their families, a pile of stones was heaped over their graves. Our custom of erecting a tombstone derives ultimately from that ancient fear; but obviously that is not the reason that we today mark the graves of our departed.

Unlike the first two books of the Bible, the third contains only a few bits of narrative. It is essentially a compendium of law. It has seemed desirable, therefore, to provide a fairly extended introduction to each section of the text before expounding it verse by verse.

The Name of the Book

At the beginning of the Christian era, or perhaps earlier, the name *Torat Kohanim,*

"The Priestly Torah," was applied to our book. It is also usually referred to in Hebrew by its first word, *Vayikra*, "And He called." The Greek translators called it *to Leuitikon*, "the Levitical book," and the Latin version of this name—Leviticus—has been generally adopted. Oddly, the Levites are mentioned in this book only in chapter 25, verses 32 through 34, though of course the priests were members of the tribe of Levi.

The Contents of the Book

Laws of sacrifice: chapters 1 through 7.

The dedication of the Tabernacle and the ordination of the priests, with certain attendant events: chapters 8 through 10.

Dietary laws: chapter 11, verses 1 through 23.

Laws of defilement and purification: chapter 11, verse 24 through chapter 15, verse 33.

The Day of Atonement: chapter 16.

Additional laws about sacrifice and food: chapter 17.

Permitted and forbidden sex relations: chapters 18 and 20.

The Law of Holiness—ethical and ritual: chapter 19.

Laws for the priesthood: chapters 21 and 22.

The Sabbath and festival calendar: chapter 23.

Two laws and an incident involving blasphemy: chapter 24.

The sabbatical and jubilee years: chapter 25.

An exhortation, containing blessings for the observance of the law and curses for its violation: chapter 26.

Laws concerning vows, gifts, and dues: chapter 27.

[1] In addition, there are a number of poetic passages and three short codes of law: Exod. 20; 21–23; 34:10–26.
[2] See General Introduction to the Torah.

Priestly Writing and Holiness Writing

The reader has already been made aware of the view that the Torah is a composite work. Though many conclusions of nineteenth-century biblical criticism have been challenged, it is hardly possible to deny the existence of three principal elements in the Pentateuch.[1] One is the Book of Deuteronomy, distinctive in viewpoint, contents, and style; it is referred to by scholars as D. The second comprises the vivid, dramatic, and moving narratives in Genesis, Exodus, and Numbers and is called J/E.[2] These books also contain extensive sections comprising a priestly document, P; and Leviticus consists altogether of priestly material. P includes a considerable amount of narrative, but it is primarily concerned with law and ritual. It is somewhat more systematic in outlook than the other documents, and its style is more precise and detailed. It can be dignified and impressive, as in the opening chapter of Genesis; but the modern reader may find tedious its concern for genealogies, the details of the structure and furnishings of the Tabernacle, and fine points of ritual law.

Though the entire Book of Leviticus is drawn from priestly sources, it is not a completely unified and ordered code. For example, it treats at length of sacrifices, but other important regulations on the subject— also from P—are found in Exodus and Numbers. The chapters on ritual defilement (11–15) do not mention the most severe type of defilement, contact with a corpse. This matter is alluded to briefly in chapter 21, verses 1 through 4, but a full exposition appears only in Numbers, chapter 19.

Even within the Book of Leviticus there is a certain lack of system. The section on sacrifice consists of two parts, chapters 6 and 7 providing additional rules for the various types of offering already discussed in chapters 1 through 5. (Chapter 17 offers still further

material on sacrifice.) Chapter 20 is largely a repetition of the laws in chapter 18.

Clearly, P is not a single seamless whole, written by one author. It is a compilation of priestly traditions drawn from various sources and, no doubt, from various periods. There are numerous discrepancies of detail; and there is some indication that, after the basic compilation was finished, additions and editorial changes were made. But the attempts of some scholars to analyze P into its component documents and establish the date of each are far from convincing.[3] Moreover, study has increasingly revealed that there was a long oral tradition behind many of the written documents. A given law may have existed for centuries before it was embodied in one of our present texts.

But, even in translation, one can detect a marked change in content, style, and mood in the second half of the book. Chapters 1 through 16 and chapter 27 are similar in matter and manner to P materials found in other books of the Torah. But chapters 17 through 26 have many distinctive characteristics. They frequently explain the purpose and intent of the laws, something rare in P. In addition to stating the reasons for individual provisions, these chapters constantly refer to their overall purpose—to maintain the holiness of the Israelite people. And holiness is understood not only in terms of ceremonial purity but especially in terms of personal and social righteousness. The divine source and sanction of all these rules is constantly emphasized by such phrases as "I the Lord am your God" after a given commandment. In their combination of moral and ritual elements and in their hortatory tone, these chapters remind us of D.[4] In short, they are a distinctive component of P, or else an entirely separate document, called by scholars the Holiness Code, H; it contains most of the Leviticus passages that appeal to the contemporary reader.

Though H is different from the other parts of the Torah, it shows many points of resemblance to the prose writings of the prophet Ezekiel. Scholars have compiled long lists of phrases that occur frequently in Ezekiel and H and seldom, if ever, in other biblical texts. It has even been suggested that Ezekiel was the author of the Holiness Code; but in fact Ezekiel's program of religious observance contradicts some regulations of Leviticus, and some of his theological ideas are also at variance with those of H. It seems, however, quite possible that H dates from the time of the prophet's activity—that is, the years following the downfall of Judah, in the sixth century B.C.E.

The present writer believes that the written documents of the Pentateuch are a crystallization of many traditions, some of them very ancient. This is also true of P. Despite a certain uniformity of style and outlook, it contains many discrepancies that indicate it is a composite of various sources. It seems probable that the priestly materials were given their present form in the fifth century B.C.E. The editors preserved without change much that was ancient, but they also made modifications and additions to meet new needs. The scapegoat law (16:8–10; 20–22) is only one of the genuinely archaic elements in P; but the priestly writing also contains passages where we meet a contrived and artificial "antiquity"—especially, the account of an elaborate shrine with a highly organized sacrificial system, completely inappropriate to desert conditions. They suggest a relatively late date. So does the sharp dis-

[3] A recent commentary on Leviticus by Karl Elliger (Tübingen: Mohr, 1966) goes to extremes in that sort of analysis and has been disregarded in the preparation of this book.

[4] Not that the P writers were indifferent to ethical considerations: see Lev. 1:10, 14; 5:20 ff., etc. But P was intended to provide a guide for ritual, not for moral conduct.

tinction in P between priests and Levites—whereas in D these two terms are synonymous.[5] The Book of Leviticus as we have it is the end product of a long and complex evolution.

Interpreters of Leviticus

For centuries Jewish children began their Bible studies with the Book of Leviticus. This strange choice was justified by the contention that pure young children should first learn about the sacrifices which were brought in purity.[6]

But adults also studied the work intensively. The rabbinic commentaries to biblical books are known as *midrashim*, and of these the one to Leviticus is among the longest and most detailed. It is called *Torat Kohanim* and also *Sifra* (*the* Book). The material is drawn largely from the expositions of the second-century Rabbi Akiba and his disciples.

The word *midrash* means "search," "interpretation"; and *midrashim* often draw inferences from the biblical text that go far beyond its plain sense. But the midrashic method of Rabbi Akiba was particularly intensive. He was convinced that every word and every letter of the Pentateuch is charged with rich and varied meaning. In *Sifra*, a legal ruling may be deduced from an "and" or a "but," thus providing biblical support for regulations hitherto known only by tradition. *Sifra* comments on nearly every verse of Leviticus in terms of both halachah, law, and haggadah, moral and religious edification.

It is probable that *Sifra* was compiled in the third century c.e. Later on, other *midrashim* to Leviticus were edited, perhaps in the sixth or seventh century. These works are almost exclusively haggadic, consisting of sermons attached to the opening sentences of different sections of the biblical book. They deal with themes of interest to the average listener who might find the details of sacrifice, and the like, rather dull and dry. Thus the sermon on the opening verse, "The LORD called to Moses," treats of prophecy and revelation; that on chapter 2, verse 1, "When a person [*nefesh*] presents," understands *nefesh* as "soul" and discusses the relation of soul and body. Though chapter 10, verse 9, prohibits the use of wine only to a priest who is about to officiate, the *midrashim* use it for a general homily on the evils of drink, containing some humorous touches. The verse, "If your brother, being in straits" (25:35), calls forth a lengthy and magnificent sermon on charity. These materials are found in a work called *Vayikra Rabbah* (roughly, "The Big Midrash to Leviticus") and in *Midrash Tanchuma* which extends over the entire Torah and exists in at least two versions. Many comments on Leviticus are also found in other *midrashim* and in the two Talmuds. Much of this material was assembled in medieval compilations, the *Yalkut Shimoni* and the *Midrash Hagadol*.

Our volume draws upon these sources as well as upon the great medieval Jewish commentators, Rashi, Ibn Ezra, and others. From *Sifra* down, they often give sound explanations of the biblical text. But, even when we find their interpretations incorrect or fanciful, they have something to teach us. We learn from them how the Torah was understood by earlier generations, who sometimes found in the text new and elevating thoughts.

We owe a great deal to the critical studies of Christian biblical scholars of the last hundred and fifty years. Their commentaries on Leviticus, however, are not among their

---

[5] See Introduction to Lev. 21.
[6] H. Schauss, *The Lifetime of the Jew* (Cincinnati: Union of American Hebrew Congregations, 1950), p. 100 and n. 114.

most successful achievements—perhaps because it was difficult for them to relate to the contents of this book. A recent commentary from which I profited is that of N. H. Snaith[7] who made extensive use of Jewish sources.

Two modern Jewish commentaries on Leviticus deserve special mention. One is the *Critical and Historical Commentary* of M. M. Kalisch[8] who was among the first Jewish scholars to utilize critical methods for the study of the Bible. Even for his age, he was too much inclined to explain age-old rites in rationalistic and moralistic terms; and his work is now largely out of date. But it is a mine of information on the history of biblical exegesis, and it contains many penetrating remarks.

The massive German commentary of David Hoffmann[9] was written from an uncompromisingly Orthodox viewpoint. But he was well acquainted with the work of the nineteenth-century Christian biblical critics, and he was frequently successful in turning their critical weapons against them. A review of this learned work was published by the Christian Bruno Baentsch, whose own commentary on Leviticus we shall cite occasionally.[10] Baentsch admitted that he had learned much from Hoffmann, despite his Orthodox approach.

Mention should also be made of two modern Hebrew commentaries on the entire Torah, including Leviticus. That of Samuel David Luzzatto[11] combines a strong commitment to tradition with considerable originality. The other, by Arnold B. Ehrlich,[12] is one of the most brilliant works of modern biblical science. Though sometimes erratic, and now partly outdated, Ehrlich's work had considerable influence on the present Torah translation.[13]

On Reading This Commentary

The translators who created the New Jewish Version provided a number of marginal notes to the translation, and they are here incorporated in the commentary and marked "T.N." for "Translator's Note." It should be observed that alternate renderings given in these notes and introduced by "Or" were considered by the Translation Committee almost as acceptable as those adopted in the text; those introduced by "Others" are well-known translations, usually found in the 1917 translation of the Jewish Publication Society, which the committee did not find acceptable.

Much of the material in Leviticus is technical, and we do not always have exact equivalents in English for the Hebrew terms. It has therefore seemed desirable to use in this commentary these Hebrew terms (after defining them) rather than the more or less approximate English renderings.

We shall also frequently employ the word "halachah," which is derived not from the Bible but from rabbinic literature. It comes from a root meaning "to go" and designates the concretely legal elements in Judaism, including civil, criminal, family, procedural, and ritual law—in contrast to matters of belief, aspiration, and idealism which cannot

7 N. H. Snaith, *Leviticus and Numbers*, The Century Bible (new edition, London: Nelson, 1967).

8 M. M. Kalisch, *A Critical and Historical Commentary on the Old Testament: Leviticus*, 2 vols. (London: Longmans Green, Reader and Dyer, 1867–1872).

9 D. Hoffmann, *Das Buch Leviticus*, 2 vols. (Berlin: M. Poppelauer, Vol. I, 1905; Vol. II, 1906).

10 B. Baentsch, *Exodus-Leviticus-Numeri* (Nowack's *Handkommentar*, Göttingen: Vandenhoeck und Ruprecht, 1903).

11 *Perush Shadal al Chamishah Chumshei Torah* (new edition, Tel Aviv: Devir, 1965).

12 *Mikra Kifeshuto* (reprinted in *The Library of Biblical Studies*, 3 vols., New York: Ktav Publishing House, 1969).

13 All the commentators mentioned in this section will be cited in the notes simply by name, it being understood that the reference is to their comment on the passage under discussion; a page reference is occasionally added.

be formulated into specific, enforceable duties. The word "halachah" can mean the entire corpus of Jewish law or a ruling on a single question.

The accepted halachah is often at variance with what seems to be the literal sense of the biblical verse on which the halachah is based. Often, indeed, there is no conflict; but frequently the rabbis go far beyond the plain intent of the text in the far-reaching and fanciful inferences they draw, and occasionally the halachah flatly negates the simple meaning of the scriptural words. (This was fully recognized by the traditional commentators. They assumed in all such cases that authentic tradition going back to Moses at Sinai required them to accept as normative an explanation that was not in accord with the usual rules of grammar and philology.)[14]

The Jewish reader needs to know not only the probable original meaning of a Bible verse but also how that verse has been understood in Jewish tradition, especially in regard to religious practice and observance. These divergent viewpoints are frequently explained in the introductions to the various sections of the ensuing commentary. Individual items are treated as follows:

[14] See Ibn Ezra's introduction to his Torah commentary.

The commentary proper cites *Sifra* and other rabbinic sources, as well as the great medieval commentaries, when these writings appear to give a correct, or at least plausible, explanation of the biblical text. Where, however, the halachah appears to go beyond or against the plain sense of Scripture, it is summarized in the section headed "Gleanings." (As a rule, such halachic summaries are not direct quotations from the sources.) The references provided in the notes are in no way exhaustive; they sometimes cite primary sources and sometimes the codification of the halachah by Maimonides and his successors. Most often, however, we rely on the explanation of a given verse in *Sifra*, in which case the reference is simply "Sifra" or is omitted altogether.

It will be seen further that the "Gleanings" are usually divided into two sections, the first containing the halachic materials, the second headed by the Hebrew term "Haggadah." This word, from a root meaning "to tell," refers to all nonlegal elements in talmudic and midrashic literature, especially those concerned with belief and with moral edification. In these sections there are more direct quotations, but often it was necessary to summarize and to explain for clarity and brevity. Included also are some selections from later Jewish literature which is not properly haggadic but is likewise edifying.

Leviticus
and Ancient Near Eastern Literature

WILLIAM W. HALLO

In the primeval garden of Genesis stood the tree of life. Man was bidden to eat of it, along with all the other trees of the garden, excepting only one, the tree of death. He did eat of it and this, "man's first disobedience," created a logical contradiction which even God could not have tolerated. Having tasted of the tree of mortality, man could not now also redeem the promise of immortality or, as the text puts it, "stretch out his hand and take also from the tree of life and eat [of it] and so live forever." Therefore he was permanently banned from the garden and destined forever after to wring a hard-earned subsistence from the soil by the sweat of his brow. The offer of sustenance without toil was withdrawn together with the promise of immortality.

But the concept of the tree of life was not abandoned; it reemerged in the Book of Proverbs as the symbol of wisdom (3:18) and justice (11:30) and in postbiblical theology as the symbol of the Bible itself. The Torah became a tree of life to those who lay hold of it, as we are reminded in the liturgy whenever the Torah scroll is returned to the Ark. What this signifies (in rabbinic exegesis) is that fear of the Lord and obedience to the Torah can still redeem a part of the primeval promise: not eternal life, but length of days; not sustenance without toil, but toil rewarded by subsistence. These reformulations are most explicit in Deuteronomy, with its almost simplistic system of rewards and punishments. But they inform the entire Torah and offer a special clue to the literary character of Leviticus.

Leviticus is the shortest of the Five Books of Moses. It is also the middle book, and its centrality in the Pentateuch is more than a mere matter of position. (It was typically the first text of the traditional *cheder*.) For all its apparent attention to archaic and obsolete priestly concerns, a far different focus emerges when the book is set against the Torah as a whole and against the literature of the surrounding Near East. Then we see that its real concern is with consumption of food (chs. 1–11) and with the related requirements of purification (chs. 12–16) and sanctification (chs. 17–27). These three broad topics provide, as it were, the warp of the book, while the woof is based on another triad: God, priests, and laity. To each are assigned very specific portions of all edibles, each receive distinct roles in purification and discrete

levels of holiness. Thus Leviticus can be regarded as a homogeneous literary work, even though we cannot prove that it ever existed as a separate book in its own right, and even though the critics differ widely in their hypotheses about the various documents and traditions that may have gone into its composition.

The Comparative Approach

After a century and more of "biblical archeology," a comparative approach to Leviticus may well begin with an appeal to those concrete material remains recovered in the excavations which throw welcome light on customs and ceremonies previously preserved only in the verbal descriptions of the biblical book. Thus, for example, the laws of the ritual bath which the Mishnah developed from the prescriptions in Leviticus 15 were found to apply to the disposition and measurements of the *mikvaot* unearthed at Masada from the time of the Second Temple (see Gleanings to 15:5 with note 12). This is startling confirmation, albeit mute. More often, the architectural and other remains are further illuminated by epigraphic finds, i.e., by monumental or archival inscriptions. Arad, for example, served as a border fortress for the Kingdom of Judah in the time of the First Temple; as such, it was privileged to have its own sanctuary (prior to the centralization of the cult at Jerusalem) complete with altar. Not only do some of its measurements and other dispositions correspond to those prescribed for the Jerusalem temple, but in or around it were found ostraca

(potsherds) inscribed with names of priestly families (e.g., Keros, Meremoth, Pashhur) known from the later books of the Bible (see note 3 to chs. 21 and 22).[1] Better even than the laconic ostraca is the evidence of literary texts. When the text (16:12) details the rules regarding the censer, it is easy to picture this cultic instrument in light, not only of the many actual censers (often in the form of a hand) excavated all over the Near East, but also of the parallel wording of texts such as the daily ritual of the Egyptian temple of Amon-Re at Karnak, which included instructions for taking the censer, laying its bowl upon its arm, and putting the incense on the fire.[2]

A word of caution is nonetheless in order before proceeding to utilize the extensive literary parallels from the Near Eastern environment. Responsible comparison must beware of false analogies by imposing the restraint of sound philology. Thus, e.g., the twelve loaves of 24:5 have long been compared to the "sweet bread" offering (*akal mutqi*) in dozens or multiples of dozens in Late Babylonian rituals. But, when the Akkadian adjective for sweet (*matqu*) was found in a lexical text as an explanation of *a-kal pa-nu*, the conclusion was hastily drawn that here was the Babylonian original of the biblical "bread of display" (the traditional "shewbread," i.e., *lechem pānîm*, Exod. 25:30; etc.). And, just as the twelve loaves of Leviticus 24 equalled the shewbread of Exodus 25, so, it was argued, the "sweet bread" of Babylonia was also called "shewbread." In fact, however, the Akkadian term must be read *a-lap-pa-nu*; it refers to a bittersweet taste; a beer of such taste; and the barley from which this beer is made. In short, there is no shewbread in Akkadian. And, if the number twelve has any significance, it should be sought, not in the Babylonian evidence which is actually later, but in the Israelite system of twelve tribes.

---

[1] Yochanan Aharoni, "The Israelite Sanctuary at Arad" in *New Directions in Biblical Archaeology*, eds. D. N. Freedman and J. C. Greenfield (Garden City: Doubleday, 1969), pp. 25–39.

[2] James B. Pritchard, ed., *Ancient Near Eastern Texts* (Princeton: Princeton University Press, 2nd ed., 1955), p. 325, n. 3. [Hereafter cited as Pritchard, *ANET.*]

The Concept of Consumption

We turn then to the main concerns of Leviticus, beginning with the "concept of consumption" as it is reflected in the cult (chs. 1–11) and epitomized in the dictum about the Aaronide priests: "For they offer the Lord's offerings by fire, the food of their God, and so must be holy" (21:6; cf. 21:8). The basic conception underlying this dictum is a widely held one in the ancient Near East: the gods, like men, need to eat in order to live, and men are there to provide for them. Already some of the oldest Mesopotamian myths justify the creation of man in these terms: the great gods, weary of the task of furnishing their own sustenance, initially force the lesser gods to labor for them, but these rebel and mankind is created to relieve them of their labors.[3] Pale reflections of the same conception linger in the mythical version of Creation in Genesis (2:4-7, 15). But when it comes to the cultic expression of this conception, Israel parts company with its Near Eastern heritage. The polytheistic cult was firmly rooted in and centered around the physical image of the deity—anthropomorphic in Mesopotamia and Syria, in Egypt theriomorphic (animal-shaped) as well. Much of the cult was devoted to what, in a pregnant phrase, has been called "the care and feeding of the gods."[4] It involved the physical presentation, to the cult statue of the deity, of real victuals twice daily and in added amounts on special days of the cultic calendar. The victuals included meat, fowl, and fish, as well as cereals, oils, and other vegetarian items, as is clear from countless records of offerings carefully drawn up by the clergy responsible for the temple accounts. Each kind of food demanded its own ceremonial, such as sprinkling for cereals and libation for oils. It was most elaborate for meats. The living animal was slaughtered and its inedible portions carefully set aside for such uses as leather-making (from the skin). The entrails, which were not considered fit for consumption, were minutely inspected for their ominous significance, and a whole "science" of divination (extispicy) developed around the interpretation of the precise configuration of lungs, intestines, and especially the liver (hepatoscopy). The edible portions were then offered to the divine statue at a table set behind drawn curtains. After the proper time had elapsed, the table was cleared and what the statue had graciously deigned to leave over was eaten by the king. The balance of the enormous daily deliveries to the temples was then distributed to the clergy for their consumption. On special festive occasions the laity too was victualled from these deliveries; they, or at least the leavings, were considered sanctified by their prior contact with the deity.

Clearly, the cultic pattern is totally different in ancient Israel, and Leviticus reflects the difference. There is no statue or other physical image of the deity and no need to "feed" it. Equally important, "there is no augury in Jacob, no divining in Israel" (Num. 23:23; cf. Lev. 19:26), hence no need to inspect the entrails of the slaughtered animal. Finally, though the priesthood was maintained by tithes and other means and received a share of the regular offerings (a practice sometimes abused as in I Samuel 2:13-16), the king was neither the principal ministrant nor the designated beneficiary of the cult which, in keeping with the emerging Israelite doctrine of collective responsibility, was an obligation on the population as a whole, or at least on all adult males. The rationale for sacrifice was correspondingly

[3] Cf. W. G. Lambert and A. R. Millard, *Atra-ḥasīs: The Babylonian Story of the Flood* (Oxford: Oxford University Press, 1969).
[4] A. Leo Oppenheim, *Ancient Mesopotamia* (Chicago: University of Chicago Press, 1964), pp. 183–198.

different. Let us begin with the meat offering.

Israelite belief involved a strict hierarchy of God, man, and world in which man ranked midway between the divine realm and the material world of nature, including plants and animals and the things made from them. The law distinguished clearly among these realms, and this was equally true of cultic as of civil legislation. Offenses against God could only be pardoned by God, offenses against human life could not be absolved by material compensation. But offenses against nature also were subject to retaliation, for it was recognized that nature had its own defenses. The spilling of animal blood was in some sense an offense against nature and courted the risk of punishment, although never on the level of human bloodshed. It was to obviate such punishment that successive provisions were made to invest the act of animal slaughtering with a measure of divine sanction (see commentary to ch. 17). The common denominator of these provisions was to turn mere slaughter into sanctification. The "sacrifice" was a sacred-making of the consumption that followed.

The levitical legislation enshrined this principle in a painstaking distribution of consumption among deity, priesthood, and laity. Repeatedly, the first eleven chapters of the book specify which parts of the animal belonged to God and which to the priests; only the balance, if any, was available to the Israelite who brought the sacrifice. This principle, once formulated, was extended to meal offerings as well, and beyond that to the secondary functions of sacrifice: though in origin designed to sanctify the very act of consumption, sacrifice ultimately served as well to sanctify other human activities and to atone for other human transgressions. While deriving many of its mechanics from ancient Near Eastern models, it thus evolved a distinctive rationale.

The Requirements of Purification

The laws of *kashrut* (ch. 11) form a logical conclusion to the legislation on consumption and are quite without parallel in the ancient Near East. They cover only foods of animal origin and form a suitable transition to the second major concern of Leviticus, namely purification (chs. 12–16). Having concluded the "instructions concerning animals" (11:46) with a short section on defilement from animal carcasses and the like, the text begins the laws of purification with a short section on defilement by the "blood of parturition" before moving on to its main concern, defilement by various biological phenomena such as skin diseases, fungus, menstruation, and genital discharges (chs. 12–15). The priestly prescriptions covering these conditions are fully analyzed in the commentary; what the modern reader most often asks is why such unsavory matters are taken up by Leviticus at all. The comparative approach supplies a suggestive answer: the ancient Near Eastern milieu was acutely sensitive to the conditions described in these chapters—not, however, primarily as a hygienic or medical problem, but for their ominous significance. Fungus-like growths in houses, for example, were interpreted in elaborate cuneiform handbooks of prognostication. Other handbooks provided appropriate rituals, not so much for treating the symptom, but for averting the (usually evil) consequences it portended. One example out of many will have to suffice. A fungus called *katarru* is treated at length in chapter 12 of *šumma ālu*, the "terrestrial omen series" (so called to distinguish it from the series devoted to astrological omens and to freak births respectively). If such a fungus is found "in a man's house, on the outer north wall, the owner of the house will die and his house will be scattered. To avert the evil, you make six axes of tamarisk and scrape away some

of the fungus with them. . . . You recite: 'Ea performed (the incantation), Ea undid (the evil).' On that day the owner of the house slaughters a red male sheep before Ishum. . . . You throw that holy water over him, and its (the portent's) evil will be dissipated."[5] Even without studying all the possible permutations on the nature, location, and significance of each fungus, or the entire ritual (including both symbolic acts and conjurational formulas) prescribed for each individual case, one can readily see that the Mesopotamian concern was rooted in the mantic world view. That is, natural (or "unnatural") phenomena were signals vouchsafed to men by the gods, an "early warning system" of evils to come. Ritual was needed to dissipate, not the fungus, but the (greater) evil that it portended. The levitical legislation was therefore perhaps a reaction to a very deep-seated popular prejudice, shared to some extent by the Israelites. Without attempting to eradicate such fear at one stroke, it wisely instituted a systematic set of rules for dealing with the symptoms that inspired it.

The legislation about the day of atonement which follows (ch. 16) would seem like an unwarranted intrusion at this point, for in its historical dimension it links up with the narrative of ch. 10, while in its legal dimension it belongs with the festal calendar of ch. 23. It should therefore probably be regarded as a special instance of defilement (in this case the forbidden encroachment by the priesthood into the sphere of the divine). To this is added the central role played by an animal in the ritual absolving the priest. From the point of view of literary structure, it thus combines the emphasis on animals in the first section of the book with that on defilements in the second and provides a fitting literary conclusion to both. Seen in this light, the central emphasis is not on the festival but on the "scapegoat." The evident "primitive" character of this ritual figure is confirmed by folkloristic parallels from all over the world, and the sophisticated cultures of the ancient Near East are conspicuously missing from these parallels.[6] True, "when the ancient Egyptians sacrificed a bull, they invoked upon its head all the evils that might otherwise befall themselves" and then "either sold the bull's head to the Greeks or cast it into the river."[7] But this is already a far cry from the physical transfer of men's sins to an animal, still preserved in a late Assyrian incantation where we read: "Take the scapegoat (mašhuldubbû), place its head upon his (the afflicted king's) head. . . . Let that spittle fall (from his mouth) into its mouth. May that king be pure, may he be clean."[8]

Possibly the earliest evidence for the institution of the scapegoat comes from the Hittite texts of Anatolia, where a sacrificial animal described as nakkuššiš is loaded with the impurities of the penitent and sent on its way.[9] The Hittite technical term was borrowed from Hurrian and appears in earlier Hurro-Akkadian texts from Nuzi and Alalakh in the more general meaning of "substitute." Etymologically, it appears to be composed of "to let go" (nakk-) and the abstract suffix (-ši), providing an interesting parallel to one of the proposed etymologies for azāzēl, the "goat that departs" (see commentary to ch. 16 with note 4) which, by

[5] Richard I. Caplice, The Akkadian Namburbi Texts: An Introduction (Sources from the Ancient Near East, Vol. 1, No. 1, 1974), p. 18. Cf. idem, Journal of Near Eastern Studies, 33, 1974, pp. 345–349. [Hereafter cited as JNES.]
[6] Cf., e. g., James G. Frazer, "Public Scapegoats," The Golden Bough (New York: Macmillan, abridged ed., 1960), ch. LVII, pp. 651–679.
[7] Ibid., p. 661.
[8] Caplice, "Namburbi Texts in the British Museum, III," Orientalia, 36 (1967), pp. 293 f.
[9] O. R. Gurney, "Magic Rituals: The Scapegoat," in Some Aspects of Hittite Religion (The Schweich Lectures of the British Academy, 1976, 1977), Lecture III, pp. 47–52. Cf. Jim Hicks, The Empire Builders (New York: Time-Life Books, 1974), pp. 105–113.

"loan-translation," became *caper emissarius* in the Vulgate and "scape-goat" in English. (The latter term was apparently coined by William Tyndale, the first great English Bible translator, in 1530).

The Laws of Sanctification

The balance of Leviticus (chs. 17–26; for 27 see below) is devoted to the laws of sanctification and may well have once constituted a discrete literary entity (see commentary). But it is artfully woven into the book almost from its opening verse (17:11), whose key verb "atone" (*kappēr*) links it to the laws of atonement in ch. 16. The verb is attested also in other Semitic languages, but only in biblical Hebrew is it so central to the cult.[10] Rites of expiation are relatively rare in older Egyptian and Mesopotamian religion which centered most of its attention on the person of the king. In Old Kingdom Egypt, the king was himself a god and the object of worship; in Mesopotamia, he was the deputy of the local or imperial deity, and it was only or largely *his* ethical conduct and cultic meticulousness that served as warrant for the common weal. With the rise of a more "personal religion" in the second millennium, the common man began to adopt the royal belief in a kind of filial relationship to his personal god or to a divine pair conceived of as his heavenly parents.[11] But the idea of a

collective, national responsibility, so intimately woven into the cult of expiation in Leviticus (e.g., 4:13), reached little further than the bland platitudes of the so-called wisdom literature in hieroglyphic and cuneiform. The contrast may best be illustrated in connection with ch. 19, "the decalogue of the Holiness Code" (see commentary to 19:3 with note 16). Although most often quoted for its lofty ethical prescriptions, the chapter nevertheless shares with the rest of Leviticus a primary preoccupation with cult and consumption. Many of its individual provisions can be closely paralleled from the ancient Near East, but in significantly different literary contexts. In New Kingdom Egypt, for example, the deceased individual was accompanied to his grave by the so-called "Book of the Dead" which replaced the earlier mortuary texts known as Pyramid Texts (Old Kingdom) and Coffin Texts (Middle Kingdom) and extended their benefits from the king and the nobility to the private individual. A standard element of these later mortuary texts was the "protestation of guiltlessness," a kind of "negative confession" with many parallels to Leviticus 19. Compare, for instance, "I have neither increased nor diminished the grain measure. . . . I have not added to the weight of the balance. I have not weakened the plummet of the scales"[12] with Lev. 19:35 f. In Mesopotamia, similar sentiments are embedded in the "Wisdom" literature, a miscellaneous category of genres addressed to and concerned with the common man. Thus the great preceptive hymn to the sun-god Shamash, patron of justice and righteousness, contrasts "the merchant who practices trickery as he holds the balances, who uses two sets of weights" with "the honest merchant who holds the balances and gives good weight" or "the merchant . . . who weighs out loans (of corn) by the minimum standard but requires a large quantity in repayment"

[10] B. A. Levine, *In the Presence of the Lord: A Study of Cult and Some Cultic Terms in Ancient Israel* (Leiden, Holland: E. J. Brill, 1974), Pt. Two and App. III, pp. 56–77, 123–127.
[11] Thorkild Jacobsen, *The Treasures of Darkness: A History of Mesopotamian Religion* (New Haven: Yale University Press, 1976), Ch. 5, pp. 145–164.
[12] Pritchard, *ANET*, p. 34.
[13] *Ibid.*, p. 388; the translation follows Lambert, *Babylonian Wisdom Literature* (Oxford: Clarendon Press, 1960), p. 133. Cf. *idem*, "Morals in Ancient Mesopotamia," *Jaarbericht van het Voorarziatisch-Egyptisch Genootschap Ex Oriente Lux*, 15 (1957–1958), pp. 184–196, for an authoritative synthesis.

with "the honest merchant who weighs out loans (of corn) by the maximum standard, thus multiplying kindness."[13] The traditional rendering of 19:16 (see commentary) finds some support in the Akkadian "Counsels of Wisdom" with its many strictures against talebearing or unnecessary involvement in the disputes of others.[14] Such advice, usually addressed to princes and courtiers, is also characteristic of Egyptian "Instructions" of all periods,[15] which share with the "Counsels" a secular setting; they are pragmatic admonitions justified by long experience rather than cultic injunctions sanctioned by divine command. Nowhere is the contrast more explicit, perhaps, than in 19:23–25 which echoes paragraph 60 of the Laws of Hammurabi[16]—only that there the tenant farmer shares the yield of the fifth year, not with God, but with the human lessor!

Having thus arrived at the sphere of Near Eastern law, one might expect to find more parallels in it to the legislation of Leviticus. Such parallels do, after all, abound with the legislation of Exodus and Deuteronomy— but only its casuistic legislation, i.e., that phrased in the typical "conditional" form of precedent- (or case-) law. That phrasing characterizes civil and criminal legislation and is largely absent in Leviticus, whose laws are mostly cultic in content (or at least in context) and apodictic (or "unconditional") in form. A good illustration is provided by the laws on sexual conduct (chs. 18 and 20), for such conduct was also a major concern of all Near Eastern case-law. On the surface there appear to be striking similarities. Cases of adultery with a consenting married woman, for example, demand that both "the adulterer and the adulteress shall be put to death" in Leviticus (20:10); in the Sumerian laws of Ur-Nammu (§ 4), the laws of Eshnunna (§ 28), Hammurabi (§§ 129, 133), the Assyrian laws (§§ 13–16, 23), and the Hittite laws (§§ 197 f.), they are likewise

"treated with the utmost gravity, the death penalty being often faced by the adulteress, her lover, or both, depending on the circumstances."[17] Forbidden marriages and incestuous relationships (Lev. 20:11–21; cf. 18:6–18) are dealt with in the Laws of Hammurabi (§§ 154–158) and the Hittite laws (§§ 189–195), homosexuality (Lev. 18:22, 20:13) in the Assyrian laws (§ 20), and bestiality (Lev. 18:23, 20:15–16) in the Hittite laws (§§ 199–200A). The Hittites condemned both incest and bestiality as ḫurkel, i.e., "illicit sex," though they provided a purification ritual and ultimately the payment of a fine to mitigate the capital punishment ordinarily mandated by the laws.[18]

In spite of their common concerns, however, the levitical and Near Eastern laws differ widely. The latter were promulgated by kings as integral parts of civil and criminal law. They formed part of the foundation of royal authority, as is clear from the repeated provision for royal intervention. In case of adultery, for example, if the aggrieved husband chooses to spare his wife, the king may spare his subject (Laws of Hammurabi § 129; cf. Assyrian laws § 15, Hittite laws § 198). The levitical laws, on the other hand, are part and parcel of the Holiness Code and, especially if considered in conjunction with ch. 19, repeatedly invoke the formulas that base the human and social relations in ques-

14 Pritchard, *ANET*, pp. 426 f.; Lambert, *Babylonian Wisdom Literature*, pp. 96–107.
15 Pritchard, *ANET*, pp. 412–425.
16 *Ibid.*, p. 169.
17 J. J. Finkelstein, "Sex Offenses in Sumerian Laws," *Journal of the American Oriental Society*, 86 (1966), p. 366. [Hereafter cited as *JAOS*.] For the passages in question see Pritchard, *ANET*, pp. 161 ff.; *ANET* (3rd. ed., 1969), p. 523.
18 H. A. Hoffner, Jr., "Incest, Sodomy, and Bestiality in the Ancient Near East," in *Orient and Occident: Essays Presented to Cyrus H. Gordon* (Alter Orient und Altes Testament, Vol. 22, 1973), pp. 81–90.

tion on the authority and holiness of God. The conclusion of the pericope, moreover, proclaims in connection with one of these formulas the very same contrast to the existing mores that is here averred: "You shall be holy to Me, for I the Lord am holy, and I have set you apart from the other peoples to be Mine" (20:26).

The next pericope (21–22) provides additional legislation for the priesthood, this time from the point of view of the Holiness Code. Only two provisions can be singled out here by way of example. The Aaronides (priestly descendants of Aaron) are to "do guard duty" for the Lord on pain of death by divine agency. This is the technical meaning of 22:9, a provision elaborated and "reformed" in Numbers 18 (see "Numbers and Ancient Near Eastern Literature"). Hittite instructions similarly hold the armed guardians of the sanctuary personally liable for various encroachments on the *sancta* within—but here their delinquencies are punished by human agency.[19]

In connection with sacrificial animals, the practice of castration is categorically prohibited (see commentary to 22:24). It may be worth noting that the evidence for castra-

tion of domesticated animals is abundant in the cuneiform sources. A recent summary of this evidence suggests that it may throw some light on the cultic terminology of the Israelites. The oft-repeated injunction that sacrificial animals be males "without blemish" (*tāmīm*; females only in Lev. 3:1, 6 and 4:28) may involve a euphemism for non-castrated in light of the Akkadian *šuklulu*, like the Hebrew word applied to sacrificial animals and meaning literally "perfect, complete." Similarly, "mutilated" in the next verse (22:25) may be a euphemism for castrated, with the further specification "they have a defect" (*mūm bām*) being a later gloss that obscured the original meaning.[20]

The cultic calendar of Leviticus has innumerable points of contact with the ancient Near East (see in detail the commentary to ch. 23). Suffice it here to emphasize the single most conspicuous point of contrast: the biblical week. True, occasional seven-day periods were observed on special occasions like the dedication of Gudea's temple at Lagash in Sumer or of Solomon's in Jerusalem (I Kings 8:65f., reading with Septuagint).[21] But no other calendar insists on the eternal and unalterable succession of seven-day periods, independent of all earthly or astronomical considerations. Originally perhaps conceived as an expression of God's sovereignty over time,[22] the Sabbath day became an inalienable rest-day and therefore a uniquely Israelite contribution to the social legislation of the world. The concept was so deeply embedded in the Israelite frame of reference that it was (secondarily) superimposed on the very notion of Creation itself, which in other respects borrowed much from Near Eastern models. Moreover, it was extended from the week to the year in the concepts of the sabbatical year and the jubilee (ch. 25). Every seventh year the land is to enjoy a Sabbath (25:2) and after "seven sabbaths of years" (25:8; New Jewish Version: "seven weeks of

[19] Jacob Milgrom, *Studies in Levitical Terminology* I (University of California Publications [in] Near Eastern Studies, Vol. 14, 1970), Ch. II; *idem*, "The Shared Custody of the Tabernacle and a Hittite Analogy," *JAOS*, 90 (1970), pp. 204–209.

[20] B. Landsberger, *The Fauna of Ancient Mesopotamia: First Part* (Materialien zum Sumerischen Lexikon, Vol. 8, No. 1, 1960), pp. 66–75. In postexilic times, the priestly author of Isaiah 56:1–8 may have relaxed some of these restrictions; see Harry M. Orlinsky, *Essays in Biblical Culture* (New York: Ktav, 1974), pp. 94–98.

[21] Cf. E. C. Kingsbury, "A Seven-Day Ritual in the Old Babylonian Cult at Larsa," *Hebrew Union College Annual*, 34 (1963), pp. 1–34, esp. p. 27. [Hereafter cited as *HUCA*.]

[22] M. Tsevat, "The Basic Meaning of the Biblical Sabbath," *Zeitschrift für die Alttestamentliche Wissenschaft*, 84 (1972), pp. 447–459.

years") a jubilee. Here, too, biblical law instituted a novel social reform, albeit not destined to spread over the world like the Sabbath itself.[23] The weekly Sabbath and the sabbatical year were wholly Israelite innovations, and, while the jubilee year may have owed something to Near Eastern precedent, this precedent was restructured (like the biblical version of Creation) by means of the sabbatical idea. Both the (an)durāru of the Akkadians[24] and their so-called mīšarum-edicts[25] provide precedents of sorts. The latter, in particular, seems to have evolved under the Hammurabi dynasty into a periodic remission of debts and freeing of debt-slaves. But this was again strictly under royal auspices and at the royal whim. It was proclaimed in the first or second year of each king's reign, and sometimes at uncertain intervals thereafter. Only the biblical legislation provided divine sanction for the institution and, at least in theory, for its predictable periodicity.[26]

Conclusion

The Holiness Code concludes (ch. 26) with a catalogue of blessings as at the end of the Covenant Code (Exod. 23:20-33) and of sanctions in the time-honored manner of the Mesopotamian law codes. An appendix on vows and related matters (ch. 27) serves to round out the book. Leviticus emerges from the structural and comparative analysis outlined above as a coherent literary work divided (like other books of the Pentateuch) into some three sections discrete in content, but unified in its insistence on the theocratic basis of its legislation. God, priesthood, and laity—the three subjects of its concern—all replace the royal focus of the Near Eastern sources with which comparisons are possible. Not the king but God is the source of law and the agency of its enforcement; not the king but the priest is the chief cultic ministrant; not the king but the "whole community of Israel" is to obey the cultic instructions and thus earn the right to consume the fat of the land.

[23] Cf. E. Neufeld, "Socio-Economic Background of Yobel and Šemiṭṭa," *Rivista degli Studi Orientali*, 33 (1958), pp. 53–124.
[24] J. Lewy, "The Biblical Institution of Dᵉrôr in the Light of Akkadian Documents," *Eretz-Israel*, 5, 1958 (Jerusalem: Israel Exploration Society), pp. 21 ff.
[25] Finkelstein, "Some New *Misharum* Material and Its Implications," in *Studies in Honor of Benno Landsberger*, ed. Hans G. Güterbock and Thorkild Jacobsen (Assyriological Studies, Vol. 16, 1965), pp. 233–246.
[26] William W. Hallo, "New Moons and Sabbaths: A Case-Study in the Contrastive Approach," *HUCA*, 48 (1977), pp. 1–18.

PART I

Laws of Sacrifice

Introduction

Today the word "sacrifice" means an act of self-deprivation. We give up something of value for the sake of a greater value: we may sacrifice a vacation to make more money, or sacrifice luxuries in order to educate our children, or sacrifice life for nation or faith. Such a sacrifice is deemed regrettable, even though necessary; if we could attain the larger end without the sacrifice, we should do so. Prudence therefore counsels us to make a sacrifice only after careful deliberation and to sacrifice no more than is needed to attain our goal.

1. Ancient Concepts of Sacrifice

That is not what the ancients meant by sacrifice. To them it was a religious rite, most often a joyous one. The offering was as large and choice as the worshiper could afford to make it. It was always a sacrifice *to* some deity or power, not—as in our usage—a sacrifice *for* some end. The sacrifice might indeed be offered in the hope of obtaining a favor, of warding off disaster, or of achieving purification from ritual defilement or sin. But just as often, perhaps more often, it was an expression of reverence and thanksgiving.

We should note that the term "sacrifice" comes from a Latin word meaning "to make something holy." The most common Hebrew equivalent is *korban*, "something brought near," i.e., to the altar [1].

2. Ancient Sacrifices

The institution of sacrifice was virtually universal among ancient peoples, going back far beyond recorded history; it still survives in some primitive cultures. Scholars have propounded various theories as to its origin: some have found the beginnings in totemism, some in ancestor worship, and so on. All such opinions are highly speculative. Sacrifice took many forms, which may have arisen separately and out of different motives. There were communal, family, and individual sacrifices; some were mandatory and offered at regular intervals, others were voluntary. Often the sacrifice took the form of a communal meal. A portion of the animal was offered to the deity, the remainder was cooked and eaten by the sacrificer and his guests who thus felt themselves in literal communion with their god.

The sacrifice was usually of food and drink, though other items, such as perfumes and incense, were sometimes offered. Bread, milk, grain, fruit, beer, wine, and other items of diet were offered by various peoples. But the most usual object of sacrifice was an animal.

It was generally believed that the supernatural powers—whether spirits of the dead, demons, or gods—have the same material needs as we and can be propitiated by satisfying those needs. An ancient Hittite text

requires priests to be neat in appearance and conscientious in practice when serving the gods, and it continues: "Are the minds of men and of the gods generally different? No! With regard to the matter with which we are dealing? No! Their minds are exactly alike" [2]. And in warning the priest not to appropriate for his own use a sheep designated for sacrifice, this text says: "Just think how the man reacts who sees his most valued possession snatched away from before his eyes" [3]. A Babylonian document gives instruction that the gods of a certain temple should be served an evening meal, a main morning meal, and a second morning meal [4]. In the Babylonian flood story, the interruption of sacrifice seems to have reduced the gods to a state of starvation for, when the survivors of the flood offered sacrifice, "the gods crowded like flies about the sacrificer" [5].

Originally, offerings were simply left at tombs, or at places regarded as haunts of the gods. In Egypt and Mesopotamia, sacrifices were usually presented to the images of the gods, later they were removed and eaten by the king or the priests. But many peoples adopted the practice of burning sacrifices, or a portion of them, on an altar. This procedure was followed in India, among the Greeks and Romans, and among some peoples of western Asia, including Israel. It suggests that the gods are sustained by inhaling the odor of the burning food. Survivals of such thinking appear in the Torah. A few passages speak of sacrifices as "the food of God" (Lev. 21:16–23; Num. 28:2); more often, they are described as providing a "pleasing odor to the Lord" (Lev. 1:9 and elsewhere).

3. Sacrifice in the Bible

Did the biblical authors intend such expressions to be taken literally? A positive answer is not easy to give. No doubt some simpleminded worshipers believed that God requires food, yet the Bible contains protests against such a notion. Psalm 50, which was presumably sung in the Temple and which commends the sacrifice of thanksgiving (v. 14), represents God as saying: "Were I hungry, I would not tell you, / for Mine is the world and all it holds. / Do I eat the flesh of bulls, / or drink the blood of he-goats?" (Ps. 50:12, 13).

Probably old forms and phraseology were retained without a clear consciousness of their original meanings. We today continue to practice ancient customs in connection with marriage, death, and mourning, and we are unaware of the primitive concepts that generated these customs. Many public ceremonies in Great Britain retain the forms and language of the period when the sovereign was an absolute monarch, though the crown today has no direct political power. Very likely the authors of Leviticus regarded sacrifice as simply an act of homage to God and not as a means of satisfying His hunger.

Israelite sacrifice, though it resembled other ancient cults in various ways, also presents striking contrasts to them. Many peoples believed that sacrifice was not merely a method of obtaining divine favor but an indispensable means of maintaining the god's vitality. The Bible, despite a few allusions to the food of God, nowhere suggests that God needs sacrifices, and it repeatedly asserts the opposite [6].

It was a common practice to connect divination with sacrifice. Omens of good or ill fortune were derived from the appearance of the organs of a sacrificed beast. The Babylonians had a whole "science" of predicting the future from such omens, especially from the size and shape of the liver [7]. Before an important undertaking, especially a battle, the Greeks and Romans would sacrifice and would inspect the entrails of the victim, to determine whether or not a

happy outcome might be expected. Nothing of this sort was found in Israelite practice.

It appears, too, that the sacrificial cult in Mesopotamia was basically a matter for the king and priests and that the common people had little to do with it. Israelite sacrifice was a more democratic affair. Provision was made for inexpensive offerings which even the poor could afford. And one of the most familiar types of sacrifice had the form of a festive meal of which the worshipers partook—a form of sacrifice unknown in Babylonia. But the more democratic tendencies are also to be found in Greek and Carthaginian practices [8].

Egyptian and Babylonian documents contain liturgical texts that had to be recited as the sacrifices were performed [9]. Biblical law makes no mention of such prescribed prayers. But we know that sacrificial rites were often accompanied by vocal and instrumental music; and many of the psalms were composed for use in the Temple [10].

Only the priestly writings provide detailed instructions for the various kinds of sacrifices [11]. But throughout the Bible sacrifice was regarded as a normal element of personal, family, and civic life. The first instance of sacrifice in the Bible is in the story of Cain and Abel; and from that point on there are constant references to the practice.

Biblical sacrifices were both communal and individual. The communal sacrifices were almost all mandatory: the burnt offerings brought daily at morning and evening and the additional sacrifices for Sabbath and holy days [12]. Some individual sacrifices were also obligatory: the paschal lamb and various sacrifices of purification. Most of the individual offerings were voluntary.

One group of biblical utterances requires special notice: the prophetic sermons that contrast the demands of ethical religion with the formal cult of sacrifice and insist on the primacy of moral conduct in individual and social life. Some of these statements are quite extreme:

"Though you offer Me burnt offerings and meal offerings, / I will not accept them, / And I will not notice your sacrifices of fat beasts . . . . But let justice roll down like water, / And righteousness like a perennial stream. Did you bring Me sacrifices and offerings in the wilderness for forty years, O people of Israel?" (Amos 5:22–25. Cf. Jer. 7:22, "When I freed your fathers from the land of Egypt, I did not speak with them nor command them concerning burnt offering or sacrifice"; see also I Sam. 15:22–23; Isa. 1:11–13; Hos. 6:6; Mic. 6:6–8.)

Some modern scholars have therefore concluded that the preexilic prophets rejected all formal worship and called for a religion of ethical conduct only.

Jewish tradition understood these utterances to be directed not against sacrifice as such, but against the substitution of ritual for morality. Sacrifice *is* acceptable, according to this view, but only when it is offered with clean hands and a pure heart. The traditional expositors were indeed compelled to interpret the prophetic teaching thus, in order to harmonize it with the authoritative requirements of the Torah. Many modern scholars regard this explanation as historically correct. The prophets, these scholars argue, could not have advocated a cultless religion; that would have been a contradiction in terms for ancient man, and perhaps for modern man as well. It is clear that many prophets, especially during and after the exile, were strongly committed to the Temple and its worship, at the same time championing ethical values.

The critics of the sacrificial system were not advocating a new *form* of worship. Isaiah and Amos spoke with strong disapproval also of the prayers and religious music of their time. Whatever their intent may have been, their critique of formal worship was not understood as an absolute rejection.

Throughout the biblical period, and for centuries thereafter, sacrifice was considered proper and necessary, when performed with sincerity and with proper regard for the other requirements of the Torah.

It requires an enormous effort of imagination on our part to understand how untold generations found the sacrificial rites inspiring. We eat much more meat than our biblical ancestors did; but it comes to us neatly prepared and packaged, and many of us do not even see it till it is ready for the table. The sights, sounds, and smells of the slaughterhouse would be very upsetting to our squeamish generation. Ancient man was not so sheltered. He lived closer to the realities of birth, life, and death. He was not unfamiliar with the slaughtering of animals and their preparation for food; and, when these activities were performed in a sacred place as part of a solemn ritual, he found them dignified and meaningful.

It was of the Temple with its sacrificial cult that the Psalmist exclaimed: "O Lord, I love Your Temple abode,/ the dwelling-place of Your presence" (Ps. 26:8).

It is to this Temple and cult that many of our favorite psalms allude (read Ps. 4, 27, 84—and 23!).

4. Talmudic Views

In the century before the Christian era, religious leadership in Palestine passed largely from the hereditary priests to a group of learned laymen known as the Pharisees. The latter had widespread popular support, and so they were able to make certain changes in Temple procedure, expressive of a more progressive religious outlook and of a democratic spirit.

But in 70 c.e. the Romans burned the Temple, and they never permitted it to be rebuilt. The sacrificial cult came to an end [13]. By that time a new institution for prayer and study, the synagogue, was fully developed, and was meeting effectively the religious needs of the Jewish people in the homeland and the Diaspora. But still the loss of the Temple was felt keenly. It was the national Shrine; and sacrifices could be performed nowhere else. Petitions for the rebuilding of the Temple and the restoration of the cult were soon added to the regular synagogue prayers.

The Rabbis, the successors of the Pharisees, introduced into the synagogue a number of practices formerly associated with the Temple. But they made no provision for "interim" sacrifices. They could have found some precedents for sacrifice outside Jerusalem despite the prohibitions of Deuteronomy (12:5–6). In the fifth century b.c.e., a Jewish military colony in Egypt had a temple of sorts. More important was the temple at Leontopolis (also in Egypt), established about 170 b.c.e. by the High Priest Onias IV whose father had been deprived of his office by the Syrian tyrant Antiochus IV. This temple remained in existence till the Romans closed it after the fall of Jerusalem. The Rabbis never acknowledged its legitimacy, but they never denounced it as wholly sinful. But when the Temple in Jerusalem was destroyed, they did not choose to follow such precedents and set up a substitute form of sacrifice.

Not that they ever consciously questioned the value of the cult. They prayed for its restoration; and they discussed the Temple ritual in fullest detail. The study of the sacrificial laws, they declared, was as acceptable to God as the actual performance of the rites [14]. When Rabbi Sheshet fasted, he prayed that the diminution of blood and fat in his body, due to the fast, might be accepted by God as equivalent to sacrificial blood and fat [15]. Rabbinic preachers depicted a heavenly temple, in which the angel Michael officiated as High Priest [16].

But some of the scholars may have felt that the day of sacrifice had passed. Perhaps this is implicit in the notion that study about sacrifice is as efficacious as bringing sacrifice. Shortly after the Temple was destroyed, it is said, the aged Rabban Johanan ben Zakkai visited its ruins in the company of his pupils. One of them bewailed the cessation of the rites that provided atonement for sin. The old sage replied, "Do not grieve, my son. We have a means of atonement that is equal to sacrifice—the doing of kind deeds. For it is said, 'I desire mercy, and not sacrifice'" (Hos. 6:6) [17]. A few centuries later, Rabbi Isaac declared that prayer takes precedence over sacrifice [18].

Still more remarkable is a parable of Rabbi Levi, a contemporary of Rabbi Isaac: The son of a king became mentally confused and fell into the habit of eating carrion. Thereupon the king ordered his servants to serve kosher meat from the same kinds of animals at his own table so that the son might regain the habit of eating proper food. Similarly, said Rabbi Levi, Israel became addicted to idolatry while in Egypt; and in the desert they still brought offerings to the goat-demons. Thereupon God said, "Let them bring regular sacrifices to Me, and they will be protected from the tendency to idolatry" [19].

5. Medieval Views

Rabbi Levi's parable may have suggested the rationalistic explanation of sacrifice offered by the philosopher Moses Maimonides (1135–1204) [20]. That famous thinker held that the sacrificial legislation was a concession to human frailty. In ancient times, sacrifice was the universal practice; the Hebrews who left Egypt could not imagine a religion without it. Had they not been permitted to bring offerings to the true God, they would inevitably have sacrificed to other deities. Biblical sacrifice was the means by which they were weaned away from heathenism and instructed in true beliefs [21]. Moreover, the animals designated for sacrifice were those held sacred by the Hindus, Egyptians, and Sabeans, which were never slaughtered by those peoples. Thus Israelite sacrifices were a repudiation of pagan superstition [22].

Such reasoning might seem to suggest that sacrifice was a temporary expedient, no longer of any value. But Maimonides drew no such conclusion. His monumental code of Jewish law includes a full exposition of the sacrificial rites, ready for use when the Messiah should arrive and the Temple be rebuilt.

Nevertheless, his explanation of sacrifice was severely criticized by the more traditionally minded. Nachmanides (on Lev. 1:9) noted that Abel and Noah brought sacrifices at a time when idolatry had not yet appeared. Basically, he objected to treating so important an element of the Torah as a mere pedagogic device. The traditionalists insisted that sacrifice must have a positive value, even though our reason is inadequate to explain it. The Kabalists found mystical, even cosmic, implications in sacrifice. And the philosopher poet, Judah Halevi, had argued, nearly a century before Maimonides, that Temple and sacrifice are indispensable for the reestablishment of a perfect relationship between God and Israel—and, through Israel, between God and mankind [23].

6. Modern Attitudes

It was only with the rise of Reform Judaism at the end of the eighteenth century that believing Jews renounced the hope of restoring sacrifice [24]. The Reformers said plainly that, whatever purpose sacrifice may have served in ancient times, it is now obsolete and without meaning for the future. They therefore eliminated from the synagogue service the traditional prayers for the

restoration of Temple and cult. Today the Conservative and Reconstructionist groups have also explicitly renounced the hope of returning to the sacrificial system; and, tacitly, so have large masses of Jews not affiliated with these modernist movements.

Even among the Orthodox, allegiance to the cult seems to be chiefly verbal, consisting of reminiscences of a distant past and hopes for a vague and distant future. Some fifty years ago, Rabbi Abraham I. Kook, the saintly leader of the Orthodox Ashkenazim of Palestine, anticipating the speedy coming of the Messiah, attempted to found a school for the practical training of priests. But the project attracted little support.

In Christianity, on the other hand, the idea of sacrifice was reinterpreted and given central importance. The death of Jesus was explained as the true sacrifice which had been foreshadowed by the animal sacrifices of the "Old Testament"; and the mass is regarded as the regular repetition of that sacrifice [25].

7. The Sacrificial Legislation of the Torah

Chapters 1 through 7 of Leviticus contain extended, but not entirely complete, instruction for the different types of sacrifice brought by individuals. (In 4:13–22, an offering for the entire community is treated.) Additional directions concerning sacrifice appear in other parts of the book as well as in priestly sections of Exodus and Numbers [26].

The present section consists of two parts. The first five chapters explain the procedures for five different kinds of offerings; then these same offerings are treated a second time in chapters 6 and 7. Characteristic of the latter section is the introductory formula, "This is the ritual of . . . ." There is some repetition in the second section, but not much; the two expositions generally supplement each other. Plainly, the editor or editors of Leviticus drew on several sources and copied down what they thought important, without recasting the material into a unified whole.

See also the discussion at Num. 28:1–30:17 ("Sacrifice as Worship") for a somewhat different emphasis.

The Olah—Burnt Offering

The first type of sacrifice discussed is called *olah*, "what goes up," i.e., goes up in smoke, because the entire animal, except for its hide, was burned on the altar. Other types of sacrifice were consumed in part by fire, and the rest was eaten by the priests, or by the priests and worshipers. In English, *olah* has for centuries been translated "burnt offering."

The *olah* had a high degree of sanctity, and it was regarded as the "standard" sacri-fice. Most required communal sacrifices were *olot*. In contrast, sacrifices made by the Greeks to the Olympian gods were always shared by the worshipers; only sacrifices made to the dread underground deities to ward off evil were presented as *holocausts*, i.e., com-pletely burned [1].

The present chapter deals with the *olah* brought by an individual as a voluntary offering.

(The first weekly portion, *Vayikra*, begins here.)

מִן־הַבָּקָר זָכָר תָּמִים יַקְרִיבֶנּוּ אֶל־פֶּתַח אֹהֶל מוֹעֵד
יַקְרִיב אֹתוֹ לִרְצֹנוֹ לִפְנֵי יְהוָה: וְסָמַךְ יָדוֹ עַל רֹאשׁ
הָעֹלָה וְנִרְצָה לוֹ לְכַפֵּר עָלָיו: וְשָׁחַט אֶת־בֶּן הַבָּקָר
לִפְנֵי יְהוָה וְהִקְרִיבוּ בְּנֵי אַהֲרֹן הַכֹּהֲנִים אֶת־הַדָּם
וְזָרְקוּ אֶת־הַדָּם עַל־הַמִּזְבֵּחַ סָבִיב אֲשֶׁר־פֶּתַח אֹהֶל

א וַיִּקְרָא אֶל־מֹשֶׁה וַיְדַבֵּר יְהוָה אֵלָיו מֵאֹהֶל מוֹעֵד
ב לֵאמֹר: דַּבֵּר אֶל־בְּנֵי יִשְׂרָאֵל וְאָמַרְתָּ אֲלֵהֶם אָדָם
כִּי־יַקְרִיב מִכֶּם קָרְבָּן לַיהוָה מִן־הַבְּהֵמָה מִן־הַבָּקָר
ג וּמִן־הַצֹּאן תַּקְרִיבוּ אֶת־קָרְבַּנְכֶם: אִם־עֹלָה קָרְבָּנוֹ

* א א' זעירא.

1] The LORD called to Moses and spoke to him from the Tent of Meeting, saying: **2]** Speak to the Israelite people, and say to them:

When any of you presents an offering of cattle to the LORD, he shall choose his offering from the herd or from the flock.

3] If his offering is a burnt offering from the herd, he shall make his offering a male without blemish. He shall bring it to the entrance of the Tent of Meeting, for acceptance in his behalf before the LORD. **4]** He shall lay his hand upon the head of the burnt offering, that it may be acceptable in his behalf, in expiation for him. **5]** The bull shall be slaughtered before the LORD; and Aaron's sons, the priests, shall offer the blood, dashing the blood against all sides of the altar which is at the entrance of the Tent of Meeting. **6]** The burnt offering shall be

1:1] *The Lord called to Moses and spoke to him.* The Hebrew order is "And He called to Moses. And the LORD said to him." This may be because this sentence continues the narrative at the end of Exodus: the divine Presence filled the Tabernacle, and so Moses would not venture to enter the Tent until God summoned him (Palestinian Targums).

From the Tent of Meeting. God called to him from the Tent and spoke to him after he entered (Rashbam).

2] *He shall choose his.* Literally, "you shall offer your" (T.N.).

From the herd. Beef cattle.

From the flock. Sheep or goats.

3] *Without blemish.* Only a healthy, normal animal was fit for sacrifice. The prophet Malachi denounced those who brought to the Temple sick, blind, or lame animals which they would not have dared present to a political ruler (Mal. 1:8).

Before the Lord. The translation follows the Targum in connecting this phrase with "acceptance in his behalf." But in chapter 1, verse 5, "before the LORD" plainly means "in the Tent, in front of the inner Shrine."

4] *Lay his hand upon the head of the burnt offering.* Thus formally designating the animal as *his* sacrifice. This ceremony was required for all quadrupeds offered by an individual, but not for communal sacrifices, and not for fowl.

In expiation for him. Other types of sacrifices are prescribed as atonement for sin (chapters 4 and 5); this is the only passage that speaks of an *olah* expiating guilt. It may preserve an old tradition otherwise unknown to us (see Gleanings).

5] *Shall be slaughtered.* Or, "he [i.e., the donor] shall slaughter." Slaughtering did not have to be performed by priests though, no doubt, the latter frequently killed the animals because of their experience in such matters. (Ezek. 44:11 assigns this duty to the Levites.) But the text explicitly requires the priests to handle the blood.

Shall offer the blood. According to tradition, they received the blood in bowls as it welled from the animal's throat; they brought it to the altar and dashed it against two opposite corners so that it spattered on all four sides [2]. This blood ceremony was regarded as the act of atonement [3].

וֹ מוֹעֵד: וְהִפְשִׁיט אֶת־הָעֹלָה וְנִתַּח אֹתָהּ לִנְתָחֶיהָ: וְנָתְנוּ
בְּנֵי אַהֲרֹן הַכֹּהֵן אֵשׁ עַל־הַמִּזְבֵּחַ וְעָרְכוּ עֵצִים עַל־
ח הָאֵשׁ: וְעָרְכוּ בְּנֵי אַהֲרֹן הַכֹּהֲנִים אֵת הַנְּתָחִים אֶת־
הָרֹאשׁ וְאֶת־הַפָּדֶר עַל־הָעֵצִים אֲשֶׁר עַל־הָאֵשׁ אֲשֶׁר
ט עַל־הַמִּזְבֵּחַ: וְקִרְבּוֹ וּכְרָעָיו יִרְחַץ בַּמָּיִם וְהִקְטִיר
הַכֹּהֵן אֶת־הַכֹּל הַמִּזְבֵּחָה עֹלָה אִשֵּׁה רֵיחַ־נִיחוֹחַ

ז לַיהֹוָה: ס וְאִם־מִן־הַצֹּאן קָרְבָּנוֹ מִן־הַכְּשָׂבִים אוֹ
יא מִן־הָעִזִּים לְעֹלָה זָכָר תָּמִים יַקְרִיבֶנּוּ: וְשָׁחַט אֹתוֹ
עַל יֶרֶךְ הַמִּזְבֵּחַ צָפֹנָה לִפְנֵי יְהֹוָה וְזָרְקוּ בְּנֵי אַהֲרֹן
יב הַכֹּהֲנִים אֶת־דָּמוֹ עַל־הַמִּזְבֵּחַ סָבִיב: וְנִתַּח אֹתוֹ לִנְתָחָיו
וְאֶת־רֹאשׁוֹ וְאֶת־פִּדְרוֹ וְעָרַךְ הַכֹּהֵן אֹתָם עַל־הָעֵצִים
יג אֲשֶׁר עַל־הָאֵשׁ אֲשֶׁר עַל־הַמִּזְבֵּחַ: וְהַקֶּרֶב וְהַכְּרָעַיִם

flayed and cut up into sections. **7]** The sons of Aaron the priest shall put fire on the altar and lay out wood upon the fire; **8]** and Aaron's sons, the priests, shall lay out the sections, with the head and the suet, on the wood that is on the fire upon the altar. **9]** Its entrails and legs shall be washed with water, and the priest shall turn the whole into smoke on the altar as a burnt offering, an offering by fire of pleasing odor to the LORD.

10] If his offering for a burnt offering is from the flock, of sheep or of goats, he shall make his offering a male without blemish. **11]** It shall be slaughtered before the LORD on the north side of the altar, and Aaron's sons, the priests, shall dash its blood against all sides of the altar. **12]** When it has been cut up into sections, the priest shall lay them out, with the head and the suet, on the wood that is on the fire upon the altar. **13]** The entrails and the legs shall

6] *Shall be flayed.* Some ancient pictures of sacrifice show an animal being burned whole on the altar [4]. But Israelite practice required the removal of the hide, the washing of the entrails, and the disjointing of the carcass before it was placed on the altar. This was also the practice of many other peoples [5]. Here, too, we could translate "he shall flay" (cf. commentary on 1:5); the work might be done by non-priests [6].

The hide became the property of the officiating priest (7:8). It was his only compensation for offering an *olah*. Of most other sacrifices, the priest received at least a portion of the meat. Israelite priests were not usually paid for their services in money. But a Phoenician temple in Marseilles had a regular schedule of tariffs posted, stating the fee in cash and in meat for each kind of animal. The priests were, however, required to forego payment if the sacrificer was poor [7].

7] *Shall put fire on the altar.* According to chapter 6, verse 6, the fire was always to be kept burning; according to chapter 9, verse 24, it was of heavenly

origin. Such discrepancies show that Leviticus was put together from a variety of sources.

8] *Shall lay out the sections.* Previous to this, the meat was salted (2:13); along with it, meal and drink offerings were placed on the altar (Num. 15:1ff.).

9] *Turn the whole into smoke.* Make sure it catches fire and is consumed.

An offering by fire. This phrase renders the Hebrew *isheh,* related to *esh,* "fire." It is a general term for all the usual forms of sacrifice.

Of pleasing odor to the Lord. See introduction to Part I, "2. Ancient Sacrifices," and cf. Gen. 8:21.

10] *From the flock.* One who cannot afford a bull may offer a less costly animal. The procedure is the same and the sacrifice is just as valid.

11] *On the north side of the altar.* This detail is not mentioned in the preceding instructions for the bull; it is understood by *Sifra* to apply to both—no doubt correctly.

יִרְחַ֣ץ בַּמָּ֑יִם וְהִקְרִ֨יב הַכֹּהֵ֤ן אֶת־הַכֹּל֙ וְהִקְטִ֣יר
הַמִּזְבֵּ֔חָה עֹלָ֛ה הֽוּא אִשֵּׁ֥ה רֵֽיחַ־נִיחֹ֖חַ לַֽיהוָֽה: פ

יד וְאִ֧ם מִן־הָע֛וֹף עֹלָ֥ה קָרְבָּנ֖וֹ לַֽיהוָ֑ה וְהִקְרִ֣יב מִן־
טו הַתֹּרִ֗ים א֛וֹ מִן־בְּנֵ֥י הַיּוֹנָ֖ה אֶת־קָרְבָּנֽוֹ: וְהִקְרִיב֤וֹ הַכֹּהֵן֙
אֶל־הַמִּזְבֵּ֔חַ וּמָלַק֙ אֶת־רֹאשׁ֔וֹ וְהִקְטִ֖יר הַמִּזְבֵּ֑חָה

טז וְנִמְצָ֣ה דָמ֔וֹ עַ֖ל קִ֣יר הַמִּזְבֵּֽחַ: וְהֵסִ֣יר אֶת־מֻרְאָת֗וֹ
בְּנֹֽצָתָ֔הּ וְהִשְׁלִ֤יךְ אֹתָהּ֙ אֵ֣צֶל הַמִּזְבֵּ֔חַ קֵ֖דְמָה אֶל־מְק֥וֹם
יז הַדָּֽשֶׁן: וְשִׁסַּ֨ע אֹת֣וֹ בִכְנָפָיו֮ לֹ֣א יַבְדִּיל֒ וְהִקְטִ֨יר אֹת֤וֹ
הַכֹּהֵן֙ הַמִּזְבֵּ֔חָה עַל־הָעֵצִ֖ים אֲשֶׁ֣ר עַל־הָאֵ֑שׁ עֹלָ֣ה ה֗וּא
אִשֵּׁ֛ה רֵ֥יחַ נִיחֹ֖חַ לַֽיהוָֽה: ס

be washed with water; the priest shall offer up and turn the whole into smoke on the altar. It is a burnt offering, an offering by fire, of pleasing odor to the LORD.

14] If his offering to the LORD is a burnt offering of birds, he shall choose his offering from turtledoves or pigeons. **15]** The priest shall bring it to the altar, pinch off its head, and turn it into smoke on the altar; and its blood shall be drained out against the side of the altar. **16]** He shall remove its crop with its contents, and cast it into the place of the ashes, at the east side of the altar. **17]** The priest shall tear it open by its wings, without severing it, and turn it into smoke on the altar, upon the wood that is on the fire. It is a burnt offering, an offering by fire, of pleasing odor to the LORD.

14] *A burnt offering of birds.* The poor worshiper was also to have the opportunity to bring an *olah.*

Pigeons. Literally, "children of a pigeon," which tradition understood as "young pigeon." This may well have been the original intent. The adult turtledove is about the same size as the young pigeon; thus, in either case, the offering would be plump and delicate-looking.

15] *Pinch off its head.* With his fingers.

And turn it into smoke. After performing the actions detailed in the ensuing clauses.

Its blood shall be drained out. The small quantity of blood made the procedure of chapter 1, verse 5,

unnecessary in the case of fowl.

16] *He shall remove its crop with its contents.* Others, "with its feathers" (T.N.). The word *notzah* is here rendered "contents" because it makes good sense in this context (so Targums) [8]. Ordinarily *notzah* means "feather." Accordingly, Rabbi Ishmael explained that an incision was to be made in the body and the crop removed with the skin and feathers covering it [9].

And cast it into the place of the ashes. The place where ashes from the altar fire were piled before removal (Lev. 6:3).

GLEANINGS

Where no reference is provided, or there is only the word Sifra, the passage is found in Sifra to the verse.

Halachah

1:2] *Any of You*

Literally, "a man of you." The word "man" implies that burnt offerings may be accepted from Gentiles [10]. The phrase "of you" forbids accepting an offering from an apostate Jew.   SIFRA

4] *Lay His Hand*

The Targums also render "hand" singular. But the Talmud inferred from Leviticus, chapter 16, verse 21, that the sacrificer must place both hands on the animal's head [11].

6] *Shall Be Flayed*

The head was not to be skinned; wool on the head of a sheep and the whiskers of a goat were to be left intact. Suet was laid over the throat to conceal the bloody cut.

7] *Shall Put Fire on the Altar*

Even though the fire was of heavenly origin, additional wood was to be placed on it before the *olah* was brought up.

11] *On the North Side of the Altar*

This instruction is repeated several times in these chapters. The halachah generalizes: All the "most holy" sacrifices—*olah*, *chatat*, *asham*—were to be slaughtered on the north side of the altar. *Shelamim*, which were of lesser holiness, might be slaughtered anywhere in the court of the Tabernacle/Temple.

15] *Pinch Off Its Head*

This operation was performed at the back of the neck, breaking the bone and severing the windpipe. For human consumption the fowl must be slaughtered by cutting the throat with a knife.

Haggadah

1:1] *The Lord Called to Moses*

Before every act of revelation, God would call, "Moses, Moses!" as at the burning bush. It was an expression of affection and of urgency. And each time Moses would respond, "Here I am."

4] *In Expiation for Him*

For what sins does the *olah* atone? For neglect of positive commandments (*Sifra*). According to another opinion, for sinful thoughts [12]. But there is a widely accepted view that a sinful intention is not accounted a sin if it is not carried out, although credit is given for good intentions that are not fulfilled [13].

16] *He Shall Remove Its Crop with Its Contents*

Birds fly about and eat seed from other men's land. Therefore the crop that held stolen food must be discarded before the fowl is offered to God. But animals eat fodder supplied by their owners, and so their inwards may be burned on the altar after they are washed.   SIFRA

Fowls are offered unplucked. Nothing is more repulsive than the smell of burning feathers; yet God commanded that the birds be offered with feathers intact so that the poor man's offering might look more impressive. A plucked bird would be small and scrawny looking [14].

17] *Pleasing Odor*

"Whether one offers much or little makes no difference, if only his heart is directed to God."

The Minchah—Meal Offering

The term *minchah* is used in the Bible for "gift" (Gen. 32:14), for "tribute" (I Kings 5:1), and for "sacrifice" in general (Gen. 4:3ff.). But in Leviticus, and elsewhere in P, it means specifically an offering prepared from grain. (In postbiblical Hebrew, *minchah* came to mean "the afternoon prayer" and, more generally, "afternoon" [1].)

This chapter deals with cereal offerings brought as separate voluntary gifts (except perhaps those treated in verses 13 through 16). Frankincense was regularly placed on such offerings. Animal sacrifices were accompanied by mandatory meal offerings—bread along with meat—for which frankincense was not required (Num. 15:1ff.) [2].

Flour and oil were the ingredients of the *minchah*. It might be uncooked, or prepared in an oven, griddle, or pan, as the donor chose. The frankincense was placed on top just before the offering was brought to the altar.

ה וְאִם־מִנְחָה עַל־הַמַּחֲבַת קָרְבָּנֶךָ מְשֻׁחִים בַּשָּׁמֶן: ס | א וְנֶ֫פֶשׁ כִּי־תַקְרִ֫יב קָרְבַּ֤ן מִנְחָה לַיהוָֹה סֹלֶת יִהְיֶה

ו פָּתוֹת אֹתָהּ פִּתִּים סֹלֶת בְּלוּלָה בַשֶּׁמֶן מַצָּה תִהְיֶה: | ב קָרְבָּנוֹ וְיָצַק עָלֶיהָ שֶׁמֶן וְנָתַן עָלֶיהָ לְבֹנָה: וֶהֱבִיאָהּ

ז וְאִם־מִנְחַת וְיָצַקְתָּ עָלֶיהָ שָׁמֶן מִנְחָה הִוא: ס | אֶל־בְּנֵי אַהֲרֹן הַכֹּהֲנִים וְקָמַ֫ץ מִשָּׁם מְלֹא קֻמְצוֹ

ח וְהֵבֵאתָ אֶת־ מַרְחֶשֶׁת קָרְבָּנֶךָ סֹלֶת בַּשֶּׁמֶן תֵּעָשֶׂה: | מִסׇּלְתָּהּ וּמִשַּׁמְנָהּ עַל כָּל־לְבֹנָתָהּ וְהִקְטִיר הַכֹּהֵן

אֶל־ הַמִּנְחָה אֲשֶׁר יֵעָשֶׂה מֵאֵלֶּה לַיהוָֹה וְהִקְרִיבָהּ | אֶת־אַזְכָּרָתָהּ הַמִּזְבֵּחָה אִשֵּׁה רֵיחַ נִיחֹחַ לַיהוָֹה:

ט מִן־הַמִּנְחָ֫ה הַכֹּהֵן וְהִגִּישָׁהּ אֶל־הַמִּזְבֵּחַ: וְהֵרִים הַכֹּהֵן | ג וְהַנּוֹתֶ֫רֶת מִן־הַמִּנְחָ֫ה לְאַהֲרֹן וּלְבָנָיו קֹדֶשׁ קָדָשִׁים

אֶת־אַזְכָּרָתָהּ וְהִקְטִיר הַמִּזְבֵּ֫חָה אִשֵּׁה רֵיחַ נִיחֹחַ | מֵאִשֵּׁי יְהוָֹה: ס וְכִי תַקְרִב קָרְבַּן מִנְחָה מַאֲפֵה

י לַיהוָֹה: וְהַנּוֹתֶ֫רֶת מִן־הַמִּנְחָ֫ה לְאַהֲרֹן וּלְבָנָיו קֹדֶשׁ | תַנּוּר סֹלֶת חַלּוֹת מַצֹּת בְּלוּלֹת בַּשֶּׁמֶן וּרְקִיקֵי מַצּוֹת

1] When a person presents an offering of meal to the LORD, his offering shall be of choice flour; he shall pour oil upon it, lay frankincense on it, 2] and present it to Aaron's sons, the priests. The priest shall scoop out of it a handful of its choice flour and oil, as well as all of its frankincense; and this token portion he shall turn into smoke on the altar, as an offering by fire, of pleasing odor to the LORD. 3] And the remainder of the meal offering shall be for Aaron and his sons, a most holy portion from the LORD's offerings by fire.

4] When you present an offering of meal baked in the oven, [it shall be of] choice flour: unleavened cakes with oil mixed in, or unleavened wafers spread with oil.

5] If your offering is a meal offering on a griddle, it shall be of choice flour with oil mixed in, unleavened. 6] Break it into bits and pour oil on it; it is a meal offering.

7] If your offering is a meal offering in a pan, it shall be made of choice flour in oil.

8] When you present to the LORD a meal offering that is made in any of these ways, it shall be brought to the priest who shall take it up to the altar. 9] The priest shall remove the token portion from the meal offering and turn it into smoke on the altar as an offering by fire, of pleasing odor to the LORD. 10] And the remainder of the meal offering shall be for Aaron and his sons, a most holy portion from the LORD's offerings by fire.

2:2] *Choice flour.* Hebrew *solet*—not "fine flour," as in earlier translations. *Solet* is meal made from the hard kernels of wheat (semolina) as is clear from Avot 5:15, "a sieve lets through the *kemach* [ordinary flour] but retains the *solet*" [3].

Frankincense. An aromatic gum obtained from Arabia (Jer. 6:20).

Token portion. Hebrew *azkarah*, from a root meaning "remember, take thought of." This portion, burned on the altar, is to bring the worshiper to mind before God.

3] *Shall be for Aaron and his sons.* Shall be eaten by the priests.

A most holy portion. Food designated as "most holy" had to be consumed inside the sacred area by priests. Food that was holy in a lesser degree (below, 7:11ff.) could be eaten outside the sacred precincts by priests and their families, as well as by lay persons who were properly purified.

4] *Oven.* Hebrew *tanur*, a cylindrical vessel of clay in which fire was kindled on a bed of pebbles. When it was well heated, the ashes were swept out and the dough was pressed against the walls of the *tanur.*

5] *Griddle.* Yielding a crisp wafer.

7] *Pan.* Yielding a soft, moist bread.

יד מֶ֑לַח ס וְאִם־תַּקְרִ֞יב מִנְחַ֣ת בִּכּוּרִ֗ים לַיהֹוָ֔ה אָבִ֞יב
קָל֤וּי בָּאֵשׁ֙ גֶּ֣רֶשׂ כַּרְמֶ֔ל תַּקְרִ֕יב אֵ֖ת מִנְחַ֥ת בִּכּוּרֶֽיךָ׃
טו וְנָתַתָּ֤ עָלֶ֙יהָ֙ שֶׁ֔מֶן וְשַׂמְתָּ֥ עָלֶ֖יהָ לְבֹנָ֑ה מִנְחָ֖ה הִֽוא׃
טז וְהִקְטִ֨יר הַכֹּהֵ֜ן אֶת־אַזְכָּרָתָ֗הּ מִגִּרְשָׂהּ֙ וּמִשַּׁמְנָ֔הּ עַ֖ל
כָּל־לְבֹנָתָ֑הּ אִשֶּׁ֖ה לַיהֹוָֽה׃ פ

יא קָדָשִׁ֖ים מֵאִשֵּׁ֣י יְהֹוָֽה׃ כָּל־הַמִּנְחָ֗ה אֲשֶׁ֤ר תַּקְרִ֙יבוּ֙
לַיהֹוָ֔ה לֹ֥א תֵעָשֶׂ֖ה חָמֵ֑ץ כִּ֤י כָל־שְׂאֹר֙ וְכָל־דְּבַ֔שׁ לֹא־
יב תַקְטִ֧ירוּ מִמֶּ֛נּוּ אִשֶּׁ֖ה לַיהֹוָֽה׃ קׇרְבַּ֥ן רֵאשִׁ֛ית תַּקְרִ֥יבוּ
יג אֹתָ֖ם לַיהֹוָ֑ה וְאֶל־הַמִּזְבֵּ֥חַ לֹא־יַעֲל֖וּ לְרֵ֥יחַ נִיחֹֽחַ׃ וְכׇל־
קׇרְבַּ֣ן מִנְחָתְךָ֮ בַּמֶּ֣לַח תִּמְלָח֒ וְלֹ֣א תַשְׁבִּ֗ית מֶ֚לַח בְּרִ֣ית
אֱלֹהֶ֔יךָ מֵעַ֖ל מִנְחָתֶ֑ךָ עַ֥ל כׇּל־קׇרְבָּנְךָ֖ תַּקְרִ֥יב

11] No meal offering that you offer to the LORD shall be made with leaven, for you must not turn into smoke any leaven or any honey as an offering by fire to the LORD. 12] You may bring them to the LORD as an offering of choice products; but they shall not be offered up on the altar for a pleasing odor. 13] You shall season your every offering of meal with salt; you shall not omit from your meal offering the salt of your covenant with God; with all your offerings you must offer salt.

14] If you bring a meal offering of first fruits to the LORD, you shall bring grain in season parched with fire, grits of the fresh ear, as your meal offering of first fruits. 15] You shall add oil to it and lay frankincense on it; it is a meal offering. 16] And the priest shall turn a token portion of it into smoke: some of the grits and oil, with all of the frankincense, as an offering by fire to the LORD.

11] *No meal offering . . . shall be made with leaven.* This may be a survival of old desert practice; the nomads generally baked their bread unleavened. Ancient customs are often retained in religious rites after they have been otherwise discarded. (For example, the Torah is read in the synagogue from a handwritten parchment scroll.) In later Jewish literature, leaven is sometimes a symbol of moral corruption or religious rebellion, but such a notion was hardly in the mind of the biblical author. Some of the cakes used in the thanksgiving sacrifice were leavened, some were not (7:12, 13). Two leavened loaves were to be offered on the Feast of Weeks (23:17). Of course, this leavened bread was not burned on the altar.

Honey. Honey is often mentioned in the Bible, especially in the familiar phrase "a land flowing with milk and honey." Many ancient peoples used it for sacrifice, and we do not know why the Torah barred it from the altar. In rabbinic literature, and possibly in some Bible passages, Hebrew *devash* designates not only bee honey but also a man-made preparation of mashed fruit. (Arabic *dibs* has the latter meaning.)

12] *An offering of choice products.* Exact meaning of Hebrew uncertain (T.N.). The obscure phrase (literally, "an offering of beginning") may allude to the first-fruit ceremony of Deuteronomy 26.

13] *Salt.* Salt, which gives flavor to food and acts as a preservative, was required not only for the *minchah* but, as the end of the verse makes plain, for all sacrifices.

The salt of your covenant with God. In ancient times, as often today, agreements were sealed with a formal meal. For men to take salt together was a symbolic way of concluding a pact. The Bible therefore describes a solemn covenant as a "covenant of salt" (Num. 18:19; II Chron. 13:5).

14] *A meal offering of first fruits.* Exactly what ceremony is meant is uncertain. Commentators have often taken this as a supplement to the law of Deuteronomy, chapter 26 (above, 2:12; see also Num. 18:13). But the halachah understood it as a reference to the new grain offering (*omer*) of Leviticus, chapter 23, verses 10 through 13.

GLEANINGS

Haggadah

2:1]   *When a Person Presents*

"Person" renders Hebrew *nefesh*, often translated "soul." A voluntary *minchah* was likely to be the gift of a poor person who could not afford anything else; all the more must we value it aright. Once, says the Midrash, a priest expressed contempt for the handful of flour a woman brought to the Temple. God rebuked him in a dream: "She offered her very soul"[4].

13]   *The Salt of Your Covenant with God*

A fanciful midrash understands the verse to mean "the covenant your God made about salt." At creation, God separated the waters above the expanse of heaven from those below it (Gen. 1:7); and the waters relegated to the lower level grieved at being so far from God's abode. So God comforted them with the promise that their briny oceans would one day provide the salt to be used on His altar [5].

Zevach Shelamim—Sacrifice of Well-Being

We come now to the sacrifice whose distinctive feature was the festive meal eaten by the sacrificer and his guests after the prescribed portions had been offered on the altar and a share had been given to the priests. But this characteristic procedure is explained only in chapter 7, verses 11ff. The present chapter deals only with the rites at the altar.

The word *zevach*, from a root meaning "to slaughter" [1], is sometimes used for sacrifice in general (Ps. 4:6, 51:19). Frequently, however, it means *zevach shelamim*, especially when it is joined with *olah* (Exod. 18:12; Deut. 12:6; Jer. 7:21). P most often uses the full term *zevach shelamim*.

The second part of the term has been traditionally associated with *shalom*, "peace,"

and the whole phrase has been translated "peace offering." But in colloquial English that expression means a gift to appease someone who has been offended—and such was not the intent of *shelamim*. Others have connected the word with another meaning of the root *shlm*, "to repay, make good," with reference to the payment of a vow (7:16). But, though some *shelamim* were brought to fulfill a vow, many were not. The rendering "sacrifice of well-being" is an educated guess: it too connects the term with *shalom* in the broader sense of "wholeness, happiness, health." In the Bible, the word has these meanings more often than that of "peace"—and it fits the festive character of the sacrifice.

765

א וְאִם־זֶבַח שְׁלָמִים קָרְבָּנוֹ אִם מִן־הַבָּקָר הוּא מַקְרִיב

ב אִם־זָכָר אִם־נְקֵבָה תָּמִים יַקְרִיבֶנּוּ לִפְנֵי יְהוָֹה: וְסָמַךְ

יָדוֹ עַל־רֹאשׁ קָרְבָּנוֹ וּשְׁחָטוֹ פֶּתַח אֹהֶל מוֹעֵד וְזָרְקוּ

בְּנֵי אַהֲרֹן הַכֹּהֲנִים אֶת־הַדָּם עַל־הַמִּזְבֵּחַ סָבִיב:

ג וְהִקְרִיב מִזֶּבַח הַשְּׁלָמִים אִשֶּׁה לַיהוָֹה אֶת־הַחֵלֶב

הַמְכַסֶּה אֶת־הַקֶּרֶב וְאֵת כָּל־הַחֵלֶב אֲשֶׁר עַל־הַקֶּרֶב:

ד וְאֵת שְׁתֵּי הַכְּלָיֹת וְאֶת־הַחֵלֶב אֲשֶׁר עֲלֵהֶן אֲשֶׁר עַל־

הַכְּסָלִים וְאֶת־הַיֹּתֶרֶת עַל־הַכָּבֵד עַל־הַכְּלָיוֹת

ה יְסִירֶנָּה: וְהִקְטִירוּ אֹתוֹ בְנֵי־אַהֲרֹן הַמִּזְבֵּחָה עַל־

הָעֹלָה אֲשֶׁר עַל־הָעֵצִים אֲשֶׁר עַל־הָאֵשׁ אִשֵּׁה רֵיחַ

נִיחֹחַ לַיהוָֹה: פ

ו וְאִם־מִן־הַצֹּאן קָרְבָּנוֹ לְזֶבַח שְׁלָמִים לַיהוָֹה זָכָר אוֹ

נְקֵבָה תָּמִים יַקְרִיבֶנּוּ: אִם־כֶּשֶׂב הוּא־מַקְרִיב אֶת־

ז קָרְבָּנוֹ וְהִקְרִיב אֹתוֹ לִפְנֵי יְהוָֹה: וְסָמַךְ אֶת־יָדוֹ עַל־

ח רֹאשׁ קָרְבָּנוֹ וְשָׁחַט אֹתוֹ לִפְנֵי אֹהֶל מוֹעֵד וְזָרְקוּ בְּנֵי

ט אַהֲרֹן אֶת־דָּמוֹ עַל־הַמִּזְבֵּחַ סָבִיב: וְהִקְרִיב מִזֶּבַח

הַשְּׁלָמִים אִשֶּׁה לַיהוָֹה חֶלְבּוֹ הָאַלְיָה תְמִימָה לְעֻמַּת

הֶעָצֶה יְסִירֶנָּה וְאֶת־הַחֵלֶב הַמְכַסֶּה אֶת־הַקֶּרֶב וְאֵת

1] If his offering is a sacrifice of well-being—

If he offers of the herd, whether a male or a female, he shall bring before the LORD one without blemish. **2]** He shall lay his hand upon the head of his offering and slaughter it at the entrance of the Tent of Meeting; and Aaron's sons, the priests, shall dash the blood against all sides of the altar. **3]** He shall then present from the sacrifice of well-being, as an offering by fire to the LORD, the fat that covers the entrails and all the fat that is about the entrails; **4]** the two kidneys and the fat that is on them, that is at the loins; and the protuberance on the liver, which he shall remove with the kidneys. **5]** Aaron's sons shall turn these into smoke on the altar, with the burnt offering which is upon the wood that is on the fire, as an offering by fire, of pleasing odor to the LORD.

6] And if his offering for a sacrifice of well-being to the LORD is from the flock, whether a male or a female, he shall offer one without blemish. **7]** If he presents a sheep as his offering, he shall bring it before the LORD **8]** and lay his hand upon the head of his offering. It shall be slaughtered before the Tent of Meeting, and Aaron's sons shall dash its blood against all sides of the altar. **9]** He shall then present, as an offering by fire to the LORD, the fat from the sacrifice of well-being: the whole broad tail, which shall be removed close to the backbone; the

---

3:1] *A sacrifice of well-being.* Others, "peace offering." Exact meaning of *shelamim* uncertain (T.N.).

3–4] *He shall present . . . the fat . . . with the kidneys.* These parts (plus the broad tail in the case of sheep, verse 9) are the ones burned on the altar, not only in the case of *shelamim*, but of all sacrifices except the *olah*—of which everything but the hide is consumed on the altar.

4] *The protuberance* [yoteret] *on the liver.* The meaning of *yoteret* has been debated. Rashi thought it was the diaphragm; but several ancient sources support the view that it was a projecting lobe of the liver [2]. Our translation follows this opinion.

9] *The whole broad tail.* In the Near East, sheep were and are of a variety having a heavy tail; it weighs ten pounds or more, and it is considered a delicacy. Herodotus (fifth century B.C.E.) tells of little carts used by the shepherds to support the tails of their sheep and prevent them from being broken; the same device is mentioned in the Mishnah some six centuries later [3].

The punctuation of the English rendering implies that the tail was among the fat portions reserved for the altar and so, by implication, forbidden as human food. This conclusion was actually drawn by the Karaite sect; but rabbinic tradition permitted the fat tail of nonsacrificial sheep to be eaten.

כָּל־הַחֵלֶב אֲשֶׁר עַל־הַקֶּרֶב: וְאֵת שְׁתֵּי הַכְּלָיֹת וְאֶת־
הַחֵלֶב אֲשֶׁר עֲלֵהֶן אֲשֶׁר עַל־הַכְּסָלִים וְאֶת־הַיֹּתֶרֶת
עַל־הַכָּבֵד עַל־הַכְּלָיֹת יְסִירֶנָּה: וְהִקְטִירוֹ הַכֹּהֵן
הַמִּזְבֵּחָה לֶחֶם אִשֶּׁה לַיהֹוָה: פ
וְאִם־עֵז קָרְבָּנוֹ וְהִקְרִיבוֹ לִפְנֵי יְהֹוָה: וְסָמַךְ אֶת־יָדוֹ
עַל־רֹאשׁוֹ וְשָׁחַט אֹתוֹ לִפְנֵי אֹהֶל מוֹעֵד וְזָרְקוּ בְּנֵי
אַהֲרֹן אֶת־דָּמוֹ עַל־הַמִּזְבֵּחַ סָבִיב: וְהִקְרִיב מִמֶּנּוּ

קָרְבָּנוֹ אִשֶּׁה לַיהֹוָה אֶת־הַחֵלֶב הַמְכַסֶּה אֶת־הַקֶּרֶב
וְאֵת כָּל־הַחֵלֶב אֲשֶׁר עַל־הַקֶּרֶב: וְאֵת שְׁתֵּי הַכְּלָיֹת
וְאֶת־הַחֵלֶב אֲשֶׁר עֲלֵהֶן אֲשֶׁר עַל־הַכְּסָלִים וְאֶת־
הַיֹּתֶרֶת עַל־הַכָּבֵד עַל־הַכְּלָיֹת יְסִירֶנָּה: וְהִקְטִירָם
הַכֹּהֵן הַמִּזְבֵּחָה לֶחֶם אִשֶּׁה לְרֵיחַ נִיחֹחַ כָּל־חֵלֶב
לַיהֹוָה: חֻקַּת עוֹלָם לְדֹרֹתֵיכֶם בְּכֹל מוֹשְׁבֹתֵיכֶם
כָּל־חֵלֶב וְכָל־דָּם לֹא תֹאכֵלוּ:   פ

fat that covers the entrails and all the fat that is about the entrails;   10] the two kidneys and the fat that is on them, that is at the loins; and the protuberance on the liver, which he shall remove with the kidneys.   11] The priest shall turn these into smoke on the altar as food, an offering by fire to the LORD.

12] And if his offering is a goat, he shall bring it before the LORD   13] and lay his hand upon its head. It shall be slaughtered before the Tent of Meeting, and Aaron's sons shall dash its blood against all sides of the altar.   14] He shall then present as his offering from it, as an offering by fire to the LORD, the fat that covers the entrails and all the fat that is about the entrails; 15] the two kidneys and the fat that is on them, that is at the loins; and the protuberance on the liver, which he shall remove with the kidneys.   16] The priest shall turn these into smoke on the altar as food, an offering by fire, of pleasing odor.

All fat is the LORD's.   17] It is a law for all time throughout the ages, in all your settlements: you must not eat any fat or any blood.

17]   *You must not eat any fat.* This categorical language could not be taken with absolute literalness. One cannot eat meat without getting some of the fat that is mixed in with the muscle. Tradition sensibly understood *chelev* in the technical sense of "prohibited fat." It is hard fat—according to Rabbi Akiba, that which is layered, covered by a membrane, and cap-

able of being peeled off [4]. Permitted fat is called *shuman.* Present-day Orthodox usage requires the slaughterer or butcher to remove all *chelev* from meat that is offered for sale. The fat of game and fowl is not forbidden.

Or any blood. See introduction to Lev. 17, "2. The Prohibition of Blood."

Chatat—Sin Offering

The previous chapters concerned sacrifices brought voluntarily. We now come to offerings that were obligatory on those who had incurred guilt. They served chiefly to expiate unintentional sins. (There are a few exceptions in chapter 5.) The law did not permit one to do a deliberate wrong and then square the account with a sacrifice. "The sacrifice of the wicked is an abomination to the LORD" (Prov. 15:8).

Ceremonial atonement for unwitting violations of the law was a psychologically sound procedure. People are often deeply disturbed if they cause harm by accident, ignorance, or oversight. The sacrifice relieved the troubled conscience. To this day, in the Yom Kippur confession, we ask forgiveness "for the sins we have sinned before You under duress or through choice . . . unwittingly or defiantly." Implicit in such a prayer is the acknowledgment that we should have shown greater care and foresight. Modern law too operates with the concepts of contributory negligence and criminal negligence.

The sacrifice prescribed in this chapter is called *chatat*, usually translated "sin offering." The translators' footnote to these words in verse 3 reads, "So traditionally; more precisely, 'offering of purgation'" [1]. Actually, the one word conveys both meanings.

The verb *chata* meant primarily "to miss the mark" [2]. The sinner is one who misses the proper objective; hence, *chata* in Scripture usually means "to commit a sin or crime." The noun *chet* means "sin" or "guilt"; the noun *chatat*, likewise meaning "sin" or "guilt," also refers to the offering that cancels out sin. Further, some forms of the verb *chata* are used for the ritual acts (especially sprinkling, Num. 19:19) which remove defilement.

In form, the *chatat* differs from other sacrifices in the special treatment of the blood of the animal. This ritual takes two forms. If the sinner is the "anointed priest," or if the offering expiates an offense of the entire community, the blood is taken into the "holy place"; some of it is sprinkled toward the inner Shrine, and some is placed on the horns of the incense altar. In such cases, the carcass of the animal is burned outside the camp. But, if the sinner is a secular ruler or a commoner, the blood is put on the horns of the main altar and the meat is eaten by the priests. In either case, the usual fat parts are burned on the altar [3].

ה רֹאשׁ הַפָּר וְשָׁחַט אֶת־הַפָּר לִפְנֵי יְהוָה: וְלָקַח הַכֹּהֵן
הַמָּשִׁיחַ מִדַּם הַפָּר וְהֵבִיא אֹתוֹ אֶל־אֹהֶל מוֹעֵד:
ו וְטָבַל הַכֹּהֵן אֶת־אֶצְבָּעוֹ בַּדָּם וְהִזָּה מִן־הַדָּם שֶׁבַע
פְּעָמִים לִפְנֵי יְהוָה אֶת־פְּנֵי פָּרֹכֶת הַקֹּדֶשׁ: וְנָתַן הַכֹּהֵן
מִן־הַדָּם עַל־קַרְנוֹת מִזְבַּח קְטֹרֶת הַסַּמִּים לִפְנֵי יְהוָה
אֲשֶׁר בְּאֹהֶל מוֹעֵד וְאֵת כָּל־דַּם הַפָּר יִשְׁפֹּךְ אֶל־

א וַיְדַבֵּר יְהוָה אֶל־מֹשֶׁה לֵּאמֹר: דַּבֵּר אֶל־בְּנֵי יִשְׂרָאֵל
לֵאמֹר נֶפֶשׁ כִּי־תֶחֱטָא בִשְׁגָגָה מִכֹּל מִצְוֹת יְהוָה אֲשֶׁר
ב לֹא תֵעָשֶׂינָה וְעָשָׂה מֵאַחַת מֵהֵנָּה: אִם הַכֹּהֵן הַמָּשִׁיחַ
יֶחֱטָא לְאַשְׁמַת הָעָם וְהִקְרִיב עַל חַטָּאתוֹ אֲשֶׁר חָטָא
ד פַּר בֶּן־בָּקָר תָּמִים לַיהוָה לְחַטָּאת: וְהֵבִיא אֶת־הַפָּר
אֶל־פֶּתַח אֹהֶל מוֹעֵד לִפְנֵי יְהוָה וְסָמַךְ אֶת־יָדוֹ עַל־

ד ד סבירין אשר לפני.

1] The LORD spoke to Moses, saying: **2]** Speak to the Israelite people thus:

When a person unwittingly incurs guilt in regard to any of the LORD's commandments about things not to be done, and does one of them—

3] If it is the anointed priest who has incurred guilt, so that blame falls upon the people, he shall offer for the sin of which he is guilty a bull of the herd without blemish as a sin offering to the LORD.   **4]** He shall bring the bull to the entrance of the Tent of Meeting, before the LORD, and lay his hand upon the head of the bull. The bull shall be slaughtered before the LORD; **5]** and the anointed priest shall take some of the bull's blood and bring it into the Tent of Meeting.   **6]** The priest shall dip his finger in the blood, and sprinkle of the blood seven times before the LORD, in front of the curtain of the Shrine.   **7]** The priest shall put some of the blood on the horns of the altar of aromatic incense, which is in the Tent of Meeting, before the LORD; and all the rest of the bull's blood he shall pour out at the base of the altar of burnt

---

4:2] *Person.* Hebrew *nefesh*, often rendered "soul." Some commentators remark that the soul is involved in every transgression, but Bachya notes that *nefesh* sometimes means the combination of soul and body, sometimes body alone (e.g., Lev. 21:1).

Incurs guilt. These words render a form of the verb *chata*, "to sin."

3] *The anointed priest.* Aaron or his successors, "the priest who is exalted [literally, great] above his fellows" (21:10). In later usage he was called *Kohen Gadol*, "High Priest." (This title appears a few times in the Bible.) Because he was the spiritual leader, his offense brought blame upon the people; because of his eminence, his offering was the largest and most costly.

As a sin offering. So traditionally; more precisely, "offering of purgation" (T.N.).

4] *Before the Lord.* See commentary on 1:3.

5] *The anointed priest.* He performed the rite on his own behalf.

Into the Tent of Meeting. Beyond the court, with its large altar, into the "holy place," containing the

altar of incense, the lamp stand, and the table for shewbread.

6] *Sprinkle.* Hebrew *hizah*, an entirely different procedure than that for other sacrifices, the blood of which was dashed (Hebrew *zarak*) from bowls against the sides of the outer altar.

In front of the curtain of the Shrine. The curtain separated the "holy place" from the "Holy of Holies" containing the ark. The priest stood some distance away and sprinkled blood in the direction of the inner Shrine; the curtain would not be stained, except by accident.

7] *On the horns of the altar.* See Exodus, chapter 30, verse 2. These four projections on the corners of an altar are mentioned in several biblical passages. (See especially I Kings 2:28, where Joab takes sanctuary by clinging to the horns of the altar.) They are also found on some ancient altars unearthed by archeologists. Their meaning is uncertain.

And all the rest of the bull's blood. . . . The blood ritual having been completed, the remaining blood is disposed of decently.

ח יְס֣וֹד מִזְבַּ֣ח הָעֹלָ֔ה אֲשֶׁר־פֶּ֖תַח אֹ֣הֶל מוֹעֵ֑ד וְאֶת־כָּל־

הַדֶּ֥שֶׁן יִשְׂרֹֽף׃ פ

חֵ֙לֶב֙ פַּ֣ר הַֽחַטָּ֔את יָרִ֣ים מִמֶּ֑נּוּ אֶת־הַחֵ֙לֶב֙ הַֽמְכַסֶּ֣ה

י וְאִ֥ם כָּל־עֲדַ֨ת יִשְׂרָאֵ֤ל יִשְׁגּוּ֙ וְנֶעְלַ֣ם דָּבָ֔ר מֵעֵינֵ֖י הַקָּהָ֑ל

ט עַל־הַקֶּ֗רֶב וְאֵת֙ כָּל־הַחֵ֙לֶב֙ אֲשֶׁ֣ר עַל־הַקֶּ֑רֶב׃ וְאֵת֙

וְעָשׂ֞וּ אַחַ֣ת מִכָּל־מִצְוֺ֣ת יְהוָ֔ה אֲשֶׁ֖ר לֹא־תֵעָשֶֽׂינָה

שְׁתֵּ֣י הַכְּלָיֹ֗ת וְאֶת־הַחֵ֙לֶב֙ אֲשֶׁ֣ר עֲלֵיהֶ֔ן אֲשֶׁ֖ר עַל־

יד וְאָשֵֽׁמוּ׃ וְנֽוֹדְעָה֙ הַֽחַטָּ֔את אֲשֶׁ֥ר חָטְא֖וּ עָלֶ֑יהָ וְהִקְרִ֣יבוּ

הַכְּסָלִ֑ים וְאֶת־הַיֹּתֶ֙רֶת֙ עַל־הַכָּבֵ֔ד עַל־הַכְּלָי֖וֹת

הַקָּהָ֡ל פַּ֣ר בֶּן־בָּקָר֩ לְחַטָּ֜את וְהֵבִ֣יאוּ אֹת֗וֹ לִפְנֵ֖י אֹ֥הֶל

י יְסִירֶֽנָּה׃ כַּאֲשֶׁ֣ר יוּרַ֔ם מִשּׁ֖וֹר זֶ֣בַח הַשְּׁלָמִ֑ים וְהִקְטִירָ֣ם

טו מוֹעֵֽד׃ וְסָמְכ֡וּ זִקְנֵ֣י הָעֵדָ֧ה אֶת־יְדֵיהֶ֛ם עַל־רֹ֥אשׁ הַפָּ֖ר

יא הַכֹּהֵ֔ן עַ֖ל מִזְבַּ֥ח הָעֹלָֽה׃ וְאֶת־ע֤וֹר הַפָּר֙ וְאֶת־כָּל־

טז לִפְנֵ֣י יְהוָ֑ה וְשָׁחַ֥ט אֶת־הַפָּ֖ר לִפְנֵ֥י יְהוָֽה׃ וְהֵבִ֞יא הַכֹּהֵ֧ן

יב בְּשָׂר֔וֹ עַל־רֹאשׁ֖וֹ וְעַל־כְּרָעָ֑יו וְקִרְבּ֖וֹ וּפִרְשֽׁוֹ׃ וְהוֹצִ֣יא

יז הַמָּשִׁ֛יחַ מִדַּ֥ם הַפָּ֖ר אֶל־אֹ֥הֶל מוֹעֵֽד׃ וְטָבַ֧ל הַכֹּהֵ֛ן

אֶת־כָּל־הַפָּ֡ר אֶל־מִח֣וּץ לַֽמַּחֲנֶה֩ אֶל־מָק֨וֹם טָה֜וֹר אֶל־

אֶצְבָּע֖וֹ מִן־הַדָּ֑ם וְהִזָּ֞ה שֶׁ֤בַע פְּעָמִים֙ לִפְנֵ֣י יְהוָ֔ה אֶת־

שֶׁ֣פֶךְ הַדֶּ֗שֶׁן וְשָׂרַ֥ף אֹת֛וֹ עַל־עֵצִ֖ים בָּאֵ֑שׁ עַל־שֶׁ֥פֶךְ

יח פְּנֵ֣י הַפָּרֹ֑כֶת׃ וּמִן־הַדָּ֞ם יִתֵּ֣ן ׀ עַל־קַרְנֹ֣ת הַמִּזְבֵּ֗חַ אֲשֶׁר֙

offering, which is at the entrance of the Tent of Meeting. 8] He shall remove all the fat from the bull of sin offering: the fat that covers the entrails and all the fat that is about the entrails; 9] the two kidneys and the fat that is on them, that is at the loins; and the protuberance on the liver, which he shall remove with the kidneys— 10] just as it is removed from the ox of the sacrifice of well-being. The priest shall turn them into smoke on the altar of burnt offering. 11] But the hide of the bull, and all its flesh, as well as its head and legs, its entrails and its dung— 12] all the rest of the bull—he shall carry to a clean place outside the camp, to the ash heap, and burn it up with wood; it shall be burned on the ash heap.

13] If it is the whole community of Israel that has erred and the matter escapes the notice of the congregation, so that they do any of the things which by the LORD's commandments ought not to be done, and thus find themselves culpable— 14] when the sin through which they incurred guilt becomes known, the congregation shall offer a bull of the herd as a sin offering, and bring it before the Tent of Meeting. 15] The elders of the community shall lay their hands upon the head of the bull before the LORD, and the bull shall be slaughtered before the LORD. 16] The anointed priest shall bring some of the blood of the bull into the Tent of Meeting, 17] and the priest shall dip his finger in the blood and sprinkle of it seven times before the LORD, in front of the curtain. 18] Some of the blood he shall put on the horns of

---

11–12] Usually the meat of the *chatat* was consumed by the priests who performed the sacrifice (6:19ff.). But obviously the High Priest should not eat of the sacrifice he brought for his own sin; so, when the blood and fat had been offered, the rest of the carcass had to be removed and burned that it might not be misused or defiled. Similarly with the *chatat* brought for the sin of all the people (4:21) [4].

12] *The ash heap.* See 6:4.

13] *The whole community of Israel.* The ancient Israelites had a strong sense of communal solidarity; they believed that the misdeeds of some members of the group, especially the leaders, could bring guilt upon all. (See especially Josh. 7; I Sam. 14:24–45.) Certainly, it was not necessary for every member of the community to violate the law before a *chatat* was required.

15] *The elders . . . shall lay their hands upon the head of the bull.* As representatives of the community, they designate the sacrifice as that of the entire people. (Most communal sacrifices were offered without this ceremony.) Otherwise, this sacrifice was performed exactly like that of the High Priest.

אֵלָיו חַטָּאתוֹ אֲשֶׁר חָטָא בָּהּ וְהֵבִיא אֶת־קָרְבָּנוֹ שְׂעִיר
עִזִּים זָכָר תָּמִים: וְסָמַךְ יָדוֹ עַל־רֹאשׁ הַשָּׂעִיר וְשָׁחַט
אֹתוֹ בִּמְקוֹם אֲשֶׁר־יִשְׁחַט אֶת־הָעֹלָה לִפְנֵי יְהֹוָה
חַטָּאת הוּא: וְלָקַח הַכֹּהֵן מִדַּם הַחַטָּאת בְּאֶצְבָּעוֹ
וְנָתַן עַל־קַרְנֹת מִזְבַּח הָעֹלָה וְאֶת־דָּמוֹ יִשְׁפֹּךְ אֶל־
יְסוֹד מִזְבַּח הָעֹלָה: וְאֶת־כָּל־חֶלְבּוֹ יַקְטִיר הַמִּזְבֵּחָה
כְּחֵלֶב זֶבַח הַשְּׁלָמִים וְכִפֶּר עָלָיו הַכֹּהֵן מֵחַטָּאתוֹ
וְנִסְלַח לוֹ:   פ

וְאִם־נֶפֶשׁ אַחַת תֶּחֱטָא בִשְׁגָגָה מֵעַם הָאָרֶץ בַּעֲשֹׂתָהּ

לִפְנֵי יְהֹוָה אֲשֶׁר בְּאֹהֶל מוֹעֵד וְאֵת כָּל־הַדָּם יִשְׁפֹּךְ
יט אֶל־יְסוֹד מִזְבַּח הָעֹלָה אֲשֶׁר־פֶּתַח אֹהֶל מוֹעֵד: וְאֵת
כ כָּל־חֶלְבּוֹ יָרִים מִמֶּנּוּ וְהִקְטִיר הַמִּזְבֵּחָה: וְעָשָׂה לַפָּר
כַּאֲשֶׁר עָשָׂה לְפַר הַחַטָּאת כֵּן יַעֲשֶׂה־לּוֹ וְכִפֶּר עֲלֵהֶם
כא הַכֹּהֵן וְנִסְלַח לָהֶם: וְהוֹצִיא אֶת־הַפָּר אֶל־מִחוּץ
לַמַּחֲנֶה וְשָׂרַף אֹתוֹ כַּאֲשֶׁר שָׂרַף אֵת הַפָּר הָרִאשׁוֹן
חַטַּאת הַקָּהָל הוּא: פ
כב אֲשֶׁר נָשִׂיא יֶחֱטָא וְעָשָׂה אַחַת מִכָּל־מִצְוֹת יְהֹוָה
כג אֱלֹהָיו אֲשֶׁר לֹא־תֵעָשֶׂינָה בִּשְׁגָגָה וְאָשֵׁם: אוֹ־הוֹדַע

the altar which is before the LORD in the Tent of Meeting, and all the rest of the blood he shall pour out at the base of the altar of burnt offering, which is at the entrance of the Tent of Meeting.   **19]** He shall remove all its fat from it and turn it into smoke on the altar.   **20]** He shall do with this bull just as is done with the [priest's] bull of sin offering; he shall do the same with it. Thus the priest shall make expiation for them, and they shall be forgiven.   **21]** He shall carry the bull outside the camp and burn it as he burned the first bull; it is the sin offering of the congregation.

22] In case it is a chieftain who incurs guilt by doing unwittingly any of the things which by the commandment of the LORD his God ought not to be done, and finds himself culpable—

23] once the sin of which he is guilty is brought to his knowledge, he shall bring as his offering a male goat without blemish.   **24]** He shall lay his hand upon the goat's head, and it shall be slaughtered at the spot where the burnt offering is slaughtered before the LORD; it is a sin offering.   **25]** The priest shall take with his finger some of the blood of the sin offering and put it on the horns of the altar of burnt offering; and the rest of its blood he shall pour out at the base of the altar of burnt offering.   **26]** All its fat he shall turn into smoke on the altar, like the fat of the sacrifice of well-being. Thus the priest shall make expiation on his behalf for his sin, and he shall be forgiven.

27] If any person from among the populace unwittingly incurs guilt by doing any of the

20] *Shall make expiation.* Hebrew *kipper.* For the meaning of this term, see introduction to Lev. 16, "5. Atonement and Return."

They shall be forgiven. From Hebrew *salach.* This verb is used in the Bible for divine forgiveness only. But, in modern Hebrew, *selichah* is the idiom for "Excuse me!"

22] *A chieftain.* Hebrew *nasi.* This term is often used for the tribal leaders (Exod. 35:27; Num. 1:10) and could refer to them here. But we should then expect a phrase like "chieftain of a tribe," or "one of the chieftains." Ezekiel, moreover, applies the word *nasi* to rulers of the Davidic family. He calls King Zedekiah

"*Nasi* of Israel" (Ezek. 21:30) and foretells the day when "My servant David shall be *nasi* in their midst" (34:24). The word here may therefore mean "king" and was so understood by *Sifra.*

Note that procedure for the *chatat* of the *nasi* and of the private citizen is markedly different from that of verses 1 through 21, aside from the lesser value of the animals offered.

24] *Where the burnt offering is slaughtered.* Cf. 1:11 (T.N.).

27] *Populace.* Literally, "people of the country" (T.N.).

כח אַחַת מִמִּצְוֺת יְהֹוָה אֲשֶׁר לֹא־תֵעָשֶׂינָה וְאָשֵׁם: אוֹ הוֹדַע אֵלָיו חַטָּאתוֹ אֲשֶׁר חָטָא וְהֵבִיא קׇרְבָּנוֹ שְׂעִירַת
כט עִזִּים תְּמִימָה נְקֵבָה עַל־חַטָּאתוֹ אֲשֶׁר חָטָא: וְסָמַךְ אֶת־יָדוֹ עַל רֹאשׁ הַחַטָּאת וְשָׁחַט אֶת־הַחַטָּאת בִּמְקוֹם
ל הָעֹלָה: וְלָקַח הַכֹּהֵן מִדָּמָהּ בְּאֶצְבָּעוֹ וְנָתַן עַל־קַרְנֹת מִזְבַּח הָעֹלָה וְאֶת־כׇּל־דָּמָהּ יִשְׁפֹּךְ אֶל־יְסוֹד הַמִּזְבֵּחַ:
לא וְאֶת־כׇּל־חֶלְבָּה יָסִיר כַּאֲשֶׁר הוּסַר חֵלֶב מֵעַל זֶבַח הַשְּׁלָמִים וְהִקְטִיר הַכֹּהֵן הַמִּזְבֵּחָה לְרֵיחַ נִיחֹחַ לַיהֹוָה וְכִפֶּר עָלָיו הַכֹּהֵן וְנִסְלַח לוֹ: פ

לב וְאִם־כֶּבֶשׂ יָבִיא קׇרְבָּנוֹ לְחַטָּאת נְקֵבָה תְמִימָה יְבִיאֶנָּה: וְסָמַךְ אֶת־יָדוֹ עַל רֹאשׁ הַחַטָּאת וְשָׁחַט אֹתָהּ
לג לְחַטָּאת בִּמְקוֹם אֲשֶׁר יִשְׁחַט אֶת־הָעֹלָה: וְלָקַח הַכֹּהֵן מִדַּם הַחַטָּאת בְּאֶצְבָּעוֹ וְנָתַן עַל־קַרְנֹת מִזְבַּח הָעֹלָה
לד וְאֶת־כׇּל־דָּמָהּ יִשְׁפֹּךְ אֶל־יְסוֹד הַמִּזְבֵּחַ: וְאֶת־כׇּל־חֶלְבָּה יָסִיר כַּאֲשֶׁר יוּסַר חֵלֶב הַכֶּשֶׂב מִזֶּבַח
לה הַשְּׁלָמִים וְהִקְטִיר הַכֹּהֵן אֹתָם הַמִּזְבֵּחָה עַל אִשֵּׁי יְהֹוָה וְכִפֶּר עָלָיו הַכֹּהֵן עַל־חַטָּאתוֹ אֲשֶׁר־חָטָא וְנִסְלַח לוֹ: פ

things which by the LORD's commandments ought not to be done, and finds himself culpable—

28] once the sin of which he is guilty is brought to his knowledge, he shall bring a female goat without blemish as his offering for the sin of which he is guilty. **29]** He shall lay his hand upon the head of the sin offering, and the sin offering shall be slaughtered at the place of the burnt offering. **30]** The priest shall take with his finger some of its blood and put it on the horns of the altar of burnt offering; and all the rest of its blood he shall pour out at the base of the altar. **31]** He shall remove all its fat, just as the fat is removed from the sacrifice of well-being; and the priest shall turn it into smoke on the altar, for a pleasing odor to the LORD. Thus the priest shall make expiation for him, and he shall be forgiven.

32] If the offering he brings as a sin offering is a sheep, he shall bring a female without blemish. **33]** He shall lay his hand upon the head of the sin offering, and it shall be slaughtered as a sin offering at the spot where the burnt offering is slaughtered. **34]** The priest shall take with his finger some of the blood of the sin offering and put it on the horns of the altar of burnt offering, and all the rest of its blood he shall pour out at the base of the altar. **35]** And all its fat he shall remove just as the fat of the sheep of the sacrifice of well-being is removed; and this the priest shall turn into smoke on the altar, over the LORD's offerings by fire. Thus the priest shall make expiation on his behalf for the sin of which he is guilty, and he shall be forgiven.

31] *For a pleasing odor to the Lord.* This formula was needed to indicate that these offerings too, though occasioned by sin, are dear to God, who welcomes the repentant (Luzzatto).

GLEANINGS

Halachah

A sin offering was required for inadvertent commission of an act forbidden by the Torah which, if deliberate, would have been punished by being "cut off from one's kin" (see commentary on 7:21). A *chatat* was not required for omission of a positive commandment. One who defiantly violated a negative law was exempt from sacrifice, for such a sacrifice would have been unavailing. His guilt could be purged away in time only by continued repentance, observance of the Day of Atonement, and the acceptance of punitive suffering, or by death [5].

4:2] *And Does One of Them*

If one committed several offenses, or repeated the same offense several times, he had to bring a *chatat* for each violation.

3] *So That Blame Falls upon the People*

Targum Pseudo-Jonathan understands: He made a mistake while bringing an offering for the people's guilt.

Bull of the Herd
A three-year-old.

12] *Outside the Camp*

In later centuries, outside the city of Jerusalem.

13] *The Whole Community of Israel*

The Rabbis, with their more developed sense of individual responsibility, were reluctant to accept the notion that the whole community must shoulder the guilt for the unknown misdeeds of a few. They therefore explained this law as referring to a case in which the Sanhedrin, the highest court, gave an erroneous legal ruling, and the people consequently violated the law without intention. The clause, *the matter escapes the notice of the congregation*, is literally "the matter is hidden from the eyes of the congregation"; and the eyes of the congregation, says *Sifra*, are the judges of the Sanhedrin. (Isa. 29:10 calls the prophets the eyes of the people.) They explained in the same way the guilt of the anointed priest (4:3) who was also authorized to issue ritual decisions and, so by an error, could lead the people to unwitting sin.

Haggadah

4:1] *When a Person Unwittingly Incurs Guilt*

Scripture says: "Whatever is in your power to do, do with all your might" (Eccles. 9:10). While you have the strength, fulfill the commandments, do charity, turn back to God. While the lamp is still burning, replenish the oil so that it does not go out. If you have sinned, do not persist in defiance; repent, and the Holy One (blessed be He) will accept you. If you have sinned a little, let it seem much to you—even if the fault was unwitting [6].

22] *In Case [Asher] . . . a Chieftain . . . Incurs Guilt*

Rabban Johanan ben Zakkai punned: Happy

(*ashre*) is the generation whose leader is manly enough to admit his sins!   SIFRA

27] *If Any Person from among the Populace . . . Incurs Guilt*

The patriarchs were able to rejoice in all the sufferings You brought upon them: for every dispensation they praised Your name. But we lack the strength to stand up under trial. When You become angry, we sin; and, when we sin, You grow angry. Do wonders for us, as You did for the patriarchs, and then we will be able to endure [7].

773

Chatat—Sin Offering; Asham—Guilt Offering

This chapter begins with four special cases that require a *chatat* (verses 1–13). Then we are introduced (verses 14–16) to another kind of sacrifice called *asham*, "guilt offering" or "penalty offering." In form, this sacrifice is identical with the *chatat* except that for the *asham* a ram is mandatory whereas, under varying circumstances, the *chatat* may be a bull, sheep, goat, fowl, or even a meal offering. In intent, however, the two sacrifices seem different. The *asham* is brought chiefly by one who has misappropriated property. He must restore what he has taken plus a 20 per cent indemnity; then by bringing an *asham* he is fully restored to divine favor.

It would be convenient if we could say that the *chatat* was brought for inadvertent of-fenses and the *asham* for deliberate misap-propriation of property. But, in fact, this chapter requires a *chatat* for withholding legal testimony, no doubt deliberately (verses 1 and 5), and an *asham* for certain unwitting transgressions (verses 17–19). These seeming inconsistencies cannot readily be brought into a coherent system, and the talmudic Rabbis had trouble with them (see Gleanings). Ap-parently the chapter is composed of tradi-tions, reflecting different periods or different priestly groups, which were assembled but not thoroughly edited.

The word *asham*, be it noted, conveys the ideas both of guilt and of punishment. The expressions "finds himself culpable," "re-alized his guilt," and "his penalty" are all forms of the same word.

ד וְאָשֵׁם: אוֹ נֶפֶשׁ כִּי תִשָּׁבַע לְבַטֵּא בִשְׂפָתַיִם לְהָרַע
אוֹ לְהֵיטִיב לְכֹל אֲשֶׁר יְבַטֵּא הָאָדָם בִּשְׁבֻעָה וְנֶעְלַם
מִמֶּנּוּ וְהוּא־יָדָע וְאָשֵׁם לְאַחַת מֵאֵלֶּה: וְהָיָה כִי־יֶאְשַׁם
ה לְאַחַת מֵאֵלֶּה וְהִתְוַדָּה אֲשֶׁר חָטָא עָלֶיהָ: וְהֵבִיא
אֶת־אֲשָׁמוֹ לַיהוָֹה עַל חַטָּאתוֹ אֲשֶׁר חָטָא נְקֵבָה מִן
הַצֹּאן כִּשְׂבָּה אוֹ־שְׂעִירַת עִזִּים לְחַטָּאת וְכִפֶּר עָלָיו

א וְנֶפֶשׁ כִּי־תֶחֱטָא וְשָׁמְעָה קוֹל אָלָה וְהוּא עֵד אוֹ רָאָה
אוֹ יָדָע אִם־לוֹא יַגִּיד וְנָשָׂא עֲוֹנוֹ: אוֹ נֶפֶשׁ אֲשֶׁר תִּגַּע
בְּכָל־דָּבָר טָמֵא אוֹ בְנִבְלַת חַיָּה טְמֵאָה אוֹ בְּנִבְלַת
בְּהֵמָה טְמֵאָה אוֹ בְּנִבְלַת שֶׁרֶץ טָמֵא וְנֶעְלַם מִמֶּנּוּ
ג וְהוּא טָמֵא וְאָשֵׁם: אוֹ כִי יִגַּע בְּטֻמְאַת אָדָם לְכֹל
טֻמְאָתוֹ אֲשֶׁר יִטְמָא בָּהּ וְנֶעְלַם מִמֶּנּוּ וְהוּא יָדָע

1] If a person incurs guilt:

When he has heard a public imprecation and—although able to testify as one who has either seen or learned of the matter—he does not give information, so that he is subject to punishment;

2] Or when a person touches any unclean thing—be it the carcass of an unclean beast or the carcass of unclean cattle or the carcass of an unclean creeping thing—and the fact has escaped him, and then, being unclean, he finds himself culpable;

3] Or when he touches human uncleanness—any such uncleanness whereby one becomes unclean—and, though he has known it, the fact has escaped him, but later he finds himself culpable;

4] Or when a person utters an oath to bad or good purpose—whatever a man may utter in an oath—and, though he has known it, the fact has escaped him, but later he finds himself culpable in any of these matters—

5] when he realizes his guilt in any of these matters, he shall confess that wherein he has sinned. **6]** And he shall bring as his penalty to the LORD, for the sin of which he is guilty, a female from the flock, sheep or goat, as a sin offering; and the priest shall make expiation on his behalf for his sin.

5:1] *When he has heard a public imprecation.* Namely, against one who withholds testimony (T.N.). Someone engaged in a lawsuit (or perhaps the court) publicly calls on those who have information about the case to appear and testify; and a curse is invoked on anyone who fails to respond. A person who withholds evidence thereby becomes a sinner and is subject to the curse. Later he has a change of heart and confesses. He must then expiate the offense with a *chatat.* "Because many decent people avoid giving testimony for fear of hurting others or of making enemies, the Torah must state plainly that failure to testify makes one liable to divine punishment" (Luzzatto).

2] *Any unclean thing . . . carcass of an unclean beast. . . .* Ritual defilement from animals is explained in 11:29ff.

3] *. . . Human uncleanness* is treated in chapters 12 through 15 and in Num. 19:11ff.

Finds himself culpable. It is not sinful to become ritually unclean; such defilement is inevitable in the ordinary course of living. Sin occurs only if one who has been defiled enters the sanctuary or eats consecrated meat without having been purified [1].

4] *Utters.* Literally, "utters with his lips" (T.N.).

An oath. Violation of oaths regarding civil claims is treated below, 5:20ff. *Sifra* therefore takes this passage, perhaps correctly, as referring to oaths of a religious character ("I swear I will fast today!") which are violated by oversight.

5–6] These verses summarize the law of chapter 4, verses 27ff., adding the requirement of a confession.

ז לְשָׁנֵי בְנֵי־יוֹנָה וְהֵבִיא אֶת־קָרְבָּנוֹ אֲשֶׁר חָטָא עֲשִׂירִת
הָאֵפָה סֹלֶת לְחַטָּאת לֹא־יָשִׂים עָלֶיהָ שֶׁמֶן וְלֹא־יִתֵּן
יב עָלֶיהָ לְבֹנָה כִּי חַטָּאת הִוא: וֶהֱבִיאָהּ אֶל־הַכֹּהֵן
וְקָמַץ הַכֹּהֵן מִמֶּנָּה מְלוֹא קֻמְצוֹ אֶת־אַזְכָּרָתָהּ
יג וְהִקְטִיר הַמִּזְבֵּחָה עַל אִשֵּׁי יְהוָה חַטָּאת הִוא: וְכִפֶּר
עָלָיו הַכֹּהֵן עַל־חַטָּאתוֹ אֲשֶׁר־חָטָא מֵאַחַת מֵאֵלֶּה
יד וְנִסְלַח לוֹ וְהָיְתָה לַכֹּהֵן כַּמִּנְחָה: ס וַיְדַבֵּר יְהוָה
טו אֶל־מֹשֶׁה לֵּאמֹר: נֶפֶשׁ כִּי־תִמְעֹל מַעַל וְחָטְאָה בִּשְׁגָגָה
מִקָּדְשֵׁי יְהוָה וְהֵבִיא אֶת־אֲשָׁמוֹ לַיהוָה אַיִל תָּמִים

ז הַכֹּהֵן מֵחַטָּאתוֹ: וְאִם־לֹא תַגִּיעַ יָדוֹ דֵּי שֶׂה וְהֵבִיא
אֶת־אֲשָׁמוֹ אֲשֶׁר חָטָא שְׁתֵּי תֹרִים אוֹ־שְׁנֵי בְנֵי־יוֹנָה
ח לַיהוָה אֶחָד לְחַטָּאת וְאֶחָד לְעֹלָה: וְהֵבִיא אֹתָם
אֶל־הַכֹּהֵן וְהִקְרִיב אֶת־אֲשֶׁר לַחַטָּאת רִאשׁוֹנָה וּמָלַק
ט אֶת־רֹאשׁוֹ מִמּוּל עָרְפּוֹ וְלֹא יַבְדִּיל: וְהִזָּה מִדַּם
הַחַטָּאת עַל־קִיר הַמִּזְבֵּחַ וְהַנִּשְׁאָר בַּדָּם יִמָּצֵה אֶל־
י יְסוֹד הַמִּזְבֵּחַ חַטָּאת הִוא: וְאֶת־הַשֵּׁנִי יַעֲשֶׂה עֹלָה
כַּמִּשְׁפָּט וְכִפֶּר עָלָיו הַכֹּהֵן מֵחַטָּאתוֹ אֲשֶׁר־חָטָא
יא וְנִסְלַח לוֹ: ס וְאִם־לֹא תַשִּׂיג יָדוֹ לִשְׁתֵּי תֹרִים אוֹ

7] But if his means do not suffice for a sheep, he shall bring to the LORD, as his penalty for that of which he is guilty, two turtledoves or two pigeons, one for a sin offering and the other for a burnt offering. 8] He shall bring them to the priest, who shall offer first the one for the sin offering, pinching its head at the nape without severing it. 9] He shall sprinkle some of the blood of the sin offering on the side of the altar, and what remains of the blood shall be drained out at the base of the altar; it is a sin offering. 10] And the second he shall prepare as a burnt offering, according to regulation. Thus the priest shall make expiation on his behalf for the sin of which he is guilty, and he shall be forgiven.

11] And if his means do not suffice for two turtledoves or two pigeons, he shall bring as his offering for that of which he is guilty a tenth of an *ephah* of choice flour for a sin offering; he shall not add oil to it or lay frankincense on it, for it is a sin offering. 12] He shall bring it to the priest, and the priest shall scoop out of it a handful as a token portion of it and turn it into smoke on the altar, with the LORD's offerings by fire; it is a sin offering. 13] Thus the priest shall make expiation on his behalf for whichever of these sins he is guilty, and he shall be forgiven. It shall belong to the priest, like the meal offering.

14] And the LORD spoke to Moses, saying:

15] When a person commits a trespass, being unwittingly remiss about any of the LORD's sacred things, he shall bring as his penalty to the LORD a ram without blemish from the flock,

7] *But if his means do not suffice for a sheep....* This section, which permits the offender to bring a less expensive *chatat* if he cannot afford the standard sacrifice, may be the direct continuation of chapter 4, verse 35, and so it applies to all sin offerings. Tradition, however, limited the concession to the cases cited in chapter 5, verses 1 through 6.

8-10] If a pair of birds is substituted, the first only is presented as a *chatat* and the procedure is a little different from that of the *olah* of fowl (1:15ff.). The latter procedure is followed for the second bird.

11] If a cereal offering is substituted, it must not have a festive character; oil and frankincense are therefore to be omitted.

13] *It shall belong to the priest, like the meal offering.* I.e., the normal *minchah* of chapter 2; after the token portion is burned, the remainder is to be eaten by the priest.

14-16] The first example of the *asham* concerns an offense which was deemed especially grave, even if unwittingly committed; the profane use of food, money, or other objects belonging to the sanctuary. Such misappropriation was called *meilah*, "trespass." An entire treatise of the Mishnah and Talmud, named *Meilah*, is based on these few verses.

מִן־הַצֹּאן בְּעֶרְכְּךָ כֶּסֶף־שְׁקָלִים בְּשֶׁקֶל־הַקֹּדֶשׁ

טו לְאָשָׁם: וְאֵת אֲשֶׁר חָטָא מִן־הַקֹּדֶשׁ יְשַׁלֵּם וְאֶת־
חֲמִישִׁתוֹ יוֹסֵף עָלָיו וְנָתַן אֹתוֹ לַכֹּהֵן וְהַכֹּהֵן יְכַפֵּר
עָלָיו בְּאֵיל הָאָשָׁם וְנִסְלַח לוֹ:   פ

יז וְאִם־נֶפֶשׁ כִּי תֶחֱטָא וְעָשְׂתָה אַחַת מִכָּל־מִצְוֹת יְהֹוָה
יח אֲשֶׁר לֹא תֵעָשֶׂינָה וְלֹא־יָדַע וְאָשֵׁם וְנָשָׂא עֲוֹנוֹ: וְהֵבִיא

אַיִל תָּמִים מִן־הַצֹּאן בְּעֶרְכְּךָ לְאָשָׁם אֶל־הַכֹּהֵן וְכִפֶּר
עָלָיו הַכֹּהֵן עַל שִׁגְגָתוֹ אֲשֶׁר־שָׁגָג וְהוּא לֹא־יָדַע וְנִסְלַח
יט לוֹ: אָשָׁם הוּא אָשֹׁם אָשַׁם לַיהֹוָה: פ

כ וַיְדַבֵּר יְהֹוָה אֶל־מֹשֶׁה לֵּאמֹר: נֶפֶשׁ כִּי תֶחֱטָא וּמָעֲלָה
מַעַל בַּיהֹוָה וְכִחֵשׁ בַּעֲמִיתוֹ בְּפִקָּדוֹן אוֹ־בִתְשׂוּמֶת
כב יָד אוֹ בְגָזֵל אוֹ עָשַׁק אֶת־עֲמִיתוֹ: אוֹ־מָצָא אֲבֵדָה

convertible into payment in silver by the sanctuary weight, as a guilt offering.   16] He shall make restitution for that wherein he was remiss about the sacred things, and he shall add a fifth part to it and give it to the priest. The priest shall make expiation on his behalf with the ram of the guilt offering, and he shall be forgiven.

17] And when a person, without knowing it, sins in regard to any of the LORD's commandments about things not to be done, and then realizes his guilt, he shall be subject to punishment. 18] He shall bring to the priest a ram without blemish from the flock, or the equivalent, as a guilt offering. The priest shall make expiation on his behalf for the error that he committed unwittingly, and he shall be forgiven.   19] It is a guilt offering; he has incurred guilt before the LORD.

20] The LORD spoke to Moses, saying: 21] When a person sins and commits a trespass against the LORD by dealing deceitfully with his fellow in the matter of a deposit or a pledge, or through robbery, or by defrauding his fellow,   22] or by finding something lost and lying

15] *A ram . . . convertible into payment in silver by the sanctuary weight.* Older translations render "according to thy valuation in silver by shekels, after the shekel of the sanctuary." (On "thy valuation," see commentary on 27:2.) The present rendering reflects the fact, known from cuneiform sources, that in ancient Near Eastern practice a money payment could be substituted for a sacrificial animal [2]. Money, of course, meant a specified weight of metal; coinage did not begin in Palestine before the fourth century B.C.E.

17–19] This paragraph is vague and perplexing. It seems to require an *asham* for inadvertent offenses, such as chapter 4 proposes to expiate with a *chatat*. The Rabbis gave a forced explanation: These verses, they say, apply to the individual who suspects, but is not sure, that he has violated a law [3] (see Gleanings).

18] *The equivalent.* I.e., in currency; cf. 5:15 (T.N.).

20–26] If by dishonest conduct one person causes financial loss to another, he must restore the full amount and pay a substantial penalty sum; then only may he bring the *asham* (cf. the similar law in Num. 5:5ff.).

21] *Sins and commits a trespass against the Lord.* To injure one's fellow man is to commit trespass against God; and "trespass" (5:15) is taking something holy for one's own use.

A pledge. Meaning of Hebrew uncertain (T.N.). The expression *tesumet yad*, "placing in [or of] the hand," occurs nowhere else in the Bible. It must refer to something entrusted to the man's care— according to Ibn Ezra, to jointly owned property.

Robbery. Hebrew *gazel*, taking something by force or threat of force.

Defrauding. Hebrew *ashak*. In this case the culprit denies wrongdoing.

אֹתוֹ בְרֹאשׁוֹ וַחֲמִשִׁתָיו יֹסֵף עָלָיו לַאֲשֶׁר הוּא לוֹ יִתְּנֶנּוּ
בְּיוֹם אַשְׁמָתוֹ: וְאֶת־אֲשָׁמוֹ יָבִיא לַיהוָה אַיִל תָּמִים
מִן־הַצֹּאן בְּעֶרְכְּךָ לְאָשָׁם אֶל־הַכֹּהֵן: וְכִפֶּר עָלָיו
הַכֹּהֵן לִפְנֵי יְהוָה וְנִסְלַח לוֹ עַל־אַחַת מִכֹּל אֲשֶׁר־
יַעֲשֶׂה לְאַשְׁמָה בָהּ:

וְכִחֵשׁ בָּהּ וְנִשְׁבַּע עַל־שָׁקֶר עַל־אַחַת מִכֹּל אֲשֶׁר־
יַעֲשֶׂה הָאָדָם לַחֲטֹא בָהֵנָּה: וְהָיָה כִּי־יֶחֱטָא וְאָשֵׁם
וְהֵשִׁיב אֶת־הַגְּזֵלָה אֲשֶׁר גָּזָל אוֹ אֶת־הָעֹשֶׁק אֲשֶׁר עָשָׁק
אוֹ אֶת־הַפִּקָּדוֹן אֲשֶׁר הָפְקַד אִתּוֹ אוֹ אֶת־הָאֲבֵדָה
אֲשֶׁר מָצָא: אוֹ מִכֹּל אֲשֶׁר־יִשָּׁבַע עָלָיו לַשָּׁקֶר וְשִׁלַּם

Haftarah Vayikra, p. 978

about it; if he swears falsely regarding any one of the various things that one may do and sin thereby—   23] when one has thus sinned and, realizing his guilt, would restore that which he got through robbery or fraud, or the deposit that was entrusted to him, or the lost thing that he found,   24] or anything else about which he swore falsely, he shall repay the principal amount and add a fifth part to it. He shall pay it to its owner when he realizes his guilt.   25] Then he shall bring to the priest, as his penalty to the LORD, a ram without blemish from the flock, or the equivalent, as a guilt offering.   26] The priest shall make expiation on his behalf before the LORD, and he shall be forgiven for whatever he may have done to draw blame thereby.

22] *If he swears falsely.* This seems to mean that, had he not perjured himself, he would be obligated only to return the misappropriated property and would be exempt from the indemnity and sacrifice.

But Rashi and Ibn Ezra understand this clause as enumerating still another category of sin—denying falsely on oath a money debt he has incurred.

25] *The equivalent.* See note on verse 18.

GLEANINGS

Halachah

The uncertainties of chapters 4 and 5 were resolved thus:

4:1] The *chatat* of chapter 4 was to be brought for inadvertent violations of negative laws, of which the deliberate violation would have entailed being "cut off from one's kin."

2] The sins enumerated in chapter 5, verses 1 through 4, entail a *chatat*, normally a sheep; but an impecunious sinner may bring an offering of lesser value. This offering is therefore traditionally called *korban oleh veyored*, "an offering that may go up or down."

3] One who is uncertain whether or not he has broken a law brings the "doubtful *asham*" of verses 17 through 19. If later he discovers that he actually did commit the offense, he must also bring a standard *chatat*.

4] The regular *asham* is brought for the cases in chapter 5, verses 15 and 16 and verses 20 through 26 also in Numbers, chapter 5, verses 5 through 9.

5:1] *When He Has Heard a Public Imprecation*

The halachah limited the penalty to those who were individually approached by the litigant and adjured to give evidence and whose failure to respond caused the litigant financial loss.

7] *But if His Means Do Not Suffice for a Sheep*

Even if he has a sheep, but needs it for his own support, he should bring a lesser offering.

16] *A Fifth Part*

According to the halachah, the indemnity is to be one-fifth, not of the principal sum, but of the total amount to be repaid. Put the other way, the principal sum is to be four-fifths of the total repaid. Thus, if the property misappropriated is worth one hundred shekels, the indemnity would be twenty-five shekels—one-fifth of the total sum (one hundred twenty-five) due the sanctuary.

Haggadah

5:16] *He Shall Make Restitution*

When the nations of the world heard this law, they said: "According to our laws, one who takes so much as a hook belonging to Caesar is to be lacerated with a plowshare; but this God is placated by a simple act of restitution. Moreover, He is more lenient about the misappropriation of what is His (He designates this as an "error," verse 15) than about robbing a human being [4].

17–19] Why should the "doubtful *asham*," brought when possibly no offense has been committed, be the costly ram while for an undoubted transgression one may offer a ewe or even fowls or flour? Because, a man might not take seriously the mere possibility of having sinned, if the Torah had not thus shown the gravity of the matter.   NACHMANIDES

21] *Commits a Sin against the Lord*

God is more concerned about the wrong done by man to his fellow than about offenses directed at Him alone. Said Rabbi Akiba: "Loans and other transactions are ordinarily consummated in the presence of witnesses; one who denies the transaction thereby denies the testimony of the witnesses. But, when one entrusts something privately to another, he wants the matter to be known only to the Third Party. And, should the recipient deny the deposit, he denies that the Third Party was present with them."   SIFRA

Said Rabbi Jose: See the blindness of him who robs or defrauds! For a trifling sum he is called sinner, liar, thief, defrauder. He must bring a costly *asham* and is forgiven only through confession and repentance. Moreover Scripture accounts him as having taken a life. Whose life? According to one opinion, that of his victim; according to another opinion, his own life. But the righteous, who are generous and give to others, are accounted as having acquired lives. They become like their Creator who revives the spirit of the lowly and oppressed [5].

Laws of Sacrifice—Olah, Minchah, Chatat

The offerings discussed in the first five chapters are now treated a second time, in the same order as before. Most of the material in this chapter and the next is new, some of it essential. See introduction to Part I, "7. The Sacrificial Legislation of the Torah."

1. The Olah—Burnt Offering

See chapter 1 which describes the procedure for the various types of *olot* in full detail. These directions are now supplemented by instructions for the care of the altar fire.

2. The Minchah—Meal Offering

Verses 7 through 11 of chapter 6 repeat the content of chapter 2, verse 11, but they spell out more fully the rules for the consumption of the *minchah* as well as the other "most holy offerings," the *chatat* and *asham*. They were to be eaten by male members of the priestly order, within the precincts of the sanctuary. (*Shelamim*, which were of lesser sanctity, could be eaten by men and women, priests and non-priests, anywhere within the camp.) Moreover, the priests' portion of the *minchah* had to be prepared without leavening.

Verses 9 through 11, which indicate that the meal offerings were to be divided among the priests, appear to contradict chapter 7, verses 9 and 10 which limit this rule to uncooked offerings, while assigning the cooked ones to the priest who presents them. Here too we see the combination of variant traditions (cf. Gleanings on 6:9).

Verses 12 through 16 introduce a new subject—the *minchah* as inaugural offering. The plain sense seems to be that the "anointed priest," i.e., High Priest, had to bring this offering when he first assumed his duties. But, from the word "regular" (Hebrew *tamid*), *Sifra* infers that the High Priest must offer this *minchah* daily. And, from the words "his sons," the conclusion was drawn that ordinary priests must bring the inaugural *minchah* once before officiating at the altar.

3. The Chatat—Sin Offering

Verses 17 through 23 give us essential information about the *chatat*. Chapter 4 had dealt only with those portions of the sacrifice that were to be burned on the altar. Now we learn that the meat was to be eaten by the priests as a "most holy" portion, except in the cases treated in chapter 4, verses 3 through 21.

(A new weekly portion, *Tzav*, begins with 6:1.)

ב וַיְדַבֵּ֥ר יְהֹוָ֖ה אֶל־מֹשֶׁ֥ה לֵּאמֹֽר: צַ֤ו אֶֽת־אַהֲרֹן֙ וְאֶת־
בָּנָ֣יו לֵאמֹ֔ר זֹ֥את תּוֹרַ֖ת הָעֹלָ֑ה הִ֣וא הָעֹלָ֡ה עַל֩
מוֹקְדָ֨ה עַל־הַמִּזְבֵּ֤חַ כָּל־הַלַּ֙יְלָה֙ עַד־הַבֹּ֔קֶר וְאֵ֥שׁ
ג הַמִּזְבֵּ֖חַ תּ֥וּקַד בּֽוֹ: וְלָבַ֨שׁ הַכֹּהֵ֜ן מִדּ֣וֹ בַ֗ד וּמִֽכְנְסֵי־בַד֮
יִלְבַּ֣שׁ עַל־בְּשָׂרוֹ֒ וְהֵרִ֣ים אֶת־הַדֶּ֗שֶׁן אֲשֶׁ֨ר תֹּאכַ֥ל הָאֵ֛שׁ
ד אֶת־הָעֹלָ֖ה עַל־הַמִּזְבֵּ֑חַ וְשָׂמ֕וֹ אֵ֖צֶל הַמִּזְבֵּֽחַ: וּפָשַׁט֙
אֶת־בְּגָדָ֔יו וְלָבַ֖שׁ בְּגָדִ֣ים אֲחֵרִ֑ים וְהוֹצִ֤יא אֶת־הַדֶּ֙שֶׁן֙
ה אֶל־מִח֣וּץ לַֽמַּחֲנֶ֔ה אֶל־מָק֖וֹם טָהֽוֹר: וְהָאֵ֨שׁ עַל־
הַמִּזְבֵּ֤חַ תּֽוּקַד־בּוֹ֙ לֹ֣א תִכְבֶּ֔ה וּבִעֵ֨ר עָלֶ֧יהָ הַכֹּהֵ֛ן

* ב מ׳ זעירא.

עֵצִ֥ים בַּבֹּ֣קֶר בַּבֹּ֑קֶר וְעָרַ֤ךְ עָלֶ֙יהָ֙ הָֽעֹלָ֔ה וְהִקְטִ֥יר
ו עָלֶ֖יהָ חֶלְבֵ֣י הַשְּׁלָמִֽים: אֵ֗שׁ תָּמִ֛יד תּוּקַ֥ד עַל־הַמִּזְבֵּ֖חַ
ז לֹ֥א תִכְבֶּֽה: ס וְזֹ֥את תּוֹרַ֖ת הַמִּנְחָ֑ה הַקְרֵ֨ב אֹתָ֤הּ
ח בְּנֵֽי־אַהֲרֹן֙ לִפְנֵ֣י יְהֹוָ֔ה אֶל־פְּנֵ֖י הַמִּזְבֵּֽחַ: וְהֵרִ֨ים מִמֶּ֜נּוּ
בְּקֻמְצ֗וֹ מִסֹּ֤לֶת הַמִּנְחָה֙ וּמִשַּׁמְנָ֔הּ וְאֵת֙ כָּל־הַלְּבֹנָ֔ה
אֲשֶׁ֖ר עַל־הַמִּנְחָ֑ה וְהִקְטִ֣יר הַמִּזְבֵּ֗חַ רֵ֧יחַ נִיחֹ֛חַ
ט אַזְכָּרָתָ֖הּ לַֽיהֹוָֽה: וְהַנּוֹתֶ֣רֶת מִמֶּ֔נָּה יֹאכְל֖וּ אַהֲרֹ֣ן וּבָנָ֑יו
מַצּ֤וֹת תֵּֽאָכֵל֙ בְּמָק֣וֹם קָדֹ֔שׁ בַּחֲצַ֥ר אֹֽהֶל־מוֹעֵ֖ד
י יֹאכְלֽוּהָ: לֹ֤א תֵאָפֶה֙ חָמֵ֔ץ חֶלְקָ֛ם נָתַ֥תִּי אֹתָ֖הּ מֵֽאִשָּׁ֑י
יא קֹ֤דֶשׁ קָֽדָשִׁים֙ הִ֔וא כַּחַטָּ֖את וְכָֽאָשָֽׁם: כָּל־זָכָ֞ר בִּבְנֵ֣י

* ח סבירין ממנה.

1] The LORD spoke to Moses, saying: 2] Command Aaron and his sons thus:

This is the ritual of the burnt offering: The burnt offering itself shall remain where it is burned upon the altar all night until morning, while the fire on the altar is kept going on it.   3] The priest shall dress in linen raiment, with linen breeches next to his body; and he shall take up the ashes to which the fire has reduced the burnt offering on the altar and place them beside the altar.   4] He shall then take off his vestments and put on other vestments, and carry the ashes outside the camp to a clean place.   5] The fire on the altar shall be kept burning, not to go out: every morning the priest shall feed wood to it, lay out the burnt offering on it, and turn into smoke the fat parts of the offerings of well-being.   6] A perpetual fire shall be kept burning on the altar, not to go out.

7] And this is the ritual of the meal offering: Aaron's sons shall present it before the LORD, in front of the altar.   8] A handful of the choice flour and oil of the meal offering shall be taken from it, with all the frankincense that is on the meal offering, and this token portion shall be turned into smoke on the altar as a pleasing odor to the LORD.   9] What is left of it shall be eaten by Aaron and his sons; it shall be eaten as unleavened cakes, in the sacred precinct; they shall eat it in the enclosure of the Tent of Meeting.   10] It shall not be baked with leaven; I have given it as their portion from My offerings by fire; it is most holy, like the sin offering and the penalty offering.   11] Only the males among Aaron's descendants may eat of it, as their

6:2] *The ritual.* Hebrew *Torah*. The older translations regularly translated this word as "law," which is often inaccurate and misleading. The present translation attempts to indicate some of the various shades of meaning; most often it renders *Torah* by "instruction."

The burnt offering itself shall remain. . . . The sacrifices were all performed during daylight hours. The altar portions of *shelamim*, *chatat*, and *asham*, consisting chiefly of fat, burned rapidly. It would take longer to consume the entire fleshy carcass of the *olah*, so these portions were left on the altar to burn through the night.

3] Each morning a priest was to clear away the debris and ashes from the altar hearth and to mend the fire.

In linen raiment. The usual four priestly vestments, tunic, sash, turban, and breeches, enumerated in Exodus 28:40-42 (*Sifra*).

6] *A perpetual fire . . . not to go out.* Such regulations were well known in Greek and Roman practice. A famous instance was the hearth in Rome tended by the vestal virgins.

אַהֲרֹן יֹאכְלֶנָּה חָק־עוֹלָם לְדֹרֹתֵיכֶם מֵאִשֵּׁי יְהֹוָה   טו וְכָל־מִנְחַת כֹּהֵן כָּלִיל תִּהְיֶה לֹא תֵאָכֵל: פ

כָּל־אֲשֶׁר־יִגַּע בָּהֶם יִקְדָּשׁ: פ   יו וַיְדַבֵּר יְהֹוָה אֶל־מֹשֶׁה לֵּאמֹר: דַּבֵּר אֶל־אַהֲרֹן וְאֶל־

יי וַיְדַבֵּר יְהֹוָה אֶל־מֹשֶׁה לֵּאמֹר: זֶה קָרְבַּן אַהֲרֹן וּבָנָיו   בָּנָיו לֵאמֹר זֹאת תּוֹרַת הַחַטָּאת בִּמְקוֹם אֲשֶׁר תִּשָּׁחֵט

אֲשֶׁר־יַקְרִיבוּ לַיהֹוָה בְּיוֹם הִמָּשַׁח אֹתוֹ עֲשִׂירִת הָאֵפָה   הָעֹלָה תִּשָּׁחֵט הַחַטָּאת לִפְנֵי יְהֹוָה קֹדֶשׁ קָדָשִׁים הִוא:

סֹלֶת מִנְחָה תָּמִיד מַחֲצִיתָהּ בַּבֹּקֶר וּמַחֲצִיתָהּ בָּעָרֶב: יט הַכֹּהֵן הַמְחַטֵּא אֹתָהּ יֹאכְלֶנָּה בְּמָקוֹם קָדֹשׁ תֵּאָכֵל

יד עַל־מַחֲבַת בַּשֶּׁמֶן תֵּעָשֶׂה מֻרְבֶּכֶת תְּבִיאֶנָּה תֻּפִינֵי מִנְחַת   בַּחֲצַר אֹהֶל מוֹעֵד: כ כֹּל אֲשֶׁר־יִגַּע בִּבְשָׂרָהּ יִקְדָּשׁ

טו פִּתִּים תַּקְרִיב רֵיחַ־נִיחֹחַ לַיהֹוָה: וְהַכֹּהֵן הַמָּשִׁיחַ תַּחְתָּיו   וַאֲשֶׁר יִזֶּה מִדָּמָהּ עַל־הַבֶּגֶד אֲשֶׁר יִזֶּה עָלֶיהָ תְּכַבֵּס

מִבָּנָיו יַעֲשֶׂה אֹתָהּ חָק־עוֹלָם לַיהֹוָה כָּלִיל תָּקְטָר: כא בְּמָקוֹם קָדֹשׁ: וּכְלִי־חֶרֶשׂ אֲשֶׁר תְּבֻשַּׁל־בּוֹ יִשָּׁבֵר וְאִם־

due for all time throughout the ages from the LORD's offerings by fire. Anything that touches these shall become holy.

12] The LORD spoke to Moses, saying: **13]** This is the offering that Aaron and his sons shall offer to the LORD on the occasion of his anointment: a tenth of an *ephah* of choice flour as a regular meal offering, half of it in the morning and half of it in the evening, **14]** shall be prepared with oil on a griddle. You shall bring it well soaked, and offer it as a meal offering of baked slices, of pleasing ordor to the LORD. **15]** And so shall the priest, anointed from among his sons to succeed him, prepare it; it is the LORD's—a law for all time—to be turned entirely into smoke. **16]** So, too, every meal offering of a priest shall be a whole offering: it shall not be eaten.

17] The LORD spoke to Moses, saying: **18]** Speak to Aaron and his sons thus: This is the ritual of the sin offering: the sin offering shall be slaughtered before the LORD, at the spot where the burnt offering is slaughtered: it is most holy. **19]** The priest who offers it as a sin offering shall eat of it; it shall be eaten in the sacred precinct, in the enclosure of the Tent of Meeting. **20]** Anything that touches its flesh shall become holy; and if any of its blood is spattered upon a garment, you shall wash the bespattered part in the sacred precinct. **21]** An earthen vessel in which it was boiled shall be broken; if it was boiled in a copper vessel, [the

---

11] *Anything that touches these shall become holy.* The translation follows the talmudic authorities and Rashi. The quality of "holiness" was thought to be transmitted by contact as an electrical charge passes from one conductor to another. Thus, if meat from a *shelamim* sacrifice came into contact with a *minchah*, it would become "most holy" and could then be eaten only by priests in the sanctuary [1].

13] *His anointment.* Or, "their anointment" (T.N.).

14] *Baked slices.* Meaning of Hebrew *tufiné* uncertain (T.N.).

18] *At the spot.* Cf. 1:11 (T.N.).

19] *The priest who offers it as a sin offering shall eat of it.* I.e., is obligated to eat of it, as the eating is

apparently part of the expiatory process. But the priests in general *may eat of it* (6:22). So Hoffmann.

20] *Anything that touches its flesh.* See commentary on 6:11.

And if any of its blood is spattered. . . . The blood had such a high degree of "holiness" that a garment on which a drop had fallen might not be taken out of the sanctuary until it had been washed.

21] *An earthen vessel . . . shall be broken.* The porous earthenware would absorb juices of the meat and, thus, part of a most holy sacrifice would be left over, violating the rule that it be eaten promptly [2]. The only remedy was to break the pottery vessel. This act, and the scouring of metal pots, had to be done inside the sacred precinct.

כב בִּכְלִי נְחֹשֶׁת בֻּשָּׁלָה וּמֹרַק וְשֻׁטַף בַּמָּיִם: כָּל־זָכָר   אֲשֶׁר יוּבָא מִדָּמָהּ אֶל־אֹהֶל מוֹעֵד לְכַפֵּר בַּקֹּדֶשׁ לֹא

כג בַּכֹּהֲנִים יֹאכַל אֹתָהּ קֹדֶשׁ קָדָשִׁים הִוא: וְכָל־חַטָּאת   תֵּאָכֵל בָּאֵשׁ תִּשָּׂרֵף: פ

vessel] shall be scoured and rinsed with water.   22] Only the males in the priestly line may eat of it: it is most holy.   23] But no sin offering may be eaten from which any blood is brought into the Tent of Meeting for expiation in the sanctuary; any such shall be consumed in fire.

23] This verse sums up chapter 4, verses 3 through 21.

GLEANINGS

Halachah

6:3] *He Shall Take Up the Ashes . . . and Place Them beside the Altar*

This removal of ashes from the altar was the first item in the daily schedule of the sanctuary [3]. According to tradition, it was a formality, only one scoopful of ashes being placed beside the altar [4]. Most of the ashes were heaped up in a pile in the center of the altar; when it grew too high to manage, one of the priests would carry the ashes out of the city [5]. This tradition is in apparent contradiction with verse 4 which seems to require the priest who removes the ashes from the altar to carry them promptly outside the camp.

19] *The Priest Who Offers It as a Sin Offering Shall Eat of It*

During the period of the Second Temple, the priests were organized in twenty-four divisions, called *mishmarot*. (I Chron. 24 ascribes this arrangement to David.) Each *mishmar* served for a week at a time, and each of its subdivisions, called a *bet av*, "father's house," served one day of that week. Against the plain sense of this and other verses, *Sifra* [6] assigns these perquisites to the entire *bet av* on duty the day the sacrifice is presented.

Haggadah

6:3] *The Priest Shall Dress in Linen Raiment*

He wore his sacred robes even to remove the ashes from the altar, to indicate his complete dedication. Not even this menial labor could impair his priestly dignity, since it was performed as a ministry to God.   BACHYA

6] *A Perpetual Fire Shall Be Kept Burning on the Altar, Not to Go Out*

This perpetual fire has served generations of

Jewish preachers as a symbol of unquenchable devotion. Marvels were related concerning it. It came forth from God's presence (9:24), and it burned continuously for 116 years, yet the thin copper sheathing of the altar never melted, and its wooden core was not charred [7]. It crouched on the altar in the shape of a lion, and it blazed as brilliantly as the sun [8].

Laws of Sacrifice—Zevach Shelamim

This far from orderly chapter is notable chiefly for basic material concerning the *shelamim* sacrifice (7:11–18, 28–34). It also contains directions, mostly repetitive, about the *asham* (7:1–10); the obligation of ritual purity for those who handle or consume sacrificial meats (7:19–21); renewed prohibition of blood and fat (7:22–26); combined with these items, more material on the perquisites of the priests; and the first references in Leviticus to the penalty of being "cut off from one's kin" (7:20 and elsewhere).

In chapter 3, directions for the *shelamim* were limited to the procedures at the altar. Here the sacrifice of well-being is treated in its essential character of a sacred meal. Two forms are distinguished: (1) the offering of thanksgiving (or acknowledgment), *todah*, and (2) the sacrifice brought in fulfillment of a vow, *neder*, or as a freewill offering, *nedavah*.

The *todah* differs from the other *shelamim* in two ways: (1) It is accompanied by an elaborate offering of bread and (2) it must be eaten on one day and the ensuing night while the other *shelamim* may be eaten over two days. No doubt other ancient peoples brought sacrifices in a spirit of gratitude, but a special category of thanksgiving offerings appears only in Israel. Great merit was attached to this sacrifice which seeks neither material nor spiritual benefit. A psalm which denies that God needs sacrifice still asserts, "He who sacrifices a thank offering honors Me" (Ps. 50:23).

Many ancient peoples were accustomed to make vows, especially in conditional form ("If I receive such-and-such a benefit, I will bring such-and-such an offering"). The vow might be the promise of a sacrifice; it is such vows that biblical authors urge us to pay promptly (Deut. 23:22ff.; Eccles. 5:3ff.) and which are mentioned in various psalms (22:26, 116:18, and others). But the Torah also deals at length with vows of abstinence in the Book of Numbers, chapters 6 and 30.

א וְזֹ֖את תּוֹרַ֣ת הָאָשָׁ֑ם קֹ֥דֶשׁ קָדָשִׁ֖ים הֽוּא: בִּמְק֗וֹם אֲשֶׁ֤ר
ב יִשְׁחֲטוּ֙ אֶת־הָ֣עֹלָ֔ה יִשְׁחֲט֖וּ אֶת־הָאָשָׁ֑ם וְאֶת־דָּמ֛וֹ יִזְרֹ֥ק
ג עַל־הַמִּזְבֵּ֖חַ סָבִֽיב: וְאֵ֛ת כָּל־חֶלְבּ֖וֹ יַקְרִ֣יב מִמֶּ֑נּוּ אֵ֚ת
ד הָ֣אַלְיָ֔ה וְאֶת־הַחֵ֖לֶב הַֽמְכַסֶּ֥ה אֶת־הַקֶּֽרֶב: וְאֵת֙ שְׁתֵּ֣י
הַכְּלָיֹ֔ת וְאֶת־הַחֵ֨לֶב֙ אֲשֶׁ֣ר עֲלֵיהֶ֔ן אֲשֶׁ֖ר עַל־הַכְּסָלִ֑ים
ה וְאֶת־הַיֹּתֶ֙רֶת֙ עַל־הַכָּבֵ֔ד עַל־הַכְּלָיֹ֖ת יְסִירֶֽנָּה: וְהִקְטִ֨יר
ו אֹתָ֤ם הַכֹּהֵן֙ הַמִּזְבֵּ֔חָה אִשֶּׁ֖ה לַיהֹוָ֑ה אָשָׁ֖ם הֽוּא: כָּל־
ז זָכָ֥ר בַּכֹּהֲנִ֖ים יֹאכְלֶ֑נּוּ בְּמָק֤וֹם קָדוֹשׁ֙ יֵֽאָכֵ֔ל קֹ֥דֶשׁ
קָדָשִׁ֖ים הֽוּא: כַּֽחַטָּאת֙ כָּֽאָשָׁ֔ם תּוֹרָ֥ה אַחַ֖ת לָהֶ֑ם
ח הַכֹּהֵ֛ן אֲשֶׁ֥ר יְכַפֶּר־בּ֖וֹ ל֣וֹ יִהְיֶֽה: וְהַ֨כֹּהֵ֔ן הַמַּקְרִ֖יב אֶת־
עֹלַ֣ת אִ֑ישׁ ע֤וֹר הָֽעֹלָה֙ אֲשֶׁ֣ר הִקְרִ֔יב לַכֹּהֵ֖ן ל֥וֹ יִהְיֶֽה:

ט וְכָל־מִנְחָ֗ה אֲשֶׁ֤ר תֵּֽאָפֶה֙ בַּתַּנּ֔וּר וְכָל־נַעֲשָׂ֥ה בַמַּרְחֶ֖שֶׁת
י וְעַל־מַֽחֲבַ֑ת לַכֹּהֵ֧ן הַמַּקְרִ֛יב אֹתָ֖הּ ל֥וֹ תִֽהְיֶֽה: וְכָל־
מִנְחָ֥ה בְלוּלָֽה־בַשֶּׁ֖מֶן וַֽחֲרֵבָ֑ה לְכָל־בְּנֵ֧י אַֽהֲרֹ֛ן תִּֽהְיֶ֖ה
אִ֥ישׁ כְּאָחִֽיו: פ

יא וְזֹ֥את תּוֹרַ֖ת זֶ֣בַח הַשְּׁלָמִ֑ים אֲשֶׁ֥ר יַקְרִ֖יב לַֽיהֹוָֽה: אִ֣ם
יב עַל־תּוֹדָה֘ יַקְרִיבֶנּוּ֒ וְהִקְרִ֣יב ׀ עַל־זֶ֣בַח הַתּוֹדָ֗ה חַלּ֤וֹת
מַצּוֹת֙ בְּלוּלֹ֣ת בַּשֶּׁ֔מֶן וּרְקִיקֵ֥י מַצּ֖וֹת מְשֻׁחִ֣ים בַּשָּׁ֑מֶן
יג וְסֹ֣לֶת מֻרְבֶּ֔כֶת חַלֹּ֖ת בְּלוּלֹ֥ת בַּשָּֽׁמֶן: עַל־חַלֹּת֙ לֶ֣חֶם
חָמֵ֔ץ יַקְרִ֖יב קָרְבָּנ֑וֹ עַל־זֶ֖בַח תּוֹדַ֥ת שְׁלָמָֽיו: וְהִקְרִ֨יב
יד מִמֶּ֤נּוּ אֶחָד֙ מִכָּל־קָרְבָּ֔ן תְּרוּמָ֖ה לַֽיהֹוָ֑ה לַכֹּהֵ֗ן הַזֹּרֵ֛ק
טו אֶת־דַּ֥ם הַשְּׁלָמִ֖ים ל֥וֹ יִהְיֶֽה: וּבְשַׂ֗ר זֶ֚בַח תּוֹדַ֣ת שְׁלָמָ֔יו

1] This is the ritual of the guilt offering: it is most holy. **2]** The guilt offering shall be slaughtered at the spot where the burnt offering is slaughtered, and the blood shall be dashed on all sides of the altar. **3]** All its fat shall be offered: the broad tail; the fat that covers the entrails; **4]** the two kidneys and the fat that is on them at the loins; and the protuberance on the liver, which shall be removed with the kidneys. **5]** The priest shall turn them into smoke on the altar as an offering by fire to the LORD; it is a guilt offering. **6]** Only the males in the priestly line may eat of it; it shall be eaten in the sacred precinct: it is most holy.

7] The guilt offering is like the sin offering. The same rule applies to both: it shall belong to the priest who makes expiation thereby. **8]** So, too, the priest who offers a man's burnt offering shall keep the skin of the burnt offering that he offered. **9]** Further, any meal offering that is baked in an oven, and any that is prepared in a pan or on a griddle, shall belong to the priest who offers it. **10]** But every other meal offering, with oil mixed in or dry, shall go to the sons of Aaron all alike.

11] This is the ritual of the sacrifice of well-being that one may offer to the LORD:

12] If he offers it for thanksgiving, he shall offer together with the sacrifice of thanksgiving unleavened cakes with oil mixed in, unleavened wafers spread with oil, and cakes of choice flour with oil mixed in, well soaked. **13]** This offering with cakes of leavened bread added, he shall offer along with his thanksgiving sacrifice of well-being. **14]** Out of this he shall offer one of each kind as a gift to the LORD; it shall go to the priest who dashes the blood of the offering of well-being. **15]** And the flesh of his thanksgiving sacrifice of well-being shall be

---

7:1] *Most holy.* Therefore the rules in verse 6 apply to it.

7] *It shall belong.* I.e., the meat and the hide.

12] *If he offers it for thanksgiving....* Three kinds of unleavened bread, plus an exceptional offering of leavened bread, accompanied the *todah.* This does not contradict the prohibition of leaven in chapter 2, verse 11, since the bread was not placed on the altar.

14] *Kind.* Literally, "offering" (T.N.).

Gift. Hebrew *terumah,* "something lifted up." *Terumah* as a technical term is rendered "heave offering" in verse 34 and frequently.

עֲוֹנָה תִּשָּׂא: וְהַבָּשָׂר אֲשֶׁר־יִגַּע בְּכָל־טָמֵא לֹא יֵאָכֵל
בָּאֵשׁ יִשָּׂרֵף וְהַבָּשָׂר כָּל־טָהוֹר יֹאכַל בָּשָׂר: וְהַנֶּפֶשׁ
אֲשֶׁר־תֹּאכַל בָּשָׂר מִזֶּבַח הַשְּׁלָמִים אֲשֶׁר לַיהוָה
וְטֻמְאָתוֹ עָלָיו וְנִכְרְתָה הַנֶּפֶשׁ הַהִוא מֵעַמֶּיהָ: וְנֶפֶשׁ
כִּי־תִגַּע בְּכָל־טָמֵא בְּטֻמְאַת אָדָם אוֹ בִּבְהֵמָה
טְמֵאָה אוֹ בְּכָל־שֶׁקֶץ טָמֵא וְאָכַל מִבְּשַׂר־זֶבַח

בְּיוֹם קָרְבָּנוֹ יֵאָכֵל לֹא־יַנִּיחַ מִמֶּנּוּ עַד־בֹּקֶר: וְאִם־
נֶדֶר אוֹ נְדָבָה זֶבַח קָרְבָּנוֹ בְּיוֹם הַקְרִיבוֹ אֶת־זִבְחוֹ
יֵאָכֵל וּמִמָּחֳרָת וְהַנּוֹתָר מִמֶּנּוּ יֵאָכֵל: וְהַנּוֹתָר מִבְּשַׂר
הַזֶּבַח בַּיּוֹם הַשְּׁלִישִׁי בָּאֵשׁ יִשָּׂרֵף: וְאִם הֵאָכֹל יֵאָכֵל
מִבְּשַׂר־זֶבַח שְׁלָמָיו בַּיּוֹם הַשְּׁלִישִׁי לֹא יֵרָצֶה הַמַּקְרִיב
אֹתוֹ לֹא יֵחָשֵׁב לוֹ פִּגּוּל יִהְיֶה וְהַנֶּפֶשׁ הָאֹכֶלֶת מִמֶּנּוּ

eaten on the day that it is offered; none of it shall be set aside until morning.
16] If, however, the sacrifice he offers is a votive or a freewill offering, it shall be eaten on the day that he offers his sacrifice, and what is left of it shall be eaten on the morrow. **17]** What is then left of the flesh of the sacrifice shall be consumed in fire on the third day. **18]** If any of the flesh of his sacrifice of well-being is eaten on the third day, it shall not be acceptable; it shall not count for him who offered it. It is an offensive thing, and the person who eats of it shall bear his guilt.

19] Flesh that touches anything unclean shall not be eaten; it shall be consumed in fire. As for other flesh, only he who is clean may eat such flesh. **20]** But the person who, in a state of uncleanness, eats flesh from the LORD's sacrifices of well-being, that person shall be cut off from his kin. **21]** When a person touches anything unclean, be it human uncleanness or an unclean animal or any unclean creature, and eats flesh from the LORD's sacrifices of well-being, that person shall be cut off from his kin.

15] *Shall be eaten on the day that it is offered.* Whereas other *shelamim* could still be eaten on the second day (7:16f.).

16] *Votive.* Brought for a vow, whether conditional or outright. The freewill offering was presumably brought without prior commitment (but see Gleanings).

17] *Shall be consumed in fire on the third day.* This rendering (instead of "What is left . . . on the third day shall be consumed in fire") follows Nachmanides who explains: The meat may be eaten during two days and the night between them. On the second night it may not be eaten, but disposal by fire does not take place till next morning.

18] *It shall not count.* I.e., improper treatment of the sacrificial meat nullifies the sacrifice. Presumably, if the offering had been brought to fulfill a vow, the worshiper would have to bring a substitute.

An offensive thing. Hebrew *pigul.* The plain sense is that eating the meat after the second day renders it *pigul* and thereby invalidates the entire sacrifice. The halachah departs completely from this plain sense (see Gleanings).

Shall bear his guilt. The expression is clarified in verses 20 and 21 as well as in chapter 19, verse 8: the offender will be "cut off from his kin."

19–21] Like ritual holiness (6:11), ritual uncleanness is transmitted by physical contact [1]. Sacred food which is accidentally defiled may not be eaten; it must be burned without ceremony. A ritually unclean person who eats consecrated food is guilty of sacrilege and subject to severe penalties. The rules stated here for *shelamim* apply to all types of consecrated food.

20] *Shall be cut off from his kin.* This expression, with variations, is found also in earlier books of the Torah, always in priestly writings [2]. Some scholars have explained the penalty as ostracism from the community, others as capital punishment [3]. But several related passages make clear that it is God who cuts off the offender from his kin (Lev. 17:10, 20:3–6). The term then refers to divine rather than human punishment, most probably premature death [4].

21] *Unclean creature.* Hebrew *sheketz*, literally, "abomination"; several manuscripts and ancient versions read *sheretz*, "swarming things" (T.N.).

כב וַיְדַבֵּר יְהוָֹה אֶל־מֹשֶׁה לֵּאמֹר: דַּבֵּר אֶל־בְּנֵי יִשְׂרָאֵל
לֵאמֹר הַמַּקְרִיב אֶת־זֶבַח שְׁלָמָיו לַיהוָֹה יָבִיא אֶת־
ל קָרְבָּנוֹ לַיהוָֹה מִזֶּבַח שְׁלָמָיו: יָדָיו תְּבִיאֶינָה אֵת אִשֵּׁי
יְהוָֹה אֶת־הַחֵלֶב עַל־הֶחָזֶה יְבִיאֶנּוּ אֵת הֶחָזֶה לְהָנִיף
לא אֹתוֹ תְּנוּפָה לִפְנֵי יְהוָֹה: וְהִקְטִיר הַכֹּהֵן אֶת־הַחֵלֶב
לב הַמִּזְבֵּחָה וְהָיָה הֶחָזֶה לְאַהֲרֹן וּלְבָנָיו: וְאֵת שׁוֹק הַיָּמִין
לג תִּתְּנוּ תְרוּמָה לַכֹּהֵן מִזִּבְחֵי שַׁלְמֵיכֶם: הַמַּקְרִיב אֶת־
דַּם הַשְּׁלָמִים וְאֶת־הַחֵלֶב מִבְּנֵי אַהֲרֹן לוֹ תִהְיֶה שׁוֹק
לד הַיָּמִין לְמָנָה: כִּי אֶת־חֲזֵה הַתְּנוּפָה וְאֵת שׁוֹק

הַשְּׁלָמִים אֲשֶׁר לַיהוָֹה וְנִכְרְתָה הַנֶּפֶשׁ הַהִוא מֵעַמֶּיהָ:
כב וַיְדַבֵּר יְהוָֹה אֶל־מֹשֶׁה לֵּאמֹר: דַּבֵּר אֶל־בְּנֵי יִשְׂרָאֵל
כג לֵאמֹר כָּל־חֵלֶב שׁוֹר וְכֶשֶׂב וָעֵז לֹא תֹאכֵלוּ: וְחֵלֶב
נְבֵלָה וְחֵלֶב טְרֵפָה יֵעָשֶׂה לְכָל־מְלָאכָה וְאָכֹל לֹא
כה תֹאכְלֻהוּ: כִּי כָּל־אֹכֵל חֵלֶב מִן־הַבְּהֵמָה אֲשֶׁר יַקְרִיב
מִמֶּנָּה אִשֶּׁה לַיהוָֹה וְנִכְרְתָה הַנֶּפֶשׁ הָאֹכֶלֶת מֵעַמֶּיהָ:
כו וְכָל־דָּם לֹא תֹאכְלוּ בְּכֹל מוֹשְׁבֹתֵיכֶם לָעוֹף
כז וְלַבְּהֵמָה: כָּל־נֶפֶשׁ אֲשֶׁר־תֹּאכַל כָּל־דָּם וְנִכְרְתָה
הַנֶּפֶשׁ הַהִוא מֵעַמֶּיהָ: פ

22] And the LORD spoke to Moses, saying: **23]** Speak to the Israelite people thus: You shall eat no fat of ox or sheep or goat. **24]** Fat from animals that died or were torn by beasts may be put to any use, but you must not eat it. **25]** If anyone eats the fat of animals from which offerings by fire may be made to the LORD, the person who eats it shall be cut off from his kin. **26]** And you must not consume any blood, either of bird or of animal, in any of your settlements. **27]** Anyone who eats blood shall be cut off from his kin.

28] And the LORD spoke to Moses, saying: **29]** Speak to the Israelite people thus: The offering to the LORD from a sacrifice of well-being must be presented by him who offers his sacrifice of well-being to the LORD: **30]** his own hands shall present the LORD's offerings by fire. He shall present the fat with the breast, the breast to be waved as a wave offering before the LORD; **31]** the priest shall turn the fat into smoke on the altar, and the breast shall go to Aaron and his sons. **32]** And the right thigh from your sacrifices of well-being you shall present to the priest as a gift; **33]** he from among Aaron's sons who offers the blood and the fat of the offering of well-being shall get the right thigh as his portion. **34]** For I have taken

23] *Fat*. I.e., hard, coarse fat (suet). Cf. 3:3-5 (T.N.). On the prohibition of fat, see commentary on 3:17. The present paragraph exempts the fat of game animals from the rule.

24] *Animals that died*. Hebrew *nevelah*, "carcass," i.e., that died a natural death. (Cf. Deut. 14:21.)

Or were torn by beasts. Hebrew *terefah*. In current usage, any nonkosher food is referred to as *terefah* (see introduction to Lev. 11:1-23, "1. A Few Definitions"; cf. Exod. 22:30).

May be put to any use. E.g., to lubricate hides.

26-27] On the prohibition of blood, see introduction to Lev. 17.

28-34] The breast and thigh of each *shelamim* sacrifice are to be given to the priest, the first as a *tenufah*, the second as a *terumah*. The old Aramaic translation (Targum) renders these terms as "raising up" and

"separation"—presumably meaning that these portions are to be lifted or removed as a special gift. The Greek renders similarly. But the rabbinic sources understood *tenufah* as "waving"; they ruled that the worshiper was to stand before the altar, holding the portions in his hands, and the priest was to move the hands of the sacrificer back and forth horizontally, and then up and down. Hence, the rendering "wave offering" found in most modern versions. But it can hardly be correct. It creates difficulties in chapter 14, verses 12 and 24, where a live lamb is the *tenufah*, and still more in Numbers, chapter 8, verse 11, where the entire tribe of Levi is to be "waved." The root of *tenufah* probably means "to be high"; the term designates either an offering that was literally lifted before the altar—a procedure known from Egyptian religion [5]—or, in a more figurative sense, a special and outstanding gift [6].

הַתְּרוּמָה לָקַחְתִּי מֵאֵת בְּנֵי־יִשְׂרָאֵל מִזִּבְחֵי שַׁלְמֵיהֶם
וָאֶתֵּן אֹתָם לְאַהֲרֹן הַכֹּהֵן וּלְבָנָיו לְחָק־עוֹלָם מֵאֵת
בְּנֵי יִשְׂרָאֵל: ‏לה זֹאת מִשְׁחַת אַהֲרֹן וּמִשְׁחַת בָּנָיו מֵאִשֵּׁי
יְהוָה בְּיוֹם הִקְרִיב אֹתָם לְכַהֵן לַיהוָה: ‏לו אֲשֶׁר צִוָּה
יְהוָה לָתֵת לָהֶם בְּיוֹם מָשְׁחוֹ אֹתָם מֵאֵת בְּנֵי יִשְׂרָאֵל

‏לו חֻקַּת עוֹלָם לְדֹרֹתָם: ‏לז זֹאת הַתּוֹרָה לָעֹלָה לַמִּנְחָה
וְלַחַטָּאת וְלָאָשָׁם וְלַמִּלּוּאִים וּלְזֶבַח הַשְּׁלָמִים: ‏לח אֲשֶׁר
צִוָּה יְהוָה אֶת־מֹשֶׁה בְּהַר סִינָי בְּיוֹם צַוֹּתוֹ אֶת־בְּנֵי
יִשְׂרָאֵל לְהַקְרִיב אֶת־קָרְבְּנֵיהֶם לַיהוָה בְּמִדְבַּר
סִינָי: פ

‏* לו סבירין כאשר.　　　　　　　　　　　　　　　　‏* לח סבירין כאשר.

the breast of wave offering and the thigh of heave offering from the Israelites, from their sacrifices of well-being, and given them to Aaron the priest and to his sons as their due from the Israelites for all time.

35] Those shall be the perquisites of Aaron and the perquisites of his sons from the LORD's offerings by fire, once they have been inducted to serve the LORD as priests; 36] these the LORD commanded to be given them, once they had been anointed, as a due from the Israelites for all time throughout the ages.

37] These are the rituals of the burnt offering, the meal offering, the sin offering, the guilt offering, the offering of ordination, and the sacrifice of well-being, 38] with which the LORD charged Moses on Mount Sinai, when He commanded that the Israelites present their offerings to the LORD, in the wilderness of Sinai.

There seems to be little, if any, difference in meaning between *tenufah* and *terumah*. The latter also comes from a root meaning "to be high." It is most often rendered "heave offering," sometimes "gift(s)" (e.g., Exod. 25:2). For *terumah* as the technical name for a tax on produce, see Numbers, chapter 18, verses 8ff.

35] *Those shall be the perquisites.* Presumably the breast and thigh. But the reference could be to all the portions assigned to the priests throughout these

chapters which formally conclude in the ensuing verses.

Perquisites. Literally, "anointment," i.e., accruing from anointment (T.N.).

Inducted. Literally, "brought forward" (T.N.).

37] *The offering of ordination.* This was actually explained in Exodus, chapter 29. But Nachmanides notes that the ordination ceremonies included all the types of sacrifices expounded in Leviticus, chapters 1 through 7.

GLEANINGS

Halachah

7:15] *The Flesh of His Thanksgiving Sacrifice ... Shall Be Eaten on the Day That It Is Offered*

Legally, it could be eaten till dawn of the second day; but the Rabbis forbid eating it after midnight, "to keep man far from sin," i.e., to allow ample margin for error [7]. This principle is also expressed in the aphorism, "Make a fence about the Torah" [8]. In modern terms: Drive ten miles an hour less than the legal limit, to make sure that you don't exceed it.

16] *A Votive or a Freewill Offering*

According to the halachah, the distinction is one of form. "I obligate myself to bring a sacrifice of well-being" is a *neder*, vow. "This sheep shall be a sacrifice of well-being" is a *nedavah*, freewill offering. In the second case, the worshiper was exempt from further obligation if the animal died, was lost, or proved defective. In the case of a vow, he would have to provide a substitute animal [9].

18] *If Any of the Flesh ... Is Eaten on the Third Day ... It Is an Offensive Thing [Pigul]*

The Targums render the verse literally; but other rabbinic interpreters [10] depart from the plain sense (as Rashbam states flatly) and explain the law of *pigul* as follows: If the officiating priest, while slaughtering the animal and dashing its blood on the altar, had *the intention* in mind that the flesh should be eaten on the third day, this wrong intention rendered the sacrifice *pigul* from the start.

It is improbable that such a rule obtained during the time of the Second Temple. Most likely it was a refinement of scholars active after 70 C.E. Why did they so radically reinterpret a plain statement? One factor, perhaps, was the question: If a sacrifice was properly performed from the start, how could it be invalidated retroactively? (This argument is raised by Rabbi Akiba in *Sifra*, though he did not consider it conclusive.) It would seem sufficient if the person who ate the food illegally were punished—by being obliged to bring a *chatat* if the act was inadvertent, by being "cut off" if it was deliberate.

A second factor was the language of chapter 19, verse 5, cited by *Sifra* on 7:17, "When you sacrifice an offering of well-being to the LORD, sacrifice it so that it may be accepted in your behalf," which was taken to mean: It must be performed with proper intent from the outset or it will not be accepted. All this is in accord with the great emphasis on intention throughout the halachah [11].

20] *Shall Be Cut Off from His Kin*

This penalty is called in rabbinic texts *karet*, "cutting off," and is the subject of a treatise of the Mishnah and Talmud entitled *Keritot*. There is general agreement that *karet* is a divinely inflicted punishment, but its exact character was debated. The view given in the commentary—that it means premature death—was held by many scholars [12]; others thought it meant that the offender would die childless [13]. Nachmanides [14] distinguished between various degrees of *karet*, depending on the crime and the criminal; the most severe form included annihilation in the world beyond the grave.

Haggadah

7:12] *If He Offers It for Thanksgiving*

"Though all sacrifices may be discontinued in the future (for, in the messianic age, men will be sinless), the offering of thanksgiving will never cease. Though all prayers may be discontinued, the prayer of thanksgiving will never cease" [15].

PART II

The Dedication of the Tabernacle
and
The Ordination of the Priests

The Divine Presence in the Sanctuary

At this point, the exposition of the laws is interrupted by a narrative section that tells of the dedication of the Tabernacle and the ordination of Aaron and his sons to the priesthood.

Directions for these rites had been given in Exodus, chapter 29, verses 1 through 37. Now we are told that they were performed by Moses acting temporarily as High Priest. After these ceremonies were conducted for seven days, Aaron and his sons assumed their duties. Their service was crowned by the visible appearance of the Divine Presence, and a miraculous flame consumed the sacrifices on the altar.

This joyous occasion was suddenly disrupted by tragedy. Two of Aaron's sons committed a ceremonial offense; and again a miraculous flame appeared, this time to take the lives of the offenders. Joined to the account of the subsequent mourning are three brief legal sections.

The general intent of these chapters is plain. They emphasize the grandeur and importance of cult and priesthood. Through the sanctuary and the sacrifices, God's nearness to His people is established and maintained. Similarly, at the dedication of Solomon's Temple, the Presence of the LORD is said to have filled the house (I Kings 3:10f.); and one report states that heavenly fire descended and consumed the sacrifices (II Chron. 7:1ff.). The terrible fate of Nadab and Abihu, Aaron's two oldest sons, underscored the need to perform the rituals strictly according to rule and stressed the accountability of the priests for the faithful discharge of their duties. The exact nature of the young men's offense, however, is obscure [1].

The chronology of the events is uncertain. Exodus, chapter 40, verses 2ff., states that Moses had the Tabernacle set up on the first day of the first month in the second year after the Exodus; and, after he had performed the various sacrifices, the Presence of the Lord became manifest. According to Leviticus, chapters 8 and 9, Moses conducted the ceremonies for seven days, but the Divine Presence did not appear until Aaron had officiated on the eighth day—and no definite dates are given. Numbers, chapter 7, moreover, reports that the chieftains of the tribes brought elaborate gifts, including sacrifices, beginning on the day when Moses set up the Tabernacle and continuing for twelve consecutive days. All these passages are from P. Evidently the priests had several traditions

on this subject which did not wholly agree. The talmudic authorities felt obligated to harmonize the apparent discrepancies. They explained that the dedication program began on the twenty-third day of the twelfth month. Moses officiated on the last seven days of that month; the eighth day of Leviticus 9:1 was the first day of the first month of Exodus 40:2 when Aaron assumed the priestly duties and the Presence of the Lord appeared. The same day, when "Moses had finished setting up the Tabernacle" (Num. 7:1)—i.e., when he had discharged his responsibilities and Aaron had taken over—the first of the tribal leaders presented his offerings (Num. 7:12) [2].

1. The Prohibition of Intoxicants

Chapter 10, verses 8–10 forbid the priests to drink any intoxicant before performing a sacred function. It is doubtful whether there is any connection between this paragraph and its context; but understandably the Rabbis tried to find one, and some of them inferred that Nadab and Abihu had been drinking before they offered the incense [3].

The restriction applied only to times when the priests were on duty. Otherwise, like other Israelites, they were free to make use of wine, which was produced and enjoyed throughout the ancient Near East.

The Bible does speak of individuals called nazirites (nezirim, "dedicated ones") who were required to abstain from wine (indeed from anything produced by the grape vine) and to leave their hair uncut. Some persons were lifelong nazirites (Samson, Judg. 13; Samuel, I Sam. 1:1; cf. Amos 2:11f.); they were apparently dedicated by their parents to this special way of life. But the priestly legislation provides that a person of either sex may make a vow to become a nazirite for a specified length of time [4]. At the end of the period, the nazirite cut his hair and

the locks were burned together with the sacrifices that he was required to bring. Thereupon he returned to his secular status (Num. 6). Because of the sacrificial element in this procedure, nazirite vows virtually ceased after the fall of the Second Temple [5].

Aside from this special case, the drinking of wine was considered normal and proper. Wine "cheers the hearts of men" (Ps. 104:15; cf. Judg. 9:13). The Bible indeed contains several warnings against drunkenness; but the tone of these passages suggests that excessive drinking was not considered sinful but rather ugly and degrading, a kind of foolish behavior that may easily lead to impropriety and even immorality (Gen. 9:20 ff.; Prov. 23:29 ff. and 31:4 ff.) The prophets who denounce drunken rulers regard their drinking as the evidence, rather than the cause, of their depravity (Isa. 5:11 ff.; Amos 2:8). The midrashim provide sermons to our Leviticus passage expounding the evils of drunkenness in general, without reference to priests; their somewhat jocular tone suggests that the Rabbis were not too seriously concerned about the problem.

Judaism has regularly employed wine in religious ceremonies from the sacrificial libations of the Bible to the traditional rites of Kiddush and Havdalah and the marriage ceremony. Few Jews are total abstainers on principle; yet the incidence of alcoholism among Jews is low, and there is a widespread belief (shared by Jews and non-Jews) that heavy drinking and intoxication are less common among Jews than in the general population. The most intensive study of the subject thus far published suggests that the drinking habits of Jews, in the United States, at least, are more like those of their neighbors than had been supposed. This study does indicate that those Jews who regularly observe the traditional home ceremonials seldom drink to excess, even though they drink frequently; whereas there is a significant in-

crease of intoxication among those Jews who have given up the traditional customs and much of the value system associated with them [6].

2. *Priestly Perquisites*

Chapter 10 verses 12–15 repeat the law (already explained in 6:7–11), concerning the sanctity of the *minchah*, cereal offering, and contrast it with the lesser sanctity of the portions assigned to the priests from sacrifices of well-being, *shelamim*. The latter, it is now made plain, may be eaten in any clean place (according to the halachah of later times, anywhere in Jerusalem), and the women of priestly families may partake of them. This section is connected to the narrative by verse 12 which was perhaps added to supply such a connection.

For an additional discussion of the prohibition of intoxicants, see commentary on Num. 6.

(A new weekly portion, *Shemini*, begins with 9:1).

עָלָיו אֶת־הַחֹשֶׁן וַיִּתֵּן אֶל־הַחֹשֶׁן אֶת־הָאוּרִים וְאֶת־
ט הַתֻּמִּים: וַיָּשֶׂם אֶת־הַמִּצְנֶפֶת עַל־רֹאשׁוֹ וַיָּשֶׂם עַל־
הַמִּצְנֶפֶת אֶל־מוּל פָּנָיו אֵת צִיץ הַזָּהָב נֵזֶר הַקֹּדֶשׁ
י כַּאֲשֶׁר צִוָּה יְהוָה אֶת־מֹשֶׁה: וַיִּקַּח מֹשֶׁה אֶת־שֶׁמֶן
הַמִּשְׁחָה וַיִּמְשַׁח אֶת־הַמִּשְׁכָּן וְאֶת־כָּל־אֲשֶׁר־בּוֹ וַיְקַדֵּשׁ
יא אֹתָם: וַיַּז מִמֶּנּוּ עַל־הַמִּזְבֵּחַ שֶׁבַע פְּעָמִים וַיִּמְשַׁח אֶת־
הַמִּזְבֵּחַ וְאֶת־כָּל־כֵּלָיו וְאֶת־הַכִּיֹּר וְאֶת־כַּנּוֹ לְקַדְּשָׁם:
יב וַיִּצֹק מִשֶּׁמֶן הַמִּשְׁחָה עַל רֹאשׁ אַהֲרֹן וַיִּמְשַׁח אֹתוֹ
לְקַדְּשׁוֹ: וַיַּקְרֵב מֹשֶׁה אֶת־בְּנֵי אַהֲרֹן וַיַּלְבִּשֵׁם כֻּתֳּנֹת
יג וַיַּחְגֹּר אֹתָם אַבְנֵט וַיַּחֲבֹשׁ לָהֶם מִגְבָּעוֹת כַּאֲשֶׁר צִוָּה

א וַיְדַבֵּר יְהוָה אֶל־מֹשֶׁה לֵּאמֹר: קַח אֶת־אַהֲרֹן וְאֶת־
בָּנָיו אִתּוֹ וְאֵת הַבְּגָדִים וְאֵת שֶׁמֶן הַמִּשְׁחָה וְאֵת פַּר
ג הַחַטָּאת וְאֵת שְׁנֵי הָאֵילִים וְאֵת סַל הַמַּצּוֹת: וְאֵת
ד כָּל־הָעֵדָה הַקְהֵל אֶל־פֶּתַח אֹהֶל מוֹעֵד: וַיַּעַשׂ מֹשֶׁה
כַּאֲשֶׁר צִוָּה יְהוָה אֹתוֹ וַתִּקָּהֵל הָעֵדָה אֶל־פֶּתַח אֹהֶל
ה מוֹעֵד: וַיֹּאמֶר מֹשֶׁה אֶל־הָעֵדָה זֶה הַדָּבָר אֲשֶׁר־צִוָּה
ו יְהוָה לַעֲשׂוֹת: וַיַּקְרֵב מֹשֶׁה אֶת־אַהֲרֹן וְאֶת־בָּנָיו
ז וַיִּרְחַץ אֹתָם בַּמָּיִם: וַיִּתֵּן עָלָיו אֶת־הַכֻּתֹּנֶת וַיַּחְגֹּר
אֹתוֹ בָּאַבְנֵט וַיַּלְבֵּשׁ אֹתוֹ אֶת־הַמְּעִיל וַיִּתֵּן עָלָיו אֶת־
ח הָאֵפֹד וַיַּחְגֹּר אֹתוֹ בְּחֵשֶׁב הָאֵפֹד וַיֶּאְפֹּד לוֹ בּוֹ: וַיָּשֶׂם

1] The LORD spoke to Moses, saying: 2] Take Aaron and his sons with him, the vestments, the anointing oil, the bull of sin offering, the two rams, and the basket of unleavened bread; 3] and assemble the whole community at the entrance of the Tent of Meeting. 4] Moses did as the LORD commanded him. And when the community was assembled at the entrance of the Tent of Meeting, 5] Moses said to the community, "This is what the LORD has commanded to be done."

6] Then Moses brought Aaron and his sons forward and washed them with water. 7] He put the tunic on him, girded him with the sash, clothed him with the robe, and put the *ephod* on him, girding him with the decorated band with which he tied it to him. 8] He put the breastpiece on him, and put into the breastpiece the Urim and Thummim. 9] And he set the headdress on his head; and on the headdress, in front, he put the gold frontlet, the holy diadem—as the LORD had commanded Moses.

10] Moses took the anointing oil and anointed the Tabernacle and all that was in it, thus consecrating them. 11] He sprinkled some of it on the altar seven times, anointing the altar, all its utensils, and the laver with its stand, to consecrate them. 12] He poured some of the anointing oil upon Aaron's head and anointed him, to consecrate him. 13] Moses then brought Aaron's sons forward, clothed them in tunics, girded them with sashes, and wound turbans upon them, as the LORD had commanded Moses.

8:3] *Assemble the whole community.* To give maximum publicity and honor to the new priesthood. Rashi, following the Midrash [7], remarks that the entire community could be accommodated at the entrance of the Tent only by a miracle. More soberly, Ibn Ezra explains that the "whole community" was represented by its leaders. See commentary on 4:13.

8] *The Urim and Thummim.* Meaning of these two words uncertain. They designate a kind of oracle. Cf. Num. 27:21 (T.N. at Exod. 28:30).

10] *Moses . . . anointed the Tabernacle. . . .* As commanded in Exod. 29:36, 30:26ff., 40:9f.

13] *Aaron's sons.* Nothing is said here about anointing the sons, though this is mentioned in Exodus 28:41; Leviticus 7:36, 10:7; and elsewhere. Perhaps the sprinkling with oil (8:30) constituted the anointment of the priests, while the High Priest was distinguished by having oil poured on his head (8:12). Otherwise, we must again assume variant traditions. Subsequent to this first ordination, there is no mention of anointment of ordinary priests, as distinguished from the High Priest [8].

אֶת אֵיל הָעֹלָה וַיִּסְמְכוּ אַהֲרֹן וּבָנָיו אֶת־יְדֵיהֶם עַל־   יד יְהֹוָה אֶת־מֹשֶׁה: וַיַּגֵּשׁ אֵת פַּר הַחַטָּאת וַיִּסְמֹךְ אַהֲרֹן

יט רֹאשׁ הָאָיִל: וַיִּשְׁחָט וַיִּזְרֹק מֹשֶׁה אֶת־הַדָּם עַל־הַמִּזְבֵּחַ   טו וּבָנָיו אֶת־יְדֵיהֶם עַל־רֹאשׁ פַּר הַחַטָּאת: וַיִּשְׁחָט וַיִּקַּח

כ סָבִיב: וְאֶת־הָאַיִל נִתַּח לִנְתָחָיו וַיַּקְטֵר מֹשֶׁה אֶת־   מֹשֶׁה אֶת־הַדָּם וַיִּתֵּן עַל־קַרְנוֹת הַמִּזְבֵּחַ סָבִיב

הָרֹאשׁ וְאֶת־הַנְּתָחִים וְאֶת־הַפָּדֶר: וְאֶת־הַקֶּרֶב וְאֶת־   בְּאֶצְבָּעוֹ וַיְחַטֵּא אֶת־הַמִּזְבֵּחַ וְאֶת־הַדָּם יָצַק אֶל־

כא הַכְּרָעַיִם רָחַץ בַּמַּיִם וַיַּקְטֵר מֹשֶׁה אֶת־כָּל־הָאַיִל   טז יְסוֹד הַמִּזְבֵּחַ וַיְקַדְּשֵׁהוּ לְכַפֵּר עָלָיו: וַיִּקַּח אֶת־כָּל־

הַמִּזְבֵּחָה עֹלָה הוּא לְרֵיחַ־נִיחֹחַ אִשֶּׁה הוּא לַיהֹוָה   הַחֵלֶב אֲשֶׁר עַל־הַקֶּרֶב וְאֵת יֹתֶרֶת הַכָּבֵד וְאֶת־שְׁתֵּי

כב כַּאֲשֶׁר צִוָּה יְהֹוָה אֶת־מֹשֶׁה: וַיַּקְרֵב אֶת־הָאַיִל הַשֵּׁנִי   יז הַכְּלָיֹת וְאֶת־חֶלְבְּהֶן וַיַּקְטֵר מֹשֶׁה הַמִּזְבֵּחָה: וְאֶת־

אֵיל הַמִּלֻּאִים וַיִּסְמְכוּ אַהֲרֹן וּבָנָיו אֶת־יְדֵיהֶם עַל־   הַפָּר וְאֶת־עֹרוֹ וְאֶת־בְּשָׂרוֹ וְאֶת־פִּרְשׁוֹ שָׂרַף בָּאֵשׁ

כג רֹאשׁ הָאָיִל: וַיִּשְׁחָט וַיִּקַּח מֹשֶׁה מִדָּמוֹ וַיִּתֵּן עַל־תְּנוּךְ   מִחוּץ לַמַּחֲנֶה כַּאֲשֶׁר צִוָּה יְהֹוָה אֶת־מֹשֶׁה: וַיַּקְרֵב

14] *He led forward the bull of sin offering.* Aaron and his sons laid their hands upon the head of the bull of sin offering, **15]** and it was slaughtered. Moses took the blood and with his finger put some on each of the horns of the altar, cleansing the altar; then he poured out the blood at the base of the altar. Thus he consecrated it and purged it.

16] Moses then took all the fat that was about the entrails, and the protuberance of the liver, and the two kidneys and their fat, and turned them into smoke on the altar. **17]** The rest of the bull, its hide, its flesh, and its dung, he put to the fire outside the camp—as the LORD had commanded Moses.

18] Then he brought forward the ram of burnt offering. Aaron and his sons laid their hands upon the ram's head, **19]** and it was slaughtered. Moses dashed the blood against all sides of the altar. **20]** The ram was cut up into sections and Moses turned the head, the sections, and the suet into smoke— **21]** the entrails and the legs having been washed with water. Moses turned all of the ram into smoke on the altar: that was a burnt offering for a pleasing odor, an offering by fire to the LORD—as the LORD had commanded Moses.

22] He brought forward the second ram, the ram of ordination. Aaron and his sons laid their hands upon the ram's head, **23]** and it was slaughtered. Moses took some of its blood and put

---

14-17] According to the rule, when the blood of a sin offering was sprinkled inside the sanctuary, the animal was burned outside the camp; if the blood was put only on the horns of the main altar, the meat was eaten by the priests (Lev. 4 and 6:17-23). But in this one case, though the blood was not taken into the sanctuary, the carcass was not eaten but burned. Perhaps this was because Moses was not technically a priest and, therefore, not able to eat a "most holy" sacrifice; or else special rules applied to this unique occasion.

15] *Thus he consecrated it and purged it.* Future printings of the Torah translation will render this sentence: "Thus he consecrated it for making expiation upon it." That is, the foregoing ritual cleansed the altar of impurity so that henceforth it would be fit for the performance of atonement rites.

22] *Ordination.* Hebrew *milluim*, literally "filling." The full term is "to fill a hand" (e.g., in 8:33). We do not know the exact force of this idiom. Some scholars have offered the guess that during the ordination ceremony the priest was handed some symbol of authority, as kings are handed a scepter during their coronation. But there is no evidence to support the guess.

אֹֽזֶן־אַהֲרֹ֛ן הַיְמָנִ֖ית וְעַל־בֹּ֣הֶן יָד֣וֹ הַיְמָנִ֑ית וְעַל־בֹּ֥הֶן

כד רַגְל֖וֹ הַיְמָנִֽית: וַיַּקְרֵ֞ב אֶת־בְּנֵ֣י אַהֲרֹ֗ן וַיִּתֵּ֨ן מֹשֶׁ֤ה מִן־

הַדָּם֙ עַל־תְּנ֤וּךְ אָזְנָם֙ הַיְמָנִ֔ית וְעַל־בֹּ֤הֶן יָדָם֙ הַיְמָנִ֔ית

וְעַל־בֹּ֖הֶן רַגְלָ֣ם הַיְמָנִ֑ית וַיִּזְרֹ֨ק מֹשֶׁ֤ה אֶת־הַדָּם֙ עַל־

כה הַמִּזְבֵּ֖חַ סָבִֽיב: וַיִּקַּ֣ח אֶת־הַחֵ֡לֶב וְאֶת־הָֽאַלְיָה֩ וְאֶֽת־

כָּל־הַחֵ֨לֶב֙ אֲשֶׁ֣ר עַל־הַקֶּ֔רֶב וְאֵת֙ יֹתֶ֣רֶת הַכָּבֵ֔ד

כו וְאֶת־שְׁתֵּ֥י הַכְּלָיֹ֖ת וְאֶת־חֶלְבְּהֶ֑ן וְאֵ֖ת שׁ֥וֹק הַיָּמִֽין: וּמִסַּ֣ל

הַמַּצּ֡וֹת אֲשֶׁר֩ לִפְנֵ֨י יְהוָ֜ה לָקַ֣ח חַלַּ֣ת מַצָּ֣ה אַחַ֗ת

וְֽחַלַּ֨ת לֶ֤חֶם שֶׁ֨מֶן֙ אַחַ֔ת וְרָקִ֖יק אֶחָ֑ד וַיָּ֨שֶׂם֙ עַל־

כז הַֽחֲלָבִ֔ים וְעַ֖ל שׁ֣וֹק הַיָּמִֽין: וַיִּתֵּ֣ן אֶת־הַכֹּ֗ל עַ֚ל כַּפֵּ֣י

אַהֲרֹ֔ן וְעַ֖ל כַּפֵּ֣י בָנָ֑יו וַיָּ֧נֶף אֹתָ֛ם תְּנוּפָ֖ה לִפְנֵ֥י יְהוָֽה:

כח וַיִּקַּ֨ח מֹשֶׁ֤ה אֹתָם֙ מֵעַ֣ל כַּפֵּיהֶ֔ם וַיַּקְטֵ֥ר הַמִּזְבֵּ֖חָה עַל־

הָֽעֹלָ֑ה מִלֻּאִ֣ים הֵ֗ם לְרֵ֤יחַ נִיחֹ֨חַ֙ אִשֶּׁ֥ה ה֖וּא לַֽיהוָֽה:

כט וַיִּקַּ֤ח מֹשֶׁה֙ אֶת־הֶ֣חָזֶ֔ה וַיְנִיפֵ֥הוּ תְנוּפָ֖ה לִפְנֵ֣י יְהוָ֑ה

מֵאֵ֣יל הַמִּלֻּאִ֗ים לְמֹשֶׁ֤ה הָיָה֙ לְמָנָ֔ה כַּאֲשֶׁ֛ר צִוָּ֥ה יְהוָ֖ה

ל אֶת־מֹשֶֽׁה: וַיִּקַּ֨ח מֹשֶׁ֜ה מִשֶּׁ֣מֶן הַמִּשְׁחָ֗ה וּמִן־הַדָּם֮ אֲשֶׁ֣ר

עַל־הַמִּזְבֵּ֒חַ֒ וַיַּ֤ז עַֽל־אַהֲרֹן֙ עַל־בְּגָדָ֔יו וְעַל־בָּנָ֖יו וְעַל־

בִּגְדֵ֣י בָנָ֣יו אִתּ֑וֹ וַיְקַדֵּ֤שׁ אֶֽת־אַהֲרֹן֙ אֶת־בְּגָדָ֔יו וְאֶת־בָּנָ֛יו

לא וְאֶת־בִּגְדֵ֥י בָנָ֖יו אִתּֽוֹ: וַיֹּ֨אמֶר מֹשֶׁ֜ה אֶל־אַהֲרֹ֣ן וְאֶל־

בָּנָ֗יו בַּשְּׁל֤וּ אֶת־הַבָּשָׂר֙ פֶּ֚תַח אֹ֣הֶל מוֹעֵ֔ד וְשָׁם֙ תֹּאכְל֣וּ

it on the ridge of Aaron's right ear, and on the thumb of his right hand, and on the big toe of his right foot. **24]** Moses then brought forward the sons of Aaron, and put some of the blood on the ridges of their right ears, and on the thumbs of their right hands, and on the big toes of their right feet; and the rest of the blood Moses dashed against every side of the altar. **25]** He took the fat—the broad tail, all the fat about the entrails, the protuberance of the liver, and the two kidneys and their fat—and the right thigh. **26]** From the basket of unleavened bread that was before the LORD, he took one cake of unleavened bread, one cake of oil bread, and one wafer, and placed them on the fat parts and on the right thigh. **27]** He placed all these on the palms of Aaron and on the palms of his sons, and waved them as a wave offering before the LORD. **28]** Then Moses took them from their hands and turned them into smoke on the altar with the burnt offering. This was an ordination offering for a pleasing odor; it was an offering by fire to the LORD. **29]** Moses took the breast and waved it as a wave offering before the LORD; it was Moses' portion of the ram of ordination—as the LORD had commanded Moses.

30] And Moses took some of the anointing oil and some of the blood that was on the altar and sprinkled it upon Aaron and upon his vestments, and also upon his sons and upon their vestments. Thus he consecrated Aaron and his vestments, and also his sons and their vestments.

31] And Moses said to Aaron and his sons: Boil the flesh at the entrance of the Tent of

---

22–29] The ram of ordination is a sacrifice of well–being, and the worshipers—here Aaron and his sons—eat its flesh. But the ritual procedure described in chapter 8, verses 26 through 29, is different from the usual rules laid down in chapter 7, verses 28 through 33, and does not seem to follow exactly the prescriptions in Exodus, chapter 29, verses 26 and 27. The ordination, a one-time event, presumably had its special rules. (On "wave," "wave offering," see commentary on 7:28–34.)

23] *On the ridge of Aaron's right ear, on the thumb of*

his right hand, and on the big toe of his right foot. Edifying explanations of this procedure have been offered (see Gleanings). But the talmudic sources refrain from moralizing; and a similar procedure was followed in purifying one who had been cured of "leprosy" (see 14:14)—in a situation where nothing "inspirational" was in place. The original intent was probably one of ritual purification; and the extremities served as a kind of summary for the entire body. The priest (or "leper") was to be cleansed of defilement "from top to toe."

Ridge. Or, "lobe" (T.N.).

יא וַיְהִי בַּיּוֹם הַשְּׁמִינִי קָרָא מֹשֶׁה לְאַהֲרֹן וּלְבָנָיו וּלְזִקְנֵי
ב יִשְׂרָאֵל: וַיֹּאמֶר אֶל־אַהֲרֹן קַח־לְךָ עֵגֶל בֶּן־בָּקָר
לְחַטָּאת וְאַיִל לְעֹלָה תְּמִימִם וְהַקְרֵב לִפְנֵי יְהוָה:
ג וְאֶל־בְּנֵי יִשְׂרָאֵל תְּדַבֵּר לֵאמֹר קְחוּ שְׂעִיר־עִזִּים
ד לְחַטָּאת וְעֵגֶל וָכֶבֶשׂ בְּנֵי־שָׁנָה תְּמִימִם לְעֹלָה: וְשׁוֹר
וָאַיִל לִשְׁלָמִים לִזְבֹּחַ לִפְנֵי יְהוָה וּמִנְחָה בְּלוּלָה
ה בַשֶּׁמֶן כִּי הַיּוֹם יְהוָה נִרְאָה אֲלֵיכֶם: וַיִּקְחוּ אֵת אֲשֶׁר
צִוָּה מֹשֶׁה אֶל־פְּנֵי אֹהֶל מוֹעֵד וַיִּקְרְבוּ כָּל־הָעֵדָה
ו וַיַּעַמְדוּ לִפְנֵי יְהוָה: וַיֹּאמֶר מֹשֶׁה זֶה הַדָּבָר אֲשֶׁר־
צִוָּה יְהוָה תַּעֲשׂוּ וְיֵרָא אֲלֵיכֶם כְּבוֹד יְהוָה: וַיֹּאמֶר

אֹתוֹ וְאֶת־הַלֶּחֶם אֲשֶׁר בְּסַל הַמִּלֻּאִים כַּאֲשֶׁר צִוֵּיתִי
לב לֵאמֹר אַהֲרֹן וּבָנָיו יֹאכְלֻהוּ: וְהַנּוֹתָר בַּבָּשָׂר וּבַלָּחֶם
לג בָּאֵשׁ תִּשְׂרֹפוּ: וּמִפֶּתַח אֹהֶל מוֹעֵד לֹא תֵצְאוּ שִׁבְעַת
יָמִים עַד יוֹם מְלֹאת יְמֵי מִלֻּאֵיכֶם כִּי שִׁבְעַת יָמִים
לד יְמַלֵּא אֶת־יֶדְכֶם: כַּאֲשֶׁר עָשָׂה בַּיּוֹם הַזֶּה צִוָּה יְהוָה
לה לַעֲשֹׂת לְכַפֵּר עֲלֵיכֶם: וּפֶתַח אֹהֶל מוֹעֵד תֵּשְׁבוּ יוֹמָם
וָלַיְלָה שִׁבְעַת יָמִים וּשְׁמַרְתֶּם אֶת־מִשְׁמֶרֶת יְהוָה וְלֹא
לו תָמוּתוּ כִּי־כֵן צֻוֵּיתִי: וַיַּעַשׂ אַהֲרֹן וּבָנָיו אֵת כָּל־
הַדְּבָרִים אֲשֶׁר־צִוָּה יְהוָה בְּיַד־מֹשֶׁה:

Haftarah Tzav, p. 983

ס ס ס

Meeting and eat it there with the bread that is in the basket of ordination—as I commanded: Aaron and his sons shall eat it; **32]** and what is left over of the flesh and the bread you shall consume in fire. **33]** You shall not go outside the entrance of the Tent of Meeting for seven days, until the day that your period of ordination is completed. For your ordination will require seven days. **34]** Everything done today, the LORD has commanded to be done [seven days], to make expiation for you. **35]** You shall remain at the entrance of the Tent of Meeting day and night for seven days, keeping the LORD's charge—that you may not die—for so I have been commanded.

    36] And Aaron and his sons did all the things that the LORD had commanded through Moses.

    1] On the eighth day Moses called Aaron and his sons, and the elders of Israel. **2]** He said to Aaron: "Take a calf of the herd for a sin offering and a ram for a burnt offering, without blemish, and bring them before the LORD. **3]** And speak to the Israelites, saying: Take a he-goat for a sin offering; a calf and a lamb, yearlings without blemish, for a burnt offering; **4]** and an ox and a ram for an offering of well-being to sacrifice before the LORD; and a meal offering with oil mixed in. For today the LORD will appear to you."

    5] They brought to the front of the Tent of Meeting the things that Moses had commanded, and the whole community came forward and stood before the LORD. **6]** Moses said: "This is what the LORD has commanded that you do, that the Presence of the LORD may appear to

---

31] *As I commanded.* Or, vocalizing *tzuveti*, "I have been commanded"; cf. verse 35 below (T.N.).

31-35] The ritual was to be repeated daily for a week.

33] *You shall not go outside.* The priests were not to absent themselves while the ceremonies were actually in progress (*Sifra*).

9:1] *On the eighth day.* I.e., of the ordination ceremonies. See introduction to this chapter. Aaron now enters on his priestly duties.

6] *The Presence of the Lord.* Hebrew *Kevod Adonai*, formerly translated "the Glory of the LORD." This

expression, found chiefly in priestly writings, designates a visible manifestation of the Divine. "The Presence of the LORD appeared . . . as a consuming fire" (Exod. 24:17). It was often accompanied by, or enveloped in, a cloud which perhaps was to protect the people from its overwhelming brilliance or from other destructive effects (Exod. 24:16). See also Ezekiel (especially 1:28), which describes the Presence as having human form, and Isaiah (6:3), "His Presence fills all the earth." Often, as here, the Presence is a sign of God's favor; but sometimes (e.g., Num. 16:19) it appears in moments of anger and punishment.

מֹשֶׁה אֶל־אַהֲרֹן קְרַב אֶל־הַמִּזְבֵּחַ וַעֲשֵׂה אֶת־חַטָּאתְךָ
וְאֶת־עֹלָתֶךָ וְכַפֵּר בַּעַדְךָ וּבְעַד הָעָם וַעֲשֵׂה אֶת־
ח קָרְבַּן הָעָם וְכַפֵּר בַּעֲדָם כַּאֲשֶׁר צִוָּה יְהוָה: וַיִּקְרַב
אַהֲרֹן אֶל־הַמִּזְבֵּחַ וַיִּשְׁחַט אֶת־עֵגֶל הַחַטָּאת אֲשֶׁר־לוֹ:
ט וַיַּקְרִבוּ בְּנֵי אַהֲרֹן אֶת־הַדָּם אֵלָיו וַיִּטְבֹּל אֶצְבָּעוֹ
בַּדָּם וַיִּתֵּן עַל־קַרְנוֹת הַמִּזְבֵּחַ וְאֶת־הַדָּם יָצַק אֶל־
י יְסוֹד הַמִּזְבֵּחַ: וְאֶת־הַחֵלֶב וְאֶת־הַכְּלָיֹת וְאֶת־הַיֹּתֶרֶת
מִן־הַכָּבֵד מִן־הַחַטָּאת הִקְטִיר הַמִּזְבֵּחָה כַּאֲשֶׁר צִוָּה
יא יְהוָה אֶת־מֹשֶׁה: וְאֶת־הַבָּשָׂר וְאֶת־הָעוֹר שָׂרַף בָּאֵשׁ
יב מִחוּץ לַמַּחֲנֶה: וַיִּשְׁחַט אֶת־הָעֹלָה וַיַּמְצִאוּ בְּנֵי אַהֲרֹן

יג אֵלָיו אֶת־הַדָּם וַיִּזְרְקֵהוּ עַל־הַמִּזְבֵּחַ סָבִיב: וְאֶת־
הָעֹלָה הִמְצִיאוּ אֵלָיו לִנְתָחֶיהָ וְאֶת־הָרֹאשׁ וַיַּקְטֵר
יד עַל־הַמִּזְבֵּחַ: וַיִּרְחַץ אֶת־הַקֶּרֶב וְאֶת־הַכְּרָעָיִם וַיַּקְטֵר
טו עַל־הָעֹלָה הַמִּזְבֵּחָה: וַיַּקְרֵב אֵת קָרְבַּן הָעָם וַיִּקַּח
אֶת־שְׂעִיר הַחַטָּאת אֲשֶׁר לָעָם וַיִּשְׁחָטֵהוּ וַיְחַטְּאֵהוּ
טז כָּרִאשׁוֹן: וַיַּקְרֵב אֶת־הָעֹלָה וַיַּעֲשֶׂהָ כַּמִּשְׁפָּט: וַיַּקְרֵב
אֶת־הַמִּנְחָה וַיְמַלֵּא כַפּוֹ מִמֶּנָּה וַיַּקְטֵר עַל־הַמִּזְבֵּחַ
יח מִלְּבַד עֹלַת הַבֹּקֶר: וַיִּשְׁחַט אֶת־הַשּׁוֹר וְאֶת־הָאַיִל
זֶבַח הַשְּׁלָמִים אֲשֶׁר לָעָם וַיַּמְצִאוּ בְּנֵי אַהֲרֹן אֶת־הַדָּם
יט אֵלָיו וַיִּזְרְקֵהוּ עַל־הַמִּזְבֵּחַ סָבִיב: וְאֶת־הַחֲלָבִים מִן־

you." **7]** Then Moses said to Aaron: "Come forward to the altar and sacrifice your sin offering and your burnt offering, making expiation for yourself and for the people; and sacrifice the people's offering and make expiation for them, as the LORD has commanded."

8] Aaron came forward to the altar and slaughtered his calf of sin offering. **9]** Aaron's sons brought the blood to him; he dipped his finger in the blood and put it on the horns of the altar; and he poured out the rest of the blood at the base of the altar. **10]** The fat, the kidneys, and the protuberance of the liver from the sin offering he turned into smoke on the altar—as the LORD had commanded Moses; **11]** and the flesh and the skin were consumed in fire outside the camp. **12]** Then he slaughtered the burnt offering. Aaron's sons passed the blood to him, and he dashed it against all sides of the altar. **13]** They passed the burnt offering to him in sections, as well as the head, and he turned it into smoke on the altar. **14]** He washed the entrails and the legs, and turned them into smoke on the altar with the burnt offering.

15] Next he brought forward the people's offering. He took the goat for the people's sin offering, and slaughtered it, and presented it as a sin offering like the previous one. **16]** He brought forward the burnt offering and sacrificed it according to regulation. **17]** He then brought forward the meal offering and, taking a handful of it, he turned it into smoke on the altar—in addition to the burnt offering of the morning. **18]** He slaughtered the ox and the ram, the people's sacrifice of well-being. Aaron's sons passed the blood to him—which he dashed against every side of the altar— **19]** and the fat parts of the ox and the ram: the broad

---

The Rabbis speak similarly of the *Shechinah*, the Divine Indwelling, but this is not necessarily something visible to the physical eye [9].

7] *Making expiation for yourself and for the people.* Until Aaron himself had been purified from guilt, he could not intercede for the people. But the Greek version, instead of "for the people," reads "for your household" (cf. 16:11); this may well be correct, since the expiation of the people is treated in the next clause.

10] *Turned into smoke.* This seems to contradict

verse 24 which tells that the sacrifices were consumed by a heavenly fire. Rashbam, followed by Luzzatto, understands "turned into smoke" to mean simply "laid the pieces on the altar ready for burning." But Hoffmann notes that on the previous days the offerings had been consumed by normal fire and that a similar fire could have been kindled on the eighth day before the heavenly fire descended.

17] *The burnt offering of the morning.* See Exodus, chapter 29, verses 38 through 46 (T.N.).

הַשּׁוֹר וּמִן־הָאַיִל הָאַלְיָה וְהַמְכַסֶּה וְהַכְּלָיֹת וְיֹתֶרֶת
הַכָּבֵד: כ וַיָּשִׂימוּ אֶת־הַחֲלָבִים עַל־הֶחָזוֹת וַיַּקְטֵר
הַחֲלָבִים הַמִּזְבֵּחָה: כא וְאֵת הֶחָזוֹת וְאֵת שׁוֹק הַיָּמִין
הֵנִיף אַהֲרֹן תְּנוּפָה לִפְנֵי יְהוָה כַּאֲשֶׁר צִוָּה מֹשֶׁה:
כב וַיִּשָּׂא אַהֲרֹן אֶת־יָדָו אֶל־הָעָם וַיְבָרְכֵם וַיֵּרֶד מֵעֲשֹׂת
כג הַחַטָּאת וְהָעֹלָה וְהַשְּׁלָמִים: וַיָּבֹא מֹשֶׁה וְאַהֲרֹן אֶל־
אֹהֶל מוֹעֵד וַיֵּצְאוּ וַיְבָרְכוּ אֶת־הָעָם וַיֵּרָא כְבוֹד־יְהוָה

* כב ידו קרי.

כד אֶל־כָּל־הָעָם: וַתֵּצֵא אֵשׁ מִלִּפְנֵי יְהוָה וַתֹּאכַל עַל־
הַמִּזְבֵּחַ אֶת־הָעֹלָה וְאֶת־הַחֲלָבִים וַיַּרְא כָּל־הָעָם
וַיָּרֹנּוּ וַיִּפְּלוּ עַל־פְּנֵיהֶם:
יא וַיִּקְחוּ בְנֵי־אַהֲרֹן נָדָב וַאֲבִיהוּא אִישׁ מַחְתָּתוֹ וַיִּתְּנוּ
בָהֵן אֵשׁ וַיָּשִׂימוּ עָלֶיהָ קְטֹרֶת וַיַּקְרִיבוּ לִפְנֵי יְהוָה
ב אֵשׁ זָרָה אֲשֶׁר לֹא צִוָּה אֹתָם: וַתֵּצֵא אֵשׁ מִלִּפְנֵי יְהוָה
ג וַתֹּאכַל אוֹתָם וַיָּמֻתוּ לִפְנֵי יְהוָה: וַיֹּאמֶר מֹשֶׁה אֶל־

tail, the covering [fat], the kidneys, and the protuberances of the livers. **20]** They laid these fat parts over the breasts; and Aaron turned the fat parts into smoke on the altar, **21]** and waved the breasts and the right thighs as a wave offering before the LORD—as Moses had commanded.

22] Aaron lifted his hands toward the people and blessed them; and he stepped down after offering the sin offering, the burnt offering, and the offering of well-being. **23]** Moses and Aaron then went inside the Tent of Meeting. When they came out, they blessed the people; and the Presence of the LORD appeared to all the people. **24]** Fire came forth from before the LORD and consumed the burnt offering and the fat parts on the altar. And all the people saw, and shouted, and fell on their faces.

1] Now Aaron's sons, Nadab and Abihu, each took his fire pan, put fire in it, and laid incense on it; and they offered before the LORD alien fire, which He had not enjoined upon them. **2]** And fire came forth from the LORD and consumed them; thus they died at the instance of the

20] *Aaron.* This word moved up from verse 21 for clarity (T.N.).

21] *Waved . . . wave offering.* See commentary on 7:28–34.

22] *He stepped down.* From the altar.

23] *Moses and Aaron then went inside the Tent of Meeting.* No reason for this is given by Scripture. *Sifra* offers two plausible explanations: Moses went in with Aaron to show him how to perform the incense offering. Or, they went in together to pray for the speedy manifestation of God's Presence.

24] *Fire came forth from before the Lord.* Either from the Presence, or (Rashbam) from the Holy of Holies. The first alternative is supported by I Kings, chapter 18, verse 38, and II Chronicles, chapter 7, verse 3.

10:1] *Each took his fire pan.* They were not presenting the regular incense offering of the morning (Exod. 30:7) which would not have required two fire pans. Evidently they were attempting something original.

Alien fire. Not from the divine flame that had descended on the altar.

Which He had not enjoined upon them. The priestly ideal is one of conformity, not of innovation.

2] *Fire came forth.* See commentary on 9:24. The wording of chapter 16, verse 2, suggests that they came too close to the Holy of Holies and the disaster followed automatically—as might happen if one touched a high tension electric wire without proper precautions.

And consumed them. They were not literally reduced to ashes for their bodies were later removed in their apparently undamaged tunics (10:5).

At the instance of the Lord. Others, "before [the LORD]" (T.N.). The Hebrew *lifne Adonai* does generally have the latter meaning (e.g., in 1:3). But commentators have recognized that sometimes it has a different force. The present translation has rendered it by such phrases as "by the grace of the LORD" (Gen. 10:7) and "with the LORD's approval" (Gen. 27:7).

אַהֲרֹן הוּא אֲשֶׁר־דִּבֶּר יְהֹוָה לֵאמֹר בִּקְרֹבַי אֶקָּדֵשׁ
ד וְעַל־פְּנֵי כָל־הָעָם אֶכָּבֵד וַיִּדֹּם אַהֲרֹן: וַיִּקְרָא מֹשֶׁה
אֶל־מִישָׁאֵל וְאֶל אֶלְצָפָן בְּנֵי עֻזִּיאֵל דֹּד אַהֲרֹן וַיֹּאמֶר
אֲלֵהֶם קִרְבוּ שְׂאוּ אֶת־אֲחֵיכֶם מֵאֵת פְּנֵי־הַקֹּדֶשׁ אֶל־
ה מִחוּץ לַמַּחֲנֶה: וַיִּקְרְבוּ וַיִּשָּׂאֻם בְּכֻתֳּנֹתָם אֶל־מִחוּץ
ו לַמַּחֲנֶה כַּאֲשֶׁר דִּבֶּר מֹשֶׁה: וַיֹּאמֶר מֹשֶׁה אֶל־אַהֲרֹן

וּלְאֶלְעָזָר וּלְאִיתָמָר בָּנָיו רָאשֵׁיכֶם אַל־תִּפְרָעוּ
וּבִגְדֵיכֶם לֹא־תִפְרֹמוּ וְלֹא תָמֻתוּ וְעַל כָּל־הָעֵדָה
יִקְצֹף וַאֲחֵיכֶם כָּל־בֵּית יִשְׂרָאֵל יִבְכּוּ אֶת־הַשְּׂרֵפָה
ז אֲשֶׁר שָׂרַף יְהֹוָה: וּמִפֶּתַח אֹהֶל מוֹעֵד לֹא תֵצְאוּ פֶּן־
תָּמֻתוּ כִּי־שֶׁמֶן מִשְׁחַת יְהֹוָה עֲלֵיכֶם וַיַּעֲשׂוּ כִּדְבַר
מֹשֶׁה: פ

LORD. **3]** Then Moses said to Aaron, "This is what the LORD meant when He said: / Through those near to Me I show Myself holy, /And assert My authority before all the people." / And Aaron was silent.

4] Moses called Mishael and Elzaphan, sons of Uzziel the uncle of Aaron, and said to them, "Come forward and carry your kinsmen away from the front of the sanctuary to a place outside the camp." **5]** They came forward and carried them out of the camp by their tunics, as Moses had ordered. **6]** And Moses said to Aaron and to his sons, Eleazar and Ithamar, "Do not bare your heads and do not rend your clothes, lest you die and anger strike the whole community. But your kinsmen, all the house of Israel, shall bewail the burning that the LORD has wrought. **7]** You must not go outside the entrance of the Tent of Meeting, lest you die, for the LORD's anointing oil is upon you." And they did as Moses had bidden.

3] *This is what the Lord meant when He said.* When and in what connection had the LORD said this? Most likely we should understand that Moses recalls an utterance, not previously recorded, which he had heard but not understood till that time. Nachmanides explains that the reference is not to a literal speech but to God's intent in decreeing the severe punishment. But other commentators sought elsewhere in the Torah for an utterance to this effect. Rashi, following the Talmud [10], cites Exodus, chapter 29, verse 43; Rashbam refers to Leviticus, chapter 21, verses 10 through 12, and understands the present verse also as a command rather than a declaration.

Through those near to Me I show Myself holy. I manifest My holiness by the strict standards I impose on those nearest to Me. Those who are called to leadership, especially religious leadership, are singled out not for privilege but for responsibility. Ibn Ezra appropriately cites Amos's challenging words to the people of Israel: "You alone have I singled out, of all the families of the earth—that is why I will call you to account for all your iniquities" (Amos 3:2).

And assert My authority. Or, "I will be glorified." Cf. Exodus 14:4 (T.N.).

And Aaron was silent. He refrained from weeping and from complaints against God. In the rabbinic phrase, he "acknowledged the justice of the decree."

4] *Mishael and Elzaphan.* Their pedigree is given in Exodus (6:18, 22). Being Levites, they were not forbidden to defile themselves by contact with the dead. Aaron, as High Priest, was explicitly forbidden to do so, whereas ordinary priests were allowed to defile themselves for near relatives (Lev. 21:2f. and 10f.). But Eleazar and Ithamar were subject to a more stringent rule because they had received the special privilege of anointment (Rashbam; similarly, Nachmanides).

6] *Do not bare your heads. . . .* Or, "dishevel your hair" (T.N.). Do not observe the customary forms of mourning [11].

ח וַיְדַבֵּר יְהוָה אֶל־אַהֲרֹן לֵאמֹר: יַיִן וְשֵׁכָר אַל־תֵּשְׁתְּ
אַתָּה וּבָנֶיךָ אִתָּךְ בְּבֹאֲכֶם אֶל־אֹהֶל מוֹעֵד וְלֹא
י תָמֻתוּ חֻקַּת עוֹלָם לְדֹרֹתֵיכֶם: וּלְהַבְדִּיל בֵּין הַקֹּדֶשׁ
יא וּבֵין הַחֹל וּבֵין הַטָּמֵא וּבֵין הַטָּהוֹר: וּלְהוֹרֹת אֶת־
בְּנֵי יִשְׂרָאֵל אֵת כָּל־הַחֻקִּים אֲשֶׁר דִּבֶּר יְהוָה אֲלֵיהֶם
בְּיַד־מֹשֶׁה: פ
יב וַיְדַבֵּר מֹשֶׁה אֶל־אַהֲרֹן וְאֶל אֶלְעָזָר וְאֶל־אִיתָמָר
בָּנָיו הַנּוֹתָרִים קְחוּ אֶת־הַמִּנְחָה הַנּוֹתֶרֶת מֵאִשֵּׁי יְהוָה
וְאִכְלוּהָ מַצּוֹת אֵצֶל הַמִּזְבֵּחַ כִּי קֹדֶשׁ קָדָשִׁים הִוא:
יג וַאֲכַלְתֶּם אֹתָהּ בְּמָקוֹם קָדוֹשׁ כִּי חָקְךָ וְחָק־בָּנֶיךָ הִוא

יד מֵאִשֵּׁי יְהוָה כִּי־כֵן צֻוֵּיתִי: וְאֵת חֲזֵה הַתְּנוּפָה וְאֵת
שׁוֹק הַתְּרוּמָה תֹּאכְלוּ בְּמָקוֹם טָהוֹר אַתָּה וּבָנֶיךָ
וּבְנֹתֶיךָ אִתָּךְ כִּי־חָקְךָ וְחָק־בָּנֶיךָ נִתְּנוּ מִזִּבְחֵי שַׁלְמֵי
טו בְנֵי יִשְׂרָאֵל: שׁוֹק הַתְּרוּמָה וַחֲזֵה הַתְּנוּפָה עַל אִשֵּׁי
הַחֲלָבִים יָבִיאוּ לְהָנִיף תְּנוּפָה לִפְנֵי יְהוָה וְהָיָה לְךָ
טז וּלְבָנֶיךָ אִתְּךָ לְחָק־עוֹלָם כַּאֲשֶׁר צִוָּה יְהוָה: וְאֵת
שְׂעִיר הַחַטָּאת דָּרֹשׁ דָּרַשׁ מֹשֶׁה וְהִנֵּה שֹׂרָף וַיִּקְצֹף
עַל־אֶלְעָזָר וְעַל־אִיתָמָר בְּנֵי אַהֲרֹן הַנּוֹתָרִים לֵאמֹר:
יז מַדּוּעַ לֹא־אֲכַלְתֶּם אֶת־הַחַטָּאת בִּמְקוֹם הַקֹּדֶשׁ כִּי
קֹדֶשׁ קָדָשִׁים הִוא וְאֹתָהּ נָתַן לָכֶם לָשֵׂאת אֶת־עֲוֹן

8] And the LORD spoke to Aaron, saying: **9]** Drink no wine or other intoxicant, you or your sons with you, when you enter the Tent of Meeting, that you may not die—it is a law for all time throughout the ages. **10]** For you must distinguish between the sacred and the profane, and between the unclean and the clean; **11]** and you must teach the Israelites all the laws which the LORD has imparted to them through Moses.

12] And Moses spoke to Aaron and to his remaining sons, Eleazar and Ithamar: Take the meal offering that is left over from the LORD's offerings by fire and eat it unleavened beside the altar, for it is most holy. **13]** You shall eat it in the sacred precinct, inasmuch as it is your due and that of your children, from the LORD's offerings by fire; for so I have been commanded. **14]** But the breast of wave offering and the thigh of heave offering you, and your sons and daughters with you, may eat in any clean place, for they have been assigned as a due to you and your children from the Israelites' sacrifices of well-being. **15]** Together with the fat of fire-offering, they must present the thigh of heave offering and the breast of wave offering, which are to be waved as a wave offering before the LORD, and which are to be your due and that of your children with you for all time—as the LORD has commanded.

16] Then Moses inquired about the goat of sin offering, and it had already been burned! He was angry with Eleazar and Ithamar, Aaron's remaining sons, and said, **17]** "Why did you not eat the sin offering in the sacred area? For it is most holy, and He has given it to you to

9] *Other intoxicant.* Hebrew *shechar,* related to *shikor,* "intoxicated." The word is either a synonym for "wine" or else refers to beer which was prepared by some ancient peoples (notably the Egyptians and Babylonians) from fermented grain. It was not, like modern beer, flavored with hops. Distilled liquors were not known in antiquity.

10–11] The priests were not only to perform rites in the sanctuary. They were also to instruct the people in their religious duties—and for this too they had to have clear heads.

16–20] This passage presents a legal point in the form of a touching dialogue.

16] *The goat of sin offering.* See commentary on 9:15.

He was angry with Eleazar and Ithamar. The Rabbis rightly note that Moses' criticism was directed equally against Aaron who, in fact, replied to the charge (*Sifra*). Moses spoke only to the sons, either out of compassion for Aaron's grief or respect for his dignity as High Priest.

17] *He has given it to you to remove the guilt of the community.* This indicates that the community's sins were not fully expiated until the priests partook of the meat of the sin offering. See commentary on 6:19.

יח הָעֵדָ֔ה לְכַפֵּ֥ר עֲלֵיהֶ֖ם לִפְנֵ֣י יְהֹוָֽה׃ הֵ֚ן לֹא־הוּבָ֣א אֶת־ הִקְרִ֜יבוּ אֶת־חַטָּאתָ֤ם וְאֶת־עֹֽלָתָם֙ לִפְנֵ֣י יְהֹוָ֔ה
דָּמָ֔הּ אֶל־הַקֹּ֖דֶשׁ פְּנִ֑ימָה אָכ֨וֹל תֹּאכְל֥וּ אֹתָ֛הּ בַּקֹּ֖דֶשׁ וַתִּקְרֶ֥אנָה אֹתִ֖י כָּאֵ֑לֶּה וְאָכַ֤לְתִּי חַטָּאת֙ הַיּ֔וֹם הַיִּיטַ֖ב
יט כַּאֲשֶׁ֥ר צִוֵּֽיתִי׃ וַיְדַבֵּ֨ר אַהֲרֹ֜ן אֶל־מֹשֶׁ֗ה הֵ֣ן הַיּ֡וֹם כ בְּעֵינֵ֥י יְהֹוָֽה׃ וַיִּשְׁמַ֣ע מֹשֶׁ֔ה וַיִּיטַ֖ב בְּעֵינָֽיו׃ פ

remove the guilt of the community and to make expiation for them before the LORD?
18] Since its blood was not brought inside the sanctuary, you should certainly have eaten it in the sanctuary, as I commanded." 19] And Aaron spoke to Moses, "See, this day they brought their sin offering and their burnt offering before the LORD, and such things have befallen me! Had I eaten sin offering today, would the LORD have approved?" 20] And when Moses heard this, he approved.

18] *Since its blood was not brought inside the sanctuary.* As is done in the case of the most solemn offerings; see 4:3–21; 16:11–17 (T.N.).

19] *And such things have befallen me!* Clearly I am not in favor with God at present. For me to eat sin offering, implying that my intercession had won forgiveness for the people, would be unsuitable (Luzzatto).

20] *And when Moses heard this, he approved.* He recognized the force of Aaron's argument. This chapter depicts Aaron with a dignity and gentleness he does not display in other narratives of the Torah. In the golden calf incident, his behavior is shabby (Exod. 32); on another occasion, he and Miriam make an unkind attack on Moses (Num. 12). Elsewhere he is the symbol of the high priesthood rather than a flesh and blood character. But here he impresses us by his mild but forthright reply to Moses—his younger brother.

GLEANINGS

Halachah

10:7] *You Must Not Go outside the Entrance of the Tent of Meeting, lest You Die*

From this verse, the general rule was inferred that any priest who leaves the sacred precinct while engaged in a sacrificial rite is guilty of a capital crime [12].

11] *You Must Teach the Israelites All the Laws*

Not only priests but all those who give instruction in matters of religious law are required to observe the prohibition against the use of alcohol. If a teacher is asked a question when he has been drinking, he must wait till the effects of the wine have had time to disappear before he renders an opinion [13].

16] *The Goat of Sin Offering*

The Rabbis held that these events occurred on the first day of the first month (see at 9:1); therefore three goats were brought as sin offerings—the goat of the people (Lev. 9:15), the goat presented by Nahshon the chieftain of Judah (Num. 7:16), and the regular sin offering for the new moon (Num. 28:15). The first two *were* eaten, for Aaron considered them exceptional sacrifices of ordination, which should be eaten even by those in mourning. But he held that the regular rule that priests should not eat sacrificial meat when in mourning should apply to the new moon sacrifice, which was to be performed through the ages. Moses thereupon admitted he had overlooked this distinction and publicly proclaimed that Aaron was in the right [14].

8:15] *For Making Expiation upon It* [*the Altar*]

Some Rabbis understood the phrase to mean "to make expiation *for it*." For, they said, when offerings for the Tabernacle were being collected, some persons may have contributed under pressure, or while they were carried away by the general enthusiasm, without really wanting to make such a gift. It was necessary to make atonement for such a possible deficiency [15].

23] *On the Ridge of Aaron's Right Ear*

"In this figure, he indicated that the fully consecrated must be pure in words and actions and in his whole life; for words are judged by hearing, the hand is the symbol of action, and the foot of the pilgrimage of life" [16].

"The ear was touched with blood, that it may be consecrated to hear the word of God; the hand, to perform the duties of the priesthood; and the foot, to walk in the path of righteousness" [17].

9:2] *Take a Calf*

Moses said to Aaron: "Brother Aaron, even though the Everpresent has forgiven your sins, you still need to put something into the mouth of Satan. Send a gift ahead of you before entering the sanctuary, lest he accuse you when you enter the sanctuary" [18].

7] *Come Forward*

Aaron was uncertain of himself, his conscience troubled over his part in the sin of the golden calf. When he looked at the altar, its horns reminded him of the calf, intensifying his embarrassment. Moses therefore bade him come forward: God would not have assigned him the priestly duties without first forgiving him. Moreover, the calf of sin offering (verse 2) was to atone for the sin of the calf.   SIFRA

22] *Aaron Lifted His Hands . . . and Blessed Them*

For the first time he uttered the threefold benediction of Numbers, chapter 6, verses 22ff. [19].

23] *They Blessed the People*

Moses said, "May it be God's will to cause His Shechinah to rest upon the work of your hands! May the LORD, the God of your fathers, increase your numbers a thousandfold and bless you, as He promised you!" They responded, "May the favor of the Lord be upon us; / let all that we put our hands to prosper, / O prosper the work of our hands" (Ps. 90:17 which is ascribed in verse 1 to Moses).

SIFRA

10:1-3] The cryptic narrative of the death of the two young men fairly cried for amplification by later preachers. Perhaps the Rabbis felt that the punishment was unduly harsh for a ritual infraction committed by inexperienced priests; yet they were sure God never acts unjustly. So they sought to solve the problem in various ways.

Most often they expanded on the sinfulness of the young men. The prohibition of wine in verses 9ff. suggested that Nadab and Abihu had been drinking before they entered the sanctuary [20]. They were also guilty of arrogance and irreverence. From Exodus (24:9ff.), it was inferred that on Sinai Nadab and Abihu had gazed boldly at the Divine Presence— as if eating and drinking!—instead of turning their eyes humbly away, as Moses had done at the burning bush (Exod. 3:6). They had refused to marry and beget children because they deemed no woman good enough for men of their exalted birth. Yet, despite their pride of ancestry, they had no respect for Moses and Aaron. "When will those old fellows die," they said, "that we may take control of the community?" [21] Had they sought the guidance of Moses, they would have avoided disaster; but they were too haughty to ask for advice [22], or even to consult each other [23]. And this list does not exhaust all the crimes with which they were charged!

Some scholars took a different approach. They declared that, except for this one offense, Nadab and Abihu were righteous men. Four times Scripture mentions their death, and each time it specifies the sin of "strange fire" to indicate that they were guilty of nothing else. No taint of corruption attached to them [24]. (The Rabbis made similar comments about the one sin that barred Moses from the promised land [25].) Though the young men employed the wrong means to bring down the Divine Presence, their motives were noble, inspired by love and joy [26]. Their punishment, by its very severity, indicates the high spiritual level they had attained.

That is why God said to them, "I will give you more honor than you gave Me. You brought in impure fire, I will slay you with a pure flame." Two threads of fire then issued from the Holy of Holies; each divided into two which entered the nostrils of the offenders and extinguished their lives. Their clothing (and, according to some, their bodies) remained intact [27]. And God grieved over their death even more than Aaron did [28].

A third approach neither vilified nor exculpated the two but actually glorified them. Philo was the most extreme advocate of this view. Nadab and Abihu, he says, had drawn nigh to God and forsaken mortal life [29]. Therefore the Bible says "They died before the Lord" [30]. They were taken up by a rush of fire unquenchable, by an undying splendor [31].

The Rabbis do not go that far, but they also speak of Nadab and Abihu as righteous men [32]. And one old story introduces the notion—unparalleled in rabbinic literature [33]—that the death of a great man may serve to consecrate a shrine: "Through those near to Me I will be sanctified" (verse 3). Moses came to Aaron and said to him, "Brother Aaron, it was told to me at Sinai: 'I am going to sanctify this House, I will sanctify it through a great man.' I always supposed that the House would be sanctified either through you or through me. Now it appears that your sons were greater than we, since it was through them that the House was sanctified." And in this assurance Aaron found comfort [34].

9] *Drink No Wine or Other Intoxicant*
A pious man had a father whose drunken habits were a source of shame to him. One rainy day the son saw a man lying in the street in a drunken stupor, with water pouring over him and urchins taunting him. And he brought his father to see the repulsive sight, hoping it might have a wholesome effect. But the father merely bent down to ask the drunkard where he could buy such potent wine! [35].

20] *And When Moses Heard This, He Approved*
He sent out a herald to proclaim, "I was mistaken about the law, and my brother Aaron instructed me." (Eleazar and Ithamar also knew the correct ruling, but they remained silent so as not to embarrass Moses.) This was one of three occasions when Moses forgot the correct halachah as a result of losing his temper [36].

PART III

Dietary Laws

Permitted and Forbidden Foods

The Dietary Laws

(See also the further discussion in commentary on Deut. 14:1–15:18.)

Most peoples have some food taboos. Naturally ones does not eat products that promptly cause sickness or discomfort, or that are too tough to chew. But foods accepted in one culture as proper and wholesome may be viewed with loathing by another culture.

Sometimes a food is avoided because people have not discovered that it is edible or because they have not learned how to prepare it. Sometimes a food is mistakenly supposed to be harmful; for a long time the tomato was thought to be poisonous. In certain cases, the rejection of a certain food—whatever its psychological origin—is institutionalized. In the United States there is not only a prejudice against eating horse meat, there are also laws forbidding its sale for human consumption and requiring the proper labeling of dog food containing horse meat. Yet in some countries people eat horse without revulsion and without harmful effects.

In many cases, dietary restrictions have been based upon, or reinforced by, religious beliefs. The Jains and Buddhists avoid the taking of life, and therefore they reject all animal food; similar attitudes were held by some individuals and groups in ancient Greece. The Hindus regard the cow as sacred, and therefore they do not eat beef. But the elaborate system of dietary laws contained in the Torah and further extended by post-biblical teachers is probably unique; certainly nothing similar was to be found in the ancient Near East.

Moreover, the motivations mentioned above do not apply to the biblical laws, which do not regard any food as inherently sacred. An animal designated for sacrifice is thereby set apart and may be eaten only by specified persons under specified circumstances—as we have already seen. Otherwise, biblically prohibited foods fall into two classes: (1) those which are restricted temporarily, such as leavened bread on Passover and untithed produce and (2) foods designated as unclean and prohibited unconditionally except in the direst emergency, to save the life of a sick or starving person.

1. A Few Definitions

Currently, food permissible according to Jewish law is called *kasher* (kosher). The word means "fit," "proper." It appears once in the Bible (Esther 8:5), where it has nothing to do with food. It is found frequently in the Talmud, often with reference to food; in later

Jewish literature, it is used chiefly in that connection.

The opposite of *kasher* in current usage is *terefah* (sometimes pronounced *treif*). The word means literally "something torn," and in the Bible it refers to an animal killed by another beast (Exod. 22:30).

The Talmud redefined the word *terefah*: it is an animal or fowl of a permitted species which is suffering from a disease, defect, or injury that would cause its death within a year [1]. An animal of a permitted species killed by another beast is called in talmudic-rabbinic literature not *terefah*, but *nevelah*, literally "carcass," "carrion." The same term is applied to an animal that has died of natural causes or has been improperly slaughtered [2].

But today a perfectly healthy animal, bird, or fish of a nonkosher species might be referred to as *terefah*, though the Bible and traditional literature designate such creatures as *tamé*, "unclean."

This word *tamé* does not mean dirty; and the opposite, *tahor*, "pure," means much more than physically clean. A creature is *tamé* because the Torah forbids its consumption. Similarly, the word *sheketz*, "abomination" (Lev. 11:10ff.), does not mean that the birds or fish in question are "naturally repulsive"; they are to be regarded as repulsive because a divine commandment forbids them.

2. The Scope of the Dietary Laws

The permanently forbidden foods are all of animal origin. Most of the prohibitions are listed in this chapter and are repeated in Deuteronomy (14:3–20) with a few omissions and additions [3]. These two passages are almost identical, in language as well as substance. The Torah contains a number of repetitions, but none as extended as this one. Since the passage seems typical of P in content and in style, it is probable that a priestly editor inserted the passage into Deuteronomy [4].

Elsewhere in the Torah there are a few other dietary rules; we have already noted the prohibition of blood and certain portions of fat. All the biblical legislation on the subject was greatly expanded by the talmudic authorities who fully developed the laws of ritual slaughtering and the rules against mixing milk and meat. A brief summary of the dietary laws as currently practiced by traditional Jews, is given in Appendix I, appearing after the final *sidrah* of Leviticus.

3. The Reason for the Dietary Laws

The Torah plainly states (Lev. 11:44ff.) that the people of Israel is sanctified by avoiding the unclean foods. But it does not explain why those foods have a defiling effect.

The Talmud divides all the commandments into two classes: (1) "those which should have been given had they not been given," i.e., moral and social laws whose value is evident, and (2) "those about which Satan and the Gentiles can raise questions," because they have no rational explanation [5]. The prohibition of pork is included in the second category. Elsewhere we read, "One should not say, 'I can't stand pork!' but rather, 'I would like to eat it, but my Father in heaven has forbidden it, and I have no choice' " [6]. And again, "What difference does it make to God whether an animal is slaughtered by cutting its throat or striking it on the back of the neck? Clearly, the commandments were given to discipline us" [7]. To this day, Orthodox teachers adhere to this position: God has imposed this regimen on us for His own reasons, and we hallow our lives by obeying Him without question [8].

Nevertheless many efforts have been made to supply a reason for these enactments. The earliest attempt we possess at a moralizing

explanation is that of Philo of Alexandria. The dietary laws, he states, are intended to teach us to control our bodily appetites. Moses did not demand Spartan self-denial; but, to discourage excessive self-indulgence, he forbade pork, the most delicious of all meats. He further prohibited the eating of carnivorous beasts and birds, in order to teach us gentleness and kindness. Philo finds a symbolic meaning in the permission to eat of animals that chew the cud and have divided hoofs: man grows in wisdom only if he repeats and chews over what he has studied and if he learns to divide and distinguish various concepts [9].

More than a thousand years after Philo, Maimonides proposed a similar view. All the commandments aim at human perfection, he declared, and the dietary laws are intended to inculcate self-control [10]. But to this he added another consideration: the idea that these regulations are also health laws. Such a view had also been propounded a little earlier by the French Bible commentator, Rabbi Samuel ben Meir (Rashbam), citing the opinions of "famous physicians" [11]. Maimonides developed the subject quite fully, with the assurance of an experienced and successful physician. All the forbidden foods, he asserts, are unwholesome [12].

Maimonides did not know that tapeworm and trichina may be transmitted through pork, that rabbits carry tularemia, and that shellfish are prone to infection and spoiling. When these facts were established by modern scientists, many persons became all the more convinced that the Mosaic ordinances were hygienic in purpose. Some of the unwary, influenced by eighteenth-century notions about "priestcraft," assumed that Moses had given religious sanction to these sound health rules in order to ensure compliance with them—deceiving the people for their own good.

One can hardly doubt that some of the dietary laws had salutary *results* in terms of health. But we have no evidence that this was their *intent*. There is no hint of such a motive in the Bible or the Talmud. Not all the prohibited foods are injurious to health; and on the other hand there is no religious sanction against the consumption of any vegetable or mineral products, though many of them are noxious.

An analogous instance is provided by the law (Exod. 30:17ff.) requiring priests to wash their hands before approaching the altar. Some time before the Christian era, the Pharisees sought to give a priestly character to all of Jewish life; they regarded the family table as a kind of altar and required all persons to wash their hands before breaking bread. The intent of this ruling was purely religious, but it must also have had the—unplanned—effect of reducing the spread of communicable disease.

The *rabbinic* laws of slaughtering, however, seem to have been designed to make the death of the animal swift and merciful. The animal is rendered unfit for food if there is a nick in the slaughtering knife or if there is delay or bungling in the slaughtering procedure [13].

Modern scholars have tried to elucidate the dietary laws of the Bible through studies in comparative religion and folklore, but these efforts have not yielded many positive results. Theories that these practices were rooted in totemism seem to be unfounded. Probably no one explanation applies to all the dietary restrictions. Some of them may have had an antipagan character.

4. The Dietary Laws in Jewish History

Though the food laws are expounded at length only in the priestly writings (including Deut. 14), they were known to other biblical writers. The old version of the Flood story

(Gen. 7:1ff., from the "J" document) tells that Noah was commanded to bring into the ark seven pairs of each species of clean animal, but only one pair each of the unclean beasts [14]. The same source reports that Israelites do not eat the thigh muscle (Gen. 32:33; see further Judg. 13:4; Ezek. 4:14). Saul displayed great concern when he was informed that the people were eating meat "with the blood." (I Sam. 14:32ff.; Isa. 65:3 and 4 and 66:17 are concerned not so much with violation of the food laws as with an obscene idolatrous cult.)

Thus some at least of the dietary rules go far back in the biblical period, perhaps even to prebiblical times. People probably observed them as a matter of course. It was only in the Hellenistic age that these laws seem to have become a burning issue. At that time, the followers of Greek culture—both Gentiles and Jews—began to sneer at all distinctive Jewish observances, especially those that required control of the appetites. The attack on Judaism by Antiochus Epiphanes was marked, among other things, by orders for the Jews to bring sacrifices of swine (I Macc. 1:47). A famous story tells how the Syrians sought to force an aged man named Eleazar to set a public example of eating pork—or even pretending to do so—and how he refused and died as a martyr (II Macc. 6). It is at this time that the pig appears to have become an object of special abhorrence to Jews. In the Bible it does not seem to be more objectionable than other forbidden animals [15].

Something of the spirit of the martyrs of the Maccabean age remained with the people in succeeding centuries, especially after the commandments of the Torah were subjected to Christian attack.

Jesus of Nazareth is reported to have said, "It is not what enters a man's mouth that defiles him; what defiles a man is what comes out of his mouth" (Matthew 15:11; Mark 7:15). But, in referring to "what enters a man's mouth," he was speaking, not of the dietary laws of the Bible, but of the Pharisaic requirement to wash the hands before eating (see above, "3. The Reason for the Dietary Laws"). There is no reason to doubt that Jesus observed the biblical food restrictions, and there is no reason to think that he called for their abrogation [16].

But the new church soon had more gentile than Jewish adherents, and it rapidly adjusted to this situation. The apostle Peter was said to have been shown in a vision that the unclean animals were no longer forbidden (Acts 10:9ff.). At a historic gathering, it was decided that gentile converts to Christianity need refrain only from the meat of idolatrous sacrifices, from blood, and from animals that had been strangled (Acts 15:20). In later centuries, Christian critics of Judaism vehemently attacked the dietary laws, with the result that Jewish resistance stiffened. Many Christians resented the unwillingness of Jews to eat in Christian homes. The desire to break down such barriers was one of the considerations that led the founders of the Reform movement to rethink the question of dietary observance.

5. *Some Modern Problems*

Those who today continue to observe the dietary laws as a matter of conscience face a number of problems, some of which concern the entire Jewish community in its internal and external relations.

The internal problem stems from the fact that, though it is a religious duty for the Orthodox Jew to avoid nonkosher food, the purveying of kosher food is not a religious function, but a commercial enterprise. To prevent conflict of interest, Jewish communities in the past engaged one or more ritual slaughterers (*shochetim*) who were communal employees and who were responsible to the

811

rabbi. They were required to examine the lungs of each animal they slaughtered and, if they found any evidence that the animal *might* not be kosher, to refer the matter to the rabbi for decision. The *shochet* did not sell meat; the meat dealer was a private entrepreneur. Even so, abuses occurred from time to time. Such difficulties have multiplied in contemporary America, where there is no unified, disciplined Jewish community—often no united Orthodox community. In New York State, it has been found necessary to establish a branch of the Department of Agriculture and Markets to police the kosher meat stores and to prosecute dealers who fraudulently sell nonkosher meat as kosher—an unfortunate obtrusion of the state into what are properly religious matters. There have also been charges of corruption and racketeering in the industry. And, while the extra supervision required should make kosher meat a trifle more expensive than comparable cuts of nonkosher meat, the difference in cost has often been so large as to discourage many persons from maintaining *kashrut* in their homes.

The external problem results from the effort in many countries to outlaw kosher slaughtering as cruel. Such efforts have often been motivated, not by compassion for animals, but by malice toward Jews. Jewish law, as we have seen, requires slaughtering to be done quickly and with a minimum of pain; and a United States federal statute recognizes *shechitah* as a humane method of slaughter.

But there is an unresolved problem, and those concerned about it are not necessarily to be dismissed as anti-Semites. The assembly line methods used in American abattoirs often involve shackling animals and hoisting them off the ground before the *shochet* comes to kill them. This procedure is questionable even from the purely ritual standpoint; it is certainly indefensible because of its cruelty.

A more humane restraining device has been invented, and the American Society for the Prevention of Cruelty to Animals has expended considerable sums to make it available to meat packers. But, despite support of this effort by national representative Jewish bodies, the new device has not been widely adopted. In the name of human decency, and for the honor of the Jewish name, the American Jewish community should insist that the improved procedure be used everywhere [17].

6. Reform Judaism and the Dietary Laws

Today the observance of *kashrut* has been made easier in many ways. Vegetable shortenings, soap made with vegetable oil, frozen kosher poultry, and prepared dinners are generally available. Many kosher butchers regularly relieve the housewife of the task of washing, salting, and rinsing meat. Yet probably only a minority of today's Jews observe the dietary laws strictly at home; still fewer observe them away from home. Large groups no longer believe these laws were divinely ordained. In Communist countries official policy makes any kind of religious observance difficult if not impossible. But even in Israel, where most of the available meat is kosher slaughtered, indifference has led to widespread disregard of the dietary laws.

American Conservative Judaism upholds *kashrut*, if not as a divine ordinance, at least as a means of inculcating Jewish distinctiveness and strengthening Jewish unity and loyalty. Its national body, the United Synagogue of America, insists that member congregations observe the dietary laws in their synagogue buildings. But only a fraction of their families maintain strictly kosher homes; and, of these, many eat nonkosher food outside their homes.

The issue of dietary observance was raised in Reform Jewish circles in the 1840s, if not

earlier, and was under discussion for some decades. In 1885, a group of distinguished Reform rabbis adopted the famous "Pittsburgh Platform"; it contained the statement: "We hold that all such Mosaic and rabbinical laws as regulate diet, priestly purity, and dress originated in ages and under the influence of ideas entirely foreign to our present mental and spiritual state. They fail to impress the modern Jew with a spirit of priestly holiness; their observance in our days is apt rather to obstruct than to further modern spiritual elevation." However, Isaac M. Wise, the chief organizer of the movement in America, publicly advocated the retention of these laws for hygienic reasons and urged that they not be made the subject of controversy and bitterness [18]. To this day a small minority of Reform Jews maintain kosher homes out of sentiment, or out of respect for Orthodox parents, or to express their solidarity with all Israel. Others avoid eating pork and shellfish, though they do not observe all the rules of *kashrut*.

The spokesmen of Reform Judaism rarely find it necessary either to attack or defend these observances. They do not regard such provisions as the literal word of God; they hold that they are no longer religiously meaningful and therefore need not be followed. But they have no quarrel with those who chose to observe the dietary laws.

Yet conscientious Reform Jews cannot disregard the subject altogether. They must help protect the right of all Jews to live by the dietary laws if they so choose—in the name both of Jewish loyalty and of religious freedom. (The national Reform Jewish bodies participate in such efforts.) They must insist

that Jewish communal institutions provide kosher food for those who desire it. And they ought to know something about these laws and their meaning.

In a larger sense, we must rethink the whole question of eating, in view of our frequent statements that Judaism deals with every aspect of human life. Is it true that "a man is what he eats"? In what sense and to what degree? Some Jews of widely varied religious backgrounds have become vegetarians on principle. Perhaps it is time to examine the question: Is it right to kill any living thing for food?

Moreover, the problem of food supply has become urgent and critical everywhere. Millions are always hungry, while others eat too much for their own good. Even in the affluent United States, large numbers are malnourished while others oscillate between gourmet cookery and reducing diets.

Judaism has encouraged the enjoyment of simple pleasures. It is a *mitzvah* to have a good Sabbath dinner, just as it is a *mitzvah* to fast on Yom Kippur. But, on the other hand, the experience of self-control is at least as educational as the experience of the latest "taste thrill." The traditional dietary laws—despite Maimonides—did not automatically generate self-control: one could gorge oneself on kosher food. Yet, in practice, adherence to *kashrut* meant for many people, not merely self-discipline, but real sacrifice. This is not to argue that we should revert to the laws of Leviticus, chapter 11; it means only that there are many religious aspects to the question of what we eat and how much, and of what there is for others to eat.

וַיְדַבֵּר יְהוָה אֶל־מֹשֶׁה וְאֶל־אַהֲרֹן לֵאמֹר אֲלֵהֶם: א

דַּבְּרוּ אֶל־בְּנֵי יִשְׂרָאֵל לֵאמֹר זֹאת הַחַיָּה אֲשֶׁר ב

תֹּאכְלוּ מִכָּל־הַבְּהֵמָה אֲשֶׁר עַל־הָאָרֶץ: כֹּל ג

מַפְרֶסֶת פַּרְסָה וְשֹׁסַעַת שֶׁסַע פְּרָסֹת מַעֲלַת גֵּרָה

בַּבְּהֵמָה אֹתָהּ תֹּאכֵלוּ: אַךְ אֶת־זֶה לֹא תֹאכְלוּ ד

מִמַּעֲלֵי הַגֵּרָה וּמִמַּפְרִסֵי הַפַּרְסָה אֶת־הַגָּמָל כִּי־

מַעֲלֵה גֵרָה הוּא וּפַרְסָה אֵינֶנּוּ מַפְרִיס טָמֵא הוּא

לָכֶם: וְאֶת־הַשָּׁפָן כִּי־מַעֲלֵה גֵרָה הוּא וּפַרְסָה לֹא ה

יַפְרִיס טָמֵא הוּא לָכֶם: וְאֶת־הָאַרְנֶבֶת כִּי־מַעֲלַת ו

גֵּרָה הוּא וּפַרְסָה לֹא הִפְרִיסָה טְמֵאָה הִוא לָכֶם:

וְאֶת־הַחֲזִיר כִּי־מַפְרִיס פַּרְסָה הוּא וְשֹׁסַע שֶׁסַע ז

פַּרְסָה וְהוּא גֵּרָה לֹא־יִגָּר טָמֵא הוּא לָכֶם: מִבְּשָׂרָם

לֹא תֹאכֵלוּ וּבְנִבְלָתָם לֹא תִגָּעוּ טְמֵאִים הֵם לָכֶם: ח

אֶת־זֶה תֹּאכְלוּ מִכֹּל אֲשֶׁר בַּמָּיִם כֹּל אֲשֶׁר־לוֹ סְנַפִּיר ט

וְקַשְׂקֶשֶׂת בַּמַּיִם בַּיַּמִּים וּבַנְּחָלִים אֹתָם תֹּאכֵלוּ:

וְכֹל אֲשֶׁר אֵין־לוֹ סְנַפִּיר וְקַשְׂקֶשֶׂת בַּיַּמִּים וּבַנְּחָלִים י

1] And the L ord spoke to Moses and Aaron, saying to them: **2]** Speak to the Israelite people thus:

These are the creatures that you may eat from among all the land animals: **3]** any animal that has true hoofs, with clefts through the hoofs, and that chews the cud—such you may eat. **4]** The following, however, of those that either chew the cud or have true hoofs, you shall not eat: the camel—although it chews the cud, it has no true hoofs: it is unclean for you; **5]** the daman—although it chews the cud, it has no true hoofs: it is unclean for you; **6]** the hare—although it chews the cud, it has no true hoofs: it is unclean for you; **7]** and the swine—although it has true hoofs, with the hoofs cleft through, it does not chew the cud: it is unclean for you. **8]** You shall not eat of their flesh or touch their carcasses; they are unclean for you.

9] These you may eat of all that live in water: anything in water, whether in the seas or in the streams, that has fins and scales—these you may eat. **10]** But anything in the seas or in the

11:1] *To Moses and Aaron.* Aaron was included in this revelation, since the priests had the duty of teaching the people to distinguish clean from unclean (10:10).

2] Permissible quadrupeds: only such may be eaten as have divided hoofs and chew the cud. That both features must be present is emphasized by the enumeration of animals that have (or appear to have) one of these characteristics, but not the other.

3] *. . . That has true hoofs.* So Ibn Ezra and others. Most interpreters take this phrase to mean "that has cloven hoofs," i.e., that two different expressions are used to emphasize the importance of the divided hoof.

　　Chews. Literally, "brings up" (T.N.).

4] *. . . The camel.* A genuine ruminant that has divided hoofs, but they are joined at the bottom by a pad.

5] *. . . The daman.* A small west Asian animal of

the hyrax family whose other members are found only in southern Africa. It looks something like a small-eared rabbit, though in fact it is distantly related to the horse and elephant. Earlier translations, "cony" and "rock badger," are misleading; "cony" is an archaic word for rabbit, and the European badger is nothing like the hyrax. This shy animal has small undivided hoofs; it does not chew the cud, but its constant munching movements give the impression that it does. The same is true of the hare (verse 6). The biblical writers were not scientific biologists.

8] *. . . Or touch their carcasses.* The wording seems to prohibit such contact absolutely. But, in view of all the law on the subject (see at 11:24, 25, 27), the sentence probably means no more than "You cannot touch their carcasses without being ritually defiled" (so Rashbam and others).

9–12] Of water creatures: Only those with fins and scales are permitted. Presumably prohibited are

מִכֹּל שֶׁרֶץ הַמַּיִם וּמִכֹּל נֶפֶשׁ הַחַיָּה אֲשֶׁר בַּמַּיִם שֶׁקֶץ טו כָּל־עֹרֵב לְמִינוֹ: וְאֵת בַּת הַיַּעֲנָה וְאֶת־הַתַּחְמָס וְאֶת־

יא הֵם לָכֶם: וְשֶׁקֶץ יִהְיוּ לָכֶם מִבְּשָׂרָם לֹא תֹאכֵלוּ   יז הַשַּׁחַף וְאֶת־הַנֵּץ לְמִינֵהוּ: וְאֶת־הַכּוֹס וְאֶת־הַשָּׁלָךְ

יב וְאֶת־נִבְלָתָם תְּשַׁקֵּצוּ: כֹּל אֲשֶׁר אֵין־לוֹ סְנַפִּיר   יח וְאֶת־הַיַּנְשׁוּף: וְאֶת־הַתִּנְשֶׁמֶת וְאֶת־הַקָּאָת וְאֶת־הָרָחָם:

יג וְקַשְׂקֶשֶׂת בַּמַּיִם שֶׁקֶץ הוּא לָכֶם: וְאֶת־אֵלֶּה תְּשַׁקְּצוּ   יט וְאֵת הַחֲסִידָה הָאֲנָפָה לְמִינָהּ וְאֶת־הַדּוּכִיפַת וְאֶת־

מִן־הָעוֹף לֹא יֵאָכְלוּ שֶׁקֶץ הֵם אֶת־הַנֶּשֶׁר וְאֶת־הַפֶּרֶס   כ הָעֲטַלֵּף: כֹּל שֶׁרֶץ הָעוֹף הַהֹלֵךְ עַל־אַרְבַּע שֶׁקֶץ

יד וְאֵת הָעָזְנִיָּה: וְאֶת־הַדָּאָה וְאֶת־הָאַיָּה לְמִינָהּ: אֵת   כא הוּא לָכֶם: אַךְ אֶת־זֶה תֹּאכְלוּ מִכֹּל שֶׁרֶץ הָעוֹף

streams that has no fins and scales, among all the swarming things of the water and among all the other living creatures that are in the water—they are an abomination for you **11]** and an abomination for you they shall remain: you shall not eat of their flesh and you shall abominate their carcasses. **12]** Everything in water that has no fins and scales shall be an abomination for you.

13] The following you shall abominate among the birds—they shall not be eaten, they are an abomination: the eagle, the vulture, and the black vulture; **14]** the kite, falcons of every variety; **15]** all varieties of raven; **16]** the ostrich, the nighthawk, the sea gull; hawks of every variety; **17]** the little owl, the cormorant, and the great owl; **18]** the white owl, the pelican, and the bustard; **19]** the stork; herons of every variety; the hoopoe, and the bat.

20] All winged swarming things, that walk on fours, shall be an abomination for you. **21]** But these you may eat among all the winged swarming things that walk on fours: all that

shellfish, amphibians, water mammals, and many fish that do not have clearly defined scales, including sharks, eels, and catfish.

13–19] The Torah does not state the characteristics of clean birds but simply gives a list of those that are forbidden. The Rabbis concluded that all those on the list are predators, and they found several anatomical traits that they have in common. "A number of these cannot be identified with certainty" (T.N.). The bat (verse 19) is, of course, a mammal, even though it flies.

Presumably all birds not included in the list are permitted, but traditional practice is much more restrictive. See Appendix I.

20–23] . . . *Winged swarming things.* The Hebrew *sheretz,* "creeping/swarming thing," is a term applied broadly to all kinds of vermin: rodents, reptiles, worms, insects, etc. (cf. verses 29 and 30). The present

verses speak of winged *sheretz,* i.e., winged insects, of which four species are singled out as permitted for eating. Every other variety of *sheretz,* with or without wings, is forbidden. Locusts and grasshoppers, cooked in various ways, are still eaten by some peoples in the Near East. Medieval halachists, uncertain about the identity of the kosher species, forbade the eating of any insects. But Kalisch, writing in the 1870s, reported that the Yemenite Jews still ate locusts [19].

20] . . . *That walk on fours.* The clause is perplexing, for all winged insects have *six* legs. Hoffmann, following Jewish tradition, understands verse 21 to mean "all that have [two additional] legs to leap with, higher than their [other] legs." This fits the fact that grasshoppers and locusts have hind legs much longer than the other four, but it hardly fits the Hebrew words of the verse [20].

הֹלֵךְ עַל־אַרְבַּע אֲשֶׁר־לוֹא כְרָעַיִם מִמַּעַל לְרַגְלָיו
לְנַתֵּר בָּהֵן עַל־הָאָרֶץ: אֶת־אֵלֶּה מֵהֶם תֹּאכֵלוּ אֶת־
הָאַרְבֶּה לְמִינוֹ וְאֶת־הַסָּלְעָם לְמִינֵהוּ וְאֶת־הַחַרְגֹּל
לְמִינֵהוּ וְאֶת־הֶחָגָב לְמִינֵהוּ: וְכֹל שֶׁרֶץ הָעוֹף אֲשֶׁר־
לוֹ אַרְבַּע רַגְלָיִם שֶׁקֶץ הוּא לָכֶם:

* כא לו קרי.

have, above their feet, jointed legs to leap with on the ground— 22] of these you may eat the following: locusts of every variety; all varieties of bald locust; crickets of every variety; and all varieties of grasshopper. 23] But all other winged swarming things that have four legs shall be an abomination for you.

22] *The following.* A number of these cannot be identified with certainty (T.N.).

GLEANING

Haggadah

11:7] . . . *The Swine—Although It Has True Hoofs, with the Hoofs Cleft Through, It Does Not Chew the Cud*

When the pig is resting, he stretches out his legs in front of him, displaying his cleft hoofs. "How kosher I am!" he seems to say, making no mention of the fact that he does not chew the cud. He symbolizes the hypocrite who parades his virtues and conceals his faults [21].

PART IV

Defilement and Purification

Defilement from Animal Carcasses

The first half of chapter 11 designates the quadrupeds, birds, fish, and insects that may and may not be eaten. The second part of the chapter deals with the effects of touching or carrying the carcasses of the forbidden creatures. Thus we come to the subject of ritual defilement and its correction, a topic that will be continued through the next four chapters. We must now examine more fully the concepts of *tamé* and *tahor*, "unclean" and "clean." We have already seen that they are not equivalent to "physically dirty" and "spic and span."

We are dealing with notions that are not peculiar to the Bible. They were common to all ancient peoples, who gave them expression in practices somewhat like those we are to examine now. Some of these ideas still survive in certain cultures, and vestiges of them remain even in our supposedly scientific civilization.

From time beyond memory, it was believed that certain places, substances, and persons carried a sort of "high charge," like an electric wire, and must be approached cautiously, if at all. The "charge" was something supernatural. Often a distinction was made between gods, who were sometimes beneficent, and demons, who were invariably hostile and destructive. The distinction was not always sharp, but it led to a distinction of ritual practice. There was a difference between places and objects that had to be avoided, because they were sacred to a deity, and those that were to be shunned as demonic. The former area is designated in Hebrew by *kadosh*, "holy," the latter by *tamé*, "unclean, impure."

In Leviticus the demonic background of the *tamé* has been all but obliterated; there are only a few allusions to primitive concepts. Generally, the laws of purity and impurity are set forth simply as God's commandments, which must be obeyed because God has ordained them. Such obedience makes Israel a holy people.

These physical concepts of the holy, the impure, and the pure are not the only ones found in Scripture. This very book of Leviticus presents a sublime concept of spiritual holiness, expressed in the noblest standards of ethical living. This advanced understanding of holiness, found also in the Prophets, will be discussed in the introduction to chapter 19. Similarly, many biblical passages assert that defilement is caused by bloodshed, idolatry, sexual immorality, and other forms of unethical behavior (see, e.g., Lev. 18:24 f.;

Jer. 2:7 f.; Ezek. 36:17 f.; Hos. 5:1–5). The contrasting word *tahor*, "pure," is also used in nonritual connections. Unalloyed gold is *tahor* (Exod. 25:31); and the Psalmist prays for a clean heart (Ps. 51:12)—that is, a spirit uncontaminated by sin or guilt.

But the present chapters treat the ritual aspects of clean and unclean. And this complex of ideas includes the notion of contagion. We saw (at 6:11) that ritual "holiness" may be transmitted by contact. The same thing is true of defilement. Both the *tamé* and the *kadosh* emit a sort of energy. But ritual purity is a neutral state and is not transmissible. A bandage is no longer sterile if it falls on the floor, yet it does not transmit its former sterility to the spot on which it falls. As with modern asepsis, so with ancient ritual, positive measures are needed to overcome defilement.

But the analogy between ancient and modern notions of contagion is far from exact. As we now understand it, infection is caused by a microorganism which, if transmitted to a new host, can grow with undiminished vigor. Ritual impurity, however, was felt to be a kind of energy which tended to grow weaker as it passed from the source to other persons or objects. In the rabbinic systematization of these laws, the source (Hebrew *av*, "father") of impurity defiles the first contact, which in turn can defile the second contact; the impurity is not transmitted farther [1].

There is indeed one form of ritual defilement of highest intensity: defilement by a human corpse. This uncleanness is transmitted for an additional stage; and the corpse is therefore called by the Rabbis "the father of fathers of impurity." This subject is mentioned only briefly in Leviticus, chapter 21, and receives full treatment in Numbers, chapter 19. The sources of impurity we shall have to deal with are: the carcasses of some of the forbidden animals (chapter 11); a

woman after childbirth (chapter 12); certain disfiguring skin diseases, as well as strange discolorations on fabrics and on the walls of houses (chapters 13 and 14); a menstruating woman, and all discharges from the human genitals, normal and abnormal (chapter 15).

Such types of defilement are clearly quite different from that discussed in the first part of chapter 11. Partaking of forbidden food is a serious violation of the law—in rabbinic terminology, "a defilement of the sacred." (So is intercourse with a menstruating woman. See 15:24, 18:19, 20:18.) But the cases enumerated in the preceding paragraph are for the most part not avoidable. Ritual impurity comes about through accident, through normal physical processes, through illness, and through actions that are in themselves proper and even commendable. One cannot remove a dead mouse from his dwelling, or tend people suffering from certain illnesses, or bury the dead, without defiling himself. The Rabbis classify such types of impurity as "defilement of the body." In general, it is not sinful to become *tamé* through them, or even to remain unpurified. (Indeed, the performance of certain ritual commands entailed defilement: Lev. 16:26 and 28; Num. 19:7, 8, and 10.) Sin occurred only when the *tamé* was brought into contact with the sacred, the *kadosh*. To enter the sacred area of the Tabernacle/Temple, or to partake of consecrated food, while in a state of impurity—that was sacrilege [2]. The priests were expected to take more stringent measures to prevent their defilement, but even for them there were certain dispensations (Lev. 21).

The laws in these chapters are detailed and technical. They were elaborated and systematized by postbiblical teachers. Not only priests, but also the lay scholars known as the Pharisees occupied themselves with these statutes. Some of the Pharisees undertook to emulate the priesthood in observing the rules

of purity. They formed *chavurot*, "societies," whose members were pledged to eat their nonsacred food in the same state of ritual purity required of the priests when they ate sacrificial meat or *terumah* ("heave offering," Num. 18:8ff.).

With the fall of the Temple, most of these laws ceased to be operative; but, in view of the lively expectation that the Temple would be rebuilt, scholars continued to study the laws, and the *chavurot* survived for many decades. The sixth section of the Mishnah, *Seder Tohorot*, containing the laws of defilement and purification, is very bulky. But after the second century C.E. it does not seem to have been studied systematically. Only the treatise *Niddah*, dealing with menstrual defilement, was provided with a *Gemara*.

בְּגָדָיו וְטָמֵא עַד־הָעֶרֶב טְמֵאִים הֵמָּה לָכֶם: ס
וְזֶה לָכֶם הַטָּמֵא בַּשֶּׁרֶץ הַשֹּׁרֵץ עַל־הָאָרֶץ הַחֹלֶד
וְהָעַכְבָּר וְהַצָּב לְמִינֵהוּ: וְהָאֲנָקָה וְהַכֹּחַ וְהַלְּטָאָה
וְהַחֹמֶט וְהַתִּנְשָׁמֶת: אֵלֶּה הַטְּמֵאִים לָכֶם בְּכָל־הַשָּׁרֶץ
כָּל־הַנֹּגֵעַ בָּהֶם בְּמֹתָם יִטְמָא עַד־הָעָרֶב: וְכֹל אֲשֶׁר־
יִפֹּל־עָלָיו מֵהֶם בְּמֹתָם יִטְמָא מִכָּל־כְּלִי־עֵץ אוֹ בֶגֶד
אוֹ־עוֹר אוֹ שָׂק כָּל־כְּלִי אֲשֶׁר־יֵעָשֶׂה מְלָאכָה בָּהֶם

כד וּלְאֵלֶּה תִּטַּמְּאוּ כָּל־הַנֹּגֵעַ בְּנִבְלָתָם יִטְמָא עַד־הָעָרֶב:
כה וְכָל־הַנֹּשֵׂא מִנִּבְלָתָם יְכַבֵּס בְּגָדָיו וְטָמֵא עַד־הָעָרֶב:
כו לְכָל־הַבְּהֵמָה אֲשֶׁר הִוא מַפְרֶסֶת פַּרְסָה וְשֶׁסַע אֵינֶנָּה
שֹׁסַעַת וְגֵרָה אֵינֶנָּה מַעֲלָה טְמֵאִים הֵם לָכֶם כָּל־הַנֹּגֵעַ
בָּהֶם יִטְמָא: וְכֹל הוֹלֵךְ עַל־כַּפָּיו בְּכָל־הַחַיָּה
הַהֹלֶכֶת עַל־אַרְבַּע טְמֵאִים הֵם לָכֶם כָּל־הַנֹּגֵעַ
בְּנִבְלָתָם יִטְמָא עַד־הָעָרֶב: וְהַנֹּשֵׂא אֶת־נִבְלָתָם יְכַבֵּס

24] And the following shall make you unclean—whoever touches their carcasses shall be unclean until evening, **25]** and whoever carries the carcasses of any of them shall wash his clothes and be unclean until evening— **26]** every animal that has true hoofs but without clefts through the hoofs, or that does not chew the cud. They are unclean for you; whoever touches them shall be unclean. **27]** Also all animals that walk on paws, among those that walk on fours, are unclean for you; whoever touches their carcasses shall be unclean until evening. **28]** And anyone who carries their carcasses shall wash his clothes and remain unclean until evening. They are unclean for you.

29] The following shall be unclean for you from among the things that swarm on the earth: the mole, the mouse, and great lizards of every variety; **30]** the gecko, the land crocodile, the lizard, the sand lizard, and the chameleon. **31]** Those are for you the unclean among all the swarming things; whoever touches them when they are dead shall be unclean until evening. **32]** And anything on which one of them falls when dead shall be unclean: be it any article of wood, or a cloth, or a skin, or a sack—any such article that can be put to use shall be dipped in

11:24] *Shall make you unclean.* By contact.

Shall be unclean until evening. As the text stands, the defiled person need not purify himself actively; he must simply avoid contact with the holy until sunset, by which time the impurity will be dissipated. That is how some modern scholars understand the passage. But *Sifra* may well be correct in understanding (on the analogy of 11:32, 17:5, and 22:6f.) that the person requires a ritual bath but is not completely purified till sunset.

25] *Whoever carries the carcasses of any of them shall wash his clothes.* Touching might mean grazing the carcass with a finger; but carrying would bring the defiling object into contact with his body and clothing, thus spreading the contagion. Here too the halachah may be correct in understanding: in addition to bathing, he must also wash his clothes; then at sundown he becomes *tahor.*

27] *That walk on paws [and have no hoofs at all].* The verse is added for the sake of completeness. Legally, the horse and bear are equally forbidden and their carcasses are equally defiling.

29–38] Defilement by the bodies of certain "creeping things." For the meaning of *sheretz,* see commentary on 11:20–23.

29] *The following.* A number of these cannot be identified with certainty (T.N.).

31] *Shall be unclean.* See commentary on 11:24.

32–38] The uncleanness of the carcass can be transmitted to various objects which can, in turn, defile still other substances, such as food.

32] *A sack.* A piece of sackcloth, a rough material, worn as a sign of mourning.

Shall be dipped in water. The chief means of ceremonial purification (see Lev. 11:25, 36, 14:5f.; Num. 19:8, 14ff., and elsewhere).

מַעְיָן וּבוֹר מִקְוֵה־מַיִם יִהְיֶה טָהוֹר וְנֹגֵעַ בְּנִבְלָתָם   לג בַּמַּיִם יוּבָא וְטָמֵא עַד־הָעֶרֶב וְטָהֵר: וְכָל־כְּלִי־חֶרֶשׂ
לז יִטְמָא: וְכִי יִפֹּל מִנִּבְלָתָם עַל־כָּל־זֶרַע זֵרוּעַ אֲשֶׁר   אֲשֶׁר־יִפֹּל מֵהֶם אֶל־תּוֹכוֹ כֹּל אֲשֶׁר בְּתוֹכוֹ יִטְמָא
לח יִזָּרֵעַ טָהוֹר הוּא: וְכִי יֻתַּן־מַיִם עַל־זֶרַע וְנָפַל   לד וְאֹתוֹ תִשְׁבֹּרוּ: מִכָּל־הָאֹכֶל אֲשֶׁר יֵאָכֵל אֲשֶׁר יָבוֹא
לט מִנִּבְלָתָם עָלָיו טָמֵא הוּא לָכֶם: ס וְכִי יָמוּת מִן   עָלָיו מַיִם יִטְמָא וְכָל־מַשְׁקֶה אֲשֶׁר יִשָּׁתֶה בְּכָל־כְּלִי
הַבְּהֵמָה אֲשֶׁר־הִיא לָכֶם לְאָכְלָה הַנֹּגֵעַ בְּנִבְלָתָהּ   לה יִטְמָא: וְכֹל אֲשֶׁר־יִפֹּל מִנִּבְלָתָם עָלָיו יִטְמָא תַּנּוּר
מ יִטְמָא עַד־הָעֶרֶב: וְהָאֹכֵל מִנִּבְלָתָהּ יְכַבֵּס בְּגָדָיו   לו וְכִירַיִם יֻתָּץ טְמֵאִים הֵם וּטְמֵאִים יִהְיוּ לָכֶם: אַךְ

water, and it shall remain unclean until evening; then it shall be clean. **33]** And if any of those falls into an earthen vessel, everything inside it shall be unclean and [the vessel] itself you shall break. **34]** As to any food that might be eaten, it shall become unclean if it came in contact with water; as to any liquid that might be drunk, it shall become unclean if it was inside any vessel. **35]** Everything on which the carcass of any of them falls shall be unclean: an oven or stove shall be smashed. They are unclean and unclean they shall remain for you. **36]** However, a spring or cistern in which water is collected shall be clean, but whoever touches such a carcass in it shall be unclean. **37]** If such a carcass falls upon seed grain that is to be sown, it is clean; **38]** but if water is put on the seed and any part of a carcass falls upon it, it shall be unclean for you.

39] If an animal that you may eat has died, anyone who touches its carcass shall be unclean until evening; **40]** anyone who eats of its carcass shall wash his clothes and remain unclean

33] *An earthen vessel . . . you shall break.* Cf. 6:21, where the pottery must be broken because it has been made *kadosh.*

34] *In contact with water.* I.e., if the food then came in contact with the carcass of any animal named in verses 29–30 (T.N.). Dry food and seeds (verse 37) are resistant to contagion; but, if they are moistened, they at once become susceptible to it.

Any liquid that might be drunk. Whereas water in springs, wells, rivers, lakes, and seas is not susceptible to ritual defilement, and indeed neutralizes ritual defilement, "drawn water" in a vessel may be defiled by the vessel itself or by some other source of impurity.

Inside any vessel. I.e., a vessel that had become contaminated by such contact (T.N.).

Verses 34 through 38 form the basis of an entire Mishnah treatise called *Machshirin,* "Things that predispose [to impurity]."

35] *Everything.* This refers back to verse 32.

An oven. See commentary on 2:4.

Stove. Hebrew *kirayim* which occurs nowhere else in the Bible. Rabbinic sources [3] describe the *kirah* as an earthenware container inside which fire was made; it had two openings on top on which pots could be placed. Being made of pottery, like the oven, it could not be purified (verse 33). Ehrlich explains the verse to mean: Though a household, which might have many pots, would ordinarily have only one oven or stove, the latter must nevertheless be smashed if it is defiled.

36–38] See commentary on 11:34.

36] *But whoever touches such a carcass in it.* Do not argue: since the spring or cistern purifies one who is already unclean, it will protect him from defilement by the carcass in the water (*Sifra*).

39–40] Not only do the carcasses of forbidden animals defile; if a permitted animal dies, or is improperly slaughtered, its carcass is a source of impurity also.

39] *Shall be unclean until evening. . . .* See commentary on 11:24 and 25.

מה נַפְשֹׁתֵיכֶם בְּכָל־הַשֶּׁרֶץ הָרֹמֵשׂ עַל־הָאָרֶץ: כִּי אֲנִי יְהוָֹה הַמַּעֲלֶה אֶתְכֶם מֵאֶרֶץ מִצְרַיִם לִהְיֹת לָכֶם לֵאלֹהִים וִהְיִיתֶם קְדֹשִׁים כִּי קָדוֹשׁ אָנִי: מו זֹאת תּוֹרַת הַבְּהֵמָה וְהָעוֹף וְכֹל נֶפֶשׁ הַחַיָּה הָרֹמֶשֶׂת בַּמָּיִם מז וּלְכָל־נֶפֶשׁ הַשֹּׁרֶצֶת עַל־הָאָרֶץ: לְהַבְדִּיל בֵּין הַטָּמֵא וּבֵין הַטָּהֹר וּבֵין הַחַיָּה הַנֶּאֱכֶלֶת וּבֵין הַחַיָּה אֲשֶׁר לֹא תֵאָכֵל:

וְטָמֵא עַד־הָעֶרֶב וְהַנֹּשֵׂא אֶת־נִבְלָתָהּ יְכַבֵּס בְּגָדָיו מא וְטָמֵא עַד־הָעָרֶב: וְכָל־הַשֶּׁרֶץ הַשֹּׁרֵץ עַל־הָאָרֶץ מב שֶׁקֶץ הוּא לֹא יֵאָכֵל: כֹּל הוֹלֵךְ עַל־גָּחוֹן וְכֹל הוֹלֵךְ עַל־אַרְבַּע עַד כָּל־מַרְבֵּה רַגְלַיִם לְכָל־הַשֶּׁרֶץ הַשֹּׁרֵץ מג עַל־הָאָרֶץ לֹא תֹאכְלוּם כִּי־שֶׁקֶץ הֵם: אַל־תְּשַׁקְּצוּ אֶת־נַפְשֹׁתֵיכֶם בְּכָל־הַשֶּׁרֶץ הַשֹּׁרֵץ וְלֹא תִטַּמְּאוּ בָּהֶם מד וְנִטְמֵתֶם בָּם: כִּי אֲנִי יְהוָה אֱלֹהֵיכֶם וְהִתְקַדִּשְׁתֶּם וִהְיִיתֶם קְדֹשִׁים כִּי קָדוֹשׁ אָנִי וְלֹא תְטַמְּאוּ אֶת־

*סב ו' רבתי והיא חצי התורה באותיות. *מן חסר א'.

Haftarah Shemini, p. 986

until evening; and anyone who carries its carcass shall wash his clothes and remain unclean until evening.

41] All the things that swarm upon the earth are an abomination; they shall not be eaten. **42]** You shall not eat, among all things that swarm upon the earth, anything that crawls on its belly, or anything that walks on fours, or anything that has many legs; for they are an abomination. **43]** You shall not draw abomination upon yourselves through anything that swarms; you shall not make yourselves unclean therewith and thus become unclean. **44]** For I the LORD am your God: you shall sanctify yourselves and be holy, for I am holy. You shall not make yourselves unclean through any swarming thing that moves upon the earth. **45]** For I the LORD am He who brought you up from the land of Egypt to be your God: you shall be holy, for I am holy.

46] These are the instructions concerning animals, birds, all living creatures that move in water, and all creatures that swarm on earth, **47]** for distinguishing between the unclean and the clean, between the living things that may be eaten and the living things that may not be eaten.

41–47] Though the eating of "creeping things" was forbidden by implication in the first half of the chapter, this prohibition is now spelled out.

42] *Belly.* Hebrew *gachon.* In Torah manuscripts, the letter *vav* in this word is written extra large, because—it is said—it is the middle letter of the entire Torah. This detail indicates the meticulous care that the scribes gave to the text.

43] *Draw abomination upon yourselves.* Make yourselves disgusting by such defilement.

And thus become unclean. The repetition is for emphasis. But the spelling of the Hebrew word is unusual; Ibn Ezra and some moderns (citing a similar

form in Job 18: 3) render it "be made stupid" (see **Gleanings**).

44] *Sanctify yourselves and be holy.* The chapter concludes by appealing to the people to raise themselves to a higher level by observing the laws just expounded. In similar terms, the Torah (Lev. 19:2) calls on them to sanctify themselves by ethical conduct.

45] Here, as often, the authority of the laws is reinforced by reference to the great historic memory of redemption from bondage.

46–47] These verses form a concluding summary, typical of priestly writing. Cf. 7:37f.

GLEANINGS

Halachah

11:31] *Those Are for You the Unclean*

From the word "those," *Sifra* infers that all other species of *sheretz*, though forbidden as food (verse 41), are not a source of defilement when dead.

34] *If It Came in Contact with Water*

The following liquids make food and seeds susceptible to uncleanness: dew, water, wine, oil, blood, milk, and honey [4].

Haggadah

11:43] *And Thus Become Unclean*

See commentary. The eating of these abominable foods causes a deterioration of the soul so that it descends from a human to a beastly level.

LUZZATTO

44] *Sanctify Yourselves and Be Holy*

With reference to both ritual and ethics, the Talmud declares: If a man defiles himself a little here below, he will be defiled still more on high, i.e., providence will give him more occasions for wrongdoing. And also: If he sanctifies himself a little here below, he will be sanctified still more on high [5].

In different terms: If one wants to be unclean, he is given the opportunity; if he wants to be clean, he receives divine support [6].

Sanctify yourself through the practice of the commandments and thus you will become holy. Such observance will help you to gain self-control so that your intelligence can govern your appetites. For our intelligence is doubly handicapped in this struggle: We have the appetites from birth, while intelligence develops slowly; and, our environment encourages us to yield to our urges, whereas intelligence is a lonely stranger in the world. BACHYA

Defilement through Childbirth

Though we now know more about the reproductive processes than any earlier generation, the birth of a baby still appears to us as something awesome, even miraculous. To prescientific man, it was an uncanny happening—especially, perhaps, since he was not well equipped to deal with the dangers that often threatened mother and child. In many cultures, childbirth was associated with the demonic, and various taboos were imposed on women in labor and after their delivery. This widespread feeling is doubtless the background of the regulations in this chapter, which declare the new mother to be ritually unclean and require sacrifices of purification.

The procedures described in this chapter lapsed with the destruction of the Second Temple. They became, however, the basis of a Christian custom, "the churching of women," still practiced in the Roman and Anglican churches. It is not mandatory; but it is considered proper for a priest to perform it on request. In some parts of Britain, there are still persons who will not admit a woman who has had a baby to their homes until she has been churched [1].

The Authorized Daily Prayer Book of the British United Synagogue (Orthodox) contains a brief service of thanksgiving for a woman after childbirth. Abrahams [2] adduces precedents for this ritual going back to fifteenth-century Germany. In American Reform practice, new parents attend a Sabbath service at which their child is publicly named. These customs have nothing to do with the ritual purification of the mother.

(A new weekly portion, *Tazria*, begins with 12:1.)

י טָהֳרָה: וּבִמְלֹאת יְמֵי טָהֳרָהּ לְבֵן אוֹ לְבַת תָּבִיא
כֶּבֶשׂ בֶּן־שְׁנָתוֹ לְעֹלָה וּבֶן־יוֹנָה אוֹ־תֹר לְחַטָּאת אֶל־
ז פֶּתַח אֹהֶל־מוֹעֵד אֶל־הַכֹּהֵן: וְהִקְרִיבוֹ לִפְנֵי יְהֹוָה
וְכִפֶּר עָלֶיהָ וְטָהֲרָה מִמְּקֹר דָּמֶיהָ זֹאת תּוֹרַת הַיֹּלֶדֶת
ח לַזָּכָר אוֹ לַנְּקֵבָה: וְאִם־לֹא תִמְצָא יָדָהּ דֵּי שֶׂה
וְלָקְחָה שְׁתֵּי־תֹרִים אוֹ שְׁנֵי בְּנֵי יוֹנָה אֶחָד לְעֹלָה
וְאֶחָד לְחַטָּאת וְכִפֶּר עָלֶיהָ הַכֹּהֵן וְטָהֵרָה: פ

פ   פ   פ

א וַיְדַבֵּר יְהֹוָה אֶל־מֹשֶׁה לֵּאמֹר: דַּבֵּר אֶל־בְּנֵי יִשְׂרָאֵל
לֵאמֹר אִשָּׁה כִּי תַזְרִיעַ וְיָלְדָה זָכָר וְטָמְאָה שִׁבְעַת
ג יָמִים כִּימֵי נִדַּת דְּוֹתָהּ תִּטְמָא: וּבַיּוֹם הַשְּׁמִינִי יִמּוֹל
ד בְּשַׂר עָרְלָתוֹ: וּשְׁלֹשִׁים יוֹם וּשְׁלֹשֶׁת יָמִים תֵּשֵׁב בִּדְמֵי
טָהֳרָה בְּכָל־קֹדֶשׁ לֹא־תִגָּע וְאֶל־הַמִּקְדָּשׁ לֹא תָבֹא
ה עַד־מְלֹאת יְמֵי טָהֳרָהּ: וְאִם־נְקֵבָה תֵלֵד וְטָמְאָה
שְׁבֻעַיִם כְּנִדָּתָהּ וְשִׁשִּׁים יוֹם וְשֵׁשֶׁת יָמִים תֵּשֵׁב עַל־דְּמֵי

1] The LORD spoke to Moses, saying: **2]** Speak to the Israelite people thus: When a woman at childbirth bears a male, she shall be unclean seven days; she shall be unclean as at the time of her menstrual infirmity.   **3]** —On the eighth day the flesh of his foreskin shall be circumcised.—   **4]** She shall remain in a state of blood purification for thirty-three days: she shall not touch any consecrated thing, nor enter the sanctuary until her period of purification is completed.   **5]** If she bears a female, she shall be unclean two weeks as during her menstruation, and she shall remain in a state of blood purification for sixty-six days.

6] On the completion of her period of purification, for either son or daughter, she shall bring to the priest, at the entrance of the Tent of Meeting, a lamb in its first year for a burnt offering, and a pigeon or a turtledove for a sin offering.   **7]** He shall offer it before the LORD and make expiation on her behalf; she shall then be clean from her flow of blood. Such are the rituals concerning her who bears a child, male or female.   **8]** If, however, her means do not suffice for a sheep, she shall take two turtledoves or two pigeons, one for a burnt offering and the other for a sin offering. The priest shall make expiation on her behalf, and she shall be clean.

12:2] *When a woman at childbirth bears.* Hebrew *tazria'*, literally, "brings forth seed" (T.N.).

She shall be unclean . . . as at the time of her menstrual infirmity. The same rules apply as during menstruation (see commentary on 15:19–23).

3] *Shall be circumcised.* The remark here is incidental. (Cf. Gen. 17:12.)

4] *In a state of blood purification.* Hebrew unclear (T.N.). Postpartum discharges do not usually continue more than a week. But their cessation does not terminate the woman's defilement, even after she has taken the ritual bath implicitly required in verse 2 (cf. commentary on 15:19); she is still forbidden to enter the sanctuary or touch sacred food.

5] If the baby is a girl, both states of the mother's impurity last twice as long. No reason is given for this rule. One guesses that, while any childbirth was regarded as uncanny and defiling, the birth of a female, who herself would one day menstruate and bear children, was considered doubly defiling. Christian commentators of former generations saw in this rule an allusion to Eve's special guilt for the "fall of man" [3].

6] *At the entrance of the Tent of Meeting.* She cannot go inside until the purification offerings have been made.

6, 7] *Sin offering . . . make expiation.* Obviously, having a baby is not a sin; it is in fact the fulfillment of a divine command (Gen. 1:18). The reference here is to ritual purgation and nothing else. See T.N. at 4:3 (T.N.).

GLEANINGS

Halachah

12:4] *In a State of Blood Purification*

The Karaite sect held that this rule also required the woman and her husband to refrain from marital relations during the entire 33/66 day period. Against this, Maimonides asserted vehemently that the couple was permitted—and indeed should be required—to resume relations after there had been a seven-day cessation of discharge. But many Rabbanite communities followed the more stringent rule [4].

Haggadah

12:6, 7] *Sin Offering. Make Expiation*

Why should the woman bring a sin offering and require expiation? While in the pain of labor, she might have vowed, "I'll never let my husband come near me again!" The offering atoned for this improper thought or word [5].

Defilement from Tzara'at

Chapters 13 and 14 are usually said to deal with leprosy, but that is begging the question. The single subject of this section is called in Hebrew *tzara'at*, a word of uncertain etymology. It designates a variety of skin ailments and is also applied to unusual changes in the appearance of fabrics and of house walls.

The Greek version of the Torah rendered *tzara'at* by *lepra*, meaning "a scaly condition." This word passed into modern languages via the Latin translation of the Bible; and, during the Middle Ages, *lepra* was identified with the disease we now call leprosy. (Formerly it was called "elephantiasis of the Greeks.")

True leprosy is now referred to as Hansen's disease (or Hansenitis), after the nineteenth-century Norwegian physician who identified the microorganism that causes it. It is not highly contagious, and it develops slowly. Among its symptoms are changes of color and growths on the skin and a loss of sensitivity to pain. In advanced cases the nose, jaw, and extremities may rot away. Modern medicine can arrest, possibly even cure, the disease; but until recent times the leper was doomed to a horrible end.

It was, then, by a mere accident of history that the usual versions of the Bible render *tzara'at* by "leprosy." The Hebrew word must include other ailments than Hansen's disease, since the recovery of the patient is regarded as possible and even likely. The only question is whether *tzara'at* ever means "leprosy." But this question cannot be answered with certainty. Medical men who have studied our chapter have suggested, variously, that it deals with eczema and psoriasis which are not contagious, of impetigo which is highly contagious, of gangrenous infections, and of true leprosy. In other biblical passages, we read of afflicted persons whose skin turned "white as snow." This description suggests an ailment called leucoderma which is disfiguring but not serious.

Such references are frequent in the biblical narratives [1]. One of the signs Moses was to give Pharaoh was to cause *tzara'at* to appear on his own hand and then disappear (Exod. 4:6ff.). Miriam was punished for her unjustified criticism of Moses by a brief attack of the ailment (Num. 12:10f.). A group of "lepers," excluded from the besieged city of Samaria, discovered that the besiegers had fled and brought the good news to the starving people (II Kings 7:3ff.). Elisha cured Naaman, a Syrian general, of

tzara'at and would take no compensation for the service. When the prophet's follower Gehazi obtained some of the reward by a ruse, Elisha declared that the "leprosy" of Naaman would cling to Gehazi and his descendants forever (II Kings 5) [2]. King Uzziah had the effrontery to offer incense on the inner altar, whereupon *tzara'at* broke out on his forehead; "the LORD had smitten him." Hastily thrust out of the Temple, he had to live out the rest of his days in isolation (II Chron. 26:16ff.).

The present translation of the Torah renders *tzara'at* by such terms as "scales" (Exod. 4:6; Num. 12:10) and "scaly [affection]" (Lev. 13:2). But, in cases where the patient is declared unclean, the terms "leprous," "leprosy," and "leper" have been retained in the effort to convey something of the horror which the Bible attaches to this affliction. For the biblical authors did not regard *tzara'at* as just one disease among others. To them it was a *nega*, "smiting," the manifestation of extreme divine displeasure. Unlike other forms of defilement, it does not merely exclude the defiled person from the sanctuary—it bars that person from all human society. It is likely that the emotional overtones attached to *tzara'at* contributed to the sense of horror and revulsion which the very word "leprosy" evokes in western culture. Hansen's disease is indeed a terrible affliction, but the thought of it upsets people more than that of other diseases just as deadly and far more infectious.

Regarding *tzara'at* as a plague, the expression of God's anger, it was natural to inquire what sin evokes this punishment. The biblical stories mentioned above suggest that it might be brought on by several different sins; and a variety of opinions is recorded by the Rabbis [3]. A favorite device of midrashic preachers was to pun on *metzora*, "leper," and *motzi ra*, "slanderer" [4]. Thus, they utilized the reading of these Torah sections as an occasion to preach against hostile talk and gossip—always an appropriate topic for a sermon.

These chapters are not concerned with medical practice as such. The priest examined suspected patients and made a diagnosis, not for the purpose of treatment, but to distinguish between *tzara'at*, which defiles, and other skin ailments that do not. The person afflicted with *tzara'at* was isolated to prevent the spread of ritual contamination but not to protect public health. Luzzatto properly notes that no provision was made for isolating other, more virulent ailments, such as bubonic plague [5]. That the intent of the laws was not hygienic appears from Leviticus, chapter 14, verse 26, which speaks of symptoms appearing on the walls of a house. Before such a house is inspected by a priest, it is to be emptied of its contents. For should he pronounce the place "unclean," everything inside it would be defiled; but household goods removed in advance remain clean!

In the same spirit, the halachists held that a person or object affected by *tzara'at* is legally unclean only from the moment when the priest makes the positive diagnosis. Therefore a person should not be examined for *tzara'at* on the eve of a festival in order not to miss the joyous celebration, and a bridegroom is permitted to postpone his examination until the marriage week is over [6]. And a gentile "leper" does not cause ritual defilement [7].

A Note on Judaism and Medicine

The role of the priest in these matters is entirely ritualistic; he does not attempt to cure *tzara'at*. In this regard, Judaism differed from some ancient and modern religions. The Greek temples of Asklepios, the god of healing, were centers of medical treatment as well as of religious observance. Among primitive peoples, medicine men have often

combined the use of medication with their rites.

The Bible says almost nothing about medical practice. The cures performed by Elijah and Elisha are presented as miracles, and similar wonder stories are told of various postbiblical personalities. In one case, Isaiah directed that an inflammation be treated with a lump of pressed figs (Isa. 38:21); but this was only after he had announced God's promise that the patient would recover. It is told of King Asa, apparently with disapproval, that, when he became ill, he did not seek the Lord but turned to the healers (II Chron. 16:12); but this probably means that he went to pagan medicine men. The Bible nowhere forbids the use of medical aid; and one who injures another physically must pay for the cure (Exod. 21:19).

Ben Sira, writing about two hundred years before the Christian era, pays a warm tribute to the physician. He urges the sick to seek medical care and, at the same time, to pray for divine help, "for from the Most High cometh healing." Indeed, God has appointed the physician for this beneficent task (Ecclus. 38).

The Talmud, which specifically asserts that the practice of medicine is sanctioned by the Torah [8], contains much medical lore [9]. The sour remark that relegates "the best of physicians to hell" [10] should not be taken too seriously; elsewhere the Talmud remarks that one who cures the sick without pay is worth as much as he gets [11].

Medieval and modern Jews have esteemed the medical profession highly. Some of the most notable teachers of Judaism have been distinguished practicing physicians, among them the poet and philosopher Judah Halevi, the philosopher and halachist Moses Maimonides, and Isaac Lampronti of Ferrara (1670–1756), the compiler of a massive talmudic encyclopedia. The contribution of Jews to the advancement of modern medical science has been outstanding.

Chapter 13 of Leviticus is full of uncertainties as to the meaning of words and phrases and as to the nature of the symptoms and the diseases discussed. Rashbam, whose commentary to the Torah was directed entirely to the plain sense of the text, says that in this chapter we cannot rely on simple grammatical exegesis nor on empirical medical knowledge. Here, for once, he is content to rely on the authority of the halachists. An entire treatise of the Mishnah, entitled Nega'im, "Plagues," is devoted to this subject.

א וַיְדַבֵּ֣ר יְהֹוָ֔ה אֶל־מֹשֶׁ֥ה וְאֶֽל־אַהֲרֹ֖ן לֵאמֹֽר: אָדָ֗ם כִּֽי־
יִהְיֶ֤ה בְעוֹר־בְּשָׂרוֹ֙ שְׂאֵ֤ת אֽוֹ־סַפַּ֨חַת֙ א֣וֹ בַהֶ֔רֶת וְהָיָ֥ה
בְעֽוֹר־בְּשָׂר֖וֹ לְנֶ֣גַע צָרָ֑עַת וְהוּבָא֙ אֶל־אַהֲרֹ֣ן הַכֹּהֵ֔ן א֚וֹ
ג אֶל־אַחַ֥ד מִבָּנָ֖יו הַכֹּֽהֲנִֽים: וְרָאָ֣ה הַכֹּהֵ֣ן אֶת־הַנֶּ֣גַע
בְּעֽוֹר־הַ֠בָּשָׂ֠ר וְשֵׂעָ֨ר בַּנֶּ֜גַע הָפַ֣ךְ ׀ לָבָ֗ן וּמַרְאֵ֤ה הַנֶּ֨גַע֙
עָמֹק֙ מֵע֣וֹר בְּשָׂר֔וֹ נֶ֥גַע צָרַ֖עַת ה֑וּא וְרָאָ֥הוּ הַכֹּהֵ֖ן
ד וְטִמֵּ֥א אֹתֽוֹ: וְאִם־בַּהֶ֩רֶת֩ לְבָנָ֨ה הִ֜וא בְּע֣וֹר בְּשָׂר֗וֹ
וְעָמֹק֙ אֵֽין־מַרְאֶ֣הָ מִן־הָע֔וֹר וּשְׂעָרָ֖ה לֹא־הָפַ֣ךְ לָבָ֑ן
ה וְהִסְגִּ֧יר הַכֹּהֵ֛ן אֶת־הַנֶּ֖גַע שִׁבְעַ֥ת יָמִֽים: וְרָאָ֣הוּ הַכֹּהֵן֮

בַּיּ֣וֹם הַשְּׁבִיעִי֒ וְהִנֵּ֤ה הַנֶּ֨גַע֙ עָמַ֣ד בְּעֵינָ֔יו לֹֽא־פָשָׂ֥ה הַנֶּ֖גַע
ו בָּע֑וֹר וְהִסְגִּיר֧וֹ הַכֹּהֵ֛ן שִׁבְעַ֥ת יָמִ֖ים שֵׁנִֽית: וְרָאָה֩ הַכֹּהֵ֨ן
אֹת֜וֹ בַּיּ֣וֹם הַשְּׁבִיעִי֮ שֵׁנִית֒ וְהִנֵּה֙ כֵּהָ֣ה הַנֶּ֔גַע וְלֹֽא־פָשָׂ֥ה
הַנֶּ֖גַע בָּע֑וֹר וְטִהֲר֤וֹ הַכֹּהֵן֙ מִסְפַּ֣חַת הִ֔וא וְכִבֶּ֥ס בְּגָדָ֖יו
ז וְטָהֵֽר: וְאִם־פָּשֹׂ֨ה תִפְשֶׂ֤ה הַמִּסְפַּ֨חַת֙ בָּע֔וֹר אַֽחֲרֵ֧י
הֵרָֽאֹת֛וֹ אֶל־הַכֹּהֵ֖ן לְטָֽהֳרָת֑וֹ וְנִרְאָ֥ה שֵׁנִ֖ית אֶל־הַכֹּהֵֽן:
ח וְרָאָה֙ הַכֹּהֵ֔ן וְהִנֵּ֛ה פָּֽשְׂתָ֥ה הַמִּסְפַּ֖חַת בָּע֑וֹר וְטִמְּא֥וֹ
הַכֹּהֵ֖ן צָרַ֥עַת הֽוּא: פ

1] The LORD spoke to Moses and Aaron, saying:
2] When a person has on the skin of his body a swelling, a rash, or a discoloration, and it develops into a scaly affection on the skin of his body, it shall be reported to Aaron the priest or to one of his sons, the priests. **3]** The priest shall examine the affection on the skin of his body: if hair in the affected patch has turned white and the affection appears to be deeper than the skin of his body, it is a leprous affection; when the priest sees it, he shall pronounce him unclean. **4]** But if it is a white discoloration on the skin of his body which does not appear to be deeper than the skin and the hair in it has not turned white, the priest shall isolate the affected person for seven days. **5]** On the seventh day the priest shall examine him, and if the affection has remained unchanged in color and the disease has not spread on the skin, the priest shall isolate him for another seven days. **6]** On the seventh day the priest shall examine him again: if the affection has faded and has not spread on the skin, the priest shall pronounce him clean. It is a rash; he shall wash his clothes, and he shall be clean. **7]** But if the rash should spread on the skin after he has presented himself to the priest and been pronounced clean, he shall present himself again to the priest. **8]** And if the priest sees that the rash has spread on the skin, the priest shall pronounce him unclean; it is leprosy.

13:1] *And Aaron.* Because the priests had to deal with cases of *tzara'at.*

2–8] First type of *tzara'at* (according to Hoffmann, the "discoloration" of verse 2). When an area of the skin of the body changes in appearance, so that it seems to be deeper than the surrounding skin, and especially if hair on this area turns white, the patient is unclean. If the symptoms are inconclusive, the patient is to be isolated for a week and examined again; this procedure may, if necessary, be repeated once more. If the patient is at any stage pronounced clean and thereafter the affection begins to spread, the priest must see him again and pronounce him unclean.

2] *Scaly affection.* Hebrew *nega'* ("plague of") *tzara'at.* The same words are translated "leprous affection" in verse 3. "Hebrew *tzara'at* is used for a variety of diseases. Where a human being is declared unclean by reason of *tzara'at,* the traditional translation 'leprosy' has been retained without regard to modern medical terminology" (T.N.). See introduction to this chapter.

It shall be reported. Or, "he shall be brought" (T.N.).

3] *Deeper than the skin of his body.* This might mean that the affection is not superficial but extends below the skin. The halachah, however, understands: Because of the change in color, the affected area seems to be lower than the rest of the skin.

י נֶגַע צָרַעַת כִּי תִהְיֶה בְּאָדָם וְהוּבָא אֶל־הַכֹּהֵן: וְרָאָה
הַכֹּהֵן וְהִנֵּה שְׂאֵת־לְבָנָה בָּעוֹר וְהִיא הָפְכָה שֵׂעָר לָבָן
יא וּמִחְיַת בָּשָׂר חַי בַּשְׂאֵת: צָרַעַת נוֹשֶׁנֶת הִוא בְּעוֹר
יב בְּשָׂרוֹ וְטִמְּאוֹ הַכֹּהֵן לֹא יַסְגִּרֶנּוּ כִּי טָמֵא הוּא: וְאִם־
פָּרוֹחַ תִּפְרַח הַצָּרַעַת בָּעוֹר וְכִסְּתָה הַצָּרַעַת אֵת
כָּל־עוֹר הַנֶּגַע מֵרֹאשׁוֹ וְעַד־רַגְלָיו לְכָל־מַרְאֵה עֵינֵי
יג הַכֹּהֵן: וְרָאָה הַכֹּהֵן וְהִנֵּה כִסְּתָה הַצָּרַעַת אֶת־כָּל־
בְּשָׂרוֹ וְטִהַר אֶת־הַנֶּגַע כֻּלּוֹ הָפַךְ לָבָן טָהוֹר הוּא:
יד וּבְיוֹם הֵרָאוֹת בּוֹ בָּשָׂר חַי יִטְמָא: וְרָאָה הַכֹּהֵן אֶת־
טו הַבָּשָׂר הַחַי וְטִמְּאוֹ הַבָּשָׂר הַחַי טָמֵא הוּא צָרַעַת
טז הוּא: אוֹ כִי יָשׁוּב הַבָּשָׂר הַחַי וְנֶהְפַּךְ לְלָבָן וּבָא אֶל־

יז הַכֹּהֵן: וְרָאָהוּ הַכֹּהֵן וְהִנֵּה נֶהְפַּךְ הַנֶּגַע לְלָבָן וְטִהַר
הַכֹּהֵן אֶת־הַנֶּגַע טָהוֹר הוּא: פ
יח וּבָשָׂר כִּי־יִהְיֶה בוֹ־בְעֹרוֹ שְׁחִין וְנִרְפָּא: וְהָיָה בִּמְקוֹם
יט הַשְּׁחִין שְׂאֵת לְבָנָה אוֹ בַהֶרֶת לְבָנָה אֲדַמְדָּמֶת וְנִרְאָה
כ אֶל־הַכֹּהֵן: וְרָאָה הַכֹּהֵן וְהִנֵּה מַרְאֶהָ שָׁפָל מִן־הָעוֹר
וּשְׂעָרָהּ הָפַךְ לָבָן וְטִמְּאוֹ הַכֹּהֵן נֶגַע־צָרַעַת הִוא
כא בַּשְּׁחִין פָּרָחָה: וְאִם יִרְאֶנָּה הַכֹּהֵן וְהִנֵּה אֵין־בָּהּ
שֵׂעָר לָבָן וּשְׁפָלָה אֵינֶנָּה מִן־הָעוֹר וְהִיא כֵהָה
כב וְהִסְגִּירוֹ הַכֹּהֵן שִׁבְעַת יָמִים: וְאִם־פָּשֹׂה תִפְשֶׂה בָּעוֹר
כג וְטִמֵּא הַכֹּהֵן אֹתוֹ נֶגַע הִוא: וְאִם־תַּחְתֶּיהָ תַּעֲמֹד
הַבַּהֶרֶת לֹא פָשָׂתָה צָרֶבֶת הַשְּׁחִין הִוא וְטִהֲרוֹ

9] When a person has a scaly affection, it shall be reported to the priest. 10] If the priest finds on the skin a white swelling which has turned some hair white, with a patch of undiscolored flesh in the swelling, 11] it is chronic leprosy on the skin of his body, and the priest shall pronounce him unclean; he need not isolate him, for he is unclean. 12] But if the eruption spreads out over the skin so that it covers all the skin of the affected person from head to foot, wherever the priest can see— 13] if the priest sees that the eruption has covered the whole body—he shall pronounce the affected person clean; he is clean, for he has turned all white. 14] But as soon as undiscolored flesh appears in it, he shall be unclean; 15] when the priest sees the undiscolored flesh, he shall pronounce him unclean. The undiscolored flesh is unclean; it is leprosy. 16] But if the undiscolored flesh again turns white, he shall come to the priest, 17] and the priest shall examine him: if the affection has turned white, the priest shall pronounce the affected person clean; he is clean.

18] When an inflammation appears on the skin of one's body and it heals, 19] and a white swelling or a white discoloration streaked with red develops where the inflammation was, he shall present himself to the priest. 20] If the priest finds that it appears lower than the rest of the skin and that the hair in it has turned white, the priest shall pronounce him unclean; it is a leprous affection that has broken out in the inflammation. 21] But if the priest finds that there is no white hair in it and it is not lower than the rest of the skin, and it is faded, the priest shall isolate him for seven days. 22] If it should spread in the skin, the priest shall pronounce him unclean; it is an affection. 23] But if the discoloration remains stationary, not having spread, it is the scar of the inflammation; the priest shall pronounce him clean.

9–17] Second type of *tzara'at* (according to Hoffmann, the "swelling" of verse 2). Here the diagnostic factor is that an abnormally white area appears on the skin, with some patches of normal color within it. A patient with these symptoms is unclean. Should the white affection spread over the entire body, the patient is clean; but he reverts to the defiled state as soon as a patch of normal skin appears. No convincing explanation of this strange rule has been offered.

9] *It shall be reported.* See T.N. above, verse 2 (T.N.).

10] *A patch of undiscolored flesh.* Others, "quick raw flesh" (T.N.).

18–23] Third type of *tzara'at.* A possible *tzara'at* developing in an inflammation, whether spontaneous or the result of an injury. The priest must distinguish between changes that indicate *tzara'at* and those caused by healing and scarring of the area.

כט וְאִישׁ אוֹ אִשָּׁה כִּי־יִהְיֶה בוֹ נָגַע בְּרֹאשׁ אוֹ בְזָקָן: ל וְרָאָה הַכֹּהֵן אֶת־הַנֶּגַע וְהִנֵּה מַרְאֵהוּ עָמֹק מִן־הָעוֹר וּבוֹ שֵׂעָר צָהֹב דָּק וְטִמֵּא אֹתוֹ הַכֹּהֵן נֶתֶק הוּא צָרַעַת הָרֹאשׁ אוֹ הַזָּקָן הוּא: לא וְכִי־יִרְאֶה הַכֹּהֵן אֶת־נֶגַע הַנֶּתֶק וְהִנֵּה אֵין־מַרְאֵהוּ עָמֹק מִן־הָעוֹר וְשֵׂעָר שָׁחֹר אֵין בּוֹ לב וְהִסְגִּיר הַכֹּהֵן אֶת־נֶגַע הַנֶּתֶק שִׁבְעַת יָמִים: וְרָאָה הַכֹּהֵן אֶת־הַנֶּגַע בַּיּוֹם הַשְּׁבִיעִי וְהִנֵּה לֹא־פָשָׂה הַנֶּתֶק וְלֹא־הָיָה בוֹ שֵׂעָר צָהֹב וּמַרְאֵה הַנֶּתֶק אֵין עָמֹק מִן־הָעוֹר: לג וְהִתְגַּלָּח וְאֶת־הַנֶּתֶק לֹא יְגַלֵּחַ וְהִסְגִּיר הַכֹּהֵן אֶת־הַנֶּתֶק שִׁבְעַת יָמִים שֵׁנִית: לד וְרָאָה הַכֹּהֵן אֶת־הַנֶּתֶק בַּיּוֹם הַשְּׁבִיעִי וְהִנֵּה לֹא־פָשָׂה הַנֶּתֶק בָּעוֹר וּמַרְאֵהוּ אֵינֶנּוּ עָמֹק מִן־הָעוֹר וְטִהַר אֹתוֹ הַכֹּהֵן וְכִבֶּס בְּגָדָיו

• לֹג נ׳ רבתי.

כד הַכֹּהֵן: ס אוֹ בָשָׂר כִּי־יִהְיֶה בְעֹרוֹ מִכְוַת־אֵשׁ וְהָיְתָה מִחְיַת הַמִּכְוָה בַּהֶרֶת לְבָנָה אֲדַמְדֶּמֶת אוֹ לְבָנָה: כה וְרָאָה אֹתָהּ הַכֹּהֵן וְהִנֵּה נֶהְפַּךְ שֵׂעָר לָבָן בַּבַּהֶרֶת וּמַרְאֶהָ עָמֹק מִן־הָעוֹר צָרַעַת הִוא בַּמִּכְוָה פָּרָחָה וְטִמֵּא אֹתוֹ הַכֹּהֵן נֶגַע צָרַעַת הִוא: כו וְאִם יִרְאֶנָּה הַכֹּהֵן וְהִנֵּה אֵין־בַּבֶּהֶרֶת שֵׂעָר לָבָן וּשְׁפָלָה אֵינֶנָּה מִן־הָעוֹר וְהִוא כֵהָה וְהִסְגִּירוֹ הַכֹּהֵן שִׁבְעַת יָמִים: כז וְרָאָהוּ הַכֹּהֵן בַּיּוֹם הַשְּׁבִיעִי אִם־פָּשֹׂה תִפְשֶׂה בָּעוֹר וְטִמֵּא הַכֹּהֵן אֹתוֹ נֶגַע צָרַעַת הִוא: כח וְאִם־תַּחְתֶּיהָ תַעֲמֹד הַבַּהֶרֶת לֹא־פָשְׂתָה בָעוֹר וְהִוא כֵהָה שְׂאֵת הַמִּכְוָה הִוא וְטִהֲרוֹ הַכֹּהֵן כִּי־צָרֶבֶת הַמִּכְוָה הִוא: פ

24] When the skin of one's body sustains a burn by fire, and the patch from the burn is a discoloration, either white streaked with red, or white, **25]** the priest shall examine it. If some hair has turned white in the discoloration, which itself appears to go deeper than the skin, it is leprosy that has broken out in the burn. The priest shall pronounce him unclean; it is a leprous affection. **26]** But if the priest finds that there is no white hair in the discoloration, and that it is not lower than the rest of the skin, and it is faded, the priest shall isolate him for seven days. **27]** On the seventh day the priest shall examine him: if it has spread in the skin, the priest shall pronounce him unclean; it is a leprous affection. **28]** But if the discoloration has remained stationary, not having spread on the skin, and it is faded, it is the swelling from the burn. The priest shall pronounce him clean, for it is the scar of the burn.

29] If a man or a woman has an affection on the head or in the beard, **30]** the priest shall examine the affection. If it appears to go deeper than the skin and there is thin yellow hair in it, the priest shall pronounce him unclean; it is a scall, a scaly eruption in the hair or beard. **31]** But if the priest finds that the scall affection does not appear to go deeper than the skin, yet there is no black hair in it, the priest shall isolate the person with the scall affection for seven days. **32]** On the seventh day the priest shall examine the affection. If the scall has not spread and no yellow hair has appeared in it, and the scall does not appear to go deeper than the skin, **33]** the person with the scall shall shave himself, but without shaving the scall; the priest shall isolate him for another seven days. **34]** On the seventh day the priest shall examine the scall. If the scall has not spread on the skin, and does not appear to go deeper than the skin, the

24-28] Similar provisions when suspicious symptoms follow a burn.

29-39] Fourth type of *tzara'at*. An affection of the scalp or of areas covered by the beard. Here, thin yellow hair is the important diagnostic factor. White hair, which in other cases indicates *tzara'at*, is not considered such an indication here, according to the halachah—no doubt because hair of the head and beard so often turns gray normally.

30] *A scall*. Hebrew *netek*, from a root meaning "tear off," probably referring to the tearing off of scabs by scratching. The word "scall" means "any scaly or scabby disease of the skin."

לה וְטָהֵר: וְאִם־פָּשֹׂה יִפְשֶׂה הַנֶּתֶק בָּעוֹר אַחֲרֵי טָהֳרָתוֹ:

לו וְרָאָהוּ הַכֹּהֵן וְהִנֵּה פָּשָׂה הַנֶּתֶק בָּעוֹר לֹא־יְבַקֵּר

לז הַכֹּהֵן לַשֵּׂעָר הַצָּהֹב טָמֵא הוּא: וְאִם־בְּעֵינָיו עָמַד
הַנֶּתֶק וְשֵׂעָר שָׁחֹר צָמַח־בּוֹ נִרְפָּא הַנֶּתֶק טָהוֹר הוּא

לח וְטִהֲרוֹ הַכֹּהֵן: ס וְאִישׁ אוֹ־אִשָּׁה כִּי־יִהְיֶה בְעוֹר־

לט בְּשָׂרָם בֶּהָרֹת בֶּהָרֹת לְבָנֹת: וְרָאָה הַכֹּהֵן וְהִנֵּה
בְעוֹר־בְּשָׂרָם בֶּהָרֹת כֵּהוֹת לְבָנֹת בֹּהַק הוּא פָּרַח

מ בָּעוֹר טָהוֹר הוּא: ס וְאִישׁ כִּי יִמָּרֵט רֹאשׁוֹ קֵרֵחַ

מא הוּא טָהוֹר הוּא: וְאִם מִפְּאַת פָּנָיו יִמָּרֵט רֹאשׁוֹ גִּבֵּחַ

מב הוּא טָהוֹר הוּא: וְכִי־יִהְיֶה בַקָּרַחַת אוֹ בַגַּבַּחַת נֶגַע
לָבָן אֲדַמְדָּם צָרַעַת פֹּרַחַת הִוא בְּקָרַחְתּוֹ אוֹ

מג בְגַבַּחְתּוֹ: וְרָאָה אֹתוֹ הַכֹּהֵן וְהִנֵּה שְׂאֵת־הַנֶּגַע לְבָנָה
אֲדַמְדֶּמֶת בְּקָרַחְתּוֹ אוֹ בְגַבַּחְתּוֹ כְּמַרְאֵה צָרַעַת עוֹר

מד בָּשָׂר: אִישׁ־צָרוּעַ הוּא טָמֵא הוּא טַמֵּא יְטַמְּאֶנּוּ הַכֹּהֵן

מה בְּרֹאשׁוֹ נִגְעוֹ: וְהַצָּרוּעַ אֲשֶׁר־בּוֹ הַנֶּגַע בְּגָדָיו יִהְיוּ
פְרֻמִים וְרֹאשׁוֹ יִהְיֶה פָרוּעַ וְעַל־שָׂפָם יַעְטֶה וְטָמֵא

מו טָמֵא יִקְרָא: כָּל־יְמֵי אֲשֶׁר הַנֶּגַע בּוֹ יִטְמָא טָמֵא הוּא
בָּדָד יֵשֵׁב מִחוּץ לַמַּחֲנֶה מוֹשָׁבוֹ: ס

priest shall pronounce him clean; he shall wash his clothes, and he shall be clean.   35] If, however, the scall should spread on the skin after he has been pronounced clean,   36] the priest shall examine him. If the scall has spread on the skin, the priest need not look for yellow hair: he is unclean.   37] But if the scall has remained unchanged in color, and black hair has grown in it, the scall is healed; he is clean. The priest shall pronounce him clean.

38] If a man or woman has the skin of the body streaked with white discolorations, 39] and the priest sees that the discolorations on the skin of the body are of a dull white, it is a tetter broken out on the skin; he is clean.

40] If a man loses the hair of his head and becomes bald, he is clean.   41] If he loses the hair on the front part of his head and becomes bald at the forehead, he is clean.   42] But if a white affection streaked with red appears on the bald part in the front or at the back of the head, it is a scaly eruption that is spreading over the bald part in the front or at the back of the head.   43] The priest shall examine him: if the swollen affection on the bald part in the front or at the back of his head is white streaked with red, like the leprosy of body skin in appearance,   44] the man is leprous; he is unclean. The priest shall pronounce him unclean; he has the affection on his head.

45] As for the person with a leprous affection, his clothes shall be rent, his hair shall be left bare, and he shall cover over his upper lip; and he shall call out, "Unclean! Unclean!"   46] He shall be unclean as long as the disease is on him. Being unclean, he shall dwell apart; his dwelling shall be outside the camp.

38–39] Harmless discolorations which do not cause defilement.

39] *Tetter* is defined as "any of various skin diseases, as eczema, characterized by itching." The word represents the Hebrew *bohak*, which occurs nowhere else in the Bible, and it probably comes from a root meaning "to be white, bright," found in postbiblical Hebrew and Aramaic.

40–43] Conditions associated with baldness. (Hebrew has two entirely different words for baldness, according to whether it starts at the front or the back of the head.) Normal baldness is not defiling; if symptoms of *tzara'at* appear in an area already bald,

the rules applied are those of the second type (verses 9ff.), not those of the fourth type.

45] *Left bare.* See T.N. at 10:6 (T.N.).

Cover over his upper lip. He was to let his head-covering hang down over his face as far as his mouth [12].

He shall call out, "Unclean! Unclean!" To warn passers-by that he is a source of defilement. The Targum paraphrases, "Do not defile yourselves!"

45–46] The "leper," adjudged to be under divine displeasure, was completely isolated and had to observe the rules of mourning (see commentary on 10:6). The "leper" had to remain outside the camp, in later times outside the walls of Jerusalem.

GLEANINGS

Halachah

13:3] *Pronounce Him Unclean*

The indispensable duty of the priest was to speak the words, "You are clean" or "You are unclean." If the priest was ignorant, he might be guided in his diagnosis by an informed layman, but it was he who had to speak the official formula.

SIFRA

6] *He Shall Wash His Clothes*

He also must take a ritual bath. Though he was not defiled, the fact that he had to undergo examination and isolation makes the ritual purification appropriate.

SIFRA

30] *A Scall*

Hebrew *netek*. Maimonides held that the falling out of a patch of hair from an area otherwise hairy (as opposed to normal balding, verses 40ff.) is sufficient evidence of *tzara'at*; Nachmanides argued that the diagnosis is not complete unless yellow hair appears. They both agree that *netek* means "falling out of hair" [13].

33] *Shall Shave Himself, without Shaving the Scall*

He is to leave two rows of hairs around the affected area so that at the end of the week it can be readily seen if the affection has spread.

SIFRA

Haggadah

13:9–17] The Rabbis were deeply aware of the paradoxical character of this rule. They represent Korah in his rebellion against the authority of Moses (Num. 16), citing this passage as proof that "the Torah is not from heaven, Moses is not a prophet, nor is Aaron a High Priest" [14].

Tzara'at of Garments

Chapter 13, verses 47–59, may be out of place. The comparable passage about *tzara'at* of houses is found at the end of chapter 14, after the directions for purifying a cured human patient.

In these verses, *tzara'at* is translated "eruptive affection." The reference seems to be to some sort of mildew or fungus; this suggestion was made in the fourteenth century by the scientifically trained Rabbi Levi ben Gershom. But some two hundred years earlier, Judah Halevi had asserted that *tzara'at* of garments and houses was not a natural phenomenon; it appeared by miracle only in the Holy Land as a sign of God's wrath at the indifferent and sinful. And Maimonides and Nachmanides agreed with him [1].

מז וְהַבֶּגֶד כִּי־יִהְיֶה בוֹ נֶגַע צָרָעַת בְּבֶגֶד צֶמֶר אוֹ בְּבֶגֶד
מח פִּשְׁתִּים: אוֹ בִשְׁתִי אוֹ בְעֵרֶב לַפִּשְׁתִּים וְלַצָּמֶר אוֹ
אֶת־הַבֶּגֶד אוֹ אֶת־הַשְּׁתִי אוֹ אֶת־הָעֵרֶב בַּצֶּמֶר אוֹ
מט בְעוֹר אוֹ בְּכָל־מְלֶאכֶת עוֹר: וְהָיָה הַנֶּגַע יְרַקְרַק אוֹ
כִּי־צָרַעַת מַמְאֶרֶת הִוא בָּאֵשׁ תִּשָּׂרֵף: וְאִם יִרְאֶה
אֲדַמְדָּם בַּבֶּגֶד אוֹ בָעוֹר אוֹ־בַשְּׁתִי אוֹ־בָעֵרֶב אוֹ
הַכֹּהֵן וְהִנֵּה לֹא־פָשָׂה הַנֶּגַע בַּבֶּגֶד אוֹ בַשְּׁתִי אוֹ בָעֵרֶב
בְּכָל־כְּלִי־עוֹר נֶגַע צָרַעַת הוּא וְהָרְאָה אֶת־הַכֹּהֵן:
נד אוֹ בְּכָל־כְּלִי־עוֹר: וְצִוָּה הַכֹּהֵן וְכִבְּסוּ אֵת אֲשֶׁר־בּוֹ
נ וְרָאָה הַכֹּהֵן אֶת־הַנָּגַע וְהִסְגִּיר אֶת־הַנֶּגַע שִׁבְעַת יָמִים:
הַנָּגַע וְהִסְגִּירוֹ שִׁבְעַת־יָמִים שֵׁנִית: וְרָאָה הַכֹּהֵן
נא וְרָאָה אֶת־הַנֶּגַע בַּיּוֹם הַשְּׁבִיעִי כִּי־פָשָׂה הַנֶּגַע בַּבֶּגֶד
אַחֲרֵי הֻכַּבֵּס אֶת־הַנֶּגַע וְהִנֵּה לֹא־הָפַךְ הַנֶּגַע אֶת־
אוֹ־בַשְּׁתִי אוֹ־בָעֵרֶב אוֹ בָעוֹר לְכֹל אֲשֶׁר־יֵעָשֶׂה הָעוֹר
עֵינוֹ וְהַנֶּגַע לֹא־פָשָׂה טָמֵא הוּא בָּאֵשׁ תִּשְׂרְפֶנּוּ פְּחֶתֶת
נב לִמְלָאכָה צָרַעַת מַמְאֶרֶת הַנֶּגַע טָמֵא הוּא: וְשָׂרַף
נו הִוא בְּקָרַחְתּוֹ אוֹ בְגַבַּחְתּוֹ: וְאִם רָאָה הַכֹּהֵן וְהִנֵּה

47] When an eruptive affection occurs in a cloth of wool or linen fabric, **48]** in the warp or in the woof of the linen or the wool, or in a skin or in anything made of skin; **49]** if the affection in the cloth or the skin, in the warp or the woof, or in any article of skin, is streaky green or red, it is an eruptive affection. It shall be shown to the priest; **50]** and the priest, after examining the affection, shall isolate the affected article for seven days. **51]** On the seventh day he shall examine the affection: if the affection has spread in the cloth—whether in the warp or the woof, or in the skin, for whatever purpose the skin may be used—the affection is a malignant eruption; it is unclean. **52]** The cloth—whether warp or woof in wool or linen, or any article of skin—in which the affection is found, shall be burned, for it is a malignant eruption; it shall be consumed in fire. **53]** But if the priest sees that the affection in the cloth—whether in warp or in woof, or in any article of skin—has not spread, **54]** the priest shall order the affected article washed, and he shall isolate it for another seven days. **55]** And if, after the affected article has been washed, the priest sees that the affection has not changed color and that it has not spread, it is unclean. It shall be consumed in fire; it is a fret, whether on its inner side or on its outer side. **56]** But if the priest sees that the affected part, after it has been washed, is faded, he shall tear it out from the cloth or skin, whether in the warp or in the

13:47] *Wool or linen.* The usual fabrics employed in biblical times.

48] *In the warp or in the woof.* "Warp" designates the threads that are set up on the loom; "woof," the threads passed around the warp threads by means of a shuttle. These terms ordinarily correspond to the Hebrew *sheti* and *erev.* But here this rendering is puzzling: How could *tzara'at* appear on the warp and not on the woof, or vice versa? Talmudic sources offer a possible solution. In talmudic times a thick thread was used for woof and a thinner one for warp [2]. This procedure may also have been followed in the biblical period. Our passage would then refer to yarns of different thickness, before or even after weaving.

49] *Green.* Or, "yellow" (T.N.).

54] *Washed.* To see if the discoloration was just an ordinary stain.

55] *Has not changed color.* Neither laundering nor the passing of time has affected it, so it is adjudged unclean even though it has not spread.

A fret. A worn spot. ("Fretfulness" is derived from this original meaning of rubbing, wearing away.) The wearing away of the fabric provided a favorable place for the development of the plague. But meaning of Hebrew *pechetet* uncertain (T.N.).

Inner side or on its outer side. Hebrew means literally "on its back-baldness or front-baldness" (cf. commentary on 13:40–43).

כְּהֶה הַנֶּגַע אַחֲרֵי הֻכַּבֵּס אֹתוֹ וְקָרַע אֹתוֹ מִן־הַבֶּגֶד אוֹ־הַשְּׁתִי אוֹ־הָעֵרֶב אוֹ־כָל־כְּלִי הָעוֹר אֲשֶׁר תְּכַבֵּס

נ״ז אוֹ מִן־הָעוֹר אוֹ מִן־הַשְּׁתִי אוֹ מִן־הָעֵרֶב׃ וְאִם־תֵּרָאֶה וְסָר מֵהֶם הַנֶּגַע וְכֻבַּס שֵׁנִית וְטָהֵר׃ זֹאת תּוֹרַת נֶגַע־

עוֹד בַּבֶּגֶד אוֹ־בַשְּׁתִי אוֹ־בָעֵרֶב אוֹ בְכָל־כְּלִי־עוֹר צָרַעַת בֶּגֶד הַצֶּמֶר אוֹ הַפִּשְׁתִּים אוֹ הַשְּׁתִי אוֹ הָעֵרֶב

נ״ח פֹּרַחַת הִוא בָּאֵשׁ תִּשְׂרְפֶנּוּ אֵת אֲשֶׁר־בּוֹ הַנָּגַע׃ וְהַבֶּגֶד אוֹ כָל־כְּלִי־עוֹר לְטַהֲרוֹ אוֹ לְטַמְּאוֹ׃

Haftarah Tazria, p. 991

woof;   **57]** and if it occurs again in the cloth—whether in warp or in woof—or in any article of skin, it is a wild growth; the affected article shall be consumed in fire.   **58]** If, however, the affection disappears from the cloth—warp or woof—or from any article of skin that has been washed, it shall be washed again, and it shall be clean.

59] This is the procedure for eruptive affections of cloth, woolen or linen, in warp or in woof, or of any article of skin, for pronouncing it clean or unclean.

58]   *It shall be washed again.* This time not a scrubbing to remove the stain, but a ceremonial dipping (so Targums).

Purification from Tzara'at

Once the priest declared the victim of tzara'at unclean, he had no further duties toward the patient until recovery. No doubt the latter and the family offered prayers and sacrifices for a cure. Moses prayed for his stricken sister (Num. 12:13).

If the leprous affection healed, the priest was summoned again to examine the patient. And when he had satisfied himself that the "plague" had disappeared, the priest conducted ceremonies to neutralize the ritual defilement—for the patient, though healed, was still *tamé*.

There were two stages to the purification. The first was performed outside the camp; the second was a sacrificial rite in the sanctuary, performed eight days later. The first part of the procedure required the use of two birds. One bird was slaughtered and its blood was utilized—but this ritual was *not* a sacrifice. It had the character of a magical act—the defilement was transferred to the second bird which was allowed to fly away, carrying the defilement with it. The intent of this ritual is something like that of the scapegoat (Lev. 16:7-10, 20ff.), as Nachmanides clearly understood [1].

The ceremony involves the use of several substances to which strong purificatory power was ascribed. Blood and fresh water are already familiar to us in this connection. Here, we encounter also cedar wood, crimson yarn, and hyssop. The reddish wood and crimson-dyed wool suggest both blood and the demonic world with which the color red has been associated through the ages (cf. conventional pictures of "the devil"). Cedar wood is also aromatic; so too is hyssop, if—as is probable—it is to be identified with Syrian marjoram. The Bible mentions it as a small plant that grows out of walls (I Kings 5:13). Perhaps it was used originally as a convenient means of sprinkling (Exod. 12:22), but it seems to have acquired a positive power to purify [2]. The Psalmist prays, "Purge me with hyssop till I am pure" (Ps. 51:9). The language is figurative, referring to moral and spiritual regeneration, but the allusion to the ritual shows that hyssop was regarded as an effective agent of purification.

The rite is then the survival of something archaic and primitive. The text does not mention anything about the demonic—only in the case of the scapegoat is there a brief allusion—and quite possibly such notions had

already vanished from the minds of those who wrote down this chapter. Customs often survive after their original motives are forgotten.

Later on, edifying explanations were offered by talmudic and more recent preachers. But the attempt to find in the rite the symbolism of spiritual regeneration is forced. The ceremonies were designed to remove a defilement that was a threat to the entire community.

The sacrifices on the eighth day also present some exceptional features. Like the woman after childbirth, the recovered "leper" must bring an offering of purgation (*chatat*) and a burnt offering. But he is also obligated to present a guilt offering (*asham*). This sacrifice is usually associated with the restitution of property that has been illegally taken (chapters 5 and 7). Its purpose here is not explained, but it is clearly of highest importance. For, whereas a poor person may substitute fowl for lambs in the case of *chatat* and *olah*, he must bring a lamb as the *asham* despite the drain on his purse. There is also a procedural novelty (verse 12).

(A new weekly portion, *Metzora*, begins with 14:1.)

הַחַיִּים: וְהִזָּה עַל הַמִּטַּהֵר מִן־הַצָּרַעַת שֶׁבַע פְּעָמִים
וְטִהֲרוֹ וְשִׁלַּח אֶת־הַצִּפֹּר הַחַיָּה עַל־פְּנֵי הַשָּׂדֶה:
וְכִבֶּס הַמִּטַּהֵר אֶת־בְּגָדָיו וְגִלַּח אֶת־כָּל־שְׂעָרוֹ וְרָחַץ
בַּמַּיִם וְטָהֵר וְאַחַר יָבוֹא אֶל־הַמַּחֲנֶה וְיָשַׁב מִחוּץ
לְאָהֳלוֹ שִׁבְעַת יָמִים: וְהָיָה בַיּוֹם הַשְּׁבִיעִי יְגַלַּח אֶת־
כָּל־שְׂעָרוֹ אֶת־רֹאשׁוֹ וְאֶת־זְקָנוֹ וְאֵת גַּבֹּת עֵינָיו וְאֶת־
כָּל־שְׂעָרוֹ יְגַלֵּחַ וְכִבֶּס אֶת־בְּגָדָיו וְרָחַץ אֶת־בְּשָׂרוֹ
בַּמַּיִם וְטָהֵר: וּבַיּוֹם הַשְּׁמִינִי יִקַּח שְׁנֵי־כְבָשִׂים תְּמִימִם
וְכַבְשָׂה אַחַת בַּת־שְׁנָתָהּ תְּמִימָה וּשְׁלֹשָׁה עֶשְׂרֹנִים
סֹלֶת מִנְחָה בְּלוּלָה בַשֶּׁמֶן וְלֹג אֶחָד שָׁמֶן: וְהֶעֱמִיד

פ פ פ

וַיְדַבֵּר יְהֹוָה אֶל־מֹשֶׁה לֵּאמֹר: זֹאת תִּהְיֶה תּוֹרַת
הַמְּצֹרָע בְּיוֹם טָהֳרָתוֹ וְהוּבָא אֶל־הַכֹּהֵן: וְיָצָא הַכֹּהֵן
אֶל־מִחוּץ לַמַּחֲנֶה וְרָאָה הַכֹּהֵן וְהִנֵּה נִרְפָּא נֶגַע־
הַצָּרַעַת מִן־הַצָּרוּעַ: וְצִוָּה הַכֹּהֵן וְלָקַח לַמִּטַּהֵר שְׁתֵּי־
צִפֳּרִים חַיּוֹת טְהֹרוֹת וְעֵץ אֶרֶז וּשְׁנִי תוֹלַעַת וְאֵזֹב:
וְצִוָּה הַכֹּהֵן וְשָׁחַט אֶת־הַצִּפּוֹר הָאֶחָת אֶל־כְּלִי־חֶרֶשׂ
עַל־מַיִם חַיִּים: אֶת־הַצִּפֹּר הַחַיָּה יִקַּח אֹתָהּ וְאֶת־עֵץ
הָאֶרֶז וְאֶת־שְׁנִי הַתּוֹלַעַת וְאֶת־הָאֵזֹב וְטָבַל אוֹתָם
וְאֵת הַצִּפֹּר הַחַיָּה בְּדַם הַצִּפֹּר הַשְּׁחֻטָה עַל הַמָּיִם

1] The LORD spoke to Moses saying: 2] This shall be the ritual for a leper at the time that he is to be cleansed.

When it has been reported to the priest,   3] the priest shall go outside the camp. If the priest sees that the leper has been healed of his scaly affection,   4] the priest shall order two live clean birds, cedar wood, crimson stuff, and hyssop to be brought for him who is to be cleansed.   5] The priest shall order one of the birds slaughtered over fresh water in an earthen vessel;   6] and he shall take the live bird, along with the cedar wood, the crimson stuff, and the hyssop, and dip them together with the live bird in the blood of the bird that was slaughtered over the fresh water.   7] He shall then sprinkle it seven times on him who is to be cleansed of the eruption and cleanse him; and he shall set the live bird free in the open country.   8] The one to be cleansed shall wash his clothes, shave off all his hair, and bathe in water; then he shall be clean. After that he may enter the camp, but he must remain outside his tent seven days.   9] On the seventh day he shall shave off all his hair—of head, beard and eyebrows. When he has shaved off all his hair, he shall wash his clothes and bathe his body in water; then he shall be clean.   10] On the eighth day he shall take two male lambs without blemish, one ewe lamb in its first year without blemish, three tenths of a measure of choice flour with oil mixed in for a meal offering, and one *log* of oil.   11] These shall be presented

14:2] *Leper*. Hebrew *metzora*. It was on this form that the Rabbis punned to connect the ailment with gossip (see introduction to Lev. 13:1–46).

It has been reported. Cf. T.N. at 13:2 (T.N.).

4] *Birds*. Hebrew *tziporim*, a term applied to small birds, such as swallows and sparrows.

5] *Slaughtered*. *Sifra* calls attention to this word, inferring, probably correctly, that the bird was to be killed by cutting its throat, not by the "pinching" used for sacrifices (1:15).

In an earthen vessel. It was probably broken after this single use (cf. 6:21, 11:33).

8] *Then he shall be clean*. He is permitted to return

to the camp/city; but the rites of purification are not finished.

Remain outside his tent. He must refrain from relations with his wife, according to tradition (see Gleanings); but the intent may be literal.

9] *He shall be clean*. But he must wait to enter the sanctuary until the sacrifices have been performed; therefore he comes only to the entrance of the Tent of Meeting (verse 11). In the days of the Second Temple, the candidate for purification stood at the Nicanor Gate, just outside the holy area.

10] *Log of oil*. Olive oil is a familiar symbol of purity. The log was a liquid measure, probably less than a pint.

הַכֹּהֵן הַמְטַהֵר אֵת הָאִישׁ הַמִּטַּהֵר וְאֹתָם לִפְנֵי יְהוָֹה:
יב פֶּתַח אֹהֶל מוֹעֵד: וְלָקַח הַכֹּהֵן אֶת־הַכֶּבֶשׂ הָאֶחָד וְהִקְרִיב אֹתוֹ לְאָשָׁם וְאֶת־לֹג הַשֶּׁמֶן וְהֵנִיף אֹתָם
יג תְּנוּפָה לִפְנֵי יְהוָֹה: וְשָׁחַט אֶת־הַכֶּבֶשׂ בִּמְקוֹם אֲשֶׁר יִשְׁחַט אֶת־הַחַטָּאת וְאֶת־הָעֹלָה בִּמְקוֹם הַקֹּדֶשׁ כִּי
יד כַּחַטָּאת הָאָשָׁם הוּא לַכֹּהֵן קֹדֶשׁ קָדָשִׁים הוּא: וְלָקַח הַכֹּהֵן מִדַּם הָאָשָׁם וְנָתַן הַכֹּהֵן עַל־תְּנוּךְ אֹזֶן הַמִּטַּהֵר הַיְמָנִית וְעַל־בֹּהֶן יָדוֹ הַיְמָנִית וְעַל־בֹּהֶן רַגְלוֹ הַיְמָנִית:
טו וְלָקַח הַכֹּהֵן מִלֹּג הַשֶּׁמֶן וְיָצַק עַל־כַּף הַכֹּהֵן
טז הַשְּׂמָאלִית: וְטָבַל הַכֹּהֵן אֶת־אֶצְבָּעוֹ הַיְמָנִית מִן הַשֶּׁמֶן אֲשֶׁר עַל־כַּפּוֹ הַשְּׂמָאלִית וְהִזָּה מִן־הַשֶּׁמֶן

יז בְּאֶצְבָּעוֹ שֶׁבַע פְּעָמִים לִפְנֵי יְהוָֹה: וּמִיֶּתֶר הַשֶּׁמֶן אֲשֶׁר עַל־כַּפּוֹ יִתֵּן הַכֹּהֵן עַל־תְּנוּךְ אֹזֶן הַמִּטַּהֵר הַיְמָנִית וְעַל־בֹּהֶן יָדוֹ הַיְמָנִית וְעַל־בֹּהֶן רַגְלוֹ הַיְמָנִית
יח עַל דַּם הָאָשָׁם: וְהַנּוֹתָר בַּשֶּׁמֶן אֲשֶׁר עַל־כַּף הַכֹּהֵן יִתֵּן עַל־רֹאשׁ הַמִּטַּהֵר וְכִפֶּר עָלָיו הַכֹּהֵן לִפְנֵי יְהוָֹה:
יט וְעָשָׂה הַכֹּהֵן אֶת־הַחַטָּאת וְכִפֶּר עַל־הַמִּטַּהֵר מִטֻּמְאָתוֹ וְאַחַר יִשְׁחַט אֶת־הָעֹלָה:
כ וְהֶעֱלָה הַכֹּהֵן אֶת־הָעֹלָה וְאֶת־הַמִּנְחָה הַמִּזְבֵּחָה וְכִפֶּר עָלָיו הַכֹּהֵן וְטָהֵר: ס
כא וְאִם־דַּל הוּא וְאֵין יָדוֹ מַשֶּׂגֶת וְלָקַח כֶּבֶשׂ אֶחָד אָשָׁם לִתְנוּפָה לְכַפֵּר עָלָיו וְעִשָּׂרוֹן סֹלֶת אֶחָד
כב בָּלוּל בַּשֶּׁמֶן לְמִנְחָה וְלֹג שָׁמֶן: וּשְׁתֵּי תֹרִים אוֹ שְׁנֵי

before the LORD, with the man to be cleansed, at the entrance of the Tent of Meeting, by the priest who performs the cleansing. **12]** The priest shall take one of the male lambs and offer it with the *log* of oil as a guilt offering, and he shall wave them as a wave offering before the LORD. **13]** The lamb shall be slaughtered at the spot in the sacred area where the sin offering and the burnt offering are slaughtered. For the guilt offering, like the sin offering, goes to the priest; it is most holy. **14]** The priest shall take some of the blood of the guilt offering, and the priest shall put it on the ridge of the right ear of him who is being cleansed, and on the thumb of his right hand, and on the big toe of his right foot. **15]** The priest shall then take some of the *log* of oil and pour it into the palm of his own left hand. **16]** And the priest shall dip his right finger in the oil that is in the palm of his left hand and sprinkle some of the oil with his finger seven times before the LORD. **17]** Some of the oil left in his palm shall be put by the priest on the ridge of the right ear of the one being cleansed, on the thumb of his right hand, and on the big toe of his right foot—over the blood of the guilt offering. **18]** The rest of the oil in his palm the priest shall put on the head of the one being cleansed. Thus the priest shall make expiation for him before the LORD. **19]** The priest shall then offer the sin offering and make expiation for the one being cleansed of his uncleanness. Lastly, the burnt offering shall be slaughtered, **20]** and the priest shall offer the burnt offering and the meal offering on the altar, and the priest shall make expiation for him. Then he shall be clean.

21] If, however, he is poor and his means are insufficient, he shall take one male lamb for a guilt offering, to be waved in expiation for him, one-tenth of a measure of choice flour with oil mixed in for a meal offering, and a *log* of oil; **22]** and two turtledoves or two pigeons, which

12] *Shall wave them as a wave offering.* See commentary on 7:28ff. According to Saadia and others [3], the priest simply led the animal around the altar.

13] *Sin offering and the burnt offering are slaughtered.* See 1:11; 4:23 (T.N.).

14–17] The priest puts blood, and later oil, on the ear, thumb, and toe of the man being cleansed. See at 8:23. The fact that the same procedure was followed for the consecration of a priest and the cleansing of a "leper" rules out moralizing explanations.

בְּנֵי יוֹנָה אֲשֶׁר תַּשִּׂיג יָדוֹ וְהָיָה אֶחָד חַטָּאת וְהָאֶחָד
כג עֹלָה: וְהֵבִיא אֹתָם בַּיּוֹם הַשְּׁמִינִי לְטָהֳרָתוֹ אֶל־הַכֹּהֵן
כד אֶל־פֶּתַח אֹהֶל־מוֹעֵד לִפְנֵי יְהוָה: וְלָקַח הַכֹּהֵן אֶת־
כֶּבֶשׂ הָאָשָׁם וְאֶת־לֹג הַשָּׁמֶן וְהֵנִיף אֹתָם הַכֹּהֵן תְּנוּפָה
כה לִפְנֵי יְהוָה: וְשָׁחַט אֶת־כֶּבֶשׂ הָאָשָׁם וְלָקַח הַכֹּהֵן מִדַּם
הָאָשָׁם וְנָתַן עַל־תְּנוּךְ אֹזֶן־הַמִּטַּהֵר הַיְמָנִית וְעַל־בֹּהֶן
כו יָדוֹ הַיְמָנִית וְעַל־בֹּהֶן רַגְלוֹ הַיְמָנִית: וּמִן־הַשָּׁמֶן יִצֹק
כז הַכֹּהֵן עַל־כַּף הַכֹּהֵן הַשְּׂמָאלִית: וְהִזָּה הַכֹּהֵן
בְּאֶצְבָּעוֹ הַיְמָנִית מִן־הַשֶּׁמֶן אֲשֶׁר עַל־כַּפּוֹ הַשְּׂמָאלִית
כח שֶׁבַע פְּעָמִים לִפְנֵי יְהוָה: וְנָתַן הַכֹּהֵן מִן־הַשֶּׁמֶן אֲשֶׁר

עַל־כַּפּוֹ עַל־תְּנוּךְ אֹזֶן הַמִּטַּהֵר הַיְמָנִית וְעַל־בֹּהֶן יָדוֹ
הַיְמָנִית וְעַל־בֹּהֶן רַגְלוֹ הַיְמָנִית עַל־מְקוֹם דַּם הָאָשָׁם:
כט וְהַנּוֹתָר מִן־הַשֶּׁמֶן אֲשֶׁר עַל־כַּף הַכֹּהֵן יִתֵּן עַל־רֹאשׁ
ל הַמִּטַּהֵר לְכַפֵּר עָלָיו לִפְנֵי יְהוָה: וְעָשָׂה אֶת־הָאֶחָד
מִן־הַתֹּרִים אוֹ מִן־בְּנֵי הַיּוֹנָה מֵאֲשֶׁר תַּשִּׂיג יָדוֹ: אֶת
לא אֲשֶׁר־תַּשִּׂיג יָדוֹ אֶת־הָאֶחָד חַטָּאת וְאֶת־הָאֶחָד עֹלָה
עַל־הַמִּנְחָה וְכִפֶּר הַכֹּהֵן עַל הַמִּטַּהֵר לִפְנֵי יְהוָה:
לב זֹאת תּוֹרַת אֲשֶׁר־בּוֹ נֶגַע צָרַעַת אֲשֶׁר לֹא־תַשִּׂיג יָדוֹ
בְּטָהֳרָתוֹ: פ

are within his means, the one to be the sin offering and the other the burnt offering. **23]** On the eighth day of his cleansing he shall bring them to the priest at the entrance of the Tent of Meeting, before the LORD. **24]** The priest shall take the lamb of guilt offering and the *log* of oil, and wave them as a wave offering before the LORD. **25]** When the lamb of guilt offering has been slaughtered, the priest shall take some of the blood of the guilt offering and put it on the ridge of the right ear of the one being cleansed, on the thumb of his right hand, and on the big toe of his right foot. **26]** The priest shall then pour some of the oil into the palm of his own left hand, **27]** and with the finger of his right hand the priest shall sprinkle some of the oil that is in the palm of his left hand seven times before the LORD. **28]** Some of the oil in his palm shall be put by the priest on the ridge of the right ear of the one being cleansed, on the thumb of his right hand, and on the big toe of his right foot, over the same places as the blood of the guilt offering; **29]** and what is left of the oil in his palm the priest shall put on the head of the one being cleansed, to make expiation for him before the LORD. **30]** He shall then offer one of the turtledoves or pigeons, depending on his means— **31]** whichever he can afford— the one as a sin offering and the other as a burnt offering, together with the meal offering. Thus the priest shall make expiation before the LORD for the one being cleansed. **32]** Such shall be the ritual for him who has a scaly affection and whose means for his cleansing are limited.

GLEANINGS

Halachah

14:5] *Slaughtered*

See commentary. The halachah also required the priest to dig a hole and bury the dead bird as soon as the blood was poured into the vessel thus stressing the nonsacrificial character of the rite (*Sifra*). Because it was not a sacrifice, this rite could be performed even after the Temple was destroyed. Rabbi Tarfon (end of first and beginning of second century C.E.), who was of priestly descent, stated that he conducted the ceremony on three occasions [4]. No later instance seems to be recorded.

7] *In the Open Country [or Field]*

Not in the direction of the sea, of a desert, or of a city. Should the bird later return, it may be eaten.

SIFRA

8] *Remain outside His Tent*

The separation of man and wife is only for this seven-day period of purification. Previously, while the man was still unclean, his wife was allowed to live with him outside the camp [5].

19] *The Meal Offering*

Not an independent *minchah* with frankincense, but simply the meal offering that regularly accompanies animal sacrifice (Num. 28:12 and elsewhere).

SIFRA

Haggadah

14:4] *Birds*

He was smitten because he engaged in gossip (see at 14:2); therefore his purification is accomplished by small birds that constantly chirp and chatter [6].

Cedar Wood . . . Hyssop

Why is the "leper" to be purified through the tallest of trees and the lowliest of plants? He was stricken because he exalted himself like the cedar; but when he abases himself like the hyssop, he will be healed [7].

Tzara'at of Houses

The phenomenon described in this section suggests some sort of fungus growth, such as mildew. It does not seem to have been common in Palestine. An early talmudic statement denies that any case of the sort ever occurred—this passage was included in the Torah only that we may acquire merit by studying it. And the scholars who questioned this assertion could offer only hearsay evidence of houses afflicted by the plague [1].

In ancient Mesopotamia, however, such manifestations were more frequent—or at least were taken more seriously. Preoccupied as they were with methods of forecasting the future, the Babylonians saw omens also in the changed appearance of buildings [2]. It may be that the appearance of *tzara'at* on garments, and even in human beings, was also utilized for divination [3].

Certainly the biblical author was dealing with what he regarded as an actual fact of experience. The law here is more severe than that for the human "leper." The latter might recover after having been declared unclean; but, if remedial measures did not check the spread of the affection in a house, all hope for a cure was abandoned and the house had to be demolished.

If the removal of stones, scraping, and replastering were effective, the house was to be purified by a rite with two birds, virtually identical with that prescribed above for the cured human being. This fact suggests that the sacrificial rites of verses 10ff. may have been an addition to the older procedure.

לג וַיְדַבֵּר יְהֹוָה אֶל־מֹשֶׁה וְאֶל־אַהֲרֹן לֵאמֹר: כִּי תָבֹאוּ
אֶל־אֶרֶץ כְּנַעַן אֲשֶׁר אֲנִי נֹתֵן לָכֶם לַאֲחֻזָּה וְנָתַתִּי נֶגַע
לד צָרַעַת בְּבֵית אֶרֶץ אֲחֻזַּתְכֶם: וּבָא אֲשֶׁר־לוֹ הַבַּיִת
לה וְהִגִּיד לַכֹּהֵן לֵאמֹר כְּנֶגַע נִרְאָה לִי בַּבָּיִת: וְצִוָּה
הַכֹּהֵן וּפִנּוּ אֶת־הַבַּיִת בְּטֶרֶם יָבֹא הַכֹּהֵן לִרְאוֹת אֶת־
לו הַנֶּגַע וְלֹא יִטְמָא כָּל־אֲשֶׁר בַּבָּיִת וְאַחַר כֵּן יָבֹא הַכֹּהֵן
לז לִרְאוֹת אֶת־הַבָּיִת: וְרָאָה אֶת־הַנֶּגַע וְהִנֵּה הַנֶּגַע
בְּקִירֹת הַבַּיִת שְׁקַעֲרוּרֹת יְרַקְרַקֹּת אוֹ אֲדַמְדַּמֹּת
לח וּמַרְאֵיהֶן שָׁפָל מִן־הַקִּיר: וְיָצָא הַכֹּהֵן מִן־הַבַּיִת אֶל־

לט פֶּתַח הַבַּיִת וְהִסְגִּיר אֶת־הַבַּיִת שִׁבְעַת יָמִים: וְשָׁב
הַכֹּהֵן בַּיּוֹם הַשְּׁבִיעִי וְרָאָה וְהִנֵּה פָּשָׂה הַנֶּגַע בְּקִירֹת
מ הַבָּיִת: וְצִוָּה הַכֹּהֵן וְחִלְּצוּ אֶת־הָאֲבָנִים אֲשֶׁר בָּהֵן
הַנֶּגַע וְהִשְׁלִיכוּ אֶתְהֶן אֶל־מִחוּץ לָעִיר אֶל־מָקוֹם
מא טָמֵא: וְאֶת־הַבַּיִת יַקְצִעַ מִבַּיִת סָבִיב וְשָׁפְכוּ אֶת־
הֶעָפָר אֲשֶׁר הִקְצוּ אֶל־מִחוּץ לָעִיר אֶל־מָקוֹם טָמֵא:
מב וְלָקְחוּ אֲבָנִים אֲחֵרוֹת וְהֵבִיאוּ אֶל־תַּחַת הָאֲבָנִים
מג וְעָפָר אַחֵר יִקַּח וְטָח אֶת־הַבָּיִת: וְאִם־יָשׁוּב הַנֶּגַע
וּפָרַח בַּבַּיִת אַחַר חִלֵּץ אֶת־הָאֲבָנִים וְאַחֲרֵי הִקְצוֹת

33] The LORD spoke to Moses and Aaron, saying:

34] When you enter the land of Canaan which I gave you as a possession, and I inflict an eruptive plague upon a house in the land you possess, 35] the owner of the house shall come and tell the priest, saying "Something like a plague has appeared upon my house." 36] The priest shall order the house cleared before the priest enters to examine the plague, so that nothing in the house may become unclean; after that the priest shall enter to examine the house. 37] If, when he examines the plague, the plague in the walls of the house is found to consist of greenish or reddish streaks, which appear to go deep into the wall, 38] the priest shall come out of the house to the entrance of the house, and close up the house for seven days. 39] On the seventh day the priest shall return. If he sees that the plague has spread on the walls of the house, 40] the priest shall order the stones with the plague in them to be pulled out and cast outside the city into an unclean place. 41] The house shall be scraped inside all around, and the coating that is scraped off shall be dumped outside the city in an unclean place. 42] They shall take other stones and replace those stones with them, and take other coating and plaster the house.

43] If the plague again breaks out in the house, after the stones have been pulled out and

---

14:34] *When you enter the land.* During the desert wanderings, the Israelites lived in tents or booths, not permanent houses.

An eruptive plague. Hebrew *nega' tzara'at.* See commentary on 13:2.

35] *Something like a plague.* The owner should not attempt a positive diagnosis which must be left to the priest (*Sifra*).

36] *Order the house cleared.* The contents of the house did not become ritually defiled until the priest declared the house infected. The owner may protect himself against loss by removing his belongings in advance of the examination (see introduction to Lev. 13:1–46).

37] *Greenish.* Or, "yellowish" (T.N.).

Reddish streaks. Meaning of Hebrew *sheka 'arurot* uncertain (T.N.).

38] *Close up the house.* Order it closed so that people know to avoid it. Verses 46 and 47 imply that it was not literally locked up.

40] *An unclean place.* Depositing this material would make the place unclean; but, presumably, it was left at a regular dump for ritually unclean materials, which those in a state of ritual purity would avoid.

41] *Coating.* Literally, "dust," "mud" (T.N.).

42] *Plaster the house.* With fresh mud. Lime plaster was known, but it was used for mortar and for caulking cisterns rather than to cover stone or wooden walls.

נא חַיִּֽים: וְלָקַח אֶת־עֵץ־הָאֶרֶז וְאֶת־הָאֵזֹב וְאֵת שְׁנִי הַתּוֹלַעַת וְאֵת הַצִּפֹּר הַחַיָּה וְטָבַל אֹתָם בְּדַם הַצִּפֹּר הַשְּׁחוּטָה וּבַמַּיִם הַחַיִּים וְהִזָּה אֶל־הַבַּיִת שֶׁבַע

נב פְּעָמִים: וְחִטֵּא אֶת־הַבַּיִת בְּדַם הַצִּפֹּר וּבַמַּיִם הַחַיִּים וּבַצִּפֹּר הַחַיָּה וּבְעֵץ הָאֶרֶז וּבָאֵזֹב וּבִשְׁנִי הַתּוֹלָעַת:

נג וְשִׁלַּח אֶת־הַצִּפֹּר הַחַיָּה אֶל־מִחוּץ לָעִיר אֶל־פְּנֵי הַשָּׂדֶה וְכִפֶּר עַל־הַבַּיִת וְטָהֵר: זֹאת הַתּוֹרָה לְכָל־

נד נֶגַע הַצָּרַעַת וְלַנָּתֶק: וּלְצָרַעַת הַבֶּגֶד וְלַבָּיִת: וְלַשְׂאֵת

נה וְלַסַּפַּחַת וְלַבֶּהָרֶת: לְהוֹרֹת בְּיוֹם הַטָּמֵא וּבְיוֹם

נו הַטָּהֹר זֹאת תּוֹרַת הַצָּרָעַת: פ

מד אֶת־הַבַּיִת וְאַחֲרֵי הַטּוֹחַ: וּבָא הַכֹּהֵן וְרָאָה וְהִנֵּה פָּשָׂה הַנֶּגַע בַּבַּיִת צָרַעַת מַמְאֶרֶת הִוא בַּבַּיִת טָמֵא הוּא:

מה וְנָתַץ אֶת־הַבַּיִת אֶת־אֲבָנָיו וְאֶת־עֵצָיו וְאֵת כָּל־עֲפַר הַבָּיִת וְהוֹצִיא אֶל־מִחוּץ לָעִיר אֶל־מָקוֹם טָמֵא:

מו וְהַבָּא אֶל־הַבַּיִת כָּל־יְמֵי הִסְגִּיר אֹתוֹ יִטְמָא עַד־

מז הָעָרֶב: וְהַשֹּׁכֵב בַּבַּיִת יְכַבֵּס אֶת־בְּגָדָיו וְהָאֹכֵל בַּבַּיִת

מח יְכַבֵּס אֶת־בְּגָדָיו: וְאִם־בֹּא יָבֹא הַכֹּהֵן וְרָאָה וְהִנֵּה לֹא־פָשָׂה הַנֶּגַע בַּבַּיִת אַחֲרֵי הִטֹּחַ אֶת־הַבָּיִת וְטִהַר

מט הַכֹּהֵן אֶת־הַבַּיִת כִּי נִרְפָּא הַנָּגַע: וְלָקַח לְחַטֵּא אֶת־הַבַּיִת שְׁתֵּי צִפֳּרִים וְעֵץ אֶרֶז וּשְׁנִי תוֹלַעַת וְאֵזֹב:

נ וְשָׁחַט אֶת־הַצִּפֹּר הָאֶחָת אֶל־כְּלִי־חֶרֶשׂ עַל־מַיִם

after the house has been scraped and replastered, **44]** the priest shall come to examine: if the plague has spread in the house, it is a malignant eruption in the house; it is unclean. **45]** The house shall be torn down—its stones and timber and all the coating on the house—and taken to an unclean place outside the city.

46] Whoever enters the house while it is closed up shall be unclean until evening. **47]** Whoever sleeps in the house must wash his clothes, and whoever eats in the house must wash his clothes.

48] If, however, the priest comes and sees that the plague has not spread in the house after the house was replastered, the priest shall pronounce the house clean, for the plague has healed. **49]** To purge the house, he shall take two birds, cedar wood, crimson stuff, and hyssop. **50]** He shall slaughter the one bird over fresh water in an earthen vessel. **51]** He shall take the cedar wood, the hyssop, the crimson stuff, and the live bird, and dip them in the blood of the slaughtered bird and the fresh water, and sprinkle on the house seven times. **52]** Having purged the house with the blood of the bird, the fresh water, the live bird, the cedar wood, the hyssop, and the crimsom stuff, **53]** he shall set the live bird free outside the city in the open country. Thus he shall make expiation for the house, and it shall be clean.

54] This is the procedure for every eruptive affection—for scalls, **55]** for an eruption on a cloth or a house, **56]** for swellings, for rashes, or for discolorations— **57]** to determine when they are unclean and when they are clean.

Such is the procedure concerning eruptions.

52, 53] *Purged. Expiation.* Clearly in a ritual sense. A house cannot be redeemed from sin.

54–57] These verses are a formal summary of the contents of chapters 13 and 14.

GLEANINGS

Halachah

14:34] *Upon a House in the Land You Possess*
The law applies only in the Land of Israel and to houses owned by Israelites.   SIFRA

46] *Whoever Enters the House*
The defiled person must take a ritual bath.   SIFRA

47] *Whoever Sleeps . . . Whoever Eats*
If he enters the building briefly, he must bathe and remain unclean until evening. If he remains long enough to eat a light meal—still more, if he stays long enough to sleep—the defilement is more severe and he must wash his garments as well.   SIFRA

Haggadah

14:34] *I Will Inflict*
Hebrew *venatati*, which can also mean "I will give." According to some haggadists, this passage is a promise. The Canaanites hid treasures in the walls of their houses. When Israel enters the land, God will send *tzara'at* upon these houses; they will have to be demolished and the Israelites will obtain the treasures [4].

Other preachers were less indulgent. Some regarded *tzara'at* of houses as a first warning to sinners. If they disregarded the warning, the plague would appear on their garments; and, if they still remained obdurate, it would afflict their bodies [5].

Still others saw this plague as the special punishment of the miser. If a person is asked for the loan of some grain or of an implement and replies meanly, "I have none," the house of that person will be visited by *tzara'at*. When the dwelling is emptied, everyone will see what the miser owns and the miser's stinginess will be publicly revealed [6].

36] *Order the House Cleared*
To protect the owner from loss. Yet the only loss would be of pottery vessels which would have to be broken; and earthenware is cheap. (For wood and metal vessels could be purified by dipping; food could be consumed while the owner was in a state of impurity.) Now, if the Torah protects a presumed sinner even from minor loss, all the more does it seek to protect the righteous against serious loss!   SIFRA

Defilement by Discharge from the Sex Organs

For ancient man, as we have seen, birth was not only awesome but frightening; it was regarded as a source of ritual impurity (chapter 12). And death was the source of the most intense defilement (Num. 19). The sexual experience, too, was viewed as uncanny and, hence, as a source of ceremonial uncleanness.

The belief that the sex act is defiling was widespread. The Roman maidens who tended the sacred fire of Vesta had to remain permanently in a virgin state. Though celibacy is alien to the Jewish outlook, we read that, immediately before the revelation at Sinai, the Israelites were directed to stay pure by washing their clothes and remaining apart from their wives (Exod. 19:4f.). And the Rabbis assert that, whereas this separation of the sexes lasted only a few days for the people, Moses—who was to be constantly the recipient of revelation—practiced continence for the rest of his life [1].

Among many peoples, warriors refrained from sexual intercourse during a campaign, not merely to conserve their physical strength, but to avoid ritual contamination. This notion is found in various biblical passages. David's soldiers are permitted to eat "holy bread" because they have been apart from women for three days (I Sam. 21:5ff.). Uriah, called home from the front, will not enter his house and sleep with his wife while his comrades are encamped in the open (II Sam. 11:11). According to the law of Deuteronomy, a soldier who has a nocturnal emission must leave the camp for a day and take a bath; at sundown he may rejoin his fellows (Deut. 23:11) [2].

Our chapter (verses 16–18) treats human semen as a source of defilement. One who has an emission, or a couple who has intercourse, or a person or object coming into contact with semen, all acquire a mild degree of uncleanness. Similar rules, often more stringent, are found among various other peoples.

Far more severe are the regulations concerning women during their monthly periods. Ancient man reacted to the phenomenon of menstruation with a horror that seems to us grotesque and hysterical, and the same is true of primitive man still today. "According to Pliny, the touch of a menstruous woman turned wine to vinegar, blighted crops, killed seedlings, blasted gardens, brought down the fruit from trees, dimmed mirrors, blunted razors, rusted iron and brass (especially at the waning of the

moon), killed bees or at least drove them from their hives, caused mares to miscarry, and so forth" [3]. Many peoples went to extreme and even cruel lengths to protect themselves against any contact with menstrual blood. The onset of puberty in females was regarded as especially dangerous, and among many tribes adolescent girls were isolated for long periods [4].

Similar superstitions were current among Jews. A talmudic statement warns against a woman passing between two men or a man passing between two women; and a further comment explains that, if the woman is at the beginning of her period, she might bring about the death of one of the men and, if at the end, she might cause them to quarrel [5]. Nachmanides asserts that animals die if they consume menstrual blood. He further reports as a matter of experience that, if a menstruating woman stares at a mirror of polished iron, drops of blood will appear on it [6].

Our chapter does not explain why blood defiles; it simply states the rules involved. This is not, however, a simple "defilement of the body"; intercourse with a woman during her menses is a "defilement of the sacred" (see introduction to Lev. 11:24–47) and is unconditionally forbidden; a violation entails the severest punishment (see 18:19 and 20:18).

In comparison with the taboos found in some societies, biblical law on this subject (verses 19–24) appears mild and rational. The woman must remain apart from her husband for seven days from the onset of her period. During this time, her person, her bedding, and anything she sits on convey ritual uncleanness. After the seven days, tradition requires her to take a ritual bath before she and her husband can share the same bed. The biblical text does not mention this immersion, but it is probably taken for granted since the bath is required for the lesser defilement of normal intercourse

(verse 18). We have called these provisions rational. This does not seem an overstatement in view of the physical difficulties many women suffer during menstruation, ranging from sleepiness to intense pain—to say nothing of the emotional tensions that often appear just before the start of the period. The law protects women from the importunities of their husbands at a time when they are not physically and emotionally ready for coitus.

The Talmud ascribed a psychological benefit to this enforced abstinence. It prevents the marital act from becoming routine; reunited after the period of "uncleanness," the couple recaptures something of the honeymoon mood [7].

The ritual bath at the end of the period may be taken either in a "source"—spring, stream, sea—or in an artificial pool known as a *mikveh* (which is also spelled *mikvah*). The laws of the *mikveh* were greatly elaborated by the rabbinic teachers (see Gleanings). They apply to all cases of defilement treated in these chapters, including the "dipping" of polluted objects. The downfall of the Temple made most laws of purity irrelevant; since then the *mikveh* has been used chiefly by married women after menstruation and by brides just before their marriage. It has, however, been regarded as an expression of piety for men to take a ritual bath, especially on the day before Yom Kippur, as a symbol of cleansing from sin.

The term *niddah*, "something to be shunned," "impurity," is applied in the Bible especially to the condition of a menstruating woman, in postbiblical literature to the woman herself. It is also the name of a tractate, in the Mishnah and Talmuds, that expounds the laws in great detail. The established halachah is in fact much more stringent than the rules as set forth in this chapter (see Gleanings).

Throughout the centuries, these laws were

conscientiously observed. A skeptic once said to Rav Kahana, "You permit a man to be alone with his wife during her period: Do you mean to say that fire can approach flax without kindling it?" The rabbi answered (by citing the words from Song of Songs 7:3, "hedged about with lilies"): The words of Torah, which are as tender as lilies, suffice to restrain them [8].

Today, however, it is certain that a large percentage of Jews do not follow the halachah strictly. This is evidenced by the fact that in many American communities there is no *mikveh* and in others the institution is maintained with great difficulty. It is probable that most Jewish couples refrain from intercourse while the wife is menstruating. The same applies, no doubt, to many non-Jewish Americans. The exaggerated fears of ancient men are not shared by all moderns, and it would be a mistake to assume a "natural revulsion." Men are not invariably finicky; and some women not only tolerate intercourse during menstruation but actively desire it [9].

This chapter also deals with defilement resulting when there is an abnormal discharge from the genitals. A man suffering from such a discharge is called *zav*, "one who flows," and the female equivalent is *zavah*. But the similarity is only in nomenclature. The *zavah* is one who continues to bleed beyond the normal period of her menses or who has bleeding at a different time of the month. (Such bleeding can be a symptom of serious ailments.) There is disagreement as to the discharge affecting the *zav*. Some students identify it as gonorrhea; others think it is only an exceptional discharge of mucus—a minor ailment called blennorrhea. The second view is supported by descriptions of the condition in rabbinic sources.

For both sexes, the "flow" entails major defilement. The patients, and anything they sleep, sit, or ride on, are a source of uncleanness until seven consecutive days pass without any discharge. Then, after a ritual bath, sacrifices of purgation must be offered.

The biblical material is not presented in the order followed in this introduction. The rather haphazard arrangement of the chapter is: verses 1–15, the *zav*; verses 16–18, defilement by semen; verses 19–24, the *niddah*; verses 25–30, the *zavah*; verses 31–33, conclusion.

וְרָחַ֥ץ בַּמַּ֖יִם וְטָמֵ֣א עַד־הָעָ֑רֶב: וְהַנֹּגֵ֖עַ בִּבְשַׂ֣ר הַזָּ֗ב ז
יְכַבֵּ֧ס בְּגָדָ֛יו וְרָחַ֥ץ בַּמַּ֖יִם וְטָמֵ֥א עַד־הָעָֽרֶב: וְכִֽי־יָרֹ֤ק ח
הַזָּב֙ בַּטָּה֔וֹר וְכִבֶּ֧ס בְּגָדָ֛יו וְרָחַ֥ץ בַּמַּ֖יִם וְטָמֵ֥א עַד־
הָעָֽרֶב: וְכָל־הַמֶּרְכָּ֗ב אֲשֶׁ֨ר יִרְכַּ֥ב עָלָ֛יו הַזָּ֖ב יִטְמָֽא: ט
וְכָל־הַנֹּגֵ֗עַ בְּכֹל֙ אֲשֶׁ֣ר יִהְיֶ֣ה תַחְתָּ֔יו יִטְמָ֖א עַד־הָעָ֑רֶב
וְהַנּוֹשֵׂ֣א אוֹתָ֔ם יְכַבֵּ֧ס בְּגָדָ֛יו וְרָחַ֥ץ בַּמַּ֖יִם וְטָמֵ֥א עַד־
הָעָֽרֶב: וְכֹ֨ל אֲשֶׁ֤ר יִגַּע־בּוֹ֙ הַזָּ֔ב וְיָדָ֖יו לֹא־שָׁטַ֣ף בַּמָּ֑יִם יא
וְכִבֶּ֧ס בְּגָדָ֛יו וְרָחַ֥ץ בַּמַּ֖יִם וְטָמֵ֥א עַד־הָעָֽרֶב: וּכְלִֽי־ יב

וַיְדַבֵּ֣ר יְהֹוָ֔ה אֶל־מֹשֶׁ֥ה וְאֶֽל־אַהֲרֹ֖ן לֵאמֹֽר: דַּבְּרוּ֙ אֶל־ א
בְּנֵ֣י יִשְׂרָאֵ֔ל וַאֲמַרְתֶּ֖ם אֲלֵהֶ֑ם אִ֣ישׁ אִ֗ישׁ כִּ֤י יִהְיֶה֙ זָ֣ב ב
מִבְּשָׂר֔וֹ זוֹב֖וֹ טָמֵ֥א הֽוּא: וְזֹ֛את תִּהְיֶ֥ה טֻמְאָת֖וֹ בְּזוֹב֑וֹ ג
רָ֣ר בְּשָׂר֞וֹ אֶת־זוֹב֗וֹ אֽוֹ־הֶחְתִּ֤ים בְּשָׂרוֹ֙ מִזּוֹב֔וֹ טֻמְאָת֖וֹ
הֽוּא: כָּל־הַמִּשְׁכָּ֗ב אֲשֶׁ֨ר יִשְׁכַּ֥ב עָלָ֛יו הַזָּ֖ב יִטְמָ֑א וְכָֽל־ ד
הַכְּלִ֕י אֲשֶׁר־יֵשֵׁ֥ב עָלָ֖יו יִטְמָֽא: וְאִ֕ישׁ אֲשֶׁ֥ר יִגַּ֖ע ה
בְּמִשְׁכָּב֑וֹ יְכַבֵּ֧ס בְּגָדָ֛יו וְרָחַ֥ץ בַּמַּ֖יִם וְטָמֵ֥א עַד־הָעָֽרֶב:
וְהַיֹּשֵׁב֙ עַל־הַכְּלִ֔י אֲשֶׁר־יֵשֵׁ֥ב עָלָ֖יו הַזָּ֑ב יְכַבֵּ֣ס בְּגָדָ֗יו ו

1] The LORD spoke to Moses and Aaron, saying: 2] Speak to the Israelite people and say to
them:

When any man has a discharge issuing from his member, he is unclean.   3] The uncleanness
from his discharge shall mean the following—whether his member runs with the discharge or is
stopped up so that there is no discharge, his uncleanness means this: 4] Any bedding on which
the one with the discharge lies shall be unclean, and every object on which he sits shall be
unclean.   5] Anyone who touches his bedding shall wash his clothes, bathe in water, and
remain unclean until evening.   6] Whoever sits on an object on which the one with the
discharge has sat shall wash his clothes, bathe in water, and remain unclean until evening.
7] Whoever touches the body of the one with the discharge shall wash his clothes, bathe in
water, and remain unclean until evening.   8] If one with a discharge spits on one who is clean,
the latter shall wash his clothes, bathe in water, and remain unclean until evening.   9] Any
means for riding which one with a discharge has mounted shall be unclean;   10] whoever
touches anything that was under him shall be unclean until evening; and whoever carries such
things shall wash his clothes, bathe in water, and remain unclean until evening.   11] If one
with a discharge, without having rinsed his hands in water, touches another person, that person
shall wash his clothes, bathe in water, and remain unclean until evening.   12] An earthen

15:1-15] For the probable nature of the discharge,
see introduction to this chapter.

2] *Member*. Literally, "flesh" (T.N.).

4-12] The virulent impurity of the *zav* is communicated to anything he touches, especially bedding,
seats, and the like, which are likely to have been in
direct contact with the affected parts and with the
discharge.

8] *Spits on one who is clean*. The halachah, logically
enough, states that the urine and feces of the *zav*
also defile (*Sifra*).

9] *Any means for riding*. A saddle, girth, or blanket—
even the wooden pommel of a saddle (*Sifra*).

11] *Without having rinsed his hands in water*. The
sentence is puzzling. It implies that, if the *zav* has
just washed his hands, he may touch another person
without defiling that person—in contradiction to the
severe rules that precede and follow. Nor is there
any indication as to how long this rinsing would
neutralize the impurity of the *zav*. The Rabbis were
compelled to depart from the plain sense of the
words (see Gleanings).

12] See commentary on 6:21f., 11:33ff.

חֶרֶשׂ אֲשֶׁר־יִגַּע־בּוֹ הַזָּב יִשָּׁבֵר וְכָל־כְּלִי־עֵץ יִשָּׁטֵף   יח וְאִשָּׁה אֲשֶׁר יִשְׁכַּב אִישׁ אֹתָהּ שִׁכְבַת־זָרַע וְרָחֲצוּ
יג בַּמָּיִם: וְכִי־יִטְהַר הַזָּב מִזּוֹבוֹ וְסָפַר לוֹ שִׁבְעַת יָמִים   בַּמַּיִם וְטָמְאוּ עַד־הָעָרֶב: פ
לְטָהֳרָתוֹ וְכִבֶּס בְּגָדָיו וְרָחַץ בְּשָׂרוֹ בְּמַיִם חַיִּים   יט וְאִשָּׁה כִּי־תִהְיֶה זָבָה דָּם יִהְיֶה זֹבָהּ בִּבְשָׂרָהּ שִׁבְעַת
יד וְטָהֵר: וּבַיּוֹם הַשְּׁמִינִי יִקַּח־לוֹ שְׁתֵּי תֹרִים אוֹ שְׁנֵי בְּנֵי   יָמִים תִּהְיֶה בְנִדָּתָהּ וְכָל־הַנֹּגֵעַ בָּהּ יִטְמָא עַד־הָעָרֶב:
יוֹנָה וּבָא לִפְנֵי יְהֹוָה אֶל־פֶּתַח אֹהֶל מוֹעֵד וּנְתָנָם   כ וְכֹל אֲשֶׁר תִּשְׁכַּב עָלָיו בְּנִדָּתָהּ יִטְמָא וְכֹל אֲשֶׁר־תֵּשֵׁב
טו אֶל־הַכֹּהֵן: וְעָשָׂה אֹתָם הַכֹּהֵן אֶחָד חַטָּאת וְהָאֶחָד   כא עָלָיו יִטְמָא: וְכָל־הַנֹּגֵעַ בְּמִשְׁכָּבָהּ יְכַבֵּס בְּגָדָיו וְרָחַץ
טז עֹלָה וְכִפֶּר עָלָיו הַכֹּהֵן לִפְנֵי יְהֹוָה מִזּוֹבוֹ: ס וְאִישׁ   כב בַּמַּיִם וְטָמֵא עַד־הָעָרֶב: וְכָל־הַנֹּגֵעַ בְּכָל־כְּלִי אֲשֶׁר־
כִּי־תֵצֵא מִמֶּנּוּ שִׁכְבַת־זָרַע וְרָחַץ בַּמַּיִם אֶת־כָּל־בְּשָׂרוֹ   תֵּשֵׁב עָלָיו יְכַבֵּס בְּגָדָיו וְרָחַץ בַּמַּיִם וְטָמֵא עַד־
יז וְטָמֵא עַד־הָעָרֶב: וְכָל־בֶּגֶד וְכָל־עוֹר אֲשֶׁר־יִהְיֶה   כג הָעָרֶב: וְאִם עַל־הַמִּשְׁכָּב הוּא אוֹ עַל־הַכְּלִי אֲשֶׁר־
עָלָיו שִׁכְבַת־זָרַע וְכֻבַּס בַּמַּיִם וְטָמֵא עַד־הָעָרֶב: כד הִוא יֹשֶׁבֶת־עָלָיו בְּנָגְעוֹ־בוֹ יִטְמָא עַד־הָעָרֶב: וְאִם

vessel which one with a discharge touches shall be broken; and any wooden implement shall be rinsed with water.

13] When one with a discharge becomes clean of his discharge, he shall count off seven days for his cleansing, wash his clothes, and bathe his body in fresh water; then he shall be clean. 14] On the eighth day he shall take two turtledoves or two pigeons and come before the LORD at the entrance of the Tent of Meeting and give them to the priest. 15] The priest shall offer them, the one as a sin offering and the other as a burnt offering. Thus the priest shall make expiation on his behalf, for his discharge, before the LORD.

16] When a man has an emission of semen, he shall bathe his whole body in water and remain unclean until evening. 17] All cloth or leather on which semen falls shall be washed in water and remain unclean until evening. 18] And if a man has carnal relations with a woman, they shall bathe in water and remain unclean until evening.

19] When a woman has a discharge, her discharge being blood from her body, she shall remain in her impurity seven days; whoever touches her shall be unclean until evening. 20] Anything that she lies on during her impurity shall be unclean; and anything that she sits on shall be unclean. 21] Anyone who touches her bedding shall wash his clothes, bathe in water, and remain unclean until evening; 22] and anyone who touches any object on which she has sat shall wash his clothes, bathe in water, and remain unclean until evening. 23] Be it the bedding or be it the object on which she has sat, on touching it he shall be unclean until evening. 24] And if a man lies with her, her impurity is communicated to him; he shall be

13] *Fresh water.* Literally, "living [i.e., running] water." The *zav* (alone among the unclean persons treated here) cannot purify himself in a *mikveh*, but he must go to a spring, stream, lake, or sea.

16] Cf. Deut. 23:11f.

18] *Carnal relations with a woman.* The English phraseology is an attempt to make passable prose out of a somewhat unusual Hebrew sentence. There is no implication that the woman is not the man's wife or that the marital act is in any way degrading or sinful.

19–24] The impurity of the menstruating woman (*niddah*). Virtually the same rules about the transmission of defilement apply to the *niddah* and the *zav*. No mention is made of a ritual bath after menstruation, but the Rabbis reasonably inferred the requirement from verse 18.

24] This verse deals only with the ritual defilement that results from intercourse with a menstruating woman. The seriousness of the offense and its punishment are stated in 18:19, 20:18.

כט לָהּ שִׁבְעַת יָמִים וְאַחַר תִּטְהָר: וּבַיּוֹם הַשְּׁמִינִי תִּקַּח־
לָהּ שְׁתֵּי תֹרִים אוֹ שְׁנֵי בְּנֵי יוֹנָה וְהֵבִיאָה אוֹתָם אֶל־
ל הַכֹּהֵן אֶל־פֶּתַח אֹהֶל מוֹעֵד: וְעָשָׂה הַכֹּהֵן אֶת־הָאֶחָד
חַטָּאת וְאֶת־הָאֶחָד עֹלָה וְכִפֶּר עָלֶיהָ הַכֹּהֵן לִפְנֵי
לא יְהוָה מִזּוֹב טֻמְאָתָהּ: וְהִזַּרְתֶּם אֶת־בְּנֵי־יִשְׂרָאֵל
מִטֻּמְאָתָם וְלֹא יָמֻתוּ בְּטֻמְאָתָם בְּטַמְּאָם אֶת־מִשְׁכָּנִי
לב אֲשֶׁר בְּתוֹכָם: זֹאת תּוֹרַת הַזָּב וַאֲשֶׁר תֵּצֵא מִמֶּנּוּ
לג שִׁכְבַת־זֶרַע לְטָמְאָה־בָהּ: וְהַדָּוָה בְּנִדָּתָהּ וְהַזָּב אֶת־
זוֹבוֹ לַזָּכָר וְלַנְּקֵבָה וּלְאִישׁ אֲשֶׁר יִשְׁכַּב עִם־טְמֵאָה:

שָׁכַב יִשְׁכַּב אִישׁ אֹתָהּ וּתְהִי נִדָּתָהּ עָלָיו וְטָמֵא
שִׁבְעַת יָמִים וְכָל־הַמִּשְׁכָּב אֲשֶׁר־יִשְׁכַּב עָלָיו
כה יִטְמָא: ס וְאִשָּׁה כִּי־יָזוּב זוֹב דָּמָהּ יָמִים רַבִּים
בְּלֹא עֶת־נִדָּתָהּ אוֹ כִי־תָזוּב עַל־נִדָּתָהּ כָּל־יְמֵי זוֹב
כו טֻמְאָתָהּ כִּימֵי נִדָּתָהּ תִּהְיֶה טְמֵאָה הִוא: כָּל־הַמִּשְׁכָּב
אֲשֶׁר־תִּשְׁכַּב עָלָיו כָּל־יְמֵי זוֹבָהּ כְּמִשְׁכַּב נִדָּתָהּ יִהְיֶה־
לָּהּ וְכָל־הַכְּלִי אֲשֶׁר תֵּשֵׁב עָלָיו טָמֵא יִהְיֶה כְּטֻמְאַת
כז נִדָּתָהּ: וְכָל־הַנּוֹגֵעַ בָּם יִטְמָא וְכִבֶּס בְּגָדָיו וְרָחַץ
כח בַּמַּיִם וְטָמֵא עַד־הָעָרֶב: וְאִם־טָהֲרָה מִזּוֹבָהּ וְסָפְרָה

Haftarah Metzora, p. 994

*כט סלרע

unclean seven days, and any bedding on which he lies shall become unclean.

25] When a woman has had a discharge of blood for many days, not at the time of her impurity, or when she has a discharge beyond her period of impurity, she shall be unclean, as though at the time of her impurity, as long as her discharge lasts: she shall be unclean. **26]** Any bedding on which she lies while her discharge lasts shall be for her like bedding during her impurity; and any object on which she sits shall become unclean, as it does during her impurity: **27]** whoever touches them shall be unclean; he shall wash his clothes, bathe in water, and remain unclean until evening.

28] When she becomes clean of her discharge, she shall count off seven days, and after that she shall be clean. **29]** On the eighth day she shall take two turtledoves or two pigeons, and bring them to the priest at the entrance of the Tent of Meeting. **30]** The priest shall offer the one as a sin offering and the other as a burnt offering; and the priest shall make expiation on her behalf, for her unclean discharge, before the LORD.

31] You shall put the Israelites on guard against their uncleanness, lest they die through their uncleanness by defiling My Tabernacle which is among them.

32] Such is the ritual concerning him who has a discharge: concerning him who has an emission of semen and becomes unclean thereby, **33]** and concerning her who is in menstrual infirmity, and concerning anyone, male or female, who has a discharge, and concerning a man who lies with an unclean woman.

Seven days. From the time of the contact, not from the beginning of her period (Sifra).

31] *Put the Israelites on guard.* Hebrew *vehizartem,* from the same root as *nazir,* nazirite, one set apart

for a sacred function. Literally, "You shall set them apart carefully from their uncleanness."

31–33] These verses conclude the section.

GLEANINGS

Halachah

15:4] *Any Bedding*

Even if the bed of the *zav* was covered by several layers of blankets, one who sat upon them would be defiled.   SIFRA

5] *Bathe in Water*

The *mikveh*—which could be used for all immersions and dippings except that of the *zav* (verse 13)—was the subject of elaborate technical rules, codified in a treatise of the Mishnah called *Mikvaot*. It must contain a minimum of forty *se'ah* of water, about twenty-four cubic feet [10]. A *mikveh* is not ritually suitable if water is constantly flowing through it [11]—another indication that these laws are not hygienic in intent. The requirements for the *mikveh* are such that an ordinary bathtub or swimming pool cannot be used for ritual purification. That these rules were already known prior to the fall of the Second Temple is indicated by the fact that the *mikveh* discovered in the ruins of Masada conforms to them [12].

11] *Without Having Rinsed His Hands in Water*

See commentary. The Rabbis understand these words to mean, "One who has not yet recovered from the impurity and taken a ritual bath." Why, then, are the hands mentioned? To indicate that, for a valid immersion, the water must cover all external parts of the body, such as the hands, but need not touch inner surfaces.   SIFRA

19] *She Shall Remain in Her Impurity Seven Days*

Because the rules of *niddah* are complicated and difficult, and the punishment for intercourse with a menstruant is so severe, the scholars and the pious Jewish women agreed, during the talmudic period, to apply the simpler but more stringent rules of the *zavah* to the *niddah* as well. The biblical law (verses 19ff.) requires abstention for seven days from the *onset* of the menstrual flow. The later regulation required the woman to count seven days from the time of the *cessation* of the flow, without further reappearance of blood, before she could take her bath and rejoin her husband [13]. A final formulation of the halachah added further stringencies, reducing still more the number of days each month when intercourse was permissible [14].

Haggadah

15:31] *Lest They Die through Their Uncleanness by Defiling My Tabernacle Which Is among Them*

Even though they are unclean, the Divine Presence still abides among them.   SIFRA

PART V

The Day of Atonement

Yom Kippur

It is impossible to exaggerate the importance of Yom Kippur in the life of the Jewish people. Even the religiously indifferent respond to its call and crowd the synagogues. To the devout it is the climax and crown of the religious year. It has inspired uplifting prayers in prose and poetry and has evoked sublime music, of which the Kol Nidre melody is only the best known example. It has changed lives. Before seeking divine forgiveness, Jews have often settled quarrels and disagreements among themselves. The Catholic Aimé Pallière began his pilgrimage to Judaism as the result of entering a synagogue on Yom Kippur afternoon. In 1913, a brilliant young German Jew named Franz Rosenzweig, who was about to adopt the Christian religion, became one of the noblest teachers and saints of modern Jewry, following a Day of Atonement spent in a small Orthodox synagogue in Berlin.

1. The Message of the Day of Atonement

The message of the day is not one of national or ethnic loyalty. It speaks to each human being and seeks to bring each person into harmony with others and with God. Non-Jews might well participate in the worship of the day without feeling alien and without forsaking their own loyalties. And yet Jews perhaps never feel so deeply Jewish as when they join with their fellow Jews in the prayers of Yom Kippur.

This holy day as we know it was created by the Jewish people in the past two thousand years. The biblical section now before us hardly suggests anything of inwardness or of moral aspiration. One may well feel disappointed when reading in Leviticus, chapter 16, the outline of a complicated sacrificial service performed by the High Priest on behalf of the community, with the people as passive spectators. At the end of the chapter—almost as an afterthought—they are commanded to fast and abstain from work on the sacred day, but nothing is said about inner contrition, self-discipline, or higher standards of conduct. For this reason, the leaders of Reform Judaism replaced this chapter, the traditional Torah reading for Yom Kippur morning, by selections from Deuteronomy, chapters 29 and 30, which they deemed more appropriate.

They retained, however, the traditional Haftarah (Isa. 57:14–58:14) which declares that fasting and formal prayer are valueless unless they lead to moral regeneration and,

above all, to the service of the weak and the unfortunate. This powerful sermon may indeed mark the beginning of the process by which the Day of Atonement was gradually transformed [1]. Most appropriate also is the afternoon Haftarah, the Book of Jonah, with its message of God's universal compassion and forgiveness.

But here we are concerned with the beginnings which seem so unpromising.

2. *The origins of Yom Kippur*

The Day of Atonement appears in the Bible only in the priestly writings. Except for an incidental allusion in Exodus (30:10), the present chapter is the first place where it is mentioned. The festival rules in other codes (Exod. 23:14ff. and 34:18–23; Deut. 16) are silent on the subject, and other biblical sources give no hint that such an observance was known. The earlier generations of biblical critics therefore inferred that Yom Kippur was a new creation of the postexilic priesthood. (The cryptic vision in Zech. 3, composed early in the postexilic period, seems to be a symbolic description of an emerging Yom Kippur ritual.)

This view no longer seems tenable, even for those who, like the present writer, believe that P in its present form was edited after the exile. So archaic a ritual, especially the scapegoat ceremony, would hardly have been invented by men who had felt the impact of the great prophets and lived through the chastening experience of the Babylonian captivity.

The Babylonians, and probably other Semitic peoples, had an elaborate new year festival which extended over ten days; on the fifth day a ceremony was performed called *kuppuru*, in which a temple was ceremonially cleansed by rubbing its walls with the body of a beheaded ram, after which the head and trunk were thrown into a river [2]. Recent scholars have theorized that there was a similar observance in ancient Israel, and they have found some evidence in the Bible to support their conjectures. If they are correct, we must further suppose that at some date these rites were detached from the new year festival and assigned to a special day, known henceforth as *Yom ha-Kippurim* [3]. This, however, remains theory. What seems sure is that the rites are ancient and that what was at first a ritual only, or primarily, for the priests later became a religious occasion for the entire community.

3. *Azazel*

The most embarrassing feature of the ancient ritual is the sending of the "scapegoat" to Azazel. The latter was probably a demonic being, residing in the desert, whose abode was regarded as a focus of impurity. Various efforts were made to avoid this embarrassment. The old Greek translation takes *azazel* as a common noun meaning "dismissal." Others rendered the word "steep mountain," or "goat that departs," or understood Azazel to be the name of a place [4].

These apologetic efforts are not convincing. For apocryphal Jewish works, composed in the last few centuries before the Christian era, tell of angels who were lured by beautiful women into lust and, ultimately, into rebellion against God. In these writings, Azazel is one of the two leaders of the rebellion. And posttalmudic documents tell a similar story about two rebel angels, Uzza and Azzael—both variations of the name Azazel [5]. These mythological stories, which must have been widely known, seem to confirm the essentially demonic character of the old biblical Azazel.

The more responsible Jewish teachers avoided the mythological notion of rebel

angels. The Talmud indeed refers frequently to Satan; but he is not, like the Satan of the New Testament, an enemy of God. He serves God as prosecutor, though at times he is overeager to get convictions. But, as we shall see, the notion of Satan as a hostile power, who must be overcome or appeased, was not entirely absent in talmudic times; and it emerged in much more open and emphatic form among the Kabalists of the Middle Ages [6].

The term "scapegoat" was apparently coined by William Tyndale, the first great English Bible translator. Thereafter, it came to be used for a person, animal, or object to which the impurity or guilt of a community was formally transferred and then removed. This concept, and the practices it inspired, is found among numberless peoples throughout the world [7]. But, in common usage today, a scapegoat is someone whom people blame for their own misfortunes, and even for their faults and sins—though the original notion of a scapegoat included the public acknowledgment by the community of its own transgressions [8].

4. The Hazards of the Yom Kippur Service

The opening verses of chapter 16 make plain that it was dangerous for the High Priest to enter the inner Shrine (Holy of Holies). The Deity was believed to be literally present, or present in a special degree, inside the Shrine, and too close an approach to divinity entailed risks. ("Man may not see Me and live," Exod. 33:20. In Greek myth, Semele was reduced to ashes when she saw Zeus in his full splendor.)

In addition to the danger of looking at God, to which the Torah plainly alludes, tradition found another hazard. Satan, it was believed, was present in the Holy of Holies, to accuse the Jews and their spokesman, the High Priest, before the divine court. This notion, suggested in Zechariah, chapter 3, is plainly expressed in many talmudic passages.

Because of these dangers, the High Priest in the days of the Second Temple would not linger in the inner Shrine so as not to worry the people waiting in the outer courts [9]. And at the close of the day he would give a banquet to his friends to celebrate his safe emergence from peril [10].

These facts serve to illuminate a controversy regarding verses 2, 12, and 13 of this chapter. The Sadducees, the priestly party, held that the High Priest should enter the Shrine carrying a firepan with incense smoking upon it. The Pharisees, the lay scholars, required him to carry the fire pan in one hand and a bowl of incense in the other; only after he had entered the Holy of Holies was he to put the incense on the burning coals. This second explanation fits the language of verses 12 and 13; yet in general it was the Sadducees who held to the literal sense of the Torah and the Pharisees who interpreted the text more freely. On this crucial point the priests must have had an ancient tradition!

This matter was explained brilliantly by Dr. Jacob Z. Lauterbach [11]. The priestly tradition, he held, sought to protect the High Priest by means of a "smoke screen." This would prevent him from seeing the Divine Presence, which could be fatal (verse 2). It would also serve to drive away Satan—in the folklore of many peoples, evil spirits are defeated by the use of smoke. The Pharisees opposed such superstitious beliefs and sent the High Priest into the sanctuary without this supposed protection. The offering of incense inside the Shrine ceased to be a security measure and was no more than one item of a prescribed ritual. But, despite this reform, the old beliefs survived to some extent.

5. Atonement and Return

In Scripture, this holy day is called the Day of the *Kippurim* (Lev. 23:27f., 25:9). The word probably comes from a root meaning "to cover up" [12]. It refers to the process by which guilt or impurity is canceled out, made nonexistent. It may be translated "expiation" which is defined as "the extinguishing of guilt by suffering or penalty." Similar words are found in other modern languages, but English has in addition the unique word, "atonement," from "at one." It designates the means by which a person estranged from God becomes at one with Him again. Though the word is peculiarly English, it expresses a biblical viewpoint. "Your sins have separated you from your God," says the prophet (Isa. 59:2); when the sin is annulled, the relationship to God is restored [13].

Kippurim and the cognate verb forms are applied in the Bible both to the canceling of guilt for moral offenses and to the purging away of ritual uncleanness (see 8:15 and 12:7 where earlier translations spoke of "atonement" for the altar and for a woman who bore a child). At the start, a clear line was not always drawn between ceremonial defilement and what we today would call sin. And, since ceremonial defilement could be corrected by ceremonial means, there was constant danger that men would rely on ritual procedures to annul moral guilt as well.

The prophets insisted that sacrificial rites alone cannot reconcile a human being to God. They held that sins are forgiven only if the sinner experiences a change of heart leading to a change of ways. They constantly urged people to turn back from evil conduct and to return to God (e.g., Ezek. 18:30; Hos. 14:2; Mal. 3:7). This theme was taken up by the talmudic and later Rabbis in their doctrine of *teshuvah*, "return"—roughly equivalent to "repentance," except that "repentance" re-fers chiefly to emotion while "return" more plainly involves action. In numberless sayings and parables, the Rabbis teach that, if a person makes the slightest attempt to change for the better, it is possible to count on a loving response from God (see Gleanings). In contrast with both biblical and later Judaism, which are concerned with the attitudes and behavior of each individual, the other religions of the ancient Near East imposed the requirements of cultic and moral purity chiefly upon the king.

Jewish literature has relatively little to say about the process of atonement and focuses rather on the turnabout, the fresh start made by a person. It is confidently expected that *teshuvah* will lead, ultimately if not always immediately (see Gleanings), to God's forgiveness. In contrast, generations of Christian theologians worked out elaborate theories of "the Atonement," endeavoring to explain how the death of Jesus operated to redeem humankind from original sin.

It is true that sacrifices were deemed to have expiatory power; but, as we have seen (chs. 4 and 5), Leviticus limits this almost entirely to unintentional violations. The Rabbis held that the blood rites of Yom Kippur atoned for unrecognized defilement of the sanctuary and its sacrifices [14]. (Where defilement was known to have occurred, the prescribed sin offering was brought at once.) The sacrifices and the ceremony of the Azazel-goat were, it is true, thought to have genuine atoning power; they were joined to the confession recited by the High Priest. But the effect of these rites was contingent on the *teshuvah* of the worshipers. According to the Mishnah, an offense against a person cannot be wiped out either by ritual or by simple contrition. The sinner must attempt to rectify the wrong and seek the good will of the injured party. Moreover, one who sins with the intention of repenting afterward, or of obtaining pardon through the Yom Kippur

rites, will not obtain forgiveness [15]. The Rabbis also held that, even after the fall of the Temple and the discontinuance of the sacrificial rites, Yom Kippur continued to have an atoning effect, when combined with *teshuvah* [16].

Shortly after the destruction, the disciples of Rabban Johanan ben Zakkai were mourning the loss of the altar as a means of atonement; thereupon the master assured them that acts of kindness and charity are equally efficacious [17]. The dictum that "*teshuvah*, prayer, and charity annul the degree of punishment" [18] was inserted into the prayer book (*Union Prayer Book*, II, pp. 256–257). Most remarkable, the lengthy confession recited on Yom Kippur in traditional synagogues (in much briefer form, *Union Prayer Book*, II, pp. 148ff.) enumerates only sins involving breach of the moral law, whereas such basic observances as Sabbath and dietary laws are not specifically mentioned [19]. Thus, the moral and spiritual aspects of the day triumphed over formal ritual.

6. *Some Problems of the Biblical Material*

Leviticus, chapter 16, presents a number of problems. It begins with the mention of the death of Nadab and Abihu and warns Aaron not to enter the Shrine without due preparation. This preparation is now de-

scribed at length. It could be (and has been) understood as the ritual to be followed whenever the High Priest chooses to enter the inner Shrine. Only much farther on (verses 29f.) do we read that this ritual is to be an annual event on a specific date (the holy day is not given a name in this chapter) and that on the day in question the people must not eat nor work. This sequence of material suggests that the observance was originally for the priesthood alone and later became a public holy day.

The festival calendar in Leviticus, chapter 23, mentions the day by name for the first time; it announces severe punishment for eating or working on the Day of Atonement. But Numbers (29:7–11) gives a list of sacrifices which does not agree with Leviticus, chapter 16. Later authorities had to harmonize the two sources (both from P). During the days of the Second Temple, the High Priest performed, not only the special Yom Kippur rites, but (on this occasion) also the regular morning and evening sacrifices of lambs and incense (Exod. 29:38ff., 30:7f.). The complete order of the day, as fixed by the halachah, is outlined in Appendix II. It became the subject of poetic compositions during the Middle Ages, and these were incorporated into various versions of the prayer book. A reinterpretation of this material appears in the *Union Prayer Book*, II, pp. 265–274.

(A new weekly portion, *Achare Mot*, begins with 16:1.)

פ פ פ

יא וַיְדַבֵּר יְהוָה אֶל־מֹשֶׁה אַחֲרֵי מוֹת שְׁנֵי בְּנֵי אַהֲרֹן
בְּקָרְבָתָם לִפְנֵי־יְהוָה וַיָּמֻתוּ: וַיֹּאמֶר יְהוָה אֶל־מֹשֶׁה
דַּבֵּר אֶל־אַהֲרֹן אָחִיךָ וְאַל־יָבֹא בְכָל־עֵת אֶל־הַקֹּדֶשׁ
מִבֵּית לַפָּרֹכֶת אֶל־פְּנֵי הַכַּפֹּרֶת אֲשֶׁר עַל־הָאָרֹן וְלֹא

י יָמוּת כִּי בֶּעָנָן אֵרָאֶה עַל־הַכַּפֹּרֶת: בְּזֹאת יָבֹא אַהֲרֹן
אֶל־הַקֹּדֶשׁ בְּפַר בֶּן־בָּקָר לְחַטָּאת וְאַיִל לְעֹלָה:
כְּתֹנֶת־בַּד קֹדֶשׁ יִלְבָּשׁ וּמִכְנְסֵי־בַד יִהְיוּ עַל־בְּשָׂרוֹ
וּבְאַבְנֵט בַּד יַחְגֹּר וּבְמִצְנֶפֶת בַּד יִצְנֹף בִּגְדֵי־קֹדֶשׁ

1] The LORD spoke to Moses after the death of the two sons of Aaron who died when they drew too close to the presence of the LORD. **2]** The LORD said to Moses:

Tell your brother Aaron that he is not to come at will into the Shrine behind the curtain, in front of the cover that is upon the ark, lest he die; for I appear in the cloud over the cover. **3]** Thus only shall Aaron enter the Shrine: with a bull of the herd for a sin offering and a ram for a burnt offering.— **4]** He shall be dressed in a sacral linen tunic, with linen breeches next to his flesh, and be girt with a linen sash, and he shall wear a linen turban. They

16.1] *After the death of the two sons of Aaron.* This phrase connects this chapter with chapter 10; the intervening sections on ritual impurity are a separate block of material.

When they drew too close. Went beyond the limits imposed on them. Ibn Ezra, following a few talmudic remarks, infers that Nadab and Abihu entered the Holy of Holies, since Aaron is now warned against doing so without proper preparation. But probably the sentence means simply, "They broke the rules and were punished; don't you break the rules or you will be punished."

2] *Your brother Aaron.* Moses was permitted to enter the Shrine at will to receive the divine revelation (Exod. 25:22; Num. 7:89); but Aaron did not have this privilege, even though he was Moses' brother (*Sifra*).

At will. Literally, "at any time" (T.N.).

For I appear in the cloud over the cover. This was understood by the Sadducees (see introduction to this chapter) to mean "I may be looked at only through the cloud of incense." The Pharisees understood the words similarly, though they postponed the placing of the incense on the coals until the High Priest had entered the Shrine [20]. This explanation is preferred by Ibn Ezra and adopted by Nachmanides. Rashi and Rashbam, however, say it refers to a divinely ordained cloud (like the pillar of cloud that led Israel through the wilderness), not to a man-made cloud of smoke.

Cover. Hebrew *kaporet.* We have seen that *kippurim,* "atonement," very likely comes from a root meaning "to cover." The word *kaporet,* presumably from the same root, could mean either "lid" or "place of atonement." The second interpretation, which goes back to the old Greek translation, is more probable [21]. The Authorized Version, following Luther, rendered "mercy seat."

The Shrine. Hebrew *kodesh,* literally, "holiness." Here, as in chapter 4, verse 6, the term designates the innermost Shrine, called "Holy of Holies" in Exodus 23:33 and elsewhere. But sometimes the whole interior of the Tabernacle is called *kodesh* (e.g., Lev. 10:4).

3] *Thus only.* In accordance with the entire ritual to be set forth. The second half of the verse mentions only one item; the bull and ram were, of course, not taken into the Shrine. In fact, the ram, as well as the one mentioned in verse 5, was not actually offered until late in the day (see verse 24).

4] *Linen tunic....* Instead of the gorgeous vestments he customarily wore (Exod. 28), the High Priest was on this occasion to wear plain white linen. The Rabbis give many explanations of this rule (see Gleanings). This priestly rule is the source of the custom for men to wear a white robe (*kittel* or *sargenes*) during the Yom Kippur service.

ה הֶם וְרָחַץ בַּמַּיִם אֶת־בְּשָׂרוֹ וּלְבֵשָׁם: וּמֵאֵת עֲדַת בְּנֵי
יִשְׂרָאֵל יִקַּח שְׁנֵי־שְׂעִירֵי עִזִּים לְחַטָּאת וְאַיִל אֶחָד
ו לְעֹלָה: וְהִקְרִיב אַהֲרֹן אֶת־פַּר הַחַטָּאת אֲשֶׁר־לוֹ
ז וְכִפֶּר בַּעֲדוֹ וּבְעַד בֵּיתוֹ: וְלָקַח אֶת־שְׁנֵי הַשְּׂעִירִם
ח וְהֶעֱמִיד אֹתָם לִפְנֵי יְהוָה פֶּתַח אֹהֶל מוֹעֵד: וְנָתַן
אַהֲרֹן עַל־שְׁנֵי הַשְּׂעִירִם גֹּרָלוֹת גּוֹרָל אֶחָד לַיהוָה
ט וְגוֹרָל אֶחָד לַעֲזָאזֵל: וְהִקְרִיב אַהֲרֹן אֶת־הַשָּׂעִיר
אֲשֶׁר עָלָה עָלָיו הַגּוֹרָל לַיהוָה וְעָשָׂהוּ חַטָּאת:

י וְהַשָּׂעִיר אֲשֶׁר עָלָה עָלָיו הַגּוֹרָל לַעֲזָאזֵל יָעֳמַד־חַי
לִפְנֵי יְהוָה לְכַפֵּר עָלָיו לְשַׁלַּח אֹתוֹ לַעֲזָאזֵל
יא הַמִּדְבָּרָה: וְהִקְרִיב אַהֲרֹן אֶת־פַּר הַחַטָּאת אֲשֶׁר־לוֹ
וְכִפֶּר בַּעֲדוֹ וּבְעַד בֵּיתוֹ וְשָׁחַט אֶת־פַּר הַחַטָּאת
יב אֲשֶׁר־לוֹ: וְלָקַח מְלֹא־הַמַּחְתָּה גַּחֲלֵי־אֵשׁ מֵעַל הַמִּזְבֵּחַ
מִלִּפְנֵי יְהוָה וּמְלֹא חָפְנָיו קְטֹרֶת סַמִּים דַּקָּה וְהֵבִיא
יג מִבֵּית לַפָּרֹכֶת: וְנָתַן אֶת־הַקְּטֹרֶת עַל־הָאֵשׁ לִפְנֵי
יְהוָה וְכִסָּה עֲנַן הַקְּטֹרֶת אֶת־הַכַּפֹּרֶת אֲשֶׁר עַל־

are sacral vestments; he shall bathe his body in water and then put them on.— 5] And from the Israelite community he shall take two he-goats for a sin offering and a ram for a burnt offering.

6] Aaron is to offer his own bull of sin offering, to make expiation for himself and for his household. 7] Aaron shall take the two he-goats and let them stand before the LORD at the entrance of the Tent of Meeting; 8] and he shall place lots upon the two goats, one marked for the LORD and the other marked for Azazel. 9] Aaron shall bring forward the goat designated by lot for the LORD, which he is to offer as a sin offering; 10] while the goat designated by lot for Azazel shall be left standing alive before the LORD, to make expiation with it and to send it off to the wilderness for Azazel.

11] Aaron shall then offer his bull of sin offering, to make expiation for himself and his household. He shall slaughter his bull of sin offering, 12] and he shall take a panful of glowing coals scooped from the altar before the LORD, and two handfuls of finely ground aromatic incense, and bring this behind the curtain. 13] He shall put the incense on the fire before the LORD, so that the cloud from the incense screens the cover that is over [the Ark of] the Pact,

5] *A ram.* The "burnt offering of the people" of verse 24.

6] *His own bull of sin offering.* Before he could make atonement for the people, he had to purge himself of sin. "Improve yourself first; then improve others" [22]. The actual sacrifice did not, however, take place until later (verse 11); so the Rabbis, reasonably enough, understood the "offering" and "expiation" mentioned here as the confession recited by the High Priest with his hands on the head of the bull [23].

7-10] The designation of the goats for the Lord and for Azazel (see introduction). According to the Mishnah [24] the goats were stationed in front of the High Priest, one to his right and one to his left. Two disks, inscribed respectively "for the Lord" and "for Azazel," had been placed in an urn. The High Priest put both hands into the urn, picked up one disk in each hand, and placed them on the heads of the goats. It was considered a good omen if the disk for the Lord came up in his right hand.

7] *Aaron.* Moved up from verse 8 for clarity (T.N.).

10-22] Sending away the scapegoat.

11] The bull of sin offering was now slaughtered; its blood was to be sprinkled in the Shrine. But first the incense rite had to be performed. Accordingly, the bowl of blood was given to a priest who stirred it constantly to keep the blood from congealing until the High Priest was ready to use it [25]

12-13] The incense rite (see introduction).

12] *Scooped from the altar before the Lord.* I.e., from the bronze altar of sacrifice at the door of the sanctuary. There was not a constant fire on the small incense altar.

יד הָעֵדֻת וְלֹא יָמוּת: וְלָקַח מִדַּם הַפָּר וְהִזָּה בְאֶצְבָּעוֹ
עַל־פְּנֵי הַכַּפֹּרֶת קֵדְמָה וְלִפְנֵי הַכַּפֹּרֶת יַזֶּה שֶׁבַע־
טו פְּעָמִים מִן־הַדָּם בְּאֶצְבָּעוֹ: וְשָׁחַט אֶת־שְׂעִיר הַחַטָּאת
אֲשֶׁר לָעָם וְהֵבִיא אֶת־דָּמוֹ אֶל־מִבֵּית לַפָּרֹכֶת וְעָשָׂה
אֶת־דָּמוֹ כַּאֲשֶׁר עָשָׂה לְדַם הַפָּר וְהִזָּה אֹתוֹ עַל־
טז הַכַּפֹּרֶת וְלִפְנֵי הַכַּפֹּרֶת: וְכִפֶּר עַל־הַקֹּדֶשׁ מִטֻּמְאֹת
בְּנֵי יִשְׂרָאֵל וּמִפִּשְׁעֵיהֶם לְכָל־חַטֹּאתָם וְכֵן יַעֲשֶׂה
יז לְאֹהֶל מוֹעֵד הַשֹּׁכֵן אִתָּם בְּתוֹךְ טֻמְאֹתָם: וְכָל־אָדָם
לֹא־יִהְיֶה בְּאֹהֶל מוֹעֵד בְּבֹאוֹ לְכַפֵּר בַּקֹּדֶשׁ עַד־

צֵאתוֹ וְכִפֶּר בַּעֲדוֹ וּבְעַד בֵּיתוֹ וּבְעַד כָּל־קְהַל
יח יִשְׂרָאֵל: וְיָצָא אֶל־הַמִּזְבֵּחַ אֲשֶׁר לִפְנֵי־יְהוָה וְכִפֶּר
עָלָיו וְלָקַח מִדַּם הַפָּר וּמִדַּם הַשָּׂעִיר וְנָתַן עַל־קַרְנוֹת
יט הַמִּזְבֵּחַ סָבִיב: וְהִזָּה עָלָיו מִן־הַדָּם בְּאֶצְבָּעוֹ שֶׁבַע
כ פְּעָמִים וְטִהֲרוֹ וְקִדְּשׁוֹ מִטֻּמְאֹת בְּנֵי יִשְׂרָאֵל: וְכִלָּה
מִכַּפֵּר אֶת־הַקֹּדֶשׁ וְאֶת־אֹהֶל מוֹעֵד וְאֶת־הַמִּזְבֵּחַ
כא וְהִקְרִיב אֶת־הַשָּׂעִיר הֶחָי: וְסָמַךְ אַהֲרֹן אֶת־שְׁתֵּי יָדָו *
עַל־רֹאשׁ הַשָּׂעִיר הַחַי וְהִתְוַדָּה עָלָיו אֶת־כָּל־עֲוֹנֹת
בְּנֵי יִשְׂרָאֵל וְאֶת־כָּל־פִּשְׁעֵיהֶם לְכָל־חַטֹּאתָם וְנָתַן

* כא ידו קרי.

lest he die.   **14]** He shall take some of the blood of the bull and sprinkle it with his finger over the cover on the east side; and in front of the cover he shall sprinkle some of the blood with his finger seven times.   **15]** He shall then slaughter the people's goat of sin offering, bring its blood behind the curtain, and do with its blood as he has done with the blood of the bull: he shall sprinkle it over the cover and in front of the cover.

16] Thus he shall purge the Shrine of the uncleanness and transgression of the Israelites, whatever their sins; and he shall do the same for the Tent of Meeting, which abides with them in the midst of their uncleanness.   **17]** When he goes in to make expiation in the Shrine, nobody else shall be in the Tent of Meeting until he comes out.

When he has made expiation for himself and his household, and for the whole congregation of Israel,   **18]** he shall go out to the altar that is before the LORD and purge it: he shall take some of the blood of the bull and of the goat and apply it to each of the horns of the altar;   **19]** and the rest of the blood he shall sprinkle on it with his finger seven times. Thus he shall cleanse it of the uncleanness of the Israelites and consecrate it.

20] When he has finished purging the Shrine, the Tent of Meeting, and the altar, the live goat shall be brought forward.   **21]** Aaron shall lay both his hands upon the head of the live goat and confess over it all the iniquities and transgressions of the Israelites, whatever their sins,

14–19] The blood rites. After offering the incense, the officiant went outside, got the bowl of bull's blood, brought it into the Shrine, and sprinkled some of the blood, once upward, seven times downward toward the ark cover. Then he went out again, the goat "for the Lord" was slaughtered, and he brought its blood into the Shrine and sprinkled it.

16] *Thus he shall purge the Shrine of the uncleanness and transgression.* The primary stress is on ritual purgation. If an individual discovered that he had entered the sacred area or eaten consecrated food while he was in a state of ritual uncleanness, he immediately brought a sin offering (5:2f.). The Yom Kippur ceremonies neutralized defilement of which

no one was aware. The reference to other sins may be a later insertion (see introduction).

And he shall do the same for the Tent of Meeting. According to the halachah [26], he brought out the bowls of blood and, standing between the incense altar and the entrance of the Shrine, he sprinkled the blood of the bull and then that of the goat toward the curtain that closed the Shrine.

18] *To the altar that is before the Lord.* This seems to mean the bronze altar of sacrifice, as in verse 12; so Ibn Ezra. But the talmudic sources (*Sifra* and others) insist that these rites are to be performed on the incense altar.

כא הַחַטָּאת יַקְטִיר הַמִּזְבֵּחָה: וְהַמְשַׁלֵּחַ אֶת־הַשָּׂעִיר
לַעֲזָאזֵל יְכַבֵּס בְּגָדָיו וְרָחַץ אֶת־בְּשָׂרוֹ בַּמָּיִם וְאַחֲרֵי־
כֵן יָבוֹא אֶל־הַמַּחֲנֶה: וְאֵת פַּר הַחַטָּאת וְאֵת שְׂעִיר
הַחַטָּאת אֲשֶׁר הוּבָא אֶת־דָּמָם לְכַפֵּר בַּקֹּדֶשׁ יוֹצִיא
אֶל־מִחוּץ לַמַּחֲנֶה וְשָׂרְפוּ בָאֵשׁ אֶת־עֹרֹתָם וְאֶת־
בְּשָׂרָם וְאֶת־פִּרְשָׁם: וְהַשֹּׂרֵף אֹתָם יְכַבֵּס בְּגָדָיו וְרָחַץ
אֶת־בְּשָׂרוֹ בַּמָּיִם וְאַחֲרֵי־כֵן יָבוֹא אֶל־הַמַּחֲנֶה: וְהָיְתָה

אֹתָם עַל־רֹאשׁ הַשָּׂעִיר וְשִׁלַּח בְּיַד־אִישׁ עִתִּי
כב הַמִּדְבָּרָה: וְנָשָׂא הַשָּׂעִיר עָלָיו אֶת־כָּל־עֲוֹנֹתָם אֶל־
כג אֶרֶץ גְּזֵרָה וְשִׁלַּח אֶת־הַשָּׂעִיר בַּמִּדְבָּר: וּבָא אַהֲרֹן
אֶל־אֹהֶל מוֹעֵד וּפָשַׁט אֶת־בִּגְדֵי הַבָּד אֲשֶׁר לָבַשׁ
כד בְּבֹאוֹ אֶל־הַקֹּדֶשׁ וְהִנִּיחָם שָׁם: וְרָחַץ אֶת־בְּשָׂרוֹ בַמַּיִם
בְּמָקוֹם קָדוֹשׁ וְלָבַשׁ אֶת־בְּגָדָיו וְיָצָא וְעָשָׂה אֶת־עֹלָתוֹ
כה וְאֶת־עֹלַת הָעָם וְכִפֶּר בַּעֲדוֹ וּבְעַד הָעָם: וְאֵת חֵלֶב

putting them on the head of the goat; and it shall be sent off to the wilderness through a designated man.   **22]** Thus the goat shall carry on it all their iniquities to an inaccessible region; and the goat shall be set free in the wilderness.

23] And Aaron shall go into the Tent of Meeting, take off the linen vestments that he put on when he entered the Shrine, and leave them there.   **24]** He shall bathe his body in water in the holy precinct and put on his vestments; then he shall come out and offer his burnt offering and the burnt offering of the people, making expiation for himself and for the people.   **25]** The fat of the sin offering he shall turn into smoke on the altar.

26] He who set the Azazel-goat free shall wash his clothes and bathe his body in water; after that he may re-enter the camp.

27] The bull of sin offering and the goat of sin offering whose blood was brought in to purge the Shrine shall be taken outside the camp; and their hides, flesh, and dung shall be consumed in fire.   **28]** He who burned them shall wash his clothes and bathe his body in water; after that he may re-enter the camp.

21] *A designated man.* Meaning of Hebrew *'itti* uncertain (T.N.). Rashbam connects *'itti* with *et,* "time," and explains: a man well acquainted with the desert trails and ready to travel them at any time.

22] *Set free.* This was not the practice in the period of the Second Temple, when the goat was toppled over a cliff to its death (see Gleanings).

23] *And leave them there.* This enigmatic passage has troubled the commentators. Surely the white robes were not left lying indefinitely in the sacred area! Is the "holy precinct" of verse 24 (the Hebrew is literally "in *a* sacred place") identical with the Tent of Meeting? Further, we must assume that other priests accompanied the High Priest to help him

bathe and change, but the text mentions only Aaron. The talmudic rabbis dealt with the passage quite radically, but their reconstruction at least makes sense (see Gleanings).

24] *And put on his vestments.* I.e., his usual vestments, called by the Rabbis "the golden garments."

   His burnt offering and the burnt offering of the people. A ram (see verses 3 and 5 above).

26–28] Those who deal with the Azazel-goat and those who burn the carcasses of the sin offerings (cf. 4:11, 12, 21; 6:23; 10:18) are ritually defiled by these powerful instruments of "de-sinning" and must purify themselves before returning to the camp.

אֶת־יָדוֹ לְכַהֵן תַּחַת אָבִיו וְלָבַשׁ אֶת־בִּגְדֵי הַבָּד בִּגְדֵי
הַקֹּדֶשׁ: לֹג וְכִפֶּר אֶת־מִקְדַּשׁ הַקֹּדֶשׁ וְאֶת־אֹהֶל מוֹעֵד
וְאֶת־הַמִּזְבֵּחַ יְכַפֵּר וְעַל הַכֹּהֲנִים וְעַל־כָּל־עַם הַקָּהָל
יְכַפֵּר: לד וְהָיְתָה־זֹּאת לָכֶם לְחֻקַּת עוֹלָם לְכַפֵּר עַל־
בְּנֵי יִשְׂרָאֵל מִכָּל־חַטֹּאתָם אַחַת בַּשָּׁנָה וַיַּעַשׂ כַּאֲשֶׁר
צִוָּה יְהוָה אֶת־מֹשֶׁה: פ

לָכֶם לְחֻקַּת עוֹלָם בַּחֹדֶשׁ הַשְּׁבִיעִי בֶּעָשׂוֹר לַחֹדֶשׁ
תְּעַנּוּ אֶת־נַפְשֹׁתֵיכֶם וְכָל־מְלָאכָה לֹא תַעֲשׂוּ הָאֶזְרָח
ל וְהַגֵּר הַגָּר בְּתוֹכְכֶם: כִּי־בַיּוֹם הַזֶּה יְכַפֵּר עֲלֵיכֶם
לְטַהֵר אֶתְכֶם מִכֹּל חַטֹּאתֵיכֶם לִפְנֵי יְהוָה תִּטְהָרוּ:
לא שַׁבַּת שַׁבָּתוֹן הִיא לָכֶם וְעִנִּיתֶם אֶת־נַפְשֹׁתֵיכֶם חֻקַּת
לב עוֹלָם: וְכִפֶּר הַכֹּהֵן אֲשֶׁר־יִמְשַׁח אֹתוֹ וַאֲשֶׁר יְמַלֵּא

29] And this shall be to you a law for all time: In the seventh month, on the tenth day of the month, you shall practice self-denial; and you shall do no manner of work, neither the citizen nor the alien who resides among you.   **30]** For on this day atonement shall be made for you to cleanse you of all your sins; you shall be clean before the LORD.   **31]** It shall be a sabbath of complete rest for you, and you shall practice self-denial; it is a law for all time.   **32]** The priest who has been anointed and ordained to serve as priest in place of his father shall make expiation. He shall put on the linen vestments, the sacral vestments.   **33]** He shall purge the innermost Shrine; he shall purge the Tent of Meeting and the altar; and he shall make expiation for the priests and for all the people of the congregation.

34] This shall be to you a law for all time: to make atonement for the Israelites for all their sins once a year.

And Moses did as the LORD had commanded him.

29–33] Obligations of the people.

29] *Practice self-denial.* Literally, "afflict yourselves." The traditional rendering "afflict your souls" is misleading; this chapter is not concerned with inner contrition. The idea of "return" appears frequently in the Bible (see introduction), but it is hardly present in this outline of formal observance. Tradition understood this self-denial as fasting, no doubt correctly (cf. Ps. 35:13, "I afflicted myself with fasting" –the new JPS translation renders simply, "I kept a fast"– and Isa. 58:3, where fasting and self-affliction are parallel).

30] This verse, summing up the intent of the observance, is repeated a number of times in the synagogue liturgy for Yom Kippur.

32] *Anointed and ordained.* In the Second Temple there was no ceremony of anointment; the High Priest was inducted into office by clothing him in the "golden vestments."

34] *And Moses did as the Lord had commanded him.* He gave the instructions to Aaron to be carried out when the Day of Atonement came around. The dedication of the Tabernacle and the death of Aaron's sons occurred in the spring (Exod. 40:17).

GLEANINGS

Halachah

16:4] *Linen Tunic*

The High Priest wore the "white vestments" for all the rites specifically connected with Yom Kippur. But for the daily offerings, morning and evening, he wore the usual "golden vestments" [27].

He Shall Bathe His Body in Water

Each time the High Priest changed from the golden to the linen vestments, or the reverse, he had to take a ritual bath. Before and after doing so, he had to wash his hands and feet from the laver. This

process occurred five times during the Yom Kippur observance [28].

6] Sin Offering

Over his own bull, the High Priest recited this confession: "O LORD, I have sinned, I have transgressed, I have rebelled against You, I and my household. O LORD, pardon the sins, transgressions, and rebellions which I and my household have committed against You; as it is written in the Torah of Your servant Moses: 'For on this day atonement shall be made for you to cleanse you of all your sins; you shall be clean before the LORD.'" The subsequent confessions were in the same form, except that the second confession also mentioned "the sons of Aaron, Your holy people," and the third (over the Azazel-goat) began "Your people Israel have sinned, have transgressed, . . . pardon the sins which Your people Israel have. . . ." In these prayers the High Priest did not address God as *Adonai* ("Lord") but actually pronounced the tetragrammaton YHWH. Each time the people heard the Name uttered (it was spoken only on this occasion), they responded, "Praised be His Name, whose glorious kingdom is forever and ever" [29].

22] Set Free in the Wilderness

See commentary. The Mishnah reports: When the lot designated the goat for Azazel, the High Priest tied a piece of crimson yarn on his head. Ten booths were set up between Jerusalem and the cliff which was known as Bet Hadura (or Bet Chadudo). At each of these stations the goat was offered food and water. When the cliff was reached, the man in charge would divide the strip of crimson wool in two: he would tie one part to the goat's horns, the other to the rock. Then he would topple the goat backward over the cliff; before the animal was half-way to the bottom, its body would be crushed [30].

The Palestinian Targum attempted to harmonize the biblical text and the tradition. It states that the man would release the goat, whereupon a violent wind would hurl the beast over the cliff.

23] And Leave Them There

See commentary. The Rabbis held that this verb is out of place. Immediately after sending the Azazel-goat away, the High Priest was to don the golden vestments and offer the two burnt offerings of verse 24—according to Nachmanides, also the regular evening burnt offering and incense. Next, he put on the linen robes once more, in order to enter the Shrine and remove the fire pan and incense bowl. Thence, he would go to a chamber in the sacred area, where he had repeatedly bathed and changed during the day, and there he would discard the linen garments. The words "and leave them there" mean merely that the vestments were to be hidden away and not used on a subsequent Yom Kippur.   SIFRA

When the rites of the day were concluded, the High Priest put on regular attire and returned home, accompanied by his friends, for whom he would hold a banquet celebrating the safe completion of his hazardous duties [31]. To this day, in many communities, some festivities are held after the fast is broken. A beautiful custom observed by some of the pious is to do a little work on the sukah, in preparation for the next holiday in the calendar [32].

29] Practice Self-Denial

On Yom Kippur one is forbidden to eat, drink, wash, anoint himself with oil, engage in sexual intercourse, or wear sandals [33]. To this day, Orthodox Jews remove their shoes in the synagogue on Yom Kippur, or wear slippers of a material other than leather. The rule of fasting is suspended when necessary for health reasons [34].

Do No Manner of Work

The same stringent laws apply as on the Sabbath, since Yom Kippur is also called Sabbath (Lev. 23:32). On all other holy days, even Rosh Hashanah, the preparation of food is permitted (Exod. 12:16), including such related tasks as lighting a fire.

32] Anointed and Ordained to Serve in Place of His Father

This indicates that the High Priest should be succeeded by his son, if the latter is qualified. But, if he is not worthy to hold the post, another priest is to be selected [35].

16:4] *Linen Tunic*

Why does the High Priest wear this simple garb on Yom Kippur, instead of his usual gorgeous vestments? (a) As an expression of humility and contrition [36]. (b) The regular vestments would be unsuitable for a ceremony of atonement, since their gold adornments would recall the sin of the golden calf [37]. (c) On this day the High Priest wears the white linen garb of the angels (Ezek. 9:2). On Yom Kippur, like the angels, we do not eat nor drink [38].

8] *For Azazel*

Nachmanides regards Azazel as representing the power of evil. *We do not offer him anything.* God controls the lot, and it is He who designates the gift for Azazel. It is as if one entertained a lord at a banquet and the lord directed that a certain dish be served to a mighty general that he might be more favorably inclined toward the host. The powers of evil are under God's control and ultimately serve His ends [39].

30] *For on This Day Atonement Shall Be Made*

Rabbi Ishmael said: There are four divisions in the matter of atonement: If one fails to observe a positive command and then repents, he is forgiven on the spot (Jer. 3:22). If he transgresses a negative command and then repents, repentance suspends punishment and Yom Kippur brings atonement (Lev. 16:30). If he commits a sin punishable by "cutting off" or by the death sentence and then repents, repentance and the Day of Atonement suspend punishment and suffering throughout the year purifies him (Ps. 89:33). But if one deliberately causes the profanation of God's name and repents, this repentance is not enough to suspend punishment nor will the Day of Atonement bring remission; rather, repentance and Yom Kippur atone for a third of the guilt, suffering atones for another third, and death, along with suffering, brings full purification (Isa. 22:14) [40].

This saying of Rabbi Ishmael was never construed as a dogma: the Rabbis generally stressed the constant availability of forgiveness to those who return: "God says to Israel. Open to Me a gate of repentance no bigger than the point of a needle, and I will open to you a gate [of forgiveness] wide enough to drive wagons and carts through" [41]. A king's son had traveled a hundred days' journey from his father. His friends advised him to return home, but he said, "I cannot, the trip is too long." Then his father sent him word, "Come back as far as your strength permits, and I will go to meet you the rest of the way." Thus God says to Israel, "Return to Me, and I will return to you" (Mal. 3:7) [42].

You Shall Be Clean before the Lord

That is, Yom Kippur will cleanse you of sins committed only before God (irreverence, neglect of prayer, ceremonial duties); but sins committed against a human being are not absolved by the Day of Atonement unless you try to correct the wrong you have done [43].

Rabbi Akiba said, "Happy are you, O Israel! Who purifies you, and before whom do you become clean? Your Father in heaven! ... As the *mikveh* cleanses the defiled, so the Holy One (blessed be He) cleanses Israel" [44].

PART VI

The Law of Holiness

Further Laws about Sacrifice and Food

This is the first chapter assigned by modern scholars to the Holiness Code (H). It does not have all the characteristic features of that document [1]; it does not, for example, specifically mention the concept of holiness, and it contains no moral injunctions. But it does give reasons for the commandments (verses 5, 11–12), and it contains some of the phraseology typical of H. It seems to have no connection with the rest of the Holiness Code which appears to be not a single, ordered document but a collection of materials all emanating from the same background and holding much the same viewpoint.

1. Secular Slaughtering Prohibited

The first part of this chapter presents a difficult problem of interpretation, even though the language is simple and clear. It demands that cattle, sheep, and goats—beasts of the species used in sacrifice—be slaughtered only at the gate of the Tabernacle so that their blood may be dashed upon the altar and the fat burned ceremonially; in short, that every such animal intended for food be brought as a *shelamim*

sacrifice. If this ritual is omitted, the person responsible is guilty of bloodshed—as if he had murdered a human being!

Now Deuteronomy (12:20ff.) provides that, after Israel has conquered and occupied the land, animals may be killed for food without sacrificial formalities, as long as the carcasses are drained of blood. The simplest explanation of this chapter, then, is that it was a temporary rule for the period of desert wandering; the Israelites were traveling in constant proximity to the Tabernacle and could easily bring their animals there and present them as sacrifices of well-being. But, after they settled in Canaan and spread over the country, frequent trips to a central Shrine (such as Shiloh and later Jerusalem) would have been burdensome; and secular slaughtering was therefore permitted. This explanation was given by Rabbi Ishmael in the second century and was adopted by later legal authorities [2]. It makes excellent sense, on the assumption that the Torah was all given through Moses, that the present chapter dates from the time of the encampment at Sinai and Deuteronomy from the end of the desert period, just before the invasion of the land.

Yet, even on this assumption, the passage presents a difficulty for it declares that "this shall be to them a law for all time" (verse 7). The Orthodox commentators are forced to restrict the application of this sentence to the immediately preceding clause: "That they may offer their sacrifices no more to the goat-demons" [3]. But, if the text is examined without preconceptions, it becomes evident that the entire provision, not just one clause, is "the law for all time" [4].

Further, we must reckon with all the many reasons for considering the Pentateuch a composite, post-Mosaic work. We cannot disregard the strong evidence that Deuteronomy was the basis for the reforms of Josiah in 621 B.C.E., when the local shrines (*bamot*) were outlawed and sacrifice was restricted to the Jerusalem Temple. This revolutionary change necessitated many adjustments. One of these concerned slaughtering. A meat meal in ancient times was a special occasion and often (or should we say, always?) took the form of a festive sacrifice performed at the local sanctuary. Now that this procedure was forbidden, and Israelites could hardly be required to travel to Jerusalem whenever they wanted meat for dinner, they were allowed to slaughter for food without sacrificial procedures.

This much is accepted by virtually all non-Orthodox scholars. From it follows the necessity of choosing one of two alternatives. Either this chapter is an old document that is explicitly repealed in Deuteronomy (12:20ff.) or it is a later document than Deuteronomy and is intended to repeal the law that permitted secular slaughtering. Both opinions have their learned supporters.

Thus Kaufmann, who regarded P as the oldest component of the Pentateuch, found in this chapter the old rule that prevailed prior to Deuteronomy, which required all slaughtering to take the form of sacrifice. But one may argue that such offerings were made at the local shrines, whereas our chapter speaks of *the* Tent of Meeting, the central sanctuary. To this Kaufmann replied that the Tent of Meeting is a symbol for any one of the local holy places [5]. This seems forced. Although P nowhere attacks the institution of *bamot*, it nowhere hints that such a multiplicity of altars is envisioned, let alone permitted. It consistently takes for granted the principle of a single sanctuary.

A more recent treatment of the subject by Jacob Milgrom [6] finds the basic intent of the law in the statement (verse 11) that blood is life. The opening verses do not state that nonsacrificial slaughter is as bad as murder, they state that it *is* murder. According to Genesis (1:29), man was supposed to be a vegetarian; and, when Noah was given permission to eat animal food, he was warned strictly against consuming blood (Gen. 9:3f.). Leviticus, chapter 17, describes the only way in which meat may be eaten without blood guilt; and it is this provision which Deuteronomy explicitly rejects [7].

This explanation is also unsatisfactory. If all nonsacrificial slaughtering was plain murder and was so regarded from time immemorial, why should the rule be further explained as a precaution against sacrifice to the goat-demons? And in fact the text does not give this as an added reason but as *the* reason for the rule.

Moreover, Genesis 9:4, according to the plain sense, allows the descendants of Noah to perform secular slaughtering as long as they do not eat of the blood—in short to do just what Deuteronomy prescribes. If H is pre-Deuteronomic and if Leviticus 17 is to limit the application of Genesis 9 imposing on Israelites restrictions from which the gentile descendants of Noah are free, one would have expected a clearer statement of the point.

The alternative possibility is that our chapter is post-Deuteronomic and is an attempt

to repeal the Deuteronomic rule. This view has been held by many of the earlier critics who regarded P—including H—as exilic or postexilic [8]. The present writer has already indicated his view that these codes preserve much ancient material but were completed in their present form no earlier than the time of the exile [9]. He thinks it probable that this chapter dates from the early post-exilic period, when the Judean community was a small remnant huddled around what was left of Jerusalem. Those who returned from Babylon looked with some distrust on the peasants who had been left on the soil when the others were deported; such people were suspected, perhaps with reason, of clinging to pagan customs. This regulation was intended to discourage those practices; perhaps also it was instituted to increase the prestige and income of the priests at the small shrine which had replaced the grand Temple of Solomon. As the Palestinian community grew in numbers and spread out over the land, this law became impracticable, the Deuteronomic practice was resumed, and our passage was understood as applying only during the desert wanderings.

This explanation appears to be the least difficult of the possibilities that have been suggested; it can hardly be called certain.

2. The Prohibition of Blood

Leviticus, chapter 3, verse 17, forbids the consumption of blood; chapter 7, verse 27, adds that violation of this rule is to be punished by *karet*. The present chapter (verses 10ff.) restates the prohibition and the penalty in strongest terms and offers an explanation of the law: the life-principle (*nefesh*, rendered "soul" in earlier translations) is in the blood—or, very probably, *is* the blood [10]. It is a sin for a human being, himself a *nefesh* (or possessed of a *nefesh*), to consume the *nefesh* even of beasts. Moreover, God has decreed that blood, as *nefesh*, shall be used on the altar to purge humankind of sin and impurity [11].

The ancients were just as much aware as we are that blood is indispensable for physical life. They thought of blood as a powerful and dangerous agent, endowed with uncanny, supernatural potencies. Many peoples have had taboos against seeing and touching blood, as well as against shedding or consuming it [12]. Yet, the biblical laws on the subject have no real parallel in the records of the ancient Near East. In Mesopotamia, sacrifice was a presentation of food already prepared; there is nothing in the Babylonian ritual texts comparable to the "dashing" of the blood of ordinary sacrifices on the altar or to the special blood rites of the *chatat* (above, chapters 1, 3, and 4) [13]. And there are only limited parallels in Greco-Roman practice [14]. Nor is there any known rule which resembles the rigorous and consistent prohibition of tasting blood—either as food or in connection with ritual—set forth in the Bible and elaborated by Jewish tradition. Our chapter requires that the blood of wild animals or fowl, which are not used in sacrifice, be drained and covered with earth (verses 13 and 14). This procedure is still followed in kosher slaughtering. Orthodox law, moreover, requires that, before meat is cooked, it must be soaked in water for a half hour, then salted and left standing for an hour, then washed again, so as to draw out all blood from the tissues [15].

That sacrificial blood has expiatory power is stated in verse 11 and is accepted doctrine in the Talmud [16]. This idea was taken up and further developed in Christianity, which taught that atonement is made for mankind through the blood of Jesus.

See further commentary on Deut. 12:20 ff. ("Blood and Meat").

א וַיְדַבֵּר יְהֹוָה אֶל־מֹשֶׁה לֵּאמֹֽר: ב דַּבֵּר אֶל־אַהֲרֹן וְאֶל־בָּנָיו וְאֶל כָּל־בְּנֵי יִשְׂרָאֵל וְאָמַרְתָּ אֲלֵיהֶם זֶה הַדָּבָר אֲשֶׁר־צִוָּה יְהֹוָה לֵאמֹֽר: ג אִישׁ אִישׁ מִבֵּית יִשְׂרָאֵל אֲשֶׁר יִשְׁחַט שׁוֹר אוֹ־כֶשֶׂב אוֹ־עֵז בַּמַּחֲנֶה אוֹ אֲשֶׁר יִשְׁחַט מִחוּץ לַמַּחֲנֶה: ד וְאֶל־פֶּתַח אֹהֶל מוֹעֵד לֹא הֱבִיאוֹ לְהַקְרִיב קָרְבָּן לַיהֹוָה לִפְנֵי מִשְׁכַּן יְהֹוָה דָּם יֵחָשֵׁב לָאִישׁ הַהוּא דָּם שָׁפָךְ וְנִכְרַת הָאִישׁ הַהוּא מִקֶּרֶב עַמּֽוֹ: ה לְמַעַן אֲשֶׁר יָבִיאוּ בְּנֵי יִשְׂרָאֵל אֶת־זִבְחֵיהֶם אֲשֶׁר הֵם זֹבְחִים עַל־פְּנֵי הַשָּׂדֶה וֶהֱבִיאֻם לַיהֹוָה אֶל־פֶּתַח אֹהֶל מוֹעֵד אֶל־הַכֹּהֵן וְזָבְחוּ זִבְחֵי שְׁלָמִים

ו לַיהֹוָה אוֹתָם: וְזָרַק הַכֹּהֵן אֶת־הַדָּם עַל־מִזְבַּח יְהֹוָה פֶּתַח אֹהֶל מוֹעֵד וְהִקְטִיר הַחֵלֶב לְרֵיחַ נִיחֹחַ לַיהֹוָֽה: ז וְלֹא־יִזְבְּחוּ עוֹד אֶת־זִבְחֵיהֶם לַשְּׂעִירִם אֲשֶׁר הֵם זֹנִים אַחֲרֵיהֶם חֻקַּת עוֹלָם תִּֽהְיֶה־זֹּאת לָהֶם לְדֹרֹתָֽם: ח וַאֲלֵהֶם תֹּאמַר אִישׁ אִישׁ מִבֵּית יִשְׂרָאֵל וּמִן־הַגֵּר אֲשֶׁר־יָגוּר בְּתוֹכָם אֲשֶׁר־יַעֲלֶה עֹלָה אוֹ־זָֽבַח: ט וְאֶל־פֶּתַח אֹהֶל מוֹעֵד לֹא יְבִיאֶנּוּ לַעֲשׂוֹת אֹתוֹ לַיהֹוָה וְנִכְרַת הָאִישׁ הַהוּא מֵעַמָּיו: י וְאִישׁ אִישׁ מִבֵּית יִשְׂרָאֵל וּמִן־הַגֵּר הַגָּר בְּתוֹכָם אֲשֶׁר יֹאכַל כָּל־דָּם וְנָתַתִּי פָנַי בַּנֶּפֶשׁ הָאֹכֶלֶת אֶת־הַדָּם וְהִכְרַתִּי אֹתָהּ מִקֶּרֶב עַמָּֽהּ:

1] The LORD spoke to Moses, saying:

2] Speak to Aaron and his sons and to all the Israelite people and say to them: This is what the LORD has commanded: **3]** If any man of the house of Israel slaughters an ox or sheep or goat in the camp, or does so outside the camp, **4]** and does not bring it to the entrance of the Tent of Meeting to present it as an offering to the LORD, before the LORD's Tabernacle, bloodguilt shall be imputed to that man: he has shed blood; that man shall be cut off from among his people. **5]** This is in order that the Israelites may bring the sacrifices which they have been making in the open—that they may bring them before the LORD, to the priest, at the entrance of the Tent of Meeting, and offer them as sacrifices of well-being to the LORD; **6]** that the priest may dash the blood against the altar of the LORD at the entrance of the Tent of Meeting, and turn the fat into smoke as a pleasing odor to the LORD; **7]** and that they may offer their sacrifices no more to the goat-demons after whom they stray. This shall be to them a law for all time, throughout the ages.

8] Say to them further: If any man of the house of Israel or of the strangers who reside among them offers a burnt offering or a sacrifice, **9]** and does not bring it to the entrance of the Tent of Meeting to offer it to the LORD, that man shall be cut off from his people.

10] And if any man of the house of Israel or of the strangers who reside among them partakes of any blood, I will set My face against the person who partakes of the blood, and I will cut him

---

17:4] *Bloodguilt shall be imputed to that man.* He is to be deemed as guilty as if he had committed homicide [17].

5] *The sacrifices which they have been making in the open.* Presumably to the goat-demons of verse 7. The traditional commentators suppose that Israel had picked up this practice in Egypt, along with other idolatrous customs. Grintz sees rather a reference to underground deities who were worshiped by night [18].

7] *Goat-demons.* Hebrew *se'irim*, which usually

means "goats." The root meaning is "hairy." Perhaps these beings were somewhat like the satyrs of Greek mythology.

A law for all time. See introduction to this chapter.

8–9] The preceding verses forbade slaughtering, even without sacrificial rites, except at the Tent of Meeting. These verses prohibit sacrificial ceremonies away from the sanctuary.

8] *Strangers who reside among them.* See commentary on 19:33ff.

10–14] On the prohibition of blood, see introduction.

יד וְכִסָּהוּ בֶּעָפָר: כִּי־נֶפֶשׁ כָּל־בָּשָׂר דָּמוֹ בְנַפְשׁוֹ הוּא
וָאֹמַר לִבְנֵי יִשְׂרָאֵל דַּם כָּל־בָּשָׂר לֹא תֹאכֵלוּ כִּי נֶפֶשׁ
כָּל־בָּשָׂר דָּמוֹ הִוא כָּל־אֹכְלָיו יִכָּרֵת: טו וְכָל־נֶפֶשׁ אֲשֶׁר
תֹּאכַל נְבֵלָה וּטְרֵפָה בָּאֶזְרָח וּבַגֵּר וְכִבֶּס בְּגָדָיו
וְרָחַץ בַּמַּיִם וְטָמֵא עַד־הָעֶרֶב וְטָהֵר: טז וְאִם לֹא יְכַבֵּס
וּבְשָׂרוֹ לֹא יִרְחָץ וְנָשָׂא עֲוֺנוֹ: פ

יא כִּי־נֶפֶשׁ הַבָּשָׂר בַּדָּם הִוא וַאֲנִי נְתַתִּיו לָכֶם עַל־
הַמִּזְבֵּחַ לְכַפֵּר עַל־נַפְשֹׁתֵיכֶם כִּי־הַדָּם הוּא בַּנֶּפֶשׁ
יְכַפֵּר: יב עַל־כֵּן אָמַרְתִּי לִבְנֵי יִשְׂרָאֵל כָּל־נֶפֶשׁ מִכֶּם
לֹא־תֹאכַל דָּם וְהַגֵּר הַגָּר בְּתוֹכְכֶם לֹא־יֹאכַל דָּם:
יג וְאִישׁ אִישׁ מִבְּנֵי יִשְׂרָאֵל וּמִן־הַגֵּר הַגָּר בְּתוֹכָם אֲשֶׁר
יָצוּד צֵיד חַיָּה אוֹ־עוֹף אֲשֶׁר יֵאָכֵל וְשָׁפַךְ אֶת־דָּמוֹ

off from among his kin.   **11]** For the life of the flesh is in the blood, and I have assigned it to you for making expiation for your lives upon the altar; it is the blood, as life, that effects expiation.   **12]** Therefore I say to the Israelite people: No person among you shall partake of blood, nor shall the stranger who resides among you partake of blood.

13] And if any Israelite or any stranger who resides among them hunts down an animal or a bird that may be eaten, he shall pour out its blood and cover it with earth.   **14]** For the life of all flesh—its blood is its life. Therefore I say to the Israelite people: You shall not partake of the blood of any flesh, for the life of all flesh is its blood. Anyone who partakes of it shall be cut off.

15] Any person, whether citizen or stranger, who eats what has died or has been torn by beasts, shall wash his clothes, bathe in water, and remain unclean until evening; then he shall be clean.   **16]** But if he does not wash [his clothes] and bathe his body, he shall bear his guilt.

13] The prohibition of blood applies even in the case of game, whereas the fat of game animals is not forbidden (7:23).

Cover it with earth. This requirement is not found in Deuteronomy 12:24.

15] *Who eats what has died [nevelah] or has been torn by beasts [terefah]* [19]. This passage repeats substantially the content of chapter 11, verses 39f. (see also commentary on 11:24f. and Gleanings).

GLEANINGS

Halachah

17:7] *That They May Offer Their Sacrifices No More to the Goat-Demons*

For the far-reaching inferences drawn by Rabbi Levi and Maimonides from this verse, see introduction to Part I, "5. Medieval Views."

15] *Who Eats What Has Died or Has Been Torn by Beasts*

The law had previously declared that defilement results not only from eating but even from touching or carrying such a carcass (11:39f.). Why then this repetition? According to *Sifra*, it refers to fowl of a clean species which have not been correctly slaughtered; eating of them causes defilement, though touching them does not.

Sex Offenses

We come at length to a topic of deep contemporary concern—sexual morality. Not that we shall find in this chapter—or in the parallel section, chapter 20, which should be read with it—a satisfactory answer to our current questions. These chapters, in fact, do not even provide an inclusive account of the biblical views about sex. They simply enumerate certain forms of sexual conduct that are forbidden and condemned.

1. Biblical Attitudes toward Sex

To understand and evaluate this material properly, we must consider how sex is treated throughout the Bible. Such an inquiry is the more necessary because many contemporary writers, in attacking laws which derive from the so-called Judeo-Christian tradition, ascribe to the Hebrew Scriptures certain attitudes that are not Jewish at all. It was Christian teachers who identified "the flesh" with sin, glorified celibacy, and regarded marriage as a concession to human frailty (see especially 1 Corinthians 7:1–9).

All this is alien to the spirit of the Hebrew Bible. At creation, it asserts, mankind was commanded to be fertile and increase (Gen.

1:28). Man is to cling to his wife so that they become one flesh (Gen. 2:24). The Bible deals frankly with many manifestations of the sex drive, licit and illicit, and recognizes its profound influence on one's emotions and behavior. The Song of Songs is a collection of explicitly erotic poems, expressive both of passion and of tenderness. In these lyrics, the man and the woman are equally open in voicing their feelings.

Very different were the attitudes of the neighbors of ancient Israel. Here we see basic differences between pagan and biblical religion. In Canaan and Mesopotamia, and somewhat differently in Egypt, a central religious element was the worship of the Mother Goddess. In the Near East she was called Astarte, Ishtar, Isis, and other names; the Greek goddesses Aphrodite and Demeter had much the same character. The Mother Goddess personified both the fertile earth and the sexual principle. Her marriage to a divine consort, called Baal and also known by various other names, was a prominent feature in both cult and myth. Some peoples celebrated this divine union by sexual orgies at the shrines or in the fields, believing that these rites increased the fertility of the soil.

877

In some places, male and female prostitutes were attached to the temples, and their earnings went into the temple treasuries. The Torah found it necessary to forbid such practices and to bar the donation of a whore's fee to the House of the Lord (Deut. 23:18).

The God of Israel has no consort and is not identified with any natural force or principle. He is Lord of nature. The reproductive process is His gift, it is not in itself divine. God's purpose is achieved by responsible use of His gift, not by mindless surrender to sensuality. The sexual impulse is not to be repressed, but it is to be controlled.

The normal sexual outlet is in marriage, which in biblical times usually took place at an early age. The forbidden manifestations of sex, as we shall see in these chapters, are adultery, incest, homosexual practices, and intercourse with animals. Moreover, sexual contact with any woman during her menstrual period—even with one's own wife—was prohibited. These laws will be fully discussed below.

Another marked difference between Israel and its neighbors concerned the practice of castration. The gelding of animals to make them more tractable has been common throughout the world. Among many peoples, notably those of the ancient Near East, the eunuch was a familiar figure. In the Phrygian cult of the "Great Mother," candidates for the priesthood castrated themselves during an orgiastic ritual, and this instance was probably not unparalleled. The Torah, however, excludes priests, suffering from any serious physical defect, from taking part in the altar service and similarly forbids the offering of a defective animal as a sacrifice. In these connections, sexual mutilation is specifically mentioned (Lev. 21:20, 22:24). A eunuch may not marry a Jewess (Deut. 23:2). But a compassionate section in a prophetic work reassures eunuchs, who are apparently here of foreign origin: By loyalty to God and His law, they may obtain "in My House / And within My walls, / A monument and a name / Better than sons or daughters" (Isa. 56:5).

From the words, "You shall have no such practices in your land" (Lev. 22:24), the rabbinic teachers concluded that castration is unconditionally forbidden; and they held that the rule applies in all countries, to human beings and to all species of animals [1].

2. Postbiblical Jewish Attitudes

The healthy affirmative attitude toward sex found in the Bible was somewhat modified in the talmudic period. This change may be due in part to Greek influence. For the Greeks were by no means unanimous in glorifying sensual indulgence. Plato, for example, speaks of the body and its functions with a certain contempt, and perhaps he was not the first of the philosophers to do so. The Cynic and Stoic schools were more emphatic in denigrating bodily functions and appetites. The Stoics taught that a sage is guided by cool reason alone; he must suppress even the tender emotions, still more the irrational and explosive passions. The Neo-Platonist thinkers advocated asceticism and may have influenced nascent Christianity.

The talmudic sources reveal such negative views to a limited extent. The Song of Songs was now interpreted as an allegory of the love between God and the people of Israel, and its primary erotic intent was indignantly rejected [2]. There was also a tendency to identify man's "evil inclination" (yetser hara) with the sexual urge—though in fact the term also includes aggressive and other sinful impulses as well. Yet the Rabbis also declared that the evil impulse is in fact "very good" since it leads man to establish a family [3]. And they called upon man to serve God with the evil impulse as well as the good [4].

There is a note of suspicion and ambiguity in some of the rabbinical pronouncements on sex. It may have been affected by economic and social conditions that compelled many persons to delay marriage, with resultant tensions [5]. Nevertheless, marriage and the having of children are still deemed a divine command; to remain a bachelor by choice was considered sinful [6]. Married couples have broad freedom in matters of sexual technique [7], and Friday night is deemed a particularly appropriate time for marital relations [8]. According to the traditional understanding of Exodus, chapter 21, verse 10, a married woman is entitled to regular satisfaction of her sexual needs, even if her husband has another wife [9]. The halachah also gave qualified approval to birth control when couples had at least two children [10]. (Of course, reliable methods of contraception were not available in premodern times.)

Medieval Jewish thinkers were more strongly affected by Greek and Christian views. Ibn Ezra (on Lev. 18:20) regards sexual activity as a necessity for physical and mental health; but sex for fun, he adds, is unworthy of an enlightened person. Maimonides adopts Aristotle's opinion that the sense of touch is degrading to our humanity. We should, he says, regard sexual intercourse with contempt and desire it only at rare intervals [11]. According to Maimonides, circumcision weakens the sexual drive and was ordained by the Torah to help man achieve self-mastery [12].

The much more conservative Nachmanides severely criticized Maimonides for adopting the ideas of the "impure Greek." A special treatise on the marital act (significantly entitled *The Letter on Holiness*, attributed to Nachmanides though not certainly by him) asserts that the act is pure and holy when properly performed, at the right time, and with the right intent. God would not have created the genitals if their function had no positive value. But a man must approach his wife with the exalted hope of producing wise and pious offspring; moreover, he should show her great consideration, so that she may fully share the joy of the sacred moment. Yet, this document too deprecates the "recreational" aspect of the sex relationship.

But, despite this modification of attitude, Jewish tradition was still far from accepting the Christian evaluation of the flesh. Characteristically, the medieval Jewish communities considered it their duty to provide dowries for poor girls and to marry them off; in Christendom, such persons were often relegated to convent life, even though they had no inclination for it.

The Jewish teachers regarded human semen as precious and not to be wasted. Nocturnal emission is not sinful, but one should avoid the fantasies that may cause it; and masturbation is strongly condemned [13].

Yet the halachah permits intercourse that will not result in conception, as when the wife is already pregnant or unable to bear children [14].

3. Modesty

Greek men regularly engaged in physical sports in the nude. Gymnasium means "place of nakedness." On some special occasions young women also appeared unclothed in public. Greek sculpture idealized the nude human body.

In contrast, Judaism insisted on modest attire for both sexes. This fact has led to the mistaken notion that Judaism is prudish. It is in fact a question as to whether sexual interest is stimulated more by exposure or by concealment. The Arabs too insist that both men and women be fully covered in public, although their literature betrays strong preoccupation with sex, including the homosexual relation.

The biblical Jewish tradition also calls for reticence in talking about sex. Not that the subject is avoided in Hebrew sources, which are forthright and free from squeamishness. Yet even in the biblical text, euphemisms are often substituted for blunter terms; in our chapter the sexual act is referred to as "uncovering the nakedness" of a person. The highly erotic material in the Song of Songs is clothed in poetic metaphors. The Rabbis likewise called for restraint of language. "Everyone knows why the bride enters the marriage chamber, but one who engages in vulgar talk brings dire punishment upon himself" [15].

Thus, Judaism through the centuries has combined an affirmative attitude toward marriage and a recognition that its physical side is good and desirable, with the acceptance of controls. The results have been highly creditable. There is always a difference between ideal and reality; and no doubt sentimentalists have on occasion exaggerated the beauty of Jewish family life. Yet, the total record is a good one in terms of family stability, child welfare, and the transmission of moral and social standards [16]. In the light of these results, even those who are most critical of traditional rules of sex morality will be well advised to examine them carefully before rejecting them as outmoded.

4. Incest

Some sort of sexual control is found in all human societies. Among the most widespread of these is the prohibition of marriage and sex relations between blood relatives. The extent of such prohibitions varies, but everywhere sexual congress between parent and child is forbidden. In ancient Egypt, marriage of brother and sister was common in the royal family, but otherwise it was prohibited. Something similar existed in ancient Persia.

It is not easy to explain the origin of these taboos. Freudian speculation about the Oedipus complex may not be universally valid, in view of the diverse forms of family structure found in various cultures. The story of Oedipus simply reveals the horror which some societies felt about sex relations between parent and child.

Moreover, the ancient peoples who formulated these rules knew nothing about genetics and did not understand the reasons why inbreeding is biologically imprudent. (The notion, once widely held, that marriage between near relatives is likely to produce mentally defective or deaf offspring is incorrect. Inbreeding simply intensifies traits already present. But, since genetic weaknesses are common, marriage even between first cousins, which is generally permitted in both religious and secular law, is risky.) In short, we know little about the origin of the laws against incest—etymologically, the word means simply "unchastity"—even though such laws are virtually universal and are rarely violated.

Biblical law forbids not only unions between close blood relatives but also, in certain cases, those between persons connected by marriage. Thus, one may not marry the widow of his father, uncle, or son. Chapter 18 of Leviticus lists the various forbidden degrees of relationship. A similar list in chapter 20 provides that those who violate these laws shall be punished by *karet* ("cutting off") [17]. The two chapters do not really complement each other, they are rather parallel versions of the same material. The biblical prohibitions were extended somewhat by rabbinic law; violation of the "secondary" rules does not, however, entail the penalty of *karet*. A table of the forbidden relationships, as defined by the halachah, is

given in Appendix III.

Several items in this list may strike us as strange. One is an omission. The union of father and daughter is not explicitly forbidden. The Rabbis had to infer it from the prohibition of a union between grandfather and granddaughter (18:10). Most likely, this omission is due to a scribal error. But perhaps intentional is the fact that, though marriage of nephew and aunt is forbidden (18:14, 20:19), there is no corresponding objection to marriage between uncle and niece. The Talmud, in fact, considers such a marriage especially meritorious [18].

Another asymmetrical provision, in verse 18 of our chapter, which has serious implications up to the present, is the prohibition of a man from marrying his wife's sister during the lifetime of the wife. This seems to bar both the polygamous marriage of two sisters and marriage to the sister of a divorced wife. Tradition understood it, reasonably enough, to allow a widower to marry his late wife's sister.

Verse 16 seems to rule out unconditionally the marriage of a man to the divorcée or widow of his brother. But Deuteronomy (25:5–10) rules that, if a man dies childless, one of his brothers must marry the widow; and the first son of the union is to be "accounted to the dead brother, that his name may not be blotted out." If the surviving brother refuses to marry his sister-in-law, he must go through a humiliating ceremony (traditionally called *chalitzah*). Thereafter, the widow may marry anyone she chooses.

The Leviticus and Deuteronomy passages are apparently in contradiction; but Jewish tradition resolved the matter without difficulty. In the case of a childless widow, the so-called levirate marriage was mandatory. But, if there were children, such a marriage was forbidden even if both parties desired it.

Moreover, later rabbinic law discouraged levirate marriage in nearly all cases preferring to deal with the situation by *chalitzah* [19].

Reform Judaism discarded *chalitzah* and permitted a childless widow to remarry without any precondition [20]. But no Reform body has officially challenged the law of verse 16, in this chapter, which forbids marriage to a deceased husband's brother. Yet many people believe such a marriage proper and desirable precisely if there are young children—the uncle who already knows and loves them is well suited to act as their father. (A similar argument has always been used to justify marriage with a deceased wife's sister.)

The issue came before the Central Conference of American Rabbis (CCAR) in 1925. Several speakers argued that justice and humanity required a Reform rabbi to officiate at the marriage of a woman to her late husband's brother. If, however, a rabbi had moral qualms about performing such a marriage, he ought in consistency to refuse to officiate when a man married his deceased wife's sister—even though the latter union is halachically permissible. The CCAR took no action in this matter; but many Reform rabbis do marry couples in either case.

5. Homosexual Behavior

(This section has been somewhat revised from the author's original text to reflect current thinking on the subject.)

Far more controversial, from the modern standpoint, is the outright condemnation of sexual relations between males (18:22)—conduct for which the death penalty is prescribed (20:13) [21]. We have no record of a death

sentence for this crime being carried out under Jewish auspices. Apparently, Christian courts executed some persons for sodomy during the Middle Ages. Up to the present, persons who commit homosexual acts are subject to severe prison sentences in many countries, including some parts of the United States—even in the case of consenting adults; but, in Canada, homosexuality has been removed from the criminal code.

Until recently, homosexuality, especially among males, has been regarded with horror as unnatural, perverted and degenerate, wherever the Jewish-Christian or Moslem outlook prevailed. The first public change of attitude in the western world was voiced chiefly by psychiatrists who called for greater compassion toward homosexuals.

In his famous 1935 letter to the concerned mother of a homosexual man, Sigmund Freud wrote, "Homosexuality is assuredly no advantage, but it is nothing to be ashamed of, no vice, no degradation, it cannot be classified as an illness." In 1974, the American Psychiatric Association deleted the term "homosexuality" from the official list of mental illnesses. Dr. Judd Marmor, past president of the American Psychiatric Association, writes, "There is no doubt that ultimately an enlightened and civilized society must rid itself of its homophobic fears and prejudices. The vast majority of homosexual men and women ask only to be accepted as human beings and allowed to live their own lives free of persecution or discrimination."

The summary and rigid condemnation of homosexual conduct found in the Hebrew Bible [22] will leave many modern readers dissatisfied. Whether the time has come to rethink our attitudes toward homosexual relationships is still debated. The subject is difficult to deal with, both because of the strong emotions it rouses and because our understanding of the matter is far from complete. The following statements, however, are probably reliable.

In many cultures there has been little or no objection to homosexual behavior. The ancient Egyptians condemned it [23], but it was widespread among the Greeks. In the Athens of Pericles and Plato, love affairs between teenage boys and older men were frequent and were even considered beneficial for the intellectual and moral development of the younger party. Even in societies that officially ban such practices, they occur more frequently than former generations supposed—or at least admitted. Homosexual behavior has often been noted among lower animals as well. The extent of homosexual activity in a given time or place is conditioned partly by social factors. It is more common where members of the opposite sex are not readily available and where prevailing standards allow for it. The reason for this is that most people cannot be sharply separated into two categories. They can respond to either heterosexual or homosexual stimulation. The exclusively heterosexual and the exclusively homosexual represent extremes; but, as a rule, people are predominantly one or the other.

We do not really know why some people have a predominantly homosexual orientation. There is no known physiological or biochemical distinction between heterosexual and homosexual persons. Homosexual men and women are rarely identifiable by the stereotypical behavior once attached to them. Nor are they more likely than the general population to exhibit neurotic symptoms or traits.

There does not appear to be any successful technique by which a homosexual orientation can be transformed into a heterosexual one, and mental health professionals rarely attempt it.

Our greatest needs at present are to gain more knowledge on the subject—knowledge which is sought objectively [24]—and to insure that individual reactions to this admittedly sensitive subject do not result in the denial of simple justice and fairness for homosexual women and men.

6. Bestiality

Sexual congress between humans and other animals has not been uncommon in rural areas. Such practices, which are unconditionally forbidden (in 18:23, 20:15 and 16), have most often been the resource of the lonely and the frustrated. Yet the theme appears in a number of pagan myths. Usually, it is a case of a woman coupling with a beast or with a god in the guise of a beast. The myth recurs in Robinson Jeffers's poem, *Roan Stallion*. In our urban society, this matter is hardly of major importance.

On adultery, see Exodus 20:13; on intercourse with a menstruant, see commentary on 15:19ff.

7. Molech Worship

Though this chapter is otherwise devoted to the subject of sexual offenses, verse 21 reads: "Do not allow any of your offspring to be offered up to Molech." The parallel in chapter 20, verses 2 through 5, though longer, is no more enlightening; it states the penalty for the offense but does not explain the offense itself.

The "conventional" account of the matter is as follows: Molech was a heathen god to whom infants were sacrificed. His worshipers called him *Melech*, "King," but in the Bible his name was provided with the vowels of *boshet*, "shame."

Human sacrifices did occur in the ancient Near East. The Moabite king, Mesha, is said (II Kings 3:27) to have sacrificed his oldest son at a time of national crisis; the text does not name the deity who received the sacrifice. One passage identifies Molech as the national god of the Ammonites (I Kings 11:7); elsewhere the Ammonite god is called Milcom. But no extrabiblical source speaks clearly of a god named *Melech*.

Deuteronomy, chapter 12, verse 31, states that the Canaanites burned their children as an offering to their gods but does not mention Molech, nor does the name appear in Deuteronomy, chapter 18, verse 10, which forbids the Israelites to make their sons and daughters "pass through the fire." Our Leviticus passages and Jeremiah (32:5) speak of giving or offering children to Molech, but not of the use of fire. Only in II Kings (23:10) are the two elements, Molech and fire, combined.

What we have called the "conventional" view derives from the assumption that all these citations mean the same thing—which is possible but far from certain.

The Talmud offers two explanations. One is that children were made to walk between two fires as a symbol of their dedication to the god. The other is that the children were tossed back and forth over a fire till they were burned [25].

Diodorus of Sicily, a Greek writer of the first century C.E., asserts that children were burned to the god Melkart ("King of the City") in Carthage which was established by colonists from northern Canaan [26]. Human sacrifice persisted for many centuries in the Roman world [27]. Yet Otto Eissfeldt, a contemporary German scholar, has presented evidence that the word *molek* was used by the Carthaginians, not as a proper name, but as the technical term for an offering made in payment of a vow [28].

An interesting, and apparently brand new, suggestion is made by Snaith in his com-

mentary. Chapters 18 and 20 are concerned almost exclusively with sex offenses. It is therefore reasonable to suppose that the Molech passages deal with a similar theme. Snaith thinks they may forbid the dedication of children as cult prostitutes. His guess is plausible but there is no evidence to support it.

All we can say with certainty is that these laws forbid the devotion of children to a pagan cult. How barbarous the form of devotion was is uncertain.

א וַיְדַבֵּר יְהוָה אֶל־מֹשֶׁה לֵּאמֹר: דַּבֵּר אֶל־בְּנֵי יִשְׂרָאֵל
ב וְאָמַרְתָּ אֲלֵהֶם אֲנִי יְהוָה אֱלֹהֵיכֶם: כְּמַעֲשֵׂה אֶרֶץ־
מִצְרַיִם אֲשֶׁר יְשַׁבְתֶּם־בָּהּ לֹא תַעֲשׂוּ וּכְמַעֲשֵׂה אֶרֶץ־
כְּנַעַן אֲשֶׁר אֲנִי מֵבִיא אֶתְכֶם שָׁמָּה לֹא תַעֲשׂוּ
ד וּבְחֻקֹּתֵיהֶם לֹא תֵלֵכוּ: אֶת־מִשְׁפָּטַי תַּעֲשׂוּ וְאֶת־חֻקֹּתַי
ה תִּשְׁמְרוּ לָלֶכֶת בָּהֶם אֲנִי יְהוָה אֱלֹהֵיכֶם: וּשְׁמַרְתֶּם

אֶת־חֻקֹּתַי וְאֶת־מִשְׁפָּטַי אֲשֶׁר יַעֲשֶׂה אֹתָם הָאָדָם וָחַי
בָּהֶם אֲנִי יְהוָה: ס אִישׁ אִישׁ אֶל־כָּל־שְׁאֵר בְּשָׂרוֹ
לֹא תִקְרְבוּ לְגַלּוֹת עֶרְוָה אֲנִי יְהוָה: ס עֶרְוַת
אָבִיךָ וְעֶרְוַת אִמְּךָ לֹא תְגַלֵּה אִמְּךָ הִוא לֹא תְגַלֶּה
עֶרְוָתָהּ: ס עֶרְוַת אֵשֶׁת־אָבִיךָ לֹא תְגַלֵּה עֶרְוַת
אָבִיךָ הִוא: ס עֶרְוַת אֲחוֹתְךָ בַת־אָבִיךָ אוֹ בַת־

1] The LORD spoke to Moses, saying: **2]** Speak to the Israelite people and say to them: I the LORD am your God. **3]** You shall not copy the practices of the land of Egypt where you dwelt, or of the land of Canaan to which I am taking you; nor shall you follow their laws. **4]** My rules alone shall you observe, and faithfully follow My laws: I the LORD am your God.

5] You shall keep My laws and My rules, by the pursuit of which man shall live: I am the LORD.

6] None of you shall come near anyone of his own flesh to uncover nakedness: I am the LORD.

7] Your father's nakedness, that is, the nakedness of your mother, you shall not uncover; she is your mother—you shall not uncover her nakedness.

8] Do not uncover the nakedness of your father's wife; it is the nakedness of your father.

18:1–5] The legal enactments are introduced by a solemn exhortation to heed the will of God, which forbids the pagan practices of both Egypt and Canaan.

3] *Nor shall you follow their laws.* Jews have always had to struggle with the question: to what extent should they adopt the ideas and practices of the outside world? Such influences are in some measure inescapable. They have affected not only those who welcomed new cultural values, the medieval Jewish philosophers and the modern Reformers for example, but also the spiritual isolationists. The custom of Yahrzeit was borrowed from the Catholics after the massacres that accompanied the First Crusade; present-day Chasidim wear garb that was fashionable among Polish Gentiles two centuries ago! In general, Judaism has been able to absorb values, ideas, and customs that are compatible with its basic outlook, while rejecting what could not be reconciled with the religious and ethical teachings of the Torah.

5] *You shall keep My laws and My rules, by the pursuit of which man shall live.* The Torah affirms life. By obeying God's law, man lives well and meaningfully and he will be rewarded by long life [29]. Nachmanides thinks the phrase refers to such legal sections as in Exodus, chapters 21 through 23, which provide for an orderly and peaceful society. Luzzatto takes it as alluding to the provisions of this chapter, the restrictions of which constitute the basis for stable and happy family life (see Gleanings).

6] *To uncover nakedness.* Here, and whenever this expression is applied to a woman, it means to have sexual intercourse with her. But when applied to a man (verses 7 and 10), it means to have intercourse with his wife. The general statement in this verse is followed by a number of specific rules.

8] *Your father's wife.* Your stepmother. A man and his wife are one flesh (Gen. 2:24), even if he should die or divorce her (T.N.).

אִמְּךָ מוֹלֶדֶת בַּיִת אוֹ מוֹלֶדֶת חוּץ לֹא תְגַלֶּה עֶרְוָתָן: ‏ ט

ס עֶרְוַת בַּת־בִּנְךָ אוֹ בַת־בִּתְּךָ לֹא תְגַלֶּה עֶרְוָתָן כִּי ‏ י

עֶרְוָתְךָ הֵנָּה: ס עֶרְוַת בַּת־אֵשֶׁת אָבִיךָ מוֹלֶדֶת ‏ יא

אָבִיךָ אֲחוֹתְךָ הִיא לֹא תְגַלֶּה עֶרְוָתָהּ: ס עֶרְוַת ‏ יב

אֲחוֹת־אָבִיךָ לֹא תְגַלֵּה שְׁאֵר אָבִיךָ הִוא: ס עֶרְוַת ‏ יג

אֲחוֹת־אִמְּךָ לֹא תְגַלֵּה כִּי־שְׁאֵר אִמְּךָ הִוא: ס עֶרְוַת ‏ יד

אֲחִי־אָבִיךָ לֹא תְגַלֵּה אֶל־אִשְׁתּוֹ לֹא תִקְרָב דֹּדָתְךָ ‏

הִוא: ס עֶרְוַת כַּלָּתְךָ לֹא תְגַלֵּה אֵשֶׁת בִּנְךָ הִוא ‏ טו

לֹא תְגַלֶּה עֶרְוָתָהּ: ס עֶרְוַת אֵשֶׁת־אָחִיךָ לֹא תְגַלֵּה ‏ טז

עֶרְוַת אָחִיךָ הִוא: ס עֶרְוַת אִשָּׁה וּבִתָּהּ לֹא תְגַלֵּה ‏ יז

אֶת־בַּת־בְּנָהּ וְאֶת־בַּת־בִּתָּהּ לֹא תִקַּח לְגַלּוֹת עֶרְוָתָהּ ‏

שַׁאֲרָה הֵנָּה זִמָּה הִוא: וְאִשָּׁה אֶל־אֲחֹתָהּ לֹא תִקָּח ‏ יח

לִצְרֹר לְגַלּוֹת עֶרְוָתָהּ עָלֶיהָ בְּחַיֶּיהָ: וְאֶל־אִשָּׁה בְּנִדַּת ‏ יט

טֻמְאָתָהּ לֹא תִקְרַב לְגַלּוֹת עֶרְוָתָהּ: וְאֶל־אֵשֶׁת ‏ כ

עֲמִיתְךָ לֹא־תִתֵּן שְׁכָבְתְּךָ לְזָרַע לְטָמְאָה־בָהּ: ‏

וּמִזַּרְעֲךָ לֹא־תִתֵּן לְהַעֲבִיר לַמֹּלֶךְ וְלֹא תְחַלֵּל אֶת־ ‏ כא

9] The nakedness of your sister—your father's daughter or your mother's, whether born into the household or outside—do not uncover their nakedness.

10] The nakedness of your son's daughter, or of your daughter's daughter—do not uncover their nakedness; for their nakedness is yours.

11] The nakedness of your father's wife's daughter, who was born into your father's household—she is your sister; do not uncover her nakedness.

12] Do not uncover the nakedness of your father's sister; she is your father's flesh.

13] Do not uncover the nakedness of your mother's sister; for she is your mother's flesh.

14] Do not uncover the nakedness of your father's brother: do not approach his wife; she is your aunt.

15] Do not uncover the nakedness of your daughter-in-law: she is your son's wife; you shall not uncover her nakedness.

16] Do not uncover the nakedness of your brother's wife; it is the nakedness of your brother.

17] Do not uncover the nakedness of a woman and her daughter; nor shall you marry her son's daughter or her daughter's daughter and uncover her nakedness: they are kindred; it is depravity.

18] Do not marry a woman as a rival to her sister and uncover her nakedness in the other's lifetime.

19] Do not come near a woman during her period of uncleanness to uncover her nakedness.

20] Do not have carnal relations with your neighbor's wife and defile yourself with her.

21] Do not allow any of your offspring to be offered up to Molech, and do not profane the name of your God: I am the LORD.

9] *Whether born into the household or outside.* The force of this clause is uncertain. The Targums explain: "Even if she is your father's daughter by a different mother, or your mother's daughter by a different father." Rashbam, Ibn Ezra, and Nachmanides interpret: "Whether born in or out of wedlock." Or, says Ibn Ezra, it could mean, "Whether she grew up in the same household or elsewhere."

10] *For their nakedness is yours.* Meaning of verse obscure (T.N.).

11] *Who was born into your father's household.* Hebrew *moledet avicha.* There is no word for "household." The meaning of the clause is obscure. It might mean: She is to be regarded as a descendant of your father, even though she is not so in fact.

18] *Do not marry a woman as a rival to her sister.* Jacob's marriage to the sisters Leah and Rachel occurred prior to the promulgation of this law at Sinai.

21] On Molech, see introduction to this chapter. On profanation of God's name, see introduction to Lev. 19.

כב שֵׁם אֱלֹהֶיךָ אֲנִי יְהֹוָה: וְאֶת־זָכָר לֹא תִשְׁכַּב מִשְׁכְּבֵי

כג אִשָּׁה תּוֹעֵבָה הִוא: וּבְכָל־בְּהֵמָה לֹא־תִתֵּן שְׁכָבְתְּךָ

לְטָמְאָה־בָהּ וְאִשָּׁה לֹא־תַעֲמֹד לִפְנֵי בְהֵמָה לְרִבְעָהּ

כד תֶּבֶל הוּא: אַל־תִּטַּמְּאוּ בְּכָל־אֵלֶּה כִּי בְכָל־אֵלֶּה

כה נִטְמְאוּ הַגּוֹיִם אֲשֶׁר־אֲנִי מְשַׁלֵּחַ מִפְּנֵיכֶם: וַתִּטְמָא

הָאָרֶץ וָאֶפְקֹד עֲוֺנָהּ עָלֶיהָ וַתָּקִא הָאָרֶץ אֶת־

כו יֹשְׁבֶיהָ: וּשְׁמַרְתֶּם אַתֶּם אֶת־חֻקֹּתַי וְאֶת־מִשְׁפָּטַי וְלֹא

תַעֲשׂוּ מִכֹּל הַתּוֹעֵבֹת הָאֵלֶּה הָאֶזְרָח וְהַגֵּר הַגָּר

כז בְּתוֹכְכֶם: כִּי אֶת־כָּל־הַתּוֹעֵבֹת הָאֵל עָשׂוּ אַנְשֵׁי־

כח הָאָרֶץ אֲשֶׁר לִפְנֵיכֶם וַתִּטְמָא הָאָרֶץ: וְלֹא־תָקִיא

הָאָרֶץ אֶתְכֶם בְּטַמַּאֲכֶם אֹתָהּ כַּאֲשֶׁר קָאָה אֶת־הַגּוֹי

כט אֲשֶׁר לִפְנֵיכֶם: כִּי כָּל־אֲשֶׁר יַעֲשֶׂה מִכֹּל הַתּוֹעֵבֹת

הָאֵלֶּה וְנִכְרְתוּ הַנְּפָשׁוֹת הָעֹשֹׂת מִקֶּרֶב עַמָּם:

ל וּשְׁמַרְתֶּם אֶת־מִשְׁמַרְתִּי לְבִלְתִּי עֲשׂוֹת מֵחֻקּוֹת

הַתּוֹעֵבֹת אֲשֶׁר נַעֲשׂוּ לִפְנֵיכֶם וְלֹא תִטַּמְּאוּ בָּהֶם אֲנִי

יְהֹוָה אֱלֹהֵיכֶם:

*כז סבירין האלה.

Haftarah Achare Mot, p. 997

22] Do not lie with a male as one lies with a woman; it is an abhorrence.

23] Do not have carnal relations with any beast and defile yourself thereby; and let no woman lend herself to a beast to mate with it; it is perversion.

24] Do not defile yourselves in any of those ways, for it is by such that the nations which I am casting out before you defiled themselves. **25]** Thus the land became defiled; and I called it to account for its iniquity, and the land spewed out its inhabitants. **26]** But you must keep My laws and My rules, and you must not do any of those abhorrent things, neither the citizen nor the stranger who resides among you; **27]** for all those abhorrent things were done by the people who were in the land before you, and the land became defiled. **28]** So let not the land spew you out for defiling it, as it spewed out the nation that came before you. **29]** All who do any of those abhorrent things—such persons shall be cut off from their people. **30]** You shall keep My charge not to engage in any of the abhorrent practices that were carried on before you, and you shall not defile yourselves through them: I the LORD am your God.

24] *Do not defile yourselves....* The chapter concludes, as it began, with an exhortation. The Land of Israel is literally the Holy Land and its sanctity would be defiled by the actions forbidden in this section.

GLEANINGS

Halachah

18:3] *Nor Shall You Follow Their Laws*

This passage forbids Jews to attend the bloody entertainments of the Roman amphitheater, to practice various superstitious customs of the gentile world, and even to imitate gentile styles of hairdressing [30].

5] *My Laws and My Rules, by the Pursuit of Which Man Shall Live*

Man is to attain life, not death, through the Torah. Therefore, when danger to life is involved, any commandment of the Torah may be disregarded, except the laws forbidding murder, idolatry, and sexual crime. But this applies only to violations in private. Public violation even of a lesser commandment would profane the name of God (see introduction to Lev. 19), and one should suffer martyrdom rather than desecrate God's name [31].

6] *None of You Shall Come near Anyone of His Flesh*

This general statement is followed by a number of specific instances. In such cases, the generalization is not held to contain more than the ensuing specific cases. We should not infer, e.g., that, because a nephew may not marry his uncle's wife (verse 14), an uncle may not marry his nephew's wife [32].

Haggadah

18:5] *My Laws and My Rules, by the Pursuit of Which Man Shall Live*

Obedience to the Torah will be rewarded by life in the world to come.   TARGUMS and SIFRA

This passage speaks not of priests, Levites, and Israelites, but of "man." The moral law is valid for all men, and the heathen who obeys the Torah is equal to the High Priest.   SIFRA

25] *The Land Became Defiled . . . and Spewed Out Its Inhabitants*

Unlike other lands, which are ruled by an angelic deputy, the Land of Israel is directly under God's providence and so is more sensitive to defilement. That is why the Canaanites were spewed out of the Holy Land whereas the Egyptians, who committed the same defiling sins, were not expelled from their country (Nachmanides).

30] *You Shall Keep My Charge*

Literally, "You shall guard My guarding." The Talmud finds in this verse the injunction to "make a fence about the Torah," i.e., to make additional restrictions which will prevent accidental violations [33] (see Gleanings, Halachah, on 7:15).

The Life of Holiness

We have reached the climactic chapter of the book, the one most often read and quoted. In American Reform practice, it is the Torah reading for Yom Kippur afternoon.

1. *Holiness*

The constant theme here is *holiness*. We have already encountered this concept, chiefly in reflections of its ancient and primitive form. Here, after summarizing such material, we shall move on to more advanced and mature conceptions of holiness, and we shall consider their implications for our own life. It will, moreover, be proper to make use of Hebrew terminology, for the word *kadosh* (plural *kedoshim*) is only roughly, but not exactly, equivalent to the English "holy." The word *kodesh*, "holiness," is often used where an adjective would be employed in English—"My holy name" (20:3) is literally "the name of My holiness." Other derivatives from the same root are: *kiddush*, "sanctification," applied especially to hallowing Sabbath and festivals over a cup of wine—but see below, "2. Sanctifying and Profaning the Name"; *kedushah*, also meaning holiness or sanctification, used especially for a series

of responses in the synagogue service; and the familiar Aramaic word *kaddish*.

a. *Kadosh* is the adjective regularly applied to divinity and divinities. In the Book of Daniel (4:5f.), the Babylonian king speaks of the "holy gods" (Aramaic *elahin kadishin*). Other biblical writings refer to angelic beings as *kedoshim* (Zech. 14:5; Ps. 9:8; Job 5:11) [1]. The God of Israel is often characterized as *kadosh*, especially by Isaiah.

b. This term, conventionally associated with deity, is also applied to places, times, objects, and procedures connected with deity. A place of worship is called *mikdash*. The innermost Shrine is *Kodesh Kodashim*, "Holy of Holies"—more exactly, "highest level of holiness." All sacrifices are holy, but some are designated as *Kodesh Kodashim*.

As the deity was regarded anciently as set apart and dangerous to approach, so it was often with places and things that were his special possession. In some Bible passages, *kadosh* has the same force as the Polynesian word *taboo* [2]. In such cases, holiness was conceived as a physical force which can pass from one object to another like an electric current with potentially destructive power.

Kodesh does not necessarily indicate an absolute taboo. The sacred places may be

approached, sacred food may be eaten, but only if special rules, especially those of ceremonial purity, are strictly observed. Disregard of these rules, intentional or otherwise, is a desecration that may lead to disastrous results.

c. This mechanical concept of "holiness" was embodied in practices treated in the earlier chapters of this book—practices that survived even after the ideas they expressed had been supplanted by a more mature concept of *kedushah*. For *kadosh* gradually came to indicate, not the physical separation of God and man, but the spiritual gap between human inadequacy and divine perfection.

In his consecration vision, Isaiah (6:3) beholds God surrounded by the *seraphim* who chant: "Holy, holy, holy! The LORD of Hosts! His presence fills all the earth!"

His immediate reaction is: "Woe is me; I am lost! / For I am a man of unclean lips / And I live among a people of unclean lips" (Isa. 6:5).

It is sinfulness, present even in speech, which makes him feel an intruder, unworthy to approach God. The prophets characterize God more often in terms of supreme righteousness than in terms of supreme power. It is Isaiah especially who calls God *Kedosh Yisrael*, "the Holy One of Israel" (e.g., 1:4).

Yet, despite the gap between God's perfection and man's limitations, God was not thought of as remote and unapproachable. A later prophet, whose words are included in the latter chapters of Isaiah, represents God as saying: "I dwell on high, in holiness, / Yet with the contrite and the lowly in spirit" (Isa. 57:15).

Most remarkable of all, our chapter summons the Israelites to imitate God and so become holy themselves.

d. This last point requires special stress in view of the great influence exercised on a generation or more of religious thinkers by the book, *The Idea of the Holy* [3]. The author,

Rudolf Otto, a Protestant theologian, was disturbed by the tendency of liberals to reduce religion to ethics. He sought to prove that man's nature has a religious aspect that was originally independent of the ethical. It is that part of us which responds to the mysterious and awesome—to the reality, at once overwhelming and fascinating, that cannot be adequately understood or rationalized. The word "holy" and its equivalents, says Otto, point to the experience of the "numinous," of a divine reality that evokes fear, awe, and submission. This experience, in its cruder and more primitive forms, is that of the uncanny, ghostly, and hair-raising. Later, as concepts of divinity are purified and elevated, ethical elements are introduced into the idea of holiness, and awe is evoked, not only by the frightening mystery, but also by the divine perfection.

It is striking that Otto, a pious Lutheran, made no mention of this chapter of Leviticus in his book. He spoke only of holiness as an emotional experience, not of *kedushah* as aspiration and task to be approached through a disciplined life. In his zeal to give religion a unique character, Otto reduced the ethical component of holiness to a mere "extra." This is not the Jewish view of the subject, as is plain from the text before us, and also from the recurrent declaration in our prayers and benedictions that God "sanctifies us through His commandments." In Judaism, religion and ethics, though not identical, are inseparable [4].

e. Chapters 18 through 20 give a clear account of holiness in life.

The prime emphasis is ethical. And the moral laws of this chapter are not mere injunctions of conformity. They call for just, humane, and sensitive treatment of others. The aged, the handicapped, and the poor are to receive consideration and courtesy. The laborer is to be promptly paid. The stranger is to be accorded the same love we

give our fellow citizens. The law is concerned, not only with overt behavior, but also with motive; vengefulness and the bearing of grudges are condemned.

Among ethical duties, that of sexual decency is singled out for particular emphasis. The Torah demands the control, not the suppression of the sexual instinct. Life is sacred. The physical process by which life is generated is to be treated responsibly.

The ethical injunctions of chapter 19 are interspersed with ritual commandments. Some of these are directed against pagan and superstitious practices deemed incompatible with biblical religion. The intent of others is not so plain. To the biblical author, these ceremonial rulings are divine ordinances with the same authority as the ethical commandments. Traditional Judaism regarded them as "royal decrees," to be observed whether or not we comprehend them (see introduction to Lev. 11:1–23).

The Jewish modernist cannot agree with this. But he can recognize that worship and ceremony, undertaken thoughtfully and reverently, can elevate personal and family life. Though he may reject older views as to the origin and authority of ritual, he may still benefit from the practice of ritual. In holy living, the ethical factor is primary, but it is not the only one. In combining moral and ceremonial commandments, the authors of the Holiness Code displayed sound understanding.

f. Such are the components of the way of life called *kadosh*. Our chapter begins with the startling declaration that by these means we can and should try to be holy like God. The same Torah that stresses the distance between His sublime perfection and our earthy limitations urges us to strive to reduce that distance. The task is endless, but it is infinitely rewarding. Rabbi Tarfon said: "Do not avoid an undertaking that has no limit or a task that cannot be completed.

It is like the case of one who was hired to take water from the sea and pour it out on the land. But, as the sea was not emptied out or the land filled with water, he became downhearted. Then someone said to him, 'Foolish fellow! Why should you be downhearted as long as you receive a dinar of gold every day as your wage?'" [5]. The pursuit of the unattainable can be a means of fulfillment.

g. The Law of Holiness is not addressed to selected individuals. It is addressed to the entire community of Israel. Its objective is not to produce a few saints, withdrawn from the world in contemplative or ascetic practices. Rather, does the Torah aim to create a holy people which displays its consecration to God's service in the normal day-to-day relations of farming, commerce, family living, and community affairs (cf. Exod. 19:6).

h. Characteristic of H is the notion of the holy land [6]. Though God rules the whole world, He is uniquely attached to, and present in, the land of Canaan, which is to be the Land of Israel. Hence, heathen practices that are tolerable elsewhere will lead to expulsion from the Land of Israel (18:24, 28; 20:22ff.). The law of the Sabbath year is imposed not only on the people but on the soil itself; failure to observe the law will have to be made up for through years of desolation (below, 26:34).

The notion that sanctity should attach to a particular geographic area may seem strange to us. Yet many find it natural for Jews to expect more of themselves than of others, to believe that a Jewish community should be a model community, and a Jewish state different from, and better than, other national states.

The idea of holiness implies that what we do and what we make of our lives matters not only to us as individuals, not only to society, but to the entire cosmos. A divine purpose runs through all existence. We can

ally ourselves to it or oppose it—or, perhaps worse, we can ignore it. This climactic chapter of the Torah deserves, not only careful reading and study, but continuing reflection on its astonishing implications.

2. Sanctifying and Profaning the Name

We have already noted the statement (18:21) that one who offers his offspring to Molech profanes the name of God. The same expression appears in chapter 19, verse 12, in connection with swearing falsely. In these contexts, the phrase seems to require no explanation. But its fuller meaning emerges elsewhere. To profane the name of God means to impair His reputation in the non-Israelite world.

Thus, Ezekiel (who, we have seen, shows affinity to the Holiness Code) declares that, when the people of Judah brought the punishment of exile upon themselves, they profaned the name of God. For the Gentiles regarded the defeat of Judah as a defeat for Judah's God as well. They supposed the people were in exile because their God was not strong enough to protect them. Therefore, to retrieve His reputation, God would purify and restore Israel. When they were back on their own soil, strong and prosperous, God's name would be "sanctified in the sight of all the peoples"—that is, the nations would recognize His power and understand that the exile was not evidence of His impotence, but of His unswerving justice (Ezek. 36:16ff.).

This concept was transformed in Rabbinic Judaism from a questionable theological proposition into a powerful moral challenge. The prestige of Israel's God among the Gentiles—the Rabbis taught—is not God's worry, it is humankind's responsibility. Jews must so live and act as to win for their God the respect of all mankind. Any behavior that brings public disgrace on Jews and Judaism is *chilul ha-Shem*, profanation of the divine Name; any action that enhances the dignity and honor of Judaism is *kiddush ha-Shem*, sanctification of the Name.

Robbing a Gentile is doubly sinful, since it adds to the sin of robbery the further sin of *chilul ha-Shem* [7]. A Jew should accept martyrdom rather than publicly violate a commandment and thus profane the name of God [8].

Kiddush ha-Shem has no connection with what we now call "public relations." It does not mean currying favor with the Gentiles. It requires us to deserve the approbation of others, whether we actually obtain it or not. The highest act of *kiddush ha-Shem* is to die for one's faith.

3. The Golden Rule

The culmination of this climactic chapter is verse 18: "Love your neighbor as yourself." It is one of several versions of what in modern times has been called "the golden rule." (We do not know when or by whom the phrase was coined.) It appears in various forms, positive and negative; but all of them demand for others the same kind of treatment we want for ourselves.

Our passage is apparently the oldest written version of the principle. When Hillel, at the beginning of the Christian era, was asked to sum up the entire Torah briefly, he replied: "What is hateful to you, do not do to your fellow" [9]. (This negative form of the golden rule was apparently proverbial in Hillel's time for it appears in practically the same words in the apocryphal book of Tobit [10].) Jesus of Nazareth, Hillel's younger contemporary, declared that the commandment of Leviticus (19:18) is second in importance only to the command to love God (Mark 12:28ff.). In the following century, Rabbi Akiba declared it to be "the great principle of the Torah" (*Sifra*).

Confucius is credited with having taught the golden rule in its negative form [11]. A more abstract version of the principle is Kant's categorical imperative: "Act only on that maxim whereby thou canst at the same time will that it should become a universal law" [12].

Some Christian apologetes have argued that the negative form of the golden rule is spiritually inferior to the positive form ascribed to Jesus: "All that you would wish that men should do unto you, do ye also unto them" (Matthew 7:12). In their zeal, they forgot that the positive form occurs first in the Torah! But, actually, there is virtually no difference in meaning between the two versions. The golden rule, it has been re-marked [13], is an instrument of criticism. It enables us to judge a proposed course of action, but it does not provide us the means of proposing a course of action; that always requires an effort of creative imagination. Regarded as a standard of judgment, the golden rule is equally effective in negative or positive form.

Some Christians have also tried to show that the saying of Jesus is more truly universal and inclusive than that of Leviticus. They argue that "neighbor" in Leviticus (19:18) means "fellow Israelite" which is true enough; but they apparently overlook the commandment of verse 34 which requires us to show the same love to a foreigner resident in the land. There is no evidence that Jesus had a broader outlook [14].

Such theoretical distinctions would in any case not be important. Our opportunity to practice the golden rule is chiefly in our relations to those who are physically near to us, our literal neighbors. In ancient times, most people had little awareness of events beyond their immediate vicinity. They had no share in major political and economic decisions.

They rarely knew even of major occurrences until the results came upon them in the form of invasion, deportation, new tax demands, and the like. Only in recent centuries, especially in our own, has the average person had the knowledge, the opportunity, and the obligation to apply the golden rule on a global scale. Today, indeed, we must consider what duties we owe to the Vietnamese, the Biafrans, the Bengalis; but that is something new. And it does not make the question of our relationships with those nearer home any less compelling.

A mechanical, though not accurate, translation of the verse might be, "You shall love to (le-) your neighbor as yourself." This circumstance has suggested to various commentators alternative interpretations of the passage. They are not grammatically justifiable, for there are numerous instances in the Bible of this construction of a direct object with le-; but they are interesting in themselves.

Thus, Ibn Ezra, noting that many commentators took "neighbor" as the direct object, preferred to render, "Love the good for your neighbor as you love it for yourself." And the modern German thinkers Hermann Cohen and Martin Buber explained, "Be loving to your fellow man, as to one who is just like you" [15].

Nachmanides held to the traditional, "Love your neighbor as yourself," but regarded the language as rhetorical exaggeration. Our nature is such that we cannot love others as much as ourselves; and the halachah does not obligate us to sacrifice our lives for others. This commandment, Nachmanides asserts, calls on us to love others as we love good for ourselves. We should free ourselves from jealousy and rejoice in our neighbor's good fortune. But we should not tolerate injustice in the name of ill-considered love.

(A new weekly portion, *Kedoshim*, begins with 19:1.)

פ   פ   פ

א וַיְדַבֵּ֥ר יְהוָ֖ה אֶל־מֹשֶׁ֥ה לֵּאמֹֽר: דַּבֵּ֞ר אֶל־כָּל־עֲדַ֧ת
בְּנֵי־יִשְׂרָאֵ֛ל וְאָמַרְתָּ֥ אֲלֵהֶ֖ם קְדֹשִׁ֣ים תִּהְי֑וּ כִּ֣י קָד֔וֹשׁ
אֲנִ֖י יְהוָ֥ה אֱלֹהֵיכֶֽם: אִ֣ישׁ אִמּ֤וֹ וְאָבִיו֙ תִּירָ֔אוּ וְאֶת־
שַׁבְּתֹתַ֖י תִּשְׁמֹ֑רוּ אֲנִ֖י יְהוָ֥ה אֱלֹהֵיכֶֽם: אַל־תִּפְנ֣וּ אֶל־

הָ֣אֱלִילִ֔ם וֵֽאלֹהֵי֙ מַסֵּכָ֔ה לֹ֥א תַעֲשׂ֖וּ לָכֶ֑ם אֲנִ֖י יְהוָ֥ה
ה אֱלֹהֵיכֶֽם: וְכִ֧י תִזְבְּח֛וּ זֶ֥בַח שְׁלָמִ֖ים לַיהוָ֑ה לִֽרְצֹנְכֶ֖ם
ו תִּזְבָּחֻֽהוּ: בְּי֧וֹם זִבְחֲכֶ֛ם יֵאָכֵ֖ל וּמִֽמָּחֳרָ֑ת וְהַנּוֹתָר֙ עַד־
ז י֣וֹם הַשְּׁלִישִׁ֔י בָּאֵ֖שׁ יִשָּׂרֵֽף: וְאִ֛ם הֵאָכֹ֥ל יֵאָכֵ֖ל בַּיּ֣וֹם
ח הַשְּׁלִישִׁ֑י פִּגּ֥וּל ה֖וּא לֹ֥א יֵרָצֶֽה: וְאֹֽכְלָיו֙ עֲוֹנ֣וֹ יִשָּׂ֔א כִּֽי־
אֶת־קֹ֥דֶשׁ יְהוָ֖ה חִלֵּ֑ל וְנִכְרְתָ֛ה הַנֶּ֥פֶשׁ הַהִ֖וא מֵעַמֶּֽיהָ:

1] The LORD spoke to Moses, saying: **2]** Speak to the whole Israelite community and say to them:

You shall be holy, for I, the LORD your God, am holy.

3] You shall each revere his mother and his father, and keep My sabbaths: I the LORD am your God.

4] Do not turn to idols or make molten gods for yourselves: I the LORD am your God.

5] When you sacrifice an offering of well-being to the LORD, sacrifice it so that it may be accepted on your behalf. **6]** It shall be eaten on the day you sacrifice it, or on the day following; but what is left by the third day must be consumed in fire. **7]** If it should be eaten on the third day, it is an offensive thing, it will not be acceptable. **8]** And he who eats of it shall bear his guilt, for he has profaned what is sacred to the LORD; that person shall be cut off from his kin.

19:2] *Speak to the whole Israelite community.* This section was proclaimed publicly because it contains so many basic laws (*Sifra*). Holiness was to be the ideal, not of a priestly caste alone, but of the entire people.

You shall be holy. See the introduction to this chapter. *Sifra* explains: "As I, God, am set apart [*parush*], so you must be set apart [*perushim*]" (this is the word rendered "Pharisees" in other contexts). Perhaps the best rendering here would be the colloquial phrase, "You shall be something special."

3] *You shall each revere his mother and his father.* It was noted already by the Rabbis [16] that the Ten Commandments are all repeated in this section, though not in the order of Exodus, chapter 20. This verse corresponds to the fifth commandment. The complete list in Leviticus, chapter 19, is as follows:

First commandment, "I the LORD am your God" (verse 4, end)

Second commandment, "You shall have no other gods" (4, beginning)

Third commandment, "You shall not swear falsely" (12)

Fourth commandment, "Remember the Sabbath day" (3)

Fifth commandment, "Honor your father and your mother" (3)

Sixth commandment, "You shall not murder" (16)

Seventh commandment, "You shall not commit adultery" (29)

Eighth commandment, "You shall not steal" (11)

Ninth commandment, "You shall not bear false witness" (16)

Tenth commandment, "You shall not covet" (18)

4] *Idols.* Hebrew *elilim.* A variety of words are used in the Hebrew Bible to designate idols. This is one of the most contemptuous of them. Perhaps it was chosen just because it sounds like the legitimate words for "God," *El* and *Elohim.* In other connections, the same word is used for "worthlessness" (Zech. 11:17; Job 13:4).

5–8] Sacrifices of well-being. See commentary and gleanings on 7:15ff. H does not expound the sacrificial law at length, though it consistently implies the importance of the cult. Perhaps this item was included because it applies to the lay worshiper rather than to the priest.

יב אִישׁ בַּעֲמִיתוֹ: וְלֹא־תִשָּׁבְעוּ בִשְׁמִי לַשָּׁקֶר וְחִלַּלְתָּ
יג אֶת־שֵׁם אֱלֹהֶיךָ אֲנִי יְהוָה: לֹא־תַעֲשֹׁק אֶת־רֵעֲךָ וְלֹא
יד תִגְזֹל לֹא־תָלִין פְּעֻלַּת שָׂכִיר אִתְּךָ עַד־בֹּקֶר: לֹא־
תְקַלֵּל חֵרֵשׁ וְלִפְנֵי עִוֵּר לֹא תִתֵּן מִכְשֹׁל וְיָרֵאתָ

ט וּבְקֻצְרְכֶם אֶת־קְצִיר אַרְצְכֶם לֹא תְכַלֶּה פְּאַת שָׂדְךָ
י לִקְצֹר וְלֶקֶט קְצִירְךָ לֹא תְלַקֵּט: וְכַרְמְךָ לֹא תְעוֹלֵל
וּפֶרֶט כַּרְמְךָ לֹא תְלַקֵּט לֶעָנִי וְלַגֵּר תַּעֲזֹב אֹתָם אֲנִי
יא יְהוָה אֱלֹהֵיכֶם: לֹא תִּגְנֹבוּ וְלֹא־תְכַחֲשׁוּ וְלֹא־תְשַׁקְּרוּ

9] When you reap the harvest of your land, you shall not reap all the way to the edges of your field, or gather the gleanings of your harvest. **10]** You shall not pick your vineyard bare, or gather the fallen fruit of your vineyard; you shall leave them for the poor and the stranger: I the LORD am your God.

11] You shall not steal; you shall not deal deceitfully or falsely with one another. **12]** You shall not swear falsely by My name, profaning the name of your God: I am the LORD.

13] You shall not defraud your neighbor. You shall not commit robbery. The wages of a laborer shall not remain with you until morning.

14] You shall not insult the deaf, or place a stumbling block before the blind. You shall fear your God: I am the LORD.

9–10] The rights of the poor at harvest time. This law appears again in chapter 23, verse 22. Deuteronomy (24:19ff.) repeats the law about the gleaning of fruit and adds that the farmer should not go back to reclaim a forgotten sheaf of grain, but it does not mention the requirement of leaving a corner of the field uncut.

This passage (and the parallels mentioned) is not an appeal to the generosity of the landowner. It confers the right to glean and to harvest the uncut edge on those who have no resources of their own. It is perhaps the oldest declaration that the disadvantaged members of the society have a right to support from that society and should not be dependent on voluntary benevolence alone—though the latter is constantly stressed as well.

Because the specific laws here apply only to an agricultural society, later tradition applied the principle involved to urban conditions (see Gleanings).

11] *You shall not deal deceitfully or falsely.* The medieval commentators disagree as to what particular practices are forbidden by the terms "deceitfully" and "falsely." But, according to most opinions, they forbid deceit concerning property entrusted to one's keeping and concerning loans and the making of fraudulent claims.

12] *Profaning the name of your God.* See the introduction to this chapter, "2. Sanctifying and Profaning the Name."

13] *Defraud.* From *ashak*, "to take advantage of, exploit, withhold something due."

Robbery. By force, in contrast to theft (by stealth). In colloquial English, we often disregard the clear legal distinction between "steal" and "rob." But the corresponding Hebrew terms, *ganav* and *gazal*, are not interchanged.

The wages of a laborer shall not remain with you until morning. Similarly Deuteronomy (24:15). *Sifra* regards this as the continuation and conclusion of the preceding sentences. To hold back the laborer's wage is to defraud him by use of superior force.

14] *You shall not insult the deaf.* Two thoughts seem to be involved: do not take advantage of the handicapped, and do not treat another person contemptuously even if you can do it with impunity.

Or place a stumbling block before the blind. Taken literally, the law seems pointless. Why should anyone commit so childish an act of cruelty? *Sifra* therefore understands the commandment figuratively: Do not give self-serving advice to one who is ignorant and inexperienced [17].

But one who sold worthless stock to a widow could argue, "I really believed it was valuable and that I was helping her to get rich." Who could prove he was insincere? Therefore, adds *Sifra*, wherever the law is something "entrusted to the heart," the Torah cautions, "You shall fear your God." He knows what your motives are!

יי רֵעֶ֖ךָ אֲנִ֥י יְהֹוָֽה׃ לֹֽא־תִשְׂנָ֥א אֶת־אָחִ֖יךָ בִּלְבָבֶ֑ךָ הוֹכֵ֤חַ
יי תּוֹכִ֙יחַ֙ אֶת־עֲמִיתֶ֔ךָ וְלֹֽא־תִשָּׂ֥א עָלָ֖יו חֵֽטְא׃ לֹֽא־תִקֹּ֤ם
וְלֹֽא־תִטֹּר֙ אֶת־בְּנֵ֣י עַמֶּ֔ךָ וְאָֽהַבְתָּ֥ לְרֵעֲךָ֖ כָּמ֑וֹךָ אֲנִ֖י

טו מֵֽאֱלֹהֶ֖יךָ אֲנִ֥י יְהֹוָֽה׃ לֹא־תַעֲשׂ֤וּ עָ֙וֶל֙ בַּמִּשְׁפָּ֔ט לֹא־
תִשָּׂ֣א פְנֵי־דָ֗ל וְלֹ֥א תֶהְדַּ֖ר פְּנֵ֣י גָד֑וֹל בְּצֶ֖דֶק תִּשְׁפֹּ֥ט
טז עֲמִיתֶֽךָ׃ לֹא־תֵלֵ֤ךְ רָכִיל֙ בְּעַמֶּ֔יךָ לֹ֥א תַעֲמֹ֖ד עַל־דַּ֣ם

15] You shall not render an unfair decision: do not favor the poor or show deference to the rich; judge your neighbor fairly.   **16]** Do not deal basely with your fellows. Do not profit by the blood of your neighbor. I am the LORD.

17] You shall not hate your kinsman in your heart. Reprove your neighbor, but incur no guilt because of him.   **18]** You shall not take vengeance or bear a grudge against your kinsfolk. Love your neighbor as yourself: I am the LORD.

15] *You shall not render an unfair decision.* The Torah repeatedly admonishes judges to uphold justice unswervingly (Exod. 23:2ff.; Deut. 1:16f.; 16:18ff.). Misguided sympathy should not lead the judge to show favoritism to the poor (Exod. 23:3).

16] *Do not deal basely with your fellows.* Others, "go about as a talebearer"; meaning of Hebrew uncertain (T.N.). This rendering is traditional. It takes the Hebrew word *rachil* as related to *rochel*, "peddler" (see commentary on verse 3, where this sentence is equated with the ninth commandment). But we do not know what *rachil* really means; and Orlinsky aptly remarks [18], "In such passages as Jeremiah 6:28 and Ezekiel 22:9, the wickedness of the people is surely more grievous than talebearing."

Do not profit by the blood of your neighbor. I.e., do not act in such a way that you profit by his death or injury; so Ehrlich. Literally, "Do not stand upon the blood of your neighbor"; precise meaning of Hebrew phrase uncertain (T.N.). Tradition explained: Do not stand by idly while your neighbor's blood is shed, do not abandon him when he is in danger (see Gleanings). Ibn Ezra takes the verse as forbidding us to associate with bloodthirsty men.

17] *You shall not hate your kinsman in your heart.* The

Torah, unlike ordinary legal codes, is concerned not only with actions but also with attitudes. It recognizes how destructive bottled-up resentment can be and cautions us against wrong feelings as well as wrong acts.

Reprove your neighbor, but incur no guilt because of him. If you think you have a justified complaint, do not brood over it but state it forthrightly. Rashi, following a hint in *Sifra*, explains: Rebuke him, but do not shame him publicly.

Or, substituting "and" for "but" (Exact force of *ve-* uncertain. T.N.), we may interpret: By giving vent to your feelings, you may save yourself from the guilt of a violent act. Or again: By pointing out your fellow's misdeeds and thus affording him the chance to make amends, you are discharging your moral obligation to him (cf. Ezek. 3:17–21).

18] *You shall not take vengeance or bear a grudge.* "A" refuses to lend his spade to "B"; "B" later refuses to lend "A" his ax—that is vengeance. But if "B" lends the ax to "A" and says, "See, I let you have it even though you wouldn't lend me your spade"— that is bearing a grudge, and it is also forbidden (*Sifra*).

Love your neighbor as yourself. See the introduction to this chapter, "3. The Golden Rule."

כא חֻפָּשָׁה: וְהֵבִיא אֶת־אֲשָׁמוֹ לַיהוָה אֶל־פֶּתַח אֹהֶל   יט יְהוָה: אֶת־חֻקֹּתַי תִּשְׁמֹרוּ בְּהֶמְתְּךָ לֹא־תַרְבִּיעַ
כב מוֹעֵד אֵיל אָשָׁם: וְכִפֶּר עָלָיו הַכֹּהֵן בְּאֵיל הָאָשָׁם   כִּלְאַיִם שָׂדְךָ לֹא־תִזְרַע כִּלְאָיִם וּבֶגֶד כִּלְאַיִם שַׁעַטְנֵז
לִפְנֵי יְהוָה עַל־חַטָּאתוֹ אֲשֶׁר חָטָא וְנִסְלַח לוֹ   כ לֹא יַעֲלֶה עָלֶיךָ: וְאִישׁ כִּי־יִשְׁכַּב אֶת־אִשָּׁה שִׁכְבַת־
מֵחַטָּאתוֹ אֲשֶׁר חָטָא: פ   זֶרַע וְהִוא שִׁפְחָה נֶחֱרֶפֶת לְאִישׁ וְהָפְדֵּה לֹא נִפְדָּתָה
אוֹ חֻפְשָׁה לֹא נִתַּן־לָהּ בִּקֹּרֶת תִּהְיֶה לֹא יוּמְתוּ כִּי־לֹא

19] You shall observe My laws.

You shall not let your cattle mate with a different kind; you shall not sow your field with two kinds of seed; you shall not put on cloth from a mixture of two kinds of material.

20] If a man has carnal relations with a woman who is a slave and has been designated for another man, but has not been redeemed or given her freedom, there shall be an indemnity; they shall not, however, be put to death, since she has not been freed. **21]** But he must bring to the entrance of the Tent of Meeting, as his guilt offering to the LORD, a ram of guilt offering. **22]** With the ram of guilt offering the priest shall make expiation for him before the LORD for the sin that he committed; and the sin that he committed will be forgiven him.

19] *My laws.* The Hebrew term for "law" here is *chukah* (elsewhere it frequently appears in the masculine form *chok*). According to the Rabbis, it designates a commandment whose purpose and meaning are not clear to us and which we must perform with simple, unquestioning obedience (introduction to this chapter, "1. Holiness"). Such in fact is the character of the provisions in this verse.

The Hebrew word *kilayim*, meaning "of two kinds," appears in each of the three clauses. Similar regulations, using the same technical term, appear in Deuteronomy (22:9–11); in the latter passage nothing is said about breeding hybrid animals, but the yoking of an ox and an ass to the same plow is forbidden. These rules seem to reflect the belief that there is something unnatural about mixing breeds. Nachmanides is quite explicit—all species were fixed at Creation; the attempt to produce a new species is a defiance of God [19]. Such notions are very strange to us who live in the post-Darwinian age.

A mixture. Hebrew *shaatnez*, a word probably of non-Hebraic origin. It is explained in Deuteronomy 22:11 as a mixture of wool and linen.

The law of *kilayim* is elaborated fully in talmudic literature; it occupies an entire treatise of the Mishnah, called *Kilayim*.

20–22] The slave woman and her lover. Biblical law prescribes the death penalty for an adulterous couple (20:10). Moreover, a woman was regarded as married —and so liable to the penalty for adultery—from the time she was engaged to a man by his payment of the bride price, even though the marriage was not yet consummated (cf. Deut. 22:23–27). The present case concerns a slave woman who is about to be set free so that she can be married. The prospective husband had not yet "redeemed" her, that is, purchased her freedom from her master; and the latter has not liberated her of his own accord. If at this point she has sex relations with another man, neither of them is subject to the death penalty for she is still a slave and therefore not legally married. Her lover must, however, pay an indemnity (probably to the prospective husband, perhaps to the owner) and then bring a guilt offering. As usual, the guilt offering is valid only after financial restitution is made (cf. 5:20–26).

20] *Indemnity.* Hebrew *bikoret*. This rendering is supported by a related word in Akkadian [20]. The older Jewish Publication Society translation, following the margin of the Revised Version, rendered "inquisition," i.e., inquiry.

כג וְכִי־תָבֹאוּ אֶל־הָאָרֶץ וּנְטַעְתֶּם כָּל־עֵץ מַאֲכָל   פִּרְיוֹ לְהוֹסִיף לָכֶם תְּבוּאָתוֹ אֲנִי יְהוָה אֱלֹהֵיכֶם:
וַעֲרַלְתֶּם עָרְלָתוֹ אֶת־פִּרְיוֹ שָׁלֹשׁ שָׁנִים יִהְיֶה לָכֶם   כו לֹא תֹאכְלוּ עַל־הַדָּם לֹא תְנַחֲשׁוּ וְלֹא תְעוֹנֵנוּ: לֹא
כד עֲרֵלִים לֹא יֵאָכֵל: וּבַשָּׁנָה הָרְבִיעִת יִהְיֶה כָּל־פִּרְיוֹ   כז תַקִּפוּ פְּאַת רֹאשְׁכֶם וְלֹא תַשְׁחִית אֵת פְּאַת זְקָנֶךָ: כח וְשֶׂרֶט
כה קֹדֶשׁ הִלּוּלִים לַיהוָה: וּבַשָּׁנָה הַחֲמִישִׁת תֹּאכְלוּ אֶת־   לָנֶפֶשׁ לֹא תִתְּנוּ בִּבְשַׂרְכֶם וּכְתֹבֶת קַעֲקַע לֹא תִתְּנוּ

23] When you enter the land and plant any tree for food, you shall regard its fruit as forbidden. Three years it shall be forbidden for you, not to be eaten. **24]** In the fourth year all its fruit shall be set aside for jubilation before the LORD; **25]** and only in the fifth year may you use its fruit—that its yield to you may be increased: I the LORD am your God.

26] You shall not eat anything with its blood. You shall not practice divination or soothsaying. **27]** You shall not round off the side-growth on your head, or destroy the side-growth of your beard. **28]** You shall not make gashes in your flesh for the dead, or incise any marks on yourselves: I am the LORD.

23–25] Prohibition of fruit of new trees. For the first three years after the tree is planted, its fruit may not be used at all; in the fourth year, the fruit must be used only for a religious celebration; thereafter, it is completely permitted. This law no doubt originated in the widespread belief that all new life—vegetable, animal, or human—belongs to the deity; giving a part of it as a redemptive offering makes the remainder available for our use. Other biblical examples are the laws of the first born (Exod. 13:2, 11ff.), the first sheaf of grain (Lev. 23:9ff.), and the first fruits (Deut. 26).

23] *Forbidden.* Hebrew root *'rl,* commonly "to be uncircumcised" (T.N.).

24] *Set aside.* Hebrew *kodesh.* On the *jubilation before the Lord,* see Gleanings.

25] *That its yield to you may be increased.* Presumably this is the reward for obeying the commandment. But the ancients knew just as well as we do that fruit trees bear little or nothing in their first few years and that stripping off the blossoms during those years makes the trees more productive later on. So perhaps these words emanate from the fruit-grower's experience as much as from the religious theories of the lawgiver.

26] *You shall not eat anything with its blood.* According to this rendering, we have one more repetition of the commandment not to consume blood (cf. 17:10ff.). But the Hebrew reads literally, "You shall not eat on

[or, with] the blood"; and various explanations have been offered.

Nachmanides connects this prohibition with the ensuing laws against divination and other heathen customs. He finds here a reference to a pagan practice in which blood was poured into a pit and people gathered around it to obtain omens for the future. This, he holds, was the sin of eating on (or, with) the blood, which the people committed according to I Sam. 14:32ff. This account is similar to what we know of Greek rites for the underground deities [21].

The Greek translation was apparently based on a different Hebrew text which read, "You shall not eat on the mountains," referring to heathen celebrations condemned by Ezekiel (18:6, 11, and 15).

Divination or soothsaying. See verse 31. (See also Deut. 18:9ff. and Ezek. 21:26). Ancient peoples had a variety of techniques for discovering the future. The Bible does not suggest that they are ineffective or fraudulent, but it bans them as idolatrous. In Israel, knowledge of the future could be sought legitimately only through prophets, through dreams, or through the sacred lot of Urim and Thummim (I Sam. 28:6).

27–28] Other forbidden pagan practices were certain ways of cutting the hair, "destroying" the beard, gashing oneself as a sign of mourning, tattooing (perhaps with heathen emblems). The wearing of side curls (*peot*) by extreme Orthodox Jews is an attempt to carry out strictly the law of verse 27.

לב אֱלֹהֵיכֶם: מִפְּנֵי שֵׂיבָה תָּקוּם וְהָדַרְתָּ פְּנֵי זָקֵן וְיָרֵאתָ
לג מֵאֱלֹהֶיךָ אֲנִי יְהוָה: ס וְכִי־יָגוּר אִתְּךָ גֵּר בְּאַרְצְכֶם
לד לֹא תוֹנוּ אֹתוֹ: כְּאֶזְרָח מִכֶּם יִהְיֶה לָכֶם הַגֵּר הַגָּר
אִתְּכֶם וְאָהַבְתָּ לוֹ כָּמוֹךָ כִּי־גֵרִים הֱיִיתֶם בְּאֶרֶץ

כט בָּכֶם אֲנִי יְהוָה: אַל־תְּחַלֵּל אֶת־בִּתְּךָ לְהַזְנוֹתָהּ וְלֹא־
ל תִזְנֶה הָאָרֶץ וּמָלְאָה הָאָרֶץ זִמָּה: אֶת־שַׁבְּתֹתַי תִּשְׁמֹרוּ
לא וּמִקְדָּשִׁי תִּירָאוּ אֲנִי יְהוָה: אַל־תִּפְנוּ אֶל־הָאֹבֹת וְאֶל־
הַיִּדְּעֹנִים אַל־תְּבַקְשׁוּ לְטָמְאָה בָהֶם אֲנִי יְהוָה

29] Do not degrade your daughter, and make her a harlot, lest the land fall into harlotry and the land be filled with depravity. **30]** You shall keep My sabbaths and venerate My sanctuary: I am the LORD.

31] Do not turn to ghosts and do not inquire of familiar spirits, to be defiled by them: I the LORD am your God.

32] You shall rise before the aged and show deference to the old; you shall fear your God: I am the LORD.

33] When a stranger resides with you in your land, you shall not wrong him. **34]** The stranger who resides with you shall be to you as one of your citizens; you shall love him as

29] *Do not degrade your daughter and make her a harlot.* This may allude to the well-attested institution of cult prostitutes whose earnings helped to maintain the temples where they plied their trade. Such practice is outlawed in Deuteronomy (23:18f.).

Lest the land fall into harlotry. That the land itself is defiled by the sins of its inhabitants is frequently stated in H (18:27ff., 20:22ff., 26:43).

31] *Ghosts . . . familiar spirits.* From remote antiquity people have turned for guidance to the spirits of the dead, and mediums still do a thriving business in supposedly civilized countries. Such practices were well known to the ancient Israelites; though banned by the Torah, they had their devotees (I Sam. 28; Isa. 8:19f.). The term "familiar spirit" means what present-day mediums call a "control," that is, a ghost with which they can readily communicate and so make contact with other persons who have died. The Rabbis, however, explain the words here rendered "ghost" and "familiar spirit" as designating different techniques for consulting the dead (*Sifra*).

32] *You shall rise before the aged.* Hebrew *sevah*, "age," "gray hair." Respect for age is demanded and praised in the Bible and in all ancient Oriental wisdom literature.

The old. Hebrew *zaken*, which also means "elder" in the sense of community leader.

Fear your God. See commentary on verse 14.

33] *When a stranger* [ger] *resides . . . in your land.* The foreigner, resident in the Land of Israel, must not only be protected against molestation but be shown positive love. Many ancient peoples had rules for the protection of aliens, generally on a basis of personal reciprocity. A Roman protected a Greek acquaintance in Rome and vice versa. (That is why Latin and the Romance languages use one word for both "host" and "guest.") But nowhere in ancient literature is there the deep concern with the feelings of the stranger which the Torah imposes on the entire community. Here and elsewhere (e.g., Exod. 22:20), the requirement is connected with the memory of Israel's own experience as aliens in Egypt. Biblical law applies in many cases to both citizen and *ger* (Num. 9:14 and elsewhere). This meant that the alien had equal rights under the law and also that he must refrain from the forbidden practices that would defile the land. But he was not required to participate in the Israelite cult.

In rabbinic sources, *ger* is used in the sense of "proselyte," and these provisions are applied specifically to those who adopt the Jewish faith. This shift reflects the great interest of the rabbinic teachers in converts who, at the beginning of the Christian era, constituted a sizeable element of the community. It does not mean that these rights were denied the unconverted Gentile who is referred to in talmudic writings as "a son of Noah."

You shall not wrong him. By taking advantage of his unfamiliarity with economic conditions and business practices, or even by unkind words (*Sifra*).

לה מִצְרָיִם אֲנִי יְהוָֹה אֱלֹהֵיכֶם: לֹא־תַעֲשׂוּ עָוֶל בַּמִּשְׁפָּט לֹ אֲשֶׁר־הוֹצֵאתִי אֶתְכֶם מֵאֶרֶץ מִצְרָיִם: וּשְׁמַרְתֶּם אֶת־
לו בַּמִּדָּה בַּמִּשְׁקָל וּבַמְּשׂוּרָה: מֹאזְנֵי צֶדֶק אַבְנֵי־צֶדֶק   כָּל־חֻקֹּתַי וְאֶת־כָּל־מִשְׁפָּטַי וַעֲשִׂיתֶם אֹתָם אֲנִי
אֵיפַת צֶדֶק וְהִין צֶדֶק יִהְיֶה לָכֶם אֲנִי יְהוָֹה אֱלֹהֵיכֶם   יְהוָֹה: פ

yourself, for you were strangers in the land of Egypt: I the LORD am your God.

35] You shall not falsify measures of length, weight, or capacity.   **36]** You shall have an honest balance, honest weights, an honest *ephah,* and an honest *hin.*

I the LORD am your God who freed you from the land of Egypt.   **37]** You shall faithfully observe all My laws and all My rules: I am the LORD.

35–36] Honest weights and measures. Integrity in business dealings is one of the components of holiness. The *ephah* was a dry measure, equivalent to about two pecks. The *hin* was a liquid measure roughly equal to an American gallon.

36] *I the Lord am your God who freed you from the*

land of Egypt. Almost the same words with which the Ten Commandments begin are set at the end of the Law of Holiness. God's reality and His redemptive works provide the authority for the exacting demands made in this chapter.

GLEANINGS

Halachah

19:3] *You Shall Each Revere His Mother and His Father, and Keep My Sabbaths*

The second clause teaches that deference to parents does not justify disobedience of the Torah; if they tell us to violate the Sabbath, we must not heed them.   SIFRA

4] *You Shall Not Reap All the Way to the Edges*

The halachah understands: One corner of each field, comprising at least one-sixtieth of its area, must be left uncut for the poor [22].

This law is treated in the section of the Mishnah called *Peah* ("corner"), together with other laws governing our obligations to the poor. Included are provisions to meet the needs of the urban poor—needs that arose as economic and social circumstances changed. The law provided for a daily distribution of food for those in immediate need of it, and for a weekly distribution of money for those who

required long-term assistance. Every effort was made to preserve the dignity of those who received charity. Regular members of the community were taxed a certain amount for the maintenance of these and other communal institutions; but all were encouraged to supplement this minimum by generous voluntary contributions [23].

11] *You Shall Not Steal*

To witness a theft and keep silent about it is also theft.   IBN EZRA

One should not steal back his own property from a thief—so as to avoid even the appearance of wrong action—but make a direct accusation and so recover what is his [24].

13] *The Wages of a Laborer Shall Not Remain with You until Morning*

The plain sense seems to be: You must pay at

900

nightfall for work done during the day. But the halachah understood the verse to mean: "You shall not hold back the wages of one hired to work [through the night] till the morning." The corresponding rule in Deuteronomy (24:15) was taken to deal with one who worked during daylight hours up to sunset. From the two passages, the conclusion was derived that one who works during the day may be paid any time during the subsequent night, anyone working at night may be paid any time the ensuing day [25]. Though this gives the employer a few more hours to pay than the biblical author seems to have intended, it still requires prompt reimbursement. There are many other provisions in the halachah for the protection of labor [26].

14] *Or Place a Stumbling Block before the Blind*
This forbids one to act in such a way as to lead the unwary to violate the Torah (*Sifra*). Therefore, one should not strike his grown son, who might be roused to return the blow or to speak disrespectfully, thus violating the injunctions of verse 3 and Exodus (21:15, 17) [27].

16] *Do Not Profit by the Blood of Your Neighbor*
This was understood to mean: Do not stand by idly when your neighbor's blood is shed. If you see someone in danger of drowning, or being attacked by robbers, or by a wild beast, you are obligated to rescue that person (*Sifra*). Further, you must not withhold testimony in a criminal case, if you have evidence that favors the accused.
SIFRA and TARGUM PSEUDO-JONATHAN

17] *Reprove Your Neighbor*
If he does not respond to your reproof, Rabbi Eliezer says: Continue to reprove him until he strikes you; Rabbi Joshua says: until he curses you; Ben Azzai says: until he insults you [28].

19] *You Shall Not Let Your Cattle Mate with a Different Kind*
One may not breed hybrid animals (such as mules), but you may keep and use them [29].

You Shall Not Sow Your Field with Two Kinds of Seed
This law likewise prohibits the grafting of

trees [30]. (Orthodox authorities have been greatly concerned that no citrons for use at Sukot should come from grafted trees.) On the other hand, it is permissible to sow vegetables between trees [31]. Though it is forbidden to plant two kinds of seeds together in a field, or to keep them growing, their products may be used. A different and more stringent law applies when mixed seeds are planted in a vineyard (Deut. 22:9) [32].

Cloth from a Mixture of Two Kinds of Material
Deuteronomy (22:11) defines *shaatnez* as a mixture of wool and linen; the halachah limits the prohibition to this one mixture. However, wool or linen may be mixed with cotton, silk, and other fibers [33]. The prohibition is only for the wearing of *shaatnez*; combinations of wool and linen may be used for any other purpose but clothing [34].

20] *Indemnity*
The halachah understood *bikoret* as "punishment," specifically, flogging for the woman; the man's punishment, the payment of indemnity and the presentation of an *asham*, is derived from the ensuing verses (*Sifra*). The Rabbis had great difficulty fitting this case into the general framework of the halachah. According to Maimonides it applies only when half the sum required for the release of the woman has been paid and when the man to whom she has been designated is a Hebrew slave [35].

24] *Set Aside for Jubilation before the Lord*
On the analogy of Deuteronomy, chapter 14, verses 22ff., the owner was required to bring the fruit to Jerusalem, where he and his family were to consume it while in a state of ritual purity [36].

26] *You Shall Not Eat Anything with its Blood*
Literally, "You shall not eat on [or, with] the blood" (see commentary). From this one verse, *Sifra* drew all the following inferences: (a) Meat may not be eaten until all the lifeblood has been drained from the carcass. (b) Sacrificial meat may not be eaten until the blood has been dashed against the altar. (c) The traditional mourner's meal is not served to relatives of one executed for a crime. (d) Judges who impose a death sentence must fast on the day of the execution.

27] *... Destroy the Side-Growth of Your Beard*

"Destroy" was understood to mean shaving with a blade. Most Orthodox authorities permit the removal of facial hair by depilatories, tweezers, scissors, clippers, or electric shavers [37]. The prohibition in this verse applies only to males.

29] *Do Not Degrade Your Daughter*

This verse forbids a father to arrange or permit a liaison for his daughter. According to Rabbi Eliezer, it also forbids the father to give his daughter in marriage to an old man. According to Rabbi Akiba, a father is obligated to arrange a marriage for his daughter when she arrives at a suitable age, so as to protect her from temptation [38].

Haggadah

19:2] *You Shall Be Holy*

The word "holy" is applied in many different connections. The angels, the heavens, the prophets, the righteous, Israel, the Sabbaths, and the sacrifices are all called *kadosh* in Scripture. You might then suppose that their holiness resembles the holiness of Him whose command brought the world into being; therefore Scripture also declares, "There is none so holy as the LORD" (I Sam. 2:2) [39].

3] *You Shall Each Revere His Father and His Mother*

The word translated "revere" also means "fear." A son ordinarily fears his father more than his mother; he honors mother more than father because she cared for him when he was little. Therefore Scripture puts mother first in this verse and puts father first in "honor your father and mother"—to teach that both parents should be revered and honored equally. SIFRA

18] *Love Your Neighbor as Yourself*

Do not say: Just as I have been humiliated, let my fellow be humiliated too; just as I have been cursed at, let my fellow be cursed at too. Said Rabbi Tanchuma: If you act thus, know whom you are humiliating—"He made him in the likeness of God" (Gen. 5:1) [40].

Out of the endless chaos of the world, one nighest thing, his neighbor, is placed before his soul and concerning this one, and well-nigh only concerning this one, he is told: He is like you! "Like you," and thus not "you." You remain You and you are to remain just that. But he is not to remain a He for you and, thus, a mere It for your You. Rather, he is like You, like your You, a You like You, an I—a soul [41].

902

Punishment of Sex Offenses

This chapter appears to be a different version of the traditions preserved in chapter 18. Aside from the section on Molech-worship (see introduction to Lev. 18), this chapter deals with virtually the same material as chapter 18, except that here the punishment of the various offenses is stated specifically. (But the severe tone of the prohibitions in chapter 18 probably implied the heavy penalties for these crimes.) This chapter also repeats (verse 6), with penalty, the prohibition against necromancy found in 19:31, and the death penalty (verse 9) for insulting a parent (stated in Exod. 21:17).

ה וְשַׂמְתִּי אֲנִי אֶת־פָּנַי בָּאִישׁ הַהוּא וּבְמִשְׁפַּחְתּוֹ וְהִכְרַתִּי
אֹתוֹ וְאֵת כָּל־הַזֹּנִים אַחֲרָיו לִזְנוֹת אַחֲרֵי הַמֹּלֶךְ
מִקֶּרֶב עַמָּם: וְהַנֶּפֶשׁ אֲשֶׁר תִּפְנֶה אֶל־הָאֹבֹת וְאֶל־
הַיִּדְּעֹנִים לִזְנוֹת אַחֲרֵיהֶם וְנָתַתִּי אֶת־פָּנַי בַּנֶּפֶשׁ הַהִוא
וְהִכְרַתִּי אֹתוֹ מִקֶּרֶב עַמּוֹ: וְהִתְקַדִּשְׁתֶּם וִהְיִיתֶם
קְדֹשִׁים כִּי אֲנִי יְהוָה אֱלֹהֵיכֶם: וּשְׁמַרְתֶּם אֶת־חֻקֹּתַי
וַעֲשִׂיתֶם אֹתָם אֲנִי יְהוָה מְקַדִּשְׁכֶם: כִּי־אִישׁ אִישׁ אֲשֶׁר
יְקַלֵּל אֶת־אָבִיו וְאֶת־אִמּוֹ מוֹת יוּמָת אָבִיו וְאִמּוֹ קִלֵּל

א וַיְדַבֵּר יְהוָה אֶל־מֹשֶׁה לֵּאמֹר: וְאֶל־בְּנֵי יִשְׂרָאֵל
תֹּאמַר אִישׁ אִישׁ מִבְּנֵי יִשְׂרָאֵל וּמִן־הַגֵּר הַגָּר
בְּיִשְׂרָאֵל אֲשֶׁר יִתֵּן מִזַּרְעוֹ לַמֹּלֶךְ מוֹת יוּמָת עַם
הָאָרֶץ יִרְגְּמֻהוּ בָאָבֶן: וַאֲנִי אֶתֵּן אֶת־פָּנַי בָּאִישׁ
הַהוּא וְהִכְרַתִּי אֹתוֹ מִקֶּרֶב עַמּוֹ כִּי מִזַּרְעוֹ נָתַן לַמֹּלֶךְ
לְמַעַן טַמֵּא אֶת־מִקְדָּשִׁי וּלְחַלֵּל אֶת־שֵׁם קָדְשִׁי: וְאִם
הַעְלֵם יַעְלִימוּ עַם הָאָרֶץ אֶת־עֵינֵיהֶם מִן־הָאִישׁ
הַהוּא בְּתִתּוֹ מִזַּרְעוֹ לַמֹּלֶךְ לְבִלְתִּי הָמִית אֹתוֹ:

1] And the LORD spoke to Moses: **2]** Say further to the Israelite people:
Any man among the Israelites, or among the strangers residing in Israel, who gives any of his offspring to Molech, shall be put to death; the people of the land shall pelt him with stones. **3]** And I will set My face against that man and will cut him off from among his people, because he gave of his offspring to Molech and so defiled My sanctuary and profaned My holy name. **4]** And if the people of the land should shut their eyes to that man when he gives of his offspring to Molech, and should not put him to death, **5]** I Myself will set My face against that man and his kin, and will cut off from among their people both him and all who follow him in going astray after Molech. **6]** And if any person turns to ghosts and familiar spirits and goes astray after them, I will set My face against that person and cut him off from among his people.

7] You shall sanctify yourselves and be holy, for I the LORD am your God. **8]** You shall faithfully observe My laws: I the LORD make you holy.

9] If any man insults his father or his mother, he shall be put to death; he has insulted his father and his mother—his bloodguilt is upon him.

20:2] *The strangers.* See commentary on 19:33.

Shall pelt him with stones. This seems to envision a mob overwhelming the offender with a shower of rocks. The halachah understands the rule differently (see Gleanings).

3] *I will set My face against that man.* I will not turn My attention away from him until he is punished.

Cut him off from among his people. See commentary on 7:21.

Defiled My sanctuary. The sanctuary would not be ritually defiled by pagan rites conducted elsewhere. Here the defilement is figurative: the reputation of the sanctuary will be stained by the misconduct of those who sometimes worship there. The meaning is therefore akin to that of "profaned My holy name" (see introduction to Lev. 19). *Sifra*, however, followed by Rashi and Nachmanides, understands *mikdashi* ("My sanctuary") to mean here "My holy people."

4] *Shut their eyes.* The phrase is in contrast with, "I will set My face against."

5] *And his kin.* The phrase seems to suggest the notion of "guilt by family relationship," a concept strongly repudiated in Deuteronomy (24:16). The rabbinic commentators explain, perhaps correctly, that the offender would not have dared commit the crime without the encouragement and protection of his family, who have thus involved themselves in his guilt. And the Targum paraphrases, "His supporters."

7] *Sanctify yourselves.* Cf. 11:44, 19:2.

8] *I the Lord make you holy.* The meaning is clarified in verse 26.

9] *If any man insults his father.* . . . See Exodus (21:17). Respect for parents is mentioned here because it strengthens family life, which the offenses next listed destroy (Hoffmann).

דָּמָיו בּֽוֹ: וְאִ֗ישׁ אֲשֶׁ֤ר יִנְאַף֙ אֶת־אֵ֣שֶׁת אִ֔ישׁ אֲשֶׁ֥ר יִנְאַ֖ף י
אֶת־אֵ֣שֶׁת רֵעֵ֑הוּ מֽוֹת־יוּמַ֥ת הַנֹּאֵ֖ף וְהַנֹּאָֽפֶת: וְאִ֗ישׁ אֲשֶׁ֤ר
יִשְׁכַּב֙ אֶת־אֵ֣שֶׁת אָבִ֔יו עֶרְוַ֥ת אָבִ֖יו גִּלָּ֑ה מֽוֹת־יֽוּמְת֥וּ יא
שְׁנֵיהֶ֖ם דְּמֵיהֶ֥ם בָּֽם: וְאִ֗ישׁ אֲשֶׁ֤ר יִשְׁכַּב֙ אֶת־כַּלָּת֔וֹ מ֥וֹת
יֽוּמְת֖וּ שְׁנֵיהֶ֑ם תֶּ֥בֶל עָשׂ֖וּ דְּמֵיהֶ֥ם בָּֽם: וְאִ֗ישׁ אֲשֶׁ֤ר יב
יִשְׁכַּב֙ אֶת־זָכָר֙ מִשְׁכְּבֵ֣י אִשָּׁ֔ה תּוֹעֵבָ֥ה עָשׂ֖וּ שְׁנֵיהֶ֑ם מ֥וֹת יג
יוּמָ֖תוּ דְּמֵיהֶ֥ם בָּֽם: וְאִ֗ישׁ אֲשֶׁ֨ר יִקַּ֧ח אֶת־אִשָּׁ֛ה וְאֶת־ יד
אִמָּ֖הּ זִמָּ֣ה הִ֑וא בָּאֵ֞שׁ יִשְׂרְפ֤וּ אֹתוֹ֙ וְאֶתְהֶ֔ן וְלֹא־תִהְיֶ֥ה
זִמָּ֖ה בְּתוֹכְכֶֽם: וְאִ֗ישׁ אֲשֶׁ֨ר יִתֵּ֧ן שְׁכָבְתּ֛וֹ בִּבְהֵמָ֖ה מ֣וֹת טו

יוּמָ֑ת וְאֶת־הַבְּהֵמָ֖ה תַּהֲרֹֽגוּ: וְאִשָּׁ֗ה אֲשֶׁ֨ר תִּקְרַ֤ב אֶל־ טו
כָּל־בְּהֵמָה֙ לְרִבְעָ֣ה אֹתָ֔הּ וְהָרַגְתָּ֥ אֶת־הָאִשָּׁ֖ה וְאֶת־
הַבְּהֵמָ֑ה מ֥וֹת יוּמָ֖תוּ דְּמֵיהֶ֥ם בָּֽם: וְאִ֣ישׁ אֲשֶׁר־יִקַּ֣ח
אֶת־אֲחֹת֡וֹ בַּת־אָבִ֣יו אֽוֹ־בַת־אִ֠מּוֹ וְרָאָ֨ה אֶת־עֶרְוָתָ֜הּ
וְהִֽיא־תִרְאֶ֤ה אֶת־עֶרְוָתוֹ֙ חֶ֣סֶד ה֔וּא וְנִ֨כְרְת֔וּ לְעֵינֵ֖י בְּנֵ֣י
עַמָּ֑ם עֶרְוַ֧ת אֲחֹת֛וֹ גִּלָּ֖ה עֲוֹנ֥וֹ יִשָּֽׂא: וְ֠אִישׁ אֲשֶׁר־יִשְׁכַּ֨ב יח
אֶת־אִשָּׁ֜ה דָּוָ֗ה וְגִלָּ֤ה אֶת־עֶרְוָתָהּ֙ אֶת־מְקֹרָ֣הּ הֶֽעֱרָ֔ה
וְהִ֕וא גִּלְּתָ֖ה אֶת־מְק֣וֹר דָּמֶ֑יהָ וְנִכְרְת֥וּ שְׁנֵיהֶ֖ם מִקֶּ֥רֶב
עַמָּֽם: וְעֶרְוַ֨ת אֲח֧וֹת אִמְּךָ֛ וַאֲח֥וֹת אָבִ֖יךָ לֹ֣א תְגַלֵּ֑ה יט

10] If a man commits adultery with a married woman, committing adultery with his neighbor's wife, the adulterer and the adulteress shall be put to death. **11]** If a man lies with his father's wife, it is the nakedness of his father that he has uncovered; the two shall be put to death—their bloodguilt is upon them. **12]** If a man lies with his daughter-in-law, both of them shall be put to death; they have committed incest—their bloodguilt is upon them. **13]** If a man lies with a male as one lies with a woman, the two of them have done an abhorrent thing; they shall be put to death—their bloodguilt is upon them. **14]** If a man marries a woman and her mother, it is depravity; both he and they shall be put to the fire, that there be no depravity among you. **15]** If a man has carnal relations with a beast, he shall be put to death; and you shall kill the beast. **16]** If a woman approaches any beast to mate with it, you shall kill the woman and the beast; they shall be put to death—their bloodguilt is upon them.

17] If a man marries his sister, the daughter of either his father or his mother, so that he sees her nakedness and she sees his nakedness, it is a disgrace; they shall be excommunicated in the sight of their kinsfolk. He has uncovered the nakedness of his sister, he shall bear his guilt. **18]** If a man lies with a woman in her infirmity and uncovers her nakedness, he has laid bare her flow and she has exposed her blood flow; both of them shall be cut off from among their people. **19]** You shall not uncover the nakedness of your mother's sister or of your

His bloodguilt is upon him. Not on those who condemn and execute him. He has only himself to blame.

10–16] On capital punishment, see Gleanings.

11–21] On forbidden sexual relations, see chapter 18.

14] *Both he and they shall be put to the fire.* The first wife entered into a completely legitimate union; it was the second, whether mother or daughter of the

first, who joined the man in an act of depravity. The word "they" must mean "the guilty one of the two." This is the view of the Talmud [1].

Put to the fire. For the procedure, see Gleanings.

15] *And you shall kill the beast.* Though it is not morally responsible, it was the unwitting cause of a human life being destroyed.

17] *Excommunicated.* Literally, "cut off" (T.N.). See commentary on 7:20.

כ אֶרֶץ זָבַת חָלָב וּדְבַשׁ אֲנִי יְהֹוָה אֱלֹהֵיכֶם אֲשֶׁר־
הִבְדַּלְתִּי אֶתְכֶם מִן־הָעַמִּים: וְהִבְדַּלְתֶּם בֵּין־הַבְּהֵמָה
הַטְּהֹרָה לַטְּמֵאָה וּבֵין־הָעוֹף הַטָּמֵא לַטָּהֹר וְלֹא־
תְשַׁקְּצוּ אֶת־נַפְשֹׁתֵיכֶם בַּבְּהֵמָה וּבָעוֹף וּבְכֹל אֲשֶׁר
תִּרְמֹשׂ הָאֲדָמָה אֲשֶׁר־הִבְדַּלְתִּי לָכֶם לְטַמֵּא: וִהְיִיתֶם
לִי קְדֹשִׁים כִּי קָדוֹשׁ אֲנִי יְהֹוָה וָאַבְדִּל אֶתְכֶם מִן־
הָעַמִּים לִהְיוֹת לִי: וְאִישׁ אוֹ־אִשָּׁה כִּי־יִהְיֶה בָהֶם אוֹב
אוֹ יִדְּעֹנִי מוֹת יוּמָתוּ בָּאֶבֶן יִרְגְּמוּ אֹתָם דְּמֵיהֶם בָּם:

Haftarah Kedoshim, p. 999

כ כִּי אֶת־שְׁאֵרוֹ הֶעֱרָה עֲו‍ֹנָם יִשָּׂאוּ: וְאִישׁ אֲשֶׁר יִשְׁכַּב
אֶת־דֹּדָתוֹ עֶרְוַת דֹּדוֹ גִּלָּה חֶטְאָם יִשָּׂאוּ עֲרִירִים
יָמֻתוּ: וְאִישׁ אֲשֶׁר יִקַּח אֶת־אֵשֶׁת אָחִיו נִדָּה הִוא עֶרְוַת
אָחִיו גִּלָּה עֲרִירִים יִהְיוּ: וּשְׁמַרְתֶּם אֶת־כָּל־חֻקֹּתַי
וְאֶת־כָּל־מִשְׁפָּטַי וַעֲשִׂיתֶם אֹתָם וְלֹא־תָקִיא אֶתְכֶם
הָאָרֶץ אֲשֶׁר אֲנִי מֵבִיא אֶתְכֶם שָׁמָּה לָשֶׁבֶת בָּהּ:
וְלֹא תֵלְכוּ בְּחֻקֹּת הַגּוֹי אֲשֶׁר־אֲנִי מְשַׁלֵּחַ מִפְּנֵיכֶם כִּי
אֶת־כָּל־אֵלֶּה עָשׂוּ וָאָקֻץ בָּם: וָאֹמַר לָכֶם אַתֶּם
תִּירְשׁוּ אֶת־אַדְמָתָם וַאֲנִי אֶתְּנֶנָּה לָכֶם לָרֶשֶׁת אֹתָהּ

father's sister, for that is laying bare one's own flesh; they shall bear their guilt.   20] If a man lies with his uncle's wife, it is his uncle's nakedness that he has uncovered. They shall bear their guilt: they shall die childless.   21] If a man marries the wife of his brother, it is indecency. It is the nakedness of his brother that he has uncovered; they shall remain childless.

22] You shall faithfully observe all My laws and all My regulations, lest the land to which I bring you to settle in spew you out.   23] You shall not follow the practices of the nation that I am driving out before you. For it is because they did all these things that I abhorred them   24] and said to you: You shall possess their land, for I will give it to you to possess, a land flowing with milk and honey. I the LORD am your God who has set you apart from other peoples.   25] So you shall set apart the clean beast from the unclean, the unclean bird from the clean. You shall not draw abomination upon yourselves through beast or bird or anything with which the ground is alive, which I have set apart for you to treat as unclean.   26] You shall be holy to Me, for I the LORD am holy, and I have set you apart from other peoples to be Mine.

27] A man or a woman who has a ghost or a familiar spirit shall be put to death; they shall be pelted with stones—their bloodguilt shall be upon them.

22–25] Cf. 18:24ff. The passages are much alike, but here (verse 25) the prohibition of unclean meats is also mentioned. This subject was treated fully in chapter 11, most of which is from P. There is no need to assume that verse 25 was inserted by a P editor.

The author of H does not detail the dietary laws, just as he does not detail the laws of sacrifice; but no doubt he considered both important.

24] *Milk and honey*. See at Exod. 3:8 and Num. 13:27.

GLEANINGS

Halachah

20:9–16] The Bible prescribes the death penalty for a number of crimes, of two classes: (1) crimes against persons, such as murder and kidnaping, and (2) acts of sacrilege, such as flagrant violation of the Sabbath, blasphemy, and the sexual offenses enumerated here. These sacrilegious acts were believed to endanger the entire community by calling down divine wrath. Never does the Bible call for the death penalty for crimes against property. In contrast, pickpockets were still hanged in England in the eighteenth century.

The talmudic rabbis, with their great concern for the sanctity of human life, were openly opposed to capital punishment. But, since they had to recognize the letter of the Torah law, they sought a variety of means to render these penal laws inoperative. Thus, in some instances, they held that the Torah referred to death by divine intervention, not to death imposed by a court. They further devised a system of technicalities to prevent the conviction of a defendant for a capital crime. This somewhat offhand approach was relatively easy for them, since the Roman government denied Jewish courts jurisdiction over capital cases.

9] *Pelt Him with Stones*
According to the halachah, the procedure for "stoning" was an orderly one. The criminal was thrown off a high platform. If the fall did not kill him, stones were to be dropped on his body till he died [2].

14] *Put to the Fire*
Not, according to the halachah, the slow agony of death at the stake. The victim's mouth was forced open and molten lead poured down his throat, killing him quickly [3].

15] *And You Shall Kill the Beast*
For, if people saw the beast in the market place, they might say, "That is the animal on account of which so-and-so was put to death." But God would not want the memory of the man's shame kept alive [4]. Moreover, the availability of the animal might tempt others to misconduct [5].

907

Laws concerning the Priests

For ancient man, the essential form of worship was sacrifice. But a sacrifice not properly performed was worse than useless—it might lead to disaster. It was essential that the cult be directed by responsible and well-informed persons.

1. The Priestly Role

Frequently, sacrifice was conducted by the head of a family or the chieftain of a tribe. In many societies the ruler was also chief priest, or the priest was also the ruler. But it was likewise a widespread practice to entrust the temples and shrines, and the rituals conducted in them, to a specially trained caste or class of priests. These functionaries often wore distinctive dress, had their special pattern of life, and received their support from the temple income. They served as intermediaries between a people and its god; they presented the offerings of the group and of individuals, and in turn they informed their people of the will of the deity. For this purpose they sometimes made use of oracular techniques, and sometimes they drew upon their extensive knowledge of religious lore and tradition.

The priestly officiants served in some communities for a limited term, in others for life. The priesthood among certain peoples was open to any qualified citizen; but, in many cases, including that of Israel, the priesthood was hereditary.

2. Israelite Priesthood

When God gave instructions for the building of the Tabernacle, He selected Aaron and his sons to serve as priests and ordained that their descendants were to inherit this prerogative forever (Exod. 25:1–29:37, especially 29:9). The rest of the tribe of Levi were assigned important tasks in the sanctuary, but in rank and sanctity they were on a lower level than their fellow Levites of Aaron's family; their duties and prerogatives are expounded at length in Numbers (3, 4, 8, and 18).

The books of Ezra, Nehemiah, and Chronicles give us considerable information about the Levites at the end of the biblical period. In the Second Temple, the Levites served as guards and as singers and instrumentalists.

But this sharp distinction between Aaronide priests and Levites of lower rank is found

only in the late books just mentioned and in the Priestly Code. It is not found in the other documents of the Pentateuch, or in the historical books of Joshua, Judges, Samuel, or Kings. The priests at Shiloh (I Sam. 2:24ff.), Nob (I Sam. 21ff.), and Jerusalem (I Kings 2:35) are not designated in these sources as descendants of Aaron. Deuteronomy constantly refers to the "levitical priests," literally, "the priests, the Levites." When "priest" or "Levite" is used alone, there is never an implied contrast between two groups. Sometimes (e.g., Deut. 18:6), "Levite" is plainly identical with "priest."

Ezekiel also uses the term "levitical priests." But he makes a distinction between the descendants of Zadok, the first priest of Solomon's Temple, and the other Levites. The latter, he asserts, had compromised with idolatry; henceforth, they are barred from sacrificial duties and, instead, must perform the menial tasks of the sanctuary. Only the loyal Zadokites are to serve at the altar (Ezek. 44:10ff.). Still later we hear for the first time that Zadok was a descendant of Aaron and of his oldest surviving son Eleazar (Ezra 7:2ff.; I Chron. 5:27ff.).

On the basis of these facts, many modern scholars have concluded that there was no distinction between the terms "priest" and "Levite" prior to the reform of King Josiah in 621 B.C.E. [1]. This reform, based on the Book of Deuteronomy, abolished all the local shrines (see Deut. 12; II Kings 22 and 23). The Deuteronomic Code (19:6ff.) promised that the priests who were deprived of office by the reform might become part of the regular Temple priesthood. But, say these scholars, the Zadokite priests, resident in Jerusalem, were able to resist this provision; they retained priestly rank for themselves and assigned a lesser rank to the newcomers. The latter became known as (nonpriestly) Levites; the Zadokite priests eventually claimed to be descendants of Aaron. And the priestly writings asserted that the distinction between priest and Levite went back to the Mosaic age.

This rather plausible theory has been attacked with considerable effectiveness by Yehezkel Kaufmann. But his own reconstruction of the history of the priesthood [2] is likewise open to criticism. In any case, the evolution must have been a long and complicated process [3].

3. *During the Second Temple*

After the return from Babylon and the rebuilding of the Temple, the priests attained greater power and prestige than at any other time before or since. There was no longer a Davidic king, and so the High Priest became the chief representative of the Jews in dealings with the great empires that successively ruled Palestine. In addition to their importance as religious officiants and political leaders, the priests were also recognized as the custodians and teachers of Torah. They constituted an aristocracy, and it was considered a high honor for Israelites to marry into a priestly family.

But qualifications for religious leadership are not always transmitted from father to son; and wealth, position, and power often corrupt those who possess them. In the days of the mad Syrian tyrant Antiochus IV (second century B.C.E.), many priests supported his effort to impose Greek customs and rites upon Jewish life; and the high priesthood fell into the hands of scoundrels who bribed and flattered the king.

But it was also priests who led the revolt against Syrian oppression—the famed Mattathias and his five sons. These Hasmoneans won the devoted support of the people. But, after the victory was won, Simon the Maccabee assumed the high priesthood, though he was not of the high priestly family, and his far from pious successors on the

throne also held the office. This greatly troubled loyal spirits. And the later Hasmonean rulers estranged the people still more by their tyranny and their intrigues.

Meantime, a new popular leadership emerged. Laymen who were respected for their learning and fervor began to challenge the spiritual authority of the priests. The laymen constituted a party which came to be known as the Pharisees (Hebrew *perushim*, "separatists," cf. commentary on 19:2). They interpreted the Torah in a democratic, humane, and often progressive manner. The priestly party came to be known as Sadducees (from their supposed ancestor Zadok/Sadok); their approach to the Torah was conservative and severe.

Not all priests were Sadducees, and not all laymen Pharisees. (In today's America, many working men are conservative and some wealthy people are Communists.) Nor did the Pharisees seek to deny the priests their position and their perquisites; they were, in fact, sticklers about paying tithes. What the Pharisees did challenge was the exclusive prerogative of the priests to interpret the Torah; and so greatly did they win popular support that in the last years of the Second Temple the priests had to perform the cult according to Pharisaic rulings (see introduction to Lev. 16, "4. The Hazards of the Yom Kippur Service").

4. *In Later Centuries*

The destruction of the Temple left the priests with little to do. The Sadducean party ceased to exist [4]. But persons of priestly origin continued to cherish the memory of their high descent. They observed many of the restrictive laws contained in our present chapters, and they were accorded certain honors by the community.

Among traditional Jews up to the present, those of priestly and Levitic descent have special rights and obligations. When the Torah is read in the synagogue, the blessing over the first subsection is recited by a *kohen*, "priest," if any such is present. The blessing for the second section is assigned to a *Levi*, "Levite." On holidays, the *kohanim* ascend the pulpit, raise their hands, and bless the congregation, in conformity with Numbers 6:22ff. Before they commence this ceremony, they leave the sanctuary to prepare themselves, and the *Levi'im* attend upon them and pour water over their hands. (Hence the tombstone of a *kohen* often bears the symbol of hands outstretched for blessing; that of a *Levi* shows a pitcher and towel.) The custom of redeeming a firstborn son (*pidyon ha-ben*) requires that a sum equivalent to five shekels of silver be given to a *kohen* by the father of the child (see Exod. 13:13).

The name *kohen* in all its forms (Cohen, Cohn, Kohn, Kagan, and others) is very common among Jews, but not all those who bear the name possess a family tradition that they are *kohanim* in fact. And many *kohanim* have nondistinctive names. The same thing applies in the case of the name Levy (Levi, Lewy, Halevy) [5].

Reform Judaism regards these distinctions, based on birth, as no longer meaningful.

5. *The Laws in Chapters 21 and 22*

This section includes a number of provisions we have already met elsewhere, here repeated or elaborated. The ancient rabbis were able to derive new legal details from these repetitions; to us, they are rather indications that the editors of Leviticus drew upon a variety of traditions and documents.

The chief new laws are the following:

a. The most severe ritual defilement is that caused by a corpse (see introduction to Lev. 11:24-47; Num. 19). It is not a sin for the ordinary Jew to defile himself by such contact, which results from the religious duty of

burying the dead or visiting the cemetery. But the priests were required to avoid such contamination. To this day, a traditional Jew who is a *kohen* will not enter a cemetery or a house where there is a corpse. The Torah makes an exception in the case of close relatives; but there are no exceptions for the High Priest who may not attend the funeral even of his own parents (21:1–4, 10–12).

b. A *kohen* may not marry a woman of bad reputation or a divorcée even of the best character. (The halachah expands this rule somewhat.) The High Priest is also forbidden to marry a widow (21:7–8, 13–15).

c. The daughter of a priest who commits an immoral act is to be burned to death (21:9). The halachah limits this rule to the case of adultery.

d. A number of physical defects are enumerated which disqualify a priest from officiating at the altar; but such persons are assigned a share of the sacrificial meats and other perquisites (21:16–24).

e. Certain of the sacred donations are explicitly set aside for consumption by priestly males (above, 6:16, 29). The other gifts may be eaten by all the permanent members of a priest's household, including slaves, but not by temporary employees. A priest's daughter who marries a layman may no longer share the sacred food; but, if she is widowed or divorced and has no children, she may resume her former status (22:10–16).

f. The physical defects that render an animal unfit for sacrifice are listed (22:17–25). In this connection, the practice of castration is categorically prohibited (verse 24). No animal is to be sacrificed until it is at least eight days old; an animal and its young are not to be sacrificed on the same day.

The conclusion of this section has been interpreted by tradition as the classic source for the duty of martyrdom.

(A new weekly portion, *Emor*, begins with 21:1.)

פ פ פ

א וַיֹּאמֶר יְהוָה אֶל־מֹשֶׁה אֱמֹר אֶל־הַכֹּהֲנִים בְּנֵי אַהֲרֹן

לֵאלֹהֵיהֶם וְלֹא יְחַלְּלוּ שֵׁם אֱלֹהֵיהֶם כִּי אֶת־אִשֵּׁי ב וְאָמַרְתָּ אֲלֵהֶם לְנֶפֶשׁ לֹא־יִטַּמָּא בְּעַמָּיו: כִּי אִם־

יְהוָה לֶחֶם אֱלֹהֵיהֶם הֵם מַקְרִיבִם וְהָיוּ קֹדֶשׁ: לִשְׁאֵרוֹ הַקָּרֹב אֵלָיו לְאִמּוֹ וּלְאָבִיו וְלִבְנוֹ וּלְבִתּוֹ

ז אִשָּׁה זֹנָה וַחֲלָלָה לֹא יִקָּחוּ וְאִשָּׁה גְּרוּשָׁה מֵאִישָׁהּ לֹא ג וּלְאָחִיו: וְלַאֲחֹתוֹ הַבְּתוּלָה הַקְּרוֹבָה אֵלָיו אֲשֶׁר לֹא־

יִקָּחוּ כִּי־קָדֹשׁ הוּא לֵאלֹהָיו: וְקִדַּשְׁתּוֹ כִּי אֶת־לֶחֶם ד הָיְתָה לְאִישׁ לָהּ יִטַּמָּא: לֹא יִטַּמָּא בַּעַל בְּעַמָּיו

אֱלֹהֶיךָ הוּא מַקְרִיב קָדֹשׁ יִהְיֶה־לָּךְ כִּי קָדוֹשׁ אֲנִי ה לְהֵחַלּוֹ: לֹא־יִקְרְחֻה קָרְחָה בְּרֹאשָׁם וּפְאַת זְקָנָם לֹא

יְהוָה מְקַדִּשְׁכֶם: וּבַת אִישׁ כֹּהֵן כִּי תֵחֵל לִזְנוֹת אֶת־ ו יְגַלֵּחוּ וּבִבְשָׂרָם לֹא יִשְׂרְטוּ שָׂרָטֶת: קְדֹשִׁים יִהְיוּ

י אָבִיהָ הִיא מְחַלֶּלֶת בָּאֵשׁ תִּשָּׂרֵף: ס וְהַכֹּהֵן הַגָּדוֹל

* ה יקרחו קרי.

1] The LORD said to Moses: Speak to the priests, the sons of Aaron, and say to them: None shall defile himself for any [dead] person among his kin, **2]** except for the relatives that are closest to him: his mother, his father, his son, his daughter, and his brother; **3]** also for a virgin sister, close to him because she has not married, for her he may defile himself. **4]** But he shall not defile himself as a kinsman by marriage, and so profane himself.

5] They shall not shave smooth any part of their heads, or cut the side-growth of their beards, or make gashes in their flesh. **6]** They shall be holy to their God and not profane the name of their God; for they offer the LORD's offerings by fire, the food of their God, and so must be holy.

7] They shall not marry a woman degraded by harlotry, nor shall they marry one divorced from her husband. For they are holy to their God **8]** and you must treat them as holy, since they offer the food of your God; they shall be holy to you, for I the LORD who sanctify you am holy.

9] When the daughter of a priest degrades herself through harlotry, it is her father whom she degrades; she shall be put to the fire.

21:2] *Relatives.* Heb. *she'ero,* literally, "his flesh."

3] *May defile himself.* See Gleanings.

4] *As a kinsman by marriage.* Literally, "as a husband among his kin"; meaning uncertain (T.N.). This rendering suggests: He is to defile himself only for certain blood relations, not for "in-laws." But *baal,* here rendered "husband," can also mean "lord, ruler"; and the verse could thus mean, "Being a lord (a man of high dignity), he shall not defile himself" [6].

5] See above, 19:27–28 and Deuteronomy 14:1, where these prohibitions apply to all Israelites. Perhaps the law was originally for priests only and, as the concept of the holy people developed, all Israelites adopted it.

6] *The food of their God.* The words were hardly meant in a literal sense by the author of Leviticus. But to preclude misunderstanding, the Targum substitutes the word "offerings" for "food."

8] *You must treat them as holy.* Yet this verse also affirms the holiness of all Israel: *I the* LORD *... sanctify you.*

9] *When the daughter of a priest degrades herself through harlotry.* The plain sense is that any act of unchastity by the daughter of a priest is punishable by a fiery death; other women were subject to death only for adultery and for what were considered perverted acts (above, 20:10–16). But the halachah limited the present rule to cases of adultery; see Gleanings.

מֵאֶחָיו אֲשֶׁר־יוּצַק עַל־רֹאשׁוֹ שֶׁמֶן הַמִּשְׁחָה וּמִלֵּא
אֶת־יָדוֹ לִלְבֹּשׁ אֶת־הַבְּגָדִים אֶת־רֹאשׁוֹ לֹא יִפְרָע
יא וּבְגָדָיו לֹא יִפְרֹם: וְעַל כָּל־נַפְשֹׁת מֵת לֹא יָבֹא
יב לְאָבִיו וּלְאִמּוֹ לֹא יִטַּמָּא: וּמִן־הַמִּקְדָּשׁ לֹא יֵצֵא וְלֹא
יְחַלֵּל אֵת מִקְדַּשׁ אֱלֹהָיו כִּי נֵזֶר שֶׁמֶן מִשְׁחַת אֱלֹהָיו
יג עָלָיו אֲנִי יְהֹוָה: וְהוּא אִשָּׁה בִבְתוּלֶיהָ יִקָּח: אַלְמָנָה
יד וּגְרוּשָׁה וַחֲלָלָה זֹנָה אֶת־אֵלֶּה לֹא יִקָּח כִּי אִם־בְּתוּלָה
טו מֵעַמָּיו יִקַּח אִשָּׁה: וְלֹא־יְחַלֵּל זַרְעוֹ בְּעַמָּיו כִּי אֲנִי
טז יְהֹוָה מְקַדְּשׁוֹ: ס וַיְדַבֵּר יְהֹוָה אֶל־מֹשֶׁה לֵּאמֹר:
יז דַּבֵּר אֶל־אַהֲרֹן לֵאמֹר אִישׁ מִזַּרְעֲךָ לְדֹרֹתָם אֲשֶׁר

יח יִהְיֶה בוֹ מוּם לֹא יִקְרַב לְהַקְרִיב לֶחֶם אֱלֹהָיו: כִּי
כָל־אִישׁ אֲשֶׁר־בּוֹ מוּם לֹא יִקְרָב אִישׁ עִוֵּר אוֹ פִסֵּחַ
יט אוֹ חָרֻם אוֹ שָׂרוּעַ: אוֹ אִישׁ אֲשֶׁר־יִהְיֶה בוֹ שֶׁבֶר רָגֶל
כ אוֹ שֶׁבֶר יָד: אוֹ־גִבֵּן אוֹ־דַק אוֹ תְּבַלֻּל בְּעֵינוֹ אוֹ גָרָב
כא אוֹ יַלֶּפֶת אוֹ מְרוֹחַ אָשֶׁךְ: כָּל־אִישׁ אֲשֶׁר־בּוֹ מוּם
מִזֶּרַע אַהֲרֹן הַכֹּהֵן לֹא יִגַּשׁ לְהַקְרִיב אֶת־אִשֵּׁי יְהֹוָה
כב מוּם בּוֹ אֵת לֶחֶם אֱלֹהָיו לֹא יִגַּשׁ לְהַקְרִיב: לֶחֶם
כג אֱלֹהָיו מִקָּדְשֵׁי הַקֳּדָשִׁים וּמִן־הַקֳּדָשִׁים יֹאכֵל: אַךְ
אֶל־הַפָּרֹכֶת לֹא יָבֹא וְאֶל־הַמִּזְבֵּחַ לֹא יִגַּשׁ כִּי־מוּם
בּוֹ וְלֹא יְחַלֵּל אֶת־מִקְדָּשַׁי כִּי אֲנִי יְהֹוָה מְקַדְּשָׁם:

10] The priest who is exalted above his fellows, on whose head the anointing oil has been poured and who has been ordained to wear the vestments, shall not bare his head or rend his vestments. 11] He shall not go in where there is any dead body; he shall not defile himself even for his father or mother. 12] He shall not go outside the sanctuary and profane the sanctuary of his God, for upon him is the distinction of the anointing oil of his God, Mine the LORD's. 13] He may marry only a woman who is a virgin. 14] A widow, or a divorced woman, or one who is degraded by harlotry—such he may not marry. Only a virgin of his own kin may he take to wife— 15] that he may not profane his offspring among his kin, for I the LORD have sanctified him.

16] The LORD spoke further to Moses: 17] Speak to Aaron and say: No man of your offspring throughout the ages who has a defect shall be qualified to offer the food of his God; 18] no one at all who has a defect shall be qualified: no man who is blind, or lame, or has a limb too short or too long; 19] no man who has a broken leg or a broken arm; 20] or who is a hunchback, or a dwarf, or who has a growth in his eye, or who has a boil-scar, or scurvy, or crushed testes. 21] No man among the offspring of Aaron the priest who has a defect shall be qualified to offer the LORD's offerings by fire; having a defect, he shall not be qualified to offer the food of his God. 22] He may eat of the food of his God, of the most holy as well as of the holy; 23] but he shall not enter behind the curtain or come near the altar, for he has a defect. He shall not profane these places sacred to Me, for I the LORD have sanctified them.

10] *The priest who is exalted.* Heb. *gadol,* "great." Occasionally in the Bible, and regularly in postbiblical literature, he is called *Kohen Gadol,* "High Priest."

Bare his head. See T.N. at 10:6 (T.N.).

12] *He shall not go outside the sanctuary.* To attend a funeral. The High Priest was not a lifelong prisoner in the Temple.

18] *Has a limb too short.* So Ibn Ezra. But Heb. *charum* is of uncertain meaning. Sifra explains: "flat-nosed" [7].

20] *Hunchback or dwarf.* These renderings, too, are far from certain, though widely adopted. Sifra understands them as referring to abnormal conditions of the eye.

23] *He shall not enter behind the curtain.* Cf. 16:1ff.

913

כד וַיְדַבֵּ֣ר מֹשֶׁ֗ה אֶֽל־אַהֲרֹ֛ן וְאֶל־בָּנָ֖יו וְאֶל־כָּל־בְּנֵ֥י
יִשְׂרָאֵֽל׃ פ

א וַיְדַבֵּ֥ר יְהוָ֖ה אֶל־מֹשֶׁ֥ה לֵּאמֹֽר׃ דַּבֵּ֨ר אֶֽל־אַהֲרֹ֜ן וְאֶל־
ב בָּנָ֗יו וְיִנָּֽזְרוּ֙ מִקָּדְשֵׁ֣י בְנֵֽי־יִשְׂרָאֵ֔ל וְלֹ֥א יְחַלְּל֖וּ אֶת־שֵׁ֣ם
ג קָדְשִׁ֑י אֲשֶׁ֣ר הֵ֥ם מַקְדִּשִׁ֖ים לִ֑י אֲנִ֖י יְהוָֽה׃ אֱמֹ֣ר אֲלֵהֶ֗ם
לְדֹרֹ֨תֵיכֶ֜ם כָּל־אִ֣ישׁ ׀ אֲשֶׁר־יִקְרַ֣ב מִכָּל־זַרְעֲכֶ֗ם אֶל־
הַקֳּדָשִׁ֞ים אֲשֶׁ֨ר יַקְדִּ֥ישׁוּ בְנֵֽי־יִשְׂרָאֵל֘ לַֽיהוָה֒ וְטֻמְאָת֣וֹ
ד עָלָ֔יו וְנִכְרְתָ֞ה הַנֶּ֤פֶשׁ הַהִוא֙ מִלְּפָנַ֣י אֲנִ֖י יְהוָֽה׃ אִ֣ישׁ
אִ֞ישׁ מִזֶּ֣רַע אַהֲרֹ֗ן וְה֤וּא צָר֙וּעַ֙ א֣וֹ זָ֔ב בַּקֳּדָשִׁים֙ לֹ֣א
יֹאכַ֔ל עַ֖ד אֲשֶׁ֣ר יִטְהָ֑ר וְהַנֹּגֵ֙עַ֙ בְּכָל־טְמֵא־נֶ֔פֶשׁ א֣וֹ

ה אִ֣ישׁ אֲשֶׁר־תֵּצֵ֥א מִמֶּ֖נּוּ שִׁכְבַת־זָ֑רַע׃ אֽוֹ־אִישׁ֙ אֲשֶׁ֣ר יִגַּ֣ע
בְּכָל־שֶׁ֗רֶץ אֲשֶׁ֣ר יִטְמָא־ל֑וֹ א֤וֹ בְאָדָם֙ אֲשֶׁ֣ר יִטְמָא־ל֔וֹ
ו לְכֹ֖ל טֻמְאָתֽוֹ׃ נֶ֚פֶשׁ אֲשֶׁ֣ר תִּגַּע־בּ֔וֹ וְטָֽמְאָ֖ה עַד־הָעָ֑רֶב
ז וְלֹ֤א יֹאכַל֙ מִן־הַקֳּדָשִׁ֔ים כִּ֥י אִם־רָחַ֥ץ בְּשָׂר֖וֹ בַּמָּֽיִם׃
וּבָ֣א הַשֶּׁ֔מֶשׁ וְטָהֵ֑ר וְאַחַר֙ יֹאכַ֣ל מִן־הַקֳּדָשִׁ֔ים כִּ֥י
ח לַחְמ֖וֹ הֽוּא׃ נְבֵלָ֤ה וּטְרֵפָה֙ לֹ֣א יֹאכַ֔ל לְטָמְאָה־בָ֑הּ
ט אֲנִ֖י יְהוָֽה׃ וְשָׁמְר֣וּ אֶת־מִשְׁמַרְתִּ֗י וְלֹֽא־יִשְׂא֤וּ עָלָיו֙ חֵ֔טְא
י וּמֵ֥תוּ ב֖וֹ כִּ֣י יְחַלְּלֻ֑הוּ אֲנִ֥י יְהוָ֖ה מְקַדְּשָֽׁם׃ וְכָל־זָ֖ר לֹא־
יֹ֣אכַל קֹ֑דֶשׁ תּוֹשַׁ֥ב כֹּהֵ֛ן וְשָׂכִ֖יר לֹא־יֹ֥אכַל קֹֽדֶשׁ׃
יא וְכֹהֵ֗ן כִּֽי־יִקְנֶ֥ה נֶ֙פֶשׁ֙ קִנְיַ֣ן כַּסְפּ֔וֹ ה֖וּא יֹ֣אכַל בּ֑וֹ וִילִ֥יד

24] Thus Moses spoke to Aaron and his sons and to all the Israelites.

1] The LORD spoke to Moses, saying: **2]** Instruct Aaron and his sons to be scrupulous about the sacred donations that the Israelite people consecrate to Me, lest they profane My holy name, Mine the LORD's. **3]** Say to them:

Throughout the ages, if any man among your offspring, while in a state of uncleanness, partakes of any sacred donation that the Israelite people may consecrate to the LORD, that person shall be cut off from before Me: I am the LORD. **4]** No man of Aaron's offspring who has an eruption or a discharge shall eat of the sacred donations until he is clean. If one touches anything made unclean by a corpse, or if a man has an emission of semen, **5]** or if a man touches any swarming thing by which he is made unclean or any human being by whom he is made unclean—whatever his uncleanness— **6]** the person who touches such shall be unclean until evening and shall not eat of the sacred donations unless he has washed his body in water. **7]** As soon as the sun sets, he shall be clean; and afterward he may eat of the sacred donations, for they are his food. **8]** He shall not eat anything that died or was torn by beasts, thereby becoming unclean: I am the LORD. **9]** They shall keep My charge, lest they incur guilt thereby and die for it, having committed profanation: I the LORD consecrate them.

10] No lay person shall eat of the sacred donations. No bound or hired laborer of a priest shall eat of the sacred donations; **11]** but a person who is a priest's property by purchase may

---

22:2] *Sacred donations.* The portions of sacrifices assigned to the priests, as well as other dues enumerated in Numbers 18:8ff. Meal offerings, sin offerings, and guilt offerings could be eaten only by males of the priestly order (6:11, 22; 7:6); the other sacred donations were shared by their households.

3] *Cut off.* As in 7:20.

4] For laws of uncleanness, see chapters 13, 15 (T.N.).

Touches anything made unclean by a corpse. Or "anyone."

8] *Anything that died or was torn by beasts.* Ezekiel

44:31 likewise states this as a rule for priests. But Exodus 22:30 and Deuteronomy 14:21 impose the prohibition on all Israel (cf. Lev. 11:39; 17:15). This is apparently another case where the entire people adopted a rule of holiness originally intended for the priesthood; cf. on 21:5.

10] *Bound or hired laborer.* The bound laborer (Heb. *toshav,* "sojourner") is most probably the "Hebrew slave" of Exodus 21:2ff. See Gleanings. Since the bound and hired laborers are not permanent members of the household, they may not eat of the sacred donations, although an out and out slave, the property of the priest (Lev. 25:44ff.), may do so.

914

בָּנָיו וְאֶל כָּל־בְּנֵי יִשְׂרָאֵל וְאָמַרְתָּ אֲלֵהֶם אִישׁ אִישׁ
מִבֵּית יִשְׂרָאֵל וּמִן־הַגֵּר בְּיִשְׂרָאֵל אֲשֶׁר יַקְרִיב קָרְבָּנוֹ
לְכָל־נִדְרֵיהֶם וּלְכָל־נִדְבוֹתָם אֲשֶׁר־יַקְרִיבוּ לַיהוָה
יט לְעֹלָה: לִרְצֹנְכֶם תָּמִים זָכָר בַּבָּקָר בַּכְּשָׂבִים
כ וּבָעִזִּים: כֹּל אֲשֶׁר־בּוֹ מוּם לֹא תַקְרִיבוּ כִּי־לֹא לְרָצוֹן
כא יִהְיֶה לָכֶם: וְאִישׁ כִּי־יַקְרִיב זֶבַח־שְׁלָמִים לַיהוָה
לְפַלֵּא־נֶדֶר אוֹ לִנְדָבָה בַּבָּקָר אוֹ בַצֹּאן תָּמִים יִהְיֶה
כב לְרָצוֹן כָּל־מוּם לֹא יִהְיֶה־בּוֹ: עַוֶּרֶת אוֹ שָׁבוּר אוֹ־
חָרוּץ אוֹ־יַבֶּלֶת אוֹ גָרָב אוֹ יַלֶּפֶת לֹא־תַקְרִיבוּ אֵלֶּה
לַיהוָה וְאִשֶּׁה לֹא־תִתְּנוּ מֵהֶם עַל־הַמִּזְבֵּחַ לַיהוָה:

יב בֵּיתוֹ הֵם יֹאכְלוּ בְלַחְמוֹ: וּבַת־כֹּהֵן כִּי תִהְיֶה לְאִישׁ
יג זָר הִוא בִּתְרוּמַת הַקֳּדָשִׁים לֹא תֹאכֵל: וּבַת־כֹּהֵן
כִּי תִהְיֶה אַלְמָנָה וּגְרוּשָׁה וְזֶרַע אֵין לָהּ וְשָׁבָה אֶל־
בֵּית אָבִיהָ כִּנְעוּרֶיהָ מִלֶּחֶם אָבִיהָ תֹּאכֵל וְכָל־זָר
יד לֹא־יֹאכַל בּוֹ: וְאִישׁ כִּי־יֹאכַל קֹדֶשׁ בִּשְׁגָגָה וְיָסַף
טו חֲמִשִׁיתוֹ עָלָיו וְנָתַן לַכֹּהֵן אֶת־הַקֹּדֶשׁ: וְלֹא יְחַלְּלוּ
אֶת־קָדְשֵׁי בְּנֵי יִשְׂרָאֵל אֵת אֲשֶׁר־יָרִימוּ לַיהוָה:
טז וְהִשִּׂיאוּ אוֹתָם עֲוֹן אַשְׁמָה בְּאָכְלָם אֶת־קָדְשֵׁיהֶם כִּי
אֲנִי יְהוָה מְקַדְּשָׁם: פ
יז וַיְדַבֵּר יְהוָה אֶל־מֹשֶׁה לֵּאמֹר: דַּבֵּר אֶל־אַהֲרֹן וְאֶל־

˚ י״נ סלרע

eat of them; and those that are born into his household may eat of his food. **12]** If a priest's daughter marries a layman, she may not eat of the sacred gifts; **13]** but if the priest's daughter is widowed or divorced and without offspring, and is back in her father's house as in her youth, she may eat of her father's food. No lay person may eat of it; **14]** but if a man eats of a sacred donation unwittingly, he shall pay the priest for the sacred donation, adding one fifth of its value. **15]** But [the priests] must not allow the Israelites to profane the sacred donations which they set aside for the LORD, **16]** or to incur guilt requiring a penalty payment, by eating such sacred donations: for it is I the LORD who make them sacred.

17] The LORD spoke to Moses, saying: **18]** Speak to Aaron and his sons, and to all the Israelite people, and say to them:

When any man of the house of Israel or of the strangers in Israel presents a burnt offering as his offering for any of the votive or any of the freewill offerings that they offer to the LORD, **19]** it must, to be acceptable in your favor, be a male without blemish, from cattle or sheep or goats. **20]** You shall not offer any that has a defect, for it will not be accepted in your favor.

21] And when a man offers, from the herd or the flock, a sacrifice of well-being to the LORD for an explicit vow or as a freewill offering, it must, to be acceptable, be without blemish: there must be no defect in it. **22]** Anything blind, or injured, or maimed, or with a wen, boil-scar, or scurvy—such you shall not offer to the LORD; you shall not put any of them on the altar

12] Cf. Numbers 18:19.

13] *And without offspring.* A child would constitute a tie with her husband's family.

14] *One fifth.* As in 5:14ff.

15] It is a responsibility of the priests to take such

precautions as will protect other Israelites from eating the sacred portions forbidden to them.

17–20] As in 1:1–3.

21] As in 3:1 and 6. In verse 22, the specific defects that disqualify the animal are listed.

Explicit. Or, "unspecified" or "extraordinary"; meaning of Hebrew *lefalé* uncertain (T.N.).

כג וְשׁוֹר וָשֶׂה שָׂרוּעַ וְקָלוּט נְדָבָה תַּעֲשֶׂה אֹתוֹ וּלְנֵדֶר

כד לֹא יֵרָצֶה: וּמָעוּךְ וְכָתוּת וְנָתוּק וְכָרוּת לֹא תַקְרִיבוּ

כה לַיהוָה וּבְאַרְצְכֶם לֹא תַעֲשׂוּ: וּמִיַּד בֶּן־נֵכָר לֹא

תַקְרִיבוּ אֶת־לֶחֶם אֱלֹהֵיכֶם מִכָּל־אֵלֶּה כִּי מָשְׁחָתָם

כו בָּהֶם מוּם בָּם לֹא יֵרָצוּ לָכֶם: ס וַיְדַבֵּר יְהוָה

כז אֶל־מֹשֶׁה לֵּאמֹר: שׁוֹר אוֹ־כֶשֶׂב אוֹ־עֵז כִּי יִוָּלֵד וְהָיָה

שִׁבְעַת יָמִים תַּחַת אִמּוֹ וּמִיּוֹם הַשְּׁמִינִי וָהָלְאָה יֵרָצֶה

כח לְקָרְבַּן אִשֶּׁה לַיהוָה: וְשׁוֹר אוֹ־שֶׂה אֹתוֹ וְאֶת־בְּנוֹ לֹא

כט תִשְׁחֲטוּ בְּיוֹם אֶחָד: וְכִי־תִזְבְּחוּ זֶבַח־תּוֹדָה לַיהוָה

ל לִרְצֹנְכֶם תִּזְבָּחוּ: בַּיּוֹם הַהוּא יֵאָכֵל לֹא־תוֹתִירוּ מִמֶּנּוּ

לא עַד־בֹּקֶר אֲנִי יְהוָה: וּשְׁמַרְתֶּם מִצְוֹתַי וַעֲשִׂיתֶם אֹתָם

לב אֲנִי יְהוָה: וְלֹא תְחַלְּלוּ אֶת־שֵׁם קָדְשִׁי וְנִקְדַּשְׁתִּי

לג בְּתוֹךְ בְּנֵי יִשְׂרָאֵל אֲנִי יְהוָה מְקַדִּשְׁכֶם: הַמּוֹצִיא

אֶתְכֶם מֵאֶרֶץ מִצְרַיִם לִהְיוֹת לָכֶם לֵאלֹהִים אֲנִי

יְהוָה: פ

as offerings by fire to the LORD.   23] You may, however, present as a freewill offering an ox or a sheep with a limb extended or contracted; but it will not be accepted for a vow.   24] You shall not offer to the LORD anything [with its testes] bruised or crushed or torn or cut. You shall have no such practices in your own land,   25] nor shall you accept such [animals] from a foreigner for offering as food for your God, for they are mutilated, they have a defect; they shall not be accepted in your favor.

26] The LORD spoke to Moses, saying: 27] When an ox or a sheep or a goat is born, it shall stay seven days with its mother, and from the eighth day on it shall be acceptable as an offering by fire to the LORD.   28] However, no animal from the herd or from the flock shall be slaughtered on the same day with its young.

29] When you sacrifice a thanksgiving offering to the LORD, sacrifice it so that it may be acceptable in your favor.   30] It shall be eaten on the same day; you shall not leave any of it until morning: I am the LORD.

31] You shall faithfully observe My commandments: I am the LORD.   32] You shall not profane My holy name, that I may be sanctified in the midst of the Israelite people—I the LORD who sanctify you,   33] I who brought you out of the land of Egypt to be your God, I the LORD.

23] This verse permits a slightly deformed animal to be used as a freewill offering, probably (but not certainly) to be offered as a sacrifice [8]. But it is the only exception to the otherwise invariable rule that sacrifices must be unblemished. The explanation given by the Rabbis is therefore not implausible—that this "freewill offering" is not to be put on the altar, but it is to be sold and the proceeds contributed to the sanctuary (Sifra). On vows and freewill offerings, see commentary on 7:16.

24] *You shall have no such practices in your own land.* I.e., mutilations (T.N.). The Hebrew wording is unusually terse; but the traditional interpretation, that the verse categorically forbids castration, is certainly correct.

26–28] Humane feeling forbids unnecessary cruelty to animals (on verse 28, cf. Deut. 22:6f.).

29–30] As in 7:15.

32] *You shall not profane My holy name.* See introduction to Lev. 19.

GLEANINGS

Halachah

21:1] *Among His Kin*

Sifra understands "his" to refer to the dead person. If the man dies among his kin, i.e., his fellow Jews, there will be someone to bury him. If, however, the priest should come upon the corpse of a Jew in a remote spot where no one else can give him proper burial, the priest would be obligated to do so even though he would become ceremonially unclean.

2] *His Relatives*

Hebrew "his flesh." This is taken to mean his wife who is not specifically mentioned in the list.

SIFRA

3] *May Defile Himself*

So Rabbi Ishmael understood. But Rabbi Akiba explained "*must* defile himself"—the priest is not merely permitted but required to take part in the funeral rites for the relatives mentioned. And so the halachah was decided [9].

7] *Degraded by Harlotry*

Hebrew *zonah va-chalalah*, literally, "a harlot and degraded." The *chalalah* is the offspring of one of the marriages forbidden in this verse, who is disqualified ("degraded") from marrying a priest (*Sifra*). *Zonah* is defined in highly technical terms to include women who for a variety of reasons may not marry a priest [10]. Priests are likewise forbidden to marry proselytes and freed slaves, who are permitted to marry other Jews.

One Divorced from Her Husband

Also one who has gone through the ceremony of *chalitzah* (see introduction to Lev. 18, "4. Incest").

For They Are Holy to Their God

And, if they contract one of these marriages, they become disqualified and lose their holiness.

8] *You Must Treat Them as Holy*

I.e., the community must, if necessary, compel the priests to preserve their status and to refrain from a disqualifying marriage.

9] *She Shall Be Put to the Fire*

See Gleanings to 20:14. Talmudic literature, however, preserved some recollection of a case when a woman was actually burned at the stake [11]. The halachah limited this law to a woman guilty of adultery. Ordinarily both parties to an adulterous union were to be punished by strangulation; but, if the woman was a betrothed virgin, her partner was to be stoned to death. If, in such case, the woman was of priestly birth, she also was to be stoned. If she was married and subject to burning, her paramour was to be strangled [12].

10] *Exalted*

The High Priest should excel his brothers in beauty, wealth, strength, wisdom, and appearance.

SIFRA

12] *He Shall Not Go outside the Sanctuary*

The High Priest may officiate in the Temple while a near relative is dead and not yet buried. Other priests may not do this; but from this verse the Rabbis deduce that no priest may leave the sanctuary without finishing a rite he has begun. If he does so, he deserves the death penalty. SIFRA

22:6–7] This rule applies only to the eating of *terumah*—nonsacrificial gifts of grain, wine, and oil received by the priests (Num. 18:12). Other sacred donations could not be eaten till the following day; and, where necessary (e.g., where 15:14f. applied), the defiled person also had to bring a purificatory offering [13].

10] *Bound [Laborer]*

According to the halachah, the "Hebrew slave" who chooses to remain in the household after his forced service is over (Exod. 21:5f.). SIFRA

23] *Contracted*

Hebrew *kalut*. According to *Sifra*, an animal whose cloven hoofs are fused so that they look like those of a horse.

24] *You Shall Have No Such Practices in Your Own Land*

Castration of men and animals is unconditionally forbidden. The phrase "in your land" does not limit the ban to the land of Israel; it implies "everything in your land," including unclean beasts. SIFRA

Haggadah

22:32] *You Shall Not Profane My Holy Name*

Though the context treats of ritual purity, tradition regarded this passage as the classical source for the law of martyrdom (see introduction to Lev. 19, "2. Sanctifying and Profaning the Name"). To prevent public profanation of God's name ("in the midst of the Israelite people"), the Jew should die rather than transgress even a minor commandment. He should offer himself unreservedly, without expectation of a miracle (Dan. 3:16ff.). Julianus and Pappus, two rebels against the Roman tyranny, were captured. The Roman officer who ordered their execution tauntingly asked them, "Why does your God not rescue you as He rescued Shadrach, Meshach, and Abed-nego?" They replied, "The three men were altogether worthy of a miracle and Nebuchadnezzar was a great king who deserved to be the instrument of a miracle. But you are a wicked ruler and do not merit such an honor, and we have incurred death for our sins. If you do not slay us, God has many other agents to punish us—lions and leopards, snakes and scorpions. But, in the end, you will be punished for our death." And the tale reports that, before the execution had taken place, orders arrived from Rome to put that officer to death. SIFRA

918

The Festival Calendar

An important feature of nearly every culture, and of nearly all religious systems, is a regular cycle of festivals and sacred occasions. These celebrations dramatize the ideals of the community and impart color and joy to its life. To most moderns, such festivals, however important and pleasurable, appear as creations of the group; their dates are fixed by custom or even by convenience. But, for ancient people (and some moderns as well), religious festivals were divinely ordained; it was urgently necessary to observe them exactly according to the god's commands and on the date he had fixed.

Festival observance is treated many times in the Torah. Short holiday calendars appear in Exodus (23:14–18 and 34:18–25) and there is a fuller statement in Deuteronomy (16:1–16). These passages speak only of the three "pilgrim festivals" [1]—Passover/Feast of Unleavened Bread, Feast of Weeks, and Feast of Booths. The present chapter lists also the New Year (though not by name) and the Day of Atonement. It is, then, the most complete biblical account of the holy days. It is supplemented in Numbers (28:1–30:1) by a detailed schedule of the sacrifices to be performed on each occasion. Moreover, Passover is discussed at length in Exodus, chapters 12 and 13, and Yom Kippur in Leviticus, chapter 16 [2].

The festivals are still of major importance to the Jews of today. They have, of course, changed greatly since biblical times. Sacrifice, the central feature of ancient worship, has long since disappeared, and many new forms of celebration have been introduced. More holidays have been added—Purim and Chanukah, the lesser occasions of Chamishah Asar Bi-Shevat and Lag Ba-Omer, and a series of fasts, notably the Ninth of Av. Here, however, we limit ourselves to the holy days commanded in the Torah and to the traditional interpretation of the biblical material [3].

1. Calendar Reckoning

Festivals have their place within some orderly reckoning of time periods. Even primitive peoples acquire some knowledge of practical astronomy. In ancient Egypt, and still more in Mesopotamia, astronomical studies were relatively advanced. And the Hebrews doubtlessly learned and borrowed much from their neighbors.

a. *The day.* Hebrew *yom*, like English "day," designates both the daylight hours and also what we call the civil day which includes nighttime [4]. The division of the day into twenty-four equal hours was probably unknown in Bible times; the night was divided into three or four watches. (In Mesopotamia, the day was divided into twelve double hours, varying in length according to the time of year.)

At what point did the civil day begin? There is some evidence that at one time the day was reckoned from sunrise to sunrise [5]. But, before the close of the biblical period, it had become standard to reckon the day from sunset to sunset, and this has been Jewish practice ever since. The Jewish day does not begin at a fixed hour—as, according to our secular practice, the civil day starts at midnight, regardless of the season. In winter, the Jewish day starts and ends earlier; in summer, later.

b. *The week.* Unlike the other units of time we are considering, the week does not clearly correspond to an astronomical phenomenon—though each phase of the moon lasts about seven days. The origin of the week has been the subject of much scholarly discussion, which has not led to many certain conclusions. So far as we know, a regular, uninterrupted cycle of seven-day units first appeared in Israel; but when and why it was introduced remains an unsettled problem. The week is certainly connected with the sacredness of the number seven and with the Sabbath. It came to the western world through Judaism and Christianity.

c. *Months and years.* As an astronomical concept, the year is the length of time in which the earth makes a circuit of the sun—a little over 365 days. Ancient peoples thought the sun moved around the earth, but they could still measure the year in terms of changing seasons, the series of equinoxes and solstices. In a calendar based on this solar year, such as the Gregorian calendar, the month is simply an arbitrary division, corresponding to no astronomical reality.

The true month (as the name, related to "moon," indicates) is the length of time in which the moon makes a circuit around the earth, readily measured from the appearance of one new moon to the next. It is a fraction over twenty-nine days; for practical purposes, therefore, lunar months are reckoned as alternately of twenty-nine and thirty days. Twelve such months add up to 354 days; a pure lunar system falls behind the sun about eleven days each year. In the Moslem calendar, which is such a system, the penitential month of Ramadan may occur at any season.

But the Israelite calendar, though it consists of lunar months, seems never to have had that character. The festivals were firmly anchored to the seasons of the agricultural year, with Passover in the spring and the Feast of Booths in the fall. There was then presumably some provision for adjusting the lunar and solar years to each other.

Centuries before the Christian era, the Babylonians had a lunisolar calendar. A watch was kept for the appearance of each new moon; when it was sighted, the king was notified, and he in turn sent orders to the temples for the proper rites to be performed. The king, moreover, would add an extra month to the year when his experts so advised, to keep the lunar calendar in balance with the solar year. As scientific knowledge advanced, the Babylonian astronomers worked out a scheme for the alternation of both twenty-nine-day and thirty-day months and for the insertion of an extra month seven times in each cyle of nineteen years. According to a recent study, this computed calendar was introduced about 481 B.C.E., after several centuries of experimentation [6].

Jewish procedure during the Second Commonwealth was much like the earlier Baby-

lonian practice. Witnesses appeared before the high court in Jerusalem to testify that they had seen the crescent moon; thereupon the court formally announced that a month had begun, and so it notified communities throughout the land by signal fires, later by messengers. Until such notice was received, people did not know whether the thirtieth day was the last of the old month or the first of the new. Diaspora Jews, who did not receive official notification, began to keep each of the sacred occasions for two days—Yom Kippur excepted—to be sure of observing them on the proper date.

The high court also determined when an extra month was to be added to the year. Their chief concern was: Would the first grain be ripe for cutting at Passover time? (See below in this introduction, "2. The Biblical Holy Days.") When necessary to assure this result, a leap year of thirteen months would be proclaimed [7].

In the fourth century C.E., the Palestinian authorities, headed by Hillel II, promulgated a mathematically computed calendar system, virtually identical with that which the Babylonians had adopted some seven centuries earlier [8]. This system, which is accurate to a high degree, is still standard in Jewish use today. It obviated the need for the two-day observance of holidays in the Diaspora; but the communities outside the land, at the advice of the Palestinian authorities, held on to their established practice, which continues among traditional Jews to the present. In the Land of Israel, the only occasion observed for two days is the Festival of the New Year [9]. Reform Judaism follows the one-day biblical rule.

d. *The names of the months.* Three ways of designating the months are found in the Bible. Most frequently, as in the present chapter, they are indicated by number. In this system, the first month is the spring month in which Passover falls.

At one time, however, the months had Hebrew or Canaanite names. At least four of them have survived. Most often mentioned is Abib (pronounced Aviv); the word means "fresh grain" and eventually acquired the general meaning "spring" (Exod. 13:4; Deut. 16:1; and elsewhere). Three other names in this series—Ziv, Bul, Ethanim—are mentioned in I Kings (6:37, 38 and 8:2).

In the Book of Esther, and sometimes in other late biblical books—Zechariah, Ezra, and Nehemiah—the ancient Babylonian month names are employed. In postbiblical times, this usage became standard and has continued to the present.

e. *Changes and controversies.* Tradition assumed that these changes of nomenclature were no more than that—that, whether the spring month was called Abib, first month, or Nisan, the calendar system was the same. Some modern scholars, too, hold this view. But there are many reasons for thinking that changes occurred also in the calendar system and in the order and character of some of the holidays. To try to trace the history of the calendar through the centuries would, however, be too complicated and hazardous an undertaking for us.

Only a few points may be noted. Our oldest document on the subject is the Gezer calendar, inscribed in old Hebrew letters on a clay tablet and said to date from the tenth century B.C.E. [10]. It is a sort of children's ditty, which does not name the months but indicates what agricultural work is performed in each of them. It starts with the olive harvest (September–October), and this may mean that the year was reckoned as beginning in the fall.

And, in fact, the day known for the last twenty centuries as the "New Year" does come in the fall; but our chapter (verse 24) locates it on the first day of the seventh month. Moreover, Exodus (12:1ff.) declares that the month of the Exodus is to be ob-

served as the first month of the year—and the emphatic language of the passage suggests that this was an innovation [11].

These data, then, suggest a shift from one calendar system to another. But the different possibility that two methods of reckoning existed side by side has also to be considered. Though the Babylonian new year was customarily celebrated in the spring, there are also reports of a similar observance in the autumn [12]. And an interesting argument has been made for the view that, in the northern kingdom the years of a king's reign were reckoned on the basis of a spring-to-spring year, while in the southern kingdom the reckoning was from fall to fall [13].

Some time during the Second Commonwealth, a sectarian group tried to introduce an entirely new—apparently solar—calendar; this attempt is recorded in two apocryphal books, Jubilees and I Enoch. These proposals seem to have influenced the group that produced the Dead Sea Scrolls, but they do not appear to have been put into practice [14].

On the controversy regarding the date of Shavuot, see "2. The Biblical Holy Days."

We should note that, though the calendar system apparently originated in Babylonia, it was adopted and promulgated by the Jewish leaders in Palestine, who claimed to hold exclusive authority in these matters. But persecution and poverty weakened the Palestinian community from the fourth century C.E. on, and the Babylonian schools became predominant in matters of halachah. Despite protests from the Land of Israel, the Babylonian scholars also regulated calendar matters. In the tenth century, a Palestinian leader named Ben Meir proposed certain departures from the usual system. In addition to substantive arguments for his position, he insisted that the regulation of the calendar was the exclusive prerogative of the Palestinian scholars. A violent conflict resulted. But eventually the authority of Babylonia

was upheld, largely through the efforts of a rising young scholar, Saadia ben Joseph, who was to become one of the greatest personalities in Jewish history [15]. Henceforth, there was no serious challenge to the accepted system. In his code of the law, Maimonides drew on the best scientific sources of his time to clarify and support the tradition.

f. *Eras*. We take it for granted that years shall be numbered consecutively from some fixed date which is thought to have marked an important starting point in history. Such fixed eras are a comparatively recent innovation. Perhaps the first of these was the Greek custom of counting from the first Olympiad, in 776 B.C.E. In earlier times, years were designated by names (as still in the traditional Chinese calendar), by names of persons who held office in successive years, or by the years of a king's reign. Biblical writers occasionally used the Exodus as a starting point for dates (e.g., I Kings 6:1).

In 312 B.C.E., a Greco-Syrian empire was established by Seleucus, one of the generals of Alexander the Great. That date was adopted throughout the Middle East as the fixed point for numbering years. This Seleucid era—the first instance of this sort—was used by Jews in legal and business documents long after Rome had swallowed up the Hellenistic states; and it was employed much later by some Oriental Jews, almost to the present.

Meantime, another scheme of chronology was developing—an attempt to date events from the creation of the world. Indications of this reckoning are found in rabbinic literature but it seems to have been accepted generally only in the tenth century C.E. This is the era presently used for Jewish religious purposes. It fixes the date of Creation as 3760 B.C.E. But, even from the Orthodox standpoint, no one is obligated to accept that date as literally correct. The universe, we agree,

is immeasurably older than such figures imply; but it is worth noting that urban civilization and recorded history did begin about four thousand years before the Christian era.

2. The Biblical Holy Days

a. *Sabbath*. See Exodus 20:8ff.

b. *Passover/Feast of Unleavened Bread*. See Exodus, chapters 12 and 13.

c. *The offering of the omer*. The Feast of Unleavened Bread was timed to coincide with the start of the grain harvest in the Land of Israel. Our chapter provides (verses 9–14) that the first grain to be cut shall be presented as a special offering at the sanctuary, together with an *olah* (the matter is mentioned nowhere else). None of the new crop may be eaten until this *omer* has been offered.

Three aspects of this law are extensively discussed in rabbinic literature. For the ruling that the offering was to be of barley and for the amount and form in which it was to be presented, see Gleanings.

Here, we must consider the heated controversy over the date when the *omer* is to be presented. According to verse 11, it is to be brought "on the day after the Sabbath." What does this mean? Jewish tradition answers: In this passage, *shabbat* means "rest day" and refers to the first day of the Matzot festival mentioned in the preceding verses. This explanation is found not only in talmudic sources but also in the Greek translation of the Torah (which here renders *shabbat* by "the first day"), Philo, and Josephus [16]. Evidently it is quite old.

But nowhere else is the term "*shabbat*" applied to a festival [17]. In this context it might well refer to the Sabbath of Passover week. A third possibility would be to identify it with the last day of the holiday.

The clarification of the point was important for two reasons. It determined when the grain harvest was to begin and especially how soon new grain could be eaten. And it fixed the date of the Feast of Weeks. For, according to verses 15 and 16, that festival was to be on the fiftieth day after the *omer* was brought. It seems that it was this second issue which led to a bitter controversy.

For there were those who insisted that *shabbat* here means the weekly Sabbath and that consequently Shavuot always falls on Sunday. This view is ascribed in talmudic literature to the Boethusians, a sect about which we have only scraps of information; apparently they were a subgroup of the Sadducees, the priestly conservatives. Probably all the Sadducees understood the verse in this way; the Karaites, who consider themselves heirs of the Sadducees, still observe Shavuot on Sunday.

The sectarian Book of Jubilees (see above, "1. Calendar Reckoning") [18], which proposes that Shavuot be celebrated on Sivan 15, clearly intended the fifty days to be counted from the last day of Passover. This procedure is also indicated in the Syriac translation of the Bible (made early in the Christian era) and is followed to this day in the practice of the Falashas—the black Jews of Ethiopia—who observe their "harvest festival" on the twelfth day of the third month [19].

Against both these interpretations, the Pharisees—the spiritual fathers of modern Judaism—upheld the view that the *shabbat* was the first day of Passover, that the *omer* must be brought the following day, Nisan 16, and that Shavuot need not fall on a Sunday. According to the present mathematical calendar, it always falls on Sivan 6. Prior to the fourth century C.E. (see "1. Calendar Reckoning"), it could fall on either the fifth, sixth, or seventh.

What motives lay behind the heated struggle of the Pharisees and Boethusians? We can only guess. No Sadducean or Boethusian documents survive. We know these sects only through their opponents. And the arguments in the Talmud for the Pharisaic

position are by no means conclusive. Orthodox scholars have understandably been at great pains to defend the tradition; Hoffmann devotes sixty pages of his commentary to the subject. Other modern scholars have been divided. Some regard the Boethusian exegesis as correct and assume that the Pharisees departed from the plain sense of the text for a purpose not stated; another view is that the Pharisees were preserving an age-old tradition from which the Boethusians tried to deviate for reasons of self-interest [20]. But none of the explanations of the controversy is entirely convincing.

d. *The omer period.* Both Leviticus (23:15ff.) and Deuteronomy (16:9–10) stress the obligation of counting off seven weeks from the formal start of the grain harvest. This biblical injunction is fulfilled literally in traditional Judaism by the ceremony of "counting the *omer.*" Each evening an appropriate benediction is pronounced, followed by the statement: "Today is the —— day of the *omer.*" This observance is also incorporated in the daily evening service of the synagogue.

The entire period from Pesach to Shavuot is known as the *omer* (or *sefirah,* "counting") period. In the course of centuries it has acquired associations that have no background in biblical law. Traditional Jews do not marry during this period, which is said to be one of mourning for persecutions that occurred in the spring. (But at what season of the year have persecutions not taken place?) Most probably this custom goes back to ancient superstitions. Also rooted in folklore are the more cheerful practices on the thirty-third day, Lag Ba-Omer [21].

e. *The Feast of Weeks (Shavuot).* This name is found in Exodus (34:22) and Deuteronomy (16:9). Exodus, chapter 23, verse 16, calls the occasion "the Feast of the Harvest," and in our chapter it is not given a name [22]. In the Talmud it is referred to as *Atzeret,* a word rendered "solemn gathering" in Leviticus (23:36) where it refers to the final day of the fall festival [23]. This name has also been explained as "closing feast." The Rabbis no doubt had that explanation in mind when they spoke of Shavuot as "the Atzeret of Pesach" [24]—thereby stressing the connection between the two festivals, one marking the beginning, the other the climax of the grain harvest.

The Bible describes Shavuot only as an agricultural festival. Later tradition regards it as the anniversary of the giving of the Torah at Sinai. According to Exodus, chapter 19, the revelation occurred early in the third month; but an explicit identification of the festival as anniversary of the revelation is not found until well after the beginning of the Christian era [25]. Thereafter, the stress on the historical meaning of the holiday overshadowed the agricultural aspect. The latter survived only in the custom of decorating the synagogue with greens and flowers. The prayers and hymns of Shavuot all glorify the Torah. And the occasion was fittingly chosen by Reform Jews for the ceremony of confirmation, at which the pledge of Sinai is renewed.

f. *Festival of the New Year (Rosh Hashanah).* For the past two thousand years, Jews have called the first day of the seventh month Rosh Hashanah, literally "the beginning of the year." But that name is not used in the Torah. Numbers (29:1) calls the occasion "the day of *teruah*" (we shall see shortly what that term means). Leviticus (23:24) calls it a "remembrance [or commemoration] of *teruah.*" In the prayer book, its usual name is the Day of Remembrance (*Yom ha-Zikaron*) [26].

The expression "*rosh hashanah*" occurs just once in the Bible—in Ezekiel (40:1), followed by the words "on the tenth day of the month" (presumably the seventh month). To avoid the obvious difficulty, the phrase

924

has usually been rendered "at the beginning of the year" rather than "on the new year." But this customary translation is questionable; the Talmud forthrightly asserts that the reference is to a jubilee year which was formally inaugurated on Yom Kippur (Lev. 25:9) [27]. The critical scholar is likely to conclude rather that Ezekiel's festival calendar differed significantly from that of Leviticus.

New year festivals were well known in the ancient Near East. In Babylonia, the new year was celebrated with great pomp and the statues of the gods were carried in procession through the city. On that day the god Marduk and other deities were said to ascend their thrones and to decree the destinies of men for the coming year. A number of modern scholars have attempted to reconstruct an ancient Israelite new year festival on the Babylonian model, citing such passages as Psalms 47, 81, and 98. And, indeed, the prayers of Rosh Hashanah still stress the kingship of God and the idea of a universal judgment. But the attempt to connect all this with prebiblical new year observances is hardly more than ingenious speculation. The Bible itself tells us little about the celebration of the first day of the seventh month.

The word "teruah" means "a loud noise"; it may be a shout (I Sam. 4:5) or it may be a blast of the ram's horn (shofar). A very ancient tradition calls for the blowing of the horn at our festival; accordingly, yom teruah (Num. 29:1) is translated in our version by "a day when the horn is sounded" and zichron teruah (Lev. 23:24) by "commemorated with loud blasts." The two phrases probably mean the same thing, but see Gleanings. In current usage, moreover, teruah denotes a throbbing blast, a kind of trill, in contrast to tekiah, a plain blast, and shevarim, a series of three short notes.

The silence of the older festival calendars about the High Holy Days and the vagueness of the statements about Rosh Hashanah even in Leviticus do not prove that these occasions were unknown before the Babylonian exile. Very probably the Festival of the New Year and the Day of Atonement rites were part of the great fall festival we now call Sukot and were included in the general commandment for that celebration. Later, these ceremonies were detached from the harvest festival and assigned to special days preceding Sukot.

The magnificent prayers and stirring ceremonies of our present new year observance are, like those of Yom Kippur, a creation of the Jewish people over many centuries.

g. *The Day of Atonement.* See chapter 16.

h. *The Feast of Booths (Sukot).* This name is found here and in Deuteronomy, chapter 16. Exodus, chapters 23 and 34, calls the autumn festival the "Feast of Ingathering." In Numbers, chapter 29, it is simply "a festival of the LORD"; and in the Talmud it is called the *Chag,* the festival par excellence [28]. It marked the close of the agricultural year, specifically of the vintage. And on the second day of the festival, ceremonies were performed—they are not mentioned in the Bible, but they were undoubtedly ancient— to evoke plentiful rains in the new agricultural season about to start. The *Chag* was an expression of grateful joy and a plea for continued blessing.

The booth is still to be seen in the Near East in a utilitarian and nonreligious context. It is a shelter built in the fields so that workers can rest, protected from the midday sun, without returning to their homes. At the height of the harvest, workers can also spend the night in the booth so as to speed up their work and finish it before the beginning of the fall rain. The ceremonial use of the sukah seems to have arisen from this custom. Later, the booth was explained as a memorial of the desert period, when the Israelites lived in frail shelters. Interestingly,

the first halt that Israel made after leaving Egypt was at a place called Succoth (Exod. 12:37).

Also characteristic of the feast are the four plants that are combined into a sort of bouquet (Lev. 23:40), the *etrog* (citron) and *lulav* (palm branch), myrtle and willow. The Karaites, who rejected talmudic tradition, understood the verse as referring to materials for the construction of the sukah; and historically they may have been right [29]. But the traditional explanation is very old. The citron and palm branch appear on Maccabean coins (about 100 B.C.E.), and so they were evidently a well-known Jewish symbol by that time.

i. *Shemini Atzeret.* The eighth (*shemini*) day of Sukot is singled out for mention in verse 36; but the point is not clear. If *atzeret* means "a solemn gathering," why is the term applied only to the last day and not also to the first day of the festival? The Talmud [30] discusses the question whether this day is a separate feast or only the conclusion of Sukot. In the traditional synagogue, moreover, the day preceding Shemini Atzeret, known as Hoshana Rabbah ("Great Hosanna"), is marked by a return to the penitential mood of Yom Kippur. These facts lend support to the view mentioned above—that the Festival of New Year and the Day of Atonement rites were originally performed at the close of the fall festival. Even after

they were transferred to their present place in the calendar, some memories of the original order survived.

Outside Israel, Shemini Atzeret also was observed for two days; and, in Babylonia, the ninth day was celebrated as Simchat Torah, the Feast of Rejoicing over the Law. On this day the annual cycle of Torah reading was completed and begun again. (In Palestine, the reading was completed only once in three years). Simchat Torah eventually became a more meaningful occasion than the biblical Shemini Atzeret, with characteristic and happy customs of its own. Reform Jewish practice has transferred some of these ceremonies to Shemini Atzeret, thus making one festival of Shemini Atzeret and Simchat Torah.

j. *New moon.* The present chapter does not discuss the celebration of the new moon; but the supplementary section enumerates the additional sacrifices for the "New Moon" day (Num. 28:11ff.). At one time, it seems, the new moon was an occasion that ranked in importance with the Sabbath (Isa. 1:13f.; Amos 8:5). Evidently our author considered it a minor occasion. In traditional Judaism, it is marked by extra prayers but not by abstention from work. Further, the advent of the new moon is solemnly announced in the synagogue on the preceding Sabbath; and a benediction is recited when the new crescent is seen.

See also commentary on Deut. 16 ("The Pilgrim Festivals in Contemporary Observance") and on Num. 28:1–30:17 ("Moon and Calendar").

ד אֵ֚לֶּה מוֹעֲדֵ֣י יְהֹוָ֔ה מִקְרָאֵ֖י קֹ֑דֶשׁ אֲשֶׁר־תִּקְרְא֥וּ אֹתָ֖ם
בְּמוֹעֲדָֽם: ה בַּחֹ֣דֶשׁ הָרִאשׁ֗וֹן בְּאַרְבָּעָ֥ה עָשָׂ֛ר לַחֹ֖דֶשׁ
בֵּ֣ין הָעַרְבָּ֑יִם פֶּ֖סַח לַיהֹוָֽה: ו וּבַחֲמִשָּׁ֨ה עָשָׂ֥ר יוֹם֙ לַחֹ֣דֶשׁ
הַזֶּ֔ה חַ֥ג הַמַּצּ֖וֹת לַיהֹוָ֑ה שִׁבְעַ֥ת יָמִ֖ים מַצּ֥וֹת תֹּאכֵֽלוּ:
ז בַּיּוֹם֙ הָֽרִאשׁ֔וֹן מִקְרָא־קֹ֖דֶשׁ יִהְיֶ֣ה לָכֶ֑ם כָּל־מְלֶ֥אכֶת
עֲבֹדָ֖ה לֹ֥א תַעֲשֽׂוּ: ח וְהִקְרַבְתֶּ֥ם אִשֶּׁ֛ה לַיהֹוָ֖ה שִׁבְעַ֥ת

א וַיְדַבֵּ֥ר יְהֹוָ֖ה אֶל־מֹשֶׁ֥ה לֵּאמֹֽר: ב דַּבֵּ֞ר אֶל־בְּנֵ֤י יִשְׂרָאֵל֙
וְאָמַרְתָּ֣ אֲלֵהֶ֔ם מוֹעֲדֵ֣י יְהֹוָ֔ה אֲשֶׁר־תִּקְרְא֥וּ אֹתָ֖ם
מִקְרָאֵ֣י קֹ֑דֶשׁ אֵ֥לֶּה הֵ֖ם מוֹעֲדָֽי: ג שֵׁ֣שֶׁת יָמִים֮ תֵּעָשֶׂ֣ה
מְלָאכָה֒ וּבַיּ֣וֹם הַשְּׁבִיעִ֗י שַׁבַּ֤ת שַׁבָּתוֹן֙ מִקְרָא־קֹ֔דֶשׁ
כָּל־מְלָאכָ֖ה לֹ֣א תַעֲשׂ֑וּ שַׁבָּ֥ת הִוא֙ לַֽיהֹוָ֔ה בְּכֹ֖ל
מוֹשְׁבֹֽתֵיכֶֽם: פ

1] The LORD spoke to Moses, saying: **2]** Speak to the Israelite people and say to them: These are My fixed times, the fixed times of the LORD, which you shall proclaim as sacred occasions.

3] On six days work may be done, but on the seventh day there shall be a sabbath of complete rest, a sacred occasion. You shall do no work; it shall be a sabbath of the LORD throughout your settlements.

4] These are the set times of the LORD, the sacred occasions, which you shall celebrate each at its appointed time: **5]** In the first month, on the fourteenth day of the month, at twilight, there shall be a passover offering to the LORD, **6]** and on the fifteenth day of that month the LORD's Feast of Unleavened Bread. You shall eat unleavened bread for seven days. **7]** The first day shall be for you a sacred occasion: you shall not work at your occupations. **8]** Seven

23:2] *To the Israelite people.* In contrast to the two preceding chapters which deal with priestly matters, the festival laws are addressed to the entire people.

Fixed times. Hebrew *moadim*. *Moed* means "appointment" and can refer either to the time or place set for a meeting. Then it comes to designate the meeting itself, especially a holy-day gathering. It is the broadest term for a religious occasion, including the High Holy Days and the minor festivals, as well as the three "pilgrim feasts" of Passover, Feast of Weeks, and Feast of Booths. (Only the latter are properly called *chagim* or *regalim*.)

3] The brief reference to the Sabbath is included apparently to preclude the notion that it had been overlooked and to stress its importance.

5] *Fourteenth day of the month, at twilight.* Hebrew *bein ha-arbayim*, literally, "between the sunsets" (see Gleanings). The language of verses 5 and 6 suggests that the evening when this sacrifice was performed was considered part of the fourteenth day and that the fifteenth—the Matzah festival—did not begin until the next morning (see "1. Calendar Reckoning").

Passover offering. Hebrew *pesach*, which in the Bible designates the sacrifice rather than the festival (see Exod. 12:11). In talmudic and later times, the entire week was known as Pesach; but the prayer

book still uses regularly the term Feast of Unleavened Bread.

6] *You shall eat unleavened bread.* Exodus (13:7) is more stringent: "No leavened bread shall be found with you, and no leaven shall be found in all your territory."

7] *You shall not work at your occupations.* Literally, "You shall do no work of labor." This phrase is used concerning all the festivals, whereas the law for Sabbath and Yom Kippur is a blunt "You shall do no work" (verses 3 and 28). What then is intended by this provision which presumably is not quite so strict? It hardly means that heavy labor is prohibited and light work allowed; buying and selling were surely not permitted. The present rendering, "You shall not work at your occupations," is likewise not altogether satisfactory; a man was hardly allowed to labor at something other than his regular job. Perhaps Nachmanides is right in referring to Exodus (12:6) which forbids work on Passover but adds, "Only what every person is to eat, that alone may be prepared for you." In short, says Nachmanides, only work involved in preparing food is permitted—as the halachah rules—and any other kind of work is forbidden as "work of labor."

בְּלוּלָה בַשֶּׁמֶן אִשֶּׁה לַיהוָה רֵיחַ נִיחֹחַ וְנִסְכֹּה יַיִן
רְבִיעִת הַהִין: וְלֶחֶם וְקָלִי וְכַרְמֶל לֹא תֹאכְלוּ עַד־
עֶצֶם הַיּוֹם הַזֶּה עַד הֲבִיאֲכֶם אֶת־קָרְבַּן אֱלֹהֵיכֶם
חֻקַּת עוֹלָם לְדֹרֹתֵיכֶם בְּכֹל מֹשְׁבֹתֵיכֶם: ס
טו וּסְפַרְתֶּם לָכֶם מִמָּחֳרַת הַשַּׁבָּת מִיּוֹם הֲבִיאֲכֶם אֶת־
עֹמֶר הַתְּנוּפָה שֶׁבַע שַׁבָּתוֹת תְּמִימֹת תִּהְיֶינָה: עַד
מִמָּחֳרַת הַשַּׁבָּת הַשְּׁבִיעִת תִּסְפְּרוּ חֲמִשִּׁים יוֹם
יז וְהִקְרַבְתֶּם מִנְחָה חֲדָשָׁה לַיהוָה: מִמּוֹשְׁבֹתֵיכֶם
תָּבִיאוּ לֶחֶם תְּנוּפָה שְׁתַּיִם שְׁנֵי עֶשְׂרֹנִים סֹלֶת

*יין ונסכו קרי

יָמִים בַּיּוֹם הַשְּׁבִיעִי מִקְרָא־קֹדֶשׁ כָּל־מְלֶאכֶת עֲבֹדָה
לֹא תַעֲשׂוּ: פ
ט וַיְדַבֵּר יְהוָה אֶל־מֹשֶׁה לֵּאמֹר: דַּבֵּר אֶל־בְּנֵי יִשְׂרָאֵל
וְאָמַרְתָּ אֲלֵהֶם כִּי־תָבֹאוּ אֶל־הָאָרֶץ אֲשֶׁר אֲנִי נֹתֵן
לָכֶם וּקְצַרְתֶּם אֶת־קְצִירָהּ וַהֲבֵאתֶם אֶת־עֹמֶר
יא רֵאשִׁית קְצִירְכֶם אֶל־הַכֹּהֵן: וְהֵנִיף אֶת־הָעֹמֶר לִפְנֵי
יְהוָה לִרְצֹנְכֶם מִמָּחֳרַת הַשַּׁבָּת יְנִיפֶנּוּ הַכֹּהֵן:
יב וַעֲשִׂיתֶם בְּיוֹם הֲנִיפְכֶם אֶת־הָעֹמֶר כֶּבֶשׂ תָּמִים בֶּן־
שְׁנָתוֹ לְעֹלָה לַיהוָה: וּמִנְחָתוֹ שְׁנֵי עֶשְׂרֹנִים סֹלֶת

days you shall make offerings by fire to the LORD. The seventh day shall be a sacred occasion: you shall not work at your occupations.

9] The LORD spoke to Moses, saying: **10]** Speak to the Israelite people and say to them: When you enter the land which I am giving to you and you reap its harvest, you shall bring the first sheaf of your harvest to the priest. **11]** He shall wave the sheaf before the LORD for acceptance in your behalf; the priest shall wave it on the day after the sabbath. **12]** On the day that you wave the sheaf, you shall offer as a burnt offering to the LORD a lamb of the first year without blemish. **13]** The meal offering with it shall be two-tenths of a measure of choice flour with oil mixed in, an offering by fire of pleasing odor to the LORD; and the libation with it shall be of wine, a quarter of a *hin*. **14]** Until that very day, until you have brought the offering of your God, you shall eat no bread or parched grain or fresh ears; it is a law for all time throughout the ages in all your settlements.

15] And from the day on which you bring the sheaf of wave offering—the day after the sabbath—you shall count off seven weeks. They must be complete: **16]** you must count until the day after the seventh week—fifty days; then you shall bring an offering of new grain to the LORD. **17]** You shall bring from your settlements two loaves of bread as a wave offering; each shall be made of two-tenths of a measure of choice flour, baked after leavening, as first fruits to the LORD. **18]** With the bread you shall present, as burnt offerings to the LORD, seven yearling lambs without blemish, one bull of the herd, and two rams, with their meal offerings

8] *Offerings by fire.* As in 1:9. This general term is used throughout the chapter, and the specific sacrifices for each occasion are detailed in Numbers (28–29).

10] *When you enter the land.* Laws concerning harvest could not be observed in the desert.

First sheaf. Hebrew *omer*. For the traditional explanation, see Gleanings.

11] *He shall wave.* See commentary on 7:28–34.

On the day after the sabbath. See "2. The Biblical Holy Days."

13] *Two-tenths of a measure.* All other such meal offerings consisted of one-tenth; perhaps it was

thought appropriate to "splurge" a bit at the time of the grain harvest. Only the usual amount of wine, however, is prescribed.

14] *You shall eat no bread or parched grain or fresh ears.* I.e., of the new crop·(T.N.). The Talmud [31] reports that merchants would bring in supplies of new grain to be put on sale as soon as the *omer* had been offered.

17] *Two loaves of bread.* This explains the *offering of new grain* in verse 16. These loaves, exceptionally, are to be leavened; they are not to be burned on the altar (cf. 2:11, 7:13). Perhaps the loaves were regarded as a thanksgiving offering and therefore leavened like those of chapter 7, verse 13.

תִּהְיֶ֫ינָה חָמֵץ תֵּאָפֶ֫ינָה בִּכּוּרִ֖ים לַיהֹוָֽה: וְהִקְרַבְתֶּ֣ם
עַל־הַלֶּ֗חֶם שִׁבְעַ֤ת כְּבָשִׂים֙ תְּמִימִם֙ בְּנֵ֣י שָׁנָ֔ה וּפַ֧ר בֶּן־
בָּקָ֛ר אֶחָ֖ד וְאֵילִ֣ם שְׁנָ֑יִם יִהְי֤וּ עֹלָה֙ לַֽיהֹוָ֔ה וּמִנְחָתָ֣ם
יח

וְנִסְכֵּיהֶ֔ם אִשֵּׁ֥ה רֵֽיחַ־נִיחֹ֖חַ לַֽיהֹוָֽה: וַעֲשִׂיתֶ֞ם שְׂעִיר־
עִזִּ֥ים אֶחָ֖ד לְחַטָּ֑את וּשְׁנֵ֧י כְבָשִׂ֛ים בְּנֵ֥י שָׁנָ֖ה לְזֶ֥בַח
יט

שְׁלָמִֽים: וְהֵנִ֣יף הַכֹּהֵ֣ן ׀ אֹתָ֡ם עַל֩ לֶ֨חֶם הַבִּכֻּרִ֜ים
תְּנוּפָה֙ לִפְנֵ֣י יְהֹוָ֔ה עַל־שְׁנֵ֖י כְּבָשִׂ֑ים קֹ֛דֶשׁ יִהְי֥וּ לַֽיהֹוָ֖ה
כ

לַכֹּהֵֽן: וּקְרָאתֶ֞ם בְּעֶ֣צֶם ׀ הַיּ֣וֹם הַזֶּ֗ה מִֽקְרָא־קֹ֙דֶשׁ֙
יִהְיֶ֣ה לָכֶ֔ם כָּל־מְלֶ֥אכֶת עֲבֹדָ֖ה לֹ֣א תַעֲשׂ֑וּ חֻקַּ֥ת עוֹלָ֛ם
כא

בְּכָל־מוֹשְׁבֹֽתֵיכֶ֖ם לְדֹרֹֽתֵיכֶֽם: וּֽבְקֻצְרְכֶ֞ם אֶת־קְצִ֣יר
אַרְצְכֶ֗ם לֹֽא־תְכַלֶּ֞ה פְּאַ֤ת שָֽׂדְךָ֙ בְּקֻצְרֶ֔ךָ וְלֶ֥קֶט
כב

קְצִֽירְךָ֖ לֹ֣א תְלַקֵּ֑ט לֶֽעָנִ֤י וְלַגֵּר֙ תַּעֲזֹ֣ב אֹתָ֔ם אֲנִ֖י
יְהֹוָ֥ה אֱלֹהֵיכֶֽם:
פ

וַיְדַבֵּ֥ר יְהֹוָ֖ה אֶל־מֹשֶׁ֥ה לֵּאמֹֽר: דַּבֵּ֛ר אֶל־בְּנֵ֥י יִשְׂרָאֵ֖ל
לֵאמֹ֑ר בַּחֹ֨דֶשׁ הַשְּׁבִיעִ֜י בְּאֶחָ֣ד לַחֹ֗דֶשׁ יִהְיֶ֤ה לָכֶם֙
כג

שַׁבָּת֔וֹן זִכְר֥וֹן תְּרוּעָ֖ה מִקְרָא־קֹֽדֶשׁ: כָּל־מְלֶ֥אכֶת
עֲבֹדָ֖ה לֹ֣א תַעֲשׂ֑וּ וְהִקְרַבְתֶּ֥ם אִשֶּׁ֖ה לַֽיהֹוָֽה: ס
כה

וַיְדַבֵּ֥ר יְהֹוָ֖ה אֶל־מֹשֶׁ֥ה לֵּאמֹֽר: אַ֡ךְ בֶּעָשׂ֣וֹר לַחֹ֩דֶשׁ֩
הַשְּׁבִיעִ֨י הַזֶּ֜ה י֧וֹם הַכִּפֻּרִ֣ים ה֗וּא מִֽקְרָא־קֹ֙דֶשׁ֙ יִהְיֶ֣ה
כו

לָכֶ֔ם וְעִנִּיתֶ֖ם אֶת־נַפְשֹֽׁתֵיכֶ֑ם וְהִקְרַבְתֶּ֥ם אִשֶּׁ֖ה לַֽיהֹוָֽה:
וְכָל־מְלָאכָה֙ לֹ֣א תַעֲשׂ֔וּ בְּעֶ֖צֶם הַיּ֣וֹם הַזֶּ֑ה כִּ֣י י֤וֹם
כח

כִּפֻּרִים֙ ה֔וּא לְכַפֵּ֣ר עֲלֵיכֶ֔ם לִפְנֵ֖י יְהֹוָ֥ה אֱלֹהֵיכֶֽם:

and libations, an offering by fire of pleasing odor to the LORD. **19]** You shall also offer one he-goat as a sin offering and two yearling lambs as a sacrifice of well-being. **20]** The priest shall wave these—the two lambs—together with the bread of first fruits as a wave offering before the LORD; they shall be holy to the LORD, for the priest. **21]** On that same day you shall hold a celebration; it shall be a sacred occasion for you; you shall not work at your occupations. This is a law for all time in all your settlements, throughout the ages.

22] And when you reap the harvest of your land, you shall not reap all the way to the edges of your field, or gather the gleanings of your harvest; you shall leave them for the poor and the stranger: I the LORD am your God.

23] The LORD spoke to Moses, saying: **24]** Speak to the Israelite people thus: In the seventh month, on the first day of the month, you shall observe complete rest, a sacred occasion commemorated with loud blasts. **25]** You shall not work at your occupations; and you shall bring an offering by fire to the LORD.

26] The LORD spoke to Moses, saying: **27]** Mark, the tenth day of this seventh month is the Day of Atonement. It shall be a sacred occasion for you: you shall practice self-denial, and you shall bring an offering by fire to the LORD; **28]** you shall do no work throughout that day. For it is a Day of Atonement, on which expiation is made on your behalf before the LORD your

18–19] These verses contain the only specific directions for animal sacrifice in this chapter. This list resembles that in Numbers (28:26ff.), but the two do not agree exactly—another instance of variant traditions in P. The halachah (*Sifra* to the verse) does not harmonize but requires both sets of offerings: those in Leviticus to accompany the loaves, those in Numbers as fixed festival sacrifices [32].

20] *The priest shall wave these—the two lambs.* Hebrew obscure (T.N.). But see commentary on Lev. 7:28–34.

22] This verse reproduces 19:9 with minor changes.

Its inclusion here reminds the worshiper that he has social as well as ritual obligations.

24] *Commemorated with loud blasts.* Hebrew *zichron teruah,* literally "a remembrance of a loud blast" (see Gleanings).

27] *Mark.* Hebrew *ach,* literally, "however, only." Luzzatto says this word is used here and in verse 39 to call attention to something unusual—fasting here, the use of *etrog* and *lulav* there.

27–32] On Yom Kippur, see chapter 16.

929

כט כִּי כָל־הַנֶּפֶשׁ אֲשֶׁר לֹא־תְעֻנֶּה בְּעֶצֶם הַיּוֹם הַזֶּה
ל וְנִכְרְתָה מֵעַמֶּיהָ: וְכָל־הַנֶּפֶשׁ אֲשֶׁר תַּעֲשֶׂה כָּל־
מְלָאכָה בְּעֶצֶם הַיּוֹם הַזֶּה וְהַאֲבַדְתִּי אֶת־הַנֶּפֶשׁ הַהִוא
לא מִקֶּרֶב עַמָּהּ: כָּל־מְלָאכָה לֹא תַעֲשׂוּ חֻקַּת עוֹלָם
לב לְדֹרֹתֵיכֶם בְּכֹל מֹשְׁבֹתֵיכֶם: שַׁבַּת שַׁבָּתוֹן הוּא לָכֶם
וְעִנִּיתֶם אֶת־נַפְשֹׁתֵיכֶם בְּתִשְׁעָה לַחֹדֶשׁ בָּעֶרֶב מֵעֶרֶב
עַד־עֶרֶב תִּשְׁבְּתוּ שַׁבַּתְּכֶם: פ
לג וַיְדַבֵּר יְהוָה אֶל־מֹשֶׁה לֵּאמֹר: דַּבֵּר אֶל־בְּנֵי יִשְׂרָאֵל
לד לֵאמֹר בַּחֲמִשָּׁה עָשָׂר יוֹם לַחֹדֶשׁ הַשְּׁבִיעִי הַזֶּה חַג
לה הַסֻּכּוֹת שִׁבְעַת יָמִים לַיהוָה: בַּיּוֹם הָרִאשׁוֹן מִקְרָא־

לו קֹדֶשׁ כָּל־מְלֶאכֶת עֲבֹדָה לֹא תַעֲשׂוּ: שִׁבְעַת יָמִים
תַּקְרִיבוּ אִשֶּׁה לַיהוָה בַּיּוֹם הַשְּׁמִינִי מִקְרָא־קֹדֶשׁ יִהְיֶה
לָכֶם וְהִקְרַבְתֶּם אִשֶּׁה לַיהוָה עֲצֶרֶת הִוא כָּל־
לז מְלֶאכֶת עֲבֹדָה לֹא תַעֲשׂוּ: אֵלֶּה מוֹעֲדֵי יְהוָה אֲשֶׁר
תִּקְרְאוּ אֹתָם מִקְרָאֵי קֹדֶשׁ לְהַקְרִיב אִשֶּׁה לַיהוָה
לח עֹלָה וּמִנְחָה זֶבַח וּנְסָכִים דְּבַר־יוֹם בְּיוֹמוֹ: מִלְּבַד
שַׁבְּתֹת יְהוָה וּמִלְּבַד מַתְּנוֹתֵיכֶם וּמִלְּבַד כָּל־נִדְרֵיכֶם
לט וּמִלְּבַד כָּל־נִדְבֹתֵיכֶם אֲשֶׁר תִּתְּנוּ לַיהוָה: אַךְ
בַּחֲמִשָּׁה עָשָׂר יוֹם לַחֹדֶשׁ הַשְּׁבִיעִי בְּאָסְפְּכֶם אֶת־
תְּבוּאַת הָאָרֶץ תָּחֹגּוּ אֶת־חַג־יְהוָה שִׁבְעַת יָמִים בַּיּוֹם

God.   **29]** Indeed, any person who does not practice self-denial throughout that day shall be cut off from his kin;   **30]** and whoever does any work throughout that day, I will cause that person to perish from among his people.   **31]** Do no work whatever; it is a law for all time, throughout the ages in all your settlements.   **32]** It shall be a sabbath of complete rest for you, and you shall practice self-denial; on the ninth day of the month at evening, from evening to evening, you shall observe this your sabbath.

33] The LORD spoke to Moses, saying: **34]** Say to the Israelite people:
On the fifteenth day of this seventh month there shall be the Feast of Booths to the LORD, [to last] seven days.   **35]** The first day shall be a sacred occasion: you shall not work at your occupations;   **36]** seven days you shall bring offerings by fire to the LORD. On the eighth day you shall observe a sacred occasion and bring an offering by fire to the LORD; it is a solemn gathering: you shall not work at your occupations.

37] Those are the set times of the LORD which you shall celebrate as sacred occasions, bringing offerings by fire to the LORD—burnt offerings, meal offerings, sacrifices, and libations, on each day what is proper to it—   **38]** apart from the sabbaths of the LORD, and apart from your gifts and from all your votive offerings and from all your freewill offerings that you give to the LORD.

39] Mark, on the fifteenth day of the seventh month, when you have gathered in the yield of your land, you shall observe the festival of the LORD [to last] seven days: a complete rest on the first day, and a complete rest on the eighth day.   **40]** On the first day you shall take the

30] *I will cause that person to perish.* This passage, says *Sifra*, clarifies the often repeated expression "so-and-so will be cut off from his kin."

32] *On the ninth day of the month at evening.* Here again is a suggestion that the new day began at daybreak rather than sundown. For the traditional explanation, see Gleanings.

34] *Booths.* Others, "Tabernacles" (T.N.).

36] *Solemn gathering.* Precise meaning of Hebrew *atzeret* uncertain (T.N.). See "2. The Biblical Holy Days." Ibn Ezra understands the root-meaning of the word as "restrain," referring to restraint from work (see also Gleanings).

37] *Those are the set times.* . . . These verses are clearly the conclusion of the festival calendar. The additional section on Sukot in verses 39–43 appears to be from another source. (On votive and freewill offerings, see commentary on 7:16.)

מ הָרִאשׁוֹן שַׁבָּתוֹן וּבַיּוֹם הַשְּׁמִינִי שַׁבָּתוֹן: וּלְקַחְתֶּם לָכֶם
בַּיּוֹם הָרִאשׁוֹן פְּרִי עֵץ הָדָר כַּפֹּת תְּמָרִים וַעֲנַף עֵץ־
עָבֹת וְעַרְבֵי־נָחַל וּשְׂמַחְתֶּם לִפְנֵי יְהוָה אֱלֹהֵיכֶם
מא שִׁבְעַת יָמִים: וְחַגֹּתֶם אֹתוֹ חַג לַיהוָה שִׁבְעַת יָמִים
בַּשָּׁנָה חֻקַּת עוֹלָם לְדֹרֹתֵיכֶם בַּחֹדֶשׁ הַשְּׁבִיעִי תָּחֹגּוּ

מב אֹתוֹ: בַּסֻּכֹּת תֵּשְׁבוּ שִׁבְעַת יָמִים כָּל־הָאֶזְרָח בְּיִשְׂרָאֵל
מג יֵשְׁבוּ בַּסֻּכֹּת: לְמַעַן יֵדְעוּ דֹרֹתֵיכֶם כִּי בַסֻּכּוֹת
הוֹשַׁבְתִּי אֶת־בְּנֵי יִשְׂרָאֵל בְּהוֹצִיאִי אוֹתָם מֵאֶרֶץ
מד מִצְרָיִם אֲנִי יְהוָה אֱלֹהֵיכֶם: וַיְדַבֵּר מֹשֶׁה אֶת־מֹעֲדֵי
יְהוָה אֶל־בְּנֵי יִשְׂרָאֵל:
פ

product of *hadar* trees, branches of palm trees, boughs of leafy trees, and willows of the brook, and you shall rejoice before the LORD your God seven days. **41]** You shall observe it as a festival of the LORD for seven days in the year; you shall observe it in the seventh month as a law for all time, throughout the ages. **42]** You shall live in booths seven days; all citizens in Israel shall live in booths, **43]** in order that future generations may know that I made the Israelite people live in booths when I brought them out of the land of Egypt, I the LORD your God.

44] So Moses declared to the Israelites the set times of the LORD.

40] *Product of hadar trees.* Others, "goodly"; exact meaning of *hadar* uncertain. Traditionally the product is understood as "citron" (T.N.). See "2. The Biblical Holy Days." All the citrus fruits were native to the Far East. The citron was the first of the family to be brought to western Asia and thence to Europe.

Leafy trees. Meaning of Hebrew *avot* uncertain (T.N.). It was understood by tradition as myrtle, the leaves of which have a "plaited" appearance, completely covering the stems.

42] *You shall live in booths.* This was understood quite literally in Jewish tradition. One was to sleep in the sukah for seven nights and take all his regular meals there. Only the circumstances of modern urban liv-

ing have compelled many observant Orthodox Jews to limit themselves to eating meals in a communal or congregational booth.

43] *That I made the Israelite people live in booths when I brought them out of the land of Egypt.* This explanation gave a Jewish historical aspect to an originally agricultural festival. According to Rashbam, the booth reminds us of our humble beginnings, and so it protects us against arrogance.

44] *So Moses declared to the Israelites the set times of the Lord.* This verse is sung during the evening service of the three major festivals (e.g., *Union Prayer Book*, I, pp. 190–191).

GLEANINGS

Halachah

23:2] *The Fixed Times of the Lord, Which You Shall Proclaim*

This means that the high court, the Sanhedrin, has the right to determine the time of the new moon—thus fixing the dates of the festivals—and to add a month to the year when necessary. Even should the earthly court make an error in these procedures, its decision is still valid and is confirmed on high.

SIFRA

5] *At Twilight*

Hebrew *bein ha-arbayim.* See commentary. The halachah required that the paschal animals be slaughtered as sacrifices in the Temple. But it must have taken hours to provide this service for the thousands of pilgrims present in Jerusalem, even with all available priests on duty. In this case, therefore, *bein ha-arbayim* was taken to mean the entire afternoon of Nisan 14, from noon on.

SIFRA

7] *You Shall Not Work at Your Occupations*

See in the commentary the citation from Nachmanides, who states the halachah.

10] *First Sheaf*

Hebrew *omer.* This word sometimes means a dry measure of about two quarts (Exod. 16:36); the halachah understands it thus here, as defining the amount of grain required for the offering. This *omer* was identified with the "meal offering of first fruits" in Leviticus (2:14); like other *minchahs*, it had to contain a fixed amount. In accordance with chapter 2, verse 14, the *omer* grain was roasted, then pounded into coarse grits before it was offered (*Sifra* on 2:14). This offering, exceptionally, was of barley, not wheat.

SIFRA

How was the cutting of the first grain performed? Representatives of the court would go out on the day before the holy day (i.e., before the first day of Passover) and tie the standing grain into bunches, so that it would be easy to cut. At the end of the holy day, the people of the nearby villages would assemble at the place, so that the harvesting should be conducted with much ceremony. When it was dark, the appointed reaper would ask, "Has the sun gone down?" and the people would reply, "Yes." This question would be asked and answered three times, and so for the following questions: "Shall I use this sickle?" "Shall I put the grain into this box?" "Shall I do it this week?" "Shall I reap?" and they would reply "Reap!" All this formality was directed against the Boethusians who denied that the grain should be cut immediately after the holy day [33].

11] *On the Day after the Sabbath*
See "2. The Biblical Holy Days."

14] *You Shall Eat No Bread*

From the new crop. Though the *omer* ceremony was discontinued after the fall of the Temple, it is still prohibited to eat of new grain until after Nisan 16.

SIFRA

17] *As First Fruits*

Once these communal first fruits had been offered, individuals might bring their own first fruits, in accordance with Deuteronomy, chapter 26 [34].

18] *You Shall Present . . . Seven Yearling Lambs*
See commentary.

932

20] *They Shall Be Holy to the Lord, for the Priest*

The holiness of the loaves consists in their being assigned to the priest for his exclusive consumption [35].

24] *Commemorated with Loud Blasts*

Hebrew *zichron teruah*, literally "a remembrance of loud blasts." During the shofar service in the synagogue, three groups of verses are recited. The first, called *malchuyot*, affirm God's sovereignty; the second, *zichronot*, speak of God's "remembering" past and present events that evoke His mercy; the third, *shofarot*, refer to blasts of the shofar on various occasions (see *Union Prayer Book*, II, pp. 78–82). The second and third sections are indicated in our verse by the words *zichron* and *teruah*. The *malchuyot* are derived from Numbers (10:10)—this passage deals with the blowing of trumpets, it contains the word "reminder" (a different form of *zichron*), and it concludes with "I the LORD am your God."   SIFRA

In traditional synagogues, the shofar is not blown on the Sabbath. In such a case, the holy day is described in the prayers by the words of our verse as "a day of *remembering* the loud blast"; when Rosh Hashanah falls on a weekday, the phrase of Numbers (29:1), *yom teruah*, "a day when the horn is sounded," is used [36].

30] *I Will Cause That Person to Perish*

See commentary.

32] *On the Ninth Day of the Month at Evening*

See commentary. Tradition understood this to

mean: Begin the fast while it is still daylight on the ninth, to make sure that you do not eat on Yom Kippur itself (*Sifra*). Similarly, one does not break his fast till well after dark, to allow margin for error.

36] *Solemn Gathering*

The commandment of the sukah does not apply to this eighth day (verse 42).

40] *Product of Hadar Trees*

The Rabbis offer several proofs that this means the citron, *etrog*. For example: It is the fruit that remains (*ha-dar*) on the tree from year to year.

SIFRA

Branches of Palm Trees

Despite the plural "branches," tradition prescribed a single *lulav*.   SIFRA

Willows of the Brook

But twigs from willows that grow elsewhere are permitted.   SIFRA

You Shall Rejoice

This is taken as a positive commandment. It is a religious obligation to eat and drink well during the festival, and mourning is forbidden throughout the holiday period [37].

42] *All Citizens*

This masculine term exempts women (as well as slaves) from the duty of living in the sukah.

SIFRA

Haggadah

23:11] *He Shall Wave the Sheaf*

Horizontally, to ward off destructive winds; up and down, to ward off harmful dews.   SIFRA

24] *In the Seventh Month, on the First Day of the Month*

Rosh Hashanah, according to a widely accepted tradition, is the anniversary of the creation of the world [38]. "This day marks the beginning of Your works; it is a memorial of the first day" (from the liturgy). It is also understood as the day of universal judgment, when the destinies of all are decided for the coming year; but the decrees are not sealed until Yom Kippur. Thereby humans are given an oppor-

tunity to repent and correct their ways; for "repentance, prayer, and charity avert the evil decree" [39].

Commemorated with Loud Blasts

The shofar is a simple horn of very ancient origin. It was used to warn people of approaching danger (Amos 3:6; Jer. 4:19, 6:1). Its shrill tone was also thought to drive away evil spirits; and Jewish tradition explains the blowing of the shofar on the new year as having the purpose (among others) of "disconcerting Satan." The latter acts as prosecutor before the heavenly court; and the shofar blast dis-

turbs him and prevents him from reading the record of Israel's sins effectively [40].

Another interpretation connected the shofar with the horn of the ram which Abraham sacrificed instead of Isaac (Gen. 22:13). The story of the "binding of Isaac" is the Torah portion for the second day of Rosh Hashanah in traditional synagogues and is read on Rosh Hashanah proper in Reform congregations. The Midrash represents God as saying to Abraham, "When your descendants sin, and they appear before Me for judgment on Rosh Hashanah, let them blow the ram's horn; this will remind Me of the piety of their ancestors and lead Me to forgive them" [41].

"Happy is the people who know the joyful shout" (Ps. 89:16). Said Rabbi Josiah: Do not other peoples know how to sound blasts? How many kinds of horns and trumpets they possess! But the verse means: Happy is the people who know how to evoke the favor of their Creator by means of the blast. For, when they blow the shofar, the Holy One (blessed be He!) arises from the throne of judgment and sits upon the throne of mercy; He is filled with compassion for them and transforms His Quality of Justice into the Quality of Mercy [42].

In contrast to these views, according to which the sound of the shofar has an influence on the demonic world, and even on the purposes of God, the rationalist Maimonides considers the impact of the ceremony on the worshiper: "The blowing of the shofar on Rosh Hashanah is an ordinance of Scripture [and must therefore be obeyed, if only for that reason]. But it also has a deeper meaning. It says to us: Awake, ye slumberers, from your slumber, and rouse yourselves from your deep sleep. Search your deeds and turn ye in repentance. Remember your Creator, ye who forget truth because of the vanity of the hour, who go astray all through the year in pursuit of trifles which can neither profit nor save. Let every one of you forsake his wicked path and his evil purpose" [43].

27] *Mark, the Tenth Day of This Seventh Month Is the Day of Atonement*

The word "*ach*" (here rendered "mark," literally, "however, only") always has a restrictive force. Here it implies that God forgives *only* those who repent.   SIFRA

36] *On the Eighth Day ... Is a Solemn Gathering [Atzeret]*

The Rabbis understand *atzeret* as coming from a root meaning "to restrain." A king once invited his children to a seven-day feast. When it was over, he was reluctant to part with them and "restrained" them to celebrate one more day with him [44].

40] *Branches of Palm Trees*

The palm was a widely accepted symbol of victory in ancient times. Apparently, there was a Roman custom for a successful litigant in a law case to leave the courtroom carrying a palm branch. So likewise, say the Rabbis, accusations are made against Israel during the Days of Awe. Have our adversaries prevailed, or have we emerged with the favor of the divine Judge? The fact that we carry the palm branch on Sukot gives the happy answer [45].

Various allegorical explanations are given of all the four plants. This is one of the most attractive: The citron is both fragrant and edible; it symbolizes those Jews who are learned in the Torah and righteous in deed. The date palm provides food, but it has no fragrance; it symbolizes those who are learned but are deficient in good acts. The myrtle is fragrant, but it yields nothing to eat; it typifies those whose conduct is exemplary but who lack knowledge of the Torah. And the willow, which offers neither nourishment nor fragrance, typifies those who are deficient both in learning and in virtue. Let them all, says God, be bound together in fellowship like a well-tied bouquet, so that the merits of each shall benefit all the others [46].

43] *That I Made the Israelite People Live in Booths When I Brought Them Out of the Land of Egypt*

See commentary. According to Rabbi Akiba, the booths in question were clouds of glory which sheltered and accompanied Israel on their desert wanderings. But Rabbi Eliezer held that the Israelites dwelt in literal booths.   SIFRA

Jewish homilists have also stressed the frail and temporary character of the sukah. We are summoned to leave our solid, seemingly permanent dwellings and live for a time in the fragile sukah, that we may become mindful of our own frailty and impermanence and of our need for divine help [47].

Oil, Bread, and the Blasphemer

This chapter consists of a number of short items that do not seem to be connected with one another.

1. Oil for the Temple Lamps

Verses 1 through 4 repeat Exodus, chapter 27, verses 20 and 21, with a few slight changes. Traditional commentators offer various reasons for the repetition. To us it is one more example of the way in which various sources were combined to form the Torah.

2. The Bread of Display

The furniture of the Tabernacle included a table overlaid with gold on which the priests were to set out "bread of display" (Exod. 25:23ff., 40:22f.). Earlier translations used "shewbread" or "showbread" for the Hebrew *lechem panim*, literally "bread of Face/Presence," a term which has been variously explained [1]. The term does not occur in this chapter, which, however, explains the procedure more fully.

There were to be twelve sizeable loaves, arranged in two rows on the table. They were to be accompanied by incense, no doubt in bowls set on either side of the rows of bread (so *Sifra*). Fresh bread was to be supplied each Sabbath; last week's loaves were to be removed and, after the incense had been burned, were to be eaten by the priests with due regard for their sanctity.

From remote antiquity, one form of offering was to set food before the image of the god, later to remove it for consumption by king or priest (see introduction to Part I, "2. Ancient Sacrifices"). Babylonian ritual also called for an offering of twelve loaves, but sometimes larger and smaller numbers were offered [2]. That the custom was ancient in Israel is attested by the story in I Samuel, chapter 21. When David fled from Saul, he came to the shrine at Nob and asked for bread. The local priest had nothing but "bread of display" which he gave to David when the latter assured him that he and his followers were in a state of ritual purity [3]. This instance from early Israelite history shows that the priestly writings—whatever the date when they were finally edited—contain very old elements.

3. The Blasphemer

Israel had been commanded (Exod. 22:27), "You shall not revile God." Now, in

935

one of the rare narrative passages of Leviticus, we read of a case where this command was violated. No one knew how to deal with the offender; so Moses sought a special revelation and was told that the criminal must die by stoning.

This is one of four episodes in the Torah in which Moses has to make a special inquiry of God before he can give a legal decision. The others are Numbers (9:6ff., 15:32ff., and 27:1ff.). These passages are discussed at length by Philo and the Rabbis who are troubled by Moses' inability to handle these cases on his own [4].

In the present instance the explanation is not difficult. The penalty for blasphemy had not yet been revealed. But the intent of the entire section remains to be explained and various possibilities suggest themselves. Was it simply to stress the sinfulness of misusing the divine name? Was it a warning of the disastrous results that may follow mixed marriage? Was it to make the legal distinction between ordinary blasphemy, punishment for which is left to God, and cases where the name YHWH is pronounced and the court must execute the offender (see verses 15f.)?

Or was it to emphasize the principle that the law applies equally to citizen and resident alien? This suggestion is supported by the presence in this chapter of other penal laws that have nothing to do with blasphemy. The penalties for murder, mayhem, and the killing of animals are repeated here, with the assertion that one standard must be applied to citizen and stranger alike.

ח לְאַזְכָּרָה אִשֶּׁה לַיהוָה: בְּיוֹם הַשַּׁבָּת בְּיוֹם הַשַּׁבָּת
יַעַרְכֶנּוּ לִפְנֵי יְהוָה תָּמִיד מֵאֵת בְּנֵי־יִשְׂרָאֵל בְּרִית
ט עוֹלָם: וְהָיְתָה לְאַהֲרֹן וּלְבָנָיו וַאֲכָלֻהוּ בְּמָקוֹם קָדֹשׁ
כִּי קֹדֶשׁ קָדָשִׁים הוּא לוֹ מֵאִשֵּׁי יְהוָה חָק־עוֹלָם: ס
י וַיֵּצֵא בֶּן־אִשָּׁה יִשְׂרְאֵלִית וְהוּא בֶּן־אִישׁ מִצְרִי בְּתוֹךְ
בְּנֵי יִשְׂרָאֵל וַיִּנָּצוּ בַּמַּחֲנֶה בֶּן הַיִּשְׂרְאֵלִית וְאִישׁ
יא הַיִּשְׂרְאֵלִי: וַיִּקֹּב בֶּן־הָאִשָּׁה הַיִּשְׂרְאֵלִית אֶת־הַשֵּׁם
וַיְקַלֵּל וַיָּבִיאוּ אֹתוֹ אֶל־מֹשֶׁה וְשֵׁם אִמּוֹ שְׁלֹמִית בַּת־
יב דִּבְרִי לְמַטֵּה־דָן: וַיַּנִּיחֻהוּ בַּמִּשְׁמָר לִפְרֹשׁ לָהֶם עַל־
פ פִּי יְהוָה:

א וַיְדַבֵּר יְהוָה אֶל־מֹשֶׁה לֵּאמֹר: צַו אֶת־בְּנֵי יִשְׂרָאֵל
וְיִקְחוּ אֵלֶיךָ שֶׁמֶן זַיִת זָךְ כָּתִית לַמָּאוֹר לְהַעֲלֹת נֵר
ג תָּמִיד: מִחוּץ לְפָרֹכֶת הָעֵדֻת בְּאֹהֶל מוֹעֵד יַעֲרֹךְ
אֹתוֹ אַהֲרֹן מֵעֶרֶב עַד־בֹּקֶר לִפְנֵי יְהוָה תָּמִיד חֻקַּת
ד עוֹלָם לְדֹרֹתֵיכֶם: עַל הַמְּנֹרָה הַטְּהֹרָה יַעֲרֹךְ אֶת־
פ הַנֵּרוֹת לִפְנֵי יְהוָה תָּמִיד:

ה וְלָקַחְתָּ סֹלֶת וְאָפִיתָ אֹתָהּ שְׁתֵּים עֶשְׂרֵה חַלּוֹת שְׁנֵי
ו עֶשְׂרֹנִים יִהְיֶה הַחַלָּה הָאֶחָת: וְשַׂמְתָּ אוֹתָם שְׁתַּיִם
מַעֲרָכוֹת שֵׁשׁ הַמַּעֲרָכֶת עַל הַשֻּׁלְחָן הַטָּהֹר לִפְנֵי
ז יְהוָה: וְנָתַתָּ עַל־הַמַּעֲרֶכֶת לְבֹנָה זַכָּה וְהָיְתָה לַלֶּחֶם

1] The LORD spoke to Moses, saying:

2] Command the Israelite people to bring you clear oil of beaten olives for lighting, to maintain lights regularly. 3] Aaron shall set them up in the Tent of Meeting outside the curtain of the Pact [to burn] from evening to morning before the LORD regularly; it is a law for all time throughout the ages. 4] He shall set up the lamps on the pure lampstand before the LORD [to burn] regularly.

5] You shall take choice flour and bake of it twelve loaves, two-tenths of a measure for each loaf. 6] Place them on the pure table before the LORD in two rows, six to a row. 7] With each row you shall place pure frankincense, which is to be a token offering for the bread, as an offering by fire to the LORD. 8] He shall arrange them before the LORD regularly every sabbath day—it is a commitment for all time on the part of the Israelites. 9] They shall belong to Aaron and his sons, who shall eat them in the sacred precinct; for they are his as most holy things from the LORD's offerings by fire, a due for all time.

10] There came out among the Israelites one whose mother was Israelite and whose father was Egyptian. And a fight broke out in the camp between that half Israelite and a certain Israelite. 11] The son of the Israelite woman pronounced the Name in blasphemy, and he was brought to Moses—now his mother's name was Shelomith daughter of Dibri of the tribe of Dan— 12] and he was placed in custody, until the decision of the LORD should be made clear to them.

24:4] *The pure lampstand* [*menorah*]. Either "the lampstand of pure gold" (so T.N. at Exod. 31:8) or "the lampstand that has been cleansed" before the lamps were refilled and replaced (Rashi).

7] In the case of ordinary cereal offerings, a token portion of meal, oil, and frankincense was burned on the altar (above, 2:2). In this case, the token portion was incense alone.

As an offering by fire. Here and in verse 9, the term refers exceptionally to the frankincense. Usually it designates any sacrifice burned on the altar.

10] *That half Israelite.* Literally, "the son of an Israelite woman" (T.N.).

12] *In custody.* The Hebrew form suggests that there was a regular detention area outside the camp for accused persons whose cases were pending. Imprisonment as punishment for a crime does not seem to have been a regular practice in ancient Israel [5].

כ כֵּן יֵעָשֶׂה לּוֹ: שֶׁבֶר תַּחַת שֶׁבֶר עַיִן תַּחַת עַיִן שֵׁן תַּחַת
כא שֵׁן כַּאֲשֶׁר יִתֵּן מוּם בָּאָדָם כֵּן יִנָּתֶן בּוֹ: וּמַכֵּה בְהֵמָה
כב יְשַׁלְּמֶנָּה וּמַכֵּה אָדָם יוּמָת: מִשְׁפַּט אֶחָד יִהְיֶה לָכֶם
כג כַּגֵּר כָּאֶזְרָח יִהְיֶה כִּי אֲנִי יְהֹוָה אֱלֹהֵיכֶם: וַיְדַבֵּר
מֹשֶׁה אֶל־בְּנֵי יִשְׂרָאֵל וַיּוֹצִיאוּ אֶת־הַמְקַלֵּל אֶל־מִחוּץ
לַמַּחֲנֶה וַיִּרְגְּמוּ אֹתוֹ אָבֶן וּבְנֵי־יִשְׂרָאֵל עָשׂוּ כַּאֲשֶׁר
צִוָּה יְהֹוָה אֶת־מֹשֶׁה:

יג וַיְדַבֵּר יְהֹוָה אֶל־מֹשֶׁה לֵּאמֹר: הוֹצֵא אֶת־הַמְקַלֵּל
אֶל־מִחוּץ לַמַּחֲנֶה וְסָמְכוּ כָל־הַשֹּׁמְעִים אֶת־יְדֵיהֶם
טו עַל־רֹאשׁוֹ וְרָגְמוּ אֹתוֹ כָּל־הָעֵדָה: וְאֶל־בְּנֵי יִשְׂרָאֵל
תְּדַבֵּר לֵאמֹר אִישׁ אִישׁ כִּי־יְקַלֵּל אֱלֹהָיו וְנָשָׂא חֶטְאוֹ:
טז וְנֹקֵב שֵׁם־יְהֹוָה מוֹת יוּמָת רָגוֹם יִרְגְּמוּ־בוֹ כָּל־הָעֵדָה
יז כַּגֵּר כָּאֶזְרָח בְּנָקְבוֹ שֵׁם יוּמָת: וְאִישׁ כִּי יַכֶּה כָּל־נֶפֶשׁ
יח אָדָם מוֹת יוּמָת: וּמַכֵּה נֶפֶשׁ־בְּהֵמָה יְשַׁלְּמֶנָּה נֶפֶשׁ
יט תַּחַת נָפֶשׁ: וְאִישׁ כִּי־יִתֵּן מוּם בַּעֲמִיתוֹ כַּאֲשֶׁר עָשָׂה

Haftarah Emor, p. 1001

13] And the LORD spoke to Moses, saying: **14]** Take the blasphemer outside the camp; and let all who were within hearing lay their hands upon his head, and let the whole community stone him.

15] And to the Israelite people speak thus: Anyone who blasphemes his God shall bear his guilt;   **16]** if he also pronounces the name LORD, he shall be put to death. The whole community shall stone him; stranger or citizen, if he has thus pronounced the Name, he shall be put to death.

17] If a man kills any human being, he shall be put to death.   **18]** One who kills a beast shall make restitution for it: life for life.   **19]** If anyone maims his fellow, as he has done so shall it be done to him: **20]** fracture for fracture, eye for eye, tooth for tooth. The injury he inflicted on another shall be inflicted on him.   **21]** He who kills a beast shall make restitution for it; but he who kills a human being shall be put to death.   **22]** You shall have one standard for stranger and citizen alike: for I the LORD am your God.

23] Moses spoke thus to the Israelites. And they took the blasphemer outside the camp and pelted him with stones. The Israelites did as the LORD had commanded Moses.

14] *Outside the camp.* The camp proper was not to be defiled by an execution.

All who were within hearing. When he uttered the blasphemy and consequently testified against him.

Lay their hands upon his head. This gesture is regularly associated with sacrifice; it appears in connection with a criminal execution only here.

17–22] For these laws, see Genesis 9:6; Exodus 21:12–14, 18–25, 35–36; and Deuteronomy 19:21. We suggested above that the repetition here may be intended to indicate that the laws apply equally to aliens. Note, however, that Exodus 21:20–21 limits the liability of one who causes the death of his slave by excessive beating; but Leviticus 24:17 rules that all homicide is punishable by death (no doubt intentional homicide is meant).

18] *One who kills a beast shall make restitution for it: life for life.* Not that one of the defendant's beasts should be killed in retaliation, but—as verse 21 indicates—that the plaintiff shall be reimbursed for his loss. So the Talmud correctly understood [6].

19] *As he has done, so shall it be done to him.* See Exodus 21:23f. and Deuteronomy 19:21 on the law of "eye for eye." There is strong reason to believe that the biblical law did not envision literal physical retaliation but rather the payment of money damages [7]. Yet the language of this verse certainly seems to refer to the infliction on the guilty party of the injury he had committed. Two facts, however, are clear. There is no record of a single instance where a Jewish court carried out such retaliation; and Jewish tradition all but unanimously understood the language as referring to financial compensation.

GLEANINGS

Haggadah

24:10] *A Fight Broke Out in the Camp*

Because the half-Israelite sneered at the immediately preceding law of the bread of display. Why should week-old bread be on the table "before the LORD," when kings enjoy bread fresh from the oven?

Another view is that the quarrel arose from the ambiguous status of the half-Israelite. He wanted to pitch his tent with his mother's tribe of Dan. But Israel had been bidden to encamp by "fathers' houses" (this is the literal rendering of the phrase given in Numbers, chapter 2, verse 2, as "ancestral houses"). So this man, the son of an Egyptian, found himself without any regular place in the camp; and in frustration he blasphemed [8].

11] *His Mother's Name Was Shelomith Daughter of Dibri*

Her name is mentioned to indicate that she was the only woman in the entire camp who entered into an improper union. Her character was indicated by her name. She said "hello" (*shalom*) to all the men and she was a chatterbox (*dabranit*, punning on Dibri) [9].

18] *Life for Life*

This is "one of the paradoxes of history. On the one hand, Judaism, the so-called religion of 'strict justice,' rejected the literal application of the law of retaliation and knew neither torture in legal procedure nor mutilation as a form of punishment. In Christian lands, on the other hand, mutilation and torture are well-nigh the indispensable accompaniments of justice from the middle of the thirteenth century down to the middle of the eighteenth, and in some countries to the middle of the nineteenth and beyond" (Hertz) [10].

Sabbatical Year and Jubilee

This chapter is a noble expression of social idealism and humanitarian concern. It presents complicated and tantalizing problems to the student of history, but its message for our time rings out with clarity and power.

1. *The Sabbatical Year*

Verses 2 through 7 prescribe that for one year in every seven the soil of the Land of Israel is to be left untilled. This seventh year is a "sabbath of the Lord." As men are to rest on the seventh day, the land is to rest in the seventh year. If the year of rest is not observed, the land will eventually have to "make up" the lost sabbaths by being laid waste (26:34, 43).

This ancient rule, recorded in the "Book of the Covenant" (Exod. 23:10f.), speaks simply of the "seventh" year and does not call it "sabbath." Now, even if the law is obeyed strictly, there will be some produce in the seventh year; grain will sprout from seed dropped during the previous harvest, and the untended vines and fruit trees will continue to bear, even though in lesser amounts. Exodus 23:11 seems to forbid the owner of the land to use such products. He must leave them to the poor and, thereafter,

to foraging beasts. Verses 6 and 7 of this chapter, though forbidding the farmer to gather this yield for his exclusive use, permit him to share in it with all the others. In the sabbatical year, the landowner and the landless pauper are to be on an equal footing. This passage appears to clarify rather than contradict the law in Exodus.

An entirely different law for the seventh year is found in Deuteronomy 15:1–10. In that year, it rules, all outstanding debts are to be canceled [1]. (Further, Deut. 31:10ff. ordains that during the Feast of Booths, in the seventh year, the Torah is to be read publicly at the central sanctuary.)

The remission of debts is called *shemitah*, from a root meaning "to let something drop." A verb from the same root is used in Exodus 23:11 for letting the land rest. (There is thus an ancient basis for the talmudic usage of calling the sabbatical year *shemitah*.) But nothing is said in Deuteronomy about letting the land lie fallow, and nothing in Leviticus about canceling debts. It is true, of course, that, in a year when agriculture was at a standstill, debtors would find it hard to meet their obligations [2].

The halachah combined the two laws. All agricultural labor was to stop (generally)

thirty days before Rosh Hashanah of the seventh year, not to be resumed until the eighth year had begun [3]; and, at the end of the seventh year, debts were to be canceled [4]. The second provision, however, did not work out in practice; and, shortly before the beginning of the Christian era, Hillel virtually abrogated it by means of a legal device called *prosbul* [5].

But the "sabbath of the land" was observed for many centuries. No information about such observance has come down from the period of the First Temple, but there is ample attestation from the centuries preceding the Common Era and thereafter.

The First Book of Maccabees reports that in a sabbatical year the city of Beth-zur surrendered to the Syrians, being unable to withstand a siege for lack of provisions (6:49). This incident is also mentioned by the historian Josephus, who also provides other references. The most interesting of these tells that Julius Caesar exempted the Palestinian Jews from certain taxes in sabbatical years [6].

The subject is treated extensively in rabbinic sources—chiefly in a treatise of the Mishnah and of the Palestinian Talmud entitled *Shevi'it*, "Seventh Year." The actual cases cited in these works make it plain that the issue was indeed a practical one. The surprising thing is not that the law was sometimes broken—many persons were suspected of trafficking in fruits of the seventh year—but that so many Jews observed it at great cost to themselves. The words, "mighty creatures who do His bidding" (Ps. 103:20), were applied by Rabbi Isaac to those who keep the sabbatical year. Who is more heroic, he asked, than one who looks out on untilled fields and unworked plantations and shares the scanty yield with others? [7]. Two generations earlier, Rabbi Yannai had authorized some agricultural work in the sabbatical year, in order to meet the exactions of Roman rulers less tolerant than Julius Caesar had

been [8]. But this was evidently an emergency measure and was not accepted as a precedent. The law of the seventh year was deemed to remain in force and is still of concern to extreme Orthodox groups in Israel. It was the subject of lively controversy when the first agricultural colonies were established; today, those who regard the law as operative meet the problem by a fictitious sale of their land to a Gentile.

The sabbatical year may have been of practical benefit in preventing exhaustion of the soil, but that was not the intent of the law. It was rather an expression of the Sabbath idea; and, like the weekly Sabbath, it has no parallel in the other cultures of the ancient Near East.

2. The Jubilee Year

a. *The law.* Beginning with verse 8, we are commanded to count off seven "weeks of years" and to consecrate the fiftieth year as a "jubilee" by sounding the ram's horn on the Day of Atonement.

The word "jubilee" (Hebrew *yovel*) might have originally meant "ram," with reference to the blast of the horn that ushers in the holy season. The Greek translation, however, rendered *yovel* by a word meaning "release"; and it has been argued that this translation is scientifically correct [9]. The Latin word *jubilum*, "wild shout," from which we get our word "jubilation," has no connection with *yovel*; but it has probably influenced the modern use of jubilee to designate a festive celebration, especially an important anniversary.

The jubilee year is marked by three chief features. First, the land is to lie fallow. According to the plain sense of Leviticus 25:8ff. and to Jewish tradition, the jubilee year follows the seventh sabbatical year—that is, there are to be two consecutive years without agricultural activity.

Second, all landed property which has been sold is to revert to its original owners, the families that received it when the land was apportioned by lot after the conquest (Josh. 13–21).

Third, Hebrew slaves are to receive their liberty.

The intent of these provisions is stated explicitly in the text. The land is God's property which He has made available for the use of His people (verse 23). It is not to be exploited for the enrichment of some individuals to the detriment of others. If need compels a person to dispose of his holding, he cannot deed it away in perpetuity, for it is not his to sell. He can sell only the number of crops to be harvested up to the next jubilee year. Further, he and the members of his family have the right to reacquire ("redeem") the property by paying a price proportionate to the number of years still to elapse before the jubilee. If it is not redeemed earlier, it reverts to the owner-family when the shofar of jubilee is sounded (verses 13–17, 25–28).

This rule did not apply to houses in walled cities, which could be sold outright; the seller had one year from the date of sale to redeem such property, after which the purchaser had an absolute title. Special laws protected the holdings of the Levites (verses 29–34).

The legislation regarding slaves is motivated by the same kind of thinking as the land law: the Israelites are God's servants and therefore should not be enslaved to any other master. If one of them is forced by poverty to accept the slave status, he is not to be treated with the same severity ordinarily suffered by slaves (verses 39ff.). He may be redeemed at any time by a relative—or by himself, if he can find the means—through payment of a sum proportionate to the time still to elapse before the next jubilee [10]. If this does not happen, he goes free in the jubilee year.

This legislation, then, expresses a constructive social purpose, rooted in the religious conviction that all wealth is God's. As a modern interpreter has put it: "Just as the Communist demand is succinctly formulated, 'None shall have property,' so the biblical formulation is 'Everyone shall have property'" [11]. To achieve this end, wealth must be periodically redistributed. The release of Hebrew slaves is part of the process, since they were most probably sold into servitude for the satisfaction of a debt. The cancellation of debts prescribed in Deuteronomy, chapter 15, had the same objective.

b. *Was the law ever practiced?* Was this inspiring proposal ever more than an idealistic vision? According to the talmudic sources, the law is in effect only when all the tribes are resident in their respective territories; it therefore fell into abeyance as soon as the trans-Jordanian tribes of Reuben and Gad were exiled [12]. There is no record that it was ever practiced during the Second Commonwealth.

Indeed, the basic assumption behind the law—namely, that at some time in the past every Israelite family had its own holding, all approximately equal—is, to put it mildly, open to question. Few historians believe that the entire land was conquered in a brief period, then systematically divided up at one time—as the Book of Joshua reports. The conquest was probably a lengthy process; various tribes and tribal coalitions invaded the country from different starting points, and at different times, and took possession of their several areas. The Book of Judges states that substantial sectors of the country remained for generations in the hands of the earlier inhabitants. The tribal territories varied greatly in size and productivity. And it is unlikely that, within the single tribes, each family got the same amount and kind of land as every other. The ideal past, which

the jubilee legislation sought to restore, probably never existed.

Our credulity is further strained by the notion that, even once in a half-century, agricultural work should have been suspended for two consecutive years. The "sabbath of the land" entailed serious hardship; two years without cultivation would have meant ruin and famine [13].

Many modern critics have therefore concluded that the jubilee law was the proposal of a high-minded theorist whose notions were admirable, but impracticable. And in fact the Torah includes a number of provisions that have an air of unreality about them; concerning several of them the Rabbis state that they never have been operative and never will be [14].

But while the law of Leviticus, chapter 25, as it stands, was probably never practiced, the Holiness writer did not create it out of nothing. Israelite and other Near Eastern traditions provided him with the material out of which he built his structure.

First, great stress was laid in Israel on the retention of family and tribal holdings. Naboth refused to sell his vineyard to King Ahab, even at a substantial profit, because he deemed it wrong to give up his ancestral heritage (I Kings 21). The obligation to redeem family property is stressed in Ruth, chapter 4. And the Torah rules that, if women inherit family property in the absence of male heirs, they must marry men of their own tribe—so that the holding is not detached from the tribal territory (Num. 36).

Second, the prophets had bitterly attacked the trend toward the concentration of landed wealth in the hands of a few (Isa. 5:8ff.; Mic. 2:2). (But it is significant that these prophets do not mention the jubilee law or complain of its violation.)

Third, we should take note of the word *deror*, "release" (verse 10). Older translations render it "liberty." The Babylonians had a term, *duraru*, also *anduraru*, which resembles *deror* both in sound and meaning. (The Babylonians got the concept from their predecessors, the Sumerians.) *Duraru* was sometimes a release of freemen who had been enslaved, sometimes the restoration of real property to its original owners, sometimes a cancellation of debts—or a combination of these [15]. So striking a parallel can hardly be accidental. The Babylonian *duraru* was not, indeed, a regularly recurring procedure. It was an exceptional act of grace on the part of a ruler. Sometimes it marked the accession of a new king. Professor Matitiahu Tsevat has suggested that, in a somewhat similar way, the sabbatical and jubilee years in Israel celebrated the renewal of the covenant between the divine King and His people [16].

At least, then, the biblical author drew on ancient traditions and memories when he formulated his proposals for economic and social reform. Beyond this statement all assertions seem speculative and unsafe. Recent years have seen a number of attempts to assert the historicity of the jubilee as an institution. But they all involve a good deal of theorizing, and they all require some departure from the plain sense of our passage (at the very least, the assumption that when our author wrote "fiftieth year," in verse 10, he meant "forty-ninth") [17].

We may note further that among various peoples the god was deemed the sole owner of the land; but the consequence was generally drawn that, for practical purposes, the land belonged to the god's earthly representative, the king, or to the priests [18]. Only the jubilee law gives a democratic application of the principle. Further, there seems to be no significant resemblance between the various procedures for the redistribution of land in former times and more recent agrarian reform, on the one hand, and the jubilee legislation on the other [19].

c. *The Book of Jubilees.* We possess a lengthy work, composed in Hebrew at some time during the Second Commonwealth, which is most often referred to as the Book of Jubilees (it was also called the Lesser Genesis) [20]. It retells the Bible story from Creation to the arrival at Mount Sinai with many changes and embellishments. The author proposed an apparently new calendar system. He also has his own scheme of biblical chronology. He divided the whole course of history into "jubilee" periods of forty-nine years each, and he dated each of the biblical incidents in such-and-such a year of such-and-such a jubilee. It is from this fact that the customary name of the book is derived. But it does not deal at all with the jubilee law. The Book of Jubilees is of great value for students of the history of the Second Commonwealth, especially of the religious ferment and sectarian conflicts of that period; but it sheds no light on this chapter of Leviticus.

d. *The influence of the jubilee law.* An Armenian code of the twelfth century put some bits of the jubilee law into practice: the rule that urban property could be redeemed only within one year after it was sold, while property outside city walls was subject to redemption for seven years—a very considerable modification [21]. Otherwise, the law as such has not been carried out; yet, it has had an enduring impact on the minds and consciences of men. It has been the inspiration of many efforts for agrarian reform and social justice.

Henry George, the American social reformer (1839–1897), whose eloquent book, *Progress and Poverty*, launched the single tax movement, acknowledged his indebtedness in a famous lecture on Moses (see Gleanings). George sought to eliminate profit from the mere ownership of land, without abolishing private enterprise. Though his system as a whole has never been put into operation, it has influenced individual legislative acts; and his passion for justice has continued to inspire those who will not accept the inequities of our present economic system as necessary and unchangeable.

It was, however, reserved for Jews to find a practical means of realizing the ideals of the biblical document. In 1897, Professor Herman Schapira proposed to the Zionist Congress that a Jewish National Fund be established for the acquisition of land in Palestine, to be operated on principles in the spirit of our chapter. The proposal was finally adopted in 1901, after Schapira's death. The Jewish National Fund (*Keren Kayemet L'Yisrael*) collected funds from Jews all over the world and began to buy land which became the inalienable property of the Jewish people. These lands were then made available for settlement by individuals and communes, for use but not for profit. Tenants may remain on the soil as long as they cultivate it properly, but they may not sell or mortgage their holdings. The fund has reclaimed much desert and swampland and has provided sites for public buildings and industrial development. Thus, a substantial fraction of the real estate of Israel was withdrawn from the speculative market; social utility was put ahead of individual aggrandizement. By its insistence on soil conservation and proper management, the Jewish National Fund was among the earliest agencies to deal seriously with the protection of natural resources.

Today we are all keenly aware of the evils and dangers inherent in a society where unconscionable wealth and unbearable poverty exist side by side and where the urge for immediate profit threatens the destruction of the environment. Thus, this chapter is of major importance to us, if not for the solutions it offers, certainly by its challenge to us to seek our own solutions to the perennial problems of poverty and injustice.

3. Slavery

The biblical legislation on slavery is not wholly consistent. There are discrepancies between the rules in this chapter and those in Exodus, chapter 21; doubtless these variations are the result of social and economic changes. The biblical writers felt a certain uneasiness about the subject (see Exod. 21). Slavery was a universal institution in the ancient world, and no one had yet proposed abolishing it. Yet some consciences in Israel were troubled by it. Nowhere in the Bible is there a reasoned defense of slavery as an institution comparable to Aristotle's detailed argument on the subject [22]. There were, it seems, some Greeks who had at least theoretical objections to slavery; but by far the strongest extant statement on the subject comes from the Jew Philo who asserted bluntly, "Servants are free by nature, no man being naturally a slave" [23]—a statement foreshadowed by Job's passionate outcry, "Did not He that made me in the womb make him?" (Job 31:15).

It is in this spirit that the Ten Commandments give the slave the right to rest on Sabbath equally with his master (Exod. 20:10; Deut. 5:14). Moreover, the Torah penalizes the slaveowner for grossly mistreating his slaves (Exod. 21:20ff.; Deut. 23:16f.). These provisions—which contrast sharply with the law of most ancient peoples that gave the master absolute power of life and death over his slaves—apply, according to the halachah, to slaves of gentile origin [24].

If the slave is of Israelite birth [25], his rights are much broader and the master's power still more restricted. The law of the "Hebrew slave" in Leviticus, chapter 25, however, is apparently in contradiction to that found in Exodus 21:1ff. and Deuter-onomy 15:12ff. and cited in Jeremiah 34:14. These passages state that the Hebrew slave is to serve six years from the time of his enslavement; then he is to receive full liberty. Our passage simply states that the Hebrew slave is to be set free in the jubilee year, if he has not been redeemed or has not found means to buy his own freedom at an earlier date. (It also requires that the slave be treated as an employee and not as a chattel, with full regard for his dignity.)

Jewish tradition attempted to reconcile the discrepancies. It held, first, that in a jubilee year all Hebrew slaves went free at once, the remainder of their six-year term being canceled. Second, the law of Exodus and Deuteronomy gave the Hebrew slave the option of remaining permanently in his master's household, as a slave in perpetuity (le῾olam, Exod. 21:6; eved olam, Deut. 15:17). The Rabbis, however, took these phrases to mean "till the jubilee," when a new era (olam) would start.

Gentile slaves, on the other hand, serve for life and pass by inheritance from parents to children (verses 44ff.). The practice of manumitting slaves, however, was not uncommon among ancient peoples, and it was practiced among Jews as well. The Rabbis are reported on occasion to have freed a slave in order to provide the tenth man for a religious quorum (minyan). Yet surprisingly, Rabbi Akiba, known as a great humanitarian, understood verse 46 to forbid the freeing of gentile slaves [26].

It is remarkable that the halachah required a master who acquired a slave of non-Jewish stock to try to convert him to Judaism. But he was not to be forcibly circumcised; if, after the lapse of a year, he still did not wish to adopt the Jewish religion, he was to be resold [27].

See also commentary on Exod. 20:19–21:36.
(A new weekly portion, *Behar*, begins with 25:1.)

פ פ פ

א וַיְדַבֵּר יְהֹוָה אֶל־מֹשֶׁה בְּהַר סִינַי לֵאמֹר: דַּבֵּר אֶל־
בְּנֵי יִשְׂרָאֵל וְאָמַרְתָּ אֲלֵהֶם כִּי תָבֹאוּ אֶל־הָאָרֶץ אֲשֶׁר
ב אֲנִי נֹתֵן לָכֶם וְשָׁבְתָה הָאָרֶץ שַׁבָּת לַיהֹוָה: שֵׁשׁ שָׁנִים
תִּזְרַע שָׂדֶךָ וְשֵׁשׁ שָׁנִים תִּזְמֹר כַּרְמֶךָ וְאָסַפְתָּ אֶת־
ג תְּבוּאָתָהּ: וּבַשָּׁנָה הַשְּׁבִיעִת שַׁבַּת שַׁבָּתוֹן יִהְיֶה לָאָרֶץ
שַׁבָּת לַיהֹוָה שָׂדְךָ לֹא תִזְרָע וְכַרְמְךָ לֹא תִזְמֹר:
ד אֵת סְפִיחַ קְצִירְךָ לֹא תִקְצוֹר וְאֶת־עִנְּבֵי נְזִירֶךָ לֹא
ה תִבְצֹר שְׁנַת שַׁבָּתוֹן יִהְיֶה לָאָרֶץ: וְהָיְתָה שַׁבַּת הָאָרֶץ

לָכֶם לְאָכְלָה לְךָ וּלְעַבְדְּךָ וְלַאֲמָתֶךָ וְלִשְׂכִירְךָ
ו וּלְתוֹשָׁבְךָ הַגָּרִים עִמָּךְ: וְלִבְהֶמְתְּךָ וְלַחַיָּה אֲשֶׁר
ז בְּאַרְצֶךָ תִּהְיֶה כָל־תְּבוּאָתָהּ לֶאֱכֹל: ס וְסָפַרְתָּ
לְךָ שֶׁבַע שַׁבְּתֹת שָׁנִים שֶׁבַע שָׁנִים שֶׁבַע פְּעָמִים וְהָיוּ
לְךָ יְמֵי שֶׁבַע שַׁבְּתֹת הַשָּׁנִים תֵּשַׁע וְאַרְבָּעִים שָׁנָה:
ח וְהַעֲבַרְתָּ שׁוֹפַר תְּרוּעָה בַּחֹדֶשׁ הַשְּׁבִעִי בֶּעָשׂוֹר
לַחֹדֶשׁ בְּיוֹם הַכִּפֻּרִים תַּעֲבִירוּ שׁוֹפָר בְּכָל־אַרְצְכֶם:
ט וְקִדַּשְׁתֶּם אֵת שְׁנַת הַחֲמִשִּׁים שָׁנָה וּקְרָאתֶם דְּרוֹר
בָּאָרֶץ לְכָל־יֹשְׁבֶיהָ יוֹבֵל הִוא תִּהְיֶה לָכֶם וְשַׁבְתֶּם

1] The LORD spoke to Moses on Mount Sinai: **2]** Speak to the Israelite people and say to them:

When you enter the land that I give you, the land shall observe a sabbath of the LORD. **3]** Six years you may sow your field and six years you may prune your vineyard and gather in the yield. **4]** But in the seventh year the land shall have a sabbath of complete rest, a sabbath of the LORD: you shall not sow your field or prune your vineyard. **5]** You shall not reap the aftergrowth of your harvest or gather the grapes of your untrimmed vines; it shall be a year of complete rest for the land. **6]** But you may eat whatever the land during its sabbath will produce—you, your male and female slaves, the hired and bound laborers who live with you, **7]** and your cattle and the beasts in your land may eat all its yield.

8] You shall count off seven weeks of years—seven times seven years—so that the period of seven weeks of years gives you a total of forty-nine years. **9]** Then you shall sound the horn loud; in the seventh month, on the tenth day of the month—the Day of Atonement—you shall have the horn sounded throughout your land **10]** and you shall hallow the fiftieth year. You shall proclaim release throughout the land for all its inhabitants. It shall be a jubilee for you:

25:1] *On Mount Sinai.* These words are a surprise; most of the laws in Leviticus were revealed in the Tent of Meeting (1:1 and elsewhere). Tradition dealt with such anomalies by the maxim, "There is no strict chronological order in the Torah" [28]. The law, presumably, was given to Moses at Sinai and, for some reason, written down in a later passage.

2] Note the parallel between the weekly Sabbath and the "sabbath of the land."

5] *Aftergrowth.* Grain that grew from seed accidentally dropped during the harvest.

Grapes of your untrimmed vines. Failure to prune vines (and trees) may reduce the yield, but fruit will still be available.

6] The owner may not harvest, store, or sell the yield, but he may share with others in consuming it (see introduction to this chapter, "1. The Sabbatical Year").

9] *The Day of Atonement.* The jubilee year begins at Rosh Hashanah, but the release goes into effect only when the shofar is sounded on Yom Kippur.

10] *You shall proclaim release.* Hebrew *deror*. This is the verse traditionally rendered, "Proclaim liberty throughout the land." But the term "release" is more precise and closer to the meaning of *duraru* (see "2. The Jubilee Year"). Moreover, the fact that this verse was inscribed on the "Liberty Bell," which announced the signing of the Declaration of Independence, might suggest to the modern reader that "liberty" here refers to national autonomy or to civil rights—neither of which was in the author's mind.

Jubilee. Hebrew *yobel*, "ram" or "ram's horn" (T.N.).

יח יְהֹוָה אֱלֹהֵיכֶם: וַעֲשִׂיתֶם אֶת־חֻקֹּתַי וְאֶת־מִשְׁפָּטַי
תִּשְׁמְרוּ וַעֲשִׂיתֶם אֹתָם וִישַׁבְתֶּם עַל־הָאָרֶץ לָבֶטַח:
יט וְנָתְנָה הָאָרֶץ פִּרְיָהּ וַאֲכַלְתֶּם לָשֹׂבַע וִישַׁבְתֶּם לָבֶטַח
כ עָלֶיהָ: וְכִי תֹאמְרוּ מַה־נֹּאכַל בַּשָּׁנָה הַשְּׁבִיעִת הֵן לֹא
כא נִזְרָע וְלֹא נֶאֱסֹף אֶת־תְּבוּאָתֵנוּ: וְצִוִּיתִי אֶת־בִּרְכָתִי
לָכֶם בַּשָּׁנָה הַשִּׁשִּׁית וְעָשָׂת אֶת־הַתְּבוּאָה לִשְׁלֹשׁ
כב הַשָּׁנִים: וּזְרַעְתֶּם אֵת הַשָּׁנָה הַשְּׁמִינִת וַאֲכַלְתֶּם מִן
הַתְּבוּאָה יָשָׁן עַד הַשָּׁנָה הַתְּשִׁיעִת עַד־בּוֹא תְּבוּאָתָהּ
כג תֹּאכְלוּ יָשָׁן: וְהָאָרֶץ לֹא תִמָּכֵר לִצְמִתֻת כִּי־לִי
כד הָאָרֶץ כִּי־גֵרִים וְתוֹשָׁבִים אַתֶּם עִמָּדִי: וּבְכֹל אֶרֶץ
כה אֲחֻזַּתְכֶם גְּאֻלָּה תִּתְּנוּ לָאָרֶץ: ס כִּי־יָמוּךְ אָחִיךָ

יא אִישׁ אֶל־אֲחֻזָּתוֹ וְאִישׁ אֶל־מִשְׁפַּחְתּוֹ תָּשֻׁבוּ: יוֹבֵל הִוא
שְׁנַת הַחֲמִשִּׁים שָׁנָה תִּהְיֶה לָכֶם לֹא תִזְרָעוּ וְלֹא
יב תִקְצְרוּ אֶת־סְפִיחֶיהָ וְלֹא תִבְצְרוּ אֶת־נְזִרֶיהָ: כִּי יוֹבֵל
הִוא קֹדֶשׁ תִּהְיֶה לָכֶם מִן־הַשָּׂדֶה תֹּאכְלוּ אֶת־
יג תְּבוּאָתָהּ: בִּשְׁנַת הַיּוֹבֵל הַזֹּאת תָּשֻׁבוּ אִישׁ אֶל־אֲחֻזָּתוֹ:
יד וְכִי־תִמְכְּרוּ מִמְכָּר לַעֲמִיתֶךָ אוֹ קָנֹה מִיַּד עֲמִיתֶךָ
טו אַל־תּוֹנוּ אִישׁ אֶת־אָחִיו: בְּמִסְפַּר שָׁנִים אַחַר הַיּוֹבֵל
תִּקְנֶה מֵאֵת עֲמִיתֶךָ בְּמִסְפַּר שְׁנֵי־תְבוּאֹת יִמְכָּר־לָךְ:
טז לְפִי רֹב הַשָּׁנִים תַּרְבֶּה מִקְנָתוֹ וּלְפִי מְעֹט הַשָּׁנִים
תַּמְעִיט מִקְנָתוֹ כִּי מִסְפַּר תְּבוּאֹת הוּא מֹכֵר לָךְ:
יז וְלֹא תוֹנוּ אִישׁ אֶת־עֲמִיתוֹ וְיָרֵאתָ מֵאֱלֹהֶיךָ כִּי אֲנִי

each of you shall return to his holding and each of you shall return to his family. **11]** That fiftieth year shall be a jubilee for you: you shall not sow, neither shall you reap the aftergrowth or harvest the untrimmed vines, **12]** for it is a jubilee. It shall be holy to you: you may only eat the growth direct from the field.

13] In this year of jubilee, each of you shall return to his holding. **14]** When you sell property to your neighbor, or buy any from your neighbor, you shall not wrong one another. **15]** In buying from your neighbor, you shall deduct only for the number of years since the jubilee; and in selling to you, he shall charge you only for the remaining crop years: **16]** the more such years, the higher the price you pay; the fewer such years, the lower the price; for what he is selling you is a number of harvests. **17]** Do not wrong one another, but fear your God; for I the LORD am your God.

18] You shall observe My laws and faithfully keep My rules, that you may live upon the land in security; **19]** the land shall yield its fruit and you shall eat your fill, and you shall live upon it in security. **20]** And should you ask, "What are we to eat in the seventh year, if we may neither sow nor gather in our crops?" **21]** I will ordain My blessing for you in the sixth year, so that it shall yield a crop sufficient for three years. **22]** When you sow in the eighth year, you will still be eating old grain of that crop; you will be eating the old until the ninth year, until its crops come in.

23] But the land must not be sold beyond reclaim, for the land is Mine; you are but strangers resident with Me. **24]** Throughout the land that you hold, you must provide for the redemption of the land.

14] *Your neighbor.* I.e., fellow Israelite; see verse 46 (T.N.).

   You shall not wrong one another. By demanding excessive payment.

21–22] It is not quite clear whether this passage refers to the sabbatical or the jubilee year. In any case, the point is that obedience to the law will be rewarded by bumper crops (see the introduction to the next chapter).

וּמָכַ֖ר מֵאֲחֻזָּת֑וֹ וּבָ֨א גֹאֲל֜וֹ אֵלָ֗יו וְגָאַל֙ אֵ֚ת אֲשֶׁר־לֹ֣א חֹמָ֔ה לַצְּמִיתֻ֛ת לַקֹּנֶ֥ה אֹת֖וֹ לְדֹרֹתָ֑יו לֹ֥א יֵצֵ֖א
מִמְכַּ֣ר אָחִֽיו׃　כוֹ וְאִ֕ישׁ כִּ֛י לֹ֥א יִֽהְיֶה־לּ֖וֹ גֹּאֵ֑ל וְהִשִּׂ֣יגָה יָד֔וֹ בַּיֹּבֵ֑ל׃ לא וּבָתֵּ֣י הַחֲצֵרִ֗ים אֲשֶׁ֨ר אֵין־לָהֶ֤ם חֹמָה֙ סָבִ֔יב
וּמָצָ֖א כְּדֵ֥י גְאֻלָּתֽוֹ׃　כז וְחִשַּׁב֙ אֶת־שְׁנֵ֣י מִמְכָּר֔וֹ וְהֵשִׁ֥יב אֶת־ עַל־שְׂדֵ֥ה הָאָ֖רֶץ יֵחָשֵׁ֑ב גְּאֻלָּה֙ תִּֽהְיֶה־לּ֔וֹ וּבַיֹּבֵ֖ל יֵצֵֽא׃
הָ֣עֹדֵ֔ף לָאִ֖ישׁ אֲשֶׁ֣ר מָֽכַר־ל֑וֹ וְשָׁ֖ב לַאֲחֻזָּתֽוֹ׃ כח וְאִם־לֹֽא־ לב וְעָרֵי֙ הַלְוִיִּ֔ם בָּתֵּ֖י עָרֵ֣י אֲחֻזָּתָ֑ם גְּאֻלַּ֥ת עוֹלָ֖ם תִּהְיֶ֥ה
מָצְאָ֣ה יָד֗וֹ דֵּי֮ הָשִׁ֣יב לוֹ֒ וְהָיָ֣ה מִמְכָּר֗וֹ בְּיַד֙ הַקֹּנֶ֣ה אֹת֔וֹ לַלְוִיִּֽם׃ לג וַאֲשֶׁ֤ר יִגְאַל֙ מִן־הַלְוִיִּ֔ם וְיָצָ֧א מִמְכַּר־בַּ֛יִת וְעִ֥יר
עַ֖ד שְׁנַ֣ת הַיֹּבֵ֑ל וְיָצָא֙ בַּיֹּבֵ֔ל וְשָׁ֖ב לַאֲחֻזָּתֽוֹ׃ ס　כט וְאִ֗ישׁ אֲחֻזָּת֖וֹ בַּיֹּבֵ֑ל כִּ֣י בָתֵּ֞י עָרֵ֣י הַלְוִיִּ֗ם הִ֚וא אֲחֻזָּתָ֔ם בְּת֖וֹךְ
כִּֽי־יִמְכֹּ֤ר בֵּית־מוֹשַׁב֙ עִ֣יר חוֹמָ֔ה וְהָיְתָ֣ה גְּאֻלָּת֔וֹ עַד־ בְּנֵ֖י יִשְׂרָאֵֽל׃ לד וּֽשְׂדֵ֛ה מִגְרַ֥שׁ עָרֵיהֶ֖ם לֹ֣א יִמָּכֵ֑ר כִּֽי־אֲחֻזַּ֥ת
תֹּ֖ם שְׁנַ֣ת מִמְכָּר֑וֹ יָמִ֖ים תִּהְיֶ֥ה גְאֻלָּתֽוֹ׃　ל וְאִ֣ם לֹֽא־יִגָּאֵ֗ל עוֹלָ֛ם ה֖וּא לָהֶֽם׃ ס　וְכִֽי־יָמ֣וּךְ אָחִ֔יךָ וּמָ֥טָה יָד֖וֹ
עַד־מְלֹ֣את ל֣וֹ שָׁנָ֣ה תְמִימָ֗ה וְ֠קָ֠ם הַבַּ֨יִת אֲשֶׁר־בָּעִ֜יר עִמָּ֑ךְ וְהֶֽחֱזַ֣קְתָּ בּ֔וֹ גֵּ֧ר וְתוֹשָׁ֛ב וָחַ֖י עִמָּ֑ךְ׃ אַל־תִּקַּ֤ח

* ל לו קרי.

25] If your brother is in straits and has to sell part of his holding, his nearest redeemer shall come and redeem what his brother has sold. 26] If a man has no one to redeem for him, but prospers and acquires enough to redeem with, 27] he shall compute the years since its sale, refund the difference to the man to whom he sold it, and return to his holding. 28] If he lacks sufficient means to recover it, what he sold shall remain with the purchaser until the jubilee; in the jubilee year it shall be released, and he shall return to his holding.

29] If a man sells a dwelling house in a walled city, it may be redeemed until a year has elapsed since its sale; the redemption period shall be a year. 30] If it is not redeemed before a full year has elapsed, the house in the walled city shall pass to the purchaser beyond reclaim throughout the ages; it shall not be released in the jubilee. 31] But houses in villages that have no encircling walls shall be classed as open country: they may be redeemed, and they shall be released through the jubilee. 32] As for the cities of the Levites, the houses in the cities they hold—the Levites shall forever have the right of redemption. 33] Such property as may be redeemed from the Levites—houses sold in a city they hold—shall be released through the jubilee; for the houses in the cities of the Levites are their holding among the Israelites. 34] But the unenclosed land about their cities cannot be sold, for that is their holding for all time.

35] If your brother, being in straits, comes under your authority, and you hold him as though

---

25] *Redeemer*. Hebrew *goʾel*. I.e., the closest relative able to redeem the land (T.N.). The close relative had the moral obligation to buy back the family holding (cf. Ruth 3:12–4:6). Originally he was also obligated to avenge the murder of a member of the family and, in this situation, was called "*goʾel* of the blood" ("blood-avenger," Deut. 19:6). Similarly, God is called the *Goʾel* of Israel (Isa. 44:6; cf. Exod. 6:6).

29] *A dwelling house in a walled city*. This was not considered tribal territory in the same sense as farm land, and therefore it might be sold in perpetuity.

32–34] *Levites*. On their status, see Numbers, chap-

ters 3 and 4. This is the only place where Leviticus mentions the Levites!

33] First half of verse obscure (T.N.). *Sifra* understands: The right of redemption applies even if the Levite sells his property to another Levite, and not only if he sells it to an ordinary Israelite.

35] Earlier translators understood the verse to mean, "If your brother is in straits and his means fail with you, you shall uphold him: he shall live by your side as a resident alien." The present rendering follows suggestions first made by Ehrlich, now supported by parallels from Mesopotamia [29].

מֵאִתּוֹ נֶשֶׁךְ וְתַרְבִּית וְיָרֵאתָ מֵאֱלֹהֶיךָ וְחֵי אָחִיךָ עִמָּךְ:
לז אֶת־כַּסְפְּךָ לֹא־תִתֵּן לוֹ בְּנֶשֶׁךְ וּבְמַרְבִּית לֹא־תִתֵּן
לח אָכְלֶךָ: אֲנִי יְהוָֹה אֱלֹהֵיכֶם אֲשֶׁר־הוֹצֵאתִי אֶתְכֶם
מֵאֶרֶץ מִצְרַיִם לָתֵת לָכֶם אֶת־אֶרֶץ כְּנַעַן לִהְיוֹת
לט לָכֶם לֵאלֹהִים: ס וְכִי־יָמוּךְ אָחִיךָ עִמָּךְ וְנִמְכַּר־
מ לָךְ לֹא־תַעֲבֹד בּוֹ עֲבֹדַת עָבֶד: כְּשָׂכִיר כְּתוֹשָׁב יִהְיֶה
מא עִמָּךְ עַד־שְׁנַת הַיֹּבֵל יַעֲבֹד עִמָּךְ: וְיָצָא מֵעִמָּךְ הוּא
וּבָנָיו עִמּוֹ וְשָׁב אֶל־מִשְׁפַּחְתּוֹ וְאֶל־אֲחֻזַּת אֲבֹתָיו יָשׁוּב:
מב כִּי־עֲבָדַי הֵם אֲשֶׁר־הוֹצֵאתִי אֹתָם מֵאֶרֶץ מִצְרַיִם לֹא

מג יִמָּכְרוּ מִמְכֶּרֶת עָבֶד: לֹא־תִרְדֶּה בוֹ בְּפָרֶךְ וְיָרֵאתָ
מד מֵאֱלֹהֶיךָ: וְעַבְדְּךָ וַאֲמָתְךָ אֲשֶׁר יִהְיוּ־לָךְ מֵאֵת הַגּוֹיִם
מה אֲשֶׁר סְבִיבֹתֵיכֶם מֵהֶם תִּקְנוּ עֶבֶד וְאָמָה: וְגַם מִבְּנֵי
הַתּוֹשָׁבִים הַגָּרִים עִמָּכֶם מֵהֶם תִּקְנוּ וּמִמִּשְׁפַּחְתָּם
אֲשֶׁר עִמָּכֶם אֲשֶׁר הוֹלִידוּ בְּאַרְצְכֶם וְהָיוּ לָכֶם
מו לַאֲחֻזָּה: וְהִתְנַחַלְתֶּם אֹתָם לִבְנֵיכֶם אַחֲרֵיכֶם לָרֶשֶׁת
אֲחֻזָּה לְעֹלָם בָּהֶם תַּעֲבֹדוּ וּבְאַחֵיכֶם בְּנֵי־יִשְׂרָאֵל
מז אִישׁ בְּאָחִיו לֹא־תִרְדֶּה בוֹ בְּפָרֶךְ: ס וְכִי תַשִּׂיג יַד
גֵּר וְתוֹשָׁב עִמָּךְ וּמָךְ אָחִיךָ עִמּוֹ וְנִמְכַּר לְגֵר תּוֹשָׁב

a resident alien, let him live by your side: **36]** do not exact from him advance or accrued interest, but fear your God. Let him live by your side as your brother. **37]** Do not lend him money at advance interest, or give him your food at accrued interest. **38]** I the LORD am your God, who brought you out of the land of Egypt, to give you the land of Canaan, to be your God.

39] If your brother under you continues in straits and must give himself over to you, do not subject him to the treatment of a slave. **40]** He shall remain under you as a hired or bound laborer; he shall serve with you only until the jubilee year. **41]** Then he and his children with him shall be free of your authority; he shall go back to his family and return to his ancestral holding.— **42]** For they are My servants, whom I freed from the land of Egypt; they may not give themselves over into servitude.— **43]** You shall not rule over him ruthlessly; you shall fear your God. **44]** Such male and female slaves as you may have—it is from the nations round about you that you may acquire male and female slaves. **45]** You may also buy them from among the children of aliens resident with you, or from their families that are among you, whom they begot in your land. These shall become your property: **46]** you may keep them as a possession for your children after you, for them to inherit as property for all time. Such you may treat as slaves. But as for your Israelite brothers, no one shall rule ruthlessly over the other.

47] If a resident alien among you has prospered, and your brother, being in straits, comes under his authority and gives himself over to the resident alien among you, or to an offshoot of

---

36] *Advance or accrued interest.* The usual word for "interest" is *neshech*, from the root "to bite"— apparently meaning the "bite" taken in advance from the total sum, as notes are commonly discounted today. This word is rendered here as "advance [interest]." "Accrued interest" is the rendering of *marbit*, "increase." It is the additional sum to be added to the principal at the time of payment.

Earlier translations employed the word "usury" which was formerly synonymous with "interest" and only later came to mean exorbitant interest. The Torah forbids taking interest in any amount from a fellow Israelite (see further on Deut. 23:21).

43] *You shall fear your God.* See commentary on 19:14.

מח עִמָּךְ אוֹ לְעֵקֶר מִשְׁפַּחַת גֵּר: אַחֲרֵי נִמְכַּר גְּאֻלָּה
מט תִּהְיֶה־לּוֹ אֶחָד מֵאֶחָיו יִגְאָלֶנּוּ: אוֹ־דֹדוֹ אוֹ בֶן־דֹּדוֹ
יִגְאָלֶנּוּ אוֹ־מִשְּׁאֵר בְּשָׂרוֹ מִמִּשְׁפַּחְתּוֹ יִגְאָלֶנּוּ אוֹ־הִשִּׂיגָה
נ יָדוֹ וְנִגְאָל: וְחִשַּׁב עִם־קֹנֵהוּ מִשְּׁנַת הִמָּכְרוֹ לוֹ עַד שְׁנַת
הַיֹּבֵל וְהָיָה כֶּסֶף מִמְכָּרוֹ בְּמִסְפַּר שָׁנִים כִּימֵי שָׂכִיר
נא יִהְיֶה עִמּוֹ: אִם־עוֹד רַבּוֹת בַּשָּׁנִים לְפִיהֶן יָשִׁיב גְּאֻלָּתוֹ

נב מִכֶּסֶף מִקְנָתוֹ: וְאִם־מְעַט נִשְׁאַר בַּשָּׁנִים עַד־שְׁנַת
נג הַיֹּבֵל וְחִשַּׁב־לוֹ כְּפִי שָׁנָיו יָשִׁיב אֶת־גְּאֻלָּתוֹ: כְּשָׂכִיר
שָׁנָה בְּשָׁנָה יִהְיֶה עִמּוֹ לֹא־יִרְדֶּנּוּ בְּפֶרֶךְ לְעֵינֶיךָ:
נד וְאִם־לֹא יִגָּאֵל בְּאֵלֶּה וְיָצָא בִּשְׁנַת הַיֹּבֵל הוּא וּבָנָיו
נה עִמּוֹ: כִּי־לִי בְנֵי־יִשְׂרָאֵל עֲבָדִים עֲבָדַי הֵם אֲשֶׁר־
הוֹצֵאתִי אוֹתָם מֵאֶרֶץ מִצְרָיִם אֲנִי יְהֹוָה אֱלֹהֵיכֶם:

an alien's family, **48]** he shall have the right of redemption even after he has given himself over. One of his brothers shall redeem him, **49]** or his uncle or his uncle's son shall redeem him, or anyone of his family who is of his own flesh shall redeem him; or, if he prospers, he may redeem himself. **50]** He shall compute with his purchaser the total from the year he gave himself over to him until the jubilee year; the price of his sale shall be applied to the number of years, as though it were for a term as a hired laborer under the other's authority. **51]** If many years remain, he shall pay back for his redemption in proportion to his purchase price; **52]** and if few years remain until the jubilee year, he shall so compute: he shall make payment for his redemption according to the years involved. **53]** He shall be under his authority as a laborer hired by the year; he shall not rule ruthlessly over him in your sight. **54]** If he has not been redeemed in any of those ways, he and his children with him shall go free in the jubilee year. **55]** For it is to Me that the Israelites are servants: they are My servants, whom I freed from the land of Egypt, I the LORD your God.

48] *He shall have the right of redemption.* If he can furnish the proper sum of money, the owner cannot refuse it and keep him in servitude.

One of his brothers shall redeem him. Cf. commentary on verse 25.

GLEANINGS

Halachah

25:8] *You Shall Count Off*

The priests are to count off the years in a formal ceremony, just as each year the days of the *omer* are counted off (see commentary on 23:15).   SIFRA

14] *You Shall Not Wrong One Another*

This rule applies not only to the present case but to all transactions. An overcharge (or under-payment) of more than one-sixth of the fair value of an article constitutes "wrong" (*ona'ah*) and may justify voiding the transaction [30].

17] *Do Not Wrong One Another*

This repetition has a purpose—it forbids *ona'ah* by words: one must not remind a penitent sinner of his former misdeeds or a convert of his heathen ancestry; one should not inquire the price of an article he does not intend to buy.   SIFRA

25–28] Redemption of property. Once he has sold it, the seller must wait a minimum of two years before attempting to redeem it.   SIFRA

29] *A Dwelling House in a Walled City*

This law applies only to cities which were in existence and had walls when Joshua conquered the country, even though the walls have since vanished. It does not apply to more recently established cities, even though they are walled now.   SIFRA

36] *Advance or Accrued Interest*

See commentary. In their treatment of the biblical material, the Rabbis make no distinction between *neshech* and *marbit*. But they apply the word *ribit* (virtually identical with *marbit*) to profit from trading in futures, which is forbidden by rabbinical ordinance [31].

39] *Do Not Subject Him to the Treatment of a Slave*

He must not be made to stand on the auction block; when sold, he must not be required to perform demeaning services for his master.   SIFRA

53] *He Shall Not Rule over Him Ruthlessly in Your Sight*

You shall not allow him to mistreat a Hebrew slave, if you observe him doing so; but you are not required to enter his house to see if he is treating the slave properly.   SIFRA

Haggadah

"Trace to its roots the cause that is thus producing want in the midst of plenty, ignorance in the midst of intelligence, aristocracy in democracy, weakness in strength—that is giving to our civilization a one-sided and unstable development, and you will find it something which this Hebrew statesman three thousand years ago perceived and guarded against. Moses saw that the real cause of the enslavement of the masses of Egypt was what has everywhere produced enslavement, the possession by a class of the land upon which and from which the whole people must live. He saw that to permit in land the same unqualified private ownership that by natural right attaches to things produced by labor would be inevitably to separate the people into the very rich and the very poor, inevitably to enslave labor....

"And, with the foresight of the philosophic states-man who legislates not for the need of a day but for all the future, he sought, in ways suited to his times and conditions, to guard against this error. Every-where in the Mosaic institutions is the land treated as the gift of the Creator to His common creatures, which no one has the right to monopolize. Every-where it is, not your estate, or your property, not the land which you bought, or the land which you conquered, but 'the land which the Lord thy God giveth thee'—'the land which the Lord lendeth thee.' And by practical legislation, by regulations to which he gave the highest sanctions, he tried to guard against the wrong that converted ancient civiliza-tions into despotisms . . . the wrong that is already filling American cities with idle men and our virgin states with tramps. . . .

"I do not say that these institutions were for their ultimate purpose the very best that might even then have been devised, for Moses had to work, as all great constructive statesmen have to work, with the tools that came to his hand and upon materials as he found them. Still less do I mean to say that forms suitable for that time and people are suitable for every time and people. I ask not veneration of the form but recognition of the spirit.

"Yet how common it is to venerate the form and to deny the spirit! There are many who believe that the Mosaic institutions were literally dictated by the Almighty, yet who would denounce as irreligious and 'communistic' any application of their spirit to the present day" (Henry George) [32].

25:40] *He Shall Remain under You as a Hired or Bound Laborer*

But though you should treat him with respect, he should regard himself humbly as a slave. SIFRA

42] *For They Are My Servants*

And so should not be subject to any of My other subjects. SIFRA

44–46] Although the Torah does not specifically command us to treat the gentile slave humanely, we should always treat him with decency and kind-ness (Maimonides) [33].

Blessings and Curses

(For a further discussion see also commentary on Deut. 27 and 28.)

Since chapter 27 takes the form of an appendix, Leviticus actually concludes with chapter 26.

1. *Tochechah*

This is the term used to describe terrible punishment or "reproof." Leviticus, chapter 26, concludes with a fervent appeal for obedience to the laws, promising bliss for the nation if they are observed and threatening terrible punishment if they are violated. The word *tochechah* is also applied to a similar exhortation in Deuteronomy, chapter 28. A shorter and less frightening homily appears in Exodus 23:20ff. In all three cases, an extensive legal section is followed by promises and threats.

This is an ancient pattern. The Babylonian Code of Hammurabi and the still older Sumerian Code of Lipit-Ishtar [1] begin by telling how the laws were promulgated; and the legal section proper is followed by the promise of blessings for those who obey these laws and by curses on those who falsify the text or violate its provisions. Just so, the various legal documents of the Torah are each introduced by an account of the Exodus and the revelation at Sinai and conclude with a *tochechah*.

In recent years, scholars have noted a similar pattern in another category of Near Eastern documents—the treaties made by powerful rulers with the vassal kings whom they "protected." Such documents promulgated by Hittite conquerors begin by reciting the benefits which the great potentate has conferred on his vassal; then the terms of the treaty are stated, followed by threats of punishment if the weaker party should violate the agreement [2].

A still more remarkable parallel is furnished by the vassal treaties of the Assyrian conqueror Esarhaddon. In view of the agreements both in the order of the curses and the language in which they are expressed, it seems certain that the author of Deuteronomy, chapter 28, borrowed from these documents [3]. Even here, the extraordinary resemblances are combined with some differences. Deuteronomy, chapter 28, begins with a promise of blessings for obedience, to which nothing in the Assyrian treaties

953

corresponds. And, though some of the striking and vivid phrases of the *tochechah* are now revealed to be conventional curses (see commentary on 26:19 and 29), the biblical author adds psychological touches (Deut. 28:65ff.) and religious references (Deut. 28:45ff. and 58ff.) to which the Assyrian documents offer no parallel [4].

Our chapter does not present such close parallels to any known document from the Near East [5], though it too contains some of the stereotyped language of the treaty curses. But here the material is worked up in a much more rhetorical fashion—and it ends with a glimmering of hope.

A review of the related biblical passages is instructive. The Exodus section (23:20ff.), which all agree is very early, is made up mostly of promises and contains few threats. Deuteronomy, chapter 28, the longest and most gruesome of these sections, ends in a mood of utter despair. (Chapters 29 and 30 of Deuteronomy contain still another *tochechah*, the most eloquent of all, in which there is an explicit promise of the spiritual renewal and then the political restoration of Israel.) Leviticus, chapter 26, concludes with a picture of ruin and dispersion, which may well reflect the actual conditions of the exilic period, yet voices the assurance that God will not abandon His people forever (see below "3. Sources of Hope").

The public reading of these threatening passages caused great uneasiness to former generations. Ordinarily it is an honor to be "called up" to recite the Torah benedictions, and those who receive this honor frequently make a gift to the synagogue in appreciation. But people avoided the privilege of being called up on the Sabbaths when the curses were read from Leviticus and Deuteronomy. The seven subsections into which the weekly Torah portion is divided, and for each of which a worshiper comes forward in the traditional synagogue to pronounce the blessings, are usually of about equal length; they rarely extend over more than twenty-five verses. But the curses in Leviticus (26:10–46) and Deuteronomy (28:7–69) are traditionally read without interruption. This arrangement served a double purpose: the disturbing passage could be completed as quickly as possible and only one reluctant worshiper had to be persuaded to say the benedictions [6].

2. The Problem of Retribution

The modern reader will likewise be stirred by the gloomy eloquence of our chapter; but his reaction will probably be quite different from that of his forebears. Almost automatically he will question the basic assumption of the chapter—that virtue and piety are requited with material benefits and wickedness with material punishment. The doctrine of earthly rewards and punishments is asserted many times in the Bible with vigor and eloquence. It was challenged irresistibly in the Book of Job and elsewhere; still, people continued to believe it because they wanted to believe it. But it cannot be rationally defended.

Let us examine the matter more closely. In Babylonian thought, the welfare of the nation was regarded as dependent on the behavior of the king. If he pleased the gods, his entire people would benefit, and, if he did not please the gods, the entire people would suffer [7]. In Israel, a more "democratic" outlook prevailed. The entire nation must assume responsibility. If it is loyal to God, it will prosper; if it is faithless, it will fall. That is the viewpoint of the present chapter and of many other biblical passages. In some cases, it is even asserted that the misdeeds of a single citizen may bring disaster on the whole community (Josh. 7).

The idea of collective responsibility was gradually modified as prophets and psalmists

recognized more fully the religious importance of the individual. This new insight led the prophet Ezekiel to an extreme and untenable version of the concept of retribution. He retained the doctrine of material rewards and punishments, and he applied it to the fate of each individual. The righteous man, he asserted, is blessed with long life and prosperity, whereas the wicked man comes to an early and evil end (Ezek. 18). He even implied (9:44ff.) that every person who died during the storming of Jerusalem deserved his fate because of prior sins! This opinion is echoed in other biblical books, notably Proverbs.

And indeed such a view appeared as the logical inference from the belief in one righteous God. One might have thought that the pagan would find less difficulty (at least in theory) with the fact of suffering, even undeserved suffering. For the many gods of paganism were deemed unstable and capricious, and some were downright hostile to man. Misfortune could then be explained as due to the malice of evil spirits or hostile godlings, to the working of inexorable fate, or (as we saw above) to the guilt of the king. Yet in fact we possess a number of Egyptian, Sumerian, and Akkadian texts which lament the misery, seemingly undeserved, that sometimes comes upon men [8]. And, if these dark realities were a difficult problem for the pagan mind, they were an even more urgent challenge to those who believed in one, all-good, creative God.

As long as people thought in terms of collective responsibility, the problem could somehow be managed. For, if a nation was predominantly righteous and therefore prosperous, even the undeserving citizens might share its good fortunes. And, if national wickedness entailed national disaster, some of the virtuous minority might get hurt in the general crash.

This form of the doctrine, moreover, contains a measure of truth. The stability of a nation depends largely on the honesty of its citizens and the justness of its institutions; moral decline can bring on political disintegration. But morality is not the only condition for national survival, perhaps not even the decisive condition. Peaceable and culturally productive peoples have been subjugated or exterminated by nations inferior to them in everything but military potential and ferocity. Who dare say that the four centuries of expropriation and genocide endured by the American Indians, the liquidation of the Baltic states by Soviet Russia, or the horrors of Auschwitz were punishments which the victims deserved?

Still less acceptable is the application of the doctrine to individual experience, as taught by Ezekiel. It can be upheld only by stubborn disregard of facts. Immoral and criminal persons may enjoy years of health, success, and honor; saintly men and women may have to bear endless agony and sorrow. The passionate eloquence with which the author of Job insisted on these realities is unanswerable. The book finally asserts that the problem of suffering is beyond human understanding. Yet at the end of the work God himself declares that Job has spoken rightly; God's reputation is not to be defended by distorting the truth (Job 42:8).

The theory of mechanical retribution, moreover, is not only mistaken but actually immoral. For, if sin is regularly followed by punishment, it follows that every misfortune is a condemnation. Job poignantly complains of the cruelty of his friends. Instead of giving him sympathy and affection in his misery, they lecture him on the need to reform his conduct (Job 19:1–21).

A few centuries after this masterpiece was written, Jewish teachers affirmed the belief in immortality and thereby provided a new approach to the problem of retribution. In an existence beyond the grave, they taught,

true justice will be meted out to righteous and wicked alike; retribution will be spiritual rather than physical. In one form or another, this has been the conviction of most Jews through the ages [9]. It is an assertion of faith which can hardly be proved or disproved.

But, concerning those realities that we can appraise here and now, at least this much may be confidently stated:

First, there is no necessary relation between a man's merits and his fortunes. A person of noblest character may be lucky or he may be miserable; a depraved individual may be lucky or he may be miserable. It is untrue to say that it always pays to be good, and it is equally untrue to say that it never pays. An honest and dependable person is usually respected and trusted; kindness to others often evokes a similar response from them. National righteousness contributes to national stability. But such results are only possibilities; they are not guaranteed.

Second, the consequences of our conduct can rarely be limited to ourselves. For good or for bad, what we do affects the lives of others, in the present and future. We cannot foresee all the effects of our decisions; we can only try to choose wisely and responsibly. Foolish and evil men have caused untold disaster; intelligent and good people have benefited all mankind. The question "Why did God let Hitler do what he did?" cannot be separated from the question "Why did God let Pasteur do what he did?"

Third, it may be that only a world like ours—a world in which we are never sure whether we will be rewarded or punished for our actions—gives us the possibility of leading a truly moral life. For the ethical decision is the decision to do the right because it is right and not for any other advantage.

3. The Sources of Hope

Our chapter, be it noted, deals not only with physical rewards and punishments but also with spiritual concerns. It alludes to the calm assurance that comes with rectitude and to the mindless terror that in moments of adversity grips those who are not sustained by a clear conscience and by the sense of God's nearness.

Toward the end of the chapter, hope is held out even for the sinful and scattered people. They must take the first step toward their redemption, by confessing their wrongdoings and turning back to God (verses 39f.). This is one of the classic passages about *teshuvah*, "return," "repentance" (see introduction to Lev. 16, "5. Atonement and Return"). Once this step is taken, God will recall and fulfill His promise to the patriarchs that their posterity shall be numerous and shall possess the land of Canaan. For Abraham, Isaac, and Jacob lived up to their side of the covenant with God; and so He is bound to keep His promise, even though the descendants of the patriarchs are not worthy.

This notion is developed in talmudic literature into the concept of *zechut avot*, "the merit of the fathers." The rabbinic version stresses not so much the obligation of God to keep His word as the great piety of the patriarchs and the love it evoked from God. The merits of the fathers, so to speak, are credited to the delinquent account of the offspring. The Rabbis utilized this doctrine with delicate tact, so as to encourage the people in times of crisis and tragedy, without undermining their own sense of moral responsibility [10].

Finally, our chapter voices a conviction that cannot be fully rationalized—God is forever the God of Israel (verse 44). And so there is always hope.

(A new weekly portion, *Bechukotai*, begins with 26:3.)

לֹא־תַעֲשׂוּ לָכֶם אֱלִילִם וּפֶסֶל וּמַצֵּבָה לֹא־תָקִימוּ
לָכֶם וְאֶבֶן מַשְׂכִּית לֹא תִתְּנוּ בְּאַרְצְכֶם לְהִשְׁתַּחֲוֺת
עָלֶיהָ כִּי אֲנִי יְהֹוָה אֱלֹהֵיכֶם: אֶת־שַׁבְּתֹתַי תִּשְׁמֹרוּ
וּמִקְדָּשִׁי תִּירָאוּ אֲנִי יְהֹוָה:

Haftarah Behar, p. 1003

פ פ פ

אִם־בְּחֻקֹּתַי תֵּלֵכוּ וְאֶת־מִצְוֺתַי תִּשְׁמְרוּ וַעֲשִׂיתֶם אֹתָם:
וְנָתַתִּי גִשְׁמֵיכֶם בְּעִתָּם וְנָתְנָה הָאָרֶץ יְבוּלָהּ וְעֵץ
הַשָּׂדֶה יִתֵּן פִּרְיוֹ: וְהִשִּׂיג לָכֶם דַּיִשׁ אֶת־בָּצִיר וּבָצִיר

יַשִּׂיג אֶת־זֶרַע וַאֲכַלְתֶּם לַחְמְכֶם לָשֹׂבַע וִישַׁבְתֶּם
לָבֶטַח בְּאַרְצְכֶם: וְנָתַתִּי שָׁלוֹם בָּאָרֶץ וּשְׁכַבְתֶּם וְאֵין
מַחֲרִיד וְהִשְׁבַּתִּי חַיָּה רָעָה מִן־הָאָרֶץ וְחֶרֶב לֹא־
תַעֲבֹר בְּאַרְצְכֶם: וּרְדַפְתֶּם אֶת־אֹיְבֵיכֶם וְנָפְלוּ
לִפְנֵיכֶם לֶחָרֶב: וְרָדְפוּ מִכֶּם חֲמִשָּׁה מֵאָה וּמֵאָה
מִכֶּם רְבָבָה יִרְדֹּפוּ וְנָפְלוּ אֹיְבֵיכֶם לִפְנֵיכֶם לֶחָרֶב:
וּפָנִיתִי אֲלֵיכֶם וְהִפְרֵיתִי אֶתְכֶם וְהִרְבֵּיתִי אֶתְכֶם
וַהֲקִימֹתִי אֶת־בְּרִיתִי אִתְּכֶם: וַאֲכַלְתֶּם יָשָׁן נוֹשָׁן וְיָשָׁן
מִפְּנֵי חָדָשׁ תּוֹצִיאוּ: וְנָתַתִּי מִשְׁכָּנִי בְּתוֹכְכֶם וְלֹא־

1] You shall not make idols for yourselves, or set up for yourselves carved images or pillars, or place figured stones in your land to worship upon, for I the LORD am your God.   2] You shall keep My sabbaths and venerate My sanctuary, Mine, the LORD's.

3] If you follow My laws and faithfully observe My commandments,   4] I will grant your rains in their season, so that the earth shall yield its produce and the trees of the field their fruit.   5] Your threshing shall overtake the vintage, and your vintage shall overtake the sowing; you shall eat your fill of bread and dwell securely in your land.

6] I will grant peace in the land, and you shall lie down untroubled by anyone; I will give the land respite from vicious beasts, and no sword shall cross your land.   7] You shall give chase to your enemies, and they shall fall before you by the sword.   8] Five of you shall give chase to a hundred, and a hundred of you shall give chase to ten thousand; your enemies shall fall before you by the sword.

9] I will look with favor upon you, and make you fertile and multiply you; and I will maintain My covenant with you.   10] You shall eat old grain long stored, and you shall have to clear out the old to make room for the new.

11] I will establish My abode in your midst, and I will not spurn you.   12] I will be ever

---

26:1] *Figured stones.* Meaning of Hebrew *maskit* uncertain (T.N.).

4] *Rains in their season.* Especially the early rain (*yoreh*), in the autumn, and the late rain (*malkosh*) shortly before harvest time in the spring.

5] *Your threshing shall overtake the vintage.* The grain harvest in the spring will be so abundant that you will be busy threshing until vintage-time at the end of the summer; and the vintage will occupy you until time for the fall sowing.

8] *Five of you shall give chase to a hundred.* With God on your side, a few of you will be able to rout many enemies. Hebrew style often uses round numbers which are not to be taken exactly (see commentary on verse 14).

9] *I will look with favor upon you.* Literally, "I will turn toward you"—like a king who turns from other affairs to reward a diligent servant (*Sifra*).

10] *You shall eat old grain long stored.* Though long stored, it will not deteriorate. Yet you will have to move some of it out of the granaries, to make room for the new crop.

11] *And I will not spurn you.* Coming after many positive blessings, this negative clause is strangely anticlimactic. If God will not spurn Israel even after they have sinned and been exiled (verse 44), why should there be need for such an assurance to those who obey the laws? Nachmanides therefore conjectured that some secret doctrine was hinted at here.

יב תִּגְעַל נַפְשִׁי אֶתְכֶם: וְהִתְהַלַּכְתִּי בְּתוֹכְכֶם וְהָיִיתִי
יג לָכֶם לֵאלֹהִים וְאַתֶּם תִּהְיוּ־לִי לְעָם: אֲנִי יְהֹוָה
אֱלֹהֵיכֶם אֲשֶׁר הוֹצֵאתִי אֶתְכֶם מֵאֶרֶץ מִצְרַיִם מִהְיֹת
לָהֶם עֲבָדִים וָאֶשְׁבֹּר מֹטֹת עֻלְּכֶם וָאוֹלֵךְ אֶתְכֶם
קוֹמְמִיּוּת: פ

יד וְאִם־לֹא תִשְׁמְעוּ לִי וְלֹא תַעֲשׂוּ אֵת כָּל־הַמִּצְוֹת
טו הָאֵלֶּה: וְאִם־בְּחֻקֹּתַי תִּמְאָסוּ וְאִם אֶת־מִשְׁפָּטַי תִּגְעַל
נַפְשְׁכֶם לְבִלְתִּי עֲשׂוֹת אֶת־כָּל־מִצְוֺתַי לְהַפְרְכֶם אֶת־

טו בְּרִיתִי: אַף־אֲנִי אֶעֱשֶׂה־זֹּאת לָכֶם וְהִפְקַדְתִּי עֲלֵיכֶם
בֶּהָלָה אֶת־הַשַּׁחֶפֶת וְאֶת־הַקַּדַּחַת מְכַלּוֹת עֵינַיִם
וּמְדִיבֹת נָפֶשׁ וּזְרַעְתֶּם לָרִיק זַרְעֲכֶם וַאֲכָלֻהוּ
יז אֹיְבֵיכֶם: וְנָתַתִּי פָנַי בָּכֶם וְנִגַּפְתֶּם לִפְנֵי אֹיְבֵיכֶם
וְרָדוּ בָכֶם שֹׂנְאֵיכֶם וְנַסְתֶּם וְאֵין־רֹדֵף אֶתְכֶם:
יח וְאִם־עַד־אֵלֶּה לֹא תִשְׁמְעוּ לִי וְיָסַפְתִּי לְיַסְּרָה אֶתְכֶם
יט שֶׁבַע עַל־חַטֹּאתֵיכֶם: וְשָׁבַרְתִּי אֶת־גְּאוֹן עֻזְּכֶם וְנָתַתִּי
כ אֶת־שְׁמֵיכֶם כַּבַּרְזֶל וְאֶת־אַרְצְכֶם כַּנְּחֻשָׁה: וְתַם לָרִיק

present in your midst: I will be your God, and you shall be My people.   13] I the LORD am your God who brought you out from the land of the Egyptians to be their slaves no more, who broke the bars of your yoke and made you walk erect.

14] But if you do not obey Me and do not observe all these commandments,   **15]** if you reject My laws and spurn My rules, so that you do not observe all My commandments and you break My covenant,   **16]** I in turn will do this to you: I will wreak misery upon you—consumption and fever, which cause the eyes to pine and the body to languish; you shall sow your seed to no purpose, for your enemies shall eat it.   **17]** I will set My face against you: you shall be routed by your enemies, and your foes shall dominate you. You shall flee though none pursues.

18] And if, for all that, you do not obey Me, I will go on to discipline you sevenfold for your sins,   **19]** and I will break your proud glory. I will make your skies like iron and your earth

---

13] *Made you walk erect.* Which you could not do till the yoke was removed.

14-45] *The curses.* "The empty-headed have declared that the curses are more numerous than the blessings, but they have not spoken truth. The blessings are uttered in broad general terms, while the curses are stated in more detail, to awe and frighten the hearers" (Ibn Ezra).

16] *Consumption and fever.* Precise nature of these ills is uncertain (T.N.). Luzzatto thinks these terms also refer to plant diseases (cf. Deut. 28:22). This view was first mentioned, but not adopted, by Ibn Ezra.

   You shall sow your seed to no purpose. It will not grow; but, if it should grow, *your enemies shall eat it* (*Sifra*).

17] *I will set My face against you.* This is the opposite of the promise in verse 9.

   You shall flee though none pursues. You will be utterly demoralized.

18] *Sevenfold for your sins.* The expression recurs in verses 21, 24, and 28. It is a characteristic way of saying "many times over" (cf. commentary on verse 8 and see Gleanings).

19] *Skies like iron.* Hot and rainless.
   Earth like copper. Hard and unproductive.
   One of the curses in the treaties of Esarhaddon reads: "May all the gods . . . turn your soil into iron so that no one may cut a furrow in it. Just as rain does not fall from a copper sky, so may there come neither rain nor dew upon your fields [11] (cf. Deut. 28:23).

בְּרִית וְנֶאֱסַפְתֶּם אֶל־עָרֵיכֶם וְשִׁלַּחְתִּי דֶבֶר בְּתוֹכְכֶם   כֹחֲכֶם וְלֹא־תִתֵּן אַרְצְכֶם אֶת־יְבוּלָהּ וְעֵץ הָאָרֶץ לֹא

כו וְנִתַּתֶּם בְּיַד־אוֹיֵב: בְּשִׁבְרִי לָכֶם מַטֵּה־לֶחֶם וְאָפוּ   כא יִתֵּן פִּרְיוֹ: וְאִם־תֵּלְכוּ עִמִּי קֶרִי וְלֹא תֹאבוּ לִשְׁמֹעַ לִי

עֶשֶׂר נָשִׁים לַחְמְכֶם בְּתַנּוּר אֶחָד וְהֵשִׁיבוּ לַחְמְכֶם   כב וְיָסַפְתִּי עֲלֵיכֶם מַכָּה שֶׁבַע כְּחַטֹּאתֵיכֶם: וְהִשְׁלַחְתִּי

כז בַּמִּשְׁקָל וַאֲכַלְתֶּם וְלֹא תִשְׂבָּעוּ: ס וְאִם־בְּזֹאת לֹא   בָכֶם אֶת־חַיַּת הַשָּׂדֶה וְשִׁכְּלָה אֶתְכֶם וְהִכְרִיתָה

כח תִשְׁמְעוּ לִי וַהֲלַכְתֶּם עִמִּי בְּקֶרִי: וְהָלַכְתִּי עִמָּכֶם   אֶת־בְּהֶמְתְּכֶם וְהִמְעִיטָה אֶתְכֶם וְנָשַׁמּוּ דַּרְכֵיכֶם:

בַּחֲמַת־קֶרִי וְיִסַּרְתִּי אֶתְכֶם אַף־אָנִי שֶׁבַע עַל־   כג וְאִם־בְּאֵלֶּה לֹא תִוָּסְרוּ לִי וַהֲלַכְתֶּם עִמִּי קֶרִי: וְהָלַכְתִּי

כט חַטֹּאתֵיכֶם: וַאֲכַלְתֶּם בְּשַׂר בְּנֵיכֶם וּבְשַׂר בְּנֹתֵיכֶם   כד אַף־אֲנִי עִמָּכֶם בְּקֶרִי וְהִכֵּיתִי אֶתְכֶם גַּם־אָנִי שֶׁבַע

ל תֹּאכֵלוּ: וְהִשְׁמַדְתִּי אֶת־בָּמֹתֵיכֶם וְהִכְרַתִּי אֶת־   כה עַל־חַטֹּאתֵיכֶם: וְהֵבֵאתִי עֲלֵיכֶם חֶרֶב נֹקֶמֶת נְקַם־

---

like copper,   **20]** so that your strength shall be spent to no purpose. Your land shall not yield its produce, nor shall the trees of the land yield their fruit.

21] And if you remain hostile toward Me and refuse to obey Me, I will go on smiting you sevenfold for your sins.   **22]** I will loose wild beasts against you, and they shall bereave you of your children and wipe out your cattle. They shall decimate you, and your roads shall be deserted.

23] And if these things fail to discipline you for Me, and you remain hostile to Me,   **24]** I too will remain hostile to you: I in turn will smite you sevenfold for your sins.   **25]** I will bring a sword against you to wreak vengeance for the covenant; and if you withdraw into your cities, I will send pestilence among you, and you shall be delivered into enemy hands.   **26]** When I break your staff of bread, ten women shall bake your bread in a single oven; they shall dole out your bread by weight and, though you eat, you shall not be satisfied.

27] But if, despite this, you disobey Me and remain hostile to Me,   **28]** I will act against you in wrathful hostility; I, for My part, will discipline you sevenfold for your sins.   **29]** You shall eat the flesh of your sons and the flesh of your daughters.   **30]** I will destroy your cult

---

20] *Your land shall not yield its produce.* It shall not yield as much as the seed you brought for planting (Sifra).

21] *Hostile.* Hebrew *keri,* found only in this chapter (see Gleanings).

25] *Vengeance for the covenant.* Which you broke by disobeying the Torah.

    You shall be delivered into enemy hands. Because you will be too weak from illness to resist.

26] *When I break your staff of bread.* As a staff supports one who walks with it, so bread sustains life. The idiom seems to have been familiar (cf. Isa. 3:1).

    In a single oven. Because fuel is in short supply (Sifra).

    Dole out your bread by weight. Rationing will be stringent.

29] *Eat the flesh of your sons.* ... Doubtless cannibalism has occurred in times of famine; but this seems to have become a literary cliché. It is a recurrent item in Esarhaddon's vassal treaties [12] and in the Scriptures (Deut. 28:53ff.; II Kings 6:25ff.; and Lam. 4:10).

30] *Your cult places.* The many idolatrous shrines in the country (see introduction to Lev. 17, "1. Secular Slaughtering Prohibited").

לה שַׁבְּתֹתֶיהָ: כָּל־יְמֵי הָשַּׁמָּה תִּשְׁבֹּת אֵת אֲשֶׁר לֹא־שָׁבְתָה
לו בְּשַׁבְּתֹתֵיכֶם בְּשִׁבְתְּכֶם עָלֶיהָ: וְהַנִּשְׁאָרִים בָּכֶם
וְהֵבֵאתִי מֹרֶךְ בִּלְבָבָם בְּאַרְצֹת אֹיְבֵיהֶם וְרָדַף אֹתָם
קוֹל עָלֶה נִדָּף וְנָסוּ מְנֻסַת־חֶרֶב וְנָפְלוּ וְאֵין רֹדֵף:
לז וְכָשְׁלוּ אִישׁ־בְּאָחִיו כְּמִפְּנֵי־חֶרֶב וְרֹדֵף אָיִן וְלֹא־תִהְיֶה
לח לָכֶם תְּקוּמָה לִפְנֵי אֹיְבֵיכֶם: וַאֲבַדְתֶּם בַּגּוֹיִם וְאָכְלָה
לט אֶתְכֶם אֶרֶץ אֹיְבֵיכֶם: וְהַנִּשְׁאָרִים בָּכֶם יִמַּקּוּ בַּעֲוֹנָם
בְּאַרְצֹת אֹיְבֵיכֶם וְאַף בַּעֲוֹנֹת אֲבֹתָם אִתָּם יִמָּקּוּ:

חַמָּנֵיכֶם וְנָתַתִּי אֶת־פִּגְרֵיכֶם עַל־פִּגְרֵי גִּלּוּלֵיכֶם
לא וְגָעֲלָה נַפְשִׁי אֶתְכֶם: וְנָתַתִּי אֶת־עָרֵיכֶם חָרְבָּה
וַהֲשִׁמּוֹתִי אֶת־מִקְדְּשֵׁיכֶם וְלֹא אָרִיחַ בְּרֵיחַ נִיחֹחֲכֶם:
לב וַהֲשִׁמֹּתִי אֲנִי אֶת־הָאָרֶץ וְשָׁמְמוּ עָלֶיהָ אֹיְבֵיכֶם
לג הַיֹּשְׁבִים בָּהּ: וְאֶתְכֶם אֱזָרֶה בַגּוֹיִם וַהֲרִיקֹתִי אַחֲרֵיכֶם
חָרֶב וְהָיְתָה אַרְצְכֶם שְׁמָמָה וְעָרֵיכֶם יִהְיוּ חָרְבָּה: אָז
לד תִּרְצֶה הָאָרֶץ אֶת־שַׁבְּתֹתֶיהָ כֹּל יְמֵי הָשַּׁמָּה וְאַתֶּם
בְּאֶרֶץ אֹיְבֵיכֶם אָז תִּשְׁבַּת הָאָרֶץ וְהִרְצָת אֶת־

places and cut down your incense stands, and I will heap your carcasses upon your lifeless fetishes.

I will spurn you.   **31]** I will lay your cities in ruin and make your sanctuaries desolate, and I will not savor your pleasing odors.   **32]** I will make the land desolate, so that your enemies who settle in it shall be appalled by it.   **33]** And you I will scatter among the nations, and I will unsheath the sword against you. Your land shall become a desolation and your cities a ruin.

34] Then shall the land make up for its sabbath years throughout the time that it is desolate and you are in the land of your enemies; then shall the land rest and make up for its sabbath years.   **35]** Throughout the time that it is desolate, it shall observe the rest that it did not observe in your sabbath years while you were dwelling upon it.   **36]** As for those of you who survive, I will cast a faintness into their hearts in the land of their enemies. The sound of a driven leaf shall put them to flight. Fleeing as though from the sword, they shall fall though none pursues.   **37]** With no one pursuing, they shall stumble over one another as before the sword. You shall not be able to stand your ground before your enemies,   **38]** but shall perish among the nations; and the land of your enemies shall consume you.

39] Those of you who survive shall be heartsick over their iniquity in the land of your

Your incense stands. Hebrew *chamanim.* This rendering was established by the unearthing of small altars or stands for offering incense, some of them bearing the word *chaman.* Scholars had previously connected the word with *chamah,* "sun," and supposed them to be some sort of solar image.

Heap your carcasses upon your lifeless fetishes. Literally, "upon the carcasses (*pigre*) of your fetishes." But Hoffmann noted that, in rabbinic Hebrew and Aramaic, the root *pgr* means "break up"; he therefore translated, "I will heap your carcasses upon the fragments of your fetishes."

31] *Your sanctuaries.* Cf. verse 30. The plural is the measure of the disloyalty—not "My sanctuary" but "your sanctuaries."

Savor your pleasing odors. Accept your sacrifices (see commentary on 1:9).

32] *Shall be appalled by it.* By the complete devastation.

33] The ultimate punishment is exile; yet even then the Israelites will be pursued by implacable enemies.

34] *Make up for its sabbath years.* This passage and verse 43 stress the importance of the sabbath year and introduce the notion that the desolation of the land is to make up for sabbath years neglected in the past. A tie is thus established between this chapter and chapter 25. There is no parallel to this idea in Deuteronomy, chapter 28, or elsewhere in the Bible.

36] The exiles will be in such constant terror that the slightest noise will stir them to panic.

38] Though the destiny of the people seems to be complete disintegration, their cause is not entirely hopeless.

39] First source of hope—The survivors acknowledge their guilt and that of their forebears.

מ נַפְשָׁם: וְאַף גַּם־זֹאת בִּהְיוֹתָם בְּאֶרֶץ אֹיְבֵיהֶם לֹא־
מְאַסְתִּים וְלֹא־גְעַלְתִּים לְכַלֹּתָם לְהָפֵר בְּרִיתִי אִתָּם
מה כִּי אֲנִי יְהוָה אֱלֹהֵיהֶם: וְזָכַרְתִּי לָהֶם בְּרִית רִאשֹׁנִים
אֲשֶׁר הוֹצֵאתִי־אֹתָם מֵאֶרֶץ מִצְרַיִם לְעֵינֵי הַגּוֹיִם
מו לִהְיוֹת לָהֶם לֵאלֹהִים אֲנִי יְהוָה: אֵלֶּה הַחֻקִּים
וְהַמִּשְׁפָּטִים וְהַתּוֹרֹת אֲשֶׁר נָתַן יְהוָה בֵּינוֹ וּבֵין בְּנֵי
יִשְׂרָאֵל בְּהַר סִינַי בְּיַד־מֹשֶׁה: פ

ס וְהִתְוַדּוּ אֶת־עֲוֺנָם וְאֶת־עֲוֺן אֲבֹתָם בְּמַעֲלָם אֲשֶׁר
מא מָעֲלוּ־בִי וְאַף אֲשֶׁר־הָלְכוּ עִמִּי בְּקֶרִי: אַף־אֲנִי אֵלֵךְ
עִמָּם בְּקֶרִי וְהֵבֵאתִי אֹתָם בְּאֶרֶץ אֹיְבֵיהֶם אוֹ־אָז
מב יִכָּנַע לְבָבָם הֶעָרֵל וְאָז יִרְצוּ אֶת־עֲוֺנָם: וְזָכַרְתִּי אֶת־
בְּרִיתִי יַעֲקוֹב וְאַף אֶת־בְּרִיתִי יִצְחָק וְאַף אֶת־בְּרִיתִי
מג אַבְרָהָם אֶזְכֹּר וְהָאָרֶץ אֶזְכֹּר: וְהָאָרֶץ תֵּעָזֵב מֵהֶם
וְתִרֶץ אֶת־שַׁבְּתֹתֶיהָ בָּהְשַׁמָּה מֵהֶם וְהֵם יִרְצוּ אֶת־
עֲוֺנָם יַעַן וּבְיַעַן בְּמִשְׁפָּטַי מָאָסוּ וְאֶת־חֻקֹּתַי גָּעֲלָה

* מב פלא ו.

enemies; more, they shall be heartsick over the iniquities of their fathers;   40] and they shall confess their iniquity and the iniquity of their fathers, in that they trespassed against Me, yea, were hostile to Me.   41] When I, in turn, have been hostile to them and have removed them into the land of their enemies, then at last shall their obdurate heart humble itself, and they shall atone for their iniquity.   42] Then will I remember My covenant with Jacob; I will remember also My covenant with Isaac, and also My covenant with Abraham; and I will remember the land.

43] For the land shall be forsaken of them, making up for its sabbath years by being desolate of them, while they atone for their iniquity; for the abundant reason that they rejected My rules and spurned My laws.   44] Yet, even then, when they are in the land of their enemies, I will not reject them or spurn them so as to destroy them, annulling My covenant with them: for I the LORD am their God.   45] I will remember in their favor the covenant with the ancients, whom I freed from the land of Egypt in the sight of the nations to be their God: I the LORD.

46] These are the laws, rules, and directions that the LORD established, through Moses on Mount Sinai, between Himself and the Israelite people.

41] *When I, in turn, have been hostile to them.* Or, taking this with what precedes: "They trespassed against Me, yea, were hostile to Me, so that I, in turn, was hostile to them and removed them... enemies. Then at last...." So Ehrlich and Hoffmann.

Obdurate. Others, "uncircumcised"; literally, "blocked" (T.N.).

42] Second source of hope—God will remember His promise to the patriarchs [13].

43] Third source of hope—God is changelessly Israel's God (cf. Mal. 3:6).

45] *The covenant with the ancients.* At Sinai. The restoration is only foreshadowed here (it is described fully in Deut. 4:29ff. and 30:1ff.).

46] *On Mount Sinai.* This concluding reference provides a connection with the beginning of chapter 25. Or perhaps we should render "at Mount Sinai" and consider the verse a conclusion to the entire Book of Leviticus, the laws of which were presumably revealed before Israel broke camp at Sinai and set forth through the desert.

GLEANINGS

Haggadah (all from Sifra)

26:4] *Rains in Their Season*

On Friday nights, when no one needs to work in the fields.

The Trees of the Field

Even those that do not now bear edible fruit will do so then.

6] *I Will Grant Peace*

For that is equal in value to all the other blessings combined.

7] *No Sword Shall Cross Your Land*

There will be no invasions, nor will an army cross your territory to reach another military objective.

8] *Five of You Shall Give Chase to a Hundred*

See commentary. The Rabbis note the change of ratio (from 5:100 to 100:10,000) and explain: The merit generated when large numbers obey the Torah increases, so to speak, in geometric proportion.

9] *I Will Maintain My Covenant with You*

I will establish a new covenant with you, written on the very hearts of the people (Jer. 31:31ff.).

17] *Your Foes Shall Dominate You*

This second clause refers to internal enemies and civil strife.

18] *Sevenfold for Your Sins*

See commentary. But in each paragraph the Rabbis endeavor to enumerate seven sins and seven corresponding plagues.

19] *Your Proud Glory*

The Temple (cf. Ezek. 24:21).

21] *Hostile*

See commentary. But *Sifra* derives *keri* from the root *krh*, "happen," and explains: If you regard My punishments as mere accidental happenings, I will treat you as of no more than incidental value.

26] *Dole Out Your Bread by Weight*

It will be of such poor quality that the loaves will crumble and the broken pieces will have to be weighed out.

32] *Your Enemies Who Settle in It Shall Be Appalled by It*

This seeming threat really contains a suggestion of hope: foreigners will never be able to settle down comfortably in the Land of Israel; only Jews can be truly at home there.

42] *Then Will I Remember My Covenant with Jacob*

Why are the patriarchs mentioned here in reverse order? To indicate that the merit even of Jacob, the youngest, is sufficient to bring about the redemption; but, if it were not sufficient, the merits of his father Isaac and grandfather Abraham would surely suffice (*Sifra* as elaborated by Rashi).

PART VII

Supplementary Laws

Vows, Gifts, and Dues

This supplementary chapter deals chiefly with gifts to the sanctuary, whether by conditional vows ("if God does such-and-such for me, I will give such-and-such") or by unconditional acts of pious gratitude. A few enigmatic verses at the end treat of certain agricultural dues.

Vows are mentioned frequently in the Bible: in narratives about Jacob (Gen. 28:20ff.), Jephthah (Judg. 11:30ff.), Hannah (I Sam. 1:11), and others; and in the legislation of Leviticus (7:16ff. and 22:17ff.) and Numbers (chapters 6 and 30). Warnings are given against rash and hasty vows (in Deut. 23:22ff. and Eccles. 5:1ff.). The present section presents laws on the subject without discussing their moral and religious implications.

Three types of gifts are treated: (1) the money equivalent of a person, *erech, erkecha*; (2) the dedication of cattle or real property, *hekdesh* [1]—such a gift being subject to redemption if the donor pays its value plus 20 per cent; (3) the irreversible gift, *cherem*.

1. Erech, erkecha

In very ancient times, persons were literally dedicated to a god. This means that they were either sacrificed, as in the case of Jephthah's daughter, or set aside for the service of the sanctuary, as in the case of Samuel. Perhaps our law developed out of the practice of redeeming dedicated persons by a money payment. But the present text indicates no such connection. It deals with a simple vow to contribute a sum equivalent to the valuation—not the value!—of a person who may be the donor, or someone else.

The amount to be contributed was determined by the age and sex of the person "valuated," according to a fixed schedule. Health and earning power were not relevant. If, however, the maker of the vow was unable to pay the fixed tariff, provision was made to give a lesser amount.

Such gifts, as well as those in the two following classes, were to be given "to the LORD." But who received them on His behalf? On this point our chapter is not clear. Verse 21 indicates that in some cases, at least, the recipient was an individual priest [2]. But a different viewpoint emerges from the interesting report in II Kings (12:5ff.).

From this passage we learn that in the days of the monarchy worshipers used to select the priest who received their gifts to the sanctuary, including "the equivalent of persons." The priests as a group were expected,

in return, to keep the Temple in repair. But the system did not work well. King Joash therefore decided—and the priests agreed—that thenceforth all donations should go into a separate fund, under the jurisdiction of the chief priest, for the maintenance of the Temple buildings.

The Rabbis interpreted our chapter in the light of this episode, and their interpretation is quite probably correct. According to the halachah, then, vowed sums, as well as the consecrated items discussed below, were applied to the maintenance of the Temple.

Verses 2 through 8 are the basis of a treatise of the Mishnah and Talmud, called *Arachin*, "Valuations."

2. *Hekdesh*

The second section of the chapter, on the consecration of cattle and real estate, treats of several different circumstances. Common to them all is the rule that, if one declares an item consecrated and later regrets his action, he can recover the property by paying its value, as assessed by a priest, plus 20 per cent.

Though the donor may regain a consecrated animal by a money payment, he cannot do so by substituting another animal, even though the second is more valuable than the first. Were he to attempt this, both animals would be consecrated. This provision (verse 10 and a similar ruling in verse 33) is the biblical basis for another treatise of the Mishnah and Talmud, called *Temurah*, "Substitution."

When the animal consecrated is of a clean species, the donor may designate it for sacrifice. Otherwise, it may be sold and the proceeds put in the fund for building maintenance. This was the regular rule if animals unsuited for the altar were donated. And gifts of real estate were usually applied to the same purpose.

On this subject, the Torah deals separately with the consecration of a house, of inherited farmland, and of land which the donor had acquired by purchase.

The value of farmland is set arbitrarily according to its area, without regard to the productiveness of the soil—just as the valuation of persons has nothing to do with their actual "sale value." The amount required to redeem such property diminishes with the approach of the jubilee year; and land that the contributor had bought from the original owner is restored to that owner when the jubilee arrives. If, however, one consecrates a field from his own ancestral holding, the law is different—and obscure (see commentary on 27:20–21).

3. *Cherem*

The third section (verses 28–30) employs the noun *cherem* and related verb forms. These words indicate something forbidden and inviolable. The Arabic word from which our English "harem" is derived is related to the Hebrew *cherem*. A slightly different form of the Arabic term is used for certain holy areas, in Mecca and elsewhere, from which non-Moslems are barred.

In the Bible, *cherem* appears most often in the context of war. It means the extermination of defeated enemies. As regards booty, *cherem* requires that the spoil must either be destroyed or put into a sacred treasury (Exod. 22:19; Num. 21:2f. with footnotes; Deut. 2:34f.; and elsewhere). If anyone appropriates an object that has been declared *cherem*, he himself becomes *cherem* and must be put to death (Deut. 7:25f.; Josh. 7:1ff.). The present Torah translation renders the root most often by "proscribe," a term, derived from Roman practice, which comes fairly close to the meaning of the Hebrew. Sometimes the root is translated "doom," as in Deuteronomy 2:34.

This background, unfortunately, does not

help much in the understanding of verse 28 which speaks of proscribing man or beast or land to the Lord. The traditional expositors held that a gift designated as *cherem* must remain forever sanctuary property—whereas ordinary consecrated gifts (*hekdesh*), if not specifically designated for sacrifice, could be sold by the sanctuary authorities or redeemed by the donor. The man proscribed is explained as a gentile slave who is thereby attached for life to the service of the sanctuary (*Sifra*). I have found no better explanation of the verse.

But the ensuing sentence states that a proscribed human being must be put to death. This cannot possibly refer to someone who was declared *cherem* by the private donor of verse 28. Unlike Roman law, the Torah never granted power of life and death to a father over his children or to a master over his slaves. For some reason, the old fierce law is repeated here: one who converts *cherem* property to his own use becomes

cherem himself and forfeits his life. (Or perhaps, as Dr. Tsevat has suggested, the verse is a warning against pronouncing a *cherem* upon a person because the consequences would be unbearable.)

It may be noted that, in later Jewish usage, *cherem* came to mean the ban pronounced by the leaders of the community on one who outraged the conscience or flouted the authority of the community. In this sense it is sometimes rendered "excommunication," though "ostracism" would be more accurate.

The end of the chapter (verses 26–27 and 30–33) deals with obligatory dues. These brief passages are largely in conflict with other passages of the Torah and present baffling problems to the student.

In general, it appears that this chapter is a collection of old materials, which, with some later additions, was appended to the Book of Leviticus after the latter was virtually completed, and that the *tochechah* was intended as the original ending of the book.

א וַיְדַבֵּ֥ר יְהֹוָ֖ה אֶל־מֹשֶׁ֥ה לֵּאמֹֽר׃ דַּבֵּ֞ר אֶל־בְּנֵ֤י יִשְׂרָאֵל֙ וְאָמַרְתָּ֣ אֲלֵהֶ֔ם אִ֕ישׁ כִּ֥י יַפְלִ֖א נֶ֑דֶר בְּעֶרְכְּךָ֥ נְפָשֹׁ֖ת לַֽיהֹוָֽה׃ וְהָיָ֤ה עֶרְכְּךָ֙ הַזָּכָ֔ר מִבֶּן֙ עֶשְׂרִ֣ים שָׁנָ֔ה וְעַ֖ד בֶּן־שִׁשִּׁ֣ים שָׁנָ֑ה וְהָיָ֣ה עֶרְכְּךָ֗ חֲמִשִּׁ֛ים שֶׁ֥קֶל כֶּ֖סֶף בְּשֶׁ֥קֶל הַקֹּֽדֶשׁ׃ וְאִם־נְקֵבָ֖ה הִ֑וא וְהָיָ֥ה עֶרְכְּךָ֖ שְׁלֹשִׁ֥ים שָֽׁקֶל׃ וְאִ֢ם מִבֶּן־חָמֵ֣שׁ שָׁנִ֗ים וְעַד֙ בֶּן־עֶשְׂרִ֣ים שָׁנָ֔ה וְהָיָ֧ה עֶרְכְּךָ֛ הַזָּכָ֖ר עֶשְׂרִ֣ים שְׁקָלִ֑ים וְלַנְּקֵבָ֖ה עֲשֶׂ֥רֶת שְׁקָלִֽים׃ וְאִ֣ם מִבֶּן־חֹ֗דֶשׁ וְעַד֙ בֶּן־חָמֵ֣שׁ שָׁנִ֔ים וְהָיָ֤ה עֶרְכְּךָ֙ הַזָּכָ֔ר חֲמִשָּׁ֥ה שְׁקָלִ֖ים כָּ֑סֶף וְלַנְּקֵבָ֣ה עֶרְכְּךָ֔ שְׁלֹ֥שֶׁת שְׁקָלִ֖ים כָּֽסֶף׃ וְאִ֨ם מִבֶּן־שִׁשִּׁ֥ים שָׁנָ֛ה וָמַ֖עְלָה

אִם־זָכָ֗ר וְהָיָ֤ה עֶרְכְּךָ֙ חֲמִשָּׁ֣ה עָשָׂ֣ר שֶׁ֔קֶל וְלַנְּקֵבָ֖ה עֲשָׂרָ֥ה שְׁקָלִֽים׃ וְאִם־מָ֣ךְ הוּא֮ מֵעֶרְכֶּךָ֒ וְהֶֽעֱמִידוֹ֙ לִפְנֵ֣י הַכֹּהֵ֔ן וְהֶעֱרִ֥יךְ אֹת֖וֹ הַכֹּהֵ֑ן עַל־פִּ֗י אֲשֶׁ֤ר תַּשִּׂיג֙ יַ֣ד הַנֹּדֵ֔ר יַעֲרִיכֶ֖נּוּ הַכֹּהֵֽן׃ ס וְאִם־בְּהֵמָ֗ה אֲשֶׁ֨ר יַקְרִ֧יבוּ מִמֶּ֛נָּה קׇרְבָּ֖ן לַֽיהֹוָ֑ה כֹּל֩ אֲשֶׁ֨ר יִתֵּ֥ן מִמֶּ֛נּוּ לַֽיהֹוָ֖ה יִֽהְיֶה־קֹּֽדֶשׁ׃ לֹ֣א יַחֲלִיפֶ֗נּוּ וְלֹֽא־יָמִ֥יר אֹת֛וֹ ט֥וֹב בְּרָ֖ע אֽוֹ־רַ֣ע בְּט֑וֹב וְאִם־הָמֵ֨ר יָמִ֤יר בְּהֵמָה֙ בִּבְהֵמָ֔ה וְהָֽיָה־ה֥וּא וּתְמוּרָת֖וֹ יִֽהְיֶה־קֹּֽדֶשׁ׃ וְאִם֙ כׇּל־בְּהֵמָ֣ה טְמֵאָ֔ה אֲשֶׁ֧ר לֹא־יַקְרִ֛יבוּ מִמֶּ֥נָּה קׇרְבָּ֖ן לַֽיהֹוָ֑ה וְהֶֽעֱמִ֥יד אֶת־הַבְּהֵמָ֖ה לִפְנֵ֥י הַכֹּהֵֽן׃ וְהֶעֱרִ֤יךְ הַכֹּהֵן֙ אֹתָ֔הּ בֵּ֥ין ט֖וֹב

* ט׳ סבירין ממנה.

1] The LORD spoke to Moses, saying:

2] Speak to the Israelite people and say to them: When a man explicitly vows to the LORD the equivalent for a human being, **3]** the following scale shall apply: If it is a male from twenty to sixty years of age, the equivalent is fifty shekels of silver by the sanctuary weight; **4]** if it is a female, the equivalent is thirty shekels. **5]** If the age is from five years to twenty years, the equivalent is twenty shekels for a male and ten shekels for a female. **6]** If the age is from one month to five years, the equivalent for a male is five shekels of silver, and the equivalent for a female is three shekels of silver. **7]** If the age is sixty years or over, the equivalent is fifteen shekels in the case of a male and ten shekels for a female. **8]** But if one cannot afford the equivalent, he shall be presented before the priest, and the priest shall assess him; the priest shall assess him according to what the vower can afford.

9] If [the vow concerns] any animal that may be brought as an offering to the LORD, any such that may be given to the LORD shall be holy. **10]** One may not exchange or substitute another for it, either good for bad, or bad for good; if one does substitute one animal for another, the thing vowed and its substitute shall both be holy. **11]** If [the vow concerns] any unclean animal which may not be brought as an offering to the LORD, the animal shall be presented before the priest, **12]** and the priest shall assess it. Whether high or low, whatever

---

27:2] *Explicitly.* See T.N. at 22:21 (T.N.).

The equivalent for a human being. Hebrew *be'erkecha nefashot.* The ending *"cha"* ordinarily indicates the possessive *"your."* Many earlier translations rendered "thy valuation." But the Hebrew construction in this chapter and in chapter 5, verse 15, precludes such a rendering. This was recognized in the Septuagint and Targums, the Talmud, and the classic Jewish commentaries.

3] *A male from twenty to sixty years of age.* Men became liable for military service when they were twenty years old (Num. 1:3).

6] *From one month to five years.* Evidently one was not to vow the equivalent of an infant less than a month old. Later Jewish law considered the viability of a child in doubt for the first month.

8] *The priest shall assess him according to what the vower can afford.* See commentary on 1:14.

9–13] The law of substitution. See introduction to this chapter, "2. Hekdesh."

11] *Unclean animal.* E.g., a horse or camel, which could be sold, and the proceeds used for upkeep of the sanctuary.

12] *High or low.* Literally, "good or bad" (T.N.).

יז מִשְּׁנַת הַיֹּבֵל יַקְדִּישׁ שָׂדֵהוּ כְּעֶרְכְּךָ יָקוּם: וְאִם־אַחַר
הַיֹּבֵל יַקְדִּישׁ שָׂדֵהוּ וְחִשַּׁב־לוֹ הַכֹּהֵן אֶת־הַכֶּסֶף עַל־
פִּי הַשָּׁנִים הַנּוֹתָרֹת עַל שְׁנַת הַיֹּבֵל וְנִגְרַע מֵעֶרְכֶּךָ:
יט וְאִם־גָּאֹל יִגְאַל אֶת־הַשָּׂדֶה הַמַּקְדִּישׁ אֹתוֹ וְיָסַף
כ חֲמִשִׁית כֶּסֶף־עֶרְכְּךָ עָלָיו וְקָם לוֹ: וְאִם־לֹא יִגְאַל
אֶת־הַשָּׂדֶה וְאִם־מָכַר אֶת־הַשָּׂדֶה לְאִישׁ אַחֵר לֹא־
כא יִגָּאֵל עוֹד: וְהָיָה הַשָּׂדֶה בְּצֵאתוֹ בַיֹּבֵל קֹדֶשׁ לַיהוָה

יב וּבֵין רַע כְּעֶרְכְּךָ הַכֹּהֵן כֵּן יִהְיֶה: וְאִם־גָּאֹל יִגְאָלֶנָּה:
יג וְיָסַף חֲמִישִׁתוֹ עַל־עֶרְכֶּךָ: וְאִישׁ כִּי־יַקְדִּשׁ אֶת־בֵּיתוֹ
קֹדֶשׁ לַיהוָה וְהֶעֱרִיכוֹ הַכֹּהֵן בֵּין טוֹב וּבֵין רָע כַּאֲשֶׁר
יד יַעֲרִיךְ אֹתוֹ הַכֹּהֵן כֵּן יָקוּם: וְאִם־הַמַּקְדִּישׁ יִגְאַל אֶת־
טו בֵּיתוֹ וְיָסַף חֲמִישִׁית כֶּסֶף־עֶרְכְּךָ עָלָיו וְהָיָה לּוֹ: וְאִם
מִשְּׂדֵה אֲחֻזָּתוֹ יַקְדִּישׁ אִישׁ לַיהוָה וְהָיָה עֶרְכְּךָ לְפִי
טז זַרְעוֹ זֶרַע חֹמֶר שְׂעֹרִים בַּחֲמִשִּׁים שֶׁקֶל כָּסֶף: אִם־

assessment is set by the priest shall stand; **13]** and if he wishes to redeem it, he must add one-fifth to its assessment.

14] If a man consecrates his house to the LORD, the priest shall assess it. Whether high or low, as the priest assesses it, so it shall stand; **15]** and if he who has consecrated his house wishes to redeem it, he must add one-fifth to the sum at which it was assessed, and it shall be his.

16] If a man consecrates to the LORD any land that he holds, its assessment shall be in accordance with its seed requirement: fifty shekels of silver to a *homer* of barley seed. **17]** If he consecrates his land as of the jubilee year, its assessment stands. **18]** But if he consecrates his land after the jubilee, the priest shall compute the price according to the years that are left until the jubilee year, and its assessment shall be so reduced; **19]** and if he who consecrated the land wishes to redeem it, he must add one-fifth to the sum at which it was assessed, and it shall pass to him. **20]** But if he does not redeem the land, and the land is sold to another, it shall no longer be redeemable: **21]** when it is released in the jubilee, the land shall be holy to the LORD, as land proscribed; it becomes the priest's holding.

16–21] Dedication of farm property. As with the valuation of persons, assessment is arbitrary. An area which requires a *homer* of barley to sow it is valued at fifty shekels of silver, regardless of the quality of the soil.

17] *Its assessment stands.* The rate just mentioned applies.

20–21] *Sifra* explains: If the donor fails to redeem his family holding and the land is sold by the Temple treasurer, it does not revert to the original owners—the donor or his heirs—in the jubilee but shall remain holy "as land proscribed." It does not, however, become the permanent property of the sanctuary but of the priests who are on duty on Yom Kippur, when the jubilee formally commences ("it becomes the priest's holding").

This explanation presents at least two difficulties. First, no indication is given as to how much time the donor has to redeem his land—for, if the Temple authorities may sell it at any time, his right of redemption is illusory. (The Bible does not mention a Temple treasurer, but verse 27 implies that someone was empowered to sell sanctuary property.) Second, the clause "and the land is sold to another" could also be rendered "and he [i.e., the donor] sells it to another." This is how Luzzatto understood the clause: if the donor consecrates the property, then sells it to someone else, the latter retains possession till the jubilee; but, because of his duplicity, the donor can never regain it. But the brief and matter-of-fact language of the verse does not suggest any such illegal, not to say immoral, action on the part of the donor. Nor does the text in any way state that the purchaser may retain the property; and indeed why should he be allowed to enjoy the use of consecrated land until the jubilee? M. Noth (*Leviticus*, English translation, p. 206) likewise understands "he sells it to another" with dishonest intent; but he finds no statement in the text as to the consequences of this sale for the buyer.

כב כִּשְׂדֵה הַחֵרֶם לַכֹּהֵן תִּהְיֶה אֲחֻזָּתוֹ: וְאִם אֶת־שְׂדֵה
מִקְנָתוֹ אֲשֶׁר לֹא מִשְּׂדֵה אֲחֻזָּתוֹ יַקְדִּישׁ לַיהוָה:
כג וְחִשַּׁב־לוֹ הַכֹּהֵן אֵת מִכְסַת הָעֶרְכְּךָ עַד שְׁנַת הַיֹּבֵל
כד וְנָתַן אֶת־הָעֶרְכְּךָ בַּיּוֹם הַהוּא קֹדֶשׁ לַיהוָה: בִּשְׁנַת
הַיּוֹבֵל יָשׁוּב הַשָּׂדֶה לַאֲשֶׁר קָנָהוּ מֵאִתּוֹ לַאֲשֶׁר־לוֹ
כה אֲחֻזַּת הָאָרֶץ: וְכָל־עֶרְכְּךָ יִהְיֶה בְּשֶׁקֶל הַקֹּדֶשׁ

כה עֶשְׂרִים גֵּרָה יִהְיֶה הַשָּׁקֶל: אַךְ־בְּכוֹר אֲשֶׁר יְבֻכַּר
לַיהוָה בִּבְהֵמָה לֹא־יַקְדִּישׁ אִישׁ אֹתוֹ אִם־שׁוֹר אִם־שֶׂה
לַיהוָה הוּא: וְאִם בַּבְּהֵמָה הַטְּמֵאָה וּפָדָה בְעֶרְכֶּךָ
וְיָסַף חֲמִשִׁתוֹ עָלָיו וְאִם־לֹא יִגָּאֵל וְנִמְכַּר בְּעֶרְכֶּךָ:
כה אַךְ כָּל־חֵרֶם אֲשֶׁר יַחֲרִם אִישׁ לַיהוָה מִכָּל־אֲשֶׁר־לוֹ
מֵאָדָם וּבְהֵמָה וּמִשְּׂדֵה אֲחֻזָּתוֹ לֹא יִמָּכֵר וְלֹא יִגָּאֵל

22] If he consecrates to the LORD land that he purchased, which is not land of his holding, **23]** the priest shall compute for him the proportionate assessment up to the jubilee year, and he shall pay the assessment as of that day, a sacred donation to the LORD. **24]** In the jubilee year the land shall revert to him from whom it was bought, whose holding the land is. **25]** All assessments shall be by the sanctuary weight, the shekel being twenty *gerahs*.

26] A firstling of animals, however, which—as a firstling—is the LORD's, cannot be consecrated by anybody; whether ox or sheep, it is the LORD's. **27]** But if it is of unclean animals, it may be ransomed at its assessment, with one-fifth added; if it is not redeemed, it shall be sold at its assessment.

28] But of all that a man owns, be it man or beast or land of his holding, nothing that he has proscribed for the LORD may be sold or redeemed; every proscribed thing is totally consecrated to the LORD. **29]** No human being who has been proscribed can be ransomed: he shall be put to death.

Thus the rendering in our translation, which agrees with the tradition, is at least as good as any, though it too leaves several questions unanswered.

22–24] These verses simply spell out the implications of chapter 25, verses 14ff. Since the donor had by his purchase acquired only the right to a number of harvests, he donates only the equivalent of those harvests.

25] *By the sanctuary weight.* These laws antedate the introduction of coinage. The biblical shekel is a weight of metal, not a stamped coin.

26–27] *Firstling.* Verse 26 states, reasonably enough, that a firstborn animal cannot be the object of a special vow since it already belongs to God. But verse 27 is a problem. For Exodus 13:13 requires that the firstling of an ass must be redeemed with a lamb; by implication, other "unclean" animals are not subject to the law of firstlings at all. Moreover, according to Jewish tradition, the firstborn animal and the redemption lamb of Exodus (13:13), as well as the redemption money for a firstborn son, are to be given to an individual priest chosen by the donor, whereas the present verse implies that the firstling belongs to the sanctuary. The traditional expositors therefore held that verse 27 is not connected with verse 26 and does not refer to firstlings; it concerns animals consecrated so that the proceeds of their sale may go to the sanctuary (cf. commentary on verse 11). But verses 26 and 27 certainly seem to belong together; from our modern standpoint, they may be a fragment of a different law about firstlings, which eventually did not prevail.

28–29] On "proscription," see above, "3. Cherem."

כט כָּל־חֵרֶם קֹדֶשׁ־קָדָשִׁים הוּא לַיהוָה: כָּל־חֵרֶם אֲשֶׁר לֹּ הַשֵּׁבֶט הָעֲשִׂירִי יִהְיֶה־קֹּדֶשׁ לַיהוָה: לֹא יְבַקֵּר בֵּין

ל יָחֳרַם מִן־הָאָדָם לֹא יִפָּדֶה מוֹת יוּמָת: וְכָל־מַעְשַׂר טוֹב לָרַע וְלֹא יְמִירֶנּוּ וְאִם־הָמֵר יְמִירֶנּוּ וְהָיָה־הוּא

הָאָרֶץ מִזֶּרַע הָאָרֶץ מִפְּרִי הָעֵץ לַיהוָה הוּא קֹדֶשׁ לֹּ וּתְמוּרָתוֹ יִהְיֶה־קֹדֶשׁ לֹא יִגָּאֵל: אֵלֶּה הַמִּצְוֺת אֲשֶׁר

לא לַיהוָה: וְאִם־גָּאֹל יִגְאַל אִישׁ מִמַּעַשְׂרוֹ חֲמִשִׁיתוֹ יֹסֵף צִוָּה יְהוָה אֶת־מֹשֶׁה אֶל־בְּנֵי יִשְׂרָאֵל בְּהַר סִינָי:

לב עָלָיו: וְכָל־מַעְשַׂר בָּקָר וָצֹאן כֹּל אֲשֶׁר־יַעֲבֹר תַּחַת

Haftarah Bechukotai, p. 1006

30] All tithes from the land, whether seed from the ground or fruit from the tree, are the LORD's; they are holy to the LORD.   31] If a man wishes to redeem any of his tithes, he must add one-fifth to them.   32] All tithes of the herd or flock—of all that passes under the shepherd's staff, every tenth one—shall be holy to the LORD.   33] He must not look out for good as against bad, or make substitution for it. If he does make substitution for it, then it and its substitute shall both be holy: it cannot be redeemed.

34] These are the commandments that the LORD gave Moses for the Israelite people on Mount Sinai.

30-33] These verses are baffling.

30] *All tithes . . . are the Lord's; they are holy to the Lord.* In this chapter, "holy to the LORD" means that something belongs either to the sanctuary or to a priest. But the extended law in Numbers (18:21ff.) assigns the tithe to the Levites. Once the latter have given a tithe of their tithe to the priests, the remainder is their property and may be consumed without any of the restrictions applicable to sacred donations! Tradition therefore identified the tithe of this verse with the tithe described in Deuteronomy (14:22ff.), known in later times as the "second tithe." This tithe remained two years out of three in the possession of the farmer, who was required to take it to Jerusalem where he, his family, and guests were to use it for a festive celebration. The identification is dubious. Deuteronomy permits the worshiper who lives far from Jerusalem, and for whom it would be a hardship to transport the produce, to substitute

money for the tithe and expend the sum on the sacred meal in Jerusalem. Nothing is said there about the additional 20 per cent specified in Leviticus 27:31.

Further, verses 32 and 33 call for a tithe of animals, which is mentioned nowhere else in the Torah! According to the Rabbis, these animals too remain in the possession of the owner and were to be consumed in a festive meal—not a sacrifice. But II Chronicles (31:6) tells of an occasion when the tithe of cattle was presented at the Temple as a sacred donation.

These laws appear to represent an entirely divergent tithe system—either a fragment of an old tradition otherwise discarded or an attempt at reform that did not succeed.

34] *These are the commandments.* Cf. 26:46. When this chapter was added on to Leviticus, the need was apparently felt to attach a new concluding verse.

GLEANINGS

Haggadah

27:7] *Fifteen Shekels in the Case of a Male and Ten Shekels for a Female*

At lower age levels, a female is assessed at either three-fifths or one-half the value of a male; but, in the upper age bracket, the woman has two-thirds the value of the man. In old age the usefulness of a man decreases more than that of a woman. "An old man in the house is a snare [nuisance], an old woman in the house is a treasure" [3].

8] *The Priest Shall Assess Him according to What the Vower Can Afford*

The maker of the vow must pay as much of the commitment as he can by the sale of his possessions; but he is not required to give up his dwelling, tools, and necessary household goods. SIFRA

11] *Unclean Animal*

See commentary. But *Sifra* explains; an animal rendered "unclean" for sacrifice through some defect.

32] *All That Passes under the Shepherd's Staff*

For counting. The animals born in a given year were to be penned and then driven out through a narrow gate. As they moved out, the owner was to count them, marking each tenth animal with a bit of red paint on the end of his staff [4].

34] *These Are the Commandments*

Emphasizing the word "these," *Sifra* declares, "Henceforth, no prophet may introduce anything new."

Yet, fortunately, the men who were responsible for this statement found the means, by interpretation and even by legislation, of developing Jewish law and thought and to keep them responsive to the needs and circumstances of each generation.

The Dietary Laws

Appendix I (to Chapter 11)

(See also the further discussion in commentary on Deut. 14:1 ff.)

The following is an outline of dietary practices as currently observed by traditional Jews.

1. Vegetable Products

Still regarded as in force are (1) the prohibition of grain from the new crop prior to the second day of Passover (see commentary on Lev. 23:9ff.); (2) the prohibition of fruit from trees during their first four years (19:23ff.—this rule is generally held to apply only in the Holy Land); (3) the prohibition during Passover of leavened food and cereals which have not been specially protected from leavening (for details, see Exod., chapter 12); (4) the prohibition of wine and brandy not made under Jewish supervision, for fear that some may have been used for libation to a heathen god. This law does not apply to beer and grain spirits.

2. Meat

The laws of Leviticus, chapter 11, and Deuteronomy, chapter 14, permit the meat of only those mammals that are horned ruminants. This essentially means beef, veal, and lamb, since goat's meat and kosher-slaughtered venison are not normally available. Of these permitted animals, the hind quarter may be eaten only if certain tendons and nerves are removed by a technique called "porging" (see commentary on Gen. 32:33).

In the United States qualified experts in this procedure are not available; the hind quarters of kosher-slaughtered animals are therefore regularly sold to nonkosher meat markets. To be fit for the use of the observant, the animal must be slaughtered in accordance with the traditional rules—by cutting the throat with a sharp knife, severing windpipe, esophagus, and jugular vein so that the blood quickly drains from the carcass.

For centuries, any Jew, man or woman, was permitted to slaughter; later, this right was restricted to qualified slaughterers (shochetim), licensed and supervised by the rabbinate of the community. The shochet, after slaughtering an animal, must inspect the lungs of the carcass, rejecting it if there is evidence of disease or if faulty slaughtering has rendered it nevelah. If he observes certain other injuries or blemishes in other places than the lungs, the animal must be rejected as terefah. Doubtful cases are referred to the rabbi.

3. Poultry

Leviticus and Deuteronomy list a number of birds, many of them predators, which may not be eaten; by implication, all other birds are permitted. But already in the talmudic period it had become the rule to eat only such birds as were certified as kosher by a specific and reliable tradition.

Today only chicken, ducks, geese, turkeys, and pigeons are regarded as proper for a kosher diet. Fowls too must be ritually slaughtered. The rules are slightly different from those for quadrupeds. Certain blemishes may render them *terefah*. But such defects are usually discovered by the housewife. The *shochet* does not inspect the fowl he has killed.

4. Salting

Because of the strict prohibition of blood, all meat, whether of quadrupeds or fowl, must be prepared in the following fashion: it is soaked in water for about half an hour, then it is thickly salted. The salt must remain on the meat for about an hour, then the meat is washed thoroughly to remove the salt—and with it any remaining blood. This process may be omitted when meat is broiled over a flame. Liver may be "koshered" only by broiling, after it has been scored with a knife and slightly salted. An egg containing a drop of "blood" must be thrown away.

5. Fish

Biblical law permits the eating of only such fish as have both fins and scales. Excluded are eels, sharks, catfish, and sturgeon among others, as well as all kinds of shellfish. The blood of fish must be washed away. Fish may be cooked with milk, but not with meat. Amphibians (e.g., frogs), reptiles, and insects are forbidden—even though the Bible permits certain species of locusts.

6. Animal Products

The eggs of forbidden fowl and the milk of forbidden mammals are likewise forbidden. For this reason, formerly, Jews would buy milk from a Gentile only if they saw him milk the animal. This refinement is nowadays observed by only a few. But Orthodox authorities still uphold the talmudic objection to cheese produced under non-Jewish auspices; for many kinds of cheeses are prepared with rennet which might come from an animal not ritually fit.

7. Milk and Meat

The commandment, "You shall not boil a kid in its mother's milk" (Exod. 23:19 and 34:26; Deut. 14:21), was understood by tradition to forbid the mixing, cooking, or eating of milk and milk products with meat and meat products. This rule was applied to the meat of poultry as well as to that of mammals but not to fish. Food containing meat is referred to as *fleischig* (or *fleischdig*); food containing milk is *milchig* (or *milchdig*); neutral foods, which may be eaten with either milk or meat, are designated *pareve* (or *minnig*).

Talmudic law requires separate utensils for milk and meat if the containers are of porous material, such as unglazed pottery or wood. (Utensils of other materials, e.g., metal, can be "koshered" and then used for either milk or meat.) Accepted custom, however, is much stricter. Though glass is admittedly nonporous and as such could be used for both milk and meat—and the same would apply to glazed china as long as it is uncracked—it is nevertheless customary to have separate dishes, tableware, and cooking utensils for *milchig* and *fleischig* foods. Two additional sets, further, are needed for Passover use.

After one has eaten meat, he is expected to wait a considerable time before eating dairy foods. This waiting period varies in different communities from one to six hours.

Order of Service for the High Priest on the Day of Atonement

Appendix II (to Chapter 16)

The following account is based on Maimonides, *Hilchot Avodat Yom ha-Kippurim*; other medieval authorities differ as to a few details.

The High Priest performed some parts of the service wearing his customary regalia (the "golden garments"); for other parts, he wore the white linen garments specified in Leviticus 16:4. For each change of costume, he had to wash his hands and feet, remove the garments he was wearing, immerse himself in a ritual bath, dry himself, don the other set of garments, and again wash his hands and feet.

1. *In Golden Garments*

Slaughter the morning *tamid* (Exod. 29:39), receive the blood, and dash it against the altar. Offer incense and tend lamps of the lampstand (Exod. 30:7). Present the parts of the *tamid* with meal offering and libation (Exod. 29:40). Sacrifice the additional offerings—a bull and seven lambs (Num. 29:8; the ram mentioned in this verse was identified by tradition with that of Lev. 16:5).

2. *In White Garments*

Confession over the bull (Lev. 16:6). Cast lots over the goats (Lev. 16:8). Second confession over the bull which is now slaughtered and the blood collected in a bowl (Lev. 16:11). Fill fire pan with coals from the altar (Lev. 16:12). Put incense into a vessel and bring the vessel and fire pan into the Holy of Holies where the incense is spread over the burning coals (Lev. 16:12–13). Recite a short prayer (Yoma 5:1). Go out, get the bowl of bull's blood, return to the Holy of Holies, and sprinkle the blood (Lev. 16:14). Go out, slaughter the goat designated "for the LORD" (known as the people's goat), receive the blood, bring it into the Holy of Holies, and sprinkle it there (Lev. 16:15). Sprinkle the blood of the bull toward the curtain (Yoma 5:4). Combine the blood of the goat and that of the bull in one bowl and use this to purge the altar of incense (Lev. 16:18–19). Make confession over the scapegoat and send it away (Lev. 16:21). Rend the carcasses of the bull and goat and remove the inner parts to be offered later (Mishnah Yoma 6:7 with commentary by Bertinoro). (The carcasses were burned outside the city. Lev. 16:27.) Read aloud, from

a scroll, chapter 16 of Leviticus. Recite by heart Numbers, chapter 29, verses 7–11. Recite eight benedictions (Mishnah Yoma 7:1).

3. *In Golden Garments*

Offer the ram of the High Priest (Lev. 16:3), that of the people (Lev. 16:5), the additional goat of sin offering (Num. 29:11), and the inner parts of the bull and goat (Mishnah Yoma 7:3 with commentary by Bertinoro). Offer the evening *tamid* (Exod. 29:41).

4. *In White Garments*

Remove the fire pan and incense vessel from the Holy of Holies (connected by tradition with Lev. 16:23).

5. *In Golden Garments*

Offer the evening incense and tend the lamps (Exod. 30:8).

Prohibited Degrees of Relationship for Marriage

Appendix III (to Chapter 18)

BIBLICAL PROHIBITIONS	TALMUDICAL EXTENSIONS

A. CONSANGUINITY

a. IN THE ASCENDING LINE

1. Mother	Grandmother (paternal as well as maternal)

b. IN THE DESCENDING LINE

2. Daughter (implied in granddaughter)	
3. Granddaughter (son's or daughter's daughter)	Son's or daughter's granddaughter

c. COLLATERAL CONSANGUINITY

4. Sister and half-sister (either born in wedlock or not)	
5. Father's sister	Grandfather's sister
6. Mother's sister	Grandmother's sister

B. AFFINITY

a. THROUGH ONE'S OWN MARRIAGE

7. Wife's mother	Wife's grandmother Wife's stepmother not strictly prohibited but objectionable
8. Wife's daughter (stepdaughter)	
9. Wife's granddaughter	
10. Wife's sister (during the lifetime of the divorced wife)	

b. THROUGH MARRIAGE OF NEAR BLOOD RELATION

11. Father's wife (stepmother)	Father's or mother's stepmother
12. Father's brother's wife	Mother's brother's wife; father's uterine brother's wife
13. Son's wife	Grandson's or great-grandson's wife
14. Brother's wife (except in the case of levirate)	

(From M. Mielziner, *The Jewish Law of Marriage and Divorce*)

הפטרות

HAFTAROT

ויקרא

Isaiah

43 : *21* — *44* : *23*

Chapters 40–66 of the Book of Isaiah are the work of an unknown author (often referred to as Deutero-Isaiah) who lived in Babylon during the days of the exile (sixth century B.C.E.). He preached unwavering trust in a God who would surely restore Israel to its homeland. Of all the prophets he is the most lyrical and his imagery the richest.

The sacrifices due to God (of which the Torah speaks) were no longer possible after Jerusalem was destroyed. Isaiah, addressing the exiles, urged them to bring instead the offerings of the heart. God, he said, would find them as acceptable as He once did those brought on the altar.

Chapter 43

מג

21] The people I formed for Myself
That they might declare My praise.

22] But you have not worshiped Me, O Jacob,
That you should be weary of Me, O Israel.

23] You have not brought Me your sheep for burnt
offerings,
Nor honored Me with your sacrifices.
I have not burdened you with meal offerings,
Nor wearied you about frankincense.

24] You have not bought Me fragrant reed with
money,
Nor sated Me with the fat of your sacrifices.
Instead, you have burdened Me with your sins,
You have wearied Me with your iniquities.

25] It is I, I who—for My own sake*ʲ*—
Wipe your transgressions away
And remember your sins no more.

26] Help me remember!
Let us join in argument,
Tell your version,
That you may be vindicated.

[21] עַם־זוּ יָצַ֣רְתִּי לִ֔י
תְּהִלָּתִ֖י יְסַפֵּֽרוּ׃

[22] וְלֹא־אֹתִ֥י קָרָ֖אתָ יַעֲקֹ֑ב
כִּֽי־יָגַ֥עְתָּ בִּ֖י יִשְׂרָאֵֽל׃

[23] לֹֽא־הֵבֵ֤יאתָ לִּי֙ שֵׂ֣ה עֹלֹתֶ֔יךָ
וּזְבָחֶ֖יךָ לֹ֣א כִבַּדְתָּ֑נִי
לֹ֤א הֶעֱבַדְתִּ֙יךָ֙ בְּמִנְחָ֔ה
וְלֹ֥א הוֹגַעְתִּ֖יךָ בִּלְבוֹנָֽה׃

[24] לֹא־קָנִ֨יתָ לִּ֤י בַכֶּ֙סֶף֙ קָנֶ֔ה
וְחֵ֥לֶב זְבָחֶ֖יךָ לֹ֣א הִרְוִיתָ֑נִי
אַ֗ךְ הֶעֱבַדְתַּ֙נִי֙ בְּחַטֹּאותֶ֔יךָ
הוֹגַעְתַּ֖נִי בַּעֲוֺנֹתֶֽיךָ׃

[25] אָנֹכִ֨י אָנֹכִ֥י ה֛וּא מֹחֶ֥ה
פְשָׁעֶ֖יךָ לְמַעֲנִ֑י
וְחַטֹּאתֶ֖יךָ לֹ֥א אֶזְכֹּֽר׃

[26] הַזְכִּירֵ֕נִי
נִשָּׁפְטָ֖ה יָ֑חַד
סַפֵּ֥ר אַתָּ֖ה
לְמַ֥עַן תִּצְדָּֽק׃

ʲ I.e., in order to put an end to the profanation of My holy name; cf. 48.9–11

27] Your earliest ancestor sinned,
And your spokesmen transgressed against Me.

28] So I profaned *ᵍ⁻*the holy princes;*⁻ᵍ*
I abandoned Jacob to proscription*ʰ*
And Israel to mockery.

Chapter 44

1] But hear, now, O Jacob My servant,
Israel whom I have chosen!

2] Thus said the LORD, your Maker,
Your Creator who has helped you since birth:
Fear not, My servant Jacob,
Jeshurun*ᵃ* whom I have chosen,

3] Even as I pour water on thirsty soil,
And rain upon dry ground,
So will I pour My spirit on your offspring,
My blessing upon your posterity.

4] And they shall sprout like*ᵇ* grass,
Like willows by watercourses.

5] One shall say, "I am the LORD's,"
Another shall use the name "Jacob,"
Another shall mark his arm "the LORD's,"*ᶜ*
And adopt the name "Israel."

6] Thus said the LORD, the King of Israel,
Their Redeemer, the LORD of Hosts:

[27] אָבִיךָ הָרִאשׁוֹן חָטָא

וּמְלִיצֶיךָ פָּשְׁעוּ בִי:

[28] וַאֲחַלֵּל שָׂרֵי קֹדֶשׁ

וְאֶתְּנָה לַחֵרֶם יַעֲקֹב

וְיִשְׂרָאֵל לְגִדּוּפִים:

מד

[1] וְעַתָּה שְׁמַע יַעֲקֹב עַבְדִּי

וְיִשְׂרָאֵל בָּחַרְתִּי בוֹ:

[2] כֹּה־אָמַר יְהוָה עֹשֶׂךָ

וְיֹצֶרְךָ מִבֶּטֶן יַעְזְרֶךָּ

אַל־תִּירָא עַבְדִּי יַעֲקֹב

וִישֻׁרוּן בָּחַרְתִּי בוֹ:

[3] כִּי אֶצָּק־מַיִם עַל־צָמֵא

וְנֹזְלִים עַל־יַבָּשָׁה

אֶצֹּק רוּחִי עַל־זַרְעֶךָ

וּבִרְכָתִי עַל־צֶאֱצָאֶיךָ:

[4] וְצָמְחוּ בְּבֵין חָצִיר

כַּעֲרָבִים עַל־יִבְלֵי־מָיִם:

[5] זֶה יֹאמַר לַיהוָה אָנִי

וְזֶה יִקְרָא בְשֵׁם־יַעֲקֹב

וְזֶה יִכְתֹּב יָדוֹ לַיהוָה

וּבְשֵׁם יִשְׂרָאֵל יְכַנֶּה:

[6] כֹּה־אָמַר יְהוָה מֶלֶךְ־יִשְׂרָאֵל

וְגֹאֲלוֹ יְהוָה צְבָאוֹת

ᵍ⁻ᵍ Emendation yields "My holy name"; see preceding note
ʰ Emendation yields "insult"

ᵃ A name for Israel; see note on Num. 23.10; cf. Deut. 32.15; 33.5, 26
ᵇ Lit. "in among"
ᶜ It was customary to mark a slave with the owner's name

I am the first and I am the last,
And there is no god but Me.

7] ^dWho like Me can announce,
Can foretell it—and match Me thereby?
Even as I told the future to an ancient people,
So let him foretell coming events to them.

8] Do not be frightened, do not be shaken!
Have I not from of old predicted to you?
I foretold, and you are My witnesses.
Is there any god, then, but Me?
"There is no other rock; I know none!"

9] The makers of idols
All work to no purpose;
And the things they treasure
Can do no good,
As they themselves can testify.
They neither look nor think,
And so they shall be shamed.

10] Who would fashion a god
Or cast a statue
That can do no good?

11] Lo, all its adherents shall be shamed;
They are craftsmen, are merely human.
Let them all assemble and stand up!
They shall be cowed, and they shall be shamed.

12] ^eThe craftsman in iron, with his tools,
Works it^f over charcoal

אֲנִי רִאשׁוֹן וַאֲנִי אַחֲרוֹן
וּמִבַּלְעָדַי אֵין אֱלֹהִים׃

7] וּמִי־כָמוֹנִי יִקְרָא
וְיַגִּידֶהָ וְיַעְרְכֶהָ לִי
מִשּׂוּמִי עַם־עוֹלָם וְאֹתִיּוֹת
וַאֲשֶׁר תָּבֹאנָה יַגִּידוּ לָמוֹ׃

8] אַל־תִּפְחֲדוּ וְאַל־תִּרְהוּ
הֲלֹא מֵאָז הִשְׁמַעְתִּיךָ
וְהִגַּדְתִּי וְאַתֶּם עֵדָי
הֲיֵשׁ אֱלוֹהַּ מִבַּלְעָדַי
וְאֵין צוּר בַּל־יָדָעְתִּי׃

9] יֹצְרֵי־פֶסֶל
כֻּלָּם תֹּהוּ
וַחֲמוּדֵיהֶם
בַּל־יוֹעִילוּ
וְעֵדֵיהֶם הֵמָּה
בַּל־יִרְאוּ וּבַל־יֵדְעוּ
לְמַעַן יֵבֹשׁוּ׃

10] מִי־יָצַר אֵל
וּפֶסֶל נָסָךְ
לְבִלְתִּי הוֹעִיל׃

11] הֵן כָּל־חֲבֵרָיו יֵבֹשׁוּ
וְחָרָשִׁים הֵמָּה מֵאָדָם
יִתְקַבְּצוּ כֻלָּם יַעֲמֹדוּ
יִפְחֲדוּ יֵבֹשׁוּ יָחַד׃

12] חָרַשׁ בַּרְזֶל מַעֲצָד
וּפָעַל בַּפֶּחָם

---

^d *Meaning of verse uncertain*
^e *The meaning of parts of vv. 12–13 is uncertain*
^f *I.e., the image he is making*

And fashions it by hammering,
Working with the strength of his arm.
Should he go hungry, his strength would ebb;
Should he drink no water, he would grow faint.

וּבְמַקָּבוֹת יִצְּרֵהוּ

וַיִּפְעָלֵהוּ בִּזְרוֹעַ כֹּחוֹ

גַּם־רָעֵב וְאֵין כֹּחַ

לֹא־שָׁתָה מַיִם וַיִּיעָף׃

13] The craftsman in wood measures with a line
And marks out a shape with a stylus;
He forms it with scraping tools,
Marking it out with a compass.
He gives it a human form,
The beauty of a man, to dwell in a shrine.

13] חָרַשׁ עֵצִים נָטָה קָו

יְתָאֲרֵהוּ בַּשֶּׂרֶד

יַעֲשֵׂהוּ בַּמַּקְצֻעוֹת

וּבַמְּחוּגָה יְתָאֲרֵהוּ

וַיַּעֲשֵׂהוּ כְּתַבְנִית אִישׁ

כְּתִפְאֶרֶת אָדָם לָשֶׁבֶת בָּיִת׃

14] For his use he cuts down cedars;
He chooses plane trees and oaks.
He sets aside trees of the forest;
Or plants firs, and the rain makes them grow.

14] לִכְרָת־לוֹ אֲרָזִים

וַיִּקַּח תִּרְזָה וְאַלּוֹן

וַיְאַמֶּץ־לוֹ בַּעֲצֵי־יָעַר

נָטַע אֹרֶן וְגֶשֶׁם יְגַדֵּל׃

15] All this serves man for fuel:
He takes some to warm himself,
And he builds a fire and bakes bread.
He also makes a god of it and worships it,
Fashions an idol and bows down to it!

15] וְהָיָה לְאָדָם לְבָעֵר

וַיִּקַּח מֵהֶם וַיָּחָם

אַף־יַשִּׂיק וְאָפָה לָחֶם

אַף־יִפְעַל־אֵל וַיִּשְׁתָּחוּ

עָשָׂהוּ פֶסֶל וַיִּסְגָּד־לָמוֹ׃

16] Part of it he burns in a fire:
On that part he roasts[g] meat,
He eats[g] the roast and is sated;
He also warms himself and cries, "Ah,
I am warm! I can feel[h] the heat!"

16] חֶצְיוֹ שָׂרַף בְּמוֹ־אֵשׁ

עַל־חֶצְיוֹ בָּשָׂר יֹאכֵל

יִצְלֶה צָלִי וְיִשְׂבָּע

אַף־יָחֹם וְיֹאמַר הֶאָח

חַמּוֹתִי רָאִיתִי אוּר׃

17] Of the rest he makes a god—his own carving!
He bows down to it, worships it;
He prays to it and cries,
"Save me, for you are my god!"

17] וּשְׁאֵרִיתוֹ לְאֵל עָשָׂה לְפִסְלוֹ

יִסְגָּד־לוֹ וְיִשְׁתַּחוּ

וְיִתְפַּלֵּל אֵלָיו וְיֹאמַר

הַצִּילֵנִי כִּי אֵלִי אָתָּה׃

---

[g] Transposing the Heb. verbs for clarity   [h] Lit. "see"

18] They have no wit or judgment:
Their eyes are besmeared, and they see not;
Their minds, and they cannot think.

19] They do not give thought,
They lack the wit and judgment to say:
"Part of it I burned in a fire;
I also baked bread on the coals,
I roasted meat and ate it—
Should I make the rest an abhorrence?
Should I bow to a block of wood?"

20] He pursues ashes!‹
A deluded mind has led him astray,
Ane he cannot save himself;
He never says to himself,
"The thing in my hand is a fraud!"

21] Remember these things, O Jacob,
For you, O Israel, are My servant:
I fashioned you, you are My servant—
O Israel, never forget Me.ʲ

22] I wipe away your sins like a cloud,
Your transgressions like mist—
Come back to Me, for I redeem you.

23] Shout, O heavens, for the LORD has acted;
Shout aloud, O depths of the earth!
Shout for joy, O mountains,
O forests with all your trees!
For the LORD has redeemed Jacob,
Has glorified Himself through Israel.

18[לֹא יָדְעוּ וְלֹא יָבִינוּ
כִּי טַח מֵרְאוֹת עֵינֵיהֶם
מֵהַשְׂכִּיל לִבֹּתָם׃

19[וְלֹא־יָשִׁיב אֶל־לִבּוֹ
וְלֹא דַעַת וְלֹא־תְבוּנָה לֵאמֹר
חֶצְיוֹ שָׂרַפְתִּי בְמוֹ־אֵשׁ
וְאַף אָפִיתִי עַל־גֶּחָלָיו לֶחֶם
אֶצְלֶה בָשָׂר וְאֹכֵל
וְיִתְרוֹ לְתוֹעֵבָה אֶעֱשֶׂה
לְבוּל עֵץ אֶסְגּוֹד׃

20[רֹעֶה אֵפֶר
לֵב הוּתַל הִטָּהוּ
וְלֹא־יַצִּיל אֶת־נַפְשׁוֹ
וְלֹא יֹאמַר
הֲלוֹא שֶׁקֶר בִּימִינִי׃

21[זְכָר־אֵלֶּה יַעֲקֹב
וְיִשְׂרָאֵל כִּי עַבְדִּי־אָתָּה
יְצַרְתִּיךָ עֶבֶד־לִי אַתָּה
יִשְׂרָאֵל לֹא תִנָּשֵׁנִי׃

22[מָחִיתִי כָעָב פְּשָׁעֶיךָ
וְכֶעָנָן חַטֹּאותֶיךָ
שׁוּבָה אֵלַי כִּי גְאַלְתִּיךָ׃

23[רָנּוּ שָׁמַיִם כִּי־עָשָׂה יְהוָה
הָרִיעוּ תַּחְתִּיּוֹת אָרֶץ
פִּצְחוּ הָרִים רִנָּה
יַעַר וְכָל־עֵץ בּוֹ
כִּי־גָאַל יְהוָה יַעֲקֹב
וּבְיִשְׂרָאֵל יִתְפָּאָר׃

ⁱ Lit. "He shepherds ashes"   ʲ Emendation yields "them," these things

982

Jeremiah was the most inward of the prophets. In his agonized visions he foresaw Jerusalem's destruction and was jailed for his preachments. When the Babylonians destroyed the city in 586 (or 585) B.C.E., he became one of the exiles and died in Egypt.

Jeremiah, preaching before the destruction of the Temple, warned his people that sacrifices alone (as commanded in the sidrah) would not mollify God's wrath unless they were accompanied by a true return to Him. Ritual without commitment was form without content.

Jeremiah

7 : 21 — 8 : 3; 9 : 22 - 23

ז

Chapter 7

21] Thus said the LORD of Hosts, the God of Israel: Add your burnt offerings to your other sacrifices and eat the meat!

22] For when I freed your fathers from the land of Egypt, I did not speak with them or command them concerning burnt offerings or sacrifice.

23] But this is what I commanded them: Do My bidding, that I may be your God and you may be My people; walk only in the way that I enjoin upon you, that it may go well with you.

24] Yet they did not listen or give ear; they followed their own counsels, the willfulness of their evil hearts. They have gone backward, not forward,

25] from the day your fathers left the land of Egypt until today. And though I kept sending all My servants, the prophets, to them[d] daily and persistently,

26] they would not listen to Me or give ear. They stiffened their necks, they acted worse than their fathers.

27] You shall say all these things to them, but they will not listen to you; you shall call to them, but they will not respond to you.

28] Then say to them: This is the nation that

---
[d] Heb. "you"

21] כֹּה אָמַר יְהֹוָה צְבָאוֹת אֱלֹהֵי יִשְׂרָאֵל עֹלוֹתֵיכֶם סְפוּ עַל־זִבְחֵיכֶם וְאִכְלוּ בָשָׂר: 22] כִּי לֹא־דִבַּרְתִּי אֶת־אֲבוֹתֵיכֶם וְלֹא צִוִּיתִים בְּיוֹם הוֹצִיאִי אוֹתָם מֵאֶרֶץ מִצְרָיִם עַל־דִּבְרֵי עוֹלָה וָזָבַח: 23] כִּי אִם־אֶת־הַדָּבָר הַזֶּה צִוִּיתִי אוֹתָם לֵאמֹר שִׁמְעוּ בְקוֹלִי וְהָיִיתִי לָכֶם לֵאלֹהִים וְאַתֶּם תִּהְיוּ־לִי לְעָם וַהֲלַכְתֶּם בְּכָל־הַדֶּרֶךְ אֲשֶׁר אֲצַוֶּה אֶתְכֶם לְמַעַן יִיטַב לָכֶם: 24] וְלֹא שָׁמְעוּ וְלֹא־הִטּוּ אֶת־אָזְנָם וַיֵּלְכוּ בְּמֹעֵצוֹת בִּשְׁרִרוּת לִבָּם הָרָע וַיִּהְיוּ לְאָחוֹר וְלֹא לְפָנִים: 25] לְמִן־הַיּוֹם אֲשֶׁר יָצְאוּ אֲבוֹתֵיכֶם מֵאֶרֶץ מִצְרַיִם עַד הַיּוֹם הַזֶּה וָאֶשְׁלַח אֲלֵיכֶם אֶת־כָּל־עֲבָדַי הַנְּבִיאִים יוֹם הַשְׁכֵּם וְשָׁלֹחַ: 26] וְלוֹא שָׁמְעוּ אֵלַי וְלֹא הִטּוּ אֶת־אָזְנָם וַיַּקְשׁוּ אֶת־עָרְפָּם הֵרֵעוּ מֵאֲבוֹתָם: 27] וְדִבַּרְתָּ אֲלֵיהֶם אֶת־כָּל־הַדְּבָרִים הָאֵלֶּה וְלֹא יִשְׁמְעוּ אֵלֶיךָ וְקָרָאתָ אֲלֵיהֶם וְלֹא יַעֲנוּכָה: 28] וְאָמַרְתָּ אֲלֵיהֶם זֶה הַגּוֹי אֲשֶׁר לוֹא־שָׁמְעוּ

would not obey the LORD their God, that would not accept rebuke. Faithfulness has perished, vanished from their mouths.

29] Shear your locks and cast them away,
Take up a lament on the heights,
For the LORD has spurned and cast off
The brood that provoked His wrath.

30] For the people of Judah have done what displeases Me—declares the LORD. They have set up their abominations in the House which is called by My name, and they have defiled it. 31] And they have built the shrines of Topheth in the Valley of Ben-hinnom to burn their sons and daughters in fire—which I never commanded, which never came to My mind.

32] Assuredly, a time is coming—declares the LORD—when men shall no longer speak of Topheth or the Valley of Ben-hinnom, but of the Valley of Slaughter; and they shall bury in Topheth until no room is left.

33] The carcasses of this people shall be food for the birds of the sky and the beasts of the earth, with none to frighten them off.

34] And I will silence in the towns of Judah and the streets of Jerusalem the sound of mirth and gladness, the voice of bridegroom and bride. For the whole land shall fall to ruin.

Chapter 8

1] At that time—declares the LORD—the bones of the kings of Judah, of its officers, of the priests, of the prophets, and of the inhabitants of Jerusalem shall be taken out of their graves

2] and exposed to the sun, the moon, and all the host of heaven which they loved and served and followed, to which they turned and bowed down. They shall not be gathered for reburial; they shall become dung upon the face of the earth. 3] And death shall be preferable to life for all

בְּקוֹל יְהוָה אֱלֹהָיו וְלֹא לָקְחוּ מוּסָר אָבְדָה
הָאֱמוּנָה וְנִכְרְתָה מִפִּיהֶם:

29 גָּזִּי נִזְרֵךְ וְהַשְׁלִיכִי
וּשְׂאִי עַל־שְׁפָיִם קִינָה
כִּי מָאַס יְהוָה וַיִּטֹּשׁ
אֶת־דּוֹר עֶבְרָתוֹ:

30 כִּי־עָשׂוּ בְנֵי־יְהוּדָה הָרַע בְּעֵינַי נְאֻם־
יְהוָה שָׂמוּ שִׁקּוּצֵיהֶם בַּבַּיִת אֲשֶׁר־נִקְרָא־שְׁמִי
עָלָיו לְטַמְּאוֹ: 31 וּבָנוּ בָּמוֹת הַתֹּפֶת אֲשֶׁר
בְּגֵיא בֶן־הִנֹּם לִשְׂרֹף אֶת־בְּנֵיהֶם וְאֶת־בְּנֹתֵיהֶם
בָּאֵשׁ אֲשֶׁר לֹא צִוִּיתִי וְלֹא עָלְתָה עַל־לִבִּי:

32 לָכֵן הִנֵּה־יָמִים בָּאִים נְאֻם־יְהוָה וְלֹא־
יֵאָמֵר עוֹד הַתֹּפֶת וְגֵיא בֶן־הִנֹּם כִּי אִם־גֵּיא
הַהֲרֵגָה וְקָבְרוּ בְתֹפֶת מֵאֵין מָקוֹם:

33 וְהָיְתָה נִבְלַת הָעָם הַזֶּה לְמַאֲכָל לְעוֹף
הַשָּׁמַיִם וּלְבֶהֱמַת הָאָרֶץ וְאֵין מַחֲרִיד:

34 וְהִשְׁבַּתִּי מֵעָרֵי יְהוּדָה וּמֵחֻצוֹת יְרוּשָׁלִַם
קוֹל שָׂשׂוֹן וְקוֹל שִׂמְחָה קוֹל חָתָן וְקוֹל כַּלָּה
כִּי לְחָרְבָּה תִּהְיֶה הָאָרֶץ:

ח

1 בָּעֵת הַהִיא נְאֻם־יְהוָה יוֹצִיאוּ אֶת־עַצְמוֹת
מַלְכֵי־יְהוּדָה וְאֶת־עַצְמוֹת שָׂרָיו וְאֶת־עַצְמוֹת
הַכֹּהֲנִים וְאֵת עַצְמוֹת הַנְּבִיאִים וְאֵת עַצְמוֹת
יוֹשְׁבֵי־יְרוּשָׁלִָם מִקִּבְרֵיהֶם: 2 וּשְׁטָחוּם לַשֶּׁמֶשׁ
וְלַיָּרֵחַ וּלְכֹל צְבָא הַשָּׁמַיִם אֲשֶׁר אֲהֵבוּם וַאֲשֶׁר
עֲבָדוּם וַאֲשֶׁר הָלְכוּ אַחֲרֵיהֶם וַאֲשֶׁר דְּרָשׁוּם
וַאֲשֶׁר הִשְׁתַּחֲווּ לָהֶם לֹא יֵאָסְפוּ וְלֹא יִקָּבֵרוּ
לְדֹמֶן עַל־פְּנֵי הָאֲדָמָה יִהְיוּ: 3 וְנִבְחַר מָוֶת

984

that are left of this wicked folk, in all the other places to which I shall banish them—declares the LORD of Hosts.

מְחַיִּים לְכֹל הַשְּׁאֵרִית הַנִּשְׁאָרִים מִן־הַמִּשְׁפָּחָה הָרָעָה הַזֹּאת בְּכָל־הַמְּקֹמוֹת הַנִּשְׁאָרִים אֲשֶׁר הִדַּחְתִּים שָׁם נְאֻם יְהוָה צְבָאוֹת:

Chapter 9

ט

22] Thus said the LORD:
Let not the wise man glory in his wisdom;
Let not the strong man glory in his strength;
Let not the rich man glory in his riches.

22] כֹּה אָמַר יְהוָה
אַל־יִתְהַלֵּל חָכָם בְּחָכְמָתוֹ
וְאַל־יִתְהַלֵּל הַגִּבּוֹר בִּגְבוּרָתוֹ
אַל־יִתְהַלֵּל עָשִׁיר בְּעָשְׁרוֹ:

23] But only in this should one glory:
In his earnest devotion to Me.
For I the LORD act with kindness,
Justice, and equity in the world;
For in these I delight
                    —declares the LORD.

23] כִּי אִם־בְּזֹאת יִתְהַלֵּל הַמִּתְהַלֵּל
הַשְׂכֵּל וְיָדֹעַ אוֹתִי
כִּי אֲנִי יְהוָה עֹשֶׂה חֶסֶד
מִשְׁפָּט וּצְדָקָה בָּאָרֶץ
כִּי־בְאֵלֶּה חָפַצְתִּי
נְאֻם־יְהוָה:

The Book of Samuel is divided into two parts. It is primarily the story of Samuel's ministry as the spiritual guide of Israel and of the reign of Israel's first two kings, Saul and David (about 1000 B.C.E.). It is history written from a theological perspective: all of Israel's fate hinges on the performance or non-performance of God's commandments.

Both sidrah and haftarah report tragic incidents connected with Tabernacle and ark, respectively. The holy precincts and objects partake of the ineffable Presence and may not be tampered with.

שמיני

Second Samuel

6 : 1 – 7 : 17

Chapter 6

1] David again assembled all the picked men of Israel, thirty thousand strong.
2] *a*Then David and all the troops that were with him set out from Baalim*b* of Judah to bring up from there the Ark of God to which the Name was attached, the name Lord of Hosts Enthroned on the Cherubim.

3] They loaded the Ark of God onto a new cart and conveyed it from the house of Abinadab which was on the hill; and Abinadab's sons, Uzzah and Ahio, guided the *c*‾new cart.

4] They conveyed it from Abinadab's house on the hill, [Uzzah walking]*d* alongside*‾c* the Ark of God and Ahio walking in front of the Ark.

5] Meanwhile, David and all the House of Israel danced before the Lord to *e*[the sound of] all kinds of cypress wood [instruments],*‾e* with lyres, harps, timbrels, sistrums, and cymbals.

ו

1] וַיֹּסֶף עוֹד דָּוִד אֶת־כָּל־בָּחוּר בְּיִשְׂרָאֵל שְׁלֹשִׁים אָלֶף: 2] וַיָּקָם וַיֵּלֶךְ דָּוִד וְכָל־הָעָם אֲשֶׁר אִתּוֹ מִבַּעֲלֵי יְהוּדָה לְהַעֲלוֹת מִשָּׁם אֵת אֲרוֹן הָאֱלֹהִים אֲשֶׁר־נִקְרָא שֵׁם שֵׁם יְהֹוָה צְבָאוֹת יֹשֵׁב הַכְּרֻבִים עָלָיו: 3] וַיַּרְכִּבוּ אֶת־אֲרוֹן הָאֱלֹהִים אֶל־עֲגָלָה חֲדָשָׁה וַיִּשָּׂאֻהוּ מִבֵּית אֲבִינָדָב אֲשֶׁר בַּגִּבְעָה וְעֻזָּא וְאַחְיוֹ בְּנֵי אֲבִינָדָב נֹהֲגִים אֶת־הָעֲגָלָה חֲדָשָׁה: 4] וַיִּשָּׂאֻהוּ מִבֵּית אֲבִינָדָב אֲשֶׁר בַּגִּבְעָה עִם אֲרוֹן הָאֱלֹהִים וְאַחְיוֹ הֹלֵךְ לִפְנֵי הָאָרוֹן: 5] וְדָוִד וְכָל־בֵּית יִשְׂרָאֵל מְשַׂחֲקִים לִפְנֵי יְהֹוָה בְּכֹל עֲצֵי בְרוֹשִׁים וּבְכִנֹּרוֹת וּבִנְבָלִים וּבְתֻפִּים וּבִמְנַעַנְעִים וּבְצֶלְצֶלִים:

---

a Vv. 2–12 are found also in I Chron. 13.5–14, with variations

b Identical with Baalah, another name for Kiriath-jearim, where the Ark had been kept (cf. I Sam. 6.21; I Chron. 13.6; Josh. 15.9)

c‾c Septuagint and 4QSam*a* read "cart alongside" (4QSam*a*=manuscript*a* of Samuel found in the fourth cave at Qumran, the site of the caves where the Bible manuscripts were found in 1949–50.)

d Cf. vv. 6–7

e‾e Cf. Kimchi; the parallel passage I Chron. 13.8 reads "with all their might and with songs"

6] But when they came to the threshing floor of Nacon, Uzzah reached out for the Ark of God and grasped it, for the oxen had stumbled.[f]
7] The LORD was incensed at Uzzah. And God struck him down on the spot [g]for his indiscretion,[g] and he died there beside the Ark of God.
8] David was distressed because the LORD had inflicted a breach upon Uzzah; and that place was named Perez-uzzah,[h] as it is still called.

9] David was afraid of the LORD that day; he said, "How can I let the Ark of the LORD come to me?"
10] So David would not bring the Ark to his place in the City of David; instead, he diverted it to the house of Obed-edom the Gittite.
11] The Ark of the LORD remained in the house of Obed-edom the Gittite three months, and the LORD blessed Obed-edom and his whole household.

12] It was reported to King David: "The LORD has blessed Obed-edom's house and all that belongs to him because of the Ark of God." [i]Thereupon David went and brought up the Ark of God from the house of Obed-edom to the City of David, amid rejoicing.
13] When the bearers of the Ark of the LORD had moved forward six paces, he sacrificed [i-i]an ox and a fatling.[i-i]
14] David whirled with all his might before the LORD; David was girt with a linen ephod.
15] Thus David and all the House of Israel brought up the Ark of the LORD with shouts and with blasts of the horn.
16] As the Ark of the LORD entered the City of David, Michal daughter of Saul looked out of the window and saw King David leaping and

6 וַיָּבֹאוּ עַד־גֹּרֶן נָכוֹן וַיִּשְׁלַח עֻזָּא אֶל אֲרוֹן הָאֱלֹהִים וַיֹּאחֶז בּוֹ כִּי שָׁמְטוּ הַבָּקָר:
7 וַיִּחַר־אַף יְהוָה בְּעֻזָּה וַיַּכֵּהוּ שָׁם הָאֱלֹהִים עַל־הַשַּׁל וַיָּמָת שָׁם עִם אֲרוֹן הָאֱלֹהִים:
8 וַיִּחַר לְדָוִד עַל אֲשֶׁר פָּרַץ יְהוָה פֶּרֶץ בְּעֻזָּה וַיִּקְרָא לַמָּקוֹם הַהוּא פֶּרֶץ עֻזָּה עַד הַיּוֹם הַזֶּה:

9 וַיִּרָא דָוִד אֶת־יְהוָה בַּיּוֹם הַהוּא וַיֹּאמֶר אֵיךְ יָבוֹא אֵלַי אֲרוֹן יְהוָה: 10 וְלֹא־אָבָה דָוִד לְהָסִיר אֵלָיו אֶת־אֲרוֹן יְהוָה עַל־עִיר דָּוִד וַיַּטֵּהוּ דָוִד בֵּית עֹבֵד־אֱדוֹם הַגִּתִּי: 11 וַיֵּשֶׁב אֲרוֹן יְהוָה בֵּית עֹבֵד אֱדֹם הַגִּתִּי שְׁלֹשָׁה חֳדָשִׁים וַיְבָרֶךְ יְהוָה אֶת־עֹבֵד אֱדֹם וְאֶת־כָּל־בֵּיתוֹ:

12 וַיֻּגַּד לַמֶּלֶךְ דָּוִד לֵאמֹר בֵּרַךְ יְהוָה אֶת־בֵּית עֹבֵד אֱדֹם וְאֶת־כָּל־אֲשֶׁר־לוֹ בַּעֲבוּר אֲרוֹן הָאֱלֹהִים וַיֵּלֶךְ דָּוִד וַיַּעַל אֶת־אֲרוֹן הָאֱלֹהִים מִבֵּית עֹבֵד אֱדֹם עִיר דָּוִד בְּשִׂמְחָה: 13 וַיְהִי כִּי צָעֲדוּ נֹשְׂאֵי אֲרוֹן־יְהוָה שִׁשָּׁה צְעָדִים וַיִּזְבַּח שׁוֹר וּמְרִיא: 14 וְדָוִד מְכַרְכֵּר בְּכָל־עֹז לִפְנֵי יְהוָה וְדָוִד חָגוּר אֵפוֹד בָּד: 15 וְדָוִד וְכָל־בֵּית יִשְׂרָאֵל מַעֲלִים אֶת־אֲרוֹן יְהוָה בִּתְרוּעָה וּבְקוֹל שׁוֹפָר: 16 וְהָיָה אֲרוֹן יְהוָה בָּא עִיר דָּוִד וּמִיכַל בַּת־שָׁאוּל נִשְׁקְפָה בְּעַד הַחַלּוֹן וַתֵּרֶא אֶת־

---

[f] Meaning of Heb. uncertain
[g-g] So Targum; I Chron. 13.10 reads "because he had laid a hand on the Ark"
[h] I.e., "the Breach of Uzzah"; cf. 5.20 and note
[i] Vv. 12b–14 are found, with variations, in I Chron. 15.25–27; vv. 15–19a, with variations, in I Chron. 15.28—16.3; vv. 19b–20a, with variations, in I Chron. 16.43
[i-i] 4QSam[a] reads "seven oxen and seven (rams)"; cf. I Chron. 15.26

whirling before the Lord; and she despised him for it.

17] They brought in the Ark of the Lord and set it up in its place inside the tent which David had pitched for it, and David sacrificed burnt offerings and offerings of well-being before the Lord.

18] When David finished sacrificing the burnt offerings and the offerings of well-being, he blessed the people in the name of the Lord of Hosts.

19] And he distributed among all the people—the entire multitude of Israel, man and woman alike—to each a loaf of bread, ᶠa cake made in a pan, and a raisin cake.ᶠ Then all the people left for their homes.

20] David went home to greet his household. And Michal daughter of Saul came out to meet David and said, "Didn't the king of Israel do him-self honor today—exposing himself today in the sight of the slavegirls of his subjects, as one of the riffraff might expose himself!"

21] David an-swered Michal, "It was before the Lord who chose me instead of your father and all his family and appointed me ruler over the Lord's people Israel! I will dance before the Lord

22] and dishonor myself even more, and be low in ᵏmy ownᵏ esteem; but among the slavegirls that you speak of I will be honored."

23] So to her dying day Michal daughter of Saul had no children.

Chapter 7

1] ᵃWhen the king was settled in his palace and the Lord had granted him safety from all the enemies around him,

2] the king said to the prophet Nathan: "Here I am dwelling in a house of cedar, while the Ark of the Lord abides in a tent!"

ᶠ⁻ᶠ Meaning of Heb. uncertain
ᵏ⁻ᵏ Septuagint reads "your"

ᵃ This chapter is found, with variations, also in I Chron. 17

הַמֶּ֤לֶךְ דָּוִד֙ מְפַזֵּ֣ז וּמְכַרְכֵּ֔ר לִפְנֵ֖י יְהוָ֑ה וַתִּ֥בֶז ל֖וֹ בְּלִבָּֽהּ׃

17] וַיָּבִ֜אוּ אֶת־אֲר֣וֹן יְהוָ֗ה וַיַּצִּ֤גוּ אֹתוֹ֙ בִּמְקוֹמ֔וֹ בְּת֣וֹךְ הָאֹ֔הֶל אֲשֶׁ֥ר נָֽטָה־ל֖וֹ דָּוִ֑ד וַיַּ֨עַל דָּוִ֜ד עֹל֧וֹת לִפְנֵ֛י יְהוָ֖ה וּשְׁלָמִֽים׃ 18] וַיְכַ֣ל דָּוִ֗ד מֵהַעֲל֥וֹת הָעוֹלָ֖ה וְהַשְּׁלָמִ֑ים וַיְבָ֣רֶךְ אֶת־הָעָ֔ם בְּשֵׁ֖ם יְהוָ֥ה צְבָאֽוֹת׃ 19] וַיְחַלֵּ֨ק לְכָל־הָעָ֜ם לְכָל־הֲמ֣וֹן יִשְׂרָאֵל֮ לְמֵאִ֣ישׁ וְעַד־אִשָּׁה֒ לְאִ֗ישׁ חַלַּ֥ת לֶ֙חֶם֙ אַחַ֔ת וְאֶשְׁפָּ֣ר אֶחָ֔ד וַאֲשִׁישָׁ֖ה אֶחָ֑ת וַיֵּ֥לֶךְ כָּל־הָעָ֖ם אִ֥ישׁ לְבֵיתֽוֹ׃

20] וַיָּ֥שָׁב דָּוִ֖ד לְבָרֵ֣ךְ אֶת־בֵּית֑וֹ וַתֵּצֵ֞א מִיכַ֣ל בַּת־שָׁא֗וּל לִקְרַ֣את דָּוִד֮ וַתֹּ֒אמֶר֒ מַה־נִּכְבַּ֨ד הַיּ֜וֹם מֶ֣לֶךְ יִשְׂרָאֵ֗ל אֲשֶׁ֨ר נִגְלָ֤ה הַיּוֹם֙ לְעֵינֵ֣י אַמְה֣וֹת עֲבָדָ֔יו כְּהִגָּל֥וֹת נִגְל֖וֹת אַחַ֥ד הָרֵקִֽים׃ 21] וַיֹּ֣אמֶר דָּוִד֮ אֶל־מִיכַל֒ לִפְנֵ֣י יְהוָ֗ה אֲשֶׁ֨ר בָּֽחַר־בִּ֤י מֵֽאָבִיךְ֙ וּמִכָּל־בֵּית֔וֹ לְצַוֺּ֥ת אֹתִ֛י נָגִ֛יד עַל־עַ֥ם יְהוָ֖ה עַל־יִשְׂרָאֵ֑ל וְשִׂחַקְתִּ֖י לִפְנֵ֥י יְהוָֽה׃ 22] וּנְקַלֹּ֤תִי עוֹד֙ מִזֹּ֔את וְהָיִ֥יתִי שָׁפָ֖ל בְּעֵינָ֑י וְעִם־הָֽאֲמָהוֹת֙ אֲשֶׁ֣ר אָמַ֔רְתְּ עִמָּ֖ם אִכָּבֵֽדָה׃ 23] וּלְמִיכַל֙ בַּת־שָׁא֔וּל לֹֽא־הָ֥יָה לָ֖הּ יָ֑לֶד עַ֖ד י֥וֹם מוֹתָֽהּ׃

ז

1] וַיְהִ֕י כִּֽי־יָשַׁ֥ב הַמֶּ֖לֶךְ בְּבֵית֑וֹ וַֽיהוָ֞ה הֵנִֽיחַ־ל֥וֹ מִסָּבִ֖יב מִכָּל־אֹיְבָֽיו׃ 2] וַיֹּ֤אמֶר הַמֶּ֙לֶךְ֙ אֶל־נָתָ֣ן הַנָּבִ֔יא רְאֵ֣ה נָ֗א אָנֹכִ֤י יוֹשֵׁב֙ בְּבֵ֣ית אֲרָזִ֔ים וַֽאֲרוֹן֙ הָֽאֱלֹהִ֔ים יֹשֵׁ֖ב בְּת֥וֹךְ הַיְרִיעָֽה׃

988

3] Nathan said to the king, "Go and do whatever you have in mind, for the LORD is with you."

4] But that same night the word of the LORD came to Nathan:

5] "Go and say to My servant David: Thus said the LORD: Are you the one to build a house for Me to dwell in?

6] From the day that I brought the people of Israel out of Egypt to this day I have not dwelt in a house, but have moved about in Tent and Tabernacle. 7] As I moved about wherever the Israelites went, did I ever reproach any of the tribal leaders[b] whom I appointed to care for My people Israel: Why have you not built Me a house of cedar?

8] "Further, say thus to My servant David: Thus said the LORD of Hosts: I took you from the pasture, from following the flock, to be ruler of My people Israel,

9] and I have been with you wherever you went, and have cut down all your enemies before you. Moreover, I will give you great renown like that of the greatest men on earth.

10] I will establish a home for My people Israel and will plant them firm, so that they shall dwell secure and shall tremble no more. Evil men shall not oppress them any more as in the past, 11] ever since I appointed chieftains over My people Israel. I will give you safety from all your enemies.

"The LORD declares to you that He, the LORD, will establish a house[c] for you.

12] When your days are done and you lie with your fathers, I will raise up your offspring after you, one of your own issue, and I will establish his kingship. 13] He shall build a house for My name, and I will establish his royal throne forever.

3 וַיֹּאמֶר נָתָן אֶל־הַמֶּלֶךְ כֹּל אֲשֶׁר בִּלְבָבְךָ לֵךְ עֲשֵׂה כִּי יְהוָה עִמָּךְ:

4 וַיְהִי בַּלַּיְלָה הַהוּא וַיְהִי דְּבַר־יְהוָה אֶל־נָתָן לֵאמֹר: 5 לֵךְ וְאָמַרְתָּ אֶל־עַבְדִּי אֶל־דָּוִד כֹּה אָמַר יְהוָה הַאַתָּה תִּבְנֶה־לִּי בַיִת לְשִׁבְתִּי: 6 כִּי לֹא יָשַׁבְתִּי בְּבַיִת לְמִיּוֹם הַעֲלֹתִי אֶת־בְּנֵי יִשְׂרָאֵל מִמִּצְרַיִם וְעַד הַיּוֹם הַזֶּה וָאֶהְיֶה מִתְהַלֵּךְ בְּאֹהֶל וּבְמִשְׁכָּן: 7 בְּכֹל אֲשֶׁר־הִתְהַלַּכְתִּי בְּכָל־בְּנֵי יִשְׂרָאֵל הֲדָבָר דִּבַּרְתִּי אֶת־אַחַד שִׁבְטֵי יִשְׂרָאֵל אֲשֶׁר צִוִּיתִי לִרְעוֹת אֶת־עַמִּי אֶת־יִשְׂרָאֵל לֵאמֹר לָמָּה לֹא בְנִיתֶם לִי בֵּית אֲרָזִים:

8 וְעַתָּה כֹּה־תֹאמַר לְעַבְדִּי לְדָוִד כֹּה אָמַר יְהוָה צְבָאוֹת אֲנִי לְקַחְתִּיךָ מִן־הַנָּוֶה מֵאַחַר הַצֹּאן לִהְיוֹת נָגִיד עַל־עַמִּי עַל־יִשְׂרָאֵל: 9 וָאֶהְיֶה עִמְּךָ בְּכֹל אֲשֶׁר הָלַכְתָּ וָאַכְרִתָה אֶת־כָּל־אֹיְבֶיךָ מִפָּנֶיךָ וְעָשִׂתִי לְךָ שֵׁם גָּדוֹל כְּשֵׁם הַגְּדֹלִים אֲשֶׁר בָּאָרֶץ: 10 וְשַׂמְתִּי מָקוֹם לְעַמִּי לְיִשְׂרָאֵל וּנְטַעְתִּיו וְשָׁכַן תַּחְתָּיו וְלֹא יִרְגַּז עוֹד וְלֹא־יֹסִיפוּ בְנֵי־עַוְלָה לְעַנּוֹתוֹ כַּאֲשֶׁר בָּרִאשׁוֹנָה: 11 וּלְמִן־הַיּוֹם אֲשֶׁר צִוִּיתִי שֹׁפְטִים עַל־עַמִּי יִשְׂרָאֵל וַהֲנִיחֹתִי לְךָ מִכָּל־אֹיְבֶיךָ וְהִגִּיד לְךָ יְהוָה כִּי־בַיִת יַעֲשֶׂה־לְּךָ יְהוָה: 12 כִּי יִמְלְאוּ יָמֶיךָ וְשָׁכַבְתָּ אֶת־אֲבֹתֶיךָ וַהֲקִימֹתִי אֶת־זַרְעֲךָ אַחֲרֶיךָ אֲשֶׁר יֵצֵא מִמֵּעֶיךָ וַהֲכִינֹתִי אֶת־מַמְלַכְתּוֹ: 13 הוּא יִבְנֶה־בַּיִת לִשְׁמִי וְכֹנַנְתִּי אֶת־כִּסֵּא מַמְלַכְתּוֹ

---

[b] Understanding shibṭe as "scepters"; so Kimchi. I Chron. 17.6 reads "chieftains"; cf. v. 11

[c] I.e., a dynasty; play on "house" (i.e., Temple) in v. 5

14] I will be a father to him, and he shall be a son to Me. When he does wrong, I will chastise him d-with the rod of men and the affliction of mortals;-d 15] but I will never withdraw My favor from him as I withdrew it from Saul, whom I removed e-to make room for you.-e

16] Your house and your kingship shall ever be secure before you;f your throne shall be established forever.''

17] Nathan spoke to David in accordance with all these words and all this prophecy.

עַד־עוֹלָֽם: 14 אֲנִי אֶהְיֶה־לּוֹ לְאָב וְהוּא יִהְיֶה־לִּי לְבֵן אֲשֶׁר בְּהַעֲוֺתוֹ וְהֹכַחְתִּיו בְּשֵׁבֶט אֲנָשִׁים וּבְנִגְעֵי בְּנֵי אָדָם: 15 וְחַסְדִּי לֹא־יָסוּר מִמֶּנּוּ כַּאֲשֶׁר הֲסִרֹתִי מֵעִם שָׁאוּל אֲשֶׁר הֲסִרֹתִי מִלְּפָנֶֽיךָ: 16 וְנֶאְמַן בֵּיתְךָ וּמַמְלַכְתְּךָ עַד־עוֹלָם לְפָנֶיךָ כִּסְאֲךָ יִהְיֶה נָכוֹן עַד־עוֹלָֽם: 17 כְּכֹל הַדְּבָרִים הָאֵלֶּה וּכְכֹל הַחִזָּיוֹן הַזֶּה כֵּן דִּבֶּר נָתָן אֶל־דָּוִֽד:

d-d I.e., only as a human father would
e-e Lit. "from before you"
f Septuagint reads "before Me," i.e., "by My favor"

990

The Book of Kings is divided into two parts. It spans four centuries and reaches from the last days of David to the destruction of the Temple by the Babylonians in 586 (or 585) B.C.E. It approaches history from a theological point of view: the story of Israel and Judah must be seen as a judgment of God on the people and its rulers.

Elisha was Elijah's successor in the role of national prophet (ninth century B.C.E.). The haftarah tells of the miraculous cure of Naaman, a prominent Gentile from abroad, who suffered from leprosy. The treatment of skin infections is the subject also of the sidrah.

תזריע

Second Kings

4 : 42 — 5 : 19

Chapter 4

42] A man came from Baal-shalishah and he brought the man of God some bread of the first reaping—twenty loaves of barley bread, and some fresh grain *ʄin his sack.ʄ* And [Elisha] said, "Give it to the people and let them eat."

43] His attendant replied, "How can I set this before a hundred men?" But he said, "Give it to the people and let them eat. For thus said the LORD: They shall eat and have some left over."

44] So he set it before them; and when they had eaten, they had some left over, as the LORD had said.

Chapter 5

1] Naaman, commander of the army of the king of Aram, was important to his lord and high in his favor, for through him the LORD had granted victory to Aram. But the man, though a great warrior, was a leper.ᵃ

2] Once, when the Arameans were out raiding, they carried off a young girl from the land of Israel, and she became an attendant to Naaman's wife.

3] She said to her mistress, "I wish Master could come before the prophet in Samaria; he would cure him of his leprosy."

4] [Naaman] went and told his lord just what the girl from the land of Israel had said.

ד

‏42] וְאִישׁ בָּא מִבַּעַל שָׁלִשָׁה וַיָּבֵא לְאִישׁ הָאֱלֹהִים לֶחֶם בִּכּוּרִים עֶשְׂרִים־לֶחֶם שְׂעֹרִים וְכַרְמֶל בְּצִקְלֹנוֹ וַיֹּאמֶר תֵּן לָעָם וְיֹאכֵלוּ:‏

‏43] וַיֹּאמֶר מְשָׁרְתוֹ מָה אֶתֵּן זֶה לִפְנֵי מֵאָה אִישׁ וַיֹּאמֶר תֵּן לָעָם וְיֹאכֵלוּ כִּי כֹה אָמַר יְהוָה אָכֹל וְהוֹתֵר: 44] וַיִּתֵּן לִפְנֵיהֶם וַיֹּאכְלוּ וַיּוֹתִרוּ כִּדְבַר יְהוָה:‏

ה

‏1] וְנַעֲמָן שַׂר־צְבָא מֶלֶךְ־אֲרָם הָיָה אִישׁ גָּדוֹל לִפְנֵי אֲדֹנָיו וּנְשֻׂא פָנִים כִּי־בוֹ נָתַן־יְהוָה תְּשׁוּעָה לַאֲרָם וְהָאִישׁ הָיָה גִּבּוֹר חַיִל מְצֹרָע:‏

‏2] וַאֲרָם יָצְאוּ גְדוּדִים וַיִּשְׁבּוּ מֵאֶרֶץ יִשְׂרָאֵל נַעֲרָה קְטַנָּה וַתְּהִי לִפְנֵי אֵשֶׁת נַעֲמָן:‏

‏3] וַתֹּאמֶר אֶל־גְּבִרְתָּהּ אַחֲלֵי אֲדֹנִי לִפְנֵי הַנָּבִיא אֲשֶׁר בְּשֹׁמְרוֹן אָז יֶאֱסֹף אֹתוֹ מִצָּרַעְתּוֹ:‏

‏4] וַיָּבֹא וַיַּגֵּד לַאדֹנָיו לֵאמֹר כָּזֹאת וְכָזֹאת דִּבְּרָה הַנַּעֲרָה אֲשֶׁר מֵאֶרֶץ יִשְׂרָאֵל:‏

ʄ-ʄ Or "on the stalk"; perhaps connected with Ugaritic bṣql   ᵃ *Cf. note on Lev. 13.3*

5] And the king of Aram said, "Go to the king of Israel, and I will send along a letter."

He set out, taking with him ten talents of silver, six thousand shekels of gold, and ten changes of clothing. 6] He brought the letter to the king of Israel. It read: "Now, when this letter reaches you, know that I have sent my courtier Naaman to you, that you may cure him of his leprosy."

7] When the king of Israel read the letter, he rent his clothes and cried, "Am I God, to deal death or give life, that this fellow writes to me to cure a man of leprosy? Just see for yourselves that he is seeking a pretext against me!"

8] When Elisha, the man of God, heard that the king of Israel had rent his clothes, he sent a message to the king: "Why have you rent your clothes? Let him come to me, and he will learn that there is a prophet in Israel."

9] So Naaman came with his horses and chariots and halted at the door of Elisha's house. 10] Elisha sent a messenger to say to him, "Go and bathe seven times in the Jordan, and your flesh shall be restored and you shall be clean." 11] But Naaman was angered and walked away. "I thought," he said, "he would surely come out to me, and would stand and invoke the LORD his God by name, and would wave his hand toward the spot, and cure the affected part.

12] Are not the Amanah and the Pharpar, the rivers of Damascus, better than all the waters of Israel? I could bathe in them and be clean!" And he stalked off in a rage.

13] But his servants came forward and spoke to him. "Sir,"[b] they said, "if the prophet told you to do something difficult, would you not do it? How much more when he has only said to you, 'Bathe and be clean.'"

וַיֹּאמֶר מֶלֶךְ־אֲרָם לֶךְ־בֹּא וְאֶשְׁלְחָה סֵפֶר [5
אֶל־מֶלֶךְ יִשְׂרָאֵל וַיֵּלֶךְ וַיִּקַּח בְּיָדוֹ עֶשֶׂר
כִּכְּרֵי־כֶסֶף וְשֵׁשֶׁת אֲלָפִים זָהָב וְעֶשֶׂר חֲלִיפוֹת
בְּגָדִים: 6 וַיָּבֵא הַסֵּפֶר אֶל־מֶלֶךְ יִשְׂרָאֵל
לֵאמֹר וְעַתָּה כְּבוֹא הַסֵּפֶר הַזֶּה אֵלֶיךָ הִנֵּה
שָׁלַחְתִּי אֵלֶיךָ אֶת־נַעֲמָן עַבְדִּי וַאֲסַפְתּוֹ
מִצָּרַעְתּוֹ: 7 וַיְהִי כִּקְרֹא מֶלֶךְ־יִשְׂרָאֵל אֶת־
הַסֵּפֶר וַיִּקְרַע בְּגָדָיו וַיֹּאמֶר הַאֱלֹהִים אָנִי
לְהָמִית וּלְהַחֲיוֹת כִּי־זֶה שֹׁלֵחַ אֵלַי לֶאֱסֹף אִישׁ
מִצָּרַעְתּוֹ כִּי אַךְ־דְּעוּ־נָא וּרְאוּ כִּי־מִתְאַנֶּה
הוּא לִי:

8 וַיְהִי כִּשְׁמֹעַ אֱלִישָׁע אִישׁ־הָאֱלֹהִים
כִּי־קָרַע מֶלֶךְ־יִשְׂרָאֵל אֶת־בְּגָדָיו וַיִּשְׁלַח אֶל
הַמֶּלֶךְ לֵאמֹר לָמָּה קָרַעְתָּ בְּגָדֶיךָ יָבֹא־נָא
אֵלַי וְיֵדַע כִּי יֵשׁ נָבִיא בְּיִשְׂרָאֵל:

9 וַיָּבֹא נַעֲמָן בְּסוּסָיו וּבְרִכְבּוֹ וַיַּעֲמֹד פֶּתַח
הַבַּיִת לֶאֱלִישָׁע: 10 וַיִּשְׁלַח אֵלָיו אֱלִישָׁע
מַלְאָךְ לֵאמֹר הָלוֹךְ וְרָחַצְתָּ שֶׁבַע־פְּעָמִים
בַּיַּרְדֵּן וְיָשֹׁב בְּשָׂרְךָ לְךָ וּטְהָר: 11 וַיִּקְצֹף
נַעֲמָן וַיֵּלַךְ וַיֹּאמֶר הִנֵּה אָמַרְתִּי אֵלַי יֵצֵא
יָצוֹא וְעָמַד וְקָרָא בְּשֵׁם־יְהוָה אֱלֹהָיו וְהֵנִיף
יָדוֹ אֶל־הַמָּקוֹם וְאָסַף הַמְּצֹרָע: 12 הֲלֹא
טוֹב אֲמָנָה וּפַרְפַּר נַהֲרוֹת דַּמֶּשֶׂק מִכֹּל מֵימֵי
יִשְׂרָאֵל הֲלֹא־אֶרְחַץ בָּהֶם וְטָהָרְתִּי וַיִּפֶן וַיֵּלֶךְ
בְּחֵמָה:

13 וַיִּגְּשׁוּ עֲבָדָיו וַיְדַבְּרוּ אֵלָיו וַיֹּאמְרוּ
אָבִי דָּבָר גָּדוֹל הַנָּבִיא דִּבֶּר אֵלֶיךָ הֲלוֹא
תַעֲשֶׂה וְאַף כִּי־אָמַר אֵלֶיךָ רְחַץ וּטְהָר:

---

[b] Lit. "(My) father"

14] So he went down and immersed himself in the Jordan seven times, as the man of God had bidden; and his flesh became like a little boy's, and he was clean. 15] Returning with his entire retinue to the man of God, he stood before him and exclaimed, "Now I know that there is no God in the whole world except in Israel! So please accept a gift from your servant."

16] But he replied, "As the LORD lives, whom I serve, I will not accept anything." He pressed him to accept, but he refused. 17] And Naaman said, "Then at least let your servant be given two muleloads of earth; for your servant will never again offer up burnt offering or sacrifice to any god, except the LORD. 18] But may the LORD pardon your servant for this: When my master enters the temple of Rimmon to bow low in worship there, and he is leaning on my arm so that I must bow low in the temple of Rimmon— when I bow low in the temple of Rimmon, may the LORD pardon your servant in this."

19] And he said to him, "Go in peace."

And he had gone some distance from him.

וַיֵּרֶד וַיִּטְבֹּל בַּיַּרְדֵּן שֶׁבַע פְּעָמִים כִּדְבַר [14
אִישׁ הָאֱלֹהִים וַיָּשָׁב בְּשָׂרוֹ כִּבְשַׂר נַעַר קָטֹן
וַיִּטְהָר: 15] וַיָּשָׁב אֶל־אִישׁ הָאֱלֹהִים הוּא
וְכָל־מַחֲנֵהוּ וַיָּבֹא וַיַּעֲמֹד לְפָנָיו וַיֹּאמֶר הִנֵּה־נָא
יָדַעְתִּי כִּי אֵין אֱלֹהִים בְּכָל־הָאָרֶץ כִּי אִם
בְּיִשְׂרָאֵל וְעַתָּה קַח־נָא בְרָכָה מֵאֵת עַבְדֶּךָ:
16] וַיֹּאמֶר חַי־יְהֹוָה אֲשֶׁר־עָמַדְתִּי לְפָנָיו אִם
אֶקָּח וַיִּפְצַר־בּוֹ לָקַחַת וַיְמָאֵן: 17] וַיֹּאמֶר
נַעֲמָן וָלֹא יֻתַּן־נָא לְעַבְדְּךָ מַשָּׂא צֶמֶד־פְּרָדִים
אֲדָמָה כִּי לוֹא־יַעֲשֶׂה עוֹד עַבְדְּךָ עֹלָה וָזֶבַח
לֵאלֹהִים אֲחֵרִים כִּי אִם־לַיהֹוָה: 18] לַדָּבָר
הַזֶּה יִסְלַח יְהֹוָה לְעַבְדֶּךָ בְּבוֹא אֲדֹנִי בֵית
רִמּוֹן לְהִשְׁתַּחֲוֹת שָׁמָּה וְהוּא נִשְׁעָן עַל־יָדִי
וְהִשְׁתַּחֲוֵיתִי בֵּית רִמֹּן בְּהִשְׁתַּחֲוָיָתִי בֵּית רִמֹּן
יִסְלַח־נָא יְהֹוָה לְעַבְדְּךָ בַּדָּבָר הַזֶּה:
19] וַיֹּאמֶר לוֹ לֵךְ לְשָׁלוֹם וַיֵּלֶךְ מֵאִתּוֹ כִּבְרַת
אָרֶץ:

v. 18 לֹא קְרִי

מצרע

The Book of Kings is divided into two parts. It spans four
centuries and reaches from the last days of David to the
destruction of the Temple by the Babylonians in 586 (or
585) B.C.E. It approaches history from a theological point
of view: the story of Israel and Judah must be seen as a
judgment of God on the people and its rulers.

The sidrah deals with skin afflictions as did the previous
Torah portion, and the haftarah (like the previous one)
brings us another tale of lepers. All illness was traced to
God's will and so were health and healing.

Second Kings

7 : 3-20

Chapter 7

3] There were four men, lepers, outside the
gate. They said to one another, "Why should we
sit here waiting for death?

4] If we decide to go
into the town, what with the famine in the town,
we shall die there; and if we just sit here, still we
die. Come, let us desert to the Aramean camp. If
they let us live, we shall live; and if they put us to
death, we shall but die."

5] They set out at twilight for the Aramean
camp; but when they came to the edge of the
Aramean camp, there was no one there.

6] For
the LORD had caused the Aramean camp to hear a
sound of chariots, a sound of horses—the din of a
huge army. They said to one another, "The king
of Israel must have hired the kings of the Hittites
and the kings of Mizraim[a] to attack us!"

7] And
they fled headlong in the twilight, abandoning
their tents and horses and asses—the [entire]
camp just as it was—as they fled for their lives.

8] When those lepers came to the edge of the
camp, they went into one of the tents and ate and
drank; then they carried off silver and gold and
clothing from there and buried it. They came back

ז

3] וְאַרְבָּעָה אֲנָשִׁים הָיוּ מְצֹרָעִים פֶּתַח
הַשַּׁעַר וַיֹּאמְרוּ אִישׁ אֶל־רֵעֵהוּ מָה אֲנַחְנוּ
יֹשְׁבִים פֹּה עַד־מָתְנוּ: 4] אִם־אָמַרְנוּ נָבוֹא
הָעִיר וְהָרָעָב בָּעִיר וָמַתְנוּ שָׁם וְאִם־יָשַׁבְנוּ
פֹה וָמָתְנוּ וְעַתָּה לְכוּ וְנִפְּלָה אֶל־מַחֲנֵה אֲרָם
אִם־יְחַיֻּנוּ נִחְיֶה וְאִם־יְמִיתֻנוּ וָמָתְנוּ:
5] וַיָּקוּמוּ בַנֶּשֶׁף לָבוֹא אֶל־מַחֲנֵה אֲרָם
וַיָּבֹאוּ עַד־קְצֵה מַחֲנֵה אֲרָם וְהִנֵּה אֵין־שָׁם
אִישׁ: 6] וַאדֹנָי הִשְׁמִיעַ אֶת־מַחֲנֵה אֲרָם
קוֹל רֶכֶב וְקוֹל סוּס קוֹל חַיִל גָּדוֹל וַיֹּאמְרוּ
אִישׁ אֶל־אָחִיו הִנֵּה שָׂכַר־עָלֵינוּ מֶלֶךְ יִשְׂרָאֵל
אֶת־מַלְכֵי הַחִתִּים וְאֶת־מַלְכֵי מִצְרַיִם לָבוֹא
עָלֵינוּ: 7] וַיָּקוּמוּ וַיָּנוּסוּ בַנֶּשֶׁף וַיַּעַזְבוּ אֶת־
אָהֳלֵיהֶם וְאֶת־סוּסֵיהֶם וְאֶת־חֲמֹרֵיהֶם הַמַּחֲנֶה
כַּאֲשֶׁר הִיא וַיָּנֻסוּ אֶל־נַפְשָׁם:
8] וַיָּבֹאוּ הַמְצֹרָעִים הָאֵלֶּה עַד־קְצֵה
הַמַּחֲנֶה וַיָּבֹאוּ אֶל־אֹהֶל אֶחָד וַיֹּאכְלוּ וַיִּשְׁתּוּ
וַיִּשְׂאוּ מִשָּׁם כֶּסֶף וְזָהָב וּבְגָדִים וַיֵּלְכוּ וַיַּטְמִנוּ

---

[a] Cf. I Kings 10.28 and note g there

and went into another tent, and they carried off what was there and buried it.

9] Then they said to one another, "We are not doing right. This is a day of good news, and we are keeping silent! If we wait until the light of morning, we shall incur guilt. Come, let us go and inform the king's palace."

10] They went and called out to the gatekeepers of the city and told them, "We have been to the Aramean camp. There is not a soul there, nor any human sound; but the horses are tethered and the asses are tethered and the tents are undisturbed."

11] The gatekeepers called out, and the news was passed on into the king's palace.

12] The king rose in the night and said to his courtiers, "I will tell you what the Arameans have done to us. They know that we are starving, so they have gone out of camp and hidden in the fields, thinking: When they come out of the town, we will take them alive and get into the town." 13] But one of the courtiers spoke up, "Let a few[b] of the remaining horses that are still here be taken—[c]they are like those that are left here of the whole multitude of Israel, out of the whole multitude of Israel that have perished[-c]—and let us send and find out."

14] They took two teams[c] of horses and the king sent them after the Aramean army, saying, "Go and find out."

15] They followed them as far as the Jordan, and found the entire road full of clothing and gear which the Arameans had thrown away in their haste; and the messengers returned and told the king.

16] The people then went out and plundered the Aramean camp. So a *seah* of choice flour sold for a shekel, and two *seahs* of barley for a shekel—as the LORD had spoken.

---

[b] Lit. "five"
[c-c] Meaning of Heb. uncertain

וַיָּשֻׁבוּ וַיָּבֹאוּ אֶל־אֹהֶל אַחֵר וַיִּשְׂאוּ מִשָּׁם וַיֵּלְכוּ וַיַּטְמִנוּ: 9 וַיֹּאמְרוּ אִישׁ אֶל־רֵעֵהוּ לֹא־כֵן אֲנַחְנוּ עֹשִׂים הַיּוֹם הַזֶּה יוֹם־בְּשֹׂרָה הוּא וַאֲנַחְנוּ מַחְשִׁים וְחִכִּינוּ עַד־אוֹר הַבֹּקֶר וּמְצָאָנוּ עָווֹן וְעַתָּה לְכוּ וְנָבֹאָה וְנַגִּידָה בֵּית הַמֶּלֶךְ: 10 וַיָּבֹאוּ וַיִּקְרְאוּ אֶל־שֹׁעֵר הָעִיר וַיַּגִּידוּ לָהֶם לֵאמֹר בָּאנוּ אֶל־מַחֲנֵה אֲרָם וְהִנֵּה אֵין־שָׁם אִישׁ וְקוֹל אָדָם כִּי אִם־הַסּוּס אָסוּר וְהַחֲמוֹר אָסוּר וְאֹהָלִים כַּאֲשֶׁר הֵמָּה: 11 וַיִּקְרָא הַשֹּׁעֲרִים וַיַּגִּידוּ בֵּית הַמֶּלֶךְ פְּנִימָה: 12 וַיָּקָם הַמֶּלֶךְ לַיְלָה וַיֹּאמֶר אֶל־עֲבָדָיו אַגִּידָה־נָּא לָכֶם אֵת אֲשֶׁר־עָשׂוּ לָנוּ אֲרָם יָדְעוּ כִּי־רְעֵבִים אֲנַחְנוּ וַיֵּצְאוּ מִן־הַמַּחֲנֶה לְהֵחָבֵה בַשָּׂדֶה לֵאמֹר כִּי־יֵצְאוּ מִן־הָעִיר וְנִתְפְּשֵׂם חַיִּים וְאֶל־הָעִיר נָבֹא: 13 וַיַּעַן אֶחָד מֵעֲבָדָיו וַיֹּאמֶר וְיִקְחוּ־נָא חֲמִשָּׁה מִן־הַסּוּסִים הַנִּשְׁאָרִים אֲשֶׁר נִשְׁאֲרוּ־בָהּ הִנָּם כְּכָל־הֲמוֹן יִשְׂרָאֵל אֲשֶׁר נִשְׁאֲרוּ־בָהּ הִנָּם כְּכָל־הֲמוֹן יִשְׂרָאֵל אֲשֶׁר־תָּמּוּ וְנִשְׁלְחָה וְנִרְאֶה: 14 וַיִּקְחוּ שְׁנֵי רֶכֶב סוּסִים וַיִּשְׁלַח הַמֶּלֶךְ אַחֲרֵי מַחֲנֵה־אֲרָם לֵאמֹר לְכוּ וּרְאוּ: 15 וַיֵּלְכוּ אַחֲרֵיהֶם עַד־הַיַּרְדֵּן וְהִנֵּה כָל־הַדֶּרֶךְ מְלֵאָה בְגָדִים וְכֵלִים אֲשֶׁר־הִשְׁלִיכוּ אֲרָם בְּחָפְזָם וַיָּשֻׁבוּ הַמַּלְאָכִים וַיַּגִּדוּ לַמֶּלֶךְ: 16 וַיֵּצֵא הָעָם וַיָּבֹזּוּ אֵת מַחֲנֵה אֲרָם וַיְהִי סְאָה־סֹלֶת בְּשֶׁקֶל וְסָאתַיִם שְׂעֹרִים בְּשֶׁקֶל כִּדְבַר יְהוָה:

17] Now the king had put the aide on whose arm he leaned in charge of the gate; and he was trampled to death in the gate by the people—just as the man of God had spoken, as he had spoken when the king came down to him.

18] For when the man of God said to the king, "This time tomorrow two *seahs* of barley shall sell at the gate of Samaria for a shekel, and a *seah* of choice flour for a shekel,"

19] the aide answered the man of God and said, "Even if the LORD made windows in the sky, could this come to pass?" And he retorted, "You shall see it with your own eyes, but you shall not eat of it."

20] That is exactly what happened to him: The people trampled him to death in the gate.

וְהַמֶּ֙לֶךְ֙ הִפְקִ֤יד אֶת־הַשָּׁלִישׁ֙ אֲשֶׁר־נִשְׁעָ֣ן [17
עַל־יָד֜וֹ עַל־הַשַּׁ֗עַר וַיִּרְמְסֻ֧הוּ הָעָ֛ם בַּשַּׁ֖עַר
וַיָּמֹ֑ת כַּאֲשֶׁ֤ר דִּבֶּר֙ אִ֣ישׁ הָאֱלֹהִ֔ים אֲשֶׁ֣ר דִּבֶּ֔ר
בְּרֶ֥דֶת הַמֶּ֖לֶךְ אֵלָֽיו: 18] וַיְהִ֗י כְּדַבֵּ֞ר אִ֣ישׁ
הָאֱלֹהִים֮ אֶל־הַמֶּ֣לֶךְ לֵאמֹר֒ סָאתַ֣יִם שְׂעֹרִ֣ים
בְּשֶׁ֗קֶל וּֽסְאָה־סֹ֙לֶת֙ בְּשֶׁ֔קֶל יִהְיֶה֙ כָּעֵ֣ת מָחָ֔ר
בְּשַׁ֖עַר שֹׁמְרֽוֹן: 19] וַיַּ֨עַן הַשָּׁלִ֜ישׁ אֶת־אִ֣ישׁ
הָאֱלֹהִים֮ וַיֹּאמַר֒ וְהִנֵּ֣ה יְהֹוָ֗ה עֹשֶׂה֙ אֲרֻבּוֹת֙
בַּשָּׁמַ֔יִם הֲיִהְיֶ֖ה כַּדָּבָ֣ר הַזֶּ֑ה וַיֹּ֗אמֶר הִנְּךָ֤ רֹאֶה֙
בְּעֵינֶ֔יךָ וּמִשָּׁ֖ם לֹ֥א תֹאכֵֽל: 20] וַֽיְהִי־ל֖וֹ כֵּ֑ן
וַיִּרְמְס֨וּ אֹת֥וֹ הָעָ֛ם בַּשַּׁ֖עַר וַיָּמֹֽת:

996

Ezekiel lived in Babylon during the days of the exile (sixth century B.C.E.) and was a master of mystic dreams and visions. Like Jeremiah and Deutero-Isaiah he fortified his people's faith in God's forgiveness, but unlike them he stressed the great need for structured ritual as a basis for a religious revival.

The Torah portion provides a detailed catalogue of forbidden sexual relations; in the haftarah, Ezekiel chastises Israel for loose sexual habits (verses 10 and 11) in addition to other transgressions. The section may be read as a vivid account of social mores of ancient times.

אחרי מות

Ezekiel

22 : 1-19

Chapter 22

1] The word of the LORD came to me:
2] Further, O mortal, *ᵃarraign, arraignᵃ* the city of bloodshed; declare to her all her abhorrent deeds!

3] Say: Thus said the Lord GOD: O city in whose midst blood is shed, so that your hour is approaching; within which fetishes are made, so that you have become unclean!

4] You stand guilty of the blood you have shed, defiled by the fetishes you have made. You have brought on your day; *ᵇyou have reached your year.ᵇ* Therefore I will make you the mockery of the nations and the scorn of all the lands.

5] Both the near and the far shall scorn you, O besmirched of name, O laden with iniquity!

6] Every one of the princes of Israel in your midst used his strength for the shedding of blood.
7] Fathers and mothers have been humiliated within you; strangers have been cheated in your midst; orphans and widows have been wronged within you.

8] You have despised My holy things and profaned My sabbaths.

9] Baseᶜ men in your midst were intent on shedding blood; in you they have eaten *ᵈupon the mountains;ᵈ* and they have practiced depravity in your midst.

ᵃ⁻ᵃ *Lit. "will you arraign, arraign"*

ᵇ⁻ᵇ *Some Babylonian mss. and ancient versions read "the time of your years has come"*

ᶜ *Meaning of Heb. uncertain*

ᵈ⁻ᵈ *I.e., in idolatry. Emendation yields "with the blood"; cf. Lev. 19.26*

כב

1] וַיְהִי דְבַר־יְהֹוָה אֵלַי לֵאמֹר: 2] וְאַתָּה בֶן־אָדָם הֲתִשְׁפֹּט הֲתִשְׁפֹּט אֶת־עִיר הַדָּמִים וְהוֹדַעְתָּהּ אֵת כָּל־תּוֹעֲבֹתֶיהָ: 3] וְאָמַרְתָּ כֹּה אָמַר אֲדֹנָי יֱהֹוִה עִיר שֹׁפֶכֶת דָּם בְּתוֹכָהּ לָבוֹא עִתָּהּ וְעָשְׂתָה גִלּוּלִים עָלֶיהָ לְטָמְאָה: 4] בְּדָמֵךְ אֲשֶׁר־שָׁפַכְתְּ אָשַׁמְתְּ וּבְגִלּוּלַיִךְ אֲשֶׁר עָשִׂית טָמֵאת וַתַּקְרִיבִי יָמַיִךְ וַתָּבוֹא עַד שְׁנוֹתָיִךְ עַל־כֵּן נְתַתִּיךְ חֶרְפָּה לַגּוֹיִם וְקַלָּסָה לְכָל־הָאֲרָצוֹת: 5] הַקְּרֹבוֹת וְהָרְחֹקוֹת מִמֵּךְ יִתְקַלְּסוּ־בָךְ טְמֵאַת הַשֵּׁם רַבַּת הַמְּהוּמָה: 6] הִנֵּה נְשִׂיאֵי יִשְׂרָאֵל אִישׁ לִזְרֹעוֹ הָיוּ בָךְ לְמַעַן שְׁפָךְ־דָּם: 7] אָב וָאֵם הֵקַלּוּ בָךְ לַגֵּר עָשׂוּ בַעֹשֶׁק בְּתוֹכֵךְ יָתוֹם וְאַלְמָנָה הוֹנוּ בָךְ: 8] קָדָשַׁי בָּזִית וְאֶת־שַׁבְּתֹתַי חִלָּלְתְּ: 9] אַנְשֵׁי רָכִיל הָיוּ בָךְ לְמַעַן שְׁפָךְ־דָּם וְאֶל־הֶהָרִים אָכְלוּ בָךְ זִמָּה עָשׂוּ בְתוֹכֵךְ:

10] In you they have un-
covered their fathers' nakedness;*e* in you they
have ravished women during their impurity.
11] They have committed abhorrent acts with
other men's wives; in their depravity they have
defiled their own daughters-in-law; in you they
have ravished their own sisters, daughters of their
fathers.

12] They have taken bribes within you
to shed blood. You have taken advance and accrued interest;*f* you have defrauded your countrymen to your profit. You have forgotten Me—
declares the Lord GOD.

13] Lo, I will strike My hands over the ill-
gotten gains that you have amassed, and over the
bloodshed that has been committed in your midst.
14] Will your courage endure, will your hands
remain firm in the days when I deal with you?
I the LORD have spoken and I will act.

15] I will
scatter you among the nations and disperse you
through the lands; I will consume the uncleanness
out of you.

16] You shall be dishonored in the
sight of nations, and you shall know that I am
the LORD.

17] The word of the LORD came to me:
18] O mortal, the House of Israel has become dross
to Me; they are all copper, tin, iron, and lead.
c-But in a crucible, the dross shall turn into silver.-*c*
19] Assuredly, thus said the Lord GOD: Because
you have all become dross, I will gather you into
Jerusalem.

10 עֶרְוַת־אָב גִּלָּה־בָּךְ טְמֵאַת הַנִּדָּה עִנּוּ־בָךְ:
11 וְאִישׁ אֶת־אֵשֶׁת רֵעֵהוּ עָשָׂה תּוֹעֵבָה וְאִישׁ
אֶת־כַּלָּתוֹ טִמֵּא בְזִמָּה וְאִישׁ אֶת־אֲחֹתוֹ בַת־
אָבִיו עִנָּה־בָךְ: 12 שֹׁחַד לָקְחוּ־בָךְ לְמַעַן
שְׁפָךְ־דָּם נֶשֶׁךְ וְתַרְבִּית לָקַחַתְּ וַתְּבַצְּעִי רֵעַיִךְ
בַּעֹשֶׁק וְאֹתִי שָׁכַחַתְּ נְאֻם אֲדֹנָי יֱהֹוִה:
13 וְהִנֵּה הִכֵּיתִי כַפִּי אֶל־בִּצְעֵךְ אֲשֶׁר
עָשִׂית וְעַל־דָּמֵךְ אֲשֶׁר הָיוּ בְּתוֹכֵךְ:
14 הֲיַעֲמֹד לִבֵּךְ אִם־תֶּחֱזַקְנָה יָדַיִךְ לַיָּמִים
אֲשֶׁר אֲנִי עֹשֶׂה אוֹתָךְ אֲנִי יְהֹוָה דִּבַּרְתִּי
וְעָשִׂיתִי: 15 וַהֲפִיצוֹתִי אוֹתָךְ בַּגּוֹיִם וְזֵרִיתִיךְ
בָּאֲרָצוֹת וַהֲתִמֹּתִי טֻמְאָתֵךְ מִמֵּךְ: 16 וְנִחַלְתְּ
בָּךְ לְעֵינֵי גוֹיִם וְיָדַעַתְּ כִּי־אֲנִי יְהֹוָה:
17 וַיְהִי דְבַר־יְהֹוָה אֵלַי לֵאמֹר: 18 בֶּן־
אָדָם הָיוּ־לִי בֵית־יִשְׂרָאֵל לְסִיג כֻּלָּם נְחֹשֶׁת
וּבְדִיל וּבַרְזֶל וְעוֹפֶרֶת בְּתוֹךְ כּוּר סִגִים כֶּסֶף
הָיוּ: 19 לָכֵן כֹּה אָמַר אֲדֹנָי יֱהֹוִה יַעַן הֱיוֹת
כֻּלְּכֶם לְסִגִים לָכֵן הִנְנִי קֹבֵץ אֶתְכֶם אֶל־תּוֹךְ
יְרוּשָׁלָ͏ִם:

---

e *I.e., have cohabited with a former wife of the father; cf. Lev. 18.7–8*   *f* *Cf. note at 18.8*
c-c *Meaning of Heb. uncertain*

Amos was a Judean shepherd and tree farmer who lived in the eighth century B.C.E. and was the first of our literary prophets. His strong emphasis on social concerns made him a favorite of the Reform movement, which saw its own social impulse as a re-creation of Amos's spirit.

The end of the sidrah delivers the stern warning that a sinful nation will be plucked from its land and delivered to its enemies. The haftarah brings us a similar warning by Amos. Yet in the end, he proclaims, God will relent and "set up again the fallen booth of David."

HAFTARAH Kedoshim

קדשים

Amos

9 : 7-15

ט

Chapter 9

7] To Me, O Israelites, you are
Just like the Ethiopians
            —declares the LORD.

True, I brought Israel up
From the land of Egypt,
But also the Philistines from Caphtor
And the Arameans from Kir.

8] Behold, the Lord GOD has His eye
Upon the sinful kingdom:
I will wipe it off
The face of the earth!
But, I will not wholly wipe out
The House of Jacob
            —declares the LORD.

9] For I will give the order
And shake the House of Israel—
Through all the nations—
As one shakes [sand] in a sieve,[b]
And not a pebble falls to the ground.

7] הֲלוֹא כִבְנֵי כֻשִׁיִּים אַתֶּם לִי

בְּנֵי יִשְׂרָאֵל

נְאֻם־יְהוָה

הֲלוֹא אֶת־יִשְׂרָאֵל הֶעֱלֵיתִי

מֵאֶרֶץ מִצְרַיִם

וּפְלִשְׁתִּיִּים מִכַּפְתּוֹר

וַאֲרָם מִקִּיר:

8] הִנֵּה עֵינֵי אֲדֹנָי יֱהֹוִה

בַּמַּמְלָכָה הַחַטָּאָה

וְהִשְׁמַדְתִּי אֹתָהּ

מֵעַל פְּנֵי הָאֲדָמָה

אֶפֶס כִּי לֹא הַשְׁמֵיד אַשְׁמִיד

אֶת־בֵּית יַעֲקֹב

נְאֻם־יְהוָה:

9] כִּי־הִנֵּה אָנֹכִי מְצַוֶּה

וַהֲנִעוֹתִי בְכָל־הַגּוֹיִם

אֶת־בֵּית יִשְׂרָאֵל

כַּאֲשֶׁר יִנּוֹעַ בַּכְּבָרָה

וְלֹא־יִפּוֹל צְרוֹר אָרֶץ:

---

[b] A coarse sieve used for cleansing grain of straw and stones, or sand of pebbles and shells

10] All the sinners of My people
Shall perish by the sword,
Who boast,
"Never shall the evil
Overtake us or come near us."

11] In that day,
I will set up again the fallen booth of David:
I will mend its breaches and set up its ruins anew.
I will build it firm as in the days of old,

12] ^{c-}So that they shall possess the rest of Edom
And all the nations once attached to My name^{-c}
—Declares the LORD who will bring this to pass.

13] A time is coming
          —declares the LORD—
When the plowman shall meet the reaper,^d
And the treader of grapes
Him who holds the [bag of] seed;
When the mountains shall drip wine
And all the hills shall wave [with grain].

14] I will restore My people Israel.
They shall rebuild ruined cities and inhabit them;
They shall plant vineyards and drink their wine;
They shall till gardens and eat their fruits.

15] And I will plant them upon their soil,
Nevermore to be uprooted
From the soil I have given them.
          —said the LORD your God.

10] בַּחֶרֶב יָמוּתוּ

כֹּל חַטָּאֵי עַמִּי

הָאֹמְרִים

לֹא־תַגִּישׁ וְתַקְדִּים בַּעֲדֵינוּ

הָרָעָה:

11] בַּיּוֹם הַהוּא

אָקִים אֶת־סֻכַּת דָּוִיד הַנֹּפֶלֶת

וְגָדַרְתִּי אֶת־פִּרְצֵיהֶן וַהֲרִסֹתָיו אָקִים

וּבְנִיתִיהָ כִּימֵי עוֹלָם:

12] לְמַעַן יִירְשׁוּ אֶת־שְׁאֵרִית אֱדוֹם

וְכָל־הַגּוֹיִם אֲשֶׁר־נִקְרָא שְׁמִי עֲלֵיהֶם

נְאֻם־יְהוָה עֹשֶׂה זֹּאת:

13] הִנֵּה יָמִים בָּאִים

נְאֻם־יְהוָה

וְנִגַּשׁ חוֹרֵשׁ בַּקֹּצֵר

וְדֹרֵךְ עֲנָבִים

בְּמֹשֵׁךְ הַזָּרַע

וְהִטִּיפוּ הֶהָרִים עָסִיס

וְכָל־הַגְּבָעוֹת תִּתְמוֹגַגְנָה:

14] וְשַׁבְתִּי אֶת־שְׁבוּת עַמִּי יִשְׂרָאֵל

וּבָנוּ עָרִים נְשַׁמּוֹת

וְיָשָׁבוּ וְנָטְעוּ כְרָמִים

וְשָׁתוּ אֶת־יֵינָם

וְעָשׂוּ גַנּוֹת וְאָכְלוּ אֶת־פְּרִיהֶם:

15] וּנְטַעְתִּים עַל־אַדְמָתָם

וְלֹא יִנָּתְשׁוּ עוֹד

מֵעַל אַדְמָתָם אֲשֶׁר נָתַתִּי לָהֶם

אָמַר יְהוָה אֱלֹהֶיךָ:

^{c-c} *I.e., the House of David shall reestablish its authority over the nations that were ruled by David*
^d *Cf. Lev. 26.5*

Ezekiel lived in Babylon during the days of the exile (sixth century B.C.E.) and was a master of mystic dreams and visions. Like Jeremiah and Deutero-Isaiah he fortified his people's faith in God's forgiveness, but unlike them he stressed the great need for structured ritual as a basis for a religious revival.

The end of the sidrah speaks of priestly duties, a theme taken up in the haftarah. Ezekiel's emphasis on the right kind of worship in the Temple provided a concrete framework for the people's hopes that the time of return and rebuilding the sanctuary would come in their own lifetime.

אמר

Ezekiel

44 : 15–31

Chapter 44

15] ᵉBut the levitical priests descended from Zadok,⁻ᵉ who maintained the service of My sanctuary when the people of Israel went astray from Me—they shall approach Me to minister to Me; they shall stand before Me to offer Me fat and blood—declares the Lord GOD.

16] They alone may enter My sanctuary and they alone shall approach My table to minister to Me; and they shall keep My charge.

17] And when they enter the gates of the inner court, they shall wear linen vestments: they shall have nothing woolen upon them when they minister inside the gates of the inner court.

18] They shall have linen turbans on their heads and linen breeches on their loins; they shall not gird themselves with anything that causes sweat.

19] When they go out to the outer court—the outer court where the people are—they shall remove the vestments in which they minister and shall deposit them in the sacred chambers;ᵈ they shall put on other garments, lest they make the people consecratedᵉ by [contact with] their vestments.

20] They shall neither shave their heads nor let their hair go untrimmed; they shall keep their hair trimmed.

21] No priest shall drink wine when he enters into the inner court.

מד

15] וְהַכֹּהֲנִים הַלְוִיִּם בְּנֵי צָדוֹק אֲשֶׁר שָׁמְרוּ אֶת־מִשְׁמֶרֶת מִקְדָּשִׁי בִּתְעוֹת בְּנֵי־יִשְׂרָאֵל מֵעָלַי הֵמָּה יִקְרְבוּ אֵלַי לְשָׁרְתֵנִי וְעָמְדוּ לְפָנַי לְהַקְרִיב לִי חֵלֶב וָדָם נְאֻם אֲדֹנָי יֱהֹוִה: 16] הֵמָּה יָבֹאוּ אֶל־מִקְדָּשִׁי וְהֵמָּה יִקְרְבוּ אֶל־שֻׁלְחָנִי לְשָׁרְתֵנִי וְשָׁמְרוּ אֶת־מִשְׁמַרְתִּי: 17] וְהָיָה בְּבוֹאָם אֶל־שַׁעֲרֵי הֶחָצֵר הַפְּנִימִית בִּגְדֵי פִשְׁתִּים יִלְבָּשׁוּ וְלֹא־יַעֲלֶה עֲלֵיהֶם צֶמֶר בְּשָׁרְתָם בְּשַׁעֲרֵי הֶחָצֵר הַפְּנִימִית וָבָיְתָה: 18] פַּאֲרֵי פִשְׁתִּים יִהְיוּ עַל־רֹאשָׁם וּמִכְנְסֵי פִשְׁתִּים יִהְיוּ עַל־מָתְנֵיהֶם לֹא יַחְגְּרוּ בַּיָּזַע: 19] וּבְצֵאתָם אֶל־הֶחָצֵר הַחִיצוֹנָה אֶל־הֶחָצֵר הַחִיצוֹנָה אֶל־הָעָם יִפְשְׁטוּ אֶת־בִּגְדֵיהֶם אֲשֶׁר הֵמָּה מְשָׁרְתִם בָּם וְהִנִּיחוּ אוֹתָם בְּלִשְׁכֹת הַקֹּדֶשׁ וְלָבְשׁוּ בְּגָדִים אֲחֵרִים וְלֹא־יְקַדְּשׁוּ אֶת־הָעָם בְּבִגְדֵיהֶם: 20] וְרֹאשָׁם לֹא יְגַלֵּחוּ וּפֶרַע לֹא יְשַׁלֵּחוּ כָּסוֹם יִכְסְמוּ אֶת־רָאשֵׁיהֶם: 21] וְיַיִן לֹא־יִשְׁתּוּ כָּל־כֹּהֵן בְּבוֹאָם אֶל־הֶחָצֵר

ᵉ⁻ᵉ *By contrast with the Levite-priests whose demotion has just been announced*

ᵈ *Cf. 42.13–14*

ᵉ *Thereby rendering the people unfit for ordinary activity*

22] They shall not marry widows[f] or divorced women; they may marry only virgins of the stock of the House of Israel, or widows who are widows of priests.

23] They shall declare to My people what is sacred and what is profane, and inform them what is clean and what is unclean.

24] In lawsuits, too, it is they who shall act as judges; they shall decide them in accordance with My rules. They shall preserve My teachings and My laws regarding all My fixed occasions; and they shall maintain the sanctity of My sabbaths.

25] [A priest] shall not defile himself by entering [a house] where there is a dead person. He shall defile himself only for father or mother, son or daughter, brother or unmarried sister. 26] After he has become clean, seven days shall be counted off for him;

27] and on the day that he reenters the inner court of the Sanctuary to minister in the Sanctuary, he shall present his sin offering—declares the Lord GOD.

28] This shall be their portion, for I am their portion; and no holding shall be given them in Israel, for I am their holding.

29] The meal offerings, sin offerings, and guilt offerings shall be consumed by them. Everything proscribed[g] in Israel shall be theirs.

30] All the choice first fruits of every kind, and all the gifts of every kind—of all your contributions—shall go to the priests. You shall further give the first of the yield of your baking[h] to the priest, that a blessing may rest upon your home.

31] Priests shall not eat anything, whether bird or animal, that died or was torn by beasts.

הַפְּנִימִית: 22] וְאַלְמָנָה וּגְרוּשָׁה לֹא-יִקְחוּ לָהֶם לְנָשִׁים כִּי אִם-בְּתוּלֹת מִזֶּרַע בֵּית יִשְׂרָאֵל וְהָאַלְמָנָה אֲשֶׁר-תִּהְיֶה אַלְמָנָה מִכֹּהֵן יִקָּחוּ:

23] וְאֶת-עַמִּי יוֹרוּ בֵּין קֹדֶשׁ לְחֹל וּבֵין-טָמֵא לְטָהוֹר יוֹדִעֻם: 24] וְעַל-רִיב הֵמָּה יַעַמְדוּ לְמִשְׁפָּט בְּמִשְׁפָּטַי יִשְׁפְּטֻהוּ וְאֶת-תּוֹרֹתַי וְאֶת-חֻקֹּתַי בְּכָל-מוֹעֲדַי יִשְׁמֹרוּ וְאֶת-שַׁבְּתוֹתַי יְקַדֵּשׁוּ:

25] וְאֶל-מֵת אָדָם לֹא יָבוֹא לְטָמְאָה כִּי אִם לְאָב וּלְאֵם וּלְבֵן וּלְבַת לְאָח וּלְאָחוֹת אֲשֶׁר לֹא-הָיְתָה לְאִישׁ יִטַּמָּאוּ: 26] וְאַחֲרֵי טָהֳרָתוֹ שִׁבְעַת יָמִים יִסְפְּרוּ-לוֹ: 27] וּבְיוֹם בֹּאוֹ אֶל הַקֹּדֶשׁ אֶל הֶחָצֵר הַפְּנִימִית לְשָׁרֵת בַּקֹּדֶשׁ יַקְרִיב חַטָּאתוֹ נְאֻם אֲדֹנָי יְהוִֹה:

28] וְהָיְתָה לָהֶם לְנַחֲלָה אֲנִי נַחֲלָתָם וַאֲחֻזָּה לֹא-תִתְּנוּ לָהֶם בְּיִשְׂרָאֵל אֲנִי אֲחֻזָּתָם: 29] הַמִּנְחָה וְהַחַטָּאת וְהָאָשָׁם הֵמָּה יֹאכְלוּם וְכָל-חֵרֶם בְּיִשְׂרָאֵל לָהֶם יִהְיֶה: 30] וְרֵאשִׁית כָּל-בִּכּוּרֵי כֹל וְכָל-תְּרוּמַת כֹּל מִכֹּל תְּרוּמוֹתֵיכֶם לַכֹּהֲנִים יִהְיֶה וְרֵאשִׁית עֲרִסוֹתֵיכֶם תִּתְּנוּ לַכֹּהֵן לְהָנִיחַ בְּרָכָה אֶל-בֵּיתֶךָ:

31] כָּל-נְבֵלָה וּטְרֵפָה מִן-הָעוֹף וּמִן-הַבְּהֵמָה לֹא יֹאכְלוּ הַכֹּהֲנִים:

[f] I.e., of laymen
[g] See Lev. 27.28
[h] See Num. 15.20–21

1002

Jeremiah was the most inward of the prophets. In his agonized visions he foresaw Jerusalem's destruction and was jailed for his preachments. When the Babylonians destroyed the city in 586 (or 585) B.C.E., he became one of the exiles and died in Egypt.

The Torah portion deals with preserving a family's title to the land. The haftarah tells us that Jeremiah had redeemed a piece of property so that it might not be lost to his family. He had thereby performed a symbolic act demonstrating his faith that Israel's bond to the land would outlast all foreign occupation.

בהר

Jeremiah

32 : 6-27

לב

Chapter 32

6] Jeremiah said: The word of the LORD came to me:

7] Hanamel, the son of your uncle Shallum, will come to you and say, "Buy my land in Anathoth, *b-*for you are next in succession to redeem it by purchase."*-b*

8] And just as the LORD had said, my cousin Hanamel came to me in the prison compound and said to me, "Please buy my land in Anathoth, in the territory of Benjamin; for the right of succession is yours, and you have the duty of redemption. Buy it." Then I knew that it was indeed the word of the LORD.

9] So I bought the land in Anathoth from my cousin Hanamel. I weighed out the money to him, seventeen shekels of silver.

10] I wrote a deed, sealed it, and had it witnessed; and I weighed out the silver on a balance.

11] I took the deed of purchase, the sealed text and the open one *c-*according to rule and law,*-c*

12] and gave the deed to Baruch son of Neriah son of Mahseiah in the presence of my kinsman Hanamel, of the witnesses *d-*who were named*-d* in the deed, and

6] וַיֹּאמֶר יִרְמְיָהוּ הָיָה דְבַר־יְהֹוָה אֵלַי לֵאמֹר: 7] הִנֵּה חֲנַמְאֵל בֶּן־שַׁלֻּם דֹּדְךָ בָּא אֵלֶיךָ לֵאמֹר קְנֵה לְךָ אֶת־שָׂדִי אֲשֶׁר בַּעֲנָתוֹת כִּי לְךָ מִשְׁפַּט הַגְּאֻלָּה לִקְנוֹת: 8] וַיָּבֹא אֵלַי חֲנַמְאֵל בֶּן־דֹּדִי כִּדְבַר יְהֹוָה אֶל־חֲצַר הַמַּטָּרָה וַיֹּאמֶר אֵלַי קְנֵה נָא אֶת־שָׂדִי אֲשֶׁר־בַּעֲנָתוֹת אֲשֶׁר בְּאֶרֶץ בִּנְיָמִין כִּי־לְךָ מִשְׁפַּט הַיְרֻשָּׁה וּלְךָ הַגְּאֻלָּה קְנֵה־לָךְ וָאֵדַע כִּי דְבַר־יְהֹוָה הוּא:

9] וָאֶקְנֶה אֶת־הַשָּׂדֶה מֵאֵת חֲנַמְאֵל בֶּן־דֹּדִי אֲשֶׁר בַּעֲנָתוֹת וָאֶשְׁקֲלָה־לּוֹ אֶת־הַכֶּסֶף שִׁבְעָה שְׁקָלִים וַעֲשָׂרָה הַכָּסֶף: 10] וָאֶכְתֹּב בַּסֵּפֶר וָאֶחְתֹּם וָאָעֵד עֵדִים וָאֶשְׁקֹל הַכֶּסֶף בְּמֹאזְנָיִם: 11] וָאֶקַּח אֶת־סֵפֶר הַמִּקְנָה אֶת־הֶחָתוּם הַמִּצְוָה וְהַחֻקִּים וְאֶת־הַגָּלוּי: 12] וָאֶתֵּן אֶת־הַסֵּפֶר הַמִּקְנָה אֶל־בָּרוּךְ בֶּן־נֵרִיָּה בֶּן־מַחְסֵיָה לְעֵינֵי חֲנַמְאֵל דֹּדִי וּלְעֵינֵי הָעֵדִים הַכֹּתְבִים בַּסֵּפֶר

---

b-b Lit. "for yours is the procedure of redemption by purchase"

c-c Force of Heb. uncertain

d-d With many mss. and ancient versions; so ancient Near Eastern practice. Other mss. and the editions read "who wrote"

all the Judeans who were sitting in the prison compound.

13] In their presence I charged Baruch as follows:

14] Thus said the Lord of Hosts, the God of Israel: "Take these documents, this deed of purchase, the sealed text and the open one, and put them into an earthen jar, so that they may last a long time."

15] For thus said the Lord of Hosts, the God of Israel: "Houses, fields, and vineyards shall again be purchased in this land."

16] But after I had given the deed to Baruch son of Neriah, I prayed to the Lord:

17] "Ah, Lord God! You made heaven and earth with Your great might and outstretched arm. Nothing is too wondrous for You!

18] You show kindness to the thousandth generation, but visit the guilt of the fathers upon their children after them. O great and mighty God whose name is Lord of Hosts, 19] wondrous in purpose and mighty in deed, whose eyes observe all the ways of men, so as to repay every man according to his ways, and with the proper fruit of his deeds!

20] You displayed signs and marvels in the land of Egypt ᵉ‑with lasting effect,‑ᵉ and won renown in Israel and among mankind to this very day.

21] You freed Your people Israel from the land of Egypt with signs and marvels, with a strong hand and an outstretched arm, and with great terror.

22] You gave them this land which You had sworn to their fathers to give them, a land flowing with milk and honey,

23] and they came and took possession of it. But they did not listen to You or follow Your Teaching; they did nothing of what You com-

הַמִּקְנֶה לְעֵינֵי כָּל־הַיְּהוּדִים הַיֹּשְׁבִים בַּחֲצַר הַמַּטָּרָה: 13 וָאֲצַוֶּה אֶת־בָּרוּךְ לְעֵינֵיהֶם לֵאמֹר: 14 כֹּה־אָמַר יְהֹוָה צְבָאוֹת אֱלֹהֵי יִשְׂרָאֵל לָקוֹחַ אֶת־הַסְּפָרִים הָאֵלֶּה אֵת סֵפֶר הַמִּקְנָה הַזֶּה וְאֵת הֶחָתוּם וְאֵת סֵפֶר הַגָּלוּי הַזֶּה וּנְתַתָּם בִּכְלִי־חָרֶשׂ לְמַעַן יַעַמְדוּ יָמִים רַבִּים: 15 כִּי כֹה אָמַר יְהֹוָה צְבָאוֹת אֱלֹהֵי יִשְׂרָאֵל עוֹד יִקָּנוּ בָתִּים וְשָׂדוֹת וּכְרָמִים בָּאָרֶץ הַזֹּאת:

16 וָאֶתְפַּלֵּל אֶל־יְהֹוָה אַחֲרֵי תִתִּי אֶת־סֵפֶר הַמִּקְנָה אֶל־בָּרוּךְ בֶּן־נֵרִיָּה לֵאמֹר: 17 אֲהָהּ אֲדֹנָי יֱהֹוִה הִנֵּה אַתָּה עָשִׂיתָ אֶת־הַשָּׁמַיִם וְאֶת־הָאָרֶץ בְּכֹחֲךָ הַגָּדוֹל וּבִזְרֹעֲךָ הַנְּטוּיָה לֹא־יִפָּלֵא מִמְּךָ כָּל־דָּבָר: 18 עֹשֶׂה חֶסֶד לַאֲלָפִים וּמְשַׁלֵּם עֲוֹן אָבוֹת אֶל־חֵיק בְּנֵיהֶם אַחֲרֵיהֶם הָאֵל הַגָּדוֹל הַגִּבּוֹר יְהֹוָה צְבָאוֹת שְׁמוֹ: 19 גְּדֹל הָעֵצָה וְרַב הָעֲלִילִיָּה אֲשֶׁר עֵינֶיךָ פְקֻחוֹת עַל־כָּל־דַּרְכֵי בְּנֵי אָדָם לָתֵת לְאִישׁ כִּדְרָכָיו וְכִפְרִי מַעֲלָלָיו: 20 אֲשֶׁר־שַׂמְתָּ אֹתוֹת וּמֹפְתִים בְּאֶרֶץ־מִצְרַיִם עַד־הַיּוֹם הַזֶּה וּבְיִשְׂרָאֵל וּבָאָדָם וַתַּעֲשֶׂה־לְּךָ שֵׁם כַּיּוֹם הַזֶּה: 21 וַתֹּצֵא אֶת־עַמְּךָ אֶת־יִשְׂרָאֵל מֵאֶרֶץ מִצְרָיִם בְּאֹתוֹת וּבְמוֹפְתִים וּבְיָד חֲזָקָה וּבְאֶזְרוֹעַ נְטוּיָה וּבְמוֹרָא גָּדוֹל: 22 וַתִּתֵּן לָהֶם אֶת־הָאָרֶץ הַזֹּאת אֲשֶׁר־נִשְׁבַּעְתָּ לַאֲבוֹתָם לָתֵת לָהֶם אֶרֶץ זָבַת חָלָב וּדְבָשׁ: 23 וַיָּבֹאוּ וַיִּרְשׁוּ אֹתָהּ וְלֹא־שָׁמְעוּ בְקוֹלֶךָ וּבְתוֹרָתְךָ לֹא הָלָכוּ אֵת כָּל־אֲשֶׁר צִוִּיתָה לָהֶם לַעֲשׂוֹת

manded them to do. Therefore You have caused all this misfortune to befall them.

24] Here are the siege-mounds, raised against the city to storm it; and the city, because of sword and famine and pestilence, is at the mercy of the Chaldeans who are attacking it. What You threatened has come to pass—as You see.

25] Yet You, Lord GOD, said to me: Buy the land for money and call in witnesses—when the city is at the mercy of the Chaldeans!"

26] Then the word of the LORD came to Jeremiah:

27] "Behold I am the LORD, the God of all flesh. Is anything too wondrous for Me?

לֹא עָשׂוּ וַתִּקְרָא אֹתָם אֵת כָּל־הָרָעָה הַזֹּאת:

24] הִנֵּה הַסֹּלְלוֹת בָּאוּ הָעִיר לְלָכְדָהּ וְהָעִיר נִתְּנָה בְּיַד הַכַּשְׂדִּים הַנִּלְחָמִים עָלֶיהָ מִפְּנֵי הַחֶרֶב וְהָרָעָב וְהַדָּבֶר וַאֲשֶׁר דִּבַּרְתָּ הָיָה וְהִנְּךָ רֹאֶה: 25] וְאַתָּה אָמַרְתָּ אֵלַי אֲדֹנָי יֱהֹוִה קְנֵה־לְךָ הַשָּׂדֶה בַּכֶּסֶף וְהָעֵד עֵדִים וְהָעִיר נִתְּנָה בְּיַד הַכַּשְׂדִּים:

26] וַיְהִי דְּבַר־יְהֹוָה אֶל־יִרְמְיָהוּ לֵאמֹר:

27] הִנֵּה אֲנִי יְהֹוָה אֱלֹהֵי כָּל־בָּשָׂר הֲמִמֶּנִּי יִפָּלֵא כָּל־דָּבָר:

Jeremiah was the most inward of the prophets. In his
agonized visions he foresaw Jerusalem's destruction and
was jailed for his preachments. When the Babylonians
destroyed the city in 586 (or 585) B.C.E., he became one
of the exiles and died in Egypt.

The sidrah presents Israel with a choice between blessings
and curses. The haftarah presents Jeremiah's assurance
that after God has punished His people the faithful can
be certain of God's favor: "Blessed is he who trusts in
the Lord."

בחקתי

Jeremiah

16 : 19 - 17 : 14

Chapter 16

טז

19] O Lord, my strength and my stronghold,
My refuge in a day of trouble,
To You nations shall come
From the ends of the earth and say:
Our fathers inherited utter delusions,
Things that are futile and worthless.

19] יְהֹוָה עֻזִּי וּמָעֻזִּי
וּמְנוּסִי בְּיוֹם צָרָה
אֵלֶיךָ גּוֹיִם יָבֹאוּ
מֵאַפְסֵי־אָרֶץ וְיֹאמְרוּ
אַךְ־שֶׁקֶר נָחֲלוּ אֲבוֹתֵינוּ
הֶבֶל וְאֵין־בָּם מוֹעִיל:

20] Can a man make gods for himself?
No-gods are they!

20] הֲיַעֲשֶׂה־לּוֹ אָדָם אֱלֹהִים
וְהֵמָּה לֹא אֱלֹהִים:

21] Assuredly, I will teach them,
Once and for all I will teach them
My power and My might.
And they shall learn that My name is Lord.

21] לָכֵן הִנְנִי מוֹדִיעָם
בַּפַּעַם הַזֹּאת אוֹדִיעֵם
אֶת־יָדִי וְאֶת־גְּבוּרָתִי
וְיָדְעוּ כִּי־שְׁמִי יְהֹוָה:

Chapter 17

יז

1] The guilt of Judah is inscribed
With a stylus of iron,
Engraved with an adamant point
On the tablet of their hearts,
ᵃ⁻And on the horns of their altars,

1] חַטַּאת יְהוּדָה כְּתוּבָה
בְּעֵט בַּרְזֶל
בְּצִפֹּרֶן שָׁמִיר חֲרוּשָׁה
עַל־לוּחַ לִבָּם
וּלְקַרְנוֹת מִזְבְּחוֹתֵיכֶם:

ᵃ⁻ᵃ *Meaning of Heb. uncertain. Emendation yields "Surely the horns of their altars / Are as a memorial against them"*

2] While their children remember⁻ᵃ
Their altars and sacred posts,
By verdant trees,
Upon lofty hills.

3] ᵇ⁻Because of the sin of your shrines
Throughout your borders,
I will make your rampart a heap in the field,
And all your treasures a spoil.⁻ᵇ

4] ᶜ⁻You will forfeit, by your own act,⁻ᶜ
The inheritance I have given you;
I will make you a slave to your enemies
In a land you have never known.
For you have kindled the flame of My wrath
Which shall burn for all time.

5] Thus said the Lord:
Cursed is he who trusts in man,
Who makes mere flesh his strength,
And turns his thoughts from the Lord.

6] He shall be like a bushᵈ in the desert,
Which does not sense the coming of good:
It is set in the scorched places of the wilderness,
In a barren land without inhabitant.

7] Blessed is he who trusts in the Lord,
Whose trust is the Lord alone.

8] He shall be like a tree planted by waters,
Sending forth its roots by a stream:
It does not sense the coming of heat,

2 כִּזְכֹּר בְּנֵיהֶם

מִזְבְּחוֹתָם וַאֲשֵׁרֵיהֶם

עַל־עֵץ רַעֲנָן

עַל גְּבָעוֹת הַגְּבֹהוֹת:

3 הֲרָרִי בַּשָּׂדֶה חֵילְךָ

כָּל־אוֹצְרוֹתֶיךָ לָבַז אֶתֵּן

בָּמֹתֶיךָ בְּחַטָּאת

בְּכָל־גְּבוּלֶיךָ:

4 וְשָׁמַטְתָּה וּבְךָ מִנַּחֲלָתְךָ

אֲשֶׁר נָתַתִּי לָךְ

וְהַעֲבַדְתִּיךָ אֶת־אֹיְבֶיךָ

בָּאָרֶץ אֲשֶׁר לֹא־יָדָעְתָּ

כִּי־אֵשׁ קְדַחְתֶּם בְּאַפִּי

עַד־עוֹלָם תּוּקָד:

5 כֹּה אָמַר יְהוָה

אָרוּר הַגֶּבֶר אֲשֶׁר יִבְטַח בָּאָדָם

וְשָׂם בָּשָׂר זְרֹעוֹ

וּמִן־יְהוָה יָסוּר לִבּוֹ:

6 וְהָיָה כְּעַרְעָר בָּעֲרָבָה

וְלֹא יִרְאֶה כִּי־יָבוֹא טוֹב

וְשָׁכַן חֲרֵרִים בַּמִּדְבָּר

אֶרֶץ מְלֵחָה וְלֹא תֵשֵׁב:

7 בָּרוּךְ הַגֶּבֶר אֲשֶׁר יִבְטַח בַּיהוָה

וְהָיָה יְהוָה מִבְטַחוֹ:

8 וְהָיָה כְּעֵץ שָׁתוּל עַל־מַיִם

וְעַל־יוּבַל יְשַׁלַּח שָׁרָשָׁיו

וְלֹא יִרְאֶה כִּי־יָבֹא חֹם

ᵇ⁻ᵇ Meaning of Heb. uncertain

ᶜ⁻ᶜ Meaning of Heb. uncertain. Emendation yields "Your hand must let go"

ᵈ Or "tamarisk"; exact meaning of Heb. uncertain

Its leaves are ever fresh;
It has no care in a year of drought,
It does not cease to yield fruit.

9] Most devious is the heart;
It is perverse—who can fathom it?

10] I the LORD probe the heart,
Search the mind—
To repay every man according to his ways,
With the proper fruit of his deeds.

11] [b-]Like a partridge hatching what she did not
lay,[-b]
So is one who amasses wealth by unjust means;
In the middle of his life it will leave him,
And in the end he will be proved a fool.

12] O Throne of Glory exalted from of old,
Our Sacred Shrine!

13] O Hope of Israel! O LORD!
All who forsake You shall be put to shame,
Those in the land who turn from You[e]
Shall be doomed[f] men,
For they have forsaken the LORD,
The Fount of living waters.

14] Heal me, O LORD, and let me be healed;
Save me, and let me be saved;
For You are my glory.

וְהָיָה עָלֵהוּ רַעֲנָן

וּבִשְׁנַת בַּצֹּרֶת לֹא יִדְאָג

וְלֹא יָמִישׁ מֵעֲשׂוֹת פֶּרִי:

9] עָקֹב הַלֵּב מִכֹּל

וְאָנֻשׁ הוּא מִי יֵדָעֶנּוּ:

10] אֲנִי יְהוָה חֹקֵר לֵב

בֹּחֵן כְּלָיוֹת

וְלָתֵת לְאִישׁ כִּדְרָכָיו

כִּפְרִי מַעֲלָלָיו:

11] קֹרֵא דָגַר וְלֹא יָלָד

עֹשֶׂה עֹשֶׁר וְלֹא בְמִשְׁפָּט

בַּחֲצִי יָמָיו יַעַזְבֶנּוּ

וּבְאַחֲרִיתוֹ יִהְיֶה נָבָל:

12] כִּסֵּא כָבוֹד מָרוֹם מֵרִאשׁוֹן

מְקוֹם מִקְדָּשֵׁנוּ:

13] מִקְוֵה יִשְׂרָאֵל יְהוָה

כָּל־עֹזְבֶיךָ יֵבֹשׁוּ

וְסוּרַי בָּאָרֶץ יִכָּתֵבוּ

כִּי עָזְבוּ מְקוֹר מַיִם־חַיִּים

אֶת־יְהוָה:

14] רְפָאֵנִי יְהוָה וְאֵרָפֵא

הוֹשִׁיעֵנִי וְאִוָּשֵׁעָה

כִּי תְהִלָּתִי אָתָּה:

[b-b] Meaning of Heb. uncertain
[e] Lit. "Me"
[f] Lit. "inscribed"; meaning of line uncertain

1008

במדבר

NUMBERS

Commentary by

W. GUNTHER PLAUT

Introducing Numbers

The Book

The Book of Numbers is composed of narrative, legislation, and archival records.

Its narrative begins at the point where Exodus leaves off. (Leviticus, which interrupts the flow of narration, consists almost entirely of legislation independent of historic precedent—with the exception of Lev. 16.) Exodus ends by relating the erection of the Tabernacle on the first day of Nisan, and Numbers starts with a census taken a month later, just a little over a year after the Children of Israel came out of Egypt. The book covers the years of the people's wanderings in the desert. However, only the beginning and closing periods of the journey are described in some detail; the thirty-eight years in which a new generation matures receive no attention at all. Biblical memory accords no further place to those who were saved from Egypt but did not prove worthy of the gift of freedom and so were condemned to die in the desert.[1]

The law given is usually case law, arising from the specific circumstances in the narrative. For instance, telling the story of the dedication of the Tabernacle occasions the statement of priestly obligations and privileges in general. From the law applicable to a particular event told in the book, the Torah proceeds to state the broader law valid for all time.

The book falls into four broad sections. The first deals with regulations promulgated at Sinai; it contains demographic and legal material of the most varied kind: from the holding of a census to the ordeal of bitter waters; from prescriptions for offerings to the use of the silver trumpets. It also includes the story of how the Tabernacle was consecrated after it had been set up (Num. 1:1–10:10).

The second part reports highlights of the early days of the march; emphasizing the various rebellions which occurred, especially the uprising of Korah, Dathan, and Abiram; and then it tells of the end of the old leadership: the deaths of Miriam and Aaron, the judgment on Moses, and the selection of Eleazar and Joshua as the new priestly and secular leaders who will bring the people into Canaan (Num. 10:11–20:1).

The third section is the "Book of Balaam," which according to some was once a separate book by that name (Num. 22:2–24:25).

The final part begins with events immediately preceding the invasion of Canaan: the elevation of Phinehas, the holding of a new census, and the first land distribution. The boundaries of the Promised Land are set and final instructions before the crossing are given (Num 25:1–36:13).

---

[1] It should be noted here that the figure thirty-eight is part of the biblical scheme which stipulates the symbolic number forty as the duration of the desert experience. H. H. Rowley has attempted to demonstrate that the total period of wanderings lasted more likely for only two years. See *From Joseph to Joshua* (London: Oxford University Press, 1950), pp. 133, 164.

Literary Aspects

In effect, the Book of Numbers tells of the end of the journey begun in Egypt or, in the wider sense, begun in the hour of creation. Everything points to this moment when Israel is at last poised to take possession of its inheritance. Based on this and other considerations, it has been suggested that the first four books of the Torah (Genesis, Exodus, Leviticus, Numbers) originally formed a four-part unit called Tetrateuch by modern scholars, while Deuteronomy, Joshua, Judges, Samuel, and Kings constituted another separate complex. Our commentary accepts this basic approach, which is discussed in greater detail in our General Introduction to the Torah. See there also for a consideration of the divine element ascribed to the text, a general overview of biblical criticism, and the likely times when the various books were composed.

While reference is made repeatedly to critical analysis as an important aid to the understanding of the Torah, the text is generally treated as a literary unit, not because it always was of one piece (it was not), but because in the final editing process it was so treated and because ever since the readers of the Torah have approached it in this fashion.

What historical accuracy in the modern sense can we ascribe to Numbers? It is not possible to answer this question precisely because the entire Torah is essentially a document of faith, that is to say, reality is viewed as an aspect of divine and human interaction. Memories and traditions of events (which we might describe as "history") were intermingled with cultic and symbolic elements. From this grew a vision of the past as it might have been and as it was later believed to have been in fact. In this way, myth and legend helped both to create and fashion "history." The need to view the biblical narrative on its own terms rather than ours has been cogently stated by George E. Mendenhall:

"The biblical narratives rarely if ever give any description of the real-life context of the event described in words. . . . As a result, every bit of data in an ancient narrative must be viewed against all the evidence we can muster for the purpose of finding the range of ideas and associations which that item of historical fact had in ancient life. It is for this reason that the comparative method is not only legitimate, it is essential. After all, every translation of the Bible into modern English is based upon an unconscious presupposition that the range of meaning of an ancient word or act compares often enough with the range of meaning of modern words to make translation possible. The extent to which we deceive ourselves in this unconscious presupposition is not known until we become aware of hitherto unknown contrasts in meaning between the two vocabularies. Biblical fundamentalism, whether Jewish or Christian, cannot learn from the past because in so many respects the defense of presently accepted ideas about religion is thought to be the only purpose of biblical narrative. It must, therefore, support ideas of comparatively recent origin—ones that usually have nothing to do with the original meaning or intention of biblical narrative because the context is so radically different."[2]

The literary aspects of Numbers are treated in greater depth in the essay by William W. Hallo which follows.

Religious Ideas

The major locale of the book is the desert, that is, the Sinai peninsula, and especially its eastern part, the Negev. The en-

[2] G. E. Mendenhall, *The Tenth Generation* (Baltimore and London: Johns Hopkins University Press, 1973), pp. 105–106.

vironment is harsh, but God deems it necessary for Israel's spiritual development. The desert is the place where the people's failures are punished, where its *Unheilsgeschichte* will prepare it for its *Heilsgeschichte*. This is the "desert motif" that underlies the Book of Numbers, which continues from where Exodus left off.[3] Israel is God's people and is therefore subject to special obligations and laws which are designed to safeguard its holiness. The book tells us how Israel continued to fall short of its divinely appointed goals; how, because of its murmurings, rebellions, and transgressions of various kinds, God was time and again disappointed in His people. Still, though individuals were punished and a whole generation was condemned to die in the wilderness, the covenant was not abrogated: the sanctuary—with its divine manifestations—remained in the midst of the camp, and God never ceased to guide and protect His chosen ones. The period of wanderings may be seen as a trial of faith, and at the end of the book there emerges the vision of a new nation which will take possession of the Holy Land and do so as a holy people.

Name

The name of the book is an English rendering of the Latin *Numeri*, which in turn was a translation of the Greek *Arithmoi*, chosen in recognition of the extensive statistical material which opens the book. The name is probably related to an earlier Hebrew appellation for the book, חֻמָּשׁ הַפְּקוּדִים (*Chumash Hapikudim*).[4] The book was occasionally also referred to by its first Hebrew word, [סֵפֶר] וַיְדַבֵּר ([*Sefer*] *Vayedaber*).[5] Its popular Hebrew name is *Bemidbar* (in the wilderness), so called after *bemidbar Sinai*, the fifth and sixth words in the opening chapter, a fitting title for a book that relates the major events from Sinai to the Plains of Moab. When the book received its separate status is still a matter of scholarly controversy.

---

[3] See Shemaryahu Talmon, "The Desert Motif," in *Biblical Motifs*, ed. Alexander Altmann (Cambridge, Mass.: Harvard University Press, 1966), pp. 31–63. Talmon calls Numbers (except for chapters 26–30) the "Book of Israel's Failings" (p. 46).

[4] See Mishnah Men. 4:3. One other book in the Pentateuch is given such a specific name unrelated to any opening word: *Torat Kohanim* (Leviticus).

[5] See Rashi on Exod. 38:26.

Numbers
and Ancient Near Eastern Literature

WILLIAM W. HALLO

A comparative literary approach to the Book of Numbers requires first of all a literary assessment of the book, and this is extraordinarily difficult. Numbers lacks the sweep and grandeur of Genesis, the theological significance of Exodus, the legislative consistency of Leviticus, the literary unity of Deuteronomy. At first glance it hardly appears to be a "book" in its own right at all. Rather it forms the conclusion of the "Tetrateuch" (Genesis–Numbers), essentially the priestly history of Israel from creation to the death of Moses. The canonical text saves the actual account of his death for the end of Deuteronomy, but probably this was an editorial change necessitated when the book was incorporated into the Pentateuch. Originally, Deuteronomy more probably constituted the beginning of a second, or Deuteronomic, history of Israel, recapitulating briefly from patriarchal times (cf. Deut. 26:5) and concluding with the Babylonian exile (II Kings 25). The Chronicler's history of Israel once more begins with Adam (I Chr. 1:1) and ends with the restoration under Ezra and Nehemiah (Neh. 13:31). Finally, Josephus retraced and updated the whole history in his *Jewish Archeology* (usually cited as *Jewish Antiquities*), chiefly for the benefit of a Hellenistic audience, much as Manetho did for

the history of Egypt, Berossos for Mesopotamia, and Philo of Byblos for Phoenicia. Thus the "Book of Numbers" as we have it starts at an apparently random point and stops short of its logical conclusion. In between it covers a seeming miscellany of narrative, legislation, and genealogy, much of it repeated either within Numbers itself or elsewhere in the historical books of the Bible.

Yet for all these literary difficulties, the book discloses aspects of literary unity and significance when subjected to closer scrutiny. We shall consider these under the generic headings already alluded to in order to arrive at a meaningful assessment of the comparative literary evidence from the surrounding Near East.

The Narrative Setting

The ostensible setting of the narrative in Numbers is a period of forty years spent in Sinai, the Negev, and Transjordan, i.e., the period of the wanderings in the desert and the beginnings of the conquest, most of the elapsed time actually being spent at Kadesh-barnea. Here a conquest of the promised land was contemplated from the south (Negev) and then abandoned, Moses and Joshua in-

stead leading a new generation through Transjordan for the assault from the east via Jericho and Ai. Whether this record, in outline or in detail, is historically accurate or not is not the issue here, but rather the literary treatment of the subject. Seen in this light, the Book of Numbers represents history according to one of its most pregnant definitions, i.e., as "the intellectual form in which a civilization renders account to itself of its past."[1] It is the image which Israel formed of that period in its history which forged it into a nation. The image may well date from an editorial hand of exilic date (sixth century B.C.E.); it was woven together from diverse and sometimes conflicting documents and oral traditions that may date as far back as the united monarchy (tenth century B.C.E.); and it purports to relate events at the end of the Bronze Age (thirteenth century B.C.E.). Unquestionably, therefore, this image was vulnerable to distortions, harmonizations, and all the other vagaries of a lengthy and complex process of literary transmission (the so-called "redactional history"). In its final form it was far removed from its sources and subject matter—several centuries further removed than was Shakespeare when he drew on Holinshed and other English chroniclers for his "histories" of early English and Scottish kings such as Lear, John, and Macbeth or, to use an example more to the point, at least as far as the *Iliad* is from the siege of Troy.

But, despite this distance from its subject, the account in Numbers did not glamorize it, or invest its actors with heroic stature, or edit away their human failings. In common with most biblical historiography, and in contrast with most of extra-biblical narrative, this phase of Israel's past was memorialized in starkly realistic terms. And not because it was

so different from the comparable phase in the history of Israel's contemporaries. On the contrary, all indications are that the Israelite wanderings formed part of a general pattern of massive migrations which swept the whole known world in the thirteenth century B.C.E. Two principal ethnic groups were involved. From the Aegean area came the Sea Peoples, collectively so called because they traveled by sea, following the coastline and settling the littoral wherever they could. These peoples have left their names scattered across the Mediterranean to this day, from Cilicia and Philistia (Palestine) in the east to Sicily, Etruria (Tuscany), and Sardinia in the west. From the Syrian and Arabian deserts, meanwhile, came waves of Semitic speaking semi-nomads, collectively known as Arameans, of whom in a larger sense the Israelites were a part. Like the Sea Peoples, they conquered new lands for permanent settlement wherever they could, in Canaan, Syria, and Babylonia. Both movements in turn displaced existing populations (wherever they did not simply absorb them), setting off a whole chain of ethnic migrations in the interior. The great empires of the time tottered under these onslaughts. Some, like the Hittites of Anatolia and the Kassites of Babylonia, came to an end. Others, like Egypt under the long-lived Rameses II and Assyria under the warlike Tukulti-Ninurta I, managed to deflect, defeat, or buy off the invaders. But the face of the ancient Near East was permanently transformed and a new age, the Iron Age, was ushered in.

If any one event may be said to have unleashed these migrations, perhaps it was the sack of Troy about 1250 B.C.E. and the subsequent fall of the Mycenaean cities of the Greek mainland. At least it was these events that found their fullest expression in subsequent literature. The *Iliad* preserves a record of the Trojan War, and both the

---

[1] J. Huizinga, "A Definition of the Concept of History," in *Philosophy and History*, ed. R. Klibansky and H. J. Paton (New York: Harper Torch, 1936), p. 9.

Odyssey and the *Aeneid* reflect the subsequent wanderings and settlement of survivors from both sides. Further east, the epic of Tukulti-Ninurta and other royal Assyrian compositions reflect some of the events of the period. Like the almost equally ancient Song of Deborah (Judg. 5), all of them are cast in the heroic mold. In truly epic terms, they celebrate the heroism and discipline of the people, the nobility and wisdom of their leaders, and the continuous and usually solicitous intervention of their gods. In short, they treat the period as a heroic age.

No such characterization applies to Numbers, though it too is said to contain an epic substratum.[2] Despite its long redactional history, it does not present a flattering tableau of Israel's past. The narratives of "The Book of Israel's Failings"[3] reveal a rebellious and stiff-necked people, suspicious of its leaders, pining for the fleshpots of Egypt (Exod. 16:3; the details of the Egyptian diet in Num. 11:5 have an uncanny resemblance to literary topoi of fertility in Egyptian texts such as the "Praise of the City Rameses"[4]), and unworthy of the Promised Land. They are accompanied by, and often enough seem entirely to consist of, a mixed multitude, described in pejorative alliteration as *erev rav* (compare our riffraff) or *asafsuf* (omnium-gatherum). Their leaders betray many moments of weakness and forfeit their own chance to enter Canaan. Even the God of Israel receives some of His most uncomplimentary portraits in Numbers, and He is only dissuaded from abandoning His people by the repeated intercession of Moses who pleads, not the merit of the Israelites, but the disgrace to God's name and fame if they are left to their just deserts. In short, the very age which saw the emergence of Israel as a people figures in this image as anything but a glorious epoch.

This characterization applies in the first instance to the period of wanderings, with their recurrent crises of deprivation and military setbacks. But even the beginnings of the conquest and settlement east of the Jordan valley lack the heroic touch in Numbers. The Assyrian royal inscriptions early developed a bombastic style glorifying deity, king, and army and dwelt lovingly on the gory details of each victorious battle. The accounts in Numbers offer a striking contrast. The report of the conquest of Sihon and his Amorite kingdom (21:21–31), for example, mentions neither Moses (as does the parallel account in Deut. 2:26–37) nor God (as this and another parallel account in Judg. 11:19–26 do). In none of the three versions is any attention lavished on the battle itself. What emerges, therefore, is a sober recital of the tribulations of migration and the harsh realities of territorial acquisition devoid of romantic embellishments. The true significance of the text must therefore be sought outside the ostensible narrative setting.

The Genealogical Framework

The traditional name for the book derived from its opening word or words (its so-called "incipit") "in the wilderness" adequately describes its ostensible setting. But the rabbinic designation, "the pentateuchal book of those numbered"—and its Greek, Latin, and modern equivalent, Numbers—more accurately points to the underlying structure dominating the text. Over and over again, we encounter lists: lists of the tribes, of their leaders, of their offerings, of their marching orders, of their numbers. These

[2] Frank M. Cross, *Canaanite Myth and Hebrew Epic* (Cambridge: Harvard University Press, 1973), especially pp. 198–206, 301–322.
[3] Shemaryahu Talmon in *Biblical Motifs*, ed. A. Altman (Cambridge: Harvard University Press, 1966), p. 46.
[4] James B. Pritchard, ed., *Ancient Near Eastern Texts* (Princeton: Princeton University Press, 2nd ed., 1955), pp. 470f. [Hereafter cited as Pritchard, *ANET*.]

lists fall into two categories, the tribal and the priestly. In the tribal lists, the number twelve is determining. This is of course likewise the number of the sons of Jacob in the patriarchal narratives of Genesis. But neither the composition nor the order of names is completely identical in the two schemes.

Some scholars have tended to regard both the constancy of the number and the variation of the order and composition as evidence for the amphictyonic character of the Israelite tribal system, i.e., a form of religious and political organization in which diverse tribes are linked to a common cult at a central sanctuary or shrine by a systematic sharing of cultic obligations rotating among the members (ideally on a basis of equality) in terms of a twelve-month calendar. Such amphictyonic leagues have long been known from classical Greece and, more recently, have been discovered in Mesopotamia at the end of the third millennium.[5]

Other scholars question the validity of these parallels, and in any case the existence of any organized tribal confederation in Israel cannot be demonstrated before the conquest of Canaan and the period of the Judges. We may therefore evade the historical issue and return to the literary one to argue that the intent of the author or editor of Numbers was to provide a necessary transition from the patriarchal biographies of Genesis to the tribal histories of Judges. The former are written entirely around individuals, the latter concern established tribes. Numbers occupies a middle ground, with each actor genealogically linked to one of the twelve sons of Jacob (this is explicit in the case of Nahshon son of Amminadab, the great-great-grandson of Judah; cf. Elishama of Ephraim) but already acting as a representative or leader of a tribe. It thus converts the sons of Jacob

into eponymous ancestors of the later tribes or, conversely speaking, provides the tribes with a convincing genealogical linkage.

The importance of genealogies has already been fully brought out in Genesis whose ten "lines" (*tōlᵉdōt*) serve as the basic literary structure of the book—a feature generally attributed to the priestly source. This structure finds its literal echo in Numbers as well (3:1); but the priestly interest in genealogies is especially revealed by the second aspect of the lists in Numbers, which is its concern with the Levites. In the genealogies and narratives of Genesis, Levi is one of the six sons born to Jacob by his first wife, Leah, and accorded equal treatment with Reuben, Simeon, and Judah. This is likewise the case in the deathbed blessings invoked on the twelve sons, or tribes, by Jacob (Gen. 49) and Moses (Deut. 33). But the tribal system of the period of the Judges (Judg. 1) differs from these formulations precisely in its treatment of the tribe of Levi, and Numbers is at pains to emphasize this difference each time it introduces one of its lists and, then, to delineate the special treatment reserved for the Levites. The comparative material can best be considered under both aspects.

We may begin with the grouping of the tribes, which is described once (Num. 2) in connection with their disposition around the Tent of Meeting and once (Num. 10) in connection with the order of march when the camp is in motion. (The significance of the "Tent of Meeting" may not have been exclusively cultic, in light of the comparative evidence, for both terms recur as loanwords outside Hebrew to describe the peculiar governmental structures of the Western Semites: "tent" [aᵓalu] in the neo-Assyrian inscriptions of Assurbanipal to identify the confederations or amphictyonies of Arabian tribes, and "meeting" [mwᶜdʷt] in the eleventh-century Egyptian tale of Wen-Amon to designate the assembly of the Phoenician city of Byblos.)

[5] William W. Hallo, "A Sumerian Amphictyony," *Journal of Cuneiform Studies*, 14 (1960), pp. 88–114.

Both times the twelve tribes are grouped in four divisions made up of three tribes each and named after the most important tribe in each. Each division is identified by a standard (*degel*) which is precisely the term that denoted the socio-military unit of mercenaries, including Jews, that served in the frontier colony of Elephantine in Egypt under the Persian Empire. And, in both the Elephantine papyri and in Numbers, the priestly families were not enrolled in any of these divisions. What Numbers describes, then, is essentially a military organization familiar from postexilic times.[6]

The order of the divisions on the march and in camp was as follows: Judah–Reuben–Ephraim–Dan. The same order, and the same individuals to represent the individual tribes, recur at the dedication of the altar (Num. 7). This chapter, apparently only a dry and repetitive catalogue of identical offerings followed by their totals, has long been regarded as a wholly artificial and secondary insertion. According to Noth, for example, "the late author thought he could emphasize the significance of these contents by painstaking detail and constant repetition."[7] But this judgment needs to be modified in light of the abundant testimony of the cuneiform archives. Such archival texts typically display identical features, including not only minute detail and endless repetition but also the same relative position of summaries and totals, specification of the standards of measure used, uniformity of types and quantities of commodities involved, and a very minimal narrative setting. They often refer to cultic occasions and are, then, a kind of descriptive ritual, i.e., a record of offerings which incidentally logs the progress of a religious ceremony. The dedication of the altar may therefore be directly dependent on an authentic archival record, albeit of a later occasion.[8]

The order of the divisions already noted recurs, more or less, in the apportioning of the land west of the Jordan (Num. 34:19–22), if allowance is made for the changes necessitated by the fact that two-and-a-half tribes were already settled in Transjordan. But a different order applies to the remaining rosters in Numbers, namely Reuben–Judah–Ephraim–Dan. In other words, Reuben and Judah (and with them two other tribes assigned to each of their respective divisions) have traded places. This alternation has been variously interpreted but, in literary terms, most probably reflects the author's intent to link the tribal structure more closely to the patriarchal narratives and genealogies in Genesis, where the relative ages of the sons of Jacob and the status of their respective mothers determine their ranking. Thus Reuben and Simon, the first-born sons of Jacob by his first wife Leah, head the list of tribal representatives sent to spy out the land (Num. 13). Their glowing reports on its fertility, especially its grapes (13:23) and milk and honey (13:27), have become clichés in art and literature but are anticipated in the description of the land of Yaa in the famous Egyptian story of Sinuhe.[9]

Essentially this sequence is also employed in the two census lists in Numbers where Reuben is even identified as the first-born of Israel (1:20; 26:5). The historical validity of these lists has usually been challenged on two grounds: one, the improbably high figures reported and, the other, the lack of documented parallels from the biblical world in general combined with the documented aversion to censuses in Israel in particular.

[6] Bezalel Porten, *Archives from Elephantine* (Berkeley: University of California Press, 1968), pp. 28–35.
[7] Martin Noth, *Numbers: A Commentary* (Philadelphia: Westminster Press, 1966), p. 63.
[8] B. A. Levine, "The Descriptive Tabernacle Texts of the Pentateuch," *Journal of the American Oriental Society*, 85 (1965), pp. 307–318. [Hereafter cited as *JAOS*.]
[9] Pritchard, *ANET*, pp. 18–22, esp. lines 80–85.

Both of these challenges can now be met, at least on the literary level. The lists do not necessarily preserve an authentic record of the time of the wanderings, but neither can they be dismissed as wholly fictional fabrications. Rather, we may be dealing, again, with archival materials (of whatever date) woven into the context of the narrative.

Specifically, it may be noted that both lists (unlike the comparable census in I Chron. 12) always include hundreds as well as thousands. In fact, then, it can be argued that the original lists used only hundreds in a numerical sense, while the word translated (and indeed understood by the redactor) as "thousands" was actually here (and demonstrably elsewhere in the Bible) a term for a military unit. This unit averaged ten men, that is, less than a modern army's platoon but well attested in ancient warfare from the *ušrātu* of Hammurabi's Babylon to the *decuriae* of Rome. On this basis the individual entries in both lists add up, not to the incredible 600,000-odd referred to in Numbers (and Exodus 12:37), but to just under 600 platoons and 6,000 men. The latter figure is not incompatible with armies of the ancient Near East. By way of example, a letter from King Shamshi-Adad of Assyria, an older contemporary of Hammurabi, to his son the viceroy of Mari, tells him to muster an army of 6,000 men from the various tribes under his rule while he himself will raise 10,000 and the allied kingdom of Eshnunna 6,000.[10]

The archives of Mari and other north Mesopotamian sites in the patriarchal period also provide extensive evidence for the existence of an elaborate technique of census-taking in connection with military service. The process is described by a technical term meaning, literally, "purification," and it clearly involved some religious rites. Each tribe or other contingent was mustered by designated representatives, and rations were allotted to all. The procedure took several months, sometimes provoked a degree of hostility, and took place at fairly lengthy intervals. Clearly, it was in part a means of maintaining central control over the half-independent tribes under the administration of the great city-states of the period.[11]

From other periods and areas of the ancient Near East, numerous "cadastral" registers indicate a general interest in vital statistics in connection with land tenure, if not for their own sake. Only one cuneiform document so far known can be described as a "birth certificate" and two others as "death certificates," but the comparative evidence strongly suggests the compatibility of the idea of a census with a tribal stage of political organization.[12]

The Legislative Context

Though an integral part of the Torah, or Law, Numbers is not primarily devoted to legislation. Laws form a significant portion of the book but they confine themselves to certain special areas dictated by the narrative and tribal framework already discussed, especially with reference to the Levites. From a literary point of view, the legislation of Numbers lacks the systematic appearance and formal unity which are generally attributed to codified law elsewhere in the Pentateuch: the Covenant Code in Exodus, the Holiness Code in Leviticus, the Deuteronomic Code in Deuteronomy, the various decalogues, anathemas, and other stereotyped formulations scattered through these three books. Instead, the legislative portions of

[10] J. M. Sasson, *The Military Establishments at Mari* (Rome: Pontifical Biblical Institute, 1969), pp. 8 f.
[11] *Ibid*.
[12] J. J. Finkelstein, *Late Old Babylonian Documents and Letters* (New Haven: Yale University Press, 1972), pp. 14–16; Edmond Sollberger in *Kramer Anniversary Volume*, ed. Barry L. Eichler *et al.* (Alter Orient und Altes Testament, Vol. 25, 1976), pp. 448 f.

Numbers are set in and directly derived from the narrative context to an extent found nowhere else. Indeed, of the thirty laws that the priestly source formulated in this narrative fashion in the first four books of the Bible, sixteen occur in Numbers, by one count.[13]

Perhaps the most explicit example of the genre is the legislation covering the inheritance of women. Following the second census (Num. 26), the daughters of Zelophehad request a ruling to cover the case of a father who, like theirs, died without male issue. Moses receives a divine response on the spot (Num. 27) and a further ruling is issued in the same matter subsequently (Num. 36). Both rulings are intended to be binding for all time; in short, they are precedent law.

It has long been observed that much of the civil legislation, both biblical and Near Eastern generally, is couched in casuistic form, i.e., as a conditional sentence. This is true of the famous code of Hammurabi and its earlier prototypes in Babylonia, of the Assyrian laws, and of the Hittite laws. It applies equally to the Covenant Code (Exod. 21 f.) and its Deuteronomic counterparts (esp. Deut. 21 f.). The identical formulation in Num. 27, combined with the narrative context, suggests that its author was aware of what modern scholarship has only gradually agreed on: that casuistic or conditional legislation was in fact conceived of as originating in a given, unique precedent. (Here then, the biblical evidence illuminates the comparative material.) This is not to say that the precedent is actual, historical fact. Rather, we may be dealing with a general predilection in ancient Near Eastern thought for deriving eternal verities from one-time occurrences in the past. Though this predilection finds its commonest expression in myth, it is reflected also in wisdom literature, and case law is often close to wisdom in spirit,

as the example of the "Solomonic judgment" (I Kings 3) reminds us.

The story of the daughters of Zelophehad is important, however, not only as a type-case, but also for its particular concern, which involves inheritance. Much of Numbers is occupied with the assignment of the Transjordanian conquests and the prospective parceling out of Canaan, regarded as the inheritance of the twelve tribes. In this context, the genealogical aspect of the tribal lists comes to the fore again, for the inheritance is treated in terms of family law. Here we may compare, not only the extensive provisions in the cuneiform law codes (above), but also the abundant testimony of documents from the actual practice of law in Mesopotamia and elsewhere, which often deal with inheritance, particularly of real estate. These show the same concern for keeping the inheritance in the family as does Num. 36, though by other means—generally allowing daughters to share in the inheritance only while unmarried or if, as priestesses of certain types, they were enjoined from having children of their own. In practice, too, the absence of male heirs was less common, given the greater willingness to resort to adoption (contrast Abraham's fear in Gen. 15:3) or concubinage. The biblical legislation, by contrast, emphasizes the blood relationship of the son and proper status of the mother. Numbers insists on the full rights of all the tribes, including those who traced their descent to the concubines of Jacob, presumably on the grounds that the sons had been adopted by his wives (Gen. 30:3).

The legislation concerning the priests and Levites is likewise embedded in the narrative context of Numbers. Again, only one example can be singled out here. The elaborate provisions for the relationship of priests and

---

[13] R. H. Pfeiffer, *Introduction to the Old Testament* (New York: Harper and Bros., 1941), pp. 250–253.

Levites to the rest of the Israelites in chapter 18 is sometimes regarded as a virtual doublet or expansion of the briefer prescriptions in earlier parts of the book. But this impression can be corrected by a detailed analysis of all Levitical terminology and its counterpart in the elaborate cultic prescriptions of the rest of the ancient Near East. In fact, it has been convincingly shown that Num. 18 intends a real change in the existing relationship of priests, Levites, and Israelites—a change evidently motivated by the terrifying experience of the Korahite plague that preceded (Num. 17). The altar and other sacred objects in the Tabernacle and its court clearly had the power to kill all who encroached on them, and to spread that retribution to the whole people. Henceforth, the officiating priests, who alone could see and employ these objects with impunity, would form a first line of defense for them. But the main guard duty fell on the Levites who, far from being priests, were armed guards sharing with the priests the custody of the sanctuary and specifically charged with preventing encroachment by laymen or unauthorized priests or Levites. Such encroachers were to be killed on the spot by the Levites on pain of death to the Levites themselves. No longer would the entire people suffer the terrible consequences of such encroachment. Narrative and legislation thus reveal the tremendous dread of those sacred objects which the priests had to employ and, together with the Levites, to guard. The considerable emoluments of the priestly and Levitical offices on which Numbers

dwells in this and other connections assume a quite reasonable aspect in this light. The possible antiquity of the underlying concept is emphasized by a Hittite analogy, "Instructions for Temple Officials," which dates from the second millennium. Here too the custody of the temple is shared between the priests, who guard the interior of the sanctuary, its court, and its entrance, and an armed guard, who protect the outside of the sacred area under the command of a priest, like the Levites of Num. 18. Both priests and guards are charged to kill any unauthorized encroacher on pain of death for themselves, the only difference being that their punishment is exacted by man, not God.[14]

Numbers and Archeology

In concentrating on the structural framework and dominant themes of Numbers, it is necessary to pass more briefly over the many individual pericopes, i.e., self-contained literary units, incorporated in the book, although these too are often illuminated by archeology and epigraphy. The antiquity of several poetic fragments, some explicitly cited from lost Hebrew works (e.g., Num. 21:14), is corroborated by various links to other Near Eastern literature. The first of the two songs of the ark (Num. 10:35 f.), for example, recurs with minor variations in the opening verse of Psalm 68, one of the most archaic items in the whole Psalter, which has been ingeniously interpreted, partly on this basis, as a catalogue of early Hebrew lyric poems cited by their incipits.[15] A comparable convention is attested, already before the end of the third millennium, in Sumerian literary bibliography, where some twenty such catalogues are now known. The poetic reproach of Aaron and Miriam (Num. 12:6–9) alludes to nocturnal visions as a means of communicating the divine will, amply testified to in the Mesopotamian repertoire of mantic tech-

[14] Pritchard, *ANET*, pp. 207–210. Cf. II Chronicles 23:7 and Jacob Milgrom, "The Shared Custody of the Tabernacle and a Hittite Analogy," *JAOS*, 90 (1970), pp. 204–209; *idem, Studies in Levitical Terminology* I (University of California Publications [in] Near Eastern Studies, Vol. 14, 1970; Berkeley: University of California Press), pp. 46–59.

[15] William F. Albright, "A Catalogue of Early Hebrew Lyric Poems (Psalm 68)," *Hebrew Union College Annual*, Vol. 23, Pt. 1 (1950–1951), pp. 1–39. [Hereafter cited as *HUCA*.]

niques such as are catalogued in the *Assyrian Dream-Book*,[16] and contrasts this with Moses' status as a favorite or intimate of the deity, expressed, as in the Ugaritic epics, by the epithet "servant [of God]." The "song of the well" (Num. 21:17 f.) has a close parallel in the poetry of the Arabian desert,[17] while the "ballad of Heshbon" (Num. 21:27–29) is so similar to Jeremiah 48:45 f. that both versions can best be assumed to go back to a common original source. Finally, the entire Balaam episode (Num. 22–24), which clearly revolves around his four prophetic oracles, may well be a narrative expansion inspired by these poems. In its derivation of Balaam from Pethor on the Euphrates and his depiction in some sense as a diviner it has Mesopotamian overtones, but a newly discovered Aramaic inscription has thrown the whole question into an entirely new light: on this seventh-century monument, Balaam the "seer of the gods" utters prophecies and, after they are rejected, curses reminiscent of the biblical parallels. The find-spot of the inscription, Tel Deir Allah, lies on the Jabbok River just east of the Jordan and has been tentatively identified with the Transjordanian Succoth which figures in the story of Gideon (Judg. 8) and elsewhere. Thus, the Balaam stories in Numbers and the newly found inscription share a common Transjordanian setting.[18]

In the story that immediately follows, that of the apostasy to Moabite idol-worship (Num. 25), Jewish tradition associated the Peor of this incident with the *bet-marzeach* or house of the funeral-feast (Jer. 16:5), whose existence is now attested epigraphically from all over the ancient world: the royal archives of Ugarit, the Jewish papyri from Elephantine, and various Semitic inscriptions from Marseilles, Athens, Petra, and Palmyra.[19] The hero of the story, Phinehas, has, like other priestly figures, a name with a patently Egyptian etymology.[20] He stays God's wrath, expressed here and repeatedly in Numbers

(e.g. 15:37, 17:9–15) as the outbreak of a plague, by instantly slaying two of the offenders, a theme echoed in the Akkadian epic of Erra, the deity who personified pestilence and the scorched-earth tactics employed against it, and who was finally appeased through the intercession of his divine attendant Ishum ("Fire").[21] As a reward, Phinehas and his descendants are promised eternal claim to priestly office and the attendant revenues; the "pact of friendship" conveying this promise is a covenant of grant well attested in the unconditional royal grants in perpetuity made in the sources from Alalakh and elsewhere in return for special zeal and devotion shown to the king.[22]

These examples are not intended to compromise the originality of the biblical text. Indeed the comparative approach helps to silhouette its distinctive features as well as those it shares with its ancient environment. Thus the absence to date of any kind of parallel to the cities of refuge (Num. 35) only highlights the uniqueness of this humane institution. But we cannot ignore the ongoing revelations of archeology. Excavations at Tanis (biblical Zoan) in Egypt, for instance, have unearthed a stela at this former Hyksos capital that celebrated the four hundredth year of its founding and used this as the basis for an "era of the city of Tanis."[23] The founding

[16] A. Leo Oppenheim, *The Interpretation of Dreams in the Ancient Near East, with a Translation of an Assyrian Dream-Book* (Transactions of the American Philosophical Society, Vol. 46, No. 3, 1956), pp. 179–373.
[17] Pfeiffer, *op. cit.*, p. 274.
[18] Jacob Hoftijzer, "The Prophet Balaam in a Sixth-Century [sic!] Aramaic Inscription," *Biblical Archaeologist*, 39 (1976), pp. 11–17.
[19] Porten, *op. cit.*, pp. 179–186.
[20] Cf., e.g., Putiel in Exod. 6:25; Hophni in I Sam. 1–4; Pashhur in Jer. 20:1–6.
[21] Luigi Cagni, *The Poem of Erra* (Sources from the Ancient Near East, Vol. 1, No. 3, 1977).
[22] Moshe Weinfeld, "The Covenant of Grant in the Old Testament and in the Ancient Near East," *JAOS*, 90 (1970), pp. 184–203, esp. pp. 201 f.
[23] Pritchard, *ANET*, pp. 252 f.

of Hebron seems to be dated by the same era (Num. 13:22). The excavations at Dibon, ancient capital of Moab (Num. 21:30; 32:34), have added materially to our knowledge of the Moabites, as have scattered epigraphic finds of Moabite inscriptions. And the rediscovery of ancient Arad has shed new light on the Midianite connections of Hobab the Kenite who guided Moses in the wilderness (Num. 10:29–32) and promises to reveal new insights into the patterns of conquest and settlement which characterized Israel's occupation of the Negev and all the Promised Land.[24]

Conclusion

In spite of its eclectic character, the Book of Numbers does constitute some kind of literary unit. By comparison with the epic records of other migrations at the end of the Bronze Age, it forms a unique repository of traditions associated with the wanderings of the Israelites and an indispensable link in the theology of Jewish history. It provides the genealogical continuity with the patriarchal traditions and the legal and moral basis for the conquests reported or anticipated. In the context of the narrative, it secures the basis for legislative precedent and innovations, with particular attention to questions of inheritance and of priestly and Levitical obligations and benefits. Though exceptionally unedifying in its portrayal of the people, and sometimes less than flattering of its human and divine leadership, it shows in both description and prescription the necessity for the purging of dissent and sinfulness, and it lays the basis for both the tribal amphictyonies of the period of the Judges and the theocratic polities that ensued. For all its free use of biblical and extra-biblical motifs, it emerges in toto as a unique compendium of Israel's image of its collective past.

[24] Yochanan Aharoni, "Nothing Early and Nothing Late: Rewriting Israel's Conquest," *Biblical Archaeologist*, 39 (1976), pp. 55–76.

PART I

Of Census and Law

In the Desert

The opening chapter sets the wilderness of Sinai as the locale and specifies the point at which the Book of Numbers begins as thirteen months after the Exodus from Egypt. In the course of the following chapters an entire generation is traversed: the Israelites who participated in the Exodus die; significant tribal changes take place; and Moses prepares to surrender the reins of leadership to his successor. Throughout, numbers and genealogies are repeatedly emphasized because they held more than historical interest for the biblical authors (see Hallo above and Commentary on Genesis, chapters 29–30). Thus, in addition to the results of the census, we are given a detailed description of the marching arrangements of the tribes. The transmission of these records may also have served the purpose (assigned by Bible scholars to the Priestly School, P) of showing the centrality of the Tabernacle. In contrast, an earlier tradition (found in Exod. 33:7 and assigned to the Elohist School, E) has the Tent located outside the encampment. (See Commentary on Exodus, chapter 40.)

Despite the detailed descriptions given, we are not entirely sure how the tribes were grouped. It is apparent that the priestly families encamped nearest the Tabernacle (see Num. 3) and that the twelve tribes were arranged in threes behind them, in the form of a quadrangle. The most important tribes—Judah, Reuben, Ephraim, Dan—gave the four camps their names. (From the importance given to Judah, scholars have concluded that the account was set down after the Assyrians had destroyed

the northern Kingdom of Israel in 721 B.C.E. and decimated its ten tribes.)
The arrangement seems to have been as follows [1].
(The first weekly portion, *Bemidbar*, begins here.)

EAST

Division of Judah

Issachar, Judah, Zebulun

Moses, Aaron and his sons

NORTH — Division of Dan — Asher, Dan, Naphtali — Merarites — TABERNACLE — Kohathites — Division of Reuben — Gad, Reuben, Simeon — SOUTH

Gershonites

Division of Ephraim

Manasseh, Ephraim, Benjamin

WEST

א וַיְדַבֵּר יְהֹוָה אֶל־מֹשֶׁה בְּמִדְבַּר סִינַי בְּאֹהֶל מוֹעֵד
בְּאֶחָד לַחֹדֶשׁ הַשֵּׁנִי בַּשָּׁנָה הַשֵּׁנִית לְצֵאתָם מֵאֶרֶץ
ב מִצְרַיִם לֵאמֹר: שְׂאוּ אֶת־רֹאשׁ כָּל־עֲדַת בְּנֵי־יִשְׂרָאֵל
לְמִשְׁפְּחֹתָם לְבֵית אֲבֹתָם בְּמִסְפַּר שֵׁמוֹת כָּל־זָכָר
ג לְגֻלְגְּלֹתָם: מִבֶּן עֶשְׂרִים שָׁנָה וָמַעְלָה כָּל־יֹצֵא צָבָא
בְּיִשְׂרָאֵל תִּפְקְדוּ אֹתָם לְצִבְאֹתָם אַתָּה וְאַהֲרֹן:
ד וְאִתְּכֶם יִהְיוּ אִישׁ אִישׁ לַמַּטֶּה אִישׁ רֹאשׁ לְבֵית־אֲבֹתָיו
ה הוּא: וְאֵלֶּה שְׁמוֹת הָאֲנָשִׁים אֲשֶׁר יַעַמְדוּ אִתְּכֶם

ו לִרְאוּבֵן אֱלִיצוּר בֶּן־שְׁדֵיאוּר: לְשִׁמְעוֹן שְׁלֻמִיאֵל בֶּן־
ז צוּרִישַׁדָּי: לִיהוּדָה נַחְשׁוֹן בֶּן־עַמִּינָדָב: לְיִשָּׂשכָר
ח נְתַנְאֵל בֶּן־צוּעָר: לִזְבוּלֻן אֱלִיאָב בֶּן־חֵלֹן: לִבְנֵי יוֹסֵף
ט לְאֶפְרַיִם אֱלִישָׁמָע בֶּן־עַמִּיהוּד לִמְנַשֶּׁה גַּמְלִיאֵל בֶּן־
יא פְּדָהצוּר: לְבִנְיָמִן אֲבִידָן בֶּן־גִּדְעֹנִי: לְדָן אֲחִיעֶזֶר
יב בֶּן־עַמִּישַׁדָּי: לְאָשֵׁר פַּגְעִיאֵל בֶּן־עָכְרָן: לְגָד אֶלְיָסָף
יד בֶּן־דְּעוּאֵל: לְנַפְתָּלִי אֲחִירַע בֶּן־עֵינָן: אֵלֶּה קְרוּאֵי
טו הָעֵדָה נְשִׂיאֵי מַטּוֹת אֲבוֹתָם רָאשֵׁי אַלְפֵי יִשְׂרָאֵל

* טו קְרוּאֵי קְרִי.

1] On the first day of the second month, in the second year following the exodus from the land of Egypt, the LORD spoke to Moses in the wilderness of Sinai, in the Tent of Meeting, saying:

2] Take a census of the whole Israelite community by the clans of its ancestral houses, listing the names, every male, head by head. 3] You and Aaron shall record them by their groups, from the age of twenty years up, all those in Israel who are able to bear arms. 4] Associated with you shall be a man from each tribe, each one the head of his ancestral house.

5] These are the names of the men who shall assist you: From Reuben, Elizur son of Shedeur. 6] From Simeon, Shelumiel son of Zurishaddai. 7] From Judah, Nahshon son of Amminadab. 8] From Issachar, Nethanel son of Zuar. 9] From Zebulun, Eliab son of Helon. 10] From the sons of Joseph: from Ephraim, Elishama son of Ammihud; from Manasseh, Gamaliel son of Pedahzur. 11] From Benjamin, Abidan son of Gideoni. 12] From Dan, Ahiezer son of Ammishaddai. 13] From Asher, Pagiel son of Ochran. 14] From Gad, Eliasaph son of Deuel. 15] From Naphtali, Ahira son of Enan. 16] Those are the elected of the assembly, the chieftains of their ancestral tribes: they are the heads of the contingents of Israel.

1:1] *Second month*. This conflicts with Exod. 38:26, which records the same overall census results but gives the time as that of the erection of the Tabernacle, which took place one month earlier, on the first day of the *first* month (see Exod. 38:26 for a discussion of the problem).

Tent of Meeting. The wilderness sanctuary, which was portable, was sometimes called Tent of Meeting (*Ohel Mo-ed*) and sometimes Tabernacle (*Mishkan*). See at Exod. 25–31.

2] *Ancestral houses*. A person's descent was traced through his or her father and back through the father's father [2]. This lineage was called "ancestral house"; it was part of a larger family (*mishpachah*) and in turn part of a tribe (*mateh*).

Every male. The census had a military overtone and, therefore, women, like minors, were not included.

3] *Twenty years*. The stipulated age for military service (Exod. 30:14).

The age of retirement was sixty; priestly service was from thirty to fifty (Num. 4:23).

5–15] *These are the names*. Tribal names are listed here in an order different from Gen. 49 and Exod. 1. Except for Amminadab and Nahshon (verse 7), these names do not occur outside Numbers. Zur and Ammi appear three times as first and second components, similar to names in other cognate traditions [3].

16] *Contingents*. אַלְפֵי (*alfe*, a plural form of אֶלֶף, *elef*). See commentary.

יז: וַיִּקַּח מֹשֶׁה וְאַהֲרֹן אֵת הָאֲנָשִׁים הָאֵלֶּה אֲשֶׁר
יח: נִקְּבוּ בְּשֵׁמוֹת: וְאֵת כָּל־הָעֵדָה הִקְהִילוּ בְּאֶחָד לַחֹדֶשׁ
הַשֵּׁנִי וַיִּתְיַלְדוּ עַל־מִשְׁפְּחֹתָם לְבֵית אֲבֹתָם בְּמִסְפַּר
יט: שֵׁמוֹת מִבֶּן עֶשְׂרִים שָׁנָה וָמַעְלָה לְגֻלְגְּלֹתָם: כַּאֲשֶׁר
צִוָּה יְהוָה אֶת־מֹשֶׁה וַיִּפְקְדֵם בְּמִדְבַּר סִינָי: ס
כ: וַיִּהְיוּ בְנֵי־רְאוּבֵן בְּכֹר יִשְׂרָאֵל תּוֹלְדֹתָם לְמִשְׁפְּחֹתָם
לְבֵית אֲבֹתָם בְּמִסְפַּר שֵׁמוֹת לְגֻלְגְּלֹתָם כָּל־זָכָר מִבֶּן
כא: עֶשְׂרִים שָׁנָה וָמַעְלָה כֹּל יֹצֵא צָבָא: פְּקֻדֵיהֶם לְמַטֵּה
רְאוּבֵן שִׁשָּׁה וְאַרְבָּעִים אֶלֶף וַחֲמֵשׁ מֵאוֹת: פ
כב: לִבְנֵי שִׁמְעוֹן תּוֹלְדֹתָם לְמִשְׁפְּחֹתָם לְבֵית אֲבֹתָם
פְּקֻדָיו בְּמִסְפַּר שֵׁמוֹת לְגֻלְגְּלֹתָם כָּל־זָכָר מִבֶּן
כג: עֶשְׂרִים שָׁנָה וָמַעְלָה כֹּל יֹצֵא צָבָא: פְּקֻדֵיהֶם לְמַטֵּה
שִׁמְעוֹן תִּשְׁעָה וַחֲמִשִּׁים אֶלֶף וּשְׁלֹשׁ מֵאוֹת: פ
כד: לִבְנֵי גָד תּוֹלְדֹתָם לְמִשְׁפְּחֹתָם לְבֵית אֲבֹתָם בְּמִסְפַּר
שֵׁמוֹת מִבֶּן עֶשְׂרִים שָׁנָה וָמַעְלָה כֹּל יֹצֵא צָבָא:

כה: פְּקֻדֵיהֶם לְמַטֵּה גָד חֲמִשָּׁה וְאַרְבָּעִים אֶלֶף וְשֵׁשׁ
מֵאוֹת וַחֲמִשִּׁים: פ
כו: לִבְנֵי יְהוּדָה תּוֹלְדֹתָם לְמִשְׁפְּחֹתָם לְבֵית אֲבֹתָם
בְּמִסְפַּר שֵׁמֹת מִבֶּן עֶשְׂרִים שָׁנָה וָמַעְלָה כֹּל יֹצֵא
כז: צָבָא: פְּקֻדֵיהֶם לְמַטֵּה יְהוּדָה אַרְבָּעָה וְשִׁבְעִים אֶלֶף
וְשֵׁשׁ מֵאוֹת: פ
כח: לִבְנֵי יִשָּׂשכָר תּוֹלְדֹתָם לְמִשְׁפְּחֹתָם לְבֵית אֲבֹתָם
בְּמִסְפַּר שֵׁמֹת מִבֶּן עֶשְׂרִים שָׁנָה וָמַעְלָה כֹּל יֹצֵא
כט: צָבָא: פְּקֻדֵיהֶם לְמַטֵּה יִשָּׂשכָר אַרְבָּעָה וַחֲמִשִּׁים
אֶלֶף וְאַרְבַּע מֵאוֹת: פ
ל: לִבְנֵי זְבוּלֻן תּוֹלְדֹתָם לְמִשְׁפְּחֹתָם לְבֵית אֲבֹתָם
בְּמִסְפַּר שֵׁמֹת מִבֶּן עֶשְׂרִים שָׁנָה וָמַעְלָה כֹּל יֹצֵא
לא: צָבָא: פְּקֻדֵיהֶם לְמַטֵּה זְבוּלֻן שִׁבְעָה וַחֲמִשִּׁים אֶלֶף
וְאַרְבַּע מֵאוֹת: פ

17] So Moses and Aaron took those men, who were designated by name, **18]** and on the first day of the second month they convoked the whole community, who were registered by the clans of their ancestral houses—the names of those aged twenty years and over being listed head by head. **19]** As the LORD had commanded Moses, so he recorded them in the wilderness of Sinai.

20] They totaled as follows: The descendants of Reuben, Israel's first-born, the registration of the clans of their ancestral house, as listed by name, head by head, all males aged twenty years and over, all who were able to bear arms— **21]** those enrolled from the tribe of Reuben: 46,500.

22] Of the descendants of Simeon, the registration of the clans of their ancestral house, their enrollment as listed by name, head by head, all males aged twenty years and over, all who were able to bear arms— **23]** those enrolled from the tribe of Simeon: 59,300.

24] Of the descendants of Gad, the registration of the clans of their ancestral house, as listed by name, aged twenty years and over, all who were able to bear arms— **25]** those enrolled from the tribe of Gad: 45,650.

26] Of the descendants of Judah, the registration of the clans of their ancestral house, as listed by name, aged twenty years and over, all who were able to bear arms— **27]** those enrolled from the tribe of Judah: 74,600.

28] Of the descendants of Issachar, the registration of the clans of their ancestral house, as listed by name, aged twenty years and over, all who were able to bear arms— **29]** those enrolled from the tribe of Issachar: 54,400.

30] Of the descendants of Zebulun, the registration of the clans of their ancestral house, as listed by name, aged twenty years and over, all who were able to bear arms— **31]** those enrolled from the tribe of Zebulun: 57,400.

לב לִבְנֵי יוֹסֵף לִבְנֵי אֶפְרַיִם תּוֹלְדֹתָם לְמִשְׁפְּחֹתָם לְבֵית
אֲבֹתָם בְּמִסְפַּר שֵׁמֹת מִבֶּן עֶשְׂרִים שָׁנָה וָמַעְלָה כֹּל
לג יֹצֵא צָבָא: פְּקֻדֵיהֶם לְמַטֵּה אֶפְרָיִם אַרְבָּעִים אֶלֶף
וַחֲמֵשׁ מֵאוֹת: פ

לד לִבְנֵי מְנַשֶּׁה תּוֹלְדֹתָם לְמִשְׁפְּחֹתָם לְבֵית אֲבֹתָם
בְּמִסְפַּר שֵׁמוֹת מִבֶּן עֶשְׂרִים שָׁנָה וָמַעְלָה כֹּל יֹצֵא
לה צָבָא: פְּקֻדֵיהֶם לְמַטֵּה מְנַשֶּׁה שְׁנַיִם וּשְׁלֹשִׁים אֶלֶף
וּמָאתָיִם: פ

לו לִבְנֵי בִנְיָמִן תּוֹלְדֹתָם לְמִשְׁפְּחֹתָם לְבֵית אֲבֹתָם
בְּמִסְפַּר שֵׁמֹת מִבֶּן עֶשְׂרִים שָׁנָה וָמַעְלָה כֹּל יֹצֵא
לז צָבָא: פְּקֻדֵיהֶם לְמַטֵּה בִנְיָמִן חֲמִשָּׁה וּשְׁלֹשִׁים אֶלֶף
וְאַרְבַּע מֵאוֹת: פ

לח לִבְנֵי דָן תּוֹלְדֹתָם לְמִשְׁפְּחֹתָם לְבֵית אֲבֹתָם בְּמִסְפַּר
שֵׁמֹת מִבֶּן עֶשְׂרִים שָׁנָה וָמַעְלָה כֹּל יֹצֵא צָבָא:

לט פְּקֻדֵיהֶם לְמַטֵּה דָן שְׁנַיִם וְשִׁשִּׁים אֶלֶף וּשְׁבַע מֵאוֹת: פ
מ לִבְנֵי אָשֵׁר תּוֹלְדֹתָם לְמִשְׁפְּחֹתָם לְבֵית אֲבֹתָם
בְּמִסְפַּר שֵׁמֹת מִבֶּן עֶשְׂרִים שָׁנָה וָמַעְלָה כֹּל יֹצֵא
מא צָבָא: פְּקֻדֵיהֶם לְמַטֵּה אָשֵׁר אֶחָד וְאַרְבָּעִים אֶלֶף
וַחֲמֵשׁ מֵאוֹת: פ

מב בְּנֵי נַפְתָּלִי תּוֹלְדֹתָם לְמִשְׁפְּחֹתָם לְבֵית אֲבֹתָם
בְּמִסְפַּר שֵׁמֹת מִבֶּן עֶשְׂרִים שָׁנָה וָמַעְלָה כֹּל יֹצֵא
מג צָבָא: פְּקֻדֵיהֶם לְמַטֵּה נַפְתָּלִי שְׁלֹשָׁה וַחֲמִשִּׁים אֶלֶף
וְאַרְבַּע מֵאוֹת: פ

מד אֵלֶּה הַפְּקֻדִים אֲשֶׁר פָּקַד מֹשֶׁה וְאַהֲרֹן וּנְשִׂיאֵי
יִשְׂרָאֵל שְׁנֵים עָשָׂר אִישׁ אִישׁ־אֶחָד לְבֵית־אֲבֹתָיו הָיוּ:
מה וַיִּהְיוּ כָל־פְּקוּדֵי בְנֵי־יִשְׂרָאֵל לְבֵית אֲבֹתָם מִבֶּן
מו עֶשְׂרִים שָׁנָה וָמַעְלָה כָּל־יֹצֵא צָבָא בְּיִשְׂרָאֵל: וַיִּהְיוּ
כָּל־הַפְּקֻדִים שֵׁשׁ־מֵאוֹת אֶלֶף וּשְׁלֹשֶׁת אֲלָפִים וַחֲמֵשׁ

32] Of the descendants of Joseph: Of the descendants of Ephraim, the registration of the clans of their ancestral house, as listed by name, aged twenty years and over, all who were able to bear arms— 33] those enrolled from the tribe of Ephraim: 40,500.

34] Of the descendants of Manasseh, the registration of the clans of their ancestral house, as listed by name, aged twenty years and over, all who were able to bear arms— 35] those enrolled from the tribe of Manasseh: 32,200.

36] Of the descendants of Benjamin, the registration of the clans of their ancestral house, as listed by name, aged twenty years and over, all who were able to bear arms— 37] those enrolled from the tribe of Benjamin: 35,400.

38] Of the descendants of Dan, the registration of the clans of their ancestral house, as listed by name, aged twenty years and over, all who were able to bear arms— 39] those enrolled from the tribe of Dan: 62,700.

40] Of the descendants of Asher, the registration of the clans of their ancestral house, as listed by name, aged twenty years and over, all who were able to bear arms— 41] those enrolled from the tribe of Asher: 41,500.

42] The descendants of Naphtali, the registration of the clans of their ancestral house, as listed by name, aged twenty years and over, all who were able to bear arms— 43] those enrolled from the tribe of Naphtali: 53,400.

44] Those are the enrollments recorded by Moses and Aaron and by the chieftains of Israel, who were twelve in number, one man to each ancestral house. 45] All the Israelites, aged twenty years and over, enrolled by ancestral houses, all those in Israel, who were able to bear arms— 46] all who were enrolled came to 603,550.

נג אֹתוֹ הַלְוִיִּם וְהוּנָּ֣ר הַקָּרֵ֔ב יוּמָת: וְחָנ֖וּ בְּנֵ֥י יִשְׂרָאֵל֙ אִ֣ישׁ
נג עַל־מַחֲנֵ֖הוּ וְאִ֥ישׁ עַל־דִּגְל֖וֹ לְצִבְאֹתָֽם: וְהַלְוִיִּ֗ם יַחֲנ֣וּ
סָבִיב֙ לְמִשְׁכַּ֣ן הָעֵדֻ֔ת וְלֹא־יִהְיֶ֣ה קֶ֔צֶף עַל־עֲדַ֖ת בְּנֵ֣י
יִשְׂרָאֵ֑ל וְשָׁמְרוּ֙ הַלְוִיִּ֔ם אֶת־מִשְׁמֶ֖רֶת מִשְׁכַּ֥ן הָעֵדֽוּת:
נד וַיַּעֲשׂ֖וּ בְּנֵ֣י יִשְׂרָאֵ֑ל כְּ֠כֹל אֲשֶׁ֨ר צִוָּ֤ה יְהֹוָה֙ אֶת־מֹשֶׁ֔ה
כֵּ֖ן עָשֽׂוּ: פ

א וַיְדַבֵּ֣ר יְהֹוָ֔ה אֶל־מֹשֶׁ֥ה וְאֶֽל־אַהֲרֹ֖ן לֵאמֹֽר: אִ֣ישׁ עַל־
דִּגְל֤וֹ בְאֹתֹת֙ לְבֵ֣ית אֲבֹתָ֔ם יַחֲנ֖וּ בְּנֵ֣י יִשְׂרָאֵ֑ל מִנֶּ֕גֶד

מז מֵא֖וֹת וַחֲמִשִּׁ֑ים וְהַ֨לְוִיִּ֔ם לְמַטֵּ֥ה אֲבֹתָ֖ם לֹ֣א הָתְפָּקְד֑וּ
בְּתוֹכָֽם: פ

מח וַיְדַבֵּ֥ר יְהֹוָ֖ה אֶל־מֹשֶׁ֥ה לֵּאמֹֽר: אַ֣ךְ אֶת־מַטֵּ֤ה לֵוִי֙ לֹ֣א
תִפְקֹ֔ד וְאֶת־רֹאשָׁ֖ם לֹ֣א תִשָּׂ֑א בְּת֖וֹךְ בְּנֵ֥י יִשְׂרָאֵֽל:

נ וְאַתָּ֡ה הַפְקֵ֣ד אֶת־הַלְוִיִּם֩ עַל־מִשְׁכַּ֨ן הָעֵדֻ֜ת וְעַ֣ל כָּל־
כֵּלָיו֮ וְעַ֣ל כָּל־אֲשֶׁר־לוֹ֒ הֵ֜מָּה יִשְׂא֣וּ אֶת־הַמִּשְׁכָּ֗ן וְאֶת־
נא כָּל־כֵּלָ֔יו וְהֵ֖ם יְשָׁרְתֻ֑הוּ וְסָבִ֥יב לַמִּשְׁכָּ֖ן יַחֲנֽוּ: וּבִנְסֹ֣עַ
הַמִּשְׁכָּ֗ן יוֹרִ֤ידוּ אֹתוֹ֙ הַלְוִיִּ֔ם וּבַחֲנֹת֙ הַמִּשְׁכָּ֔ן יָקִ֥ימוּ

47] The Levites, however, were not recorded among them by their ancestral tribe. 48] For the LORD had spoken to Moses, saying: 49] Do not on any account enroll the tribe of Levi or take a census of them with the Israelites. 50] You shall put the Levites in charge of the Tabernacle of the Pact, all its furnishings, and everything that pertains to it: they shall carry the Tabernacle and all its furnishings, and they shall tend it; and they shall camp around the Tabernacle. 51] When the Tabernacle is to set out, the Levites shall take it down, and when the Tabernacle is to be pitched, the Levites shall set it up; any outsider who encroaches shall be put to death. 52] The Israelites shall encamp troop by troop, each man with his division and each under his standard. 53] The Levites, however, shall camp around the Tabernacle of the Pact, that wrath may not strike the Israelite community; the Levites shall stand guard around the Tabernacle of the Pact.

54] The Israelites did accordingly; just as the LORD had commanded Moses, so they did.

1] The LORD spoke to Moses and Aaron saying: 2] The Israelites shall camp each with his standard, under the banners of their ancestral house; they shall camp around the Tent of Meeting at a distance.

47] *The Levites, however.* On their special position, see chapters 8, 10, and 18. They were not to fight wars, an exemption still observed for rabbis, rabbinical students, and clergymen in Israel and other countries.

50] *Tabernacle of the Pact.* Where the Ark with the Tablets was kept.

51] *Any outsider.* Rendered "layman" in Exod. 29:33. The term refers to someone who is not a Levite or not commissioned to assist [4].

Shall be put to death. According to one Jewish tradition, God rather than a human court would look to the punishment [5].

2:2] *Standard.* דֶּגֶל (*degel*). The custom of distinguishing tribes and armies by some ensign appears to be of great antiquity and was common among Egyptians, Babylonians, Assyrians, and other nations. The *degel* signified a distinct military unit; sometimes it depicted an animal figure, e.g., the Roman eagle. What the Israelite standards showed is no longer known; whatever they were, the very omission of their description suggests that everyone was familiar with them.

The term *degel* also came to mean the division distinguished by the standard, here apparently each group of three tribes. Such usage occurs elsewhere, e.g., in the Elephantine papyri [6].

Banners. אֹתֹת (*otot*), possibly colored flags. The Midrash suggests that the flags were embroidered and that the colors resembled the precious stones in the priestly breastplate [7].

The Midrash also believes that other nations learned the institution of colored flags from Israel.

Camp . . . at a distance. To avoid encroachment on the Tent. Josh. 3:4 stipulates the distance as 2,000 cubits, or about 3,000 feet. In later Jewish tradition this became the distance one was permitted to walk on the Sabbath outside the city limits [8].

יד וּשְׁלֹשׁ מֵאוֹת: וּמַטֵּה גָּד וְנָשִׂיא לִבְנֵי גָד אֶלְיָסָף בֶּן

רְעוּאֵל: וּצְבָאוֹ וּפְקֻדֵיהֶם חֲמִשָּׁה וְאַרְבָּעִים אֶלֶף

טו וְשֵׁשׁ מֵאוֹת וַחֲמִשִּׁים: כָּל־הַפְּקֻדִים לְמַחֲנֵה רְאוּבֵן

טז מְאַת אֶלֶף וְאֶחָד וַחֲמִשִּׁים אֶלֶף וְאַרְבַּע־מֵאוֹת

וַחֲמִשִּׁים לְצִבְאֹתָם וּשְׁנִיִם יִסָּעוּ: ס וְנָסַע אֹהֶל־

יז מוֹעֵד מַחֲנֵה הַלְוִיִּם בְּתוֹךְ הַמַּחֲנֹת כַּאֲשֶׁר יַחֲנוּ כֵּן

יח יִסָּעוּ אִישׁ עַל־יָדוֹ לְדִגְלֵיהֶם: ס דֶּגֶל מַחֲנֵה

אֶפְרַיִם לְצִבְאֹתָם יָמָּה וְנָשִׂיא לִבְנֵי אֶפְרַיִם אֱלִישָׁמָע

יט בֶּן־עַמִּיהוּד: וּצְבָאוֹ וּפְקֻדֵיהֶם אַרְבָּעִים אֶלֶף וַחֲמֵשׁ

כ מֵאוֹת: וְעָלָיו מַטֵּה מְנַשֶּׁה וְנָשִׂיא לִבְנֵי מְנַשֶּׁה גַּמְלִיאֵל

כא בֶּן־פְּדָהצוּר: וּצְבָאוֹ וּפְקֻדֵיהֶם שְׁנַיִם וּשְׁלֹשִׁים אֶלֶף

כב וּמָאתָיִם: וּמַטֵּה בִּנְיָמִן וְנָשִׂיא לִבְנֵי בִנְיָמִן אֲבִידָן בֶּן

כג גִּדְעֹנִי: וּצְבָאוֹ וּפְקֻדֵיהֶם חֲמִשָּׁה וּשְׁלֹשִׁים אֶלֶף

כד וְאַרְבַּע מֵאוֹת: כָּל־הַפְּקֻדִים לְמַחֲנֵה אֶפְרַיִם מְאַת

אֶלֶף וּשְׁמֹנַת־אֲלָפִים וּמֵאָה לְצִבְאֹתָם וּשְׁלִשִׁים

י סָבִיב לְאֹהֶל־מוֹעֵד יַחֲנוּ: וְהַחֹנִים קֵדְמָה מִזְרָחָה

דֶּגֶל מַחֲנֵה יְהוּדָה לְצִבְאֹתָם וְנָשִׂיא לִבְנֵי יְהוּדָה

ד נַחְשׁוֹן בֶּן־עַמִּינָדָב: וּצְבָאוֹ וּפְקֻדֵיהֶם אַרְבָּעָה

ה וְשִׁבְעִים אֶלֶף וְשֵׁשׁ מֵאוֹת: וְהַחֹנִים עָלָיו מַטֵּה

ו יִשָּׂשכָר וְנָשִׂיא לִבְנֵי יִשָּׂשכָר נְתַנְאֵל בֶּן־צוּעָר: וּצְבָאוֹ

וּפְקֻדָיו אַרְבָּעָה וַחֲמִשִּׁים אֶלֶף וְאַרְבַּע מֵאוֹת:

ז מַטֵּה זְבוּלֻן וְנָשִׂיא לִבְנֵי זְבוּלֻן אֱלִיאָב בֶּן־חֵלֹן:

ח וּצְבָאוֹ וּפְקֻדָיו שִׁבְעָה וַחֲמִשִּׁים אֶלֶף וְאַרְבַּע מֵאוֹת:

ט כָּל־הַפְּקֻדִים לְמַחֲנֵה יְהוּדָה מְאַת אֶלֶף וּשְׁמֹנִים אֶלֶף

וְשֵׁשֶׁת־אֲלָפִים וְאַרְבַּע־מֵאוֹת לְצִבְאֹתָם רִאשֹׁנָה

יִסָּעוּ: ס דֶּגֶל מַחֲנֵה רְאוּבֵן תֵּימָנָה לְצִבְאֹתָם

יא וְנָשִׂיא לִבְנֵי רְאוּבֵן אֱלִיצוּר בֶּן־שְׁדֵיאוּר: וּצְבָאוֹ

יב וּפְקֻדָיו שִׁשָּׁה וְאַרְבָּעִים אֶלֶף וַחֲמֵשׁ מֵאוֹת: וְהַחֹנִם

עָלָיו מַטֵּה שִׁמְעוֹן וְנָשִׂיא לִבְנֵי שִׁמְעוֹן שְׁלֻמִיאֵל בֶּן־

יג צוּרִישַׁדָּי: וּצְבָאוֹ וּפְקֻדֵיהֶם תִּשְׁעָה וַחֲמִשִּׁים אֶלֶף

3] Camped on the front, or east side: the standard of the division of Judah, troop by troop. Chieftain of the Judites: Nahshon son of Amminadab. **4]** His troop, as enrolled: 74,600. **5]** Camping next to it: The tribe of Issachar. Chieftain of the Issacharites: Nethanel son of Zuar. **6]** His troop, as enrolled: 54,400. **7]** The tribe of Zebulun. Chieftain of the Zebulun-ites: Eliab son of Helon. **8]** His troop, as enrolled: 57,400. **9]** The total enrolled in the division of Judah: 186,400, for all troops. These shall march first.

10] On the south: the standard of the division of Reuben, troop by troop. Chieftain of the Reubenites: Elizur son of Shedeur. **11]** His troop, as enrolled: 46,500. **12]** Camping next to it: The tribe of Simeon. Chieftain of the Simeonites: Shelumiel son of Zurishaddai. **13]** His troop, as enrolled: 59,300. **14]** And the tribe of Gad. Chieftain of the Gadites: Eliasaph son of Reuel. **15]** His troop, as enrolled: 45,650. **16]** The total enrolled in the division of Reuben: 151,450, for all troops. These shall march second.

17] Then, midway between the divisions, the Tent of Meeting, the division of the Levites, shall move. As they camp, so they shall march, each in position, by their standards. **18]** On the west: the standard of the division of Ephraim, troop by troop. Chieftain of the Ephraimites: Elishama son of Ammihud. **19]** His troop, as enrolled: 40,500.

20] Next to it: The tribe of Manasseh. Chieftain of the Manassites: Gamaliel son of Pedahzur. **21]** His troop, as enrolled: 32,200 **22]** And the tribe of Benjamin. Chieftain of the Benjaminites: Abidan son of Gideoni. **23]** His troop, as enrolled: 35,400. **24]** The total enrolled in the division of Ephraim: 108,100 for all troops. These shall march third.

14] *Reuel.* In Num. 1:14 and 10:20 he is called Deuel.

17] *The Levites.* How they marched is not clear, and in Num. 10:13–28 the procedure is somewhat different.

כה יִסָּעוּ: ס דֶּגֶל מַחֲנֵה דָן צָפֹנָה לְצִבְאֹתָם וְנָשִׂיא
כו לִבְנֵי דָן אֲחִיעֶזֶר בֶּן־עַמִּישַׁדָּי: וּצְבָאוֹ וּפְקֻדֵיהֶם שְׁנַיִם
כז וְשִׁשִּׁים אֶלֶף וּשְׁבַע מֵאוֹת: וְהַחֹנִים עָלָיו מַטֵּה אָשֵׁר
כח וְנָשִׂיא לִבְנֵי אָשֵׁר פַּגְעִיאֵל בֶּן־עָכְרָן: וּצְבָאוֹ
כט וּפְקֻדֵיהֶם אֶחָד וְאַרְבָּעִים אֶלֶף וַחֲמֵשׁ מֵאוֹת: וּמַטֵּה
ל נַפְתָּלִי וְנָשִׂיא לִבְנֵי נַפְתָּלִי אֲחִירַע בֶּן־עֵינָן: וּצְבָאוֹ
לא וּפְקֻדֵיהֶם שְׁלֹשָׁה וַחֲמִשִּׁים אֶלֶף וְאַרְבַּע מֵאוֹת: כָּל־
הַפְּקֻדִים לְמַחֲנֵה דָן מְאַת אֶלֶף וְשִׁבְעָה וַחֲמִשִּׁים

אֶלֶף וְשֵׁשׁ מֵאוֹת לָאַחֲרֹנָה יִסְעוּ לְדִגְלֵיהֶם: פ
לב אֵלֶּה פְּקוּדֵי בְנֵי־יִשְׂרָאֵל לְבֵית אֲבֹתָם כָּל־פְּקוּדֵי
הַמַּחֲנֹת לְצִבְאֹתָם שֵׁשׁ־מֵאוֹת אֶלֶף וּשְׁלֹשֶׁת אֲלָפִים
לג וַחֲמֵשׁ מֵאוֹת וַחֲמִשִּׁים: וְהַלְוִיִּם לֹא הָתְפָּקְדוּ בְּתוֹךְ
לד בְּנֵי יִשְׂרָאֵל כַּאֲשֶׁר צִוָּה יְהוָה אֶת־מֹשֶׁה: וַיַּעֲשׂוּ בְּנֵי
יִשְׂרָאֵל כְּכֹל אֲשֶׁר־צִוָּה יְהוָה אֶת־מֹשֶׁה כֵּן־חָנוּ
לְדִגְלֵיהֶם וְכֵן נָסָעוּ אִישׁ לְמִשְׁפְּחֹתָיו עַל־בֵּית
אֲבֹתָיו: פ

25] On the north: the standard of the division of Dan, troop by troop. Chieftain of the Danites: Ahiezer son of Ammishaddai. 26] His troop, as enrolled: 62,700. 27] Camping next to it: The tribe of Asher. Chieftain of the Asherites: Pagiel son of Ochran. 28] His troop, as enrolled: 41,500. 29] And the tribe of Naphtali. Chieftain of the Naphtalites: Ahira son of Enan. 30] His troop, as enrolled: 53,400. 31] The total enrolled in the division of Dan: 157,600. These shall march last, by their standards.

32] Those are the enrollments of the Israelites by ancestral houses. The total enrolled in the divisions, for all troops: 603,550. 33] The Levites, however, were not recorded among the Israelites, as the LORD had commanded Moses.

34] The Israelites did accordingly; just as the LORD had commanded Moses, so they camped by their standards, and so they marched, each with his clan according to his ancestral house.

The Census Figures

The text gives the total number of male Israelites over the age of twenty as 603,550, which agrees exactly with the figure given in Exod. 38:26. It agrees rather closely with the results of a second census (Num. 26) and corresponds to the more general 600,000 presented in Exod. 12:37 and Num. 11:21. But these numbers raise many difficulties both because of their size and because of other statistics recorded in the Bible (for instance, the notation in Num. 3:43 that there were only 22,273 first-born children among this multitude). Ancient and modern scholars have wrestled with these difficulties, but without definitive results. Their opinions range from calling the biblical statistics pure invention (including the suggestion of symbolic representation) to defending all details and harmonizing all discrepancies[1] [10].

The most obvious problem is presented by the figure of some 600,000 arms-bearing men, which would suggest that about two million Israelites wandered in the desert. The logistics of so large a migration exceeds the bounds of likelihood and has led some traditional interpreters to posit that the Israelites spread not only through Sinai but through the whole Arabian peninsula. Others point out that the Negev could sustain a much larger population in earlier days than in later times and that we should not judge conditions from the present aridity of the southland. But the intimacy portrayed in many of the accounts of the wanderings and in the leaders' relationships with the people does not seem to allow for millions of Israelites in the desert. Still, we must take into account the persistence with which biblical tradition presents the figure of 600,000 and that (as Martin Noth has pointed out [11]) the statistics appear "uncontrived."

The key to the puzzle may well lie in the Hebrew word *elef* (אֶלֶף) which here and elsewhere is translated as "thousand," the meaning it has in contemporary usage. But it is possible that in earlier days *elef* did not have such a precise numerical value. Just as *revavot* (רְבָבוֹת) is often taken to convey "tens of thousands," so *elef* may originally have been an indefinite term, probably some social tribal unit, representing a value far below a thousand. In fact, in Num. 1:16 our translation renders the word not as "thousands" but as "contingents."

In time this meaning of *elef* was lost or reinterpreted and "one thousand" was the only sense understood. For in the days of the monarchy, when the old tribal-federal structure had given way to a more centralized military establishment, the army had units of one thousand men with an officer appointed by the crown. By this time, the old figures and terms were comprehended in the light of current experience which would explain the large figures in the transmitted text [12].

Thus, the tribe of Reuben is said to have enrolled "46 *elef* 500" fighting men and usually this is understood to mean 46,500 persons. But, by reading *elef* as "contingent," we would translate verse 21 as: "Those enrolled from the tribe of Reuben: 46 contingents [=] 500." Applying this method to the other tribes, we would read each figure this way: the "thousands" represent contingents, the hundreds the actual muster of fighting men. Therefore, Judah would have had 600 men in arms, Zebulun 400. Gad and Asher would have contributed the most, 650 each. Altogether the Israelite fighting force

---

[1] Kautzsch and Cazelles suggest (by dint of *gematria*) that 603 is meant to present the numerical value of בְּנֵי יִשְׂרָאֵל (*Bene Yisrael*) [9].

would have amounted to 5,550 men. Fighting forces of such size compare well with other ancient armies, as attested in Mari and elsewhere. (See Hallo's essay.)

This theory, while it does not solve all other difficulties, would suggest a total of about 20,000 Israelites in the desert. The interpretation also gives due credit to the care with which traditions were transmitted. We may no longer fully understand their meaning (nor, in this case, was this meaning fully understood when the Bible was committed to writing), but we do well to take the tradition itself seriously.

GLEANINGS

In the Wilderness (Num. 1:1)

What an unlikely place to meet God! How quickly we decide, when we are faced with uncongenial circumstances, that we are not likely to be able to communicate with God! How often do we quickly and glibly defend our spiritual obtuseness by pointing to unfavorable conditions and situations!

This book reminds us that there is no condition, there is no circumstance, there is no travail in which people cannot hear the voice of God if they are determined to hear it.

Out of the desert, with all of its dangers, came the Torah, which is our proudest possession and gives to our group-life as Jews its most authentic character and to all humanity the most valid promise of continuing creative contributions to the total fund of human understanding. That voice spoke in the desert.   M. ADLER [13]

Torah and Wilderness

Why was the Torah given in the wilderness? Because the desert is open and accessible to all mankind, as it is said (Isa. 55:1): "Let everyone who is thirsty come for water" (i.e., for Torah).

Why was the Torah not given in the Promised Land? So that no one tribe would have a preferred claim. Moreover, as the Torah came from a land neither sown nor tilled, so Torah scholars should live without sowing or tilling, that is, they should be relieved of the yoke of earning a living.   MIDRASH [14]

The wilderness is the most miserable of all places. Having received the Torah there, Israel could take its Torah to the deprived of the earth, and from lowliness ascend to the heights.

CHASIDIC [15]

Who preserves Torah? He who makes himself like the desert: set apart from the world.

MIDRASH [16]

To Both

Eighteen times it says in the Torah (as in Num. 2:2) that God addressed Moses and Aaron equally. This became a model for the *Shemoneh-esreh*, the Eighteen Benedictions of the traditional prayer service.   MIDRASH [17]

Counting People

There was until quite recently an ambivalence toward counting people and toward knowing their ages. For there was a feeling that knowing a person's "number" was equivalent to knowing his essence, and such knowledge was ultimately a divine prerogative (e.g., knowing when "someone's number was up"). However important a census might be, it had to have divine sanction, and if it did not—as in David's time—the consequences could be catastrophic (II Sam. 24). A latter-day reflection of this ambivalence was the hesitation of Jews to keep an exact record of their own years or the habit of counting people in their presence by saying, "Not one, not two,

not three . . ."—as if to tell God that they were not really presuming on His privileges.

Another aspect of this ambivalence toward numbering is the idea that it sets a limit. Growth and blessing appear unlimited only so long as their limits are not known; they become circumscribed when "numbered" [18]. Such "knowledge is death" [19].

A Census

When the Children of Israel are numbered for a proper purpose, their numbers are preserved (as here), but, when they are not, their numbers are diminished (as in II Sam. 24).   MIDRASH [20].

A Numbering

Because the love of them is before Him, He counts them every hour. When they went out of Egypt He counted them and when they transgressed with the golden calf He counted them. . . .

When He came to put upon them His *Shechinah* He counted them. . . .   RASHI [21]

The Lord of Hosts He counts them, counts them
   every hour,
Each single, irreplaceable dear head,
Beloved ones in freedom and in sin;
He numbers them amongst the living and the
   dead.

And when to each the moment of His giving
   comes,
The moment of indwelling in each compassed
   soul,
He counts, that love should not except
The least and most unworthy from life's goal.

That none be missing then, His love
Each solitary life to number and to count
Remembers, fearing one be strayed
When the *Shechinah* rests upon the mount.

A. K. BLANK [22]

Priestly Service

These two chapters treat of the composition and duties of the priestly families not mentioned in the previous section. We hear first of the family of Aaron, then of the remainder of the Levites, and finally of the first-born of the Israelites, who are assigned to divine service. Chapter 4 records additional census figures, but these relate specifically to service in the Tabernacle.

It will be noted that the duties of the priests appear to be very limited. They are not depicted as leaders and guides; and their function is un-assuming—in a sense, negative: they are held responsible for protecting the holy things from unauthorized personnel. For by definition and Hebrew usage the sacred is separate and holiness is apartness.*

(A new weekly portion, *Naso*, begins with 4:21.)

---

* This is the frequent meaning of קָדוֹשׁ (*kadosh*). Thus Sinai is holy in that it is unap-proachable (Exod. 19:23); the Sabbath is set aside and declared holy (Gen. 2:3).

וְהַעֲמַדְתָּ אֹתוֹ לִפְנֵי אַהֲרֹן הַכֹּהֵן וְשֵׁרְתוּ אֹתוֹ:   א וְאֵלֶּה תּוֹלְדֹת אַהֲרֹן וּמֹשֶׁה בְּיוֹם דִּבֶּר יְהֹוָה אֶת־מֹשֶׁה

ז וְשָׁמְרוּ אֶת־מִשְׁמַרְתּוֹ וְאֶת־מִשְׁמֶרֶת כָּל־הָעֵדָה לִפְנֵי   בְּהַר סִינָי: ב וְאֵלֶּה שְׁמוֹת בְּנֵי־אַהֲרֹן הַבְּכֹר נָדָב

ח אֹהֶל מוֹעֵד לַעֲבֹד אֶת־עֲבֹדַת הַמִּשְׁכָּן: וְשָׁמְרוּ אֶת־   ג וַאֲבִיהוּא אֶלְעָזָר וְאִיתָמָר: אֵלֶּה שְׁמוֹת בְּנֵי אַהֲרֹן

כָּל־כְּלֵי אֹהֶל מוֹעֵד וְאֶת־מִשְׁמֶרֶת בְּנֵי יִשְׂרָאֵל לַעֲבֹד   ד הַכֹּהֲנִים הַמְּשֻׁחִים אֲשֶׁר־מִלֵּא יָדָם לְכַהֵן: וַיָּמָת נָדָב

ט אֶת־עֲבֹדַת הַמִּשְׁכָּן: וְנָתַתָּה אֶת־הַלְוִיִּם לְאַהֲרֹן וּלְבָנָיו   וַאֲבִיהוּא לִפְנֵי יְהֹוָה בְּהַקְרִבָם אֵשׁ זָרָה לִפְנֵי יְהֹוָה

י נְתוּנִם נְתוּנִם הֵמָּה לוֹ מֵאֵת בְּנֵי יִשְׂרָאֵל: וְאֶת־אַהֲרֹן   בְּמִדְבַּר סִינַי וּבָנִים לֹא־הָיוּ לָהֶם וַיְכַהֵן אֶלְעָזָר

וְאֶת־בָּנָיו תִּפְקֹד וְשָׁמְרוּ אֶת־כְּהֻנָּתָם וְהַזָּר הַקָּרֵב   וְאִיתָמָר עַל־פְּנֵי אַהֲרֹן אֲבִיהֶם: פ

יוּמָת: פ   ה וַיְדַבֵּר יְהֹוָה אֶל־מֹשֶׁה לֵּאמֹר: הַקְרֵב אֶת־מַטֵּה לֵוִי

1] This is the line of Aaron and Moses at the time that the LORD spoke with Moses on Mount Sinai. **2]** These were the names of Aaron's sons: Nadab the first-born and Abihu, Eleazar, and Ithamar; **3]** those were the names of Aaron's sons, the anointed priests who were ordained for priesthood. **4]** But Nadab and Abihu died by the will of the LORD, when they offered alien fire before the LORD in the wilderness of Sinai; and they left no sons. So it was Eleazar and Ithamar who served as priests in the lifetime of their father Aaron.

5] The LORD spoke to Moses, saying: **6]** Advance the tribe of Levi and place them in attendance upon Aaron the priest to serve him. **7]** They shall perform duties for him and for the whole community before the Tent of Meeting, doing the work of the Tabernacle. **8]** They shall take charge of all the furnishings of the Tent of Meeting—a duty on behalf of the Israelites—doing the work of the Tabernacle. **9]** You shall assign the Levites to Aaron and to his sons: they are formally assigned to him from among the Israelites. **10]** You shall make Aaron and his sons responsible for observing their priestly duties; and any outsider who encroaches shall be put to death.

3:1] *This is the line.* תּוֹלְדֹת (*toledot*), a genealogical formula which—especially in Genesis (see Gen. 2:4)—often serves as an introduction to a new section.

3] *Ordained.* The Hebrew implies an act of sacred investiture, saying that the priests' hands were filled, possibly referring to a ceremony in which they received some token to have or hold. See at Exod. 27:41.

The Akkadian has the expression "to fill into the hand," in the sense of "to appoint" [1].

4] *By the will of the Lord.* Better "before the Lord," relating it more clearly to Lev. 10:1–7 where the story of their death is told.

Left no sons. Else they would have inherited the priesthood and would be mentioned here. See also I Chron. 24:2.

6] *Tribe of Levi.* Its members are to serve the Aaronide priests (*Kohanim*, singular *Kohen* [2]), doing the more menial tasks (see Num. 3:9; 18:6). The distinction of three classes of Jews—the priestly *Kohen*, the Levite, and the plain Israelite—

survived the destruction of the Second Temple in a number of observances and customs: at the reading of the Torah, "A priest reads first, and after him a Levite, and after him an Israelite—in the interest of peace" [3]; at the Passover table three pieces of matzah placed on the plate were popularly named for the three classes of Jews. Historically, however, the top and bottom matzot at the Seder table represented the "double bread" לֶחֶם מִשְׁנֶה (*lechem mishneh*) prescribed for representing the "bread of affliction" [4].

In attendance. On their persons. In traditional synagogues to this day, Levites help wash the Aaronide *Kohanim* before they mount the rostrum for the priestly benediction of Num. 6:22 ff.

9] *Formally assigned.* The Hebrew has a legal flavor achieved by the mechanism of repeating the word "assigned": *netunim netunim*. According to B. A. Levine, the term denotes that the Levites had the status of a guild, similar to organizations existing in Ugarit [5].

10] *Outsider.* See Num. 1:51.

יא וַיְדַבֵּ֥ר יְהוָ֖ה אֶל־מֹשֶׁ֥ה לֵּאמֹֽר: וַאֲנִ֞י הִנֵּ֧ה לָקַ֣חְתִּי אֶת־
הַלְוִיִּ֗ם מִתּוֹךְ֙ בְּנֵ֣י יִשְׂרָאֵ֔ל תַּ֥חַת כָּל־בְּכ֖וֹר פֶּ֣טֶר רֶ֑חֶם
יב מִבְּנֵ֣י יִשְׂרָאֵ֑ל וְהָ֥יוּ לִ֖י הַלְוִיִּֽם: כִּ֣י לִי֮ כָּל־בְּכוֹר֒ בְּיוֹם֩
הַכֹּתִ֨י כָל־בְּכ֜וֹר בְּאֶ֣רֶץ מִצְרַ֗יִם הִקְדַּ֨שְׁתִּי לִ֤י כָל־
בְּכוֹר֙ בְּיִשְׂרָאֵ֔ל מֵאָדָ֖ם עַד־בְּהֵמָ֑ה לִ֣י יִהְי֔וּ אֲנִ֖י
יג יְהוָֽה: פ

יד וַיְדַבֵּ֤ר יְהוָה֙ אֶל־מֹשֶׁ֔ה בְּמִדְבַּ֥ר סִינַ֖י לֵאמֹֽר: פְּקֹד֙
אֶת־בְּנֵ֣י לֵוִ֔י לְבֵ֥ית אֲבֹתָ֖ם לְמִשְׁפְּחֹתָ֑ם כָּל־זָכָ֛ר מִבֶּן־
טו חֹ֥דֶשׁ וָמַ֖עְלָה תִּפְקְדֵֽם: וַיִּפְקֹ֥ד אֹתָ֛ם מֹשֶׁ֖ה עַל־פִּ֣י
טז יְהוָ֑ה כַּאֲשֶׁ֖ר צֻוָּֽה: וַיִּֽהְיוּ־אֵ֥לֶּה בְנֵֽי־לֵוִ֖י בִּשְׁמֹתָ֑ם גֵּרְשׁ֕וֹן
יז וּקְהָ֖ת וּמְרָרִֽי: וְאֵ֛לֶּה שְׁמ֥וֹת בְּנֵֽי־גֵרְשׁ֖וֹן לְמִשְׁפְּחֹתָ֑ם

יח לִבְנִ֖י וְשִׁמְעִ֑י: וּבְנֵ֣י קְהָ֗ת לְמִשְׁפְּחֹתָ֔ם עַמְרָ֥ם וְיִצְהָ֖ר
יט חֶבְר֣וֹן וְעֻזִּיאֵ֑ל וּבְנֵ֤י מְרָרִי֙ לְמִשְׁפְּחֹתָ֔ם מַחְלִ֖י וּמוּשִׁ֑י
כ אֵ֥לֶּה הֵ֛ם מִשְׁפְּחֹ֥ת הַלֵּוִ֖י לְבֵ֥ית אֲבֹתָֽם: לְגֵרְשׁ֗וֹן
כא מִשְׁפַּ֙חַת֙ הַלִּבְנִ֔י וּמִשְׁפַּ֖חַת הַשִּׁמְעִ֑י אֵ֣לֶּה הֵ֔ם מִשְׁפְּחֹ֖ת
כב הַגֵּרְשֻׁנִּֽי: פְּקֻדֵיהֶם֙ בְּמִסְפַּ֣ר כָּל־זָכָ֔ר מִבֶּן־חֹ֖דֶשׁ
וָמָ֑עְלָה פְּקֻ֣דֵיהֶ֔ם שִׁבְעַ֥ת אֲלָפִ֖ים וַחֲמֵ֥שׁ מֵאֽוֹת:
כג מִשְׁפְּחֹ֖ת הַגֵּרְשֻׁנִּ֑י אַחֲרֵ֧י הַמִּשְׁכָּ֛ן יַחֲנ֖וּ יָֽמָּה: וּנְשִׂ֥יא בֵֽית־
כד אָ֛ב לַגֵּרְשֻׁנִּ֖י אֶלְיָסָ֥ף בֶּן־לָאֵֽל: וּמִשְׁמֶ֤רֶת בְּנֵֽי־גֵרְשׁוֹן֙
כה בְּאֹ֣הֶל מוֹעֵ֔ד הַמִּשְׁכָּ֖ן וְהָאֹ֑הֶל מִכְסֵ֕הוּ וּמָסַ֕ךְ פֶּ֖תַח
כו אֹ֥הֶל מוֹעֵֽד: וְקַלְעֵ֣י הֶֽחָצֵ֗ר וְאֶת־מָסַךְ֙ פֶּ֣תַח הֶֽחָצֵ֔ר
אֲשֶׁ֧ר עַל־הַמִּשְׁכָּ֛ן וְעַל־הַמִּזְבֵּ֖חַ סָבִ֑יב וְאֵת֙ מֵֽיתָרָ֔יו

11] The LORD spoke to Moses, saying: **12]** I hereby take the Levites from among the Israelites in place of all the first-born, the first issue of the womb among the Israelites: the Levites shall be Mine. **13]** For every first-born is Mine: at the time that I smote every first-born in the land of Egypt, I consecrated every first-born in Israel, man and beast, to Myself, to be Mine, the LORD's.

14] The LORD spoke to Moses in the wilderness of Sinai, saying: **15]** Record the Levites by ancestral house and by clan; record every male among them from the age of one month up. **16]** So Moses recorded them at the command of the LORD, as he was bidden. **17]** These were the sons of Levi by name: Gershon, Kohath, and Merari. **18]** These were the names of the sons of Gershon by clan: Libni and Shimei. **19]** The sons of Kohath by clan: Amram and Izhar, Hebron and Uzziel. **20]** The sons of Merari by clan: Mahli and Mushi.

These were the clans of the Levites within their ancestral houses:

21] To Gershon belonged the clan of the Libnites and the clan of the Shimeites; those were the clans of the Gershonites. **22]** The recorded entries of all their males from the age of one month up, as recorded, came to 7,500. **23]** The clans of the Gershonites were to camp behind the Tabernacle, to the west. **24]** The chieftain of the ancestral house of the Gershonites was Eliasaph son of Lael. **25]** The duties of the Gershonites in the Tent of Meeting comprised: the tabernacle, the tent, its covering, and the screen for the entrance of the Tent of Meeting; **26]** the hangings of the enclosure, the screen for the entrance of the enclosure which surrounds the Tabernacle, the cords thereof, and the altar—all the service connected with these.

13] *Mine, the Lord's.* An emphatic formula; literally, "I am the Lord."

15] *Record the Levites.* The census may be compared to Exod. 6:16–19 and to Num. 26:58 where some differences occur.

Age of one month. In Jewish tradition a child must live a month before being considered fully viable, a *ben kayama* [6]. Neither funeral nor mourning practices are observed if the child has not reached this age, and the child is considered as if stillborn [7].

25] *Tabernacle.* Apparently distinguished here from the "Tent." See Num. 1:1.

לד אֵלֶּה הֵם מִשְׁפְּחֹת מְרָרִי: וּפְקֻדֵיהֶם בְּמִסְפַּר כָּל־זָכָר
לה מִבֶּן־חֹדֶשׁ וָמָעְלָה שֵׁשֶׁת אֲלָפִים וּמָאתָיִם: וּנְשִׂיא בֵית־
אָב לְמִשְׁפַּחַת מְרָרִי צוּרִיאֵל בֶּן־אֲבִיחָיִל עַל יֶרֶךְ
לו הַמִּשְׁכָּן יַחֲנוּ צָפֹנָה: וּפְקֻדַּת מִשְׁמֶרֶת בְּנֵי מְרָרִי קַרְשֵׁי
הַמִּשְׁכָּן וּבְרִיחָיו וְעַמֻּדָיו וַאֲדָנָיו וְכָל־כֵּלָיו וְכֹל
לז עֲבֹדָתוֹ: וְעַמֻּדֵי הֶחָצֵר סָבִיב וְאַדְנֵיהֶם וִיתֵדֹתָם
לח וּמֵיתְרֵיהֶם: וְהַחֹנִים לִפְנֵי הַמִּשְׁכָּן קֵדְמָה לִפְנֵי אֹהֶל־
מוֹעֵד מִזְרָחָה מֹשֶׁה וְאַהֲרֹן וּבָנָיו שֹׁמְרִים מִשְׁמֶרֶת
הַמִּקְדָּשׁ לְמִשְׁמֶרֶת בְּנֵי יִשְׂרָאֵל וְהַזָּר הַקָּרֵב יוּמָת:
לט כָּל־פְּקוּדֵי הַלְוִיִּם אֲשֶׁר פָּקַד מֹשֶׁה וְאַהֲרֹן עַל־פִּי
יְהוָה לְמִשְׁפְּחֹתָם כָּל־זָכָר מִבֶּן־חֹדֶשׁ וָמַעְלָה שְׁנַיִם

כז לְכֹל עֲבֹדָתוֹ: ס וְלִקְהָת מִשְׁפַּחַת הָעַמְרָמִי
וּמִשְׁפַּחַת הַיִּצְהָרִי וּמִשְׁפַּחַת הַחֶבְרֹנִי וּמִשְׁפַּחַת
כח הָעָזִּיאֵלִי אֵלֶּה הֵם מִשְׁפְּחֹת הַקְּהָתִי: בְּמִסְפַּר כָּל־
זָכָר מִבֶּן־חֹדֶשׁ וָמָעְלָה שְׁמֹנַת אֲלָפִים וְשֵׁשׁ מֵאוֹת
כט שֹׁמְרֵי מִשְׁמֶרֶת הַקֹּדֶשׁ: מִשְׁפְּחֹת בְּנֵי־קְהָת יַחֲנוּ עַל
ל יֶרֶךְ הַמִּשְׁכָּן תֵּימָנָה: וּנְשִׂיא בֵית־אָב לְמִשְׁפְּחֹת
לא הַקְּהָתִי אֱלִיצָפָן בֶּן־עֻזִּיאֵל: וּמִשְׁמַרְתָּם הָאָרֹן
וְהַשֻּׁלְחָן וְהַמְּנֹרָה וְהַמִּזְבְּחֹת וּכְלֵי הַקֹּדֶשׁ אֲשֶׁר
לב יְשָׁרְתוּ בָּהֶם וְהַמָּסָךְ וְכֹל עֲבֹדָתוֹ: וּנְשִׂיא נְשִׂיאֵי הַלֵּוִי
אֶלְעָזָר בֶּן־אַהֲרֹן הַכֹּהֵן פְּקֻדַּת שֹׁמְרֵי מִשְׁמֶרֶת
לג הַקֹּדֶשׁ: לִמְרָרִי מִשְׁפַּחַת הַמַּחְלִי וּמִשְׁפַּחַת הַמּוּשִׁי

27] To Kohath belonged the clan of the Amramites, the clan of the Izharites, the clan of the Hebronites, and the clan of the Uzzielites; those were the clans of the Kohathites. 28] All the listed males from the age of one month up came to 8,600, attending to the duties of the sanctuary. 29] The clans of the Kohathites were to camp along the south side of the Tabernacle. 30] The chieftain of the ancestral house of the Kohathite clans was Elizaphan son of Uzziel. 31] Their duties comprised: the ark, the table, the lampstand, the altars, and the sacred utensils that were used with them, and the screen—all the service connected with these. 32] The head chieftain of the Levites was Eleazar son of Aaron the priest, in charge of those attending to the duties of the sanctuary.

33] To Merari belonged the clan of the Mahlites and the clan of the Mushites; those were the clans of Merari. 34] The recorded entries of all their males from the age of one month up came to 6,200. 35] The chieftain of the ancestral house of the clans of Merari was Zuriel son of Abihail. They were to camp along the north side of the Tabernacle. 36] The assigned duties of the Merarites comprised: the planks of the Tabernacle, its bars, posts, and sockets, and all its furnishings—all the service connected with these; 37] also the posts around the enclosure, and their sockets, pegs, and cords.

38] Those who were to camp before the Tabernacle, in front—before the Tent of Meeting, on the east—were Moses and Aaron and his sons, attending to the duties of the sanctuary, as a duty on behalf of the Israelites; and any outsider who encroached was to be put to death. 39] All the Levites who were recorded, whom at the LORD's command Moses and Aaron recorded by their clans, all the males from the age of one month up, came to 22,000.

27] *Amramites.* The descendants of Moses' father Amram.

30] *Kohathite clans.* Who had the most important duties.

31] *Screen.* The screening curtain, see Num. 4:5.

39] *And Aaron.* The Hebrew vocalized text has diacritical dots above the name. What was intended thereby is not clear; perhaps the reading of the name was to be omitted as it is in the Syriac and Samaritan versions. According to the Rabbis it meant that Aaron was not included in the levitical census [8].

מ וְעֶשְׂרִים אָלֶף: ס וַיֹּאמֶר יְהוָה אֶל־מֹשֶׁה פְּקֹד כָּל־
בְּכֹר זָכָר לִבְנֵי יִשְׂרָאֵל מִבֶּן־חֹדֶשׁ וָמָעְלָה וְשָׂא אֵת
מא מִסְפַּר שְׁמֹתָם: וְלָקַחְתָּ אֶת־הַלְוִיִּם לִי אֲנִי יְהוָה תַּחַת
כָּל־בְּכֹר בִּבְנֵי יִשְׂרָאֵל וְאֵת בֶּהֱמַת הַלְוִיִּם תַּחַת כָּל־
מב בְּכוֹר בְּבֶהֱמַת בְּנֵי יִשְׂרָאֵל: וַיִּפְקֹד מֹשֶׁה כַּאֲשֶׁר צִוָּה
מג יְהוָה אֹתוֹ אֶת־כָּל־בְּכוֹר בִּבְנֵי יִשְׂרָאֵל: וַיְהִי כָל־
בְּכוֹר זָכָר בְּמִסְפַּר שֵׁמֹת מִבֶּן־חֹדֶשׁ וָמַעְלָה
לִפְקֻדֵיהֶם שְׁנַיִם וְעֶשְׂרִים אֶלֶף שְׁלֹשָׁה וְשִׁבְעִים
וּמָאתָיִם:
מד וַיְדַבֵּר יְהוָה אֶל־מֹשֶׁה לֵּאמֹר: קַח אֶת־הַלְוִיִּם תַּחַת
כָּל־בְּכוֹר בִּבְנֵי יִשְׂרָאֵל וְאֶת־בֶּהֱמַת הַלְוִיִּם תַּחַת
מו בְּהֶמְתָּם וְהָיוּ־לִי הַלְוִיִּם אֲנִי יְהוָה: וְאֵת פְּדוּיֵי

הַשְּׁלֹשָׁה וְהַשִּׁבְעִים וְהַמָּאתַיִם הָעֹדְפִים עַל־הַלְוִיִּם
מז מִבְּכוֹר בְּנֵי יִשְׂרָאֵל: וְלָקַחְתָּ חֲמֵשֶׁת חֲמֵשֶׁת שְׁקָלִים
לַגֻּלְגֹּלֶת בְּשֶׁקֶל הַקֹּדֶשׁ תִּקָּח עֶשְׂרִים גֵּרָה הַשָּׁקֶל:
מח וְנָתַתָּה הַכֶּסֶף לְאַהֲרֹן וּלְבָנָיו פְּדוּיֵי הָעֹדְפִים בָּהֶם:
מט וַיִּקַּח מֹשֶׁה אֵת כֶּסֶף הַפִּדְיוֹם מֵאֵת הָעֹדְפִים עַל
נ פְּדוּיֵי הַלְוִיִּם: מֵאֵת בְּכוֹר בְּנֵי יִשְׂרָאֵל לָקַח אֶת־
הַכֶּסֶף חֲמִשָּׁה וְשִׁשִּׁים וּשְׁלֹשׁ מֵאוֹת וָאֶלֶף בְּשֶׁקֶל
נא הַקֹּדֶשׁ: וַיִּתֵּן מֹשֶׁה אֶת־כֶּסֶף הַפְּדֻיִם לְאַהֲרֹן וּלְבָנָיו
עַל־פִּי יְהוָה כַּאֲשֶׁר צִוָּה יְהוָה אֶת־מֹשֶׁה:
פ
ד וַיְדַבֵּר יְהוָה אֶל־מֹשֶׁה וְאֶל־אַהֲרֹן לֵאמֹר: נָשֹׂא אֶת־
רֹאשׁ בְּנֵי קְהָת מִתּוֹךְ בְּנֵי לֵוִי לְמִשְׁפְּחֹתָם לְבֵית

*נא חסר ר.

40] The LORD said to Moses: Record every first-born male of the Israelite people from the age of one month up, and make a list of their names; 41] and take the Levites for Me the LORD, in place of every first-born among the Israelite people, and the cattle of the Levites in place of every first-born among the cattle of the Israelites. 42] So Moses recorded all the first-born among the Israelites, as the LORD had commanded him. 43] All the first-born males as listed by name, recorded from the age of one month up, came to 22,273.

44] The LORD spoke to Moses, saying: 45] Take the Levites in place of all the first-born among the Israelite people, and the cattle of the Levites in place of their cattle; and the Levites shall be Mine, the LORD's. 46] And as the redemption price of the 273 Israelite first-born over and above the number of the Levites, 47] take five shekels per head—take this by the sanctuary weight, twenty *gerahs* to the shekel— 48] and give the money to Aaron and his sons as the redemption price for those who are in excess. 49] So Moses took the redemption money from those over and above the ones redeemed by the Levites; 50] he took the money from the first-born of the Israelites, 1,365 sanctuary shekels. 51] And Moses gave the redemption money to Aaron and his sons at the LORD's bidding, as the LORD had commanded Moses.

1] The LORD spoke to Moses and Aaron, saying:
2] Take a [separate] census of the Kohathites among the Levites, by the clans of their

40] *Record every first-born male.* He is considered to belong to God. Moses previously surrendered 22,273 first-born Israelites to the Lord and received 22,000 Levites in their stead. He therefore has to be compensated for the difference of 273 (verse 46). (It is clear that the explanation given in the commentary to the previous unit, with regard to the census, does not apply here. When the text was fixed in its present form the Hebrew *elef* was here understood as "thousand," and not as "contingent.")

41] *Cattle.* This provision appears to contradict Num. 18:15, 17, where the rule is stated that only unclean animals are to be redeemed. The Talmud, in order to resolve the contradiction, applies chapter 3 to clean animals only [9].

Gray suggests emending בֶּהֱמַת (*behemat*, cattle of) to בְּכוֹר (*bechor*, first-born) [10].

47] *Sanctuary weight.* Amounting to a little less than half an ounce of silver per shekel.

48] *Those who are in excess.* Referring to the 273; see at verse 40. The Rabbis suggest that the procedure described was based on drawing lots [11].

ט תֵּחַשׁ וְשָׂמוּ אֶת־בַּדָּיו: וְלָקְחוּ בֶּגֶד תְּכֵלֶת וְכִסּוּ אֶת־   ג אֲבֹתָם: מִבֶּן שְׁלֹשִׁים שָׁנָה וָמַעְלָה וְעַד בֶּן־חֲמִשִּׁים

מְנֹרַת הַמָּאוֹר וְאֶת־נֵרֹתֶיהָ וְאֶת־מַלְקָחֶיהָ וְאֶת־   שָׁנָה כָּל־בָּא לַצָּבָא לַעֲשׂוֹת מְלָאכָה בְּאֹהֶל מוֹעֵד:

מַחְתֹּתֶיהָ וְאֵת כָּל־כְּלֵי שַׁמְנָהּ אֲשֶׁר יְשָׁרְתוּ־לָהּ בָּהֶם: ד זֹאת עֲבֹדַת בְּנֵי־קְהָת בְּאֹהֶל מוֹעֵד קֹדֶשׁ הַקֳּדָשִׁים:

י וְנָתְנוּ אֹתָהּ וְאֶת־כָּל־כֵּלֶיהָ אֶל־מִכְסֵה עוֹר תַּחַשׁ וְנָתְנוּ   ה וּבָא אַהֲרֹן וּבָנָיו בִּנְסֹעַ הַמַּחֲנֶה וְהוֹרִדוּ אֵת פָּרֹכֶת

יא עַל־הַמּוֹט: וְעַל מִזְבַּח הַזָּהָב יִפְרְשׂוּ בֶּגֶד תְּכֵלֶת   ו הַמָּסָךְ וְכִסּוּ־בָהּ אֵת אֲרֹן הָעֵדֻת: וְנָתְנוּ עָלָיו כְּסוּי

וְכִסּוּ אֹתוֹ בַּמִּכְסֵה עוֹר תַּחַשׁ וְשָׂמוּ אֶת־בַּדָּיו: עוֹר תַּחַשׁ וּפָרְשׂוּ בֶגֶד־כְּלִיל תְּכֵלֶת מִלְמָעְלָה וְשָׂמוּ

יב וְלָקְחוּ אֶת־כָּל־כְּלֵי הַשָּׁרֵת אֲשֶׁר יְשָׁרְתוּ־בָם בַּקֹּדֶשׁ   ז בַּדָּיו: וְעַל שֻׁלְחַן הַפָּנִים יִפְרְשׂוּ בֶּגֶד תְּכֵלֶת וְנָתְנוּ

וְנָתְנוּ אֶל־בֶּגֶד תְּכֵלֶת וְכִסּוּ אוֹתָם בְּמִכְסֵה עוֹר תַּחַשׁ   עָלָיו אֶת־הַקְּעָרֹת וְאֶת־הַכַּפֹּת וְאֶת־הַמְּנַקִּיֹּת וְאֵת

יג וְנָתְנוּ עַל־הַמּוֹט: וְדִשְּׁנוּ אֶת־הַמִּזְבֵּחַ וּפָרְשׂוּ עָלָיו בֶּגֶד   ח קְשׂוֹת הַנָּסֶךְ וְלֶחֶם הַתָּמִיד עָלָיו יִהְיֶה: וּפָרְשׂוּ

יד אַרְגָּמָן: וְנָתְנוּ עָלָיו אֶת־כָּל־כֵּלָיו אֲשֶׁר יְשָׁרְתוּ עָלָיו   עֲלֵיהֶם בֶּגֶד תּוֹלַעַת שָׁנִי וְכִסּוּ אֹתוֹ בְּמִכְסֵה עוֹר

ancestral house,   **3]** from the age of thirty years up to the age of fifty, all who are subject to service, to perform tasks for the Tent of Meeting.   **4]** This is the responsibility of the Kohathites in the Tent of Meeting: the most sacred objects.

5] At the breaking of camp, Aaron and his sons shall go in and take down the screening curtain and cover the Ark of the Pact with it.   **6]** They shall lay a covering of dolphin skin over it and spread a cloth of pure blue on top; and they shall put its poles in place.

7] Over the table of display they shall spread a blue cloth; they shall place upon it the bowls, the ladles, the jars, and the libation jugs; and the regular bread shall rest upon it.   **8]** They shall spread over these a crimson cloth which they shall cover with a covering of dolphin skin; and they shall put the poles in place.

9] Then they shall take a blue cloth and cover the lampstand for lighting, with its lamps, its tongs, and its fire pans, as well as all the oil vessels that are used in its service.   **10]** They shall put it and all its furnishings into a covering of dolphin skin, which they shall then place on a carrying frame.

11] Next they shall spread a blue cloth over the altar of gold and cover it with a covering of dolphin skin; and they shall put its poles in place.   **12]** They shall take all the service vessels with which the service in the sanctuary is performed, put them into a blue cloth and cover them with a covering of dolphin skin, which they shall then place on a carrying frame.   **13]** They shall remove the ashes from the [copper] altar and spread a purple cloth over it.   **14]** Upon it

---

4:3] *Age of thirty years.* In Num. 8:23–26 the minimum age for being counted in this separate census is twenty-five, in I Chron. 23:24–27 it is twenty. The Rabbis explain the difference by positing that there was an additional period of apprenticeship and also a need for an expanded work force in the Temple [12].

6] *Dolphin skin.* The translation represents a reasonable guess, the precise meaning of *tachash* being unknown. See at Exod. 25:5.
Others suggest goat skin [13].
   Blue. A color which was usually obtained from certain kinds of shellfish. The Phoenicians were

famous for a cloth in this hue. Colors appear to be used symbolically in biblical writings (e.g., Exod. 24:10), although the nature of such symbolism remains often in doubt [14]. On the use of blue in *tzitzit*, see commentary on Num. 15.

7] *Regular bread.* The bread which was regularly presented (so New English Bible) and which is described in Exod. 25:30.

8] *Crimson.* The color was obtained from the bodies of certain worms and insects which were dried and ground into powder.

11] *Altar of gold.* Described in Exod. 30:1–6.

בָּהֶם אֶת־הַמַּחְתֹּת אֶת־הַמִּזְלָגֹת וְאֶת־הַיָּעִים וְאֶת־
הַמִּזְרָקֹת כֹּל כְּלֵי הַמִּזְבֵּחַ וּפָרְשׂוּ עָלָיו כְּסוּי עוֹר
טו תַּחַשׁ וְשָׂמוּ בַדָּיו: וְכִלָּה אַהֲרֹן וּבָנָיו לְכַסֹּת אֶת־
הַקֹּדֶשׁ וְאֶת־כָּל־כְּלֵי הַקֹּדֶשׁ בִּנְסֹעַ הַמַּחֲנֶה וְאַחֲרֵי־כֵן
יָבֹאוּ בְנֵי־קְהָת לָשֵׂאת וְלֹא־יִגְּעוּ אֶל־הַקֹּדֶשׁ וָמֵתוּ
טז אֵלֶּה מַשָּׂא בְנֵי־קְהָת בְּאֹהֶל מוֹעֵד: וּפְקֻדַּת אֶלְעָזָר
בֶּן־אַהֲרֹן הַכֹּהֵן שֶׁמֶן הַמָּאוֹר וּקְטֹרֶת הַסַּמִּים וּמִנְחַת
הַתָּמִיד וְשֶׁמֶן הַמִּשְׁחָה פְּקֻדַּת כָּל־הַמִּשְׁכָּן וְכָל־אֲשֶׁר־
בּוֹ בְּקֹדֶשׁ וּבְכֵלָיו:

פ

יז וַיְדַבֵּר יְהוָה אֶל־מֹשֶׁה וְאֶל־אַהֲרֹן לֵאמֹר: אַל־
יח תַּכְרִיתוּ אֶת־שֵׁבֶט מִשְׁפְּחֹת הַקְּהָתִי מִתּוֹךְ הַלְוִיִּם:
יט וְזֹאת עֲשׂוּ לָהֶם וְחָיוּ וְלֹא יָמֻתוּ בְּגִשְׁתָּם אֶת־קֹדֶשׁ

הַקֳּדָשִׁים אַהֲרֹן וּבָנָיו יָבֹאוּ וְשָׂמוּ אוֹתָם אִישׁ אִישׁ
כ עַל־עֲבֹדָתוֹ וְאֶל־מַשָּׂאוֹ: וְלֹא־יָבֹאוּ לִרְאוֹת כְּבַלַּע
אֶת־הַקֹּדֶשׁ וָמֵתוּ:

Haftarah Bemidbar, p. 1252

פ פ פ

כב וַיְדַבֵּר יְהוָה אֶל־מֹשֶׁה לֵּאמֹר: נָשֹׂא אֶת־רֹאשׁ בְּנֵי
כג גֵרְשׁוֹן גַּם־הֵם לְבֵית אֲבֹתָם לְמִשְׁפְּחֹתָם: מִבֶּן שְׁלֹשִׁים
שָׁנָה וָמַעְלָה עַד בֶּן־חֲמִשִּׁים שָׁנָה תִּפְקֹד אוֹתָם כָּל־
כד הַבָּא לִצְבֹא צָבָא לַעֲבֹד עֲבֹדָה בְּאֹהֶל מוֹעֵד: זֹאת
כה עֲבֹדַת מִשְׁפְּחֹת הַגֵּרְשֻׁנִּי לַעֲבֹד וּלְמַשָּׂא: וְנָשְׂאוּ אֶת־
יְרִיעֹת הַמִּשְׁכָּן וְאֶת־אֹהֶל מוֹעֵד מִכְסֵהוּ וּמִכְסֵה
הַתַּחַשׁ אֲשֶׁר־עָלָיו מִלְמָעְלָה וְאֶת־מָסַךְ פֶּתַח אֹהֶל
כו מוֹעֵד: וְאֵת קַלְעֵי הֶחָצֵר וְאֶת־מָסַךְ פֶּתַח שַׁעַר

---

they shall place all the vessels that are used in its service: the fire pans, the flesh hooks, the scrapers, and the basins—all the vessels of the altar—and over it they shall spread a covering of dolphin skin; and they shall put its poles in place.

15] When Aaron and his sons have finished covering the sacred objects and all the furnishings of the sacred objects at the breaking of camp, only then shall the Kohathites come and lift them, so that they do not come in contact with the sacred objects and die. These things in the Tent of Meeting shall be the porterage of the Kohathites.

16] Responsibility shall rest with Eleazar son of Aaron the priest for the lighting oil, the aromatic incense, the regular meal offering, and the anointing oil—responsibility for the whole Tabernacle and for everything consecrated that is in it or in its vessels.

17] The LORD spoke to Moses and Aaron, saying: **18]** Do not let the group of Kohathite clans be cut off from the Levites. **19]** Do this with them, that they may live and not die when they approach the most sacred objects: let Aaron and his sons go in and assign each of them to his duties and to his porterage. **20]** But let not [the Kohathites] go inside and witness the dismantling of the sanctuary, lest they die.

21] The LORD spoke to Moses, saying: **22]** Take [further] a census of the Gershonites, by their ancestral house and by their clans. **23]** Record them from the age of thirty years up to the age of fifty, all who are subject to service in the performance of tasks for the Tent of Meeting. **24]** These are the duties of the Gershonite clans as to labor and porterage: **25]** they shall carry the cloths of the Tabernacle, the Tent of Meeting with its covering, the covering of dolphin skin that is on top of it, and the screen for the entrance of the Tent of Meeting; **26]** the hangings of the enclosure, the screen at the entrance of the gate of the

---

15] *When Aaron . . . porterage of the Kohathites.* This continues verse 4, making verses 5–14 an insert. Also, verse 18 seems to continue verse 15, altogether suggesting a disordered text.

20] *Witness the dismantling.* Others, "look at the sacred objects even for a moment" (for this was likened to seeing God, which was a capital offense, I Sam. 6:19) [15].

עֲבֹדַת מִשְׁפַּחַת בְּנֵי מְרָרִי לְכָל־עֲבֹדָתָם בְּאֹהֶל   הֶחָצֵר אֲשֶׁר עַל־הַמִּשְׁכָּן וְעַל־הַמִּזְבֵּחַ סָבִיב וְאֵת

לד מוֹעֵד בְּיַד אִיתָמָר בֶּן־אַהֲרֹן הַכֹּהֵן: וַיִּפְקֹד מֹשֶׁה   מֵיתְרֵיהֶם וְאֶת־כָּל־כְּלֵי עֲבֹדָתָם וְאֵת כָּל־אֲשֶׁר יֵעָשֶׂה

וְאַהֲרֹן וּנְשִׂיאֵי הָעֵדָה אֶת־בְּנֵי הַקְּהָתִי לְמִשְׁפְּחֹתָם   כז לָהֶם וְעָבָדוּ: עַל־פִּי אַהֲרֹן וּבָנָיו תִּהְיֶה כָּל־עֲבֹדַת

לה וּלְבֵית אֲבֹתָם: מִבֶּן שְׁלֹשִׁים שָׁנָה וָמַעְלָה וְעַד בֶּן   בְּנֵי הַגֵּרְשֻׁנִּי לְכָל־מַשָּׂאָם וּלְכֹל עֲבֹדָתָם וּפְקַדְתֶּם

חֲמִשִּׁים שָׁנָה כָּל־הַבָּא לַצָּבָא לַעֲבֹדָה בְּאֹהֶל מוֹעֵד: כח עֲלֵהֶם בְּמִשְׁמֶרֶת אֵת כָּל־מַשָּׂאָם: זֹאת עֲבֹדַת

לו וַיִּהְיוּ פְקֻדֵיהֶם לְמִשְׁפְּחֹתָם אַלְפַּיִם שְׁבַע מֵאוֹת   מִשְׁפְּחֹת בְּנֵי הַגֵּרְשֻׁנִּי בְּאֹהֶל מוֹעֵד וּמִשְׁמַרְתָּם בְּיַד

לז וַחֲמִשִּׁים: אֵלֶּה פְקוּדֵי מִשְׁפְּחֹת הַקְּהָתִי כָּל־הָעֹבֵד   כט אִיתָמָר בֶּן־אַהֲרֹן הַכֹּהֵן: ס בְּנֵי מְרָרִי לְמִשְׁפְּחֹתָם

בְּאֹהֶל מוֹעֵד אֲשֶׁר פָּקַד מֹשֶׁה וְאַהֲרֹן עַל־פִּי יְהוָה   ל לְבֵית־אֲבֹתָם תִּפְקֹד אֹתָם: מִבֶּן שְׁלֹשִׁים שָׁנָה וָמַעְלָה

לח בְּיַד־מֹשֶׁה: ס וּפְקוּדֵי בְּנֵי גֵרְשׁוֹן לְמִשְׁפְּחוֹתָם   וְעַד בֶּן־חֲמִשִּׁים שָׁנָה תִּפְקְדֵם כָּל־הַבָּא לַצָּבָא לַעֲבֹד

לט וּלְבֵית אֲבֹתָם: מִבֶּן שְׁלֹשִׁים שָׁנָה וָמַעְלָה וְעַד בֶּן   לא אֶת־עֲבֹדַת אֹהֶל מוֹעֵד: וְזֹאת מִשְׁמֶרֶת מַשָּׂאָם לְכָל־

חֲמִשִּׁים שָׁנָה כָּל־הַבָּא לַצָּבָא לַעֲבֹדָה בְּאֹהֶל מוֹעֵד: עֲבֹדָתָם בְּאֹהֶל מוֹעֵד קַרְשֵׁי הַמִּשְׁכָּן וּבְרִיחָיו

מ וַיִּהְיוּ פְּקֻדֵיהֶם לְמִשְׁפְּחֹתָם לְבֵית אֲבֹתָם אַלְפַּיִם וְשֵׁשׁ   לב וְעַמּוּדָיו וַאֲדָנָיו: וְעַמּוּדֵי הֶחָצֵר סָבִיב וְאַדְנֵיהֶם

מאות וּשְׁלֹשִׁים: אֵלֶּה פְקוּדֵי מִשְׁפְּחֹת בְּנֵי גֵרְשׁוֹן כָּל־   וִיתֵדֹתָם וּמֵיתְרֵיהֶם לְכָל־כְּלֵיהֶם וּלְכֹל עֲבֹדָתָם

הָעֹבֵד בְּאֹהֶל מוֹעֵד אֲשֶׁר פָּקַד מֹשֶׁה וְאַהֲרֹן עַל־פִּי   לג וּבְשֵׁמֹת תִּפְקְדוּ אֶת־כְּלֵי מִשְׁמֶרֶת מַשָּׂאָם: זֹאת

---

enclosure that surrounds the Tabernacle, the cords thereof, and the altar, and all their service equipment and all their accessories; and they shall perform the service. 27] All the duties of the Gershonites, all their porterage and all their service, shall be performed on orders from Aaron and his sons; you shall make them responsible for attending to all their porterage. 28] Those are the duties of the Gershonite clans for the Tent of Meeting; they shall attend to them under the direction of Ithamar son of Aaron the priest.

29] As for the Merarites, you shall record them by the clans of their ancestral house; 30] you shall record them from the age of thirty years up to the age of fifty, all who are subject to service in the performance of the duties for the Tent of Meeting. 31] These are their porterage tasks in connection with their various duties for the Tent of Meeting: the planks, the bars, the posts, and the sockets of the Tabernacle; 32] all the posts around the enclosure and their sockets, pegs, and cords—all these furnishings and their service: you shall list by name the objects that are their porterage tasks. 33] Those are the duties of the Merarite clans, pertaining to their various duties in the Tent of Meeting under the direction of Ithamar son of Aaron the priest.

34] So Moses, Aaron, and the chieftains of the community recorded the Kohathites by the clans of their ancestral house, 35] from the age of thirty years up to the age of fifty, all who were subject to service for work relating to the Tent of Meeting. 36] Those recorded by their clans came to 2,750. 37] That was the enrollment of the Kohathite clan, all those who performed duties relating to the Tent of Meeting, whom Moses and Aaron recorded at the command of the LORD through Moses.

38] The Gershonites who were recorded by the clans of their ancestral house, 39] from the age of thiry years up to the age of fifty, all who were subject to service for work relating to the Tent of Meeting— 40] those recorded by the clans of their ancestral house came to 2,630. 41] That was the enrollment of the Gershonite clans, all those performing duties relating to the Tent of Meeting whom Moses and Aaron recorded at the command of the LORD.

מז וּלְבֵית אֲבֹתָם: מִבֶּן שְׁלֹשִׁים שָׁנָה וָמַעְלָה וְעַד בֶּן־
חֲמִשִּׁים שָׁנָה כָּל־הַבָּא לַעֲבֹד עֲבֹדַת עֲבֹדָה וַעֲבֹדַת
מח מַשָּׂא בְּאֹהֶל מוֹעֵד: וַיִּהְיוּ פְּקֻדֵיהֶם שְׁמֹנַת אֲלָפִים
מט וַחֲמֵשׁ מֵאוֹת וּשְׁמֹנִים: עַל־פִּי יְהוָה פָּקַד אוֹתָם בְּיַד־
מֹשֶׁה אִישׁ אִישׁ עַל־עֲבֹדָתוֹ וְעַל־מַשָּׂאוֹ וּפְקֻדָיו אֲשֶׁר־
צִוָּה יְהוָה אֶת־מֹשֶׁה:
פ

מב יְהוָה: וּפְקוּדֵי מִשְׁפְּחֹת בְּנֵי מְרָרִי לְמִשְׁפְּחֹתָם לְבֵית
מג אֲבֹתָם: מִבֶּן שְׁלֹשִׁים שָׁנָה וָמַעְלָה וְעַד בֶּן־חֲמִשִּׁים
מד שָׁנָה כָּל־הַבָּא לַצָּבָא לַעֲבֹדָה בְּאֹהֶל מוֹעֵד: וַיִּהְיוּ
מה פְקֻדֵיהֶם לְמִשְׁפְּחֹתָם שְׁלֹשֶׁת אֲלָפִים וּמָאתָיִם: אֵלֶּה
פְקוּדֵי מִשְׁפְּחֹת בְּנֵי מְרָרִי אֲשֶׁר פָּקַד מֹשֶׁה וְאַהֲרֹן
מו עַל־פִּי יְהוָה בְּיַד־מֹשֶׁה: כָּל־הַפְּקֻדִים אֲשֶׁר פָּקַד
מֹשֶׁה וְאַהֲרֹן וּנְשִׂיאֵי יִשְׂרָאֵל אֶת־הַלְוִיִּם לְמִשְׁפְּחֹתָם

* סם סבירין כאשר.

42] The enrollment of the Merarite clans by the clans of their ancestral house, 43] from the age of thirty years up to the age of fifty, all who were subject to service for work relating to the Tent of Meeting— 44] those recorded by their clans came to 3,200. 45] That was the enrollment of the Merarite clans which Moses and Aaron recorded at the command of the LORD through Moses.

46] All the Levites whom Moses, Aaron, and the chieftains of Israel recorded by the clans of their ancestral houses, 47] from the age of thirty years up to the age of fifty, all who were subject to duties of service and porterage relating to the Tent of Meeting— 48] those recorded came to 8,580. 49] Each one was given responsibility for his service and porterage at the command of the LORD through Moses, and each was recorded as the LORD had commanded Moses.

48] 8,580. Far too large a number considering the limited work required. In line with the explanation offered above, we would best understand: eight contingents amounting to 580 persons. Rashi's suggestion [16] that verse 47 refers to music during sacrificial offerings is forced and does not satisfactorily account for thousands of participants.

The First-Born

(See commentary on Gen. 25, for a discussion of primogeniture.)

"Every first-born is Mine," says the text (Num. 3:13) and explains that, when God smote the first-born in Egypt, He set aside as His own every first-born in Israel, both of man and beast. Since the consecration of all Israelite first-born to the service of God was not feasible because they were too many, a substitution was arranged by which the Levites were to be considered as substitutes for the first-born among the people. To this day, the practice of redeeming the first-born (*pidyon ha-ben*) has its place in Jewish tradition. It reenacts the ancient substitution by having the father of the child "purchase" his son from a priest.[1]

It is no longer clear how the original idea of God's special relationship with and ownership of the first-born arose and how it was exemplified in prebiblical days, but it is likely that it was related to primitive customs of sacrificing children to a divinity. This is reflected in God's final punishment of Pharaoh's Egypt, which consisted of claiming its first-born. It is probable that child sacrifice was at one time not completely unknown in Israel; the story of Jephthah's daughter (Judg. 11:30 ff.) shows that it was still a possibility in the eleventh century B.C.E. However, the practice was apparently rare and was soon abandoned, being considered an abomination.[2] The story of the Akedah (Gen. 22) shows God rejecting the sacrifice of Abraham's son and instead providing a ram as the offering. The divine claim was restricted to the first fruits of the land (which were to be set aside as holy and to be dedicated to the service of God) and in the human realm this claim was expressed through priestly substitution. The Midrash says that originally all Israelite first-born were priests, but after the sin with the golden calf the service in the sanctuary was confined to Levites [18].

The first-born not only has an obligating relationship to God, he also has corresponding privileges. He has the right to a special portion of the inheritance and he succeeds as head of the family [19]. Yet, although Deuteronomic law specifically prohibits the abridgment of the inheritance rights of the first-born (Deut. 21:15–17) and treats such rights, by implication, as inherent, God's choice remains free and outside these legal provisions: Jacob, Joseph, Moses, and David are second- or late-born. Biblical literature frequently dwells on the contrast between siblings, and more often than not God chooses the younger as if to emphasize that natural order is not equivalent to nor always reflective of divine preference. God's blessing rests on whom He chooses and whom He judges to be worthy. The accident of first birth may assure earthly goods but not the gifts of the spirit.

---

[1] The ceremony is described and discussed in commentary to 17:16–18:32.

[2] Remnants of such practices are recorded in II Kings 3:27 (Mesha of Moab sacrificing his heir) and hinted at in Micah 6:7. It is not certain, however, that the custom of passing a child through fire (II Kings 16:3; 17:17; 21:6) involved actual sacrifice [17].

GLEANINGS

These Are the Names

This statement occurs twice (3:2 and 3) to impress on us that even after their anointment to the priesthood the sons of Aaron did not receive new names as is the custom among some other nations and religions. Anointment did not change the essential nature or capacity of the priest.   EGLEI TAL [20]

God Grieved

The deaths of Nadab and Abihu are recorded here (Num. 3:4) and in other passages (Lev. 10:2; 16:1; Num. 26:61; I Chron. 24:2). This teaches that God felt grieved for them, for the sons of Aaron were dear to Him.   MIDRASH [21]

Humility

Eleazar, son of the High Priest, merited a special notation (4:16), for the work there specified was done by himself. Though it was menial labor, he did not leave it to others. When a man thinks much of the glory of Heaven and little of his own, both the glory of Heaven and his own are magnified. Hence, his name is forever enshrined in these pages.   MIDRASH [22]

The Most Sacred Objects

What a contrast to modern life! We brazenly dare to touch anything and make bold to tear the mystery from everything. Reverence for the things of God must be given a relevance to the things of men, until the sacred puts a halo around the secular.   A. G. BUTZER [23]

Blue Cloth

Note that the accouterments were colorful, not drab. Judaism never was without its esthetic side.

Retirement

Priestly service which consisted largely of singing terminated at age fifty, for after that the capacity to sing well declines sharply.

MIDRASH [24]

Aaron before Moses

It says (Num. 3:1): "This is the line of Aaron and Moses," even though Moses is usually mentioned first and is the one with whom the Torah tradition originates. But, while in monarchy and priesthood hereditary succession obtains, it does not in matters of prophecy. Even as Aaron could not bequeath his gifts to Moses, so Moses could not transmit his own.   A. B. EHRLICH [25]

[Ehrlich ends his comment with his customary hint: "He who understands will know what I mean." The implication is that each generation is on its own in this respect.]

The Sin

Originally the Temple service devolved upon the first-born but, when they committed the sin of the golden calf, the Levites, inasmuch as they had not erred in the matter of the calf, were privileged to enter in their stead.   MIDRASH [26]

Halachah

R. Simeon b. Gamaliel says: Any child who does not live thirty days has not completed his embryonic period of months but is a miscarriage. Why does he hold this view? R. Simeon b. Gamaliel's opinion rests on the language of the Torah, inasmuch as the Omnipresent ordered the first-born to be numbered for the purpose of

redemption only thirty days after their birth (Num. 3:40).   MIDRASH [27]

All the Levites (Num. 4:46)

After having enumerated the Levites in single families—the families of the sons of Kohath separately, the family of the sons of Gershon separately, and the family of the sons of Merari separately—Scripture recapitulates and sums up all their numbers together. This is to tell you that all of them were regarded by God with equal love.   MIDRASH [28]

Origin of the Levites

The origin of the Levites is a still unsolved problem. Early in the history of Israel there was a secular tribe called Levi, famed for its violence (Gen. 34:25–31; 49:5–7). We do not know whether it lost its territory and was transformed into the landless tribe of sanctuary attendants, or whether after some particularly violent episode it was wiped out and a religious order with the same name came to be regarded as a tribe in its place.

J. STURDY [29]

Laws of Holiness—The Ordeal

At first sight the laws contained in this section have little relation to each other: they deal with persons excluded from the camp because they are ritually unclean; with priests receiving offerings from a confessed robber; and with the procedures to be followed when a woman is accused by her husband of having committed adultery. The events discussed are themselves ordinary though somewhat infrequent; they happen to people in their everyday lives. The thread connecting these laws is the awareness of God's pervasive presence, which demands that the camp remain ritually pure and therefore holy. They function to restore a transgressor to the community and to assure the purity of family relationships. The sacred is never divorced from the ordinary because God's people stand constantly before Him.

מַ֤עַל בַּֽיהֹוָה֙ וְאָֽשְׁמָ֔ה הַנֶּ֖פֶשׁ הַהִ֑וא׃ וְהִתְוַדּ֗וּ אֶת־
חַטָּאתָם֙ אֲשֶׁ֣ר עָשׂ֔וּ וְהֵשִׁ֤יב אֶת־אֲשָׁמוֹ֙ בְּרֹאשׁ֔וֹ
וַֽחֲמִֽישִׁת֖וֹ יֹסֵ֣ף עָלָ֑יו וְנָתַ֕ן לַֽאֲשֶׁ֥ר אָשַׁ֖ם לֽוֹ׃ וְאִם־אֵ֨ין
לָאִ֜ישׁ גֹּאֵ֗ל לְהָשִׁ֤יב הָֽאָשָׁם֙ אֵלָ֔יו הָֽאָשָׁ֛ם הַמּוּשָׁ֥ב
לַֽיהֹוָ֖ה לַכֹּהֵ֑ן מִלְּבַ֗ד אֵ֚יל הַכִּפֻּרִ֔ים אֲשֶׁ֥ר יְכַפֶּר־בּ֖וֹ
עָלָֽיו׃ וְכָל־תְּרוּמָ֞ה לְכָל־קׇדְשֵׁ֧י בְנֵֽי־יִשְׂרָאֵ֛ל אֲשֶׁר־
יַקְרִ֥יבוּ לַכֹּהֵ֖ן ל֥וֹ יִֽהְיֶֽה׃ וְאִ֥ישׁ אֶת־קֳדָשָׁ֖יו ל֣וֹ יִֽהְי֑וּ אִ֛ישׁ
אֲשֶׁר־יִתֵּ֥ן לַכֹּהֵ֖ן ל֥וֹ יִֽהְיֶֽה׃ פ

וַיְדַבֵּ֥ר יְהֹוָ֖ה אֶל־מֹשֶׁ֥ה לֵּאמֹֽר׃ צַ֚ו אֶת־בְּנֵ֣י יִשְׂרָאֵ֔ל
וִֽישַׁלְּחוּ֙ מִן־הַֽמַּחֲנֶ֔ה כָּל־צָר֖וּעַ וְכָל־זָ֑ב וְכֹ֖ל טָמֵ֥א
לָנָ֑פֶשׁ׃ מִזָּכָ֤ר עַד־נְקֵבָה֙ תְּשַׁלֵּ֔חוּ אֶל־מִח֥וּץ לַֽמַּחֲנֶ֖ה
תְּשַׁלְּח֑וּם וְלֹ֤א יְטַמְּאוּ֙ אֶת־מַֽחֲנֵיהֶ֔ם אֲשֶׁ֥ר אֲנִ֖י שֹׁכֵ֥ן
בְּתוֹכָֽם׃ וַיַּֽעֲשׂוּ־כֵן֙ בְּנֵ֣י יִשְׂרָאֵ֔ל וַיְשַׁלְּח֣וּ אוֹתָ֔ם אֶל־
מִח֖וּץ לַֽמַּחֲנֶ֑ה כַּֽאֲשֶׁ֨ר דִּבֶּ֤ר יְהֹוָה֙ אֶל־מֹשֶׁ֔ה כֵּ֥ן עָשׂ֖וּ
בְּנֵ֥י יִשְׂרָאֵֽל׃ פ

וַיְדַבֵּ֥ר יְהֹוָ֖ה אֶל־מֹשֶׁ֥ה לֵּאמֹֽר׃ דַּבֵּר֮ אֶל־בְּנֵ֣י יִשְׂרָאֵל֒
אִ֣ישׁ אֽוֹ־אִשָּׁ֗ה כִּ֤י יַֽעֲשׂוּ֙ מִכָּל־חַטֹּ֣את הָֽאָדָ֔ם לִמְעֹ֥ל

1] The LORD spoke to Moses saying: **2]** Instruct the Israelites to remove from camp anyone with an eruption or a discharge and anyone defiled by a corpse. **3]** Remove male and female alike; put them outside the camp so that they do not defile the camp of those in whose midst I dwell.

4] The Israelites did so, putting them outside the camp; as the LORD had spoken to Moses, so the Israelites did.

5] The LORD spoke to Moses, saying: **6]** Speak to the Israelites: When a man or woman commits any wrong toward a fellow man, thus breaking faith with the LORD, and that person realizes his guilt, **7]** he shall confess the wrong that he has done. He shall make restitution in the principal amount and add one-fifth to it, giving it to him whom he has wronged. **8]** If the man has no kinsman to whom restitution can be made, the amount repaid shall go to the LORD for the priest—in addition to the ram of expiation with which expiation is made on his behalf. **9]** So, too, any gift among the sacred donations that the Israelites offer shall be the priest's. **10]** And each shall retain his sacred donations: each priest shall keep what is given to him.

5:2] *Eruption.* A general term, probably covering a number of diseases, amongst them the dreaded leprosy (see at Lev. 13 and 14). The illness (*tzaraᶜat*) was considered to create a state of ritual impurity and therefore the removal of the offending person was more than a health measure. Here, as in all diseases, God's corrective justice was seen at work [1].

Later tradition saw *tzaraᶜat* as a punishment for eleven sins and also related it to the sin of the golden calf.

Discharge. An abnormal flow resulting either from disease (such as gonorrhea or blennorrhea) or from natural causes (like continued mucous emission, prolonged or untimely menstruation, or postnatal flux); see Lev. 15:2 ff.; Deut. 23:11 ff.; and the introduction to Lev. 15 [2].

In Maimonides's time (twelfth century), all menstruating women were kept in a separate house.

Defiled by a corpse. Defiled by having touched a dead body (see Num. 19:11 ff.).

3] *Remove.* The law was later applied as follows: people afflicted by *tzaraᶜat* were not to come into Jerusalem; those with a discharge were barred from the Temple Mount; and those defiled by a corpse from the Temple itself [3].

6] *Thus breaking faith with the Lord.* A fundamental statement underlying Torah laws: the injury is done to God as well as to man. Cf. Lev. 5:21.

7] *Confess.* Publicly.

8] *Kinsman.* גּוֹאֵל (*go-el*), who redeems the family property; see Lev. 25:25 and Ruth 4:1–6. The Rabbis applied this rule to a proselyte who died without leaving a Jewish family behind [4].

In addition. Besides the regular sacrifice, which goes to the priest; Lev. 7:7.

יא וַיְדַבֵּ֥ר יְהוָ֖ה אֶל־מֹשֶׁ֥ה לֵּאמֹֽר: דַּבֵּר֙ אֶל־בְּנֵ֣י יִשְׂרָאֵ֔ל
וְאָמַרְתָּ֖ אֲלֵהֶ֑ם אִ֥ישׁ אִישׁ֙ כִּֽי־תִשְׂטֶ֣ה אִשְׁתּ֔וֹ וּמָעֲלָ֥ה ב֖וֹ
יג מָֽעַל: וְשָׁכַ֨ב אִ֥ישׁ אֹתָהּ֮ שִׁכְבַת־זֶרַע֒ וְנֶעְלַם֙ מֵעֵינֵ֣י
אִישָׁ֔הּ וְנִסְתְּרָ֖ה וְהִ֣יא נִטְמָ֑אָה וְעֵד֙ אֵ֣ין בָּ֔הּ וְהִ֖וא לֹ֥א
יד נִתְפָּֽשָׂה: וְעָבַ֨ר עָלָ֧יו רֽוּחַ־קִנְאָ֛ה וְקִנֵּ֥א אֶת־אִשְׁתּ֖וֹ וְהִ֣וא
נִטְמָ֑אָה אֽוֹ־עָבַ֨ר עָלָ֤יו רֽוּחַ־קִנְאָה֙ וְקִנֵּ֣א אֶת־אִשְׁתּ֔וֹ
טו וְהִ֖יא לֹ֣א נִטְמָֽאָה: וְהֵבִ֨יא הָאִ֣ישׁ אֶת־אִשְׁתּוֹ֮ אֶל־הַכֹּהֵן֒
וְהֵבִ֤יא אֶת־קָרְבָּנָהּ֙ עָלֶ֔יהָ עֲשִׂירִ֥ת הָאֵיפָ֖ה קֶ֣מַח

שְׂעֹרִ֑ים לֹֽא־יִצֹ֨ק עָלָ֜יו שֶׁ֗מֶן וְלֹֽא־יִתֵּ֤ן עָלָיו֙ לְבֹנָ֔ה כִּֽי־
טז מִנְחַ֤ת קְנָאֹת֙ ה֔וּא מִנְחַ֥ת זִכָּר֖וֹן מַזְכֶּ֥רֶת עָוֹֽן: וְהִקְרִ֥יב
יז אֹתָ֖הּ הַכֹּהֵ֑ן וְהֶֽעֱמִדָ֖הּ לִפְנֵ֥י יְהוָֽה: וְלָקַ֧ח הַכֹּהֵ֛ן מַ֥יִם
קְדֹשִׁ֖ים בִּכְלִי־חָ֑רֶשׂ וּמִן־הֶֽעָפָ֗ר אֲשֶׁ֤ר יִֽהְיֶה֙ בְּקַרְקַ֣ע
יח הַמִּשְׁכָּ֔ן יִקַּ֥ח הַכֹּהֵ֖ן וְנָתַ֥ן אֶל־הַמָּֽיִם: וְהֶֽעֱמִ֨יד הַכֹּהֵ֥ן
אֶת־הָֽאִשָּׁה֮ לִפְנֵ֣י יְהוָה֒ וּפָרַע֙ אֶת־רֹ֣אשׁ הָֽאִשָּׁ֔ה וְנָתַ֣ן
עַל־כַּפֶּ֗יהָ אֵ֚ת מִנְחַ֣ת הַזִּכָּר֔וֹן מִנְחַ֥ת קְנָאֹ֖ת הִ֑וא וּבְיַ֣ד
יט הַכֹּהֵ֣ן יִֽהְי֔וּ מֵ֥י הַמָּרִ֖ים הַֽמְאָֽרֲרִֽים: וְהִשְׁבִּ֨יעַ אֹתָ֜הּ

11] The LORD spoke to Moses, saying: **12]** Speak to the Israelite people and say to them: If any man's wife has gone astray and broken faith with him **13]** in that a man has had carnal relations with her unbeknown to her husband, and she keeps secret the fact that she has defiled herself without being forced, and there is no witness against her— **14]** but a fit of jealousy comes over him and he is wrought up about the wife who has defiled herself; or if a fit of jealousy comes over one and he is wrought up about his wife although she has not defiled herself— **15]** the man shall bring his wife to the priest. And he shall bring as an offering for her one-tenth of an *ephah* of barley flour. No oil shall be poured upon it and no frankincense shall be laid on it, for it is a meal offering of jealousy, a meal offering of remembrance which recalls wrongdoing.

16] The priest shall bring her forward and have her stand before the LORD. **17]** The priest shall take sacral water in an earthen vessel and, taking some of the earth that is on the floor of the Tabernacle, the priest shall put it into the water. **18]** After he has made the woman stand before the LORD, the priest shall bare the woman's head and place upon her hands the meal offering of remembrance, which is a meal offering of jealousy. And in the priest's hands shall be the water of bitterness that induces the spell. **19]** The priest shall adjure the woman, saying to

10] *Each.* Each priest. Others, each one who brings offerings [5].

12] *If any man's wife has gone astray.* In prophetic writing, Israel is depicted as the faithless wife who has betrayed God (see, for instance, Hos. 1 and 2; Ezek. 16 and 22).

13] *Unbeknown to her husband.* The Rabbis extend this to a husband who conceals his knowing of the act for the time being [6].

   Without being forced. She had not been raped [7]. Another reading: "without being discovered in the act" [8].

14] *Fit of jealousy.* In order to protect the wife, the Rabbis stipulated that the husband must have

warned her in front of witnesses not to communicate with the corespondent. They also instituted procedures to induce the wife to confess [9].

15] *One-tenth of an ephah.* About 7 pints.

16] *Before the Lord.* It later became customary to institute this procedure in the so-called Nicanor Gate of the Temple [10].

17] *Sacral water.* Kept in a laver in the Tabernacle.

18] *Water of bitterness.* It is not clear whether the water was actually bitter or whether the expression is figurative [11]. In any case, it is God, not the water, who punishes the guilty.

הַכֹּהֵן וְאָמַר אֶל־הָאִשָּׁה אִם־לֹא שָׁכַב אִישׁ אֹתָךְ וְאִם־
לֹא שָׂטִית טֻמְאָה תַּחַת אִישֵׁךְ הִנָּקִי מִמֵּי הַמָּרִים
הַמְאָרְרִים הָאֵלֶּה: וְאַתְּ כִּי שָׂטִית תַּחַת אִישֵׁךְ וְכִי
נִטְמֵאת וַיִּתֵּן אִישׁ בָּךְ אֶת־שְׁכָבְתּוֹ מִבַּלְעֲדֵי אִישֵׁךְ:
וְהִשְׁבִּיעַ הַכֹּהֵן אֶת־הָאִשָּׁה בִּשְׁבֻעַת הָאָלָה וְאָמַר
הַכֹּהֵן לָאִשָּׁה יִתֵּן יְהֹוָה אוֹתָךְ לְאָלָה וְלִשְׁבֻעָה בְּתוֹךְ
עַמֵּךְ בְּתֵת יְהֹוָה אֶת־יְרֵכֵךְ נֹפֶלֶת וְאֶת־בִּטְנֵךְ צָבָה:
וּבָאוּ הַמַּיִם הַמְאָרְרִים הָאֵלֶּה בְּמֵעַיִךְ לַצְבּוֹת בֶּטֶן
וְלַנְפִּל יָרֵךְ וְאָמְרָה הָאִשָּׁה אָמֵן אָמֵן: וְכָתַב אֶת־
הָאָלֹת הָאֵלֶּה הַכֹּהֵן בַּסֵּפֶר וּמָחָה אֶל־מֵי הַמָּרִים:

כד וְהִשְׁקָה אֶת־הָאִשָּׁה אֶת־מֵי הַמָּרִים הַמְאָרְרִים וּבָאוּ
כה בָהּ הַמַּיִם הַמְאָרְרִים לְמָרִים: וְלָקַח הַכֹּהֵן מִיַּד
הָאִשָּׁה אֵת מִנְחַת הַקְּנָאֹת וְהֵנִיף אֶת־הַמִּנְחָה לִפְנֵי
כו יְהֹוָה וְהִקְרִיב אֹתָהּ אֶל־הַמִּזְבֵּחַ: וְקָמַץ הַכֹּהֵן מִן
הַמִּנְחָה אֶת־אַזְכָּרָתָהּ וְהִקְטִיר הַמִּזְבֵּחָה וְאַחַר יַשְׁקֶה
כז אֶת־הָאִשָּׁה אֶת־הַמָּיִם: וְהִשְׁקָהּ אֶת־הַמַּיִם וְהָיְתָה אִם־
נִטְמְאָה וַתִּמְעֹל מַעַל בְּאִישָׁהּ וּבָאוּ בָהּ הַמַּיִם
הַמְאָרְרִים לְמָרִים וְצָבְתָה בִטְנָהּ וְנָפְלָה יְרֵכָהּ
כח וְהָיְתָה הָאִשָּׁה לְאָלָה בְּקֶרֶב עַמָּהּ: וְאִם־לֹא נִטְמְאָה
כט הָאִשָּׁה וּטְהֹרָה הִוא וְנִקְּתָה וְנִזְרְעָה זָרַע: וְאֹת תּוֹרַת

her "If no man has lain with you, if you have not gone astray in defilement while married to your husband, be immune to harm from this water of bitterness that induces the spell. 20] But if you have gone astray while married to your husband and have defiled yourself, if a man other than your husband has had carnal relations with you"— 21] here the priest shall administer the curse of adjuration to the woman, as the priest goes on to say to the woman— "may the LORD make you a curse and an imprecation among your people, as the LORD causes your thigh to sag and your belly to distend; 22] may this water that induces the spell enter your body, causing the belly to distend and the thigh to sag." And the woman shall say, "Amen, amen!"

23] The priest shall put these curses down in writing and rub it off into the water of bitterness. 24] He is to make the woman drink the water of bitterness that induces the spell, so that the spell-inducing water may enter into her to bring on bitterness. 25] Then the priest shall take from the woman's hand the meal offering of jealousy, wave the meal offering before the LORD, and present it on the altar. 26] The priest shall scoop out of the meal offering a token part of it and turn it into smoke on the altar. Lastly, he shall make the woman drink the water.

27] Once he has made her drink the water—if she has defiled herself by breaking faith with her husband, the spell-inducing water shall enter into her to bring on bitterness, so that her belly shall distend and her thigh shall sag; and the woman shall become a curse among her people. 28] But if the woman has not defiled herself and is pure, she shall be unharmed and able to retain seed.

21] *Thigh to sag.* The meaning is not certain. "Thigh" is probably a euphemism for the sexual organ (see Gen. 24:2). The expression might also refer to dropsy of the ovaries, thus implying the threat of sterility.

22] *Amen, amen.* The Hebrew affirmation means "So be it!" or the (now archaic) exclamation "Faith!" The woman's amen signified her agreement to the oath just spoken.

A Hittite soldier's oath also demanded this affirmation [12].

23] *In writing.* Verses 23–26 may have been retained from another ritual. Ezekiel (2:9–3:3) tells of the prophet eating a scroll as a symbolic gesture.

28] *Retain seed.* The exonerated wife will receive the blessing of fertility as compensation for her humiliation [13]. Another interpretation is that she will "return to her husband" [14].

לֹא הַקְּנָאֹת אֲשֶׁר תִּשְׂטֶה אִשָּׁה תַּחַת אִישָׁהּ וְנִטְמָאָה: אוֹ

אִישׁ אֲשֶׁר תַּעֲבֹר עָלָיו רוּחַ קִנְאָה וְקִנֵּא אֶת־אִשְׁתּוֹ

וְהֶעֱמִיד אֶת־הָאִשָּׁה לִפְנֵי יְהֹוָה וְעָשָׂה לָהּ הַכֹּהֵן אֵת

לֹא כָּל־הַתּוֹרָה הַזֹּאת: וְנִקָּה הָאִישׁ מֵעָוֹן וְהָאִשָּׁה הַהִוא

תִּשָּׂא אֶת־עֲוֹנָהּ:   פ

29] This is the ritual in cases of jealousy, when a woman goes astray while married to her husband and defiles herself, 30] or when a fit of jealousy comes over a man and he is wrought up over his wife: the woman shall be made to stand before the LORD and the priest shall carry out all this ritual with her. 31] The man shall be clear of guilt; but that woman shall suffer for her guilt.

29] *This is the ritual.* Verses 29 and 30 are a summary of the preceding [15].

31] *The man shall be clear.* Of any sin relating to her humiliation or death [16].

Ordeals

The procedure described in verses 11–31 is generally referred to as an "ordeal." The term covers a variety of methods for ascertaining divine judgment through tests administered to persons suspected of certain crimes. Here the suspicions of a jealous husband may be proved or disproved by giving his wife a mixture of sacred water, earth from the floor of the Tabernacle, and the script of curses, and by observing the results of this ministration.

Ordeals of jealousy were known in the ancient Near East, though not in the precise form preserved here, and there were parallels in many other cultures. The Babylonian Code of Hammurabi (about 1750 B.C.E.) has the following provision for a water ordeal:

"If a seignior's wife was accused by her husband, but she was not caught while lying with another man, she shall make affirmation by God and return to her house. If the finger was pointed at the wife of a seignior because of another man, but she has not been caught while lying with the other man, she shall throw herself into the river for the sake of her husband"[1] [18].

In Mari, there existed a water ordeal with an oral adjuration, and there too (as in our text) water was mixed with earth. In the Hittite instruction for Temple officials, a person suspected of having shortchanged the gods had to drink a sacred potion. It may well be that among the West Semites ordeal by water was practiced in the absence of conclusive evidence.

Many kinds of ordeals were in use among Greeks and Romans, and some of them persisted in Europe until well into modern times. The accused might have to walk barefoot over hot coals or to pass through fire—if he was unharmed he was deemed guilty; if harmed, declared innocent. One water test (often used on a suspected witch) involved throwing the accused, who was bound or weighted down, into a river; floating would indicate guilt, sinking and drowning were (belated) signs of innocence. In Japanese tradition the woman was made to drink water in which a certain paper had been dipped. Similar customs are still to be found in parts of Africa [19].

The Ordeal in Jewish Law

The Torah gives the male partner clear prerogatives by laying the burden of proof of innocence on the woman. And, while both the wife and her adulterous lover were subject to capital punishment if guilty (Lev. 20:10; Deut. 22:22), no reverse ordeal was instituted: a wife suspecting her husband of infidelity had no recourse. The standards were not the same and men were allowed to be polygamous. The woman was "set aside" (mekudeshet), the husband was not. Mishnah and Talmud treated of the ordeal extensively in the tractate Sotah ("faithless wife").

One major problem inherent in the law of ordeal is the underlying assumption that by invoking the procedure a husband could force God to make the truth known. No other Torah law is dependent on such a divine manifestation. According to the Rabbis, an immediate response was expected to the test[2] [20]. Its use was an exception to the talmudic principle that one should not rely on the occurrence of miracles.[3] According to Nachmanides, it was effective only as long

---

[1] The wife submitted herself to the water ordeal, with the river acting as the divine judge. The river ordeal obtained in other cases as well [17].

[2] In another case, Moses made the Children of Israel drink water mixed with dust from the golden calf (Exod. 32:20), but the Bible does not tell whether this was done to reveal the guilty. Rashi, based on the Talmud, assumes that this was the case.

[3] אֵין סוֹמְכִין עַל הַנֵּס (ein somchin al hanes) based on Rabba's Aramaic saying [21].

1054

as the majority of Israel did God's will—which is vague enough to suggest that this remnant of prebiblical times had no permanent place in an imperfect society [22]. In fact, at the time of the destruction of the Second Temple, moral fibers loosened to such an extent that R. Johanan ben Zakkai abolished the test altogether [23].

The law of ordeal implies that fidelity is an essential element in marriage and that jealousy is a legitimate sentiment, for trust is the foundation of the marital covenant. As in all situations involving private or public trust, the parties must not only *be* faithful but also *appear* to be worthy of confidence.

GLEANINGS

Allusions

One may see in Num. 5:2 a series of allusions. The words "remove from camp" allude to Israel's exile, and the rest of the verse lists the transgressions which will cause the exile to be imposed: "eruption" alludes to idolatry; "discharge" to immorality; and "defiled by a corpse" to the shedding of blood which defiles the land. For these transgressions the Temple was destroyed.   MIDRASH [24]

Wrong toward a Fellow Man (Num. 5:6)

It is possible to sin against God without sinning against man (see Ps. 51:4–6), but all sins against man are also sins against God.

G. B. GRAY [25]

Proselytes

Who are the people that have no relatives able to speak for them and take up their cause (Num. 5:8)? They are the proselytes whom the Torah means to protect especially, for proselytes are beloved and as important as Israelites.

MIDRASH [26]

Fools

Fools believe that the money which they have lying in their coffers is theirs, while the money they give away to charity is theirs no longer. Actually, quite the reverse is true. Only those possessions which are given away for sacred purposes remain one's property ("each shall retain his sacred donation," Num. 5:10). But those possessions which a man greedily amasses for himself are not his at all. Such gains will not remain with him for longer than a fleeting moment.

CHASIDIC [27]

Exclusion

The exclusion of one who has had an eruption affirms the principle of social purity; of the one who had an issue, the need for sexual purity; and the exclusion of the dead underscores that God can be served only by life.

S. R. HIRSCH [28]

The Reward of Modesty

The accused wife shall drink the water of ordeal and depart, awaiting the reward of her modesty or the extreme penalty of her incontinence; for if she has been falsely accused she may hope for seed and children, disregarding all apprehensions and anxieties on the subject of barrenness and childlessness.   PHILO [29]

A Christian Midrash

[From the trial of Joseph and Mary when her pregnancy became obvious.] And the High Priest said: "Give back the virgin whom you have received from the temple of the Lord." And Joseph wept bitterly. And the High Priest said: "I will give you to drink the water of the conviction of the Lord, and it will make manifest your sins before your eyes." And the High Priest took it and gave it to Joseph to drink and sent him into the wilderness; and he came back whole. And he made Mary also drink and sent her into the wilderness; and she also returned whole. And all the people marveled, because the water had not revealed any sin in them. And the High Priest said: "If the Lord God has not made manifest your sins, neither do I condemn you." And he released them. And Joseph took Mary and departed to his house, rejoicing and glorifying the God of Israel.   PROTEVANGELIUM OF JAMES [30]

Two Betrayals

The text (Num. 5:12) which is translated, "If any man's wife has gone astray . . ." literally says: "If a man's, a man's wife has gone astray. . . ." Why this repetition? To indicate that she has in fact betrayed twice: her husband and her God who commanded not to commit adultery.

MIDRASH [31]

Vows of Abstinence

The subject of vows (נְדָרִים, *nedarim*; singular נֶדֶר, *neder*) occurs frequently in the Torah and other biblical books. For instance, Jacob vows that the Lord will be his God under stated conditions (Gen. 28:20); Jephthah vows that he will bring a certain sacrifice if God gives him victory (Judg. 11:30 ff.); and the Psalmist sings: "I will perform unto You my vows, which my lips have uttered and my mouth has spoken when I was in distress" (Ps. 66:13). General rules about vows are found in Lev. 27; vows of women are treated in Num. 30; and a talmudic tractate, Nedarim, is devoted to vows in general. Vows also play a role in other literatures from the ancient Near East [1].

The chapter before us deals with the particular mode of vowing in which a person pledged himself to certain kinds of abstinence for religious purposes and was called a nazirite (נָזִיר, *nazir*, see at verse 2). Such vows, undertaken to gain divine favor or to express gratitude for it, were common among many cultures and are still found today. While the regulations of this section (which deal both with the observance and the conclusion of naziriteship) are the only reference in the Torah to the practice, later sections of the Bible show it to have been widespread. In addition to avoiding alcohol and contact with the dead, the nazirite also had to let his hair grow in order to fulfill his vow: he would not merely observe his vow privately, by abstaining, he would also constantly testify to his special position by his appearance. Long hair was thus a sign of holiness, a symbolism meaningful in various cultures and ages.

א וַיְדַבֵּר יְהוָֹה אֶל־מֹשֶׁה לֵּאמֹר: דַּבֵּר אֶל־בְּנֵי יִשְׂרָאֵל
וְאָמַרְתָּ אֲלֵהֶם אִישׁ אוֹ־אִשָּׁה כִּי יַפְלִא לִנְדֹּר נֶדֶר
ג נָזִיר לְהַזִּיר לַיהוָֹה: מִיַּיִן וְשֵׁכָר יַזִּיר חֹמֶץ יַיִן וְחֹמֶץ
שֵׁכָר לֹא יִשְׁתֶּה וְכָל־מִשְׁרַת עֲנָבִים לֹא יִשְׁתֶּה וַעֲנָבִים
ד לַחִים וִיבֵשִׁים לֹא יֹאכֵל: כֹּל יְמֵי נִזְרוֹ מִכֹּל אֲשֶׁר
ה יֵעָשֶׂה מִגֶּפֶן הַיַּיִן מֵחַרְצַנִּים וְעַד־זָג לֹא יֹאכֵל: כָּל־
יְמֵי נֶדֶר נִזְרוֹ תַּעַר לֹא־יַעֲבֹר עַל־רֹאשׁוֹ עַד־מְלֹאת
הַיָּמִם אֲשֶׁר־יַזִּיר לַיהוָֹה קָדֹשׁ יִהְיֶה גַּדֵּל פֶּרַע שְׂעַר
ו רֹאשׁוֹ: כָּל־יְמֵי הַזִּירוֹ לַיהוָֹה עַל־נֶפֶשׁ מֵת לֹא יָבֹא:

ז לְאָבִיו וּלְאִמּוֹ לְאָחִיו וּלְאַחֹתוֹ לֹא־יִטַּמָּא לָהֶם בְּמֹתָם
ח כִּי נֵזֶר אֱלֹהָיו עַל־רֹאשׁוֹ: כֹּל יְמֵי נִזְרוֹ קָדֹשׁ הוּא
ט לַיהוָֹה: וְכִי־יָמוּת מֵת עָלָיו בְּפֶתַע פִּתְאֹם וְטִמֵּא רֹאשׁ
נִזְרוֹ וְגִלַּח רֹאשׁוֹ בְּיוֹם טָהֳרָתוֹ בַּיּוֹם הַשְּׁבִיעִי יְגַלְּחֶנּוּ:
י וּבַיּוֹם הַשְּׁמִינִי יָבִא שְׁתֵּי תֹרִים אוֹ שְׁנֵי בְּנֵי יוֹנָה אֶל־
יא הַכֹּהֵן אֶל־פֶּתַח אֹהֶל מוֹעֵד: וְעָשָׂה הַכֹּהֵן אֶחָד
לְחַטָּאת וְאֶחָד לְעֹלָה וְכִפֶּר עָלָיו מֵאֲשֶׁר חָטָא עַל־
יב הַנָּפֶשׁ וְקִדַּשׁ אֶת־רֹאשׁוֹ בַּיּוֹם הַהוּא: וְהִזִּיר לַיהוָֹה
אֶת־יְמֵי נִזְרוֹ וְהֵבִיא כֶּבֶשׂ בֶּן־שְׁנָתוֹ לְאָשָׁם וְהַיָּמִים

1] The LORD spoke to Moses, saying: **2]** Speak to the Israelites and say to them: If anyone, man or woman, explicitly utters a nazirite's vow, to set himself apart for the LORD, **3]** he shall abstain from wine and any other intoxicant; he shall not drink vinegar of wine or of any other intoxicant, neither shall he drink anything in which grapes have been steeped, nor eat grapes fresh or dried. **4]** Throughout his term as nazirite, he may not eat anything that is obtained from the grapevine, even seeds or skin.

5] Throughout the term of his vow as nazirite, no razor shall touch his head; it shall remain consecrated until the completion of his term as nazirite of the LORD, the hair of his head being left to grow untrimmed. **6]** Throughout the term that he has set apart for the LORD, he shall not go in where there is a dead person. **7]** Even if his father or mother, or his brother or sister should die, he must not defile himself for them, since hair set apart for his God is upon his head: **8]** throughout his term as nazirite he is consecrated to the LORD.

9] If a person dies suddenly near him, defiling his consecrated hair, he shall shave his head on the day he becomes clean; he shall shave it on the seventh day. **10]** On the eighth day he shall bring two turtledoves or two pigeons to the priest, at the entrance of the Tent of Meeting. **11]** The priest shall offer one as a sin offering and the other as a burnt offering, and make expiation on his behalf for the guilt that he incurred through the corpse. That same day he shall reconsecrate his head **12]** and rededicate to the LORD his term as nazirite; and he shall bring a

---

6:2] *Or woman.* Queen Helena of Adiabene (first century C.E.), a convert to Judaism, observed the vows for many years in gratitude for her son Izates's safe return from war [2]. (See Num. 30:3 ff. on the general treatment of women's vows.)

Explicitly. The Hebrew is not clear; cf. Lev. 22:21.

Nazirite. From a root meaning either "set aside," "dedicate," or "curse."

3] *Any other intoxicant.* The exact meaning of these and some other terms describing alcoholic beverages is uncertain.

5] *It shall remain consecrated.* The hair [3].

7] *Even if . . . should die.* Similar restrictions were placed on the High Priest.

See Lev. 10:6; 21:5; Ezek. 44:20 to compare the stringency of nazirite vows with other priestly rules.

Hair. The Hebrew reads *nezer* (consecration). The symbol of this consecration is the hair on his head. (Cf. Lev. 21:12.)

9] *Dies suddenly.* Such contact with the dead made the nazirite unclean and made continuation of his term impossible; see Num. 19:14-16.

He shall shave it. And, according to rabbinic tradition, bury it because it was now considered defiled [4]. At the completion of the term, however, the hair was burned (verse 18).

יג הָרִאשֹׁנִים יִפֹּלוּ כִּי טָמֵא נִזְרוֹ: וְזֹאת תּוֹרַת הַנָּזִיר בְּיוֹם מְלֹאת יְמֵי נִזְרוֹ יָבִיא אֹתוֹ אֶל־פֶּתַח אֹהֶל
יד מוֹעֵד: וְהִקְרִיב אֶת־קָרְבָּנוֹ לַיהוָה כֶּבֶשׂ בֶּן־שְׁנָתוֹ תָמִים אֶחָד לְעֹלָה וְכַבְשָׂה אַחַת בַּת־שְׁנָתָהּ תְּמִימָה
טו לְחַטָּאת וְאַיִל־אֶחָד תָּמִים לִשְׁלָמִים: וְסַל מַצּוֹת סֹלֶת חַלֹּת בְּלוּלֹת בַּשֶּׁמֶן וּרְקִיקֵי מַצּוֹת מְשֻׁחִים בַּשָּׁמֶן
טז וּמִנְחָתָם וְנִסְכֵּיהֶם: וְהִקְרִיב הַכֹּהֵן לִפְנֵי יְהוָה וְעָשָׂה
יז אֶת־חַטָּאתוֹ וְאֶת־עֹלָתוֹ: וְאֶת־הָאַיִל יַעֲשֶׂה זֶבַח שְׁלָמִים לַיהוָה עַל סַל הַמַּצּוֹת וְעָשָׂה הַכֹּהֵן אֶת־
יח מִנְחָתוֹ וְאֶת־נִסְכּוֹ: וְגִלַּח הַנָּזִיר פֶּתַח אֹהֶל מוֹעֵד אֶת־

רֹאשׁ נִזְרוֹ וְלָקַח אֶת־שְׂעַר רֹאשׁ נִזְרוֹ וְנָתַן עַל־הָאֵשׁ
יט אֲשֶׁר־תַּחַת זֶבַח הַשְּׁלָמִים: וְלָקַח הַכֹּהֵן אֶת־הַזְּרֹעַ בְּשֵׁלָה מִן־הָאַיִל וְחַלַּת מַצָּה אַחַת מִן־הַסַּל וּרְקִיק מַצָּה אֶחָד וְנָתַן עַל־כַּפֵּי הַנָּזִיר אַחַר הִתְגַּלְּחוֹ אֶת־
כ נִזְרוֹ: וְהֵנִיף אוֹתָם הַכֹּהֵן תְּנוּפָה לִפְנֵי יְהוָה קֹדֶשׁ הוּא לַכֹּהֵן עַל חֲזֵה הַתְּנוּפָה וְעַל שׁוֹק הַתְּרוּמָה
כא וְאַחַר יִשְׁתֶּה הַנָּזִיר יָיִן: זֹאת תּוֹרַת הַנָּזִיר אֲשֶׁר יִדֹּר קָרְבָּנוֹ לַיהוָה עַל־נִזְרוֹ מִלְּבַד אֲשֶׁר־תַּשִּׂיג יָדוֹ כְּפִי נִדְרוֹ אֲשֶׁר יִדֹּר כֵּן יַעֲשֶׂה עַל תּוֹרַת נִזְרוֹ: פ

lamb in its first year as a penalty offering. The previous period shall be void, since his consecrated hair was defiled.

13] This is the ritual for the nazirite: On the day that his term as nazirite is completed, he shall be brought to the entrance of the Tent of Meeting. 14] As his offering to the LORD he shall present: one male lamb in its first year, without blemish, for a burnt offering; one ewe lamb in its first year, without blemish, for a sin offering; one ram without blemish for an offering of well-being; 15] a basket of unleavened cakes of choice flour with oil mixed in, and unleavened wafers spread with oil; and the proper meal offerings and libations.

16] The priest shall present them before the LORD and offer the sin offering and the burnt offering. 17] He shall offer the ram as a sacrifice of well-being to the LORD, together with the basket of unleavened cakes; the priest shall also offer the meal offerings and the libations. 18] The nazirite shall then shave his consecrated hair, at the entrance of the Tent of Meeting, and take the locks of his consecrated hair and put them on the fire that is under the sacrifice of well-being.

19] The priest shall take the shoulder of the ram when it has been boiled, one unleavened cake from the basket, and one unleavened wafer, and place them on the hands of the nazirite after he has shaved his consecrated hair. 20] The priest shall wave them as a wave offering before the LORD; and this shall be a sacred donation for the priest, in addition to the breast of the wave offering and the thigh of heave offering. After that the nazirite may drink wine.

21] Such is the obligation of a nazirite; except that he who vows an offering to the LORD of what he can afford beyond his nazirite requirements must do exactly according to the vow which he has made beyond his obligation as a nazirite.

12] *Penalty.* Because of his carelessness.

14] *He shall present.* Four types of offerings: a burnt offering (always a male animal, given in gratitude); an expiational offering (always a female animal); a well-being or peace offering (either a male or female animal, brought in celebration of the fulfillment of the vow); and a meal offering. This range of sacrifices underlines the importance which the Torah ascribed to the naziriteship [5].

18] *Locks . . . on the fire.* They were burned not as a sacrifice but to prevent an object of consecration from being profaned [6].

21] *What he can afford.* Tradition obligated the friends of the nazirite to provide the offerings when he was too poor [7].

The Nazirite

The Torah treats naziriteship as an already existing institution: it does not deal with reasons for taking vows but, rather, with the way in which a person is to conduct himself once he has become a nazirite.

The basic rules are clear and relatively simple: the nazirite was to abstain from alcohol, not to cut his hair, and not to defile his special status of holiness by contact with the dead. These rules resemble the restrictions placed on the High Priest, although naziriteship did not bestow priestly status on the devotee. The nazirite was subject to the stringent laws of what may be described as an informal holy order. It was entered voluntarily, but once the pledge was made the nazirite was not free to alter the conditions or to disregard the obligations incurred until they were fulfilled. Parents, however, could obligate their children, even those not yet born. Famous biblical cases are Samson (Judg. 13:5), Samuel (I Sam. 1:11),[1] and possibly the Rechabite sect (Jer. 35).[2] The Christian Scriptures indicate that John the Baptist was a nazir[3] and that Paul placed himself temporarily under the rules of abstinence [8]. The Mishnah and Talmud devote much space to the practice [9], and it was so well known in ancient Israel that Lev. 25:5 and 11 could use nazir as a figurative term.[4]

The period of naziriteship varied. It could last a limited time (as our text presupposes), in which case the Rabbis set thirty days as the minimum time for such an observance [10]. But naziriteship could also last for life (as with Samson and Samuel), in which case custom distinguished between the strict category of "Samson-nazir," who would never cut his hair, and the less stringent obligation of "life-nazir," who could thin it once a year to keep it from becoming too burdensome [11].

In later times naziriteship met with disfavor, for Jewish tradition frowned increasingly on asceticism. To be sure, there were at all times individuals who by means of prolonged fasting, study, and prayer sought to achieve closer communion with God, but ascetic practice never again became institutionalized as it did in Christianity with its various kinds of holy orders and the assumption of celibacy by priests and others. A talmudic passage already chides the nazir for denying himself the luxury of wine and adds: "How much greater therefore the sin of one who denies himself any necessities of life" [12]. Even someone who fasted longer than required was considered a sinner [13].

Alcohol and Hair
(See also at Lev. 8:1 ff.)

The two major elements of the nazirite vow relate to wine and hair, and both of these forms of abstinence occur in a sufficient number of other cultures to suggest that a pervasive symbolism obtains here.

Alcohol. Throughout history intoxicants have received cultural, religious, and often legal attention. The debilitating effects of alcohol were well known, for wine was in universal use in the Near East and the Mediterranean basin (northern cultures developed other sources for the production of alcohol). What was not fully understood, however, was the physiological cause for the irrational behavior of the drinker, and it is likely that alcohol was originally deemed to contain or

---

[1] So the Septuagint; the Masoretic text knows only of the vow not to cut Samuel's hair.

[2] The Rechabites were a small sect in the days of the First Temple. They did not drink wine, but whether they observed full nazirite restrictions is not clear.

[3] Note also that John's birth is announced by an angel much like in Samuel's case.

[4] It appears in the English translation as "untrimmed vine."

spawn supernatural powers which were in competition with the gods. The English expression "spirits" for alcohol testifies to this ancient belief [14]. The Torah places the use and abuse of wine at the beginning of man's history (Gen. 9:20 ff.), and the Bible makes repeated reference to the effects of drink (e.g., Prov. 20:1; Eccles. 10:17). Later Jewish tradition counseled moderation but never total abstinence, and this moderation became an aspect of Jewish social mores. Even the Dead Sea brotherhoods, with all their strict rules of admission and conduct, made no mention in their scriptures of nazirite abstention. Among Jews, total abstainers from alcohol were looked upon as exceptions, and the practices of whole religious communities which corresponded in this respect to nazirites (such as Moslems or some modern Protestant sects) found no normative response among Jews. The Rechabites were a notable exception [15].

Hair. Throughout history the hair of the head has been important to people. Men and women have usually considered it as the crown of the visible self, the most malleable part of their external personality; they have beautified it, shaped or colored it, and have on occasion removed or hidden it. Already in biblical times, cutting a man's beard against his will (as was done by the Nazis to Jews) or a woman's hair as punishment (as was done in France and Northern Ireland by partisans to those accused of collaboration)

represented the ultimate in public humiliation (II Sam. 10:4; Isa. 3:17). Where hair was or is cut or shaved voluntarily (as by Buddhist, Roman Catholic, and ancient Egyptian priests), the act symbolizes consecration. And so does the reverse: a nazirite, a medieval king,[5] or a hermit set themselves aside for special purposes and their hair signified their status.

Frequently, hirsute appearance has symbolized personal integrity [16]. In cultures favoring short hair, the growing of long hair may indicate a rebellious spirit or a different value system. Not long ago the expression "long hair" meant classic or esoteric taste in the arts. In postbiblical Judaism earlocks and beard were deemed worthy of special attention. To this day, the Jew observant of biblical tradition (Lev. 19:27; 21:5) will not let a razor come upon the corners of his beard [17]. Detailed halachic regulations govern the methods of trimming the beard,[6] and a Chasid is distinguished by his earlocks (*pe-ot*). By their appearance, the observant aim to testify to membership in a people who, all of them, are consecrated to God. In light of these ancient identifications of hair with separateness and holiness, we can better understand the profound unease with which, in our century, young people's preoccupation with short or (later) long hair was greeted by their elders, for more than mere appearance was at stake.

---

[5] The royal crown was probably originally a fillet, and not by accident a Hebrew term for diadem is נֵזֶר (*nezer*, from the same root as *nazir*).

[6] For instance, allowing electric shavers, because they operate like scissors (which are permitted) and not like razor blades (which are forbidden).

GLEANINGS

Abstinence in Islam

The general Moslem prohibition of wine, which was only gradually made stringent by the prophet, may have found a starting point in the opposition to wine among some of the Arabs. The commentators, in accordance with the prevailing theory in Islam, have interpreted the passages in the Koran as a prohibition of all intoxicants.   G. B. GRAY [18]

Hair

It is a common belief that the hair is part of the man's vital being. If the one main object is to keep the man's power and vitality at the full, the hair is never shorn; if the object is to present the deity with part of man's life, the hair is a suitable means of achieving this. The practice is in no way peculiar to the Hebrews, nor is the origin to be sought in peculiar Hebrew beliefs.

G. B. GRAY [19]

Against Nature

The Sages say that he who "sits and fasts," that is, one who fasts longer than the law requires, is a sinner. Also, if he fasts and makes no spiritual progress, or if the fast has no deeper effect on him, then he has afflicted himself without purpose and therefore is considered a sinner. The same is true for other forms of abstinence.

KETAV SOFER [20]

Antisocial

Our Rabbis frowned upon persons who would renounce their worldly privileges and possessions without affording their neighbors to share their part in it, as such an attitude will result in abstention from the permissible benefits of life. They saw in it an impediment for realizing goodness in this world by weakening necessary spiritual fortitude. They condemned in it an antisocial attitude, a relation towards the community which is alien to the spirit of Judaism. He who separates himself from the benefits of life, who thinks that the mortal's lot is altogether a bad thing (as would appear from Eccles. 1:13), must needs come to make light of the striving for perfection of the human race. Any chain is only as strong as its weakest link; if he belittles the value of the individual, what may be expected of the community at large? If man will deny himself to provide his own wants, who will take care of the needs of others? Therefore, they rejected those who afflict themselves with asceticism because they were convinced that he who is occupied with his ascetic indulgence will have no mind for the needs of his neighbor.   SIMON FEDERBUSH [21]

In Praise of Nazirites

(Why does a nazirite have to bring a sin offering after he has meticulously fulfilled his vows?) Because when he completes his time as a nazir he sins against his own soul, for until then he was set aside for God's service. Now that he returns to the desires of the world, he requires atonement.   NACHMANIDES [22]

From the Mishnah

If a man said: "I will be a nazirite," and his fellow heard and said: "I, too," [and another heard and said:] "I, too," they all become nazirites. If the first was released [from his vow], they are all released; if the last was released, the last is released but the others all remain bound. If a man said: "I will be a nazirite," and his fellow heard and said: "Let my mouth be as his mouth!" or "Let my hair be as his hair!" he becomes a nazirite. [If he said:] "I will be a nazirite," and his wife heard and said: "I, too," he may revoke her vow but his own remains binding. [If she said:] "I will be a nazirite," and her husband heard her and said: "I, too," he cannot revoke her vow [23].

The Priestly Benediction

The three phrases that comprise verses 24, 25, and 26 in this brief segment have come to be known as the *Birkat Kohanim*, or Priestly Benediction, which J. H. Hertz called "the crown and seal of the whole sacred order" [1]. The Hebrew text has a distinct rhythmic structure, which rises from three to five to seven words (see Gleanings). In each phrase, following an opening verb couched in the future tense, the divine name יהוה stands in second place; the second section of the first two blessings consists of a single verb, while in the third blessing it broadens to a strong finale. The benediction evokes the image of a king and his court: the sovereign bestows favors on his subjects and grants them the blessings of his friendship.

In Lev. 9:22 Aaron is recorded as having raised his hands and blessed the people, but the words of his blessing are not given. In early days, these verses in Numbers may have served for individual benedictions only—such as for nazirites who had fulfilled their vows, hence the juxtaposition of the blessings with the section on nazirites—but in time the act became directed toward the community at large and was incorporated into Jewish and Christian worship. In modern times, Liberal and Conservative Jewish practices have reversed the historic trend and have once again allowed the blessings to serve individual purposes as well.

כב וַיְדַבֵּר יְהוָה אֶל־מֹשֶׁה לֵּאמֹר: דַּבֵּר אֶל־אַהֲרֹן וְאֶל־ כד פָּנָיו אֵלֶיךָ וִיחֻנֶּךָּ: ס יִשָּׂא יְהוָה פָּנָיו אֵלֶיךָ וְיָשֵׂם
בָּנָיו לֵאמֹר כֹּה תְבָרֲכוּ אֶת־בְּנֵי יִשְׂרָאֵל אָמוֹר כו לְךָ שָׁלוֹם: ס וְשָׂמוּ אֶת־שְׁמִי עַל־בְּנֵי יִשְׂרָאֵל וַאֲנִי
כה לָהֶם: ס יְבָרֶכְךָ יְהוָה וְיִשְׁמְרֶךָ: ס יָאֵר יְהוָה אֲבָרֲכֵם: ס

22] The LORD spoke to Moses: **23]** Speak to Aaron and his sons: Thus shall you bless the people of Israel. Say to them:

24] The LORD bless you and keep you!

25] The LORD deal kindly and graciously with you!

26] The LORD bestow His favor upon you and grant you peace!

27] Thus they shall link My name with the people of Israel, and I will bless them.

6:23] *Thus.* Rabbinic tradition held that this word commanded that the benediction be spoken precisely in this fashion, that is to say, in Hebrew [2].

24] *Bless you.* With material goods, according to the explanation of the Rabbis, who interpreted each blessing to confer different benefits [3].

Keep you. Compare Ps. 121:7: "The Lord keep you from all evil, may He keep your soul."

Others interpret this as referring to material blessings too [4].

25] *Deal kindly.* Or, "make His face to shine," that is, to experience the radiance of the divine presence.

Graciously. The Midrash interprets: give you grace in the eyes of men [5].

26] *Bestow His favor.* Others, "lift up His countenance."

In contrast, a "fallen countenance" betokens disfavor or anger (see Gen. 4:5, 6).

Peace. Or, wholeness, an internal, emotional benefit. Others translate *shalom* as friendship.

But in Lev. 26:6 a similar expression denotes external peace, i.e., absence of strife.

27] *Link My name.* Or, "put My name." The Hebrew is couched in a somewhat alliterative form: שָׂמוּ—שְׁמִי (*samu—shemi*) [6].

In the Sephardic rite, verse 27 is also part of the benediction.

How the Blessing Was Spoken

The use of the threefold benediction has varied with times and circumstances. At one time all Levites, and not only the priests, were entitled to speak the blessing (Deut. 10:8). Before the First Temple was built King David blessed his people (although it is not stated that he or the Levites used the threefold benediction, II Sam. 6:18), even as Solomon did after he finished building the sanctuary (II Kings 8:55).

In the days of the Second Temple the priests intoned the sacred formula every day at the morning sacrifice, or (perhaps occasionally) at the end of services: "And the people besought the Lord Most High in prayer before Him who is merciful, till the order of the worship of the Lord was ended; so they completed His service. Then Simon came down and lifted up his hands over the whole congregation of the sons of Israel to pronounce the blessing of the Lord with his lips and to glory in His name" [7]. The divine name was pronounced in the Temple proper while in the synagogues in the country the word Adonai[1] was substituted [8].

In prevailing Ashkenazic practice of the Orthodox, the blessings are pronounced only on the holy days. Those members whose families have by name or tradition preserved the memory of their priestly status[2] leave the service in order to wash themselves or be assisted in the washing by members of levitical families.[3] When they return they mount the rostrum (which used to be called *duchan* and from which came the common term *duchanen* for the act of blessing). They cover themselves with their prayer shawls so that they might concentrate on the holiness of the moment and also so that the congregation not be distracted by looking at their faces and by seeing them as people they know in everyday life, rather than as representatives of an ancient clan.[4] They lift their hands and spread their fingers to create a simile of the Hebrew letter ש (*shin*, the first letter of *Shaddai*, Almighty). The benediction is then intoned in a special sing-song which is meant to impress the listeners with the awesomeness of the moment. The *Kitzur Shulchan Aruch*, a popular halachic handbook, describes the procedure as follows:

"They raise their hands toward their shoulders and spread them out, and separate their fingers so that there be five open spaces between them; thus, between each two fingers there is one open space, and between two fingers and the thumb there is another open space, the same with the other hand, making four open spaces, and between the two thumbs there is also an open space, which makes five open spaces. When the priests bless the people they should neither look around nor divert their thoughts, but their eyes should be directed downward as when praying. The people should pay attention to the benedictions, and they should face the priests, but they should not gaze at them, nor should the priests themselves gaze at their hands. Thus they have made it a custom to let the folds of their prayer shawls drop over their faces and hands, and the congre-

---

[1] On Adonai as a substitute for יהוה, see commentary on Gen. 2.

[2] They are called *Kohanim*, plural form of *Kohen*, priest. Generally, families with such names as Cohn, Kahn, Cowan, Kagan, Katz will have preserved the family tradition of priestly descent.

[3] Their names are usually derivatives like Levin, Lewin, Lewissohn, and, of course, Levy.

[4] In the course of time many superstitions grew up about these customs. It was widely believed that looking at the *Kohanim* during the blessing would cause blindness. The Zohar, quoting R. Jose, gives this reason: "It matters because the Divine Name is reflected in the fingers of the priests' hands, so that although people cannot see the *Shechinah* they ought not to look towards the hands of the priests, as that would indicate irreverence towards the *Shechinah*" [9].

gation do likewise in order not to gaze [at the priests]" [10].

In Reform and Conservative synagogues the pronouncement of the blessings is no longer restricted to *Kohanim*; rabbis now often conclude various ritual occasions, services, or weddings with the benediction (or they use other formulas, such as Ps. 90:17). In Christian churches, ministers pronounce the words on similar occasions.

The Power to Bless

The Torah specifies that the benediction is to be spoken by the priests and that, upon their pronouncement, God will bless them. This appears to suggest that the threefold blessing has special qualities in that it forces the hand of God: a human word, delivered by the right person in the right manner, will call forth a predictable divine response.[5] Such ritual acts are probably known to most religious systems. The Christian concept of the nature and effect of the sacraments is of a similar order. The priest administers them in the proper fashion and the recipient is thereby related to the divine presence.

Biblical and postbiblical tradition knows of other instances where the special qualities of the one who blesses provide benefits to the one who is blessed. Most prominent among these is a father's blessing, when he dispenses both earthly and heavenly benefits as a last testament (see commentary on Gen. 27) [11]. These traditions go back to very ancient times and clearly rest on the belief that a priest (or a father) is endowed with spiritual prerogatives not available to others.

These persons, then, are by their inheritance, relationship, training, dedication, or ordination believed to have certain special powers. They become the transmitters of human aspiration (as when a rabbi or minister is asked to speak words of invocation), or the initiators or channels of divine grace (as in benedictions and sacraments). The difficulties raised by these suppositions have long been recognized. Not only is the borderline of religious magic uncomfortably close, but the assumptions of permanent special status in relationship to God are difficult to accept.

In consequence, a modern reading of the benediction would tend to divest it of the quality of cause-and-effect and see it as a prayer instead, a position already proposed by the Rashbam [12]. Thus priests, kings, rabbis, ministers, fathers, or grandfathers attempt to represent their own aspirations as well as those for whom they pray. God's presence becomes a common hope rather than a certainty, similar to the blessing which is greeting and prayer: "The Lord be with you" [6](Ruth 2:4). The rhythmic strength of the threefold prayer opens the heart of those who pronounce and those who hear it, and God in turn will grant His blessing in accordance with His own will.

---

[5] But see Exod. 20:21: God will bless those whom He himself causes to call on Him. There it appears that God initiates the blessing which will be granted when man responds to Him.

[6] It is, of course, possible to argue that God, having promised to bless when the priests pronounce the benediction, is certain to stand by His promise. He is a faithful God who honors the covenant of which this section is a part.

GLEANINGS

Terse and Beautiful

The priestly blessing gives terse and beautiful expression to the thought that Israel owes all to God who shields His people from all harm and grants them all things necessary for their welfare.

G. B. GRAY [13]

Three-Five-Seven

The first blessing has three words, the second five, the third seven. They remind us of the foundation for all blessings: the three Patriarchs, the five books of the Torah, and the seven Heavens.

BACHYA [14]

Perhaps—though there are doubts—this ascent (3–5–7) includes also the number of letters in the blessing: 15–20–25, for a total of 60, the basis of the sexagesimal system of ancient Babylon. But there is reason to believe that older manuscripts had slightly different spellings. CASSUTO [15]

I Will Bless

Israel said to God: "Why do you tell the priests to bless us? We desire Your blessing alone!" Said the Holy One: "Although I have told the priests to bless you, I shall stand in their company to give effect to the benediction." Therefore, at the end of the section it states explicitly (verse 27): "I will bless them." MIDRASH [16]

What Is Best

Man does not always know what is best for him, therefore I shall bless him in accordance with My knowledge. BIUR

What We Ask

The first blessing is material, the second spiritual, the third combines both.

N. LEIBOWITZ [17]

"May God bless thee," with possessions; "and keep thee," from these possessions possessing thee. May God guard thee from sin and shield thee from all destructive influences that so often follow in the wake of earthly prosperity.

J. H. HERTZ [18]

Why do we ask God first to bless us and then keep or guard us? Because, if He does give us material blessings we need to be protected from the evil results such prosperity may bring.

CHASIDIC [19]

Peace

שָׁלוֹם [*shalom*] has a much wider meaning [than abstinence from strife] and involves prosperity, good health, wholeness, and completeness in every way. N. H. SNAITH [20]

Peace is a precious thing, since for all the deeds and meritorious acts which our father Abraham accomplished the only reward given to him was peace, as it says: "You shall go to your fathers in peace" (Gen. 15:15).

You find likewise that the Torah was compared above all to peace, as it says: "All her paths are peace" (Prov. 3:17). Thus also you find that the Holy One, blessed be He, comforts Jerusalem above all with the promise of peace, for it says: "And My people shall abide in a peaceable habitation" (Isa. 37:18). MIDRASH [21]

Peace, say the Rabbis, is one of the pillars of the world; without it the social order could not exist. Therefore let a man do his utmost to promote it. Thus it is that the greatest Sages made a point of being the first to salute passersby in the street. Peace is the burthen of the prayer with which every service in the synagogue concludes:

"May He who makes peace in His high heavens grant peace unto us!" The Jew who is true to himself will labor with special energy in the cause of peace. The war-loving Jew is a contradiction in terms. Only the peace-loving Jew is a true follower of his Prophets who set universal brotherhood in the forefront of their pictures of coming happiness for mankind, predicting the advent of a Golden Age when nations should not lift up sword against nation, nor learn war any more. M. JOSEPH [22]

A Blessing of the Dead Sea Brotherhood

When they enter into that covenant [at the ceremony of initiation], the priests and the Levites are to pronounce a blessing upon the God of salvation and upon all that He does to make known His truth; and all that enter the covenant are to say after them: Amen, amen. . . . Then the priests are to invoke a blessing on all that have cast their lot with God, that walk blamelessly in all their ways; and they are to say: May He bless you with all good and keep you from all evil, and illumine your heart with insight into the things of life, and grace you with knowledge of things eternal, and lift up His gracious coun-

tenance towards you to grant you peace everlasting. MANUAL OF DISCIPLINE [23]

The Practice in the Temple

They pronounced the blessing over the people as a single blessing; in the provinces it was pronounced as three blessings, but in the Temple as a single blessing. In the Temple they pronounced the Name as it was written, but in the provinces by a substituted word. In the provinces the priests raised their hands as high as their shoulders, but in the Temple above their heads, excepting the High Priest, who raised his hands only as high as the frontlet. R. Judah says: "The High Priest also raised his hand above the frontlet, for it is written, 'Aaron lifted up his hands toward the people and blessed them' " (Lev. 9:22). MISHNAH [24]

Parental Blessings

It is an old custom on the eve of the Sabbath for sons to receive this blessing: "God make you like Ephraim and Manasseh."

Daughters are blessed with this formula: "God make you like Sarah, Rebekah, Rachel, and Leah."

Princely and Priestly Things

Chapter 7 deals with the princely offerings brought for the dedication of the Tabernacle.* These were presented according to the tribal order detailed in chapter 2, with the animals being offered first, then the gold and silver vessels. The chapter is marked by elaborate repetition which here and elsewhere in the Bible represents a form of literary or legal style and which seems to reflect the prototype of an "archival document" [1]. Since the Rabbis sought deeper reasons why the Torah would treat what appeared to be a minor aspect of ancient desert history at such extraordinary length and in such loving detail, the Midrash accords this chapter particular attention, finding special meaning in each offering (for examples, see commentary and Gleanings).

Chapter 8, which begins a new weekly portion in the synagogue cycle, first describes the lighting of the golden candlestick in the Tabernacle and then turns to the Levites and their status in the hierarchy of service.

(A new weekly portion, *Beha'alotecha*, begins with 8:1.)

* For a description of Temple dedications in later centuries, see I Kings 8:62; II Chron. 7:5 (First Temple); Neh. 12:43 (Second Temple); I Macc. 4:52 (rededication of Second Temple).

ז אוֹתָם אֶל־הַלְוִיִּם: אֵת שְׁתֵּי הָעֲגָלוֹת וְאֵת אַרְבַּעַת
ח הַבָּקָר נָתַן לִבְנֵי גֵרְשׁוֹן כְּפִי עֲבֹדָתָם: וְאֵת אַרְבַּע
הָעֲגָלֹת וְאֵת שְׁמֹנַת הַבָּקָר נָתַן לִבְנֵי מְרָרִי כְּפִי
ט עֲבֹדָתָם בְּיַד אִיתָמָר בֶּן־אַהֲרֹן הַכֹּהֵן: וְלִבְנֵי קְהָת
לֹא נָתָן כִּי־עֲבֹדַת הַקֹּדֶשׁ עֲלֵהֶם בַּכָּתֵף יִשָּׂאוּ:
י וַיַּקְרִיבוּ הַנְּשִׂאִים אֵת חֲנֻכַּת הַמִּזְבֵּחַ בְּיוֹם הִמָּשַׁח
אֹתוֹ וַיַּקְרִיבוּ הַנְּשִׂיאִם אֶת־קָרְבָּנָם לִפְנֵי הַמִּזְבֵּחַ:
יא וַיֹּאמֶר יְהוָה אֶל־מֹשֶׁה נָשִׂיא אֶחָד לַיּוֹם נָשִׂיא אֶחָד
יב לַיּוֹם יַקְרִיבוּ אֶת־קָרְבָּנָם לַחֲנֻכַּת הַמִּזְבֵּחַ: ס וַיְהִי
הַמַּקְרִיב בַּיּוֹם הָרִאשׁוֹן אֶת־קָרְבָּנוֹ נַחְשׁוֹן בֶּן־עַמִּינָדָב

א וַיְהִי בְּיוֹם כַּלּוֹת מֹשֶׁה לְהָקִים אֶת־הַמִּשְׁכָּן וַיִּמְשַׁח
אֹתוֹ וַיְקַדֵּשׁ אֹתוֹ וְאֶת־כָּל־כֵּלָיו וְאֶת־הַמִּזְבֵּחַ וְאֶת־כָּל־
ב כֵּלָיו וַיִּמְשָׁחֵם וַיְקַדֵּשׁ אֹתָם: וַיַּקְרִיבוּ נְשִׂיאֵי יִשְׂרָאֵל
רָאשֵׁי בֵּית אֲבֹתָם הֵם נְשִׂיאֵי הַמַּטֹּת הֵם הָעֹמְדִים
ג עַל־הַפְּקֻדִים: וַיָּבִיאוּ אֶת־קָרְבָּנָם לִפְנֵי יְהוָה שֵׁשׁ־
עֶגְלֹת צָב וּשְׁנֵי עָשָׂר בָּקָר עֲגָלָה עַל־שְׁנֵי הַנְּשִׂאִים
ד וְשׁוֹר לְאֶחָד וַיַּקְרִיבוּ אוֹתָם לִפְנֵי הַמִּשְׁכָּן: וַיֹּאמֶר
ה יְהוָה אֶל־מֹשֶׁה לֵּאמֹר: קַח מֵאִתָּם וְהָיוּ לַעֲבֹד אֶת־
עֲבֹדַת אֹהֶל מוֹעֵד וְנָתַתָּה אוֹתָם אֶל־הַלְוִיִּם אִישׁ כְּפִי
י עֲבֹדָתוֹ: וַיִּקַּח מֹשֶׁה אֶת־הָעֲגָלֹת וְאֶת־הַבָּקָר וַיִּתֵּן

1] On the day that Moses finished setting up the Tabernacle, he anointed and consecrated it and all its furnishings, as well as the altar and its utensils. When he had anointed and consecrated them, 2] the chieftains of Israel, the heads of ancestral houses, namely, the chieftains of the tribes, those who were in charge of enrollment, drew near 3] and brought their offering before the LORD: six draught carts and twelve oxen, a cart for every two chieftains and an ox for each one.

When they had brought them before the Tabernacle, 4] the LORD said to Moses: 5] Accept these from them for use in the service of the Tent of Meeting, and give them to the Levites according to their respective services.

6] Moses took the carts and the oxen and gave them to the Levites. 7] Two carts and four oxen he gave to the Gershonites, as required for their service, 8] and four carts and eight oxen he gave to the Merarites, as required for their service—under the direction of Ithamar son of Aaron the priest. 9] But to the Kohathites he did not give any; since theirs was the service of the [most] sacred objects, their porterage was by shoulder.

10] The chieftains also brought the dedication offering for the altar upon its being anointed. As the chieftains were presenting their offerings before the altar, 11] the LORD said to Moses: Let them present their offerings for the dedication of the altar, one chieftain each day.

12] The one who presented his offering on the first day was Nahshon son of Amminadab of

7:1] *On the day that Moses finished setting up the Tabernacle.* According to Exod. 40:17 this was the first day of the first month of the second year of the Exodus. In point of time sequence this passage precedes the opening chapter of Numbers (which begins a month later) and connects it directly with the end of Exodus [2].

9] *By shoulder.* Without the aid of carts. Hence King David gave rise to a grave offense when he caused a wagon to be used to transport the ark, and he later made certain that he would not repeat the same error (II Sam. 6:3 ff. and I Chron. 15:11 ff.) [3].

י לְמַטֵּה יְהוּדָה: וְקָרְבָּנוֹ קַעֲרַת־כֶּסֶף אַחַת שְׁלֹשִׁים
וּמֵאָה מִשְׁקָלָהּ מִזְרָק אֶחָד כֶּסֶף שִׁבְעִים שֶׁקֶל בְּשֶׁקֶל
הַקֹּדֶשׁ שְׁנֵיהֶם מְלֵאִים סֹלֶת בְּלוּלָה בַשֶּׁמֶן לְמִנְחָה:
יד כַּף אַחַת עֲשָׂרָה זָהָב מְלֵאָה קְטֹרֶת: פַּר אֶחָד בֶּן
טו בָּקָר אַיִל אֶחָד כֶּבֶשׂ־אֶחָד בֶּן־שְׁנָתוֹ לְעֹלָה: שָׂעִיר־
טז עִזִּים אֶחָד לְחַטָּאת: וּלְזֶבַח הַשְּׁלָמִים בָּקָר שְׁנַיִם
אֵילִם חֲמִשָּׁה עַתּוּדִים חֲמִשָּׁה כְּבָשִׂים בְּנֵי־שָׁנָה חֲמִשָּׁה
זֶה קָרְבַּן נַחְשׁוֹן בֶּן־עַמִּינָדָב: פ

יח בַּיּוֹם הַשֵּׁנִי הִקְרִיב נְתַנְאֵל בֶּן־צוּעָר נְשִׂיא יִשָּׂשכָר:
יט הִקְרִב אֶת־קָרְבָּנוֹ קַעֲרַת־כֶּסֶף אַחַת שְׁלֹשִׁים וּמֵאָה
מִשְׁקָלָהּ מִזְרָק אֶחָד כֶּסֶף שִׁבְעִים שֶׁקֶל בְּשֶׁקֶל
הַקֹּדֶשׁ שְׁנֵיהֶם מְלֵאִים סֹלֶת בְּלוּלָה בַשֶּׁמֶן לְמִנְחָה:
כ כַּף אַחַת עֲשָׂרָה זָהָב מְלֵאָה קְטֹרֶת: פַּר אֶחָד בֶּן
כב בָּקָר אַיִל אֶחָד כֶּבֶשׂ־אֶחָד בֶּן־שְׁנָתוֹ לְעֹלָה: שָׂעִיר־
כג עִזִּים אֶחָד לְחַטָּאת: וּלְזֶבַח הַשְּׁלָמִים בָּקָר שְׁנַיִם

אֵילִם חֲמִשָּׁה עַתֻּדִים חֲמִשָּׁה כְּבָשִׂים בְּנֵי־שָׁנָה חֲמִשָּׁה
זֶה קָרְבַּן נְתַנְאֵל בֶּן־צוּעָר: פ
כד בַּיּוֹם הַשְּׁלִישִׁי נָשִׂיא לִבְנֵי זְבוּלֻן אֱלִיאָב בֶּן־חֵלֹן:
כה קָרְבָּנוֹ קַעֲרַת־כֶּסֶף אַחַת שְׁלֹשִׁים וּמֵאָה מִשְׁקָלָהּ
מִזְרָק אֶחָד כֶּסֶף שִׁבְעִים שֶׁקֶל בְּשֶׁקֶל הַקֹּדֶשׁ
כו שְׁנֵיהֶם מְלֵאִים סֹלֶת בְּלוּלָה בַשֶּׁמֶן לְמִנְחָה: כַּף
כז אַחַת עֲשָׂרָה זָהָב מְלֵאָה קְטֹרֶת: פַּר אֶחָד בֶּן־בָּקָר
כח אַיִל אֶחָד כֶּבֶשׂ־אֶחָד בֶּן־שְׁנָתוֹ לְעֹלָה: שְׂעִיר־עִזִּים
כט אֶחָד לְחַטָּאת: וּלְזֶבַח הַשְּׁלָמִים בָּקָר שְׁנַיִם אֵילִם
חֲמִשָּׁה עַתֻּדִים חֲמִשָּׁה כְּבָשִׂים בְּנֵי־שָׁנָה חֲמִשָּׁה זֶה
קָרְבַּן אֱלִיאָב בֶּן־חֵלֹן: פ
ל בַּיּוֹם הָרְבִיעִי נָשִׂיא לִבְנֵי רְאוּבֵן אֱלִיצוּר בֶּן
לא שְׁדֵיאוּר: קָרְבָּנוֹ קַעֲרַת־כֶּסֶף אַחַת שְׁלֹשִׁים וּמֵאָה
מִשְׁקָלָהּ מִזְרָק אֶחָד כֶּסֶף שִׁבְעִים שֶׁקֶל בְּשֶׁקֶל
הַקֹּדֶשׁ שְׁנֵיהֶם מְלֵאִים סֹלֶת בְּלוּלָה בַשֶּׁמֶן לְמִנְחָה:

the tribe of Judah. **13]** His offering: one silver bowl weighing 130 shekels and one silver basin of 70 shekels by the sanctuary weight, both filled with choice flour with oil mixed in, for a meal offering; **14]** one gold ladle of 10 shekels, filled with incense; **15]** one bull of the herd, one ram, and one lamb in its first year, for a burnt offering; **16]** one goat for a sin offering; **17]** and for his sacrifice of well-being: two oxen, five rams, five he-goats, and five yearling lambs. That was the offering of Nahshon son of Amminadab.

18] On the second day, Nethanel son of Zuar, chieftain of Issachar, made his offering. **19]** He presented as his offering: one silver bowl weighing 130 shekels and one silver basin of 70 shekels by the sanctuary weight, both filled with choice flour with oil mixed in, for a meal offering; **20]** one gold ladle of 10 shekels, filled with incense; **21]** one bull of the herd, one ram, and one lamb in its first year, for a burnt offering; **22]** one goat for a sin offering; **23]** and for his sacrifice of well-being: two oxen, five rams, five he-goats, and five yearling lambs. That was the offering of Nethanel son of Zuar.

24] On the third day, it was the chieftain of the Zebulunites, Eliab son of Helon. **25]** His offering: one silver bowl weighing 130 shekels and one silver basin of 70 shekels by the sanctuary weight, both filled with choice flour with oil mixed in, for a meal offering; **26]** one gold ladle of 10 shekels, filled with incense; **27]** one bull of the herd, one ram, and one lamb in its first year, for a burnt offering; **28]** one goat for a sin offering; **29]** and for his sacrifice of well-being: two oxen, five rams, five he-goats, and five yearling lambs. That was the offering of Eliab son of Helon.

30] On the fourth day, it was the chieftain of the Reubenites, Elizur son of Shedeur. **31]** His offering: one silver bowl weighing 130 shekels and one silver basin of 70 shekels by the sanctuary weight, both filled with choice flour with oil mixed in, for a meal offering; **32]** one

לב כַּף אַחַת עֲשָׂרָה זָהָב מְלֵאָה קְטֹרֶת: פַּר אֶחָד בֶּן־
לד בָּקָר אַיִל אֶחָד כֶּבֶשׂ־אֶחָד בֶּן־שְׁנָתוֹ לְעֹלָה: שְׂעִיר־
לה עִזִּים אֶחָד לְחַטָּאת: וּלְזֶבַח הַשְּׁלָמִים בָּקָר שְׁנַיִם
אֵילִם חֲמִשָּׁה עַתֻּדִים חֲמִשָּׁה כְּבָשִׂים בְּנֵי־שָׁנָה חֲמִשָּׁה
זֶה קָרְבַּן אֱלִיצוּר בֶּן־שְׁדֵיאוּר: פ

לו בַּיּוֹם הַחֲמִישִׁי נָשִׂיא לִבְנֵי שִׁמְעוֹן שְׁלֻמִיאֵל בֶּן־
לז צוּרִישַׁדָּי: קָרְבָּנוֹ קַעֲרַת־כֶּסֶף אַחַת שְׁלֹשִׁים וּמֵאָה
מִשְׁקָלָהּ מִזְרָק אֶחָד כֶּסֶף שִׁבְעִים שֶׁקֶל בְּשֶׁקֶל
הַקֹּדֶשׁ שְׁנֵיהֶם מְלֵאִים סֹלֶת בְּלוּלָה בַשֶּׁמֶן לְמִנְחָה:
לח כַּף אַחַת עֲשָׂרָה זָהָב מְלֵאָה קְטֹרֶת: פַּר אֶחָד בֶּן־
לט/מ בָּקָר אַיִל אֶחָד כֶּבֶשׂ־אֶחָד בֶּן־שְׁנָתוֹ לְעֹלָה: שְׂעִיר־
מא עִזִּים אֶחָד לְחַטָּאת: וּלְזֶבַח הַשְּׁלָמִים בָּקָר שְׁנַיִם
אֵילִם חֲמִשָּׁה עַתֻּדִים חֲמִשָּׁה כְּבָשִׂים בְּנֵי־שָׁנָה חֲמִשָּׁה
זֶה קָרְבַּן שְׁלֻמִיאֵל בֶּן־צוּרִישַׁדָּי: פ

מב בַּיּוֹם הַשִּׁשִּׁי נָשִׂיא לִבְנֵי גָד אֶלְיָסָף בֶּן־דְּעוּאֵל: קָרְבָּנוֹ

לג קְעֲרַת־כֶּסֶף אַחַת שְׁלֹשִׁים וּמֵאָה מִשְׁקָלָהּ מִזְרָק אֶחָד
כֶּסֶף שִׁבְעִים שֶׁקֶל בְּשֶׁקֶל הַקֹּדֶשׁ שְׁנֵיהֶם מְלֵאִים
סֹלֶת בְּלוּלָה בַשֶּׁמֶן לְמִנְחָה: כַּף אַחַת עֲשָׂרָה זָהָב
לד מְלֵאָה קְטֹרֶת: פַּר אֶחָד בֶּן־בָּקָר אַיִל אֶחָד כֶּבֶשׂ־
אֶחָד בֶּן־שְׁנָתוֹ לְעֹלָה: שְׂעִיר־עִזִּים אֶחָד לְחַטָּאת:
מו וּלְזֶבַח הַשְּׁלָמִים בָּקָר שְׁנַיִם אֵילִם חֲמִשָּׁה עַתֻּדִים
חֲמִשָּׁה כְּבָשִׂים בְּנֵי־שָׁנָה חֲמִשָּׁה זֶה קָרְבַּן אֶלְיָסָף
בֶּן־דְּעוּאֵל: פ

מח בַּיּוֹם הַשְּׁבִיעִי נָשִׂיא לִבְנֵי אֶפְרָיִם אֱלִישָׁמָע בֶּן־
מט עַמִּיהוּד: קָרְבָּנוֹ קַעֲרַת־כֶּסֶף אַחַת שְׁלֹשִׁים וּמֵאָה
מִשְׁקָלָהּ מִזְרָק אֶחָד כֶּסֶף שִׁבְעִים שֶׁקֶל בְּשֶׁקֶל
הַקֹּדֶשׁ שְׁנֵיהֶם מְלֵאִים סֹלֶת בְּלוּלָה בַשֶּׁמֶן לְמִנְחָה:
נ כַּף אַחַת עֲשָׂרָה זָהָב מְלֵאָה קְטֹרֶת: פַּר אֶחָד בֶּן־
נב בָּקָר אַיִל אֶחָד כֶּבֶשׂ־אֶחָד בֶּן־שְׁנָתוֹ לְעֹלָה: שְׂעִיר־
נג עִזִּים אֶחָד לְחַטָּאת: וּלְזֶבַח הַשְּׁלָמִים בָּקָר שְׁנַיִם

gold ladle of 10 shekels, filled with incense;   **33]** one bull of the herd, one ram, and one lamb in its first year, for a burnt offering;   **34]** one goat for a sin offering;   **35]** and for his sacrifice of well-being: two oxen, five rams, five he-goats, and five yearling lambs. That was the offering of Elizur son of Shedeur.

36] On the fifth day, it was the chieftain of the Simeonites, Shelumiel son of Zurishaddai. **37]** His offering: one silver bowl weighing 130 shekels and one silver basin of 70 shekels by the sanctuary weight, both filled with choice flour with oil mixed in, for a meal offering;   **38]** one gold ladle of 10 shekels, filled with incense;   **39]** one bull of the herd, one ram, and one lamb in its first year, for a burnt offering;   **40]** one goat for a sin offering;   **41]** and for his sacrifice of well-being: two oxen, five rams, five he-goats, and five yearling lambs. That was the offering of Shelumiel son of Zurishaddai.

42] On the sixth day, it was the chieftain of the Gadites, Eliasaph son of Deuel.   **43]** His offering: one silver bowl weighing 130 shekels and one silver basin of 70 shekels by the sanctuary weight, both filled with choice flour with oil mixed in, for a meal offering;   **44]** one gold ladle of 10 shekels, filled with incense;   **45]** one bull of the herd, one ram, and one lamb in its first year, for a burnt offering;   **46]** one goat for a sin offering;   **47]** and for his sacrifice of well-being: two oxen, five rams, five he-goats, and five yearling lambs. That was the offering of Eliasaph son of Deuel.

48] On the seventh day, it was the chieftain of the Ephraimites, Elishama son of Ammihud. **49]** His offering: one silver bowl weighing 130 shekels and one silver basin of 70 shekels by the sanctuary weight, both filled with choice flour with oil mixed in, for a meal offering;   **50]** one gold ladle of 10 shekels, filled with incense;   **51]** one bull of the herd, one ram, and one lamb in its first year, for a burnt offering;   **52]** one goat for a sin offering;   **53]** and for his sacrifice

48] *On the seventh day.* Even though individual sacrifice was not ordinarily brought on the Sabbath.

אֵילִם חֲמִשָּׁה עַתֻּדִים חֲמִשָּׁה כְּבָשִׂים בְּנֵי־שָׁנָה חֲמִשָּׁה
זֶה קָרְבַּן אֱלִישָׁמָע בֶּן־עַמִּיהוּד: פ

נד בַּיּוֹם הַשְּׁמִינִי נָשִׂיא לִבְנֵי מְנַשֶּׁה גַּמְלִיאֵל בֶּן־פְּדָהצוּר:
נה קָרְבָּנוֹ קַעֲרַת־כֶּסֶף אַחַת שְׁלֹשִׁים וּמֵאָה מִשְׁקָלָהּ מִזְרָק אֶחָד כֶּסֶף שִׁבְעִים שֶׁקֶל בְּשֶׁקֶל הַקֹּדֶשׁ
נו שְׁנֵיהֶם מְלֵאִים סֹלֶת בְּלוּלָה בַשֶּׁמֶן לְמִנְחָה: כַּף
נז אַחַת עֲשָׂרָה זָהָב מְלֵאָה קְטֹרֶת: פַּר אֶחָד בֶּן־בָּקָר
נח אַיִל אֶחָד כֶּבֶשׂ־אֶחָד בֶּן־שְׁנָתוֹ לְעֹלָה: שְׂעִיר־עִזִּים
נט אֶחָד לְחַטָּאת: וּלְזֶבַח הַשְּׁלָמִים בָּקָר שְׁנַיִם אֵילִם חֲמִשָּׁה עַתֻּדִים חֲמִשָּׁה כְּבָשִׂים בְּנֵי־שָׁנָה חֲמִשָּׁה זֶה קָרְבַּן גַּמְלִיאֵל בֶּן־פְּדָהצוּר: פ
ס בַּיּוֹם הַתְּשִׁיעִי נָשִׂיא לִבְנֵי בִנְיָמִן אֲבִידָן בֶּן־גִּדְעֹנִי:
סא קָרְבָּנוֹ קַעֲרַת־כֶּסֶף אַחַת שְׁלֹשִׁים וּמֵאָה מִשְׁקָלָהּ מִזְרָק אֶחָד כֶּסֶף שִׁבְעִים שֶׁקֶל בְּשֶׁקֶל הַקֹּדֶשׁ
סב שְׁנֵיהֶם מְלֵאִים סֹלֶת בְּלוּלָה בַשֶּׁמֶן לְמִנְחָה: כַּף

סג אַחַת עֲשָׂרָה זָהָב מְלֵאָה קְטֹרֶת: פַּר אֶחָד בֶּן־בָּקָר
סד אַיִל אֶחָד כֶּבֶשׂ־אֶחָד בֶּן־שְׁנָתוֹ לְעֹלָה: שְׂעִיר־עִזִּים
סה אֶחָד לְחַטָּאת: וּלְזֶבַח הַשְּׁלָמִים בָּקָר שְׁנַיִם אֵילִם חֲמִשָּׁה עַתֻּדִים חֲמִשָּׁה כְּבָשִׂים בְּנֵי־שָׁנָה חֲמִשָּׁה זֶה קָרְבַּן אֲבִידָן בֶּן־גִּדְעֹנִי: פ
סו בַּיּוֹם הָעֲשִׂירִי נָשִׂיא לִבְנֵי דָן אֲחִיעֶזֶר בֶּן־עַמִּישַׁדָּי:
סז קָרְבָּנוֹ קַעֲרַת־כֶּסֶף אַחַת שְׁלֹשִׁים וּמֵאָה מִשְׁקָלָהּ מִזְרָק אֶחָד כֶּסֶף שִׁבְעִים שֶׁקֶל בְּשֶׁקֶל הַקֹּדֶשׁ
סח שְׁנֵיהֶם מְלֵאִים סֹלֶת בְּלוּלָה בַשֶּׁמֶן לְמִנְחָה: כַּף
סט אַחַת עֲשָׂרָה זָהָב מְלֵאָה קְטֹרֶת: פַּר אֶחָד בֶּן־בָּקָר
ע אַיִל אֶחָד כֶּבֶשׂ־אֶחָד בֶּן־שְׁנָתוֹ לְעֹלָה: שְׂעִיר־עִזִּים
עא אֶחָד לְחַטָּאת: וּלְזֶבַח הַשְּׁלָמִים בָּקָר שְׁנַיִם אֵילִם חֲמִשָּׁה עַתֻּדִים חֲמִשָּׁה כְּבָשִׂים בְּנֵי־שָׁנָה חֲמִשָּׁה זֶה קָרְבַּן אֲחִיעֶזֶר בֶּן־עַמִּישַׁדָּי: פ

of well-being: two oxen, five rams, five he-goats, and five yearling lambs. That was the offering of Elishama son of Ammihud.

54] On the eighth day, it was the chieftain of the Manassites, Gamaliel son of Pedahzur. **55]** His offering: one silver bowl weighing 130 shekels and one silver basin of 70 shekels by the sanctuary weight, both filled with choice flour with oil mixed in, for a meal offering; **56]** one gold ladle of 10 shekels, filled with incense; **57]** one bull of the herd, one ram, and one lamb in its first year, for a burnt offering; **58]** one goat for a sin offering; **59]** and for his sacrifice of well-being: two oxen, five rams, five he-goats, and five yearling lambs. That was the offering of Gamaliel son of Pedahzur.

60] On the ninth day, it was the chieftain of the Benjaminites, Abidan son of Gideoni. **61]** His offering: one silver bowl weighing 130 shekels and one silver basin of 70 shekels by the sanctuary weight, both filled with choice flour with oil mixed in, for a meal offering; **62]** one gold ladle of 10 shekels, filled with incense; **63]** one bull of the herd, one ram, and one lamb in its first year, for a burnt offering; **64]** one goat for a sin offering; **65]** and for his sacrifice of well-being: two oxen, five rams, five he-goats, and five yearling lambs. That was the offering of Abidan son of Gideoni.

66] On the tenth day, it was the chieftain of the Danites, Ahiezer son of Ammishaddai. **67]** His offering: one silver bowl weighing 130 shekels and one silver basin of 70 shekels by the sanctuary weight, both filled with choice flour with oil mixed in, for a meal offering; **68]** one gold ladle of 10 shekels, filled with incense; **69]** one bull of the herd, one ram, and one lamb in its first year, for a burnt offering; **70]** one goat for a sin offering; **71]** and for his sacrifice of well-being: two oxen, five rams, five he-goats, and five yearling lambs. That was the offering of Ahiezer son of Ammishaddai.

עע בְּיוֹם עַשְׁתֵּי עָשָׂר יוֹם נָשִׂיא לִבְנֵי אָשֵׁר אֲשֶׁר פַּגְעִיאֵל בֶּן

עג עָכְרָן: קָרְבָּנֹו קַעֲרַת־כֶּסֶף אַחַת שְׁלֹשִׁים וּמֵאָה
מִשְׁקָלָהּ מִזְרָק אֶחָד כֶּסֶף שִׁבְעִים שֶׁקֶל בְּשֶׁקֶל
הַקֹּדֶשׁ שְׁנֵיהֶם מְלֵאִים סֹלֶת בְּלוּלָה בַשֶּׁמֶן לְמִנְחָה:

עה כַּף אַחַת עֲשָׂרָה זָהָב מְלֵאָה קְטֹרֶת: פַּר אֶחָד
בֶּן־בָּקָר אַיִל אֶחָד כֶּבֶשׂ־אֶחָד בֶּן־שְׁנָתֹו לְעֹלָה:

עו שְׂעִיר־עִזִּים אֶחָד לְחַטָּאת: וּלְזֶבַח הַשְּׁלָמִים בָּקָר
שְׁנַיִם אֵילִם חֲמִשָּׁה עַתֻּדִים חֲמִשָּׁה כְּבָשִׂים בְּנֵי־
שָׁנָה חֲמִשָּׁה זֶה קָרְבַּן פַּגְעִיאֵל בֶּן־עָכְרָן: פ

עח בְּיוֹם שְׁנֵים־עָשָׂר יוֹם נָשִׂיא לִבְנֵי נַפְתָּלִי אֲחִירַע בֶּן

עט עֵינָן: קָרְבָּנֹו קַעֲרַת־כֶּסֶף אַחַת שְׁלֹשִׁים וּמֵאָה
מִשְׁקָלָהּ מִזְרָק אֶחָד כֶּסֶף שִׁבְעִים שֶׁקֶל בְּשֶׁקֶל
הַקֹּדֶשׁ שְׁנֵיהֶם מְלֵאִים סֹלֶת בְּלוּלָה בַשֶּׁמֶן לְמִנְחָה:

פ כַּף אַחַת עֲשָׂרָה זָהָב מְלֵאָה קְטֹרֶת: פַּר אֶחָד בֶּן־

פב בָּקָר אַיִל אֶחָד כֶּבֶשׂ־אֶחָד בֶּן־שְׁנָתֹו לְעֹלָה: שְׂעִיר־

עג עִזִּים אֶחָד לְחַטָּאת: וּלְזֶבַח הַשְּׁלָמִים בָּקָר שְׁנַיִם
אֵילִם חֲמִשָּׁה עַתֻּדִים חֲמִשָּׁה כְּבָשִׂים בְּנֵי־שָׁנָה חֲמִשָּׁה
זֶה קָרְבַּן אֲחִירַע בֶּן־עֵינָן: פ

פד וְזֹאת חֲנֻכַּת הַמִּזְבֵּחַ בְּיוֹם הִמָּשַׁח אֹתֹו מֵאֵת נְשִׂיאֵי
יִשְׂרָאֵל קַעֲרֹת כֶּסֶף שְׁתֵּים עֶשְׂרֵה מִזְרְקֵי־כֶסֶף שְׁנֵים

פה עָשָׂר כַּפֹּות זָהָב שְׁתֵּים עֶשְׂרֵה: שְׁלֹשִׁים וּמֵאָה
הַקְּעָרָה הָאַחַת כֶּסֶף וְשִׁבְעִים הַמִּזְרָק הָאֶחָד כֹּל
כֶּסֶף הַכֵּלִים אַלְפַּיִם וְאַרְבַּע־מֵאֹות בְּשֶׁקֶל הַקֹּדֶשׁ:

פו כַּפֹּות זָהָב שְׁתֵּים־עֶשְׂרֵה מְלֵאֹת קְטֹרֶת עֲשָׂרָה עֲשָׂרָה
הַכַּף בְּשֶׁקֶל הַקֹּדֶשׁ כָּל־זְהַב הַכַּפֹּות עֶשְׂרִים וּמֵאָה:

פז כָּל־הַבָּקָר לָעֹלָה שְׁנֵים עָשָׂר פָּרִים אֵילִם שְׁנֵים־עָשָׂר
כְּבָשִׂים בְּנֵי־שָׁנָה שְׁנֵים עָשָׂר וּמִנְחָתָם וּשְׂעִירֵי עִזִּים

פח שְׁנֵים עָשָׂר לְחַטָּאת: וְכֹל בְּקַר זֶבַח הַשְּׁלָמִים
עֶשְׂרִים וְאַרְבָּעָה פָּרִים אֵילִם שִׁשִּׁים עַתֻּדִים שִׁשִּׁים
כְּבָשִׂים בְּנֵי־שָׁנָה שִׁשִּׁים זֹאת חֲנֻכַּת הַמִּזְבֵּחַ אַחֲרֵי

72] On the eleventh day, it was the chieftain of the Asherites, Pagiel son of Ochran. **73]** His offering: one silver bowl weighing 130 shekels and one silver basin of 70 shekels by the sanctuary weight, both filled with choice flour with oil mixed in, for a meal offering; **74]** one gold ladle of 10 shekels, filled with incense; **75]** one bull of the herd, one ram, and one lamb in its first year, for a burnt offering; **76]** one goat for a sin offering; **77]** and for his sacrifice of well-being: two oxen, five rams, five he-goats, and five yearling lambs. That was the offering of Pagiel son of Ochran.

78] On the twelfth day, it was the chieftain of the Naphtalites, Ahira son of Enan. **79]** His offering: one silver bowl weighing 130 shekels and one silver basin of 70 shekels by the sanctuary weight, both filled with choice flour with oil mixed in, for a meal offering; **80]** one gold ladle of 10 shekels, filled with incense; **81]** one bull of the herd, one ram, and one lamb in its first year, for a burnt offering; **82]** one goat for a sin offering; **83]** and for his sacrifice of well-being: two oxen, five rams, five he-goats, and five yearling lambs. That was the offering of Ahira son of Enan.

84] This was the dedication offering for the altar from the chieftains of Israel upon its being anointed: silver bowls, 12; silver basins, 12; gold ladles, 12. **85]** Silver per bowl, 130; per basin, 70. Total silver of vessels, 2,400 sanctuary shekels. **86]** The 12 gold ladles filled with incense—10 sanctuary shekels per ladle—total gold of the ladles, 120.

87] Total of herd animals for burnt offerings, 12 bulls; of rams, 12; of yearling lambs, 12— with their proper meal offerings; of goats for sin offerings, 12. **88]** Total of herd animals for sacrifices of well-being, 24 bulls; of rams, 60; of he-goats, 60; of yearling lambs, 60. That was the dedication offering for the altar after its anointing.

ד אֶת־מֹשֶׁה: וְזֶה מַעֲשֵׂה הַמְּנֹרָה מִקְשָׁה זָהָב עַד־יְרֵכָהּ
עַד־פִּרְחָהּ מִקְשָׁה הִוא כַּמַּרְאֶה אֲשֶׁר הֶרְאָה יְהוָה
אֶת־מֹשֶׁה כֵּן עָשָׂה אֶת־הַמְּנֹרָה: פ

ה וַיְדַבֵּר יְהוָה אֶל־מֹשֶׁה לֵּאמֹר: קַח אֶת־הַלְוִיִּם מִתּוֹךְ
ו בְּנֵי יִשְׂרָאֵל וְטִהַרְתָּ אֹתָם: וְכֹה־תַעֲשֶׂה לָהֶם לְטַהֲרָם
ז הַזֵּה עֲלֵיהֶם מֵי חַטָּאת וְהֶעֱבִירוּ תַעַר עַל־כָּל־
ח בְּשָׂרָם וְכִבְּסוּ בִגְדֵיהֶם וְהִטֶּהָרוּ: וְלָקְחוּ פַּר בֶּן־בָּקָר
וּמִנְחָתוֹ סֹלֶת בְּלוּלָה בַשָּׁמֶן וּפַר־שֵׁנִי בֶן־בָּקָר תִּקַּח

פט הַמָּשַׁח אֹתוֹ: וּבְבֹא מֹשֶׁה אֶל־אֹהֶל מוֹעֵד לְדַבֵּר אִתּוֹ
וַיִּשְׁמַע אֶת־הַקּוֹל מִדַּבֵּר אֵלָיו מֵעַל הַכַּפֹּרֶת אֲשֶׁר
עַל־אֲרֹן הָעֵדֻת מִבֵּין שְׁנֵי הַכְּרֻבִים וַיְדַבֵּר אֵלָיו:

Haftarah Naso, p. 1256   פ פ פ

א וַיְדַבֵּר יְהוָה אֶל־מֹשֶׁה לֵּאמֹר: דַּבֵּר אֶל־אַהֲרֹן
וְאָמַרְתָּ אֵלָיו בְּהַעֲלֹתְךָ אֶת־הַנֵּרֹת אֶל־מוּל פְּנֵי
י הַמְּנוֹרָה יָאִירוּ שִׁבְעַת הַנֵּרוֹת: וַיַּעַשׂ כֵּן אַהֲרֹן אֶל־
מוּל פְּנֵי הַמְּנוֹרָה הֶעֱלָה נֵרֹתֶיהָ כַּאֲשֶׁר צִוָּה יְהוָה

89] When Moses went into the Tent of Meeting to speak with Him, he would hear the Voice addressing him from above the cover that was on top of the Ark of the Pact between the two cherubim; thus He spoke to him.

1] The LORD spoke to Moses, saying: **2]** Speak to Aaron and say to him, "When you mount the lamps, let the seven lamps give light at the front of the lampstand." **3]** Aaron did so; he mounted the lamps at the front of the lampstand, as the LORD had commanded Moses—·

4] Now this is how the lampstand was made: it was hammered work of gold, hammered from base to petal. According to the pattern that the LORD had shown Moses, so was the lampstand made.

5] The LORD spoke to Moses, saying: **6]** Take the Levites from among the Israelites and cleanse them. **7]** This is what you shall do to them to cleanse them: sprinkle on them water of purification, and let them go over their whole body with a razor, and wash their clothes; thus they shall be cleansed. **8]** Let them take a bull of the herd, and with it a meal offering of choice flour with oil mixed in, and you take a second bull of the herd for a sin offering.

89] *He would hear the Voice.* As he had been promised in Exod. 25:22. After the Tabernacle was dedicated, it became the place where Moses usually approached God [4].

Between the two cherubim. The winged figures described in Exod. 25:18 ff.

8:2] *Mount the lamps.* As provided for in Exod. 25:31–40. The actual lighting was entrusted to Aaron.

The lampstand. מְנוֹרָה (*menorah*); its lights were mounted in front, apparently to shed light on the table and the shew bread. A representation of the Temple menorah, stemming from the first century B.C.E., has been found, presumably the work of one who had actually seen it. J. Gutmann claims that modern Reformers first introduced the seven-branched menorah into their synagogues to show that they no longer believed in a messianic restoration of the Temple [5]. The menorah is now generally found in Jewish houses of worship and has become the national symbol of Israel.

6] *Cleanse them.* The Levites were only cleansed, not consecrated like the priests.

7] *Water of purification.* Possibly this refers to the water which was mingled with the ashes of the red cow, the laws of which are set down in Num. 19:9 [6].

Their whole body with a razor. This is what certain physically afflicted people had to do (Lev. 14:8), and it emphasizes that the Torah considers the Levites spiritually separated from the rest of the people, even as lepers and others were separated bodily. On the other hand, a nazirite who had been defiled only shaved his head (Num. 6:9). Egyptian priests shaved their bodies every second day for hygienic reasons, especially to avoid lice [7].

Wash their clothes. For the sake of purification, a procedure well known in the ancient Near East. The Pharaoh's court included an official royal launderer and a man entitled "Chief Launderer of the Palace" [8].

ט לְחַטָּאת: וְהִקְרַבְתָּ֙ אֶת־הַלְוִיִּ֔ם לִפְנֵ֖י אֹ֥הֶל מוֹעֵ֑ד
י וְהִקְהַלְתָּ֔ אֶֽת־כָּל־עֲדַ֖ת בְּנֵ֣י יִשְׂרָאֵ֑ל וְהִקְרַבְתָּ֤ אֶת־הַלְוִיִּם֙ לִפְנֵ֣י יְהֹוָ֔ה וְסָמְכ֧וּ בְנֵֽי־יִשְׂרָאֵ֛ל אֶת־יְדֵיהֶ֖ם עַל־הַלְוִיִּֽם:
יא וְהֵנִיף֩ אַהֲרֹ֨ן אֶת־הַלְוִיִּ֤ם תְּנוּפָה֙ לִפְנֵ֣י יְהֹוָ֔ה מֵאֵ֖ת בְּנֵ֣י יִשְׂרָאֵ֑ל וְהָי֕וּ לַעֲבֹ֖ד אֶת־עֲבֹדַ֥ת יְהֹוָֽה:
יב וְהַלְוִיִּם֙ יִסְמְכ֣וּ אֶת־יְדֵיהֶ֔ם עַ֖ל רֹ֣אשׁ הַפָּרִ֑ים וַעֲשֵׂ֞ה אֶת־הָאֶחָ֣ד חַטָּ֗את וְאֶת־הָאֶחָד֙ עֹלָ֣ה לַֽיהֹוָ֔ה לְכַפֵּ֖ר עַל־הַלְוִיִּֽם:
יג וְהַֽעֲמַדְתָּ֙ אֶת־הַלְוִיִּ֔ם לִפְנֵ֥י אַהֲרֹ֖ן וְלִפְנֵ֣י בָנָ֑יו וְהֵנַפְתָּ֥ אֹתָ֖ם תְּנוּפָ֥ה לַֽיהֹוָֽה: וְהִבְדַּלְתָּ֙ אֶת־הַלְוִיִּ֔ם
יד מִתּ֖וֹךְ בְּנֵ֣י יִשְׂרָאֵ֑ל וְהָ֥יוּ לִ֖י הַלְוִיִּֽם: וְאַחֲרֵי־כֵ֗ן יָבֹ֙אוּ֙

הַלְוִיִּ֔ם לַעֲבֹ֖ד אֶת־אֹ֣הֶל מוֹעֵ֑ד וְטִֽהַרְתָּ֣ אֹתָ֔ם וְהֵנַפְתָּ֥ אֹתָ֖ם תְּנוּפָֽה: כִּי֩ נְתֻנִ֨ים נְתֻנִ֥ים הֵ֙מָּה֙ לִ֔י מִתּ֖וֹךְ בְּנֵ֣י יִשְׂרָאֵ֑ל תַּ֩חַת֩ פִּטְרַ֨ת כָּל־רֶ֜חֶם בְּכ֥וֹר כֹּל֙ מִבְּנֵ֣י יִשְׂרָאֵ֔ל לָקַ֥חְתִּי אֹתָ֖ם לִֽי: כִּ֣י לִ֤י כָל־בְּכוֹר֙ בִּבְנֵ֣י יִשְׂרָאֵ֔ל בָּאָדָ֖ם וּבַבְּהֵמָ֑ה בְּי֗וֹם הַכֹּתִ֤י כָל־בְּכוֹר֙ בְּאֶ֣רֶץ מִצְרַ֔יִם הִקְדַּ֥שְׁתִּי אֹתָ֖ם לִֽי: וָאֶקַּ֙ח֙ אֶת־הַלְוִיִּ֔ם תַּ֥חַת כָּל־בְּכ֖וֹר בִּבְנֵ֣י יִשְׂרָאֵֽל: וָאֶתְּנָ֨ה אֶת־הַלְוִיִּ֜ם נְתֻנִ֣ים לְאַהֲרֹ֣ן וּלְבָנָ֗יו מִתּוֹךְ֙ בְּנֵ֣י יִשְׂרָאֵ֔ל לַעֲבֹ֞ד אֶת־עֲבֹדַ֤ת בְּנֵֽי־יִשְׂרָאֵל֙ בְּאֹ֣הֶל מוֹעֵ֔ד וּלְכַפֵּ֖ר עַל־בְּנֵ֣י יִשְׂרָאֵ֑ל וְלֹ֨א יִהְיֶ֜ה בִּבְנֵ֤י יִשְׂרָאֵל֙ נֶ֔גֶף בְּגֶ֥שֶׁת בְּנֵֽי־

9] You shall bring the Levites forward before the Tent of Meeting. Assemble the whole Israelite community, **10]** and bring the Levites forward before the LORD. Let the Israelites lay their hands upon the Levites, **11]** and let Aaron designate the Levites before the LORD as a wave offering from the Israelites, that they may perform the service of the LORD. **12]** The Levites shall now lay their hands upon the heads of the bulls; one shall be offered to the LORD as a sin offering and the other as a burnt offering, to make expiation for the Levites.

13] You shall place the Levites in attendance upon Aaron and his sons, and designate them as a wave offering to the LORD. **14]** Thus you shall set the Levites apart from among the Israelites, and the Levites shall be Mine. **15]** Thereafter the Levites shall be qualified for the service of the Tent of Meeting, once you have cleansed them and designated them as a wave offering. **16]** For they are formally assigned to Me from among the Israelites: I have taken them for Myself in place of all the first issue of the womb, of all the first-born of the Israelites. **17]** For every first-born among the Israelites, man as well as beast, is Mine; I consecrated them to Myself at the time that I smote every first-born in the land of Egypt. **18]** Now I take the Levites instead of every first-born of the Israelites; **19]** and from among the Israelites I formally assign the Levites to Aaron and his sons, to perform the service for the Israelites in the Tent of Meeting and to make expiation for the Israelites, so that no plague may afflict the Israelites for coming too near the sanctuary.

9] *Assemble the whole Israelite community.* In their presence the Levites will be symbolically "offered" to God (as if they were a sacrifice) by the laying on of hands and by "waving" (see verse 11).

10] *Let the Israelites* [that is, their representatives] *lay their hands.* סָמְכוּ (*samechu*), from which comes the word סְמִיכָה (*semichah*, ordination). Aaron "lays his hands" on the Levites (ordains them), while they "fill their hands" (are being ordained). See commentary on Num. 3:3.

11] *Wave offering.* The nature of the motion is variously described: moving the hands horizontally and vertically; or moving forward toward the altar (symbolizing the offering) and moving backward (the return of the offering by God); or the Levites being led toward or around the Holy of Holies [9].

The rendering "wave" is not felicitous, though it has talmudic backing. Originally a simple "lifting up" was probably involved, as if to show the offering to God; see commentary on Exod. 29:24 and Lev. 7:28.

14] *Set the Levites apart.* The general qualifications of the Levites are once more summarized.

19] *Formally assign.* See at Num. 3:9.

Make expiation. Or, "atonement." Some say the word *kapper* (כַּפֵּר) here doubles in its non-religious sense of "cover," and that the Levites acted as a cover or screen between the sacred place and the common people [10].

כ יִשְׂרָאֵל אֶל־הַקֹּדֶשׁ: וַיַּעַשׂ מֹשֶׁה וְאַהֲרֹן וְכָל־עֲדַת
בְּנֵי־יִשְׂרָאֵל לַלְוִיִּם כְּכֹל אֲשֶׁר־צִוָּה יְהוָה אֶת־מֹשֶׁה

כא לַלְוִיִּם כֵּן־עָשׂוּ לָהֶם בְּנֵי יִשְׂרָאֵל: וַיִּתְחַטְּאוּ הַלְוִיִּם
וַיְכַבְּסוּ בִּגְדֵיהֶם וַיָּנֶף אַהֲרֹן אֹתָם תְּנוּפָה לִפְנֵי יְהוָה

כב וַיְכַפֵּר עֲלֵיהֶם אַהֲרֹן לְטַהֲרָם: וְאַחֲרֵי־כֵן בָּאוּ הַלְוִיִּם
לַעֲבֹד אֶת־עֲבֹדָתָם בְּאֹהֶל מוֹעֵד לִפְנֵי אַהֲרֹן וְלִפְנֵי
בָנָיו כַּאֲשֶׁר צִוָּה יְהוָה אֶת־מֹשֶׁה עַל־הַלְוִיִּם כֵּן עָשׂוּ

כג לָהֶם: ס וַיְדַבֵּר יְהוָה אֶל־מֹשֶׁה לֵּאמֹר: זֹאת אֲשֶׁר
כד לַלְוִיִּם מִבֶּן חָמֵשׁ וְעֶשְׂרִים שָׁנָה וָמַעְלָה יָבוֹא לִצְבֹא
כה צָבָא בַּעֲבֹדַת אֹהֶל מוֹעֵד: וּמִבֶּן חֲמִשִּׁים שָׁנָה יָשׁוּב
כו מִצְּבָא הָעֲבֹדָה וְלֹא יַעֲבֹד עוֹד: וְשֵׁרֵת אֶת־אֶחָיו
בְּאֹהֶל מוֹעֵד לִשְׁמֹר מִשְׁמֶרֶת וַעֲבֹדָה לֹא יַעֲבֹד כָּכָה
תַּעֲשֶׂה לַלְוִיִּם בְּמִשְׁמְרֹתָם: פ

20] Moses, Aaron, and the whole Israelite community did with the Levites accordingly; just as the LORD had commanded Moses in regard to the Levites, so the Israelites did with them. 21] The Levites purified themselves and washed their clothes; and Aaron designated them as a wave offering before the LORD, and Aaron made expiation for them to cleanse them. 22] Thereafter, the Levites were qualified to perform their service in the Tent of Meeting, under Aaron and his sons. As the LORD had commanded Moses in regard to the Levites, so they did to them.

23] The LORD spoke to Moses, saying: 24] This is the rule for the Levites. From twenty-five years of age up they shall participate in the work force in the service of the Tent of Meeting; 25] but at the age of fifty they shall retire from the work force and shall serve no more. 26] They may assist their brother Levites at the Tent of Meeting by standing guard, but they shall perform no labor. Thus you shall deal with the Levites in regard to their duties.

21] *Purified.* Literally, "unsinned."
24] *From twenty-five years.* Num. 4:3, 23, 30 put the age at thirty. Perhaps the first five years were a probationary period, or the Levites were used in guard service as they were after they reached the age of fifty (verse 26). The tasks entrusted to the Levites were thought to require maturity as well as physical fitness [11].

The Symbolic Context

Levites play an important role in the complex relationship between God and Israel. Basic to this relationship is the belief that all of Israel's first-born sons belong to God (Num. 8:13–17). Because God accepts the Levites as substitutes, they are set aside in a special way. However, He does not keep them for Himself but surrenders them, so to speak, to the priests. Hereafter, the Levites serve the priests. This service, then, is a double substitution: it represents God's claim on the Levites, which in turn derives from their substitution for all the first-born. We must therefore approach these passages with the understanding that biblical men saw the levitic and priestly duties in a symbolic context that included their own first-born sons and thus involved them directly and significantly in the acts described. What appears as ritual history to us was religious reality of high meaning to them.[1]

This explains the lavish attention that the Midrash pays to chapter 7. Its treatment of Nahshon, who brought his offering on the first day (Num. 7:12) may serve as one example. It is noted, for instance, that Nahshon alone of all the leaders is not called a chieftain. The reason given by the Midrash is that he might be tempted to exalt himself over his brethren since he is assigned to the sacrifice of the first day. Hence his title was purposefully omitted.

The same reason is given in an interpretation of verse 13, which in the Hebrew literally says: "*And* his offering . . ." (rather than merely "His offering"). The additional "and," which would be appropriate for the subsequent offerings, was inserted (according to the Midrash) so that Nahshon could not boast by saying "I was the first." For, were he to boast nonetheless, people could point to the "and" to indicate that he was in fact the last [12].

Another example from the Midrash: The Torah mentions three offerings (Num. 7:45) because of Israel's three merits during their slavery in Egypt: they did not change their names; they preserved Hebrew as their language; and they were chaste [13].

Added to all other considerations, tradition saw the Tabernacle and its service as a new stage in God's relationship to Israel (see Commentary on Exodus, chapters 25 ff.). This idea is expressed in the midrashic saying that in Adam's time the Divine Presence departed from this world, but when the Tabernacle was erected it returned. In fact, the Rabbis compared the day on which the Tabernacle was reared up to the day on which the world was created [14]. The Tabernacle signified that God's Presence dwelt in the midst of His beloved people.

---

[1] An interesting reflection of such substitutional practice persists into modern days. In traditional Judaism a first-born son is obligated to fast on the day before Passover but is permitted to substitute for the fast a form of talmudic study.

GLEANINGS

On Their Shoulders (Num. 7:9)

It seems to me, as I read this verse and re-read it, that we are being told not only about a detail of transportation but that we are also being instructed in a very important matter. When it comes to the very heart of religion, we must not try to find—and cannot really find—a substitute for our own shoulders. We cannot transfer to anybody else, or to anything else, the obligations that rest exclusively upon ourselves. There are things that others cannot do for us.

The Bene Kehat—the "family that carried the ark"—had a challenging responsibility. They had to carry it upon their own bodies; they had to feel its weight; they could not seek means to make the burden easier. Religion, too, is a burden, and it is also a discipline. Anyone who seeks to carry a faith easily, shouldering no special tasks, making no distinctive sacrifices, will have a religion that is neither true nor helpful.

M. ADLER [15]

God's Love

God fills the heaven and the earth, yet out of love for His people He contracts His glory as if He actually dwelt between the cherubim.

MIDRASH [16]

Each One

Seeing that the offerings of the princes were all identical and in the same amount, why should Scripture mention the offerings of each prince separately? Because each of them brought his offering of his own accord, not in order to ape the others, but solely of his own free will.

CHASIDIC [17]

The Voice (Num. 7:89)

The word "addressing" (מְדַבֵּר, *midaber*) is a rare reflexive form, as if God were speaking to Himself and Moses overhearing Him. (מְדַבֵּר is understood as if מִתְדַּבֵּר.)

RASHI [18]

[Another explanation: The Masoretes purposely did not punctuate מְדַבֵּר, in order to minimize the possibility that "the Voice" would be identified with a divine person apart from God.]

Vayehi (וַיְהִי)

The Midrash expounded at length on the opening word of Num. 7, which in older translations was rendered "And it came to pass...." The expression was taken to indicate that something radically new had happened.

Rab expounded: Something that had never happened from the time the world was created until then took place on that day. From the time when the world was created until that moment the *Shechinah* had never dwelt in this lower world. It only did this from the moment when the Tabernacle was erected and thenceforward. For this reason it says *Vayehi*: it was an innovation. R. Shimon bar Yochai said it was something that, having already been in existence, had ceased and now returned to its previous state. You find that from the beginning of the world's creation the *Shechinah* had dwelt in this lower world; but, once the *Shechinah* departed at the time when Adam sinned, it did not descend again until the Tabernacle had been erected.

MIDRASH [19]

Before the Tabernacle was set up the world was unstable, but when the Tabernacle was erected the world was firmly established.

MIDRASH [20]

The Second Passover; the Cloud;
the Silver Trumpets

Three separate matters are dealt with in this section: the celebration of a "Second Passover" for those prevented from observing it at its proper time; a detailed description of the cloud that signified God's presence in the camp; and the use of the silver trumpets for secular and religious occasions.

It will be noted that the section begins by specifying the time of the divine instruction as the first new moon of the second year after the Exodus, that is to say, in the first month of that year.* As mentioned before, this historical note—introducing a legal prescription—is characteristic of the Book of Numbers, but the time itself is one month earlier than the time at which Numbers opens in chapter 1. This obvious difficulty led the Rabbis to establish the principle (since then applied in numerous other places) of אֵין מֻקְדָם וּמְאֻחָר בַּתּוֹרָה, "There is no before or after in the Torah" [1]. In their view the book had to be seen as whole, and sequence or placement were not to be judged by ordinary measures. This principle made it possible to explain other scriptural problems of a similar nature and it was justified by the fundamental conviction that the Torah was of divine origin and hence could not be approached like creations of human hands.

---

* The Israelites were therefore still at Mt. Sinai, since they did not leave from there until the twentieth day of the second month (see Num. 10:11).

הַהוּא וַיִּקְרְב֕וּ לִפְנֵ֥י מֹשֶׁ֖ה וְלִפְנֵ֣י אַהֲרֹ֑ן בַּיּ֥וֹם הַהֽוּא׃
ז וַיֹּאמְר֨וּ הָאֲנָשִׁ֜ים הָהֵ֗מָּה אֵלָיו֙ אֲנַ֣חְנוּ טְמֵאִ֖ים לְנֶ֣פֶשׁ
אָדָ֑ם לָ֣מָּה נִגָּרַ֗ע לְבִלְתִּ֡י הַקְרִב֩ אֶת־קָרְבַּ֨ן יְהֹוָ֜ה
בְּמֹעֲד֔וֹ בְּת֖וֹךְ בְּנֵ֥י יִשְׂרָאֵֽל׃ ח וַיֹּ֥אמֶר אֲלֵהֶ֖ם מֹשֶׁ֑ה עִמְד֣וּ
וְאֶשְׁמְעָ֔ה מַה־יְצַוֶּ֥ה יְהֹוָ֖ה לָכֶֽם׃ פ

ט וַיְדַבֵּ֥ר יְהֹוָ֖ה אֶל־מֹשֶׁ֥ה לֵּאמֹֽר׃ י דַּבֵּ֛ר אֶל־בְּנֵ֥י יִשְׂרָאֵ֖ל
לֵאמֹ֑ר אִ֣ישׁ אִ֣ישׁ כִּֽי־יִהְיֶֽה־טָמֵ֣א ׀ לָנֶ֗פֶשׁ אוֹ֩ בְדֶ֨רֶךְ
רְחֹקָ֜הׁ לָכֶ֗ם א֚וֹ לְדֹרֹ֣תֵיכֶ֔ם וְעָ֥שָׂה פֶ֖סַח לַיהֹוָֽה׃
יא בַּחֹ֨דֶשׁ הַשֵּׁנִ֜י בְּאַרְבָּעָ֨ה עָשָׂ֥ר י֛וֹם בֵּ֥ין הָעַרְבַּ֖יִם יַעֲשׂ֣וּ
אֹת֑וֹ עַל־מַצּ֥וֹת וּמְרֹרִ֖ים יֹאכְלֻֽהוּ׃ יב לֹֽא־יַשְׁאִ֤ירוּ מִמֶּ֙נּוּ֙

א וַיְדַבֵּ֣ר יְהֹוָ֣ה אֶל־מֹשֶׁ֣ה בְמִדְבַּר־סִינַ֡י בַּשָּׁנָ֣ה הַשֵּׁנִ֡ית
לְצֵאתָ֞ם מֵאֶ֧רֶץ מִצְרַ֛יִם בַּחֹ֥דֶשׁ הָרִאשׁ֖וֹן לֵאמֹֽר׃
ב וְיַעֲשׂ֧וּ בְנֵֽי־יִשְׂרָאֵ֛ל אֶת־הַפָּ֖סַח בְּמוֹעֲדֽוֹ׃ ג בְּאַרְבָּעָ֣ה
עָשָֽׂר־י֠וֹם בַּחֹ֨דֶשׁ הַזֶּ֜ה בֵּ֧ין הָעַרְבַּ֛יִם תַּעֲשׂ֥וּ אֹת֖וֹ
בְּמֹעֲד֑וֹ כְּכׇל־חֻקֹּתָ֛יו וּכְכׇל־מִשְׁפָּטָ֖יו תַּעֲשׂ֥וּ אֹתֽוֹ׃
ד וַיְדַבֵּ֥ר מֹשֶׁ֛ה אֶל־בְּנֵ֥י יִשְׂרָאֵ֖ל לַעֲשֹׂ֥ת הַפָּֽסַח׃ ה וַיַּעֲשׂ֣וּ
אֶת־הַפֶּ֡סַח בָּרִאשׁ֡וֹן בְּאַרְבָּעָה֩ עָשָׂ֨ר י֥וֹם לַחֹ֛דֶשׁ בֵּ֥ין
הָעַרְבַּ֖יִם בְּמִדְבַּ֣ר סִינָ֑י כְּ֠כֹ֠ל אֲשֶׁ֨ר צִוָּ֤ה יְהֹוָה֙ אֶת־
מֹשֶׁ֔ה כֵּ֥ן עָשׂ֖וּ בְּנֵ֥י יִשְׂרָאֵֽל׃ ו וַיְהִ֣י אֲנָשִׁ֗ים אֲשֶׁ֨ר הָי֤וּ
טְמֵאִים֙ לְנֶ֣פֶשׁ אָדָ֔ם וְלֹא־יָכְל֥וּ לַעֲשֹׂת־הַפֶּ֖סַח בַּיּ֣וֹם

<small>* ו סבירין ויהיו</small>

1] The LORD spoke to Moses in the wilderness of Sinai, on the first new moon of the second year following the exodus from the land of Egypt, saying: **2]** Let the Israelite people offer the passover sacrifice at its set time: **3]** you shall offer it on the fourteenth day of this month, at twilight, at its set time; you shall offer it in accordance with all its rules and rites.

4] Moses instructed the Israelites to offer the passover sacrifice; **5]** and they offered the passover sacrifice in the first month, on the fourteenth day of the month, at twilight, in the wilderness of Sinai. Just as the LORD had commanded Moses, so the Israelites did.

6] But there were some men who were unclean by reason of a corpse and could not offer the passover sacrifice on that day. Appearing that same day before Moses and Aaron, **7]** those men said to them, "Unclean though we are by reason of a corpse, why must we be debarred from presenting the LORD's offering at its set time with the rest of the Israelites?" **8]** Moses said to them, "Stand by, and let me hear what instructions the LORD gives about you."

9] And the LORD spoke to Moses, saying: **10]** Speak to the Israelite people, saying: When any of you or of your posterity who are defiled by a corpse or are on a long journey would offer a passover sacrifice to the LORD, **11]** they shall offer it in the second month, on the fourteenth day of the month, at twilight. They shall eat it with unleavened bread and bitter herbs,

9:1] *The Lord spoke.* It is possible to understand the Hebrew as a pluperfect: "The Lord had spoken." This would avoid the difficulty (noted above) regarding the time sequence by making this verse a recapitulation of an earlier statement. Biblical critics generally assign 9:1 ff. to one source, and chapters 1–6 to another.

2] *At its set time.* As already set forth in Exod. 12.

3] *At twilight.* Literally, "between the evenings." The exact time span was a matter of rabbinic controversy. The time to light Sabbath candles on Friday afternoon is before twilight.

According to the Samaritans and Karaites the time was between sunset and darkness; according to Josephus it was between three and five p.m. ("the ninth to eleventh hours") [2].

4] *To offer the passover sacrifice.* According to some this was the only time they did so in the wilderness, for Exod. 12:25 commands its observance first in Egypt and then again only after the Israelites enter Canaan [3]. The Passover celebration at this time may have been understood as part of the ceremonies dedicating the Tabernacle.

6] *Unclean . . . and could not offer.* As Lev. 7:20–21 expressly forbids.

10] *Long journey.* Literally, "far" journey. On the Masoretic dot over the word "long," see commentary below.

11] *Unleavened bread and bitter herbs.* As prescribed in Exod. 12:8.

הַמִּשְׁכָּן כִּסָּה הֶעָנָן אֶת־הַמִּשְׁכָּן לְאֹהֶל הָעֵדֻת וּבָעֶרֶב   עַד־בֹּקֶר וְעֶצֶם לֹא יִשְׁבְּרוּ־בוֹ כְּכָל־חֻקַּת הַפֶּסַח
יִהְיֶה עַל־הַמִּשְׁכָּן כְּמַרְאֵה־אֵשׁ עַד־בֹּקֶר: כֵּן יִהְיֶה   יַעֲשׂוּ אֹתוֹ: וְהָאִישׁ אֲשֶׁר־הוּא טָהוֹר וּבְדֶרֶךְ לֹא־הָיָה
תָמִיד הֶעָנָן יְכַסֶּנּוּ וּמַרְאֵה־אֵשׁ לָיְלָה: וּלְפִי הֵעָלֹת   וְחָדַל לַעֲשׂוֹת הַפֶּסַח וְנִכְרְתָה הַנֶּפֶשׁ הַהִוא מֵעַמֶּיהָ
הֶעָנָן מֵעַל הָאֹהֶל וְאַחֲרֵי כֵן יִסְעוּ בְּנֵי יִשְׂרָאֵל   כִּי קָרְבַּן יְהֹוָה לֹא הִקְרִיב בְּמֹעֲדוֹ חֶטְאוֹ יִשָּׂא
וּבִמְקוֹם אֲשֶׁר יִשְׁכָּן־שָׁם הֶעָנָן שָׁם יַחֲנוּ בְּנֵי יִשְׂרָאֵל: הָאִישׁ הַהוּא: וְכִי־יָגוּר אִתְּכֶם גֵּר וְעָשָׂה פֶסַח לַיהֹוָה
עַל־פִּי יְהֹוָה יִסְעוּ בְּנֵי יִשְׂרָאֵל וְעַל־פִּי יְהֹוָה יַחֲנוּ כָּל־   כְּחֻקַּת הַפֶּסַח וּכְמִשְׁפָּטוֹ כֵּן יַעֲשֶׂה חֻקָּה אַחַת יִהְיֶה
יְמֵי אֲשֶׁר יִשְׁכֹּן הֶעָנָן עַל־הַמִּשְׁכָּן יַחֲנוּ: וּבְהַאֲרִיךְ   לָכֶם וְלַגֵּר וּלְאֶזְרַח הָאָרֶץ: ס וּבְיוֹם הָקִים אֶת־

12] and they shall not leave any of it over until morning. They shall not break a bone of it. They shall offer it in strict accord with the law of the passover sacrifice. 13] But if a man who is clean and not on a journey refrains from offering the passover sacrifice, that person shall be cut off from his kin, for he did not present the LORD's offering at its set time; that man shall bear his guilt.

14] And when a stranger who resides with you would offer a passover sacrifice to the LORD, he must offer it in accordance with the rules and rites of the passover sacrifice. There shall be one law for you, whether stranger or citizen of the country.

15] On the day that the Tabernacle was set up, the cloud covered the Tabernacle, the Tent of the Pact; and in the evening it rested over the Tabernacle in the likeness of fire until morning. 16] It was always so: the cloud covered it, appearing as fire by night. 17] And whenever the cloud lifted from the Tent, the Israelites would set out accordingly; and at the spot where the cloud settled, there the Israelites would make camp. 18] On a sign from the LORD the Israelites broke camp, and on a sign from the LORD they made camp: they remained

12] *Not break a bone.* See Exod. 12:46. Critics consider these provisions as belonging originally to two separate festivals, the Feast of Passover and the Feast of Matzot.

In strict accord. The Second Passover is to be observed like the first, but the Rabbis ruled that it was not subject to *all* the laws of the first Passover; thus, leavened bread did not need to be removed from the house [4]. An observance of the Second Passover is described in II Chron. 30.

The law. Repeated here because of the exception which follows [5].

13] *Cut off from his kin.* Or, according to rabbinic tradition, punished by God, through death without offspring or through some other means [6]. See at Exod. 31:14.

14] *Stranger.* גֵּר (*ger*), a resident alien (the Hebrew verb גּוּר, means "to reside"). He had all the rights and legal protections of a citizen (אֶזְרַח)

but had to submit to circumcision if he wanted to participate in the Passover rites (Exod. 12:48–49). Later on, *ger* (especially *ger tzedek*) became the term for proselyte, which is also current usage.

15] *The cloud.* Other biblical passages speak of the cloud preceding Israel on its journeys (Exod. 13:21); guiding it (Exod. 40:34–38); standing in front of the Tabernacle (Exod. 33:7–11). The reason for this detailed passage containing previously stated information is not clear [7].

Tabernacle, the Tent of the Pact. The terms appear here to be used synonymously. But traditional interpreters understood "Tabernacle" to mean the whole structure and "Tent of the Pact" that portion where the ark was kept and where alone the cloud rested [8]. Also see at Exod. 40.

18] *On a sign.* That is, on God's command. The passage makes it clear that no other independent power was involved [9].

יח וַיְדַבֵּר יְהוָה אֶל־מֹשֶׁה לֵּאמֹר: עֲשֵׂה לְךָ שְׁתֵּי

חֲצוֹצְרֹת כֶּסֶף מִקְשָׁה תַּעֲשֶׂה אֹתָם וְהָיוּ לְךָ לְמִקְרָא

הָעֵדָה וּלְמַסַּע אֶת־הַמַּחֲנוֹת: וְתָקְעוּ בָּהֵן וְנוֹעֲדוּ

אֵלֶיךָ כָּל־הָעֵדָה אֶל־פֶּתַח אֹהֶל מוֹעֵד: וְאִם־בְּאַחַת

יִתְקָעוּ וְנוֹעֲדוּ אֵלֶיךָ הַנְּשִׂיאִים רָאשֵׁי אַלְפֵי יִשְׂרָאֵל:

וּתְקַעְתֶּם תְּרוּעָה וְנָסְעוּ הַמַּחֲנוֹת הַחֹנִים קֵדְמָה:

וּתְקַעְתֶּם תְּרוּעָה שֵׁנִית וְנָסְעוּ הַמַּחֲנוֹת הַחֹנִים תֵּימָנָה

תְּרוּעָה יִתְקְעוּ לְמַסְעֵיהֶם: וּבְהַקְהִיל אֶת־הַקָּהָל

תִּתְקְעוּ וְלֹא תָרִיעוּ: וּבְנֵי אַהֲרֹן הַכֹּהֲנִים יִתְקְעוּ

בַּחֲצֹצְרוֹת וְהָיוּ לָכֶם לְחֻקַּת עוֹלָם לְדֹרֹתֵיכֶם:

הֶעָנָן עַל־הַמִּשְׁכָּן יָמִים רַבִּים וְשָׁמְרוּ בְנֵי־יִשְׂרָאֵל

אֶת־מִשְׁמֶרֶת יְהוָה וְלֹא יִסָּעוּ: וְיֵשׁ אֲשֶׁר יִהְיֶה הֶעָנָן

יָמִים מִסְפָּר עַל־הַמִּשְׁכָּן עַל־פִּי יְהוָה יַחֲנוּ וְעַל־פִּי

יְהוָה יִסָּעוּ: וְיֵשׁ אֲשֶׁר יִהְיֶה הֶעָנָן מֵעֶרֶב עַד־בֹּקֶר

וְנַעֲלָה הֶעָנָן בַּבֹּקֶר וְנָסָעוּ אוֹ יוֹמָם וָלַיְלָה וְנַעֲלָה

הֶעָנָן וְנָסָעוּ: אוֹ־יֹמַיִם אוֹ־חֹדֶשׁ אוֹ־יָמִים בְּהַאֲרִיךְ

הֶעָנָן עַל־הַמִּשְׁכָּן לִשְׁכֹּן עָלָיו יַחֲנוּ בְנֵי־יִשְׂרָאֵל וְלֹא

יִסָּעוּ וּבְהֵעָלֹתוֹ יִסָּעוּ: עַל־פִּי יְהוָה יַחֲנוּ וְעַל־פִּי

יְהוָה יִסָּעוּ אֶת־מִשְׁמֶרֶת יְהוָה שָׁמְרוּ עַל־פִּי יְהוָה

בְּיַד־מֹשֶׁה: פ

encamped as long as the cloud stayed over the Tabernacle. **19]** When the cloud lingered over the Tabernacle many days, the Israelites observed the LORD's mandate and did not journey on. **20]** At such times as the cloud rested over the Tabernacle for but a few days, they remained encamped on a sign from the LORD, and broke camp on a sign from the LORD. **21]** And at such times as the cloud stayed from evening until morning, they broke camp as soon as the cloud lifted in the morning. Day or night, whenever the cloud lifted, they would break camp. **22]** Whether it was two days or a month or a year—however long the cloud lingered over the Tabernacle—the Israelites remained encamped and did not set out; only when it lifted did they break camp. **23]** On a sign from the LORD they made camp and on a sign from the LORD they broke camp; they observed the LORD's mandate at the LORD's bidding through Moses.

1] The LORD spoke to Moses, saying: **2]** Have two silver trumpets made; make them of hammered work. They shall serve you to summon the community and to set the divisions in motion. **3]** When both are blown in long blasts, the whole community shall assemble before you at the entrance of the Tent of Meeting; **4]** and if only one is blown, the chieftains, heads of Israel's contingents, shall assemble before you. **5]** But when you sound short blasts, the divisions encamped on the east shall move forward; **6]** and when you sound short blasts a second time, those encamped on the south shall move forward. Thus short blasts shall be blown for setting them in motion, **7]** while to convoke the congregation you shall blow long blasts, not short ones. **8]** The trumpets shall be blown by Aaron's sons, the priests.

22] *A year.* Here, not an exact span but an indefinite expression; literally, "(many) days" [10]. Compare Lev. 25:29; I Sam. 27:7.

10:2] *Trumpets.* Their sound supplemented the visible sign of the cloud. They were about three to four feet long, straight, with flaring ends. A reproduction may be seen on the Arch of Titus in Rome and on a coin from Bar Kochba's time [11]. Such trumpets were for centuries used in St. Peter's Basilica at papal masses.

3] *Long blasts.* This is the traditional interpretation, but the Hebrew meaning is uncertain. In the synagogue ritual, *tekiah* denotes a single blast, *teruah* a series of staccato blasts [12].

וּבְרָאשֵׁי חָדְשֵׁיכֶם וּתְקַעְתֶּם בַּחֲצֹצְרֹת עַל עֹלֹתֵיכֶם   ט וְכִי־תָבֹאוּ מִלְחָמָה בְּאַרְצְכֶם עַל־הַצַּר הַצֹּרֵר אֶתְכֶם

וְעַל זִבְחֵי שַׁלְמֵיכֶם וְהָיוּ לָכֶם לְזִכָּרוֹן לִפְנֵי אֱלֹהֵיכֶם   וַהֲרֵעֹתֶם בַּחֲצֹצְרֹת וְנִזְכַּרְתֶּם לִפְנֵי יְהוָה אֱלֹהֵיכֶם

אֲנִי יְהוָה אֱלֹהֵיכֶם: פ   י וְנוֹשַׁעְתֶּם מֵאֹיְבֵיכֶם: וּבְיוֹם שִׂמְחַתְכֶם וּבְמוֹעֲדֵיכֶם

ט צ׳ פתוחה.

This shall be for you an institution for all time throughout the ages. **9]** When you are at war in your own land against an aggressor who attacks you, you shall sound short blasts on the trumpets, that you may be remembered before the LORD your God and be delivered from your enemies. **10]** And on your joyous occasions, your fixed festivals and new moon days, you shall sound the trumpets over your burnt offerings and your sacrifices of well-being. They shall be a reminder of you before the LORD your God: I the LORD am your God.

9] *Remembered before the Lord.* As if it were a prayer. Another interpretation: Because you will have done according to God's command [13].

10] *Joyous occasions.* As, for instance, when David removed the ark (I Chron. 15:24) or when Solomon dedicated the Temple (II Chron. 5:12).

Fixed festivals. Those enumerated in Lev. 23 and Num. 28.

The Development of Law

The passages concerned with the Second Passover afford us a special opportunity to observe the development of biblical and postbiblical law. The Passover rites have two sources, joining more ancient traditions involving the sacrifice of an animal to a more recent institution based on the use of unleavened bread [14]. After the destruction of the Temple in 70 C.E. the tradition of eating unleavened bread became the center of the Jewish holy day week; today only the Samaritans continue the sacrificial rites, which they hold on Mt. Gerizim near Shechem. Christians consider Jesus as the paschal lamb and partake of the sacrifice symbolically through communion.

The institution of the Second Passover was clearly an adjustment to certain recurring situations. For instance, the original law had made no allowance for someone's uncleanness or for his inability to bring the sacrifice due to absence from the sanctuary. In the time of Hezekiah's reforms (after the destruction of the Kingdom of Israel in 721 B.C.E.), a Second Passover was observed for reasons not stated in the Torah, namely, "because the priests had not sanctified themselves in sufficient number, neither had the people gathered themselves together in Jerusalem" (II Chron. 30:3). It appears that the supplementary law was applied in a time of political and religious reconstruction, but beyond this the intrabiblical record does not disclose how widely or frequently the law was observed. We only know that, in general, ritual practice was lax during the earlier centuries.

The development of the law did not cease here. The Torah specifies that persons on a long journey are privileged to observe the Passover a month later. Since a person's inability to go to Jerusalem was not always a matter of being too far away, the word "long" (or "far") was interpreted by the Rabbis both literally and figuratively. The Mishnah extended the reasons for absence to error and constraint and said categorically that "long journey" was equivalent to any place outside the Temple [15]. Biblical manuscripts were provided with a special notation in the form of a dot ("diacritical point") over the last letter of the word "long" (רְחֹקָה). It showed the reader that while the text said one thing it should be understood differently.[1]

This was an extreme method of dealing with situations which could no longer be covered by the letter of the law. Since a new law could not be formulated nor the current law changed (Deut. 4:2), amendments and developments took place on the basis of the written word—even if, as here, the word was denied its original meaning. This method of legal growth was the foundation for the halachah, the system of Jewish law, and it worked as long as the rabbis felt free to mold the law in accordance with the demands of the time. Halachah ran into serious difficulties only in modern times when the rabbis no longer considered themselves qualified to interpret the law freely. This absence of a vigorous adaptive process in the turbulent days following the emancipation gave rise to the Reform movement (nineteenth century), which opened new avenues for reinterpretation. At the same time this development could not help but weaken the respect for the underlying postbiblical law, though this had not been the intent of the Reformers.

---

[1] There are ten places in the Torah and five in the rest of the Bible which have diacritical points added [16].

GLEANINGS

The Stranger

It is a feature of Israelite law that the resident alien shall be subject to the same laws as the native Israelite. He is the newcomer. Special care has to be taken that he not be deprived of human rights because, like the widow and fatherless, he has no protector. He can share the privileges, but he also has to obey the rules.

N. H. SNAITH [17]

Unpredictable

Will and purpose behind the cloud were entirely unpredictable. Sometimes there was a long stay, sometimes the rest was for a few days only. That was the school of wandering in the desert, in which we were to learn for all time to accept what God demands, however incomprehensible His guidance. S. R. HIRSCH [18]

Trumpet and Cloud

The cloud was a visual, the trumpets an auditive reminder of God's presence. Somehow Jewish instinct never quite trusted the witness of the eyes. Moses performed signs, but these could be duplicated—what he *said* could not. At Sinai the emphasis was not so much on what the people saw but, more importantly, on what they heard. The true key word of Judaism is not *re-eh* (see) but *shema* (hear). The cloud is gone, the sound of the shofar remains.

The Sound of the Shofar

In ancient Israel the sound of the ram's horn announced the beginning of a new month and all the solemn moments of the year. But, when the new moon of the seventh month came to be observed as the New Year [Rosh Hashanah], it gathered to itself new and deeper meanings.

In time it came to commemorate the creation of the world; to recall the binding of Isaac and the covenant at Sinai; to celebrate God's kingship over the universe; to warn of his judgment upon all men, demanding of them repentance and rededication; and to proclaim the ultimate triumph of good over evil.

The shofar, then, reminds us of our responsibilities as human beings, created in God's image, and as members of the house of Israel, whose task it is to be a kingdom of priests and a holy people. GATES OF REPENTANCE [19]

The stirring sound of the shofar proclaimed the covenant at Mount Sinai which bound Israel to God as a kingdom of priests and a holy people. Ever since that distant day, the voice of the shofar has resounded through the habitations of Israel awakening high allegiance to God and His commandments. At the new moon, on joyous festivals as well as on solemn days of fasting and repentance, and in the jubilee year when liberty was proclaimed throughout the land, our fathers hearkened to the tones of the ram's horn and recalled their obligation to serve the Lord with all their heart and with all their strength. Thus do we, their children, prepare to hearken now to the solemn sound of the shofar. May it summon us to struggle against the forces of evil within our hearts and in the world. Let it arouse within us the will to righteousness and strengthen our trust in God's justice and love. May it direct our thoughts to the day when the shofar will sound for the redemption of all mankind.

UNION PRAYER BOOK [20]

PART II

A People Wandering

Of Rebels and Prophets

The Torah now turns to the wanderings in the wilderness that will be the subject matter of the next ten chapters (until 20:13). The order of the march is set forth and the people move on, only to exhibit feelings of deep unrest.

The theme of rebellion against God runs like a thread through the Torah and much of the Bible, especially the prophetic books. It begins with the first man, who rebelled by tasting the fruits of knowledge. It continues in the rebellion of Cain, the uprising of the generation of Babel, and in time becomes a recurrent feature of Israel's relationship to its covenantal Partner. Here, the popular rebellion is based on general dissatisfaction (verses 1–3) and then focuses on the boredom of eating manna day after day (verses 4 ff.). The so-called "riffraff" is blamed for stimulating the dissatisfaction of the people.

In the ensuing tension Moses realizes that he needs assistance. The seventy men who are chosen become not merely deputized administrators but also purveyors of prophecy. While a zealous Joshua urges his master to restrict such competition, Moses rejects a narrow interpretation of prophetic privilege.

יא וַיְהִי בַּשָּׁנָה הַשֵּׁנִית בַּחֹדֶשׁ הַשֵּׁנִי בְּעֶשְׂרִים בַּחֹדֶשׁ
יב נַעֲלָה הֶעָנָן מֵעַל מִשְׁכַּן הָעֵדֻת וַיִּסְעוּ בְנֵי־יִשְׂרָאֵל לְמַסְעֵיהֶם מִמִּדְבַּר סִינָי וַיִּשְׁכֹּן הֶעָנָן בְּמִדְבַּר פָּארָן:
יג וַיִּסְעוּ בָּרִאשֹׁנָה עַל־פִּי יְהֹוָה בְּיַד־מֹשֶׁה: וַיִּסַּע דֶּגֶל מַחֲנֵה בְנֵי־יְהוּדָה בָּרִאשֹׁנָה לְצִבְאֹתָם וְעַל־צְבָאוֹ
יד נַחְשׁוֹן בֶּן־עַמִּינָדָב: וְעַל־צְבָא מַטֵּה בְּנֵי יִשָּׂשכָר
טו נְתַנְאֵל בֶּן־צוּעָר: וְעַל־צְבָא מַטֵּה בְּנֵי זְבוּלֻן אֱלִיאָב
טז בֶּן־חֵלֹן: וְהוּרַד הַמִּשְׁכָּן וְנָסְעוּ בְנֵי־גֵרְשׁוֹן וּבְנֵי מְרָרִי
יז נֹשְׂאֵי הַמִּשְׁכָּן: וְנָסַע דֶּגֶל מַחֲנֵה רְאוּבֵן לְצִבְאֹתָם
יח וְעַל־צְבָאוֹ אֱלִיצוּר בֶּן־שְׁדֵיאוּר: וְעַל־צְבָא מַטֵּה בְּנֵי

כ שִׁמְעוֹן שְׁלֻמִיאֵל בֶּן־צוּרִישַׁדָּי: וְעַל־צְבָא מַטֵּה בְּנֵי־
כא גָד אֶלְיָסָף בֶּן־דְּעוּאֵל: וְנָסְעוּ הַקְּהָתִים נֹשְׂאֵי הַמִּקְדָּשׁ
כב וְהֵקִימוּ אֶת־הַמִּשְׁכָּן עַד־בֹּאָם: וְנָסַע דֶּגֶל מַחֲנֵה בְנֵי־אֶפְרַיִם לְצִבְאֹתָם וְעַל־צְבָאוֹ אֱלִישָׁמָע בֶּן־עַמִּיהוּד:
כג וְעַל־צְבָא מַטֵּה בְּנֵי מְנַשֶּׁה גַּמְלִיאֵל בֶּן־פְּדָהצוּר:
כד וְעַל־צְבָא מַטֵּה בְּנֵי בִנְיָמִן אֲבִידָן בֶּן־גִּדְעוֹנִי: וְנָסַע
כה דֶּגֶל מַחֲנֵה בְנֵי־דָן מְאַסֵּף לְכָל־הַמַּחֲנֹת לְצִבְאֹתָם
כו וְעַל־צְבָאוֹ אֲחִיעֶזֶר בֶּן־עַמִּישַׁדָּי: וְעַל־צְבָא מַטֵּה בְּנֵי
כז אָשֵׁר פַּגְעִיאֵל בֶּן־עָכְרָן: וְעַל־צְבָא מַטֵּה בְּנֵי נַפְתָּלִי
כח אֲחִירַע בֶּן־עֵינָן: אֵלֶּה מַסְעֵי בְנֵי־יִשְׂרָאֵל לְצִבְאֹתָם

11] In the second year, on the twentieth day of the second month, the cloud lifted from the Tabernacle of the Pact **12]** and the Israelites set out on their journeys from the wilderness of Sinai. The cloud came to rest in the wilderness of Paran.

13] When the march was to begin, at the LORD's bidding through Moses, **14]** the first standard to set out, troop by troop, was the division of Judah. In command of its troop was Nahshon son of Amminadab; **15]** in command of the tribal troop of Issachar, Nethanel son of Zuar; **16]** and in command of the tribal troop of Zebulun, Eliab son of Helon.

17] Then the Tabernacle would be taken apart; and the Gershonites and the Merarites, who carried the Tabernacle, would set out.

18] The next standard to set out, troop by troop, was the division of Reuben. In command of its troop was Elizur son of Shedeur; **19]** in command of the tribal troop of Simeon, Shelumiel son of Zurishaddai; **20]** and in command of the tribal troop of Gad, Eliasaph son of Deuel.

21] Then the Kohathites, who carried the sacred objects, would set out; and by the time they arrived, the Tabernacle would be set up again.

22] The next standard to set out, troop by troop, was the division of Ephraim. In command of its troop was Elishama son of Ammihud; **23]** in command of the tribal troop of Manasseh, Gamaliel son of Pedahzur; **24]** and in command of the tribal troop of Benjamin, Abidan son of Gideoni.

25] Then, as the rear guard of all the divisions, the standard of the division of Dan would set out, troop by troop. In command of its troop was Ahiezer son of Ammishaddai; **26]** in command of the tribal troop of Asher, Pagiel son of Ochran; **27]** and in command of the tribal troop of Naphtali, Ahira son of Enan.

28] Such was the Israelites' order of march, as they marched troop by troop.

10:12] *Wilderness of Paran.* The central and north- ern part of the Sinai peninsula and the central Negev. It is not clear where precisely in this area the people were.

אֹתָֽנוּ כִּ֣י עַל־כֵּ֤ן יָדַ֙עְתָּ֙ חֲנֹתֵ֣נוּ בַּמִּדְבָּ֔ר וְהָיִ֥יתָ לָּ֖נוּ   כט וַיִּסָּֽעוּ: ס וַיֹּ֣אמֶר מֹשֶׁ֗ה לְ֠חֹבָ֠ב בֶּן־רְעוּאֵ֣ל הַמִּדְיָנִ֣י

לב לְעֵינָֽיִם: וְהָיָ֖ה כִּי־תֵלֵ֣ךְ עִמָּ֑נוּ וְהָיָ֣ה הַטּ֣וֹב הַה֗וּא   חֹתֵ֣ן מֹשֶׁ֔ה נֹסְעִ֣ים ׀ אֲנַ֗חְנוּ אֶל־הַמָּקוֹם֙ אֲשֶׁ֣ר אָמַ֣ר

לג אֲשֶׁ֨ר יֵיטִ֧יב יְהֹוָ֛ה עִמָּ֖נוּ וְהֵטַ֥בְנוּ לָֽךְ: וַיִּסְעוּ֙ מֵהַ֣ר יְהֹוָ֔ה   יְהֹוָ֔ה אֹת֖וֹ אֶתֵּ֣ן לָכֶ֑ם לְכָ֤ה אִתָּ֙נוּ֙ וְהֵטַ֣בְנוּ לָ֔ךְ כִּֽי־יְהֹוָ֥ה

דֶּ֚רֶךְ שְׁלֹ֣שֶׁת יָמִ֔ים וַאֲר֧וֹן בְּרִית־יְהֹוָ֛ה נֹסֵ֥עַ לִפְנֵיהֶ֖ם   ל דִּבֶּר־ט֖וֹב עַל־יִשְׂרָאֵֽל: וַיֹּ֣אמֶר אֵלָ֔יו לֹ֣א אֵלֵ֑ךְ כִּ֧י אִם־

לד דֶּ֚רֶךְ שְׁלֹ֣שֶׁת יָמִ֔ים לָת֥וּר לָהֶ֖ם מְנוּחָֽה: וַעֲנַ֧ן יְהֹוָ֛ה   לא אֶל־אַרְצִ֥י וְאֶל־מֽוֹלַדְתִּ֖י אֵלֵֽךְ: וַיֹּ֕אמֶר אַל־נָ֖א תַּעֲזֹ֣ב

29] Moses said to Hobab son of Reuel the Midianite, Moses' father-in-law, "We are setting out for the place of which the LORD has said, 'I will give it to you.' Come with us and we will be generous with you; for the LORD has promised to be generous to Israel."

30] "I will not go," he replied to him, "but will return to my native land." **31]** He said, "Please do not leave us, inasmuch as you know where we should camp in the wilderness and can be our guide. **32]** So if you come with us, we will extend to you the same bounty that the LORD grants us."

33] They marched from the mountain of the LORD a distance of three days. The Ark of the Covenant of the LORD traveled in front of them on that three days' journey to seek out a resting place for them; **34]** and the LORD's cloud kept above them by day, as they moved on from camp.

29] *Hobab son of Reuel.* The phrase "Moses' father-in-law" could refer to either Hobab or Reuel. In either case this contradicts the account in Exod. 2:18, 21, naming Jethro as the son of Reuel the father-in-law of Moses. Jewish tradition generally held that Hobab was another name for Jethro, just as Horeb was taken to be another name for Sinai. Critics distinguish a Hobab tradition (here and in Judg. 4:11) and a Jethro tradition (in Exodus).

According to the Midrash, where the problem is discussed in detail, Moses' father-in-law had seven names. For instance, in Judg. 1:16 the name is given as Keni [1]. See further at Exod. 2:18, 21.

30] *I . . . will return to my native land.* That is, to Midian. Scholars are divided over its location. Some find it in the southern Sinai peninsula, others locate it in northwest Arabia, at the east side of the Gulf of Akaba, and also consider this area to be the locale of the Horeb tradition (see verse 29) [2]. Still others consider "Midian" not necessarily as a place name but as signifying the land over which the people called Midianites had control. The Midianites later teamed up with Moab and were destroyed (Num. 22:4, 7).

31] *Guide.* Literally, "eyes." Hobab's assistance reflects an alliance of Israel and the Kenites, a Midianite subgroup to whom Hobab belonged (Judg. 4:11).

33] *In front.* According to verse 21 the Kohathites, who carried the ark, traveled in the middle of the camp train. Various attempts have been made to resolve the contradiction, but possibly verses 33–36 represent a fragment from another source (see verse 35).

The Rabbis held that a second ark was involved, which carried the broken Tablets [3]; Ibn Ezra, that this account represents a singular occasion; Luzzatto took it figuratively: though the ark traveled in Israel's midst, it was as if it led them on the march.

יהוָה וַתִּשְׁקַע הָאֵשׁ: וַיִּקְרָא שֵׁם־הַמָּקוֹם הַהוּא
תַּבְעֵרָה כִּי־בָעֲרָה בָם אֵשׁ יְהוָה: וְהָאסַפְסֻף אֲשֶׁר
בְּקִרְבּוֹ הִתְאַוּוּ תַּאֲוָה וַיָּשֻׁבוּ וַיִּבְכּוּ גַּם בְּנֵי יִשְׂרָאֵל
וַיֹּאמְרוּ מִי יַאֲכִלֵנוּ בָּשָׂר: זָכַרְנוּ אֶת־הַדָּגָה אֲשֶׁר־
נֹאכַל בְּמִצְרַיִם חִנָּם אֵת הַקִּשֻּׁאִים וְאֵת הָאֲבַטִּחִים
וְאֶת־הֶחָצִיר וְאֶת־הַבְּצָלִים וְאֶת־הַשּׁוּמִים: וְעַתָּה
נַפְשֵׁנוּ יְבֵשָׁה אֵין כֹּל בִּלְתִּי אֶל־הַמָּן עֵינֵינוּ: וְהַמָּן

עֲלֵיהֶם יוֹמָם בְּנָסְעָם מִן־הַמַּחֲנֶה: * י ס וַיְהִי בִּנְסֹעַ
הָאָרֹן וַיֹּאמֶר מֹשֶׁה קוּמָה יְהוָה וְיָפֻצוּ אֹיְבֶיךָ וְיָנֻסוּ
מְשַׂנְאֶיךָ מִפָּנֶיךָ: וּבְנֻחֹה יֹאמַר שׁוּבָה יְהוָה רִבְבוֹת
אַלְפֵי יִשְׂרָאֵל: ז   פ
וַיְהִי הָעָם כְּמִתְאֹנְנִים רַע בְּאָזְנֵי יְהוָה וַיִּשְׁמַע יְהוָה
וַיִּחַר אַפּוֹ וַתִּבְעַר־בָּם אֵשׁ יְהוָה וַתֹּאכַל בִּקְצֵה
הַמַּחֲנֶה: וַיִּצְעַק הָעָם אֶל־מֹשֶׁה וַיִּתְפַּלֵּל מֹשֶׁה אֶל־

* ד א' נחה.   * לה לו נון הפוכה.
                                            * לו ובנחה קרי.

35] When the ark was to set out, Moses would say: Advance, O LORD! / May Your enemies be scattered, / And may Your foes flee before You!

36] And when it halted, he would say: / Return, O LORD, / You who are Israel's myriads of thousands!

1] The people took to complaining bitterly before the LORD. The LORD heard and was incensed: a fire of the LORD broke out against them, ravaging the outskirts of the camp. **2]** The people cried out to Moses. Moses prayed to the LORD, and the fire died down. **3]** That place was named Taberah, because a fire of the LORD had broken out against them.

4] The riffraff in their midst felt a gluttonous craving; and the Israelites, moreover, wept and said, "If only we had meat to eat! **5]** We remember the fish that we used to eat free in Egypt, the cucumbers, the melons, the leeks, the onions, and the garlic. **6]** Now our gullets are shrivelled. There is nothing at all! Nothing but this manna to look to!"

35] *Moses would say.* The same inverted letter (*nun*) encloses the Hebrew verses 35 and 36, suggesting that they were somehow transposed. The Mishnah considers these two verses to contain the minimum number of letters (85) required to make a scroll sacred [4]; and Rabbi Judah ha-Nasi (compiler of the Mishnah, second century C.E.) took the two verses to be a separate book, thereby making Numbers consist of three books and the whole Torah of seven and explaining the verse in Prov. 9:1, which speaks of Wisdom (traditionally interpreted as Torah) hewing out her "seven pillars" [5]. Variants of verse 35 can be found in Pss. 68:2 and 132:8 [6].

The two sayings are included in the synagogue's traditional Torah service, at the beginning and the end.

36] *You who are.* Others, "Return, O Lord, unto the ten thousands of the families of Israel!"

11:3] *Taberah.* From the root בער, to burn.

4] *Riffraff.* The English translation conveys the onomatopoetic Hebrew term *asafsuf*, literally, "people gathered together," that is, a mixed multitude not bound by tribal ties.

In Exod. 12:38 the mixed multitude is called *erev rav*, "omnium-gatherum." The nature of both expressions underscores the oral character of the underlying tradition. Targum Onkelos uses the same Aramaic word (ערברבין) for both.

If only we had meat. Evidently the story comes from a source that was not aware of the tradition of Israelites owning cattle in the desert.

Rashi suggests they were really asking for a miracle; Nachmanides, that they ate some cattle but knew it would not have sufficed.

5] *Fish . . . free.* An exaggerated expression, meaning that it cost very little. The Israelites here apparently describe the diet of the Egyptian working class. While the cry is ostensibly for meat only, it is for variety also. In a talmudic discussion it is suggested that the remembrance of Egyptian delicacies was a euphemism for the sexual license in which they had indulged [7].

ח כְּזַרְעַ־גַּד הוּא וְעֵינוֹ כְּעֵין הַבְּדֹלַח: שָׁטוּ הָעָם וְלָקְטוּ
וְטָחֲנוּ בָרֵחַיִם אוֹ דָכוּ בַּמְּדֹכָה וּבִשְּׁלוּ בַּפָּרוּר וְעָשׂוּ
ט אֹתוֹ עֻגוֹת וְהָיָה טַעְמוֹ כְּטַעַם לְשַׁד הַשָּׁמֶן: וּבְרֶדֶת
י הַטַּל עַל־הַמַּחֲנֶה לָיְלָה יֵרֵד הַמָּן עָלָיו: וַיִּשְׁמַע מֹשֶׁה
אֶת־הָעָם בֹּכֶה לְמִשְׁפְּחֹתָיו אִישׁ לְפֶתַח אָהֳלוֹ וַיִּחַר־
יא אַף יְהוָה מְאֹד וּבְעֵינֵי מֹשֶׁה רָע: וַיֹּאמֶר מֹשֶׁה אֶל־
יְהוָה לָמָה הֲרֵעֹתָ לְעַבְדֶּךָ וְלָמָּה לֹא־מָצָתִי חֵן
יב בְּעֵינֶיךָ לָשׂוּם אֶת־מַשָּׂא כָּל־הָעָם הַזֶּה עָלָי: הֶאָנֹכִי
הָרִיתִי אֵת כָּל־הָעָם הַזֶּה אִם־אָנֹכִי יְלִדְתִּיהוּ כִּי־

תֹאמַר אֵלַי שָׂאֵהוּ בְחֵיקֶךָ כַּאֲשֶׁר יִשָּׂא הָאֹמֵן אֶת־
יג הַיֹּנֵק עַל הָאֲדָמָה אֲשֶׁר נִשְׁבַּעְתָּ לַאֲבֹתָיו: מֵאַיִן לִי
בָּשָׂר לָתֵת לְכָל־הָעָם הַזֶּה כִּי־יִבְכּוּ עָלַי לֵאמֹר תְּנָה־
יד לָּנוּ בָשָׂר וְנֹאכֵלָה: לֹא־אוּכַל אָנֹכִי לְבַדִּי לָשֵׂאת
טו אֶת־כָּל־הָעָם הַזֶּה כִּי כָבֵד מִמֶּנִּי: וְאִם־כָּכָה אַתְּ־
עֹשֶׂה לִּי הָרְגֵנִי נָא הָרֹג אִם־מָצָאתִי חֵן בְּעֵינֶיךָ וְאַל־
אֶרְאֶה בְּרָעָתִי: פ
טז וַיֹּאמֶר יְהוָה אֶל־מֹשֶׁה אֶסְפָה־לִּי שִׁבְעִים אִישׁ מִזִּקְנֵי
יִשְׂרָאֵל אֲשֶׁר יָדַעְתָּ כִּי־הֵם זִקְנֵי הָעָם וְשֹׁטְרָיו וְלָקַחְתָּ

* יא חסר א'

7] Now the manna was like coriander seed, and in color it was like bdellium. 8] The people would go about and gather it, grind it between millstones or pound it in a mortar, boil it in a pot, and make it into cakes. It tasted like rich cream. 9] When the dew fell on the camp at night, the manna would fall upon it.

10] Moses heard the people weeping, every clan apart, each person at the entrance of his tent. The LORD was very angry, and Moses was distressed. 11] And Moses said to the LORD, "Why have You dealt ill with Your servant, and why have I not enjoyed Your favor, that You have laid the burden of all this people upon me? 12] Did I conceive all this people, did I bear them, that You should say to me, 'Carry them in your bosom as a nurse carries an infant,' to the land that You have promised on oath to their fathers? 13] Where am I to get meat to give to all this people, when they whine before me and say, 'Give us meat to eat!' 14] I cannot carry all this people by myself, for it is too much for me. 15] If You would deal thus with me, kill me rather, I beg You, and let me see no more of my wretchedness!"

16] Then the LORD said to Moses, "Gather for Me seventy of Israel's elders of whom you have experience as elders and officers of the people, and bring them to the Tent of Meeting and let them take their place with you. 17] I will come down and speak with you there, and I will draw upon the spirit that is on you and put it upon them; they shall share the burden of the

7] *Manna*. See Exod. 16:14 ff.

Coriander seed. An umbelliferous plant. The gray-white seeds are spicy and are nowadays eaten mixed with bread and sweets.

Bdellium. A resinous gum (see Gen. 2:18).

10] *The people weeping*. The rebellion had now apparently spread to every clan.

11] *The burden*. Moses had not wanted the leadership in the first place (Exod. 4:10 ff.) and never ceased to consider it burdensome.

15] *My wretchedness*. The Masorah preserves the tradition that this is one of eighteen places where the scribes changed the text to avoid disrespect, for Moses had really said either "*their* wretchedness" (that is, he did not want to see the misfortunes which would befall the people) or "*Your*

wretchedness" (ascribing evil to God) [8].

16] *Seventy...elders*. The seventy elders appointed previously (Exod. 18:13–27) seem to have served in a judicial function primarily, while here the burden of leadership is shared, suggesting a distribution of administrative duties. Most likely the accounts of these appointments come from different traditions.

The Midrash harmonizes the matter by holding that the original seventy elders had died in the fire of Taberah [9]. Luke 10:1–20 seems to be based on the account in chapter 11. The Septuagint has the number as seventy-two, perhaps adding Eldad and Medad rather than including them. The Letter of Aristeas suggests that the Septuagint was created by seventy-two translators, six elders from each tribe.

יז אֹתָם אֶל־אֹהֶל מוֹעֵד וְהִתְיַצְּבוּ שָׁם עִמָּךְ: וְיָרַדְתִּי
וְדִבַּרְתִּי עִמְּךָ שָׁם וְאָצַלְתִּי מִן־הָרוּחַ אֲשֶׁר עָלֶיךָ
וְשַׂמְתִּי עֲלֵיהֶם וְנָשְׂאוּ אִתְּךָ בְּמַשָּׂא הָעָם וְלֹא־תִשָּׂא
אַתָּה לְבַדֶּךָ: יח וְאֶל־הָעָם תֹּאמַר הִתְקַדְּשׁוּ לְמָחָר
וַאֲכַלְתֶּם בָּשָׂר כִּי בְּכִיתֶם בְּאָזְנֵי יְהוָה לֵאמֹר מִי
יַאֲכִלֵנוּ בָּשָׂר כִּי־טוֹב לָנוּ בְּמִצְרָיִם וְנָתַן יְהוָה לָכֶם
בָּשָׂר וַאֲכַלְתֶּם: יט לֹא יוֹם אֶחָד תֹּאכְלוּן וְלֹא יוֹמָיִם
וְלֹא חֲמִשָּׁה יָמִים וְלֹא עֲשָׂרָה יָמִים וְלֹא עֶשְׂרִים
יוֹם: כ עַד חֹדֶשׁ יָמִים עַד אֲשֶׁר־יֵצֵא מֵאַפְּכֶם וְהָיָה
לָכֶם לְזָרָא יַעַן כִּי־מְאַסְתֶּם אֶת־יְהוָה אֲשֶׁר בְּקִרְבְּכֶם
וַתִּבְכּוּ לְפָנָיו לֵאמֹר לָמָּה זֶּה יָצָאנוּ מִמִּצְרָיִם: כא וַיֹּאמֶר

מֹשֶׁה שֵׁשׁ־מֵאוֹת אֶלֶף רַגְלִי הָעָם אֲשֶׁר אָנֹכִי בְּקִרְבּוֹ
וְאַתָּה אָמַרְתָּ בָּשָׂר אֶתֵּן לָהֶם וְאָכְלוּ חֹדֶשׁ יָמִים:
כב הֲצֹאן וּבָקָר יִשָּׁחֵט לָהֶם וּמָצָא לָהֶם אִם אֶת־כָּל־דְּגֵי
הַיָּם יֵאָסֵף לָהֶם וּמָצָא לָהֶם: פ
כג וַיֹּאמֶר יְהוָה אֶל־מֹשֶׁה הֲיַד יְהוָה תִּקְצָר עַתָּה תִרְאֶה
הֲיִקְרְךָ דְבָרִי אִם־לֹא: כד וַיֵּצֵא מֹשֶׁה וַיְדַבֵּר אֶל־הָעָם
אֵת דִּבְרֵי יְהוָה וַיֶּאֱסֹף שִׁבְעִים אִישׁ מִזִּקְנֵי הָעָם
וַיַּעֲמֵד אֹתָם סְבִיבֹת הָאֹהֶל: כה וַיֵּרֶד יְהוָה בֶּעָנָן
וַיְדַבֵּר אֵלָיו וַיָּאצֶל מִן־הָרוּחַ אֲשֶׁר עָלָיו וַיִּתֵּן עַל־
שִׁבְעִים אִישׁ הַזְּקֵנִים וַיְהִי כְּנוֹחַ עֲלֵיהֶם הָרוּחַ
וַיִּתְנַבְּאוּ וְלֹא יָסָפוּ: כו וַיִּשָּׁאֲרוּ שְׁנֵי־אֲנָשִׁים בַּמַּחֲנֶה שֵׁם

people with you, and you shall not bear it alone. **18]** And say to the people: Be ready for tomorrow and you shall eat meat, for you have kept whining before the LORD and saying, 'If only we had meat to eat! Indeed, we were better off in Egypt!' The LORD will give you meat and you shall eat. **19]** You shall eat not one day, not two, not even five days or ten or twenty, **20]** but a whole month, until it comes out of your nostrils and becomes loathsome to you. For you have rejected the LORD who is among you, by whining before Him and saying, 'Oh, why did we ever leave Egypt!'"

21] But Moses said, "The people who are with me number six hundred thousand men; yet You say, 'I will give them enough meat to eat for a whole month.' **22]** Could enough flocks and herds be slaughtered to suffice them? Or could all the fish of the sea be gathered for them to suffice them?" **23]** And the LORD answered Moses, "Is there a limit to the LORD's power? You shall soon see whether what I have said happens to you or not!"

24] Moses went out and reported the words of the LORD to the people. He gathered seventy of the people's elders and stationed them around the Tent. **25]** Then the LORD came down in a cloud and spoke to him; He drew upon the spirit that was on him and put it upon the seventy elders. And when the spirit rested upon them they spoke in ecstasy, but did not continue.

26] Two men, one named Eldad and the other Medad, had remained in camp; yet the spirit

17] *I will come down.* One of ten times in Torah where God is said to descend from on high [10].

Draw upon the spirit that is on you. אָצַלְתִּי (atzalti), whence the word אֲצִילוּת (atzilut), emanation. (See also Gen. 27:36.)

21] *But Moses . . . whole month.* His faith is no longer firm, an indication of his waning capacities. Rashi considered Moses' response here an error as grave as that committed later at Meribah, for which he was severely punished (Num. 20:2 ff.), but there his lack of faith was displayed in public, and not in private as here.

However, the prevailing tenor of traditional Jewish comment is to exculpate Moses [11].

23] *Is there a limit . . .?* Literally, "Is the Lord's hand too short?"

25] *Spoke in ecstasy.* Others, "prophesied." The root נבא appears to be related to Akkadian *nabû*, to call. The נָבִיא (navi), prophet, is one who is called to announce God's will.

One may also note that the Hebrew text uses the verb "prophesy" here in the reflexive mode, which might hint at the writer's desire to convey that the elders only acted like, but were not real, prophets.

But did not continue. The Hebrew is ambiguous and could also mean "did not stop" [12].

הָאֶחָד וְשֵׁם הַשֵּׁנִי מֵידָד וַתָּנַח עֲלֵהֶם הָרוּחַ
וְהֵמָּה בַּכְּתֻבִים וְלֹא יָצְאוּ הָאֹהֱלָה וַיִּתְנַבְּאוּ בַּמַּחֲנֶה:
כז וַיָּרָץ הַנַּעַר וַיַּגֵּד לְמֹשֶׁה וַיֹּאמַר אֶלְדָּד וּמֵידָד
מִתְנַבְּאִים בַּמַּחֲנֶה: כח וַיַּעַן יְהוֹשֻׁעַ בִּן־נוּן מְשָׁרֵת מֹשֶׁה
מִבְּחֻרָיו וַיֹּאמַר אֲדֹנִי מֹשֶׁה כְּלָאֵם: כט וַיֹּאמֶר לוֹ מֹשֶׁה
הַמְקַנֵּא אַתָּה לִי וּמִי יִתֵּן כָּל־עַם יְהוָה נְבִיאִים כִּי־יִתֵּן
יְהוָה אֶת־רוּחוֹ עֲלֵיהֶם: ל וַיֵּאָסֵף מֹשֶׁה אֶל־הַמַּחֲנֶה הוּא
וְזִקְנֵי יִשְׂרָאֵל: לא וְרוּחַ נָסַע מֵאֵת יְהוָה וַיָּגָז שַׂלְוִים מִן־
הַיָּם וַיִּטֹּשׁ עַל־הַמַּחֲנֶה כְּדֶרֶךְ יוֹם כֹּה וּכְדֶרֶךְ יוֹם כֹּה

לב סְבִיבוֹת הַמַּחֲנֶה וּכְאַמָּתַיִם עַל־פְּנֵי הָאָרֶץ: וַיָּקָם
הָעָם כָּל־הַיּוֹם הַהוּא וְכָל־הַלַּיְלָה וְכֹל יוֹם הַמָּחֳרָת
וַיַּאַסְפוּ אֶת־הַשְּׂלָו הַמַּמְעִיט אָסַף עֲשָׂרָה חֳמָרִים
לג וַיִּשְׁטְחוּ לָהֶם שָׁטוֹחַ סְבִיבוֹת הַמַּחֲנֶה: הַבָּשָׂר עוֹדֶנּוּ
בֵּין שִׁנֵּיהֶם טֶרֶם יִכָּרֵת וְאַף יְהוָה חָרָה בָעָם וַיַּךְ
לד יְהוָה בָּעָם מַכָּה רַבָּה מְאֹד: וַיִּקְרָא אֶת־שֵׁם־הַמָּקוֹם
הַהוּא קִבְרוֹת הַתַּאֲוָה כִּי־שָׁם קָבְרוּ אֶת־הָעָם
לה הַמִּתְאַוִּים: מִקִּבְרוֹת הַתַּאֲוָה נָסְעוּ הָעָם חֲצֵרוֹת וַיִּהְיוּ
בַּחֲצֵרוֹת:
פ

* לֶב הַשְּׂלָו קְרִי.

rested upon them—they were among those recorded, but they had not gone out to the Tent—and they spoke in ecstasy in the camp. **27]** A youth ran out and told Moses, saying, "Eldad and Medad are acting the prophet in the camp!" **28]** And Joshua son of Nun, Moses' attendant from his youth, spoke up and said, "My lord Moses, restrain them!" **29]** But Moses said to him, "Are you wrought up on my account? Would that all the LORD's people were prophets, that the LORD put His spirit upon them!" **30]** Moses then re-entered the camp together with the elders of Israel.

31] A wind from the LORD started up, swept quail from the sea and strewed them over the camp, about a day's journey on this side and about a day's journey on that side, all around the camp, and some two cubits deep on the ground. **32]** The people set to gathering quail all that day and night and all the next day—even he who gathered least had ten *homers*—and they spread them out all around the camp. **33]** The meat was still between their teeth, not yet chewed, when the anger of the LORD blazed forth against the people and the LORD struck the people with a very severe plague. **34]** That place was named Kibroth-hattaavah, because the people who had the craving were buried there.

35] Then the people set out from Kibroth-hattaavah for Hazeroth.

28] *Joshua.* Previously he had been reported as one who "would not stir out of the tent" (Exod. 33:11); here he becomes an active partisan.

31] *Quail.* שְׂלָיו (*selav*), similar to Arabic *salwa.* The birds belong to the partridge family, the African species migrating to Europe and breeding on plains and marshes [13]. Compare Exod. 16 for an earlier rebellion which was answered with the appearance of quail.

32] *Ten homers.* Estimated by some at 100 bushels; by others at half that amount (see Num. 15:4); by still others at "a donkey's load"—relating חֹמֶר (*chomer*) to חֲמוֹר (*chamor*), donkey [14].

The *chomer* (חֹמֶר) should not be confused with the *omer* (עֹמֶר). A *chomer* had 100 *omers.*

They spread them out. To let them dry, which was an Egyptian custom with fish as well [15].

It is possible, however, that the text may have read יִשְׁחֲטוּ (*yishchetu*), slaughtered, instead of יִשְׁטְחוּ (*yishtechu*), spread out, as it does in the Syriac version.

33] *Not yet chewed.* The meaning of the Hebrew is not certain.

A very severe plague. They choked on their greed.

34] *Kibroth-hattaavah.* Meaning "graves of craving"; either those who lusted were buried here or their craving was, so that they no longer desired meat [16].

Conversely, of course, the name (already in existence) may have given rise to this etiological tale.

The Fleshpots of Egypt

The cry of the rebels was for meat and variety, not for food as such, for there was no hunger among the people. Meat was the object of momentary craving; but after this was satisfied—or more than satisfied—the underlying problems which had caused the rebellion still remained. Satiety, boredom, lack of challenge, and the inconveniences of nomad existence were seeds of discontent as potent as want and poverty. A surfeit of manna and meat would not for long cover the lack of inner resources among the people. Long years of slavery had produced a generation that could not adjust its dreams of freedom to reality. Ultimately it was the God of freedom whom the murmurers rejected when they cried, "Oh, why did we ever leave Egypt!" (Num. 11:20). It would not be long before that whole generation would be pronounced unfit to enter the Promised Land (Num. 14).

The rebellion was fomented, so we are told, by the "riffraff." This was surely the judgment of later generations and designed to exculpate the majority of the people, who were thus shown to have been misled by worthless agitators. When a rebellion succeeds, it is called a revolution and its leaders are heroes; when it fails, it and its instigators are given derogatory names. Not infrequently such political and moral depravity is then explained as having originated with foreign elements [17], "probably foreigners who joined the camp" [18]. The "riffraff" recalls the *erev rav*, the "mixed multitude" at the time of the Exodus (Exod. 12:38), a designation for the disadvantaged people from the bottom of Egypt's social heap who joined themselves to the liberated Israelites.[1] But it is unlikely that these camp followers could have caused widespread unrest unless there was popular sentiment for it. As usual under such circumstances, it was the mass of people who suffered ("a very severe plague"), and not merely the rebel leaders or those who had made the dissatisfaction vocal.

Prophetic Power

The brief segment of verses 24–30 gives us an insight into the Torah's conception of how men are endowed with supernatural powers. We hear of the seventy elders speaking "in ecstasy" after God "drew" on Moses' spirit and "put it" on them. They had their moment of divine rapture "but did not continue" (verse 25). Taking the text at its word, the idea is that, instead of endowing the seventy independently with "the spirit," God took a portion from Moses and gave it to them. It was in every way a sharing of authority, both human and divine, and in both cases the supply was limited. Even though later interpretations stressed that Moses could yield the gift of godly grace without diminishing his own—they compared Moses to a candle from which light is taken without thereby reducing its power—the Torah had a less "spiritualized" and more practical view of the situation. As long as Moses, Aaron, and Miriam were the only recipients of divine knowledge their authority was unquestioned; as soon as the seventy were called, the unique status of the three was impaired. This is why it did not prove possible to have so large a group acting the prophet; having done so once they did not continue and presumably confined their activities to purely administrative matters.

But there remained Eldad and Medad who had not joined in the mass ecstasy at the Tent and who continued their special prophetic behavior—possibly by speaking in trance or by ecstatic dance or song [20]. We do not know why they separated them-

---

[1] Another interpretation of "riffraff" is that it was a collective term for other Semite clans [19].

selves,[2] but evidently Moses' chief aide, Joshua, considered them a source of dangerous competition to his master. Significantly Moses himself took the opposite view and welcomed their novel status. "Would that all the Lord's people were prophets," he says in gentle rebuke to his zealous serv-

ant. For Moses is secure in his own relationship with God and convinced that only as more and more people experience the blessing of the Divine Presence can the dream of a holy people be realized.[3] The great man is able to share; the lesser leader feels impelled to protect his status at all times.

---

[2] The Midrash says it was out of modesty [21].

[3] B. Halevi holds that the story originated with or reinforced a later prophetic school which emphasized that prophecy could not and should not be

restrained by authority (represented by Joshua's plea). Hence, with Rashi, he interprets כְּלָאֵם (in verse 28) as תְּנֵם אֶל בֵּית כֶּלֶא (put them in jail) [22].

GLEANINGS

The Stranger

The kindness shown to Hobab should be shown to all who join themselves to Israel.

MIDRASH [23]

Ecstasy and Prophecy

The ecstatic is moved by a will to experience ecstasies. He is in quest of what is not promised and what does not spontaneously communicate itself, and he must ever anew strive to attain his goal by means of various stimulants. Dramatic gestures, dance, music, alcohol, opium, hashish, the drinking of water of a sacred well, or of the blood of an animal, induce the state of rapture which enables man to transcend the barriers of self. The prophet, on the other hand, is not moved by a will to experience prophecy. What he achieves comes against his will. He does not pant for illumination. He does not call for it; he is called upon. God comes upon the prophet before the prophet seeks the coming of God.

Ecstasy is motivated by man's concern for God, by his will to be illumined. Prophecy, to the prophet's mind, is motivated by God's concern for man, by God's will that the prophet illumine his people. A. J. HESCHEL [24]

[Heschel's analysis does not cover all cases. In II Kings 3:15 Elisha arranges for a prophecy; and

in Isa. 6:9 f. God's command to the prophet appears to be the opposite of illumination.]

Seventy Elders

The gathering of righteous men is a boon to them and to the world. MISHNAH [25]

The elders are referred to in the singular (אִישׁ, ish, rather than אֲנָשִׁים, anashim) because they were special, singular men. MIDRASH [26]

Flesh

It says that the "riffraff" and the Israelites felt a gluttonous craving for meat (Num. 11:4). This is a figure of speech. For the people had cattle for food; and their memories were of fish and vegetables (verse 5). What they desired was human flesh, that is, sexual excess, even incest.

MIDRASH [27]

Fish

They remembered that fish was free in Egypt. Free? Even straw could be obtained only by hard labor! They were free only of mitzvot, for in those days they did not have to worry about the laws of the Torah, and this they remembered with nostalgia.

JONATHAN BEN UZZIEL [28]

Halachah

The text provides that the flocks and herds "be slaughtered" but that fish of the sea "be gathered" (Num. 11:22). The Rabbis used this as a proof text to show why fish did not have to be ritually slaughtered like cattle and fowl.

TALMUD [29]

Moses Sinned

Moses asked God to kill him (Num. 11:15), a cry uttered in despair. He should not have allowed his lips to pass such a prayer for it betokened a diminution of his respect for life. Therefore he was punished by having part of his spiritual substance removed from him. From this we learn that no man should curse himself.

I. HOROWITZ [30]

Parent and Nurse

Three points emerge. Both God and Moses are angry with the people. Moses blames God for having laid on him the burden of nursing these refractory children. And he feels unable to carry the burden alone. A fourth point, that if God cannot do better than this He had better kill him, is a startling rhetorical flourish with which he emphasizes his complaints. This is the only time that we have an image of Moses as a parent or nurse of the Children of Israel; the very rarity of the image suggests that it is used in extreme exasperation and it looks therefore as though we have here a genuine tradition of Moses' being driven at one point nearly to despair by the people's lack of discipline and self-control.

D. DAICHES [31]

They Tested Him

To test God was in their mind
   when they demanded food for themselves.
They spoke against God saying:
   "Can God spread a feast in the wilderness?
True, He struck the rock and waters flowed,
   streams gushed forth;
   but can He provide bread?
Can He supply His people with meat?"
God heard and He raged;
   fire broke out against Jacob,
   anger flared up at Israel,
   because they did not put their trust in God,
   did not rely on His deliverance.

PSALMS 78:17–22

Of Prophecy and Punishment

The previous chapter dealt with prophecy. God took some of His gifts from Moses and imparted them to other leaders. Joshua perceived clearly that the unique position of Moses was fundamentally altered and tried to prevent the change—in vain, for Moses would have no part of it. The change occurred, the leader's authority was now shared.

Chapter 11 is the Torah's first intimation that Moses has passed his zenith and that the slow and painful descent has begun. In the course of the rebellions that follow each other in quick succession, Moses is judged unfit to bring the people into the Promised Land. But it is God alone who determines His relationship with the aging Moses and, when all is said and done, Moses remains His friend; he alone among all men can speak with his Master face to face. Though others cavil at this, the leader continues to enjoy divine protection, and his detractors and opponents experience divine wrath. This is the background of the intrafamilial rebellion of Aaron and Miriam in chapter 12 and of the rebellion of Korah in chapter 16.

יא וַתְּדַבֵּר מִרְיָם וְאַהֲרֹן בְּמֹשֶׁה עַל־אֹדוֹת הָאִשָּׁה

ב הַכֻּשִׁית אֲשֶׁר לָקָח כִּי־אִשָּׁה כֻשִׁית לָקָח: וַיֹּאמְרוּ הֲרַק אַךְ־בְּמֹשֶׁה דִּבֶּר יְהֹוָה הֲלֹא גַּם־בָּנוּ דִבֵּר וַיִּשְׁמַע

ג יְהֹוָה: וְהָאִישׁ מֹשֶׁה עָנָו מְאֹד מִכֹּל הָאָדָם אֲשֶׁר עַל־

ד פְּנֵי הָאֲדָמָה: ס וַיֹּאמֶר יְהֹוָה פִּתְאֹם אֶל־מֹשֶׁה וְאֶל־אַהֲרֹן וְאֶל־מִרְיָם צְאוּ שְׁלָשְׁתְּכֶם אֶל־אֹהֶל מוֹעֵד

ה וַיֵּצְאוּ שְׁלָשְׁתָּם: וַיֵּרֶד יְהֹוָה בְּעַמּוּד עָנָן וַיַּעֲמֹד פֶּתַח

י הָאֹהֶל וַיִּקְרָא אַהֲרֹן וּמִרְיָם וַיֵּצְאוּ שְׁנֵיהֶם: וַיֹּאמֶר שִׁמְעוּ־נָא דְבָרָי אִם־יִהְיֶה נְבִיאֲכֶם יְהֹוָה בַּמַּרְאָה אֵלָיו אֶתְוַדָּע בַּחֲלוֹם אֲדַבֶּר־בּוֹ: לֹא־כֵן עַבְדִּי מֹשֶׁה בְּכָל־בֵּיתִי נֶאֱמָן הוּא: פֶּה אֶל־פֶּה אֲדַבֶּר־בּוֹ וּמַרְאֶה וְלֹא בְחִידֹת וּתְמֻנַת יְהֹוָה יַבִּיט וּמַדּוּעַ לֹא יְרֵאתֶם לְדַבֵּר בְּעַבְדִּי בְמֹשֶׁה: וַיִּחַר־אַף יְהֹוָה בָּם וַיֵּלַךְ: וְהֶעָנָן סָר מֵעַל הָאֹהֶל וְהִנֵּה מִרְיָם מְצֹרַעַת כַּשָּׁלֶג

v ג עניו קרי.

When they were in Hazeroth, **1]** Miriam and Aaron spoke against Moses because of the Cushite woman he had married: "He married a Cushite woman!"

2] They said, "Has the LORD spoken only through Moses? Has He not spoken through us as well?" The LORD heard it. **3]** Now Moses was a very humble man, more so than any other man on earth. **4]** Suddenly the LORD called to Moses, Aaron, and Miriam, "Come out, you three, to the Tent of Meeting." So the three of them went out. **5]** The LORD came down in a pillar of cloud, stopped at the entrance of the Tent, and called out, "Aaron and Miriam!" The two of them came forward; **6]** and He said, "Hear these My words: When a prophet of the LORD arises among you, I make Myself known to him in a vision, I speak with him in a dream. **7]** Not so with My servant Moses; he is trusted throughout My household. **8]** With him I speak mouth to mouth, plainly and not in riddles, and he beholds the likeness of the LORD. How then did you not shrink from speaking against My servant Moses!" **9]** Still incensed with them, the LORD departed.

10] As the cloud withdrew from the Tent, there was Miriam stricken with snow-white scales! When Aaron turned toward Miriam, he saw that she was stricken with scales.

When they were in Hazeroth. The new translation groups these words with chapter 12 because they appear to introduce the subsequent passage and could be considered a bridge.

12:1] *Cushite woman.* The reference seems to be to a Sudanese or Ethiopian wife he had taken in addition to the Midianite Zipporah. Whether the marriage itself gave rise to talk is not clear, but in any case the gossip is only the pretext for the real issue, namely, Moses' prophetic standing.

But some, like Ibn Ezra, believe that "Cushite woman" refers to Zipporah. Cross sees in the accusation a slur on the standing of the "Moses priesthood," which flourished at Shiloh and Dan, while the Aaronides were centered at Bethel and Jerusalem [1].

2] *Only through Moses?* This is the crux of the sibling rebellion. Like Aaron, Miriam too wants to expand her prophetic status (Exod. 15:20).

3] *A very humble man.* As Ibn Ezra points out, he had not sought his special status.

6] *When a prophet.* The Hebrew is not clear.

7] *My servant Moses.* A phrase of endearment used also for the Patriarchs and later for David.
In Ugaritic epics, too, an intimate of the deity is called "ṣervant" as a term of endearment.
He is trusted. He can approach Me at any time and remains My chosen leader and confidant.

8] *Mouth to mouth.* Not mouth to ear or mouth to soul; nor by nocturnal vision (usual as a mantic technique in Mesopotamian tradition). Moses is literally "inspirited," inspired in the direct sense [2].
The likeness of the Lord. But even Moses does not behold the Lord himself, whom no man can see and live (Exod. 33:18–24).

10] *Snow-white scales.* See Lev. 13:2–3.

יא וַיִּפֶן אַהֲרֹן אֶל־מִרְיָם וְהִנֵּה מְצֹרָעַת: וַיֹּאמֶר אַהֲרֹן
אֶל־מֹשֶׁה בִּי אֲדֹנִי אַל־נָא תָשֵׁת עָלֵינוּ חַטָּאת אֲשֶׁר
יב נוֹאַלְנוּ וַאֲשֶׁר חָטָאנוּ: אַל־נָא תְהִי כַּמֵּת אֲשֶׁר בְּצֵאתוֹ
יג מֵרֶחֶם אִמּוֹ וַיֵּאָכֵל חֲצִי בְשָׂרוֹ: וַיִּצְעַק מֹשֶׁה אֶל־יְהֹוָה
לֵאמֹר אֵל נָא רְפָא נָא לָהּ:   פ

יד וַיֹּאמֶר יְהֹוָה אֶל־מֹשֶׁה וְאָבִיהָ יָרֹק יָרַק בְּפָנֶיהָ הֲלֹא
תִכָּלֵם שִׁבְעַת יָמִים תִּסָּגֵר שִׁבְעַת יָמִים מִחוּץ לַמַּחֲנֶה
טו וְאַחַר תֵּאָסֵף: וַתִּסָּגֵר מִרְיָם מִחוּץ לַמַּחֲנֶה שִׁבְעַת
טז יָמִים וְהָעָם לֹא נָסַע עַד־הֵאָסֵף מִרְיָם: וְאַחַר נָסְעוּ
הָעָם מֵחֲצֵרוֹת וַיַּחֲנוּ בְּמִדְבַּר פָּארָן:

Haftarah Beha'alotecha, p. 1259

11] And Aaron said to Moses, "O my lord, account not to us the sin which we committed in our folly. 12] Let her not be as one dead, who emerges from his mother's womb with half his flesh eaten away." 13] So Moses cried out to the LORD, saying, "O God, pray heal her!"

14] But the LORD said to Moses, "If her father spat in her face, would she not bear her shame for seven days? Let her be shut out of camp for seven days, and then let her be readmitted." 15] So Miriam was shut out of camp seven days; and the people did not march on until Miriam was readmitted. 16] After that the people set out from Hazeroth and encamped in the wilderness of Paran.

12] *As one dead.* That is, like a still-born child. According to the Rabbis, this sentence originally read slightly differently: instead of "his mother's womb," the verse read "our mother's womb," but was altered by the Scribes out of respect for Jochebed [3].

16] *Paran.* See at Num. 10:12.

The Uniqueness of Moses

The brief account in chapter 12 sets forth in unmistakable terms the unique position of Moses as God's chief steward. He is older and diminished in physical and even intellectual and spiritual strength, but the characteristics that distinguish him from other prophets are as pronounced as ever. Some of these are specifically noted here, others become clear when we consider the particular prophetic endowment of Moses as the Torah conceives of it [4].

Other prophets receive the divine message in dreams or visions (verses 6–8); their apprehension of God is shrouded; and the message itself is symbolic or filled with riddles. "Not so with My servant Moses": he needs no visions or dreams; he is fully awake and in command of his intellectual powers; and he beholds the glory of God directly, though even he cannot see His face (Exod. 33:18–23). The divine speech is clear and unmistakable to him—no hidden meanings need to be discovered, no similes need be translated into everyday language. Further differences emerge as we study the biblical record: unlike many prophets, Moses did not go into a trance, and trembling, physical weakness, or mental detachment were not aspects of his meetings with God. Unlike others, he did not have to await the visitation of the Presence but could seek it at will.

Jewish tradition adds one further distinction: while other prophets, after their vision, returned to their normal existence and resumed marital relations, Moses did not do so; he kept himself apart in dwelling and by sexual abstinence. The Torah gives no warrant for this assumption of monk-like behavior, but the Rabbis concluded that even for Moses sexual intercourse would have been incompatible with his readiness for instant divine communication. Indeed, all the people were bidden to abstain from such relationships when they prepared themselves to receive the covenant (Exod. 19:15). According to the Rabbis, Moses' abstinence was construed by Miriam and Aaron as excessive and demonstrative piety, and it was to this they referred when they talked about the Cushite woman [5].

In sum, Moses was the unique friend of God and, as a trusted confidant, had access to the divine mansion. In him, a true and worthy servant of God, humility and strength were finely balanced. Properly, the final verses of the Torah dwell on his uniqueness: "Never again did there arise in Israel a prophet like Moses" (Deut. 34:10).

How Aaron Was Punished

At first reading of the story it appears that Miriam is punished and Aaron is not, although clearly Aaron is a co-offender. In fact, his offense is more serious, for he is the High Priest and second only to Moses. In the biblical scheme, punishment could not bypass the chief offender. Therefore, we should expect that Aaron not only be disciplined but disciplined more severely than Miriam.

This is precisely what the story conveys, for while Miriam is punished corporally Aaron is punished mentally. In his case, the mental suffering is far more intense than its physical counterpart. Aaron doubtlessly undergoes great anguish not only because of the divine rebuke—in the eyes of the Torah a severe chastisement in itself [6]—but also he suffers keenly from guilt when he sees his sister disfigured hideously while he who had committed the same offense apparently is let off free. The hurt of seeing a dear one suffer is often far greater than one's own physical agony.

But the worst punishment is yet to come. Aaron has pretended to be the equal of his younger brother and now has to humble himself utterly. "Oh, my lord!" he says to

Moses and then begs his forgiveness and asks him to intercede with God. Humiliation is added to mental suffering and guilt.

Miriam's pain is short-lived and like most physical ailments quickly forgotten once she is healed. But Aaron's punishment does not end when the incident is over and probably leaves deep scars. Miriam's illness is a warning to the people at large that slander and rebellion are evil, but the sight of Aaron, the High Priest, bowing down before Moses and begging his pardon is a warning no less potent and surely more memorable [7].

Black Is Beautiful

Cushite is a figurative term for "beautiful," for the numerical value of the letters in כּוּשִׁית is equal to those in יְפַת מַרְאֶה. All acknowledged her beauty even as they acknowledged her blackness.   RASHI

[Based on the rendering of כּוּשִׁית in the Targum. Both words add up to 736: כ = 20, ו = 6, שׁ = 300, י = 10, ת = 400.]

Hallo points out that "Black Is Beautiful" was a part of Jewish understanding before it became a slogan of black liberation in North America. [8].

A Very Humble Man

He was so called because while God heard the slander and gossip about Moses the latter himself paid no attention.   MIDRASH [9]

"O God, Pray Heal Her"

Moses knew how to pray. At one time he stood before God for forty days and forty nights; here he says but a few words. From this you may learn that there is a time to say long prayers and a time to say short ones.   MIDRASH [10]

Rule of Conduct

Why did God separate Moses when he spoke about him to Miriam and Aaron? To teach us that one should never speak more than part of a man's praise to his face.   TALMUD [11]

Moses "Beholds the Likeness of God" (Num. 12:8)

If commentators on God's speech to Aaron and Miriam are of the opinion that even strictly historical consideration would have to deal with a primacy on the part of Moses, "admittedly while rejecting any arrogation to him of an entirely different kind of revelation," this can be assented to for the time being. Nevertheless, we should not regard the speech of God as though it were a free composition aiming at the glorification of Moses. Behind this speech, it seems to me, is concealed some reminiscence, albeit a faded one, of the man who recognized his God, the God who is present at every time in the way in which He is present—who recognized Him in his natural appearances "visually," and who experienced His word as breathed into his innermost self. That is classically Israelite in character but is nonetheless unique in its purity and strength. And, even if we were not to read anything about it, we would still have to postulate an experience of the kind as underlying such words and such a deed.   M. BUBER [12]

Irony

(Miriam had complained about the black wife whom Moses had married. Now she was "stricken with snow-white scales.")

Was this an example of divine irony? Perhaps the implication is: "She's too dark for you, is she? If you prefer whiteness, I'll make you whiter than ever."   D. DAICHES [13]

Trial and Condemnation

The Israelites' first opportunity to enter the Promised Land now approaches. It was understood by tradition that the divine promise of possession could not be realized without a military struggle, for warfare and occupation were the context in which the widespread population movements at the end of the Bronze Age took place.

Spies, or scouts, are first sent out to explore the land—to collect information about the strengths and weaknesses of its military, economic, and natural resources—and on their return they give conflicting interpretations of what they saw. That in itself is not surprising, for the various parts of Canaan differ considerably: "The coastal plain has abundant water resources and fertile soils; the hills of the lowlands are well suited for vineyards and olive groves. The central mountains were covered by forests in antiquity, and some of the wide valleys intersecting them from east to west are among the most fertile parts of the country. As against this 'rich land' there is the 'poor': the Negev, the Judean desert, and parts of the Jordan valley. The spies, who traveled along the mountains,* saw before their eyes the typical landscape of Canaan: on the one hand, fields of corn, orchards, and woods; and on the other—east of the watershed—barren grey hills, dry and desolate, the few green spots between them only serving to emphasize their desert character" [1]. The people, on hearing the various assessments of the land, choose to believe the pessimists rather than the optimists and in despair make ready to return

* See the accompanying map.

to Egypt. God is now convinced that the generation of the Exodus is unfit for true independence; it will be condemned to wander in the desert and will not be permitted to occupy Canaan. An attempt to stay the divine judgment fails, and a belated show of courage has disastrous consequences.

The story exhibits a number of internal difficulties and contradictions. Biblical critics see two distinct accounts: one from the P tradition which has the spies exploring the whole land, and another from the J/E tradition which relates a somewhat simpler expedition (see commentary).

(A new weekly portion, *Shelach-Lecha*, begins with 13:1.)

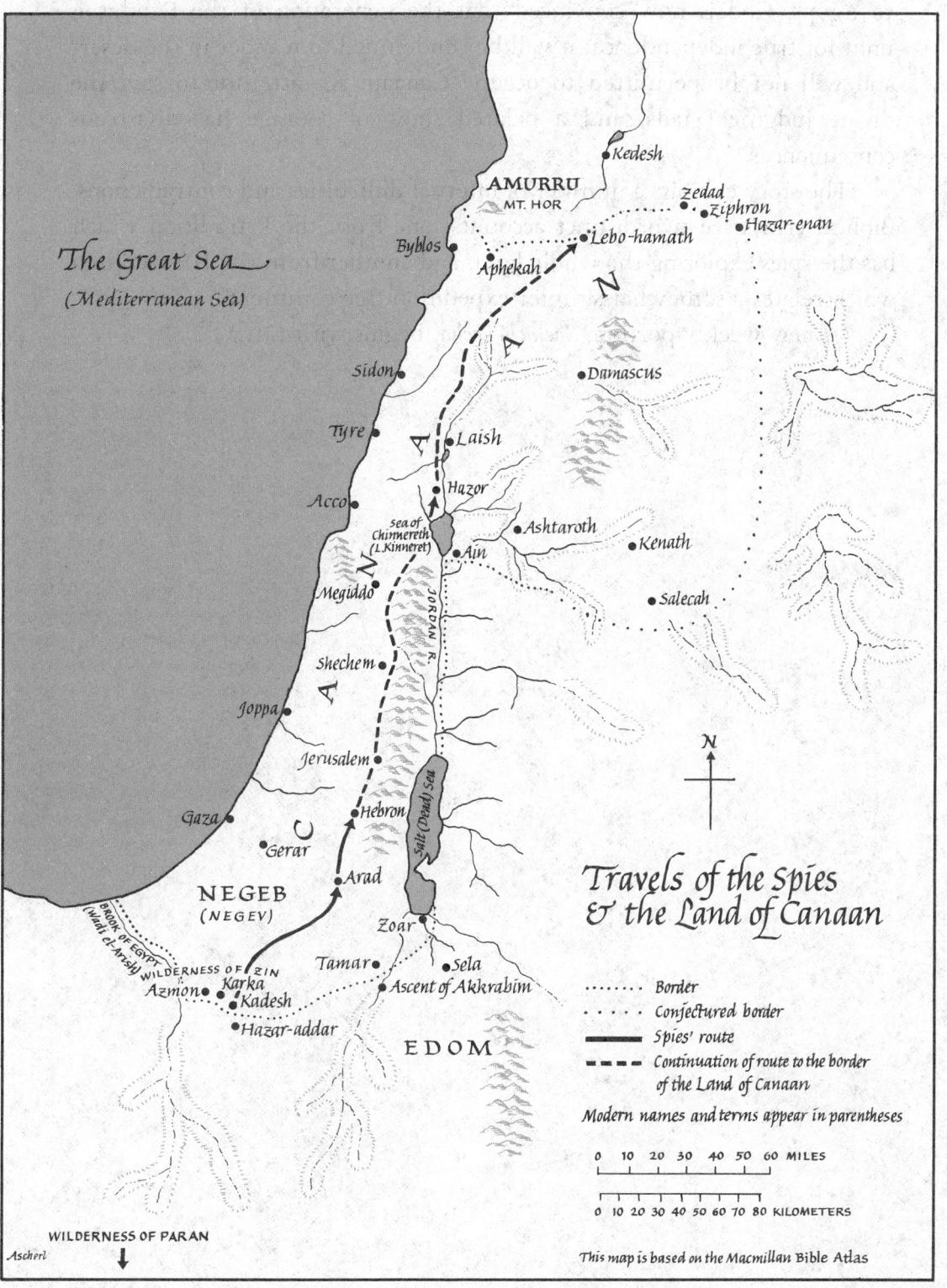

The Great Sea
(Mediterranean Sea)

Kedesh

AMURRU
MT. HOR

Zedad
Ziphron
Hazar-enan

Byblos
Aphekah
Lebo-hamath

Sidon
Damascus

Tyre
Laish

Acco
Hazor

Sea of
Chinnereth
(L.Kinneret)
Ain

Ashtaroth
Kenath

Megiddo
JORDAN R.
Salecah

Shechem

Joppa

Jerusalem

Gaza
Hebron

Gerar
Salt (Dead) Sea

Arad
Zoar

NEGEB
(NEGEV)

Tamar
Sela
Ascent of Akkrabim

WILDERNESS OF ZIN
Karka
Azmon
Kadesh

BROOK OF EGYPT
(Wadi el-Arish)

Hazar-addar

EDOM

N

Travels of the Spies
& the Land of Canaan

.... Border

• • • • • • Conjectured border

━━━━━ Spies' route

▬ ▬ ▬ Continuation of route to the border
of the Land of Canaan

Modern names and terms appear in parentheses

0 10 20 30 40 50 60 MILES

0 10 20 30 40 50 60 70 80 KILOMETERS

This map is based on the Macmillan Bible Atlas

Ascherl

WILDERNESS OF PARAN
↓

1106

ח בֶּן־יוֹסֵף: לְמַטֵּה אֶפְרַיִם הוֹשֵׁעַ בִּן־נוּן: לְמַטֵּה בִנְיָמִן
י פַּלְטִי בֶּן־רָפוּא: לְמַטֵּה זְבוּלֻן גַּדִּיאֵל בֶּן־סוֹדִי:
יא־יב לְמַטֵּה יוֹסֵף לְמַטֵּה מְנַשֶּׁה גַּדִּי בֶּן־סוּסִי: לְמַטֵּה דָן
יג עַמִּיאֵל בֶּן־גְּמַלִּי: לְמַטֵּה אָשֵׁר סְתוּר בֶּן־מִיכָאֵל:
יד־טו לְמַטֵּה נַפְתָּלִי נַחְבִּי בֶּן־וָפְסִי: לְמַטֵּה גָד גְּאוּאֵל בֶּן־
מָכִי: אֵלֶּה שְׁמוֹת הָאֲנָשִׁים אֲשֶׁר־שָׁלַח מֹשֶׁה לָתוּר
טז אֶת־הָאָרֶץ וַיִּקְרָא מֹשֶׁה לְהוֹשֵׁעַ בִּן־נוּן יְהוֹשֻׁעַ: וַיִּשְׁלַח
יז אֹתָם מֹשֶׁה לָתוּר אֶת־אֶרֶץ כְּנָעַן וַיֹּאמֶר אֲלֵהֶם עֲלוּ
יח זֶה בַּנֶּגֶב וַעֲלִיתֶם אֶת־הָהָר: וּרְאִיתֶם אֶת־הָאָרֶץ מַה־

פ פ פ

א וַיְדַבֵּר יְהוָה אֶל־מֹשֶׁה לֵּאמֹר: שְׁלַח־לְךָ אֲנָשִׁים וְיָתֻרוּ
אֶת־אֶרֶץ כְּנַעַן אֲשֶׁר־אֲנִי נֹתֵן לִבְנֵי יִשְׂרָאֵל אִישׁ אֶחָד
אִישׁ אֶחָד לְמַטֵּה אֲבֹתָיו תִּשְׁלָחוּ כֹּל נָשִׂיא בָהֶם:
ב וַיִּשְׁלַח אֹתָם מֹשֶׁה מִמִּדְבַּר פָּארָן עַל־פִּי יְהוָה כֻּלָּם
ג אֲנָשִׁים רָאשֵׁי בְנֵי־יִשְׂרָאֵל הֵמָּה: וְאֵלֶּה שְׁמוֹתָם לְמַטֵּה
ד רְאוּבֵן שַׁמּוּעַ בֶּן־זַכּוּר: לְמַטֵּה שִׁמְעוֹן שָׁפָט בֶּן־חוֹרִי:
ה־ו לְמַטֵּה יְהוּדָה כָּלֵב בֶּן־יְפֻנֶּה: לְמַטֵּה יִשָּׂשכָר יִגְאָל

1] The LORD spoke to Moses, saying, **2]** "Send men to scout the land of Canaan, which I am giving to the Israelite people; send one man from each of their ancestral tribes, each one a chieftain among them." **3]** So Moses, by the LORD's command, sent them out from the wilderness of Paran, all the men being leaders of the Israelites. **4]** And these were their names:

From the tribe of Reuben, Shammua son of Zaccur. **5]** From the tribe of Simeon, Shaphat son of Hori. **6]** From the tribe of Judah, Caleb son of Jephunneh. **7]** From the tribe of Issachar, Igal son of Joseph. **8]** From the tribe of Ephraim, Hosea son of Nun. **9]** From the tribe of Benjamin, Palti son of Rafu. **10]** From the tribe of Zebulun, Gaddiel son of Sodi. **11]** From the tribe of Joseph, namely, the tribe of Manasseh, Gaddi son of Susi. **12]** From the tribe of Dan, Ammiel son of Gemalli. **13]** From the tribe of Asher, Sethur son of Michael. **14]** From the tribe of Naphtali, Nahbi son of Vophsi. **15]** From the tribe of Gad, Geuel son of Machi. **16]** Those were the names of the men whom Moses sent to scout the land; but Moses changed the name of Hosea son of Nun to Joshua.

17] When Moses sent them to scout the land of Canaan, he said to them, "Go up there into the Negeb and on into the hill country, **18]** and see what kind of country it is. Are the people

---

13:2] *Send men.* Here, God gives Moses the order, while Deut. 1:22 relates that the sending was done not at God's behest but at the people's. The Rabbis harmonized the two passages by suggesting that the special verb form for "send" (שְׁלַח־לְךָ) could be understood as "go ahead, send them," indicating God's permission rather than a direct order to send spies [2].

16] *Moses changed the name of Hosea.* The change involves the addition of the letter י (Y), which with the letter ה (H) forms the first part of יהוה (YHVH) and symbolizes Joshua's future role as

Israel's leader. This part (יה, YH) is sometimes used by itself for the Divine Name (as in Exod. 15:2) and frequently as a suffix to human names (as in אליה Elijah).

In Neh. 8:17, Joshua is called by yet a third name, Jeshua (which was also the Hebrew name of Jesus). Ehrlich explains the name change as an attempt by a later biblical tradition to harmonize the stories of the spies [3].

17] *Negeb.* Now commonly spelled Negev, the southern part of modern Israel. It was partially fertile in biblical days and contained twenty-nine cities (Josh. 15:21–32) [4].

כב אֶת־הָאָרֶץ מִמִּדְבַּר־צִן עַד־רְחֹב לְבֹא חֲמָת: וַיַּעֲלוּ
בַנֶּגֶב וַיָּבֹא עַד־חֶבְרוֹן וְשָׁם אֲחִימָן שֵׁשַׁי וְתַלְמַי יְלִידֵי
הָעֲנָק וְחֶבְרוֹן שֶׁבַע שָׁנִים נִבְנְתָה לִפְנֵי צֹעַן מִצְרָיִם:
כג וַיָּבֹאוּ עַד־נַחַל אֶשְׁכֹּל וַיִּכְרְתוּ מִשָּׁם זְמוֹרָה וְאֶשְׁכּוֹל
עֲנָבִים אֶחָד וַיִּשָּׂאֻהוּ בַמּוֹט בִּשְׁנָיִם וּמִן־הָרִמֹּנִים וּמִן
כד הַתְּאֵנִים: לַמָּקוֹם הַהוּא קָרָא נַחַל אֶשְׁכּוֹל עַל אֹדוֹת
* כב סבירין ויבאו.

הוּא וְאֶת־הָעָם הַיּשֵׁב עָלֶיהָ הֶחָזָק הוּא הֲרָפֶה הַמְעַט
יט הוּא אִם־רָב: וּמָה הָאָרֶץ אֲשֶׁר־הוּא ישֵׁב בָּהּ הֲטוֹבָה
הִוא אִם־רָעָה וּמָה הֶעָרִים אֲשֶׁר־הוּא יוֹשֵׁב בָּהֵנָּה
כ הַבְּמַחֲנִים אִם בְּמִבְצָרִים: וּמָה הָאָרֶץ הַשְּׁמֵנָה הִוא
אִם־רָזָה הֲיֵשׁ־בָּהּ עֵץ אִם־אַיִן וְהִתְחַזַּקְתֶּם וּלְקַחְתֶּם
כא מִפְּרִי הָאָרֶץ וְהַיָּמִים יְמֵי בִּכּוּרֵי עֲנָבִים: וַיַּעֲלוּ וַיָּתֻרוּ

who dwell in it strong or weak, few or many? **19]** Is the country in which they dwell good or bad? Are the towns they live in open or fortified? **20]** Is the soil rich or poor? Is it wooded or not? And take pains to bring back some of the fruit of the land."—Now it happened to be the season of the first ripe grapes.

21] They went up and scouted the land, from the wilderness of Zin to Rehob, at Lebo-hamath. **22]** They went up into the Negeb and came to Hebron, where lived Ahiman, Sheshai, and Talmai, the Anakites.—Now Hebron was founded seven years before Zoan of Egypt.— **23]** They reached the wadi Eshcol, and there they cut down a branch with a single cluster of grapes—it had to be borne on a carrying frame by two of them—and some pomegranates and figs. **24]** That place was named the wadi Eshcol because of the cluster that the Israelites cut down there.

20] *First ripe grapes*. At the end of July.

21] *From the wilderness of Zin*. In the northern Negev. From there the spies went to Lebo-hamath (or "the entrance to Hamath"), a mountain pass in eastern Lebanon, north of Damascus. The surveyed region was well settled at the beginning of the second millennium B.C.E., and again during the period of the Israel-Judah monarchies. It featured grazing and agriculture and abutted popular caravan routes. The spies followed the road through sparsely inhabited mountain areas west of the Jordan and avoided the more densely settled coastal plain and low lands.

22] *Anakites*. Possibly a word of Hebrew origin, meaning "long necks" (because the men may have worn necklaces [5]) or "powerful ones." More probably the Anakites were identical with the Iy'aneks found in Egyptian execration texts from 2000 B.C.E., where they were called rebels [6]. And there is a third possibility: Anak may be a word of Philistine-Mycenean origin meaning "mastery" [7].

"Anakites" was long understood to denote "giants." However, anthropology provides no evidence that men of unusual stature lived in Palestine during this period; even so, the reason for the tradition is fairly clear. "The existing dolmens and the size and strength of the Canaanite fortresses suggest that only giants could have built them. We find this same idea among the Greeks, who reported that the huge walls of their ancient cities had been built by the Cyclopes, giant artisans from Asia Minor. This tradition has led to the expression 'Cyclopean' masonry, to describe the huge blocks used in constructing some ancient cities" [8].

Hebron. Elsewhere also called Kiriath-arba (Gen. 23:2), some seventeen miles south of Jerusalem. The cave of Machpelah, where the Patriarchs were buried, is located there. Hebron was an old city, having been founded before the year 2000 B.C.E. Josephus called it the oldest city in Palestine [9].

Others put the time around 1800 B.C.E. [10] or even much later, about 1400 B.C.E., when Zoan was rebuilt after an earlier destruction [11].

23] *Wadi Eshcol*. Literally, "Cluster Wadi," a city known for its orchards, probably near Hebron. Because it is unlikely that the spies carried the fruit with them on their way north, this account is assigned by critics to a source which did not know of a northern expedition (see commentary).

כט עֲמָלֵק יוֹשֵׁב בְּאֶרֶץ הַנֶּגֶב וְהַחִתִּי וְהַיְבוּסִי וְהָאֱמֹרִי
יוֹשֵׁב בָּהָר וְהַכְּנַעֲנִי יוֹשֵׁב עַל-הַיָּם וְעַל יַד הַיַּרְדֵּן:
ל וַיַּהַס כָּלֵב אֶת-הָעָם אֶל-מֹשֶׁה וַיֹּאמֶר עָלֹה נַעֲלֶה
לא וְיָרַשְׁנוּ אֹתָהּ כִּי-יָכוֹל נוּכַל לָהּ: וְהָאֲנָשִׁים אֲשֶׁר-עָלוּ
עִמּוֹ אָמְרוּ לֹא נוּכַל לַעֲלוֹת אֶל-הָעָם כִּי-חָזָק הוּא
לב מִמֶּנּוּ: וַיֹּצִיאוּ דִּבַּת הָאָרֶץ אֲשֶׁר תָּרוּ אֹתָהּ אֶל-בְּנֵי
יִשְׂרָאֵל לֵאמֹר הָאָרֶץ אֲשֶׁר עָבַרְנוּ בָהּ לָתוּר אֹתָהּ
אֶרֶץ אֹכֶלֶת יוֹשְׁבֶיהָ הִוא וְכָל-הָעָם אֲשֶׁר-רָאִינוּ

כה הָאֶשְׁכּוֹל אֲשֶׁר-כָּרְתוּ מִשָּׁם בְּנֵי יִשְׂרָאֵל: וַיָּשֻׁבוּ מִתּוּר
כו הָאָרֶץ מִקֵּץ אַרְבָּעִים יוֹם: וַיֵּלְכוּ וַיָּבֹאוּ אֶל-מֹשֶׁה
וְאֶל-אַהֲרֹן וְאֶל-כָּל-עֲדַת בְּנֵי-יִשְׂרָאֵל אֶל-מִדְבַּר
פָּארָן קָדֵשָׁה וַיָּשִׁיבוּ אֹתָם דָּבָר וְאֶת-כָּל-הָעֵדָה
כז וַיַּרְאוּם אֶת-פְּרִי הָאָרֶץ: וַיְסַפְּרוּ-לוֹ וַיֹּאמְרוּ בָּאנוּ
אֶל-הָאָרֶץ אֲשֶׁר שְׁלַחְתָּנוּ וְגַם זָבַת חָלָב וּדְבַשׁ הִוא
כח וְזֶה-פִּרְיָהּ: אֶפֶס כִּי-עַז הָעָם הַיֹּשֵׁב בָּאָרֶץ וְהֶעָרִים
בְּצֻרוֹת גְּדֹלֹת מְאֹד וְגַם-יְלִדֵי הָעֲנָק רָאִינוּ שָׁם:

25] At the end of forty days they returned from scouting the land. 26] They went straight to Moses and Aaron and the whole Israelite community at Kadesh in the wilderness of Paran, and they made their report to them and to the whole community, as they showed them the fruit of the land. 27] This is what they told him: "We came to the land you sent us to; it does indeed flow with milk and honey, and this is its fruit. 28] However, the people who inhabit the country are powerful, and the cities are fortified and very large; moreover, we saw the Anakites there. 29] Amalekites dwell in the Negeb region; Hittites, Jebusites, and Amorites inhabit the hill country; and Canaanites dwell by the Sea and along the Jordan."

30] Caleb hushed the people before Moses and said, "Let us by all means go up, and we shall gain possession of it, for we shall surely overcome it."

31] But the men who had gone up with him said, "We cannot attack that people, for it is stronger than we." 32] Thus they spread calumnies among the Israelites about the land they

25] *Forty days.* A round or perhaps symbolic number that occurs elsewhere in the Torah. The forty days of the spies' wanderings are enlarged to forty years' wanderings, which will be the punishment meted out to Israel.

26] *Kadesh.* Also called Kadesh-barnea (Num. 32:8) or Meribah of Kadesh (Num. 27:14), located about fifty miles south of Beer-sheba. The place becomes the Israelites' chief base for the next thirty-eight years, until the time of conquest. Kadesh means "holy," and many biblical scholars believe that Mt. Sinai was the name of a holy mountain in this area. (For a full discussion of the location of Sinai, see commentary on Exod. 19.)

27] *Milk and honey.* It has long been assumed that this phrase denoted both nomadic and agricultural products, which, to a wandering people, signified

ultimate wealth, like nectar and ambrosia in the Greek tradition.

This view has lately been challenged by N. Hareuveni, who holds that "milk and honey" was originally an idiom conveying "an abundance of wild animals." In his opinion, the spies did not bring back a laudatory report by speaking of "milk and honey," but one which warned the people that the land was overrun by wild beasts who constantly threatened to "devour its settlers" (verse 32). In later centuries, when the text was finalized, the original meaning of the phrase was no longer understood [12]. (See also Gleanings.)

29] *Hill country.* Later called Hills of Judea or West Bank.

31] *We cannot attack.* The walls of ancient Canaanite cities were thirty to fifty feet high and sometimes fifteen feet thick.

לי בְּתוֹכָהּ אַנְשֵׁי מִדּוֹת: וְשָׁם רָאִינוּ אֶת־הַנְּפִילִים בְּנֵי
עֲנָק מִן־הַנְּפִלִים וַנְּהִי בְעֵינֵינוּ כַּחֲגָבִים וְכֵן הָיִינוּ
בְּעֵינֵיהֶם:
א וַתִּשָּׂא כָּל־הָעֵדָה וַיִּתְּנוּ אֶת־קוֹלָם וַיִּבְכּוּ הָעָם בַּלָּיְלָה
ב הַהוּא: וַיִּלֹּנוּ עַל־מֹשֶׁה וְעַל־אַהֲרֹן כֹּל בְּנֵי יִשְׂרָאֵל
וַיֹּאמְרוּ אֲלֵהֶם כָּל־הָעֵדָה לוּ־מַתְנוּ בְּאֶרֶץ מִצְרַיִם אוֹ
ג בַּמִּדְבָּר הַזֶּה לוּ־מָתְנוּ: וְלָמָה יְהוָה מֵבִיא אֹתָנוּ אֶל־
הָאָרֶץ הַזֹּאת לִנְפֹּל בַּחֶרֶב נָשֵׁינוּ וְטַפֵּנוּ יִהְיוּ לָבַז
ד הֲלוֹא טוֹב לָנוּ שׁוּב מִצְרָיְמָה: וַיֹּאמְרוּ אִישׁ אֶל־אָחִיו

ה נִתְּנָה רֹאשׁ וְנָשׁוּבָה מִצְרָיְמָה: וַיִּפֹּל מֹשֶׁה וְאַהֲרֹן עַל־
ו פְּנֵיהֶם לִפְנֵי כָּל־קְהַל עֲדַת בְּנֵי יִשְׂרָאֵל: וִיהוֹשֻׁעַ
בִּן־נוּן וְכָלֵב בֶּן־יְפֻנֶּה מִן־הַתָּרִים אֶת־הָאָרֶץ קָרְעוּ
ז בִּגְדֵיהֶם: וַיֹּאמְרוּ אֶל־כָּל־עֲדַת בְּנֵי־יִשְׂרָאֵל לֵאמֹר
הָאָרֶץ אֲשֶׁר עָבַרְנוּ בָהּ לָתוּר אֹתָהּ טוֹבָה הָאָרֶץ
ח מְאֹד מְאֹד: אִם־חָפֵץ בָּנוּ יְהוָה וְהֵבִיא אֹתָנוּ אֶל־
הָאָרֶץ הַזֹּאת וּנְתָנָהּ לָנוּ אֶרֶץ אֲשֶׁר־הִוא זָבַת חָלָב
ט וּדְבָשׁ: אַךְ בַּיהוָה אַל־תִּמְרֹדוּ וְאַתֶּם אַל־תִּירְאוּ אֶת־
עַם הָאָרֶץ כִּי לַחְמֵנוּ הֵם סָר צִלָּם מֵעֲלֵיהֶם וַיהוָה

had scouted, saying, "The country that we traversed and scouted is one that devours its settlers. All the people that we saw in it are men of great size; **33]** we saw the Nephilim there—the Anakites are part of the Nephilim—and we looked like grasshoppers to ourselves, and so we must have looked to them."

1] The whole community broke into loud cries, and the people wept that night. **2]** All the Israelites railed against Moses and Aaron. "If only we had died in the land of Egypt," the whole community shouted at them, "or if only we might die in this wilderness! **3]** Why is the LORD taking us to that land to fall by the sword? Our wives and children will be carried off! It would be better for us to go back to Egypt!" **4]** And they said to one another, "Let us head back for Egypt."

5] Then Moses and Aaron fell on their faces before all the assembled congregation of the Israelites. **6]** And Joshua son of Nun and Caleb son of Jephunneh, of those who had scouted the land, rent their clothes **7]** and exhorted the whole Israelite community: "The land that we traversed and scouted is an exceedingly good land. **8]** If the LORD is pleased with us, He will bring us into that land, a land that flows with milk and honey, and give it to us; **9]** only you must not rebel against the LORD. Have no fear then of the people of the country, for they are our prey: their protection has departed from them, but the LORD is with us. Have no fear of

32] *Devours its settlers.* This negative judgment is assigned by critics to the P tradition, in contrast to the J/E tradition, which has the spies speak of a land of milk and honey (but see at verse 27). It has also been suggested that "devours" was a reference to practices of cannibalism amongst the Canaanites or that it denoted an abundance of warfare. (See also the similar expression in Lev. 26:38.)

33] *Nephilim.* Demi-gods or giants (see Gen. 6:4).

Grasshoppers. Locusts in their hopping stage; some species are expressly permitted as food in Lev. 11:21–22.

14:4] *Let us head back.* Or, "let us appoint a captain and turn back."

5] *Fell on their faces.* Their apparent despair fore-

shadows their growing inability to exercise effective leadership—a prelude to the events related in chapter 20.

6] *Joshua . . . and Caleb.* They, instead of Moses and Aaron, step forward to exhort the people.

Rent their clothes. As a sign of mourning. Traditional Judaism to this day provides for rending one's garment (or a symbolic substitute, like a ribbon) at the burial of a close relative.

9] *Our prey.* Literally, "our food" or "our bread."

Their protection. A figurative rendering of the literal "their shadow" (see Gleanings).

Bachya suggests that צִלָּם (*tzilam*) refers to God, as in Ps. 121:5; Luzzatto that it refers to what provides shade, hence "protection."

כְּאִישׁ אֶחָד וְאָמְרוּ הַגּוֹיִם אֲשֶׁר־שָׁמְעוּ אֶת־שִׁמְעֲךָ

טו לֵאמֹר: מִבִּלְתִּי יְכֹלֶת יְהֹוָה לְהָבִיא אֶת־הָעָם הַזֶּה אֶל־הָאָרֶץ אֲשֶׁר־נִשְׁבַּע לָהֶם וַיִּשְׁחָטֵם בַּמִּדְבָּר:

טז,יז וְעַתָּה יִגְדַּל־נָא כֹּחַ אֲדֹנָי כַּאֲשֶׁר דִּבַּרְתָּ לֵאמֹר: יְהֹוָה אֶרֶךְ אַפַּיִם וְרַב־חֶסֶד נֹשֵׂא עָוֹן וָפָשַׁע וְנַקֵּה לֹא יְנַקֶּה פֹּקֵד עֲוֹן אָבוֹת עַל־בָּנִים עַל־שִׁלֵּשִׁים וְעַל־רִבֵּעִים:

יט סְלַח־נָא לַעֲוֹן הָעָם הַזֶּה כְּגֹדֶל חַסְדֶּךָ וְכַאֲשֶׁר

כ נָשָׂאתָה לָעָם הַזֶּה מִמִּצְרַיִם וְעַד־הֵנָּה: וַיֹּאמֶר יְהֹוָה

כא סָלַחְתִּי כִּדְבָרֶךָ: וְאוּלָם חַי־אָנִי וְיִמָּלֵא כְבוֹד־יְהֹוָה

כב אֶת־כָּל־הָאָרֶץ: כִּי כָל־הָאֲנָשִׁים הָרֹאִים אֶת־כְּבֹדִי וְאֶת־אֹתֹתַי אֲשֶׁר־עָשִׂיתִי בְמִצְרַיִם וּבַמִּדְבָּר וַיְנַסּוּ אֹתִי

כג זֶה עֶשֶׂר פְּעָמִים וְלֹא שָׁמְעוּ בְּקוֹלִי: אִם־יִרְאוּ אֶת־

י אֹתָם אֶל־תִּירָאֵם: וַיֹּאמְרוּ כָּל־הָעֵדָה לִרְגּוֹם אֹתָם בָּאֲבָנִים וּכְבוֹד יְהֹוָה נִרְאָה בְּאֹהֶל מוֹעֵד אֶל־כָּל־בְּנֵי יִשְׂרָאֵל: פ

יא וַיֹּאמֶר יְהֹוָה אֶל־מֹשֶׁה עַד־אָנָה יְנַאֲצֻנִי הָעָם הַזֶּה וְעַד־אָנָה לֹא־יַאֲמִינוּ בִי בְּכֹל הָאֹתוֹת אֲשֶׁר עָשִׂיתִי

יב בְּקִרְבּוֹ: אַכֶּנּוּ בַדֶּבֶר וְאוֹרִשֶׁנּוּ וְאֶעֱשֶׂה אֹתְךָ לְגוֹי־

יג גָּדוֹל וְעָצוּם מִמֶּנּוּ: וַיֹּאמֶר מֹשֶׁה אֶל־יְהֹוָה וְשָׁמְעוּ מִצְרַיִם כִּי־הֶעֱלִיתָ בְכֹחֲךָ אֶת־הָעָם הַזֶּה מִקִּרְבּוֹ:

יד וְאָמְרוּ אֶל־יוֹשֵׁב הָאָרֶץ הַזֹּאת שָׁמְעוּ כִּי־אַתָּה יְהֹוָה בְּקֶרֶב הָעָם הַזֶּה אֲשֶׁר־עַיִן בְּעַיִן נִרְאָה אַתָּה יְהֹוָה וַעֲנָנְךָ עֹמֵד עֲלֵהֶם וּבְעַמֻּד עָנָן אַתָּה הֹלֵךְ לִפְנֵיהֶם

טו יוֹמָם וּבְעַמּוּד אֵשׁ לָיְלָה: וְהֵמַתָּה אֶת־הָעָם הַזֶּה

---

them!''   **10]** As the whole community threatened to pelt them with stones, the Presence of the LORD appeared in the Tent of Meeting to all the Israelites.

11] And the LORD said to Moses, "How long will this people spurn Me, and how long will they have no faith in Me despite all the signs that I have performed in their midst?   **12]** I will strike them with pestilence and disown them, and I will make of you a nation far more numerous than they!"   **13]** But Moses said to the LORD, "When the Egyptians, from whose midst You brought up this people in Your might, hear the news,   **14]** they will tell it to the inhabitants of that land. Now they have heard that You, O LORD, are in the midst of this people; that You, O LORD, appear in plain sight when Your cloud rests over them and when You go before them in a pillar of cloud by day and in a pillar of fire by night.   **15]** If then You slay this people to a man, the nations who have heard Your fame will say,   **16]** 'It must be because the LORD was powerless to bring that people into the land which He had promised them on oath that He slaughtered them in the wilderness.'   **17]** Therefore, I pray, let my Lord's forbearance be great, as You have declared, saying,   **18]** 'The LORD! slow to anger and abounding in kindness; forgiving iniquity and transgression; yet not remitting all punishment, but visiting the iniquity of fathers upon children, upon the third and fourth generations.' **19]** Pardon, I pray, the iniquity of this people according to Your great kindness, as You have forgiven this people ever since Egypt."

  20] And the LORD said, "I pardon, as you have asked.   **21]** Nevertheless, as I live and as the LORD's Presence fills the whole world,   **22]** none of the men who have seen My Presence and the signs that I have performed in Egypt and in the wilderness, and who have tried Me these many times and have disobeyed Me,   **23]** shall see the land that I promised on oath to their

---

13–14] It may be that the two verses are in disarray, but such "confusion" may be a device to convey the high emotion of Moses [13].

18] *The Lord . . . generations.* A partial quotation of Exod. 34:6–7.

19–20] The verses are quoted in the Yom Kippur eve liturgy, immediately after the Kol Nidre.

22] *Tried Me these many times.* Literally, "ten times"; see Gen. 31:41. Rabbi Judah (second century C.E.) enumerates ten instances when Israel tried God: twice at the Red Sea; twice each with complaints about water, manna, and quails; once with the golden calf; and once in the wilderness of Paran [14].

הָאָרֶץ אֲשֶׁר נִשְׁבַּעְתִּי לַאֲבֹתָם וְכָל־מְנַאֲצַי לֹא
כד יִרְאוּהָ: וְעַבְדִּי כָלֵב עֵקֶב הָיְתָה רוּחַ אַחֶרֶת עִמּוֹ
וַיְמַלֵּא אַחֲרָי וַהֲבִיאֹתִיו אֶל־הָאָרֶץ אֲשֶׁר־בָּא שָׁמָּה
כה וְזַרְעוֹ יוֹרִשֶׁנָּה: וְהָעֲמָלֵקִי וְהַכְּנַעֲנִי יוֹשֵׁב בָּעֵמֶק מָחָר
פְּנוּ וּסְעוּ לָכֶם הַמִּדְבָּר דֶּרֶךְ יַם־סוּף: פ

כו וַיְדַבֵּר יְהוָה אֶל־מֹשֶׁה וְאֶל־אַהֲרֹן לֵאמֹר: עַד־מָתַי
לָעֵדָה הָרָעָה הַזֹּאת אֲשֶׁר הֵמָּה מַלִּינִים עָלָי אֶת־
תְּלֻנּוֹת בְּנֵי יִשְׂרָאֵל אֲשֶׁר הֵמָּה מַלִּינִים עָלַי שָׁמָעְתִּי:
כח אֱמֹר אֲלֵהֶם חַי־אָנִי נְאֻם־יְהוָה אִם־לֹא כַּאֲשֶׁר
כט דִּבַּרְתֶּם בְּאָזְנָי כֵּן אֶעֱשֶׂה לָכֶם: בַּמִּדְבָּר הַזֶּה יִפְּלוּ

פִּגְרֵיכֶם וְכָל־פְּקֻדֵיכֶם לְכָל־מִסְפַּרְכֶם מִבֶּן עֶשְׂרִים
ל שָׁנָה וָמָעְלָה אֲשֶׁר הֲלִינֹתֶם עָלָי: אִם־אַתֶּם תָּבֹאוּ אֶל־
הָאָרֶץ אֲשֶׁר נָשָׂאתִי אֶת־יָדִי לְשַׁכֵּן אֶתְכֶם בָּהּ כִּי אִם־
לא כָּלֵב בֶּן־יְפֻנֶּה וִיהוֹשֻׁעַ בִּן־נוּן: וְטַפְּכֶם אֲשֶׁר אֲמַרְתֶּם
לָבַז יִהְיֶה וְהֵבֵיאתִי אֹתָם וְיָדְעוּ אֶת־הָאָרֶץ אֲשֶׁר
לב מְאַסְתֶּם בָּהּ: וּפִגְרֵיכֶם אַתֶּם יִפְּלוּ בַּמִּדְבָּר הַזֶּה:
לג וּבְנֵיכֶם יִהְיוּ רֹעִים בַּמִּדְבָּר אַרְבָּעִים שָׁנָה וְנָשְׂאוּ
לד אֶת־זְנוּתֵיכֶם עַד־תֹּם פִּגְרֵיכֶם בַּמִּדְבָּר: בְּמִסְפַּר
הַיָּמִים אֲשֶׁר־תַּרְתֶּם אֶת־הָאָרֶץ אַרְבָּעִים יוֹם יוֹם
לַשָּׁנָה יוֹם לַשָּׁנָה תִּשְׂאוּ אֶת־עֲוֹנֹתֵיכֶם אַרְבָּעִים שָׁנָה
* לֹא מלא י׳

fathers; none of those who spurn Me shall see it.   **24]** But My servant Caleb, because he was imbued with a different spirit and remained loyal to Me—him will I bring into the land which he entered, and his offspring shall hold it as a possession.   **25]** Now the Amalekites and the Canaanites occupy the valleys. Start out, then, tomorrow and march into the wilderness by way of the Sea of Reeds."

  26] The LORD spoke further to Moses and Aaron,   **27]** "How much longer shall that wicked community keep muttering against Me? Very well, I have heeded the incessant muttering of the Israelites against Me.   **28]** Say to them: 'As I live,' says the LORD, 'I will do to you just as you have urged Me.   **29]** In this very wilderness shall your carcasses drop. Of all of you who were recorded in your various lists from the age of twenty years up, you who mutter against Me,   **30]** not one shall enter the land in which I swore to settle you—save Caleb son of Jephunneh and Joshua son of Nun.   **31]** Your children who, you said, would be carried off—these will I allow to enter; they shall know the land that you have rejected.   **32]** But your carcasses shall drop in this wilderness,   **33]** while your children roam the wilderness for forty years, suffering for your faithlessness, until the last of your carcasses is down in the wilderness.   **34]** You shall bear your punishment for forty years corresponding to the number of days—forty days—that you scouted the land: a year for each day. Thus you shall

24] *Caleb.* Since Joshua's name is omitted, critics see here a Caleb tradition, as distinguished from a Joshua-and-Caleb tradition (see commentary).

25] *March into the wildnerness.* There the Israelites will remain until the next generation has grown to maturity.

  Sea of Reeds. The location of the sea is in doubt; see commentary on Exod. 13:17.

26] *Spoke further.* God now details what He has already stated in general terms. Scholars consider this verse to introduce the Joshua-and-Caleb tradition.

28] *"As I live," says the Lord.* (חַי אָנִי נְאֻם יְהוָה)

While the two halves of this expression occur in the Torah only once again (the first in verse 21 above; the second in Gen. 22:16), they were favored idioms in Ezekiel and Jeremiah: נְאֻם יְהוָה is found sixteen times in the former and 162 times in the latter.

30] *I swore.* Literally, "raised My hand."

33] *Forty years.* Forty is sometimes used as a round number and here too might indicate "a long time." Since the next thirty-eight years are passed over in silence, some scholars believe that only two years of wandering were involved.

  See also 13:25 on "forty days."

לד וִידַעְתֶּם אֶת־תְּנוּאָתִי: אֲנִי יְהֹוָה דִּבַּרְתִּי אִם־לֹא זֹאת
אֶעֱשֶׂה לְכָל־הָעֵדָה הָרָעָה הַזֹּאת הַנּוֹעָדִים עָלָי
לה בַּמִּדְבָּר הַזֶּה יִתַּמּוּ וְשָׁם יָמֻתוּ: וְהָאֲנָשִׁים אֲשֶׁר־שָׁלַח
מֹשֶׁה לָתוּר אֶת־הָאָרֶץ וַיָּשֻׁבוּ וַיַּלִּונוּ עָלָיו אֶת־כָּל־
לו הָעֵדָה לְהוֹצִיא דִבָּה עַל־הָאָרֶץ: וַיָּמֻתוּ הָאֲנָשִׁים
לז מוֹצִאֵי דִבַּת־הָאָרֶץ רָעָה בַּמַּגֵּפָה לִפְנֵי יְהֹוָה: וִיהוֹשֻׁעַ
לח בִּן־נוּן וְכָלֵב בֶּן־יְפֻנֶּה הָיוּ מִן־הָאֲנָשִׁים הָהֵם הַהֹלְכִים
לט לָתוּר אֶת־הָאָרֶץ: וַיְדַבֵּר מֹשֶׁה אֶת־הַדְּבָרִים הָאֵלֶּה
מ אֶל־כָּל־בְּנֵי יִשְׂרָאֵל וַיִּתְאַבְּלוּ הָעָם מְאֹד: וַיַּשְׁכִּמוּ

* לו וילינו קרי.

בַּבֹּקֶר וַיַּעֲלוּ אֶל־רֹאשׁ־הָהָר לֵאמֹר הִנֶּנּוּ וְעָלִינוּ אֶל־
מא הַמָּקוֹם אֲשֶׁר־אָמַר יְהֹוָה כִּי חָטָאנוּ: וַיֹּאמֶר מֹשֶׁה
לָמָּה זֶּה אַתֶּם עֹבְרִים אֶת־פִּי יְהֹוָה וְהִוא לֹא תִצְלָח:
מב אַל־תַּעֲלוּ כִּי אֵין יְהֹוָה בְּקִרְבְּכֶם וְלֹא תִּנָּגְפוּ לִפְנֵי
מג אֹיְבֵיכֶם: כִּי הָעֲמָלֵקִי וְהַכְּנַעֲנִי שָׁם לִפְנֵיכֶם וּנְפַלְתֶּם
בֶּחָרֶב כִּי־עַל־כֵּן שַׁבְתֶּם מֵאַחֲרֵי יְהֹוָה וְלֹא־יִהְיֶה
מד יְהֹוָה עִמָּכֶם: וַיַּעְפִּלוּ לַעֲלוֹת אֶל־רֹאשׁ הָהָר וַאֲרוֹן
מה בְּרִית־יְהֹוָה וּמֹשֶׁה לֹא־מָשׁוּ מִקֶּרֶב הַמַּחֲנֶה: וַיֵּרֶד
הָעֲמָלֵקִי וְהַכְּנַעֲנִי הַיֹּשֵׁב בָּהָר הַהוּא וַיַּכּוּם וַיַּכְּתוּם
עַד־הַחָרְמָה: פ

know what it means to thwart Me. **35]** I the LORD have spoken: Thus will I do to all that wicked band that has banded together against Me: in this very wilderness they shall die to the last man.'"

36] As for the men whom Moses sent to scout the land, those who came back and caused the whole community to mutter against him by spreading calumnies about the land— **37]** those who spread such calumnies about the land died of plague, by the will of the LORD. **38]** Of those men who had gone to scout the land, only Joshua son of Nun and Caleb son of Jephunneh survived.

39] When Moses repeated these words to all the Israelites, the people were overcome by grief. **40]** Early next morning they set out toward the crest of the hill country, saying, "We are prepared to go up to the place that the LORD has spoken of, for we were wrong." **41]** But Moses said, "Why do you transgress the LORD's command? This will not succeed. **42]** Do not go up, lest you be routed by your enemies, for the LORD is not in your midst. **43]** For the Amalekites and the Canaanites will be there to face you, and you will fall by the sword, inasmuch as you have turned from following the LORD and the LORD will not be with you."

44] Yet defiantly they marched to the crest of the hill country, though neither the LORD's Ark of the Covenant nor Moses stirred from the camp. **45]** And the Amalekites and the Canaanites who dwelt in that hill country came down and dealt them a shattering blow at Hormah.

40] *We are prepared.* But it is now too late; the judgment has been pronounced.

45] *Hormah.* Probably near today's Arad in the Negev. Folk etymology related the name to "destruction" (Num. 21:3; Judg. 1:17), or to חֵרֶם (cherem), ban.

The Morality of Conquest

The Torah is based on the concept that God chose the people of Israel as His servants and that He reserved Canaan for them as their habitat. It was not their homeland; it was to become theirs by conquest and occupation. In this respect Israel does not differ from other nations and their historical experience. Much of history tells how peoples migrated and took possession of new lands. The old inhabitants were usually assimilated, and only rarely were they driven off.[1] But Israel viewed its conquest and possession of the land primarily as a suprahistorical event, as a consequence of divine providence. Only when God was with the people could they succeed; if, as is related at the end of this section, He withdrew His support, failure was sure to follow. Therefore, the occupation was not seen in heroic perspective, but always as a foundation for ethical and religious obligations. The morality of the forcible displacement of the Canaanites was never raised by the Torah, and neither was the morality of war as such.[2] The biblical tradition considered warfare a normal aspect of life (although universal peace was the ultimate ideal; Isa. 11:6–9). The overriding idea was that the Promised Land was to be conquered at the behest of God, who had decided on this course for reasons He did not reveal.

But, while occupation as such was not a moral issue, the methods of warfare were (see Deut. 20 and 21). Even more important, the continued possession of the land was seen in terms of a moral trust. Israel would keep the land only so long as the nation kept faith with God. Only a righteous Israel was entitled to inhabit the land, for it was God's and was itself holy. This imposed the obligation of moral living on the Children of Israel, something not demanded to this extent of any other nation in the world. Israel's tenure of the land was therefore considered conditional.[3] This unique concept is found in Torah and Prophets and received its most vivid expression in the recurring theme of exile-and-return. The Bible makes God responsible for Israel's being in the land but makes Israel responsible for remaining there and, later, for creating the conditions for return.

Two Traditions

Biblical scholars see in chapters 13 and 14 two distinct traditions that in the course of time became joined in the present text. One (ascribed to J/E sources) deals with a rebellion against God and features Caleb; the other (P tradition) describes a rebellion against the leadership of Moses and Aaron and features Hosea-Joshua. Following the analysis of Gray [16], the two traditions can be separated as follows:

1. J/E: Moses dispatches Caleb and others from Kadesh to scout the land of Canaan. They go only as far as Hebron and Nahal Eshcol and cut a sample cluster of grapes. When they return to Kadesh, they show the fruit and report that they saw a land flowing

---

[1] The biblical injunction to drive out the original inhabitants of Canaan was in fact never carried out.

[2] It was later on raised by the Rabbis who distinguished "religious wars" (מִלְחֲמוֹת מִצְוָה), "obligation wars" (מִלְחֲמוֹת חוֹבָה), and wars which had no religious significance (מִלְחֲמוֹת רְשׁוּת) [15].

[3] However, in one place, Gen. 15:16, the Torah suggests that a native nation will lose possession of Canaan because of its own sins, and Amos 1:3 ff. applies the yardstick of sin and punishment to various nations. Conversely, Edom's possession of its land was also confirmed by divine fiat (Deut. 2:5), and Amos 9:7 considers the dwelling places of the Philistines and Arameans as willed specifically by God.

with milk and honey but held by strong inhabitants. Caleb hushes the dismay of the people and is optimistic about Israel's chances, but the other spies say there are giants in the land. The people react bitterly and want to return to Egypt. God is angry with them; Moses appeases Him; but a divine judgment is passed on that entire generation, except for Caleb. The Children of Israel now repent and make their futile attack on the Canaanites and Amalekites.[4]

2. P: God commands Moses to send spies. They are dispatched from Paran; all of them are princes whose names are listed in detail. Moses changes Hosea's name to Joshua. The spies explore the land all the way north to the mountains of Lebanon. After forty days they return and give a pessimistic assessment of the land: "It devours its settlers." The people weep at this report and rebel against Moses and Aaron, demanding a return to Egypt. The leaders prostrate themselves in silence, while Joshua and Caleb defend them. The people threaten to stone them, but God appears at the Tent. He passes a sentence of wandering and death for all over the age of twenty, except Joshua and Caleb.[5]

The two traditions tell the same basic story but differ in important details. In one version, only the southern part of Canaan is explored; in the other, a report of the whole land is given. One records a futile war, the other includes genealogical material usually associated with the priestly writings. In the latter, God is manifested at the sanctuary, while in the former He uses Moses as His intermediary. Caleb is a hero in both sources, but Joshua figures only in P.

---

[4] 13:7–23, 26–32; 14:11–25, 39–45; see also Deut. 1:23 ff.   [5] 13:1–17, 25, 26, 32; 14:1, 2, 5–10, 26–39.

GLEANINGS

The Climate of Canaan

Small as it is, Palestine has always had the advantages of many kinds of climate, owing in part to the variety of the terrain. In general, the land resembles the drier parts of southern California, but everything is on a much smaller scale. Mount Hermon in the north, which is over 9,000 feet high, tends to be cold, whereas just over one hundred miles to the south, in the Jordan Valley, Jericho swelters in tropical heat. Jerusalem, although less than fifteen miles to the southwest of Jericho, is almost 4,000 feet higher, and its inhabitants have usually found its climate temperate. There is another important element, the winds. The winds from the east are usually hot and dry, coming as they do from the desert. Those from the north, on the other hand, and especially from the west across the Mediterranean, are much more gentle, bringing with them cool air and rain. The all-important rainy season usually begins in October and ends in March or April.　　　　　　　　　　　H. ORLINSKY [17]

How to Tell

How could the spies tell whether the Canaanites were strong or weak (Num. 13:18)? Moses had instructed them: "If the people dwell in open communities they are strong, for they are confident of their own strength; if in fortified cities, they are weak and their hearts timid."

MIDRASH [18]

Slander

In their report the spies began by speaking well of the land, saying it flowed with milk and honey, and then they went on to talk of its bad points. That is how slanderers talk about people.

MIDRASH [19]

First, the Negev

Moses sent the spies first to the Negev, the poorest part of Canaan. This was calculated psychology: like a shrewd merchant he showed his less valuable wares first.　　　MIDRASH [20]

The Real Mission

The Land of Promise was not merely a geographical acquisition, not merely the name of a place. It represented their future. The twelve men were not sent to explore a land: they were sent on a mission to explore the future of a people.

M. ADLER [21]

The Silent Ones Died Also

All Israelites over twenty years of age were condemned to die in the desert, even those who silently disagreed with the majority and favored Joshua and Caleb. Why? Because they did not speak up.　　　　　　　　　MIDRASH [22]

A Land That Devours Its Settlers (Num. 13:32)

Ill fares the land, to hastening ills a prey,
Where wealth accumulates and men decay.

O. GOLDSMITH [23]

Milk and Honey

What did those scouts actually see? Modern archeology provides us with certain clues. The early inhabitants of the land of Canaan lived mostly in the valleys and plains which had plenty of water and rich soil. There, extensive agriculture was easily developed.

In contrast to these valleys, many hills and slopes were covered with wild thickets and forests and were, therefore, uninhabited. Wild goats foraged there on the natural food supply, providing the "flow of milk." (Goat milk was com-

monly used in biblical times.) These same thickets and bushes also produced many varieties of flowers which fed wild bees, who made the "honey flow." What the scouts saw was indeed a "land of milk and honey" *precisely because* it was forest wilderness inhabited by wild goats and bees who thrived on the profusion of wild undergrowth.   N. HAREUVENI [24]

How Much Longer? (Num. 14:27)

There are limits even to the patience of God. Man cries, "How long, Lord?" and God responds, "How long, man?"   INTERPRETER'S BIBLE [25]

The Real Sin

The spies said: "We cannot attack that people for it is stronger than we." (Num. 13:31). "Than we" מִמֶּנּוּ (*mimenu*), could also be understood "than He." What the spies suggested was that even God could not overcome the Canaanites. Israel was punished for this lack of faith in God, not for disbelief in its own strength.

                                                    TALMUD [26]

Shadows

They are called "protection" (Num. 14:9) and their absence betokens disaster. In Jewish folklore the absence of a shadow on Hoshana Rabbah (the seventh day of Tabernacles), and in central European Christian folklore on Christmas eve, indi-

cated that the person would die the following year [27].

Tishah b'Av

God's judgment that the rebellious generation would die in the desert was issued on the ninth day of Av. It was the first of the evil events which befell Israel on this calendar day.

                                                  MISHNAH [28]

[The others mentioned: the destruction of the First and Second Temples, the destruction of Bethar (second century B.C.E.), and the ploughing up of Jerusalem.]

Continuity

The generation of the Exodus does not die in one day, and those who will conquer Canaan do not appear suddenly the next morning. There might have been a "miracle": the instantaneous death of a multitude and an immediate resurgence. But here as well God assures the historical continuity and contemporaneousness of old men who grow older and new men who are growing up. Those who died in the desert do not disappear before the living: they lead them for a time, which may differ in length but is nonetheless real, to the very threshold of the Promised Land.

                                                  A. NEHER [29]

Various Laws; Fringes

The Torah now presents a variety of laws, among them the rule regarding chalah (setting aside a portion of the dough), which is still observed by very traditional Jews, though in an altered manner [1]. The chapter also treats of the effects of inadvertent sin and the punishment for those who break the Sabbath ordinances. It repeats the principles by which strangers are to be treated and finally states the law of fringes (*tzitzit*), which has found its major application in the use of the prayer shawl (talit).

א וַיְדַבֵּר יְהֹוָה אֶל־מֹשֶׁה לֵּאמֹר: דַּבֵּר אֶל־בְּנֵי יִשְׂרָאֵל וְאָמַרְתָּ אֲלֵהֶם כִּי תָבֹאוּ אֶל־אֶרֶץ מוֹשְׁבֹתֵיכֶם אֲשֶׁר ב אֲנִי נֹתֵן לָכֶם: וַעֲשִׂיתֶם אִשֶּׁה לַיהֹוָה עֹלָה אוֹ־זֶבַח לְפַלֵּא־נֶדֶר אוֹ בִנְדָבָה אוֹ בְּמֹעֲדֵיכֶם לַעֲשׂוֹת רֵיחַ ג נִיחֹחַ לַיהֹוָה מִן־הַבָּקָר אוֹ מִן־הַצֹּאן: וְהִקְרִיב הַמַּקְרִיב קָרְבָּנוֹ לַיהֹוָה מִנְחָה סֹלֶת עִשָּׂרוֹן בָּלוּל ד בִּרְבִעִית הַהִין שָׁמֶן: וְיַיִן לַנֶּסֶךְ רְבִיעִית הַהִין תַּעֲשֶׂה ה עַל־הָעֹלָה אוֹ לַזָּבַח לַכֶּבֶשׂ הָאֶחָד: אוֹ לָאַיִל תַּעֲשֶׂה מִנְחָה סֹלֶת שְׁנֵי עֶשְׂרֹנִים בְּלוּלָה בַשֶּׁמֶן שְׁלִשִׁית הַהִין:

ז וְיַיִן לַנֶּסֶךְ שְׁלִשִׁית הַהִין תַּקְרִיב רֵיחַ־נִיחֹחַ לַיהֹוָה: ח וְכִי־תַעֲשֶׂה בֶן־בָּקָר עֹלָה אוֹ־זֶבַח לְפַלֵּא־נֶדֶר אוֹ־ ט שְׁלָמִים לַיהֹוָה: וְהִקְרִיב עַל־בֶּן־הַבָּקָר מִנְחָה סֹלֶת שְׁלֹשָׁה עֶשְׂרֹנִים בָּלוּל בַּשֶּׁמֶן חֲצִי הַהִין: וְיַיִן תַּקְרִיב יא לַנֶּסֶךְ חֲצִי הַהִין אִשֵּׁה רֵיחַ־נִיחֹחַ לַיהֹוָה: כָּכָה יֵעָשֶׂה לַשּׁוֹר הָאֶחָד אוֹ לָאַיִל הָאֶחָד אוֹ־לַשֶּׂה בַכְּבָשִׂים יב אוֹ בָעִזִּים: כַּמִּסְפָּר אֲשֶׁר תַּעֲשׂוּ כָּכָה תַּעֲשׂוּ יג לָאֶחָד כְּמִסְפָּרָם: כָּל־הָאֶזְרָח יַעֲשֶׂה־כָּכָה אֶת־ יד אֵלֶּה לְהַקְרִיב אִשֵּׁה רֵיחַ־נִיחֹחַ לַיהֹוָה: וְכִי־יָגוּר

1] The LORD spoke to Moses, saying: **2]** Speak to the Israelite people and say to them: When you enter the land which I am giving you to settle in,   **3]** and would present an offering by fire to the LORD from the herd or from the flock, be it burnt offering or sacrifice, in fulfillment of a vow explicitly uttered, or as a freewill offering, or at your fixed occasions, producing an odor pleasing to the LORD:

4] The person who presents the offering to the LORD shall bring as a meal offering: a tenth of a measure of choice flour with a quarter of a *hin* of oil mixed in.   **5]** You shall also offer, with the burnt offering or the sacrifice, a quarter of a *hin* of wine as a libation for each sheep.

6] In the case of a ram, you shall present as a meal offering: two-tenths of a measure of choice flour with a third of a *hin* of oil mixed in;   **7]** and a third of a *hin* of wine as a libation— as an offering of pleasing odor to the LORD.

8] And if it is an animal from the herd that you offer to the LORD as a burnt offering or as a sacrifice, in fulfillment of a vow explicitly uttered or as an offering of well-being,   **9]** there shall be offered a meal offering along with the animal: three-tenths of a measure of choice flour with half a *hin* of oil mixed in;   **10]** and as libation you shall offer half a *hin* of wine—these being offerings by fire of pleasing odor to the LORD.

11] Thus shall be done with each ox, with each ram, and with any sheep or goat,   **12]** as many as you offer; you shall do thus with each one, as many as there are.   **13]** Every citizen, when presenting an offering by fire of pleasing odor to the LORD, shall do so with them.

15:3] *Burnt offering or sacrifice.* On these and other types of offerings see introduction to Leviticus.

    Explicitly uttered. See Lev. 22:21.

    An odor pleasing to the Lord. The image of God liking the smell of sacrifice is today hard to appreciate, because modern civilization has devalued the sense of smell. See commentary on Gen. 8:21.

4] *The person . . . shall bring.* A sacrifice comparable to a human meal is prescribed, that is, one with pleasant accouterments, wine, and oil.

The amounts here specified may be compared to those listed in Ezek. 46:5 ff., where, however, they apply to princely offerings.

    Tenth of a measure. Possibly the meaning of the Hebrew *isaron* (connecting it with עֶשֶׂר, *eser*, ten), which has the same content as an *omer*. The exact modern equivalents of this and other measures are much in dispute.

    Hin. A liquid measure. How the libation was to be offered is not specified in the Torah.

    One source: it was at the foot of the altar [2].

וְאָמַרְתָּ אֲלֵהֶם בְּבֹאֲכֶם אֶל־הָאָרֶץ אֲשֶׁר אֲנִי מֵבִיא   אֶתְכֶם גֵּר אוֹ אֲשֶׁר־בְּתוֹכְכֶם לְדֹרֹתֵיכֶם וְעָשָׂה אִשֶּׁה

אֶתְכֶם שָׁמָּה: וְהָיָה בַּאֲכָלְכֶם מִלֶּחֶם הָאָרֶץ תָּרִימוּ   יט רֵיחַ נִיחֹחַ לַיהוָה כַּאֲשֶׁר תַּעֲשׂוּ כֵּן יַעֲשֶׂה: הַקָּהָל

תְרוּמָה לַיהוָה: רֵאשִׁית עֲרִסֹתֵכֶם חַלָּה תָּרִימוּ   חֻקָּה אַחַת לָכֶם וְלַגֵּר הַגָּר חֻקַּת עוֹלָם לְדֹרֹתֵיכֶם

תְרוּמָה כִּתְרוּמַת גֹּרֶן כֵּן תָּרִימוּ אֹתָהּ: מֵרֵאשִׁית   כא כָּכֶם כַּגֵּר יִהְיֶה לִפְנֵי יְהוָה: תּוֹרָה אַחַת וּמִשְׁפָּט אֶחָד

עֲרִסֹתֵיכֶם תִּתְּנוּ לַיהוָה תְּרוּמָה לְדֹרֹתֵיכֶם: ס וְכִי   כב יִהְיֶה לָכֶם וְלַגֵּר הַגָּר אִתְּכֶם: פ

תִשְׁגּוּ וְלֹא תַעֲשׂוּ אֵת כָּל־הַמִּצְוֹת הָאֵלֶּה אֲשֶׁר־דִּבֶּר   וַיְדַבֵּר יְהוָה אֶל־מֹשֶׁה לֵּאמֹר: דַּבֵּר אֶל־בְּנֵי יִשְׂרָאֵל

14] And when, throughout the ages, a stranger who has taken up residence with you, or one who lives among you, would present an offering by fire of pleasing odor to the LORD—as you do, so shall it be done by   **15]** the rest of the congregation. There shall be one law for you and for the resident stranger; it shall be a law for all time throughout the ages. You and the stranger shall be alike before the LORD;   **16]** the same ritual and the same rule shall apply to you and to the stranger who resides among you.

17] The LORD spoke to Moses, saying: **18]** Speak to the Israelite people and say to them: When you enter the land to which I am taking you   **19]** and you eat of the bread of the land, you shall set some aside as a gift to the LORD: **20]** as the first yield of your baking, you shall set aside a loaf as a gift; you shall set it aside as a gift like the gift from the threshing floor.   **21]** You shall make a gift to the LORD from the first yield of your baking, throughout the ages.

22] If you unwittingly fail to observe any one of the commandments which the LORD has

---

14] *A stranger.* גֵּר (*ger*). The equality of native and stranger in civil law and most ceremonial laws is often stressed in the Torah. See Num. 9:14; 15:15–16, 29.

14–15] *So shall it be done . . . congregation.* The Hebrew text is obscure.

19] *Bread of the land.* According to the Mishnah this applies to the five species—wheat, barley, spelt, oats, and rye—from which bread was made [3].

20] *Baking.* The meaning of the Hebrew עֲרִיסָה (*arisah*) is uncertain. The Mishnah says that, if a minimum of one *omer* of flour is used, a professional baker must set 1/48 aside, while someone baking for home use owes twice the amount, or 1/24 [4].

Loaf. חַלָּה (*chalah*), a thick loaf (distinct from the thin loaf, רְקִיק, *rekik*, of Lev. 2:4), the portion set aside for the priest. This duty is one of the positive commandments incumbent on women and was applied not only to those in the Land of Israel but to Jews everywhere (after the destruction of the Temple the portion set aside was thrown into the fire instead of being given to the priest) [5]. According to the Mishnah, women must not neglect the laws relevant to chalah, menstruation, and Sabbath lights [6].

The chalah used by Jews at Sabbath and holy day meals is not associated with this law of setting aside a portion, but with Exod. 25:30; 29:23. The thick-thin distinction also prevailed in Babylonian sacrifices [7].

22] *If you unwittingly.* The principle here stated has no apparent connection with the preceding, and the offerings provided for in verses 24 ff. differ from those in Lev. 4 and 5. The Rabbis explained this as follows: the passages in Numbers deal with the consequences of idolatry, those in Leviticus with all other sins. Other interpreters applied the two sets of laws to sins of omission and commission, respectively [8].

כג יְהוָה אֶל־מֹשֶׁה: אֵת כָּל־אֲשֶׁר צִוָּה יְהוָה אֲלֵיכֶם בְּיַד־
מֹשֶׁה מִן־הַיּוֹם אֲשֶׁר צִוָּה יְהוָה וָהָלְאָה לְדֹרֹתֵיכֶם:
כד וְהָיָה אִם מֵעֵינֵי הָעֵדָה נֶעֶשְׂתָה לִשְׁגָגָה וְעָשׂוּ כָל־
הָעֵדָה פַּר בֶּן־בָּקָר אֶחָד לְעֹלָה לְרֵיחַ נִיחֹחַ לַיהוָה
וּמִנְחָתוֹ וְנִסְכּוֹ כַּמִּשְׁפָּט וּשְׂעִיר־עִזִּים אֶחָד לְחַטָּת:
כה וְכִפֶּר הַכֹּהֵן עַל־כָּל־עֲדַת בְּנֵי יִשְׂרָאֵל וְנִסְלַח לָהֶם
כִּי־שְׁגָגָה הִוא וְהֵם הֵבִיאוּ אֶת־קָרְבָּנָם אִשֶּׁה לַיהוָה
וְחַטָּאתָם לִפְנֵי יְהוָה עַל־שִׁגְגָתָם: כו וְנִסְלַח לְכָל־עֲדַת
בְּנֵי יִשְׂרָאֵל וְלַגֵּר הַגָּר בְּתוֹכָם כִּי לְכָל־הָעָם
בִּשְׁגָגָה: ס כז וְאִם־נֶפֶשׁ אַחַת תֶּחֱטָא בִשְׁגָגָה וְהִקְרִיבָה
עֵז בַּת־שְׁנָתָהּ לְחַטָּאת: כח וְכִפֶּר הַכֹּהֵן עַל־הַנֶּפֶשׁ הַשֹּׁגֶגֶת

כט בְּחֶטְאָהּ בִשְׁגָגָה לִפְנֵי יְהוָה לְכַפֵּר עָלָיו וְנִסְלַח לוֹ:
ל הָאֶזְרָח בִּבְנֵי יִשְׂרָאֵל וְלַגֵּר הַגָּר בְּתוֹכָם תּוֹרָה אַחַת
יִהְיֶה לָכֶם לָעֹשֶׂה בִּשְׁגָגָה: וְהַנֶּפֶשׁ אֲשֶׁר־תַּעֲשֶׂה בְּיָד
רָמָה מִן־הָאֶזְרָח וּמִן־הַגֵּר אֶת־יְהוָה הוּא מְגַדֵּף
לא וְנִכְרְתָה הַנֶּפֶשׁ הַהִוא מִקֶּרֶב עַמָּהּ: כִּי דְבַר־יְהוָה
בָּזָה וְאֶת־מִצְוָתוֹ הֵפַר הִכָּרֵת תִּכָּרֵת הַנֶּפֶשׁ הַהִוא
עֲוֹנָה בָהּ:   פ
לב וַיִּהְיוּ בְנֵי־יִשְׂרָאֵל בַּמִּדְבָּר וַיִּמְצְאוּ אִישׁ מְקֹשֵׁשׁ עֵצִים
לג בְּיוֹם הַשַּׁבָּת: וַיַּקְרִיבוּ אֹתוֹ הַמֹּצְאִים אֹתוֹ מְקֹשֵׁשׁ
לד עֵצִים אֶל־מֹשֶׁה וְאֶל־אַהֲרֹן וְאֶל כָּל־הָעֵדָה: וַיַּנִּיחוּ
לה אֹתוֹ בַּמִּשְׁמָר כִּי לֹא פֹרַשׁ מַה־יֵּעָשֶׂה לוֹ: ס וַיֹּאמֶר

* כד חסר א׳.
* כח ה׳ רפה.
* לא ה׳ רפה.

declared to Moses 23] —anything that the LORD has enjoined upon you through Moses—from the day that the LORD gave the commandment and on through the ages:

24] If this was done unwittingly, through the inadvertence of the community, the whole community shall present one bull of the herd as a burnt offering of pleasing odor to the LORD, with its proper meal offering, and one he-goat as a sin offering. 25] The priest shall make expiation for the whole Israelite community and they shall be forgiven; for it was an error, and for their error they have brought their offering, an offering by fire to the LORD and their sin offering before the LORD. 26] The whole Israelite community and the stranger residing among them shall be forgiven, for it happened to the entire people through error.

27] In case it is an individual who has sinned unwittingly, he shall offer a she-goat in its first year as a sin offering. 28] The priest shall make expiation before the LORD on behalf of the person who erred, for he sinned unwittingly, making such expiation for him that he may be forgiven. 29] For the citizen among the Israelites and for the stranger who resides among them—you shall have one ritual for anyone who acts in error.

30] But the person, be he citizen or stranger, who acts defiantly reviles the LORD; that person shall be cut off from among his people. 31] Because he has spurned the word of the LORD and violated His commandment, that person shall be cut off—he bears his guilt.

32] Once, when the Israelites were in the wilderness, they came upon a man gathering wood on the sabbath day. 33] Those who found him as he was gathering wood brought him before Moses, Aaron, and the whole community. 34] He was placed in custody, for it had not been

30] *Defiantly.* Literally, "with upraised hand," possibly referring to a clenched fist or similar gesture denoting public protest.

This is similar to the interpretation of the Targum: "He who acts arrogantly" (בְּרֵישׁ גְּלֵי).

Cut off. See at Num. 9:13.

31] *He bears his guilt.* Until he has repented [9].

32] *Gathering wood.* Probably in order to make a

fire, which was forbidden on the Sabbath; Exod. 35:3.

The Rabbis identified the offender as Zelophehad, hence the later plea of his five daughters (Num. 27:1 ff.) [10].

34] *What should be done to him.* In what manner the death penalty (decreed in Exod. 31:14 for the Sabbath violator) was to be administered.

יְהֹוָה אֶל־מֹשֶׁה מוֹת יוּמַת הָאִישׁ רָגוֹם אֹתוֹ בָאֲבָנִים
לה כָּל־הָעֵדָה מִחוּץ לַמַּחֲנֶה: וַיֹּצִיאוּ אֹתוֹ כָּל־הָעֵדָה
אֶל־מִחוּץ לַמַּחֲנֶה וַיִּרְגְּמוּ אֹתוֹ בָּאֲבָנִים וַיָּמֹת כַּאֲשֶׁר
צִוָּה יְהֹוָה אֶת־מֹשֶׁה: פ
לח וַיֹּאמֶר יְהֹוָה אֶל־מֹשֶׁה לֵּאמֹר: דַּבֵּר אֶל־בְּנֵי יִשְׂרָאֵל
וְאָמַרְתָּ אֲלֵהֶם וְעָשׂוּ לָהֶם צִיצִת עַל־כַּנְפֵי בִגְדֵיהֶם
לט לְדֹרֹתָם וְנָתְנוּ עַל־צִיצִת הַכָּנָף פְּתִיל תְּכֵלֶת: וְהָיָה

לָכֶם לְצִיצִת וּרְאִיתֶם אֹתוֹ וּזְכַרְתֶּם אֶת־כָּל־מִצְוֹת
יְהֹוָה וַעֲשִׂיתֶם אֹתָם וְלֹא־תָתוּרוּ אַחֲרֵי לְבַבְכֶם
מ וְאַחֲרֵי עֵינֵיכֶם אֲשֶׁר־אַתֶּם זֹנִים אַחֲרֵיהֶם: לְמַעַן
תִּזְכְּרוּ וַעֲשִׂיתֶם אֶת־כָּל־מִצְוֹתָי וִהְיִיתֶם קְדֹשִׁים
מא לֵאלֹהֵיכֶם: אֲנִי יְהֹוָה אֱלֹהֵיכֶם אֲשֶׁר הוֹצֵאתִי אֶתְכֶם
מֵאֶרֶץ מִצְרַיִם לִהְיוֹת לָכֶם לֵאלֹהִים אֲנִי יְהֹוָה
אֱלֹהֵיכֶם:

Haftarah Shelach-Lecha, p. 1262

specified what should be done to him.   **35]** Then the LORD said to Moses, "The man shall be put to death: the whole community shall pelt him with stones outside the camp."   **36]** So the whole community took him outside the camp and stoned him to death—as the LORD had commanded Moses.

37] The LORD said to Moses, as follows: **38]** Speak to the Israelite people and instruct them to make for themselves fringes on the corners of their garments throughout the ages; let them attach a cord of blue to the fringe at each corner.   **39]** That shall be your fringe; look at it and recall all the commandments of the LORD and observe them, so that you do not follow your heart and eyes in your lustful urge.   **40]** Thus you shall be reminded to observe all My commandments and to be holy to your God.   **41]** I the LORD am your God, who brought you out of the land of Egypt to be your God: I, the LORD your God.

35] *Stones*. According to the Rabbis, the Torah specifies four types of execution by the courts: stoning, burning, by the sword, and strangling [11]; and two by divine action: "extirpation" (*karet*) and "death by Heaven" [12].

36] *The whole community*. The witnesses stoned him, while the whole community took responsibility by watching [13].

38] *Fringes*. צִיצִית (*tzitzit*). In Deut. 22:12 fringes are called *gedilim*. See commentary.

Blue. Prescribed only in this passage [14].

The Law of Fringes

The embellishment of garments with tassels or fringes appears to be older than the Bible and may be seen in pictorial representations of other peoples.[1] It is therefore possible that the biblical tradition tried to infuse a common custom with a religious dimension. Deut. 22:12 provides that the fringes be worn on the four corners of the garment (that is, two in front and two in back). They were to be looked at, which was taken to mean that they should be visible,[2] and hence observant Jews could at once be recognized by their fringes. *Tzitzit* were often attached to an outer mantle that resembled the Roman *pallium*. During the persecutions in the Middle Ages, Jews hid their *tzitzit* by attaching them to a small, four-cornered cloth with an opening in the middle that could be slipped over the head and worn under the outer garment. Traditionally observant Jewish men, especially Chasidim, still wear such "four corners" (*arba kanfot*, also called *talit katan*, i.e., small talit) and, with ancient fears now gone, often make sure that its fringes are visible [17].

Fringes are also attached to the prayer shawl or talit, generally donned by men at morning services. During the reading of Num. 15:37–42, one of several selections that follow the recital of Deut. 6:4 (the *Shema*), the worshiper will take hold of the fringes, look at them to fulfill the biblical command, and then kiss them.

The *Kitzur Shulchan Aruch*, which lists the essentials of the halachah, says:

"The precept relating to fringes is great, because Scriptures weighed it and ascribed to it all the commandments, as it is said: 'Look upon it and recall all the commandments of the Lord' (verse 39). Therefore every Jew must be careful to wear a *talit katan* all day. This must be made of white lamb's wool, about three-fourths of a cubit in length and half a cubit in width; others hold that it must be a cubit square. Every man should also be careful to have a big talit with fringes, to wrap himself in while praying, and he should be particular to possess a handsome talit. Every religious act must be done in the handsomest way, as it is written: 'This is my God, and I will glorify Him,' and it is explained to mean: Become proud before Him when performing His commandments.

"Even fringes that fell off and were removed from the talit must not be thrown into a rubbish heap, because it is forbidden to despise a precept. Some people are particular to hide such fringes in a book and to make a book mark out of them, because, since a holy precept was once performed therewith, let another precept be performed with them. One must not make any unworthy use of an old talit which he does not use any longer for the performances of any precept" [18].

Women are exempt from wearing *tzitzit*,

---

[1] Finds from Mari show that fringes (*sisiktu*) and locks of hair represented the whole person (note that in Ezek. 8:3 *tzitzit* means "lock of hair"). They were required as verifications from laymen who had experienced visions and wanted to transmit them as prophetic reports. Fringes and locks of hair were also used in legal contexts as occasional substitutes for seals in signing clay documents [15].

[2] A. Milgram calls attention to a historic controversy about this aspect of the commandment: "The talmudic authorities interpreted the phrase 'look upon it' (Num. 15:39) to imply that the talit was to be worn only at daytime. A blind man was therefore obligated to put on the talit at prayer even though he could not 'look upon it.' The Karaites, however, in their literalness, removed the phrase from its context, which clearly indicates that it is a garment and is therefore to be worn, and ruled that the *tzitzit* were to be hung up on a wall, so that every one might 'look upon' them" [16].

because the law demanding that one "look upon it" depends on a certain fixed time and women are generally excused from such laws [19].

The thread of blue that is commanded (verse 38) was increasingly hard to come by since the exact color dye from snails could be obtained only with great difficulty. Hence the Rabbis suspended the obligation[3] [21], and since then the fringes on the talit and talit katan were customarily made of white threads only.[4] Lately, it has been claimed that the snails from which the blue color was produced are now identifiable and available once more, and therefore some individuals, especially among the Chasidim, have reintroduced blue threads made from the dye of these snails into their tzitzit. So far this practice has not found wide acceptance.

Reform Jews have by and large abandoned the use of the talit, although those participating in the service on the pulpit usually wear it. The fringed stole worn by Christian officiants is a direct descendant of the talit.

[3] However J. Z. Lauterbach has argued that the abandonment of blue threads had a theological reason. The Rabbis wanted to combat the idea that the blue thread reflected an actual heavenly throne which was blue in color [20].

[4] In fact, Rabbi Meir held the omission of a white thread to be a more serious transgression since everyone could easily obtain white threads [22].

Chalah

The commandment of chalah follows a section which, according to the Rabbis, speaks of idolatry. Therefore it may be said that anyone who observes the commandment of chalah is as if he had repudiated idolatry. Why? Because the man who sets aside chalah believes that all possessions are from the Lord, while the pagan regards his possessions as having been obtained by his own might, by "the work of man's hands" (Ps. 115:3). These are the idols which are destroyed by observing the commandment of chalah.   CHASIDIC [23]

Make a Gift to the Lord from the First Yield (Num. 15:21)

It says "from the first yield of your baking," which one may interpret as "one's early years" [cf., the English expression "half-baked," denoting immaturity]. Do not wait until you become old to serve the Lord; give Him some of your early manhood as well.   CHASIDIC [24]

Early Failure

How observant were the Israelites in the desert? Note that they observed but one single Sabbath and already violated the second.
                                MIDRASH [25]

Gematria

The Jews' search for a logical correlation between the talit and the commandments of God was rewarded with intriguing discoveries. The numerical value of the word *tzitzit* is 600.[5] Each of the fringes contains 8 threads and 5 knots, making a total of 613. This number corresponds to the 613 commandments contained in the Torah.

It was also noted that in making the fringes one winds the long thread around the other threads between the 5 knots 7, 8, 11, and 13 times respectively. The first three numbers equal 26, which is the numerical value of the Tetragrammaton (יהוה). The remaining number 13 equals the numerical value of the word "one" אֶחָד (*echad*) —the last word in the opening verse of the *Shema*. The fringes of the talit thus, not only remind the Jew of the 613 divine commandments, but also underscore the central doctrine of Judaism, that the Lord is One.   A. MILGRAM [26]

Blue

Blue is for the sea, the sea suggests the heavens, and the heavens suggest the throne of glory.
                                MIDRASH [27]

Christian Scriptures

Jesus, like all observant Jews of his time, wore *tzitzit* but warned against "hypocrites" who went about "with broad phylacteries and large tassels."
                                [28]

Look at It (Num. 15:39)

The word "it" (*oto*) could also mean "Him" [there being no neutral gender in Hebrew]. Hence, while looking at the fringe and remembering His commandments, one merits beholding God, as it were.   TALMUD [29]

Do Not Follow Your Heart (Num. 15:39)

When a man learns much, prays much, and thinks "I am truly pious," he transgresses the command, "Do not follow your heart and your eye in your lustful urge." Let him look at the *tzitzit* and remember who he is.   CHASIDIC [30]

---

[5] In the numerical use of the Hebrew alphabet ציצית equals 600: צ=90 (used twice), י=10(used twice), and ת=400.

The Rebellion of Korah, Dathan, and Abiram

The Torah now turns to the most serious rebellion that faced Moses and Aaron during the forty years of wanderings through the desert. The rebellion is led by Korah, Dathan, and Abiram, and like the other uprisings it ends in failure. God comes to the aid of His chosen leaders and destroys their opponents dramatically: some are literally swallowed by the earth, others are burned, and still others are struck by a plague.

The reader will notice that the story shifts its emphasis several times from Korah to Dathan and Abiram. Apparently two traditions were joined together.* One tells of an antilevitic revolt by Korah, which features the issue of priestly succession; the other of a civil uprising against Moses, which was led by Dathan and Abiram. The two stories eventually became one, and the person of Korah emerges as the chief villain.

The King James Bible, The New English Bible, and other Christian translations (following the Septuagint's version) differ in chapter and verse arrangements from the Hebrew text: they assign fifty verses to chapter 16 and therefore shorten chapter 17 by fifteen verses, making 17:1 equivalent to 17:16 in our version.

(A new weekly portion, *Korah*, begins with 16:1.)

---

*Note also that Num. 27:3 speaks only of Korah and Deut. 11:6 and Ps. 106:17 only of Dathan and Abiram.

פ פ פ

א וַיִּקַּח קֹרַח בֶּן־יִצְהָר בֶּן־קְהָת בֶּן־לֵוִי וְדָתָן וַאֲבִירָם
ב בְּנֵי אֱלִיאָב וְאוֹן בֶּן־פֶּלֶת בְּנֵי רְאוּבֵן: וַיָּקֻמוּ לִפְנֵי
מֹשֶׁה וַאֲנָשִׁים מִבְּנֵי־יִשְׂרָאֵל חֲמִשִּׁים וּמָאתָיִם נְשִׂיאֵי
ג עֵדָה קְרִאֵי מוֹעֵד אַנְשֵׁי־שֵׁם: וַיִּקָּהֲלוּ עַל־מֹשֶׁה וְעַל־
אַהֲרֹן וַיֹּאמְרוּ אֲלֵהֶם רַב־לָכֶם כִּי כָל־הָעֵדָה כֻּלָּם
קְדֹשִׁים וּבְתוֹכָם יְהֹוָה וּמַדּוּעַ תִּתְנַשְּׂאוּ עַל־קְהַל
ד יְהֹוָה: וַיִּשְׁמַע מֹשֶׁה וַיִּפֹּל עַל־פָּנָיו: וַיְדַבֵּר אֶל־קֹרַח
ה וְאֶל־כָּל־עֲדָתוֹ לֵאמֹר בֹּקֶר וְיֹדַע יְהֹוָה אֶת־אֲשֶׁר־לוֹ
וְאֶת־הַקָּדוֹשׁ וְהִקְרִיב אֵלָיו וְאֵת אֲשֶׁר יִבְחַר־בּוֹ
ו יַקְרִיב אֵלָיו: זֹאת עֲשׂוּ קְחוּ־לָכֶם מַחְתּוֹת קֹרַח וְכָל־

ז עֲדָתוֹ: וּתְנוּ בָהֵן אֵשׁ וְשִׂימוּ עֲלֵיהֶן קְטֹרֶת לִפְנֵי
יְהֹוָה מָחָר וְהָיָה הָאִישׁ אֲשֶׁר־יִבְחַר יְהֹוָה הוּא הַקָּדוֹשׁ
ח רַב־לָכֶם בְּנֵי לֵוִי: וַיֹּאמֶר מֹשֶׁה אֶל־קֹרַח שִׁמְעוּ־נָא
ט בְּנֵי לֵוִי: הַמְעַט מִכֶּם כִּי־הִבְדִּיל אֱלֹהֵי יִשְׂרָאֵל
אֶתְכֶם מֵעֲדַת יִשְׂרָאֵל לְהַקְרִיב אֶתְכֶם אֵלָיו לַעֲבֹד
אֶת־עֲבֹדַת מִשְׁכַּן יְהֹוָה וְלַעֲמֹד לִפְנֵי הָעֵדָה
י לְשָׁרְתָם: וַיַּקְרֵב אֹתְךָ וְאֶת־כָּל־אַחֶיךָ בְנֵי־לֵוִי אִתָּךְ
יא וּבִקַּשְׁתֶּם גַּם־כְּהֻנָּה: לָכֵן אַתָּה וְכָל־עֲדָתְךָ הַנֹּעָדִים
יב עַל־יְהֹוָה וְאַהֲרֹן מַה־הוּא כִּי תַלִּינוּ עָלָיו: וַיִּשְׁלַח
מֹשֶׁה לִקְרֹא לְדָתָן וְלַאֲבִירָם בְּנֵי אֱלִיאָב וַיֹּאמְרוּ
יג לֹא נַעֲלֶה: הַמְעַט כִּי הֶעֱלִיתָנוּ מֵאֶרֶץ זָבַת חָלָב

יא תלינו קרי.

1] Now Korah, son of Izhar son of Kohath son of Levi, betook himself, along with Dathan and Abiram sons of Eliab, and On son of Peleth—descendants of Reuben— **2]** to rise up against Moses, together with two hundred and fifty Israelites, chieftains of the community, chosen in the assembly, men of repute. **3]** They combined against Moses and Aaron and said to them, "You have gone too far! For all the community are holy, all of them, and the LORD is in their midst. Why then do you raise yourselves above the LORD's congregation?"

4] When Moses heard this, he fell on his face. **5]** Then he spoke to Korah and all his company, saying, "Come morning, the LORD will make known who is His and who is holy, and will grant him access to Himself; He will grant access to the one He has chosen. **6]** Do this: You, Korah and all your band, take fire pans, **7]** and tomorrow put fire in them and lay incense on them before the LORD. Then the man whom the LORD chooses, he shall be the holy one. You have gone too far, sons of Levi!"

8] Moses said further to Korah, "Hear me, sons of Levi. **9]** Is it not enough for you that the God of Israel has set you apart from the community of Israel and given you access to Him, to perform the duties of the LORD's Tabernacle, and to minister to the community and serve them? **10]** Thus He has advanced you and all your fellow Levites with you; yet you seek the priesthood too! **11]** Truly, it is against the LORD that you and all your company have banded together. For who is Aaron that you should rail against him?"

12] Moses sent for Dathan and Abiram, sons of Eliab; but they said, "We will not

16:1] *Betook himself.* A speculative translation to render as closely as possible the Hebrew וַיִּקַּח (*vayikach*), which means "he took" but does not say what he took.

Ibn Ezra: "took men"; others emend וַיִּקַּח to read וַיָּקָם (*vayakam*), he rose, or וַיָּקַח (*vayekach*), he was impudent. One free translation reads: "he challenged the authority of Moses" [1].

On son of Peleth. He is not otherwise mentioned in the story or in the rest of the Bible. Critics believe On to be a textual corruption, especially since in Num. 26:5, 8–9, Eliab is listed as the

son of Pallu, son of Reuben, suggesting that Peleth should be read Pallu, while "and On" should be emended or omitted.

4] *Fell on his face.* Usually done in prayer, but here either in humility or powerlessness.

6] *Your band.* Literally, "his" band.

Fire pans. Bronze containers for live coals and incense (see Lev. 16:12).

11] *Who is Aaron.* Why rail against him—was he not appointed by God himself?

12] *We will not come!* Literally, "we will not

וּדְבַשׁ לַהֲמִיתֵנוּ בַּמִּדְבָּר כִּי־תִשְׂתָּרֵר עָלֵינוּ גַּם־

יד הִשְׂתָּרֵר: אַף לֹא אֶל־אֶרֶץ זָבַת חָלָב וּדְבַשׁ הֲבִיאֹתָנוּ

וַתִּתֶּן־לָנוּ נַחֲלַת שָׂדֶה וָכָרֶם הַעֵינֵי הָאֲנָשִׁים הָהֵם

טו תְּנַקֵּר לֹא נַעֲלֶה: וַיִּחַר לְמֹשֶׁה מְאֹד וַיֹּאמֶר אֶל־יְהֹוָה

אַל־תֵּפֶן אֶל־מִנְחָתָם לֹא חֲמוֹר אֶחָד מֵהֶם נָשָׂאתִי

טז וְלֹא הֲרֵעֹתִי אֶת־אַחַד מֵהֶם: וַיֹּאמֶר מֹשֶׁה אֶל־קֹרַח

אַתָּה וְכָל־עֲדָתְךָ הֱיוּ לִפְנֵי יְהֹוָה אַתָּה וָהֵם וְאַהֲרֹן

יז מָחָר: וּקְחוּ אִישׁ מַחְתָּתוֹ וּנְתַתֶּם עֲלֵיהֶם קְטֹרֶת

וְהִקְרַבְתֶּם לִפְנֵי יְהֹוָה אִישׁ מַחְתָּתוֹ חֲמִשִּׁים וּמָאתַיִם

יח מַחְתֹּת וְאַתָּה וְאַהֲרֹן אִישׁ מַחְתָּתוֹ: וַיִּקְחוּ אִישׁ מַחְתָּתוֹ

וַיִּתְּנוּ עֲלֵיהֶם אֵשׁ וַיָּשִׂימוּ עֲלֵיהֶם קְטֹרֶת וַיַּעַמְדוּ פֶּתַח

יט אֹהֶל מוֹעֵד וּמֹשֶׁה וְאַהֲרֹן: וַיַּקְהֵל עֲלֵיהֶם קֹרַח אֶת־

כָּל־הָעֵדָה אֶל־פֶּתַח אֹהֶל מוֹעֵד וַיֵּרָא כְבוֹד־יְהֹוָה

כ אֶל־כָּל־הָעֵדָה: ס וַיְדַבֵּר יְהֹוָה אֶל־מֹשֶׁה וְאֶל־

כא אַהֲרֹן לֵאמֹר: הִבָּדְלוּ מִתּוֹךְ הָעֵדָה הַזֹּאת וַאֲכַלֶּה

כב אֹתָם כְּרָגַע: וַיִּפְּלוּ עַל־פְּנֵיהֶם וַיֹּאמְרוּ אֵל אֱלֹהֵי

הָרוּחֹת לְכָל־בָּשָׂר הָאִישׁ אֶחָד יֶחֱטָא וְעַל כָּל־הָעֵדָה

כג תִּקְצֹף: ס וַיְדַבֵּר יְהֹוָה אֶל־מֹשֶׁה לֵּאמֹר: דַּבֵּר

אֶל־הָעֵדָה לֵאמֹר הֵעָלוּ מִסָּבִיב לְמִשְׁכַּן־קֹרַח דָּתָן

כה וַאֲבִירָם: וַיָּקָם מֹשֶׁה וַיֵּלֶךְ אֶל־דָּתָן וַאֲבִירָם וַיֵּלְכוּ

come! **13]** Is it not enough that you brought us from a land flowing with milk and honey to have us die in the wilderness, that you would also lord it over us? **14]** Even if you had brought us to a land flowing with milk and honey, and given us possession of fields and vineyards, should you gouge out those men's eyes? We will not come!" **15]** Moses was much aggrieved and he said to the LORD, "Pay no regard to their oblation. I have not taken the ass of any one of them, nor have I wronged any one of them."

16] And Moses said to Korah, "Tomorrow, you and all your company appear before the LORD, you and they and Aaron. **17]** Each of you take his fire pan and lay incense on it, and each of you bring his fire pan before the LORD, two hundred and fifty fire pans; you and Aaron also [bring] your fire pans." **18]** Each of them took his fire pan, put fire in it, laid incense on it, and took his place at the entrance of the Tent of Meeting, as did Moses and Aaron. **19]** Korah gathered the whole community against them at the entrance of the Tent of Meeting.

Then the Presence of the LORD appeared to the whole community, **20]** and the LORD spoke to Moses and Aaron, saying, **21]** "Stand back from this community that I may annihilate them in an instant!" **22]** But they fell on their faces and said, "O God, Source of the breath of all flesh! When one man sins, will You be wrathful with the whole community?"

23] The LORD spoke to Moses, saying, **24]** "Speak to the community and say: Withdraw from about the abodes of Korah, Dathan, and Abiram."

25] Moses rose and went to Dathan and Abiram, the elders of Israel following him. **26]** He

ascend." Going to a holy place is generally described by עלה (alah). Going up to the bimah to participate in the Torah service or going to settle in Israel are acts called aliyah.

14] *Gouge out those men's eyes?* An idiomatic expression similar to the English "throw dust in their eyes," or "blind them to the true facts" [2]. Others, "hoodwink" [3]; "fool us" [4].

15] *Their oblation.* Which they will doubtlessly offer with demonstrative piety. Moses' first defense before God is against what he considers Dathan's and Abiram's implied accusation of corruption.

Samuel makes a similar but more elaborate defense (I Sam. 12:3).

19] *Korah gathered the whole community.* The people did not necessarily side with him but readily came out to watch his attack on the establishment. As Num. 17:6 indicates, however, some dissatisfaction was rife among them. By not backing Moses and Aaron they exposed themselves to divine retribution.

22] *Source.* Literally, "God."

לא הָאֵלֶּה אֶת־יְהֹוָה: וַיְהִי כְּכַלֹּתוֹ לְדַבֵּר אֵת כָּל־הַדְּבָרִים הָאֵלֶּה וַתִּבָּקַע הָאֲדָמָה אֲשֶׁר תַּחְתֵּיהֶם:
לב וַתִּפְתַּח הָאָרֶץ אֶת־פִּיהָ וַתִּבְלַע אֹתָם וְאֶת־בָּתֵּיהֶם וְאֵת כָּל־הָאָדָם אֲשֶׁר לְקֹרַח וְאֵת כָּל־הָרְכוּשׁ: וַיֵּרְדוּ
לג הֵם וְכָל־אֲשֶׁר לָהֶם חַיִּים שְׁאֹלָה וַתְּכַס עֲלֵיהֶם הָאָרֶץ וַיֹּאבְדוּ מִתּוֹךְ הַקָּהָל: וְכָל־יִשְׂרָאֵל אֲשֶׁר
לד סְבִיבֹתֵיהֶם נָסוּ לְקֹלָם כִּי אָמְרוּ פֶּן־תִּבְלָעֵנוּ הָאָרֶץ:
לה וְאֵשׁ יָצְאָה מֵאֵת יְהֹוָה וַתֹּאכַל אֵת הַחֲמִשִּׁים וּמָאתַיִם אִישׁ מַקְרִיבֵי הַקְּטֹרֶת: ס

יז וַיְדַבֵּר יְהֹוָה אֶל־מֹשֶׁה לֵּאמֹר: אֱמֹר אֶל־אֶלְעָזָר בֶּן־אַהֲרֹן הַכֹּהֵן וְיָרֵם אֶת־הַמַּחְתֹּת מִבֵּין הַשְּׂרֵפָה וְאֶת־

כו אַחֲרָיו זִקְנֵי יִשְׂרָאֵל: וַיְדַבֵּר אֶל־הָעֵדָה לֵאמֹר סוּרוּ נָא מֵעַל אָהֳלֵי הָאֲנָשִׁים הָרְשָׁעִים הָאֵלֶּה וְאַל־תִּגְּעוּ
כז בְּכָל־אֲשֶׁר לָהֶם פֶּן־תִּסָּפוּ בְּכָל־חַטֹּאתָם: וַיֵּעָלוּ מֵעַל מִשְׁכַּן־קֹרַח דָּתָן וַאֲבִירָם מִסָּבִיב וְדָתָן וַאֲבִירָם יָצְאוּ נִצָּבִים פֶּתַח אָהֳלֵיהֶם וּנְשֵׁיהֶם וּבְנֵיהֶם וְטַפָּם:
כח וַיֹּאמֶר מֹשֶׁה בְּזֹאת תֵּדְעוּן כִּי־יְהֹוָה שְׁלָחַנִי לַעֲשׂוֹת
כט אֵת כָּל־הַמַּעֲשִׂים הָאֵלֶּה כִּי־לֹא מִלִּבִּי: אִם־כְּמוֹת כָּל־הָאָדָם יְמֻתוּן אֵלֶּה וּפְקֻדַּת כָּל־הָאָדָם יִפָּקֵד
ל עֲלֵיהֶם לֹא יְהֹוָה שְׁלָחָנִי: וְאִם־בְּרִיאָה יִבְרָא יְהֹוָה וּפָצְתָה הָאֲדָמָה אֶת־פִּיהָ וּבָלְעָה אֹתָם וְאֶת־כָּל־אֲשֶׁר לָהֶם וְיָרְדוּ חַיִּים שְׁאֹלָה וִידַעְתֶּם כִּי נִאֲצוּ הָאֲנָשִׁים

addressed the community, saying, "Move away from the tents of these wicked men and touch nothing that belongs to them, lest you be wiped out for all their sins." **27]** So they withdrew from about the abodes of Korah, Dathan, and Abiram.

Now Dathan and Abiram had come out and they stood at the entrance of their tents, with their wives, their children, and their little ones. **28]** And Moses said, "By this you shall know that it was the LORD who sent me to do all these things; that they are not of my own devising: **29]** if these men die as all men do, if their lot be the common fate of all mankind, it was not the LORD who sent me. **30]** But if the LORD brings about something unheard-of, so that the ground opens its mouth wide and swallows them up with all that belongs to them, and they go down alive into Sheol, you shall know that these men have spurned the LORD." **31]** Scarcely had he finished speaking all these words when the ground under them burst asunder, **32]** and the earth opened its mouth and swallowed them up with their households, all Korah's people and all their possessions. **33]** They went down alive into Sheol, with all that belonged to them; the earth closed over them and they vanished from the midst of the congregation. **34]** All Israel around them fled at their shrieks, for they said, "The earth might swallow us!"

35] And a fire went forth from the LORD and consumed the two hundred and fifty men offering the incense.

1] The Lord spoke to Moses, saying: **2]** Order Eleazar son of Aaron the priest to remove the fire pans—for they have become sacred—from among the charred remains; and scatter the

26] *Move away.* When Moses talks authoritatively, the people follow him by habit or instinct and abandon the rebels.

32] *Opened its mouth.* An expression usually reserved to indicate speech. The Hebrew ear detected here a special dimension: it was as if the earth itself spoke in judgment [5]. The text does not specify the location.

All Korah's people. His household. But according to Num. 26:11 his children did not die.

33] *Sheol.* The abode of the dead, thought of as a region below the earth (see Gen. 37:35, which speaks of going down to Sheol) [6].

17:2] *Become sacred.* קָדֵשׁוּ (kadeshu), set aside, unfit for ordinary use.

הָאֵשׁ וָהֵלְאָה כִּי קָדֵשׁוּ: אֵת מַחְתּוֹת הַחַטָּאִים
הָאֵלֶּה בְּנַפְשֹׁתָם וְעָשׂוּ אֹתָם רִקֻּעֵי פַחִים צִפּוּי
לַמִּזְבֵּחַ כִּי־הִקְרִיבֻם לִפְנֵי־יְהֹוָה וַיִּקְדָּשׁוּ וְיִהְיוּ לְאוֹת
לִבְנֵי יִשְׂרָאֵל: וַיִּקַּח אֶלְעָזָר הַכֹּהֵן אֵת מַחְתּוֹת
הַנְּחֹשֶׁת אֲשֶׁר הִקְרִיבוּ הַשְּׂרֻפִים וַיְרַקְּעוּם צִפּוּי
לַמִּזְבֵּחַ: זִכָּרוֹן לִבְנֵי יִשְׂרָאֵל לְמַעַן אֲשֶׁר לֹא־יִקְרַב
אִישׁ זָר אֲשֶׁר לֹא מִזֶּרַע אַהֲרֹן הוּא לְהַקְטִיר קְטֹרֶת
לִפְנֵי יְהֹוָה וְלֹא־יִהְיֶה כְקֹרַח וְכַעֲדָתוֹ כַּאֲשֶׁר דִּבֶּר
יְהֹוָה בְּיַד־מֹשֶׁה לוֹ: פ

וַיִּלֹּנוּ כָּל־עֲדַת בְּנֵי־יִשְׂרָאֵל מִמָּחֳרָת עַל־מֹשֶׁה וְעַל־
אַהֲרֹן לֵאמֹר אַתֶּם הֲמִתֶּם אֶת־עַם יְהֹוָה: וַיְהִי
בְּהִקָּהֵל הָעֵדָה עַל־מֹשֶׁה וְעַל־אַהֲרֹן וַיִּפְנוּ אֶל־אֹהֶל
מוֹעֵד וְהִנֵּה כִסָּהוּ הֶעָנָן וַיֵּרָא כְּבוֹד יְהֹוָה: וַיָּבֹא מֹשֶׁה

וְאַהֲרֹן אֶל־פְּנֵי אֹהֶל מוֹעֵד: ס וַיְדַבֵּר יְהֹוָה אֶל־
מֹשֶׁה לֵּאמֹר: הֵרֹמּוּ מִתּוֹךְ הָעֵדָה הַזֹּאת וַאֲכַלֶּה אֹתָם
כְּרָגַע וַיִּפְּלוּ עַל־פְּנֵיהֶם: וַיֹּאמֶר מֹשֶׁה אֶל־אַהֲרֹן קַח
אֶת־הַמַּחְתָּה וְתֶן־עָלֶיהָ אֵשׁ מֵעַל הַמִּזְבֵּחַ וְשִׂים קְטֹרֶת
וְהוֹלֵךְ מְהֵרָה אֶל־הָעֵדָה וְכַפֵּר עֲלֵיהֶם כִּי־יָצָא
הַקֶּצֶף מִלִּפְנֵי יְהֹוָה הֵחֵל הַנָּגֶף: וַיִּקַּח אַהֲרֹן כַּאֲשֶׁר
דִּבֶּר מֹשֶׁה וַיָּרָץ אֶל־תּוֹךְ הַקָּהָל וְהִנֵּה הֵחֵל הַנֶּגֶף
בָּעָם וַיִּתֵּן אֶת־הַקְּטֹרֶת וַיְכַפֵּר עַל־הָעָם: וַיַּעֲמֹד בֵּין־
הַמֵּתִים וּבֵין הַחַיִּים וַתֵּעָצַר הַמַּגֵּפָה: וַיִּהְיוּ הַמֵּתִים
בַּמַּגֵּפָה אַרְבָּעָה עָשָׂר אֶלֶף וּשְׁבַע מֵאוֹת מִלְּבַד
הַמֵּתִים עַל־דְּבַר־קֹרַח: וַיָּשָׁב אַהֲרֹן אֶל־מֹשֶׁה אֶל־
פֶּתַח אֹהֶל מוֹעֵד וְהַמַּגֵּפָה נֶעֱצָרָה: פ

coals abroad.   3] [Remove] the fire pans of those who have sinned at the cost of their lives, and let them be made into hammered sheets as plating for the altar—for once they have been used for offering to the LORD, they have become sacred—and let them serve as a warning to the people of Israel.   4] Eleazar the priest took the copper fire pans which had been used for offering by those who died in the fire; and they were hammered into plating for the altar,   5] as the LORD had ordered him through Moses. It was to be a reminder to the Israelites, so that no outsider—one not of Aaron's offspring—should presume to offer incense before the LORD and suffer the fate of Korah and his band.

6] Next day the whole Israelite community railed against Moses and Aaron, saying, "You two have brought death upon the LORD's people!"   7] But as the community gathered against them, Moses and Aaron turned toward the Tent of Meeting; the cloud had covered it and the Presence of the LORD appeared.

8] When Moses and Aaron reached the Tent of Meeting,   9] the Lord spoke to Moses, saying,   10] "Remove yourselves from this community, that I may annihilate them in an instant." They fell on their faces.   11] Then Moses said to Aaron, "Take the fire pan, and put on it fire from the altar. Add incense and take it quickly to the community and make expiation for them. For wrath has gone forth from the LORD: the plague has begun!"   12] Aaron took it, as Moses had ordered, and ran to the midst of the congregation, where the plague had begun among the people. He put on the incense and made expiation for the people;   13] he stood between the dead and the living until the plague was checked.   14] Those who died of the plague came to fourteen thousand and seven hundred, aside from those who died on account of Korah.   15] Aaron then returned to Moses at the entrance of the Tent of Meeting, since the plague was checked.

3] *Remove.* The Hebrew is obscure.

6] *The whole Israelite community railed.* The dis-content aroused by the rebels was apparently widespread and involved over 14,000 people.

Two Traditions

Bible critics ascribe the difficulties of this section to a joining of two traditions. While a clear division is no longer possible, there appears to be a Korah rebellion that is directed against Aaron and levitic privilege and an anti-Moses uprising led by Dathan and Abiram. The former is assigned to the P source and the latter to the J/E source.[1]

The first story tells of Korah and 250 men who complain about the special religious status of the Levites. There is a contest involving censers; Korah's people come to the Tent and are consumed by fire; their censers are taken away, destroyed, and symbolically refashioned; the 14,000 people who support the rebellion or who are unhappy with Korah's punishment are killed by a plague. The story appears to reflect a struggle for priestly privilege. Once upon a time (as attested by Psalms) Korah's people were full priests and singers, but after a power struggle they were reduced to doorkeepers.[2]

The second tradition tells of the rebellion of Dathan and Abiram, and members of the tribe of Reuben, against the civil authority of Moses. They refuse a confrontation with him. Moses appeals to the community, which backs him up and withdraws from the rebels, who in turn are swallowed by the earth. This story may represent the memory of an intertribal struggle. Originally the tribe of Reuben was very important, but in time it was dislodged from its original preeminence. This is also reflected in the Jacob tale, where the first-born Reuben is passed over in favor of others.

The Rabbis attempted in ingenious fashion to harmonize the various difficulties and apparent discrepancies that arose from the interweaving of the two traditions. The talmudic discussion reveals the extent of their speculation in this matter. For instance, inasmuch as verses 31–32 speak of the earth swallowing Korah's men but do not mention Korah himself, some say that the earth swallowed Korah's tent but that he was not in it; others that Korah was burned and that his ashes were swallowed; or that he died afterwards in the plague [8].

The Punishment

There were numerous rebellions in the desert, and they were directed against either God or His emissary. In each case the rebels were reported to have died of plague, or fire, or in battle. Only twice, when the position of Moses was severely attacked, was there unusual punishment: by cleaving the earth, as in this story, and by leprosy, when Miriam and Aaron challenged their brother (Num. 12). In the people's uprisings against God the consequences do not lie outside the human realm, but in the challenges to Moses the punishments are supernatural.

The intent of this biblical tradition is clear—to underline in the strongest terms the political and spiritual supremacy of the priests, and their successors, who were shown to have unequivocal divine sanction. A rebellion against them and Moses as their leader was in fact a rebellion against God. Those who demurred were therefore exposed to divine wrath, which was demonstrably severe in behalf of His servant. God could take care of His own status, so to speak, and therefore needed only the usual forms of retribution; but, when His authority was

---

[1] P: comprising Num. 16:1a, 2–7, 18–24, 27, 35; 17:6–15. Some see a substratum, possibly from the D-source, comprising Num. 16:8–11, 16, 17; 17:1–5.

J/E: comprising 16:1b, 12–15, 25–34.

[2] See Pss. 42–49; 84; 85; 87; 88. The status reduction is seen by some to be reflected in Pss. 42:5 and 84:11. Cross considers the story to be late because it covers over the conflict between the Aaronide and Mushite (i.e., Moses') priestly clans and sees them as already reunited [7].

challenged indirectly and more subtly by undermining His human representatives, the punishment took on unusual and memorable form. "The earth opened its mouth" is a vivid image reminiscent of Gen. 4:11, which also depicts the earth as an active participant in the drama, speeding the condemned to their abode in the netherworld. (Characteristically of Numbers, this story is followed in chapters 17 and 18 by legislation that sets forth once and for all what the priestly and levitical duties are to be.)

Over the years the Korah story assumed great importance. Rabbis of mishnaic and talmudic times viewed themselves as direct spiritual descendants of Moses, and they interpreted the punishment of Korah as a warning to their own contemporaries who challenged the divine sanctity of rabbinic teaching. However, since a repetition of biblical miracles could not be counted on, the Rabbis threatened their challengers with eternal damnation—for instance, when they declared that those who did not believe in resurrection would have no share in the world-to-come. It is in this light that we must see the assertion of Rabbi Akiba that Korah not only was punished in the desert but excluded from divine grace for all time to come [9]. This is also the meaning of the rabbinic tradition that Korah argued with Moses about ritual fringes and other halachic matters and attacked the sense and logic of the Torah, which is to say he battled not merely Moses but the God of Moses.[3] God stood behind His chosen leader then, and in the centuries to come He would stand behind the leaders who followed Moses and taught in His name.

Korah's Argument

Korah's rebellion was directed against the leadership of Moses.[4] Superficially, his act may appear to be the usual attempt by someone out of power to displace the incumbent rulers. But the Bible's very silence about his motives directs our attention away from Korah's true intention to his stated argument.

Korah said: "All the community are holy. . . . Why then do you raise yourselves above the Lord's congregation?" The question implies the challenge: If God is in our midst, then whoever is leading us will have His support. Or, going further (though this is not expressed): If we are all holy, what need is there for someone like Moses to instruct us, or why is there need for laws to make us holy? Since the people are holy, commandments from without are not necessary [13].

Note that Moses and Aaron make no answer to the first part of Korah's statement, that is, the reference to communal holiness. They refer only to the latter ("Why do you raise yourselves . . . ?"), leaving it to God to reaffirm their embattled leadership. He raised them to high position and He will answer the rebels, as indeed He does.

But the question still seeks its answer. Ultimately, as Buber emphasizes, the question Korah asked poses an insoluble contradiction [14]: for holiness can never be fully realized within history, yet the people are to act as if it can be or even as if it has

---

[3] This inference is drawn from the fact that the law of fringes (end of Num. 15) immediately precedes the Korah story [10]. According to another tradition, Korah commented on the difficult provision in Lev. 13:12–13 (which declares as "clean" a person totally covered by a certain skin disease). The paradox led him to declare: "The Torah is not from Heaven; Moses is not His prophet nor Aaron His priest" [11]. Another midrash, commenting on Num. 16:33 (which tells that Korah's people went alive into Sheol), speculates that Korah was kept alive so that he might forever shout, "Moses was right!" [12].

[4] Using Korah and Moses as the chief protagonists of the story now found in the received Torah text.

been realized. This is the biblical way of dealing with a divine impasse and it became the normative way of Jewish tradition. Korah's argument turns on the eternal tension between authority and freedom. Like many demagogues after him, Korah offered himself as a fitting guardian of the spirit of freedom. But while the people might have accepted the offer of substitute leadership, God did not.

The argument Korah presented was not blotted out with the drastic divine response, and neither was Korah's name. His family continued to serve with high distinction; no less a person than the prophet Samuel was his descendant (I Chron. 6:16 ff.); ten psalms were composed by the sons of Korah; and his offspring functioned in the Temple courts. Like Korah's argument, they refused to disappear [15].

GLEANINGS

Even the Children and Little Ones (Num. 16:27)

Why were innocent children drawn into a rebellion not of their making? This teaches the grievousness of strife, for, while an earthly court does not punish minors, the Heavenly Court makes even suckling infants bear the consequences of their fathers' sins.   RASHI

Korah's Grievance

It was a case of family jealousy. Since the priesthood and political leadership had already been taken by Aaron and Moses, sons of Amram (Kohath's oldest son), Korah felt that at least the leadership of the clan should have gone to him, who was the son of Izhar, Kohath's second son. Instead, the appointment had gone to Elizaphan (Num. 3:30), son of Uzziel, who was Kohath's fourth and youngest son (Exod. 6:18).

MIDRASH [16]

Moses Fell on His Face (Num. 16:4)

Why not Aaron too, who also was the object of rebellion (Num. 16:3) and in two other places is shown as having been clearly involved in the controversy (16:22; 17:10)? Because it was Aaron's priesthood which was primarily at stake, and he did not want to play the partisan.

HAYIM DOV CHAVEL [17]

These Wicked Men (Num. 16:26)

There are four types of the wicked (רָשָׁע): one who contemplates violence against a fellow-man (even though he may not carry it out); one who borrows but does not pay back; one who is arrogant and does not respect his superiors; and one who is prone to cause strife. Dathan and Abiram fell into both latter categories.

MIDRASH [18]

When One Man Sins (Num. 16:22)

Usually, when people in a province rebel against the king, the latter's legions come and carry out an indiscriminate massacre. But God knows the secret intentions of men and therefore does not punish the whole community for one man's sins.   MIDRASH [19]

And Korah Betook Himself (Num. 16:1)

Korah failed because he wanted to seize greatness and strength for himself with his own hands. Greatness is good only if it is bestowed on a man by Heaven: man cannot go out and take it for himself.   CHASIDIC [20]

Not in Heaven's Name

Every controversy that is in the name of Heaven shall in the end lead to a permanent result, but every controversy that is not in the name of Heaven shall not lead to a permanent result. Which controversy was in the name of Heaven? The controversy of Hillel and Shammai. And which was not in the name of Heaven? The controversy of Korah and all his company.

ETHICS OF THE FATHERS [21]

The Quarrel

Korah quarreled with peace, and he who quarrels with peace quarrels with the Holy Name.   ZOHAR [22]

Literary Notes

Note the subtleties of play and counterplay in challenge and response. Korah says, "You have gone too far"; in response Moses takes up the same phrase. And when he says, "Is it not enough for you..." the rebels respond with his words as if to say, "We too can do it."   I. ARAMA [23]

Of Priests, Levites, and Israelites

The rebellion of Korah and the devastation which followed it raised the question of the special position of priests and Levites. Theirs was the awesome duty of guarding the sanctuary from unqualified trespass. Therefore, the Torah now sets forth a detailed list of their tasks and ensuing privileges and underlines that they will exist "for all time" (Num. 18:8). The exalted position of Aaron's family is buttressed by a divine miracle—the blossoming of his rod. Then the gift offerings in which the priests participate are listed, among them the first fruits of the harvest and the redemption proceeds of the human first-born, a practice which has persisted into our present day. (For a detailed discussion of the priesthood, see commentary on Lev. 21 and 22; on primogeniture, see commentary on Gen. 25:27 ff.).

Probably the distinction between ordinary Israelites, priests, and Levites had not yet hardened at the time of Korah's rebellion (Korah could still claim "All the community are holy"), but subsequently the boundaries between them were clearly defined. Two classes of guards now protected the sacred precincts from all outsiders: priests, who were the chief officers and who also had access to the inner court, and Levites, who worked under their command. This kind of division is very old; a Hittite temple manual of the second millennium B.C.E. makes similar provisions and distinctions, and there too trespass by unauthorized persons is punishable by death—reflecting the deep sense of awe in which holy places were held [1].

In Christian versions Num. 17:16–18:32 comprises Num. 17:1–18:32.

כב וַיַּנַּח מֹשֶׁה אֶת־הַמַּטֹּת לִפְנֵי יְהוָה בְּאֹהֶל הָעֵדֻת: וַיְהִי
מִמָּחֳרָת וַיָּבֹא מֹשֶׁה אֶל־אֹהֶל הָעֵדוּת וְהִנֵּה פָּרַח
מַטֵּה־אַהֲרֹן לְבֵית לֵוִי וַיֹּצֵא פֶרַח וַיָּצֵץ צִיץ וַיִּגְמֹל
כד שְׁקֵדִים: וַיֹּצֵא מֹשֶׁה אֶת־כָּל־הַמַּטֹּת מִלִּפְנֵי יְהוָה אֶל־
כָּל־בְּנֵי יִשְׂרָאֵל וַיִּרְאוּ וַיִּקְחוּ אִישׁ מַטֵּהוּ:
פ
כה וַיֹּאמֶר יְהוָה אֶל־מֹשֶׁה הָשֵׁב אֶת־מַטֵּה אַהֲרֹן לִפְנֵי
הָעֵדוּת לְמִשְׁמֶרֶת לְאוֹת לִבְנֵי־מֶרִי וּתְכַל תְּלוּנֹתָם
כו מֵעָלַי וְלֹא יָמֻתוּ: וַיַּעַשׂ מֹשֶׁה כַּאֲשֶׁר צִוָּה יְהוָה אֹתוֹ
פ   כֵּן עָשָׂה:
כז וַיֹּאמְרוּ בְּנֵי יִשְׂרָאֵל אֶל־מֹשֶׁה לֵאמֹר הֵן גָּוַעְנוּ אָבַדְנוּ
כח כֻּלָּנוּ אָבָדְנוּ: כֹּל הַקָּרֵב הַקָּרֵב אֶל־מִשְׁכַּן יְהוָה

טז וַיְדַבֵּר יְהוָה אֶל־מֹשֶׁה לֵּאמֹר: דַּבֵּר אֶל־בְּנֵי יִשְׂרָאֵל
וְקַח מֵאִתָּם מַטֶּה מַטֶּה לְבֵית אָב מֵאֵת כָּל־נְשִׂיאֵהֶם
לְבֵית אֲבֹתָם שְׁנֵים עָשָׂר מַטּוֹת אִישׁ אֶת־שְׁמוֹ תִּכְתֹּב
יח עַל־מַטֵּהוּ: וְאֵת שֵׁם אַהֲרֹן תִּכְתֹּב עַל־מַטֵּה לֵוִי כִּי
יט מַטֶּה אֶחָד לְרֹאשׁ בֵּית אֲבוֹתָם: וְהִנַּחְתָּם בְּאֹהֶל
כ מוֹעֵד לִפְנֵי הָעֵדוּת אֲשֶׁר אִוָּעֵד לָכֶם שָׁמָּה: ❊ וְהָיָה
הָאִישׁ אֲשֶׁר אֶבְחַר־בּוֹ מַטֵּהוּ יִפְרָח וַהֲשִׁכֹּתִי מֵעָלַי
אֶת־תְּלֻנּוֹת בְּנֵי יִשְׂרָאֵל אֲשֶׁר הֵם מַלִּינִם עֲלֵיכֶם:
כא וַיְדַבֵּר מֹשֶׁה אֶל־בְּנֵי יִשְׂרָאֵל וַיִּתְּנוּ אֵלָיו כָּל־
נְשִׂיאֵיהֶם מַטֶּה לְנָשִׂיא אֶחָד מַטֶּה לְנָשִׂיא אֶחָד לְבֵית
אֲבֹתָם שְׁנֵים עָשָׂר מַטּוֹת וּמַטֵּה אַהֲרֹן בְּתוֹךְ מַטּוֹתָם:

❊ כ חצי הספר בפסוקים

16] The LORD spoke to Moses, saying: **17]** Speak to the Israelite people and take from them—from the chieftains of their ancestral houses—one staff for each chieftain of an ancestral house: twelve staffs in all. Inscribe each man's name on his staff,   **18]** there being one staff for each head of an ancestral house; also inscribe Aaron's name on the staff of Levi.   **19]** Deposit them in the Tent of Meeting before the Pact, where I meet with you.   **20]** The staff of the man whom I choose shall sprout, and I will rid Myself of the incessant mutterings of the Israelites against you.

21] Moses spoke thus to the Israelites. Their chieftains gave him a staff for each chieftain of an ancestral house, twelve staffs in all; among these staffs was that of Aaron.   **22]** Moses deposited the staffs before the LORD, in the Tent of the Pact.   **23]** The next day Moses entered the Tent of the Pact, and there the staff of Aaron of the house of Levi had sprouted: it had brought forth sprouts, produced blossoms, and borne almonds.   **24]** Moses then brought out all the staffs from before the LORD to all the Israelites; each identified and recovered his staff.

25] The LORD said to Moses, "Put Aaron's staff back before the Pact, as a lesson to rebels, so that their mutterings against Me may cease, lest they die."   **26]** This Moses did; just as the LORD had commanded him, so he did.

27] But the Israelites said to Moses, "Lo, we perish! We are lost, all of us lost!   **28]** Every-

17:17] *Staff.* A stick carried by the leaders (see commentary). A word play (or term extension) is involved here: מַטֶּה (*mateh*) doubles for "staff" and "tribe."

Twelve staffs in all. For the twelve tribes, including the tribe of Levi [2]. Others, Levi's staff, with Aaron's name on it, was a thirteenth staff, because Joseph's two sons, Ephraim and Manasseh, were counted separately [3].

19] *Before the Pact.* Before the Ark of the Covenant or Pact. The Christian Scriptures (Hebrews 9:4) record that in the ark were kept "the golden pot that had manna, Aaron's rod, and the Tables of the Covenant."

23] *Almonds.* Rapid flowering is characteristic of the almond tree. In Jeremiah's dedication to his prophetic mission, the almond branch, שָׁקֵד (*shaked*), symbolizes the speedy coming to pass of the words that God will put into his mouth: "For I am watching over [שֹׁקֵד, *shoked*] My word to perform it" (Jer. 1:12). According to a later Jewish tradition, the staff of the Messiah will be an almond branch [4].

27] *Lo, we perish!* Previous experience leads the people to believe that another disaster is about to follow [5].

ה יִקְרַב אֲלֵיכֶם: וּשְׁמַרְתֶּם אֵת מִשְׁמֶרֶת הַקֹּדֶשׁ וְאֵת   ס   יָמוּת הַאִם תַּמְנוּ לִגְוֺעַ:

מִשְׁמֶרֶת הַמִּזְבֵּחַ וְלֹא־יִהְיֶה עוֹד קֶצֶף עַל־בְּנֵי   א וַיֹּאמֶר יְהוָה אֶל־אַהֲרֹן אַתָּה וּבָנֶיךָ וּבֵית־אָבִיךָ אִתָּךְ

יִשְׂרָאֵל: וַאֲנִי הִנֵּה לָקַחְתִּי אֶת־אֲחֵיכֶם הַלְוִיִּם מִתּוֹךְ   תִּשְׂאוּ אֶת־עֲוֺן הַמִּקְדָּשׁ וְאַתָּה וּבָנֶיךָ אִתָּךְ תִּשְׂאוּ אֶת־

בְּנֵי יִשְׂרָאֵל לָכֶם מַתָּנָה נְתֻנִים לַיהוָה לַעֲבֹד אֶת־   ב עֲוֺן כְּהֻנַּתְכֶם: וְגַם אֶת־אַחֶיךָ מַטֵּה לֵוִי שֵׁבֶט אָבִיךָ

ז עֲבֹדַת אֹהֶל מוֹעֵד: וְאַתָּה וּבָנֶיךָ אִתְּךָ תִּשְׁמְרוּ אֶת־   הַקְרֵב אִתָּךְ וְיִלָּווּ עָלֶיךָ וִישָׁרְתוּךָ וְאַתָּה וּבָנֶיךָ אִתָּךְ

כְּהֻנַּתְכֶם לְכָל־דְּבַר הַמִּזְבֵּחַ וּלְמִבֵּית לַפָּרֹכֶת   ג לִפְנֵי אֹהֶל הָעֵדֻת: וְשָׁמְרוּ מִשְׁמַרְתְּךָ וּמִשְׁמֶרֶת כָּל־

וַעֲבַדְתֶּם עֲבֹדַת מַתָּנָה אֶתֵּן אֶת־כְּהֻנַּתְכֶם וְהַזָּר   הָאֹהֶל אַךְ אֶל־כְּלֵי הַקֹּדֶשׁ וְאֶל־הַמִּזְבֵּחַ לֹא יִקְרָבוּ

הַקָּרֵב יוּמָת: פ   ד וְלֹא־יָמֻתוּ גַם־הֵם גַּם־אַתֶּם: וְנִלְווּ עָלֶיךָ וְשָׁמְרוּ אֶת־

ח וַיְדַבֵּר יְהוָה אֶל־אַהֲרֹן וַאֲנִי הִנֵּה נָתַתִּי לְךָ אֶת־   מִשְׁמֶרֶת אֹהֶל מוֹעֵד לְכֹל עֲבֹדַת הָאֹהֶל וְזָר לֹא־

---

one who so much as ventures near the LORD's Tabernacle must die. Alas, we are doomed to perish!"

1] The LORD said to Aaron: You with your sons and the ancestral house under your charge shall bear any guilt connected with the sanctuary; you and your sons alone shall bear any guilt connected with your priesthood. **2]** You shall associate with yourself your kinsmen the tribe of Levi, your ancestral tribe, to be attached to you and to minister to you and to your sons under your charge before the Tent of the Pact. **3]** They shall discharge their duties to you and to the Tent as a whole, but they must not have any contact with the furnishings of the Shrine or with the altar, lest both they and you die. **4]** They shall be attached to you and discharge the duties of the Tent of Meeting, all the service of the Tent; but no outsider shall intrude upon you **5]** as you discharge the duties connected with the Shrine and the altar, that wrath may not again strike the Israelites.

6] I hereby take your fellow Levites from among the Israelites; they are assigned to you in dedication to the LORD, to do the work of the Tent of Meeting; **7]** while you and your sons under your charge shall be careful to perform your priestly duties in everything pertaining to the altar and to what is behind the curtain. I make your priesthood a service of dedication; any outsider who encroaches shall be put to death.

8] The LORD spoke further to Aaron: I hereby give you charge of My gifts, all the sacred donations of the Israelites; I grant them to you and to your sons as a perquisite, a due for all

---

18:1] *Bear any guilt.* You will be held responsible: the Levites for the sanctuary and Aaron's family for the specific tasks of the priesthood. You must not be laggard in your guardianship and let others trespass.

According to the Talmud, both guardian and trespasser would incur the death penalty [6].

2] *To be attached.* יִלָּווּ (yilavu), a word play on the name לֵוִי (Levi); see Gen. 29:34.

3] *Furnishings of the Shrine.* The holy vessels, the shew bread (or bread of display), the candlestick, altar, and ark.

6] *Assigned to you in dedication.* The Hebrew words מַתָּנָה and נְתֻנִים are from the same root and refer to the status of the Levites as a Temple guild, which worked under the direction of the priesthood; see at Num. 3:9 [7].

8] *Perquisite.* See Lev. 7:35 [8]. The priests, having no land, received their support in kind. Rabbis and ministers often had similar arrangements up to recent times.

מִשְׁמֶ֣רֶת תְּרוּמֹתַ֗י לְכָל־קָדְשֵׁי֙ בְנֵֽי־יִשְׂרָאֵ֔ל לְךָ֧

ט נְתַתִּ֣ים לְמָשְׁחָ֗ה וּלְבָנֶ֛יךָ לְחָק־עוֹלָ֖ם׃ זֶ֣ה יִהְיֶ֥ה לְךָ֛

מִקֹּ֥דֶשׁ הַקֳּדָשִׁ֖ים מִן־הָאֵ֑שׁ כָּל־קָרְבָּנָ֡ם לְֽכָל־מִנְחָתָם֩

וּֽלְכָל־חַטָּאתָ֨ם וּֽלְכָל־אֲשָׁמָ֜ם אֲשֶׁ֥ר יָשִׁ֣יבוּ לִ֔י קֹ֣דֶשׁ

י קׇֽדָשִׁ֥ים לְךָ֛ ה֖וּא וּלְבָנֶֽיךָ׃ בְּקֹ֣דֶשׁ הַקֳּדָשִׁ֖ים

יא תֹּאכְלֶ֑נּוּ כָּל־זָכָר֙ יֹאכַ֣ל אֹת֔וֹ קֹ֖דֶשׁ יִֽהְיֶה־לָּֽךְ׃ וְזֶה־לְּךָ֞

תְּרוּמַ֣ת מַתָּנָ֡ם לְכָל־תְּנוּפֹת֩ בְּנֵ֨י יִשְׂרָאֵ֜ל לְךָ֧ נְתַתִּ֣ים

וּלְבָנֶ֧יךָ וְלִבְנֹתֶ֛יךָ אִתְּךָ֖ לְחָק־עוֹלָ֑ם כָּל־טָה֥וֹר

יב בְּבֵיתְךָ֖ יֹאכַ֥ל אֹתֽוֹ׃ כֹּ֚ל חֵ֣לֶב יִצְהָ֔ר וְכָל־חֵ֖לֶב תִּיר֣וֹשׁ

יג וְדָגָ֑ן רֵאשִׁיתָ֛ם אֲשֶׁר־יִתְּנ֥וּ לַֽיהֹוָ֖ה לְךָ֥ נְתַתִּֽים׃ בִּכּוּרֵ֞י

כָּל־אֲשֶׁ֣ר בְּאַרְצָ֗ם אֲשֶׁר־יָבִ֛יאוּ לַֽיהֹוָ֖ה לְךָ֣ יִהְיֶ֑ה כָּל־

יד טָה֥וֹר בְּבֵיתְךָ֖ יֹאכְלֶֽנּוּ׃ כָּל־חֵ֥רֶם בְּיִשְׂרָאֵ֖ל לְךָ֥ יִהְיֶֽה׃

time.   **9]** This shall be yours from the most holy sacrifices, the offerings by fire: every such offering that they render to Me as most holy sacrifices, namely, every meal offering, sin offering, and penalty offering of theirs, shall belong to you and your sons.   **10]** You shall partake of them as most sacred donations: only males may eat them; you shall treat them as consecrated.

11] This, too, shall be yours: the heave offerings of their gifts, all the wave offerings of the Israelites, I give to you, to your sons, and to the daughters that are with you, as a due for all time; everyone of your household who is clean may eat it.

12] All the best of the new oil, wine, and grain—the choice parts that they present to the LORD—I give to you.   **13]** The first fruits of everything in their land, that they bring to the LORD, shall be yours; everyone of your household who is clean may eat them.   **14]** Everything that has been proscribed in Israel shall be yours.   **15]** The first issue of the womb of every

9] *Offerings by fire.* The meaning of the Hebrew is uncertain.

10] *Only males.* Only they could partake of meal, sin, and penalty offerings, while heave offerings and first fruits could be shared by the women in the priestly family. The former offerings related to the forgiveness of sins and, in a male-oriented religion, only males were priests and could therefore participate.

11] *Who is clean.* Ritually clean, for the process of eating was a sacred function.

12] *All the best.* Literally, "the fat." The Hebrew idiom has entered English parlance through the expression "fat of the land" (Gen. 45:18), i.e., the choicest. The Torah does not specify the amount that the Israelites were to offer in this instance. The Mishnah suggests that someone who contributed 1/40 was considered generous (1/30 ac-

cording to the stricter rules of Shammai); 1/50 was thought average; and 1/60 was held parsimonious [9]. To this day some observant Jews will take a portion of anything new (e.g., a bottle of soft drink) and, in order to observe the command, spill or spoil a portion, there being no Temple priest to receive it.

13] *First fruits.* For details of the presentation, see Deut. 26:2–11.

Of everything. But the actual practice was to offer only "from the seven kinds," the fruit for which the land was famous: wheat, barley, wine, figs, pomegranates, olive oil, dates (including date honey) [10].

14] *Proscribed.* Everything dedicated to the sanctuary was banned from private use and could not be redeemed; see Lev. 27:28.

כ הוּא לִפְנֵי יְהוָה לְךָ וּלְזַרְעֲךָ אִתָּךְ: וַיֹּאמֶר יְהוָה אֶל־
אַהֲרֹן בְּאַרְצָם לֹא תִנְחָל וְחֵלֶק לֹא־יִהְיֶה לְךָ בְּתוֹכָם
כא אֲנִי חֶלְקְךָ וְנַחֲלָתְךָ בְּתוֹךְ בְּנֵי יִשְׂרָאֵל: ס וְלִבְנֵי
לֵוִי הִנֵּה נָתַתִּי כָּל־מַעֲשֵׂר בְּיִשְׂרָאֵל לְנַחֲלָה חֵלֶף
עֲבֹדָתָם אֲשֶׁר־הֵם עֹבְדִים אֶת־עֲבֹדַת אֹהֶל מוֹעֵד:
כב וְלֹא־יִקְרְבוּ עוֹד בְּנֵי יִשְׂרָאֵל אֶל־אֹהֶל מוֹעֵד לָשֵׂאת
כג חֵטְא לָמוּת: וְעָבַד הַלֵּוִי הוּא אֶת־עֲבֹדַת אֹהֶל מוֹעֵד
וְהֵם יִשְׂאוּ עֲו‍ֹנָם חֻקַּת עוֹלָם לְדֹרֹתֵיכֶם וּבְתוֹךְ בְּנֵי
כד יִשְׂרָאֵל לֹא יִנְחֲלוּ נַחֲלָה: כִּי אֶת־מַעְשַׂר בְּנֵי־יִשְׂרָאֵל
אֲשֶׁר יָרִימוּ לַיהוָה תְּרוּמָה נָתַתִּי לַלְוִיִּם לְנַחֲלָה עַל־
כֵּן אָמַרְתִּי לָהֶם בְּתוֹךְ בְּנֵי יִשְׂרָאֵל לֹא יִנְחֲלוּ נַחֲלָה: פ

טו כָּל־פֶּטֶר רֶחֶם לְכָל־בָּשָׂר אֲשֶׁר־יַקְרִיבוּ לַיהוָה
בָּאָדָם וּבַבְּהֵמָה יִהְיֶה־לָּךְ אַךְ פָּדֹה תִפְדֶּה אֵת
בְּכוֹר הָאָדָם וְאֵת בְּכוֹר־הַבְּהֵמָה הַטְּמֵאָה תִּפְדֶּה:
טז וּפְדוּיָו מִבֶּן־חֹדֶשׁ תִּפְדֶּה בְּעֶרְכְּךָ כֶּסֶף חֲמֵשֶׁת
שְׁקָלִים בְּשֶׁקֶל הַקֹּדֶשׁ עֶשְׂרִים גֵּרָה הוּא: אַךְ בְּכוֹר־
יז שׁוֹר אוֹ־בְכוֹר כֶּשֶׂב אוֹ־בְכוֹר עֵז לֹא תִפְדֶּה קֹדֶשׁ
הֵם אֶת־דָּמָם תִּזְרֹק עַל־הַמִּזְבֵּחַ וְאֶת־חֶלְבָּם תַּקְטִיר
יח אִשֶּׁה לְרֵיחַ נִיחֹחַ לַיהוָה: וּבְשָׂרָם יִהְיֶה־לָּךְ כַּחֲזֵה
יט הַתְּנוּפָה וּכְשׁוֹק הַיָּמִין לְךָ יִהְיֶה: כֹּל תְּרוּמֹת
הַקֳּדָשִׁים אֲשֶׁר יָרִימוּ בְנֵי־יִשְׂרָאֵל לַיהוָה נָתַתִּי לְךָ
וּלְבָנֶיךָ וְלִבְנֹתֶיךָ אִתְּךָ לְחָק־עוֹלָם בְּרִית מֶלַח עוֹלָם

being, man or beast, that is offered to the LORD, shall be yours; but you shall have the first-born of man redeemed, and you shall also have the firstling of unclean animals redeemed. **16]** Take as their redemption price, from the age of one month up, the money equivalent of five shekels by the sanctuary weight, which is twenty *gerahs*. **17]** But the firstlings of cattle, sheep, or goats may not be redeemed; they are consecrated. You shall dash their blood against the altar, and turn their fat into smoke as an offering by fire for a pleasing odor to the LORD. **18]** But their meat shall be yours: it shall be yours like the breast of wave offering and like the right thigh.

19] All the sacred gifts that the Israelites set aside for the LORD I give to you, to your sons, and to the daughters that are with you, as a due for all time. It shall be an everlasting covenant of salt before the LORD for you and for your offspring as well. **20]** And the LORD said to Aaron: You shall, however, have no territorial share among them or own any portion in their midst; I am your portion and your share among the Israelites.

21] And to the Levites I hereby give all the tithes in Israel as their share in return for the services that they perform, the services of the Tent of Meeting. **22]** Henceforth, Israelites shall not trespass on the Tent of Meeting, and thus incur guilt and die: **23]** only Levites shall perform the services of the Tent of Meeting; others would incur guilt. It is a law for all time throughout the ages. But they shall have no territorial share among the Israelites; **24]** for it is the tithes set aside by the Israelites as a gift to the LORD that I give to the Levites as their share. Therefore I have said concerning them: They shall have no territorial share among the Israelites.

15] *First-born of man.* He, too, belonged to God (Exod. 13:2, 12–15), but he was to be redeemed instead of sacrificed. (See at Num. 3:13 ff.).

16] *Their redemption price.* Referring to humans. For animals, see Exod. 34:19 f.

19] *Covenant of salt.* Probably meaning an everlasting covenant (see Lev. 2:13; II Chron. 13:5). The expression seems to derive from the use of salt as a preservative; similarly in Rashi, "because salt does not decay."

Among expressions based on the use of salt are these: "eating someone's salt" (as in Ezra 4:14), meaning his hospitality or entering his service—hence "salary," from the Latin *sal*; "salt of the earth" (from the Christian Scriptures, Matthew 5:13), the finest, rarest [11].

20] *I am your portion.* Both spiritually and materially.

21] *Tithes.* מַעֲשֵׂר (*ma'aser*), the tenth, from *eser*, ten.

ל תְּרוּמַת יְהוָה מִכָּל־חֶלְבּוֹ אֶת־מִקְדְּשׁוֹ מִמֶּנּוּ: וְאָמַרְתָּ אֲלֵהֶם בַּהֲרִימְכֶם אֶת־חֶלְבּוֹ מִמֶּנּוּ וְנֶחְשַׁב לַלְוִיִּם

לא כִּתְבוּאַת גֹּרֶן וְכִתְבוּאַת יָקֶב: וַאֲכַלְתֶּם אֹתוֹ בְּכָל־מָקוֹם אַתֶּם וּבֵיתְכֶם כִּי־שָׂכָר הוּא לָכֶם חֵלֶף

לב עֲבֹדַתְכֶם בְּאֹהֶל מוֹעֵד: וְלֹא־תִשְׂאוּ עָלָיו חֵטְא בַּהֲרִימְכֶם אֶת־חֶלְבּוֹ מִמֶּנּוּ וְאֶת־קָדְשֵׁי בְנֵי־יִשְׂרָאֵל לֹא תְחַלְּלוּ וְלֹא תָמוּתוּ:

כה וַיְדַבֵּר יְהוָה אֶל־מֹשֶׁה לֵּאמֹר: וְאֶל־הַלְוִיִּם תְּדַבֵּר וְאָמַרְתָּ אֲלֵהֶם כִּי־תִקְחוּ מֵאֵת בְּנֵי־יִשְׂרָאֵל אֶת־הַמַּעֲשֵׂר אֲשֶׁר נָתַתִּי לָכֶם מֵאִתָּם בְּנַחֲלַתְכֶם וַהֲרֵמֹתֶם

כז מִמֶּנּוּ תְּרוּמַת יְהוָה מַעֲשֵׂר מִן־הַמַּעֲשֵׂר: וְנֶחְשַׁב לָכֶם

כח תְּרוּמַתְכֶם כַּדָּגָן מִן־הַגֹּרֶן וְכַמְלֵאָה מִן־הַיָּקֶב: כֵּן תָּרִימוּ גַם־אַתֶּם תְּרוּמַת יְהוָה מִכֹּל מַעְשְׂרֹתֵיכֶם אֲשֶׁר תִּקְחוּ מֵאֵת בְּנֵי יִשְׂרָאֵל וּנְתַתֶּם מִמֶּנּוּ אֶת־תְּרוּמַת

כט יְהוָה לְאַהֲרֹן הַכֹּהֵן: מִכֹּל מַתְּנֹתֵיכֶם תָּרִימוּ אֵת כָּל־

Haftarah Korah, p. 1265

25] The LORD spoke to Moses, saying: **26]** Speak to the Levites and say to them: When you receive from the Israelites their tithes, which I have assigned to you as your share, you shall remove from them one-tenth of the tithe as a gift to the LORD. **27]** This shall be accounted to you as your contribution. As with the new grain from the threshing floor or the flow from the vat, **28]** so shall you on your part set aside a gift for the LORD from all the tithes that you receive from the Israelites; and from them you shall bring the gift for the LORD to Aaron the priest. **29]** You shall set aside all gifts due to the LORD from everything that is donated to you, from each thing its best portion, the part thereof that is to be consecrated.

30] Say to them further: When you have removed the best part from it, you Levites may consider it the same as the yield of threshing floor or vat. **31]** You and your households may eat it anywhere, for it is your recompense for your services in the Tent of Meeting. **32]** You will incur no guilt through it, once you have removed the best part from it; but you must not profane the sacred donations of the Israelites, lest you die.

26] *Gift to the Lord.* The Levites too must tithe from what they receive. Thus they give to the priests "a tithe of the tithe" [12]. (For a full discussion of tithes see at Deut. 14:22.)

32] *The best part.* Which was to be given to the priests. Nonobservance was a capital offense.

The Flowering Rod

When the Israelites prepared for the first Passover and for the Exodus from Egypt, they were bidden to have their loins girded, their sandals on their feet, and their staffs in their hands (Exod. 12:11). Such staffs, rods, or sticks may therefore be said to have been in common use for work (as for shepherds), for support in walking, or for defense against animals and even people. In addition to such practical uses, rods have also been symbols of authority and office throughout history. (Examples are the scepter of a monarch, the mace of the speaker in Parliament, the baton of a symphony conductor.) In such cases the staffs were often made of special materials and were elaborately decorated. Aaron's staff, which had figured prominently in connection with various miracles in Egypt—it had turned into a serpent and it had been the signal for turning the Nile into blood and for bringing on the plagues of frogs and lice (Exod. 7:9 ff.)—was probably a fairly ordinary stick fashioned from a branch with his name inscribed on it to distinguish it from the rods submitted by the other tribal leaders.

The Torah interprets the overnight budding of Aaron's rod as a miracle. As such, it becomes part of the tradition found in many nations that tells of sticks suddenly come into bloom. For instance, among the Greeks and Romans, Pausanias relates that Hercules leaned his club against the image of Hermes, and the club which was made of wild olive wood struck root in the ground and sprouted afresh. While Jewish postbiblical tradition does not extend the story of the flowering rod beyond this single occurrence, Christian patrology and later legends utilize the theme repeatedly, as with the stick of Joseph of Arimathea, the staff of Desiderius, and others.

Pidyon ha-Ben—Redemption of the First-Born

The Torah stipulates that the first-born male child is to be redeemed. According to Snaith:

"The principle that lies behind the whole idea of first fruits and the first-born is that all increase of every kind belongs to God, and this must be acknowledged by the presentation at the Shrine of the first of the fruits and the first that is born. These are not 'given,' but 'presented,' since they are God's already. Thus at all harvest festivals, modern equally with ancient, the harvest-gifts are God's gifts to men and not man's gifts to God. When all this has been acknowledged in the first-fruits ceremony, God permits men to use the rest for sustenance and enjoyment" [13].

Jewish tradition developed a set ritual for the redemption of the first-born son, and its essentials are still widely observed. Following are some of the laws and customs that apply [14]. They amplify the simple central act whereby the father presents his son symbolically to a descendant of a priestly family, a *Kohen* (see at Num. 3:6), and then receives the child back in exchange for the redemption price of five dollars (formerly *selaim*). Appropriate formulas embellish and formalize the ceremony.

Time: the thirty-first day,[1] preferably during day light. If it is a Sabbath or holy day, the *pidyon* is postponed until night, for it involves a monetary transaction. (In contrast, circumcision takes place on such days.)

First-born means the mother's first-born; if a man marries several times, the law may apply each time.

Responsibility rests on the father, not the mother. If the father has died, a rabbinic court must redeem the child. If redemption

---

[1] After the child has completed thirty days of life, when he is considered a viable person.

has been neglected, the child must redeem himself when of age. If either the father or the mother is the child of a priestly or levitic family, the first-born need not generally be redeemed.

Money: The priest may return the money if he chooses, and nowadays it is often understood that he will do so or give the money to charity.

Feast: It is customary to celebrate the event with a festive repast.

Many Jews feel that the ceremony is either empty or anachronistic with its legal phrases and ancient formulations and with the participation of someone who holds a sacred position by virtue of descent. Most Reform Jews have abandoned the ceremony because they have rejected all matters relating to priestly privilege as being no longer applicable. It is well to remember, however, that the *Kohen* represents not so much himself as the claim that God has on the first-born son in Jewish tradition: the child belongs to Him and His service, for God spared Israel's first-born in the night of the Exodus. There is, therefore, a direct line between the redemption from Egypt and the redemption of a Jewish child, between the first-born then and those of today (see Exod. 13:2). The idea that the child belongs to God first and foremost is at the heart of the *pidyon ha-ben*, and this realization can be a sobering and important experience for the parents who set out to raise their first child.

GLEANINGS

Flowering Rods

Christian hagiography knows several parallels. In the year 253, it is related, a certain Desiderius was designated by God as the chosen successor of the bishop of Langres. Since he could not be identified, a delegation was sent to Rome to seek counsel. On the return journey they met a laborer of that name driving a cart. He dismounted and stuck his staff into the ground. At once it blossomed. Somewhat similarly, in the fifth century, St. Orans was offered the bishopric of Auch, which he at first declined. His staff, however, rooted itself in solid rock and then blossomed, revealing that he was indeed chosen of God. The same story was told also concerning the election of Paul of Reims to the see of Trois-Chateaux.

T. H. GASTER [15]

Aaron's Rod

Some say that it was the staff which had been in the hand of Judah; others say that it was the staff that had been in the hand of Moses. Others again say that Moses took a beam and, cutting it into twelve planks, said to the princes: "Take your sticks every one of you from the same beam." He did it in order that they should not say that Aaron's rod was fresh and that this was the reason why it flowered.

Why almonds and not pomegranates, or nuts? Because Israel was compared to the two latter. [In Song of Songs 4:13 and 6:11, rabbinic interpretation identifies the young woman of the poem as Israel.] That same staff was held in the hand of every king until the Temple was destroyed, and then it was [divinely] hidden away. That same staff also is destined to be held in the hand of the King Messiah (may it be speedily in our days!); as it says, "The Lord will stretch forth from Zion your mighty staff, hold sway over your enemies!" (Ps. 110:2). MIDRASH [16]

A Retelling

He [Moses] called the multitude to a congregation and patiently heard what apology they had to make for themselves, without opposing them, and this lest he should embitter the multitude: he only desired the heads of the tribes to bring their rods, with the names of their tribes inscribed upon them, and that he should receive the priesthood in whose rod God should give a sign. This was agreed to. So the rest brought their rods, as did Aaron also who had written the tribe of Levi on his rod. These rods Moses laid up in the Tabernacle of God. On the next day he brought out the rods, which were known from one another by those who brought them, they having distinctly noted them, as had the multitude also; and, as to the rest, in the same form Moses had received them, in that they saw them still; but they also saw buds and branches grown out of Aaron's rod, with ripe fruits upon them: they were almonds, the rod having been cut out of that tree. The people were so amazed at this strange sight that, though Moses and Aaron were before under some degree of hatred, they now laid that hatred aside and began to admire the judgment of God concerning them, so that hereafter they applauded what God had decreed and permitted Aaron to enjoy the priesthood peaceably. And thus God ordained him priest several times, and he retained that honor without further disturbance. And hereby this sedition of the Hebrews, which had been a great one and had lasted a great while, was at last composed.

JOSEPHUS [17]

God's Due

Restore to God His due in tithe and time;
A tithe purloin'd cankers the whole estate.

G. HERBERT [18]

1143

The Red Cow; Laws of Purification

The rules regarding the red heifer are often called the most mysterious laws of the Torah. They prescribe a process of purification for anyone who has been in contact with a dead body. This is accomplished through sprinkling a person with the ashes of an unblemished red heifer. The sprinkling, done on the third and seventh days after such contact, has a cleansing effect, but those who handle the ashes are unclean until nightfall. The Rabbis sought in vain to plumb the rationale of these rules and came to the conclusion that they were instituted to test Israel's unconditional obedience (see Gleanings).

Except for Num. 31:19–24, where the practice seems to be assumed, the Hebrew Bible lacks any further reference to the rite. It is mentioned in Christian Scriptures (Hebrews 9:13) and treated elaborately in rabbinic writings. Josephus records the tradition that upon Miriam's death, which is related immediately after this section (Num. 20:1), those who buried her were cleansed by the ashes of the first red cow used for this purpose [1]. The joining of the legislation in this chapter to the notation of Miriam's death thus appears deliberate.

(A new weekly portion, *Chukat*, begins with this, 19:1.)

י דָּמָהּ עַל־פִּרְשָׁהּ יִשְׂרֹף: וְלָקַח הַכֹּהֵן עֵץ אֶרֶז וְאֵזוֹב
ז וּשְׁנִי תוֹלָעַת וְהִשְׁלִיךְ אֶל־תּוֹךְ שְׂרֵפַת הַפָּרָה: וְכִבֶּס
בְּגָדָיו הַכֹּהֵן וְרָחַץ בְּשָׂרוֹ בַּמַּיִם וְאַחַר יָבֹא אֶל־
ח הַמַּחֲנֶה וְטָמֵא הַכֹּהֵן עַד־הָעָרֶב: וְהַשֹּׂרֵף אֹתָהּ יְכַבֵּס
בְּגָדָיו בַּמַּיִם וְרָחַץ בְּשָׂרוֹ בַּמָּיִם וְטָמֵא עַד־הָעָרֶב:
ט וְאָסַף אִישׁ טָהוֹר אֵת אֵפֶר הַפָּרָה וְהִנִּיחַ מִחוּץ
לַמַּחֲנֶה בְּמָקוֹם טָהוֹר וְהָיְתָה לַעֲדַת בְּנֵי־יִשְׂרָאֵל
י לְמִשְׁמֶרֶת לְמֵי נִדָּה חַטָּאת הִוא: וְכִבֶּס הָאֹסֵף אֶת־
אֵפֶר הַפָּרָה אֶת־בְּגָדָיו וְטָמֵא עַד־הָעָרֶב וְהָיְתָה לִבְנֵי

פ   פ   פ   פ

א וַיְדַבֵּר יְהֹוָה אֶל־מֹשֶׁה וְאֶל־אַהֲרֹן לֵאמֹר: זֹאת חֻקַּת
הַתּוֹרָה אֲשֶׁר־צִוָּה יְהֹוָה לֵאמֹר דַּבֵּר אֶל־בְּנֵי
יִשְׂרָאֵל וְיִקְחוּ אֵלֶיךָ פָרָה אֲדֻמָּה תְּמִימָה אֲשֶׁר אֵין־
ב בָּהּ מוּם אֲשֶׁר לֹא־עָלָה עָלֶיהָ עֹל: וּנְתַתֶּם אֹתָהּ אֶל־
ג אֶלְעָזָר הַכֹּהֵן וְהוֹצִיא אֹתָהּ אֶל־מִחוּץ לַמַּחֲנֶה וְשָׁחַט
אֹתָהּ לְפָנָיו: וְלָקַח אֶלְעָזָר הַכֹּהֵן מִדָּמָהּ בְּאֶצְבָּעוֹ
ד וְהִזָּה אֶל־נֹכַח פְּנֵי אֹהֶל־מוֹעֵד מִדָּמָהּ שֶׁבַע פְּעָמִים:
ה וְשָׂרַף אֶת־הַפָּרָה לְעֵינָיו אֶת־עֹרָהּ וְאֶת־בְּשָׂרָהּ וְאֶת־

1] The LORD spoke to Moses and Aaron, saying: **2]** This is the ritual law that the LORD has commanded:

Instruct the Israelite people to bring you a red cow without blemish, in which there is no defect and on which no yoke has been laid. **3]** You shall give it to Eleazar the priest. It shall be taken outside the camp and slaughtered in his presence. **4]** Eleazar the priest shall take some of its blood with his finger and sprinkle it seven times toward the front of the Tent of Meeting. **5]** The cow shall be burned in his sight—its hide, flesh, and blood shall be burned, its dung included— **6]** and the priest shall take cedar wood, hyssop, and crimson stuff, and throw them into the fire consuming the cow. **7]** The priest shall wash his garments and bathe his body in water; after that the priest may re-enter the camp, but he shall be unclean until evening. **8]** He who performed the burning shall also wash his garments in water, bathe his body in water, and be unclean until evening. **9]** A man who is clean shall gather up the ashes of the cow and deposit them outside the camp in a clean place, to be kept for water of lustration for the Israelite community. It is for cleansing. **10]** He who gathers up the ashes of the cow shall also wash his clothes and be unclean until evening.

This shall be a permanent law for the Israelites and for the strangers who reside among you.

19:2] *Ritual law.* חֻקַּת הַתּוֹרָה (*chukat ha-Torah*) is an unusual expression, the only other occurrence being in Num. 31:21.

Red cow. פָּרָה אֲדֻמָּה (*parah adumah*), a heifer, of unspecified age.

The Rabbis allowed it up to three years of age; R. Meir up to five years [2].

Without blemish, in which there is no defect. Taken by Jewish tradition to mean a totally red cow [3].

No yoke. This condition is not required for other animal sacrifices (see also Deut. 21:3).

4] *Seven times.* Seven is a favorite biblical number in connection with matters of holiness. Seven days will make the person clean.

5] *Its dung included.* That is, included with its intestines.

6] *Cedar wood.* Wood from the mightiest of trees.

Hyssop. Considered the lowliest of plants because it grows in crevices (see I Kings 5:13). The exact identity of the biblical hyssop is in doubt; perhaps it is *majorana syriaca*, a species of marjoram [4].

Crimson stuff. Obtained from the scarlet worm.

9] *To be kept.* Rabbinic tradition records that the ashes were stored in the Temple [5].

Lustration. That is, purification. The term נִדָּה (*nidah*) is also and primarily used for the impurity incurred by a menstruating woman.

It is for cleansing. From sin.

יא יִשְׂרָאֵל וְלַגֵּר הַגָּר בְּתוֹכָם לְחֻקַּת עוֹלָם: הַנֹּגֵעַ בְּמֵת עַל־פְּנֵי הַשָּׂדֶה בַּחֲלַל־חֶרֶב אוֹ בְמֵת אוֹ־בְעֶצֶם אָדָם

יב לְכָל־נֶפֶשׁ אָדָם וְטָמֵא שִׁבְעַת יָמִים: הוּא יִתְחַטָּא־בוֹ אוֹ בְקֶבֶר יִטְמָא שִׁבְעַת יָמִים: וְלָקְחוּ לַטָּמֵא מֵעֲפַר בַּיּוֹם הַשְּׁלִישִׁי וּבַיּוֹם הַשְּׁבִיעִי יִטְהָר וְאִם־לֹא יִתְחַטָּא שְׂרֵפַת הַחַטָּאת וְנָתַן עָלָיו מַיִם חַיִּים אֶל־כֶּלִי:

יג בַּיּוֹם הַשְּׁלִישִׁי וּבַיּוֹם הַשְּׁבִיעִי לֹא יִטְהָר: כָּל־הַנֹּגֵעַ וְלָקַח אֵזוֹב וְטָבַל בַּמַּיִם אִישׁ טָהוֹר וְהִזָּה עַל־הָאֹהֶל בְּמֵת בְּנֶפֶשׁ הָאָדָם אֲשֶׁר־יָמוּת וְלֹא יִתְחַטָּא אֶת־מִשְׁכַּן וְעַל־כָּל־הַכֵּלִים וְעַל־הַנְּפָשׁוֹת אֲשֶׁר הָיוּ־שָׁם וְעַל־ יְהוָה טִמֵּא וְנִכְרְתָה הַנֶּפֶשׁ הַהוּא מִיִּשְׂרָאֵל כִּי מֵי נִדָּה הַנֹּגֵעַ בָּעֶצֶם אוֹ בֶחָלָל אוֹ בַמֵּת אוֹ בַקָּבֶר: וְהִזָּה

יד לֹא־זֹרַק עָלָיו טָמֵא יִהְיֶה עוֹד טֻמְאָתוֹ בוֹ: זֹאת הַטָּהֹר עַל־הַטָּמֵא בַּיּוֹם הַשְּׁלִישִׁי וּבַיּוֹם הַשְּׁבִיעִי הַתּוֹרָה אָדָם כִּי־יָמוּת בְּאֹהֶל כָּל־הַבָּא אֶל־הָאֹהֶל וְחִטְּאוֹ בַּיּוֹם הַשְּׁבִיעִי וְכִבֶּס בְּגָדָיו וְרָחַץ בַּמַּיִם וְטָהֵר

טו וְכָל־אֲשֶׁר בָּאֹהֶל יִטְמָא שִׁבְעַת יָמִים: וְכֹל כְּלִי פָתוּחַ בָּעֶרֶב: וְאִישׁ אֲשֶׁר־יִטְמָא וְלֹא יִתְחַטָּא וְנִכְרְתָה הַנֶּפֶשׁ

טז אֲשֶׁר אֵין־צָמִיד פָּתִיל עָלָיו טָמֵא הוּא: וְכֹל אֲשֶׁר־יִגַּע הַהוּא מִתּוֹךְ הַקָּהָל כִּי אֶת־מִקְדַּשׁ יְהוָה טִמֵּא מֵי נִדָּה

11] He who touches the corpse of any human being shall be unclean for seven days.   12] He shall cleanse himself with it on the third day and on the seventh day, and then be clean; if he fails to cleanse himself on the third and seventh days, he shall not be clean.   13] Whoever touches a corpse, the body of a person who has died, and does not cleanse himself, defiles the LORD's Tabernacle; that person shall be cut off from Israel. Since the water of lustration was not dashed on him, he remains unclean; his uncleanness is still upon him.

14] This is the procedure: When a person dies in a tent, whoever enters the tent and whoever is in the tent shall be unclean seven days;   15] and every open vessel, with no lid fastened down, shall be unclean.   16] And in the open, anyone who touches a person who was killed or who died naturally, or human bone, or a grave, shall be unclean seven days. 17] Some of the ashes from the fire of cleansing shall be taken for the unclean person, and fresh water shall be added to them in a vessel.   18] A person who is clean shall take hyssop, dip it in the water, and sprinkle on the tent and on all the vessels and people who were there, or on him who touched the bones or the person who was killed or died naturally or the grave.   19] The clean person shall sprinkle it upon the unclean person on the third day and on the seventh day, thus cleansing him by the seventh day. He shall then wash his clothes and bathe in water, and at nightfall he shall be clean.   20] If anyone who has become unclean fails to cleanse himself, that person shall be cut off from the congregation, for he has defiled the LORD's sanctuary. The water of lustration was not dashed on him: he is unclean.

11] *Human being.* If he touches a dead animal that is forbidden for food he is impure until sunset (Lev. 11:24, 25, 27 ff.).

14] *Tent.* Rabbinic law extended the wilderness law to houses and shelters [6].

15] *Every open vessel.* Its contents were considered contaminated.

20] *Shall be cut off.* The exact meaning of this penalty (*karet*), which is frequently prescribed in the Torah, is not clear. Some believe it to have been a form of ostracism or exile; others see in it a prescription for judicial execution. Postbiblical tradition held that *karet* signified that God himself would punish the offender, usually through premature death and childlessness. (See further at Exod. 12:16 and 31:14.)

כא לְאֹזְרַק עָלָיו טָמֵא הוּא: וְהָיְתָה לָהֶם לְחֻקַּת עוֹלָם   כב עַד־הָעֶרֶב: וְכָל אֲשֶׁר־יִגַּע־בּוֹ הַטָּמֵא יִטְמָא וְהַנֶּפֶשׁ
וּמַזֵּה מֵי־הַנִּדָּה יְכַבֵּס בְּגָדָיו וְהַנֹּגֵעַ בְּמֵי הַנִּדָּה יִטְמָא   הַנֹּגַעַת תִּטְמָא עַד־הָעֶרֶב: פ

21] That shall be for them a law for all time. Further, he who sprinkled the water of lustration shall wash his clothes; and whoever touches the water of lustration shall be unclean until evening.   22] Whatever that unclean person touches shall be unclean; and the person who touches him shall be unclean until evening.

22] *Whatever that unclean person touches.* This includes touching another person.

The Red Cow

The need to be cleansed after touching a corpse reflects an ancient and universal fear of the dead, whose spirits were believed capable of injuring the community. While the ritual of the red cow is doubtlessly based on prebiblical practices—an old Canaanite epic tells of the death of the god of fertility, who went to the underworld and there copulated with a heifer [7]—the Torah here appears to reinterpret old practices in accordance with its own religious views. At the core of these stands the idea that Israel is a holy people and that holiness demands a state of physical and spiritual purity. Israelites must eat clean food, and if they touch anything upon which a taboo rests, like dead humans and dead animals unfit for food, they become tainted and must wait until a certain period has elapsed to have their pristine condition restored, which often requires the performance of special rites. These, however, are not sacrificial in nature, for sacrifice is needed only when spiritual impurity has been incurred through sin.

The ashes were mixed with water that was especially fortified with symbolic additives, although we cannot be sure of their original meaning. The use of such liquids for purification is not restricted to this ritual: Moses made the people drink a mixture of water and the ashes of the golden calf (Exod. 32:20); and persons affected with certain skin diseases as well as "leprous" houses must be cleansed with waters fortified by cedar wood, crimson stuff, and hyssop (Lev. 14:4, 49–52). The special waters used during the ordeal of jealousy also belong in this category (Num. 5:11 ff.). Immersion in water had ritual and sometimes supernatural significance (as in the case of Naaman being cured by immersion in the Jordan River), for water was considered the cleansing agent par excellence and helped to remove cultic impurity.

The insistence of the Bible on the red color is unexplained. The Christian Scriptures apparently saw in it an evocation of blood and compared the blood of Christ to the red cow in that it removed spiritual defilement ("dead works"; Hebrews 9:13–14).

Most difficult of all the aspects of the rite is the provision that handling the ashes rendered impure, while the ashes themselves made pure. A midrash relates that a Gentile once came to R. Johanan ben Zakkai and asked about the reason for the ritual. The rabbi gave him a rational answer but later admitted to his students that a mystery was involved, for in and of themselves the dead were not impure nor the ashes purifying. "But," said the Sage, "this is what God has decreed, and you may not transgress His law" [8]. The puzzlement over the contradiction has persisted to this day, and we may well speculate whether this rite of ancient origin does not reflect the inherent and hence persistent contradiction between life and death. They are eternally linked and eternally in tension, and whoever touches them touches both purity and impurity at the same time.

GLEANINGS

Shabbat Parah

(On one of the Sabbaths before Passover the chapter on the red cow [parah] is read in traditional synagogues in addition to the regular weekly portion, and the Sabbath is therefore called *Shabbat Parah*.) The special reading is to commemorate the purification of the unclean so that they may be enabled to bring the Passover sacrifice in a state of purity.   J. H. HERTZ [9]

Nine Times

The ritual of burning the red cow was enacted only nine times: once by Moses, once by Ezra, and seven times thereafter.   MISHNAH [10]

Solomon's Wisdom

Solomon was wiser than all men, but when it came to the section of the red cow he admitted: "I said, 'I will get wisdom,' but it was far from me."   MIDRASH [11]

A Mystery

Four Torah laws cannot be explained by human reason but, being divine, demand implicit obedience: to marry one's brother's widow (Deut. 25:5); not to mingle wool and linen in a garment (Deut. 22:11); to perform the rites of the scapegoat (Lev. 16:26, 34); and the red cow. Satan comes and criticizes these statutes as irrational. Know therefore that it was the Creator of the world, the One and Only, who instituted them.   MIDRASH [12]

Halachah

A *Kohen* (priest) may not be in contact with the dead except his own relatives (Lev. 21:2-4).

Num. 19:14 extends "contact" to entering a tent in which a dead body is kept, and the Rabbis interpreted this to apply to any overhang or enclosure [13]. For this reason, Orthodox rabbis of priestly descent will stand outside at the open door when officiating at funeral services held in a mortuary chapel but are generally able to go to the internment because the graves are in the open.

The old custom of whitewashing graves probably served to call attention to them so they would not be accidentally touched [14].

Allegory

The mixture of water and ashes reminds men of what elements they consist, for knowledge of oneself is the most wholesome form of purification.   PHILO [15]

The spotlessness of the cow and her death outside the camp suggested to Christian interpreters the story of Jesus; red, the color of the blood of the passion; the cedar, hope; the hyssop, faith; the scarlet, charity. The dead who make men unclean are man's dead works.   AUGUSTINE [16]

Retold

And when Moses said to his people, "Verily, God bids you sacrifice a cow," they said, "Are you making a jest of us?" He said, "God keep me from being one of the foolish." They said, "Call on your Lord for us that He would make plain to us what she is." He said, "God says, 'She is a cow neither old nor young, but of the middle age—between the two,' do therefore what you are bidden."

They said, "Call on your Lord for us, that He

would make plain to us what is her color." He said, "God says, 'She is a fawn-colored cow; her color is very bright; she rejoices the beholders.' "

They said, "Call on your Lord for us that He would make plain to us what cow it is—for to us cows are alike—and verily, if God please, we shall be guided rightly."

He said, "God says, 'She is a cow not worn by ploughing the earth or watering the field, sound, no blemish in her.' " They said, "Now you have brought the truth." Then they sacrificed her; yet nearly had they done it not.   KORAN [17]

Blemish

The red cow was to be without blemish and without having borne a yoke. Similarly, if a man thinks he is without blemish we may be sure he has never accepted the yoke of Heaven. For if he had he would know that he had many faults.

CHASIDIC [18]

Homilies

Though the rite of the red heifer may in some ways resemble the mixing of medicines, it has no human origin but is divine, established by a decree of God which must be obeyed without cavil. Differing with this significance of the rite, another commentator sees the red heifer as a symbolic expiation for Israel's misdeed in regard to the golden calf.

Other commentators, by means of allegorical interpretation, see in the rites of the red heifer a prefiguring of Israel's experience in Egypt, Babylon, Media, Greece, and Rome and a prefiguring of Rome's ultimate destruction. Still others see Israel unruly as a heifer and so punished and exiled but, finally, through the merit of Israel's devout men, delivered, cleansed by God himself, and restored to Jerusalem. There, in the time-to-come, God, dispensing with the red heifer, will himself cleanse Israel of their sins [19].

Thirty-Eight Years Later

We now approach the opening scene in the last act of the drama that describes Israel's forty years in the desert. The preceding chapters told of events in the second year after the Children of Israel left Egypt (Num. 1:1; 9:1). At this point, the end of the wandering comes into view. Miriam's and Aaron's deaths are reported. Elsewhere we learn that Aaron died forty years after leaving Egypt (Num. 33:38), but we do not know what happened in the intervening thirty-eight years. The Torah is silent about them. The old generation has died or is dying, a new one has grown up. There is little further to be said about those who loved the security of slavery more than the uncertain freedom that was offered them. The focus begins to shift to their children—but not before we learn the fate of their three leaders, of whom the prophet said that God had sent them to Israel to help Him accomplish the redemption from Egypt (Micah 6:4).

Of these, Moses is of course by far the most important. The remainder of Numbers and all of Deuteronomy treat him as the towering father of his people. Yet he, too, is marked by age and belongs to the past. He fails seriously when he deals with the uprising at Meribah and God pronounces the inevitable judgment: Moses, like the others of his generation, is to die without entering the Promised Land.

ז וַיְדַבֵּר יְהוָה אֶל־מֹשֶׁה לֵּאמֹר: קַח אֶת־הַמַּטֶּה וְהַקְהֵל אֶת־הָעֵדָה אַתָּה וְאַהֲרֹן אָחִיךָ וְדִבַּרְתֶּם אֶל־הַסֶּלַע לְעֵינֵיהֶם וְנָתַן מֵימָיו וְהוֹצֵאתָ לָהֶם מַיִם מִן־הַסֶּלַע וְהִשְׁקִיתָ אֶת־הָעֵדָה וְאֶת־בְּעִירָם: ט וַיִּקַּח מֹשֶׁה אֶת־הַמַּטֶּה מִלִּפְנֵי יְהוָה כַּאֲשֶׁר צִוָּהוּ: י וַיַּקְהִלוּ מֹשֶׁה וְאַהֲרֹן אֶת־הַקָּהָל אֶל־פְּנֵי הַסָּלַע וַיֹּאמֶר לָהֶם שִׁמְעוּ־נָא הַמֹּרִים הֲמִן־הַסֶּלַע הַזֶּה נוֹצִיא לָכֶם מָיִם: יא וַיָּרֶם מֹשֶׁה אֶת־יָדוֹ וַיַּךְ אֶת־הַסֶּלַע בְּמַטֵּהוּ פַּעֲמָיִם וַיֵּצְאוּ מַיִם רַבִּים וַתֵּשְׁתְּ הָעֵדָה וּבְעִירָם: ס יב וַיֹּאמֶר יְהוָה אֶל־מֹשֶׁה וְאֶל־אַהֲרֹן יַעַן לֹא־הֶאֱמַנְתֶּם בִּי לְהַקְדִּישֵׁנִי לְעֵינֵי בְּנֵי יִשְׂרָאֵל לָכֵן לֹא תָבִיאוּ אֶת־הַקָּהָל הַזֶּה

א וַיָּבֹאוּ בְנֵי־יִשְׂרָאֵל כָּל־הָעֵדָה מִדְבַּר־צִן בַּחֹדֶשׁ הָרִאשׁוֹן וַיֵּשֶׁב הָעָם בְּקָדֵשׁ וַתָּמָת שָׁם מִרְיָם וַתִּקָּבֵר שָׁם: ב וְלֹא־הָיָה מַיִם לָעֵדָה וַיִּקָּהֲלוּ עַל־מֹשֶׁה וְעַל־אַהֲרֹן: ג וַיָּרֶב הָעָם עִם־מֹשֶׁה וַיֹּאמְרוּ לֵאמֹר וְלוּ גָוַעְנוּ בִּגְוַע אַחֵינוּ לִפְנֵי יְהוָה: ד וְלָמָה הֲבֵאתֶם אֶת־קְהַל יְהוָה אֶל־הַמִּדְבָּר הַזֶּה לָמוּת שָׁם אֲנַחְנוּ וּבְעִירֵנוּ: ה וְלָמָה הֶעֱלִיתֻנוּ מִמִּצְרַיִם לְהָבִיא אֹתָנוּ אֶל־הַמָּקוֹם הָרָע הַזֶּה לֹא מְקוֹם זֶרַע וּתְאֵנָה וְגֶפֶן וְרִמּוֹן וּמַיִם אַיִן לִשְׁתּוֹת: ו וַיָּבֹא מֹשֶׁה וְאַהֲרֹן מִפְּנֵי הַקָּהָל אֶל־פֶּתַח אֹהֶל מוֹעֵד וַיִּפְּלוּ עַל־פְּנֵיהֶם וַיֵּרָא כְבוֹד־יְהוָה אֲלֵיהֶם: פ

1] The Israelites arrived in a body at the wilderness of Zin on the first new moon, and the people stayed at Kadesh. Miriam died there and was buried there.

2] The community was without water, and they joined against Moses and Aaron. **3]** The people quarrelled with Moses, saying, "If only we had perished when our brothers perished at the instance of the LORD! **4]** Why have you brought the LORD's congregation into this wilderness for us and our beasts to die there? **5]** Why did you make us leave Egypt to bring us to this wretched place, a place with no grain or figs or vines or pomegranates? There is not even water to drink!"

6] Moses and Aaron came away from the congregation to the entrance of the Tent of Meeting, and fell on their faces. The Presence of the LORD appeared to them, **7]** and the LORD spoke to Moses, saying, **8]** "You and your brother Aaron take the rod and assemble the community, and before their very eyes order the rock to yield its water. Thus you shall produce water for them from the rock and provide drink for the congregation and their beasts."

9] Moses took the rod from before the LORD, as He had commanded him. **10]** Moses and Aaron assembled the congregation in front of the rock; and he said to them, "Listen, you rebels, shall we get water for you out of this rock?" **11]** And Moses raised his hand and struck the rock twice with his rod. Out came copious water, and the community and their beasts drank.

12] But the LORD said to Moses and Aaron, "Because you did not trust Me enough to affirm My sanctity in the sight of the Israelite people, therefore you shall not lead this congregation into the land that I have given them." **13]** Those are the Waters of Meribah—meaning that

---

20:1] *Zin.* See Num. 13:21.

Kadesh. See Num. 13:26.

Miriam died. No official mourning period was observed for her, as would be the case for Aaron (verse 29).

3] *When our brothers perished.* Those belonging to the generation of the Exodus from Egypt [1].

8] *The rod.* Either that of Aaron, which had

blossomed (Num. 17:25), or that of Moses, with which he had struck the rock once before (Exod. 17:5, 6).

Order the rock. At the earlier incident Moses had been commanded to strike the rock physically; here he is to order it verbally. No reason is given for the difference in commands.

To yield its water. The rock, as will subsequently become evident, contained water within.

אֶל־הָאָרֶץ אֲשֶׁר־נָתַתִּי לָהֶם: הֵמָּה מֵי מְרִיבָה אֲשֶׁר־
רָבוּ בְנֵי־יִשְׂרָאֵל אֶת־יְהֹוָה וַיִּקָּדֵשׁ בָּם: ס וַיִּשְׁלַח
מֹשֶׁה מַלְאָכִים מִקָּדֵשׁ אֶל־מֶלֶךְ אֱדוֹם כֹּה אָמַר
אָחִיךָ יִשְׂרָאֵל אַתָּה יָדַעְתָּ אֵת כָּל־הַתְּלָאָה אֲשֶׁר
מְצָאָתְנוּ: וַיֵּרְדוּ אֲבֹתֵינוּ מִצְרַיְמָה וַנֵּשֶׁב בְּמִצְרַיִם
יָמִים רַבִּים וַיָּרֵעוּ לָנוּ מִצְרַיִם וְלַאֲבֹתֵינוּ: וַנִּצְעַק
אֶל־יְהֹוָה וַיִּשְׁמַע קֹלֵנוּ וַיִּשְׁלַח מַלְאָךְ וַיֹּצִאֵנוּ מִמִּצְרָיִם
וְהִנֵּה אֲנַחְנוּ בְקָדֵשׁ עִיר קְצֵה גְבוּלֶךָ: נַעְבְּרָה־נָּא
בְאַרְצֶךָ לֹא נַעֲבֹר בְּשָׂדֶה וּבְכֶרֶם וְלֹא נִשְׁתֶּה מֵי

בְּאֵר דֶּרֶךְ הַמֶּלֶךְ נֵלֵךְ לֹא נִטֶּה יָמִין וּשְׂמֹאול עַד
אֲשֶׁר־נַעֲבֹר גְּבֻלֶךָ: וַיֹּאמֶר אֵלָיו אֱדוֹם לֹא תַעֲבֹר בִּי
פֶּן־בַּחֶרֶב אֵצֵא לִקְרָאתֶךָ: וַיֹּאמְרוּ אֵלָיו בְּנֵי־יִשְׂרָאֵל
בַּמְסִלָּה נַעֲלֶה וְאִם־מֵימֶיךָ נִשְׁתֶּה אֲנִי וּמִקְנַי וְנָתַתִּי
מִכְרָם רַק אֵין־דָּבָר בְּרַגְלַי אֶעֱבֹרָה: וַיֹּאמֶר לֹא
תַעֲבֹר וַיֵּצֵא אֱדוֹם לִקְרָאתוֹ בְּעַם כָּבֵד וּבְיָד חֲזָקָה:
וַיְמָאֵן אֱדוֹם נְתֹן אֶת־יִשְׂרָאֵל עֲבֹר בִּגְבֻלוֹ וַיֵּט
יִשְׂרָאֵל מֵעָלָיו: פ

‎יח פלא ו.

the Israelites quarrelled with the LORD—through which He affirmed His sanctity.

14] From Kadesh, Moses sent messengers to the king of Edom: "Thus says your brother Israel: You know all the hardships that have befallen us; **15]** that our ancestors went down to Egypt, that we dwelt in Egypt a long time, and that the Egyptians dealt harshly with us and our ancestors. **16]** We cried to the LORD and He heard our plea, and He sent a messenger who freed us from Egypt. Now we are in Kadesh, the town on the border of your territory. **17]** Allow us, then, to cross your country. We will not pass through fields or vineyards, and we will not drink water from wells. We will follow the king's highway, turning off neither to the right nor to the left until we have crossed your territory."

18] But Edom answered him, "You shall not pass through us, else we will go out against you with the sword." **19]** "We will keep to the beaten track," the Israelites said to them, "and if we or our cattle drink your water, we will pay for it. We ask only for passage on foot—it is but a small matter." **20]** But they replied, "You shall not pass through!" And Edom went out against them in heavy force, strongly armed. **21]** So Edom would not let Israel cross their territory, and Israel turned away from them.

13] *Waters of Meribah.* Meaning "waters of strife," in the sense that these were waters of ordeal in the juridical sense (note that an alternate name of the Kadesh oasis is *Ein Mishpat,* "well of judgment").

Affirmed His sanctity. This appears to contradict verse 12 directly and is taken by Bible critics as support for the idea that the story originally had been somewhat different. They suggest that the leaders committed some serious sin that was later edited away (see commentary). The traditional interpretation is that God affirmed His sanctity by punishing Moses and Aaron [2]. 14] *Edom.* On the east side of the Red Sea. The mountains of the area are still called הָרֵי אֱדוֹם (*Hare Edom*) in Israeli cartography.

Your brother Israel. Alluding to the relationship of Israel (Jacob) and Edom (Esau), Gen. 25:25. The close linkage is noted elsewhere, e.g., Deut. 2:4; 23:8.

16] *Messenger.* This refers either to an angel or to Moses [3].

17] *To cross your country.* From south to north, to reach the eastern bank of the Jordan.

King's highway. It led from the Gulf of Akaba in the south up through Edom to Damascus. The highway and the fortifications abutting it were destroyed in later centuries, and the road was rebuilt about 108 C.E. by the Roman Emperor Trajan.

כב וַיִּסְעוּ מִקָּדֵשׁ וַיָּבֹאוּ בְנֵי־יִשְׂרָאֵל כָּל־הָעֵדָה הֹר הָהָר:
כג וַיֹּאמֶר יְהֹוָה אֶל־מֹשֶׁה וְאֶל־אַהֲרֹן בְּהֹר הָהָר עַל־
כד גְּבוּל אֶרֶץ־אֱדוֹם לֵאמֹר: יֵאָסֵף אַהֲרֹן אֶל־עַמָּיו כִּי
לֹא יָבֹא אֶל־הָאָרֶץ אֲשֶׁר נָתַתִּי לִבְנֵי יִשְׂרָאֵל עַל
כה אֲשֶׁר־מְרִיתֶם אֶת־פִּי לְמֵי מְרִיבָה: קַח אֶת־אַהֲרֹן
כו וְאֶת־אֶלְעָזָר בְּנוֹ וְהַעַל אֹתָם הֹר הָהָר: וְהַפְשֵׁט אֶת־
אַהֲרֹן אֶת־בְּגָדָיו וְהִלְבַּשְׁתָּם אֶת־אֶלְעָזָר בְּנוֹ וְאַהֲרֹן

כז יֵאָסֵף וּמֵת שָׁם: וַיַּעַשׂ מֹשֶׁה כַּאֲשֶׁר צִוָּה יְהֹוָה וַיַּעֲלוּ
כח אֶל־הֹר הָהָר לְעֵינֵי כָּל־הָעֵדָה: וַיַּפְשֵׁט מֹשֶׁה אֶת־
אַהֲרֹן אֶת־בְּגָדָיו וַיַּלְבֵּשׁ אֹתָם אֶת־אֶלְעָזָר בְּנוֹ וַיָּמָת
אַהֲרֹן שָׁם בְּרֹאשׁ הָהָר וַיֵּרֶד מֹשֶׁה וְאֶלְעָזָר מִן־הָהָר:
כט וַיִּרְאוּ כָּל־הָעֵדָה כִּי גָוַע אַהֲרֹן וַיִּבְכּוּ אֶת־אַהֲרֹן
שְׁלֹשִׁים יוֹם כֹּל בֵּית יִשְׂרָאֵל: ס

22] Setting out from Kadesh, the Israelites arrived in a body at Mount Hor. 23] At Mount Hor, on the boundary of the land of Edom, the LORD said to Moses and Aaron, 24] "Let Aaron be gathered to his kin: he is not to enter the land that I have given to the Israelite people, because you disobeyed my command about the waters of Meribah. 25] Take Aaron and his son Eleazar and bring them up on Mount Hor. 26] Strip Aaron of his vestments and put them on his son Eleazar. There Aaron shall be gathered unto the dead."

27] Moses did as the LORD had commanded. They ascended Mount Hor in the sight of the whole community. 28] Moses stripped Aaron of his vestments and put them on his son Eleazar, and Aaron died there on the summit of the mountain. When Moses and Eleazar came down from the mountain, 29] the whole community knew that Aaron had breathed his last. All the house of Israel bewailed Aaron thirty days.

23] *Mount Hor*. According to the context it lay on the boundary of Edom, hence it was often identified with Jebel Nebi Harun ("mountain of the prophet Aaron"), some fifty miles south of the Dead Sea [4]. It is more likely, however, that "boundary" is to be taken more broadly and that Mount Hor (possibly like Sinai) was in the neighborhood of Kadesh where the people "arrived in a body" after turning back from Edom. Deut. 10:6 records a different tradition: there, Aaron is reported to have been buried at Moserah.

24] *Let Aaron be gathered to his kin*. He will die.

The expression was first used for Jacob (Gen. 49:33).

26] *Gathered unto the dead*. Literally, "gathered and died."

28] *Moses stripped Aaron*. Approaching death was not hidden from the dying.

29] *Thirty days*. The same period was later on observed for Moses (Deut. 34:8). This period remains important in Jewish mourning practice. Mourning for seventy days, observed after Jacob's death, was an Egyptian custom (see at Gen. 50:3).

The Second Murmuring

This is the second murmuring to take place at Meribah, the first being reported in Exod. 17:1–7, and in both instances water is miraculously provided from a rock. Bible critics have, therefore, suggested that we have here two versions of the same story. However, such a conclusion is highly speculative. It is equally likely that a return to the old resting place, which had seen a popular upheaval many years before, evoked memories and frustrations and led to a renewed complaint against the leaders who seemed to keep Israel forever in the desert. In fact, the focus here is less on the discontent of the people and more on the failure of leadership. It is in every sense a tragic tale which in its utter brevity raises serious questions about the sin of Moses and Aaron.

The Sin

Because of rebelliousness and lack of faith, the generation of the Exodus died in the wilderness. Now the same punishment is pronounced on its leaders, Moses and Aaron. However, the precise nature of the sin they committed is not clearly specified. The Torah says only that they did not trust God enough to affirm His sanctity (verse 12).

Most commentators see this lack of trust expressed in the manner by which Moses and Aaron executed God's demand to bring water to the thirsty people [5]. They were to have *ordered* the rock to yield water (verse 8), but Moses instead *struck* the rock twice with his rod, and the people were given water in this fashion. According to this explanation, the miracle was to have lain in the power of the word spoken to the inanimate stone in God's name. Instead, Moses performed a physical act—not only once but twice—thereby revealing his lack of trust in the divine word[1] [7]. Other interpreters stress the apparent anger of the leaders. Moses says: "Listen, you rebels," thus addressing his own people in anger—but leadership and wrath do not go together [8]. Others note that Moses and Aaron say: "Shall *we* get water for you out of this rock?" thereby appearing to emphasize their own rather than God's role in the miracle[2] [10]. Still others take the Meribah incident to be merely the occasion for pronouncing judgment and consider the sins of Aaron and Moses worthy of the severe punishment to have been committed previously (Aaron's with the golden calf; Moses' with the spies)[3] [12].

None of these explanations (except the last, which however finds no warrant in the story itself) satisfies the question of how a minor transgression committed in frustration and justifiable anger could wipe out a lifetime of merit and service. Seen as an isolated incident, the punishment does not fit the crime. Neither striking the rock rather than speaking to it with confidence nor saying "we" instead of "God" is sufficient reason to keep Moses and Aaron from entering the Promised Land. However, the Torah does not question God's justice. Therefore some feel that the real sin of the brothers was edited out, in order to safeguard their reputation [13]. While that is a possibility, it cannot be proved. Moreover, the text *as it is* does contain the answer.

We must look at the story in the full context of the brothers' role as leaders of the people. On previous occasions when members of the generation of the Exodus had murmured, Moses had known how to

---

[1] The Koran, however, speaks of God asking Moses to strike the rock and, after he proceeds to do this, of twelve fountains opening up [6].

[2] Or that the sin lay in Moses likening his own powers to those of God [9].

[3] One midrash suggests that Moses' real sin lay in his having slain the taskmaster in Egypt [11].

deal with them. Now, at Meribah, it was the new generation, born or raised in freedom, who longed for an Egypt it had never seen or only dimly remembered and who still preferred the imagined comforts of the land of slavery to the trials of liberty.

To Moses and Aaron this regression must have come as a monstrous shock. It was as if their whole life's work, almost forty years of it, was wasted. In their younger days the two leaders would have recovered quickly and would have known how to meet the crisis, but somehow this time it was too much for them. In former days they had acted, now they were stunned into silence. They simply gave up and retreated to the sanctuary; they gave no reproof to the people and made no plea for assistance from God. They met the crisis with resignation and silence, two broken men seeking refuge at the door of the Tent [14].

Here lies the answer to the riddle. The faith that Moses and Aaron broke was their faith in the continuity of God's promise to an undeserving and rebellious people. In former days the brothers would have staunchly stood their ground, now the disillusionment of old age rendered them mute and passive. The Psalmist calls Moses a man of embittered spirit.[4] At Meribah of Kadesh, the rock of "strife and holiness," the ancient leadership was shattered. It broke because a new age demanded new vision, new faith, and undiminished capacity to sanctify the God of Israel to the people of Israel. If the Torah implies sin on the part of Moses and Aaron, it can only be the sin of failure: for leaders are always held responsible for the performance of those they lead. Both Moses and Aaron apparently considered the divine judgment to be just and knew it to be irreversible. Aaron never raised his voice concerning it and Moses did it once and then ever so briefly (Deut. 3:23–25).[5]

Miriam is dead; soon Aaron will join her, and so will Moses before the end of that year. A new set of younger leaders is about to take their places and to guide the new generation of the people into the Promised Land.

Aaron the Man

What kind of person was the man Aaron who emerges from the biblical record? The Torah provides us with enough information so that we may attempt to picture him.

He held high office, the highest cultic position the fledgling community could offer. Yet even here he was, as in everything else, second to his younger brother Moses, and in a society that laid much store by the rights and privileges of the first-born this must at times have been a hard burden for Aaron to bear. It was almost always "Moses and Aaron" and rarely the other way around; it was Moses who transmitted the Torah to the people; it was Moses who invested Aaron with his duties, who led the people in war, and judged them in peace. Aaron would have been more than human if feelings of jealousy and frustration had not overcome him from time to time, and in a memorable—and for him psychologically disastrous—incident he joined his sister Miriam in an attempt to contest the supremacy of Moses (see Num. 12).

The fact is that Aaron did not possess his brother's stature. When he should have stood his ground firmly at the incident of the golden calf he failed, and no whitewashing by later generations can obliterate the clear

---

[4] Assuming that הֵמְרוּ (himru) in Ps. 106:33 can be understood as if it were הֵמֵרוּ (hemeru), the verse would say: "They embittered his spirit and he spoke rashly."

[5] However, the Midrash lists many attempts by Moses to stay the divine judgment [15].

biblical record in this regard (see commentary on Exodus 32). At best his attitude then was ambiguous, and perhaps ambiguity and ambivalence were part of his character. He was, on the other hand, a man who evidently filled his office with dignity and who bore the bitter blow of losing two of his sons with remarkable stoicism and strength (see Leviticus 10:1–7). The Rabbis preserved a tradition that Aaron was distinguished by his devotion to teaching and his ability to make peace between his fellow men. Hillel said: "Be of the disciples of Aaron, loving peace and pursuing peace, loving your fellow men and bringing them near to the Torah" [16]. In the fond remembrance of his people this became his lasting image (see further in Gleanings). The death of Aaron, says a midrash, was as painful to God as was the breaking of the Tablets. That midrash is a grateful people's tribute to one of its great leaders, the first of the priestly line, and a human being we can understand, forgive, and love [17].

GLEANINGS

Death of the Just
Why does the story of Miriam's death follow directly the chapter of the red cow? To teach us that even as the ashes of the red cow cleanse from transgression, so does the death of the just.
TALMUD [18]

Blood
The first time Moses struck the rock, it brought forth blood. It cried to God who said to Moses: "Even a rock needs to be treated justly. You should have talked to it before you struck it."
MIDRASH [19]

The Wandering Rock
Ancient legend told that the rock containing water followed Israel through the desert for forty years [20].

Christian Scriptures preserve this tradition by comparing the rock of Meribah to Christ, "the same supernatural rock that accompanied their travels" [21].

Great Men
Judaism teaches that the greater the man the stricter the standard by which he is judged, and, if he does not measure up, the greater will be his guilt and punishment.   S. R. HIRSCH [22]

The Whole Community Knew (Num. 20:29)
What does this mean? When Moses returned from the mountain after Aaron had died, the people accused him of having killed his brother. Only through God's miraculous intervention was Moses relieved of the charge, and only then "the whole community knew" that Aaron had breathed his last.   MIDRASH [23]

Aaron's Death
The righteous are informed of the day of their death so that they may hand the crown to their children.   MIDRASH [24]

To meet death as Aaron met it, at the end of a good life, is to die on top of the mountain, in sight of the Promised Land.
INTERPRETER'S BIBLE [25]

The Peacemaker
Of Aaron it says that "all the house of Israel" bewailed him (verse 29), while of Moses it merely says that "the Israelites" bewailed him (Deut. 34:8). In this way the Torah tells Aaron's praise as a peacemaker [26].

According to rabbinic legend Aaron would go from house to house and, whenever he found one

who did not know how to recite the *Shema*, he taught him to recite it. He did not, however, restrict his activities to "establishing peace between God and man," but strove to establish peace between man and his fellow. If he discovered that two men had fallen out, he hastened first to the one, then to the other, saying to each: "If you only knew how he with whom you quarreled regrets his action!" Aaron would thus speak to each separately, until both the former enemies would mutually forgive each other, and as soon as they were again face to face greet each other as friends [27]. This kindness of his led many a sinner to reform, who at the moment when he was about to commit a sin thought to himself, "How shall I be able to lift up my eyes to Aaron's face, I, to whom Aaron was so kind!"

J. H. HERTZ [28]

Aaron in Christian Literature

As the ancestor and founder of the one priesthood entitled to offer acceptable sacrifice to God, Aaron was taken as a paradigm for Christ in the New Testament and later Christian tradition: he offers sacrifice, mediates between the people and God, and ministers in the Holy of Holies. The typology is developed especially in the Epistle to the Hebrews, which stresses the superiority of Jesus' perfect sacrifice to the animal sacrifices of the Aaronic priesthood. Jesus, the high priest of the New Covenant, is foreshadowed by Aaron, the high priest of the Old Covenant, but Christ's priesthood, which is "after the order of Melchizedek," supersedes and replaces the inferior priesthood of Aaron [29].

Influenced by this distinction, the Mormons distinguished in their hierarchy between a lesser, Aaronic priesthood, and the office of high priest which is according to the order of Melchizedek[30].

Aaron in Islamic Tradition

Aaron (called Harun) is depicted on the whole like the biblical figure, though not as head of the priestly tribe. Similar to the midrashic tradition he is exonerated and made an onlooker and administrator rather than a participant in the incident of the golden calf. The people are misled by "Samiri" (either a Samaritan or Samael, an incarnation of Satan).

Wandering and Warfare

This section (which ends the portion חֻקַּת, *Chukat*) deals with events following the retreat from the borders of Edom. There is another outbreak of discontent and subsequent punishment. Three military engagements end in victory, over Arad, over the Amorites, and over Bashan. The latter two campaigns loomed large in the folk memory of subsequent centuries; the Psalmist (136:17–22) celebrates them as victories over "mighty kings." This is hardly surprising, for the territories then conquered became Israel's first permanent possessions and the major dwelling place of two and one-half tribes (see Num. 32).

These stories, told without particular theological overtones, present serious difficulties, for the text contains fragmentary and somewhat obscure quotations, and the places it mentions often cannot be identified, especially since the *Book of the Wars of the Lord*, to which the Torah refers (verse 14) and which might have elucidated the text, has not been preserved. Still, the general setting is not in doubt: Israel's battles took place in Transjordan [1].

בֵּאלֹהִים וּבְמֹשֶׁה לָמָה הֶעֱלִיתֻנוּ מִמִּצְרַיִם לָמוּת   א וַיִּשְׁמַע הַכְּנַעֲנִי מֶלֶךְ־עֲרָד יֹשֵׁב הַנֶּגֶב כִּי בָּא יִשְׂרָאֵל
בַּמִּדְבָּר כִּי אֵין לֶחֶם וְאֵין מַיִם וְנַפְשֵׁנוּ קָצָה בַּלֶּחֶם   דֶּרֶךְ הָאֲתָרִים וַיִּלָּחֶם בְּיִשְׂרָאֵל וַיִּשְׁבְּ מִמֶּנּוּ שֶׁבִי:
הַקְּלֹקֵל: וַיְשַׁלַּח יְהוָה בָּעָם אֵת הַנְּחָשִׁים הַשְּׂרָפִים י   ב וַיִּדַּר יִשְׂרָאֵל נֶדֶר לַיהוָה וַיֹּאמַר אִם־נָתֹן תִּתֵּן אֶת־
וַיְנַשְּׁכוּ אֶת־הָעָם וַיָּמָת עַם־רָב מִיִּשְׂרָאֵל: וַיָּבֹא הָעָם   ג הָעָם הַזֶּה בְּיָדִי וְהַחֲרַמְתִּי אֶת־עָרֵיהֶם: וַיִּשְׁמַע יְהוָה
אֶל־מֹשֶׁה וַיֹּאמְרוּ חָטָאנוּ כִּי־דִבַּרְנוּ בַיהוָה וָבָךְ   בְּקוֹל יִשְׂרָאֵל וַיִּתֵּן אֶת־הַכְּנַעֲנִי וַיַּחֲרֵם אֶתְהֶם וְאֶת־
הִתְפַּלֵּל אֶל־יְהוָה וְיָסֵר מֵעָלֵינוּ אֶת־הַנָּחָשׁ וַיִּתְפַּלֵּל   פ   עָרֵיהֶם וַיִּקְרָא שֵׁם־הַמָּקוֹם חָרְמָה:
מֹשֶׁה בְּעַד הָעָם: וַיֹּאמֶר יְהוָה אֶל־מֹשֶׁה עֲשֵׂה לְךָ ח   ד וַיִּסְעוּ מֵהֹר הָהָר דֶּרֶךְ יַם־סוּף לִסְבֹב אֶת־אֶרֶץ
שָׂרָף וְשִׂים אֹתוֹ עַל־נֵס וְהָיָה כָּל־הַנָּשׁוּךְ וְרָאָה אֹתוֹ   ה אֱדוֹם וַתִּקְצַר נֶפֶשׁ־הָעָם בַּדָּרֶךְ: וַיְדַבֵּר הָעָם

1] When the Canaanite, king of Arad, who dwelt in the Negeb, learned that Israel was coming by the way of Atharim, he engaged Israel in battle and took some of them captive. 2] Then Israel made a vow to the LORD and said, "If You deliver this people into our hand, we will proscribe their towns." 3] The LORD heeded Israel's plea and delivered up the Canaanites; and they and their cities were proscribed. So that place was named Hormah.

4] They set out from Mount Hor by the road to the Sea of Reeds to skirt the land of Edom. But the people grew restive on the journey, 5] and the people spoke against God and against Moses, "Why did you make us leave Egypt to die in the wilderness? There is no bread and no water, and we have come to loathe this miserable food." 6] The LORD sent *seraph* serpents among the people. They bit the people and many of the Israelites died. 7] The people came to Moses and said, "We sinned by speaking against the LORD and against you. Intercede with the LORD to take away the serpents from us!" And Moses interceded for the people. 8] Then the LORD said to Moses, "Make a *seraph* figure and mount it on a standard. And if anyone who is

21:1] *Arad.* Located twenty-five miles east of Beer-sheba and twenty miles southeast of Hebron, near Masada and the Dead Sea. The king of Arad heard of the Israelites' intentions, moved southward, and attacked them near Mount Hor [2]. In 1961 a modern city was built a short distance east of the ancient mound and given the old name of Arad [3].

The way of Atharim. The location is not known. Many understand Atharim as *Hatarim* (הַתָּרִים, "the scouts"), referring to the route of the spies (Num. 13:21–25) [4].

2] *We will proscribe.* We will utterly destroy them, reserving no booty except what is to be deposited in the sanctuary as an offering.

3] *Hormah.* "Proscription" or "destruction," see Num. 14:45. However, in Josh. 12:14, Arad and Hormah appear as different places.

4] *Sea of Reeds.* Others, "Red Sea" (see Exod. 10:19). The text suggests that the people started in a southwesterly direction and then turned east.

5] *This miserable food.* The manna [5].

6] *Seraph serpents.* Others, "fiery serpents," suggesting that שָׂרָף (*saraf*) comes from the root meaning "to burn." Perhaps they were serpents whose bite inflamed the skin [6]; the exact meaning remains uncertain. Seraph was the name given to a winged celestial being (Isa. 6:2).

ט וָחָי: וַיַּעַשׂ מֹשֶׁה נְחַשׁ נְחֹשֶׁת וַיְשִׂמֵהוּ עַל־הַנֵּס וְהָיָה
אִם־נָשַׁךְ הַנָּחָשׁ אֶת־אִישׁ וְהִבִּיט אֶל־נְחַשׁ הַנְּחֹשֶׁת וָחָי:
י וַיִּסְעוּ בְּנֵי יִשְׂרָאֵל וַיַּחֲנוּ בְּאֹבֹת: וַיִּסְעוּ מֵאֹבֹת וַיַּחֲנוּ
בְּעִיֵּי הָעֲבָרִים בַּמִּדְבָּר אֲשֶׁר עַל־פְּנֵי מוֹאָב מִמִּזְרַח
יא הַשָּׁמֶשׁ: מִשָּׁם נָסָעוּ וַיַּחֲנוּ בְּנַחַל זָרֶד: מִשָּׁם נָסָעוּ וַיַּחֲנוּ

מֵעֵבֶר אַרְנוֹן אֲשֶׁר בַּמִּדְבָּר הַיֹּצֵא מִגְּבֻל הָאֱמֹרִי כִּי
יד אַרְנוֹן גְּבוּל מוֹאָב בֵּין מוֹאָב וּבֵין הָאֱמֹרִי: עַל־כֵּן
יֵאָמַר בְּסֵפֶר מִלְחֲמֹת יְהוָה אֶת־וָהֵב בְּסוּפָה וְאֶת־
טו הַנְּחָלִים אַרְנוֹן: וְאֶשֶׁד הַנְּחָלִים אֲשֶׁר נָטָה לְשֶׁבֶת עָר
טז וְנִשְׁעַן לִגְבוּל מוֹאָב: וּמִשָּׁם בְּאֵרָה הִוא הַבְּאֵר אֲשֶׁר

bitten looks at it, he shall recover." **9]** Moses made a copper serpent and mounted it on a standard; and when anyone was bitten by a serpent, he would look at the copper serpent and recover.

10] The Israelites marched on and encamped at Oboth. **11]** They set out from Oboth and encamped at Iye-abarim, in the wilderness bordering on Moab to the east. **12]** From there they set out and encamped at the wadi Zered. **13]** From there they set out and encamped beyond the Arnon, that is, in the wilderness that extends from the territory of the Amorites. For the Arnon is the boundary of Moab, between Moab and the Amorites. **14]** Therefore the Book of the Wars of the LORD speaks of "...Waheb in Suphah, and the wadis: the Arnon **15]** with its tributary wadis, stretched along the settled country of Ar, hugging the territory of Moab...."

16] And from there to Beer, which is the well where the LORD said to Moses, "Assemble the

9] *Copper serpent.* Such a serpent was found at various excavations. The incident took place near Punon, an important copper mine in antiquity.

Mounted it on a standard. In later centuries the mounted serpent was idolized by the people and therefore destroyed by Hezekiah (eighth century B.C.E.; II Kings 18:4). Some scholars consider the desert story to be etiological, that is, designed to explain the origin of the serpent cult in Israel [7].

And recover. Tales of the healing influence of serpents are found in other cultural traditions; for instance, Asclepius, the Greek god of healing, appeared in the form of a serpent; and, similarly, the medical symbol commonly in use today (*caduceus*) features two serpents.

10] *Oboth.* "Water skins," probably the name of an oasis south of the Dead Sea; some identify it with today's Ain el-Weiba. The Israelites circumvented Edom and were on their way northward, on the eastern side of the Jordan.

11] *Iye-abarim.* "Ruins of Abarim." This location too has not been identified. Abarim is the name of a mountain range northeast of the Dead Sea.

12] *Wadi Zered.* Probably Wadi el-Hesa (brook of willows), which runs from east to west into the southern corner of the Dead Sea.

13] *Arnon.* Today's Wadi el-Mujib, running east to west and emptying into the Dead Sea's east side. The land of the Amorites lay north of the Arnon, Moab south of it; Edom in turn was south of Moab, and Ammon northeast of the Amorites.

14] *Book of the Wars of the Lord.* See commentary. This is also the title of a famous medieval work by Ralbag (Gersonides).

15] *Ar.* Possibly the capital of Moab, often identified with a city later called Areopolis [8].

16] *And from there* [they set out] *to Beer.* The name means simply "well," which suggests that it was so widely known in the area that it needed no further identification.

אָמַר יְהוָֹה לְמֹשֶׁה אֱסֹף אֶת־הָעָם וְאֶתְּנָה לָהֶם
מָיִם: ס יז אָז יָשִׁיר יִשְׂרָאֵל אֶת־הַשִּׁירָה הַזֹּאת עֲלִי
בְאֵר עֱנוּ־לָהּ: יח בְּאֵר חֲפָרוּהָ שָׂרִים כָּרוּהָ נְדִיבֵי הָעָם
בִּמְחֹקֵק בְּמִשְׁעֲנֹתָם וּמִמִּדְבָּר מַתָּנָה: יט וּמִמַּתָּנָה
נַחֲלִיאֵל וּמִנַּחֲלִיאֵל בָּמוֹת: כ וּמִבָּמוֹת הַגַּיְא אֲשֶׁר
בִּשְׂדֵה מוֹאָב רֹאשׁ הַפִּסְגָּה וְנִשְׁקָפָה עַל־פְּנֵי
הַיְשִׁימֹן
פ
כא וַיִּשְׁלַח יִשְׂרָאֵל מַלְאָכִים אֶל־סִיחֹן מֶלֶךְ־הָאֱמֹרִי
כב לֵאמֹר: אֶעְבְּרָה בְאַרְצֶךָ לֹא נִטֶּה בְּשָׂדֶה וּבְכֶרֶם

לֹא נִשְׁתֶּה מֵי בְאֵר בְּדֶרֶךְ הַמֶּלֶךְ נֵלֵךְ עַד אֲשֶׁר־
כג נַעֲבֹר גְּבֻלֶךָ: וְלֹא־נָתַן סִיחֹן אֶת־יִשְׂרָאֵל עֲבֹר
בִּגְבֻלוֹ וַיֶּאֱסֹף סִיחֹן אֶת־כָּל־עַמּוֹ וַיֵּצֵא לִקְרַאת
יִשְׂרָאֵל הַמִּדְבָּרָה וַיָּבֹא יָהְצָה וַיִּלָּחֶם בְּיִשְׂרָאֵל:
כד וַיַּכֵּהוּ יִשְׂרָאֵל לְפִי־חָרֶב וַיִּירַשׁ אֶת־אַרְצוֹ מֵאַרְנֹן
עַד־יַבֹּק עַד־בְּנֵי עַמּוֹן כִּי עַז גְּבוּל בְּנֵי עַמּוֹן: כה וַיִּקַּח
יִשְׂרָאֵל אֵת כָּל־הֶעָרִים הָאֵלֶּה וַיֵּשֶׁב יִשְׂרָאֵל בְּכָל־
כו עָרֵי הָאֱמֹרִי בְּחֶשְׁבּוֹן וּבְכָל־בְּנֹתֶיהָ: כִּי חֶשְׁבּוֹן עִיר
סִיחֹן מֶלֶךְ הָאֱמֹרִי הִוא וְהוּא נִלְחַם בְּמֶלֶךְ מוֹאָב

people that I may give them water." **17]** Then Israel sang this song: Spring up, O well—sing to it— / **18]** The well which the chieftains dug, / Which the nobles of the people started / With maces, with their own staffs. / And from Midbar to Mattanah, **19]** and from Mattanah to Nahaliel, and from Nahaliel to Bamoth, **20]** and from Bamoth to the valley that is in the country of Moab, at the peak of Pisgah, overlooking the wasteland.

21] Israel now sent messengers to Sihon king of the Amorites, saying, **22]** "Let me pass through your country. We will not turn off into fields or vineyards, and we will not drink water from wells. We will follow the king's highway until we have crossed your territory."
23] But Sihon would not let Israel pass through his territory. Sihon gathered all his people and went out against Israel in the wilderness. He came to Jahaz and engaged Israel in battle.
24] But Israel put them to the sword, and took possession of their land, from the Arnon to the Jabbok, as far as [Az] of the Ammonites, for Az marked the boundary of the Ammonites.
25] Israel took all those towns. And Israel settled in all the towns of the Amorites, in Heshbon and all its dependencies.

26] Now Heshbon was the city of Sihon king of the Amorites, who had fought against a former king of Moab and taken all his land from him as far as the Arnon. **27]** Therefore the

17] *Then Israel sang this song.* This formula is similar to the one that introduces the Song of the Sea (*Shirat ha-Yam*, Exod. 15:1). In later centuries the Song at the Well was sung in the Temple of Jerusalem every third Sabbath at the *Minchah* sacrificial service and *Shirat ha-Yam* on the intervening two Sabbaths [9].

18] *With maces . . . staffs.* It appears that a symbolic ceremony was involved [10].

Midbar. "Wilderness." The phrase is not clear, and neither are some of the place names in verse 19.

20] *Pisgah.* A location in the Abarim mountains, opposite Jericho, east of the northern tip of the Dead Sea. Moses later viewed Canaan from Pisgah and died there (Deut. 34:1, 5).

21] *Sihon king of the Amorites.* He had issued the same refusal as Edom (20:14 ff.). But while the Israelites circumvented Edom's borders they decided to fight Sihon and, later, Og (verse 33).

23] *Jahaz.* The precise location is not known.

24] *Jabbok.* The river at which Jacob wrestled with the mysterious angel (Gen. 32:23 ff.). The stream is now called Wadi Zarka; it empties into the Jordan from the east.

25] *Heshbon.* "Reckoning," located opposite Jericho, about twenty miles east of the Jordan.

26] *Taken all his land.* Israel took the land from the Amorites and not from Moab, whose possessions they were not to acquire because it was assigned to Lot's descendants (Deut. 2:9, 10) [11].

לב בְּאֶרֶץ הָאֱמֹרִי: וַיִּשְׁלַח מֹשֶׁה לְרַגֵּל אֶת־יַעְזֵר וַיִּלְכְּדוּ
לג בְּנֹתֶיהָ וַיּוֹרֶשׁ אֶת־הָאֱמֹרִי אֲשֶׁר־שָׁם: וַיִּפְנוּ וַיַּעֲלוּ
דֶּרֶךְ הַבָּשָׁן וַיֵּצֵא עוֹג מֶלֶךְ־הַבָּשָׁן לִקְרָאתָם הוּא
לד וְכָל־עַמּוֹ לַמִּלְחָמָה אֶדְרֶעִי: וַיֹּאמֶר יְהֹוָה אֶל־מֹשֶׁה
אַל־תִּירָא אֹתוֹ כִּי בְיָדְךָ נָתַתִּי אֹתוֹ וְאֶת־כָּל־עַמּוֹ
וְאֶת־אַרְצוֹ וְעָשִׂיתָ לּוֹ כַּאֲשֶׁר עָשִׂיתָ לְסִיחֹן מֶלֶךְ
לה הָאֱמֹרִי אֲשֶׁר יוֹשֵׁב בְּחֶשְׁבּוֹן: וַיַּכּוּ אֹתוֹ וְאֶת־בָּנָיו וְאֶת־

* לב ווֹרֶשׁ קרי

כז הָרִאשׁוֹן וַיִּקַּח אֶת־כָּל־אַרְצוֹ מִיָּדוֹ עַד־אַרְנֹן: עַל־כֵּן
יֹאמְרוּ הַמֹּשְׁלִים בֹּאוּ חֶשְׁבּוֹן תִּבָּנֶה וְתִכּוֹנֵן עִיר
כח סִיחוֹן: כִּי־אֵשׁ יָצְאָה מֵחֶשְׁבּוֹן לֶהָבָה מִקִּרְיַת סִיחֹן
כט אָכְלָה עָר מוֹאָב בַּעֲלֵי בָּמוֹת אַרְנֹן: אוֹי־לְךָ מוֹאָב
אָבַדְתָּ עַם־כְּמוֹשׁ נָתַן בָּנָיו פְּלֵיטִם וּבְנֹתָיו בַּשְּׁבִית
ל לְמֶלֶךְ אֱמֹרִי סִיחוֹן: וַנִּירָם אָבַד חֶשְׁבּוֹן עַד־דִּיבֹן
לא וַנַּשִּׁים עַד־נֹפַח אֲשֶׁר עַד־מֵידְבָא: וַיֵּשֶׁב יִשְׂרָאֵל

bards would recite: "Come to Heshbon, it is built firm; / Sihon's city is well founded. / **28]** For fire went forth from Heshbon, / Flame from Sihon's city, / Consuming Ar of Moab, / The lords of Bamoth by the Arnon. / **29]** Woe to you, O Moab! / You are undone, O people of Chemosh! / His sons are rendered fugitive / And his daughters captive / By an Amorite king, Sihon." / **30]** Yet we have cast them down utterly, / Heshbon along with Dibon; / We have wrought desolation at Nophah, / Which is hard by Medeba.

31] So Israel occupied the land of the Amorites. **32]** Then Moses sent to spy out Jazer, and they captured its dependencies and dispossessed the Amorites who were there.

33] They marched on and went up the road to Bashan, and Og king of Bashan, with all his people, came out to Edrei to engage them in battle. **34]** But the LORD said to Moses, "Do not fear him, for I give him and all his people and his land into your hand. You shall do to him as you did to Sihon king of the Amorites who dwelt in Heshbon." **35]** They defeated him and

27] *The bards.* Possibly professional Amorite singers [12], or a quotation from another, no longer extant source [13].

29] *Chemosh.* God of the Moabites to whom Solomon later erected a shrine (I Kings 11:7).

The name of Chemosh appears on the Moabite stone of King Mesha [14]. Kaufmann emphasizes that the biblical passage does not imply *admission* that Chemosh is a living god [15].

30] *Yet we have cast them down.* Or, "we have ploughed up" [16]; the Hebrew cannot be translated with certainty.

Which (אֲשֶׁר), *asher.* In most Torah texts, the letter *resh* in *asher* has a masoretic dot over it, possibly to suggest that the ר ought to be omitted. In that case the text would read "a fire (אֵשׁ, *esh*) up to Medeba" [17].

Medeba. A city on the main north-south highway, south of Heshbon and east of the Dead Sea. It was later assigned to the territory of Reuben (Josh. 13:9, 16) and figured in the Maccabean war (second century B.C.E.; I Macc. 9:35 ff.). A map of Palestine was excavated in a sixth-century C.E. church in Medeba.

32] *Dispossessed.* This translation follows the masoretic notation that the text is to be understood as וַיּוֹרֶשׁ (*vayoresh*) dispossessed, rather than וַיִּירַשׁ (*vayirash*) inherited.

33] *Bashan.* A fruitful plain by the Yarmuk River. The story is told in greater detail in Deut. 3:1 ff.

Edrei. Today's Dar'a, about thirty miles east of Lake Kinneret (or Sea of Galilee). Thus the Transjordanian territories from the Dead Sea to Kinneret were now in Israel's hands.

כָּל־עַמּוֹ עַד־בִּלְתִּי הִשְׁאִיר־לוֹ שָׂרִיד וַיִּירְשׁוּ אֶת־   יא   וַיִּסְעוּ בְּנֵי יִשְׂרָאֵל וַיַּחֲנוּ בְּעַרְבוֹת מוֹאָב מֵעֵבֶר

אַרְצוֹ:   לְיַרְדֵּן יְרֵחוֹ:

Haftarah Chukat, p. 1268

his sons and all his people, until no remnant was left him; and they took possession of his
country.   **1]** The Israelites then marched on and encamped in the steppes of Moab, across the
Jordan from Jericho.

22:1] *Marched on.* Having extended its hold to
the north, Israel's main force returned and concentrated further south, in the Aravah opposite
Jericho (the first mention of that city in the
Torah). This stopping place is the last before the
invasion under Joshua. It is the setting for the story
of Balaam, which follows; and it is here that
Phinehas is elevated to the high priesthood and
from here that Moses goes up to Mount Pisgah
to die.

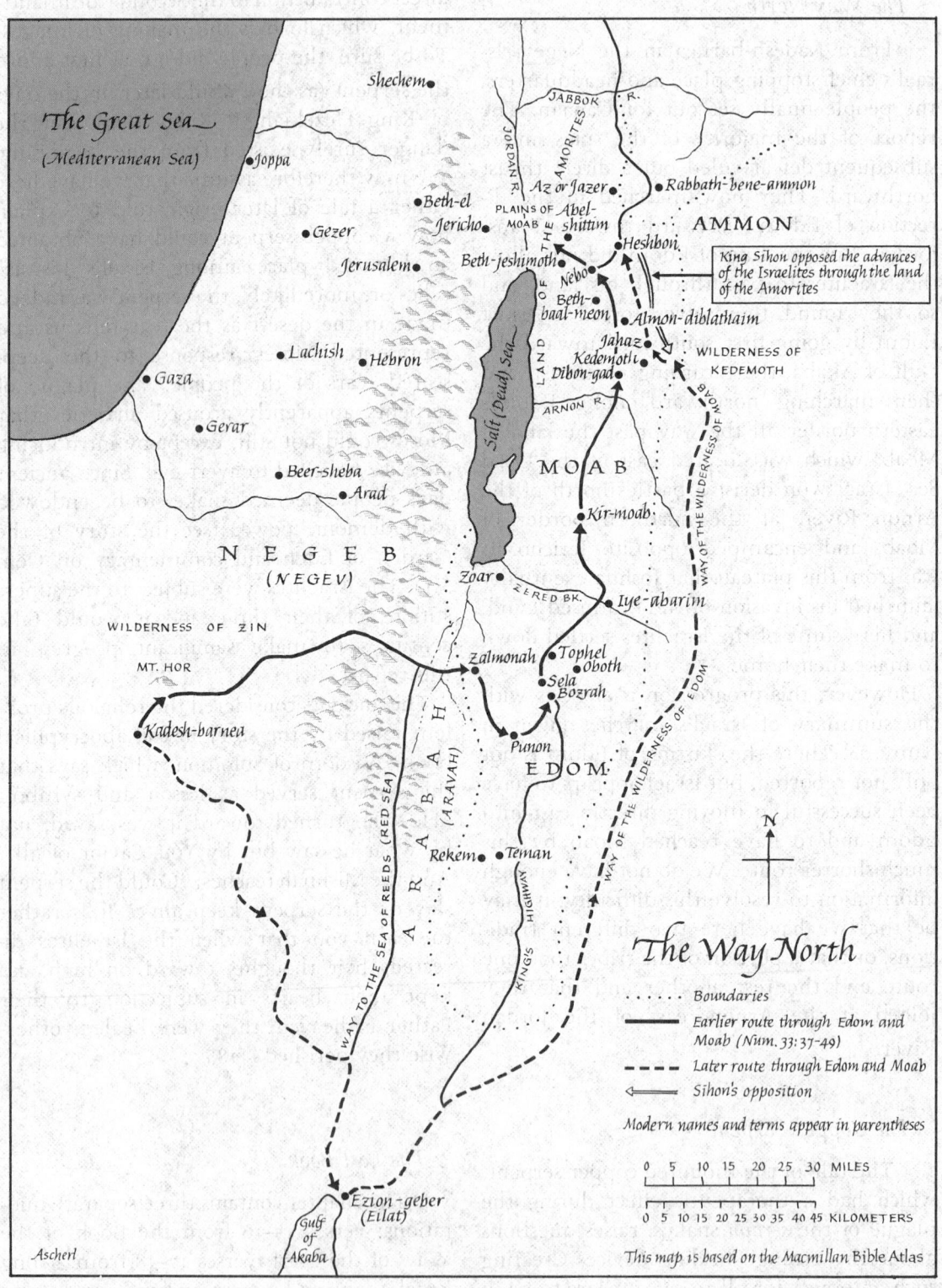

The Great Sea
(Mediterranean Sea)

Shechem

JABBOK R.

THE AMORITES

JORDAN R.

Joppa

Az or Jazer
Rabbath-bene-ammon

Beth-el
Jericho
PLAINS OF MOAB
Abel-shittim
AMMON

Gezer
Jerusalem
Beth-jeshimoth
Heshbon

King Sihon opposed the advances of the Israelites through the land of the Amorites

Nebo
Beth-baal-meon
Almon-diblathaim

LAND OF THE AMORITES

Lachish
Hebron
Jahaz
Kedemoth
Dibon-gad
WILDERNESS OF KEDEMOTH

Gaza
Salt (Dead) Sea
ARNON R.

Gerar

Beer-sheba
Arad
MOAB

WAY OF THE WILDERNESS OF MOAB

NEGEB
(NEGEV)
Zoar
Kir-moab

ZERED BK.
Iye-abarim

WILDERNESS OF ZIN

MT. HOR
Zalmonah
Tophel
Oboth

Sela
Bozrah

Kadesh-barnea
Punon
EDOM

WAY OF THE WILDERNESS OF EDOM

A R A B A H
(ARAVAH)

Rekem
Teman

WAY TO THE SEA OF REEDS (RED SEA)

KING'S HIGHWAY

N

The Way North

· · · · · · Boundaries

─────── Earlier route through Edom and
         Moab (Num. 33: 37-49)

─ ─ ─ ─ Later route through Edom and Moab

⇐   Sihon's opposition

Modern names and terms appear in parentheses

0 5 10 15 20 25 30 MILES

0 5 10 15 20 25 30 35 40 45 KILOMETERS

Ezion-geber
(Eilat)

Gulf
of
Akaba

Ascherl

This map is based on the Macmillan Bible Atlas

The Way North

From Kadesh-barnea in the Negev, Israel's chief stopping place and headquarters, the people finally set out for Canaan. The report of the majority of the spies and a subsequent defeat ruled out a direct thrust northward. They now marched in the direction of Edom, eastward toward Transjordan. But the king of Edom did not allow the Israelites to pass through his land, and so they found themselves forced to skirt Edom by going first southward toward the Gulf of Akaba, there turning northeast, and then marching northward along Edom's eastern border all the way past the land of Moab, which was located east of the Dead Sea. Israel won decisive battles north of the Arnon River, at the northern border of Moab, and encamped opposite Jericho. It was from this plateau that Joshua eventually launched his invasion of the Promised Land, and here some of the Israelites settled down to make their home.

However, this progression is at odds with the summary of Israel's marches given in Num. 33. There the skirting of Edom is not only not reported, but Israel appears to have been successful in moving directly east into Edom and to have reached Moab by this much shorter route. We do not have enough information to resolve this difficulty; it may be that we have here two different traditions, or that a portion of the tribes took one route and the rest another and that they joined at the Arnon, east of the Jordan River.

The Copper Serpent

The tale of the mounted copper serpent, which had a therapeutic effect during the plague of the *seraph* snakes, raises questions about this strange healing device. Creating such an object for all to see appears to be in direct contradiction to the Second Commandment, which forbids the making of images. To be sure, the people did not at first adore the serpent (as they would later, in the days of King Hezekiah, II Kings 18:4), but the danger surely existed from the beginning. We may therefore assume that we have here either a tale of later origin told to explain how a copper serpent could have obtained an honored place among Israel's historic relics or, more likely, the serpent was indeed made in the desert as the text tells us and represented Moses' response to the deep-seated fears of the people. The plague of serpents apparently aroused anxieties that Moses could not still, except by introducing a device believed to avert evil. Since ancient days people deemed snakes to be endowed with demonic power (see the story of the Garden of Eden and commentary on Gen. 3:1). The Israelites were subject to the superstitions of their time, and it would take centuries to make significant progress in this regard.

The ancients considered the religious problem raised by the story in the apocryphical book, Wisdom of Solomon, which says that the serpent served as lesson and symbol: "He who turned toward it was saved, not by what he saw but by You, Savior of all." And the Mishnah teaches: "Could the serpent slay or the serpent keep alive? It is rather to teach you that when the Israelites directed their thoughts toward on high and kept their hearts in subjection to their Father in heaven, they were healed; otherwise they perished" [18].

The Lost Book

The chapter contains three separate quotations: verses 15–16 from the Book of the Wars of the Lord; verses 17–18 from a song Israel sang; and verses 27–30 from a song

the bards would recite.[1] It is possible that all three quotations (and perhaps also verses 19 and 20) stem from an extrabiblical collection called the Book of the Wars of the Lord, which has since been lost. Scholars generally assume that it contained poems in praise of God's prowess and His protection of Israel in times of armed struggle. Though the book is mentioned nowhere else in the Bible and no other references to it have been discovered so far, its citation in the text lends support to the assumption that in the composition of the Torah ancient written and oral sources were used.[2]

Elsewhere the Bible makes reference to a Book of Jashar (Josh. 10:12, 13; II Sam. 1:19–27) and quotes from it; this book too has been lost.[3] It is not unlikely that other poems or fragmentary sections of the Bible may have come from these and similar collections even though the biblical text does not identify them as its sources. Thus, the Song of Moses (Exod. 15) may first have been preserved in another book; and the chapters of Balaam's oracles (Num. 22–24) may originally have been a separate entity that only later was incorporated in the Torah (see introduction).

The existence of such ancient works would testify to a long literary tradition among the Israelites. This would also explain why the excerpts preserved in this chapter are somewhat obscure, for the course of transmission—first oral and then written—must have covered many centuries.

[1] It may be that Jeremiah has such a song in mind when he re-creates the images to which Num. 21:27–30 refer. His text reads like a variant of the Torah's citation (or perhaps both reflect a common source): For fire went forth from Heshbon, / Flame from the midst of Sihon, / Consuming the brow of Moab, / The pate of the people of Shaon. / Woe to you, O Moab! / The people of Chemosh are undone, / For your sons are carried off into captivity, / Your daughters into exile (Jer. 48:45 f.).

[2] The Septuagint and Targum Yerushalmi held, however, that the "Book" here referred to was the Torah itself and translated accordingly. Of modern scholars, Tur-Sinai denies that the text refers to the existence of a separate book [19].

[3] Some scholars believe that the Book of Jashar is merely another name for the Book of the Wars of the Lord. [20].

GLEANINGS

Allegories

The serpent represents patient endurance (the copper symbolizing strength) which overcomes pleasure.   PHILO [21]

In the Christian Scriptures, looking on the serpent is a symbol for believing in the Messiah [22].

Humility and Repentance

No sooner had the people rebelled against Moses than they repented and even asked him to pray for them, and he in turn did not hesitate to respond (21:7). From this we learn both the humility of Moses and the power of repentance; and also that he who is being sincerely asked to forgive should not stay angry.   MIDRASH [23]

Then Israel Sang (Num. 21:17)

At the Reed Sea it said that in addition to Israel "Moses sang" (Exod. 15:1). Why did he not also sing here, at the well? Because he had been punished on account of the well (Num. 20:2–13), and no man praises his executioner.

MIDRASH [24]

In the Wilderness

The "well" is a symbol for Torah. If so, why was it given in the wilderness? So that all men should have access to it.   MIDRASH [25]

Similarly, in Num. 21:18 וּמִמִּדְבָּר מַתָּנָה can be understood as "and from the wilderness a gift." This teaches that he who makes himself accessible like the wilderness receives the gift of Torah.

TALMUD [26]

Chieftains and Nobles

The well symbolizes Torah; the chieftains who dug it symbolize the scholars who search deeply into Torah; the nobles who started it symbolize the generous people who support the scholars and thus themselves have a share in Torah.   THE GAON OF VILNA [27]

Mohammed's Arrow

It is told that the prophet once used an arrow to scrape the sand, and water flowed freely [28].

Og

He was a giant, a left-over from the Rephaim of old (Deut. 3:11). In the whole world there was none so difficult to overcome as Og.

MIDRASH [29]

The Serpent

This bronze serpent very probably in fact goes back in Jerusalem to pre-Israelite times and was a fertility symbol in the temple of the Jebusites in Jerusalem. Several other bronze serpent images have been found in Palestine, for instance, at Gezer, Hazor, and Megiddo; one has recently been discovered in the excavation of a temple at Timnah in the Aravah, near Elat, dated to about 1200–900 B.C. and assumed to be Midianite in origin, so it was known in the wilderness area as well as in Palestine. But the story here looks like an explanatory story built upon the existence of the snake in the Temple in Jerusalem. While Hezekiah must have recognized its Canaanite origin and destroyed it for this reason, it was earlier regarded as legitimate but in need of explanation, and so the story we have was developed. The serpent moves from its fertility context to being understood as having healing and protective properties for those bitten by snakes and so is a sign of the Lord's protective power.

J. STURDY [30]

PART III

The Story of Balaam

The tale of Balaam is one of those intriguing portions of the Torah that appear simple and straightforward on the surface yet are complex when studied in detail. A pagan soothsayer is engaged by King Balak of Moab to curse the Israelites in order to impede their further progress. Balaam agrees, but God thwarts the design and instead causes him to bless Israel.

The story is told in prose and poetry: there are four oracles; a miracle when an animal sees what man cannot; a slowly building drama, with God as both Balaam's confidant and counterfoil; and Balaam himself, the pagan who is on speaking terms with the Lord of Israel, a man driven by a force he cannot control, whose oracles can be said to summarize the revelation of God's purpose for Israel [1]. The prophet Micah saw the Balaam story as a counterpoint to that of the Exodus: At the beginning of the wandering God manifested His love for Israel by thwarting Pharaoh; forty years later and at the gates of the Promised Land He opposed the last foe so that Israel "might know the righteous acts of the Lord" (Micah 6:4, 5). The special quality of this story encouraged the talmudic opinion that it was a separate book of the Bible, making Seven Books of Moses: Genesis, Exodus, Leviticus, Numbers 1–21, Balaam (Num. 22–24), Numbers 25–end, and Deuteronomy [2]. It is a tale of great charm, humor, moving poetry, and particular literary quality. The device of repetition is used to heighten the suspense, and the final words reverberate in chords of majestic prophecy.

Furthermore, the story has numerous difficulties and apparent contradictions. Some passages associate Balaam with Midian, most others with Moab.* God allows Balaam to go but is angry at him for going; the prophet appears as both the servant and the enemy of God (see Num. 31:7, 18). This lack of unity suggests that the tale was inspired by the four oracle-poems, which are of older origin.

Bible critics usually find two primary sources, J and E, on which they believe the story to be based. For instance, some assign the tale of the speaking ass to J, as an interlude in the E story. The rabbinic as well as Christian estimates of Balaam vary but slightly: he is usually seen as the villain, though occasionally he emerges as a tragic figure.

* However, O. Eissfeldt has argued that this very association betokened the existence of a Midianite empire encompassing Moab, so that "elders of Midian" (Num. 22:4) could indeed be found in Moab and that the explanation of Targum Jonathan—that the king of Moab was a Midianite—could reflect historic fact [3].

The Story of Balaam

The opening of the story seems to promise a clear and dramatic encounter between the would-be cursers and Israel. But when Balaam accepts the invitation issued by King Balak of Moab, both his acceptance and God's role in bringing it about (or in failing to prevent it) are ambiguous. And the dream-like quality which colors the tale with the appearance of the divine messenger who is seen only by Balaam's ass is reinforced when the animal suddenly speaks wryly and sarcastically to its master. So when Balaam arrives at the king's court, the stage is set for a more complex and surprising conflict.

Balaam delivers four prophecies in place of the curses desired and expected by Balak. In the first two he proclaims that he is speaking in the name of God; both times Balak fails to grasp that his intention has been thwarted. Blinded by his preconceptions, he thinks that mechanical preparations for the oracles were incomplete and that, if proper arrangements can be made, the desired curses will be pronounced.

Balaam's oracles are cast in poetic form. They sing of Israel, its place among nations, and its relationship to God. These poems are put into Balaam's mouth as a direct divine inspiration, which makes them an authentic expression of the Torah; for this is how biblical tradition saw the fate and future of the people of Israel.

In the first oracle Balaam speaks of Israel's nature, of its protection from curse and foe; in the second oracle of God's unalterable promise to Israel and His continuing presence in its midst. When challenged a third time to curse, Balaam sings of the beauty of Israel's habitation and predicts

that Israel will be victorious over its enemies. Before he returns to his home, he prophesies once again: first legitimizing his own special connection with the Almighty and then predicting the downfall of Moab as well as that of some neighboring nations. Thus the circle closes: Balak seeks to curse and is cursed in turn.

"Had he rested content with Balaam's first refusal, he would merely have lost the assistance he hoped to derive from a powerful curse; he sends again, and Balaam comes to bless, and so to range against him the very forces with which he wished to be allied" [1].

The text contains a number of philological difficulties that cannot be resolved with certainty. Because of their technical nature, they will not be noted or treated in detail.

(A new weekly portion, *Balak*, begins with 22:2.)

ס ס ס

אֶת־הָעָם הַזֶּה כִּי־עָצוּם הוּא מִמֶּנִּי אוּלַי אוּכַל נַכֶּה־   ב וַיַּרְא בָּלָק בֶּן־צִפּוֹר אֵת כָּל־אֲשֶׁר־עָשָׂה יִשְׂרָאֵל

בּוֹ וַאֲגָרְשֶׁנּוּ מִן־הָאָרֶץ כִּי יָדַעְתִּי אֵת אֲשֶׁר־תְּבָרֵךְ   ג לָאֱמֹרִי: וַיָּגָר מוֹאָב מִפְּנֵי הָעָם מְאֹד כִּי רַב־הוּא

מְבֹרָךְ וַאֲשֶׁר תָּאֹר יוּאָר: ז וַיֵּלְכוּ זִקְנֵי מוֹאָב וְזִקְנֵי   ד וַיָּקָץ מוֹאָב מִפְּנֵי בְּנֵי יִשְׂרָאֵל: וַיֹּאמֶר מוֹאָב אֶל־זִקְנֵי

מִדְיָן וּקְסָמִים בְּיָדָם וַיָּבֹאוּ אֶל־בִּלְעָם וַיְדַבְּרוּ אֵלָיו   מִדְיָן עַתָּה יְלַחֲכוּ הַקָּהָל אֶת־כָּל־סְבִיבֹתֵינוּ כִּלְחֹךְ

דִּבְרֵי בָלָק: ח וַיֹּאמֶר אֲלֵיהֶם לִינוּ פֹה הַלַּיְלָה וַהֲשִׁבֹתִי   הַשּׁוֹר אֵת יֶרֶק הַשָּׂדֶה וּבָלָק בֶּן־צִפּוֹר מֶלֶךְ לְמוֹאָב

אֶתְכֶם דָּבָר כַּאֲשֶׁר יְדַבֵּר יְהוָה אֵלָי וַיֵּשְׁבוּ שָׂרֵי־   ה בָּעֵת הַהִוא: וַיִּשְׁלַח מַלְאָכִים אֶל־בִּלְעָם בֶּן־בְּעוֹר

מוֹאָב עִם־בִּלְעָם: ט וַיָּבֹא אֱלֹהִים אֶל־בִּלְעָם וַיֹּאמֶר   פְּתוֹרָה אֲשֶׁר עַל־הַנָּהָר אֶרֶץ בְּנֵי־עַמּוֹ לִקְרֹא־לוֹ

מִי הָאֲנָשִׁים הָאֵלֶּה עִמָּךְ: י וַיֹּאמֶר בִּלְעָם אֶל־   לֵאמֹר הִנֵּה עַם יָצָא מִמִּצְרַיִם הִנֵּה כִסָּה אֶת־עֵין

הָאֱלֹהִים בָּלָק בֶּן־צִפֹּר מֶלֶךְ מוֹאָב שָׁלַח אֵלָי: י הָאָרֶץ וְהוּא יֹשֵׁב מִמֻּלִי: וְעַתָּה לְכָה־נָּא אָרָה־לִּי

יא הִנֵּה הָעָם הַיֹּצֵא מִמִּצְרַיִם וַיְכַס אֶת־עֵין הָאָרֶץ עַתָּה

2] Balak son of Zippor saw all that Israel had done to the Amorites.

3] Moab was alarmed because that people was so numerous. Moab dreaded the Israelites,

4] and Moab said to the elders of Midian, "Now this horde will lick clean all that is about us as an ox licks up the grass of the field."

Balak son of Zippor, who was king of Moab at that time, 5] sent messengers to Balaam son of Beor in Pethor, which is by the Euphrates, in the land of his kinsfolk, to invite him, saying, "There is a people that came out of Egypt; it hides the earth from view, and it is settled next to me. 6] Come then, put a curse upon this people for me, since they are too numerous for me; perhaps I can thus defeat them and drive them out of the land. For I know that he whom you bless is blessed indeed, and he whom you curse is cursed."

7] The elders of Moab and the elders of Midian, versed in divination, set out. They came to Balaam and gave him Balak's message. 8] He said to them, "Spend the night here, and I shall reply to you as the LORD may instruct me." So the Moabite dignitaries stayed with Balaam.

9] God came to Balaam and said, "What do these people want of you?" 10] Balaam said to God, "Balak son of Zippor, king of Moab, sent me this message: 11] Here is a people that

---

22:2] *Balak son of Zippor.* Balak lived about 1300 B.C.E., when the Semitic tribes of the area had merged into several kingdoms which battled nomadic peoples such as Israel.

4] *Elders of Midian.* According to Targum Jonathan, Balak was a Midianite who had become king of Moab, a not unlikely assumption in view of recent research.

5] *Balaam son of Beor.* A "Bela son of Beor" is mentioned in Gen. 36:32 but, despite the similarity (בֶּלַע—בִּלְעָם), the identity is doubtful.

The name Balaam is characteristic of the second millennium B.C.E.; a Bil-amma was known in the fifteenth century [2].

Pethor . . . by the Euphrates. Literally, "by the river." An inscription of the ninth century B.C.E.

mentions a Mesopotamian town of Pitru [3]. Other biblical versions have "by the river in the land of Ammon" (reading עַמּוֹן instead of עַמּוֹ); this reading would place Balaam's residence closer to Moab and reduce the length of his journey.

Others hold that the present text is accurate and that *ammo* should be rendered not as "his kinsfolk" but read as Amau since there were such a people in Mesopotamia [4].

7] *Elders . . . versed in divination.* Colleagues whom it would be hard to refuse [5].

9] *What do these people want of you?* A rhetorical question to which God already knows the answer. Compare Gen. 4:9, "Where is your brother Abel?"

לְכָה קָבָה־לִּי אֹתוֹ אוּלַי אוּכַל לְהִלָּחֶם בּוֹ וְגֵרַשְׁתִּיו:
יב וַיֹּאמֶר אֱלֹהִים אֶל־בִּלְעָם לֹא תֵלֵךְ עִמָּהֶם לֹא תָאֹר
אֶת־הָעָם כִּי בָרוּךְ הוּא: וַיָּקָם בִּלְעָם בַּבֹּקֶר וַיֹּאמֶר
אֶל־שָׂרֵי בָלָק לְכוּ אֶל־אַרְצְכֶם כִּי מֵאֵן יְהוָה לְתִתִּי
לַהֲלֹךְ עִמָּכֶם: וַיָּקוּמוּ שָׂרֵי מוֹאָב וַיָּבֹאוּ אֶל־בָּלָק
טו וַיֹּאמְרוּ מֵאֵן בִּלְעָם הֲלֹךְ עִמָּנוּ: וַיֹּסֶף עוֹד בָּלָק שְׁלֹחַ
שָׂרִים רַבִּים וְנִכְבָּדִים מֵאֵלֶּה: וַיָּבֹאוּ אֶל־בִּלְעָם
וַיֹּאמְרוּ לוֹ כֹּה אָמַר בָּלָק בֶּן־צִפּוֹר אַל־נָא תִמָּנַע
מֵהֲלֹךְ אֵלָי: כִּי־כַבֵּד אֲכַבֶּדְךָ מְאֹד וְכֹל אֲשֶׁר־תֹּאמַר
אֵלַי אֶעֱשֶׂה וּלְכָה־נָּא קָבָה־לִּי אֵת הָעָם הַזֶּה: וַיַּעַן
בִּלְעָם וַיֹּאמֶר אֶל־עַבְדֵי בָלָק אִם־יִתֶּן־לִי בָלָק מְלֹא
בֵיתוֹ כֶּסֶף וְזָהָב לֹא אוּכַל לַעֲבֹר אֶת־פִּי יְהוָה אֱלֹהָי

יט לַעֲשׂוֹת קְטַנָּה אוֹ גְדוֹלָה: וְעַתָּה שְׁבוּ נָא בָזֶה גַּם־אַתֶּם
כ הַלַּיְלָה וְאֵדְעָה מַה־יֹּסֵף יְהוָה דַּבֵּר עִמִּי: וַיָּבֹא
אֱלֹהִים אֶל־בִּלְעָם לַיְלָה וַיֹּאמֶר לוֹ אִם־לִקְרֹא לְךָ
בָּאוּ הָאֲנָשִׁים קוּם לֵךְ אִתָּם וְאַךְ אֶת־הַדָּבָר אֲשֶׁר־
אֲדַבֵּר אֵלֶיךָ אֹתוֹ תַעֲשֶׂה: וַיָּקָם בִּלְעָם בַּבֹּקֶר וַיַּחֲבֹשׁ
כב אֶת־אֲתֹנוֹ וַיֵּלֶךְ עִם־שָׂרֵי מוֹאָב: וַיִּחַר־אַף אֱלֹהִים
כִּי־הוֹלֵךְ הוּא וַיִּתְיַצֵּב מַלְאַךְ יְהוָה בַּדֶּרֶךְ לְשָׂטָן לוֹ
וְהוּא רֹכֵב עַל־אֲתֹנוֹ וּשְׁנֵי נְעָרָיו עִמּוֹ: וַתֵּרֶא הָאָתוֹן
אֶת־מַלְאַךְ יְהוָה נִצָּב בַּדֶּרֶךְ וְחַרְבּוֹ שְׁלוּפָה בְּיָדוֹ
וַתֵּט הָאָתוֹן מִן־הַדֶּרֶךְ וַתֵּלֶךְ בַּשָּׂדֶה וַיַּךְ בִּלְעָם אֶת־
כד הָאָתוֹן לְהַטֹּתָהּ הַדָּרֶךְ: וַיַּעֲמֹד מַלְאַךְ יְהוָה בְּמִשְׁעוֹל
כה הַכְּרָמִים גָּדֵר מִזֶּה וְגָדֵר מִזֶּה: וַתֵּרֶא הָאָתוֹן אֶת־

came out from Egypt and hides the earth from view. Come now and curse them for me; perhaps I can engage them in battle and drive them off." **12]** But God said to Balaam, "Do not go with them. You must not curse that people, for they are blessed."

13] Balaam arose in the morning, and said to Balak's dignitaries, "Go back to your own country, for the LORD will not let me go with you." **14]** The Moabite dignitaries left, and they came to Balak and said, "Balaam refused to come with us."

15] Then Balak sent other dignitaries, more numerous and distinguished than the first. **16]** They came to Balaam and said to him, "Thus says Balak son of Zippor: Please do not refuse to come to me. **17]** I will reward you richly and I will do anything you ask of me. Only come and damn this people for me." **18]** Balaam replied to Balak's officials, "Though Balak were to give me his house full of silver and gold, I could not do anything, big or little, contrary to the command of the LORD my God. **19]** So you, too, stay here overnight, and let me find out what else the LORD may say to me." **20]** That night God came to Balaam and said to him, "If these men have come to invite you, you may go with them. But whatever I command you, that you shall do."

21] When he arose in the morning, Balaam saddled his ass and departed with the Moabite dignitaries. **22]** But God was incensed at his going; so an angel of the LORD placed himself in his way as an adversary.

He was riding on his she-ass, with his two servants alongside, **23]** when the ass caught sight of the angel of the LORD standing in the way, with his drawn sword in his hand. The ass swerved from the road and went into the fields; and Balaam beat the ass to turn her back onto the road. **24]** The angel of the LORD then stationed himself in a lane between the vineyards,

22] *God was incensed.* According to many scholars this belongs to the J source, the preceding verses to E. According to Nachmanides, God was angry at Balaam for going without revealing to Balak's messengers the divine command in its full mean-ing. Instead, he left them hoping that he might be able to curse Israel after all.

An adversary. שָׂטָן (satan). The term later came to represent the adversary in the divine court (see Job 1:6 ff.; 2:1 ff.).

מַלְאַ֤ךְ יְהֹוָה֙ וַתִּלָּחֵ֔ץ אֶל־הַקִּ֕יר וַתִּלְחַ֛ץ אֶת־רֶ֥גֶל
בִּלְעָ֖ם אֶל־הַקִּ֑יר וַיֹּ֖סֶף לְהַכֹּתָֽהּ: וַיּ֥וֹסֶף מַלְאַךְ־יְהֹוָ֖ה כו
עֲב֑וֹר וַֽיַּעֲמֹד֙ בְּמָק֣וֹם צָ֔ר אֲשֶׁ֛ר אֵֽין־דֶּ֥רֶךְ לִנְט֖וֹת יָמִ֥ין
וּשְׂמֹֽאול: וַתֵּ֤רֶא הָֽאָתוֹן֙ אֶת־מַלְאַ֣ךְ יְהֹוָ֔ה וַתִּרְבַּ֖ץ תַּ֣חַת כז
בִּלְעָ֑ם וַיִּֽחַר־אַ֣ף בִּלְעָ֔ם וַיַּ֥ךְ אֶת־הָאָת֖וֹן בַּמַּקֵּֽל:
וַיִּפְתַּ֥ח יְהֹוָ֖ה אֶת־פִּ֣י הָֽאָת֑וֹן וַתֹּ֤אמֶר לְבִלְעָם֙ מֶֽה־ כח
עָשִׂ֣יתִי לְךָ֔ כִּ֣י הִכִּיתַ֔נִי זֶ֖ה שָׁלֹ֥שׁ רְגָלִֽים: וַיֹּ֤אמֶר בִּלְעָם֙ כט
לָ֣אָת֔וֹן כִּ֥י הִתְעַלַּ֖לְתְּ בִּ֑י ל֤וּ יֶשׁ־חֶ֙רֶב֙ בְּיָדִ֔י כִּ֥י עַתָּ֖ה
הֲרַגְתִּֽיךְ: וַתֹּ֨אמֶר הָֽאָת֜וֹן אֶל־בִּלְעָ֗ם הֲלוֹא֙ אָֽנֹכִ֣י ל
אֲתֹֽנְךָ֗ אֲשֶׁר־רָכַ֙בְתָּ֙ עָלַ֔י מֵעֽוֹדְךָ֖ עַד־הַיּ֣וֹם הַזֶּ֑ה
הַֽהַסְכֵּ֣ן הִסְכַּ֔נְתִּי לַעֲשׂ֥וֹת לְךָ֖ כֹּ֑ה וַיֹּ֖אמֶר לֹֽא: וַיְגַ֣ל לא
* כן פלא ו׳

יְהֹוָ֞ה אֶת־עֵינֵ֣י בִלְעָ֗ם וַיַּ֞רְא אֶת־מַלְאַ֤ךְ יְהֹוָה֙ נִצָּ֣ב
בַּדֶּ֔רֶךְ וְחַרְבּ֥וֹ שְׁלֻפָ֖ה בְּיָד֑וֹ וַיִּקֹּ֥ד וַיִּשְׁתַּ֖חוּ לְאַפָּֽיו:
וַיֹּ֤אמֶר אֵלָיו֙ מַלְאַ֣ךְ יְהֹוָ֔ה עַל־מָ֗ה הִכִּ֙יתָ֙ אֶת־אֲתֹ֣נְךָ֔ לב
זֶ֖ה שָׁל֣וֹשׁ רְגָלִ֑ים הִנֵּ֤ה אָֽנֹכִי֙ יָצָ֣אתִי לְשָׂטָ֔ן כִּֽי־יָרַ֥ט
הַדֶּ֖רֶךְ לְנֶגְדִּֽי: וַתִּרְאַ֙נִי֙ הָֽאָת֔וֹן וַתֵּ֣ט לְפָנַ֔י זֶ֖ה שָׁלֹ֣שׁ לג
רְגָלִ֑ים אוּלַי֙ נָטְתָ֣ה מִפָּנַ֔י כִּ֥י עַתָּ֛ה גַּם־אֹתְכָ֥ה הָרַ֖גְתִּי
וְאוֹתָ֥הּ הֶֽחֱיֵֽיתִי: וַיֹּ֨אמֶר בִּלְעָ֜ם אֶל־מַלְאַ֤ךְ יְהֹוָה֙ לד
חָטָ֔אתִי כִּ֣י לֹ֤א יָדַ֙עְתִּי֙ כִּ֣י אַתָּ֛ה נִצָּ֥ב לִקְרָאתִ֖י בַּדָּ֑רֶךְ
וְעַתָּ֛ה אִם־רַ֥ע בְּעֵינֶ֖יךָ אָשׁ֥וּבָה לִּֽי: וַיֹּ֩אמֶר֩ מַלְאַ֨ךְ לה
יְהֹוָ֜ה אֶל־בִּלְעָ֗ם לֵ֚ךְ עִם־הָ֣אֲנָשִׁ֔ים וְאֶ֗פֶס אֶת־הַדָּבָ֛ר
אֲשֶׁר־אֲדַבֵּ֥ר אֵלֶ֖יךָ אֹת֣וֹ תְדַבֵּ֑ר וַיֵּ֥לֶךְ בִּלְעָ֖ם עִם־שָׂרֵ֥י

---

with a fence on either side. **25]** The ass, seeing the angel of the LORD, pressed herself against the wall and squeezed Balaam's foot against the wall; so he beat her again. **26]** Once more the angel of the LORD moved forward and stationed himself on a spot so narrow that there was no room to swerve right or left. **27]** When the ass now saw the angel of the LORD, she lay down under Balaam; and Balaam was furious and beat the ass with his stick.

28] Then the LORD opened the ass's mouth, and she said to Balaam, "What have I done to you that you have beaten me these three times?" **29]** Balaam said to the ass, "You have made a mockery of me! If I had a sword with me, I'd kill you." **30]** The ass said to Balaam, "Look, I am the ass that you have been riding all along until this day! Have I been in the habit of doing thus to you?" And he answered, "No."

31] Then the LORD uncovered Balaam's eyes, and he saw the angel of the LORD standing in the way, his drawn sword in his hand; thereupon he bowed right down to the ground. **32]** The angel of the LORD said to him, "Why have you beaten your ass these three times? It is I who came out as an adversary, for the errand is obnoxious to me. **33]** And when the ass saw me, she shied away because of me those three times. If she had not shied away from me, you are the one I should have killed, while sparing her." **34]** Balaam said to the angel of the LORD, "I erred because I did not know that you were standing in my way. If you still disapprove, I will turn back." **35]** But the angel of the LORD said to Balaam, "Go with the men. But you must say nothing except what I tell you." So Balaam went on with Balak's dignitaries.

28] *Opened the ass's mouth.* The only other instance in the Bible of an animal speaking is the serpent's address to Eve in the Garden of Eden (Gen. 3:1) [6].

31] *Right down to the ground.* The Hebrew is more expressive: "prostrated himself to his nostrils."

32] *Obnoxious.* The meaning of the Hebrew is uncertain.

36] *Ir-moab.* Apparently meant to indicate the northeast corner of Moab; others read "Ar of Moab," referring to the old capital, or "the city of Moab," i.e., its chief city [7]. The location of these incidents in relation to Israel's encampment near the Dead Sea and the known boundaries of Moab presents unresolved difficulties.

לו בָּלָק: וַיִּשְׁמַע בָּלָק כִּי־בָא בִלְעָם וַיֵּצֵא לִקְרָאתוֹ
אֶל־עִיר מוֹאָב אֲשֶׁר עַל־גְּבוּל אַרְנֹן אֲשֶׁר בִּקְצֵה
לז הַגְּבוּל: וַיֹּאמֶר בָּלָק אֶל־בִּלְעָם הֲלֹא שָׁלֹחַ שָׁלַחְתִּי
אֵלֶיךָ לִקְרֹא־לָךְ לָמָּה לֹא־הָלַכְתָּ אֵלָי הַאֻמְנָם לֹא
לח אוּכַל כַּבְּדֶךָ: וַיֹּאמֶר בִּלְעָם אֶל־בָּלָק הִנֵּה־בָאתִי
אֵלֶיךָ עַתָּה הֲיָכֹל אוּכַל דַּבֵּר מְאוּמָה הַדָּבָר אֲשֶׁר
לט יָשִׂים אֱלֹהִים בְּפִי אֹתוֹ אֲדַבֵּר: וַיֵּלֶךְ בִּלְעָם עִם־בָּלָק
מ וַיָּבֹאוּ קִרְיַת חֻצוֹת: וַיִּזְבַּח בָּלָק בָּקָר וָצֹאן וַיְשַׁלַּח
מא לְבִלְעָם וְלַשָּׂרִים אֲשֶׁר אִתּוֹ: וַיְהִי בַבֹּקֶר וַיִּקַּח בָּלָק
אֶת־בִּלְעָם וַיַּעֲלֵהוּ בָּמוֹת בָּעַל וַיַּרְא מִשָּׁם קְצֵה הָעָם:

א וַיֹּאמֶר בִּלְעָם אֶל־בָּלָק בְּנֵה־לִי בָזֶה שִׁבְעָה מִזְבְּחֹת
ב וְהָכֵן לִי בָּזֶה שִׁבְעָה פָרִים וְשִׁבְעָה אֵילִים: וַיַּעַשׂ
בָּלָק כַּאֲשֶׁר דִּבֶּר בִּלְעָם וַיַּעַל בָּלָק וּבִלְעָם פָּר
ג וָאַיִל בַּמִּזְבֵּחַ: וַיֹּאמֶר בִּלְעָם לְבָלָק הִתְיַצֵּב עַל־
עֹלָתֶךָ וְאֵלְכָה אוּלַי יִקָּרֵה יְהוָה לִקְרָאתִי וּדְבַר
ד מַה־יַּרְאֵנִי וְהִגַּדְתִּי לָךְ וַיֵּלֶךְ שֶׁפִי: וַיִּקָּר אֱלֹהִים אֶל־
בִּלְעָם וַיֹּאמֶר אֵלָיו אֶת־שִׁבְעַת הַמִּזְבְּחֹת עָרַכְתִּי
ה וָאַעַל פָּר וָאַיִל בַּמִּזְבֵּחַ: וַיָּשֶׂם יְהוָה דָּבָר בְּפִי בִלְעָם
ו וַיֹּאמֶר שׁוּב אֶל־בָּלָק וְכֹה תְדַבֵּר: וַיָּשָׁב אֵלָיו וְהִנֵּה
נִצָּב עַל־עֹלָתוֹ הוּא וְכָל־שָׂרֵי מוֹאָב: וַיִּשָּׂא מְשָׁלוֹ

36] When Balak heard that Balaam was coming, he went out to meet him at Ir-moab, which is on the Arnon border, at its farthest point. **37]** Balak said to Balaam, "When I first sent to invite you, why didn't you come to me? Am I really unable to reward you?" **38]** But Balaam said to Balak, "And now that I have come to you, have I the power to speak freely? I can utter only the word that God puts into my mouth."

39] Balaam went with Balak and they came to Kiriath-huzoth. **40]** Balak sacrificed oxen and sheep, and had them served to Balaam and the dignitaries with him. **41]** In the morning Balak took Balaam up to Bamoth-baal. From there he could see a portion of the people.

1] Balaam said to Balak, "Build me seven altars here and have seven bulls and seven rams ready here for me." **2]** Balak did as Balaam directed; and Balak and Balaam offered up a bull and a ram on each altar. **3]** Then Balaam said to Balak, "Stay here beside your offerings while I am gone. Perhaps the LORD will grant me a manifestation, and whatever He reveals to me I will tell you." And he went off alone.

4] God manifested Himself to Balaam, who said to Him, "I have set up the seven altars and offered up a bull and a ram on each altar." **5]** And the LORD put a word in Balaam's mouth and said, "Return to Balak and speak thus."

6] So he returned to him and found him standing beside his offerings, and all the Moabite **dignitaries with him. 7]** He took up his theme, and said: / From Aram has Balak brought me, /

39] *Kiriath-huzoth.* "City of streets," of unknown location.

40] *Had them served.* When sacrifices were brought the major portion of the offering was usually eaten by both the offering party and the priests. It is possible that in very ancient days meat was consumed only on such occasions [8].

41] *Bamoth-baal.* Meaning "height [for the worship] of Baal." It was deemed important to see the object that was to be cursed.

23:1] *Seven.* The sacred number par excellence which probably derived its status from the then observed seven planets [9].

3] *He went off alone.* Others, "he went off limping" (as a result of his foot being crushed against the wall); "he went [to] the height" [10].

4] *God manifested Himself.* Literally, "God fell in with Balaam," וַיִּקָּר (*vayikar*), a word play on יָקְרֶה (*yikareh*) and לִקְרָאתִי (*likrati*) in the preceding verse. Rashi, following dominant Jewish tradition, took this expression to be purposely derisive, indicating that God had a lesser relationship with Balaam than what He would have had with a true prophet.

תְּרָאֶנּוּ מִשָּׁם אֶפֶס קָצֵהוּ תִרְאֶה וְכֻלּוֹ לֹא תִרְאֶה

וְקָבְנוֹ־לִי מִשָּׁם: יד וַיִּקָּחֵהוּ שְׂדֵה צֹפִים אֶל־רֹאשׁ הַפִּסְגָּה

וַיִּבֶן שִׁבְעָה מִזְבְּחֹת וַיַּעַל פָּר וָאַיִל בַּמִּזְבֵּחַ: טו וַיֹּאמֶר

אֶל־בָּלָק הִתְיַצֵּב כֹּה עַל־עֹלָתֶךָ וְאָנֹכִי אִקָּרֶה כֹּה:

טז וַיִּקָּר יְהוָה אֶל־בִּלְעָם וַיָּשֶׂם דָּבָר בְּפִיו וַיֹּאמֶר שׁוּב

אֶל־בָּלָק וְכֹה תְדַבֵּר: יז וַיָּבֹא אֵלָיו וְהִנּוֹ נִצָּב עַל־עֹלָתוֹ

וְשָׂרֵי מוֹאָב אִתּוֹ וַיֹּאמֶר לוֹ בָּלָק מַה־דִּבֶּר יְהוָה:

יח וַיִּשָּׂא מְשָׁלוֹ וַיֹּאמַר קוּם בָּלָק וּשֲׁמָע הַאֲזִינָה עָדַי בְּנוֹ

צִפֹּר: יט לֹא אִישׁ אֵל וִיכַזֵּב וּבֶן־אָדָם וְיִתְנֶחָם הַהוּא

אָמַר וְלֹא יַעֲשֶׂה וְדִבֶּר וְלֹא יְקִימֶנָּה: כ הִנֵּה בָרֵךְ

וַיֹּאמֶר מִן־אֲרָם יַנְחֵנִי בָלָק מֶלֶךְ־מוֹאָב מֵהַרְרֵי־קֶדֶם

ה לְכָה אָרָה־לִּי יַעֲקֹב וּלְכָה זֹעֲמָה יִשְׂרָאֵל: מָה אֶקֹּב

ט לֹא קַבֹּה אֵל וּמָה אֶזְעֹם לֹא זָעַם יְהוָה: כִּי־מֵרֹאשׁ

צֻרִים אֶרְאֶנּוּ וּמִגְּבָעוֹת אֲשׁוּרֶנּוּ הֶן־עָם לְבָדָד יִשְׁכֹּן

וּבַגּוֹיִם לֹא יִתְחַשָּׁב: י מִי מָנָה עֲפַר יַעֲקֹב וּמִסְפָּר אֶת־

רֹבַע יִשְׂרָאֵל תָּמֹת נַפְשִׁי מוֹת יְשָׁרִים וּתְהִי אַחֲרִיתִי

כָּמֹהוּ: יא וַיֹּאמֶר בָּלָק אֶל־בִּלְעָם מֶה עָשִׂיתָ לִי לָקֹב

אֹיְבַי לְקַחְתִּיךָ וְהִנֵּה בֵּרַכְתָּ בָרֵךְ: יב וַיַּעַן וַיֹּאמַר הֲלֹא

אֵת אֲשֶׁר יָשִׂים יְהוָה בְּפִי אֹתוֹ אֶשְׁמֹר לְדַבֵּר:

יג וַיֹּאמֶר אֵלָיו בָּלָק לְךָ־נָּא אִתִּי אֶל־מָקוֹם אַחֵר אֲשֶׁר

* יש חסר ה'.

Moab's king from the hills of the East: / Come, curse me Jacob, / Come, tell Israel's doom! / **8]** How can I damn whom God has not damned, / How doom when the LORD has not doomed? / **9]** As I see them from the mountain tops, / Gaze on them from the heights, / There is a people that dwells apart, / Not reckoned among the nations. / **10]** Who can count the dust of Jacob, / Number the dust-cloud of Israel? / May I die the death of the upright, / May my fate be like theirs!

11] Then Balak said to Balaam, "What have you done to me? Here I brought you to damn my enemies, and instead you have blessed them!" **12]** He replied, "I can only repeat faithfully what the LORD puts in my mouth." **13]** Then Balak said to him, "Come with me to another place from which you can see them—you will see only a portion of them; you will not see all of them—and damn them for me from there." **14]** With that, he took him to Sedeh-zophim, on the summit of Pisgah. He built seven altars and offered a bull and a ram on each altar. **15]** And [Balaam] said to Balak, "Stay here beside your offerings, while I seek a manifestation yonder."

16] The LORD manifested Himself to Balaam and put a word in his mouth, saying, "Return to Balak and speak thus." **17]** He went to him and found him standing beside his offerings, and the Moabite dignitaries with him. Balak asked him, "What did the LORD say?" **18]** And he took up his theme, and said: / Up, Balak, attend, / Give ear unto me, son of Zippor! / **19]** God is not man to be capricious, / Or mortal to change His mind. / Would He speak and not act, / Promise and not fulfill? / **20]** My message was to bless: / When He blesses, I cannot

10] *Dust of Jacob.* The couplet is figurative for "Who can bewitch Jacob?"—dust being used in magical rites of Mesopotamia [11].

Death of the upright. יְשָׁרִים (*yesharim*), according to some a word play on יְשֻׁרוּן (*yeshurun*), a name for Israel, Deut. 32:15. Others point to the same parallel יָשָׁר—אַחֲרִית in Ps. 37:37 and Prov. 14:12 [12]. No reference to afterlife is intended by this expression.

13] *To another place.* A change of place was believed to change one's fortune.

14] *Sedeh-zophim.* "Look-out spot."

16] *Manifested.* See above at verse 4. Here a word play on אִקָּרֶה (*ikareh*) in the preceding verse.

19] *Mortal.* Literally, "son of man," an expression frequently found in Ezekiel and in the Christian Scriptures.

אֶל־מָקוֹם אַחֵר אוּלַי יִישַׁר בְּעֵינֵי הָאֱלֹהִים וְקַבֹּתוֹ
לִי מִשָּׁם: וַיִּקַּח בָּלָק אֶת־בִּלְעָם רֹאשׁ הַפְּעוֹר הַנִּשְׁקָף
עַל־פְּנֵי הַיְשִׁימֹן: וַיֹּאמֶר בִּלְעָם אֶל־בָּלָק בְּנֵה־לִי
בָזֶה שִׁבְעָה מִזְבְּחֹת וְהָכֵן לִי בָּזֶה שִׁבְעָה פָרִים
וְשִׁבְעָה אֵילִם: וַיַּעַשׂ בָּלָק כַּאֲשֶׁר אָמַר בִּלְעָם וַיַּעַל
פָּר וָאַיִל בַּמִּזְבֵּחַ:

וַיַּרְא בִּלְעָם כִּי טוֹב בְּעֵינֵי יְהוָֹה לְבָרֵךְ אֶת־יִשְׂרָאֵל
וְלֹא־הָלַךְ כְּפַעַם־בְּפַעַם לִקְרַאת נְחָשִׁים וַיָּשֶׁת אֶל־
הַמִּדְבָּר פָּנָיו: וַיִּשָּׂא בִלְעָם אֶת־עֵינָיו וַיַּרְא אֶת־
יִשְׂרָאֵל שֹׁכֵן לִשְׁבָטָיו וַתְּהִי עָלָיו רוּחַ אֱלֹהִים:

כא לְקַחְתִּי וּבֵרֵךְ וְלֹא אֲשִׁיבֶנָּה: לֹא־הִבִּיט אָוֶן בְּיַעֲקֹב
וְלֹא־רָאָה עָמָל בְּיִשְׂרָאֵל יְהוָֹה אֱלֹהָיו עִמּוֹ וּתְרוּעַת
כב מֶלֶךְ בּוֹ: אֵל מוֹצִיאָם מִמִּצְרָיִם כְּתוֹעֲפֹת רְאֵם לוֹ:
כג כִּי לֹא־נַחַשׁ בְּיַעֲקֹב וְלֹא־קֶסֶם בְּיִשְׂרָאֵל כָּעֵת יֵאָמֵר
כד לְיַעֲקֹב וּלְיִשְׂרָאֵל מַה־פָּעַל אֵל: הֶן־עָם כְּלָבִיא יָקוּם
וְכַאֲרִי יִתְנַשָּׂא לֹא יִשְׁכַּב עַד־יֹאכַל טֶרֶף וְדַם־חֲלָלִים
כה יִשְׁתֶּה: וַיֹּאמֶר בָּלָק אֶל־בִּלְעָם גַּם־קֹב לֹא תִקֳּבֶנּוּ
כו גַּם־בָּרֵךְ לֹא תְבָרֲכֶנּוּ: וַיַּעַן בִּלְעָם וַיֹּאמֶר אֶל־בָּלָק
הֲלֹא דִּבַּרְתִּי אֵלֶיךָ לֵאמֹר כֹּל אֲשֶׁר־יְדַבֵּר יְהוָֹה
כז אֹתוֹ אֶעֱשֶׂה: וַיֹּאמֶר בָּלָק אֶל־בִּלְעָם לְכָה־נָּא אֶקָּחֲךָ

reverse it. / **21]** No harm is in sight for Jacob, / No woe in view for Israel. / The LORD their God is with them, / And their King's acclaim in their midst. / **22]** God who freed them from Egypt / Is for them like the horns of the wild ox. / **23]** Lo, there is no augury in Jacob, / No divining in Israel: / Jacob is told at once, / Yea Israel, what God has planned. / **24]** Lo, a people that rises like a lion, / Leaps up like the king of beasts, / Rests not till it has feasted on prey / And drunk the blood of the slain.

25] Thereupon Balak said to Balaam, "Don't curse them and don't bless them!" **26]** In reply, Balaam said to Balak, "But I told you: Whatever the LORD says, that I must do." **27]** Then Balak said to Balaam, "Come now, I will take you to another place. Perhaps God will deem it right that you damn them for me there." **28]** Balak took Balaam to the peak of Peor, which overlooks the wasteland. **29]** Balaam said to Balak, "Build me here seven altars, and have seven bulls and seven rams ready for me here." **30]** Balak did as Balaam said: he offered up a bull and a ram on each altar.

1] Now Balaam, seeing that it pleased God to bless Israel, did not, as on previous occasions, go in search of omens, but turned his face toward the wilderness. **2]** As Balaam looked up and saw Israel encamped tribe by tribe, the spirit of God came upon him. **3]** Taking up his theme,

22] *God who freed them from Egypt.* Balaam here introduces a subtle correction of Balak's statement that Israel was "a people come out of Egypt" (Num. 22:5), as if it had come out without God's help [13].

Horns of the wild ox. The animal uses them both for protection and attack, and God's power is pictured in like terms. The same imagery is used in Deut. 33:17.

The Babylonian King Hammurabi described himself as "a fiery wild ox who gores his foes." And, in the ancient Near East, gods were frequently depicted with horns or wearing horned crowns. In one bas-relief at Ugarit, Baal is shown with the horns of an ox (aurochs, now an extinct species) [14].

23] *There is no augury in Jacob.* Possibly a parenthetical note by the Torah editor, with reference to the prohibition of augury, Deut. 18:10–15 [15].

The King James and Revised Standard Versions have "against Jacob." It is also possible to take the phrase as an aside by Balaam meaning, "What I do here is useless anyway."

24] *Rises like a lion.* A bas-relief from the ninth century B.C.E. in Mesopotamia depicts a rising lion [16].

28] *Peor.* Its precise location is unknown.

24:1] *In search of omens.* He no longer looked for special manifestations, as before (Num. 23:3, 15).

ג וַיִּשָּׂא מְשָׁלוֹ וַיֹּאמַר נְאֻם בִּלְעָם בְּנוֹ בְעֹר וּנְאֻם הַגֶּבֶר
ד שְׁתֻם הָעָיִן: נְאֻם שֹׁמֵעַ אִמְרֵי־אֵל אֲשֶׁר מַחֲזֵה שַׁדַּי
ה יֶחֱזֶה נֹפֵל וּגְלוּי עֵינָיִם: מַה־טֹּבוּ אֹהָלֶיךָ יַעֲקֹב
ו מִשְׁכְּנֹתֶיךָ יִשְׂרָאֵל: כִּנְחָלִים נִטָּיוּ כְּגַנֹּת עֲלֵי נָהָר
ז כַּאֲהָלִים נָטַע יְהוָה כַּאֲרָזִים עֲלֵי־מָיִם: יִזַּל־מַיִם
מִדָּלְיָו וְזַרְעוֹ בְּמַיִם רַבִּים וְיָרֹם מֵאֲגַג מַלְכּוֹ וְתִנַּשֵּׂא
ח מַלְכֻתוֹ: אֵל מוֹצִיאוֹ מִמִּצְרַיִם כְּתוֹעֲפֹת רְאֵם לוֹ
יֹאכַל גּוֹיִם צָרָיו וְעַצְמֹתֵיהֶם יְגָרֵם וְחִצָּיו יִמְחָץ:
ט כָּרַע שָׁכַב כַּאֲרִי וּכְלָבִיא מִי יְקִימֶנּוּ מְבָרְכֶיךָ בָּרוּךְ

י וְאֹרְרֶיךָ אָרוּר: וַיִּחַר־אַף בָּלָק אֶל־בִּלְעָם וַיִּסְפֹּק
אֶת־כַּפָּיו וַיֹּאמֶר בָּלָק אֶל־בִּלְעָם לָקֹב אֹיְבַי
יא קְרָאתִיךָ וְהִנֵּה בֵּרַכְתָּ בָרֵךְ זֶה שָׁלֹשׁ פְּעָמִים: וְעַתָּה
בְּרַח־לְךָ אֶל־מְקוֹמֶךָ אָמַרְתִּי כַּבֵּד אֲכַבֶּדְךָ וְהִנֵּה
יב מְנָעֲךָ יְהוָה מִכָּבוֹד: וַיֹּאמֶר בִּלְעָם אֶל־בָּלָק הֲלֹא
גַּם אֶל־מַלְאָכֶיךָ אֲשֶׁר־שָׁלַחְתָּ אֵלַי דִּבַּרְתִּי לֵאמֹר:
יג אִם־יִתֶּן־לִי בָלָק מְלֹא בֵיתוֹ כֶּסֶף וְזָהָב לֹא אוּכַל
לַעֲבֹר אֶת־פִּי יְהוָה לַעֲשׂוֹת טוֹבָה אוֹ רָעָה מִלִּבִּי
יד אֲשֶׁר־יְדַבֵּר יְהוָה אֹתוֹ אֲדַבֵּר: וְעַתָּה הִנְנִי הוֹלֵךְ

he said: / Word of Balaam son of Beor, / Word of the man whose eye is true, / **4]** Word of him who hears God's speech, / Who beholds visions from the Almighty, / Prostrate, but with eyes unveiled: / **5]** How fair are your tents, O Jacob, / Your dwellings, O Israel! / **6]** Like palm groves that stretch out, / Like gardens beside a river, / Like aloes planted by the LORD, / Like cedars beside the water; / **7]** Their boughs drip with moisture, / Their roots have abundant water. / Their king shall rise above Agag, / Their kingdom shall be exalted. / **8]** God who freed them from Egypt / Is for them like the horns of the wild ox. / They shall devour enemy nations, / Crush their bones, / And smash their arrows. / **9]** They crouch, they lie down like a lion, / Like the king of beasts; who dare rouse them? / Blessed are they who bless you, / Accursed they who curse you!

10] Enraged at Balaam, Balak struck his hands together. "I called you," Balak said to Balaam, "to damn my enemies, and instead you have blessed them these three times! **11]** Back with you at once to your own place! I was going to reward you richly, but the LORD has denied you the reward." **12]** Balaam replied to Balak, "But I even told the messengers you sent to me, **13]** 'Though Balak were to give me his house full of silver and gold, I could not of my own accord do anything good or bad contrary to the LORD's command. What the LORD says, that I must say.' **14]** And now, as I go back to my people, let me inform you of

---

3] *Whose eye is true.* Or, "whose eye is closed," but who can see truly when God reveals the truth to him [17].

4] *Almighty.* שַׁדַּי (*Shaddai*), a term of uncertain meaning. See at Gen. 17:1.

Prostrate. Moffat translates: "Sleeping but awake in soul."

Some say that the description bears marked resemblance to an epileptic convulsion.

5] *How fair.* Others, "how goodly," "how lovely" [18]. The physical image of Israel is the reflection of its spiritual being. The phrase has been incorporated into Jewish liturgy and is recited on entering the synagogue [19].

6] *Aloes.* The African variety yielded drugs or potions; the Indian, perfume.

Like cedars beside the water. This is poetic license, for cedars grow on heights. The repetition in these verses of references to water and moisture underlines their preciousness in the Near East. In Arab parlance, "the prosperous are a well-watered meadow and their life is a moistened one" [20].

7] *Their roots.* Literally, "seeds." Israel's posterity will have strength and victory.

Agag. Either a general name for Amalekite kings (like "Pharaoh" for Egyptian rulers), or a later insertion referring to Saul's capture of Agag (I Sam. 15:8, 32, 33).

9] *Blessed are they . . . curse you!* The same thought as in Gen. 12:3 and 27:29.

לְעַמִּי לְכָה אִיעָצְךָ אֲשֶׁר יַעֲשֶׂה הָעָם הַזֶּה לְעַמְּךָ ׃ וְקַרְקַר כָּל־בְּנֵי־שֵׁת ׃ וְהָיָה אֱדוֹם יְרֵשָׁה וְהָיָה יְרֵשָׁה יד

בְּאַחֲרִית הַיָּמִים ׃ וַיִּשָּׂא מְשָׁלוֹ וַיֹּאמַר נְאֻם בִּלְעָם שֵׂעִיר אֹיְבָיו וְיִשְׂרָאֵל עֹשֶׂה חָיִל ׃ וְיֵרְדְּ מִיַּעֲקֹב טו

בְּנוֹ בְעֹר וּנְאֻם הַגֶּבֶר שְׁתֻם הָעָיִן ׃ נְאֻם שֹׁמֵעַ אִמְרֵי וְהֶאֱבִיד שָׂרִיד מֵעִיר ׃ וַיַּרְא אֶת־עֲמָלֵק וַיִּשָּׂא מְשָׁלוֹ טז

אֵל וְיֹדֵעַ דַּעַת עֶלְיוֹן מַחֲזֵה שַׁדַּי יֶחֱזֶה נֹפֵל וּגְלוּי וַיֹּאמַר רֵאשִׁית גּוֹיִם עֲמָלֵק וְאַחֲרִיתוֹ עֲדֵי אֹבֵד ׃

עֵינָיִם ׃ אֶרְאֶנּוּ וְלֹא עַתָּה אֲשׁוּרֶנּוּ וְלֹא קָרוֹב דָּרַךְ וַיַּרְא אֶת־הַקֵּינִי וַיִּשָּׂא מְשָׁלוֹ וַיֹּאמַר אֵיתָן מוֹשָׁבֶךָ יז

כּוֹכָב מִיַּעֲקֹב וְקָם שֵׁבֶט מִיִּשְׂרָאֵל וּמָחַץ פַּאֲתֵי מוֹאָב וְשִׂים בַּסֶּלַע קִנֶּךָ ׃ כִּי אִם־יִהְיֶה לְבָעֵר קָיִן עַד־מָה

* יח פלרע

what this people will do to your people in days to come." **15]** He took up his theme, and said: / Word of Balaam son of Beor, / Word of the man whose eye is true, / **16]** Word of him who hears God's speech, / Who obtains knowledge from the Most High, / And beholds visions from the Almighty, / Prostrate, but with eyes unveiled: / **17]** What I see for them is not yet, / What I behold will not be soon: / A star rises from Jacob, / A meteor comes forth from Israel; / It smashes the brow of Moab, / The foundation of all children of Seth. / **18]** Edom becomes a possession, / Yea, Seir a possession of its enemies; / But Israel is triumphant. / **19]** A victor issues from Jacob / To wipe out what is left of Ir. / **20]** He saw Amalek and, taking up his theme, he said: / A leading nation is Amalek; / But its fate is to perish forever. / **21]** He saw the Kenites and, taking up his theme, he said: / Though your abode be secure, / And your nest be set among cliffs, / **22]** Yet shall Kain be consumed, / When Asshur takes you captive. /

17] *A star rises from Jacob.* Various interpretations have taken this to be a prophetic reference to David [21]; to the Messiah to come [22]; to Bar Kochba, the leader of the anti-Roman revolt that took place between 132 and 135 C.E. [23]; and to Jesus [24]. The verse also played a role among the Dead Sea sects [25]. Gaster reads the oracle as an astrological forecast (see Gleanings). The best interpretation is suggested by Gevirtz: *Kochav* here does not mean "star" but "host" or "army" (compare the cognate Arabic *kaukabun*, "multitude"), and the parallel *shevet* would then be used in the ordinary sense of "tribe." Hence the couplet reads: "A host rises from Jacob, / A tribe comes forth from Israel" [26].

Meteor. שֵׁבֶט (*shevet*). In view of the preceding, "tribe" is a better rendering.

Children of Seth. Meaning "children of men." Seth was Adam's third son (Gen. 4:25), from whom all men were believed to have descended (Noah was of his line). The oracle sees Israel defeating all enemies, however many and however strong.

In a similar phrase in Jer. 48:45, שֵׁת (*shet*) is supplanted by שָׁאוֹן (*shaon*); therefore Ehrlich suggests that the oracle of Balaam should read "children of Shaon," meaning all those bent on war [27].

18] *Seir.* A name for Edom (Gen. 14:6; Judg. 5:4).

21] *Your nest.* קִנֶּךָ (*kinecha*), a word play on קֵנִי (*keni*) and קַיִן (*kayin*) [28].

22] *Kain.* The name of Adam's first-born, קַיִן (Cain), but here used as a parallel to Seth and standing for the Kenite people who were traditional friends of Israel (Moses' father-in-law was from that tribe). This prophecy is, therefore, not inimical in nature but rather sadly contemplative: Alas, Asshur (Assyria) will destroy our friends.

כג אַשּׁוּר תִּשְׁבֶּךָ: וַיִּשָּׂא מְשָׁלוֹ וַיֹּאמַר אוֹי מִי יִחְיֶה מִשֻּׂמוֹ כה עֲדֵי אֹבֵד: וַיָּקָם בִּלְעָם וַיֵּלֶךְ וַיָּשָׁב לִמְקֹמוֹ וְגַם־בָּלָק

כד אֵל: וְצִים מִיַּד כִּתִּים וְעִנּוּ אַשּׁוּר וְעִנּוּ־עֵבֶר וְגַם־הוּא הָלַךְ לְדַרְכּוֹ: פ

23] He took up his theme and said: / Alas, who can survive except God has willed it! /
24] Ships come from the quarter of Kittim; / They subject Asshur, subject Eber. / They, too, shall perish forever.
25] Then Balaam set out on his journey back home; and Balak also went his way.

24] *Kittim . . . Asshur . . . Eber.* Kittim elsewhere stands for the western maritime nations [29], but here more likely a foreign power from far away that will subdue the eastern peoples: the Assyrians and those "beyond" the Euphrates [30].

The Septuagint translates עֵבֶר (*ever*) as "Hebrews," which has biblical precedent but is not likely in this context.

Curses

Among ancient and primitive peoples, a curse was more than an expressed wish for evil, it was also considered a method of translating such harmful efforts into reality. Curses were usually (though not always) pronounced in the name of a god or demon or other-worldly being, and the potency of the imprecation lay precisely in the fact that it aroused against a person those forces which were normally beyond human control or resistance and which could be countered only by more powerful beings of the same order [31].

The belief in the power of the curse was current among the Babylonians, who relied on professional sorcerers to curse their enemies before a battle; it was also current among the Israelites. The Bible reports several cases. When children mocked the prophet Elisha, he "cursed them in the name of the Lord. And there came forth two she-bears out of the wood and tore forty and two children of them" (II Kings 2:23, 24). The invocation of a curse also played a pivotal role in the ordeal of jealousy, when the words of the curse were rubbed from the scroll into the bitter water, which was then drunk by a woman accused of adultery (Num. 5:11-29). Josephus reports that in the first century B.C.E. Hyrcanus II summoned Onias to curse Aristobulus II and his followers [32]. Similarly, the supporters of Mohammed invited a famous poet to curse their foes before the battle of Bedr [33].

The Torah approaches the act of pronouncing fateful words—both for evil and for good—with great seriousness. When a man like Balaam, to whom the story ascribes powerful spiritual gifts, made ready to invoke a curse, even God viewed his intent with alarm and made sure that pejoratives would be turned into blessings. In a sense, Balaam possessed a portion of God's power (just as the elders had obtained some part of Moses' prophetic capacity[1]) and he could apply it either for the benefit or to the detriment of Israel. The Rabbis, uncomfortable with the magic aspects of cursing, considered an execration to be a form of prayer: the curser asking God with dramatic insistence to respond to his wish. Effect and cause became intermingled in the process; what remained was the conviction that there is great power in the spoken word affecting both speaker and hearer, and especially so when the word issues from a prophet whose linkage to the Divine Presence is alive and real.

The Speaking Ass

Traditional Jewish and Christian interpreters have considered the ass which opened its mouth to rebuke its master as a religious wonder, and its speech a miracle designed to magnify God's name and to demonstrate His special love for Israel. It is God who gives speech and controls it both in man and beast [34]. Maimonides, on the other hand, tried to rationalize the intent of the text, postulating that Balaam experienced the episode as a vision and that it therefore did not really happen [35]. His view gained few adherents, for indeed the text seems clear and not at all concerned with later philosophical doubts about God's impact on nature.[2] Rather, it utilizes its imagery to drive home a point of far greater importance, namely, that a great and proud man was incapable of seeing what a dumb beast could

[1] Num. 11:17. On the question of whether Balaam can be considered a prophet in the biblical sense, see commentary on "Balaam—Prophet or Sorcerer?"

[2] An intermediate view was taken by Luzzatto. According to him, the text does not state outright that the ass made human sounds, but only that it conveyed to Balaam the presence of God in a manner *as if* it had spoken the words which are recorded.

behold and that however exalted a human being—or however close to God—his vision was limited and his sureness frail. The main burden of the story, which is full of irony and subtle humor, is not in fact the *speaking* but the *seeing* ass, contrasted with the prophet who looks and yet is blind. Over against both of them stands their Creator, and in their common creatureliness they are bound to the ultimate purposes of God.

A People Apart

Few prophecies have been borne out as accurately as Balaam's vision of Israel in the passing of time: "A people that dwells apart, not reckoned among the nations."[3] For better or for worse, Balaam's forecast has become an incontrovertible historical fact. In the Western world men are commonly divided into two unlikely portions, Gentiles and Jews—one the overwhelming multitude of men; the other, in comparison, an infinitesimal group. On the face of it, this is a ludicrous division, with no meaningful quantitative basis, yet its qualitative force remains unabated. At its worst, the setting apart of the Jew has meant ghettoization, disenfranchisement, anti-Semitism, and finally the holocaust. At its best, it has signified the attempt to render an entire people holy, its voluntary submission to God and Torah, the development of hundreds of thousands of students and scholars, the pursuit of knowledge as a sacred discipline, and the unabashed proclamation of an apparently impossible goal—to hasten the kingdom of God through human effort.

The concept of "a people apart" is not, however, merely an observable experience in history. Balaam's prophecy and its subsequent development in Jewish thought have raised it to the level of doctrine. Here history and theology have reinforced each other: what life showed to be a fact was believed to have been God's plan from the beginning, and this belief in turn caused Jews (as well as Christians who also believed this, but with different emphasis) to consider apartness as normal, acceptable, and even desirable.

But there have been those Jews, especially in modern times, who have denied the continuing validity of Balaam's vision. They see it as part of the (to them, objectionable) doctrine of the Chosen People, and they consider such teaching contrary to the ideals of an egalitarian society. Others, driven by social pressures, have assimilated themselves to the environment in which they live and have consciously or otherwise minimized their traditional apartness. Not surprisingly, such forces for leveling the division between Jew and Gentile exist in the State of Israel as well. Its citizens want to be reckoned among the nations, they want to be treated as part of and not apart from the community of men. Yet both in Israel and the Diaspora there remains the overwhelming conviction that political nationhood is only a device for security and survival and that the fate of the people of Israel in all their habitations is ultimately tied to the mysteries of a suprahistoric will. For the believers in the reality of the covenant the vision of Balaam has not lost its force; they view apartness as a necessary means of self-realization and of serving the ends of their Divine Master. Hence, as the people of God, they must carry "the burden of singularity" [37].

[3] This is the traditional rendering of Num. 23:9. S. Gevirtz has argued—on the basis of considerable evidence—that the Hebrew text originally conveyed something radically different. According to him, "not reckoned among the nations" should read "among the nations resides secure" [36]. However, our commentary is based on the unamended text; for, whatever Balaam's oracle meant to convey, two thousand years and more of Jewish comment have read the passage as it now appears.

Balaam—Prophet or Sorcerer?

Despite the obviously intimate relationship which the text describes as existing between God and Balaam, traditional Jewish and Christian opinions almost unvaryingly see the man who blessed Israel and foresaw the doom of its enemies as a sorcerer, a man who loved money more than truth and who ended up in hell.[4] The reasons for this pejorative judgment are found not so much in the "Book of Balaam" (Num. 22:2–24:25) as in later passages in Numbers, Deuteronomy, and Joshua, which shed a negative light on him.

Deuteronomy 23:6 says that "God refused to heed Balaam," suggesting that the latter had intended to carry out Balak's wish. Joshua 13:22 calls Balaam a soothsayer or sorcerer (קֹסֵם, kosem) and notes that he was slain by the Israelites in their war with the Midianites. Numbers 31:16 makes Balaam responsible for inducing Israel to go "whoring," an incident reported at the conclusion and failure of his mission to curse. This combination of statements already caused an early translator of the Torah to speak of "Balaam the wicked"[5] [40], and this remains, with few exceptions, the assessment of his character. He is variously called proud, insolent, cunning, hypocritical, false, ungrateful, treacherous, cruel, blasphemous, deceiving, and sanctimonious [41].

There are, however, other voices. Thus, a talmudic passage admits that he was a prophet at first and states that only later did he forsake God and turn magician. This would explain the biblical statement that God put His word in Balaam's mouth, for, says the Talmud, the divine command was to him like a fishhook, that is to say, Balaam attempted to break loose from God [42]. Another rabbinic interpretation goes even further. Commenting on the assessment of Moses by the Torah that "never again did there arise in Israel a prophet like Moses" (Deut. 34:10), a midrash says that, while none did arise in Israel, among the other nations there did, and that was Balaam son of Beor [43].

Still another midrash, coming to the heart of the problem, which is the prophetic status of a pagan, says: God gave prophecy to men like Balaam and Job so that they might turn people toward Him and also that other nations should not have cause to say that God was accessible only to Israel[6] [47]. Ibn Ezra agrees that in any case Balaam's prophecy had the stamp of truth [48], a consideration that renders somewhat academic the question of whether the term נָבִיא (navi, prophet) can be applied to Balaam [49]. The most complimentary view of Balaam is put forth by M. M. Kalisch who describes him as something of a saint: "firm and inexorable . . . solely an instrument of Omnipotence . . . like a mysterious spirit from a higher and nobler world" [50].

There is, finally, the interpretation of Balaam advanced by W. F. Albright, which differs radically from all others. On the basis of his reading of the text (with some vocalizations changed), he comes to the conclusion that "Balaam was really a North-Syrian diviner from the Euphrates Valley, that he

---

[4] The Rabbis interpreted "home" in Num. 24:25 (which says that Balaam went "back home"—in Hebrew literally "to his place") to mean hell, which was "home" to him, "his place" [38].

[5] He also interpreted Balaam's building of seven altars as an attempt to induce Israel to commit idolatry [39].

[6] Similar thoughts have been expressed in connection with the giving of the Torah to Israel: God had offered it first to other nations [44]; the Torah was given in the desert because the desert is accessible to all [45]; and prophecy, like Torah, was available to all [46].

became a convert to Yahwism [Israel's faith], and that he later abandoned Israel and joined the Midianites in fighting against the Yahwists." In this reading, Balaam's oracles are those not of an unwilling adversary but of a convert and so they speak with all the fervor of a man who has discovered a new faith [51].

But even keeping the text as it is, there is another and far simpler explanation of the biblical intent. The three chapters containing the story of Balaam are in fact indifferent to a judgment either of Balaam's character or of his religion. They focus not on him but on the God of Israel who loves and protects His people. They take it for granted that God is heard by anyone to whom He wishes to make Himself known; a religious parochialism that would question the authenticity of such a communication is foreign to the tradition that produced this story. In fact, the very power of Israel's Lord lies in His capacity to reach beyond Israel; the fates of Moab and Assyria rest in His hand as surely as the fate of His chosen people. His servants may be Jethro and Balaam as well as Moses and Aaron. The text, then, is less the tale of a pagan, be he prophet or sorcerer, than a paean of God and His affection for the Children of Israel.[7]

---

[7] G. B. Gray makes this point strongly: "It is hardly overstating the case to say that Balaam is an accident and is not of the essence of the story" [52].

GLEANINGS

The Tongue

Why did Balak compare Israel to an ox licking the grass (Num. 22:4)? Because the ox uses his tongue to conquer, and so does Israel, a people who conquer with the power of the tongue and the word. As Israel relies on words of prayer and blessing, so Balak wanted Balaam to counteract his foes with words of curses.   MIDRASH [53]

Freedom

At first Balaam was told not to go, but when he insisted he was given permission by God. From this you learn that God lets a man go the way which his heart desires.

TALMUD; MIDRASH [54]

Balaam Insisted

Even though he knew that cursing Israel was against the will of God he insisted on trying and thus risked his own destruction. Thus it is always with Israel's enemies.   M. HACOHEN [55]

The Second Time

With respect to God, "once" means once and for all; and he who, like Balaam, after God's first word, tries to find out whether this rule does really apply also to him will be punished. For if we do not take God's first unequivocal word as being sufficient ("Do not go with them"), then the next time God will without fail speak the words of the demon that is within us ("You may go").   F. ROSENZWEIG [56][8]

Balaam and Abraham

We are told that "when he arose in the morning, Balaam saddled his ass" (verse 21). A similar expression is used by Abraham when he prepared to sacrifice his son Isaac. But there is a difference. Abraham tried to do God's will, yet God did not permit the full execution of his intent. Since Balaam tried to oppose God's will, how much less likely that God would permit him and his like to succeed in their aim to destroy Israel.

CHASIDIC [57]

---

[8] Rosenzweig finds the theme of doing it again, of "resuming," to be pervasive in the Balaam story.

Balaam Saddled the Ass (Num. 22:21)

A man of his status did this himself? It was because he hated Israel and, as the saying goes, "hatred causes a man to forget his dignity."

RASHI

Created before Time

The mouth (i.e., the speech) of Balaam's ass belonged to ten things fashioned at the end of the sixth day of creation, on the borderline of the first Sabbath.   ETHICS OF THE FATHERS [58]

This idea about the time of creation has also been applied to the mouth of the earth that swallowed Korah (Num. 16:32) and the mouth of the well (Num. 21:6).

The Fathers of the Mishnah, who taught that Balaam's ass was created on the eve of the Sabbath, in the twilight, were not fantastic fools, but subtle philosophers, discovering the reign of universal law through the exceptions, the miracles that had to be created specially and were still a part of the order of the world, bound to appear in due time much as apparently erratic comets are.

I. ZANGWILL [59]

Parallels

The belief that animals can descry spirits is virtually universal. In the *Odyssey*, when the goddess Athene appears to Odysseus, the dogs of the swineherd Eumaios perceive her presence, though the hero's son Telemachos does not. On the race course at Olympia, says Pausanias, there was an altar at which the horses regularly shied, because they saw the ghost of a hero who was buried nearby. Certain dogs, declares Pliny, had the faculty of seeing fauns invisible to men.

T. H. GASTER [60]

Why Animals Don't Speak

The wisdom of animals often puts man to shame; but gifted with speech they would become unfit to serve. Hence God arranged for them to be mute.   MIDRASH [61]

The Ass Died

As soon as it had finished speaking the ass died so that people should not say, "This is the animal which spoke," and make it an object of reverence.   MIDRASH [62]

A Laughing Stock

Balaam wants to correct God's plan for the world and is blinder than his own beast; he wants to overcome God's resistance but must yield to his animal; he wants to spoil a whole people with his word and his anger is helpless before the ass; he wants to prance before the great and becomes a laughing stock before his servants.

S. R. HIRSCH

To Bless and Curse

Balaam did not have it in his power either to bless or to curse. The blessing was redundant— God had already blessed—and the curse ineffective. Why then did God prevent him from cursing? Because he foresaw Israel's future sins and punishments. He did not want the nations to say: "It was Balaam's curse which caused it."

YALKUT ME'AM LO'EZ [63]

To This Day

Trust in and fear of curses have not been confined to ancient or even medieval times. To this day we speak of a thing or a person as cursed, that is, as permanently delivered over to ill fortune; burning a person in effigy is an expression of this popular and persistent belief.

Come, Curse Me Jacob (Num. 23:7)

The expression starts by saying "come, curse me...." Balak unwittingly invites Balaam to curse him. This teaches that he who curses, curses himself.   MIDRASH [64]

Not Like the Nations

The secret of Israel's survival is that it has gone its own way, regardless of what other nations might think or say in praise or scorn.

CHASIDIC [65]

A People That Dwells Apart (Num. 23:9)

Israel will live in a physically definable land as עַם (am), a people, a social community. Its greatness will not be as גּוֹי (goy), nation, a political body seeking power amongst other nations.

S. R. HIRSCH

How to Die

Balaam's wish to "*die* the death of the upright" (Num. 23:10) was a mistaken wish. Rather, he should have aspired to *live* like the righteous.

CHASIDIC [66]

No Harm Is in Sight for Jacob (Num. 23:21)

This could also be rendered: "He [God] sees no iniquity in Jacob." There are times when God shuts His eyes to Israel's sins and considers its merits instead.

MIDRASH [67]

Basing himself on this interpretation the Berditchever Rebbe said: "A Jew who imitates God will search out the good in Israel." And R. Aaron of Karlin said: "I wish I could love the righteous as much as a truly righteous man can love the sinners of our people" [68].

The use of this verse in the traditional New Year's liturgy [69], the prominent use in the prayer book of Num. 24:5 ("How fair are your tents..."), and the frequent approbations which Balaam's sayings received in Jewish tradition are based on the maxim: "Receive the truth from whoever speaks it."

B. H. EPSTEIN [70]

The Will of God

The hidden inner side of all these strange happenings is now brought out into the open. A prophetic word lays bare the will of God which is hidden from human eyes, the will that is continuously at work in and behind those projects that men may devise for themselves. The blessing of God sets limits to the effect of the darkest and bitterest curses.

G. VON RAD [71]

Alone

The Jew will be what he was. For his anchorpoint is the awesome, hidden Other One who Himself dwells alone. Aloneness is the existential burden of the Jew. He is, as tradition and meaning convey, *kadosh*, holy and separate at once.

Separateness is the yoke of the Jew. It demands a heavy price; it demands it of all and of each. It tears the soul with longing for the embracing friendship of the nations, and it drives us back to the lonely post of waiting. It aims its beam into the heart of every Jew, searing some and illuminating others. Our psyche is burned by desire and rejection, by forgetting and remembering, by openness and withdrawal.

W. G. PLAUT [72]

Tribe by Tribe (Num. 24:2)

Balaam noticed the peculiar arrangement of Israel's tents: the doors were so placed that no one would disturb his neighbor's privacy.

TALMUD [73]

The arrangement by families showed the inner strength of the people.

S. R. HIRSCH

Balaam's Vision

The Rabbis say that Balaam was blind in one eye.[9] How so? Each man has two eyes: with one he sees the greatness of God, with the other his own smallness. Balaam had an eye to see the former but was blind to the latter.

CHASIDIC [75]

Prostrate

It says that Balaam prophesied while lying prostrate (Num. 24:5). True prophecy is indeed impossible unless a man humbles himself.

CHASIDIC [76]

What Balaam Saw

What did Balaam see that caused him to say: "How fair are your tents, O Jacob...."? He saw their schools.

TARGUM JONATHAN [77]

Note that it says מַה טֹבוּ (*mah tovu*), literally, "how good." He saw moral, not esthetic, beauty.

MALBIM [78]

Instead of reading "your tents" (*mishkenotecha*), you might read "your forfeits" (*mashkenotecha*), for tent and temple were to be forfeited by Israel when they sinned.

MIDRASH [79]

---

[9] Based on the fact that Num. 24:3 says "eye" rather than "eyes" [74].

Astrology

Balaam's references to star and meteor arose out of his predilection for astrology.[10] At the core lay the ancient notion that everything on earth had its counterpart in heaven. In accordance with this idea the Mesopotamians developed an elaborate celestial geography. The north, or right side of the sky, was characterized as Subartu or Gutium; the south, or left side, as Akkad; the west, or upper reaches, as Amurru or Syria; the east, or lower reaches, as Elam. Accordingly, a phenomenon appearing in any one of these quarters betokened the fate or fortune of the corresponding quarter on earth. What Balaam means, then, is that a comet, wandering star, or even meteor has appeared in the quarter of the heavens representing Israel and is heading toward the outskirts of that which answers to Moab, where it will eventually "strike."

T. H. GASTER [80]

Mark of the Prophet

The prophet does not mediate between God and man, he does not receive revelation in order to pass it on; rather . . . God speaks as "I" directly from within him. . . . He no sooner opens his mouth than God already speaks. Hardly has he uttered his "Thus saith the Lord," or the even briefer, even more hurried "Oracle of the Lord"— which even dispenses with the verbal form— before God has already taken possession of his lips.

F. ROSENZWEIG [81]

Balaam in Moslem Tradition

While Balaam is not mentioned by name in the Koran, a passage in Sura VII is often interpreted to refer to him. There, and in later Moslem tradition, he is depicted as an evil-doer incarnate, and various folktales were told about him. Here, too, the influence of the Midrash can be clearly discerned [82].

[10] This comment is based on rendering שֵׁבֶט as "meteor," see at Num. 24:17.

PART IV

At the Gates of the Promised Land

Following the interlude of the Balaam story, the Torah takes up the tale of Israel's preparations for the eventual occupation of the Promised Land. After the battles reported in chapter 21, the people encamp at Shittim, east of the Jordan, opposite Jericho.

As so frequently in the Book of Numbers, the Torah ties legal and ritual prescriptions to various incidents: the permanent right of the family of Phinehas to the priesthood rewards his severity against immoral behavior; the laws of female inheritance are presented in connection with the specific case of the daughters of Zelophehad; a military engagement with the Midianites leads the text to state general laws on warfare; and, finally, a review of the wanderings is the occasion for delineating the borders of the Promised Land and providing for the establishment of cities of refuge.

In all likelihood Numbers once ended with the story of the death of Moses. But when Deuteronomy was later on added to the Tetrateuch and made the fifth and concluding book in the Torah, the tale of Moses' last days was transferred to the concluding portion of Deuteronomy, where it is found today.

Punishment and Reward

At Shittim, their last way station, the Israelites become involved with women from Moab and follow them in immoral and idolatrous practices. According to a later reference (Num. 31:16), this was a plot suggested by Balaam, even though neither the "Book of Balaam" nor the incident itself suggests this connection. What his intended curses were meant to accomplish came to pass through leading the people into sin.

The drastic punishment that ensues is highlighted by a dramatic act of indignation: Phinehas, Aaron's grandson and the son of the incumbent High Priest, Eleazar, executes an Israelite who publicly flouts the moral code with a Midianite woman. For this act Phinehas and his descendants are awarded the hereditary and permanent priesthood in Israel. The very distinction here conferred for what at first appears to be but another example meant to strengthen the bases of Israel's moral behavior suggests that this was considered an event of crucial significance. "It was counted to him for righteousness unto all generations forever" (Ps. 106:31) [1].

Bible critics generally distinguish between two parts of the story: one relating the incident with the Moab women (verses 1–5; J/E-source), the other telling of the public act of immorality with a Midianite rather than a Moabite partner (verses 6–18; P-source). Whatever the nature of the composition, it is important to realize that the story itself has numerous parallels in antiquity in which a person who has shown exemplary devotion to a king is rewarded with a royal grant in perpetuity. It is probable

1191

that the Egyptian origin of Phinehas's name (see at verse 7) is a reflection of the existence of similar tales outside of Israel [2].

The announcement of God's reward in verse 10 begins a new weekly portion, *Pinchas* (of which Phinehas is the traditional English equivalent).

שְׁפְטֵי יִשְׂרָאֵל הִרְגוּ אִישׁ אֲנָשָׁיו הַנִּצְמָדִים לְבַעַל א וַיֵּשֶׁב יִשְׂרָאֵל בַּשִּׁטִּים וַיָּחֶל הָעָם לִזְנוֹת אֶל־בְּנוֹת
פְּעוֹר: י וְהִנֵּה אִישׁ מִבְּנֵי יִשְׂרָאֵל בָּא וַיַּקְרֵב אֶל־אֶחָיו ב מוֹאָב: וַתִּקְרֶאןָ לָעָם לְזִבְחֵי אֱלֹהֵיהֶן וַיֹּאכַל הָעָם
אֶת־הַמִּדְיָנִית לְעֵינֵי מֹשֶׁה וּלְעֵינֵי כָּל־עֲדַת בְּנֵי ג וַיִּשְׁתַּחֲווּ לֵאלֹהֵיהֶן: וַיִּצָּמֶד יִשְׂרָאֵל לְבַעַל פְּעוֹר
יִשְׂרָאֵל וְהֵמָּה בֹכִים פֶּתַח אֹהֶל מוֹעֵד: וַיַּרְא פִּינְחָס ד וַיִּחַר־אַף־יְהוָה בְּיִשְׂרָאֵל: וַיֹּאמֶר יְהוָה אֶל־מֹשֶׁה קַח
בֶּן־אֶלְעָזָר בֶּן־אַהֲרֹן הַכֹּהֵן וַיָּקָם מִתּוֹךְ הָעֵדָה וַיִּקַּח אֶת־כָּל־רָאשֵׁי הָעָם וְהוֹקַע אוֹתָם לַיהוָה נֶגֶד הַשָּׁמֶשׁ
ח רֹמַח בְּיָדוֹ: וַיָּבֹא אַחַר אִישׁ־יִשְׂרָאֵל אֶל־הַקֻּבָּה ה וְיָשֹׁב חֲרוֹן אַף־יְהוָה מִיִּשְׂרָאֵל: וַיֹּאמֶר מֹשֶׁה אֶל־

1] While Israel was staying at Shittim, the people profaned themselves by whoring with the Moabite women, 2] who invited the people to the sacrifices for their god. The people partook of them and worshiped that god. 3] Thus Israel attached itself to Baal-peor, and the LORD was incensed with Israel. 4] The LORD said to Moses, "Take all the ringleaders and have them publicly impaled before the LORD, so that the LORD's wrath may turn away from Israel." 5] So Moses said to Israel's officials, "Each of you slay those of his men who attached themselves to Baal-peor."

6] Just then one of the Israelites came and brought a Midianite woman over to his companions, in the sight of Moses and of the whole Israelite community who were weeping at the entrance of the Tent of Meeting. 7] When Phinehas, son of Eleazar son of Aaron the priest, saw this, he left the assembly and, taking a spear in his hand, 8] he followed the Israelite into the chamber and stabbed both of them, the Israelite and the woman, through the

25:1] *Shittim.* "Acacias," also referred to as Abel-shittim ("mourning at the acacias," Num. 33:49), northeast of the Dead Sea [3].

Josephus speaks of palm forests at a site called Abila in his day [4].

Profaned. Others, "began." Both meanings are possible. A similar doubt exists with regard to הוּחַל in Gen. 4:26.

3] *Attached itself.* וַיִּצָּמֶד (vayitzamed) is related to צֶמֶד (tzemed, pair).

The basic meaning of the root *tzmd* in Semitic languages is "(to/the) yoke." The image evoked here is that of the whole people binding itself voluntarily to Baal-peor like two oxen in a team.

Baal-peor. The local deity; the national Moabite god was Chemosh (21:29). The worship was apparently licentious [5].

4] *Publicly.* Literally, "in the face of the sun," that is, in the sight of everyone.

Impaled. Others, "hanged" [6]. According to Rashi, the offender was hanged only after he had

been killed by stoning (which was the general punishment for idolatry) [7]. New English Bible understands: "hurl them down to their death" [8].

6] *One of the Israelites.* His name and that of his companion are given in verse 14. Apparently his act was one of particularly brazen defiance.

Weeping. Either because of the executions or the plague noted later.

7] *Phinehas.* A name of Egyptian origin, like that of Moses. Its meaning was "the Nubian" or "the Negro." He was later a leader in the war against the Midianites and an important figure after the tribes crossed into Canaan under Joshua. A hillside in Ephraim was named after him—or perhaps some of the tales about Phinehas were told to explain how Givat Pinchas got its name (Josh. 24:33).

8] *Into the chamber . . . through the belly.* The Hebrew word play would be better rendered "into the private chamber . . . through the private parts" [9].

יד תַּחַת אֲשֶׁר קִנֵּא לֵאלֹהָיו וַיְכַפֵּר עַל־בְּנֵי יִשְׂרָאֵל: וְשֵׁם
אִישׁ יִשְׂרָאֵל הַמֻּכֶּה אֲשֶׁר הֻכָּה אֶת־הַמִּדְיָנִית זִמְרִי
טו בֶּן־סָלוּא נְשִׂיא בֵית־אָב לַשִּׁמְעֹנִי: וְשֵׁם הָאִשָּׁה הַמֻּכָּה
הַמִּדְיָנִית כָּזְבִּי בַת־צוּר רֹאשׁ אֻמּוֹת בֵּית־אָב
בְּמִדְיָן הוּא: פ
טז וַיְדַבֵּר יְהוָה אֶל־מֹשֶׁה לֵּאמֹר: צָרוֹר אֶת־הַמִּדְיָנִים
יז וְהִכִּיתֶם אוֹתָם: כִּי צֹרְרִים הֵם לָכֶם בְּנִכְלֵיהֶם אֲשֶׁר־
נִכְּלוּ לָכֶם עַל־דְּבַר־פְּעוֹר וְעַל־דְּבַר כָּזְבִּי בַת־נְשִׂיא
מִדְיָן אֲחֹתָם הַמֻּכָּה בְיוֹם־הַמַּגֵּפָה עַל־דְּבַר־פְּעוֹר:

וַיִּדְקֹר אֶת־שְׁנֵיהֶם אֵת אִישׁ יִשְׂרָאֵל וְאֶת־הָאִשָּׁה אֶל־
ט קֳבָתָהּ וַתֵּעָצַר הַמַּגֵּפָה מֵעַל בְּנֵי יִשְׂרָאֵל: וַיִּהְיוּ
הַמֵּתִים בַּמַּגֵּפָה אַרְבָּעָה וְעֶשְׂרִים אָלֶף:

Haftarah Balak, p. 1272

פ פ פ

יא וַיְדַבֵּר יְהוָה אֶל־מֹשֶׁה לֵּאמֹר: פִּינְחָס בֶּן־אֶלְעָזָר
בֶּן־אַהֲרֹן הַכֹּהֵן הֵשִׁיב אֶת־חֲמָתִי מֵעַל בְּנֵי־יִשְׂרָאֵל
בְּקַנְאוֹ אֶת־קִנְאָתִי בְּתוֹכָם וְלֹא־כִלִּיתִי אֶת־בְּנֵי־
יב יִשְׂרָאֵל בְּקִנְאָתִי: לָכֵן אֱמֹר הִנְנִי נֹתֵן לוֹ אֶת־בְּרִיתִי
יג שָׁלוֹם: וְהָיְתָה לּוֹ וּלְזַרְעוֹ אַחֲרָיו בְּרִית כְּהֻנַּת עוֹלָם

belly. Then the plague against the Israelites was checked.   9] Those who died of the plague numbered twenty-four thousand.

10] The LORD spoke to Moses, saying,   11] "Phinehas, son of Eleazar son of Aaron the priest, has turned back My wrath from the Israelites by displaying among them his passion for Me, so that I did not wipe out the Israelite people in My passion.   12] Say, therefore, 'I grant him My pact of friendship.   13] It shall be for him and his descendants after him a pact of priesthood for all time, because he took impassioned action for his God, thus making expiation for the Israelites.'"

14] The name of the Israelite who was killed, the one who was killed with the Midianite woman, was Zimri son of Salu, chieftain of a Simeonite ancestral house.   15] The name of the Midianite woman who was killed was Cozbi daughter of Zur; he was the tribal head of an ancestral house in Midian.

16] The LORD spoke to Moses, saying,   17] "Assail the Midianites and defeat them—
18] for they assailed you by the trickery they practiced against you—because of the affair of Peor and because of the affair of their kinswoman Cozbi, daughter of the Midianite chieftain, who was killed at the time of the plague on account of Peor."

9] *Died of the plague.* This verse is the starting point of G. E. Mendenhall's thesis [10]; see commentary.

12] *My pact of friendship.* Meaning "My promise." Others, "My covenant of peace." This is one of many such "covenants of grants" found in the Bible. God bestows such grants out of grace (*chesed*) or, as here, in return for meritorious deeds. By contrast, a conditional grant requires reciprocal performance and can be abrogated for failure to comply. These covenants have parallels in ancient Near East literature [11].

Some suggest that the text ought to read שִׁלּוּם (*shilum*, reward) instead of שָׁלוֹם (*shalom*). The translation would then read: "I will grant to Phinehas the covenant of priesthood as reward."

15] *Cozbi.* "Voluptuous," here in a sexual sense.

17] *Assail the Midianites.* They were close allies of the Moabites. According to the tradition transmitted here and amplified by Num. 31, Balaam counselled that the only way to overcome the Israelites was to incite them "by trickery" to immorality and idolatry [12].

The Moral and Historical Problem

The Torah states that the crown of God's favor was bestowed on Phinehas, and that because he had shown himself zealous his descendants would inherit the priesthood forever. This presents the reader with the serious moral question of how such a priceless reward could be given for an act of killing.

By postbiblical and especially contemporary standards the deed and its rewards appear to have an unwarranted relationship. But the story is biblical and must be appreciated in its own context. To begin with, Phinehas is rewarded not so much for slaying the transgressors as for saving his people from God's destructive wrath.[1] But, even if we assume that the text concentrates on the former merit, we must remember that the Moabite fertility cult was to the Israelites the incarnation of evil and the mortal enemy of their religion. At a crucial moment in its formative history, Israel's very purpose and existence were challenged. The strict moral code of a new nation was put to its first public test.

According to Mendenhall, it is likely that the plague (mentioned in verse 9 as an apparent consequence of Israel's immorality) was in fact the context in which the original incident took place [14]. An epidemic of serious proportions ravaged large portions of the ancient Near East at that time, possibly it was the bubonic plague. The Israelites were suddenly infected with the disease through their contact with the Moabites or Midianites. Zimri boldly followed a pagan precedent for dealing with such a mysterious affliction; and by his public act he urged his fellow Israelites to engage in prostitution rites as a means of warding off the plague. The result was that the disease spread more rapidly.

Phinehas did not act out of superior medical knowledge. He saw in Zimri's act an open breach of the covenant, a flagrant return to the practices that the compact at Sinai had forsworn. There was no precedent in the brief history of the people to determine how to deal with such a religious and moral emergency. Mendenhall makes it appear plausible that this was the first incident in which God's power over life and death (in a juridical sense) passed to the people. Phinehas's impulsive deed was not merely a kind of battlefield execution but reflected his apprehension that the demands of God needed human realization and required a memorable and dramatic example against permissiveness in the religious realm. The Torah, by obviously approving strongly, implies that this was the proper way to halt further religious disintegration and to repair the breach of the covenant.[2]

---

[1] A remote parallel may be found in the Babylonian Irra-Epic, composed about 1100 B.C.E. It tells how Irra, the pestilence deity, was angered by mankind and unleashed destruction against Babylonia until appeased [13].

[2] While this approval limited ancient commentators in their attitude toward Phinehas, they could express themselves more freely with regard to a similar incident, the killing of an Egyptian overseer by Moses (Exod. 2:11–12). In that instance, the Bible records no judgment, neither in approval nor disapproval, but one tradition speculates that this killing was the real reason Moses was denied entrance into the Holy Land. Opposing this, another opinion holds that the reason for Moses' grave remaining unknown is that he had left it to Phinehas to restore Israel's purity and had not himself acted quickly [15]. The latter opinion conforms more to the realities of the historical background: it was precisely the demonstrative display of ethical supremacy that distinguished Phinehas, even as it had distinguished a younger Moses in Egypt.

The Priesthood

(For a full discussion of the priesthood in Israel, see commentary on Lev. 21 and 22.)

In the earliest days the Patriarchs offered sacrifices on altars they had built themselves (Gen. 8:20; 12:8; 22:9; 26:25; 35:7). Kings, too, though not belonging to the priestly class, brought offerings (e.g., David in I Sam. 24:25 and Solomon in I Kings 3:15), and this privilege (or duty) may have devolved on every head of a family. In the course of time, however, the Levites—and among them a particular clan, the Zadokites of the family of Aaron—absorbed the priestly functions. How this happened, and whether this was an old tradition, is not altogether clear. The three major biblical records dealing with the priesthood speak of "the priests the Levites" (especially in Deuteronomy); "the priests the sons of Aaron" (especially in Leviticus and Numbers); and "the priests the Levites, the sons of Zadok" (in Ezekiel). Scholars generally assume these statements to reflect distinct stages in the evolution of the priesthood.

It appears from Gen. 34 and 49 that in patriarchal days Levi was a secular tribe, but that in time, perhaps because Moses himself was a Levite, special duties of a priestly nature accrued to the tribe. Their leading family, the descendants of Eli, was almost wiped out by the Philistines, at Aphek where Phinehas, too, was killed (I Sam. 4:10 f.), and a while later King Saul caused all the priests of Nob to be massacred, with only Abiathar escaping (I Sam. 22:11–23). He and Zadok were reinstated by David as priests in Jerusalem. Zadok participated actively in the political power struggle and backed Solomon who succeeded to the throne, while Abiathar supported the claims of Adonijah and was subsequently exiled. All the Jerusalem priests from that time on until the Babylonian exile were of the Zadokite clan, and this tradition was reinforced by Ezekiel and, most likely, by the story of Phinehas whose ancestry the Zadokites claimed.

The struggle for priestly hegemony is reflected by Ezekiel (44:4–14), when he castigates non-Zadokite Levites for their idolatrous practices, and by Zechariah (3:1–9), when he recounts the priestly conflict in dramatic language. An echo of the ascent of the Zadokites to preeminence may be heard in the Dead Sea Scrolls which refer to them in especially laudatory terms as "the sons of Zadok, the priests, who keep the covenant and who seek His will" [16].

In sum, if the Phinehas tradition goes back to desert days as the Torah has it, his family did not achieve its due until centuries later. However, it seems more likely that the connection between Phinehas and the everlasting priesthood became an etiological relationship after the Zadokites emerged as the inheritors of the priesthood. It was then that its supporters sought ancient warrants for such an exalted position and traced their genealogy back to a man who had proved his zeal for the Lord of Israel in an earlier time.[3]

---

[3] For this genealogy, see Ezek. 7:1–6; I Chron. 5:35 ff. There are also Torah sections that give the family of Ithamar (Phinehas's uncle) special priestly rights: Lev. 10:6, 12, 16; Num. 3:1–4.

GLEANINGS

Wait

Why does the first part of the story (verses 1–9) belong to one weekly portion and the last part (verses 10–15) to another? To teach us that in matters of divine zeal one should not expect immediate rewards.　　　　M. HACOHEN [17]

Rewards

Because Phinehas had taken the spear with his arm, prayed with his mouth, and struck the sinners in their innards, the Torah (Deut. 18:3) provides that the priests receive the sacrificial gifts of shoulder, cheekbone, and maw.

TARGUM JONATHAN [18]

The parts given to the priests were *zeroa* (the right shoulder), the *lechayayim* (the cheeks), and the *kevah* (the maw of any domesticated animal). According to Aristophanes [19], the maw was considered a great delicacy.

Legality

Phinehas acted meritoriously only because he punished the transgression in flagranto, in the act. Had he done it afterwards it would have been murder.　　　　S. R. HIRSCH [20]

Heroism

The real merit of Phinehas lay in his willingness to expose and deal with immorality though it was perpetrated by two prominent persons like Zimri and Cozbi [21].

A Legend

Phinehas did not really die but reemerged in a miraculous transformation like the prophet Elijah, who also slew idolators (I Kings 18).

MIDRASH [22]

The legend is derived from the fact that שָׁלוֹם (peace) is written with a small ו, which suggested the reading שָׁלֵם (whole): Phinehas passed "whole" into heaven. Note that the story of Elijah is read as the Haftarah (the prophetic portion added to the weekly Torah reading) on the Sabbath when the story of Phinehas is the assigned Torah selection.

Reputation

Why does the Torah note that Zimri was head of a clan (verse 14)? To teach that when a man tarnishes his reputation his whole family is affected.　　　　MIDRASH [23]

Peace

As a reward Phinehas received God's *berit shalom*, literally, His covenant of peace. Great was this gift for the world is maintained by peace, and the Torah is peace itself, as it is said: "All her paths are peace" (Prov. 3:17).　　　MIDRASH [24]

Responsibility

The offending ringleaders who were punished (verse 4) were in fact chief officials [25]. Though they themselves did not sin, they allowed the immorality to go unchecked, hence they too bore the consequences.　　　　MIDRASH [26]

Another interpretation: Phinehas's merit lay in

his willingness to assume responsibility when Moses, Aaron, and the seventy elders were slow to act. CHASIDIC [27]

Self-Defense

The command "Assail the Midianites..." (verse 17) was a proof-text for the right to self-defense. Thus the maxim: "If a man comes to kill you, kill him first." MIDRASH [28]

Incense and Prayer

Phinehas, like Aaron, stayed a plague (Num. 25:10). But, while of Phinehas it says (Ps. 106:30–31) that it was accounted to him for righteousness ever after, Aaron received no such praise. Why? Because Aaron used incense to implore God, and Phinehas used prayer.

Incense was a ritual, bound to an institution; prayer is available to all, and forever. CHASIDIC [29]

Of Census and Women's Inheritance

The second census, coming immediately before the Midianite war and the invasion of the Promised Land, serves to put the people in a state of alert. The statistics differ in significant respects from those recorded in Num. 1, a difference only partially explained by the lapse of time (see commentary). The projected allotment of the land causes the five daughters of Zelophehad to plead equal treatment for themselves and raises the question of inheritance by women. The latter is a prime example of how a law developed for a specific occasion became the foundation for a statement of general law (Num. 35). The law underscores the Torah's intent to keep the allotments within family and tribe, if possible (Num. 27:8–11).

Moses is then bidden to prepare for death and Joshua is appointed his successor.

פ ‏ וַיְהִי אַחֲרֵי הַמַּגֵּפָה: ‏ יט
שְׁלֹשָׁה וְאַרְבָּעִים אֶלֶף וּשְׁבַע מֵאוֹת וּשְׁלֹשִׁים:

א ‏ וַיֹּאמֶר יְהֹוָה אֶל־מֹשֶׁה וְאֶל אֶלְעָזָר בֶּן־אַהֲרֹן הַכֹּהֵן
וּבְנֵי פַלּוּא אֱלִיאָב: וּבְנֵי אֱלִיאָב נְמוּאֵל וְדָתָן ח

ב ‏ לֵאמֹר: שְׂאוּ אֶת־רֹאשׁ כָּל־עֲדַת בְּנֵי־יִשְׂרָאֵל מִבֶּן
וַאֲבִירָם הוּא־דָתָן וַאֲבִירָם קְרוּאֵי הָעֵדָה אֲשֶׁר הִצּוּ

עֶשְׂרִים שָׁנָה וָמַעְלָה לְבֵית אֲבֹתָם כָּל־יֹצֵא צָבָא
עַל־מֹשֶׁה וְעַל־אַהֲרֹן בַּעֲדַת־קֹרַח בְּהַצֹּתָם עַל־יְהֹוָה:

ג ‏ בְּיִשְׂרָאֵל: וַיְדַבֵּר מֹשֶׁה וְאֶלְעָזָר הַכֹּהֵן אֹתָם בְּעַרְבֹת
וַתִּפְתַּח הָאָרֶץ אֶת־פִּיהָ וַתִּבְלַע אֹתָם וְאֶת־קֹרַח בְּמוֹת י

ד ‏ מוֹאָב עַל־יַרְדֵּן יְרֵחוֹ לֵאמֹר: מִבֶּן עֶשְׂרִים שָׁנָה
הָעֵדָה בַּאֲכֹל הָאֵשׁ אֵת חֲמִשִּׁים וּמָאתַיִם אִישׁ וַיִּהְיוּ

וָמָעְלָה כַּאֲשֶׁר צִוָּה יְהֹוָה אֶת־מֹשֶׁה וּבְנֵי יִשְׂרָאֵל
לְנֵס: וּבְנֵי־קֹרַח לֹא־מֵתוּ: ס בְּנֵי שִׁמְעוֹן לְמִשְׁפְּחֹתָם יא־יב

ה ‏ הַיֹּצְאִים מֵאֶרֶץ מִצְרָיִם: רְאוּבֵן בְּכוֹר יִשְׂרָאֵל בְּנֵי
לִנְמוּאֵל מִשְׁפַּחַת הַנְּמוּאֵלִי לְיָמִין מִשְׁפַּחַת הַיָּמִינִי

רְאוּבֵן חֲנוֹךְ מִשְׁפַּחַת הַחֲנֹכִי לְפַלּוּא מִשְׁפַּחַת
לְיָכִין מִשְׁפַּחַת הַיָּכִינִי: לְזֶרַח מִשְׁפַּחַת הַזַּרְחִי לְשָׁאוּל יג

ו ‏ הַפַּלֻּאִי: לְחֶצְרֹן מִשְׁפַּחַת הַחֶצְרוֹנִי לְכַרְמִי מִשְׁפַּחַת
מִשְׁפַּחַת הַשָּׁאוּלִי: אֵלֶּה מִשְׁפְּחֹת הַשִּׁמְעֹנִי שְׁנַיִם יד

ז ‏ הַכַּרְמִי: אֵלֶּה מִשְׁפְּחֹת הָרֻאוּבֵנִי וַיִּהְיוּ פְקֻדֵיהֶם
וְעֶשְׂרִים אֶלֶף וּמָאתָיִם: ס בְּנֵי גָד לְמִשְׁפְּחֹתָם טו

* ס קריאי קרי.

19] When the plague was over,   **1]** the LORD said to Moses and to Eleazar son of Aaron the priest,   **2]** "Take a census of the whole Israelite community from the age of twenty years up, by their ancestral houses, all Israelites able to bear arms."   **3]** So Moses and Eleazar the priest, on the steppes of Moab, at the Jordan near Jericho, gave instructions about them, namely, **4]** those from twenty years up, as the LORD had commanded Moses.

The descendants of the Israelites who came out of the land of Egypt were:

5] Reuben, Israel's first-born. Descendants of Reuben: [Of] Enoch, the clan of the Enochites; of Pallu, the clan of the Palluites;   **6]** of Hezron, the clan of the Hezronites; of Carmi, the clan of the Carmites.   **7]** Those are the clans of the Reubenites. The persons enrolled came to 43,730.

8] Born to Pallu: Eliab.   **9]** The sons of Eliab were Nemuel, and Dathan and Abiram. These are the same Dathan and Abiram, chosen in the assembly, who agitated against Moses and Aaron as part of Korah's band when they agitated against the LORD.   **10]** Whereupon the earth opened its mouth and swallowed them up with Korah—when that band died, when the fire consumed the two hundred and fifty men—and they became an example.   **11]** The sons of Korah, however, did not die.

12] Descendants of Simeon by their clans: Of Nemuel, the clan of the Nemuelites; of Jamin, the clan of the Jaminites; of Jachin, the clan of the Jachinites;   **13]** of Zerah, the clan of the Zerahites; of Saul, the clan of the Saulites.   **14]** Those are the clans of the Simeonites; [persons enrolled:] 22,200.

25:19] *When the plague was over.* The Masorah puts a space between this clause and the rest of the sentence, thereby making verse 19 a literary bridge.

The two other instances of such annotation in the Torah are Gen. 35:22 and Deut. 2:8. See Gen. 2:4, another example of a literary bridge.

26:3, 4] *So Moses . . . Lord had commanded Moses.* The Hebrew is obscure.

9, 10] *Dathan and Abiram . . . Korah.* Referring to the events told in Num. 16.

11] *Did not die.* This apparently contradicts Num. 16:32 and stems probably from a different tradition. Descendants of Korah are mentioned also in verse 58 and are listed as the authors of eleven psalms (Pss. 42; 44–49; 84; 85; 87; 88), though it is not certain that the Korah of these psalms is the same as the Korah of Num. 16. The descendants of Dathan and Abiram, however, perished.

לְצָפוֹן מִשְׁפַּחַת הַצְּפוֹנִי לְחַגִּי מִשְׁפַּחַת הַחַגִּי לְשׁוּנִי
טז מִשְׁפַּחַת הַשּׁוּנִי: לְאָזְנִי מִשְׁפַּחַת הָאָזְנִי לְעֵרִי מִשְׁפַּחַת
יז הָעֵרִי: לַאֲרוֹד מִשְׁפַּחַת הָאֲרוֹדִי לְאַרְאֵלִי מִשְׁפַּחַת
יח הָאַרְאֵלִי: אֵלֶּה מִשְׁפְּחֹת בְּנֵי־גָד לִפְקֻדֵיהֶם אַרְבָּעִים
יט אֶלֶף וַחֲמֵשׁ מֵאוֹת: ס בְּנֵי יְהוּדָה עֵר וְאוֹנָן וַיָּמָת
כ עֵר וְאוֹנָן בְּאֶרֶץ כְּנָעַן: וַיִּהְיוּ בְנֵי־יְהוּדָה לְמִשְׁפְּחֹתָם
לְשֵׁלָה מִשְׁפַּחַת הַשֵּׁלָנִי לְפֶרֶץ מִשְׁפַּחַת הַפַּרְצִי לְזֶרַח
כא מִשְׁפַּחַת הַזַּרְחִי: וַיִּהְיוּ בְנֵי־פֶרֶץ לְחֶצְרֹן מִשְׁפַּחַת
כב הֶחָמוּלִי לְחָמוּל מִשְׁפַּחַת הֶחָמוּלִי: אֵלֶּה מִשְׁפְּחֹת
יְהוּדָה לִפְקֻדֵיהֶם שִׁשָּׁה וְשִׁבְעִים אֶלֶף וַחֲמֵשׁ
כג מֵאוֹת: ס בְּנֵי יִשָּׂשכָר לְמִשְׁפְּחֹתָם תּוֹלָע מִשְׁפַּחַת
כד הַתּוֹלָעִי לְפֻוָה מִשְׁפַּחַת הַפּוּנִי: לְיָשׁוּב מִשְׁפַּחַת
כה הַיָּשׁוּבִי לְשִׁמְרֹן מִשְׁפַּחַת הַשִּׁמְרֹנִי: אֵלֶּה מִשְׁפְּחֹת

יִשָּׂשכָר לִפְקֻדֵיהֶם אַרְבָּעָה וְשִׁשִּׁים אֶלֶף וּשְׁלֹשׁ
כו מֵאוֹת: ס בְּנֵי זְבוּלֻן לְמִשְׁפְּחֹתָם לְסֶרֶד מִשְׁפַּחַת
הַסַּרְדִּי לְאֵלוֹן מִשְׁפַּחַת הָאֵלֹנִי לְיַחְלְאֵל מִשְׁפַּחַת
כז הַיַּחְלְאֵלִי: אֵלֶּה מִשְׁפְּחֹת הַזְּבוּלֹנִי לִפְקֻדֵיהֶם שִׁשִּׁים
כח אֶלֶף וַחֲמֵשׁ מֵאוֹת: ס בְּנֵי יוֹסֵף לְמִשְׁפְּחֹתָם מְנַשֶּׁה
כט וְאֶפְרָיִם: בְּנֵי מְנַשֶּׁה לְמָכִיר מִשְׁפַּחַת הַמָּכִירִי וּמָכִיר
ל הוֹלִיד אֶת־גִּלְעָד לְגִלְעָד מִשְׁפַּחַת הַגִּלְעָדִי: אֵלֶּה
בְּנֵי גִלְעָד אִיעֶזֶר מִשְׁפַּחַת הָאִיעֶזְרִי לְחֵלֶק מִשְׁפַּחַת
לא הַחֶלְקִי: וְאַשְׂרִיאֵל מִשְׁפַּחַת הָאַשְׂרִאֵלִי וְשֶׁכֶם
לב מִשְׁפַּחַת הַשִּׁכְמִי: וּשְׁמִידָע מִשְׁפַּחַת הַשְּׁמִידָעִי וְחֵפֶר
לג מִשְׁפַּחַת הַחֶפְרִי: וּצְלָפְחָד בֶּן־חֵפֶר לֹא־הָיוּ לוֹ בָּנִים
כִּי אִם־בָּנוֹת וְשֵׁם בְּנוֹת צְלָפְחָד מַחְלָה וְנֹעָה חָגְלָה
לד מִלְכָּה וְתִרְצָה: אֵלֶּה מִשְׁפְּחֹת מְנַשֶּׁה וּפְקֻדֵיהֶם שְׁנַיִם

15] Descendants of Gad by their clans: Of Zephon, the clan of the Zephonites; of Haggi, the clan of the Haggites; of Shuni, the clan of the Shunites; **16]** of Ozni, the clan of the Oznites; of Eri, the clan of the Erites; **17]** of Arod, the clan of the Arodites; of Areli, the clan of the Arelites. **18]** Those are the clans of Gad's descendants; persons enrolled: 40,500.

19] Born to Judah: Er and Onan. Er and Onan died in the land of Canaan.

20] Descendants of Judah by their clans: Of Shelah, the clan of the Shelanites; of Perez, the clan of the Perezites; of Zerah, the clan of the Zerahites. **21]** Descendants of Perez: of Hezron, the clan of the Hezronites; of Hamul, the clan of the Hamulites. **22]** Those are the clans of Judah; persons enrolled: 76,500.

23] Descendants of Issachar by their clans: [Of] Tola, the clan of the Tolaites; of Puvah, the clan of the Punites; **24]** of Jashub, the clan of the Jashubites; of Shimron, the clan of the Shimronites. **25]** Those are the clans of Issachar; persons enrolled: 64,300.

26] Descendants of Zebulun by their clans: Of Sered, the clan of the Seredites; of Elon, the clan of the Elonites; of Jahleel, the clan of the Jahleelites. **27]** Those are the clans of the Zebulunites; persons enrolled: 60,500.

28] The sons of Joseph were Manasseh and Ephraim—by their clans.

29] Descendants of Manasseh: Of Machir, the clan of the Machirites.—Machir begot Gilead.—Of Gilead, the clan of the Gileadites. **30]** These were the descendants of Gilead: [Of] Iezer, the clan of the Iezerites; of Helek, the clan of the Helekites; **31]** [of] Asriel, the clan of the Asrielites; [of] Shechem, the clan of the Shechemites; **32]** [of] Shemida, the clan of the Shemidaites; [of] Hepher, the clan of the Hepherites. **33]** —Now Zelophehad son of Hepher had no sons, only daughters.The names of Zelophehad's daughters were Mahlah, Noah, Hoglah, Milcah, and Tirzah.— **34]** Those are the clans of Manasseh; persons enrolled: 52,700.

19] *Died in the land of Canaan.* Before the family settled in Egypt (see Gen. 38:7, 10; 46:12).

לה וַחֲמִשִּׁים אֶלֶף וּשְׁבַע מֵאוֹת: ס אֵלֶּה בְנֵי־אֶפְרַיִם֙ לְמִשְׁפְּחֹתָ֔ם לְשׁוּתֶ֗לַח מִשְׁפַּ֙חַת֙ הַשֻּׁ֣תַלְחִ֔י לְבֶ֕כֶר

לו מִשְׁפַּ֣חַת הַבַּכְרִ֑י לְתַ֕חַן מִשְׁפַּ֖חַת הַתַּחֲנִֽי: וְאֵ֖לֶּה בְּנֵ֣י

לז שׁוּתָ֑לַח לְעֵרָ֕ן מִשְׁפַּ֖חַת הָעֵרָנִֽי: אֵ֣לֶּה מִשְׁפְּחֹ֤ת בְּנֵֽי־אֶפְרַ֙יִם֙ לִפְקֻ֣דֵיהֶ֔ם שְׁנַ֥יִם וּשְׁלֹשִׁ֛ים אֶ֖לֶף וַחֲמֵ֣שׁ מֵא֑וֹת

לח אֵ֥לֶּה בְנֵֽי־יוֹסֵ֖ף לְמִשְׁפְּחֹתָֽם: ס בְּנֵ֣י בִנְיָמִן֮ לְמִשְׁפְּחֹתָ֒ם֒ לְבֶ֗לַע מִשְׁפַּ֙חַת֙ הַבַּלְעִ֔י לְאַשְׁבֵּ֕ל מִשְׁפַּ֖חַת

לט הָֽאַשְׁבֵּלִ֑י לַֽאֲחִירָ֕ם מִשְׁפַּ֖חַת הָאֲחִירָמִֽי: לִשְׁפוּפָ֕ם

מ מִשְׁפַּ֣חַת הַשּׁוּפָמִ֑י לְחוּפָ֕ם מִשְׁפַּ֖חַת הַֽחוּפָמִֽי: וַיִּהְי֤וּ בְנֵי־בֶ֙לַע֙ אַ֣רְדְּ וְנַֽעֲמָ֔ן מִשְׁפַּ֙חַת֙ הָֽאַרְדִּ֔י לְנַֽעֲמָ֕ן

מא מִשְׁפַּ֖חַת הַֽנַּעֲמִֽי: אֵ֥לֶּה בְנֵֽי־בִנְיָמִ֖ן לְמִשְׁפְּחֹתָ֑ם וּפְקֻ֣דֵיהֶ֔ם חֲמִשָּׁ֧ה וְאַרְבָּעִ֛ים אֶ֖לֶף וְשֵׁ֥שׁ מֵאֽוֹת: ס

מב אֵ֤לֶּה בְנֵי־דָן֙ לְמִשְׁפְּחֹתָ֔ם לְשׁוּחָ֕ם מִשְׁפַּ֖חַת הַשּׁוּחָמִ֑י

מג אֵ֛לֶּה מִשְׁפְּחֹ֥ת דָּ֖ן לְמִשְׁפְּחֹתָֽם: כָּל־מִשְׁפְּחֹ֥ת הַשּׁוּחָמִ֖י

לִפְקֻ֣דֵיהֶ֔ם אַרְבָּעָ֧ה וְשִׁשִּׁ֛ים אֶ֖לֶף וְאַרְבַּ֥ע מֵאֽוֹת: ס

מד בְּנֵ֣י אָשֵׁר֮ לְמִשְׁפְּחֹתָ֒ם֒ לְיִמְנָ֗ה מִשְׁפַּ֙חַת֙ הַיִּמְנָ֔ה לְיִשְׁוִ֕י

מה מִשְׁפַּ֖חַת הַיִּשְׁוִ֑י לִבְרִיעָ֕ה מִשְׁפַּ֖חַת הַבְּרִיעִֽי: לִבְנֵ֣י בְרִיעָ֔ה לְחֶ֕בֶר מִשְׁפַּ֖חַת הַֽחֶבְרִ֑י לְמַ֙לְכִּיאֵ֔ל מִשְׁפַּ֖חַת

מו הַמַּלְכִּֽיאֵלִֽי: וְשֵׁ֥ם בַּת־אָשֵׁ֖ר שָֽׂרַח: אֵ֛לֶּה מִשְׁפְּחֹ֥ת בְּנֵֽי־

מז אָשֵׁ֖ר לִפְקֻ֣דֵיהֶ֑ם שְׁלֹשָׁ֧ה וַֽחֲמִשִּׁ֛ים אֶ֖לֶף וְאַרְבַּ֥ע

מח מֵאֽוֹת: ס בְּנֵ֣י נַפְתָּלִי֮ לְמִשְׁפְּחֹתָ֒ם֒ לְיַ֙חְצְאֵ֔ל מִשְׁפַּ֙חַת֙

מט הַיַּחְצְאֵלִ֔י לְגוּנִ֕י מִשְׁפַּ֖חַת הַגּוּנִֽי: לְיֵ֕צֶר מִשְׁפַּ֖חַת הַיִּצְרִ֑י

נ לְשִׁלֵּ֕ם מִשְׁפַּ֖חַת הַשִּׁלֵּמִֽי: אֵ֛לֶּה מִשְׁפְּחֹ֥ת נַפְתָּלִ֖י לְמִשְׁפְּחֹתָ֑ם וּפְקֻ֣דֵיהֶ֔ם חֲמִשָּׁ֧ה וְאַרְבָּעִ֛ים אֶ֖לֶף וְאַרְבַּ֥ע

נא מֵאֽוֹת: אֵ֗לֶּה פְּקוּדֵי֙ בְּנֵ֣י יִשְׂרָאֵ֔ל שֵׁשׁ־מֵא֥וֹת אֶ֖לֶף וָאָ֑לֶף שְׁבַ֥ע מֵא֖וֹת וּשְׁלֹשִֽׁים: פ

נב וַיְדַבֵּ֥ר יְהֹוָ֖ה אֶל־מֹשֶׁ֥ה לֵּאמֹֽר: לָאֵ֗לֶּה תֵּחָלֵ֥ק הָאָ֛רֶץ

נד בְּנַחֲלָ֖ה בְּמִסְפַּ֣ר שֵׁמֽוֹת: לָרַ֗ב תַּרְבֶּה֙ נַֽחֲלָת֔וֹ וְלַמְעַט֙

35] These are the descendants of Ephraim by their clans: Of Shuthelah, the clan of the Shuthelahites; of Becher, the clan of the Becherites; of Tahan, the clan of the Tahanites. **36]** These are the descendants of Shuthelah: Of Eran, the clan of the Eranites. **37]** Those are the clans of Ephraim's descendants; persons enrolled: 32,500.

Those are the descendants of Joseph by their clans.

38] The descendants of Benjamin by their clans: Of Bela, the clan of the Belaites; of Ashbel, the clan of the Ashbelites; of Ahiram, the clan of the Ahiramites; **39]** of Shephupham, the clan of the Shuphamites; of Hupham, the clan of the Huphamites. **40]** The sons of Bela were Ard and Naaman: [Of Ard,] the clan of the Ardites; of Naaman, the clan of the Naamanites. **41]** Those are the descendants of Benjamin by their clans; persons enrolled: 45,600.

42] These are the descendants of Dan by their clans: Of Shuham, the clan of the Shuhamites. Those are the clans of Dan, by their clans. **43]** All the clans of the Shuhamites; persons enrolled: 64,400.

44] Descendants of Asher by their clans: Of Imnah, the clan of the Imnites; of Ishvi, the clan of the Ishvites; of Beriah, the clan of the Beriites. **45]** Of the descendants of Beriah: Of Heber, the clan of the Heberites; of Malchiel, the clan of the Malchielites. **46]** —The name of Asher's daughter was Serah.— **47]** These are the clans of Asher's descendants; persons enrolled: 53,400.

48] Descendants of Naphtali by their clans: Of Jahzeel, the clan of the Jahzeelites; of Guni, the clan of the Gunites; **49]** of Jezer, the clan of the Jezerites; of Shillem, the clan of the Shillemites. **50]** Those are the clans of the Naphtalites, clan by clan; persons enrolled: 45,400.

51] This is the enrollment of the Israelites: 601,730.

52] The Lord spoke to Moses, saying, **53]** "Among these shall the land be apportioned as shares, according to the listed names: **54]** with larger groups increase the share, with smaller groups reduce the share. Each is to be assigned its share according to its enrollment. **55]** The

נה תַּמְעִיט נַחֲלָתוֹ אִישׁ לְפִי פְקֻדָיו יֻתַּן נַחֲלָתוֹ: אַךְ־
בְּגוֹרָל יֵחָלֵק אֶת־הָאָרֶץ לִשְׁמוֹת מַטּוֹת־אֲבֹתָם יִנְחָלוּ:
נו עַל־פִּי הַגּוֹרָל תֵּחָלֵק נַחֲלָתוֹ בֵּין רַב לִמְעָט: ס
נז וְאֵלֶּה פְקוּדֵי הַלֵּוִי לְמִשְׁפְּחֹתָם לְגֵרְשׁוֹן מִשְׁפַּחַת
הַגֵּרְשֻׁנִּי לִקְהָת מִשְׁפַּחַת הַקְּהָתִי לִמְרָרִי מִשְׁפַּחַת
נח הַמְּרָרִי: אֵלֶּה מִשְׁפְּחֹת לֵוִי מִשְׁפַּחַת הַלִּבְנִי מִשְׁפַּחַת
הַחֶבְרֹנִי מִשְׁפַּחַת הַמַּחְלִי מִשְׁפַּחַת הַמּוּשִׁי מִשְׁפַּחַת
נט הַקָּרְחִי וּקְהָת הוֹלִד אֶת־עַמְרָם: וְשֵׁם אֵשֶׁת עַמְרָם
יוֹכֶבֶד בַּת־לֵוִי אֲשֶׁר יָלְדָה אֹתָהּ לְלֵוִי בְּמִצְרָיִם
וַתֵּלֶד לְעַמְרָם אֶת־אַהֲרֹן וְאֶת־מֹשֶׁה וְאֵת מִרְיָם
ס אֲחֹתָם: וַיִּוָּלֵד לְאַהֲרֹן אֶת־נָדָב וְאֶת־אֲבִיהוּא אֶת־
סא אֶלְעָזָר וְאֶת־אִיתָמָר: וַיָּמָת נָדָב וַאֲבִיהוּא בְּהַקְרִיבָם
סב אֵשׁ זָרָה לִפְנֵי יְהוָה: וַיִּהְיוּ פְקֻדֵיהֶם שְׁלֹשָׁה וְעֶשְׂרִים
אֶלֶף כָּל־זָכָר מִבֶּן־חֹדֶשׁ וָמָעְלָה כִּי לֹא הָתְפָּקְדוּ

בְּתוֹךְ בְּנֵי יִשְׂרָאֵל כִּי לֹא־נִתַּן לָהֶם נַחֲלָה בְּתוֹךְ בְּנֵי
סג יִשְׂרָאֵל: אֵלֶּה פְּקוּדֵי מֹשֶׁה וְאֶלְעָזָר הַכֹּהֵן אֲשֶׁר
פָּקְדוּ אֶת־בְּנֵי יִשְׂרָאֵל בְּעַרְבֹת מוֹאָב עַל יַרְדֵּן יְרֵחוֹ:
סד וּבְאֵלֶּה לֹא־הָיָה אִישׁ מִפְּקוּדֵי מֹשֶׁה וְאַהֲרֹן הַכֹּהֵן
סה אֲשֶׁר פָּקְדוּ אֶת־בְּנֵי יִשְׂרָאֵל בְּמִדְבַּר סִינָי: כִּי־אָמַר
יְהוָה לָהֶם מוֹת יָמֻתוּ בַּמִּדְבָּר וְלֹא־נוֹתַר מֵהֶם אִישׁ
כִּי אִם־כָּלֵב בֶּן־יְפֻנֶּה וִיהוֹשֻׁעַ בִּן־נוּן: ס
א וַתִּקְרַבְנָה בְּנוֹת צְלָפְחָד בֶּן־חֵפֶר בֶּן־גִּלְעָד בֶּן־מָכִיר
בֶּן־מְנַשֶּׁה לְמִשְׁפְּחֹת מְנַשֶּׁה בֶן־יוֹסֵף וְאֵלֶּה שְׁמוֹת
ב בְּנֹתָיו מַחְלָה נֹעָה וְחָגְלָה וּמִלְכָּה וְתִרְצָה: וַתַּעֲמֹדְנָה
לִפְנֵי מֹשֶׁה וְלִפְנֵי אֶלְעָזָר הַכֹּהֵן וְלִפְנֵי הַנְּשִׂיאִם וְכָל־
ג הָעֵדָה פֶּתַח אֹהֶל־מוֹעֵד לֵאמֹר: אָבִינוּ מֵת בַּמִּדְבָּר
וְהוּא לֹא־הָיָה בְּתוֹךְ הָעֵדָה הַנּוֹעָדִים עַל־יְהוָה
ד בַּעֲדַת־קֹרַח כִּי־בְחֶטְאוֹ מֵת וּבָנִים לֹא־הָיוּ לוֹ: לָמָּה

land, moreover, is to be apportioned by lot; and the allotment shall be made according to the listings of their ancestral tribes. **56]** Each portion shall be assigned by lot, whether for larger or smaller groups."

57] This is the enrollment of the Levites by their clans: Of Gershon, the clan of the Gershonites; of Kohath, the clan of the Kohathites; of Merari, the clan of the Merarites. **58]** These are the clans of Levi: The clan of the Libnites, the clan of the Hebronites, the clan of the Mahlites, the clan of the Mushites, the clan of the Korahites.—Kohath begot Amram. **59]** The name of Amram's wife was Jochebed daughter of Levi, who was born to Levi in Egypt; she bore to Amram Aaron and Moses and their sister Miriam. **60]** To Aaron were born Nadab and Abihu, Eleazar and Ithamar. **61]** Nadab and Abihu died when they offered alien fire before the LORD.— **62]** Their enrollment of 23,000 comprised all males from a month up. They were not part of the regular enrollment of the Israelites, since no share was assigned to them among the Israelites.

63] These are the persons enrolled by Moses and Eleazar the priest who registered the Israelites on the steppes of Moab, at the Jordan near Jericho. **64]** Among these there was not one of those enrolled by Moses and Aaron the priest when they recorded the Israelites in the wilderness of Sinai. **65]** For the LORD had said of them, "They shall die in the wilderness." Not one of them survived, except Caleb son of Jephunneh and Joshua son of Nun.

1] The daughters of Zelophehad, of Manassite family—son of Hepher son of Gilead son of Machir son of Manasseh son of Joseph—came forward. The names of the daughters were Mahlah, Noah, Hoglah, Milcah, and Tirzah. **2]** They stood before Moses, Eleazar the priest, the chieftains, and the whole assembly, at the entrance of the Tent of Meeting, and they said, **3]** "Our father died in the wilderness. He was not one of the faction, Korah's faction, which banded together against the LORD, but died for his own sin; and he has left no

27:3] *Died for his own sin.* The meaning is not clear. Perhaps: He was judged by God for an un-specified sin and was punished to die without sons [1].

יִוָּרַע שֵׁם־אָבִינוּ מִתּוֹךְ מִשְׁפַּחְתּוֹ כִּי אֵין לוֹ בֵּן תְּנָה־
לָּנוּ אֲחֻזָּה בְּתוֹךְ אֲחֵי אָבִינוּ: וַיַּקְרֵב מֹשֶׁה אֶת־מִשְׁפָּטָן
לִפְנֵי יְהוָה: פ

וַיֹּאמֶר יְהוָה אֶל־מֹשֶׁה לֵּאמֹר: כֵּן בְּנוֹת צְלָפְחָד
דֹּבְרֹת נָתֹן תִּתֵּן לָהֶם אֲחֻזַּת נַחֲלָה בְּתוֹךְ אֲחֵי אֲבִיהֶם
וְהַעֲבַרְתָּ אֶת־נַחֲלַת אֲבִיהֶן לָהֶן: וְאֶל־בְּנֵי יִשְׂרָאֵל
תְּדַבֵּר לֵאמֹר אִישׁ כִּי־יָמוּת וּבֵן אֵין לוֹ וְהַעֲבַרְתֶּם
אֶת־נַחֲלָתוֹ לְבִתּוֹ: וְאִם־אֵין לוֹ בַּת וּנְתַתֶּם אֶת־נַחֲלָתוֹ
לְאֶחָיו: וְאִם־אֵין לוֹ אַחִים וּנְתַתֶּם אֶת־נַחֲלָתוֹ לַאֲחֵי
אָבִיו: וְאִם־אֵין אַחִים לְאָבִיו וּנְתַתֶּם אֶת־נַחֲלָתוֹ
לִשְׁאֵרוֹ הַקָּרֹב אֵלָיו מִמִּשְׁפַּחְתּוֹ וְיָרַשׁ אֹתָהּ וְהָיְתָה
* ה ג' רבתי.

לִבְנֵי יִשְׂרָאֵל לְחֻקַּת מִשְׁפָּט כַּאֲשֶׁר צִוָּה יְהוָה אֶת־
מֹשֶׁה: פ

וַיֹּאמֶר יְהוָה אֶל־מֹשֶׁה עֲלֵה אֶל־הַר הָעֲבָרִים הַזֶּה
וּרְאֵה אֶת־הָאָרֶץ אֲשֶׁר נָתַתִּי לִבְנֵי יִשְׂרָאֵל: וְרָאִיתָה
אֹתָהּ וְנֶאֱסַפְתָּ אֶל־עַמֶּיךָ גַּם־אָתָּה כַּאֲשֶׁר נֶאֱסַף אַהֲרֹן
אָחִיךָ: כַּאֲשֶׁר מְרִיתֶם פִּי בְּמִדְבַּר־צִן בִּמְרִיבַת
הָעֵדָה לְהַקְדִּישֵׁנִי בַמַּיִם לְעֵינֵיהֶם הֵם מֵי־מְרִיבַת
קָדֵשׁ מִדְבַּר־צִן: ס וַיְדַבֵּר מֹשֶׁה אֶל־יְהוָה לֵאמֹר:
יִפְקֹד יְהוָה אֱלֹהֵי הָרוּחֹת לְכָל־בָּשָׂר אִישׁ עַל־
הָעֵדָה: אֲשֶׁר־יֵצֵא לִפְנֵיהֶם וַאֲשֶׁר יָבֹא לִפְנֵיהֶם וַאֲשֶׁר
יוֹצִיאֵם וַאֲשֶׁר יְבִיאֵם וְלֹא תִהְיֶה עֲדַת יְהוָה כַּצֹּאן

sons. **4]** Let not our father's name be lost to his clan just because he had no son! Give us a holding among our father's kinsmen!"

5] Moses brought their case before the LORD.

6] And the LORD said to Moses, **7]** "The plea of Zelophehad's daughters is just: you should give them a hereditary holding among their father's kinsmen; transfer their father's share to them.

8] "Further, speak to the Israelite people as follows: 'If a man dies without leaving a son, you shall transfer his property to his daughter. **9]** If he has no daughter, you shall assign his property to his brothers. **10]** If he has no brothers, you shall assign his property to his father's brothers. **11]** If his father had no brothers, you shall assign his property to his nearest relative in his own clan, and he shall inherit it.' This shall be the law of procedure for the Israelites, in accordance with the LORD's command to Moses."

12] The LORD said to Moses, "Ascend these heights of Abarim and view the land that I have given to the Israelite people. **13]** When you have seen it, you too shall be gathered to your kin, just as your brother Aaron was. **14]** For, in the wilderness of Zin, when the community was contentious, you disobeyed My command to uphold My sanctity in their sight by means of the water." Those are the Waters of Meribath-kadesh, in the wilderness of Zin.

15] Moses spoke to the LORD, saying, **16]** "Let the LORD, Source of the breath of all flesh, appoint someone over the community **17]** who shall go out before them and come in before them, and who shall take them out and bring them in, so that the LORD's community may not be

---

12] *Heights of Abarim.* The mountains beyond the Jordan (see Num. 21:11; "beyond" is written from the point of view of people already dwelling in Canaan, west of the Jordan). The place was probably Jebel en-Neba (Mount Nebo, Deut. 32:49), 2,740 feet high. From this elevation one can see wide stretches of the land west of the river.

14] *Meribath-kadesh.* Or Meribah, referring to the events told in Num. 20.

15] *Moses spoke.* In apparent resignation. Later tradition, however, had Moses argue his case vigorously with God [2].

17] *Who shall go out.* Who shall lead them in all matters and whom the people shall follow.

יהֹוָה עַל־פִּיו יֵצְאוּ וְעַל־פִּיו יָבֹאוּ הוּא וְכָל־בְּנֵי־
יִשְׂרָאֵל אִתּוֹ וְכָל־הָעֵדָה: וַיַּעַשׂ מֹשֶׁה כַּאֲשֶׁר צִוָּה
יְהֹוָה אֹתוֹ וַיִּקַּח אֶת־יְהוֹשֻׁעַ וַיַּעֲמִדֵהוּ לִפְנֵי אֶלְעָזָר
הַכֹּהֵן וְלִפְנֵי כָּל־הָעֵדָה: וַיִּסְמֹךְ אֶת־יָדָיו עָלָיו וַיְצַוֵּהוּ
כַּאֲשֶׁר דִּבֶּר יְהֹוָה בְּיַד־מֹשֶׁה: פ

יח אֲשֶׁר אֵין־לָהֶם רֹעֶה: וַיֹּאמֶר יְהֹוָה אֶל־מֹשֶׁה קַח־לְךָ
אֶת־יְהוֹשֻׁעַ בִּן־נוּן אִישׁ אֲשֶׁר־רוּחַ בּוֹ וְסָמַכְתָּ אֶת־
יט יָדְךָ עָלָיו: וְהַעֲמַדְתָּ אֹתוֹ לִפְנֵי אֶלְעָזָר הַכֹּהֵן וְלִפְנֵי
כ כָּל־הָעֵדָה וְצִוִּיתָה אֹתוֹ לְעֵינֵיהֶם: וְנָתַתָּה מֵהוֹדְךָ
עָלָיו לְמַעַן יִשְׁמְעוּ כָּל־עֲדַת בְּנֵי יִשְׂרָאֵל: וְלִפְנֵי
כא אֶלְעָזָר הַכֹּהֵן יַעֲמֹד וְשָׁאַל לוֹ בְּמִשְׁפַּט הָאוּרִים לִפְנֵי

like sheep that have no shepherd." 18] And the LORD answered Moses, "Single out Joshua son of Nun, an inspired man, and lay your hand upon him. 19] Have him stand before Eleazar the priest and before the whole community, and commission him in their sight. 20] Invest him with some of your authority, so that the whole Israelite community may obey. 21] But he shall present himself to Eleazar the priest, who shall on his behalf seek the decision of the Urim before the LORD. By such instruction they shall go out and by such instruction they shall come in, he and all the Israelites, the whole community."

22] Moses did as the LORD commanded him. He took Joshua and had him stand before Eleazar the priest and before the whole community. 23] He laid his hands upon him and commissioned him—as the LORD had spoken through Moses.

18] *Lay your hand upon him.* Thereby symbolically transmitting the powers of leadership. This practice, called *semichah*, became prominent in Jewish and Christian traditions for rabbinic and clerical ordination [3]. The same term is also used for consecrating a sacrificial animal (Exod. 29:10; Lev. 1:4).

20] *Some of your authority.* Have him share it even now, before your death. Others interpret this to mean that Joshua would receive only a portion of Moses' authority [4].

This is the only occurrence of *hod* in the Torah.

21] *Urim.* Usually mentioned with Thummim, objects used for ascertaining God's will (see at Exod. 28:30). It is not clear what place they had in the scheme of biblical tradition, which usually frowns on divination, nor precisely how they were used. Here it appears that, while Moses never needed such devices for communicating with God, Joshua will require them, implying also that he will need the assistance of Eleazar.

23] *He laid his hands upon him.* On the nature of this ceremony, see at Exod. 29:10.

The Second Census

Thirty-nine years have passed since the first desert census was taken (Num. 1). That census produced a total of 5,500 fighting men, understanding the Hebrew word *elef* not to mean "thousand," as in our English translation, but as "contingent" or "unit." Thus, Reuben numbered not 46,500 men but "46 units [amounting to] 500 men" [5]. Setting the census figures of chapters 1 and 26 next to each other, we obtain this picture:

Comparison of Desert Censuses

Tribe	Traditional Counting (*elef* = 1,000 men)		Revised Counting (*elef* = unit)	
	First Census	Second Census	First Census	Second Census
Reuben	46,500	43,730	500	730
Simeon	59,300	22,200	300	200
Gad	45,650	40,500	650	500
Judah	74,600	76,500	600	500
Issachar	54,400	64,300	400	300
Zebulun	57,400	60,500	400	500
Manasseh	32,200	52,700	200	700
Ephraim	40,500	32,500	500	500
Benjamin	35,400	45,600	400	600
Dan	67,700	64,400	700	400
Asher	41,500	53,400	500	400
Naphtali	53,400	45,400	400	400
Levi*	22,000	23,000	(no fighting men)	

---

* The priestly tribe was numbered separately. See Num. 3:39 and 26:62.

Comparing the first two columns, we note a dramatic decrease in Simeon and significant increases in a number of tribes, especially in Manasseh, with the totals of the two counts diverging by only about 1,000. In this "traditional" method of counting, how can the far-reaching tribal shifts be explained? It is not likely they would have occurred in the course of thirty-nine years, and it is possible that either the accounts stem from different traditions or that they were set down at different times, at a much later date, when the internal composition of the people of Israel had greatly changed.

But if we take columns three and four to be the proper interpretation of the Hebrew text, only Manasseh shows a substantial difference with an increase of 250 per cent. The other differences can be explained on the basis of natural increase or decrease, considering the wars Israel had fought and the plagues it had suffered. No conclusion regarding Manasseh can be reached on the basis of the available information. Nor do we know exactly why the census was taken at this juncture. It may have had military implications since the invasion was at hand, or it may have served the purposes of land distribution, or both.

The Laws of Inheritance

Old practice dictated that land was inherited through the male line only. If a man died without sons, his brother was to marry the widow and their son would become the heir. Still, there would be cases when such procedure could not apply, and the law promulgated for the daughters of Zelophehad covers one such exception: when there were no sons, nor sons who left offspring, the women could inherit, but with the stipulation that they married within their own tribes (see Num. 36).[1]

Later Jewish law set down the order of inheritance in this manner:

> Sons and their offspring;
> Daughters and their offspring;

---

[1] As so often in Numbers, that law is set forth in connection with a narrative. Note also that, in Job 42:15, his daughters are listed as heirs despite the existence of sons [6].

The father;
Brothers and their offspring;
Sisters and their offspring;
The paternal grandfather;
Paternal uncles and their offspring;
Paternal sisters and their offspring;
The paternal great-grandfather, etc. [7].

Furthermore, the husband was added as an heir, but the wife did not inherit from the husband. The first obligation incumbent on the estate was to provide for unmarried daughters. The principle was: they must be supported even if the sons are thereby reduced to beggary [8].

GLEANINGS

The Census

Every time Israel stumbled they were subjected to a census.   MIDRASH [9]

Only the Men

The decree that except for Joshua and Caleb all Israelites over twenty who had left Egypt should die in the desert extended only to the men.[2] The women were spared, for they had preserved the spirit of law and morality.

MIDRASH [10]

Like a Candle

Moses laying his hands on Joshua may be compared to one candle lighting another. No light is lost to the former.   MIDRASH [11]

Joshua

Part of the new leader's greatness lay in his willingness to perform any, even menial, tasks. Also, he would petition forcefully for the needs of the community.   MIDRASH [12]

A Man

It says literally, "appoint a man (אִישׁ) over the community" (Num. 27:15). Moses asked for a man among men; a man, not a superman; a man, not a burning zealot like Phinehas.

CHASIDIC [13]

God characterizes Joshua as "an inspired man" (Num. 27:18). Literally, it says "a man in whom there is spirit"—because only he who knows his own spirit can have knowledge of the needs of others.   CHASIDIC [14]

Qualities of a Leader

The Torah describes the new leader as one who would "go out" before the people and "come in before them" (Num. 27:17). A true leader must "go out" before his people and not trail behind them. He must lead them and not constantly look back to see what they want.

One can also understand this to mean that a leader of people must take care to "take them out" from corruption and "bring them in" to holiness, lest he himself be dragged down to their level.   CHASIDIC [15]

---

[2] This was deduced from the expression in verse 65, "not one of them survived,"
which reads literally, "not a man amongst them survived."

1207

Offerings; Festivals; Vows of Women

The sacrificial ritual for all festival occasions is now described in detail; it resembles closely the prescriptions in Lev. 23 and, less so, Ezek. 45:18 ff.[1] In this calendar the sacred number seven is much in evidence, suggesting an ancient symbolism inherent in the system (see Gleanings and Commentary on Genesis, chapter 2).[2] What connection this section has with the preceding is not clear. Malbim suggests that its insertion here implied that Joshua, unlike Moses, was to assume only military and civil control, while religious practices were to be removed from his authority.

The daily offerings were at the heart of the Temple worship and are treated in a special mishnaic treatise ("Tamid").[3] Traditional Judaism developed these rules and preserved them as potentially significant even after the destruction of the Second Temple, for the belief was (and among some Jews still is) that these would be reinstituted once God caused the Temple to be rebuilt. Consequently, selections from these chapters are still given a special place in all but Reform synagogues: Num. 28:1–15 are read on the new moon, and portions of chapters 28 and 29 constitute additional readings (from the second scroll) on festivals and intermediate days.

---

[1] See commentary on Lev. 23 for a detailed treatment of the festivals.

[2] The prescriptions contained in this section resemble those of archival documents (such as in Num. 7) and may have been abstracted from an earlier record to be restated here as general rules [1].

[3] For a full discussion of the sacrificial ritual, see Commentary on Leviticus, chapters 1–7, especially Lev. 7:16 ff.

The detailed sacrificial section is followed at once by laws concerning vows, especially vows of women. Some scholars believe these prescriptions were originally placed after the rules dealing with female inheritance (Num. 27), while Ibn Ezra suggests that they belong more properly after chapter 32. However, their present position may be due to the fact that the last verse of chapter 29 mentions votive *offerings* and for mnemotechnical reasons votive *pronouncements* were then treated. A mishnaic treatise ("Nedarim") is devoted to the subject of vows.

(A new weekly portion, *Matot*, begins with 30:2.)

א וַיְדַבֵּ֥ר יְהוָ֖ה אֶל־מֹשֶׁ֥ה לֵּאמֹֽר: צַ֚ו אֶת־בְּנֵ֣י יִשְׂרָאֵ֔ל
וְאָמַרְתָּ֖ אֲלֵהֶ֑ם אֶת־קָרְבָּנִ֨י לַחְמִ֜י לְאִשַּׁ֗י רֵ֚יחַ נִֽיחֹחִ֔י
ג תִּשְׁמְר֕וּ לְהַקְרִ֥יב לִ֖י בְּמוֹעֲדֽוֹ: וְאָמַרְתָּ֣ לָהֶ֔ם זֶ֚ה
הָֽאִשֶּׁ֔ה אֲשֶׁ֥ר תַּקְרִ֖יבוּ לַיהוָ֑ה כְּבָשִׂ֨ים בְּנֵֽי־שָׁנָ֧ה תְמִימִ֛ם
ד שְׁנַ֥יִם לַיּ֖וֹם עֹלָ֥ה תָמִֽיד: אֶת־הַכֶּ֥בֶשׂ אֶחָ֖ד תַּעֲשֶׂ֣ה
בַבֹּ֑קֶר וְאֵת֙ הַכֶּ֣בֶשׂ הַשֵּׁנִ֔י תַּעֲשֶׂ֖ה בֵּ֥ין הָעַרְבָּֽיִם:
ה וַעֲשִׂירִ֧ית הָאֵיפָ֛ה סֹ֖לֶת לְמִנְחָ֑ה בְּלוּלָ֛ה בְּשֶׁ֥מֶן כָּתִ֖ית
ו רְבִיעִ֥ת הַהִֽין: עֹלַ֣ת תָּמִ֔יד הָעֲשֻׂיָ֖ה בְּהַ֣ר סִינַ֔י לְרֵ֣יחַ

ז נִיחֹ֙חַ֙ אִשֶּׁ֣ה לַֽיהוָ֔ה וְנִסְכּוֹ֙ רְבִיעִ֣ת הַהִ֔ין לַכֶּ֖בֶשׂ הָֽאֶחָ֑ד
ח בַּקֹּ֗דֶשׁ הַסֵּ֛ךְ נֶ֥סֶךְ שֵׁכָ֖ר לַֽיהוָֽה: וְאֵת֙ הַכֶּ֣בֶשׂ הַשֵּׁנִ֔י
תַּעֲשֶׂ֖ה בֵּ֣ין הָעַרְבָּ֑יִם כְּמִנְחַ֨ת הַבֹּ֤קֶר וּכְנִסְכּוֹ֙ תַּֽעֲשֶׂ֔ה
אִשֵּׁ֛ה רֵ֥יחַ נִיחֹ֖חַ לַֽיהוָֽה: פ
ט וּבְיוֹם֙ הַשַּׁבָּ֔ת שְׁנֵֽי־כְבָשִׂ֥ים בְּנֵֽי־שָׁנָ֖ה תְּמִימִ֑ם וּשְׁנֵ֣י
י עֶשְׂרֹנִ֗ים סֹ֧לֶת מִנְחָ֛ה בְּלוּלָ֥ה בַשֶּׁ֖מֶן וְנִסְכּֽוֹ: עֹלַ֣ת שַׁבַּ֥ת
בְּשַׁבַּתּ֖וֹ עַל־עֹלַ֥ת הַתָּמִ֖יד וְנִסְכָּֽהּ: פ

ט י הב׳ פתוחה.

1] The LORD spoke to Moses, saying: **2]** Command the Israelite people and say to them: Be punctilious in presenting to Me at stated times the offerings of food due Me, as offerings by fire of pleasing odor to Me.

3] Say to them: These are the offerings by fire that you are to present to the LORD: As a regular burnt offering every day, two yearling lambs without blemish. **4]** You shall offer one lamb in the morning, and the other lamb you shall offer at twilight. **5]** And as a meal offering, there shall be a tenth of an *ephah* of choice flour with a quarter of a *hin* of beaten oil mixed in **6]** —the regular burnt offering instituted at Mount Sinai—an offering by fire of pleasing odor to the LORD.

7] The libation with it shall be a quarter of a *hin* for each lamb, to be poured in the sacred precinct as an offering of fermented drink to the LORD. **8]** The other lamb you shall offer at twilight, preparing the same meal offering and libation as in the morning—an offering by fire of pleasing odor to the LORD.

9] On the sabbath day: two yearling lambs without blemish, together with two-tenths of a measure of choice flour with oil mixed in as a meal offering, and with the proper libation— **10]** a burnt offering for every sabbath, in addition to the regular burnt offering and its libation.

28:2] *Due Me.* Literally, "My offering, My food." The expression reflects a prebiblical notion that the deity actually consumed the sacrifice. It survives here as a technical idiom.

Pleasing odor. Another old idiom meaning "acceptable" (see commentary on Gen. 8:21). In the Gilgamesh epic the gods are depicted as smelling the savor of the sacrifice and crowding around it "like flies" [2].

3] *You are to present.* From common funds; the responsibility belongs to the whole community (see Neh. 10:33).

Regular. תָּמִיד (*tamid,* "always" or "forever"); cf. Lev. 6:13. Hence the name of the mishnaic

treatise dealing with offerings. In the eighth century B.C.E. animals were offered in the morning and grain in the evening (see II Kings 16:15).

5] *Ephah . . . hin.* See at Num. 15:4.

6] *Instituted at Mount Sinai.* See Exod. 29:38–41.

7] *Fermented drink.* The Akkadian cognate term signified "beer."

9] *On the sabbath day.* An additional offering (*musaf*) was brought on the Sabbath. In the traditional synagogue, the *musaf* prayer (coming after the Torah reading on Shabbat, new moon, and holy day) is a remembrance of this sacrifice.

יא וּבְרָאשֵׁי֙ חָדְשֵׁיכֶ֔ם תַּקְרִ֥יבוּ עֹלָ֖ה לַיהֹוָ֑ה פָּרִ֨ים בְּנֵֽי־
בָקָ֤ר שְׁנַ֙יִם֙ וְאַ֣יִל אֶחָ֔ד כְּבָשִׂ֧ים בְּנֵי־שָׁנָ֛ה שִׁבְעָ֖ה
יב תְּמִימִֽם: וּשְׁלֹשָׁ֣ה עֶשְׂרֹנִ֗ים סֹ֤לֶת מִנְחָה֙ בְּלוּלָ֣ה בַשֶּׁ֔מֶן
לַפָּ֖ר הָֽאֶחָ֑ד וּשְׁנֵ֣י עֶשְׂרֹנִ֗ים סֹ֤לֶת מִנְחָה֙ בְּלוּלָ֣ה בַשֶּׁ֔מֶן
יג לָאַ֖יִל הָֽאֶחָֽד: וְעִשָּׂרֹ֣ן עִשָּׂר֗וֹן סֹ֤לֶת מִנְחָה֙ בְּלוּלָ֣ה
בַשֶּׁ֔מֶן לַכֶּ֖בֶשׂ הָֽאֶחָ֑ד עֹלָה֙ רֵ֣יחַ נִיחֹ֔חַ אִשֶּׁ֖ה לַֽיהֹוָֽה:
יד וְנִסְכֵּיהֶ֗ם חֲצִ֣י הַהִ֣ין יִֽהְיֶ֣ה לַפָּ֡ר וּשְׁלִישִׁ֣ת הַהִ֣ין לָאַ֡יִל
וּרְבִיעִ֣ת הַהִין֩ לַכֶּ֨בֶשׂ יָ֑יִן זֹ֣את עֹלַ֥ת חֹ֙דֶשׁ֙ בְּחָדְשׁ֔וֹ
טו לְחָדְשֵׁ֖י הַשָּׁנָֽה: וּשְׂעִ֨יר עִזִּ֥ים אֶחָ֛ד לְחַטָּ֖את לַֽיהֹוָ֑ה
טז עַל־עֹלַ֧ת הַתָּמִ֛יד יֵֽעָשֶׂ֖ה וְנִסְכּֽוֹ: ס וּבַחֹ֣דֶשׁ הָרִאשׁ֗וֹן
בְּאַרְבָּעָ֨ה עָשָׂ֥ר י֛וֹם לַחֹ֖דֶשׁ פֶּ֣סַח לַֽיהֹוָֽה: וּבַֽחֲמִשָּׁ֡ה

עָשָׂ֣ר יֽוֹם֩ לַחֹ֨דֶשׁ הַזֶּ֜ה חָ֗ג שִׁבְעַ֤ת יָמִים֙ מַצּ֣וֹת יֵֽאָכֵֽל:
יז בַּיּ֥וֹם הָֽרִאשׁ֖וֹן מִקְרָא־קֹ֑דֶשׁ כׇּל־מְלֶ֥אכֶת עֲבֹדָ֖ה לֹ֥א
יח תַֽעֲשֽׂוּ: וְהִקְרַבְתֶּ֨ם אִשֶּׁ֤ה עֹלָה֙ לַֽיהֹוָ֔ה פָּרִ֧ים בְּנֵֽי־בָקָ֛ר
שְׁנַ֖יִם וְאַ֣יִל אֶחָ֑ד וְשִׁבְעָ֤ה כְבָשִׂים֙ בְּנֵ֣י שָׁנָ֔ה תְּמִימִ֖ם
יט יִֽהְי֥וּ לָכֶֽם: וּמִ֨נְחָתָ֔ם סֹ֖לֶת בְּלוּלָ֣ה בַשָּׁ֑מֶן שְׁלֹשָׁ֣ה
עֶשְׂרֹנִ֞ים לַפָּ֗ר וּשְׁנֵ֧י עֶשְׂרֹנִ֛ים לָאַ֖יִל תַּֽעֲשֽׂוּ: עִשָּׂר֤וֹן
כ עִשָּׂרוֹן֙ תַּֽעֲשֶׂ֔ה לַכֶּ֖בֶשׂ הָֽאֶחָ֑ד לְשִׁבְעַ֖ת הַכְּבָשִֽׂים:
כב וּשְׂעִ֥יר חַטָּ֖את אֶחָ֑ד לְכַפֵּ֖ר עֲלֵיכֶֽם: מִלְּבַד֙ עֹלַ֣ת
כג הַבֹּ֔קֶר אֲשֶׁ֖ר לְעֹלַ֣ת הַתָּמִ֑יד תַּֽעֲשׂ֖וּ אֶת־אֵֽלֶּה: כָּאֵ֜לֶּה
כד תַּֽעֲשׂ֤וּ לַיּוֹם֙ שִׁבְעַ֣ת יָמִ֔ים לֶ֛חֶם אִשֵּׁ֥ה רֵֽיחַ־נִיחֹ֖חַ לַֽיהֹוָ֑ה
כה עַל־עוֹלַ֧ת הַתָּמִ֛יד יֵֽעָשֶׂ֖ה וְנִסְכּֽוֹ: וּבַיּוֹם֙ הַשְּׁבִיעִ֔י

11] On your new moons you shall present a burnt offering to the LORD: two bulls of the herd, one ram, and seven yearling lambs, without blemish. **12]** As meal offering for each bull: three-tenths of a measure of choice flour with oil mixed in. As meal offering for each ram: two-tenths of a measure of choice flour with oil mixed in. **13]** As meal offering for each lamb: a tenth of a measure of fine flour with oil mixed in. Such shall be the burnt offering of pleasing odor, an offering by fire to the LORD. **14]** Their libations shall be: half a *hin* of wine for a bull, a third of a *hin* for a ram, and a quarter of a *hin* for a lamb. That shall be the monthly burnt offering for each new moon of the year. **15]** And there shall be one goat as a sin offering to the LORD, to be offered in addition to the regular burnt offering and its libation.

16] In the first month, on the fourteenth day of the month, there shall be a passover sacrifice to the LORD, **17]** and on the fifteenth day of that month a festival. Unleavened bread shall be eaten for seven days. **18]** The first day shall be a sacred occasion: you shall not work at your occupations. **19]** You shall present an offering by fire, a burnt offering, to the LORD: two bulls of the herd, one ram, and seven yearling lambs—see that they are without blemish. **20]** The meal offering with them shall be of choice flour with oil mixed in: prepare three-tenths of a measure for a bull, two-tenths for a ram; **21]** and for each of the seven lambs prepare one-tenth of a measure. **22]** And there shall be one goat for a sin offering, to make expiation in your behalf. **23]** You shall present these in addition to the morning portion of the regular burnt offering. **24]** You shall offer the like daily for seven days as food, an offering by fire of pleasing odor to the LORD; they shall be offered, with their libations, in addition to the regular burnt offering. **25]** And the seventh day shall be a sacred occasion for you: you shall not work at your occupations.

11] *New moons.* The sacrificial provisions resemble those prescribed for Passover, but otherwise the new moon observance is not detailed in the Torah.

16] *On the fourteenth day.* The sacrifice was offered at sunset, and on the next day it was eaten. Critics see this as a combination of two originally separate festivals (Passover and the Feast of Unleavened Bread; see commentary on Exod. 12).

18] *Not work at your occupations.* Food may be prepared. Unlike Shabbat, when food may not be prepared.

מִקְרָא־קֹדֶשׁ יִהְיֶה לָכֶם כָּל־מְלֶאכֶת עֲבֹדָה לֹא
תַעֲשׂוּ: ס וּבְיוֹם הַבִּכּוּרִים בְּהַקְרִיבְכֶם מִנְחָה
חֲדָשָׁה לַיהוָה בְּשָׁבֻעֹתֵיכֶם מִקְרָא־קֹדֶשׁ יִהְיֶה לָכֶם
כָּל־מְלֶאכֶת עֲבֹדָה לֹא תַעֲשׂוּ: וְהִקְרַבְתֶּם עוֹלָה
לְרֵיחַ נִיחֹחַ לַיהוָה פָּרִים בְּנֵי־בָקָר שְׁנַיִם אַיִל אֶחָד
שִׁבְעָה כְבָשִׂים בְּנֵי שָׁנָה: וּמִנְחָתָם סֹלֶת בְּלוּלָה בַשֶּׁמֶן
שְׁלֹשָׁה עֶשְׂרֹנִים לַפָּר הָאֶחָד שְׁנֵי עֶשְׂרֹנִים לָאַיִל
הָאֶחָד: עִשָּׂרוֹן עִשָּׂרוֹן לַכֶּבֶשׂ הָאֶחָד לְשִׁבְעַת
הַכְּבָשִׂים: שְׂעִיר עִזִּים אֶחָד לְכַפֵּר עֲלֵיכֶם: מִלְּבַד
עֹלַת הַתָּמִיד וּמִנְחָתוֹ תַּעֲשׂוּ תְּמִימִם יִהְיוּ־לָכֶם
וְנִסְכֵּיהֶם: פ

וּבַחֹדֶשׁ הַשְּׁבִיעִי בְּאֶחָד לַחֹדֶשׁ מִקְרָא־קֹדֶשׁ יִהְיֶה
לָכֶם כָּל־מְלֶאכֶת עֲבֹדָה לֹא תַעֲשׂוּ יוֹם תְּרוּעָה
יִהְיֶה לָכֶם: וַעֲשִׂיתֶם עֹלָה לְרֵיחַ נִיחֹחַ לַיהוָה פַּר
בֶּן־בָּקָר אֶחָד אַיִל אֶחָד כְּבָשִׂים בְּנֵי־שָׁנָה שִׁבְעָה
תְּמִימִם: וּמִנְחָתָם סֹלֶת בְּלוּלָה בַשֶּׁמֶן שְׁלֹשָׁה עֶשְׂרֹנִים
לַפָּר שְׁנֵי עֶשְׂרֹנִים לָאָיִל: וְעִשָּׂרוֹן אֶחָד לַכֶּבֶשׂ הָאֶחָד
לְשִׁבְעַת הַכְּבָשִׂים: וּשְׂעִיר־עִזִּים אֶחָד חַטָּאת לְכַפֵּר
עֲלֵיכֶם: מִלְּבַד עֹלַת הַחֹדֶשׁ וּמִנְחָתָהּ וְעֹלַת הַתָּמִיד
וּמִנְחָתָהּ וְנִסְכֵּיהֶם כְּמִשְׁפָּטָם לְרֵיחַ נִיחֹחַ אִשֶּׁה
לַיהוָה: ס וּבֶעָשׂוֹר לַחֹדֶשׁ הַשְּׁבִיעִי הַזֶּה מִקְרָא־
קֹדֶשׁ יִהְיֶה לָכֶם וְעִנִּיתֶם אֶת־נַפְשֹׁתֵיכֶם כָּל־מְלָאכָה

26] On the day of the first fruits, your Feast of Weeks, when you bring an offering of new grain to the LORD, you shall observe a sacred occasion: you shall not work at your occupations. **27]** You shall present a burnt offering of pleasing odor to the LORD: two bulls of the herd, one ram, seven yearling lambs. **28]** The meal offering with them shall be of choice flour with oil mixed in, three-tenths of a measure for a bull, two-tenths for a ram, **29]** and one-tenth for each of the seven lambs. **30]** And there shall be one goat for expiation in your behalf. **31]** You shall present them—see that they are without blemish—with their libations, in addition to the regular burnt offering and its meal offering.

1] In the seventh month, on the first day of the month, you shall observe a sacred occasion: you shall not work at your occupations. You shall observe it as a day when the horn is sounded. **2]** You shall present a burnt offering of pleasing odor to the LORD: one bull of the herd, one ram, and seven yearling lambs, without blemish. **3]** The meal offering with them—choice flour with oil mixed in—shall be: three-tenths of a measure for a bull, two-tenths for a ram, **4]** and one-tenth for each of the seven lambs. **5]** And there shall be one goat for a sin offering, to make expiation in your behalf— **6]** in addition to the burnt offering of the new moon with its meal offering and the regular burnt offering with its meal offering, each with its libation as prescribed, offerings by fire of pleasing odor to the LORD.

7] On the tenth day of the same seventh month you shall observe a sacred occasion when you shall practice self-denial. You shall do no work. **8]** You shall present to the LORD a burnt

---

26] *Feast of Weeks.* שָׁבֻעוֹת (Shavuot). Also called Pentecost (Greek for "fiftieth day" after Pesach). According to Jewish tradition, the sacrifices ordered here are in addition to those prescribed in Lev. 23:18–21 [3].

29:1] *A sacred occasion.* Rosh Hashanah, the religious new year, as it later became known.

A day when the horn is sounded. Trumpets were blown on all festivals and new moons (Num. 10:10), but on the new year a different kind of

blast (*teruah*) was heard, the exact nature of which was much debated in talmudic days [4]. In time, the ram's horn (*shofar*) became the horn for this occasion.

7] *Tenth day.* Called Day of Atonement (*Yom ha-Kippurim*) in Lev. 23:26.

Self-denial. Primarily by abstaining from food.

No work. Of any kind; a stricter prohibition than for the other holy days on which only occupational labor is prohibited.

עָשָׂר פָּרִים שְׁנֵי עֶשְׂרֹנִים לָאַיִל הָאֶחָד לִשְׁנֵי הָאֵילִם:　　ח לֹא תַעֲשׂוּ: וְהִקְרַבְתֶּם עֹלָה לַיהוָה רֵיחַ נִיחֹחַ פַּר
טו וְעִשָּׂרוֹן עִשָּׂרוֹן לַכֶּבֶשׂ הָאֶחָד לְאַרְבָּעָה עָשָׂר　　בֶּן־בָּקָר אֶחָד אַיִל אֶחָד כְּבָשִׂים בְּנֵי־שָׁנָה שִׁבְעָה
טז כְּבָשִׂים: וּשְׂעִיר־עִזִּים אֶחָד חַטָּאת מִלְּבַד עֹלַת　　ט תְּמִימִם יִהְיוּ לָכֶם: וּמִנְחָתָם סֹלֶת בְּלוּלָה בַשָּׁמֶן
יז הַתָּמִיד מִנְחָתָהּ וְנִסְכָּהּ: ס וּבַיּוֹם הַשֵּׁנִי פָּרִים בְּנֵי־　　שְׁלֹשָׁה עֶשְׂרֹנִים לַפָּר שְׁנֵי עֶשְׂרֹנִים לָאַיִל הָאֶחָד:
בָקָר שְׁנֵים עָשָׂר אֵילִם שְׁנָיִם כְּבָשִׂים בְּנֵי־שָׁנָה　　י עִשָּׂרוֹן עִשָּׂרוֹן לַכֶּבֶשׂ הָאֶחָד לְשִׁבְעַת הַכְּבָשִׂים:
יח אַרְבָּעָה עָשָׂר תְּמִימִם: וּמִנְחָתָם וְנִסְכֵּיהֶם לַפָּרִים　　יא שְׂעִיר־עִזִּים אֶחָד חַטָּאת מִלְּבַד חַטַּאת הַכִּפֻּרִים
יט לָאֵילִם וְלַכְּבָשִׂים בְּמִסְפָּרָם כַּמִּשְׁפָּט: וּשְׂעִיר־　　יב וְעֹלַת הַתָּמִיד וּמִנְחָתָהּ וְנִסְכֵּיהֶם: ס וּבַחֲמִשָּׁה
עִזִּים אֶחָד חַטָּאת מִלְּבַד עֹלַת הַתָּמִיד וּמִנְחָתָהּ　　עָשָׂר יוֹם לַחֹדֶשׁ הַשְּׁבִיעִי מִקְרָא־קֹדֶשׁ יִהְיֶה לָכֶם
כ וְנִסְכֵּיהֶם: ס וּבַיּוֹם הַשְּׁלִישִׁי פָּרִים עַשְׁתֵּי־עָשָׂר　　כָּל־מְלֶאכֶת עֲבֹדָה לֹא תַעֲשׂוּ וְחַגֹּתֶם חַג לַיהוָה
אֵילִם שְׁנָיִם כְּבָשִׂים בְּנֵי־שָׁנָה אַרְבָּעָה עָשָׂר תְּמִימִם:　　יג שִׁבְעַת יָמִים: וְהִקְרַבְתֶּם עֹלָה אִשֵּׁה רֵיחַ נִיחֹחַ לַיהוָה
כא וּמִנְחָתָם וְנִסְכֵּיהֶם לַפָּרִים לָאֵילִם וְלַכְּבָשִׂים　　פָּרִים בְּנֵי־בָקָר שְׁלֹשָׁה עָשָׂר אֵילִם שְׁנַיִם כְּבָשִׂים
כב בְּמִסְפָּרָם כַּמִּשְׁפָּט: וּשְׂעִיר חַטָּאת אֶחָד מִלְּבַד עֹלַת　　יד בְּנֵי־שָׁנָה אַרְבָּעָה עָשָׂר תְּמִימִם יִהְיוּ: וּמִנְחָתָם סֹלֶת
כג הַתָּמִיד וּמִנְחָתָהּ וְנִסְכָּהּ: ס וּבַיּוֹם הָרְבִיעִי פָּרִים　　בְּלוּלָה בַשֶּׁמֶן שְׁלֹשָׁה עֶשְׂרֹנִים לַפָּר הָאֶחָד לִשְׁלֹשָׁה

offering of pleasing odor: one bull of the herd, one ram, seven yearling lambs; see that they are without blemish.　**9]** The meal offering with them—of choice flour with oil mixed in—shall be: three-tenths of a measure for a bull, two-tenths for the one ram,　**10]** one-tenth for each of the seven lambs.　**11]** And there shall be one goat for a sin offering, in addition to the sin offering of expiation and the regular burnt offering with its meal offering, each with its libation.

12] On the fifteenth day of the seventh month, you shall observe a sacred occasion: you shall not work at your occupations.—Seven days you shall observe a festival of the LORD.— **13]** You shall present a burnt offering, an offering by fire of pleasing odor to the LORD: thirteen bulls of the herd, two rams, fourteen yearling lambs; they shall be without blemish. **14]** The meal offerings with them—of choice flour with oil mixed in—shall be: three-tenths of a measure for each of the thirteen bulls, two-tenths for each of the two rams,　**15]** and one-tenth for each of the fourteen lambs.　**16]** And there shall be one goat for a sin offering—in addition to the regular burnt offering, its meal offering and libation.

17] Second day: Twelve bulls of the herd, two rams, fourteen yearling lambs, without blemish;　**18]** the meal offerings and libations for the bulls, rams, and lambs, in the quantities prescribed;　**19]** and one goat for a sin offering—in addition to the regular burnt offering, its meal offering and libations.

20] Third day: Eleven bulls, two rams, fourteen yearling lambs, without blemish;　**21]** the meal offerings and libations for the bulls, rams, and lambs, in the quantities prescribed; **22]** and one goat for a sin offering—in addition to the regular burnt offering, its meal offering and libation.

12] *Fifteenth day.* The Feast of Tabernacles (Sukot). The harvest festival was by its nature the most joyous of all celebrations and its importance was underlined by the great number of sacrifices prescribed. (The command to dwell in booths or tabernacles is found in Lev. 23:42.)

כג　עֲשָׂרָה אֵילִם שְׁנַיִם כְּבָשִׂים בְּנֵי־שָׁנָה אַרְבָּעָה עָשָׂר

כד　תְּמִימִם: מִנְחָתָם וְנִסְכֵּיהֶם לַפָּרִים לָאֵילִם וְלַכְּבָשִׂים

כה　בְּמִסְפָּרָם כַּמִּשְׁפָּט: וּשְׂעִיר־עִזִּים אֶחָד חַטָּאת מִלְּבַד

כו　עֹלַת הַתָּמִיד מִנְחָתָהּ וְנִסְכָּהּ: ס וּבַיּוֹם הַחֲמִישִׁי

פָּרִים תִּשְׁעָה אֵילִם שְׁנַיִם כְּבָשִׂים בְּנֵי־שָׁנָה אַרְבָּעָה

כז　עָשָׂר תְּמִימִם: וּמִנְחָתָם וְנִסְכֵּיהֶם לַפָּרִים לָאֵילִם

כח　וְלַכְּבָשִׂים בְּמִסְפָּרָם כַּמִּשְׁפָּט: וּשְׂעִיר חַטָּאת אֶחָד

כט　מִלְּבַד עֹלַת הַתָּמִיד וּמִנְחָתָהּ וְנִסְכָּהּ: ס וּבַיּוֹם

הַשִּׁשִּׁי פָּרִים שְׁמֹנָה אֵילִם שְׁנַיִם כְּבָשִׂים בְּנֵי־שָׁנָה

ל　אַרְבָּעָה עָשָׂר תְּמִימִם: וּמִנְחָתָם וְנִסְכֵּיהֶם לַפָּרִים

לא　לָאֵילִם וְלַכְּבָשִׂים בְּמִסְפָּרָם כַּמִּשְׁפָּט: וּשְׂעִיר חַטָּאת

אֶחָד מִלְּבַד עֹלַת הַתָּמִיד מִנְחָתָהּ וּנְסָכֶיהָ: ס

לב　וּבַיּוֹם הַשְּׁבִיעִי פָּרִים שִׁבְעָה אֵילִם שְׁנַיִם כְּבָשִׂים

לג　בְּנֵי־שָׁנָה אַרְבָּעָה עָשָׂר תְּמִימִם: וּמִנְחָתָם וְנִסְכֵּהֶם

לַפָּרִים לָאֵילִם וְלַכְּבָשִׂים בְּמִסְפָּרָם כְּמִשְׁפָּטָם:

לד　וּשְׂעִיר חַטָּאת אֶחָד מִלְּבַד עֹלַת הַתָּמִיד מִנְחָתָהּ

לה　וְנִסְכָּהּ: ס בַּיּוֹם הַשְּׁמִינִי עֲצֶרֶת תִּהְיֶה לָכֶם כָּל־

לו　מְלֶאכֶת עֲבֹדָה לֹא תַעֲשׂוּ: וְהִקְרַבְתֶּם עֹלָה אִשֵּׁה

רֵיחַ נִיחֹחַ לַיהוָה פַּר אֶחָד אַיִל אֶחָד כְּבָשִׂים בְּנֵי־

לז　שָׁנָה שִׁבְעָה תְּמִימִם: מִנְחָתָם וְנִסְכֵּיהֶם תְּמִימִם לַפָּר לָאַיִל

לח　וְלַכְּבָשִׂים בְּמִסְפָּרָם כַּמִּשְׁפָּט: וּשְׂעִיר חַטָּאת אֶחָד

לט　מִלְּבַד עֹלַת הַתָּמִיד וּמִנְחָתָהּ וְנִסְכָּהּ: אֵלֶּה תַּעֲשׂוּ

לַיהוָה בְּמוֹעֲדֵיכֶם לְבַד מִנִּדְרֵיכֶם וְנִדְבֹתֵיכֶם

לְעֹלֹתֵיכֶם וּלְמִנְחֹתֵיכֶם וּלְנִסְכֵּיכֶם וּלְשַׁלְמֵיכֶם:

* לֹא חסר י׳

23] Fourth day: Ten bulls, two rams, fourteen yearling lambs, without blemish; **24]** the meal offerings and libations for the bulls, rams, and lambs, in the quantities prescribed; **25]** and one goat for a sin offering—in addition to the regular burnt offering, its meal offering and libation.

26] Fifth day: Nine bulls, two rams, fourteen yearling lambs, without blemish; **27]** the meal offerings and libations for the bulls, rams, and lambs, in the quantities prescribed; **28]** and one goat for a sin offering—in addition to the regular burnt offering, its meal offering and libation.

29] Sixth day: Eight bulls, two rams, fourteen yearling lambs, without blemish; **30]** the meal offerings and libations for the bulls, rams, and lambs, in the quantities prescribed; **31]** and one goat for a sin offering—in addition to the regular burnt offering, its meal offering and libations.

32] Seventh day: Seven bulls, two rams, fourteen yearling lambs, without blemish; **33]** the meal offerings and libations for the bulls, rams, and lambs, in the quantities prescribed; **34]** and one goat for a sin offering—in addition to the regular burnt offering, its meal offering and libation.

35] On the eighth day you shall hold a solemn gathering; you shall not work at your occupations. **36]** You shall present a burnt offering, an offering by fire of pleasing odor to the LORD: one bull, one ram, seven yearling lambs, without blemish; **37]** the meal offerings and libations for the bull, the ram, and the lambs, in the quantities prescribed; **38]** and one goat for a sin offering—in addition to the regular burnt offering, its meal offering and libation.

39] All these you shall offer to the LORD at the stated times, in addition to your votive and freewill offerings, be they burnt offerings, meal offerings, libations, or offerings of well-

---

35] *Solemn gathering.* עֲצֶרֶת (*atzeret*). The observance took place on the eighth day (*shemini*), hence the name Shemini Atzeret for the festival. It equalled Rosh Hashanah and Yom Kippur in the number of sacrifices.

39] *All these you shall offer.* As communal obligations, regardless of any additional private sacrifices.

אָסְרָה עַל־נַפְשָׁהּ יָקוּם: וְאִם־הֵנִ֨יא אָבִ֤יהָ אֹתָהּ֙ בְּי֣וֹם י
שָׁמְע֔וֹ כָּל־נְדָרֶ֣יהָ וֶֽאֱסָרֶ֗יהָ אֲשֶׁר־אָסְרָ֛ה עַל־נַפְשָׁ֖הּ
לֹ֣א יָק֑וּם וַֽיהֹוָה֙ יִֽסְלַח־לָ֔הּ כִּֽי־הֵנִ֥יא אָבִ֖יהָ אֹתָֽהּ:
וְאִם־הָי֤וֹ תִֽהְיֶה֙ לְאִ֔ישׁ וּנְדָרֶ֖יהָ עָלֶ֑יהָ א֚וֹ מִבְטָ֣א שְׂפָתֶ֔יהָ ח
אֲשֶׁ֥ר אָסְרָ֖ה עַל־נַפְשָֽׁהּ: וְשָׁמַ֥ע אִישָׁ֛הּ בְּי֥וֹם שָׁמְע֖וֹ
וְהֶֽחֱרִ֣ישׁ לָ֑הּ וְקָ֣מוּ נְדָרֶ֗יהָ וֶֽאֱסָרֶ֛הָ אֲשֶׁר־אָסְרָ֥ה עַל־
נַפְשָׁ֖הּ יָקֻֽמוּ: וְ֠אִ֠ם בְּי֨וֹם שְׁמֹ֤עַ אִישָׁהּ֙ יָנִ֣יא אוֹתָ֔הּ וְהֵפֵ֗ר ט
אֶת־נִדְרָהּ֙ אֲשֶׁ֣ר עָלֶ֔יהָ וְאֵת֙ מִבְטָ֣א שְׂפָתֶ֔יהָ אֲשֶׁ֥ר
אָסְרָ֖ה עַל־נַפְשָׁ֑הּ וַֽיהֹוָ֖ה יִֽסְלַח־לָֽהּ: וְנֵ֥דֶר אַלְמָנָ֖ה
וּגְרוּשָׁ֑ה כֹּ֛ל אֲשֶׁר־אָסְרָ֥ה עַל־נַפְשָׁ֖הּ יָק֥וּם עָלֶֽיהָ:

וַיֹּ֤אמֶר מֹשֶׁה֙ אֶל־בְּנֵ֣י יִשְׂרָאֵ֔ל כְּכֹ֛ל אֲשֶׁר־צִוָּ֥ה יְהֹוָ֖ה א
אֶת־מֹשֶֽׁה:

Haftarah Pinchas, p. 1275

פ פ פ

וַיְדַבֵּ֤ר מֹשֶׁה֙ אֶל־רָאשֵׁ֣י הַמַּטּ֔וֹת לִבְנֵ֥י יִשְׂרָאֵ֖ל לֵאמֹ֑ר ב
זֶ֣ה הַדָּבָ֔ר אֲשֶׁ֖ר צִוָּ֥ה יְהֹוָֽה: אִישׁ֩ כִּֽי־יִדֹּ֨ר נֶ֜דֶר לַֽיהֹוָ֗ה ג
אֽוֹ־הִשָּׁ֤בַע שְׁבֻעָה֙ לֶאְסֹ֤ר אִסָּר֙ עַל־נַפְשׁ֔וֹ לֹ֥א יַחֵ֖ל
דְּבָר֑וֹ כְּכָל־הַיֹּצֵ֥א מִפִּ֖יו יַֽעֲשֶֽׂה: וְאִשָּׁ֕ה כִּֽי־תִדֹּ֥ר נֶ֖דֶר ד
לַֽיהֹוָ֑ה וְאָסְרָ֥ה אִסָּ֛ר בְּבֵ֥ית אָבִ֖יהָ בִּנְעֻרֶֽיהָ: וְשָׁמַ֨ע ה
אָבִ֜יהָ אֶת־נִדְרָ֗הּ וֶֽאֱסָרָהּ֙ אֲשֶׁ֣ר אָסְרָ֣ה עַל־נַפְשָׁ֔הּ
וְהֶֽחֱרִ֥ישׁ לָ֖הּ אָבִ֑יהָ וְקָ֙מוּ֙ כָּל־נְדָרֶ֔יהָ וְכָל־אִסָּ֛ר אֲשֶׁר־

being. **1]** So Moses spoke to the Israelites just as the LORD had commanded Moses.

2] Moses spoke to the heads of the Israelite tribes, saying: This is what the LORD has commanded:

3] If a man makes a vow to the LORD or takes an oath imposing an obligation on himself, he shall not break his pledge; he must carry out all that has crossed his lips.

4] If a woman makes a vow to the LORD and assumes an obligation while still in her father's household by reason of her youth, **5]** and her father learns of her vow or her self-imposed obligation and offers no objection, all her vows shall stand and every self-imposed obligation shall stand. **6]** But if her father restrains her on the day he finds out, none of her vows or self-imposed obligations shall stand; and the LORD will forgive her, since her father restrained her.

7] If she should marry while her vow or the commitment to which she bound herself is still in force, **8]** and her husband learns of it and offers no objection on the day he finds out, her vows shall stand and her self-imposed obligations shall stand. **9]** But if her husband restrains her on the day that he learns of it, he thereby annuls her vow which was in force or the commitment to which she bound herself; and the LORD will forgive her. **10]** —The vow of a widow or of a divorced woman, however, whatever she has imposed on herself, shall be

30:1] *So Moses.* In Christian Bibles this verse is counted as verse 40 of chapter 29; hence their verse numbering in chapter 30 differs by one from the texts commonly used by Jews.

It should be noted that all chapter divisions are of medieval Christian origin and do not go back to the Masoretic tradition.

2] *To the heads.* And not to all Israel as usual. Jewish tradition suggested that the law was not originally made public so as to discourage the practice of vowing [5].

3] *Vow . . . obligation.* The former represents a promise to do, the latter a promise to abstain.

Crossed his lips. Silent intent is not sufficient, it must literally "come out of his mouth." But what one says must correspond to what one means: "His word remains void until mouth and heart agree" [6].

4] *By reason of her youth.* No provision is made for a mature woman still under her father's jurisdiction. The omission is due to the generally prevailing custom of early marriages.

6] *The Lord will forgive her.* If she now breaks her vow, even if she did not know it had been cancelled [7].

יא וְאִם־בֵּית אִישָׁהּ נָדָרָה אוֹ־אָסְרָה אִסָּר עַל־נַפְשָׁהּ
יב בִּשְׁבֻעָה: וְשָׁמַע אִישָׁהּ וְהֶחֱרִשׁ לָהּ לֹא הֵנִיא אֹתָהּ וְקָמוּ כָּל־נְדָרֶיהָ וְכָל־אִסָּר אֲשֶׁר־אָסְרָה עַל־נַפְשָׁהּ
יג יָקוּם: וְאִם־הָפֵר יָפֵר אֹתָם בְּיוֹם שָׁמְעוֹ כָּל־מוֹצָא שְׂפָתֶיהָ לִנְדָרֶיהָ וּלְאִסַּר נַפְשָׁהּ לֹא יָקוּם
יד אִישָׁהּ הֲפֵרָם וַיהוָה יִסְלַח־לָהּ: כָּל־נֵדֶר וְכָל־שְׁבֻעַת
טו אִסָּר לְעַנֹּת נָפֶשׁ אִישָׁהּ יְקִימֶנּוּ וְאִישָׁהּ יְפֵרֶנּוּ: וְאִם־

הַחֲרֵשׁ יַחֲרִישׁ לָהּ אִישָׁהּ מִיּוֹם אֶל־יוֹם וְהֵקִים אֶת־כָּל־נְדָרֶיהָ אוֹ אֶת־כָּל־אֱסָרֶיהָ אֲשֶׁר עָלֶיהָ הֵקִים אֹתָם כִּי־הֶחֱרִשׁ לָהּ בְּיוֹם שָׁמְעוֹ: וְאִם־הָפֵר יָפֵר אֹתָם אַחֲרֵי שָׁמְעוֹ וְנָשָׂא אֶת־עֲוֹנָהּ: אֵלֶּה הַחֻקִּים אֲשֶׁר צִוָּה יְהוָה אֶת־מֹשֶׁה בֵּין אִישׁ לְאִשְׁתּוֹ בֵּין־אָב לְבִתּוֹ בִּנְעֻרֶיהָ בֵּית אָבִיהָ: פ

binding upon her.— **11]** So, too, if, while in her husband's household, she makes a vow or imposes an obligation on herself by oath, **12]** and her husband learns of it, yet offers no objection—thus failing to restrain her—all her vows shall stand and all her self-imposed obligations shall stand. **13]** But if her husband does annul them on the day he finds out, then nothing that has crossed her lips shall stand, whether vows or self-imposed obligations. Her husband has annulled them, and the LORD will forgive her. **14]** Every vow and every sworn obligation of self-denial may be upheld by her husband or annulled by her husband. **15]** If her husband offers no objection from that day to the next, he has upheld all the vows or obligations she has assumed: he has upheld them by offering no objection on the day he found out. **16]** But if he annuls them after [the day] he finds out, he shall bear her guilt.

17] Those are the laws that the LORD enjoined upon Moses as between a man and his wife, and as between a father and his daughter while in her father's household by reason of her youth.

14] *Self-denial.* To abstain from food and drink, not washing herself, not adorning herself, and the like. According to the Rabbis, only such obligations may be annulled by the husband [8].

16] *He shall bear her guilt.* If she now breaks her vow to fulfill his wishes.

Moon and Calendar

The ritual calendar presented in this section and Lev. 23 is oriented to the phases of the moon (hence the common term lunar calendar, in contrast to solar or sun-based calendar). To this day the Jewish festival cycle preserves the biblical arrangement, and all holy days are calculated by the revolutions of the moon around the earth. The Jewish year consists of twelve such cycles, each of which takes about 29½ days to accomplish. Thus, the months have either 29 or 30 days, and twelve such months add up to 354 days. Since this total is 11 days short of the 365 days of the sun year, a lunar calendar of 354 days would fall back further and further in relation to the solar cycle, so that in time the festivals would no longer be related to the natural seasons. After a few years the fall harvest holy days (Sukot) would recede into late, then early summer, then into spring, and so forth. In order to avoid this, a special leap month is inserted every two or three years—7 leap years in 19 years—which keeps the festivals within their proper seasons. (The Moslem calendar has no such correction, and thus the festival month of Ramadan moves through the entire solar year.) The popular notion that Jewish festivals "move about" is proper only in relation to the sun cycle, on which the civil calendar is based. They are, however, quite fixed in the lunar calendar: Rosh Hashanah always falls on the first day of Tishri and Passover always on the fifteenth day of Nisan.

In biblical times, a lunar calendar had obvious advantages, for it was possible for everyone to observe the waxing and waning of the moon and thus to know the advent of festivals. The appearance of the new moon was an important event in biblical days and was celebrated with great emphasis, even though no record of the exact nature of the celebration has been preserved (we only know that work was prohibited; Amos 8:5).

In contradistinction, the Sabbath had no relation whatsoever to any celestial bodies or cycles; it occurred inexorably week after week. It is not surprising, therefore, that such an observance had a difficult time establishing itself in a pastoral and agricultural society oriented to the cyclical manifestations of the heavens. For many centuries the festival of the new moon seems to have competed in importance with the Sabbath (see Isa. 1:13), and only slowly did the latter assert its dominance in Jewish life.

To this day, however, the arrival of the new moon, which signals the beginning of a new month in the calendar, is observed in Jewish ritual; special prayers are recited, and the new moon's reappearance is announced in the synagogue on the preceding Sabbath.

(There is considerable evidence that prior to the Babylonian exile Israel followed a solar calendar, oriented to the seasons, with months of thirty days; see Gleanings.)

Sacrifice as Worship

(For an extensive discussion of sacrifice as well as a somewhat different point of view, see Commentary on Leviticus, introduction to chapters 1–7.)

With the exception of the remnant who hope for God's reestablishment of the old Temple worship and prepare themselves for its possible advent in our time, most people would consider the sacrificial cult described in these chapters and elsewhere in the Bible as a "primitive" means of approaching the Creator. (This is so despite the fact that the traditional Jewish service continues to include prayers for the reestablishment of the cult; but the maintenance of such prayer formulas arises more from an Orthodox unwillingness to change the prayer book than from the worshipers' adherence to such beliefs and hopes.) While a simple dismissal of animal sacrifice as "primitive" may satisfy our sense

of modern superiority, it does not give consideration to the underlying purposes of the old practices.

Private sacrifice was meant to place the offerer into a meaningful and direct relationship with God. This was accomplished by bringing the prescribed food (animal or plant) to a sacred place, consuming it there in an atmosphere of holy ritual, and at the same time sharing a portion of the sacrifice with the priests. In the case of animal offerings the procedure was basically this: instead of slaughtering the animal privately and eating it privately (as was the overwhelming practice everywhere), it was killed at a special spot, its meat was shared with representatives of the Temple, and it was consumed in an atmosphere of gratitude, exaltation, repentance, or other sentiment appropriate to the occasion for the sacrifice. Frequently such cultic meals were the only occasions on which the worshipers would or could afford to eat meat. While certain sacrifices were thought to derive religious validity from the mere act of offering them, those which were brought for the purpose of atonement required repentance and amends; and without these the sacrifice was considered worthless [9]. Public offerings like those prescribed for holy days were to reflect the awareness of the whole community that God dwelt in its midst.

What do moderns consider "primitive" about such rituals? Doubtless, the pre-biblical origins of sacrifice go back to beliefs that the gods desired the food for their consumption. But the Torah itself no longer gives any warrant for the continuation of such beliefs, and Ps. 50:8 ff. expressly disavows them. Most likely it is the public nature of the ancient slaughtering process that is repellent to current tastes. We prefer to hide the procedure behind the walls of abattoirs where the animals are killed in a fashion no less bloody, but without making it

necessary for the consumer to witness the life-and-death cycle which goes into his pleasurable nourishment. Moreover, even when we share with others in the eating process, we do not generally experience any of the genuinely worthy emotions which were usually engendered by the sacrifices of old. In the root meaning of the English word, we do not "sacrifice" (i.e., render holy) anything when we eat.

This does not mean that our age ought to be ready for any reconsideration of cultic sacrifice. It does suggest that when seen in its own context the biblical order of animal offerings was a genuine form of worship that cannot be quickly dismissed with prejudicial contemporary judgments.

The Status of Women

In the wide span covered by the biblical tradition, the status of women varies from time to time. Still, it may be said that throughout the Bible, and especially in the narrative sections, they are given important and highly sympathetic treatment. Women like Miriam, Deborah, Ruth, and Esther are clearly heroines on a par with men.

However, such treatment does not basically alter the inferior social and legal position of females throughout the ancient Near East. While the Torah records a number of laws in which men and women are treated equally (for instance, as regards reverence for parents; punishment in cases of incest; and dietary observances), it is on the whole male-oriented. The male has rights the female does not enjoy. She is to be wife and mother, invested with inherent dignity, to be sure, but by law and social order relegated to a second-class status comparable to that of minors. The second chapter of Genesis perpetuates the tradition that the male was created first and that, in opposition to the subsequent biological order, woman was fashioned from him: she was of him

and therefore forever must belong to him.

The daughters of Zelophehad are accorded special treatment—but only so long as they fulfill the primary purpose of preserving the integrity of tribe and land (Num. 36:6), reflecting the fact that men always remained members of their tribe, while women might in effect join another tribe by marriage. Chapter 30 clearly indicates the general biblical view of women's status: it limits their competence even when it comes to such personal matters as vows. Later Jewish law sought to meliorate the legal disadvantages of the female and to give her wider protection in matters of marriage, divorce, and inheritance. While it equalized the responsibility of both sexes with regard to negative ("You shall not . . .") commandments, it found itself incapable of breaking through the framework of certain restrictions. Even now, Orthodox practice provides that it is the man who betrothes the woman and who sanctifies her in marriage—and not vice versa. Consequently it is he who must divorce her, and without his consent the marriage generally cannot be dissolved. To this day the signature of a youthful male is valid on a document while that of a mature woman is not.

Such disabilities are in part traceable to the Bible, but in effect go much beyond it. Male dominance of human affairs is rooted in prehistoric developments and is found to have been nearly universal. There have been occasional instances of matriarchal social orders and tales of fabled Amazons (such as those reputed to have lived near the Black Sea or in South America), but these exceptions pale in comparison with history's pervasive male orientation. The biblical record deals with the realities of its age (as in the matter of slavery). It does so, however, with the underlying assumption that, while religious rites revolve around men, the religious impulse and God's relationship to women are neither prejudiced nor affected. In matters of human dignity, faith, and ethical behavior, the Bible knows only of human beings without respect to their sexual differences.

GLEANINGS

Food for God

The Torah has God say, literally, "My food" (Num. 28:2). But does God need food? Rather, it means, your offerings of charity constitute His "food."   CHASIDIC [10]

Does God Need Atonement?

The text speaks of a "sin offering to the Lord" (Num. 28:15), which could also be understood as an "offering in behalf of the Lord." But does God need atonement? In a manner of speaking, He does: He himself atones for making the moon smaller and paler than the sun. (This is an oblique way of suggesting that God atones for Israel's sufferings, for Israel is compared to the moon, pale during history's daylight hours, and shining only in its nighttime.)   MIDRASH [11]

But another tradition, bypassing allegory, says: God needs no atonement from man, nor does He need sacrifices. These opportunities were instituted for man's benefit only.   MIDRASH [12]

Seven

The numbers of animals to be offered on Sukot are in multiples of seven: seventy bullocks, ninety-eight lambs, fourteen rams, seven goats. Comments the Talmud: the seventy bullocks serve as atonement for the seventy nations of the world (implying Israel's responsibility for humanity's sins); and the ninety-eight lambs serve to avert the ninety-eight curses in Deut. 28:15–68. [13]

Tradition

The daily sacrifice was to be offered in the morning (Num. 28:4), but no such provision was made for the Sabbath. This is why Jews go to the synagogue early every day, but on the Sabbath they delay.[1]   SHULCHAN ARUCH [15]

The Nature of Sacrifice

Sacrifice was the external expression of man's personal response to a personal God. It was not a mechanical, magic gesture with an efficacy unrelated to the interior dispositions of the one offering it. If sacrifice was not motivated by sincere interior dispositions, it was empty formalism, a mocking of true divine-human relationship. . . . Israelite sacrifice was not a simple concept: It was not uniquely the offering of a *gift* to God to acknowledge His dominion, nor uniquely a *means of effecting union* with Him, nor uniquely an *act of expiation*. Simultaneously it was all three and more.   J. J. CASTELOT [16]

The People Always

Moses spoke "to the heads of the tribes, to the Children of Israel" (so literally Num. 30:2). From this you may learn that when speaking to leaders one must keep in mind the people.[2]

CHASIDIC [18]

---

[1] The Sephardim do not have this tradition [14].
[2] The same verse, with its special mention of leaders, serves in another context as a legal warrant for learned men ("heads") to annul a person's rash vow [17].

Mornings and Evenings

Sacrifices are symbols of repentance. There-fore, even as sacrifices are offered early and late, man must repent both mornings and evenings.

CHASIDIC [19]

For You

The Torah speaks of *"your* new moons" (Num. 28:11). Rabbi Akiba said: When new moons and festivals are celebrated in a way that they are only "yours" (that is, man's) and not also God's and celebrated for His sake, then God says: "I hate *your* new moons and festivals" (Isa. 1:14), even though elsewhere He says: "These are *My* festivals" (Lev. 23:2).   MIDRASH [20]

Obligations of Men and Women

All positive commandments which must be fulfilled at a certain time are obligatory on men, but not on women (e.g., listening to the shofar sounds at the Rosh Hashanah service), but if they do not depend on a fixed time they must be ob-served by men and women alike (like returning a lost article or fixing a mezuzah to the doorpost). But negative commandments, whether dependent on a fixed time or not, are obligatory on both men and women alike (e.g., not working on Shabbat or abstaining from forbidden foods).[3] [21]

Solar and Lunar Calendars

We can assume that at first the solar calendar was used. With the return from Babylonian exile, the lunar calendar was used, with reliance on the testimony of witnesses and the actual day on which the moon was sighted was declared new moon. Toward the end of the Second Tem-ple, the day the witnesses testified was also eligible to be Rosh Chodesh although the moon was sighted on another day. This was done only under special circumstances and for a specific reason— the sacrifices. After the destruction of the Temple, the day of testimony was always declared new moon except for the months of Tishri and Nisan because of the holidays. Rabban Gamaliel (first century C.E.) began relying on calculations though he did not abolish the witnesses. In the days of Ulla (third century C.E.) the festivals were inten-tionally shifted around to prevent them from coming on certain days of the week.

MENACHEM RAAB [22]

---

[3] There are exceptions to these general rules; for instance, women too must eat matzah on the Seder night, and they are exempt from certain rules about touching dead bodies.

War and First Settlement

Chapter 31 deals with Moses' last military enterprise, the campaign against the Midianites. The Midianites are described as the instigators of the immoralities at Baal-peor, and the war against them is set down as a divinely imposed obligation (Num. 25:16, 17). The priest Phinehas rather than Joshua is placed in command, for the struggle becomes more than a fight for living space; it assumes religious character as "the Lord's vengeance" (Num. 31:3), since the command to exterminate the Midianites is ascribed to God.

Once the war is won, the first permanent settlement takes place. Chapter 32 tells why the tribes of Gad, Reuben, and one-half of Manasseh desire to stay in this area, east of the Jordan, and describes the conditions under which they are allowed to do so. The land at issue is the area forming the major portion of modern Transjordan (formerly the Hashemite Kingdom of Jordan), with its capital of Amman, just east of the lands the ancient Israelites captured and settled. The biblical boundaries stretched from the Arnon River to the Sea of Galilee. East of it was the land of Ammon; north of it, Amurru (from which a portion known as Gilead was also taken); and to the south, Moab. In the time of David and Solomon (about 300 years later), the Israelites briefly extended their trans-Jordanian possessions to the north, to include the Golan Heights, and to the east, to areas beyond today's Amman.

The interest in preserving the statistics of the war booty is but one example of the great attention to records apparent throughout the book.

וְאֶת־צוּר וְאֶת־חוּר וְאֶת־רֶבַע חֲמֵשֶׁת מַלְכֵי מִדְיָן וְאֵת   א וַיְדַבֵּר יְהֹוָה אֶל־מֹשֶׁה לֵּאמֹר: נְקֹם נִקְמַת בְּנֵי יִשְׂרָאֵל

בִּלְעָם בֶּן־בְּעוֹר הָרְגוּ בֶּחָרֶב: וַיִּשְׁבּוּ בְנֵי־יִשְׂרָאֵל   ט   ב מֵאֵת הַמִּדְיָנִים אַחַר תֵּאָסֵף אֶל־עַמֶּיךָ: וַיְדַבֵּר מֹשֶׁה

אֶת־נְשֵׁי מִדְיָן וְאֶת־טַפָּם וְאֵת כָּל־בְּהֶמְתָּם וְאֶת־כָּל־   ג אֶל־הָעָם לֵאמֹר הֵחָלְצוּ מֵאִתְּכֶם אֲנָשִׁים לַצָּבָא

מִקְנֵיהֶם וְאֶת־כָּל־חֵילָם בָּזָזוּ: וְאֵת כָּל־עָרֵיהֶם   י   ד וְיִהְיוּ עַל־מִדְיָן לָתֵת נִקְמַת־יְהֹוָה בְּמִדְיָן: אֶלֶף לַמַּטֶּה

בְּמוֹשְׁבֹתָם וְאֵת כָּל־טִירֹתָם שָׂרְפוּ בָּאֵשׁ: וַיִּקְחוּ אֶת־   יא   אֶלֶף לַמַּטֶּה לְכֹל מַטּוֹת יִשְׂרָאֵל תִּשְׁלְחוּ לַצָּבָא:

כָּל־הַשָּׁלָל וְאֵת כָּל־הַמַּלְקוֹחַ בָּאָדָם וּבַבְּהֵמָה: ה וַיִּמָּסְרוּ מֵאַלְפֵי יִשְׂרָאֵל אֶלֶף לַמַּטֶּה שְׁנֵים־עָשָׂר אֶלֶף

וַיָּבִאוּ אֶל־מֹשֶׁה וְאֶל־אֶלְעָזָר הַכֹּהֵן וְאֶל־עֲדַת בְּנֵי־   יב   ו חֲלוּצֵי צָבָא: וַיִּשְׁלַח אֹתָם מֹשֶׁה אֶלֶף לַמַּטֶּה לַצָּבָא

יִשְׂרָאֵל אֶת־הַשְּׁבִי וְאֶת־הַמַּלְקוֹחַ וְאֶת־הַשָּׁלָל אֶל־   אֹתָם וְאֶת־פִּינְחָס בֶּן־אֶלְעָזָר הַכֹּהֵן לַצָּבָא וּכְלֵי

הַמַּחֲנֶה אֶל־עַרְבֹת מוֹאָב אֲשֶׁר עַל־יַרְדֵּן יְרֵחוֹ: ס   ז הַקֹּדֶשׁ וַחֲצֹצְרוֹת הַתְּרוּעָה בְּיָדוֹ: וַיִּצְבְּאוּ עַל־מִדְיָן

וַיֵּצְאוּ מֹשֶׁה וְאֶלְעָזָר הַכֹּהֵן וְכָל־נְשִׂיאֵי הָעֵדָה   יג   ח כַּאֲשֶׁר צִוָּה יְהֹוָה אֶת־מֹשֶׁה וַיַּהַרְגוּ כָּל־זָכָר: וְאֶת־

לִקְרָאתָם אֶל־מִחוּץ לַמַּחֲנֶה: וַיִּקְצֹף מֹשֶׁה עַל   יד   מַלְכֵי מִדְיָן הָרְגוּ עַל־חַלְלֵיהֶם אֶת־אֱוִי וְאֶת־רֶקֶם

1] The LORD spoke to Moses, saying, **2]** "Avenge the Israelite people on the Midianites; then you shall be gathered to your kin."

3] Moses spoke to the people, saying, "Let men be picked out from among you for a campaign, and let them fall upon Midian to wreak the LORD's vengeance on Midian. **4]** You shall dispatch on the campaign a thousand from every one of the tribes of Israel."

5] So a thousand from each tribe were furnished from the divisions of Israel, twelve thousand picked for the campaign. **6]** Moses dispatched them on the campaign, a thousand from each tribe, with Phinehas son of Eleazar serving as priest on the campaign, equipped with the sacred utensils and the trumpets for sounding the blasts. **7]** They took the field against Midian, as the LORD had commanded Moses, and slew every male. **8]** Along with their other victims, they slew the kings of Midian: Evi, Rekem, Zur, Hur, and Reba, the five kings of Midian. They also put Balaam son of Beor to the sword.

9] The Israelites took the women and children of the Midianites captive, and seized as booty all their beasts, all their herds, and all their wealth. **10]** And they destroyed by fire all the towns in which they were settled, and their encampments. **11]** They gathered all the spoil and all the booty, man and beast, **12]** and they brought the captives, the booty, and the spoil to Moses, Eleazar the priest, and the whole Israelite community, at the camp in the steppes of Moab, at the Jordan near Jericho.

13] Moses, Eleazar the priest, and all the chieftains of the community came out to meet them outside the camp. **14]** Moses became angry with the commanders of the army, the officers of

---

31:4] *A thousand from every one of the tribes.* Each tribe furnished an *elef*, which is here and elsewhere translated as "a thousand," but more likely means "contingent" or "unit" of varying size (see commentary to 1:1–2:34).

6] *Phinehas.* Whose demonstrated zeal (Num. 25:7) made him a fitting symbol of the real purpose of the campaign.

The sacred utensils. Perhaps the Ark of the Covenant or the holy garments with the Urim and Thummim [1].

8] *Balaam.* Like the passage in Josh. 13:22, this verse and verse 16 are apparently from a tradition other than the main Balaam story (Num. 22 ff.), which reports that the prophet returned to his native land (Num. 24:25) and not to Midian.

Ibn Ezra harmonizes these accounts by saying that Balaam must have gone to Midian on some other occasion.

10] *The towns.* Better, "protected encampments," the Midianites being nomads who had no towns.

פְּקוּדֵי הֶחָיִל שָׂרֵי הָאֲלָפִים וְשָׂרֵי הַמֵּאוֹת הַבָּאִים

וְכָל־כְּלִי־עֵץ תִּתְחַטָּאוּ: ס וַיֹּאמֶר אֶלְעָזָר הַכֹּהֵן כא

יד מִצְּבָא הַמִּלְחָמָה: וַיֹּאמֶר אֲלֵיהֶם מֹשֶׁה הַחִיִּיתֶם כָּל־

אֶל־אַנְשֵׁי הַצָּבָא הַבָּאִים לַמִּלְחָמָה זֹאת חֻקַּת הַתּוֹרָה

טו נְקֵבָה: הֵן הֵנָּה הָיוּ לִבְנֵי יִשְׂרָאֵל בִּדְבַר בִּלְעָם

אֲשֶׁר־צִוָּה יְהוָה אֶת־מֹשֶׁה: אַךְ אֶת־הַזָּהָב וְאֶת־הַכָּסֶף כב

לִמְסָר־מַעַל בַּיהוָה עַל־דְּבַר־פְּעוֹר וַתְּהִי הַמַּגֵּפָה

אֶת־הַנְּחֹשֶׁת אֶת־הַבַּרְזֶל אֶת־הַבְּדִיל וְאֶת־הָעֹפָרֶת:

יז בַּעֲדַת יְהוָה: וְעַתָּה הִרְגוּ כָל־זָכָר בַּטָּף וְכָל־אִשָּׁה

כָּל־דָּבָר אֲשֶׁר־יָבֹא בָאֵשׁ תַּעֲבִירוּ בָאֵשׁ וְטָהֵר אַךְ כג

יז יֹדַעַת אִישׁ לְמִשְׁכַּב זָכָר הֲרֹגוּ: וְכֹל הַטַּף בַּנָּשִׁים

בְּמֵי נִדָּה יִתְחַטָּא וְכֹל אֲשֶׁר לֹא־יָבֹא בָּאֵשׁ תַּעֲבִירוּ

יח אֲשֶׁר לֹא־יָדְעוּ מִשְׁכַּב זָכָר הַחֲיוּ לָכֶם: וְאַתֶּם חֲנוּ

בַמָּיִם: וְכִבַּסְתֶּם בִּגְדֵיכֶם בַּיּוֹם הַשְּׁבִיעִי וּטְהַרְתֶּם כד

מִחוּץ לַמַּחֲנֶה שִׁבְעַת יָמִים כֹּל הֹרֵג נֶפֶשׁ וְכֹל נֹגֵעַ

וְאַחַר תָּבֹאוּ אֶל־הַמַּחֲנֶה: ס וַיֹּאמֶר יְהוָה אֶל־מֹשֶׁה כה

בֶּחָלָל תִּתְחַטְּאוּ בַּיּוֹם הַשְּׁלִישִׁי וּבַיּוֹם הַשְּׁבִיעִי אַתֶּם

לֵּאמֹר: שָׂא אֵת רֹאשׁ מַלְקוֹחַ הַשְּׁבִי בָּאָדָם וּבַבְּהֵמָה: כו

כ וּשְׁבִיכֶם: וְכָל־בֶּגֶד וְכָל־כְּלִי־עוֹר וְכָל־מַעֲשֵׂה עִזִּים

אַתָּה וְאֶלְעָזָר הַכֹּהֵן וְרָאשֵׁי אֲבוֹת הָעֵדָה: וְחָצִיתָ כז

thousands and the officers of hundreds, who had come back from the military campaign.
15] Moses said to them, "You have spared every female!   16] Yet they are the very ones who, at the bidding of Balaam, induced the Israelites to trespass against the LORD in the matter of Peor, so that the LORD's community was struck by the plague.   17] Now, therefore, slay every male among the children, and slay also every woman who has known a man carnally;   18] but spare every young woman who has not had carnal relations with a man.

19] "You shall then stay outside the camp seven days; every one among you or among your captives who has slain a person or touched a corpse shall cleanse himself on the third and seventh days.   20] You shall also cleanse every cloth, every article of skin, everything made of goats' hair, and every object of wood."

21] Eleazar the priest said to the troops who had taken part in the fighting, "This is the ritual law that the LORD has enjoined upon Moses: 22] Gold and silver, copper, iron, tin and lead   23] —any article that can withstand fire—these you shall pass through fire and they shall be clean, except that they must be cleansed with water of lustration; and anything that cannot withstand fire you must pass through water.   24] On the seventh day you shall wash your clothes and be clean, and after that you may enter the camp."

25] The LORD said to Moses: 26] "You and Eleazar the priest and the family heads of the community take an inventory of the booty that was captured, man and beast,   27] and divide

17] *Has known a man carnally*. She was not to live since she might have been one of the seducers of Baal-peor (Num. 25:1–5). The virgins were spared; they would be married to Israelites and absorbed into the mainstream of religion and culture. There was at this time no prohibition against marriages with non-Israelites.

Another interpretation says that those old enough to have had sexual relations were included

in the ban [2].

23] *They shall be clean*. Having become defiled through contact with the dead.

Water of lustration. Described in Num. 19:12 ff. Jewish tradition, maintaining that only vessels used for food were included in this regulation [3]. took these rules as the basis for the rules governing the *kashering* of utensils (see Gleanings).

את־הַמַּלְק֗וֹחַ בֵּ֚ין תֹּפְשֵׂ֣י הַמִּלְחָמָ֔ה הַיֹּצְאִ֖ים לַצָּבָ֑א
כח וּבֵ֖ין כָּל־הָעֵדָֽה: וַהֲרֵמֹתָ֨ מֶ֜כֶס לַיהֹוָ֗ה מֵאֵ֣ת אַנְשֵׁ֣י
הַמִּלְחָמָה֮ הַיֹּצְאִ֣ים לַצָּבָא֒ אֶחָ֣ד נֶ֔פֶשׁ מֵחֲמֵ֖שׁ הַמֵּא֑וֹת
מִן־הָֽאָדָם֙ וּמִן־הַבָּקָ֔ר וּמִן־הַחֲמֹרִ֖ים וּמִן־הַצֹּֽאן:
כט מִמַּֽחֲצִיתָ֖ם תִּקָּ֑חוּ וְנָֽתַתָּ֛ה לְאֶלְעָזָ֥ר הַכֹּהֵ֖ן תְּרוּמַ֥ת
ל יְהֹוָֽה: וּמִמַּֽחֲצִ֨ת בְּנֵֽי־יִשְׂרָאֵ֜ל תִּקַּ֣ח ׀ אֶחָ֣ד ׀ אָחֻ֣ז מִן־
הַֽחֲמִשִּׁ֗ים מִן־הָֽאָדָ֧ם מִן־הַבָּקָ֛ר מִן־הַֽחֲמֹרִ֖ים וּמִן־הַצֹּ֑אן
מִכָּל־הַבְּהֵמָ֑ה וְנָֽתַתָּ֤ה אֹתָם֙ לַֽלְוִיִּ֔ם שֹֽׁמְרֵ֕י מִשְׁמֶ֖רֶת
לא מִשְׁכַּ֣ן יְהֹוָֽה: וַיַּ֣עַשׂ מֹשֶׁ֔ה וְאֶלְעָזָ֖ר הַכֹּהֵ֑ן כַּֽאֲשֶׁ֛ר צִוָּ֥ה
לב יְהֹוָ֖ה אֶת־מֹשֶֽׁה: וַיְהִי֙ הַמַּלְק֔וֹחַ יֶ֣תֶר הַבָּ֔ז אֲשֶׁ֥ר בָּֽזְז֖וּ
עַ֣ם הַצָּבָ֑א צֹ֗אן שֵׁשׁ־מֵא֥וֹת אֶ֛לֶף וְשִׁבְעִ֥ים אָ֖לֶף
לג וַֽחֲמֵ֥שֶׁת אֲלָפִֽים: וּבָקָ֕ר שְׁנַ֥יִם וְשִׁבְעִ֖ים אָ֑לֶף: וַֽחֲמֹרִ֕ים

לה אֶחָ֥ד וּשְׁלֹשִׁ֖ים אָ֑לֶף: וְנֶ֣פֶשׁ אָדָ֔ם מִן־הַנָּשִׁ֕ים אֲשֶׁ֥ר לֹֽא־
יָֽדְע֖וּ מִשְׁכַּ֣ב זָכָ֑ר כָּל־נֶ֕פֶשׁ שְׁנַ֥יִם וּשְׁלֹשִׁ֖ים אָֽלֶף:
לו וַתְּהִי֙ הַמֶּֽחֱצָ֔ה חֵ֕לֶק הַיֹּֽצְאִ֖ים בַּצָּבָ֑א מִסְפַּ֣ר הַצֹּ֗אן
שְׁלֹשׁ־מֵא֥וֹת אֶ֛לֶף וּשְׁלֹשִׁ֥ים אֶ֖לֶף וְשִׁבְעַ֥ת אֲלָפִ֖ים
לז וַֽחֲמֵ֥שׁ מֵאֽוֹת: וַיְהִ֧י הַמֶּ֣כֶס לַיהֹוָ֖ה מִן־הַצֹּ֑אן שֵׁ֥שׁ מֵא֖וֹת
לח חָמֵ֥שׁ וְשִׁבְעִֽים: וְהַ֨בָּקָ֔ר שִׁשָּׁ֥ה וּשְׁלֹשִׁ֖ים אָ֑לֶף וּמִכְסָ֥ם
לט לַֽיהֹוָ֖ה שְׁנַ֥יִם וְשִׁבְעִֽים: וַֽחֲמֹרִ֕ים שְׁלֹשִׁ֥ים אֶ֖לֶף וַֽחֲמֵ֣שׁ
מ מֵא֑וֹת וּמִכְסָ֥ם לַֽיהֹוָ֖ה אֶחָ֥ד וְשִׁשִּֽׁים: וְנֶ֣פֶשׁ אָדָ֔ם שִׁשָּׁ֥ה
מא עָשָׂ֖ר אָ֑לֶף וּמִכְסָ֣ם לַֽיהֹוָ֔ה שְׁנַ֥יִם וּשְׁלֹשִׁ֖ים נָֽפֶשׁ: וַיִּתֵּ֣ן
מֹשֶׁ֗ה אֶת־מֶ֨כֶס֙ תְּרוּמַ֣ת יְהֹוָ֔ה לְאֶלְעָזָ֖ר הַכֹּהֵ֑ן כַּֽאֲשֶׁ֛ר
מב צִוָּ֥ה יְהֹוָ֖ה אֶת־מֹשֶֽׁה: וּמִֽמַּֽחֲצִ֖ית בְּנֵ֣י יִשְׂרָאֵ֑ל אֲשֶׁ֤ר
חָצָ֣ה מֹשֶׁ֔ה מִן־הָֽאֲנָשִׁ֖ים הַצֹּֽבְאִֽים: וַתְּהִ֛י מֶֽחֱצַ֥ת הָֽעֵדָ֖ה

the booty equally between the combatants who engaged in the campaign and the rest of the community. **28]** You shall exact a levy for the LORD: in the case of the warriors who engaged in the campaign, one item in five hundred, of persons, oxen, asses, and sheep, **29]** shall be taken from their half-share and given to Eleazar the priest as a contribution to the LORD; **30]** and from the half-share of the other Israelites you shall withhold one in every fifty human beings as well as cattle, asses, and sheep—all the animals—and give them to the Levites, who attend to the duties of the LORD's Tabernacle."

31] Moses and Eleazar the priest did as the LORD commanded Moses. **32]** The amount of booty, other than the spoil that the troops had plundered, came to 675,000 sheep, **33]** 72,000 head of cattle, **34]** 61,000 asses, **35]** and a total of 32,000 human beings, namely, the women who had not had carnal relations.

36] Thus, the half-share of those who had engaged in the campaign [was as follows]: The number of sheep was 337,500, **37]** and the LORD's levy from the sheep was 675; **38]** the cattle came to 36,000, from which the LORD's levy was 72; **39]** the asses came to 30,500, from which the LORD's levy was 61. **40]** And the number of human beings was 16,000, from which the LORD's levy was 32. **41]** Moses gave the contributions levied for the LORD to Eleazar the priest, as the LORD had commanded Moses.

42] As for the half-share of the other Israelites, which Moses withdrew from the men who

---

27] *Divide the booty equally.* This applied only to captured women and cattle, not to other booty, such as food, clothing, and trinkets, which the soldiers would keep (verse 53). The practice is mentioned again in connection with one of David's battles and is there described as having been instituted by him. No mention is made of the Torah law (I Sam. 30:24, 25).

28] *You shall exact.* Although the warriors kept some booty and shared it equally, they needed to

pay only one-tenth of the tax levied on those who stayed at home. The Koran provides that one-fifth of the spoils are to be dedicated [4].

30] *One in every fifty.* The mathematical or symbolic system doubtlessly inherent in many of the figures here becomes again apparent: the proportion 1:50 is the same as 12 units to 600 units, which left Egypt (or 12,000: 600,000 in the traditional rendering).

מִדְּהַצֹּאן שְׁלֹשׁ־מֵאוֹת אֶלֶף וּשְׁלֹשִׁים אֶלֶף שִׁבְעַת

טַבַּעַת עָגִיל וְכוּמָז לְכַפֵּר עַל־נַפְשֹׁתֵינוּ לִפְנֵי יְהוָה:

מד אֲלָפִים וַחֲמֵשׁ מֵאוֹת: וּבָקָר שִׁשָּׁה וּשְׁלֹשִׁים אֶלֶף:

נא וַיִּקַּח מֹשֶׁה וְאֶלְעָזָר הַכֹּהֵן אֶת־הַזָּהָב מֵאִתָּם כָּל כְּלִי

מה וַחֲמֹרִים שְׁלֹשִׁים אֶלֶף וַחֲמֵשׁ מֵאוֹת: וְנֶפֶשׁ אָדָם שִׁשָּׁה

נב מַעֲשֶׂה: וַיְהִי כָּל־זְהַב הַתְּרוּמָה אֲשֶׁר הֵרִימוּ לַיהוָה

מו עָשָׂר אָלֶף: וַיִּקַּח מֹשֶׁה מִמַּחֲצִת בְּנֵי־יִשְׂרָאֵל אֶת־

שִׁשָּׁה עָשָׂר אֶלֶף שְׁבַע־מֵאוֹת וַחֲמִשִּׁים שָׁקֶל מֵאֵת

הָאָחֻז אֶחָד מִן־הַחֲמִשִּׁים מִן־הָאָדָם וּמִן־הַבְּהֵמָה וַיִּתֵּן

נג שָׂרֵי הָאֲלָפִים וּמֵאֵת שָׂרֵי הַמֵּאוֹת: אַנְשֵׁי הַצָּבָא בָּזְזוּ

אֹתָם לַלְוִיִּם שֹׁמְרֵי מִשְׁמֶרֶת מִשְׁכַּן יְהוָה כַּאֲשֶׁר צִוָּה

נד אִישׁ לוֹ: וַיִּקַּח מֹשֶׁה וְאֶלְעָזָר הַכֹּהֵן אֶת־הַזָּהָב מֵאֵת

מח יְהוָה אֶת־מֹשֶׁה: וַיִּקְרְבוּ אֶל־מֹשֶׁה הַפְּקֻדִים אֲשֶׁר

שָׂרֵי הָאֲלָפִים וְהַמֵּאוֹת וַיָּבִאוּ אֹתוֹ אֶל־אֹהֶל מוֹעֵד

מט לְאַלְפֵי הַצָּבָא שָׂרֵי הָאֲלָפִים וְשָׂרֵי הַמֵּאוֹת: וַיֹּאמְרוּ

זִכָּרוֹן לִבְנֵי־יִשְׂרָאֵל לִפְנֵי יְהוָה: פ

אֶל־מֹשֶׁה עֲבָדֶיךָ נָשְׂאוּ אֶת־רֹאשׁ אַנְשֵׁי הַמִּלְחָמָה

נ אֲשֶׁר בְּיָדֵנוּ וְלֹא־נִפְקַד מִמֶּנּוּ אִישׁ: וַנַּקְרֵב אֶת־קָרְבַּן

א וּמִקְנֶה רַב הָיָה לִבְנֵי רְאוּבֵן וְלִבְנֵי־גָד עָצוּם מְאֹד

יְהוָה אִישׁ אֲשֶׁר מָצָא כְלִי־זָהָב אֶצְעָדָה וְצָמִיד

וַיִּרְאוּ אֶת־אֶרֶץ יַעְזֵר וְאֶת־אֶרֶץ גִּלְעָד וְהִנֵּה הַמָּקוֹם

ב מְקוֹם מִקְנֶה: וַיָּבֹאוּ בְנֵי־גָד וּבְנֵי רְאוּבֵן וַיֹּאמְרוּ אֶל־

had taken the field, **43]** that half-share of the community consisted of 337,500 sheep, **44]** 36,000 head of cattle, **45]** 30,500 asses, **46]** and 16,000 human beings. **47]** From this half-share of the Israelites, Moses withheld one in every fifty humans and animals; and he gave them to the Levites, who attended to the duties of the LORD's Tabernacle, as the LORD had commanded Moses.

48] The commanders of the troop divisions, the officers of thousands and the officers of hundreds, approached Moses. **49]** They said to Moses, "Your servants have made a check of the warriors in our charge, and not one of us is missing. **50]** So we have brought as an offering to the LORD such articles of gold as each of us came upon: armlets, bracelets, signet rings, earrings, and pendants, that expiation may be made for our persons before the LORD." **51]** Moses and Eleazar the priest accepted the gold from them, all kinds of wrought articles. **52]** All the gold that was offered by the officers of thousands and the officers of hundreds as a contribution to the LORD came to 16,750 shekels. **53]** —But in the ranks everyone kept his booty for himself.— **54]** So Moses and Eleazar the priest accepted the gold from the officers of thousands and the officers of hundreds and brought it to the Tent of Meeting, as a reminder in behalf of the Israelites before the LORD.

1] The Reubenites and the Gadites owned cattle in very great numbers. Noting that the lands of Jazer and Gilead were a region suitable for cattle, **2]** the Gadites and the Reubenites came to Moses, Eleazar the priest, and the chieftains of the community, and said, **3]** "Ataroth,

50] *Pendants.* Jewelry was highly regarded by nomads such as the Midianites, for it was transportable wealth.

The term כּוּמָז (*kumaz*) also occurs in the story of the building of the Tabernacle (Exod. 35:22). The King James Version translates "tablets," the Revised Standard Version "beads."

Expiation. For what is not stated—perhaps for the general slaughter in which they had engaged [5]. (See Gleanings.)

54] *As a reminder.* See Exod. 30:16. The gold was probably fashioned into sacred vessels [6].

32:1] *Jazer.* A little west of today's Amman.

Gilead. A name given to various areas east of the Jordan, between the Dead Sea and the Sea of Galilee. In this verse it seems to refer to areas south of the Jabbok River, and in verse 39 to land farther north.

משֶׁה וְאֶל־אֶלְעָזָר הַכֹּהֵן וְאֶל־נְשִׂיאֵי הָעֵדָה לֵאמֹר:

יוַיִּחַר־אַף יְהֹוָה בַּיּוֹם הַהוּא
עֲטָרוֹת וְדִיבֹן וְיַעְזֵר וְנִמְרָה וְחֶשְׁבּוֹן וְאֶלְעָלֵה וּשְׂבָם

אֲשֶׁר־נָתַן לָהֶם יְהֹוָה:

יאוַיִּשָּׁבַע לֵאמֹר אִם־יִרְאוּ הָאֲנָשִׁים הָעֹלִים מִמִּצְרַיִם
וּנְבוֹ וּבְעֹן: דהָאָרֶץ אֲשֶׁר הִכָּה יְהֹוָה לִפְנֵי עֲדַת

מִבֶּן עֶשְׂרִים שָׁנָה וָמַעְלָה אֵת הָאֲדָמָה אֲשֶׁר נִשְׁבַּעְתִּי
יִשְׂרָאֵל אֶרֶץ מִקְנֶה הִוא וְלַעֲבָדֶיךָ מִקְנֶה: ס

לְאַבְרָהָם לְיִצְחָק וּלְיַעֲקֹב כִּי לֹא־מִלְאוּ אַחֲרָי:
הוַיֹּאמְרוּ אִם־מָצָאנוּ חֵן בְּעֵינֶיךָ יֻתַּן אֶת־הָאָרֶץ הַזֹּאת

יבבִּלְתִּי כָלֵב בֶּן־יְפֻנֶּה הַקְּנִזִּי וִיהוֹשֻׁעַ בִּן־נוּן כִּי מִלְאוּ
לַעֲבָדֶיךָ לַאֲחֻזָּה אַל־תַּעֲבִרֵנוּ אֶת־הַיַּרְדֵּן: יוַיֹּאמֶר

אַחֲרֵי יְהֹוָה: יגוַיִּחַר־אַף יְהֹוָה בְּיִשְׂרָאֵל וַיְנִעֵם בַּמִּדְבָּר
משֶׁה לִבְנֵי־גָד וְלִבְנֵי רְאוּבֵן הַאַחֵיכֶם יָבֹאוּ לַמִּלְחָמָה

אַרְבָּעִים שָׁנָה עַד־תֹּם כָּל־הַדּוֹר הָעֹשֶׂה הָרַע בְּעֵינֵי
זוְאַתֶּם תֵּשְׁבוּ פֹה: וְלָמָּה תְנִיאוּן אֶת־לֵב בְּנֵי יִשְׂרָאֵל

יהֹוָה: ידוְהִנֵּה קַמְתֶּם תַּחַת אֲבֹתֵיכֶם תַּרְבּוּת אֲנָשִׁים
מֵעֲבֹר אֶל־הָאָרֶץ אֲשֶׁר־נָתַן לָהֶם יְהֹוָה: חכֹּה עָשׂוּ

חַטָּאִים לִסְפּוֹת עוֹד עַל חֲרוֹן אַף־יְהֹוָה אֶל־יִשְׂרָאֵל:
אֲבֹתֵיכֶם בְּשָׁלְחִי אֹתָם מִקָּדֵשׁ בַּרְנֵעַ לִרְאוֹת אֶת־

טוכִּי תְשׁוּבֻן מֵאַחֲרָיו וְיָסַף עוֹד לְהַנִּיחוֹ בַּמִּדְבָּר
הָאָרֶץ: טוַיַּעֲלוּ עַד־נַחַל אֶשְׁכּוֹל וַיִּרְאוּ אֶת־הָאָרֶץ

וְשִׁחַתֶּם לְכָל־הָעָם הַזֶּה: ס טזוַיִּגְּשׁוּ אֵלָיו וַיֹּאמְרוּ
וַיָּנִיאוּ אֶת־לֵב בְּנֵי יִשְׂרָאֵל לְבִלְתִּי־בֹא אֶל־הָאָרֶץ

גִּדְרֹת צֹאן נִבְנֶה לְמִקְנֵנוּ פֹּה וְעָרִים לְטַפֵּנוּ: יזוַאֲנַחְנוּ
נֵחָלֵץ חֻשִׁים לִפְנֵי בְּנֵי יִשְׂרָאֵל עַד אֲשֶׁר אִם־הֲבִיאֹנֻם

יז תניאון קרי.

Dibon, Jazer, Nimrah, Heshbon, Elealeh, Sebam, Nebo, and Beon— 4] the land that the LORD has conquered for the community of Israel is cattle country, and your servants have cattle. 5] It would be a favor to us," they continued, "if this land were given to your servants as a holding; do not move us across the Jordan."

6] Moses replied to the Gadites and the Reubenites, "Are your brothers to go to war while you stay here? 7] Why will you turn the minds of the Israelites from crossing into the land which the LORD has given them? 8] That is what your fathers did when I sent them from Kadesh-barnea to survey the land. 9] After going up to the wadi Eshcol and surveying the land, they turned the minds of the Israelites from invading the land that the LORD had given them. 10] Thereupon the LORD was incensed and He swore, 11] 'None of the men from twenty years up who came out of Egypt shall see the land that I promised on oath to Abraham, Isaac and Jacob, for they did not remain loyal to Me— 12] none except Caleb son of Jephunneh the Kenizzite and Joshua son of Nun, for they remained loyal to the LORD.' 13] The LORD was incensed at Israel, and for forty years He made them wander in the wilderness, until the whole generation that had provoked the LORD's displeasure was gone. 14] And now you, a breed of sinful men, have replaced your fathers, to add still further to the LORD's wrath against Israel. 15] If you turn away from Him and He abandons them once more in the wilderness, you will bring calamity upon all this people."

16] Then they stepped up to him and said, "We will build here sheepfolds for our flocks and towns for our children. 17] And we will hasten as shock-troops in the van of the Israelites

3] *Ataroth, Dibon . . . and Beon.* Some of these cities were recaptured from Israel by King Mesha of Moab (ninth century B.C.E.) amidst a great massacre. The record of this campaign was inscribed by the king on a stone, which was discovered in 1868 and which is so far the most extensive single record of the Moabite language (closely related to Hebrew) [7].

Heshbon. See Num. 21:25.

4] *Cattle country.* To this day it is extolled in an Arab proverb [8].

8] *What your fathers did.* As related in Num. 13 and 14.

12] *Kenizzite.* A clan later absorbed into the tribe of Judah.

אֶל־מְקוֹמָם וְיָשַׁב טַפֵּנוּ בְּעָרֵי הַמִּבְצָר מִפְּנֵי יֹשְׁבֵי
יח הָאָרֶץ: לֹא נָשׁוּב אֶל־בָּתֵּינוּ עַד הִתְנַחֵל בְּנֵי יִשְׂרָאֵל
יט אִישׁ נַחֲלָתוֹ: כִּי לֹא נִנְחַל אִתָּם מֵעֵבֶר לַיַּרְדֵּן וָהָלְאָה
כִּי בָאָה נַחֲלָתֵנוּ אֵלֵינוּ מֵעֵבֶר הַיַּרְדֵּן מִזְרָחָה: פ
כ וַיֹּאמֶר אֲלֵיהֶם מֹשֶׁה אִם־תַּעֲשׂוּן אֶת־הַדָּבָר הַזֶּה אִם־
כא תֵּחָלְצוּ לִפְנֵי יְהוָה לַמִּלְחָמָה: וְעָבַר לָכֶם כָּל־חָלוּץ
אֶת־הַיַּרְדֵּן לִפְנֵי יְהוָה עַד הוֹרִישׁוֹ אֶת־אֹיְבָיו מִפָּנָיו:
כב וְנִכְבְּשָׁה הָאָרֶץ לִפְנֵי יְהוָה וְאַחַר תָּשֻׁבוּ וִהְיִיתֶם נְקִיִּם
מֵיְהוָה וּמִיִּשְׂרָאֵל וְהָיְתָה הָאָרֶץ הַזֹּאת לָכֶם לַאֲחֻזָּה
כג לִפְנֵי יְהוָה: וְאִם־לֹא תַעֲשׂוּן כֵּן הִנֵּה חֲטָאתֶם לַיהוָה
כד וּדְעוּ חַטַּאתְכֶם אֲשֶׁר תִּמְצָא אֶתְכֶם: בְּנוּ־לָכֶם עָרִים
לְטַפְּכֶם וּגְדֵרֹת לְצֹנַאֲכֶם וְהַיֹּצֵא מִפִּיכֶם תַּעֲשׂוּ:

כה וַיֹּאמֶר בְּנֵי־גָד וּבְנֵי רְאוּבֵן אֶל־מֹשֶׁה לֵאמֹר עֲבָדֶיךָ
כו יַעֲשׂוּ כַּאֲשֶׁר אֲדֹנִי מְצַוֶּה: טַפֵּנוּ נָשֵׁינוּ מִקְנֵנוּ וְכָל־
כז בְּהֶמְתֵּנוּ יִהְיוּ־שָׁם בְּעָרֵי הַגִּלְעָד: וַעֲבָדֶיךָ יַעַבְרוּ
כָּל־חֲלוּץ צָבָא לִפְנֵי יְהוָה לַמִּלְחָמָה כַּאֲשֶׁר אֲדֹנִי
כח דֹּבֵר: וַיְצַו לָהֶם מֹשֶׁה אֵת אֶלְעָזָר הַכֹּהֵן וְאֵת יְהוֹשֻׁעַ
בִּן־נוּן וְאֶת־רָאשֵׁי אֲבוֹת הַמַּטּוֹת לִבְנֵי יִשְׂרָאֵל: כט וַיֹּאמֶר
מֹשֶׁה אֲלֵהֶם אִם־יַעַבְרוּ בְנֵי־גָד וּבְנֵי־רְאוּבֵן אִתְּכֶם
אֶת־הַיַּרְדֵּן כָּל־חָלוּץ לַמִּלְחָמָה לִפְנֵי יְהוָה וְנִכְבְּשָׁה
הָאָרֶץ לִפְנֵיכֶם וּנְתַתֶּם לָהֶם אֶת־אֶרֶץ הַגִּלְעָד
ל לַאֲחֻזָּה: וְאִם־לֹא יַעַבְרוּ חֲלוּצִים אִתְּכֶם וְנֹאחֲזוּ
לא בְתֹכְכֶם בְּאֶרֶץ כְּנָעַן: וַיַּעֲנוּ בְנֵי־גָד וּבְנֵי רְאוּבֵן
לֵאמֹר אֵת אֲשֶׁר דִּבֶּר יְהוָה אֶל־עֲבָדֶיךָ כֵּן נַעֲשֶׂה:

* כה סבירין ויאמרו.

until we have established them in their home, while our children stay in the fortified towns because of the inhabitants of the land. 18] We will not return to our homes until every one of the Israelites is in possession of his portion. 19] But we will not have a share with them in the territory beyond the Jordan, for we have received our share on the east side of the Jordan."

20] Moses said to them, "If you do this, if you go to battle as shock-troops, at the instance of the LORD, 21] and every shock-fighter among you crosses the Jordan, at the instance of the LORD, until He has dispossessed His enemies before Him, 22] and the land has been subdued, at the instance of the LORD, and then you return—you shall be clear before the LORD and before Israel; and this land shall be your holding under the LORD. 23] But if you do not do so, you will have sinned against the LORD; and know that your sin will overtake you. 24] Build towns for your children and sheepfolds for your flocks, but do what you have promised."

25] The Gadites and the Reubenites answered Moses, "Your servants will do as my lord commands. 26] Our children, our wives, our flocks, and all our other livestock will stay behind in the towns of Gilead; 27] while your servants, all those recruited for war, cross over, at the instance of the LORD, to engage in battle—as my lord orders."

28] Then Moses gave instructions concerning them to Eleazar the priest, Joshua son of Nun, and the family heads of the Israelite tribes. 29] Moses said to them, "If every shock-fighter among the Gadites and the Reubenites crosses the Jordan with you to do battle, at the instance of the LORD, and the land is subdued before you, you shall give them the land of Gilead as a holding. 30] But if they do not cross over with you as shock-troops, they shall receive holdings among you in the land of Canaan."

31] The Gadites and the Reubenites said in reply, "Whatever the LORD has spoken concerning your servants, that we will do. 32] We ourselves will cross over as shock-troops, at the

---

21] *Shock-fighter.* חָלוּץ (*chalutz*), in contemporary Hebrew "a pioneer" [9]. Others read "armed" [10], although Gad and Reuben were not armed more than the others. The New English Bible has "drafted."

23] *Sin will overtake you.* Compare the similar image in God's warning to Cain (Gen. 4:7).

31] *In reply.* They now affirmed their promises publicly.

לב נַחְנוּ נַעֲבֹר חֲלוּצִים לִפְנֵי יְהוָה אֶרֶץ כְּנָעַן וְאִתָּנוּ
לג אֲחֻזַּת נַחֲלָתֵנוּ מֵעֵבֶר לַיַּרְדֵּן: וַיִּתֵּן לָהֶם מֹשֶׁה לִבְנֵי־
גָד וְלִבְנֵי רְאוּבֵן וְלַחֲצִי שֵׁבֶט מְנַשֶּׁה בֶן־יוֹסֵף אֶת־
מַמְלֶכֶת סִיחֹן מֶלֶךְ הָאֱמֹרִי וְאֶת־מַמְלֶכֶת עוֹג מֶלֶךְ
הַבָּשָׁן הָאָרֶץ לְעָרֶיהָ בִּגְבֻלֹת עָרֵי הָאָרֶץ סָבִיב:
לד וַיִּבְנוּ בְנֵי־גָד אֶת־דִּיבֹן וְאֶת־עֲטָרֹת וְאֵת עֲרֹעֵר: וְאֶת־
לה עַטְרֹת שׁוֹפָן וְאֶת־יַעְזֵר וְיָגְבֳהָה: וְאֶת־בֵּית נִמְרָה
לו וְאֶת־בֵּית הָרָן עָרֵי מִבְצָר וְגִדְרֹת צֹאן: וּבְנֵי רְאוּבֵן

לז בָּנוּ אֶת־חֶשְׁבּוֹן וְאֶת־אֶלְעָלֵא וְאֵת קִרְיָתָיִם: וְאֶת־נְבוֹ
וְאֶת־בַּעַל מְעוֹן מוּסַבֹּת שֵׁם וְאֶת־שִׂבְמָה וַיִּקְרְאוּ
בְשֵׁמֹת אֶת־שְׁמוֹת הֶעָרִים אֲשֶׁר בָּנוּ: וַיֵּלְכוּ בְּנֵי מָכִיר
בֶּן־מְנַשֶּׁה גִּלְעָדָה וַיִּלְכְּדֻהָ וַיּוֹרֶשׁ אֶת־הָאֱמֹרִי אֲשֶׁר־
בָּהּ: וַיִּתֵּן מֹשֶׁה אֶת־הַגִּלְעָד לְמָכִיר בֶּן־מְנַשֶּׁה וַיֵּשֶׁב
בָּהּ: וְיָאִיר בֶּן־מְנַשֶּׁה הָלַךְ וַיִּלְכֹּד אֶת־חַוֹּתֵיהֶם וַיִּקְרָא
אֶתְהֶן חַוֹּת יָאִיר: וְנֹבַח הָלַךְ וַיִּלְכֹּד אֶת־קְנָת וְאֶת־
בְּנֹתֶיהָ וַיִּקְרָא לָה נֹבַח בִּשְׁמוֹ:

Haftarah Matot, p. 1278

instance of the LORD, into the land of Canaan; and we shall keep our hereditary holding across the Jordan."

33] So Moses assigned to them—to the Gadites, the Reubenites, and the half-tribe of Manasseh son of Joseph—the kingdom of Sihon king of the Amorites and the kingdom of Og king of Bashan, the land with its various cities and the territories of their surrounding towns. **34]** The Gadites rebuilt Dibon, Ataroth, Aroer, **35]** Atroth-shophan, Jazer, Jogbehah, **36]** Beth-nimrah, and Beth-haran as fortified towns or as enclosures for flocks. **37]** The Reubenites rebuilt Heshbon, Elealeh, Kiriathaim, **38]** Nebo, Baal-meon—some names being changed—and Sibmah; they gave [their own] names to towns that they rebuilt. **39]** The descendants of Machir son of Manasseh went to Gilead and captured it, dispossessing the Amorites who were there; **40]** so Moses gave Gilead to Machir son of Manasseh, and he settled there. **41]** Jair son of Manasseh went and captured their villages, which he renamed Havvoth-jair. **42]** And Nobah went and captured Kenath and its dependencies, renaming it Nobah after himself.

32] *Across the Jordan.* That is (seen from Canaan), Transjordan.

33] *Half-tribe of Manasseh.* Who had not previously figured in the discussion; possibly a later addition to explain Manasseh's presence on the east bank.

34] *Gadites rebuilt.* The cities named had been destroyed during the war.

Aroer. In the southeast corner of the territory under discussion, where one would have expected the tribe of Reuben. Perhaps some of the towns changed hands [11].

39] *Went to Gilead.* Apparently on a special campaign of their own, penetrating farther north. Some scholars consider verses 39–42 as a separate tradition, perhaps a fragment from an account of conquests after Moses' death [12].

41] *Their villages.* The text should probably read "[he] captured Havvoth-ham which he renamed Havvoth-jair," reading חַוֹּת הָם for חַוֹּתֵיהֶם. הָם (Ham) is listed as a town in Gen. 14:5.

42] *Nobah.* A family of the tribe of Manasseh, not otherwise identified.

The Slaying of the Prisoners

The text reports the killing of all Midianite males by the Israelites and then, at the express behest of Moses, the further dispatch of all women who might have had a share in the sexual orgies referred to in chapter 25. This report contains historical and moral problems of a high order.

Note first that the war itself is hardly dealt with; the emphasis is on cultic matters—purification and the division of spoils. Note further that, while the enemy is massacred, not one Israelite is reported missing (Num. 31:49), which leads to the assumption that this section is not an actual report but a schematic reconstruction of events long past, with the aim of showing how God had protected His people and how, in return, certain things were owed to Him. The nonhistorical aspects of this account may also be seen in the listing of extraordinarily large numbers of people slain and booty captured. Finally, though "every male" was said to have been killed, such was far from the actual fact. At most only a portion of the Midianites could have been killed, for not only did they not disappear as a nation, but they dominated Israel a relatively short time thereafter (see Josh. 6–8). In sum, then, the details of the Midianite war may be said to constitute a form of biblical interpretation of the past [13].

However, this exacerbates the moral question. For if the extermination of the Midianites did not in fact take place, or at least not to the extent detailed in the text, what would move the authors of the Torah to write as though it had taken place? How can the idea of slaughtering so many prisoners be reconciled with the humanitarian ideals and the deep sense of compassion that are the very heart of the Torah?

The matter puzzled the ancients as well.

A midrash attempts to relieve God of responsibility and comments that Moses' anger brought him to sin, implying that it was not God but Moses who issued the fatal command concerning the Midianite women, and that God punished him for it.[1] Exempting God from responsibility does not, however, explain why the text, by its silence, appears to condone the procedure.

The fact is that, as in the matter of slavery and the status of women, the Torah speaks within the context of its time. It accepts certain matters as "normal"—and wars, with their slaughter and cruelties, belong to them. The Torah does, however, require of men who had killed a ritual atonement—a unique provision in any human code [15]—and it introduces certain meliorating rules. (These may be compared to the various Geneva conventions of modern times applying themselves not to war as such but to the treatment of prisoners and civilians whose fate is to be bettered in conflicts still to occur.) To be sure, prophetic vision looked to a time when all wars would be abolished, but such a vision addressed itself to post-history or at best to the distant future. The realities have not changed greatly to this day, except that in many ways modern war may have increased the cruelties practiced in ancient, more "primitive" times.

The biblical account, which, as indicated, represents a reconstruction of history, is to be seen as a statement of what should have happened rather than what actually happened. It doubtlessly came from an age when Israel had trouble with the native inhabitants of its conquered territories and when widespread immorality was ascribed to these components of the population. The wilderness history thus became a retroactive judgment by a later age: if the injunctions

---

[1] The punishment is said to have consisted of God's entrusting the laws of cleansing to Eleazar rather than to Moses (see Num. 31:14), which cannot be taken seriously as the intent of the text [14].

of Moses had been followed there would have been fewer troubles in the centuries to follow. The great leader, it was implied, knew that idolatry and sexual excess often went together, and he had given the prescription for dealing with the problem root

and branch. The passages recorded in chapter 31 are concerned primarily with Israel's purity and reflect the belief that as long as idolaters were a significant part of the population the purposes of the Law could never be fully achieved.[2]

[2] This same belief also underlies the biblical injunction to exterminate the native peoples in Canaan,

which command was, of course, never carried out in actual history.

GLEANINGS

Responsibility

Why did Moses become angry with the officers and not with the common soldiers (Num. 31:14)? To teach us that in every generation corruption is the responsibility of the leaders.

MIDRASH [16]

Halachah on Kashrut

The Orthodox laws concerning the fitness of eating vessels are based on the provisions of Num. 31:21–23. They provide, for instance, that in order to *kasher* certain utensils, such as spits used in fire, these should be brought to white heat ("pass through fire"); dishes and similar articles used for hot liquid or moist food should be cleansed in boiling water; and utensils used for cold foods only are to be rinsed or soaked. [17]

Halachah on Marriage

On the basis of verse 15 (which exempts female children from the decree), Rabbi Shimon bar Yochai declared: a child converted by herself when three years or younger (as, for instance, a gentile baby adopted into a Jewish family today) is a fit mate for a priest who otherwise is forbidden to marry converts. [18]

Why Moses Became Angry

The accusation leveled by Moses against Reuben and Gad (Num. 32:6 ff.) seems intemperate, especially in view of what follows, for the tribes were not at all lacking in responsibility. Says Isaac Arama (fifteenth century C.E.): "One would think that Moses ought to have apologized for having mistaken their motive. Why did he not do so? Because his anger was in fact justified. He saw their real motives: they had found a good living and did not want to give it up. The spiritual import of the Promised Land meant nothing to them. They considered settlement a purely economic matter—anywhere. They spoke in pragmatic terms while Moses no fewer than four times reminded them of God's share in the Land" [19]. Therefore the Midrash comments: they became fond of their material possessions and loved their money, settling outside the Land, and in the end they were the first to be exiled (I Chron. 5:26)[3] [21].

B. S. JACOBSON [22]

Things before People

God said to Reuben and Gad: since you mention your cattle before your children (Num. 32:16) you will find no blessing in your wealth.[4]

MIDRASH [23]

[3] However, there is another tradition that stresses the eagerness and humility of Reuben and Gad. This is based on the shortened Hebrew form for "we" in verse 32, implying that the two tribes made

themselves small [20].

[4] The Midrash notes that Moses corrected them, putting the children first (verse 24).

Appearance

The Torah commands Reuben and Gad to be "clear before the Lord and before Israel" (Num. 32:22). The idea contained in this phrase became a great moral maxim among the Rabbis. "Man should be clear not only before God but also in the estimation of his fellowmen." A man should avoid doing even those things that appear wrong.

J. H. HERTZ [24]

Halachah on Conditional Contracts

The way the land was given to Reuben and Gad on the condition that they fulfill their promise became the foundation for the Jewish law of conditional contracts (tenaim). The four basic principles are: the condition must be stated twice, once positively and once negatively (as Moses did); the positive condition must precede the negative; the "if" must precede the "what"; and the condition must be fulfillable.

SHULCHAN ARUCH [25]

Review of the Wanderings;
Boundaries of Canaan

Forty-two way stations are listed in the recapitulation of the forty years of wandering. The order of some of these halting places is at variance with what is told in Num. 21, and a number of these places cannot be securely located. The list begins with the Exodus and reviews the long journey in the manner of an archival record. The major divisions are the following:

From Rameses (Egypt) to the Sinai desert (verses 5–15 and compare Num. 10:11)—one year.

In the Sinai and Zin deserts (verses 16–36)—thirty-eight years.

From Kadesh (Zin desert) to the Plains of Moab (verses 37–49)—fortieth year [1]. (See the map at chapter 21.)

Following these divisions, the section describes the projected boundaries of the land to be invaded and tells how the Israelites are to deal with the native peoples. Rules governing the apportionment of the land and the appointment of supervisors are then set down. Only Joshua and Caleb remain of the old guard; the other names are all new, for a new generation with its own leadership has grown up. With some exceptions, the listing of the tribes proceeds from the south to the north of the forthcoming settlement.

(The last weekly portion, *Mas'ey*, begins with 33:1.)

פ פ פ

א אֵלֶּה מַסְעֵי בְנֵי־יִשְׂרָאֵל אֲשֶׁר יָצְאוּ מֵאֶרֶץ מִצְרָיִם
ב לְצִבְאֹתָם בְּיַד־מֹשֶׁה וְאַהֲרֹן: וַיִּכְתֹּב מֹשֶׁה אֶת־
מוֹצָאֵיהֶם לְמַסְעֵיהֶם עַל־פִּי יְהֹוָה וְאֵלֶּה מַסְעֵיהֶם
ג לְמוֹצָאֵיהֶם: וַיִּסְעוּ מֵרַעְמְסֵס בַּחֹדֶשׁ הָרִאשׁוֹן
בַּחֲמִשָּׁה עָשָׂר יוֹם לַחֹדֶשׁ הָרִאשׁוֹן מִמָּחֳרַת הַפֶּסַח
יָצְאוּ בְנֵי־יִשְׂרָאֵל בְּיָד רָמָה לְעֵינֵי כָּל־מִצְרָיִם:
ד וּמִצְרַיִם מְקַבְּרִים אֵת אֲשֶׁר הִכָּה יְהֹוָה בָּהֶם כָּל־
ה בְּכוֹר וּבֵאלֹהֵיהֶם עָשָׂה יְהֹוָה שְׁפָטִים: וַיִּסְעוּ בְנֵי־
ו יִשְׂרָאֵל מֵרַעְמְסֵס וַיַּחֲנוּ בְּסֻכֹּת: וַיִּסְעוּ מִסֻּכֹּת וַיַּחֲנוּ

ז בְאֵתָם אֲשֶׁר בִּקְצֵה הַמִּדְבָּר: וַיִּסְעוּ מֵאֵתָם וַיָּשָׁב
עַל־פִּי הַחִירֹת אֲשֶׁר עַל־פְּנֵי בַּעַל צְפוֹן וַיַּחֲנוּ לִפְנֵי
ח מִגְדֹּל: וַיִּסְעוּ מִפְּנֵי הַחִירֹת וַיַּעַבְרוּ בְתוֹךְ־הַיָּם
הַמִּדְבָּרָה וַיֵּלְכוּ דֶּרֶךְ שְׁלֹשֶׁת יָמִים בְּמִדְבַּר אֵתָם
ט וַיַּחֲנוּ בְּמָרָה: וַיִּסְעוּ מִמָּרָה וַיָּבֹאוּ אֵילִמָה וּבְאֵילִם
שְׁתֵּים עֶשְׂרֵה עֵינֹת מַיִם וְשִׁבְעִים תְּמָרִים וַיַּחֲנוּ־שָׁם:
י וַיִּסְעוּ מֵאֵילִם וַיַּחֲנוּ עַל־יַם־סוּף: וַיִּסְעוּ מִיַּם־סוּף
יא יב וַיַּחֲנוּ בְּמִדְבַּר־סִין: וַיִּסְעוּ מִמִּדְבַּר־סִין וַיַּחֲנוּ בְּדָפְקָה:
יג וַיִּסְעוּ מִדָּפְקָה וַיַּחֲנוּ בְּאָלוּשׁ: וַיִּסְעוּ מֵאָלוּשׁ וַיַּחֲנוּ
יד בִּרְפִידִם וְלֹא־הָיָה שָׁם מַיִם לָעָם לִשְׁתּוֹת: וַיִּסְעוּ

1] These were the marches of the Israelites who started out from the land of Egypt, troop by troop, in the charge of Moses and Aaron. 2] Moses recorded the starting points of their various marches as directed by the LORD. Their marches, by starting points, were as follows:

3] They set out from Rameses in the first month, on the fifteenth day of the first month. It was on the morrow of the passover offering that the Israelites started out boldly, in plain view of all the Egyptians. 4] The Egyptians meanwhile were burying those among them whom the LORD had struck down, every first-born—whereby the LORD executed judgment on their gods.

5] The Israelites set out from Rameses and encamped at Succoth. 6] They set out from Succoth and encamped at Etham, which is on the edge of the wilderness. 7] They set out from Etham and turned about toward Pi-hahiroth, which faces Baal-zephon, and they encamped before Migdol. 8] They set out from Pene-hahiroth and passed through the sea into the wilderness; and they made a three-days' journey in the wilderness of Etham and encamped at Marah. 9] They set out from Marah and came to Elim. There were twelve springs in Elim and seventy palm trees, so they encamped there. 10] They set out from Elim and encamped by the Sea of Reeds. 11] They set out from the Sea of Reeds and encamped in the wilderness of Sin. 12] They set out from the wilderness of Sin and encamped at Dophkah. 13] They set out from Dophkah and encamped at Alush. 14] They set out from Alush and encamped at Rephidim; it was there that the people had no water to

33:2] As directed. A subclause to "various marches." But according to Nachmanides it was the recording of the wanderings by Moses which was directed by God, so that Israel might always remember the guiding hand of God.

3] Rameses. Which as slaves in Egypt they had helped to build (Exod. 1:11).

6] Edge of the wilderness. Called wilderness of Shur in Exod. 15:22.

8] Pene-hahiroth. In Exod. 14:2, Pi-hahiroth; also in Num. elsewhere.

14] Rephidim. The battle with the Amalekites (Exod. 17:8) that took place here is not mentioned, nor are the giving of manna and the revelation at Sinai. Perhaps these events were so well known that they did not need a special note [2]. Modern Rephidim is in the Sinai peninsula, not far from the Suez Canal, and not the likely spot for the ancient battle with Amalek.

טו מֵרְפִידִם וַיַּחֲנוּ בְּמִדְבַּר סִינָי: וַיִּסְעוּ מִמִּדְבַּר סִינָי
טז וַיַּחֲנוּ בְּקִבְרֹת הַתַּאֲוָה: וַיִּסְעוּ מִקִּבְרֹת הַתַּאֲוָה וַיַּחֲנוּ
יז בַּחֲצֵרֹת: וַיִּסְעוּ מֵחֲצֵרֹת וַיַּחֲנוּ בְּרִתְמָה: וַיִּסְעוּ
כ מֵרִתְמָה וַיַּחֲנוּ בְּרִמֹּן פָּרֶץ: וַיִּסְעוּ מֵרִמֹּן פָּרֶץ וַיַּחֲנוּ
כא בְּלִבְנָה: וַיִּסְעוּ מִלִּבְנָה וַיַּחֲנוּ בְּרִסָּה: וַיִּסְעוּ מֵרִסָּה
כב וַיַּחֲנוּ בִּקְהֵלָתָה: וַיִּסְעוּ מִקְּהֵלָתָה וַיַּחֲנוּ בְּהַר שָׁפֶר:
כג וַיִּסְעוּ מֵהַר שָׁפֶר וַיַּחֲנוּ בַּחֲרָדָה: וַיִּסְעוּ מֵחֲרָדָה וַיַּחֲנוּ
כד בְּמַקְהֵלֹת: וַיִּסְעוּ מִמַּקְהֵלֹת וַיַּחֲנוּ בְּתָחַת: וַיִּסְעוּ
כה מִתָּחַת וַיַּחֲנוּ בְּתָרַח: וַיִּסְעוּ מִתָּרַח וַיַּחֲנוּ בְּמִתְקָה:
כו וַיִּסְעוּ מִמִּתְקָה וַיַּחֲנוּ בְּחַשְׁמֹנָה: וַיִּסְעוּ מֵחַשְׁמֹנָה וַיַּחֲנוּ
כז בְּמֹסֵרוֹת: וַיִּסְעוּ מִמֹּסֵרוֹת וַיַּחֲנוּ בִּבְנֵי יַעֲקָן: וַיִּסְעוּ
לא מִבְּנֵי יַעֲקָן וַיַּחֲנוּ בְּחֹר הַגִּדְגָּד: וַיִּסְעוּ מֵחֹר הַגִּדְגָּד

לה וַיַּחֲנוּ בְּיָטְבָתָה: וַיִּסְעוּ מִיָּטְבָתָה וַיַּחֲנוּ בְּעַבְרֹנָה:
לו וַיִּסְעוּ מֵעַבְרֹנָה וַיַּחֲנוּ בְּעֶצְיֹן גָּבֶר: וַיִּסְעוּ מֵעֶצְיֹן גָּבֶר
לז וַיַּחֲנוּ בְמִדְבַּר צִן הִוא קָדֵשׁ: וַיִּסְעוּ מִקָּדֵשׁ וַיַּחֲנוּ בְּהֹר
לח הָהָר בִּקְצֵה אֶרֶץ אֱדוֹם: וַיַּעַל אַהֲרֹן הַכֹּהֵן אֶל הֹר
הָהָר עַל פִּי יְהוָה וַיָּמָת שָׁם בִּשְׁנַת הָאַרְבָּעִים לְצֵאת
בְּנֵי יִשְׂרָאֵל מֵאֶרֶץ מִצְרַיִם בַּחֹדֶשׁ הַחֲמִישִׁי בְּאֶחָד
לט לַחֹדֶשׁ: וְאַהֲרֹן בֶּן שָׁלֹשׁ וְעֶשְׂרִים וּמְאַת שָׁנָה בְּמֹתוֹ
מ בְּהֹר הָהָר: ס וַיִּשְׁמַע הַכְּנַעֲנִי מֶלֶךְ עֲרָד וְהוּא
יֹשֵׁב בַּנֶּגֶב בְּאֶרֶץ כְּנָעַן בְּבֹא בְּנֵי יִשְׂרָאֵל: וַיִּסְעוּ מֵהֹר
מא הָהָר וַיַּחֲנוּ בְּצַלְמֹנָה: וַיִּסְעוּ מִצַּלְמֹנָה וַיַּחֲנוּ בְּפוּנֹן:
מג וַיִּסְעוּ מִפּוּנֹן וַיַּחֲנוּ בְּאֹבֹת: וַיִּסְעוּ מֵאֹבֹת וַיַּחֲנוּ בְּעִיֵּי
מד הָעֲבָרִים בִּגְבוּל מוֹאָב: וַיִּסְעוּ מֵעִיִּים וַיַּחֲנוּ בְּדִיבֹן

drink. **15]** They set out from Rephidim and encamped in the wilderness of Sinai. **16]** They set out from the wilderness of Sinai and encamped at Kibroth-hattaavah. **17]** They set out from Kibroth-hattaavah and encamped at Hazeroth. **18]** They set out from Hazeroth and encamped at Rithmah. **19]** They set out from Rithmah and encamped at Rimmon-perez. **20]** They set out from Rimmon-perez and encamped at Libnah. **21]** They set out from Libnah and encamped at Rissah. **22]** They set out from Rissah and encamped at Kehelath. **23]** They set out from Kehelath and encamped at Mount Shepher. **24]** They set out from Mount Shepher and encamped at Haradah. **25]** They set out from Haradah and encamped at Makheloth. **26]** They set out from Makheloth and encamped at Tahath. **27]** They set out from Tahath and encamped at Terah. **28]** They set out from Terah and encamped at Mithkah. **29]** They set out from Mithkah and encamped at Hashmonah. **30]** They set out from Hashmonah and encamped at Moseroth. **31]** They set out from Moseroth and encamped at Bene-jaakan. **32]** They set out from Bene-jaakan and encamped at Hor-haggidgad. **33]** They set out from Hor-haggidgad and encamped at Jotbath. **34]** They set out from Jotbath and encamped at Abronah. **35]** They set out from Abronah and encamped at Ezion-geber. **36]** They set out from Ezion-geber and encamped in the wilderness of Zin, that is, Kadesh. **37]** They set out from Kadesh and encamped at Mount Hor, on the edge of the land of Edom.

38] Aaron the priest ascended Mount Hor at the command of the LORD and died there, in the fortieth year after the Israelites had left the land of Egypt, on the first day of the fifth month. **39]** Aaron was a hundred and twenty-three years old when he died on Mount Hor. **40]** And the Canaanite, king of Arad, who dwelt in the Negeb, in the land of Canaan, learned of the coming of the Israelites.

41] They set out from Mount Hor and encamped at Zalmonah. **42]** They set out from Zalmonah and encamped at Punon. **43]** They set out from Punon and encamped at Oboth. **44]** They set out from Oboth and encamped at Iye-abarim, in the territory of Moab. **45]** They

---

35] *Ezion-geber.* At the head of the Gulf of Aqaba. Glueck identified it as Elath (modern Eilat), but it is now believed to have been the island of Jazirat-Farun. See also Deut. 2:8 [3].

מה   גָּד: וַיִּסְעוּ מִדִּיבֹן גָּד וַיַּחֲנוּ בְּעַלְמֹן דִּבְלָתָיְמָה: וַיִּסְעוּ
מֵעַלְמֹן דִּבְלָתָיְמָה וַיַּחֲנוּ בְּהָרֵי הָעֲבָרִים לִפְנֵי נְבוֹ:

מו   וַיִּסְעוּ מֵהָרֵי הָעֲבָרִים וַיַּחֲנוּ בְּעַרְבֹת מוֹאָב עַל יַרְדֵּן

מז   יְרֵחוֹ: וַיַּחֲנוּ עַל־הַיַּרְדֵּן מִבֵּית הַיְשִׁמֹת עַד אָבֵל

מח   הַשִּׁטִּים בְּעַרְבֹת מוֹאָב: ס וַיְדַבֵּר יְהוָֹה אֶל־מֹשֶׁה

מט   בְּעַרְבֹת מוֹאָב עַל־יַרְדֵּן יְרֵחוֹ לֵאמֹר: דַּבֵּר אֶל־בְּנֵי

נ   יִשְׂרָאֵל וְאָמַרְתָּ אֲלֵהֶם כִּי אַתֶּם עֹבְרִים אֶת־הַיַּרְדֵּן

נא   אֶל־אֶרֶץ כְּנָעַן: וְהוֹרַשְׁתֶּם אֶת־כָּל־יֹשְׁבֵי הָאָרֶץ

נב   מִפְּנֵיכֶם וְאִבַּדְתֶּם אֵת כָּל־מַשְׂכִּיֹּתָם וְאֵת כָּל־צַלְמֵי

נג   מַסֵּכֹתָם תְּאַבֵּדוּ וְאֵת כָּל־בָּמוֹתָם תַּשְׁמִידוּ: וְהוֹרַשְׁתֶּם
אֶת־הָאָרֶץ וִישַׁבְתֶּם־בָּהּ כִּי לָכֶם נָתַתִּי אֶת־הָאָרֶץ

יד   לָרֶשֶׁת אֹתָהּ: וְהִתְנַחַלְתֶּם אֶת־הָאָרֶץ בְּגוֹרָל
לְמִשְׁפְּחֹתֵיכֶם לָרַב תַּרְבּוּ אֶת־נַחֲלָתוֹ וְלַמְעַט תַּמְעִיט
אֶת־נַחֲלָתוֹ אֶל אֲשֶׁר־יֵצֵא לוֹ שָׁמָּה הַגּוֹרָל לוֹ יִהְיֶה

טו   לְמַטּוֹת אֲבֹתֵיכֶם תִּתְנֶחָלוּ: וְאִם־לֹא תוֹרִישׁוּ אֶת־
יֹשְׁבֵי הָאָרֶץ מִפְּנֵיכֶם וְהָיָה אֲשֶׁר תּוֹתִירוּ מֵהֶם
לְשִׂכִּים בְּעֵינֵיכֶם וְלִצְנִינִם בְּצִדֵּיכֶם וְצָרֲרוּ אֶתְכֶם

נו   עַל־הָאָרֶץ אֲשֶׁר אַתֶּם יֹשְׁבִים בָּהּ: וְהָיָה כַּאֲשֶׁר
דִּמִּיתִי לַעֲשׂוֹת לָהֶם אֶעֱשֶׂה לָכֶם: פ

לד   וַיְדַבֵּר יְהוָֹה אֶל־מֹשֶׁה לֵּאמֹר: צַו אֶת־בְּנֵי יִשְׂרָאֵל
וְאָמַרְתָּ אֲלֵהֶם כִּי־אַתֶּם בָּאִים אֶל־הָאָרֶץ כְּנָעַן זֹאת
הָאָרֶץ אֲשֶׁר תִּפֹּל לָכֶם בְּנַחֲלָה אֶרֶץ כְּנַעַן

---

set out from Iyim and encamped at Dibon-gad. **46]** They set out from Dibon-gad and encamped at Almon-diblathaim. **47]** They set out from Almon-diblathaim and encamped in the hills of Abarim, before Nebo. **48]** They set out from the hills of Abarim and encamped in the steppes of Moab, at the Jordan near Jericho; **49]** they encamped by the Jordan from Beth-jeshimoth as far as Abel-shittim, in the steppes of Moab.

50] In the steppes of Moab, at the Jordan near Jericho, the LORD spoke to Moses, saying: **51]** Speak to the Israelite people and say to them: When you cross the Jordan into the land of Canaan, **52]** you shall dispossess all the inhabitants of the land; you shall destroy all their figured objects; you shall destroy all their molten images, and you shall demolish all their cult places. **53]** And you shall take possession of the land and settle in it, for I have given the land to you to possess it. **54]** You shall apportion the land among yourselves by lot, clan by clan: with larger groups increase the share, with smaller groups reduce the share. Wherever the lot falls for anyone, that shall be his. You shall have your portions according to your ancestral tribes. **55]** But if you do not dispossess the inhabitants of the land, those whom you allow to remain shall be stings in your eyes and thorns in your sides, and they shall harass you in the land in which you live; **56]** so that I will do to you what I planned to do to them.

1] The LORD spoke to Moses, saying: **2]** Instruct the Israelite people and say to them: When you enter the land of Canaan, this is the land that shall fall to you as your portion, the land of Canaan with its various boundaries:

52] *Figured objects.* Used for idolatrous purposes (see Lev. 26:1).

Cult places. Or, "high places." Such sacred locales on hill tops were common in many lands as earthly counterparts of divine habitats [4]. The Prophets inveighed against the continued use of these old places of pagan worship.

55] *If you do not.* An addendum explaining why the people of Israel after their settlement were in constant difficulties: they had not in fact dispossessed the native peoples.

34:2] *Fall to you as your portion.* When later on you cast it by lot.

י לִגְבֻלֹתֶיהָ: וְהָיָה לָכֶם פְּאַת־נֶגֶב מִמִּדְבַּר־צִן עַל־יְדֵי
אֱדוֹם וְהָיָה לָכֶם גְּבוּל נֶגֶב מִקְצֵה יָם־הַמֶּלַח קֵדְמָה:
ד וְנָסַב לָכֶם הַגְּבוּל מִנֶּגֶב לְמַעֲלֵה עַקְרַבִּים וְעָבַר צִנָה
וְהָיָה תּוֹצְאֹתָיו מִנֶּגֶב לְקָדֵשׁ בַּרְנֵעַ וְיָצָא חֲצַר־אַדָּר
ה וְעָבַר עַצְמֹנָה: וְנָסַב הַגְּבוּל מֵעַצְמוֹן נַחְלָה מִצְרָיִם
ו וְהָיוּ תוֹצְאֹתָיו הַיָּמָּה: וּגְבוּל יָם וְהָיָה לָכֶם הַיָּם
הַגָּדוֹל וּגְבוּל זֶה־יִהְיֶה לָכֶם גְּבוּל יָם: וְזֶה־יִהְיֶה לָכֶם
ז גְּבוּל צָפוֹן מִן־הַיָּם הַגָּדֹל תְּתָאוּ לָכֶם הֹר הָהָר:
ח מֵהֹר הָהָר תְּתָאוּ לְבֹא חֲמָת וְהָיוּ תּוֹצְאֹת הַגְּבֻל
ט צְדָדָה: וְיָצָא הַגְּבֻל זִפְרֹנָה וְהָיוּ תוֹצְאֹתָיו חֲצַר עֵינָן
י זֶה־יִהְיֶה לָכֶם גְּבוּל צָפוֹן: וְהִתְאַוִּיתֶם לָכֶם לִגְבוּל
יא קֵדְמָה מֵחֲצַר עֵינָן שְׁפָמָה: וְיָרַד הַגְּבֻל מִשְּׁפָם
* ד וְהָיוּ קרי.

הָרִבְלָה מִקֶּדֶם לָעָיִן וְיָרַד הַגְּבֻל וּמָחָה עַל־כֶּתֶף
יב יָם־כִּנֶּרֶת קֵדְמָה: וְיָרַד הַגְּבוּל הַיַּרְדֵּנָה וְהָיוּ תוֹצְאֹתָיו
יָם הַמֶּלַח זֹאת תִּהְיֶה לָכֶם הָאָרֶץ לִגְבֻלֹתֶיהָ סָבִיב:
יג וַיְצַו מֹשֶׁה אֶת־בְּנֵי יִשְׂרָאֵל לֵאמֹר זֹאת הָאָרֶץ אֲשֶׁר
תִּתְנַחֲלוּ אֹתָהּ בְּגוֹרָל אֲשֶׁר צִוָּה יְהוָה לָתֵת לְתִשְׁעַת
הַמַּטּוֹת וַחֲצִי הַמַּטֶּה: כִּי לָקְחוּ מַטֵּה בְנֵי הָראוּבֵנִי
יד לְבֵית אֲבֹתָם וּמַטֵּה בְנֵי־הַגָּדִי לְבֵית אֲבֹתָם וַחֲצִי
טו מַטֵּה מְנַשֶּׁה לָקְחוּ נַחֲלָתָם: שְׁנֵי הַמַּטּוֹת וַחֲצִי
הַמַּטֶּה לָקְחוּ נַחֲלָתָם מֵעֵבֶר לְיַרְדֵּן יְרֵחוֹ קֵדְמָה
מִזְרָחָה: פ
טז וַיְדַבֵּר יְהוָה אֶל־מֹשֶׁה לֵּאמֹר: אֵלֶּה שְׁמוֹת הָאֲנָשִׁים
יז אֲשֶׁר־יִנְחֲלוּ לָכֶם אֶת־הָאָרֶץ אֶלְעָזָר הַכֹּהֵן וִיהוֹשֻׁעַ

3] Your southern sector shall extend from the wilderness of Zin alongside Edom. Your southern boundary shall start on the east from the tip of the Dead Sea. 4] Your boundary shall then turn to pass south of the ascent of Akrabbim and continue to Zin, and its limits shall be south of Kadesh-barnea, reaching Hazar-addar and continuing to Azmon. 5] From Azmon the boundary shall turn toward the Wadi of Egypt and terminate at the Sea.

6] For the western boundary you shall have the coast of the Great Sea; that shall serve as your western boundary.

7] This shall be your northern boundary: Draw a line from the Great Sea to Mount Hor; 8] from Mount Hor draw a line to Lebo-hamath, and let the boundary reach Zedad. 9] The boundary shall then run to Ziphron and terminate at Hazar-enan. That shall be your northern boundary.

10] For your eastern boundary you shall draw a line from Hazar-enan to Shepham. 11] From Shepham the boundary shall descend to Riblah on the east side of Ain; from there the boundary shall continue downward and abut on the eastern slopes of the Sea of Chinnereth. 12] The boundary shall then descend along the Jordan and terminate at the Dead Sea.

That shall be your land as defined by its boundaries on all sides.

13] Moses instructed the Israelites, saying: This is the land you are to receive by lot as your hereditary portion, which the LORD has commanded to be given to the nine and a half tribes. 14] For the Reubenite tribe by its ancestral houses, the Gadite tribe by its ancestral houses, and the half-tribe of Manasseh have already received their portions: 15] those two and a half tribes have received their portions across the Jordan, opposite Jericho, on the east, the orient side.

16] The LORD spoke to Moses, saying: 17] These are the names of the men through whom the land shall be apportioned for you: Eleazar the priest and Joshua son of Nun. 18] And you

4] *Zin.* At the northern end of the Aravah; it may also have been called by names like Tamara, Ir ha-Temarim, Sin, and others [5].

יח בִּדְנוֹן: וְנָשִׂיא אֶחָד נָשִׂיא אֶחָד מִמַּטֶּה תִּקְחוּ לִנְחֹל
כה בֶּן־שִׁפְטָן: וּלְמַטֵּה בְנֵי־זְבוּלֻן נָשִׂיא אֱלִיצָפָן בֶּן־
יט אֶת־הָאָרֶץ: וְאֵלֶּה שְׁמוֹת הָאֲנָשִׁים לְמַטֵּה יְהוּדָה כָּלֵב
כו פַּרְנָךְ: וּלְמַטֵּה בְנֵי־יִשָּׂשכָר נָשִׂיא פַּלְטִיאֵל בֶּן־עַזָּן:
כ בֶּן־יְפֻנֶּה: וּלְמַטֵּה בְּנֵי שִׁמְעוֹן שְׁמוּאֵל בֶּן־עַמִּיהוּד:
כז וּלְמַטֵּה בְנֵי־אָשֵׁר נָשִׂיא אֲחִיהוּד בֶּן־שְׁלֹמִי: וּלְמַטֵּה
כא לְמַטֵּה בִנְיָמִן אֱלִידָד בֶּן־כִּסְלוֹן: וּלְמַטֵּה בְנֵי־דָן נָשִׂיא
כח בְנֵי־נַפְתָּלִי נָשִׂיא פְּדַהְאֵל בֶּן־עַמִּיהוּד: אֵלֶּה
כב בֻּקִּי בֶּן־יָגְלִי: לִבְנֵי יוֹסֵף לְמַטֵּה בְנֵי־מְנַשֶּׁה נָשִׂיא
כט אֲשֶׁר צִוָּה יְהֹוָה לְנַחֵל אֶת־בְּנֵי־יִשְׂרָאֵל בְּאֶרֶץ
כג חַנִּיאֵל בֶּן־אֵפֹד: וּלְמַטֵּה בְנֵי־אֶפְרַיִם נָשִׂיא קְמוּאֵל
כד   כְּנָעַן: פ

shall also take a chieftain from each tribe through whom the land shall be apportioned.
19] These are the names of the men: from the tribe of Judah: Caleb son of Jephunneh.
20] From the Simeonite tribe: Samuel son of Ammihud.   21] From the tribe of Benjamin:
Elidad son of Chislon.   22] From the Danite tribe: a chieftain, Bukki son of Jogli.   23] For
the descendants of Joseph: from the Manassite tribe: a chieftain, Hanniel son of Ephod;
24] and from the Ephraimite tribe: a chieftain, Kemuel son of Shiphtan.   25] From the
Zebulunite tribe: a chieftain, Elizaphan son of Parnach.   26] From the Issacharite tribe: a
chieftain, Paltiel son of Azzan.   27] From the Asherite tribe: a chieftain, Ahihud son of
Shelomi.   28] From the Naphtalite tribe: a chieftain, Pedahel son of Ammihud.

29] It was these whom the LORD designated to allot portions to the Israelites in the land of
Canaan.

The Boundaries of the Promised Land
(See the map at chapter 13.)

Several times the Torah projects the outlines of the Promised Land. Of these, the description in Num. 34:1-12 is the most detailed and can be identified with reasonable accuracy.[1]

The southern border ran from the lower end of the Dead Sea southwest to what today would be the middle of Israel's Negev, turning northwest toward the Brook of Egypt (Wadi el-Arish) at the sea.

The Mediterranean provided the western border, stretching from Wadi el-Arish all the way to what is now northern Lebanon, at Byblos.

The northern border ran eastward about 100 miles to a spot deep inside modern Syria, east of Damascus.

The eastern border is the most difficult to identify precisely, especially since desert areas were involved. It appears to have stretched southward from the northern boundary near Damascus and after about fifty miles turned west, where it met the southern end of the Lake of Galilee, and from there the Jordan and the Dead Sea formed the eastern line.

This territory was never for any extended time in the full control of the Israelites. Twice only did their sovereignty extend over the entire area—under David and Solomon (tenth century B.C.E.) and under Alexander Jannai (100 B.C.E.)—and once nearly so, under Jeroboam II (eighth century B.C.E.).

It has been suggested that inasmuch as the Canaan of history was generally quite different from the land described here, we should read the chapter as an idealized projection: the borders as outlined were to delineate Canaan as it ought to have been or ought to become. This interpretation has been accorded unexpected prominence in modern days, for it has been taken by some Jews as a biblically approved desideratum for fixing Israel's borders, and by Arabs as a cogent reason for fearing "Israeli expansionism."

However, such an interpretation—both ancient and modern—is erroneous, for the biblical text did not intend to make an idealized projection. In the context of the thirteenth pre-Christian century it used the term "Canaan" for the old Egyptian province of Syria-Palestine, which for centuries had been under the domination of the Pharaohs. About 1270 B.C.E., that is, at about the time when Israel was poised to invade the land, Rameses II signed a treaty with the king of the Hittites under which the Egyptian holdings were frozen to comprise the area delineated in this chapter. Thus "Canaan" was not a projection but rather a stereotype used in its day, and the borders set forth were in effect the old borders of this Egyptian province [6]. (Similar instances of geopolitical shorthand are found frequently in history; for instance, "America" today usually refers not to the continent but to the United-States.)

The territory east of the Jordan claimed by the two and one-half tribes was not included in the description, for it was not part of the Egyptian sphere of influence, and, besides, its settled population was sparse.

In fact, as we survey the many descriptions of the Land of Israel, both as Promised Land and as actually occupied space over the course of many centuries, from patriarchal to Roman times, we may distinguish five different conceptions of what constituted the land: Canaan as promised to the Patriarchs; Canaan plus the territory conquered by Moses (Transjordan); Joshua's Land of Israel;

---

[1] It is also smaller than the areas described in Gen. 15:16 and Deut. 11:24, both of which speak of the Euphrates as the eastern border. Scholars ascribe the boundaries of Num. 34 to the P tradition.

the land of actual settlement subsequent to Joshua; and the kingdoms of Israel from David on [7]. The Promised Land was both more and less than later historical conquests and settlements. It was more in that it foresaw Israel's sole occupancy of the land, unshared by the indigenous nations which were to have been (but were not) driven out; it was less in that Transjordan was never part of the Promise (so that it may be assumed that this tradition preceded the conquest by Moses).

GLEANINGS

Prefiguration

The section begins by detailing the marches which the people had undertaken, as well as their various starting points. In later generations there would be many marches and starting points for Israel—a strong reason why this portion should be studied and restudied.　　　M. HACOHEN [8]

Precious

The Holy One said: "Both the land and the people of Israel are precious to Me. I shall bring a precious people into a precious land: you both fit each other."　　　MIDRASH [9]

Unbound

Why, in the recital of the journeys, was the revelation at Sinai left out? Because once the Torah was given it became timeless and cut loose from any one place: every moment is its moment and every place its place.　　　M. HACOHEN [10]

Halachah

There are laws which are applicable only in the Promised Land and others which are operative everywhere. The boundaries mentioned in Chapter 34 determine whether or not one is inside Eretz Yisrael in the halachic sense.　　　TALMUD [11]

The Lot

Only space, not blessings, were covered by the lot. The blessings inherent in the land would have to await a later time.　　　CHASIDIC [12]

Entering the Land

The main purpose of occupying Canaan was to lead a holy life there and to preserve the sanctity of the land by keeping the Torah and its commandments. Without the Torah the Land of Israel is no more important than any other.　　　CHASIDIC [13]

Why the Stations Were Enumerated

Apparently this is an enumeration that is quite useless. But the need for this was very great. For all miracles are certain in the opinion of one who has seen them: however, at a future time their story becomes a mere traditional narrative, and there is a possibility for the hearer to consider it untrue. It is well known that it is impossible and inconceivable that a miracle lasts permanently throughout the succession of generations so that all men can see it. Now one of the miracles of the Law, and one of the greatest among them, is the sojourn of Israel for forty years in the desert and the finding of the manna there every day. For that desert was, as is stated in Scripture, a place "wherein were serpents, fiery serpents, and scorpions, and thirsty ground where there was no water" [Deut. 8:15]. Those are places that are very remote from cultivated land and unnatural for man; "it is no place of seed or of figs or of vines or of pomegranates" [Num. 20:5], and so on. It is also said of it that it is a land "that no man passed through" [Zech. 7:14], and so on. The text of the Torah states: "Ye have not eaten bread, neither have ye drunk wine or strong drink" [Deut. 29:5], and so on. All these are manifest visible miracles. Now God, may He be exalted, knew that in the future what happens to traditional narratives would happen to those

1240

miracles: People would think that [the Children of Israel] sojourned in a desert that was near to cultivated land and in which man can live, like the deserts inhabited at present by the Arabs, or that it consisted of places in which it was possible to till and to reap or to feed on plants that were to be found there, or that it was natural for the manna always to come down in those places, or that there were wells of water in those places. Therefore all these fancies are rebutted and the traditional relation of all these miracles is confirmed through the enumeration of those stations, so that men to come could see them and thus know how great was the miracle constituted by the sojourn of the human species in those places for forty years. MAIMONIDES [14]

Levitical Towns; Cities of Refuge

In the allotment of the land no distinction was made between the tribes which derived their origin from Jacob's two wives and those which traced themselves to his concubines. They were all children of Israel and, by adoptive legal process or historical accession, of equal status. The Levites too were to get their share. Even though other Torah passages emphasize that the Levites were to be landless and Num. 18 specifically provides for their support to compensate them for their landlessness, and while Deuteronomy speaks of them as people who need protection similar to strangers, orphans, and widows, Num. 35 does make a land allotment to them. Some scholars believe that the provisions of this chapter, which assign forty-eight towns west and east of the Jordan to the Levites, were never fully carried out and that in effect the Levites were scattered among the tribes, without significant holdings of their own.* But it has been shown that for a short time during the time of David and Solomon levitical towns played an important socio-political role and that levitical families lived in these cities at some time [3]. Among these were six cities that served as "cities of refuge," an arrangement reflecting ancient concepts of law and justice (see commentary).

The sanctuary cities are also treated in Deuteronomy (4:41–43 and 19:1–13). While the language differs, the rules are substantially the same. Both versions apparently accommodated the disappearance of local altars which previously had served as places of refuge.

---

* They describe the provisions as "fictitious" [1] and "wishful thinking on the part of the P-editors" [2].

The last chapter of Numbers returns to a specific case in the history of the tribe of Manasseh, the daughters of Zelophehad, whose names and ancestry are once again stated (see chapter 27). The reason for concluding the book in this fashion is not altogether clear, but it may reflect the Torah's pervasive genealogical interest: there are ten generations from Adam to Noah; ten generations from Noah to Terah (Abraham's father); and ten generations from Abraham to the daughters of Zelophehad. The end of the wanderings is thus related to creation, and Genesis and Numbers are placed into a unified structure.

א וַיְדַבֵּ֣ר יְהוָ֔ה אֶל־מֹשֶׁ֑ה בְּעַֽרְבֹ֥ת מוֹאָ֖ב עַל־יַרְדֵּ֥ן יְרֵחֽוֹ
ב לֵאמֹֽר׃ צַו֮ אֶת־בְּנֵ֣י יִשְׂרָאֵל֒ וְנָתְנ֣וּ לַלְוִיִּ֗ם מִֽנַּחֲלַ֧ת
אֲחֻזָּתָ֛ם עָרִ֖ים לָשָׁ֑בֶת וּמִגְרָ֗שׁ לֶֽעָרִים֙ סְבִיבֹֽתֵיהֶ֔ם
ג תִּתְּנ֖וּ לַלְוִיִּֽם׃ וְהָי֧וּ הֶעָרִ֛ים לָהֶ֖ם לָשָׁ֑בֶת וּמִגְרְשֵׁיהֶ֗ם
ד יִֽהְי֤וּ לִבְהֶמְתָּם֙ וְלִרְכֻשָׁ֔ם וּלְכֹ֖ל חַיָּתָֽם׃ וּמִגְרְשֵׁ֣י
הֶֽעָרִ֗ים אֲשֶׁ֤ר תִּתְּנוּ֙ לַלְוִיִּ֔ם מִקִּ֤יר הָעִיר֙ וָח֔וּצָה אֶ֖לֶף
ה אַמָּ֥ה סָבִֽיב׃ וּמַדֹּתֶ֞ם מִח֣וּץ לָעִ֗יר אֶת־פְּאַת־קֵ֣דְמָה
אַלְפַּ֪יִם בָּֽאַמָּ֟ה וְאֶת־פְּאַת־נֶ֩גֶב֩ אַלְפַּ֨יִם בָּֽאַמָּ֜ה וְאֶת־
פְּאַת־יָ֣ם ׀ אַלְפַּ֣יִם בָּֽאַמָּ֗ה וְאֵ֨ת פְּאַ֥ת צָפ֛וֹן אַלְפַּ֥יִם

*בָּֽאַמָּ֖ה וְהָעִ֣יר בַּתָּ֑וֶךְ זֶ֚ה יִהְיֶ֣ה לָהֶ֔ם מִגְרְשֵׁ֖י הֶעָרִֽים׃
ו וְאֵ֣ת הֶֽעָרִ֗ים אֲשֶׁ֤ר תִּתְּנוּ֙ לַלְוִיִּ֔ם אֵ֚ת שֵׁשׁ־עָרֵ֣י הַמִּקְלָ֔ט
אֲשֶׁ֣ר תִּתְּנ֔וּ לָנֻ֥ס שָׁ֖מָּה הָרֹצֵ֑חַ וַעֲלֵיהֶ֣ם תִּתְּנ֔וּ אַרְבָּעִ֥ים
ז וּשְׁתַּ֖יִם עִֽיר׃ כָּל־הֶֽעָרִ֗ים אֲשֶׁ֤ר תִּתְּנוּ֙ לַלְוִיִּ֔ם אַרְבָּעִ֥ים
ח וּשְׁמֹנֶ֖ה עִ֑יר אֶתְהֶ֖ן וְאֶת־מִגְרְשֵׁיהֶֽן׃ וְהֶֽעָרִ֗ים אֲשֶׁ֣ר תִּתְּנ֞וּ
מֵאֲחֻזַּ֣ת בְּנֵֽי־יִשְׂרָאֵ֗ל מֵאֵ֤ת הָרַב֙ תַּרְבּ֔וּ וּמֵאֵ֥ת הַמְעַ֖ט
תַּמְעִ֑יטוּ אִ֗ישׁ כְּפִ֤י נַֽחֲלָתוֹ֙ אֲשֶׁ֣ר יִנְחָ֔לוּ יִתֵּ֥ן מֵעָרָ֖יו
לַלְוִיִּֽם׃
פ

*ה סבירין לכם׃

1] The LORD spoke to Moses in the steppes of Moab at the Jordan near Jericho, saying: **2]** Instruct the Israelite people to assign, out of the holdings apportioned to them, towns for the Levites to dwell in; you shall also assign to the Levites pasture land around their towns. **3]** The towns shall be theirs to dwell in, and the pasture shall be for the cattle they own and all their other beasts. **4]** The town pasture that you are to assign to the Levites shall extend a thousand cubits outside the town wall all around. **5]** You shall measure off two thousand cubits outside the town on the east side, two thousand on the south side, two thousand on the west side, and two thousand on the north side, with the town in the center. That shall be the pasture for their towns.

6] The towns that you assign to the Levites shall comprise the six cities of refuge which you are to set aside for a manslayer to flee to, to which you shall add forty-two towns. **7]** Thus the total of the towns that you assign to the Levites shall be forty-eight towns, with their pasture. **8]** In setting aside towns from the holdings of the Israelites, take more from the larger groups and less from the smaller, so that each assigns towns to the Levites in proportion to the share it receives.

35:4] *Town pasture.* To be added to the city property assigned to the Levites. In this verse the extent of the pasture land appears to be half of that given in the next verse, which has suggested to some that there was something like a "common cubit" as distinguished from a "holy cubit." But M. Greenberg has shown that no such assumption needs to be made and that this prescription represented a practical solution to the general problem of levitical landlessness [4].

5] *Two thousand cubits.* In rabbinic law this rule became the foundation for the law on Sabbath limits for walking: one may walk within a circumference of 2,000 cubits of a city (*techum Shabbat*). By a legal device known as *eruv* the limit can be extended farther by 2,000 cubits, or about one-half mile (a cubit being the average distance

from the elbow to the tip of the middle finger, about 18 inches). The matter became a point of issue in the rabbinic controversy with the Karaites who refused to allow this verse to extend the specific prohibition of Exod. 16:29: "Let no man leave his place on the seventh day."

6] *Six cities of refuge.* Of which three were to lie east of the Jordan (verse 14).

In contemporary Hebrew מִקְלָט means "shelter," especially "air raid shelter."

8] *More from the larger groups.* A statement of fair share distribution on which most modern tax systems are based. Thus, the Naphtalites are less numerous than the Ephraimites and Gadites (see commentary on 25:19 ff.) and therefore contribute fewer cities (Josh. 21).

This rule presents a problem to those who in-

ט מִקְלָט תִּהְיֶינָה: לִבְנֵי יִשְׂרָאֵל וְלַגֵּר וְלַתּוֹשָׁב בְּתוֹכָם תִּהְיֶינָה שֵׁשׁ־הֶעָרִים הָאֵלֶּה לְמִקְלָט לָנוּס שָׁמָּה כָּל־ טז מַכֵּה־נֶפֶשׁ בִּשְׁגָגָה: וְאִם־בִּכְלִי בַרְזֶל הִכָּהוּ וַיָּמֹת רֹצֵחַ הוּא מוֹת יוּמַת הָרֹצֵחַ: וְאִם בְּאֶבֶן יָד אֲשֶׁר־ יז יָמוּת בָּהּ הִכָּהוּ וַיָּמֹת רֹצֵחַ הוּא מוֹת יוּמַת הָרֹצֵחַ: יח אוֹ בִּכְלִי עֵץ־יָד אֲשֶׁר־יָמוּת בּוֹ הִכָּהוּ וַיָּמֹת רֹצֵחַ הוּא יט מוֹת יוּמַת הָרֹצֵחַ: גֹּאֵל הַדָּם הוּא יָמִית אֶת־הָרֹצֵחַ כ בְּפִגְעוֹ־בוֹ הוּא יְמִתֶנּוּ: וְאִם־בְּשִׂנְאָה יֶהְדָּפֶנּוּ אוֹ־

ט וַיְדַבֵּר יְהוָה אֶל־מֹשֶׁה לֵּאמֹר: דַּבֵּר אֶל־בְּנֵי יִשְׂרָאֵל י וְאָמַרְתָּ אֲלֵהֶם כִּי אַתֶּם עֹבְרִים אֶת־הַיַּרְדֵּן אַרְצָה יא כְּנָעַן: וְהִקְרִיתֶם לָכֶם עָרִים עָרֵי מִקְלָט תִּהְיֶינָה לָכֶם וְנָס שָׁמָּה רֹצֵחַ מַכֵּה־נֶפֶשׁ בִּשְׁגָגָה: וְהָיוּ לָכֶם יב הֶעָרִים לְמִקְלָט מִגֹּאֵל וְלֹא יָמוּת הָרֹצֵחַ עַד־עָמְדוֹ יג לִפְנֵי הָעֵדָה לַמִּשְׁפָּט: וְהֶעָרִים אֲשֶׁר תִּתֵּנוּ שֵׁשׁ־עָרֵי יד מִקְלָט תִּהְיֶינָה לָכֶם: אֵת שְׁלֹשׁ הֶעָרִים תִּתְּנוּ מֵעֵבֶר לַיַּרְדֵּן וְאֵת שְׁלֹשׁ הֶעָרִים תִּתְּנוּ בְּאֶרֶץ כְּנָעַן עָרֵי

9] The LORD spoke further to Moses: **10]** Speak to the Israelite people and say to them: When you cross the Jordan into the land of Canaan,   **11]** you shall provide yourselves with places to serve you as cities of refuge to which a manslayer who has killed a person unintentionally may flee.   **12]** The cities shall serve you as a refuge from the avenger, so that the manslayer may not die unless he has stood trial before the assembly.

13] The towns that you thus assign shall be six cities of refuge in all.   **14]** Three cities shall be set aside beyond the Jordan, and the other three shall be set aside in the land of Canaan: they shall serve as cities of refuge.   **15]** These six cities shall serve the Israelites and the resident aliens among them for refuge, so that anyone who kills a person unintentionally may flee there.

16] Anyone, however, who strikes another with an iron object so that death results is a murderer; the murderer must be put to death.   **17]** If he struck him with a stone tool that could cause death, and death resulted, he is a murderer; the murderer must be put to death.   **18]** Similarly, if the object with which he struck him was a wooden tool that could cause death, and death resulted, he is a murderer; the murderer must be put to death.   **19]** The blood-avenger himself shall put the murderer to death; it is he who shall put him to death upon encounter.   **20]** So, too, if he pushed him in hate or hurled something at him on purpose and

terpret the census figures in the traditional way (understanding *elef* to mean "thousand"), for then Naphtali is *more* numerous than Gad and Ephraim.

12] *Avenger.* Also called "blood avenger" (verses 19, 21); literally, "redeemer," the next of kin. See Lev. 25:25 and commentary.

13] *Six cities.* Rabbinic tradition said that, while all levitical cities were suitable for refuge, in only the six named specifically was the community obliged to take care of the refugee [5]. The six cities were: Kedesh (Naphtali), Shechem (Ephraim), and Hebron (Judah) on the west side; Bezer (Reuben), Ramoth (Gad), and Golan (Manasseh) on the east side (Josh. 20:7, 8).

14] *Three cities shall be . . . beyond the Jordan.* The reason for making two and one-half tribes bear a share equal to the other nine and one-half appears to be based on geographic necessity: one was to be in feasible reach of refuge everywhere in the country. Rashi suggests that the incidence of manslaughter was high in the open areas of Gilead [6]. But Deut. 19:9 suggests that three more cities west of the Jordan might be added.

16] *Iron object.* Which was considered prima facie evidence of intent to kill.

17, 18] *Tool.* Literally, "of the hand," that is, large enough to fill the hand and therefore a potentially fatal weapon [7].

כא הִשְׁלִיךְ עָלָיו בִּצְדִיָּה וַיָּמֹת: אוֹ בְאֵיבָה הִכָּהוּ בְיָדוֹ
וַיָּמֹת מוֹת־יוּמַת הַמַּכֶּה רֹצֵחַ הוּא גֹּאֵל הַדָּם יָמִית
כב אֶת־הָרֹצֵחַ בְּפִגְעוֹ־בוֹ: וְאִם־בְּפֶתַע בְּלֹא־אֵיבָה הֲדָפוֹ
כג אוֹ־הִשְׁלִיךְ עָלָיו כָּל־כְּלִי בְּלֹא צְדִיָּה: אוֹ בְכָל־אֶבֶן
אֲשֶׁר־יָמוּת בָּהּ בְּלֹא רְאוֹת וַיַּפֵּל עָלָיו וַיָּמֹת וְהוּא
כד לֹא־אוֹיֵב לוֹ וְלֹא מְבַקֵּשׁ רָעָתוֹ: וְשָׁפְטוּ הָעֵדָה בֵּין
כה הַמַּכֶּה וּבֵין גֹּאֵל הַדָּם עַל הַמִּשְׁפָּטִים הָאֵלֶּה: וְהִצִּילוּ
הָעֵדָה אֶת־הָרֹצֵחַ מִיַּד גֹּאֵל הַדָּם וְהֵשִׁיבוּ אֹתוֹ הָעֵדָה
אֶל־עִיר מִקְלָטוֹ אֲשֶׁר־נָס שָׁמָּה וְיָשַׁב בָּהּ עַד־מוֹת
כו הַכֹּהֵן הַגָּדֹל אֲשֶׁר־מָשַׁח אֹתוֹ בְּשֶׁמֶן הַקֹּדֶשׁ: וְאִם־יָצֹא
יֵצֵא הָרֹצֵחַ אֶת־גְּבוּל עִיר מִקְלָטוֹ אֲשֶׁר יָנוּס שָׁמָּה:

כז וּמָצָא אֹתוֹ גֹּאֵל הַדָּם מִחוּץ לִגְבוּל עִיר מִקְלָטוֹ
כח וְרָצַח גֹּאֵל הַדָּם אֶת־הָרֹצֵחַ אֵין לוֹ דָּם: כִּי בְעִיר
מִקְלָטוֹ יֵשֵׁב עַד־מוֹת הַכֹּהֵן הַגָּדֹל וְאַחֲרֵי מוֹת הַכֹּהֵן
כט הַגָּדֹל יָשׁוּב הָרֹצֵחַ אֶל־אֶרֶץ אֲחֻזָּתוֹ: וְהָיוּ אֵלֶּה
לָכֶם לְחֻקַּת מִשְׁפָּט לְדֹרֹתֵיכֶם בְּכֹל מוֹשְׁבֹתֵיכֶם:
ל כָּל־מַכֵּה־נֶפֶשׁ לְפִי עֵדִים יִרְצַח אֶת־הָרֹצֵחַ וְעֵד אֶחָד
לא לֹא־יַעֲנֶה בְנֶפֶשׁ לָמוּת: וְלֹא־תִקְחוּ כֹפֶר לְנֶפֶשׁ רֹצֵחַ
לב אֲשֶׁר־הוּא רָשָׁע לָמוּת כִּי־מוֹת יוּמָת: וְלֹא־תִקְחוּ כֹפֶר
לָנוּס אֶל־עִיר מִקְלָטוֹ לָשׁוּב לָשֶׁבֶת בָּאָרֶץ עַד־מוֹת
לג הַכֹּהֵן: וְלֹא־תַחֲנִיפוּ אֶת־הָאָרֶץ אֲשֶׁר אַתֶּם בָּהּ כִּי
הַדָּם הוּא יַחֲנִיף אֶת־הָאָרֶץ וְלָאָרֶץ לֹא־יְכֻפַּר לַדָּם

death resulted, 21] or if he struck him with his hand in enmity and death resulted, the assailant shall be put to death; he is a murderer. The blood-avenger shall put the murderer to death upon encounter.

22] But if he pushed him without malice aforethought or hurled any object at him unintentionally, 23] or inadvertently dropped upon him any deadly object of stone, and death resulted—though he was not an enemy of his and did not seek his harm— 24] in such cases the assembly shall decide between the slayer and the blood-avenger. 25] The assembly shall protect the manslayer from the blood-avenger, and the assembly shall restore him to the city of refuge to which he fled, and there he shall remain until the death of the high priest who was anointed with the sacred oil. 26] But if the manslayer ever goes outside the limits of the city of refuge to which he has fled, 27] and the blood-avenger comes upon him outside the limits of his city of refuge, and the blood-avenger kills the manslayer, there is no bloodguilt on his account. 28] For he must remain inside his city of refuge until the death of the high priest; after the death of the high priest, the manslayer may return to his land holding.

29] Such shall be your law of procedure throughout the ages in all your settlements.

30] If anyone kills a person, the manslayer may be executed only on the evidence of witnesses; the testimony of a single witness against a person shall not suffice for a sentence of death. 31] You may not accept a ransom for the life of a murderer who is guilty of a capital crime; he must be put to death. 32] Nor may you accept ransom in lieu of flight to a city of refuge, enabling one to return to live on his land before the death of the priest. 33] You shall not pollute the land in which you live; for blood pollutes the land, and the land can have no expiation for blood that is shed on it, except by the blood of him who shed it. 34] You shall

24] *The assembly.* Of the community in whose boundaries the slaying had occurred.

30] *Witnesses.* At least two (Deut. 17:6).

32] *Ransom.* Permissible for other injuries but paid in cases of death only when caused by an animal (Exod. 21:29, 30). The Koran permits ransom for life [8].

33] *Blood pollutes the land.* Jer. (3:1) uses the same expression for adultery.

עַל נַחֲלַת הַמַּטֶּה אֲשֶׁר תִּהְיֶינָה לָהֶם וּמִנַּחֲלַת מַטֵּה
ה אֲבֹתֵינוּ יִגָּרַע נַחֲלָתָן: וַיְצַו מֹשֶׁה אֶת־בְּנֵי יִשְׂרָאֵל עַל־
ו פִּי יְהוָה לֵאמֹר כֵּן מַטֵּה בְנֵי־יוֹסֵף דֹּבְרִים: זֶה הַדָּבָר
אֲשֶׁר־צִוָּה יְהוָה לִבְנוֹת צְלָפְחָד לֵאמֹר לַטּוֹב
בְּעֵינֵיהֶם תִּהְיֶינָה לְנָשִׁים אַךְ לְמִשְׁפַּחַת מַטֵּה אֲבִיהֶם
ז תִּהְיֶינָה לְנָשִׁים: וְלֹא־תִסֹּב נַחֲלָה לִבְנֵי יִשְׂרָאֵל מִמַּטֶּה
אֶל־מַטֶּה כִּי אִישׁ בְּנַחֲלַת מַטֵּה אֲבֹתָיו יִדְבְּקוּ בְּנֵי
ח יִשְׂרָאֵל: וְכָל־בַּת יֹרֶשֶׁת נַחֲלָה מִמַּטּוֹת בְּנֵי יִשְׂרָאֵל
לְאֶחָד מִמִּשְׁפַּחַת מַטֵּה אָבִיהָ תִּהְיֶה לְאִשָּׁה לְמַעַן
ט יִירְשׁוּ בְּנֵי יִשְׂרָאֵל אִישׁ נַחֲלַת אֲבֹתָיו: וְלֹא־תִסֹּב
נַחֲלָה מִמַּטֶּה לְמַטֶּה אַחֵר כִּי־אִישׁ בְּנַחֲלָתוֹ יִדְבְּקוּ
י מַטּוֹת בְּנֵי יִשְׂרָאֵל: כַּאֲשֶׁר צִוָּה יְהוָה אֶת־מֹשֶׁה כֵּן

לד אֲשֶׁר שֻׁפַּךְ־בָּהּ כִּי־אִם בְּדַם שֹׁפְכוֹ: וְלֹא תְטַמֵּא אֶת־
הָאָרֶץ אֲשֶׁר אַתֶּם יֹשְׁבִים בָּהּ אֲשֶׁר אֲנִי שֹׁכֵן בְּתוֹכָהּ
כִּי אֲנִי יְהוָה שֹׁכֵן בְּתוֹךְ בְּנֵי יִשְׂרָאֵל: פ

לו א וַיִּקְרְבוּ רָאשֵׁי הָאָבוֹת לְמִשְׁפַּחַת בְּנֵי־גִלְעָד בֶּן־מָכִיר
בֶּן־מְנַשֶּׁה מִמִּשְׁפְּחֹת בְּנֵי יוֹסֵף וַיְדַבְּרוּ לִפְנֵי מֹשֶׁה
ב וְלִפְנֵי הַנְּשִׂאִים רָאשֵׁי אָבוֹת לִבְנֵי יִשְׂרָאֵל: וַיֹּאמְרוּ
אֶת־אֲדֹנִי צִוָּה יְהוָה לָתֵת אֶת־הָאָרֶץ בְּנַחֲלָה בְּגוֹרָל
לִבְנֵי יִשְׂרָאֵל וַאדֹנִי צֻוָּה בַיהוָה לָתֵת אֶת־נַחֲלַת
ג צְלָפְחָד אָחִינוּ לִבְנֹתָיו: וְהָיוּ לְאֶחָד מִבְּנֵי שִׁבְטֵי בְנֵי־
יִשְׂרָאֵל לְנָשִׁים וְנִגְרְעָה נַחֲלָתָן מִנַּחֲלַת אֲבֹתֵינוּ וְנוֹסַף
עַל נַחֲלַת הַמַּטֶּה אֲשֶׁר תִּהְיֶינָה לָהֶם וּמִגֹּרַל נַחֲלָתֵנוּ
ד יִגָּרֵעַ: וְאִם־יִהְיֶה הַיֹּבֵל לִבְנֵי יִשְׂרָאֵל וְנוֹסְפָה נַחֲלָתָן

not defile the land in which you live, in which I Myself abide, for I the LORD abide among the Israelite people.

1] The family heads in the clan of the descendants of Gilead son of Machir son of Manasseh, one of the Josephite clans, came forward and appealed to Moses and the chieftains, family heads of the Israelites. **2]** They said, "The LORD commanded my lord to assign the land to the Israelites as shares by lot, and my lord was further commanded by the LORD to assign the share of our kinsman Zelophehad to his daughters. **3]** Now, if they marry persons from another Israelite tribe, their share will be cut off from our ancestral portion and be added to the portion of the tribe into which they marry; thus our allotted portion will be diminished. **4]** And even when the Israelites observe the jubilee, their share will be added to that of the tribe into which they marry, and their share will be cut off from the ancestral portion of our tribe."

5] So Moses, at the LORD's bidding, instructed the Israelites, saying: "The plea of the Josephite tribe is just. **6]** This is what the LORD has commanded concerning the daughters of Zelophehad: They may marry anyone they wish, provided they marry into a clan of their father's tribe. **7]** No inheritance of the Israelites may pass over from one tribe to another, but the Israelites must remain bound each to the ancestral portion of his tribe. **8]** Every daughter among the Israelite tribes who inherits a share must marry someone from a clan of her father's tribe, in order that every Israelite may keep his ancestral share. **9]** Thus no inheritance shall pass over from one tribe to another, but the Israelite tribes shall remain bound each to its portion."

36:3] *If they marry.* Outside the tribe. The children of such unions will follow the fathers' ancestry, and thus the property inherited from the mothers will now be vested in another tribe.

4] *The jubilee.* See Lev. 25:10 ff. The rule applies only to sale of property, not to inheritance.

8] *Every daughter.* The law was now extended to all tribes but apparently not applied later on. The Talmud explains this by holding that the law was meant only temporarily, for the time prior to the occupation of the land [9].

עָשׂוּ בְּנוֹת צְלָפְחָד: וַתִּהְיֶינָה מַחְלָה תִרְצָה וְחָגְלָה יא

וּמִלְכָּה וְנֹעָה בְּנוֹת צְלָפְחָד לִבְנֵי דֹדֵיהֶן לְנָשִׁים:

מִמִּשְׁפְּחֹת בְּנֵי־מְנַשֶּׁה בֶן־יוֹסֵף הָיוּ לְנָשִׁים וַתְּהִי נַחֲלָתָן יב

עַל־מַטֵּה מִשְׁפַּחַת אֲבִיהֶן: אֵלֶּה הַמִּצְוֹת וְהַמִּשְׁפָּטִים יג

אֲשֶׁר צִוָּה יְהֹוָה בְּיַד־מֹשֶׁה אֶל־בְּנֵי יִשְׂרָאֵל בְּעַרְבֹת

מוֹאָב עַל יַרְדֵּן יְרֵחוֹ:

Haftarah Mas'ey, p. 1282

10] The daughters of Zelophehad did as the LORD had commanded Moses: **11]** Mahlah, Tirzah, Hoglah, Milcah, and Noah, Zelophehad's daughters, were married to sons of their uncles, **12]** marrying into clans of descendants of Manasseh son of Joseph; and so their share remained in the tribe of their father's clan.

13] These are the commandments and regulations that the LORD enjoined upon the Israelites, through Moses, on the steppes of Moab, at the Jordan near Jericho.

13] *On the steppes of Moab.* A postscript to the section of laws beginning with Num. 27. It resembles the concluding sentence of Leviticus.

The Blood Avenger

The basic provisions of chapter 35 are these: When a man killed someone unintentionally he could find security by fleeing to one of the six levitical cities. The blood avenger [10], who as next of kin to the slain person had the traditional task of hunting down the killer, could not violate the sanctuary of these cities. A trial would be held in the locale where the slaying occurred,[1] and, if lack of malice aforethought was established, the manslayer would be sent back to the city of refuge to stay there securely until the death of the reigning High Priest. The institutionalization of such asylum may be the earliest of its kind, though in a general way such arrangements had parallels in other cultures: general amnesties were and still are frequent on the occasion of a new monarch or after a coup d'état; and Roman temples as well as medieval churches served as sanctuaries (note the dual use of the term) for murderers. The distinguishing features of the biblical provisions are the restriction of asylum to the unintentional slayer and the connection of the institution with the death of the High Priest. The link between these two characteristics was the fundamental postulate that homicide—even if accidental—could not be expiated by ransom like other transgressions. Only death could compensate for the loss of life, and thus the death of the High Priest became the symbol of communal expiation.

It is clear that these rules arose from social traditions that knew of family feuds as normal consequences of manslaughter. The go-el was charged by his family to be not only avenger but redeemer, which is the strict meaning of the word. In the event of the depletion of family life by the loss of blood, the go-el had a responsibility to secure for the family an equivalent of that loss by other blood. "His mission was not vengeance, but equity. He was not an avenger, but a redeemer, a restorer, a balancer" [11]. The biblical law reckoned with this tradition and therefore insisted here and elsewhere that only the person involved in the killing was to be held responsible. "He who sins shall die; the son shall not be responsible for the sins of his father, neither the father for those of his son" (Ezek. 18:20). With the Torah's establishment of judicial rules and processes, the law was generally taken out of the hands of private persons. But the privileges of the avenger were so firmly rooted among the people that the provisions for the cities of refuge must be looked upon as a gradual and intermediate shift from private to public law enforcement.[2] In fact, the Torah still granted the avenger the right to kill when his victim left the city of refuge (verse 27).

The institution of sanctuary had three purposes. It was a protective measure, to give everyone the opportunity to let passions cool (so specifically Deut. 19:6). It served further as a punishment for the manslayer, because exile constituted a form of social death.[3] The third and in some ways most important

---

[1] This is apparent from verse 25, which states that "the assembly shall restore him to the city of refuge to which he had fled."

[2] This development may also be seen in the generally misunderstood passage Exod. 21:23–25 ("eye for eye"). No talion was involved; rather, the law provided for fines (the value of an eye for an eye), which moved such cases from the realm of private to the domain of public criminal law (see Commentary on Exodus).

[3] Later Jewish law made certain, however, that the city of refuge would take proper care of the exile and even provide for his spiritual sustenance [12]. Maimonides speaks of the need to have the man's teacher exiled with him and the students exiled with their teacher [13]. We do not know to what extent such rules were actually observed in ancient days.

purpose was to contain and isolate the sin that had been committed, for killing was understood to contaminate the community. Confining the manslayer thus had the double function of containing the manslayer until the time of final expiation and keeping the body social from further contamination. Since ultimately only death could expiate the sin, it was not until the High Priest had died that the process was completed and full expiation extended to the manslayer himself [14]. The killing of a human being, though it occurred without evil intent, was a moral injury to the total community. The holy people had a special God-relationship that was founded on zealous regard for the sanctity of every life.

GLEANINGS

Numbers

There were six cities of refuge and altogether forty-eight levitical cities. This compared to the *Shema*: the six Hebrew words of the sentence "Hear O Israel," and the forty-eight of the paragraph, "You shall love the Lord your God . . ." which follows.⁴ Just as ancient man could find succor in the levitical cities when he had sinned, so today one may find surcease in "the city of *Shema*." CHASIDIC [15]

Intent

The regulations concerning the cities of refuge emphasized that in matters of commandments and transgressions it is intent which counts.
BACHYA [16]

Hope for the Righteous

If God made sure that manslayers be treated with equity, how much more so will He take care of the righteous! MIDRASH [17]

No Share

Why did the Levites have no share in the land? Because, according to the Sages, the Levites did not suffer slavery in Egypt, and the Land of Israel is one of the things which can be acquired only by suffering. Only he who has suffered exile and persecution will truly inherit the land.

M. HACOHEN [18]

Joy

There were no greater days of joy in Israel than the end of Yom Kippur and the fifteenth day of Av, when it was the custom for young marriageable people to meet each other. Why on the fifteenth of Av? Because on that day later authorities had given permission for intertribal marriages and had declared that the biblical prohibitions applied only to the generation which had settled the land.

YALKUT ME'AM LO'EZ [19]

Moses' Vision

So the Prophet remains in the wilderness, buries his own generation, and trains up a new one. Year after year passes, and he never grows weary of repeating to this growing generation the laws of righteousness that must guide its life in the land of its future; never tires of recalling the glorious past in which these laws were fashioned. The past and the future are the Prophet's whole life, each completing the other. In the present he sees nothing but a wilderness, a life far removed from his ideal; and therefore he looks before and after. He lives in the future world of his vision and seeks strength in the past out of which that vision-world is quarried.

Forty years are gone, and the new generation is about to emerge from its vagabond life in the wilderness and take up the broken thread of the national task, when the Prophet dies, and another man assumes the leadership and brings the people to its land.

AHAD HA-AM [20]

⁴ The reference is to the Hebrew text of Deut. 6:4–9, referred to as *Shema*.

HAFTAROT

במדבר

Hosea

2 : 1-22

Hosea lived in the Northern Kingdom (Israel) in the
eighth century B.C.E. He frequently spoke of his people's
relationship to God as that of a wife to a husband who
had cast her out for her transgressions. But God still
loved Israel, the prophet preached, and would take her
back if she repented.

The opening chapter of Numbers gives account of Israel's
numbers in the wilderness, and the opening of Hosea's
parable speaks of the multitudes of the people who are as
"the sands of the sea." Though they have forsaken God
He will take them back in faithfulness and espouse Israel
unto Him forever.

ב

Chapter 2

1] ^aThe number of the people of Israel shall
be like that of the sands of the sea, which cannot
be measured or counted; and instead of being told,
"You are Not-My-People,"^b they shall be called
Children-of-the-Living-God.

2] The people of
Judah and the people of Israel shall assemble
together and appoint one head over them; and
they shall rise from the ground^c—for marvelous
shall be ^dthe day of Jezreel!^{-d}

3] Oh, call^e your brothers "My People,"
And your sisters "Lovingly Accepted"!

4] Rebuke^e your mother, rebuke her—
For she is not My wife
And I am not her husband—

And let her put away her harlotry from her face
And her adultery from between her breasts.

5] Else will I strip her naked
And leave her as on the day she was born:

1] וְהָיָה מִסְפַּר בְּנֵי־יִשְׂרָאֵל כְּחוֹל הַיָּם
אֲשֶׁר לֹא־יִמַּד וְלֹא יִסָּפֵר וְהָיָה בִּמְקוֹם אֲשֶׁר
יֵאָמֵר לָהֶם לֹא־עַמִּי אַתֶּם יֵאָמֵר לָהֶם בְּנֵי
אֵל־חָי: 2 וְנִקְבְּצוּ בְּנֵי־יְהוּדָה וּבְנֵי־יִשְׂרָאֵל
יַחְדָּו וְשָׂמוּ לָהֶם רֹאשׁ אֶחָד וְעָלוּ מִן־הָאָרֶץ
כִּי גָדוֹל יוֹם יִזְרְעֶאל:

3 אִמְרוּ לַאֲחֵיכֶם עַמִּי
וְלַאֲחוֹתֵיכֶם רֻחָמָה:

4 רִיבוּ בְאִמְּכֶם רִיבוּ
כִּי־הִיא לֹא אִשְׁתִּי
וְאָנֹכִי לֹא אִישָׁהּ
וְתָסֵר זְנוּנֶיהָ מִפָּנֶיהָ
וְנַאֲפוּפֶיהָ מִבֵּין שָׁדֶיהָ:

5 פֶּן־אַפְשִׁיטֶנָּה עֲרֻמָּה
וְהִצַּגְתִּיהָ כְּיוֹם הִוָּלְדָהּ

^a Vv. 1–3 anticipate the conclusion of the chapter
^b See 1.9
^c Meaning, perhaps, "from their wretched condition," or "to ascendancy over the land'
^{d-d} I.e., the day when the name Jezreel will convey a promise (2.23–25) instead of a
threat (1.4–5)
^e The Lord addresses Hosea and his fellow North Israelites; see 1.9. The mother is
the nation; her children the individual North Israelites

And I will make her like a wilderness,
Render her like desert land,
And let her die of thirst.

6] I will also disown her children;
For they are now a harlot's brood,

7] In that their mother has played the harlot,
She that conceived them has acted shamelessly—
Because she thought,
"I will go after my lovers,
Who supply my bread and my water,
My wool and my linen,
My oil and my drink."

8] Assuredly,
I will hedge up her/ roads with thorns
And raise walls against her,
And she shall not find her paths.

9] Pursue her lovers as she will,
She shall not overtake them;
And seek them as she may,
She shall never find them.
Then she will say,
"I will go and return
To my first husband,
For then I fared better than now."

10] And she did not consider this:
It was I who bestowed on her
The new grain and wine and oil;
I who lavished silver on her
And gold—which they used for Baal.

11] Assuredly,
I will take back My new grain in its time

וְשַׂמְתִּ֙יהָ כַּמִּדְבָּ֔ר

וְשַׁתִּ֖הָ כְּאֶ֣רֶץ צִיָּ֑ה

וַהֲמִתִּ֖יהָ בַּצָּמָֽא׃

6 וְאֶת־בָּנֶ֖יהָ לֹ֣א אֲרַחֵ֑ם

כִּֽי־בְנֵ֥י זְנוּנִ֖ים הֵֽמָּה׃

7 כִּ֤י זָֽנְתָה֙ אִמָּ֔ם

הֹבִ֖ישָׁה הֽוֹרָתָ֑ם

כִּ֣י אָֽמְרָ֗ה

אֵלְכָ֞ה אַחֲרֵ֣י מְאַהֲבַ֗י נֹֽתְנֵ֤י לַחְמִי֙ וּמֵימַ֔י

צַמְרִ֣י וּפִשְׁתִּ֔י

שַׁמְנִ֖י וְשִׁקּוּיָֽי׃

8 לָכֵ֛ן

הִנְנִי־שָׂ֥ךְ אֶת־דַּרְכֵּ֖ךְ בַּסִּירִ֑ים

וְגָֽדַרְתִּי֙ אֶת־גְּדֵרָ֔הּ

וּנְתִיבוֹתֶ֖יהָ לֹ֥א תִמְצָֽא׃

9 וְרִדְּפָ֤ה אֶת־מְאַהֲבֶ֙יהָ֙

וְלֹֽא־תַשִּׂ֣יג אֹתָ֔ם

וּבִקְשָׁ֖תַם וְלֹ֣א תִמְצָ֑א

וְאָֽמְרָ֗ה

אֵלְכָ֤ה וְאָשׁ֙וּבָה֙

אֶל־אִישִׁ֣י הָֽרִאשׁ֔וֹן

כִּ֣י ט֥וֹב לִ֛י אָ֖ז מֵעָֽתָּה׃

10 וְהִיא֙ לֹ֣א יָֽדְעָ֔ה

כִּ֤י אָֽנֹכִי֙ נָתַ֣תִּי לָ֔הּ

הַדָּגָן֙ וְהַתִּיר֣וֹשׁ וְהַיִּצְהָ֔ר

וְכֶ֣סֶף הִרְבֵּ֥יתִי לָ֖הּ

וְזָהָ֖ב עָשׂ֥וּ לַבָּֽעַל׃

11 לָכֵ֣ן אָשׁ֗וּב וְלָֽקַחְתִּ֤י דְגָנִי֙ בְּעִתּ֔וֹ

/ Heb. "your." Vv. 8–9 would read well after v. 15

1253

And My new wine in its season,
And I will snatch away My wool and My linen
That serve to cover her nakedness.

12] Now will I uncover her shame
In the very sight of her lovers,
And none shall save her from Me.

13] And I will end all her rejoicing:
Her festivals, new moons, and sabbaths—
All her festive seasons.

14] I will lay waste her vines and her fig trees,
Which she thinks are a fee
She received from her lovers;
I will turn them into brushwood,
And beasts of the field shall devour them.

15] Thus will I punish her
For the days of the Baalim,
On which she brought them offerings;
When, decked with earrings and jewels,
She would go after her lovers,
Forgetting Me
           —declares the LORD.

16] Assuredly,
I will speak coaxingly to her
And lead her through the wilderness*g*
And speak to her tenderly.

17] I will give her her vineyards from there,
And the Valley of Achor*h* as a *i-*plowland of hope.*-i*

---

g I.e., her ravaged land (see vv. 5, 10–11, 14); so Ibn Ezra
h A desolate region; cf. Isa. 65.10; see further Josh. 7.25–26
i-i Connecting petach with pitach "to plow" (see Isa. 28.24). Meaning of Heb. uncertain; others "door of hope"

וְתִירוֹשִׁי בְּמוֹעֲדוֹ

וְהִצַּלְתִּי צַמְרִי וּפִשְׁתִּי

לְכַסּוֹת אֶת־עֶרְוָתָהּ׃

[12] וְעַתָּה אֲגַלֶּה אֶת־נַבְלֻתָהּ

לְעֵינֵי מְאַהֲבֶיהָ

וְאִישׁ לֹא־יַצִּילֶנָּה מִיָּדִי׃

[13] וְהִשְׁבַּתִּי כָּל־מְשׂוֹשָׂהּ

חַגָּהּ חָדְשָׁהּ וְשַׁבַּתָּהּ

וְכֹל מוֹעֲדָהּ׃

[14] וַהֲשִׁמֹּתִי גַּפְנָהּ וּתְאֵנָתָהּ

אֲשֶׁר אָמְרָה

אֶתְנָה הֵמָּה לִי

אֲשֶׁר נָתְנוּ־לִי מְאַהֲבָי

וְשַׂמְתִּים לְיַעַר

וַאֲכָלָתַם חַיַּת הַשָּׂדֶה׃

[15] וּפָקַדְתִּי עָלֶיהָ

אֶת־יְמֵי הַבְּעָלִים

אֲשֶׁר תַּקְטִיר לָהֶם

וַתַּעַד נִזְמָהּ וְחֶלְיָתָהּ

וַתֵּלֶךְ אַחֲרֵי מְאַהֲבֶיהָ

וְאֹתִי שָׁכְחָה

נְאֻם־יְהֹוָה׃

[16] לָכֵן הִנֵּה אָנֹכִי מְפַתֶּיהָ

וְהֹלַכְתִּיהָ הַמִּדְבָּר

וְדִבַּרְתִּי עַל־לִבָּהּ׃

[17] וְנָתַתִּי לָהּ אֶת־כְּרָמֶיהָ מִשָּׁם

וְאֶת־עֵמֶק עָכוֹר לְפֶתַח תִּקְוָה

There she shall respond as in the days of her youth,
When she came up from the land of Egypt.

18] And in that day
                —declares the Lord—
You will call [Me] Ishi,*i*
And no more will you call Me Baali.*i*

19] For I will remove the names of the Baalim
    from her mouth,
And they shall nevermore be mentioned by name.

20] In that day, I will make a covenant for
them with the beasts of the field, the birds of the
air, and the creeping things of the ground; I will
also banish*k* bow, sword, and war from the land.
Thus I will let them lie down in safety.

21] And I will espouse you forever:
I will espouse you *l*with righteousness and justice,
And with goodness and mercy,

22] And I will espouse you with faithfulness;*-l*
Then you shall be devoted to the Lord.

וְעָנְתָה שָּׁמָּה כִּימֵי נְעוּרֶיהָ

וּכְיוֹם עֲלוֹתָהּ מֵאֶרֶץ־מִצְרָיִם:

18] וְהָיָה בַיּוֹם־הַהוּא

נְאֻם־יְהֹוָה

תִּקְרְאִי אִישִׁי

וְלֹא־תִקְרְאִי־לִי עוֹד בַּעְלִי:

19] וַהֲסִרֹתִי אֶת־שְׁמוֹת הַבְּעָלִים מִפִּיהָ

וְלֹא־יִזָּכְרוּ עוֹד בִּשְׁמָם:

20] וְכָרַתִּי לָהֶם בְּרִית בַּיּוֹם הַהוּא עִם־חַיַּת
הַשָּׂדֶה וְעִם־עוֹף הַשָּׁמַיִם וְרֶמֶשׂ הָאֲדָמָה וְקֶשֶׁת
וְחֶרֶב וּמִלְחָמָה אֶשְׁבּוֹר מִן־הָאָרֶץ וְהִשְׁכַּבְתִּים
לָבֶטַח:

21] וְאֵרַשְׂתִּיךְ לִי לְעוֹלָם

וְאֵרַשְׂתִּיךְ לִי בְּצֶדֶק וּבְמִשְׁפָּט

וּבְחֶסֶד וּבְרַחֲמִים:

22] וְאֵרַשְׂתִּיךְ לִי בֶּאֱמוּנָה

וְיָדַעַתְּ אֶת־יְהֹוָה:

---

i Both Ishi *and* Baali *mean "my husband," but the latter also means "my Baal"*
k Lit. "break"
l-l As the bride price which the Bridegroom will pay, He will confer these qualities
   on her, so that she will never offend again

After Joshua's initial conquest of Canaan a number of leaders ("Judges") guided the troubled and often disunited tribes during the twelfth and eleventh centuries B.C.E. Their military and personal adventures are recounted in the 21 chapters which portray the protracted difficulties Israel encountered in its attempt to make the Promised Land its own.

The subject of vows is treated in the sidrah, and the haftarah tells of events leading up to the birth of Samson who was a nazirite, that is, bound by vows to lead a special life. He broke his vows and paid for it with his life.

נשא

Judges
13 : 2-25

יג

Chapter 13

2] There was a certain man from Zorah, of the stock of Dan, whose name was Manoah. His wife was barren and had borne no children. 3] An angel of the LORD appeared to the woman and said to her, "You are barren and have borne no children; but you shall conceive and bear a son. 4] Now be careful not to drink wine or other intoxicant, or to eat anything unclean.

5] For you are going to conceive and bear a son; let no razor touch his head, for the boy is to be a nazirite to God from the womb on. He shall be the first to deliver Israel from the Philistines."

6] The woman went and told her husband, "A man of God came to me; he looked like an angel of God, very frightening. I did not ask him where he was from, nor did he tell me his name. 7] He said to me, 'You are going to conceive and bear a son. Drink no wine or other intoxicant, and eat nothing unclean, for the boy is to be a nazirite to God from the womb to the day of his death!' "

8] Manoah pleaded with the LORD. "Oh, my Lord!" he said, "please let the man of God that You sent come to us again, and let him instruct us how to act with the child that is to be born."

2 וַיְהִי אִישׁ אֶחָד מִצָּרְעָה מִמִּשְׁפַּחַת הַדָּנִי וּשְׁמוֹ מָנוֹחַ וְאִשְׁתּוֹ עֲקָרָה וְלֹא יָלָדָה: 3 וַיֵּרָא מַלְאַךְ־יְהוָה אֶל־הָאִשָּׁה וַיֹּאמֶר אֵלֶיהָ הִנֵּה־נָא אַתְּ־עֲקָרָה וְלֹא יָלַדְתְּ וְהָרִית וְיָלַדְתְּ בֵּן: 4 וְעַתָּה הִשָּׁמְרִי נָא וְאַל־תִּשְׁתִּי יַיִן וְשֵׁכָר וְאַל־תֹּאכְלִי כָּל־טָמֵא: 5 כִּי הִנָּךְ הָרָה וְיֹלַדְתְּ בֵּן וּמוֹרָה לֹא־יַעֲלֶה עַל־רֹאשׁוֹ כִּי־נְזִיר אֱלֹהִים יִהְיֶה הַנַּעַר מִן־הַבָּטֶן וְהוּא יָחֵל לְהוֹשִׁיעַ אֶת־יִשְׂרָאֵל מִיַּד־פְּלִשְׁתִּים:

6 וַתָּבֹא הָאִשָּׁה וַתֹּאמֶר לְאִישָׁהּ לֵאמֹר אִישׁ הָאֱלֹהִים בָּא אֵלַי וּמַרְאֵהוּ כְּמַרְאֵה מַלְאַךְ הָאֱלֹהִים נוֹרָא מְאֹד וְלֹא שְׁאִלְתִּיהוּ אֵי־מִזֶּה הוּא וְאֶת־שְׁמוֹ לֹא־הִגִּיד לִי: 7 וַיֹּאמֶר לִי הִנָּךְ הָרָה וְיֹלַדְתְּ בֵּן וְעַתָּה אַל־תִּשְׁתִּי יַיִן וְשֵׁכָר וְאַל־תֹּאכְלִי כָּל־טֻמְאָה כִּי־נְזִיר אֱלֹהִים יִהְיֶה הַנַּעַר מִן־הַבֶּטֶן עַד־יוֹם מוֹתוֹ:

8 וַיֶּעְתַּר מָנוֹחַ אֶל־יְהוָה וַיֹּאמַר בִּי אֲדוֹנָי אִישׁ הָאֱלֹהִים אֲשֶׁר שָׁלַחְתָּ יָבוֹא־נָא עוֹד אֵלֵינוּ וְיוֹרֵנוּ מַה־נַּעֲשֶׂה לַנַּעַר הַיּוּלָּד:

9] God heeded Manoah's plea, and the angel of God came to the woman again. She was sitting in the field and her husband Manoah was not with her.

10] The woman ran in haste to tell her husband. She said to him, "The man who came to me before[a] has just appeared to me." 11] Manoah promptly followed his wife. He came to the man and asked him: "Are you the man who spoke to my wife?" "Yes," he answered. 12] Then Manoah said, "May your words soon come true! What rules shall be observed for the boy?"

13] The angel of the Lord said to Manoah, "The woman must abstain from all the things against which I warned her.

14] She must not eat anything that comes from the grapevine, or drink wine or other intoxicant, or eat anything unclean. She must observe all that I commanded her."

15] Manoah said to the angel of the Lord, "Let us detain you and prepare a kid for you." 16] But the angel of the Lord said to Manoah, "If you detain me, I shall not eat your food; and if you present a burnt offering, offer it to Lord."— For Manoah did not know that he was an angel of the Lord.

17] So Manoah said to the angel of the Lord, "What is your name? We should like to honor you when your words come true." 18] The angel said to him, "You must not ask for my name; it is unknowable!"

19] Manoah took the kid and the meal offering and offered them up on the rock to the Lord; [b]and a marvelous thing happened[b] while Manoah and his wife looked on.

20] As the flames leaped up from the altar toward the sky, the angel of the Lord ascended in the flames of the altar, while Manoah and his wife looked on; and they flung themselves on their faces to the ground.—

9] וַיִּשְׁמַ֥ע הָאֱלֹהִ֖ים בְּק֣וֹל מָנ֑וֹחַ וַיָּבֹ֣א מַלְאַךְ֩ הָאֱלֹהִ֨ים ע֜וֹד אֶל־הָאִשָּׁ֗ה וְהִיא֙ יוֹשֶׁ֣בֶת בַּשָּׂדֶ֔ה וּמָנ֥וֹחַ אִישָׁ֖הּ אֵ֥ין עִמָּֽהּ׃ 10] וַתְּמַהֵר֙ הָֽאִשָּׁ֔ה וַתָּ֖רָץ וַתַּגֵּ֣ד לְאִישָׁ֑הּ וַתֹּ֣אמֶר אֵלָ֔יו הִנֵּ֨ה נִרְאָ֤ה אֵלַי֙ הָאִ֔ישׁ אֲשֶׁר־בָּ֥א בַיּ֖וֹם אֵלָֽי׃ 11] וַיָּ֛קָם וַיֵּ֥לֶךְ מָנ֖וֹחַ אַחֲרֵ֣י אִשְׁתּ֑וֹ וַיָּבֹא֙ אֶל־הָאִ֔ישׁ וַיֹּ֣אמֶר ל֗וֹ הַאַתָּ֥ה הָאִ֛ישׁ אֲשֶׁר־דִּבַּ֥רְתָּ אֶל־הָאִשָּׁ֖ה וַיֹּ֥אמֶר אָֽנִי׃ 12] וַיֹּ֣אמֶר מָנ֔וֹחַ עַתָּ֖ה יָבֹ֣א דְבָרֶ֑יךָ מַה־יִּהְיֶ֥ה מִשְׁפַּט־הַנַּ֖עַר וּמַעֲשֵֽׂהוּ׃ 13] וַיֹּ֛אמֶר מַלְאַ֥ךְ יְהוָ֖ה אֶל־מָנ֑וֹחַ מִכֹּ֛ל אֲשֶׁר־אָמַ֥רְתִּי אֶל־הָאִשָּׁ֖ה תִּשָּׁמֵֽר׃ 14] מִכֹּ֣ל אֲשֶׁר־יֵצֵא֩ מִגֶּ֨פֶן הַיַּ֜יִן לֹ֣א תֹאכַ֗ל וְיַ֤יִן וְשֵׁכָר֙ אַל־תֵּ֔שְׁתְּ וְכָל־טֻמְאָ֖ה אַל־תֹּאכַ֑ל כֹּ֥ל אֲשֶׁר־צִוִּיתִ֖יהָ תִּשְׁמֹֽר׃

15] וַיֹּ֥אמֶר מָנ֖וֹחַ אֶל־מַלְאַ֣ךְ יְהוָ֑ה נַעְצְרָה־נָּ֣א אוֹתָ֔ךְ וְנַעֲשֶׂ֥ה לְפָנֶ֖יךָ גְּדִ֥י עִזִּֽים׃ 16] וַיֹּאמֶר֩ מַלְאַ֨ךְ יְהוָ֜ה אֶל־מָנ֗וֹחַ אִם־תַּעְצְרֵ֙נִי֙ לֹא־אֹכַ֣ל בְּלַחְמֶ֔ךָ וְאִם־תַּעֲשֶׂ֣ה עֹלָ֔ה לַיהוָ֖ה תַּעֲלֶ֑נָּה כִּ֚י לֹא־יָדַ֣ע מָנ֔וֹחַ כִּֽי־מַלְאַ֥ךְ יְהוָ֖ה הֽוּא׃ 17] וַיֹּ֧אמֶר מָנ֛וֹחַ אֶל־מַלְאַ֥ךְ יְהוָ֖ה מִ֣י שְׁמֶ֑ךָ כִּֽי־יָבֹ֥א דברך[דְבָרְךָ֖] וְכִבַּדְנֽוּךָ׃ 18] וַיֹּ֤אמֶר לוֹ֙ מַלְאַ֣ךְ יְהוָ֔ה לָ֥מָּה זֶּ֖ה תִּשְׁאַ֣ל לִשְׁמִ֑י וְהוּא־פֶֽלִאי׃

19] וַיִּקַּ֨ח מָנ֜וֹחַ אֶת־גְּדִ֤י הָעִזִּים֙ וְאֶת־הַמִּנְחָ֔ה וַיַּ֥עַל עַל־הַצּ֖וּר לַֽיהוָ֑ה וּמַפְלִ֣א לַעֲשׂ֔וֹת וּמָנ֥וֹחַ וְאִשְׁתּ֖וֹ רֹאִֽים׃ 20] וַיְהִי֩ בַעֲל֨וֹת הַלַּ֜הַב מֵעַ֣ל הַמִּזְבֵּ֗חַ הַשָּׁמַ֔יְמָה וַיַּ֥עַל מַלְאַךְ־יְהוָ֖ה בְּלַ֣הַב הַמִּזְבֵּ֑חַ וּמָנ֤וֹחַ וְאִשְׁתּוֹ֙ רֹאִ֔ים וַיִּפְּל֥וּ עַל־פְּנֵיהֶ֖ם

[a] Lit. "in the day"   [b-b] Meaning of Heb. uncertain

21] The angel of the LORD never appeared again to Manoah and his wife.—Manoah then realized that it had been an angel of the LORD.

22] And Manoah said to his wife, "We shall surely die, for we have seen a divine being."

23] But his wife said to him, "Had the LORD meant to take our lives, He would not have accepted a burnt offering and meal offering from us, nor let us see all these things; and He would not have made such an announcement to us."

24] The woman bore a son, and she named him Samson. The boy grew up, and the LORD blessed him.

25] The spirit of the LORD first moved him in the encampment of Dan, between Zorah and Eshtaol.

21] וְלֹא־יָסַף עוֹד מַלְאַךְ יְהוָה לְהֵרָאֹה אֶל־מָנוֹחַ וְאֶל־אִשְׁתּוֹ אָז יָדַע מָנוֹחַ כִּי־מַלְאַךְ יְהוָה הוּא: 22] וַיֹּאמֶר מָנוֹחַ אֶל־אִשְׁתּוֹ מוֹת נָמוּת כִּי אֱלֹהִים רָאִינוּ: 23] וַתֹּאמֶר לוֹ אִשְׁתּוֹ לוּ חָפֵץ יְהוָה לַהֲמִיתֵנוּ לֹא־לָקַח מִיָּדֵנוּ עֹלָה וּמִנְחָה וְלֹא הֶרְאָנוּ אֶת־כָּל־אֵלֶּה וְכָעֵת לֹא הִשְׁמִיעָנוּ כָּזֹאת:

24] וַתֵּלֶד הָאִשָּׁה בֵּן וַתִּקְרָא אֶת־שְׁמוֹ שִׁמְשׁוֹן וַיִּגְדַּל הַנַּעַר וַיְבָרְכֵהוּ יְהוָה: 25] וַתָּחֶל רוּחַ יְהוָה לְפַעֲמוֹ בְּמַחֲנֵה־דָן בֵּין צָרְעָה וּבֵין אֶשְׁתָּאֹל:

Zechariah preached in Palestine after the exiles had returned from Babylon and, under Zerubbabel's and the
High Priest Joshua's leaderships, had begun to rebuild
the Temple. When the project lagged, the prophet exhorted
his people to persist and maintain the vision of a great
sanctuary dedicated to the worship of God.

In Zechariah's vision, a candlestick symbolizes the mystery
of divine illumination (this connects the haftarah with the
Torah portion's beginning). The symbolism represents a
warning to Zerubbabel: It will be the spirit of his governor-
ship that will prevail, not its trappings of power. Verses
4:1–7 are also used on First Shabbat Chanukah.

בהעלתך

Zechariah
2:14–4:7

ב

Chapter 2

14] Shout for joy, Fair Zion! For lo, I come;
and I will dwell in your midst—declares the LORD.
15] In that day many nations will attach themselves to the LORD and become His*f* people, and
He*g* will dwell in your midst. Then you will know
that I was sent to you by the LORD of Hosts.

16] The LORD will *h*take Judah to Himself as
His portion*-h* in the Holy Land, and He will choose
Jerusalem once more.

17] Be silent, all flesh, before the LORD!
For He is roused from His holy habitation.

14] רָנִּי וְשִׂמְחִי בַּת־צִיּוֹן כִּי הִנְנִי־בָא וְשָׁכַנְתִּי
בְתוֹכֵךְ נְאֻם־יְהֹוָה: 15 וְנִלְווּ גוֹיִם רַבִּים אֶל
יְהֹוָה בַּיּוֹם הַהוּא וְהָיוּ לִי לְעָם וְשָׁכַנְתִּי בְתוֹכֵךְ
וְיָדַעַתְּ כִּי־יְהֹוָה צְבָאוֹת שְׁלָחַנִי אֵלָיִךְ:
16] וְנָחַל יְהֹוָה אֶת־יְהוּדָה חֶלְקוֹ עַל אַדְמַת
הַקֹּדֶשׁ וּבָחַר עוֹד בִּירוּשָׁלָיִם:
17] הַס כָּל־בָּשָׂר מִפְּנֵי יְהֹוָה
כִּי נֵעוֹר מִמְּעוֹן קָדְשׁוֹ:

Chapter 3

1] He further showed me Joshua, the high
priest, standing before the angel of the LORD, and
the Accuser*a* standing at his right to accuse him.
2] But [the angel of] the LORD said to the Accuser,
"The LORD rebuke you, O Accuser; may the LORD
who has chosen Jerusalem rebuke you! For this is
a brand plucked from the fire."*b*

3] Now Joshua
was clothed in filthy garments when he stood
before the angel.

ג

1] וַיַּרְאֵנִי אֶת־יְהוֹשֻׁעַ הַכֹּהֵן הַגָּדוֹל עֹמֵד
לִפְנֵי מַלְאַךְ יְהֹוָה וְהַשָּׂטָן עֹמֵד עַל־יְמִינוֹ
לְשִׂטְנוֹ: 2 וַיֹּאמֶר יְהֹוָה אֶל־הַשָּׂטָן יִגְעַר יְהֹוָה
בְּךָ הַשָּׂטָן וְיִגְעַר יְהֹוָה בְּךָ הַבֹּחֵר בִּירוּשָׁלָיִם
הֲלוֹא זֶה אוּד מֻצָּל מֵאֵשׁ: 3 וִיהוֹשֻׁעַ הָיָה
לָבֻשׁ בְּגָדִים צוֹאִים וְעֹמֵד לִפְנֵי הַמַּלְאָךְ:

f Heb. "My"
g Heb. "I"
h-h Emendation yields "allot to Judah its portion"; cf. Num. 34.17
a Others "Satan"
b Joshua's father (Hag. 1.1; I Chron. 5.40–41) was exiled and his grandfather executed
(II Kings 25.18–21) by the Babylonians, but Joshua returned

4] The latter spoke up and said to his attendants, "Take the filthy garments off him!" And he said to him, "See, I have removed your guilt from you, and you shall be clothed in [priestly] robes."

5] Then he[c] gave the order, "Let a pure[d] diadem be placed on his head." And they placed the pure diadem on his head and clothed him in [priestly] garments,[e] as the angel of the LORD stood by.

6] And the angel of the LORD charged Joshua as follows:

7] "Thus said the LORD of Hosts: If you walk in My paths and keep My charge, you in turn will rule My House and guard My courts, and I will permit you to move about among these attendants.

8] Hearken well, O High Priest Joshua, you and your fellow priests sitting before you! For those men are a sign that I am going to bring My servant the Branch.[f]

9] For mark well this stone which I place before Joshua, a single stone with seven eyes.[g] I will execute its engraving—declares the LORD— and I will remove that country's guilt in a single day.

10] In that day —declares the LORD of Hosts—you will be inviting each other to the shade of vines and fig trees."

Chapter 4

1] The angel who talked with me came back and woke me as a man is wakened from sleep. 2] He said to me, "What do you see?" And I answered, "I see a lampstand all of gold, with a bowl above it. The lamps on it are seven in

4 וַיַּעַן וַיֹּאמֶר אֶל־הָעֹמְדִים לְפָנָיו לֵאמֹר הָסִירוּ הַבְּגָדִים הַצֹּאִים מֵעָלָיו וַיֹּאמֶר אֵלָיו רְאֵה הֶעֱבַרְתִּי מֵעָלֶיךָ עֲוֹנֶךָ וְהַלְבֵּשׁ אֹתְךָ מַחֲלָצוֹת: 5 וָאֹמַר יָשִׂימוּ צָנִיף טָהוֹר עַל רֹאשׁוֹ וַיָּשִׂימוּ הַצָּנִיף הַטָּהוֹר עַל רֹאשׁוֹ וַיַּלְבִּשֻׁהוּ בְּגָדִים וּמַלְאַךְ יְהוָה עֹמֵד: 6 וַיָּעַד מַלְאַךְ יְהוָה בִּיהוֹשֻׁעַ לֵאמֹר: 7 כֹּה־אָמַר יְהוָה צְבָאוֹת אִם־בִּדְרָכַי תֵּלֵךְ וְאִם אֶת־מִשְׁמַרְתִּי תִשְׁמֹר וְגַם־אַתָּה תָּדִין אֶת־בֵּיתִי וְגַם תִּשְׁמֹר אֶת־חֲצֵרָי וְנָתַתִּי לְךָ מַהְלְכִים בֵּין הָעֹמְדִים הָאֵלֶּה: 8 שְׁמַע־נָא יְהוֹשֻׁעַ הַכֹּהֵן הַגָּדוֹל אַתָּה וְרֵעֶיךָ הַיֹּשְׁבִים לְפָנֶיךָ כִּי־אַנְשֵׁי מוֹפֵת הֵמָּה כִּי־הִנְנִי מֵבִיא אֶת־עַבְדִּי צֶמַח: 9 כִּי הִנֵּה הָאֶבֶן אֲשֶׁר נָתַתִּי לִפְנֵי יְהוֹשֻׁעַ עַל־ אֶבֶן אַחַת שִׁבְעָה עֵינָיִם הִנְנִי מְפַתֵּחַ פִּתֻּחָהּ נְאֻם יְהוָה צְבָאוֹת וּמַשְׁתִּי אֶת־עֲוֹן הָאָרֶץ־הַהִיא בְּיוֹם אֶחָד: 10 בַּיּוֹם הַהוּא נְאֻם יְהוָה צְבָאוֹת תִּקְרְאוּ אִישׁ לְרֵעֵהוּ אֶל־תַּחַת גֶּפֶן וְאֶל־תַּחַת תְּאֵנָה:

ד

1 וַיָּשָׁב הַמַּלְאָךְ הַדֹּבֵר בִּי וַיְעִירֵנִי כְּאִישׁ אֲשֶׁר־יֵעוֹר מִשְּׁנָתוֹ: 2 וַיֹּאמֶר אֵלַי מָה אַתָּה רֹאֶה וָאֹמַר רָאִיתִי וְהִנֵּה מְנוֹרַת זָהָב כֻּלָּהּ וְגֻלָּהּ עַל־רֹאשָׁהּ וְשִׁבְעָה נֵרֹתֶיהָ עָלֶיהָ שִׁבְעָה

c Heb. "I"

d I.e., ritually pure

e Joshua has now been rendered fit to associate with the heavenly beings (v. 7); cf. Isa. 6.6–8

f I.e., the future king of David's line. See 6.12; Jer. 23.5–6; 33.15–16; cf. Isa. 11.1

g Meaning of Heb. uncertain. The stone apparently symbolizes the God-given power of the future Davidic ruler; see below 4.6–7

number, and the ᵃlamps above it have⁻ᵃ seven pipes;

> 3] and by it are two olive trees, one on the right of the bowl and one on its left." 4] I, in turn, asked the angel who talked with me, "What do those things mean, my lord?" 5] "Do you not know what those things mean?" asked the angel who talked with me; and I said, "No, my lord."

> 6] Then he explained to me as follows:ᵇ

"This is the word of the LORD to Zerubbabel:ᶜ Not by might, nor by power, but by My spiritᵈ— said the LORD of Hosts. 7] Whoever you are, O great mountain in the path of Zerubbabel, turn into level ground! For he shall produce that excellent stone; it shall be greeted with shouts of 'Beautiful! Beautiful!' "

וְשִׁבְעָה מוּצָקוֹת לַנֵּרוֹת אֲשֶׁר עַל־רֹאשָׁהּ:
3] וּשְׁנַיִם זֵיתִים עָלֶיהָ אֶחָד מִימִין הַגֻּלָּה וְאֶחָד עַל־שְׂמֹאלָהּ: 4] וָאַעַן וָאֹמַר אֶל־הַמַּלְאָךְ הַדֹּבֵר בִּי לֵאמֹר מָה אֵלֶּה אֲדֹנִי: 5] וַיַּעַן הַמַּלְאָךְ הַדֹּבֵר בִּי וַיֹּאמֶר אֵלַי הֲלוֹא יָדַעְתָּ מָה־הֵמָּה אֵלֶּה וָאֹמַר לֹא אֲדֹנִי: 6] וַיַּעַן וַיֹּאמֶר אֵלַי לֵאמֹר

זֶה דְּבַר־יְהֹוָה אֶל־זְרֻבָּבֶל לֵאמֹר לֹא בְחַיִל וְלֹא בְכֹחַ כִּי אִם־בְּרוּחִי אָמַר יְהֹוָה צְבָאוֹת: 7] מִי־אַתָּה הַר־הַגָּדוֹל לִפְנֵי זְרֻבָּבֶל לְמִישֹׁר וְהוֹצִיא אֶת־הָאֶבֶן הָרֹאשָׁה תְּשֻׁאוֹת חֵן חֵן לָהּ:

ᵃ⁻ᵃ *Emendation yields "bowl above it has"*

ᵇ *The explanation is given in the last sentence of v. 10*

ᶜ *A grandson of King Jehoiachin (I Chron. 3.17–19) and the secular head of the repatriated community (Hag. 1.1)*

ᵈ *I.e., Zerubbabel will succeed by means of spiritual gifts conferred upon him by the LORD; cf. Isa. 11.2 ff.*

Joshua became Moses' successor and led the conquest of the Promised Land. While his name is attached to the 24 chapters which recount the campaign, the book is likely of much later origin. It portrays history essentially as a judgment of God.

Both sidrah and haftarah tell that spies were sent out to explore the land. Joshua himself participated in the earlier adventure and, on returning, failed to convince the people of the feasibility of the conquest. Now that he is the people's leader his messengers can at last prepare the long awaited campaign.

שלח-לך

Joshua

2 : 1-24

ב

Chapter 2

1] Joshua son of Nun secretly sent two spies from Shittim, saying, "Go, reconnoiter the region of Jericho." So they set out, and they came to the house of a harlot named Rahab and lodged there. 2] The king of Jericho was told, "Some men have come here tonight, Israelites, to spy out the country."

3] The king of Jericho thereupon sent orders to Rahab: "Produce the men who came to you and entered your house, for they have come to spy out the whole country."

4] The woman, however, had taken the two men and hidden them. "It is true," she said, "the men did come to me, but I didn't know where they were from. 5] And at dark, when the gate was about to be closed, the men left; and I don't know where the men went. Quick, go after them, for you can overtake them."—

6] Now she had taken them up to the roof and hidden them under some stalks of flax which she had lying on the roof.— 7] So the men pursued them in the direction of the Jordan down to the fords; and no sooner had the pursuers gone out than the gate was shut behind them.

8] ᵃ‑The spies‑ᵃ had not yet gone to sleep when she came up to them on the roof.

ᵃ‑ᵃ Heb. "They"

1] וַיִּשְׁלַ֣ח יְהוֹשֻֽׁעַ־בִּן־נ֠וּן מִֽן־הַשִּׁטִּ֞ים שְׁנַֽיִם־אֲנָשִׁ֤ים מְרַגְּלִים֙ חֶ֣רֶשׁ לֵאמֹ֔ר לְכ֛וּ רְא֥וּ אֶת־הָאָ֖רֶץ וְאֶת־יְרִיח֑וֹ וַיֵּ֨לְכ֜וּ וַ֠יָּבֹאוּ בֵּֽית־אִשָּׁ֥ה זוֹנָ֛ה וּשְׁמָ֥הּ רָחָ֖ב וַיִּשְׁכְּבוּ־שָֽׁמָּה׃ 2] וַיֵּ֣אָמַ֔ר לְמֶ֥לֶךְ יְרִיח֖וֹ לֵאמֹ֑ר הִנֵּ֣ה אֲ֠נָשִׁים בָּ֣אוּ הֵ֧נָּה הַלַּ֛יְלָה מִבְּנֵ֥י יִשְׂרָאֵ֖ל לַחְפֹּ֥ר אֶת־הָאָֽרֶץ׃ 3] וַיִּשְׁלַ֗ח מֶ֣לֶךְ יְרִיח֔וֹ אֶל־רָחָ֖ב לֵאמֹ֑ר ה֠וֹצִ֛יאִי הָאֲנָשִׁ֤ים הַבָּאִ֨ים אֵלַ֜יִךְ אֲשֶׁר־בָּ֣אוּ לְבֵיתֵ֗ךְ כִּ֚י לַחְפֹּ֣ר אֶת־כׇּל־הָאָ֖רֶץ בָּֽאוּ׃ 4] וַתִּקַּ֧ח הָֽאִשָּׁ֛ה אֶת־שְׁנֵ֥י הָאֲנָשִׁ֖ים וַֽתִּצְפְּנ֑וֹ וַתֹּ֣אמֶר ׀ כֵּ֗ן בָּ֤אוּ אֵלַי֙ הָֽאֲנָשִׁ֔ים וְלֹ֥א יָדַ֖עְתִּי מֵאַ֥יִן הֵֽמָּה׃ 5] וַיְהִ֨י הַשַּׁ֜עַר לִסְגּ֗וֹר בַּחֹ֙שֶׁךְ֙ וְהָאֲנָשִׁ֣ים יָצָ֔אוּ לֹ֣א יָדַ֔עְתִּי אָ֥נָה הָלְכ֖וּ הָֽאֲנָשִׁ֑ים רִדְפ֤וּ מַהֵר֙ אַחֲרֵיהֶ֔ם כִּ֖י תַשִּׂיגֽוּם׃ 6] וְהִ֖יא הֶעֱלָ֣תַם הַגָּ֑גָה וַֽתִּטְמְנֵם֙ בְּפִשְׁתֵּ֣י הָעֵ֔ץ הָעֲרֻכ֥וֹת לָ֖הּ עַל־הַגָּֽג׃ 7] וְהָאֲנָשִׁ֗ים רָדְפ֤וּ אַֽחֲרֵיהֶם֙ דֶּ֣רֶךְ הַיַּרְדֵּ֔ן עַ֖ל הַֽמַּעְבְּר֑וֹת וְהַשַּׁ֣עַר סָגָ֔רוּ אַחֲרֵ֕י כַּאֲשֶׁ֥ר יָצְא֖וּ הָרֹדְפִ֥ים אַחֲרֵיהֶֽם׃ 8] וְהֵ֖מָּה טֶ֣רֶם יִשְׁכָּב֑וּן וְהִ֛יא עָלְתָ֥ה עֲלֵיהֶ֖ם

1262

9] She said to the men, "I know that the LORD has given the country to you, because dread of you has fallen upon us, and all the inhabitants of the land are quaking before you.

10] For we have heard how the LORD dried up the waters of the Sea of Reeds for you when you left Egypt, and what you did to Sihon and Og, the two Amorite kings across the Jordan, whom you doomed.[b]

11] When we heard about it, we lost heart, and no man had any more spirit left because of you; for the LORD your God is the only God in heaven above and on earth below.

12] Now, since I have shown loyalty to you, swear to me by the LORD that you in turn will show loyalty to my family. Provide me with a reliable sign

13] that you will spare the lives of my father and mother, my brothers and sisters, and all who belong to them, and save us from death."

14] The men answered her, "Our persons are pledged for yours, even to death! If you do not disclose this mission of ours, we will show you true loyalty when the LORD gives us the land."

15] She let them down by a rope through the window—for her dwelling was at the outer side of the city wall and she lived in the actual wall. 16] She said to them, "Make for the hills, so that the pursuers may not come upon you. Stay there in hiding three days, until the pursuers return; then go your way."

17] But the men warned her, "We will be released from this oath which you have made us take

18] [unless,] when we invade the country, you tie this length of crimson cord to the window through which you let us down. Bring your father,

עַל־הַגָּג: 9 וַתֹּאמֶר אֶל־הָאֲנָשִׁים יָדַעְתִּי כִּי נָתַן יְהֹוָה לָכֶם אֶת־הָאָרֶץ וְכִי־נָפְלָה אֵימַתְכֶם עָלֵינוּ וְכִי נָמֹגוּ כָּל־יֹשְׁבֵי הָאָרֶץ מִפְּנֵיכֶם:

10 כִּי שָׁמַעְנוּ אֵת אֲשֶׁר־הוֹבִישׁ יְהֹוָה אֶת־מֵי יַם־סוּף מִפְּנֵיכֶם בְּצֵאתְכֶם מִמִּצְרָיִם וַאֲשֶׁר עֲשִׂיתֶם לִשְׁנֵי מַלְכֵי הָאֱמֹרִי אֲשֶׁר בְּעֵבֶר הַיַּרְדֵּן לְסִיחֹן וּלְעוֹג אֲשֶׁר הֶחֱרַמְתֶּם אוֹתָם:

11 וַנִּשְׁמַע וַיִּמַּס לְבָבֵנוּ וְלֹא־קָמָה עוֹד רוּחַ בְּאִישׁ מִפְּנֵיכֶם כִּי יְהֹוָה אֱלֹהֵיכֶם הוּא אֱלֹהִים בַּשָּׁמַיִם מִמַּעַל וְעַל־הָאָרֶץ מִתָּחַת: 12 וְעַתָּה הִשָּׁבְעוּ־נָא לִי בַּיהֹוָה כִּי־עָשִׂיתִי עִמָּכֶם חָסֶד וַעֲשִׂיתֶם גַּם־אַתֶּם עִם־בֵּית אָבִי חֶסֶד וּנְתַתֶּם לִי אוֹת אֱמֶת: 13 וְהַחֲיִתֶם אֶת־אָבִי וְאֶת־ אִמִּי וְאֶת־אַחַי וְאֶת־אַחְיוֹתַי וְאֵת כָּל־אֲשֶׁר לָהֶם וְהִצַּלְתֶּם אֶת־נַפְשֹׁתֵינוּ מִמָּוֶת: 14 וַיֹּאמְרוּ לָהּ הָאֲנָשִׁים נַפְשֵׁנוּ תַחְתֵּיכֶם לָמוּת אִם לֹא תַגִּידוּ אֶת־דְּבָרֵנוּ זֶה וְהָיָה בְּתֵת יְהֹוָה לָנוּ אֶת־הָאָרֶץ וְעָשִׂינוּ עִמָּךְ חֶסֶד וֶאֱמֶת:

15 וַתּוֹרִדֵם בַּחֶבֶל בְּעַד הַחַלּוֹן כִּי בֵיתָהּ בְּקִיר הַחוֹמָה וּבַחוֹמָה הִיא יוֹשָׁבֶת: 16 וַתֹּאמֶר לָהֶם הָהָרָה לֵּכוּ פֶּן־יִפְגְּעוּ בָכֶם הָרֹדְפִים וְנַחְבֵּתֶם שָׁמָּה שְׁלֹשֶׁת יָמִים עַד שֹׁב הָרֹדְפִים וְאַחַר תֵּלְכוּ לְדַרְכְּכֶם:

17 וַיֹּאמְרוּ אֵלֶיהָ הָאֲנָשִׁים נְקִיִּם אֲנַחְנוּ מִשְּׁבֻעָתֵךְ הַזֶּה אֲשֶׁר הִשְׁבַּעְתָּנוּ: 18 הִנֵּה אֲנַחְנוּ בָאִים בָּאָרֶץ אֶת־תִּקְוַת חוּט הַשָּׁנִי הַזֶּה תִּקְשְׁרִי בַּחַלּוֹן אֲשֶׁר הוֹרַדְתֵּנוּ בּוֹ וְאֶת־אָבִיךְ

---

[b] I.e., *placed under* cherem, *which meant the annihilation of the inhabitants. Cf. Deut.* 2.34 *ff.*

your mother, your brothers, and all your family together in your house;

19] and if anyone ventures outside the doors of your house, his blood will be on his head, and we shall be clear. But if a hand is laid on anyone who remains in the house with you, his blood shall be on our heads. 20] And if you disclose this mission of ours, we shall likewise be released from the oath which you made us take."

21] She replied, "Let it be as you say."

She sent them on their way, and they left; and she tied the crimson cord to the window.

22] They went straight to the hills and stayed there three days, until the pursuers turned back. And so the pursuers, searching all along the road, did not find them.

23] Then the two men came down again from the hills and crossed over. They came to Joshua son of Nun and reported to him all that had happened to them.

24] They said to Joshua, "The Lord has delivered the whole land into our power; in fact, all the inhabitants of the land are quaking before us."

וְאֶת־אִמֵּךְ וְאֶת־אַחַיִךְ וְאֵת כָּל־בֵּית אָבִיךְ תַּאַסְפִי אֵלַיִךְ הַבָּיְתָה: 19] וְהָיָה כֹּל אֲשֶׁר־יֵצֵא מִדַּלְתֵי בֵיתֵךְ הַחוּצָה דָּמוֹ בְרֹאשׁוֹ וַאֲנַחְנוּ נְקִיִּם וְכֹל אֲשֶׁר יִהְיֶה אִתָּךְ בַּבַּיִת דָּמוֹ בְרֹאשֵׁנוּ אִם־יָד תִּהְיֶה־בּוֹ: 20] וְאִם־תַּגִּידִי אֶת־דְּבָרֵנוּ זֶה וְהָיִינוּ נְקִיִּם מִשְּׁבֻעָתֵךְ אֲשֶׁר הִשְׁבַּעְתָּנוּ: 21] וַתֹּאמֶר כְּדִבְרֵיכֶם כֶּן־הוּא וַתְּשַׁלְּחֵם וַיֵּלֵכוּ וַתִּקְשֹׁר אֶת־תִּקְוַת הַשָּׁנִי בַּחַלּוֹן:

22] וַיֵּלְכוּ וַיָּבֹאוּ הָהָרָה וַיֵּשְׁבוּ שָׁם שְׁלֹשֶׁת יָמִים עַד־שָׁבוּ הָרֹדְפִים וַיְבַקְשׁוּ הָרֹדְפִים בְּכָל־הַדֶּרֶךְ וְלֹא מָצָאוּ:

23] וַיָּשֻׁבוּ שְׁנֵי הָאֲנָשִׁים וַיֵּרְדוּ מֵהָהָר וַיַּעַבְרוּ וַיָּבֹאוּ אֶל־יְהוֹשֻׁעַ בִּן־נוּן וַיְסַפְּרוּ־לוֹ אֵת כָּל־הַמֹּצְאוֹת אוֹתָם: 24] וַיֹּאמְרוּ אֶל־יְהוֹשֻׁעַ כִּי נָתַן יְהוָה בְּיָדֵנוּ אֶת־כָּל־הָאָרֶץ וְגַם־נָמֹגוּ כָּל־יֹשְׁבֵי הָאָרֶץ מִפָּנֵינוּ:

The Book of Samuel is divided into two parts. It is primarily the story of Samuel's ministry as the spiritual guide
of Israel and of the reign of Israel's first two kings, Saul
and David (about 1000 B.C.E.). It is history written from
a theological perspective: all of Israel's fate hinges on the
performance or non-performance of God's commandments.

In the sidrah, Korah and his followers try to displace the
aging Moses; in the haftarah, the people demand that
the aging Samuel choose a king as his successor. But,
while Moses leaves the judgment of his performance to
God, Samuel delivers himself of a spirited defense of his
incumbency—and then yields to the people's request.

קרח

First Samuel
11 : 14–12 : 22

Chapter 11

14] Samuel said to the people, "Come, let us
go to Gilgal and there inaugurate the monarchy."
15] So all the people went to Gilgal, and there at
Gilgal they declared Saul king before the LORD.
They offered sacrifices of well-being there before
the LORD; and Saul and all the men of Israel held
a great celebration there.

Chapter 12

1] Then Samuel said to all Israel, "I have
yielded to you in all you have asked of me and
have set a king over you.

2] Henceforth the king
will be your leader.

"As for me, I have grown old and gray—but
my sons are still with you—and I have been your
leader from my youth to this day.

3] Here I am!
Testify against me, in the presence of the LORD
and in the presence of His anointed one: Whose
ox have I taken, or whose ass have I taken? Whom
have I defrauded or whom have I robbed?
From whom have I taken a bribe ᵃ⁻to look the
other way?⁻ᵃ I will return it to you."

4] They re-
sponded, "You have not defrauded us, and you
have not robbed us, and you have taken nothing
from anyone."

5] He said to them, "The LORD

יא

14] וַיֹּ֤אמֶר שְׁמוּאֵל֙ אֶל־הָעָ֔ם לְכ֖וּ וְנֵלְכָ֣ה
הַגִּלְגָּ֑ל וּנְחַדֵּ֥שׁ שָׁ֖ם הַמְּלוּכָֽה׃ 15] וַיֵּלְכ֣וּ כָל־
הָעָ֣ם הַגִּלְגָּ֗ל וַיַּמְלִ֨כוּ שָׁ֤ם אֶת־שָׁאוּל֙ לִפְנֵ֣י יְהֹוָה֙
בַּגִּלְגָּ֔ל וַיִּזְבְּחוּ־שָׁ֛ם זְבָחִ֥ים שְׁלָמִ֖ים לִפְנֵ֣י יְהֹוָ֑ה
וַיִּשְׂמַ֨ח שָׁ֜ם שָׁא֛וּל וְכָל־אַנְשֵׁ֥י יִשְׂרָאֵ֖ל עַד־מְאֹֽד׃

יב

1] וַיֹּ֤אמֶר שְׁמוּאֵל֙ אֶל־כָּל־יִשְׂרָאֵ֔ל הִנֵּ֤ה
שָׁמַ֨עְתִּי֙ בְקֹֽלְכֶ֔ם לְכֹ֥ל אֲשֶׁר־אֲמַרְתֶּ֖ם לִ֑י
וָאַמְלִ֥יךְ עֲלֵיכֶ֖ם מֶֽלֶךְ׃ 2] וְעַתָּ֞ה הִנֵּ֥ה הַמֶּ֣לֶךְ ׀
מִתְהַלֵּ֣ךְ לִפְנֵיכֶ֗ם וַֽאֲנִי֙ זָקַ֣נְתִּי וָשַׂ֔בְתִּי וּבָנַ֖י הִנָּ֣ם
אִתְּכֶ֑ם וַֽאֲנִי֙ הִתְהַלַּ֣כְתִּי לִפְנֵיכֶ֔ם מִנְּעֻרַ֖י עַד־
הַיּ֥וֹם הַזֶּֽה׃ 3] הִנְנִ֣י עֲנ֣וּ בִ֗י נֶ֤גֶד יְהֹוָה֙ וְנֶ֣גֶד
מְשִׁיח֒וֹ אֶת־שׁוֹר֩ ׀ מִ֨י לָקַ֜חְתִּי וַֽחֲמ֣וֹר מִ֣י לָקַ֗חְתִּי
וְאֶת־מִ֤י עָשַׁ֨קְתִּי֙ אֶת־מִ֣י רַצּ֔וֹתִי וּמִיַּד־מִי֙ לָקַ֣חְתִּי
כֹ֗פֶר וְאַעְלִ֥ים עֵינַ֖י בּ֑וֹ וְאָשִׁ֖יב לָכֶֽם׃
4] וַיֹּ֣אמְר֔וּ לֹ֥א עֲשַׁקְתָּ֖נוּ וְלֹ֣א רַצּוֹתָ֑נוּ וְלֹֽא־
לָקַ֥חְתָּ מִיַּד־אִ֖ישׁ מְאֽוּמָה׃ 5] וַיֹּ֣אמֶר אֲלֵיהֶ֗ם

ᵃ⁻ᵃ Septuagint reads "or a pair of sandals? [Cf. Amos 2.6] Testify against me"

then is witness, and His anointed is witness, [b]to your admission[b] this day that you have found nothing in my possession." They[c] responded, "He is!"

6] Samuel said to the people, [d]"The Lord [is witness], He who appointed[d] Moses and Aaron and who brought your fathers out of the land of Egypt.

7] Come, stand before the Lord while I cite against you all the kindnesses that the Lord has done to you and your fathers.

8] "When Jacob came to Egypt,[e] . . . your fathers cried out to the Lord, and the Lord sent Moses and Aaron, who brought your fathers out of Egypt and settled them in this place.

9] But they forgot the Lord their God; so He delivered them into the hands of Sisera the military commander of Hazor, into the hands of the Philistines, and into the hands of the king of Moab; and these made war upon them.

10] They cried to the Lord, 'We are guilty, for we have forsaken the Lord and worshiped the Baalim and the Ashtaroth. Oh, deliver us from our enemies and we will serve you.'

11] And the Lord sent Jerubbaal and Bedan[f] and Jephthah and Samuel, and delivered you from the enemies around you; and you dwelt in security.

12] But when you saw that Nahash king of the Ammonites was advancing against you, you said to me, 'No, we must have a king reigning over us'—though the Lord your God is your King.

13] "Well, the Lord has set a king over you! Here is the king that you have chosen, that you have asked for.

עֵד יְהוָה בָּכֶם וְעֵד מְשִׁיחוֹ הַיּוֹם הַזֶּה כִּי לֹא מְצָאתֶם בְּיָדִי מְאוּמָה וַיֹּאמֶר עֵד׃

6] וַיֹּאמֶר שְׁמוּאֵל אֶל־הָעָם יְהוָה אֲשֶׁר עָשָׂה אֶת־מֹשֶׁה וְאֶת־אַהֲרֹן וַאֲשֶׁר הֶעֱלָה אֶת־אֲבֹתֵיכֶם מֵאֶרֶץ מִצְרָיִם׃ 7] וְעַתָּה הִתְיַצְּבוּ וְאִשָּׁפְטָה אִתְּכֶם לִפְנֵי יְהוָה אֵת כָּל־צִדְקוֹת יְהוָה אֲשֶׁר־עָשָׂה אִתְּכֶם וְאֶת־אֲבֹתֵיכֶם׃

8] כַּאֲשֶׁר־בָּא יַעֲקֹב מִצְרָיִם וַיִּזְעֲקוּ אֲבֹתֵיכֶם אֶל־יְהוָה וַיִּשְׁלַח יְהוָה אֶת־מֹשֶׁה וְאֶת־אַהֲרֹן וַיּוֹצִיאוּ אֶת־אֲבוֹתֵיכֶם מִמִּצְרַיִם וַיֹּשִׁבוּם בַּמָּקוֹם הַזֶּה׃ 9] וַיִּשְׁכְּחוּ אֶת־יְהוָה אֱלֹהֵיהֶם וַיִּמְכֹּר אֹתָם בְּיַד סִיסְרָא שַׂר־צְבָא חָצוֹר וּבְיַד־פְּלִשְׁתִּים וּבְיַד מֶלֶךְ מוֹאָב וַיִּלָּחֲמוּ בָּם׃ 10] וַיִּזְעֲקוּ אֶל־יְהוָה וַיֹּאמְרוּ חָטָאנוּ כִּי עָזַבְנוּ אֶת־יְהוָה וַנַּעֲבֹד אֶת־הַבְּעָלִים וְאֶת־הָעַשְׁתָּרוֹת וְעַתָּה הַצִּילֵנוּ מִיַּד אֹיְבֵינוּ וְנַעַבְדֶךָ׃ 11] וַיִּשְׁלַח יְהוָה אֶת־יְרֻבַּעַל וְאֶת־בְּדָן וְאֶת־יִפְתָּח וְאֶת־שְׁמוּאֵל וַיַּצֵּל אֶתְכֶם מִיַּד אֹיְבֵיכֶם מִסָּבִיב וַתֵּשְׁבוּ בֶּטַח׃ 12] וַתִּרְאוּ כִּי־נָחָשׁ מֶלֶךְ בְּנֵי־עַמּוֹן בָּא עֲלֵיכֶם וַתֹּאמְרוּ לִי לֹא כִּי־מֶלֶךְ יִמְלֹךְ עָלֵינוּ וַיהוָה אֱלֹהֵיכֶם מַלְכְּכֶם׃

13] וְעַתָּה הִנֵּה הַמֶּלֶךְ אֲשֶׁר בְּחַרְתֶּם אֲשֶׁר שְׁאֶלְתֶּם וְהִנֵּה נָתַן יְהוָה עֲלֵיכֶם מֶלֶךְ׃

[b-b] Lit. "against you"

[c] Heb. "he"

[d-d] Meaning of Heb. uncertain

[e] Septuagint adds "the Egyptians oppressed them"

[f] Septuagint "Barak"

14] "If you will revere the LORD, worship Him, and obey Him, and will not flout the LORD's command, if both you and the king who reigns over you will follow the LORD your God, [well and good].

15] But if you do not obey the LORD and you flout the LORD's command, the hand of the LORD will strike you *d-as it did your fathers.-d*

16] "Now stand by and see the marvelous thing that the LORD will do before your eyes. 17] It is the season of the wheat harvest.*g* I will pray to the LORD and He will send thunder and rain; then you will take thought and realize what a wicked thing you did in the sight of the LORD when you asked for a king."

18] Samuel prayed to the LORD, and the LORD sent thunder and rain that day, and the people stood in awe of the LORD and of Samuel.

19] The people all said to Samuel, "Intercede for your servants with the LORD your God that we may not die, for we have added to all our sins the wickedness of asking for a king."

20] But Samuel said to the people, "Have no fear. You have, indeed, done all those wicked things. Do not, however, turn away from the LORD your God, but serve the LORD with all your heart.

21] Do not turn away to follow worthless things, which can neither profit nor save but are worthless.

22] For the sake of His great name, the LORD will never abandon His people, seeing that the LORD undertook to make you His people. . . ."

[14 אִם־תִּירְא֣וּ אֶת־יְהֹוָ֗ה וַעֲבַדְתֶּ֤ם אֹתוֹ֙ וּשְׁמַעְתֶּ֣ם בְּקֹל֔וֹ וְלֹ֥א תַמְר֖וּ אֶת־פִּ֣י יְהֹוָ֑ה וִהְיִתֶ֣ם גַּם־אַתֶּ֗ם וְגַם־הַמֶּ֙לֶךְ֙ אֲשֶׁ֣ר מָלַ֣ךְ עֲלֵיכֶ֔ם אַחַ֖ר יְהֹוָ֥ה אֱלֹהֵיכֶֽם: 15 וְאִם־לֹ֤א תִשְׁמְעוּ֙ בְּק֣וֹל יְהֹוָ֔ה וּמְרִיתֶ֖ם אֶת־פִּ֣י יְהֹוָ֑ה וְהָיְתָ֧ה יַד־יְהֹוָ֛ה בָּכֶ֖ם וּבַאֲבֹתֵיכֶֽם:

16 גַּם־עַתָּ֣ה הִֽתְיַצְּב֗וּ וּרְא֛וּ אֶת־הַדָּבָ֥ר הַגָּד֖וֹל הַזֶּ֑ה אֲשֶׁ֣ר יְהֹוָ֔ה עֹשֶׂ֖ה לְעֵינֵיכֶֽם: 17 הֲל֤וֹא קְצִיר־חִטִּים֙ הַיּ֔וֹם אֶקְרָא֙ אֶל־יְהֹוָ֔ה וְיִתֵּ֥ן קֹל֖וֹת וּמָטָ֑ר וּדְע֣וּ וּרְא֗וּ כִּֽי־רָעַתְכֶ֤ם רַבָּה֙ אֲשֶׁ֤ר עֲשִׂיתֶם֙ בְּעֵינֵ֣י יְהֹוָ֔ה לִשְׁא֥וֹל לָכֶ֖ם מֶֽלֶךְ:

18 וַיִּקְרָ֤א שְׁמוּאֵל֙ אֶל־יְהֹוָ֔ה וַיִּתֵּ֧ן יְהֹוָ֛ה קֹלֹ֥ת וּמָטָ֖ר בַּיּ֣וֹם הַה֑וּא וַיִּירָ֨א כָל־הָעָ֥ם מְאֹ֛ד אֶת־יְהֹוָ֖ה וְאֶת־שְׁמוּאֵֽל: 19 וַיֹּאמְר֣וּ כָל־הָעָ֣ם אֶל־שְׁמוּאֵ֗ל הִתְפַּלֵּ֧ל בְּעַד־עֲבָדֶ֛יךָ אֶל־יְהֹוָ֥ה אֱלֹהֶ֖יךָ וְאַל־נָמ֑וּת כִּֽי־יָסַ֤פְנוּ עַל־כָּל־חַטֹּאתֵ֙ינוּ֙ רָעָ֔ה לִשְׁאֹ֥ל לָ֖נוּ מֶֽלֶךְ: 20 וַיֹּ֧אמֶר שְׁמוּאֵ֣ל אֶל־הָעָם֮ אַל־תִּירָאוּ֒ אַתֶּ֣ם עֲשִׂיתֶ֔ם אֵ֥ת כָּל־הָרָעָ֖ה הַזֹּ֑את אַ֗ךְ אַל־תָּס֙וּרוּ֙ מֵאַחֲרֵ֣י יְהֹוָ֔ה וַעֲבַדְתֶּ֥ם אֶת־יְהֹוָ֖ה בְּכָל־לְבַבְכֶֽם: 21 וְלֹ֖א תָּס֑וּרוּ כִּ֣י ׀ אַחֲרֵ֣י הַתֹּ֗הוּ אֲשֶׁ֧ר לֹֽא־יוֹעִ֛ילוּ וְלֹ֥א יַצִּ֖ילוּ כִּי־תֹ֥הוּ הֵֽמָּה: 22 כִּ֠י לֹֽא־יִטֹּ֤שׁ יְהֹוָה֙ אֶת־עַמּ֔וֹ בַּעֲב֖וּר שְׁמ֣וֹ הַגָּד֑וֹל כִּ֣י הוֹאִ֣יל יְהֹוָ֔ה לַעֲשׂ֥וֹת אֶתְכֶ֛ם ל֖וֹ לְעָֽם:

---

d-d Meaning of Heb. uncertain

g When thunderstorms do not occur in the Land of Israel

After Joshua's initial conquest of Canaan a number of leaders ("Judges") guided the troubled and often disunited tribes during the twelfth and eleventh centuries B.C.E. Their military and personal adventures are recounted in the 21 chapters which portray the protracted difficulties Israel encountered in its attempt to make the Promised Land its own.

The sidrah recounts Israel's campaign against Arad and the vow the people made when the campaign began. The haftarah records how Jephthah, one of the judges, made a vow which he believed obligated him to sacrifice his daughter. The text reports the terrible dilemma but does not definitively state that she was indeed sacrificed.

חקת

Judges
11 : 1-33

Chapter 11

1] Jephthah the Gileadite was an able warrior, who was the son of a prostitute. Jephthah's father was Gilead;

2] but Gilead also had sons by his wife, and when the wife's sons grew up, they drove Jephthah out. They said to him, "You shall have no share in our father's property, for you are the son of an outsider."[a]

3] So Jephthah fled from his brothers and settled in the Tob country. Men of low character gathered about Jephthah and went out raiding with him.

4] Some time later, the Ammonites went to war against Israel.

5] And when the Ammonites attacked Israel, the elders of Gilead went to bring Jephthah back from the Tob country.

6] They said to Jephthah, "Come be our chief, so that we can fight the Ammonites."

7] Jephthah replied to the elders of Gilead, "You are the very people who rejected me and drove me out of my father's house. How can you come to me now when you are in trouble?"

8] The elders of Gilead said to Jephthah, "Honestly, we have now turned back to you. If you come with us and fight the Ammonites, you shall be our commander over all the inhabitants of Gilead."

9] Jephthah said to the elders of Gilead, "[Very well,] if you bring

---

[a] Lit. *"another woman"*

יא

1] וְיִפְתָּח הַגִּלְעָדִי הָיָה גִּבּוֹר חַיִל וְהוּא בֶּן אִשָּׁה זוֹנָה וַיּוֹלֶד גִּלְעָד אֶת־יִפְתָּח: 2] וַתֵּלֶד אֵשֶׁת־גִּלְעָד לוֹ בָּנִים וַיִּגְדְּלוּ בְנֵי־הָאִשָּׁה וַיְגָרְשׁוּ אֶת־יִפְתָּח וַיֹּאמְרוּ לוֹ לֹא־תִנְחַל בְּבֵית־אָבִינוּ כִּי בֶן־אִשָּׁה אַחֶרֶת אָתָּה: 3] וַיִּבְרַח יִפְתָּח מִפְּנֵי אֶחָיו וַיֵּשֶׁב בְּאֶרֶץ טוֹב וַיִּתְלַקְּטוּ אֶל־יִפְתָּח אֲנָשִׁים רֵיקִים וַיֵּצְאוּ עִמּוֹ:

4] וַיְהִי מִיָּמִים וַיִּלָּחֲמוּ בְנֵי־עַמּוֹן עִם־יִשְׂרָאֵל: 5] וַיְהִי כַּאֲשֶׁר־נִלְחֲמוּ בְנֵי־עַמּוֹן עִם־יִשְׂרָאֵל וַיֵּלְכוּ זִקְנֵי גִלְעָד לָקַחַת אֶת־יִפְתָּח מֵאֶרֶץ טוֹב: 6] וַיֹּאמְרוּ לְיִפְתָּח לְכָה וְהָיִיתָה לָּנוּ לְקָצִין וְנִלָּחֲמָה בִּבְנֵי עַמּוֹן: 7] וַיֹּאמֶר יִפְתָּח לְזִקְנֵי גִלְעָד הֲלֹא אַתֶּם שְׂנֵאתֶם אוֹתִי וַתְּגָרְשׁוּנִי מִבֵּית אָבִי וּמַדּוּעַ בָּאתֶם אֵלַי עַתָּה כַּאֲשֶׁר צַר לָכֶם: 8] וַיֹּאמְרוּ זִקְנֵי גִלְעָד אֶל־יִפְתָּח לָכֵן עַתָּה שַׁבְנוּ אֵלֶיךָ וְהָלַכְתָּ עִמָּנוּ וְנִלְחַמְתָּ בִּבְנֵי עַמּוֹן וְהָיִיתָ לָּנוּ לְרֹאשׁ לְכֹל יֹשְׁבֵי גִלְעָד: 9] וַיֹּאמֶר יִפְתָּח אֶל־זִקְנֵי גִלְעָד אִם

me back to fight the Ammonites and the LORD delivers them to me, I am to be your commander."

10] And the elders of Gilead answered Jephthah, "The LORD Himself shall be witness between us: we will do just as you have said."

11] Jephthah went with the elders of Gilead, and the people made him their commander and chief. And Jephthah repeated all these terms before the LORD at Mizpah.

12] Jephthah then sent messengers to the king of the Ammonites, saying, "What have you against me that you have come to make war on my country?"

13] The king of the Ammonites replied to Jephthah's messengers, "When Israel came from Egypt, they seized the land which is mine, from the Arnon to the Jabbok as far as the Jordan. Now, then, restore it peaceably."

14] Jephthah again sent messengers to the king of the Ammonites.

15] He said to him, "Thus said Jephthah: Israel did not seize the land of Moab or the land of the Ammonites. 16] When they left Egypt, Israel traveled through the wilderness to the Sea of Reeds and went on to Kadesh.

17] Israel then sent messengers to the king of Edom, saying, 'Allow us to cross your country.' But the king of Edom would not consent. They also sent a mission to the king of Moab, and he refused. So Israel, after staying at Kadesh,

18] traveled on through the wilderness, skirting the land of Edom and the land of Moab. They kept to the east of the land of Moab until they encamped on the other side of the Arnon; and, since Moab ends at the Arnon, they never entered Moabite territory.

מְשִׁיבִים אַתֶּם אוֹתִי לְהִלָּחֵם בִּבְנֵי עַמּוֹן וְנָתַן יְהוָה אוֹתָם לְפָנָי אָנֹכִי אֶהְיֶה לָכֶם לְרֹאשׁ:

10] וַיֹּאמְרוּ זִקְנֵי־גִלְעָד אֶל־יִפְתָּח יְהוָה יִהְיֶה שֹׁמֵעַ בֵּינוֹתֵינוּ אִם־לֹא כִדְבָרְךָ כֵּן נַעֲשֶׂה:

11] וַיֵּלֶךְ יִפְתָּח עִם־זִקְנֵי גִלְעָד וַיָּשִׂימוּ הָעָם אוֹתוֹ עֲלֵיהֶם לְרֹאשׁ וּלְקָצִין וַיְדַבֵּר יִפְתָּח אֶת־כָּל־דְּבָרָיו לִפְנֵי יְהוָה בַּמִּצְפָּה:

12] וַיִּשְׁלַח יִפְתָּח מַלְאָכִים אֶל־מֶלֶךְ בְּנֵי עַמּוֹן לֵאמֹר מַה־לִּי וָלָךְ כִּי־בָאתָ אֵלַי לְהִלָּחֵם בְּאַרְצִי: 13] וַיֹּאמֶר מֶלֶךְ בְּנֵי־עַמּוֹן אֶל מַלְאֲכֵי יִפְתָּח כִּי־לָקַח יִשְׂרָאֵל אֶת־אַרְצִי בַּעֲלוֹתוֹ מִמִּצְרַיִם מֵאַרְנוֹן וְעַד הַיַּבֹּק וְעַד הַיַּרְדֵּן וְעַתָּה הָשִׁיבָה אֶתְהֶן בְּשָׁלוֹם:

14] וַיּוֹסֶף עוֹד יִפְתָּח וַיִּשְׁלַח מַלְאָכִים אֶל־מֶלֶךְ בְּנֵי עַמּוֹן: 15] וַיֹּאמֶר לוֹ כֹּה אָמַר יִפְתָּח לֹא־לָקַח יִשְׂרָאֵל אֶת־אֶרֶץ מוֹאָב וְאֶת־אֶרֶץ בְּנֵי עַמּוֹן: 16] כִּי בַּעֲלוֹתָם מִמִּצְרָיִם וַיֵּלֶךְ יִשְׂרָאֵל בַּמִּדְבָּר עַד־יַם־סוּף וַיָּבֹא קָדֵשָׁה: 17] וַיִּשְׁלַח יִשְׂרָאֵל מַלְאָכִים אֶל־מֶלֶךְ אֱדוֹם לֵאמֹר אֶעְבְּרָה־נָּא בְאַרְצֶךָ וְלֹא שָׁמַע מֶלֶךְ אֱדוֹם וְגַם אֶל־מֶלֶךְ מוֹאָב שָׁלַח וְלֹא אָבָה וַיֵּשֶׁב יִשְׂרָאֵל בְּקָדֵשׁ: 18] וַיֵּלֶךְ בַּמִּדְבָּר וַיָּסָב אֶת־אֶרֶץ אֱדוֹם וְאֶת־אֶרֶץ מוֹאָב וַיָּבֹא מִמִּזְרַח־שֶׁמֶשׁ לְאֶרֶץ מוֹאָב וַיַּחֲנוּן בְּעֵבֶר אַרְנוֹן וְלֹא־בָאוּ בִּגְבוּל מוֹאָב כִּי אַרְנוֹן גְּבוּל מוֹאָב:

1269

19] "Then Israel sent messengers to King Sihon of the Amorites, the king of Heshbon. Israel said to him, 'Allow us to cross through your country to our homeland.'

20] But Sihon would not trust Israel to pass through his territory. Sihon mustered all his troops, and they encamped at Jahaz; he engaged Israel in battle.

21] But the LORD, the God of Israel, delivered Sihon and all his troops into Israel's hands, and they defeated them; and Israel took possession of all the land of the Amorites, the inhabitants of that land. 22] Thus they occupied all the territory of the Amorites from the Arnon to the Jabbok and from the wilderness to the Jordan.

23] "Now, then, the LORD, the God of Israel, dispossessed the Amorites before His people Israel; and should you possess their land? 24] Do you not hold what Chemosh your god gives you to possess? So we will hold on to everything that the LORD our God has given us to possess.

25] "Besides, are you any better than Balak son of Zippor, king of Moab? Did he start a quarrel with Israel or go to war with them?

26] "While Israel has been occupying Heshbon and its dependencies, and Aroer and its dependencies, and all the towns along the Arnon for three hundred years, why have you not tried to recover them all this time?

27] I have done you no wrong; yet you are doing me harm and making war on me. May the LORD, who judges, decide today between the Israelites and the Ammonites!"

28] But the king of the Ammonites paid no heed to the message that Jephthah sent him.

19] וַיִּשְׁלַ֥ח יִשְׂרָאֵ֖ל מַלְאָכִ֑ים אֶל־סִיחֹ֣ון מֶֽלֶךְ־הָאֱמֹרִ֖י מֶ֣לֶךְ חֶשְׁבֹּ֑ון וַיֹּ֤אמֶר לֹו֙ יִשְׂרָאֵ֔ל נַעְבְּרָה־נָּ֥א בְאַרְצְךָ֖ עַד־מְקֹומִֽי׃ 20] וְלֹא־הֶאֱמִ֨ין סִיחֹ֤ון אֶת־יִשְׂרָאֵל֙ עֲבֹ֣ר בִּגְבֻלֹ֔ו וַיֶּאֱסֹ֤ף סִיחֹון֙ אֶת־כָּל־עַמֹּ֔ו וַֽיַּחֲנ֖וּ בְּיָ֑הְצָה וַיִּלָּ֖חֶם עִם־יִשְׂרָאֵֽל׃ 21] וַ֠יִּתֵּן יְהוָ֨ה אֱלֹהֵֽי־יִשְׂרָאֵ֜ל אֶת־סִיחֹ֤ון וְאֶת־כָּל־עַמֹּו֙ בְּיַ֣ד יִשְׂרָאֵ֔ל וַיַּכּ֑וּם וַיִּירַשׁ֙ יִשְׂרָאֵ֔ל אֵ֚ת כָּל־אֶ֣רֶץ הָאֱמֹרִ֔י יֹושֵׁ֖ב הָאָ֥רֶץ הַהִֽיא׃ 22] וַיִּ֣ירְשׁ֔וּ אֵ֖ת כָּל־גְּב֣וּל הָאֱמֹרִ֑י מֵֽאַרְנֹון֙ וְעַד־הַיַּבֹּ֔ק וּמִן־הַמִּדְבָּ֖ר וְעַד־הַיַּרְדֵּֽן׃

23] וְעַתָּ֞ה יְהוָ֣ה ׀ אֱלֹהֵ֣י יִשְׂרָאֵ֗ל הֹורִישׁ֙ אֶת־הָ֣אֱמֹרִ֔י מִפְּנֵ֖י עַמֹּ֣ו יִשְׂרָאֵ֑ל וְאַתָּ֖ה תִּירָשֶֽׁנּוּ׃ 24] הֲלֹ֞א אֵ֣ת אֲשֶׁ֧ר יֹורִֽישְׁךָ֛ כְּמֹ֥ושׁ אֱלֹהֶ֖יךָ אֹותֹ֣ו תִירָ֑שׁ וְאֵת֩ כָּל־אֲשֶׁ֨ר הֹורִ֜ישׁ יְהוָ֧ה אֱלֹהֵ֛ינוּ מִפָּנֵ֖ינוּ אֹותֹ֥ו נִירָֽשׁ׃

25] וְעַתָּ֗ה הֲטֹ֥וב טֹוב֙ אַתָּ֔ה מִבָּלָ֥ק בֶּן־צִפֹּ֖ור מֶ֣לֶךְ מֹואָ֑ב הֲרֹ֥וב רָב֙ עִם־יִשְׂרָאֵ֔ל אִם־נִלְחֹ֥ם נִלְחַ֖ם בָּֽם׃

26] בְּשֶׁ֣בֶת יִ֠שְׂרָאֵל בְּחֶשְׁבֹּ֨ון וּבִבְנֹותֶ֜יהָ וּבְעַרְעֹ֣ור וּבִבְנֹותֶ֗יהָ וּבְכָל־הֶֽעָרִים֙ אֲשֶׁר֙ עַל־יְדֵ֣י אַרְנֹ֔ון שְׁלֹ֥שׁ מֵאֹ֖ות שָׁנָ֑ה וּמַדּ֥וּעַ לֹֽא־הִצַּלְתֶּ֖ם בָּעֵ֥ת הַהִֽיא׃ 27] וְאָֽנֹכִי֙ לֹֽא־חָטָ֣אתִי לָ֔ךְ וְאַתָּ֞ה עֹשֶׂ֥ה אִתִּ֛י רָעָ֖ה לְהִלָּ֣חֶם בִּ֑י יִשְׁפֹּ֨ט יְהוָ֤ה הַשֹּׁפֵט֙ הַיֹּ֔ום בֵּ֚ין בְּנֵ֣י יִשְׂרָאֵ֔ל וּבֵ֖ין בְּנֵ֥י עַמֹּֽון׃

28] וְלֹ֣א שָׁמַ֔ע מֶ֖לֶךְ בְּנֵ֣י עַמֹּ֑ון אֶל־דִּבְרֵ֣י יִפְתָּ֔ח אֲשֶׁ֥ר שָׁלַ֖ח אֵלָֽיו׃

29] Then the spirit of the Lord came upon Jephthah. He marched through Gilead and Manasseh, passing Mizpeh of Gilead; and from Mizpeh of Gilead he crossed over [to] the Ammonites. 30] And Jephthah made the following vow to the Lord: "If you deliver the Ammonites into my hands,

31] then whatever comes out of the door of my house to meet me on my safe return from the Ammonites shall be the Lord's and shall be offered by me as a burnt offering."

32] Jephthah crossed over to the Ammonites and attacked them, and the Lord delivered them into his hands. 33] He utterly routed them—from Aroer as far as Minnith, twenty towns—all the way to Abel-cheramin. So the Ammonites submitted to the Israelites.

29] וַתְּהִי עַל־יִפְתָּח רוּחַ יְהֹוָה וַיַּעֲבֹר אֶת־הַגִּלְעָד וְאֶת־מְנַשֶּׁה וַיַּעֲבֹר אֶת־מִצְפֵּה גִלְעָד וּמִמִּצְפֵּה גִלְעָד עָבַר בְּנֵי עַמּוֹן: 30] וַיִּדַּר יִפְתָּח נֶדֶר לַיהֹוָה וַיֹּאמַר אִם־נָתוֹן תִּתֵּן אֶת־בְּנֵי עַמּוֹן בְּיָדִי: 31] וְהָיָה הַיּוֹצֵא אֲשֶׁר יֵצֵא מִדַּלְתֵי בֵיתִי לִקְרָאתִי בְּשׁוּבִי בְשָׁלוֹם מִבְּנֵי עַמּוֹן וְהָיָה לַיהֹוָה וְהַעֲלִיתִיהוּ עוֹלָה:

32] וַיַּעֲבֹר יִפְתָּח אֶל־בְּנֵי עַמּוֹן לְהִלָּחֶם בָּם וַיִּתְּנֵם יְהֹוָה בְּיָדוֹ: 33] וַיַּכֵּם מֵעֲרוֹעֵר וְעַד־בּוֹאֲךָ מִנִּית עֶשְׂרִים עִיר וְעַד אָבֵל כְּרָמִים מַכָּה גְדוֹלָה מְאֹד וַיִּכָּנְעוּ בְּנֵי עַמּוֹן מִפְּנֵי בְּנֵי יִשְׂרָאֵל:

Micah was a contemporary of Isaiah (late eighth century
B.C.E.). He witnessed the destruction of the Northern
Kingdom and predicted a like fate for Judah and Jerusalem
unless the people and their leaders would amend their
sinful ways.

Micah reminds his people of God's beneficences, including
His guidance of Balaam who had come to curse Israel
(this passage connects the haftarah with the sidrah).
What is required is not so much the bringing of sacrifices;
rather, a turning of the heart: "Only to do justice, to love
goodness, and to walk modestly with your God."

HAFTARAH Balak

בלק

Micah

5 : 6 – 6 : 8

Chapter 5

ה

6] The remnant of Jacob shall be,
In the midst of the many peoples,
Like dew from the LORD,
Like droplets on grass—
Which do not look to any man
Nor place their hope in mortals.

6] וְהָיָה שְׁאֵרִית יַעֲקֹב
בְּקֶרֶב עַמִּים רַבִּים
כְּטַל מֵאֵת יְהֹוָה
כִּרְבִיבִים עֲלֵי־עֵשֶׂב
אֲשֶׁר לֹא־יְקַוֶּה לְאִישׁ
וְלֹא יְיַחֵל לִבְנֵי אָדָם:

7] The remnant of Jacob
Shall be among the nations,
In the midst of the many peoples,
Like a lion among beasts of the wild,
Like a fierce lion among flocks of sheep,
Which tramples wherever it goes
And rends, with none to deliver.

7] וְהָיָה שְׁאֵרִית יַעֲקֹב בַּגּוֹיִם
בְּקֶרֶב עַמִּים רַבִּים
כְּאַרְיֵה בְּבַהֲמוֹת יַעַר
כִּכְפִיר בְּעֶדְרֵי־צֹאן
אֲשֶׁר אִם־עָבַר וְרָמַס
וְטָרַף וְאֵין מַצִּיל:

8] Your hand shall prevail over your foes,
And all your enemies shall be cut down!

8] תָּרֹם יָדְךָ עַל־צָרֶיךָ
וְכָל־אֹיְבֶיךָ יִכָּרֵתוּ:

9] In that day
              —declares the LORD—
I will destroy the horses in your midst
And wreck your chariots.

9] וְהָיָה בַיּוֹם־הַהוּא
נְאֻם־יְהֹוָה
וְהִכְרַתִּי סוּסֶיךָ מִקִּרְבֶּךָ
וְהַאֲבַדְתִּי מַרְכְּבֹתֶיךָ:

10] I will destroy the cities of your land
And demolish all your fortresses.

10] וְהִכְרַתִּי עָרֵי אַרְצֶךָ
וְהָרַסְתִּי כָּל־מִבְצָרֶיךָ:

11] I will destroy the sorcery you practice,
And you shall have no more soothsayers.

12] I will destroy your idols
And the sacred pillars in your midst;
And no more shall you bow down
To the work of your hands.

13] I will tear down the sacred posts in your midst
And destroy your cities.[g]

14] In anger and wrath
Will I wreak retribution
On the nations[h] that have not obeyed.

Chapter 6

1] Hear what the LORD is saying:
Come, present [My] case before the mountains,
And let the hills hear you pleading.

2] Hear, you mountains, the case of the LORD—
[a]You firm[a] foundations of the earth!
For the LORD has a case against His people,
He has a suit against Israel.

3] "My people!
What wrong have I done you?
What hardship have I caused you?
Testify against Me.
4] In fact,
I brought you up from the land of Egypt,
I redeemed you from the house of bondage,
And I sent before you
Moses, Aaron, and Miriam.

11 וְהִכְרַתִּי כְשָׁפִים מִיָּדֶךָ
וּמְעוֹנְנִים לֹא יִהְיוּ־לָךְ:

12 וְהִכְרַתִּי פְסִילֶיךָ
וּמַצֵּבוֹתֶיךָ מִקִּרְבֶּךָ
וְלֹא־תִשְׁתַּחֲוֶה עוֹד
לְמַעֲשֵׂה יָדֶיךָ:

13 וְנָתַשְׁתִּי אֲשֵׁירֶיךָ מִקִּרְבֶּךָ
וְהִשְׁמַדְתִּי עָרֶיךָ:

14 וְעָשִׂיתִי בְּאַף וּבְחֵמָה נָקָם
אֶת־הַגּוֹיִם אֲשֶׁר לֹא שָׁמֵעוּ:

ו

1 שִׁמְעוּ־נָא אֵת אֲשֶׁר־יְהֹוָה אֹמֵר
קוּם רִיב אֶת־הֶהָרִים
וְתִשְׁמַעְנָה הַגְּבָעוֹת קוֹלֶךָ:

2 שִׁמְעוּ הָרִים אֶת־רִיב יְהֹוָה
וְהָאֵתָנִים מֹסְדֵי אָרֶץ
כִּי רִיב לַיהֹוָה עִם־עַמּוֹ
וְעִם־יִשְׂרָאֵל יִתְוַכָּח:

3 עַמִּי מֶה־עָשִׂיתִי לָךְ
וּמָה הֶלְאֵתִיךָ עֲנֵה בִי:

4 כִּי הֶעֱלִתִיךָ מֵאֶרֶץ מִצְרַיִם
וּמִבֵּית עֲבָדִים פְּדִיתִיךָ
וָאֶשְׁלַח לְפָנֶיךָ
אֶת־מֹשֶׁה אַהֲרֹן וּמִרְיָם:

---

[g] *Emendation yields "idols"*
[h] *Emendation yields "arrogant"*

[a-a] *Emendation yields "Give ear, you"*

5] "My people,
Remember what Balak king of Moab
Plotted against you,
And how Balaam son of Beor
Responded to him.
[Recall your passage]
From Shittim to Gilgal[b]—
And you will recognize
The gracious acts of the LORD."

6] With what shall I approach the LORD,
Do homage to God on high?
Shall I approach Him with burnt offerings,
With calves a year old?

7] Would the LORD be pleased with thousands of
     rams,
With myriads of streams of oil?
Shall I give my firstborn for my transgression,
The fruit of my body for my sins?

8] "He has told you, O man, what is good,
And what the LORD requires of you:
Only to do justice
And to love goodness,
And [c]to walk modestly with your God;[c]

עַמִּי זְכָר־נָא 5]
מַה־יָּעַץ בָּלָק מֶלֶךְ מוֹאָב
וּמֶה־עָנָה אֹתוֹ
בִּלְעָם בֶּן־בְּעוֹר
מִן־הַשִּׁטִּים עַד־הַגִּלְגָּל
לְמַעַן דַּעַת צִדְקוֹת יְהֹוָה:

בַּמָּה אֲקַדֵּם יְהֹוָה 6]
אִכַּף לֵאלֹהֵי מָרוֹם
הַאֲקַדְּמֶנּוּ בְעוֹלוֹת
בַּעֲגָלִים בְּנֵי שָׁנָה:

הֲיִרְצֶה יְהֹוָה בְּאַלְפֵי אֵילִים 7]
בְּרִבְבוֹת נַחֲלֵי־שָׁמֶן
הַאֶתֵּן בְּכוֹרִי פִּשְׁעִי
פְּרִי בִטְנִי חַטַּאת נַפְשִׁי:

הִגִּיד לְךָ אָדָם מַה־טּוֹב 8]
וּמָה־יְהֹוָה דּוֹרֵשׁ מִמְּךָ
כִּי אִם־עֲשׂוֹת מִשְׁפָּט
וְאַהֲבַת חֶסֶד
וְהַצְנֵעַ לֶכֶת עִם־אֱלֹהֶיךָ:

---

[b] I.e., the crossing of the Jordan; see Josh. 3.1, 14–4.19
[c-c] Or "It is prudent to serve your God"

The Book of Kings is divided into two parts. It spans four centuries and reaches from the last days of David to the destruction of the Temple by the Babylonians in 586 (or 585) B.C.E. It approaches history from a theological point of view: the story of Israel and Judah must be seen as a judgment of God on the people and its rulers.

The sidrah speaks of the zeal of Pinchas (Phinehas) who defended public morality and was rewarded with the crown of priesthood for his descendants. The haftarah recounts the devotion of Elijah the prophet (ninth century B.C.E.) who was rewarded with the everlasting affection of Israel's generations.

פנחס

First Kings

18 : 46 – 19 : 21

Chapter 18

46] The hand of the LORD had come upon Elijah. *ⁱHe tied up his skirts⁻ⁱ* and ran in front of Ahab all the way to Jezreel.

יח

46] וְיַד־יְהֹוָה הָיְתָה אֶל־אֵלִיָּהוּ וַיְשַׁנֵּס מָתְנָיו וַיָּרָץ לִפְנֵי אַחְאָב עַד־בֹּאֲכָה יִזְרְעֶאלָה:

Chapter 19

1] When Ahab told Jezebel all that Elijah had done and how he had put all the prophetsᵃ to the sword,

2] Jezebel sent a messenger to Elijah, saying, *ᵇ"Thus and more may the gods do⁻ᵇ* if by this time tomorrow I have not made you like one of them."

3] Frightened,ᶜ he fled at once for his life. He came to Beersheba, which is in Judah, and left his servant there;

4] he himself went a day's journey into the wilderness. He came to a broom bush and sat down under it, and prayed that he might die. "Enough!" he cried. "Now, O Lord, take my life, for I am no better than my fathers."

יט

1] וַיַּגֵּד אַחְאָב לְאִיזֶבֶל אֵת כָּל־אֲשֶׁר עָשָׂה אֵלִיָּהוּ וְאֵת כָּל־אֲשֶׁר הָרַג אֶת־כָּל־הַנְּבִיאִים בֶּחָרֶב: 2] וַתִּשְׁלַח אִיזֶבֶל מַלְאָךְ אֶל־אֵלִיָּהוּ לֵאמֹר כֹּה־יַעֲשׂוּן אֱלֹהִים וְכֹה יוֹסִפוּן כִּי־כָעֵת מָחָר אָשִׂים אֶת־נַפְשְׁךָ כְּנֶפֶשׁ אַחַד מֵהֶם:

3] וַיַּרְא וַיָּקָם וַיֵּלֶךְ אֶל־נַפְשׁוֹ וַיָּבֹא בְּאֵר שֶׁבַע אֲשֶׁר לִיהוּדָה וַיַּנַּח אֶת־נַעֲרוֹ שָׁם: 4] וְהוּא־הָלַךְ בַּמִּדְבָּר דֶּרֶךְ יוֹם וַיָּבֹא וַיֵּשֶׁב תַּחַת רֹתֶם אֶחָד וַיִּשְׁאַל אֶת־נַפְשׁוֹ לָמוּת וַיֹּאמֶר רַב עַתָּה יְהֹוָה קַח נַפְשִׁי כִּי־לֹא־טוֹב אָנֹכִי מֵאֲבֹתָי:

ⁱ⁻ⁱ *Lit. "He bound up his loins"*   ᵃ *Of Baal; see 18.40*
ᵇ⁻ᵇ *A formula of imprecation. Many Heb. mss. and Septuagint add "to me"*
ᶜ *So many Heb. mss. and Septuagint; most mss. and the editions read "And he saw and"*

5] He lay down and fell asleep under a broom bush. Suddenly an angel touched him and said to him, "Arise and eat."

6] He looked about; and there, beside his head, was a cake baked on hot stones and a jar of water! He ate and drank, and lay down again.

7] The angel of the LORD came a second time and touched him and said, "Arise and eat, or the journey will be too much for you." 8] He arose and ate and drank; and with the strength from that meal he walked forty days and forty nights as far as the mountain of God at Horeb.

9] There he went into a cave, and there he spent the night.

Then the word of the LORD came to him. He said to him, "Why are you here, Elijah?" 10] He replied, "I am moved by zeal for the LORD, the God of Hosts, for the Israelites have forsaken Your covenant, torn down Your altars, and put Your prophets to the sword. I alone am left, and they are out to take my life."

11] "Come out," He called, "and stand on the mountain before the LORD."

And lo, the LORD passed by. There was a great and mighty wind, splitting mountains and shattering rocks by the power of the LORD; but the LORD was not in the wind. After the wind—an earthquake; but the LORD was not in the earthquake. 12] After the earthquake—fire; but the LORD was not in the fire. And after the fire—a soft murmuring sound.[d]

13] When Elijah heard it, he wrapped his mantle about his face and went out and stood at the entrance of the cave. Then a voice addressed him: "Why are you here, Elijah?" 14] He answered, "I am moved by zeal for the LORD, the God of Hosts; for the Israelites have forsaken Your covenant, torn down Your altars, and have put Your prophets to the sword. I alone am left, and they are out to take my life."

5] וַיִּשְׁכַּב וַיִּישַׁן תַּחַת רֹתֶם אֶחָד וְהִנֵּה־זֶה מַלְאָךְ נֹגֵעַ בּוֹ וַיֹּאמֶר לוֹ קוּם אֱכוֹל: 6] וַיַּבֵּט וְהִנֵּה מְרַאֲשֹׁתָיו עֻגַת רְצָפִים וְצַפַּחַת מָיִם וַיֹּאכַל וַיֵּשְׁתְּ וַיָּשָׁב וַיִּשְׁכָּב: 7] וַיָּשָׁב מַלְאַךְ יְהֹוָה שֵׁנִית וַיִּגַּע־בּוֹ וַיֹּאמֶר קוּם אֱכֹל כִּי רַב מִמְּךָ הַדָּרֶךְ: 8] וַיָּקָם וַיֹּאכַל וַיִּשְׁתֶּה וַיֵּלֶךְ בְּכֹחַ הָאֲכִילָה הַהִיא אַרְבָּעִים יוֹם וְאַרְבָּעִים לַיְלָה עַד הַר הָאֱלֹהִים חֹרֵב:

9] וַיָּבֹא שָׁם אֶל־הַמְּעָרָה וַיָּלֶן שָׁם וְהִנֵּה דְבַר־יְהֹוָה אֵלָיו וַיֹּאמֶר לוֹ מַה־לְּךָ פֹה אֵלִיָּהוּ: 10] וַיֹּאמֶר קַנֹּא קִנֵּאתִי לַיהֹוָה אֱלֹהֵי צְבָאוֹת כִּי־עָזְבוּ בְרִיתְךָ בְּנֵי יִשְׂרָאֵל אֶת־מִזְבְּחֹתֶיךָ הָרָסוּ וְאֶת־נְבִיאֶיךָ הָרְגוּ בֶחָרֶב וָאִוָּתֵר אֲנִי לְבַדִּי וַיְבַקְשׁוּ אֶת־נַפְשִׁי לְקַחְתָּהּ: 11] וַיֹּאמֶר צֵא וְעָמַדְתָּ בָהָר לִפְנֵי יְהֹוָה וְהִנֵּה יְהֹוָה עֹבֵר וְרוּחַ גְּדוֹלָה וְחָזָק מְפָרֵק הָרִים וּמְשַׁבֵּר סְלָעִים לִפְנֵי יְהֹוָה לֹא בָרוּחַ יְהֹוָה וְאַחַר הָרוּחַ רַעַשׁ לֹא בָרַעַשׁ יְהֹוָה: 12] וְאַחַר הָרַעַשׁ אֵשׁ לֹא בָאֵשׁ יְהֹוָה וְאַחַר הָאֵשׁ קוֹל דְּמָמָה דַקָּה: 13] וַיְהִי כִּשְׁמֹעַ אֵלִיָּהוּ וַיָּלֶט פָּנָיו בְּאַדַּרְתּוֹ וַיֵּצֵא וַיַּעֲמֹד פֶּתַח הַמְּעָרָה וְהִנֵּה אֵלָיו קוֹל וַיֹּאמֶר מַה־לְּךָ פֹה אֵלִיָּהוּ: 14] וַיֹּאמֶר קַנֹּא קִנֵּאתִי לַיהֹוָה אֱלֹהֵי צְבָאוֹת כִּי־עָזְבוּ בְרִיתְךָ בְּנֵי יִשְׂרָאֵל אֶת־מִזְבְּחֹתֶיךָ הָרָסוּ וְאֶת־נְבִיאֶיךָ הָרְגוּ בֶחָרֶב וָאִוָּתֵר אֲנִי לְבַדִּי וַיְבַקְשׁוּ אֶת־נַפְשִׁי לְקַחְתָּהּ:

[d] Others "a still, small voice"

15] The Lord said to him, "Go back by the way you came, [and] on to the wilderness of Damascus. When you get there, anoint Hazael as king of Aram.

16] Also anoint Jehu son of Nimshi as king of Israel, and anoint Elisha son of Shaphat of Abel-meholah to succeed you as prophet.

17] Whoever escapes the sword of Hazael shall be slain by Jehu, and whoever escapes the sword of Jehu shall be slain by Elisha. 18] I will leave in Israel only seven thousand—every knee that has not knelt to Baal and every mouth that has not kissed him."

19] He set out from there and came upon Elisha son of Shaphat as he was plowing. There were twelve yoke of oxen ahead of him, and he was with the twelfth. Elijah came over to him and threw his mantle over him.

20] He left the oxen and ran after Elijah, saying: "Let me kiss my father and mother good-bye, and I will follow you." And he answered him, "Go back. What have I done to you?"[e]

21] He turned back from him and took the yoke of oxen and slaughtered them; he boiled [f]their meat[f] with the gear[g] of the oxen and gave it to the people, and they ate. Then he arose and followed Elijah and became his attendant.

וַיֹּאמֶר יְהוָה אֵלָיו לֵךְ שׁוּב לְדַרְכְּךָ 15
מִדְבַּרָה דַמָּשֶׂק וּבָאתָ וּמָשַׁחְתָּ אֶת־חֲזָאֵל לְמֶלֶךְ
עַל־אֲרָם: 16 וְאֵת יֵהוּא בֶן־נִמְשִׁי תִּמְשַׁח
לְמֶלֶךְ עַל־יִשְׂרָאֵל וְאֶת־אֱלִישָׁע בֶּן־שָׁפָט מֵאָבֵל
מְחוֹלָה תִּמְשַׁח לְנָבִיא תַּחְתֶּיךָ: 17 וְהָיָה
הַנִּמְלָט מֵחֶרֶב חֲזָאֵל יָמִית יֵהוּא וְהַנִּמְלָט
מֵחֶרֶב יֵהוּא יָמִית אֱלִישָׁע: 18 וְהִשְׁאַרְתִּי
בְיִשְׂרָאֵל שִׁבְעַת אֲלָפִים כָּל־הַבִּרְכַּיִם אֲשֶׁר
לֹא־כָרְעוּ לַבַּעַל וְכָל־הַפֶּה אֲשֶׁר לֹא־נָשַׁק לוֹ:

19 וַיֵּלֶךְ מִשָּׁם וַיִּמְצָא אֶת־אֱלִישָׁע בֶּן־שָׁפָט
וְהוּא חֹרֵשׁ שְׁנֵים־עָשָׂר צְמָדִים לְפָנָיו וְהוּא
בִּשְׁנֵים הֶעָשָׂר וַיַּעֲבֹר אֵלִיָּהוּ אֵלָיו וַיַּשְׁלֵךְ
אַדַּרְתּוֹ אֵלָיו: 20 וַיַּעֲזֹב אֶת־הַבָּקָר וַיָּרָץ
אַחֲרֵי אֵלִיָּהוּ וַיֹּאמֶר אֶשְּׁקָה־נָּא לְאָבִי וּלְאִמִּי
וְאֵלְכָה אַחֲרֶיךָ וַיֹּאמֶר לוֹ לֵךְ שׁוּב כִּי מֶה
עָשִׂיתִי לָךְ: 21 וַיָּשָׁב מֵאַחֲרָיו וַיִּקַּח אֶת־
צֶמֶד הַבָּקָר וַיִּזְבָּחֵהוּ וּבִכְלִי הַבָּקָר בִּשְּׁלָם
הַבָּשָׂר וַיִּתֵּן לָעָם וַיֹּאכֵלוּ וַיָּקָם וַיֵּלֶךְ אַחֲרֵי
אֵלִיָּהוּ וַיְשָׁרְתֵהוּ:

---

[e] I.e., I am not stopping you
[f-f] Lit. "them, the flesh"
[g] I.e., using it as firewood; cf. II Sam. 24.22

Jeremiah was the most inward of the prophets. In his agonized visions he foresaw Jerusalem's destruction and was jailed for his preachments. When the Babylonians destroyed the city in 586 (or 585) B.C.E., he became one of the exiles and died in Egypt.

If you go back on your obligation to God your sin will overtake you, Jeremiah the prophet warned his people. This is the basic message he delivered to his generation and reflects the teaching of the Torah in this week's sidrah. It is the first of two "sermons of rebuke" selected for two successive Sabbaths.

מטות

Jeremiah

1 : 1–2 : 3

Chapter 1

א

1] The words of Jeremiah son of Hilkiah, one of the priests at Anathoth in the territory of Benjamin.

2] The word of the LORD came to him in the days of King Josiah son of Amon of Judah, in the thirteenth year of his reign, 3] and throughout the days of King Jehoiakim son of Josiah of Judah, and until the end of the eleventh year of King Zedekiah son of Josiah of Judah, when Jerusalem went into exile in the fifth month.

1] דִּבְרֵי יִרְמְיָהוּ בֶּן־חִלְקִיָּהוּ מִן־הַכֹּהֲנִים אֲשֶׁר בַּעֲנָתוֹת בְּאֶרֶץ בִּנְיָמִן: 2] אֲשֶׁר הָיָה דְבַר־יְהוָה אֵלָיו בִּימֵי יֹאשִׁיָּהוּ בֶן־אָמוֹן מֶלֶךְ יְהוּדָה בִּשְׁלֹשׁ־עֶשְׂרֵה שָׁנָה לְמָלְכוֹ: 3] וַיְהִי בִּימֵי יְהוֹיָקִים בֶּן־יֹאשִׁיָּהוּ מֶלֶךְ יְהוּדָה עַד־תֹּם עַשְׁתֵּי־עֶשְׂרֵה שָׁנָה לְצִדְקִיָּהוּ בֶן־יֹאשִׁיָּהוּ מֶלֶךְ יְהוּדָה עַד־גְּלוֹת יְרוּשָׁלִַם בַּחֹדֶשׁ הַחֲמִישִׁי:

4] The word of the LORD came to me:

5] Before I created you in the womb, I selected you;
Before you were born, I consecrated you;
I appointed you a prophet concerning the nations.

6] I replied:
Ah, Lord GOD!
I don't know how to speak,
For I am still a boy.

7] And the LORD said to me:
Do not say, "I am still a boy,"
But go wherever I send you
And speak whatever I command you.

4] וַיְהִי דְבַר־יְהוָה אֵלַי לֵאמֹר:

5] בְּטֶרֶם אֶצּוֹרְךָ בַבֶּטֶן יְדַעְתִּיךָ וּבְטֶרֶם תֵּצֵא מֵרֶחֶם הִקְדַּשְׁתִּיךָ נָבִיא לַגּוֹיִם נְתַתִּיךָ:

6] וָאֹמַר אֲהָהּ אֲדֹנָי יְהוִה הִנֵּה לֹא־יָדַעְתִּי דַּבֵּר כִּי־נַעַר אָנֹכִי:

7] וַיֹּאמֶר יְהוָה אֵלַי אַל־תֹּאמַר נַעַר אָנֹכִי כִּי עַל־כָּל־אֲשֶׁר אֶשְׁלָחֲךָ תֵּלֵךְ וְאֵת כָּל־אֲשֶׁר אֲצַוְּךָ תְּדַבֵּר:

8] Have no fear of them,
For I am with you to deliver you
      —declares the Lord.

9] The Lord put out His hand and touched my mouth, and the Lord said to me: Herewith I put My words into your mouth.

10] See, I appoint you this day
Over nations and kingdoms:
To uproot and to pull down,
To destroy and to overthrow,
To build and to plant.

11] The word of the Lord came to me: What do you see, Jeremiah? I replied: I see a branch of an almond tree.[a]

12] The Lord said to me:
You have seen right,
For I am watchful[b] to bring My word to pass.

13] And the word of the Lord came to me a second time: What do you see? I replied:
I see a steaming pot,
[c]Tipped away from the north.[c]

14] And the Lord said to me:
From the north shall disaster break loose
Upon all the inhabitants of the land!

15] For I am summoning all the peoples
    of the kingdoms of the north
         —declares the Lord.

8 אַל־תִּירָא מִפְּנֵיהֶם
כִּי־אִתְּךָ אֲנִי לְהַצִּלֶךָ
נְאֻם־יְהוָה:

9 וַיִּשְׁלַח יְהוָה אֶת־יָדוֹ וַיַּגַּע עַל־פִּי וַיֹּאמֶר
יְהוָה אֵלַי הִנֵּה נָתַתִּי דְבָרַי בְּפִיךָ:

10 רְאֵה הִפְקַדְתִּיךָ הַיּוֹם הַזֶּה
עַל־הַגּוֹיִם וְעַל־הַמַּמְלָכוֹת
לִנְתוֹשׁ וְלִנְתוֹץ
וּלְהַאֲבִיד וְלַהֲרוֹס
לִבְנוֹת וְלִנְטוֹעַ:

11 וַיְהִי דְבַר־יְהוָה אֵלַי לֵאמֹר מָה־אַתָּה
רֹאֶה יִרְמְיָהוּ וָאֹמַר מַקֵּל שָׁקֵד אֲנִי רֹאֶה:

12 וַיֹּאמֶר יְהוָה אֵלַי
הֵיטַבְתָּ לִרְאוֹת
כִּי־שֹׁקֵד אֲנִי עַל־דְּבָרִי לַעֲשֹׂתוֹ:

13 וַיְהִי דְבַר־יְהוָה אֵלַי שֵׁנִית לֵאמֹר
מָה אַתָּה רֹאֶה
וָאֹמַר סִיר נָפוּחַ אֲנִי רֹאֶה
וּפָנָיו מִפְּנֵי צָפוֹנָה:

14 וַיֹּאמֶר יְהוָה אֵלַי
מִצָּפוֹן תִּפָּתַח הָרָעָה
עַל כָּל־יֹשְׁבֵי הָאָרֶץ:

15 כִּי הִנְנִי קֹרֵא
לְכָל־מִשְׁפְּחוֹת מַמְלְכוֹת צָפוֹנָה
נְאֻם־יְהוָה

[a] Heb. shaked
[b] Heb. shoked
[c-c] Meaning of Heb. uncertain

They shall come, and shall each set up a throne
Before the gates of Jerusalem,
Against its walls round about,
And against all the towns of Judah.

וּבָ֗אוּ וְנָֽתְנוּ֩ אִ֨ישׁ כִּסְא֜וֹ

פֶּ֣תַח ׀ שַׁעֲרֵ֣י יְרוּשָׁלַ֗ם

וְעַ֤ל כָּל־חֽוֹמֹתֶ֨יהָ֙ סָבִ֔יב

וְעַ֖ל כָּל־עָרֵ֥י יְהוּדָֽה:

16] And I will argue My case against them[d]
For all their wickedness:
They have forsaken Me
And sacrificed to other gods
And worshiped the works of their hands.

16] וְדִבַּרְתִּ֤י מִשְׁפָּטַי֙ אוֹתָ֔ם

עַ֖ל כָּל־רָעָתָ֑ם

אֲשֶׁ֣ר עֲזָב֗וּנִי

וַֽיְקַטְּרוּ֙ לֵֽאלֹהִ֣ים אֲחֵרִ֔ים

וַיִּֽשְׁתַּחֲו֖וּ לְמַעֲשֵׂ֥י יְדֵיהֶֽם:

17] So you, gird up your loins,
Arise and speak to them
All that I command you.
Do not break down before them,
Lest I break you before them.

17] וְאַתָּה֙ תֶּאְזֹ֣ר מָתְנֶ֔יךָ

וְקַמְתָּ֙ וְדִבַּרְתָּ֣ אֲלֵיהֶ֔ם

אֵ֛ת כָּל־אֲשֶׁ֥ר אָנֹכִ֖י אֲצַוֶּ֑ךָּ

אַל־תֵּחַת֙ מִפְּנֵיהֶ֔ם

פֶּֽן־אֲחִתְּךָ֖ לִפְנֵיהֶֽם:

18] I make you this day
A fortified city,
And an iron pillar,
And bronze walls
Against the whole land—
Against Judah's kings and officers,
And against its priests and citizens.[e]

18] וַאֲנִ֞י הִנֵּ֧ה נְתַתִּ֣יךָ הַיּ֗וֹם

לְעִ֣יר מִבְצָ֞ר

וּלְעַמּ֥וּד בַּרְזֶ֛ל

וּלְחֹמ֥וֹת נְחֹ֖שֶׁת

עַל־כָּל־הָאָ֑רֶץ

לְמַלְכֵ֤י יְהוּדָה֙ לְשָׂרֶ֔יהָ

לְכֹהֲנֶ֖יהָ וּלְעַ֥ם הָאָֽרֶץ:

19] They will attack you,
But they shall not overcome you;
For I am with you—declares the LORD—to save
    you.

19] וְנִלְחֲמ֥וּ אֵלֶ֖יךָ

וְלֹא־י֣וּכְלוּ לָ֑ךְ

כִּֽי־אִתְּךָ֥ אֲנִ֛י נְאֻם־יְהוָ֖ה לְהַצִּילֶֽךָ:

---

[d] I.e., against Jerusalem and Judah
[e] Lit. "the people of the land"

Chapter 2

1] The word of the Lord came to me, saying,

2] Go proclaim to Jerusalem: Thus said the Lord:
I accounted to your favor
The devotion of your youth,
Your love as a bride—
How you followed Me in the wilderness,
In a land not sown.

3] Israel was holy to the Lord,
The first fruits of His harvest.
All who ate of it were held guilty;
Disaster befell them
          —declares the Lord.

1] וַיְהִי דְבַר־יְהֹוָה אֵלַי לֵאמֹר:

2] הָלֹךְ וְקָרָאתָ בְאָזְנֵי יְרוּשָׁלַ͏ִם לֵאמֹר

כֹּה אָמַר יְהֹוָה

זָכַרְתִּי לָךְ חֶסֶד נְעוּרַיִךְ

אַהֲבַת כְּלוּלֹתָיִךְ

לֶכְתֵּךְ אַחֲרַי בַּמִּדְבָּר

בְּאֶרֶץ לֹא זְרוּעָה:

3] קֹדֶשׁ יִשְׂרָאֵל לַיהֹוָה

רֵאשִׁית תְּבוּאָתֹה כָּל־אֹכְלָיו יֶאְשָׁמוּ

רָעָה תָּבֹא אֲלֵיהֶם

נְאֻם־יְהֹוָה:

Jeremiah was the most inward of the prophets. In his agonized visions he foresaw Jerusalem's destruction and was jailed for his preachments. When the Babylonians destroyed the city in 586 (or 585) B.C.E., he became one of the exiles and died in Egypt.

The selection presents another of Jeremiah's "sermons of rebuke" and follows the previous haftarah. He predicts disaster for a society that has forsaken God and His law, even as the sidrah warns Israel against defiling the land by violence.

מסעי

Jeremiah

2 : 4–28; 3 : 4; 4 : 1–2

ב

Chapter 2

4] Hear the word of the LORD, O House of Jacob,
Every clan of the House of Israel!

5] Thus said the LORD:
What wrong did your fathers find in Me
That they abandoned Me
And went after delusion and were deluded?

6] They never asked themselves, "Where is the LORD,
Who brought us up from the land of Egypt,
Who led us through the wilderness,
A land of deserts and pits,
A land of drought and darkness,
A land no man had traversed,
Where no human being had dwelt?"

7] I brought you to this country of farm land
To enjoy its fruit and its bounty;
But you came and defiled My land,
You made My possession abhorrent.

8] The priests never asked themselves, "Where is the LORD?"
The guardians of the Teaching ignored Me;

4] שִׁמְע֥וּ דְבַר־יְהֹוָ֖ה בֵּ֣ית יַעֲקֹ֑ב
וְכָל־מִשְׁפְּח֖וֹת בֵּ֥ית יִשְׂרָאֵֽל:

5] כֹּ֣ה ׀ אָמַ֣ר יְהֹוָ֗ה
מַה־מָּצְא֨וּ אֲבוֹתֵיכֶ֥ם בִּי֙ עָ֔וֶל
כִּ֥י רָחֲק֖וּ מֵעָלָ֑י
וַיֵּלְכ֛וּ אַחֲרֵ֥י הַהֶ֖בֶל וַיֶּהְבָּֽלוּ:

6] וְלֹ֣א אָמְר֔וּ אַיֵּ֖ה יְהֹוָ֑ה
הַמַּעֲלֶ֤ה אֹתָ֨נוּ֙ מֵאֶ֣רֶץ מִצְרַ֔יִם
הַמּוֹלִ֤יךְ אֹתָ֨נוּ֙ בַּמִּדְבָּ֔ר
בְּאֶ֨רֶץ עֲרָבָ֤ה וְשׁוּחָה֙
בְּאֶ֨רֶץ צִיָּה֙ וְצַלְמָ֔וֶת
בְּאֶ֗רֶץ לֹא־עָ֤בַר בָּהּ֙ אִ֔ישׁ
וְלֹא־יָשַׁ֥ב אָדָ֖ם שָֽׁם:

7] וָאָבִ֤יא אֶתְכֶם֙ אֶל־אֶ֣רֶץ הַכַּרְמֶ֔ל
לֶאֱכֹ֥ל פִּרְיָ֖הּ וְטוּבָ֑הּ
וַתָּבֹ֨אוּ֙ וַתְּטַמְּא֣וּ אֶת־אַרְצִ֔י
וְנַחֲלָתִ֥י שַׂמְתֶּ֖ם לְתוֹעֵבָֽה:

8] הַכֹּהֲנִ֗ים לֹ֤א אָמְרוּ֙ אַיֵּ֣ה יְהֹוָ֔ה
וְתֹפְשֵׂ֤י הַתּוֹרָה֙ לֹ֣א יְדָע֔וּנִי

1282

The rulers[a] rebelled against Me,
And the prophets prophesied by Baal
And followed what can do no good.

9] Oh, I will go on accusing you
    —declares the LORD—
And I will accuse your children's children!

10] Just cross over to the isles of the Kittim and
  look,
Send to Kedar and observe carefully;
See if aught like this has ever happened:

11] Has any nation changed its gods
Even though they are no-gods?
But My people has exchanged its glory
For what can do no good.

12] Be appalled, O heavens, at this;
Be horrified, utterly dazed!
     —says the LORD.

13] For My people have done a twofold wrong:
They have forsaken Me, the Fount of living waters,
And hewed them out cisterns, broken cisterns,
Which cannot even hold water.

14] Is Israel a bondman,
Is he a home-born slave?
Then why is he given over to plunder?

15] Lions have roared over him,
Have raised their cries.
They have made his land a waste,
His cities desolate, without inhabitants.

וְהָרֹעִים פָּשְׁעוּ בִי

וְהַנְּבִיאִים נִבְּאוּ בַבַּעַל

וְאַחֲרֵי לֹא־יוֹעִלוּ הָלָכוּ:

9] לָכֵן עֹד אָרִיב אִתְּכֶם

נְאֻם־יְהוָֹה

וְאֶת־בְּנֵי בְנֵיכֶם אָרִיב:

10] כִּי עִבְרוּ אִיֵּי כִתִּיִּים וּרְאוּ

וְקֵדָר שִׁלְחוּ וְהִתְבּוֹנְנוּ מְאֹד

וּרְאוּ הֵן הָיְתָה כָּזֹאת:

11] הַהֵימִיר גּוֹי אֱלֹהִים

וְהֵמָּה לֹא אֱלֹהִים

וְעַמִּי הֵמִיר כְּבוֹדוֹ

בְּלוֹא יוֹעִיל:

12] שֹׁמּוּ שָׁמַיִם עַל־זֹאת

וְשַׂעֲרוּ חָרְבוּ מְאֹד

נְאֻם־יְהוָֹה:

13] כִּי־שְׁתַּיִם רָעוֹת עָשָׂה עַמִּי

אֹתִי עָזְבוּ מְקוֹר מַיִם חַיִּים

לַחְצֹב לָהֶם בֹּארֹות

בֹּארֹת נִשְׁבָּרִים

אֲשֶׁר לֹא־יָכִלוּ הַמָּיִם:

14] הַעֶבֶד יִשְׂרָאֵל

אִם־יְלִיד בַּיִת הוּא

מַדּוּעַ הָיָה לָבַז:

15] עָלָיו יִשְׁאֲגוּ כְפִרִים

נָתְנוּ קוֹלָם

וַיָּשִׁיתוּ אַרְצוֹ לְשַׁמָּה

עָרָיו נִצְּתוּ מִבְּלִי יֹשֵׁב:

---

[a] Lit. "shepherds"; cf. 3.15; 23.1 ff.

16] Those, too, in Noph and Tahpanhes[b]
[c-]Will lay bare[-c] your head.

17] See, [d-]that is the price you have paid
For forsaking the LORD your God[-d]
[c-]While He led you in the way.[-c]

18] What, then, is the good of your going to Egypt
To drink the waters of the Nile?
And what is the good of your going to Assyria
To drink the waters of the Euphrates?

19] Let your misfortune reprove you,
Let your afflictions rebuke you;
Mark well how bad and bitter it is
That you forsake the LORD your God,
That awe for Me is not in you
          —declares the Lord GOD of Hosts.

20] For long ago you[e] broke your yoke,
Tore off your yoke-bands,
And said, "I will not work!"[f]
On every high hill and under every verdant tree,
You recline as a whore.

21] I planted you with noble vines,
All with choicest seed;
Alas, I find you changed
Into a base, an alien vine!

טז] גַּם־בְּנֵי־נֹף וְתַחְפַּנְחֵס
יִרְעוּךְ קָדְקֹד:

יז] הֲלוֹא־זֹאת תַּעֲשֶׂה־לָּךְ
עׇזְבֵךְ אֶת־יְהוָה אֱלֹהַיִךְ
בְּעֵת מוֹלִכֵךְ בַּדָּרֶךְ:

יח] וְעַתָּה מַה־לָּךְ לְדֶרֶךְ מִצְרַיִם
לִשְׁתּוֹת מֵי שִׁחוֹר
וּמַה־לָּךְ לְדֶרֶךְ אַשּׁוּר
לִשְׁתּוֹת מֵי נָהָר:

יט] תְּיַסְּרֵךְ רָעָתֵךְ
וּמְשֻׁבוֹתַיִךְ תּוֹכִחֻךְ
וּדְעִי וּרְאִי כִּי־רַע וָמָר
עׇזְבֵךְ אֶת־יְהוָה אֱלֹהָיִךְ
וְלֹא פַחְדָּתִי אֵלַיִךְ
נְאֻם־אֲדֹנָי יְהוִה צְבָאוֹת:

כ] כִּי מֵעוֹלָם שָׁבַרְתִּי עֻלֵּךְ
נִתַּקְתִּי מוֹסְרוֹתַיִךְ
וַתֹּאמְרִי לֹא אֶעֱבוֹר
כִּי עַל־כָּל־גִּבְעָה גְבֹהָה
וְתַחַת כָּל־עֵץ רַעֲנָן
אַתְּ צֹעָה זֹנָה:

כא] וְאָנֹכִי נְטַעְתִּיךְ שֹׂרֵק
כֻּלֹּה זֶרַע אֱמֶת
וְאֵיךְ נֶהְפַּכְתְּ לִי
סוּרֵי הַגֶּפֶן נׇכְרִיָּה:

---

[b] *Cities in Egypt. The Egyptians, like the Assyrians, will prove a disappointment;*
  cf. v. 36
[c-c] *Meaning of Heb. uncertain*
[d-d] *Lit. "that is what your forsaking the LORD your God is doing to you"*
[e] *For the form, cf. shakamti, Judg. 5.7; others "I"*
[f] *Following the ketib; qere "transgress"*

22] Though you wash with natron
And use much lye,
Your guilt is ingrained before Me
                    —declares the Lord GOD.

23] How can you say, "I am not defiled,
I have not gone after the Baalim"?
Look at your deeds in the Valley,[g]
Consider what you have done!
Like a lustful she-camel,
[c-]Restlessly running about,[-c]

24] Or like a wild ass used to the desert,
Snuffing the wind in her eagerness,
Whose passion none can restrain,
None that seek her need grow weary—
In her season, they'll find her!

25] Save your foot from going bare,
And your throat from thirst.
But you say, "It is no use.
No, I love the strangers,[h]
And after them I must go."

26] Like a thief chagrined when he is caught,
So is the House of Israel chagrined—
They, their kings, their officers,
And their priests and prophets.

27] They said to wood, "You are my father,"
To stone, "You gave birth to me,"
While to Me they turned their backs
And not their faces.

[22] כִּי אִם־תְּכַבְּסִי בַּנֶּתֶר
וְתַרְבִּי־לָךְ בֹּרִית
נִכְתָּם עֲוֺנֵךְ לְפָנַי
נְאֻם אֲדֹנָי יְהֹוִה:

[23] אֵיךְ תֹּאמְרִי לֹא נִטְמֵאתִי
אַחֲרֵי הַבְּעָלִים לֹא הָלַכְתִּי
רְאִי דַרְכֵּךְ בַּגַּיְא
דְּעִי מֶה עָשִׂית
בִּכְרָה קַלָּה מְשָׂרֶכֶת דְּרָכֶיהָ:

[24] פֶּרֶה לִמֻּד מִדְבָּר
בְּאַוַּת נַפְשָׁהּ שָׁאֲפָה רוּחַ
תַּאֲנָתָהּ מִי יְשִׁיבֶנָּה
כָּל־מְבַקְשֶׁיהָ לֹא יִיעָפוּ
בְּחָדְשָׁהּ יִמְצָאוּנְהָ:

[25] מִנְעִי רַגְלֵךְ מִיָּחֵף
וּגְרוֺנֵךְ מִצִּמְאָה
וַתֹּאמְרִי נוֺאָשׁ
לוֺא כִּי־אָהַבְתִּי זָרִים
וְאַחֲרֵיהֶם אֵלֵךְ:

[26] כְּבֹשֶׁת גַּנָּב כִּי יִמָּצֵא
כֵּן הֹבִישׁוּ בֵּית יִשְׂרָאֵל
הֵמָּה מַלְכֵיהֶם שָׂרֵיהֶם
וְכֹהֲנֵיהֶם וּנְבִיאֵיהֶם:

[27] אֹמְרִים לָעֵץ אָבִי אַתָּה
וְלָאֶבֶן אַתְּ יְלִדְתָּנוּ
כִּי־פָנוּ אֵלַי עֹרֶף
וְלֹא פָנִים

[g] I.e., of Hinnom; cf. 7.31–32; 32.35
[c-c] Meaning of Heb. uncertain
[h] I.e., other gods

But in their hour of calamity they cry,
"Arise and save us!"

28] And where are those gods
You made for yourself?
Let them arise and save you, if they can,
In your hour of calamity.
For your gods have become, O Judah,
As many as your towns!

Chapter 3

4] Just now you called to Me, "Father!
You are the Guide of my youth. . . ."

Chapter 4

1] If you return, O Israel

—declares the LORD—

If you return to Me,
If you remove your abominations from My
    presence
And do not waver,

2] And ᵃ⁻swear, "As the LORD lives,"⁻ᵃ
In sincerity, justice, and righteousness—
Nations shall bless themselves by youᵇ
And praise themselves by you.ᵇ

וּבְעֵת רָעָתָם יֹאמְרוּ

קוּמָה וְהוֹשִׁיעֵנוּ:

28] וְאַיֵּה אֱלֹהֶיךָ אֲשֶׁר עָשִׂיתָ לָּךְ

יָקוּמוּ אִם־יוֹשִׁיעוּךָ בְּעֵת רָעָתֶךָ

כִּי מִסְפַּר עָרֶיךָ

הָיוּ אֱלֹהֶיךָ יְהוּדָה:

ג

4] הֲלוֹא מֵעַתָּה קָרָאתִי לִי אָבִי

אַלּוּף נְעֻרַי אָתָּה:

ד

1] אִם־תָּשׁוּב יִשְׂרָאֵל

נְאֻם־יְהֹוָה

אֵלַי תָּשׁוּב

וְאִם־תָּסִיר שִׁקּוּצֶיךָ מִפָּנַי

וְלֹא תָנוּד:

2] וְנִשְׁבַּעְתָּ חַי־יְהֹוָה

בֶּאֱמֶת בְּמִשְׁפָּט וּבִצְדָקָה

וְהִתְבָּרְכוּ בוֹ גּוֹיִם

וּבוֹ יִתְהַלָּלוּ:

ᵃ⁻ᵃ *I.e., profess the worship of the* LORD
ᵇ *Heb.* "him"

DEUTERONOMY

Commentary by

W. GUNTHER PLAUT

Introducing Deuteronomy

DUDLEY WEINBERG ז"ל *and W. GUNTHER PLAUT*[1]

Name

Deuteronomy is the fifth of the five books of the Torah. The name is derived from the Greek and means "second law," which is the way the Septuagint translated the expression *mishneh ha-torah* in 17:18 (our translation renders these words as "a copy of this Teaching"). As in the other books of the Torah, the Hebrew name is taken from the first sentence of chapter 1; it is known as דְּבָרִים (*devarim*, words), for the book begins by saying, "These are the words...."

Content

Deuteronomy is presented as a series of farewell speeches by Moses and ends with a description of his death. With few exceptions the book exhibits an integrated flow of narrative, exhortation, liturgy, law, and poetry. It addresses itself to Israel at a crucial period of its history and aims at national solutions which will guarantee the achievement of the nation's highest goals: peace, prosperity, and security—both material and spiritual—under the suzerainty of the One God.

The book may be divided in a number of ways. One possibility is taking the text as being organized around four titles: 1:4; 4:44; 28:69; and 33:1. A more frequent division, which has been adopted in this commentary, distinguishes five parts: a prologue which reviews the past and a first sermon which stresses Israel's relationship to God (chapters 1:1–4:43); a second, long discourse which presents laws of ritual and civil character and a long catalogue of consequences (chapters 4:44–11:25); a third discourse (chapters 11:26–28:69); a final appeal and farewell by Moses (chapters 29–33); and a brief epilogue describing the leader's death (chapter 34).

In presenting the text in such a manner, one should remember that the need for systematizing which modern people feel when they approach a subject did not exist in the same way in ancient days. One of the reasons for this difference lies in the fact that today we *read* the material, while the early traditions of Israel were transmitted at first in *oral* form. Such transmission required aids to memory—and these might consist of assonances, word plays, and other mnemotechnical devices.[2] Or again, the text might be governed by its relationship to older, pre-existing traditions. In any case, one should at all times be on guard against judging these matters from a contemporary point of view. For instance, it has been claimed that Moses'

---

[1] When Rabbi Dudley Weinberg died in 1976, he left behind the draft of an introduction to his planned commentary on Deuteronomy. I have incorporated many of his notes, in this introduction, as a memorial to a dear friend and unique spiritual leader.

[2] For example, 22:13–29 deals with the actual or putative loss of virginity and related circumstances of sexual intercourse. In the midst of these laws (in verse 22) the subject of adultery is briefly introduced, and then the text returns to its former concerns.

first sermon elaborates on the first commandment and that the subsequent text deals with the rest of the Decalogue. Such analysis may satisfy the modern inquirer, but it has little to do with the structure of the ancient text.

Characteristics

That text, however, does have some overriding characteristics, and it features certain subjects which are either unique to Deuteronomy or which, by style and emphasis, give it a particular flavor. At the core stands the covenantal concept: At Horeb,[3] God concluded a pact with Israel and the mutuality of their intentions and obligations flows from this covenant.

God is One and is Israel's Master; He is to be the people's object of love and undivided loyalty. Idolatry is decried time and again and so are magic and the dark arts of the sorcerer. "You shall love the Lord your God" (6:5) spells out Israel's basic obligation which is amplified by a set of ordinances that the people must carefully observe. If they love and obey God, He will raise them above the nations, not because Israel is superior to other peoples, but because Israel is in possession of a special teaching. Torah makes Israel unique, and the Giver of Torah will protect this unequalled covenantal partner. But should the latter break the oath of loyalty, the direst consequences will occur, and both heaven and earth are called upon to witness these awesome threats.

The unique God and His unique people—the theme is not altogether new, for it forms the subject of the revelation at Horeb-Sinai (Exod. 19 and 20). In Deuteronomy, however, monotheism is central and God's Chosen Ones are time and again reminded that theirs is an unequalled opportunity. Their task is not easy and it is weighted with warnings of certain retribution for misdeeds. But the people are not adrift on an uncharted sea; they have guides to help them.

First and foremost among these is the Book itself, open and accessible to all who care to learn its teachings. Torah is not an esoteric doctrine beyond the people's reach; rather, it is "very close to you, in your mouth and in your heart, to observe it" (30:14).

Then there is Moses, friend and intimate of God whose representative he is. He is more than a transmitter of the divine word; he is prophet, intermediary, and fiery advocate for his people. Exodus and Numbers hint at his special status which at times approaches the level of semidivinity—such as the glow that emanates from his face (Exod. 34:29–33). In Deuteronomy, these supernatural traits of Moses are less in evidence, but his importance as leader and interpreter is stressed more than in the other books. In fact, Moses is shown to be surprisingly unhesitating in emphasizing his own role.

Finally, there are the priests who will aid the people in their quest of divine favor. They belong to the family of Aaron the Levite and have a variety of functions. Prime amongst these is the singular privilege of officiating at the central sanctuary. No longer may the people bring sacrifices at various shrines; now only one altar is permitted to them. The centralization of the cult is an important characteristic of Deuteronomy, and a contemplation of the reasons for this rule leads us squarely into a consideration of the origins of the book as a whole.

Time and Authorship

Our commentary holds that Deuteronomy, like the whole Torah, was the result of many centuries of growth, a fusion of sources

---

[3] In Deuteronomy, God's mountain is generally called Horeb rather than Sinai. In the other books of the Torah, Horeb is traced to E, and Sinai to J and P. The close relation of Deuteronomy to the (northern)

and traditions, orally transmitted at first and then committed to writing. Nowhere can this development be followed more clearly than in the composition of Deuteronomy, for it is the only one of the five books of the Torah which enjoys a fairly unambiguous historical setting.

A radical religious reformation, which was carried out in 621 B.C.E. by King Josiah who reigned in Judah from 640–608, is reported in II Kings 22 and 23. This reformation displayed a remarkable resemblance to certain provisions which occur only in Deuteronomy. Some of these provisions differ with or at least vary from legislation which is contained in the other Torah books. For example, Josiah abolished the ancient practice of worshiping and offering sacrifices at the "high places" and established the Temple in Jerusalem as the sole sanctuary in which sacrifices could be properly offered. Deuteronomy is the only book of the Torah which contains legislation to that effect. Similarly, the prohibition of the worship of the heavenly bodies was stringently forbidden by Josiah. This too is a matter with which Deuteronomy is much concerned (17:3). Further, Deuteronomy 16:1–8 requires that Passover be celebrated in Jerusalem, while Exodus 12 provides that it be observed at home. Josiah arranged Passover to be celebrated in Jerusalem in accordance with the law in Deuteronomy; and II Kings 23:22 f. records that such a Passover had not been celebrated during the entire period of the judges and of the monarchy, which is to say, for nearly four centuries.

According to the account in II Kings 22 and 23, King Josiah's reform was predicated on the discovery of a document called "Book of Teaching" (*Sefer ha-Torah*). This "Book of Teaching" is reported to have been found by the High Priest Hilkiah while the Temple was being repaired on orders of the king (II Kings 22:8). Precisely what this book was is not stated; however, the intriguing correspondence between the account of Josiah's reform and the Book of Deuteronomy is heightened by the fact that the expression "Book of Teaching" occurs nowhere else except in Deuteronomy and refers to Deuteronomy itself (29:20).

II Kings 23:1–2 describes that King Josiah assembled the leadership and the people of Judah and how they entered into a covenant with God, pledging themselves to abide loyally by the rules set down in the newly discovered book. The language of this passage is highly reminiscent of several passages in Deuteronomy in which the people are summoned to pledge their devotion and loving loyalty to God (e.g., 10:12–11:32 and 29:9–30:20).

What was the "Book of Teaching" which was discovered during the reign of Josiah and which provided the platform for his religious revolution in 621 B.C.E.? While biblical scholars are agreed that Josiah's "book" was not precisely the same text which is contained in Deuteronomy as we know it today, they are also largely agreed that there is an inescapable connection between the two. Modern scholars speculate about the exact contents of Josiah's "book," but most agree that it contained the core of what subsequently, through a continuing process of addition and editing, ultimately became our Book of Deuteronomy.

Assuming that the account of the discovery of the Torah book in II Kings 22:8 is historically accurate (or at least reflects a genuinely historical situation), we still are faced with some unanswered questions. How did the book which the High Priest Hilkiah "discovered" during the process of Temple repair come to be "hidden"? When and by whom was it written?

E-source is observable elsewhere as well. See further footnotes 5 and 10.

A significant clue is found in the biblical account of an earlier reform, similar to that which Josiah undertook. It occurred under the sponsorship of King Hezekiah who reigned in Judah from 715–687 B.C.E.[4] He too had mounted an assault against idolatry and the places and objects of idolatrous worship (II Kings 18:3–6). He too had attempted to centralize worship in the Jerusalem Temple (II Kings 18:22). Hezekiah's reform may well have been the occasion for the composition—or at least the beginning of the composition—of the Torah book whose discovery later helped to prompt and to provide the program for King Josiah's reform.

It is possible that the fall of Samaria and the Northern Kingdom, which occurred a few years before Hezekiah's accession, contributed to the monarch's reform. Northerners may have brought a basic document with them when they fled to Jerusalem—for Deuteronomy does indeed show affinity to the E-tradition which is believed to hail from the North. The centralization of the cult which was to have distinguished the shrine of Shechem now focused on Jerusalem.[5]

In addition, the reforms of Hezekiah were closely related to his foreign policy and constituted an aspect of his rebellion against his Assyrian overlords—a rebellion that caused the invasion of Judah by Sennacherib, in 701 B.C.E. For instance, the centralization of the cult which Hezekiah undertook increased his access to large amounts of money deposited in the Temple treasury. This in turn made him assume a greater degree of political independence, but, while the Assyrians quelled his insurrection, his religious reforms remained in place during his lifetime.

A radical change occurred during the reign of his successors, Manasseh and Amon, especially since Assyria—under the kingship of Esarhaddon—obtained a stature of great power and extended its suzerainty as far west and south as Egypt and as far east as Elam.[6] Perhaps it was Manasseh's desire to conform more closely to the religious practices of his masters (though they did not apparently require such adjustments from their vassals); perhaps his and Amon's personal inclinations played a role—at any rate, in their reigns idolatrous practices were reintroduced, and an idol was placed in the Temple itself. Manasseh supported the Assyrians, tentatively at first and then vigorously, and his policy was carried on by his son Amon. Two years after his accession Amon was murdered, possibly by religious traditionalists or possibly by an anti-Assyrian conspiracy, or perhaps a combination of these forces. The result was the installation of Josiah as king who in stages reformed the cult and at the same time managed to distance himself from Assyria, which was now entering into a period of political weakness. The climax of Josiah's reforms was the discovery of Deuteronomy and the spread of his ideas into cities of the former Northern Kingdom of Israel. This was possible because Assyria had already lost effective control of Judah and her neighboring territories.

What then can we say about the time of Deuteronomy's composition?

It is possible to assume that some traditions in the book were quite old and that they

---

[4] There is some controversy over the year of his ascendancy to the throne; some scholars put it somewhat earlier.

[5] So Jacob Milgrom, *HUCA*, 47 (1976), pp. 1–17, on the basis of linguistic terminology. According to his reconstruction, the book was reworked by P (after the reversal of Manasseh) and in this new form became state law under Josiah. M. Or, *Beth Mikra*, 73 (1978), pp. 218–220, adds the observation that the *sefer* found by Hilkiah probably contained chapters (scrolls?) from Exodus.

[6] This development may be followed in the essay of Carl D. Evans, "Judah's Foreign Policy from Hezekiah to Josiah," *Scripture in Context: Essays on the Comparative Method*, ed. C. D. Evans, W. W. Hallo, J. B. White (Pittsburgh Theological Monograph Series, vol. 34, 1980; Pittsburgh: Pickwick Press).

were subsequently molded to fit the special needs of changing times. Thus, the centralization of the cult in Jerusalem under Hezekiah may have been one consequence of the destruction of the Northern Kingdom in 721 B.C.E., a few years before the king ascended the throne. The emphasis on the Aaronide priesthood may have been the result of a power struggle among priestly families; while the strong exhorting voice calling the people to the worship of the One God may have belonged to an "underground" movement during the reigns of Manasseh and Amon. In Josiah's time, a full hundred years after the Northern Kingdom was destroyed and its people led away by the Assyrians, a religious revival combined with favorable political circumstances to bring forth a document which may have been the core of what we have come to know as the Book of Deuteronomy.[7]

What of Moses?

The Book of Deuteronomy begins with the assertion that Moses was delivering his final summary address to the people in the land of Moab (present-day Kingdom of Jordan) as they were about to cross the Jordan River to take possession of the land which had for so long been promised them and in which Israel would at last find rest and security. That this assertion, which is frequently repeated in Deuteronomy, is a fiction seems obvious. It is not Moses who is the speaker or the preacher in Deuteronomy, although the ultimate inspiration for much that is said in Deuteronomy may well be traced back to him. Nor are the auditors of the Deuteronomic preacher the survivors

of the wilderness experience which was about to achieve its culmination in Israel's homecoming. The fiction, however, speaks its own truth, and in that sense it is no fiction at all. If the conviction of modern scholarship concerning the time of Deuteronomy's composition is correct—and both historical and archeological evidence seems to confirm that conviction—then the "fiction" addresses itself to a real life situation which existed during the later period of the monarchy in Judah. That it does so, in terms of principles which were derived from ancient traditions which transcended the immediately addressed situation, was essential to the role of Deuteronomy in the development of biblical and postbiblical Judaism. The "fiction" of Deuteronomy was a summons to do God's will whenever it was heard; instruction from the past called forth a response in the present. The period of Josiah's reign, like the situation of the Israelites on the Steppes of Moab, was one marked by radical renewal, hope, and change. It too seemed like the fulfillment of a promise and was surely so understood by those who lived through it and attempted to interpret its meaning both at the time itself and in retrospect.

At the same time, the very persistence of Moses in the awareness of the people and of the compilers and preservers of their traditions lend enormous weight to the conviction that the real and historical Moses, difficult as the recovery of his genuine biography may be, was the true generator of the religion of Israel, the effective founder of the people of Israel, the inspired genius whose insights and career in many ways shaped the ideal, not only of the Jewish people, but of the entire Western world. While Deuteronomy did not flow directly from the pen of Moses, it did in part flow from his spirit. Why else would the actual authors of Deuteronomy have attributed their Torah book to him? Why else would

[7] The document which Hilkiah and Shaphan brought to Josiah must have been much shorter than the present Deuteronomy, for it had two readings in one day and possibly three (II Kings 22:8–10; 23:1–2).

the ultimate compilers of the entire Torah text have presented Moses as its earthly author and as God's chosen messenger whose mission was to proclaim His uniqueness and unity and to bring Israel into covenant with Him alone? Moses is not diminished by critical historical and literary analysis of the biblical text. If anything, his stature is enlarged and his life, although we may know very little of its details, looms large in history and especially in the consciousness of his people for whom he became *Mosheh Rabbenu*, Moses our teacher.

And what of the divine role in the text? This question has been discussed at some length in our commentary on Exodus 19 and in the General Introduction to the Torah. We hold that the Torah is a record of Israel's striving to meet God and understand His will. In centuries of search, of finding and forgetting, of inspiration and desperation, God touched the soul of His people and the sparks of these meetings burn in the pages of the Torah. Deuteronomy is such a record of encounters, and it clearly stands—more than the other Torah books—in the tradition of Israel's prophets. When the prophets proclaimed, "Thus says the Lord," it was not a gratuitous attribution by the speaker; it was felt as reality and partook of it. Last but not least, as time went on, the belief that indeed God had spoken through Moses gained a firm hold and this belief developed its own dynamism, shaping the fate of a believing people. They *knew* what God wanted of them and tried to carry out His will as best they could.

Relation to Other Torah Books

Were the other Torah books already formulated when Deuteronomy came into being? The question cannot be answered with certainty; in fact, nowhere do scholars disagree more widely than in the dating of

the various strands that went into the making of the Torah.[8]

As indicated above,[9] this commentary proceeds from the theory that major elements of the J, E, and P-traditions were already in existence when the D-texts were first formulated, representing partly an expansion, partly a departure from the former.[10] It is possible and even likely that Deuteronomy's core (chapters 5–26, 28) was set down as a book before the other four books of the Torah were formulated as distinct documents. When eventually they were, there came into existence a "Tetrateuch" (four books) which stood side by side with Deuteronomy. The latter was then enlarged with a prologue (chapters 1–4), an insert (chapter 27), and a concluding section (chapters 29–34). In this form the Book of Deuteronomy was joined to the Tetrateuch to form the Pentateuch (five books) or Torah, thereby bringing the major traditions concerning Moses together in one large work.[11]

Literary Aspects

As indicated, narrative, exhortation, liturgy, law, and poetry form the literary genres of the book. Narration occurs at the

---

[8] Concise surveys may be found in Kenneth A. Kitchen, *Ancient Orient and Old Testament* (London: Tyndale Press, 1966), pp. 112–138; Roland de Vaux, *The Bible and the Ancient Near East* (Darton, Longman, and Todd, 1972), pp. 31–48; on Deuteronomy, see Moshe Weinfeld, *Encyclopaedia Judaica*, Vol. 5, cols. 1574 ff.; N. Lohfink, *Interpreter's Dictionary of the Bible*, Supplement, pp. 229 ff.

[9] See General Introduction to the Torah.

[10] The formulation of the Sabbath commandment (5:15) represents an expansion; the permission to eat meat at profane occasions, away from a sacrificial context (12:15), represents a departure from former practice.

[11] In Deuteronomy, however, the word תּוֹרָה (translated as "teaching") refers to Deuteronomy, not to the Pentateuch (which in this form did not yet exist).

beginning and end and in chapter 27, and poetry only in chapter 32. Sometimes an exhortation has a narrative reference point, such as the passage in which Israel is asked to remember forever what Amalek had done, and the text then briefly recounts the relevant events (25:17–19). There is liturgy, such as the thanksgiving ritual and recitation (chapter 26) and the reenactment of a covenantal ceremony marked by blessings and curses (chapter 27). All these materials, including many of the laws, are couched in a language which is different from that found in the other books of the Torah. The sentences are marked by more clauses, and the phrases have often a poetic quality, featuring a kind of prose meter with assonances which give the text a special rhythm and sense of ceremony.[12]

The style is highly rhetorical, the speaker pleads and urges, threatens and comforts, exhorts and, at the last, invokes the very heavens to be his witnesses.[13] The text has all the earmarks of preaching and uses a series of key expressions such as: "Hear, O Israel"; "do not try the Lord"; "be careful, then"; "give heed"; "remember"; "guard yourselves." The phrases are sometimes long and repetitive, but this only serves to heighten the oratorical effect of the whole.

[12] Lohfink, *Interpreter's Dictionary of the Bible*, p. 229. In classical languages this is called "artistic prose."
[13] The technical term by which this style is often described is "parenesis" (from the Greek *ainos*, speech), a type of exhortation.
[14] See especially M. Weinfeld, *Deuteronomy and the Deuteronomic School* (Oxford: Clarendon Press, 1972). Peake's *Commentary on the Bible* (London: Thomas Nelson and Sons, 1962), p. 269, says: "Just as Genesis to Numbers is the P-Bible, so Deuteronomy to II Kings is the D-Bible."
[15] The former opinion is expounded by Gerhard von Rad, the latter by George E. Mendenhall.
[16] On casuistic and apodictic law see A. Alt, *Essays on Old Testament History and Religion* (Garden City: Doubleday, 1968), and the survey by R. Sonsino, *Journal of Reform Judaism* (Summer 1979), pp. 117–123.

Special grammatical forms—such as the ending *un* in the plural imperfect of the third person—add the flavor of the unusual. The closest parallels are found in the prose style of Jeremiah and in the so-called "Early Prophets," that is, the books from Joshua to Kings. The affinity of this latter group to Deuteronomy has caused many scholars to say that it came from a "Deuteronomic school," whose theological interests were distinct from and were somewhat at variance with those who produced the Tetrateuch.[14] But scholarly agreement ends here. Some hold that the Deuteronomic school was centered in rural areas, among the Levites, while others detect telling parallels with the kind of "wisdom language" known at the court and in the city.[15]

The core of Deuteronomy (chapters 5–26) consists of laws which have their parallels in other ancient Near Eastern codes. They consist of casuistic and apodictic law. The former is much more frequent and states the cases and conditions under which the law is to be operative, for instance: "When you take the field against your enemies . . ." (20:1). Apodictic law is stated without conditional clauses, as in the Decalogue and elsewhere: "You shall not have in your pouch alternate weights" (25:13), or "You shall not boil a kid in its mother's milk" (14:21).[16]

How do these laws relate to the Book of the Covenant which is generally considered the oldest of the legal codes in the Torah (Exod. 21–23)? The Deuteronomist, though fully conversant with this code, yet departs from it significantly. Compare, for instance, the way a Hebrew slave is to be treated. Both Exodus 21:2–6 and Deuteronomy 15:12–18 agree on the need to free such a servant at the end of six years but disagree on whether the slave is entitled to compensation. Exodus says no, Deuteronomy (which extends the law also to female slaves) says yes. In this and similar instances, the Deuteronomist

clearly amends older laws, especially those which have a moral and religious underpinning.[17] The majority of the casuistic laws in Exodus are not mentioned at all in Deuteronomy, probably because these belonged to a corpus of law common to the neighboring nations which the Deuteronomic circle expected to remain operative.[18] For the whole framework of the covenant bears a close resemblance to Hittite suzerain-vassal treaties of the second millennium and neo-Assyrian treaties of the time when Deuteronomy germinated.[19]

In sum, Deuteronomy is the heir of old traditions which it molded in accordance with new social and political needs and did so in a prophetic spirit which gave it the urgency of religious imperatives. As time went on, these characteristics especially impressed themselves on the soul of Israel, for they made clear that even the smallest rule had the purpose of purifying the Lord's people and that the nation as a whole, collectively, had a responsibility for the future. The ringing cadences were believed to have been the words of Moses, the greatest figure of Israel's past, and were thereby given added stature. God himself was seen to stand behind leader and law. When Deuteronomy was at last joined to the Tetrateuch and became the fifth book of the Torah, it continued the saga which had started with Creation, had proceeded to the fashioning of Israel, and, with the death of Moses, now completed the first stage of a universal history. Israel, as God's co-worker, was to be forever ready to help the Creator perfect the work of His hands. Torah was the way, and a willing people thereby held the key both to its own fate and to the future of the world.

[17] Already Rashi, in his commentary on the Exodus passages, recognized the expanding nature of the Deuteronomic law.

[18] The revolutionary nature of Deuteronomic law is propounded by Weinfeld, *Deuteronomy*, *passim*, who holds that the book came to replace rather than complement the older law. Two other radical theorists may be mentioned. Ellis Rivkin, *The Shaping of Jewish History* (New York: Charles Scribner's Sons, 1971), considers Deuteronomy as an attempt to end prophetic privilege and install Moses as the one unequalled prophet whose words were immutable. This revolution failed, for Jeremiah and Ezekiel continued independently to interpret the divine will. But another, later revolution succeeded, that of a group of anonymous leaders who installed the Aaronides as God's sole priests and did so by creating the Pentateuch and thus saved a disintegrating YHWH religion (pp. 17–41). Morton Smith, *Palestinian Parties and Politics That Shaped the Old Testament* (New York and London: Columbia University Press, 1971), on the other hand, considers Deuteronomy to have been a religious and political success. It represented the "God Alone" party which taught God's jealous love for Israel. In doing so it altered older traditions, proclaimed Israel to be a separate people, and established monotheism as Israel's religion (pp. 48–56).

[19] This aspect is discussed in greater detail in William W. Hallo's essay, which follows. See there also for a discussion on kingship in Deuteronomy.

Deuteronomy
and Ancient Near Eastern Literature

WILLIAM W. HALLO

Deuteronomy occupies a unique position in the Hebrew Bible and in the history of biblical scholarship. More nearly than any other biblical book, it can lay claim to having been a book in its own right before it was incorporated into the canon; it is the least hypothetical of the documents which the documentary hypothesis claims as the original components of the Pentateuch. Deuteronomy, or at least its central core (here Parts II and III), preserves in its essence the "book of the law" found by Hilkiah the High Priest and turned over to King Josiah of Judah in the eighteenth year of his reign (621 B.C.E.) according to one of the most fundamental tenets of modern biblical criticism.

But beyond this there is little scholarly agreement. The authorship of Deuteronomy has been variously attributed to the priestly circles that found it; to the prophetic movement whose influence is said to be evident in it; to the royal court that needed it to counter precisely the exclusive prophetic claims to speak for God; to the party of scribes and wise men who wanted a new morality based on universal norms, or contrariwise to a zealous group of exiles from the defeated northern kingdom of Israel striving to preserve pre-monarchic traditions and purify them from the corrupting cosmopolitanism of the surrounding world.

In formal and stylistic terms, too, Deuteronomy has been subject to very divergent modern interpretations: as a lengthy sermon on the theme of collective responsibility; as the libretto of a recurrent cultic ceremony celebrating the renewal of the covenant; as a lawbook superseding or supplementing the "Covenant Code" of Exodus; as a declaration of independence from human (Assyrian) overlordship and of vassalage instead to God; as an integral and concluding part of the Pentateuch or contrariwise as the introduction to the "Deuteronomic" history of the Former Prophets (Joshua through Kings).[1]

These and other issues will probably never be resolved by appeal to the biblical text alone. Here as elsewhere, the comparative and archeological evidence must be thrown into the balance. It will be marshaled here in accordance with the structural analysis of the text offered in the commentary and with the literary genres adduced in the various proposed comparisons.

[1] Moshe Weinfeld, "Deuteronomy—The Present State of Inquiry," *Journal of Biblical Literature*, 86 (1967), pp. 249–262 [hereafter cited as *JBL*]; idem, *Deuteronomy and the Deuteronomic School* (Oxford, 1972).

Deuteronomy as Homily

Ostensibly the Book of Deuteronomy presents itself to us in the guise of a homily, i.e., a religious discourse addressed to a congregation. Indeed, with the exception of a few narrative introductions, inserts, and transitions, all of the book is phrased in the first person as a direct address by Moses or, rather, as three successive sermons (chs. 1–4, 5–28, 29–31),[2] a song (32), and a blessing of the twelve tribes (33). Only the concluding notice of Moses' death (34) falls outside this framework (see below).

Such a framework is unique in biblical literature. All the other narratives involving Moses and the legislation attributed to him are phrased in the third person, and this is generally true of the other historical figures in the Bible. Only the literary prophets speak in the first person, but their biographies tend to retreat behind the transcendental events and messages that are their primary concern. Even apocalyptic and apocryphal literature, although more receptive to the "autobiographical" style, did not follow the model of Deuteronomy. On the contrary, the Temple Scroll recently edited from the finds at Qumran took pains to eliminate all references to Moses and rephrased the Deuteronomic record in third person terms.[3]

The parenetic or hortatory style of Deuteronomy seems, in fact, less at home in Israel than in Greece, where rhetoric first evolved as a fine art in the orations of an Isocrates or a Demosthenes, and where historians like Thucydides and Xenophon sprinkled their narratives with lengthy speeches and exhortations, not, to be sure, claiming to be verbatim transcripts of the original words, but aspiring in an imaginative way to suggest what the protagonists, given their character and the circumstances, might have said on a given occasion. There are, as a result, scholars who would like to see Greek models as inspiring the literary structure and legislative content of the Book of Deuteronomy.[4] In comparative terms, this represents a "minimalist" view. As usual, it is open to challenge.

For in point of fact the style of Deuteronomy is not so much oratorical or autobiographical as pseudo-autobiographical. That is to say, the figure of Moses is presented in such colorless terms that it is clearly no more than a literary device for supporting the thread of injunction and narrative. Only a truly "maximalist" position would take the Mosaic authorship of the book literally. More specifically, the choice of Moses for this literary purpose is evidently dictated by the intention of imparting the highest possible authority to a legislative program by attributing it to the great lawgiver himself. In this respect, the most suggestive literary models are to be found, not in the contemporary west, but in the older Near East.

In Egypt, where every official tended to decorate his tomb with an autobiographical obituary,[5] there early evolved a sophisticated form of fictitious narrative in the first person, the most famous examples being the tales of Sinuhe and Wen-Amon.[6] And in more blatantly pseudepigraphical autobiography, the great leaders of a hoary antiquity are made to speak in texts that are patently of much later date, and pretend to furnish either an eye-witness account of their "own"

---

[2] In the present commentary, chs. 1–4 are treated as a prologue and 5–28 as two separate discourses (5–11 and 12–28, with ch. 27 as an insert).

[3] Baruch A. Levine, "The Temple Scroll," *Bulletin of the American Schools of Oriental Research*, 232 (1978), pp. 5–23. [Hereafter cited as *BASOR*.]

[4] Morton Smith, "East Mediterranean Law Codes of the Early Iron Age," *H. L. Ginsberg Volume* (*Eretz-Israel*, 14, Jerusalem, 1978), pp. 38–43.

[5] See the examples in James B. Pritchard, *Ancient Near Eastern Texts* (3rd ed., Princeton, 1969), pp. 227 f., 230, 233 f., 329 f. [Hereafter cited as Pritchard, *ANET*.]

[6] *Ibid.*, pp. 18–22 and 25–29 respectively.

time or an accurate prophecy of the then future (already past), or both in succession. The tradition of seven lean years is preserved in a Ptolemaic text thus attributed to Pharaoh Djoser of the Old Kingdom.[7]

But the genre is most at home in the literature of Babylonia and Assyria, where the tradition of first person royal inscriptions went back to the beginnings of the second millennium, and easily spawned fictitious royal autobiographies by imitation. The great kings of the Akkad dynasty were cast in this role, notably Sargon and Naram-Sin, but also some less celebrated rulers of the later third and second millennia. The authority of these ancient worthies was presumably invoked in order to enhance the credibility of the texts attributed to them, just as in the case of Deuteronomy.[8]

Deuteronomy as Cult Libretto

But if such pseudo-autobiographies provide a model of sorts for the form and the framework of the book, we must look further for the source of its particular function. The words attributed to Moses in Deuteronomy are addressed by him to the entire people of Israel as it prepared to cross the Jordan into the Promised Land. They therefore assume a definite purpose, a programmatic function. Their intent is to lay down a virtual constitution for the people when they take possession of the land. The Decalogue and some of the laws previously given in the wilderness are repeated or supplemented to the accompaniment of reiterated exhortations of a general requirement to do God's will and a specific new injunction to prepare to centralize the entire cult at a single place of God's choosing.

Such cultic centralization, although "anticipating" the ultimate role of Jerusalem and possible Mesopotamian analogies,[9] also reflects the older realities of Israel's past, the tradition of primary shrines that had united the tribes on the cultic plane ever since the conquest and settlement of the Promised Land, even while they remained largely fragmented on the political plane. Shechem, Shilo, Bethel, and Gilgal appear to have played this role successively in the period of the Judges and Samuel,[10] although recent opinion questions this reconstruction.[11] All of them are located in the central highlands today referred to variously as "Samaria" or the "West Bank" which were then occupied by the "Rachel tribes"—Benjamin, Ephraim, and (half of) Manasseh. They were thus relatively accessible to the more outlying tribes on the coast, in the Galilee, Transjordan, and Judea, but they were clearly in the territory of the later northern kingdom and shared its particular interests.[12]

Such a "northern" bias has been detected also in the theology of Deuteronomy. The conspicuous stress on the love-relationship between God and Israel shows affinities with

[7] *Ibid.*, pp. 31 f.
[8] *Ibid.*, p. 119; cf. A. K. Grayson, *Babylonian Historical-Literary Texts* (Toronto Semitic Texts and Studies, 3, 1975), pp. 7–9.
[9] Weinfeld, "Cult Centralization in Israel in the Light of Neo-Babylonian Analogy," *Journal of Near Eastern Studies*, 23 (1964), pp. 202–212. [Hereafter cited as *JNES*.]
[10] George W. Anderson, "Israelite Amphictyonies," *Translating and Understanding the Old Testament*, ed. H. T. Frank and W. L. Reed (1970), pp. 135–151.
[11] Roland de Vaux, "Was There an Israelite Amphictyony?" *Biblical Archaeology Review*, 3/2 (1977), pp. 40–47. Cf. already Harry M. Orlinsky, "The Tribal System of Israel and Related Groups in the Period of the Judges," *Studies and Essays in Honor of Abraham A. Neuman* (1962), pp. 375–387; reprinted in *Oriens Antiquus*, 1 (1962), pp. 11–20, and in *Essays in Biblical Culture and Biblical Translation* (1974), pp. 66–77. (See there, p. 77, for additional references.)
[12] J. H. Hayes and J. M. Miller, eds., *Israelite and Judaean History* (Philadelphia: The Westminster Press, 1977), pp. 297—308; Jacob Weingreen, "The Theory of the Amphictyony in Pre-Monarchial Israel," *Journal of the Ancient Near Eastern Society*, 5 (1973), pp. 427–434.

the northern prophet Hosea.[13] The outspoken opposition to idolatry reflects, like that of the "Elohistic" or northern source of the Tetrateuch, the greater exposure of the cosmopolitan north to indigenous and foreign polytheistic cults. The use of "place" (māqōm) to identify (any) sacred locale is in marked distinction to the southern "height" (bāmā) in this sense. (In post-biblical Hebrew, "the place" even became a substitute for the divine name.) Above all, the stress on God's name contrasts with the central role of God's glory in the priestly source.[14]

It has therefore been argued that the Book of Deuteronomy reflects an attempt by the prophetic circles in the north to elevate Moses to the status of the first and greatest prophet (cf., e.g., Hosea 12:14; Deut. 18:18), and to picture him as mediator for a cult ceremony at which the covenant was established or renewed. Indeed, Deuteronomy would be the libretto of such a ceremony, while passages such as Joshua 24 would represent shorter synopses together with stage directions.

But even on this uniquely Israelite interpretation of the overall function of the book, essential elements in it owe something to Near Eastern precedent. The amphictyonic principle, named for the classical Greek leagues of Delos, Delphi, etc., has been detected also in King Solomon's provisioning system (I Kings 4:7–19) and at the court of his younger Egyptian contemporary Sheshonq I (the biblical Shishak), though it is debated who copied it from whom;[15] its earliest manifestation may go back to the end of the third millennium in Sumer.[16] The notion of "establishing the name," so central to Deuteronomy, echoes earlier Sumerian, Akkadian, and Phoenician idioms, where it refers to acquiring legitimacy or fame, especially by the king.[17] This analogy suggests that a traditional royal prerogative was here being bestowed on God. And the "place" of God's choosing with which this name is invariably linked in Deuteronomy is similarly evocative of the cult places literally referred to as the "place where the king stands."[18] Thus the conception of Deuteronomy as the text of a periodic cultic renewal of the covenant by the tribes of Israel finds some support in the comparative data.

Deuteronomy as Lawbook

The core of Deuteronomy is formed by its legislation, repeating and supplementing the Covenant Code in Exodus, the Holiness Code in Leviticus, and scattered priestly laws in Numbers. The Greek (and English) name of the whole book, based on the Hebrew of 17:18 (cf. also Joshua 8:32), reflects the central importance of this "repetition of the law" (New Jewish Version: "a copy of this Teaching"). And the phrase "as God commanded/promised/swore," repeated more than thirty times in the text, sounds like a

[13] For other interpretations of the relationship, see William L. Moran, "The Ancient Near Eastern Background of the Love of God in Deuteronomy," *Catholic Biblical Quarterly*, 25 (1963), pp. 77–87; J. W. McKay, "Man's Love of God in Deuteronomy and the Father/Teacher-Son/Pupil Relationship," *Vetus Testamentum*, 22 (1972), pp. 426–435. [Hereafter cited as *VT*.]

[14] E. W. Nicholson, *Deuteronomy and Tradition* (Philadelphia: Fortress Press, 1967); *idem*, "The Centralisation of the Cult in Deuteronomy," *VT*, 13 (1963), pp. 380–389.

[15] D. B. Redford, "Studies in Relations between Palestine and Egypt during the First Millennium B.C. I. The Taxation System of Solomon," *Studies on the Ancient Palestinian World* (Toronto Semitic Texts and Studies, 2, 1972), pp. 141–156. Alberto R. Green, "Israelite Influence at Shishak's Court?" *BASOR*, 233 (1979), pp. 59–62.

[16] William W. Hallo, "A Sumerian Amphictyony," *Journal of Cuneiform Studies*, 14 (1960), pp. 88–114. [Hereafter cited as *JCS*.]

[17] Shalom M. Paul, "Psalm 72:5—A Traditional Blessing for the Long Life of the King," *JNES*, 31 (1972), p. 354.

[18] Richard S. Ellis, "Mountains and Rivers," *Bibliotheca Mesopotamica*, 7 (Malibu, 1977), pp. 29–34.

recurrent footnote, alluding to the previous formulations in the rest of the Pentateuch.[19]

But the "Deuteronomic code" is not only the most crucial portion of the book, it is also the oldest or, more precisely, the portion most explicitly indebted to older models. This is true in the first place of the overall structure of the material. Like the other biblical codes and, more particularly, like their cuneiform antecedents, the Deuteronomic code is encased within a prologue and epilogue, the former largely hortatory in character, the latter prominently featuring catalogues of blessings for compliance and curses for non-compliance with the code. The internal arrangement of the individual laws proceeds generally from the cultic legislation (chs. 12–14) to criminal, civil, and procedural law (15–25), each grouped in broad legal categories which, according to a new interpretation, follow the order of topics in the Decalogue in ch. 5, whose provisions are conspicuously not repeated here.[20]

A similar order (albeit in reverse) and comparable groupings were already imposed on the Laws of Hammurabi by the scholars of his time or a little later.[21] More telling still is the testimony of individual enactments, adduced here by way of illustration only.

At its outset, the code provides for the centralization of the cult, but mitigates the new law by allowing "profane slaughter" outside the central sanctuary (12:21; cf. 12:15) thus maintaining the distinction from sacred slaughter which set Israel apart from its neighbors.[22] The specific prohibition against the consumption of pork (14:8) was based on the unclean character of the pig, not, as elsewhere in the ancient world, on its sacred nature and cultic uses, attested occasionally also by biblical allusions[23] and by bones and artistic representations uncovered by excavations at Palestinian sites which were under Egyptian or Assyrian rule or influence.[24]

The laws of the sabbatical year (ch. 15) elaborate on those of Leviticus 25 and like them represent an essentially Israelite institutionalization of what had at best been vaguely comparable precedents in the Old Babylonian dynasty of Hammurabi.[25] His son Samsu-iluna and his descendant Ammisaduqa promulgated edicts which appear to have provided for remission of certain debts and release of certain debt-slaves, but not at regular intervals.[26]

The judiciary envisaged in Deuteronomy has been compared to the reform of King Jehoshaphat of Judah (ca. 870–850 B.C.E.) as described in II Chronicles 19:4–11 (see commentary to 16:18–20 and 17:8–13). But both enactments, involving priests as well as judges in an elaborate hierarchy, have an analogy of sorts in the Edict of Horemheb (late fourteenth century B.C.E.), last pharaoh of the great Eighteenth Dynasty in Egypt's empire period.[27] The law of the king which follows (17:14–20; cf. I Samuel 8:9, 11; 10:25)

---

[19] J. Milgrom, "Profane Slaughter and the Composition of Deuteronomy," *Hebrew Union College Annual*, 47 (1976), pp. 1–17.

[20] Stephen A. Kaufman, "The Structure of the Deuteronomic Law," *Maarav*, 1 (1979), pp. 105–158.

[21] J. J. Finkelstein, "A Late Old Babylonian Copy of the Law of Hammurapi," *JCS*, 21 (1967), pp. 39–48.

[22] Hallo, "The Concept of Consumption," in essay to Commentary on Leviticus.

[23] J. M. Sasson, "Isaiah LXVI, 3–4a," *VT*, 26 (1976), pp. 199–207.

[24] De Vaux, "The Sacrifice of Pigs in Palestine and in the Ancient Near East," in de Vaux, *The Bible and the Ancient Near East*, translated by D. McHugh (Garden City: Doubleday, 1971), ch. 14, pp. 252–269; Alfred von Rohr Sauer, "The Cultic Role of the Pig in Ancient Times," *In Memoriam Paul Kahle*, ed. Matthew Black and Georg Fohrer (Beiheft zur Zeitschrift für die alttestamentliche Wissenschaft, 103, 1968), pp. 201–207.

[25] Hallo, "The Laws of Sanctification," in essay to Commentary on Leviticus.

[26] Finkelstein, "The Edict of Ammiṣaduqa: A New Text," *Revue d'Assyriologie et d'Archéologie Orientale*, 63 (1969), pp. 45–64. [Hereafter cited as *RA*.]

[27] Kurt Pflüger, "The Edict of King Haremhab," *JNES*, 5 (1946), pp. 260–268.

may similarly have drawn its immediate inspiration from a specific Judean reign, but again its ultimate antecedents have been sought in Canaanite political practice, notably in respect of conscription for military services and public works and of royal control over real and movable property and over the tithing of income.[28]

The issue of "prophetic credentials" is taken up next (18:9–22; cf. already ch. 13) and silhouetted against the multifarious divination techniques encountered among the indigenous populations. Of all these techniques, the most intriguing may be that of interrogating "ghosts and familiar spirits," almost invariably linked together throughout the Hebrew Bible. The translations of these terms sound quite colorless in English, but in the Septuagint they appear as engastrímythos, literally stomach-talker or ventriloquist, and terato-skópos, literally diviner by prodigies or monstrous births, revealing something of their long history still dimly familiar to the Hellenistic world. New evidence, especially in Hittite, suggests that the "ghosts" in question were conjured up out of pits dug in the ground to the accompaniment of elaborate rituals.[29] As for teratoscopy (even if it is a mistranslation in Greek), this practice of divining the future from monstrous deformities encountered (or imagined) at the birth of infants or (more often) of domesticated animals was highly developed in ancient Mesopotamia. Not only were such freak births duly reported to the court, but elaborate cuneiform handbooks systematically interpreted the centuries of observations of such births and the "results" that had attended them.[30]

The cities of refuge (19:1–13) were an essentially unique Israelite innovation. Although the concept of asylum was familiar to the classical world in connection with temples and specifically altars, and the very word asylum comes from the Greek word for "inviolable," yet the notion of whole cities set aside for the purpose (cf. Numbers 35; Joshua 20 f.; I Chronicles 6) was strange to Greek ears and translated with a term borrowed from the language of banishment and exile. In Deuteronomy, where the cities are chosen on the basis of their location and not of their sacred character (as Levitical cities), the contrast with the classical world is even more conspicuous. But there may be a remote precedent in Mesopotamian lore, where the distant forest is described as a city on the one hand and on the other as a place of detention, protection, refuge, or sanctuary.[31]

The cities of refuge were primarily designed to break the traditional chain of blood-vengeance, a motive sometimes attributed also to the legislation regarding unsolved homicide, which is found only in Deuteronomy (21:1–9). The alleged parallels from Nuzi similarly apply the principle of collective liability, but only in cases of burglary or the killing of livestock.[32] Closer precedents are found, rather, in the Hittite laws. Here the earlier version of paragraph 6 provides for compensation to the heir of the victim from the owner of the land on which

[28] I. Mendelsohn, "Samuel's Denunciation of Kingship in the Light of the Akkadian Documents from Ugarit," *BASOR*, 143 (1956), pp. 17–27. Cf. also John Gray, "Canaanite Kingship in Theory and Practice," *VT*, 2 (1952), pp. 193–220.

[29] Harry A. Hoffner, Jr., "Second Millennium Antecedents to the Hebrew 'ôb," *JBL*, 86 (1967), pp. 384–401; idem; "The Hittites and Hurrians," *Peoples of Old Testament Times*, ed. D. J. Wiseman (Oxford, 1973), pp. 197–228; esp. p. 216.

[30] Erle Leichty, *The Omen Series Šumma Izbu* (Texts from Cuneiform Sources, 4, New York, 1970).

[31] Hallo, "Notes from the Babylonian Collection I: Nungal in the Egal," *JCS*, 31 (1979), pp. 161–165.

[32] Cyrus H. Gordon, "An Akkadian Parallel to Deuteronomy 21:1 ff.," *RA*, 33 (1936), pp. 1–6. "Biblical Customs and the Nuzu Tablets," *Biblical Archaeologist*, 3 (1940), pp. 1–12; reprinted in *The Biblical Archaeologist Reader*, 2 (1964), ed. D. N. Freedman and E. F. Campbell, Jr., pp. 21–33.

the body is found. But the later version provides, as in Deuteronomy, for the contingency that it was found in open country between settlements, in which event the nearest settlement (within stated limits) bears the responsibility.[33]

The treatment of female captives (21:10–14) is again unparalleled in the other biblical codes. The Deuteronomic provision directs the woman to shave her hair, clip her nails, and change her garment before entering her new state as wife of her captor. This is in keeping with the symbolic role which hair, nails, and (the fringes of one's) garment play elsewhere in the Bible and in the earlier Near East. They are, in effect, the personality in effigy or in miniature. In Mesopotamia, fingernails or fringes were used to validate a contract (in the absence of a seal),[34] and the hair and fringes to "identify" a witness who reported a dream of ominous significance to the court.[35] Shaving off the peculiar hairdo required of slaves was also an element in the ceremony of manumission.

Deuteronomy condemns as "abhorrent to the Lord" more offenses than any of the other biblical codes, though Proverbs is also familiar with the concept. Abominations, sins, or taboos against this or that deity are common clichés likewise in Sumerian wisdom literature and in Akkadian religious texts.

But, while the taboo concept was thus common to Israelites and Mesopotamians, they had very different notions of what constituted a taboo. In Israel, the very practices most sacred to foreign deities were often regarded as abominations to God. One of the practices condemned in these terms is transvestism, the adoption of clothes of the opposite sex (22:5). This appears to be a direct reaction to an aspect of the cult of the Canaanite goddess Ashtarte and her Mesopotamian equivalents Ishtar and Inanna, or to its more innocent literary and dramatic reflexes ("travesty").[36] Much the same could be said in regard to cultic prostitution (23:18 f.).[37]

Absent such explicit reaction against practices sanctioned or even commanded by Near Eastern usage, much of the specifically Deuteronomic legislation was of a more obviously humanitarian cast, and therefore not "justified" in specific terms. Indeed, it often paralleled traditional Near Eastern usage as documented in literature and records if not specifically in law. This "humanitarianism" extends in the first place to animals, as in the prohibition against yoking of ox and ass together (22:10), not found in the comparable rules about "unnatural mixtures" in Leviticus 19:19, but reminiscent of the proverbial juxtaposition of ox and ass in Sumerian literature (e.g., Lugalbanda Epic, 164 f.). The prohibition against muzzling the threshing oxen was already observed by the early Sumerians according to actual account texts on the one hand (see commentary to 25:4) and the so-called "Farmer's Almanac" on the other; this didactic collection of agricultural lore also seems already to provide for leaving the gleanings of the harvest (cf. 24:19 f.) for the destitute.[38] The prohibition against interest between fellow-Israelites (23:20 f.) seems less a case of xenophobia than of a time-honored practice of waiving interest in cases of "a loan between gentlemen" attested in a four-

---

[33] Pritchard, *ANET*, p. 189; H. A. Hoffner, Jr., "Some Contributions of Hittitology to Old Testament Study," *Tyndale Bulletin*, 20 (1969), pp. 27–55.

[34] Ferris J. Stephens, "The Ancient Significance of Ṣiṣith," *JBL*, 50 (1931), pp. 59–70.

[35] Pritchard, *ANET*, pp. 623–626; 629–632; esp. letters a, b, m, n, p.

[36] W. H. Ph. Römer, "Randbemerkungen zur Travestie von Deut. 22,5," *Studies ... Beek* (Studia Semitica Neerlandica, 16, 1974), pp. 217–222.

[37] E. M. Yamauchi, "Cultic Prostitution," in *Orient and Occident: Essays Presented to Cyrus H. Gordon* (Alter Orient und Altes Testament, Vol. 22, 1973), pp. 213–222.

[38] Samuel N. Kramer, *The Sumerians* (Chicago: The University of Chicago Press, 1963), pp. 296 f., 342.

teenth- or thirteenth-century letter found at Ugarit.[39]

Legislation regarding women is prominent in Deuteronomy, providing additional protection as well as further constraints not found in the comparable provisions of earlier biblical or Near Eastern codes, but sometimes attested as customary law by the testimony of actual court cases. Thus the elaborate protection of the bride against unjustified aspersions on her virginity (22:13–19) is paralleled by a dossier of contracts and litigation regarding just such a case from eighteenth-century Babylonia.[40] The penalty exacted from the wife embroiled with her husband's antagonist (25:11 f.) seems less excessive in light of the clear precedent in the notoriously cruel Assyrian laws as codified about the end of the twelfth century B.C.E., or of the even earlier but less certain parallel alleged from a court case at fifteenth-century Nuzi.[41] Such parallels could be multiplied at will by additional examples.

Deuteronomy as Covenant

Libraries and archives thus furnish a wealth of detail about the customary and statutory law of the ancient Near East, and its preservation and reemergence in the legal formulations of Deuteronomy. But these essentially isolated relics from a remote antiquity cannot serve to date and evaluate the book as such. For this purpose, we must look rather to the peroration of Moses' homily (27–31), which at one time may have concluded the original book. The idea of setting up large stones and coating them with plaster before inscribing them (27:2) is now attested by archeological finds from the eighth century B.C.E. in the northern Sinai[42] and in Transjordan.[43] The latter find also features a long list of curses and assigns a prominent role to Shagar-and-Ishtar as a composite goddess of fertility (and the starry

heavens) which is echoed by the cognate nouns for "offspring" and "calving" in the catalogue of blessings and curses in ch. 28 (4, 18, 51; cf. 7:13).

But the closest connections of this catalogue are with the treaties imposed on their vassals by the Assyrian kings of the first millennium, most notably Esarhaddon (680–669 B.C.E.). In numerous exemplars dated three years before his death, he adjured each of his Iranian vassals to fealty to himself and, after his demise, to his designated successor, on pain of suffering a lengthy succession of fearsome curses.[44] Some of these curses occur in virtually identical form and even in the same order in Deuteronomy.[45] And the efficacy of such curses was described in what has been aptly termed "one of the most striking parallels . . . between cuneiform and biblical literature in any period."[46]

When it is remembered that the entire reign of Esarhaddon fell within the long reign of Manasseh; that this ruler was (by necessity if not by choice)[47] a particularly loyal vassal

[39] Pritchard, ANET, p. 629.
[40] Hallo, "The Slandered Bride," Studies Presented to A. Leo Oppenheim (Chicago, 1964), pp. 95–105.
[41] Pritchard, ANET, p. 181, 8; Gordon, "A New Akkadian Parallel to Deuteronomy 25:11–12," The Journal of the Palestine Oriental Society, 15 (1935), pp. 29–34.
[42] Ze'ev Meshel and Carol Meyers, "The Name of God in the Wilderness of Zin," Biblical Archaeologist 39 (1976), pp. 6–10; Meshel, "Did Yahweh Have a Consort? The New Religious Inscriptions from the Sinai," Biblical Archaeology Review, 5/2 (1979), pp. 24–35.
[43] Jacob Hoftijzer, "The Prophet Balaam in a 6th-Century [sic] Aramaic Inscription," Biblical Archaeologist, 39 (1976), pp. 11–17; cf. B. A. Levine, "The Deir ʿAlla Plaster Inscriptions" (in press).
[44] Pritchard, ANET, pp. 534, 541. See also Gleanings to ch. 28.
[45] Weinfeld, "Traces of Assyrian Treaty Formulae in Deuteronomy," Biblica, 46 (1965), pp. 417–427; R. Frankena, "The Vassal-Treaties of Esarhaddon and the Dating of Deuteronomy," Oudtestamentische Studiën, 14 (1965), pp. 122–154.
[46] Moran, op. cit., p. 83, referring to the Annals of Assurbanipal (ANET, p. 300, lines 11–16) compared with Deut. 29:23–25.
[47] Carl D. Evans, "Judah's Foreign Policy from Heze-

of Assyria; and that the Assyrians concluded vassal treaties with their western neighbors not unlike those preserved for their vassals on the eastern frontier[48]—then it is tempting to conclude that the kingdom of Judah became only too familiar, under Manasseh, with the form of such treaties. What the anti-Assyrian party did, on this assumption, was to employ this form to declare Judah's independence of Assyria and its allegiance to God.

This interpretation of matters holds good whether the form was original to Assyria or to some antecedent Syrian tradition, and whether the declaration was drafted under Hezekiah or Manasseh or Josiah, as variously proposed. But it fits best the situation in Josiah's eighteenth year when the "book of the law" was discovered in the Temple (II Kings 22–23). For by then Assyria was in retreat; Judah had recovered much of the territory of the old northern kingdom; and Josiah was ready to apply a "pattern of usurpation" known as early as Old Babylonian times in Mesopotamia that included, among other steps, shifting allegiance from a foreign king to the deity of one's own nation or city.[49] The same device was still employed in Maccabean times in Israel and in Renaissance times in Europe.[50]

Deuteronomy as History

The original core of Deuteronomy can thus be defined by its literary affinities to external models, but that core was successively embedded in larger biblical contexts by the editorial addition of the miscellaneous appendices that now conclude the book. Of these the earliest may well have been the notice of Joshua's appointment to succeed Moses (31:14 f.) followed, first in prose (vv. 16–30) and then in poetry (ch. 32), by classic formulations of the Deuteronomistic view of history: that adherence to the covenant promises national weal, while apostasy ensures disaster. This doctrine reflects a cyclical view of history which far antedates Deuteronomy, and in which periods of prosperity and disaster follow each other in inevitable succession, often in consequence of the cultic piety displayed or, on the contrary, withheld by a given king with respect to a particular deity or shrine. Where Deuteronomy differed was in extending the obligations from the exclusively cultic sphere to the whole realm of legal and ethical norms, and from the sole figure of the king to the nation as a whole.

Deuteronomy's doctrine of collective responsibility so thoroughly informed the historical books that follow it in the canon (Joshua through Kings) that it is reasonable to reconstruct a stage when they were editorially linked together by the passages in question. If so, however, the link was broken again by the insertion of the blessing of Moses (ch. 33), an ancient poem that may have been designed to parallel the equally ancient poem at the end of Genesis (Gen. 49) and thus to confer on Deuteronomy the same kind of literary and religious status that Genesis already enjoyed. The notice of Moses' death (ch. 34) probably originally belonged at the end of Numbers as the conclusion of a "triteuch" consisting of Exodus-Leviticus-Numbers or of a "tetrateuch" running from Genesis to Numbers. Its removal to the end of Deuteronomy allowed that book to serve as the conclusion of the

kiah to Josiah," in *Scripture in Context: Essays on the Comparative Method*, ed. Evans, Hallo, and John B. White (Pittsburgh Theological Monograph Series 34, 1980), pp. 157–178.

[48] Cf. *ANET*, pp. 532–534.

[49] Hallo and William K. Simpson, *The Ancient Near East: A History* (New York: Harcourt Brace Jovanovich, Inc., 1971), pp. 86 f. and n. 48.

[50] Marco Treves, "The Reign of God in the Old Testament," *VT*, 19 (1969), pp. 230–243.

biography of Moses and, ultimately, of the whole Pentateuch.

The successive stages of literary history which eventually produced the Book of Deuteronomy can thus be reconstructed with some degree of probability. Each of them reveals formal and functional ties to the literature of the surrounding Near East, and each adds new dimensions that together lend the book its distinctive character.

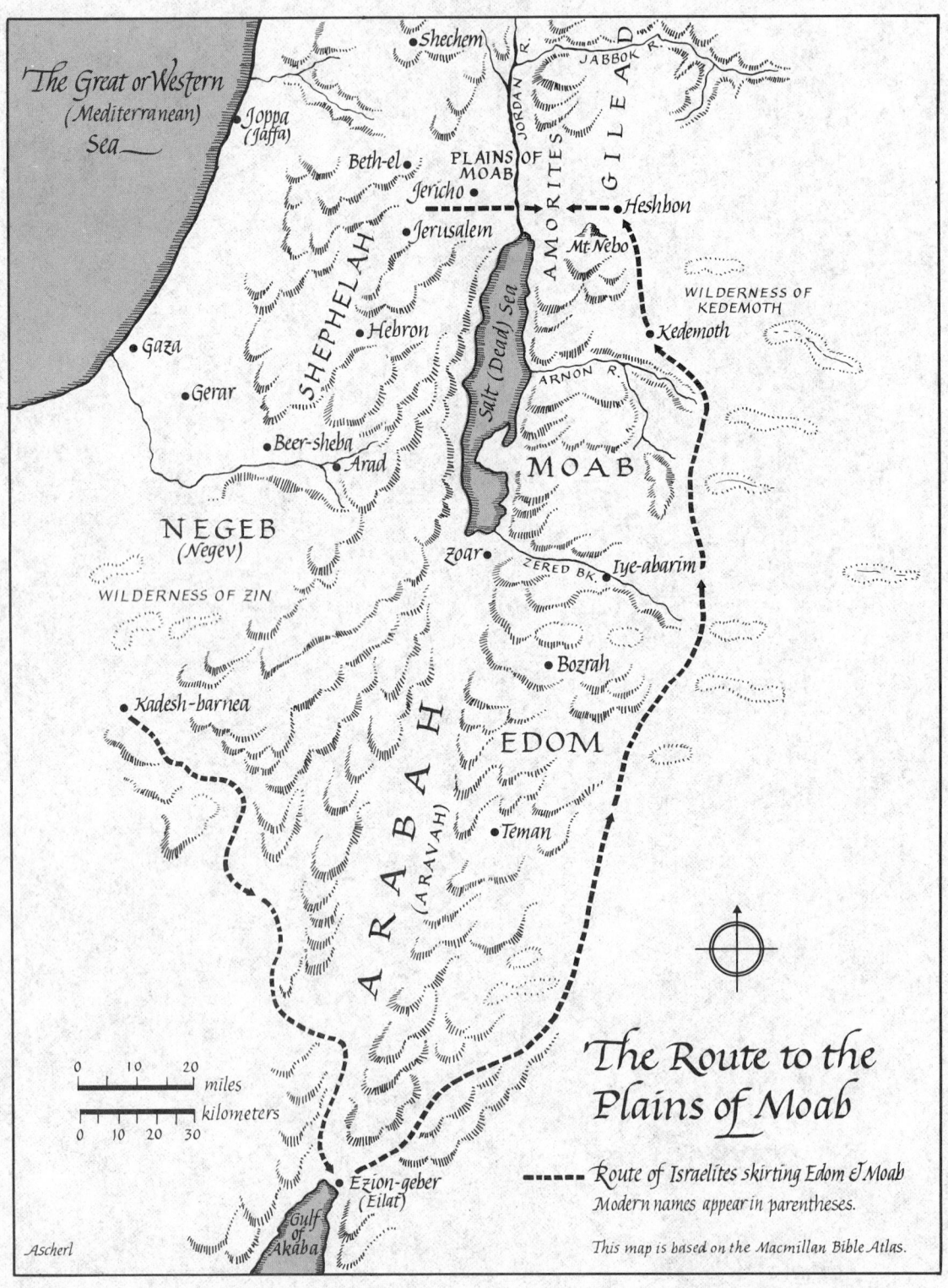

The Great or Western
(Mediterranean)
Sea

•Shechem

JORDAN R.

JABBOK R.

GILEAD

•Joppa
(Jaffa)

Beth-el•

PLAINS OF
MOAB

•Jericho

Jerusalem•

AMORITES

•Heshbon

Mt. Nebo

SHEPHELAH

•Gaza

•Gerar

Hebron•

Salt (Dead) Sea

WILDERNESS OF
KEDEMOTH

•Kedemoth

ARNON R.

•Beer-sheba

•Arad

MOAB

NEGEB
(Negev)

WILDERNESS OF ZIN

Zoar•

ZERED BK.

•Iye-abarim

•Bozrah

•Kadesh-barnea

EDOM

ARABAH
(ARAVAH)

•Teman

The Route to the
Plains of Moab

Ezion-geber•
(Eilat)

– – – – Route of Israelites skirting Edom & Moab
Modern names appear in parentheses.

Gulf
or
Akaba

This map is based on the Macmillan Bible Atlas.

Ascherl

0   10   20 miles

0 10 20 30 kilometers

PART I

Prologue

FIRST DISCOURSE

The prologue to Deuteronomy (Chapters 1–4:43) prepares the stage for the instructions, laws, warnings, blessings, and curses that Moses delivers to the Children of Israel. It is set in the time immediately preceding his death; the place where he delivers them is the plateau of Moab, east of Jericho, across the Jordan River (see map).

The prologue recalls the historical preambles of certain ancient Near Eastern treaties.* It can be conveniently divided into four parts: (1) recounting time and place (1:1–5); (2) first review of Israel's wanderings in the desert and God's unceasing care (1:6–45); (3) continued review and Moses' own part in the people's unfolding history (1:46–3:29); (4) summation (4:1–43).

Most of the content of the prologue represents a recounting of events well known to the readers of Exodus, Leviticus, and especially Numbers, and both the similarities and the differences in these accounts have a bearing on how one may judge the origin and composition of the Book of Deuteronomy as a whole (see "Introducing Deuteronomy").

The prologue states at once that what follows was spoken by Moses. This commentary takes the view (discussed earlier, see introduction) that, while Mosaic traditions may be at the core of the book, the text itself was composed many centuries later. Both prologue and epilogue were written from a post-Mosaic and cis-Jordanian point of view. But by the time they were set down the name and figure of Moses were firmly identified with the events described and the laws bearing his name were believed to have originated with God. These ascriptions developed their own dynamics and in time became sacred history which had a decisive effect on the minds and hearts of subsequent generations.

---

* These treaties—like those made by Assyrian King Esarhaddon in 672 B.C.E.—specify the parties to the treaty; the past benefits bestowed by the suzerain and his rights to exclusive loyalty and obedience; and finally the blessings which arise from compliance as well as the consequences which will follow any noncompliance. The basis of Deuteronomy is the treaty-covenant between God and Israel, upon whom He lavishes His protective love. Israel's faithfulness to the covenant will assure this protection in perpetuity [1]. (See also W. W. Hallo's essay above.)

The Setting

The introductory section provides the setting; like the rest of the prologue it reveals little of the thrust and fervor of the later chapters of
Deuteronomy.* A matter-of-fact recital plays down the high emotions,
the triumphs, and tragedies of Israel's past. Only later on will the text
move from this low-keyed historical review to an ever-greater intensity
of rhetoric.

(The weekly portion, *Devarim*, begins here.)

---

* This suggests that the entire introductory portion of Deuteronomy (chapters 1–4)
   is from a tradition other than that which produced the book's main portion.

בְּאַרְבָּעִים שָׁנָה בְּעַשְׁתֵּי־עָשָׂר חֹדֶשׁ בְּאֶחָד לַחֹדֶשׁ   אֵלֶּה הַדְּבָרִים אֲשֶׁר דִּבֶּר מֹשֶׁה אֶל־כָּל־יִשְׂרָאֵל   א

דִּבֶּר מֹשֶׁה אֶל־בְּנֵי יִשְׂרָאֵל כְּכֹל אֲשֶׁר צִוָּה יְהֹוָה   בְּעֵבֶר הַיַּרְדֵּן בַּמִּדְבָּר בָּעֲרָבָה מוֹל סוּף בֵּין־פָּארָן

אֹתוֹ אֲלֵהֶם: אַחֲרֵי הַכֹּתוֹ אֵת סִיחֹן מֶלֶךְ הָאֱמֹרִי   ד   וּבֵין־תֹּפֶל וְלָבָן וַחֲצֵרֹת וְדִי זָהָב: אַחַד עָשָׂר יוֹם   ב

אֲשֶׁר יוֹשֵׁב בְּחֶשְׁבּוֹן וְאֵת עוֹג מֶלֶךְ הַבָּשָׁן אֲשֶׁר־יוֹשֵׁב   מֵחֹרֵב דֶּרֶךְ הַר־שֵׂעִיר עַד קָדֵשׁ בַּרְנֵעַ: וַיְהִי   ג

1] These are the words that Moses addressed to all Israel on the other side of the Jordan.— Through the wilderness, in the Arabah near Suph, between Paran and Tophel, Laban, Hazeroth, and Di-zahab,   **2]** it is eleven days from Horeb to Kadesh-barnea by the Mount Seir route.—   **3]** It was in the fortieth year, on the first day of the eleventh month, that Moses addressed the Israelites in accordance with the instructions that the LORD had given him for them,   **4]** after he had defeated Sihon king of the Amorites who dwelt in Heshbon, and Og

1:1] *Words.* דְּבָרִים (*devarim*), here in the broad sense of "discourse" and referring to the whole book.

On the other side of the Jordan. The Hebrew בְּעֵבֶר has a more general meaning: "The region by the Jordan" [1].

Arabah. (Aravah) The depression that runs from Lake Kinneret to the Gulf of Akaba. In the Torah, as in modern Israel, the name is attached only to the valley south of the Dead Sea.

Near Suph. The geographical references that follow are difficult to identify. Thus Suph means "reed," but most likely there were no reeds in Moab where verse 5 places the speaker; similarly, Hazeroth is known to us as a place in the Sinai peninsula only (see Num. 33:17); and the otherwise unknown Di-zahab might mean a place where gold (*zahav*) was found, except that we have no records of gold finds in the area.

The Midrash suggests that the place names were symbolic expressions. For instance, Di-zahab was seen to refer to the place where Israel sinned with the golden calf [2].

2] *Eleven days . . . by the Mount Seir route.* If Mount Horeb (Sinai) is today's Jebel Musa, a journey of eleven days' travel by foot would traverse 160 miles (256 km) to Kadesh-barnea; while a route via Seir (east of the Aravah) would consume more time. The mountain where the covenant was proclaimed is usually called Horeb in Deuteronomy and in the source called E; while in J and P its name is Sinai (see our Commentary on Exodus).

Malbim interprets "eleven days" to mean the time it took Moses to deliver his message at the places mentioned.

Kadesh-barnea. Excavations suggest that in all likelihood it lay some 50 miles (80 km) south of Beer-sheba. It was the Israelites' headquarters for most of their forty years of wandering.

3] *Eleventh month.* Shevat, counting from the spring season, i.e., the month of Nisan.

4] *Sihon king of the Amorites.* See the story told in Num. 21:21–31. Amorites here refers to an ethnic group that inhabited Transjordan. See also verse 6.

Heshbon. East of Jericho.

Og king of Bashan. See Num. 21:33 ff. Bashan is the area northeast of Lake Kinneret and north of the Yarmuk River.

Ashtaroth (and) Edrei. The Hebrew text does not contain the word "and," but that two different places were meant is clear from Josh. 12:4; 13:12, 31. Ashtaroth can be identified with today's Tel Ashtarah, 15 miles north of Der'a, which is 30 miles east of Lake Kinneret.

ה בְּעַשְׁתָּרֹת בְּאֶדְרֶעִי: בְּעֵבֶר הַיַּרְדֵּן בְּאֶרֶץ מוֹאָב   הוֹאִיל מֹשֶׁה בֵּאֵר אֶת־הַתּוֹרָה הַזֹּאת לֵאמֹר:

king of Bashan who dwelt at Ashtaroth [and] Edrei.   **5]** On the other side of the Jordan, in the
land of Moab, Moses undertook to expound this Teaching. He said:

5] *Moab.* The land east of the Dead Sea.

Moses undertook. The Hebrew הוֹאִיל has the
connotation of doing it gladly, or eagerly.

This Teaching. תּוֹרָה (*torah*) has a number of
meanings. It can (especially in the plural, *torot*)
describe a set of laws; here it most likely refers to

the whole Book of Deuteronomy.

Today the most frequent meaning is the Pentateuch, i.e., the Five Books of Moses; and finally
Torah (without the article) refers to the entire
body of Jewish law and lore.

These Are the Words

In its earliest days, Torah represented essentially an oral tradition. Even after it was committed to writing, the majority of the people were not literate and therefore received the tradition primarily through the spoken word. To them, words indicated the beginning of God's creative process—"God said, 'Let there be light,' and there was light"—and the Ten Words proclaimed at Sinai were understood as a direct continuation of this process: even as words were instrumental in the world's creation, so were they in the creation and perfection of the Creator's people. And since the words that Moses had spoken (or was believed to have spoken) were taken to be a resonance of the divine will, those who transmitted them made certain that they would be preserved as accurately as possible. Even when new and revolutionary ideas were introduced in these traditions [3] the old words were carefully guarded. This led frequently to textual contradictions, but in time these were considered as merely apparent, not real, for Deuteronomy and all of the Torah were seen as the single emanation of the divine mind. A proper understanding would therefore explain any perceived inconsistencies.

There were other variations as well, which were entirely due to the problems of physical transmission and which led to textual discrepancies, so that even after the words were fixed in written form different manuscripts testified to different oral traditions. The Torah scrolls which nowadays are entirely uniform in content are based on the prescriptions of the so-called Masoretes ("transmitters"), who flourished in Palestine in the eighth to tenth centuries C.E., and whose rules as to what constituted the best tradition became accepted among Jews.[1] On the whole, it is remarkable how faithfully all sacred texts were preserved, and this was especially true of the most sacred of all, the Torah. Great and loving care was lavished on transmitting it faithfully, and we may assume that a similar degree of faithfulness was brought to bear on its earlier, oral transmission.

In the introduction above, the problem of the origin and the historic context of Deuteronomy were discussed at some length. Whatever was the content of the book found by King Josiah, we may be certain that much of the manuscript was based on oral traditions which reached back into earlier times. The history of Judaism, and especially of its beginnings, was bound up in words spoken and heard, expressed and interpreted, and the capacity to hear and understand was the essential counterpart of speech. Characteristically, the *Shema* ("Hear, O Israel! The Lord is our God, the Lord alone." Deut. 6:4) became a central expression of Israel's faith. Thus, when the Book of Deuteronomy opens with the phrase "These are the words," it places the human ability to formulate moral concepts and to heed their command at the head of the message that Moses delivered to his people.

---

[1] Since by that time Christianity was already launched on its own independent course, Christian manuscripts and translations were based on Hebrew sources which occasionally differed to some degree (though generally not in a significant manner) from the norm established later by the Masoretes.

GLEANINGS

All

We are told that Moses addressed his words to "all Israel" (verse 1). How could he address so large a multitude and be heard?

A traditional view held that a miracle made this possible (similar to the way Judah's voice was said to have carried through all Egypt when he spoke in behalf of Benjamin) [4]. But another commentator, calling our attention to the fact that "all Israel" frequently occurs in Deuteronomy, notes especially 31:11–12, where the preceding verses describe "all Israel" to consist of Joshua, the elders, and the priests, i.e., the notables who bore responsibility for the people. It was these whom Moses addressed.

SOLOMON EPHRAIM LENCICZ [5]

These

The opening word of Deuteronomy is אֵלֶּה (eleh, these). By way of gematria,[2] אלה adds up to 36. Tradition has it that the world is sustained by thirty-six righteous persons,[3] even as it is sustained by "these" words of Torah.

ITTURE TORAH [7]

Bees

דְּבָרִים (devarim, words) may be vocalized to read דְּבֹרִים (devorim, bees). Just as bee's honey is sweet and its sting sharp, so are the words of Torah.　　　MIDRASH [8]

Before and After

When Moses was younger he thought of himself as a man of few words (Exod. 4:10), but after he had received the Torah he changed and spoke about it often and at length.　　MIDRASH [9]

Reproof

(Deuteronomy contains many words of reproof which were repeated frequently in various ways.) Moses spoke as he did because he knew himself to be near death, for otherwise a leader ought not to reprove and reprove again and again.

RASHI

(When a preacher was reminded of Rashi's comment he replied: When I preach I feel as if each day is my dying day.) [10]

Moses, the friend of Israel, rebuked the people, while Balaam, the enemy of Israel, blessed the people (Num., chs. 22–24). Thus the authenticity of both was beyond question.　　MIDRASH [11]

Twice and Once

Twice we are told that Moses *reiterated* the substance of the Torah ("These are the words," verse 1; "Moses addressed . . . ," verse 3), and once that he *explained* the teaching (verse 5). In this you may find a hint of the traditional prescription to prepare oneself for the reading of the text of the weekly scriptural portion by studying it twice in the original Hebrew and once in the Aramaic exposition (called Targum).

CHASIDIC [12]

Moses and Elijah

It says that "Moses undertook to expound" (verse 5). One can rearrange the letters הוֹאִיל (undertook) to read אליהו (Elijah). In time to come, Elijah, the forerunner of the Messiah, will explain difficult questions left unexpounded by Moses.　　　CHASIDIC [13]

---

[2] A Hebrew term derived from the Greek and related by some to our "geometry" but more likely from *grammateiae*, "script," rather than *ge*, "earth," and *metria*, "measurement" [6]. It describes a method which connects a word with the numerical value of its letters. Thus אלה equals 36 (א=1, ל=30, ה=5).

[3] In the Hebrew system of writing numbers, 36 is ל"ו (lamed-vav); hence the thirty-six righteous are called "lamed-vavniks."

First Review

Moses prefaces his exposition of the Torah by recollecting the history of Israel during the forty years in the wilderness. In this review he includes his own role, especially his inability to enter the Promised Land. Along with the generation already dead, he bears the sting of God's displeasure and stern judgment.

In addressing Israel, Moses says "you" both to those in his hearing who will be allowed to cross over into Canaan and also to those who already perished in the desert. For in his view, what happened to the fathers is an integral part of the children's fate; the obligations of Sinai undertaken by the forebears are binding upon their descendants. Moses will express this thought later on more succinctly: "I make this covenant, with its sanctions, not with you alone, but both with those who are standing here with us this day before the Lord our God and with those who are not with us here this day," that is, with those not yet born (29:13-14). This chronological continuum, combined with the idea of collective, national responsibility for the covenant, is the framework upon which Deuteronomy rests (see further below).

It should be noted that, although the sin of idolatry is prominently mentioned in later chapters, here in the prologue it is the sin of losing faith which Moses singles out. In his review of the wanderings this failure is the target of his critique, one which is constantly before his mind, for he too shares its consequences.

יְהוָ֧ה אֱלֹהֵ֛ינוּ דִּבֶּ֥ר אֵלֵ֖ינוּ בְּחֹרֵ֣ב לֵאמֹ֑ר רַב־לָכֶ֥ם ו
שֶׁ֖בֶת בָּהָ֥ר הַזֶּֽה: פְּנ֣וּ וּסְע֣וּ לָכֶ֗ם וּבֹ֜אוּ הַ֣ר הָאֱמֹרִי֮ ז
וְאֶל־כָּל־שְׁכֵנָיו֒ בָּעֲרָבָ֥ה בָהָ֛ר וּבַשְּׁפֵלָ֥ה וּבַנֶּ֖גֶב וּבְח֣וֹף
הַיָּ֑ם אֶ֤רֶץ הַֽכְּנַעֲנִי֙ וְהַלְּבָנ֔וֹן עַד־הַנָּהָ֥ר הַגָּדֹ֖ל נְהַר־
פְּרָֽת: רְאֵ֛ה נָתַ֥תִּי לִפְנֵיכֶ֖ם אֶת־הָאָ֑רֶץ בֹּ֚אוּ וּרְשׁ֣וּ ח
אֶת־הָאָ֗רֶץ אֲשֶׁ֨ר נִשְׁבַּ֤ע יְהוָה֙ לַאֲבֹֽתֵיכֶ֔ם לְאַבְרָהָ֥ם
לְיִצְחָ֖ק וּֽלְיַעֲקֹ֑ב לָתֵ֣ת לָהֶ֔ם וּלְזַרְעָ֖ם אַחֲרֵיהֶֽם:
וָאֹמַ֣ר אֲלֵכֶ֔ם בָּעֵ֥ת הַהִ֖וא לֵאמֹ֑ר לֹא־אוּכַ֥ל לְבַדִּ֖י ט
שְׂאֵ֥ת אֶתְכֶֽם: יְהוָ֥ה אֱלֹהֵיכֶ֖ם הִרְבָּ֣ה אֶתְכֶ֑ם וְהִנְּכֶ֣ם י

הַיּ֔וֹם כְּכוֹכְבֵ֥י הַשָּׁמַ֖יִם לָרֹֽב: יְהוָ֞ה אֱלֹהֵ֣י אֲבֽוֹתֵכֶ֗ם יא
יֹסֵ֧ף עֲלֵיכֶ֛ם כָּכֶ֖ם אֶ֣לֶף פְּעָמִ֑ים וִיבָרֵ֣ךְ אֶתְכֶ֔ם
כַּאֲשֶׁ֖ר דִּבֶּ֥ר לָכֶֽם: אֵיכָ֥ה אֶשָּׂ֖א לְבַדִּ֑י טָרְחֲכֶ֥ם יב
וּמַֽשַּׁאֲכֶ֖ם וְרִֽיבְכֶֽם: הָב֣וּ לָ֠כֶם אֲנָשִׁ֨ים חֲכָמִ֧ים וּנְבֹנִ֛ים יג
וִֽידֻעִ֖ים לְשִׁבְטֵיכֶ֑ם וַאֲשִׂימֵ֖ם בְּרָאשֵׁיכֶֽם: וַתַּעֲנ֖וּ אֹתִ֑י יד
וַתֹּ֣אמְר֔וּ טֽוֹב־הַדָּבָ֥ר אֲשֶׁר־דִּבַּ֖רְתָּ לַעֲשֽׂוֹת: וָאֶקַּ֞ח טו
אֶת־רָאשֵׁ֣י שִׁבְטֵיכֶ֗ם אֲנָשִׁ֤ים חֲכָמִים֙ וִֽידֻעִ֔ים וָאֶתֵּ֥ן
אֹתָ֖ם רָאשִׁ֣ים עֲלֵיכֶ֑ם שָׂרֵ֨י אֲלָפִ֜ים וְשָׂרֵ֣י מֵא֗וֹת
וְשָׂרֵ֤י חֲמִשִּׁים֙ וְשָׂרֵ֣י עֲשָׂרֹ֔ת וְשֹׁטְרִ֖ים לְשִׁבְטֵיכֶֽם:

6] The LORD our God spoke to us at Horeb, saying: You have stayed long enough at this mountain. **7]** Start out and make your way to the hill country of the Amorites and to all their neighbors in the Arabah, the hill country, the Shephelah, the Negeb, the seacoast, the land of the Canaanites, and the Lebanon, as far as the Great River, the river Euphrates. **8]** See, I place the land at your disposal. Go, take possession of the land that the LORD swore to your fathers, Abraham, Isaac, and Jacob, to give to them and to their offspring after them.

9] Thereupon I said to you, "I cannot bear the burden of you by myself. **10]** The LORD your God has multiplied you until you are today as numerous as the stars in the sky.— **11]** May the LORD, the God of your fathers, increase your numbers a thousandfold, and bless you as He promised you.— **12]** How can I bear unaided the trouble of you, and the burden, and the bickering! **13]** Pick from each of your tribes men who are wise, discerning, and experienced, and I will appoint them as your heads." **14]** You answered me and said, "What you propose to do is good." **15]** So I took your tribal leaders, wise and experienced men, and appointed them heads over you: chiefs of thousands, chiefs of hundreds, chiefs of fifties, and

1:6] *The Lord our God.* The combination of God's personal name (YHVH) and the generic appellation (Elohim) occurs frequently in Deuteronomy. About the meaning of YHVH, see at Exod. 6; on Elohim, see at Exod. 3 and Gen. 2.

7] *Hill country of the Amorites.* In Assyrian sources, the areas of Syria and Palestine appear as lands of the Amorites; in Deuteronomy the term is more restricted. See verse 4.

Shephelah. "Lowlands," the western foothills of the Judean mountains. The cities in this area are listed in Josh. 15:33–44.

Negeb. נֶגֶב (Negev), the southland; today the term covers the area from Beer-sheba to Eilat.

Euphrates. The text has in mind the territory occupied in Solomonic days. See further at 11:24.

8] *See.* The word is frequently employed in Deuteronomy as an introduction; it begins the *sidrah* רְאֵה (11:26). Compare the English "Look here...."

Swore to your fathers. Abraham, Isaac, and Jacob (see Gen. 15:18; 26:3 f.; 28:13 f.).

9] *Thereupon.* In another tradition, what is related here took place before the revelation at Sinai, and at the advice of Jethro (Exod. 18).

11] *May the Lord ...* An interjection; similar to expressions like "My father, may he rest in peace," or "... may he live to 120 years."

13] *Pick.* In this version the people—not, as recorded in Numbers, God or Moses—chose the spies.

Experienced. Or, "known to you (for their ability)" [1].

טו וָאֲצַוֶּה אֶת־שֹׁפְטֵיכֶם בָּעֵת הַהִוא לֵאמֹר שָׁמֹעַ בֵּין
אֲחֵיכֶם וּשְׁפַטְתֶּם צֶדֶק בֵּין־אִישׁ וּבֵין־אָחִיו וּבֵין גֵּרוֹ:
טז לֹא־תַכִּירוּ פָנִים בַּמִּשְׁפָּט כַּקָּטֹן כַּגָּדֹל תִּשְׁמָעוּן לֹא
תָגוּרוּ מִפְּנֵי־אִישׁ כִּי הַמִּשְׁפָּט לֵאלֹהִים הוּא וְהַדָּבָר
יז אֲשֶׁר יִקְשֶׁה מִכֶּם תַּקְרִבוּן אֵלַי וּשְׁמַעְתִּיו: וָאֲצַוֶּה
אֶתְכֶם בָּעֵת הַהִוא אֵת כָּל־הַדְּבָרִים אֲשֶׁר תַּעֲשׂוּן:
יט וַנִּסַּע מֵחֹרֵב וַנֵּלֶךְ אֵת כָּל־הַמִּדְבָּר הַגָּדוֹל וְהַנּוֹרָא
הַהוּא אֲשֶׁר רְאִיתֶם דֶּרֶךְ הַר הָאֱמֹרִי כַּאֲשֶׁר צִוָּה

כ יְהֹוָה אֱלֹהֵינוּ אֹתָנוּ וַנָּבֹא עַד קָדֵשׁ בַּרְנֵעַ: וָאֹמַר
אֲלֵכֶם בָּאתֶם עַד־הַר הָאֱמֹרִי אֲשֶׁר־יְהֹוָה אֱלֹהֵינוּ
כא נֹתֵן לָנוּ: רְאֵה נָתַן יְהֹוָה אֱלֹהֶיךָ לְפָנֶיךָ אֶת־הָאָרֶץ
עֲלֵה רֵשׁ כַּאֲשֶׁר דִּבֶּר יְהֹוָה אֱלֹהֵי אֲבֹתֶיךָ לָךְ
כב אַל־תִּירָא וְאַל־תֵּחָת: וַתִּקְרְבוּן אֵלַי כֻּלְּכֶם וַתֹּאמְרוּ
נִשְׁלְחָה אֲנָשִׁים לְפָנֵינוּ וְיַחְפְּרוּ־לָנוּ אֶת־הָאָרֶץ
וְיָשִׁבוּ אֹתָנוּ דָּבָר אֶת־הַדֶּרֶךְ אֲשֶׁר נַעֲלֶה־בָּהּ וְאֵת
כג הֶעָרִים אֲשֶׁר נָבֹא אֲלֵיהֶן: וַיִּיטַב בְּעֵינַי הַדָּבָר

chiefs of tens, and officials for your tribes.   **16]** I further charged your magistrates as follows, "Hear out your fellow men, and decide justly between any man and a fellow Israelite or a stranger.   **17]** You shall not be partial in judgment: hear out low and high alike. Fear no man, for judgment is God's. And any matter that is too difficult for you, you shall bring to me and I will hear it."   **18]** Thus I instructed you, at that time, about the various things that you should do.

    19] We set out from Horeb and traveled the great and terrible wilderness that you saw, along the road to the hill country of the Amorites, as the LORD our God had commanded us. When we reached Kadesh-barnea,   **20]** I said to you, "You have come to the hill country of the Amorites which the LORD our God is giving to us.   **21]** See, the LORD your God has placed the land at your disposal. Go up, take possession, as the LORD, the God of your fathers, promised you. Fear not and be not dismayed."

    22] Then all of you came to me and said, "Let us send men ahead to reconnoiter the land for us and bring back word on the route we shall follow and the cities we shall come to."   **23]** I

16] *Magistrates.* Rendered "judges" in the biblical Book of Judges. No special responsibility for them was recorded in Exodus, where they were treated like other officials. On the other hand, the Exodus account (18:13 ff.) gives the credit for instituting the judicial system to Jethro, Moses' father-in-law, while the Deuteronomic version overlooks Jethro. Verses 16 and 17 establish basic principles of justice based on complete equality.

    Hear out. From this the Talmud derived the rule that a judge should not listen to one party before the other one has arrived [2].

17] *Low and high alike.* Lower and upper classes are to be treated without distinction. Another un-

derstanding: Give equal attention to all cases, whether involving small or large amounts [3].

    Fear no man. When truth is at stake.

19] *Kadesh-barnea.* See at 1:2.

21] *See.* The Hebrew here changes from plural to singular, a stylistic device frequent in the book.

22] *You came to me.* In Num. 13 the initiative was God's, and the fault lay in part with the spies who discouraged the people, while here the people alone are to blame.

  Hoffmann reconciles the differences by seeing Moses in Numbers as a historian and in Deuteronomy as a moralist.

וָאֶקַּח מִכֶּם שְׁנֵים עָשָׂר אֲנָשִׁים אִישׁ אֶחָד לַשָּׁבֶט:

כד וַיִּפְנוּ וַיַּעֲלוּ הָהָרָה וַיָּבֹאוּ עַד־נַחַל אֶשְׁכֹּל וַיְרַגְּלוּ

כה אֹתָהּ: וַיִּקְחוּ בְיָדָם מִפְּרִי הָאָרֶץ וַיּוֹרִדוּ אֵלֵינוּ וַיָּשִׁבוּ אֹתָנוּ דָבָר וַיֹּאמְרוּ טוֹבָה הָאָרֶץ אֲשֶׁר־יְהוָה

כו אֱלֹהֵינוּ נֹתֵן לָנוּ: וְלֹא אֲבִיתֶם לַעֲלֹת וַתַּמְרוּ אֶת־

כז פִּי יְהוָה אֱלֹהֵיכֶם: וַתֵּרָגְנוּ בְאָהֳלֵיכֶם וַתֹּאמְרוּ בְּשִׂנְאַת יְהוָה אֹתָנוּ הוֹצִיאָנוּ מֵאֶרֶץ מִצְרָיִם לָתֵת

כח אֹתָנוּ בְּיַד הָאֱמֹרִי לְהַשְׁמִידֵנוּ: אָנָה אֲנַחְנוּ עֹלִים אַחֵינוּ הֵמַסּוּ אֶת־לְבָבֵנוּ לֵאמֹר עַם גָּדוֹל וָרָם מִמֶּנּוּ עָרִים גְּדֹלֹת וּבְצוּרֹת בַּשָּׁמָיִם וְגַם־בְּנֵי עֲנָקִים רָאִינוּ

* כח פלרע

כט שָׁם: וָאֹמַר אֲלֵכֶם לֹא־תַעַרְצוּן וְלֹא־תִירְאוּן מֵהֶם:

ל יְהוָה אֱלֹהֵיכֶם הַהֹלֵךְ לִפְנֵיכֶם הוּא יִלָּחֵם לָכֶם

לא כְּכֹל אֲשֶׁר עָשָׂה אִתְּכֶם בְּמִצְרַיִם לְעֵינֵיכֶם: וּבַמִּדְבָּר אֲשֶׁר רָאִיתָ אֲשֶׁר נְשָׂאֲךָ יְהוָה אֱלֹהֶיךָ כַּאֲשֶׁר יִשָּׂא־אִישׁ אֶת־בְּנוֹ בְּכָל־הַדֶּרֶךְ אֲשֶׁר הֲלַכְתֶּם עַד־בֹּאֲכֶם

לב עַד־הַמָּקוֹם הַזֶּה: וּבַדָּבָר הַזֶּה אֵינְכֶם מַאֲמִינִם

לג בַּיהוָה אֱלֹהֵיכֶם: הַהֹלֵךְ לִפְנֵיכֶם בַּדֶּרֶךְ לָתוּר לָכֶם מָקוֹם לַחֲנֹתְכֶם בָּאֵשׁ לַיְלָה לַרְאֹתְכֶם בַּדֶּרֶךְ אֲשֶׁר

לד תֵּלְכוּ־בָהּ וּבֶעָנָן יוֹמָם: וַיִּשְׁמַע יְהוָה אֶת־קוֹל

לה דִּבְרֵיכֶם וַיִּקְצֹף וַיִּשָּׁבַע לֵאמֹר: אִם־יִרְאֶה אִישׁ

approved of the plan, and so I selected twelve of your men, one from each tribe. **24]** They made for the hill country, came to the wadi Eshcol, and spied it out. **25]** They took some of the fruit of the land with them and brought it down to us. And they gave us this report, "It is a good land that the LORD our God is giving to us."

26] Yet you refused to go up, and flouted the command of the LORD your God. **27]** You sulked in your tents and said, "It is because the LORD hates us that He brought us out of the land of Egypt, to hand us over to the Amorites to wipe us out. **28]** What kind of place are we going to? Our kinsmen have taken the heart out of us, saying, 'We saw there a people stronger and taller than we, large cities with walls sky-high, and even Anakites.'"

29] I said to you, "Have no dread or fear of them. **30]** None other than the LORD your God, who goes before you, will fight for you, just as He did for you in Egypt before your very eyes, **31]** and in the wilderness, where you saw how the LORD your God carried you, as a man carries his son, all the way that you traveled until you came to this place. **32]** Yet for all that, you have no faith in the LORD your God, **33]** who goes before you on your journeys—to scout the place where you are to encamp—in fire by night and in cloud by day, in order to guide you on the route you are to follow."

34] When the LORD heard your loud complaint, He was angry. He vowed: **35]** Not one of

23] *I approved.* God's role in the scheme is not a part of Moses' story; hence many scholars find this to be added proof of different traditions.

24] *Wadi Eshcol.* Probably somewhere in the vicinity of Hebron; see also Num. 13:23–24.

27] *You sulked.* Others, "murmured."

28] *Walls sky-high.* So they appeared to the nomads.

Anakites. In popular mythology a people of gigantic stature, but anthropology provides no evidence that such people lived in Palestine in

biblical times; see our commentary on Num. 13:22.

31] *As a man carries his son.* The image of God as father and Israel as child recurs in Deut. 8:5 and 32:11, and elsewhere in the Bible. A similar image depicts God carrying Israel as on eagles' wings (Exod. 19:4).

32] *Yet for all that.* Despite God's proven care you did not believe His promise [4].

מ יָבֹ֣אוּ שָׁ֔מָּה וְלָהֶ֣ם אֶתְּנֶ֔נָּה וְהֵ֖ם יִֽרָשֽׁוּהָ׃ וְאַתֶּ֖ם פְּנ֣וּ
מא לָכֶ֑ם וּסְע֥וּ הַמִּדְבָּ֖רָה דֶּ֥רֶךְ יַם־סֽוּף׃ וַֽתַּעֲנ֣וּ וַתֹּאמְר֣וּ
אֵלַ֗י חָטָ֘אנוּ֮ לַֽיהוָה֒ אֲנַ֤חְנוּ נַֽעֲלֶה֙ וְנִלְחַ֔מְנוּ כְּכֹ֥ל
אֲשֶׁר־צִוָּ֖נוּ יְהוָ֣ה אֱלֹהֵ֑ינוּ וַֽתַּחְגְּר֗וּ אִ֚ישׁ אֶת־כְּלֵ֣י
מב מִלְחַמְתּ֔וֹ וַתָּהִ֖ינוּ לַעֲלֹ֥ת הָהָֽרָה׃ וַיֹּ֨אמֶר יְהוָ֜ה אֵלַ֗י
אֱמֹ֤ר לָהֶם֙ לֹ֤א תַֽעֲלוּ֙ וְלֹא־תִלָּ֣חֲמ֔וּ כִּ֥י אֵינֶ֖נִּי בְּקִרְבְּכֶ֑ם
מג וְלֹ֥א תִנָּֽגְפ֖וּ לִפְנֵ֣י אֹיְבֵיכֶֽם׃ וָֽאֲדַבֵּ֥ר אֲלֵיכֶ֖ם וְלֹ֣א
שְׁמַעְתֶּ֑ם וַתַּמְר֗וּ אֶת־פִּ֣י יְהוָ֔ה וַתָּזִ֖דוּ וַתַּעֲל֥וּ הָהָֽרָה׃

בָֽאֲנָשִׁ֣ים הָאֵ֔לֶּה הַדּ֥וֹר הָרָ֖ע הַזֶּ֑ה אֵ֚ת הָאָ֣רֶץ הַטּוֹבָ֔ה
לז אֲשֶׁ֣ר נִשְׁבַּ֔עְתִּי לָתֵ֖ת לַאֲבֹֽתֵיכֶֽם׃ זֽוּלָתִ֞י כָּלֵ֤ב בֶּן־
יְפֻנֶּה֙ ה֣וּא יִרְאֶ֔נָּה וְלֽוֹ־אֶתֵּ֧ן אֶת־הָאָ֛רֶץ אֲשֶׁ֥ר דָּֽרַךְ־בָּ֖הּ
לז וּלְבָנָ֑יו יַ֕עַן אֲשֶׁ֥ר מִלֵּ֖א אַחֲרֵ֥י יְהוָֽה׃ גַּם־בִּי֙ הִתְאַנַּ֣ף
לח יְהוָ֔ה בִּגְלַלְכֶ֖ם לֵאמֹ֑ר גַּם־אַתָּ֖ה לֹא־תָבֹ֥א שָֽׁם׃ יְהוֹשֻׁ֣עַ
בִּן־נ֗וּן הָעֹמֵ֤ד לְפָנֶ֙יךָ֙ ה֣וּא יָ֣בֹא שָׁ֔מָּה אֹת֣וֹ חַזֵּ֔ק כִּי־
לט ה֖וּא יַנְחִלֶ֣נָּה אֶת־יִשְׂרָאֵֽל׃ וְטַפְּכֶ֞ם אֲשֶׁ֣ר אֲמַרְתֶּ֗ם לָבַ֣ז
יִֽהְיֶ֔ה וּ֠בְנֵיכֶם אֲשֶׁ֨ר לֹא־יָדְע֤וּ הַיּוֹם֙ ט֣וֹב וָרָ֔ע הֵ֖מָּה

* לח מלעיל.

---

these men, this evil generation, shall see the good land that I swore to give to your fathers—
36] none except Caleb son of Jephunneh; he shall see it, and to him and his descendants will I
give the land on which he set foot, because he remained loyal to the LORD.

37] Because of you the LORD was incensed with me too, and He said: You shall not enter it
either.   **38]** Joshua son of Nun, who attends you, he shall enter it. Imbue him with strength,
for he shall allot it to Israel.   **39]** Moreover, your little ones who you said would be carried
off, your children who do not yet know good from bad, they shall enter it; to them will I give it
and they shall possess it.   **40]** As for you, turn about and march into the wilderness, toward
the Sea of Reeds.

41] You replied to me, saying, "We stand guilty before the LORD. We will go up now and
fight, just as the LORD our God commanded us." And you all girded yourselves with war gear
and recklessly started for the hill country.   **42]** But the LORD said to me: Warn them, "Do not
go up and do not fight, since I am not in your midst; else you will be routed by your
enemies."   **43]** I spoke to you, but you would not listen; you flouted the LORD's command and

---

36] *None except Caleb.* Clearly a tradition different
from Num. 14:6–7, 30, where both Caleb and
Joshua are named as the dissenters (assigned to
the P-source, in contrast to Num. 14:24, which is
ascribed to J/E and singles out only Caleb). In
Deuteronomy Caleb alone is distinguished for his
faith, whereas Joshua's selection as the successor
of Moses and his entrance into the Land (verse 38)
are not connected with this incident.

On *which he set foot.* Hebron and vicinity; see
Josh. 14:13 ff.

37] *Incensed with me too.* Num. 20 reported the
condemnation of Moses to have taken place at

Meribah, at the incident of the rock, during the
thirty-ninth year of wandering. But here Moses
appears to have been punished at Kadesh-barnea,
in the second year, for the sins of the people or
for some other unreported reason [5].

39] *Your children.* Who were under twenty years
of age; see at 2:14.

From this the Rabbis inferred that youths under
twenty were not punished for transgressions
judged by the divine court [6].

41] *Recklessly.* The Hebrew word occurs nowhere
else in the Bible; the translation is suggested by
the context.

מד וַיֵּצֵא הָאֱמֹרִי הַיֹּשֵׁב בָּהָר הַהוּא לִקְרַאתְכֶם וַיִּרְדְּפוּ
אֶתְכֶם כַּאֲשֶׁר תַּעֲשֶׂינָה הַדְּבֹרִים וַיַּכְּתוּ אֶתְכֶם
מה בְּשֵׂעִיר עַד־חָרְמָה: וַתָּשֻׁבוּ וַתִּבְכּוּ לִפְנֵי יְהֹוָה וְלֹא־
שָׁמַע יְהֹוָה בְּקֹלְכֶם וְלֹא הֶאֱזִין אֲלֵיכֶם:

willfully marched into the hill country. **44]** Then the Amorites who lived in those hills came out against you like so many bees and chased you, and they crushed you at Hormah in Seir. **45]** Again you wept before the LORD; but the LORD would not heed your cry or give ear to you.

44] *At Hormah in Seir.* With several ancient versions one should read "from Seir to Hormah" (מִשֵּׂעִיר instead of בְּשֵׂעִיר). Seir was the name most frequently applied to the Edomite mountains east of the Aravah; here it means probably a mountain near Jerusalem (see Josh. 15:10). Hormah was a place in the general vicinity of Beersheba; both the meaning of the name and the exact location are in doubt (see at Num. 21:3).

The Nature of Jewish Law

At the very beginning of Moses' recollections stands a brief statement on the principles of judicial procedure (verses 16 and 17); the courts must deal justly; give both sides a fair hearing; make no distinction between people of great or little status;[1] and apply one standard to Israelite citizen and resident alien when they have a lawsuit with each other.

These principles are then drawn together by enunciating their common basis: "judgment is God's." Biblical legislation assumes the divine origin of the law and covers its content as well as its administration. The law is of one piece and does not, therefore, know of any distinction between moral, ritual, and mere "legal" norms. What Israel must do is revealed and willed by God.[2] Transgression of His will is sinful and fraught with consequences human and divine; morality, ritual, and law are part of one single structure and are indistinguishable in the Torah and the Prophets. The latter often laid heavy emphasis on ethical behavior, but in doing so they did not negate the unified nature of Israelite law. This unity was developed and carried over into that highly complex system of later Jewish law which, when eventually codified in Mishnah and Talmud, became known as halachah, the way in which a Jew was to order his life in accordance with divine will, as understood by the Rabbis in subsequent centuries.

Traditional Jewish law to this day maintains this view of halachah; in it there are no distinctions (except for the purpose of systematic organization) that separate the laws governing the relations between God and the individual from those between human beings, or ritual from civil and criminal law. Thus, fasting on Yom Kippur and loving one's neighbor are both commanded in the halachah; the latter mitzvah is no more "ethical" than the former, for both are considered emanating from one divine source, and therefore halachah is, by its very nature, "ethical."

Reform Judaism brought a different perspective to Jewish law. While recognizing that the Torah presented the unitary principle of law as "God's judgment," it could not overlook either that human hands shaped the Torah or the human contribution made in later centuries to its development. In doing so it attempted to distinguish between various laws and gave a higher priority to moral norms than to ritual demands. The teachings of the Prophets became especially important to Reform because they stressed above all the need for social ethics and moral attitudes, and in turn the ritual aspects of halachah took a distinctly secondary place. Still, Reform always perceived its practices and perspectives to be guided by the biblical injunction: Whatever we do must be just, for justice is the will of God.

From the days of the formulation of the Torah this obligation has rested on every individual as well as on the whole people. God's judgment falls on all Israel if too many of its leaders and members transgress His law. The Jewish "ought" is at the same time personal and collective, for the nation has been and remains a partner to the covenant, the covenant which was concluded between the Lord and the totality of Israel who proclaimed: "All that the Lord has spoken we will do!" (Exod. 19:8)

---

[1] The text has also been understood as referring to matters of large and small financial consideration; see note on verse 17.

[2] Non-Israelites too must observe certain basic, self-evident laws (called by Tradition the Noahide laws); see our commentary on Gen. 8:15–9:29.

Two Generations

A striking feature of Moses' oration is the way in which he addressed the generation about to enter the Land. Clearly, his warnings were addressed to people whose fathers and mothers had perished in the wilderness, because by their lack of faith they had shown themselves unworthy of God's trust. But while Moses spoke to the people before him and recited to them the sins of the past, he slipped into a remarkable identification of past and present. In recounting the crucial incident of the spies (which eventually led to the condemnation of the old generation) he might have been expected to say: "Then all of them came to me and said . . ." (verse 22), or "They refused to go up . . ." (verse 26), or "I said to them . . ." (verse 29). But in every case, instead of using "them" and "they," Moses used "you," addressing the new generation as if *they* had been the sinners, who must now be cautioned not to repeat the earlier transgression.

This appears to be more than a stylistic peculiarity. Even as the text changes frequently from plural to singular and back again—thus reflecting the close relation between individual and collective responsibility—so it views Israel's past and present as a single continuum. The covenant was originally concluded with those now dead, but its force continued unabated and it will apply to future generations as well: "I make this covenant . . . both with those who are standing here with us this day before the Lord our God and with those who are not with us here this day" (29:13–14). The history of the Jewish people possessed then, and has continued to exhibit, a quality which identifies past and present, in that the obligations of the people are in fact a-historical. They are not bound by time.

Therefore, when Moses begins his exhortations, his prologue deals not with idolatry (a theme to which he will later insistently turn) but rather with lack of faith and trust. Once before the people had stood at the gates of Canaan but had disbelieved God's promise; Moses now cautions them not to repeat the same sin. For this reason he does not single out the incident of the golden calf, which had loomed so large as a virtual abandonment of the covenant; rather, he begins with the challenge to the present generation to trust God's providence. "You" made a fatal error once before, he says, don't do it again. You are now the fathers and mothers of Israel, and in the future our people will identify with you as you do with your own forebears. Your responsibility is therefore not to yourselves alone, it is to the generations yet unborn who will be able to say even as you do now: "*We* stood at Sinai."[3]

---

[3] See also the words of the Haggadah: In every generation, each person should feel as though he himself/she herself had gone forth from Egypt, as it is said (Exod. 13:8), "because of what the Lord did *for me* when *I* went free from Egypt."

Blessing and Reproof

Moses begins his exhortation with a blessing (verse 11), in order to make his reproof more palatable. M. HACOHEN [7]

One of the reasons Jerusalem was destroyed was that people did not reprove one another. TALMUD [8]

How

Three uttered their prophecy by using the word אֵיכָה (*echah*, how):

Moses, who said: "How can I alone bear the trouble of you" (verse 12);

Isaiah, who said: "How has the faithful city become a harlot" (1:21); and

Jeremiah, who said: "How does the city sit solitary" (Lam. 1:1).[4]

The Sages connected all three "hows" by bringing them into a liturgical relationship with one another. They arranged the Book of Lamentations, which deals with the destruction of the Temple, to be read on the 9th of Av; and the passages from Deuteronomy and Isaiah to be the scriptural readings for the Sabbath before Tishah b'Av.

The Stranger

It says "Decide justly between any man ... or a stranger" (verse 16). The Hebrew reads literally *"his* stranger"—as if the stranger lived in his house and was therefore doubly dependent on him. The following story is based on this reading.

The wife of a rabbi prepared to lodge a complaint against her maid. The rabbi accompanied his wife to the magistrate. Was this not beneath his dignity? she asked. His answer: No, I intend to represent the maid who, being "our" stranger, needs someone to take her part so that justice will be done. AFTER J. H. HERTZ

Seven Qualities

Judges must exhibit seven qualities: they must be wise, discerning, and experienced[5] (verse 13); they must be capable, fear God, be trustworthy, and spurn ill-gotten gain (Exod. 18:21). MAIMONIDES [9]

"Experienced" (verse 13) means that they must be in close contact with the people, which is to say, they must love them. ITTURE TORAH [10]

Decide Justly (verse 16)

וּשְׁפַטְתֶּם צֶדֶק could be understood to mean "judge righteousness." There are times when the way righteousness is executed needs itself judging and weighing in the balance. CHASIDIC [11]

The Judgment of Moses

Why in verse 37 does Moses say that he was punished *because of the people*, while in Num. 20 it is recounted how he was punished for *his own particular sin*? The answer is that God was incensed with him as with everyone else, except Joshua and Caleb, when He judged Israel as unfit to enter the Land. Moses was one of the people and suffered their fate, but God waited for a propitious time to announce His judgment to Moses.[6] YALKUT ME'AM LO'EZ [12]

---

[4] Tradition ascribed the authorship of Lamentations to Jeremiah.

[5] See verse 15, for an alternate understanding of יְדֵעִים.

[6] This represents one of many rabbinic and post-rabbinic attempts to explain why the apparently minor transgression related in Num. 20 brought on such drastic divine retribution (see our commentary on that chapter).

The Secret of Moses' Blessing

Students of the text delighted to find hidden connections. Thus, they asked, how could Moses bestow a blessing of thousandfold power (verse 11)? They argued in this way:

In gematria the letters in Moses equal the letters in El Shaddai (a name for God: משה and אל שדי both add up to 345).[7] Now the letters in אל שדי when written out fully look thus: יוד, דלת, שין, למד, אלף. Add these letters together and you find they amount to 999! Moses loved Israel with divine love and thus, adding his own benediction, he could bestow this extravagant thousandfold blessing.   CHASIDIC [13]

[7] מ=40, ש=300, ה=5;   א=1, ל=30, ש=300, ד=4, י=10.

Second Review

The purpose of the long recital with which Moses begins his exhortation is to lay before the people a clear view of their fate, a fate closely tied to the will of God. He recalls how they wandered in the desert for forty years, thirty-eight of which were punishment for their fathers' lack of trust in God; how the Guardian of Israel had brought the old generation out of Egypt in a display of wonders and terrors never experienced by any other nation; how He had taken them to Sinai and told them what they needed to do so that they might merit divine approval and enter the Promised Land—and how they had proven themselves unworthy of the divine trust. They acted cowardly when given the opportunity to conquer the land, their cowardice springing from their lack of faith that God would sustain them. Their failure was a failure of nerve: to believe in the saving power of the Lord. In consequence, the whole generation of the Exodus was condemned to die in the wilderness, and Moses himself was included in the judgment. Like the captain of a sinking ship, he was to perish with his people whom he had not prepared properly for their task.

The section ends with Moses recounting how his own plea, to be allowed to enter the Promised Land, was rejected by God. With this the prologue comes to an end, and in chapter 4 we will read the beginning of Moses' first major oration.

It is important to view this recital also in the light of ancient Near Eastern treaty patterns. These usually contained a declaration that granted land and rule to the vassal and then, as here, proceeded to a description of the land and its boundaries [1].

(A new weekly portion, *Va'etchanan*, begins with 3:23.)

מו וַתֵּשְׁבוּ בְקָדֵשׁ יָמִים רַבִּים כַּיָּמִים אֲשֶׁר יְשַׁבְתֶּם:

א וַנֵּפֶן וַנִּסַּע הַמִּדְבָּרָה דֶּרֶךְ יַם־סוּף כַּאֲשֶׁר דִּבֶּר

יְהֹוָה אֵלָי וַנָּסָב אֶת־הַר־שֵׂעִיר יָמִים רַבִּים: ס

ב יְהֹוָה אֵלַי לֵאמֹר: רַב־לָכֶם סֹב אֶת־הָהָר הַזֶּה פְּנוּ

ג לָכֶם צָפֹנָה: וְאֶת־הָעָם צַו לֵאמֹר אַתֶּם עֹבְרִים

ד בִּגְבוּל אֲחֵיכֶם בְּנֵי־עֵשָׂו הַיֹּשְׁבִים בְּשֵׂעִיר וְיִירְאוּ

ה מִכֶּם וְנִשְׁמַרְתֶּם מְאֹד: אַל־תִּתְגָּרוּ בָם כִּי לֹא־אֶתֵּן

לָכֶם מֵאַרְצָם עַד מִדְרַךְ כַּף־רָגֶל כִּי־יְרֻשָּׁה לְעֵשָׂו

נָתַתִּי אֶת־הַר שֵׂעִיר: אֹכֶל תִּשְׁבְּרוּ מֵאִתָּם בַּכֶּסֶף

וַאֲכַלְתֶּם וְגַם־מַיִם תִּכְרוּ מֵאִתָּם בַּכֶּסֶף וּשְׁתִיתֶם:

כִּי יְהֹוָה אֱלֹהֶיךָ בֵּרַכְךָ בְּכֹל מַעֲשֵׂה יָדֶךָ יָדַע

לֶכְתְּךָ אֶת־הַמִּדְבָּר הַגָּדֹל הַזֶּה זֶה אַרְבָּעִים שָׁנָה

יְהֹוָה אֱלֹהֶיךָ עִמָּךְ לֹא חָסַרְתָּ דָּבָר: וַנַּעֲבֹר מֵאֵת

אַחֵינוּ בְנֵי־עֵשָׂו הַיֹּשְׁבִים בְּשֵׂעִיר מִדֶּרֶךְ הָעֲרָבָה

46] Thus, after you had remained at Kadesh all that long time, **1]** we marched back into the wilderness, toward the Sea of Reeds, as the LORD had spoken to me, and skirted the hill country of Seir a long time.

2] Then the LORD said to me: **3]** You have been skirting this hill country long enough; now turn north. **4]** And charge the people as follows: You will be passing through the territory of your kinsmen, the descendants of Esau, who live in Seir. Though they will be afraid of you, be very careful **5]** not to start a fight with them. For I will not give you of their land so much as a foot can tread on; I have given the hill country of Seir as a possession to Esau. **6]** What food you eat you shall obtain from them for money; even the water you drink you shall procure from them for money. **7]** Indeed, the LORD your God has blessed you in all your undertakings. He has watched over your wanderings through this great wilderness; the LORD your God has been with you these past forty years: you have lacked nothing.

8] We then moved on, away from our kinsmen, the descendants of Esau, who live in Seir, away from the road of the Arabah, away from Elath and Ezion-geber; and we marched on in

2:1] *Toward the Sea of Reeds.* Its location is disputed; see our commentary on Exod. 13:18.

4] *Territory of your kinsmen.* The report in Num. 20:14 ff. differs: there, Edom is depicted as having refused Israel its request to pass through.

Traditional interpreters explain the discrepancy in this way: the account in Numbers tells of what happened thirty-eight years before, in Deuteronomy of what happened recently; according to this view the Edomites had altered their policies. Another interpretation denies that Seir (Esau) is identical with Edom [2].

5] *Seir as a possession to Esau.* While Moab and Ammon were bequeathed to Lot (in that Moab and Ammon were traced back to Lot, Gen. 19:37–38). Israel was not the only people to receive its land as a divine patrimony.

8] *We then moved on.* Marching from the northern end of the Gulf of Akaba through the Aravah toward the southern end of the Dead Sea; from there turning eastward, then north again toward Moab.

Ezion-geber. Its original location is in doubt. For a time it was believed to have been near or identical with Elath (modern Eilat); but lately the island of Jazirat-Farun, in the northern end of the Gulf of Akaba, has been accepted as the more likely site [3]. See also at Num. 33:35.

Tradition prescribes that in the writing of the Torah a space be inserted between Ezion-geber and the words following. Why the Masoretes introduced this is not clear. Perhaps at one time a new sentence started here.

מֵאֵילַת וּמֵעֶצְיֹן גָּבֶר ס וַנֵּפֶן וַנַּעֲבֹר דֶּרֶךְ מִדְבַּר
ט מוֹאָב: וַיֹּאמֶר יְהוָה אֵלַי אַל־תָּצַר אֶת־מוֹאָב וְאַל־
תִּתְגָּר בָּם מִלְחָמָה כִּי לֹא־אֶתֵּן לְךָ מֵאַרְצוֹ יְרֻשָּׁה
י כִּי לִבְנֵי־לוֹט נָתַתִּי אֶת־עָר יְרֻשָּׁה: הָאֵמִים לְפָנִים
יא יָשְׁבוּ בָהּ עַם גָּדוֹל וְרַב וָרָם כָּעֲנָקִים: רְפָאִים
יֵחָשְׁבוּ אַף־הֵם כָּעֲנָקִים וְהַמֹּאָבִים יִקְרְאוּ לָהֶם
יב אֵמִים: וּבְשֵׂעִיר יָשְׁבוּ הַחֹרִים לְפָנִים וּבְנֵי עֵשָׂו
יִירָשׁוּם וַיַּשְׁמִידוּם מִפְּנֵיהֶם וַיֵּשְׁבוּ תַחְתָּם כַּאֲשֶׁר

עָשָׂה יִשְׂרָאֵל לְאֶרֶץ יְרֻשָּׁתוֹ אֲשֶׁר־נָתַן יְהוָה לָהֶם:
יג עַתָּה קֻמוּ וְעִבְרוּ לָכֶם אֶת־נַחַל זֶרֶד וַנַּעֲבֹר אֶת־
יד נַחַל זָרֶד: וְהַיָּמִים אֲשֶׁר־הָלַכְנוּ מִקָּדֵשׁ בַּרְנֵעַ עַד
אֲשֶׁר־עָבַרְנוּ אֶת־נַחַל זֶרֶד שְׁלֹשִׁים וּשְׁמֹנֶה שָׁנָה עַד־
תֹּם כָּל־הַדּוֹר אַנְשֵׁי הַמִּלְחָמָה מִקֶּרֶב הַמַּחֲנֶה
טו כַּאֲשֶׁר נִשְׁבַּע יְהוָה לָהֶם: וְגַם יַד־יְהוָה הָיְתָה בָּם
טז לְהֻמָּם מִקֶּרֶב הַמַּחֲנֶה עַד תֻּמָּם: וַיְהִי כַאֲשֶׁר־תַּמּוּ
יז כָּל־אַנְשֵׁי הַמִּלְחָמָה לָמוּת מִקֶּרֶב הָעָם: ס וַיְדַבֵּר

the direction of the wilderness of Moab. **9]** And the LORD said to me: Do not harass the Moabites or engage them in war. For I will not give you any of their land as a possession; I have given Ar as a possession to the descendants of Lot.—

10] It was formerly inhabited by the Emim, a people great and numerous, and as tall as the Anakites. **11]** Like the Anakites, they are counted as Rephaim; but the Moabites call them Emim. **12]** Similarly, Seir was formerly inhabited by the Horites; but the descendants of Esau dispossessed them, wiping them out and settling in their place, just as Israel did in the land they were to possess, which the LORD had given to them.—
13] Up now! Cross the wadi Zered!

So we crossed the wadi Zered. **14]** The time that we spent in travel from Kadesh-barnea until we crossed the wadi Zered was thirty-eight years, until that whole generation of warriors had perished from the camp, as the LORD had sworn concerning them. **15]** Indeed, the hand of the LORD struck them, to root them out from the camp to the last man.

16] When all the warriors among the people had died off, **17]** the LORD spoke to me,

9] *Ar.* An important Moabite city.

10] *Formerly.* Verses 10–12 are an editorial aside, as if written in parentheses.

Emim. They are here listed as "Rephaim" (while in Gen. 14:5 they were thought to be distinct from them). The explanation has the flavor of folk memory and popular commentary. See further in W. W. Hallo's essay, above.

13] *Up now!* Moses resumes his recital of past events.

Wadi Zered. A stream near the Moabite border; its identity is in doubt.

14] *Thirty-eight years.* As in the Book of Numbers, no statement is made about any happenings during this period. The generation of the Exodus died and so did the knowledge of their latter-day lives,

for now it was their children who constituted Israel's future and the chronicler's attention shifts to them. Tradition fixed the 15th of Av as the date when Israel was given permission to proceed to Canaan, and for centuries the day was celebrated with great joy [4].

On that day the marriageable women dressed in white and danced with the young men, inviting them to choose their partners for marriage. It was also the day of wood-offering, when priests and people brought firewood to the altar for use at sacrifices.

Whole generation of warriors had perished. "Warriors" is not to be understood technically as if only males perished. Rather, the word should be understood as "people over twenty," which conforms with Num. 14:21 ff.

...

יח יְהוָ֥ה אֵלַ֖י לֵאמֹ֑ר אַתָּ֨ה עֹבֵ֥ר הַיּ֛וֹם אֶת־גְּב֥וּל מוֹאָ֖ב
יט אֶת־עָֽר: וְקָרַבְתָּ֗ מ֚וּל בְּנֵ֣י עַמּ֔וֹן אַל־תְּצֻרֵ֖ם וְאַל־
תִּתְגָּ֣ר בָּ֑ם כִּ֣י לֹֽא־אֶ֠תֵּן מֵאֶ֨רֶץ בְּנֵֽי־עַמּ֤וֹן לְךָ֙ יְרֻשָּׁ֔ה
כ כִּֽי־לִבְנֵי־ל֖וֹט נְתַתִּ֥יהָ יְרֻשָּֽׁה: אֶֽרֶץ־רְפָאִ֥ים תֵּחָשֵׁ֖ב
אַף־הִ֑וא רְפָאִ֤ים יָֽשְׁבוּ־בָהּ֙ לְפָנִ֔ים וְהָ֣עַמֹּנִ֔ים יִקְרְא֥וּ
כא לָהֶ֖ם זַמְזֻמִּֽים: עַ֣ם גָּד֥וֹל וְרַ֛ב וָרָ֖ם כָּעֲנָקִ֑ים וַיַּשְׁמִידֵ֤ם
כב יְהוָה֙ מִפְּנֵיהֶ֔ם וַיִּֽירָשֻׁ֖ם וַיֵּשְׁב֣וּ תַחְתָּֽם: כַּאֲשֶׁ֣ר עָשָׂ֗ה
לִבְנֵ֤י עֵשָׂו֙ הַיֹּֽשְׁבִ֣ים בְּשֵׂעִ֔יר אֲשֶׁ֤ר הִשְׁמִיד֙ אֶת־הַחֹרִ֜י

מִפְּנֵיהֶ֗ם וַיִּֽירָשֻׁם֙ וַיֵּֽשְׁב֣וּ תַחְתָּ֔ם עַ֖ד הַיּ֥וֹם הַזֶּֽה:
כג וְהָֽעַוִּ֛ים הַיֹּֽשְׁבִ֥ים בַּחֲצֵרִ֖ים עַד־עַזָּ֑ה כַּפְתֹּרִים֙ הַיֹּֽצְאִ֣ים
כד מִכַּפְתּ֔וֹר הִשְׁמִיד֖וּם וַיֵּשְׁב֥וּ תַחְתָּֽם: ק֣וּמוּ סְּע֗וּ וְעִבְרוּ֘
אֶת־נַ֣חַל אַרְנֹן֒ רְאֵ֣ה נָתַ֣תִּי בְ֠יָדְךָ אֶת־סִיחֹ֨ן מֶֽלֶךְ־
חֶשְׁבּ֧וֹן הָֽאֱמֹרִ֛י וְאֶת־אַרְצ֖וֹ הָחֵ֣ל רָ֑שׁ וְהִתְגָּ֥ר בּ֖וֹ
כה מִלְחָמָֽה: הַיּ֣וֹם הַזֶּ֗ה אָחֵל֙ תֵּ֤ת פַּחְדְּךָ֙ וְיִרְאָ֣תְךָ֔ עַל־
פְּנֵי֙ הָֽעַמִּ֔ים תַּ֖חַת כָּל־הַשָּׁמָ֑יִם אֲשֶׁ֤ר יִשְׁמְעוּן֙ שִׁמְעֲךָ֔
כו וְרָֽגְז֥וּ וְחָל֖וּ מִפָּנֶֽיךָ: וָֽאֶשְׁלַ֤ח מַלְאָכִים֙ מִמִּדְבַּ֣ר

* כד ס׳ דנוסה.

saying: **18]** You are now passing through the territory of Moab, through Ar.   **19]** You will then be close to the Ammonites; do not harass them or start a fight with them. For I will not give any part of the land of the Ammonites to you as a possession; I have given it as a possession to the descendants of Lot.—

20] It, too, is counted as Rephaim country. It was formerly inhabited by Rephaim, whom the Ammonites call Zamzummim,   **21]** a people great and numerous and as tall as the Anakites. The LORD wiped them out, so that [the Ammonites] dispossessed them and settled in their place,   **22]** as He did for the descendants of Esau who live in Seir, when He wiped out the Horites before them, so that they dispossessed them and settled in their place, as is still the case.   **23]** So, too, with the Avvim who dwelt in villages in the vicinity of Gaza: the Caphtorim, who came from Crete, wiped them out and settled in their place.—

24] Up! Set out across the wadi Arnon! See, I give into your power Sihon the Amorite, king of Heshbon, and his land. Begin the occupation: engage him in battle.   **25]** This day I begin to put the dread and fear of you upon the peoples everywhere under heaven, so that they shall tremble and quake because of you whenever they hear you mentioned.

26] Then I sent messengers from the wilderness of Kedemoth to Sihon king of Heshbon with

19] *Land of the Ammonites.* In the area of today's Amman, east of the Jordan, northeast of the Dead Sea. To the south of it was Moab and further south was Edom.

20] *It, too.* Verses 20–23 are another editorial aside.

Zamzummim. Likely identical with the Zuzim of Gen. 14:5. It has been suggested that the name imitated some speech habit of the people (compare the Greek *barbaros* and Latin *barbarus* as terms for foreign people).

23] *Avvim.* A people not further identified. Their land was not to be conquered by Israel until the end of Joshua's life (Josh. 13:3).

Gaza. About 50 miles (80 km) south of Tel Aviv-Jaffa. An important town on the road from Mesopotamia to Egypt, mentioned already in the el-Amarna letters of fourteenth century B.C.E.

Caphtorim who came from Crete. Literally, "from Caphtor." The identity of Caphtor and Crete is a longstanding assumption, but without final proof. Some believe Caphtor to mean Cappadocia, an area in today's eastern Turkey.

24] *Up!* Moses resumes his narrative.

Begin the occupation. The meaning of רָשׁ (rash) is deduced from the context.

26] *I sent messengers.* Rehearsing the story told in Num. 21:21 ff.

Kedemoth. Not mentioned previously. It appears in Josh. 13:18 and I Chron. 6:64 as located in the territory of Reuben (east of the Jordan River).

וַיֹּאמֶר יְהוָֹה אֵלַי רְאֵה הַחִלֹּתִי תֵּת לְפָנֶיךָ　לא
אֶת־סִיחֹן וְאֶת־אַרְצוֹ הָחֵל רָשׁ לָרֶשֶׁת אֶת־אַרְצוֹ:
וַיֵּצֵא סִיחֹן לִקְרָאתֵנוּ הוּא וְכָל־עַמּוֹ לַמִּלְחָמָה יָהְצָה:　לב
וַיִּתְּנֵהוּ יְהוָֹה אֱלֹהֵינוּ לְפָנֵינוּ וַנַּךְ אֹתוֹ וְאֶת־בָּנָו* וְאֶת־　לג
כָּל־עַמּוֹ: וַנִּלְכֹּד אֶת־כָּל־עָרָיו בָּעֵת הַהִוא וַנַּחֲרֵם　לד
אֶת־כָּל־עִיר מְתִם וְהַנָּשִׁים וְהַטָּף לֹא הִשְׁאַרְנוּ שָׂרִיד:
רַק הַבְּהֵמָה בָּזַזְנוּ לָנוּ וּשְׁלַל הֶעָרִים אֲשֶׁר לָכָדְנוּ:　לה
מֵעֲרֹעֵר אֲשֶׁר עַל־שְׂפַת־נַחַל אַרְנֹן וְהָעִיר אֲשֶׁר　לו
בַּנַּחַל וְעַד־הַגִּלְעָד לֹא הָיְתָה קִרְיָה אֲשֶׁר שָׂגְבָה

*לו בָּנָיו קרי.

קְדֵמוֹת אֶל־סִיחוֹן מֶלֶךְ חֶשְׁבּוֹן דִּבְרֵי שָׁלוֹם לֵאמֹר:
אֶעְבְּרָה בְאַרְצֶךָ בַּדֶּרֶךְ בַּדֶּרֶךְ אֵלֵךְ לֹא אָסוּר　כז
יָמִין וּשְׂמֹאול: אֹכֶל בַּכֶּסֶף תַּשְׁבִּרֵנִי וְאָכַלְתִּי וּמַיִם　כח
בַּכֶּסֶף תִּתֶּן־לִי וְשָׁתִיתִי רַק אֶעְבְּרָה בְרַגְלָי: כַּאֲשֶׁר　כט
עָשׂוּ־לִי בְּנֵי עֵשָׂו הַיֹּשְׁבִים בְּשֵׂעִיר וְהַמּוֹאָבִים הַיֹּשְׁבִים
בְּעָר עַד אֲשֶׁר־אֶעֱבֹר אֶת־הַיַּרְדֵּן אֶל־הָאָרֶץ אֲשֶׁר־
יְהוָֹה אֱלֹהֵינוּ נֹתֵן לָנוּ: וְלֹא אָבָה סִיחֹן מֶלֶךְ חֶשְׁבּוֹן　ל
הַעֲבִרֵנוּ בּוֹ כִּי־הִקְשָׁה יְהוָֹה אֱלֹהֶיךָ אֶת־רוּחוֹ
וְאִמֵּץ אֶת־לְבָבוֹ לְמַעַן תִּתּוֹ בְיָדְךָ כַּיּוֹם הַזֶּה: ס

*כז פלא ו.

an offer of peace, as follows, **27]** "Let me pass through your country. I will keep strictly to the highway, turning off neither to the right nor to the left. **28]** What food I eat you will supply for money, and what water I drink you will furnish for money; just let me pass through— **29]** as the descendants of Esau who dwell in Seir did for me, and the Moabites who dwell in Ar—that I may cross the Jordan into the land that the LORD our God is giving us."

30] But Sihon king of Heshbon would not let us pass through, because the LORD had stiffened his will and hardened his heart in order to deliver him into your power—as is now the case. **31]** And the LORD said to me: See, I begin by placing Sihon and his land at your disposal. Begin the occupation; take possession of his land.

32] Sihon with all his men took the field against us at Jahaz, **33]** and the LORD our God delivered him to us and we defeated him and his sons and all his men. **34]** At that time we captured all his towns, and we doomed every town—men, women, and children—leaving no survivor. **35]** We retained as booty only the cattle and the spoil of the cities that we captured. **36]** From Aroer on the edge of the Arnon valley, including the town in the valley itself, to Gilead, not a city was too mighty for us; the LORD our God delivered everything to

27] *Keep strictly to the highway.* Literally, "I will keep to the highway, to the highway"—and will not stray from it.

28] *Pass through.* The story resembles the account in Num. 20:18 ff. as far as the payments are concerned, but it differs in that it does not seem to know of the delegation which was sent and the refusal it met. Another version of the account appears in Judg. 11:19–22.

30] *Stiffened his will.* Like Pharaoh's. On the theological problem—how God can restrict a person's free will and yet punish him as if he were free—see our commentary on Exod. 4:19–6:1.

32] *At Jahaz.* According to the Mesha stone, it was located not far from Dibon. Mesha, king of Moab, erected the stele to commemorate his victory over Israel (ninth century B.C.E.).

34] *We doomed.* Or, "proscribed" (so translated in Num. 21:2), meaning: We utterly destroyed them, reserving no booty except what was to be deposited in the sanctuary as an offering, and taking no prisoners. What was to be doomed could not be sold or redeemed; Lev. 27:28.

35] *We retained...the cattle.* But, when later on Jericho was conquered under Joshua's leadership, cattle too were doomed (Josh. 6:21). Amalek was to be treated in like manner (I Sam. 15:3).

36] *Aroer.* About 10 miles (16 km) from the Dead Sea.

אֶת־כָּל־עָרָיו בָּעֵת הַהִוא לֹא הָיְתָה קִרְיָה אֲשֶׁר לֹא־לָקַחְנוּ מֵאִתָּם שִׁשִּׁים עִיר כָּל־חֶבֶל אַרְגֹּב מַמְלֶכֶת עוֹג בַּבָּשָׁן: כָּל־אֵלֶּה עָרִים בְּצֻרֹת חוֹמָה גְבֹהָה דְּלָתַיִם וּבְרִיחַ לְבַד מֵעָרֵי הַפְּרָזִי הַרְבֵּה מְאֹד: וַנַּחֲרֵם אוֹתָם כַּאֲשֶׁר עָשִׂינוּ לְסִיחֹן מֶלֶךְ חֶשְׁבּוֹן הַחֲרֵם כָּל־עִיר מְתִם הַנָּשִׁים וְהַטָּף: וְכָל־הַבְּהֵמָה וּשְׁלַל הֶעָרִים בַּזּוֹנוּ לָנוּ: וַנִּקַּח בָּעֵת הַהִוא אֶת־הָאָרֶץ מִיַּד שְׁנֵי מַלְכֵי הָאֱמֹרִי אֲשֶׁר בְּעֵבֶר הַיַּרְדֵּן מִנַּחַל אַרְנֹן עַד־הַר חֶרְמוֹן: צִידֹנִים יִקְרְאוּ לְחֶרְמוֹן שְׂרִיֹן וְהָאֱמֹרִי יִקְרְאוּ־לוֹ שְׂנִיר: כָּל עָרֵי

מִמֶּנּוּ אֶת־הַכֹּל נָתַן יְהוָה אֱלֹהֵינוּ לְפָנֵינוּ: רַק אֶל־אֶרֶץ בְּנֵי־עַמּוֹן לֹא קָרָבְתָּ כָּל־יַד נַחַל יַבֹּק וְעָרֵי הָהָר וְכֹל אֲשֶׁר־צִוָּה יְהוָה אֱלֹהֵינוּ: וַנֵּפֶן וַנַּעַל דֶּרֶךְ הַבָּשָׁן וַיֵּצֵא עוֹג מֶלֶךְ־הַבָּשָׁן לִקְרָאתֵנוּ הוּא וְכָל־עַמּוֹ לַמִּלְחָמָה אֶדְרֶעִי: וַיֹּאמֶר יְהוָה אֵלַי אַל־תִּירָא אֹתוֹ כִּי בְיָדְךָ נָתַתִּי אֹתוֹ וְאֶת־כָּל־עַמּוֹ וְאֶת־אַרְצוֹ וְעָשִׂיתָ לּוֹ כַּאֲשֶׁר עָשִׂיתָ לְסִיחֹן מֶלֶךְ הָאֱמֹרִי אֲשֶׁר יוֹשֵׁב בְּחֶשְׁבּוֹן: וַיִּתֵּן יְהוָה אֱלֹהֵינוּ בְּיָדֵנוּ גַּם אֶת־עוֹג מֶלֶךְ־הַבָּשָׁן וְאֶת־כָּל־עַמּוֹ וַנַּכֵּהוּ עַד־בִּלְתִּי הִשְׁאִיר־לוֹ שָׂרִיד: וַנִּלְכֹּד

us. **37]** But you did not encroach upon the land of the Ammonites, all along the wadi Jabbok and the towns of the hill country, just as the LORD our God had commanded.

1] We made our way up the road toward Bashan, and Og king of Bashan with all his men took the field against us at Edrei. **2]** But the LORD said to me: Do not fear him, for I am delivering him and all his men and his country into your power, and you will do to him as you did to Sihon king of the Amorites, who lived in Heshbon.

3] So the LORD our God also delivered into our power Og king of Bashan, with all his men, and we dealt them such a blow that no survivor was left. **4]** At that time we captured all his towns; there was not a town that we did not take from them: sixty towns, the whole district of Argob, the kingdom of Og in Bashan **5]** —all those towns were fortified with high walls, gates, and bars—apart from a great number of unwalled towns. **6]** We doomed them as we had done in the case of Sihon king of Heshbon; we doomed every town—men, women, and children— **7]** and retained as booty all the cattle and the spoil of the towns.

8] Thus we seized, at that time, from the two Amorite kings, the country beyond the Jordan, from the wadi Arnon to Mount Hermon (**9)** Sidonians call Hermon Sirion, and the Amorites call it Senir), **10]** all the towns of the Tableland and the whole of Gilead and Bashan as far as

37] *Wadi Jabbok.* It divided the tribe of Gad, on its south side, from one-half the tribe of Manasseh on the north. The story of Jacob's wrestling with the angel and his meeting with Esau was located here (Gen. 32:23).

3:1] *We made our way.* The war against Og was recounted in Num. 21:33 ff.

Bashan. See at Deut. 1:4.

4] *Sixty towns.* Probably a round figure meaning "many towns" [5].

Argob. Josephus identified it with Jaulan (Golan) [6].

5] *Unwalled towns.* See also Ezek. 38:11.

8] *Beyond the Jordan.* On this expression see at Deut. 1:1.

From the wadi Arnon. Which flows into the Dead Sea, near its middle.

To Mount Hermon. The highest peak in the northern mountains adjacent to Palestine, 9,232 feet (2,797 meters) high.

9] *Sidonians call.* Clearly an editorial aside and therefore bracketed in the English text. The Sidonians were often called Phoenicians; Sidon was a port city south of today's Beirut.

10] *Tableland.* The plains of Moab.

הַמִּישֹׁר וְכָל־הַגִּלְעָד וְכָל־הַבָּשָׁן עַד־סַלְכָה וְאֶדְרֶעִי

יא עָרֵי מַמְלֶכֶת עוֹג בַּבָּשָׁן: כִּי רַק־עוֹג מֶלֶךְ הַבָּשָׁן
נִשְׁאַר מִיֶּתֶר הָרְפָאִים הִנֵּה עַרְשׂוֹ עֶרֶשׂ בַּרְזֶל הֲלֹה
הִוא בְּרַבַּת בְּנֵי עַמּוֹן תֵּשַׁע אַמּוֹת אָרְכָּהּ וְאַרְבַּע

יב אַמּוֹת רָחְבָּהּ בְּאַמַּת־אִישׁ: וְאֶת־הָאָרֶץ הַזֹּאת יָרַשְׁנוּ
בָּעֵת הַהִוא מֵעֲרֹעֵר אֲשֶׁר־עַל־נַחַל אַרְנֹן וַחֲצִי הַר־

יג הַגִּלְעָד וְעָרָיו נָתַתִּי לָרֻאוּבֵנִי וְלַגָּדִי: וְיֶתֶר הַגִּלְעָד

וְכָל־הַבָּשָׁן מַמְלֶכֶת עוֹג נָתַתִּי לַחֲצִי שֵׁבֶט הַמְנַשֶּׁה
כֹּל חֶבֶל הָאַרְגֹּב לְכָל־הַבָּשָׁן הַהוּא יִקָּרֵא אֶרֶץ

יד רְפָאִים: יָאִיר בֶּן־מְנַשֶּׁה לָקַח אֶת־כָּל־חֶבֶל אַרְגֹּב
עַד־גְּבוּל הַגְּשׁוּרִי וְהַמַּעֲכָתִי וַיִּקְרָא אֹתָם עַל־שְׁמוֹ

טו אֶת־הַבָּשָׁן חַוֹּת יָאִיר עַד הַיּוֹם הַזֶּה: וּלְמָכִיר נָתַתִּי

טז אֶת־הַגִּלְעָד: וְלָרֻאוּבֵנִי וְלַגָּדִי נָתַתִּי מִן־הַגִּלְעָד וְעַד־
נַחַל אַרְנֹן תּוֹךְ הַנַּחַל וּגְבֻל וְעַד יַבֹּק הַנַּחַל גְּבוּל

‪*‬ יא כְּתִיב בַּה׳.

Salcah and Edrei, the towns of Og's kingdom in Bashan.— **[11]** Only Og king of Bashan was left of the remaining Rephaim. His bedstead, an iron bedstead, is now in Rabbah of the Ammonites; it is nine cubits long and four cubits wide, by the standard cubit!)

12] And this is the land which we apportioned at that time: The part from Aroer along the wadi Arnon, with part of the hill country of Gilead and its towns, I assigned to the Reubenites and the Gadites. **13]** The rest of Gilead, and all of Bashan under Og's rule—the whole Argob district, all that part of Bashan which is called Rephaim country—I assigned to the half-tribe of Manasseh. **14]** Jair son of Manasseh received the whole Argob district (that is, Bashan) as far as the boundary of the Geshurites and the Maacathites, and named it after himself, Havvoth-jair—as is still the case. **15]** To Machir I assigned Gilead. **16]** And to the Reubenites and the Gadites I assigned the part from Gilead down to the wadi Arnon, the middle of the wadi being the boundary, and up to the wadi Jabbok, the boundary of the Ammonites.

Salcah. The city is generally identified with modern Salkhad, southeast of Edrei (see at Deut. 1:4).

11] *Only Og.* This folkloric note pictures Og as the survivor of a race of giants (similarly in Josh. 12:4 and 13:12).
Some believe that "bedstead" was a euphemism for Og's sarcophagus.
Rabbah. Also called Rabbat-B'nei-Ammon. In the Hellenistic period it was one of several cities named Philadelphia (after Ptolemy Philadelphos). Today it is the site of Jordan's capital, Amman.
Standard cubit. Literally, "a man's cubit," possibly figured from the tip of the middle finger to the end of the elbow, similar to the way a yard was figured before it became fixed definitively. There were several cubits, none of which can be precisely reconstructed. The legendary bed was

some thirteen to sixteen feet long and six to seven feet wide [7].

12] *This is the land.* The description proceeds from south to north in verses 12–13, and in reverse in verses 14–16. Reuben had settled in the southernmost portion, south and east of the Dead Sea; Gad settled north of it, and Manasseh occupied the rich land north of Gad, now located mostly in Syria.

14] *Geshurites and Maacathites.* Two Canaanite tribes dwelling in the western part of Manasseh's territory, that is, in the Golan.
Havvoth-jair. Literally, "villages of Jair." According to Num. 32:39 ff. and other passages, the area was known as Gilead.
15] *Machir.* The only son of Manasseh (Jacob's grandson) is here used to represent the tribe.

יהוָה אֱלֹהֵיכֶם לִשְׁנֵי הַמְּלָכִים הָאֵלֶּה כֵּן־יַעֲשֶׂה יהוָה
כב לְכָל־הַמַּמְלָכוֹת אֲשֶׁר אַתָּה עֹבֵר שָׁמָּה: לֹא תִּירָאוּם
כִּי יהוָה אֱלֹהֵיכֶם הוּא הַנִּלְחָם לָכֶם:

Haftarah Devarim, p. 1590

ס ס ס

כג וָאֶתְחַנַּן אֶל־יהוָה בָּעֵת הַהִוא לֵאמֹר: אֲדֹנָי יְהוִה
כד אַתָּה הַחִלּוֹתָ לְהַרְאוֹת אֶת־עַבְדְּךָ אֶת־גָּדְלְךָ וְאֶת־
יָדְךָ הַחֲזָקָה אֲשֶׁר מִי־אֵל בַּשָּׁמַיִם וּבָאָרֶץ אֲשֶׁר־
כה יַעֲשֶׂה כְמַעֲשֶׂיךָ וְכִגְבוּרֹתֶךָ: אֶעְבְּרָה־נָּא וְאֶרְאֶה אֶת־
הָאָרֶץ הַטּוֹבָה אֲשֶׁר בְּעֵבֶר הַיַּרְדֵּן הָהָר הַטּוֹב הַזֶּה
כו וְהַלְּבָנֹן: וַיִּתְעַבֵּר יהוָה בִּי לְמַעַנְכֶם וְלֹא שָׁמַע

יז בְּנֵי עַמּוֹן: וְהָעֲרָבָה וְהַיַּרְדֵּן וּגְבֻל מִכִּנֶּרֶת וְעַד
יָם הָעֲרָבָה יָם הַמֶּלַח תַּחַת אַשְׁדֹּת הַפִּסְגָּה מִזְרָחָה:
יח וָאֲצַו אֶתְכֶם בָּעֵת הַהִוא לֵאמֹר יהוָה אֱלֹהֵיכֶם
נָתַן לָכֶם אֶת־הָאָרֶץ הַזֹּאת לְרִשְׁתָּהּ חֲלוּצִים תַּעַבְרוּ
יט לִפְנֵי אֲחֵיכֶם בְּנֵי־יִשְׂרָאֵל כָּל־בְּנֵי־חָיִל: רַק נְשֵׁיכֶם
וְטַפְּכֶם וּמִקְנֵכֶם יָדַעְתִּי כִּי־מִקְנֶה רַב לָכֶם יֵשְׁבוּ
כ בְּעָרֵיכֶם אֲשֶׁר נָתַתִּי לָכֶם: עַד אֲשֶׁר־יָנִיחַ יהוָה
לַאֲחֵיכֶם כָּכֶם וְיָרְשׁוּ גַם־הֵם אֶת־הָאָרֶץ אֲשֶׁר יהוָה
אֱלֹהֵיכֶם נֹתֵן לָהֶם בְּעֵבֶר הַיַּרְדֵּן וְשַׁבְתֶּם אִישׁ
כא לִירֻשָּׁתוֹ אֲשֶׁר נָתַתִּי לָכֶם: וְאֶת־יְהוֹשׁוּעַ צִוֵּיתִי בָּעֵת
הַהִוא לֵאמֹר עֵינֶיךָ הָרֹאֹת אֵת כָּל־אֲשֶׁר עָשָׂה

* כ סבורין לכם.

17] [We also seized] the Arabah, from the foot of the slopes of Pisgah on the east, to the edge of the Jordan, and from Chinnereth down to the sea of the Arabah, the Dead Sea.

18] At that time I charged you, saying, "The LORD your God has given you this country to possess. You must go as shocktroops, warriors all, at the head of your Israelite kinsmen. **19]** Only your wives, children, and livestock—I know that you have much livestock—shall be left in the towns I have assigned to you, **20]** until the LORD has granted your kinsmen a haven such as you have, and they too have taken possession of the land that the LORD your God is giving them, beyond the Jordan. Then you may return each to the homestead that I have assigned to him."

21] I also charged Joshua at that time, saying, "You have seen with your own eyes all that the LORD your God has done to these two kings; so shall the LORD do to all the kingdoms into which you shall cross over. **22]** Do not fear them, for it is the LORD your God who will battle for you."

23] I pleaded with the LORD at that time, saying, **24]** "O Lord GOD, You who let Your servant see the first works of Your greatness and Your mighty hand, You whose powerful deeds no god in heaven or on earth can equal! **25]** Let me, I pray, cross over and see the good land on the other side of the Jordan, that good hill country, and the Lebanon." **26]** But the

17] *Pisgah.* A mountain range northeast of the Dead Sea, where later on Moses will die (34:1–5).

Chinnereth. A city from which Lake Kinneret (also called Sea of Galilee or Lake Tiberias) received its name.

Dead Sea. Literally, "Salt Sea," the lowest spot on earth. Its water is heavily salinated and only microscopic life exists in it.

18] *I charged you.* I charged the two and a half tribes.

Shock-troops. חֲלוּצִים (*chalutzim*). In modern Hebrew the term has come to mean "pioneers."

19] *I know that you have.* The kind of interjection a speaker is likely to make.

24] *O Lord God.* אֲדֹנָי יֱהֹוִה. Usually יהוה is voweled יְהֹוָה, but when following the word Adonai its voweling is that of אֱלֹהִים (*Elohim*), and the two words are pronounced *Adonai Elohim*.

No god in heaven. There is none whom others call "god" who can equal Israel's Lord (see further at Exod. 20:3).

25] *Hill country.* The Judean hills.

וְחַזְּקֵהוּ וְאַמְּצֵהוּ כִּי־הוּא יַעֲבֹר לִפְנֵי הָעָם הַזֶּה　　אֵלָי וַיֹּאמֶר יְהוָה אֵלַי רַב־לָךְ אַל־תּוֹסֶף דַּבֵּר
כט וְהוּא יַנְחִיל אוֹתָם אֶת־הָאָרֶץ אֲשֶׁר תִּרְאֶה: וַנֵּשֶׁב　　כו אֵלַי עוֹד בַּדָּבָר הַזֶּה: עֲלֵה רֹאשׁ הַפִּסְגָּה וְשָׂא
בַּגַּיְא מוּל בֵּית פְּעוֹר:　　עֵינֶיךָ יָמָּה וְצָפֹנָה וְתֵימָנָה וּמִזְרָחָה וּרְאֵה בְעֵינֶיךָ
פ　　כז כִּי־לֹא תַעֲבֹר אֶת־הַיַּרְדֵּן הַזֶּה: וְצַו אֶת־יְהוֹשֻׁעַ

LORD was wrathful with me on your account and would not listen to me. The LORD said to me, "Enough! Never speak to Me of this matter again! 27] Go up to the summit of Pisgah and gaze about, to the west, the north, the south, and the east. Look at it well, for you shall not go across yonder Jordan. 28] Give Joshua his instructions, and inbue him with strength and courage, for he shall go across at the head of this people and he shall allot to them the land that you may only see."

29] Meanwhile we stayed on in the valley near Beth-peor.

26] *The Lord was wrathful.* וַיִּתְעַבֵּר is a word play on אֶעְבְּרָה (verse 25): God's anger is a response to Moses' plea.

The Lord said to me. The interplay between God and Moses was greatly expanded by the Midrash; see Gleanings at chapter 34.

29] *Beth-peor.* Where Israel sinned with the women of Moab (Num. 25:1 ff.) and where Moses will be buried (Deut. 34:6). It probably was near Heshbon, but the exact location is unknown.

Variant Traditions

The stories here related are found also in the Book of Numbers, and there is general agreement between these accounts. However, in Moses' recollections a series of colorful and informative asides are included, which deal in part with history and geography and in part with folklore, such as the remarkable bedstead of Og. Another and important difference is the role assigned to Caleb and Joshua. The Deuteronomic account of Israel's faithlessness singles out Caleb alone as the one who by his demonstrated faith had merited the right to enter Canaan. He had opposed the majority and had insisted that Israel could overcome all obstacles if only they trusted God's word. Joshua too was spared, not because (as in Num. 14:6) he had stood with Caleb against the multitude, but because he was Moses' lieutenant and he alone was trained to lead the nation.

Another difference is the way Moses was punished. In Deuteronomy, Moses suffered exclusion from Canaan because, as a leader, he shared his people's fate. In Numbers, Moses was punished for his individual sin—though what precisely the sin was is not clear (see Commentary on Numbers, chapter 20). Further differences occur in the descriptions of Israel's relationship with Edom and Moab (see at 2:4 and 2:28).

In all these cases it is apparent that there were variant traditions about Israel's wanderings which in time were joined. Their confluence—in a process that lasted many hundreds of years—resulted eventually in the text as we have it now. In general, the Deuteronomic account of Israel's wanderings is more detailed, more given to relating folklore, and more hortatory than Numbers, for its primary aim is to give moral instructions. Yet despite these differences the basic stories are the same. After the disastrous incident with the spies when Israel had refused to go forward, the people wandered about the Negev and the Sinai peninsula, and not until the old generation had died did they prepare for a new thrust. During their fortieth year in the wilderness they went northward, taking a route to the east of the Aravah, through the hills and plains of today's Kingdom of Jordan. They skirted Edom (east of the Negev) on its eastern side and then attacked the realms of Sihon and Og, conquering them and settling two and a half tribes on their territories. These wars mark the end of Israel's wanderings for, when Moses will have finished his last instructions and will have died east of the Jordan, his successor Joshua will lead the people into Canaan and begin the long struggle to occupy the whole land—a struggle that was not to be finished until the time of David and Solomon, more than two hundred years later.

God's Realm

In two important passages the second chapter concerns itself with the extension of God's realm beyond Israel. The influence that God has over Israel's fate is of course the foundation of all biblical thinking about Him. It is taken for granted that God's power was unlimited as far as His chosen ones were concerned; He could and did destroy Israel's enemies when it pleased Him. The whole Exodus story was a demonstration of His might and a paean to His glory. God and Israel were the focus; the Egyptians and other nations appeared to merit God's attention only in relation to Israel.[1]

---

[1] This is so, even though there is never any question that God created the nations; see Gen. 10 and 11. Only once in the first four books of the Torah is there another dimension, when it is said that the inhabit-

Now, in 2:5 and 2:19, a new note is struck. Israel is specifically instructed not to touch Edom and Ammon, for these are given as inalienable possessions to their inhabitants: Edom to the descendants of Esau (Isaac's older son and Jacob's brother), and Ammon to the offspring of Lot (Abraham's nephew). To be sure, this makes the Edomites and Ammonites Israel's kinsmen, but it is not the relationship alone that causes God to concern himself with them. After all, Moab too, like Ammon, is pictured as Lot's inheritance (stained though it was, Gen. 19:37–38), but Moab's land is never considered sacrosanct. It is subject to conquest like all of Canaan whose inhabitants are by divine preordination destined to be conquered by the Israelites.

The permanent allotment of the lands of Edom and Ammon to their inhabitants introduces a concept which later prophets (especially the Second Isaiah) stressed with great force: it is God's unique quality that He holds sway over all the nations, cares for them, and judges them. He is the one single God, He is God alone (Deut. 6:4), and there is no power beside Him. Other gods are false, and their adoration futile. Here, then, monotheism is proclaimed in its full force, and the Book of Deuteronomy devotes much space to its proclamation. Deut. 2:5 and 2:19 are notations made on the canvas of Israel's story and they hint at the fuller development which Moses will give to the theme of the all-embracing One God of the world.

ants of Canaan will forfeit the land because of their misdeeds—implying that otherwise they had a di-

vine right of possession. Not until Deuteronomy, however, does this dimension come into full view.

GLEANINGS

Alive or Dead
The word מְתִים (men) is very similar to the word מֵתִים (dead). This shows that the difference between alive and dead is small, it is merely the position of the dots under the מ.

ITTURE TORAH [8]

Va'etchanan
The opening word of the weekly portion (3:23) is a form which suggests a reflexive sense, such as "I got myself to plead."

Said the Rabbi of Tsans, in like manner: "Before I begin to pray, I pray that I may be able to pray." [9]

At That Time (Deut. 3:23)
Moses prayed "at that time." When is "that time" for prayer? Any time, and not when it appears convenient. Moses prayed then and there—learn from him.

ISRAEL SALANTER [10]

Gematria
According to tradition, Moses spoke 515 prayers for וָאֶתְחַנַּן equals 515 by gematria, and so does תְּפִלָּה (prayer). Now, if God is present in prayer (add יהוה = 26) you obtain 541, a number equivalent to the letters in יִשְׂרָאֵל (Israel).[2] If Israel clings to God in prayer, it will gain true life.

CHATAM SOFER [11]

2 וֹ=6, אֿ=1, תֿ=400, חֿ=8, נֿ=50 (twice);
תֿ=400, פֿ=80, לֿ=30, הֿ=5;

יֿ=10, הֿ=5, וֿ=6, הֿ=5;
יֿ=10, שֿ=300, רֿ=200, אֿ=1; לֿ=30.

Note that the word for song (שִׁירָה) also adds up to 515,[3] for song and prayer go together.

M. HACOHEN [12]

What Moses Saw

Moses saw "the good land" (3:25), that is, the good *in* the land, unlike the spies who saw the bad in it.

CHASIDIC [13]

Moses encompassed with his gaze more than Joshua or his successor would actually tread upon. His vision was larger than subsequent reality.

M. HACOHEN [14]

That Good Hill Country (Deut. 3:25)

Throughout the Hebrew Scripture we find a deep love of mountains and mountain scenery. The Rabbis even introduced a special blessing to be recited on beholding lofty mountains.[4] Thus the Psalmist sang: "I turn my eyes to the mountains; from where will my help come?" (121:1)

AFTER J. H. HERTZ

Enough! (Deut. 3:26)

According to a midrash, Moses failed to understand God's judgment and even ventured to say: "If that is the way it is to be, then all men are alike and there is no difference between the righteous and the sinner, and all is accidental."[5] God cut him short and said "Enough! Never speak to Me of this matter again!"

TANCHUMA [15]

"Enough!" is a warning which implies man's need to realize that all he can do is do his part; this is enough. Man cannot ever hope to fulfill all his human wishes. He must accept whatever gratification comes from his particular role in the work of achieving God's will, even if he will not taste the fruit of his labor.

THE BIBLE READER [16]

---

[3] שׁ=300, יִ=10, רִ=200, הָ=5

[4] "Blessed are You, Lord God, Ruler of the universe, Author of the work of Creation."

[5] This is similar to the midrashic interpretation given to Gen. 4 by Jonathan ben Uzziel, who ascribes the same outburst to Cain; see our Commentary on Genesis, chapter 4, Gleanings.

Summary: To Observe the Law

Moses now proceeds from a consideration of the past to a summary of the fundamental requirements which God asks of Israel. Such a resumé could have stood at the end of the book; its placement here appears as an intrusion in a text that perhaps once continued directly with the second discourse starting with verse 44. This intrusion is emphasized by the further addition of three verses (41–43) dealing with cities of refuge, a subject that has no connection with what precedes or follows.

The summary sets forth the completeness of Torah as well as its uniqueness, qualities that characterize the treaty-covenant between God and Israel, with the Torah serving as the instrument ratifying this relationship. The first part of chapter 4 is itself cast in this covenantal framework and may be said to be, in this respect, a miniature of the whole Book of Deuteronomy:* It has a prologue (verses 1–8); it specifies the parties and how they came to make the covenant (9–14); it sets forth the request for undivided loyalty to the King (15–18); it issues warnings, with a first intimation of future exile (19–29); it sets forth rewards (30–31) [1].

The recital of the treaty is climaxed by an eloquent statement of God's power and an appeal to observe the law "that it may go well with you and your children" (verse 40).

---

* A similar and more complete parallel to the treaty form will be found below, in chapter 29. See also Hallo's essay above.

ד וְאַתֶּם הַדְּבֵקִים בַּיהוָה אֱלֹהֵיכֶם חַיִּים כֻּלְּכֶם הַיּוֹם:
ה רְאֵה לִמַּדְתִּי אֶתְכֶם חֻקִּים וּמִשְׁפָּטִים כַּאֲשֶׁר צִוַּנִי
יְהוָה אֱלֹהָי לַעֲשׂוֹת כֵּן בְּקֶרֶב הָאָרֶץ אֲשֶׁר אַתֶּם
ו בָּאִים שָׁמָּה לְרִשְׁתָּהּ: וּשְׁמַרְתֶּם וַעֲשִׂיתֶם כִּי הִוא
חָכְמַתְכֶם וּבִינַתְכֶם לְעֵינֵי הָעַמִּים אֲשֶׁר יִשְׁמְעוּן
אֵת כָּל־הַחֻקִּים הָאֵלֶּה וְאָמְרוּ רַק עַם־חָכָם וְנָבוֹן
ז הַגּוֹי הַגָּדוֹל הַזֶּה: כִּי מִי־גוֹי גָּדוֹל אֲשֶׁר־לוֹ אֱלֹהִים
קְרֹבִים אֵלָיו כַּיהוָה אֱלֹהֵינוּ בְּכָל־קָרְאֵנוּ אֵלָיו:

א וְעַתָּה יִשְׂרָאֵל שְׁמַע אֶל־הַחֻקִּים וְאֶל־הַמִּשְׁפָּטִים אֲשֶׁר
אָנֹכִי מְלַמֵּד אֶתְכֶם לַעֲשׂוֹת לְמַעַן תִּחְיוּ וּבָאתֶם
וִירִשְׁתֶּם אֶת־הָאָרֶץ אֲשֶׁר יְהוָה אֱלֹהֵי אֲבֹתֵיכֶם נֹתֵן
ב לָכֶם: לֹא תֹסִפוּ עַל־הַדָּבָר אֲשֶׁר אָנֹכִי מְצַוֶּה אֶתְכֶם
וְלֹא תִגְרְעוּ מִמֶּנּוּ לִשְׁמֹר אֶת־מִצְוֹת יְהוָה אֱלֹהֵיכֶם
ג אֲשֶׁר אָנֹכִי מְצַוֶּה אֶתְכֶם: עֵינֵיכֶם הָרֹאֹת אֵת אֲשֶׁר־
עָשָׂה יְהוָה בְּבַעַל פְּעוֹר כִּי כָל־הָאִישׁ אֲשֶׁר הָלַךְ
אַחֲרֵי בַעַל־פְּעוֹר הִשְׁמִידוֹ יְהוָה אֱלֹהֶיךָ מִקִּרְבֶּךָ:

1] And now, O Israel, give heed to the laws and rules which I am instructing you to observe, so that you may live to enter and occupy the land that the LORD, the god of your fathers, is giving you.   2] You shall not add anything to what I command you or take anything away from it, but keep the commandments of the LORD your God that I enjoin upon you.   3] You saw with your own eyes what the LORD did in the matter of Baal-peor, that the LORD your God wiped out from among you every person who followed Baal-peor;   4] while you, who held fast to the LORD your God, are all alive today.

5] See, I have imparted to you laws and rules, as the LORD my God has commanded me, for you to abide by in the land which you are about to invade and occupy.   6] Observe them faithfully, for that will be proof of your wisdom and discernment to other peoples, who on hearing of all these laws will say, "Surely, that great nation is a wise and discerning people."   7] For what great nation is there that has a god so close at hand as is the LORD our

4:1] *Laws and rules.* The Torah frequently places *chukim* and *mishpatim* next to each other, but the distinction between them is not fully established. A number of theories have been developed: (1) that *chukim* deal with the basic relationship of man to God, the world, and himself, and *mishpatim* with man's relation to his fellow man, as expressed in civil and criminal law; (2) that the reasons for *mishpatim* are clear, whereas those for *chukim* are hidden (for instance, why the consumption of pork is prohibited [2]); (3) that *chukim* are those laws that restrict our sensual life and aim at creating a people of personal purity (for instance, laws of *kashrut* or those defining sexual transgressions [3]); (4) and, most likely, that *mishpatim* represents case law and *chukim* apodictic law, "engraved" for all time. See further our commentary on Exod. 21:1.

So that you may live. The offer of rewards is an important aspect of the covenant model and there-

fore a normal accompaniment of the law, though doing God's will for His sake rather than for reward is a higher form of human response.

3] *The matter of Baal-peor.* Baal-peor, a local Moabite deity whom many Israelites worshiped in a moment of weakness (Num. 25:1–5). The sinful practices may have been sexual orgies.

4] *You . . . held fast.* This phrase was taken into the liturgy and is recited in traditional services before the blessings over the Torah.

6] *Observe them faithfully.* Literally, "observe and do them," a juxtaposition which has led tradition to identify "observe" as the duty to study, which complements the duty to "do" [4].

7] *A god so close at hand.* אֱלֹהִים is constructed with the plural קְרֹבִים suggesting that one should understand "god(s)" and not "God." But this conclusion is not compelling, for in Gen. 20:13 the same construction occurs, but clearly God (and not any god) is meant [5].

ח וּמִ֣י גּ֣וֹי גָּד֔וֹל אֲשֶׁר־ל֛וֹ חֻקִּ֥ים וּמִשְׁפָּטִ֖ים צַדִּיקִ֑ם
כְּכֹל֙ הַתּוֹרָ֣ה הַזֹּ֔את אֲשֶׁ֧ר אָנֹכִ֛י נֹתֵ֥ן לִפְנֵיכֶ֖ם הַיּֽוֹם:
ט רַ֡ק הִשָּׁ֣מֶר לְךָ֩ וּשְׁמֹ֨ר נַפְשְׁךָ֜ מְאֹ֗ד פֶּן־תִּשְׁכַּ֣ח אֶת־
הַדְּבָרִ֣ים אֲשֶׁר־רָא֣וּ עֵינֶ֗יךָ וּפֶן־יָס֙וּרוּ֙ מִלְּבָ֣בְךָ֔ כֹּ֖ל
י יְמֵ֣י חַיֶּ֑יךָ וְהוֹדַעְתָּ֥ם לְבָנֶ֖יךָ וְלִבְנֵ֣י בָנֶ֑יךָ: י֗וֹם אֲשֶׁ֣ר
עָמַ֣דְתָּ לִפְנֵי֩ יְהֹוָ֨ה אֱלֹהֶ֜יךָ בְּחֹרֵ֗ב בֶּאֱמֹ֨ר יְהֹוָ֜ה
אֵלַ֗י הַקְהֶל־לִי֙ אֶת־הָעָ֔ם וְאַשְׁמִעֵ֖ם אֶת־דְּבָרָ֑י אֲשֶׁ֨ר
יִלְמְד֜וּן לְיִרְאָ֣ה אֹתִ֗י כׇּל־הַיָּמִים֙ אֲשֶׁ֨ר הֵ֤ם חַיִּים֙
יא עַל־הָ֣אֲדָמָ֔ה וְאֶת־בְּנֵיהֶ֖ם יְלַמֵּדֽוּן: וַתִּקְרְב֥וּן וַתַּעַמְדֽוּן

God whenever we call upon Him?   8] Or what great nation has laws and rules as perfect as all this Teaching that I set before you this day?

9] But take utmost care and watch yourselves scrupulously, so that you do not forget the things that you saw with your own eyes and so that they do not fade from your mind as long as you live. And make them known to your children and to your children's children: 10] The day you stood before the LORD your God at Horeb, when the LORD said to me, "Gather the people to Me that I may let them hear My words, in order that they may learn to revere Me as long as they live on earth, and may so teach their children." 11] You came forward and stood at the foot of the mountain. The mountain was ablaze with flames to the very skies, dark with densest clouds. 12] The LORD spoke to you out of the fire; you heard the sound of words but perceived no shape—nothing but a voice. 13] He declared to you the covenant which He commanded you to observe, the Ten Commandments; and He inscribed them on two tablets of stone. 14] At the same time the LORD commanded me to impart to you laws and rules for you to observe in the land which you are about to cross into and occupy.

15] For your own sake, therefore, be most careful—since you saw no shape when the LORD

9] *Your mind.* The Hebrew says literally "your heart," for the heart was thought to be the seat of intelligence.

10] *You stood.* Moses identifies his audience with the previous generation (see above, commentary on 1:6–46, "Two Generations").

Gather the people. "Assemble" would be better, as a parallel to 9:10; 10:4; 18:16, where יוֹם הַקָּהָל is rendered as "day of the Assembly."

Revere Me. This does not convey the full meaning of the word. In the biblical view, man's relationship to God goes beyond reverence. יָרֵא means to stand in awe and deference, amazement, trembling, and fear.

11] *The very skies.* Literally, "heart of heaven."

13] *The covenant.* בְּרִית (berit) denotes the fundamental relationship of God with Israel; see below, verse 37, and our commentary on Exod. 19:1–25, "The Covenant."

Ten Commandments. They represent the covenant but are not identical with it. On the term, see at Exod. 20.

14] *To impart to you.* Moses conveys all divine laws to Israel as God's intermediary, with the exception of the Ten Commandments, which are, at least in part, transmitted directly by God.

הַבַּרְזֶל מִמִּצְרָיִם לִהְיוֹת לוֹ לְעַם נַחֲלָה כַּיּוֹם הַזֶּה:
כא וַיהוָה הִתְאַנַּף־בִּי עַל־דִּבְרֵיכֶם וַיִּשָּׁבַע לְבִלְתִּי עָבְרִי
אֶת־הַיַּרְדֵּן וּלְבִלְתִּי־בֹא אֶל־הָאָרֶץ הַטּוֹבָה אֲשֶׁר
כב יְהוָה אֱלֹהֶיךָ נֹתֵן לְךָ נַחֲלָה: כִּי אָנֹכִי מֵת בָּאָרֶץ
הַזֹּאת אֵינֶנִּי עֹבֵר אֶת־הַיַּרְדֵּן וְאַתֶּם עֹבְרִים וִירִשְׁתֶּם
כג אֶת־הָאָרֶץ הַטּוֹבָה הַזֹּאת: הִשָּׁמְרוּ לָכֶם פֶּן־תִּשְׁכְּחוּ
אֶת־בְּרִית יְהוָה אֱלֹהֵיכֶם אֲשֶׁר כָּרַת עִמָּכֶם וַעֲשִׂיתֶם
לָכֶם פֶּסֶל תְּמוּנַת כֹּל אֲשֶׁר צִוְּךָ יְהוָה אֱלֹהֶיךָ:
כד כִּי יְהוָה אֱלֹהֶיךָ אֵשׁ אֹכְלָה הוּא אֵל קַנָּא: פ

* כן סבורין כאשר.

טו מִתּוֹךְ הָאֵשׁ: פֶּן־תַּשְׁחִתוּן וַעֲשִׂיתֶם לָכֶם פֶּסֶל תְּמוּנַת
טז כָּל־סָמֶל תַּבְנִית זָכָר אוֹ נְקֵבָה: תַּבְנִית כָּל־בְּהֵמָה
אֲשֶׁר בָּאָרֶץ תַּבְנִית כָּל־צִפּוֹר כָּנָף אֲשֶׁר תָּעוּף
יז בַּשָּׁמָיִם: תַּבְנִית כָּל־רֹמֵשׂ בָּאֲדָמָה תַּבְנִית כָּל־דָּגָה
יח אֲשֶׁר־בַּמַּיִם מִתַּחַת לָאָרֶץ: וּפֶן־תִּשָּׂא עֵינֶיךָ הַשָּׁמַיְמָה
וְרָאִיתָ אֶת־הַשֶּׁמֶשׁ וְאֶת־הַיָּרֵחַ וְאֶת־הַכּוֹכָבִים כֹּל
צְבָא הַשָּׁמַיִם וְנִדַּחְתָּ וְהִשְׁתַּחֲוִיתָ לָהֶם וַעֲבַדְתָּם אֲשֶׁר
חָלַק יְהוָה אֱלֹהֶיךָ אֹתָם לְכֹל הָעַמִּים תַּחַת כָּל־
כ הַשָּׁמָיִם: וְאֶתְכֶם לָקַח יְהוָה וַיּוֹצִא אֶתְכֶם מִכּוּר

your God spoke to you at Horeb out of the fire— **16]** not to act wickedly and make for yourselves a sculptured image in any likeness whatever: the form of a man or a woman, **17]** the form of any beast on earth, the form of any winged bird that flies in the sky, **18]** the form of anything that creeps on the ground, the form of any fish that is in the waters below the earth. **19]** And when you look up to the sky and behold the sun and the moon and the stars, the whole heavenly host, you must not be lured into bowing down to them or serving them. These the LORD your God allotted to the other peoples everywhere under heaven; **20]** but you the LORD took and brought out of Egypt, that iron blast furnace, to be His very own people, as is now the case.

21] Now the LORD was angry with me on your account and swore that I should not cross the Jordan and enter the good land that the LORD your God is giving you as a heritage. **22]** For I must die in this land; I shall not cross the Jordan. But you will cross and take possession of that good land. **23]** Take care, then, not to forget the covenant that the LORD your God concluded with you, and not to make for yourselves a sculptured image in any likeness, against which the LORD your God has enjoined you. **24]** For the LORD your God is a consuming fire, an impassioned God.

16] *Sculptured image.* For the purpose of idolatry.

18] *Waters below the earth.* The ancients believed the earth to be flat and resting on water.

19] *Sun and the moon.* Which were worshiped in various countries. Thus the moon god was adored in Ur, whence Abraham's family came.

Allotted to the other peoples. This appears to suggest that non-Israelites are permitted to worship such deities, and that in this sense everything has its origin with God, even the practice of idolatry, which He has allotted to other nations [6].

The Talmud adds, however, that idolaters—by yielding to the opportunity—are causing their own destruction. Luzzatto considered the text to stress God's way of leading men upward.

20] *His very own people.* עַם נַחֲלָה, literally, "people of (His) inheritance." In 7:6 and 14:2 Israel is called סְגֻלָּה, (His) treasured people. On the concept of chosenness see at Exod. 19:5.

21] *And swore.* This was not related in Num. 20:12. See above, commentary on 2:1–3:29, "Variant Traditions," on the two traditions about the punishment of Moses.

Tradition harmonizes the discrepancy by saying that the judgment in Numbers was pronounced by God in the form of an oath [7].

24] *Impassioned God.* Older translations had "jealous"; see at Exod. 20:5.

כה כִּי־תוֹלִיד בָּנִים וּבְנֵי בָנִים וְנוֹשַׁנְתֶּם בָּאָרֶץ וְהִשְׁחַתֶּם וַעֲשִׂיתֶם פֶּסֶל תְּמוּנַת כֹּל וַעֲשִׂיתֶם הָרַע בְּעֵינֵי

כו יְהוָה־אֱלֹהֶיךָ לְהַכְעִיסוֹ: הַעִידֹתִי בָכֶם הַיּוֹם אֶת־הַשָּׁמַיִם וְאֶת־הָאָרֶץ כִּי־אָבֹד תֹּאבֵדוּן מַהֵר מֵעַל הָאָרֶץ אֲשֶׁר אַתֶּם עֹבְרִים אֶת־הַיַּרְדֵּן שָׁמָּה לְרִשְׁתָּהּ לֹא־תַאֲרִיכֻן יָמִים עָלֶיהָ כִּי הִשָּׁמֵד תִּשָּׁמֵדוּן:

כז וְהֵפִיץ יְהוָה אֶתְכֶם בָּעַמִּים וְנִשְׁאַרְתֶּם מְתֵי מִסְפָּר

כח בַּגּוֹיִם אֲשֶׁר יְנַהֵג יְהוָה אֶתְכֶם שָׁמָּה: וַעֲבַדְתֶּם־שָׁם אֱלֹהִים מַעֲשֵׂה יְדֵי אָדָם עֵץ וָאֶבֶן אֲשֶׁר לֹא־יִרְאוּן

כט וְלֹא יִשְׁמְעוּן וְלֹא יֹאכְלוּן וְלֹא יְרִיחֻן: וּבִקַּשְׁתֶּם מִשָּׁם אֶת־יְהוָה אֱלֹהֶיךָ וּמָצָאתָ כִּי תִדְרְשֶׁנּוּ בְּכָל־

ל לְבָבְךָ וּבְכָל־נַפְשֶׁךָ: בַּצַּר לְךָ וּמְצָאוּךָ כֹּל הַדְּבָרִים הָאֵלֶּה בְּאַחֲרִית הַיָּמִים וְשַׁבְתָּ עַד־יְהוָה אֱלֹהֶיךָ

לא וְשָׁמַעְתָּ בְּקֹלוֹ: כִּי אֵל רַחוּם יְהוָה אֱלֹהֶיךָ לֹא יַרְפְּךָ וְלֹא יַשְׁחִיתֶךָ וְלֹא יִשְׁכַּח אֶת־בְּרִית אֲבֹתֶיךָ

לב אֲשֶׁר נִשְׁבַּע לָהֶם: כִּי שְׁאַל־נָא לְיָמִים רִאשֹׁנִים אֲשֶׁר־הָיוּ לְפָנֶיךָ לְמִן־הַיּוֹם אֲשֶׁר בָּרָא אֱלֹהִים אָדָם עַל־הָאָרֶץ וּלְמִקְצֵה הַשָּׁמַיִם וְעַד־קְצֵה הַשָּׁמָיִם

25] Should you, when you have begotten children and children's children and are long established in the land, act wickedly and make for yourselves a sculptured image in any likeness, causing the LORD your God displeasure and vexation,   **26]** I call heaven and earth this day to witness against you that you shall soon perish from the land which you are crossing the Jordan to occupy; you shall not long endure in it, but shall be utterly wiped out.   **27]** The LORD will scatter you among the peoples, and only a scant few of you shall be left among the nations to which the LORD will drive you.   **28]** There you will serve man-made gods of wood and stone, that cannot see or hear or eat or smell.

29] But if you search there for the LORD your God, you will find Him, if only you seek Him with all your heart and soul—   **30]** when you are in distress because all these things have befallen you and, in the end, return to the LORD your God and obey Him.   **31]** For the LORD your God is a compassionate God: He will not fail you nor will He let you perish; He will not forget the covenant which He made on oath with your fathers.

32] You have but to inquire about bygone ages that came before you, ever since God created man on earth, from one end of heaven to the other: has anything as grand as this ever happened,

25] *Should you.* Traditional interpreters take this to be a prophecy, critical scholars as a passage arising out of some devastating experience.

Long established. Literally, "grown old"; when you will have lost your spiritual keenness.

26] *I call heaven and earth.* A frequent expression in Deuteronomy, having legal force as in vassal treaties. Heaven and earth function as witnesses [8]. See also at 32:1.

28] *There you will serve.* In exile Israel will be forced to practice the very idolatry they had voluntarily chosen in Canaan.

29] *But if you search . . . you will find.* The image of searching and finding is found in Jer. 29:13 and Isa. 55:6.

30] *In the end.* The expression projects Israel's return to God in the course of time; it does not here have the posthistorical sense that later prophets gave it.

31] *A compassionate God.* See at Exod. 34:6.

32] *Ever since God created man.* From this, the halachah derived restrictions about inquiries into what happened *before* creation and into the nature of heaven and hell [9].

הֲנִהְיָה כַּדָּבָר הַגָּדוֹל הַזֶּה אוֹ הֲנִשְׁמַע כָּמֹהוּ:

לי הֲשָׁמַע עָם קוֹל אֱלֹהִים מְדַבֵּר מִתּוֹךְ־הָאֵשׁ כַּאֲשֶׁר־
לד שָׁמַעְתָּ אַתָּה וַיֶּחִי: אוֹ הֲנִסָּה אֱלֹהִים לָבוֹא לָקַחַת
לוֹ גוֹי מִקֶּרֶב גּוֹי בְּמַסֹּת בְּאֹתֹת וּבְמוֹפְתִים וּבְמִלְחָמָה
וּבְיָד חֲזָקָה וּבִזְרוֹעַ נְטוּיָה וּבְמוֹרָאִים גְּדֹלִים כְּכֹל
אֲשֶׁר־עָשָׂה לָכֶם יְהֹוָה אֱלֹהֵיכֶם בְּמִצְרַיִם לְעֵינֶיךָ:
לה אַתָּה הָרְאֵתָ לָדַעַת כִּי יְהֹוָה הוּא הָאֱלֹהִים אֵין
עוֹד מִלְבַדּוֹ: מִן־הַשָּׁמַיִם הִשְׁמִיעֲךָ אֶת־קֹלוֹ לְיַסְּרֶךָּ
וְעַל־הָאָרֶץ הֶרְאֲךָ אֶת־אִשּׁוֹ הַגְּדוֹלָה וּדְבָרָיו שָׁמַעְתָּ
לז מִתּוֹךְ הָאֵשׁ: וְתַחַת כִּי אָהַב אֶת־אֲבֹתֶיךָ וַיִּבְחַר

בְּזַרְעוֹ אַחֲרָיו וַיּוֹצִאֲךָ בְּפָנָיו בְּכֹחוֹ הַגָּדֹל מִמִּצְרָיִם:
לח לְהוֹרִישׁ גּוֹיִם גְּדֹלִים וַעֲצֻמִים מִמְּךָ מִפָּנֶיךָ לַהֲבִיאֲךָ
לט לָתֶת־לְךָ אֶת־אַרְצָם נַחֲלָה כַּיּוֹם הַזֶּה: וְיָדַעְתָּ הַיּוֹם
וַהֲשֵׁבֹתָ אֶל־לְבָבֶךָ כִּי יְהֹוָה הוּא הָאֱלֹהִים בַּשָּׁמַיִם
מ מִמַּעַל וְעַל־הָאָרֶץ מִתָּחַת אֵין עוֹד: וְשָׁמַרְתָּ אֶת־
חֻקָּיו וְאֶת־מִצְוֹתָיו אֲשֶׁר אָנֹכִי מְצַוְּךָ הַיּוֹם אֲשֶׁר
יִיטַב לְךָ וּלְבָנֶיךָ אַחֲרֶיךָ וּלְמַעַן תַּאֲרִיךְ יָמִים
עַל־הָאֲדָמָה אֲשֶׁר יְהֹוָה אֱלֹהֶיךָ נֹתֵן לְךָ
כָּל־הַיָּמִים: פ

• לֹא כָּךְ צָרִיךְ לִבְטֹא.

or has its like ever been known? **33]** Has any people heard the voice of a god speaking out of a fire, as you have, and survived? **34]** Or has any god ventured to go and take for himself one nation from the midst of another by prodigious acts, by signs and portents, by war, by a mighty and outstretched arm and awesome power, as the LORD your God did for you in Egypt before your very eyes? **35]** It has been clearly demonstrated to you that the LORD alone is God; there is none beside Him. **36]** From the heavens He let you hear His voice to discipline you; on earth He let you see His great fire; and from amidst that fire you heard His words. **37]** And because He loved your fathers, He chose their offspring after them; He Himself, in His great might, led you out of Egypt, **38]** to drive from your path nations greater and more populous than you, to take you into their land and give it to you as a heritage, as is still the case. **39]** Know therefore this day and keep in mind that the LORD alone is God in heaven above and on earth below; there is no other. **40]** Observe His laws and commandments, which I enjoin upon you this day, that it may go well with you and your children after you, and that you may long remain in the land that the LORD your God is giving you for all time.

33] *And survived.* Ordinarily human beings cannot behold the Divine and live (Exod. 33:20). Only Israel was granted moments of exception (Exod. 20:19).

34] *Outstretched arm.* See Exod. 6:6.

35] *Clearly demonstrated.* Literally, "you have been shown to know." The phrase has entered the liturgy for Shemini Atzeret-Simchat Torah [10].

37] *Because He loved your fathers.* The love was an unconditional grant extended to Abraham, Isaac, and Jacob and remained so for their descendants. But Deuteronomy made the grant of land dependent on Israel's compliance with the law [11].

Their offspring. Literally, "his offspring," referring either to the Fathers as a collective or to one of them, possibly Jacob, who gave the people his name [12].

38] *As is still the case.* Referring to the abiding love of God.

Von Rad reads the phrase as applying to Israel's occupation of the land and says that the editor "forgot the fiction that it was Moses speaking" [13].

39] *Know therefore.* The sentence has entered the daily liturgy and concludes the first paragraph of the *Aleinu* [14].

מא אָז יַבְדִּיל מֹשֶׁה שָׁלֹשׁ עָרִים בְּעֵבֶר הַיַּרְדֵּן מִזְרְחָה שָׁמֶשׁ: מב לָנֻס שָׁמָּה רוֹצֵחַ אֲשֶׁר יִרְצַח אֶת־רֵעֵהוּ בִּבְלִי־דַעַת וְהוּא לֹא־שֹׂנֵא לוֹ מִתְּמֹל שִׁלְשֹׁם וְנָס

מג אֶל־אַחַת מִן־הֶעָרִים הָאֵל וָחָי: אֶת־בֶּצֶר בַּמִּדְבָּר בְּאֶרֶץ הַמִּישֹׁר לָרֻאוּבֵנִי וְאֶת־רָאמֹת בַּגִּלְעָד לַגָּדִי וְאֶת־גּוֹלָן בַּבָּשָׁן לַמְנַשִּׁי:

* סב סבורין האלה.
* מג כן צריך לבטא.

41] Then Moses set aside three cities on the east side of the Jordan,   **42]** to which a manslayer could escape, one who unwittingly slew a fellow man without having been hostile to him in the past; he could flee to one of these cities and live: **43]** Bezer, in the wilderness in the Tableland, belonging to the Reubenites; Ramoth, in Gilead, belonging to the Gadites; and Golan, in Bashan, belonging to the Manassites.

41] *Then Moses set aside.* According to Num. 35:10 ff. (see commentary there) six cities of refuge were to be set aside, three of them on the eastern side of the Jordan where three tribes had already settled. The Talmud speculates that the sparsely populated eastern territories needed as many cities of refuge as the rest of the country together because of the high incidence of crime [15]. Already Hosea called Gilead a land "covered with footprints of blood" (6:8).

43] *Bezer . . . Ramoth . . . Golan.* Their precise location is not known. Bezer was southeast of the Dead Sea; Ramoth, near today's Amman; Golan, somewhere on the Golan Heights.

Neither Add Nor Detract

One of the laws which in time assumed crucial significance reads: "You shall not add anything to what I command you or take anything away from it ..." (4:2). It is possible that such an injunction was at first directed to the scribes, warning them to keep the text exactly as they found it, with its apparent contradictions, mistakes in spelling, duplications, and incomprehensible passages. A similar rule was already in effect in ancient Egypt, a thousand years prior to the Exodus, and is also reflected in the Akkadian Epic of Erra. There it is said of the poet who had been taught a poem that "he left nothing out nor did he add a single line" [16]. In Jeremiah's vision the prophet was cautioned not to leave out a single word when he transmitted divine instruction; and a proverb, in exalting God's teaching, said, "Add not to His words." Two other passages clearly established the rule as applying to the essence of God's work and word: Koheleth proclaimed that whatever God did was "for ever," and another passage in Deuteronomy enjoined the Israelites to be careful and observe only what they had been taught, neither more nor less.[1]

In later centuries, both 4:2 and 13:1 became proof texts for limiting changes in and interpretations of the Torah laws. Special note was taken of the fact that 4:2 is phrased in the plural while 13:1 is couched in the singular. Thus the former was understood to be addressed to the leaders of the community who were warned not to pass off their injunctions as equivalent to the Torah itself and to let the people know at all times what was of rabbinic and what of pentateuchal origin (מִדְּרַבָּנָן and מִדְּאוֹרַיְיתָא) [17]. On the other hand, 13:1 was seen to address itself

to each individual, exhorting him to complete and meticulous observance [18]. But rabbinic law was not in itself seen as innovative, it only made the intent of the Torah "clearer" (though often it did so innovatively).

Another reading of the two verses became even more important, for it understood 4:2 as prohibiting changes in the number of the commandments—there were according to tradition 613 mitzvot in the Torah—so that there should not be 612 or 614; and 13:1 was seen to mean that each individual mitzvah was to be carried out as specified and was not to be tampered with.[2] Thus, since an authoritative interpretation of the laws of phylacteries had arrived at four paragraphs that were to be inscribed on the parchment, this was to remain an unalterable rule, as were four double threads in the ritual fringes [19]. Moreover, the general rule was declared applicable both in Eretz Yisrael and in the Diaspora.

The Course of Jewish Law

To be sure, no community could survive and grow without an organic development of its laws. Halachah—the body of written and oral law—became the instrument by which the Jewish people ordered their lives. While the Written Torah remained unchanged and unchangeable, the Oral Torah interpreted it, thereby expanding and contracting it in accordance with the needs of new times. The Rabbis created a set of guidelines that spelled out the possibilities of such interpretation; for instance, they determined how analogies were to be used, how legal inferences were to be made, or how the repetition of certain laws affected their content. At first, out of deference to the strict injunc-

---

[1] Jer. 26:2; Prov. 30:6; Eccles. 3:14; Deut. 13:1.
[2] This became particularly important because the Christian church had declared these and similar provisions of the Torah as no longer binding, for in its view the "Old Covenant" (at Sinai) had been set aside by the "New Covenant" (through Jesus).

tions of Deut. 4:2 and 13:1, none of these rabbinic rules and their conclusions was permitted to be written down, but by the year 200 C.E. this restriction was abandoned and the basic code of Jewish life was committed to writing. The result was the Mishnah, which combined into its six sections[3] every aspect of Jewish living, from the regulation of the liturgy to civil and criminal law to family purity. Now the Mishnah became the foundation for legal discussions in the academies and for decisions in the courts, and after three more centuries two bodies of recorded debates and decisions were assembled: one in Palestine (the Palestinian or Jerusalem Talmud—"talmud" meaning study or learning) and the other in Babylon (the Babylonian Talmud). The latter became the commanding, fundamental document for all subsequent ages. It is a vast-ranging commentary on the Mishnah, but it does not usually adhere strictly to the subject at hand and instead covers every conceivable area of human knowledge, Jewish law, popular custom, theological and moral considerations—all arranged rather loosely, reflecting the unstructured discussions of the Sages rather than the rigorous systematizing of an editor.

The Talmud now was the edifice in which Jewish life dwelt, and at once it itself became the object of study, comment, and argument. Scholars wrote legal opinions (responsa) and composed commentaries, and in time abstracts appeared that attempted to summarize all previous contributions to talmudic knowledge and to set down clearly what laws a Jew ought to observe. Of these attempts the code of Maimonides (twelfth century) achieved the greatest authority and deeply influenced Jewish practice during the following centuries, until the appearance of Joseph Karo's *Shulchan Aruch* (sixteenth century). From then on the latter was universally considered the authoritative handbook of Jewish law and life. After its appearance it quickly became the object of scholarly commentary; it was considered extensively in responsa and continues in this capacity until today. Most of the halachah it contains is represented in both its biblical and its rabbinic provisions as binding, for it is taken to be the will of God.

This system was by nature highly conservative, since the Torah, being considered divine, was in principle unamendable, and even the most ingenious interpretation could not alter a rule beyond a certain point. Moreover, the Oral Torah, too, shared in the divine nature of the law and therefore in its resistance to change. Still, the process worked well enough as long as Jews lived in a basically conservative and frequently restricted environment, where faith and custom provided the framework of existence. But with the beginning of Enlightenment, at the end of the eighteenth century, Western Jewry left its traditional habitat, both physically and culturally, and this placed enormous strains on the halachah. Its guardians were highly defensive and refused to find legal justifications for even the most minor changes. In consequence, an increasing number of Jews looked for means of adjusting the law to an emerging modern industrial society. The result was the development of Reform Judaism, which amended the law while assuring the preservation of its spirit. The new movement saw its greatest advance in North America, where at the beginning of the twentieth century its members discarded many of the 613 mitzvot, even when they were explicitly stated in or founded on the Written Torah. For them,

[3] *Zeraim* (Seeds), *Mo-ed* (Feasts), *Nashim* (Women), *Nezikin* (Damages), *Kodashim* (Hallowed Things), *Tohorot* (Cleanness).

the provisions of Deut. 4:2 and 13:1 had ceased to be operative, especially—though not exclusively—in the area of ritual practice.[4] Their emphasis was on the moral component of Judaism, which they found championed by the biblical prophets.

Reform Judaism thus largely separated itself from halachic Judaism, which has continued to be vigorously represented by Orthodoxy. Conservatism occupies a middle ground; it stands with Reform in recognizing the human and therefore changeable aspect of the law, while it tries to effect these changes within the framework of the halachah. There has also been a turn toward a greater incorporation of halachic principles within the Reform movement, albeit on a basis that allows for individual decision within the framework of a mitzvah system [20]. The rules laid down by the Deuteronomist have thus experienced a long and varied development, and they continue to be at issue in contemporary Judaism.[5]

---

[4] Such as the careful observance of dietary laws, the wearing of fringes, or rules pertaining to the descendants of priestly families.

[5] In fact, the nature of mitzvah and its theological foundations are a serious problem to Reform Judaism and have been the subject of varying interpretations [21].

GLEANINGS

Never Closed

It says (verse 7) that God is close at hand whenever Israel does call on Him. To "call" on God means to pray, which teaches that the gates of prayer are never closed.   MIDRASH [22]

The Uniqueness of Torah (verse 8)

When other nations follow their laws they are merely law-abiding; when Israel observes the Torah it is at the same time engaged in the praise of God.   CHASIDIC [23]

But Take Utmost Care (verse 9)

Moses warns Israel, the very people who were vouchsafed great miracles, against idolatry. From this you may learn that however pious a person is he is always in potential danger of idolatry and should never fully trust himself.

Literally, verse 9 reads, "Only watch yourself and watch your soul scrupulously."[6] Why the dual warning to both "watch *yourself*" and "watch your *soul* scrupulously"? The word "yourself" refers to your body to which you need give only ordinary attention, and there is little doubt that you will do so. But, when it comes to your soul, you are likely to neglect it, hence "watch your soul scrupulously."   CHASIDIC [24]

The Chain of Generations

Torah is to be taught to children and children's children (verse 9). He who teaches his child Torah is considered as if he taught Torah not only to his child but to his child's children and their children, to the end of time.

A grandchild taught by his grandfather is considered as if he had received the Torah at Sinai.

TALMUD [25]

---

[6] The word נַפְשֶׁךָ is a Hebrew idiom for "your self," but it is here interpreted literally as if it meant "your soul."

The Image

Verse 23 reads strangely in the Hebrew, for in effect it warns us not to make a sculptured image of His mitzvot! It means that mitzvot should not become like idols of wood and stone, without soul and spirit.　　　　CHASIDIC [26]

Gematria

Verses 25 and following contain the prediction that Israel will fall away from God and then be exiled. This will happen when the people are "long established" (וְנוֹשַׁנְתֶּם) in the Land. The Hebrew letters of the word add up to 852[7]—the number of years Israel would dwell in the Land. Actually, however, the people were exiled already after 850 years, that is, two years ahead of the prediction. By not letting the time run out to its full length God avoided also bringing the full force of verse 26 to bear on them, namely, that they would be "utterly wiped out."　　　　RASHI [27]

Searching and Finding (verse 29)

Every promise found in the Torah also contains a command. Thus the promise "The Lord your God is bringing you into a good land..." (8:7) entails the command to go and settle in the Promised Land. So here: "If you search" implies the mitzvah to search without delay.　　　　M. HACOHEN [28]

Distress

In the Hebrew of verse 30 the words "when you are in distress"—בַּצַּר לְךָ—are phrased in the singular (לְךָ, not לָכֶם). Distress confined to an individual is true distress.[8]　　　　MIDRASH [30]

This Day

We are to know God "this day" (verse 39), meaning the duty to rediscover every day that the Lord is God.　　　　CHASIDIC [31]

---

[7] וּ= 6, נ= 50, וּ= 6, שׁ=300, נ=50, תּ=400, ם=40.

[8] Note the proverb: "Distress shared by the community is in itself half a consolation"[29].

PART II

Second Discourse

With the second discourse, the Book of Deuteronomy rises to its heights of oratory. Moses appears as the preacher par excellence, his exhortations are issued with increased insistence. Time and again his commands, issued in God's name, are accompanied by promises as well as imprecations: if the Children of Israel obey the Lord all will be well with them, but, if they leave the path of Torah and mitzvot, disaster will overtake them. In the first discourse, God's past protection was cited as the chief warrant for Israel's compliance with His will; now the law itself is repeated in essence and held up as a unique guide to ethical behavior. God is the focus of exclusive adoration and the seat of ethical concern, and thus the foundations of ethical monotheism (as it has come to be known) are linked to Moses.* "Hear, O Israel" is the ringing address thrice repeated, and "You shall love the Lord your God" stands forth as the opening theme of the discourse. Again it is the nation as a whole which is held responsible for the actions of its members: the measure of their individual adherence to the covenant forms the basis for God's judgment on all Israel, for good and for evil.

While there is general agreement that Moses' first discourse ended with 4:43 (the postscript about the cities of refuge), there is no agreement as to where the second discourse begins and where it ends. Thus, verses 44 to the end of chapter 4 are obviously an introduction of some kind, but this introduction is at once followed by another one (5:1) which appears to be unrelated to it. It may therefore be that 4:44–49 belonged somewhere else, possibly at the beginning of the whole Book of Deuteronomy [1]. Further, the address itself is seen by some to extend up to and including chapter 26 and by others to reach even farther, to 30:20. The majority of scholars, however, believe 11:25 to be the termination of this discourse, a division we have adopted.

Its content can be broadly divided as follows: (1) general introduction, describing the locus (4:44–49); the Decalogue, with introductory and concluding exhortations (chapter 5); (2) the *Shema*, with introduction and follow-up (6:1–19); duty to rehearse the Exodus from Egypt (6:20–25);

---

* See "Introducing Deuteronomy" on the controversy whether Moses' ideas preceded those of the Prophets and were incorporated in Deuteronomy or whether the book was to a large extent the consequence of later teaching, with Moses' name linked to it to give it added authority.

(3) warning not to be tempted by mixed marriage and idolatry (chapter 7); (4) duty not to forget God's goodness toward Israel (chapter 8); (5) recollection of the golden calf episode, of the fashioning of the second tablets, of Israel's stubbornness (9:1–10:11); (6) further exhortation to faith (10:12–11:25).

Again and again Moses recounts God's continuing care for His people and Israel's consequent obligation to obey His will. For Israel is not an ordinary nation; it has a special relationship with the Lord, and out of this relationship comes its potential for holiness and love. It is its task to make the potential actual, and thus the love of God becomes a command, centered upon the Holy One who is the protecting as well as demanding partner of the covenant. (The Deuteronomic view of history is discussed in W. W. Hallo's essay, above.)

The Decalogue

After a brief introduction the second discourse presents a recollection of the covenant at Horeb and of the Ten Commandments. Inasmuch as the Decalogue has been discussed in detail in Exodus 20, the notes below will summarize the earlier commentary and then discuss the differences between the two versions. These differences are most pronounced in the Sabbath commandment, which gives the need for human (instead of God's) rest as the reason for observance.

Traditional commentaries explain the divergencies as purposeful, in that the two versions together are seen to reveal the full meaning of the divine will. This commentary, on the other hand, understands the Exodus Decalogue to represent one sacred tradition and the one in Deuteronomy, another. This explains also why the former speaks of the revelation having taken place at Sinai while the latter places it at Horeb.[1] The latter also stresses the great role that Moses played in the transmission, for his position as intermediary between God and the people is an important aspect of the Deuteronomic version. (On this aspect, see introduction, above.)

It has been suggested that the Decalogue was at one stage of Israel's history part of a sacral recital. If so, it ceased to have this function when the synagogue service was fixed. The Decalogue did not become part of the obligatory daily liturgy, although it is included as an additional reading in Reform, Conservative, and Orthodox prayer books. Perhaps this ambivalent status arose from the fear that the Ten Commandments

[1] On the significance of this difference, see our commentary on Exod. 3:1.

might be considered the heart of Judaism and that the other mitzvot could be disregarded.[2] Once this caution was fully understood the unique position of the Decalogue was given its due emphasis, and it became customary for the congregation to rise in respect when the Ten Words were read from the Torah.[3]

[2] Such a view was held by the Karaitic sect.   [3] In the weekly portions *Yitro* and *Va'etchanan* and on the festival of Shavuot.

מד וְזֹאת הַתּוֹרָה אֲשֶׁר־שָׂם מֹשֶׁה לִפְנֵי בְּנֵי יִשְׂרָאֵל: מט הַר שִׂיאֹן הוּא חֶרְמוֹן: וְכָל־הָעֲרָבָה עֵבֶר הַיַּרְדֵּן
מה אֵלֶּה הָעֵדֹת וְהַחֻקִּים וְהַמִּשְׁפָּטִים אֲשֶׁר דִּבֶּר מֹשֶׁה   מִזְרָחָה וְעַד יָם הָעֲרָבָה תַּחַת אַשְׁדֹּת הַפִּסְגָּה: פ
מו אֶל־בְּנֵי יִשְׂרָאֵל בְּצֵאתָם מִמִּצְרָיִם: בְּעֵבֶר הַיַּרְדֵּן   א וַיִּקְרָא מֹשֶׁה אֶל־כָּל־יִשְׂרָאֵל וַיֹּאמֶר אֲלֵהֶם שְׁמַע
בַּגַּיְא מוּל בֵּית פְּעוֹר בְּאֶרֶץ סִיחֹן מֶלֶךְ הָאֱמֹרִי   יִשְׂרָאֵל אֶת־הַחֻקִּים וְאֶת־הַמִּשְׁפָּטִים אֲשֶׁר אָנֹכִי דֹּבֵר
אֲשֶׁר יוֹשֵׁב בְּחֶשְׁבּוֹן אֲשֶׁר הִכָּה מֹשֶׁה וּבְנֵי יִשְׂרָאֵל   בְּאָזְנֵיכֶם הַיּוֹם וּלְמַדְתֶּם אֹתָם וּשְׁמַרְתֶּם לַעֲשֹׂתָם:
מז בְּצֵאתָם מִמִּצְרָיִם: וַיִּירְשׁוּ אֶת־אַרְצוֹ וְאֶת־אֶרֶץ עוֹג   ב יְהֹוָה אֱלֹהֵינוּ כָּרַת עִמָּנוּ בְּרִית בְּחֹרֵב: לֹא אֶת־
מֶלֶךְ־הַבָּשָׁן שְׁנֵי מַלְכֵי הָאֱמֹרִי אֲשֶׁר בְּעֵבֶר הַיַּרְדֵּן   אֲבֹתֵינוּ כָּרַת יְהֹוָה אֶת־הַבְּרִית הַזֹּאת כִּי אִתָּנוּ
מח מִזְרַח שָׁמֶשׁ: מֵעֲרֹעֵר אֲשֶׁר עַל־שְׂפַת־נַחַל אַרְנֹן וְעַד־   ד אֲנַחְנוּ אֵלֶּה פֹה הַיּוֹם כֻּלָּנוּ חַיִּים: פָּנִים בְּפָנִים

44] This is the Teaching that Moses set before the Israelites: **45]** these are the exhortations, laws, and rules that Moses addressed to the people of Israel, after they had left Egypt, **46]** beyond the Jordan, in the valley at Beth-peor, in the land of Sihon king of the Amorites, who dwelt in Heshbon, whom Moses and the Israelites defeated after they had left Egypt. **47]** They had taken possession of his country and that of Og king of Bashan—the two kings of the Amorites who were on the east side of the Jordan, **48]** from Aroer on the banks of the wadi Arnon, as far as Mount Sion, that is, Hermon; **49]** also the whole Arabah on the east side of the Jordan, as far as the Sea of the Arabah, at the foot of the slopes of Pisgah.

1] Moses summoned all the Israelites and said to them: Hear, O Israel, the laws and rules that I proclaim to you this day! Study them and observe them faithfully!

2] The LORD our God made a covenant with us at Horeb. **3]** It was not with our fathers that the LORD made this covenant, but with us, the living, every one of us who is here today. **4]** Face to face the LORD spoke to you on the mountain out of the fire— **5]** I stood

---

4:44] *This is the Teaching.* וְזֹאת הַתּוֹרָה (*vezot ha-Torah*). This general term is replaced in verse 45 (which forms an introduction from another source) by "exhortations, laws, and norms."

Verse 44 is recited at synagogue services as the Torah scroll is lifted up and shown to the congregation; it is followed by the words:

עַל־פִּי יְהֹוָה בְּיַד־מֹשֶׁה

"At the command of the Lord through Moses" (Num. 4:37).

46] *Land of Sihon.* Victories over Sihon and Og loomed large in the memory of the people, for they established the nation's military competence and constituted the opening phase in the conquest of the Promised Land (see 1:4; 3:2).

48] *Aroer.* See 2:36; 3:8.

Mount Sion. (שִׂיאֹן) Probably a name for Mount Hermon and not to be confused with Zion (צִיּוֹן). The Sidonians called it Sirion; see 3:9.

49] *Pisgah.* The introduction to the discourse ends with a reference to the place where Moses will die.

5:1] *Hear, O Israel.* First of the several times this address is issued. Perhaps it was at one time a formal call to assembly.

3] *Not with our fathers.* That is to say, not with them alone, who are now dead, but also with us, the living. Such elliptical style occurs in other places as well. (On the idea that the covenant bound also those not present, see below, at 29:13.)

4] *Face to face.* This tradition stands in contrast to what the next verse and also verses 20 ff. state, namely, that Moses was God's spokesman.

Nachmanides (Moses ben Nachman Gerondi) reconciles the contradiction by repeating the tradition that Israel heard only the first two commandments directly from God, and the Talmud suggests that God was like the Torah reader at a worship service and Moses the translator and interpreter [1].

כׇּל־תְּמוּנָ֔ה אֲשֶׁ֤ר בַּשָּׁמַ֙יִם֙ מִמַּ֔עַל וַאֲשֶׁ֥ר בָּאָ֖רֶץ מִתָּ֑חַת
וַאֲשֶׁ֥ר בַּמַּ֖יִם מִתַּ֣חַת לָאָ֑רֶץ לֹֽא־תִשְׁתַּחֲוֶ֥ה לָהֶ֖ם וְלֹ֣א
תׇעׇבְדֵ֑ם כִּ֣י אָנֹכִ֞י יְהֹוָ֤ה אֱלֹהֶ֙יךָ֙ אֵ֣ל קַנָּ֔א פֹּ֠קֵד עֲוֺ֨ן
אָב֧וֹת עַל־בָּנִ֛ים וְעַל־שִׁלֵּשִׁ֥ים וְעַל־רִבֵּעִ֖ים לְשֹׂנְאָ֑י וְעֹ֥שֶׂה
חֶ֖סֶד לַאֲלָפִ֑ים לְאֹהֲבַ֖י וּלְשֹׁמְרֵ֥י מִצְוֺתָֽו׃ ס

ה דִּבֶּ֣ר יְהֹוָ֧ה עִמָּכֶ֛ם בָּהָ֖ר מִתּ֣וֹךְ הָאֵ֑שׁ אָנֹכִ֞י עֹמֵ֨ד
בֵּין־יְהֹוָ֤ה וּבֵֽינֵיכֶם֙ בָּעֵ֣ת הַהִ֔וא לְהַגִּ֥יד לָכֶ֖ם אֶת־
דְּבַ֣ר יְהֹוָ֑ה כִּ֤י יְרֵאתֶם֙ מִפְּנֵ֣י הָאֵ֔שׁ וְלֹֽא־עֲלִיתֶ֥ם
י בָּהָ֖ר לֵאמֹֽר׃ ס אָֽנֹכִי֙ יְהֹוָ֣ה אֱלֹהֶ֔יךָ אֲשֶׁ֧ר
הֽוֹצֵאתִ֛יךָ מֵאֶ֥רֶץ מִצְרַ֖יִם מִבֵּ֣ית עֲבָדִ֑ים לֹֽא־יִהְיֶ֥ה
ח לְךָ֛ אֱלֹהִ֥ים אֲחֵרִ֖ים עַל־פָּנָֽיַ׃ לֹֽא־תַעֲשֶֽׂה־לְךָ֣ פֶ֣סֶל

between the LORD and you at that time to convey the LORD's words to you, for you were afraid of the fire and did not go up the mountain—saying:

6] I the LORD am your God who brought you out of the land of Egypt, the house of bondage: **7]** You shall have no other gods beside Me.

8] You shall not make for yourself a sculptured image, any likeness of what is in the heavens above, or on the earth below, or in the waters below the earth. **9]** You shall not bow down to them or serve them. For I the LORD your God am an impassioned God, visiting the guilt of the fathers upon the children, upon the third and upon the fourth generations of those who reject Me, **10]** but showing kindness to the thousandth generation of those who love Me and keep My commandments.

5] *You were afraid.* As recounted in Exod. 20:15–18.

   And did not go up. Here, Israel's fear is given as reason. In Exod. 19:12, 13, 23, it was because of God's warning, reflecting two different traditions.

6] *I the Lord.* Rather, "I am the Lord. . . ." Jewish tradition generally considered this verse, and this verse alone, as the first commandment. It serves also as a preamble in the manner of ancient Near Eastern proclamations. God's claim on His people is as Redeemer, not Creator, and, though it is meant for the whole community, it is (in Hebrew) addressed to the individual Israelite.

7] *You shall have no other gods beside Me.* The opening phrase of the second commandment which extends through verse 10. The singularity of God is a central theme of Deuteronomy, "the commandment of all commandments, in its rigor without parallel in religious history" [2]. It establishes God's exclusive right to Israel's loyalty.

8] *A sculptured image, any likeness.* With the intent to adore it. Though idols were not generally identified as actual gods, they represented them in surrogate fashion: Images were given "life" in special mouth-opening ceremonies, which were renewed periodically by mouth washing. The idols were "fed," and there is evidence that they were buried when damaged. In contrast, יְהֹוָה could not be represented in any form since the world itself was His creation. This commandment does not prohibit plastic works as such, else verse 9 would be unnecessary. Still, the strict construction given to this commandment by the Jews (and by Moslems as well) prevented them for many centuries from developing the sculptured arts freely (see further our commentary on Exod. 20:4).

9] *Impassioned God.* Denoting passion rather than possessiveness (so in the older rendering "jealous God").

יא לֹא תִשָּׂא אֶת־שֵׁם־יְהוָֹה אֱלֹהֶיךָ לַשָּׁוְא כִּי לֹא יְנַקֶּה יְהוָֹה אֵת אֲשֶׁר־יִשָּׂא אֶת־שְׁמוֹ לַשָּׁוְא: ס שָׁמוֹר אֶת־יוֹם הַשַּׁבָּת לְקַדְּשׁוֹ כַּאֲשֶׁר צִוְּךָ יְהוָֹה אֱלֹהֶיךָ: יג שֵׁשֶׁת יָמִים תַּעֲבֹד וְעָשִׂיתָ כָּל־מְלַאכְתֶּךָ: וְיוֹם הַשְּׁבִיעִי שַׁבָּת לַיהוָֹה אֱלֹהֶיךָ לֹא־תַעֲשֶׂה כָל־

מְלָאכָה אַתָּה וּבִנְךָ־וּבִתֶּךָ וְעַבְדְּךָ־וַאֲמָתֶךָ וְשׁוֹרְךָ וַחֲמֹרְךָ וְכָל־בְּהֶמְתֶּךָ וְגֵרְךָ אֲשֶׁר בִּשְׁעָרֶיךָ לְמַעַן יָנוּחַ עַבְדְּךָ וַאֲמָתְךָ כָּמוֹךָ: יד וְזָכַרְתָּ כִּי־עֶבֶד הָיִיתָ בְּאֶרֶץ מִצְרַיִם וַיֹּצִאֲךָ יְהוָֹה אֱלֹהֶיךָ מִשָּׁם בְּיָד חֲזָקָה וּבִזְרֹעַ נְטוּיָה עַל־כֵּן צִוְּךָ יְהוָֹה אֱלֹהֶיךָ

11] You shall not swear falsely by the name of the LORD your God; for the LORD will not clear one who swears falsely by His name.

12] Observe the sabbath day and keep it holy, as the LORD your God has commanded you. 13] Six days you shall labor and do all your work, 14] but the seventh day is a sabbath of the LORD your God: you shall not do any work—you, your son or your daughter, your male or female slave, your ox or your ass, or any of your cattle, or the stranger in your settlements, so that your male and female slave may rest as you do. 15] Remember that you were a slave in the land of Egypt and the LORD your God freed you from there with a mighty hand and an outstretched arm; therefore the LORD your God has commanded you to observe the sabbath day.

11] *Not swear falsely.* The commandment may originally have referred to a custom of swearing "by the life of God," and that therefore such an oath demanded extreme caution [3]. However, the meaning of the Hebrew is in doubt; it may not at all relate to swearing falsely but to taking God's name in vain or to abusing it—forbidding magical, profane, or even casual use of the divine name. Proponents of the latter interpretation point out that the ninth commandment, which deals with false witness, implies the prohibition of swearing falsely.

The second commandment dealt with the misuse of image, the third turns to the misuse of God's name—a transition from the visual to the verbal. The divine name is part of the divine essence; hence care must be taken lest one diminish the sanctity of God by misusing His name. Jewish tradition subsequently introduced severe restrictions in any pronouncement of the Name (see our commentary on Exodus 20:7).

12] *Observe.* שָׁמוֹר (shamor); in the Exodus version the opening word of the fourth commandment is זָכוֹר (zachor, remember). Tradition treats this difference as purposeful and suggests that "remember" refers to positive acts, like sanctification

through candles and wine and Sabbath joy, and "observe" to abstinence from any form of labor. The commandment is the only one that exhibits significant differences between the two versions, and, although critical scholars believe them to be due to varying traditions, rabbinic opinion insisted that the Deuteronomic version was in some miraculous fashion proclaimed together with the text reported in Exodus 20 [4]. Both שָׁמוֹר and זָכוֹר are infinitives absolute serving as imperatives (compare the German *Aufpassen!*). On the origins of the Sabbath and its observance in history see at Exodus 20.

Keep it holy. By setting it apart. In Jewish tradition the expression לְקַדְּשׁוֹ implies the duty to sanctify the Sabbath with a benediction (*Kiddush*).

As the Lord your God has commanded you. This phrase is not found in the Exodus version.

14] *Not do any work.* Jewish tradition defined this in detail, developing a catalogue of thirty-nine main types of prohibited labor (see commentary at Exod. 20:10).

15] *Remember.* The reason given for the commandment constitutes the main difference from Exodus. See below.

ט״ לַעֲשׂוֹת אֶת־יוֹם הַשַּׁבָּת: ס   כַּבֵּד אֶת־אָבִיךָ   אֱלֹהֶיךָ נָתַן לָךְ: ס   לֹא תִּרְצָח: ס   וְלֹא

וְאֶת־אִמֶּךָ כַּאֲשֶׁר צִוְּךָ יְהוָה אֱלֹהֶיךָ לְמַעַן יַאֲרִיכֻן   תִּנְאָף: ס   וְלֹא תִּגְנֹב: ס   וְלֹא־תַעֲנֶה בְרֵעֲךָ עֵד

יָמֶיךָ וּלְמַעַן יִיטַב לָךְ עַל הָאֲדָמָה אֲשֶׁר־יְהוָה   יח שָׁוְא: ס   וְלֹא תַחְמֹד אֵשֶׁת רֵעֶךָ ס   וְלֹא תִתְאַוֶּה

16] Honor your father and your mother, as the LORD your God has commanded you, that you may long endure, and that you may fare well, in the land that the LORD your God is giving you.

17] You shall not murder. / You shall not commit adultery. / You shall not steal. / You shall not bear false witness against your neighbor.

18] You shall not covet your neighbor's wife. You shall not crave your neighbor's house, or

16] *Honor your father and your mother.* The fifth commandment in Jewish tradition, it completes the first tablet, which deals mainly with the relationship of humans to God. The commandment makes the honor given to parents a prerequisite for Israel's continued stay in the Holy Land.

And that you may fare well. The phrase is not found in Exodus.

17] *You shall not murder.* See commentary on Exod. 20:13. The older translation was "You shall not kill." But while in English there is a distinction between "kill" (which may be authorized by the state or be accidental) and "murder" (which is unauthorized and malicious), the Hebrew רָצַח cannot be clearly distinguished from the more frequent הָרַג [5]. However, the commandment deals obviously with homicide, and hence those supporting pacifism or the abolition of capital punishment cannot justifiably base themselves on this word but must look to other reasons.

You shall not commit adultery. This, like the commandment that follows, is connected with the preceding by the conjunctive וְ, linking the injunctions stylistically more closely than in Exodus 20 where the וְ is absent. The seventh commandment and the eighth and ninth are in this version part of verse 17, while in other versions they are separate, thus giving the chapter three additional verses. (This alternate counting is indicated below by bracketed numbers.)

The command raises the purity of family life to the highest level of importance. In time this became a distinguishing aspect of Israel's social structure, complementing the honor rendered to parents and the sense of responsibility felt for all members of the family. The commandment applies to men and women: both are punished when found guilty of adultery (Lev. 20:10), the man having violated someone else's marriage; the woman, her own (for men could enter multiple marriages while women could not).

You shall not steal. The Rabbis interpreted the eighth commandment as referring to the theft of persons and Lev. 19:11 to the theft of property [6].

You shall not bear false witness. The prohibition covers not only the act of witnessing in court, it addresses itself also to the character of a person. Lying injures both liar and society and when practiced in judicial proceedings is doubly injurious. Says a midrash: "Everything in the world was created by God except the art of lying" [7].

The text here uses שָׁוְא instead of שֶׁקֶר as in Exodus. The difference appears to be stylistic only.

18] [21] *You shall not covet your neighbor's wife.* "Wife" is placed here before "house"; in Exodus the order is reversed, "house" being understood as "household" (of which the wife was considered a part). Here, the wife is clearly distinguished from material possessions others might crave. The commandment is the most inward of the Ten Words.

You shall not crave. תִתְאַוֶּה (titaveh), a stylistic variance of תַחְמֹד (tachmod, covet).

Your neighbor's house. A neighbor's possessions are ready-at-hand objects for what people covet.

It has been suggested that this command was a

יֹסְפִים אֲנַחְנוּ לִשְׁמֹעַ אֶת־קוֹל יְהֹוָה אֱלֹהֵינוּ עוֹד

כג וָמָתְנוּ: כִּי מִי כָל־בָּשָׂר אֲשֶׁר שָׁמַע קוֹל אֱלֹהִים

כד חַיִּים מְדַבֵּר מִתּוֹךְ־הָאֵשׁ כָּמֹנוּ וַיֶּחִי: קְרַב אַתָּה

וּשֲׁמָע אֵת כָּל־אֲשֶׁר יֹאמַר יְהֹוָה אֱלֹהֵינוּ וְאַתְּ תְּדַבֵּר

אֵלֵינוּ אֵת כָּל־אֲשֶׁר יְדַבֵּר יְהֹוָה אֱלֹהֵינוּ אֵלֶיךָ

כה וְשָׁמַעְנוּ וְעָשִׂינוּ: וַיִּשְׁמַע יְהֹוָה אֶת־קוֹל דִּבְרֵיכֶם

בְּדַבֶּרְכֶם אֵלָי וַיֹּאמֶר יְהֹוָה אֵלַי שָׁמַעְתִּי אֶת־קוֹל

דִּבְרֵי הָעָם הַזֶּה אֲשֶׁר דִּבְּרוּ אֵלֶיךָ הֵיטִיבוּ כָּל־אֲשֶׁר

כו דִּבֵּרוּ: מִי־יִתֵּן וְהָיָה לְבָבָם זֶה לָהֶם לְיִרְאָה אֹתִי

וְלִשְׁמֹר אֶת־כָּל־מִצְוֹתַי כָּל־הַיָּמִים לְמַעַן יִיטַב לָהֶם

יט לְרֵעֶךָ: ס אֶת־הַדְּבָרִים הָאֵלֶּה דִּבֶּר יְהֹוָה אֶל־

כָּל־קְהַלְכֶם בָּהָר מִתּוֹךְ הָאֵשׁ הֶעָנָן וְהָעֲרָפֶל קוֹל

גָּדוֹל וְלֹא יָסָף וַיִּכְתְּבֵם עַל־שְׁנֵי לֻחֹת אֲבָנִים וַיִּתְּנֵם

כ אֵלָי: וַיְהִי כְּשָׁמְעֲכֶם אֶת־הַקּוֹל מִתּוֹךְ הַחֹשֶׁךְ וְהָהָר

בֹּעֵר בָּאֵשׁ וַתִּקְרְבוּן אֵלַי כָּל־רָאשֵׁי שִׁבְטֵיכֶם

כא וְזִקְנֵיכֶם: וַתֹּאמְרוּ הֵן הֶרְאָנוּ יְהֹוָה אֱלֹהֵינוּ אֶת־

כְּבֹדוֹ וְאֶת־גָּדְלוֹ וְאֶת־קֹלוֹ שָׁמַעְנוּ מִתּוֹךְ הָאֵשׁ הַיּוֹם

כב הַזֶּה רָאִינוּ כִּי־יְדַבֵּר אֱלֹהִים אֶת־הָאָדָם וָחָי: וְעַתָּה

לָמָּה נָמוּת כִּי תֹאכְלֵנוּ הָאֵשׁ הַגְּדֹלָה הַזֹּאת אִם־

* כד הם׳ בקמץ.

his field, or his male or female slave, or his ox, or his ass, or anything that is your neighbor's.

19] The LORD spoke those words—those and no more—to your whole congregation at the mountain, with a mighty voice out of the fire and the dense clouds. He inscribed them on two tablets of stone, which He gave to me. **20]** When you heard the voice out of the darkness, while the mountain was ablaze with fire, you came up to me, all your tribal heads and elders, **21]** and said, "The LORD our God has just shown us His majestic Presence, and we have heard His voice out of the fire; we have seen this day that man may live though God has spoken to him. **22]** Let us not die, then, for this fearsome fire will consume us; if we hear the voice of the LORD our God any longer, we shall die. **23]** For what mortal ever heard the voice of the living God speak out of the fire, as we did, and lived? **24]** You go closer and hear all that the LORD our God says, and then you tell us everything that the LORD our God tells you, and we will willingly do it."

25] The LORD heard the plea that you made to me, and the LORD said to me, "I have heard the plea that this people made to you; they did well to speak thus. **26]** May they always be of such mind, to revere Me and follow all My commandments, that it may go well with them and

warning issued to a nomadic or seminomadic community not to become entirely sedentary [8].

Or his field. These words are not in the Exodus version.

19] [22] *Those words.* The Decalogue.

Those and no more. Our translation connects these words (וְלֹא יָסָף), which are found at the end of the phrase, to "The Lord spoke those words"; but others understand that after the Ten Commandments had been proclaimed God no longer spoke "with a mighty voice out of the fire and the

dense clouds" [9].

He inscribed them. As told in Exod. 32:16 and in Deut. 9:9–10.

22] [25] *Let us not die.* See 4:33.

26] [29] *May they . . . be.* The verse is clearly based on the assumption that human beings possess the freedom to follow or not to follow God's commands [10]; see below.

To revere. The Hebrew is stronger, it conveys also a sense of awe and fear. (See above, at 4:10.)

כז וְלִבְנֵיהֶם לְעֹלָם: לֵךְ אֱמֹר לָהֶם שׁוּבוּ לָכֶם
כח לְאָהֳלֵיכֶם: וְאַתָּה פֹּה עֲמֹד עִמָּדִי וַאֲדַבְּרָה אֵלֶיךָ
אֵת כָּל־הַמִּצְוָה וְהַחֻקִּים וְהַמִּשְׁפָּטִים אֲשֶׁר תְּלַמְּדֵם
וְעָשׂוּ בָאָרֶץ אֲשֶׁר אָנֹכִי נֹתֵן לָהֶם לְרִשְׁתָּהּ:

כט וּשְׁמַרְתֶּם לַעֲשׂוֹת כַּאֲשֶׁר צִוָּה יְהוָֹה אֱלֹהֵיכֶם אֶתְכֶם
ל לֹא תָסֻרוּ יָמִין וּשְׂמֹאל: בְּכָל־הַדֶּרֶךְ אֲשֶׁר צִוָּה
יְהוָֹה אֱלֹהֵיכֶם אֶתְכֶם תֵּלֵכוּ לְמַעַן תִּחְיוּן וְטוֹב
לָכֶם וְהַאֲרַכְתֶּם יָמִים בָּאָרֶץ אֲשֶׁר תִּירָשׁוּן:

with their children forever! **27]** Go, say to them, 'Return to your tents.' **28]** But you remain here with Me, and I will give you the whole Instruction—the laws and the rules—which you shall impart to them, for them to observe in the land that I am giving them to possess.''

29] Be careful, then, to do as the LORD your God has commanded you. Do not turn aside to the right or to the left: **30]** follow only the path that the LORD your God has enjoined upon you, so that you may thrive and that it may go well with you, and that you may long endure in the land you are to occupy.

27] [30] *Return to your tents.* From which the people had been absent for three days (Exod. 19:15). 28] [31] *The whole Instruction.* In the Torah, מִצְוָה (*mitzvah*) describes that which God has commanded; the Rabbis determined that there were 613 such Torah mitzvot [11].

Which you shall impart. Jewish tradition finds here its warrant for the basic belief that God's will was transmitted authentically by Moses and his successors when they interpreted (and interpret) the mitzvot of the Torah.

To observe in the land. A large portion of the positive commandments in Deuteronomy could be observed only in the Land of Israel [12].

The Commandment of Social Conscience

Both versions of the Sabbath commandment state the reason why the day has been specially set aside and they state it differently. In Exodus, Israel is bidden to imitate God the Creator: even as He rested on the seventh day so must His chosen ones. Once a week they are to reenact the creative process and thus renew their own creative power. Here, in Deuteronomy, the duty to observe the Sabbath is linked not to God the Creator but to God the Redeemer. In remembering its own liberation from Egyptian slavery, Israel is to recall that all servants are human and therefore must extend the duty and privilege of Sabbath rest to them as well. Week after week the humanity of the servant is brought into the focus of social conscience. In consequence, Judaism became a religion in which social justice, equity, and decency occupied a central position.

In Genesis (2:1–3) the Sabbath is shown to be the seal of Creation and becomes God's sanctified time as well; in Exodus 20 the fourth commandment makes the day Israel's sanctified time, a supernaturally defined span that depends on no celestial or terrestrial occurrence. Even as God "renews daily the work of creation," so Israel renews weekly its awareness and appreciation of this ongoing process. In Deuteronomy, on the other hand, the Sabbath is founded, not on prehistoric creation, but on the historic creation of His people from the mire of slavery, and thus the day is humanized and its humanization is extended to all members of Israel's society. Exodus proclaims Israel's freedom from the tyranny of time; Deuteronomy, from human tyranny—and both proclamations rest in the sovereignty of God.

The day then, in remembrance and observance, is anchored in God's kingship, His manifestation outside and inside history. In Exodus the day's foundation is universal, in Deuteronomy it is bound up with Israel's experience; in Exodus the day's observance is aimed at rekindling human awe before the miracle of existence, in Deuteronomy the quality of gratitude is the focus, and out of this gratitude arises the obligation to safeguard the humanity of others.[1] Yet, on another level, the two foundations of the Sabbath—creation and redemption—are joined by the mortar of revelation. The Sabbath *Kiddush* praises God as the Giver of mitzvot (i.e., the God of Revelation) who assigned the day to Israel as a reminder of the work of creation and a remembrance of the Exodus from Egypt.

We do not know whether the Sabbath was observed in Israel long before the fourth commandment raised its celebration to the status of divinely ordained duty. It is, however, likely that the original phrasing of the commandment was simply, "Observe (or, remember) the Sabbath day to keep it holy," and that two different yet related traditions arose, each of which gave the day its own special foundation. In the confluence of these traditions the unique character of the Jewish Sabbath was shaped, a day linking heaven and earth, the creation of the world and that of Israel, the creature of eternity and of history, the focus on self and on others. The Sabbath proclaims God's sovereignty over time, and in both Exodus and Deuteronomy Israel is bidden to extend this mastery,

---

[1] The very term *tzedakah*, which describes the act of caring for the less privileged, contains the dual elements of human charity and divinely sanctioned obligation. It should be emphasized, however, that social concern is found in other books of the Torah as well; see, for instance, our commentary on the Covenant Code, Exod. 21:1 ff.

viewed through the prism of creation and redemption, to the realm of human practice. The Sabbath thus helped to mold Israel's consciousness of both time and humanity [13].

The Doctrine of Free Will

The chapter contains a verse (5:26) which in time became the proof text for the doctrine of human free will. Moses reports God as *hoping* that Israel would always revere Him and follow His commandments.[2] This obviously implies that God does not *know* whether or not Israel will do His will, for Israel—like all humanity—is free to obey or not to obey. It is the theme first touched upon in the story of the Garden of Eden and of Cain and Abel, and then drawn into question in the Exodus story of Pharaoh whose heart was "hardened" by God. But here, in Deuteronomy, the biblical text is unequivocal, for all that God can do is hope. He can guide, urge, and even threaten Israel, but He cannot force it to walk the right path. In the realm of nature rigid laws exist that determine the relationship between cause and effect, but no such laws prevail in the ethical realm. The doctrine was expressed pithily in the talmudic saying, "Everything is determined by Heaven, except the fear of Heaven" [14]. God cannot command the moral will of His children. In this view, then, there appears to be a limit to God's foreknowledge; He may be omniscient in all other ways, but He cannot determine what decisions human beings will make.[3]

But granting that humans are free, is God also? Can He make choices that do not square with human conceptions of justice and yet, simply because they are divine choices, claim ethical rightness on a higher level? An early discussion of this problem was posed by the story of Akiba's martyrdom. Because he insisted on teaching Torah, despite an imperial Roman decree forbidding it, he was sentenced to death and flayed alive. When Moses (being shown Akiba's fate in a vision) questioned God's apparent acquiescence in Akiba's martyrdom, God replied: "Silent! Such is My will" [17]. Ultimately, although we can—and even must—question God (as did Abraham and Job), we cannot penetrate the mystery of His will. We may (as the philosopher Saadia did) suppose that God and humanity are bound by the same laws of justice, but we cannot hope to understand the reason for many divine choices. This limitation is an aspect of our mortality, and our concern must be focused on the *quality* of our human choices, believing that we are indeed free to determine it.

---

[2] In the Hebrew text God says מִי־יִתֵּן, literally, "Who might grant" that Israel be of such a mind. Says Biur: God too can express a wish of this kind, for freedom of will was given to man.

[3] Rabbi Akiba, however, taught that while there is human free will God already knows what the outcome will be: "Everything is foreseen, yet freedom of choice exists" [15]. According to a thoroughly mechanistic view of life, moral freedom is an illusion, however. No one is ever really free to do anything, for everyone is programed by heredity, training, environment, electrical and chemical stimuli, etc., to act in strictly predictable fashion—*if* we had all the information available to make the prediction. Judaism rejects this approach and holds to the premise that there is a realm, however narrow, where human beings are free to make ethical choices. The medieval philosopher Abraham Ibn Daud considered divine ignorance in this respect to be a defect of creation. On the other hand, Bachya ibn Pakuda, who wrote a popular treatise on the ethical life (*Duties of the Heart*), believed that, even if God himself had determined our human choices in advance, we still had to act *as if* true freedom of will existed [16].

GLEANINGS

The Refuge

Why does the opening statement of Moses' discourse ("This is the Teaching," 4:44) come immediately after the rules for manslayer and blood avenger (4:41–43)? Even as the latter cannot pursue as long as the former has found refuge in one of the special "cities of refuge," so the Angel of Death cannot slay as long as a person is in his "city of refuge," that is, while studying Torah. It was told that the Angel of Death found Rabbi Chisda sitting on a branch of a tree, immersed in his studies, and because of this had no power over him. But when the branch broke Chisda interrupted his studies and in that moment the Angel of Death overcame him.

BASED ON THE TALMUD [18]

Face to Face

Moses recalls that God spoke to Israel "face to face." One would expect the expression פָּנִים אֶל פָּנִים, but it says פָּנִים בְּפָנִים (literally, "face *in* face"), expressing even greater directness. The Presence is not only turned to the other, but penetrates into the other.   S. R. HIRSCH [19]

Grandeur

The Decalogue belongs to humanity's truly great possessions, and one ought to speak of it only in the simplest words, since no encomium can describe it. It is the core and soul of Moses' lifework, the cornerstone of Israel's religion, and, through it, the fundamental law for the ethical development of humanity.   E. AUERBACH [20]

Critique of Moses

Moses should not have said "I stood between the Lord and you" (5:5), for in so saying he was thinking of his own importance and became not a link but a barrier. Only God can utter "I."

But is there no moment when there is room for the human "I"? There is. When the Evil Impulse whispers "You are unworthy to fulfill the precepts of the Torah," answer: "I *am* worthy."

CHASIDIC [21]

I Am the Lord Your God (5:6)

The suffix ךָ[4] refers to Israel collectively, and at the same time to each Israelite individually. The Midrash says: Even as thousands look at a great portrait and each one feels that it looks at *him*, so every Israelite at Horeb felt that the Divine Voice was addressing him.   J. H. HERTZ [22]

Oaths

The last letters of תִשָּׂא אֶת־שֵׁם are the anagram of אֱמֶת. Not only are false oaths prohibited, true ones too ought to be avoided.

CHASIDIC [23]

(This play on letters was meant to find scriptural warrant for the prevailing practice not to testify under oath—even when this entailed severe financial loss—for fear of using God's name for mundane purposes.)

God's Possession

Sabbath is the day that belongs to God in a special way, a day not desecrated by human usage. Not a word is said about observing it in a cultic fashion. Hence one may speculate that in Israel's older days abstinence from "using" the day was the main observance, whereby the day was demonstratively "returned to God."

G. VON RAD [24]

---

[4] אֱלֹהֶיךָ, "your (singular) God," not אֱלֹהֵיכֶם, "your (plural) God."

The Feast of Creation

The Sabbath is the feast of creation, but of a creation wrought for the sake of redemption. The feast instituted at the close of creation is creation's meaning and goal.　　　　F. ROSENZWEIG [25]

Observe the Sabbath Day

The word שָׁמוֹר means "Keep in mind" (as in Gen. 37:11). All week one should keep the Sabbath in mind.　　　　CHASIDIC [26]

But another interpretation holds the opposite view: "Remember" (Exodus version) the Sabbath during the week and "observe" it (Deuteronomy version) when it occurs.

Together

"Remember" and "Observe" (that is, both versions of the Sabbath commandment) were miraculously pronounced together by God, though the human mouth and ear cannot duplicate it.

RASHI [27]

So also in the Sabbath hymn, *Lecha Dodi*, "Observe" and "Remember": the One God caused us to hear them as one single word.

Even after Death

Parents should be honored even after their death. A meritorious child can redeem an unworthy parent, so that child and parent may dwell together in *Gan Eden*.　　　　ZOHAR [28]

Return to Your Tents (5:27)

"Here at Sinai," says God, "you showed Me reverence; now let Me see what you do when you return home."　　　　CHASIDIC [29]

How to Teach

God asks Moses to remain with Him (5:28). The Hebrew literally says to "stand" with Him. A teacher while teaching should stand or sit with dignity. God, so to speak, was himself "standing" with Moses while teaching him.　　　　TALMUD [30]

The Shema

Moses had opened his second discourse with a restatement of the Decalogue; now he turns to the major theme of the address, the elaboration of the second commandment, "You shall have no other gods before Me." He begins his ringing appeal with *Shema Yisrael*, words that have become deeply imbedded in the consciousness of Jews, however far away they may be from the traditions of their faith. "Hear, O Israel" and "You shall love the Lord your God" are the cornerstones of Judaism's edifice, which have been given added exposure through Christianity and Islam. In the Gospels the love of God is quoted as one of two pillars of human obligation [1], and in Islam the declaration "There is no god but Allah" is a rewording of the *Shema* and, as in Jewish tradition, it has become the watchword of its faith.

The *Shema* (the expression sometimes encompasses only verse 4, sometimes verses 4–9, and, in the liturgy, these plus additional Torah selections) has been called "Judaism's greatest contribution to the religious thought of mankind" [2], the source from which Judaism time and again drew its strength for inspiration and rejuvenation [3], "the great text of monotheism" [4]. It derived its importance both from its intrinsic meaning and from the place it assumed in Jewish liturgy and history. Repeated morning and night, as well as in moments of gravest crisis and at death's door, it has sustained every generation of Jews and deepened their commitment to the One saving and caring God. Yet, despite the centrality which the *Shema* has been accorded in Jewish tradition, its exact meaning (therefore, its translation) is not entirely certain, nor is the reason for the particular

1364

writing of its Hebrew text (the third letters of the first and last words are enlarged). We have here, as perhaps nowhere else in the Torah in like degree, an example of original text and later tradition coalescing and impinging upon each other to a remarkable degree, raising four verses, inconspicuously imbedded in Moses' discourse, to a position of eminence rivaled only by the Ten Commandments.

The *Shema* is followed by three brief "sermons," verses 10–15, 16–19, and 20–25. There are some scholars who believe that the original Book of Deuteronomy began here and extended through chapter 11.

א וְזֹאת הַמִּצְוָה הַחֻקִּים וְהַמִּשְׁפָּטִים אֲשֶׁר צִוָּה יְהֹוָה אֱלֹהֵיכֶם לְלַמֵּד אֶתְכֶם לַעֲשׂוֹת בָּאָרֶץ אֲשֶׁר אַתֶּם

ב עֹבְרִים שָׁמָּה לְרִשְׁתָּהּ: לְמַעַן תִּירָא אֶת־יְהֹוָה אֱלֹהֶיךָ לִשְׁמֹר אֶת־כָּל־חֻקֹּתָיו וּמִצְוֹתָיו אֲשֶׁר אָנֹכִי מְצַוְּךָ אַתָּה וּבִנְךָ וּבֶן־בִּנְךָ כֹּל יְמֵי חַיֶּיךָ וּלְמַעַן

ג יַאֲרִכֻן יָמֶיךָ: וְשָׁמַעְתָּ יִשְׂרָאֵל וְשָׁמַרְתָּ לַעֲשׂוֹת אֲשֶׁר יִיטַב לְךָ וַאֲשֶׁר תִּרְבּוּן מְאֹד כַּאֲשֶׁר דִּבֶּר

יְהֹוָה אֱלֹהֵי אֲבֹתֶיךָ לָךְ אֶרֶץ זָבַת חָלָב וּדְבָשׁ: פ

ד שְׁמַע יִשְׂרָאֵל יְהֹוָה אֱלֹהֵינוּ יְהֹוָה אֶחָד:

ה וְאָהַבְתָּ אֵת יְהֹוָה אֱלֹהֶיךָ בְּכָל־לְבָבְךָ וּבְכָל־נַפְשְׁךָ וּבְכָל־מְאֹדֶךָ: וְהָיוּ הַדְּבָרִים הָאֵלֶּה אֲשֶׁר אָנֹכִי

ו מְצַוְּךָ הַיּוֹם עַל־לְבָבֶךָ: וְשִׁנַּנְתָּם לְבָנֶיךָ וְדִבַּרְתָּ בָּם בְּשִׁבְתְּךָ בְּבֵיתֶךָ וּבְלֶכְתְּךָ בַדֶּרֶךְ וּבְשָׁכְבְּךָ

ז וּבְקוּמֶךָ: וּקְשַׁרְתָּם לְאוֹת עַל־יָדֶךָ וְהָיוּ לְטֹטָפֹת בֵּין

1] And this is the Instruction—the laws and the rules—that the LORD your God has commanded [me] to impart to you, to be observed in the land which you are about to cross into and occupy, **2]** so that you, your son, and your son's son may revere the LORD your God and follow, as long as you live, all His laws and commandments which I enjoin upon you, to the end that you may long endure. **3]** Obey, O Israel, willingly and faithfully, that it may go well with you and that you may increase greatly [in] a land flowing with milk and honey, as the LORD, the God of your fathers, spoke to you.

4] Hear, O Israel! The LORD is our God, the LORD alone. **5]** You shall love the LORD your God with all your heart and with all your soul and with all your might. **6]** Take to heart these instructions with which I charge you this day. **7]** Impress them upon your children. Recite them when you stay at home and when you are away, when you lie down and when you get

6:1] *Instruction.* מִצְוָה (*mitzvah*) here covers laws (חֻקִּים, *chukim*) and rules (מִשְׁפָּטִים, *mishpatim*), but other translations are possible, making *mitzvah* a coordinate of the other terms and covering a specific type of legislation [5].

2] *Revere.* See comment on 5:26.

3] *Willingly and faithfully.* A free translation, literally, "If you listen and are careful to do."

A land flowing with milk and honey. Ibn Ezra suggests that this phrase should be connected with the end of verse 1. On the meaning of "milk and honey," see at Exod. 3:8 and Num. 13:27.

4] *The Lord is our God, the Lord alone.* In this translation of the *Shema* two affirmations are made: one, that the Divinity is Israel's God, and two, that it is He alone and no one else. Other translations render "The Lord our God, the Lord is One" (stressing the unity of God) or "The Lord our God is one Lord" (that is, neither divisible nor to be coupled with other deities, like Zeus with Jupiter) [6].

5] *Your heart.* Your intellect.

Your soul. Your affective capacity; see above, at 4:29.

The Talmud understands "your soul" to mean "your life": we are obligated to love God even if He takes our life [7]. The story of Rabbi Akiba's death is a dramatic example of such love; see Gleanings below.

Your might. Your physical strength.

However, according to tradition this means one's material possessions [8]. The Rabbis ruled that while there is a limit to the obligation to lay down one's life (it needs to be done only to avoid committing murder, incest, and idolatry), there is no such limitation on the amount of money that must be sacrificed in order to avoid violations of the Torah law. (Under ordinary circumstances people were to contribute no more than 20 per cent of their substance [9].)

7] *Impress.* Others, "teach diligently." Our translation derives וְשִׁנַּנְתָּם from שׁנן, to sharpen, to make an incision, a meaning reflected precisely by the German *einschärfen.* But perhaps a better derivation is from שָׁנָה, repeat, and the rendition therefore should be "Recite (or repeat) them to your children" [10].

ט עֵינֶיךָ: וּכְתַבְתָּם עַל־מְזוּזֹת בֵּיתֶךָ וּבִשְׁעָרֶיךָ: ס

י וְהָיָה כִּי־יְבִיאֲךָ יְהֹוָה אֱלֹהֶיךָ אֶל־הָאָרֶץ אֲשֶׁר נִשְׁבַּע לַאֲבֹתֶיךָ לְאַבְרָהָם לְיִצְחָק וּלְיַעֲקֹב לָתֶת לָךְ

יא עָרִים גְּדֹלֹת וְטֹבֹת אֲשֶׁר לֹא־בָנִיתָ: וּבָתִּים מְלֵאִים כָּל־טוּב אֲשֶׁר לֹא־מִלֵּאתָ וּבֹרֹת חֲצוּבִים אֲשֶׁר לֹא־חָצַבְתָּ כְּרָמִים וְזֵיתִים אֲשֶׁר לֹא־נָטָעְתָּ וְאָכַלְתָּ

יב וְשָׂבָעְתָּ: הִשָּׁמֶר לְךָ פֶּן־תִּשְׁכַּח אֶת־יְהֹוָה אֲשֶׁר

יג הוֹצִיאֲךָ מֵאֶרֶץ מִצְרַיִם מִבֵּית עֲבָדִים: אֶת־יְהֹוָה אֱלֹהֶיךָ תִּירָא וְאֹתוֹ תַעֲבֹד וּבִשְׁמוֹ תִּשָּׁבֵעַ: לֹא

יד תֵלְכוּן אַחֲרֵי אֱלֹהִים אֲחֵרִים מֵאֱלֹהֵי הָעַמִּים אֲשֶׁר

טו סְבִיבוֹתֵיכֶם: כִּי אֵל קַנָּא יְהֹוָה אֱלֹהֶיךָ בְּקִרְבֶּךָ פֶּן־יֶחֱרֶה אַף־יְהֹוָה אֱלֹהֶיךָ בָּךְ וְהִשְׁמִידְךָ מֵעַל

up.   8] Bind them as a sign on your hand and let them serve as a symbol on your forehead;   9] inscribe them on the doorposts of your house and on your gates.

10] When the LORD your God brings you into the land which He swore to your fathers, Abraham, Isaac, and Jacob, to give you—great and flourishing cities which you did not build,   11] houses full of all good things which you did not fill, hewn cisterns which you did not hew, vineyards and olive groves which you did not plant—and you eat your fill,   12] take heed that you do not forget the LORD who freed you from the land of Egypt, the house of bondage.   13] Revere only the LORD your God and worship Him alone, and swear only by His name.   14] Do not follow other gods, any gods of the peoples about you   15] —for the LORD your God in your midst is an impassioned God—lest the anger of the LORD your God blaze forth against you and He wipe you off the face of the earth.

8] *Sign on your hand.* Originally this was a figure of speech, but Jewish tradition interpreted it to command the wearing of hand-phylacteries (*tefillin shel yad*; see commentary on Exod. 13:9).

Symbol on your forehead. טֹטָפֹת (*totafot*) may have derived originally from women's ornaments, as shown on Nimrud ivories [11]. This injunction too was understood literally as the command to wear head-phylacteries (*tefillin shel rosh*; see commentary on Exod. 13:16).

The two sets of tefillin consist of small boxes to which leather straps are attached for affixing the boxes to hand and head during morning worship. The boxes contain parchments with the *Shema* and other scriptural selections inscribed on them. (For details, see Commentary on Exodus, chapter 13.)

9] *Inscribe them on the doorposts.* Jewish tradition takes this to be a command to put a *mezuzah* on the doors of one's dwelling [12]. *Mezuzah* is the Hebrew word for the doorpost itself but has given its name to the small container and its parchment,

on which are written the words of Deut. 6:4–9 and 11:13–21.

10] *Great and flourishing cities.* This was a view of Canaan as seen from the outside.

11] *You eat your fill.* Medieval commentators were greatly puzzled with this verse since it appeared to give the Israelites permission to eat the Canaanites' (non-kosher) food [13]. The words are cited in the *Birkat ha-Mazon* (Grace after Meals).

13] *Worship Him.* In Hebrew, עבד denoted originally physical service and later spiritual (worship) service as well. (The same dual meaning of the word service is found in English, in the Aramaic *pelach*, and the Latin-based cultivate-cult.)

Swear only by His Name. And by none other. The word "only" is not in the Hebrew text but is implied [14].

15] *Impassioned God.* On this, see at Exod. 20:5.

Lest . . . He wipe you off. Spoken as a hyperbole to emphasize the seriousness of the consequence.

טו פְּנֵי הָאֲדָמָה: ס לֹא תְנַסּוּ אֶת־יְהוָה אֱלֹהֵיכֶם
יז כַּאֲשֶׁר נִסִּיתֶם בַּמַּסָּה: שָׁמוֹר תִּשְׁמְרוּן אֶת־מִצְוֹת
יח יְהוָה אֱלֹהֵיכֶם וְעֵדֹתָיו וְחֻקָּיו אֲשֶׁר צִוָּךְ: וְעָשִׂיתָ
הַיָּשָׁר וְהַטּוֹב בְּעֵינֵי יְהוָה לְמַעַן יִיטַב לָךְ וּבָאתָ
וְיָרַשְׁתָּ אֶת־הָאָרֶץ הַטֹּבָה אֲשֶׁר־נִשְׁבַּע יְהוָה לַאֲבֹתֶיךָ:
יט לַהֲדֹף אֶת־כָּל־אֹיְבֶיךָ מִפָּנֶיךָ כַּאֲשֶׁר דִּבֶּר
כ יְהוָה: ס כִּי־יִשְׁאָלְךָ בִנְךָ מָחָר לֵאמֹר מָה
הָעֵדֹת וְהַחֻקִּים וְהַמִּשְׁפָּטִים אֲשֶׁר צִוָּה יְהוָה אֱלֹהֵינוּ
כא אֶתְכֶם: וְאָמַרְתָּ לְבִנְךָ עֲבָדִים הָיִינוּ לְפַרְעֹה

כב בְּמִצְרָיִם וַיֹּצִיאֵנוּ יְהוָה מִמִּצְרַיִם בְּיָד חֲזָקָה: וַיִּתֵּן
יְהוָה אוֹתֹת וּמֹפְתִים גְּדֹלִים וְרָעִים בְּמִצְרַיִם
כג בְּפַרְעֹה וּבְכָל־בֵּיתוֹ לְעֵינֵינוּ: וְאוֹתָנוּ הוֹצִיא מִשָּׁם
לְמַעַן הָבִיא אֹתָנוּ לָתֶת לָנוּ אֶת־הָאָרֶץ אֲשֶׁר נִשְׁבַּע
כד לַאֲבֹתֵינוּ: וַיְצַוֵּנוּ יְהוָה לַעֲשׂוֹת אֶת־כָּל־הַחֻקִּים
הָאֵלֶּה לְיִרְאָה אֶת־יְהוָה אֱלֹהֵינוּ לְטוֹב לָנוּ כָּל־
כה הַיָּמִים לְחַיֹּתֵנוּ כְּהַיּוֹם הַזֶּה: וּצְדָקָה תִּהְיֶה־לָּנוּ כִּי־
נִשְׁמֹר לַעֲשׂוֹת אֶת־כָּל־הַמִּצְוָה הַזֹּאת לִפְנֵי יְהוָה
אֱלֹהֵינוּ כַּאֲשֶׁר צִוָּנוּ:

16] Do not try the LORD your God, as you did at Massah. **17]** Be sure to keep the commandments, exhortations, and laws which the LORD your God has enjoined upon you. **18]** Do what is right and good in the sight of the LORD, that it may go well with you and that you may be able to occupy the good land which the LORD your God promised on oath to your fathers, **19]** and that your enemy may be driven out before you, as the LORD has spoken.

20] When, in time to come, your son asks you, "What mean the exhortations, laws, and rules which the LORD our God has enjoined upon you?" **21]** you shall say to your son, "We were slaves to Pharaoh in Egypt and the LORD freed us from Egypt with a mighty hand. **22]** The LORD wrought before our eyes marvelous and destructive signs and portents in Egypt, against Pharaoh and all his household; **23]** and us He freed from there, that He might take us and give us the land that He had promised on oath to our fathers. **24]** Then the LORD commanded us to observe all these laws, to revere the LORD our God, for our lasting good and for our survival, as is now the case. **25]** It will be therefore to our merit before the LORD our God to observe faithfully this whole Instruction, as He has commanded us."

16] *Massah.* "Trial," see Exod. 17:1 ff. Israel had grumbled about the dearth of water and had dared Moses to provide a miracle—thereby "trying" God himself.

18] *Do what is right and good.* The Rabbis developed an important ethical principle from this verse, holding that it was not sufficient to do the "right" or legal thing, but that one needed to go beyond and do also what was "good" or moral. See below, Gleanings [15].

20] *Your son asks you.* The question has been taken into the Passover Haggadah and is ascribed to the Wise Son. The answer he receives in verse 21 is similar to the one given the Simple Son (Exod. 13:14). See also Gleanings below.

25] *Merit.* צְדָקָה (*tzedakah*), a word usually denoting "right" or "just" action, but occasionally meaning "merit" as here and in Gen. 15:6, Deut. 24:13. Those who acknowledge God are counted as being "right" in their relation to Him [16].

The words "in the sight of the Lord" appear later in the Hebrew text but are moved up in the translation for better understanding.

The Shema—Its Meaning

The six words of the *Shema* (6:4) have become the best-known words in Judaism's liturgy, the "watchword" of Israel's faith, and this despite the fact that their precise meaning is not clear at all. In the Hebrew text, after the opening call "Hear, O Israel," the affirmation itself states tersely: "Lord our God Lord *echad*." The uncertainty of the meaning arises from the absence of punctuation and the nature of juxtaposing these Hebrew words without an explicative verb, as well as from the various emphases that can be ascribed to the word *echad*: one, alone, unique. Thus, the text can be understood to say:

יהוה is our God, and יהוה alone;

יהוה is our God, one indivisible יהוה;

יהוה our God is a unique יהוה;

יהוה is our God, יהוה is unique (in His extraordinariness).

Despite these variant meanings—or perhaps because of them!—the words assumed a position of centrality in Jewish thinking and liturgical practice, and this position became assured and hallowed through Rabbi Akiba's martyrdom (see Gleanings). Since that time Jews have repeated the *Shema* on countless other occasions as they sanctified God's name through their death; and they continue to speak the six words (usually with the words that follow and other selections; see further below) at prayer services throughout the year, affix them to their doorposts, and inscribe them on their phylacteries.

While in earliest days the existence of other gods was accepted by Israel, the uniqueness of the Lord became an article of faith as time went on: יְהֹוָה not only was Israel's personal guardian, He was also superior to all other deities—if in fact these could be said to exist at all (an idea that had been discarded by the time Deuteronomy was codified). God was now acknowledged as singular or unique or extraordinary, who in His wisdom had bound himself to the people Israel. In repeating the *Shema* the Jew directed himself to this special relationship, he gloried in it, and pledged his very life to witness to the Holy One. Jewish devotional manuals often advised the worshiper to keep the possibility of martyrdom in mind and, in reciting the watchword as well as the words following it, to concentrate on God's incomparable greatness as Creator and Giver of the Torah. Thus, Alexander Suskind of Grodno suggested that one remember these thoughts:

"I believe with perfect faith, pure and true, that You are one and unique and that You have created all worlds, upper and lower, without end, and You are in past, present, and future. I make You King over each of my limbs that it might keep and perform the precepts of Your holy Torah and I make You King over my children and children's children to the end of time. I will, therefore, command my children and grandchildren to accept the yoke of Your Kingdom, Divinity, and Lordship upon themselves, and I will command them to command their children, in turn, up to the last generation to accept, all of them, the yoke of Your Kingdom, Divinity, and Lordship" [17].

The *Shema* thus came to be like a precious gem, in that the light of faith made its words sparkle with rich brilliance of varied colors. Negatively, it underscored the Jew's opposition to polytheism and pagan ethics, to the dualism of the Zoroastrians, the pantheism of the Greeks, and the trinitarianism of the Christians. Positively, the One God was seen to imply one humanity and therefore demanded the brotherhood of all; it spoke of the world as the stage for the ethical life and linked monotheism and morality. It meant that God undergirded all laws for nature and for mankind; hence heaven and earth as well as human history were His

domain. And, if humanity found itself still unredeemed, God's presence would reach beyond history into the time of messianic redemption: "The Lord shall reign over all the earth; on that day the Lord shall be One and His name shall be One" (Zech. 14:9; cf. Zeph. 3:9).[1] These principles were seen by generations of Jews as rays shining forth from the *Shema*, as from a diamond set into a crown of faith and proven true and enduring in human history.

The Love of God [18]

It is one of the characteristics of Deuteronomy that it stresses the duty to love God as well as to acknowledge Him as Israel's savior, the singular Deity in the world who rules it in solitary splendor. "You must love the Lord your God with all your heart and with all your soul and with all your might"—this is the great theme to which the book returns time and again. The duty presupposes, by its nature, a reciprocal relationship, for God loves Israel and has loved it since patriarchal days—a love freely extended to a people whom He chose mysteriously, inexplicably (4:37; 7:7–8). But no love—neither divine nor human—can exist in a vacuum; without mutual loyalty its roots dry up and its flowers wither. And since God is by nature a faithful God (אֵל נֶאֱמָן), it is *Israel's* loyalty which needs to be nurtured and strengthened. As in marriage, love rests on loyalty and trust, and although love itself cannot be forced [19] the uniquely desirable relationship it engenders is constantly held up to Israel. In that sense, it becomes a "must"

for disenchanted love often turns to anger, and even the Divine Lover is caught in this tension of opposites.[2] Hosea, Jeremiah, and the Second Isaiah, as well as the rabbinic view of the Song of Songs, saw God and Israel in a quasi-conjugal relationship: bliss is in store for the bride (identified with Israel) who deserves the love of her bridegroom (God), but woe to her if she betrays her trust. She will be cast out, thrust into darkness, and only a merciful lover, remembering their past affection, can restore her to her former position (see Hosea 2; Jeremiah 2, 3, 31:2–6; Isaiah 49:14–54:8).

The duty to love God is on occasion coupled with the caution to fear Him (so in 10:12 and in 11:13–21, which constitutes the second paragraph in the morning and evening *Shema*). Both love and fear can motivate us to do God's will, but of the two, according to the Rabbis, love is superior; still, fear needs to be instilled in those whose moral development is imperfect[3] [22].

How then can one love God? From ancient to modern times writers have given much attention to this question. The Midrash holds that we best express this love when we conduct ourselves in such a manner as to make God beloved by others [23]. It is our attention to the mitzvot that will make us as well as others aware of the One in Whose name they are performed, and, the greater our devotion and concentration upon the mitzvah and its Giver, the more likely we will be to enter into the context of pure love. For, while love as such cannot be the subject of command, actions leading to love—

---

[1] This phrase culminates the Aleinu (or "Adoration") and occurs in all three daily prayer services.

[2] Such tension is expressed also in ancient Near Eastern vassal-suzerain treatises, where political loyalty was generally expressed by the term "love" [20].

[3] It should be kept in mind, however, as B. J. Bam-

berger has shown [21], that neither "love" nor "fear," as we use the terms today, is a proper rendering of the biblical terms אַהֲבָה and יִרְאָה. They indicate action more than an inward state, overt demonstrations of loyalty to God, and hence are two sides of the same coin. Both together denote what we would call "active religion."

both ours and others'—can be. Each mitzvah done in the right spirit is an act of loving God. It can be done everywhere and anywhere, wherever the opportunity for mitzvot exists, and it is, therefore, not exclusively the consequence of spiritual contemplation.[4] "You must love the Lord your God" is the command to do godly deeds, which will vouchsafe the capacity and will to love the Lover of Israel.

The Shema in Jewish Liturgy

As indicated above, the single line of the *Shema* (6:4) holds a position of importance in Jewish practice unparalleled by any other verse. It is recited at evening and morning services on various occasions, on retiring at night and at the end of Yom Kippur, where it is almost at once followed by the sevenfold exclamation "The Lord is God!" (I Kings 18:39). It is a custom among Orthodox Jews to cover the eyes while saying the words, in order to increase one's concentration and to linger on the last letter (ד) which is written large in the Hebrew text. (But the *Shema* need not be said in Hebrew; one's obligation is fulfilled by saying it in any language.) The Talmud prescribes that the sentence be spoken clearly and precisely; the fires of hell, it says with metaphoric emphasis, are cooled for those who observe this rule [25].

Already at an early time it became a custom to read verse 4 twice daily together with verses 5–9 as well as nine other verses from chapter 11 (13–21), and five from Numbers (15:37–41).[5] These readings together became known as the *Shema* in a liturgical sense and were surrounded by benedictions extolling God as Creator, faithful Lover, and Protector of Israel. Tradition prescribed the hours during which the *Shema* had to be recited: the evening prayers were to be said between nightfall and dawn, and the morning *Shema* from dawn on until one-quarter of the day had passed [27].

It was natural that so important a text became the subject of controversy and special practices. The schools of Hillel and Shammai (at the beginning of the Common Era) argued over the bodily position one ought to assume while reciting the *Shema*. Shammai held that verse 7 was to be taken literally: at night speak the words lying down, and in the morning standing up; while Hillel (whose teaching prevailed) ruled that one should not change one's position during the recital [28]. Reform practice provides for the congregation to stand in order to emphasize the importance of the *Shema*, while in Orthodox and most Conservative synagogues it is recited sitting down.[6] Another difference has developed around the response customarily made to the public proclamation of the *Shema*: "Praised be the Lord's name for ever and ever." In Reform synagogues this response is spoken or sung aloud, in others it is said *sotto voce*, except on Yom Kippur.

And, finally, traditional prayer books provide that an individual person preface the

---

[4] The medieval moralist Bachya ibn Pakuda was one of the minority who believed that the love of God could be achieved only if one divorced himself from worldly pursuits. "What does the love of God consist of? The soul's complete surrender of its own accord to the Creator in order to cleave to His supernal light . . . then it will become completely preoccupied with His service and have no place for any other thought, sending forth not even one of the limbs of its body on any other service but that drawn to by His will;

loosening the tongue but to make mention of Him and praise Him out of love of Him and longing for Him" [24].

[5] In Reform services, the latter two paragraphs are omitted and only two verses (Num. 15:40–41) are recited to conclude Deut. 6:4–9 [26].

[6] However, congregations stand for the *Shema* during special parts of a service which in themselves require standing: the *Musaf Kedushah*, the Torah service, and the concluding proclamations of Yom Kippur.

Shema with the three words *El Melech ne-eman* (O God, faithful King!). This practice seems to have been instituted in order to raise the number of words found in the three paragraphs of the *Shema* (which amounts to two hundred forty-five) to two hundred forty-eight, thus equaling the number of positive mitzvot in the Torah—another indication that these words were seen to be at the heart of the Jewish faith.

GLEANINGS

The Death of Rabbi Akiba (about 138 C.E.)

The wicked government (the Romans) issued a decree forbidding the Jews to study and practice the Torah. Pappus ben Judah came and found Rabbi Akiba publicly bringing gatherings together and occupying himself with the Torah. He said to him: "Akiba, are you not afraid of the government?" He replied: "I will answer you with a parable. A fox was once walking alongside a river, and he saw fishes going in swarms from one place to another. He said to them: 'From what are you fleeing?' They replied: 'From the nets cast for us by men.' He said to them: 'Would you like to come up on to the dry land so that you and I can live together in the way that my ancestors lived with your ancestors?' They replied: 'Are you the one that they call the cleverest of animals? You are not clever but foolish. If we are afraid in the element in which we live, how much more in the element in which we would die!' So it is with us. If such is our condition when we sit and study the Torah, of which it is written, 'For that is your life and the length of your days' (Deut. 30:20), if we go and neglect it how much worse off we shall be!"

It is related that soon afterward Rabbi Akiba was arrested and thrown into prison, and Pappus ben Judah was also arrested and imprisoned next to him. He said to him: "Pappus, who brought you here?" He replied: "Happy are you, Rabbi Akiba, that you have been seized for busying yourself with the Torah! Alas for Pappus who has been seized for busying himself with idle things!" When Rabbi Akiba was taken out for execution, it was the hour for the recital of the *Shema* and, while they combed his flesh with iron combs, he was accepting upon himself the kingship of heaven.[7]

His disciples said to him: "Our teacher, even to this point?" He said to them: "All my days I have been troubled by this verse, 'with all your soul,' which I interpret 'even if He takes your soul.' I said: When shall I have the opportunity of fulfilling this? Now that I have the opportunity shall I not fulfill it?" He prolonged the word *echad*[8] until he expired while saying it. A heavenly voice went forth and proclaimed: "Happy are you, Akiba, that your soul has departed with the word *echad!*"   TALMUD [29]

Hearing and Seeing

Israel's original knowledge rested on seeing ("You have been *shown* that you might know," 4:35), by being made eyewitnesses to the revelation at Sinai. Since that time, however, tradition rests on hearing and not on a continuation of natural phenomena—hence, "*Hear*, O Israel!"

AFTER S. R. HIRSCH [30]

---

[7] Meaning, he recited the *Shema*.

[8] The last word of verse 4.

Why are the last letters of שְׁמַע and אֶחָד written large in all Torah scrolls? We no longer know the reason, but the following have been suggested:

To remind us to concentrate on the thought that lies between the ע and the ד;

The large ע: so that one should read שְׁמַע and not שֶׁמָּא ("Perhaps, O Israel . . .");

The large ד: so that one should read אֶחָד and not אַחֵר ("another").[9]

Together, ע and ד read עֵד (*ed*, witness), to emphasize that the Jew who pronounces the *Shema* witnesses to the Holy One.　SFORNO AND OTHERS

God's Glory

God said to Israel, "My children, everything I have created I have created in pairs: heaven and earth, sun and moon, Adam and Eve, this world and the world-to-come. But My glory is one and unique in the world—hence '. . . the Lord alone.'"
　MIDRASH [31]

One

He is One. Nobody will dispute that this doctrine is absolutely necessary for complete devotion, admiration, and love toward God. For devotion, admiration, and love spring from the superiority of one over all else.　SPINOZA [32]

Thou art One, the beginning of all computation, the base of all construction.

Thou art One, and in the mystery of Thy Oneness the wise of heart are astonished, for they know not what it is.

Thou art One, and Thy Oneness neither diminishes nor increases, neither lacks nor exceeds.

Thou art One, but not as the one that is counted or owned, for number and chance cannot reach Thee, nor attribute, nor form.

Thou art One, but my mind is too feeble to set Thee a law or a limit, and therefore I say: "I will take heed to my ways, that I sin not with my tongue."

Thou art One, and Thou art exalted above abasement and falling—not like a man, who falls when he is alone.
　SOLOMON IBN GABIROL [33]

Modern Jewish monotheistic belief has been so thoroughly explored in the previous centuries that a consensus has emerged among believers as to what it implies and what it rejects. Judaism stands or falls on the rejection of polytheism as it is compatible with dualism or trinitarianism. . . . Moderns will be sceptical, to say the least, regarding the kabbalistic systems and will regard chasidic pantheism as logically obscure. The believing Jew still recites the *Shema* as plying the pure monotheistic doctrine on which Judaism as a religion is based.　L. JACOBS [34]

He is the One, and therefore man must decide for Him, in contrast to and over and against all else, and must serve Him only and no power of nature or fate. . . . It is the grasp of this singular Reality, the awareness of this singular Truth, this will and courage to decide for the One and Only, rather than the multiple and the many, which is the soul of monotheism.　LEO BAECK [35]

A Doctrine of Faith

I believe with perfect faith that the Creator, blessed be His name, is One only and that there is no unity in any manner like His, and that He alone is our God, who was, is, and will be.
　MAIMONIDES [36]

In poetic form, the principle appears as the second stanza of the hymn *Yigdal*, by Meir Leoni (based on Maimonides):

One He is, no unity like His,
Mysterious and unending in His unity.

---

[9] Conversely, in Exod. 34:14 the ר is written large, so that one should not read אֶחָד, which instead of "Do not bow down to any other god" would be perverted into: "Do not bow down to the One God."

To Love God

The meaning of the love of God is that a man should be longing and yearning after the nearness of God, blessed be He, and striving to reach His holiness, in the same manner as he would pursue any object for which he feels a strong passion. He should feel that bliss and delight in mentioning His name, in uttering His praises, and in occupying himself with the words of the Torah, which a lover feels toward the wife of his youth, or the father toward his only son.   LUZZATTO [37]

This is the way the Psalmist describes his yearning:
Like a hind crying for water,
My soul cries for You, O God;
My soul thirsts for God, the living God....
PSALM 42:2–3

Man cannot love God as he loves another human being. Love of God involves a holy fear or reverence (6:13), and it expresses itself in that devoted and single-minded loyalty which issues in wholehearted and obedient service. The love of God without obedience is not love.

G. E. WRIGHT [38]

"You must love the Lord" means to do His commandments out of love, and "with all your heart" challenges us to do it with both our good and evil inclinations.[10]   MIDRASH [39]

What, then, is the way to love Him and revere Him? When man contemplates His works and His wonderful, great creatures and fathoms through them His inestimable and boundless wisdom, he will immediately love, and praise, and exalt, and will be seized by a keen longing passion to know Him—as David said: "My soul thirsts for God, the living God" (Ps. 42:3).

What is suitable love? To love God with an exceedingly great and very intense love until one's soul is knit with the love of God and one is constantly obsessed by it. As in a state of love-sickness, in which the mind cannot be diverted from the beloved, the lover is constantly obsessed by his love, lying down or rising up, eating or drinking.

Even more so will the lovers of God experience this constant obsession in their heart, as we are bidden to love "with all your heart and with all your soul," and as Solomon expressed allegorically "I am love-sick" (Song of Songs 5:8); the entire Song of Songs is, in fact, an allegorical expression of this love.   MAIMONIDES [40]

Defiant Love

The story was told of a man who had lost his wife and children in a pogrom. He addressed God as follows: "Master of the universe, You have done much to make me forsake my faith. Know then that in spite of it all I am a Jew, and a Jew I will remain, and nothing You will yet do to me will avail You anything and turn me away from loving You."   SHELOMO IBN VERGA [41]

Unity and Love

The juxtaposition of verse 4 (God's unity) and verse 5 (the love of God) suggests that, when we recognize Him as One, we are challenged to love Him as the source of all that happens to us—both good and evil.   MALBIM [42]

Sequence

It says (6:6) "Take to heart" and then (6:7) "Impress them upon your children." Only when you yourself take them to heart will you be able to impress them upon your children, as the saying is, "Words that come from the heart can enter the heart."   ALSHECH [43]

A Difficulty

How is it possible to command the love of God when it is dependent on an inner urge? Suppose such an urge is absent? However, every person has the potential somewhere buried within him, hence the commandment means to bolster the spirit so that the slumbering love of God may be uncovered.   SEFAT EMET [44]

The Commandment

Of course, love cannot be commanded. No third party can command it or extort it. No third party can, but the One can. The commandment

---

[10] This is derived from the word לְבָבְךָ (rather than לְבְּךָ, which has only one ב).

to love can only proceed from the mouth of the Lover. Only the Lover can and does say: love me! —and He really does so. In His mouth the commandment to love is not a strange commandment; it is none other than the voice of love itself. The love of the Lover has, in fact, no word to express itself other than the commandment.

F. ROSENZWEIG [45]

Love People First

Three times the Torah asks us to love: twice, in Leviticus (19:18, 34), we are commanded to love human beings; then, in Deuteronomy, our love is directed toward God. Only after we have learned to love people can we come to love God.

CHASIDIC [46]

Before beginning one's prayers one should concentrate on the thought of loving one's fellow creatures.   ISAAC BEN SOLOMON LURIA (HA-ARI) [47]

Our God (Deut. 6:4)

The "our" appears to limit God's universality. Hence we must take special care to proclaim His unity.   YALKUT SHIMONI [48]

He is "our God" now, and not yet the God of all nations, but in the future He will be "the Lord alone."   RASHI [49]

Sharpen

The duty to "impress" means to teach in-

decisively, to sharpen the intellect of one's child on the words of Torah.   ZOHAR [50]

Do Not Try the Lord (Deut. 6:16)

This means: Do not test one of God's prophets by challenging him to perform miracles.

MAIMONIDES [51]

Do What Is Right and Good (Deut. 6:18)

(The Rabbis did not consider "right" and "good" as synonyms. Rather, they took "good" to be an extension and widening of "right.")

This is a new command, not implied in any previous mitzvah. It means the (moral) obligation to go, when necessary, beyond what is (legally) required of us.   RASHI [52]

According to one opinion, Jerusalem was destroyed because its inhabitants acted merely according to the letter of the law and did not go beyond it.   TALMUD [53]

The Wise and the Wicked Sons

(The Haggadah assigns the question of 6:20 to the Wise Son,[11] but—according to the Masorah —he too says "you" like the Wicked Son. What then is the distinction?)

The Wise Son says "you" because the law was enjoined before his own time; at the same time he acknowledges that God stands behind the law. The Wicked Son (Exod. 12:26) does not acknowledge the latter.   TOSEFET BERACHAH [55]

---

11 The Haggadah distinguishes the Wise Son from the Wicked in that the former identifies with his people while the latter does not. (He says, "What does this mean to *you*," excluding himself [54].)

Dealing with Idolatry

The seventh chapter addresses the chief religious problem of the anticipated occupation of Canaan: how is Israel to deal with the idolaters
and idolatries they will find in the land? For the first time since Egypt,
the people will be exposed to and come in close contact with a foreign
culture that will be a potential snare to the invaders, whose own religious
practices are not as yet firmly established. The rules for occupation are
therefore extreme in their simplicity: those who endanger Israel's spiritual
survival are to be destroyed; mixed marriage with the inhabitants is to
be avoided; the pagan images and their sanctuaries are to be demolished.
If Israel will follow these prescriptions, all will be well and blessings will
attend it, but, if not, the very destruction due the enemy will be visited
on Israel itself. God will prove himself both faithful and vengeful, as circumstances demand, for His Chosen People stand in an ambience not duplicated elsewhere and unrelated to their power or their numbers.

These provisions have to be seen and understood in their own context
and must not be judged by the need and experience of a later age. Only
when we consider them as applicable to our own time does contemporary
judgment become opportune. The clash of cultures is a problem in contemporary Israel, and so is the frequent occurrence of mixed marriages
in the Diaspora, while idolatry, with which the ancients were greatly
concerned, is no longer an issue. Still, this subject raises questions about
the God whom the Torah depicts as desiring the death of idolaters and
who commands "Show them no pity!"

(A new weekly portion, *Ekev*, begins with 7:12.)

א כִּי יְבִיאֲךָ יְהוָה אֱלֹהֶיךָ אֶל־הָאָרֶץ אֲשֶׁר־אַתָּה בָא־
שָׁמָּה לְרִשְׁתָּהּ וְנָשַׁל גּוֹיִם־רַבִּים מִפָּנֶיךָ הַחִתִּי
וְהַגִּרְגָּשִׁי וְהָאֱמֹרִי וְהַכְּנַעֲנִי וְהַפְּרִזִּי וְהַחִוִּי וְהַיְבוּסִי
ב שִׁבְעָה גוֹיִם רַבִּים וַעֲצוּמִים מִמֶּךָּ: וּנְתָנָם יְהוָה
אֱלֹהֶיךָ לְפָנֶיךָ וְהִכִּיתָם הַחֲרֵם תַּחֲרִים אֹתָם לֹא־

ג תִכְרֹת לָהֶם בְּרִית וְלֹא תְחָנֵּם: וְלֹא תִתְחַתֵּן בָּם
בִּתְּךָ לֹא־תִתֵּן לִבְנוֹ וּבִתּוֹ לֹא־תִקַּח לִבְנֶךָ:
ד כִּי־יָסִיר אֶת־בִּנְךָ מֵאַחֲרַי וְעָבְדוּ אֱלֹהִים אֲחֵרִים
ה וְחָרָה אַף־יְהוָה בָּכֶם וְהִשְׁמִידְךָ מַהֵר: כִּי־אִם־כֹּה
תַעֲשׂוּ לָהֶם מִזְבְּחֹתֵיהֶם תִּתֹּצוּ וּמַצֵּבֹתָם תְּשַׁבֵּרוּ

1] When the LORD your God brings you to the land that you are about to invade and occupy, and He dislodges many nations before you—the Hittites, Girgashites, Amorites, Canaanites, Perizzites, Hivites, and Jebusites, seven nations much larger than you— 2] and the LORD your God delivers them to you and you defeat them, you must doom them to destruction: grant them no terms and give them no quarter. 3] You shall not intermarry with them: do not give your daughters to their sons or take their daughters for your sons. 4] For they will turn your children away from Me to worship other gods, and the LORD's anger will blaze forth against you and He will promptly wipe you out. 5] Instead, this is what you shall do to them: you shall tear down their altars, smash their pillars, cut down their sacred posts, and consign their images to the fire.

7:1] *Hittites.* The great Hittite empire of Anatolia (central Turkey) collapsed about the time of the Israelite conquest of Canaan (about 1200 B.C.E.) and its survivors fled into northern Syria. There they formed city-states jointly with Arameans invading from the south. (These are the Hittites referred to in neo-Assyrian inscriptions.) In the Bible, "Hittites" is more often than not used as an ideological pejorative with little specific ethnic content (compare the use of Ishmaelite, Midianite, Medanite; see our Commentary on Genesis, chapter 37) [1].

Girgashites. They are not known in sources outside the Bible. According to the Midrash the Israelites did not, however, encounter them during their conquest, for the Girgashites were said to have emigrated to Africa [2].

Amorites. See at 1:4, 7.

Canaanites. Here apparently a term for those natives who had no other tribal loyalty. In other contexts "Canaanites" is a general word for the inhabitants of the land.

Perizzites. Living in central Canaan, around Bethel and Shechem (see Josh. 17:15; Judg. 1:4 f.). The name may indicate "people who dwell in the open countryside" (see 3:5).

Hivites. They also lived near Shechem, and around Gibeon (Gen. 34:2; Josh. 9:7; 11:19).

Jebusites. Who lived in and around Jebus, which was the old name for Jerusalem. The Jebusites were not dislodged until King David's time, a little before 1000 B.C.E. (II Sam. 5:6).

Seven nations. This is the only time in the Torah that all the seven are listed together.

2] *Doom them to destruction.* On the problem raised by this verse and verse 16, see commentary below, "The Treatment of Conquered Nations."

4] *Away from Me.* Moses speaks here like a prophet, as if with God's voice.

5] *Their altars.* Such altars have been unearthed by archeologists [3].

Pillars. A row of some ten free-standing slabs was found at Gezer [4]. Most likely they represented seats of the deity. It has been suggested that the "memorial chapel" at Hazor was destroyed by the Israelites to fulfill this commandment [5].

Sacred posts. Usually made of wood, these *asherim* (dedicated to the goddess Asherah) were found near altar sites and represented sacred trees.

בְּיָ֤ד חֲזָקָה֙ וַיִּפְדְּךָ֔ מִבֵּ֣ית עֲבָדִ֔ים מִיַּ֖ד פַּרְעֹ֥ה מֶֽלֶךְ־

מִצְרָֽיִם: וְיָ֣דַעְתָּ֔ כִּֽי־יְהֹוָ֥ה אֱלֹהֶ֖יךָ ה֣וּא הָאֱלֹהִ֑ים הָאֵל֙

הַנֶּֽאֱמָ֔ן שֹׁמֵ֧ר הַבְּרִ֣ית וְהַחֶ֗סֶד לְאֹהֲבָ֛יו וּלְשֹׁמְרֵ֥י

מִצְוֺתָ֖ו לְאֶ֥לֶף דּֽוֹר: וּמְשַׁלֵּ֧ם לְשֹׂנְאָ֛יו אֶל־פָּנָ֖יו

לְהַאֲבִיד֑וֹ לֹ֤א יְאַחֵר֙ לְשֹׂנְא֔וֹ אֶל־פָּנָ֖יו יְשַׁלֶּם־לֽוֹ:

וְשָׁמַרְתָּ֨ אֶת־הַמִּצְוָ֜ה וְאֶת־הַֽחֻקִּ֣ים וְאֶת־הַמִּשְׁפָּטִ֗ים

אֲשֶׁ֨ר אָנֹכִ֧י מְצַוְּךָ֛ הַיּ֖וֹם לַעֲשׂוֹתָֽם:

וַאֲשֵׁירֵהֶ֖ם תְּגַדֵּע֑וּן וּפְסִילֵיהֶ֖ם תִּשְׂרְפ֣וּן בָּאֵ֑שׁ: כִּ֣י

עַ֤ם קָדוֹשׁ֙ אַתָּ֔ה לַיהֹוָ֖ה אֱלֹהֶ֑יךָ בְּךָ֞ בָּחַ֣ר ׀ יְהֹוָ֣ה

אֱלֹהֶ֗יךָ לִהְי֥וֹת לוֹ֙ לְעַ֣ם סְגֻלָּ֔ה מִכֹּל֙ הָֽעַמִּ֔ים אֲשֶׁ֖ר

עַל־פְּנֵ֥י הָאֲדָמָֽה: לֹ֣א מֵֽרֻבְּכֶ֞ם מִכָּל־הָֽעַמִּים֮ חָשַׁ֣ק

יְהֹוָ֣ה בָּכֶם֒ וַיִּבְחַ֣ר בָּכֶ֑ם כִּֽי־אַתֶּ֥ם הַמְעַ֖ט מִכָּל־

הָעַמִּֽים: כִּי֩ מֵאַֽהֲבַ֨ת יְהֹוָ֜ה אֶתְכֶ֗ם וּמִשָּׁמְר֤וֹ אֶת־

הַשְּׁבֻעָה֙ אֲשֶׁ֣ר נִשְׁבַּ֣ע לַאֲבֹֽתֵיכֶ֔ם הוֹצִ֧יא יְהֹוָ֛ה אֶתְכֶ֖ם

ט סצותיו ק׳

Haftarah Va'etchanan, p. 1595

6] For you are a people consecrated to the LORD your God: of all the peoples on earth the LORD your God chose you to be His treasured people.   7] It is not because you are the most numerous of peoples that the LORD set His heart on you and chose you—indeed, you are the smallest of peoples;   8] but it was because the LORD loved you and kept the oath He made to your fathers that the LORD freed you with a mighty hand and rescued you from the house of bondage, from the power of Pharaoh king of Egypt.

9] Know, therefore, that only the LORD your God is God, the steadfast God who keeps His gracious covenant to the thousandth generation of those who love Him and keep His commandments.   10] but who instantly requites with destruction those who reject Him— never slow with those who reject Him, but requiting them instantly.   11] Therefore, observe faithfully the Instruction—the laws and the rules—with which I charge you today.

6] *His treasured people.* עַם סְגֻלָּה (*am segullah*), a term probably related to the Akkadian *sikilfu* (property) or *sugullu* (cattle, which was usually a person's main possession; see further at Exod. 19:5). According to Buber, the term meant "a possession which is withdrawn from general family property because one invidividual has a special relation to it and a special claim on it" [6].

7] *Not because you are the most numerous.* God operates sometimes in contradiction to what the "natural" order appears to suggest or demand; "an act of paradoxical divine love" [7].

Chose you. On the concept of the Chosen People, see at Exod. 19.

8] *The Lord loved you.* His love is the foundation of the command to love Him.

9] *Steadfast God.* הָאֵל הַנֶּאֱמָן (*ha-el ha-ne-eman*), see at verse 12.

Thousandth generation. The Hebrew לְאֶלֶף דּוֹר is a stylistic variance of לַאֲלָפִים in the Ten Commandments (Exod. 20:6 and Deut. 5:10).

10] *Instantly.* Literally, "to their faces," that is, while they can see and experience it.

11] *Therefore.* The sentence repeats the introduction of chapter 6, bringing this section to a close (and also the *sidrah Va'etchanan* which ends here).

תִּהְיֶה מִכָּל־הָעַמִּים לֹא־יִהְיֶה בְךָ עָקָר וַעֲקָרָה
טו וּבִבְהֶמְתֶּךָ: וְהֵסִיר יְהוָֹה מִמְּךָ כָּל־חֹלִי וְכָל־מַדְוֵי
מִצְרַיִם הָרָעִים אֲשֶׁר יָדַעְתָּ לֹא יְשִׂימָם בָּךְ וּנְתָנָם
טז בְּכָל־שֹׂנְאֶיךָ: וְאָכַלְתָּ אֶת־כָּל־הָעַמִּים אֲשֶׁר יְהוָֹה
אֱלֹהֶיךָ נֹתֵן לָךְ לֹא־תָחוֹס עֵינְךָ עֲלֵיהֶם וְלֹא תַעֲבֹד
יז אֶת־אֱלֹהֵיהֶם כִּי־מוֹקֵשׁ הוּא לָךְ: ס כִּי תֹאמַר
בִּלְבָבְךָ רַבִּים הַגּוֹיִם הָאֵלֶּה מִמֶּנִּי אֵיכָה אוּכַל

פ פ פ

יב וְהָיָה עֵקֶב תִּשְׁמְעוּן אֵת הַמִּשְׁפָּטִים הָאֵלֶּה וּשְׁמַרְתֶּם
וַעֲשִׂיתֶם אֹתָם וְשָׁמַר יְהוָֹה אֱלֹהֶיךָ לְךָ אֶת־הַבְּרִית
יג וְאֶת־הַחֶסֶד אֲשֶׁר נִשְׁבַּע לַאֲבֹתֶיךָ: וַאֲהֵבְךָ וּבֵרַכְךָ
וְהִרְבֶּךָ וּבֵרַךְ פְּרִי־בִטְנְךָ וּפְרִי־אַדְמָתֶךָ דְּגָנְךָ
וְתִירֹשְׁךָ וְיִצְהָרֶךָ שְׁגַר־אֲלָפֶיךָ וְעַשְׁתְּרֹת צֹאנֶךָ עַל
יד הָאֲדָמָה אֲשֶׁר־נִשְׁבַּע לַאֲבֹתֶיךָ לָתֶת לָךְ: בָּרוּךְ

12] And if you do obey these rules and observe them faithfully, the LORD your God will maintain for you the gracious covenant that He made on oath with your fathers: **13]** He will love you and bless you and multiply you; He will bless the issue of your womb and the produce of your soil, your new grain and wine and oil, the calving of your herd and the lambing of your flock, in the land that He swore to your fathers to give you.   **14]** You shall be blessed above all other peoples: there shall be no sterile male or female among you or among your livestock.   **15]** The LORD will ward off from you all sickness; He will not bring upon you any of the dreadful diseases of Egypt, about which you know, but will inflict them upon all your enemies.

16] You shall destroy all the peoples that the LORD your God delivers to you, showing them no pity. And you shall not worship their gods, for that would be a snare to you.   **17]** Should you say to yourselves, "These nations are more numerous than we; how can we dispossess

12] *And if you do.* The new *sidrah Ekev* is named after the second Hebrew word, עֵקֶב, literally, "on the heel of," i.e., in consequence of your obeisance. The catalogue of blessings that begins here and reaches to verse 24 more than counterbalances the brief warnings in verses 4 and 10 (a full catalogue of blessings and curses is presented in chapter 28). It becomes clear—and this remains a prominent theme of Deuteronomy—that God's execution of the covenantal terms depends on Israel. He is the unchanging, faithful God, and therefore Israel's fate for good or evil depends essentially on the people itself.

The blessings present the familiar recital of protection, fertility of body and soil, health and victory [8].

13] *Calving.* עַשְׁתְּרֹת (*ashterot*), a word related to

Ashtoreth, a Canaanite goddess concerned with fertility.

14] *No sterile male or female.* A hyperbolic expression, not to be understood literally.

15] *Dreadful diseases of Egypt.* Probably a reference to dysentery, ophthalmia, and especially elephantiasis; the last was called by the Roman historian Pliny "the particular Egyptian disease" [9].

16] *Destroy.* Literally, "eat," "consume." The idiom occurs also in Num. 13:32 (where the spies report that Canaan "consumes" its inhabitants). In Num. 14:9, the potential enemy is called "our bread," that is, our prey.

Showing them no pity. See commentary below.

יח לְהוֹרִישָׁם: לֹא תִירָא מֵהֶם זָכֹר תִּזְכֹּר אֵת אֲשֶׁר־

מְעַט לֹא תוּכַל כַּלֹּתָם מַהֵר פֶּן־תִּרְבֶּה עָלֶיךָ חַיַּת

יט עָשָׂה יְהֹוָה אֱלֹהֶיךָ לְפַרְעֹה וּלְכָל־מִצְרָיִם: הַמַּסֹּת

הַשָּׂדֶה: וּנְתָנָם יְהֹוָה אֱלֹהֶיךָ לְפָנֶיךָ וְהָמָם מְהוּמָה כג

הַגְּדֹלֹת אֲשֶׁר־רָאוּ עֵינֶיךָ וְהָאֹתֹת וְהַמֹּפְתִים וְהַיָּד

גְדֹלָה עַד הִשָּׁמְדָם: וְנָתַן מַלְכֵיהֶם בְּיָדֶךָ וְהַאֲבַדְתָּ כד

הַחֲזָקָה וְהַזְּרֹעַ הַנְּטוּיָה אֲשֶׁר הוֹצִאֲךָ יְהֹוָה אֱלֹהֶיךָ

אֶת־שְׁמָם מִתַּחַת הַשָּׁמָיִם לֹא־יִתְיַצֵּב אִישׁ בְּפָנֶיךָ

כֵּן־יַעֲשֶׂה יְהֹוָה אֱלֹהֶיךָ לְכָל־הָעַמִּים אֲשֶׁר־אַתָּה יָרֵא

עַד הִשְׁמִדְךָ אֹתָם: פְּסִילֵי אֱלֹהֵיהֶם תִּשְׂרְפוּן בָּאֵשׁ כה

מִפְּנֵיהֶם: וְגַם אֶת־הַצִּרְעָה יְשַׁלַּח יְהֹוָה אֱלֹהֶיךָ בָּם כ

לֹא־תַחְמֹד כֶּסֶף וְזָהָב עֲלֵיהֶם וְלָקַחְתָּ לָךְ פֶּן תִּוָּקֵשׁ

עַד־אֲבֹד הַנִּשְׁאָרִים וְהַנִּסְתָּרִים מִפָּנֶיךָ: לֹא תַעֲרֹץ כא

בּוֹ כִּי תוֹעֲבַת יְהֹוָה אֱלֹהֶיךָ הוּא: וְלֹא־תָבִיא תוֹעֵבָה כו

מִפְּנֵיהֶם כִּי־יְהֹוָה אֱלֹהֶיךָ בְּקִרְבֶּךָ אֵל גָּדוֹל וְנוֹרָא:

אֶל־בֵּיתֶךָ וְהָיִיתָ חֵרֶם כָּמֹהוּ שַׁקֵּץ תְּשַׁקְּצֶנּוּ וְתַעֵב

כב וְנָשַׁל יְהֹוָה אֱלֹהֶיךָ אֶת־הַגּוֹיִם הָאֵל מִפָּנֶיךָ מְעַט

תְּתַעֲבֶנּוּ כִּי־חֵרֶם הוּא:
פ

* כב סבורין האלה.

them?" **18]** You need have no fear of them. You have but to bear in mind what the LORD your God did to Pharaoh and all the Egyptians: **19]** the wondrous acts that you saw with your own eyes, the signs and the portents, the mighty hand, and the outstretched arm by which the LORD your God liberated you. Thus will the LORD your God do to all the peoples you now fear. **20]** The LORD your God will also send a plague against them, until those who are left in hiding perish before you. **21]** Do not stand in dread of them, for the LORD your God is in your midst, a great and awesome God.

22] The LORD your God will dislodge those peoples before you little by little; you will not be able to put an end to them at once, else the wild beasts would multiply to your hurt. **23]** The LORD your God will deliver them up to you, throwing them into utter panic until they are wiped out. **24]** He will deliver their kings into your hand, and you shall obliterate their name from under the heavens; no man shall stand up to you, until you have wiped them out.

25] You shall consign the images of their gods to the fire; you shall not covet the silver and gold on them and keep it for yourselves, lest you be ensnared thereby; for that is abhorrent to the LORD your God. **26]** You must not bring an abhorrent thing into your house, or you will be proscribed like it; you must reject it as abominable and abhorrent, for it is proscribed.

20] *Plague.* Others, "hornet," "panic." See at Exod. 23:28.

22] *Little by little.* This is the same prediction found in Exod. 23:29–30 and explains ex-post-facto why God decided not to make the conquest easy. The actual and full acquisition took several hundred years, and the native population was assimilated and not driven off or killed.

In the Book of Judges, various reasons are given for the gradual rather than quick occupation: God wanted to punish Israel (2:3); to test Israel (3:1, 4); to make a new generation taste war (3:2).

25] *Silver and gold on them.* Nothing was to be used that was at any time connected with the idols.

The Treatment of Conquered Nations

The Torah instructs the Israelites to "doom" the idolatrous nations in Canaan and to show them no pity. This provision is in stark contrast to the pervasive humaneness of the book, and therefore attempts of various kinds have been made to explain or defend this harshness and to make clear how a loving and caring God could be seen to issue such edicts.

An early attempt was made in talmudic days. The Hebrew for "show them no pity" (לֹא תְחָנֵּם) was read as "do not grant them [land]," as if the text read לֹא תַחֲנֵם, that is, do not sell real estate to them—a rendering which leaned on the warning in Exod. 23:33 not to let them dwell "in your land" [10]. But even if one would deem this interpretation feasible (which it is not, in view of the clear Masoretic text), one could not argue away the provision of Deut. 20:16 which, using another word, unequivocally says, "You shall not let a soul remain alive."

The text has further been defended on the grounds of necessity: unless the native people were done away with, they would ensnare Israel with their idolatrous practices, and the maintenance of the Sinaitic covenant was a task overshadowing all else. God's plans for humanity could not and cannot be measured by human considerations. To emphasize this point, S. R. Hirsch interpreted the twice-issued injunction of verses 2 and 16 to show that repetition was needed because it went so much against the sensibilities of the Israelites [11]. However, no student of history can easily accept such a reading, for all too many humans have fallen victim to inquisitors and crusading warriors who pretended to act out of the highest religious motives.

And already in talmudic times the notion was rejected that an Almighty God would agree to wipe idolatry off the face of the earth, though He had the power to do so.

One comes closer to an understanding of the Torah if one abandons efforts to shield it from criticism and sees it in the light of its own time, its values, and standards.[1] "The custom to 'dedicate' an enemy to the deity, or to ban him, or after a victory to annihilate him, is told us of various Near Eastern nations[2] as well as of the Greeks, Romans, Celts, and Germans. Since the sensitivities of the ancients were not offended by the rigor of this procedure, Moses could use this harsh war practice as a means to shield Israel from pagan infection" [13].

But even this interpretation does not do the text full justice, for it ascribes to Moses a point of view which may not have been his at all. Moreover, and most important: the unyielding tenor of these provisions stands in sharp contrast to the fact that such a policy of annihilation was never carried out—the Canaanites were *not* annihilated. In fact, in Judg. 3:1, God himself is said to have abrogated His original command (see above, at verse 22). Later, in retrospect—taking Deuteronomy to be a post-settlement and not a Mosaic document—the reader was told that the rampant idolatry which characterized Israel's history for centuries could have been avoided had the native peoples been destroyed. Note that the sermon warns the Israelites not to intermarry with the idolaters —the very idolaters who were supposed to be doomed!

A proper understanding, then, would view these passages as retrojections of what could and might have been, and the senti-

---

[1] This approach is easier for the liberal who sees the Torah as a human document than for a fundamentalist who considers it the word of God.

[2] The Mesha stone (ninth century B.C.E.) tells of Nebo's 7,000 Israelites—"men, boys, women, girls, and maidservants"—being "devoted" to Ashtar-Chemosh [12].

ments were acceptable in view of the common practices of the times.

Mixed Marriage

The practice of encouraging endogamy (marriage within the group) was not unique to Israel, but, because the Jewish people down to the present age have generally supported it and have discouraged exogamy (marriage out of the group), the purpose and desirability of such practices continue to be debated. It is important, however, to avoid the projection of latter-day religious, psychological, and sociological opinions onto the discussion of the biblical text.

An example of such projection is the talmudic discussion of the warning in verse 3, not to intermarry with the sons and daughters of the seven Canaanite nations. The Talmud, proceeding from the practice of avoiding marriage with *any* other nation and assuming that such was already the case in biblical days, reasoned as follows: Since marriage with unconverted Gentiles of any kind was prohibited, verse 3 could only mean to issue an additional restriction, namely, not to marry Canaanites, *even if converted* [14]. This is similar to the discussion about Abraham's observance of the prohibition of mixing milk and meat, which is postbiblical, and rests on biblical law which is post-Abrahamitic [15].

There is no question that endogamy was encouraged amongst the Israelites from earliest days on. This may be gathered from the stories of Abraham (instructing his servant to find a wife for his son from his own family) or Rebekah (whose unhappiness over Esau's marriages to foreign women was especially recorded; Gen. 26:34–35). But, at the same time, exogamous alliances did take place throughout the early centuries of Israel's existence; thus, Moses, Solomon, and Ahab took foreign wives, as did the tribal forefathers Simeon and Joseph. Not until the time of Ezra, that is, about 400 B.C.E., after the exiles' return from Babylon, were such marriages deemed socially and politically so undesirable that they had to be dissolved (see Ezra 9). In this phase of history, the consolidation of religious commitment through strictly enforced endogamy appeared as a necessary policy, one which persisted thereafter into modern times.[3]

We may assume, therefore, that Deuteronomy attempted to codify a principle but that as in other matters the actual carrying out of the law fell far short of the ideal. At stake was the religious purity of both people and land, buttressed by the conviction that only a nation totally consecrated to God could be His partner in the covenant. For it was not enough for Israel to merely exist and survive with a national identity; it was to be a special people, a "holy nation"—and therefore only families in whose midst God and Torah-conscious generations would be reared could be entrusted with this task. The prohibition against out-marriages[4] *was religious* in nature, it had nothing to do with racial ideas, and with superiority only in the sense that Israel had a unique relation with the Holy One which needed to be protected at all costs [16].

Endogamous marriage represented no problems for Diaspora Jews in host societies that disapproved of or forbade mixed marriages. But, when such restraints were removed and Jews themselves became less

---

[3] The Book of Ruth may have been written to counteract this development and may have been written as a defense of exogamy.

[4] See further, for instance, Num. 25:1 ff.; 31:15 f.; Josh. 23:7; Judg. 3:6; I Kings 2:1.

attentive to traditional ways, the rate of exogamous marriages increased sharply. Once exogamous patterns become established they develop their own dynamic thrust. While the great majority of Jews continue to endorse the old biblical prohibitions, at least in theory, there is no agreement on how to treat the actual spread of mixed marriages and how to keep their offspring in the Jewish fold. In the Reform movement especially, the discussion of means and ends has been vigorous, with no resolution in sight [17]. The problem is ultimately an expression of the tension of contrasting tendencies in Jewish history: its expanding and contracting heartbeats, the broadening and the narrowing of peoplehood. Together they give the biblical concern an abiding relevancy.

Mixed Marriage

Though the halachah prohibits mixed marriage for both men and women and does not recognize such marriages as religiously valid, it considers the children of Jewish mothers and gentile (unconverted) fathers as Jewish, and the offspring of Jewish fathers and gentile (unconverted) mothers as gentile.[5]

Reform Judaism, though it too continues to discourage mixed marriages, recognizes their validity once they have been contracted and accepts the offspring of these unions as Jewish if the parents—and, later, the children themselves—affirm their Jewish identity [19].

Today

In the Hebrew text the words "observe" and "today" stand together, לַעֲשׂוֹתָם הַיּוֹם, as a reminder to observe God's commandments today and not to delay them until tomorrow (that is, after death).   TALMUD [20]

Observe Them Faithfully (Deut. 7:12)

Israel's obedience is required for the totality of Torah, and not for one command in preference to another. No mitzvah is "superior" or "inferior": "Be heedful of a light precept as of a grave one, for you do not know the measure of reward for each command."   MISHNAH AND MIDRASH [21]

The Last Mitzvah

The Baal Shem Tov explained the opening words of the *sidrah* וְהָיָה עֵקֶב (verse 12), as if they meant "and the end shall be . . . ."[6] Therefore, he concluded, consider every mitzvah as the last you will be able to perform in your life.

M. HACOHEN [22]

Plural and Singular (verse 12)

The warning "If, then, *you* obey . . ." is in Hebrew couched in the plural, but the reward, "God will keep with *you* the gracious covenant," in the singular. One can warn all, but only individuals can perform the mitzvah and merit the reward.   CHASIDIC [23]

Halachah

(Verse 25 commands the destruction of heathen images. Does this include pagan antiques?)

If the pagans themselves have abandoned or mutilated their idols they have destroyed their status as forbidden images and the statues may be acquired or kept. An idolater can abrogate the status of an idol, an Israelite cannot.

TALMUD [24]

The Sanctity of One's Home (verse 26)

The prohibition to bring idols into one's house implies the prohibition to sell the house to an idolater. (However, this obtains only in Eretz Yisrael.)   TALMUD [25]

---

[5] The proof text (a combination of verses 3 and 4) is interpreted this way: the Hebrew of verse 4 begins with a masculine construction, saying literally "when *he* (the gentile husband) turns your son away from Me." Thus, though the child has a gentile father (and a Jewish mother), he is still called "your son" (i.e., an acknowledged Jew). For lack of the reverse expression, the child of a gentile mother is regarded as gentile [18].

[6] Understanding עֵקֶב to mean "end" (literally, "heel").

The Good Life

The discourse now turns to the inner dimensions of Israel's existence. If it is lived in accordance with God's will, its material rewards will be readily apparent, but these will not tell the whole story. Moses hopes that Israel will come to understand the munificence of God and the generous protection He has afforded His children and will appreciate that their good fortune is due primarily to Him and not to their own power. The forty long years they spent in the desert were a necessary education for them, so that they might learn that human dependence on God must be total, that "man does not live on bread alone, but that man may live on anything that the Lord decrees" (8:3). Thus it is not only Israel's actions that are important, but also its state of mind, its humility, its feeling of essential powerlessness in the face of the Lord's might.

The land Israel will inherit (or, in Josianic days,[1] land already inherited) is called "a good land" (8:7), whose wealth is described in detail. That very wealth, however, has its dangers, and Israel is warned that affluence is likely to engender false pride. Once again, the by now familiar threat is repeated: If despite God's favors in past and present the people turn to other gods, the divine wrath will be unleashed and Israel "shall certainly perish" (8:19).

A brief postscript (9:1–5) emphasizes once more that it was God whose will bestowed the land on Israel and that a contributing factor in Israel's

---

[1] In the seventh century B.C.E., when Deuteronomy was most likely composed (see introduction).

successful occupation of the land was the wickedness of the native peoples, their immorality and idolatry, which caused them to lose their title to the Holy Land.[2] This statement implies, of course, that Israel too will possess Canaan only as long as it justifies God's trust and does not defile the sacredness of the soil.

[2] The idea that possession of Canaan depends on the morality of the inhabitants is found also in Gen. 15:16 and Lev. 18:24 ff.

א כָּל־הַמִּצְוָ֗ה אֲשֶׁ֨ר אָֽנֹכִ֧י מְצַוְּךָ֛ הַיּ֖וֹם תִּשְׁמְר֣וּן לַֽעֲשׂ֑וֹת לְמַ֨עַן תִּֽחְי֜וּן וּרְבִיתֶ֗ם וּבָאתֶם֙ וִֽירִשְׁתֶּ֣ם אֶת־הָאָ֔רֶץ

ב אֲשֶׁר־נִשְׁבַּ֥ע יְהֹוָ֖ה לַֽאֲבֹֽתֵיכֶֽם: וְזָֽכַרְתָּ֣ אֶת־כָּל־הַדֶּ֗רֶךְ אֲשֶׁ֨ר הֹֽלִֽיכְךָ֜ יְהֹוָ֧ה אֱלֹהֶ֛יךָ זֶ֛ה אַרְבָּעִ֥ים שָׁנָ֖ה בַּמִּדְבָּ֑ר לְמַ֨עַן עַנֹּֽתְךָ֜ לְנַסֹּֽתְךָ֗ לָדַ֜עַת אֶת־אֲשֶׁ֤ר

ג בִּֽלְבָֽבְךָ֙ הֲתִשְׁמֹ֣ר מִצְוֹתָ֖ו אִם־לֹֽא: וַיְעַנְּךָ֘ וַיַּרְעִבֶ֒ךָ֒ וַיַּֽאֲכִֽלְךָ֤ אֶת־הַמָּן֙ אֲשֶׁ֣ר לֹֽא־יָדַ֔עְתָּ וְלֹ֥א יָֽדְע֖וּן אֲבֹתֶ֑יךָ לְמַ֣עַן הֽוֹדִֽיעֲךָ֗ כִּ֠י לֹ֣א עַל־הַלֶּ֤חֶם לְבַדּוֹ֙ יִֽחְיֶ֣ה הָֽאָדָ֔ם

ד כִּ֛י עַל־כָּל־מוֹצָ֥א פִֽי־יְהֹוָ֖ה יִֽחְיֶ֣ה הָֽאָדָ֑ם: שִׂמְלָֽתְךָ֞

לֹ֤א בָֽלְתָה֙ מֵֽעָלֶ֔יךָ וְרַגְלְךָ֖ לֹ֣א בָצֵ֑קָה זֶ֖ה אַרְבָּעִ֥ים

ה שָׁנָֽה: וְיָֽדַעְתָּ֖ עִם־לְבָבֶ֑ךָ כִּ֠י כַּֽאֲשֶׁ֨ר יְיַסֵּ֥ר אִישׁ֙ אֶת־

ו בְּנ֔וֹ יְהֹוָ֥ה אֱלֹהֶ֖יךָ מְיַסְּרֶֽךָּ: וְשָׁ֣מַרְתָּ֔ אֶת־מִצְוֹ֖ת

ז יְהֹוָ֣ה אֱלֹהֶ֑יךָ לָלֶ֥כֶת בִּדְרָכָ֖יו וּלְיִרְאָ֥ה אֹתֽוֹ: כִּ֚י יְהֹוָ֣ה אֱלֹהֶ֔יךָ מְבִֽיאֲךָ֖ אֶל־אֶ֣רֶץ טוֹבָ֑ה אֶ֚רֶץ נַ֣חֲלֵי

ח מַ֔יִם עֲיָנֹת֙ וּתְהֹמֹ֔ת יֹֽצְאִ֥ים בַּבִּקְעָ֖ה וּבָהָֽר: אֶ֚רֶץ חִטָּ֣ה וּשְׂעֹרָ֔ה וְגֶ֥פֶן וּתְאֵנָ֖ה וְרִמּ֑וֹן אֶֽרֶץ־זֵ֥ית שֶׁ֖מֶן

ט וּדְבָֽשׁ: אֶ֗רֶץ אֲשֶׁ֨ר לֹ֤א בְמִסְכֵּנֻת֙ תֹּֽאכַל־בָּ֣הּ לֶ֔חֶם לֹֽא־תֶחְסַ֥ר כֹּ֖ל בָּ֑הּ אֶ֚רֶץ אֲשֶׁ֤ר אֲבָנֶ֨יהָ֙ בַרְזֶ֔ל

* ב מצותיו ק׳.

1] You shall faithfully observe all the Instruction that I enjoin upon you today, that you may thrive and increase and be able to occupy the land which the LORD promised on oath to your fathers.

2] Remember the long way that the LORD your God has made you travel in the wilderness these past forty years, that He might test you by hardships to learn what was in your hearts: whether you would keep His commandments or not. **3]** He subjected you to the hardship of hunger and then gave you manna to eat, which neither you nor your fathers had ever known, in order to teach you that man does not live on bread alone, but that man may live on anything that the LORD decrees. **4]** The clothes upon you did not wear out, nor did your feet swell these forty years. **5]** Bear in mind that the LORD your God disciplines you just as a man disciplines his son. **6]** Therefore keep the commandments of the LORD your God: walk in His ways and revere Him.

7] For the LORD your God is bringing you into a good land, a land with streams and springs and fountains issuing from plain and hill; **8]** a land of wheat and barley, of vines, figs, and pomegranates, a land of olive trees and honey; **9]** a land where you may eat food without stint, where you will lack nothing; a land whose rocks are iron and from whose hills you can

8:2] *That He might test you by hardships.* Literally, "in order to afflict you for the purpose of testing you." The same word עַנּוֹת (anot, afflict) is used for the hardships imposed on Israel by the Egyptians (Exod. 1:11). In Egypt the afflictions were the work of an oppressor; in the desert they were instituted by God for Israel's sake.

3] *Manna.* See Exodus, chapter 16. Whatever explanations of the natural background of this food may be offered (such as believing it to have been an exudation and secretion by symbiotic insects living on tamarisks), the Torah perceived of manna as a supernatural gift. The test referred to in the preceding verse consisted of seeing

whether Israel could accommodate itself to continued dependence on God [1].

4] *Clothes . . . did not wear out.* A hyperbole describing God's miraculous care.

The Rabbis, however, understood this verse literally: If God could provide manna He could (and did) make the clothes of children grow along with them [2].

8] *A land of wheat and barley.* They continue to be the two chief field crops grown in the land today.

9] *Whose rocks are iron.* The reference is unclear, for iron was not mined in Canaan but was imported.

וּמֵהֲרָרֶיהָ תַּחְצֹב נְחֹשֶׁת: וְאָכַלְתָּ וְשָׂבָעְתָּ וּבֵרַכְתָּ
אֶת־יְהֹוָה אֱלֹהֶיךָ עַל־הָאָרֶץ הַטֹּבָה אֲשֶׁר נָתַן־לָךְ:
יא הִשָּׁמֶר לְךָ פֶּן־תִּשְׁכַּח אֶת־יְהֹוָה אֱלֹהֶיךָ לְבִלְתִּי שְׁמֹר
מִצְוֹתָיו וּמִשְׁפָּטָיו וְחֻקֹּתָיו אֲשֶׁר אָנֹכִי מְצַוְּךָ הַיּוֹם:
יב פֶּן־תֹּאכַל וְשָׂבָעְתָּ וּבָתִּים טֹבִים תִּבְנֶה וְיָשָׁבְתָּ:
יג וּבְקָרְךָ וְצֹאנְךָ יִרְבְּיֻן וְכֶסֶף וְזָהָב יִרְבֶּה־לָּךְ וְכֹל
יד אֲשֶׁר־לְךָ יִרְבֶּה: וְרָם לְבָבֶךָ וְשָׁכַחְתָּ אֶת־יְהֹוָה
אֱלֹהֶיךָ הַמּוֹצִיאֲךָ מֵאֶרֶץ מִצְרַיִם מִבֵּית עֲבָדִים:
טו הַמּוֹלִיכְךָ בַּמִּדְבָּר הַגָּדֹל וְהַנּוֹרָא נָחָשׁ שָׂרָף וְעַקְרָב
וְצִמָּאוֹן אֲשֶׁר אֵין־מָיִם הַמּוֹצִיא לְךָ מַיִם מִצּוּר
טז הַחַלָּמִישׁ: הַמַּאֲכִלְךָ מָן בַּמִּדְבָּר אֲשֶׁר לֹא־יָדְעוּן

אֲבֹתֶיךָ לְמַעַן עַנֹּתְךָ וּלְמַעַן נַסֹּתֶךָ לְהֵיטִבְךָ
יז בְּאַחֲרִיתֶךָ: וְאָמַרְתָּ בִּלְבָבֶךָ כֹּחִי וְעֹצֶם יָדִי עָשָׂה
יח לִי אֶת־הַחַיִל הַזֶּה: וְזָכַרְתָּ אֶת־יְהֹוָה אֱלֹהֶיךָ כִּי הוּא
הַנֹּתֵן לְךָ כֹּחַ לַעֲשׂוֹת חָיִל לְמַעַן הָקִים אֶת־בְּרִיתוֹ
אֲשֶׁר־נִשְׁבַּע לַאֲבֹתֶיךָ כַּיּוֹם הַזֶּה: פ
יט וְהָיָה אִם־שָׁכֹחַ תִּשְׁכַּח אֶת־יְהֹוָה אֱלֹהֶיךָ וְהָלַכְתָּ
אַחֲרֵי אֱלֹהִים אֲחֵרִים וַעֲבַדְתָּם וְהִשְׁתַּחֲוִיתָ לָהֶם
כ הַעִדֹתִי בָכֶם הַיּוֹם כִּי אָבֹד תֹּאבֵדוּן: כַּגּוֹיִם אֲשֶׁר
יְהֹוָה מַאֲבִיד מִפְּנֵיכֶם כֵּן תֹּאבֵדוּן עֵקֶב לֹא תִשְׁמְעוּן
בְּקוֹל יְהֹוָה אֱלֹהֵיכֶם:

mine copper. **10]** When you have eaten your fill, give thanks to the LORD your God for the good land which He has given you.

11] Take care lest you forget the LORD your God and fail to keep His commandments, His rules, and His laws, which I enjoin upon you today. **12]** When you have eaten your fill, and have built fine houses to live in, **13]** and your herds and flocks have multiplied, and your silver and gold have increased, and everything you own has prospered, **14]** beware lest your heart grow haughty and you forget the LORD your God—who freed you from the land of Egypt, the house of bondage; **15]** who led you through the great and terrible wilderness with its *seraph* serpents and scorpions, a parched land with no water in it, who brought forth water for you from the flinty rock; **16]** who fed you in the wilderness with manna, which your fathers had never known, in order to test you by hardships only to benefit you in the end— **17]** and you say to yourselves, "My own power and the might of my own hand have won this wealth for me." **18]** Remember that it is the LORD your God who gives you the power to get wealth, in fulfillment of the covenant that He made on oath with your fathers, as is still the case.

19] If you do forget the LORD your God and follow other gods to serve them or bow down to them, I warn you this day that you shall certainly perish; **20]** like the nations that the LORD will cause to perish before you, so shall you perish—because you did not heed the LORD your God.

10] *Give thanks.* The obligation to thank God after the conclusion of a meal (בִּרְכַּת הַמָּזוֹן) is based on this verse (see Gleanings).

15] *Seraph serpents.* The meaning of "seraph" is uncertain; some render it "fiery," a presumed ref-erence to snake bites that caused an inflammation of the skin. See at Num. 21:6.

18] *As is still the case.* Moses emphasizes that the covenant continues to exist.

א שְׁמַע יִשְׂרָאֵל אַתָּה עֹבֵר הַיּוֹם אֶת־הַיַּרְדֵּן לָבֹא לָרֶשֶׁת גּוֹיִם גְּדֹלִים וַעֲצֻמִים מִמֶּךָּ עָרִים גְּדֹלֹת וּבְצֻרֹת בַּשָּׁמָיִם: ב עַם־גָּדוֹל וָרָם בְּנֵי עֲנָקִים אֲשֶׁר אַתָּה יָדַעְתָּ וְאַתָּה שָׁמַעְתָּ מִי יִתְיַצֵּב לִפְנֵי בְּנֵי עֲנָק: ג וְיָדַעְתָּ הַיּוֹם כִּי יְהֹוָה אֱלֹהֶיךָ הוּא הָעֹבֵר לְפָנֶיךָ אֵשׁ אֹכְלָה הוּא יַשְׁמִידֵם וְהוּא יַכְנִיעֵם לְפָנֶיךָ וְהוֹרַשְׁתָּם וְהַאֲבַדְתָּם מַהֵר כַּאֲשֶׁר דִּבֶּר יְהֹוָה לָךְ: ד אַל־תֹּאמַר בִּלְבָבְךָ בַּהֲדֹף יְהֹוָה אֱלֹהֶיךָ אֹתָם מִלְּפָנֶיךָ לֵאמֹר בְּצִדְקָתִי הֱבִיאַנִי יְהֹוָה לָרֶשֶׁת אֶת־הָאָרֶץ הַזֹּאת וּבְרִשְׁעַת הַגּוֹיִם הָאֵלֶּה יְהֹוָה מוֹרִישָׁם מִפָּנֶיךָ: ה לֹא בְצִדְקָתְךָ וּבְיֹשֶׁר לְבָבְךָ אַתָּה בָא לָרֶשֶׁת אֶת־אַרְצָם כִּי בְּרִשְׁעַת הַגּוֹיִם הָאֵלֶּה יְהֹוָה אֱלֹהֶיךָ מוֹרִישָׁם מִפָּנֶיךָ וּלְמַעַן הָקִים אֶת־הַדָּבָר אֲשֶׁר נִשְׁבַּע יְהֹוָה לַאֲבֹתֶיךָ לְאַבְרָהָם לְיִצְחָק וּלְיַעֲקֹב:

1] Hear, O Israel! You are about to cross the Jordan to invade and dispossess nations greater and more populous than you: great cities with walls sky-high; 2] a people great and tall, the Anakites, of whom you have knowledge; for you have heard it said, "Who can stand up to the children of Anak?" 3] Know then this day that none other than the LORD your God is crossing at your head, a devouring fire; it is He who will wipe them out. He will subdue them before you, that you may quickly dispossess and destroy them, as the LORD promised you. 4] And when the LORD your God has thrust them from your path, say not to yourselves, "The LORD has enabled me to occupy this land because of my virtues"; it is rather because of the wickedness of those nations that the LORD is dispossessing them before you. 5] It is not because of your virtues and your rectitude that you will be able to occupy their country, but because of the wickedness of those nations the LORD your God is dispossessing them before you, and in order to fulfill the oath that the LORD made to your fathers, Abraham, Isaac, and Jacob.

9:1] *Walls sky-high.* See at 1:28.

2] *Anakites of whom you have knowledge.* Because the messengers who spied out the land told you about them; see Num. 13:28; Deut. 1:28.

3] *A devouring fire.* A figure of speech recalling the image of the pillar of fire that led the people by night (Exod. 40:38).

Quickly. In 7:22, Israel was told that the land could be conquered only "little by little." The two promises may be examples of different foci: in the earlier passage the emphasis was on the explanation of failure; here the stress is on anticipated success.

Most modern scholars see the two verses as arising from different sources; similarly, the Book of Joshua stresses the quickness of the conquest, and the Book of Judges its slowness.

4] *Rather because of the wickedness of those nations.* The phrase duplicates verse 5 and may be the erroneous addition of a scribe; it is missing in the Septuagint. See also above, footnote 2.

Not on Bread Alone

The saying "Man does not live on bread alone" (8:3) is firmly ensconced in the English language, but the meaning which those who quote it wish to convey thereby is not at all what the Torah itself expresses. Popularly spoken, the quotation only encompasses the first part of the sentence and has come to mean: human beings are not fulfilled by material things alone; there is another, spiritual dimension of life which makes it truly worthwhile. The full text hardly allows for this interpretation,[1] though what it means precisely may be in some doubt.

There is no question about the broader meaning of the text: God taught you in the wilderness that He could meet your needs by whatever means He chose. He gave you manna to show you that you would be sustained through His providence, whether you had bread or not. This time He sent manna, another time He could choose to care for you in a different way. Such is the general import of the statement; it fits the context which relates God's desire to educate His people in a true understanding of their own limitations on the one hand and His limitless power on the other [3].

There is another dimension to the Hebrew text. Literally, the second half of the verse says that man lives עַל כָּל־מוֹצָא פִי־יְהֹוָה, "by any product of God's mouth." Our translation renders the idiom properly as "anything that the Lord decrees," that is, God's word and will are the cause of every material thing, just as the world itself came into being by His word. The process of creation was dependent on God's word (Gen. 1), and so is Israel, whom He has fashioned.[2]

Chastisements of Love

In stating that God tried Israel by hardships in the wilderness (8:2–3) the Torah enunciates an important principle of faith. When Israel suffered, it says, it suffered because God in His very love of Israel so willed it. The Psalmist put it this way:

Happy is the man whom You discipline,
  O Lord . . .
To give him tranquillity in times of
  misfortune.

(94:12–13)

or:

It was good for me that I was humbled,
so that I might learn Your laws.

(119:71)

By chastisements of love (יִסּוּרִין שֶׁל אַהֲבָה, yisurin shel ahavah), as tradition came to call them, a loving Father educates and purifies His children. In doing so, He too may be said to experience suffering, to weep over the bitter effects of the afflictions He himself has brought about; nonetheless He must do what divine necessity demands [4].

In postbiblical and early medieval times this doctrine came to explain the realities of human suffering in general and Israel's calamities in particular. It allowed for the protests of a Job who questioned the justice of God, but who in the end surrendered to the superior wisdom of the One before whom he stood in awe though he could not fathom His design. This, so the doctrine held, was Israel's fate. Chosen by divine decision it had become God's stake in the perfection of the human race, and, if the Children of Israel had to endure sufferings to merit this choice, it was worth the price. This teaching, while it

---

[1] It should be noted, however, that Ibn Ezra comes close to it when he says that human beings are sustained by what emanates from the heavenly spheres (עֶלְיוֹנִים) and these emanations are of a spiritual nature.

[2] An Egyptian source speaks of the god Ptah, "who maintains all humans with his food, in whose power are length of days, fate, and riches; one lives from that which issues from his mouth."

offered a total defense of God, also demanded total faith and to a significant extent had to surrender the human understanding of what constituted justice on this earth.

Maimonides's opposition to this teaching did much to weaken its hold on rabbinic and popular belief [5]. He distinguished between three types of suffering: (1) those caused by natural causes, like earthquakes—they are part of our physical existence which itself is ultimately destructible; (2) those caused by social corruption, like wars—these are society's burden and responsibility; and, finally, (3) that suffering we bring upon ourselves. In this analysis *yisurin shel ahavah* have no place at all and were therefore to be rejected as a general explanation of injustice, evil, and suffering—even though in some few instances, such as the case stated in Deut. 8:2–3, they were accepted as an authentic interpretation of divine and human reality.

Nowadays, after Auschwitz, the broader doctrine has disappeared; manifestly it could not be held that a benevolent God caused the destruction of six million of His people for their own good. In the light of such changes in the nature of belief, the abiding validity of the biblical statement itself must also be drawn into the question. In the To-rah's telling, Moses believed God to have been a disciplining Father to Israel, an interpretation which we today need not find compelling. This theology, cogent for many centuries, will hardly convince the modern reader whose concept of God differs from the Bible's premise of an all-powerful Lord who deals with His people as they deserve and He determines.

The Source of Wealth

In no small measure the discourse presents a severe indictment of Israel's society. While it is phrased as a warning of something that will happen in the future, the history of Deuteronomy suggests a different setting: brought to light (and probably written) during the reign of King Josiah, the book meant to address first and foremost its own time. If therefore Moses is portrayed as speaking of the corrosive effects of affluence (8:11 ff.) we may see in this a comment on conditions prevailing in Judah in the seventh century B.C.E. Then, as many times later, physical well-being led people to regard their own power as the chief source of their wealth. In doing so they lost sight of its ultimate wellspring, the gracious providence of God. In ringing terms the sermon calls the people to greater humility and lessened pride: "Remember that it is the Lord your God who gives you the power to get wealth" (8:18).

It was also a time when the Promised Land was seen to have richly provided for its inhabitants. Its agriculture was flourishing, and even the Negev had its share of productive communities. Its hills were amply forested, the water supply was sufficient, and a modicum of mineral resources had been tapped. It was, as the Torah states emphatically, "a good land" (verse 7), and it would continue to be a source of blessing if its inhabitants would see themselves as stewards of God's gift and remain worthy of it by dint of their faithful observance of the covenant.

GLEANINGS

Grace before and after Meals

8:10 is the proof text for the בִּרְכַּת הַמָּזוֹן (*Birkat ha-Mazon*, the blessings spoken at the conclusion of a meal). The Rabbis extended the obligation and ruled that one should bless Him beforehand as well [6]. The purpose of these mitzvot is to make one realize that nature and human effort alone do not fully sustain us. Hence it was considered a sacrilege to "enjoy the gifts of this world without a benediction" [7].

Before the Meal

The halachah greatly elaborated on the variety of prayers which were to be said on different occasions, especially before a meal. The benedictions over bread and wine are the most frequently used, in fact, saying "*Ha-Motzi*"[3] became a term for pronouncing any prior blessing over food. Having spoken the *berachah* over bread one need not say blessings for other foods in the ensuing meal, except if one drinks wine over which the customary *berachah* should always be said—even if one drinks it in the middle of the meal [8].

After the Meal

According to the halachah, these blessings are obligatory if one has eaten as little as a *shiur zayit*, the measure of an olive; but the full grace is said only if some bread has been consumed. The blessings speak of God's grace, of gratitude for the Land of Israel as well as other signs of divine goodness, of Jerusalem to be rebuilt, and of hope for messianic redemption. Deut. 8:10 is recited in an early part of this litany of thanks, which may be spoken in any language. A shortened form of the *Birkat ha-Mazon* is provided for those occasions when no bread was eaten or when it is not feasible to recite the entire version. Conservative and Reform synagogues have published such briefer forms of grace for public occasions, as do the (Reform) *Shabbat Manual* and *Gates of the House* for home use. The Reform Haggadah features both the shorter and longer versions [9].

Doubled

By blessing God we double our enjoyment of the food.　　　　　　　JUDAH HALEVI [10]

On Bread (Deut. 8:3)

Note that it says *on* and not *by* bread alone. Man is bidden not to stake his life merely on gaining a livelihood: eating in order to work, working in order to eat. His true purpose should be learning in order to teach, observe, do, and uphold Torah in truth and faith.　　CHATAM SOFER [11]

Satisfaction

Your readiness to thank God after a meal is part of having "eaten your fill" (8:10).

The command addresses itself not merely to those who have satisfied their hunger but also, and especially, to those who are habitually well sated.　　　　　　　　　　　CHASIDIC [12]

Lest Your Heart Grow Haughty (Deut. 8:14)

The greatest haughtiness is that of excessive piety.　　　　　　　　　　CHASIDIC [13]

Even Now

The translation says that God "*freed* you from the land of Egypt" (8:14), but the Hebrew reads literally "*frees* you"[4] even now. It is a reminder

---

[3] So called after the key verb in the *berachah* over bread: הַמּוֹצִיא לֶחֶם מִן הָאָרֶץ, "Who brings forth bread from the earth" (based on Ps. 104:14).

[4] הַמּוֹצִיאֲךָ (present participle) instead of הוֹצִיאֲךָ (past tense).

that God's liberation of His people has never ceased.　　　　　　　　　　　　CHASIDIC [14]

Insensitivity

In addressing Israel, Moses tells them, "You are about to cross the Jordan" (9:1). Thereby he hinted that they, but not he himself, would be so privileged, and he hoped that they might intercede for him with God. However, the people failed him; they were insensitive to his plea.

MIDRASH [15]

The Stiff-Necked People

oses continues his appeal to the people by reminding them of their repeated trespasses. Of these, the incident of the golden calf stands out as a particularly odious offense against God, and Moses recalls it in some detail in order to buttress his main point: the Israelites are a stiff-necked people and God's favor has been bestowed upon them not because of their merits but rather despite their moral failures.

As befits an oration, it is weighted with judgmental epithets like "provoked," "sinful," "wicked," "defiant." The account is personal and emotional, quite in contrast to the tale in Exodus 32 which speaks in detached, objective tones.

Perhaps more than at any other time, Moses stresses his own role as intermediary between God and the people. Had it not been for him, he says, there would have been nothing to stop the avenging anger of the Lord against both Israel and Aaron. This emphasis on the leader's unique role is a distinguishing aspect of Deuteronomy. It is in fact presented with such insistence that later commentators wondered about the presumed modesty of the man Moses.

The disquisition is interrupted by four verses, 10:6–9. While Moses' address speaks of "I" and "we," the interlude switches to the impersonal "they." The passage brings us an important notation on the function of the Levites which rounds out what we have learned about them in other parts of the Torah.

וְאַרְבָּעִים לַיְלָה לֶחֶם לֹא אָכַלְתִּי וּמַיִם לֹא שָׁתִיתִי:
יַיִּתֵּן יְהֹוָה אֵלַי אֶת־שְׁנֵי לוּחֹת הָאֲבָנִים כְּתֻבִים
בְּאֶצְבַּע אֱלֹהִים וַעֲלֵיהֶם כְּכָל־הַדְּבָרִים אֲשֶׁר דִּבֶּר
יְהֹוָה עִמָּכֶם בָּהָר מִתּוֹךְ הָאֵשׁ בְּיוֹם הַקָּהָל: וַיְהִי
מִקֵּץ אַרְבָּעִים יוֹם וְאַרְבָּעִים לָיְלָה נָתַן יְהֹוָה אֵלַי
אֶת־שְׁנֵי לֻחֹת הָאֲבָנִים לֻחוֹת הַבְּרִית: וַיֹּאמֶר יְהֹוָה
אֵלַי קוּם רֵד מַהֵר מִזֶּה כִּי שִׁחֵת עַמְּךָ אֲשֶׁר הוֹצֵאתָ
מִמִּצְרָיִם סָרוּ מַהֵר מִן־הַדֶּרֶךְ אֲשֶׁר צִוִּיתִם עָשׂוּ
לָהֶם מַסֵּכָה: וַיֹּאמֶר יְהֹוָה אֵלַי לֵאמֹר רָאִיתִי אֶת־

וַיָדַעְתָּ כִּי לֹא בְצִדְקָתְךָ יְהֹוָה אֱלֹהֶיךָ נֹתֵן
לְךָ אֶת־הָאָרֶץ הַטּוֹבָה הַזֹּאת לְרִשְׁתָּהּ כִּי עַם־
קְשֵׁה־עֹרֶף אָתָּה: זְכֹר אַל־תִּשְׁכַּח אֵת אֲשֶׁר־
הִקְצַפְתָּ אֶת־יְהֹוָה אֱלֹהֶיךָ בַּמִּדְבָּר לְמִן־הַיּוֹם אֲשֶׁר־
יָצָאתָ מֵאֶרֶץ מִצְרַיִם עַד־בֹּאֲכֶם עַד־הַמָּקוֹם הַזֶּה
מַמְרִים הֱיִיתֶם עִם־יְהֹוָה: וּבְחֹרֵב הִקְצַפְתֶּם אֶת־
יְהֹוָה וַיִּתְאַנַּף יְהֹוָה בָּכֶם לְהַשְׁמִיד אֶתְכֶם: בַּעֲלֹתִי
הָהָרָה לָקַחַת לוּחֹת הָאֲבָנִים לוּחֹת הַבְּרִית אֲשֶׁר־
כָּרַת יְהֹוָה עִמָּכֶם וָאֵשֵׁב בָּהָר אַרְבָּעִים יוֹם

6] Know, then, that it is not for any virtue of yours that the LORD your God is giving you this good land to occupy; for you are a stiffnecked people. **7]** Remember, never forget, how you provoked the LORD your God to anger in the wilderness: from the day that you left the land of Egypt until you reached this place, you have continued defiant toward the LORD.

8] At Horeb you so provoked the LORD that the LORD was angry enough with you to have destroyed you. **9]** I had ascended the mountain to receive the tablets of stone, the Tablets of the Covenant that the Lord had made with you, and I stayed on the mountain forty days and forty nights, eating no bread and drinking no water. **10]** And the LORD gave me the two tablets of stone inscribed by the finger of God, with the exact words that the LORD had addressed to you out of the fire on the day of the Assembly.

11] At the end of those forty days and forty nights, the LORD gave me the two tablets of stone, the Tablets of the Covenant. **12]** And the LORD said to me, "Hurry, go down from here at once, for the people whom you brought out of Egypt have acted wickedly; they have been quick to stray from the path that I enjoined upon them; they have made themselves a molten image." **13]** The LORD further said to me, "I see that this is a stiffnecked

---

9:6] *Stiffnecked people.* Moses quotes the judgment issued by God at the incident of the golden calf (Exod. 32:9).

The Yom Kippur liturgy includes a congregational confession that we are still a stiff-necked people.

8] *At Horeb.* Where the most notable of the rebellions took place, the incident of the golden calf (Exod. 32–34). The murmurings at Marah and Massah had happened earlier.

You . . . provoked. Moses addresses either the survivors of these events or the whole people whom he identifies with the past; see above, on Deut. 1:22.

10] *Day of the Assembly.* When the people stood at Horeb (or Sinai). The expression is rare; it occurs again in 10:4 and 18:16.

11] *The Lord gave me.* A repetition of verse 10, a stylistic device not uncommon in the Torah and in ancient Near Eastern literature. It may be best to translate verse 11 in the pluperfect: "Now when the Lord had given me. . . ."

Tablets of the Covenant. On which the Ten Commandments were inscribed.

12] *A molten image.* A calf (verse 16).

הָעָם הַזֶּה וְהִנֵּה עַם־קְשֵׁה־עֹרֶף הוּא: הֶרֶף מִמֶּנִּי יד

וְאַשְׁמִידֵם וְאֶמְחֶה אֶת־שְׁמָם מִתַּחַת הַשָּׁמָיִם וְאֶעֱשֶׂה

אוֹתְךָ לְגוֹי־עָצוּם וָרָב מִמֶּנּוּ: וָאֵפֶן וָאֵרֵד מִן־הָהָר טו

וְהָהָר בֹּעֵר בָּאֵשׁ וּשְׁנֵי לוּחֹת הַבְּרִית עַל שְׁתֵּי יָדָי:

וָאֵרֶא וְהִנֵּה חֲטָאתֶם לַיהוָה אֱלֹהֵיכֶם עֲשִׂיתֶם לָכֶם טז

עֵגֶל מַסֵּכָה סַרְתֶּם מַהֵר מִן־הַדֶּרֶךְ אֲשֶׁר־צִוָּה יְהוָה

אֶתְכֶם: וָאֶתְפֹּשׂ בִּשְׁנֵי הַלֻּחֹת וָאַשְׁלִכֵם מֵעַל שְׁתֵּי יז

יָדָי* וָאֲשַׁבְּרֵם לְעֵינֵיכֶם: וָאֶתְנַפַּל לִפְנֵי יְהוָה

כָּרִאשֹׁנָה אַרְבָּעִים יוֹם וְאַרְבָּעִים לַיְלָה לֶחֶם לֹא

אָכַלְתִּי וּמַיִם לֹא שָׁתִיתִי עַל כָּל־חַטַּאתְכֶם אֲשֶׁר

חֲטָאתֶם לַעֲשׂוֹת הָרַע בְּעֵינֵי יְהוָה לְהַכְעִיסוֹ: כִּי

יָגֹרְתִּי מִפְּנֵי הָאַף וְהַחֵמָה אֲשֶׁר קָצַף יְהוָה עֲלֵיכֶם

לְהַשְׁמִיד אֶתְכֶם וַיִּשְׁמַע יְהוָה אֵלַי גַּם בַּפַּעַם הַהִוא:

וּבְאַהֲרֹן הִתְאַנַּף יְהוָה מְאֹד לְהַשְׁמִידוֹ וָאֶתְפַּלֵּל כ

גַּם־בְּעַד אַהֲרֹן בָּעֵת הַהִוא: וְאֶת־חַטַּאתְכֶם אֲשֶׁר־ כא

* יד קמץ בטרחא

people.   14] Let Me alone and I will destroy them and blot out their name from under heaven, and I will make you a nation far more numerous than they."

15] I started down the mountain, a mountain ablaze with fire, the two Tablets of the Covenant in my two hands.   16] I saw how you had sinned against the LORD your God: you had made yourselves a molten calf; you had been quick to stray from the path that the LORD had enjoined upon you.   17] Thereupon I gripped the two tablets and flung them away with both my hands, smashing them before your eyes.   18] I threw myself down before the LORD—eating no bread and drinking no water forty days and forty nights, as before—because of the great wrong you had committed, doing what displeased the LORD and vexing Him.   19] For I was in dread of the LORD's fierce anger against you, which moved Him to wipe you out. And that time, too, the LORD gave heed to me.—   20] Moreover, the LORD was angry enough with Aaron to have destroyed him; so I also interceded for Aaron at that time.—   21] As for that

14] *Let Me alone.* The exclamation must be understood as a challenge to Moses to appease the divine anger, though Moses has not yet pleaded Israel's case [1]. The parallel passage in Exod. 32:10 uses a different idiom (הַנִּיחָה לִי instead of הֶרֶף מִמֶּנִּי) to express the same meaning.

15] *I started down.* God had told Moses what was happening in the camp, and now Moses sees for himself. The repetition may be compared to the prayer which Abraham's servant delivers and which is then essentially repeated as it is realized in fact (Gen. 24).

17] *Smashing them.* Since the covenant had been broken by the people, the "Tablets of the Covenant" were no longer applicable. The smashing was a vivid reflection of the people's defection, comparable to the later custom of tearing up a contract when its terms have been violated.

The Rabbis disagreed on whether Moses was justified in destroying God's handiwork; see at Exodus 32, Gleanings.

18] *As before.* Moses had fasted for forty days and nights in the mountain; now—on reaching the tribes below—he commenced a second period of abstinence, in order to plead the people's cause and to expiate their sins. Later on he will ascend again and begin a third period of fasting after which he will descend once more, this time with the second tablets. The three times forty days and nights of self-abnegation amount to a total of one hundred twenty, paralleling the one hundred twenty years of Moses' life (on this figure see Gen. 6:3 and commentary there) [2].

19] *And that time, too.* As at Marah (Exod. 15:25) and Massah (Exod. 17:1 ff.).

20] *I also interceded for Aaron.* Neither God's judgment of Aaron nor Moses' intercession is found in the Exodus account.

עֲשִׂיתֶם אֶת־הָעֵגֶל לְקַחְתִּי וָאֶשְׂרֹף אֹתוֹ ׀ בָּאֵשׁ וָאֶכֹּת כא לְהַשְׁמִיד אֶתְכֶם: וָאֶתְפַּלֵּל אֶל־יְהֹוָה וָאֹמַר אֲדֹנָי
אֹתוֹ טָחוֹן הֵיטֵב עַד אֲשֶׁר־דַּק לְעָפָר וָאַשְׁלִךְ אֶת־ יְהֹוָה אַל־תַּשְׁחֵת עַמְּךָ וְנַחֲלָתְךָ אֲשֶׁר פָּדִיתָ בְּגָדְלֶךָ
כב עֲפָרוֹ אֶל־הַנַּחַל הַיֹּרֵד מִן־הָהָר: וּבְתַבְעֵרָה וּבְמַסָּה כב אֲשֶׁר־הוֹצֵאתָ מִמִּצְרַיִם בְּיָד חֲזָקָה: זְכֹר לַעֲבָדֶיךָ
וּבְקִבְרֹת הַתַּאֲוָה מַקְצִפִים הֱיִיתֶם אֶת־יְהֹוָה: לְאַבְרָהָם לְיִצְחָק וּלְיַעֲקֹב אַל־תֵּפֶן אֶל־קְשִׁי הָעָם
כג וּבִשְׁלֹחַ יְהֹוָה אֶתְכֶם מִקָּדֵשׁ בַּרְנֵעַ לֵאמֹר עֲלוּ הַזֶּה וְאֶל־רִשְׁעוֹ וְאֶל־חַטָּאתוֹ: פֶּן־יֹאמְרוּ הָאָרֶץ אֲשֶׁר
וּרְשׁוּ אֶת־הָאָרֶץ אֲשֶׁר נָתַתִּי לָכֶם וַתַּמְרוּ אֶת־פִּי הוֹצֵאתָנוּ מִשָּׁם מִבְּלִי יְכֹלֶת יְהֹוָה לַהֲבִיאָם אֶל־
יְהֹוָה אֱלֹהֵיכֶם וְלֹא הֶאֱמַנְתֶּם לוֹ וְלֹא שְׁמַעְתֶּם הָאָרֶץ אֲשֶׁר־דִּבֶּר לָהֶם וּמִשִּׂנְאָתוֹ אוֹתָם הוֹצִיאָם
כד בְּקֹלוֹ: מַמְרִים הֱיִיתֶם עִם־יְהֹוָה מִיּוֹם דַּעְתִּי אֶתְכֶם: לַהֲמִתָם בַּמִּדְבָּר: וְהֵם עַמְּךָ וְנַחֲלָתֶךָ אֲשֶׁר הוֹצֵאתָ
כה וָאֶתְנַפַּל לִפְנֵי יְהֹוָה אֵת אַרְבָּעִים הַיּוֹם וְאֶת־ בְּכֹחֲךָ הַגָּדֹל וּבִזְרֹעֲךָ הַנְּטוּיָה: פ
אַרְבָּעִים הַלַּיְלָה אֲשֶׁר הִתְנַפָּלְתִּי כִּי־אָמַר יְהֹוָה

<small>* כד מ' קטנה.</small>

sinful thing you had made, the calf, I took it and put it to the fire; I broke it to bits and ground it thoroughly until it was fine as dust, and I threw its dust into the brook that comes down from the mountain.

22] Again you provoked the LORD at Taberah, and at Massah, and at Kibroth-hattaavah.

23] And when the LORD sent you on from Kadesh-barnea, saying, "Go up and occupy the land that I am giving you," you flouted the command of the LORD your God; you did not put your trust in Him and did not obey Him.

24] As long as I have known you, you have been defiant toward the LORD.

25] When I lay prostrate before the LORD those forty days and forty nights, because the LORD was determined to destroy you, **26]** I prayed to the LORD and said, "O Lord GOD, do not annihilate Your very own people, whom You redeemed in Your majesty and whom You freed from Egypt with a mighty hand. **27]** Give thought to Your servants, Abraham, Isaac, and Jacob, and pay no heed to the stubbornness of this people, its wickedness, and its sinfulness. **28]** Else the country from which You freed us will say, 'It was because the LORD was powerless to bring them into the land that He had promised them, and because He hated them, that He brought them out to have them die in the wilderness.' **29]** Yet they are Your very own people, whom You freed with Your great might and Your outstretched arm."

21] *Brook that comes down.* This too is not in Exodus; there, Moses made Israel swallow the ground-up calf mixed with water, which is not mentioned here.

22] *At Taberah.* See Num. 11:1 ff.

At Massah. See Exod. 17:2 ff. The first rebellion, at Marah, is not mentioned.

At Kibroth-hattaavah. See Num. 11:4–34.

23] *From Kadesh-barnea.* From where the spies were sent out; their negative report caused the people to rebel (see Deut. 1:22 ff. and Num. 13–14).

25] *Those forty days and forty nights.* Literally, "the forty days and forty nights that I lay prostrate."

28] *Country . . . will say.* The country's *people* will say: similar ellipses are common in English (e.g., "the whole town will talk").

It may be noted that the Hebrew noun (הָאָרֶץ) is in the feminine singular and the verb (יֹאמְרוּ) in the masculine plural.

הַדְּבָרִים אֲשֶׁר דִּבֶּר יְהֹוָה אֲלֵיכֶם בָּהָר מִתּוֹךְ א בָּעֵת הַהִוא אָמַר יְהֹוָה אֵלַי פְּסָל־לְךָ שְׁנֵי־לוּחֹת

הָאֵשׁ בְּיוֹם הַקָּהָל וַיִּתְּנֵם יְהֹוָה אֵלָי: ה וָאֵפֶן וָאֵרֵד אֲבָנִים כָּרִאשֹׁנִים וַעֲלֵה אֵלַי הָהָרָה וְעָשִׂיתָ לְּךָ

מִן־הָהָר וָאָשִׂם אֶת־הַלֻּחֹת בָּאָרוֹן אֲשֶׁר עָשִׂיתִי וַיִּהְיוּ ב אֲרוֹן עֵץ: וְאֶכְתֹּב עַל־הַלֻּחֹת אֶת־הַדְּבָרִים אֲשֶׁר

שָׁם כַּאֲשֶׁר צִוַּנִי יְהֹוָה: ו וּבְנֵי יִשְׂרָאֵל נָסְעוּ מִבְּאֵרֹת הָיוּ עַל־הַלֻּחֹת הָרִאשֹׁנִים אֲשֶׁר שִׁבַּרְתָּ וְשַׂמְתָּם

בְּנֵי־יַעֲקָן מוֹסֵרָה שָׁם מֵת אַהֲרֹן וַיִּקָּבֵר שָׁם וַיְכַהֵן ג בָּאָרוֹן: וָאַעַשׂ אֲרוֹן עֲצֵי שִׁטִּים וָאֶפְסֹל שְׁנֵי־לֻחֹת

אֶלְעָזָר בְּנוֹ תַּחְתָּיו: ז מִשָּׁם נָסְעוּ הַגֻּדְגֹּדָה וּמִן־הַגֻּדְגֹּדָה אֲבָנִים כָּרִאשֹׁנִים וָאַעַל הָהָרָה וּשְׁנֵי הַלֻּחֹת בְּיָדִי:

יָטְבָתָה אֶרֶץ נַחֲלֵי־מָיִם: ח בָּעֵת הַהִוא הִבְדִּיל יְהֹוָה ד וַיִּכְתֹּב עַל־הַלֻּחֹת כַּמִּכְתָּב הָרִאשׁוֹן אֵת עֲשֶׂרֶת

* ב פתח באתנח.

1] Thereupon the LORD said to me, "Carve out two tablets of stone like the first, and come up to Me on the mountain; and make an ark of wood. 2] I will inscribe on the tablets the commandments that were on the first tablets which you smashed, and you shall deposit them in the ark."

3] I made an ark of acacia wood and carved out two tablets of stone like the first; I took the two tablets with me and went up the mountain. 4] The LORD inscribed on the tablets the same text as on the first, the Ten Commandments that He addressed to you on the mountain out of the fire on the day of the Assembly; and the LORD gave them to me. 5] Then I left and went down from the mountain, and I deposited the tablets in the ark that I had made, where they still are, as the LORD had commanded me.

6] From Beeroth-bene-jaakan the Israelites marched to Moserah. Aaron died there and was buried there; and his son Eleazar became priest in his stead. 7] From there they marched to Gudgod, and from Gudgod to Jotbath, a region of running brooks.

8] At that time the LORD set apart the tribe of Levi to carry the Ark of the LORD's Covenant,

10:1] *Ark of wood.* In Exod. 34:1 we are told that the ark was made *after* Moses returned from his second ascent, and not before. Rashi therefore assumed that the Deuteronomy passage indicates that a temporary ark was made and served as a receptacle until the permanent one was ready [3]. Others read the account as a telescoped version of the Exodus story [4].

5] *Where they still are.* This translation does not render the sense of the Hebrew, which says: "And they remained there"—clearly an anachronism that betrays the late date of the composition.

In Deuteronomic times the tablets were kept in the ark which stood in the Holy of Holies in the Temple where Solomon had brought it (I Kings 8:9).

6] *From Beeroth-bene-jaakan.* This passage poses a number of further problems: it suddenly interrupts the flow of the discourse; in Num. 33:31–33 the way stations are recounted in different order; and in Num. 20:22 ff. and 33:38 Aaron was said to have died at Mt. Hor and not at Moserah.

a. Placement in the text. This is best explained by considering the passage a mnemotechnical insertion: the preceding subject had been the restoration of God's favor to Israel after the incident with the golden calf, which involved Aaron and (in the Exodus account) stressed the loyalty of the Levites. Hence the notation in verses 6–9 rounds out the recital [5].

b. Order of way stations. Most likely a variant tradition is represented here, characterized also by the mention of Gudgod, which in Num. 33:31–32 is called Hor-haggidgad.

אֶת־שֵׁבֶט הַלֵּוִי לָשֵׂאת אֶת־אֲרוֹן בְּרִית־יְהֹוָה לַעֲמֹד
לִפְנֵי יְהֹוָה לְשָׁרְתוֹ וּלְבָרֵךְ בִּשְׁמוֹ עַד הַיּוֹם הַזֶּה:
עַל־כֵּן לֹא־הָיָה לְלֵוִי חֵלֶק וְנַחֲלָה עִם־אֶחָיו יְהֹוָה
הוּא נַחֲלָתוֹ כַּאֲשֶׁר דִּבֶּר יְהֹוָה אֱלֹהֶיךָ לוֹ: וְאָנֹכִי
עָמַדְתִּי בָהָר כַּיָּמִים הָרִאשֹׁנִים אַרְבָּעִים יוֹם

וְאַרְבָּעִים לַיְלָה וַיִּשְׁמַע יְהֹוָה אֵלַי גַּם בַּפַּעַם הַהִוא
לֹא־אָבָה יְהֹוָה הַשְׁחִיתֶךָ: וַיֹּאמֶר יְהֹוָה אֵלַי קוּם
לֵךְ לְמַסַּע לִפְנֵי הָעָם וְיָבֹאוּ וְיִירְשׁוּ אֶת־הָאָרֶץ
אֲשֶׁר־נִשְׁבַּעְתִּי לַאֲבֹתָם לָתֵת לָהֶם: פ

to stand in attendance upon the LORD, and to bless in His name, as is still the case.   9] That is why the Levites have received no hereditary portion along with their kinsmen: the LORD is their portion, as the LORD your God spoke concerning them.

10] I had stayed on the mountain, as I did the first time, forty days and forty nights; and the LORD heeded me once again: the LORD agreed not to destroy you.   11] And the LORD said to me, "Up, resume the march at the head of the people, that they may invade and occupy the land that I swore to their fathers to give them."

c. Aaron's death. Conventional harmonizers say that Moserah lay in the vicinity of or at the foot of a mountain range called Hor, hence no conflict exists with what is recorded in Numbers. Other scholars consider this divergence as another evidence that variant traditions are involved.

9] *No hereditary portion.* Meaning, no land. The Levites were maintained by offerings which people brought to the Temple.

10] *I had stayed on the mountain.* After ascending with the new tablets. The second stay, like the first, lasted forty days and nights.

Defiance

"As long as I have known you, you have been defiant toward the Lord." These words of Moses are the prophet's ringing indictment of his people (9:24). They are, in his eyes, a stiff-necked lot, prone to sin, provoking God to anger, ungrateful for His many mercies—altogether undeserving of His continuing concern. Only because of their forefathers' merit and the pledge God had made to them, has He not abandoned Israel. If in his own lifetime Moses had cause to be disillusioned with the people he led, how much more so the Deuteronomist who, centuries later, could look back on a nation's record steeped in idolatry, social injustice, and continued disregard of the covenant. It was a dismal picture, calling forth the prophetic ire with which the text bristles.

It cannot be denied that the words here attributed to and projected onto Moses have a deeply pessimistic strain within them. He exhorts his people, but he already knows that they will not heed him. Their obduracy appears to be part of their nature. That nonetheless he (like God himself) persists in loving them is in the end not explicable in rational terms: they belong to each other for good and for evil, and he will fight for them whether they deserve it or not.

In viewing this tension-filled relationship, one must keep in mind that while Israel is the immediate focus there is also a larger perspective. For, throughout the Torah, Israel has a paradigmatic quality, which is to say that as God's people they represent humanity as a whole. At times their fate is even linked to the cosmos itself. Thus, the Israelites' wilderness sojourn, during which they were sustained by God, reenacts humanity's experience in Eden; the building of the Tabernacle parallels (in the key words used) the creation of the world; and Israel's observance of Shabbat rehearses the climactic moments of creation. Similarly, Israel's defiance of God is but an acting out of what the Torah judges to be the general character of man, "how every plan devised by his mind was nothing but evil all the time" (Gen. 6:5). Torah and Prophets may in fact be seen as responding to this condition by providing Israel and humanity with an opportunity to overcome it through covenant and mitzvot.

The stiff-neckedness of Israel is therefore a particular distillation of the spirit of defiance built into the human species. If there is to be any hope for the latter it will only be because Israel begins to fulfill its obligations and responds to the terms of the covenant [6].

The Intermediary

It has become a fundamental aspect of Jewish teaching—in contrast to Christianity's—that people neither need nor can use an intermediary in their relationship with God (see I Sam. 2:25). However, this principle most decidedly did not apply when it came to the position that Moses occupied as a mediator between God and Israel. According to Moses' own account, it was *his* intervention that procured God's forgiveness, it was *his* advocacy then and at other times which saved the people from the effects of divine anger. This puts Moses, the man who could speak with God face to face and who returned from these encounters with their afterglow imprinted on his brow, into a category that can only be described as superhuman, even semidivine.

This special status is underscored by the symbolic use of numbers. Even as Moses will live to the age of a hundred twenty—the ideal life span of biblical tradition—so his entreaties before God lasted one hundred twenty days. During this time of "perfection" he received the commandments and pleaded Israel's cause, all the while observing a total fast which, as tradition pointed out, meant that he was sustained by divine food.

But these superhuman capacities and attributes were counterbalanced by the man's thorough humanity. He had human foibles. The Rabbis wondered why Moses felt impelled to reveal his special role, that is, why he had spoken about his intercession when the people never needed to know about it. Quite clearly, he *wanted* them to know what he had done and was not satisfied to keep them in ignorance of his accomplishments. This was hardly an admirable trait, for which the Sages valiantly tried to find an acceptable explanation (see Gleanings, below).

Despite this, the man Moses has remained somewhat remote. In the consciousness of his people, he is *Mosheh Rabbenu*, Moses our teacher (the only prophet so called), the prophet or rabbi par excellence. But the term conveys awe rather than affection. He was human, to be sure, but his humanity was of a kind that touched the edge of the Divine. After him, in the mainstream of Jewish history, all prophets abided fully in the human realm. God might use them to reach the people, but the people no longer needed them to reach their God. (See further below, commentary on chapter 34.)

A Note on the Levites (Deut. 10:8–9)

The text specifies four duties and privileges which were assigned to "the Levites."[1] The term itself has both a larger and a narrower meaning: it refers sometimes to the whole tribe which includes and features the priests, and at other times only to the non-priestly Levites who assisted the priests in

various ways. In Deuteronomy "Levites" generally means levitical *priests* (thus, 31:9 speaks of "the priests, sons of Levi, who carried the Ark of the Lord's Covenant"), and we may therefore assume that in our passage too the *priests* are meant. Their first duty was to carry the Ark;[2] secondly, they were to "stand in attendance upon the Lord," that is, to officiate at cultic functions, like sacrifices; thirdly, they were to bless the people in God's name, a duty specifically assigned to priests in Num. 6:23. A fourth duty, listed not here but farther on (Deut. 33:10), consisted of burning the incense. The Levites were landless and were considered "God's portion" (Num. 18:20). Their sustenance came, so to speak, from the Lord's table: they received their share of the contributions that the people brought to the Temple in both money and kind (see Deut. 18:1–8).

In time, "Levites" came to mean only the non-priests who sang at the Temple service and otherwise attended the priests and performed menial tasks in the sanctuary. The priests themselves were of the levitical family of Zadok and traced their ancestry to Aaron. This development was the result of a long struggle of various factions and families. In 70 C.E. when the Temple was destroyed, most levitical functions, both priestly and non-priestly, ceased, though Jews remained careful to preserve their descent from these families, for in traditional practice some halachic and liturgical rules still apply to them. Reform Judaism no longer observes distinctions of this kind.

---

[1] For a fuller treatment of the Levites, their service and history, see our commentaries on Lev. 21–22 and Exod. 29 (Gleanings).

[2] But in Num. 3:31 and 4:15 this task is given to the non-priestly family of the Kohathites—clearly a different tradition, which reflects changes that over the centuries occurred in the Temple service.

GLEANINGS

Confession

Our God, God of our ancestors, grant that our prayers may reach You. Do not be deaf to our pleas, for we are not so arrogant and stiffnecked as to say before You, Lord our God and God of all ages, we are perfect and have not sinned; rather do we confess: we have gone astray, we have sinned, we have transgressed.

We are arrogant, brutal, careless, destructive, egocentric, false, greedy, heartless, insolent, and joyless. Our sins are an alphabet of woe.

LITURGY FOR THE DAY OF ATONEMENT [7]

To Know

Better a sinner who knows he is a sinner than a righteous man who knows he is righteous.

CHASIDIC [8]

In Praise of Stubbornness

Why are the Patriarchs mentioned in connection with Israel's stubbornness (Deut. 9:27)? Because they too possessed a measure of it. For without it neither they nor their descendants could have stood up to the whole world.

ISAAC ELIJAH LANDAU [9]

Yom ha-Kahal (Deut. 9:10)

The day of the giving of the Torah was called "Day of Assembly," because never before or after had the people assembled in such unity of spirit.

BASED ON THE ZOHAR [10]

The Order Is All-important

In 10:1 God commanded (in literal translation): "Carve out for yourself . . ."—פְּסָל־לְךָ. In

the second commandment (5:8) it says: "(You shall not make) for yourself a sculptured image"—(לֹא תַעֲשֶׂה לְךָ פֶסֶל). Note that, in one, לְךָ follows פֶסֶל and, in the other, it precedes it. From this you may learn that when לְךָ (yourself) comes first it leads to idolatry; when second, to the Tablets of the Law.

CHASIDIC [11]

Both Sets

According to tradition, both the broken and whole sets of the tablets were kept in the ark [12]. From this we learn that one should respect a scholar who has forgotten his learning through adverse circumstances (age, troubles, illness).

TALMUD [13]

Replace Them

God said to Moses: You were the intermediary between Me and My people. You broke the tablets (which were entrusted to you) and you must replace them, "carve out two tablets of stone like the first."[3]

MIDRASH [14]

A Time to Cast Away

It says: "There is . . . a time to every purpose under the heaven . . . a time to cast away stones and a time to gather stones together" (Eccles. 3:1, 5). This is applicable to Moses: there was a time for him to cast away tablets and a time to hew new ones.

MIDRASH [15]

Small מ

In some manuscripts the first מ of מַמְרִים (defiant, Deut. 9:24) is written small[4] to hint that, though Moses accused the people of defiance, he

---

[3] The Midrash connects this with the halachah which rules that, when a cask is broken before delivery to the buyer, the middleman must replace it.

[4] Though not in the Masoretic text; see Minchat Shai.

himself took part of the blame.[5]

CHASIDIC [16]

A Question

Why did Moses tell the people about his prayer and God's answer? Did this not serve to aggrandize himself, inasmuch as without his telling no one would ever have known about it! He needed to teach us a lesson, namely, that when one prays for others such prayer is more likely to be answered than prayer for one's own sake. Note that, when Moses prayed for himself and asked that God reverse the judgment and let him enter the Promised Land, the Lord cut him off by saying "Enough!" (Deut. 3:26) But, when he prayed for Israel for forty days and nights, God let him be and in the end He relented.

This is what the Talmud means when it says: He who prolongs his prayer will not have it return empty.

YALKUT YEHUDAH [17]

---

[5] This is based on Rashi's comment on 1:13, where the Masoretic text reads ואשימם and Rashi's text ואשמם (without י; which could be understood as "their guilt"). This suggested to Rashi that when a people sins the guilt rests first and foremost with its leaders.

The Good Land

The discourse continues with an exhortation along familiar lines: Israel must revere and love God and God only, for He is their proven guardian and savior. Special emphasis is now placed on the land which will be Israel's, for it is not like other lands. It is particularly blessed by being fertile, gifted with ample water, and not subject to the climatic vagaries of Egypt. The text looks at the land from the east side of the Jordan and sees it—with its expanse from north to south—touching the Mediterranean. This is one of several geographic descriptions of the Promised Land given by the Torah and suggests that there were different conceptions of what actual area the Promise was to encompass. In general, "Canaan" was a stereotypical expression used to describe the old borders of the Egyptian province (for a detailed discussion, see our commentary on Num. 34).

The discourse emphasizes once more the Israelite's duty to love the stranger and again gives as the reason for this mitzvah the people's servitude in Egypt.

יב וְעַתָּה יִשְׂרָאֵל מָה יְהוָֹה אֱלֹהֶיךָ שֹׁאֵל מֵעִמָּךְ כִּי אִם־לְיִרְאָה אֶת־יְהוָֹה אֱלֹהֶיךָ לָלֶכֶת בְּכָל־דְּרָכָיו וּלְאַהֲבָה אֹתוֹ וְלַעֲבֹד אֶת־יְהוָֹה אֱלֹהֶיךָ בְּכָל־לְבָבְךָ	טו וּמַלְתֶּם אֵת עָרְלַת לְבַבְכֶם וְעָרְפְּכֶם לֹא תַקְשׁוּ עוֹד: טז כִּי יְהוָֹה אֱלֹהֵיכֶם הוּא אֱלֹהֵי הָאֱלֹהִים וַאֲדֹנֵי
יג וּבְכָל־נַפְשֶׁךָ: לִשְׁמֹר אֶת־מִצְוֹת יְהוָֹה וְאֶת־חֻקֹּתָיו אֲשֶׁר אָנֹכִי מְצַוְּךָ הַיּוֹם לְטוֹב לָךְ: יד הֵן לַיהוָֹה אֱלֹהֶיךָ הַשָּׁמַיִם וּשְׁמֵי הַשָּׁמָיִם הָאָרֶץ וְכָל־אֲשֶׁר־בָּהּ:	הָאֲדֹנִים הָאֵל הַגָּדֹל הַגִּבֹּר וְהַנּוֹרָא אֲשֶׁר לֹא־יִשָּׂא פָנִים וְלֹא יִקַּח שֹׁחַד: יז עֹשֶׂה מִשְׁפַּט יָתוֹם וְאַלְמָנָה וְאֹהֵב גֵּר לָתֶת לוֹ לֶחֶם וְשִׂמְלָה: יח וַאֲהַבְתֶּם אֶת־הַגֵּר
טו רַק בַּאֲבֹתֶיךָ חָשַׁק יְהוָֹה לְאַהֲבָה אוֹתָם וַיִּבְחַר בְּזַרְעָם אַחֲרֵיהֶם בָּכֶם מִכָּל־הָעַמִּים כַּיּוֹם הַזֶּה:	כִּי־גֵרִים הֱיִיתֶם בְּאֶרֶץ מִצְרָיִם: יט אֶת־יְהוָֹה אֱלֹהֶיךָ תִּירָא אֹתוֹ תַעֲבֹד וּבוֹ תִדְבָּק וּבִשְׁמוֹ תִּשָּׁבֵעַ: הוּא

v. כ קמץ בז״ק.

12] And now, O Israel, what does the LORD your God demand of you? Only this: to revere the LORD your God, to walk only in His paths, to love Him, and to serve the LORD your God with all your heart and soul, 13] keeping the LORD's commandments and laws, which I enjoin upon you today, for your good. 14] Mark, the heavens to their uttermost reaches belong to the LORD your God, the earth and all that is on it! 15] Yet it was to your fathers that the LORD was drawn in His love for them, so that He chose you, their lineal descendants, from among all peoples—as is now the case. 16] Cut away, therefore, the thickening about your hearts and stiffen your necks no more. 17] For the LORD your God is God supreme and Lord supreme, the great, the mighty, and the awesome God, who shows no favor and takes no bribe, 18] but upholds the cause of the fatherless and the widow, and befriends the stranger, providing him with food and clothing.— 19] You too must befriend the stranger, for you were strangers in the land of Egypt.

20] You must revere the LORD your God: only Him shall you worship, to Him shall you hold fast, and by His name shall you swear. 21] He is your glory and He is your God, who

10:12] *Revere.* See above, at 4:10, on יָרֵא in its basic meaning of fear and trembling. In this verse, both fear and love are combined to form the most desirable relationship with God (see commentary on 6:1–25, "The Love of God").

13] *Your good.* The Torah unhesitatingly holds out rewards for obeisance to God. Maimonides considered this approach a necessary educational device [1].

14] *To their uttermost reaches.* Literally, "and the heaven of heavens."

16] *Cut away . . . the thickening.* Older translations had "circumcise the foreskin of your hearts." "Circumcise" was an idiom used also in regard to lips and ears.

17] *God supreme and Lord supreme.* Literally, "the God of gods and the Lord of lords."

Great . . . mighty . . . awesome. These attributes of God are quoted in the daily liturgy, in the first paragraph of the *Tefillah* or main prayer.

Takes no bribe. Do not consider your sacrifice as a means of influencing God's will.

18] *The stranger.* גֵּר (ger), a resident alien who was a free person but without political rights, who would generally be someone from another land or district. The Rabbis differentiated between such a person (later called *ger toshav*, resident alien) and a *ger tzedek* (righteous alien) who had converted to Judaism [2].

19] *For you were strangers.* See commentary below.

תְּהִלָּתֶךָ וְהוּא אֱלֹהֶיךָ אֲשֶׁר־עָשָׂה אִתְּךָ אֶת־הַגְּדֹלֹת
כב וְאֶת־הַנּוֹרָאֹת הָאֵלֶּה אֲשֶׁר רָאוּ עֵינֶיךָ: בְּשִׁבְעִים
נֶפֶשׁ יָרְדוּ אֲבֹתֶיךָ מִצְרָיְמָה וְעַתָּה שָׂמְךָ יְהוָה
אֱלֹהֶיךָ כְּכוֹכְבֵי הַשָּׁמַיִם לָרֹב:
א וְאָהַבְתָּ אֵת יְהוָה אֱלֹהֶיךָ וְשָׁמַרְתָּ מִשְׁמַרְתּוֹ וְחֻקֹּתָיו
ב וּמִשְׁפָּטָיו וּמִצְוֹתָיו כָּל־הַיָּמִים: וִידַעְתֶּם הַיּוֹם כִּי
לֹא אֶת־בְּנֵיכֶם אֲשֶׁר לֹא־יָדְעוּ וַאֲשֶׁר לֹא־רָאוּ אֶת־
מוּסַר יְהוָה אֱלֹהֵיכֶם אֶת־גָּדְלוֹ אֶת־יָדוֹ הַחֲזָקָה
ג וּזְרֹעוֹ הַנְּטוּיָה: וְאֶת־אֹתֹתָיו וְאֶת־מַעֲשָׂיו אֲשֶׁר עָשָׂה

בְּתוֹךְ מִצְרַיִם לְפַרְעֹה מֶלֶךְ־מִצְרַיִם וּלְכָל־אַרְצוֹ:
ד וַאֲשֶׁר עָשָׂה לְחֵיל מִצְרַיִם לְסוּסָיו וּלְרִכְבּוֹ אֲשֶׁר
הֵצִיף אֶת־מֵי יַם־סוּף עַל־פְּנֵיהֶם בְּרָדְפָם אַחֲרֵיכֶם
ה וַיְאַבְּדֵם יְהוָה עַד הַיּוֹם הַזֶּה: וַאֲשֶׁר עָשָׂה לָכֶם
בַּמִּדְבָּר עַד־בֹּאֲכֶם עַד־הַמָּקוֹם הַזֶּה: וַאֲשֶׁר עָשָׂה
ו לְדָתָן וְלַאֲבִירָם בְּנֵי אֱלִיאָב בֶּן־רְאוּבֵן אֲשֶׁר פָּצְתָה
הָאָרֶץ אֶת־פִּיהָ וַתִּבְלָעֵם וְאֶת־בָּתֵּיהֶם וְאֶת־אָהֳלֵיהֶם
וְאֵת כָּל־הַיְקוּם אֲשֶׁר בְּרַגְלֵיהֶם בְּקֶרֶב כָּל־יִשְׂרָאֵל:
ז כִּי עֵינֵיכֶם הָרֹאֹת אֵת כָּל־מַעֲשֵׂה יְהוָה הַגָּדֹל אֲשֶׁר

wrought for you those marvelous, awesome deeds that you saw with your own eyes. **22]** Your ancestors went down to Egypt seventy persons in all; and now the LORD your God has made you as numerous as the stars of heaven.

1] Love, therefore, the LORD your God, and always keep His charge, His laws, His rules, and His commandments.

2] Take thought this day that it was not your children, who neither experienced nor witnessed the lesson of the LORD your God—His majesty, His mighty hand, His outstretched arm; **3]** the signs and the deeds that He performed in Egypt against Pharaoh king of Egypt and all his land; **4]** what He did to Egypt's army, its horses and chariots; how the LORD rolled back upon them the waters of the Sea of Reeds when they were pursuing you, thus destroying them once and for all; **5]** what He did for you in the wilderness before you arrived in this place; **6]** and what He did to Dathan and Abiram, sons of Eliab son of Reuben, when the earth opened her mouth and swallowed them, along with their households, their tents, and every living thing in their train, from amidst all Israel— **7]** but that it was you who saw with your own eyes all the marvelous deeds that the LORD performed.

22] *Seventy persons.* So Exod. 1:5.

11:1] *Keep His charge.* The Hebrew style is distinct in that it uses the same root for both verb and noun: וְשָׁמַרְתָּ מִשְׁמַרְתּוֹ. The word מִשְׁמֶרֶת has also the meaning of "being on watch," conveying here that God's command is like a treasure to be watched.

The same idiom occurs also in Gen. 26:5.

2] *Take thought.* The Hebrew syntax is not clear. Our English translation takes the passage from the second half of verse 2 to verse 6 as an apposition to explain what "the lesson" is. Verse 7 then concludes the first half of verse 2 [3].

Lesson. The word מוּסָר (*musar*) later came primarily to mean ethical teaching in general.

4] *Once and for all.* An idiomatic rendering of the literal "unto this day" [4].

6] *Dathan and Abiram.* Who were leaders in the revolt against Moses. There were two traditions, one ascribing the initiative to Dathan and Abiram, the other naming Korah as the ring leader (see our commentary on Num. 16; the Deuteronomist follows the former tradition and omits the mention of Korah).

This omission is explained by the Sages in two ways: one, that only Dathan and Abiram were swallowed by the earth, but not Korah; or that, since Korah's sons were still alive (Num. 26:11), Moses did not wish to offend them by mentioning their father's sin [5].

עֹבְרִים שָׁמָּה לְרִשְׁתָּהּ אֶרֶץ הָרִים וּבְקָעֹת לִמְטַר
הַשָּׁמַיִם תִּשְׁתֶּה־מָּיִם: אֶרֶץ אֲשֶׁר־יְהוָה אֱלֹהֶיךָ דֹּרֵשׁ
אֹתָהּ תָּמִיד עֵינֵי יְהוָה אֱלֹהֶיךָ בָּהּ מֵרֵשִׁית הַשָּׁנָה
וְעַד אַחֲרִית שָׁנָה: ס וְהָיָה אִם־שָׁמֹעַ תִּשְׁמְעוּ
אֶל־מִצְוֹתַי אֲשֶׁר אָנֹכִי מְצַוֶּה אֶתְכֶם הַיּוֹם לְאַהֲבָה
אֶת־יְהוָה אֱלֹהֵיכֶם וּלְעָבְדוֹ בְּכָל־לְבַבְכֶם וּבְכָל־
נַפְשְׁכֶם: וְנָתַתִּי מְטַר־אַרְצְכֶם בְּעִתּוֹ יוֹרֶה וּמַלְקוֹשׁ
וְאָסַפְתָּ דְגָנֶךָ וְתִירֹשְׁךָ וְיִצְהָרֶךָ: וְנָתַתִּי עֵשֶׂב בְּשָׂדְךָ

עָשָׂה: וּשְׁמַרְתֶּם אֶת־כָּל־הַמִּצְוָה אֲשֶׁר אָנֹכִי מְצַוְּךָ
הַיּוֹם לְמַעַן תֶּחֶזְקוּ וּבָאתֶם וִירִשְׁתֶּם אֶת־הָאָרֶץ אֲשֶׁר
אַתֶּם עֹבְרִים שָׁמָּה לְרִשְׁתָּהּ: וּלְמַעַן תַּאֲרִיכוּ יָמִים
עַל־הָאֲדָמָה אֲשֶׁר נִשְׁבַּע יְהוָה לַאֲבֹתֵיכֶם לָתֵת לָהֶם
וּלְזַרְעָם אֶרֶץ זָבַת חָלָב וּדְבָשׁ: ס כִּי הָאָרֶץ
אֲשֶׁר אַתָּה בָא־שָׁמָּה לְרִשְׁתָּהּ לֹא כְאֶרֶץ מִצְרַיִם
הִוא אֲשֶׁר יְצָאתֶם מִשָּׁם אֲשֶׁר תִּזְרַע אֶת־זַרְעֲךָ
וְהִשְׁקִיתָ בְרַגְלְךָ כְּגַן הַיָּרָק: וְהָאָרֶץ אֲשֶׁר אַתֶּם

*יב חסר א'.

8] Keep, therefore, all the Instruction that I enjoin upon you today, so that you may have the strength to invade and occupy the land which you are about to cross into and occupy, **9]** and that you may long endure upon the soil which the LORD swore to your fathers to give to them and to their descendants, a land flowing with milk and honey.

10] For the land which you are about to invade and occupy is not like the land of Egypt from which you have come. There the grain you sowed had to be watered by your own labors, like a vegetable garden; **11]** but the land you are about to cross into and occupy, a land of hills and valleys, soaks up its water from the rains of heaven. **12]** It is a land which the LORD your God looks after, on which the LORD your God always keeps His eye, from year's beginning to year's end.

13] If, then, you obey the commandments that I enjoin upon you this day, loving the LORD your God and serving Him with all your heart and soul, **14]** I will grant the rain for your land in season, the early rain and the late. You shall gather in your new grain and wine and oil—

15] I will also provide grass in the fields for your cattle—and thus you shall eat your

---

10] *By your own labors.* The translation understands the literal "by your foot" figuratively, thereby sidestepping speculation about the irrigation methods used by the Egyptians (such as: they carried the water from the river on their shoulders and transported it on foot).

11] *Soaks up.* Retains it without wasteful runoffs or flooding. The comparison is made for hortatory purposes and therefore employs exaggeration.

13–21] These verses are the fourth selection inscribed on phylacteries because mention is made of binding these admonitions to hand and fore-

head (verse 18). The passage is also recited in the traditional daily liturgy as the second section of the *Shema*, after Deut. 6:4–9.

The Mishnah explains that this order is instituted so that a person might first accept the yoke of the Kingdom of heaven (Deut. 6) and then the yoke of the mitzvot (Deut. 11) [6].

14] *I will grant.* Moses speaks in God's stead. However, the Samaritan text has "*He* will grant."

Early rain and the late. The former falls in late October and early November, the latter in late March and early April. The height of the rainy season occurs in December and January.

כִּימֵי הַשָּׁמַיִם עַל־הָאָרֶץ: ס כִּי אִם־שָׁמֹר כב
תִּשְׁמְרוּן אֶת־כָּל־הַמִּצְוָה הַזֹּאת אֲשֶׁר אָנֹכִי מְצַוֶּה
אֶתְכֶם לַעֲשֹׂתָהּ לְאַהֲבָה אֶת־יְהֹוָה אֱלֹהֵיכֶם לָלֶכֶת
בְּכָל־דְּרָכָיו וּלְדָבְקָה־בוֹ: וְהוֹרִישׁ יְהֹוָה אֶת־כָּל־ כג
הַגּוֹיִם הָאֵלֶּה מִלִּפְנֵיכֶם וִירִשְׁתֶּם גּוֹיִם גְּדֹלִים
וַעֲצֻמִים מִכֶּם: כָּל־הַמָּקוֹם אֲשֶׁר תִּדְרֹךְ כַּף־רַגְלְכֶם כד
בּוֹ לָכֶם יִהְיֶה מִן־הַמִּדְבָּר וְהַלְּבָנוֹן מִן־הַנָּהָר נְהַר־
פְּרָת וְעַד הַיָּם הָאַחֲרוֹן יִהְיֶה גְּבֻלְכֶם: לֹא־יִתְיַצֵּב כה
אִישׁ בִּפְנֵיכֶם פַּחְדְּכֶם וּמוֹרַאֲכֶם יִתֵּן יְהֹוָה אֱלֹהֵיכֶם
עַל־פְּנֵי כָל־הָאָרֶץ אֲשֶׁר תִּדְרְכוּ־בָהּ כַּאֲשֶׁר דִּבֶּר
לָכֶם:

לְבְהֶמְתֶּךָ וְאָכַלְתָּ וְשָׂבָעְתָּ: הִשָּׁמְרוּ לָכֶם פֶּן־יִפְתֶּה טו
לְבַבְכֶם וְסַרְתֶּם וַעֲבַדְתֶּם אֱלֹהִים אֲחֵרִים
וְהִשְׁתַּחֲוִיתֶם לָהֶם: וְחָרָה אַף־יְהֹוָה בָּכֶם וְעָצַר אֶת־ טז
הַשָּׁמַיִם וְלֹא־יִהְיֶה מָטָר וְהָאֲדָמָה לֹא תִתֵּן אֶת־
יְבוּלָהּ וַאֲבַדְתֶּם מְהֵרָה מֵעַל הָאָרֶץ הַטֹּבָה אֲשֶׁר
יְהֹוָה נֹתֵן לָכֶם: וְשַׂמְתֶּם אֶת־דְּבָרַי אֵלֶּה עַל־לְבַבְכֶם יז
וְעַל־נַפְשְׁכֶם וּקְשַׁרְתֶּם אֹתָם לְאוֹת עַל־יֶדְכֶם וְהָיוּ
לְטוֹטָפֹת בֵּין עֵינֵיכֶם: וְלִמַּדְתֶּם אֹתָם אֶת־בְּנֵיכֶם יח
לְדַבֵּר בָּם בְּשִׁבְתְּךָ בְּבֵיתֶךָ וּבְלֶכְתְּךָ בַדֶּרֶךְ
וּבְשָׁכְבְּךָ וּבְקוּמֶךָ: וּכְתַבְתָּם עַל־מְזוּזוֹת בֵּיתֶךָ יט
וּבִשְׁעָרֶיךָ: לְמַעַן יִרְבּוּ יְמֵיכֶם וִימֵי בְנֵיכֶם עַל כ
הָאֲדָמָה אֲשֶׁר נִשְׁבַּע יְהֹוָה לַאֲבֹתֵיכֶם לָתֵת לָהֶם כא

Haftarah Ekev, p. 1599

fill. **16]** Take care not to be lured away to serve other gods and bow to them. **17]** For the LORD's anger will flare up against you, and He will shut up the skies so that there will be no rain and the ground will not yield its produce; and you will soon perish from the good land that the LORD is giving you.

18] Therefore impress these My words upon your very heart: bind them as a sign on your hand and let them serve as a symbol on your forehead, **19]** and teach them to your children— reciting them when you stay at home and when you are away, when you lie down and when you get up; **20]** and inscribe them on the doorposts of your house and on your gates— **21]** to the end that you and your children may endure, in the land that the LORD swore to your fathers to give to them, as long as there is a heaven over the earth.

22] If, then, you faithfully keep all this Instruction that I command you, loving the LORD your God, walking in all His ways, and holding fast to Him, **23]** the LORD will dislodge before you all these nations: you will dispossess nations greater and more numerous than you. **24]** Every spot on which your foot treads shall be yours; your territory shall extend from the wilderness to the Lebanon and from the River—the Euphrates—to the Western Sea. **25]** No man shall stand up to you: the LORD your God will put the dread and the fear of you over the whole land in which you set foot, as He promised you.

16] *Take care.* It has been suggested that verses 13–15 ought to be read as depending on the clause "If then" and that only in verse 16 the resolution occurs. This would, however, not alter the Torah's apparent idea that rainfall is granted or withheld at God's will. See also chapter 28 [7].

17] *The Lord's anger will flare up.* The description

of punishment is as hyperbolic as the promise of plenty.

18] *Your very heart.* Literally, "your heart and soul."

Symbol on your forehead. See at Deut. 6:8.

24] *Western Sea.* The Mediterranean.

Why Love the Stranger?

In an oft-quoted talmudic passage, R. Eliezer comments on the surprising fact that Scripture asks us no fewer than thirty-six times to love[1] the stranger [8]. This is the more noteworthy when one compares this with other ancient Near Eastern records. There, the protection of *widows* and *orphans* was well entrenched (care of these was a cliché for the humane conduct of kings), but not the concern for *strangers*, which is unique to the Torah. The frequency of this repetition suggests that aliens had a difficult time and that instead of finding acceptance and friendship (let alone love) they experienced rejection. Similarly, the duty to love God was repeated so often because the Israelites continued to be steeped in idolatry. The command "You must love (or befriend) the stranger" must be appreciated in this light.

The Torah gives two explicitly stated reasons for this mitzvah. One, which occurs only once, calls on the Israelite's compassion: "You shall not oppress a stranger, *for you know the feelings of the stranger*, having yourselves been strangers in the land of Egypt" (Exod. 23:9). But, while this reminder of past bitter experience could be expected to create empathy amongst those who had actually been slaves, it was certainly less potent for their descendants.[2]

The second, and related, reason is purely historical and is stated time and again: You were strangers once, and were mistreated, therefore do not do to others what was done to your forefathers. But could this rehearsal of ancient history be expected to produce moral rectitude? Aside from the obvious weakness of this type of motivation, should we not expect the Torah to tell us the real reason for treating the stranger decently is that it is the right and moral thing to do?

That, in fact, is what the Torah does tell us, albeit in its own way which, as so often, is implicit rather than explicit. To be sure, the reference to slavery in Egypt is cast in historical terms, as many commentators pointed out [9], but it is also "religious" in the deepest sense. Nachmanides therefore says: The reminder that we were slaves in Egypt draws our attention to the fact that God hears the cry of the oppressed and saves them as He saved Israel in Egypt [10]. The reference to the Exodus is the Torah's standard method of eliciting Israel's awareness of God's overarching presence, and in two places the text emphasizes it clearly. One, in Lev. 19:34, says: "You shall love him (the stranger) as yourself, for you were strangers in the land of Egypt: *I the Lord am your God*." The other is found in the text above (Deut. 10:17–19): "For the Lord your God is God supreme and Lord supreme, the great, the mighty, and the awesome God who ... befriends the stranger, providing him with food and clothing. You too must befriend the stranger, for you were strangers in the land of Egypt."

In the Torah's view, ethics belongs in the

---

[1] Our translation of verses 18 and 19 renders the Hebrew word אָהַב as "befriend," but in Lev. 19:34 it retains the more usual "love," probably because it would be awkward to say that one should "befriend a stranger as oneself." The commandment intends that we should disregard the strangeness of the גֵּר as much as possible and make him feel welcome, that is, *befriend* him. Asking us to *love* him, in the ordinary sense of the English word, would hardly be realistic. (See also Rosenzweig in Gleanings.)

[2] Another Deuteronomic law (26:5–9) and subsequent tradition (as expressed in the Haggadah) required the Israelite to identify himself with the Egyptian experience, and the command to love the stranger was thereby given added emphasis. But the question remains how this identification could be achieved to the point where it decisively influenced social attitudes and actions.

realm of religion because God sets the standards of human behavior. Thus, the esteem for and love of the stranger is a reflection of our love of God [11]. In the alien we are first and foremost bidden to discover the presence of the redeeming God and thereby to reinforce our bonds with all humanity.

On the Geography of the Land

This commentary assumes that the text of Deuteronomy reflects a time when the Israelites had long been settled in the land and therefore were well familiar with its advantages and shortcomings (see introduction). When therefore, toward the end of his discourse, Moses is pictured as extolling the physical features of Canaan, we may take this to be a judgment based on experience, made at the time of King Josiah and not, as a fundamentalist view of the Torah would have it, an assessment made from a trans-Jordanian perspective, before the conquest under Joshua. It is noteworthy, then, that the land is said to possess a natural superiority to Egypt, in that it needs a minimum of care because of its rainfall and the retentive condition of the soil; and also in that, instead of the Egyptian flatlands, it possesses an amplitude of hills, valleys, and rivers. This judgment—especially if allowance is made for the poetic license expected in the context of Moses' address—remains an accurate description of Israel's geographic features.

Contrary to popular impression, the average annual rainfall in the land does not differ from that found in temperate zones. The difference lies in the intensity of the rain per hour and its distribution: it falls during forty to sixty days in a season stretching from October to April, while in temperate climes precipitation occurs over some one hundred eighty days spread over twelve months [12]. A further difference lies in the uneven distribution of the rain over the face of the land: in the southern desert there is less than

30 mm. (1.2 in.) rain per annum, while in northern Galilee there may be up to 1,100 mm. (44 in.). The forested areas of Judea and Samaria have a consistently high amount of precipitation. Since in antiquity the forests were far more widespread and the top soil had not yet eroded to the extent it did in later centuries, runoffs must have been fewer and much of the land was deserving of the description that it soaked up the rainwater (Deut. 11:11).

The major geographical feature of the land is its location at the edge of the earth's longest rift valley, which runs from the Zambesi in Central Africa to the Ural Mountains in Soviet Russia, 6,000 km. (3,700 miles) long, forming one vast basin containing primarily streams that do not discharge into the sea. Thus, 70 percent of the rivers and wadis in the mountains girding Israel run into the rift valley. Its lowest point, the Dead Sea, is the lowest surface area on earth.

Moses calls Canaan "a land of hills and valleys." In its topography it is not unlike Greece or Switzerland, where people live in relative proximity to one another, yet—because of the mountains—are also separate and prone to keep individual traditions and dialects alive. The long endurance of tribal differences in Israel was in part a function of its geography.

The land was further distinguished in that it was the land bridge connecting the two major cultural and political centers of the ancient Near East, Egypt and Mesopotamia. The Via Maris (as it was known later on) ran along the Mediterranean, and the King's Highway on the east side of the Jordan. Armies traversed these roads and often fought for them and the cities that guarded their access. In the process, religious and other cultural influences from north and south fructified its people. But ultimately it was neither the natural nor the geopolitical advantages which gave the land its distinc-

tion; rather, it was the conviction of its people that they were possessing it as God's gift. To them, it was a supranatural possession whose title could be revoked if the covenant on which it was based was breached—an eternal yet conditional gift, a land "on which the Lord your God always keeps His eye, from year's beginning to year's end" (Deut.

11:12). It reaches, in the words of this exhortation, all the way to the Euphrates, an idealized conception of its extent, or a hope that the days of Solomon's reign would return.[3]

On this note of promise and vision the second discourse of Moses reaches its conclusion.

---

[3] See further at Deut. 2:7 and Commentary on Numbers, chapter 34. P. Diepold distinguishes three Deuteronomic concepts of the extent of the land: a cis-Jordanian, a trans-Jordanian, and a Euphrates tradition [13].

GLEANINGS

And Now (Deut. 10:12)

Whenever the Torah begins an admonition with "And now . . ." (וְעַתָּה) it implies the need for repentance.   MIDRASH [14]

What . . . (10:12)

"What is it that the Lord your God demands of you?" The "what" (מָה) denotes humility, as when Moses and Aaron say "What are we?" (Exod. 16:7).[4] Hence, in our text too: Humility is *what* the Lord requires.   THE BAAL SHEM TOV [15]

Only This . . . (10:12)

God asks "only" reverence, from which we learn that everything is in the power of heaven except man's reverence for God (i.e., the "only" must be supplied by man).   TALMUD [16]

Commented the chasidic leader, Levi Yitzchak of Berditchev, always a staunch defender of Israel: In those days, reverence for God was a small matter for the people (hence the text says "only this"), because they had seen the great deeds of the Lord. And he confronted God: "Give our generation the likes of the Exodus and see how for us too reverence for You will be a small matter!" [17]

Love and Fear[5]

Both are commanded, and only if one serves Him out of both motivations does one serve Him fully.   ISAAC ALFASI [18]

A popular saying went: "Fear without love is incomplete; love without fear is nothing."

A Contradiction

Since we are commanded to make Shabbat a delight (Isa. 58:13), why are congregations exposed to Shabbat sermons which reprove the people and sadden the heart? Because such admonition is called a circumcision of the heart (Deut. 10:16), and we are taught that circumcision is a command to be observed even on Shabbat.   CHASIDIC [19]

God Supreme (10:17)

The Hebrew literally calls Him "God of gods and Lord of lords," because He is beyond any description and conception we might have of His divinity.   CHASIDIC [20]

Neighbor and Stranger

He is "like you" ("as yourself," Lev. 19:18), and thus not "you." You remain you and are to

---

[4] One Torah translation renders the verse "*Who* are we. . . ."

[5] Understanding "fear" as "reverence" (יִרְאָה); see above, at 10:12.

remain just that. But he is not to remain a He for you, and thus a mere It for you. Rather he is like You, like your You, a You like You, an I—a soul.

F. ROSENZWEIG [21]

Animals First

In Deut. 11:15 the Torah speaks first of God providing grass for cattle and then says "thus you shall eat your fill." From this, Rabbi Judah taught, in the name of Rav: A person is forbidden to eat until he has fed his cattle.

TALMUD [22]

Responsibility

In the *Shema* the command to teach the children is addressed to the individual (וְשִׁנַּנְתָּם, Deut. 6:7), while here it is phrased in the plural (וְלִמַּדְתֶּם אֹתָם, Deut. 11:19). From this you learn that the primary responsibility for education rests with the parents, the secondary with the community.

BASED ON THE TALMUD [23]

The Mountains

It is a little land, Canaan, small and slender as scarcely any other historical land. It stretches down from the mountains to the sea and from the mountains to the river. Not the river, which is more boundary than internal influence, but the mountains give the land its determining line. It is a land with a spine, similar to Italy. From the south to the north stretch mountains. In the south, the outposts lie between the Sea of Salt (into which runs the downward-flowing Jordan) and the Great Sea, the Mediterranean; while, in the north, the white mountains of Lebanon form a terminus. Occasionally, in the course of the centuries, the boundaries advanced; but the land always remained small. Everything that occurred in it had an intimacy; only that which was outside seemed distant.[6]

LEO BAECK [24]

[6] Baeck here refers to the spiritual state of Israel.

PART III

Third Discourse

While the second discourse was essentially an elaboration of the first and second commandments—stressing the love, respect, and unique adoration due the God of Israel—the text now—comprising the third discourse—turns to other considerations which may be divided into two broad categories: ritual (moral) and civil (social) laws, plus an epilogue. Some of these appear elsewhere in the Torah, others are found only here. For instance, the passages dealing with false prophets occur only in Deuteronomy, whereas rules of permitted and forbidden foods can be found also in Leviticus.

Ritual and Moral Laws
   Worship in a central place, 12:1–28
   Further injunctions against idolatry, 12:29–13:19; 16:21–17:7
   Self-mutilation, 14:1–2
   Permitted and forbidden foods, 14:3–21
   Tithes, 14:22–29
   Release, 15:1–18
   Firstlings, 15:19–23
   Holy days, 16:1–17
   Kindness to animals, 22:1–4, 6–8; 25:4
   Unnatural mixtures, 22:5, 9–11
   Fringes, 22:12
   Unchastity, 22:13–29
   Ostracism, 23:1–9
   Holiness of the camp, 23:10–15
   Temple prostitution, 23:18–19
   Skin affection, 24:8–9
   Amalek, 25:17–19

Civil, Criminal, and Social Laws
   Debts, prevention of poverty, 15:1–11
   Laws of slavery, 15:12–18
   Judges and courts, 16:18–20
   Election of a king, 17:14–20
   Priests and Levites, 18:1–8
   Prophets, 18:9–22 (also in ch. 13)
   Cities of refuge, 19:1–13

Encroachment, 19:14
False testimony, 19:15–21
Rules of war, 20:1–20
Unsolved murder, 21:1–9
Punishment by hanging, 21:22–23
Marriage to captive woman, 21:10–24
Primogeniture, 21:15–17
Rebellious son, 21:18–21
Runaway slaves, 23:16–17
Interest charges, 23:20–21
Vows, 23:22–24
Neighbor's rights, 23:25–26
Remarriage, 24:1–4
Exemption from war service, 24:5
Pledges, 24:6, 10–13, 17–18
Kidnaping, 24:7
Wages, 24:14–15
Personal responsibility, 24:16
Strangers, orphans, and widows, 24:17–22
Excessive punishment, 25:1–3
Levirate marriage, 25:5–10
Assault, 25:11–12
Weights and measures, 25:13–16

Epilogue
Exhortation, chapter 26
Pronouncement of blessings and curses, chapters 27–28.

In depicting the bulk of Deuteronomic legislation in this fashion we need to remember that the Torah itself did not deal with such categories of law. Often certain passages obtained their present position as an aid to memory rather than for systematic reasons in the modern sense. But it is noteworthy that, unlike in Mesopotamian codes, laws regarding *persons* generally precede laws of *property*, with procedural regulations following or interspersed.

The Divine Command

Many commentators consider the last seven verses of chapter 11 as the conclusion of the second discourse and not, as we do here, as the beginning of the third. Our reason is primarily literary: the discourse thus opens with the command to pronounce blessings and curses on Mount Gerizim and Mount Ebal, respectively; and, in chapter 27, at the end of the discourse, this command is repeated and treated in detail. The formal, dramatic invocation of the Divine Presence constitutes the framework for the code of special laws which forms the bulk of Deuteronomy. Our division is supported by the rabbinic provision that a new weekly portion (*Re'eh*) begins with 11:26.

ס ס ס

כו רְאֵ֗ה אָנֹכִ֛י נֹתֵ֥ן לִפְנֵיכֶ֖ם הַיּ֑וֹם בְּרָכָ֖ה וּקְלָלָֽה: אֶת־
הַבְּרָכָ֑ה אֲשֶׁ֣ר תִּשְׁמְע֔וּ אֶל־מִצְוֺת֙ יְהֹוָ֣ה אֱלֹֽהֵיכֶ֔ם אֲשֶׁ֧ר
כז אָנֹכִ֛י מְצַוֶּ֥ה אֶתְכֶ֖ם הַיּֽוֹם: וְהַקְּלָלָ֗ה אִם־לֹ֤א תִשְׁמְעוּ֙
אֶל־מִצְוֺת֙ יְהֹוָ֣ה אֱלֹֽהֵיכֶ֔ם וְסַרְתֶּ֣ם מִן־הַדֶּ֔רֶךְ אֲשֶׁ֧ר
אָנֹכִ֛י מְצַוֶּ֥ה אֶתְכֶ֖ם הַיּ֑וֹם לָלֶ֗כֶת אַחֲרֵ֛י אֱלֹהִ֥ים
כח אֲחֵרִ֖ים אֲשֶׁ֥ר לֹֽא־יְדַעְתֶּֽם: ס וְהָיָ֗ה כִּ֤י יְבִֽיאֲךָ֙
יְהֹוָ֣ה אֱלֹהֶ֔יךָ אֶל־הָאָ֕רֶץ אֲשֶׁר־אַתָּ֥ה בָא־שָׁ֖מָּה

ל לְרִשְׁתָּ֑הּ וְנָתַתָּ֤ה אֶת־הַבְּרָכָה֙ עַל־הַ֣ר גְּרִזִ֔ים וְאֶת־
הַקְּלָלָ֖ה עַל־הַ֥ר עֵיבָֽל: הֲלֹא־הֵ֜מָּה בְּעֵ֣בֶר הַיַּרְדֵּ֗ן
אַחֲרֵי֙ דֶּ֚רֶךְ מְב֣וֹא הַשֶּׁ֔מֶשׁ בְּאֶ֙רֶץ֙ הַֽכְּנַעֲנִ֔י הַיֹּשֵׁ֖ב
לא בָּעֲרָבָ֑ה מ֥וּל הַגִּלְגָּ֖ל אֵ֥צֶל אֵלוֹנֵ֥י מֹרֶֽה: כִּ֤י אַתֶּם֙
עֹבְרִ֣ים אֶת־הַיַּרְדֵּ֔ן לָבֹא֙ לָרֶ֣שֶׁת אֶת־הָאָ֔רֶץ אֲשֶׁר־
יְהֹוָ֥ה אֱלֹֽהֵיכֶ֖ם נֹתֵ֣ן לָכֶ֑ם וִֽירִשְׁתֶּ֥ם אֹתָ֖הּ וִֽישַׁבְתֶּם־בָּֽהּ:
לב וּשְׁמַרְתֶּ֣ם לַעֲשׂ֔וֹת אֵ֥ת כָּל־הַֽחֻקִּ֖ים וְאֶת־הַמִּשְׁפָּטִ֑ים
אֲשֶׁ֧ר אָנֹכִ֛י נֹתֵ֥ן לִפְנֵיכֶ֖ם הַיּֽוֹם:

26] See, this day I set before you blessing and curse: **27]** blessing, if you obey the commandments of the LORD your God which I enjoin upon you this day; **28]** and curse, if you do not obey the commandments of the LORD your God, but turn away from the path which I enjoin upon you this day and follow other gods, whom you have not experienced. **29]** When the LORD your God brings you into the land which you are about to invade and occupy, you shall pronounce the blessing at Mount Gerizim and the curse at Mount Ebal.— **30]** Both are on the other side of the Jordan, beyond the west road which is in the land of the Canaanites who dwell in the Arabah—near Gilgal, by the terebinths of Moreh.

31] For you are about to cross the Jordan to invade and occupy the land which the LORD your God is giving to you. When you have occupied it and are settled in it, **32]** take care to observe all the laws and rules that I have set before you this day.

11:26] *I set before you.* Affirming free choice.

27-28] *Blessing . . . curse.* Details of the procedure are given at the end of the discourse, 27:12 ff. Mount Gerizim (called by the Arabs Jebel al-Tur, 2,849 ft. or 855 m. high) lies to the south of Shechem (modern Nablus), while Mount Ebal (Jebel Islamiya, 3,077 ft. or 923 m. high) is to the north. Gerizim has numerous springs arising at its foot and is the more fertile of the two. Its choice as the mountain of blessing may go back to an old tradition that regarded Shechem rather than Sinai and Jerusalem as the chief locale of God's presence. This explains the Samaritan claim that Gerizim is superior in sanctity to Jerusalem [1].

28] *Experienced.* The word יָדַע describes some-times intellectual apprehension and at other times an intimate, living relationship; see Hosea 13:4 and, in sexual respects, Gen. 4:1 (and our commentary to Gen. 2:25–3:24, "Sexual Interpretation").

30] *Canaanites who dwell in the Arabah—near Gilgal.* The name Gilgal (suggesting rolled stones that formed a marker or monument) was probably applied to several sacred places in Canaan. Similarly, Arabah (or Aravah) may have been used in various senses; Driver suggests that here it meant an area near Jericho where a Gilgal was located, a place that could be seen from the heights of Moab [2].

Terebinths of Moreh. Noted in Gen. 12:6 as standing near Shechem.

GLEANINGS

Singular

The *sidrah* begins with the word "See," which in the Hebrew (רְאֵה) is in the singular. Thereafter, however, the text switches to the plural. The reason is that, while the commandments are set before the whole people (hence the plural address), each individual must "see" and decide whether to obey or disobey.   AFTER BACHYA [3]

This Day (Deut. 11:26)

This signified that the mitzvah of Gerizim and Ebal was to be performed at once, and not after total possession of the land had been achieved. It emphasized that Israel was to live in the land only for the sake of doing mitzvot.

RALBAG (GERSONIDES) [4]

I Set before You Blessing and Curse

Hence the saying: "Sword and book came down from Heaven together." God said: If you observe what is written in the Book you will be saved from the sword, but if not it will slay you.

MIDRASH [5]

In laying two choices before us, God urges us to choose the good and helps us if we strive to achieve it. For He does not deal with us in accordance with strict justice.   MIDRASH [6]

The choice between blessing and curse does not permit of a compromise. They are two opposites between which one must choose.

SFORNO [7]

It says "blessing, if you obey" (verse 27)—it is enough to obey, for this will inevitably lead to the performance of mitzvot. But regarding the curse the text speaks differently. It adds to "curse, if you do not obey" (verse 28) the words, "but turn away." For failure to obey or hear does not always and necessarily lead to actual sin.   CHASIDIC [8]

The words are so couched as to make clear that every acknowledgment of idolatry is tantamount to a denial of the Torah, and every denial of idolatry is an acknowledgment of the Torah.

MIDRASH [9]

Two Mountains

Gerizim and Ebal are two peaks of the Ephraim range of mountains which still show a striking contrast in their appearance. Gerizim to the south of the valley of Shechem presents a smiling green slope rising in fruit-covered terraces to its summit; Ebal on the north side, steep, barren, and bleak, slightly higher than Gerizim. The two mounts lying next to each other form accordingly a most telling instructive picture of blessing and curse. They both rise on one and the same soil, both are watered by one and the same fall of rain and dew, the same air breathes over both of them, the same pollen wafts over both of them, and yet Ebal remains in barren bleakness while Gerizim is clad to its summit in embellishment of vegetation. In the same way, blessing and curse are not conditional on external circumstances but on our own inner receptivity for the one or the other, on our behavior towards that which is to bring blessing.   S. R. HIRSCH [10]

The Central Sanctuary

Moses' third discourse begins with a fundamental tenet which characterizes the Book of Deuteronomy: the overriding need for a central sanctuary. In order to achieve a centralization of sacrificial worship, all other sites and altars were to be dismantled and destroyed. This provision constituted an important development in the religious life of the people: it was part of the constant fight against idolatry, for it struck at the persistence of local pagan cults; and it was also a stage in the unification of the nation in which the central sanctuary played a significant role.

This raised some ancillary problems, chief among them the custom of eating meat only on sacrificial occasions. Since such consumption had taken place in the context of sacrificial worship in various localities, which were at all times in reach of every person, a central sanctuary would prevent an Israelite from eating meat most of the time. Hence the law specifies at once that, while sacrifice would be centralized, the consumption of meat would not. But other offerings, such as firstlings, must be brought to the central site.

The section ends with a warning not to give way to curiosity about foreign religious practices, and with a repetition of the injunction not to add to or detract from the law as presented. In most English versions, 13:1 is reckoned as belonging to chapter 12 (making it 12:32; actually, the verse is a bridge between the two chapters).

אֵלֶּה הַחֻקִּים וְהַמִּשְׁפָּטִים אֲשֶׁר תִּשְׁמְרוּן לַעֲשׂוֹת בָּאָרֶץ אֲשֶׁר נָתַן יְהֹוָה אֱלֹהֵי אֲבֹתֶיךָ לְךָ לְרִשְׁתָּהּ כָּל־הַיָּמִים אֲשֶׁר־אַתֶּם חַיִּים עַל־הָאֲדָמָה: אַבֵּד תְּאַבְּדוּן אֶת־כָּל־הַמְּקֹמוֹת אֲשֶׁר עָבְדוּ־שָׁם הַגּוֹיִם אֲשֶׁר אַתֶּם יֹרְשִׁים אֹתָם אֶת־אֱלֹהֵיהֶם עַל־הֶהָרִים הָרָמִים וְעַל־הַגְּבָעוֹת וְתַחַת כָּל־עֵץ רַעֲנָן: וְנִתַּצְתֶּם אֶת־מִזְבְּחֹתָם וְשִׁבַּרְתֶּם אֶת־מַצֵּבֹתָם וַאֲשֵׁרֵיהֶם תִּשְׂרְפוּן בָּאֵשׁ וּפְסִילֵי אֱלֹהֵיהֶם תְּגַדֵּעוּן וְאִבַּדְתֶּם אֶת־שְׁמָם מִן־הַמָּקוֹם הַהוּא: לֹא־תַעֲשׂוּן כֵּן לַיהֹוָה אֱלֹהֵיכֶם: כִּי אִם־אֶל־הַמָּקוֹם אֲשֶׁר־יִבְחַר יְהֹוָה אֱלֹהֵיכֶם מִכָּל־שִׁבְטֵיכֶם לָשׂוּם אֶת־שְׁמוֹ שָׁם לְשִׁכְנוֹ תִדְרְשׁוּ וּבָאתָ שָׁמָּה: וַהֲבֵאתֶם שָׁמָּה עֹלֹתֵיכֶם וְזִבְחֵיכֶם וְאֵת מַעְשְׂרֹתֵיכֶם וְאֵת תְּרוּמַת יֶדְכֶם וְנִדְרֵיכֶם וְנִדְבֹתֵיכֶם וּבְכֹרֹת בְּקַרְכֶם וְצֹאנְכֶם: וַאֲכַלְתֶּם־שָׁם לִפְנֵי יְהֹוָה אֱלֹהֵיכֶם וּשְׂמַחְתֶּם בְּכֹל מִשְׁלַח יֶדְכֶם אַתֶּם וּבָתֵּיכֶם אֲשֶׁר בֵּרַכְךָ יְהֹוָה

1] These are the laws and rules which you must carefully observe in the land that the LORD, God of your fathers, is giving you to possess, as long as you live on earth. **2]** You must destroy all the sites at which the nations you are to dispossess worshiped their gods, whether on lofty mountains and on hills or under any luxuriant tree. **3]** Tear down their altars, smash their pillars, put their sacred posts to the fire, and cut down the images of their gods, obliterating their name from that site. **4]** Do not worship the LORD your God in like manner, **5]** but look only to the site that the LORD your God will choose amidst all your tribes as His habitation, to establish His name there. There you are to go, **6]** and there you are to bring your burnt offerings and other sacrifices, your tithes and contributions, your votive and freewill offerings, and the firstlings of your herds and flocks. **7]** Together with your households, you shall feast there before the LORD your God, happy in all the undertakings in which the LORD your God has blessed you.

12:1] *Laws and rules.* See at 4:1.

Live on earth. Others apply the expression *al ha-adamah* to the land of Israel only [1] (see further in Gleanings).

2] *Lofty mountains . . . hills.* These were traditional places of pagan worship, but in biblical religion, too, elevated places play an important role: Mt. Sinai, Mt. Nebo, Mt. Zion. Driver suggested that in such places one was believed closer to the Divinity [2].

Tree. Sacred trees also were frequent worship sites, and it is likely that the *menorah* was a stylized tree (see commentary on Exod. 25:31 ff.).

3] *Altars . . . pillars.* Rashi suggests that the former consisted of many stones, the latter of single slabs.

Sacred posts. They were called *asherim* because they were dedicated to Asherah (see at 7:5). The command to destroy pagan sites and objects was considered obligatory only in Eretz Yisrael and not, for obvious reasons, outside the Land [3].

4] *In like manner.* That is, on mountains or under trees.

6] *There you are to bring.* Seven kinds of offerings are mentioned:

a. Burnt offerings. The *olah* was consumed entirely by fire (see verse 27); older translations used the term holocaust, "wholly burnt."

b. Other sacrifices. *Zevach*, an offering of which only the blood and some other parts were sacrificed, the rest was eaten; such sacrifices were usually thanks or peace offerings. (A detailed discussion of sacrifices may be found in our Commentary on Leviticus, in the introduction to Part I, "Laws of Sacrifice.")

c. Tithes. The *ma-aser* (from עֶשֶׂר, *eser*, ten) was the tenth of cattle or produce set aside for the Levites and the socially disadvantaged (see at 14:22 ff.) [4].

d. Contributions. *Terumah* ("heave offering") was a general levy brought on the three pilgrim festivals and for special occasions, such as contri-

אֱלֹהֵיכֶם אַתֶּם וּבְנֵיכֶם וּבְנֹתֵיכֶם וְעַבְדֵיכֶם
וְאַמְהֹתֵיכֶם וְהַלֵּוִי אֲשֶׁר בְּשַׁעֲרֵיכֶם כִּי אֵין לוֹ חֵלֶק
וְנַחֲלָה אִתְּכֶם: הִשָּׁמֶר לְךָ פֶּן־תַּעֲלֶה עֹלֹתֶיךָ בְּכָל־
מָקוֹם אֲשֶׁר תִּרְאֶה: כִּי אִם־בַּמָּקוֹם אֲשֶׁר־יִבְחַר יְהוָה
בְּאַחַד שְׁבָטֶיךָ שָׁם תַּעֲלֶה עֹלֹתֶיךָ וְשָׁם תַּעֲשֶׂה כֹּל
אֲשֶׁר אָנֹכִי מְצַוֶּךָּ: רַק בְּכָל־אַוַּת נַפְשְׁךָ תִּזְבַּח
וְאָכַלְתָּ בָשָׂר כְּבִרְכַּת יְהוָה אֱלֹהֶיךָ אֲשֶׁר נָתַן־לְךָ
בְּכָל־שְׁעָרֶיךָ הַטָּמֵא וְהַטָּהוֹר יֹאכְלֶנּוּ כַּצְּבִי וְכָאַיָּל:
רַק הַדָּם לֹא תֹאכֵלוּ עַל־הָאָרֶץ תִּשְׁפְּכֶנּוּ כַּמָּיִם:

אֱלֹהֶיךָ: לֹא תַעֲשׂוּן כְּכֹל אֲשֶׁר אֲנַחְנוּ עֹשִׂים פֹּה
הַיּוֹם אִישׁ כָּל־הַיָּשָׁר בְּעֵינָיו: כִּי לֹא־בָאתֶם עַד־
עָתָּה אֶל־הַמְּנוּחָה וְאֶל־הַנַּחֲלָה אֲשֶׁר־יְהוָה אֱלֹהֶיךָ
נֹתֵן לָךְ: וַעֲבַרְתֶּם אֶת־הַיַּרְדֵּן וִישַׁבְתֶּם בָּאָרֶץ אֲשֶׁר־
יְהוָה אֱלֹהֵיכֶם מַנְחִיל אֶתְכֶם וְהֵנִיחַ לָכֶם מִכָּל־
אֹיְבֵיכֶם מִסָּבִיב וִישַׁבְתֶּם־בֶּטַח: וְהָיָה הַמָּקוֹם
אֲשֶׁר־יִבְחַר יְהוָה אֱלֹהֵיכֶם בּוֹ לְשַׁכֵּן שְׁמוֹ שָׁם שָׁמָּה
תָבִיאוּ אֵת כָּל־אֲשֶׁר אָנֹכִי מְצַוֶּה אֶתְכֶם עוֹלֹתֵיכֶם
וְזִבְחֵיכֶם מַעְשְׂרֹתֵיכֶם וּתְרֻמַת יֶדְכֶם וְכֹל מִבְחַר
נִדְרֵיכֶם אֲשֶׁר תִּדְּרוּ לַיהוָה: וּשְׂמַחְתֶּם לִפְנֵי יְהוָה

8] You shall not act at all as we now act here, every man as he pleases, **9]** because you have not yet come to the allotted haven that the LORD your God is giving you. **10]** When you cross the Jordan and settle in the land that the LORD your God is allotting to you, and He grants you safety from all your enemies around you and you live in security, **11]** then you must bring everything that I command you to the site where the LORD your God will choose to establish His name: your burnt offerings and other sacrifices, your tithes and contributions, and all the choice votive offerings that you vow to the LORD. **12]** And you shall rejoice before the LORD your God with your sons and daughters and with your male and female slaves, along with the Levite of your settlement, for he has no territorial allotment among you.

13] Take care not to sacrifice your burnt offerings in any place you like, **14]** but only in the place which the LORD will choose in one of your tribal territories. There you shall sacrifice your burnt offerings and there you shall observe all that I enjoin upon you. **15]** But whenever you desire, you may slaughter and eat meat in any of your settlements, according to the blessing which the LORD your God has granted you. The unclean and the clean alike may partake of it, as of the gazelle and the deer. **16]** But you must not partake of the blood; you shall pour it out on the ground like water.

---

butions for the building of a sanctuary.

However, in talmudic literature, *terumah* referred mostly to portions given to the priests.

e. Votive offerings. Made to fulfill a vow (*neder*). On the importance and treatment of vows see our commentary on Num. 30:1–16.

f. Freewill offerings. A *nedavah* was a sacrifice made voluntarily, because the worshiper wanted to offer it.

The term has persisted in modern Hebrew and in Yiddish to describe charitable gifts.

g. Firstlings. *Bikkurim*, the first yield of herd and field belonged to God. See below at 15:19.

8] *As we now act here.* These words may be a critique of conditions prevailing in later days (see

Judg. 17:6; 21:25).

12] *Levite of your settlement.* The original idea of settling the Levites in forty-eight special cities apparently never materialized. Instead, levitical families lived in all communities and served in the central sanctuary on a rotating basis.

15] *The unclean and the clean.* In the ritual sense. Thus, a woman in her menstrual period was considered unclean, and afterwards, her ablutions performed, she was clean.

The gazelle and the deer. Which are permitted for food but not for sacrifice. Similarly, an animal with a blemish which disqualified it for sacrifice but not for food would be included in this rule [5].

16] *Partake of the blood.* See commentary below.

יז לֹא־תוּכַל לֶאֱכֹל בִּשְׁעָרֶיךָ מַעְשַׂר דְּגָנְךָ וְתִירֹשְׁךָ
וְיִצְהָרֶךָ וּבְכֹרֹת בְּקָרְךָ וְצֹאנֶךָ וְכָל־נְדָרֶיךָ אֲשֶׁר
יח תִּדֹּר וְנִדְבֹתֶיךָ וּתְרוּמַת יָדֶךָ: כִּי אִם־לִפְנֵי יְהוָה
אֱלֹהֶיךָ תֹּאכְלֶנּוּ בַּמָּקוֹם אֲשֶׁר יִבְחַר יְהוָה אֱלֹהֶיךָ
בּוֹ אַתָּה וּבִנְךָ וּבִתֶּךָ וְעַבְדְּךָ וַאֲמָתֶךָ וְהַלֵּוִי אֲשֶׁר
בִּשְׁעָרֶיךָ וְשָׂמַחְתָּ לִפְנֵי יְהוָה אֱלֹהֶיךָ בְּכֹל מִשְׁלַח
יט יָדֶךָ: הִשָּׁמֶר לְךָ פֶּן־תַּעֲזֹב אֶת־הַלֵּוִי כָּל־יָמֶיךָ עַל־
כ אַדְמָתֶךָ: ס כִּי־יַרְחִיב יְהוָה אֱלֹהֶיךָ אֶת־גְּבֻלְךָ
כַּאֲשֶׁר דִּבֶּר־לָךְ וְאָמַרְתָּ אֹכְלָה בָשָׂר כִּי־תְאַוֶּה
נַפְשְׁךָ לֶאֱכֹל בָּשָׂר בְּכָל־אַוַּת נַפְשְׁךָ תֹּאכַל בָּשָׂר:
כא כִּי־יִרְחַק מִמְּךָ הַמָּקוֹם אֲשֶׁר יִבְחַר יְהוָה אֱלֹהֶיךָ
לָשׂוּם שְׁמוֹ שָׁם וְזָבַחְתָּ מִבְּקָרְךָ וּמִצֹּאנְךָ אֲשֶׁר נָתַן
יְהוָה לְךָ כַּאֲשֶׁר צִוִּיתִךָ וְאָכַלְתָּ בִּשְׁעָרֶיךָ בְּכֹל

כב אַוַּת נַפְשֶׁךָ: אַךְ כַּאֲשֶׁר יֵאָכֵל אֶת־הַצְּבִי וְאֶת־הָאַיָּל
כג כֵּן תֹּאכְלֶנּוּ הַטָּמֵא וְהַטָּהוֹר יַחְדָּו יֹאכְלֶנּוּ: רַק
חֲזַק לְבִלְתִּי אֲכֹל הַדָּם כִּי הַדָּם הוּא הַנָּפֶשׁ וְלֹא־
כד תֹאכַל הַנֶּפֶשׁ עִם־הַבָּשָׂר: לֹא תֹּאכְלֶנּוּ עַל־הָאָרֶץ
כה תִּשְׁפְּכֶנּוּ כַּמָּיִם: לֹא תֹּאכְלֶנּוּ לְמַעַן יִיטַב לְךָ
וּלְבָנֶיךָ אַחֲרֶיךָ כִּי־תַעֲשֶׂה הַיָּשָׁר בְּעֵינֵי יְהוָה: רַק
כו קָדָשֶׁיךָ אֲשֶׁר־יִהְיוּ לְךָ וּנְדָרֶיךָ תִּשָּׂא וּבָאתָ אֶל־
כז הַמָּקוֹם אֲשֶׁר־יִבְחַר יְהוָה: וְעָשִׂיתָ עֹלֹתֶיךָ הַבָּשָׂר
וְהַדָּם עַל־מִזְבַּח יְהוָה אֱלֹהֶיךָ וְדַם־זְבָחֶיךָ יִשָּׁפֵךְ
כח עַל־מִזְבַּח יְהוָה אֱלֹהֶיךָ וְהַבָּשָׂר תֹּאכֵל: שְׁמֹר
וְשָׁמַעְתָּ אֵת כָּל־הַדְּבָרִים הָאֵלֶּה אֲשֶׁר אָנֹכִי מְצַוֶּךָּ
לְמַעַן יִיטַב לְךָ וּלְבָנֶיךָ אַחֲרֶיךָ עַד־עוֹלָם כִּי תַעֲשֶׂה
הַטּוֹב וְהַיָּשָׁר בְּעֵינֵי יְהוָה אֱלֹהֶיךָ: כט כִּי־יַכְרִית

* כא חסר י׳.

17] You may not partake in your settlements of the tithes of your new grain or wine or oil, or of the firstlings of your herds and flocks, or of any of the votive offerings that you vow, or of your freewill offerings, or of your contributions.   **18]** These you must consume before the LORD your God in the place that the LORD your God will choose—you and your son and your daughter, your male and female slaves, and the Levite in your settlements—happy before the LORD your God in all your undertakings.   **19]** Be sure not to neglect the Levite as long as you live in your land.

20] When the LORD enlarges your territory, as He has promised you, and you say, "I shall eat some meat," for you have the urge to eat meat, you may eat meat whenever you wish.   **21]** If the place where the LORD has chosen to establish His name is too far from you, you may slaughter any of the cattle or sheep that the LORD gives you, as I have instructed you; and you may eat to your heart's content in your settlements.   **22]** Eat it, however, as the gazelle and the deer are eaten: the unclean may eat it together with the clean.   **23]** But make sure that you do not partake of the blood; for the blood is the life, and you must not consume the life with the flesh.   **24]** You must not partake of it; you must pour it out on the ground like water: **25]** you must not partake of it, in order that it may go well with you and with your descendants to come, for you will be doing what is right in the sight of the LORD.

26] But such sacred and votive donations as you may have shall be taken by you to the site that the LORD will choose.   **27]** You shall offer your burnt offerings, both the flesh and the blood, on the altar of the LORD your God; and of your other sacrifices, the blood shall be poured out on the altar of the LORD your God, and you shall eat the flesh.

28] Be careful to heed all these commandments which I enjoin upon you; thus it will go well with you and with your descendants after you forever, for you will be doing what is good and right in the sight of the LORD your God.

20] *I shall eat some meat.* What follows gives a strong hortatory
cast to the injunctions previously issued.

יְהוָה אֱלֹהֶיךָ אֶת־הַגּוֹיִם אֲשֶׁר אַתָּה בָא־שָׁמָּה לָרֶשֶׁת

ל אוֹתָם מִפָּנֶיךָ וְיָרַשְׁתָּ אֹתָם וְיָשַׁבְתָּ בְּאַרְצָם: הִשָּׁמֶר

לְךָ פֶּן־תִּנָּקֵשׁ אַחֲרֵיהֶם אַחֲרֵי הִשָּׁמְדָם מִפָּנֶיךָ וּפֶן־

תִּדְרֹשׁ לֵאלֹהֵיהֶם לֵאמֹר אֵיכָה יַעַבְדוּ הַגּוֹיִם הָאֵלֶּה

לא אֶת־אֱלֹהֵיהֶם וְאֶעֱשֶׂה־כֵּן גַּם־אָנִי: לֹא־תַעֲשֶׂה כֵן

לַיהוָה אֱלֹהֶיךָ כִּי כָל־תּוֹעֲבַת יְהוָה אֲשֶׁר שָׂנֵא

עָשׂוּ לֵאלֹהֵיהֶם כִּי גַם אֶת־בְּנֵיהֶם וְאֶת־בְּנֹתֵיהֶם

יִשְׂרְפוּ בָאֵשׁ לֵאלֹהֵיהֶם:

א אֵת כָּל־הַדָּבָר אֲשֶׁר אָנֹכִי מְצַוֶּה אֶתְכֶם אֹתוֹ

תִשְׁמְרוּ לַעֲשׂוֹת לֹא־תֹסֵף עָלָיו וְלֹא תִגְרַע מִמֶּנּוּ: פ

29] When the LORD your God has cut down before you the nations which you are about to invade and dispossess, and you have dispossessed them and settled in their land, 30] beware of being lured into their ways after they have been wiped out before you! Do not inquire about their gods, saying, "How did those nations worship their gods? I too will follow those practices." 31] You shall not act thus toward the LORD your God, for they perform for their gods every abhorrent act that the LORD detests; they even offer up their sons and daughters in fire to their gods. 1] Be careful to observe only that which I enjoin upon you: neither add to it nor take away from it.

31] *Even . . . their sons and daughters.* Tradition took the word גַּם (*gam*, "even," but normally meaning "also") to imply that sacrificing one's parents also fell under the prohibition. In various pagan cultures infirm parents were abandoned to wild animals or otherwise disposed of.

The Centralization of Worship

Traditional interpreters of the Torah aver that the rules, which demand that all sacrifices must be brought to a central sanctuary, anticipate the settlement of Israel in the land. This commentary, however, holds that these regulations are the record of religious developments which took place after the settlement and the results of which the Book of Deuteronomy attempted to codify [6].

In the early days after the conquest, cultic as well as political life was completely decentralized and tribal organizations were the seats of power. With the establishment of the monarchy (just before the year 1000 B.C.E.) a centralized authority began to emerge, but tribal autonomy continued to exist for a long time. In religious matters, too, centralization was slow to come. People worshiped at local shrines, and often they would adopt cultic practices devoted to the local deity and combine them with the worship of Israel's God. This was natural, for there was a belief common to the peoples of the ancient Near East that the gods of a country could not be ignored with impunity. A syncretistic approach to religion—which was prominent especially among the Greeks and, later, the Romans—was a feature of Israel's worship in the early centuries of settlement in Canaan.

In this proliferation of centers, some like Shechem, Shiloh, and Beth-el achieved special status, but they remained local or, at most, regional sanctuaries. With the unification of the tribes under David and the establishment of Jerusalem as the political center of the nation, the drive toward religious centralization also gained strength.[1] In the centuries that followed, unified politics and centralized religious worship became mutually supportive.

However, the process of religious centralization received a setback when the nation split into two kingdoms, Israel and Judah, so that even within Judah (where the Temple of Jerusalem was located) local worship practices persisted and sacrifices continued to be offered at sacred shrines and *bamot* ("heights"). People would come to these various places with their meat and grain offerings and share them with the priestly attendants. In addition, other pagan practices were popular with significant numbers of Israelites, as is shown by the story of the prophet Elijah's contest with four hundred priests of Baal. Toward the latter part of the eighth century King Hezekiah abolished the *bamot*, but they were reintroduced by Manasseh (II Kings 21:3), until Josiah did away with them once and for all (II Kings 23). It was under his rule that the text of a book was found which scholars generally identify with Deuteronomy or its prototype. The text became normative for the cult and called for centralized worship as the will of God. As a concession, the eating of meat was permitted outside the sanctuary, but Jerusalem and its Temple, built by King Solomon three hundred thirty-five years before, became thereafter the focal point of the people's political and religious existence.[2]

---

[1] From what political foundations this unification developed is a matter of scholarly dispute. One theory posits a league (amphictyony) based at first on six "Leah" tribes, which were later—after the arrival of the "Joseph" group from Egypt—expanded into a twelve-member league. David placed his central shrine in Jerusalem because it was neutral territory and therefore less likely to have tribal opposition. Opponents of this theory point to the absence of any mention of the league in the books of Judges and Samuel, and to the purely hypothetical nature of the "Leah" group [7].

[2] Jerusalem is not mentioned in Deuteronomy or the rest of the Torah. Only after the Deuteronomic reform (see introduction) was this central worship place firmly ensconced in the Jerusalemic Temple.

Blood and Meat

Three times the Torah deals with the non-sacrificial, everyday consumption of meat (Gen. 9:4; Lev., chapter 17; Deut. 12:20 ff.). Clearly, these passages reveal a development of attitudes, but precisely what this development was is a matter of scholarly controversy.[3]

The eating of animal flesh is probably a late stage in human evolution. Originally humanity was vegetarian; the Creation account reflects this in that it permits the consumption of plants but is silent on animals, which are specifically allowed only after the Flood (Gen. 1:29; 9:4). The idea persisted that blood was the seat of life and had a mysterious quality, and that therefore it was not to be eaten under any circumstances. It was to be poured on the ground where primal earth received it back, or dashed against the altar where, so to speak, God himself accepted it. Only in the latter case could the meat be consumed, for the altar was God's table, where the food could be shared with Him through His representatives. Thus, all slaughter for food had to be sacral in nature.[4]

This rule was feasible as long as sacrifices could be brought to local shrines accessible to the people. But, when the cult was centralized in the Deuteronomic reformation, provision had to be made for those who could not reach the sanctuary to consume meat in a non-sacral way. Such profane slaughter—limited to animals unfit for sacrifice—was therefore now permitted (12:15).

This in turn led to the practice of draining blood from the profanely slaughtered animal to the greatest degree possible, which in post-biblical days resulted in elaborate rules for ritual slaughtering (*shechitah*), and the washing, salting, and soaking of meat prior to eating it [11].

When the Temple was destroyed in 586 B.C.E. these rules lapsed, and when the exiles returned to Palestine they may have reinstituted local shrines where sacrifices could be offered. After the rebuilding of the Temple this proliferation of worship places conflicted once again with the needs of the central authority, and in time the old Deuteronomic rules were reasserted and remained in force during the existence of the Second Temple, until it was burned by the Romans in the year 70 C.E. Thereafter, rabbinic law created a body of rules that prescribe precisely what constitutes *kasher* (that is, ritually clean or permissible) meat.[5]

Do Not Inquire

The Torah states in Deut. 12:30 that Israelites are not to inquire about pagan religions and ask, "How did those nations worship their gods?" Such inquiry, it was feared, might lead to imitative idolatrous practices. If Israel was to be purged from paganism, it was best to prohibit the very knowledge of such dangerous ways. This intellectual isolation led in time to a concept of non-Israelite and, later, non-Jewish religions that was not always in consonance with the facts. In this way, it has been suggested, the Torah itself

---

[3] For a detailed analysis, see our Commentary on Leviticus, chapter 17 and H. C. Brichto's study of slaughter, sacrifice, blood, and atonement [8].

[4] According to Brichto, "slaughter on other than a duly designated altar, thus failing acknowledgment of God's lordship over all life, constituted a taboo" [9]. Jacob Milgrom finds the use of the term זבח to offer a clue to the question when and how Deuteronomy

was composed. Elsewhere in the Torah and in cognate languages זבח bears a sacral connotation; but now, in Deut. 12:15 and 21, it is used for profane occasions as well because such slaughter had been previously the custom in northern Israel [10].

[5] For the Reform view on *kashrut*, see commentaries on Deut. 14:1–15:23, "Dietary Law," and on Lev. 11:1–23.

came to view Canaanite worship in a one-dimensional way and decried it as a complete abomination in the eyes of God. The purpose of this view was clear: In order to establish God as the Supreme Ruler of Israel, all other religious practices and ideologies were ruled out of bounds and their very knowledge considered inadmissible [12].

In the history of nations such protectionism has often been the policy of religious as well as political orthodoxies. Thus, the Inquisition proscribed certain books as dangerous to the Catholic faith and created an Index which, in theory at least, exists to this day. The traditional view of the Torah law under discussion has been that it was instituted as a temporary educational measure needed until the worship of God was firmly established. But, in effect, this protective approach remained operative in postbiblical times as well. A number of "unorthodox" books were excluded from the official biblical canon and of most of them no Hebrew originals survive. They were probably destroyed; some are known to us in other languages (mostly Greek), and of others, perhaps many, no trace remains. Even today, certain Orthodox Jewish communities attempt to isolate their members from access to non-Orthodox writings—both Jewish and non-Jewish; and a strictly Orthodox Jew will not enter a church for any reason whatsoever, lest such a visit violate the injunction "Do not inquire about their gods."

Liberal Jews—like liberals in general—take a different view: they consider the biblical law as no longer applicable in the modern context. They affirm the independence of the human spirit and the freedom of intellectual inquiry. To be sure, unlimited inquiry carries certain risks, but these are worth the price, for the freedom of knowledge is, for liberals, a requisite for a fully free human existence.

GLEANINGS

Inside and Outside

The Torah instructs us about laws which we are to "observe in the land . . ." (12:1). From this you might gather that all commandments are valid only in Eretz Yisrael—therefore the verse says "as long as you live on earth."[6] From this you might conclude that all commandments are valid both inside and outside Eretz Yisrael—hence it says "observe in the land." Since the rule both includes and excludes, one must look at the context. Matters that are personal (such as the prohibition of idolatry) must be observed everywhere, while others (such as the erasure of idolatry) relate only to the Land. MIDRASH [13]

Utterly

The Hebrew prescription of verse 2 ("You must destroy all the sites") carries an emphasis which might be rendered "You must destroy *utterly* all the sites." From this we learn that when idolatry is to be uprooted it is to be done root and branch. TALMUD [14]

Halachah

Verse 3 prescribes that the names of the pagan gods are to be obliterated, and verse 4 that God (and, by implication, His name) is to be treated differently. These verses became the proof texts for a number of halachic rules, known as the rules of מוֹחֵק (*mochek*, erasing).

Thus, books containing God's name were not to be destroyed but either to be buried or to be stored away (hence the preservation of many ancient manuscripts in storage places called *genizot*).

Further, the Divine Name, once written, must not be erased. A prefix may be erased (as in לַיהוָה), but not a suffix (as in אֱלֹהֶיךָ). Seven divine names fall under this rule: יְהוָה (YHVH), אֲדֹנָי (Adonai), אֵל (El), אֱלֹהַּ (Eloha), אֱלֹהִים (Elohim), שַׁדַּי (Shaddai), and צְבָאוֹת (Tzeva-ot, though, strictly speaking, this is not a divine name). SHULCHAN ARUCH [15]

Eating Flesh

Although humans have unlimited rule over animals, they must restrain themselves from enjoying "the life" of the animal (that is, its blood). We need special strength for this restraint, hence verse 23 says רַק חֲזַק, which literally means "only be strong." D. HOFFMANN [16]

The Levite

(Verse 19 admonishes Israel not to neglect the Levites.) They are the living nerves and arteries coming out from the centerpoint of the sanctuary by means of which the members are kept in spiritual connection with the brain and heart of the nation. They are the representatives of the sanctuary of the Torah in the midst of the people. Amongst a nation actively engaged in agriculture, cattle breeding, and the industries associated with them, such unproductive members of the community as the Levites could easily fall into disrepute, be looked on as a burden to the community, and remain unrespected and undervalued in their vital importance for the spiritual, moral, and national well-being of the nation. Hence the repeated admonition not to neglect the Levite; the duration of your remaining on your own soil is essentially dependent on the esteem and respect you give the Levite, and the influence you allow him to have on your spiritual and moral development. S. R. HIRSCH [17]

---

[6] The Midrash thus translates the end of verse 1, as does our version. Another rendering is "as long as you live in that land." The Hebrew text permits either interpretation.

False Prophets

The section before us deals with *the* basic problem in prophecy: how to distinguish between the authentic and inauthentic address. The Torah both accepts and rejects what would appear to be the obvious test: Are the prophecies realized as predicted or not?[1] It was clear that even a pretender could chance on a proper anticipation of the future, and in that case how would one know whether the prophets derived their inspiration from God, their own imagination, or from a demonic source? The question itself precluded an unambiguous answer. Even so, there had to be some criterion that would enable the people to distinguish between true and false prophecy. The Torah suggests that the dividing line between the two was loyalty to God. Negatively, if the pretending prophet counseled disobedience of the divine command or even idolatry, then he was *ipso facto* a pretender, regardless of the accuracy of his predictions. Positively, only someone remaining within the ambience of the mitzvot could be considered a true *navi*—but this was where the question rested. After all, an ultimate test of authenticity could be secured only by a divine proclamation, heard by all the people, which would designate a certain person to be God's true servant to whom one needed to listen. Postbiblical Jewish tradition was greatly intrigued by the intractability of the problem and attempted to elucidate what the Torah itself had left vague.[2]

---

[1] Deut. 18:21–22 versus 13:3. While these passages likely came from two different traditions, their juxtaposition in the Torah underlines the ambiguities of prophecy.

[2] In postbiblical times, chapter 13 served, for Jews, as a warning against heresies and, for Christians, as veiled predictions of the appearance of Jesus.

The section falls into three parts. The first deals with the signs a prophet might give; the second, with the possibility that close relatives might lead one astray; and the third, with the fate to be visited on a whole community that has defected. In the last instance, the punishment was to be extreme: total extermination, including even the cattle.

In the notations that follow, the numbers in double brackets refer to the versions where our verse 1 is their 12:32 (as explained previously); thus, 13:2] [1] means that in our text the sentence is in verse 2, in other versions it is in verse 1.

יְהֹוָה אֱלֹהֵיכֶם תֵּלֵכוּ וְאֹתוֹ תִירָאוּ וְאֶת־מִצְוֹתָיו
תִּשְׁמֹרוּ וּבְקֹלוֹ תִשְׁמָעוּ וְאֹתוֹ תַעֲבֹדוּ וּבוֹ תִדְבָּקוּן:
וְהַנָּבִיא הַהוּא אוֹ חֹלֵם הַחֲלוֹם הַהוּא יוּמָת כִּי
דִבֶּר־סָרָה עַל־יְהֹוָה אֱלֹהֵיכֶם הַמּוֹצִיא אֶתְכֶם מֵאֶרֶץ
מִצְרַיִם וְהַפֹּדְךָ מִבֵּית עֲבָדִים לְהַדִּיחֲךָ מִן־הַדֶּרֶךְ
אֲשֶׁר צִוְּךָ יְהֹוָה אֱלֹהֶיךָ לָלֶכֶת בָּהּ וּבִעַרְתָּ הָרָע
מִקִּרְבֶּךָ: ס   כִּי יְסִיתְךָ אָחִיךָ בֶן־אִמֶּךָ אוֹ־בִנְךָ

ב כִּי־יָקוּם בְּקִרְבְּךָ נָבִיא אוֹ חֹלֵם חֲלוֹם וְנָתַן אֵלֶיךָ
ג אוֹת אוֹ מוֹפֵת: וּבָא הָאוֹת וְהַמּוֹפֵת אֲשֶׁר־דִּבֶּר
אֵלֶיךָ לֵאמֹר נֵלְכָה אַחֲרֵי אֱלֹהִים אֲחֵרִים אֲשֶׁר
ד לֹא־יְדַעְתָּם וְנָעָבְדֵם: לֹא תִשְׁמַע אֶל־דִּבְרֵי הַנָּבִיא
הַהוּא אוֹ אֶל־חוֹלֵם הַחֲלוֹם הַהוּא כִּי מְנַסֶּה יְהֹוָה
אֱלֹהֵיכֶם אֶתְכֶם לָדַעַת הֲיִשְׁכֶם אֹהֲבִים אֶת־יְהֹוָה
ה אֱלֹהֵיכֶם בְּכָל־לְבַבְכֶם וּבְכָל־נַפְשְׁכֶם: אַחֲרֵי

*ה קמץ בז"ק.   *ו קמץ ברביעי

2] If there appears among you a prophet or a dream-diviner and he gives you a sign or a portent, **3]** saying, "Let us follow and worship another god"—whom you have not experienced—even if the sign or portent that he named to you comes true, **4]** do not heed the words of that prophet or that dream-diviner. For the LORD your God is testing you to see whether you really love the LORD your God with all your heart and soul. **5]** Follow none but the LORD your God, and revere none but Him; observe His commandments alone, and heed only His orders; worship none but Him, and hold fast to Him. **6]** As for that prophet or dream-diviner, he shall be put to death; for he urged disloyalty to the LORD your God—who freed you from the land of Egypt and who redeemed you from the house of bondage—to make you stray from the path that the LORD your God commanded you to follow. Thus you will sweep out evil from your midst.

7] If your brother, your own mother's son, or your son or daughter, or the wife of your

13:2] [1] *Prophet.* The Hebrew נָבִיא (navi) probably is related to the Akkadian nabû, to call, to summon. Akkadian kings were frequently described as "summoned" by a god, and in this sense the Hebrew may be meant (i.e., navi would be a passive participle). But some believe navi to be an active participle, and hence to have the meaning "speaker" or "announcer" (of God's message, not his own, though he phrases his master's thoughts) [1].

The English "prophet" derives from the Greek prophetes, meaning one who speaks out for a god. The popular understanding that a prophet is one who foretells the future does therefore not properly describe the full meaning of the term. The navi received his message in many ways, such as in dreams or visions or by direct address, but only Moses, Israel's foremost prophet, regularly communicated face to face with the Divine (Num. 12:6–8).

Dream-diviner. An accepted profession in Egypt (see our commentary on Gen. 39:1–40:23,

"Dreams"). Though its practitioners existed in Israel it did not gain the approbation of the Torah. (While Joseph and Daniel did interpret dreams, they did so only ad hoc, at the behest of foreign potentates.)

3] [2] *Experienced.* The word יָדַע is here used in its widest sense; more than intellectual knowledge is involved. See Deut. 11:28.

6] [5] *Put to death.* The manner of execution is not specified. The Rabbis ruled that it was to be by stoning [2].

Disloyalty. The Hebrew סָרָה derives either from סָרַר (to be defiant; as in Deut. 21:18) or סוּר (to stray).

Sweep out evil. An expression characteristic of Deuteronomy.

7] [6] *Your own mother's son.* Who, in biblical times, was the true "blood brother." Sister and brother who had a mother in common could not marry, but, if they had only a father in common,

אוֹ־בִתְּךָ֩ אוֹ־אֵ֨שֶׁת חֵיקֶ֜ךָ אוֹ רֵֽעֲךָ֗ אֲשֶׁ֣ר כְּנַפְשְׁךָ֘   יֹּ   מֵאֶ֤רֶץ מִצְרַ֙יִם֙ מִבֵּ֣ית עֲבָדִ֔ים וְכָל־יִשְׂרָאֵ֖ל יִשְׁמְע֣וּ

בַּסֵּ֣תֶר לֵאמֹ֑ר נֵֽלְכָ֗ה וְנַֽעַבְדָה֙ אֱלֹהִ֣ים אֲחֵרִ֔ים אֲשֶׁר֙   וְיִרָא֑וּן וְלֹֽא־יוֹסִ֣פוּ לַֽעֲשׂ֗וֹת כַּדָּבָ֥ר הָרָ֛ע הַזֶּ֖ה

לֹ֤א יָדַ֙עְתָּ֙ אַתָּ֣ה וַאֲבֹתֶ֔יךָ: מֵֽאֱלֹהֵ֣י הָֽעַמִּ֗ים אֲשֶׁר֙   יג   בְּקִרְבֶּֽךָ: ס   כִּֽי־תִשְׁמַ֞ע בְּאַחַ֣ת עָרֶ֗יךָ אֲשֶׁר֩ יְהֹוָ֨ה

סְבִיבֹ֣תֵיכֶ֔ם הַקְּרֹבִ֣ים אֵלֶ֔יךָ א֖וֹ הָֽרְחֹקִ֣ים מִמֶּ֑ךָּ מִקְצֵ֥ה   יד   אֱלֹהֶ֛יךָ נֹתֵ֥ן לְךָ֖ לָשֶׁ֣בֶת שָׁ֑ם לֵאמֹֽר: יָֽצְא֞וּ אֲנָשִׁ֤ים

הָאָ֖רֶץ וְעַד־קְצֵ֥ה הָאָֽרֶץ: לֹֽא־תֹאבֶ֣ה ל֗וֹ וְלֹ֤א תִשְׁמַ֤ע   טו   בְּנֵֽי־בְלִיַּ֙עַל֙ מִקִּרְבֶּ֔ךָ וַיַּדִּ֛יחוּ אֶת־יֹֽשְׁבֵ֥י עִירָ֖ם לֵאמֹ֑ר

אֵלָ֔יו וְלֹֽא־תָח֤וֹס עֵֽינְךָ֙ עָלָ֔יו וְלֹֽא־תַחְמֹ֖ל וְלֹֽא־תְכַסֶּ֥ה   נֵֽלְכָ֗ה וְנַֽעַבְדָ֛ה אֱלֹהִ֥ים אֲחֵרִ֖ים אֲשֶׁ֥ר לֹֽא־יְדַעְתֶּֽם:

עָלָֽיו: כִּ֤י הָרֹג֙ תַּֽהַרְגֶ֔נּוּ יָֽדְךָ֛ תִּֽהְיֶה־בּ֥וֹ בָרִֽאשׁוֹנָ֖ה   טו   וְדָֽרַשְׁתָּ֧ וְחָֽקַרְתָּ֛ וְשָֽׁאַלְתָּ֖ הֵיטֵ֑ב וְהִנֵּ֤ה אֱמֶת֙ נָכ֣וֹן

לַֽהֲמִית֑וֹ וְיַ֥ד כָּל־הָעָ֖ם בָּאַֽחֲרֹנָֽה: וּסְקַלְתּ֥וֹ בָֽאֲבָנִ֖ים   הַדָּבָ֔ר נֶֽעֶשְׂתָ֛ה הַתּֽוֹעֵבָ֥ה הַזֹּ֖את בְּקִרְבֶּֽךָ: הַכֵּ֣ה תַכֶּ֗ה

וָמֵ֑ת כִּ֣י בִקֵּ֗שׁ לְהַדִּֽיחֲךָ֙ מֵעַל֙ יְהֹוָ֣ה אֱלֹהֶ֔יךָ הַמּֽוֹצִיאֲךָ֣   אֶת־יֹֽשְׁבֵ֞י הָעִ֤יר הַהִוא֙ לְפִי־חָ֔רֶב הַֽחֲרֵ֥ם אֹתָ֛הּ וְאֶת־

bosom, or your closest friend entices you in secret, saying, "Come let us worship other gods"— whom neither you nor your fathers have experienced— **8]** from among the gods of the peoples around you, either near to you or distant, anywhere from one end of the earth to the other: **9]** do not assent or give heed to him. Show him no pity or compassion, and do not shield him; **10]** but take his life. Let your hand be the first against him to put him to death, and the hand of the rest of the people thereafter. **11]** Stone him to death, for he sought to make you stray from the LORD your God, who brought you out of the land of Egypt, out of the house of bondage. **12]** Thus all Israel will hear and be afraid, and such evil things will not be done again in your midst.

13] If you hear it said, of one of the towns that the LORD your God is giving you to dwell in, **14]** that some scoundrels from among you have gone and subverted the inhabitants of their town, saying "Come let us worship other gods"—whom you have not experienced— **15]** you shall investigate and inquire and interrogate thoroughly. If it is true, the fact is established—that abhorrent thing was perpetrated in your midst— **16]** put the inhabitants of that town to the sword and put its cattle to the sword. Doom it and all that is in it to

they could (as Tamar suggested to her half brother Amnon in David's time, II Sam. 13:13).

The Samaritan version reads, "the son of your father or the son of your mother."

9] [8] *Do not shield him.* As you ordinarily would shield a relative.

10] [9] *Take his life.* After due trial [3].

A number of scholars, following the Septuagint, emend הָרֹג תַּֽהַרְגֶנּוּ to הַגֵּד תַּגִּידוּ: "but report him" [4].

Let your hand be the first. As in the case of witnesses, Deut. 17:7.

11] [10] *Stone him.* Considered the most severe form of punishment, commensurate with the offense of idolatry.

14] [13] *Scoundrels.* בְּנֵֽי־בְלִיַּעַל (bene veliya-al). The term is not a proper name, as the King James Version and Christian Scriptures suggest [5].

15] [14] *Investigate . . . inquire . . . interrogate.* From this verse, and from 17:4 and 19:18, the Rabbis established that seven questions were to be asked of witnesses in criminal cases [6].

16] [15] *Put . . . to the sword.* A proper idiomatic translation of לְפִי־חָרֶב; the King James Version rendered literally, "to the edge of the sword," whence the English idiom.

Doom it. See at 7:2. The town that had offended against God was forfeited to Him. However, there is no record that such a case ever occurred in Israel's history. (See also Gleanings.)

רַחֲמִים וְרִחַמְךָ וְהִרְבֶּךָ כַּאֲשֶׁר נִשְׁבַּע לַאֲבֹתֶיךָ: ‏ כָּל־אֲשֶׁר־בָּהּ וְאֶת־בְּהֶמְתָּהּ לְפִי־חָרֶב: וְאֶת־כָּל־

יט כִּי תִשְׁמַע בְּקוֹל יְהוָה אֱלֹהֶיךָ לִשְׁמֹר אֶת־כָּל־ שְׁלָלָהּ תִּקְבֹּץ אֶל־תּוֹךְ רְחֹבָהּ וְשָׂרַפְתָּ בָאֵשׁ אֶת־הָעִיר

מִצְוֹתָיו אֲשֶׁר אָנֹכִי מְצַוְּךָ הַיּוֹם לַעֲשׂוֹת הַיָּשָׁר בְּעֵינֵי וְאֶת־כָּל־שְׁלָלָהּ כָּלִיל לַיהוָה אֱלֹהֶיךָ וְהָיְתָה תֵּל

יְהוָה אֱלֹהֶיךָ: ‏ עוֹלָם לֹא תִבָּנֶה עוֹד: וְלֹא־יִדְבַּק בְּיָדְךָ מְאוּמָה

מִן־הַחֵרֶם לְמַעַן יָשׁוּב יְהוָה מֵחֲרוֹן אַפּוֹ וְנָתַן־לְךָ

destruction: **17]** gather all its spoil into the open square, and burn the town and all its spoil as a holocaust to the LORD your God. And it shall remain an everlasting ruin, never to be rebuilt. **18]** Let nothing that has been doomed stick to your hand, in order that the LORD may turn from His blazing anger and show you compassion, and in His compassion increase you as He promised your fathers on oath— **19]** for you will be heeding the LORD your God, obeying all His commandments which I enjoin upon you this day, doing what is right in the sight of the LORD your God.

17] [16] *An everlasting ruin.* תֵּל עוֹלָם (*tel olam*). *Tel*, like its cognates in Akkadian (*tillu*) and Arabic (*tel* or *tal*), means heap or mound but was applied particularly to the characteristic man-made hills which to this day dot the surface of the entire Near East and constitute the superimposed strata of successive levels of human occupation at any given site, each leveled after destruction by natural or human agency. The term generally identifies archeological sites in Arabic-speaking countries (e.g. Tel el Amarna in Egypt), but Tel Aviv (lit-erally, "Mound of Spring") in Israel is named after the Babylonian city mentioned by Ezekiel (3:15; cf. Ezra 2:59 and Nehemiah 7:61).

18] [17] *Stick to your hand.* As with Achan ben Carmi and associates, an incident that nearly en-gulfed all the people in disaster (Josh. 7:1 ff.).

Turn from His blazing anger. Kindled by the city's transgression.

And show you compassion. The whole nation has become infected by the idolatry of one of its cities and therefore stands in need of God's mercy.

Prophets

One must be careful to distinguish between the original meaning of *navi* and the overtones which the accepted and common translation "prophet" has given it (see above, at verse 2). Moses, as Israel's first and most important *navi*, was primarily the announcer and interpreter of the divine will, and only in the later chapters of the book does he speak to the people of their future.

The Bible has no special word to describe a false prophet; both the true servant of God and the pretender are called *navi*.[1] The absence of a clearly distinct terminology reflects the basic difficulty of distinguishing between the two, and in fact farther on (18:21) the Torah formulates the anticipated question: "And should you ask yourselves, 'How can we know that the oracle was not spoken by the Lord?'" The text then proceeds to give the answer: If the future bears out the *navi*'s words, he is authentic (provided he remains within the ambience of the mitzvot), and, if it does not, he is a pretender. This appears to be the basic guideline, and, as chapter 13 makes clear, there are exceptions and cautions which are not easy to apply. Also, even if in the course of time a prediction does come true, how can the hearer know this at the time the prophecy is made? (The case of Hananiah illustrates this problem.[2]) And, to complicate matters even further, authentic prophets too occasionally prove to be wide of the mark. (See, for instance, Zechariah's prediction of Zerubbabel's success, which was not borne out in subsequent history; Zech. 4:6–7.) Not surprisingly, then, the Torah supplies an ambiguous answer to the problem, and, in the end, the good sense of the people must be relied on to clarify the matter.

In order to understand the Torah texts properly it is important to keep in mind that the true business of prophecy was not to predict the future but to confront Israel with the consequences of various alternatives [7]. Further, one must distinguish between the *theory* of the Deuteronomic laws and their practical *application*. In theory, there were the tests of which the text speaks, but, in practice, biblical prophecy usually disregarded them, for it was the larger message which needed to be borne out by experience rather than the details.[3]

Still, there are subsidiary questions raised by the text. For instance, how could a false prophet perform "signs and portents" in the first instance? A number of answers were suggested by tradition:

1. Such a prophet was once a true *navi* but subsequently defected, like Hananiah ben Azzur (Jer. 28) [9].

2. The pretender imitates the true *navi* and "steals his words" [10].

3. There are many who can make accurate

---

[1] The Septuagint introduces the term *pseudoprophetes*, and rabbinic literature speaks of נְבִיאֵי שֶׁקֶר (*nevi-e sheker*), "falsehood purveyors."

[2] Jer. 28. Jeremiah himself, in opposing Hananiah, had therefore no way of disproving the latter's predictions on the spot. The dramatic tests in which Moses (Num. 16) and Elijah (I Kings 18) engaged remain rare exceptions. Equally rare was the application of the criterion set up by Deut. 13. The inauthentic prophet generally spoke as if God himself had sent him; he did not speak in a strange god's name (exceptions are found in I Kings 18; Jer. 2:8; 23:13).

[3] Both in principle and practice, Deuteronomic credentials of prophecy differed from Babylonian mantic. The latter's predictions could not be disproved by experience—at worst, the observations on which such predictions were based might require refinement. It is also noteworthy that, while biblical credentials could (at least in theory) claim total accuracy, moderns would be highly uncomfortable with and suspicious of such "uncanny" prediction [8].

predictions on the basis of natural observation [11].

4. Some people have certain clairvoyant powers [12].

Why were these problems altogether raised by and included in the text? Did they reflect a contemporary set of circumstances which made the guidelines in chapters 13 and 18 necessary? Among the suggestions identifying the historical life situation for these passages (the "Sitz im Leben") are these:

1. There was a religious offensive by Canaanite prophets in the ninth century B.C.E., the time of Elijah (I Kings 18:19).

2. The Baal priests of Samaria undertook a drive for expanded influence at a later time (II Kings 10:23).

3. The Torah seeks to counter the consequences of the Assyrian conquest of the northern kingdom, which introduced heathen practices on a wide scale (after 722 B.C.E.).

The ambiguities which the passages on the false prophets present may be said to be inherent in every case when humans experience—or believe they experience—a contact with the Divine. How could Jacob tell at first whether it was a demon or an angel who was confronting him in the middle of the night? And on what did he base his judgment when he says afterward that it had been a divine being (Gen. 32:31)? God's presence is elusive, and those who say they speak in His name must be tested by their whole message, their proven loyalties, and their character—and even then we may reach the wrong conclusions. Ultimately it must be the people, in their ongoing history, who will distinguish true from false.

GLEANINGS

A Case of Medieval Censorship

A comment on verse 2 by the Baal ha-Turim[4] led to an interesting intervention by the Christian censor. Israel is warned against a false prophet "among you" (בְּקִרְבְּךָ). Said the Baal ha-Turim: "This, by way of gematria [13], hints at 'that woman' (זוּ הָאִשָּׁה; in both cases the sum of letters amounts to 324)." This was the commentator's way of referring to Mary, mother of Jesus.

He then applied the same method to the words "among you a prophet" (בְּקִרְבְּךָ נָבִיא) and continued: "This hints at 'the woman and her son' (זוּ הָאִשָּׁה וּבְנָהּ; in both cases the sum is 387)."

The censor caught the comment, which implied that Jesus was one of the false prophets, and excised everything after the words, "This by way of gematria . . ." and in this way—bereft of all meaning—subsequent editions of the Baal ha-Turim's comment were printed thereafter.[5]

Signs and Portents

According to my religious teaching, miracles are not the distinguishing marks of Truth and do not provide moral certainty about the divine mission of the prophet. For seducers and false prophets too can perform signs, whether through magic, secret arts, or perhaps a misuse of a gift given to them for a good purpose. MOSES MENDELSSOHN [14]

---

[4] Jacob ben Asher; he is called "Baal ha-Turim" because of his great halachic work, the *Arba-ah Turim.*

[5] So to this day the most popular of all rabbinic Bibles, the *Mikra'ot Gedolot.* A similar reference to Jesus was also seen to be implied in verse 7, which speaks of "your own mother's son" but does not mention the father.

The Lord . . . Is Testing You (verse 4)

The victorious spread and world dominion of Christianity were at all times a testing for Israel's loyalty to and affection for God and His Torah. Israel has persisted and, in the future, will not waver in its faith.　　　　　D. HOFFMANN [15]

Falsifiers

Even as one who falsifies *human* words (i.e., as a witness in a court case) is guilty of death, how much more so is one who falsifies *divine* words.
　　　　　　　　　　　　　　　　　MIDRASH [16]

Punishment

The Rabbis explained the references to false prophets in chapters 13 and 18 as follows:

A false prophet is one who prophesies what he has not heard and what was not spoken to him; he is executed by man.[6] But one who suppresses his prophecy (like Jonah) or one who ignores the words of a prophet,[7] or a prophet who violates his own words,[8]—his death is caused by Heaven, as it is said, "I Myself will call him to account" (Deut. 18:19).　　　　　MISHNAH [18]

One and Many

The injunction in verse 5 (not to follow other gods) is couched in the plural, and in Deut. 10:20 in the singular. There are times when defection from God remains a personal matter, but in times of upheaval the whole community is affected and one must act as part of it to save the religion.
　　　　　　　　　　　　　　　　　CHASIDIC [19]

Far and Near

The Hebrew for "Follow . . . the Lord" (verse 5) reads literally "Go *after* the Lord," using the term אַחֲרֵי for "after." This is used when the object is far, and אַחַר when it is near. Why then is אַחַר

not used here when one is asked to be close to God?

Because only when one walks אַחֲרֵי God, deeming oneself far from Him, does one merit to be close.　　　　　　　　　　　　CHASIDIC [20]

How?

Is it really possible to "follow" God, who is described (Deut. 9:3) as a "devouring fire"? Rather, you should follow His attributes: as He clothes the naked, so must you; as He visits the sick, comforts the mourners, and buries the dead, so must you.　　　　　　　　　　　　TALMUD [21]

Jerusalem

The holy city was not included in the expression "one of the towns" (verse 13), for Jerusalem was established first and foremost as God's habitation, not man's.　　　　　RASHI [22]

(According to the Talmud, this is one of ten distinctions of Jerusalem [23].)

Never

The destruction of a whole community because of idolatry (verses 13 ff.) never occurred nor will it ever occur. The sole purpose of the warning is that it might be studied and that one might receive reward for such study.　　　TOSEFTA [24]

Not to Heed

Anyone who summons us to violate the Torah, adducing signs and wonders in his favor, even if he causes the sun, moon, and stars to stand still as in the days of Joshua, we must pay no heed to him. Whatever success attends him, whatever wealth, honor, and praise he enjoys, we are not to believe his message or subscribe to his teachings, since truth cannot be established by miracles or any visual spectacle.　　　N. LEIBOWITZ [25]

---

[6] The former case is illustrated by Zedekiah ben Chenaanah (I Kings 22:11) and the latter by Hananiah (Jer. 28:1 ff.) [17].

[7] See I Kings 20:35-36.　　[8] See I Kings 13.

Of Food, Tithes, and Social Equity

Israel is to become "a kingdom of priests and a holy nation" (Exod. 19:6). The Torah stresses time and again that this end can be reached only if the people acquire a state of purity and create a society of justice, equity, and love. The section before us deals with pathways that lead to this goal and makes it clear that ritual (the method of Israel's striving for purity) and ethics are two equally necessary approaches, for one sustains the other. Ritual acts serve as the framework of ethical behavior, and ethical impulses are in constant need of symbolic reinforcements. Thus, there is a natural relationship between laws of ritual cleanliness in eating and the rules of tithing that govern the nation's care for the Levites and the poor.

Most of the laws in this segment have been stated elsewhere in the Torah. The dietary rules especially and those dealing with the year of remission have been dealt with extensively in Leviticus.* Particular note will, however, be made of the biblical and postbiblical aversion to the swine.

In general, the Deuteronomic emphasis, as revealed in this section, is both on personal holiness (for we must always remember that we are children of God, verse 1) and on humanitarian concerns (for as His children we are responsible for others). This double perspective governs the Jewish understanding of *tzedakah*, its reasons and its benefits (see commentary on 16:18–18:8, "The Pursuit of Justice").

* See commentary on Lev. 11:1–23; 25:1–55; and Appendix I.

פַּרְסָה וְשֹׁסַעַת שֶׁסַע שְׁתֵּי פְרָסוֹת מַעֲלַת גֵּרָה   בָּנִים אַתֶּם לַיהוָה אֱלֹהֵיכֶם לֹא תִתְגֹּדְדוּ וְלֹא־

בַּבְּהֵמָה אֹתָהּ תֹּאכֵלוּ: אַךְ אֶת־זֶה לֹא תֹאכְלוּ   תָשִׂימוּ קָרְחָה בֵּין עֵינֵיכֶם לָמֵת: כִּי עַם קָדוֹשׁ אַתָּה

מִמַּעֲלֵי הַגֵּרָה וּמִמַּפְרִיסֵי הַפַּרְסָה הַשְּׁסוּעָה אֶת־   לַיהוָה אֱלֹהֶיךָ וּבְךָ בָּחַר יְהוָה לִהְיוֹת לוֹ לְעַם

הַגָּמָל וְאֶת־הָאַרְנֶבֶת וְאֶת־הַשָּׁפָן כִּי־מַעֲלֵה גֵרָה   סְגֻלָּה מִכֹּל הָעַמִּים אֲשֶׁר עַל־פְּנֵי הָאֲדָמָה: ס

הֵמָּה וּפַרְסָה לֹא הִפְרִיסוּ טְמֵאִים הֵם לָכֶם: וְאֶת־   לֹא תֹאכַל כָּל־תּוֹעֵבָה: זֹאת הַבְּהֵמָה אֲשֶׁר תֹּאכֵלוּ

הַחֲזִיר כִּי־מַפְרִיס פַּרְסָה הוּא וְלֹא גֵרָה טָמֵא הוּא   שׁוֹר שֵׂה כְשָׂבִים וְשֵׂה עִזִּים: אַיָּל וּצְבִי וְיַחְמוּר

לָכֶם מִבְּשָׂרָם לֹא תֹאכֵלוּ וּבְנִבְלָתָם לֹא תִגָּעוּ: ס   וְאַקּוֹ וְדִישֹׁן וּתְאוֹ וָזָמֶר: וְכָל־בְּהֵמָה מַפְרֶסֶת

1] You are children of the LORD your God. You shall not gash yourselves or shave the front of your heads because of the dead. 2] For you are a people consecrated to the LORD your God: the LORD your God chose you from among all other peoples on earth to be His treasured people.

3] You shall not eat anything abhorrent. 4] These are the animals that you may eat: the ox, the sheep, and the goat; 5] the deer, the gazelle, the roebuck, the wild goat, the ibex, the antelope, the mountain sheep, 6] and any other animal that has true hoofs which are cleft in two and brings up the cud—such you may eat. 7] But the following, which do bring up the cud or have true hoofs which are cleft through, you may not eat: the camel, the hare, and the daman—for although they bring up the cud, they have no true hoofs—they are unclean for you; 8] also the swine—for although it has true hoofs, it does not bring up the cud—is unclean for you. You shall not eat of their flesh or touch their carcasses.

14:1] *Gash yourselves.* Similarly in Lev. 19:28, though with a different Hebrew terminology. Jeremiah makes repeated references to the practice (Jer. 16:6; 41:5; 47:5) [1].

Or shave. Addressed in Lev. 21:5 to the priests only, but here to everybody. In Lev. 19:28 the general rule goes on to forbid the practice of tattooing.

Because of the dead. Apparently these customs were primarily mourning rites.

3] *You shall not eat.* Essentially the same rules as in Lev. 11:2–20.

Abhorrent. The Torah calls certain foods "abhorrent" not because they are naturally abhorrent to humans but because they are prohibited to Israel. Tradition considered the dietary laws to have two main functions: to separate and distinguish Israel from the nations and to sanctify it through special discipline [2]. (See further in Gleanings.) The word תּוֹעֵבָה (to-evah) is generally used to proscribe Canaanite practices [3].

4] *These . . . you may eat.* The permission covers the then most commonly domesticated animals, except pigs and camels, and clearly aims to exclude predators. The text proceeds from individual examples to the general definition, while in Lev. 11:3 only the latter is stated. Scholars differ in their assessment of this difference; some hold it to be due to different sources, others to the proven need for elaboration. Not all the animals enumerated in the text can be identified with certainty, but it may be assumed that the terms described creatures very familiar to the Israelites in Canaan.

5] *Ibex.* A type of wild goat with curved horns.

7] *Hare.* It does not in fact chew the cud, but because of its constant munching appears to do so.

Daman. A shy small animal of the hyrax family. It too gives the appearance of bringing up the cud. The biblical statements are based on the zoological knowledge of the time.

8] *Swine.* The prohibition covers both the wild boar and the domesticated pig. See further commentary below.

ט אֵ֣תָּה תֹּאכְלוּ֮ מִכֹּ֣ל אֲשֶׁ֣ר בַּמָּ֑יִם כֹּ֧ל אֲשֶׁר־ל֛וֹ סְנַפִּ֥יר

י וְקַשְׂקֶ֖שֶׂת תֹּאכֵ֑לוּ וְכֹ֡ל אֲשֶׁ֣ר אֵֽין־לוֹ֩ סְנַפִּ֨יר וְקַשְׂקֶ֜שֶׂת

יא לֹ֣א תֹאכֵ֔לוּ טָמֵ֥א ה֖וּא לָכֶֽם׃ ס כָּל־צִפּ֥וֹר טְהֹרָ֖ה

יב תֹּאכֵֽלוּ׃ וְזֶ֕ה אֲשֶׁ֥ר לֹֽא־תֹאכְל֖וּ מֵהֶ֑ם הַנֶּ֥שֶׁר וְהַפֶּ֖רֶס

יג וְהָֽעָזְנִיָּֽה׃ וְהָרָאָה֙ וְאֶת־הָ֣אַיָּ֔ה וְהַדַּיָּ֖ה לְמִינָֽהּ׃ וְאֶת

יד כָּל־עֹרֵ֖ב לְמִינֽוֹ׃ וְאֵ֤ת בַּ֣ת הַֽיַּעֲנָ֔ה וְאֶת־הַתַּחְמָ֖ס וְאֶת־

טז הַשַּׁ֥חַף וְאֶת־הַנֵּ֖ץ לְמִינֵֽהוּ׃ אֶת־הַכּ֥וֹס וְאֶת־הַיַּנְשׁ֖וּף

יז וְהַתִּנְשָֽׁמֶת׃ וְהַקָּאָ֥ת וְאֶת־הָֽרָחָ֖מָה וְאֶת־הַשָּׁלָֽךְ׃

יח וְהַֽחֲסִידָ֣ה וְהָאֲנָפָ֖ה לְמִינָ֑הּ וְהַדּֽוּכִיפַ֖ת וְהָעֲטַלֵּֽף׃

יט וְכֹל֙ שֶׁ֣רֶץ הָע֔וֹף טָמֵ֥א ה֖וּא לָכֶ֑ם לֹ֖א יֵאָכֵֽלוּ׃ כָּל־

כא עוֹף֥ טָה֖וֹר תֹּאכֵֽלוּ׃ לֹ֣א תֹאכְל֣וּ כָל־נְבֵלָה֮ לַגֵּ֣ר

אֲשֶׁר־בִּשְׁעָרֶ֣יךָ תִּתְּנֶ֣נָּה וַאֲכָלָ֗הּ א֤וֹ מָכֹר֙ לְנָכְרִ֔י כִּ֣י

9] These you may eat of all that live in water: you may eat anything that has fins and scales. **10]** But you may not eat anything that has no fins and scales: it is unclean for you.

11] You may eat any clean bird. **12]** The following you may not eat: the eagle, the vulture, and the black vulture; **13]** the kite, the falcon, and the buzzard of any variety; **14]** every variety of raven; **15]** the ostrich, the nighthawk, the sea gull, and the hawk of any variety; **16]** the little owl, the great owl, and the white owl; **17]** the pelican, the bustard, and the cormorant; **18]** the stork, any variety of heron, the hoopoe, and the bat.

19] All winged swarming things are unclean for you: they may not be eaten. **20]** You may eat only clean winged creatures.

21] You shall not eat anything that has died a natural death; give it to the stranger in your

---

9] *Live in water.* A condensation of Lev. 11:9–12. The reason for the rule is not clear; its application prohibits shell fish, eels, lampreys, and water mammals.

11] *Clean bird.* As in Lev. 11:13–19. What constitutes "clean" is not stated, only the unclean birds are enumerated.

The Rabbis attempted to find general rules that could be said to govern the Torah's distinctions. They considered those birds clean which had an extra talon, a craw, and a detachable stomach lining. As for the prohibitions, the rules seem to aim at excluding all predators, as in the case of mammals. The list of permitted birds nowadays includes chicken, goose, duck, turkey, and varieties of the pigeon family. Other birds, though not prohibited by the Bible, have generally been disallowed by common practice and rabbinic rulings. These rules are not, however, universally observed; thus the house sparrow is permitted in some localities but proscribed in others [4].

12] *The eagle.* The identification of a number of the birds that follow is speculative.

13] *The kite.* This word illustrates the difficulties of the Hebrew text. The translation assumes רָאָה

(ra-ah, a word otherwise unknown) to be a scribal error for דָּאָה (da-ah, Lev. 11:14), for ר and ד are easily mistaken for one another. In that case, what meaning has דַּיָּה (dayah) in the same verse? It is translated as "buzzard" but may be another scribal variant.

15] *The ostrich.* Which survives now only in Africa, but in biblical times apparently inhabited Canaan.

18] *The bat.* Then believed to be a bird [5].

19] *All winged swarming things.* The reference is probably to forbidden varieties of locusts; compare Lev. 11:20–23 and commentary there [6].

21] *Died a natural death.* An animal that was not slaughtered. As with the Torah's dietary rules in general, this too was less a hygienic than a ritual provision, though it did have salubrious side effects.

Give it to the stranger. Who is not part of the ritual community. The נָכְרִי (nochri) is the occasional visitor, while the גֵּר (ger) is a resident alien who does share in a number of ritual occasions; hence the provisions for the ger are different (Lev. 17:15). This distinction between the two kinds of non-Israelites is important, for it makes it clear beyond question that the permission to

עַם קָדוֹשׁ אַתָּה לַיהוָה אֱלֹהֶיךָ לֹא־תְבַשֵּׁל גְּדִי
בַּחֲלֵב אִמּוֹ: פ

כִּי לֹא תוּכַל שְׂאֵתוֹ כִּי־יִרְחַק מִמְּךָ הַמָּקוֹם אֲשֶׁר
יִבְחַר יְהוָה אֱלֹהֶיךָ לָשׂוּם שְׁמוֹ שָׁם כִּי יְבָרֶכְךָ

כב עַשֵּׂר תְּעַשֵּׂר אֵת כָּל־תְּבוּאַת זַרְעֶךָ הַיֹּצֵא הַשָּׂדֶה
כג שָׁנָה שָׁנָה: וְאָכַלְתָּ לִפְנֵי יְהוָה אֱלֹהֶיךָ בַּמָּקוֹם אֲשֶׁר־

כה יְהוָה אֱלֹהֶיךָ: וְנָתַתָּה בַּכָּסֶף וְצַרְתָּ הַכֶּסֶף בְּיָדְךָ
יִבְחַר לְשַׁכֵּן שְׁמוֹ שָׁם מַעְשַׂר דְּגָנְךָ תִּירֹשְׁךָ וְיִצְהָרֶךָ

וְהָלַכְתָּ אֶל־הַמָּקוֹם אֲשֶׁר יִבְחַר יְהוָה אֱלֹהֶיךָ בּוֹ:
וּבְכֹרֹת בְּקָרְךָ וְצֹאנֶךָ לְמַעַן תִּלְמַד לְיִרְאָה אֶת־

כו וְנָתַתָּה הַכֶּסֶף בְּכֹל אֲשֶׁר־תְּאַוֶּה נַפְשְׁךָ בַּבָּקָר
כד יְהוָה אֱלֹהֶיךָ כָּל־הַיָּמִים: וְכִי־יִרְבֶּה מִמְּךָ הַדֶּרֶךְ

וּבַצֹּאן וּבַיַּיִן וּבַשֵּׁכָר וּבְכֹל אֲשֶׁר תִּשְׁאָלְךָ נַפְשֶׁךָ
וְאָכַלְתָּ שָּׁם לִפְנֵי יְהוָה אֱלֹהֶיךָ וְשָׂמַחְתָּ אַתָּה

community to eat, or you may sell it to a foreigner. For you are a people consecrated to the LORD your God.

You shall not boil a kid in its mother's milk.

22] You shall set aside every year a tenth part of all the yield of your sowing that is brought from the field. **23]** You shall consume the tithes of your new grain and wine and oil, and the firstlings of your herds and flocks, in the presence of the LORD your God, in the place where He will choose to establish His name, so that you may learn to revere the LORD your God forever. **24]** Should the distance be too great for you, should you be unable to transport them, because the place where the LORD your God has chosen to establish His name is far from you and because the LORD your God has blessed you, **25]** you may convert them into money. Wrap up the money and take it with you to the place that the LORD your God has chosen, **26]** and spend the money on anything you want—cattle, sheep, wine, or other intoxicant, or anything you may desire. And you shall feast there, in the presence of the LORD your God, and rejoice with your household.

give the *nochri* meat from a dead but not slaughtered animal was purely ritual in nature. The *nochri*, as a religious outsider, could receive food that was ritually unfit for the Israelite, even as the former was allowed to eat pork but the latter was not.

You shall not boil. This prohibition occurs twice more in the Torah, and in exactly the same formulation (Exod. 23:19, 34:26; see there for commentary). The purpose of the law is not clear; it probably was to counteract certain idolatrous practices. Rabbinic Judaism developed the command into a cornerstone of dietary law and saw it as a prohibition of eating milk and meat products together—a meaning entirely extraneous to the text.

22] *Tenth part.* The tithe; the English word derives from Old English *teogothian,* "tenth." See commentary below.

Of all the yield. Commentators differed on the extent of the command. Some took verse 22 to state an all-inclusive principle; others saw it limited by verse 23 and therefore applicable only to new grain, wine, and oil [7].

23] *And the firstlings.* They are not subject to tithing, but are to be eaten at the sanctuary (Deut. 12:17–18).

24] *Because the Lord . . . has blessed you.* With abundant crops.

26] *Other intoxicant.* שֵׁכָר (*shechar;* whence the word *shikor,* drunk). Drinking alcohol in moderation was approved, but incontinence was strongly condemned. Thus, Isaiah castigates those "who chase liquor from early in the morning" (Isa. 5:11).

שָׁמוֹט כָּל־בַּעַל מַשֵּׁה יָדוֹ אֲשֶׁר יַשֶּׁה בְּרֵעֵהוּ לֹא־
יִגֹּשׂ אֶת־רֵעֵהוּ וְאֶת־אָחִיו כִּי־קָרָא שְׁמִטָּה לַיהוָה:
אֶת־הַנָּכְרִי תִּגֹּשׂ וַאֲשֶׁר יִהְיֶה לְךָ אֶת־אָחִיךָ תַּשְׁמֵט
יָדֶךָ: אֶפֶס כִּי לֹא יִהְיֶה־בְּךָ אֶבְיוֹן כִּי־בָרֵךְ יְבָרֶכְךָ
יְהוָה בָּאָרֶץ אֲשֶׁר יְהוָה אֱלֹהֶיךָ נֹתֵן לְךָ נַחֲלָה
לְרִשְׁתָּהּ: רַק אִם־שָׁמוֹעַ תִּשְׁמַע בְּקוֹל יְהוָה אֱלֹהֶיךָ
לִשְׁמֹר לַעֲשׂוֹת אֶת־כָּל־הַמִּצְוָה הַזֹּאת אֲשֶׁר אָנֹכִי
מְצַוְּךָ הַיּוֹם: כִּי־יְהוָה אֱלֹהֶיךָ בֵּרַכְךָ כַּאֲשֶׁר דִּבֶּר־

כז וּבֵיתֶךָ: וְהַלֵּוִי אֲשֶׁר־בִּשְׁעָרֶיךָ לֹא תַעַזְבֶנּוּ כִּי אֵין
כח לוֹ חֵלֶק וְנַחֲלָה עִמָּךְ: ס מִקְצֵה שָׁלֹשׁ שָׁנִים
     תּוֹצִיא אֶת־כָּל־מַעְשַׂר תְּבוּאָתְךָ בַּשָּׁנָה הַהִוא וְהִנַּחְתָּ
כט בִּשְׁעָרֶיךָ: וּבָא הַלֵּוִי כִּי אֵין־לוֹ חֵלֶק וְנַחֲלָה עִמָּךְ
     וְהַגֵּר וְהַיָּתוֹם וְהָאַלְמָנָה אֲשֶׁר בִּשְׁעָרֶיךָ וְאָכְלוּ וְשָׂבֵעוּ
     לְמַעַן יְבָרֶכְךָ יְהוָה אֱלֹהֶיךָ בְּכָל־מַעֲשֵׂה יָדְךָ אֲשֶׁר
     תַּעֲשֶׂה: ס
טו א מִקֵּץ שֶׁבַע־שָׁנִים תַּעֲשֶׂה שְׁמִטָּה: וְזֶה דְּבַר הַשְּׁמִטָּה

27] But do not neglect the Levite in your community, for he has no hereditary portion as you have.   28] Every third year you shall bring out the full tithe of your yield of that year, but leave it within your settlements.   29] Then the Levite, who has no hereditary portion as you have, and the stranger, the fatherless, and the widow in your settlements shall come and eat their fill, so that the LORD your God may bless you in all the enterprises you undertake.

1] Every seventh year you shall practice remission of debts.   2] This shall be the nature of the remission: every creditor shall remit the due that he claims from his neighbor; he shall not dun his neighbor or kinsman, for the remission proclaimed is of the LORD.   3] You may dun the foreigner; but you must remit whatever is due you from your kinsmen.

4] There shall be no needy among you—since the LORD your God will bless you in the land which the LORD your God is giving you as a hereditary portion—   5] if only you heed the LORD your God and take care to keep all this Instruction that I enjoin upon you this day.   6] For the LORD your God will bless you as He has promised you: you will extend loans

28] *Every third year.* Tradition understood this to mean *"at the end of* every third year"; the sabbatical year—when nothing came in—was omitted from the counting, so that there were two tithing cycles in every seven-year period.

29] *The Levite.* He is listed with the poor, since he has no field allotment of his own.

15:1] *Every seventh year.* Understood as *"at the end of* every seventh year"; parallel to 14:28 [8].
   Remission of debts. The term שְׁמִטָּה (shemitah) has the root meaning "to let drop." The rendering here as "remission of debts" is derived from the context, for shemitah has a wider meaning; see Exod. 23:10 and commentary there. On the release effected by the jubilee year, see Lev. 25 and commentary there.
   Just how much of the law was ever enforced, even in early days, is not certain; its abuses were eventually circumvented in the first century C.E.

by Hillel, through the device of *prosbul* [9]. Even before that time the remission did not cover such debts as wages owed, loans secured by pledges, or merchandise bought on credit.

3] *Dun the foreigner.* The *nochri,* as occasional visitor or tradesman, was not part of the community subject to *shemitah.* The verse makes clear that the law of remission had a ritual as well as a commercial dimension. See above, on 14:21.

4] *There shall be no needy.* To be understood as an exhortation: "There shouldn't really be any needy among you" (in which case *shemitah* for debts would be unnecessary). The Torah was in no doubt, however, that poverty would in fact continue to exist (see verses 7 ff., and expressly verse 11).

6] *You will extend loans.* A figure of speech describing the extent of Israel's material well-being.

יא וּבְכֹל מִשְׁלַח יָדֶךָ: כִּי לֹא־יֶחְדַּל אֶבְיוֹן מִקֶּרֶב
הָאָרֶץ עַל־כֵּן אָנֹכִי מְצַוְּךָ לֵאמֹר פָּתֹחַ תִּפְתַּח
אֶת־יָדְךָ לְאָחִיךָ לַעֲנִיֶּךָ וּלְאֶבְיֹנְךָ בְּאַרְצֶךָ: ס
יב כִּי־יִמָּכֵר לְךָ אָחִיךָ הָעִבְרִי אוֹ הָעִבְרִיָּה וַעֲבָדְךָ שֵׁשׁ
יג שָׁנִים וּבַשָּׁנָה הַשְּׁבִיעִת תְּשַׁלְּחֶנּוּ חָפְשִׁי מֵעִמָּךְ: וְכִי־
יד תְשַׁלְּחֶנּוּ חָפְשִׁי מֵעִמָּךְ לֹא תְשַׁלְּחֶנּוּ רֵיקָם: הַעֲנֵיק
תַּעֲנִיק לוֹ מִצֹּאנְךָ וּמִגָּרְנְךָ וּמִיִּקְבֶךָ אֲשֶׁר בֵּרַכְךָ
טו יְהוָה אֱלֹהֶיךָ תִּתֶּן־לוֹ: וְזָכַרְתָּ כִּי עֶבֶד הָיִיתָ בְּאֶרֶץ
מִצְרַיִם וַיִּפְדְּךָ יְהוָה אֱלֹהֶיךָ עַל־כֵּן אָנֹכִי מְצַוְּךָ
טז אֶת־הַדָּבָר הַזֶּה הַיּוֹם: וְהָיָה כִּי־יֹאמַר אֵלֶיךָ לֹא
אֵצֵא מֵעִמָּךְ כִּי אֲהֵבְךָ וְאֶת־בֵּיתֶךָ כִּי־טוֹב לוֹ

לְךָ וְהַעֲבַטְתָּ גּוֹיִם רַבִּים וְאַתָּה לֹא תַעֲבֹט וּמָשַׁלְתָּ
ז בְּגוֹיִם רַבִּים וּבְךָ לֹא יִמְשֹׁלוּ: ס כִּי־יִהְיֶה בְךָ
אֶבְיוֹן מֵאַחַד אַחֶיךָ בְּאַחַד שְׁעָרֶיךָ בְּאַרְצְךָ אֲשֶׁר
יְהוָה אֱלֹהֶיךָ נֹתֵן לָךְ לֹא תְאַמֵּץ אֶת־לְבָבְךָ וְלֹא
ח תִקְפֹּץ אֶת־יָדְךָ מֵאָחִיךָ הָאֶבְיוֹן: כִּי־פָתֹחַ תִּפְתַּח אֶת־
יָדְךָ לוֹ וְהַעֲבֵט תַּעֲבִיטֶנּוּ דֵּי מַחְסֹרוֹ אֲשֶׁר יֶחְסַר לוֹ:
ט הִשָּׁמֶר לְךָ פֶּן־יִהְיֶה דָבָר עִם־לְבָבְךָ בְלִיַּעַל לֵאמֹר
קָרְבָה שְׁנַת־הַשֶּׁבַע שְׁנַת הַשְּׁמִטָּה וְרָעָה עֵינְךָ בְּאָחִיךָ
הָאֶבְיוֹן וְלֹא תִתֵּן לוֹ וְקָרָא עָלֶיךָ אֶל־יְהוָה וְהָיָה בְךָ
י חֵטְא: נָתוֹן תִּתֵּן לוֹ וְלֹא־יֵרַע לְבָבְךָ בְּתִתְּךָ לוֹ כִּי
בִּגְלַל הַדָּבָר הַזֶּה יְבָרֶכְךָ יְהוָה אֱלֹהֶיךָ בְּכָל־מַעֲשֶׂךָ

---

to many nations, but require none yourself; you will dominate many nations, but they will not dominate you.

7] If, however, there is a needy person among you, one of your kinsmen in any of your settlements in the land that the LORD your God is giving you, do not harden your heart and shut your hand against your needy kinsman. **8]** Rather, you must open your hand and lend him sufficient for whatever he needs. **9]** Beware lest you harbor the base thought, "The seventh year, the year of remission, is approaching," so that you are mean to your needy kinsman and give him nothing. He will cry out to the LORD against you, and you will incur guilt. **10]** Give to him readily and have no regrets when you do so, for in return the LORD your God will bless you in all your efforts and in all your undertakings. **11]** For there will never cease to be needy ones in your land, which is why I command you: open your hand to the poor and needy kinsman in your land.

12] If a fellow Hebrew, man or woman, is sold to you, he shall serve you six years, and in the seventh year you shall set him free. **13]** When you set him free, do not let him go empty-handed: **14]** Furnish him out of the flock, threshing floor, and vat, with which the LORD your God has blessed you. **15]** Bear in mind that you were slaves in the land of Egypt and the LORD your God redeemed you; therefore I enjoin this commandment upon you today.

16] But should he say to you, "I do not want to leave you"—for he loves you and your

---

7] *If, however.* If you will not heed God's commands, then there *will* be needy among you. In that case, let debt remission—which is still the subject in view—assist your social conscience.

9] *The seventh year.* "The septenary" would be a more accurate rendering of the Hebrew, which describes the seventh year in terms of the time span it completes.

11] *Never cease to be needy.* A realistic appraisal of

Israel's limited capacity to live in all respects as a holy people.

12] *Serve you six years.* This parallels Exod. 21:2 ff. in most respects. Note the equal treatment of the bondwoman and the emphasis on gifts to be given at the time of release. Lev. 25:39–46 adds rules on the release of slaves in the jubilee year [10].

16] *But should he say.* Disdaining his freedom.

כ וְלֹא תָגֹז בְּכוֹר צֹאנֶךָ: לִפְנֵי יְהוָה אֱלֹהֶיךָ תֹאכְלֶנּוּ שָׁנָה בְשָׁנָה בַּמָּקוֹם אֲשֶׁר־יִבְחַר יְהוָה אַתָּה וּבֵיתֶךָ: כא וְכִי־יִהְיֶה בוֹ מוּם פִּסֵּחַ אוֹ עִוֵּר כֹּל מוּם רָע לֹא תִזְבָּחֶנּוּ לַיהוָה אֱלֹהֶיךָ: כב בִּשְׁעָרֶיךָ תֹאכְלֶנּוּ הַטָּמֵא וְהַטָּהוֹר יַחְדָּו כַּצְּבִי וְכָאַיָּל: כג רַק אֶת־דָּמוֹ לֹא תֹאכֵל עַל־הָאָרֶץ תִּשְׁפְּכֶנּוּ כַּמָּיִם: פ

יז עַמֶּךָ: וְלָקַחְתָּ אֶת־הַמַּרְצֵעַ וְנָתַתָּה בְאָזְנוֹ וּבַדֶּלֶת וְהָיָה לְךָ עֶבֶד עוֹלָם וְאַף לַאֲמָתְךָ תַּעֲשֶׂה־כֵּן: יח לֹא־יִקְשֶׁה בְעֵינֶךָ בְּשַׁלֵּחֲךָ אֹתוֹ חָפְשִׁי מֵעִמָּךְ כִּי מִשְׁנֶה שְׂכַר שָׂכִיר עֲבָדְךָ שֵׁשׁ שָׁנִים וּבֵרַכְךָ יְהוָה אֱלֹהֶיךָ בְּכֹל אֲשֶׁר תַּעֲשֶׂה: יט כָּל־הַבְּכוֹר אֲשֶׁר יִוָּלֵד בִּבְקָרְךָ וּבְצֹאנְךָ הַזָּכָר תַּקְדִּישׁ לַיהוָה אֱלֹהֶיךָ לֹא תַעֲבֹד בִּבְכֹר שׁוֹרֶךָ

household and is happy with you— **17]** you shall take an awl and put it through his ear into the door, and he shall become your slave in perpetuity. Do the same with your female slave. **18]** When you do set him free, do not feel aggrieved; for in the six years he has given you double the service of a hired man. Moreover, the LORD your God will bless you in all you do.

19] You shall consecrate to the LORD your God all male firstlings that are born in your herd and in your flock: you must not work your firstling ox or shear your firstling sheep. **20]** You and your household shall eat it annually before the LORD your God in the place that the LORD will choose. **21]** But if it has a defect, lameness or blindness, any serious defect, you shall not sacrifice it to the LORD your God. **22]** Eat it in your settlements, the unclean among you no less than the clean, just like the gazelle and the deer. **23]** Only you must not partake of its blood; you shall pour it out on the ground like water.

17] *Take an awl.* Targum Yerushalmi adds, "publicly, in the court house," which brings the law in line with the parallel passage in Exod. 21:6.

In Middle Assyrian laws the piercing of the ear is listed as a punishment for failing to report a harlot's improper attire [11].

In perpetuity. In order to reconcile this provision with the laws of the jubilee year (Lev. 25), tradition interpreted "in perpetuity" to mean "until the jubilee" [12].

18] *Do not feel aggrieved.* As will likely be the case. Jeremiah in fact scolds the people for their unwillingness to heed the command (34:14).

19] *All male firstlings.* A postscript as well as a bridge to the laws of Passover which follow. The firstlings of animals have their parallel in the firstlings of produce, and the Passover sacrifice recalls that Israel's first-born children are God's possession.

The provisions agree generally with other Torah passages (Exod. 13:11 ff.; Lev. 27:26 ff.; Num. 18:15 ff.). However, there are differences; e.g., in Numbers the firstlings belong to the priests.

20] *Shall eat.* In a sacrificial ceremony, as verse 21 makes clear.

22] *Like the gazelle and the deer.* This refers to the statement in Deut. 12:15 (see there).

Tithes

The command to yield a tenth of one's sustenance to God is rooted in the recognition that He is its source and, that even as He has a special concern for the Levites and the poor, so we too must show it to them. According to Deut. 14:22 ff. tithing was an annual process, and its portions were to be consumed at the sanctuary, but, if the distance from one's home was too great, the produce could be converted into money, and with the proceeds the food for the feast could be purchased at the locale of the sanctuary. Every third year, however, the tithe was kept in the home community and distributed to the Levites and the poor, who depended on such contributions. This procedure differs significantly from that set forth in Num. 18:21. There, tithes are to be given to the Levites who in turn will tithe to the priests.[1]

Scholars have attempted to elucidate the historical development of tithing from the different provisions in Numbers and Deuteronomy, and from the mention made of it in Genesis. It seems certain that the concept of contributing some portion of one's increase as an expression of gratitude to God was very old, reaching into pastoral days (Jacob vows to tithe if God will protect him, Gen. 28:22; see also Gen. 14:20) and finding its parallels in Ugaritic and Mesopotamian practice, where tithes were known as *ma'saru* and *ešrētu* (later: *ešrû*) respectively [13].

An understanding of sequential developments, however, depends on whether Deuteronomic law preceded the law in Numbers, or vice versa. If Deuteronomy is considered older, then it would appear that tithing was at first a social institution, and that in time it became sacralized; the secular aspect being reflected in Deuteronomy, and the sacral, with its emphasis on ritual and priests, in Numbers, chapter 18. If, on the other hand, Numbers has the older tradition, then tithing began as a tax for the maintenance of the sanctuary and later became secularized as a social levy.[2]

During the period of the Second Temple, tithes were no longer given to the Levites and instead were transmitted directly to the priests, since there were relatively small numbers of Levites in attendance at the sanctuary. One talmudic opinion saw this altered procedure as a divine punishment for the Levites because so few of them had returned with Ezra from the Babylonian exile [15]. Still later, it became a custom among the pious to tithe voluntarily even from their grain purchases (though only the farmer who grew the produce was obligated to tithe), inasmuch as there was grave suspicion that farmers were lax in their observance of the law. The halachah concerning tithing is contained in a number of mishnaic and Palestinian talmudic treatises, notably *Terumot, Demai, Ma'aserot,* and *Ma'aser Sheni.*

In medieval times the church levied special tithes on Jewish communities and also applied the biblical prescription to its own faithful. The great European cathedrals were paid for to a large extent by these levies, which were obligatory in many states until the French Revolution. The Eastern Ortho-

---

[1] The Rabbis harmonized the difference by stipulating three tithes: the first tithe was to go to the Levites; a second (*ma-aser sheni*) was to be eaten at the sanctuary by the owner of the land; and a third (*masar ani,* "tithe of the poor") was raised every third year and sixth year, in which case it took the place of the *ma-aser sheni.* The tithe of produce and animals mentioned in Lev. 27:30–33 was considered as referring to the Deuteronomic law (see commentary in Leviticus).

[2] Our commentary takes the latter position (see introduction) [14].

dox churches never adopted tithing, while Mormons and Seventh Day Adventists practice it to this day.

Dietary Laws

1. *General Rules.*[3] The biblical regulations provide that although all plants are permitted as food not all animals are.

Allowed are:

Four-legged land animals with parted hooves and a regurgitative digestion; fish that have fins and scales (other water animals are forbidden); birds, except those expressly forbidden (mostly predators); some insects.

Forbidden are:

Animals that have died other than by slaughter; a kid boiled in its mother's milk; *sheretz* (swarming or creeping things) like insects and worms with some exceptions; by application, reptiles and amphibians.

Rabbinic tradition developed a complex system of *kashrut* from these basic laws (to which must of course be added the rules of Passover and of fast days).

2. *Purpose.* Five reasons have been identified as underlying the Torah's dietary laws:[4]

a. They were to distinguish the Israelites from their Canaanite neighbors and, later, from the nations. Indeed, such separation became a major consequence of *kashrut* observance.

b. The laws constituted a rigorous discipline by which Israel was to consecrate itself to God.

c. *Kashrut* promotes human hygiene. This position was held by Maimonides and Nachmanides but vigorously opposed by others, notably by Abarbanel (see Gleanings).

d. The main skein that runs through these laws is to arouse in us a sense of hesitation,

even guilt, concerning the consumption of meat—a point of view expressed by Rabbi Abraham Kook (see Gleanings).

e. *Kashrut* expresses an aspect of holiness in that it aims at completeness (see further in Gleanings).

It is likely that a number of such purposes, separately or together, added to already existing taboos and helped to form the biblical system, which must be taken in its entirety as an approach to holiness. It was part and parcel of sacred practice without which Israel could not function in its relation to God. The individual laws now found in the Torah had developed over a long time, and in similar fashion later centuries shaped them further into the observances and rules that now form the body of traditional *kashrut*. Reform Jews, in their eclectic approach to halachah, have generally abandoned most biblical and postbiblical restrictions on the consumption of meat, but many still observe the prohibition of eating pork and (less so) shell fish; others take upon themselves the laws of *kashrut* as a personal discipline; and still others observe such practices as a sign of solidarity with fellow Jews. Where food is served in Reform synagogues, the *biblical* rules set forth above are usually observed, while *postbiblical* rules are applied but rarely.

3. *The Prohibition of Pork.* Among all the laws one prohibition stands out and, indeed, in Jewish history assumed special significance: the biblical and postbiblical aversion to the eating of swine's flesh.

It appears from Isaiah 65:4 and 66:3, 17 that during exilic times in Babylonia some Israelites brought swine's blood as an oblation in sacrifices and consumed its meat on such occasions. However, such illicit sacrifices were exceptional [16]. The Egyptians ate or

---

[3] For a detailed discussion, see commentary on Lev. 11; see there also for a consideration of the contemporary liberal view of these laws.

[4] But see the comment of von Rad (below, in Gleanings), which cautions us not to search too deeply for such reasons.

sacrificed swine at full-moon festivals as, according to their mythology, the god Seth was identified with the swine. In Ugarit, the animal was apparently a symbol of strength; among the Greeks the pig was the most frequently sacrificed animal, and Adonis was called the swine-god. In pre-Israelite times in Canaan, the animal was freely raised and consumed, but on the whole there is no evidence that the pig was widely adored among Israel's neighbors.

What brought about the particularly strong aversion in Israel cannot be determined with certainty. In Maccabean times (second century B.C.E.) it had become a strong symbol of anti-Judaism (I Macc. 1:44–50; II Macc. 6:18 ff.); in Christian Scriptures swine were connected with demons [17];

and in talmudic times the ill effects of pork consumption were well known. A proverb said that when ten diseases descended on the world the pig took nine. Swine were despised for their reputed filthy habits, were compared to dogs (which enjoyed low esteem in early days), and a folk saying went: "A gold ring in a swine's snout is like a pretty woman without sense" (Prov. 11:22) [18].

While other nations and religions also forbade the eating of pigs (notably Islam; see Gleanings), nowhere did the prohibition become so invested with emotional weight as in Jewish tradition. Jews were bidden to abstain both from eating pork and from rearing the animal for profit [19], but in modern times the observance of these injunctions has weakened, both in and outside Israel.

GLEANINGS

Children

It says (Deut. 14:1): "You are children of the Lord your God." Rabbi Judah said: You are called His children only if your behavior makes you worthy of the ascription; Rabbi Meir said: You are called His children even if you are unworthy.

TALMUD [20]

The Kite

It is called רָאָה (ra-ah) because the root signals that it sees extraordinarily well. Said a chasidic rabbi about an enemy of Israel: "The Rabbis said that a kite can fly in Babylon and see carcasses in Israel." That kind of bird was already declared unclean by the Torah. ITTURE TORAH [21]

The Way

The Torah says that tithing will lead to a reverence of God. Some come to revere God through observance of Torah, and others come to Torah through reverence. CHASIDIC [22]

Too Far

When is "the place . . . far from you" (verse 24)? When the commandments of the Torah are a burden to you, then God—who is called "the Place of the World"—becomes too far for you.

ALSHECH [23]

Wrap It Up

Why does the Torah have to say "Wrap up the money" (verse 25; the prescription is unnecessary, for people would do it anyway)? To suggest that we should always "wrap up" our money so that we may rule over it, and not it over us.

CHASIDIC [24]

On Tzedakah (Deut. 15:7–11)

Though the giving of tzedakah is a positive commandment, no blessing is spoken when one gives. For the gift may be rejected and the blessing would have been spoken in vain. RASHBA [25]

Even those who do not give from the heart and give only because of shame or social pressure are accounted as having given *tzedakah*. Many give less than they ought and more than they want.

MEIR BAR-ILAN [26]

The reward for giving will come in the next world; in this world the reward is the joy of performing the mitzvah.   KETAV SOFER [27]

In the Hebrew, the command to open our hands to the needy (Deut. 15:8) is constructed in the "doubling" or emphatic form. Why twice? To teach that one should give twice: once before and once after being asked.   M. HACOHEN [28]

From the indefinite tense (the infinitive) you may learn that there is no limit on the times that *tzedakah* needs to be repeated.   S. R. HIRSCH [29]

On Dietary Laws

The contemporary reader must not understand this material to represent mere "externalities," which obstruct true piety. On the contrary, it is their very function to serve it. Such rites are rooted in a holistic view that understands what happens in form also to happen in content, and the spiritual to express itself in material, external matters. And, further, he must restrain himself from asking too much about the "reason" and symbolism of the rites—something we are wont to do. Rites remain remarkably stable, while their spiritual context will frequently change.

G. VON RAD [30]

Be it far from me to believe the way they speculate because, if I would accept that, then the divine Torah would be nothing but a kind of abridged hygienic or medico-dietary manual. That is not the way of the divine Torah and the profundity of its purpose. Moreover, do we not see peoples "eating pork, and the detestable thing, and the mouse" (Isa. 66:17), all sorts of fowl and unclean fish, yet sane and sound, a model of health? Then, again, there are quite a number of harmful creatures, like snake, viper, asp, and scorpion, which are not listed in the text. Even among the plants there are some harmful ones, deathly poisonous; yet we find no injunctions in the Torah against eating them. It all sums up to one conclusion: the divine Torah does not intend to legislate healthful prescription but rather cares for promoting the welfare of our soul. The Torah does not employ any terms like harmful, or bad for your health or digestion, but abominable, detestable, impure, unclean, tainted, in order to teach: the dietary laws are not given merely for the protection of the body, but to guard man's spirit, his soul.

ABARBANEL [31]

(Rabbi Kook proceeds from the general idea that humanity was originally vegetarian and that the permission to kill animals for food was a divine and only temporary concession. We are not to forget that when we eat meat we have destroyed life, and in this way he interprets the command in Lev. 17:13 to pour out the blood of the animal and cover it with earth.)

Cover the blood! Hide your shame! These actions will bear fruit and ultimately educate mankind. The mute protest will, when the time is ripe, be transformed into a mighty shout and succeed in its aim. The very nature of the principles of ritual slaughter, with their specific rules and regulations designed to reduce pain, create the atmosphere that you are not dealing with a helpless unprotected object, with an inanimate automat, but with a living soul.   A. KOOK [32]

The Holy Days

In six other places does the Torah prescribe the celebration of holy days: three times in Exodus (chapters 12 and 13 in connection with the institution of Passover; 23:14–18; 34:18–25); twice in Leviticus (chapter 16, which deals with the Day of Atonement; and chapter 23); and once in Numbers (28:1–30:1, where the sacrificial order of the holy days is set forth in detail). Here, in Deuteronomy, neither the New Year nor the Day of Atonement is mentioned; the emphasis is on the three pilgrim celebrations—שָׁלֹשׁ רְגָלִים, *shalosh regalim*: Passover (Pesach), Pentecost (Shavuot), and Tabernacles (Sukot)*—all of which require a visit to the central sanctuary.

The pilgrimage itself is a characteristic feature of Deuteronomy, an aspect of its basic aim to make the Temple in Jerusalem the central point of the national cult. Thus, the Passover sacrifice is no longer to be consumed at home or at local shrines, and the festival now combines the originally separate traditions of *pesach* and *matzot*. Regarding Sukot, the absence of any mention of *lulav* and *etrog* or of the wilderness experience—contained in the Leviticus passages—is due either to the Deuteronomic focus on the central sanctuary as the locus of God's presence or to varying traditions about the celebration of the festival.

The term חַג (*chag*), which is in this section affixed to the festivals, is related to the Arabic *haj*, or *hag*, which denotes the required Moslem pilgrimage to Mecca and a title given to someone who has made such a pilgrimage.

---

* On the history of the Pesach festival, see our Commentary on Exodus, chapter 12; and on Shavuot and Sukot, our Commentary on Leviticus, chapter 23.

א שָׁמוֹר֙ אֶת־חֹ֣דֶשׁ הָֽאָבִ֔יב וְעָשִׂ֣יתָ פֶּ֔סַח לַֽיהֹוָ֖ה אֱלֹהֶ֑יךָ
כִּ֞י בְּחֹ֣דֶשׁ הָֽאָבִ֗יב הוֹצִ֨יאֲךָ֜ יְהֹוָ֧ה אֱלֹהֶ֛יךָ מִמִּצְרַ֖יִם
ג לָֽיְלָה: וְזָבַ֥חְתָּ פֶּ֛סַח לַֽיהֹוָ֥ה אֱלֹהֶ֖יךָ צֹ֣אן וּבָקָ֑ר
בַּמָּקוֹם֙ אֲשֶׁר־יִבְחַ֣ר יְהֹוָ֔ה לְשַׁכֵּ֥ן שְׁמ֖וֹ שָֽׁם: לֹא־
תֹּאכַ֤ל עָלָיו֙ חָמֵ֔ץ שִׁבְעַ֥ת יָמִ֛ים תֹּֽאכַל־עָלָ֥יו מַצּ֖וֹת

לֶ֣חֶם עֹ֑נִי כִּ֣י בְחִפָּז֗וֹן יָצָ֙אתָ֙ מֵאֶ֣רֶץ מִצְרַ֔יִם לְמַ֣עַן
תִּזְכֹּר֮ אֶת־י֣וֹם צֵֽאתְךָ֘ מֵאֶ֣רֶץ מִצְרַ֔יִם כֹּ֖ל יְמֵ֥י חַיֶּֽיךָ:
ד וְלֹֽא־יֵֽרָאֶ֨ה לְךָ֥ שְׂאֹ֛ר בְּכָל־גְּבֻֽלְךָ֖ שִׁבְעַ֣ת יָמִ֑ים וְלֹֽא־
יָלִ֣ין מִן־הַבָּשָׂ֗ר אֲשֶׁ֨ר תִּזְבַּ֥ח בָּעֶ֛רֶב בַּיּ֥וֹם הָֽרִאשׁ֖וֹן
ה לַבֹּֽקֶר: לֹ֥א תוּכַ֖ל לִזְבֹּ֣חַ אֶת־הַפָּ֑סַח בְּאַחַ֖ד שְׁעָרֶ֑יךָ

1] Observe the month of Abib and offer a passover sacrifice to the LORD your God, for it was in the month of Abib, at night, that the LORD your God freed you from Egypt. 2] You shall slaughter the passover sacrifice for the LORD your God, from the flock and the herd, in the place where the LORD will choose to establish His name. 3] You shall not eat anything leavened with it; for seven days thereafter you shall eat unleavened bread, bread of distress— for you departed from the land of Egypt hurriedly—so that you may remember the day of your departure from the land of Egypt as long as you live. 4] For seven days no leaven shall be found with you in all your territory, and none of the flesh of what you slaughter on the evening of the first day shall be left until morning.

5] You are not permitted to slaughter the passover sacrifice in any of the settlements that the

16:1] *Observe the month of Abib.* חֹדֶשׁ (chodesh, month) means, strictly speaking, "new moon"— making it likely that Passover was once observed on the first day of the month; see at Exod. 12:2 [1].

אָבִיב (aviv) is the old name for the spring month and reflects the Canaanite calendar. Later on, the month became known as Nisan, from *Nisanu* in the Babylonian calendar.

2] *From the flock and the herd.* That is, from sheep and goats (the "flock") and cattle (the "herd"). Exod. 12:3 specifically commands to take a lamb but says nothing about cattle. This difference is evidence of a development from an earlier practice (reflected in Exodus), after wider agricultural options had become available to a well-settled community (reflected in Deuteronomy).

The contrast of the two passages caused the Rabbis a good deal of difficulty, and their various attempts at reconciliation provide an example of their methods: (1) a lamb was to be sacrificed in Egypt; cattle were permitted later [2]; (2) the sacrifice commanded in Exodus was obligatory, the one in Deuteronomy provided an additional voluntary opportunity [3]; (3) the lamb was obligatory for Passover; cattle were used for peace offerings or were consumed at the *minchah* sacri-

fice when the obligatory *pesach* was insufficient for the company [4].

3] *Anything leavened.* חָמֵץ (chametz). What precisely fell under this prohibition became the subject of elaborate halachic rulings (see further at Exod. 12:15).

Unleavened bread. מַצּוֹת (matzot, plural form of *matzah*) were used also on occasions other than Passover; see Lev. 2:4 f. [5].

Bread of distress. Or, "bread of affliction," לֶחֶם עֹנִי (lechem oni). Early in the Passover Seder the leader lifts up the matzah and says, in Aramaic, "This is the bread of affliction" (הָא לַחְמָא עַנְיָא).

4] *No leaven.* Here called שְׂאֹר (se-or), and not *chametz* as in verse 3, a variation in language but not in meaning.

But, according to the Talmud, this betokens a purposeful difference [6].

Shall be found with you. The Rabbis interpreted "with you" (לְךָ, lecha) to cover only "your own leaven in all your territory" and not leaven belonging to others [7].

From this was developed the halachic device of selling one's leavened materials before Pass-

אֲשֶׁר־יְהוָה אֱלֹהֶיךָ נֹתֵן לָךְ: כִּי אִם־אֶל־הַמָּקוֹם תֹּאכַל מַצּוֹת וּבַיּוֹם הַשְּׁבִיעִי עֲצֶרֶת לַיהוָה אֱלֹהֶיךָ ׳
אֲשֶׁר־יִבְחַר יְהוָה אֱלֹהֶיךָ לְשַׁכֵּן שְׁמוֹ שָׁם תִּזְבַּח אֶת־ לֹא תַעֲשֶׂה מְלָאכָה: ס שִׁבְעָה שָׁבֻעֹת תִּסְפָּר־לָךְ ט
הַפֶּסַח בָּעָרֶב כְּבוֹא הַשֶּׁמֶשׁ מוֹעֵד צֵאתְךָ מִמִּצְרָיִם: מֵהָחֵל חֶרְמֵשׁ בַּקָּמָה תָּחֵל לִסְפֹּר שִׁבְעָה שָׁבֻעוֹת
וּבִשַּׁלְתָּ וְאָכַלְתָּ בַּמָּקוֹם אֲשֶׁר יִבְחַר יְהוָה אֱלֹהֶיךָ ז וְעָשִׂיתָ חַג שָׁבֻעוֹת לַיהוָה אֱלֹהֶיךָ מִסַּת נִדְבַת יָדְךָ ׳
בּוֹ וּפָנִיתָ בַבֹּקֶר וְהָלַכְתָּ לְאֹהָלֶיךָ: שֵׁשֶׁת יָמִים ח אֲשֶׁר תִּתֵּן כַּאֲשֶׁר יְבָרֶכְךָ יְהוָה אֱלֹהֶיךָ: וְשָׂמַחְתָּ ׳׳

LORD your God is giving you; **6]** but at the place where the LORD your God will choose to establish His name, there alone shall you slaughter the passover sacrifice, in the evening, at sundown, the time of day when you departed from Egypt. **7]** You shall cook and eat it at the place which the LORD your God will choose; and in the morning you may start back on your journey home. **8]** After eating unleavened bread six days, you shall hold a solemn gathering for the LORD your God on the seventh day: you shall do no work.

9] You shall count off seven weeks; start to count the seven weeks when the sickle is first put to the standing grain. **10]** Then you shall observe the Feast of Weeks for the LORD your God, offering your freewill contribution according as the LORD your God has blessed you. **11]** You

over to a non-Jew, which permitted the seller to keep them in his house during the festival.

On the evening of the first day. The eve before Passover.

6] *In the evening, at sundown.* Similar to Exod. 12:6, "at twilight." According to Rashi this meant "from 6 P.M. on" [8], while Josephus reported 9 to 11 P.M. as the time when his contemporaries celebrated.

The latter's estimate that the number of Passover pilgrims in Jerusalem was 2,700,000 [9] represents a wild exaggeration.

The time of day. מוֹעֵד (mo-ed) might also mean "the season (of the year)"; so the old JPS translation.

7] *Start back.* The plain text suggests that the journey toward home started on the first day of the festival. It follows that, at the time of the formulation of the text, travel on a holy day was permitted [10]. However, this conclusion did not agree with rabbinic teaching, and, since it considered the halachah to be in total conformity with the Torah, it had to reconcile the text with the

rabbinic prohibition. Among the harmonizing interpretations were these: (1) the Torah meant the *second* day of Passover, which in Israel is not observed as a holy day [11]; (2) in the morning the people started back to their inns, either inside or on the outskirts of Jerusalem, where they stayed the night and then went home on the second day [12]; (3) the journey home started on the last, not the first, day [13].

8] *Solemn gathering.* עֲצֶרֶת (atzeret). It is also called מִקְרָא קֹדֶשׁ in Num. 29:12 and חַג in Exod. 13:7. The various terms appear to be interchangeable, though some scholars think they represent various stages of development (see further at Lev. 23:36).

9] *Count off seven weeks.* Rabbinic tradition starts the count on the second day of Passover, which constituted a controversy with the Karaites; see commentary at Lev. 23.

10] *Feast of Weeks.* חַג שָׁבֻעוֹת (Chag Shavuot), also called חַג הַקָּצִיר (Chag ha-Katzir, Harvest Festival) in Exod. 23:16 and in Num. 28:26 יוֹם הַבִּכּוּרִים (Yom ha-Bikkurim, Day of the First Fruits).

לִפְנֵי יְהוָה אֱלֹהֶיךָ אַתָּה וּבִנְךָ וּבִתֶּךָ וְעַבְדְּךָ וַאֲמָתֶךָ   בִּשְׁעָרֶיךָ: שִׁבְעַת יָמִים תָּחֹג לַיהוָה אֱלֹהֶיךָ בַּמָּקוֹם

וְהַלֵּוִי אֲשֶׁר בִּשְׁעָרֶיךָ וְהַגֵּר וְהַיָּתוֹם וְהָאַלְמָנָה אֲשֶׁר   אֲשֶׁר־יִבְחַר יְהוָה כִּי יְבָרֶכְךָ יְהוָה אֱלֹהֶיךָ בְּכָל־

בְּקִרְבֶּךָ בַּמָּקוֹם אֲשֶׁר יִבְחַר יְהוָה אֱלֹהֶיךָ לְשַׁכֵּן   תְּבוּאָתְךָ וּבְכֹל מַעֲשֵׂה יָדֶיךָ וְהָיִיתָ אַךְ שָׂמֵחַ: שָׁלוֹשׁ

שְׁמוֹ שָׁם: וְזָכַרְתָּ כִּי־עֶבֶד הָיִיתָ בְּמִצְרָיִם וְשָׁמַרְתָּ   פְּעָמִים בַּשָּׁנָה יֵרָאֶה כָל־זְכוּרְךָ אֶת־פְּנֵי יְהוָה אֱלֹהֶיךָ

וְעָשִׂיתָ אֶת־הַחֻקִּים הָאֵלֶּה: בַּמָּקוֹם אֲשֶׁר יִבְחָר בְּחַג הַמַּצּוֹת וּבְחַג הַשָּׁבֻעוֹת

חַג הַסֻּכֹּת תַּעֲשֶׂה לְךָ שִׁבְעַת יָמִים בְּאָסְפְּךָ מִגָּרְנְךָ   וּבְחַג הַסֻּכּוֹת וְלֹא יֵרָאֶה אֶת־פְּנֵי יְהוָה רֵיקָם: אִישׁ

וּמִיִּקְבֶךָ: וְשָׂמַחְתָּ בְּחַגֶּךָ אַתָּה וּבִנְךָ וּבִתֶּךָ וְעַבְדְּךָ   כְּמַתְּנַת יָדוֹ כְּבִרְכַּת יְהוָה אֱלֹהֶיךָ אֲשֶׁר נָתַן־לָךְ:

וַאֲמָתְךָ וְהַלֵּוִי וְהַגֵּר וְהַיָּתוֹם וְהָאַלְמָנָה אֲשֶׁר

Haftarah Re'eh, p. 1604

---

shall rejoice before the LORD your God with your son and daughter, your male and female slave, the Levite in your communities, and the stranger, the fatherless, and the widow in your midst, at the place where the LORD your God will choose to establish His name. **12]** Bear in mind that you were slaves in Egypt, and take care to obey these laws.

13] After the ingathering from your threshing floor and your vat, you shall hold the Feast of Booths for seven days. **14]** You shall rejoice in your festival, with your son and daughter, your male and female slave, the Levite, the stranger, the fatherless, and the widow in your communities. **15]** You shall hold festival for the LORD your God seven days, in the place that the LORD will choose; for the LORD your God will bless all your crops and all your undertakings, and you shall have nothing but joy.

16] Three times a year—on the Feast of Unleavened Bread, on the Feast of Weeks, and on the Feast of Booths—all your males shall appear before the LORD your God in the place that He will choose. They shall not appear before the LORD empty-handed, **17]** but each with his own gift, according to the blessing that the LORD your God has bestowed upon you.

13] *Feast of Booths.* חַג הַסֻּכּוֹת (*Chag ha-Sukot*). No reason for the booths is given, as in Lev. 23:43, namely, that the Israelites dwelt in booths when they were in the wilderness. In Exod. 23:16 the festival is called חַג הָאָסִיף (*Chag ha-Asif*), Ingathering or Harvest Feast, and in I Kings 8:2 and 65 it is simply called הֶחָג (*He-Chag*, The Festival).

    Seven days. From the 15th to the 21st of Tishri. According to Lev. 23:36 and Num. 29:35, the festival concludes with an eighth day observance (*Shemini Atzeret*).

15] *Nothing but joy.* On Passover the people went home after the opening observance; on Sukot they stayed all week.

    The opening of verse 14 and the conclusion of

verse 15 have become a Hebrew folk song: וְשָׂמַחְתָּ בְּחַגֶּךָ וְהָיִיתָ אַךְ שָׂמֵחַ (*Vesamachta bechagecha vehayita ach same-ach*).

16] *Three times a year.* A résumé; see Exod. 23:17. The Israelites were promised that during these pilgrimages no enemy would attack their homes (Exod. 34:23).

    Here the term שָׁלֹשׁ פְּעָמִים (*shalosh pe-amim*) is used, while at other times it is שָׁלֹשׁ רְגָלִים (*shalosh regalim*). The words are plural forms of foot (*regel*) and sole (*pa-am*), and from the rhythmic beat of foot and sole the plurals came to mean "times." Popular etymology later understood the term שָׁלֹשׁ רְגָלִים to have arisen because one went to Jerusalem on foot.

The Pilgrim Festivals in Contemporary Observance

1. *In General.* In Deuteronomy the festivals of Pesach, Shavuot, and Sukot were to be celebrated at the central sanctuary. After its final destruction, in 70 C.E., the celebrations returned to their places of origin, the Jewish homes, and to the new local sanctuaries, the synagogues. The following will set forth in brief outline how contemporary Jews in the Diaspora—and especially Reform Jews—observe these holy days. No attempt will be made to explain the complex halachah that surrounds them today or the details of liturgy characterizing the observances in home and synagogue. It will be clear that the holy days have traversed a long road from biblical to postbiblical days, from medieval to modern times. The Pilgrim Festivals are no longer what they were; they have changed greatly, and there is every reason to believe that they will continue to do so, inside and outside Israel, as long as the Jewish people exhibit a goodly measure of religious dynamism.

Some features are common to all three festivals. They all ask the Jew to alter the patterns of daily existence and set these days aside for worship with family and community and for rejoicing at special celebrations. However, many Jews in the Diaspora continue to work on these holy days and thereby are denied the full enjoyment of their blessings.

While the Torah specifies the precise number of days that each festival is to be observed—Pesach, seven days; Shavuot, one day; Sukot, eight days—the uncertainty of determining the calendar led in ancient days to an extension of these durations. In order not to violate the festival, Diaspora Jews (who did not have the benefit of the monthly announcement of the new moon, made by the Sanhedrin) added an additional day to each. Thus, Pesach was celebrated for eight days, Shavuot for two, and Sukot for nine—the ninth day in effect a second-day Shemini Atzeret, now called Simchat Torah. (In Israel, the three festivals continue to be observed according to the biblical reckoning, and Reform Jews everywhere do likewise, holding that, with the calendar permanently fixed, the cautionary additional days of the Diaspora are no longer required.)

The liturgy for these holy days is enriched by certain additions, chief amongst them the solemn recital and (in traditional synagogues) the enactment of the Priestly Benediction,[1] the Hallel Psalms (113–118), and Yizkor, a special memorial prayer. Also, particular Torah and Haftarah readings are assigned to each festival.

2. *Pesach.* The Jewish home celebration par excellence, Pesach rehearses the birth of the covenant people and celebrates the glories of freedom. The festival begins in the evening of the fourteenth day of Nisan with the Seder, a unique occasion for religious sharing with family, friends, and guests; for enhancing the meaning of Judaism and rejoicing in its beauty; and for a personal experience of the mysterious unfolding of God's role in history and of the wonder of our redemption, past, present, and future.

The Seder is essentially a home celebration, but many synagogues have instituted communal observances in order to accommodate those who cannot celebrate in their homes. Liberal Jews generally do not follow the minutiae with which rabbinic tradition has surrounded the holy day week; as in every other respect, their observance will vary widely, as will the degree of their abstinence from all leaven. They understand the customs and rituals of Pesach to be symbolic reminders of the holy day's underlying

---

[1] In Israel and among Sephardic Jews, however, the benediction is enacted every Shabbat as well.

1451

purpose, which remains in the words of the Haggadah,[2] that each generation should consider itself as having been redeemed. Pesach provides the opportunity for reliving the story of liberation, which has its roots in history and makes its urgent demands on the present.

3. *Shavuot.* The festival is observed seven weeks after the second day of Pesach, on the sixth day of Sivan, and has come to signify the day when God revealed His law at Sinai. At first, Shavuot was an agricultural celebration, the Festival of the First Fruits; its identification with the communication of the Ten Commandments (which are read as a Torah selection in the synagogue) came at a later time. The Festival of the First Fruits plays some renewed role in Israel, but the major connection of this aspect with today's observance lies in the reading of the Book of Ruth (which is set at the season of reaping the early harvest).

The festival suffered diminished attention in modern times, until Reform leaders began to fix Confirmation for that day. Thus, in an annual reenactment of the drama at Sinai, young people take upon themselves the obligations of partnership in the covenant and say, "All that the Lord has spoken we will do." As Confirmation day, Shavuot has once again been given a place of honor in the liberal observance.

4. *Sukot.* It is likely that in early days Sukot marked the beginning of the religious year; later it became the major agricultural festival, celebrating the bringing in of the harvest. Its theme is gratitude for God's bounty, and its name betokens its major ritual: the building of *sukot*, frail booths, which are to remind the Jew of the deprivations of the wilderness years as well as of God's providential care. The number of liberal Jews who build their own *sukot* at home is growing, though the primary place of observing the mitzvah still is in the synagogue. Sukot begins on the fifteenth day of Tishri. On the last day, Simchat Torah, the annual Torah reading cycle is completed and begun again at once. The joy exhibited when all the scrolls are removed from the ark and taken around the sanctuary is testimony to the abiding strength of Torah as well as to the deep commitment to study it and make it relevant in one's everyday life.[3]

In modern times Sukot served as the inspiration for the Canadian and American Thanksgivings (the former observed in October, the latter in November).

---

[2] The order of service provided for the Seder.

[3] The observance of Sukot is enhanced by the use of *lulav* (palm, myrtle, and willow) and *etrog* (a citrus fruit).

GLEANINGS

Exodus

Passover! A nation has been commemorating for thousands of years the day of its Exodus from the house of bondage. Throughout all the atrocities of enslavement and despotism, of inquisition, forced conversion, and massacre, the Jewish nation carries in its heart the yearning for freedom and gives this craving a folk expression which shall not pass over a single soul in Israel, a single downtrodden, pauperized soul!

From fathers to sons, throughout all the generations, the Exodus from Egypt is related as a personal reminiscence, thereby retaining its original luster. "In every generation every man must regard himself as if he personally were redeemed from Egypt."

This is the peak of historic consciousness, and history has no greater example of a fusion of individual with group than this ancient pedagogic command. . . . I do not know of any other ancient memory so entirely a symbol of our present and future as the "memory of the Exodus from Egypt."　BERL KATZENELSON [14]

The Season of Joy

However burdensome the Passover minutiae, especially in regard to the prohibition of leaven, became to the Jewish household, the predominant feature was always an exuberance of joy. In the darkest days of medievalism the synagogue and home resounded with song and thanksgiving, and the young imbibed the joy and comfort of their elders through the beautiful symbols of the feast and the richly adorned tale of the deliverance (the Haggadah). The Passover feast with its "night of divine watching" endowed the Jew ever anew with endurance during the dark night of medieval tyranny and with faith in "the Keeper of Israel who slumbereth not nor sleepeth." Moreover, as the springtide of nature fills each creature with joy and hope, so Israel's feast of redemption promises the great day of liberty to those who still chafe under the yoke of oppression.

K. KOHLER [15]

The Center

The center of the Jewish Passover is not the Jewish people as such. Its annual return does not resemble a patriotic festival like the fourteenth of July (in France), the glory of which deserves enthusiasm and even sacrifice. So little is the Seder a national festival that the Haggadah does not even mention the name of Moses the Liberator. No human exploit is indicated. But what is shown as necessary is that the Jew should become conscious of his Jewishness. Not that the members of a nation should unite to celebrate a national liberation, but that the very ideas of liberation and redemption should be removed from the sphere of abstract thought and be considered from the point of view of an experience, which differs from all others, the experience of the Jewish people in Egypt. In all ages, it is the duty of each man to think of himself as one who had himself come out of Egypt.　A. NEHER [16]

Where Is That Mountain?

Where is that mountain of which we read in the
    Bible—
Sinai—on which the Torah was given to Israel?
Perhaps it is in Egypt
where the wild Israelites left the little idols
of the sons of Jacob, the little idols
which stood in the corners of the tents
and rode with the rider
under the saddlecloth; perhaps it is in Egypt—

a land of such affliction
three thousand years or so afterwards
we speak of it to this day.
Blessed are You, Lord, God of the universe,
Who has kept us alive.

Where is that mountain of which we read in the
        Bible—
Sinai—on which the Torah was given to Israel?
Perhaps it is in Palestine;
for Sinai was built out of skeletons
of much suffering,
in which the lives of the Israelites
were like the sands—
that become in the centuries rock, ledges of rock,
a mountain, and at last
the Law,
cut into tables of stone.
Blessed are You, God, King of the universe,
Who has kept Israel alive.

                              CHARLES REZNIKOFF [17]

Rejoice on Shavuot (Deut. 16:11)

    Do not rejoice merely in what the earth yields
to you, but rather let earth and heaven be joined:
the beautiful blessing is of the earth, the holiness
is of heaven. God brings blessings to you, and you
should raise yourself toward Him in sanctity.

                              YISRAEL ELDAD [18]

Compassion

    Why is joy commanded for Shavuot and
Sukot, but not for Pesach? Why is the full *Hallel*
said on Sukot, but only the half *Hallel* on Pesach?
Because of the Egyptians who died, as it says: "Do
not rejoice when your enemy falls" (Prov. 24:17).[4]

                              YALKUT SHIMONI [20]

You Shall Have Nothing but Joy (Deut. 16:15)

    This is not a command but rather a statement
meant to create confidence that even though you
may start rejoicing in poor circumstances you will
end it in well-being.   AFTER RASHI

The verse means: "Let no worries intrude."

                              SFORNO

The expression "nothing but" (אַךְ, *ach*) is a "diminishing" term [21] and here it means: On the
first day we are commanded to take a *lulav*, build
a *sukah*, and to rejoice; for six days to have a
sukah and joy; and on the eighth day "nothing
but joy."   THE GAON OF VILNA [22]

[4] This is a parallel to the talmudic story of God si-
lencing the angels who wanted to rejoice over the
death of the Egyptians, saying: "The work of My
hands is drowning in the sea, and you want to
sing . . . !" [19]

Administration of Law and State, I

The weekly portion *Shofetim*—"magistrates"—begins (at 16:18) an extensive segment dealing with the ethical and administrative norms for providing the community with a suitable structure. The rules imply that, if these provisions are carried out in the spirit of the Torah, Israel will have come closer to the ideal of being God's kingdom of priests. That is the ultimate objective, which is to say that the mere pragmatic suitability of administrative arrangements is not the only reason they are included in the Torah.

The text deals with officials, judicial procedures, and appeals, with monarchy and priesthood. There are also two unconnected inserts on deviant worship practices (16:21 and 17:1) which may at one time have had their place with chapter 13.*

The section shows that the original tribal system had now developed into a centralized one; it roots the monarchy in divine approval; it confirms the judicial status of the Levites; and altogether shows how an older desert-bred people, geared for war, had become a settled society with a civil organization.

* Tradition explains the placement by comparing an unjust judge to an idol [1].

ס   ס   ס

מוֹם כֹּל דָּבָר רָע כִּי תוֹעֲבַת יְהוָה אֱלֹהֶיךָ הוּא: ס

יח שֹׁפְטִים וְשֹׁטְרִים תִּתֶּן־לְךָ בְּכָל־שְׁעָרֶיךָ אֲשֶׁר יְהוָה
אֱלֹהֶיךָ נֹתֵן לְךָ לִשְׁבָטֶיךָ וְשָׁפְטוּ אֶת־הָעָם מִשְׁפַּט־

ב כִּי־יִמָּצֵא בְקִרְבְּךָ בְּאַחַד שְׁעָרֶיךָ אֲשֶׁר־יְהוָה אֱלֹהֶיךָ
נֹתֵן לָךְ אִישׁ אוֹ־אִשָּׁה אֲשֶׁר יַעֲשֶׂה אֶת־הָרַע בְּעֵינֵי

יט צֶדֶק: לֹא־תַטֶּה מִשְׁפָּט לֹא תַכִּיר פָּנִים וְלֹא־תִקַּח
שֹׁחַד כִּי הַשֹּׁחַד יְעַוֵּר עֵינֵי חֲכָמִים וִיסַלֵּף דִּבְרֵי

ג יְהוָה־אֱלֹהֶיךָ לַעֲבֹר בְּרִיתוֹ: וַיֵּלֶךְ וַיַּעֲבֹד אֱלֹהִים
אֲחֵרִים וַיִּשְׁתַּחוּ לָהֶם וְלַשֶּׁמֶשׁ אוֹ לַיָּרֵחַ אוֹ לְכָל־

כ צַדִּיקִים: צֶדֶק צֶדֶק תִּרְדֹּף לְמַעַן תִּחְיֶה וְיָרַשְׁתָּ

ד צְבָא הַשָּׁמַיִם אֲשֶׁר לֹא־צִוִּיתִי: וְהֻגַּד־לְךָ וְשָׁמַעְתָּ
וְדָרַשְׁתָּ הֵיטֵב וְהִנֵּה אֱמֶת נָכוֹן הַדָּבָר נֶעֶשְׂתָה

כא אֶת־הָאָרֶץ אֲשֶׁר־יְהוָה אֱלֹהֶיךָ נֹתֵן לָךְ: ס לֹא־
תִטַּע לְךָ אֲשֵׁרָה כָּל־עֵץ אֵצֶל מִזְבַּח יְהוָה אֱלֹהֶיךָ

ה הַתּוֹעֵבָה הַזֹּאת בְּיִשְׂרָאֵל: וְהוֹצֵאתָ אֶת־הָאִישׁ הַהוּא
אוֹ אֶת־הָאִשָּׁה הַהִוא אֲשֶׁר עָשׂוּ אֶת־הַדָּבָר הָרַע

כב אֲשֶׁר תַּעֲשֶׂה־לָּךְ: וְלֹא־תָקִים לְךָ מַצֵּבָה אֲשֶׁר שָׂנֵא
יְהוָה אֱלֹהֶיךָ: ס

הַזֶּה אֶל־שְׁעָרֶיךָ אֶת־הָאִישׁ אוֹ אֶת־הָאִשָּׁה וּסְקַלְתָּם

א לֹא־תִזְבַּח לַיהוָה אֱלֹהֶיךָ שׁוֹר וָשֶׂה אֲשֶׁר יִהְיֶה בוֹ

ו בָּאֲבָנִים וָמֵתוּ: עַל־פִּי שְׁנַיִם עֵדִים אוֹ שְׁלֹשָׁה

18] You shall appoint magistrates and officials for your tribes, in all the settlements that the Lord your God is giving you, and they shall govern the people with due justice.   **19]** You shall not judge unfairly: you shall show no partiality; you shall not take bribes, for bribes blind the eyes of the discerning and upset the plea of the just.   **20]** Justice, justice shall you pursue, that you may thrive and occupy the land that the Lord your God is giving you.

21] You shall not set up a sacred post—any kind of pole beside the altar of the Lord your God that you may make—   **22]** or erect a stone pillar; for such the Lord your God detests.

1] You shall not sacrifice to the Lord your God an ox or a sheep that has any defect of a serious kind, for that is abhorrent to the Lord your God.

2] If there is found among you, in one of the settlements which the Lord your God is giving you, a man or woman who has affronted the Lord your God and transgressed His covenant—   **3]** turning to the worship of other gods and bowing down to them, to the sun or the moon or any of the heavenly host, something I never commanded—   **4]** and you have been informed or have learned of it, then you shall make a thorough inquiry. If it is true, the fact is established, that abhorrent thing was perpetrated in Israel,   **5]** you shall take the man or the woman who did that wicked thing out to the public place, and you shall stone them, man or woman, to death.—   **6]** A person shall be put to death only on the testimony of two or more witnesses; he

16:18] *In all the settlements.* See commentary below.

19] *Plea of the just.* Of those who are in the right.

21] *Sacred post.* An *asherah*; see at Deut. 7:5.

17:1] *Defect of a serious kind.* The underlying idea is that God is to be served with what is perfect. Specific blemishes are enumerated in Lev. 22:17 ff. See also Hallo's essay in Leviticus.

3] *Sun . . . moon . . . heavenly host.* Solar and astral religion was widespread in the ancient Near East and publicly practiced by Manasseh (II Kings 21:3; II Chron. 33:3 ff.).

4] *The fact is established.* Through proper trial.

5] *Stone them.* As in Deut. 13:11.

6] *Two or more witnesses.* The Hebrew reads literally "two or three." From the unusual "absolute" use of the word שְׁנַיִם (rather than the construct שְׁנֵי עֵדִים as in Deut. 19:15, where civil matters are at issue), the Rabbis concluded that in criminal cases the two witnesses had to testify that they both as a pair had seen the crime committed [2].

וְעָשִׂ֗יתָ עַל־פִּ֤י הַדָּבָר֙ אֲשֶׁ֣ר יַגִּ֣ידוּ לְךָ֔ מִן־הַמָּק֣וֹם
הַה֔וּא אֲשֶׁ֖ר יִבְחַ֣ר יְהוָ֑ה וְשָׁמַרְתָּ֣ לַעֲשׂ֔וֹת כְּכֹ֖ל אֲשֶׁ֥ר
יוֹר֗וּךָ׃ עַל־פִּ֤י הַתּוֹרָה֙ אֲשֶׁ֣ר יוֹר֔וּךָ וְעַל־הַמִּשְׁפָּ֛ט
אֲשֶׁר־יֹאמְר֥וּ לְךָ֖ תַּעֲשֶׂ֑ה לֹ֣א תָס֗וּר מִן־הַדָּבָ֛ר אֲשֶׁר־
יַגִּ֥ידֽוּ לְךָ֖ יָמִ֥ין וּשְׂמֹֽאל׃ וְהָאִ֞ישׁ אֲשֶׁר־יַעֲשֶׂ֣ה בְזָד֗וֹן
לְבִלְתִּ֞י שְׁמֹ֤עַ אֶל־הַכֹּהֵן֙ הָעֹמֵ֞ד לְשָׁ֤רֶת שָׁם֙ אֶת־יְהוָ֣ה
אֱלֹהֶ֔יךָ א֖וֹ אֶל־הַשֹּׁפֵ֑ט וּמֵת֙ הָאִ֣ישׁ הַה֔וּא וּבִֽעַרְתָּ֥
הָרָ֖ע מִיִּשְׂרָאֵֽל׃ וְכָל־הָעָ֖ם יִשְׁמְע֣וּ וְיִרָ֑אוּ וְלֹ֥א יְזִיד֖וּן

עֵדִ֖ים יוּמַ֣ת הַמֵּ֑ת לֹ֥א יוּמַ֖ת עַל־פִּ֥י עֵ֥ד אֶחָֽד׃
יַ֣ד הָעֵדִ֞ים תִּֽהְיֶה־בּ֤וֹ בָרִֽאשֹׁנָה֙ לַהֲמִית֔וֹ וְיַ֥ד כָּל־הָעָ֖ם
בָּאַחֲרֹנָ֑ה וּבִֽעַרְתָּ֥ הָרָ֖ע מִקִּרְבֶּֽךָ׃ פ
כִּ֣י יִפָּלֵא֩ מִמְּךָ֨ דָבָ֜ר לַמִּשְׁפָּ֗ט בֵּֽין־דָּ֨ם לְדָ֜ם בֵּֽין־דִּ֣ין
לְדִ֗ין וּבֵ֥ין נֶ֨גַע֙ לָנֶ֔גַע דִּבְרֵ֥י רִיבֹ֖ת בִּשְׁעָרֶ֑יךָ וְקַמְתָּ֣
וְעָלִ֔יתָ אֶל־הַמָּק֔וֹם אֲשֶׁ֥ר יִבְחַ֛ר יְהוָ֥ה אֱלֹהֶ֖יךָ בּֽוֹ׃
וּבָאתָ֗ אֶל־הַכֹּהֲנִים֙ הַלְוִיִּ֔ם וְאֶל־הַשֹּׁפֵ֔ט אֲשֶׁ֥ר יִהְיֶ֖ה
בַּיָּמִ֣ים הָהֵ֑ם וְדָרַשְׁתָּ֙ וְהִגִּ֣ידוּ לְךָ֔ אֵ֖ת דְּבַ֥ר הַמִּשְׁפָּֽט׃

must not be put to death on the testimony of a single witness.— **7]** Let the hands of the witnesses be the first against him to put him to death, and the hands of the rest of the people thereafter. Thus you will sweep out evil from your midst.

8] If a case is too baffling for you to decide, be it a controversy over homicide, civil law, or assault—matters of dispute in your courts—you shall promptly repair to the place which the LORD your God will have chosen, **9]** and appear before the levitical priests, or the magistrate in charge at the time, and present your problem. When they have announced to you the verdict in the case, **10]** you shall carry out the verdict that is announced to you from that place which the LORD chose, observing scrupulously all their instructions to you. **11]** You shall act in accordance with the instructions given you and the ruling handed down to you; you must not deviate from the verdict that they announce to you either to the right or to the left. **12]** Should a man act presumptuously and disregard the priest charged with serving there the LORD your God, or the magistrate, that man shall die. Thus you will sweep out evil from Israel: **13]** all the people will hear and be afraid and will not act presumptuously again.

7] *Witnesses be the first.* Perhaps this involved a symbolic act on their part, or they were to be the first to do the actual killing.

8] *Promptly repair.* The text uses the word עָלָה, to "go up," probably because Jerusalem lies on elevated ground.

In a figurative sense, *aliyah,* "going up," means today immigration to Israel.

9] *Levitical priests.* Literally, "the priests (who are) the Levites"; they are to serve as a higher court. The expression suggests that at the time of Deuteronomy not all priests were Levites and that this section reflects the power struggle which in time led to the unquestioned assumption of priestly duties and privileges by the Zadokites, a levitical family. Later on, the Zadokites invoked Aaron as their ancestor to legitimate their status. (See further at Num. 25.)

Or the magistrate. He presided in non-ritual matters.

But a traditional source maintained that priests participated in every case, and that a magistrate ruled alone only if no priest was available or if he was unfit and therefore not qualified to judge [3].

11] *Instructions.* *Ha-torah,* understood in the broad sense.

12] *A man.* It is not clear who this man is, whether a litigant or someone else, and what the punishable offense might be [4].

Act. From this word, tradition ruled that *teaching* alone was not punishable, only if criminal *action* resulted from it was the penalty invoked [5]. This also meant that unconventional thought was not subject to prosecution.

יָשִׁיב אֶת־הָעָם מִצְרַ֫יְמָה לְמַ֫עַן הַרְבּ֣וֹת ס֑וּס וַֽיהוָ֗ה

אָמַ֣ר לָכֶ֔ם לֹ֥א תֹסִפ֛וּן לָשׁ֥וּב בַּדֶּ֖רֶךְ הַזֶּ֥ה עֽוֹד׃

יז וְלֹ֤א יַרְבֶּה־לּוֹ֙ נָשִׁ֔ים וְלֹ֥א יָס֖וּר לְבָב֑וֹ וְכֶ֣סֶף וְזָהָ֗ב

לֹ֥א יַרְבֶּה־לּ֖וֹ מְאֹֽד׃ יח וְהָיָ֣ה כְשִׁבְתּ֔וֹ עַ֖ל כִּסֵּ֣א מַמְלַכְתּ֑וֹ

וְכָ֨תַב ל֜וֹ אֶת־מִשְׁנֵ֨ה הַתּוֹרָ֤ה הַזֹּאת֙ עַל־סֵ֔פֶר מִלִּפְנֵ֖י

יט הַכֹּהֲנִ֥ים הַלְוִיִּֽם׃ וְהָיְתָ֣ה עִמּ֔וֹ וְקָ֥רָא ב֖וֹ כָּל־יְמֵ֣י

יד ע֗וֹד ס כִּֽי־תָבֹ֣א אֶל־הָאָ֗רֶץ אֲשֶׁ֨ר יְהוָ֤ה אֱלֹהֶ֙יךָ֙

נֹתֵ֣ן לָ֔ךְ וִֽירִשְׁתָּ֖הּ וְיָשַׁ֣בְתָּה בָּ֑הּ וְאָמַרְתָּ֗ אָשִׁ֤ימָה עָלַ֙י֙

טו מֶ֔לֶךְ כְּכָל־הַגּוֹיִ֖ם אֲשֶׁ֥ר סְבִיבֹתָֽי׃ שׂ֣וֹם תָּשִׂ֤ים עָלֶ֙יךָ֙

מֶ֔לֶךְ אֲשֶׁ֥ר יִבְחַ֛ר יְהוָ֥ה אֱלֹהֶ֖יךָ בּ֑וֹ מִקֶּ֣רֶב אַחֶ֗יךָ

תָּשִׂ֤ים עָלֶ֙יךָ֙ מֶ֔לֶךְ לֹ֣א תוּכַ֗ל לָתֵ֤ת עָלֶ֙יךָ֙ אִ֣ישׁ נָכְרִ֔י

טז אֲשֶׁ֥ר לֹֽא־אָחִ֖יךָ הֽוּא׃ רַק֩ לֹא־יַרְבֶּה־לּ֨וֹ סוּסִ֜ים וְלֹֽא־

יֵשׁ סְבִירִין בָּהּ

14] If, after you have entered the land that the LORD your God has given you, and occupied it and settled in it, you decide, "I will set a king over me, as do all the nations about me," **15]** you shall be free to set a king over yourself, one chosen by the LORD your God. Be sure to set as king over yourself one of your own people; you must not set a foreigner over you, one who is not your kinsman. **16]** Moreover, he shall not keep many horses or send people back to Egypt to add to his horses, since the LORD has warned you, "You must not go back that way again." **17]** And he shall not have many wives, lest his heart go astray; nor shall he amass silver and gold to excess.

18] When he is seated on his royal throne, he shall have a copy of this Teaching written for him on a scroll by the levitical priests. **19]** Let it remain with him and let him read in it all his

15] *Of your own people.* This is paralleled in the Constitution of the United States, which provides that only a native-born American may be president.

16] *Many horses.* A criticism of Solomon who kept fourteen hundred horses (I Kings 10:26 ff.). Horses were imported into Canaan and Egypt by the invading Hyksos in the middle of the second millennium B.C.E. and were primarily used for war chariots, not for ordinary drayage. The Mishnah limits the king to using them for chariots; the Targum considers three horses one too many [6].

Send people back. It has been suggested that this was to discourage the dispatch of mercenary soldiers to Egypt in exchange for horses, and that such Hebrew soldiers became the nucleus of the Elephantine colony [7].

You must not go back. For permanent settlement; commercial trade was permitted [8].

17] *Many wives.* Another criticism of Solomon who "loved many foreign women" and built altars for their deities (I Kings 11). These worship sites

were destroyed in the Josianic-Deuteronomic reformation (II Kings 23:13).

However, polygamy itself was not prohibited and was practiced in biblical times and later [9]; it was proscribed in Christian-ruled countries by a decree of Rabbenu Gershom (Germany, 1000 C.E.) and by law in modern Israel.

18] *Copy of this Teaching.* The Book of Deuteronomy. The Septuagint derived the title of the book from this verse, and Maimonides that of his major halachic work (*Mishneh Torah*).

A scroll. סֵפֶר (*sefer*); written on papyrus or leather and rolled up, but the term covered other inscriptions as well.

Written . . . by the levitical priests. The conjunction מִלִּפְנֵי could also mean that the copy was to be made from a copy *before*, that is, in possession of the priests; see I Sam. 10:25, where the prophet is recorded to have written down the law of the kingdom and "laid it up before the Lord." (See also Josh. 8:32. However, the author of the Samuel passage, reporting events of the eleventh century B.C.E., apparently did not know of any Torah prescription to that effect.)

מֵאֵת זֹבְחֵי הַזֶּבַח אִם־שׁוֹר אִם־שֶׂה וְנָתַן לַכֹּהֵן הַזְּרֹעַ
וְהַלְּחָיַיִם וְהַקֵּבָה: רֵאשִׁית דְּגָנְךָ תִּירֹשְׁךָ וְיִצְהָרֶךָ
וְרֵאשִׁית גֵּז צֹאנְךָ תִּתֶּן־לּוֹ: כִּי בוֹ בָּחַר יְהֹוָה אֱלֹהֶיךָ
מִכָּל־שְׁבָטֶיךָ לַעֲמֹד לְשָׁרֵת בְּשֵׁם־יְהֹוָה הוּא וּבָנָיו
כָּל־הַיָּמִים: ס וְכִי־יָבֹא הַלֵּוִי מֵאַחַד שְׁעָרֶיךָ
מִכָּל־יִשְׂרָאֵל אֲשֶׁר־הוּא גָּר שָׁם וּבָא בְּכָל־אַוַּת נַפְשׁוֹ
אֶל־הַמָּקוֹם אֲשֶׁר־יִבְחַר יְהֹוָה: וְשֵׁרֵת בְּשֵׁם יְהֹוָה
אֱלֹהָיו כְּכָל־אֶחָיו הַלְוִיִּם הָעֹמְדִים שָׁם לִפְנֵי יְהֹוָה:
חֵלֶק כְּחֵלֶק יֹאכֵלוּ לְבַד מִמְכָּרָיו עַל־הָאָבוֹת: ס

חַיָּיו לְמַעַן יִלְמַד לְיִרְאָה אֶת־יְהֹוָה אֱלֹהָיו לִשְׁמֹר
אֶת־כָּל־דִּבְרֵי הַתּוֹרָה הַזֹּאת וְאֶת־הַחֻקִּים הָאֵלֶּה
לַעֲשֹׂתָם: לְבִלְתִּי רוּם־לְבָבוֹ מֵאֶחָיו וּלְבִלְתִּי סוּר
מִן־הַמִּצְוָה יָמִין וּשְׂמֹאול לְמַעַן יַאֲרִיךְ יָמִים עַל־
מַמְלַכְתּוֹ הוּא וּבָנָיו בְּקֶרֶב יִשְׂרָאֵל: ס
לֹא־יִהְיֶה לַכֹּהֲנִים הַלְוִיִּם כָּל־שֵׁבֶט לֵוִי חֵלֶק וְנַחֲלָה
עִם־יִשְׂרָאֵל אִשֵּׁי יְהֹוָה וְנַחֲלָתוֹ יֹאכֵלוּן: וְנַחֲלָה לֹא־
יִהְיֶה־לּוֹ בְּקֶרֶב אֶחָיו יְהֹוָה הוּא נַחֲלָתוֹ כַּאֲשֶׁר
דִּבֶּר־לוֹ: ס וְזֶה יִהְיֶה מִשְׁפַּט הַכֹּהֲנִים מֵאֵת הָעָם

> כ סלא ו׳

life, so that he may learn to revere the LORD his God, to observe faithfully every word of this Teaching as well as these laws. **20]** Thus he will not act haughtily toward his fellows or deviate from the Instruction to the right or to the left, to the end that he and his descendants may reign long in the midst of Israel.

1] The levitical priests, the whole tribe of Levi, shall have no territorial portion with Israel. They shall live only off the LORD's offerings by fire as their portion, **2]** and shall have no portion among their brother tribes: the LORD is their portion, as He promised them.

3] This then shall be the priests' due from the people: Everyone who offers a sacrifice, whether an ox or a sheep, must give the shoulder, the cheeks, and the stomach to the priest. **4]** You shall also give him the first fruits of your new grain and wine and oil, and the first shearing of your sheep. **5]** For the LORD your God has chosen him and his descendants, out of all your tribes, to be in attendance for service in the name of the LORD for all time.

6] If a Levite would go, from any of the settlements throughout Israel where he has been residing, to the place that the LORD has chosen, he may do so whenever he pleases. **7]** He may serve in the name of the LORD his God like all his fellow Levites who are there in attendance before the LORD. **8]** They shall receive equal shares of the dues, without regard to personal gifts or patrimonies.

20] *Not act haughtily.* As if the law bound the people but not him.

18:1] *No territorial portion.* Based on the literal "no portion nor inheritance." Tradition understood: no portion in booty, no inheritance in land [10].

Their portion. Understanding the Hebrew "its portion" as the tribe's. The subject is treated in Lev. 7:31 ff.; see also Num. 18:18 ff.

3] *Shoulder . . . cheeks . . . stomach.* The reason for selecting these parts is not clear; see Gleanings for a homiletical interpretation.

The passages in Leviticus and Numbers prescribe breast and right thigh, a difference which the Mishnah tried to reconcile [11].

4] *First fruits.* רֵאשִׁית (reshit), which tradition distinguished from *reshit bikkurim* (Exod. 23:19; 34:26).

First shearing. From which clothes would be made; this was not previously mentioned.

5] *Him and his descendants.* Levi and those presumed to be his descendants, that is, all Levites.

7] *He may serve.* He is free to move anywhere and retain his privileges.

8] *Without regard.* The Hebrew as it stands is obscure and the translation speculative.

The Administration of Justice

1. *Background.* The judicial structure envisaged by Deuteronomy reflects a well-settled, centrally governed society, but at the same time stages of earlier tribal and more fluid conditions may be detected. The very opening phrase (16:18), "You shall appoint ...," still roots ultimate administrative power in the people rather than the king, and the admonitions administered to the ruler (17:18–19) are to remind him that his decisions are limited by old religious norms. Deuteronomy here continues the process of secularizing the state while retaining, as every evolutionary society must, important vestiges of former stages.[1]

In former days, justice had been administered by elders who in difficult matters inquired of God's representatives, the priests. According to the report in II Chron. 19:5–11, King Jehoshaphat, in the ninth century B.C.E., reorganized the system of placing judges in all fortified cities of Judah and created a mixed priestly-secular tribunal in Jerusalem. It appears that our section codifies his reforms. Later, in Roman times, each city had seven judicial officers, with two levitical attendants [12].

2. *The Supreme Court.* Our text (17:8 ff.) speaks of a high court which was to be the final authority in both religious and civil matters. The court, later called Sanhedrin,[2] was divided into the Small Sanhedrin of twenty-three judges and the Grand Sanhedrin of seventy-one. The latter was the Supreme Court of the state.[3] Its powers were considerable; its decisions had the force of law; it ratified the appointments of high priest and king; and its permission was required if the king wanted to engage in a non-obligatory war. Because the court's rulings were frequently innovative, it was in effect also a limited legislative body.[4]

Its main functions were to rule on cultic affairs, such as levitical and priestly duties; it determined the monthly calendar on the basis of testimony at the time of each new moon; it had final authority with respect to the Temple area; and it made sure that the royal Torah scrolls contained the authentic text. In addition, the Sanhedrin was the supreme court in capital cases and in all religious matters that affected the stability of society, such as the impeachment of the High Priest. Inevitably, there were power struggles between court, king, and High Priest, all of whom were used—and often pitted against one another—by the Roman rulers. It was the genius of the Jewish people that despite all political struggles and internal as well as external upheavals the principles of justice which the Torah enunciates were never lost sight of. In the end, when Temple and state were destroyed, the law survived and its principles remained the undergirding framework of Jewish life.

The Monarchy

Not until the prophet Samuel crowned Saul king of Israel, in the eleventh century B.C.E., did the monarchical system of government make its appearance in Jewish history. Samuel himself had opposed the introduction of the monarchy and had presented his argu-

---

[1] This view assumes that Deuteronomy came from a later time than Numbers; see introduction and also commentary on 14:1–15:23, where this conclusion determines how one views the history of tithing.

[2] From the Greek *synedrion*, meaning a council or meeting.

[3] However, rabbinic and Greek sources do not agree on the nature of the Sanhedrin, and its history is a subject of scholarly debate.

[4] Similarly, the American Senate, which is primarily a legislative body, has on occasion important judicial functions (as in the case of impeachments) and must agree to certain appointments and the conduct of war.

ments to the people (I Sam. 8), but he eventually yielded to their desire.[5] The theocracy that was envisaged from early days on did not require a king,[6] but once he was enthroned his powers were wide, much like those among neighboring peoples. The aim of Deuteronomy was therefore to emphasize that for both king and people there existed a superior divine law and that the rulership of Israel was an aspect of carrying out God's covenantal plan. Hence, the king, though he was chosen by the people, was believed to occupy his place only "by grace of God" (the expression is part of a British monarch's title to this day) [15].   In Israel this was more than a formal ascription; it had deep roots in the way God's supreme rulership was understood. And because of this the prophet Nathan could stand up to King David, or Elijah to King Ahab; and indeed because of this the whole institution of prophecy as a critique of state and society became possible.

For underlying the organization of the community was the conviction that Israel was a kingdom of priests, all of whom had access to God. To speak in modern terms, the monarchy in ancient Israel was "constitutional": the Torah was the constitution and God was the King of Kings, including Israel's.

The Pursuit of Justice

"Justice, justice shall you pursue" (18:20) is the distillation of the Torah's prescription for the social ordering of society. No people gave as much loving attention to the overriding importance of law equitably administered and enforced as did Israel. This special concern earned the Jews a reputation for "legalism"—a negative judgment that missed the essence of the biblical and postbiblical understanding of justice.

Human justice has as its goal the establishment of divine equity: it is *tikun olam*, a contribution to the world's perfection. In biblical thought, law did not exist for its own sake; it had its roots in God's will for Israel. To pursue justice meant therefore that one strove to love God, and neither was achievable without the other. Even the Almighty himself needed both justice and love to sustain the world, a principle which tradition saw expressed in the two major names for God: *Elohim*, representing the quality of justice, and *Adonai*, that of love and mercy.[7] But while love, whether of God or of His creatures, resists circumscription, justice admits of and requires firmer delineation. Justice can be ordered, at least to some extent, while love cannot. The achievement of a just society represents a practical goal, and its pursuit may succeed in engendering love as well; a loving society, however, will remain an ideal if it is not founded on law.

Jewish law came to be known as halachah, "the way to go" to fulfill the divine intent. Giving meticulous attention to its minutiae was to be doing His will, and, while in time this preoccupation often became extreme, its ultimate purpose was never in question: it was and remained to carry out Israel's oblition under the covenant to perfect the kingdom of the Almighty. Conversely, to act with lovingkindness was to act justly, for such was one's obligation. *Tzedek*, the word for justice, and *tzedakah*, the word for giving to others, express the same objective. In the Jewish conception, one does not give "charity" merely out of the love of one's heart; one gives *tzedakah*, that which is required be-

[5] Tradition explains this by claiming that what Samuel opposed was not the monarchy per se, but only Israel's desire to be like other nations [13].

[6] However, rabbinic literature contains extensive controversies on this subject [14].

[7] See commentary on Gen. 2.

cause of being a Jew and because of being human. To give in a loving spirit is of course the highest rung, but giving in any frame of mind satisfies at least the requirements of justice, or of restoring a God-willed balance to the human realm.

(Midrashic and halachic interpretations of the key phrase abound; see Gleanings below.)

GLEANINGS

Magistrates and Officials

Rabbi Eliezer ben Shamua said: Only if there are officials (who can enforce the judgment) can judges function.　　　　　MIDRASH [16]

It Matters

Do not think: What difference does it make if we pervert justice to acquit our friend or wrest the judgment of the poor or respect the person of the rich? Therefore it says: "You judge for God, not for man" (II Chron. 19:6). Consider what you do, and conduct yourselves in every judgment as if the Holy One blessed be He were standing before you. This is the meaning of the phrase: "He is with you in giving judgment" (*ibid.*).

RASHI [17]

Justice, Justice, Shall You Pursue

The principle applies both to a judgment and to a compromise: the latter too must be guided by justice.　　　　　TALMUD [18]

The double emphasis means: Justice under any circumstance, whether to your profit or loss, whether in word or in action, whether to Jew or non-Jew. It also means: Do not use unjust means to secure justice.　　BACHYA BEN ASHER [19]

"Justice" is repeated because in matters of justice one may never stand still.
The pursuit of justice is the beginning of justice.
Do justly so that justice be engendered.

CHASIDIC [20]

The double promise of verse 20 ("that you may thrive and occupy the land") means: To pursue the goal of justice unceasingly with all devotion is

Israel's great task in order that its physical and political existence be secured. The significant truth is thereby laid down, that the possession of the land comes into question every minute, and has to be constantly merited afresh (i.e., through justice) by a Jewish state.　　S. R. HIRSCH [21]

No Sacred Post

The prohibition of 16:21 led to the rule that no tree be planted nor house be built on the Temple mount.　　　　　MAIMONIDES [22]

Formerly and Now

In the days of the ancestors God was pleased to have them erect stone pillars, but no longer, since the Canaanites used them for their pagan rituals.　　　　　RASHI [23]

Already Dead

In Deut. 17:6 the Hebrew reads literally: "The dead shall be put to death." The wicked are called dead even when still alive.　　TALMUD [24]

You Shall Act in Accordance with the Instructions Given You (Deut. 17:11)

The Sages used this as a proof text to justify the blessings which state that God "has commanded us"—to read the Scroll of Esther, to kindle the Shabbat and Chanukah lights[8]—even though there is no record of His command. But "the instructions given you" tell us to follow the Sages.　　　　　MAIMONIDES [25]

You Must Not Deviate . . . either to the Right or to the Left (Deut. 17:11)

(This phrase became the subject of numerous discussions in rabbinic literature. Some said that

[8] We say: . . . וְצִוָּנוּ לְהַדְלִיק נֵר . . .

one must heed the Sages even if they tell us that right is left and left is right, but others held that we need not follow them if we are certain that they are wrong.)

Rabban Gamliel had calculated the new moon for Tishri to fall on one day, while Rabbi Joshua had reckoned it for another day. R. Gamliel, exercising the prerogatives of his office, ordered R. Joshua to come to him with money and walking stick on a day which the latter had calculated to be Yom Kippur, the 10th of Tishri (on which carrying money and stick would be forbidden). After much agonizing, R. Joshua obeyed. R. Gamliel kissed him and said: "Come in peace, my master and my disciple; my master in wisdom, and my disciple because you accepted my words."

MISHNAH [26]

On Monarchy

(Is monarchy a concession made by the Torah or is it a necessary institution? In the controversy alluded to above, none took a stronger anti-monarchical position than the medieval statesman and commentator Abarbanel.)

Even if we should admit that a king is beneficial and necessary for other peoples for the improvement and maintenance of political order—which actually is contrary to the truth—such reasoning does not apply to making kingship necessary for Israel. The general proposition advances three arguments in favor of kingship: (1) as supreme commander of their armed forces, to give them help and comfort against the enemy and to fight for their country; (2) as supreme legislative authority, to provide them with constitution and laws as the occasion warrants it; (3) as supreme judicial tribunal, to sentence and punish, as called for by the circumstances. For these three functions, Israel has no need to appoint a king.[9]

ABARBANEL [27]

Shoulder, Cheek, and Stomach

These were awarded to the priests in honor of Phinehas: the shoulder because he took his spear in his hand (Num. 25:7); the cheek because his prayer averted a plague (Ps. 106:30); and the stomach because of his deed (Num. 25:8).

TALMUD [28]

Another explanation: The cheeks are the first part of the animal; the shoulder the first part of its extremities; and the stomach the first of its inner parts. The object of the command is to strengthen the moral quality of generosity and to weaken the appetite for eating and acquisition.

MAIMONIDES [29]

[9] Abarbanel's reasons: God is Israel's supreme commander; Israel has Torah and halachah; and Israel needs no king to establish justice in its midst.

Administration of Law and State, II

In the continued list of laws dealing with the welfare of the community, cultic and judicial matters stand side by side. The Torah makes no distinction between them; both are seen to pertain equally to the fulfillment of Israel's covenantal obligations. Thus, the removal of a sorcerer and the isolation (and protection) of a manslayer in a city of refuge maintain the standards of purity incumbent on the nation. Doing the "right" thing is essential for Israel, and in this perception law is religion and religion is law. This biblical view carried over into rabbinic language, which used the word דָּת (*dat*, law) also to denote religion, and into the halachah, which did not generally distinguish between various kinds of mitzvot.

The segment before us treats of authentic and inauthentic prophets and of the various proscribed kinds of magic. It goes on to state the rules pertaining to the cities of refuge, which parallel but do not duplicate the regulations at the end of the Book of Numbers. A comparison between these two sets of laws makes it possible to retrace the history of this institution. Finally, there is additional criminal and civil law, ending with a repetition of the so-called *lex talionis*.

ט כִּי אַתָּה בָּא אֶל־הָאָרֶץ אֲשֶׁר־יְהוָה אֱלֹהֶיךָ נֹתֵן לָךְ
י לֹא־תִלְמַד לַעֲשׂוֹת כְּתוֹעֲבֹת הַגּוֹיִם הָהֵם: לֹא־יִמָּצֵא
בְךָ מַעֲבִיר בְּנוֹ־וּבִתּוֹ בָּאֵשׁ קֹסֵם קְסָמִים מְעוֹנֵן
יא וּמְנַחֵשׁ וּמְכַשֵּׁף: וְחֹבֵר חָבֶר וְשֹׁאֵל אוֹב וְיִדְּעֹנִי
יב וְדֹרֵשׁ אֶל־הַמֵּתִים: כִּי־תוֹעֲבַת יְהוָה כָּל־עֹשֵׂה אֵלֶּה

וּבִגְלַל הַתּוֹעֵבֹת הָאֵלֶּה יְהוָה אֱלֹהֶיךָ מוֹרִישׁ אוֹתָם
יג מִפָּנֶיךָ: תָּמִים תִּהְיֶה עִם יְהוָה אֱלֹהֶיךָ: כִּי הַגּוֹיִם
הָאֵלֶּה אֲשֶׁר אַתָּה יוֹרֵשׁ אוֹתָם אֶל־מְעֹנְנִים וְאֶל־
יד קֹסְמִים יִשְׁמָעוּ וְאַתָּה לֹא כֵן נָתַן לְךָ יְהוָה אֱלֹהֶיךָ:

ᵛ יֵשׁ בְּקָצָת סְפָרִים הת' רַבָּתִי.

9] When you enter the land that the LORD your God is giving you, you shall not learn to imitate the abhorrent practices of those nations.   **10]** Let no one be found among you who consigns his son or daughter to the fire, or who is an augur, a soothsayer, a diviner, a sorcerer,   **11]** one who casts spells, or one who consults ghosts or familiar spirits, or one who inquires of the dead.   **12]** For anyone who does such things is abhorrent to the LORD, and it is because of these abhorrent things that the LORD your God is dispossessing them before you.   **13]** You must be wholehearted with the LORD your God.   **14]** Those nations that you are about to dispossess do indeed resort to soothsayers and augurs; to you, however, the LORD your God has not assigned the like.

18:9] *Abhorrent practices.* Particular examples are enumerated in the following. All of them constitute breaches in the trust relationship between Israel and God.

10] *Consigns ... to the fire.* "Consigns" is a non-committal translation of מַעֲבִיר; for it is not clear whether this means that the child was actually burnt [1] or was passed between two fires [2]. The prohibition was understood to be directed against the worship of Molech, which was expressly forbidden in Lev. 20:2–5 and 18:21 (see commentary there). In any case, the injunction encompasses certain abhorrent Canaanite cultic practices [3].

Augur. Who predicts from the entrails of animals or from the flight of birds.

Soothsayer. The meaning of the Hebrew is uncertain [4].

Diviner. Forbidden also in Lev. 19:26. The Midrash thought a מְנַחֵשׁ to be someone who observed omens at certain times, like new moon, Shabbat eve, or end of Shabbat [5]. The old Jewish custom of not starting new ventures on such occasions is probably related to this.

Sorcerer. מְכַשֵּׁף (*mechashef*) was and has remained the general term for one who uses dark powers.

11] *Casts spells.* According to rabbinic tradition,

a snake charmer [6]. Driver understands the root חבר in the usual meaning "connect," "tie together," and renders "one who ties magic knots" [7].

Consults ghosts. Like the witch of En-dor (I Sam. 28). The Septuagint had a realistic view of how ghosts were "consulted" and translated the Hebrew as *engastrimythos* (ventriloquist).

Familiar spirits. Better, following the Septuagint, one who divines by means of freak or monstrous births, a practice well known in Mesopotamia.

Inquires of the dead. A general prohibition of necromancy. One practice was to consult from skulls of the deceased.

12] *Is dispossessing them.* One of the instances which specify that moral conduct was a condition for possession of the land and its absence a reason for expulsion. This applied primarily to Israel, but occasionally, as here, to the other dwellers in the land as well.

13] *Wholehearted.* Noah` (Gen. 6:9) and Abraham (Gen. 17:1) are called "blameless." The Hebrew תָּמִים (*tamim*, wholehearted, blameless) is related to תָּם (*tam*, simple). Israel is to have simple, undivided loyalty to God, unsullied by magic practices.

14] *To you, however.* To Israel are given other means of ascertaining how to face the future: the

טו נָבִיא מִקִּרְבְּךָ מֵאַחֶיךָ כָּמֹנִי יָקִים לְךָ יְהוָה אֱלֹהֶיךָ

טז אֵלָיו תִּשְׁמָעוּן: כְּכֹל אֲשֶׁר־שָׁאַלְתָּ מֵעִם יְהוָה
אֱלֹהֶיךָ בְּחֹרֵב בְּיוֹם הַקָּהָל לֵאמֹר לֹא אֹסֵף לִשְׁמֹעַ
אֶת־קוֹל יְהוָה אֱלֹהָי וְאֶת־הָאֵשׁ הַגְּדֹלָה הַזֹּאת לֹא־

יז אֶרְאֶה עוֹד וְלֹא אָמוּת: וַיֹּאמֶר יְהוָה אֵלָי הֵיטִיבוּ

יח אֲשֶׁר דִּבֵּרוּ: נָבִיא אָקִים לָהֶם מִקֶּרֶב אֲחֵיהֶם כָּמוֹךָ
וְנָתַתִּי דְבָרַי בְּפִיו וְדִבֶּר אֲלֵיהֶם אֵת כָּל־אֲשֶׁר

יט אֲצַוֶּנּוּ: וְהָיָה הָאִישׁ אֲשֶׁר לֹא־יִשְׁמַע אֶל־דְּבָרַי אֲשֶׁר

כ יְדַבֵּר בִּשְׁמִי אָנֹכִי אֶדְרֹשׁ מֵעִמּוֹ: אַךְ הַנָּבִיא אֲשֶׁר

יָזִיד לְדַבֵּר דָּבָר בִּשְׁמִי אֵת אֲשֶׁר לֹא־צִוִּיתִיו לְדַבֵּר
וַאֲשֶׁר יְדַבֵּר בְּשֵׁם אֱלֹהִים אֲחֵרִים וּמֵת הַנָּבִיא

כא הַהוּא: וְכִי תֹאמַר בִּלְבָבֶךָ אֵיכָה נֵדַע אֶת־הַדָּבָר

כב אֲשֶׁר לֹא־דִבְּרוֹ יְהוָה: אֲשֶׁר יְדַבֵּר הַנָּבִיא בְּשֵׁם
יְהוָה וְלֹא־יִהְיֶה הַדָּבָר וְלֹא יָבוֹא הוּא הַדָּבָר אֲשֶׁר
לֹא־דִבְּרוֹ יְהוָה בְּזָדוֹן דִּבְּרוֹ הַנָּבִיא לֹא תָגוּר מִמֶּנּוּ:

א כִּי־יַכְרִית יְהוָה אֱלֹהֶיךָ אֶת־הַגּוֹיִם אֲשֶׁר יְהוָה
אֱלֹהֶיךָ נֹתֵן לְךָ אֶת־אַרְצָם וִירִשְׁתָּם וְיָשַׁבְתָּ בְּעָרֵיהֶם

שו קמץ בז״ק.

15] The LORD your God will raise up for you a prophet from among your own people, like myself; him you shall heed. **16]** This is just what you asked of the LORD your God at Horeb, on the day of the Assembly, saying, "Let me not hear the voice of the LORD my God any longer or see this wondrous fire any more, lest I die." **17]** Whereupon the LORD said to me, "They have done well in speaking thus. **18]** I will raise up a prophet for them from among their own people, like yourself: I will put My words in his mouth and he will speak to them all that I command him; **19]** and if anybody fails to heed the words he speaks in My name, I Myself will call him to account. **20]** But any prophet who presumes to speak in My name an oracle which I did not command him to utter, or who speaks in the name of other gods—that prophet shall die." **21]** And should you ask yourselves, "How can we know that the oracle was not spoken by the LORD?"— **22]** if the prophet speaks in the name of the LORD and the oracle does not come true, that oracle was not spoken by the LORD; the prophet has uttered it presumptuously: do not stand in dread of him.

1] When the LORD your God has cut down the nations whose land the LORD your God is giving you, and you have dispossessed them and settled in their towns and homes, **2]** you shall

Urim and Thummim, the priests, and prophets to whom the text now turns.

15] *A prophet . . . like myself.* This and verse 18 are the only instances where Moses refers to himself as נָבִיא (navi); in the last verse but two in the Torah he is so called also by the author.

Von Rad suggests that the contrast between mantic and prophet "is the result of persistent thought by Israel about the uniqueness of prophetic revelation" [8].

17] *They have done well.* See at Deut. 5:25; the statement differs from the account in Exod. 20:15–18.

19] *I Myself will call him to account.* According to tradition, this means that the punishment will be by divine judgment, and not by human agency. Perhaps he will die prematurely [9].

21] *How can we know . . . ?* See the discussion in chapter 13. Jeremiah, in his confrontation with the self-styled prophet Hananiah, predicted the death of the latter, and indeed Hananiah died that year (Jer. 28). But such ready proof of inauthenticity was rarely at hand.

The Torah distinguished between two types of false prophets: one, who *thought* he spoke in God's name; and the other, who *deliberately* prophesied in the name of false gods. Chapter 13 deals with the latter, the text above with the former.

19:1] *Settled in their towns and homes.* In Deut. 12:29 it says "settled in their land."

ב וּבְבָתֵּיהֶם: שָׁלוֹשׁ עָרִים תַּבְדִּיל לָךְ בְּתוֹךְ אַרְצְךָ
ג אֲשֶׁר יְהוָה אֱלֹהֶיךָ נֹתֵן לְךָ לְרִשְׁתָּהּ: תָּכִין לְךָ הַדֶּרֶךְ וְשִׁלַּשְׁתָּ אֶת־גְּבוּל אַרְצְךָ אֲשֶׁר יַנְחִילְךָ יְהוָה אֱלֹהֶיךָ וְהָיָה לָנוּס שָׁמָּה כָּל־רֹצֵחַ:
ד וְזֶה דְּבַר הָרֹצֵחַ אֲשֶׁר יָנוּס שָׁמָּה וָחָי אֲשֶׁר יַכֶּה אֶת־רֵעֵהוּ בִּבְלִי־דַעַת וְהוּא לֹא־שֹׂנֵא לוֹ מִתְּמֹל שִׁלְשֹׁם:
ה וַאֲשֶׁר יָבֹא אֶת־רֵעֵהוּ בַיַּעַר לַחְטֹב עֵצִים וְנִדְּחָה יָדוֹ בַגַּרְזֶן לִכְרֹת הָעֵץ וְנָשַׁל הַבַּרְזֶל מִן־הָעֵץ וּמָצָא אֶת־רֵעֵהוּ וָמֵת הוּא יָנוּס אֶל־אַחַת הֶעָרִים־הָאֵלֶּה וָחָי:
ו פֶּן־יִרְדֹּף גֹּאֵל הַדָּם אַחֲרֵי הָרֹצֵחַ כִּי יֵחַם לְבָבוֹ וְהִשִּׂיגוֹ כִּי־יִרְבֶּה הַדֶּרֶךְ וְהִכָּהוּ נָפֶשׁ וְלוֹ אֵין מִשְׁפַּט־מָוֶת
ז כִּי לֹא שֹׂנֵא הוּא לוֹ מִתְּמוֹל שִׁלְשׁוֹם: עַל־כֵּן אָנֹכִי מְצַוְּךָ לֵאמֹר שָׁלֹשׁ עָרִים תַּבְדִּיל לָךְ: וְאִם־יַרְחִיב
ח יְהוָה אֱלֹהֶיךָ אֶת־גְּבֻלְךָ כַּאֲשֶׁר נִשְׁבַּע לַאֲבֹתֶיךָ וְנָתַן
ט לְךָ אֶת־כָּל־הָאָרֶץ אֲשֶׁר דִּבֶּר לָתֵת לַאֲבֹתֶיךָ: כִּי־תִשְׁמֹר אֶת־כָּל־הַמִּצְוָה הַזֹּאת לַעֲשֹׂתָהּ אֲשֶׁר אָנֹכִי מְצַוְּךָ הַיּוֹם לְאַהֲבָה אֶת־יְהוָה אֱלֹהֶיךָ וְלָלֶכֶת בִּדְרָכָיו כָּל־הַיָּמִים וְיָסַפְתָּ לְךָ עוֹד שָׁלֹשׁ עָרִים עַל הַשָּׁלֹשׁ הָאֵלֶּה: וְלֹא יִשָּׁפֵךְ דָּם נָקִי בְּקֶרֶב אַרְצְךָ

set aside three cities in the land that the LORD your God is giving you to possess. **3]** You shall survey the distances, and divide into three parts the territory of the country that the LORD your God has allotted to you, so that any manslayer may have a place to flee to. **4]**—Now this is the case of the manslayer who may flee there and live: one who has killed another unwittingly, without having been his enemy in the past. **5]** For instance, a man goes with his neighbor into a grove to cut wood; as his hand swings the ax to cut down a tree, the ax-head flies off the handle and strikes the other so that he dies. That man shall flee to one of these cities and live.—

6] Otherwise, when the distance is great, the blood-avenger, pursuing the manslayer in hot anger, may overtake him and kill him; yet he did not incur the death penalty, since he had never been the other's enemy. **7]** That is why I command you: set aside three cities.

8] And when the LORD your God enlarges your territory, as He swore to your fathers, and gives you all the land that He promised to give your fathers— **9]** if you faithfully observe all this Instruction which I enjoin upon you this day, to love the LORD your God and to walk in His ways at all times—then you shall add three more towns to those three. **10]** Thus blood of the

From the addition "and homes" tradition adduced that Israel was permitted to dwell in Canaanite homes despite their having harbored idolatrous practices [10].

3] *Divide into three parts.* So that all Israelites would have relatively easy access to the cities of refuge, and the situation noted in verse 6 would not occur.

Any manslayer. Who has killed unintentionally.

5] *And live.* After he has explained his case to the elders of the city; see Josh. 20:4.

6] *The blood-avenger.* He represents a leftover of an earlier state of judicial practice. He was usually the slain person's nearest kinsman, who, by killing the manslayer, would redress the balance of life. Should he in fact succeed in doing so, he would be guiltless, even if the alleged manslayer would later be found to have been innocent; in that case the whole community was considered at fault for not providing a place to which the accused could have fled in time.

9] *You shall add.* Either a repetition of the command in verse 2, or added for emphasis, or referring to the East Jordanian cities which Moses had set aside (Deut. 4:41–43). In that case there was a total of nine cities of refuge [11].

אֲשֶׁר יְהֹוָה אֱלֹהֶיךָ נֹתֵן לְךָ נַחֲלָה וְהָיָה עָלֶיךָ
דָּמִים: פ

יא וְכִי־יִהְיֶה אִישׁ שֹׂנֵא לְרֵעֵהוּ וְאָרַב לוֹ וְקָם עָלָיו
יב וְהִכָּהוּ נֶפֶשׁ וָמֵת וְנָס אֶל־אַחַת הֶעָרִים הָאֵל: וְשָׁלְחוּ
זִקְנֵי עִירוֹ וְלָקְחוּ אֹתוֹ מִשָּׁם וְנָתְנוּ אֹתוֹ בְּיַד גֹּאֵל
יג הַדָּם וָמֵת: לֹא־תָחוֹס עֵינְךָ עָלָיו וּבִעַרְתָּ דַם־הַנָּקִי
יד מִיִּשְׂרָאֵל וְטוֹב לָךְ: ס לֹא תַסִּיג גְּבוּל רֵעֲךָ

אֲשֶׁר גָּבְלוּ רִאשֹׁנִים בְּנַחֲלָתְךָ אֲשֶׁר תִּנְחַל בָּאָרֶץ
טו אֲשֶׁר יְהֹוָה אֱלֹהֶיךָ נֹתֵן לְךָ לְרִשְׁתָּהּ: ס לֹא־
יָקוּם עֵד אֶחָד בְּאִישׁ לְכָל־עָוֹן וּלְכָל־חַטָּאת בְּכָל־
חֵטְא אֲשֶׁר יֶחֱטָא עַל־פִּי שְׁנֵי עֵדִים אוֹ עַל־פִּי
טז שְׁלֹשָׁה־עֵדִים יָקוּם דָּבָר: כִּי־יָקוּם עֵד־חָמָס בְּאִישׁ
יז לַעֲנוֹת בּוֹ סָרָה: וְעָמְדוּ שְׁנֵי־הָאֲנָשִׁים אֲשֶׁר־לָהֶם
הָרִיב לִפְנֵי יְהֹוָה לִפְנֵי הַכֹּהֲנִים וְהַשֹּׁפְטִים אֲשֶׁר

* יא סבירין האלה.

innocent will not be shed, bringing bloodguilt upon you in the land that the LORD your God is allotting to you.

11] If, however, a man who is his neighbor's enemy lies in wait for him and sets upon him and strikes him a fatal blow and then flees to one of these towns,   **12]** the elders of his town shall have him brought back from there and shall hand him over to the blood-avenger to be put to death;   **13]** you must show him no pity. Thus you will purge Israel of the blood of the innocent, and it will go well with you.

14] You shall not move your neighbor's landmarks, set up by previous generations, in the property that will be allotted to you in the land that the LORD your God is giving you to possess.

15] A single witness may not validate against a person any guilt or blame for any offense that may be committed; a case can be valid only on the testimony of two witnesses or more.   **16]** If a man appears against another to testify maliciously and gives false testimony against him,   **17]** the two parties to the dispute shall appear before the LORD, before the priests or

12] *Hand him over.* After a trial. Apparently the avenger functioned as a prosecutor.

13] *Blood of the innocent.* Which "pollutes the land" and cannot be cleansed "except by the blood of him who shed it" (Num. 35:33). Manslaughter did not permit of ransom (Exod. 21:12; Lev. 24:21; only when an animal had killed was it permitted, Exod. 21:30).

14] *Your neighbor's landmarks.* Their removal constituted an act of theft that was included in the imprecations pronounced on Mount Ebal (Deut. 27:17). Archeologists have found many boundary stones in Canaan as well as in Greece and Mesopotamia.

Set up by previous generations. By the רִאשֹׁנִים (rishonim), the early settlers. The translation projects the application of the law into the future, hence it speaks of property "that *will be* allotted

to you." But it is more likely that the verse addressed itself to conditions which had developed during the settlement and aimed at protecting impoverished or otherwise weakened farmers.

The Rabbis extended the law into the ethical realm, to prohibit an infringement of someone's honor and livelihood (see Gleanings).

15] *A single witness.* He was insufficient in criminal (as well as in most civil) cases; see Deut. 17:6; Num. 35:30.

Guilt . . . blame . . . offense. Stylistic variations which tradition, however, took to convey different meanings.

16] *Testify maliciously.* Literally, "a witness of violence," that is, who is doing violence to someone by perverting the truth.

17] *The two parties.* According to the Talmud, the two witnesses [12].

כ וְהַנִּשְׁאָרִים יִשְׁמְע֖וּ וְיִרָ֑אוּ וְלֹא־יֹסִ֣פוּ לַעֲשׂ֣וֹת ע֗וֹד
כא כַּדָּבָ֥ר הָרָ֛ע הַזֶּ֖ה בְּקִרְבֶּֽךָ: וְלֹ֥א תָח֖וֹס עֵינֶ֑ךָ נֶ֣פֶשׁ
בְּנֶ֣פֶשׁ עַ֤יִן בְּעַ֙יִן֙ שֵׁ֣ן בְּשֵׁ֔ן יָ֥ד בְּיָ֖ד רֶ֥גֶל בְּרָֽגֶל: ס

יח יִהְי֥וּ בַיָּמִ֖ים הָהֵ֑ם וְדָרְשׁ֤וּ הַשֹּׁפְטִים֙ הֵיטֵ֔ב וְהִנֵּ֥ה עֵד־
יט שֶׁ֙קֶר֙ הָעֵ֔ד שֶׁ֖קֶר עָנָ֣ה בְאָחִֽיו: וַעֲשִׂ֣יתֶם ל֗וֹ כַּאֲשֶׁ֥ר
זָמַ֛ם לַעֲשׂ֥וֹת לְאָחִ֖יו וּבִֽעַרְתָּ֥ הָרָ֖ע מִקִּרְבֶּֽךָ:

* יט הטעם נסוג אחור.

magistrates in authority at the time,   **18]** and the magistrates shall make a thorough investigation. If the man who testified is a false witness, if he has testified falsely against his fellow man,   **19]** you shall do to him as he schemed to do to his fellow. Thus you will sweep out evil from your midst;   **20]** others will hear and be afraid, and such evil things will not again be done in your midst.   **21]** Nor must you show pity: life for life, eye for eye, tooth for tooth, hand for hand, foot for foot.

19] *As he schemed.* Pharisees and Sadducees debated when this was to be applied. The latter held that the false witness was to be killed only if the person against whom he testified had already been executed; the Pharisees, only if the accused was still alive. The reason for this Pharisaic opinion was in turn debated by the Talmud and later commentators [13].

21] *Life for life.* Commonly referred to as *lex talionis*; for commentary see at Exod. 21:23 ff. The best current understanding of this law is that actual talion was not at all intended; rather, the provision represented an instance of public law developing from the private pursuit of justice and that compensation was intended.

More on the Cities of Refuge

Places of refuge,[1] where offenders against the law could find sanctuary, were not entirely unknown in the Mediterranean area, but the elaborate development of the institution was unique to Israel [14].

The original place was a shrine or altar, and the Book of Kings reports two such cases. In one, Adonijah, after his failed usurpation of the throne, fled to the altar where he held on to the horns; whereupon, after King Solomon promised him immunity, he left free and unmolested. In the other, Joab too fled to the Tabernacle, but in his instance Solomon did not respect the sanctuary and had the general killed (I Kings 1:50–53; 2:28–34). Apparently, Joab was considered an intentional manslayer to whom the law of refuge did not apply (Exod. 21:14).

The legislation that we find in the Torah is of a later time. In earlier days, any law breaker could repair to the altar and there find refuge, whether he be an escaped slave, a debtor, or a political offender. The Torah laws came to restrict this privilege to the unintentional manslayer, and in time the town in which the shrine was located was considered an extended place of sanctuary. For the manslayer, confinement to such a city was tantamount to punishment by exile, which ended when the High Priest died. The reason for this termination may have been that his death was deemed an expiation for all the unrequited deaths that had occurred during his regime.

The desire to centralize the cult in Jerusalem led to a reduction and thereafter abolition of outlying shrines, and the six cities—no longer identified as part of the forty-eight levitical cities as in Num. 35—became secular, judicial places of refuge, and no longer did the death of the High Priest play a role. In this way an old institution was transformed to meet changing conditions. We do not know for how long thereafter it enjoyed a viable existence.[2]

Magic and Mantic

Deut. 18:10–11 deal with two distinct types of practices, with magic and mantic.

Magic may be defined as a practice that attempts to utilize mysterious forces which are not controlled (in biblical terms) by God or (in scientific terms) by natural laws. Mantic is the art of divination. By knowing the secrets of certain signs, the practitioner "divines"—that is, he acts with godlike knowledge, but, unlike the purveyor of magic, he does not manipulate the suprahuman or human realms, he only interprets them. Of magic practitioners our chapter mentions those who manipulate gods, nature, and men: sorcerers and spell casters. It further mentions two types of mantic purveyors:

1. Those who consult the past (by getting in touch with the dead, or ghosts, or familiar spirits).

2. Those who predict the future (augurs, soothsayers, diviners, astrologers, dream interpreters, and false prophets who claim to represent God but base their pronouncements on illegitimate sources).

The biblical text decried these activities because they were unauthorized and not because they were believed to have no substance. When God played a role the practice

---

[1] The term עָרֵי מִקְלָט is not found in Deuteronomy but restricted to Numbers. For the basic discussion, see at Num. 35:9–34; also Exod. 21:12–14; see also at Deut. 4:41–43.

[2] One obtains a different view if Deuteronomy is believed to be older than Numbers, as many scholars aver (see "Introducing Deuteronomy").

was approved; thus Joseph and Daniel were considered inspired interpreters of dreams; Moses and Aaron were given special "signs" by God himself. The witch of En-dor whom King Saul consulted engaged in an illegal but not an impossible enterprise. Josiah, who had much to do with the codification of Deuteronomy, was a strong opponent of magic and mantic practices, which had been commonplace in the days of Jezebel and Manasseh (II Kings 9:22; 21:6; II Chron. 34:3–7).

Biblical opposition restrained but could not eradicate these activities, and belief in their efficacy persisted into medieval and even modern days. Especially in the Middle Ages, superstitious beliefs and practices of many kinds had as firm a hold on Jews as on their environment, although on the whole they were not experienced as a threat to Judaism, and witch hunts remained confined to the Christian community. Because mystical texts often utilized magic (and sometimes, mantic) concepts and presuppositions, mysticism itself has been viewed with suspicion, but often unfairly so, for in the history of religion the borderline between the authentic and inauthentic has on occasion become blurred. Belief in magic and mantic has waxed and waned, and, since the full mastery of reality must remain beyond human grasp, there will always be those who will attempt to enhance their power and knowledge by resorting to putative forces not subject to the revealed will of God or ordinary laws of nature [15].

GLEANINGS

Astrology

A dichotomy of powers between the gods and a realm beside or beyond them is implicit in all astrology. On the one hand, the heavenly bodies are living gods; therefore, astral phenomena are understood to reflect mythological events. But, besides the gods, immutable laws are operative as well. The influence of the stars follows natural and eternal laws. Within this framework the gods live out their lives. Hence the astral signs can be taken as both divine decisions and fixed laws of the metadivine realm. Because of the growing tendency toward stressing the latter scientific aspect, astrology was able eventually to separate itself entirely from the belief in gods. In Hellenistic times, it was grounded on a doctrine of cosmic sympathy, the mysterious interconnection of all phenomena whose signs are written in the heavens. For many centuries, it was deeply rooted even in the Christian and Jewish worlds. In paganism, however, it served as one of the expressions of the primary, fundamental subjection of the gods to the laws of a higher realm.   Y. KAUFMANN [16]

Magic in Egypt

Egypt was permeated with magical beliefs. It developed an enormous literature on the subject and a ramified manufacture of magical objects. Magic was called upon at every turn in life: to ward off spirits of the dead, demons, scorpions, serpents, wild beasts, fire, rain, injury, sickness, and enemies; to protect women in childbirth and newborn infants; and to ensure the dying man happiness beyond the grave. The gods have an important role as teachers of magical arts to men. Their names, uttered in spells or written on charms, are a chief means of conjuring. They themselves are regarded as charged with the same powers as are found in magical objects and devices. The dead king who "devours the gods" fills his belly with their power and knowledge. Moreover, the gods practice magic in their own right; man merely imitates them.

Y. KAUFMANN [17]

Magic in Biblical and Hellenic Religion

In truth, there is a clear distinction regarding

the concept of power between the prophetic-biblical-Jewish ideology and the magical-mystic belief of the Hellenistic world. The might of God is revealed, in the Bible, in the act of creation, and in the historical Providence with which He watched over His people, which serves as a source of hope to those who love and revere Him. The power remains even when He manifests himself—the power of an invisible God, who is immaterial. On the other hand, in the Hellenistic world the power was conceived as something impersonal, which was found in people and substance. It was a visible and material power. Magical acts were a concomitant of the nature of idolatry. Idolatry, in all its forms, believed in the existence of a source of power apart from the godhead, for it did not recognize a god who transcended the existential system that controlled everything and whose will was absolute. Magic flows from the desire to utilize these forces, and idolatry associates man with the deity in the need for magic. Nor does the fact that there was also opposition to sorcery and sorcerers affect the position. Idolatry forbade injurious magic, especially in the case of a rejected and defeated religion.   E. URBACH [18]

You Must Be Wholehearted with the Lord Your God (Deut. 18:13)

Even if no one sees you in your inner chamber and you are only "with your God," you must be wholehearted with Him.   ALSHECH [19]

The ת in תָּמִים (wholehearted) is written large. For if you walk wholehearted with God it is as if you sustained the Torah from א to ת.

BAAL HA-TURIM [20]

Five biblical verses convey the essence of Judaism:

"You must be wholehearted with the Lord your God" (Deut. 18:13).

"I have set the Lord always before me" (Ps. 16:8).

"You shall love your neighbor as yourself" (Lev. 19:18).

"In all your ways acknowledge Him" (Prov. 3:6).

"To walk humbly with your God" (Micah 6:8).

In Hebrew, the opening letters of these verses form the word תְּשׁוּבָה, repentance.   CHASIDIC [21]

Only in Israel

The prophet whom God will raise up must be "from among your own people" (Deut. 18:15). This means also that he must arise in the Land of Israel.   MIDRASH [22]

Cities of Refuge

Everything must be done so that the cities can be reached easily; this includes building roads and making them level.   MAIMONIDES [23]

Moving the Landmark (Deut. 19:14)

The law follows the warning (verse 13) to purge the land of innocent blood. Moving a landmark defiles the land like spilled blood.

D. HOFFMANN [24]

Why is the law necessary when we are already commanded "You shall not steal"? In order to make clear that any infringement of a neighbor's rights is included. The law also prohibits selling one's family graves, even those as yet unoccupied; and it forbids changing the words of a teacher which are pronounced in his name.

MIDRASH [25]

Administration of Law and State, III

Inevitably, the laws regulating the administration of the community return to the subject of war which was then, as it still is, a major means of arranging and rearranging human affairs. These Deuteronomic laws— Hoffmann calls them rules for preserving life, which therefore well fit the context of this section [1]—are designed to check the barbarity of war and "to bring it under the influence of the higher moral spirit of Israel's religion, and to secure recognition for the claims of morality and moderation" [2].

In this connection, the text deals with exemptions from the duty to serve, with the disposition of booty, the treatment of captive nations, and ecologic restrictions. The latter rules—unequaled in intent until modern conventions of war—became the starting point for extensive discussions on human responsibility toward the environment. Together with previous and subsequent passages on the subject of war (Deut. 7:16 ff.; 9:1 ff.; 31:3 ff.), the regulations form a body of "war sermons," as von Rad has described them [3]. They are followed by a prescription belonging to the leftovers of earlier times: the procedures to be observed when a community has a case of unsolved manslaughter on its hands. The cleansing ritual requires a heifer to be sacrificed in a particular way, and the juxtaposition of these rules to those of war emphasizes that all killing defiles the covenantal people whose purity needs constant watching and, when necessary, restoration.

א כִּי־תֵצֵא לַמִּלְחָמָה עַל־אֹיְבֶךָ וְרָאִיתָ סוּס וָרֶכֶב עַם
רַב מִמְּךָ לֹא תִירָא מֵהֶם כִּי־יְהֹוָה אֱלֹהֶיךָ עִמָּךְ
ב הַמַּעַלְךָ מֵאֶרֶץ מִצְרָיִם: וְהָיָה כְּקָרָבְכֶם אֶל־
ג הַמִּלְחָמָה וְנִגַּשׁ הַכֹּהֵן וְדִבֶּר אֶל־הָעָם: וְאָמַר אֲלֵהֶם
שְׁמַע יִשְׂרָאֵל אַתֶּם קְרֵבִים הַיּוֹם לַמִּלְחָמָה עַל־

אֹיְבֵיכֶם אַל־יֵרַךְ לְבַבְכֶם אַל־תִּירְאוּ וְאַל־תַּחְפְּזוּ
ד וְאַל־תַּעַרְצוּ מִפְּנֵיהֶם: כִּי יְהֹוָה אֱלֹהֵיכֶם הַהֹלֵךְ
עִמָּכֶם לְהִלָּחֵם לָכֶם עִם־אֹיְבֵיכֶם לְהוֹשִׁיעַ אֶתְכֶם:
ה וְדִבְּרוּ הַשֹּׁטְרִים אֶל־הָעָם לֵאמֹר מִי־הָאִישׁ אֲשֶׁר
בָּנָה בַיִת־חָדָשׁ וְלֹא חֲנָכוֹ יֵלֵךְ וְיָשֹׁב לְבֵיתוֹ פֶּן־יָמוּת

1] When you take the field against your enemies, and see horses and chariots—forces larger than yours—have no fear of them, for the LORD your God, who brought you from the land of Egypt, is with you. **2]** Before you join battle, the priest shall come forward and address the troops. **3]** He shall say to them, "Hear, O Israel! You are about to join battle with your enemy. Let not your courage falter. Do not be in fear, or in panic, or in dread of them. **4]** For it is the LORD your God who marches with you to do battle for you against your enemy, to bring you victory."

5] Then the officials shall address the troops, as follows, "Is there anyone who has built a new house but has not dedicated it? Let him go back to his home, lest he die in battle and

20:1] *When you take the field.* Most likely, these rules applied only to certain types of war, not to life-and-death defensive struggles (see commentary below).

Horses and chariots. Used by the Egyptians and Assyrians; because of the success they vouchsafed, the Israelites too desired to possess them, although their first reliance should have been on God. Isaiah (31:1) inveighs against "those who go down to Egypt for help and rely on horses," and the Psalmist (20:8) says: "They call on chariots, they call on horses, but we call on the name of the Lord our God." See also Deut. 17:16.

2] *The priest.* Tradition called him "the priest anointed for war," a specialist whose status was comparable to that of the High Priest [4].

3] *Hear, O Israel!* The formulaic opening of his address stresses its ritual nature.

4] *God who marches with you.* Either a figure of speech or a reference to the ark which was carried into battle.

A rabbinic scholar held that there were always two arks: one with the tablets of the Ten Commandments which stayed behind and one with the broken tablets which went with the army [5].

5] *Then the officials.* Representing the king. The people are addressed first by the most important personage, the priest; then by the officials; and finally the lowest in this order, the army commanders, take over (verse 9).

Is there anyone . . .? The exemptions follow an order of ever greater anxiety: the home builder, the farmer (who works four years before he harvests), the newly married, and lastly the coward. In the Maccabean wars these prescriptions were recorded to have been carried out (in the second century B.C.E., I Macc. 3:56).

According to the Talmud, those who claimed an exemption had to submit proof, much like a conscientious objector under American law [6].

Let him go back. Tradition saw this as a command: he *had* to go back, for his anxiety would prove infectious (verse 8). Also, most men in such positions would be too embarrassed to exercise their option [7].

According to von Rad, the reason lay elsewhere: it was believed that someone who had to dedicate a thing was threatened by demons who were dangerous for others as well [8].

בַּמִּלְחָמָה וְאִישׁ אַחֵר יַחְנְכֶנּוּ: וּמִי־הָאִישׁ אֲשֶׁר־נָטַע
כֶּרֶם וְלֹא חִלְּלוֹ יֵלֵךְ וְיָשֹׁב לְבֵיתוֹ פֶּן־יָמוּת בַּמִּלְחָמָה
וְאִישׁ אַחֵר יְחַלְּלֶנּוּ: וּמִי־הָאִישׁ אֲשֶׁר אֵרַשׂ אִשָּׁה וְלֹא
לְקָחָהּ יֵלֵךְ וְיָשֹׁב לְבֵיתוֹ פֶּן־יָמוּת בַּמִּלְחָמָה וְאִישׁ
אַחֵר יִקָּחֶנָּה: וְיָסְפוּ הַשֹּׁטְרִים לְדַבֵּר אֶל־הָעָם
וְאָמְרוּ מִי־הָאִישׁ הַיָּרֵא וְרַךְ הַלֵּבָב יֵלֵךְ וְיָשֹׁב לְבֵיתוֹ
וְלֹא יִמַּס אֶת־לְבַב אֶחָיו כִּלְבָבוֹ: וְהָיָה כְּכַלֹּת
הַשֹּׁטְרִים לְדַבֵּר אֶל־הָעָם וּפָקְדוּ שָׂרֵי צְבָאוֹת

בְּרֹאשׁ הָעָם: ס כִּי־תִקְרַב אֶל־עִיר לְהִלָּחֵם
עָלֶיהָ וְקָרָאתָ אֵלֶיהָ לְשָׁלוֹם: וְהָיָה אִם־שָׁלוֹם תַּעַנְךָ
וּפָתְחָה לָךְ וְהָיָה כָּל־הָעָם הַנִּמְצָא־בָהּ יִהְיוּ לְךָ
לָמַס וַעֲבָדוּךָ: וְאִם־לֹא תַשְׁלִים עִמָּךְ וְעָשְׂתָה עִמְּךָ
מִלְחָמָה וְצַרְתָּ עָלֶיהָ: וּנְתָנָהּ יְהֹוָה אֱלֹהֶיךָ בְּיָדֶךָ
וְהִכִּיתָ אֶת־כָּל־זְכוּרָהּ לְפִי־חָרֶב: רַק הַנָּשִׁים וְהַטַּף
וְהַבְּהֵמָה וְכֹל אֲשֶׁר יִהְיֶה בָעִיר כָּל־שְׁלָלָהּ תָּבֹז לָךְ
וְאָכַלְתָּ אֶת־שְׁלַל אֹיְבֶיךָ אֲשֶׁר נָתַן יְהֹוָה אֱלֹהֶיךָ לָךְ:

another dedicate it. **6]** Is there anyone who has planted a vineyard but has never harvested it? Let him go back to his home, lest he die in battle and another initiate it. **7]** Is there anyone who has paid the bride-price for a wife, but who has not yet married her? Let him go back to his home, lest he die in battle and another marry her." **8]** The officials shall go on addressing the troops and say, "Is there anyone afraid and disheartened? Let him go back to his home, lest the courage of his comrades flag like his." **9]** When the officials have finished addressing the troops, army commanders shall assume command of the troops.

10] When you approach a town to attack it, you shall offer it terms of peace. **11]** If it responds peaceably and lets you in, all the people present there shall serve you at forced labor. **12]** If it does not surrender to you, but would join battle with you, you shall lay siege to it; **13]** and when the LORD your God delivers it into your hand, you shall put all its males to the sword. **14]** You may, however, take as your booty the women, the children, and the livestock, and everything in the town—all its spoil—and enjoy the use of the spoil of your enemy which the LORD your God gives you.

6] *Who . . . has never harvested.* Literally, "profaned," that is, he has not yet removed it from sacred restrictions to his own private use, which could take place only after four years had elapsed since planting (Lev. 19:23–25).

7] *Paid the bride-price.* He was considered legally married, though he had not as yet lived with his wife. The fully married also had a one-year exemption (Deut. 24:5). The ceremony of betrothal was once entirely separate from the marriage; in the traditional wedding of today the two are joined and the ritual begins with a "betrothal blessing," בְּרְכַּת אֵירוּסִין.

Let him go back. According to the Mishnah, the man had to perform noncombatant service, like helping to provide food and water for the army and repairing the roads [9].

In the modern American army, the draft was first directed to the unmarried, but being newly married provided no special exemption.

9] *When the officials have finished.* After the ritual, the physical preparations for war begin.

10] *Approach a town.* Which lies outside of Canaan, according to verses 15–16.

Terms of peace. A euphemism for "call to surrender."

11] *Forced labor.* The likely meaning is that the city, through its people, was to perform certain tasks, not that individual citizens were to be impressed.

12] *Lay siege.* This consisted of constructing siege works (see verse 20), such as building mounds for the scaling of the city's walls, attempts to burn the gates (usually made of wood), and to starve the population.

טו כֵּן תַּעֲשֶׂה לְכָל־הֶעָרִים הָרְחֹקֹת מִמְּךָ מְאֹד אֲשֶׁר
טז לֹא־מֵעָרֵי הַגּוֹיִם־הָאֵלֶּה הֵנָּה: רַק מֵעָרֵי הָעַמִּים
הָאֵלֶּה אֲשֶׁר יְהוָה אֱלֹהֶיךָ נֹתֵן לְךָ נַחֲלָה לֹא תְחַיֶּה
יז כָּל־נְשָׁמָה: כִּי־הַחֲרֵם תַּחֲרִימֵם הַחִתִּי וְהָאֱמֹרִי
הַכְּנַעֲנִי וְהַפְּרִזִּי הַחִוִּי וְהַיְבוּסִי כַּאֲשֶׁר צִוְּךָ יְהוָה
יח אֱלֹהֶיךָ: לְמַעַן אֲשֶׁר לֹא־יְלַמְּדוּ אֶתְכֶם לַעֲשׂוֹת כְּכֹל
תּוֹעֲבֹתָם אֲשֶׁר עָשׂוּ לֵאלֹהֵיהֶם וַחֲטָאתֶם לַיהוָה
יט אֱלֹהֵיכֶם: ס כִּי־תָצוּר אֶל־עִיר יָמִים רַבִּים

לְהִלָּחֵם עָלֶיהָ לְתָפְשָׂהּ לֹא־תַשְׁחִית אֶת־עֵצָהּ לִנְדֹּחַ
עָלָיו גַּרְזֶן כִּי מִמֶּנּוּ תֹאכֵל וְאֹתוֹ לֹא תִכְרֹת כִּי
כ הָאָדָם עֵץ הַשָּׂדֶה לָבֹא מִפָּנֶיךָ בַּמָּצוֹר: רַק עֵץ
אֲשֶׁר־תֵּדַע כִּי לֹא־עֵץ מַאֲכָל הוּא אֹתוֹ תַשְׁחִית
וְכָרָתָּ וּבָנִיתָ מָצוֹר עַל־הָעִיר אֲשֶׁר־הִוא עֹשָׂה עִמְּךָ
מִלְחָמָה עַד רִדְתָּהּ: פ
א כִּי־יִמָּצֵא חָלָל בָּאֲדָמָה אֲשֶׁר יְהוָה אֱלֹהֶיךָ נֹתֵן לְךָ

15] Thus you shall deal with all towns that lie very far from you; towns that do not belong to nations hereabout.   16] In the towns of the latter peoples, however, which the LORD your God is giving you as a heritage, you shall not let a soul remain alive.   17] No, you must proscribe them—the Hittites and the Amorites, the Canaanites and the Perizzites, the Hivites and the Jebusites—as the LORD your God has commanded you,   18] lest they lead you into doing all the abhorrent things that they have done for their gods and you stand guilty before the LORD your God.

19] When in your war against a city you have to besiege it a long time in order to capture it, you must not destroy its trees, wielding the ax against them. You may eat of them, but you must not cut them down. Are trees of the field human to withdraw before you into the besieged city?   20] Only trees which you know do not yield food may be destroyed; you may cut them down for constructing siegeworks against the city that is waging war on you, until it has been reduced.

1] If, in the land that the LORD your God is giving you to possess, someone slain is found

---

15] *Very far from you.* Lying outside of Canaan.

16] *Not let a soul remain alive.* See at Deut. 7:2. This is a retrospective command: had you done this you would not have lapsed into idolatry. In the actual invasion no wholesale extermination of the local population took place, although such a procedure would not have offended against the usual practice of the times.

17] *Proscribe them.* Put them under the ban, for they belong to God and are therefore unfit for human use; see at Lev. 27:29. The Girgashites, mentioned in Deut. 7:1, are not listed here. Tradition explained the omission by speculating that this people had meanwhile, in anticipation of Israel's invasion, migrated to Africa [10].

19] *You must not cut them down.* Forbidding deforestation, which was a common practice in ancient warfare (similar to defoliation in modern

days) [11]. However, a scorched-earth policy was carried out by the Israelites in a campaign against the Moabites, and the exception was said to have been ordered by God himself; II Kings 3:19.

Are trees ... human ...? Meaning, you are warring against people, not trees.

The Hebrew was understood by some as a positive statement: "a human being is (like) a tree," which stresses his close dependence on vegetation [12].

20] *Until it has been reduced.* Tradition took this as a proof text that a siege could be continued even on the Sabbath [13].

21:1] *Someone slain.* חָלָל (*chalal*) is of the same root as חִלֵּל (*chilel*, profane). Killing soils the land and must be expiated either by the death of the culprit or, if he is not identified, by a special procedure.

ג לְרִשְׁתָּהּ נֹפֵל בַּשָּׂדֶה לֹא נוֹדַע מִי הִכָּהוּ: וְיָצְאוּ
זְקֵנֶיךָ וְשֹׁפְטֶיךָ וּמָדְדוּ אֶל־הֶעָרִים אֲשֶׁר סְבִיבֹת
הֶחָלָל: וְהָיָה הָעִיר הַקְּרֹבָה אֶל־הֶחָלָל וְלָקְחוּ זִקְנֵי
הָעִיר הַהִוא עֶגְלַת בָּקָר אֲשֶׁר לֹא־עֻבַּד בָּהּ אֲשֶׁר
לֹא־מָשְׁכָה בְּעֹל: וְהוֹרִדוּ זִקְנֵי הָעִיר הַהִוא אֶת־
הָעֶגְלָה אֶל־נַחַל אֵיתָן אֲשֶׁר לֹא־יֵעָבֵד בּוֹ וְלֹא
יִזָּרֵעַ וְעָרְפוּ־שָׁם אֶת־הָעֶגְלָה בַּנָּחַל: וְנִגְּשׁוּ הַכֹּהֲנִים
בְּנֵי לֵוִי כִּי בָם בָּחַר יְהוָה אֱלֹהֶיךָ לְשָׁרְתוֹ וּלְבָרֵךְ

ו בְּשֵׁם יְהוָה וְעַל־פִּיהֶם יִהְיֶה כָּל־רִיב וְכָל־נָגַע: וְכֹל
זִקְנֵי הָעִיר הַהִוא הַקְּרֹבִים אֶל־הֶחָלָל יִרְחֲצוּ אֶת־
יְדֵיהֶם עַל־הָעֶגְלָה הָעֲרוּפָה בַנָּחַל: וְעָנוּ וְאָמְרוּ
יָדֵינוּ לֹא שָׁפְכֻה אֶת־הַדָּם הַזֶּה וְעֵינֵינוּ לֹא רָאוּ:
ח כַּפֵּר לְעַמְּךָ יִשְׂרָאֵל אֲשֶׁר־פָּדִיתָ יְהוָה וְאַל־תִּתֵּן דָּם
ט נָקִי בְּקֶרֶב עַמְּךָ יִשְׂרָאֵל וְנִכַּפֵּר לָהֶם הַדָּם: וְאַתָּה
תְּבַעֵר הַדָּם הַנָּקִי מִקִּרְבֶּךָ כִּי־תַעֲשֶׂה הַיָּשָׁר בְּעֵינֵי
יְהוָה:

Haftarah Shofetim, p. 1607

ז שפכו קרי.

---

lying in the open, the identity of the slayer not being known, **2]** your elders and magistrates shall go out and measure the distances from the corpse to the nearby towns. **3]** The elders of the town nearest to the corpse shall then take a heifer which has never been worked, which has never pulled in a yoke; **4]** and the elders of that town shall bring the heifer down to a rugged wadi, which is not tilled or sown. There, in the wadi, they shall break the heifer's neck. **5]** The priests, sons of Levi, shall come forward; for the LORD your God has chosen them to minister to Him and to pronounce blessing in the name of the LORD, and every lawsuit and case of assault is subject to their ruling. **6]** Then all the elders of the town nearest to the corpse shall wash their hands over the heifer whose neck was broken in the wadi. **7]** And they shall make this declaration: "Our hands did not shed this blood, nor did our eyes see it done. **8]** Absolve, O LORD, Your people Israel whom You redeemed, and do not let guilt for the blood of the innocent remain among Your people Israel." And they will be absolved of bloodguilt. **9]** Thus you will remove from your midst guilt for the blood of the innocent, for you will be doing what is right in the sight of the LORD.

2] *Your elders and magistrates.* Originally, these came from the nearest cities; later they were drawn from cities with courts and from Jerusalem [14].

3] *A heifer.* Similar to one that was offered as a firstling; Deut. 15:19.

4] *Rugged wadi.* Others, "wadi running with water" or "rough valley" [15].

Not tilled or sown. Similar to the restrictions for the heifer.

They. The magistrates. For the meaning of the ritual, see commentary below.

5] *The priests.* Up to this point they have not been mentioned. The text has better continuity without this verse; most likely, it is a later addition.

Case of assault. Or, "of skin affection," see Deut. 17:8 and 24:8.

6] *Wash their hands.* The ritual of purification symbolized their innocence. Thus Psalm 26:6: "I wash my hands in innocence" (see also Ps. 73:13). Hence also the English expression "to wash one's hands of a matter."

7] *Our hands did not shed.* The elders speak in the name of the community.

8] *Absolve.* כַּפֵּר (*kapper*); the same root appears in the word (Yom) Kippur. The purpose of the process is to restore the city to its condition of guiltlessness.

The Conduct of War

In the biblical view, warfare was unavoidable and sometimes necessary [16]; universal peace was envisioned for posthistorical days (Micah 4:3). Until then, God's people too had to fight, and in such struggles, if they were righteous in purpose and conduct, God's assistance was anticipated. For, since Israel's existence in this world was bound up with God's will, the nation's wars were ultimately His wars: they were holy struggles. Hence, the preparations for war were ritualized, as were the distribution of booty and the treatment of the enemy, and the fight itself was directed by the One who was called "Lord of Hosts." The priest (verse 2) was a kind of antique army chaplain, but his service was not designed to assist the individual soldier; rather, he aimed at binding the fighting men to the purposes of God, and thus he literally "consecrated" or "sanctified" the war. Hence his status approached that of the High Priest [17].

The concept that wars could serve the deity was an old one and not unique to Israel. The "Israel dimension" grew out of specific historic experiences which were seen as manifestations of God's will, as judgments on His own people and on other nations, the divine element operating in the unfolding of history. It is likely that the ritual which developed, and which is codified in our chapter, also had a pragmatic effect in that it helped to unify the nation, for it reminded Israel of its spiritual destiny and spurred it on to greater national devotion.

Later tradition distinguished between various kinds of war and coined a special terminology to describe them. The conquest of the land as well as a defensive war that was fought to assure Israel's survival was called "obligatory" (*milchemet mitzvah*) [18], whereas any other war—such as a preemptive struggle—was merely optional (*milchemet reshut*). The Deuteronomic law of military exemptions was considered applicable only to the optional war; in a battle for survival no one was excused from serving, not even a bridegroom; he had to go forth from the bridal chamber to do his share in the war [19].

How closely these rules were observed in practice is hard to say; they were doubtlessly at one time part of the cult and faded away when Israel's independence was destroyed.

The Uses of Nature

The text says: "When in your war against a city you have to besiege it a long time in order to capture it, *you must not destroy its trees*, wielding the ax against them. . . . Are trees of the field human to withdraw before you into the besieged city?" The prohibition applied to food-yielding trees only; others were permitted for the construction of siege works (Deut. 20:19–20) [20].

These verses are clearly a limitation on the principle enunciated in Gen. 1:28 that humanity may utilize ("master") the earth's resources to the fullest. For "the earth is the Lord's with all that it holds" (Ps. 24:1), and God reminds His creatures that they must operate within certain laws—for their own benefit as well as that of nature. The Torah had no literal equivalent of our "ecology," but the interdependence of creation and humanity and the dependence of both on God were part of its world view. The institution of the sabbatical year, when the farmer was to let the fields lie fallow so that they might recuperate, not only represented the insights of agricultural experience but had above all a socio-religious dimension. The poor and the stranger were to benefit from this seventh-year cessation, and thereby God reasserted His ownership of the land.

The Rabbis expanded the biblical law considerably and created a whole category of actions that fell under the prohibition of wastefulness, which they called בַּל־תַּשְׁחִית

(*bal tashchit*).[1] They ruled that the law against cutting down a fruit tree, by extension, also forbade drawing off its sap for the sake of destruction, and thus defoliation of such trees would also be considered contrary to the spirit of the law. When a tree is cut down, as the saying goes, its voice of pain resounds throughout the world.

The halachah went still further. It ruled that spoliation of fruit was forbidden, as was diverting the flow of a river to cause distress to a besieged city; and Maimonides formulated the rules of tradition as follows: All needless destruction is included in this prohibition; for instance, whoever burns a garment, or breaks a vessel needlessly, contravenes the command "You must not destroy" [21]. A talmudic opinion even stated that someone who could get along on corn but insisted on eating wheat (a rarer commodity), or someone who could drink mead but drank wine instead, infringed on the ordinance of *bal tashchit* [22]. For creation was seen as an ongoing process, and humans at all times were God's co-partners in safeguarding its potential. The Torah uses the example of behavior during warfare to demonstrate the importance of this principle.

Unsolved Manslaughter

The expiatory ritual for unsolved manslaughter, contained in 21:1–9, undoubtedly went back to very ancient times, and there are Hittite laws resembling the Torah in this respect. Underlying these provisions was the concept that murder stained the land and that without the punishment of the guilty the cultic purity of the community was impaired. The community nearest the place of the evil deed was considered responsible,[2] and a heifer was chosen to ward off the wrath of the Divine. Once the ritual was completed, God's assurance of forgiveness was obtained and the community's purity restored [23].

The expiation ceremony is complemented by Lev. 4:13–15 (provision for cleansing the community from some unspecified sin) and Num., chapter 19 (dealing with the sacrifice of the red heifer). The three passages apparently arose in different ages but served the same general purpose. Traditional commentators considered the law in Leviticus as the overarching rule and the provisions in Numbers and Deuteronomy as specific examples.

They also found the ritual of the *eglah arufah* (the broken-necked heifer) to have had a practical value. Hoffmann reasoned that it would attract so much public attention and interest that the level of communal responsibility would be raised by this procedure as much as by the execution of the apprehended murderer. Abarbanel said that its shock value would prevent the people from forgetting the act and would keep alive the search for the offender [24]. The Mishnah reports that the procedure ceased when crimes of murder multiplied to such a degree that the ritual was no longer feasible [25].

---

[1] A variant of the phrase in verse 19: *lo tashchit*, "you must not destroy."

[2] See Gleanings for the talmudic controversy on why the nearest city was thus singled out.

GLEANINGS

Only with Justice

Why do the prescriptions concerning warfare follow the rules of justice in the preceding chapter? To teach that Israel will succeed in war only if it practices justice.　　　　RASHI [26]

Have No Fear (Deut. 20:1)

This is one of the 365 negative commands of the Torah. One who exhibits fear is answerable for the loss of life he occasions by his attitude.

MAIMONIDES [27]

He who fears humans is likely to have forgotten God.　　　　TRADITIONAL [28]

Enemies

God delivers not only from human enemies (20:4) but also helps us to victory in the battle against the evil impulse.　　　　CHASIDIC [29]

Peace

The greatness of peace may be seen from Scripture. Even when it deals with war it commands: When you make war, first proclaim peace (20:10).

Great is peace, for God has placed it in heaven itself, as it is said: "He makes peace in His high places" (Job 25:2).　　　　MIDRASH [30]

Two Views on War

After World War I, in 1924, the Central Conference of American Rabbis resolved:

We believe that war is morally indefensible.

But after World War II, in 1955, the emphasis changed:

We reject the spreading cancer of despair that wracks the soul of mankind with the anguish of inevitable war [31].

Priorities

From the order in which the exemptions from service are listed (20:5–7), one may conclude that a man first ought to build a house, then plant a vineyard, and then proceed to marry.

TALMUD [32]

Homilies

The three exemptions may be likened to a person's return to his religious roots:

To his faith, that is, when a person has acquired its foundations but has not yet lived by it.

To the commandments, that is, if he observes them but not yet for God's sake.

To the Torah, that is, if he engages in its study but not yet for its own sake.

YALKUT ME'AM LO'EZ [33]

The officials ask: "Is there anyone afraid . . . ?" (20:8) This means: . . . of the sins he has committed.　　　　MISHNAH [34]

It also refers to someone constantly preoccupied with his guilt.　　　　CHASIDIC [35]

Eglah Arufah (the heifer whose neck is broken, 21:1 ff.)

The ritual of expiating an unsolved murder occasioned an interesting controversy between the Palestinian and Babylonian Rabbis. It concerned the declaration by the elders of the town nearest the scene of the crime who state (verse 7): "Our hands did not shed this blood, nor did our eyes see it done." But was there ever any suspicion that it was the elders who were the slayers?

The Palestinian Rabbis took this to refer to the unknown slayer, meaning: No one came within our jurisdiction whom we neglected to bring to justice. The Babylonian Rabbis referred the text

to the victim, meaning: No one came within our jurisdiction for whom we failed to provide protection or whom we left without a livelihood.

MISHNAH [36]

Thus responsibility for wrongdoing does not only lie with the perpetrator himself and even with the accessory. Lack of proper care and attention is also criminal. Whoever keeps to his own quiet corner and refuses to have anything to do with the "evil world," who observes oppression and violence but does not stir a finger in protest, cannot proclaim with a clear conscience that "our hands have not shed this blood."

N. LEIBOWITZ [37]

Low-Key

If Scripture's call to mankind to safeguard the earth is too restrained for the liking of today's ecological activists, we might bear in mind that the Bible originated in an era when nature worship and the adoration of natural forces and phenomena were prevalent. The Bible fought against this Zeitgeist and strove to implant in its audience an awareness of the worth of the human being, a recognition of the preciousness in the eyes of the Lord of human suffering and human happiness. "Man was created in the image of God" and he was not to be broken by fear of the forces of nature or by the tyranny of nature cults. Viewed in this context, the concern of the biblical tradition for nature had to be formulated, of necessity, in a low-keyed message. But the concern was clearly and unmistakably there. Woven into the narrative, written into specific laws, it is remarkable evidence that the Bible is truly our life and the length of our days, that we may dwell on the land which destiny has provided for us (Deut. 30:20).

E. G. FREUDENSTEIN [38]

The Social Weal, I

The section before us contains a series of diverse laws. Most of them (to speak in modern terms) aim at impressing moral values on the social structure so that Israel may in every respect be worthy of being God's people. Others, such as the law of fringes, deal with the special status of Israel as God's people or, as in the laws against unnatural mixtures, with the need to preserve the intent of creation.

The following subjects are treated: rights of women who are captives of war or who no longer enjoy their husbands' love; treatment of a defiant, rebellious son; burial of an executed criminal; consideration for the property of others; unnatural mixtures—among people, crops, animals, and clothing materials; consideration for animals; fringes.

According to Maimonides, the new weekly portion, *Ki Tetze*, which begins here with 21:10, contains seventy-two mitzvot. One of these—dealing with a mother bird and her young—became the center of a famous dispute over the justice of God (see commentary).

ס   ס   ס

י כִּי־תֵצֵא לַמִּלְחָמָה עַל־אֹיְבֶיךָ וּנְתָנוֹ יְהֹוָה אֱלֹהֶיךָ
יא בְּיָדֶךָ וְשָׁבִיתָ שִׁבְיוֹ: וְרָאִיתָ בַּשִּׁבְיָה אֵשֶׁת יְפַת־תֹּאַר
יב וְחָשַׁקְתָּ בָהּ וְלָקַחְתָּ לְךָ לְאִשָּׁה: וַהֲבֵאתָהּ אֶל־תּוֹךְ
בֵּיתֶךָ וְגִלְּחָה אֶת־רֹאשָׁהּ וְעָשְׂתָה אֶת־צִפָּרְנֶיהָ:
יג וְהֵסִירָה אֶת־שִׂמְלַת שִׁבְיָהּ מֵעָלֶיהָ וְיָשְׁבָה בְּבֵיתֶךָ
וּבָכְתָה אֶת־אָבִיהָ וְאֶת־אִמָּהּ יֶרַח יָמִים וְאַחַר כֵּן

יד תָּבוֹא אֵלֶיהָ וּבְעַלְתָּהּ וְהָיְתָה לְךָ לְאִשָּׁה: וְהָיָה אִם־
לֹא חָפַצְתָּ בָּהּ וְשִׁלַּחְתָּהּ לְנַפְשָׁהּ וּמָכֹר לֹא־תִמְכְּרֶנָּה
בַּכֶּסֶף לֹא־תִתְעַמֵּר בָּהּ תַּחַת אֲשֶׁר עִנִּיתָהּ: ס
טו כִּי־תִהְיֶיןָ לְאִישׁ שְׁתֵּי נָשִׁים הָאַחַת אֲהוּבָה וְהָאַחַת
שְׂנוּאָה וְיָלְדוּ־לוֹ בָנִים הָאֲהוּבָה וְהַשְּׂנוּאָה וְהָיָה הַבֵּן
טז הַבְּכֹר לַשְּׂנִיאָה: וְהָיָה בְּיוֹם הַנְחִילוֹ אֶת־בָּנָיו אֵת
אֲשֶׁר־יִהְיֶה לוֹ לֹא יוּכַל לְבַכֵּר אֶת־בֶּן־הָאֲהוּבָה עַל־

10] When you take the field against your enemies, and the LORD your God delivers them into your power and you take some of them captive, **11]** and you see among the captives a beautiful woman and you desire her and would take her to wife, **12]** you shall bring her into your house, and she shall trim her hair, pare her nails, **13]** and discard her captive's garb. She shall spend a month's time in your house lamenting her father and mother; after that you may come to her and possess her, and she shall be your wife. **14]** Then, should you no longer want her, you must release her outright. You must not sell her for money: since you had your will of her, you must not enslave her.

15] If a man has two wives, one loved and the other unloved, and both the loved and the unloved have borne him sons, but the first-born is the son of the unloved one— **16]** when he wills his property to his sons, he may not treat as first-born the son of the loved one in disregard

---

21:10–14] It should be noted that these verses present ideal and theoretical, rather than practical, legislation. Actual warfare, then and always, gave vent to humanity's basest impulses; killing, rape, and looting were, and remain, its ambience. The Torah must be seen to have here a meliorating purpose, a statement of how God's people, if war became their lot, *should* behave.

Although the text does not say so, later tradition took it to apply to non-obligatory wars, as in Deut. 20:1. Verses 10–14 appear to belong directly after 20:20, where they may have stood at one time. The permission to marry a captive did not extend to Canaanite women, who were not permitted to Israelites (Deut. 7:3).

12] *Trim her hair.* Others, "shave her head." The procedure signified a change in the woman's status.

The custom persists among some Orthodox women who cut off their hair prior to marriage.

Pare her nails. Many understand this in the opposite sense: "let her nails grow." Commentators have suggested various reasons for the law, such as control of certain idolatrous practices [1].

Note that traditional Jewish law provides generally that a person must bury or burn the parings of nails [2].

13] *Month's time.* To adjust, like a mourner, to her changed status; cf. Num. 20:29; Deut. 34:8.

15] *Two wives.* The Bible permitted polygamy, though the law indicates that multiple marriage would likely lead to serious problems. Rachel and Leah, Hannah and Peninnah were examples of the "loved" and "unloved" wives (Gen. 29:30–31; I Sam. 1).

The first-born. Under the prevailing rule of primogeniture, the first-born son had certain rights: he inherited a double portion and succeeded the father as head of the family. He could sell his birthright (as Esau did, Gen. 25:29 ff.) or he could be deprived of it by his father (as Reuben was, Gen. 49:3–4), but only for cause, and not because he was the son of an unloved mother. In that sense, his mother had a stake in seeing her son's prerogatives maintained.

פְּנֵי בֶן־הַשְּׂנוּאָה הַבְּכֹר: כִּי אֶת־הַבְּכֹר בֶּן־הַשְּׂנוּאָה יז

יַכִּיר לָתֶת לוֹ פִּי שְׁנַיִם בְּכֹל אֲשֶׁר־יִמָּצֵא לוֹ כִּי־הוּא

רֵאשִׁית אֹנוֹ לוֹ מִשְׁפַּט הַבְּכֹרָה: ס כִּי־יִהְיֶה לְאִישׁ יח

בֵּן סוֹרֵר וּמוֹרֶה אֵינֶנּוּ שֹׁמֵעַ בְּקוֹל אָבִיו וּבְקוֹל אִמּוֹ

וְיִסְּרוּ אֹתוֹ וְלֹא יִשְׁמַע אֲלֵיהֶם: וְתָפְשׂוּ בוֹ אָבִיו יט

וְאִמּוֹ וְהוֹצִיאוּ אֹתוֹ אֶל־זִקְנֵי עִירוֹ וְאֶל־שַׁעַר מְקֹמוֹ:

וְאָמְרוּ אֶל־זִקְנֵי עִירוֹ בְּנֵנוּ זֶה סוֹרֵר וּמֹרֶה אֵינֶנּוּ כ

שֹׁמֵעַ בְּקֹלֵנוּ זוֹלֵל וְסֹבֵא: וּרְגָמֻהוּ כָּל־אַנְשֵׁי עִירוֹ כא

בָאֲבָנִים וָמֵת וּבִעַרְתָּ הָרָע מִקִּרְבֶּךָ וְכָל־יִשְׂרָאֵל

יִשְׁמְעוּ וְיִרָאוּ: ס וְכִי־יִהְיֶה בְאִישׁ חֵטְא מִשְׁפַּט־ כב

מָוֶת וְהוּמָת וְתָלִיתָ אֹתוֹ עַל־עֵץ: לֹא־תָלִין נִבְלָתוֹ כג

עַל־הָעֵץ כִּי־קָבוֹר תִּקְבְּרֶנּוּ בַּיּוֹם הַהוּא כִּי־קִלְלַת

אֱלֹהִים תָּלוּי וְלֹא תְטַמֵּא אֶת־אַדְמָתְךָ אֲשֶׁר יְהוָה

אֱלֹהֶיךָ נֹתֵן לְךָ נַחֲלָה: ס

of the son of the unloved one who is older. **17]** Instead, he must accept the first-born, the son of the unloved one, and allot to him a double portion of all he possesses; since he is the first fruit of his vigor, the birthright is his due.

18] If a man has a wayward and defiant son, who does not heed his father or mother and does not obey them even after they discipline him, **19]** his father and mother shall take hold of him and bring him out to the elders of his town at the public place of his community. **20]** They shall say to the elders of his town, "This son of ours is disloyal and defiant; he does not heed us. He is a glutton and a drunkard." **21]** Thereupon the men of his town shall stone him to death. Thus you will sweep out evil from your midst: all Israel will hear and be afraid.

22] If a man is guilty of a capital offense and is put to death, and you impale him on a stake, **23]** you must not let his corpse remain on the stake overnight, but must bury him the same day. For an impaled body is an affront to God: you shall not defile the land that the LORD your God is giving you to possess.

17] *Double portion.* Effectively, "two-thirds."

18] *A wayward and defiant son.* This harsh procedure takes to an extreme the provisions found elsewhere in the Torah, where death is provided for those who strike or curse their parents (Exod. 21:15, 17; Lev. 20:9; Deut. 27:16); although, if "cursing" parents is to be understood as "insulting" them, the treatment of the wayward son would appear less extreme. But there is a possibility that the law is to be seen primarily as a warning, and a Sage of the Talmud flatly declared that the conditions which would cause a court to decree the death penalty "never occurred and never will occur" [3]. A biblical proverb suggests that a defiant son will have a bad end, but it does not refer to a trial:

The eye that mocks at his father,/ And despises to obey his mother,/ The ravens of the valley shall pick it out,/ And the young vultures shall eat it (Prov. 30:17).

20] *A glutton and a drunkard.* Prov. 23:20–21 warn:

Be not among winebibbers,/ Among gluttonous eaters of flesh;/ For the drunkard and the glutton shall come to poverty,/ And drowsiness shall clothe a man with rags.

22] *Impale him on a stake.* Or, "hang him on a gibbet" (New English Bible) or "on a tree" (old JPS translation). The impaling was not itself a form of execution and probably took place only after the offender's execution by other means. The passage may have been placed here because the previous law specified death by stoning, and it is now stated that impaling must follow the stoning.

23] *Bury him the same day.* Tradition expanded this to all burials [4]. See commentary.

Affront to God. Because even the lowliest criminal bears the divine image.

Others translate as "is accursed of God" [5].

גֵּבֶר שִׂמְלַת אִשָּׁה כִּי תוֹעֲבַת יְהוָֹה אֱלֹהֶיךָ כָּל־
עֹשֵׂה אֵלֶּה: פ

י כִּי יִקָּרֵא קַן־צִפּוֹר לְפָנֶיךָ בַּדֶּרֶךְ בְּכָל־עֵץ אוֹ
עַל־הָאָרֶץ אֶפְרֹחִים אוֹ בֵיצִים וְהָאֵם רֹבֶצֶת עַל־
הָאֶפְרֹחִים אוֹ עַל־הַבֵּיצִים לֹא־תִקַּח הָאֵם עַל־
הַבָּנִים: שַׁלֵּחַ תְּשַׁלַּח אֶת־הָאֵם וְאֶת־הַבָּנִים תִּקַּח־לָךְ
לְמַעַן יִיטַב לָךְ וְהַאֲרַכְתָּ יָמִים: ס כִּי תִבְנֶה
בַּיִת חָדָשׁ וְעָשִׂיתָ מַעֲקֶה לְגַגֶּךָ וְלֹא־תָשִׂים דָּמִים

א לֹא־תִרְאֶה אֶת־שׁוֹר אָחִיךָ אוֹ אֶת־שֵׂיוֹ נִדָּחִים
ב וְהִתְעַלַּמְתָּ מֵהֶם הָשֵׁב תְּשִׁיבֵם לְאָחִיךָ: וְאִם־לֹא
קָרוֹב אָחִיךָ אֵלֶיךָ וְלֹא יְדַעְתּוֹ וַאֲסַפְתּוֹ אֶל־תּוֹךְ
בֵּיתֶךָ וְהָיָה עִמְּךָ עַד דְּרֹשׁ אָחִיךָ אֹתוֹ וַהֲשֵׁבֹתוֹ לוֹ:
ג וְכֵן תַּעֲשֶׂה לַחֲמֹרוֹ וְכֵן תַּעֲשֶׂה לְשִׂמְלָתוֹ וְכֵן תַּעֲשֶׂה
לְכָל־אֲבֵדַת אָחִיךָ אֲשֶׁר־תֹּאבַד מִמֶּנּוּ וּמְצָאתָהּ לֹא
ד תוּכַל לְהִתְעַלֵּם: ס לֹא־תִרְאֶה אֶת־חֲמוֹר אָחִיךָ
אוֹ שׁוֹרוֹ נֹפְלִים בַּדֶּרֶךְ וְהִתְעַלַּמְתָּ מֵהֶם הָקֵם תָּקִים
ה עִמּוֹ: ס לֹא־יִהְיֶה כְלִי־גֶבֶר עַל־אִשָּׁה וְלֹא־יִלְבַּשׁ

1] If you see your fellow's ox or sheep gone astray, do not ignore it; you must take it back to your fellow.   **2]** If your fellow does not live near you or you do not know who he is, you shall bring it home and it shall remain with you until your fellow claims it; then you shall give it back to him.   **3]** You shall do the same with his ass; you shall do the same with his garment; and so too shall you do with anything that your fellow loses and you find: you must not remain indifferent.

4] If you see your fellow's ass or ox fallen on the road, do not ignore it; you must help him raise it.

5] A woman must not put on man's apparel, nor shall a man wear woman's clothing; for whoever does these things is abhorrent to the LORD your God.

6] If, along the road, you chance upon a bird's nest, in any tree or on the ground, with fledglings or eggs and the mother sitting over the fledglings or on the eggs, do not take the mother together with her young.   **7]** Let the mother go, and take only the young, in order that you may fare well and have a long life.

8] When you build a new house, you shall make a parapet for your roof, so that you do not

---

22:1] *Your fellow's ox.* In Exod. 23:4, "your enemy's," that is, someone of your own people who is your enemy. While either verse could be a broadening of the other, it is likely that we have here two versions of a common law of concern.

2] *Does not live near you.* He lives so far that restoration of the animal would become an undue burden.

4] *Fallen on the road.* The animal must be helped not only for the sake of the owner but for its own sake. This concern is in Jewish tradition called "(concern for the) distress of living creatures" (*tza-ar ba-alei chayim*). See commentary and compare Exod. 23:5.

5] *Man's apparel.* The Hebrew is more general and says "man's gear." (See further in Gleanings.)

Abhorrent. The Hebrew term suggests that transvestism was considered not so much a sexual deviation as an idolatrous practice.

6] *Do not take the mother.* Commentators have suggested various reasons for this law; see commentary.

7] *Have a long life.* The premature death of a lad who observed the commandment caused a second-century C.E. rabbi to lose his faith; see commentary.

8] *Make a parapet.* Modern building codes have similar regulations.

ט בְּבֵיתֶךָ כִּי־יִפֹּל הַנֹּפֵל מִמֶּנּוּ: לֹא־תִזְרַע כַּרְמְךָ
כִּלְאָיִם פֶּן־תִּקְדַּשׁ הַמְלֵאָה הַזֶּרַע אֲשֶׁר תִּזְרָע
י וּתְבוּאַת הַכָּרֶם: ס לֹא־תַחֲרֹשׁ בְּשׁוֹר־וּבַחֲמֹר

יא יַחְדָּו: לֹא תִלְבַּשׁ שַׁעַטְנֵז צֶמֶר וּפִשְׁתִּים יַחְדָּו: ס
יב גְּדִלִים תַּעֲשֶׂה־לָּךְ עַל־אַרְבַּע כַּנְפוֹת כְּסוּתְךָ אֲשֶׁר
תְּכַסֶּה־בָּהּ: ס

* ט קמץ בז"ק.

bring bloodguilt on your house if anyone should fall from it.

9] You shall not sow your vineyard with a second kind of seed, else the crop—from the seed you have sown—and the yield of the vineyard may not be used. **10]** You shall not plow with an ox and an ass together. **11]** You shall not wear cloth combining wool and linen.

12] You shall make tassels on the four corners of the garment with which you cover yourself.

9] *Second kind of seed.* Verses 9–11 reflect the biblical aversion to interfering with the established order of nature—in stark contrast with the objectives of modern technology. See further commentary on Lev. 19:19. The Hebrew term כִּלְאָיִם (kil'ayim) is the name of a tractate in Mishnah and Palestinian Talmud, where more than sixty different plants are mentioned, providing thereby an important source for the knowledge of ancient agriculture.

May not be used. Literally, "lest it become sacred," i.e., set aside for God's use. Tradition provided that the yield be burned.

10] *An ox and an ass together.* A law unique to the Torah, which here wants to protect the weaker animal and to prevent the mixing of species, even at work.

Tradition expanded the provision to all animals of different kinds [6].

11] *Wool and linen.* The mixture is called שַׁעַטְנֵז (sha-atnez), a word of unknown origin. The verse may be taken as an explanation of Lev. 19:19 (see commentary there). Since priests, on the other hand, *had* to wear garments made of wool and

linen, this law may be seen to aim at separating the holy from the profane. See further at Exod. 28:15 [7].

12] *Tassels.* Here called *gedilim*, while in Num. 15:37 ff. they are called *tzitzit*; see commentary there. The tassels serve as reminders of God's ever-presence.

Because the command followed directly on the prohibition of *sha-atnez*, the Talmud reasoned that the Torah permitted woolen tassels to be attached to linen garments [8].

Four corners. The normal garment was square or oblong and had four corners. When in time different (tailored) clothes were adopted, the law was believed not to apply to them and, in order to fulfill the commandment, a special four-cornered cloth with tassels (called *talit*) was donned during prayer. There are also observant Jews who at all times wear a "four-corners" garment (called *arba kanfot*), a square cloth with tassels and with a hole in the middle which is slipped over the head and is regularly worn as part of one's clothing (usually as an undergarment). Certain groups of Orthodox Jews make sure that the fringes are seen at all times.

Burying the Dead

Quick burial of the deceased was a matter of great concern in the ancient Near East except in Egypt, where embalming was practiced. The natural process of decomposition was accelerated by the warm climate, and an abundance of birds and other animals that would feed on the cadavers demanded an early burial. One of the curses with which a wayward Israel is threatened is precisely this: "Your carcasses shall become food for all the birds of the sky and all the beasts of the earth, with none to frighten them off" (Deut. 28:26; see also Jer. 22:19).

The sight of unburied bodies was considered an offense not only against human dignity but against God himself. Even a criminal who had been impaled (or hanged) was to be interred before sunset "for an impaled body is an affront to God: you shall not defile the land that the Lord your God is giving you to possess" (Deut. 21:23).

In the biblical conception of afterlife[1] there was room to believe that in death one could be united with the past, especially if one would be buried in the ancestral plot. The acquisition of such a site, usually or frequently a cave, was therefore of prime concern for Abraham after his wife's death, and the Hittites from whom he purchased Machpelah were well aware of his need and exacted an exorbitant price from him (see Gen. 23:15 and our commentary there). Jacob, though he lived in Egypt for seventeen years and died there, was conveyed back to the cave of Machpelah, and Joseph implored his family not to leave his bones behind when the people would depart from Egypt (Gen. 50:25). Such burial assured the dead that they would "sleep with their fathers" and "be gathered to their kin" (I Kings 11:43; Gen. 25:8).

The Bible neither reports nor requires a distinct ritual for interment; the only prescription is contained in Deut 21:23; expressed negatively, it commands not to leave the hanged person overnight, positively, to bury him the same day.[2] Coffins were not used, though in later centuries important personages were placed in stone sarcophagi.[3] The custom of burning the dead (cremation) was not acceptable as a proper way of disposing of the dead.

The story of Saul's death provides an important exception, for the burning of his mutilated body by his followers was done to forestall further indignities, and the remains were buried thereafter (I Sam. 31:12; the account in I Chron. 10:12 omits the burning). To be sure, one of the means of execution prescribed by the Torah was burning the condemned,[4] but it is likely that, once death had occurred, the body was buried and, at most, only the entrails were consumed by fire [11]. In sum, the Bible reflects a deep-rooted respect for the human body, which even in death must be treated with care and consideration. To do so was to honor God in whose image humanity had been created.

Regard for Animals

The passage which commands that a mother bird should be let go, while her young may be taken from the nest (Deut. 22:6–7), is characteristic of the Torah's concern for the feelings and needs of animals.[5]

---

[1] The existence of this belief has been conclusively demonstrated by C. H. Brichto [9].

[2] Jewish tradition expanded the command by way of an *a fortiori* argument to every dead person: If this consideration was to be shown a criminal, how much more so to others [10].

[3] Current practice in Israel prescribes burial in shrouds, without the use of coffins.

[4] On the procedure of burning the condemned, see Gleanings to Lev. 20, "Put to the Fire."

[5] This was the opinion of Maimonides who wrote: "If the mother is let go or escapes of her own ac-

Though it takes for granted that certain animals may be sacrificed and used for food—a recognition of the universal law of survival[6]—it also makes clear that God's mercy extends to all of His creation.

Thus, ox and ass are not to plow under the same yoke (Deut. 22:10; see above); ox, ass, and all cattle are made beneficiaries of Sabbath rest (Deut. 5:14); an animal and its young may not be slaughtered on the same day (Lev. 22:28); an ox is not to be muzzled while threshing the corn (Deut. 25:4), so that it may not be tortured by its inability to satisfy its hunger; the sabbatical year has as one of its purposes to give both persons and beasts a chance to harvest the fallow fields (Lev. 25:6–7); and Balaam's unjust harshness toward his ass is criticized by God's messenger (Num. 22:32). The final line in the Book of Jonah sums up this divine concern: in a rhetorical question God proclaims that His mercy extends to beasts as well as to innocent human beings.

Later Jewish tradition greatly expanded on the need to prevent cruelty to animals and to avoid as much as possible causing "pain to living things" (*tza-ar ba-alei chayim*). The elaborate laws governing ritual slaughter were in part designed to kill as quickly as possible (see Commentary on Leviticus, chapter 11); and Deut. 11:15, which mentions cattle before people, was interpreted to mean that an owner had to feed his animals before he could sit down to eat [13]. Human beings are to imitate their Creator:

for even as He is merciful so must they practice lovingkindness to all living creatures.

Reward and Punishment

In biblical thought—and especially in the Book of Deuteronomy—God is believed to reward those who do His will and punish those who defy it.[7] Deut. 28 presents a long list of blessings and an even longer one of curses that will be the divine responses to and consequences of Israel's behavior.[8] The fifth commandment promises those who honor father and mother that they will "long endure" in the land that God gives to them (Deut. 5:16). The same reward is held out to those who observe the command concerning the bird's nest, which appears to emphasize the importance the Torah ascribed to this particular rule (Deut. 22:6–7). Although later interpreters tried to soften the unequivocal nature of this promise,[9] its original intent cannot be in doubt: long years on this earth are proof of God's favor.

To be sure, the righteous did not always appear to prosper, nor did the wicked always seem to be the targets of divine wrath. Questions about God's justice were already asked in biblical days—the entire Book of Job is devoted to this problem of "theodicy"—and they have been asked ever since. Because God's ways are not fully disclosed to man, those who did and do take the biblical promises literally are themselves often subjected to severe trials of their faith. Rabbi Elisha ben Abuyah (second century C.E.)

---

cord she will not be pained by seeing that the young are taken away. In most cases this will lead to people leaving everything alone, for what may be taken is in most cases not fit to be eaten" [12]. But others, like Nachmanides, argued that the purpose of the Torah law was not regard for animals as such, but rather to educate human beings in kindness.

[6] Note, however, that the opening chapters of Genesis portray humans as vegetarians; only later, after

the Flood, are they given permission to eat meat. See our commentary on Gen. 1:30.

[7] For a fuller treatment of this subject, see commentary on Lev. 26 and on Deut. 28.

[8] For other examples, see, e.g., Deut. 11:13–21 and Lev. 23.

[9] By saying, for instance, that the "life" referred to was not of this world but beyond the grave and that, in fact, the reward for the fulfillment of precepts

observed a young lad who, at his father's behest, had approached a bird's nest. The boy followed the Torah to the letter, driving away the mother bird and taking her offspring. But, instead of being rewarded with long life for honoring his father and respecting the law of the bird's nest, the lad fell to his death. Elisha thereupon denied that God ruled with justice and defected from traditional Judaism. His colleagues referred to him henceforth as *Acher*, "the other one," thereby avoiding to pronounce his name [16].

Through the story of Acher, the command concerning the bird's nest became a focal point of discussions on biblical theology. It may be doubted that the reward here held out was ever meant to be taken literally; rather, from the beginning, it was primarily hortatory: Do as God says, and He will reward you in His way. But there was no doubt that a reward was to be expected for an observant individual or for Israel as a people. The specifics might be unclear or temporarily unobservable, but biblical faith was unyielding in its assertion that human deeds were subject to divine judgment and its consequences.

does not occur in this world [14]. "The reward of a good deed is (another) good deed, and the consequence of sin is (further) sin" [15].

GLEANINGS

The Real War

The rules of war also apply to a person's war on his evil impulse, which can be overcome and taken prisoner. Hence the Rabbis praise the greatness of those who by repentance turn their sins into the opposite.   ISAIAH HURWITZ [17]

The Torah's language (Deut. 21:10) is in the singular, for it directs itself to the fact that a man has no greater enemy than the evil impulse.

THE BAAL SHEM TOV [18]

The Wayward and Defiant Son (Deut. 21:18)

(A tradition says that this law was never operative.[10]) If so, why was it written in the Torah? To study (more) and to obtain reward therefrom.

TALMUD [19]

This reminds us that it is the way of the wicked to teach their habits to others.   CHASIDIC [20]

Hebrew law insisted on respect being paid to parents, and Hebrew moralists did not hesitate to commend the rod as a salutary instrument of education; but the father's authority—though, at least in an earlier age, he could sell his daughter into slavery—was not despotic: he had not, as at Rome, power of life and death over his son; where (as in the case here contemplated) vice and insubordination became intolerable, he could not take the law into his own hands, he must appeal to the decision of an impartial tribunal.

S. D. DRIVER [21]

Even more than the rights of children, the rights of parents are guarded by the Torah, which values highly respect for authority.

D. HOFFMANN [22]

Bury the Criminal

It says: "An impaled body is an affront to

[10] Note, for instance, that in Prov. 30:17 defiance of parents is not characterized as punishable by law, but it is merely said to lead to a bad end.

1489

God" (Deut. 21:23). This is similar to two brothers, one of whom was a king and the other a criminal. When the latter was convicted and hanged, people who saw him thought that he was the king. (The meaning of the parable: man is created in God's image.)   TALMUD [23]

Your Fellow's Ox

In Exod. 23:4, the command is to restore the animal to an *enemy*, here (Deut. 22:1), to one's *fellow*. Why the different verbiage? When you return the animal to an enemy and extinguish your hatred you will be returning it to your fellow.

BACHYA

The final summation is that "you must not remain indifferent" (Deut. 22:3). The Talmud permits certain exceptions to the command as, for instance, when the finder is aged or a sage; but when a human being is lost exceptions do not apply.   AKIBA EGER [24]

Transvestism (Deut. 22:5)

The Torah forbids the wearing of apparel customary for the opposite sex. From this rule, tradition concluded that "man's apparel" included implements of war, and a midrash explained that this was the reason for Jael killing Sisera with tent pin and mallet (Judg. 4:17–21), because as a woman she was not supposed to wield a man's weapon [25].

This also meant that women were precluded from joining the army [26]; note the present-day controversy in Israel over women's exemption from the military. According to Targum Jonathan the rule implied further that women were forbidden the wearing of talit and tefillin (prayer shawl and phylacteries); but the Talmud disagreed and said that women, while exempt from the duty, were not prohibited from using them [27].

On the island of Cos, says Plutarch, priests of Hercules dressed as women; while, in Rome, men who participated in the vernal mysteries of that god did likewise. So too in the cult of Dionysus, males often adopted feminine costume, just as at the annual festival of Oschophoria boys were attired as girls and, at the Skirophoria, men were garbed like women. The same practice is attested also in connection with the cult of Leukippos in Crete. . . .

The origin of the custom is disputed. According to some scholars, it is a method of assimilating the worshiper to the person of the deity (though it is difficult then to explain why the devotees of the male Hercules affected feminine attire). According to others, it is a form of disguise, designed to foil demons and similar noxious spirits. Probably, as Frazer has observed, there is no single origin for all the examples of this practice; in some, the former idea comes into play; in others, the latter. It has also been suggested that, in cases where men wear women's clothes in the performance of magical rites, this reflects the widespread belief that magic (especially when it aims at promoting fertility) is primarily the province of the female sex, and that—at least in some instances—the usage may go back to a time when priesthood was in the hands of women. Also, . . . transvestism is a well-known symptom of sexual abnormality . . . frequently associated with religious psychosis.

T. GASTER [28]

Operations to correct the problem of transvestism and bisexuality are the subject of various halachic opinions. Generally speaking, elective surgery is frowned upon because of the danger attendant upon it, but there may be cases where exceptions could apply [29].

The Bird's Nest

Why does the Hebrew for "let the mother go" use the verb twice?[11] If you chance on a nest the second time, do not say, "I have already performed the mitzvah." You must fulfill it every time it comes your way.   MIDRASH [30]

The Torah promises long life to those who observe this mitzvah, which is easy to fulfill in that it demands no effort or sacrifice. How much more

---

[11] 22:7 reads שַׁלֵּחַ תְּשַׁלַּח.

1490

so, by implication, does the promise extend to those who do difficult mitzvot.　　RASHI [31]

As It Might Have Been

(In this fictional treatment the author pictures Elisha ben Abuyah [see above], accompanied by other Sages, witnessing the death of a boy who died while fulfilling the command of bird's nest—even though the Torah promised long life to those who observe it.)

Elisha trembled from head to foot. A cold perspiration covered him. Nausea writhed through his entrails.

The scene he had just witnessed brought with sudden vividness to his mind the tragedy that had befallen Meir's children.[12] The two pictures merged into a unity, insane and incredible. A wild protest stormed up in him against the horror of it, its senseless waste of life, its wanton cruelty.

The Sages turned and slowly mounted the slope together, talking meanwhile, trying to restore their confidence, to solidify a crumbling universe. At first, Elisha did not listen, so stunned was he, so dazed his senses. But, as his mind recovered from its initial disorganization, he heard one of them say, "He will have his length of days. God is just. It is hard to understand, but let us remember that there is a better world, in which it is all day, a day that stretches for eternity."

At once Elisha knew the answer to the question he had never ventured to face before.

A great negation crystallized in him. The veil of deception dissolved before his eyes. The only belief he still cherished disintegrated as had all the others. The last tenuous chord that bound him to his people was severed.

And when the Sages droned on, their words buzzing like flies, revulsion swept Elisha. He could no longer tolerate their deliberate blindness. In cold desperation he silenced them.

"It is all a lie," he said with a terrible quiet in his voice. "There is no reward. There is no Judge. There is no judgment. For there is no God."

The wind blew in from the sea across horror-stricken faces. The sun, weltering so long in its own blood, died slowly.

MILTON STEINBERG [32]

Yoking Ox and Ass Together (Deut. 22:10)

Why was this prohibition instituted? Because, say some, the ass does not have the strength of an ox (and thus would be worked beyond its capacity); others hold that, because the ox chews its cud and the ass does not, the latter would suffer, seeing (as it thinks) that the ox eats all day. But God, being merciful to all His creatures, wants to save them from suffering unduly [33].

---

[12] His friend, Rabbi Meir, had lost two young children.

The Social Weal, II

Now follow various civil and criminal laws which, as always, aim at raising the level of the people's communal and individual purity. Just as the Torah's ritual prescriptions were related to this objective, so were those laws which are nowadays called moral and/or secular: together they are the basis for making Israel a fit partner in God's covenant.

The subjects covered in this section are: sexual relationships, their civil and criminal aspects and consequences (divorce, *mamzerut*, prostitution); relations with Ammonites, Moabites, and Edomites; physical hygiene as an aspect of ritual purity; escaped slaves; protection of the weak; taking interest; pledges and loans; treatment of laborers; fulfilling one's vow; kidnaping; affirmation of the principle of personal responsibility.

The laws are not arranged in accordance with any perceivable system; occasionally it is clear that two subjects are placed in sequence as an aid to memory, but at other times the reason is not clear. The family law here presented reflects an extended kinship structure and is most likely quite ancient.

בָּתֵּי וּפָרְשׂוּ הַשִּׂמְלָה לִפְנֵי זִקְנֵי הָעִיר: וְלָקְחוּ זִקְנֵי
הָעִיר־הַהִוא אֶת־הָאִישׁ וְיִסְּרוּ אֹתוֹ: וְעָנְשׁוּ אֹתוֹ מֵאָה
כֶסֶף וְנָתְנוּ לַאֲבִי הַנַּעֲרָה כִּי הוֹצִיא שֵׁם רָע עַל
בְּתוּלַת יִשְׂרָאֵל וְלוֹ־תִהְיֶה לְאִשָּׁה לֹא־יוּכַל לְשַׁלְּחָהּ
כָּל־יָמָיו: ס וְאִם־אֱמֶת הָיָה הַדָּבָר הַזֶּה לֹא־
נִמְצְאוּ בְתוּלִים לַנַּעֲרָ: וְהוֹצִיאוּ אֶת־הַנַּעֲרָ אֶל־פֶּתַח
בֵּית־אָבִיהָ וּסְקָלוּהָ אַנְשֵׁי עִירָהּ בָּאֲבָנִים וָמֵתָה כִּי־
עָשְׂתָה נְבָלָה בְּיִשְׂרָאֵל לִזְנוֹת בֵּית אָבִיהָ וּבִעַרְתָּ

יח

יט

כ

כא

כִּי־יִקַּח אִישׁ אִשָּׁה וּבָא אֵלֶיהָ וּשְׂנֵאָהּ: וְשָׂם לָהּ
עֲלִילֹת דְּבָרִים וְהוֹצִיא עָלֶיהָ שֵׁם רָע וְאָמַר אֶת־
הָאִשָּׁה הַזֹּאת לָקַחְתִּי וָאֶקְרַב אֵלֶיהָ וְלֹא־מָצָאתִי
לָהּ בְּתוּלִים: וְלָקַח אֲבִי הַנַּעֲרָ וְאִמָּהּ וְהוֹצִיאוּ
אֶת־בְּתוּלֵי הַנַּעֲרָ אֶל־זִקְנֵי הָעִיר הַשָּׁעְרָה: וְאָמַר
אֲבִי הַנַּעֲרָ אֶל־הַזְּקֵנִים אֶת־בִּתִּי נָתַתִּי לָאִישׁ הַזֶּה
לְאִשָּׁה וַיִּשְׂנָאֶהָ: וְהִנֵּה־הוּא שָׂם עֲלִילֹת דְּבָרִים
לֵאמֹר לֹא־מָצָאתִי לְבִתְּךָ בְּתוּלִים וְאֵלֶּה בְּתוּלֵי

יג

יד

טו

טז

יז

*כ, כא רה קרי.
*טו, טז הנערה קרי.

13] A man marries a woman and cohabits with her. Then he takes an aversion to her **14]** and makes up charges against her and defames her, saying, "I married this woman; but when I approached her, I found that she was not a virgin." **15]** In such a case, the girl's father and mother shall produce the evidence of the girl's virginity before the elders of the town at the gate. **16]** And the girl's father shall say to the elders, "I gave this man my daughter to wife, but he has taken an aversion to her; **17]** so he has made up charges, saying, 'I did not find your daughter a virgin.' But here is the evidence of my daughter's virginity!" And they shall spread out the cloth before the elders of the town. **18]** The elders of that town shall then take the man and flog him, **19]** and they shall fine him a hundred [shekels of] silver and give it to the girl's father; for the man has defamed a virgin in Israel. Moreover, she shall remain his wife; he shall never have the right to divorce her.

20] But if the charge proves true, the girl was found not to have been a virgin, **21]** then the girl shall be brought out to the entrance of her father's house, and the men of the town shall stone her to death; for she did a shameful thing in Israel, committing fornication while under

---

22:13] *Takes an aversion.* See commentary below.

14] *She was not a virgin.* The woman was expected to be a virgin, but no stigma for premarital sexual activity was attached to the man. The evidence of bleeding from a ruptured hymen was taken as proof of virginity; see next verse. (On virginity, see at Exod. 22:15.)

15] *The girl's.* The unvocalized text reads נער, which could mean young man, but the word is read נַעֲרָה, girl. This defective spelling occurs throughout the Torah (except in verse 19, which has the expected נערה).

Evidence. Usually blood-stained sheets; their examination by the family was an important post-nuptial ceremony, prevalent in Eastern Europe

and North Africa (and probably elsewhere) well into the twentieth century.

18] *Flog him.* Tradition stipulated that, while forty stripes were the norm, only thirty-nine should be administered, lest an error occur and the punishment be excessive [1].

19] *A hundred (shekels of) silver.* That is, twice the amount of the dowry stipulated in the case of one who had seduced a virgin (verse 29). Slander was considered a most serious offense.

Give it to the girl's father. He was the head of the family that had been offended by the husband's action [2].

21] *To the entrance of her father's house.* Her family shared in her disgrace for she had not been properly supervised.

כה וְאִם־בַּשָּׂדֶה יִמְצָא הָאִישׁ אֶת־הַנַּעֲרָ הַמְאֹרָשָׂה וְהֶחֱזִיק־
בָּהּ הָאִישׁ וְשָׁכַב עִמָּהּ וּמֵת הָאִישׁ אֲשֶׁר־שָׁכַב עִמָּהּ
כו לְבַדּוֹ: וְלַנַּעֲרָ לֹא־תַעֲשֶׂה דָבָר אֵין לַנַּעֲרָ חֵטְא
מָוֶת כִּי כַּאֲשֶׁר יָקוּם אִישׁ עַל־רֵעֵהוּ וּרְצָחוֹ נֶפֶשׁ
כז כֵּן הַדָּבָר הַזֶּה: כִּי בַשָּׂדֶה מְצָאָהּ צָעֲקָה הַנַּעֲרָ
הַמְאֹרָשָׂה וְאֵין מוֹשִׁיעַ לָהּ: ס כח כִּי־יִמְצָא אִישׁ
נַעֲרָ בְתוּלָה אֲשֶׁר לֹא־אֹרָשָׂה וּתְפָשָׂהּ וְשָׁכַב עִמָּהּ
כט וְנִמְצָאוּ: וְנָתַן הָאִישׁ הַשֹּׁכֵב עִמָּהּ לַאֲבִי הַנַּעֲרָ חֲמִשִּׁים

כג הָרָע מִקִּרְבֶּךָ: ס כי־יִמָּצֵא אִישׁ שֹׁכֵב עִם־אִשָּׁה
בְעֻלַת־בַּעַל וּמֵתוּ גַּם־שְׁנֵיהֶם הָאִישׁ הַשֹּׁכֵב עִם־הָאִשָּׁה
כג וְהָאִשָּׁה וּבִעַרְתָּ הָרָע מִיִּשְׂרָאֵל: ס כִּי יִהְיֶה נַעֲרָ
בְתוּלָה מְאֹרָשָׂה לְאִישׁ וּמְצָאָהּ אִישׁ בָּעִיר וְשָׁכַב
כד עִמָּהּ: וְהוֹצֵאתֶם אֶת־שְׁנֵיהֶם אֶל־שַׁעַר הָעִיר הַהִוא
וּסְקַלְתֶּם אֹתָם בָּאֲבָנִים וָמֵתוּ אֶת־הַנַּעֲרָ עַל־דְּבַר
אֲשֶׁר לֹא־צָעֲקָה בָעִיר וְאֶת־הָאִישׁ עַל־דְּבַר אֲשֶׁר־
עִנָּה אֶת־אֵשֶׁת רֵעֵהוּ וּבִעַרְתָּ הָרָע מִקִּרְבֶּךָ: ס
* כג–כט רח קרי.

her father's authority. Thus you will sweep away evil from your midst.

22] If a man is found lying with another man's wife, both of them—the man and the woman with whom he lay—shall die. Thus you will sweep away evil from Israel.

23] In the case of a virgin who is engaged to a man—if a man comes upon her in town and lies with her, **24]** you shall take the two of them out to the gate of that town and stone them to death: the girl because she did not cry for help in the town, and the man because he violated his neighbor's wife. Thus you will sweep away evil from your midst. **25]** But if the man comes upon the engaged girl in the open country, and the man lies with her by force, only the man who lay with her shall die, **26]** but you shall do nothing to the girl. The girl did not incur the death penalty, for this case is like that of a man attacking another and murdering him. **27]** He came upon her in the open; though the engaged girl cried for help, there was no one to save her.

28] If a man comes upon a virgin who is not engaged and he seizes her and lies with her, and they are discovered, **29]** the man who lay with her shall pay the girl's father fifty [shekels of]

22] *Shall die.* The Ten Commandments forbid adultery, without stipulating the penalty. Here, capital punishment is specified but not its exact nature (nor is it in Lev. 20:10). In Ezekiel's time the culprits were stoned to death (Ezek. 16:40), which is most likely what the Torah intended.

Ibn Ezra deduces this from the proximity of verse 21, where stoning is commanded; but the Talmud, basing itself on linguistic analogy, opined that, whenever מִיתָה without specification was used, strangulation was intended [3].

23] *Engaged to a man.* That is, one for whom a bride-price had been paid; see 20:7. Such a woman was considered as if already married, and therefore, if another man had intercourse with her, the two had committed adultery. Sexual relations

with a virgin who was not engaged had civil but not criminal consequences; see verse 28 and Exod. 22:15.

In town. Where, so it was presumed, her cry for help would be heard.

However, later Jewish authorities were inclined to believe a woman who claimed that she had resisted her attacker or that resistance would have resulted in certain death (which likelihood constituted a valid excuse) [4].

28] *A virgin who is not engaged.* The same principle is stated in Exod. 22:15-16, except that there no fixed bride-price is stipulated. Deuteronomy may reflect a later social structure where money had already become an important measure of values.

ג כֶּסֶף וְלוֹ־תִהְיֶה לְאִשָּׁה תַּחַת אֲשֶׁר עִנָּה לֹא־יוּכַל שַׁלְּחָהּ כָּל־יָמָיו: ס

א לֹא־יִקַּח אִישׁ אֶת־אֵשֶׁת אָבִיו וְלֹא יְגַלֶּה כְּנַף

ב אָבִיו: ס לֹא־יָבֹא פְצוּעַ־דַּכָּא וּכְרוּת שָׁפְכָה בִּקְהַל

ג יְהוָה: ס לֹא־יָבֹא מַמְזֵר בִּקְהַל יְהוָה גַּם דּוֹר

ד עֲשִׂירִי לֹא־יָבֹא לוֹ בִּקְהַל יְהוָה: ס לֹא־יָבֹא עַמּוֹנִי וּמוֹאָבִי בִּקְהַל יְהוָה גַּם דּוֹר עֲשִׂירִי לֹא־יָבֹא לָהֶם

ה בִּקְהַל יְהוָה עַד־עוֹלָם: עַל־דְּבַר אֲשֶׁר לֹא־קִדְּמוּ

---

silver, and she shall be his wife. Because he has violated her, he can never have the right to divorce her.

1] No man shall marry his father's former wife, so as to remove his father's garment.

2] No one whose testes are crushed or whose member is cut off shall be admitted into the congregation of the LORD.

3] No one misbegotten shall be admitted into the congregation of the LORD; none of his descendants, even in the tenth generation, shall be admitted into the congregation of the LORD.

4] No Ammonite or Moabite shall be admitted into the congregation of the LORD; none of their descendants, even in the tenth generation, shall ever be admitted into the congregation of the LORD, **5]** because they did not meet you with food and water on your journey after you

---

29] *She shall be his wife.* If her father agrees (Exod. 22:16).

Divorce her. Literally, "send her away," i.e., to her father's house.

23:1] Some versions have this verse as 22:30 (for instance, King James, New Standard Version, New English Bible), and their numberings of chapter 23 are noted in brackets.

Father's former wife. The prohibition is stated as part of a catalogue of incestual relationships in Lev. 18:8 and 20:11. It is not clear why here, in Deuteronomy, only this and no other close sexual relationship is proscribed, and why no punishment is here indicated as in Leviticus. If Leviticus is the older book, then there must have been a special reason to single out this offense; if Deuteronomy is older, it may be that this particular union was deemed acceptable by some, and the law made sure that it was ranked with the other and long acknowledged sexual taboos.

Remove his father's garment. The opposite of "spreading his garment," which meant taking a woman as a wife; see Ruth 3:9; Ezek. 16:8. By marrying his father's former wife, the son substituted himself for his father. The imagery also has sexual overtones, as in the story of Noah and

his sons (Gen. 9:20 ff.).

2] [1] *Whose testes are crushed.* By an operation, in order to make him a eunuch. This prohibition aimed at preserving Israel's purity and was meant as an attack on an existing institution [5]. Eunuchs had frequently positions of honor and influence; see I Sam. 8:15; Jer. 38:7; Isa. 56:4 f.

3] [2] *Misbegotten.* The meaning of the biblical מַמְזֵר (*mamzer*) is unclear. Later, tradition explained it to mean the offspring of a prohibited union. Leviticus, 18:6–20 and 20:10–21 [6], lists the various forbidden relationships. See commentary there.

4] [3] *Ammonite or Moabite.* Israel's traditional enemies: hostility toward them continued into Deuteronomic times (however, in Deut. 2:29, Moab is spoken of favorably). In prophetic literature the Moabites are called haughty (see, for instance, Isa. 16:6) and the Ammonites, cruel (Amos 1:13).

Shall ever be admitted. The proscription was not strictly observed—Ruth was a Moabitess!—and the Rabbis ruled that the law applied to Moab's men only, not to its women [7].

ה בָּנִים אֲשֶׁר־יִוָּלְדוּ לָהֶם דּוֹר שְׁלִישִׁי יָבֹא לָהֶם בִּקְהַל
יְהוָה: ס י כִּי־תֵצֵא מַחֲנֶה עַל־אֹיְבֶיךָ וְנִשְׁמַרְתָּ
מִכֹּל דָּבָר רָע: יא כִּי־יִהְיֶה בְךָ אִישׁ אֲשֶׁר לֹא־יִהְיֶה
טָהוֹר מִקְּרֵה־לָיְלָה וְיָצָא אֶל־מִחוּץ לַמַּחֲנֶה לֹא
יָבֹא אֶל־תּוֹךְ הַמַּחֲנֶה: יב וְהָיָה לִפְנוֹת־עֶרֶב יִרְחַץ בַּמָּיִם
וּכְבֹא הַשֶּׁמֶשׁ יָבֹא אֶל־תּוֹךְ הַמַּחֲנֶה: יג וְיָד תִּהְיֶה לְּךָ
מִחוּץ לַמַּחֲנֶה וְיָצָאתָ שָׁמָּה חוּץ: יד וְיָתֵד תִּהְיֶה לְּךָ

אֶתְכֶם בַּלֶּחֶם וּבַמַּיִם בַּדֶּרֶךְ בְּצֵאתְכֶם מִמִּצְרָיִם
וַאֲשֶׁר שָׂכַר עָלֶיךָ אֶת־בִּלְעָם בֶּן־בְּעוֹר מִפְּתוֹר
ו אֲרַם נַהֲרַיִם לְקַלְלֶךָ: וְלֹא־אָבָה יְהוָה אֱלֹהֶיךָ לִשְׁמֹעַ
אֶל־בִּלְעָם וַיַּהֲפֹךְ יְהוָה אֱלֹהֶיךָ לְּךָ אֶת־הַקְּלָלָה
ז לִבְרָכָה כִּי אֲהֵבְךָ יְהוָה אֱלֹהֶיךָ: לֹא־תִדְרֹשׁ שְׁלֹמָם
ח וְטֹבָתָם כָּל־יָמֶיךָ לְעוֹלָם: ס לֹא־תְתַעֵב אֲדֹמִי
כִּי אָחִיךָ הוּא לֹא־תְתַעֵב מִצְרִי כִּי־גֵר הָיִיתָ בְאַרְצוֹ:

left Egypt, and because they hired Balaam son of Beor, from Pethor of Aram-naharaim, to curse you.— 6] But the LORD your God refused to heed Balaam; instead, the LORD your God turned the curse into a blessing for you, for the LORD your God loves you.— 7] You shall never concern yourself with their welfare or benefit as long as you live.

8] You shall not abhor an Edomite, for he is your kinsman. You shall not abhor an Egyptian, for you were a stranger in his land. 9] Children born to them may be admitted into the congregation of the LORD in the third generation.

10] When you go out as a troop against your enemies, be on your guard against anything untoward. 11] If anyone among you has been rendered unclean by a nocturnal emission, he must leave the camp, and he must not re-enter the camp. 12] Toward evening he shall bathe in water, and at sundown he may re-enter the camp. 13] Further, there shall be an area for you outside the camp, where you may relieve yourself. 14] With your gear you shall have a

---

5] [4] *Balaam*. The reference is to Num. 22–24.

Pethor of Aram-naharaim. In Num. 22:5, "Pethor . . . by the Euphrates"; here, the location is given more generally: "Aram of Mesopotamia" (*naharaim* meaning "two rivers," that is, Tigris and Euphrates).

7] [6] *You shall never concern yourself*. And, of course, make no alliances with them—possibly a remembrance of the bad experience David had with them (II Sam. 10).

Driver suggests that the emotional quarantine ordered in verse 7 had the effect of preventing active national hatred. We do not hate people in whom we have no interest.

8] [7] *Edomite . . . your kinsman*. He was perceived as a descendant of Esau, Jacob's brother; Gen. 36:1.

You shall not abhor an Egyptian. If Israelites had reason to abhor any nation, it would expectably be Egypt, the nation that had enslaved them. Yet, Egypt was not to be remembered with aversion.

Possibly, there was a psycho-historical echo of guilt in Israel's relationship with Egypt, going back to the days when Joseph and his family had been servants of an exploitative Pharaoh [8].

9] [8] *In the third generation*. Of residence in Israel.

11] [10] *Nocturnal emission*. Such emission was considered ritually polluting; see Lev. 15:16.

13] [12] *An area*. Hebrew יָד (*yad*), a word which usually means "hand" and sometimes "memorial" (as in *yad vashem*, Isa. 56:5).

עַל־אֲזֵנֶךָ וְהָיָה בְּשִׁבְתְּךָ חוּץ וְחָפַרְתָּה בָהּ וְשַׁבְתָּ
וְכִסִּיתָ אֶת־צֵאָתֶךָ: כִּי יְהוָה אֱלֹהֶיךָ מִתְהַלֵּךְ בְּקֶרֶב
מַחֲנֶךָ לְהַצִּילְךָ וְלָתֵת אֹיְבֶיךָ לְפָנֶיךָ וְהָיָה מַחֲנֶיךָ
קָדוֹשׁ וְלֹא־יִרְאֶה בְךָ עֶרְוַת דָּבָר וְשָׁב מֵאַחֲרֶיךָ: ס
לֹא־תַסְגִּיר עֶבֶד אֶל־אֲדֹנָיו אֲשֶׁר־יִנָּצֵל אֵלֶיךָ מֵעִם
אֲדֹנָיו: עִמְּךָ יֵשֵׁב בְּקִרְבְּךָ בַּמָּקוֹם אֲשֶׁר־יִבְחַר בְּאַחַד
שְׁעָרֶיךָ בַּטּוֹב לוֹ לֹא תּוֹנֶנּוּ: ס לֹא־תִהְיֶה קְדֵשָׁה
מִבְּנוֹת יִשְׂרָאֵל וְלֹא־יִהְיֶה קָדֵשׁ מִבְּנֵי יִשְׂרָאֵל:

יד

לֹא־תָבִיא אֶתְנַן זוֹנָה וּמְחִיר כֶּלֶב בֵּית יְהוָה אֱלֹהֶיךָ
לְכָל־נֶדֶר כִּי תוֹעֲבַת יְהוָה אֱלֹהֶיךָ גַּם־שְׁנֵיהֶם: ס
לֹא־תַשִּׁיךְ לְאָחִיךָ נֶשֶׁךְ כֶּסֶף נֶשֶׁךְ אֹכֶל נֶשֶׁךְ כָּל־
דָּבָר אֲשֶׁר יִשָּׁךְ: לַנָּכְרִי תַשִּׁיךְ וּלְאָחִיךָ לֹא תַשִּׁיךְ
לְמַעַן יְבָרֶכְךָ יְהוָה אֱלֹהֶיךָ בְּכֹל מִשְׁלַח יָדֶךָ עַל־
הָאָרֶץ אֲשֶׁר־אַתָּה בָא־שָׁמָּה לְרִשְׁתָּהּ: ס כִּי־תִדֹּר
נֶדֶר לַיהוָה אֱלֹהֶיךָ לֹא תְאַחֵר לְשַׁלְּמוֹ כִּי־דָרֹשׁ
יִדְרְשֶׁנּוּ יְהוָה אֱלֹהֶיךָ מֵעִמָּךְ וְהָיָה בְךָ חֵטְא: וְכִי

יט

כ

כא

כב

כג

spike, and when you have squatted you shall dig a hole with it and cover up your excrement. **15]** Since the LORD your God moves about in your camp to protect you and to deliver your enemies to you, let your camp be holy; let Him not find anything unseemly among you and turn away from you.

16] You shall not turn over to his master a slave who seeks refuge with you from his master. **17]** He shall live with you in any place he may choose among the settlements in your midst, wherever he pleases; you must not ill-treat him.

18] No Israelite woman shall be a cult prostitute, nor shall any Israelite man be a cult prostitute. **19]** You shall not bring the fee of a whore or the pay of a dog into the house of the LORD your God in fulfillment of any vow, for both are abhorrent to the LORD your God.

20] You shall not deduct interest from loans to your countryman, whether in money or food or anything else that can be deducted as interest. **21]** You may deduct interest from loans to foreigners; but do not deduct any from loans to your countryman—so that the LORD your God may bless you in all your undertakings in the land which you are about to invade and occupy.

22] When you make a vow to the LORD your God, do not put off fulfilling it, for the LORD your God will require it of you, and you will have incurred guilt; **23]** whereas you incur no

16] [15] *A slave.* Who came to you from abroad [9]. The Talmud asserted that this rule obtained also when the owner abroad was an Israelite [10].

18] [17] *Cult prostitute.* Sexual orgies were a well-known part of many peoples' fertility rites and took place even in Jerusalem, until King Josiah put an end to them (II Kings 23:7) [11].

19] [18] *Dog.* Here used as a pejorative, to describe a male prostitute. The simile is found in a Phoenician inscription also [12]. Dogs were not domesticated in biblical times and were considered wild beasts.

20] [19] *Deduct interest.* See commentary below. נֶשֶׁךְ (*neshech*) is related to the word for "bite," the interest being seen as taking a bite out of the capital. (Note also the English expression "tax bite.") Lev. 25:36–37 introduced the additional terms *tarbit* ("increase") and *marbit*, translated as "accrued interest," to be paid at the time of the loan's repayment; *neshech* is rendered as "advance interest."

22] [21] *A vow to the Lord.* Either by promising Him something, or by calling on Him as a witness. "Better not to vow than to vow and not fulfill it" (Eccles. 5:3–4). See Num. 30.

כד תֶחְדַּל לִנְדֹּר לֹא־יִהְיֶה בְךָ חֵטְא: מוֹצָא שְׂפָתֶיךָ
תִּשְׁמֹר וְעָשִׂיתָ כַּאֲשֶׁר נָדַרְתָּ לַיהוָה אֱלֹהֶיךָ נְדָבָה
כה אֲשֶׁר דִּבַּרְתָּ בְּפִיךָ: ס כִּי תָבֹא בְּכֶרֶם רֵעֶךָ
וְאָכַלְתָּ עֲנָבִים כְּנַפְשְׁךָ שָׂבְעֶךָ וְאֶל־כֶּלְיְךָ לֹא
כו תִתֵּן: ס כִּי תָבֹא בְּקָמַת רֵעֶךָ וְקָטַפְתָּ מְלִילֹת
בְּיָדֶךָ וְחֶרְמֵשׁ לֹא תָנִיף עַל קָמַת רֵעֶךָ: ס
א כִּי־יִקַּח אִישׁ אִשָּׁה וּבְעָלָהּ וְהָיָה אִם־לֹא תִמְצָא־חֵן
בְּעֵינָיו כִּי־מָצָא בָהּ עֶרְוַת דָּבָר וְכָתַב לָהּ סֵפֶר
ב כְּרִיתֻת וְנָתַן בְּיָדָהּ וְשִׁלְּחָהּ מִבֵּיתוֹ: וְיָצְאָה מִבֵּיתוֹ

ג וְהָלְכָה וְהָיְתָה לְאִישׁ־אַחֵר: וּשְׂנֵאָהּ הָאִישׁ הָאַחֲרוֹן
וְכָתַב לָהּ סֵפֶר כְּרִיתֻת וְנָתַן בְּיָדָהּ וְשִׁלְּחָהּ מִבֵּיתוֹ
אוֹ כִי יָמוּת הָאִישׁ הָאַחֲרוֹן אֲשֶׁר־לְקָחָהּ לוֹ לְאִשָּׁה:
ד לֹא־יוּכַל בַּעְלָהּ הָרִאשׁוֹן אֲשֶׁר־שִׁלְּחָהּ לָשׁוּב לְקַחְתָּהּ
לִהְיוֹת לוֹ לְאִשָּׁה אַחֲרֵי אֲשֶׁר הֻטַּמָּאָה כִּי־תוֹעֵבָה
הִוא לִפְנֵי יְהוָה וְלֹא תַחֲטִיא אֶת־הָאָרֶץ אֲשֶׁר יְהוָה
אֱלֹהֶיךָ נֹתֵן לְךָ נַחֲלָה: ס כִּי־יִקַּח אִישׁ אִשָּׁה
ה חֲדָשָׁה לֹא יֵצֵא בַּצָּבָא וְלֹא־יַעֲבֹר עָלָיו לְכָל־
דָּבָר נָקִי יִהְיֶה לְבֵיתוֹ שָׁנָה אֶחָת וְשִׂמַּח אֶת־אִשְׁתּוֹ

guilt if you refrain from vowing. **24]** You must fulfill what has crossed your lips and perform what you have voluntarily vowed to the LORD your God, having made the promise with your own mouth.

25] When you enter your neighbor's vineyard, you may eat your fill of the grapes, as many as you want; but you must not put any in your vessel. **26]** When you find yourself amid your neighbor's standing grain, you may pluck ears with your hand; but you must not put a sickle to your neighbor's grain.

1] A man takes a wife and possesses her. She fails to please him because he finds something obnoxious about her, and he writes her a bill of divorcement, hands it to her, and sends her away from his house; **2]** she leaves his household and becomes the wife of another man; **3]** then this latter man rejects her, writes her a bill of divorcement, hands it to her, and sends her away from his house; or the man who married her last dies. **4]** Then the first husband who divorced her shall not take her to wife again, since she has been defiled—for that would be abhorrent to the LORD. You must not bring sin upon the land which the LORD your God is giving you as a heritage.

5] When a man has taken a bride, he shall not go out with the army or be assigned to it for any purpose; he shall be exempt one year for the sake of his household, to give happiness to the woman he has married.

25] [24] *When you enter.* Verses 25 and 26 may refer to the law of Lev. 19:9 and 10, which are meant to keep the poor from starving. Or the verses may be seen as continuing the theme of verses 20 and 21: your possessions are never fully your own and must be shared.

The Rabbis debated whether the law applied without restriction, even to a passer-by [13].

24:1] *Bill of divorcement.* Literally, "a document of cutting off." Both the conclusion of an agreement (see Deut. 29:13; and Commentary on Genesis, chapter 16) and its dissolution were described by the word כָּרֵת.

4] *She has been defiled.* For her first husband. She is disqualified because her second marriage appears now as a promiscuous interlude. According to Nachmanides, the prohibition was intended to prevent wife swapping.

5] *He shall be exempt.* This appears to be an extension of Deut. 20:5 ff. There the exemption applies to a betrothed man, here also to one who is newly married.

יא לַעֲבֹט עֲבֹטוֹ: בַּחוּץ תַּעֲמֹד וְהָאִישׁ אֲשֶׁר אַתָּה
יב נֹשֶׁה בוֹ יוֹצִיא אֵלֶיךָ אֶת־הַעֲבוֹט הַחוּצָה: וְאִם־אִישׁ
יג עָנִי הוּא לֹא תִשְׁכַּב בַּעֲבֹטוֹ: הָשֵׁב תָּשִׁיב לוֹ אֶת־
הָעֲבוֹט כְּבוֹא הַשֶּׁמֶשׁ וְשָׁכַב בְּשַׂלְמָתוֹ וּבֵרֲכֶךָּ וּלְךָ
יד תִּהְיֶה צְדָקָה לִפְנֵי יְהֹוָה אֱלֹהֶיךָ: ס לֹא־תַעֲשֹׁק
שָׂכִיר עָנִי וְאֶבְיוֹן מֵאַחֶיךָ אוֹ מִגֵּרְךָ אֲשֶׁר בְּאַרְצְךָ
טו בִּשְׁעָרֶיךָ: בְּיוֹמוֹ תִתֵּן שְׂכָרוֹ וְלֹא־תָבוֹא עָלָיו הַשֶּׁמֶשׁ

א אֲשֶׁר־לָקָח: לֹא־יַחֲבֹל רֵחַיִם וָרָכֶב כִּי־נֶפֶשׁ הוּא
ב חֹבֵל: ס כִּי־יִמָּצֵא אִישׁ גֹּנֵב נֶפֶשׁ מֵאֶחָיו מִבְּנֵי
יִשְׂרָאֵל וְהִתְעַמֶּר־בּוֹ וּמְכָרוֹ וּמֵת הַגַּנָּב הַהוּא וּבִעַרְתָּ
ג הָרָע מִקִּרְבֶּךָ: ס הִשָּׁמֶר בְּנֶגַע־הַצָּרַעַת לִשְׁמֹר
מְאֹד וְלַעֲשׂוֹת כְּכֹל אֲשֶׁר־יוֹרוּ אֶתְכֶם הַכֹּהֲנִים הַלְוִיִם
ד כַּאֲשֶׁר צִוִּיתִם תִּשְׁמְרוּ לַעֲשׂוֹת: זָכוֹר אֵת אֲשֶׁר־עָשָׂה
יְהֹוָה אֱלֹהֶיךָ לְמִרְיָם בַּדֶּרֶךְ בְּצֵאתְכֶם מִמִּצְרָיִם: ס
ה כִּי־תַשֶּׁה בְרֵעֲךָ מַשַּׁאת מְאוּמָה לֹא־תָבֹא אֶל־בֵּיתוֹ

6] A handmill or an upper millstone shall not be taken in pawn, for that would be taking someone's life in pawn.

7] If a man is found to have kidnaped a fellow Israelite, enslaving him or selling him, that kidnaper shall die; thus you will sweep out evil from your midst.

8] In cases of a skin affection be most careful to do exactly as the levitical priests instruct you. Take care to do as I have commanded them. **9]** Remember what the LORD your God did to Miriam on the journey after you left Egypt.

10] When you make a loan of any sort to your neighbor, you must not enter his house to seize his pledge. **11]** You must remain outside, while the man to whom you made the loan brings the pledge out to you. **12]** If he is a needy man, you shall not go to sleep in his pledge; **13]** you must return the pledge to him at sundown, that he may sleep in his cloth and bless you; and it will be to your merit before the LORD your God.

14] You shall not abuse a needy and destitute laborer, whether a fellow countryman or a stranger in one of the communities of your land. **15]** You must pay him his wages on the same

6] *Handmill.* Which consists of an upper and lower millstone. The injunction means: every family needs its handmill for making bread; therefore do not take it or any part of it away.

The Hebrew is alliterative and therefore easily memorable: רֵחַיִם—רֶכֶב (rechayim—rechev).

7] *Kidnaped.* Compare Exod. 21:16. In biblical days the profit from kidnaping lay in selling the captive, today it comes from having him ransomed.

The Rabbis applied the commandment "You shall not steal" to the theft of persons: see at Deut. 5:17.

8] *Skin affection.* Older translations have "leprosy"; see Lev., chapters 13 and 14. The priests dealt with the physiological aspects of the illness as part of ritual impurity.

9] *Miriam.* A reference to the incident recounted in Num. 12.

The verse has been taken as one proof that Leviticus and Numbers are older than Deuteronomy. This is however not conclusive, for the references may be to well-known traditions rather than to fixed texts [14].

10] *You must not enter.* That is, the lender [15]. Compare Exod. 22:25–26, which is less specific.

12] *Sleep in his pledge.* Do not use or keep his garment, which he gave you as a pledge [16].

15] *You must pay him.* An elaboration of the principle laid down in Lev. 19:13; but this too does not give us warrant to say that Leviticus is the older book; see above at verse 8.

כִּי עָנִי הוּא וְאֵלָיו הוּא נֹשֵׂא אֶת־נַפְשׁוֹ וְלֹא־יִקְרָא

עָלֶיךָ אֶל־יְהֹוָה וְהָיָה בְךָ חֵטְא: ס לֹא־יוּמְתוּ

אָבוֹת עַל־בָּנִים וּבָנִים לֹא־יוּמְתוּ עַל־אָבוֹת אִישׁ

בְּחֶטְאוֹ יוּמָתוּ: ס לֹא תַטֶּה מִשְׁפַּט גֵּר יָתוֹם וְלֹא

תַחֲבֹל בֶּגֶד אַלְמָנָה: וְזָכַרְתָּ כִּי עֶבֶד הָיִיתָ בְּמִצְרַיִם

וַיִּפְדְּךָ יְהֹוָה אֱלֹהֶיךָ מִשָּׁם עַל־כֵּן אָנֹכִי מְצַוְּךָ לַעֲשׂוֹת

אֶת־הַדָּבָר הַזֶּה: ס כִּי תִקְצֹר קְצִירְךָ בְשָׂדֶךָ

וְשָׁכַחְתָּ עֹמֶר בַּשָּׂדֶה לֹא־תָשׁוּב לְקַחְתּוֹ לַגֵּר לַיָּתוֹם

וְלָאַלְמָנָה יִהְיֶה לְמַעַן יְבָרֶכְךָ יְהֹוָה אֱלֹהֶיךָ בְּכֹל

מַעֲשֵׂה יָדֶיךָ: ס כִּי תַחְבֹּט זֵיתְךָ לֹא תְפָאֵר

אַחֲרֶיךָ לַגֵּר לַיָּתוֹם וְלָאַלְמָנָה יִהְיֶה: כִּי תִבְצֹר

כַּרְמְךָ לֹא תְעוֹלֵל אַחֲרֶיךָ לַגֵּר לַיָּתוֹם וְלָאַלְמָנָה

יִהְיֶה: וְזָכַרְתָּ כִּי־עֶבֶד הָיִיתָ בְּאֶרֶץ מִצְרַיִם עַל־כֵּן

אָנֹכִי מְצַוְּךָ לַעֲשׂוֹת אֶת־הַדָּבָר הַזֶּה: ס

---

day, before the sun sets, for he is needy and urgently depends on it; else he will cry to the LORD against you and you will incur guilt.

16] Parents shall not be put to death for children, nor children be put to death for parents: a person shall be put to death only for his own crime.

17] You shall not subvert the rights of the stranger or the fatherless; you shall not take a widow's garment in pawn. **18]** Remember that you were a slave in Egypt and that the LORD your God redeemed you from there; therefore do I enjoin you to observe this commandment.

19] When you reap the harvest in your field and overlook a sheaf in the field, do not turn back to get it; it shall go to the stranger, the fatherless, and the widow—in order that the LORD your God may bless you in all your undertakings.

20] When you beat down the fruit of your olive trees, do not go over them again; that shall go to the stranger, the fatherless, and the widow. **21]** When you gather the grapes of your vineyard, do not pick it over again; that shall go to the stranger, the fatherless, and the widow. **22]** Always remember that you were a slave in the land of Egypt; therefore do I enjoin you to observe this commandment.

16] *Only for his own crime.* See commentary below.

17] *A widow's garment.* Generally, anyone's garment may be taken in pledge, but not a widow's.

19] *When you reap.* It is an undergirding principle of the Torah that every citizen shares in the responsibility for easing the life of the poor, and the abolition of poverty is considered the mark of an ideal society (Deut. 15:4). God himself demands justice for the disadvantaged, who thus ground their claim in more than human charity. Compare

Lev. 19:9 f. and 23:22.

Verses 19–21 present certain problems that traditional commentators discussed in great detail. If the reason for the law had a social purpose, they said, the poor were hardly protected, for they had to depend on the owner's inadvertence. Furthermore, the mitzvah can be carried out only if one is forgetful; hence it does not emanate entirely from free will. Therefore, the true intent of these laws was seen to be the molding of character: people should learn not to want every last piece of produce and profit.

The Prohibition of Taking Interest
(Deut. 23:20-21)

In the ancient Near East, interest charges were well known in societies where the social structure had become sufficiently complex. Thus, in the second millennium B.C.E., Babylonian law permitted 20 percent interest on money and 33 1/3 percent on grain [17]. In Greece and Rome, on the other hand, the taking of interest was considered improper; Aristotle considered money a naturally barren commodity and incapable of reproducing itself—hence interest, as its quasi-offspring, was seen by him to be contrary to nature [18].

Torah law, here as well as in Exod. 22:24 and Lev. 25:35-37, added a moral dimension. Loans were originally extended not for commercial but for charitable purposes, and to connect charity with profit appeared as highly improper. Ezekiel (18:13) condemns it bitterly, and the Psalmist (15:5) praises the person who has never lent on interest. But these statements refer to social, not commercial relationships. To foreigners who were in the land presumably for the purpose of trading, the ancient Near Eastern rules applied, permitting (and expecting) interest.

The sentiment against taking interest from one's people persisted into postbiblical days and was in fact expanded by the Rabbis. A person refraining from charging it was praised as one who had accepted the yoke of the Kingdom of Heaven. In time, however, legal subterfuges were approved that permitted interest taking, in order to accommodate changed economic conditions [19]. The medieval Christian church prohibited its believers from taking interest for any purpose, thus leaving the development of commercial capital to the Jews in its midst, and creating thereby the image of the Jew as a greedy moneylender. He was held up to obloquy for such activity, while at the same time the lending process in which he engaged was both encouraged and needed by the ruling power.[1]

Current economic policy does not distinguish effectively between loans for personal reasons, including need, and for commercial enterprises. Today it is often the poor who have no access to free-loan societies or credit unions and, therefore, pay exorbitant interest rates for desperately needed funds—a total reversal of the original intent of the Torah.

Divorce

In biblical as well as talmudic law, it was the man who acquired a wife[2] and who, when it pleased him, sent her away. In only two instances was this male prerogative restricted: when a husband had falsely accused his wife of having had prenuptial intercourse and when a man had slept with a virgin who had not been engaged to someone else (Deut. 22:19; 22:29). Otherwise, except for incest and adultery, the man was free to do as he wanted, for the law reflected a social tradition that was male-oriented and which permitted polygamy.

The bill of divorcement was an instrument created to testify that the woman was entitled to marry again. We no longer know its precise content, but there is every reason to believe that the get of the Talmud, which is in use until this day, was itself based on a long tradition (see below, for the text of a get). Its core is the husband's declaration that the woman is no longer his wife and therefore free to marry another man. In Hosea's simile the formula was "She is not my wife, neither am I her husband" (Hos.

---

[1] The term "usury" was formerly a synonym for interest and later came to mean excessive interest.

[2] She is mekudeshet, sanctified, consecrated, literally "set aside" for him.

2:4), and in Sumerian practice a similar statement was made, probably first as an oral declaration which was then attested to in the written instrument. The Bible does not speak of a financial settlement for the divorcée, but the prevalence of such an arrangement in Mesopotamian law makes it likely that it was taken for granted by the Bible as part of the proceedings [20].

Despite the ease with which a man could send away his wife,[3] permanent union was the biblical ideal and divorce was considered a necessary evil. It occurred probably most frequently when the marriage failed to produce an offspring, it being believed that in such an instance the woman was the infertile partner. On the other hand, one may conclude from Exod. 21:10–11 that a wife had the right to leave her husband if he refused her proper sustenance and the fulfillment of sexual obligations.

A divorced woman returned to her father's house and did not keep her children, who remained with her husband. Also, she was forbidden to a priest (Lev. 21:7), and it may be assumed that divorce was considered a severe reflection on the woman and produced a significant reduction of her social status. In the fifth century B.C.E., divorces became frequent; whether or not this was related to Ezra's injunction to have Israelite men divorce their foreign wives is hard to say (cf. Malachi 2:13–16; Ezra 10:3 ff.).[4] In later centuries, divorce became relatively rare, and when it occurred it carried with it a serious social stigma. Only in more recent days has divorce once again been accepted by Jews as an aspect of the complexities of marriage. But the ideal enunciated by Koheleth has remained normative: "Enjoy life with the wife whom you love, during all the days of your transient existence which have been apportioned to you under the sun: for that is your reward of life and labor that are yours under the sun" (Eccles. 9:9).

Individual and Collective Responsibility
(Deut. 24:16)

The very insistence of the Deuteronomic law, that "a person shall be put to death only for his own crime," indicates the need for counteracting certain then prevailing conditions. Indeed, the Bible records a number of incidents that bear this out. In one, Joshua exacts punishment from a whole family (7:24–25); in another, David vows that Joab's murder of Abner will be avenged on the former's clan (II Sam. 3:29); in a third, David surrenders to the Gibeonites members of Saul's family to be killed for acts which Saul committed many years before (II Sam. 21:1 ff.). In contrast, King Amaziah is specifically commended for observing the Torah of Moses, and the writer takes pains to quote the Torah verse verbatim (II Kings 14:6; II Chron. 25:4). Amaziah reigned in Judea in the eighth century B.C.E., and his commendation indicates that the old principle of individual responsibility, enunciated in our passage, was at last taking root in practice.[5] During the days of the Babylonian exile, the prophet Ezekiel (chapter 18)

---

[3] Deut. 24:1 gives the man this right if he finds anything obnoxious in his wife—whether the reason was sexual, behavioral, or whatever. The schools of Hillel and Shammai had a controversy on this matter [21].
[4] Prevailing scholarly opinion places Malachi before Ezra, and hence the former's statement that God detests divorce is independent of Ezra's later procedures. Sirach (second century B.C.E.) encouraged men to terminate their marriages if their wives were ill-spoken and not responsive to correction (Sirach 25:25 f.). In the time of Josephus (first century C.E.), divorces still must have been frequent; "people have many reasons," he wrote [22], a fact attested to by the Mishnah a hundred years later [23].
[5] By the time the books of Kings and Chronicles were composed, Deuteronomy had encoded the old principle, which could now be quoted.

1502

further elaborated on this idea, which became a cornerstone of Israel's conception of justice.

How does the doctrine of individual responsibility relate to the second commandment which states that God will visit the sins of the fathers on the third and fourth generations (Deut. 5:9)? In the latter case, says Driver, "the reference is to the providence of God, operating naturally through the normal constitution of society: children are linked to their parents by ties, physical and social, from which they cannot free themselves; and they suffer, not because they are *guilty* of their fathers' sins, but because by the self-acting operation of natural laws their fathers' sins entail disgrace and misfortune upon them" [24]. The Deuteronomic law, on the other hand, deals with action by a *human* judicial agency and forbids the punishment of children for crimes they have not committed.[6]

---

[6] It may be noted that the law of Deuteronomy became in the halachah a proof text for criminal court procedure. The text implies, so it was held, that parents and children were not to testify against each other in capital matters, a principle then extended to other relatives [25].

GLEANINGS

She Did Not Cry for Help (Deut. 22:24)

This teaches that a person needs to cry for help, for the cry makes God a partner to one's fate.   AFTER SEFAT EMET [26]

Gear and Ear

It says (Deut. 23:14): "With your gear . . . cover up." Do not read "your gear" (אֲזֵנְךָ) but "your ear" (אָזְנְךָ). For when a person hears dirty talk he should cover his ears.   TALMUD [27]

Divorce Law

From the Code of Hammurabi: If a seignor wishes to divorce his wife who did not bear him children, he shall give her money to the full amount of the marriage price and he shall also make good to her the dowry which she brought from her father's house, and then he may divorce her. If he is a peasant, he shall give her one-third mina of silver [28].

From the Halachah: After fixing the time, place, and identities of husband and wife, the bill of divorcement (*get*) says (in excerpt):

"I (the husband) do willingly consent, being under no constraint, to release, set free, and put aside you, my wife . . . in order that you may have permission and authority for yourself to go and marry any man you may desire. No person may hinder you from this day onward, and you are permitted to any man. This shall be for you a bill of dismissal, a letter of release,

and a document of freedom, in accordance with the laws of Moses and Israel."

SHULCHAN ARUCH [29]

Slander

The plague comes to us because we indulge in slander. See what happened to Miriam: she slandered Moses and the plague attacked her (Num. 12). Therefore, the instruction about treating a skin affection (Deut. 24:8) is followed by "Remember what the Lord your God did to Miriam" (verse 9).

R. Yochanan said: If you slander strangers you will end up slandering your own. Let the pious Miriam be a warning to all slanderers.

MIDRASH [30]

You Shall Not Take a Widow's Garment in Pawn (Deut. 24:17)

The Rabbis argued whether it was the intent of the Torah to protect a *poor* widow, or whether the language of the text precluded a consideration of the Torah's intent, and hence the taking of *any* widow's garment was prohibited. The latter interpretation was adopted, and the principle established that one should investigate the Torah's (that is, God's) intent only in matters which were not halachic [31].

When You . . . Overlook a Sheaf (Deut. 24:19)

Even though a person has no deliberate intention of performing a mitzvah, yet he is considered as having performed it (he has overlooked a sheaf and lets it be). How much more meritorious is one who deliberately does a mitzvah.

TOSEFTA [32]

The Social Weal, III

The two chapters that follow complete the book's social, legal, ethical, and ritual prescriptions. They touch on many different areas but are, as always, united by religious concerns.

Socio-legal subjects covered are: obligation to marry the widow of one's deceased brother; honest weights; treatment of Amalek; excessive punishment; unseemly fight.

Ethico-ritual rules: muzzling an ox (kindness to animals); thanksgiving; tithing.

The section ends with an exhortation to observe the covenant which obligates both God and Israel.

(A new weekly portion, *Ki Tavo*, begins with 26:1.)

א כִּי־יִהְיֶה רִיב בֵּין אֲנָשִׁים וְנִגְּשׁוּ אֶל־הַמִּשְׁפָּט וּשְׁפָטוּם
הַחוּצָה לְאִישׁ זָר יְבָמָהּ יָבֹא עָלֶיהָ וּלְקָחָהּ לוֹ
וְהִצְדִּיקוּ אֶת־הַצַּדִּיק וְהִרְשִׁיעוּ אֶת־הָרָשָׁע: וְהָיָה אִם־ ב
לְאִשָּׁה וְיִבְּמָהּ: וְהָיָה הַבְּכוֹר אֲשֶׁר תֵּלֵד יָקוּם עַל־ י
בִּן הַכּוֹת הָרָשָׁע וְהִפִּילוֹ הַשֹּׁפֵט וְהִכָּהוּ לְפָנָיו כְּדֵי
שֵׁם אָחִיו הַמֵּת וְלֹא־יִמָּחֶה שְׁמוֹ מִיִּשְׂרָאֵל: וְאִם־לֹא
רִשְׁעָתוֹ בְּמִסְפָּר: אַרְבָּעִים יַכֶּנּוּ לֹא יֹסִיף פֶּן־יֹסִיף ג
יַחְפֹּץ הָאִישׁ לָקַחַת אֶת־יְבִמְתּוֹ וְעָלְתָה יְבִמְתּוֹ
לְהַכֹּתוֹ עַל־אֵלֶּה מַכָּה רַבָּה וְנִקְלָה אָחִיךָ לְעֵינֶיךָ:
הַשַּׁעְרָה אֶל־הַזְּקֵנִים וְאָמְרָה מֵאֵן יְבָמִי לְהָקִים
לֹא־תַחְסֹם שׁוֹר בְּדִישׁוֹ: ס כִּי־יֵשְׁבוּ אַחִים יַחְדָּו ה
לְאָחִיו שֵׁם בְּיִשְׂרָאֵל לֹא אָבָה יַבְּמִי: וְקָרְאוּ־לוֹ
וּמֵת אַחַד מֵהֶם וּבֵן אֵין־לוֹ לֹא־תִהְיֶה אֵשֶׁת־הַמֵּת
זִקְנֵי־עִירוֹ וְדִבְּרוּ אֵלָיו וְעָמַד וְאָמַר לֹא חָפַצְתִּי

1] When there is a dispute between men and they go to law, and a decision is rendered declaring the one in the right and the other in the wrong— **2]** if the guilty one is to be flogged, the magistrate shall have him lie down and be given lashes in his presence, by count, as his guilt warrants. **3]** He may be given up to forty lashes, but not more, lest being flogged further, to excess, your brother be degraded before your eyes.

4] You shall not muzzle an ox while it is threshing.

5] When brothers dwell together and one of them dies and leaves no son, the wife of the deceased shall not be married to a stranger, outside the family. Her husband's brother shall unite with her: take her as his wife and perform the levir's duty. **6]** The first son that she bears shall be accounted to the dead brother, that his name may not be blotted out in Israel. **7]** But if the man does not want to marry his brother's widow, his brother's widow shall appear before the elders in the gate and declare, "My husband's brother refuses to establish a name in Israel for his brother; he will not perform the duty of a levir." **8]** The elders of his town shall then summon him and talk to him. If he insists, saying, "I do not want to

---

25:2] *To be flogged.* בִּן הַכּוֹת (bin hakot). *Bin* is a variant of *ben* and usually means "son" (as with Joshua bin Nun); but when it precedes a noun which is not a name, as here, it has the meaning "subject to (flogging)."

The Aramaic equivalent is *bar*: thus, *bar mitzvah* means "subject to mitzvah."

3] *Up to forty lashes.* The words "up to" are not in the Hebrew text and were inserted to comply with the halachic understanding of the verse that thirty-nine blows should be the limit. See at Deut. 22:18. (See further in Gleanings.)

4] *Not muzzle.* Rather, you must allow the animal to eat at will [1].

While it is threshing. The animal was tied to a pivot and walked in circles treading the corn. This method of threshing is still used in countries with nonmechanized agriculture.

Driver calls the law "another example of the humanity which is characteristic of Deuteronomy."

5] *When brothers dwell together.* On common family property.

Her husband's brother shall . . . perform the levir's duty. The word "levir" is the Latin for "husband's brother," hence the particular relationship and its consequences are called "levirate." The text takes a knowledge of "the levir's duty" for granted and only describes what happens if a brother is unwilling to fulfill it.

A talmudic treatise *Yevamot* deals with the halachah arising from these prescriptions. (See further in commentary below.)

6] *Shall be accounted.* In apportioning the inheritance [2].

טו לְקַחְתָּהּ: וְנִגְּשָׁה יְבִמְתּוֹ אֵלָיו לְעֵינֵי הַזְּקֵנִים וְחָלְצָה
נַעֲלוֹ מֵעַל רַגְלוֹ וְיָרְקָה בְּפָנָיו וְעָנְתָה וְאָמְרָה
כָּכָה יֵעָשֶׂה לָאִישׁ אֲשֶׁר לֹא־יִבְנֶה אֶת־בֵּית
י אָחִיו: וְנִקְרָא שְׁמוֹ בְּיִשְׂרָאֵל בֵּית חֲלוּץ הַנָּעַל: ס
יא כִּי־יִנָּצוּ אֲנָשִׁים יַחְדָּו אִישׁ וְאָחִיו וְקָרְבָה אֵשֶׁת
הָאֶחָד לְהַצִּיל אֶת־אִישָׁהּ מִיַּד מַכֵּהוּ וְשָׁלְחָה יָדָהּ
יב וְהֶחֱזִיקָה בִּמְבֻשָׁיו: וְקַצֹּתָה אֶת־כַּפָּהּ לֹא תָחוֹס

יג עֵינֶךָ: ס לֹא־יִהְיֶה לְךָ בְּכִיסְךָ אֶבֶן וָאָבֶן גְּדוֹלָה
יד וּקְטַנָּה: לֹא־יִהְיֶה לְךָ בְּבֵיתְךָ אֵיפָה וְאֵיפָה גְּדוֹלָה
טו וּקְטַנָּה: אֶבֶן שְׁלֵמָה וָצֶדֶק יִהְיֶה־לָּךְ אֵיפָה שְׁלֵמָה
וָצֶדֶק יִהְיֶה־לָּךְ לְמַעַן יַאֲרִיכוּ יָמֶיךָ עַל הָאֲדָמָה
טז אֲשֶׁר־יְהֹוָה אֱלֹהֶיךָ נֹתֵן לָךְ: כִּי תוֹעֲבַת יְהֹוָה
אֱלֹהֶיךָ כָּל־עֹשֵׂה אֵלֶּה כֹּל עֹשֵׂה עָוֶל: פ
יז זָכוֹר אֵת אֲשֶׁר־עָשָׂה לְךָ עֲמָלֵק בַּדֶּרֶךְ בְּצֵאתְכֶם

marry her," **9]** his brother's widow shall go up to him in the presence of the elders, pull the sandal off his foot, spit in his face, and make this declaration: Thus shall be done to the man who will not build up his brother's house! **10]** And he shall go in Israel by the name of "the family of the unsandaled one."

11] If two men get into a fight with each other, and the wife of one comes up to save her husband from his antagonist and puts out her hand and seizes him by his genitals, **12]** you shall cut off her hand; show no pity.

13] You shall not have in your pouch alternate weights, larger and smaller. **14]** You shall not have in your house alternate measures, a larger and a smaller. **15]** You must have completely honest weights and completely honest measures, if you are to endure long on the soil that the LORD your God is giving you. **16]** For everyone who does those things, everyone who deals dishonestly, is abhorrent to the LORD your God.

17] Remember what Amalek did to you on your journey, after you left Egypt— **18]** how,

9] *Pull the sandal off.* Hebrew חָלְצָה (*chaltzah*); hence the ceremony is known as *chalitzah.*

11] *His genitals.* Literally, "his shame parts" (compare the Latin *pudenda*).

Cut off her hand. A punishment not otherwise decreed in the Torah. In the laudable effort to save her husband the woman used what were considered impermissible means. In this conflict of personal need (to defend her husband) with public morality the Torah opted to support the latter. Compare the endorsement given to Phinehas, who responded violently against sexual license; Num. 25:1 ff. (On the question of talion, and the expression "hand for hand," see at Deut. 19:21.)

A talmudic discussion suggests that the law did not apply when the woman's action was the only recourse to save her husband, and that in any case a fine was exacted in lieu of mutilation [3].

13] *Weights.* אֶבֶן (*even*) means generally "stone," for stones often served as weights.

Larger and smaller. One for buying and one for selling. Compare Lev. 19:35.

14] *Measures.* אֵיפָה (*efah*) was a measure for both dry and liquid substances; it was equal to about 36 litres (8 gallons) [4].

17] *Remember what Amalek did.* The reference is to the events reported in Exod. 17:8–13; see our commentary there. In Deuteronomic days, Amalek—a group of Nomadic tribes in the Negev and Sinai—no longer threatened the Israelites, but the memory of their first battle stamped Amalek forever as the archenemy whose weakened condition was doubtlessly seen as just retribution.

Verses 17–19 form an additional Torah reading on the Sabbath before Purim, which is called *Shabbat Zachor* after the first word in verse 17, *zachor,* remember.

ו אֲשֶׁר יִבְחַר יְהוָה אֱלֹהֶיךָ לְשַׁכֵּן שְׁמוֹ שָׁם: וּבָאתָ
אֶל־הַכֹּהֵן אֲשֶׁר יִהְיֶה בַּיָּמִים הָהֵם וְאָמַרְתָּ אֵלָיו
הִגַּדְתִּי הַיּוֹם לַיהוָה אֱלֹהֶיךָ כִּי־בָאתִי אֶל־הָאָרֶץ
אֲשֶׁר נִשְׁבַּע יְהוָה לַאֲבֹתֵינוּ לָתֶת לָנוּ: וְלָקַח הַכֹּהֵן
הַטֶּנֶא מִיָּדֶךָ וְהִנִּיחוֹ לִפְנֵי מִזְבַּח יְהוָה אֱלֹהֶיךָ:
ה וְעָנִיתָ וְאָמַרְתָּ לִפְנֵי יְהוָה אֱלֹהֶיךָ אֲרַמִּי אֹבֵד אָבִי
וַיֵּרֶד מִצְרַיְמָה וַיָּגָר שָׁם בִּמְתֵי מְעָט וַיְהִי־שָׁם לְגוֹי
גָּדוֹל עָצוּם וָרָב: וַיָּרֵעוּ אֹתָנוּ הַמִּצְרִים וַיְעַנּוּנוּ
וַיִּתְּנוּ עָלֵינוּ עֲבֹדָה קָשָׁה: וַנִּצְעַק אֶל־יְהוָה אֱלֹהֵי
אֲבֹתֵינוּ וַיִּשְׁמַע יְהוָה אֶת־קֹלֵנוּ וַיַּרְא אֶת־עָנְיֵנוּ וְאֶת־

יח מִמִּצְרָיִם: אֲשֶׁר קָרְךָ בַּדֶּרֶךְ וַיְזַנֵּב בְּךָ כָּל־הַנֶּחֱשָׁלִים
יט אַחֲרֶיךָ וְאַתָּה עָיֵף וְיָגֵעַ וְלֹא יָרֵא אֱלֹהִים: וְהָיָה
בְּהָנִיחַ יְהוָה אֱלֹהֶיךָ לְךָ מִכָּל־אֹיְבֶיךָ מִסָּבִיב בָּאָרֶץ
אֲשֶׁר יְהוָה־אֱלֹהֶיךָ נֹתֵן לְךָ נַחֲלָה לְרִשְׁתָּהּ תִּמְחֶה
אֶת־זֵכֶר עֲמָלֵק מִתַּחַת הַשָּׁמָיִם לֹא תִּשְׁכָּח:

Haftarah Ki Tetze, p. 1612

פ　פ　פ

א וְהָיָה כִּי־תָבוֹא אֶל־הָאָרֶץ אֲשֶׁר יְהוָה אֱלֹהֶיךָ נֹתֵן
ב לְךָ נַחֲלָה וִירִשְׁתָּהּ וְיָשַׁבְתָּ בָּהּ: וְלָקַחְתָּ מֵרֵאשִׁית
כָּל־פְּרִי הָאֲדָמָה אֲשֶׁר תָּבִיא מֵאַרְצְךָ אֲשֶׁר יְהוָה
אֱלֹהֶיךָ נֹתֵן לָךְ וְשַׂמְתָּ בַטֶּנֶא וְהָלַכְתָּ אֶל־הַמָּקוֹם

undeterred by fear of God, he surprised you on the march, when you were famished and weary, and cut down all the stragglers in your rear.　**19]** Therefore, when the LORD your God grants you safety from all your enemies around you, in the land that the LORD your God is giving you as a hereditary portion, you shall blot out the memory of Amalek from under heaven. Do not forget!

1] When you enter the land that the LORD your God is giving you as a heritage, and you occupy it and settle in it,　**2]** you shall take some of every first fruit of the soil, which you harvest from the land that the LORD your God is giving you, put it in a basket and go to the place where the LORD your God will choose to establish His name.　**3]** You shall go to the priest in charge at that time and say to him, "I acknowledge this day before the LORD your God that I have entered the land which the LORD swore to our fathers to give us."

4] The priest shall take the basket from your hand and set it down in front of the altar of the LORD your God.

5] You shall then recite as follows before the LORD your God: "My father was a fugitive Aramean. He went down to Egypt with meager numbers and sojourned there; but there he became a great and very populous nation.　**6]** The Egyptians dealt harshly with us and oppressed us; they imposed heavy labor upon us.　**7]** We cried to the LORD, the God of our fathers, and the LORD heard our plea and saw our plight, our misery, and our

18]　*Undeterred by fear of God.* Which has no national limitation and obligates other peoples as well [5].

Stragglers in your rear. This aspect is not mentioned in Exodus.

The word נֶחֱשָׁלִים (*necheshalim,* translated as "stragglers") was probably נֶחֱלָשִׁים (*nechelashim,* enfeebled). Hence: those left behind. Such transpositions occurred frequently and sometimes the

transposed word remained as a variant of the original. Thus, the usual word for "lamb" is כֶּבֶשׂ (*keves*), but כֶּשֶׂב (*kesev*) also occurs. Or note עָיֵף (*ayef,* tired) and its variant יָעֵף (*ya-ef*).

26:3]　*The Lord your God.* The speaker says "your God" in deference to the priest.

But the Septuagint has "my God."

5]　*Fugitive Aramean.* See commentary below.

ח עֲמָלֵנוּ וְאֶת־לַחֲצֵנוּ: וַיּוֹצִאֵנוּ יְהוָֹה מִמִּצְרַיִם בְּיָד
חֲזָקָה וּבִזְרֹעַ נְטוּיָה וּבְמֹרָא גָּדֹל וּבְאֹתוֹת וּבְמֹפְתִים:
ט וַיְבִאֵנוּ אֶל־הַמָּקוֹם הַזֶּה וַיִּתֶּן־לָנוּ אֶת־הָאָרֶץ הַזֹּאת
י אֶרֶץ זָבַת חָלָב וּדְבָשׁ: וְעַתָּה הִנֵּה הֵבֵאתִי אֶת־
רֵאשִׁית פְּרִי הָאֲדָמָה אֲשֶׁר־נָתַתָּה לִּי יְהוָֹה וְהִנַּחְתּוֹ
לִפְנֵי יְהוָֹה אֱלֹהֶיךָ וְהִשְׁתַּחֲוִיתָ לִפְנֵי יְהוָֹה אֱלֹהֶיךָ:
יא וְשָׂמַחְתָּ בְכָל־הַטּוֹב אֲשֶׁר נָתַן־לְךָ יְהוָֹה אֱלֹהֶיךָ
יב וּלְבֵיתֶךָ אַתָּה וְהַלֵּוִי וְהַגֵּר אֲשֶׁר בְּקִרְבֶּךָ: ס כִּי

תְכַלֶּה לַעְשֵׂר אֶת־כָּל־מַעְשַׂר תְּבוּאָתְךָ בַּשָּׁנָה
הַשְּׁלִישִׁת שְׁנַת הַמַּעֲשֵׂר וְנָתַתָּה לַלֵּוִי לַגֵּר לַיָּתוֹם
יג וְלָאַלְמָנָה וְאָכְלוּ בִשְׁעָרֶיךָ וְשָׂבֵעוּ: וְאָמַרְתָּ לִפְנֵי
יְהוָֹה אֱלֹהֶיךָ בִּעַרְתִּי הַקֹּדֶשׁ מִן־הַבַּיִת וְגַם נְתַתִּיו
לַלֵּוִי וְלַגֵּר לַיָּתוֹם וְלָאַלְמָנָה כְּכָל־מִצְוָתְךָ אֲשֶׁר
יד צִוִּיתָנִי לֹא־עָבַרְתִּי מִמִּצְוֹתֶיךָ וְלֹא שָׁכָחְתִּי: לֹא־
אָכַלְתִּי בְאֹנִי מִמֶּנּוּ וְלֹא־בִעַרְתִּי מִמֶּנּוּ בְּטָמֵא וְלֹא־
נָתַתִּי מִמֶּנּוּ לְמֵת שָׁמַעְתִּי בְּקוֹל יְהוָֹה אֱלֹהָי עָשִׂיתִי

oppression. **8]** The LORD freed us from Egypt by a mighty hand, by an outstretched arm and awesome power, and by signs and portents. **9]** He brought us to this place and gave us this land, a land flowing with milk and honey. **10]** Wherefore I now bring the first fruits of the soil which You, O LORD, have given me."

You shall leave it before the LORD your God and bow low before the LORD your God. **11]** And you shall enjoy, together with the Levite and the stranger in your midst, all the bounty that the LORD your God has bestowed upon you and your household.

12] When you have set aside in full the tenth part of your yield—in the third year, the year of the tithe—and have given it to the Levite, the stranger, the fatherless, and the widow, that they may eat their fill in your settlements, **13]** you shall declare before the LORD your God: "I have cleared out the consecrated portion from the house; and I have given it to the Levite, the stranger, the fatherless, and the widow, just as You commanded me; I have neither transgressed nor neglected any of Your commandments: **14]** I have not eaten of it while in mourning; I have not cleared out any of it while I was unclean, and I have not deposited any of it with the dead. I have obeyed the LORD my God; I have done just as You commanded

9] *Milk and honey.* See at Deut. 6:3.

10] *You shall leave it.* The basket which you have brought (verse 4).

11] *You shall enjoy.* At a festive meal, to which the Levites as well as strangers were to be invited. The offering itself belonged to the priests; Deut. 18:4.

12] *When you have set aside.* The duty of tithing was set forth in Deut. 14:28–29; see there. The gift was followed by a formal declaration of religious compliance.

This confessional litany, called *Viddui Ma-aser* (confession of tithing), was in later centuries as-

signed to the eve of the last day of Passover in the fourth and seventh years of the sabbatical cycle and pronounced in the Temple in Jerusalem [6].

14] *While in mourning.* That is, while unclean through contact with the dead, and before the necessary ablutions had been made (cf. Hos. 9:4).

The translation is one of several that have been suggested, in part because what follows deals with the dead. But Rashbam understands: I did not (eat of it myself) for my own benefit (cf. the Hebrew text of Job 20:10).

Deposited any of it with the dead. As was done in Egypt, where food was buried with the dead for their journey in the afterlife. Such practices appear to have continued in Israel for many centuries [7].

טו כְּכֹל אֲשֶׁר צִוִּיתָנִי: הַשְׁקִיפָה מִמְּעוֹן קָדְשְׁךָ מִן
הַשָּׁמַיִם וּבָרֵךְ אֶת־עַמְּךָ אֶת־יִשְׂרָאֵל וְאֵת הָאֲדָמָה
אֲשֶׁר נָתַתָּה לָנוּ כַּאֲשֶׁר נִשְׁבַּעְתָּ לַאֲבֹתֵינוּ אֶרֶץ
טז זָבַת חָלָב וּדְבָשׁ: ס הַיּוֹם הַזֶּה יְהֹוָה אֱלֹהֶיךָ
מְצַוְּךָ לַעֲשׂוֹת אֶת־הַחֻקִּים הָאֵלֶּה וְאֶת־הַמִּשְׁפָּטִים
וְשָׁמַרְתָּ וְעָשִׂיתָ אוֹתָם בְּכָל־לְבָבְךָ וּבְכָל־נַפְשֶׁךָ:

יז אֶת־יְהֹוָה הֶאֱמַרְתָּ הַיּוֹם לִהְיוֹת לְךָ לֵאלֹהִים וְלָלֶכֶת
בִּדְרָכָיו וְלִשְׁמֹר חֻקָּיו וּמִצְוֺתָיו וּמִשְׁפָּטָיו וְלִשְׁמֹעַ
יח בְּקֹלוֹ: וַיהֹוָה הֶאֱמִירְךָ הַיּוֹם לִהְיוֹת לוֹ לְעַם סְגֻלָּה
יט כַּאֲשֶׁר דִּבֶּר־לָךְ וְלִשְׁמֹר כָּל־מִצְוֺתָיו: וּלְתִתְּךָ עֶלְיוֹן
עַל כָּל־הַגּוֹיִם אֲשֶׁר עָשָׂה לִתְהִלָּה וּלְשֵׁם וּלְתִפְאָרֶת
וְלִהְיֹתְךָ עַם־קָדֹשׁ לַיהֹוָה אֱלֹהֶיךָ כַּאֲשֶׁר דִּבֵּר:

me.   **15]** Look down from Your holy abode, from heaven, and bless Your people Israel and the soil You have given us, a land flowing with milk and honey, as You swore to our fathers."

16] The LORD your God commands you this day to observe these laws and rules; observe them faithfully with all your heart and soul.   **17]** You have affirmed this day that the LORD is your God, that you will walk in His ways, that you will observe His laws and commandments and rules, and that you will obey Him.   **18]** And the LORD has affirmed this day that you are, as He promised you, His treasured people which shall observe all His commandments, **19]** and that He will set you, in fame and renown and glory, high above all the nations that He has made; and that you shall be, as He promised, a holy people to the LORD your God.

16] *Observe these laws*. Of chapters 12–26; a final exhortation.

17] *You have affirmed*. As, in return, has God; verse 18. This mutuality is expressed by the causal

form (otherwise unknown) of the word אָמַר. God causes Israel's affirmation and Israel's acceptance causes God's.

18] *His treasured people*. See on Deut. 7:6.

Chalitzah

The duty to preserve both the name and inheritance of a deceased and childless brother by marrying his widow ("the levir's duty") was apparently deeply rooted in Israel's tradition. The Torah text takes both its knowledge and its practice for granted and addresses itself only to the case of a recalcitrant brother and to the public ceremony (*chalitzah*) which was highlighted by pulling off his sandal and by spitting in his face. The symbolism of the procedure appears to have legal, psychological, and sexual overtones which doubtlessly were at one time clearly understood.

Thus, documents found in Nuzi (Mesopotamia) show that a shoe was used for effecting certain legal transactions, and "lifting the foot" symbolized the release of property[1] [8].

The Book of Ruth (4:7) remembers: "Now this was the custom in former time in Israel concerning redeeming and concerning exchanging, to confirm all things: a man drew off his shoe, and gave it to his neighbor; and this was the attestation in Israel."[2] But, in addition to representing possession, feet and shoes seem to have represented also certain sexual meanings. In Arabic, a woman is sometimes referred to as "a sandal," and by covering or uncovering his feet a man would convey an erotic message. Similarly, the act of spitting may originally not have been designed to humiliate the brother, but rather to have evoked an image of the semen he had withheld, even as did the act of unshoeing [9].

Levirate marriages were performed for many centuries, well into Mishnaic times (second century C.E.) [10]. But there was increasing doubt whether they were socially desirable, especially in view of the express statement in Lev. 18:16 which forbids a man to marry his brother's wife, classifying such a union with other incestuous relationships. The levirate law permits such marriage and, in fact, demands it when the widow has no children, but the exception does not fully relieve the sense of aversion which Lev. 18 expresses. Therefore, in the course of time, *chalitzah* appeared as a more desirable alternative and its practice, a priority over levirate marriage. Ultimately, the Rabbis made *chalitzah* a requirement and forbade levirate unions, save in exceptional cases. A ruling in the State of Israel states that the Torah law had to be set aside because "most levirs do not undergo levirate marriage for the sake of fulfilling a mitzvah, and also to preserve peace and harmony in the State of Israel by keeping the laws of Torah uniform for all" [11]. Still, the halachah continues to consider a widow whose brother-in-law has not yet released her through *chalitzah* as unmarriageable, and this has produced a number of hardship cases.[3] Orthodox rabbis —despite their concern for the widow—have found themselves unable to resolve the obvious contradiction: the widow depends on a brother-in-law to release her from the effects of a law that has been officially declared inoperative.[4]

Reform Judaism has drawn the logical

---

[1] Nowadays, surrendering a key would be a comparable symbolic act.

[2] Some centuries later, the glove of the right hand had taken the place of the shoe, as the Targum to Ruth 4:7 attests. The procedure recorded in the Book of Ruth diverges from the Torah, but the issue was of a somewhat different nature, which apparently demanded different practices.

[3] For instance, the brother-in-law may be a minor who cannot perform *chalitzah* until he is legally capable to do so.

[4] They have meliorated the Torah demand that the widow spit in the levir's face (she now spits on the ground), but they have not been able to overcome a levir's unavailability or unwillingness to perform *chalitzah*.

conclusion: It views levirate marriage as an undesirable norm for modern society and therefore considers *chalitzah* no longer necessary.

Thanksgiving

While the festival of Sukot represented the national religious thanksgiving festival (on which the American and Canadian holidays are based), the Torah orders a personal expression of gratitude as well and prescribes the exact words that are to be spoken on such an occasion (26:5–11). Although this is one of the few instances in the Torah where liturgical pronouncements are fixed—another example is the priestly benediction, Num. 6:22–27—its meaning is not clear.

The Israelite is to come to the sanctuary and, so to speak, identify himself historically. He is to begin by saying אֲרַמִּי אֹבֵד אָבִי—three words, none of which is unambiguous in this context. אֲרַמִּי (Arami) usually means "Aramean"; אֹבֵד (oved) could mean "lost" or "losing," but also "cause to be lost"; אָבִי (avi) means "my father" or "my ancestor."

Our translation has "My father was a fugitive Aramean"—which could be a reference to Abraham (who, when he left Haran, could be said to have been an Aramean) or, more likely, to Jacob (who fled from Laban); but the problem is that Abraham was not a fugitive and Jacob no Aramean.

Other translations have "The Aramean (tried to) cause my father to be lost (i.e., to be destroyed)." The Aramean was seen to be Laban, and the "father" was Jacob, whom Laban attempted to undo.

These are complex grammatical questions that render an undisputed interpretation impossible—but then perhaps such is not necessary to obtain. The Torah is repeatedly ambiguous. Here, thanksgiving is to be rooted in the past, with its glories and its difficulties. The facts of near destruction in ages gone by (or in recent memory, as the case may be) were set down as necessary recollections for an Israelite's thanksgiving. Whether the danger to survival came to an Abraham or to a Jacob, whether the ancestor was threatened or merely lost (physically? spiritually?) is less important than that the past needed to be seen as impinging on the present, and that God's beneficent guidance needed to be rehearsed from generation to generation. The very opaqueness of the language may in fact have prevented the obligation from being identified with the remote past only and instead served to render it of continuing significance [12].

GLEANINGS

Flogging (Deut. 25:1–3)

The number of lashes to be administered is "up to forty lashes but no more." (Therefore, only thirty-nine strokes are given so that a mistake in counting may not lead to excessive punishment.)

If the scourged person dies, the one administering the lashes is not culpable, but if he gave even one stroke too many he is culpable and subject to exile.

Excessive beating would cause "your brother" to be degraded in your eyes. After having been flogged he is like your brother.[5] MISHNAH [14]

A magistrate must watch the flogging to make sure that the culprit can still bear the lashes.

MIDRASH [15]

Those appointed to administer the lashes should be weak in body but strong in understanding.

TALMUD [16]

If we look into the place in the Torah in which the law of flogging occurs and its close connection with the law of not muzzling an ox (which follows it), then the tendency of the teaching here is not so much on flogging as a punishment as it is directed to its limitation. In the laws preceding (24:20 ff.), kindness and consideration are demanded for the socially deprived, and, in the law following (25:4), considerate behavior is demanded even for animals. So here, when a person is to be disciplined, the court is commanded to exercise watchful consideration. S. R. HIRSCH [17]

Two Times

The word "everyone" occurs twice in 25:16 (which deals with dishonesty). Dishonesty would be a sin even if there were no Torah command (Cain's murder of Abel was a sin even though there was not yet any law), for it is self-evident. Hence it says "everyone," to make clear that the law includes even those who do not know of its existence. KETAV SOFER [18]

When

(The opening word of 26:1, וְהָיָה, was construed by the Rabbis to indicate a sense of joy, and was applied by them to every occurrence of the word.)

Settling in Eretz Yisrael is one of the gifts vouchsafed to Israel, in recompense for its suffering.

Y. L. EGER [19]

Past and Present

In 26:5 the expression "fugitive" (אֹבֵד) is a present participle. Persecution of Israel existed long ago and has not ceased in our day.

CHASIDIC [20]

Reciprocity

God's "bringing" Israel into the land and "bringing" the first fruits are set into a mutual relationship that is stressed in the prayer itself (26:9–10): "*He brought* us to this place. . . . Wherefore *I now bring* the first fruits of the soil." Thus is expressed the reciprocity between God and the individual members of the people.

M. BUBER [21]

---

[5] The Mishnah states further that if the flogged person befouls himself no further strokes are administered. It was also noted that the numerical value of "your brother" (אָחִיךָ) is 39: א =1, ח =8, י =10, כ =20 [13].

Blessings and Curses, I

It is at once apparent that the following section differs from the preceding one, for directives in the second person now give way to a third person framework. Furthermore, the chapter interrupts the flow of chapters 26–28, and it is likely that it once stood after chapter 28.* Such a position would give it the literary function of ending Part III of the Book of Deuteronomy: at its beginning (11:26 ff.) the blessings and curses on Mount Gerizim and Mount Ebal were assigned their role, and now, at the end, this role would be described in detail. Blessings and curses thus form the framework for the special laws contained in Part III, even as a short catalogue of blessings concludes the Book of the Covenant (Exod. 23:20 ff.), and a list of blessings and curses follows the Holiness Code (Lev. 26).

The preparations for the ritual fall into four parts: (1) inscribing the law on stone tablets and placing them on Mount Ebal; (2) erecting the altar; (3) sacrifice and meal of rejoicing by the people; (4) pronouncement of the curses by the Levites and acknowledgment by the people.

For a discussion of blessings and curses, see commentary below and Gleanings to Introduction to Part III.

* But von Rad believes that ch. 28 once followed after 27:10. He calls the twelve laws of 27:15–26 "the Shechem Dodecalogue, the oldest list of prohibitions in the Bible" [1].

ה וּבָנִיתָ שָּׁם מִזְבֵּחַ לַיהוָה אֱלֹהֶיךָ מִזְבַּח אֲבָנִים לֹא־
ו תָנִיף עֲלֵיהֶם בַּרְזֶל: אֲבָנִים שְׁלֵמוֹת תִּבְנֶה אֶת־
מִזְבַּח יְהוָה אֱלֹהֶיךָ וְהַעֲלִיתָ עָלָיו עוֹלֹת לַיהוָה
ז אֱלֹהֶיךָ: וְזָבַחְתָּ שְׁלָמִים וְאָכַלְתָּ שָּׁם וְשָׂמַחְתָּ לִפְנֵי
ח יְהוָה אֱלֹהֶיךָ: וְכָתַבְתָּ עַל־הָאֲבָנִים אֶת־כָּל־דִּבְרֵי
הַתּוֹרָה הַזֹּאת בָּאֵר הֵיטֵב: ס

ט וַיְדַבֵּר מֹשֶׁה וְהַכֹּהֲנִים הַלְוִיִּם אֶל־כָּל־יִשְׂרָאֵל לֵאמֹר
הַסְכֵּת וּשְׁמַע יִשְׂרָאֵל הַיּוֹם הַזֶּה נִהְיֵיתָ לְעָם לַיהוָה
י אֱלֹהֶיךָ: וְשָׁמַעְתָּ בְּקוֹל יְהוָה אֱלֹהֶיךָ וְעָשִׂיתָ אֶת־
יא מִצְוֹתָו וְאֶת־חֻקָּיו אֲשֶׁר אָנֹכִי מְצַוְּךָ הַיּוֹם: ס   וַיְצַו

א וַיְצַו מֹשֶׁה וְזִקְנֵי יִשְׂרָאֵל אֶת־הָעָם לֵאמֹר שָׁמֹר
ב אֶת־כָּל־הַמִּצְוָה אֲשֶׁר אָנֹכִי מְצַוֶּה אֶתְכֶם הַיּוֹם: וְהָיָה
בַּיּוֹם אֲשֶׁר תַּעַבְרוּ אֶת־הַיַּרְדֵּן אֶל־הָאָרֶץ אֲשֶׁר־
יְהוָה אֱלֹהֶיךָ נֹתֵן לָךְ וַהֲקֵמֹתָ לְךָ אֲבָנִים גְּדֹלוֹת
ג וְשַׂדְתָּ אֹתָם בַּשִּׂיד: וְכָתַבְתָּ עֲלֵיהֶן אֶת־כָּל־דִּבְרֵי
הַתּוֹרָה הַזֹּאת בְּעָבְרֶךָ לְמַעַן אֲשֶׁר תָּבֹא אֶל־הָאָרֶץ
אֲשֶׁר־יְהוָה אֱלֹהֶיךָ נֹתֵן לְךָ אֶרֶץ זָבַת חָלָב וּדְבַשׁ
ד כַּאֲשֶׁר דִּבֶּר יְהוָה אֱלֹהֵי־אֲבֹתֶיךָ לָךְ: וְהָיָה בְּעָבְרְכֶם
אֶת־הַיַּרְדֵּן תָּקִימוּ אֶת־הָאֲבָנִים הָאֵלֶּה אֲשֶׁר אָנֹכִי
מְצַוֶּה אֶתְכֶם הַיּוֹם בְּהַר עֵיבָל וְשַׂדְתָּ אוֹתָם בַּשִּׂיד:

יא מצותיו קרי.

1] Moses and the elders of Israel charged the people, saying: Observe all the Instruction that I enjoin upon you this day. **2]** As soon as you have crossed the Jordan into the land that the LORD your God is giving you, you shall set up large stones. Coat them with plaster **3]** and inscribe upon them all the words of this Teaching. When you cross over to invade the land that the LORD your God is giving you, a land flowing with milk and honey, as the LORD, the God of your fathers, promised you— **4]** upon crossing the Jordan, you shall set up these stones, about which I charge you this day, on Mount Ebal, and coat them with plaster. **5]** There, too, you shall build an altar to the LORD your God, an altar of stones. Do not wield an iron tool over them; **6]** you must build the altar of the LORD your God of unhewn stones. You shall offer on it burnt offerings to the LORD your God, **7]** and you shall sacrifice there offerings of well-being and eat them, rejoicing before the LORD your God. **8]** And on those stones you shall inscribe every word of this Teaching most distinctly.

9] Moses and the levitical priests spoke to all Israel, saying: Silence! Hear, O Israel! Today you have become the people of the LORD your God: **10]** Heed the LORD your God and observe His commandments and His laws, which I enjoin upon you this day. **11]** Thereupon

---

27:2] *As soon as you have crossed.* The prescriptions that follow were not precisely observed by Joshua; thus Mount Gerizim is not mentioned as having a role in his ceremonies—despite the specific statement that Joshua carried out the law of Moses (Josh. 8:30 ff.). One cannot explain this discrepancy with certainty; one possibility is that the author of Deuteronomy (who lived centuries after Joshua and probably later also than the compilation of the Book of Joshua) wanted to point out that the conquest of the land had not always followed divine prescriptions and had, in fact, significantly digressed from them (as also in the matter of extirpating the pagans).

The construction of verses 2–4 is difficult and the translation uncertain.

Coat them with plaster. And afterwards inscribe them, according to Egyptian practice. This method preserved the inscription better than an incision in the stone, which often weathered badly [2].

3] *This Teaching.* According to Josh. 8:32, this appears to mean the Book of Deuteronomy; see also at Deut. 1:5.

Josephus: only the blessings and curses were inscribed [3]; Mishnah: the whole Torah [4]; Saadia: the essential teachings of Torah [5].

9] *Levitical priests.* See at 18:1.

יג מֹשֶׁה֙ אֶת־הָעָ֔ם בַּיּ֥וֹם הַה֖וּא לֵאמֹֽר׃ ׳אֵ֣לֶּה יַֽעַמְד֞וּ
לְבָרֵ֤ךְ אֶת־הָעָם֙ עַל־הַ֣ר גְּרִזִ֔ים בְּעָבְרְכֶ֖ם אֶת־הַיַּרְדֵּ֑ן
יג שִׁמְעוֹן֙ וְלֵוִ֣י וִֽיהוּדָ֔ה וְיִשָּׂשכָ֖ר וְיוֹסֵ֥ף וּבִנְיָמִֽן׃ וְאֵ֛לֶּה
יַעַמְד֥וּ עַל־הַקְּלָלָ֖ה בְּהַ֣ר עֵיבָ֑ל רְאוּבֵן֙ גָּ֣ד וְאָשֵׁ֔ר
יד וּזְבוּלֻ֖ן דָּ֥ן וְנַפְתָּלִֽי׃ וְעָנ֣וּ הַלְוִיִּ֗ם וְאָֽמְר֛וּ אֶל־כָּל־אִ֥ישׁ

טו יִשְׂרָאֵ֖ל ק֣וֹל רָֽם׃ ס אָר֣וּר הָאִ֡ישׁ אֲשֶׁ֣ר יַעֲשֶׂה֩
פֶ֨סֶל וּמַסֵּכָ֜ה תּוֹעֲבַ֣ת יְהֹוָ֗ה מַעֲשֵׂ֛ה יְדֵ֥י חָרָ֖שׁ וְשָׂ֣ם
בַּסָּ֑תֶר וְעָנ֧וּ כָל־הָעָ֛ם וְאָמְר֖וּ אָמֵֽן׃ ס אָר֣וּר
טז מַקְלֶ֥ה אָבִ֖יו וְאִמּ֑וֹ וְאָמַ֥ר כָּל־הָעָ֖ם אָמֵֽן׃ ס אָר֣וּר
יז מַסִּ֖יג גְּב֣וּל רֵעֵ֑הוּ וְאָמַ֥ר כָּל־הָעָ֖ם אָמֵֽן׃ ס אָר֣וּר

Moses charged the people, saying: **12]** After you have crossed the Jordan, the following shall stand on Mount Gerizim when the blessing for the people is spoken: Simeon, Levi, Judah, Issachar, Joseph, and Benjamin.   **13]** And for the curse, the following shall stand on Mount Ebal: Reuben, Gad, Asher, Zebulun, Dan, and Naphtali.   **14]** The Levites shall then proclaim in a loud voice to all the men of Israel:

15] Cursed be the man who makes a sculptured or molten image, abhorred by the LORD, a craftman's handiwork, and sets it up in secret.—And all the people shall respond, Amen.

16] Cursed be he who insults his father or mother.—And all the people shall say, Amen.

17] Cursed be he who moves his neighbor's landmark.—And all the people shall say, Amen.

12] *The following shall stand.* Not only is the construction of verses 12 and 13 uncertain, but also the role of the participants in the proceedings. It appears that the representatives of the tribes (not the tribes themselves) stood in their assigned places and that the Levites were represented along with all the others while the blessings were spoken (verse 12). Other Levites, possibly the priestly members, spoke the blessings and the curses, but only the latter function is specifically relegated to them (verse 14) [6].

On Mount Gerizim. For the blessing, only tribes who derived their ancestry from the children of Leah and Rachel are assigned. The mountain became the Samaritans' chief place of worship, surpassing Mount Zion in sanctity.

13] *On Mount Ebal.* For the curses, the four putative descendants of Jacob's handmaidens, Bilhah and Zilpah, are selected, plus Reuben (who lost his birthright, Gen. 49:4), and Zebulun, possibly because as Leah's youngest he was chosen to equalize the two sides of six tribes each.

15–26] The twelve curses enumerated here have no equivalent blessings, but because blessings *were* spoken (verse 12) it may be that they were the reverse of the curses. Thus, the first blessing might have been: "Blessed be the man who does not make objects to be used for idolatry" [7].

It is likely that these reprehensible actions were chosen because they would generally be committed in secret and remain unpunished by human courts [8]. The people assumed collective responsibility for such acts, of which the first and last concern a person's relationship with God (that is, with His incorporeality and His Torah) and the others with the purity of the family and with moral behavior in various respects. It is noteworthy that four of the twelve address sexual matters. Possibly these curses were at one time part of a liturgical function and were later inserted into Deuteronomy [9].

15] *Amen.* Repeated after every curse, it is a declamation of spiritual assent.

The Hebrew is of the same root as *emunah* ("faith"); compare the (archaic) English expression "In faith!" (See also at Num. 5:22.)

16] *Insults.* מַקְלֶה (*makleh*), literally, "makes light of," the direct opposite of *kibed* ("honors"), literally, "gives weight to." In Exod. 21:17 and Lev. 20:9 the term is *mekalel*, "curses" or "reviles" one's parents; thus, the Deuteronomic prohibition goes much farther.

17] *Landmark.* See at Deut. 19:14.

יט מַשְׁגֶּה עִוֵּר בַּדָּרֶךְ וְאָמַר כָּל־הָעָם אָמֵן: ס   כג   אָמֵן: ס   אָרוּר שֹׁכֵב עִם־חֹתַנְתּוֹ וְאָמַר כָּל־הָעָם
מַטֶּה מִשְׁפַּט גֵּר־יָתוֹם וְאַלְמָנָה וְאָמַר כָּל־הָעָם   כד   אָמֵן: ס   אָרוּר מַכֵּה רֵעֵהוּ בַּסָּתֶר וְאָמַר כָּל־
כ אָרוּר שֹׁכֵב עִם־אֵשֶׁת אָבִיו כִּי גִלָּה כְּנַף   כה   הָעָם אָמֵן: ס   אָרוּר לֹקֵחַ שֹׁחַד לְהַכּוֹת נֶפֶשׁ
כא אָבִיו וְאָמַר כָּל־הָעָם אָמֵן: ס   אָרוּר שֹׁכֵב עִם־   כו   דָּם נָקִי וְאָמַר כָּל־הָעָם אָמֵן: ס   אָרוּר אֲשֶׁר
כב כָּל־בְּהֵמָה וְאָמַר כָּל־הָעָם אָמֵן: ס   אָרוּר שֹׁכֵב   לֹא־יָקִים אֶת־דִּבְרֵי הַתּוֹרָה־הַזֹּאת לַעֲשׂוֹת אוֹתָם
עִם־אֲחֹתוֹ בַּת־אָבִיו אוֹ בַת־אִמּוֹ וְאָמַר כָּל־הָעָם   וְאָמַר כָּל־הָעָם אָמֵן: פ

18] Cursed be he who misdirects a blind person on his way.—And all the people shall say, Amen.

19] Cursed be he who subverts the rights of the stranger, the fatherless, and the widow.—And all the people shall say, Amen.

20] Cursed be he who lies with his father's wife, for he has removed his father's garment.—And all the people shall say, Amen.

21] Cursed be he who lies with any beast.—And all the people shall say, Amen.

22] Cursed be he who lies with his sister, whether daughter of his father or of his mother.—And all the people shall say, Amen.

23] Cursed be he who lies with his mother-in-law.—And all the people shall say, Amen.

24] Cursed be he who strikes down his neighbor in secret.—And all the people shall say, Amen.

25] Cursed be he who accepts a bribe in the case of the murder of an innocent person.—And all the people shall say, Amen.

26] Cursed be he who will not uphold the terms of this Teaching and observe them.—And all the people shall say, Amen.

18] *Who misdirects a blind person.* Cf. Lev. 19:14, "who places a stumbling block before the blind."

19] *Rights of the stranger.* So Deut. 24:17 and elsewhere in the Torah.

20] *Lies with his father's wife.* That is, his stepmother.

Removed his father's garment. See at Deut. 23:1.

21] *Lies with any beast.* Commits sodomy; see Exod. 22:18.

22] *Lies with his sister.* That is, his half sister; see Lev. 18:9; 20:17. In earlier days, down to David's time, such a relationship was permitted; see II Sam. 13:13; Gen. 20:12 (Abraham and Sarah were children of the same father but not of the same mother).

24] *Strikes down.* Kills; equivalent to the sixth commandment (Deut. 5:17).

Tradition applied this to killing someone's reputation [10].

In secret. He may escape human law, but he will not escape God's.

25] *Accepts a bribe.* In order to let the murderer go free; or to let an innocent person be slain instead. The text is ambiguous; it is also unclear whether the injunction is directed to a judge or a witness.

26] *This Teaching.* The Book of Deuteronomy. Prevailing tradition took it to mean the whole Torah [11].

Blessings and Curses[1]

Blessings and curses were closely bound to a belief in the power of speech, and both were frequently amplified by precisely circumscribed acts. Where such formulae and actions were deemed to have an independent and inevitable efficacy, which would force extra-human agencies to conform to the will of the invoker, the participants were operating in the realm of magic. Where, on the other hand, such acts were essentially submissions to the Divine, who was called upon to ratify them, blessings and curses acquired religious legitimacy. They were and are, then, forms of prayer, and thus the biblical prescriptions regarding them are to be understood. Nonetheless, the dividing line between magic and religion cannot always be clearly drawn; for instance, when Isaac said to Esau that he had already given his primary blessing away (Gen. 27:37), he spoke from a context which ascribed to his words a non-cancellable quality. The blessings and curses on Mount Gerizim and Mount Ebal had a clearly didactic purpose: they aimed at guiding the hearers to live in accordance with God's law. When God himself blessed or cursed, He could invoke himself ("By Myself I swear"; Gen. 22:16), but usually His words were tantamount to actions, for a realization of the divine will was inherent in the divine word.

Blessings and curses were usually delineated in detail; they must be executed precisely to evoke in speaker and hearer the kind of awe which would put them in touch with the supernatural Presence. They featured key words as well as special motions—such as laying on and lifting of hands, or destroying a document on which the curse was written.

While the Bible knows only one expression for blessing (*barech*, *berachah*), a number of words are used for cursing. The chief terms are *arur* (as in the chapter before us; it appears to have an operational, liturgical aspect: "cursed be he who . . ."); *alah* (which may be said to be the formulation of the curse); and *kilel* (a broad term, describing attitudes and actions; the noun *kelalah* is the usual opposite of *berachah*) [12].

Curses were included in Hittite vassal treaties; and all oaths that people swore (and swear) may be seen to contain an element of self-cursing. Thus Ruth swore that she would stay with Naomi and added that God should punish her if she broke her oath (Ruth 1:17). The legal sphere maintains to this day the connection between oath and self-curse, for the person who swears falsely thereby assumes voluntarily the consequences of the law. God too swears, although in His case the aspect of self-cursing assumes a different quality. When He invokes himself He implies: I would not be God if what I say will not come to pass.

A noteworthy aspect of the litany prescribed for the two mountains is its overt and implied emphasis on acts committed in secret. "There is a superb element in Israel's commitment, in a solemn moment, to the righteous will of God above all spheres of life, especially to a will which is operative precisely when man believes himself to be alone with himself. Israel makes itself the executor of this divine will by carrying it into the secret pathways of life" [13].

---

[1] This subject is also dealt with in our commentaries on Genesis, chapter 48, Numbers 6:22–27, and Leviticus, chapter 26.

GLEANINGS

A New Covenant

Three covenants did God conclude with Israel: one after the Exodus, one at Sinai, and one at this time, for the Sinaitic covenant had been abrogated by the sin of the golden calf. Therefore Moses says (verse 9): "Today you have become the people of the Lord your God."

HIZKUNI [14]

Monuments

The nations erect monuments to memorialize their conquests, victories, and heroes. Israel is to inscribe on stone the words of Torah.

ABARBANEL [15]

Stones

Expose a human "stone"[2] to God's teaching and it will be shattered.   TALMUD [16]

The power of Torah is so great that even stones are moved by it.   CHASIDIC [17]

Why the Nations Lost the Promised Land

The Torah was inscribed on the stones in seventy languages, but the nations chose to disregard it. Had they accepted it they would have been accepted into the covenant and would not have lost the Land.   TALMUD [18]

Even if they had accepted only the seven Noahide laws they would not have been driven out.

S. R. HIRSCH [19]

Secret and Public

All curses refer to secret transgressions. For public offenders there is hope of repentance; for hypocrites there is none.   CHASIDIC [20]

Misdirecting the Blind

Those too are cursed who give poor advice to the ignorant or who cause others to sin.

D. HOFFMANN [21]

The Meaning of the Curses

All blessing is denied to him who outwardly plays the pious man devoted to God but in secret denies the exclusive existence of One God and His Rule; who outwardly is respectful to his parents but inwardly considers himself vastly superior to them; who in the eyes of men preserves the reputation of an honest man but, where it is unobserved, does not hesitate to injure the rights of his neighbor to his own advantage; who is full of enthusiasm for the welfare of his neighbors, in the presence of clever and intelligent people, but pushes short-sighted and blind people into misfortune; who grovels before the powerful but denies the weak and helpless their rights; pretends to be a highly respectable member of society, to wallow in sexual licentiousness in intimate privacy (verses 20–23); who does not dig a dagger into his neighbor but, under the cloak of conversation, murders his happiness, his peace, and his honor; who enjoys the highest confidence in his community but misuses it in secret corruption; finally, also one who, even if he lives correctly and dutifully for himself, still looks with indifference on the abandonment of the duties of the Torah in his immediate and wider circles.

S. R. HIRSCH [22]

---

[2] That is, a person who has a heart of stone.

Blessings and Curses, II

The chapter before us contains an awesome array of curses that dwarf the catalogue of blessings preceding them. However, this imbalance should not be surprising, for in the Torah specific negative commandments far outnumber specific positive ones,[1] for in general it is more usual to create codes of forbidden than of desirable behavior. What sets chapter 28 aside are its detail and the expanse of its imaginative projection: whatever blessing or curse would be real to the biblical age here finds its place. The Torah promises and it threatens, and here as elsewhere it is unabashedly realistic: it assumes that, while pure love of God and His commandments is the highest rung, such height of total devotion for its own sake can be scaled only by the fewest; the majority will need earthly rewards and punishments held up before their eyes.[2]

Attempts have been made by some scholars to distinguish three catalogues of curses, starting in verses 15, 45, and 58. Others would find a "core" of blessings and curses which were greatly expanded later on. Thus, von Rad has reconstructed what he believes to be an original body of curses, with a clearly agricultural basis [2]. In any case, the whole chapter bears a striking resemblance to the vassal treaties of the Assyrian King Esar-

[1] Ibn Ezra (on Lev. 26:13) makes the point that "blessings are uttered in broad general terms, while curses are stated in greater detail, to awe and frighten the hearers."

[2] Maimonides sought to meliorate this idea of automatic rewards and punishments—especially as far as rainfall and drought were concerned—by terming it a necessary device in the education of a people emerging from idolatry; see also above, at chapter 11 [1].

haddon (see Commentary on Leviticus, chapter 26, and Gleanings below). The Assyrian and Hebrew texts are broadly contemporary, and there is general scholarly agreement that the former influenced the latter. In the Assyrian model, of course, there is a triangle of suzerain, vassal, and deity, while in the covenant between God and Israel only the Sovereign and His vassal are partners. The former lays down conditions and states what He will do if the latter complies or fails to comply. The catalogue of chapter 28 therefore must be seen as part of the Torah's everpresent view of Israel as a covenanted community [3].

אֶת־אֹיְבֶיךָ הַקָּמִים עָלֶיךָ נִגָּפִים לְפָנֶיךָ בְּדֶרֶךְ אֶחָד
יֵצְאוּ אֵלֶיךָ וּבְשִׁבְעָה דְרָכִים יָנוּסוּ לְפָנֶיךָ: יְצַו
יְהוָה אִתְּךָ אֶת־הַבְּרָכָה בַּאֲסָמֶיךָ וּבְכֹל מִשְׁלַח יָדֶךָ
וּבֵרַכְךָ בָּאָרֶץ אֲשֶׁר־יְהוָה אֱלֹהֶיךָ נֹתֵן לָךְ: יְקִימְךָ
יְהוָה לוֹ לְעַם קָדוֹשׁ כַּאֲשֶׁר נִשְׁבַּע־לָךְ כִּי תִשְׁמֹר
אֶת־מִצְוֹת יְהוָה אֱלֹהֶיךָ וְהָלַכְתָּ בִּדְרָכָיו: וְרָאוּ כָּל־
עַמֵּי הָאָרֶץ כִּי שֵׁם יְהוָה נִקְרָא עָלֶיךָ וְיָרְאוּ מִמֶּךָּ:
וְהוֹתִרְךָ יְהוָה לְטוֹבָה בִּפְרִי בִטְנְךָ וּבִפְרִי בְהֶמְתְּךָ

א וְהָיָה אִם־שָׁמוֹעַ תִּשְׁמַע בְּקוֹל יְהוָה אֱלֹהֶיךָ לִשְׁמֹר
לַעֲשׂוֹת אֶת־כָּל־מִצְוֹתָיו אֲשֶׁר אָנֹכִי מְצַוְּךָ הַיּוֹם וּנְתָנְךָ
ב יְהוָה אֱלֹהֶיךָ עֶלְיוֹן עַל כָּל־גּוֹיֵי הָאָרֶץ: וּבָאוּ עָלֶיךָ
כָל־הַבְּרָכוֹת הָאֵלֶּה וְהִשִּׂיגֻךָ כִּי תִשְׁמַע בְּקוֹל יְהוָה
ג אֱלֹהֶיךָ: בָּרוּךְ אַתָּה בָּעִיר וּבָרוּךְ אַתָּה בַּשָּׂדֶה:
ד בָּרוּךְ פְּרִי־בִטְנְךָ וּפְרִי אַדְמָתְךָ וּפְרִי בְהֶמְתֶּךָ שְׁגַר
ה אֲלָפֶיךָ וְעַשְׁתְּרוֹת צֹאנֶךָ: בָּרוּךְ טַנְאֲךָ וּמִשְׁאַרְתֶּךָ:
ו בָּרוּךְ אַתָּה בְּבֹאֶךָ וּבָרוּךְ אַתָּה בְּצֵאתֶךָ: יִתֵּן יְהוָה
ז

1] Now, if you obey the LORD your God, to observe faithfully all His commandments which I enjoin upon you this day, the LORD your God will set you high above all the nations of the earth. 2] All these blessings shall come upon you and take effect, if you will but heed the word of the LORD your God:

3] Blessed shall you be in the city and blessed shall you be in the country.

4] Blessed shall be the issue of your womb, the produce of your soil, and the offspring of your cattle, the calving of your herd and the lambing of your flock.

5] Blessed shall be your basket and your kneading bowl.

6] Blessed shall you be in your comings and blessed shall you be in your goings.

7] The LORD will put to rout before you the enemies who attack you; they will march out against you by a single road, but flee from you by many roads. 8] The LORD will ordain blessings for you upon your barns and upon all your undertakings: He will bless you in the land which the LORD your God is giving you. 9] The LORD will establish you as His holy people, as He swore to you, if you keep the commandments of the LORD your God and walk in His ways. 10] And all the peoples of the earth shall see that the LORD's name is proclaimed over you, and they shall stand in fear of you. 11] The LORD will give you abounding prosperity in the issue of your womb, the offspring of your cattle, and the produce of your soil in the land

28:2] *Blessings shall . . . take effect.* Literally, "shall overtake you." They are pictured as having an independent existence. Compare Ps. 23:6, "goodness and mercy shall pursue me."

3] *Blessed.* Six general blessings—counting verse 4 to contain three different blessings—are enumerated, corresponding to the six tribes that bless. (Similarly, six general curses, verses 16-19, may be seen to precede the rest.)

5] *Your basket.* For gathering the produce.

Your kneading bowl. Which utilizes the blessings that were gathered in the basket.

7] *Many roads.* Literally, "seven," often used in a broad sense; compare the English use of "dozen" or "hundred."

9] *Holy people.* עַם קָדוֹשׁ (*am kadosh*). In Exod. 19:6 Israel is called גּוֹי קָדוֹשׁ (*goy kadosh*) but, while homilies have been woven around this difference, the expressions appear to have conveyed the same meaning.

10] *Is proclaimed over you.* That is, Israel belongs to God, and God lends His name to Israel; compare Isa. 4:1, "Only let us be called by Your name."

הַיּוֹם וּבָאוּ עָלֶיךָ כָּל־הַקְּלָלוֹת הָאֵלֶּה וְהִשִּׂיגוּךָ:   וּבִפְרִי אַדְמָתֶךָ עַל הָאֲדָמָה אֲשֶׁר נִשְׁבַּע יְהֹוָה

טז אָרוּר אַתָּה בָּעִיר וְאָרוּר אַתָּה בַּשָּׂדֶה: אָרוּר טַנְאֲךָ   יב לַאֲבֹתֶיךָ לָתֶת לָךְ: יִפְתַּח יְהֹוָה לְךָ אֶת־אוֹצָרוֹ

יז וּמִשְׁאַרְתֶּךָ: אָרוּר פְּרִי־בִטְנְךָ וּפְרִי אַדְמָתְךָ שְׁגַר   הַטּוֹב אֶת־הַשָּׁמַיִם לָתֵת מְטַר־אַרְצְךָ בְּעִתּוֹ וּלְבָרֵךְ

יח אֲלָפֶיךָ וְעַשְׁתְּרֹת צֹאנֶךָ: אָרוּר אַתָּה בְּבֹאֶךָ וְאָרוּר   אֵת כָּל־מַעֲשֵׂה יָדֶךָ וְהִלְוִיתָ גּוֹיִם רַבִּים וְאַתָּה לֹא

יט אַתָּה בְּצֵאתֶךָ: יְשַׁלַּח יְהֹוָה בְּךָ אֶת־הַמְּאֵרָה אֶת־   יג תִלְוֶה: וּנְתָנְךָ יְהֹוָה לְרֹאשׁ וְלֹא לְזָנָב וְהָיִיתָ רַק

כ הַמְּהוּמָה וְאֶת־הַמִּגְעֶרֶת בְּכָל־מִשְׁלַח יָדְךָ אֲשֶׁר   לְמַעְלָה וְלֹא תִהְיֶה לְמָטָּה כִּי־תִשְׁמַע אֶל־מִצְוֹת

תַּעֲשֶׂה עַד הִשָּׁמֶדְךָ וְעַד־אֲבָדְךָ מַהֵר מִפְּנֵי רֹעַ   יְהֹוָה אֱלֹהֶיךָ אֲשֶׁר אָנֹכִי מְצַוְּךָ הַיּוֹם לִשְׁמֹר וְלַעֲשׂוֹת:

מַעֲלָלֶיךָ אֲשֶׁר עֲזַבְתָּנִי: יַדְבֵּק יְהֹוָה בְּךָ אֶת־הַדָּבֶר   יד וְלֹא תָסוּר מִכָּל־הַדְּבָרִים אֲשֶׁר אָנֹכִי מְצַוֶּה אֶתְכֶם

כא עַד כַּלֹּתוֹ אֹתְךָ מֵעַל הָאֲדָמָה אֲשֶׁר־אַתָּה בָא־   הַיּוֹם יָמִין וּשְׂמֹאול לָלֶכֶת אַחֲרֵי אֱלֹהִים אֲחֵרִים

כב שָׁמָּה לְרִשְׁתָּהּ: יַכְּכָה יְהֹוָה בַּשַּׁחֶפֶת וּבַקַּדַּחַת   לְעָבְדָם:
פ

וּבַדַּלֶּקֶת וּבַחַרְחֻר וּבַחֶרֶב וּבַשִּׁדָּפוֹן וּבַיֵּרָקוֹן   טו וְהָיָה אִם־לֹא תִשְׁמַע בְּקוֹל יְהֹוָה אֱלֹהֶיךָ לִשְׁמֹר

כג וּרְדָפוּךָ עַד אָבְדֶךָ: וְהָיוּ שָׁמֶיךָ אֲשֶׁר עַל־רֹאשְׁךָ   לַעֲשׂוֹת אֶת־כָּל־מִצְוֹתָיו וְחֻקֹּתָיו אֲשֶׁר אָנֹכִי מְצַוְּךָ

---

that the LORD swore to your fathers to give you. **12]** The LORD will open for you His bounteous store, the heavens, to provide rain for your land in season and to bless all your undertakings. You will be creditor to many nations, but debtor to none.

13] The LORD will make you the head, not the tail; you will always be at the top and never at the bottom—if only you obey and faithfully observe the commandments of the LORD your God which I enjoin upon you this day, **14]** and do not deviate to the right or to the left from any of the commandments that I enjoin upon you this day and turn to the worship of other gods.

15] But if you do not obey the LORD your God to observe faithfully all His commandments and laws which I enjoin upon you this day, all these curses shall come upon you and take effect:

16] Cursed shall you be in the city and cursed shall you be in the country.

17] Cursed shall be your basket and your kneading bowl.

18] Cursed shall be the issue of your womb and the produce of your soil, the calving of your herd and the lambing of your flock.

19] Cursed shall you be in your comings and cursed shall you be in your goings.

20] The LORD will let loose against you calamity, panic, and frustration in all the enterprises you undertake, so that you shall soon be utterly wiped out because of your evildoing in forsaking Me. **21]** The LORD will make pestilence cling to you, until He has put an end to you in the land which you are invading to occupy. **22]** The LORD will strike you with consumption, fever, and inflammation, with scorching heat and drought, with blight and mildew; they shall hound you until you perish. **23]** The skies above your head shall be copper

---

12] *Creditor.* See at 15:6.

17] *Your basket.* Verses 17 and 18 correspond to verses 5 and 4, respectively.

20] *The Lord will let loose.* The Rabbis counted 98 specific curses, twice the number enumerated in Leviticus 26 [4].

22] *Consumption.* The meaning of this and the following afflictions is not always certain.

Drought. חֶרֶב (*cherev*) usually means sword; originally the text was probably read חֹרֶב (*chorev*), which means drought, as, e.g., in Judg. 6:37.

כד נְחֹשֶׁת וְהָאָרֶץ אֲשֶׁר־תַּחְתֶּיךָ בַּרְזֶל: יִתֵּן יְהוָה אֶת־
מְטַר אַרְצְךָ אָבָק וְעָפָר מִן־הַשָּׁמַיִם יֵרֵד עָלֶיךָ
כה עַד הִשָּׁמְדָךְ: יִתֶּנְךָ יְהוָה נִגָּף לִפְנֵי אֹיְבֶיךָ בְּדֶרֶךְ
אֶחָד תֵּצֵא אֵלָיו וּבְשִׁבְעָה דְרָכִים תָּנוּס לְפָנָיו
כו וְהָיִיתָ לְזַעֲוָה לְכֹל מַמְלְכוֹת הָאָרֶץ: וְהָיְתָה נִבְלָתְךָ
לְמַאֲכָל לְכָל־עוֹף הַשָּׁמַיִם וּלְבֶהֱמַת הָאָרֶץ וְאֵין
כז מַחֲרִיד: יַכְּכָה יְהוָה בִּשְׁחִין מִצְרַיִם וּבַעְפֹלִים וּבַגָּרָב
כח וּבֶחָרֶס אֲשֶׁר לֹא־תוּכַל לְהֵרָפֵא: יַכְּכָה יְהוָה בְּשִׁגָּעוֹן
כט וּבְעִוָּרוֹן וּבְתִמְהוֹן לֵבָב: וְהָיִיתָ מְמַשֵּׁשׁ בַּצָּהֳרַיִם

* כז וּבַטְּחוֹרִים קרי.

כַּאֲשֶׁר יְמַשֵּׁשׁ הָעִוֵּר בָּאֲפֵלָה וְלֹא תַצְלִיחַ אֶת־
דְּרָכֶיךָ וְהָיִיתָ אַךְ עָשׁוּק וְגָזוּל כָּל־הַיָּמִים וְאֵין
ל מוֹשִׁיעַ: אִשָּׁה תְאָרֵשׂ וְאִישׁ אַחֵר יִשְׁגָּלֶנָּה בַּיִת תִּבְנֶה
לא וְלֹא־תֵשֵׁב בּוֹ כֶּרֶם תִּטַּע וְלֹא תְחַלְּלֶנּוּ: שׁוֹרְךָ טָבוּחַ
לְעֵינֶיךָ וְלֹא תֹאכַל מִמֶּנּוּ חֲמֹרְךָ גָּזוּל מִלְּפָנֶיךָ
וְלֹא יָשׁוּב לָךְ צֹאנְךָ נְתֻנוֹת לְאֹיְבֶיךָ וְאֵין לְךָ מוֹשִׁיעַ:
לב בָּנֶיךָ וּבְנֹתֶיךָ נְתֻנִים לְעַם אַחֵר וְעֵינֶיךָ רֹאוֹת וְכָלוֹת
לג אֲלֵיהֶם כָּל־הַיּוֹם וְאֵין לְאֵל יָדֶךָ: פְּרִי אַדְמָתְךָ
וְכָל־יְגִיעֲךָ יֹאכַל עַם אֲשֶׁר לֹא־יָדָעְתָּ וְהָיִיתָ רַק

* ל יִשְׁכָּבֶנָּה קרי.

and the earth under you iron.   **24]** The LORD will make the rain of your land dust, and sand shall drop on you from the sky, until you are wiped out.

25] The LORD will put you to rout before your enemies; you shall march out against them by a single road, but flee from them by many roads; and you shall become a horror to all the kingdoms of the earth.   **26]** Your carcasses shall become food for all the birds of the sky and all the beasts of the earth, with none to frighten them off.

27] The LORD will strike you with the Egyptian inflammation, with hemorrhoids, boil-scars, and itch, from which you shall never recover.

28] The LORD will strike you with madness, blindness, and dismay.   **29]** You shall grope at noon as a blind man gropes in the dark; you shall not prosper in your ventures, but shall be constantly abused and robbed, with none to give help.

30] If you pay the bride-price for a wife, another man shall enjoy her. If you build a house, you shall not live in it. If you plant a vineyard, you shall not harvest it.   **31]** Your ox shall be slaughtered before your eyes, but you shall not eat of it; your ass shall be seized in front of you, and it shall not be returned to you; your flock shall be delivered to your enemies, with none to help you.   **32]** Your sons and daughters shall be delivered to another people, while you look on; and your eyes shall strain for them constantly, but you shall be helpless.   **33]** A people you do not know shall eat up the produce of your soil and all your gains; you shall be abused and

27] *Egyptian inflammation.* Likely a reference to a group of diseases considered prominent in Egypt: elephantiasis, dysentery, ophthalmia; see Deut. 7:15. Others believe the expression to refer to the plagues, see Exod. 15:26; especially the disease of boils, Exod. 9:9–10.

Hemmorrhoids. The Hebrew text says עֳפָלִים, but tradition, considering this too indelicate a word for communal reading, substituted טְחֹרִים. Today both words serve to describe the affliction with which the Philistines were reported to have been struck by divine fiat (I Sam. 5:6 ff.).

28] *Dismay.* Better, "confusion," the third of the afflictions of the mind: one cannot think, see straight, or understand.

30] *Enjoy her.* Another euphemism substituted for the written text which says "violate her"; compare verse 27. The three deprivations listed here refer to pleasures so basic that a man was excused from army service in order to enjoy them; Deut. 20:5 ff.

32] *Helpless.* Or, "powerless." The word אֵל (*el*) means usually a (or the) divinity, but sometimes it also means "power," as in Gen. 31:29.

33] *A people you do not know.* More idiomatically: "... you have not even heard of."

מא גְּבוּלְךָ וְשֶׁמֶן לֹא תָסוּךְ כִּי יִשַּׁל זֵיתֶךָ: בָּנִים וּבָנוֹת
מב תּוֹלִיד וְלֹא־יִהְיוּ לָךְ כִּי יֵלְכוּ בַּשֶּׁבִי: כָּל־עֵצְךָ
מג וּפְרִי אַדְמָתֶךָ יְיָרֵשׁ הַצְּלָצַל: הַגֵּר אֲשֶׁר בְּקִרְבְּךָ
יַעֲלֶה עָלֶיךָ מַעְלָה מָּעְלָה וְאַתָּה תֵרֵד מַטָּה מָּטָּה:
מד הוּא יַלְוְךָ וְאַתָּה לֹא תַלְוֶנּוּ הוּא יִהְיֶה לְרֹאשׁ
מה וְאַתָּה תִּהְיֶה לְזָנָב: וּבָאוּ עָלֶיךָ כָּל־הַקְּלָלוֹת הָאֵלֶּה
וּרְדָפוּךָ וְהִשִּׂיגוּךָ עַד הִשָּׁמְדָךְ כִּי־לֹא שָׁמַעְתָּ בְּקוֹל
יְהוָה אֱלֹהֶיךָ לִשְׁמֹר מִצְוֺתָיו וְחֻקֹּתָיו אֲשֶׁר צִוָּךְ:
מו וְהָיוּ בְךָ לְאוֹת וּלְמוֹפֵת וּבְזַרְעֲךָ עַד־עוֹלָם: תַּחַת
אֲשֶׁר לֹא־עָבַדְתָּ אֶת־יְהוָה אֱלֹהֶיךָ בְּשִׂמְחָה וּבְטוּב

לד עָשׁוּק וְרָצוּץ כָּל־הַיָּמִים: וְהָיִיתָ מְשֻׁגָּע מִמַּרְאֵה עֵינֶיךָ
לה אֲשֶׁר תִּרְאֶה: יַכְּכָה יְהוָה בִּשְׁחִין רָע עַל־הַבִּרְכַּיִם
וְעַל־הַשֹּׁקַיִם אֲשֶׁר לֹא־תוּכַל לְהֵרָפֵא מִכַּף רַגְלְךָ
לו וְעַד קָדְקֳדֶךָ: יוֹלֵךְ יְהוָה אֹתְךָ וְאֶת־מַלְכְּךָ אֲשֶׁר
תָּקִים עָלֶיךָ אֶל־גּוֹי אֲשֶׁר לֹא־יָדַעְתָּ אַתָּה וַאֲבֹתֶיךָ
לז וְעָבַדְתָּ שָּׁם אֱלֹהִים אֲחֵרִים עֵץ וָאָבֶן: וְהָיִיתָ לְשַׁמָּה
לְמָשָׁל וְלִשְׁנִינָה בְּכֹל הָעַמִּים אֲשֶׁר־יְנַהֶגְךָ יְהוָה שָׁמָּה:
לח זֶרַע רַב תּוֹצִיא הַשָּׂדֶה וּמְעַט תֶּאֱסֹף כִּי יַחְסְלֶנּוּ
לט הָאַרְבֶּה: כְּרָמִים תִּטַּע וְעָבָדְתָּ וְיַיִן לֹא־תִשְׁתֶּה וְלֹא
מ תֶאֱגֹר כִּי תֹאכְלֶנּוּ הַתֹּלָעַת: זֵיתִים יִהְיוּ לְךָ בְּכָל־

downtrodden continually,   **34]** until you are driven mad by what your eyes behold.   **35]** The LORD will afflict you at the knees and thighs with a severe inflammation, from which you shall never recover—from the sole of your foot to the crown of your head.

36] The LORD will drive you, and the king you have set over you, to a nation unknown to you or your fathers, where you shall serve other gods, of wood and stone.   **37]** You shall be a consternation, a proverb, and a byword among all the peoples to which the LORD will drive you.

38] Though you take much seed out to the field, you shall gather in little, for the locust shall consume it.   **39]** Though you plant vineyards and till them, you shall have no wine to drink or store, for the worm shall devour them.   **40]** Though you have olive trees throughout your territory, you shall have no oil for anointment, for your olives shall drop off.   **41]** Though you beget sons and daughters, they shall not remain with you, for they shall go into captivity.   **42]** The cricket shall take over all the trees and produce of your land.

43] The stranger in your midst shall rise above you higher and higher, while you sink lower and lower: **44]** he shall be your creditor, but you shall not be his; he shall be the head and you the tail.

45] All these curses shall befall you; they shall pursue you and overtake you, until you are wiped out, because you did not heed the LORD your God and keep the commandments and laws that He enjoined upon you.   **46]** They shall serve as signs and proofs against you and your offspring for all time.   **47]** Because you would not serve the LORD your God in joy and

---

35] *From the sole of your foot.* Compare Job 2:7. The English idiom reverses the order: "from head to toe."

36] *Will drive you.* After the defeat of the northern kingdom in 721 B.C.E. and the ensuing exile, everyone knew the terror of this threat.

42] *Cricket.* צְלָצַל (*tzelatzal*), an onomatopoetic word that evokes a whirring sound.

43] *The stranger in your midst.* A temporary resi-

dent who would usually be there to conduct commercial affairs. He was not subject to Jewish law (though he enjoyed its protection) and hence would be exempt from the punishment allotted to the community.

45] *All these curses.* This appears to be the beginning of an originally separate catalogue of maledictions.

46] *For all time.* Not in the literal sense, for repentance was always possible; Deut. 30:1 ff.

מח לְבַב מֶרֶב כֹּל: וְעָבַדְתָּ אֶת־אֹיְבֶיךָ אֲשֶׁר יְשַׁלְּחֶנּוּ
יְהוָה בָּךְ בְּרָעָב וּבְצָמָא וּבְעֵירֹם וּבְחֹסֶר כֹּל וְנָתַן
מט עֹל בַּרְזֶל עַל־צַוָּארֶךָ עַד הִשְׁמִידוֹ אֹתָךְ: יִשָּׂא יְהוָה
עָלֶיךָ גּוֹי מֵרָחֹק מִקְצֵה הָאָרֶץ כַּאֲשֶׁר יִדְאֶה הַנָּשֶׁר
נ גּוֹי אֲשֶׁר לֹא־תִשְׁמַע לְשֹׁנוֹ: גּוֹי עַז פָּנִים אֲשֶׁר לֹא־
נא יִשָּׂא פָנִים לְזָקֵן וְנַעַר לֹא יָחֹן: וְאָכַל פְּרִי בְהֶמְתְּךָ
וּפְרִי־אַדְמָתְךָ עַד הִשָּׁמְדָךְ אֲשֶׁר לֹא־יַשְׁאִיר לְךָ
דָּגָן תִּירוֹשׁ וְיִצְהָר שְׁגַר אֲלָפֶיךָ וְעַשְׁתְּרֹת צֹאנֶךָ
נב עַד הַאֲבִידוֹ אֹתָךְ: וְהֵצַר לְךָ בְּכָל־שְׁעָרֶיךָ עַד
רֶדֶת חֹמֹתֶיךָ הַגְּבֹהֹת וְהַבְּצֻרוֹת אֲשֶׁר אַתָּה בֹּטֵחַ

בָּהֵן בְּכָל־אַרְצֶךָ וְהֵצַר לְךָ בְּכָל־שְׁעָרֶיךָ בְּכָל־
נג אַרְצְךָ אֲשֶׁר נָתַן יְהוָה אֱלֹהֶיךָ לָךְ: וְאָכַלְתָּ פְרִי־
בִטְנְךָ בְּשַׂר בָּנֶיךָ וּבְנֹתֶיךָ אֲשֶׁר נָתַן־לְךָ יְהוָה אֱלֹהֶיךָ
נד בְּמָצוֹר וּבְמָצוֹק אֲשֶׁר־יָצִיק לְךָ אֹיְבֶךָ: הָאִישׁ הָרַךְ
בְּךָ וְהֶעָנֹג מְאֹד תֵּרַע עֵינוֹ בְאָחִיו וּבְאֵשֶׁת חֵיקוֹ
נה וּבְיֶתֶר בָּנָיו אֲשֶׁר יוֹתִיר: מִתֵּת לְאַחַד מֵהֶם מִבְּשַׂר
בָּנָיו אֲשֶׁר יֹאכֵל מִבְּלִי הִשְׁאִיר־לוֹ כֹּל בְּמָצוֹר
נו וּבְמָצוֹק אֲשֶׁר יָצִיק לְךָ אֹיִבְךָ בְּכָל־שְׁעָרֶיךָ: הָרַכָּה
בְּךָ וְהָעֲנֻגָּה אֲשֶׁר לֹא־נִסְּתָה כַף־רַגְלָהּ הַצֵּג עַל־
הָאָרֶץ מֵהִתְעַנֵּג וּמֵרֹךְ תֵּרַע עֵינָהּ בְּאִישׁ חֵיקָהּ

gladness over the abundance of everything,   **48]** you shall have to serve—in hunger and thirst, naked and lacking everything—the enemies whom the LORD will let loose against you. He will put an iron yoke upon your neck until He has wiped you out.

  49] The LORD will bring a nation against you from afar, from the end of the earth, which will swoop down like the eagle—a nation whose language you do not understand,   **50]** a ruthless nation, that will show the old no regard and the young no mercy.   **51]** It shall devour the offspring of your cattle and the produce of your soil, until you have been wiped out, leaving you nothing of new grain, wine, or oil, of the calving of your herds and the lambing of your flocks, until it has brought you to ruin.   **52]** It shall shut you up in all your towns throughout your land until every mighty, towering wall in which you trust has come down. And when you are shut up in all your towns throughout your land that the LORD your God has given you,   **53]** you shall eat your own issue, the flesh of your sons and daughters that the LORD your God has given you, because of the desperate straits to which your enemy shall reduce you.   **54]** He who is most tender and fastidious among you shall be too mean to his brother and the wife of his bosom and the children he has spared   **55]** to share with any of them the flesh of the children that he eats, because he has nothing else left as a result of the desperate straits to which your enemy shall reduce you in all your towns.   **56]** And she who is most tender and dainty among you, so tender and dainty that she would never venture to set a foot on the ground, shall begrudge the husband of her bosom, and her son and her daughter,   **57]** the

49–50] This catalogue has the earmarks of exilic experience, especially the vivid description of the conqueror in verse 50. The lack of compassion for the aged is ascribed to the Babylonians by Isa. 47:6 and Lam. 4:16; 5:12.

53] *You shall eat.* That this actually happened is attested by Lam. 2:20 and 4:10 (see also commentary on Lev. 26:29 and Jer. 19:9). An Assyrian inscription from Uruk says: "We consumed the flesh of our sons and daughters" [5]. See further at verse 57.

56] *Tender and dainty.* She did not walk but was carried. The image is applied by Isa. 47:1 to Babylon: "O Fair Chaldea; / Nevermore shall they call you / The tender and dainty one."

וּבְבָנֶה וּבְבִתֶּה: וּבְשִׁלְיָתָהּ הַיּוֹצֵת מִבֵּין רַגְלֶיהָ
וּבְבָנֶיהָ אֲשֶׁר תֵּלֵד כִּי־תֹאכְלֵם בְּחֹסֶר־כֹּל בַּסֵּתֶר
בְּמָצוֹר וּבְמָצוֹק אֲשֶׁר יָצִיק לְךָ אֹיִבְךָ בִּשְׁעָרֶיךָ:

נח אִם־לֹא תִשְׁמֹר לַעֲשׂוֹת אֶת־כָּל־דִּבְרֵי הַתּוֹרָה הַזֹּאת
הַכְּתֻבִים בַּסֵּפֶר הַזֶּה לְיִרְאָה אֶת־הַשֵּׁם הַנִּכְבָּד
נט וְהַנּוֹרָא הַזֶּה אֵת יְהֹוָה אֱלֹהֶיךָ: וְהִפְלָא יְהֹוָה אֶת־
מַכֹּתְךָ וְאֵת מַכּוֹת זַרְעֶךָ מַכּוֹת גְּדֹלֹת וְנֶאֱמָנוֹת
ס וָחֳלָיִם רָעִים וְנֶאֱמָנִים: וְהֵשִׁיב בְּךָ אֵת כָּל־מַדְוֵה
סא מִצְרַיִם אֲשֶׁר יָגֹרְתָּ מִפְּנֵיהֶם וְדָבְקוּ בָּךְ: גַּם כָּל־
חֳלִי וְכָל־מַכָּה אֲשֶׁר לֹא כָתוּב בְּסֵפֶר הַתּוֹרָה
סב הַזֹּאת יַעְלֵם יְהֹוָה עָלֶיךָ עַד הִשָּׁמְדָךְ: וְנִשְׁאַרְתֶּם
בִּמְתֵי מְעָט תַּחַת אֲשֶׁר הֱיִיתֶם כְּכוֹכְבֵי הַשָּׁמָיִם
‏* סב קמץ בז״ק.

סז לָרֹב כִּי־לֹא שָׁמַעְתָּ בְּקוֹל יְהֹוָה אֱלֹהֶיךָ: וְהָיָה
כַּאֲשֶׁר־שָׂשׂ יְהֹוָה עֲלֵיכֶם לְהֵיטִיב אֶתְכֶם וּלְהַרְבּוֹת
אֶתְכֶם כֵּן יָשִׂישׂ יְהֹוָה עֲלֵיכֶם לְהַאֲבִיד אֶתְכֶם
וּלְהַשְׁמִיד אֶתְכֶם וְנִסַּחְתֶּם מֵעַל הָאֲדָמָה אֲשֶׁר־אַתָּה
סד בָא־שָׁמָּה לְרִשְׁתָּהּ: וֶהֱפִיצְךָ יְהֹוָה בְּכָל־הָעַמִּים
מִקְצֵה הָאָרֶץ וְעַד־קְצֵה הָאָרֶץ וְעָבַדְתָּ שָּׁם אֱלֹהִים
אֲחֵרִים אֲשֶׁר לֹא־יָדַעְתָּ אַתָּה וַאֲבֹתֶיךָ עֵץ וָאָבֶן:
סה וּבַגּוֹיִם הָהֵם לֹא תַרְגִּיעַ וְלֹא־יִהְיֶה מָנוֹחַ לְכַף־
רַגְלֶךָ וְנָתַן יְהֹוָה לְךָ שָׁם לֵב רַגָּז וְכִלְיוֹן עֵינַיִם
סו וְדַאֲבוֹן נָפֶשׁ: וְהָיוּ חַיֶּיךָ תְּלֻאִים לְךָ מִנֶּגֶד וּפָחַדְתָּ
סז לַיְלָה וְיוֹמָם וְלֹא תַאֲמִין בְּחַיֶּיךָ: בַּבֹּקֶר תֹּאמַר

afterbirth that issues from between her legs and the babies she bears; she shall eat them secretly, because of utter want, in the desperate straits to which your enemy shall reduce you in your towns.

58] If you fail to observe faithfully all the terms of this Teaching that are written in this book, to reverence this honored and awesome Name, the LORD your God, **59]** the LORD will inflict extraordinary plagues upon you and your offspring, strange and lasting plagues, malignant and chronic diseases. **60]** He will bring back upon you all the sicknesses of Egypt which you dreaded so, and they shall cling to you. **61]** Moreover, the LORD will bring upon you all the other diseases and plagues that are not mentioned in this book of Teaching, until you are wiped out. **62]** You shall be left a scant few, after having been as numerous as the stars in the skies, because you did not heed the command of the LORD your God. **63]** And as the LORD once delighted in making you prosperous and many, so will the LORD now delight in causing you to perish and in wiping you out; you shall be torn from the land which you are about to invade and occupy.

64] The LORD will scatter you among all the peoples from one end of the earth to the other, and there you shall serve other gods, wood and stone, whom neither you nor your ancestors have experienced. **65]** Yet even among those nations you shall find no peace, nor shall your foot find a place to rest. The LORD will give you there an anguished heart and eyes that pine and a despondent spirit. **66]** The life you face shall be precarious; you shall be in terror, night and day, with no assurance of survival. **67]** In the morning you shall say, "If only it were

57] *Afterbirth.* This occurred during the siege of Samaria in the ninth century B.C.E. (II Kings 6:28).

58] *If you fail.* A third catalogue of curses.

59] *Lasting.* Literally, "true," that is, not apparent or temporary diseases.

66] *No assurance.* The same use of the root אמן as in verse 59, but with a negative modifier.

סט לַעֲבָדִים וְלִשְׁפָחוֹת וְאֵין קֹנֶה: ס אֵלֶּה דִבְרֵי
הַבְּרִית אֲשֶׁר־צִוָּה יְהֹוָה אֶת־מֹשֶׁה לִכְרֹת אֶת־בְּנֵי
יִשְׂרָאֵל בְּאֶרֶץ מוֹאָב מִלְּבַד הַבְּרִית אֲשֶׁר־כָּרַת
אִתָּם בְּחֹרֵב:

מִי־יִתֵּן עֶרֶב וּבָעֶרֶב תֹּאמַר מִי־יִתֵּן בֹּקֶר מִפַּחַד
לְבָבְךָ אֲשֶׁר תִּפְחָד וּמִמַּרְאֵה עֵינֶיךָ אֲשֶׁר תִּרְאֶה:
סח וֶהֱשִׁיבְךָ יְהֹוָה מִצְרַיִם בָּאֳנִיּוֹת בַּדֶּרֶךְ אֲשֶׁר אָמַרְתִּי
לְךָ לֹא־תֹסִיף עוֹד לִרְאֹתָהּ וְהִתְמַכַּרְתֶּם שָׁם לְאֹיְבֶיךָ

* סו קמץ בז"ק.

evening!" and in the evening you shall say, "If only it were morning!"—because of what your
heart shall dread and your eyes shall see. **68]** The LORD will send you back to Egypt in
galleys, by a route which I told you you should not see again. There you shall offer yourselves
for sale to your enemies as male and female slaves, but none will buy.

69] These are the terms of the covenant which the LORD commanded Moses to conclude
with the Israelites in the land of Moab, in addition to the covenant which He had made with
them at Horeb.

68] *Back to Egypt.* The ultimate threat.

None will buy. The ultimate humiliation: people will avoid you as cursed (a comparable English
idiom would be "You will be a drug on the
market").

69] *These are the terms.* A postscript to the preceding and also an introduction to what follows.

Such bridges occur repeatedly in the Torah; see
at Gen. 2:4.

Conclude . . . in the land of Moab. Meaning, in
Moab the covenant was affirmed. The Deuteronomic code ends here.

In some versions verse 69 is noted as the first
verse of chapter 29.

Comparisons and Uses

The catalogue invites comparisons with Exod. 23:20 ff. and Lev. 26:3 ff.

The Exodus passages are significantly different in that they are a notable exception to the expected preponderance of curses over blessings: the former are contained in a simple verse (verse 21) while the latter hold out fertility, health, and success in greater detail. The treatment in Leviticus bears a general resemblance to Deut. 28, and in some instances both have similar formulations. Nonetheless, the differences in style and wording are greater than the affinities; the Leviticus passages seem closer to Ezekiel, and Deut. 28 closer to Jeremiah.

It is most probable, therefore, that the three catalogues stem from three different traditions all of which elaborate on the consequences of God's covenant with His people [6]. It should also be noted that the Hebrew text directs itself to the individual Israelite rather than to the people as a whole, an approach often found in the Torah. The individual is considered responsible for the community; it is through his or her actions that the covenant is confirmed or endangered.

Jewish tradition has held that at one time or another all the curses of chapter 28 were fulfilled; still, Israel survived because it never totally forgot its God [7]. It became the custom, when the annual cycle of Torah readings would reach this chapter, to call up a volunteer for the curses (sometimes the synagogue's contract with the sexton included his obligation to "volunteer"). Such a person would often be called up, not in customary fashion, by his name, but rather as "He who wishes" [8]. The chapter itself would be read without interruption and in a low voice, a rule that applies also to the reading of Lev. 26:14–43. This practice reflects an old fear that, if one spoke too loudly of possible adversity, it might, in mysterious fashion, be invited to happen. In Reform services, the chapter is rarely, if ever, read in its entirety.

1529

Despite

The promise of blessings (verse 2) is followed by the caution "if you heed" (verse 3). We are bidden to heed God *despite* the blessings.

CHASIDIC [9]

Blessed

"Blessed be you in the city" (verse 6) was interpreted by the Rabbis to mean that one should be part of a community and live close to a synagogue.

TALMUD [10]

In Your Comings . . . Your Goings (verse 6)

May you leave this world as you entered it: without sin.

TALMUD [11]

Another explanation: May your descendants not dishonor you.

MIDRASH [12]

Only if you leave this world in righteousness can you be said to have been blessed—and this can be said only of the fewest. For the majority, the rabbinic assessment applies that humanity would have been better off had it not been created at all.

CHATAM SOFER [13]

A Holy People (verse 9)

In the Book of Exodus (19:6), when calling Israel a holy people, the Torah uses the term *goy kadosh*. Here, at the end of the desert wandering, they are called *am kadosh*. In forty years they had progressed from *goy*, a nation like other nations, to *am*, a people with a spiritual purpose.

W. G. P.

The Nations

The Torah foresees that "all the peoples of the earth" will come to see God's glory (verse 10). The Hebrew (*amei ha-aretz*) can also be understood as "ignorant peoples of the earth,"[1] implying that it is Israel's task to bring God's knowledge to them.

THE GAON OF VILNA [14]

Gematria

The curses in chapter 28 contain 676 letters (in the Hebrew text), even as the word רָעוֹת *ra-ot*, evil occurrences) has the value of 676.[2]

Now note that God's holy name יְהֹוָה has the value of 26,[3] and 26 x 26 is 676. The hidden meaning is: The Torah threatens with רָעוֹת, but from all of them יְהֹוָה will rescue us.

CHASIDIC [15]

The Difference

In the curses of verses 17 and 18 "your basket and your kneading bowl" come before "the issue of your womb," that is, the material comes before the personal evil. In the corresponding blessings of verses 4 and 5 the order is reversed. When blessing, God begins with us; when cursing, He begins with our possessions. So He did also with Job.

D. HOFFMANN [16]

Never

The maledictions pronounced on Israel (especially the threat that the people will be "utterly wiped out," verse 20) are conditional; they take effect only if all of Israel, as a whole nation, de-

---

[1] In postbiblical Hebrew, *am ha-aretz* was understood as "peasant" and became a pejorative, the common term for a person ignorant of Torah and/or negligent in observing certain laws.

[2] ר=200; ע=70; ו=6; ת=400; added together they make 676.

[3] י=10; ה=5; ו=6; ה=5; together they make 26.

fects from the covenant. This is a degree of deterioration which has never taken place.

S. R. HIRSCH [17]

Joy of Service

We are castigated for failing to rejoice in God's service (verse 47), as it is said: "Let the heart of them rejoice that seek the Lord" (I Chron. 16:10). Someone searching for a lost article rejoices only when he finds it, but seekers after God rejoice even in the search.　　CHASIDIC [18]

You Shall Eat Your Own Issue (verse 53)

The text should be understood, not only in the dreadful literal sense, but also as applying to parents who are forced to eat their children's food and are cursed because of their dependence on them.　　CHASIDIC [19]

Horrors of War

(Describing scenes during the Roman siege of Jerusalem, 70 C.E.) It was now a miserable case, and a sight that would justly bring tears into our eyes, how men stood as to their food, while the more powerful had more than enough, and the weaker were lamenting (for want of it). But famine overcomes all other passions, and it is destructive to nothing so much as to modesty; for what was otherwise worthy of reverence was in this case despised; insomuch that wives pulled the very morsels that their husbands were eating out of their very mouths, as did children to fathers, and what was still more to be pitied, so did the mothers do to their infants; and, when those that were most dear were perishing under their hands, they were not ashamed to take from them the very last drops that might preserve their lives; and, while they ate after this manner, yet were they not concealed in so doing.　　JOSEPHUS [20]

Past and Future

"In the morning you shall say, 'If only it were evening'" (verse 67), expressing a desperate wish for a better future. This is the way the Targum Yerushalmi understands the Hebrew. But the text can also be rendered as referring to the past: "If only it were (still yesterday) evening." This is the Talmud's way of reading [21], expressing the wish for a return of the past. For, reasons the Talmud, we know at least how things *were*, while we do not know how they *will be*—they might turn out to be worse.

Deuteronomy and Esarhaddon

Deuteronomy [22]

28:32:　And the heavens over your head shall be brass, and the earth under you shall be iron.

28:27:　The Lord will smite you with Egyptian inflammation . . . and with scars from which you shall never recover.

28:28-9:　The Lord will smite you with madness and blindness, and confusion of mind, and you shall grope at noonday as the blind gropes in the darkness; and you shall not prosper in your ways, and you shall only be oppressed and robbed continually, and there shall be none to help you.

Esarhaddon [23]

528-31:　May they (the gods) make your ground like iron so that no one can plough (cut) it. Just as rain does not fall from a brazen heaven, so may rain and dew not come upon your fields and pastures.

419-20:　May Sin . . . the light of heaven and earth clothe you with leprosy; may he not order your entering into the presence of the gods or king.

422-4:　May Shamash . . . not render you a just judgment (not give you a reliable decision); may he deprive you of the sight of your eyes (so that) they will wander about in darkness.

Deuteronomy

28:26: Your corpses shall be food for all birds of the heaven and for beasts of the earth.

28:30: You shall betroth a wife, and another man shall lie with her.

28:32: Your sons and your daughters shall be given to another people.

28:33: A nation which you have not known shall eat up the fruits of your ground and of your labors. . . .

Esarhaddon

425-7: May Ninurta . . . fell you with his swift arrow; may he fill the steppe with your corpses; may he feed your flesh to the vulture (and) the jackal.

428-9: May Venus, the brightest of stars, make your wives lie in your enemy's lap while your eyes look (at them).

429-30a: May your sons not be masters of your house.

430b: May a foreign enemy divide all your goods.

PART IV

Final Appeal and Farewell

With chapter 28 the Deuteronomic code came to its conclusion. Its last verse, 69,* serves as a bridge to what follows: a summation of Israel's history highlighted by the establishment of the covenant and, in covenantal style, a recapitulation of blessings and curses, with heaven and earth invoked as witnesses to this formal restatement.

Joshua is now formally appointed as the successor of Moses, and the book ends, much like the Book of Genesis, on a poetic note. A song comprises chapter 32, and a blessing, chapter 33. Then, in chapter 34, follows a brief epilogue telling of Moses' death.

The section contains two important theological statements: that future generations too will be bound by the covenant and that the book which testifies to it is openly accessible to all Israel and is not a hidden document in the possession of a special caste.

It has been noted that the section contains a number of words not found elsewhere in Deuteronomy. Examples are: לְמַעַן תַּשְׂכִּילוּ, in the sense of "that you may succeed" (29:8); אָלָה, "oath" or "sanction" (frequently in ch. 29); וַיִּתְּשֵׁם, "uprooted them" (29:27). Such linguistic variances suggest to some that these chapters came from a separate source which was later joined to the bulk of Deuteronomy. However, the integration of these chapters into the main text is such that they now form an essential part of the whole. They give the latter its literary climax and leave hearer and reader with a prophetic vision.

* In some versions (like King James, Revised Standard Version, New English Bible), Deut. 28:69 forms the first verse of chapter 29, and thus our 29:1 becomes their 29:2, etc. When referring to any verses for chapter 29, the latter method of counting will be listed in brackets, following our method of counting, i.e., 29:1 [2], 29:2 [3], etc.

The Last Oration

The final address of Moses follows the pattern made familiar by previous orations: the deeds of God are recounted as are the obligations arising therefrom for His subjects; the Sovereign's exclusive right to their loyalty is established, followed by a catalogue of consequential rewards and punishments. The address thus follows the outline of treaties between ruler and ruled which were encountered in Hittite and neo-Assyrian documents and which the Torah covenant reflects repeatedly.* The last oration does, however, present a novel feature (for Deuteronomy) in the reason given for the repetition of the covenantal framework: Israel had heretofore not fully understood the extent of God's works, because it had not had "a mind to understand or eyes to see or ears to hear" (29:3 [4])—a thought expressed in a similar way by Isaiah in his vision of God (6:9–10).

The address is characterized by broad and sweeping vigor, its words couched in striking prose, its images rich in compelling allusions. It lays down an enduring foundation for Israel's religion in that the Torah is declared to be valid for all generations, freely accessible to every member of the people, and not, as among other nations, the possession of a privileged few. The importance of these statements caused the liturgists of the Reform movement to include readings from chapter 29 in the afternoon service of Yom Kippur [1].

---

* See W. W. Hallo's essay. Von Rad calls verses 15–20 a mini-covenant and suggests that this may at one time have been the last part of Deuteronomy.

Style and choice of words distinguish the address from earlier orations. Some believe it to be a product of the Babylonian exile, when the punishments here predicted had already become bitter reality [2].

(A new weekly portion, *Nitzavim*, begins with 29:9 [10].)

וְשֵׁכָר לֹא שְׁתִיתֶם לְמַעַן תֵּדְעוּ כִּי אֲנִי יְהוָה
אֱלֹהֵיכֶם: וַתָּבֹאוּ אֶל־הַמָּקוֹם הַזֶּה וַיֵּצֵא סִיחֹן מֶלֶךְ־
חֶשְׁבּוֹן וְעוֹג מֶלֶךְ־הַבָּשָׁן לִקְרָאתֵנוּ לַמִּלְחָמָה וַנַּכֵּם:
וַנִּקַּח אֶת־אַרְצָם וַנִּתְּנָהּ לְנַחֲלָה לָרֻאוּבֵנִי וְלַגָּדִי וְלַחֲצִי
שֵׁבֶט הַמְנַשִּׁי: וּשְׁמַרְתֶּם אֶת־דִּבְרֵי הַבְּרִית הַזֹּאת
וַעֲשִׂיתֶם אֹתָם לְמַעַן תַּשְׂכִּילוּ אֵת כָּל־אֲשֶׁר תַּעֲשׂוּן:

Haftarah Ki Tavo, p. 1614

פ   פ   פ

אַתֶּם נִצָּבִים הַיּוֹם כֻּלְּכֶם לִפְנֵי יְהוָה אֱלֹהֵיכֶם

וַיִּקְרָא מֹשֶׁה אֶל־כָּל־יִשְׂרָאֵל וַיֹּאמֶר אֲלֵהֶם אַתֶּם
רְאִיתֶם אֵת כָּל־אֲשֶׁר עָשָׂה יְהוָה לְעֵינֵיכֶם בְּאֶרֶץ
מִצְרַיִם לְפַרְעֹה וּלְכָל־עֲבָדָיו וּלְכָל־אַרְצוֹ: הַמַּסּוֹת
הַגְּדֹלֹת אֲשֶׁר רָאוּ עֵינֶיךָ הָאֹתֹת וְהַמֹּפְתִים הַגְּדֹלִים
הָהֵם: וְלֹא־נָתַן יְהוָה לָכֶם לֵב לָדַעַת וְעֵינַיִם לִרְאוֹת
וְאָזְנַיִם לִשְׁמֹעַ עַד הַיּוֹם הַזֶּה: וָאוֹלֵךְ אֶתְכֶם אַרְבָּעִים
שָׁנָה בַּמִּדְבָּר לֹא־בָלוּ שַׂלְמֹתֵיכֶם מֵעֲלֵיכֶם וְנַעַלְךָ
לֹא־בָלְתָה מֵעַל רַגְלֶךָ: לֶחֶם לֹא אֲכַלְתֶּם וְיַיִן

1] Moses summoned all Israel and said to them:

You have seen all that the LORD did before your very eyes in the land of Egypt, to Pharaoh and to all his courtiers and to his whole country: **2]** the wondrous feats that you saw with your own eyes, those prodigious signs and marvels. **3]** Yet to this day the LORD has not given you a mind to understand or eyes to see or ears to hear.

4] I led you through the wilderness forty years; the clothes on your back did not wear out, nor did the sandals on your feet; **5]** you had no bread to eat and no wine or other liquor to drink—that you might know that I the LORD am your God.

6] When you reached this place, Sihon king of Heshbon and Og king of Bashan came out to engage us in battle, but we defeated them. **7]** We took their land and gave it to the Reubenites, the Gadites, and the half-tribe of Manasseh as their heritage. **8]** Therefore observe faithfully all the terms of this covenant, that you may succeed in all that you undertake.

9] You stand this day, all of you, before the LORD your God—your tribal heads, your elders

---

29:3] [4] *The Lord has not given you a mind.* Despite all His labors in your behalf He could not make you appreciate Him. The idea appears to stem from a time of religious regression.

Traditional commentators wrestled with the problem posed by the text. Ibn Ezra said that the Torah here reasserts that God is the first giver of insight, and Maimonides stated that God is thus shown as the ultimate cause even of free choice [3].

Eyes . . . ears. Israel failed as a witness to God's deeds.

4] [5] *I led you.* A repetition of Deut. 8:2 ff., where the objective of God's action was said to be the education of Israel, to teach it that "man does not live on bread alone."

Note also the Hebrew terminology for "led": here it is a form of הָלַךְ not, as in Exodus and

Numbers, of יָצָא and עָלָה.

5] [6] *Bread . . . wine . . . liquor.* These ordinary accoutrements of life were not available and only God sustained you.

I the Lord am your God. A formulaic ending to the statement.

6] [7] *Sihon . . . Og.* See at 2:32 ff., 3:1 ff.

8] [9] *That you may succeed.* That you may after all understand God's marvelous deeds for you.

9] [10] *You stand this day.* The introduction which provides the setting for a ceremony of reaffirmation. The words "this day" are repeated six times in the oration and lend it rising emphasis.

רָאשֵׁיכֶם שִׁבְטֵיכֶם זִקְנֵיכֶם וְשֹׁטְרֵיכֶם כֹּל אִישׁ י֜   יְהֹוָה אֱלֹהֵינוּ וְאֵת אֲשֶׁר אֵינֶנּוּ פֹּה עִמָּנוּ הַיּוֹם: כִּי־
יִשְׂרָאֵל: טַפְּכֶם נְשֵׁיכֶם וְגֵרְךָ אֲשֶׁר בְּקֶרֶב מַחֲנֶיךָ י   אַתֶּם יְדַעְתֶּם אֵת אֲשֶׁר־יָשַׁבְנוּ בְּאֶרֶץ מִצְרָיִם וְאֵת
מֵחֹטֵב עֵצֶיךָ עַד שֹׁאֵב מֵימֶיךָ: לְעׇבְרְךָ בִּבְרִית יא   אֲשֶׁר־עָבַרְנוּ בְּקֶרֶב הַגּוֹיִם אֲשֶׁר עֲבַרְתֶּם: וַתִּרְאוּ
יְהֹוָה אֱלֹהֶיךָ וּבְאָלָתוֹ אֲשֶׁר יְהֹוָה אֱלֹהֶיךָ כֹּרֵת   אֶת־שִׁקּוּצֵיהֶם וְאֵת גִּלֻּלֵיהֶם עֵץ וָאֶבֶן כֶּסֶף וְזָהָב
עִמְּךָ הַיּוֹם: לְמַעַן הָקִים־אֹתְךָ הַיּוֹם לוֹ לְעָם וְהוּא יב   אֲשֶׁר עִמָּהֶם: פֶּן־יֵשׁ בָּכֶם אִישׁ אוֹ־אִשָּׁה אוֹ מִשְׁפָּחָה
יִהְיֶה־לְּךָ לֵאלֹהִים כַּאֲשֶׁר דִּבֶּר־לָךְ וְכַאֲשֶׁר נִשְׁבַּע   אוֹ־שֵׁבֶט אֲשֶׁר לְבָבוֹ פֹנֶה הַיּוֹם מֵעִם יְהֹוָה אֱלֹהֵינוּ
לַאֲבֹתֶיךָ לְאַבְרָהָם לְיִצְחָק וּלְיַעֲקֹב: וְלֹא אִתְּכֶם יג   לָלֶכֶת לַעֲבֹד אֶת־אֱלֹהֵי הַגּוֹיִם הָהֵם פֶּן־יֵשׁ בָּכֶם
לְבַדְּכֶם אָנֹכִי כֹּרֵת אֶת־הַבְּרִית הַזֹּאת וְאֶת־הָאָלָה   שֹׁרֶשׁ פֹּרֶה רֹאשׁ וְלַעֲנָה: וְהָיָה בְּשׇׁמְעוֹ אֶת־דִּבְרֵי
הַזֹּאת: כִּי אֶת־אֲשֶׁר יֶשְׁנוֹ פֹּה עִמָּנוּ עֹמֵד הַיּוֹם לִפְנֵי יד   הָאָלָה הַזֹּאת וְהִתְבָּרֵךְ בִּלְבָבוֹ לֵאמֹר שָׁלוֹם יִהְיֶה־

and your officials, all the men of Israel, **10]** your children, your wives, even the stranger within your camp, from woodchopper to waterdrawer— **11]** to enter into the covenant of the LORD your God, which the LORD your God is concluding with you this day, with its sanctions; **12]** to the end that He may establish you this day as His people and be your God, as He promised you and as He swore to your fathers, Abraham, Isaac, and Jacob. **13]** I make this covenant, with its sanctions, not with you alone, **14]** but both with those who are standing here with us this day before the LORD our God and with those who are not with us here this day.

15] Well you know that we dwelt in the land of Egypt and that we passed through the midst of various other nations; **16]** and you have seen the detestable things and the fetishes of wood and stone, silver and gold, that they keep. **17]** Perchance there is among you some man or woman, or some clan or tribe, whose heart is even now turning away from the LORD our God to go and worship the gods of those nations—perchance there is among you a stock sprouting poison weed and wormwood. **18]** When such a one hears the words of these sanctions, he may fancy himself immune, thinking, "I shall be safe, though I follow my own wilful heart"—

10] [11] *Woodchopper . . . waterdrawer.* Lowly occupations; the Gibeonites were condemned to fill these tasks forever (Josh. 9:21 ff.). The expressions likely described declassed persons in Israel's midst.

In literary English, "hewers of wood and drawers of water" has come to stand for menial service.

Because one might have expected a contrast instead, which would have expressed the thought that everyone "from the lowest to the highest" was present, it has been suggested that both "woodchopper" and "waterdrawer" had figurative meanings, the former a reference to Abraham (who took wood for the sacrifice of Isaac), the latter referring to Elijah (who used water in his contest with the Baal priests) [4].

11] [12] *To enter into the covenant.* The verb is עָבַר, which usually means "to pass over," an image reminiscent of the "covenant between the pieces," Gen. 15.

The usual verb for concluding a pact is כָּרַת; other expressions are עָמַד (II Kings 23:3) and בָּא (II Chron. 15:12).

13] [14] *Not with you alone.* Compare Deut. 5:3 and commentary below.

17] [18] *Wormwood.* A bitter herb, genus *artemisia*.

18] [19] *Fancy himself immune.* Literally, "bless himself" and thereby ward off the curse.

לִי כִּי בִּשְׁרִרוּת לִבִּי אֵלֵךְ לְמַעַן סְפוֹת הָרָוָה אֶת־
יט הַצְּמֵאָה: לֹא־יֹאבֶה יְהֹוָה סְלֹחַ לוֹ כִּי אָז יֶעְשַׁן
אַף־יְהֹוָה וְקִנְאָתוֹ בָּאִישׁ הַהוּא וְרָבְצָה בּוֹ כָּל־הָאָלָה
הַכְּתוּבָה בַּסֵּפֶר הַזֶּה וּמָחָה יְהֹוָה אֶת־שְׁמוֹ מִתַּחַת
כ הַשָּׁמָיִם: וְהִבְדִּילוֹ יְהֹוָה לְרָעָה מִכֹּל שִׁבְטֵי יִשְׂרָאֵל
כְּכֹל אָלוֹת הַבְּרִית הַכְּתוּבָה בְּסֵפֶר הַתּוֹרָה הַזֶּה:
כא וְאָמַר הַדּוֹר הָאַחֲרוֹן בְּנֵיכֶם אֲשֶׁר יָקוּמוּ מֵאַחֲרֵיכֶם
וְהַנָּכְרִי אֲשֶׁר יָבֹא מֵאֶרֶץ רְחוֹקָה וְרָאוּ אֶת־מַכּוֹת
הָאָרֶץ הַהִוא וְאֶת־תַּחֲלֻאֶיהָ אֲשֶׁר־חִלָּה יְהֹוָה בָּהּ:
כב גָּפְרִית וָמֶלַח שְׂרֵפָה כָל־אַרְצָהּ לֹא תִזָּרַע וְלֹא
תַצְמִחַ וְלֹא־יַעֲלֶה בָהּ כָּל־עֵשֶׂב כְּמַהְפֵּכַת סְדֹם

וַעֲמֹרָה אַדְמָה וּצְבֹיִּם אֲשֶׁר הָפַךְ יְהֹוָה בְּאַפּוֹ
כג וּבַחֲמָתוֹ: וְאָמְרוּ כָּל־הַגּוֹיִם עַל־מֶה עָשָׂה יְהֹוָה כָּכָה
כד לָאָרֶץ הַזֹּאת מֶה חֳרִי הָאַף הַגָּדוֹל הַזֶּה: וְאָמְרוּ
עַל אֲשֶׁר עָזְבוּ אֶת־בְּרִית יְהֹוָה אֱלֹהֵי אֲבֹתָם אֲשֶׁר
כה כָּרַת עִמָּם בְּהוֹצִיאוֹ אֹתָם מֵאֶרֶץ מִצְרָיִם: וַיֵּלְכוּ
וַיַּעַבְדוּ אֱלֹהִים אֲחֵרִים וַיִּשְׁתַּחֲווּ לָהֶם אֱלֹהִים אֲשֶׁר
כו לֹא־יְדָעוּם וְלֹא חָלַק לָהֶם: וַיִּחַר־אַף יְהֹוָה בָּאָרֶץ
הַהִוא לְהָבִיא עָלֶיהָ אֶת־כָּל־הַקְּלָלָה הַכְּתוּבָה
כז בַּסֵּפֶר הַזֶּה: וַיִּתְּשֵׁם יְהֹוָה מֵעַל אַדְמָתָם בְּאַף וּבְחֵמָה
וּבְקֶצֶף גָּדוֹל וַיַּשְׁלִכֵם אֶל־אֶרֶץ אַחֶרֶת כַּיּוֹם הַזֶּה:

* כג וצביים קרי.

to the utter ruin of moist and dry alike. **19]** The LORD will never forgive him; rather will the LORD's anger and passion rage against that man, till every sanction recorded in this book comes down upon him, and the LORD blots out his name from under heaven.

20] The LORD will single them out from all the tribes of Israel for misfortune, in accordance with all the sanctions of the covenant recorded in this book of Teaching. **21]** And later generations will ask—the children who succeed you, and foreigners who come from distant lands and see the plagues and diseases that the LORD has inflicted upon that land, **22]** all its soil devastated by sulfur and salt, beyond sowing and producing, no grass growing in it, just like the upheaval of Sodom and Gomorrah, Admah and Zeboiim, which the LORD overthrew in His fierce anger— **23]** all nations will ask, "Why did the LORD do thus to this land? Wherefore that awful wrath?" **24]** They will be told, "Because they forsook the covenant that the LORD, God of their fathers, made with them when He freed them from the land of Egypt; **25]** they turned to the service of other gods and worshiped them, gods whom they had not experienced and whom He had not allotted to them. **26]** So the LORD was incensed at that land and brought upon it all the curses recorded in this book. **27]** The LORD uprooted them from their soil in anger, fury, and great wrath, and cast them into another land, as is still the case."

In medieval mystical practice, pronouncing the secret name of God was believed to have an immunizing effect.

Moist and dry. Meaning, "everything." The combination of contrasting terms to express a totality is called "merism"; compare "good and bad" in Gen. 2:17, and the English "young and old" [5].

20] [21] *Single them out.* Hebrew, "it," that is, a tribe or clan with its members. It may be that the verse is a reference to the near destruction of one

of the tribes (perhaps Simeon, which no longer appears in the blessing of Moses; see ch. 33).

22] [23] *Sulfur.* Older versions had "brimstone."
Upheaval of Sodom. As told in Gen. 19:24 ff.

25] [26] *Not allotted to them.* See above, at 4:19–20.

27] [28] *Cast them.* וַיַּשְׁלִכֵם is marked by a large ל in handwritten Torah scrolls. The reason for this tradition is not known.

The Mishnah applied the phrase to the Ten

כח הַנִּסְתָּרֹת לַיהוָה אֱלֹהֵינוּ וְהַנִּגְלֹת לָנוּ וּלְבָנֵינוּ עַד־
עוֹלָם לַעֲשׂוֹת אֶת־כָּל־דִּבְרֵי הַתּוֹרָה הַזֹּאת: ס

א וְהָיָה כִי־יָבֹאוּ עָלֶיךָ כָּל־הַדְּבָרִים הָאֵלֶּה הַבְּרָכָה
וְהַקְּלָלָה אֲשֶׁר נָתַתִּי לְפָנֶיךָ וַהֲשֵׁבֹתָ אֶל־לְבָבֶךָ בְּכָל־
ב הַגּוֹיִם אֲשֶׁר הִדִּיחֲךָ יְהוָה אֱלֹהֶיךָ שָׁמָּה: וְשַׁבְתָּ עַד־
יְהוָה אֱלֹהֶיךָ וְשָׁמַעְתָּ בְקֹלוֹ כְּכֹל אֲשֶׁר־אָנֹכִי מְצַוְּךָ
הַיּוֹם אַתָּה וּבָנֶיךָ בְּכָל־לְבָבְךָ וּבְכָל־נַפְשֶׁךָ:
ג וְשָׁב יְהוָה אֱלֹהֶיךָ אֶת־שְׁבוּתְךָ וְרִחֲמֶךָ וְשָׁב וְקִבֶּצְךָ
ד מִכָּל־הָעַמִּים אֲשֶׁר הֱפִיצְךָ יְהוָה אֱלֹהֶיךָ שָׁמָּה: אִם־

יִהְיֶה נִדַּחֲךָ בִּקְצֵה הַשָּׁמָיִם מִשָּׁם יְקַבֶּצְךָ יְהוָה
ה אֱלֹהֶיךָ וּמִשָּׁם יִקָּחֶךָ: וֶהֱבִיאֲךָ יְהוָה אֱלֹהֶיךָ אֶל־
הָאָרֶץ אֲשֶׁר־יָרְשׁוּ אֲבֹתֶיךָ וִירִשְׁתָּהּ וְהֵיטִבְךָ וְהִרְבְּךָ
ו מֵאֲבֹתֶיךָ: וּמָל יְהוָה אֱלֹהֶיךָ אֶת־לְבָבְךָ וְאֶת־לְבַב
זַרְעֶךָ לְאַהֲבָה אֶת־יְהוָה אֱלֹהֶיךָ בְּכָל־לְבָבְךָ וּבְכָל־
ז נַפְשְׁךָ לְמַעַן חַיֶּיךָ: וְנָתַן יְהוָה אֱלֹהֶיךָ אֵת כָּל־הָאָלוֹת
הָאֵלֶּה עַל־אֹיְבֶיךָ וְעַל־שֹׂנְאֶיךָ אֲשֶׁר רְדָפוּךָ: וְאַתָּה
ח תָשׁוּב וְשָׁמַעְתָּ בְּקוֹל יְהוָה וְעָשִׂיתָ אֶת־כָּל־מִצְוֹתָיו
ט אֲשֶׁר אָנֹכִי מְצַוְּךָ הַיּוֹם: וְהוֹתִירְךָ יְהוָה אֱלֹהֶיךָ

28] Concealed acts concern the LORD our God; but with overt acts, it is for us and our children ever to apply all the provisions of this Teaching.

1] When all these things befall you—the blessing and the curse that I have set before you—and you take them to heart amidst the various nations to which the LORD your God has banished you, **2]** and you return to the LORD your God, and you and your children heed His command with all your heart and soul, just as I enjoin upon you this day, **3]** then the LORD your God, will restore your fortunes and take you back in love. He will bring you together again from all the peoples where the LORD your God has scattered you. **4]** Even if your outcasts are at the ends of the world, from there the LORD your God will gather you, from there He will fetch you. **5]** And the LORD your God will bring you to the land which your fathers occupied, and you shall occupy it; and He will make you more prosperous and more numerous than your fathers.

6] Then the LORD your God will open up your heart and the hearts of your offspring to love the LORD your God with all your heart and soul, in order that you may live. **7]** The LORD your God will inflict all those curses upon the enemies and foes who persecuted you. **8]** You, however, will again heed the LORD and obey all His commandments which I enjoin upon you this day. **9]** And the LORD your God will grant you abounding prosperity in all your

Tribes exiled by the Assyrians. They were punished in accordance with the Torah's threat and (according to R. Akiba) will also have no share in the world-to-come [6].

28] [29] *Concealed acts.* The verse is not connected with the preceding and appears to be a later insertion; note that it speaks of "us" instead of "them." Perhaps it was at first a congregational response to the Torah reading and then became part of the text [7].

For us and our children. Tradition prescribes

eleven dots to be placed over these words. On this and the meaning of the verse, see commentary below.

30:4] *Ends of the world.* Literally, "of the heavens." See also the excerpt from Ps. 139 in Gleanings.

6] *Open up.* Literally, "circumcise"; compare 10:16, where Israel is bidden to "cut away the thickening" of its heart. Here, the verse adds the concept of God assisting in the process of repentance.

בְּכֹל מַעֲשֵׂה יָדֶךָ בִּפְרִי בִטְנְךָ וּבִפְרִי בְהֶמְתְּךָ
וּבִפְרִי אַדְמָתְךָ לְטֹבָה כִּי יָשׁוּב יְהֹוָה לָשׂוּשׂ
עָלֶיךָ לְטוֹב כַּאֲשֶׁר־שָׂשׂ עַל־אֲבֹתֶיךָ: כִּי תִשְׁמַע
בְּקוֹל יְהֹוָה אֱלֹהֶיךָ לִשְׁמֹר מִצְוֹתָיו וְחֻקֹּתָיו
הַכְּתוּבָה בְּסֵפֶר הַתּוֹרָה הַזֶּה כִּי תָשׁוּב אֶל־יְהֹוָה
אֱלֹהֶיךָ בְּכָל־לְבָבְךָ וּבְכָל־נַפְשֶׁךָ: ס כִּי הַמִּצְוָה
הַזֹּאת אֲשֶׁר אָנֹכִי מְצַוְּךָ הַיּוֹם לֹא־נִפְלֵאת הִוא
מִמְּךָ וְלֹא־רְחֹקָה הִוא: לֹא בַשָּׁמַיִם הִוא לֵאמֹר
מִי יַעֲלֶה־לָּנוּ הַשָּׁמַיְמָה וְיִקָּחֶהָ לָּנוּ וְיַשְׁמִעֵנוּ אֹתָהּ
וְנַעֲשֶׂנָּה: וְלֹא־מֵעֵבֶר לַיָּם הִוא לֵאמֹר מִי יַעֲבָר־לָנוּ
אֶל־עֵבֶר הַיָּם וְיִקָּחֶהָ לָּנוּ וְיַשְׁמִעֵנוּ אֹתָהּ וְנַעֲשֶׂנָּה:
כִּי־קָרוֹב אֵלֶיךָ הַדָּבָר מְאֹד בְּפִיךָ וּבִלְבָבְךָ
לַעֲשֹׂתוֹ: ס רְאֵה נָתַתִּי לְפָנֶיךָ הַיּוֹם אֶת־הַחַיִּים
וְאֶת־הַטּוֹב וְאֶת־הַמָּוֶת וְאֶת־הָרָע: אֲשֶׁר אָנֹכִי מְצַוְּךָ

הַיּוֹם לְאַהֲבָה אֶת־יְהֹוָה אֱלֹהֶיךָ לָלֶכֶת בִּדְרָכָיו
וְלִשְׁמֹר מִצְוֹתָיו וְחֻקֹּתָיו וּמִשְׁפָּטָיו וְחָיִיתָ וְרָבִיתָ
וּבֵרַכְךָ יְהֹוָה אֱלֹהֶיךָ בָּאָרֶץ אֲשֶׁר־אַתָּה בָא־שָׁמָּה
לְרִשְׁתָּהּ: וְאִם־יִפְנֶה לְבָבְךָ וְלֹא תִשְׁמָע וְנִדַּחְתָּ
וְהִשְׁתַּחֲוִיתָ לֵאלֹהִים אֲחֵרִים וַעֲבַדְתָּם: הִגַּדְתִּי
לָכֶם הַיּוֹם כִּי אָבֹד תֹּאבֵדוּן לֹא־תַאֲרִיכֻן יָמִים
עַל־הָאֲדָמָה אֲשֶׁר אַתָּה עֹבֵר אֶת־הַיַּרְדֵּן לָבוֹא
שָׁמָּה לְרִשְׁתָּהּ: הַעִדֹתִי בָכֶם הַיּוֹם אֶת־הַשָּׁמַיִם וְאֶת־
הָאָרֶץ הַחַיִּים וְהַמָּוֶת נָתַתִּי לְפָנֶיךָ הַבְּרָכָה וְהַקְּלָלָה
וּבָחַרְתָּ בַּחַיִּים לְמַעַן תִּחְיֶה אַתָּה וְזַרְעֶךָ: לְאַהֲבָה
אֶת־יְהֹוָה אֱלֹהֶיךָ לִשְׁמֹעַ בְּקֹלוֹ וּלְדָבְקָה־בוֹ כִּי הוּא
חַיֶּיךָ וְאֹרֶךְ יָמֶיךָ לָשֶׁבֶת עַל־הָאֲדָמָה אֲשֶׁר נִשְׁבַּע
יְהֹוָה לַאֲבֹתֶיךָ לְאַבְרָהָם לְיִצְחָק וּלְיַעֲקֹב לָתֵת לָהֶם:

Haftarah Nitzavim, p. 1618

undertakings, in the issue of your womb, the offspring of your cattle, and the produce of your soil. For the LORD will again delight in your well-being, as He did in that of your fathers, **10]** since you will be heeding the LORD your God and keeping His commandments and laws that are recorded in this book of the Teaching—once you return to the LORD your God with all your heart and soul.

11] Surely, this Instruction which I enjoin upon you this day is not too baffling for you, nor is it beyond reach. **12]** It is not in the heavens, that you should say, "Who among us can go up to the heavens and get it for us and impart it to us, that we may observe it?" **13]** Neither is it beyond the sea, that you should say, "Who among us can cross to the other side of the sea and get it for us and impart it to us, that we may observe it?" **14]** No, the thing is very close to you, in your mouth and in your heart, to observe it.

15] See, I set before you this day life and prosperity, death and adversity. **16]** For I command you this day, to love the LORD your God, to walk in His ways, and to keep His commandments, His laws, and His rules, that you may thrive and increase, and that the LORD your God may bless you in the land which you are about to invade and occupy. **17]** But if your heart turns away and you give no heed, and are lured into the worship and service of other gods, **18]** I declare to you this day that you shall certainly perish; you shall not long endure on the soil which you are crossing the Jordan to invade and occupy. **19]** I call heaven and earth to witness against you this day: I have put before you life and death, blessing and curse. Choose life—if you and your offspring would live— **20]** by loving the LORD your God, heeding His commands, and holding fast to Him. For thereby you shall have life and shall long endure upon the soil that the LORD your God swore to Abraham, Isaac, and Jacob to give to them.

14] *In your mouth.* As you retell the commands of Torah. Oral transmission was of supreme importance since not many people could read.

Commitment for the Future

"I make this covenant ... with those who are standing here ... and with those who are not here with us this day" (29:13, 14). The reference is to future generations: they too are committed to the covenant, even though they had no voice in concluding it. This concept is essential to the continuity of Torah and of the people who are its bearers; it was expressed at the beginning of Deuteronomy and is now restated near the end (see commentary on 1:6–46, "Two Generations").[1]

That the present can and does commit the future to some extent is unquestionable. We are who we are because of our ancestors and of their achievements and failures. The fifteenth-century commentator Isaac Abarbanel compared Israel to a debtor: even as his estate is responsible for an unpaid loan, so Israel remains in debt to God for its liberation from Egypt and the gift of Eretz Yisrael. This is what the Midrash meant when it said that the souls of all the generations were present when the covenant was concluded.

But may a child not reject its inheritance? May a future Israel not choose to abandon God and Torah? It will not do so and it cannot, Abarbanel avowed—and Jewish history to this day has upheld this judgment. Already Ezekiel's strong affirmation may have referred to this question: "As I live—declares the Lord God—I *will* reign over you ... I *will* bring you into the bond of the covenant" (Ezek. 20:33 ff.). Individuals can defect; the people as a whole cannot [8].

The Accessibility of Torah

The Torah belongs to, and therefore is the responsibility of, all the people. Clearly, the words of Deut. 30:11–14 emphasize this principle and at the same time reject the notion that Torah is secret lore, accessible only to a chosen few.

Israel had its priests, but, unlike those of Egypt's temples or of Greece's oracle places, their knowledge of God's law was not exclusive. Because of their training, knowledge, and position, their decisions had superior weight (as did those of the Rabbis in post-biblical history). However, Israel's priests dealt at all times with a law and a tradition available to all. This is the obvious meaning of verse 12: "(The Torah) is not in the heavens, that you should say, 'Who among us can go up to the heavens and get it for us and impart it to us, that we may observe it?'" The text provides its own affirmation: "No, the thing is very close to you, in your mouth and in your heart, to observe it" (verse 14).

In the religious traditions of antiquity such a commitment to universal accessibility was unique, and it had an even more profound effect on the Jewish people as the centuries passed. The study of Torah became the supreme preoccupation of the Jew; none was too humble to be excluded from the mitzvah of learning and none too prominent to be excused from it. It was a command, averred the Mishnah, that outweighed all others, for everything flowed from it [9].

The Torah, said a second-century Sage, speaks in a language that human beings can grasp [10]; it deals with the overt, not the hidden. Only the latter belongs to the realm of God, while the realm of Torah is open and accessible to all. This is the meaning implied in Deut. 29:28,[2] and stated unequivo-

---

[1] The text seems to assume that the future generations are those born into the nation as well as those who will join it voluntarily. The nation as a whole may need to reaffirm the covenant from time to time, while individuals are bound by their history and their people.

[2] The Talmud records a controversy on this verse between R. Yehudah and R. Nehemiah. Both took

cally by the Psalmist (115:16):

> The heavens belong to the Lord,
> But the earth He gave over to man.

The Torah makes clear that, though there are limits to human knowledge, these limits do not apply to the will of God as revealed in the Torah. Interpretation and elucidation may be needed, but these will be supplied by Israel and not by God.

Turning Back

In its first ten phrases Chapter 30 contains an idea fundamental to the Book of Deuteronomy and to biblical thought in general. Seven times the text uses forms of the word שוב (shuv, turn),[3] a stylistic device that underscores the central thought: If Israel turns back to the God it has forsaken, God will graciously receive it back in turn.

In Deuteronomy the concept of turning is squarely rooted in the covenant relationship between God, the suzerain, and Israel, the servant and vassal. In Egypt, Israel had exchanged the lordship of Pharaoh for the mastery of God and, at Sinai, had confirmed the new allegiance dramatically. However, on entering the Land, exposed to the influence of Canaanite religions, Israel's loyalty to its suzerain had wavered and even lapsed. The people had strayed from single allegiance and turned to other gods, and it is such straying—and the need for turning back—that forms the subject of our chapter.

This modality of the suzerain-vassal relationship governs the Deuteronomic idea of God's covenant with Israel. When Israel breaches the covenant God turns away and surrenders His people to misfortune. When Israel returns to Him, He too returns and "repents of His anger."[4] The reaffirmation of the covenant, which is the subject of chapters 29 and 30, thus contains an element of mutuality in its provision for restoration: the covenant may be broken, but it will not be abrogated, for the possibility of mutual return keeps it alive.

This view of turn and return (expressed by the term "shuv") antedates the formulation of the Deuteronomic text and most likely had its roots in earlier centuries, when the Sinaitic covenant still found its echo in the suzerain-vassal treaties of the ancient Near East. In Hosea (eighth century, B.C.E.), a shift is observable: now the covenant is likened to marriage, and though the wife is still subject to her master—the Hebrew for husband is ba-al, master—the old suzerain-vassal typology begins to pale. Turning is now identified with an attitude of the heart as much as a national show of loyalty, and the prophets, especially Hosea and Jeremiah, insistently address themselves to this theme. The need for a new national heart becomes a cornerstone of Israel's religious perceptions.

Turning back begins in Deuteronomy and Prophets as a possibility and challenge for all Israel and inevitably thereby becomes an obligation and opportunity for each indi-

---

Deut. 29:28 to refer to sin, the former stating that God holds Israel responsible for all sins committed by members of the people, even when these sins are hidden, whereas the latter said that all Israel was responsible only for overt transgressions. The verse was believed to have a concealed meaning hinted at by the Masoretes who placed diacritical dots over eleven letters of the phrase: [11] לנו ולבנינו עד עולם.

[3] The English translation does not convey this seven-fold occurrence. Forms of שוב are found in verse 1 ("take them"); verse 2 ("return"); verse 3 ("restore," "bring again"); verse 8 ("you will again"); verse 9 ("the Lord will again"); and verse 10 ("return"). This multiple use of שוב occurs also in Psalm 126, verse 1 ("restores"),and again in verse 4.

[4] The Midrash goes even further and says that God goes into exile with Israel and returns with it; see Gleanings below.

vidual (see, e.g., Jer. 36:3). The word *"teshu-vah"* does not yet occur in biblical writing in the meaning of repentance; when it appears in rabbinic sources—after the destruction of the Temple and the sacrificial cult [12]—it deals usually with an *individual's* (rather than the whole people's) transgression. God stands ready to forgive a sinner if he or she truly repents. In the order of the universe such repentance is seen to be of primal importance: of the seven things created by God even before Creation, says the Talmud, Torah stood first and repentance second.[5]

Nowhere is the difference between the spiritual life and its material counterpart more clearly seen than in the possibility of turning. In the world of nature the principle of irreversibility obtains: events move in one direction only, and once they have happened they cannot be undone. Not so with repentance: it provides for turning back the clock through a joining of human will and divine acceptance. In that sense one can understand the saying of one Sage who proclaimed the repentant sinner to be superior to one who had never sinned [14]. He meant that the reversible life of the spirit was more significant than the irreversible sweep of the rest of existence. That is why Yom Kippur became Jewry's most important holy day and the ever-present possibility of *teshuvah*, a cornerstone of Judaism.

---

[5] The other five are paradise, hell, the throne of glory, the temple, and the name of the Messiah. The inclusion of each of these is derived from a different biblical verse. That of repentance is derived from Psalm 90:2–3: "Before You brought forth the earth and the world . . . You decreed, 'Return, you mortals!' " [13].

GLEANINGS

Curses and Repentance

Chapter 28 (with its imprecations) precedes chapters 29 and 30 (which extol turning back). The object of chapter 28 is to lead Israel to repent.

SEFAT EMET [15]

Concealed and Revealed (Deut. 29:28)

The final time of redemption is concealed but not its beginning, for it begins with Israel's repentance: "It is for us and our children ever to apply. . . ." KETAV SOFER [16]

There are those who transgress secretly but perform mitzvot in public, and others who transgress openly but perform mitzvot secretly.

CHASIDIC [17]

Return

In both 30:2 and 30:10 the Torah says "return to the Lord," but the Hebrew has a subtle difference: in verse 2 the word "to" is עַד, in verse 10 it is אֶל.[6] The latter signifies a higher form of repentance, for it adds "with all your heart and soul."

MALBIM [18]

Do not read עַד (to) but עֵד (witness). When you return you will be witness to the possibility of repentance. CHASIDIC [19]

God Will Return Your Captivity (Deut. 30:3)

The word "return"[7] in this translation functions as a transitive verb, but in the Hebrew the word appears to be intransitive (שָׁב). If understood in this fashion, one would see the text to say that God himself dwells in exile with Israel

and "will return with (אֶת) your captivity."

RASHI [20]

Liturgy

It is customary to pronounce special blessings on the Sabbath before the arrival of the new moon (Birkat ha-Chodesh). The only exception is Shabbat Nitzavim (when Deut. 29:9 ff. is read), which is always the last Sabbath in the month of Elul, just before the arrival of Rosh Hashanah.

Why this omission? Because on this Sabbath God himself blesses the new month and the new year. CHASIDIC [21]

Torah Can Be Learned (Deut. 30:11)

Fools attempt to learn the whole Torah all at once, and when they fail they give up altogether. The wise study a little every day.

MIDRASH [22]

Astrology

When we are told that the Torah is not in the heavens (30:12), we are to understand that it is not found among the astrologers. MIDRASH [23]

The Reach of God

Psalm 139:7–10 speak poetically of the omnipresence of God, expanding on the theme of Deut. 30:4.

If I ascend to heaven, You are there;
If I descend to Sheol, You are there too.
If I take wing with the dawn to come to rest on the western horizon, even there Your hand will be guiding me, Your right hand be holding me fast.

---

[6] Only Buber-Rosenzweig's translation transmits this distinction, rendering עַד as hin (turn toward Him) and אֶל as um (turn back to Him).

[7] This is an alternate understanding for "restore" your fortunes.

Moses Prepares for Death

The discourses are now concluded and the Torah turns to the narrative of Moses' last days: his preparations for death, the appointment of Joshua as his successor, and the final instructions he issues to Joshua and the Levites. Then, in chapters 32 and 33, two poems follow—one a song, the other a blessing—and, in chapter 34, the account of the leader's death, which concludes the book.

Chapter 31 does not present a straightforward account. After introductory words of parting (verses 1–8), Moses charges the priests to write down the teaching and to have it read to the people once every seven years, during the Feast of Booths.

Then, with verse 14, a section begins that clearly did not originally form part of the account. It interrupts the story (which continues in verse 24) and contains Hebrew terms not otherwise found in Deuteronomy.*

(Chapter 31 constitutes a complete weekly Torah portion, *Vayelech*, the shortest in the Torah.)

---

* Examples are: Tent of Meeting, verse 14; alien gods, verse 16; break My covenant, verses 16, 20; hide My countenance, verse 17; plan (*yetzer*, as in Gen. 6:5), verse 21.

ד פ פ פ

א וַיֵּלֶךְ מֹשֶׁה וַיְדַבֵּר אֶת־הַדְּבָרִים הָאֵלֶּה אֶל־כָּל־

יְהֹוָה: וְעָשָׂה יְהֹוָה לָהֶם כַּאֲשֶׁר עָשָׂה לְסִיחוֹן וּלְעוֹג
ב יִשְׂרָאֵל: וַיֹּאמֶר אֲלֵהֶם בֶּן־מֵאָה וְעֶשְׂרִים שָׁנָה אָנֹכִי

מַלְכֵי הָאֱמֹרִי וּלְאַרְצָם אֲשֶׁר הִשְׁמִיד אֹתָם: וּנְתָנָם
הַיּוֹם לֹא־אוּכַל עוֹד לָצֵאת וְלָבוֹא וַיהֹוָה אָמַר אֵלַי

יְהֹוָה לִפְנֵיכֶם וַעֲשִׂיתֶם לָהֶם כְּכָל־הַמִּצְוָה אֲשֶׁר
ג לֹא תַעֲבֹר אֶת־הַיַּרְדֵּן הַזֶּה: יְהֹוָה אֱלֹהֶיךָ הוּא

צִוִּיתִי אֶתְכֶם: חִזְקוּ וְאִמְצוּ אַל־תִּירְאוּ וְאַל־תַּעַרְצוּ
עֹבֵר לְפָנֶיךָ הוּא־יַשְׁמִיד אֶת־הַגּוֹיִם הָאֵלֶּה מִלְּפָנֶיךָ

מִפְּנֵיהֶם כִּי יְהֹוָה אֱלֹהֶיךָ הוּא הַהֹלֵךְ עִמָּךְ לֹא
וִירִשְׁתָּם יְהוֹשֻׁעַ הוּא עֹבֵר לְפָנֶיךָ כַּאֲשֶׁר דִּבֶּר

יַרְפְּךָ וְלֹא יַעַזְבֶךָּ: ס וַיִּקְרָא מֹשֶׁה לִיהוֹשֻׁעַ
וַיֹּאמֶר אֵלָיו לְעֵינֵי כָל־יִשְׂרָאֵל חֲזַק וֶאֱמָץ כִּי אַתָּה

1] Moses went and spoke these things to all Israel. **2]** He said to them:
I am now one hundred and twenty years old, I can no longer be active. Moreover, the LORD has said to me, "You shall not go across yonder Jordan." **3]** The LORD your God Himself will cross over at your head; and He will wipe out those nations from your path and you shall dispossess them.—Joshua is the one who shall cross at your head, as the LORD has spoken.—

4] The LORD will do to them as He did to Sihon and Og, kings of the Amorites, and to their countries, when He wiped them out. **5]** The LORD will deliver them up to you, and you shall deal with them in full accordance with the Instruction that I have enjoined upon you. **6]** Be strong and resolute, be not in fear or in dread of them; for the LORD your God Himself marches with you: He will not fail you or forsake you.

7] Then Moses called Joshua and said to him in the sight of all Israel: Be strong and resolute,

---

31:1] *Moses went and spoke.* Proceeded to speak. A similar English idiom is, "went ahead and spoke."

These things. Of which he had spoken before (so the Septuagint), or of which he was about to speak. Such ambiguity is frequently found in the Torah in sentences that constitute a bridge between two accounts; see, for instance, Gen. 2:4.

2] *One hundred and twenty years old.* He spanned three generations of forty years each. One hundred and twenty is a figure which, as the multiple of the first five whole numbers ($1 \times 2 \times 3 \times 4 \times 5$), came to represent in the Torah the ideal of longevity. It also combines the decimal and duo-decimal systems (10×12). (A popular Jewish wish is, "May you live to 120 years.")

The two men who preceded and succeeded Moses in his leadership, Joseph and Joshua, fell short of his age, both dying at 110 (the ideal life span in Egypt), a figure which was also a symbolic construct: $5^2 + 6^2 + 7^2$. Similarly, Abraham, Isaac, and Jacob were said to have reached ages of struc-

tured length: Abraham, 175 (7×5^2); Isaac, 180 (5×6^2); Jacob, 147 (3×7^2) [1].

Be active. Literally, "come and go." But he was not senile, see Deut. 34:7.

Moreover. A better rendering of וַ would be "in any case." Even were I still in full strength I could not lead you across the Jordan. So, while Joshua will now stand at your head, your real leader, as always, will be God.

4] *Sihon and Og.* Compare Deut. 3:21. On Sihon's fate see 2:32 ff.; on Og's, 3:1 ff.

5] *The Instruction that I have enjoined.* Referring to Deut. 7:1 ff., where intermarriage with these nations is prohibited and their destruction demanded.

7] *In the sight of all Israel.* That is, publicly.

Be strong and resolute. חֲזַק וֶאֱמָץ (*chazak ve-ematz*). Here, Moses says this to Joshua; God will be heard to repeat these words to Joshua after

יג אֶת־הַתּוֹרָ֣ה הַזֹּ֑את נֶ֥גֶד כׇּל־יִשְׂרָאֵ֖ל בְּאׇזְנֵיהֶֽם: הַקְהֵ֣ל
אֶת־הָעָ֡ם הָֽאֲנָשִׁ֣ים וְהַנָּשִׁים֩ וְהַטַּ֨ף וְגֵרְךָ֜ אֲשֶׁ֣ר בִּשְׁעָרֶ֗יךָ
לְמַ֨עַן יִשְׁמְע֜וּ וּלְמַ֣עַן יִלְמְד֗וּ וְיָֽרְאוּ֙ אֶת־יְהֹוָ֣ה אֱלֹֽהֵיכֶ֔ם
יד וְשָֽׁמְר֣וּ לַעֲשׂ֔וֹת אֶת־כׇּל־דִּבְרֵ֖י הַתּוֹרָ֥ה הַזֹּֽאת: וּבְנֵיהֶ֞ם
אֲשֶׁ֣ר לֹֽא־יָֽדְע֗וּ יִשְׁמְעוּ֙ וְלָ֣מְד֔וּ לְיִרְאָ֖ה אֶת־יְהֹוָ֣ה
אֱלֹֽהֵיכֶ֑ם כׇּל־הַיָּמִ֗ים אֲשֶׁ֨ר אַתֶּ֤ם חַיִּים֙ עַל־הָ֣אֲדָמָ֔ה
אֲשֶׁ֨ר אַתֶּ֜ם עֹבְרִ֧ים אֶת־הַיַּרְדֵּ֛ן שָׁ֖מָּה לְרִשְׁתָּֽהּ: פ

יד וַיֹּ֨אמֶר יְהֹוָ֜ה אֶל־מֹשֶׁ֗ה הֵ֣ן קָרְב֣וּ יָמֶ֘יךָ֮ לָמוּת֒ קְרָ֣א
אֶת־יְהוֹשֻׁ֗עַ וְהִֽתְיַצְּב֛וּ בְּאֹ֥הֶל מוֹעֵ֖ד וַאֲצַוֶּ֑נּוּ וַיֵּ֤לֶךְ מֹשֶׁה֙

ח תָב֣וֹא אֶת־הָעָ֗ם אֶל־הָאָ֙רֶץ֙ אֲשֶׁ֣ר נִשְׁבַּ֣ע יְהֹוָ֣ה
לַאֲבֹתָ֖ם לָתֵ֣ת לָהֶ֑ם וְאַתָּ֖ה תַּנְחִילֶ֥נָּה אוֹתָֽם: וַֽיהֹוָ֡ה
ה֣וּא הַהֹלֵ֣ךְ לְפָנֶ֔יךָ ה֚וּא יִהְיֶ֣ה עִמָּ֔ךְ לֹ֥א יַרְפְּךָ֖ וְלֹ֣א
ט יַֽעַזְבֶ֑ךָּ לֹ֥א תִירָ֖א וְלֹ֥א תֵחָֽת: וַיִּכְתֹּ֣ב מֹשֶׁה֮ אֶת־
הַתּוֹרָ֣ה הַזֹּאת֒ וַֽיִּתְּנָ֗הּ אֶל־הַכֹּֽהֲנִים֙ בְּנֵ֣י לֵוִ֔י הַנֹּ֣שְׂאִ֔ים
אֶת־אֲר֖וֹן בְּרִ֣ית יְהֹוָ֑ה וְאֶל־כׇּל־זִקְנֵ֖י יִשְׂרָאֵֽל: וַיְצַ֤ו
י מֹשֶׁה֙ אוֹתָ֣ם לֵאמֹ֔ר מִקֵּ֣ץ ׀ שֶׁ֣בַע שָׁנִ֗ים בְּמֹעֵ֛ד שְׁנַ֥ת
יא הַשְּׁמִטָּ֖ה בְּחַ֥ג הַסֻּכּֽוֹת: בְּב֣וֹא כׇל־יִשְׂרָאֵ֗ל לֵרָאוֹת֙
אֶת־פְּנֵי֙ יְהֹוָ֣ה אֱלֹהֶ֔יךָ בַּמָּק֖וֹם אֲשֶׁ֣ר יִבְחָ֑ר תִּקְרָ֞א

for it is you who shall go with this people into the land that the LORD swore to their fathers to give them, and it is you who shall apportion it to them. **8]** And the LORD Himself will go before you. He will be with you; He will not fail you or forsake you. Fear not and be not dismayed!

9] Moses wrote down this Teaching and gave it to the priests, sons of Levi, who carried the Ark of the LORD's Covenant, and to all the elders of Israel.

10] And Moses instructed them as follows: Every seventh year, the year set for remission, at the Feast of Booths, **11]** when all Israel comes to appear before the LORD your God in the place which He will choose, you shall read this Teaching aloud in the presence of all Israel. **12]** Gather the people—men, women, children, and the strangers in your communities —that they may hear and so learn to revere the LORD your God and to observe faithfully every word of this Teaching. **13]** Their children, too, who have not had the experience, shall hear and learn to revere the LORD your God as long as they live in the land which you are about to cross the Jordan to occupy.

14] The LORD said to Moses: The time is drawing near for you to die. Call Joshua and

Moses' death; and the people too will address them to their new leader (Josh. 1:6, 9, 18).

It is you. And not I, Moses.

9] *Wrote down this Teaching.* That is, the Book of Deuteronomy. But older commentators believed this to refer to the whole Torah and considered it proof that the Torah was the work of Moses.

To the priests . . . and to all the elders. He gave it to both the religious and civil authorities. The book was thus expressly removed from an exclusively priestly domain.

10] *Every seventh year.* Meaning, at the end of every seven years; see at Deut. 15:1 [2].

At the Feast of Booths. On Sukot, one of the three festivals when Israelites were bidden to make a pilgrimage to the sanctuary (16:16).

The Mishnah records that the reading took place at the end of the first day, and, if the first fell on the Sabbath, on the second day [3].

11] *You shall read.* This was applied to those who held supreme responsibility; at one time it was a priest like Ezra (see Neh. 8) or the High Priest [4], at other times a king like Josiah (II Kings 23).

The Mishnah reports that King Agrippa stood up and read the following passages from Deuteronomy: 1:1–6:6; 11:13 ff.; 14:22 ff.; 17:14 ff.; 26:12 ff.; chapters 27 and 28 [5].

12] *And the strangers.* Josephus reports that the slaves, too, were in attendance at the public reading [6].

This verse and the first part of verse 13 form the opening of a Torah service in *Gates of Prayer* [7].

13] *Their children, too.* Compare 29:10.

כִּי פָנָ֤ה אֶל־אֱלֹהִים֙ אֲחֵרִ֔ים: וְעַתָּ֗ה כִּתְב֤וּ לָכֶם֙
אֶת־הַשִּׁירָ֣ה הַזֹּ֔את וְלַמְּדָ֥הּ אֶת־בְּנֵֽי־יִשְׂרָאֵ֖ל שִׂימָ֣הּ
בְּפִיהֶ֑ם לְמַ֨עַן תִּהְיֶה־לִּ֜י הַשִּׁירָ֥ה הַזֹּ֛את לְעֵ֖ד בִּבְנֵ֥י
יִשְׂרָאֵֽל: כִּֽי־אֲבִיאֶ֜נּוּ אֶל־הָאֲדָמָ֣ה אֲשֶׁר־נִשְׁבַּ֣עְתִּי
לַאֲבֹתָיו֮ זָבַ֣ת חָלָ֣ב וּדְבַשׁ֒ וְאָכַ֤ל וְשָׂבַע֙ וְדָשֵׁ֔ן וּפָנָ֞ה
אֶל־אֱלֹהִ֤ים אֲחֵרִים֙ וַעֲבָד֔וּם וְנִאֲצ֖וּנִי וְהֵפֵ֥ר אֶת־
בְּרִיתִֽי: וְהָיָ֠ה כִּֽי־תִמְצֶ֨אןָ אֹת֜וֹ רָע֤וֹת רַבּוֹת֙ וְצָר֔וֹת
וְ֠עָנְתָה הַשִּׁירָ֨ה הַזֹּ֤את לְפָנָיו֙ לְעֵ֔ד כִּ֛י לֹ֥א תִשָּׁכַ֖ח
מִפִּ֣י זַרְע֑וֹ כִּ֧י יָדַ֣עְתִּי אֶת־יִצְר֗וֹ אֲשֶׁ֨ר ה֤וּא עֹשֶׂה֙
הַיּ֔וֹם בְּטֶ֣רֶם אֲבִיאֶ֔נּוּ אֶל־הָאָ֖רֶץ אֲשֶׁ֥ר נִשְׁבָּֽעְתִּי:

וִיהוֹשֻׁ֔עַ וַיִּֽתְיַצְּב֖וּ בְּאֹ֣הֶל מוֹעֵֽד: וַיֵּרָ֧א יְהֹוָ֛ה בָּאֹ֖הֶל
בְּעַמּ֣וּד עָנָ֑ן וַיַּעֲמֹ֛ד עַמּ֥וּד הֶעָנָ֖ן עַל־פֶּ֥תַח הָאֹֽהֶל:
וַיֹּ֨אמֶר יְהֹוָ֜ה אֶל־מֹשֶׁ֗ה הִנְּךָ֤ שֹׁכֵב֙ עִם־אֲבֹתֶ֔יךָ וְקָם֩
הָעָ֨ם הַזֶּ֜ה וְזָנָ֣ה ׀ אַחֲרֵ֣י ׀ אֱלֹהֵ֣י נֵֽכַר־הָאָ֗רֶץ אֲשֶׁ֨ר ה֤וּא
בָא־שָׁ֨מָּה֙ בְּקִרְבּ֔וֹ וַעֲזָבַ֕נִי וְהֵפֵר֙ אֶת־בְּרִיתִ֔י אֲשֶׁ֥ר
כָּרַ֖תִּי אִתּֽוֹ: וְחָרָ֣ה אַפִּ֣י ב֣וֹ בַיּוֹם־הַ֠הוּא וַעֲזַבְתִּ֞ים
וְהִסְתַּרְתִּ֤י פָנַי֙ מֵהֶ֔ם וְהָיָ֣ה לֶאֱכֹ֔ל וּמְצָאֻ֛הוּ רָע֥וֹת
רַבּ֖וֹת וְצָר֑וֹת וְאָמַר֙ בַּיּ֣וֹם הַה֔וּא הֲלֹ֗א עַ֣ל כִּֽי־אֵ֤ין
אֱלֹהַי֙ בְּקִרְבִּ֔י מְצָא֖וּנִי הָרָע֣וֹת הָאֵ֑לֶּה: וְאָנֹכִ֗י הַסְתֵּ֨ר
אַסְתִּ֤יר פָּנַי֙ בַּיּ֣וֹם הַה֔וּא עַ֥ל כָּל־הָרָעָ֖ה אֲשֶׁ֥ר עָשָׂ֑ה

present yourselves in the Tent of Meeting, that I may instruct him. Moses and Joshua went and presented themselves in the Tent of Meeting. **15]** The LORD appeared in the Tent, in a pillar of cloud, the pillar of cloud having come to rest at the entrance of the tent.

16] The LORD said to Moses: You are soon to lie with your fathers. This people will thereupon go astray after the alien gods in their midst, in the land which they are about to enter; they will forsake Me and break My covenant which I made with them. **17]** Then My anger will flare up against them, and I will abandon them and hide My countenance from them. They shall be ready prey; and many evils and troubles shall befall them. And they shall say on that day, "Surely it is because our God is not in our midst that these evils have befallen us." **18]** Yet I will keep My countenance hidden on that day, because of all the evil they have done in turning to other gods. **19]** Therefore, write down this poem and teach it to the people of Israel; put it in their mouths, in order that this poem may be My witness against the people of Israel. **20]** When I bring them into the land flowing with milk and honey that I promised on oath to their fathers, and they eat their fill and grow fat and turn to other gods and serve them, spurning Me and breaking My covenant, **21]** and the many evils and troubles befall them— then this poem shall confront them as a witness, since it will never be lost from the mouth of their offspring. For I know what plans they are devising even now, before I bring them into the land that I promised on oath.

16] *Go astray.* The Hebrew זָנָה evokes the image of adultery; compare Hos. 3:1.

According to Driver, the verse was at first meant literally and only afterwards, metaphorically [8].

17] *Hide My countenance.* See commentary below. The expression occurs nowhere else in the Torah but is found in Isaiah (8:17), Micah (3:4), and Psalms (e.g., 30:8).

God is not in our midst. Blaming God for not protecting His people.

19] *Write down.* Phrased in Hebrew in the plural,

as if addressed to Moses and Joshua, or to all the people [9]. Moses, however, is reported as doing the actual writing (verse 22).

This poem. Or, "song," which is contained in chapter 32.

May be My witness. That I warned them. Yet God already knows that Israel will transgress the law; see commentary below.

21] *Plans they are devising.* God knows their יֵצֶר, their inclination to do evil, for it is indigenous to human nature (Gen. 6:5).

כב וַיִּכְתֹּב מֹשֶׁה אֶת־הַשִּׁירָה הַזֹּאת בַּיּוֹם הַהוּא וַיְלַמְּדָהּ
כג אֶת־בְּנֵי יִשְׂרָאֵל: וַיְצַו אֶת־יְהוֹשֻׁעַ בִּן־נוּן וַיֹּאמֶר חֲזַק
וֶאֱמָץ כִּי אַתָּה תָּבִיא אֶת־בְּנֵי יִשְׂרָאֵל אֶל־הָאָרֶץ
כד אֲשֶׁר־נִשְׁבַּעְתִּי לָהֶם וְאָנֹכִי אֶהְיֶה עִמָּךְ: וַיְהִי כְּכַלּוֹת
מֹשֶׁה לִכְתֹּב אֶת־דִּבְרֵי הַתּוֹרָה־הַזֹּאת עַל־סֵפֶר עַד
כה תֻּמָּם: וַיְצַו מֹשֶׁה אֶת־הַלְוִיִּם נֹשְׂאֵי אֲרוֹן בְּרִית־יְהוָה
כו לֵאמֹר: לָקֹחַ אֵת סֵפֶר הַתּוֹרָה הַזֶּה וְשַׂמְתֶּם אֹתוֹ
מִצַּד אֲרוֹן בְּרִית־יְהוָה אֱלֹהֵיכֶם וְהָיָה־שָׁם בְּךָ לְעֵד:
כז כִּי אָנֹכִי יָדַעְתִּי אֶת־מֶרְיְךָ וְאֶת־עָרְפְּךָ הַקָּשֶׁה הֵן

בְּעוֹדֶנִּי חַי עִמָּכֶם הַיּוֹם מַמְרִים הֱיִתֶם עִם־יְהֹוָה
כח וְאַף כִּי־אַחֲרֵי מוֹתִי: הַקְהִילוּ אֵלַי אֶת־כָּל־זִקְנֵי
שִׁבְטֵיכֶם וְשֹׁטְרֵיכֶם וַאֲדַבְּרָה בְאָזְנֵיהֶם אֵת הַדְּבָרִים
כט הָאֵלֶּה וְאָעִידָה בָּם אֶת־הַשָּׁמַיִם וְאֶת־הָאָרֶץ: כִּי
יָדַעְתִּי אַחֲרֵי מוֹתִי כִּי־הַשְׁחֵת תַּשְׁחִתוּן וְסַרְתֶּם מִן
הַדֶּרֶךְ אֲשֶׁר צִוִּיתִי אֶתְכֶם וְקָרָאת אֶתְכֶם הָרָעָה
בְּאַחֲרִית הַיָּמִים כִּי־תַעֲשׂוּ אֶת־הָרַע בְּעֵינֵי יְהֹוָה
ל לְהַכְעִיסוֹ בְּמַעֲשֵׂה יְדֵיכֶם: וַיְדַבֵּר מֹשֶׁה בְּאָזְנֵי כָּל־
קְהַל יִשְׂרָאֵל אֶת־דִּבְרֵי הַשִּׁירָה הַזֹּאת עַד תֻּמָּם:

Haftarah Vayelech, p. 1623

22] That day, Moses wrote down this poem and taught it to the Israelites.

23] And He charged Joshua son of Nun: Be strong and resolute: for you shall bring the Israelites into the land which I promised them on oath, and I will be with you.

24] When Moses had put down in writing the words of this Teaching to the very end, **25]** Moses charged the Levites who carried the Ark of the Covenant of the LORD, saying: **26]** Take this book of Teaching and place it beside the Ark of the Covenant of the LORD your God, and let it remain there as a witness against you. **27]** Well I know how defiant and stiffnecked you are: even now, while I am still alive in your midst, you have been defiant toward the LORD; how much more, then, when I am dead! **28]** Gather to me all the elders of your tribes and your officials, that I may speak all these words to them and that I may call heaven and earth to witness against them. **29]** For I know that, when I am dead, you will act wickedly and turn away from the path which I enjoined upon you, and that in time to come misfortune will befall you for having done evil in the sight of the LORD and vexed Him by your deeds.

30] Then Moses recited the words of this poem to the very end, in the hearing of the whole congregation of Israel:

23] *I will be with you.* As if I were alive. The expression gives Moses' speech a suprahuman tinge.

24] *When Moses . . . .* This would follow best after verse 13 and probably stood there originally.

25] *The Levites.* That is, the priests among them; see verse 9.

26] *Take.* The Hebrew here uses an infinitive absolute (לָקֹחַ) instead of an imperative; found also, e.g., in the Decalogue (Deut. 5:12, שָׁמוֹר, and Exod. 20:8, זָכוֹר).

Contemporary languages have similar grammatical expressions; compare the German *Aufpassen!*

Place it [the book] beside the Ark. According to I Sam. 6:8, 11, 15, it was placed there in a container (*argaz*), and Targum Yerushalmi says that it was a box (*kufsa*).

Rabbi Meir (second century C.E.) had a tradition, however, that the book was kept inside the ark, with the tablets [10].

As a witness against you. As a written document fortifying what was at that time an essentially oral tradition.

27] *Well I know.* From forty years of bitter experience in leading a recalcitrant people.

28] *Heaven and earth.* As ultimate witnesses, representing the infinite and the finite. Moses' song will start with invoking these two again (ch. 32).

Two Theological Questions

1. *God's Knowledge and Human Freedom.* In verses 16 ff. God is depicted as telling Moses of Israel's future defection, as already knowing that the people will rebel against Him and that the fearful consequences of which chapter 28 had told will come to pass. If, in fact, it could be said that God anticipates the future, of what significance would human free will be? Why would God warn Israel to heed His law when He knew that they would refuse to do so? The problem is of a similar order as the confrontation between Egypt's Pharaoh and Moses: the latter pleaded with the ruler to let Israel go, but God had already informed Moses that his pleas would fall on barren ground and that God had arranged for the Pharaoh's destruction.[1]

Traditional Judaism attempted to solve the apparent contradiction between divine foreknowledge and human freedom by maintaining that while free will was given God's omniscience included a complete knowledge of human nature and the course of action people would adopt.[2]

However, when Deuteronomy was composed, these questions were not raised at all. Israel had already rebelled and suffered grievous consequences. The text does not theologize about it; rather, it phrases its judgment in the form of a prophecy which in effect has God say, "I told you so.[3] You have been proven to be stiff-necked and there–fore invited My punishment." The book never doubts that Israel could have acted differently, but the unhappy facts of history made speculation over what might have happened useless. The Torah leaves the matter there, and only later on were theological questions extrapolated from the text.

2. *The Hidden God.* Instead of showing compassion, the Torah says, God will hide himself when Israel sins; that is, He will be impervious to Israel's suffering and its cries for help (verses 17 and 18). From the Deuteronomic point of view—with national transgression and its consequences already having happened—the passages serve to explain God's inaction. They imply that He could have saved His people but chose not to do so, for when Israel breached the covenant God was released from His obligations as Israel's guardian and sovereign. This approach is the basic view of all prophets: Israel's misfortunes are traceable to its own misdeeds. Not God but Israel itself is to blame; God, though omnipotent, is exculpated. A repentant Israel will, however, find Him willing to reestablish the covenant on its old foundations. The wife who has gone astray will be taken back by a Husband who has never lost His love for her.

While medieval Jewish thought accepted these premises, modern post-Auschwitz thinkers have been unable to follow. They no longer believed in a God who could have saved His people from the gas chambers but chose to look away and hide His face. The Holocaust could not be understood as the monstrous result of putative sins that

---

[1] See our Commentary on Exodus, chapter 4.

[2] This conclusion is paralleled, though from a different perspective, by the view of contemporary Behaviorists who consider human action to be determined by the interaction of genetic and environmental factors. The Mishnaic phrasing was, "Everything is foreseen, nonetheless free will is given," or "Everything is in the hands of God except the fear of God" [11]. Nachmanides calls God's foreknowledge "Knowledge in potential."

[3] Prophets and Deuteronomy vigorously asserted that Israel's misfortunes were punishments from God and not—as antiprophetic parties suggested—from the Queen of Heaven or other deities that had been neglected (see Jer. 44:18).

Israel had committed. There remained only one alternative—short of either total disbelief or a defiant "Yet will I believe"—and that was to give up the idea of an omnipotent God. Rather, one needed to see Him as limited by human freedom. God is hidden as long as the world chooses to be alienated from Him; humanity, to whom He gave the choice to act for good or for evil, shuts Him out or lets Him in. Not God hides His face, we hide it. He took a chance on us when He created us free, and He, like us, must bear the consequences of human action. To phrase this in Deuteronomic terms: He hides himself because He must [12].

Joshua, Moses' Successor

The Torah gives us some insight into the type of person who inherited the mantle of leadership from Moses. The Book of Joshua, of course, greatly enlarges this picture.

Joshua (whom another tradition calls Hoshea), son of Nun, was an Ephraimite who had three functions assigned to him: he was Moses' personal attendant who accompanied him on his ascent of Mount Sinai; he was the guardian of the Tent; and he was a military commander who fought Amalek and whose military capacity made him the logical man to head the people in their campaign of conquering Canaan. He had previously earned his spurs by standing—at great personal risk—with Caleb against the majority of the spies; against them he proclaimed his belief that the conquest would be successful (Num. 14:6–10). He would live to be one hundred ten years, like Joseph. Thus the man who caused Israel to leave the Land was accorded the same life span as the man who would bring them back (see above, at verse 2).

Joshua became the leader of his people in a crucial time. He was now the head of the confederated tribes, he himself leading the Joseph tribe. As Moses' successor he too will be called "the servant of the Lord" and he too will be addressed by God, but he will not be God's intimate. "No personal experience to be compared with that of Moses can be glimpsed anywhere," wrote Buber [13].

In the Torah, then, Joshua is a loyal aide of his master, zealous for him and for God, courageous in defending his convictions, and successful in battle. He and Caleb were privileged to experience both the Exodus from Egypt and the conquest of the Land; that he was not like Moses does not diminish his greatness. To be chosen as the successor of the founder was in itself the mark of divine favor. For him it must have been a moment fraught with anxiety; for Moses, the investiture must have carried both regret and nostalgia. Both Joshua and Moses were human, and in their humanity they experienced the trauma of transition (see further in Gleanings).

God Knew

Before God brought Israel into the Promised Land He knew of its future sin and misery. If then, despite this, He gave the land He had promised the Fathers to their children, the latter may rest assured that the promise in the song of Moses will at some time be fulfilled.

D. HOFFMANN [14]

Liturgical

The weekly portion *Vayelech* (chapter 31) is almost always combined with the preceding one, *Nitzavim*. They are read separately only when between Rosh Hashanah and Sukot there are two Sabbaths neither of which coincides with a holy day.

הֵן

(In verse 14, when God tells Moses that death is near, He begins by saying הֵן, *hen*, "behold.")

In decreeing his death, God honored Moses by beginning with the word הֵן, the same word Moses had used in paying honor to God (Deut. 10:14).

MIDRASH [15]

The Judgment

Moses said to God: "Master of the universe, must I die after my eyes have witnessed all Your glory and power?" God replied: "What man can live and not see death (Ps. 89:49)? Were there men comparable to Abraham, Isaac, and Jacob? Yet they had to die."

And, though there was none like Moses who spoke with the Creator face to face, God said

(verse 14): "The time is drawing near for you to die."

MIDRASH [16]

Envy

Moses did not want to die.[4] But, when at the investiture of Joshua the two men went into the Tabernacle and the Cloud separated them, God spoke to Joshua alone. Afterwards Moses asked, "What did He say to you?"

Joshua replied: "When God spoke with you, did I come to know?"[5]

Thereupon Moses turned to God and told Him he was ready to die. "Better to die a hundred times than to experience even one moment of envy," he said. That is what Solomon meant: "Jealousy is cruel as the grave" (Song of Songs 8:6).

MIDRASH [17]

Joshua's Investiture

Then Joshua knelt, and Moses placed his hands upon his head and called out:

"The spirit which God put into me, I put into thee. Go in strength, and let thy might increase."

And Moses knelt by the side of Joshua and lifted his hands to heaven and prayed aloud:

"I thank Thee, O God, the God of our fathers, that Thou hast granted it to me to see the leader of Israel before Thou didst close mine eyes. And I implore Thee, God of our fathers, to strengthen his hands and to be with him as Thou hast been with me until this day."

Then he rose from his knees and called out to the people:

---

[4] More on this theme below, Gleanings on ch. 34.   [5] But another understanding is: "When God spoke with you, I knew (without asking)."

"See your leader, Joshua: Him shall ye obey!"

But among the people there was a heavyhearted silence. No tumult was raised, and no voice was heard save that of Joshua, which lamented:

"My lord, my teacher, my father!"

SHOLEM ASCH [18]

The Hidden Countenance

(After God has warned Israel against turning to alien gods, verse 16, He says that He will hide His face, verse 17.)

People will turn to man-made means to solve their problems rather than to Me—hence My countenance will be hidden.　　SFORNO [19]

Resurrection

In traditional commentaries, verse 16 became one of the proof texts for the teaching of resurrection from death. This was based on the Hebrew sequence of the words . . . הִנְּךָ שֹׁכֵב עִם אֲבֹתֶיךָ וְקָם

—literally, "You are soon to lie with your fathers and will rise . . . ."[6]

According to the Talmud, וְקָם is one of the words in the Torah where it is doubtful whether it is to be read with what precedes or with what follows, or perhaps (as here) with both [20].

Every Israelite

It says "Write down this poem"[7] (verse 19). Now the Hebrew for "write down" is phrased in the plural, implying that it is addressed to all Israel. Each Israelite has the obligation to write a scroll of the Torah (or, if he cannot do it himself, have one written in his name).　　TALMUD [21]

This Poem May Be My Witness (verse 19)

But does God require a witness? Rather, the poem was to remind God not to judge Israel too harshly. For, though He knew their nature (verse 21), He still chose them to be His people.

MALBIM [22]

---

[6] Our translation does not reflect this reading; rather, it follows the plain sense and places a period after "your fathers" (the Masoretic punctuation places an *etnachta*—similar to a semicolon—after "your fathers").

[7] "This poem" was taken to mean the whole Torah, since according to the halachah no one was permitted to copy merely parts of it.

The Song of Moses

The Bible ascribes three songs to Moses, of which two are in the Torah: one delivered after Israel's rescue from the Reed Sea, at the beginning of the desert wanderings (Exod. 15), and the other here, at the end. These two poems may therefore be seen to frame the wilderness experience, and though on the surface they appear to serve different purposes—the first a thanksgiving hymn, the second a poem of the future—they both deal with Israel's survival. At the sea, the physical existence of the nation was assured, but the forty years that followed put its spiritual future in doubt. Now, at the borders of the Promised Land, Moses celebrates the eventual realization of God's will for His people. He sings a hymn of hope to an Israel that will prevail in spirit as well as in body.*

The poem warns; it instructs; it gives hope. Israel's past history has amply demonstrated God's love and care, and these will not be found wanting in the future. Rebellion against His law may put Israel in dire straits, but in the end God will be shown not to have forgotten the people He had created. At the close of the recital, Moses is bidden to ascend Mount Nebo and prepare for death.

(Chapter 32 comprises the weekly portion *Ha'azinu*.)

---

* Psalm 90, which is also ascribed to Moses, is a prayer which shows some linguistic affinity to Deut. 32, e.g., יוֹמָת in Ps. 90:15 and Deut. 32:2 [1].

צַדִּיק וְיָשָׁר הֽוּא: אֵל אֱמוּנָה וְאֵין עָ֫וֶל   פ פ פ

דּוֹר עִקֵּשׁ וּפְתַלְתֹּֽל: שִׁחֵת לוֹ לֹא בָּנָיו מוּמָם ה   הַאֲזִ֥ינוּ הַשָּׁמַ֖יִם וַאֲדַבֵּ֑רָה   וְתִשְׁמַ֥ע הָאָ֖רֶץ אִמְרֵי־פִֽי: א

עַם נָבָל וְלֹא חָכָם   הֲֽ לַיהֹוָה תִּגְמְלוּ־זֹאת י   יַעֲרֹ֤ף כַּמָּטָר֙ לִקְחִ֔י   תִּזַּ֥ל כַּטַּ֖ל אִמְרָתִ֑י ב

הֽוּא עָשְׂךָ֖ וַֽיְכֹנְנֶֽךָ:   הֲלוֹא־הוּא אָבִיךָ קָּנֶךָ   כִּשְׂעִירִ֣ם עֲלֵי־דֶ֔שֶׁא   וְכִרְבִיבִ֖ים עֲלֵי־עֵֽשֶׂב:

בִּינוּ שְׁנוֹת דֹּר־וָדֹר   זְכֹר יְמוֹת עוֹלָם י   הָב֥וּ גֹ֖דֶל לֵאלֹהֵֽינוּ:   כִּ֛י שֵׁ֥ם יְהֹוָ֖ה אֶקְרָ֑א ג

זְקֵנֶיךָ֖ וְיֹֽאמְרוּ־לָֽךְ:   שְׁאַל אָבִיךָ וְיַגֵּדְךָ   כִּ֥י כָל־דְּרָכָ֖יו מִשְׁפָּ֑ט   הַצּוּר֙ תָּמִ֣ים פׇּעֳל֔וֹ ד

*ו ה' רבתי והיא תיבה לעצמה.

1] Give ear, O heavens, let me speak; / Let the earth hear the words I utter! / 2] May my discourse come down as the rain, / My speech distill as the dew, / Like showers on young growth, / Like droplets on the grass. / 3] For the name of the LORD I proclaim; / Give glory to our God!

4] The Rock!—His deeds are perfect, / Yea, all His ways are just; / A faithful God, never false, / True and upright is He. / 5] Children unworthy of Him, / That crooked and twisted generation— / Their baseness has played Him false. / 6] Do you thus requite the LORD, / O dull and witless people? / Is not He the Father who created you, / Fashioned you and made you endure!

7] Remember the days of old, / Consider the years of ages past; / Ask your father, he will

---

32:1] *Give ear.* Heaven and earth are both fit audience and witness to the song. Isaiah 1:2 uses the same imagery.

2] *My discourse.* Others, "My doctrine." In Proverbs (4:2) the Torah is called by this term: "For I have given you good doctrine"—a phrase that is recited at the end of the Torah service [2].

Like droplets on the grass. So will God's teachings nourish the soul of Israel.

3] *Give glory to our God.* These words too have become part of the Torah service in the synagogue [3].

4] *The Rock!* הַצּוּר (Ha-Tzur). God is repeatedly so called in the poem, the term denoting rugged steadfastness (compare the English idiom "like a rock"). Jewish and Christian liturgies frequently use this ascription; for instance: Rock of Israel, Rock of Ages, my Rock and my Redeemer.

In syntax, the use of a noun by which the subject is identified with the qualities inherent in it is called *casus pendens* [4]; compare Ps. 18:31, "God!— His way is perfect." The Hebrew liturgy also em-

ploys this kind of address-and-description; for instance, "the King!" [5], "the Good One," and "the Compassionate One" [6].

5] *Children unworthy.* Literally, "non-children," in contrast to the faithful Father. The rendering is but one of several of the obscure Hebrew text. Old JPS translation had: "Is corruption His? No; His children's is the blemish."

6] *Do you thus requite the Lord.* The Hebrew has an enlarged and detached ה prefixed to the divine name (though manuscripts vary on this). The reason is not clear; see Gleanings.

7] *Remember the days of old.* With Moses as the presumed speaker, the reference would be to patriarchal days [7]; in the later listener, the early days of nationhood might be evoked. In either case, the phrase testifies to history as a predominantly oral tradition.

Ages past. דֹּר־וָדֹר (dor va-dor), literally, "generation upon generation."

Jewish morning and afternoon prayers quote the expression in the *Amidah*: "To all generations we will make known Your greatness" [8].

ח בְּהַנְחֵל עֶלְיוֹן גּוֹיִם · · · בְּהַפְרִידוֹ בְּנֵי אָדָם · · · יַצֵּב גְּבֻלֹת עַמִּים · · · לְמִסְפַּר בְּנֵי יִשְׂרָאֵל׃ · · · יַפְרֵשׂ כְּנָפָיו יִקָּחֵהוּ · · · יִשָּׂאֵהוּ עַל־אֶבְרָתוֹ׃

ט כִּי חֵלֶק יְהֹוָה עַמּוֹ · · · יַעֲקֹב חֶבֶל נַחֲלָתוֹ׃ · · · יְהֹוָה בָּדָד יַנְחֶנּוּ · · · וְאֵין עִמּוֹ אֵל נֵכָר׃

י יִמְצָאֵהוּ בְּאֶרֶץ מִדְבָּר · · · וּבְתֹהוּ יְלֵל יְשִׁמֹן · · · יַרְכִּבֵהוּ עַל־בָּמֳותֵי אָרֶץ · · · וַיֹּאכַל תְּנוּבֹת שָׂדָי · · · יְסֹבְבֶנְהוּ יְבוֹנְנֵהוּ · · · יִצְּרֶנְהוּ כְּאִישׁוֹן עֵינוֹ׃ · · · וַיֵּנִקֵהוּ דְבַשׁ מִסֶּלַע · · · וְשֶׁמֶן מֵחַלְמִישׁ צוּר׃

יא כְּנֶשֶׁר יָעִיר קִנּוֹ · · · עַל־גּוֹזָלָיו יְרַחֵף · · · חֶמְאַת בָּקָר וַחֲלֵב צֹאן · · · עִם־חֵלֶב כָּרִים · · · וְאֵילִים בְּנֵי־בָשָׁן וְעַתּוּדִים · · · עִם־חֵלֶב כִּלְיוֹת חִטָּה

*יֵ׳ ו׳ יתירה. · · · קמץ בו׳׳ק.

inform you, / Your elders, they will tell you: / **8]** When the Most High gave nations their homes / And set the divisions of man, / He fixed the boundaries of peoples / In relation to Israel's numbers. / **9]** For the LORD's portion is His people, / Jacob His own allotment.

10] He found him in a desert region, / In an empty howling waste. / He engirded him, watched over him, / Guarded him as the pupil of His eye. / **11]** Like an eagle who rouses his nestlings, / Gliding down to his young, / So did He spread His wings and take him, / Bear him along on His pinions; / **12]** The LORD alone did guide him, / No alien god at His side.

13] He set him atop the highlands, / To feast on the yield of the earth; / He fed him honey from the crag, / And oil from the flinty rock, / **14]** Curd of kine and milk of flocks; / With the best of lambs and rams, / Bulls of Bashan and he-goats; / With the very finest wheat— /

8] *Gave nations their homes.* As set forth in Gen. 10. It was a fundamental belief that God had divided the earth among the nations [9]. A similar thought is expressed in Ps. 74:17.

In relation to Israel's numbers. For Israel was central in God's plan—an idea absent from Gen. 10. The Septuagint had a different Hebrew text, reading "in relation to the children of God." Revised Standard Version, New English Bible, New American Bible, and others follow this reading, which has a parallel in a Dead Sea fragment [10].

9] *The Lord's portion.* Israel belonged to God, as His treasured people (Deut. 7:6).

10] *He found him.* God is pictured as having discovered Israel in the desert (so also Hosea 9:10). Von Rad calls this a "foundling tradition," comparable to a patriarchal and Exodus tradition [11]. Jeremiah (2:2) reverses the image: Israel followed God into the wilderness.

An empty howling waste. תֹהוּ (tohu) recalls the second verse of Genesis, which says that at Creation the earth was tohu. As God created the earth from nothingness, so He created Israel and brought it out of the wasteland.

The adjective "howling" may refer to the voices of night animals or to a belief that the desert was inhabited by shrieking demons [12].

Pupil of His eye. Others, "apple of His eye"; the core which appears to be black (see Prov. 7:2). The word אִישׁוֹן (ishon) has also been taken as a diminutive of אִישׁ (ish, man), the miniature reflection of oneself that may be seen in another's eye [13].

This diminutive reflection is also the basic meaning of the English word "pupil."

11] *Like an eagle.* Compare Exod. 19:4.

Rouses his nestlings. To feed them as well as to teach them how to fly; so did God tend Israel in its youth. (See further in Gleanings.)

12] *The Lord alone.* The same word בָּדָד (badad) as used in Balaam's saying that Israel dwells "apart" (Num. 23:9); in both cases uniqueness and separateness go together. See further the comment on Jeshurun in verse 15.

13] *Honey . . . oil.* Both were found abundantly in ancient Canaan.

14] *Curd . . . . lambs . . . rams . . . . bulls . . . he-goats.* Mainstays of a people that domesticated animals.

Very finest wheat. Literally, "the kidney fat of wheat." The Hebrew idiom used the word "fat"

צוּר יְלָדְךָ תֶּשִׁי   לֹא שְׂעָרוּם אֲבֹתֵיכֶם: וַיִּשְׁמַן יְשֻׁרוּן וַיִּבְעָט   וְדָם־עֵנָב תִּשְׁתֶּה־חָמֶר:

וַיַּרְא יְהֹוָה וַיִּנְאָץ   וַתִּשְׁכַּח אֵל מְחֹלְלֶךָ:   וַיִּטֹּשׁ אֱלוֹהַּ עָשָׂהוּ   שָׁמַנְתָּ עָבִיתָ כָּשִׂיתָ

וַיֹּאמֶר אַסְתִּירָה פָנַי מֵהֶם   מִכַּעַס בָּנָיו וּבְנֹתָיו: יַקְנִאֻהוּ בְּזָרִים   וַיְנַבֵּל צוּר יְשֻׁעָתוֹ:

כִּי דוֹר תַּהְפֻּכֹת הֵמָּה   אֶרְאֶה מָה אַחֲרִיתָם   יִזְבְּחוּ לַשֵּׁדִים לֹא אֱלֹהַּ   בְּתוֹעֵבֹת יַכְעִיסֻהוּ:

הֵם קִנְאוּנִי בְלֹא־אֵל   בָּנִים לֹא־אֵמֻן בָּם: חֲדָשִׁים מִקָּרֹב בָּאוּ   אֱלֹהִים לֹא יְדָעוּם

And foaming grape-blood was your drink.

15] So Jeshurun grew fat and kicked— / You grew fat and gross and coarse— / He forsook the God who made him / And spurned the Rock of his support. / **16]** They incensed Him with alien things, / Vexed Him with abominations. / **17]** They sacrificed to demons, no-gods, / Gods they had never known, / New ones, who came but lately, / Who stirred not your fathers' fears. / **18]** You neglected the Rock that begot you, / Forgot the God who brought you forth.

19] The LORD saw and was vexed / And spurned His sons and His daughters. / **20]** He said: / I will hide My countenance from them, / And see how they fare in the end. / For they are a treacherous breed, / Children with no loyalty in them. / **21]** They incensed Me with

to describe the best of a thing, whence the English expression "fat of the land" (compare also "cream of the crop").

Wheat . . . grape-blood. Products of an agricultural society. The poetic catalogue reflects a nation settled in its land.

15] *Jeshurun.* A poetic name for Israel, here occurring for the first time in the Torah. Even as *badad* in verse 12 evoked Balaam's use of it (Num. 23:9), so Balaam's *ashurenu* in that same verse is here paralleled by *jeshurun.*

Ibn Ezra traces the name Jeshurun to *yashar,* right, straight.

And kicked. Like a stubborn, spoiled mule.

Coarse. The meaning of the Hebrew is not certain. An Arabic word of similar sound means "to be gorged with food," which would fit here.

Rock of his support. Or, "of his salvation." The phrase appears in the opening of a popular Chanukah hymn, *Ma-oz Tzur Yeshuati.*

17] *Demons.* שֵׁדִים (*shedim*) is translated better as "demigods" to whom human sacrifices were offered, as Ps. 106:37 attests (the only other occurrence of *shedim* in the Bible).

The word is of Akkadian origin where it de-

scribed a good and friendly spirit, a protective power [14].

No-gods. Who are adored by the no-children of verse 5 (see comment there).

New ones. Who turn out to be mere fads.

Who stirred not your fathers' fears. The meaning of the Hebrew is uncertain. Better, based on parallels to Arabic *sha-ara* and Aramaic *se-ar:* "whom your fathers did not know" (or "acknowledge"; so New English Bible).

18] *Brought you forth.* In travail, like a mother. The same feminine imagery is evoked also in Ps. 90:2, "Before You brought forth the earth and the world. . . ."

In the Masoretic text the י of תֶּשִׁי is written small. The reason, Ibn Ezra suggests, is that the י was a later addition and the word originally read תֶּשׁ (from the root נשה, forget, neglect), similar to תֵּט in Prov. 4:5.

19] *And His daughters.* Their mention is unusual when speaking of God.

20] *Hide My countenance.* See above, at 31:17.

Treacherous. Better, "perverse"; the Hebrew means, literally, "upside down."

No loyalty. Parallel to the no-gods and no-folk in the next verse.

גַּם־בָּחוּר֙ גַּם־בְּתוּלָ֔ה	וּמֵחֲדָרִ֖ים אֵימָ֑ה	וַאֲנִ֥י אַקְנִיאֵ֖ם בְּלֹא־עָ֑ם	כָּעֲס֖וּנִי בְּהַבְלֵיהֶ֑ם
אָמַ֖רְתִּי אַפְאֵיהֶ֑ם	כב יוֹנֵק֙ עִם־אִ֣ישׁ שֵׂיבָֽה׃	כִּי־אֵ֙שׁ֙ קָדְחָ֣ה בְאַפִּ֔י	כג בְּג֤וֹי נָבָ֖ל אַכְעִיסֵֽם׃
לוּלֵ֗י כַּ֚עַס אוֹיֵ֣ב אָג֔וּר	כד אַשְׁבִּ֤יתָה מֵֽאֱנ֣וֹשׁ זִכְרָ֔ם	וַתֹּ֙אכַל֙ אֶ֣רֶץ וִֽיבֻלָ֔הּ	וַתִּיקַ֙ד֙ עַד־שְׁא֣וֹל תַּחְתִּ֔ית
פֶּֽן־יֹאמְרוּ֙ יָדֵ֣נוּ רָ֔מָה	פֶּֽן־יְנַכְּר֖וּ צָרֵ֑ימוֹ	אַסְפֶּ֥ה עָלֵ֖ימוֹ רָע֑וֹת	כה וַתְּלַהֵ֖ט מֽוֹסְדֵ֥י הָרִֽים׃
כִּֽי־ג֛וֹי אֹבַ֥ד עֵצ֖וֹת הֵ֑מָּה	וְלֹ֥א יְהוָ֖ה פָּעַ֥ל כָּל־זֹֽאת׃	מְזֵ֥י רָעָ֖ב וּלְחֻ֣מֵי רֶ֑שֶׁף	חִצַּ֖י אֲכַלֶּה־בָּֽם׃
ל֚וּ חָכְמ֣וּ יַשְׂכִּ֔ילוּ זֹ֑את	וְאֵ֥ין בָּהֶ֖ם תְּבוּנָֽה׃	וְשֶׁן־בְּהֵמֹת֙ אֲשַׁלַּח־בָּ֔ם	וְקֶ֖טֶב מְרִירִ֑י
אֵיכָ֞ה יִרְדֹּ֤ף אֶחָד֙ אֶ֔לֶף	ל יָבִ֖ינוּ לְאַחֲרִיתָֽם׃	מִח֥וּץ תְּשַׁכֶּל־חֶ֖רֶב	כה עִם־חֲמַ֥ת זֹחֲלֵ֖י עָפָֽר׃

no-gods, / Vexed Me with their futilities; / I'll incense them with a no-folk, / Vex them with a nation of fools. / **22]** For a fire has flared in My wrath / And burned to the bottom of Sheol, / Has consumed the earth and its increase, / Eaten down to the base of the hills. / **23]** I will sweep misfortunes on them, / Use up My arrows on them: / **24]** Wasting famine, ravaging plague, / Deadly pestilence, and fanged beasts / Will I let loose against them, / With venomous creepers in dust. / **25]** The sword shall deal death without, / As shall the terror within, / To youth and maiden alike, / The suckling as well as the aged. / **26]** I might have reduced them to naught, / Made their memory cease among men, / **27]** But for fear of the taunts of the foe, / Their enemies who might misjudge / And say, "Our own hand has prevailed; / None of this was wrought by the LORD!"

28] For they are a folk void of sense, / Lacking in all discernment. / **29]** Were they wise, they would think upon this, / Gain insight into their future: / **30]** "How could one have

---

21] *Futilities.* Idols that are nothing but a "puff," which is the meaning of *hevel*; see Eccles. 1:2 (where *hevel* is translated as "vanity").

No-folk. Meaning either a people who are hardly worth mentioning or who are so uncivilized that they do not deserve the name "people." The poet may not have had any particular nation in mind, his statement meaning that when the time came God would use even barbarians for His purpose.

Fools. The word נָבָל is in assonance with הֶבֶל in the same verse.

22] *A fire.* Meaning, God's jealousy.

Sheol. A mythical place whither the dead were believed to descend. It is mentioned frequently in the Bible but is not further defined.

Eaten down. A parallel to "burned to the bottom."

23] *I will sweep.* The translation follows Ibn Ezra (who derives the word from ספה); others understand "heap" (from אסף) or "add" (from יסף).

24] *Wasting famine.* The seven threats of misfortune may be an echo of the seven evil spirits noted in Mesopotamian texts [15]. They are couched in difficult poetic language. Compare also Job 3:5 (and commentaries thereon).

26] *Reduced them.* The meaning of the Hebrew is uncertain. The translation supposes that אַפְאֵיהֶם is related to פֵּאָה (corner), hence: the leftover in the corner of the field.

27] *But for fear.* God's honor needs protection, and He "fears" that His enemies might misjudge His power.

The ascription of such a feeling to God is called anthropopathic, while the ascription of human form or action is termed anthropomorphic (see at verse 40).

28] *For they are.* There is no way of telling whether this refers to Israel's enemies or to Israel itself, but the former view fits the context better [16].

29] *Were they wise.* The enemies would come to understand that God does not permanently for-

וּשְׁנַ֖יִם יָנִ֣יסוּ רְבָבָ֑ה אִם־לֹ֤א כִּֽי־צוּרָ֣ם מְכָרָ֔ם לְעֵ֖ת תָּמ֣וּט רַגְלָ֑ם כִּ֥י קָר֛וֹב י֥וֹם אֵידָ֖ם

לא וַֽיהוָ֖ה הִסְגִּירֵֽם׃ כִּ֛י לֹ֥א כְצוּרֵ֖נוּ צוּרָ֑ם לי וְחָ֖שׁ עֲתִדֹ֥ת לָֽמוֹ׃ כִּֽי־יָדִ֤ין יְהוָה֙ עַמּ֔וֹ

לב וְאֹיְבֵ֖ינוּ פְּלִילִֽים׃ כִּֽי־מִגֶּ֤פֶן סְדֹם֙ גַּפְנָ֔ם וְעַל־עֲבָדָ֖יו יִתְנֶחָ֑ם כִּ֤י יִרְאֶה֙ כִּי־אָ֣זְלַת יָ֔ד

לג וּמִשַּׁדְמֹ֖ת עֲמֹרָ֑ה עֲנָבֵ֨מוֹ֙ עִנְּבֵי־ר֔וֹשׁ לי וְאָ֖פֵס עָצ֥וּר וְעָזֽוּב׃ וְאָמַ֖ר אֵ֥י אֱלֹהֵֽימוֹ

לי אַשְׁכְּלֹ֥ת מְרֹרֹ֖ת לָֽמוֹ׃ חֲמַ֥ת תַּנִּינִ֖ם יֵינָ֑ם לה צ֖וּר חָסָ֥יוּ בֽוֹ׃ אֲשֶׁ֨ר חֵ֤לֶב זְבָחֵ֨ימוֹ֙ יֹאכֵ֔לוּ

לד הֲלֹא־ה֖וּא כָּמֻ֣ס עִמָּדִ֑י יִשְׁתּ֖וּ יֵ֣ין נְסִיכָ֑ם יָק֖וּמוּ וְיַעְזְרֻכֶ֑ם

לה לִ֤י נָקָם֙ וְשִׁלֵּ֔ם חָתֻ֖ם בְּאוֹצְרֹתָֽי׃ לי יְהִ֥י עֲלֵיכֶ֖ם סִתְרָֽה׃ רְא֣וּ עַתָּ֗ה כִּ֣י אֲנִ֤י אֲנִי֙ ה֔וּא

routed a thousand, / Or two put ten thousand to flight, / Unless their Rock had sold them, / The LORD had given them up?" / **31]** For their rock is not like our Rock, / In our enemies' own estimation.

32] Ah! The vine for them is from Sodom, / From the vineyards of Gomorrah; / The grapes for them are poison, / A bitter growth their clusters. / **33]** Their wine is the venom of asps, / The pitiless poison of vipers. / **34]** Lo, I have it all put away, / Sealed up in My storehouses, / **35]** To be My vengeance and recompense, / At the time that their foot falters. / Yea, their day of disaster is near, / And destiny rushes upon them.

36] For the LORD will vindicate His people / And take revenge for His servants, / When He sees that their might is gone, / And neither bond nor free is left. / **37]** He will say: Where are their gods, / The rock in whom they sought refuge, / **38]** Who ate the fat of their offerings / And drank their libation wine? / Let them rise up to your help, / And let them be a shield unto you! / **39]** See, then, that I, I am He; / There is no god beside Me. / I deal death and give life;

sake His people. (If Israel is the subject: it would appreciate the necessity of God's chastisements.)

The phrase is frequently recited as part of the Reform Jewish funeral service.

30] *Had sold them.* Into servitude.

31] *In our enemies' own estimation.* A parenthetical aside [17].

32] *The vine.* Here used as a symbol of corruption.
Poison. רֹשׁ, the same as רֹאשׁ in the next verse.

34] *Put away.* God uses the enemy now, but his true character is not forgotten.
כָּמֻס (kamus) is understood to mean כָּנֻס (kanus), stored up.

35] *To be My vengeance.* This accords with the Masoretic reading, but the text is likely corrupt. לִי נָקָם probably was לְיוֹם נָקָם, "against the day of

vengeance"—which fits with the preceding verse (so the Septuagint, the Samaritan version, New American Bible, and New English Bible).

Old JPS and Revised Standard Version render "vengeance is Mine."

36] *And take revenge.* Or, "He will repent himself" (that is, change His mind; so translated in Num. 23:19); the phrase is repeated in Ps. 135:14.
Neither bond nor free. Meaning, "no one." A merism, similar to "moist and dry," 29:18; see comment there.

37] *He will say.* Again, the subject is not clear; it is either God or the enemy. The former view appears more in consonance with the flow of the poem [18].

39] *I, I am He.* Compare Isa. 43:11, "I, I am the Lord" (where the fuller form אָנֹכִי is used, instead of אֲנִי, as here).

אֲנִי אָמִית וַאֲחַיֶּה   וְאֵין אֱלֹהִים עִמָּדִי

וְאֵין מִיָּדִי מַצִּיל: מָחַצְתִּי וַאֲנִי אֶרְפָּא

וְאָמַרְתִּי חַי אָנֹכִי לְעֹלָם: מ כִּי־אֶשָּׂא אֶל־שָׁמַיִם יָדִי

וְתֹאחֵז בְּמִשְׁפָּט יָדִי   מא אִם־שַׁנּוֹתִי בְּרַק חַרְבִּי

וְלִמְשַׂנְאַי אֲשַׁלֵּם: אָשִׁיב נָקָם לְצָרָי

וְחַרְבִּי תֹּאכַל בָּשָׂר   מב אַשְׁכִּיר חִצַּי מִדָּם

מֵרֹאשׁ פַּרְעוֹת אוֹיֵב: מִדַּם חָלָל וְשִׁבְיָה

כִּי דַם־עֲבָדָיו יִקּוֹם   מג הַרְנִינוּ גוֹיִם עַמּוֹ

וְכִפֶּר אַדְמָתוֹ עַמּוֹ:   וְנָקָם יָשִׁיב לְצָרָיו

פ

מד וַיָּבֹא מֹשֶׁה וַיְדַבֵּר אֶת־כָּל־דִּבְרֵי הַשִּׁירָה־הַזֹּאת בְּאָזְנֵי
מה הָעָם הוּא וְהוֹשֵׁעַ בִּן־נוּן: וַיְכַל מֹשֶׁה לְדַבֵּר אֶת־
כָּל־הַדְּבָרִים הָאֵלֶּה אֶל־כָּל־יִשְׂרָאֵל: מו וַיֹּאמֶר אֲלֵהֶם
שִׂימוּ לְבַבְכֶם לְכָל־הַדְּבָרִים אֲשֶׁר אָנֹכִי מֵעִיד בָּכֶם
הַיּוֹם אֲשֶׁר תְּצַוֻּם אֶת־בְּנֵיכֶם לִשְׁמֹר לַעֲשׂוֹת אֶת־
מז כָּל־דִּבְרֵי הַתּוֹרָה הַזֹּאת: כִּי לֹא־דָבָר רֵק הוּא
מִכֶּם כִּי־הוּא חַיֵּיכֶם וּבַדָּבָר הַזֶּה תַּאֲרִיכוּ יָמִים
עַל־הָאֲדָמָה אֲשֶׁר אַתֶּם עֹבְרִים אֶת־הַיַּרְדֵּן שָׁמָּה
לְרִשְׁתָּהּ:

פ

/ I wounded and I will heal: / None can deliver from My hand. / **40]** Lo, I raise My hand to heaven / And say: As I live forever, / **41]** When I whet My flashing blade / And My hand lays hold on judgment, / Vengeance will I wreak on My foes, / Will I deal to those who reject Me. / **42]** I will make drunk My arrows with blood— / As My sword devours flesh— / Blood of the slain and the captive / From the long-haired enemy chiefs.

43] O nations, acclaim His people! / For He'll avenge the blood of His servants, / Wreak vengeance on His foes, / And cleanse the land of His people.

44] Moses came, together with Hosea son of Nun, and recited all the words of this poem in the hearing of the people.

45] And when Moses finished reciting all these words to all Israel, **46]** he said to them: Take to heart all the words with which I have warned you this day. Enjoin them upon your children, that they may observe faithfully all the terms of this Teaching. **47]** For this is not a trifling thing for you: it is your very life; through it you shall long endure on the land which you are to occupy upon crossing the Jordan.

40] *I raise My hand to heaven.* An anthropomorphism that would be deemed an "inappropriate" expression today.

41] *Flashing blade.* Literally, "lightning of My blade" (or sword).

The image entered the "Battle Hymn of the Republic": "I have seen the fearful lightning of His terrible swift sword."

42] *With blood.* The poet describes God's victory in the accepted terms of ancient warfare.

And the captive. Who were often slain.

Long-haired enemy chiefs. Perhaps referring to the no-folk (verse 21) who had a wild appearance. The Hebrew for long-haired, *par-ot*, is in clear assonance with *par-oh*, Pharaoh, Israel's arch-enemy.

Note, however, that such wild hair had the poet's approval (Judg. 5:2), if it signified the dedication of a *nazir*.

43] *Cleanse the land.* Polluted by the enemy (or polluted by Israel's idolatry).

45] *All these words.* In the Book of Deuteronomy; but traditional interpreters take it as a reference to the whole Torah.

47] *Not a trifling thing.* Literally, "not empty."

מֵת אַהֲרֹן אָחִיךָ בְּהֹר הָהָר וַיֵּאָסֶף אֶל־עַמָּיו:
נא עַל אֲשֶׁר מְעַלְתֶּם בִּי בְּתוֹךְ בְּנֵי יִשְׂרָאֵל בְּמֵי־מְרִיבַת
קָדֵשׁ מִדְבַּר־צִן עַל אֲשֶׁר לֹא־קִדַּשְׁתֶּם אוֹתִי בְּתוֹךְ
נב בְּנֵי יִשְׂרָאֵל: כִּי מִנֶּגֶד תִּרְאֶה אֶת־הָאָרֶץ וְשָׁמָּה לֹא
תָבוֹא אֶל־הָאָרֶץ אֲשֶׁר־אֲנִי נֹתֵן לִבְנֵי יִשְׂרָאֵל:

מח וַיְדַבֵּר יְהוָה אֶל־מֹשֶׁה בְּעֶצֶם הַיּוֹם הַזֶּה לֵאמֹר:
מט עֲלֵה אֶל־הַר הָעֲבָרִים הַזֶּה הַר־נְבוֹ אֲשֶׁר בְּאֶרֶץ
מוֹאָב אֲשֶׁר עַל־פְּנֵי יְרֵחוֹ וּרְאֵה אֶת־אֶרֶץ כְּנַעַן
נ אֲשֶׁר אֲנִי נֹתֵן לִבְנֵי יִשְׂרָאֵל לַאֲחֻזָּה: וּמֻת בָּהָר
אֲשֶׁר אַתָּה עֹלֶה שָׁמָּה וְהֵאָסֵף אֶל־עַמֶּיךָ כַּאֲשֶׁר־

Haftarah Ha'azinu, p. 1626

48] That very day the LORD spoke to Moses: **49]** Ascend these heights of Abarim to Mount Nebo, which is in the land of Moab facing Jericho, and view the land of Canaan which I am giving the Israelites as their holding. **50]** You shall die on the mountain that you are about to ascend, and shall be gathered to your kin, as your brother Aaron died on Mount Hor and was gathered to his kin; **51]** for you both broke faith with Me among the Israelite people, at the waters of Meribath-kadesh in the wilderness of Zin, by failing to uphold My sanctity among the Israelite people. **52]** You may view the land from a distance, but you shall not enter it— the land that I am giving to the Israelite people.

49] *Abarim.* The mountain range "beyond (the river Jordan)," seen from the perspective of Canaan. Nebo was one peak in this range. Verses 48–52 are similar to Num. 27:12–14 and probably came from the same tradition. They were not originally part of Deuteronomy but placed here to provide the book with a sequential arrangement. One may assume that the story of the death of Moses (chapter 34) was at first told at the end of Numbers.

50] *To your kin.* The plural form of עַם (*am*, people); an English equivalent would be "your folks."

Mount Hor. Its location is uncertain; some believe it to be near Petra; others, near Kadesh-barnea. Compare Num. 20:22 ff.

However, in Deut. 10:6 Aaron is reported to have died at Moserah. This may be a different tradition, or Moserah may have been a place in the area of Mount Hor.

51] *For you both broke faith.* This recalls the story told in Num. 20 where the failure of Moses and Aaron, during a rebellion, led God to pronounce the judgment of death on the two leaders (see commentary there). In Deut. 3:26 and 4:21 Moses ascribes the cause of his punishment not to his own doings but to Israel's sin; on this difference see commentary on chapter 3, above.

Wilderness of Zin. In the area of Kadesh-barnea.

The Poem—Its Setting

Like the Song at the Sea (Exod. 15), the poem of Deut. 32 is also called *Shirah* (Deut. 31:30), though it is more often referred to as *Ha-azinu* ("Give ear"), the opening Hebrew word. In the affection of subsequent generations it stood close to the former,[1] but, whereas the *Shirah* at the Reed Sea is most likely of ancient origin, *Ha-azinu* has a distinctly later setting.[2]

Israel appears to be well settled in the Land, the Exodus from Egypt lies in the distant past. At the Reed Sea, idolatry had not been an issue; here it is, for centuries of intimate contact with pagan peoples have led Israel to dilute its exclusive allegiance to the One God. Apparently, the nation has suffered a series of major disasters, which the poem, in prophetic fashion, explains as just punishments for Israel's sins. The song has its parallels in Psalms 78, 105, 106 and, in prose, in Ezekiel 20. An exact time for the composition cannot be fixed; on linguistic grounds one finds the writings of Jeremiah and Ezekiel most closely related. However, since the poem does not mention exile as one of Israel's misfortunes, one may assume that its composition preceded the destruction of the Northern Kingdom by the Assyrians and the subsequent exile of the Ten Tribes.

The matter is complicated by distinctly archaic expressions and unusual ideas, such as feeding Israel on curd and honey, or the people being found by God in the desert, or the nations being numbered according to Israel's hosts.

Structure of the Poem

Ancient Hebrew poetry does not know rhyme, though it does use assonance; it is characterized primarily by rhythm, meter, parallelism, and repetition. The forty-three verses of our poem are mostly two-liners, each with two parts, the second of which is parallel to and reinforces the content of the first. Most lines have three accents (though there are a few variations). The translation of the first line reflects the Hebrew rhythm:

> Give ear, O heaven, let me speak;
> Let the earth hear the words I utter.

According to Masoretic rule, the lines are written in a special way: each line contains two phrase-parts which are separated by a central space. In Torah manuscripts the poem is thus written in two columns, a somewhat simpler arrangement than that prescribed for the *Shirah* of Exod. 15 (see there).

The structure of the poem was discussed as early as in talmudic days. The Talmud divided it into six sections, but this was done in part to provide necessary divisions for the different readers who were called to the Torah. The divisions are verses 1–6, 7–12, 13–18, 19–28, 29–39, 40–43 and are remembered by the acrostic הזי״ו לך, the opening letters of each section.[3]

Our analysis [21] shows the following:

There is a prologue (1–3) and an epilogue (40–44). Between them stands the main body of the poem, its thirty-six verses falling into three parts of twelve verses each: 4–15, 16–27, 28–39. Verses 15 and 27 (which end the first two sections) are transitions to

---

[1] According to Maimonides, at least one of the two poems is to be recited at daily services [19].

[2] The "ancient origin" of Exod. 15 is, however, disputed by some scholars, and so is our rendering of

the background of Deut. 32. For instance, it has been suggested that the chapter reflects the fall of Samaria and that it belongs to exilic days.

[3] Readings 7 and 8 consist of verses 44–47 and 48–52, in the prose section which follows the poem [20].

what follows. The poem then has this structure:

1–3: prologue, calling on heaven and earth, and exalting God; 4–15: part 1, God's love for Israel; 16–27: part 2, Israel's ingratitude; 28–39: part 3, indictment of the nations and their eventual fate; 40–44: epilogue, heaven is again called as witness, and God is once more exalted.

The flow of the song is marked by a degree of repetition that gives it special intensity. Thus, the image of the discourse as life-giving rain appears four times in verse 2, as does the justice of God in verse 3. Six times in the poem the Lord is called Rock; there are no-children, no-gods, and no-folk, and the listener is strongly impressed that evil deeds will beget bitter consequences. The song has a triangular construction: its promises and warnings move between the three polarities of God, Israel, and the nations. Each depends on the actions and thoughts of the others; none—not even God himself—is seen as fully independent. In fact, this interdependence holds the poem together and almost demands that the heavens themselves become witnesses of Moses' rousing discourse.

The Ambivalence of God

At the heart of the poem stands an idea which, while not unique to the Bible, is here presented with special force. In the Torah it is expressed also in Gen. 6:5–7, and it is part of Hosea's thought (6:4; 11:8 f.). In these passages, as in the poem's verses 26–35, God is depicted as ambivalent about His course of action (note comment on verse 36). In Genesis, He is shown to have realized that the creation of humanity had been an error, and therefore He decided to destroy it—but not completely. Noah represents the door of compassion which God leaves open for himself. Hosea has God ask himself, "How can I give you up, O Ephraim? How surrender you, O Israel?" and then provides His own answer, "I have had a change of heart. . . . I will not act on My wrath."

In Moses' song, it is not compassion that motivates God; rather, it is His honor that must be protected. Israel is both endangered and saved because it is close to Him and is thereby involved in His needs as well. God must be seen to be God, and if Israel endangers His majesty it must suffer the consequences. At the same time, it will be rescued from perdition because God cannot allow Israel to be destroyed. The fate of the covenant people is thus forever hammered out on the anvil of history, for the ambivalence of the Divine Partner makes Israel the object both of love and of anger. The nations are the tools of God's action, but His goal is to create an evermore loyal and observant Israel. Thus does the song explain the relationship, and in the mouth of Moses it becomes a statement of fundamental belief [22].

GLEANINGS

Discourse and Speech

Of discourse, Moses says that it should come down as rain (that is, in abundance); but of speech, that it should "distill" (verse 2). Torah is discourse par excellence and it should be plentiful, but its teaching should be short and "distilled." Thus the Talmud says, "One should always teach with brevity."   ABARBANEL [23]

The ה

(Verse 6 begins with a ה which is detached from the word that follows.) This ה is the end of Moses' signature. If one takes the first letters of verses 1–6 (ה, י, כ, ה, ש, ה), they add up to 345 by way of gematria which represents the value of the letters in Moses' name (משה). In this way Moses affixed his name to the book, ending his "signature" with the detached ה.

MIDRASH [24]

Dull and Witless People (verse 6)

Why are two adjectives used to describe Israel's folly? Note the distinction Jeremiah makes when he says (16:11): "They deserted Me and did not keep My commandments," on which the Talmud elaborates by having God say: "Would that they forsook Me but kept My Torah, for its light would lead them to return to Me [25]. But if they are without Torah who will lead them back?"

This is what Moses meant: "Dull"—without knowledge of God; and "witless" (or wisdomless)—without the redeeming wisdom of Torah.

CHAFETZ CHAYIM [26]

Another interpretation: Targum Onkelos interprets "dull and witless people" as a nation that received the Torah but did not thereby become wise. Now the Midrash uses the word נָבָל (na-val, dull) to mean "inferior variety" and says: Death, prophecy, and divine wisdom have inferior varieties. Sleep resembles but is not like death, and so are dreams an inferior reflection of prophecy, and Torah of divine wisdom [27]. Hence a people that is naval is one that though it has received Torah falls short of divine wisdom and is לֹא חָכָם (lo chacham, witless).   THE GAON OF VILNA [28]

Ask Your Father (verse 7)

This verse was used as a proof text to support the words "who has commanded us to kindle the Chanukah lights." Whence do we know that God commanded us to do this? From this verse, for your father (and your teachers) will tell you of God's miracles and thereby will obligate you.

TALMUD [29]

In Relation to Israel's Numbers (verse 8)

The plain text was taken to mean that the seventy nations who peopled the earth were a macro-image of the seventy souls whom Jacob brought to Egypt [30].

Like an Eagle (verse 11)

The simile has its foundation in the habits of the bird.

Two parent eagles were teaching their offspring, two young birds, the maneuvers of flight. Rising from the top of a mountain, they at first made small circles and the young imitated them; they paused on their wings waiting till they had made their first flight, holding them on their expanded wings when they appeared exhausted, and then took a second and larger gyration, always rising toward the sun, and enlarging their

circle of flight, so as to make a gradually ascending spiral.   S. D. DRIVER [31]

Jeshurun Grew Fat and Kicked (verse 15)

Generally, Jeshurun is an attribute of praise, indicating a higher rung of Israel's striving. That is the problem: when Israel reaches the rung where it is worthy of being called Jeshurun, it becomes proud and kicks.   CHASIDIC [32]

No-gods (verse 21)

They are called perverse because they turn God's good will into anger.   RASHI

Another interpretation: Israel perverts אֵל (God) into its opposite לֹא (no) and therefore is called "a treacherous breed" (verse 20), literally a perverse breed that turns everything upside down, like אֵל into לֹא.   CHASIDIC [33]

Promise and Fulfillment

In the beginning, at the burning bush, God said (Exod. 3:14): "I will be what I will be,"[4] meaning "I will redeem you from slavery and bring you into your own land." Now, in sight of the Promised Land, He speaks in the present tense, as the God who has fulfilled His promise: "I, I am He" (verse 39).   CHATAM SOFER [34]

An Ascent

In bidding Moses to prepare for death, God says to him, "Ascend these heights" (verse 48), for it was to be a true ascent for Moses, not a descent.   MIDRASH [35]

---

[4] This is one of the understandings of that verse, based on the construction of אֶהְיֶה אֲשֶׁר אֶהְיֶה in what appears to be the future tense (see commentary on Exod. 3).

The Blessing of Moses

Jacob had blessed his sons before his death (Gen. 49), and, in the tradition of Jacob, so does Moses now bless his people. He looks at each tribe and prays for its well-being in the light of its characteristics, inclinations, and capacities. The blessing, a poem like Jacob's testament, is both prayer and prophecy. A comparison of these two blessings, as well as a consideration of the age of the poem, will be found below, in the commentary.

The blessing is quite unlike the song of Moses that precedes it (in chapter 32). There, God stood at the center; here, it is Israel that commands the hearer's attention. The song directed itself forcefully to the danger of idolatry and to God's ensuing wrath; the blessing overlooks both subjects entirely. The song soared in exciting and memorable phrases; the blessing, in comparison, is a calm assessment of Israel's past and future. In Hebrew manuscripts the blessing is set in prose form, yet its sentences clearly display a poetic rhythm. Its language has an antique flavor; some of its words are either rare or unique in the Bible; and a number of phrases are obscure and the text is not always in order. The structure of the blessing is as follows: verse 1: superscription; verses 2–5: establishing the blessing's foundation—God's kingship over Israel; verses 6–25: the catalogue of blessings; verses 26–29: conclusion, which returns to the beginning in that it extols God, the Protector of Israel.

Because verses 2–5 and 26–29 contain no blessings, some scholars have

suggested that these phrases did not originally form a part of the text. However, as in a covenant (on which the blessings are ultimately founded), an exordium and a matching conclusion are necessary. They frame the main text perfectly, and there is no convincing reason to suppose them to be later additions.

(Chapter 33 begins the Torah's last weekly portion, *Vezot ha-Berachah*, so called after the opening words.)

קָדְשָׁיו בְּיָדֶךָ וְהֵם תֻּכּוּ לְרַגְלֶךָ יִשָּׂא מִדַּבְּרֹתֶיךָ:
ד תּוֹרָה צִוָּה־לָנוּ מֹשֶׁה מוֹרָשָׁה קְהִלַּת יַעֲקֹב:
ה וַיְהִי בִישֻׁרוּן מֶלֶךְ בְּהִתְאַסֵּף רָאשֵׁי עָם יַחַד שִׁבְטֵי
י יִשְׂרָאֵל: יְחִי רְאוּבֵן וְאַל־יָמֹת וִיהִי מְתָיו מִסְפָּר: ס

‏ב תרין פילין קרי‎.

‏פ פ פ‎

א וְזֹאת הַבְּרָכָה אֲשֶׁר בֵּרַךְ מֹשֶׁה אִישׁ הָאֱלֹהִים אֶת־
ב בְּנֵי יִשְׂרָאֵל לִפְנֵי מוֹתוֹ: וַיֹּאמַר יְהֹוָה מִסִּינַי בָּא
וְזָרַח מִשֵּׂעִיר לָמוֹ הוֹפִיעַ מֵהַר פָּארָן וְאָתָה מֵרִבְבֹת
ג קֹדֶשׁ מִימִינוֹ אֵשׁ דָּת לָמוֹ: אַף חֹבֵב עַמִּים כָּל־

1] This is the blessing with which Moses, the man of God, bade the Israelites farewell before he died. **2]** He said: The LORD came from Sinai; / He shone upon them from Seir; / He appeared from Mount Paran, / And approached from Ribeboth-kodesh, / Lightning flashing at them from His right. / **3]** Lover, indeed, of the people, / Their hallowed are all in Your hand. / They followed in Your steps, / Accepting Your pronouncements, / **4]** When Moses charged us with the Teaching / As the heritage of the congregation of Jacob. / **5]** Then He became King in Jeshurun, / When the heads of the people assembled, / The tribes of Israel together.

6] May Reuben live and not die, / Though few be his numbers.

33:1] *The man of God.* The expression occurs nowhere else in the Torah, but it does in Josh. 14:6, Psalms 90:1, Ezra 3:2, I Chron. 23:14, and II Chron. 30:16, in reference to Moses and in reference to others repeatedly in the rest of the Bible.

2] *Came from Sinai.* To reveal himself. Sinai was, so to speak, "God's mountain."

Seir . . . Mount Paran. Mountain ranges adjacent to the Negev. As the sun rises over the mountains so does God's glory rise over Israel.

Ribeboth-kodesh. A place otherwise unknown. With the Septuagint, one should probably read Meribath-kadesh, which occurs a few verses earlier, in 32:51, and provides a good parallel to Seir and Paran.

Lightning flashing. The Masorah ruled that the single word אֵשְׁדָּת be read as two words אֵשׁ דָּת, but the meaning is thereby not made any clearer. Probably, we have here another place name, in parallel with Seir, Paran, and Meribath-kadesh (Ribeboth-kodesh).

From His right. The right hand denotes strength, as in Exod. 15:6, "Your right hand, O Lord, glorious in power, Your right hand, O Lord, shatters the foe!"

Lover, indeed. Verses 3–5 are obscure, and many emendations have been offered to make sense out of what is evidently a corrupt text [1]. The above translation apostrophizes God; another possibility is to take Moses as the one who is called lover of his people [2]. Such an understanding would produce a better meaning: "O lover of the people, all His (God's) holy ones were in your care; they followed in your footsteps, accepted your pronouncements. Then the Torah with which Moses charged us became the heritage of the congregation of Jacob, and he (Moses) became king in Jeshurun, when the heads of the people assembled the tribes of Israel together."

4] *Moses charged us.* The phrase entered the Jewish prayer book. In the Ashkenazic *siddur* it is part of the child's morning prayer, in the Sephardic and Reform rituals, it is recited during the Torah service.

In *Gates of Prayer*, however, the text is changed to read: "The Torah commanded us by God through Moses. . . ." [3].

5] *Jeshurun.* See at 32:15.

6] *May Reuben live.* Reuben was Jacob's first-born and came first also in the Patriarch's testament (Gen. 49:3). This blessing lacks the introduction provided for the others. A line such as "Of Reuben he said" probably preceded it. For the meaning and historical setting, see commentary below.

ז וְזֹאת לִיהוּדָה֒ וַיֹּאמַר֒ שְׁמַ֤ע יְהֹוָה֙ ק֣וֹל יְהוּדָ֔ה וְאֶל־
עַמּ֖וֹ תְּבִיאֶ֑נּוּ יָדָיו֙ רָ֣ב ל֔וֹ וְעֵ֥זֶר מִצָּרָ֖יו תִּהְיֶֽה׃ פ

ח וּלְלֵוִ֣י אָמַ֔ר תֻּמֶּ֥יךָ וְאוּרֶ֖יךָ לְאִ֣ישׁ חֲסִידֶ֑ךָ אֲשֶׁ֤ר

ט נִסִּיתוֹ֙ בְּמַסָּ֔ה תְּרִיבֵ֖הוּ עַל־מֵ֣י מְרִיבָֽה׃ הָאֹמֵ֞ר לְאָבִ֤יו
וּלְאִמּוֹ֙ לֹ֣א רְאִיתִ֔יו וְאֶת־אֶחָיו֙ לֹ֣א הִכִּ֔יר וְאֶת־בָּנָ֖ו

לֹ֣א יָדָ֔ע כִּ֤י שָֽׁמְרוּ֙ אִמְרָתֶ֔ךָ וּבְרִיתְךָ֖ יִנְצֹֽרוּ׃ יוֹר֤וּ
מִשְׁפָּטֶ֙יךָ֙ לְיַעֲקֹ֔ב וְתוֹרָתְךָ֖ לְיִשְׂרָאֵ֑ל יָשִׂ֤ימוּ קְטוֹרָה֙
יא בְּאַפֶּ֔ךָ וְכָלִ֖יל עַל־מִזְבְּחֶ֑ךָ בָּרֵ֤ךְ יְהֹוָה֙ חֵיל֔וֹ וּפֹ֥עַל
יָדָ֖יו תִּרְצֶ֑ה מְחַ֤ץ מָתְנַ֙יִם֙ קָמָ֔יו וּמְשַׂנְאָ֖יו מִן־יְקוּמֽוּן׃ ס

ט בניו קרי

7] And this he said of Judah: / Hear, O LORD, the voice of Judah / And restore him to his people. / Though his own hands strive for him, / Help him against his foes.

8] And of Levi he said: / Let Your Thummim and Urim / Be with Your faithful one, / Whom You tested at Massah, / Challenged at the waters of Meribah; **9]** Who said of his father and mother, / "I consider them not." / His brothers he disregarded, / Ignored his own children / Your precepts alone they observed, / And kept Your covenant. / **10]** They shall teach Your norms to Jacob / And Your instructions to Israel. / They shall offer You incense to savor / And whole-offerings on Your altar. / **11]** Bless, O LORD, his substance, / And favor his undertakings. / Smite the loins of his foes; / Let his enemies rise no more.

7] *His own hands.* If רָב is understood as an imperative, a better reading emerges: "Strengthen his hands for him"; for the verse is clearly meant as a plea to other tribes for greater support of a weakened or perhaps separated tribe (see below).

It is possible, however, that the first part of verse 7 once referred to Simeon (who has no blessing at all) [4], and the second part (perhaps plus verse 11) to Judah. Later, after Simeon had been absorbed into Judah, its name was dropped from the blessing.

8] *Thummim and Urim.* Oracular devices, usually named in reverse order (Exod. 28:30; Lev. 8:8). Neither their origin nor the meaning of the terms is known. The devices were stones carried by the High Priest and the blind choice of one of them was believed to reveal God's will. With the rise of prophecy they gradually fell into disuse; see details in our commentary on Exod. 28.

The hope which Moses expresses is that the devices, which are in Levi's (the priestly tribe's) charge, might be truly effective.

Whom You tested. The note about the waters of Massah ("test") and Meribah ("strife") is apparently a reference to the incident reported in Exod. 17. But there it was the people of Israel who tested God. Perhaps Moses' recollection indicates that the Levites (who are not mentioned in the Exodus passage) had been part of the rebellious multitude but later became God's staunchest servants (see verse 9).

Driver suggests that the Massah-Meribah episode of the blessing has another event in mind which was not reported in the Torah [5]. The text has word plays on both Massah and Meribah.

9] *I consider them not.* Meaning that, in their utter devotion to God, they slew defectors in the golden calf episode without regard to family association (Exod. 32:27 ff.).

10] *They shall teach.* The Levites had both ritual and educational functions. The latter were in post-biblical times taken over first by scribes and then by rabbis.

Incense to savor. Literally, "they shall place incense in Your nostril" (cf. Gen. 8:21), an anthropomorphism quite acceptable in biblical times and experienced in the same fashion as references to God's eye or ear. There was an altar for offering incense and another for bringing sacrifices.

11] *Smite the loins.* This does not seem to fit the Levites. The whole verse may have belonged to a blessing directed to Judah; see above, at verse 7.

טו לְבִנְיָמִ֣ן אָמַ֔ר יְדִ֣יד יְהֹוָ֔ה יִשְׁכֹּ֥ן לָבֶ֖טַח עָלָ֑יו חֹפֵ֤ף יִ יָֽרְחִֽים: וּמֵרֹ֖אשׁ הַרְרֵי־קֶ֑דֶם וּמִמֶּ֖גֶד גִּבְע֥וֹת עוֹלָֽם:
יג עָלָיו֙ כָּל־הַיּ֔וֹם וּבֵ֥ין כְּתֵפָ֖יו שָׁכֵֽן: ס וּלְיוֹסֵ֣ף אָמַ֔ר טו וּמִמֶּ֗גֶד אֶ֙רֶץ֙ וּמְלֹאָ֔הּ וּרְצ֥וֹן שֹֽׁכְנִ֖י סְנֶ֑ה תָּב֙וֹאתָה֙
מְבֹרֶ֥כֶת יְהֹוָ֖ה אַרְצ֑וֹ מִמֶּ֤גֶד שָׁמַ֙יִם֙ מִטָּ֔ל וּמִתְּה֖וֹם יז לְרֹ֣אשׁ יוֹסֵ֔ף וּלְקָדְקֹ֖ד נְזִ֣יר אֶחָ֑יו: בְּכ֨וֹר שׁוֹר֜וֹ הָדָ֣ר
יד רֹבֶ֥צֶת תָּֽחַת: וּמִמֶּ֛גֶד תְּבוּאֹ֥ת שָׁ֑מֶשׁ וּמִמֶּ֖גֶד גֶּ֥רֶשׁ ל֗וֹ וְקַרְנֵ֤י רְאֵם֙ קַרְנָ֔יו בָּהֶ֗ם עַמִּ֛ים יְנַגַּ֥ח יַחְדָּ֖ו אַפְסֵי־

12] Of Benjamin he said: / Beloved of the LORD, / He rests securely beside Him; / Ever does He protect him, / As he rests between His shoulders.

13] And of Joseph he said: / Blessed of the LORD be his land / With the bounty of dew from heaven, / And of the deep that couches below; / **14]** With the bounteous yield of the sun, / And the bounteous crop of the moons; / **15]** With the best from the ancient mountains, / And the bounty of hills immemorial; / **16]** With the bounty of earth and its fullness, / And the favor of the Presence in the Bush. / May these rest on the head of Joseph, / On the crown of the elect of his brothers. / **17]** Like a firstling bull in his majesty, / He has horns like the horns of the wild-ox; / With them he gores the peoples, / The ends of the earth one and all. / These are

12] *Benjamin . . . beloved of the Lord.* So called because Jerusalem was located in its territory. Thus God "dwells amid his (Benjamin's) slopes"—a translation preferable to "he (Benjamin) rests between His (God's) shoulders."

According to aggadic tradition, the courts of the Temple were located in the allotted territory of Judah, the Temple itself in Benjamin's. At the time of the division of the land, Jerusalem had belonged to the Jebusites, and after its conquest by David it straddled the border between the two tribes [6]. The text has a better meaning if חֹפֵף ("protect") is understood as "spread His wings"; creating the image that God, like an eagle guarding its young, has Benjamin rest between His shoulders; see this simile in 32:11 [7].

13] *Dew from heaven.* A better reading (following the Targum and Hebrew manuscripts) would substitute מֵעַל ("from above") for מִטַּל ("with dew"). The text would then say: "With the bounty of heaven above," which would be similar to the blessing bestowed on Joseph by Jacob (Gen. 49:25).

Deep that couches. The subterranean waters re pictured as a monster; תְּהוֹם (tehom, deep) re-lls the dragon Tiamat of Mesopotamian lore our commentary on Gen. 1:2 and Gleanings eon).

14] *Yield of the sun.* On whose warmth the harvest depends [8]. New English Bible translates: "ripened by the sun."

Crop of the moons. That is, of the changing seasons; but it is possible that the expression reflects a belief in the power of the moon to influence some crops [9].

15] *Hills immemorial.* Or, "everlasting hills," an image also found in Jacob's blessing (Gen. 49:26).

16] *Presence in the Bush.* Or, "Dweller in the Bush," a reference to Moses' perceiving God as speaking out of the burning bush (Exod. 3:1 ff.). The catalogue of nature's blessings (verses 13–15) is climaxed by the privilege of God's presence.

Rest on the head of Joseph. This and the remainder of the verse are almost identical with Gen. 49:26.

For this reason, too, תָּבוֹאתָה (tavotah, "rest on" or "come upon"), which has no grammatical precedent, should be altered to תִּהְיֶין (tiheyena, "shall be") as in Gen. 49:26.

17] *Firstling bull.* An image of strength. The Canaanite chief deity was called "Bull-El."

Horns of the wild-ox. The re-em was a large-horned species (aurochs) which has since become

בָּרוּךְ מַרְחִיב גָּד כְּלָבִיא שָׁכֵן וְטָרַף זְרוֹעַ אַף־ אֶרֶץ וְהֵם רִבְבוֹת אֶפְרַיִם וְהֵם אַלְפֵי מְנַשֶּׁה: ס
כא קָדְקֹד: וַיַּרְא רֵאשִׁית לוֹ כִּי־שָׁם חֶלְקַת מְחֹקֵק יח וְלִזְבוּלֻן אָמַר שְׂמַח זְבוּלֻן בְּצֵאתֶךָ וְיִשָּׂשכָר בְּאֹהָלֶיךָ:
סָפוּן וַיֵּתֵא רָאשֵׁי עָם צִדְקַת יְהוָה עָשָׂה וּמִשְׁפָּטָיו יט עַמִּים הַר־יִקְרָאוּ שָׁם יִזְבְּחוּ זִבְחֵי־צֶדֶק כִּי שֶׁפַע
כב עִם־יִשְׂרָאֵל: ס וּלְדָן אָמַר דָּן גּוּר אַרְיֵה יְזַנֵּק יַמִּים יִינָקוּ וּשְׂפֻנֵי טְמוּנֵי חוֹל: ס וּלְגָד אָמַר כ

the myriads of Ephraim, / Those are the thousands of Manasseh.

18] And of Zebulun he said: / Rejoice, O Zebulun, on your journeys, / And Issachar, in your tents. / **19]** They invite their kin to the mountain, / Where they offer sacrifices of success. / For they draw from the riches of the sea / And the hidden hoards of the sand.

20] And of Gad he said: / Blessed be He who enlarges Gad! / Poised is he like a lion / To tear off arm and scalp. / **21]** He chose for himself the best, / For there is the portion of the revered chieftain, / Where the heads of the people come. / He executed the LORD's judgments / And His decisions for Israel.

22] And of Dan he said: / Dan is a lion's whelp / That leaps forth from Bashan.

extinct. Its strength is described in Job 39:9–12. The Psalmist sings (92:11): "You raise my horn high like that of a wild-ox."

These . . . those. Each brother is represented by one of the horns.

18] *On your journeys.* On your voyages by ship; Zebulun's territory lay along the sea (compare Gen. 49:13).

Issachar, in your tents. Issachar was profitably engaged in agriculture, but in Gen. 49:14–15 its life of ease is criticized.

Later Jewish tradition took "tents" to mean "Torah"; in the same way as Balaam's blessing was interpreted: "How fair are your tents, O Jacob" (Num. 24:5) [10].

19] *They invite their kin.* עַמִּים (amim) could also mean "(other) peoples." Both Zebulun and Issachar were rich and apparently celebrated their success with an annual festivity to which kin or other neighboring people were invited.

To the mountain. Perhaps Mount Carmel or Mount Tabor.

Tradition took this to be a reference to the Temple mount in Jerusalem [11].

Sea . . . sand. The Jerusalem Targum speculates that part of their enterprises consisted of producing a much desired purple dye from mussels, and of making glass from the sand. Such glass

making is attested to by Josephus as well as Greek and Roman sources [12].

20] *Enlarges Gad.* Which had its extensive territories east of the Jordan.

Like a lion. In I Chron. 12:9 the Gadites are described as "mighty men of valor, men trained for war, that could handle shield and spear; whose faces were like the faces of lions. . . ."

21] The verse is obscure and all translations are speculative. The sense seems to be that Gad obtained an extra portion because of its devotion to God, and because it helped Israel in its conquest of Canaan after having obtained its own land at an earlier time (Num. 32; Josh. 22).

"The revered chieftain" was by tradition taken to be Moses, and "the portion" a reference to his unknown burial place [13].

22] *Dan is a lion's whelp.* In Jacob's blessing Judah is so described (Gen. 49:9), while Dan is compared to a serpent (49:17). Both lion and serpent attack suddenly. Dan's chief city was Laish, a poetic name for "lion."

Leaps forth from Bashan. An area east of Lake Kinneret. The story of Dan's settlement is told in Judg. 18. The Song of Songs (4:8) speaks of lion's dens in the area of Mount Hermon.

כג מִן־הַבָּשָׁן: וּלְנַפְתָּלִי אָמַר נַפְתָּלִי שְׂבַע רָצוֹן וּמָלֵא   כח אוֹיֵב וַיֹּאמֶר הַשְׁמֵד: וַיִּשְׁכֹּן יִשְׂרָאֵל בֶּטַח בָּדָד
כד בִּרְכַּת יְהוָה יָם וְדָרוֹם יְרָשָׁה: ס וּלְאָשֵׁר אָמַר   עֵין יַעֲקֹב אֶל־אֶרֶץ דָּגָן וְתִירוֹשׁ אַף־שָׁמָיו יַעַרְפוּ
בָּרוּךְ מִבָּנִים אָשֵׁר יְהִי רְצוּי אֶחָיו וְטֹבֵל בַּשֶּׁמֶן   כט טָל: אַשְׁרֶיךָ יִשְׂרָאֵל מִי כָמוֹךָ עַם נוֹשַׁע בַּיהוָה
כה רַגְלוֹ: בַּרְזֶל וּנְחֹשֶׁת מִנְעָלֶךָ וּכְיָמֶיךָ דָּבְאֶךָ:   מָגֵן עֶזְרֶךָ וַאֲשֶׁר־חֶרֶב גַּאֲוָתֶךָ וְיִכָּחֲשׁוּ אֹיְבֶיךָ לָךְ
כו אֵין כָּאֵל יְשֻׁרוּן רֹכֵב שָׁמַיִם בְּעֶזְרֶךָ וּבְגַאֲוָתוֹ שְׁחָקִים: וְאַתָּה עַל־בָּמוֹתֵימוֹ תִדְרֹךְ: ס
כז מְעֹנָה אֱלֹהֵי קֶדֶם וּמִתַּחַת זְרֹעֹת עוֹלָם וַיְגָרֶשׁ מִפָּנֶיךָ

23] And of Naphtali he said: / O Naphtali, sated with favor / And full of the LORD's blessing, / Take possession on the west and south.

24] And of Asher he said: / Most blessed of sons be Asher; / May he be the favorite of his brothers, / May he dip his foot in oil. / **25]** May your doorbolts be iron and copper, / And your security last all your days. / **26]** O Jeshurun, there is none like God, / Riding through the heavens to help you, / Through the skies in His majesty. / **27]** The ancient God is a refuge, / A support are the arms everlasting. / He drove out the enemy before you / By His command: Destroy! / **28]** Thus Israel dwells in safety, / Untroubled is Jacob's abode, / In a land of grain and wine, / Under heavens dripping dew. / **29]** O happy Israel! Who is like you, / A people delivered by the LORD, / Your protecting Shield, your Sword triumphant! / Your enemies shall come cringing before you, / And you shall tread on their backs.

23] *West and south.* Of Lake Kinneret, that is, the upper and lower Galilee. The Valley of Jezreel was then and is today the country's bread basket.

24] *Asher.* The name itself connotes happiness; see verse 29 and Ps. 1:1, "Happy is the man. . . ."

Dip his foot in oil. Olive trees abounded in Galilee.

A popular saying was: "It is easier to raise olives in Galilee than a child in the Land of Israel" [14].

25] *Your doorbolts.* The translation of this verse is speculative, although it seems clear that Moses' blessing hopes to secure Asher from the attack of enemies.

26] *Riding through the heavens.* Compare Ps. 68:34, ". . . who rides the ancient highest heavens," an expression with parallels in Ugaritic literature [15].

27] *A support are the arms everlasting.* Similar to the older translations which had "underneath are the everlasting arms." But the meaning of the whole verse is not certain, and various emendations have been proposed which yield quite different interpretations.

In the traditional ritual of the synagogue, this verse begins the last annual reading from the Torah, which takes place on Simchat Torah. The person given the honor of reciting the blessings over it is called *Chatan Torah* (Bridegroom of the Torah).

28] *Untroubled is Jacob's abode.* Or, "Jacob's fountain." Note that the word "untroubled" (Hebrew בָּדָד, *badad*) has the basic meaning "apart," isolation being regarded as an assurance of survival. (See also above, at 33:12.)

Ein Yaacov ("Fountain of Jacob") is the title of a well-known collection of tales and interpretations culled from the Talmud.

29] *Tread on their backs.* Literally, "on their high places," that is, you will triumph over them [16].

Comparisons

Three times in the Bible the nature and fate of the tribes are the subject of poetic creation: in the testament of Jacob (Gen. 49), in the blessing of Moses (Deut. 33), in the song of Deborah (Judg. 5). The blessing ascribed to Moses and its historic setting will be understood more clearly if one compares it with the passages in Genesis and Judges.

Name of Tribe and Location	Genesis Chapter 49	Judges Chapter 5	Deuteronomy Chapter 33
Reuben East of Jordan, near Dead Sea	First-born; powerful, but no longer the leader	Indifferent to national crisis, though not without internal conflict	Near extinction
Simeon Central Negev	Described as violent; in danger of being scattered	No mention (Josh. 15:26 ff. shows that Simeonite cities are now absorbed into Judah; cf. Josh. 19:1-7)	No mention
Judah Northern Negev	The leading tribe; strong; seat of kings	No mention	Weak, separated from rest of people; in need of help[1]
Levi No territory	Behavior condemned; priesthood not mentioned	No mention	Praise for its courage and priestly role (which, however, is not yet assured)
Benjamin Jerusalem and north	Warlike; a "ravenous wolf"	Supported Deborah	Beloved; secure; wars are over
Joseph[2] Highlands around Samaria; half of Manasseh lies east of Jordan	Strong; blessed by God	Leading contributor to Deborah's victory	Blessed greatly; strong

[1] But see commentary above, at verse 7.
[2] In Genesis and Deuteronomy, Ephraim and Manasseh are represented by their eponymous father, Joseph.

Name of Tribe and Location	Genesis Chapter 49	Judges Chapter 5	Deuteronomy Chapter 33
Zebulun Western Jezreel, reaching to the sea	Seafaring	Holds marshal's staff; risked its life for Israel	Seafaring; successful
Issachar Eastern Jezreel	Rich lands; criticized for serving others	Supported Deborah	Agricultural; successful; not criticized
Gad East of Jordan	Strongest tribe east of Jordan, involved in warfare	Called "Gilead"; did not support Deborah	Highly praised; warlike; expansionist
Dan Originally south of Jaffa, but migrated to northernmost Galilee	Aggressive; "shall judge his people" (possibly a reference to Samson)	Did not support Deborah; went on sea expedition instead	Aggressive; strong (possible reference to Samson)
Naphtali Northern Galilee, along Lake Kinneret	Compared to a roaming hind with fawns	Praised for its contribution	Rich; "sated with favor"
Asher Southern and western Galilee	Rich	No mention	"Most blessed"; rich olive orchards; but needs secure borders

Analysis

As explained in our commentary on Gen. 49, the testament of Jacob came probably from the time of the Judges, before 1000 B.C.E., not too far removed from the particular events that gave rise to the song of Deborah. The tribes were already in Canaan but neither securely settled nor as yet united into a nation; they differed widely from one another and seem to have been bound together by faith rather than blood. The sup-

position of a common ancestry served to strengthen their still tenuous ties.

In contrast, the blessing ascribed to Moses originated in an era of greater security, which would place it several centuries later, after the monarchy had been established. Intertribal rivalries are not mentioned; no criticism is leveled against any tribe; nor is idolatry an issue. Israel is now a nation, and God—who is not mentioned in Jacob's blessing—is exalted as the people's savior, and

because of Him Israel's future looks bright. This makes it probable that the poem was a hymn of national thanksgiving, perhaps recited at some ritual function, and later put into the mouth of Moses and appended to the Book of Deuteronomy.

The words spoken about Judah may give us a further key to the blessing's location in history. The tribe of Judah (which by this time had incorporated Simeon) had become separated from the rest of the nation,[3] which may be a reference to the division of the united kingdom after the death of Solomon. The song was sung in Judah and was in part a plea to the north to reunite the nation. It may have been about 900 B.C.E., a time when the Levites had already assumed an important place in the cultic system. Not unlike a prophecy, the blessing is the bearer of future hopes. Placed in the mouth of Moses it becomes "much more than an empty wish; it contains creative words which are capable of fashioning the future" [17].

For unknown reasons, the blessing suffered considerably in its early stages of transmission, resulting in a number of textual corruptions that add to the already difficult text with its antique poetic language. The poem has none of the fervor of the song of Moses; rather, it speaks to a community which on the whole enjoys material prosperity and is still secure in its relation to God. Idolatrous practices have not as yet roused the poet's ire, as they have in the song. The latter comes to us from a subsequent age when disaster had overtaken the nation—a far cry from the fairly idyllic picture drawn in the blessing.

---

[3] Reading verse 7 as we have it now.

GLEANINGS

From Criticism to Praise

(The interpretations that follow are based on the traditional assumption that Moses himself authored the blessing.)

Moses had always rebuked his people, but in the end he gives them words of hope. The Prophets learned from him.   MIDRASH [18]

Another explanation: One should connect Deut. 1:1 ("These are the words...") with 33:1 ("This is the blessing..."). Moses begins with "These are the words" (of criticism and exhortation) and ends with "This is the blessing" (containing only praise). This teaches that even in Moses' harshest words was contained the promise of blessing.

M. HACOHEN [19]

Why does Moses speak of himself as "the man of God"? To indicate that, though he spoke the blessing, the inspiration came from God.

S. R. HIRSCH [20]

Another explanation: Up 'til now Moses had been very humble, but when about to die he felt that future generations would not know who he was. He therefore reasoned: "If not now, when?"   CHASIDIC [21]

Another explanation: God had said to Moses that the hour of his death had come (31:14). Then Moses said: "All these years I have rebuked Israel, I want to leave them with a blessing." Thereupon Satan came and tried to prevent him, but Moses cast him down and blessed Israel despite him.

MIDRASH [22]

Only Israel

"The Lord came from Sinai... Seir... Paran" (verse 2). This is a reminder that the Torah was offered also to other nations who, however, refused it when they heard some of its laws. Only Israel accepted, and unconditionally so.

MIDRASH [23]

Another explanation: God spoke "from Sinai" in Hebrew; "from Seir" in Latin; "from Mount Paran" in Arabic; "from Ribeboth-kodesh" in Aramaic. For God offered the Torah to all nations.

MIDRASH [24]

The Threefold Cord

"This..." in verse 1 refers to the Torah, which is in itself a blessing. Why then does the text go on to speak of God and Moses? To indicate that all three participated in the blessing, and to bear out what Koheleth said (Eccles. 4:12): "A three-fold cord is not quickly broken."

MIDRASH [25]

Friendship

The Sages warn us that one should not try a friend too much, lest envy or even hatred ensue. One exception to this rule is God: His friends will always "rest securely beside Him" (verse 12).

A. I. KOOK [26]

The Portion of the Revered Chieftain (verse 21)

This refers to the grave of Moses, for, though Moses died on Mount Nebo (which is in the terri-

tory of Reuben), the angels transferred him to the portion of Gad and the Lord buried him there. The grave of Moses was one of the ten things created by God on the sixth day of Creation, at dusk, before the Sabbath [27].

MIDRASH [28]

Alone

(Taking בָּדָד, in verse 28, to mean "alone" rather than "untroubled.") Other nations rely on treaties for their safety. Israel is not secured in this way, but only by its trust in God.

M. HACOHEN [29]

PART V

Epilogue

THE DEATH OF MOSES

End and Beginning

The brief last chapter of Deuteronomy reports the death of the great leader. God shows him the Land of Promise, and the viewing of the land is both a vision of the future and an assurance that the faithful God will carry out what He swore to the Ancestors. The Torah concludes with the passing of Moses, but in the person of his successor the forward thrust of Israel's history is secured. While Joshua is not another Moses—"Never again did there arise in Israel a prophet like Moses" (verse 10)—he will be a competent leader for changing times. The only constant is God himself; because of Him the end of one era is at once the beginning of a new one. Generations may change, the God of the covenant remains the same.

In tone and style, the final verses of the book are bereft of the emotion that had erupted in the song of Moses, and neither do they contain the imagery of the blessing. The account is straightforward, and the final judgment of Moses' greatness speaks merely in terms of comparison: he was, and will remain, superior to all others who are gifted with prophecy; but the nature of his greatness will have to be culled from his life's story, not from a final assessment.

Traditional opinions varied on the authorship of chapter 34. According to one, the whole Torah was written by Moses, including all the last chapter; according to another, Joshua wrote verses 5–12; while Ibn Ezra assigned all the chapter to Joshua. He advanced two reasons: the use of the third person in chapter 34 and the silence of the text on any final return of Moses from the mountain [1]. This bold assertion later on helped to

open the door for those who doubted the Mosaic authorship of other passages as well.

Modern scholars, too, though arguing from different premises, are divided on the authorship of these verses, which may at one time have stood at the end of Numbers or followed after Deut. 32:52 (the blessing being a later insertion into the text; see above, commentary on ch. 33) [2]. But such an investigation into the literary origins of the chapter is likely to remain inconclusive. For a variety of traditions have here been brought together, and this amalgam forms in itself a fitting conclusion to the Torah as we now have it in its totality. For, though the whole book was the product of different times and sources, it became in the course of centuries one book, the repository of Israel's faith and of its struggle with and for God. The final chapter now concludes this one great story or, rather, the story of its genesis and growth. The future will unfold new chapters, and the Book of Joshua will begin their recitation.

וַיַּעַל מֹשֶׁה מֵעַרְבֹת מוֹאָב אֶל־הַר נְבוֹ רֹאשׁ הַפִּסְגָּה אֲשֶׁר עַל־פְּנֵי יְרֵחוֹ וַיַּרְאֵהוּ יְהֹוָה אֶת־כָּל־הָאָרֶץ אֶת־ הַגִּלְעָד עַד־דָּן: וְאֵת כָּל־נַפְתָּלִי וְאֶת־אֶרֶץ אֶפְרַיִם וּמְנַשֶּׁה וְאֵת כָּל־אֶרֶץ יְהוּדָה עַד הַיָּם הָאַחֲרוֹן: וְאֶת־הַנֶּגֶב וְאֶת־הַכִּכָּר בִּקְעַת יְרֵחוֹ עִיר הַתְּמָרִים

עַד־צֹעַר: וַיֹּאמֶר יְהֹוָה אֵלָיו זֹאת הָאָרֶץ אֲשֶׁר נִשְׁבַּעְתִּי לְאַבְרָהָם לְיִצְחָק וּלְיַעֲקֹב לֵאמֹר לְזַרְעֲךָ אֶתְּנֶנָּה הֶרְאִיתִיךָ בְעֵינֶיךָ וְשָׁמָּה לֹא תַעֲבֹר: וַיָּמָת שָׁם מֹשֶׁה עֶבֶד־יְהֹוָה בְּאֶרֶץ מוֹאָב עַל־פִּי יְהֹוָה: וַיִּקְבֹּר אֹתוֹ בַגַּי בְּאֶרֶץ מוֹאָב מוּל בֵּית פְּעוֹר וְלֹא־

1] Moses went up from the steppes of Moab to Mount Nebo, to the summit of Pisgah, opposite Jericho, and the LORD showed him the whole land: Gilead as far as Dan; 2] all Naphtali; the land of Ephraim and Manasseh; the whole land of Judah as far as the Western Sea; 3] the Negeb; and the Plain—the valley of Jericho, the city of palm trees—as far as Zoar. 4] And the LORD said to him, "This is the land of which I swore to Abraham, Isaac, and Jacob, 'I will give it to your offspring.' I have let you see it with your own eyes, but you shall not cross there."

5] So Moses the servant of the LORD died there, in the land of Moab, at the command of the LORD. 6] He buried him in the valley in the land of Moab, near Beth-peor; and no one knows

34:1] *Steppes of Moab.* The river Jordan is flanked on both sides by fertile flatlands, which on the east were called the steppes of Moab.

Mount Nebo . . . Pisgah. Possibly one and the same mountain, but given different names by different traditions. Or, Pisgah may have meant a mountain range, and Mount Nebo, the peak on which Moses died. Today, the name Mount Nebo is attached to an elevation that rises 2,643 feet (805.5 meters) above sea level; it provides a good view of much of central Israel.

The Lord showed him. There is no vantage point from which the whole land can be seen, but one should note that the report flavors the natural with the supernatural. Similarly, it serves no purpose to attempt a reading of the text that would allow for a naturalistic interpretation.

An example of the latter is to understand "as far as Dan" (עַד דָּן) as "toward Dan."

Gilead. The area east and southeast of Lake Kinneret.

Dan. The area of Mount Hermon which became the location of the tribe after it migrated northward (see above, at 33:22).

2] *Naphtali.* Located west of Lake Kinneret.

Ephraim . . . Manasseh . . . Judah. The area west of the Jordan between Kinneret and the Dead Sea. (Part of Manasseh dwelt east of the Jordan.)

This section of the country was in 1948 occupied by the Hashemite Kingdom of Jordan and generally referred to as West Bank. In 1967, control of the area was wrested from the Jordanians by Israel and called *Yehudah ve-Shomron* (i.e., Judah and Samaria).

Western Sea. The Mediterranean. Neither this nor Mount Hermon is visible from Mount Nebo.

3] *The Plain.* The text notes its chief city, Jericho. Its biblical name was *Kikar* ("Round") because the area around Jericho has the appearance of a deep dish. Its fertility was vividly described by Josephus [3].

Zoar. The place to which Lot fled after the destruction of Sodom and Gomorrah, Gen. 19:20 ff. According to Josephus, Zoar was located southeast of the Dead Sea (an area that today is part of Saudi Arabia) [4].

4] *You shall not cross there.* The Midrash embellished this brief account and told of Moses' resistance to God's judgment; see Gleanings below.

5] *At the command of the Lord.* Literally, "by the mouth of the Lord," whence the tradition arose that Moses died by a divine kiss [5].

6] *He buried him.* That is, God buried Moses. But the Hebrew construction could also be under-

ידע איש את־קברתו עד היום הזה: ומשה בן־   י
מאה ועשרים שנה במתו לא־כהתה עינו ולא־נס
לחה: ויבכו בני ישראל את־משה בערבת מואב   ח
שלשים יום ויתמו ימי בכי אבל משה: ויהושע בן־   ט
נון מלא רוח חכמה כי־סמך משה את־ידיו עליו
וישמעו אליו בני־ישראל ויעשו כאשר צוה יהוה

את־משה: ולא־קם נביא עוד בישראל כמשה אשר   י
ידעו יהוה פנים אל־פנים: לכל־האתת והמופתים   יא
אשר שלחו יהוה לעשות בארץ מצרים לפרעה
ולכל־עבדיו ולכל־ארצו: ולכל היד החזקה ולכל   יב
המורא הגדול אשר עשה משה לעיני כל־ישראל:

Haftarah Vezot ha-Berachah, p. 1631

his burial place to this day. **7]** Moses was a hundred and twenty years old when he died; his eyes were undimmed and his vigor unabated. **8]** And the Israelites bewailed Moses in the steppes of Moab for thirty days.

The period of wailing and mourning for Moses came to an end. **9]** Now Joshua son of Nun was filled with the spirit of wisdom because Moses had laid his hands upon him; and the Israelites heeded him, doing as the LORD had commanded Moses.

10] Never again did there arise in Israel a prophet like Moses—whom the LORD singled out, face to face, **11]** for the various signs and portents that the LORD sent him to display in the land of Egypt, against Pharaoh and all his courtiers and his whole country, **12]** and for all the great might and awesome power that Moses displayed before all Israel.

stood as "someone buried him," meaning "he was buried." This would suggest that the burial place was once known and later forgotten [6].

Ibn Ezra, basing himself on a rabbinic saying, understood "Moses buried himself," that is, he went away to die [7].

Near Beth-peor. Its location is not certain; it was somewhere east of Jericho. See at Deut. 3:29.

7] *A hundred and twenty years old.* On the symbolism of this figure, see at Deut. 31:2. Moses had been eighty years old at the time of the Exodus (Exod. 7:7).

His vigor. לחֹה (*lechoh*) occurs only here. It is probably related to *lach* (moist) and was meant as a reference to Moses' unabated (possibly sexual) capacity.

Note the opposite English idiom for an old person, "dried up."

8] *Thirty days.* As was done for Aaron; Num. 20:29. The period has remained significant in Jewish mourning practices. (See further in Gleanings.)

Wailing and mourning. The two went together; wailing was an externalized expression of grief and complemented other mourning customs.

9] *Had laid his hands.* סָמַך (*samach*), whence *semichah*, the general term for ordination; see at Num. 27:18 ff.

10] *Face to face.* This was the most important aspect of Moses' singularity (see at Num. 12:8). Deuteronomy once probably ended here.

11] *Various signs.* Most likely a later addition which recalls the Exodus as the central experience of Moses' and Israel's existence.

Moses—Man and Legend

In Jewish tradition he is called *Mosheh Rabbenu*, Moses our teacher. The cognomen combines affection and awe: he is Israel's own teacher par excellence. He was not called the lawgiver, for the law was believed to be of God. The pages of the Torah tell us what kind of man he was, and the fertile imagination of the nation he loved embellished this picture with many legends. The book was named after him[1] because he was its transmitter, not because he was its creator. With the written text, so this tradition further avers, God also gave him the Oral Law, interpretations which would be arrived at by compenent scholars in centuries to come, 'til the end of time. The revelation at Sinai encompassed the totality of the divine law and was called Torah in its wider sense. It revealed what God wanted of His people, and this will was made known to Moses, His servant and our teacher. Thus the traditional view.

A scholarly historical assessment is of needs more complex. It too proceeds from the biblical text, for it is the only source of information about Moses available to us. But, since the Torah itself is the repository of various traditions from different times, the "historical Moses" cannot be securely recovered. Scholars generally agree that Moses was indeed a historical figure who led a people of slaves out of Egypt and who gave them a religious and legal constitution. He was a man identified with the desert, with Sinai and/or Horeb, and not with Canaan itself, which for him never moved from promise to fulfillment. All else about Moses is conjectural, and so far all attempts to separate fact from later legend, or to find the Mosaic core of the Torah legislation, have failed to produce anything approaching a scholarly consensus.

What kind of person emerges when we take the Torah as a whole, without regard to its literary history? Curiously, though Moses dominates the four books from Exodus to Deuteronomy, and many incidents are reported about him, his personality remains somewhat distant. He is human but at the same time more than human; he is alive and at once statuesque, like a sculpture cast in resplendent marble. He sins, yet the nature of his sin is unclear; while in Numbers his own shortcomings cause God's judgment on him, in Deuteronomy he is said to have been punished because of Israel's transgressions. He is called a meek or humble man, yet he is wrathful like God; he is submissive to his Master, yet stands up to Him in defense of Israel for whom he is prepared to surrender his life. We cannot discern any of his feelings toward his wife and children, toward Aaron, his brother and constant co-worker, or toward Joshua, his successor.[2] He has unique access to the Divine Presence and is so secure in this relationship that when Eldad and Medad act as prophets he is not jealous of them. Above all, he loves his people; his severest castigations are rendered out of love. He assumes many roles: lawgiver, founder of the national cult, military leader, and mouthpiece of God. Not surprisingly, later generations stood in awe of him, and his very greatness prevented them from embracing him as they did David or Elijah. His towering stature bestrides the history of Israel, and thereby the history of Western civilization. He is a commanding personage in Christian and

---

[1] The term *Torat Mosheh* is already found in the Bible, e.g., Mal. 3:22; Dan. 9:11.

[2] But others' feelings toward him are occasionally recorded, see e.g., Num. 12:1 ff.

Moslem traditions and through them has helped to shape the canons of law and morality. The last verses of Deuteronomy, which report his death, are thus also prologue to the further history of Israel as well as of humanity.

(For a canvas of characterizations, see Gleanings.)

GLEANINGS

The Death of Moses

(Many of the following stories are taken from the Midrash "The Death of Moses our Teacher," which was composed to be recited on Simchat Torah, when the annual reading cycle is concluded and commenced once again. For further midrashim, see Gleanings on ch. 31.)

When Moses saw that death was imminent he said to Israel: "I have given you much trouble by teaching you Torah and mitzvot—forgive me!" They said: "Our teacher and master, you are forgiven."

Then they said: "We too have angered you often and given you much trouble, forgive us too!" He said: "You are forgiven" [8].

(The Midrash records in detail how solicitous Moses was about his successor and how he served him publicly.)

Moses did everything to ensure that Joshua was installed as Israel's leader. But, when the divine cloud descended and separated him from God and Joshua, he thought: Better a hundred deaths than feeling jealous even once!

As he was about to die his wisdom was given to Joshua. Then Moses said to God: "Until this moment I desired life, now my life is in Your hands" [9].

(Moses entered into a prolonged argument with God, giving reasons why he should not die.)

God said: "You must die because you did not sanctify Me."[3]

Moses responded: "You deal with Your creatures in mercy and forgive them once, twice, even three times—but not me!"

Said God: "You committed six sins, still I did not accuse you."

"You refused Me when I asked you to deliver your people" (Exod. 4:13).

"You accused Me of making things worse for Israel and of not having delivered the people" (Exod. 5:23).

"You tested Me twice" (in the uprising of Korah, Num. 16:29, 30).

"You slandered your people when you said: 'Listen, you rebels!'" (Num. 20:10), "and again when you called them 'a breed of sinful men'" (Num. 32:14) [10].

Moses had to die because he had slain the Egyptian taskmaster (Exod. 2:11 ff.).

God: "Did I tell you to slay the Egyptian?"

Moses: "But You killed all the first-born in Egypt!"

God: "Do you resemble Me? I cause people to die and I also revive them" [11].

Ten times is Moses' death mentioned in the Bible: eight times in Deuteronomy and twice in the Book of Joshua. For ten times it was decreed that Moses should not enter Eretz Yisrael, though the judgment was not sealed until the Court on High declared: "You shall not go across yonder Jordan" (Deut. 3:27). But Moses was unconcerned, thinking: Israel has committed many sins, yet whenever I prayed for them God answered me.

When God saw that Moses made light of the decree and did not engage in prayer, He swore to himself that Moses would not enter the Land and sealed the decree.

Moses now donned sackcloth and commenced to pray. He drew a circle and said: "I will not move until You alter the judgment." But God

---

[3] The reference is to the story told in Numbers 20.

ordered all the gates of heaven to be shut to Moses' prayer [12].

God decreed that not even Moses' bones would cross into the Promised Land. But, Moses objected, would not the bones of Joseph accompany the people? God then accused Moses of not having acknowledged his ancestry when he was called an Egyptian (Exod. 2:19), whereas Joseph had acted differently (Gen. 41:12–16) [13].

Moses prayed in fact 515 times for a reversal of the judgment. Whence do we know this? From Deut. 3:23, "I pleaded with the Lord at that time. . . ." The Hebrew for "I pleaded" is וָאֶתְחַנַּן, the letters of which add up to 515.[4] At last God relented and allowed him at least to *view* the land [14].

Moses continued to plead his case.
"If I cannot go into the Land, let me become like one of the beasts of the field that eat its grass and drink its water and live and enjoy the world; or let me fly about like a bird gathering its food— only let my soul be like one of them."
God then said: "Enough! Never speak of this matter again!" [15].

In that hour God said: "I have heard your prayer, I Myself will bury you" [16].

When God kissed Moses and took away his soul[5] He wept, as it were. So did the heavens and the earth [17].

Why did God busy himself with Moses' burial? Because, when at the time of the Exodus everyone was looking for gold and silver, Moses looked for the coffin of Joseph. When he found it he himself carried it on his shoulders. Thus he helped to fulfill the oath of Gen. 50:25 [18].

Moses died on the seventh day of Adar and dur-

ing each hour of the day God informed him how many more hours he had to live [19].

In his view of the Land Moses had also glimpsed the future, even the time of resurrection[6] [20].

The grave of Moses is concealed from human eyes so that it would not be turned into a place of adoration [21].

Israel is called "holy" (Lev. 19:2 and elsewhere), but not Moses, not in the Torah nor in later Jewish parlance.[7]

Face to Face
Then slowly the aged
God bowed down His aged face to the aged
    mortal.
Withdrew him out of himself in kisses
into his older age. And with hands of creation
swiftly remounted to the mountain, until it
    amounted
to nothing more than the others, lightly
    surmounting
human conjecture.   R. M. RILKE [23]

The Life of Moses
The term "prophet" when used with reference both to Moses and to the others is ambiguous. The same applies, in my opinion, to his miracles and to the miracles of others. . . . For instance, Moses' apprehension was not like that of the Patriarchs, but greater.   MAIMONIDES [24]

I have conceived the idea of writing the life of Moses, who, according to the account of some persons, was the lawgiver of the Jews, but according to others only an interpreter of the sacred laws, the greatest and most perfect man that ever lived, having a desire to make his character fully known to those who ought not to remain in ignorance respecting him, for the glory of the laws which he left behind him has reached over the

[4] ו=6; א=1; ת=400; ח=8; נ=50; ן=50.
[5] See above, at verse 5.
[6] Based on reading יָם (sea, Deut. 34:2) as יוֹם (day).
[7] The expression "Holy Moses" is not traceable to

Jewish sources. It appeared first in 1855 "as an oath or expletive" and later as an expression of "surprise or amazement" [22].

whole world, and has penetrated to the very furthest limits of the universe... though the historians who have flourished among the Greeks have not chosen to think him worthy of mention.

PHILO [25]

Moses and Aaron

Of Moses it says that "the Israelites" wept for him (בְּנֵי יִשְׂרָאֵל, verse 8), but of Aaron that "*all the house of Israel*" did (כָּל בֵּית יִשְׂרָאֵל, Num. 20:29). This means that only the men bewailed Moses, and both men and women mourned for Aaron, because the latter had made peace between people, and thousands of children, born to parents reconciled by him, bore his name.   MIDRASH [26]

Formerly I felt little affection for Moses, probably because the Hellenic spirit was dominant within me, and I could not pardon the Jewish lawgiver for his intolerance of images and every sort of plastic representation. I failed to see that, despite his hostile attitude to art, Moses was himself a great artist, gifted with the true artist's spirit. Only in him, as in his Egyptian neighbors, the artistic spirit was exercised solely upon the colossal and the indestructible. But, unlike the Egyptians, he did not shape his works out of bricks or granite. His pyramids were built of men, his obelisks hewn out of human material. A feeble race of shepherds he transformed into a people bidding defiance to the centuries—a great, eternal, holy people, God's people, an exemplar to all other peoples, the prototype of mankind; he created Israel. With greater justice than the Roman poet could this artist, the son of Amram and Yochebed the midwife, boast of having erected a monument more enduring than brass.

HEINE [27]

Moses did not establish the religious relationship between the Bene Yisrael and YHVH. He was not the first to utter that "primal sound" in enthusiastic astonishment. That may have been done by somebody long before who, driven by an irresistible force along a new road, now felt himself to be preceded along that road by "Him," the invisible one who permitted himself to be seen. But it was Moses who, on this religious relationship, established a covenant between the God and

"His people." Nothing of such a kind can be imagined except on the assumption that a relation which had come down from ancient times has been melted in the fire of some new personal experience. The foundation takes place before the assembled host; the experience is undergone in solitude.

M. BUBER [28]

Hosea and Jeremiah have found sublime words to celebrate the indissoluble union between God and Israel. Feeling the full weight of this union, Moses has a deeper sense of his own indestructible attachment to Israel. He is the only one of all the men in the Bible for whom God offers to let Israel disappear and to begin history with another people. Moses refuses. In spite of the immense risks, he wishes to continue history with this people, and it is this people which will continue in history. What an absurd undertaking, contrary to the clarity of God and the realities of the situation! However, the decision of Moses is as obstinate as it is far-reaching. Today we recognize its immediate and unalterable consequences in the reassertion of the Jewish people, whose very existence seems contrary to reason and who do not fit into the ordinary scheme of things.   A. NEHER [29]

Moses was a man, a human being. He was not a saint, an ascetic, one who had stripped himself of all ordinary human feelings; equally, he was not a hero in the sense in which that word was ordinarily understood in ancient times. Certainly he was in no way a demigod. He is indeed presented as a figure of incomparable greatness. But the neat and exact precision with which the dividing line between him and God is always made clear is one of the most admirable features of these narratives. There was nothing divine about Moses. Therefore neither the men of his own time nor the men of later times ever offered to him such worship as is offered to God alone. He was "the man Moses."

G. VON RAD [30]

The fact that Moses himself is not shown as having lived to participate in the conquest of the Promised Land proper may well reflect, as well as the historical fact that the leader of the fugitives from Egypt who welded them into a people and gave them divinely sanctioned laws lived and died

before the real conquest of Palestine was begun, the belief that the stern and bloody business of conquering a country, even if done in the implementation of a divine promise and in the interests of a divinely ordained way of life, was not the job of the lawgiver himself. . . . Moses is trapped between his ideals and the harsh practicalities involved in carrying them out. That is a not unjustifiable reading of the story as it is given to us in the biblical text.   D. DAICHES [31]

His passion for social justice, his struggle for national liberation, his triumphs and disappointments, his poetic inspiration, his gifts as a strategist and his organizational genius, his complex relationship with God and His people, his requirements and promises, his condemnations and blessings, his bursts of anger, his silences, his efforts to reconcile the law with compassion, authority with integrity—no individual, ever, anywhere, accomplished so much for so many people in so many different domains. His influence is boundless, it reverberates beyond time.   E. WIESEL [32]

Falasha Legend

(The Falashas are an ethnic group in Ethiopia who are part of the Jewish people and of its early traditions.)

God informed Moses that he would die on a Friday. Accordingly, Moses put on his shrouds every Friday and waited for the Angel of Death. . . . He saw three angels, who assumed the appearance of three young men, busying themselves with the digging of a grave. "For whom is the grave?" asked Moses. "For the beloved of God," was the reply. "If so," said Moses, "I will assist you in your work." The angels rejoined: "We know not whether the grave is big enough. Wouldst thou go down into it? The person to be buried therein is of thy size." As soon as Moses descended into the grave, he was met there by the Angel of Death, who greeted him with the words: "Peace unto thee, O Moses the son of Amram!" Moses replied: "Peace be with thee"—and he died. The angels then buried him in the grave in which he met death [33].

The Wonder

I do not pretend to understand the mystery of human transformation, the moment when the response of a man to the world about him throws upon his mind a new and wondrous light concerning the nature of our species and binds him to a vision of the future to which he gives over his life. . . . In the person of Moses was developed the paradigm of the Israelite prophet, the individual through whom God speaks to and acts upon man.

CHAIM POTOK [34]

הפטרות

HAFTAROT

דברים

Isaiah

1 : 1— 27

א

Isaiah is the foremost name among the prophets. A member of the royal household in Jerusalem, he preached for some forty years in the latter part of the eighth century B.C.E., warning king and people to trust God rather than the might of their armies. Though Isaiah's name is attached to the whole book, chapters 40 to 66 stem from an unknown later prophet of exilic times.

The opening of the Book of Deuteronomy shows Moses placing the story of his people into the context of God's providence. The leader reproves Israel time and again and so does Isaiah in his sermons. The haftarah is always read on the Sabbath before the ninth day of Av (Tishah b'Av) which is known as Shabbat Chazon, after the first word of the text.

Chapter 1

1] The prophecies of Isaiah son of Amoz, who prophesied concerning Judah and Jerusalem in the reigns of Uzziah, Jotham, Ahaz, and Hezekiah, kings of Judah.

1] חֲזוֹן יְשַׁעְיָהוּ בֶן־אָמוֹץ אֲשֶׁר חָזָה עַל־יְהוּדָה וִירוּשָׁלָ͏ִם בִּימֵי עֻזִּיָּהוּ יוֹתָם אָחָז יְחִזְקִיָּהוּ מַלְכֵי יְהוּדָה:

2] Hear, O heavens, and give ear, O earth,
For the LORD has spoken:
"I reared children and brought them up—
And they have rebelled against Me!

2] שִׁמְעוּ שָׁמַיִם וְהַאֲזִינִי אֶרֶץ
כִּי יְהֹוָה דִּבֵּר
בָּנִים גִּדַּלְתִּי וְרוֹמַמְתִּי
וְהֵם פָּשְׁעוּ בִי:

3] An ox knows its owner,
An ass its master's crib:
Israel does not know,
My people takes no thought."

3] יָדַע שׁוֹר קֹנֵהוּ
וַחֲמוֹר אֵבוּס בְּעָלָיו
יִשְׂרָאֵל לֹא יָדַע
עַמִּי לֹא הִתְבּוֹנָן:

4] Ah, sinful nation!
People laden with iniquity!
Brood of evildoers!
Depraved children!
They have forsaken the LORD,
Spurned the Holy One of Israel,
Turned their backs [on Him].

4] הוֹי גּוֹי חֹטֵא
עַם כֶּבֶד עָו‍ֹן
זֶרַע מְרֵעִים
בָּנִים מַשְׁחִיתִים
עָזְבוּ אֶת־יְהֹוָה
נִאֲצוּ אֶת־קְדוֹשׁ יִשְׂרָאֵל
נָזֹרוּ אָחוֹר:

5] Why do you seek further beatings,
That you continue to offend?

5] עַל־מֶה תֻכּוּ עוֹד
תּוֹסִיפוּ סָרָה

Every head is ailing,
And every heart is sick.

6] From head to foot
No spot is sound:
All bruises, and welts,
And festering sores—
Not pressed out, not bound up,
Not softened with oil.

7] Your land is a waste,
Your cities burnt down;
Before your eyes, the yield of your soil
Is consumed by strangers—
A wasteland ᵃ⁻as overthrown by strangers!⁻ᵃ

8] Fairᵇ Zion is left
Like a booth in a vineyard,
Like a hut in a cucumber field,
Like a city beleaguered.

9] Had not the LORD of Hosts
Left us some survivors,
We should be like Sodom,
Another Gomorrah.

10] Hear the word of the LORD,
You chieftains of Sodom;
Give ear to our God's instruction,
You folk of Gomorrah!

11] "What need have I of all your sacrifices?"
Says the LORD.

כָּל־רֹאשׁ לָחֳלִי

וְכָל־לֵבָב דַּוָּי׃

6] מִכַּף־רֶגֶל וְעַד־רֹאשׁ

אֵין־בּוֹ מְתֹם

פֶּצַע וְחַבּוּרָה

וּמַכָּה טְרִיָּה

לֹא־זֹרוּ וְלֹא חֻבָּשׁוּ

וְלֹא רֻכְּכָה בַּשָּׁמֶן׃

7] אַרְצְכֶם שְׁמָמָה

עָרֵיכֶם שְׂרֻפוֹת אֵשׁ

אַדְמַתְכֶם לְנֶגְדְּכֶם

זָרִים אֹכְלִים אֹתָהּ

וּשְׁמָמָה כְּמַהְפֵּכַת זָרִים׃

8] וְנוֹתְרָה בַת־צִיּוֹן

כְּסֻכָּה בְכָרֶם

כִּמְלוּנָה בְמִקְשָׁה

כְּעִיר נְצוּרָה׃

9] לוּלֵי יְהֹוָה צְבָאוֹת

הוֹתִיר לָנוּ שָׂרִיד כִּמְעָט

כִּסְדֹם הָיִינוּ

לַעֲמֹרָה דָּמִינוּ׃

10] שִׁמְעוּ דְבַר־יְהֹוָה

קְצִינֵי סְדֹם

הַאֲזִינוּ תּוֹרַת אֱלֹהֵינוּ

עַם עֲמֹרָה׃

11] לָמָּה־לִּי רֹב־זִבְחֵיכֶם

יֹאמַר יְהֹוָה

ᵃ⁻ᵃ *Emendation yields "like Sodom overthrown"*
ᵇ *Lit. "Daughter"*

"I am sated with burnt offerings of rams, | שָׂבַעְתִּי עֹלוֹת אֵילִים

And suet of fatlings, | וְחֵלֶב מְרִיאִים

And blood of bulls; | וְדַם פָּרִים וּכְבָשִׂים

And I have no delight | וְעַתּוּדִים לֹא חָפָצְתִּי:

In lambs and he-goats.

12] That you come to appear before Me— | 12] כִּי תָבֹאוּ לֵרָאוֹת פָּנָי

Who asked that ᵉᵉof you? | מִי־בִקֵּשׁ זֹאת מִיֶּדְכֶם

Trample My courts | רְמֹס חֲצֵרָי:

13] no more; | 13] לֹא תוֹסִיפוּ הָבִיא מִנְחַת־שָׁוְא

Bringing oblations is futile,ᵉ | קְטֹרֶת תּוֹעֵבָה הִיא לִי

Incense is offensive to Me. | חֹדֶשׁ וְשַׁבָּת קְרֹא מִקְרָא

New moon and sabbath, | לֹא־אוּכַל אָוֶן וַעֲצָרָה:

Proclaiming of solemnities,

ᵈ⁻Assemblies with iniquity,⁻ᵈ

I cannot abide.

14] Your new moons and fixed seasons | 14] חָדְשֵׁיכֶם וּמוֹעֲדֵיכֶם שָׂנְאָה נַפְשִׁי

Fill Me with loathing; | הָיוּ עָלַי לָטֹרַח

They are become a burden to Me, | נִלְאֵיתִי נְשֹׂא:

I cannot endure them.

15] And when you lift up your hands, | 15] וּבְפָרִשְׂכֶם כַּפֵּיכֶם

I will turn My eyes away from you; | אַעְלִים עֵינַי מִכֶּם

Though you pray at length, | גַּם כִּי־תַרְבּוּ תְפִלָּה

I will not listen. | אֵינֶנִּי שֹׁמֵעַ

Your hands are stained with crime— | יְדֵיכֶם דָּמִים מָלֵאוּ:

16] Wash yourselves clean; | 16] רַחֲצוּ הִזַּכּוּ

Put your evil doings | הָסִירוּ רֹעַ מַעַלְלֵיכֶם

Away from My sight. | מִנֶּגֶד עֵינָי

Cease to do evil; | חִדְלוּ הָרֵעַ:

17] Learn to do good. | 17] לִמְדוּ הֵיטֵב

Devote yourselves to justice; | דִּרְשׁוּ מִשְׁפָּט

ᵉ⁻Aid the wronged.⁻ᵉ | אַשְּׁרוּ חָמוֹץ

Uphold the rights of the orphan; | שִׁפְטוּ יָתוֹם

Defend the cause of the widow. | רִיבוּ אַלְמָנָה:

ᵉ⁻ᵉ *Others "of you, to trample My courts?* | 13] *Bring no more vain oblations"*

ᵈ⁻ᵈ *Septuagint "Fast and assembly"; cf. Joel 1.14*   ᵉ⁻ᵉ *Meaning of Heb. uncertain*

18] Come, ᵉ‑ᵉ let us reach an understanding ᵉ‑ᵉ
                   —says the LORD.
Be your sins like crimson,
They can turn snow-white;
Be they red as dyed wool,
They can become like fleece.

19] If, then, you agree and give heed,
You will eat the good things of the earth;

20] But if you refuse and disobey,
ᶠ‑ᶠ You will be devoured [by] the sword. ᶠ‑ᶠ —
For it was the LORD who spoke.

21] Alas, she has become a harlot,
The faithful city
That was filled with justice,
Where righteousness dwelt—
But now murderers.

22] Your⁹ silver has turned to dross;
ᵉ‑ᵉ Your wine is cut with water. ᵉ‑ᵉ

23] Your rulers are rogues
And cronies of thieves,
Every one avid for presents
And greedy for gifts;
They do not judge the case of the orphan,
And the widow's cause never reaches them.

24] Assuredly, this is the declaration
Of the Sovereign, the LORD of Hosts,
The Mighty One of Israel:

18] לְכוּ־נָא וְנִוָּכְחָה

יֹאמַר יְהֹוָה

אִם־יִהְיוּ חֲטָאֵיכֶם כַּשָּׁנִים

כַּשֶּׁלֶג יַלְבִּינוּ

אִם־יַאְדִּימוּ כַתּוֹלָע

כַּצֶּמֶר יִהְיוּ:

19] אִם־תֹּאבוּ וּשְׁמַעְתֶּם

טוּב הָאָרֶץ תֹּאכֵלוּ:

20] וְאִם־תְּמָאֲנוּ וּמְרִיתֶם

חֶרֶב תְּאֻכְּלוּ

כִּי פִּי יְהֹוָה דִּבֵּר:

21] אֵיכָה הָיְתָה לְזוֹנָה

קִרְיָה נֶאֱמָנָה

מְלֵאֲתִי מִשְׁפָּט

צֶדֶק יָלִין בָּהּ

וְעַתָּה מְרַצְּחִים:

22] כַּסְפֵּךְ הָיָה לְסִיגִים

סָבְאֵךְ מָהוּל בַּמָּיִם:

23] שָׂרַיִךְ סוֹרְרִים

וְחַבְרֵי גַּנָּבִים

כֻּלּוֹ אֹהֵב שֹׁחַד

וְרֹדֵף שַׁלְמֹנִים

יָתוֹם לֹא יִשְׁפֹּטוּ

וְרִיב אַלְמָנָה לֹא־יָבוֹא אֲלֵיהֶם:

24] לָכֵן נְאֻם הָאָדוֹן יְהֹוָה צְבָאוֹת

אֲבִיר יִשְׂרָאֵל

ᵉ‑ᵉ *Meaning of Heb. uncertain*
ᶠ‑ᶠ *Or "You will be fed the sword"*
⁹ *I.e., Jerusalem's*

"Ah, I will get satisfaction from My foes;
I will wreak vengeance on My enemies!

25] I will turn My hand against you,
And smelt out your dross h-as with lye,-h
And remove your slag:

26] I will restore your magistrates as of old,
And your counselors as of yore.
After that you shall be called
City of Righteousness, Faithful City."

27] ʿZion shall be saved in the judgment;
Her repentant ones, in the retribution.ⁱ

הוֹי אֶנָּחֵם מִצָּרַי
וְאִנָּקְמָה מֵאוֹיְבָי:
25] וְאָשִׁיבָה יָדִי עָלַיִךְ
וְאֶצְרֹף כַּבֹּר סִגָּיִךְ
וְאָסִירָה כָּל־בְּדִילָיִךְ:
26] וְאָשִׁיבָה שֹׁפְטַיִךְ כְּבָרִאשֹׁנָה
וְיֹעֲצַיִךְ כְּבַתְּחִלָּה
אַחֲרֵי־כֵן יִקָּרֵא לָךְ
עִיר הַצֶּדֶק
קִרְיָה נֶאֱמָנָה:
27] צִיּוֹן בְּמִשְׁפָּט תִּפָּדֶה
וְשָׁבֶיהָ בִּצְדָקָה:

h-h Emendation yields "in a crucible"; cf. 48.10
i Others "Zion shall be saved by justice, / Her repentant ones by righteousness"
i For this meaning cf. 5.16; 10.22

Chapters 40–66 of the Book of Isaiah are the work of an unknown author (often referred to as Deutero-Isaiah) who lived in Babylon during the days of the exile (sixth century B.C.E.). He preached unwavering trust in a God who would surely restore Israel to its homeland. Of all the prophets he is the most lyrical and his imagery the richest.

The Torah portion contains the Shema, the framework of Israel's love for God. In turn, divine love is the subject of Isaiah's message of comfort. The haftarah is always read on the Sabbath after Tishah b'Av and its first words of consolation have given the Sabbath its name, Shabbat Nachamu.

ואתחנן

Isaiah

40 : 1–26

מ

Chapter 40

1] Comfort, oh, comfort My people,
Says your God.

א] נַחֲמוּ נַחֲמוּ עַמִּי
יֹאמַר אֱלֹהֵיכֶם:

2] Speak tenderly to Jerusalem,
And declare to her
That her term of service is over,
That her iniquity is expiated;
For she has received at the hand of the LORD
Double for all her sins.

ב] דַּבְּרוּ עַל־לֵב יְרוּשָׁלַ͏ִם
וְקִרְאוּ אֵלֶיהָ
כִּי מָלְאָה צְבָאָהּ
כִּי נִרְצָה עֲוֺנָהּ
כִּי לָקְחָה מִיַּד יְהֹוָה
כִּפְלַיִם בְּכָל־חַטֹּאתֶיהָ:

3] A voice rings out:
"Clear in the desert
A road for the LORD!
Level in the wilderness
A highway for our God!

ג] קוֹל קוֹרֵא
בַּמִּדְבָּר פַּנּוּ דֶּרֶךְ יְהֹוָה
יַשְּׁרוּ בָּעֲרָבָה
מְסִלָּה לֵאלֹהֵינוּ:

4] Let every valley be raised,
Every hill and mount made low.
Let the rugged ground become level
And the ridges become a plain.

ד] כָּל־גֶּיא יִנָּשֵׂא
וְכָל־הַר וְגִבְעָה יִשְׁפָּלוּ
וְהָיָה הֶעָקֹב לְמִישׁוֹר
וְהָרְכָסִים לְבִקְעָה:

5] The Presence of the LORD shall appear,
And all flesh, as one, shall behold—
For the LORD Himself has spoken."

ה] וְנִגְלָה כְּבוֹד יְהֹוָה
וְרָאוּ כָל־בָּשָׂר יַחְדָּו
כִּי פִּי יְהֹוָה דִּבֵּר:

6] A voice rings out: "Proclaim!"
ᵃ‾Another asks,‾ᵃ "What shall I proclaim?"
"All flesh is grass,
All its goodness like flowers of the field:

6] קוֹל אֹמֵר קְרָא
וְאָמַר מָה אֶקְרָא
כָּל־הַבָּשָׂר חָצִיר
וְכָל־חַסְדּוֹ כְּצִיץ הַשָּׂדֶה:

7] Grass withers, flowers fade
When the breath of the LORD blows on them.
Indeed, man is but grass:

7] יָבֵשׁ חָצִיר נָבֵל צִיץ
כִּי רוּחַ יְהוָה נָשְׁבָה בּוֹ
אָכֵן חָצִיר הָעָם:

8] Grass withers, flowers fade—
But the word of our God is always fulfilled!"

8] יָבֵשׁ חָצִיר נָבֵל צִיץ
וּדְבַר אֱלֹהֵינוּ יָקוּם לְעוֹלָם:

9] Ascend a lofty mountain,
O herald of joy to Zion;
Raise your voice with power,
O herald of joy to Jerusalem—
Raise it, have no fear;
Announce to the cities of Judah:
Behold your God!

9] עַל הַר־גָּבֹהַ עֲלִי־לָךְ
מְבַשֶּׂרֶת צִיּוֹן
הָרִימִי בַכֹּחַ קוֹלֵךְ
מְבַשֶּׂרֶת יְרוּשָׁלִָם
הָרִימִי אַל־תִּירָאִי
אִמְרִי לְעָרֵי יְהוּדָה
הִנֵּה אֱלֹהֵיכֶם:

10] Behold, the Lord GOD comes in might,
And His arm wins triumph for Him;
See, His rewardᵇ is with Him,
His recompense before Him.

10] הִנֵּה אֲדֹנָי יְהוִה בְּחָזָק יָבוֹא
וּזְרֹעוֹ מֹשְׁלָה לוֹ
הִנֵּה שְׂכָרוֹ אִתּוֹ
וּפְעֻלָּתוֹ לְפָנָיו:

11] Like a shepherd He pastures His flock:
He gathers the lambs in His arms
And carries them in His bosom;
Gently He drives the mother sheep.

11] כְּרֹעֶה עֶדְרוֹ יִרְעֶה
בִּזְרֹעוֹ יְקַבֵּץ טְלָאִים
וּבְחֵיקוֹ יִשָּׂא עָלוֹת יְנַהֵל:

12] Who measured the waters with the hollow of
his hand,
And gauged the skies with a span,
And meted earth's dust with a measure,ᶜ

12] מִי־מָדַד בְּשָׁעֳלוֹ מַיִם
וְשָׁמַיִם בַּזֶּרֶת תִּכֵּן
וְכָל בַּשָּׁלִשׁ עֲפַר הָאָרֶץ

ᵃ‾ᵃ 1QIsᵃ and Septuagint read "And I asked." (1QIsᵃ = manuscriptᵃ of Isaiah found
in the first cave of Qumran, the site of the caves where the Bible manuscripts were
found in 1949–50.)
ᵇ The reward and recompense to the cities of Judah; cf. Jer. 31.14, 16
ᶜ Heb. shalish "third," probably a third of an ephah

And weighed the mountains with a scale
And the hills with a balance?

וְשָׁקַל בַּפֶּ֫לֶס הָרִים
וּגְבָעוֹת בְּמֹאזְנָֽיִם:

13] Who has plumbed the mind of the LORD,
What man could tell Him His plan?

13 מִֽי־תִכֵּן אֶת־ר֣וּחַ יְהֹוָ֑ה
וְאִישׁ עֲצָתוֹ יוֹדִיעֶֽנּוּ:

14] Whom did He consult, and who taught Him,
Guided Him in the way of right?
Who guided Him in knowledge
And showed Him the path of wisdom?

14 אֶת־מִי נוֹעַץ וַיְבִינֵהוּ
וַֽיְלַמְּדֵהוּ בְּאֹרַח מִשְׁפָּט
וַֽיְלַמְּדֵהוּ דַעַת
וְדֶרֶךְ תְּבוּנוֹת יוֹדִיעֶֽנּוּ:

15] The nations are but a drop in a bucket,
Reckoned as dust on a balance;
The very coastlands He lifts like motes.

15 הֵן גּוֹיִם כְּמַר מִדְּלִי
וּכְשַׁחַק מֹאזְנַיִם נֶחְשָׁ֑בוּ
הֵן אִיִּים כַּדַּק יִטּֽוֹל:

16] Lebanon is not fuel enough,
Nor its beasts enough for sacrifice.

16 וּלְבָנוֹן אֵין דֵּי בָּעֵ֑ר
וְחַיָּתוֹ אֵין דֵּי עוֹלָֽה:

17] All nations are as naught in His sight;
He accounts them as less than nothing.

17 כָּל־הַגּוֹיִם כְּאַיִן נֶגְדּ֑וֹ
מֵאֶפֶס וָתֹהוּ נֶחְשְׁבוּ־לֽוֹ:

18] To whom, then, can you liken God,
What form compare to Him?

18 וְאֶל־מִי תְּדַמְּיוּן אֵ֑ל
וּמַה־דְּמוּת תַּֽעַרְכוּ־לֽוֹ:

19] The idol? A woodworker shaped it,
And a smith overlaid it with gold,
d-Forging links of silver.-d

19 הַפֶּסֶל נָסַךְ חָרָ֑שׁ
וְצֹרֵף בַּזָּהָב יְרַקְּעֶ֑נּוּ
וּרְתֻקוֹת כֶּסֶף צוֹרֵֽף:

20] As a gift, he chooses the mulberrye—
A wood that does not rot—
Then seeks a skillful woodworker
To make a firm idol,
That will not topple.

20 הַֽמְסֻכָּן תְּרוּמָה עֵץ
לֹֽא־יִרְקַב יִבְחָ֑ר
חָרָשׁ חָכָם יְבַקֶּשׁ־ל֔וֹ
לְהָכִין פֶּסֶל לֹא יִמּֽוֹט:

21] Do you not know?
Have you not heard?

21 הֲלוֹא תֵֽדְעוּ
הֲלוֹא תִשְׁמָ֔עוּ

---

d-d Meaning of Heb. uncertain
e Heb. mesukan; according to a Jewish tradition, preserved by Jerome, a kind of
  wood; a similar word denotes a kind of wood in Akkadian

Have you not been told
From the very first?
Have you not discerned
^{d-}How the earth was founded?^{-d}

22] It is He who is enthroned above the vault of
    the earth,
So that its inhabitants seem as grasshoppers;
Who spread out the skies like gauze,
Stretched them out like a tent to dwell in.

23] He brings potentates to naught,
Makes rulers of the earth as nothing.

24] Hardly are they planted,
Hardly are they sown,
Hardly has their stem
Taken root in earth,
When He blows upon them and they dry up,
And the storm bears them off like straw.

25] To whom, then, can you liken Me,
To whom can I be compared?
                   —says the Holy One.

26] Lift high your eyes and see:
Who created these?
He who sends out their host by count,
Who calls them each by name:
Because of His great might and vast power,
Not one fails to appear.

הֲלוֹא הֻגַּד מֵרֹאשׁ לָכֶם
הֲלוֹא הֲבִינֹתֶם מוֹסְדוֹת הָאָרֶץ:
22 הַיֹּשֵׁב עַל־חוּג הָאָרֶץ
וְיֹשְׁבֶיהָ כַּחֲגָבִים
הַנּוֹטֶה כַדֹּק שָׁמַיִם
וַיִּמְתָּחֵם כָּאֹהֶל לָשָׁבֶת:
23 הַנּוֹתֵן רוֹזְנִים לְאָיִן
שֹׁפְטֵי אֶרֶץ כַּתֹּהוּ עָשָׂה:
24 אַף בַּל־נִטָּעוּ
אַף בַּל־זֹרָעוּ
אַף בַּל־שֹׁרֵשׁ
בָּאָרֶץ גִּזְעָם
וְגַם נָשַׁף בָּהֶם וַיִּבָשׁוּ
וּסְעָרָה כַּקַּשׁ תִּשָּׂאֵם:
25 וְאֶל־מִי תְדַמְּיוּנִי וְאֶשְׁוֶה
יֹאמַר קָדוֹשׁ:
26 שְׂאוּ־מָרוֹם עֵינֵיכֶם וּרְאוּ
מִי־בָרָא אֵלֶּה
הַמּוֹצִיא בְמִסְפָּר צְבָאָם
לְכֻלָּם בְּשֵׁם יִקְרָא
מֵרֹב אוֹנִים וְאַמִּיץ כֹּחַ
אִישׁ לֹא נֶעְדָּר:

^{d-d} *Meaning of Heb. uncertain*

עֵקֶב

Chapters 40–66 of the Book of Isaiah are the work of an unknown author (often referred to as Deutero-Isaiah) who lived in Babylon during the days of the exile (sixth century B.C.E.). He preached unwavering trust in a God who would surely restore Israel to its homeland. Of all the prophets he is the most lyrical and his imagery the richest.

Isaiah speaks of God as both loving and just. He punishes Israel for its sins, yet He takes it back in compassion— "Lo, the Lord God will help me." In the Torah reading, Moses too sets forth the way in which God will deal with His people. This is the second Sabbath of consolation after Tishah b'Av.

Isaiah

49 : 14 — 51 : 3

מט

Chapter 49

14] Zion says,
"The Lord has forsaken me,
My Lord has forgotten me."

14] וַתֹּאמֶר צִיּוֹן
עֲזָבַנִי יְהֹוָה
וַאדֹנָי שְׁכֵחָנִי:

15] Can a woman forget her baby,
Or disown the child of her womb?
Though she might forget,
I never could forget you.

15] הֲתִשְׁכַּח אִשָּׁה עוּלָהּ
מֵרַחֵם בֶּן־בִּטְנָהּ
גַּם־אֵלֶּה תִשְׁכַּחְנָה
וְאָנֹכִי לֹא אֶשְׁכָּחֵךְ:

16] See, I have engraved you
On the palms of My hands,
Your walls are ever before Me.

16] הֵן עַל־כַּפַּיִם חַקֹּתִיךְ
חוֹמֹתַיִךְ נֶגְדִּי תָּמִיד:

17] Swiftly your children are coming;
Those who ravaged and ruined you shall leave
    you.

17] מִהֲרוּ בָּנָיִךְ
מְהָרְסַיִךְ וּמַחֲרִיבַיִךְ מִמֵּךְ יֵצֵאוּ:

18] Look up all around you and see:
They are all assembled, are come to you!
As I live
                        —declares the Lord—
You shall don them all like jewels,
Deck yourself with them like a bride.

18] שְׂאִי־סָבִיב עֵינַיִךְ וּרְאִי
כֻּלָּם נִקְבְּצוּ בָאוּ־לָךְ
חַי־אָנִי
נְאֻם־יְהֹוָה
כִּי כֻלָּם כָּעֲדִי תִלְבָּשִׁי
וּתְקַשְּׁרִים כַּכַּלָּה:

19] As for your ruins and desolate places
And your land laid waste—

19] כִּי חָרְבֹתַיִךְ וְשֹׁמְמֹתַיִךְ
וְאֶרֶץ הֲרִסֻתֵךְ

You shall soon be crowded with settlers,
While destroyers stay far from you.

20] The children *you thought you had lost*
Shall yet say in your hearing,
"The place is too crowded for me;
Make room for me to settle."

21] And you will say to yourself,
"Who bore these for me
When I was bereaved and barren,
Exiled and disdained*—*
By whom, then, were these reared?
I was left all alone—
And where have these been?"

22] Thus said the Lord GOD:
I will raise My hand to nations
And lift up My ensign to peoples;
And they shall bring your sons in their bosoms,
And carry your daughters on their backs.

23] Kings shall tend your children,
Their queens shall serve you as nurses.
They shall bow to you, face to the ground,
And lick the dust of your feet.
And you shall know that I am the LORD—
Those who trust in Me shall not be shamed.

24] Can spoil be taken from a warrior,
Or captives retrieved from a victor?

25] Yet thus said the LORD:
Captives shall be taken from a warrior

כִּי עַתָּה תֵּצְרִי מִיּוֹשֵׁב
וְרָחֲקוּ מְבַלְּעָיִךְ:

20 עוֹד יֹאמְרוּ בְאׇזְנַיִךְ
בְּנֵי שִׁכֻּלָיִךְ
צַר־לִי הַמָּקוֹם
גְּשָׁה־לִּי וְאֵשֵׁבָה:

21 וְאָמַרְתְּ בִּלְבָבֵךְ
מִי יָלַד־לִי אֶת־אֵלֶּה
וַאֲנִי שְׁכוּלָה וְגַלְמוּדָה
גֹּלָה וְסוּרָה
וְאֵלֶּה מִי גִדֵּל
הֵן אֲנִי נִשְׁאַרְתִּי לְבַדִּי
אֵלֶּה אֵיפֹה הֵם:

22 כֹּה־אָמַר אֲדֹנָי יְהֹוִה
הִנֵּה אֶשָּׂא אֶל־גּוֹיִם יָדִי
וְאֶל־עַמִּים אָרִים נִסִּי
וְהֵבִיאוּ בָנַיִךְ בְּחֹצֶן
וּבְנֹתַיִךְ עַל־כָּתֵף תִּנָּשֶׂאנָה:

23 וְהָיוּ מְלָכִים אֹמְנַיִךְ
וְשָׂרוֹתֵיהֶם מֵינִיקֹתַיִךְ
אַפַּיִם אֶרֶץ יִשְׁתַּחֲווּ־לָךְ
וַעֲפַר רַגְלַיִךְ יְלַחֵכוּ
וְיָדַעַתְּ כִּי־אֲנִי יְהֹוָה
אֲשֶׁר לֹא־יֵבֹשׁוּ קֹוָי:

24 הֲיֻקַּח מִגִּבּוֹר מַלְקוֹחַ
וְאִם־שְׁבִי צַדִּיק יִמָּלֵט:

25 כִּי־כֹה אָמַר יְהֹוָה
גַּם־שְׁבִי גִבּוֹר יֻקָּח

---

e–e Lit. "of your bereavement"   *f Meaning of Heb. uncertain*

And spoil shall be retrieved from a tyrant;
For *I* will contend with your adversaries,
And *I* will deliver your children.

וּמַלְק֥וֹחַ עָרִ֖יץ יִמָּלֵ֑ט

וְאֶת־יְרִיבֵךְ֙ אָנֹכִ֣י אָרִ֔יב

וְאֶת־בָּנַ֖יִךְ אָנֹכִ֥י אוֹשִֽׁיעַ׃

26] I will make your oppressors eat their own
flesh,
They shall be drunk with their own blood as with
wine.
And all mankind shall know
That I the LORD am your Savior,
The Mighty One of Jacob, your Redeemer.

26 וְהַאֲכַלְתִּ֤י אֶת־מוֹנַ֙יִךְ֙ אֶת־בְּשָׂרָ֔ם

וְכֶעָסִ֖יס דָּמָ֣ם יִשְׁכָּר֑וּן

וְיָדְע֣וּ כָל־בָּשָׂ֗ר

כִּ֣י אֲנִ֤י יְהֹוָה֙ מוֹשִׁיעֵ֔ךְ

וְגֹאֲלֵ֖ךְ אֲבִ֥יר יַעֲקֹֽב׃

Chapter 50

 נ

1] Thus said the LORD:
*a*Where is the bill of divorce
Of your mother whom I dismissed?
And which of My creditors was it
To whom I sold you off?
You were only sold off for your sins,
And your mother dismissed for your crimes.

1 כֹּ֣ה ׀ אָמַ֣ר יְהֹוָ֗ה

אֵ֣י זֶ֠ה סֵ֣פֶר כְּרִית֤וּת אִמְּכֶם֙

אֲשֶׁ֣ר שִׁלַּחְתִּ֔יהָ

א֚וֹ מִ֣י מִנּוֹשַׁ֔י

אֲשֶׁר־מָכַ֥רְתִּי אֶתְכֶ֖ם ל֑וֹ

הֵ֤ן בַּעֲוֺנֹֽתֵיכֶם֙ נִמְכַּרְתֶּ֔ם

וּבְפִשְׁעֵיכֶ֖ם שֻׁלְּחָ֥ה אִמְּכֶֽם׃

2] Why, when I came, was no one there,
Why, when I called, would none respond?
Is my arm, then, too short to rescue,
Have I not the power to save?
With a mere rebuke I dry up the sea,
And turn rivers into desert.
Their fish stink from lack of water;
They lie dead *b*of thirst.*b*

2 מַדּ֜וּעַ בָּ֣אתִי וְאֵ֣ין אִ֗ישׁ

קָרָ֙אתִי֙ וְאֵ֣ין עוֹנֶ֔ה

הֲקָצ֨וֹר קָצְרָ֤ה יָדִי֙ מִפְּד֔וּת

וְאִם־אֵֽין־בִּ֥י כֹ֖חַ לְהַצִּ֑יל

הֵ֣ן בְּגַעֲרָתִ֞י אַחֲרִ֣יב יָ֗ם

אָשִׂ֤ים נְהָרוֹת֙ מִדְבָּ֔ר

תִּבְאַ֤שׁ דְּגָתָם֙ מֵאֵ֣ין מַ֔יִם

וְתָמֹ֖ת בַּצָּמָֽא׃

3] I clothe the skies in blackness
And make their raiment sackcloth.

3 אַלְבִּ֥ישׁ שָׁמַ֖יִם קַדְר֑וּת

וְשַׂ֖ק אָשִׂ֥ים כְּסוּתָֽם׃

---

a The mother (the country) has not been formally divorced, nor the children (the people) sold because of poverty. Therefore there is no obstacle to their restoration
b-b Change of vocalization yields "on the parched ground"; cf. 44.3

4] ᵉ⁻The Lord GOD gave me a skilled tongue,
To know how to speak timely words to the
     weary.⁻ᵉ
Morning by morning, He rouses,
He rouses my ear
To give heed like disciples.

5] The Lord GOD opened my ears,
And I did not disobey,
I did not run away.

6] I offered my back to the floggers,
And my cheeks to those who tore out my hair.
I did not hide my face
From insult and spittle.

7] But the Lord GOD will help me—
Therefore I feel no disgrace;
Therefore I have set my face like flint,
And I know I shall not be shamed.

8] My Vindicator is at hand—
Who dare contend with me?
Let us stand up together!ᵈ
Who would be my opponent?
Let him approach me!

9] Lo, the Lord GOD will help me—
Who can get a verdict against me?
They shall all wear out like a garment,
The moth shall consume them.

10] Who among you reveres the LORD
And heeds the voice of His servant?—

4 אֲדֹנָי יְהוִה נָתַן לִי לְשׁוֹן לִמּוּדִים
לָדַעַת לָעוּת אֶת־יָעֵף דָּבָר
יָעִיר בַּבֹּקֶר בַּבֹּקֶר
יָעִיר לִי אֹזֶן
לִשְׁמֹעַ כַּלִּמּוּדִים׃

5 אֲדֹנָי יְהוִה פָּתַח־לִי אֹזֶן
וְאָנֹכִי לֹא מָרִיתִי
אָחוֹר לֹא נְסוּגֹתִי׃

6 גֵּוִי נָתַתִּי לְמַכִּים
וּלְחָיַי לְמֹרְטִים
פָּנַי לֹא הִסְתַּרְתִּי
מִכְּלִמּוֹת וָרֹק׃

7 וַאדֹנָי יְהוִה יַעֲזָר־לִי
עַל־כֵּן לֹא נִכְלָמְתִּי
עַל־כֵּן שַׂמְתִּי פָנַי כַּחַלָּמִישׁ
וָאֵדַע כִּי־לֹא אֵבוֹשׁ׃

8 קָרוֹב מַצְדִּיקִי
מִי־יָרִיב אִתִּי
נַעַמְדָה יָּחַד
מִי־בַעַל מִשְׁפָּטִי
יִגַּשׁ אֵלָי׃

9 הֵן אֲדֹנָי יְהוִה יַעֲזָר־לִי
מִי־הוּא יַרְשִׁיעֵנִי
הֵן כֻּלָּם כַּבֶּגֶד יִבְלוּ
עָשׁ יֹאכְלֵם׃

10 מִי בָכֶם יְרֵא יְהוָה
שֹׁמֵעַ בְּקוֹל עַבְדּוֹ

ᵉ⁻ᵉ *Meaning of Heb. uncertain*
ᵈ *I.e., as opponents in court; cf. Num. 35.12*

Though he walk in darkness
And have no light,
Let him trust in the name of the LORD
And rely upon his God.

11] But you are all kindlers of fire,
ᵉ⁻Girding onᵉ firebrands.
Walk by the blaze of your fire,
By the brands that you have lit!
This has come to you from My hand:
ᵉ⁻You shall lie down in pain.⁻ᵉ

Chapter 51

1] Listen to Me, you who pursue justice,
You who seek the LORD:
Look to the rock you were hewn from,
To the quarry you were dug from.

2] Look back to Abraham your father
And to Sarah who brought you forth.
For he was only one when I called him,
But I blessed him and made him many.

3] Truly the LORD has comforted Zion,
Comforted all her ruins;
He has made her wilderness like Eden,
Her desert like the Garden of the LORD.
Gladness and joy shall abide there,
Thanksgiving and the sound of music.

אֲשֶׁר הָלַךְ חֲשֵׁכִים

וְאֵין נֹגַהּ לוֹ

יִבְטַח בְּשֵׁם יְהֹוָה

וְיִשָּׁעֵן בֵּאלֹהָיו:

11] הֵן כֻּלְּכֶם קֹדְחֵי אֵשׁ

מְאַזְּרֵי זִיקוֹת

לְכוּ בְּאוּר אֶשְׁכֶם

וּבְזִיקוֹת בִּעַרְתֶּם

מִיָּדִי הָיְתָה־זֹּאת לָכֶם

לְמַעֲצֵבָה תִּשְׁכָּבוּן:

נא

1] שִׁמְעוּ אֵלַי

רֹדְפֵי צֶדֶק

מְבַקְשֵׁי יְהֹוָה

הַבִּיטוּ אֶל־צוּר חֻצַּבְתֶּם

וְאֶל־מַקֶּבֶת בּוֹר נֻקַּרְתֶּם:

2] הַבִּיטוּ אֶל־אַבְרָהָם אֲבִיכֶם

וְאֶל־שָׂרָה תְּחוֹלֶלְכֶם

כִּי־אֶחָד קְרָאתִיו

וַאֲבָרְכֵהוּ וְאַרְבֵּהוּ:

3] כִּי־נִחַם יְהֹוָה צִיּוֹן

נִחַם כָּל־חָרְבֹתֶיהָ

וַיָּשֶׂם מִדְבָּרָהּ כְּעֵדֶן

וְעַרְבָתָהּ כְּגַן־יְהֹוָה

שָׂשׂוֹן וְשִׂמְחָה יִמָּצֵא בָהּ

תּוֹדָה וְקוֹל זִמְרָה:

ᵉ⁻ᵉ Emendation yields "Lighters of"
ᵉ⁻ᵉ Meaning of Heb. uncertain

ראה

Isaiah

54 : 11 — 55 : 5

*Chapters 40–66 of the Book of Isaiah are the work of an
unknown author (often referred to as Deutero-Isaiah)
who lived in Babylon during the days of the exile (sixth
century B.C.E.). He preached unwavering trust in a God
who would surely restore Israel to its homeland. Of all the
prophets he is the most lyrical and his imagery the richest.*

*Even as the sidrah sets before Israel the choice between
blessing and curse, so does Isaiah assure his people that
though the curse has been visited on Israel the time for
blessing will now be at hand. This is the third haftarah
of consolation read after Tishah b'Av.*

נד

Chapter 54

11] Unhappy, storm-tossed one, uncomforted!
I will lay carbuncles[d] as your building stones
And make your foundations of sapphires.

[11] עֲנִיָּה סֹעֲרָה לֹא נֻחָמָה
הִנֵּה אָנֹכִי מַרְבִּיץ בַּפּוּךְ אֲבָנַיִךְ
וִיסַדְתִּיךְ בַּסַּפִּירִים:

12] I will make your battlements of rubies,
Your gates of precious stones,
The whole encircling wall of gems.

[12] וְשַׂמְתִּי כַּדְכֹד שִׁמְשֹׁתַיִךְ
וּשְׁעָרַיִךְ לְאַבְנֵי אֶקְדָּח
וְכָל־גְּבוּלֵךְ לְאַבְנֵי־חֵפֶץ:

13] And all your children shall be disciples of the
    LORD,
And great shall be the happiness of your children;

[13] וְכָל־בָּנַיִךְ לִמּוּדֵי יְהֹוָה
וְרַב שְׁלוֹם בָּנָיִךְ:

14] You shall be established through righteousness.
You shall be safe from oppression,
And shall have no fear;
From ruin, and it shall not come near you.

[14] בִּצְדָקָה תִּכּוֹנָנִי
רַחֲקִי מֵעֹשֶׁק
כִּי־לֹא תִירָאִי
וּמִמְּחִתָּה כִּי לֹא־תִקְרַב אֵלָיִךְ:

15] 'Surely no harm can be done
Without My consent:
Whoever would harm you
Shall fall because of you.

[15] הֵן גּוֹר יָגוּר
אֶפֶס מֵאוֹתִי
מִי־גָר אִתָּךְ
עָלַיִךְ יִפּוֹל:

16] It is I who created the smith
To fan the charcoal fire

[16] הִנֵּה אָנֹכִי בָּרָאתִי חָרָשׁ
נֹפֵחַ בְּאֵשׁ פֶּחָם

---

[d] *Taking* puch *as a by-form of* nofech; *so already Rashi*
[e] *Meaning of verse uncertain*

And produce the tools for his work;
So it is I who create
The instruments of havoc.

17] No weapon formed against you
Shall succeed.
And every tongue that contends with you at law
You shall defeat.
Such is the lot of the servants of the LORD.
Such their triumph through Me
—declares the LORD.

Chapter 55

1] Ho, all who are thirsty,
Come for water,
Even if you have no money;
Come, buy food and eat:
Buy food without money,
Wine and milk without cost.

2] Why do you spend money for what is not
    bread,
Your earnings for what does not satisfy?
Give heed to Me,
And you shall eat choice food
And enjoy the richest viands.

3] Incline your ear and come to Me;
Hearken, and you shall be revived.
And I will make with you an everlasting covenant,
The enduring loyalty promised to David.

4] ª⁻As I made him a leaderᵇ of peoples,
A prince and commander of peoples,

ª⁻ª Cf. II Sam. 22.44–45 || Ps. 18.44–45
ᵇ Cf. Targum; others "witness"

וּמוֹצִיא כְלִי לְמַעֲשֵׂהוּ

וְאָנֹכִי בָּרָאתִי

מַשְׁחִית לְחַבֵּל:

17] כָּל־כְּלִי יוּצַר עָלַיִךְ

לֹא יִצְלָח

וְכָל־לָשׁוֹן תָּקוּם־אִתָּךְ לַמִּשְׁפָּט

תַּרְשִׁיעִי זֹאת נַחֲלַת עַבְדֵי יְהֹוָה

וְצִדְקָתָם מֵאִתִּי

נְאֻם־יְהֹוָה:

נה

1] הוֹי כָּל־צָמֵא

לְכוּ לַמַּיִם

וַאֲשֶׁר אֵין־לוֹ כָּסֶף

לְכוּ שִׁבְרוּ וֶאֱכֹלוּ

וּלְכוּ שִׁבְרוּ בְּלוֹא־כֶסֶף

וּבְלוֹא מְחִיר יַיִן וְחָלָב:

2] לָמָּה תִשְׁקְלוּ־כֶסֶף בְּלוֹא־לֶחֶם

וִיגִיעֲכֶם בְּלוֹא לְשָׂבְעָה

שִׁמְעוּ שָׁמוֹעַ אֵלַי

וְאִכְלוּ־טוֹב

וְתִתְעַנַּג בַּדֶּשֶׁן נַפְשְׁכֶם:

3] הַטּוּ אָזְנְכֶם וּלְכוּ אֵלַי

שִׁמְעוּ וּתְחִי נַפְשְׁכֶם

וְאֶכְרְתָה לָכֶם בְּרִית עוֹלָם

חַסְדֵי דָוִד הַנֶּאֱמָנִים:

4] הֵן עֵד לְאוּמִּים נְתַתִּיו

נָגִיד וּמְצַוֵּה לְאֻמִּים:

5] So you shall summon a nation you did not
   know,
And a nation that did not know you
Shall come running to you⁻ᵃ—
For the sake of the Lord your God,
The Holy One of Israel who has glorified you.

‏[5 הֵן גּוֹי לֹא־תֵדַע תִּקְרָא
‏וְגוֹי לֹא־יְדָעוּךָ אֵלֶיךָ יָרוּצוּ
‏לְמַעַן יְהֹוָה אֱלֹהֶיךָ
‏וְלִקְדוֹשׁ יִשְׂרָאֵל כִּי פֵאֲרָךְ:

Chapters 40–66 of the Book of Isaiah are the work of an
unknown author (often referred to as Deutero-Isaiah)
who lived in Babylon during the days of the exile (sixth
century B.C.E.). He preached unwavering trust in a God
who would surely restore Israel to its homeland. Of all the
prophets he is the most lyrical and his imagery the richest.

In his fourth message of consolation read after Tishah
b'Av, Isaiah speaks in ringing words of God's forgiveness
of Israel's sins, chief amongst which loomed the command
contained in the sidrah: "Justice, justice shall you pursue."

שפטים

Isaiah

51 : 12 — 52 : 12

נא

Chapter 51

12] I, I am He who comforts you!
What ails you that you fear
Man who must die,
Mortals who fare like grass?

[12 אָנֹכִי אָנֹכִי הוּא מְנַחֶמְכֶם
מִי־אַתְּ וַתִּירְאִי
מֵאֱנוֹשׁ יָמוּת
וּמִבֶּן־אָדָם חָצִיר יִנָּתֵן:

13] You have forgotten the LORD your Maker,
Who stretched out the skies and made firm the
earth!
And you live all day in constant dread
Because of the rage of an oppressor
Who is aiming to cut [you] down.
Yet of what account is the rage of an oppressor?

[13 וַתִּשְׁכַּח יְהוָה עֹשֶׂךָ
נוֹטֶה שָׁמַיִם וְיֹסֵד אָרֶץ
וַתְּפַחֵד תָּמִיד כָּל־הַיּוֹם
מִפְּנֵי חֲמַת הַמֵּצִיק
כַּאֲשֶׁר כּוֹנֵן לְהַשְׁחִית
וְאַיֵּה חֲמַת הַמֵּצִיק:

14] *g*Quickly the crouching one is freed;
He is not cut down and slain,
And he shall not want for food.

[14 מִהַר צֹעֶה לְהִפָּתֵחַ
וְלֹא־יָמוּת לַשַּׁחַת
וְלֹא יֶחְסַר לַחְמוֹ:

15] For I the LORD your God—
Who stir up the sea into roaring waves,
Whose name is LORD of Hosts—

[15 וְאָנֹכִי יְהוָה אֱלֹהֶיךָ
רֹגַע הַיָּם וַיֶּהֱמוּ גַּלָּיו
יְהוָה צְבָאוֹת שְׁמוֹ:

16] *h*Have put My words in your mouth
And sheltered you with My hand;*–h*

[16 וָאָשִׂם דְּבָרַי בְּפִיךָ
וּבְצֵל יָדִי כִּסִּיתִיךָ

---

g Meaning of verse uncertain. Emendation yields (cf. Jer. 11.19; Job 14.7–9) "Quickly
   the tree buds anew; | It does not die though cut down, | And its sap does not fail"
h-h I.e., I have chosen you to be a prophet-nation; cf. 49.2; 59.21

I, who planted^i the skies and made firm the earth,
Have said to Zion: You are My people!

לְנְטֹעַ שָׁמַיִם וְלִיסֹד אָרֶץ

וְלֵאמֹר לְצִיּוֹן עַמִּי־אָתָּה:

17] Rouse, rouse yourself!
Arise, O Jerusalem,
You who from the LORD's hand
Have drunk the cup of His wrath,
You who have drained to the dregs
The bowl, the cup of reeling!

17] הִתְעוֹרְרִי הִתְעוֹרְרִי

קוּמִי יְרוּשָׁלַם

אֲשֶׁר שָׁתִית מִיַּד יְהוָה

אֶת־כּוֹס חֲמָתוֹ

אֶת־קֻבַּעַת כּוֹס הַתַּרְעֵלָה

שָׁתִית מָצִית:

18] She has none to guide her
Of all the sons she bore;
None takes her by the hand,
Of all the sons she reared.^j

18] אֵין מְנַהֵל לָה

מִכָּל־בָּנִים יָלָדָה

וְאֵין מַחֲזִיק בְּיָדָהּ

מִכָּל־בָּנִים גִּדֵּלָה:

19] These two things have befallen you:
Wrack and ruin—who can console you?
Famine and sword—^k how shall I^k comfort you?

19] שְׁתַּיִם הֵנָּה קֹרְאֹתַיִךְ

מִי יָנוּד לָךְ

הַשֹּׁד וְהַשֶּׁבֶר

וְהָרָעָב וְהַחֶרֶב

מִי אֲנַחֲמֵךְ:

20] Your sons lie in a swoon
At the corner of every street—
Like an antelope caught in a net—
Drunk with the wrath of the LORD,
With the rebuke of your God.

20] בָּנַיִךְ עֻלְּפוּ

שָׁכְבוּ בְּרֹאשׁ כָּל־חוּצוֹת

כְּתוֹא מִכְמָר

הַמְלֵאִים חֲמַת־יְהוָה

גַּעֲרַת אֱלֹהָיִךְ:

21] Therefore,
Listen to this, unhappy one,
Who are drunk, but not with wine!

21] לָכֵן

שִׁמְעִי־נָא זֹאת עֲנִיָּה

וּשְׁכֻרַת וְלֹא מִיָּיִן:

22] Thus said the LORD, your Lord,
Your God who champions His people:

22] כֹּה־אָמַר אֲדֹנַיִךְ יְהוָה

וֵאלֹהַיִךְ יָרִיב עַמּוֹ

---

^i Emendation yields "stretched out"; cf. Syriac version and v. 13
^j To guide a drunken parent home was a recognized filial duty in ancient Canaan and Egypt
^k-k Several ancient versions render "who can"

Herewith I take from your hand
The cup of reeling,[1]
The bowl, the cup of My wrath;
You shall never drink it again.

הִנֵּה לָקַחְתִּי מִיָּדֵךְ
אֶת־כּוֹס הַתַּרְעֵלָה
אֶת־קֻבַּעַת כּוֹס חֲמָתִי
לֹא־תוֹסִיפִי לִשְׁתּוֹתָהּ עוֹד:

23] I will put it in the hands of your tormentors,
Who have commanded you,
"Get down, that we may walk over you"—
So that you made your back like the ground,
Like a street for passers-by.

[23 וְשַׂמְתִּיהָ בְּיַד־מוֹגַיִךְ
אֲשֶׁר־אָמְרוּ לְנַפְשֵׁךְ
שְׁחִי וְנַעֲבֹרָה
וַתָּשִׂימִי כָאָרֶץ גֵּוֵךְ
וְכַחוּץ לַעֹבְרִים:

Chapter 52

נב

1] Awake, awake, O Zion!
Clothe yourself in splendor;
Put on your robes of majesty,
Jerusalem, holy city!
For the uncircumcised and the unclean
Shall never enter you again.

[1 עוּרִי עוּרִי
לִבְשִׁי עֻזֵּךְ צִיּוֹן
לִבְשִׁי בִּגְדֵי תִפְאַרְתֵּךְ
יְרוּשָׁלַ͏ִם עִיר הַקֹּדֶשׁ
כִּי לֹא יוֹסִיף יָבֹא־בָךְ עוֹד
עָרֵל וְטָמֵא:

2] Arise, shake off the dust,
Sit [on your throne], Jerusalem!
Loose the bonds from your neck,
O captive one, Fair Zion!

[2 הִתְנַעֲרִי מֵעָפָר
קוּמִי שְּׁבִי יְרוּשָׁלָ͏ִם
הִתְפַּתְּחִי מוֹסְרֵי צַוָּארֵךְ
שְׁבִיָּה בַּת־צִיּוֹן:

3] For thus said the Lord:
You were sold for no price,
And shall be redeemed without money.

[3 כִּי־כֹה אָמַר יְהוָֹה
חִנָּם נִמְכַּרְתֶּם
וְלֹא בְכֶסֶף תִּגָּאֵלוּ:

4] For thus said the Lord God:
Of old, My people went down
To Egypt to sojourn there;

[4 כִּי כֹה אָמַר אֲדֹנָי יֱהוִֹה
מִצְרַיִם יָרַד־עַמִּי בָרִאשֹׁנָה
לָגוּר שָׁם

---

[1] A figure of speech for a dire fate; cf. Jer. 25.15 ff.

But Assyria has robbed them,
Giving nothing in return.[a]
5] What therefore do I gain here?
        —declares the LORD—
For My people has been carried off for nothing,
Their mockers howl
        —declares the LORD—
And constantly, unceasingly,
My name is reviled.

6] Assuredly, My people shall learn My name,
Assuredly [they shall learn] on that day
That I, the one who promised,
Am now at hand.

7] How welcome on the mountain
Are the footsteps of the herald
Announcing happiness,
Heralding good fortune,
Announcing victory,
Telling Zion, "Your God is King!"

8] Hark!
Your watchmen raise their voices,
As one they shout for joy;
For every eye shall behold
The LORD's return to Zion.

9] Raise a shout together,
O ruins of Jerusalem!
For the LORD will comfort His people,
Will redeem Jerusalem.

10] The LORD will bare His holy arm
In the sight of all the nations,

וְאַשּׁוּר בְּאֶפֶס עֲשָׁקוֹ׃

5] וְעַתָּה מַה־לִּי־פֹה
נְאֻם־יְהוָה
כִּי־לֻקַּח עַמִּי חִנָּם
מֹשְׁלָיו יְהֵילִילוּ
נְאֻם־יְהוָה
וְתָמִיד כָּל־הַיּוֹם
שְׁמִי מִנֹּאָץ׃

6] לָכֵן יֵדַע עַמִּי שְׁמִי
לָכֵן בַּיּוֹם הַהוּא
כִּי־אֲנִי־הוּא הַמְדַבֵּר הִנֵּנִי׃

7] מַה־נָּאווּ עַל־הֶהָרִים
רַגְלֵי מְבַשֵּׂר
מַשְׁמִיעַ שָׁלוֹם
מְבַשֵּׂר טוֹב
מַשְׁמִיעַ יְשׁוּעָה
אֹמֵר לְצִיּוֹן מָלַךְ אֱלֹהָיִךְ׃

8] קוֹל צֹפַיִךְ נָשְׂאוּ קוֹל
יַחְדָּו יְרַנֵּנוּ
כִּי עַיִן בְּעַיִן יִרְאוּ
בְּשׁוּב יְהוָה צִיּוֹן׃

9] פִּצְחוּ רַנְּנוּ יַחְדָּו
חָרְבוֹת יְרוּשָׁלִָם
כִּי־נִחַם יְהוָה עַמּוֹ
גָּאַל יְרוּשָׁלָםִ׃

10] חָשַׂף יְהוָה אֶת־זְרוֹעַ קָדְשׁוֹ
לְעֵינֵי כָּל־הַגּוֹיִם

---

[a] *Whereas the Israelites themselves sought hospitality in Egypt, Assyria (i.e., the Chaldean Empire) has exiled them by force*

And the very ends of earth shall see
The victory of our God.

11] Turn, turn away, touch naught unclean
As you depart from there;
Keep pure, as you go forth from there,
You who bear the vessels of the LORD!^b

12] For you will not depart in haste,
Nor will you leave in flight;
For the LORD is marching before you,
The God of Israel is your rear guard.

וְרָאוּ כָּל־אַפְסֵי־אָרֶץ
אֵת יְשׁוּעַת אֱלֹהֵינוּ:
11] סוּרוּ סוּרוּ צְאוּ מִשָּׁם
טָמֵא אַל־תִּגָּעוּ
צְאוּ מִתּוֹכָהּ
הִבָּרוּ נֹשְׂאֵי כְּלֵי יְהֹוָה:
12] כִּי לֹא בְחִפָּזוֹן תֵּצֵאוּ
וּבִמְנוּסָה לֹא תֵלֵכוּן
כִּי־הֹלֵךְ לִפְנֵיכֶם יְהֹוָה
וּמְאַסִּפְכֶם אֱלֹהֵי יִשְׂרָאֵל:

^b Cf. Ezra 1.7–8; 5.14–15

Chapters 40–66 of the Book of Isaiah are the work of an unknown author (often referred to as Deutero-Isaiah) who lived in Babylon during the days of the exile (sixth century B.C.E.). He preached unwavering trust in a God who would surely restore Israel to its homeland. Of all the prophets he is the most lyrical and his imagery the richest.

The end of the sidrah with its message of hope is reflected in the Isaianic message of consolation, the fifth haftarah of comfort after Tishah b'Av. Whatever may have happened, God's love for Israel is unshakable: "The mountains may move . . . my loyalty shall never move from you." This message was chosen also as part of the haftarah for sidrah Noach.

כי תצא

Isaiah

54 : 1- 10

נד

Chapter 54

1] Shout, O barren one,
You who bore no child!
Shout aloud for joy,
You who did not travail!
For the children of the wife forlorn
Shall outnumber those of the espoused
—said the LORD.

2] Enlarge the site of your tent,
a-Extend the size of your dwelling,-*a*
Do not stint!
Lengthen the ropes, and drive the pegs firm.

3] For you shall spread out to the right and the left;
Your offspring shall dispossess nations!*b*
And shall people the desolate towns.

4] Fear not, you shall not be shamed;
Do not cringe, you shall not be disgraced.
For you shall forget
The reproach of your youth,
And remember no more
The shame of your widowhood.

5] For He who made you will espouse you—
His name is "LORD of Hosts";
The Holy One of Israel will redeem you,
Who is called "God of all the Earth."

[1] רָנִּי עֲקָרָה לֹא יָלָדָה
פִּצְחִי רִנָּה וְצַהֲלִי לֹא־חָלָה
כִּי־רַבִּים בְּנֵי־שׁוֹמֵמָה
מִבְּנֵי בְעוּלָה אָמַר יְהֹוָה:

[2] הַרְחִיבִי מְקוֹם אׇהֳלֵךְ
וִירִיעוֹת מִשְׁכְּנוֹתַיִךְ יַטּוּ אַל־תַּחְשֹׂכִי
הַאֲרִיכִי מֵיתָרַיִךְ וִיתֵדֹתַיִךְ חַזֵּקִי:

[3] כִּי־יָמִין וּשְׂמֹאול תִּפְרֹצִי
וְזַרְעֵךְ גּוֹיִם יִירָשׁ
וְעָרִים נְשַׁמּוֹת יוֹשִׁיבוּ:

[4] אַל־תִּירְאִי כִּי־לֹא תֵבוֹשִׁי
וְאַל־תִּכָּלְמִי כִּי־לֹא תַחְפִּירִי
כִּי בֹשֶׁת עֲלוּמַיִךְ תִּשְׁכָּחִי
וְחֶרְפַּת אַלְמְנוּתַיִךְ לֹא תִזְכְּרִי־עוֹד:

[5] כִּי בֹעֲלַיִךְ עֹשַׂיִךְ
יְהֹוָה צְבָאוֹת שְׁמוֹ
וְגֹאֲלֵךְ קְדוֹשׁ יִשְׂרָאֵל
אֱלֹהֵי כׇל־הָאָרֶץ יִקָּרֵא:

---

a-a Lit. "Let the cloths of your dwelling extend"
b I.e., the foreigners who had occupied regions from which Israelites had been exiled; cf. II Kings 17.24

6] The Lord has called you back
As a wife forlorn and forsaken.
Can one cast off the wife of his youth?
         —said your God.

7] For a little while I forsook you.
But with vast love I will bring you back.

8] In slight anger, for a moment,
I hid My face from you;
But with kindness everlasting
I will take you back in love
         —said the Lord your Redeemer.

9] For this to Me is like the waters[c] of Noah:
As I swore that the waters of Noah
Nevermore would flood the earth,
So I swear that I will not
Be angry with you or rebuke you.

10] For the mountains may move
And the hills be shaken,
But my loyalty shall never move from you,
Nor My covenant of friendship be shaken
         —said the Lord, who takes you back in love.

6 כִּי־כְאִשָּׁה עֲזוּבָה

וַעֲצוּבַת רוּחַ קְרָאָךְ יְהוָה

וְאֵשֶׁת נְעוּרִים

כִּי תִמָּאֵס אָמַר אֱלֹהָיִךְ:

7 בְּרֶגַע קָטֹן עֲזַבְתִּיךְ

וּבְרַחֲמִים גְּדֹלִים אֲקַבְּצֵךְ:

8 בְּשֶׁצֶף קֶצֶף הִסְתַּרְתִּי פָנַי רֶגַע מִמֵּךְ

וּבְחֶסֶד עוֹלָם רִחַמְתִּיךְ

אָמַר גֹּאֲלֵךְ יְהוָה:

9 כִּי־מֵי נֹחַ זֹאת לִי

אֲשֶׁר נִשְׁבַּעְתִּי מֵעֲבֹר מֵי־נֹחַ

עוֹד עַל־הָאָרֶץ

כֵּן נִשְׁבַּעְתִּי

מִקְּצֹף עָלַיִךְ וּמִגְּעָר־בָּךְ:

10 כִּי הֶהָרִים יָמוּשׁוּ

וְהַגְּבָעוֹת תְּמוּטֶינָה

וְחַסְדִּי מֵאִתֵּךְ לֹא־יָמוּשׁ

וּבְרִית שְׁלוֹמִי לֹא תָמוּט

אָמַר מְרַחֲמֵךְ יְהוָה:

_____

[c] Other Heb. mss. and the ancient versions read "days"

כי תבוא

Chapters 40–66 of the Book of Isaiah are the work of an unknown author (often referred to as Deutero-Isaiah) who lived in Babylon during the days of the exile (sixth century B.C.E.). He preached unwavering trust in a God who would surely restore Israel to its homeland. Of all the prophets he is the most lyrical and his imagery the richest.

The haftarah, sixth in the series of the Isaianic messages of consolation, is a counterweight to the bitter catalogue of threats and curses which climax the sidrah. The depressing mood of the latter is lifted by Isaiah's ringing call, "Arise, shine, for your light has dawned."

Isaiah
60 : 1-22

ס

Chapter 60

1] Arise, shine, for your light has dawned;
The Presence of the LORD has shone upon you!

2] Behold! Darkness shall cover the earth,
And thick clouds the peoples;
But upon you the LORD will shine,
And His Presence be seen over you.

3] And nations shall walk by your light;
Kings, by your shining radiance.

4] Raise your eyes and look about:
They have all gathered and come to you.
Your sons shall be brought from afar,
Your daughters like babes on shoulders.

5] As you behold, you will glow;
Your heart will throb and thrill—
For the wealth of the sea[a] shall pass on to you,
The riches of nations shall flow to you.

6] Dust clouds of camels shall cover you,
Dromedaries of Midian and Ephah.

1] קוּמִי אוֹרִי כִּי־בָא אוֹרֵךְ

וּכְבוֹד יְהֹוָה עָלַיִךְ זָרָח:

2] כִּי־הִנֵּה הַחֹשֶׁךְ יְכַסֶּה־אֶרֶץ

וַעֲרָפֶל לְאֻמִּים

וְעָלַיִךְ יִזְרַח יְהֹוָה

וּכְבוֹדוֹ עָלַיִךְ יֵרָאֶה:

3] וְהָלְכוּ גוֹיִם לְאוֹרֵךְ

וּמְלָכִים לְנֹגַהּ זַרְחֵךְ:

4] שְׂאִי סָבִיב עֵינַיִךְ וּרְאִי

כֻּלָּם נִקְבְּצוּ בָאוּ־לָךְ

בָּנַיִךְ מֵרָחוֹק יָבֹאוּ

וּבְנֹתַיִךְ עַל־צַד תֵּאָמַנָה:

5] אָז תִּרְאִי וְנָהַרְתְּ

וּפָחַד וְרָחַב לְבָבֵךְ

כִּי־יֵהָפֵךְ עָלַיִךְ הֲמוֹן יָם

חֵיל גּוֹיִם יָבֹאוּ לָךְ:

6] שִׁפְעַת גְּמַלִּים תְּכַסֵּךְ

בִּכְרֵי מִדְיָן וְעֵיפָה

---

[a] *Emendation yields "coastlands"*

They all shall come from Sheba;
They shall bear gold and frankincense,
And shall herald the glories of the LORD.

7] All the flocks of Kedar shall be assembled for
    you,
The rams of Nebaioth shall serve your needs;
They shall be welcome offerings on My altar,
And I will add glory to My glorious House.

8] Who are these that float like a cloud,
Like doves to their cotes?

9] *b*Behold, the coastlands await me,*-b*
With *c*ships of Tarshish*-c* in the lead,
To bring your sons from afar,
And their*d* silver and gold as well—
For the name of the LORD your God,
For the Holy One of Israel, who has glorified you.

10] Aliens shall rebuild your walls,
Their kings shall wait upon you—
For in anger I struck you down,
But in favor I take you back.

11] Your gates shall always stay open—
Day and night they shall never be shut—
To let in the wealth of the nations,
With their kings in procession.

12] For the nation or the kingdom
That does not serve you shall perish;
Such nations shall be destroyed.

כֻּלָּם מִשְּׁבָא יָבֹאוּ

זָהָב וּלְבוֹנָה יִשָּׂאוּ

וּתְהִלֹּת יְהֹוָה יְבַשֵּׂרוּ:

7 כָּל־צֹאן קֵדָר יִקָּבְצוּ לָךְ

אֵילֵי נְבָיוֹת יְשָׁרְתוּנֶךְ

יַעֲלוּ עַל־רָצוֹן מִזְבְּחִי

וּבֵית תִּפְאַרְתִּי אֲפָאֵר:

8 מִי־אֵלֶּה כָּעָב תְּעוּפֶינָה

וְכַיּוֹנִים אֶל־אֲרֻבֹּתֵיהֶם:

9 כִּי־לִי אִיִּים יְקַוּוּ

וׇאֳנִיּוֹת תַּרְשִׁישׁ בָּרִאשֹׁנָה

לְהָבִיא בָנַיִךְ מֵרָחוֹק

כַּסְפָּם וּזְהָבָם אִתָּם

לְשֵׁם יְהֹוָה אֱלֹהַיִךְ

וְלִקְדוֹשׁ יִשְׂרָאֵל כִּי פֵאֲרָךְ:

10 וּבָנוּ בְנֵי־נֵכָר חֹמֹתַיִךְ

וּמַלְכֵיהֶם יְשָׁרְתוּנֶךְ

כִּי בְקִצְפִּי הִכִּיתִיךְ

וּבִרְצוֹנִי רִחַמְתִּיךְ:

11 וּפִתְּחוּ שְׁעָרַיִךְ תָּמִיד

יוֹמָם וָלַיְלָה לֹא יִסָּגֵרוּ

לְהָבִיא אֵלַיִךְ חֵיל גּוֹיִם

וּמַלְכֵיהֶם נְהוּגִים:

12 כִּי־הַגּוֹי וְהַמַּמְלָכָה

אֲשֶׁר לֹא־יַעַבְדוּךְ יֹאבֵדוּ

וְהַגּוֹיִם חָרֹב יֶחֱרָבוּ:

b-b Emendation yields "The vessels of the coastlands are gathering"
c-c Probably a type of large ship
d I.e., of the people of the coastlands

13] The majesty of Lebanon shall come to you—
Cypress and pine and box—
To adorn the site of My Sanctuary,
To glorify the place where My feet rest.

14] Bowing before you, shall come
The children of those who tormented you;
Prostrate at the soles of your feet
Shall be all those who reviled you;
And you shall be called
"City of the LORD,
Zion of the Holy One of Israel."

15] Whereas you have been forsaken,
Rejected, with none passing through,
I will make you a pride everlasting,
A joy for age after age.

16] You shall suck the milk of the nations,
Suckle at royal breasts.ᵉ
And you shall know
That I the LORD am your Savior,
I, The Mighty One of Jacob, am your Redeemer.

17] Instead of copper I will bring gold,
Instead of iron I will bring silver;
Instead of wood, copper;
And instead of stone, iron.
And I will appoint Well-being as your
    government,
Prosperity as your officials.

18] The cry "Violence!"
Shall no more be heard in your land,
Nor "Wrack and ruin!"
Within your borders.
And you shall name your walls "Victory"
And your gates "Renown."

כְּבוֹד הַלְּבָנוֹן אֵלַיִךְ יָבוֹא [13
בְּרוֹשׁ תִּדְהָר וּתְאַשּׁוּר יַחְדָּו
לְפָאֵר מְקוֹם מִקְדָּשִׁי
וּמְקוֹם רַגְלַי אֲכַבֵּד:

וְהָלְכוּ אֵלַיִךְ שְׁחוֹחַ [14
בְּנֵי מְעַנַּיִךְ
וְהִשְׁתַּחֲווּ עַל־כַּפּוֹת רַגְלַיִךְ
כָּל־מְנַאֲצָיִךְ
וְקָרְאוּ לָךְ עִיר יְהֹוָה
צִיּוֹן קְדוֹשׁ יִשְׂרָאֵל:

תַּחַת הֱיוֹתֵךְ עֲזוּבָה [15
וּשְׂנוּאָה וְאֵין עוֹבֵר
וְשַׂמְתִּיךְ לִגְאוֹן עוֹלָם
מְשׂוֹשׂ דּוֹר וָדוֹר:

וְיָנַקְתְּ חֲלֵב גּוֹיִם [16
וְשֹׁד מְלָכִים תִּינָקִי
וְיָדַעַתְּ כִּי אֲנִי יְהֹוָה
מוֹשִׁיעֵךְ וְגֹאֲלֵךְ אֲבִיר יַעֲקֹב:

תַּחַת הַנְּחֹשֶׁת אָבִיא זָהָב [17
וְתַחַת הַבַּרְזֶל אָבִיא כֶסֶף
וְתַחַת הָעֵצִים נְחֹשֶׁת
וְתַחַת הָאֲבָנִים בַּרְזֶל
וְשַׂמְתִּי פְקֻדָּתֵךְ שָׁלוֹם
וְנֹגְשַׂיִךְ צְדָקָה:

לֹא־יִשָּׁמַע עוֹד חָמָס בְּאַרְצֵךְ [18
שֹׁד וָשֶׁבֶר בִּגְבוּלָיִךְ
וְקָרָאת יְשׁוּעָה חוֹמֹתַיִךְ
וּשְׁעָרַיִךְ תְּהִלָּה:

ᵉ Lit. "breasts of kings" or "breasts of kingdoms"

1616

19] No longer shall you need the sun
For light by day,
Nor the shining of the moon
For radiance [by night*/];
For the LORD shall be your light everlasting,
Your God shall be your glory.

20] Your sun shall set no more,
Your moon no more withdraw;
For the LORD shall be a light to you forever,
And your days of mourning shall be ended.

21] And your people, all of them righteous,
Shall possess the land for all time;
They are the shoot that I planted,
My handiwork in which I glory.

22] The smallest shall become a clan;
The least, a mighty nation.
I the LORD will speed it in due time.

19] לֹא־יִהְיֶה־לָּךְ עוֹד הַשֶּׁמֶשׁ
לְאוֹר יוֹמָם
וּלְנֹגַהּ הַיָּרֵחַ לֹא־יָאִיר לָךְ
וְהָיָה־לָּךְ יְהֹוָה לְאוֹר עוֹלָם
וֵאלֹהַיִךְ לְתִפְאַרְתֵּךְ:

20] לֹא־יָבוֹא עוֹד שִׁמְשֵׁךְ
וִירֵחֵךְ לֹא יֵאָסֵף
כִּי יְהֹוָה יִהְיֶה־לָּךְ לְאוֹר עוֹלָם
וְשָׁלְמוּ יְמֵי אֶבְלֵךְ:

21] וְעַמֵּךְ כֻּלָּם צַדִּיקִים
לְעוֹלָם יִירְשׁוּ אָרֶץ
נֵצֶר מַטָּעַי מַעֲשֵׂה יָדַי לְהִתְפָּאֵר:

22] הַקָּטֹן יִהְיֶה לָאֶלֶף
וְהַצָּעִיר לְגוֹי עָצוּם
אֲנִי יְהֹוָה בְּעִתָּהּ אֲחִישֶׁנָּה:

---

*/ So 1QIsᵃ, Septuagint, and Targum. (1QIsᵃ=manuscriptᵃ of Isaiah found
in the first cave of Qumran, the site of the caves where the Bible manuscripts were
found in 1949–50.)

נצבים

Isaiah

61 : 10 — 63 : 9

Chapters 40–66 of the Book of Isaiah are the work of an unknown author (often referred to as Deutero-Isaiah) who lived in Babylon during the days of the exile (sixth century B.C.E.). He preached unwavering trust in a God who would surely restore Israel to its homeland. Of all the prophets he is the most lyrical and his imagery the richest.

The seventh Isaianic message of consolation is usually read on the Sabbath before Rosh Hashanah. It ties in with the holy day season and with the sidrah which challenges Israel to make a choice for life and for God. "As a bridegroom rejoices over his bride," Isaiah sings, "so will God rejoice over you."

Chapter 61

10] I greatly rejoice in the LORD,
My whole being exults in my God.
For He has clothed me with garments of triumph,
Wrapped me in a robe of victory,
Like a bridegroom adorned with a turban,
Like a bride bedecked with her finery.

11] For as the earth brings forth her growth
And a garden makes the seed shoot up,
So the Lord GOD will make
Victory and renown shoot up
In the presence of all the nations.

Chapter 62

1] For the sake of Zion I will not be silent,
For the sake of Jerusalem I will not be still,
Till her victory emerge resplendent
And her triumph like a flaming torch.

2] Nations shall see your victory,
And every king your majesty;
And you shall be called by a new name
Which the LORD Himself shall bestow.

סא

10] שׂוֹשׂ אָשִׂישׂ בַּיהֹוָה
תָּגֵל נַפְשִׁי בֵּאלֹהַי
כִּי הִלְבִּישַׁנִי בִּגְדֵי־יֶשַׁע
מְעִיל צְדָקָה יְעָטָנִי
כֶּחָתָן יְכַהֵן פְּאֵר
וְכַכַּלָּה תַּעְדֶּה כֵלֶיהָ:

11] כִּי כָאָרֶץ תּוֹצִיא צִמְחָהּ
וּכְגַנָּה זֵרוּעֶיהָ תַצְמִיחַ
כֵּן אֲדֹנָי יֱהֹוִה יַצְמִיחַ
צְדָקָה וּתְהִלָּה נֶגֶד כָּל־הַגּוֹיִם:

סב

1] לְמַעַן צִיּוֹן לֹא אֶחֱשֶׁה
וּלְמַעַן יְרוּשָׁלַ͏ִם לֹא אֶשְׁקוֹט
עַד־יֵצֵא כַנֹּגַהּ צִדְקָהּ
וִישׁוּעָתָהּ כְּלַפִּיד יִבְעָר:

2] וְרָאוּ גוֹיִם צִדְקֵךְ
וְכָל־מְלָכִים כְּבוֹדֵךְ
וְקֹרָא לָךְ שֵׁם חָדָשׁ
אֲשֶׁר פִּי יְהֹוָה יִקֳּבֶנּוּ:

3] You shall be a glorious crown
In the hand of the LORD,
And a royal diadem
In the palm of your God.
4] Nevermore shall you be called "Forsaken,"
Nor shall your land be called "Desolate";
But you shall be called "I delight in her,"
And your land "Espoused."
For the LORD takes delight in you,
And your land shall be espoused.

5] As a youth espouses a maiden,
*-*Your sons-* shall espouse you;
And as a bridegroom rejoices over his bride,
So will your God rejoice over you.

6] Upon your walls, O Jerusalem,
I have set watchmen,
Who shall never be silent
By day or by night.
O you, the LORD's remembrancers,[b]
Take no rest

7] And give no rest to Him,
Until He establish Jerusalem
And make her renowned on earth.

8] The LORD has sworn by His right hand,
By His mighty arm:
Nevermore will I give your new grain
To your enemies for food,
Nor shall foreigners drink the new wine
For which you have labored.

3 וְהָיִ֛יתְ עֲטֶ֥רֶת תִּפְאֶ֖רֶת בְּיַד־יְהוָ֑ה
וּצְנִ֥יף מְלוּכָ֖ה בְּכַף־אֱלֹהָֽיִךְ׃
4 לֹא־יֵאָמֵר֩ לָ֨ךְ ע֜וֹד עֲזוּבָ֗ה
וּלְאַרְצֵךְ֙ לֹא־יֵאָמֵ֥ר עוֹד֙ שְׁמָמָ֔ה
כִּ֣י לָ֗ךְ יִקָּרֵא֙ חֶפְצִי־בָ֔הּ
וּלְאַרְצֵ֖ךְ בְּעוּלָ֑ה
כִּֽי־חָפֵ֤ץ יְהוָה֙ בָּ֔ךְ
וְאַרְצֵ֖ךְ תִּבָּעֵֽל׃
5 כִּֽי־יִבְעַ֤ל בָּחוּר֙ בְּתוּלָ֔ה
יִבְעָל֖וּךְ בָּנָ֑יִךְ
וּמְשׂ֤וֹשׂ חָתָן֙ עַל־כַּלָּ֔ה
יָשִׂ֥ישׂ עָלַ֖יִךְ אֱלֹהָֽיִךְ׃
6 עַל־חוֹמֹתַ֣יִךְ יְרוּשָׁלִַ֗ם
הִפְקַ֙דְתִּי֙ שֹֽׁמְרִ֔ים
כָּל־הַיּ֧וֹם וְכָל־הַלַּ֛יְלָה תָּמִ֖יד
לֹ֣א יֶחֱשׁ֑וּ
הַמַּזְכִּרִים֙ אֶת־יְהוָ֔ה
אַל־דֳּמִ֖י לָכֶֽם׃
7 וְאַֽל־תִּתְּנ֥וּ דֳמִ֖י ל֑וֹ
עַד־יְכוֹנֵ֞ן וְעַד־יָשִׂ֧ים אֶת־יְר֛וּשָׁלִַ֖ם
תְּהִלָּ֥ה בָּאָֽרֶץ׃
8 נִשְׁבַּ֧ע יְהוָ֛ה בִּֽימִינ֖וֹ
וּבִזְר֣וֹעַ עֻזּ֑וֹ
אִם־אֶתֵּן֩ אֶת־דְּגָנֵ֨ךְ ע֤וֹד
מַֽאֲכָל֙ לְאֹ֣יְבַ֔יִךְ
וְאִם־יִשְׁתּ֤וּ בְנֵֽי־נֵכָר֙ תִּ֣ירוֹשֵׁ֔ךְ
אֲשֶׁ֖ר יָגַ֥עַתְּ בּֽוֹ׃

- Change of vocalization yields "He who rebuilds you"
[b] I.e., the watchmen just mentioned

9] But those who harvest it shall eat it
And give praise to the LORD;
And those who gather it shall drink it
In My sacred courts.

10] Pass through, pass through the gates!
Clear the road for the people;
Build up, build up the highway,
Remove the rocks!
Raise an ensign over the peoples!

11] See, the LORD has proclaimed
To the end of the earth:
Announce to Fair Zion,
Your Deliverer is coming!
See, his reward is with Him,
His recompense before Him.[c]

12] And they shall be called, "The Holy People,
The Redeemed of the LORD,"
And you shall be called, "Sought Out,
A City Not Forsaken."

9] כִּי מְאַסְפָיו יֹאכְלֻהוּ

וְהִלְלוּ אֶת־יְהֹוָה

וּמְקַבְּצָיו יִשְׁתֻּהוּ

בְּחַצְרוֹת קָדְשִׁי:

10] עִבְרוּ עִבְרוּ בַּשְּׁעָרִים

פַּנּוּ דֶּרֶךְ הָעָם

סֹלּוּ סֹלּוּ הַמְסִלָּה

סַקְּלוּ מֵאֶבֶן

הָרִימוּ נֵס עַל־הָעַמִּים:

11] הִנֵּה יְהֹוָה הִשְׁמִיעַ

אֶל־קְצֵה הָאָרֶץ

אִמְרוּ לְבַת־צִיּוֹן

הִנֵּה יִשְׁעֵךְ בָּא

הִנֵּה שְׂכָרוֹ אִתּוֹ

וּפְעֻלָּתוֹ לְפָנָיו:

12] וְקָרְאוּ לָהֶם עַם־הַקֹּדֶשׁ

גְּאוּלֵי יְהֹוָה

וְלָךְ יִקָּרֵא דְרוּשָׁה

עִיר לֹא נֶעֱזָבָה:

Chapter 63

1] Who is this coming from Edom,
In crimsoned garments from Bozrah—
[Who is] this, majestic in attire,
[a-]Pressing forward[-a] in His great might?
"It is I, who contend victoriously,
[b-]Powerful to give triumph."[-b]

סג

1] מִי־זֶה בָּא מֵאֱדוֹם

חֲמוּץ בְּגָדִים מִבָּצְרָה

זֶה הָדוּר בִּלְבוּשׁוֹ

צֹעֶה בְּרֹב כֹּחוֹ

אֲנִי מְדַבֵּר בִּצְדָקָה

רַב לְהוֹשִׁיעַ:

---

[c] The recompense to the cities of Judah; cf. Jer. 31.14, 16

[a-a] Meaning of Heb. uncertain; emendation yields "striding"

[b-b] Change of vocalization yields "Who contest triumphantly"; cf. 19.20

2] Why is your clothing so red,
Your garments like his who treads grapes?[c]

3] "I trod out a vintage alone;
[d-Of the peoples-d] no man was with Me.
I trod them down in My anger,
Trampled them in My rage;
Their life-blood[e] bespattered My garments,
And all My clothing was stained.

4] For I had planned a day of vengeance,
And My year of redemption arrived.

5] Then I looked, but there was none to help;
I stared, but there was none to aid—
So My own arm wrought the triumph,
And [f-My own rage-f] was My aid.

6] I trampled peoples in My anger,
[g-I made them drunk with-g] My rage,
And I hurled their glory to the ground."

7] I will recount the kind acts of the LORD,
The praises of the LORD—
For all that the LORD has wrought for us,
The vast bounty to the House of Israel
That He bestowed upon them
According to His mercy and His great kindness.

8] He thought: Surely they are My people,
Children who will not play false.
[h-So He was their Deliverer.

מַדּוּעַ אָדֹם לִלְבוּשֶׁךָ [2
וּבְגָדֶיךָ כְּדֹרֵךְ בְּגַת:

פּוּרָה דָּרַכְתִּי לְבַדִּי [3
וּמֵעַמִּים אֵין־אִישׁ אִתִּי
וְאֶדְרְכֵם בְּאַפִּי
וְאֶרְמְסֵם בַּחֲמָתִי
וְיֵז נִצְחָם עַל־בְּגָדַי
וְכָל־מַלְבּוּשַׁי אֶגְאָלְתִּי:

כִּי יוֹם נָקָם בְּלִבִּי [4
וּשְׁנַת גְּאוּלַי בָּאָה:

וְאַבִּיט וְאֵין עֹזֵר [5
וְאֶשְׁתּוֹמֵם וְאֵין סוֹמֵךְ
וַתּוֹשַׁע לִי זְרֹעִי
וַחֲמָתִי הִיא סְמָכָתְנִי:

וְאָבוּס עַמִּים בְּאַפִּי [6
וַאֲשַׁכְּרֵם בַּחֲמָתִי
וְאוֹרִיד לָאָרֶץ נִצְחָם:

חַסְדֵי יְהוָה אַזְכִּיר [7
תְּהִלֹּת יְהוָה
כְּעַל כֹּל אֲשֶׁר־גְּמָלָנוּ יְהוָה
וְרַב־טוּב לְבֵית יִשְׂרָאֵל
אֲשֶׁר־גְּמָלָם כְּרַחֲמָיו
וּכְרֹב חֲסָדָיו:

וַיֹּאמֶר אַךְ־עַמִּי הֵמָּה [8
בָּנִים לֹא יְשַׁקֵּרוּ
וַיְהִי לָהֶם לְמוֹשִׁיעַ:

---

[c] Lit. "in a press"   [d-d] Emendation yields "Peoples, and...."   [e] Meaning of Heb. uncertain
[f-f] Many mss. read vetzidkati "My victorious [right hand]"; cf. 59.16
[g-g] Many mss. and Targum read "I shattered them in"; cf. 14.25
[h-h] Ancient versions read "So He was their Deliverer | 9] In all their troubles. | No

9] In all their troubles He was troubled,
And the angel of His Presence delivered them.ᴬ
In His love and pity
He Himself redeemed them,
Raised them, and exalted them
All the days of old.

[9 בְּכָל־צָרָתָם לוֹ צָר
וּמַלְאַךְ פָּנָיו הוֹשִׁיעָם
בְּאַהֲבָתוֹ וּבְחֶמְלָתוֹ
הוּא גְאָלָם
וַיְנַטְּלֵם וַיְנַשְּׂאֵם
כָּל־יְמֵי עוֹלָם:

[so ketiv] *angel or messenger, / His own Presence delivered them." Cf. Deut.* 4.37
which yields "He Himself"

וילך

Chapters 40–66 of the Book of Isaiah are the work of an unknown author (often referred to as Deutero-Isaiah) who lived in Babylon during the days of the exile (sixth century B.C.E.). He preached unwavering trust in a God who would surely restore Israel to its homeland. Of all the prophets he is the most lyrical and his imagery the richest.

The prophecy, last of the haftarot of consolation, contains the heart of Deutero-Isaiah's message: "Seek the Lord while He can be found"; "Observe what is right and do what is just, for soon My salvation shall come." It is a fitting introduction to the new year. The same haftarah is read on the afternoon of Tishah b'Av and introduces a note of hope.

Isaiah

55 : 6 — 56 : 8

נה

Chapter 55

6] Seek the LORD while He can be found,
Call to Him while He is near.

7] Let the wicked give up his ways,
The sinful man his plans;
Let him turn back to the LORD,
And He will pardon him;
To our God,
For He freely forgives.

8] For My plans are not your plans,
Nor are My ways[e] your ways[e]
     —declares the LORD.

9] But as the heavens are high above the earth,
So are My ways[e] high above your ways[e]
And My plans above your plans.

10] For as the rain or snow drops from heaven
And returns not there,
But soaks the earth
And makes it bring forth vegetation,
Yielding [d]seed for sowing and bread for eating,[d]

[6] דִּרְשׁ֥וּ יְהֹוָ֖ה בְּהִמָּצְא֑וֹ
קְרָאֻ֖הוּ בִּֽהְיוֹת֥וֹ קָרֽוֹב:

[7] יַעֲזֹ֤ב רָשָׁע֙ דַּרְכּ֔וֹ
וְאִ֥ישׁ אָ֖וֶן מַחְשְׁבֹתָ֑יו
וְיָשֹׁ֤ב אֶל־יְהֹוָה֙ וִֽירַחֲמֵ֔הוּ
וְאֶל־אֱלֹהֵ֖ינוּ כִּֽי־יַרְבֶּ֥ה לִסְלֽוֹחַ:

[8] כִּ֣י לֹ֤א מַחְשְׁבוֹתַי֙ מַחְשְׁב֣וֹתֵיכֶ֔ם
וְלֹ֥א דַרְכֵיכֶ֖ם דְּרָכָ֑י
נְאֻ֖ם יְהֹוָֽה:

[9] כִּֽי־גָבְה֥וּ שָׁמַ֖יִם מֵאָ֑רֶץ
כֵּ֣ן גָּבְה֤וּ דְרָכַי֙ מִדַּרְכֵיכֶ֔ם
וּמַחְשְׁבֹתַ֖י מִמַּחְשְׁבֹֽתֵיכֶֽם:

[10] כִּ֡י כַּֽאֲשֶׁ֣ר יֵרֵד֩ הַגֶּ֨שֶׁם וְהַשֶּׁ֜לֶג מִן־הַשָּׁמַ֗יִם
וְשָׁ֙מָּה֙ לֹ֣א יָשׁ֔וּב
כִּ֚י אִם־הִרְוָ֣ה אֶת־הָאָ֔רֶץ
וְהֽוֹלִידָ֖הּ וְהִצְמִיחָ֑הּ
וְנָ֤תַן זֶ֙רַע֙ לַזֹּרֵ֔עַ וְלֶ֖חֶם לָֽאֹכֵֽל:

---

[e] *Emendation yields "words"; cf. v. 11 and 40.8*
[d-d] *Lit. "seed for the sower and bread for the eater"*

11] So is the word that issues from My mouth:
It does not come back to Me unfulfilled,
But performs what I purpose,
Achieves what I sent it to do.

12] Yea, you shall leaveᵉ in joy and be led home
secure.
Before you, mount and hill shall shout aloud,
And all the trees of the field shall clap their hands.

13] Instead of the brier, a cypress shall rise;
Instead of the nettle, a myrtle shall rise.
These shall stand as a testimony to the LORD,
As an everlasting sign that shall not perish.

Chapter 56

1] Thus said the LORD:
Observe what is right and do what is just;
For soon My salvation shall come,
And My deliverance be revealed.

2] Happy is the man who does this,
The man who holds fast to it:
Who keeps the sabbath and does not profane it,
And stays his hand from doing any evil.

3] Let not the foreigner say,
Who has attached himself to the LORD,
"The LORD will keep me apart from His people";
And let not the eunuch say,
"I am a withered tree."

4] For thus said the LORD:
"As regards the eunuchs who keep My sabbaths,

נו

11] כֵּן יִהְיֶה דְבָרִי אֲשֶׁר יֵצֵא מִפִּי
לֹא־יָשׁוּב אֵלַי רֵיקָם
כִּי אִם־עָשָׂה אֶת־אֲשֶׁר חָפַצְתִּי
וְהִצְלִיחַ אֲשֶׁר שְׁלַחְתִּיו׃

12] כִּי־בְשִׂמְחָה תֵצֵאוּ וּבְשָׁלוֹם תּוּבָלוּן
הֶהָרִים וְהַגְּבָעוֹת יִפְצְחוּ לִפְנֵיכֶם רִנָּה
וְכָל־עֲצֵי הַשָּׂדֶה יִמְחֲאוּ־כָף׃

13] תַּחַת הַנַּעֲצוּץ יַעֲלֶה בְרוֹשׁ
וְתַחַת הַסִּרְפַּד יַעֲלֶה הֲדַס
וְהָיָה לַיהוָה לְשֵׁם
לְאוֹת עוֹלָם לֹא יִכָּרֵת׃

11] כֹּה אָמַר יְהוָה
שִׁמְרוּ מִשְׁפָּט וַעֲשׂוּ צְדָקָה
כִּי־קְרוֹבָה יְשׁוּעָתִי לָבוֹא
וְצִדְקָתִי לְהִגָּלוֹת׃

21] אַשְׁרֵי אֱנוֹשׁ יַעֲשֶׂה־זֹּאת
וּבֶן־אָדָם יַחֲזִיק בָּהּ
שֹׁמֵר שַׁבָּת מֵחַלְּלוֹ
וְשֹׁמֵר יָדוֹ מֵעֲשׂוֹת כָּל־רָע׃

31] וְאַל־יֹאמַר בֶּן־הַנֵּכָר
הַנִּלְוָה אֶל־יְהוָה לֵאמֹר
הַבְדֵּל יַבְדִּילַנִי יְהוָה מֵעַל עַמּוֹ
וְאַל־יֹאמַר הַסָּרִיס
הֵן אֲנִי עֵץ יָבֵשׁ׃

41] כִּי־כֹה אָמַר יְהוָה
לַסָּרִיסִים אֲשֶׁר יִשְׁמְרוּ אֶת־שַׁבְּתוֹתַי

ᵉ I.e., leave the Babylonian exile

1624

Who have chosen what I desire
And hold fast to My covenant—

5] I will give them, in My House
And within My walls,
A monument and a name
Better than sons or daughters.
I will give them an everlasting name
Which shall not perish.

6] As for the foreigners
Who attach themselves to the LORD,
To minister to Him.
And to love the name of the LORD,
To be His servants—
All who keep the sabbath and do not profane it,
And who hold fast to My covenant—

7] I will bring them to My sacred mount
And let them rejoice in My house of prayer.
Their burnt offerings and sacrifices
Shall be welcome on My altar;
For My House shall be called
A house of prayer for all peoples."

8] Thus declares the Lord GOD,
Who gathers the dispersed of Israel:
"I will gather still more to those already
    gathered."

וּבָחֲרוּ בַּאֲשֶׁר חָפָצְתִּי

וּמַחֲזִיקִים בִּבְרִיתִי:

5] וְנָתַתִּי לָהֶם בְּבֵיתִי

וּבְחוֹמֹתַי

יָד וָשֵׁם

טוֹב מִבָּנִים וּמִבָּנוֹת

שֵׁם עוֹלָם אֶתֶּן־לוֹ

אֲשֶׁר לֹא יִכָּרֵת:

6] וּבְנֵי הַנֵּכָר

הַנִּלְוִים עַל־יְהֹוָה לְשָׁרְתוֹ

וּלְאַהֲבָה אֶת־שֵׁם יְהֹוָה

לִהְיוֹת לוֹ לַעֲבָדִים

כָּל־שֹׁמֵר שַׁבָּת מֵחַלְּלוֹ

וּמַחֲזִיקִים בִּבְרִיתִי:

7] וַהֲבִיאוֹתִים אֶל־הַר קָדְשִׁי

וְשִׂמַּחְתִּים בְּבֵית תְּפִלָּתִי

עוֹלֹתֵיהֶם וְזִבְחֵיהֶם

לְרָצוֹן עַל־מִזְבְּחִי

כִּי בֵיתִי בֵּית־תְּפִלָּה יִקָּרֵא

לְכָל־הָעַמִּים:

8] נְאֻם אֲדֹנָי יֱהֹוִה

מְקַבֵּץ נִדְחֵי יִשְׂרָאֵל

עוֹד אֲקַבֵּץ עָלָיו לְנִקְבָּצָיו:

האזינו

Second Samuel

22 : 1-51

The Book of Samuel is divided into two parts. It is primarily the story of Samuel's ministry as the spiritual guide of Israel and of the reign of Israel's first two kings, Saul and David (about 1000 B.C.E.). It is history written from a theological perspective: all of Israel's fate hinges on the performance or non-performance of God's commandments.

The sidrah records the "Song of Moses," the haftarah a prayer of David (which is repeated, with minor changes, as Psalm 18). The mood befits the time of the High Holy Days: "In my anguish I called on the Lord . . . my cry entered His ears." The prayer serves also as the haftarah for the seventh day of Pesach.

Chapter 22

כב

1] *David addressed the words of this song to the LORD, after the LORD had saved him from the hands of all his enemies and from the hands of Saul.

1] וַיְדַבֵּר דָּוִד לַיהֹוָה אֶת־דִּבְרֵי הַשִּׁירָה הַזֹּאת בְּיוֹם הִצִּיל יְהֹוָה אֹתוֹ מִכַּף כָּל־אֹיְבָיו וּמִכַּף שָׁאוּל:

2] He said:
O LORD, my crag, my fastness, my deliverer!

2] וַיֹּאמַר
יְהֹוָה סַלְעִי וּמְצֻדָתִי וּמְפַלְטִי־לִי:

3] O ᵇ⁻God, the rock⁻ᵇ wherein I take shelter:
My shield, my ᶜ⁻mighty champion,⁻ᶜ my fortress and refuge!
My savior, You who rescue me from violence!

3] אֱלֹהֵי צוּרִי אֶחֱסֶה־בּוֹ
מָגִנִּי וְקֶרֶן יִשְׁעִי
מִשְׂגַּבִּי וּמְנוּסִי
מֹשִׁעִי מֵחָמָס תֹּשִׁעֵנִי:

4] ᵈ⁻All praise! I called on the LORD,⁻ᵈ
And I was delivered from my enemies.

4] מְהֻלָּל אֶקְרָא יְהֹוָה
וּמֵאֹיְבַי אִוָּשֵׁעַ:

5] For the breakers of Death encompassed me,
The torrents of Belialᵉ terrified me;

5] כִּי אֲפָפֻנִי מִשְׁבְּרֵי־מָוֶת
נַחֲלֵי בְלִיַּעַל יְבַעֲתֻנִי:

6] The snares of Sheol encircled me,
The toils of Death engulfed me.

6] חֶבְלֵי שְׁאוֹל סַבֻּנִי
קִדְּמֻנִי מֹקְשֵׁי־מָוֶת:

ᵃ This poem occurs again as Ps. 18, with a number of variations, some of which are cited in the following notes

ᵇ⁻ᵇ Lit. "the God of my rock"; Ps. 18.3 "my God, my rock"

ᶜ⁻ᶜ Lit. "horn of rescue"

ᵈ⁻ᵈ Construction of Heb. uncertain

ᵉ I.e., the nether world, like "Death" and "Sheol"

7] In my anguish I called on the LORD,
Cried out to my God;
In His abode*ʲ* He heard my voice,
My cry entered His ears.

8] Then the earth rocked and quaked,
The foundations of heaven*ᵍ* shook—
Rocked by His indignation.

9] Smoke went up from His nostrils,
From His mouth came devouring fire;
Live coals blazed forth from Him.

10] He bent the sky and came down,
Thick cloud beneath His feet.

11] He mounted a cherub and flew;
*ʰ*He was seen*ʰ* on the wings of the wind.

12] He made pavilions of darkness about Him,
Dripping clouds, huge thunderheads;

13] In the brilliance before Him
Blazed fiery coals.

14] The LORD thundered forth from heaven,
The Most High sent forth His voice;

15] He let loose bolts, and scattered them;*ⁱ*
Lightning and, put them to rout.

16] The bed of the sea was exposed,
The foundations of the world were laid bare
By the mighty roaring of the LORD,
At the blast of the breath of His nostrils.

בְּצַר־לִי אֶקְרָא יְהֹוָה [7
וְאֶל־אֱלֹהַי אֶקְרָא
וַיִּשְׁמַע מֵהֵיכָלוֹ קוֹלִי
וְשַׁוְעָתִי בְּאָזְנָיו:

וַיִּתְגָּעַשׁ וַתִּרְעַשׁ הָאָרֶץ [8
מוֹסְדוֹת הַשָּׁמַיִם יִרְגָּזוּ
וַיִּתְגָּעֲשׁוּ כִּי־חָרָה לוֹ:

עָלָה עָשָׁן בְּאַפּוֹ [9
וְאֵשׁ מִפִּיו תֹּאכֵל
גֶּחָלִים בָּעֲרוּ מִמֶּנּוּ:

וַיֵּט שָׁמַיִם וַיֵּרַד [10
וַעֲרָפֶל תַּחַת רַגְלָיו:

וַיִּרְכַּב עַל־כְּרוּב וַיָּעֹף [11
וַיֵּרָא עַל־כַּנְפֵי־רוּחַ:

וַיָּשֶׁת חֹשֶׁךְ סְבִיבֹתָיו סֻכּוֹת [12
חַשְׁרַת־מַיִם עָבֵי שְׁחָקִים:

מִנֹּגַהּ נֶגְדּוֹ [13
בָּעֲרוּ גַּחֲלֵי־אֵשׁ:

יַרְעֵם מִן־שָׁמַיִם יְהֹוָה [14
וְעֶלְיוֹן יִתֵּן קוֹלוֹ:

וַיִּשְׁלַח חִצִּים וַיְפִיצֵם [15
בָּרָק וַיָּהֹם:

וַיֵּרָאוּ אֲפִקֵי יָם [16
יִגָּלוּ מֹסְדוֹת תֵּבֵל
בְּגַעֲרַת יְהֹוָה
מִנִּשְׁמַת רוּחַ אַפּוֹ:

ʲ Lit. "Temple"
ᵍ Ps. 18.8 "mountains"
ʰ⁻ʰ Ps. 18.11 "Gliding"
ⁱ I.e., the enemies in v. 4

17] He reached down from on high, He took me,
Drew me out of the mighty waters;ⁱ

18] He rescued me from my enemy so strong,
From foes too mighty for me.

19] They attacked me on my day of calamity,
But the LORD was my stay.

20] He brought me out to freedom,
He rescued me because He was pleased with me.

21] The LORD rewarded me according to my
merit,
He requited the cleanness of my hands.

22] For I have kept the ways of the LORD
And have not been guilty before my God;

23] I am mindful of all His rules
And have not departed from His laws.

24] I have been blameless before Him,
And have guarded myself against sinning—

25] And the LORD has requited my merit,
According to my purity in His sight.

26] With the loyal You deal loyally;
With the blameless hero,^k blamelessly.

27] With the pure You act in purity,
And with the perverse You are wily.

28] To humble folk You give victory,
^{l-}And You look with scorn on the haughty.^{-l}

29] You, O LORD, are my lamp;
The LORD lights up my darkness.

יְשָׁלַ֤ח מִמָּר֨וֹם יִקָּחֵ֔נִי [17
יַֽמְשֵׁ֗נִי מִמַּ֥יִם רַבִּֽים:

יַצִּילֵ֗נִי מֵאֹֽיְבִ֥י עָ֑ז [18
מִ֝שֹּׂנְאַ֗י כִּ֣י אָמְצ֥וּ מִמֶּֽנִּי:

יְקַדְּמֻ֥נִי בְּי֣וֹם אֵידִ֑י [19
וַיְהִ֖י יְהֹוָ֣ה מִשְׁעָ֣ן לִֽי:

וַיֹּצֵ֣א לַמֶּרְחָ֣ב אֹתִ֑י [20
יְחַלְּצֵ֗נִי כִּי־חָ֥פֵֽץ בִּֽי:

יִגְמְלֵ֣נִי יְהֹוָ֣ה כְּצִדְקָתִ֑י [21
כְּבֹ֥ר יָ֝דַ֗י יָשִׁ֥יב לִֽי:

כִּ֣י שָׁ֭מַרְתִּי דַּרְכֵ֣י יְהֹוָ֑ה [22
וְלֹ֥א רָ֝שַׁ֗עְתִּי מֵאֱלֹהָֽי:

כִּ֣י כָל־מִשְׁפָּטָ֣יו לְנֶגְדִּ֑י [23
וְ֝חֻקֹּתָ֗יו לֹֽא־אָסוּר מִמֶּֽנָּה:

וָאֱהִ֣י תָמִ֣ים ל֑וֹ [24
וָ֝אֶשְׁתַּמְּרָ֗ה מֵעֲוֺנִֽי:

וַיָּֽשֶׁב־יְהֹוָ֣ה לִ֣י כְּצִדְקָתִ֑י [25
כְּ֝בֹרִ֗י לְנֶ֣גֶד עֵינָֽיו:

עִם־חָסִ֥יד תִּתְחַסָּ֑ד [26
עִם־גְּב֥וֹר תָּמִ֥ים תִּתַּמָּֽם:

עִם־נָבָ֥ר תִּתְבָּרָ֑ר [27
וְעִם־עִ֝קֵּ֗שׁ תִּתְפַּתָּֽל:

וְאֶת־עַ֣ם עָנִ֣י תּוֹשִׁ֑יעַ [28
וְעֵינֶ֖יךָ עַל־רָמִ֣ים תַּשְׁפִּֽיל:

כִּֽי־אַתָּ֥ה נֵרִ֣י יְהֹוָ֑ה [29
וַֽיהֹוָ֖ה יַגִּ֣יהַּ חׇשְׁכִּֽי:

ⁱ Cf. v. 5
^k Ps. 18.26 "man"
^{l-l} Lit. "And lower Your eyes on the haughty"; Ps. 18.28 "But haughty eyes You
humble"

30] With You, I can rush a barrier,[m]
With my God, I can scale a wall.

כִּי בְכָה אָרוּץ גְּדוּד [30
בֵּאלֹהַי אֲדַלֶּג־שׁוּר:

31] The way of God is perfect,
The word of the Lord is pure.
He is a shield to all who take refuge in Him.

הָאֵל תָּמִים דַּרְכּוֹ [31
אִמְרַת יְהֹוָה צְרוּפָה
מָגֵן הוּא לְכֹל הַחֹסִים בּוֹ:

32] Yea, who is a god except the Lord,
Who is a rock except God—

כִּי מִי־אֵל מִבַּלְעֲדֵי יְהֹוָה [32
וּמִי צוּר מִבַּלְעֲדֵי אֱלֹהֵינוּ:

33] The God, [n]my mighty stronghold,[n]
Who kept[o] my path secure;

הָאֵל מָעוּזִּי חָיִל [33
וַיַּתֵּר תָּמִים דַּרְכִּי:

34] Who made my legs like a deer's,
And set me firm on the[p] heights;

מְשַׁוֶּה רַגְלַי כָּאַיָּלוֹת [34
וְעַל בָּמֹתַי יַעֲמִידֵנִי:

35] Who trained my hands for battle,
So that my arms can bend a bow of bronze!

מְלַמֵּד יָדַי לַמִּלְחָמָה [35
וְנִחַת קֶשֶׁת־נְחוּשָׁה זְרֹעֹתָי:

36] You have granted me the shield of Your
protection
[q]And Your providence has made me great.[q]

וַתִּתֶּן־לִי מָגֵן יִשְׁעֶךָ [36
וַעֲנֹתְךָ תַּרְבֵּנִי:

37] You have let me stride on freely,
And my feet have not slipped.

תַּרְחִיב צַעֲדִי תַּחְתֵּנִי [37
וְלֹא מָעֲדוּ קַרְסֻלָּי:

38] I pursued my enemies and wiped them out,
I did not turn back till I destroyed them.

אֶרְדְּפָה אֹיְבַי וָאַשְׁמִידֵם [38
וְלֹא אָשׁוּב עַד־כַּלּוֹתָם:

39] I destroyed them, I struck them down;
They rose no more, they lay at my feet.

וָאֲכַלֵּם וָאֶמְחָצֵם וְלֹא יְקוּמוּן [39
וַיִּפְּלוּ תַּחַת רַגְלָי:

40] You have girt me with strength for battle,
Brought low my foes before me,

וַתַּזְרֵנִי חַיִל לַמִּלְחָמָה [40
תַּכְרִיעַ קָמַי תַּחְתֵּנִי:

41] Made my enemies turn tail before me,
My foes—and I wiped them out.

וְאֹיְבַי תַּתָּה לִּי עֹרֶף [41
מְשַׂנְאַי וָאַצְמִיתֵם:

---

[m] Cf. post-biblical gedudiyot, "walls," Aramaic gudda, "wall"
[n-n] Ps. 18.33 "who girded me with might"
[o] Meaning of Heb. uncertain; Ps. 18.33 "made"
[p] Taking bamotai as a poetic form of bamot; cf. Hab. 3.19; others "my"
[q-q] Meaning of Heb. uncertain

42] They looked,ʳ but there was none to deliver;
To the Lord, but He answered them not.

אֵלֹ־יְהוָה וְלֹא עָנָם׃   [42 יִשְׁעוּ וְאֵין מֹשִׁיעַ

43] I pounded them like dust of the earth,
Stamped, crushed them like dirt of the streets.

כְּטִיט־חוּצוֹת אֲדִקֵּם אֶרְקָעֵם׃   [43 וְאֶשְׁחָקֵם כַּעֲפַר־אָרֶץ

44] You have rescued me from the strife of
      peoples,ˢ
ᵗ˙Kept me to beᵗ a ruler of nations;
Peoples I knew not must serve me.

עַם לֹא־יָדַעְתִּי יַעַבְדֻנִי׃   [44 וַתְּפַלְּטֵנִי מֵרִיבֵי עַמִּי
תְּשִׁמְרֵנִי לְרֹאשׁ גּוֹיִם

45] Aliens have cringed before me,
Paid me homage at the mere report of me.

לִשְׁמוֹעַ אֹזֶן יִשָּׁמְעוּ לִי׃   [45 בְּנֵי נֵכָר יִתְכַּחֲשׁוּ־לִי

46] Aliens have lost courage
�q˙And come trembling out of their fastnesses.˙�q

וְיַחְגְּרוּ מִמִּסְגְּרוֹתָם׃   [46 בְּנֵי נֵכָר יִבֹּלוּ

47] The Lord lives! Blessed is my rock!
Exalted be God, the rock
Who gives me victory;

וְיָרֻם אֱלֹהֵי צוּר יִשְׁעִי׃   [47 חַי־יְהוָה וּבָרוּךְ צוּרִי

48] The God who has vindicated me
And made peoples subject to me,

וּמֹרִיד עַמִּים תַּחְתֵּנִי׃   [48 הָאֵל הַנֹּתֵן נְקָמֹת לִי

49] Rescued me from my enemies,
Raised me clear of my foes,
Saved me from lawless men!

מֵאִישׁ חֲמָסִים תַּצִּילֵנִי׃   [49 וּמוֹצִיאִי מֵאֹיְבָי
וּמִקָּמַי תְּרוֹמְמֵנִי

50] For this I sing Your praise among the nations
And hymn Your name:

וּלְשִׁמְךָ אֲזַמֵּר׃   [50 עַל־כֵּן אוֹדְךָ יְהוָה בַּגּוֹיִם

51] ᵘ˙Tower of victory˙ᵘ to His king,
Who deals graciously with His anointed,
With David and his offspring evermore.

וְעֹשֶׂה־חֶסֶד לִמְשִׁיחוֹ   [51 מַגְדִּיל יְשׁוּעוֹת מַלְכּוֹ
לְדָוִד וּלְזַרְעוֹ עַד־עוֹלָם׃

ʳ Ps. 18.42 "cried"
ˢ So some mss. and the Septuagint; most mss. and the printed editions "my people"
ᵗ⁻ᵗ Ps. 18.44 "made me"
 q⁻q Meaning of Heb. uncertain
ᵘ⁻ᵘ Ketiv Ps. 18.51 reads "Who accords wondrous victories"

Joshua became Moses' successor and led the conquest of the Promised Land. While his name is attached to the 24 chapters which recount the campaign, the book is likely of much later origin. It portrays history essentially as a judgment of God.

The end of the Torah cycle leads directly into the story of Joshua and of the conquest of the land under his leadership. Moses had encouraged Joshua to be "strong and resolute," and with these same words the new leader addresses his people.

וזאת הברכה

Joshua

1 : 1-18

Chapter 1

א

1] After the death of Moses the servant of the LORD, the LORD said to Joshua son of Nun, Moses' attendant:

2] "My servant Moses is dead. Prepare to cross the Jordan, together with all this people, into the land which I am giving to the Israelites. 3] Every spot on which your foot treads I give to you, as I promised Moses.

4] Your territory shall extend from the wilderness and the Lebanon to the Great River, the River Euphrates [on the east] —the whole Hittite country—and up to the Mediterranean[a] Sea on the west.

5] No man shall be able to resist you as long as you live. As I was with Moses, so I will be with you; I will not fail you or forsake you.

6] "Be strong and resolute, for you shall apportion to this people the land that I swore to their fathers to give them.

7] But you must be very strong and resolute to observe faithfully all the Teaching that My servant Moses enjoined upon you. Do not deviate from it to the right or to the left, that you may be successful wherever you go.

8] Let not this Book of the Teaching cease from

[1] וַיְהִ֗י אַחֲרֵ֛י מ֥וֹת מֹשֶׁ֖ה עֶ֣בֶד יְהוָ֑ה וַיֹּ֤אמֶר יְהוָה֙ אֶל־יְהוֹשֻׁ֣עַ בִּן־נ֔וּן מְשָׁרֵ֥ת מֹשֶׁ֖ה לֵאמֹֽר: [2] מֹשֶׁ֥ה עַבְדִּ֖י מֵ֑ת וְעַתָּה֩ ק֨וּם עֲבֹ֜ר אֶת־הַיַּרְדֵּ֣ן הַזֶּ֗ה אַתָּה֙ וְכָל־הָעָ֣ם הַזֶּ֔ה אֶל־הָאָ֕רֶץ אֲשֶׁ֧ר אָנֹכִ֛י נֹתֵ֥ן לָהֶ֖ם לִבְנֵ֥י יִשְׂרָאֵֽל: [3] כָּל־מָק֗וֹם אֲשֶׁ֨ר תִּדְרֹ֧ךְ כַּף־רַגְלְכֶ֛ם בּ֖וֹ לָכֶ֣ם נְתַתִּ֑יו כַּאֲשֶׁ֥ר דִּבַּ֖רְתִּי אֶל־מֹשֶֽׁה: [4] מֵהַמִּדְבָּ֨ר וְהַלְּבָנ֜וֹן הַזֶּ֗ה וְעַד־הַנָּהָ֤ר הַגָּדוֹל֙ נְהַר־פְּרָ֔ת כֹּ֚ל אֶ֣רֶץ הַֽחִתִּ֔ים וְעַד־הַיָּ֥ם הַגָּד֖וֹל מְב֣וֹא הַשָּׁ֑מֶשׁ יִֽהְיֶ֖ה גְּבוּלְכֶֽם: [5] לֹֽא־יִתְיַצֵּ֥ב אִישׁ֙ לְפָנֶ֔יךָ כֹּ֖ל יְמֵ֣י חַיֶּ֑יךָ כַּאֲשֶׁ֨ר הָיִ֤יתִי עִם־מֹשֶׁה֙ אֶהְיֶ֣ה עִמָּ֔ךְ לֹ֥א אַרְפְּךָ֖ וְלֹ֥א אֶעֶזְבֶֽךָּ: [6] חֲזַ֖ק וֶאֱמָ֑ץ כִּ֣י אַתָּ֗ה תַּנְחִיל֙ אֶת־הָעָ֣ם הַזֶּ֔ה אֶת־הָאָ֕רֶץ אֲשֶׁר־נִשְׁבַּ֥עְתִּי לַאֲבוֹתָ֖ם לָתֵ֥ת לָהֶֽם: [7] רַ֣ק חֲזַ֣ק וֶֽאֱמַ֣ץ מְאֹ֗ד לִשְׁמֹ֤ר לַעֲשׂוֹת֙ כְּכָל־הַתּוֹרָ֗ה אֲשֶׁ֤ר צִוְּךָ֙ מֹשֶׁ֣ה עַבְדִּ֔י אַל־תָּס֥וּר מִמֶּ֖נּוּ יָמִ֣ין וּשְׂמֹ֑אול לְמַ֣עַן תַּשְׂכִּ֔יל בְּכֹ֖ל אֲשֶׁ֥ר תֵּלֵֽךְ: [8] לֹֽא־יָמ֡וּשׁ סֵפֶר֩ הַתּוֹרָ֨ה הַזֶּ֜ה מִפִּ֗יךָ

---

[a] Heb. "Great"

your lips, but recite it day and night, so that you may observe faithfully all that is written in it. Only then will you prosper in your undertakings and only then will you be successful.

9] "I charge you: Be strong and resolute; do not be terrified or dismayed, for the LORD your God is with you wherever you go."

10] Joshua thereupon gave orders to the officials of the people:

11] "Go through the camp and charge the people thus: Get provisions ready, for in three days' time you are to cross the Jordan, in order to enter and occupy the land which the LORD your God is giving you as a possession."

12] Then Joshua said to the Reubenites, the Gadites, and the half-tribe of Manasseh,

13] "Remember what Moses the servant of the LORD enjoined upon you, when he said: 'The LORD your God is granting you a haven; He is assigning this territory to you.'

14] Let your wives, children, and livestock remain in the land which Moses assigned to you *b-on this side of-b* the Jordan; but every one of your fighting men shall go across armed*c* in the van of your kinsmen. And you shall assist them

15] until the LORD has given your kinsmen a haven, such as you have, and they too have gained possession of the land which the LORD your God has assigned to them. Then you may return to the land on the east side of the Jordan, which Moses the servant of the LORD assigned to you as your possession, and you may occupy it."

16] They answered Joshua, "We will do everything you have commanded us and we will go wherever you send us.

וְהָגִ֤יתָ בּוֹ֙ יוֹמָ֣ם וָלַ֔יְלָה לְמַ֙עַן֙ תִּשְׁמֹ֣ר לַעֲשׂ֔וֹת כְּכָל־הַכָּת֖וּב בּ֑וֹ כִּי־אָ֛ז תַּצְלִ֥יחַ אֶת־דְּרָכֶ֖ךָ וְאָ֥ז תַּשְׂכִּֽיל׃

9 הֲל֤וֹא צִוִּיתִ֙יךָ֙ חֲזַ֣ק וֶאֱמָ֔ץ אַֽל־תַּעֲרֹ֖ץ וְאַל־תֵּחָ֑ת כִּ֤י עִמְּךָ֙ יְהוָ֣ה אֱלֹהֶ֔יךָ בְּכֹ֖ל אֲשֶׁ֥ר תֵּלֵֽךְ׃

10 וַיְצַ֣ו יְהוֹשֻׁ֔עַ אֶת־שֹׁטְרֵ֥י הָעָ֖ם לֵאמֹֽר׃

11 עִבְר֣וּ ׀ בְּקֶ֣רֶב הַֽמַּחֲנֶ֗ה וְצַוּ֤וּ אֶת־הָעָם֙ לֵאמֹ֔ר הָכִ֥ינוּ לָכֶ֖ם צֵדָ֑ה כִּ֞י בְּע֣וֹד ׀ שְׁלֹ֣שֶׁת יָמִ֗ים אַתֶּם֙ עֹֽבְרִים֙ אֶת־הַיַּרְדֵּ֣ן הַזֶּ֔ה לָבוֹא֙ לָרֶ֣שֶׁת אֶת־הָאָ֔רֶץ אֲשֶׁר֙ יְהוָ֣ה אֱלֹֽהֵיכֶ֔ם נֹתֵ֥ן לָכֶ֖ם לְרִשְׁתָּֽהּ׃

12 וְלָרֽאוּבֵנִי֙ וְלַגָּדִ֔י וְלַחֲצִ֖י שֵׁ֣בֶט הַֽמְנַשֶּׁ֑ה אָמַ֥ר יְהוֹשֻׁ֖עַ לֵאמֹֽר׃ 13 זָכוֹר֙ אֶת־הַדָּבָ֔ר אֲשֶׁ֨ר צִוָּ֥ה אֶתְכֶ֛ם מֹשֶׁ֥ה עֶֽבֶד־יְהוָ֖ה לֵאמֹ֑ר יְהוָ֤ה אֱלֹֽהֵיכֶם֙ מֵנִ֣יחַ לָכֶ֔ם וְנָתַ֥ן לָכֶ֖ם אֶת־הָאָ֥רֶץ הַזֹּֽאת׃ 14 נְשֵׁיכֶ֣ם טַפְּכֶם֮ וּמִקְנֵיכֶם֒ יֵֽשְׁבוּ֙ בָּאָ֔רֶץ אֲשֶׁ֨ר נָתַ֥ן לָכֶ֛ם מֹשֶׁ֖ה בְּעֵ֣בֶר הַיַּרְדֵּ֑ן וְאַתֶּם֩ תַּעַבְר֨וּ חֲמֻשִׁ֜ים לִפְנֵ֣י אֲחֵיכֶ֗ם כֹּ֚ל גִּבּוֹרֵ֣י הַחַ֔יִל וַעֲזַרְתֶּ֖ם אוֹתָֽם׃ 15 עַ֠ד אֲשֶׁר־יָנִ֨יחַ יְהוָ֥ה ׀ לַֽאֲחֵיכֶם֮ כָּכֶם֒ וְיָרְשׁ֣וּ גַם־הֵ֔מָּה אֶת־הָאָ֕רֶץ אֲשֶׁר־יְהוָ֥ה אֱלֹֽהֵיכֶ֖ם נֹתֵ֣ן לָהֶ֑ם וְשַׁבְתֶּ֞ם לְאֶ֤רֶץ יְרֻשַּׁתְכֶם֙ וִירִשְׁתֶּ֣ם אוֹתָ֔הּ אֲשֶׁ֣ר ׀ נָתַ֣ן לָכֶ֗ם מֹשֶׁה֙ עֶ֣בֶד יְהוָ֔ה בְּעֵ֥בֶר הַיַּרְדֵּ֖ן מִזְרַ֥ח הַשָּֽׁמֶשׁ׃

16 וַֽיַּעֲנ֔וּ אֶת־יְהוֹשֻׁ֖עַ לֵאמֹ֑ר כֹּ֤ל אֲשֶׁר־צִוִּיתָ֙נוּ֙ נַֽעֲשֶׂ֔ה וְאֶֽל־כָּל־אֲשֶׁ֥ר תִּשְׁלָחֵ֖נוּ נֵלֵֽךְ׃

b-b Lit. "across"

c Meaning of Heb. uncertain

17] We will obey you just as we obeyed Moses; let but the Lord your God be with you as He was with Moses!

18] Any man who flouts your commands and does not obey every order you give him shall be put to death. Only be strong and resolute!"

כֹּל אֲשֶׁר־שָׁמַעְנוּ אֶל־מֹשֶׁה כֵּן נִשְׁמַע [17
אֵלֶיךָ רַק יִהְיֶה יְהוָה אֱלֹהֶיךָ עִמָּךְ כַּאֲשֶׁר
הָיָה עִם־מֹשֶׁה: 18] כָּל־אִישׁ אֲשֶׁר־יַמְרֶה אֶת־
פִּיךָ וְלֹא־יִשְׁמַע אֶת־דְּבָרֶיךָ לְכֹל אֲשֶׁר־תְּצַוֶּנּוּ
יוּמָת רַק חֲזַק וֶאֱמָץ:

The haftarah is taken from three prophets—Hosea, Micah, and Joel. It begins with Hosea's call on Israel to return to God (hence the name given to the Sabbath); then follow three verses from Micah that assure us of God's readiness to forgive our sins; and, finally, the selection from Joel pictures the fullness of God's forgiving grace.

The three prophets may have been contemporaries (eighth century B.C.E.); in any case they speak to the same spiritual condition of Israel: the people are in dread danger of destruction because of having forsaken God. But repentance will move Him to grant forgiveness to His people.

HAFTARAH Shabbat Shuvah

שבת שובה

Hosea

14 : 2 - 10

Chapter 14

יד

2] Return, O Israel, to the LORD your God,
For you have fallen because of your sin.

3] Take words with you
And return to the LORD.
Say to Him:
ᵃ"Forgive all guilt
And accept what is good;
Instead of bulls we will pay
[The offering of] our lips.*ᵃ*

4] Assyria shall not save us,
No more will we ride on steeds;*ᵇ*
Nor ever again will we call
Our handiwork our god,
Since in You alone orphans find pity!"

5] I will heal their affliction,*ᶜ*
Generously will I take them back in love;
For My anger has turned away from them.*ᵈ*

[2] שׁוּבָה יִשְׂרָאֵל עַד יְהוָה אֱלֹהֶיךָ
כִּי כָשַׁלְתָּ בַּעֲוֺנֶךָ:

[3] קְחוּ עִמָּכֶם דְּבָרִים
וְשׁוּבוּ אֶל־יְהוָה
אִמְרוּ אֵלָיו
כָּל־תִּשָּׂא עָוֺן
וְקַח־טוֹב
וּנְשַׁלְּמָה פָרִים שְׂפָתֵינוּ:

[4] אַשּׁוּר לֹא יוֹשִׁיעֵנוּ
עַל־סוּס לֹא נִרְכָּב
וְלֹא־נֹאמַר עוֹד
אֱלֹהֵינוּ לְמַעֲשֵׂה יָדֵינוּ
אֲשֶׁר־בְּךָ יְרֻחַם יָתוֹם:

[5] אֶרְפָּא מְשׁוּבָתָם
אֹהֲבֵם נְדָבָה
כִּי שָׁב אַפִּי מִמֶּנּוּ:

ᵃ⁻ᵃ Meaning of Heb. uncertain
ᵇ I.e., we will no longer depend on an alliance with Egypt; cf. II Kings 18.24 || Isa. 36.9; Isa. 30.16
ᶜ For this meaning of meshuvah see Jer. 2.19; 3.22
ᵈ Heb. "him"

6] I will be to Israel like dew;
He shall blossom like the lily,
He shall strike root like a ᵉ‾Lebanon tree.‾ᵉ

אֶהְיֶה כַטַּל לְיִשְׂרָאֵל [6

יִפְרַח כַּשּׁוֹשַׁנָּה

וְיַךְ שָׁרָשָׁיו כַּלְּבָנוֹן:

7] His boughs shall spread out far,
His beauty shall be like the olive tree's,
His fragrance like that of Lebanon.

יֵלְכוּ יֹנְקוֹתָיו [7

וִיהִי כַזַּיִת הוֹדוֹ

וְרֵיחַ לוֹ כַּלְּבָנוֹן:

8] They who sit in his shade shall be revived:
They shall bring to life new grain,
They shall blossom like the vine;
His scent shall be like the wine of Lebanon.ᶠ

יָשֻׁבוּ יֹשְׁבֵי בְצִלּוֹ [8

יְחַיּוּ דָגָן וְיִפְרְחוּ כַגָּפֶן

זִכְרוֹ כְּיֵין לְבָנוֹן:

9] Ephraim [shall say]:
"What more have I to do with idols?
When I respond and look to Him,
I become like a verdant cypress."
ᵃ‾Your fruit is provided by Me.‾ᵃ

אֶפְרַיִם [9

מַה־לִּי עוֹד לַעֲצַבִּים

אֲנִי עָנִיתִי וַאֲשׁוּרֶנּוּ

אֲנִי כִּבְרוֹשׁ רַעֲנָן

מִמֶּנִּי פֶּרְיְךָ נִמְצָא:

10] He who is wise will consider these words,
He who is prudent will take note of them.
For the paths of the LORD are smooth;
The righteous can walk on them,
While sinners stumble on them.

מִי חָכָם וְיָבֵן אֵלֶּה [10

נָבוֹן וְיֵדָעֵם

כִּי־יְשָׁרִים דַּרְכֵי יְהֹוָה

וְצַדִּקִים יֵלְכוּ בָם

וּפֹשְׁעִים יִכָּשְׁלוּ בָם:

ᵉ‾ᵉ Emendation yields "poplar"
ᶠ Emendation yields "Helbon"; cf. Ezek. 27.18
ᵃ‾ᵃ Meaning of Heb. uncertain

Micah

7 : 18-20

Chapter 7

18] Who is a God like You,
Forgiving iniquity
And remitting transgression;
Who has not maintained His wrath forever
Against the remnant of His own people,
Because He loves graciousness!

19] He will take us back in love;
He will cover up our iniquities,
You will hurl all our[i] sins
Into the depths of the sea.

20] You will keep faith with Jacob,
Loyalty to Abraham,
As You promised on oath to our fathers
In days gone by.

ז

‏18] מִי־אֵל כָּמוֹךָ‎
‏נֹשֵׂא עָוֹן וְעֹבֵר עַל־פֶּשַׁע‎
‏לִשְׁאֵרִית נַחֲלָתוֹ‎
‏לֹא־הֶחֱזִיק לָעַד אַפּוֹ‎
‏כִּי־חָפֵץ חֶסֶד הוּא׃‎
‏19] יָשׁוּב יְרַחֲמֵנוּ‎
‏יִכְבֹּשׁ עֲוֹנֹתֵינוּ‎
‏וְתַשְׁלִיךְ בִּמְצֻלוֹת יָם‎
‏כָּל־חַטֹּאותָם׃‎
‏20] תִּתֵּן אֱמֶת לְיַעֲקֹב‎
‏חֶסֶד לְאַבְרָהָם‎
‏אֲשֶׁר־נִשְׁבַּעְתָּ לַאֲבֹתֵינוּ‎
‏מִימֵי קֶדֶם׃‎

Joel

2 : 15-27

Chapter 2

15] Blow a horn in Zion,
Solemnize a fast,
Proclaim an assembly!

16] Gather the people,
Bid the congregation purify themselves.[d]

ב

‏15] תִּקְעוּ שׁוֹפָר בְּצִיּוֹן קַדְּשׁוּ־צוֹם‎
‏קִרְאוּ עֲצָרָה׃‎
‏16] אִסְפוּ־עָם‎
‏קַדְּשׁוּ קָהָל‎

---

[i] Heb. "their"   [d] Cf. Exod. 19.10; Zeph. 1.7

Bring together the old,
Gather the babes
And the sucklings at the breast;
Let the bridegroom come out of his chamber,
The bride from her canopied couch.

17] Between the portico and the altar,
Let the priests, the LORD's ministers, weep
And say:
"Oh, spare Your people, LORD!
Let not Your possession become a mockery,
To be taunted by nations!
Let not the peoples say,
'Where is their God?'"

18] Then the LORD was roused
On behalf of His land
And had compassion
Upon His people.
19] In response to His people
The LORD declared:
"I will grant you the new grain,
The new wine, and the new oil,
And you shall have them in abundance.
Nevermore will I let you be
A mockery among the nations.

20] I will drive the northerner*e* far from you,
I will thrust it into a parched and desolate land—
Its van to the Eastern Sea*f*
And its rear to the Western Sea;*g*
And the stench of it shall go up,
And the foul smell rise."
For [the LORD] shall work great deeds.

קִבְצוּ זְקֵנִים אִסְפוּ עוֹלָלִים וְיֹנְקֵי שָׁדָיִם

יֵצֵא חָתָן מֵחֶדְרוֹ

וְכַלָּה מֵחֻפָּתָהּ:

17] בֵּין הָאוּלָם וְלַמִּזְבֵּחַ

יִבְכּוּ הַכֹּהֲנִים מְשָׁרְתֵי יְהוָה

וְיֹאמְרוּ

חוּסָה יְהוָה עַל־עַמֶּךָ

וְאַל־תִּתֵּן נַחֲלָתְךָ לְחֶרְפָּה

לִמְשָׁל־בָּם גּוֹיִם

לָמָּה יֹאמְרוּ בָעַמִּים

אַיֵּה אֱלֹהֵיהֶם:

18] וַיְקַנֵּא יְהוָה לְאַרְצוֹ

וַיַּחְמֹל עַל־עַמּוֹ:

19] וַיַּעַן יְהוָה וַיֹּאמֶר לְעַמּוֹ

הִנְנִי שֹׁלֵחַ לָכֶם אֶת־הַדָּגָן

וְהַתִּירוֹשׁ וְהַיִּצְהָר

וּשְׂבַעְתֶּם אֹתוֹ

וְלֹא־אֶתֵּן אֶתְכֶם עוֹד

חֶרְפָּה בַּגּוֹיִם:

20] וְאֶת־הַצְּפוֹנִי אַרְחִיק מֵעֲלֵיכֶם

וְהִדַּחְתִּיו אֶל־אֶרֶץ צִיָּה וּשְׁמָמָה

אֶת־פָּנָיו אֶל־הַיָּם הַקַּדְמֹנִי

וְסֹפוֹ אֶל־הַיָּם הָאַחֲרוֹן

וְעָלָה בָאְשׁוֹ

וְתַעַל צַחֲנָתוֹ

כִּי הִגְדִּיל לַעֲשׂוֹת:

e I.e., the locusts. Emendation yields "My multitude"; cf. "nation" (1.6), "horde,"
 "army," and "host" (2.2, 5, 11, and 25)
f The Dead Sea
g The Mediterranean Sea

21] Fear not, O soil, rejoice and be glad;
For the LORD has wrought great deeds.

אַל־תִּֽירְאִי אֲדָמָה [21]

גִּילִי וּשְׂמָחִי

כִּֽי־הִגְדִּיל יְהֹוָה לַעֲשֽׂוֹת׃

22] Fear not, O beasts of the field,
For the pastures in the wilderness
Are clothed with grass.
The trees have borne their fruit;
Fig tree and vine
Have yielded their strength.

אַל־תִּֽירְאוּ בַּהֲמוֹת שָׂדַי [22]

כִּי דָשְׁאוּ נְאוֹת מִדְבָּר

כִּֽי־עֵץ נָשָׂא פִרְיוֹ

תְּאֵנָה וָגֶפֶן נָתְנוּ חֵילָֽם׃

23] O children of Zion, be glad,
Rejoice in the LORD your God.
For He has given you the early rain in [His]
    kindness,
Now He makes the rain fall [as] formerly—
The early rain and the late—

וּבְנֵי צִיּוֹן [23]

גִּילוּ וְשִׂמְחוּ בַּֽיהֹוָה אֱלֹֽהֵיכֶם

כִּֽי־נָתַן לָכֶם אֶת־הַמּוֹרֶה לִצְדָקָה

וַיּוֹרֶד לָכֶם גֶּשֶׁם

מוֹרֶה וּמַלְקוֹשׁ בָּרִאשֽׁוֹן׃

24] And threshing floors shall be piled with grain,
And vats shall overflow with new wine and oil.

וּמָלְאוּ הַגֳּרָנוֹת בָּר [24]

וְהֵשִׁיקוּ הַיְקָבִים תִּירוֹשׁ וְיִצְהָֽר׃

25] "I will repay you *h*-for the years-*h*
Consumed by swarms and hoppers,
By grubs and locusts,
The great army I let loose against you.

וְשִׁלַּמְתִּי לָכֶם אֶת־הַשָּׁנִים [25]

אֲשֶׁר אָכַל הָאַרְבֶּה

הַיֶּלֶק וְהֶחָסִיל וְהַגָּזָם

חֵילִי הַגָּדוֹל אֲשֶׁר שִׁלַּחְתִּי בָּכֶֽם׃

26] And you shall eat your fill
And praise the name of the LORD your God
Who dealt so wondrously with you—
My people shall be shamed no more.

וַאֲכַלְתֶּם אָכוֹל וְשָׂבוֹעַ [26]

וְהִלַּלְתֶּם אֶת־שֵׁם יְהֹוָה אֱלֹֽהֵיכֶם

אֲשֶׁר־עָשָׂה עִמָּכֶם לְהַפְלִיא

וְלֹא־יֵבֹשׁוּ עַמִּי לְעוֹלָֽם׃

27] And you shall know
That I am in the midst of Israel:
That I the LORD am your God
And there is no other.
And My people shall be shamed no more."

וִידַעְתֶּם כִּי בְקֶרֶב יִשְׂרָאֵל אָנִי [27]

וַאֲנִי יְהֹוָה אֱלֹֽהֵיכֶם וְאֵין עוֹד

וְלֹא־יֵבֹשׁוּ עַמִּי לְעוֹלָֽם׃

h-h Emendation yields "double what was"

*Zechariah preached in Palestine after the exiles had re-
turned from Babylon and, under Zerubbabel's and the
High Priest Joshua's leaderships, had begun to rebuild
the Temple. When the project lagged, the prophet exhorted
his people to persist and maintain the vision of a great
sanctuary dedicated to the worship of God.*

*Verse 16 speaks of the observance of Sukot in Zechariah's
time. His is an apocalyptic vision that sees the final vindication of Israel.*

יום ראשון של סכות

Zechariah

14: 7–9, 16–21

יד

Chapter 14

7] But there shall be a continuous day—only
the LORD knows when—of neither day nor night,
and there shall be light at eventide.

8] In that day, fresh water shall flow from
Jerusalem, part of it to the Eastern Sea*d* and part
to the Western Sea,*e* throughout the summer and
winter.

9] And the LORD shall be king over all the
earth; in that day there shall be one LORD with
one name.*f*

7] וְהָיָה יוֹם־אֶחָד הוּא יִוָּדַע לַיהוָה לֹא־יוֹם
וְלֹא־לָיְלָה וְהָיָה לְעֵת־עֶרֶב יִהְיֶה־אוֹר:

8] וְהָיָה בַּיּוֹם הַהוּא יֵצְאוּ מַיִם־חַיִּים
מִירוּשָׁלַ͏ִם חֶצְיָם אֶל־הַיָּם הַקַּדְמוֹנִי וְחֶצְיָם
אֶל־הַיָּם הָאַחֲרוֹן בַּקַּיִץ וּבָחֹרֶף יִהְיֶה:

9] וְהָיָה יְהוָה לְמֶלֶךְ עַל־כָּל־הָאָרֶץ בַּיּוֹם
הַהוּא יִהְיֶה יְהוָה אֶחָד וּשְׁמוֹ אֶחָד:

. . .

16] All who survive of all those nations that
came up against Jerusalem shall make a pilgrimage year by year to bow low to the King LORD
of Hosts and to observe the Feast of Booths.

17] Any of the earth's communities that does not
make the pilgrimage to Jerusalem to bow low to
the King LORD of Hosts shall receive no rain.

18] However, if the community of Egypt does
not make this pilgrimage, it shall not be visited
by the same affliction with which the LORD will

16] וְהָיָה כָּל־הַנּוֹתָר מִכָּל־הַגּוֹיִם הַבָּאִים
עַל־יְרוּשָׁלָ͏ִם וְעָלוּ מִדֵּי שָׁנָה בְשָׁנָה לְהִשְׁתַּחֲוֺת
לְמֶלֶךְ יְהוָה צְבָאוֹת וְלָחֹג אֶת־חַג הַסֻּכּוֹת:

17] וְהָיָה אֲשֶׁר לֹא־יַעֲלֶה מֵאֵת מִשְׁפְּחוֹת הָאָרֶץ
אֶל־יְרוּשָׁלַ͏ִם לְהִשְׁתַּחֲוֺת לְמֶלֶךְ יְהוָה צְבָאוֹת
וְלֹא עֲלֵיהֶם יִהְיֶה הַגָּשֶׁם: 18] וְאִם־מִשְׁפַּחַת
מִצְרַיִם לֹא־תַעֲלֶה וְלֹא בָאָה וְלֹא עֲלֵיהֶם
תִּהְיֶה הַמַּגֵּפָה אֲשֶׁר יִגֹּף יְהוָה אֶת־הַגּוֹיִם אֲשֶׁר

---

d I.e., the Dead Sea; cf. Joel 2.20

e I.e., the Mediterranean Sea; cf. Joel 2.20

f I.e., the LORD alone shall be worshiped and shall be invoked by His true name

strike the other nations that do not come up to observe the Feast of Booths.[i]

19] Such shall be the punishment of Egypt and of all other nations that do not come up to observe the Feast of Booths.

20] In that day, even the bells on the horses shall be inscribed "Holy to the LORD." The metal pots in the House of the LORD shall be like the basins before the altar;

21] indeed, every metal pot in Jerusalem and in Judah shall be holy to the LORD of Hosts. And all those who sacrifice shall come and take of these to boil [their sacrificial meat] in; in that day there shall be no more traders[k] in the House of the LORD of Hosts.

Ezekiel lived in Babylon during the days of the exile (sixth century B.C.E.) and was a master of mystic dreams and visions. Like Jeremiah and Deutero-Isaiah he fortified his people's faith in God's forgiveness, but unlike them he stressed the great need for structured ritual as a basis for a religious revival.

Though Israel is deserving of punishment, its enemies— symbolized by Gog and Magog—will in the end suffer destruction at God's hand.

Chapter 38

18] On that day, when Gog sets foot on the soil of Israel—declares the Lord GOD—My raging anger shall flare up.

19] For I have decreed in My indignation and in My blazing wrath: On that day, a terrible earthquake shall befall the land of Israel.

20] The fish of the sea, the birds of the sky, the beasts of the field, all creeping things that move on the ground, and every human being on earth shall quake before Me. Mountains shall be overthrown, cliffs shall topple, and every wall shall crumble to the ground.

לֹא יַעֲלוּ לָחֹג אֶת־חַג הַסֻּכּוֹת: 19] וְזֹאת תִּהְיֶה חַטַּאת מִצְרָיִם וְחַטַּאת כָּל־הַגּוֹיִם אֲשֶׁר לֹא יַעֲלוּ לָחֹג אֶת־חַג הַסֻּכּוֹת:

20] בַּיּוֹם הַהוּא יִהְיֶה עַל־מְצִלּוֹת הַסּוּס קֹדֶשׁ לַיהוָה וְהָיָה הַסִּירוֹת בְּבֵית יְהוָה כַּמִּזְרָקִים לִפְנֵי הַמִּזְבֵּחַ: 21] וְהָיָה כָל־סִיר בִּירוּשָׁלַ͏ִם וּבִיהוּדָה קֹדֶשׁ לַיהוָה צְבָאוֹת וּבָאוּ כָּל־הַזֹּבְחִים וְלָקְחוּ מֵהֶם וּבִשְּׁלוּ בָהֶם וְלֹא־יִהְיֶה כְנַעֲנִי עוֹד בְּבֵית־יְהוָה צְבָאוֹת בַּיּוֹם הַהוּא:

HAFTARAH
Chol ha-Mo'ed Sukot

חול המועד סכות
Ezekiel
38 : 18 — 39 : 7

לח

18] וְהָיָה בַּיּוֹם הַהוּא בְּיוֹם בּוֹא גוֹג עַל־ אַדְמַת יִשְׂרָאֵל נְאֻם אֲדֹנָי יֱהוִה תַּעֲלֶה חֲמָתִי בְּאַפִּי: 19] וּבְקִנְאָתִי בְאֵשׁ־עֶבְרָתִי דִּבַּרְתִּי אִם־לֹא בַּיּוֹם הַהוּא יִהְיֶה רַעַשׁ גָּדוֹל עַל אַדְמַת יִשְׂרָאֵל: 20] וְרָעֲשׁוּ מִפָּנַי דְּגֵי הַיָּם וְעוֹף הַשָּׁמַיִם וְחַיַּת הַשָּׂדֶה וְכָל־הָרֶמֶשׂ הָרֹמֵשׂ עַל־הָאֲדָמָה וְכֹל הָאָדָם אֲשֶׁר עַל־פְּנֵי הָאֲדָמָה וְנֶהֶרְסוּ הֶהָרִים וְנָפְלוּ הַמַּדְרֵגוֹת וְכָל־חוֹמָה לָאָרֶץ תִּפּוֹל:

---

[i] Because Egypt is not dependent on rain, it will suffer some other punishment, presumably that described in v. 12

[k] To sell ritually pure vessels

21] ^{d-}I will then summon the sword against him throughout My mountains^{-d}—declares the Lord GOD—and every man's sword shall be turned against his brother. 22] I will punish him with pestilence and with bloodshed; and I will pour torrential rain, hailstones, and sulfurous fire upon him and his hordes and the many peoples with him.

23] Thus will I manifest My greatness and My holiness, and make Myself known in the sight of many nations. And they shall know that I am the LORD.

Chapter 39

1] And you, O mortal, prophesy against Gog and say: Thus said the Lord GOD: I am going to deal with you, O Gog, chief prince of Meshech and Tubal!

2] I will turn you around and ^{a-}drive you on,^{-a} and I will take you from the far north and lead you toward the mountains of Israel. 3] I will strike your bow from your left hand and I will loosen the arrows from your right hand. 4] You shall fall on the mountains of Israel, you and all your battalions and the peoples who are with you; and I will give you as food to carrion birds of every sort and to the beasts of the field, 5] as you lie in the open field. For I have spoken—declares the Lord GOD.

6] And I will send a fire against Magog and against those who dwell secure in the coastlands. And they shall know that I am the LORD.

7] I will make My holy name known among My people Israel, and never again will I let My holy name be profaned. And the nations shall know that I the LORD am holy in Israel.

---

^{d-d} *Meaning of Heb. uncertain*

^{a-a} *Meaning of Heb. uncertain*

21] וְקָרָ֥אתִי עָלָ֛יו לְכָל־הָרַ֖י חֶ֗רֶב נְאֻם֙ אֲדֹנָ֣י יְהוִ֔ה חֶ֥רֶב אִ֖ישׁ בְּאָחִ֥יו תִּֽהְיֶֽה: 22] וְנִשְׁפַּטְתִּ֥י אִתּ֖וֹ בְּדֶ֣בֶר וּבְדָ֑ם וְגֶ֣שֶׁם שׁוֹטֵף֩ וְאַבְנֵ֨י אֶלְגָּבִ֜ישׁ אֵ֣שׁ וְגָפְרִ֗ית אַמְטִ֤יר עָלָיו֙ וְעַל־אֲגַפָּ֔יו וְעַל־עַמִּ֥ים רַבִּ֖ים אֲשֶׁ֥ר אִתּֽוֹ: 23] וְהִתְגַּדִּלְתִּי֙ וְהִתְקַדִּשְׁתִּ֔י וְנ֣וֹדַעְתִּ֔י לְעֵינֵ֖י גּוֹיִ֣ם רַבִּ֑ים וְיָדְע֖וּ כִּֽי־אֲנִ֥י יְהוָֽה:

לט

1] וְאַתָּ֤ה בֶן־אָדָם֙ הִנָּבֵ֣א עַל־גּ֔וֹג וְאָ֣מַרְתָּ֔ כֹּ֥ה אָמַ֖ר אֲדֹנָ֣י יְהוִ֑ה הִנְנִ֤י אֵלֶ֙יךָ֙ גּ֔וֹג נְשִׂ֕יא רֹ֥אשׁ מֶ֖שֶׁךְ וְתֻבָֽל: 2] וְשֹׁבַבְתִּ֙יךָ֙ וְשִׁשֵּׁאתִ֔יךָ וְהַעֲלִיתִ֖יךָ מִיַּרְכְּתֵ֣י צָפ֑וֹן וַהֲבִאוֹתִ֖יךָ עַל־הָרֵ֥י יִשְׂרָאֵֽל: 3] וְהִכֵּיתִ֥י קַשְׁתְּךָ֖ מִיַּ֣ד שְׂמֹאולֶ֑ךָ וְחִצֶּ֕יךָ מִיַּ֥ד יְמִינְךָ֖ אַפִּֽיל: 4] עַל־הָרֵ֨י יִשְׂרָאֵ֜ל תִּפּ֗וֹל אַתָּה֙ וְכָל־אֲגַפֶּ֔יךָ וְעַמִּ֖ים אֲשֶׁ֣ר אִתָּ֑ךְ לְעֵ֨יט צִפּ֧וֹר כָּל־כָּנָ֛ף וְחַיַּ֥ת הַשָּׂדֶ֖ה נְתַתִּ֥יךָ לְאָכְלָֽה: 5] עַל־פְּנֵ֥י הַשָּׂדֶ֖ה תִּפּ֑וֹל כִּ֚י אֲנִ֣י דִבַּ֔רְתִּי נְאֻ֖ם אֲדֹנָ֥י יְהוִֽה: 6] וְשִׁלַּחְתִּי־אֵ֣שׁ בְּמָג֔וֹג וּבְיֹשְׁבֵ֥י הָאִיִּ֖ים לָבֶ֑טַח וְיָדְע֖וּ כִּֽי־אֲנִ֥י יְהוָֽה: 7] וְאֶת־שֵׁ֨ם קָדְשִׁ֜י אוֹדִ֗יעַ בְּת֣וֹךְ עַמִּ֣י יִשְׂרָאֵ֔ל וְלֹֽא־אַחֵ֥ל אֶת־שֵׁם־קָדְשִׁ֖י ע֑וֹד וְיָדְע֣וּ הַגּוֹיִ֗ם כִּֽי־אֲנִ֤י יְהוָה֙ קָד֖וֹשׁ בְּיִשְׂרָאֵֽל:

Joshua became Moses' successor and led the conquest of the Promised Land. While his name is attached to the 24 chapters which recount the campaign, the book is likely of much later origin. It portrays history essentially as a judgment of God.

The end of the Torah cycle leads directly into the story of Joshua and of the conquest of the land under his leadership. Moses had encouraged Joshua to be "strong and resolute," and with these same words the new leader addresses his people.

עצרת – שמחת תורה

Joshua

1 : 1-18

Chapter 1

א

1] After the death of Moses the servant of the LORD, the LORD said to Joshua son of Nun, Moses' attendant:

א[וַיְהִי אַחֲרֵי מוֹת מֹשֶׁה עֶבֶד יְהֹוָה וַיֹּאמֶר יְהֹוָה אֶל־יְהוֹשֻׁעַ בִּן־נוּן מְשָׁרֵת מֹשֶׁה לֵאמֹר:

2] "My servant Moses is dead. Prepare to cross the Jordan, together with all this people, into the land which I am giving to the Israelites. 3] Every spot on which your foot treads I give to you, as I promised Moses.

2] מֹשֶׁה עַבְדִּי מֵת וְעַתָּה קוּם עֲבֹר אֶת־הַיַּרְדֵּן הַזֶּה אַתָּה וְכָל־הָעָם הַזֶּה אֶל־הָאָרֶץ אֲשֶׁר אָנֹכִי נֹתֵן לָהֶם לִבְנֵי יִשְׂרָאֵל: 3] כָּל־מָקוֹם אֲשֶׁר תִּדְרֹךְ כַּף־רַגְלְכֶם בּוֹ לָכֶם נְתַתִּיו כַּאֲשֶׁר דִּבַּרְתִּי אֶל־מֹשֶׁה: 4] מֵהַמִּדְבָּר

4] Your territory shall extend from the wilderness and the Lebanon to the Great River, the River Euphrates [on the east] —the whole Hittite country—and up to the Mediterranean[a] Sea on the west.

וְהַלְּבָנוֹן הַזֶּה וְעַד־הַנָּהָר הַגָּדוֹל נְהַר־פְּרָת כֹּל אֶרֶץ הַחִתִּים וְעַד־הַיָּם הַגָּדוֹל מְבוֹא הַשֶּׁמֶשׁ יִהְיֶה גְּבוּלְכֶם: 5] לֹא־יִתְיַצֵּב אִישׁ

5] No man shall be able to resist you as long as you live. As I was with Moses, so I will be with you; I will not fail you or forsake you.

לְפָנֶיךָ כֹּל יְמֵי חַיֶּיךָ כַּאֲשֶׁר הָיִיתִי עִם־מֹשֶׁה אֶהְיֶה עִמָּךְ לֹא אַרְפְּךָ וְלֹא אֶעֶזְבֶךָּ:

6] "Be strong and resolute, for you shall apportion to this people the land that I swore to their fathers to give them.

6] חֲזַק וֶאֱמָץ כִּי אַתָּה תַּנְחִיל אֶת־הָעָם הַזֶּה אֶת־הָאָרֶץ אֲשֶׁר־נִשְׁבַּעְתִּי לַאֲבוֹתָם לָתֵת לָהֶם: 7] רַק חֲזַק וֶאֱמַץ מְאֹד לִשְׁמֹר לַעֲשׂוֹת

7] But you must be very strong and resolute to observe faithfully all the Teaching that My servant Moses enjoined upon you. Do not deviate from it to the right or to the left, that you may be successful wherever you go.

כְּכָל־הַתּוֹרָה אֲשֶׁר צִוְּךָ מֹשֶׁה עַבְדִּי אַל־תָּסוּר מִמֶּנּוּ יָמִין וּשְׂמֹאול לְמַעַן תַּשְׂכִּיל בְּכֹל אֲשֶׁר תֵּלֵךְ: 8] לֹא־יָמוּשׁ סֵפֶר הַתּוֹרָה הַזֶּה מִפִּיךָ

8] Let not this Book of the Teaching cease from

---

[a] Heb. "Great"

your lips, but recite it day and night, so that you may observe faithfully all that is written in it. Only then will you prosper in your undertakings and only then will you be successful.

9] "I charge you: Be strong and resolute; do not be terrified or dismayed, for the LORD your God is with you wherever you go."

10] Joshua thereupon gave orders to the officials of the people:

11] "Go through the camp and charge the people thus: Get provisions ready, for in three days' time you are to cross the Jordan, in order to enter and occupy the land which the LORD your God is giving you as a possession."

12] Then Joshua said to the Reubenites, the Gadites, and the half-tribe of Manasseh,

13] "Remember what Moses the servant of the LORD enjoined upon you, when he said: 'The LORD your God is granting you a haven; He is assigning this territory to you.'

14] Let your wives, children, and livestock remain in the land which Moses assigned to you b-on this side of-b the Jordan; but every one of your fighting men shall go across armedᶜ in the van of your kinsmen. And you shall assist them

15] until the LORD has given your kinsmen a haven, such as you have, and they too have gained possession of the land which the LORD your God has assigned to them. Then you may return to the land on the east side of the Jordan, which Moses the servant of the LORD assigned to you as your possession, and you may occupy it."

16] They answered Joshua, "We will do everything you have commanded us and we will go wherever you send us.

וְהָגִיתָ בּוֹ יוֹמָם וָלַיְלָה לְמַעַן תִּשְׁמֹר לַעֲשׂוֹת כְּכָל־הַכָּתוּב בּוֹ כִּי־אָז תַּצְלִיחַ אֶת־דְּרָכֶךָ וְאָז תַּשְׂכִּיל:

9 הֲלוֹא צִוִּיתִיךָ חֲזַק וֶאֱמָץ אַל־תַּעֲרֹץ וְאַל־תֵּחָת כִּי עִמְּךָ יְהוָה אֱלֹהֶיךָ בְּכֹל אֲשֶׁר תֵּלֵךְ:

10 וַיְצַו יְהוֹשֻׁעַ אֶת־שֹׁטְרֵי הָעָם לֵאמֹר:

11 עִבְרוּ בְּקֶרֶב הַמַּחֲנֶה וְצַוּוּ אֶת־הָעָם לֵאמֹר הָכִינוּ לָכֶם צֵידָה כִּי בְּעוֹד שְׁלֹשֶׁת יָמִים אַתֶּם עֹבְרִים אֶת־הַיַּרְדֵּן הַזֶּה לָבוֹא לָרֶשֶׁת אֶת־הָאָרֶץ אֲשֶׁר יְהוָה אֱלֹהֵיכֶם נֹתֵן לָכֶם לְרִשְׁתָּהּ:

12 וְלָראוּבֵנִי וְלַגָּדִי וְלַחֲצִי שֵׁבֶט הַמְנַשֶּׁה אָמַר יְהוֹשֻׁעַ לֵאמֹר: 13 זָכוֹר אֶת־הַדָּבָר אֲשֶׁר צִוָּה אֶתְכֶם מֹשֶׁה עֶבֶד־יְהוָה לֵאמֹר יְהוָה אֱלֹהֵיכֶם מֵנִיחַ לָכֶם וְנָתַן לָכֶם אֶת־הָאָרֶץ הַזֹּאת: 14 נְשֵׁיכֶם טַפְּכֶם וּמִקְנֵיכֶם יֵשְׁבוּ בָּאָרֶץ אֲשֶׁר נָתַן לָכֶם מֹשֶׁה בְּעֵבֶר הַיַּרְדֵּן וְאַתֶּם תַּעַבְרוּ חֲמֻשִׁים לִפְנֵי אֲחֵיכֶם כֹּל גִּבּוֹרֵי הַחַיִל וַעֲזַרְתֶּם אוֹתָם: 15 עַד אֲשֶׁר־יָנִיחַ יְהוָה לַאֲחֵיכֶם כָּכֶם וְיָרְשׁוּ גַם־הֵמָּה אֶת־הָאָרֶץ אֲשֶׁר־יְהוָה אֱלֹהֵיכֶם נֹתֵן לָהֶם וְשַׁבְתֶּם לְאֶרֶץ יְרֻשַּׁתְכֶם וִירִשְׁתֶּם אוֹתָהּ אֲשֶׁר נָתַן לָכֶם מֹשֶׁה עֶבֶד יְהוָה בְּעֵבֶר הַיַּרְדֵּן מִזְרַח הַשָּׁמֶשׁ:

16 וַיַּעֲנוּ אֶת־יְהוֹשֻׁעַ לֵאמֹר כֹּל אֲשֶׁר־צִוִּיתָנוּ נַעֲשֶׂה וְאֶל־כָּל־אֲשֶׁר תִּשְׁלָחֵנוּ נֵלֵךְ:

---

b-b Lit. "across"

ᶜ Meaning of Heb. uncertain

17] We will obey you just as we obeyed Moses; let but the Lord your God be with you as He was with Moses!

18] Any man who flouts your commands and does not obey every order you give him shall be put to death. Only be strong and resolute!"

כְּכֹל אֲשֶׁר־שָׁמַעְנוּ אֶל־מֹשֶׁה כֵּן נִשְׁמַע [17] אֵלֶיךָ רַק יִהְיֶה יְהֹוָה אֱלֹהֶיךָ עִמָּךְ כַּאֲשֶׁר הָיָה עִם־מֹשֶׁה: [18] כָּל־אִישׁ אֲשֶׁר־יַמְרֶה אֶת־ פִּיךָ וְלֹא־יִשְׁמַע אֶת־דְּבָרֶיךָ לְכֹל אֲשֶׁר־תְּצַוֶּנּוּ יוּמָת רַק חֲזַק וֶאֱמָץ:

The selection of this haftarah for Chanukah was meant as an emphasis that the festival had above all spiritual content: not military power but God's spirit is the abiding source of victory.

Zechariah preached in Palestine after the exiles had returned from Babylon and, under Zerubbabel's and the High Priest Joshua's leaderships, had begun to rebuild the Temple. When the project lagged, the prophet exhorted his people to persist and maintain the vision of a great sanctuary dedicated to the worship of God.

הפטרה לשבת חנכה (א)

Zechariah

4:1-7

ד

Chapter 4

1] The angel who talked with me came back and woke me as a man is wakened from sleep. 2] He said to me, "What do you see?" And I answered, "I see a lampstand all of gold, with a bowl above it. The lamps on it are seven in number, and the a-lamps above it have-a seven pipes; 3] and by it are two olive trees, one on the right of the bowl and one on its left."

4] I, in turn, asked the angel who talked with me, "What do those things mean, my lord?"

5] "Do you not know what those things mean?" asked the angel who talked with me; and I said, "No, my lord."

6] Then he explained to me as follows:b

"This is the word of the LORD to Zerubbabel:c Not by might, nor by power, but by My spiritd— said the LORD of Hosts.

7] Whoever you are, O great mountain in the path of Zerubbabel, turn into level ground! For he shall produce that excellent stone; it shall be greeted with shouts of 'Beautiful! Beautiful!' "

1] וַיָּשָׁב הַמַּלְאָךְ הַדֹּבֵר בִּי וַיְעִירֵנִי כְּאִישׁ אֲשֶׁר־יֵעוֹר מִשְּׁנָתוֹ: 2] וַיֹּאמֶר אֵלַי מָה אַתָּה רֹאֶה וָאֹמַר רָאִיתִי וְהִנֵּה מְנוֹרַת זָהָב כֻּלָּהּ וְגֻלָּהּ עַל־רֹאשָׁהּ וְשִׁבְעָה נֵרֹתֶיהָ עָלֶיהָ שִׁבְעָה וְשִׁבְעָה מוּצָקוֹת לַנֵּרוֹת אֲשֶׁר עַל־רֹאשָׁהּ: 3] וּשְׁנַיִם זֵיתִים עָלֶיהָ אֶחָד מִימִין הַגֻּלָּה וְאֶחָד עַל־שְׂמֹאלָהּ: 4] וָאַעַן וָאֹמַר אֶל־הַמַּלְאָךְ הַדֹּבֵר בִּי לֵאמֹר מָה אֵלֶּה אֲדֹנִי: 5] וַיַּעַן הַמַּלְאָךְ הַדֹּבֵר בִּי וַיֹּאמֶר אֵלַי הֲלוֹא יָדַעְתָּ מָה־הֵמָּה אֵלֶּה וָאֹמַר לֹא אֲדֹנִי: 6] וַיַּעַן וַיֹּאמֶר אֵלַי לֵאמֹר

זֶה דְּבַר־יְהֹוָה אֶל־זְרֻבָּבֶל לֵאמֹר לֹא בְחַיִל וְלֹא בְכֹחַ כִּי אִם־בְּרוּחִי אָמַר יְהֹוָה צְבָאוֹת: 7] מִי־אַתָּה הַר־הַגָּדוֹל לִפְנֵי זְרֻבָּבֶל לְמִישֹׁר וְהוֹצִיא אֶת־הָאֶבֶן הָרֹאשָׁה תְּשֻׁאוֹת חֵן חֵן לָהּ:

a-a Emendation yields "bowl above it has"

b The explanation is given in the last sentence of v. 10

c A grandson of King Jehoiachin (I Chron. 3.17–19) and the secular head of the repatriated community (Hag. 1.1)

d I.e., Zerubbabel will succeed by means of spiritual gifts conferred upon him by the LORD; cf. Isa. 11.2 ff.

The Book of Kings is divided into two parts. It spans four centuries and reaches from the last days of David to the destruction of the Temple by the Babylonians in 586 (or 585) B.C.E. It approaches history from a theological point of view: the story of Israel and Judah must be seen as a judgment of God on the people and its rulers.

Ten candlesticks of gold are an important feature of the dedication of the Solomonic Temple, which is here—in the manner of ancient archival records—repeated in detail.

הפטרה לשבת חנכה (ב)

First Kings

7 : 40–50

ז

Chapter 7

40] Hiram also made the lavers, the scrapers, and the sprinkling bowls.

So Hiram finished all the work that he had been doing for King Solomon on the House of the LORD:

41] the two columns, the two globes of the capitals upon the columns; and the two pieces of network to cover the two globes of the capitals upon the columns;

42] the 400 pomegranates for the two pieces of network, two rows of pomegranates for each network, to cover the two globes of the capitals upon the columns;

43] the ten stands and the ten lavers upon the stands;
44] the one tank with the twelve oxen underneath the tank;

45] the pails, the scrapers, and the sprinkling bowls. All those vessels in the House of the LORD which Hiram made for King Solomon were of burnished bronze.

46] The king had them cast ⁿ‑ⁿin earthen molds,‑ⁿ in the plain of the Jordan between Succoth and Zarethan.
47] Solomon left all the vessels [unweighed] because of their very great quantity; the weight of the bronze was not reckoned.

40 וַיַּעַשׂ חִירוֹם אֶת־הַכִּיֹּרוֹת וְאֶת־הַיָּעִים וְאֶת־הַמִּזְרָקוֹת וַיְכַל חִירָם לַעֲשׂוֹת אֶת־כָּל־הַמְּלָאכָה אֲשֶׁר עָשָׂה לַמֶּלֶךְ שְׁלֹמֹה בֵּית יְהוָה: 41 עַמֻּדִים שְׁנַיִם וְגֻלֹּת הַכֹּתָרֹת אֲשֶׁר־עַל־רֹאשׁ הָעַמּוּדִים שְׁתָּיִם וְהַשְּׂבָכוֹת שְׁתַּיִם לְכַסּוֹת אֶת־שְׁתֵּי גֻּלֹּת הַכֹּתָרֹת אֲשֶׁר עַל־רֹאשׁ הָעַמּוּדִים: 42 וְאֶת־הָרִמֹּנִים אַרְבַּע מֵאוֹת לִשְׁתֵּי הַשְּׂבָכוֹת שְׁנֵי־טוּרִים רִמֹּנִים לַשְּׂבָכָה הָאֶחָת לְכַסּוֹת אֶת־שְׁתֵּי גֻּלֹּת הַכֹּתָרֹת אֲשֶׁר עַל־פְּנֵי הָעַמּוּדִים: 43 וְאֶת־הַמְּכֹנוֹת עָשֶׂר וְאֶת־הַכִּיֹּרֹת עֲשָׂרָה עַל־הַמְּכֹנוֹת: 44 וְאֶת־הַיָּם הָאֶחָד וְאֶת־הַבָּקָר שְׁנֵים־עָשָׂר תַּחַת הַיָּם: 45 וְאֶת־הַסִּירוֹת וְאֶת־הַיָּעִים וְאֶת־הַמִּזְרָקוֹת וְאֵת כָּל־הַכֵּלִים הָאֵלֶּה אֲשֶׁר עָשָׂה חִירָם לַמֶּלֶךְ שְׁלֹמֹה בֵּית יְהוָה נְחֹשֶׁת מְמֹרָט: 46 בְּכִכַּר הַיַּרְדֵּן יְצָקָם הַמֶּלֶךְ בְּמַעֲבֵה הָאֲדָמָה בֵּין סֻכּוֹת וּבֵין צָרְתָן: 47 וַיַּנַּח שְׁלֹמֹה אֶת־כָּל־הַכֵּלִים מֵרֹב מְאֹד מְאֹד לֹא נֶחְקַר מִשְׁקַל הַנְּחֹשֶׁת:

ⁿ‑ⁿ Lit. "in the thick of the earth"

48] And Solomon made all the furnishings that were in the House of the LORD: the altar, of gold; the table for the bread of display, of gold; 49] the lampstands—five on the right side and five on the left—in front of the Shrine, of solid gold; and the petals, lamps, and tongs, of gold; 50] the basins, snuffers, sprinkling bowls, ladles, and fire pans, of solid gold; and the hinge sockets for the doors of the innermost part of the House, the Holy of Holies, and for the doors of the Great Hall of the House, of gold.

מח] וַיַּעַשׂ שְׁלֹמֹה אֵת כָּל־הַכֵּלִים אֲשֶׁר בֵּית יְהוָה אֵת מִזְבַּח הַזָּהָב וְאֶת־הַשֻּׁלְחָן אֲשֶׁר עָלָיו לֶחֶם הַפָּנִים זָהָב: מט] וְאֶת־הַמְּנֹרוֹת חָמֵשׁ מִיָּמִין וְחָמֵשׁ מִשְּׂמֹאול לִפְנֵי הַדְּבִיר זָהָב סָגוּר וְהַפֶּרַח וְהַנֵּרֹת וְהַמֶּלְקַחַיִם זָהָב: נ] וְהַסִּפּוֹת וְהַמְזַמְּרוֹת וְהַמִּזְרָקוֹת וְהַכַּפּוֹת וְהַמַּחְתּוֹת זָהָב סָגוּר וְהַפֹּתוֹת לְדַלְתוֹת הַבַּיִת הַפְּנִימִי לְקֹדֶשׁ הַקֳּדָשִׁים לְדַלְתֵי הַבַּיִת לַהֵיכָל זָהָב:

The Book of Kings is divided into two parts. It spans four centuries and reaches from the last days of David to the destruction of the Temple by the Babylonians in 586 (or 585) B.C.E. It approaches history from a theological point of view: the story of Israel and Judah must be seen as a judgment of God on the people and its rulers.

The haftarah, in the spirit of the day, speaks of funds collected for the ancient Temple. The building had fallen into disrepair and the people's offerings were used to pay the carpenters and other laborers in the work of repair.

HAFTARAH Shekalim

שקלים

Second Kings

12 : 5-16

יב

Chapter 12

5] Jehoash said to the priests, "All the money, current money, brought into the House of the LORD as sacred donations—ᵃ‑any money a man may pay as the money equivalent of persons,‑ᵃ or any other money that a man may be minded to bring to the House of the LORD—

6] let the priests receive it, each from his benefactor; they, in turn, shall make repairs on the House, wherever damage may be found."

7] But in the twenty-third year of King Jehoash, [it was found that] the priests had not made the repairs on the House.

ה] וַיֹּאמֶר יְהוֹאָשׁ אֶל־הַכֹּהֲנִים כֹּל כֶּסֶף הַקֳּדָשִׁים אֲשֶׁר־יוּבָא בֵית־יְהוָה כֶּסֶף עוֹבֵר אִישׁ כֶּסֶף נַפְשׁוֹת עֶרְכּוֹ כָּל־כֶּסֶף אֲשֶׁר יַעֲלֶה עַל לֶב־אִישׁ לְהָבִיא בֵּית יְהוָה: ו] יִקְחוּ לָהֶם הַכֹּהֲנִים אִישׁ מֵאֵת מַכָּרוֹ וְהֵם יְחַזְּקוּ אֶת־בֶּדֶק הַבַּיִת לְכֹל אֲשֶׁר־יִמָּצֵא שָׁם בָּדֶק:

ז] וַיְהִי בִּשְׁנַת עֶשְׂרִים וְשָׁלֹשׁ שָׁנָה לַמֶּלֶךְ יְהוֹאָשׁ לֹא־חִזְּקוּ הַכֹּהֲנִים אֶת־בֶּדֶק הַבָּיִת:

ᵃ‑ᵃ See Lev. 27.2–8

8] So King Jehoash summoned the priest Jehoiada and the other priests and said to them, "Why have you not kept the House in repair? Now do not accept money from your benefactors any more, but have it donated for the repair of the House."

9] The priests agreed that they would neither accept money from the people nor make repairs on the House.

10] And the priest Jehoiada took a chest and bored a hole in its lid. He placed it at the right side of the altar as one entered the House of the LORD, and the priestly guards of the threshold deposited there all the money that was brought into the House of the LORD.

11] Whenever they saw that there was much money in the chest, the royal scribe and the high priest would come up and put the money accumulated in the House of the LORD into bags, and they would count it. 12] Then they would deliver the money *b-that was weighed out-b* to the overseers of the work, who were in charge of the House of the LORD. These, in turn, used to pay the carpenters and the laborers who worked on the House of the LORD, 13] and the masons and the stonecutters. They also paid for wood and for quarried stone with which to make the repairs on the House of the LORD, and for every other expenditure that had to be made in repairing the House. 14] However, no silver bowls and no snuffers, basins, or trumpets—no vessels of gold or silver—were made at the House of the LORD from the money brought into the House of the LORD; 15] this was given only to the overseers of the work for the repair of the House of the LORD. 16] No check was kept on the men to whom the money was delivered to pay the workers; for they dealt honestly.

8 וַיִּקְרָא֩ הַמֶּ֨לֶךְ יְהוֹאָ֜שׁ לִיהוֹיָדָ֤ע הַכֹּהֵן֙ וְלַכֹּ֣הֲנִ֔ים וַיֹּ֣אמֶר אֲלֵהֶ֔ם מַדּ֛וּעַ אֵינְכֶ֥ם מְחַזְּקִ֖ים אֶת־בֶּ֣דֶק הַבָּ֑יִת וְעַתָּ֗ה אַל־תִּקְחוּ־כֶ֙סֶף֙ מֵאֵ֣ת מַכָּֽרֵיכֶ֔ם כִּֽי־לְבֶ֥דֶק הַבַּ֖יִת תִּתְּנֻֽהוּ׃ 9 וַיֵּאֹ֖תוּ הַכֹּֽהֲנִ֑ים לְבִלְתִּ֤י קְחַת־כֶּ֙סֶף֙ מֵאֵ֣ת הָעָ֔ם וּלְבִלְתִּ֥י חַזֵּ֖ק אֶת־בֶּ֥דֶק הַבָּֽיִת׃

10 וַיִּקַּ֞ח יְהוֹיָדָ֤ע הַכֹּהֵן֙ אֲר֣וֹן אֶחָ֔ד וַיִּקֹּ֥ב חֹ֖ר בְּדַלְתּ֑וֹ וַיִּתֵּ֣ן אֹת֡וֹ אֵ֣צֶל הַמִּזְבֵּ֣חַ מִיָּמִ֡ין בְּבוֹא־אִישׁ֩ בֵּ֨ית יְהוָ֜ה וְנָֽתְנוּ־שָׁ֗מָּה הַכֹּֽהֲנִים֙ שֹֽׁמְרֵ֣י הַסַּ֔ף אֶת־כָּל־הַכֶּ֖סֶף הַמּוּבָ֥א בֵית־יְהוָֽה׃ 11 וַֽיְהִי֙ כִּרְאוֹתָ֔ם כִּֽי־רַ֥ב הַכֶּ֖סֶף בָּֽאָר֑וֹן וַיַּ֨עַל סֹפֵ֤ר הַמֶּ֙לֶךְ֙ וְהַכֹּהֵ֣ן הַגָּד֔וֹל וַיָּצֻ֙רוּ֙ וַיִּמְנ֔וּ אֶת־הַכֶּ֖סֶף הַנִּמְצָ֥א בֵית־יְהוָֽה׃ 12 וְנָתְנוּ֙ אֶת־הַכֶּ֣סֶף הַֽמְתֻכָּ֔ן עַל־יְדֵי֙ עֹשֵׂ֣י הַמְּלָאכָ֔ה הַמֻּפְקָדִ֖ים בֵּ֣ית יְהוָ֑ה וַיּוֹצִיאֻ֜הוּ לְחָרָשֵׁ֤י הָעֵץ֙ וְלַבֹּנִ֔ים הָעֹשִׂ֖ים בֵּ֥ית יְהוָֽה׃ 13 וְלַגֹּֽדְרִים֙ וּלְחֹצְבֵ֣י הָאֶ֔בֶן וְלִקְנ֤וֹת עֵצִים֙ וְאַבְנֵ֣י מַחְצֵ֔ב לְחַזֵּ֖ק אֶת־בֶּ֣דֶק בֵּית־יְהוָ֑ה וּלְכֹ֛ל אֲשֶׁר־יֵצֵ֥א עַל־הַבַּ֖יִת לְחָזְקָֽה׃ 14 אַךְ֩ לֹ֨א יֵעָשֶׂ֜ה בֵּ֣ית יְהוָ֗ה סִפּ֥וֹת כֶּ֙סֶף֙ מְזַמְּר֤וֹת מִזְרָקוֹת֙ חֲצֹ֣צְר֔וֹת כָּל־כְּלִ֥י זָהָ֖ב וּכְלִי־כָ֑סֶף מִן־הַכֶּ֖סֶף הַמּוּבָ֥א בֵית־יְהוָֽה׃ 15 כִּֽי־לְעֹשֵׂ֥י הַמְּלָאכָ֖ה יִתְּנֻ֑הוּ וְחִזְּקוּ־ב֖וֹ אֶת־בֵּ֥ית יְהוָֽה׃ 16 וְלֹ֧א יְחַשְּׁב֣וּ אֶת־הָֽאֲנָשִׁ֗ים אֲשֶׁ֨ר יִתְּנ֤וּ אֶת־הַכֶּ֙סֶף֙ עַל־יָדָ֔ם לָתֵ֖ת לְעֹשֵׂ֣י הַמְּלָאכָ֑ה כִּ֥י בֶאֱמֻנָ֖ה הֵ֥ם עֹשִֽׂים׃

b-b Meaning of Heb. uncertain

The Sabbath derives its name from Deuteronomy 25:17, the injunction to "remember" (zachor) the misdeeds of Amalek. Shabbat Zachor always precedes the celebration of Purim.

The Book of Esther represents most likely a combination of history and romance and belongs to the latest compositions found in the Bible (probably early second century B.C.E.). Its underlying theme is the providential, though sometimes hidden, care of God for His people who are saved from seemingly inevitable destruction.

Esther

7 : 1-10; 8 : 15-17

Chapter 7

1] So the king and Haman came to banquet with Esther the queen.

2] And the king said again unto Esther on the second day at the banquet of wine: "Whatever your petition, queen Esther, it shall be granted you; and whatever your request, even to the half of the kingdom, it shall be performed."

3] Then Esther the queen answered and said: "If I have found favor in your sight, O king, and if it please the king, let my life be given me at my petition, and my people at my request;

4] for we are sold, I and my people, to be destroyed, to be slain, and to perish. But if we had been sold for bondmen and bondwomen, I had held my peace, for the adversary is not worthy that the king be endamaged."

5] Then spoke the king Ahasuerus and said unto Esther the queen: "Who is he, and where is he, that does presume in his heart to do so?"

6] And Esther said: "An adversary and an enemy, even this wicked Haman." Then Haman was terrified before the king and the queen.

7] And the king arose in his wrath from the banquet of wine and went into the palace garden; but Haman remained to make request for his life to Esther the queen; for he saw that there was evil determined against him by the king.

8] Then the king returned out of the palace garden into the place of the banquet of wine; and Haman was fallen upon the couch whereon Esther was. Then said the king: "Will he even force the queen before me in

ז

1] וַיָּבֹא הַמֶּלֶךְ וְהָמָן לִשְׁתּוֹת עִם־אֶסְתֵּר הַמַּלְכָּה: 2] וַיֹּאמֶר הַמֶּלֶךְ לְאֶסְתֵּר גַּם בַּיּוֹם הַשֵּׁנִי בְּמִשְׁתֵּה הַיַּיִן מַה־שְּׁאֵלָתֵךְ אֶסְתֵּר הַמַּלְכָּה וְתִנָּתֵן לָךְ וּמַה־בַּקָּשָׁתֵךְ עַד־חֲצִי הַמַּלְכוּת וְתֵעָשׂ: 3] וַתַּעַן אֶסְתֵּר הַמַּלְכָּה וַתֹּאמַר אִם־מָצָאתִי חֵן בְּעֵינֶיךָ הַמֶּלֶךְ וְאִם־עַל־הַמֶּלֶךְ טוֹב תִּנָּתֶן־לִי נַפְשִׁי בִּשְׁאֵלָתִי וְעַמִּי בְּבַקָּשָׁתִי: 4] כִּי נִמְכַּרְנוּ אֲנִי וְעַמִּי לְהַשְׁמִיד לַהֲרוֹג וּלְאַבֵּד וְאִלּוּ לַעֲבָדִים וְלִשְׁפָחוֹת נִמְכַּרְנוּ הֶחֱרַשְׁתִּי כִּי אֵין הַצָּר שֹׁוֶה בְּנֵזֶק הַמֶּלֶךְ: 5] וַיֹּאמֶר הַמֶּלֶךְ אֲחַשְׁוֵרוֹשׁ וַיֹּאמֶר לְאֶסְתֵּר הַמַּלְכָּה מִי הוּא זֶה וְאֵי־זֶה הוּא אֲשֶׁר־מְלָאוֹ לִבּוֹ לַעֲשׂוֹת כֵּן: 6] וַתֹּאמֶר אֶסְתֵּר אִישׁ צַר וְאוֹיֵב הָמָן הָרָע הַזֶּה וְהָמָן נִבְעַת מִלִּפְנֵי הַמֶּלֶךְ וְהַמַּלְכָּה: 7] וְהַמֶּלֶךְ קָם בַּחֲמָתוֹ מִמִּשְׁתֵּה הַיַּיִן אֶל־גִּנַּת הַבִּיתָן וְהָמָן עָמַד לְבַקֵּשׁ עַל־נַפְשׁוֹ מֵאֶסְתֵּר הַמַּלְכָּה כִּי רָאָה כִּי־כָלְתָה אֵלָיו הָרָעָה מֵאֵת הַמֶּלֶךְ: 8] וְהַמֶּלֶךְ שָׁב מִגִּנַּת הַבִּיתָן אֶל־בֵּית מִשְׁתֵּה הַיַּיִן וְהָמָן נֹפֵל עַל־הַמִּטָּה אֲשֶׁר אֶסְתֵּר עָלֶיהָ וַיֹּאמֶר הַמֶּלֶךְ הֲגַם לִכְבּוֹשׁ אֶת־הַמַּלְכָּה עִמִּי

the house?'' As the word went out of the king's mouth, they covered Haman's face.

9] Then said Harbonah, one of the chamberlains that were before the king: "Behold also, the gallows fifty cubits high, which Haman has made for Mordecai, who spoke good for the king, stands in the house of Haman." And the king said: "Hang him thereon."

10] So they hanged Haman on the gallows that he had prepared for Mordecai. Then was the king's wrath assuaged.

Chapter 8

15] And Mordecai went forth from the presence of the king in royal apparel of blue and white, and with a great crown of gold, and with a robe of fine linen and purple; and the city of Shushan shouted and was glad.

16] The Jews had light and gladness, and joy and honor.

17] And in every province, and in every city, whithersoever the king's commandment and his decree came, the Jews had gladness and joy, a feast and a good day. And many from among the peoples of the land became Jews; for the fear of the Jews was fallen upon them.

בַּבַּיִת הַדָּבָר יָצָא מִפִּי הַמֶּלֶךְ וּפְנֵי הָמָן חָפוּ: 9 וַיֹּאמֶר חַרְבוֹנָה אֶחָד מִן־הַסָּרִיסִים לִפְנֵי הַמֶּלֶךְ גַּם הִנֵּה־הָעֵץ אֲשֶׁר־עָשָׂה הָמָן לְמָרְדֳּכַי אֲשֶׁר דִּבֶּר־טוֹב עַל־הַמֶּלֶךְ עֹמֵד בְּבֵית הָמָן גָּבֹהַּ חֲמִשִּׁים אַמָּה וַיֹּאמֶר הַמֶּלֶךְ תְּלֻהוּ עָלָיו: 10 וַיִּתְלוּ אֶת־הָמָן עַל־הָעֵץ אֲשֶׁר־הֵכִין לְמָרְדֳּכַי וַחֲמַת הַמֶּלֶךְ שָׁכָכָה:

ח

15 וּמָרְדֳּכַי יָצָא מִלִּפְנֵי הַמֶּלֶךְ בִּלְבוּשׁ מַלְכוּת תְּכֵלֶת וָחוּר וַעֲטֶרֶת זָהָב גְּדוֹלָה וְתַכְרִיךְ בּוּץ וְאַרְגָּמָן וְהָעִיר שׁוּשָׁן צָהֲלָה וְשָׂמֵחָה: 16 לַיְּהוּדִים הָיְתָה אוֹרָה וְשִׂמְחָה וְשָׂשֹׂן וִיקָר: 17 וּבְכָל־מְדִינָה וּמְדִינָה וּבְכָל־עִיר וָעִיר מְקוֹם אֲשֶׁר דְּבַר־הַמֶּלֶךְ וְדָתוֹ מַגִּיעַ שִׂמְחָה וְשָׂשֹׂן לַיְּהוּדִים מִשְׁתֶּה וְיוֹם טוֹב וְרַבִּים מֵעַמֵּי הָאָרֶץ מִתְיַהֲדִים כִּי־נָפַל פַּחַד־הַיְּהוּדִים עֲלֵיהֶם:

Ezekiel

36 : 22-36

לו

Ezekiel lived in Babylon during the days of the exile (sixth century B.C.E.) and was a master of mystic dreams and visions. Like Jeremiah and Deutero-Isaiah he fortified his people's faith in God's forgiveness, but unlike them he stressed the great need for structured ritual as a basis for a religious revival.

The Torah portion which gives the Sabbath its name (Numbers 19:1–9) refers to the right of individual purification, and Ezekiel uses the same symbolism for the cleansing of all Israel.

Chapter 36

22] Say to the House of Israel: Thus said the Lord GOD: Not for your sake will I act, O House of Israel, but for My holy name, which you have caused to be profaned among the nations to which you have come.

23] I will sanctify My great name which has been profaned among the nations—among whom you have caused it to be profaned. And the nations shall know that I am the LORD—declares the Lord GOD—when I manifest My holiness before their eyes through you. 24] I will take you from among the nations and gather you from all the countries, and I will bring you back to your own land.

25] I will sprinkle clean water upon you, and you shall be clean: I will cleanse you from all your uncleanness and from all your fetishes.

26] And I will give you a new heart and put a new spirit into you: I will remove the heart of stone from your body and give you a heart of flesh;

27] and I will put My spirit into you. Thus I will cause you to follow My laws and faithfully to observe My rules.

28] Then you shall dwell in the land which I gave to your fathers, and you shall be My people and I will be your God.

29] And when I have delivered you from all your uncleanness, I will summon the grain and make it abundant, and I will not bring famine upon you.

30] I will make the fruit of your trees and the crops of your fields abundant, so that you shall never again be humiliated before the nations because of famine.

22] לָכֵ֞ן אֱמֹ֣ר לְבֵֽית־יִשְׂרָאֵ֗ל כֹּ֤ה אָמַר֙ אֲדֹנָ֣י יְהֹוִ֔ה לֹ֧א לְמַעַנְכֶ֛ם אֲנִ֥י עֹשֶׂ֖ה בֵּ֣ית יִשְׂרָאֵ֑ל כִּ֤י אִם־לְשֵׁם־קׇדְשִׁי֙ אֲשֶׁ֣ר חִלַּלְתֶּ֔ם בַּגּוֹיִ֖ם אֲשֶׁר־בָּ֥אתֶם שָֽׁם: 23] וְקִדַּשְׁתִּ֞י אֶת־שְׁמִ֣י הַגָּד֗וֹל הַֽמְחֻלָּל֙ בַּגּוֹיִ֔ם אֲשֶׁ֥ר חִלַּלְתֶּ֖ם בְּתוֹכָ֑ם וְיָדְע֣וּ הַגּוֹיִ֗ם כִּֽי־אֲנִ֣י יְהֹוָ֔ה נְאֻם֙ אֲדֹנָ֣י יְהֹוִ֔ה בְּהִקׇּדְשִׁ֥י בָכֶ֖ם לְעֵינֵיהֶֽם: 24] וְלָקַחְתִּ֤י אֶתְכֶם֙ מִן־הַגּוֹיִ֔ם וְקִבַּצְתִּ֥י אֶתְכֶ֖ם מִכׇּל־הָאֲרָצ֑וֹת וְהֵבֵאתִ֥י אֶתְכֶ֖ם אֶל־אַדְמַתְכֶֽם: 25] וְזָרַקְתִּ֧י עֲלֵיכֶ֛ם מַ֥יִם טְהוֹרִ֖ים וּטְהַרְתֶּ֑ם מִכֹּ֧ל טֻמְאֽוֹתֵיכֶ֛ם וּמִכׇּל־גִּלּ֥וּלֵיכֶ֖ם אֲטַהֵ֥ר אֶתְכֶֽם: 26] וְנָתַתִּ֤י לָכֶם֙ לֵ֣ב חָדָ֔שׁ וְר֥וּחַ חֲדָשָׁ֖ה אֶתֵּ֣ן בְּקִרְבְּכֶ֑ם וַהֲסִ֨רֹתִ֜י אֶת־לֵ֤ב הָאֶ֙בֶן֙ מִבְּשַׂרְכֶ֔ם וְנָתַתִּ֥י לָכֶ֖ם לֵ֥ב בָּשָֽׂר: 27] וְאֶת־רוּחִ֖י אֶתֵּ֣ן בְּקִרְבְּכֶ֑ם וְעָשִׂ֗יתִי אֵ֤ת אֲשֶׁר־בְּחֻקַּי֙ תֵּלֵ֔כוּ וּמִשְׁפָּטַ֥י תִּשְׁמְר֖וּ וַעֲשִׂיתֶֽם: 28] וִֽישַׁבְתֶּ֣ם בָּאָ֔רֶץ אֲשֶׁ֥ר נָתַ֖תִּי לַאֲבֹֽתֵיכֶ֑ם וִהְיִ֤יתֶם לִי֙ לְעָ֔ם וְאָ֣נֹכִ֔י אֶהְיֶ֥ה לָכֶ֖ם לֵאלֹהִֽים: 29] וְהוֹשַׁעְתִּ֣י אֶתְכֶ֔ם מִכֹּ֖ל טֻמְאֽוֹתֵיכֶ֑ם וְקָרָ֤אתִי אֶל־הַדָּגָן֙ וְהִרְבֵּיתִ֣י אֹת֔וֹ וְלֹא־אֶתֵּ֥ן עֲלֵיכֶ֖ם רָעָֽב: 30] וְהִרְבֵּיתִי֙ אֶת־פְּרִ֣י הָעֵ֔ץ וּתְנוּבַ֖ת הַשָּׂדֶ֑ה לְמַ֗עַן אֲשֶׁ֨ר לֹ֤א תִקְח֣וּ ע֔וֹד חֶרְפַּ֥ת רָעָ֖ב בַּגּוֹיִֽם:

31] Then you
shall recall your evil ways and your base conduct,
and you shall loathe yourselves for your iniquities
and your abhorrent practices.

32] Not for your
sake will I act—declares the Lord GOD—take good
note! Be ashamed and humiliated because of your
ways, O House of Israel!

33] Thus said the Lord GOD: When I have
cleansed you of all your iniquities, I will people
your settlements, and the ruined places shall be
rebuilt;

34] and the desolate land, after lying
waste in the sight of every passerby, shall again
be tilled.

35] And men shall say, "That land,
once desolate, has become like the garden of
Eden; and the cities, once ruined, desolate, and
ravaged, are now populated and fortified."
36] And the nations that are left around you shall
know that I the LORD have rebuilt the ravaged
places and replanted the desolate land. I the LORD
have spoken and will act.

[31] וּזְכַרְתֶּם֙ אֶת־
דַּרְכֵיכֶ֣ם הָרָעִ֗ים וּמַעַלְלֵיכֶם֙ אֲשֶׁ֣ר לֹֽא־
טוֹבִ֔ים וּנְקֹֽטֹתֶם֙ בִּפְנֵיכֶ֔ם עַ֖ל עֲוֺנֹ֣תֵיכֶ֑ם וְעַ֖ל
תּוֹעֲבֹֽתֵיכֶֽם: [32] לֹ֧א לְמַֽעַנְכֶ֣ם אֲנִֽי־עֹשֶׂ֗ה נְאֻם֙
אֲדֹנָ֣י יֱהֹוִ֔ה יִוָּדַ֖ע לָכֶ֑ם בּ֧וֹשׁוּ וְהִכָּֽלְמ֛וּ מִדַּרְכֵיכֶ֖ם
בֵּ֥ית יִשְׂרָאֵֽל:

[33] כֹּ֤ה אָמַר֙ אֲדֹנָ֣י יֱהֹוִ֔ה בְּיוֹם֙ טַֽהֲרִ֣י אֶתְכֶ֔ם
מִכֹּ֖ל עֲוֺנֹֽתֵיכֶ֑ם וְהֽוֹשַׁבְתִּי֙ אֶת־הֶ֣עָרִ֔ים וְנִבְנ֖וּ
הֶחֳרָבֽוֹת: [34] וְהָאָ֥רֶץ הַנְּשַׁמָּ֖ה תֵּֽעָבֵ֑ד תַּ֗חַת
אֲשֶׁ֤ר הָֽיְתָה֙ שְׁמָמָ֔ה לְעֵינֵ֖י כׇּל־עוֹבֵֽר:
[35] וְאָֽמְר֗וּ הָאָ֤רֶץ הַלֵּ֙זוּ֙ הַנְּשַׁמָּ֔ה הָֽיְתָ֖ה כְּגַן־
עֵ֑דֶן וְהֶֽעָרִ֧ים הֶֽחֳרֵב֛וֹת וְהַֽנְשַׁמּ֥וֹת וְהַנֶּֽהֱרָס֖וֹת
בְּצוּר֥וֹת יָשָֽׁבוּ: [36] וְיָֽדְע֣וּ הַגּוֹיִ֗ם אֲשֶׁ֣ר יִשָּֽׁאֲרוּ֮
סְבִיבֽוֹתֵיכֶם֒ כִּ֣י ׀ אֲנִ֣י יְהֹוָ֗ה בָּנִ֙יתִי֙ הַנֶּֽהֱרָס֔וֹת
נָטַ֖עְתִּי הַנְּשַׁמָּ֑ה אֲנִ֥י יְהֹוָ֖ה דִּבַּ֥רְתִּי וְעָשִֽׂיתִי:

Ezekiel lived in Babylon during the days of the exile (sixth century B.C.E.) and was a master of mystic dreams and visions. Like Jeremiah and Deutero-Isaiah he fortified his people's faith in God's forgiveness, but unlike them he stressed the great need for structured ritual as a basis for a religious revival.

The haftarah details the leader's obligations for arranging the Passover sacrifice. He had to bring a sin offering in his own behalf as well as in behalf of the entire people. Thus, their shortcomings were symbolically declared to be also his responsibility.

הַחֹדֶשׁ

Ezekiel

45 : 16-25

Chapter 45

16] In this contribution, the entire population must join with the prince in Israel.

17] But the burnt offerings, the meal offerings, and the libations on festivals, new moons, sabbaths—all fixed occasions—of the House of Israel shall be the obligation of the prince; he shall provide the sin offerings, the meal offerings, the burnt offerings, and the offerings of well-being, to make expiation for the House of Israel.

18] Thus said the LORD GOD: On the first day of the first month, you shall take a bull of the herd without blemish, and you shall cleanse the Sanctuary.

19] The priest shall take some of the blood of the sin offering and apply it to the doorposts of the Temple, to the four corners of the ledge[h] of the altar, and to the doorposts of the gate of the inner court.

20] You shall do the same [i]on the seventh day of the month[i] to purge the Temple from uncleanness caused by unwitting or ignorant persons.

21] On the fourteenth day of the first month you shall have the passover sacrifice; and during a festival of seven days unleavened bread shall be eaten.

22] On that day, the prince shall provide a bull of sin offering on behalf of himself and of the entire population;

מה

16] כָּל הָעָם הָאָרֶץ יִהְיוּ אֶל־הַתְּרוּמָה הַזֹּאת לַנָּשִׂיא בְּיִשְׂרָאֵל:

17] וְעַל־הַנָּשִׂיא יִהְיֶה הָעוֹלוֹת וְהַמִּנְחָה וְהַנֶּסֶךְ בַּחַגִּים וּבֶחֳדָשִׁים וּבַשַּׁבָּתוֹת בְּכָל־מוֹעֲדֵי בֵּית יִשְׂרָאֵל הוּא־יַעֲשֶׂה אֶת־הַחַטָּאת וְאֶת־הַמִּנְחָה וְאֶת־הָעוֹלָה וְאֶת־הַשְּׁלָמִים לְכַפֵּר בְּעַד בֵּית־יִשְׂרָאֵל:

18] כֹּה־אָמַר אֲדֹנָי יֱהוִֹה בָּרִאשׁוֹן בְּאֶחָד לַחֹדֶשׁ תִּקַּח פַּר־בֶּן־בָּקָר תָּמִים וְחִטֵּאתָ אֶת־הַמִּקְדָּשׁ: 19] וְלָקַח הַכֹּהֵן מִדַּם הַחַטָּאת וְנָתַן אֶל־מְזוּזַת הַבַּיִת וְאֶל־אַרְבַּע פִּנּוֹת הָעֲזָרָה לַמִּזְבֵּחַ וְעַל־מְזוּזַת שַׁעַר הֶחָצֵר הַפְּנִימִית:

20] וְכֵן תַּעֲשֶׂה בְּשִׁבְעָה בַחֹדֶשׁ מֵאִישׁ שֹׁגֶה וּמִפֶּתִי וְכִפַּרְתֶּם אֶת־הַבָּיִת:

21] בָּרִאשׁוֹן בְּאַרְבָּעָה עָשָׂר יוֹם לַחֹדֶשׁ יִהְיֶה לָכֶם הַפָּסַח חָג שְׁבֻעוֹת יָמִים מַצּוֹת יֵאָכֵל: 22] וְעָשָׂה הַנָּשִׂיא בַּיּוֹם הַהוּא בַּעֲדוֹ

[h] *Meaning of Heb. uncertain*
[i-i] *Septuagint reads "in the seventh month"*

23] and during the seven days of the festival, he shall provide daily—for seven days—seven bulls and seven rams, without blemish, for a burnt offering to the LORD, and one goat daily for a sin offering.

24] He shall provide a meal offering of an *ephah*[k] for each bull and an *ephah* for each ram, with a *hin* of oil to every *ephah*.

25] So, too, during the festival of the seventh month, for seven days from the fifteenth day on, he shall provide the same sin offerings, burnt offerings, meal offerings, and oil.

Malachi is a descriptive term meaning "My messenger," and this name is attached to the last of the prophetic books. While the identity of the prophet remains unknown, his writings appear to be contemporary with Nehemiah who rebuilt the Temple after the people's return from exile, in the middle of the fifth century B.C.E.

Malachi's oration, the very last in the prophetic books, is a defense of God. It is not God who has changed but Israel, the prophet says, and the day of judgment is at hand. It will be the final Great Day of the Lord (hence the name of the Sabbath) and will be heralded by the prophet Elijah.

Chapter 3

4] Then the offerings of Judah and Jerusalem shall be pleasing to the LORD as in the days of yore and in the years of old.

5] But [first] I will step forward to contend against you, and I will act as a relentless accuser against those who have no fear of Me: who practice sorcery, who commit adultery, who swear falsely, who cheat laborers of their hire, and who subvert [the cause of] the widow, orphan, and stranger—said the LORD of Hosts.

6] [c]For I am the LORD—I have not changed; and you are the children of Jacob—you have not ceased to be.

[k] *Of choice flour*
[c] *Vv. 6–12 resume the thought of 1.2–5*

וּבְעַד כָּל־עַם הָאָרֶץ פַּר חַטָּאת: 23] וְשִׁבְעַת יְמֵי־הֶחָג יַעֲשֶׂה עוֹלָה לַיהוָה שִׁבְעַת פָּרִים וְשִׁבְעַת אֵילִם תְּמִימִם לַיּוֹם שִׁבְעַת הַיָּמִים וְחַטָּאת שְׂעִיר עִזִּים לַיּוֹם: 24] וּמִנְחָה אֵיפָה לַפָּר וְאֵיפָה לָאַיִל יַעֲשֶׂה וְשֶׁמֶן הִין לָאֵיפָה: 25] בַּשְּׁבִיעִי בַּחֲמִשָּׁה עָשָׂר יוֹם לַחֹדֶשׁ בֶּחָג יַעֲשֶׂה כָאֵלֶּה שִׁבְעַת הַיָּמִים כַּחַטָּאת כָּעֹלָה וְכַמִּנְחָה וְכַשָּׁמֶן:

HAFTARAH Shabbat ha-Gadol

שבת הגדול

Malachi
3 : 4-24

ג

4] וְעָרְבָה לַיהוָה מִנְחַת יְהוּדָה וִירוּשָׁלָ͏ִם כִּימֵי עוֹלָם וּכְשָׁנִים קַדְמֹנִיּוֹת: 5] וְקָרַבְתִּי אֲלֵיכֶם לַמִּשְׁפָּט וְהָיִיתִי עֵד מְמַהֵר בַּמְכַשְּׁפִים וּבַמְנָאֲפִים וּבַנִּשְׁבָּעִים לַשָּׁקֶר וּבְעֹשְׁקֵי שְׂכַר־שָׂכִיר אַלְמָנָה וְיָתוֹם וּמַטֵּי־גֵר וְלֹא יְרֵאוּנִי אָמַר יְהוָה צְבָאוֹת:

6] כִּי אֲנִי יְהוָה לֹא שָׁנִיתִי וְאַתֶּם בְּנֵי־יַעֲקֹב לֹא כְלִיתֶם:

7] From the very days of your fathers you have turned away from My laws and have not observed them. Turn back to Me, and I will turn back to you—said the LORD of Hosts. But you ask, "How shall we turn back?" 8] Ought man to defraud[d] God? Yet you are defrauding Me. And you ask, "How have we been defrauding You?" In tithe and contribution.[e] 9] You are suffering from a curse, yet you go on defrauding Me—the whole nation of you. 10] Bring the full tithe into the storehouse,[f] and let there be food in My House, and thus put Me to the test—said the LORD of Hosts. I will surely open the floodgates of the sky for you and pour down boundless blessing;

11] and I will banish the locusts[g] from you, so that they will not destroy the yield of your soil; and your vines in the field shall no longer miscarry—said the LORD of Hosts.

12] And all the nations shall account you happy, for you shall be the most desired of lands—said the LORD of Hosts.

13] You have spoken hard words against Me—said the LORD. But you ask, "What have we been saying among ourselves against You?"

14] You have said, "It is useless to serve God. What have we gained by keeping His charge and walking in abject awe of the LORD of Hosts? 15] And so, we account the arrogant happy: they have indeed done evil and endured; they have indeed dared God and escaped."

16] In this vein have those who revere the LORD been talking to one another. The LORD has heard and noted it, and a scroll of remembrance has been written at His behest concerning those who revere the LORD and esteem His name.

17] And on the day that I am preparing, said the LORD of Hosts, they shall be My treasured possession; I will be tender toward them as a man is tender toward a son who ministers to him.

7] לְמִימֵי אֲבֹתֵיכֶם סַרְתֶּם מֵחֻקַּי וְלֹא שְׁמַרְתֶּם שׁוּבוּ אֵלַי וְאָשׁוּבָה אֲלֵיכֶם אָמַר יְהֹוָה צְבָאוֹת וַאֲמַרְתֶּם בַּמֶּה נָשׁוּב: 8] הֲיִקְבַּע אָדָם אֱלֹהִים כִּי אַתֶּם קֹבְעִים אֹתִי וַאֲמַרְתֶּם בַּמֶּה קְבַעֲנוּךָ הַמַּעֲשֵׂר וְהַתְּרוּמָה: 9] בַּמְּאֵרָה אַתֶּם נֵאָרִים וְאֹתִי אַתֶּם קֹבְעִים הַגּוֹי כֻּלּוֹ: 10] הָבִיאוּ אֶת־כָּל־הַמַּעֲשֵׂר אֶל־בֵּית הָאוֹצָר וִיהִי טֶרֶף בְּבֵיתִי וּבְחָנוּנִי נָא בָּזֹאת אָמַר יְהֹוָה צְבָאוֹת אִם־לֹא אֶפְתַּח לָכֶם אֵת אֲרֻבּוֹת הַשָּׁמַיִם וַהֲרִיקֹתִי לָכֶם בְּרָכָה עַד־בְּלִי־דָי: 11] וְגָעַרְתִּי לָכֶם בָּאֹכֵל וְלֹא־יַשְׁחִת לָכֶם אֶת־פְּרִי הָאֲדָמָה וְלֹא־תְשַׁכֵּל לָכֶם הַגֶּפֶן בַּשָּׂדֶה אָמַר יְהֹוָה צְבָאוֹת: 12] וְאִשְּׁרוּ אֶתְכֶם כָּל־הַגּוֹיִם כִּי־תִהְיוּ אַתֶּם אֶרֶץ חֵפֶץ אָמַר יְהֹוָה צְבָאוֹת:

13] חָזְקוּ עָלַי דִּבְרֵיכֶם אָמַר יְהֹוָה וַאֲמַרְתֶּם מַה־נִּדְבַּרְנוּ עָלֶיךָ: 14] אֲמַרְתֶּם שָׁוְא עֲבֹד אֱלֹהִים וּמַה־בֶּצַע כִּי שָׁמַרְנוּ מִשְׁמַרְתּוֹ וְכִי הָלַכְנוּ קְדֹרַנִּית מִפְּנֵי יְהֹוָה צְבָאוֹת: 15] וְעַתָּה אֲנַחְנוּ מְאַשְּׁרִים זֵדִים גַּם־נִבְנוּ עֹשֵׂי רִשְׁעָה גַּם בָּחֲנוּ אֱלֹהִים וַיִּמָּלֵטוּ: 16] אָז נִדְבְּרוּ יִרְאֵי יְהֹוָה אִישׁ אֶל־רֵעֵהוּ וַיַּקְשֵׁב יְהֹוָה וַיִּשְׁמָע וַיִּכָּתֵב סֵפֶר זִכָּרוֹן לְפָנָיו לְיִרְאֵי יְהֹוָה וּלְחֹשְׁבֵי שְׁמוֹ: 17] וְהָיוּ לִי אָמַר יְהֹוָה צְבָאוֹת לַיּוֹם אֲשֶׁר אֲנִי עֹשֶׂה סְגֻלָּה וְחָמַלְתִּי עֲלֵיהֶם כַּאֲשֶׁר יַחְמֹל אִישׁ עַל־בְּנוֹ הָעֹבֵד אֹתוֹ:

---

[d] Heb. kaba, a play on the name of Jacob (v. 6); cf. Gen. 27.36

[e] I.e., the contributions to the priests from the new grain, oil, and wine; see Num. 18.12

[f] I.e., the public storehouse; see Neh. 13.10–13   [g] Lit. "devourer"

18] And you shall come to see the difference between the righteous and the wicked, between him who has served the Lord and him who has not served Him.

19] For lo! That day is at hand, burning like an oven. All the arrogant and all the doers of evil shall be straw, and the day that is coming—said the Lord of Hosts—shall burn them to ashes and leave of them neither stock nor boughs. 20] But for you who revere My name a sun of victory shall rise ʰ⁻to bring healing.⁻ʰ You shall go forth and stamp like stall-fed calves,

21] and you shall trample the wicked to a pulp, for they shall be dust beneath your feet on the day that I am preparing—said the Lord of Hosts.

22] Be mindful of the Teaching of My servant Moses, whom I charged at Horeb with laws and rules for all Israel.

23] Lo, I will send the prophet Elijah to you before the coming of the awesome, fearful day of the Lord.

24] He shall reconcile fathers with sons and sons with their fathers, so that, when I come, I do not strike the whole land with utter destruction.

Lo, I will send the prophet Elijah to you before the coming of the awesome, fearful day of the Lord.

18[וְשַׁבְתֶּם

וּרְאִיתֶם בֵּין צַדִּיק לְרָשָׁע בֵּין עֹבֵד אֱלֹהִים לַאֲשֶׁר לֹא עֲבָדוֹ:

19 כִּי־הִנֵּה הַיּוֹם בָּא בֹּעֵר כַּתַּנּוּר וְהָיוּ כָל־זֵדִים וְכָל־עֹשֵׂה רִשְׁעָה קַשׁ וְלִהַט אֹתָם הַיּוֹם הַבָּא אָמַר יְהוָה צְבָאוֹת אֲשֶׁר לֹא־יַעֲזֹב לָהֶם שֹׁרֶשׁ וְעָנָף: 20 וְזָרְחָה לָכֶם יִרְאֵי שְׁמִי שֶׁמֶשׁ צְדָקָה וּמַרְפֵּא בִּכְנָפֶיהָ וִיצָאתֶם וּפִשְׁתֶּם כְּעֶגְלֵי מַרְבֵּק: 21 וְעַסּוֹתֶם רְשָׁעִים כִּי־יִהְיוּ אֵפֶר תַּחַת כַּפּוֹת רַגְלֵיכֶם בַּיּוֹם אֲשֶׁר אֲנִי עֹשֶׂה אָמַר יְהוָה צְבָאוֹת:

22 זִכְרוּ תּוֹרַת מֹשֶׁה עַבְדִּי אֲשֶׁר צִוִּיתִי אוֹתוֹ בְחֹרֵב עַל־כָּל־יִשְׂרָאֵל חֻקִּים וּמִשְׁפָּטִים: 23 הִנֵּה אָנֹכִי שֹׁלֵחַ לָכֶם אֵת אֵלִיָּה הַנָּבִיא לִפְנֵי בּוֹא יוֹם יְהוָה הַגָּדוֹל וְהַנּוֹרָא: 24 וְהֵשִׁיב לֵב־אָבוֹת עַל־בָּנִים וְלֵב בָּנִים עַל־אֲבוֹתָם פֶּן־אָבוֹא וְהִכֵּיתִי אֶת־הָאָרֶץ חֵרֶם:

הִנֵּה אָנֹכִי שֹׁלֵחַ לָכֶם אֵת אֵלִיָּה הַנָּבִיא לִפְנֵי בּוֹא יוֹם יְהוָה הַגָּדוֹל וְהַנּוֹרָא:

ʰ⁻ʰ Lit. "with healing in the corners of its garments"; others "with healing in its wings"

First Day of Pesach

Chapters 40–66 of the Book of Isaiah are the work of an unknown author (often referred to as Deutero-Isaiah) who lived in Babylon during the days of the exile (sixth century B.C.E.). He preached unwavering trust in a God who would surely restore Israel to its homeland. Of all the prophets he is the most lyrical and his imagery the richest.

Isaiah reminds his people of God's protection throughout their history and cites the salvation at the sea as a prime example. This providential care makes Israel God's eternal witness.

Isaiah

43 : 1–15

Chapter 43

מג

1] But now thus said the LORD
Who created you, O Jacob,
Who formed you, O Israel:
Fear not, for I will redeem you;
I have singled you out by name,
You are Mine.

1] וְעַתָּה כֹּה־אָמַר יְהוָֹה
בֹּרַאֲךָ יַעֲקֹב
וְיֹצֶרְךָ יִשְׂרָאֵל
אַל־תִּירָא כִּי גְאַלְתִּיךָ
קָרָאתִי בְשִׁמְךָ
לִי־אָתָּה:

2] When you pass through water,
I will be with you;
Through streams,
They shall not overwhelm you.
When you walk through fire,
You shall not be scorched;
Through flame,
It shall not burn you.

2] כִּי־תַעֲבֹר בַּמַּיִם
אִתְּךָ אָנִי
וּבַנְּהָרוֹת
לֹא יִשְׁטְפוּךָ
כִּי־תֵלֵךְ בְּמוֹ־אֵשׁ
לֹא תִכָּוֶה
וְלֶהָבָה
לֹא תִבְעַר־בָּךְ:

3] For I the LORD am your God,
The Holy One of Israel, your Savior.
I give Egypt as a ransom for you,
Ethiopia and Saba in exchange for you.

3] כִּי אֲנִי יְהוָֹה אֱלֹהֶיךָ
קְדוֹשׁ יִשְׂרָאֵל מוֹשִׁיעֶךָ
נָתַתִּי כָפְרְךָ מִצְרַיִם
כּוּשׁ וּסְבָא תַּחְתֶּיךָ:

4] Because you are precious to Me,
And honored, and I love you,

4] מֵאֲשֶׁר יָקַרְתָּ בְעֵינַי
נִכְבַּדְתָּ וַאֲנִי אֲהַבְתִּיךָ

I give men in exchange for you
And peoples in your stead.

5] Fear not, for I am with you:
I will bring your folk from the East,
Will gather you out of the West;

6] I will say to the North, "Give back!"
And to the South, "Do not withhold!
Bring My sons from afar,
And My daughters from the end of the earth—

7] All who are linked to My name,
Whom I have created,
Formed, and made for My glory—

8] Setting free that people,
Blind though it has eyes
And deaf though it has ears."

9] All the nations assemble as one,
The peoples gather.
Who among them declared this,
Foretold to us the things that have happened?
Let them produce their witnesses and be
    vindicated,
That men, hearing them, may say, "It is true!"[a]

10] My witnesses are *you*
            —declares the LORD—
My servant, whom I have chosen.
To the end that you[b] may take thought,
And believe in Me,
And understand that I am He:

וְאֶתֵּן אָדָם תַּחְתֶּיךָ
וּלְאֻמִּים תַּחַת נַפְשֶׁךָ:

5] אַל־תִּירָא כִּי־אִתְּךָ אָנִי
מִמִּזְרָח אָבִיא זַרְעֶךָ
וּמִמַּעֲרָב אֲקַבְּצֶךָּ:

6] אֹמַר לַצָּפוֹן תֵּנִי
וּלְתֵימָן אַל־תִּכְלָאִי
הָבִיאִי בָנַי מֵרָחוֹק
וּבְנוֹתַי מִקְצֵה הָאָרֶץ:

7] כֹּל הַנִּקְרָא בִשְׁמִי
וְלִכְבוֹדִי בְּרָאתִיו
יְצַרְתִּיו אַף־עֲשִׂיתִיו:

8] הוֹצִיא עַם־עִוֵּר
וְעֵינַיִם יֵשׁ
וְחֵרְשִׁים וְאָזְנַיִם לָמוֹ:

9] כָּל־הַגּוֹיִם נִקְבְּצוּ יַחְדָּו
וְיֵאָסְפוּ לְאֻמִּים
מִי בָהֶם יַגִּיד זֹאת
וְרִאשֹׁנוֹת יַשְׁמִיעֻנוּ
יִתְּנוּ עֵדֵיהֶם וְיִצְדָּקוּ
וְיִשְׁמְעוּ וְיֹאמְרוּ אֱמֶת:

10] אַתֶּם עֵדַי
נְאֻם־יְהוָֹה
וְעַבְדִּי אֲשֶׁר בָּחָרְתִּי
לְמַעַן תֵּדְעוּ וְתַאֲמִינוּ לִי
וְתָבִינוּ כִּי־אֲנִי הוּא

---

[a] I.e., that the other nations' gods are real
[b] Emendation yields "they"

1658

Before Me no god was formed,
And after Me none shall exist—

11] None but Me, the LORD.
Beside Me, none can grant triumph.

12] I alone foretold the deliverance
And I brought it to pass;
I announced it,
And no strange god was among you.
So you are My witnesses

—declares the LORD—

And I am God.

13] Ever since day was, I am He;
None can deliver from My hand.
When I act, who can reverse it?

14] Thus said the LORD,
Your Redeemer, the Holy One of Israel:
For your sake ᶜ⁻I send to Babylon;
I will bring down all [her] bars,
And the Chaldeans shall raise their voice in
     lamentation.⁻ᶜ

15] I am your Holy One, the LORD,
Your King, the Creator of Israel.

לְפָנַי֙ לֹא־נ֣וֹצַר אֵ֔ל

וְאַחֲרַ֖י לֹ֥א־יִהְיֶֽה׃

11] אָנֹכִ֥י אָנֹכִ֖י יְהֹוָ֑ה

וְאֵ֥ין מִבַּלְעָדַ֖י מוֹשִֽׁיעַ׃

12] אָנֹכִ֞י הִגַּ֤דְתִּי

וְהוֹשַׁ֙עְתִּי֙

וְהִשְׁמַ֔עְתִּי

וְאֵ֥ין בָּכֶ֖ם זָ֑ר

וְאַתֶּ֥ם עֵדַ֛י

נְאֻם־יְהֹוָ֖ה

וַֽאֲנִי־אֵֽל׃

13] גַּם־מִיּוֹם֙ אֲנִ֣י ה֔וּא

וְאֵ֥ין מִיָּדִ֖י מַצִּ֑יל

אֶפְעַ֖ל וּמִ֥י יְשִׁיבֶֽנָּה׃

14] כֹּֽה־אָמַ֧ר יְהֹוָ֛ה

גֹּאַלְכֶ֖ם קְד֣וֹשׁ יִשְׂרָאֵ֑ל

לְמַעַנְכֶ֞ם שִׁלַּ֣חְתִּי בָבֶ֗לָה

וְהוֹרַדְתִּ֤י בָֽרִיחִים֙ כֻּלָּ֔ם

וְכַשְׂדִּ֖ים בׇּאֳנִיּ֥וֹת רִנָּתָֽם׃

15] אֲנִ֥י יְהֹוָ֖ה קְדֽוֹשְׁכֶ֑ם

בּוֹרֵ֥א יִשְׂרָאֵ֖ל מַלְכְּכֶֽם׃

ᶜ⁻ᶜ *Meaning of Heb. uncertain*

Ezekiel lived in Babylon during the days of the exile (sixth century B.C.E.) and was a master of mystic dreams and visions. Like Jeremiah and Deutero-Isaiah he fortified his people's faith in God's forgiveness, but unlike them he stressed the great need for structured ritual as a basis for a religious revival.

Even as God gave life to the enslaved in Egypt so will He give life to His people in exile. To express this hope, Ezekiel evokes the image of dry bones being brought to life by God.

חול המועד פסח

Ezekiel

37: 1-14

לז

Chapter 37

1] The hand of the Lord came upon me. He took me out by the spirit of the Lord and set me down in the valley. It was full of bones.

2] He led me all around them; there were very many of them spread over the valley, and they were very dry.

3] He said to me, "O mortal, can these bones live again?" I replied, "O Lord God, only You know."

4] And He said to me, "Prophesy over these bones and say to them: O dry bones, hear the word of the Lord!

5] Thus said the Lord God to these bones: I will cause breath to enter you and you shall live again.

6] I will lay sinews upon you, and cover you with flesh, and form skin over you. And I will put breath into you, and you shall live again. And you shall know that I am the Lord!"

7] I prophesied as I had been commanded. And while I was prophesying, suddenly there was a sound of rattling, and the bones came together, bone to matching bone.

8] I looked, and there were sinews on them, and flesh had grown, and skin had formed over them; but there was no breath in them.

9] Then He said to me, "Prophesy to the breath, prophesy, O mortal! Say to the breath: Thus said the Lord God: Come, O breath, from the four winds, and breathe into these slain, that they may live again."

1] הָיְתָה עָלַי יַד־יְהֹוָה וַיּוֹצִאֵנִי בְרוּחַ יְהֹוָה וַיְנִיחֵנִי בְּתוֹךְ הַבִּקְעָה וְהִיא מְלֵאָה עֲצָמוֹת:

2] וְהֶעֱבִירַנִי עֲלֵיהֶם סָבִיב סָבִיב וְהִנֵּה רַבּוֹת מְאֹד עַל־פְּנֵי הַבִּקְעָה וְהִנֵּה יְבֵשׁוֹת מְאֹד:

3] וַיֹּאמֶר אֵלַי בֶּן־אָדָם הֲתִחְיֶינָה הָעֲצָמוֹת הָאֵלֶּה וָאֹמַר אֲדֹנָי יֱהֹוִה אַתָּה יָדָעְתָּ:

4] וַיֹּאמֶר אֵלַי הִנָּבֵא עַל־הָעֲצָמוֹת הָאֵלֶּה וְאָמַרְתָּ אֲלֵיהֶם הָעֲצָמוֹת הַיְבֵשׁוֹת שִׁמְעוּ דְּבַר־יְהֹוָה: 5] כֹּה אָמַר אֲדֹנָי יֱהֹוִה לָעֲצָמוֹת הָאֵלֶּה הִנֵּה אֲנִי מֵבִיא בָכֶם רוּחַ וִחְיִיתֶם:

6] וְנָתַתִּי עֲלֵיכֶם גִּדִים וְהַעֲלֵתִי עֲלֵיכֶם בָּשָׂר וְקָרַמְתִּי עֲלֵיכֶם עוֹר וְנָתַתִּי בָכֶם רוּחַ וִחְיִיתֶם וִידַעְתֶּם כִּי־אֲנִי יְהֹוָה:

7] וְנִבֵּאתִי כַּאֲשֶׁר צֻוֵּיתִי וַיְהִי־קוֹל כְּהִנָּבְאִי וְהִנֵּה־רַעַשׁ וַתִּקְרְבוּ עֲצָמוֹת עֶצֶם אֶל־עַצְמוֹ:

8] וְרָאִיתִי וְהִנֵּה עֲלֵיהֶם גִּדִים וּבָשָׂר עָלָה וַיִּקְרַם עֲלֵיהֶם עוֹר מִלְמָעְלָה וְרוּחַ אֵין בָּהֶם: 9] וַיֹּאמֶר אֵלַי הִנָּבֵא אֶל־הָרוּחַ הִנָּבֵא בֶן־אָדָם וְאָמַרְתָּ אֶל־הָרוּחַ כֹּה־אָמַר אֲדֹנָי יֱהֹוִה מֵאַרְבַּע רוּחוֹת בֹּאִי הָרוּחַ וּפְחִי בַּהֲרוּגִים

1660

10] I prophesied as He commanded me. The breath entered them, and they came to life and stood up on their feet, a vast multitude.

11] And He said to me: O mortal, these bones are the whole House of Israel. They say, "Our bones are dried up, our hope is gone; we are doomed."

12] Prophesy, therefore, and say to them: Thus said the Lord GOD: I am going to open your graves and lift you out of the graves, O My people, and bring you to the land of Israel.

13] You shall know, O My people, that I am the LORD when I have opened your graves and lifted you out of your graves.

14] I will put My breath into you and you shall live again, and I will set you upon your own soil. Then you shall know that I the LORD have spoken and have acted—declares the LORD.

הָאֵ֖לֶּה וַיִּֽחְיֽוּ׃ 10 וְהִנַּבֵּ֙אתִי֙ כַּאֲשֶׁ֣ר צִוָּ֔נִי וַתָּבוֹא֩ בָהֶ֨ם הָר֜וּחַ וַיִּֽחְי֗וּ וַיַּֽעַמְדוּ֙ עַל־רַגְלֵיהֶ֔ם חַ֖יִל גָּד֥וֹל מְאֹ֥ד מְאֹֽד׃

11 וַיֹּ֣אמֶר אֵלַ֔י בֶּן־אָדָ֕ם הָעֲצָמ֣וֹת הָאֵ֔לֶּה כָּל־בֵּ֥ית יִשְׂרָאֵ֖ל הֵ֑מָּה הִנֵּ֣ה אֹמְרִ֗ים יָבְשׁ֧וּ עַצְמוֹתֵ֛ינוּ וְאָבְדָ֥ה תִקְוָתֵ֖נוּ נִגְזַ֥רְנוּ לָֽנוּ׃

12 לָכֵן֩ הִנָּבֵ֨א וְאָמַרְתָּ֜ אֲלֵיהֶ֗ם כֹּֽה־אָמַר֮ אֲדֹנָ֣י יְהוִה֒ הִנֵּה֩ אֲנִ֨י פֹתֵ֜חַ אֶת־קִבְרֽוֹתֵיכֶ֗ם וְהַעֲלֵיתִ֥י אֶתְכֶ֛ם מִקִּבְרֽוֹתֵיכֶ֖ם עַמִּ֑י וְהֵבֵאתִ֥י אֶתְכֶ֖ם אֶל־אַדְמַ֥ת יִשְׂרָאֵֽל׃

13 וִֽידַעְתֶּ֖ם כִּֽי־אֲנִ֣י יְהוָ֑ה בְּפִתְחִ֣י אֶת־קִבְרֽוֹתֵיכֶ֗ם וּבְהַעֲלוֹתִ֥י אֶתְכֶ֛ם מִקִּבְרֽוֹתֵיכֶ֖ם עַמִּֽי׃

14 וְנָתַתִּ֨י רוּחִ֤י בָכֶם֙ וִֽחְיִיתֶ֔ם וְהִנַּחְתִּ֥י אֶתְכֶ֖ם עַל־אַדְמַתְכֶ֑ם וִֽידַעְתֶּ֞ם כִּֽי־אֲנִ֧י יְהוָ֛ה דִּבַּ֥רְתִּי וְעָשִׂ֖יתִי נְאֻם־יְהוָֽה׃

Seventh Day of Pesach

The Book of Samuel is divided into two parts. It is primarily the story of Samuel's ministry as the spiritual guide
of Israel and of the reign of Israel's first two kings, Saul
and David (about 1000 B.C.E.). It is history written from
a theological perspective: all of Israel's fate hinges on the
performance or non-performance of God's commandments.

David's prayer on his deliverance from the hand of Saul
is read on the seventh day of Pesach to recall once again
the gratitude which Israel felt and feels for its deliverance
from Egypt.

יום שביעי של פסח

Second Samuel

22 : 1-51

כב

Chapter 22

1] *a*David addressed the words of this song to
the Lord, after the Lord had saved him from the
hands of all his enemies and from the hands of
Saul.

1] וַיְדַבֵּ֨ר דָּוִ֜ד לַֽיהוָ֗ה אֶת־דִּבְרֵ֛י הַשִּׁירָ֥ה
הַזֹּ֖את בְּי֨וֹם הִצִּ֤יל יְהוָה֙ אֹת֔וֹ מִכַּ֥ף כָּל־אֹיְבָ֖יו
וּמִכַּ֥ף שָׁאֽוּל׃

2] He said:
O Lord, my crag, my fastness, my deliverer!

2] וַיֹּאמַ֑ר

יְהוָ֛ה סַֽלְעִ֥י וּמְצֻדָתִ֖י וּמְפַלְטִי־לִֽי׃

3] O *b*-God, the rock*-b* wherein I take shelter:
My shield, my *c*-mighty champion,*-c* my fortress
and refuge!
My savior, You who rescue me from violence!

3] אֱלֹהֵ֥י צוּרִ֖י אֶחֱסֶה־בּ֑וֹ

מָגִנִּ֞י וְקֶ֣רֶן יִשְׁעִ֗י

מִשְׂגַּבִּי֙ וּמְנוּסִ֔י

מֹשִׁעִ֕י מֵחָמָ֖ס תֹּשִׁעֵֽנִי׃

4] *d*-All praise! I called on the Lord,*-d*
And I was delivered from my enemies.

4] מְהֻלָּ֖ל אֶקְרָ֣א יְהוָ֑ה

וּמֵאֹיְבַ֖י אִוָּשֵֽׁעַ׃

5] For the breakers of Death encompassed me,
The torrents of Belial*e* terrified me;

5] כִּ֥י אֲפָפֻ֖נִי מִשְׁבְּרֵי־מָ֑וֶת

נַֽחֲלֵ֥י בְלִיַּ֖עַל יְבַעֲתֻֽנִי׃

6] The snares of Sheol encircled me,
The toils of Death engulfed me.

6] חֶבְלֵ֥י שְׁא֖וֹל סַבֻּ֑נִי

קִדְּמֻ֖נִי מֹקְשֵׁי־מָֽוֶת׃

---

a This poem occurs again as Ps. 18, with a number of variations, some of which are
   cited in the following notes
b-b Lit. "the God of my rock"; Ps. 18.3 "my God, my rock"
c-c Lit. "horn of rescue"
d-d Construction of Heb. uncertain
e I.e., the nether world, like "Death" and "Sheol"

7] In my anguish I called on the LORD,
Cried out to my God;
In His abode*ƒ* He heard my voice,
My cry entered His ears.

בְּצַר־לִי אֶקְרָא יְהֹוָה [7
וְאֶל־אֱלֹהַי אֶקְרָא
וַיִּשְׁמַע מֵהֵיכָלוֹ קוֹלִי
וְשַׁוְעָתִי בְּאָזְנָיו:

8] Then the earth rocked and quaked,
The foundations of heaven*ᵍ* shook—
Rocked by His indignation.

וַיִּתְגָּעַשׁ וַתִּרְעַשׁ הָאָרֶץ [8
מוֹסְדוֹת הַשָּׁמַיִם יִרְגָּזוּ
וַיִּתְגָּעֲשׁוּ כִּי־חָרָה לוֹ:

9] Smoke went up from His nostrils,
From His mouth came devouring fire;
Live coals blazed forth from Him.

עָלָה עָשָׁן בְּאַפּוֹ [9
וְאֵשׁ מִפִּיו תֹּאכֵל
גֶּחָלִים בָּעֲרוּ מִמֶּנּוּ:

10] He bent the sky and came down,
Thick cloud beneath His feet.

וַיֵּט שָׁמַיִם וַיֵּרַד [10
וַעֲרָפֶל תַּחַת רַגְלָיו:

11] He mounted a cherub and flew;
*ʰ*He was seen*⁻ʰ* on the wings of the wind.

וַיִּרְכַּב עַל־כְּרוּב וַיָּעֹף [11
וַיֵּרָא עַל־כַּנְפֵי־רוּחַ:

12] He made pavilions of darkness about Him,
Dripping clouds, huge thunderheads;

וַיָּשֶׁת חֹשֶׁךְ סְבִיבֹתָיו סֻכּוֹת [12
חַשְׁרַת־מַיִם עָבֵי שְׁחָקִים:

13] In the brilliance before Him
Blazed fiery coals.

מִנֹּגַהּ נֶגְדּוֹ [13
בָּעֲרוּ גַּחֲלֵי־אֵשׁ:

14] The LORD thundered forth from heaven,
The Most High sent forth His voice;

יַרְעֵם מִן־שָׁמַיִם יְהֹוָה [14
וְעֶלְיוֹן יִתֵּן קוֹלוֹ:

15] He let loose bolts, and scattered them;*ⁱ*
Lightning and, put them to rout.

וַיִּשְׁלַח חִצִּים וַיְפִיצֵם [15
בָּרָק וַיָּהֹם:

16] The bed of the sea was exposed,
The foundations of the world were laid bare
By the mighty roaring of the LORD,
At the blast of the breath of His nostrils.

וַיֵּרָאוּ אֲפִקֵי יָם [16
יִגָּלוּ מֹסְדוֹת תֵּבֵל
בְּגַעֲרַת יְהֹוָה
מִנִּשְׁמַת רוּחַ אַפּוֹ:

ƒ *Lit. "Temple"*
ᵍ *Ps. 18.8 "mountains"*
ʰ⁻ʰ *Ps. 18.11 "Gliding"*
ⁱ *I.e., the enemies in v. 4*

17] He reached down from on high, He took me,
Drew me out of the mighty waters;[j]

18] He rescued me from my enemy so strong,
From foes too mighty for me.

19] They attacked me on my day of calamity,
But the Lord was my stay.

20] He brought me out to freedom,
He rescued me because He was pleased with me.

21] The Lord rewarded me according to my
merit,
He requited the cleanness of my hands.

22] For I have kept the ways of the Lord
And have not been guilty before my God;

23] I am mindful of all His rules
And have not departed from His laws.

24] I have been blameless before Him,
And have guarded myself against sinning—

25] And the Lord has requited my merit,
According to my purity in His sight.

26] With the loyal You deal loyally;
With the blameless hero,[k] blamelessly.

27] With the pure You act in purity,
And with the perverse You are wily.

28] To humble folk You give victory,
[l-]And You look with scorn on the haughty.[-l]

29] You, O Lord, are my lamp;
The Lord lights up my darkness.

יְשָׁלַ֤ח מִמָּרוֹם֙ יִקָּחֵ֔נִי 17[

יַֽמְשֵׁ֖נִי מִמַּ֥יִם רַבִּֽים׃

יַצִּילֵ֗נִי מֵאֹיְבִ֥י עָ֑ז 18[

מִ֝שֹּׂנְאַ֗י כִּ֣י אָמְצ֥וּ מִמֶּֽנִּי׃

יְקַדְּמֻ֖נִי בְּי֣וֹם אֵידִ֑י 19[

וַֽיְהִי־יְהוָ֖ה מִשְׁעָ֥ן לִֽי׃

וַיֹּצֵ֣א לַמֶּרְחָ֣ב אֹתִ֑י 20[

יְ֝חַלְּצֵ֗נִי כִּי־חָ֥פֵֽץ בִּֽי׃

יִגְמְלֵ֤נִי יְהוָה֙ כְּצִדְקָתִ֔י 21[

כְּבֹ֥ר יָדַ֖י יָשִׁ֥יב לִֽי׃

כִּ֣י שָׁמַ֔רְתִּי דַּרְכֵ֖י יְהוָ֑ה 22[

וְלֹ֥א רָשַׁ֖עְתִּי מֵאֱלֹהָֽי׃

כִּ֣י כָל־מִשְׁפָּטָ֣יו לְנֶגְדִּ֑י 23[

וְחֻקֹּתָ֖יו לֹא־אָס֥וּר מִמֶּֽנָּה׃

וָאֶהְיֶ֣ה תָמִ֣ים ל֑וֹ 24[

וָֽאֶשְׁתַּמְּרָ֖ה מֵעֲוֺנִֽי׃

וַיָּ֖שֶׁב יְהוָ֥ה לִ֣י כְּצִדְקָתִ֑י 25[

כְּבֹרִ֖י לְנֶ֥גֶד עֵינָֽיו׃

עִם־חָסִ֥יד תִּתְחַסָּ֑ד 26[

עִם־גְּב֥וֹר תָּמִ֥ים תִּתַּמָּֽם׃

עִם־נָבָ֥ר תִּתָּבָ֑ר 27[

וְעִם־עִקֵּ֖שׁ תִּתַּפָּֽל׃

וְאֶת־עַ֥ם עָנִ֖י תּוֹשִׁ֑יעַ 28[

וְעֵינֶ֖יךָ עַל־רָמִ֥ים תַּשְׁפִּֽיל׃

כִּֽי־אַתָּ֥ה נֵירִ֖י יְהוָ֑ה 29[

וַֽיהוָ֖ה יַגִּ֥יהַּ חָשְׁכִּֽי׃

---

[j] Cf. v. 5

[k] Ps. 18.26 "man"

[l-l] Lit. "And lower Your eyes on the haughty"; Ps. 18.28 "But haughty eyes You
humble"

30] With You, I can rush a barrier,[m]
With my God, I can scale a wall.

כִּי בְכָה אָרֻץ גְּדוּד [30]

בֵּאלֹהַי אֲדַלֶּג־שׁוּר:

31] The way of God is perfect,
The word of the LORD is pure.
He is a shield to all who take refuge in Him.

הָאֵל תָּמִים דַּרְכּוֹ [31]

אִמְרַת יְהוָה צְרוּפָה

מָגֵן הוּא לְכֹל הַחֹסִים בּוֹ:

32] Yea, who is a god except the LORD,
Who is a rock except God—

כִּי מִי־אֵל מִבַּלְעֲדֵי יְהוָה [32]

וּמִי צוּר מִבַּלְעֲדֵי אֱלֹהֵינוּ:

33] The God, [n]my mighty stronghold,[n]
Who kept[o] my path secure;

הָאֵל מָעוּזִּי חָיִל [33]

וַיַּתֵּר תָּמִים דַּרְכִּי:

34] Who made my legs like a deer's,
And set me firm on the[p] heights;

מְשַׁוֶּה רַגְלַי כָּאַיָּלוֹת [34]

וְעַל בָּמֹתַי יַעֲמִדֵנִי:

35] Who trained my hands for battle,
So that my arms can bend a bow of bronze!

מְלַמֵּד יָדַי לַמִּלְחָמָה [35]

וְנִחַת קֶשֶׁת־נְחוּשָׁה זְרֹעֹתָי:

36] You have granted me the shield of Your
protection
[q]And Your providence has made me great.[q]

וַתִּתֶּן־לִי מָגֵן יִשְׁעֶךָ [36]

וַעֲנֹתְךָ תַרְבֵּנִי:

37] You have let me stride on freely,
And my feet have not slipped.

תַּרְחִיב צַעֲדִי תַחְתֵּנִי [37]

וְלֹא מָעֲדוּ קַרְסֻלָּי:

38] I pursued my enemies and wiped them out,
I did not turn back till I destroyed them.

אֶרְדְּפָה אֹיְבַי וָאַשְׁמִידֵם [38]

וְלֹא אָשׁוּב עַד־כַּלּוֹתָם:

39] I destroyed them, I struck them down;
They rose no more, they lay at my feet.

וָאֲכַלֵּם וָאֶמְחָצֵם וְלֹא יְקוּמוּן [39]

וַיִּפְּלוּ תַּחַת רַגְלָי:

40] You have girt me with strength for battle,
Brought low my foes before me,

וַתַּזְרֵנִי חַיִל לַמִּלְחָמָה [40]

תַּכְרִיעַ קָמַי תַּחְתֵּנִי:

41] Made my enemies turn tail before me,
My foes—and I wiped them out.

וְאֹיְבַי תַּתָּה לִי עֹרֶף [41]

מְשַׂנְאַי וָאַצְמִיתֵם:

[m] Cf. post-biblical gedudiyot, "walls," Aramaic gudda, "wall"
[n-n] Ps. 18.33 "who girded me with might"
[o] Meaning of Heb. uncertain; Ps. 18.33 "made"
[p] Taking bamotai as a poetic form of bamot; cf. Hab. 3.19; others "my"
[q-q] Meaning of Heb. uncertain

42] They looked,[r] but there was none to deliver;
To the LORD, but He answered them not.

42] יִשְׁעוּ וְאֵין מֹשִׁיעַ
אֶל־יְהוָה וְלֹא עָנָם:

43] I pounded them like dust of the earth,
Stamped, crushed them like dirt of the streets.

43] וְאֶשְׁחָקֵם כַּעֲפַר־אָרֶץ
כְּטִיט־חוּצוֹת אֲדִקֵּם אֶרְקָעֵם:

44] You have rescued me from the strife of
    peoples,[s]
[t]Kept me to be[t] a ruler of nations;
Peoples I knew not must serve me.

44] וַתְּפַלְּטֵנִי מֵרִיבֵי עַמִּי
תִּשְׁמְרֵנִי לְרֹאשׁ גּוֹיִם
עַם לֹא־יָדַעְתִּי יַעַבְדֻנִי:

45] Aliens have cringed before me,
Paid me homage at the mere report of me.

45] בְּנֵי נֵכָר יִתְכַּחֲשׁוּ־לִי
לִשְׁמוֹעַ אֹזֶן יִשָּׁמְעוּ לִי:

46] Aliens have lost courage
[q]And come trembling out of their fastnesses.[q]

46] בְּנֵי נֵכָר יִבֹּלוּ
וְיַחְגְּרוּ מִמִּסְגְּרוֹתָם:

47] The LORD lives! Blessed is my rock!
Exalted be God, the rock
Who gives me victory;

47] חַי־יְהוָה וּבָרוּךְ צוּרִי
וְיָרֻם אֱלֹהֵי צוּר יִשְׁעִי:

48] The God who has vindicated me
And made peoples subject to me,

48] הָאֵל הַנֹּתֵן נְקָמֹת לִי
וּמֹרִיד עַמִּים תַּחְתֵּנִי:

49] Rescued me from my enemies,
Raised me clear of my foes,
Saved me from lawless men!

49] וּמוֹצִיאִי מֵאֹיְבָי
וּמִקָּמַי תְּרוֹמְמֵנִי
מֵאִישׁ חֲמָסִים תַּצִּילֵנִי:

50] For this I sing Your praise among the nations
And hymn Your name:

50] עַל־כֵּן אוֹדְךָ יְהוָה בַּגּוֹיִם
וּלְשִׁמְךָ אֲזַמֵּר:

51] [u]Tower of victory[u] to His king,
Who deals graciously with His anointed,
With David and his offspring evermore.

51] מִגְדּוֹל יְשׁוּעוֹת מַלְכּוֹ
וְעֹשֶׂה חֶסֶד לִמְשִׁיחוֹ
לְדָוִד וּלְזַרְעוֹ עַד־עוֹלָם:

---

[r] Ps. 18.42 "cried"

[s] So some mss. and the Septuagint; most mss. and the printed editions "my people"

[t-t] Ps. 18.44 "made me"

[q-q] Meaning of Heb. uncertain

[u-u] Ketiv Ps. 18.51 reads "Who accords wondrous victories"

The Book of Samuel is divided into two parts. It is primarily the story of Samuel's ministry as the spiritual guide
of Israel and of the reign of Israel's first two kings, Saul
and David (about 1000 B.C.E.). It is history written from
a theological perspective: all of Israel's fate hinges on the
performance or non-performance of God's commandments.

David's lament over the slain King Saul and his son
Jonathan expresses our sorrow on this day of Holocaust
remembrance: "Your glory, O Israel, lies slain on your
heights; how have the mighty fallen!"

II Samuel

1 : 17 – 27

Chapter 1

17] And David intoned this dirge over Saul
and his son Jonathan—

18] *a*⁻He ordered the Ju-
dites to be taught [The Song of the] Bow.⁻*a* It is
recorded in the Book of Jashar.*c*

19] Your glory, O Israel,
Lies slain on your heights;
How have the mighty fallen!

20] Tell it not in Gath,
Do not proclaim it in the streets of Ashkelon,
Lest the daughters of the Philistine rejoice,
Lest the daughters of the uncircumcised exult.

21] O hills of Gilboa—
Let there be no dew or rain on you,
d⁻Or bountiful fields,⁻*d*
For there the shield of warriors lay rejected,
The shield of Saul,
Polished with oil no more.

א

[17] וַיְקֹנֵן דָּוִד אֶת־הַקִּינָה הַזֹּאת עַל־שָׁאוּל
וְעַל־יְהוֹנָתָן בְּנוֹ: 18] וַיֹּאמֶר לְלַמֵּד בְּנֵי־
יְהוּדָה קָשֶׁת הִנֵּה כְתוּבָה עַל־סֵפֶר הַיָּשָׁר:

[19] הַצְּבִי יִשְׂרָאֵל
עַל־בָּמוֹתֶיךָ חָלָל
אֵיךְ נָפְלוּ גִבּוֹרִים:

[20] אַל־תַּגִּידוּ בְגַת
אַל־תְּבַשְּׂרוּ בְּחוּצֹת אַשְׁקְלוֹן
פֶּן־תִּשְׂמַחְנָה בְּנוֹת פְּלִשְׁתִּים
פֶּן־תַּעֲלֹזְנָה בְּנוֹת הָעֲרֵלִים:

[21] הָרֵי בַגִּלְבֹּעַ
אַל־טַל וְאַל־מָטָר עֲלֵיכֶם
וּשְׂדֵי תְרוּמֹת
כִּי שָׁם נִגְעַל מָגֵן גִּבּוֹרִים
מָגֵן שָׁאוּל
בְּלִי מָשִׁיחַ בַּשָּׁמֶן:

---

a⁻a Meaning of Heb. uncertain

c Presumably a collection of war songs

d⁻d Meaning of Heb. uncertain. Emendation yields "springs from the deep"; cf. Ugaritic
    shr'thmtm, and see Gen. 7.11; 8.2

22] From the blood of slain,
From the fat of warriors—
The bow of Jonathan
Never turned back;
The sword of Saul
Never withdrew empty.

23] Saul and Jonathan,
Beloved and cherished,
Never parted
In life or in death!
They were swifter than eagles,
They were stronger than lions!

24] Daughters of Israel,
Weep over Saul,
Who clothed you in crimson and finery,
Who decked your robes with jewels of gold.

25] How have the mighty fallen
In the thick of battle—
Jonathan, slain on your heights!

26] I grieve for you,
My brother Jonathan,
You were most dear to me.
Your love was wonderful to me
More than the love of women.

27] How have the mighty fallen,
The ᵉ‑ʸweapons of warᵉ‑ʸ perished!

[22] מִדַּם חֲלָלִים
מֵחֵלֶב גִּבּוֹרִים
קֶשֶׁת יְהוֹנָתָן
לֹא נָשׂוֹג אָחוֹר
וְחֶרֶב שָׁאוּל
לֹא תָשׁוּב רֵיקָם:

[23] שָׁאוּל וִיהוֹנָתָן
הַנֶּאֱהָבִים וְהַנְּעִימִם
בְּחַיֵּיהֶם וּבְמוֹתָם
לֹא נִפְרָדוּ
מִנְּשָׁרִים קַלּוּ
מֵאֲרָיוֹת גָּבֵרוּ:

[24] בְּנוֹת יִשְׂרָאֵל
אֶל־שָׁאוּל בְּכֶינָה
הַמַּלְבִּשְׁכֶם שָׁנִי עִם־עֲדָנִים
הַמַּעֲלֶה עֲדִי זָהָב עַל לְבוּשְׁכֶן:

[25] אֵיךְ נָפְלוּ גִבֹּרִים
בְּתוֹךְ הַמִּלְחָמָה
יְהוֹנָתָן עַל־בָּמוֹתֶיךָ חָלָל:

[26] צַר־לִי עָלֶיךָ
אָחִי יְהוֹנָתָן
נָעַמְתָּ לִּי מְאֹד
נִפְלְאַתָה אַהֲבָתְךָ לִי
מֵאַהֲבַת נָשִׁים:

[27] אֵיךְ נָפְלוּ גִבּוֹרִים
וַיֹּאבְדוּ כְּלֵי מִלְחָמָה:

ᵉ‑ʸ *I.e., Saul and Jonathan*

Chapters 40–66 of the Book of Isaiah are the work of an unknown author (often referred to as Deutero-Isaiah) who lived in Babylon during the days of the exile (sixth century B.C.E.). He preached unwavering trust in a God who would surely restore Israel to its homeland. Of all the prophets he is the most lyrical and his imagery the richest.

Our hope for the State of Israel is expressed in this Isaianic vision: "Nations shall walk by your light."

יום העצמאות

Isaiah

60 : 1-22

Chapter 60

ס

1] Arise, shine, for your light has dawned;
The Presence of the LORD has shone upon you!

[1 קוּמִי אוֹרִי כִּי-בָא אוֹרֵךְ
וּכְבוֹד יְהֹוָה עָלַיִךְ זָרָח:

2] Behold! Darkness shall cover the earth,
And thick clouds the peoples;
But upon you the LORD will shine,
And His Presence be seen over you.

[2 כִּי-הִנֵּה הַחֹשֶׁךְ יְכַסֶּה-אֶרֶץ
וַעֲרָפֶל לְאֻמִּים
וְעָלַיִךְ יִזְרַח יְהֹוָה
וּכְבוֹדוֹ עָלַיִךְ יֵרָאֶה:

3] And nations shall walk by your light;
Kings, by your shining radiance.

[3 וְהָלְכוּ גוֹיִם לְאוֹרֵךְ
וּמְלָכִים לְנֹגַהּ זַרְחֵךְ:

4] Raise your eyes and look about:
They have all gathered and come to you.
Your sons shall be brought from afar,
Your daughters like babes on shoulders.

[4 שְׂאִי סָבִיב עֵינַיִךְ וּרְאִי
כֻּלָּם נִקְבְּצוּ בָאוּ-לָךְ
בָּנַיִךְ מֵרָחוֹק יָבֹאוּ
וּבְנֹתַיִךְ עַל-צַד תֵּאָמַנָה:

5] As you behold, you will glow;
Your heart will throb and thrill—
For the wealth of the sea[a] shall pass on to you,
The riches of nations shall flow to you.

[5 אָז תִּרְאִי וְנָהַרְתְּ
וּפָחַד וְרָחַב לְבָבֵךְ
כִּי-יֵהָפֵךְ עָלַיִךְ הֲמוֹן יָם
חֵיל גּוֹיִם יָבֹאוּ לָךְ:

6] Dust clouds of camels shall cover you,
Dromedaries of Midian and Ephah.

[6 שִׁפְעַת גְּמַלִּים תְּכַסֵּךְ
בִּכְרֵי מִדְיָן וְעֵיפָה

a Emendation yields "coastlands"

1669

They all shall come from Sheba;
They shall bear gold and frankincense,
And shall herald the glories of the Lord.

כֻּלָּם מִשְּׁבָא יָבֹאוּ
זָהָב וּלְבוֹנָה יִשָּׂאוּ
וּתְהִלֹּת יְהוָה יְבַשֵּׂרוּ:

7] All the flocks of Kedar shall be assembled for
    you,
The rams of Nebaioth shall serve your needs;
They shall be welcome offerings on My altar,
And I will add glory to My glorious House.

7] כָּל־צֹאן קֵדָר יִקָּבְצוּ לָךְ
אֵילֵי נְבָיוֹת יְשָׁרְתוּנֶךָ
יַעֲלוּ עַל־רָצוֹן מִזְבְּחִי
וּבֵית תִּפְאַרְתִּי אֲפָאֵר:

8] Who are these that float like a cloud,
Like doves to their cotes?

8] מִי־אֵלֶּה כָּעָב תְּעוּפֶינָה
וְכַיּוֹנִים אֶל־אֲרֻבֹּתֵיהֶם:

9] ᵇ⁻Behold, the coastlands await me,⁻ᵇ
With ᶜ⁻ships of Tarshish⁻ᶜ in the lead,
To bring your sons from afar,
And their ᵈ silver and gold as well—
For the name of the Lord your God,
For the Holy One of Israel, who has glorified you.

9] כִּי־לִי אִיִּים יְקַוּוּ
וָאֳנִיּוֹת תַּרְשִׁישׁ בָּרִאשֹׁנָה
לְהָבִיא בָנַיִךְ מֵרָחוֹק
כַּסְפָּם וּזְהָבָם אִתָּם
לְשֵׁם יְהוָה אֱלֹהַיִךְ
וְלִקְדוֹשׁ יִשְׂרָאֵל כִּי פֵאֲרָךְ:

10] Aliens shall rebuild your walls,
Their kings shall wait upon you—
For in anger I struck you down,
But in favor I take you back.

10] וּבָנוּ בְנֵי־נֵכָר חֹמֹתַיִךְ
וּמַלְכֵיהֶם יְשָׁרְתוּנֶךָ
כִּי בְקִצְפִּי הִכִּיתִיךְ
וּבִרְצוֹנִי רִחַמְתִּיךְ:

11] Your gates shall always stay open—
Day and night they shall never be shut—
To let in the wealth of the nations,
With their kings in procession.

11] וּפִתְּחוּ שְׁעָרַיִךְ תָּמִיד
יוֹמָם וָלַיְלָה לֹא יִסָּגֵרוּ
לְהָבִיא אֵלַיִךְ חֵיל גּוֹיִם
וּמַלְכֵיהֶם נְהוּגִים:

12] For the nation or the kingdom
That does not serve you shall perish;
Such nations shall be destroyed.

12] כִּי־הַגּוֹי וְהַמַּמְלָכָה
אֲשֶׁר לֹא־יַעַבְדוּךְ יֹאבֵדוּ
וְהַגּוֹיִם חָרֹב יֶחֱרָבוּ:

ᵇ⁻ᵇ *Emendation yields "The vessels of the coastlands are gathering"*
ᶜ⁻ᶜ *Probably a type of large ship*
ᵈ *I.e., of the people of the coastlands*

13] The majesty of Lebanon shall come to you—
Cypress and pine and box—
To adorn the site of My Sanctuary,
To glorify the place where My feet rest.

14] Bowing before you, shall come
The children of those who tormented you;
Prostrate at the soles of your feet
Shall be all those who reviled you;
And you shall be called
"City of the LORD,
Zion of the Holy One of Israel."

15] Whereas you have been forsaken,
Rejected, with none passing through,
I will make you a pride everlasting,
A joy for age after age.

16] You shall suck the milk of the nations,
Suckle at royal breasts.ᵉ
And you shall know
That I the LORD am your Savior,
I, The Mighty One of Jacob, am your Redeemer.

17] Instead of copper I will bring gold,
Instead of iron I will bring silver;
Instead of wood, copper;
And instead of stone, iron.
And I will appoint Well-being as your
     government,
Prosperity as your officials.

18] The cry "Violence!"
Shall no more be heard in your land,
Nor "Wrack and ruin!"
Within your borders.
And you shall name your walls "Victory"
And your gates "Renown."

כְּבוֹד הַלְּבָנוֹן אֵלַיִךְ יָבוֹא [13
בְּרוֹשׁ תִּדְהָר וּתְאַשּׁוּר יַחְדָּו
לְפָאֵר מְקוֹם מִקְדָּשִׁי
וּמְקוֹם רַגְלַי אֲכַבֵּד:

וְהָלְכוּ אֵלַיִךְ שְׁחוֹחַ [14
בְּנֵי מְעַנַּיִךְ
וְהִשְׁתַּחֲווּ עַל־כַּפּוֹת רַגְלַיִךְ
כָּל־מְנַאֲצָיִךְ
וְקָרְאוּ לָךְ עִיר יְהֹוָה
צִיּוֹן קְדוֹשׁ יִשְׂרָאֵל:

תַּחַת הֱיוֹתֵךְ עֲזוּבָה [15
וּשְׂנוּאָה וְאֵין עוֹבֵר
וְשַׂמְתִּיךְ לִגְאוֹן עוֹלָם
מְשׂוֹשׂ דּוֹר וָדוֹר:

וְיָנַקְתְּ חֲלֵב גּוֹיִם [16
וְשֹׁד מְלָכִים תִּינָקִי
וְיָדַעַתְּ כִּי־אֲנִי יְהֹוָה
מוֹשִׁיעֵךְ וְגֹאֲלֵךְ אֲבִיר יַעֲקֹב:

תַּחַת הַנְּחֹשֶׁת אָבִיא זָהָב [17
וְתַחַת הַבַּרְזֶל אָבִיא כֶסֶף
וְתַחַת הָעֵצִים נְחֹשֶׁת
וְתַחַת הָאֲבָנִים בַּרְזֶל
וְשַׂמְתִּי פְקֻדָּתֵךְ שָׁלוֹם
וְנֹגְשַׂיִךְ צְדָקָה:

לֹא־יִשָּׁמַע עוֹד חָמָס בְּאַרְצֵךְ [18
שֹׁד וָשֶׁבֶר בִּגְבוּלָיִךְ
וְקָרָאת יְשׁוּעָה חוֹמֹתַיִךְ
וּשְׁעָרַיִךְ תְּהִלָּה:

ᵉ Lit. "breasts of kings" or "breasts of kingdoms"

1671

19] No longer shall you need the sun
For light by day,
Nor the shining of the moon
For radiance [by night*];
For the Lord shall be your light everlasting,
Your God shall be your glory.

20] Your sun shall set no more,
Your moon no more withdraw;
For the Lord shall be a light to you forever,
And your days of mourning shall be ended.

21] And your people, all of them righteous,
Shall possess the land for all time;
They are the shoot that I planted,
My handiwork in which I glory.

22] The smallest shall become a clan;
The least, a mighty nation.
I the Lord will speed it in due time.

[19] לֹא־יִהְיֶה־לָּךְ עוֹד הַשֶּׁמֶשׁ

לְאוֹר יוֹמָם

וּלְנֹגַהּ הַיָּרֵחַ לֹא־יָאִיר לָךְ

וְהָיָה־לָּךְ יְהוָה לְאוֹר עוֹלָם

וֵאלֹהַיִךְ לְתִפְאַרְתֵּךְ:

[20] לֹא־יָבוֹא עוֹד שִׁמְשֵׁךְ

וִירֵחֵךְ לֹא יֵאָסֵף

כִּי יְהוָה יִהְיֶה־לָּךְ לְאוֹר עוֹלָם

וְשָׁלְמוּ יְמֵי אֶבְלֵךְ:

[21] וְעַמֵּךְ כֻּלָּם צַדִּיקִים

לְעוֹלָם יִירְשׁוּ אָרֶץ

נֵצֶר מַטָּעַי מַעֲשֵׂה יָדַי לְהִתְפָּאֵר:

[22] הַקָּטֹן יִהְיֶה לָאֶלֶף

וְהַצָּעִיר לְגוֹי עָצוּם

אֲנִי יְהוָה בְּעִתָּהּ אֲחִישֶׁנָּה:

*So 1QIsᵃ, Septuagint, and Targum ›   (1QIsᵃ=manuscriptᵃ of Isaiah found
in the first cave of Qumran, the site of the caves where the Bible manuscripts were
found in 1949–50.)

Chapters 40–66 of the Book of Isaiah are the work of an unknown author (often referred to as Deutero-Isaiah) who lived in Babylon during the days of the exile (sixth century B.C.E.). He preached unwavering trust in a God who would surely restore Israel to its homeland. Of all the prophets he is the most lyrical and his imagery the richest.

The holy day celebrates God's choice of Israel to receive the Torah at Sinai, and the prophecy chosen for this day expands on this election: God's people will "teach the true way to the nations."

Isaiah

42 : 1–12

Chapter 42

מב

1] This is My servant, whom I uphold,
My chosen one, in whom I delight.
I have put My spirit upon him,
He shall teach the true way to the nations.

2] He shall not cry out or shout aloud,
Or make his voice heard in the streets.

3] ᵃ⁻He shall not break even a bruised reed,
Or snuff out even a dim wick.⁻ᵃ
He shall bring forth the true way.

4] He shall not grow dim or be bruised
Till he has established the true way on earth;
And the coastlands shall await his teaching.

5] Thus said God the LORD,
Who created the heavens and stretched them out,
Who spread out the earth and what it brings
     forth,
Who gave breath to the people upon it
And life to those who walk thereon:

6] I the LORD, in My grace, have summoned you,
And I have grasped you by the hand.

1] הֵ֤ן עַבְדִּי֙ אֶתְמָךְ־בּ֔וֹ
בְּחִירִ֖י רָצְתָ֣ה נַפְשִׁ֑י
נָתַ֤תִּי רוּחִי֙ עָלָ֔יו
מִשְׁפָּ֖ט לַגּוֹיִ֥ם יוֹצִֽיא׃

2] לֹ֥א יִצְעַ֖ק וְלֹ֣א יִשָּׂ֑א
וְלֹֽא־יַשְׁמִ֥יעַ בַּח֖וּץ קוֹלֽוֹ׃

3] קָנֶ֤ה רָצוּץ֙ לֹ֣א יִשְׁבּ֔וֹר
וּפִשְׁתָּ֥ה כֵהָ֖ה לֹ֣א יְכַבֶּ֑נָּה
לֶאֱמֶ֖ת יוֹצִ֥יא מִשְׁפָּֽט׃

4] לֹ֤א יִכְהֶה֙ וְלֹ֣א יָר֔וּץ
עַד־יָשִׂ֥ים בָּאָ֖רֶץ מִשְׁפָּ֑ט
וּלְתוֹרָת֖וֹ אִיִּ֥ים יְיַחֵֽלוּ׃

5] כֹּֽה־אָמַ֞ר הָאֵ֣ל ׀ יְהֹוָ֗ה
בּוֹרֵ֤א הַשָּׁמַ֙יִם֙ וְנ֣וֹטֵיהֶ֔ם
רֹקַ֥ע הָאָ֖רֶץ וְצֶאֱצָאֶ֑יהָ
נֹתֵ֤ן נְשָׁמָה֙ לָעָ֣ם עָלֶ֔יהָ
וְר֖וּחַ לַהֹלְכִ֥ים בָּֽהּ׃

6] אֲנִ֧י יְהֹוָ֛ה קְרָאתִ֥יךָֽ בְצֶ֖דֶק
וְאַחְזֵ֣ק בְּיָדֶ֑ךָ

ᵃ⁻ᵃ *Or "A bruised reed, he shall not be broken; | A dim wick, he shall not be snuffed out"*

I created you, and appointed you
A ^bcovenant-people,^{-b} ^{c-}a light of nations^{-c}—

וְאֶצָּרְךָ וְאֶתֶּנְךָ

לִבְרִית עָם לְאוֹר גּוֹיִם:

7] ^{d-}Opening eyes deprived of light,^{-d}
Rescuing prisoners from confinement,
From the dungeon those who sit in darkness.

[7 לִפְקֹחַ עֵינַיִם עִוְרוֹת

לְהוֹצִיא מִמַּסְגֵּר אַסִּיר

מִבֵּית כֶּלֶא יֹשְׁבֵי חֹשֶׁךְ:

8] I am the LORD, that is My name;
I will not yield My glory to another,
Nor My renown to idols.

[8 אֲנִי יְהֹוָה הוּא שְׁמִי

וּכְבוֹדִי לְאַחֵר לֹא־אֶתֵּן

וּתְהִלָּתִי לַפְּסִילִים:

9] See, the things once predicted have come,
And now I foretell new things,
Announce to you ere they sprout up.

[9 הָרִאשֹׁנוֹת הִנֵּה־בָאוּ

וַחֲדָשׁוֹת אֲנִי מַגִּיד

בְּטֶרֶם תִּצְמַחְנָה אַשְׁמִיעַ אֶתְכֶם:

10] Sing to the LORD a new song,
His praise from the ends of the earth—
^{e-}You who sail the sea and you creatures in it,
You coastlands^{-e} and their inhabitants!

[10 שִׁירוּ לַיהֹוָה שִׁיר חָדָשׁ

תְּהִלָּתוֹ מִקְצֵה הָאָרֶץ

יוֹרְדֵי הַיָּם וּמְלֹאוֹ

אִיִּים וְיֹשְׁבֵיהֶם:

11] Let the desert and its towns cry aloud,
The villages where Kedar dwells;
Let Sela's inhabitants shout,
Call out from the peaks of the mountains.

[11 יִשְׂאוּ מִדְבָּר וְעָרָיו

חֲצֵרִים תֵּשֵׁב קֵדָר

יָרֹנּוּ יֹשְׁבֵי סֶלַע

מֵרֹאשׁ הָרִים יִצְוָחוּ:

12] Let them do honor to the LORD,
And tell His glory in the coastlands.

[12 יָשִׂימוּ לַיהֹוָה כָּבוֹד

וּתְהִלָּתוֹ בָּאִיִּים יַגִּידוּ:

^{b-b} Lit. "covenant of a people"; meaning of Heb. uncertain
^{c-c} See 49.6; "light": i.e., the agent of good fortune
^{d-d} An idiom meaning "freeing the imprisoned"; cf. 61.1
^{e-e} Emendation yields "Let the sea roar and its creatures, |The coastlands...." Cf.
Ps. 98.7

תשעה באב – שחרית

Jeremiah

8 : 13 — 9 : 23

ח

Jeremiah was the most inward of the prophets. In his agonized visions he foresaw Jerusalem's destruction and was jailed for his preachments. When the Babylonians destroyed the city in 586 (or 585) B.C.E., he became one of the exiles and died in Egypt.

The last line of the haftarah summarizes the depth of Israel's lament, a passage chosen by tradition to express the people's cry over the bitterness of exile.

Chapter 8

13] ^a"I will make an end of them"^a
     —declares the L<small>ORD</small>:
No grapes left on the vine,
No figs on the fig tree,
The leaves all withered;
^bWhatever I have given them is gone.^b

13] אָסֹף אֲסִיפֵם

נְאֻם־יְהֹוָה

אֵין עֲנָבִים בַּגֶּפֶן

וְאֵין תְּאֵנִים בַּתְּאֵנָה

וְהֶעָלֶה נָבֵל

וָאֶתֵּן לָהֶם יַעַבְרוּם:

14] Why are we sitting by?
Let us gather into the fortified cities
And meet our doom there.
For the L<small>ORD</small> our God has doomed us,
He has made us drink a bitter draft.
Because we sinned against the L<small>ORD</small>.

14] עַל־מָה אֲנַחְנוּ יֹשְׁבִים

הֵאָסְפוּ וְנָבוֹא אֶל־עָרֵי הַמִּבְצָר

וְנִדְּמָה־שָּׁם

כִּי יְהֹוָה אֱלֹהֵינוּ הֲדִמָּנוּ

וַיַּשְׁקֵנוּ מֵי־רֹאשׁ

כִּי חָטָאנוּ לַיהֹוָה:

15] We hoped for good fortune, but no happiness
  came;
For a time of relief—instead there is terror!

15] קַוֵּה לְשָׁלוֹם וְאֵין טוֹב

לְעֵת מַרְפֵּה וְהִנֵּה בְעָתָה:

16] The snorting of their horses was heard from
  Dan;
At the loud neighing of their steeds
The whole land quaked.
They came and devoured the land and what was
  in it,
The towns and those who dwelt in them.

16] מִדָּן נִשְׁמַע נַחְרַת סוּסָיו

מִקּוֹל מִצְהֲלוֹת אַבִּירָיו

רָעֲשָׁה כָּל־הָאָרֶץ

וַיָּבוֹאוּ וַיֹּאכְלוּ אֶרֶץ וּמְלוֹאָהּ

עִיר וְיֹשְׁבֵי בָהּ:

---

^{a-a} *Meaning of Heb. uncertain; change of vocalization yields "Their fruit harvest has been gathered in"*
^{b-b} *Meaning of Heb. uncertain*

17] Lo, I will send serpents against you,
Adders that cannot be charmed,
And they shall bite you
— — — — — — — — —declares the LORD.

18] *b-*When in grief I would seek comfort,*-b*
My heart is sick within me.

19] *c-*"Is not the LORD in Zion,
Is not her King within her?
Why then did they anger Me with their images,
With alien futilities?"
Hark! The outcry of my poor people
From the land far and wide:

20] "Harvest is past,
Summer is gone,
But we have not been saved."

21] Because my people is shattered I am shattered;
I am dejected, seized by desolation.

22] Is there no balm in Gilead,
Can no physician be found?
Why has healing not yet
Come to my poor people?

23] Oh, that my head were water,
My eyes a fount of tears!
Then would I weep day and night
For the slain of my poor people.

17] כִּי הִנְנִי מְשַׁלֵּחַ בָּכֶם נְחָשִׁים
צִפְעֹנִים אֲשֶׁר אֵין־לָהֶם לָחַשׁ
וְנִשְּׁכוּ אֶתְכֶם
נְאֻם־יְהוָֹה:

18] מַבְלִיגִיתִי עֲלֵי יָגוֹן
עָלַי לִבִּי דַוָּי:

19] הִנֵּה־קוֹל שַׁוְעַת בַּת־עַמִּי
מֵאֶרֶץ מַרְחַקִּים
הַיהוָה אֵין בְּצִיּוֹן
אִם־מַלְכָּהּ אֵין בָּהּ
מַדּוּעַ הִכְעִסוּנִי בִּפְסִלֵיהֶם
בְּהַבְלֵי נֵכָר:

20] עָבַר קָצִיר
כָּלָה קָיִץ
וַאֲנַחְנוּ לוֹא נוֹשָׁעְנוּ:

21] עַל־שֶׁבֶר בַּת־עַמִּי הָשְׁבָּרְתִּי
קָדַרְתִּי שַׁמָּה הֶחֱזִקָתְנִי:

22] הַצֳרִי אֵין בְּגִלְעָד
אִם־רֹפֵא אֵין שָׁם
כִּי מַדּוּעַ לֹא עָלְתָה אֲרֻכַת
בַּת־עַמִּי:

23] מִי־יִתֵּן רֹאשִׁי מַיִם
וְעֵינִי מְקוֹר דִּמְעָה
וְאֶבְכֶּה יוֹמָם וָלַיְלָה
אֵת חַלְלֵי בַת־עַמִּי:

b-b Meaning of Heb. uncertain
c Here God is speaking

ט

1] Oh, to be in the desert,
At an encampment for wayfarers!
Oh, to leave my people,
To go away from them—
For they are all adulterers,
A band of rogues.

[1] מִי־יִתְּנֵנִי בַמִּדְבָּר

מְלוֹן אֹרְחִים

וְאֶעֶזְבָה אֶת־עַמִּי

וְאֵלְכָה מֵאִתָּם

כִּי כֻלָּם מְנָאֲפִים

עֲצֶרֶת בֹּגְדִים:

2] They bend their tongues like bows;
They are valorous in the land
For treachery, not for honesty;
They advance from evil to evil.
And they do not heed Me
            —declares the LORD.

[2] וַיַּדְרְכוּ אֶת־לְשׁוֹנָם קַשְׁתָּם

שֶׁקֶר וְלֹא לֶאֱמוּנָה

גָּבְרוּ בָאָרֶץ

כִּי מֵרָעָה אֶל־רָעָה יָצָאוּ

וְאֹתִי לֹא־יָדָעוּ

נְאֻם־יְהוָה:

3] Beware, every man of his friend!
Trust not even a brother!
For every brother takes advantage,
Every friend ᵃ⁻is base in his dealings.⁻ᵃ

[3] אִישׁ מֵרֵעֵהוּ הִשָּׁמֵרוּ

וְעַל־כָּל־אָח אַל־תִּבְטָחוּ

כִּי כָל־אָח עָקוֹב יַעְקֹב

וְכָל־רֵעַ רָכִיל יַהֲלֹךְ:

4] One man cheats the other,
They will not speak truth;
They have trained their tongues to speak falsely;
ᵇ⁻They wear themselves out working iniquity.

[4] וְאִישׁ בְּרֵעֵהוּ יְהָתֵלּוּ

וֶאֱמֶת לֹא יְדַבֵּרוּ

לִמְּדוּ לְשׁוֹנָם דַּבֶּר־שֶׁקֶר

הַעֲוֵה נִלְאוּ:

5] You dwell in the midst of deceit.
In their deceit,⁻ᵇ they refuse to heed Me
            —declares the LORD.

[5] שִׁבְתְּךָ בְּתוֹךְ מִרְמָה

בְּמִרְמָה מֵאֲנוּ דַעַת־אוֹתִי

נְאֻם־יְהוָה:

6] Assuredly, thus said the LORD of Hosts:
Lo, I shall smelt and assay them—
ᵇ⁻For what else can I do because of My poor
    people?⁻ᵇ

[6] לָכֵן כֹּה אָמַר יְהוָה צְבָאוֹת

הִנְנִי צוֹרְפָם וּבְחַנְתִּים

כִּי־אֵיךְ אֶעֱשֶׂה מִפְּנֵי בַת־עַמִּי:

ᵃ⁻ᵃ Others "go about as a talebearer among"; meaning of Heb. unknown
ᵇ⁻ᵇ Meaning of Heb. uncertain

7] Their tongue is a sharpened arrow,
They use their mouths to deceive.
One speaks to his fellow in friendship,
But lays an ambush for him in his heart.

8] Shall I not punish them for such deeds?
— says the LORD —
Shall I not bring retribution
On such a nation as this?

9] For the mountains I take up weeping and
    wailing,
For the pastures in the wilderness, a dirge.
They are laid waste; no man passes through,
And no sound of cattle is heard.
Birds of the sky and beasts as well
Have fled and are gone.

10] I will turn Jerusalem into rubble,
Into dens for jackals;
And I will make the towns of Judah
A desolation without inhabitants.

11] What man is so wise
That he understands this?
To whom has the LORD's mouth spoken,
So that he can explain it:
Why is the land in ruins,
Laid waste like a wilderness,
With none passing through?

12] The LORD replied: Because they forsook
the Teaching I had set before them. They did not
obey Me and they did not follow it,
13] but
followed their own willful heart and followed

7] חֵץ שָׁחוּט לְשׁוֹנָם

מִרְמָה דִבֵּר

בְּפִיו שָׁלוֹם אֶת־רֵעֵהוּ יְדַבֵּר

וּבְקִרְבּוֹ יָשִׂים אָרְבּוֹ:

8] הַעַל־אֵלֶּה לֹא־אֶפְקָד־בָּם

נְאֻם־יְהֹוָה

אִם בְּגוֹי אֲשֶׁר־כָּזֶה

לֹא תִתְנַקֵּם נַפְשִׁי:

9] עַל־הֶהָרִים אֶשָּׂא בְכִי וָנֶהִי

וְעַל־נְאוֹת מִדְבָּר קִינָה

כִּי נִצְּתוּ מִבְּלִי־אִישׁ עֹבֵר

וְלֹא שָׁמְעוּ קוֹל מִקְנֶה

מֵעוֹף הַשָּׁמַיִם וְעַד־בְּהֵמָה

נָדְדוּ הָלָכוּ:

10] וְנָתַתִּי אֶת־יְרוּשָׁלַםִ לְגַלִּים

מְעוֹן תַּנִּים

וְאֶת־עָרֵי יְהוּדָה

אֶתֵּן שְׁמָמָה מִבְּלִי יוֹשֵׁב:

11] מִי־הָאִישׁ הֶחָכָם

וְיָבֵן אֶת־זֹאת

וַאֲשֶׁר דִּבֶּר פִּי־יְהֹוָה אֵלָיו

וְיַגִּדָה

עַל־מָה אָבְדָה הָאָרֶץ

נִצְּתָה כַמִּדְבָּר

מִבְּלִי עֹבֵר:

12] וַיֹּאמֶר יְהֹוָה עַל־עָזְבָם אֶת־תּוֹרָתִי אֲשֶׁר
נָתַתִּי לִפְנֵיהֶם וְלֹא־שָׁמְעוּ בְקוֹלִי וְלֹא־הָלְכוּ
בָהּ: 13] וַיֵּלְכוּ אַחֲרֵי שְׁרִרוּת לִבָּם וְאַחֲרֵי

the Baalim, as their fathers had taught them. 14] Assuredly, thus said the LORD of Hosts, the God of Israel: I am going to feed that people wormwood and make them drink a bitter draft.

15] I will scatter them among nations which they and their fathers never knew; and I will dispatch the sword after them until I have consumed them.

16] Thus said the LORD of Hosts:
Listen!
Summon the dirge-singers, let them come;

17] Send for the skilled women, let them come.
Let them quickly start a wailing for us,
That our eyes may run with tears,
Our pupils flow with water.

18] For the sound of wailing
Is heard from Zion:
How we are despoiled!
How greatly we are shamed!
Ah, we must leave our land,
Abandon[c] our dwellings!

19] Hear, O women, the word of the LORD,
Let your ears receive the word of His mouth,
And teach your daughters wailing,
And one another lamentation.

20] For death has climbed through our windows,
Has entered our fortresses,
To cut off babes from the streets,
Young men from the squares.

הַבְּעָלִים אֲשֶׁר לִמְּדוּם אֲבוֹתָם: 14] לָכֵן כֹּה־אָמַר יְהוָה צְבָאוֹת אֱלֹהֵי יִשְׂרָאֵל הִנְנִי מַאֲכִילָם אֶת־הָעָם הַזֶּה לַעֲנָה וְהִשְׁקִיתִים מֵי־רֹאשׁ: 15] וַהֲפִצוֹתִים בַּגּוֹיִם אֲשֶׁר לֹא יָדְעוּ הֵמָּה וַאֲבוֹתָם וְשִׁלַּחְתִּי אַחֲרֵיהֶם אֶת־הַחֶרֶב עַד כַּלּוֹתִי אוֹתָם:

16] כֹּה אָמַר יְהוָה צְבָאוֹת
הִתְבּוֹנְנוּ
וְקִרְאוּ לַמְקוֹנְנוֹת וּתְבוֹאֶינָה
וְאֶל־הַחֲכָמוֹת שִׁלְחוּ וְתָבוֹאנָה:

17] וּתְמַהֵרְנָה וְתִשֶּׂנָה עָלֵינוּ נֶהִי
וְתֵרַדְנָה עֵינֵינוּ דִּמְעָה
וְעַפְעַפֵּינוּ יִזְּלוּ־מָיִם:

18] כִּי קוֹל נְהִי
נִשְׁמַע מִצִּיּוֹן
אֵיךְ שֻׁדָּדְנוּ
בֹּשְׁנוּ מְאֹד
כִּי־עָזַבְנוּ אָרֶץ
כִּי הִשְׁלִיכוּ מִשְׁכְּנוֹתֵינוּ:

19] כִּי־שְׁמַעְנָה נָשִׁים דְּבַר־יְהוָה
וְתִקַּח אָזְנְכֶם דְּבַר־פִּיו
וְלַמֵּדְנָה בְנֹתֵיכֶם נֶהִי
וְאִשָּׁה רְעוּתָהּ קִינָה:

20] כִּי־עָלָה מָוֶת בְּחַלּוֹנֵינוּ
בָּא בְּאַרְמְנוֹתֵינוּ
לְהַכְרִית עוֹלָל מִחוּץ
בַּחוּרִים מֵרְחֹבוֹת:

c Lit. "They abandoned"

21] Speak thus—says the LORD:
The carcasses of men shall lie
Like dung upon the fields,
Like sheaves behind the reaper,
With none to pick them up.

22] Thus said the LORD:
Let not the wise man glory in his wisdom;
Let not the strong man glory in his strength;
Let not the rich man glory in his riches.

23] But only in this should one glory:
In his earnest devotion to Me.
For I the LORD act with kindness,
Justice, and equity in the world;
For in these I delight
                              —declares the LORD.

[21 דַּבֵּר כֹּה נְאֻם־יְהֹוָה

וְנָפְלָה נִבְלַת הָאָדָם

כְּדֹמֶן עַל־פְּנֵי הַשָּׂדֶה

וּכְעָמִיר מֵאַחֲרֵי הַקּוֹצֵר

וְאֵין מְאַסֵּף:

[22 כֹּה אָמַר יְהֹוָה

אַל־יִתְהַלֵּל חָכָם בְּחָכְמָתוֹ

וְאַל־יִתְהַלֵּל הַגִּבּוֹר בִּגְבוּרָתוֹ

אַל־יִתְהַלֵּל עָשִׁיר בְּעָשְׁרוֹ:

[23 כִּי אִם־בְּזֹאת יִתְהַלֵּל הַמִּתְהַלֵּל

הַשְׂכֵּל וְיָדֹעַ אוֹתִי

כִּי אֲנִי יְהֹוָה עֹשֶׂה חֶסֶד

מִשְׁפָּט וּצְדָקָה בָּאָרֶץ

כִּי־בְאֵלֶּה חָפַצְתִּי

נְאֻם־יְהֹוָה:

Chapters 40–66 of the Book of Isaiah are the work of an unknown author (often referred to as Deutero-Isaiah) who lived in Babylon during the days of the exile (sixth century B.C.E.). He preached unwavering trust in a God who would surely restore Israel to its homeland. Of all the prophets he is the most lyrical and his imagery the richest.

On the afternoon of Tishah b'Av a note of hope is introduced in the words of Deutero-Isaiah: God's promise of salvation will come as surely as the rain will cause the earth to bring forth its fruit.

HAFTARAH
Tishah b'Av (Afternoon)

תשעה באב – מנחה

Isaiah
55 : 6 — 56 : 8

נה

Chapter 55

6] Seek the LORD while He can be found,
Call to Him while He is near.

‎6] דִּרְשׁוּ יְהוָה בְּהִמָּצְאוֹ
קְרָאֻהוּ בִּהְיוֹתוֹ קָרוֹב:

7] Let the wicked give up his ways,
The sinful man his plans;
Let him turn back to the LORD,
And He will pardon him;
To our God,
For He freely forgives.

‎7] יַעֲזֹב רָשָׁע דַּרְכּוֹ
וְאִישׁ אָוֶן מַחְשְׁבֹתָיו
וְיָשֹׁב אֶל־יְהוָה וִירַחֲמֵהוּ
וְאֶל־אֱלֹהֵינוּ כִּי־יַרְבֶּה לִסְלוֹחַ:

8] For My plans are not your plans,
Nor are My ways[e] your ways[e]
                    —declares the LORD.

‎8] כִּי לֹא מַחְשְׁבוֹתַי מַחְשְׁבוֹתֵיכֶם
וְלֹא דַרְכֵיכֶם דְּרָכָי
נְאֻם יְהוָה:

9] But as the heavens are high above the earth,
So are My ways[e] high above your ways[e]
And My plans above your plans.

‎9] כִּי־גָבְהוּ שָׁמַיִם מֵאָרֶץ
כֵּן גָּבְהוּ דְרָכַי מִדַּרְכֵיכֶם
וּמַחְשְׁבֹתַי מִמַּחְשְׁבֹתֵיכֶם:

10] For as the rain or snow drops from heaven
And returns not there,
But soaks the earth
And makes it bring forth vegetation,
Yielding [d]seed for sowing and bread for eating,[d]

‎10] כִּי כַּאֲשֶׁר יֵרֵד הַגֶּשֶׁם וְהַשֶּׁלֶג מִן־הַשָּׁמַיִם
וְשָׁמָּה לֹא יָשׁוּב
כִּי אִם־הִרְוָה אֶת־הָאָרֶץ
וְהוֹלִידָהּ וְהִצְמִיחָהּ
וְנָתַן זֶרַע לַזֹּרֵעַ וְלֶחֶם לָאֹכֵל:

[e] Emendation yields "words"; cf. v. 11 and 40.8
[d-d] Lit. "seed for the sower and bread for the eater"

11] So is the word that issues from My mouth:
It does not come back to Me unfulfilled,
But performs what I purpose,
Achieves what I sent it to do.

12] Yea, you shall leave^e in joy and be led home
    secure.
Before you, mount and hill shall shout aloud,
And all the trees of the field shall clap their hands.

13] Instead of the brier, a cypress shall rise;
Instead of the nettle, a myrtle shall rise.
These shall stand as a testimony to the Lord,
As an everlasting sign that shall not perish.

Chapter 56

1] Thus said the Lord:
Observe what is right and do what is just;
For soon My salvation shall come,
And My deliverance be revealed.

2] Happy is the man who does this,
The man who holds fast to it:
Who keeps the sabbath and does not profane it,
And stays his hand from doing any evil.

3] Let not the foreigner say,
Who has attached himself to the Lord,
"The Lord will keep me apart from His people";
And let not the eunuch say,
"I am a withered tree."

4] For thus said the Lord:
"As regards the eunuchs who keep My sabbaths,

11 כֵּן יִֽהְיֶ֣ה דְבָרִי֮ אֲשֶׁ֣ר יֵצֵ֣א מִפִּי֒
לֹֽא־יָשׁ֥וּב אֵלַ֖י רֵיקָ֑ם
כִּ֤י אִם־עָשָׂה֙ אֶת־אֲשֶׁ֣ר חָפַ֔צְתִּי
וְהִצְלִ֖יחַ אֲשֶׁ֥ר שְׁלַחְתִּֽיו׃

12 כִּֽי־בְשִׂמְחָ֣ה תֵצֵ֔אוּ וּבְשָׁל֖וֹם תּֽוּבָל֑וּן
הֶהָרִ֣ים וְהַגְּבָע֗וֹת יִפְצְח֤וּ לִפְנֵיכֶם֙ רִנָּ֔ה
וְכָל־עֲצֵ֥י הַשָּׂדֶ֖ה יִמְחֲאוּ־כָֽף׃

13 תַּ֤חַת הַֽנַּעֲצוּץ֙ יַעֲלֶ֣ה בְר֔וֹשׁ
וְתַ֥חַת הַסִּרְפַּ֖ד יַעֲלֶ֣ה הֲדַ֑ס
וְהָיָ֤ה לַֽיהוָה֙ לְשֵׁ֔ם
לְא֥וֹת עוֹלָ֖ם לֹ֥א יִכָּרֵֽת׃

נו

1 כֹּ֚ה אָמַ֣ר יְהוָ֔ה
שִׁמְר֥וּ מִשְׁפָּ֖ט וַעֲשׂ֣וּ צְדָקָ֑ה
כִּֽי־קְרוֹבָ֤ה יְשֽׁוּעָתִי֙ לָב֔וֹא
וְצִדְקָתִ֖י לְהִגָּלֽוֹת׃

2 אַשְׁרֵ֤י אֱנוֹשׁ֙ יַעֲשֶׂה־זֹּ֔את
וּבֶן־אָדָ֖ם יַחֲזִ֣יק בָּ֑הּ
שֹׁמֵ֤ר שַׁבָּת֙ מֵֽחַלְּל֔וֹ
וְשֹׁמֵ֥ר יָד֖וֹ מֵעֲשׂ֥וֹת כָּל־רָֽע׃

3 וְאַל־יֹאמַ֣ר בֶּן־הַנֵּכָ֗ר
הַנִּלְוָ֤ה אֶל־יְהוָה֙ לֵאמֹ֔ר
הַבְדֵּ֧ל יַבְדִּילַ֛נִי יְהוָ֖ה מֵעַ֣ל עַמּ֑וֹ
וְאַל־יֹאמַר֙ הַסָּרִ֔יס
הֵ֥ן אֲנִ֖י עֵ֥ץ יָבֵֽשׁ׃

4 כִּי־כֹ֣ה ׀ אָמַ֣ר יְהוָ֗ה
לַסָּֽרִיסִים֙ אֲשֶׁ֤ר יִשְׁמְרוּ֙ אֶת־שַׁבְּתוֹתַ֔י

---

^{e} I.e., leave the Babylonian exile

Who have chosen what I desire
And hold fast to My covenant—

וּבָחֲרוּ בַּאֲשֶׁר חָפָצְתִּי

וּמַחֲזִיקִים בִּבְרִיתִי:

5] I will give them, in My House
And within My walls,
A monument and a name
Better than sons or daughters.
I will give them an everlasting name
Which shall not perish.

5 וְנָתַתִּי לָהֶם בְּבֵיתִי

וּבְחוֹמֹתַי

יָד וָשֵׁם

טוֹב מִבָּנִים וּמִבָּנוֹת

שֵׁם עוֹלָם אֶתֶּן־לוֹ

אֲשֶׁר לֹא יִכָּרֵת:

6] As for the foreigners
Who attach themselves to the LORD,
To minister to Him.
And to love the name of the LORD,
To be His servants—
All who keep the sabbath and do not profane it,
And who hold fast to My covenant—

6 וּבְנֵי הַנֵּכָר

הַנִּלְוִים עַל־יְהֹוָה לְשָׁרְתוֹ

וּלְאַהֲבָה אֶת־שֵׁם יְהֹוָה

לִהְיוֹת לוֹ לַעֲבָדִים

כָּל־שֹׁמֵר שַׁבָּת מֵחַלְּלוֹ

וּמַחֲזִיקִים בִּבְרִיתִי:

7] I will bring them to My sacred mount
And let them rejoice in My house of prayer.
Their burnt offerings and sacrifices
Shall be welcome on My altar;
For My House shall be called
A house of prayer for all peoples."

7 וַהֲבִיאוֹתִים אֶל־הַר קָדְשִׁי

וְשִׂמַּחְתִּים בְּבֵית תְּפִלָּתִי

עוֹלֹתֵיהֶם וְזִבְחֵיהֶם

לְרָצוֹן עַל־מִזְבְּחִי

כִּי בֵיתִי בֵּית־תְּפִלָּה יִקָּרֵא

לְכָל־הָעַמִּים:

8] Thus declares the Lord GOD,
Who gathers the dispersed of Israel:
"I will gather still more to those already
    gathered."

8 נְאֻם אֲדֹנָי יֱהֹוִה

מְקַבֵּץ נִדְחֵי יִשְׂרָאֵל

עוֹד אֲקַבֵּץ עָלָיו לְנִקְבָּצָיו:

1683

Shabbat Rosh Chodesh

שבת ראש חדש

Isaiah
66 : 1–13, 23

Chapters 40–66 of the Book of Isaiah are the work of an unknown author (often referred to as Deutero-Isaiah) who lived in Babylon during the days of the exile (sixth century B.C.E.). He preached unwavering trust in a God who would surely restore Israel to its homeland. Of all the prophets he is the most lyrical and his imagery the richest.

Isaiah contrasts the earnest searchers after God with those who mock Him with despicable rites. But it is the former who will experience the Lord's mercy upon Zion. The last verse of the haftarah is the reason why the selection is read whenever a Sabbath coincides with the new moon.

Chapter 66

1] Thus said the LORD:
The heaven is My throne
And the earth is My footstool:
Where could you build a house for Me,
What place could serve as My abode?

2] All this was made by My hand,
And thus it all came into being
            —declares the LORD.
Yet to such a one I look:
To the poor and broken-hearted,
Who is concerned about My word.

3] ᵃAs for those who slaughter oxen and slay
   humans,
Who sacrifice sheep and immolateᵇ dogs,
Who present as oblation the blood of swine,
Who offerᶜ incense and worship false gods—
Just as they have chosen their ways
And take pleasure in their abominations,

סו

[1] כֹּה אָמַר יְהֹוָה

הַשָּׁמַיִם כִּסְאִי

וְהָאָרֶץ הֲדֹם רַגְלָי

אֵי־זֶה בַיִת אֲשֶׁר תִּבְנוּ־לִי

וְאֵי־זֶה מָקוֹם מְנוּחָתִי:

[2] וְאֶת־כָּל־אֵלֶּה יָדִי עָשָׂתָה

וַיִּהְיוּ כָל־אֵלֶּה

נְאֻם־יְהֹוָה

וְאֶל־זֶה אַבִּיט

אֶל־עָנִי וּנְכֵה־רוּחַ

וְחָרֵד עַל־דְּבָרִי:

[3] שׁוֹחֵט הַשּׁוֹר מַכֵּה־אִישׁ

זוֹבֵחַ הַשֶּׂה עֹרֵף כֶּלֶב

מַעֲלֵה מִנְחָה דַּם־חֲזִיר

מַזְכִּיר לְבֹנָה מְבָרֵךְ אָוֶן

גַּם־הֵמָּה בָּחֲרוּ בְּדַרְכֵיהֶם

וּבְשִׁקּוּצֵיהֶם נַפְשָׁם חָפֵצָה:

ᵃ Vv. 3–4 refer to practitioners of idolatrous rites; cf. v. 17 and 57.5–8; 65.1–12

ᵇ Lit. "break the necks of"

ᶜ Heb. mazkir refers to giving the "token portion" (azkarah); cf. Lev. 2.2

4] So will I choose to mock them,
To bring on them the very thing they dread.
For I called and none responded,
I spoke and none paid heed.
They did what I hold evil
And chose what I do not want.

5] Hear the word of the Lord,
You who are concerned about His word!
Your kinsmen who hate you,
Who spurn you because of Me,[d] are saying,
"Let the Lord manifest His Presence,
So that we may look upon your joy."
But theirs shall be the shame.

6] Hark, tumult from the city,
Thunder from the Temple!
It is the thunder of the Lord
As He deals retribution to His foes.

7] Before she labored, she was delivered;
Before her pangs came, she bore a son.

8] Who ever heard the like?
Who ever witnessed such events?
Can a land pass through travail
In a single day?
Or is a nation born
All at once?
Yet Zion travailed
And at once bore her children!

גַּם־אֲנִ֞י אֶבְחַ֣ר בְּתַעֲלֻלֵיהֶ֗ם [4

וּמְגֽוּרֹתָם֙ אָבִ֣יא לָהֶ֔ם

יַ֤עַן קָרָ֙אתִי֙ וְאֵ֣ין עוֹנֶ֔ה

דִּבַּ֖רְתִּי וְלֹ֣א שָׁמֵ֑עוּ

וַיַּעֲשׂ֤וּ הָרַע֙ בְּעֵינַ֔י

וּבַאֲשֶׁ֥ר לֹֽא־חָפַ֖צְתִּי בָּחָֽרוּ׃

שִׁמְעוּ֙ דְּבַר־יְהוָ֔ה [5

הַחֲרֵדִ֖ים אֶל־דְּבָר֑וֹ

אָמְרוּ֩ אֲחֵיכֶ֨ם שֹׂנְאֵיכֶ֜ם

מְנַדֵּיכֶ֗ם לְמַ֤עַן שְׁמִי֙

יִכְבַּ֣ד יְהוָ֔ה

וְנִרְאֶ֥ה בְשִׂמְחַתְכֶ֖ם

וְהֵ֥ם יֵבֹֽשׁוּ׃

ק֣וֹל שָׁאוֹן֙ מֵעִ֔יר [6

ק֖וֹל מֵהֵיכָ֑ל

ק֣וֹל יְהוָ֔ה

מְשַׁלֵּ֥ם גְּמ֖וּל לְאֹיְבָֽיו׃

בְּטֶ֥רֶם תָּחִ֖יל יָלָ֑דָה [7

בְּטֶ֨רֶם יָב֥וֹא חֵ֛בֶל לָ֖הּ

וְהִמְלִ֥יטָה זָכָֽר׃

מִֽי־שָׁמַ֣ע כָּזֹ֔את [8

מִ֥י רָאָ֖ה כָּאֵ֑לֶּה

הֲי֤וּחַל אֶ֙רֶץ֙

בְּי֣וֹם אֶחָ֔ד

אִם־יִוָּ֥לֵֽד גּ֖וֹי

פַּ֣עַם אֶחָ֑ת

כִּֽי־חָ֛לָה גַּם־יָלְדָ֥ה צִיּ֖וֹן

אֶת־בָּנֶֽיהָ׃

---

[d] Lit. "My name"

9] Shall I who bring on labor not bring about
   birth?
                              —says the LORD.
   Shall I who cause birth shut the womb?
                              —said your GOD.

10] Rejoice with Jerusalem and be glad for her,
    All you who love her!
    Join in her jubilation,
    All you who mourned over her—

11] That you may suck from her breast
    Consolation to the full,
    That you may draw from her bosom^e
    Glory to your delight.

12] For thus said the LORD:
    I will extend to her
    Prosperity like a stream,
    The wealth of nations
    Like a wadi in flood;
    And you shall drink of it.
    You shall be carried on shoulders
    And dandled upon knees.

13] As a mother comforts her son
    So I will comfort you;
    You shall find comfort in Jerusalem.

        . . .

23] And new moon after new moon,
    And sabbath after sabbath,
    All flesh shall come to worship Me
                              —said the LORD.

9] הַאֲנִי אַשְׁבִּיר וְלֹא אוֹלִיד

יֹאמַר יְהֹוָה

אִם־אֲנִי הַמּוֹלִיד וְעָצַרְתִּי

אָמַר אֱלֹהָיִךְ:

10] שִׂמְחוּ אֶת־יְרוּשָׁלַם וְגִילוּ בָהּ

כָּל־אֹהֲבֶיהָ

שִׂישׂוּ אִתָּהּ מָשׂוֹשׂ

כָּל־הַמִּתְאַבְּלִים עָלֶיהָ:

11] לְמַעַן תִּינְקוּ וּשְׂבַעְתֶּם

מִשֹּׁד תַּנְחֻמֶיהָ

לְמַעַן תָּמֹצּוּ וְהִתְעַנַּגְתֶּם

מִזִּיז כְּבוֹדָהּ:

12] כִּי־כֹה אָמַר יְהֹוָה

הִנְנִי נֹטֶה־אֵלֶיהָ

כְּנָהָר שָׁלוֹם

וּכְנַחַל שׁוֹטֵף כְּבוֹד גּוֹיִם

וִינַקְתֶּם עַל־צַד תִּנָּשֵׂאוּ

וְעַל־בִּרְכַּיִם תְּשָׁעֳשָׁעוּ:

13] כְּאִישׁ אֲשֶׁר אִמּוֹ תְּנַחֲמֶנּוּ

כֵּן אָנֹכִי אֲנַחֶמְכֶם

וּבִירוּשָׁלַם תְּנֻחָמוּ:

        . . .

23] וְהָיָה מִדֵּי־חֹדֶשׁ בְּחָדְשׁוֹ

וּמִדֵּי שַׁבָּת בְּשַׁבַּתּוֹ

יָבוֹא כָל־בָּשָׂר לְהִשְׁתַּחֲוֹת לְפָנַי

אָמַר יְהֹוָה:

---

^e Cf. Akkadian zizu, Arabic zizat "udder"

The Book of Samuel is divided into two parts. It is primarily the story of Samuel's ministry as the spiritual guide of Israel and of the reign of Israel's first two kings, Saul and David (about 1000 B.C.E.). It is history written from a theological perspective: all of Israel's fate hinges on the performance or non-performance of God's commandments.

The haftarah is read whenever a Sabbath immediately precedes the new moon. The tale begins with David's friend Jonathan saying, "Tomorrow will be the new moon . . .," and is a tribute to their friendship which was maintained despite the fact that Jonathan's father, King Saul, sought David's life.

מחר חדש

First Samuel

20 : 18-42

Chapter 20

18] Jonathan said to him, "Tomorrow will be the new moon; and you will be missed when your seat remains vacant.[h]

19] So the day after tomorrow, go down [i]all the way[i] to the place where you hid [i]the other time,[i] and stay close to the Ezel stone.

20] Now I will shoot three arrows to one side of it, as though I were shooting at a mark,

21] and I will order the boy to go and find the arrows. If I call to the boy, 'Hey! the arrows are on this side of you,' be reassured[k] and come, for you are safe and there is no danger—as the LORD lives!

22] But if, instead, I call to the lad, 'Hey! the arrows are beyond you,' then leave, for the LORD has sent you away.

23] As for the promise we made to each other,[l] may the LORD be [witness] between you and me forever."

24] David hid in the field. The new moon came, and the king sat down to partake of the meal.

25] When the king took his usual place on the seat by the wall, Jonathan rose[m] and Abner sat down at Saul's side; but David's place remained vacant.

כ

18 וַיֹּֽאמֶר־ל֥וֹ יְהוֹנָתָ֖ן מָחָ֣ר חֹ֑דֶשׁ וְנִפְקַ֕דְתָּ כִּ֥י יִפָּקֵ֖ד מוֹשָׁבֶֽךָ׃ 19 וְשִׁלַּשְׁתָּ֙ תֵּרֵ֣ד מְאֹ֔ד וּבָאתָ֙ אֶל־הַמָּק֔וֹם אֲשֶׁר־נִסְתַּ֥רְתָּ שָּׁ֖ם בְּי֣וֹם הַֽמַּעֲשֶׂ֑ה וְיָ֣שַׁבְתָּ֔ אֵ֖צֶל הָאֶ֥בֶן הָאָֽזֶל׃ 20 וַאֲנִ֕י שְׁלֹ֥שֶׁת הַחִצִּ֖ים צִדָּ֣ה אוֹרֶ֑ה לְשַֽׁלַּֽח־לִ֖י לְמַטָּרָֽה׃ 21 וְהִנֵּה֙ אֶשְׁלַ֣ח אֶת־הַנַּ֔עַר לֵ֖ךְ מְצָ֣א אֶת־הַחִצִּ֑ים אִם־אָמֹר֩ אֹמַ֨ר לַנַּ֜עַר הִנֵּ֥ה הַחִצִּ֣ים ׀ מִמְּךָ֣ וָהֵ֗נָּה קָחֶ֧נּוּ ׀ וָבֹ֛אָה כִּֽי־שָׁל֥וֹם לְךָ֛ וְאֵ֥ין דָּבָ֖ר חַי־יְהוָֽה׃ 22 וְאִם־כֹּ֤ה אֹמַר֙ לָעֶ֔לֶם הִנֵּ֥ה הַחִצִּ֖ים מִמְּךָ֣ וָהָ֑לְאָה לֵ֕ךְ כִּ֥י שִֽׁלַּחֲךָ֖ יְהוָֽה׃ 23 וְהַ֨דָּבָ֔ר אֲשֶׁ֥ר דִּבַּ֖רְנוּ אֲנִ֣י וָאָ֑תָּה הִנֵּ֧ה יְהוָ֛ה בֵּינִ֥י וּבֵֽינְךָ֖ עַד־עוֹלָֽם׃

24 וַיִּסָּתֵ֥ר דָּוִ֖ד בַּשָּׂדֶ֑ה וַיְהִ֣י הַחֹ֔דֶשׁ וַיֵּ֧שֶׁב הַמֶּ֛לֶךְ אֶל־הַלֶּ֖חֶם לֶאֱכֽוֹל׃ 25 וַיֵּ֣שֶׁב הַ֠מֶּלֶךְ עַל־מֽוֹשָׁב֞וֹ כְּפַ֣עַם ׀ בְּפַ֗עַם אֶל־מוֹשַׁב֙ הַקִּ֔יר וַיָּ֙קָם֙ יְה֣וֹנָתָ֔ן וַיֵּ֥שֶׁב אַבְנֵ֖ר מִצַּ֣ד שָׁא֑וּל וַיִּפָּקֵ֖ד

---

[h] At the festal meal [i-i] Lit. "very much"

[i-i] Lit. "on the day of the incident"; see 19.2 ff.

[k] Lit. "accept it" [l] See vv. 12–17

[m] Force of Heb. uncertain; Septuagint "faced him"

26] That day, however, Saul said nothing. "It's accidental," he thought. ⁿ-"He must be unclean and not yet cleansed."-ⁿ

27] But on the day after the new moon, the second day, David's place was vacant again. So Saul said to his son Jonathan, "Why didn't the son of Jesseᵒ come to the meal yesterday or today?"

28] Jonathan answered Saul, "David begged leave of me to go to Bethlehem.

29] He said, 'Please let me go, for we are going to have a family feast in our town and my brother has summoned me to it. Do me a favor, let me slip away to see my kinsmen.' That is why he has not come to the king's table."

30] Saul flew into a rage against Jonathan. "You son of a perverse, rebellious woman!" he shouted. "I know that you side with the son of Jesse—to your shame, and to the shame of your mother's nakedness!

31] For as long as the son of Jesse lives on earth, neither you nor your kingship will be secure. Now then, have him brought to me, for he is marked for death."
32] But Jonathan spoke up and said to his father, "Why should he be put to death? What has he done?"

33] At that, Saul threwᵖ his spear at him to strike him down; and Jonathan realized that his father was determined to do away with David.

34] Jonathan rose from the table in a rage. He ate no food on the second day of the new moon, because he was grieved about David, and because his father had humiliated him.

35] In the morning, Jonathan went out into the open for the meeting with David, accompanied by a young boy.

36] He said to the boy, "Run ahead and find the arrows that I shoot." And

26 וְלֹא־דִבֶּר שָׁאוּל מְאוּמָה מְקוֹם דָּוִד: בַּיּוֹם הַהוּא כִּי אָמַר מִקְרֶה הוּא בִּלְתִּי טָהוֹר הוּא כִּי־לֹא טָהוֹר: 27 וַיְהִי מִמָּחֳרַת הַחֹדֶשׁ הַשֵּׁנִי וַיִּפָּקֵד מְקוֹם דָּוִד וַיֹּאמֶר שָׁאוּל אֶל יְהוֹנָתָן בְּנוֹ מַדּוּעַ לֹא־בָא בֶן־יִשַׁי גַּם תְּמוֹל גַּם הַיּוֹם אֶל־הַלָּחֶם: 28 וַיַּעַן יְהוֹנָתָן אֶת־שָׁאוּל נִשְׁאֹל נִשְׁאַל דָּוִד מֵעִמָּדִי עַד־בֵּית לָחֶם: 29 וַיֹּאמֶר שַׁלְּחֵנִי נָא כִּי זֶבַח מִשְׁפָּחָה לָנוּ בָּעִיר וְהוּא צִוָּה־לִי אָחִי וְעַתָּה אִם־מָצָאתִי חֵן בְּעֵינֶיךָ אִמָּלְטָה נָּא וְאֶרְאֶה אֶת־אֶחָי עַל־כֵּן לֹא־בָא אֶל־שֻׁלְחַן הַמֶּלֶךְ:

30 וַיִּחַר־אַף שָׁאוּל בִּיהוֹנָתָן וַיֹּאמֶר לוֹ בֶּן נַעֲוַת הַמַּרְדּוּת הֲלוֹא יָדַעְתִּי כִּי־בֹחֵר אַתָּה לְבֶן־יִשַׁי לְבָשְׁתְּךָ וּלְבֹשֶׁת עֶרְוַת אִמֶּךָ: 31 כִּי כָל־הַיָּמִים אֲשֶׁר בֶּן־יִשַׁי חַי עַל־הָאֲדָמָה לֹא תִכּוֹן אַתָּה וּמַלְכוּתֶךָ וְעַתָּה שְׁלַח וְקַח אֹתוֹ אֵלַי כִּי בֶן־מָוֶת הוּא: 32 וַיַּעַן יְהוֹנָתָן אֶת־שָׁאוּל אָבִיו וַיֹּאמֶר אֵלָיו לָמָּה יוּמַת מֶה עָשָׂה: 33 וַיָּטֶל שָׁאוּל אֶת־הַחֲנִית עָלָיו לְהַכֹּתוֹ וַיֵּדַע יְהוֹנָתָן כִּי־כָלָה הִיא מֵעִם אָבִיו לְהָמִית אֶת־דָּוִד: 34 וַיָּקָם יְהוֹנָתָן מֵעִם הַשֻּׁלְחָן בָּחֳרִי־אָף וְלֹא־אָכַל בְּיוֹם־הַחֹדֶשׁ הַשֵּׁנִי לֶחֶם כִּי נֶעְצַב אֶל־דָּוִד כִּי הִכְלִמוֹ אָבִיו:

35 וַיְהִי בַבֹּקֶר וַיֵּצֵא יְהוֹנָתָן הַשָּׂדֶה לְמוֹעֵד דָּוִד וְנַעַר קָטֹן עִמּוֹ: 36 וַיֹּאמֶר לְנַעֲרוֹ רֻץ מְצָא־נָא אֶת־הַחִצִּים אֲשֶׁר אָנֹכִי מוֹרֶה הַנַּעַר

ⁿ-ⁿ *Heb. construction unclear*
ᵒ *To refer to a person merely as "the son (ben) of . . ." is slighting; cf. 10.11; 20:30, 31; Isa. 7:4*
ᵖ *As in 18.11, change of vocalization yields "raised"*

as the boy ran, he shot the arrows past him.
37] When the boy came to the place where the
arrows shot by Jonathan had fallen, Jonathan
called out to the boy, "Hey, the arrows are beyond
you!"

38] And Jonathan called after the boy,
"Quick, hurry up. Don't stop!" So Jonathan's
boy gathered the arrows and came back to his
master.—

39] The boy suspected nothing; only
Jonathan and David knew the arrangement.—
40] Jonathan handed the gear to his boy and told
him, "Take these back to the town."

41] When
the boy got there, David *emerged from his
concealment at*ᵠ the Negeb.ʳ He flung himself
face down on the ground and bowed low three
times. They kissed each other and wept together;
David wept the longer.

42] Jonathan said to David, "Go in peace! For
we two have sworn to each other in the name of
the LORD: 'May the LORD be [witness] between
you and me, and between your offspring and
mine, forever!'"

רָץ וְהוּא־יָרָה הַחֵצִי לְהַעֲבִרוֹ: 37] וַיָּבֹא
הַנַּעַר עַד־מְקוֹם הַחֵצִי אֲשֶׁר יָרָה יְהוֹנָתָן
וַיִּקְרָא יְהוֹנָתָן אַחֲרֵי הַנַּעַר וַיֹּאמֶר הֲלוֹא הַחֵצִי
מִמְּךָ וָהָלְאָה: 38] וַיִּקְרָא יְהוֹנָתָן אַחֲרֵי הַנַּעַר
מְהֵרָה חוּשָׁה אַל־תַּעֲמֹד וַיְלַקֵּט נַעַר יְהוֹנָתָן
אֶת־הַחֵצִי וַיָּבֹא אֶל־אֲדֹנָיו: 39] וְהַנַּעַר לֹא
יָדַע מְאוּמָה אַךְ יְהוֹנָתָן וְדָוִד יָדְעוּ אֶת־הַדָּבָר:
40] וַיִּתֵּן יְהוֹנָתָן אֶת־כֵּלָיו אֶל־הַנַּעַר אֲשֶׁר־לוֹ
וַיֹּאמֶר לוֹ לֵךְ הָבֵיא הָעִיר: 41] הַנַּעַר בָּא
וְדָוִד קָם מֵאֵצֶל הַנֶּגֶב וַיִּפֹּל לְאַפָּיו אַרְצָה
וַיִּשְׁתַּחוּ שָׁלֹשׁ פְּעָמִים וַיִּשְּׁקוּ אִישׁ אֶת־רֵעֵהוּ
וַיִּבְכּוּ אִישׁ אֶת־רֵעֵהוּ עַד־דָּוִד הִגְדִּיל:

42] וַיֹּאמֶר יְהוֹנָתָן לְדָוִד לֵךְ לְשָׁלוֹם אֲשֶׁר
נִשְׁבַּעְנוּ שְׁנֵינוּ אֲנַחְנוּ בְּשֵׁם יְהוָה לֵאמֹר יְהוָה
יִהְיֶה בֵּינִי וּבֵינֶךָ וּבֵין זַרְעִי וּבֵין זַרְעֲךָ עַד
עוֹלָם:

ᵠ⁻ᵠ Lit. "rose up from beside"   ʳ Identical with the "Ezel Stone," v. 19

Genesis

Creation GEN. 1:1—2:3

1. See *Interpreter's Dictionary* (4 vols., plus supplementary vol., New York and Nashville: Abingdon, 1962–1976), Vol. I, p. 728, and literature cited on p. 732. On בְּרֵאשִׁית see the study by Menahem Naor, *Beth Mikra*, 46, 3 (June 1971), pp. 306 ff.

2. See *Notes on the New Translation of the Torah*, ed. Harry M. Orlinsky (Philadelphia: Jewish Publication Society, 1969), especially on Philo's influence on the interpretation of this verse. [Hereafter this work will be referred to as JPS *Notes*.]

The translation here follows the Septuagint; Targum. Also see Hag. 12a for what was created on the first day.

3. See A. Jeremias, *Das Alte Testament* (Leipzig: J. C. Hinrich, 1916), pp. 49 ff., for a detailed analysis; also T. Friedman, *Beth Mikra*, 82, 4 (1980), pp. 309 ff., who supports the meaning of "spirit" in the sense of "power."

4. Compare Isa. 51:9, 10; Ps. 89:11; Job 26:10–12; and also rabbinic sources, e.g., B. B. 74b.

5. So Jonathan ben Uzziel; San. 38b; Ibn Ezra. Luzzatto: an Aramaism; Nachmanides: God and Earth together; Pirke de-R. Eliezer 11: God addresses the Torah. Also, cf. Epistle of Barnabas 5:5; 6:12, where God is represented as consulting Christ.

6. Mishnah Yeb. 6:6. See J. M. Epstein, *Aruch ha-Shulchan*, Even ha-Ezer 1:11.

7. See Rashi; Ibn Ezra.

8. See Arnold B. Ehrlich, *Mikra Kifeshuto* (New York: Ktav, 1969), *ad* 12:3; H. M. Orlinsky, *Ancient Israel* (Ithaca: Cornell University Press, 1954), pp. 27–29.

9. Gerhard von Rad, *Genesis: A Commentary* (Philadelphia: Westminster Press, 1961), p. 114.

10. *From Adam to Noah* (Jerusalem: Magnes Press, 1961), p. 304.

11. *Hebrew Union College Annual*, 39 (1968), p. 37. [Hereafter this journal is cited as *HUCA*.]

12. Gen. R. 1:1, 2; 12:2.

13. See Abarbanel.

14. Gen. R. 8:10.

15. Maimonides, *Guide of the Perplexed*, I, 52–53. For a linguistic study of the terms "image" and "likeness," see J. Maxwell Miller, *Journal of Biblical Literature*, 99 (September 1972), pp. 289–304. [Hereafter this journal is cited as *JBL*.]

16. Sifre Deuteronomy, Ekev, 49, ed. M. Friedmann; similarly Sotah 14a.

17. Leo Baeck, *Das Wesen des Judentums* (5th ed.; Frankfurt: J. Kauffmann, 1922), p. 166; Eng. ed.: *The Essence of Judaism* (rev. ed.; New York: Schocken, 1948), p. 152.

18. Cassuto, *A Commentary on the Book of Genesis*, 2 parts (Jerusalem: Magnes Press, 1961, 1964), *passim*. Some have taken this theory to extremes. For instance, the letters in ויאמר אלהים ("and God said"), when taken at their numerical value, amount to 343, which is 7 x 7 x 7. For an explanation of *gematria*, see Gleanings to Gen. 14:1–24, "Three Hundred Eighteen Retainers."

19. Revelations 1:10.

20. Gen. R. 9:2.

21. Gottfried von Leibnitz, *Théodicée* 1:8. Compare Voltaire's satire on "the best of all possible worlds" in *Candide*, Ch. 1.

22. Benno Jacob, *Das erste Buch der Tora*, *Genesis* (Berlin: Schocken, 1934).

23. Franz Rosenzweig, *Stern der Erlösung* (2d ed.; Frankfurt: J. Kauffmann, 1930), pp. 196 f. Eng. ed.: *The Star of Redemption*, trans. William W. Hallo (New York: Holt, Rinehart & Winston, 1970–1971), pp. 154, 311. [Hereafter reference is to Eng. ed.]

24. *Ethics of the Fathers* 3:18.

25. Mishnah San. 4:5.

26. *Ibid.*

27. Martin Buber, *Die chassidischen Bücher* (Berlin: Schocken, 1927), p. 157.

28. *Ancient Near Eastern Texts*, ed. James B. Pritchard (2nd ed., Princeton: Princeton University Press, 1955), pp. 60 f. [Hereafter cited as Pritchard, *ANET*.]

29. *Interpreter's Dictionary*, Vol. I, p. 726.

30. Karl Barth, *Church Dogmatics* (Edinburgh: T. & T. Clark, 1958), Vol. III, p. 215.

31. Rosenzweig, *Star of Redemption*, pp. 313 f.

32. R. Simchah Bunam, quoted by Louis I. Newman, *The Hasidic Anthology* (New York: Bloch, 1944), p. 61.

33. Robert Gordis, *Congress bi-Weekly*, 38, 5 (April 1971), p. 12. Man as God's co-partner: Sab. 10a. Further on ecology and Jewish tradition, see J. I. Helfand, *Judaism*, 20, 3 (Summer 1971), pp. 330–335.

34. Fackenheim, Emil L., *Tradition and Change*, ed. A. L. Jamison (Syracuse: Syracuse University Press, 1978), pp. 226 f. Based on the midrash in Gen. R. 8:5.

Man in Eden GEN. 2:4–24

1. See JPS *Notes*.

2. See Theodor H. Gaster, *Myth, Legend and Custom in the Old Testament* (New York: Harper & Row, 1969), p. 27.

3. *Ibid.*; also see D. Ershal, *Beth Mikra*, 40, 1 (December 1969), pp. 100 ff.

4. Yeb. 63a; also see Ibn Ezra on Exod. 1:1.

5. Pritchard, *ANET*, "Enuma Elish," pp. 60 f.

6. *Ibid.*, "Enki and Ninhursag," p. 38.

7. Rashi, based on San. 38a–b.

8. B. Jacob, with reference to Ps. 139:16.

9. Gen. R. 8:1.

10. There probably was a separate midrashic collection about the original Adam, which has survived only in comments and quotations, interpretations and speculations, found in other sources. Among these are the writings of Philo, the Christian Scriptures, the Gnostics; Mishnah and Talmud; the writings of Islam and the Druse; and medieval Jewish mystical books.

See Gershom Scholem, *On the Kabbalah and Its Symbolism* (New York: Schocken, 1965), pp. 159–165. For a modern interpretation, see Joseph B. Soloveitchik, *Tradition*, 7, 2 (Summer 1965), pp. 5 f.

11. Philo, summarized by Samuel Sandmel, *Philo's Place in Judaism* (New York: Ktav, 1971), pp. xxi, 100.

12. Shakespeare, *The Merchant of Venice*, Act 4, Scene 1.

13. Buber, *Werke* (Munich: Kösel Verlag, 1964), Vol. II, p. 877.

14. Unpublished manuscript. By permission of the author.

15. "From Depatriarchalizing in Biblical Interpretation," *Journal of the American Academy of Religion*, XLI, I (March 1973), pp. 30–48. The article reevaluates the role of woman in the Genesis story.

16. Ber. 61a.

17. Gen. R. 9:7.

The Expulsion from Eden GEN. 3

1. Wisdom of Solomon 2:24. But it has also been held that the serpent deceives in order to give man his humanity; see K. A. Joines, *Serpent Symbolism in the Old Testament* (Haddonfield, England: Haddon House, 1974), p. 30.

2. See JPS *Notes*.

3. Gen. R. 15:7.

4. Buber, *The Prophetic Faith* (New York: Macmillan, 1949), p. 90.

5. Pes. 118a.

6. See E. O. James, *The Tree of Life* (Leiden, Holland: E. J. Brill, 1966), for a full treatment of this subject.

7. II Esdras 7:118; but, in contrast, see Baruch 4:1·

8. Romans 5:12, 18.

9. A merism, see at Deut. 29:18. Compare JPS *Notes* and von Rad, *Genesis*, p. 79. See also the discussion by W. Malcolm Clark, *JBL*, 88 (September 1969), pp. 266–278.

10. Consult *Interpreter's Dictionary*, Vol. II, p. 235, under "Fall" for bibliography.

11. Maimonides, *Guide*, I, 2.

12. Rashi on Gen. 4:1; see Gen. R. 22:2.

13. For a summary of opinions, see John A. Bailey, *JBL*, 89 (June 1970), pp. 144 ff.

14. See Rosenzweig, *Star of Redemption*, p. 266.
15. Friedrich von Schiller, from his poem *Kassandra*.
16. Compare Mech. to Exod. 14:29.
17. Tanch. Vayeshev 46b; Gen. R. 9:5 (based on a tradition that R. Meir had a Torah scroll in which Gen. 1:31 read טוב מות instead of טוב מְאֹד, or which had a marginal note to that effect).
18. Sab. 55b.
19. Pritchard, *ANET*, "Gilgamesh," p. 75.
20. Philo, *On the Creation of the World*, 56.
21. San. 29a.
22. C. F. von Weizsäcker, quoted in V. Gollancz, *Man and God* (Boston: Houghton Mifflin, 1951), pp. 190 f.
23. Tanch. Tazri'a 1:9.
24. Pirke de-R. Eliezer 14.

25. John Milton, *Paradise Lost*, opening stanzas.
26. Henry S. Slonimsky, *Essays* (Cincinnati, Ohio: Hebrew Union College Press, 1967), p. 53.
27. Erub. 13b.
28. Moshe Mordecai Epstein, quoted in *Ma'yanah shel Torah*, ed. Alexander Zusia Friedman (5 vols., Tel Aviv: Pe'er, 1955–1956), Vol. I, p. 26; Eng. trans.: *Wellsprings of Torah* (2 vols., New York: Judaica Press, 1969), p. 11. The passage is a comment on Rashi, *ad loc.*
29. *Joseph and His Brothers*, trans. H. T. Lowe-Porter (New York: Alfred A. Knopf, 1966), p. 27.
30. Louis Ginzberg, *The Legends of the Jews* (Philadelphia: Jewish Publication Society, 1909–1946), Vol. V, p. 97, note 70.
31. *Ariel*, 36 (1974), pp. 74, 78.

Cain and Abel GEN. 4

1. This theory has been elaborately developed and illustrated by Gaster, *Myth*, pp. 51 ff.
2. See JPS *Notes*.
3. So Ephraim A. Speiser, *Genesis* (Garden City: Doubleday, 1964), *ad loc.*; also New English Bible.
4. Similarly, Targum Yerushalmi.
5. Compare II Chron. 1:2, for a similar ellipsis.
6. Compare Maimonides, Hilch. Rotse'ach 1:4.
7. See JPS *Notes*.
8. Stanley Gevirtz, *JBL*, 96 (1977), pp. 570 f.
9. For a complete analysis of this difficult passage, see Samuel Sandmel, *HUCA*, 32 (1961), pp. 19 ff.
10. S. R. Hirsch and others.
11. Cyrus H. Gordon, *Before the Bible* (New York: Harper & Row, 1962), p. 16. Rabbinic sources deal with the whole question of Cain's repentance. See Lev. R. 10:5; Tanch. 1:25; and literature quoted in Louis Ginzberg, *Legends*, Vol. V, p. 141, note 26. For a comprehensive discussion, see C. D. Gvaryahu, *Beth Mikra*, 32, 1 (October 1967), pp. 27 ff. The Koran,

too, speaks of Cain's repentance, Sura V:36 (The Table).
12. Yehezkel Kaufmann, *The Religion of Israel* (Chicago: University of Chicago Press, 1960), p. 295.
13. Gen. R. 22:9.
14. Hul. 7b; see also R. Simchah Bunam, quoted in *Ma'yanah shel Torah*, Vol. I, p. 31.
15. Also see Gen. R. 22:8.
16. Ben Sira 15:12. [This work is sometimes referred to as Sirach.]
17. *Ethics of the Fathers* 4:1.
18. Maimonides, Hilch. Teshuvah 5:4.
19. Mishnah San. 4:5. See Maimonides, Hilch. Rotse'ach 4:9; and Rashi.
20. Avot de-R. Nathan 31, also quoted in the Koran, Sura V:36 (The Table).
21. Mordecai M. Kaplan, unpublished manuscript.
22. Elie Wiesel, *A Beggar in Jerusalem* (New York: Random House, 1970), p. 111.
23. Westermann, *Genesis* 1–11 (Darmstadt: Wissenschaftliche Buchhandlung, 1972), p. 59.

Primeval Man GEN. 5:1—6:8

1. See B. B. 17a. Buber (*Werke*, Vol. II, p. 887) denies, however, that the expression "walked with God" is a moral judgment in either Enoch's or Moses' case but means these men were able to participate in God's governance, His own "movement."

2. See JPS *Notes*; see also Westermann, *Genesis*, pp. 68–76.
3. See Enoch 6–8; see also Ginzberg, *Legends*, Vol. V, p. 153, note 57.
4. Julian Morgenstern, *HUCA*, 14 (1939), pp. 29–40, 114 ff.

5. Bernard Bamberger, *Fallen Angels* (Philadelphia: Jewish Publication Society, 1952), p. 263, note 1.

6. So Mendelssohn; Hirsch.

7. So various midrashim, e.g., Sifre Beha'alotecha 86; Rashi; Ibn Ezra; B. Jacob. See also Augustine who derives the Civitas Dei from the children of Seth, and Civitas Terrestra from Cain.

8. The figure 120 occurs frequently in the Bible; see Num. 7:86; I Kings 9:14; 10:10; II Chron. 5:12. See also the use of 120,000 in Judg. 8:10; I Kings 8:63; I Chron. 12:37; II Chron. 7:5; 28:6.

9. Rashi. The whole subject of these numbers is explored by E. Dhorme, *Revue Biblique*, 33 (1924), pp. 532–556; 35 (1926), pp. 66–82; 223–239; 532–556.

10. Morgenstern, *HUCA*, 14 (1939), p. 85.

11. *Rediscovering Judaism*, ed. A. J. Wolf (Chicago: Quadrangle Press, 1965), editor's essay, pp. 142 ff.

12. Gen. R. 23:3.

13. See W. W. Hallo, *Journal of Cuneiform Studies*, 23, 3 (1971), pp. 57–67.

14. Speiser, *Genesis*, p. 41.

15. Luzzatto, following Radak.

16. Kaplan, unpublished manuscript.

17. Jer. Ned. 9:4, 41c, which portrays the Torah as saving Israel.

18. M. M. Kasher, in *Encyclopedia of Biblical Interpretation* (New York: American Biblical Encyclopedic Society, 1953), Vol. I, p. 245. Also see Nachmanides and Bachya; and Rabad, Commentary on Sifra Kedoshim 4:12.

19. Avot de-R. Nathan 31; San. 37a (see Munich manuscript and Dikduke Sofrim). Quoted also in the Koran, Sura V:36 (The Table), in connection with Abel's death.

20. Based on Gen. R. 26:7.

The Flood GEN. 6:9—8:14

1. So Rashi who cites a similar use of אֶת in Exod. 9:33 and I Kings 15:23.

2. For a summary of such attempts, see W. H. Stiebing, Jr., *Biblical Archaeological Review* [hereafter referred to as *BAR*], 2, 2 (1976), pp. 1 ff.

3. See San. 108b; Ginzberg, *Legends*, Vol. V, p. 175, note 20.

4. Tanch. Bereshit 12; San. 108a. Further references in Ginzberg, *Legends*, Vol. V, p. 173, notes 15, 17.

5. Sefer ha-Yashar.

6. Compare Matthew 24:37 ff.; Luke 17:26 ff.

7. I Peter 3:20–21. See Jack P. Lewis, *A Study of the Interpretation of Noah and the Flood in Jewish and Christian Literature* (Leiden: E. J. Brill, 1968). For another understanding, see H. H. Cohen, *The Drunkenness of Noah* (University, Ala.: University of Alabama Press, 1974), pp. 13–30: The crime consisted of acquiring the father's sexual prowess by seeing him in an act of intercourse. F. W. Bassett, *Vetus Testamentum* [hereafter cited as *VT*] (Leiden: E. J. Brill, 21, 1971, pp. 232–237), suggests that Ham slept with Noah's wife, making Canaan the fruit of incest.

8. San. 108a.

9. See Gordis, *Congress bi-Weekly*, pp. 9 ff.

10. See Ginzberg, *Legends*, Vol. V, p. 180, note 32.

11. Pritchard, *ANET*, "Atrahasis," p. 104. For a fuller analysis of the relationship between Bible and ancient Near East, see T. Frymer-Kensky, *BAR*, 4, 4 (1978), pp. 32–41. For parallels in the Agean area, see H. H. Cohen, *Drunkenness*, pp. 97–116.

12. Pritchard, *ANET*, "Gilgamesh," pp. 94 f.

13. *Ibid.*, p. 93.

14. Tanchuma; Midrash ha-Gadol; San. 108a–b; and Ginzberg, *Legends*, Vol. V, p. 174, note 19, where old Christian sources are also cited.

15. Koran, Sura VII:57–62 (Al Araf).

16. Morris Adler, *The Voice Still Speaks* (New York: Bloch, 1969), pp. 19, 21. The most scathing assessment of Noah's character was written by D. Garnett, *Two by Two—A Story of Survival* (New York: Atheneum, 1964); see also Mark Twain, *Letters from the Earth* (Greenwich: Fawcett, 1963).

17. Buber, *Werke*, Vol. II, p. 884.

After the Flood GEN. 8:15—9:29

1. See Targum. The anthropomorphism of this expression was discussed by the Church Father Clementine, *Homilies* 3:39. R. Rendtorff (*Kerygma und Dogma*, 7 [1961], pp. 69–78) sees in 8:21 the original end of the Urgeschichte, with blessing now taking the place of the Eden curse (Gen. 3).

2. Pritchard, *ANET*, "Gilgamesh," p. 95.

3. See Mishnah B. K. 1:4.

4. Speiser.

5. Compare Malbim; Cassuto.

6. San. 70a.

7. Pesikta Zutarti; see also Radak.

8. Ned. 31a.

9. San. 56b.

10. San. 56a–b; Maimonides, Hilch. Melachim 8:11, 9:1 ff.; Judah Halevi, *Kuzari* 3:73.

11. Acts 15:20, 29.

12. H. Revel, *Universal Jewish Encyclopedia* (New York: Universal Jewish Encyclopedia Inc., 1939–1943), Vol. VIII, pp. 227–228. Hermann Cohen, in *Die Religion der Vernunft aus den Quellen des Judentums* (Leipzig: G. Fock, 1919, pp. 143 f.), has shown how Hugo Grotius and others developed the rabbinic approach to Noahide law into a system of natural law.

13. Samuel Atlas, *Dimensions*, 1, 2 (1967), p. 22.

14. Yore De'ah 66 ff. See also Acts 15:29; and Koran, Sura II:168, v. 4.

15. See Saadia; Rashi. For a divergent view, see Ibn Ezra.

16. Pes. 25a–b; San. 74a.

17. San. 57b.

18. San. 59b; cf. Maharsha; Yeb. 62a.

19. San. 70a.

20. John Skinner, *Genesis* (New York: Scribner's, 1910), *ad loc.*

21. Quoted in *Itture Torah*, comp. and ed., Aaron Jacob Greenberg (Tel Aviv: Yavneh, from 1965), Vol. I, p. 76.

The Nations GEN. 10

1. Targum Yerushalmi.

2. See also the connection of Cushan and Midian in Hab. 3:7.

3. Speiser.

4. Rabbi Meir of Rothenburg, Responsum No. 27. For a fuller discussion, see Solomon B. Freehof, *A Treasury of Responsa* (Philadelphia: Jewish Publication Society, 1963), pp. 216 ff., with a responsum by Ezekiel Landau. Also see Lev. 17:13.

5. William Foxwell Albright, *Journal of Near Eastern Studies* [hereafter cited as *JNES*], 3 (1944), pp. 254 f.

6. Speiser.

7. Erub. 53a; Sifre Bechukotai 2.

8. Midrash ha-Gadol 11:28; Gen. R. 38:13. There is also a special midrash dealing with Nimrod and Abraham: A. Jellinek, *Bet ha-Midrash* 1:25 ff.

9. Following Targum Jonathan.

10. Kaplan, unpublished manuscript.

11. Borowitz, *Journal of Ecumenical Studies*, 8, 3 (Summer 1971), p. 566.

Babel and after: The End of Prehistory GEN. 11:1–26

1. Pritchard, *ANET*, pp. 68 f.

2. Herodotus, *History*, Vol. I, p. 179.

3. See W. F. Albright, *JBL*, 43 (1924), pp. 363–393, esp. p. 385.

4. But Albright, in *Yahweh and the Gods of Canaan* (Garden City, N. Y.: Doubleday, 1968, p. 99), denies that the biblical tower can have referred to Etemenanki.

5. So Josephus, *The Jewish Antiquities*, trans. William Whiston (New York: Al Burt Co., n.d.), I, 4:1; B. Jacob; Cassuto.

6. B. Jacob, commentary, *ad loc.*

7. André Parrot, *The Tower of Babel* (London: SCM Press, 1955).

8. See the analysis by C. D. Gvaryahu, *Beth Mikra*, 32, 1 (October 1967), pp. 27–36.

9. A. Koestler, in accepting the Sonning Prize, University of Copenhagen, quoted in *Toronto Globe and Mail* (May 6, 1968), p. 7.

10. Gen. R. 38:7.

11. Tanch. Noah 18; Rashi.

12. See also Cassuto on Gen. 11:5 who calls the verse "a satirical allusion."

13. Midrash ha-Gadol 11:3.

14. See also Apocalypse of Baruch (Greek version) 3:5.

15. Midrash ha-Gadol 11:9; Rashi.

16. John Ruskin, *Lecture on Architecture and Paint-*

ing, quoted in Solomon Goldman, *In the Beginning* (Philadelphia: Jewish Publication Society, 1949), p. 518.

17. Edna St. Vincent Millay, *Conversation at Midnight* (New York: Harper & Row, 1937), p. 100.

18. See Gordon, *Before Columbus* (New York: Crown, 1971), pp. 164 f. He also brings interesting parallels from the Central American (Mayan) *Popol Vuh*.

19. *Journal of Ecumenical Studies*, 8, 3 (Summer 1971), pp. 565 f.

Part III *The Line of Terah. Abraham*

1. William F. Albright and Nelson Glueck choose the earlier age; Ephraim A. Speiser and Cyrus H. Gordon, the later. Westermann, *Genesis*, introduction to chs. 12–50, agrees that there is a historic foundation, without assigning a definite time. Stiebing, *BAR*, 1, 2 (1975), pp. 17 ff., finds the data too uncertain to reach definite conclusions. But John van Seters denies all claims of historicity. On the basis of excavations at Beer-Sheva, Ze'ev Herzog, *BAR*, 6, 6 (1980), pp. 12 ff., suggests that the stories originated during the thirteenth to the eleventh centuries B.C.E., i.e., the period of early settlement in Canaan.

2. Von Rad, *Genesis*, p. 166. But the whole depiction of the nomadic nature of pre-Israelite existence has been drawn into question by N. K. Gottwald, *BAR*, 4, 2 (1978), pp. 2 ff.

3. Kaufmann, *Religion of Israel*, pp. 221 ff.

4. *Hebrew Origins* (New York: Harper and Brothers, rev. ed., 1950), pp. 184 ff.

The Call of Abraham GEN. 11:27—12:9

1. "What befell him also befell his descendants"; Tanch. Lech Lecha 9.

2. See, e.g., Gen. R. 84: 5; Ibn Ezra on Gen. 9:18, 31:42.

3. Gordon, *Before the Bible*, p. 287.

4. See Nachmanides.

5. See Hermann Gunkel, *Genesis* (Göttingen: Vandenhoeck & Ruprecht, 1901), *ad loc.*; Speiser.

6. See *Entsiklopedyah Mikra'it* (Jerusalem: Mosad Bialik, from 1955), Vol. I, cols. 328–329.

7. Spinoza, *Theological Tractate* 8.

8. Maharal (commentary on Rashi). For a Christian point of view, see von Rad, *Genesis*, pp. 155 f.

9. Kaufmann, *Religion of Israel*, p. 60.

10. Avot de-R. Nathan 33; Pirke de-R. Eliezer 26; Gunkel, *Genesis*, p. 164.

11. A. M. Klein, *Poems* (Philadelphia: Jewish Publication Society, 1944), p. 46.

12. Gen. R. 38:13 *et al.*, especially *Ma'aseh Avraham Avinu* (Jellinek, *Bet ha-Midrash* 1:25 ff.); Jubilees 11, 12, 20. Philo considered Abraham's opposition to the Babylonian astrologers the reason for his emigration. The Koran, Sura XXI:53 (The Prophets), utilizes these tales. On the astral religion of Terah, see J. Leroy, *HUCA*, 18 (1944), p. 443; 19 (1945), p. 448; and L. R. Bailey, *HUCA*, 42 (1971), pp. 106 ff. and note 45.

13. Buber, *Prophetic Faith*, p. 88.

14. Millay, *Conversation at Midnight*, pp. 43, 46.

15. *Itture Torah*, Vol. I, p. 83.

16. Gen. R. 39:2.

17. Philo, *On the Migration of Abraham*, 9.

18. Kaufmann, *Religion of Israel*, p. 222.

19. *Joseph and His Brothers*, pp. 6–7.

Wanderings GEN. 12:10—13:18

1. Nelson Glueck, *The River Jordan* (Philadelphia: Jewish Publication Society, 1946), p. 73.

2. See Earle Bennett Cross, *The Hebrew Family: A Study in Historical Sociology* (Chicago: University of Chicago Press, 1927).

3. This interpretation is proposed by Speiser, *Genesis*, pp. 91 ff. See also Sandmel, *JBL*, 80 (June 1961), pp. 105–122. However, Samuel Greengus, *HUCA*, 46 (1976), pp. 1–31, has shown that this theory has serious defects, adoption being reserved for the lower classes and not connected with marriage.

4. Radak; Sforno; Luzzatto.

5. Nachmanides.

6. Josephus, *Antiquities*, I, 8:1, 2.

7. Gunkel.

8. Klaus Koch, *The Growth of the Biblical Tradition* (New York: Scribner's, 1969), p. 127.

9. Pes. 25b; San. 74a.

10. N. Avigad and Y. Yadin, *A Genesis Apocryphon* (Jerusalem: Magnes Press of the Hebrew University, 1956), cols. 20:6 f. (For the Christian Scriptures, see Romans 4:19; 9:9; Hebrews 11:11; I Peter 3:6.) The quotation is a small part of an extravagant descrip-tion of Sarah's beauty. Also see the tale in Gen. R. 40:5 which is similar to the opening story in the *Arabian Nights*.

11. Henry Wadsworth Longfellow, *The Divine Tragedy*, The First Passover, III.

12. Quoted in M. M. Kasher, *Torah Shelemah* (3rd ed., New York; beginning with Vol. 20, Jerusalem: Machon Torah Shelemah, from 1949), 12:145, 565. [Hereafter this work will be referred to as *TS*.]

13. As told by Ginzberg, *Legends*, Vol. I, pp. 221–222.

14. Vol. XI, p. 57.

The War of the Four against the Five GEN. 14

1. The majority of scholars assume a historical incident, but some deny it, especially Gunkel, *Genesis*, pp. 262 ff. See *Biblical Motifs*, ed. Alexander Altmann (Cambridge, Mass.: Harvard University Press, 1966), Michael C. Astour, pp. 65 ff. There is a dispute also over the usual assumption of different sources. For instance, Engnell, *A Rigid Scrutiny*, ed. J. T. Willis (Nashville: Vanderbilt University Press, 1969, p. 54, note 6), strongly maintains the unity of 14:17 and 18. See the analysis by Westermann, *Genesis*, pp. 244 f.

2. See J. Simons, *The Geographical and Topographical Texts of the Old Testament* (Leiden: E. J. Brill, 1959), p. 86.

3. See *BAR*, 5, 6 (1979), pp. 52 f.

4. See *Entsiklopedyah Mikra'it*, Vol. III, p. 272.

5. So Gordon, *JNES*, 13 (1954), p. 57.

6. Glueck, *River Jordan*, p. 74.

7. So Gordon, *Before the Bible*, p. 286.

8. So Albright, *Yahweh and the Gods of Canaan*, who further supports the theory that Eber and Arab are essentially the same terms.

9. This difference is stressed by Moshe Greenberg, "Hab/piru and Hebrews," *World History of the Jewish People*, ed. Benjamin Mazar (New Brunswick: Rutgers University Press, 1970), Vol. II, pp. 188 ff. He con-cludes that Habiru and Ivri describe different groups. However, see Roland de Vaux, *JNES*, 27 (1968), pp. 221–228, who discusses the "ethnic" theory.

10. For a study of terms and relationships, see Greenberg, *loc. cit.*; Mary Gray, *HUCA*, 29 (1958), pp. 135–202; George E. Mendenhall, *The Tenth Generation* (Baltimore and London: Johns Hopkins University, 1973), pp. 121–144.

11. See also Gen. 39:14; 41:12 where Joseph is called a Hebrew, or coming from the land of the Hebrews (Gen. 40:15).

12. Compare Adonizedek; Josh. 10:1. See Roy A. Rosenberg, *HUCA*, 36 (1965), pp. 161 ff.

13. Hebrews 5:6–11.

14. Hebrews 7:1–3.

15. Targum. See also Josephus, *Antiquities*, I, 10:2.

16. See further, *Interpreter's Dictionary*, Vol. III, p. 343; and Ginzberg, *Legends*, Vol. V, p. 225, note 102.

17. Lev. R. 28:4.

18. Gen. R. 42:8.

19. Quoted in Mordecai Hacohen, *Al ha-Torah* (Jerusalem: Reuben Mass, 1962), Vol. I, p. 48.

20. *Joseph and His Brothers*, p. 288.

The Covenant between the Pieces; The Birth of Ishmael GEN. 15—16

1. Albright, *Yahweh and the Gods of Canaan*, pp. 65–66.

2. Romans 4:2, 3; Galatians 3:6–11.

3. James 2:23–26.

4. See Simons, *Geographical and Topographical Texts*, pp. 15 ff. Kaufmann, *Religion of Israel*, pp. 201 ff., dis-tinguishes a series of different conceptions about the shape of the Promised Land in the Bible. For a full discussion of this subject, see Num. 34:1 ff.

5. Gen. R. 45:2.

6. Pritchard, *ANET*, Code of Hammurabi 146, p. 172.

7. Quoted by Speiser, *Genesis*, p. 120.

8. On the question of concubine and slave wife, see Louis Epstein, *Marriage Laws in the Bible and Talmud* (Cambridge, Mass.: Harvard University Press, 1942), pp. 55 ff.

9. Compare Wellhausen; Tur-Sinai.

10. Nahum Sarna, *Understanding Genesis* (New York: McGraw-Hill, 1966), p. 127.

11. See James Frazer, quoted in Gaster, *Myth*, pp. 140 ff., where arguments for various theories are marshaled. For Greek parallels, see Gordon, *Before the Bible*, p. 96.

12. Koran, Sura IV:124 (The Women).

13. Brichto, *HUCA*, 39 (1968), pp. 44 f.

14. John Ruskin, *Fors Clavigera*, Letter 65, quoted in Goldman, *In the Beginning*, p. 541.

15. Leo Baeck, *This People Israel* (Philadelphia: Jewish Publication Society, 1965), p. 12.

16. Note on *Shulchan Aruch*, Even ha-Ezer 1:3 and 154:6. The relevant law is based on Yeb. 64a and Tosefta Yeb. 8:4. For a detailed treatment, see P. Dickstein, *Dine nisu'in vegerushin* (Tel Aviv: Yavneh, 1956), Ch. XI.

17. Pritchard, *ANET*, p. 353.

The Covenant of Circumcision GEN. 17

1. Speiser.

2. R. H. 16b.

3. So Rashi.

4. So Gen. R. 47:4.

5. Zohar 1:93b.

6. For a general survey of the practice, see *Encyclopedia of Religion and Ethics*, ed. James Hastings (New York: Scribner's, 1924–1927), Vol. III, pp. 659 ff., under "Circumcision." Also Morgenstern, *Rites of Birth, Marriage, Death and Kindred Occasions* (Cincinnati, Ohio: Hebrew Union College Press, 1966), pp. 48 ff.; Charles Weiss, *Journal of Sex Research*, 2, 2 (1966), pp. 69–88, discusses psychoanalytic dimensions.

7. Herodotus, *History*, Vol. II, 36, 104; Maimonides, *Guide*, II, 49.

8. Mishnah Nid. 5:3; Jer. Ned. 3 to end (38b).

9. Tanch. Lech Lecha 20.

10. Gen. R. 11:6. Also see Ned. 31b; Rashi; Baruch Epstein, *Torah Temimah* on Gen. 17:1.

11. See Isserles to *Shulchan Aruch*, Yoreh De'ah 335:10.

12. See Freehof, *Reform Jewish Practice* (Cincinnati, Ohio: Hebrew Union College Press, 1944), Vol. II, pp. 113 f.

13. See the discussion in Sab. 132a; Freehof, *Reform Responsa* (Cincinnati, Ohio: Hebrew Union College Press, 1960), pp. 90 ff.

14. Freehof, *Current Reform Responsa* (Cincinnati, Ohio: Hebrew Union College Press, 1963), p. 95.

15. The laws are conveniently summarized in Hyman Goldin, *HaMadrikh* (rev. ed., New York: Hebrew Publishing Company, 1956), pp. 27 ff.

16. Pes. R. 23:4.

The Messengers GEN. 18:1–15

1. Maimonides, *Guide*, II, 42. For a Greek parallel to the tale, see Homer, *Odyssey*, XVII, 485 ff.; also see, Gunkel, *Genesis*, p. 200.

2. B. M. 87a.

3. Nachmanides.

4. Luzzatto.

5. Gen. R. 48:14.

6. But see Ginzberg, *Legends*, Vol. V, p. 235, note 140.

7. Ovid, *Fasti*, V, 493–544.

8. Also see Bamberger, *Fallen Angels*, passim.

9. Gordon, *Before the Bible*, p. 291.

10. B. M. 86b.

11. Midrash ha-Gadol, Vayera 1.

12. Shev. 35b; Sab. 127a; and Rashi on 18:3.

13. Avot de-R. Nathan 13; Gen. R. 48:13.

14. The original source of the story is not known. See Bamberger, *Proselytism in the Talmudic Period* (Cincinnati, Ohio: Hebrew Union College Press, 1939), p. 209, note 17.

15. Based on the quotation in *On Jewish Learning*, ed. Nahum Glatzer (New York: Schocken, 1955), p. 124.

16. B. M. 87a. See also Yeb. 65b.

Sodom and Gomorrah GEN. 18:16—19:38

1. Mishnah Bik. 1:4 and Bertinoro thereto; differently, Jer. Bik. 1:4, 64a. Also see Tosafot to B. B. 81a; Maimonides, Hilch. Bikkurim 4:3, and his letter to the convert Obadiah.

2. See Gleanings and notes 10 and 11.

3. On this subject, see Arthur Marmorstein, *The Doctrine of Merits in Old Rabbinical Literature* (London: Jew's College, 1920).

4. Mishnah San. 1:6.

5. Pirke de-R. Eliezer 25; Zohar Vayera 108b–109a.

6. Gen. R. 49:6.

7. Sheldon H. Blank, *Prophetic Faith in Isaiah* (New York: Harper & Row, 1958), pp. 199 ff.

8. See Gen. R. 50:9.

9. See Zohar, *loc. cit.*; Pirke de-R. Eliezer 25; Sefer ha-Yashar 62 on the legend of a "procrustean bed" in Sodom.

10. Wisdom of Solomon 10:6–8. Deuteronomy 29:23 mentions four cities (adding Admah and Zeboiim), while Wisdom and other ancient sources also count Zoar in the number, making it five altogether.

11. *Views of the Biblical World* (Chicago and New York: Jordan Publishing Company, 1959–1961), Vol. I, pp. 60–61; Josephus, *Antiquities*, I, 11:4; *idem, The Jewish War*, trans. William Whiston (New York: Al Burt Co., n.d.), IV, 8:4.

Crises GEN. 20—21

1. Jer. Meg. 1:9, 71d.

2. See Rashi; Rashbam; Sforno.

3. Hallo, *Journal of the American Oriental Society*, 88 (1968), pp. 71–89. [Hereafter cited as *JAOS*.]

4. Ket. 60a; II Macc. 7:29.

5. See Rashi; note rejoinder of Nachmanides.

6. Pritchard, *ANET*, p. 160.

7. Maimonides, *Guide*, I, 44.

8. Speiser.

9. Ta'an. 14b.

10. Zvi Adar, *The Biblical Narrative* (Jerusalem: World Zionist Organization, 1959), p. 123.

11. Gen. R. 52:13.

12. See Galatians 4:21–5:1.

13. *Handwörterbuch des Islam*, ed. A. J. Wensick and H. J. Kramer (Leiden: E. J. Brill, 1941), under "Islam."

14. Koran, Sura XIX:55 (Mary). Enoch (Idris) is described in the same fashion. It may be noted that both here and in Sura XXI:85 (The Prophets) Enoch is listed *after* Ishmael.

15. Gen. R. 53:14.

16. See Ginzberg, *Legends*, Vol. V, p. 248, note 225.

17. Louis Isaac Rabinowitz, *Jerusalem Post* (November 3, 1969), p. 13.

18. As told by Ginzberg, *Legends*, Vol. I, p. 239, based on Gen. R. 45:5–8, 46:3, and other sources; see Ginzberg, Vol. V, pp. 232–233, notes 122 and 123.

19. Zvi Adar, *Biblical Narrative*, p. 123.

The Akedah GEN. 22

1. Gen. R. 56:8.

2. See Josephus, *Antiquities*, I, 13:2; Jubilees 18:13.

3. Speiser.

4. Reproduced in *From Adam to Daniel*, ed. G. Cornfeld (New York: Macmillan, 1962), p. 75.

5. Compare Euripides' play, *Iphigenia at Aulis*. On the use of the Akedah in ancient decorations, see Bernard Goldman, *The Sacred Portal* (Detroit: Wayne State University Press, 1966), pp. 53 ff.

6. Eduard Meyer, *Die Israeliten und ihre Nachbarstämme* (Halle: M. Niemeyer, 1906), p. 241.

7. Jer. Sotah 5:8, 20c. This was, however, a minority opinion. The majority held that Job was a contemporary of Moses; see B. B. 14b.

8. See Morgenstern, *Rites*, p. 182.

9. John 3:16.

10. Robert Graves and Raphael Patai, *Hebrew Myths* (London: Cassel, 1963–1964), p. 176.

11. Hebrews 11:17–19; James 2:21 f.

12. Zohar 1:119b.

13. IV Macc. 14:20.

14. *Ethics of the Fathers* 5:3; Pirke de-R. Eliezer 26.

15. Maimonides, *Guide*, III, 24; Nachmanides. See also Nehama Leibowitz, *Iyyunim Besefer Bereshit* (Jerusalem: Ha-Histradrut ha-Tsiyonit ha-Olamit, 1966). p. 134.

16. Rosenzweig, *Star of Redemption*, p. 266.

17. Gen. R. 56:8; see also Rashi and Bachya on text.

18. Gen. R. 56:8.

19. See Ta'an. 16a and Tosafot. Also Shalom Spiegel, *The Last Trial* (Philadelphia: Jewish Publication Society, 1968), who devotes an entire volume to this tradition.

20. Based on the midrashim cited in previous note.

21. Divre Hayim 9, quoted in *Itture Torah*, Vol. I, p. 161.

22. R. H. 16a where the ceremony is described.

23. Shulchan Aruch shel ha-Rav, quoted by Shmuel Y. Agnon, *Days of Awe* (New York: Schocken, 1965), pp. 68–69.

24. Saadia, quoted by Agnon, *Days of Awe*, pp. 71–72.

25. Ikkarim 3:36, based on San. 89b and Rashi.

26. *Musaf* service.

27. Koran, Sura XXXVII:100–109 (The Ranks).

28. Kaplan, unpublished manuscript.

29. S. R. Driver, *Genesis* (New York: Edwin S. Gorham, 1904), p. 222.

30. Erich Auerbach, *Mimesis* (Garden City, N. Y.: Doubleday, 1957), pp. 6–7.

31. Sören Kierkegaard, *Fear and Trembling* (Princeton, N.J.: Princeton University Press, 1945), pp. xvi, 89–90.

32. Fackenheim, *Quest for Past and Future* (Bloomington: Indiana University Press, 1968), pp. 64 f.

33. Wellisch, *Isaac and Oedipus* (London: Routledge and Kegan Paul, 1954), pp. 114 ff.

34. Quoted by N. M. Waldman, *Reconstructionist* (October 1978), pp. 13 ff.

The Death of Sarah GEN. 23

1. *Interpreter's Dictionary*, Supplement, p. 412; M. Noth, *Uberlieferungsgeschichte des Pentateuchs* (Stuttgart: W. Kohlhammer, 2nd ed., 1960), p. 170; different, von Rad, *ad loc.*

2. Compare Herbert Petschow, *Journal of Cuneiform Studies*, 19, 4 (1965), pp. 103 ff.; Gene M. Tucker, *JBL*, 85 (March 1966), pp. 77 ff.

3. The antiquity of the grave stones is discussed by Yosef Breslavi, *Beth Mikra*, 36, 1 (January 1969), pp. 50 ff.

4. Gen. R. 58:1; Midrash ha-Gadol.

5. Gen. R. 79:7.

6. San. 91a.

7. *TS*, Vol. IV, p. 918, note 5.

8. *Ibid.*; Midrash Mishle 31. See also Ginzberg, *Legends*, Vol. V, p. 258.

9. M. K. 27b.

10. Avot de-R. Nathan 44.

11. *Itture Torah*, Vol. I, p. 180.

12. See *Encyclopaedia Judaica*, Vol. 11, cols. 670–674.

Rebekah at the Well GEN. 24:1—25:18

1. See *Jewish Encyclopedia* (New York: Funk & Wagnalls, 1901–1906), Vol. VIII, pp. 335 ff., for polygamy and monogamy in Jewish history.

2. So Speiser. For a different interpretation, see R. D. Freedman, *BAR*, 2, 2 (1976), pp. 3–4.

3. Nachmanides.

4. Mishnah Ket. 5:2.

5. Gen. R. 61:4; Rashi. Ibn Ezra denies this.

6. Gen. R. 68:4.

7. Sotah 2a.

8. Medieval commentators discussed this problem in detail: cf., especially, Abarbanel, *ad loc.*; Nachmanides at the end of *sidrah* בֹּא; Maimonides, Hilch. Akkum 11:4; and Rabad's critique thereon.

9. Based on Stanley Gevirtz.

10. Sarna, *Understanding Genesis*, pp. 84–85.

11. Gen. R. 65:9, 59:6.

12. Compare Rashi; Hacohen, *Al ha-Torah*, Vol. I, p. 69.

13. As told by Ginzberg, *Legends*, Vol. I, pp. 305–306, based on "The Testament of Abraham," a pseudepigraphic work.

The Twins GEN. 25:19–34

1. Pritchard, *ANET*, "Gilgamesh," p. 74.
2. Speiser; Cassuto.
3. Jeremias, *Das Alte Testament*, p. 315.
4. *Ibid.*, p. 316.
5. Tur-Sinai.
6. So B. Jacob.
7. Reference and sources in Sarna, *Understanding Genesis*, pp. 185 ff.
8. Compare *TS 1037:210.*
9. Rashbam; Sforno; but see Nachmanides.
10. So, especially, Gunkel, *ad loc.* The term "gamesmanship" is applied by Speiser.
11. See Rashi; Sforno.
12. So von Rad.
13. Gen. R. 63:6 ff.
14. Ginzberg, *Legends*, Vol. V, p. 278, note 51.
15. John Bunyan, *The Pilgrim's Progress*, quoted by S. Goldman, *In the Beginning*, p. 596.
16. Roger Williams, letter to Major Mason, June 22, 1670, quoted in S. Goldman, *In the Beginning*, p. 399.
17. Sarna, *Understanding Genesis*, p. 188.
18. So Cassuto, See *Entsiklopedyah Mikra'it*, Vol. III, p. 722.
19. IV Esdras 6:8–10.
20. Maurice Samuel, *Certain People of the Book* (New York: Alfred A. Knopf, 1955), p. 163.
21. Henry E. Kagan, lecture delivered at UAHC Biennial, Chicago, November 16, 1963.

The Life of Isaac GEN. 26

1. Speiser.
2. She was so characterized by Samuel, *Certain People of the Book*, pp. 130–185. Also see p. 275. For a characterization of Isaac, see also Adar, *Biblical Narrative*, pp. 70 ff.
3. Leibowitz, *Iyyunim*, p. 183.
4. Hacohen, *Al ha-Torah*, Vol. I, p. 80.
5. Adler, *The Voice Still Speaks*, p. 105.
6. R. Beer-Hofmann, *Jacob's Dream*, trans. I. B. Wynn (Philadelphia: Jewish Publication Society, 1946), p. 85.

Isaac Blesses His Sons GEN. 27:1—28:9

1. Similarly Radak.
2. Malbim.
3. Sforno; Rashbam.
4. So also Nachmanides and Rashbam.
5. Stanley Gevirtz, *Patterns in the Early Poetry of Israel* (Chicago: University of Chicago Press, 1963), pp. 35–47.
6. Gunkel, *ad loc.*
7. See de Vaux, *Genèse* (Paris: Les Editions du Cerf, 1953), p. 125, note d.
8. Zohar, Genesis 145a.
9. See Tanch. Toledot 171.
10. See the detailed discussion by W. Gunther Plaut, *Journal of the Central Conference of American Rabbis* [hereafter cited as *CCAR Journal*] (June 1960), pp. 30 ff.
11. See Thomas Mann, *Joseph and His Brothers*, p. 131. Similarly, Samuel, *Certain People of the Book*, p. 166.
12. See Naphtali Berlin in his comment on Gen. 24:65.
13. *Entsiklopedyah Mikra'it*, Vol. II, p. 357; see *ibid.* for literature. Also see *Interpreter's Dictionary*, Vol. I, pp. 446 ff.
14. Samuel E. Karff, manuscript work, by permission.
15. Amy K. Blank, *The Spoken Choice* (Cincinnati, Ohio: Hebrew Union College Press, 1959); pp. 11 ff.
16. De Vaux, *Genèse*, p. 126.
17. Gen. R. 65:20; Bachya; Malbim.
18. Gen. R. 65:19.

Jacob's Dream GEN. 28:10–22

1. On the parallels to this image, see *Interpreter's Dictionary*, Vol. I, p. 130, under "Angel"; H. A. Hoffner, Jr., *JBL*, 86 (December 1967), p. 397. Note that the staircase of the Babylonian *zikkurrat* is called *simmiltu*, possibly—by transposition—from the same root as *sulam*. For a different interpretation (*sulam* as "way" to the Bethel sanctuary of later days), see C. Houtman, *VT*, 27 (1977), pp. 337–351.

2. See Kaufmann, *Religion of Israel*, p. 259.

3. So, e.g., Malbim.

4. Gen. R. 70:4. See the commentary of Z. W. Einhorn (Maharzu).

5. On the subject of vows in Psalms, see especially H. Gunkel and J. Begrich, *Einleitung in die Psalmen* (Göttingen: Vandenhoek & Ruprecht, 1933), pp. 247–250.

6. Gen. R. 68:12. See the commentary of S. Straschun (Hareshash), note 6.

7. Gen. R. 68:12; Lev. R. 29:2.

8. John Ruskin, *The Crown of Wild Olive*, quoted by S. Goldman, *In the Beginning*, p. 611.

9. Gen. R. 68:9; Pirke de-R. Eliezer 35.

10. Pirke de-R. Eliezer 35.

11. Quoted by Hacohen, *Al ha-Torah*, Vol. I, pp. 91 f.

12. Beer-Hofmann, *Jacob's Dream*, pp. 170 f.

13. *Heaven Take My Hand* (Toronto: McClelland and Stewart, 1968), pp. 20 f.

Jacob in Haran GEN. 29—30

1. Compare Homer, *Iliad*, XII, 451.

2. Targum: "pleasing eyes"; similarly S.R. Hirsch.

3. Speiser.

4. Buber and Rosenzweig, *Die Schrift und ihre Verdeutschung* (Berlin: Schocken, 1936), pp. 224 ff. See also above, commentary to Gen. 27:1–28:9.

5. Also see Rabinowitz, *Jerusalem Post* (November 28, 1968; January 13 and January 20, 1970).

6. See also JPS *Notes*.

7. Speiser. In Gen. 44:5, 15, Joseph is also reported to have practiced divination.

8. See JPS *Notes*.

9. Martin Noth, *The History of Israel* (New York: Harper & Row, 1956), pp. 85 ff., suggests the existence of an amphictyony, but this is disputed by others. See also John Bright, "Early Israel," in *Old Testament Issues*, ed. Sandmel (New York-Evanston-London: Harper & Row, 1968), pp. 159 ff.

10. See Otto Eissfeldt, *The Old Testament* (New York: Harper & Row, 1965), p. 40, with further references. See also above, commentary to Gen. 49:1–27.

11. See Gen. R. 73:10.

12. See Bachya on Gen. 30:38.

13. Midrash Lekach Tov.

14. John Calvin, *Commentaries*, trans. John King (Grand Rapids, Mich.: Eerdmans, 1948–1950), Vol. II, p. 128.

15. Von Rad, *Genesis*, p. 268.

16. Midrash Yelammedenu and Midrash Lekach Tov.

17. Gaster, *Myth*, p. 200.

Jacob's Departure from Haran GEN. 31:1—32:3

1. Rashi.

2. See JPS *Notes*.

3. Jer. Sab. 17a.

4. Nachmanides; see also B. Jacob.

5. Pritchard, *ANET*, p. 177. For an actual court case in Hurrian law, see Hallo, *JAOS*, 87 (1967), p. 64, note 1.

6. Gordon, *Before the Bible*, pp. 249 ff. See also above, note to Gen. 2:24.

7. See Driver.

8. Josephus, *Antiquities*, XVIII, 9:5.

9. Moshe Greenberg, *JBL*, 81 (1962), pp. 239 ff.; so also Gunkel, *Genesis*, pp. 344 ff. On the etymology of תְּרָפִים see Hoffner, Jr., *JNES*, 27, 1 (1968), pp. 61 ff.

10. Speiser, *Genesis*, p. 250.

11. So Gen. R. 74:5.

12. So Rashbam; Ibn Ezra; based on Tanch. Vayetze 12.

13. B. M. 93b.

14. Gaster, *Myth*, p. 201.

15. Quoted, *ibid.*, p. 204.

16. Vergil, *Aeneid*, II, 293 f.

Jacob Becomes Israel GEN. 32:4—33:17

1. So Speiser; see JPS *Notes*.
2. See also Nachmanides and Sforno on Gen. 32:21.
3. So J. L. Benor, *Beth Mikra*, 58 (1974), pp. 435–440.
4. For a different interpretation, see S. Gevirtz, *HUCA*, 46 (1976), pp. 50–54, who sees *gid ha-nasheh* as a hint at Gad and Manasseh.
5. El-Amarna letters and Ugarit.
6. For Mesopotamian and Greek parallels, cf. Gunkel, *Genesis*, pp. 363 f.; Graves and Patai, *Hebrew Myths*, pp. 227 f.
7. Compare Shakespeare, *Hamlet*, Act I, Scene 1; Plautus, *Amphitryon*, Act I, Scene 3.
8. Morgenstern, *Book of Genesis*, pp. 270 ff.; Maimonides, *Guide*, II, 42; also Ralbag, commentary, *ad loc.*; and Milch. ha-Shem 6.
9. Abarbanel.
10. Koran, Sura III:87 (The Family of Imran).
11. Quoted in *Ma'yanah shel Torah*, Vol. I, p. 148.
12. Quoted in *Itture Torah*, Vol. I, p. 293.
13. Kaplan, unpublished manuscript.
14. The ambiguity recurs in II Sam. 24:1 and I Chron.

21:1. Compare Gen. R. 77:3 (the man was Esau's protective angel) and sources quoted in *TS*, 32:116, note (he was Samael). In Beer-Hofmann, *Jacob's Dream*, angels as well as Samael wrestle with him. See also A. J. Wolf, *CCAR Journal* (October 1961), p. 47; von Rad, *Genesis*, p. 316.
15. Based on Gen. R. 76:2.
16. Based on Sifre Beha'alotecha.
17. Gen. R. 78:9.
18. Hul. 89b ff.; Yoreh De'ah 65:5–7.
19. Jessie Sampter, *Brand Plucked from the Fire* (Philadelphia: Jewish Publication Society, 1937), p. 170.
20. From *An Anthology of American Negro Literature*, ed. S. C. Watkins (New York: Modern Library, 1944), p. 144.
21. Fineman, *Jacob* (New York: Random House, 1941), pp. 179–180.
22. "A Jungian Midrash on Jacob's Dream," *Reconstructionist*, October 1976, pp. 22–23.
23. *Psychoanalysis and the Bible* (New York: Bloch Publishing Co., 1974), p. 52.

The Rape of Dinah GEN. 33:18—34:31

1. See JPS *Notes*.
2. Rashi and Rashbam favor the latter interpretation.
3. See Gen. R. 80:12.
4. Gen. R. 80:11; B. B. 15b; Pirke de-R. Eliezer 38.
5. B. Jacob. Gunkel, in line with his general assessment of biblical morality, thinks that the Torah relates the incident "with satisfaction," *ad* Gen. 34:28. See also W. R. Bowie, *Interpreter's Bible* (New York

and Nashville: Abingdon, 1957), *ad loc.*
6. See Midrash ha-Chefetz 9; in *TS*, 34:59.
7. Judith 9:2 ff.
8. Koh. R. 10:8; Tanch. Vayishlach 5.
9. Johann Wolfgang von Goethe, Letter to Sara von Grothuss, 1812; quoted in S. Goldman, *In the Beginning*, p. 634.
10. *Jacob*, pp. 208–209.

Births and Deaths GEN. 35—36

1. On this see B. Gemser, *O. T. Studien*, 12 (1958), pp. 1 ff.
2. See E. C. Kingsbury, *HUCA*, 38 (1967), p. 136.
3. See Orach Chayim, Yoreh De'ah 282.
4. J-source, Ch. 28; E-source, Ch. 35.
5. J. H. Hertz.
6. B. Jacob, *Genesis*, p. 664.
7. Note Gen. R. 82:10; also Rashi; Biur.

8. M. Tsevat, *HUCA*, 33 (1962), pp. 107 ff.
9. So the Samaritan version; Hertz. At Mari, a major tribe was known as "Sons of the South" (*Maru-Yamina*).
10. D. Cohen, *Beth Mikra*, 73 (1978), pp. 239–241.
11. Meg. 4:10.
12. Sab. 55b. Note the parallel in the *Iliad*, Vol. IX, 446 ff.

13. Rashi.

14. For a full discussion of this question, see de Vaux, *Revue Biblique*, 74 (1967), pp. 481–503.

15. See JPS *Notes*.

16. See Jer. Ber. 8:5, 12b; Pes. 54a; and Rabbenu Tam's comment on B. B. 115b.

17. Driver.

18. B. Jacob.

19. Midrash Or ha-Afelah 9, quoted in *TS*, 35: 110.

20. Jer. Shek. 2:5, 47a; and Gen. R. 82:10.

21. Abraham Isaac Kuk, *Iggerot Re'ayah* (1st ed., Jerusalem: Hotsa'at Yerushalayim, 1923), Vol. I, p. 190.

22. Beer-Hofmann, *Jacob's Dream*, pp. 60–61.

23. Morgenstern, *Book of Genesis*, p. 229.

24. *Joseph and His Brothers*, p. 94.

Part V *The Line of Jacob*

1. For an extensive analysis of the entire story, see Donald B. Redford, *A Study of the Biblical Story of Joseph* (Leiden: E. J. Brill, 1970).

2. Aristotle's term is "Peripety" which, when combined with "Discovery" (as in the Joseph story), produces the most effective drama; see *Poetics*, XII. This theme is stressed also by N. Tucker; *Beth Mikra*, 77 (1979), pp. 170–179. For a literary analysis of the Joseph story, see K. Seybold, *Literary Interpretations of Biblical Narratives*, ed. Kenneth R. R. Gros Louis (New York and Nashville: Abingdon Press, 1974), pp. 59 ff.

Young Joseph GEN. 37

1. Gunkel. See JPS *Notes* for a summary of interpretations. Also Gaster, *Myth*, p. 216, who believes it was a coat of extra length reaching to the ankles.

2. Sotah 11a.

3. J. Vergote, *Joseph en Egypte* (Louvain: Publications Universitaires, 1959), pp. 146 ff.

4. For a detailed analysis, see Plaut, *CCAR Journal* (April 1969), pp. 65 ff. See also Gen. R. 84:18. The Joseph story is retold, with special additions, in the Koran, Sura XII:2–19 (Joseph, Peace Be on Him); for an excerpt, see Gleanings, "The Story in Moslem Tradition."

5. Sura XII:2–19 (Joseph, Peace Be on Him).

Tamar GEN. 38

1. Compare Gen. R. 85:1.

2. Targum; Rashi.

3. See Even ha-Ezer 9:1.

4. So I. Robinson, *JBL*, 96 (1977), p. 569. For a different interpretation, see G. Bitton, *Beth Mikra*, 75 (1978), pp. 478–479.

5. Herodotus, *History*, Vol. I, 199, tells of the widespread observance of this custom in Babylonia.

6. This is explained by Michael C. Astour, *JBL*, 85 (1966), pp. 185 ff.

7. Graves and Patai, *Hebrew Myths*, p. 247, quote also an Ethiopian seduction tale.

8. So Rashbam; Radak; Hizkuni.

9. Compare Midrash Lekach Tov.

10. *Commentary* magazine, December 1975, p. 76, see also J. Goldin, *JBL*, 96 (1977), pp. 27–44; H. Gilad, *Beth Mikra*, 64 (1975), pp. 127–128.

11. *TS*, 38:6–8.

12. *Shulchan Aruch*, Even ha-Ezer 165:1; see also *Encyclopaedia Judaica*, Vol. 11, cols. 122 ff.

13. F. Delitzsch, quoted by von Rad, *Genesis*, p. 35, note.

14. As told by Ginzberg, *Legends*, Vol. II, pp. 35–36.

15. *A Study of the Biblical Story of Joseph*, p. 18.

Joseph in Egypt GEN. 39—40

1. T. O. Lambdin, *JAOS*, 73 (1953), pp. 145 ff.
2. See *Interpreter's Dictionary*, Vol. II, p. 667; J. van Seters, *The Hyksos* (New Haven and London: Yale University Press, 1966).
3. Gordon, *Before the Bible*, p. 114.
4. Compare Orlinsky, *Ancient Israel*, pp. 32 ff.
5. So Ibn Ezra; Radak; Hizkuni; and others. In Gen. R. 86:6 "bread" has a sexual connotation.
6. Sefer ha-Yashar.
7. Abarbanel and Sforno make this point. Gunkel, *Genesis*, citing Diodorus, suggests that castration would have been another and more likely punishment.
8. See Vergote, *Joseph en Egypte*, pp. 35 ff.
9. Compare W. Kornfeld, *Revue Biblique*, 57 (1950), pp. 92 ff.
10. San. 56a–b; see commentary to 8:15–9:29; see Rashi on Gen. 39:9.
11. See Ber. 55b.
12. Pritchard, *ANET*, p. 495. See also Oppenheim on interpretation of dreams in the ancient Near East, *Transactions of the American Philosophical Society*, 46, 3 (1956). And see "Mesopotamia" in *Entsiklopedyah Mikra'it*, Vol. V, cols. 59 ff.
13. See Ber. 55–57.
14. *TS*, 39:18 ff.
15. Midrash ha-Gadol; Zohar 1:246a; Rashi; Abarbanel.
16. *TS*, 39:18 ff.; Gen. R. 98:20. On the *shalshelet* and other rare accents in the light of Midrash, see D. B. Weisberg, *Jewish Quarterly Review*, 57 (1966), p. 64. See also note to Gen. 24:12.
17. Midrash Or ha-Afelah.
18. Pritchard, *ANET*, p. 24.

The Elevation of Joseph: The Brothers' First Visit GEN. 41—42

1. Targum Onkelos.
2. See *Joseph et Aseneth*, ed. M. Philonenko (Leiden: E. J. Brill, 1968); *Jewish Encyclopedia*, Vol. II, pp. 172 ff.
3. Gen. R 84:7.
4. Pritchard, *ANET*, pp. 31–32. The record claims to stem from the Pharaoh Djoser (*ca.* 2800 B.C.E.).
5. After Sefer ha-Yashar.
6. Gen. R. 91:1 preserved this implication.
7. Ruth Brin, *A Rag of Love* (Minneapolis, Minn.: Emmett, 1969), p. 41.

The Second Visit GEN. 43:1—44:17

1. Compare Maimonides, *Guide*, III, 40.
2. Biur; Luzzatto.
3. Herodotus, *History*, Vol. I, 241.
4. Compare von Rad.
5. For further references, see the survey in *Jewish Encyclopedia*, Vol. IV, pp. 623–624.
6. San. 65b. See also Maimonides, Hilch. Akkum 11:4; and Kesef Mishneh, *ad loc*.
7. Midrash ha-Gadol.
8. Quoted by Gunkel.
9. Berachot, end.
10. *Certain People of the Book*, pp. 309–310.

Joseph Reveals His Identity GEN. 44:18—45:15

1. B. Jacob.
2. Pritchard, *ANET*, p. 259.
3. Rashi; Nachmanides *et al.*
4. Rashi.
5. See commentary to 41:1–42:38.
6. Gen. R. 21:6.
7. This emphasis is made by Josephus, *Antiquities*, II, 6:7; Jubilees 42:25; and sources quoted in *TS*, 44:14.
8. Gen. R. 93:6.
9. *Itture Torah*, Vol. I, p. 389.
10. Gen. R. 93:7; Rashi; and see Alshech.
11. *Antiquities*, II, 6:8.

Jacob Goes to Egypt GEN. 45:16—46:27

1. Sforno.
2. See Hul. 90b.
3. Rashi and Ibn Ezra.
4. Rashbam.
5. See sources quoted in *TS*, 45:88 on midrashic elaborations of this scene.
6. Compare B. Jacob.
7. Zohar Vayechi 226a; Chochmat Adam 157:9. Nowadays the mitzvah of closing the eyes is usually fulfilled by the burial society. Mishnah Sab. 23:5 prohibits such closing on the Sabbath.
8. Rashbam; Hizkuni; Sforno. See also JPS *Notes*.
9. See JPS *Notes* for a discussion of this counting.
10. Midrash ha-Gadol; Sefer ha-Yashar.
11. Speiser.
12. Compare Gen. R. 94:9 for a sample of how the Midrash dealt with the problem.
13. Midrash ha-Gadol; Midrash Lekach Tov; see also von Rad, *Genesis*, p. 397.
14. Sforno follows this line of reasoning.
15. *Ethics of the Fathers* 3:16.
16. Mech. Pischa 14.
17. Zohar Vayigash 1:210a.
18. See, e.g., Ber. 5a; San. 101a,b; Ta'an. 8a.
19. Zohar Vayigash 210a.
20. Midrash Lekach Tov; cf. Nachmanides.
21. Reported in the name of R. Simeon (Avot de-R. Nathan 30) and R. Hiya (Gen. R. 94:3).
22. Mech. Shira 3.
23. *On Joseph*, 42.

Jacob in Egypt GEN. 46:28—47:27

1. So, e.g., B. Jacob.
2. See T. Reinach, *Textes des Auteurs Grecs et Romains Relatifs au Judaisme* (Paris: Ernest Leroux, 1895), p. 23.
3. Rashi, following Gen. R. 95:4.
4. Ehrlich; Speiser.
5. See the use of the term in Prov. 30:8, 31:15. On priestly privilege in antiquity, see Diodorus, *Historical Library*, Vol. I, 54, 73 f.; Herodotus, *History*, Vol. II, 168 f.
6. See Speiser.
7. Hertz.
8. Von Rad, *Genesis*, p. 404.
9. See, e.g., Gunkel.
10. I Macc. 10:30; other details in Driver, *Genesis*, ad loc.
11. Speiser, *Genesis*, p. 353.
12. See Plaut, *CCAR Journal* (October 1961), pp. 29 ff.
13. Gen. R. 95:3; Rashi; *Itture Torah*, p. 420.
14. Amy K. Blank, *Spoken Choice*, pp. 21, 25, excerpts.
15. *Democracy Reborn*, quoted by S. Goldman, *In the Beginning*, pp. 685 f.
16. *On Joseph*, 43.

The Blessing of Ephraim and Manasseh GEN. 47:28—48:22

1. Bachya; Midrash ha-Gadol.
2. So Midrash ha-Gadol; Nachmanides; Bachya.
3. So Rashi, following the Talmud, Meg. 16b.
4. So Ibn Ezra; Sforno. See Tanch. Vayechi 3.
5. Midrash Aggadah.
6. Also in Hebrews 11:21.
7. See *TS* and Driver, *Genesis*, ad loc.
8. The textual translation "crossing his hands" follows the Septuagint. See JPS *Notes* for further discussion and references.
9. O. Procksch, *Die Genesis übersetz und erklärt* (Leipzig: A. Deichert, 1913), ad loc.
10. B. Jacob, in reference to Josh. 24:32, which states that Joseph was buried at Shechem, "in the parcel of ground which Jacob bought," and that this property became the inheritance of the children of Joseph.
11. Jubilees 34:1–9 notes such a tradition which may itself be an outflow of Gen. 48:22.
12. So Abarbanel; Ehrlich. See also John 4:5.
13. Mech. Beshalach 3.
14. Gen. R. 97:6.
15. Midrash ha-Chefetz.
16. Gittin 13a.
17. Quoted in *Wellsprings of Torah*, pp. 93–94.
18. *Ibid.*, p. 95.

Jacob's Testament GEN. 49:1–27

1. Compare Gevirtz, *Patterns*, pp. 35 ff.
2. Compare Jeremias, *Das Alte Testament*, pp. 343 ff.
3. Josh. 19:1; Judg. 1:3.
4. See the discussion in JPS *Notes*.
5. So Hizkuni; Delitzsch; B. Jacob.
6. Following Rashi. On this passage and the verses to follow (Gen. 49:5–7, 8–12), see the discussion by C. M. Carmichael, *JBL*, 88 (December 1969), Part IV, pp. 435–444.
7. The translation follows Rashi and Tanchuma. The derivation from the Greek, there suggested, is however in error. Compare Mitchell Dahood, *Catholic Biblical Quarterly*, 23 (1961), pp. 54–56, who translates "circumcision blades."
8. Isa. 18:7; Ps. 68:30, 76:12 have the word שַׁי meaning tribute or present. See also Gen. R. 97 (new version). There exists a large body of literature devoted to an interpretation of this single phrase; cf. Driver, *Genesis*, pp. 410 ff.; Gunkel, Skinner, and B. Jacob, *ad loc.*; also Eissfeldt, Supplement to *VT*, 4 (1957), pp. 138–147. For a contemporary interpretation, see Monford Harris, in *Rediscovering Judaism*, ed. Wolf, pp. 99 ff.
9. See Targum Onkelos; San. 98b; Gen. R. 97 (new version); Zohar 1:25b.
10. Matthew 21:5, in connection with Zech. 9:9.
11. Yalkut Shimoni 161.
12. Ibn Ezra; Radak *et al.* Ehrlich thinks that Gen. 49:18 is an ejaculation by the falling rider.
13. Delitzsch.
14. See JPS *Notes* for discussion and reference.
15. Jer. Hor. 2:5, 46d; Gen. R. 98:20.
16. Compare Rashbam.
17. S. Gevirtz, *HUCA*, 46 (1976), pp. 35 ff.
18. Mann, *I Believe*, ed. Clifton Fadiman (New York: Simon and Schuster, 1939), pp. 189–194.
19. Koran, Sura XII:37–40 (Joseph, Peace Be on Him).
20. Bowie, *Interpreter's Bible*, pp. 821–822.
21. *Certain People of the Book*, pp. 344–345.

The Deaths of Jacob and Joseph GEN. 49:28—50:26

1. Herodotus, *History*, Vol. II, 86 ff.; Diodorus, *Historical Library*, Vol. I, 72, 91.
2. See B. Jacob.
3. Jer. M. K. 3:5, 82c. See also Gen. R. 100:7.
4. Josh. 24:29. See Speiser; Gaster, *Myth*, p. 222.
5. Driver, *Genesis*, p. 400.
6. Von Rad, *Genesis*, pp. 428 ff.
7. Thomas More, *Godly Meditation*, quoted by S. Goldman, *In the Beginning*, p. 700.
8. Yeb. 65b; Gen. R. 100:8. See also B. M. 87a.
9. Midrash Lekach Tov.
10. After Sotah 13a, b; Mech. to Exod. 13:19.
11. *On Joseph*, 44.

Exodus

Part I *Prologue*

1. Exod. R. 1:12. See Phyllis Trible, *Religion in Life*, Vol. 44 (1975), pp. 7–13.

2. See Hugo Gressmann, *Die Anfänge Israels* (Göttingen: Vandenhoeck und Ruprecht, 1914), p. 23.

3. *Literary Interpretations of Biblical Narratives*, ed. Kenneth R. R. Gros Louis (New York and Nashville: Abingdon, 1974), pp. 81 f.

Israel in Egypt EXOD. 1:1–22

1. See the counting of Rashi and Ibn Ezra, commentaries on Gen. 46:26, 27. S. R. Driver in his commentary (4th ed., Cambridge, England: Cambridge University Press, 1918), p. 5, assigns the genealogy and verses 13 and 14 to the P-source. For an opposite view, see the commentaries of Benno Jacob (offset only, Berlin) and Umberto Cassuto (Jerusalem: Magnes Press), *ad loc.*

2. Exod. R. 1:8.

3. Sotah 11a; Moshe Greenberg, *Understanding Exodus* (New York: Behrman House, 1969), p. 21, translates as "emigrate": Pharaoh is concerned over Israel's leaving the country.

4. D. B. Redford, *Vetus Testamentum* [hereafter cited as *VT*] (Leiden, Holland: E. J. Brill), 13 (1963), pp. 401–418; see also E. P. Uphill, *Journal of Near Eastern Studies* [hereafter cited as *JNES*], 27 (1968), pp. 291–316.

5. Opinions of the commentators are divided. A midrash (Sotah 11b; Exod. R. 1:13) suggests that the two women were Jochebed and Miriam (or Elisheba).

6. See commentary on Gen. 11:27–12:9, "The Call of Abraham"; George E. Mendenhall, *The Tenth Generation* (Baltimore and London: Johns Hopkins University Press, 1973), pp. 122–141, for a recent summary of the Habiru problem; also M. Greenberg, "Habpiru and Hebrews," *World History of the Jewish People*, ed. B. Mazar (New Brunswick, N.J.: Rutgers University Press, 1970), Vol. II (on Patriarchs), pp. 188–200.

7. Exod. R. 1:34.

8. *Moses and the Vocation of the Jewish People* (New York and London: Harper/Longmans, 1959), p. 73.

9. *Itture Torah*, comp. and ed. Aaron Jacob Greenberg (Tel Aviv: Yavneh, from 1965), Vol. III, p. 8.

10. Exod. R. 1:6.

11. *Torah Shelemah* [hereafter cited as *TS*], M. M. Kasher (3rd ed., from 1949: partial English edition, *Encyclopedia of Biblical Interpretation*. New York: American Biblical Encyclopedia Society, from 1953), Vol. 8, p. 12.

12. Ascribed to Levi Yitzchak of Berditchev, *Itture Torah*, Vol. III, p. 9.

13. Exod. R. 1:11.

14. Commentary to 9:27.

15. Exod. R. 1:18; for more elaborate midrashim, see *TS*, Vol. 8, pp. 49–50. See also Josephus, *The Jewish Antiquities*, trans. William Whiston (New York: Al Burt Co., n.d.), II, 2:9.

16. *Itture Torah*, Vol. III, p. 10.

17. *Ibid.*, p. 11.

18. *Ibid.*, pp. 73 f.

19. *The Collected Poems of A. M. Klein* (Toronto: McGraw-Hill Ryerson, 1974), p. 143.

20. Louis Ginzberg, *The Legends of the Jews* (7 vols., Philadelphia: Jewish Publication Society, 1909–1946), Vol. V, pp. 413 f., n. 106. [Hereafter cited as Ginzberg, *Legends.*]

1. Gerhard von Rad, *Moses* (New York: Association Press, 1959), pp. 8–9.

2. For other comparative material, see Theodor H. Gaster, *Myth, Legend and Custom in the Old Testament* (New York: Harper and Row, 1969), pp. 224–230, 380–382. For views of Moses' ancestry, see Abba Hillel Silver, *Moses and the Original Torah* (New York: Macmillan Co., 1961), pp. 16, 69 ff. The attempt of Sigmund Freud, *Moses and Monotheism* (London: Hogarth Press, 1939), to prove that Moses was an Egyptian prince who defected has not found scholarly support.

3. Elias Auerbach, *Moses* (Amsterdam: G. J. A. Ruys, 1953), pp. 104 ff., believes Aaron and Miriam to have been siblings to each other but not to Moses and that the relationship noted in 2:4 was added later.

4. Midrash ha-Gadol. See also Martin Buber, *Moses* (Oxford and London: East and West Library, 1947), p. 36.

5. *Ancient Near Eastern Texts*, ed. James B. Pritchard (3rd ed., Princeton: Princeton University Press, 1969), pp. 448, 475. [Hereafter cited as Pritchard, *ANET*.]

6. Cf. Arnold B. Ehrlich, *Mikra Kifeshuto* (rev. ed., New York: Ktav, 1969), and Cassuto who emphasize that the Hebrew suggests talion.

7. Otto Eissfeldt, *Journal of Biblical Literature* [hereafter cited as *JBL*], 87 (1968), pp. 383–393.

8. H. H. Rowley, *Moses and the Decalogue* (Manchester, England: Manchester University Press, 1951), pp. 159–160, suggests that Jochebed, Moses' mother, may have been of Midianite descent.

9. See Driver; Martin Noth, *Exodus: A Commentary* (English ed., Philadelphia: Westminster Press, 1962), p. 37. William Foxwell Albright, *Catholic Biblical Quarterly* [hereafter cited as *CBQ*], 25 (1963), pp. 6–11, believed that Reuel was the name of a clan, perhaps a Kenite subgroup of the Midianites.

10. This point is made strongly by Samuel Sandmel in his biographical novel of Moses, *Alone on Top of the Mountain* (Garden City: Doubleday, 1973). See also M. Greenberg, *Exodus*, p. 49.

11. N. H. Tur-Sinai, *Peshuto shel Mikra* (Jerusalem: Kiryat Sefer, 1962), makes this point but suggests that וַיֵּרָא be emended to וַיֵּרָא and וַיִּוָּדַע אֱלֹהִים to

וַיִּוָּדַע אֲלֵיהֶם "And God appeared to the Israelites and He was known by them."

12. M. Greenberg, *Exodus*, p. 55.

13. Elie Wiesel, *Messengers of God* (New York: Random House, 1975), p. 181.

14. Ahad Ha-Am, *Essays, Letters, Memoirs*, ed. Leon Simon (Oxford and London: East and West Library, 1956), p. 107.

15. See Sotah 12a; Exod. R. 1:20.

16. Pap. Jumilhac, quoted by M. Greenberg, *Exodus*, p. 40.

17. Pritchard, *ANET*, p. 119. On the whole legend, see Brevard S. Childs, *JBL*, 84 (1965), pp. 109–122.

18. Strabo, quoted in Gaster, *Myth*, p. 228. See pp. 224–230 for a large collection of similar stories.

19. *Ibid.*, p. 229.

20. Commentary on 2:3.

21. *TS*, Vol. 8, pp. 70–71.

22. Exod. R. 1:26. The midrash has also entered Moslem literature through commentaries on the Koran, Sura XX:28, 29 (Ta. Ha.). A summary of other Moslem interpretations of the life of Moses may be found in August Wünsche, *Aus Israels Lehrhallen* (Leipzig: Eduard Pfeiffer, 1907), Vol. I, pp. 163 ff.

23. *On the Life of Moses*, 6.

24. *Antiquities*, II, 9:6.

25. Acts 7:22.

26. *The Book of Exodus: A Critical, Theological Commentary* (Philadelphia: Westminster Press, 1974), pp. 44 f.

27. *Ad loc.*

28. "Thou Shalt Have No Other Gods Before Me," *The Ten Commandments*, ed. A. L. Robinson (New York: Simon and Schuster, 1944), p. 3.

29. "Petirat Mosheh Rabbenu," *Bet ha-Midrash*, ed. A. Jellinek (Jerusalem: Bamberger and Wahrmann, 1938), Vol. I, p. 119.

30. Sura XXVIII:13–18 (The Story).

31. Mechilta Shirata 1.

32. Exod. R. 1:27.

33. Seder Eliyahu Rabbah 21.

34. *Moses*, pp. 112–113.

35. *Moses and the Original Torah*, p. 34.

36. *A Passover Haggadah*, prepared by the Central Conference of American Rabbis, ed. Herbert Bronstein, illust. Leonard Baskin (New York: Grossman Publishers, 1974), p. 43.

1. Pritchard, *ANET*, pp. 159, 164.

2. See M. Greenberg, *Exodus*, pp. 101–102.

3. J. Philip Hyatt, *Exodus*, New Century Bible Series (Greenwood, S.C.: Attic Press, 1971), p. 71; *Interpreter's Dictionary of the Bible* [hereafter cited as *IDB*] (4 vols., New York and Nashville: Abingdon, 1962; supp. vol., 1976), Vol. IV, pp. 376 ff.; Yehezkel Kaufmann, *The Religion of Israel*, trans. and abridg. Moshe Greenberg (Chicago: University of Chicago Press, 1960), pp. 242 ff.; Frederick W. Winnett, *The Mosaic Tradition* (Toronto: University of Toronto Press, 1949), pp. 71 ff. The Midrash says that Sinai had five or even six names (Exod. R. 2:4; Num. R. 1:7).

4. So Childs, *JBL*, 84 (1965), pp. 109 ff.

5. Josh. 5:15; Ber. 62b. For comparative literature, see Gaster, *Myth*, pp. 231 f.

6. Pritchard, *ANET*, p. 19. However, Nogah Ha-reuveni, *Teva va-Aretz*, Vol. 17, No. 2 (1975), pp. 71–73, argues that "milk and honey" were originally derogatory terms. See at Num. 13:27.

7. Ephraim A. Speiser, *World History of the Jewish People* (on Canaanites and Amorites), pp. 168 f.; J. van Seters, *VT*, 22 (1972) (on Amorites and Hittites), pp. 64–81.

8. Exod. R. 3:14; see also Buber, *Moses*, p. 47.

9. See *Notes on the New Translation of the Torah* [hereafter cited as *JPS Notes*], ed. Harry M. Orlinsky (Philadelphia: Jewish Publication Society, 1969); M. Greenberg, *Exodus*, pp. 76 f.; Noth, *Exodus*, p. 42, believes that something is missing in the text.

10. Buber, *Moses*, p. 61.

11. Mechilta de-R. Shimon.

12. Similarly, New English Bible [hereafter cited as NEB]: "unless he is compelled." Differently, B. Jacob: "not even by threats."

13. See the response of Josephus to Manetho: *Contra Apionem* (*Against Apion*), I, 26:236–250; D. J. Silver, *Jewish Quarterly Review* [hereafter cited as *JQR*], new series, 64(2), pp. 123–153.

14. So B. Jacob; Cassuto; M. Greenberg.

15. So Jeffrey H. Tigay, *Gratz College Annual of Jewish Studies*, Vol. 3 (1974), pp. 29–42. The Midrash told of an incident in his childhood when he burnt his tongue.

16. Ber. 64a; see also at Gen. 44:17.

17. Rashi on 6:1; San. 111a; see also discussion of this problem by Nachmanides in his commentary on 5:22.

18. For comparative traditions and sources, see Gaster, *Myth*, pp. 232 ff.

19. Homer, *Odyssey*, XVI:172; X:238.

20. See also Exod. R. 3:8; also W. G. Plaut, *Journal of the Central Conference of American Rabbis* [hereafter cited as *CCAR Journal*] (October 1960), pp. 18–21.

21. For a survey of the use of divine names in the Bible, see M. H. Segal, *The Pentateuch* (Jerusalem: Magnes Press, 1967), pp. 103–123.

22. This question was raised by Maimonides, *Guide of the Perplexed*, I, 63.

23. See Exod. R. 3:6, quoting R. Isaac's opinion; Maimonides, *Guide*, I, 65; Joseph Albo, *Sefer ha-Ikkarim*, II:27; B. Jacob, *ad loc.*; Driver, pp. 40 f. For a survey of interpretations, see M. Reisel, *The Mysterious Name of YHWH* (Assen: Van Gorcum, 1957), pp. 12 ff.; Hyatt, pp. 75–78. Childs, *Exodus*, pp. 60 ff., interprets "I am there, wherever it may be . . . I am really there." The formula would not express the indefiniteness of God but His actuality.

24. Exod. R. 3:6; Midrash ha-Gadol on 3:14. The aspect of God's opaqueness or hiddenness is also stressed by *Pirke de-R. Eliezer*, English ed. Gerald Friedlander (reprint, New York: Hermon Press, 1965), 40; Nachmanides; Malbim; Auerbach, *Moses*, pp. 41–42; G. von Rad, *Old Testament Theology* (2 vols., New York: Harper and Row, 1962), Vol. 1, pp. 193 f.; *idem, Moses*, pp. 20 f.; Ludwig Koehler-Walter Baumgartner, *Lexicon in Veteris Testamenti Libros: Hebrew-Aramaic Lexicon* (Grand Rapids: Eerdmans, 1951–1953), p. 16: "verhüllende Selbstbezeichnung"; Childs, *Exodus*, p. 76: "both an answer and the refusal of an answer." Compare also Gressmann, p. 32: "I am called—what I am called"; Tur-Sinai, *ad loc.* Sandmel, *Alone on Top of the Mountain*, pp. 37 f., goes even farther and sees in God's answer not theology but a bit of wry humor, designed to help Moses over his fright.

25. Exod. R. 2:2.

26. Exod. R. 2:5.

27. *On the Life of Moses*, 12.

28. Nehama Leibowitz, *Studies in the Weekly Sidrah* (Jerusalem: World Zionist Organization, 1960), "Shemot," 5719 Annual.

29. Exod. R. 2:5.

30. *TS*, Vol. 8, p. 123.

31. Exod. R. 2:6.

32. *Itture Torah*, Vol. III, p. 28.

33. Exod. R. 2:5.

34. *Itture Torah*, Vol. III, p. 28.

35. *Ibid*., p. 32.

36. Midrash ha-Gadol on 3:14.

37. *On the Life of Moses*, 14.

38. *The Religion of Israel*, p. 224.

39. Exod. R. 3:7; see Pes. 50a; Kid. 71a.

40. *Wellsprings of Torah*, ed. N. L. Alpert (2 vols., New York: Judaica Press, 1969), Vol. I, p. 112.

41. Commentary on 4:15 f.

42. *Itture Torah*, Vol. III, p. 38.

43. Exod. R. 3:12; see also *Yalkut Me'am Lo'ez* (11 vols., Jerusalem: Or Chadash, 1967–1971) on 4:1.

44. Exod. R. 3:13.

45. *Wellsprings*, Vol. I, p. 111.

46. R. Simchah Bunam, *Itture Torah*, Vol. III, p. 38.

47. Sura XX:12–35 (Ta. Ha.).

Return   EXOD. 4:19—6:1

1. Exod. R. 5:2; further literature in Ginzberg, *Legends*, Vol. V, p. 404, n. 69. The tradition of Moses being forty years old on his flight from Pharaoh is found in Sifre Deut. 357; also Christian Scriptures, Acts 7:23. The number forty and its multiples are used frequently in the Torah and fit into a schematic numerical structure; see at Gen. 6:3. Nachmanides emphasizes that much time elapsed between verses 18 and 19.

2. John 12:14–15. See also Matthew 2:19–21 for further parallels between the Jesus and Moses stories. The same image appears also in Ugaritic literature.

3. The Samaritan version places this verse with the last plague.

4. So B. Jacob.

5. Ibn Ezra; Luzzatto; Driver.

6. Moses: so Rashi and most commentators; the child: so Jonathan ben Uzziel; M. Greenberg; cf. also the discussion in Ned. 31b–32a.

7. Jonathan ben Uzziel suggests that the foreskin was thrust at the feet of the attacking angel in order to propitiate him.

8. *Bonner Biblische Beiträge*, I (1951), pp. 120–128; see also T. C. Mitchell, *VT*, 19 (1969), pp. 93–112, on the distinction, if any, between חָתָן and חֹתֵן.

9. Noth, *Exodus*, p. 51, and others suggest that this "Aaron passage" was added later.

10. A photographic reproduction may be seen in *Views of the Biblical World* (5 vols., Chicago and New York: Jordan Publishing Co., 1959–1961), Vol. I, p. 128.

11. See Cassuto, p. 61; also Gaster, *Myth*, pp. 234, 384, for comparative stories from other sources.

12. *Moses*, pp. 58 f.

13. On the general subject of circumcision, see Charles Weiss, *The Journal of Sex Research*, Vol. 2, No. 2 (July 1966), pp. 69–88. Gressmann, p. 37, and Driver, *ad loc.*, believe that the original story told of Moses' circumcision on his wedding night; for other references, see Buber, *Moses*, p. 209, n. 54. Tur-Sinai would read לְמוֹהֶלֶת (a female circumciser, i.e., Zipporah) for לְמוּלֹת.

14. Theodor Reik, *Mystery on the Mountain* (New York: Harper and Bros., 1959), p. 115.

15. *Hebrew Union College Annual* [hereafter cited as *HUCA*], 34 (1963), pp. 35–70.

16. Georg Beer-Kurt Galling, commentary on Exodus (Tübingen, Germany: J. B. C. Mohr, 1939), p. 38.

17. Rashi; Ibn Ezra; Targum Onkelos speaks of an "angel from the Lord." This position is essentially supported by J. L. Benor, *Beth Mikra*, 58, 3 (April–June 1974), pp. 435–440, on the basis of Arabic parallels; also Childs, *Exodus*, p. 104.

18. *TS*, Vol. 8, p. 198, n.

19. Samson Raphael Hirsch.

20. For a similar view, see Hans Kosmala, *VT*, 12 (1962), pp. 14–28.

21. Exod. R. 13:3; 11:1, 2. For a more detailed discussion and literature, see W. G. Plaut, *CCAR Journal* (October 1962), pp. 18–23; Cassuto, pp. 56–57; and especially F. Hesse, *Das Verstockungsproblem im Alten Testament* (Berlin: A. Töpelmann, 1955), who stresses God's freedom and Israel's redemption as the predominant themes.

22. *Journal of Bible and Religion*, Vol. 32 (1964), pp. 355–358.

23. Exod. R. 9:8.

24. Mechilta Amalek 3.
25. Exod. R. 5:15.
26. R. Simchah Bunam, *Itture Torah*, Vol. III, p. 42.
27. *Ibid.*, p. 44.

28. *Ibid.*, p. 45.
29. *Ibid.*, p. 46.
30. From Sura XXVIII:33–35 (The Story) and XXVI: 15–23 (The Poets).

The Second Revelation EXOD. 6:2—7:13

1. See A. Malamat, *Journal of the American Oriental Society* [hereafter cited as *JAOS*], 88 (1968), pp. 170 f.
2. So Driver; Cassuto.
3. See M. Greenberg, pp. 130–131; Cassuto, p. 76.
4. Kaufmann, *The Religion of Israel*, pp. 221 ff.; also see Gleanings. Similarly, Auerbach, *Moses*, pp. 217 ff.; Childs, *Exodus*, p. 64; the theory is denied by M. H. Segal, *The Pentateuch*, pp. 125 ff. See also Sigmund Mowinckel, *HUCA*, 32 (1961), p. 126; Cassuto, *ad loc.*; David Daiches, *Moses* (New York: Praeger Publishers, 1975), pp. 50 f.
5. Only rarely has the pronunciation Jehovah been given scholarly endorsement; one exception is J. Neubauer, *Bibelwissenschaftliche Irrungen* (Berlin: Louis Lamm, 1917), who bases his opinion on Jerusalem Talmud San. 10:1, describing the controversy between the Rabbanites and the Samaritans over the pronunciation. M. S. Enslin, *The Prophet from Nazareth* (New York: Schocken, 1968), p. 19, n. 7, calls the vocalization Jehovah an "orthoepic monstrosity."
6. See W. F. Albright, *From the Stone Age to Christianity* (2nd ed., Baltimore and London: Johns Hopkins University Press, 1946), pp. 196–199.
7. So M. Reisel, *The Mysterious Name of YHWH*. He relates יהוה to הואהא in the Manual of Discipline and perceives a development from Yahuwah to Yehuah or Yahuah. See especially pp. 34 ff. and 74 f.
8. So W. von Soden, *Welt des Orients*, Vol. III,

No. 3 (1966), pp. 177–187, who arrives at this conclusion after an exhaustive analysis of verb forms in Babylonian and Canaanite languages.
9. See S. Mowinckel, *HUCA*, 32 (1961), pp. 128 ff.; Buber, *Moses*, pp. 50 f.; Martin Buber-Franz Rosenzweig, *Die Schrift und ihre Verdeutschung* (Berlin: Schocken, 1936), pp. 184 ff.
10. So Hyatt, *Exodus*, pp. 78–81, with a concise summary of various themes.
11. So Beer-Galling, p. 31; the *El du Yahwi* derivation is suggested by Frank Moore Cross, Jr., *Harvard Theological Review*, LV (1962), pp. 225–258.
12. *Al ha-Torah* (5 vols., Jerusalem: Reuben Mass, 1962), Vol. II, pp. 167–168.
13. The interpretation is based on the use of וַיְדַבֵּר and וַיֹּאמֶר in direct contiguity; Exod. R. 6:1; Mak. 11a.
14. Quoted in *The Hasidic Anthology*, ed. Louis I. Newman (New York: Bloch, 1944), p. 307, n. 2.
15. Jerusalem Talmud Pes. 10:1; 37b–c. For a modern study of these various terms, see J. Wijngaards, *VT*, 15 (1965), pp. 191–202; see also B. S. Childs, Supplement to *VT*, 14 (1967), pp. 30–39.
16. *Itture Torah*, Vol. III, p. 51; Hayyim Schauss, *The Jewish Festivals* (Cincinnati: Union of American Hebrew Congregations, 1938), pp. 80, 81, 295, n. 82.
17. *Wellsprings*, Vol. I, p. 120; *Itture Torah*, Vol. III, p. 57.
18. Exod. R. 7:5; based on B.B. 110a.
19. *The Religion of Israel*, pp. 223, 225.

Part III *Confrontation and Exodus*

1. This has been explored by David Daube, *The Exodus Pattern in the Bible* (London: Faber and Faber, 1963), pp. 73 ff.

2. See S. R. Hirsch on 7:15.
3. M. Greenberg, *Exodus*, p. 204. Similarly, Hyatt, pp. 336–345, who calls the plagues "theological events," i.e., signs and wonders.

4. "The Admonitions of Ipuwer," Pritchard, *ANET*, pp. 441 ff. (for an excerpt, see Gleanings to 7:14–9:12, "Egyptian Parallel"). See also Barbara Bell, *American Journal of Archeology*, Vol. 75 (1971), pp. 1–26, who connects a prolonged drought and the onset of a "Dark Age" with this text.

5. See the analysis by Childs, *Exodus*, pp. 130 ff.

6. *Collected Poems*, p. 143.

The First Six Plagues EXOD. 7:14—9:12

1. *Interpreter's Bible* [hereafter cited as *IB*] (12 vols., New York and Nashville: Abingdon, 1952), Vol. I, pp. 899–900.

2. For the arrangement in our translation, see *JPS Notes*.

3. *On the Life of Moses*, 19.

4. Luke 11:20. Other references in Gaster, *Myth*, p. 236.

5. So Noth, *Exodus*, p. 78.

6. See, for instance, Mordecai M. Kaplan, *Judaism as a Civilization* (New York: Macmillan, 1934), p. 98. So also David Hume (*Essay on Miracles*) who held that miracles were a violation of the laws of nature.

7. *Theologico-Political Treatise*, 6.

8. B.M. 59b. For an analysis of this legend, see Izhak England, *Tradition*, Vol. 15, Nos. 1–2 (1975), pp. 137–152. On the significance of miracles for talmudic Judaism, see Alexander Guttmann, *HUCA*, 20 (1947), pp. 363–406.

9. *Ethics of the Fathers* 5:6; Exod. R. 21:6; Maimonides, *Guide*, II, 25.

10. *Summa Theologica*, I, 110:4.

11. *City of God*, 21:8.

12. *God in Search of Man* (Philadelphia: Jewish Publication Society, 1956), p. 43; similarly, Buber, *Moses*, pp. 61 ff. See also Gleanings. For a discussion of modern scientific attitudes toward "miracles," see W. G. Plaut, *Judaism and the Scientific Spirit* (New York: Union of American Hebrew Congregations, 1962), pp. 39–45.

13. See M. Greenberg, *Exodus*, pp. 201–202, citing the investigations of G. Hort; Driver, pp. 57–58, 62; on Catholic exegesis, see *Jerome Bible Commentary*, eds. R. E. Brown, J. A. Fitzmyer, R. E. Murphy (Englewood Cliffs, N.J.: Prentice-Hall, 1968), *ad loc*. See also the comprehensive articles in *IDB*, Vol. III, pp. 392–402, and *Encyclopaedia Judaica* (16 vols., Jerusalem: Keter, 1972), Vol. 12, cols. 73 ff.

14. Quoted by Driver, p. 58.

15. *Between God and Man*, ed. F. A. Rothschild (New York: Free Press, 1959), p. 65.

16. *Moses*, p. 77.

17. Exod. R. 11:6. For a discussion of God stiffening Pharaoh's heart, see introduction to Part III.

18. *Itture Torah*, Vol. III, pp. 66–67.

19. Commentary on Exod. 7:28.

20. Exod. R. 10:6.

21. *Wellsprings*, Vol. I, pp. 122–123.

22. Pritchard, *ANET*, pp. 441 f.

The Last Four Plagues EXOD. 9:13—11:10

1. See Driver.

2. M. Greenberg, *Exodus*, p. 161.

3. So Abarbanel.

4. See Daube, *Exodus Pattern*, pp. 47 ff., 62 ff.

5. *Ibid.*, pp. 55 ff. For a different view, see G. W. Coats, *VT*, 18 (1968), pp. 450–457, who considers the secret escape with spoils as an independent theme.

6. *Moses*, pp. 73 f.

7. M. Greenberg, *Exodus*, p. 182.

8. Pritchard, *ANET*, p. 444. This manuscript belongs to the time of Moses.

9. *Wellsprings*, Vol. I, p. 127, quoting the Gerer Rav.

10. Abraham Samuel Benjamin Wolf Sofer, quoted in *Itture Torah*, Vol. III, p. 84.

11. *The Hasidic Anthology*, ed. Newman, p. 118, n. 4.

12. *Itture Torah*, Vol. III, p. 81.

13. *Ibid.*

14. *Moses*, p. 68.

15. Commentary on Exodus, p. 135.

16. *Prophetic Faith in Isaiah* (New York: Harper and Bros., 1958), p. 136. Blank stresses that the universal element—the extension of God's recognition to the whole world—connects the signs of the redemption tale in Egypt with prophetic preachments, especially in Isaiah and Ezekiel.

Passover and Deliverance   EXOD. 12:1–42

1. See Noth, *Exodus*, p. 94.

2. Driver, p. 87.

3. See Rashi; Nachmanides; Ibn Ezra; and Pes. 58a ff.

4. Mishnah Pes. 10:5 and *A Passover Haggadah* hold the view that the custom was symbolic; Ivan Engnell, *A Rigid Scrutiny*, ed. John T. Willis (Nashville: Vanderbilt University Press, 1969), p. 189, that it was prophylactic in nature.

5. So the Midrash, Mechilta Pischa 7. In support of this view, see T. F. Glasson, *Journal of Theological Studies*, new series, 10 (1959), pp. 79–84.

6. Engnell, *Rigid Scrutiny*, p. 190; Buber, *Moses*, p. 71, compares this origin to that of חג (festival), a word also connected with the meaning "to dance."

7. See Rashi who follows Mechilta Pischa 8 and Pes. 120a and 28b.

8. Mechilta Pischa 8.

9. See Matitiahu Tsevat, *HUCA*, 32 (1961), pp. 196–201; also the studies by Julian Morgenstern, *HUCA*, 8–9 (1931), pp. 16–22, 33–58, and W. Zimmerli, *Zeitschrift für die alttestamentliche Wissenschaft* [hereafter cited as *ZAW*], Vol. 66 (1954), pp. 9–19. A talmudic tractate, Keritot, is devoted to this subject.

10. See Meg. 7b.

11. Cf. Noth, *Exodus*, p. 97.

12. See, for instance, Mechilta Pischa 13; Rashi; Nachmanides.

13. Daube, *Exodus Patterns*, pp. 55 ff.; see also Jubilees 48:18.

14. See commentary on Numbers, chs. 1 and 26; for a survey of the literature, see G. E. Mendenhall, *JBL*, 77 (1958), pp. 52–66.

15. See W. G. Plaut, *CCAR Journal* (June 1964), pp. 36–38.

16. Exod. R. 18:11; see also Mechilta Pischa 14 and Septuagint.

17. Exod. R. 15:1 holds that the time of enslavement was shortened rather than lengthened.

18. *Bulletin of the American Schools of Oriental Research* [hereafter cited as *BASOR*], 58 (1935), pp. 10–18.

19. *Peshuto shel Mikra*, Vol. I, on Gen. 16:16; *Bibliotheca Orientalis*, Vol. 18 (1961), pp. 16–17; similarly, C. Shedl, *Bibliotheca Orientalis*, Vol. 18 (1961), pp. 218–219.

20. *The Jewish War*, trans. William Whiston (New York: Al Burt Co., n.d.), VI, 9:3.

21. *IB*, Vol. I, p. 922; on the whole problem, see *Entsiklopedyah Mikra'it* (Jerusalem: Mosad Bialik, from 1955), Vol. V, p. 227.

22. Sporadically, the sacrificial cult continued for some time; see A. Guttmann, *HUCA*, 38 (1967), pp. 137–148.

23. For an assessment of the spiritual differences between the Samaritan and Jewish Passovers, see André Neher, *Moses*, pp. 127–128.

24. J. P. Hyatt, *Numbers*, pp. 144–146.

25. Buber, *Moses*, p. 72; see also *IDB*, Vol. III, p. 664. Details of the Temple sacrifice are described in the Mishnah (Pes. 5:1 ff.).

26. See Commentary on Numbers, ch. 3.

27. So, for instance, Robert H. Pfeiffer, *Religion in the Old Testament* (New York: Harper and Bros., 1961), p. 167, based on the argument first put forth by Wellhausen; the other view is prominently presented by H. J. Kraus, *Evangelische Theologie*, Vol. 18 (1958), pp. 47–67.

28. See the article "Jesus" in *Encyclopaedia Judaica*, Vol. 10, cols. 10 ff., and the literature mentioned there.

29. See Mishnah Pes. 10:5; *A Passover Haggadah*.

30. See the discussion in *Jerome Bible Commentary*, p. 425; *IB*, Vol. I, pp. 916 ff.; Childs, *Exodus*, pp. 209 ff.

31. See also Lev. 23:15 ff. and the standard encyclopedias under "Easter."

32. Exod. R. 15:2.
33. Exod. R. 17:2.
34. See Mechilta Pischa 13.
35. Quoted in *Wellsprings*, Vol. I, p. 130.

36. Mechilta Pischa 13.
37. *Moses*, pp. 72-73.

Addenda to the Passover Observance   EXOD. 12:43—13:16

1. Pes. 96b.
2. See the discussion in JPS *Notes* and B. Jacob.
3. John 19:36. *Jerome Bible Commentary*, p. 53, calls the Torah passage "an anti-type to the scene on Golgotha."
4. So Ibn Ezra. For a discussion of the relevant laws in Exodus, Numbers, and Deuteronomy, see Kaufmann, *The Religion of Israel*, pp. 187 ff.
5. M. E. L. Mallowan, *Nimrud and Its Remains* (London: Collins, 1966), Vol. 2, figures 458, 549. On the etymology of *totafot*, see E. A. Speiser, *JQR*, new series, 48 (1959), pp. 208–217, who derives it from a Sumerian-Akkadian word.
6. Primarily from Men. 34a–37b and Mechilta Pischa 17.
7. San. 88b.
8. Matthew 23:5. See further Erub. 96a; *Entsiklo-pedyah Mikra'it*, Vol. III, col. 376.
9. Ber. 6a, with reference to Deut. 28:10.

10. *Mishneh Torah* [also cited as *Yad*], Hilch. Tefillin, 4:25, 26.
11. *Yad, Hilch. Chametz u-matzah* 6:1.
12. J: *Jerome Bible Commentary*, p. 53; D: Noth, *Exodus*, pp. 99–101; *IB*, p. 924.
13. See commentary on Gen. 1:1–2:3, "God in Genesis."
14. Orach Chayim 32:41.
15. *Aruch ha-Shulchan* 32:74.
16. Orach Chayim 38:7; Isserles Resp. 132; *Aruch ha-Shulchan* 38:9 f.
17. For an overview of the subject, see *Encyclopaedia Judaica* (on Tefillin) and *Jewish Encyclopedia*, ed. I. Singer (12 vols., New York: Funk and Wagnalls, 1901–1904) (on Phylacteries). For the basic laws, see Maimonides, *Yad*, Hilch. Tefillin.
18. See Mechilta Pischa 16.
19. Based on Mechilta Pischa 18.
20. *Hilch. Tefillin* 4:25; see also Meg. 28a.
21. Mechilta Pischa 13.

Rescue at the Sea   EXOD. 13:17—14:31

1. See Noth, *Exodus*, p. 105, for a critical analysis; N. H. Snaith, *VT*, 15 (1965), pp. 395–398.
2. See Mechilta Beshalach 1.
3. See M. H. Pope, *Bulletin of the American Oriental Society*, 200 (December 1970), pp. 56–61, who explains that the stallions were stampeded by a mare let loose in their midst; cf. Song of Songs 1:9 and Pritchard, *ANET*, p. 241, n. 37.
4. See Yigael Yadin, *The Art of Warfare in Biblical Lands* (London: Weidenfeld and Nicolson, 1963), pp. 112 f.
5. But Ibn Ezra finds this explanation unlikely, for God had already assured Moses that He would help. Hence he interprets "Why do you cry . . .?" as "Why do you (Israel) cry . . .?"; only He addresses the rebuke to Moses as the leader and spokesman.

6. So Driver.
7. Exod. R. 22:2.
8. See the extensive analysis by H. M. Orlinsky, Supplement to *VT*, 14 (1967), pp. 1 ff.
9. *IB*, Vol. I, p. 931.
10. Hugo Gressmann, *Die Anfänge Israels*, p. 58.
11. Commentary on Exod. 13:21. See further, *Encyclopaedia Judaica*, Vol. 13, cols. 523–524.
12. *The Tenth Generation*, pp. 32–66.
13. J. Edgar Park, *IB*, Vol. I, p. 929.
14. For examples of detailed analysis, see Gressmann, p. 55; Noth, *Exodus*, p. 119.
15. *Antiquities*, II, 16:5; Gaster, *Myth*, quoting Fraser, pp. 237 ff.
16. *Moses*, pp. 75, 77, 79.
17. For a survey, see *Encyclopaedia Judaica*, Vol. 6,

cols. 1048 ff.; G. I. Davies, *VT*, 22 (1972), pp. 152–163; M. Harel, *Mas'ey Sinai* (Tel Aviv: Am Oved, 1968). See also *IDB*, supplement, pp. 304 ff. Zvi Ilam, *Beth Mikra*, 78, 3 (April–June 1979), pp. 278–282, makes a strong case for Mt. Sinai being Sarbit el-Chadam, northwest of Jebel Musa, near the Gulf of Suez.

18. Mechilta Beshalach 1.

19. *Ibid.*, 4; Exod. R. 21:3, 5, 8.

20. Exod. R. 21:10.

21. Based on Mechilta Amalek 3.

22. *Itture Torah*, Vol. III, p. 109; based on the Talmud, Meg. 10b.

23. *Wellsprings*, Vol. I, p. 134.

24. *Ibid.*

25. *Ma'yanah shel Torah*, ed. Alexander Zusia Friedman (5 vols., Tel Aviv: Pe'er, 1955–1956), Vol. II, p. 62.

26. *Itture Torah*, Vol. III, p. 115; based on Exod. R. 21:5.

27. *Itture Torah*, p. 119.

28. See *Ethics of the Fathers* 5:6.

29. *The Star of Redemption*, trans. W. W. Hallo (New York: Holt, Rinehart and Winston, 1970–1971), introduction to Part II; the quotation is from p. 111.

30. *Al ha-Torah*, Vol. II, p. 193.

31. See Carl Van Doren, *Benjamin Franklin* (New York: Viking Press, 1938), p. 553.

32. Quoted in *The Hasidic Anthology*, ed. Newman, p. 343.

33. See the sources quoted in Ginzberg, *Legends*, Vol. VI, p. 10, n. 54.

34. Meg. 10b; San. 39b.

35. Prepared by the Central Conference of American Rabbis, ed. Bronstein, illust. Baskin, p. 49.

Shirah—The Song at the Sea   EXOD. 15:1–21

1. See Mechilta Shirata (or "Shirta," according to another reading) 7, giving other examples as well.

2. Driver, p. 129. An extensive Hebrew commentary and detailed literary assessment and analysis of the song has been written by Luzzatto in his commentary on the Torah.

3. Mechilta Shirata 9.

4. For a detailed analysis, see Driver, pp. 130–131. Aage Bentzen, *Introduction to the Old Testament* (Copenhagen: G.E.C. Gad, 1948), Vol. I, p. 163, sees the poem as part of an annual enthronement rite of God, celebrated in the Solomonic Temple.

5. *Canaanite Myth and Hebrew Epic* (Cambridge, Mass.: Harvard University Press, 1973), pp. 121 ff.; 156 ff. The Mosaic origin of the poem is also defended by Judah Goldin, *The Song at the Sea* (New Haven and London: Yale University Press, 1971), pp. 34 ff.; see there for a discussion of divergent opinions.

6. Eccles. 3:4; see also Jer. 31:3; Lam. 5:15.

7. See Judg. 11:34 (Jephthah); I Sam. 18:6 (Saul).

8. I Kings 18:26 (Baal priests).

9. See Suk. 51b, 53a.

10. In early rabbinic times wooing was done on the 15th of Av and on Yom Kippur: Mishnah Ta'an. 4:8.

11. Mass. Soferim 20:2.

12. See also Sotah 30b where the response is compared to "Halleluyah" in the recitation of the Hallel psalms; see also there for dissenting views. Luzzatto (*ad verse* 1) compares the recitation to Ps. 136 and its repetition of "For His mercy endures forever."

13. Jerusalem Meg. 3:7; 74b; see also Babylonian Meg. 16b.

14. *Yad*, Hilch. Sefer Torah, 8 (end).

15. *Ad verse* 1.

16. Mechilta Shirata 1; elaborated in Zohar Beshalach 54a.

17. Exod. R. 23:4.

18. Mechilta Shirata 3.

19. From the rhymed translation by Nina Salamon, *Selected Poems of Judah Halevi* (Philadelphia: Jewish Publication Society, 1928), p. 171.

20. *Itture Torah*, Vol. III, p. 126; *The Hasidic Anthology*, ed. Newman, p. 146 (similarly, also S. R. Hirsch).

21. Pritchard, *ANET*, pp. 130–131. Whether or not this is a hymn or perhaps a song encouraging Baal to rise up and act is in doubt; see T. Gaster, *Thespis* (New York: Henry Schuman, 1950), pp. 161 f.

22. *Moses*, p. 95.

23. *Selected Essays of Ahad Ha-Am*, transl. and ed. Leon Simon (Philadelphia: Jewish Publication Society, 1912), p. 320.

1. See Noth, *Exodus*, p. 131.

2. See the comparative material in Gaster, *Myth*, pp. 241–242; Driver, pp. 142–143.

3. See Sifra 140 on Lev. 18:4.

4. So Ibn Ezra.

5. Mishnah Men. 10:1–3.

6. Compare II Corinthians 8:15.

7. See also Hebrews 9:4.

8. Quoted by B. Jacob, pp. 683–684.

9. *IDB*, Vol. III, p. 260; pictures, *ibid.*, Vol. II, p. 255; also *Views of the Biblical World*, Vol. I, p. 149. See also the detailed discussion in Driver, pp. 153–154; B. Jacob, pp. 683–694; Bodenheimer, *Biblical Archaeologist*, 10 (1947), pp. 2–6.

10. For detailed parallels, see Gaster, *Myth*, pp. 242–243. B. Jacob, p. 687, stresses the connection between matzah and manna.

11. On this theme, which Daube calls the "desert typology," see Hallo's essay, n. 25. Shemaryahu Talmon, *Biblical Motifs*, ed. Alexander Altmann (Cambridge, Mass.: Harvard University Press, 1966), pp. 31–64, emphasizes that the desert was not a goal in itself but only a means of establishing a more perfect relationship between God and Israel.

12. Vol. III, p. 129.

13. The Maggid of Mezeritz, *ibid.*, p. 133; based on Sforno.

14. Mechilta Vayassa 1. The biblical passage drawn upon for "forgetting" is Deut. 8:19.

15. *Yalkut Shimoni* I:258.

16. Mechilta Vayassa 5. See also Rashi.

17. Mechilta Vayassa 2.

18. *Ethics of the Fathers* 5:6; also Mechilta Vayassa 6.

19. Exod. R. 25:12. In Sab. 118b, R. Shimon bar Yochai stipulates two sabbaths.

20. Also S. R. Hirsch.

21. *Antiquities*, III, 1:6.

22. *On the Life of Moses*, 36. For a Christian interpretation, see John 6:30–35; also I Corinthians 10:3; Revelations 2:17.

23. *Exodus*, pp. 285 f.

Foes and Friends EXOD. 17:1—18:27

1. This may also be the sign referred to by Ezek. 9:14; cf. Beer-Galling, p. 93, who calls the attitude of Moses a particular *Gebetsgebärde*; W. W. Hallo, *JBL*, 77 (1958), pp. 324–328; and the expression "X marks the spot." *IB*, Vol. I, p. 960, interprets the cross as an "intersection of the divine and human."

2. Josephus, *Antiquities*, III, 2:4, and Rashi on verse 10 ·

3. So Ehrlich and, in an extensive analysis, Childs, *Exodus*, pp. 311 f.

4. Noth, *Exodus*, p. 146, suggests that the name "Jethro" in this chapter is a later addition and that originally he was referred to only as Moses' father-in-law.

5. Tur-Sinai suggests that the original might have read something like this:

כִּי בֹ[יָדוֹ הַחֲזָקָה הֵפֵר כָּל] דָּבָר אֲשֶׁר זָדוּ עֲלֵיהֶם

"For with His mighty hand He brought to naught all that they had schemed against them."

6. Mechilta Amalek 2.

7. *Commentary* magazine (January 1962), pp. 63 f.

8. *Pesikta Rabbati* 12, Hebrew ed. M. Friedmann (reprint, Tel Aviv, 1963); English ed. William G. Braude (New Haven: Yale University Press, 1968); Josephus, *Antiquities*, III, 2:1.

9. *Pesikta de-R. Kahana* 27, English ed. William G. Braude–Israel J. Kapstein (Philadelphia: Jewish Publication Society, 1975).

10. This point is made by Cassuto, p. 212. On the possibility of the excavations at Arad shedding light on the Kenite connection, see B. Mazar, *JNES*, 24 (1965), pp. 297–303.

11. Mechilta Vayassa 7.

12. Targum Jonathan to Num. 21:19; Num. R. 19:25, 26; Christian Scriptures applied this to Jesus, I Corinthians 10:4.

13. *Itture Torah*, Vol. III, p. 138.

14. Mechilta Amalek 1.

15. Mishnah R.H. 3:8.

16. *Itture Torah*, Vol. III, p. 140.

17. Based on Mechilta Amalek 1.

18. *On the Life of Moses*, 39.

19. Mechilta Amalek 3.

Part V *Revelation and Commandment*

1. Foreword to Solomon Goldman, *The Ten Commandments* (Chicago: University of Chicago Press, 1956), p. xv.

2. *This People Israel* (Philadelphia: Jewish Publication Society, 1965), p. 77.

3. Sab. 88b, where it also related that Moses captured the Torah from the angels; see also Exod. R. 28:1.

4. Exod. R. 29:9.

5. Exod. R. 28:6; also 5:9; *Wellsprings*, Vol. I, p. 150 (Siftey Kohen).

6. *Moses*, trans. Maurice Samuel (New York: G. P. Putnam's Sons, 1951), p. 234.

7. In *The Shavuot Anthology*, ed. Philip Goodman (Philadelphia: Jewish Publication Society, 1974), p. 180.

8. *Ibid.*, pp. 188 ff. (excerpts).

At Sinai EXOD. 19:1–25

1. Driver, p. 176.

2. The basic controversy relates to von Rad's theory that there were two separate Exodus and Sinai traditions; for a critical analysis, see Childs, *Exod.*, pp. 337 ff.; on internal difficulties of the text, see Noth, *Exodus*, pp. 153 ff.

3. S. Asch, *Moses*, p. 233.

4. Mechilta Bachodesh 2.

5. Biblical critics assign the covenant in ch. 24 to the J/E-source; the one in ch. 6 to P.

6. So W. W. Hallo, *JAOS*, 87 (1967), p. 64, n. 1. M. Greenberg, *JAOS*, 71 (1951), pp. 172–174, derives *segullah* from another Akkadian word.

7. The comparisons with ancient Near Eastern records have been set forth persuasively by Mendenhall; see, e.g., his article in *IDB*, Vol. I, pp. 714 ff. See also *IB*, Vol. I, pp. 354 ff.; also D. J. McCarthy, *CBQ*, 23 (1965), pp. 217–240. The resemblance to vassal treaties is denied by Hyatt, *Exodus*, pp. 196–199, who believes such parallels to have been unknown to Israel.

8. *The Religion of Israel*, pp. 233–234.

9. A full discussion of the viewpoint of W. G. Plaut may be found in his *The Case for the Chosen People* (Garden City: Doubleday, 1965).

10. Chief among the Jewish critics of the concept is Mordecai M. Kaplan; see, e.g., *The Future of the American Jew* (New York: Macmillan, 1948), pp. 211 ff.

11. Sab. 88a. See also *Yalkut Me'am Lo'ez* on 19:8. The midrash is quoted in the Koran, Sura VII:170 (Al Araf).

12. This point is strongly made in Tanch. Yitro (end).

13. Pritchard, *ANET*, p. 206.

14. Tanch. Yitro 9 and Mechilta Bachodesh 1.

15. Exod. R. 28:2.

16. Suk. 5a; see also Exod. R. 28:1, Mechilta Bachodesh 4.

17. Based on Mechilta Bachodesh 4.

18. On 19:5 and 6.

19. *Itture Torah*, Vol. III, p. 154. See there also for the statement that Israel will be God's beloved even after all the nations acknowledge Him as their ruler.

20. Mechilta Bachodesh 4.

21. *Ibid.*, 9. See further Ginzberg, *Legends*, Vol. VI, p. 31, n. 183.

22. Mechilta Bachodesh 5; Ginzberg, *Legends*, Vol. VI, p. 31, n. 181.

23. Midrash Aseret ha-Dibrot 68; Ginzberg, *Legends*, Vol. VI, p. 35, n. 196.

24. Mechilta Bachodesh 5.

25. *Al ha-Torah*, Vol. II, p. 215.

26. *Ibid.*, p. 216.

27. *Itture Torah*, Vol. III, p. 160.

28. Sifre Deut. 79b (Ekev 41); see also Solomon Schechter, *Some Aspects of Rabbinic Theology* (New York: Macmillan, 1909), pp. 109 ff.

29. Quoted in *Al ha-Torah*, Vol. II, p. 215. (In *Itture Torah*, Vol. III, p. 155, the same comment is credited to a chasidic source, but the latter clearly copies the Gaon.)

30. *Die Religion der Vernunft aus den Quellen des Judentums* (Leipzig: Gustav Fock, 1919), p. 97.

31. *Man Is Not Alone* (Philadelphia: Jewish Publication Society, 1966), p. 195.

32. *This People Israel*, p. 62.

33. *The Case for the Chosen People*, pp. 94–95.

34. *The Spoken Choice* (Cincinnati: Hebrew Union College Press, 1959), p. 33.

1. Cassuto, pp. 234–235. See also Gleanings.

2. See General Introduction to the Torah, "How the Torah Came to Be Written."

3. J. Ryder Smith, *The Religion of the Hebrews* (London, 1935), p. 33.

4. For a further discussion, see Buber, *Moses*, pp. 119 ff.

5. *Moses and the Decalogue*, pp. 101–102; Albright also strongly supports the Mosaic connection with these laws (*From the Stone Age to Christianity*, pp. 196 ff.).

6. Shev. 20b.

7. See Mechilta Bachodesh 8; Maimonides (*Sefer ha-Mitzvot*), who lists fifteen mitzvot altogether, counts verse 2 as the first of the positive and verse 3 as the first of the negative commandments. For a full discussion, see S. H. Weingarten, *Beth Mikra*, 59 (1974), pp. 549–571.

8. See, e.g., Mak. 23b–24a.

9. Acts 7:53; Galatians 3:19; Hebrews 2:2.

10. Rosenzweig, Letter to Martin Buber, 1925, *Briefe* (Berlin: Schocken, 1935), p. 535; Gershom Scholem, *Commentary* magazine (November 1964), p. 39; Maimonides, *Guide*, II, 33, a view with which Abarbanel vigorously disagrees.

11. W. J. Harrelson, *IDB*, Vol. IV, p. 572.

12. *The Tenth Generation*, pp. 211 f.

13. Kid. 30b; see the detailed discussion of this subject by S. R. Hirsch.

14. Yoma 53b–54a; II Maccabees 2:1–8.

15. See *Views of the Biblical World*, Vol. I, pp. 153 and 154.

16. Ber. 12a.

17. For an extended discussion of the Decalogue, see M. Greenberg–D. Kadosh, *Encyclopaedia Judaica*, Vol. 5, cols. 1435–1449; Goldman, *The Ten Commandments*; also H. H. Rowley, *Bulletin of the John Rylands Society*, Vol. 34 (1951–1952), pp. 81–118.

18. Mishnah Tamid 5:1.

19. דִּבְּרוֹת is the plural of the noun which occurs in Jer. 5:13. עֲשֶׂרֶת הַדִּבְּרוֹת is found in Ber. 12a; Sab. 86b *et al.*

20. Midrash ha-Gadol. Further on this word, see E. Ben-Yehuda, *Dictionary and Thesaurus of the Hebrew Language* (New York and London: Thomas Yoseloff, 1960), Vol. I, p. 318.

21. Pritchard, *ANET*, pp. 164, 320.

22. So Kaufmann, *The Religion of Israel*, pp. 221 ff., against the traditional biblical critics who see the Prophets as the originators and refiners of monotheism.

23. Goldman, *Ten Commandments*, p. 143. So Mechilta Bachodesh 6: "unsearched and uncounted."

24. See the discussion in JPS *Notes*; Childs, *Exodus*, pp. 409 ff. NEB takes a middle ground and translates "wrong use."

25. Von Rad, *Theology*, Vol. 1, pp. 175 f.; see also the credo in Deut. 26:5 ff.

26. Midrash ha-Gadol.

27. Mechilta Bachodesh 6.

28. For a detailed treatment of this subject, see Joseph Gutmann, *HUCA*, 32 (1962), pp. 161–174; Israel Abrahams in *No Graven Images*, ed. J. Gutmann (New York: Ktav, 1971), pp. 19–35; *idem, Graven*, pp. 3–8. On Islam, see there, p. 16, n. 10, with further literature.

29. See also G. W. Ahlström, *VT*, 25 (1975), pp. 106–109, where literature on this subject is cited.

30. *Moses*, p. 26.

31. *On the Ten Commandments*, 17. The best Greek tradition frowned on swearing; similar traditions were found among the Persians and Scythians; see Goldman, *Ten Commandments*, pp. 159–160.

32. Mechilta Bachodesh 6 widens the prohibition by forbidding anyone even to assume the obligation to take an oath in the future. See further *Jewish Encyclopedia*, Vol. IX, pp. 365 ff., on oaths in civil and criminal cases.

33. *Summa Theologica*, quoted by Goldman, *Ten Commandments*, pp. 83 f.

34. *Ibid.*, p. 84.

35. *Ibid.*

36. Quoted in *Pentateuch and Haftorahs*, ed. Joseph H. Hertz (Oxford: Oxford University Press, 1929), Vol. 1, p. 401.

37. Exod. R. 28:6.

38. Midrash Aseret ha-Dibrot, introduction.

39. *Min ha-Torah* (5 vols., Jerusalem: Reuben Mass, 1972), Vol. II, p. 464.

40. Mak. 23b–24a. This also reflects the tradition to count "I the Lord..." (verse 2) as the first commandment.

41. *Expostulation* L:384.

42. Sura CXLI (The Unity).

43. Mechilta Bachodesh 6.
44. *Ibid.*

45. Quoted in *The Hasidic Anthology*, ed. Newman, p. 193.

The Decalogue—The Sabbath EXOD. 20:8–11

1. J. H. Hertz, *Pentateuch and Haftorahs*, p. 297.
2. Mechilta Bachodesh 7; Maimonides, *Yad*, Hilch. Shabbat 29:1; *Shulchan Aruch*, Orach Chayim 273.
3. Midrash ha-Gadol (see Gleanings).
4. The basic text is found in Mishnah Sab. 7:2.
5. See *IDB*, Vol. IV, pp. 135 ff.
6. Acknowledgment is made to W. W. Hallo for calling my attention to these distinctions (private communication).
7. *ZAW*, Vol. 84, No. 4 (1972), pp. 447–459.
8. Erub. 51a.
9. This phrasing was Ahad Ha-Am's, *Al Parashat Derachim*, III, 30. It was based on earlier statements such as Abraham Ibn Ezra's אִגֶּרֶת שַׁבָּת (Iggeret Shabbat).
10. For fasting after an ominous dream, see Ber. 31b; *Shulchan Aruch*, Orach Chayim 288:4.
11. For a liberal approach to Shabbat observance, see *A Shabbat Manual*, published for the Central Conference of American Rabbis (New York: Ktav, 1972); for a poetic traditional appreciation, A. J. Heschel, *The Sabbath* (Philadelphia: Jewish Publication Society, 1951); for a representative collection of Sabbath materials, old and new, Abraham E. Millgram, *Sabbath Anthology* (Philadelphia: Jewish Publication Society, 1965).

12. *Histories*, II, 4, quoted in Theodore Reinach, *Textes d'Auteurs Grecs et Romains Relatifs au Judaisme* (Paris: E. Leroux, 1895), pp. 305–306.
13. Quoted, *ibid.*, p. 262.
14. *Treatise on Superstition*, 8; quoted in T. Reinach, p. 136.
15. *Contra Apionem*, 2:40.
16. See Koran, Sura XVI:125 (The Bee).
17. Koran, Sura XCIV:9–10 (The Assembly).
18. Mechilta Bachodesh 7.
19. Mechilta Shabbata 1.
20. *On the Creation of the World*, 30.
21. Gen. R. 11:8. See further Ginzberg, *Legends*, Vol. VI, p. 41, n. 221.
22. Quoted in *Sefer ha-Shabbat*, ed. Y. L. Baruch (Tel Aviv: Devir, 1967), p. 26.
23. Exod. R. 25:11.
24. Alphabet of Rabbi Akiba (older version), ז״ג ש״ת.
25. Midrash ha-Gadol.
26. *On the Ten Commandments*, 20.
27. Quoted in *A Shabbat Manual*, p. 76.
28. *Ibid.*, p. 80.
29. *Ibid.*, p. 79.

The Decalogue—The Fifth to Tenth Commandments; Postscript EXOD. 20:12–18

1. So J. J. Stamm, *Theologische Zeitschrift*, 1 (1945), pp. 81–90.
2. E.g., Philo, *On the Ten Commandments*, 12; Christian Scriptures, Luke 18:20.
3. Driver.
4. See *Jerome Bible Commentary*.
5. So Nachmanides; Bachya; Luzzatto. Ibn Ezra takes an opposite view.
6. See JPS *Notes*.
7. Nachmanides: The test was to accustom Israel to faith; S. R. Hirsch: It was to see whether Israel was capable of hearing the rest of the Torah directly or only through Moses.
8. A similar position is taken by Plato, *Laws*,

4:717 C–D: Parental honor is second only to that due to gods and demi-gods; Aristotle, *Nichomachean Ethics*, IX:2, 8: "honor such as given to the gods."
9. See Mechilta Bachodesh 8.
10. Pritchard, *ANET*, p. 175, Code of Hammurabi 195.
11. See H. C. Brichto, *HUCA*, 44 (1973), pp. 1–54.
12. So Ibn Ezra; Luzzatto.
13. *The Tenth Generation*, p. 218, n. 6.
14. *Torah Commentary* on Gen. 8:15–9:29. The prohibition of adultery also belongs to these so-called Noahide laws. See the talmudic discussion in San. 56–58.
15. See Maimonides, *Yad*, Hilch. Rotse'ach 2:2;

commentary on Gen. 8:15–9:29.

16. Mishnah Mak. 1:10.

17. Even ha-Ezer 1:10.

18. Mechilta Nezikim 5; San. 86a; Maimonides, *Yad*, Hilch. Genevah 9:1.

19. This interpretation is suggested by Bachya. See also Ibn Ezra and the discussion by N. Leibowitz, *Iyyunim Chadashim Besefer Shemot* (Jerusalem: World Zionist Organization, 1973), pp. 243–247.

20. *Pesikta Rabbati* 24.

21. Commentary on the Ten Commandments, reprinted in *TS*, Vol. 16, pp. 183 ff. (citation from p. 186); see further n. 5, Torah commentary of Saadia (Jerusalem: Mosad Harav Kook, 1963), *ad loc*.

22. Midrash on the Ten Commandments.

23. Mechilta Bachodesh 8.

24. *Ibid*.

25. Midrash on the Ten Commandments; see also A. Z. 23b–24a. The story has several variants.

26. Pritchard, *ANET*, p. 150.

27. Exod. R. 47:6; Mechilta Bachodesh 8.

28. Hul. 94a.

29. *Ethics of the Fathers* 4:1.

30. Based on the interpretation of R. Akiba who opposes the opinion of R. Ishmael, Mechilta Bachodesh 9.

31. *On the Ten Commandments*, 11.

32. *TS*, Vol. 16, p. 143, n. 455. (However, in Mechilta Bachodesh 9, Israel is lauded for its reluctance.)

33. *Ibid*.

Part VI *Laws*

1. Cassuto, pp. 264, 312, denies that 24:7 refers to the law code alone.

2. For extensive analyses of various theories, see Beer-Galling, pp. 121 ff., and Henri Cazelles, *Etudes sur le Code d'Alliance* (Paris: Letouzey et Ane, 1946). Cazelles proposes the East-of-Jordan theory; Albright, *From the Stone Age to Christianity*, p. 204, places the origin well into the period of the divided kingdom (900 to 800 B.C.E.), seeing Canaanite influence in the laws; Segal, *Pentateuch*, pp. 39–41, sees patriarchal roots clearly established; while, at the other end of the scale, Morgenstern [*HUCA*, 5 (1927–1928), pp. 1 ff.; 7 (1930), pp. 19 ff.; 8 (1931–1932), pp. 1 ff., 741 ff.] tries to demonstrate a protracted editorial process down to postexilic times; and R. H. Pfeiffer, *Introduction to the Old Testament* (New York: Harper and Bros., 1948), pp. 213 ff., holds that both codes in Exodus and Deuteronomy come from a common Canaanite, post-Mosaic source.

3. For a comprehensive survey, see *Entsiklopedyah Mikra'it*, Vol. V, pp. 587–614; for a quick-reference comparative chart, Childs, *Exodus*, pp. 462–463.

4. See the chart in Pfeiffer, *Introduction to the Old Testament*, p. 214.

5. *Moses and the Original Torah*, p. 134.

Laws on Worship, Serfdom, Injuries EXOD. 20:19—21:36

1. On the various problems contained in this verse, see Leibowitz, *Iyyunim*, pp. 256–261.

2. B. D. Eerdmans, *The Religion of Israel* (Leiden, Holland: University Press, 1947), pp. 27 ff.

3. See the exhaustive study by Baruch A. Levine, *In the Presence of the Lord* (Leiden, Holland: E. J. Brill, 1974), on this and the other sacrifices detailed in the Torah.

4. So Cassuto.

5. Driver; Beer-Galling.

6. See Driver for the suggestion that the original ceremony involved bringing out the household gods or images.

7. Noth, *Exodus*, p. 178.

8. See Mechilta Nezikin 2; Josephus, *Antiquities*, IV, 8:28.

9. See S. M. Paul, *JNES*, 28 (1969), pp. 48–53.

10. In his analysis of the code, Hyatt, *Exodus*, pp. 217–224, considers מוֹת יוּמָת to signify punishment arising from native Israel (rather than assimilated) law.

11. Pritchard, *ANET*, p. 176, Code of Hammurabi 249 provides also for an act of God in the case of an ox.

12. Driver reports that in Moslem tradition fleeing to a tomb was equivalent to seeking the shelter of an altar.

13. The excavation at Beer-Sheba is described and pictured by Yohanan Aharoni, *Biblical Archaeology Review*, Vol. I, No. 1 (1975), pp. 1 ff.

14. See Gleanings. For parallels from Greek law, see Driver.

15. Mishnah San. 11:1; also Pritchard, *ANET*, p. 167, Code of Hammurabi 14.

16. So Cassuto who considers מְקַלֵּל here to be the opposite of כַּבֵּד in the Decalogue. See further JPS *Notes*.

17. See Mechilta Nezikin 5; Mishnah San. 7:8; Mishnah Shev. 4:13. The verse is cited by Jesus in an argument with the Pharisees (Matthew 15:4).

18. Pritchard, *ANET*, p. 175, Code of Hammurabi 206.

19. See Plutarch, *Cato*, 21.

20. Speiser, *JBL*, 83 (1963), pp. 301–306.

21. Pritchard, *ANET*, p. 175, Code of Hammurabi 199; *ibid.*, p. 189, Hittite code 8.

22. For a complete survey of comparative laws, see Gaster, *Myth*, pp. 243–250; also Driver.

23. Mechilta Nezikin 10; Rashi.

24. See *IDB*, Vol. IV, pp. 383–390; *Entsiklopedyah Mikra'it*, Vol. VI, pp. 2–19.

25. On the term and its changing meaning, see H. M. Orlinsky, Supplement to *VT*, 14 (1967), pp. 1 ff.

26. Cohen, *Louis Ginzberg Jubilee Volume* (English section, New York: American Academy for Jewish Research, 1945), pp. 113–132; Talmud: B.K. 87b, based on Mishnah B.K. 8:3. N. P. Lemche, *VT*, 25 (1975), pp. 129–144, also maintains a sociological meaning for *Ivri*.

27. See also Morgenstern, *HUCA*, 7 (1930), p. 81, n. 82.

28. Pritchard, *ANET*, p. 163, Eshnunna 42–47; *ibid.*, p. 189, Hittite code 7.

29. Ibn Ezra on verse 24, quoting Saadia; see Mechilta Nezikin 8; for further reference: Mishnah

B.K. 8:1 and the discussion in the Talmud, B.K. 83b; S. R. Hirsch on verse 25. Only Josephus, *Antiquities*, IV, 8:35, records an opposite view: He claims that in his time the injured had a choice between retribution and compensation, but this claim is not supported by other sources. See also B. S. Jackson, *VT*, 23 (1973), pp. 273–304.

30. See A. S. Diamond, *Iraq*, Vol. 19 (1957), pp. 151–155; B. Rosenkrantz, *Zeitschrift für Assyriologie*, Vol. 44 (1938), pp. 210–214; J. K. Mikliszanski, *JBL*, 66 (1947), pp. 295–310; J. J. Finkelstein, *Journal of Cuneiform Studies*, 15 (1961), pp. 91–104.

31. For a survey of rabbinic law, see *TS*, Vol. 17, pp. 258–270.

32. *On Special Laws*, 3.

33. See Finkelstein, *Temple Law Quarterly*, 46 (1973), pp. 169–290.

34. Reprinted in Gaster, *Myth*, pp. 243 ff., with other comparative legislation and Gaster's comments, p. 253. See also Plato, *Laws*, IX, 12:873D–874A.

35. Exod. R. 30:2; *TS*, Vol. 16, p. 176.

36. Noth, *Exodus*, p. 177.

37. Mechilta Bachodesh 11.

38. Mishnah Middot 3:4; also Mechilta, *loc. cit.*

39. Exod. R. 30:20.

40. Based on Mechilta Nezikin I.

41. *Al ha-Torah*, Vol. II, p. 220, quoting B.M. 30b (לְעָבְדוּ לִפְנִים מִשּׁוּרַת הַדִּין).

42. *Toledot Yitzchak*, quoted in M. Hacohen, *Min ha-Torah*, Vol. II, p. 476.

43. *Yad*, Hilch. Avadim 9:8.

44. Pritchard, *ANET*, p. 175.

45. *Ibid.*, p. 189.

46. *Ibid.*, p. 163.

47. *Ibid.*, p. 176.

48. Speech in Springfield, Illinois, July 16, 1852, *Lincoln's Complete Works* (New York: F. D. Tandy Co., 1905), Vol. II, p. 176.

Laws on Property and Moral Behavior EXOD. 21:37—23:9

1. *The Tenth Generation*, p. 4.

2. Pritchard, *ANET*, p. 166, Code of Hammurabi 8.

3. See H. Limet, *Orientalia*, 38 (1969), pp. 520–532.

4. Plato, *Laws*, 9:874B.

5. See Mechilta Nezikin 13; San. 72a–b.

6. See the discussion in JPS *Notes*.

7. Mechilta Nezikin 15; Mishnah B.M. 93 ff.

8. Mechilta Nezikin understands הָאֱלֹהִים to mean "judges."

9. *Ibid.*

10. Compare Pritchard, *ANET*, p. 176, Code of Hammurabi 244.

11. Pritchard, *ANET*, p. 185.

12. So Mechilta Nezikin 17. The translation used follows Ehrlich.

13. Pritchard, *ANET*, p. 166, Code of Hammurabi 2; *ibid.*, p. 184, Middle Assyrian law A47. S. D. Walters, *Journal of Cuneiform Studies*, 23 (1970), pp. 28–38, 123, suggests varying degrees of social unrest for the varying treatments of sorcery.

14. Pritchard, *ANET*, p. 199, Hittite laws 187–188, 199. H. A. Hoffner, *Alter Orient und Altes Testament*, Vol. 22 (1973), pp. 81–90, suggests that this difference may have been due to different degrees of kinship with these animals; see also Cazelles, *Etudes*, p. 76.

15. For a full discussion, see R. P. Maloney, *CBQ*, 36, 1 (1974), pp. 1–20; see also *IDB*, Vol. I, p. 809.

16. *Antiquities*, IV, 8, 10. Similarly, the translation "judges" (suggested by S. R. Hirsch and others) should be rejected. The parallel would be weak and the Hebrew should then have to read אֶת הָאֱלֹהִים.

17. So, for instance, S. R. Hirsch; J. H. Hertz, *Pentateuch and Haftorahs*.

18. So B. Jacob.

19. Cassuto, *ad loc.*; so also Albright, *Yahweh and the Gods of Canaan* (Garden City: Doubleday, 1968), p. 104.

20. See *Encyclopaedia Judaica*, Vol. 16, col. 490.

21. See further at Lev. 19:33. The Talmud B.M. 59b notes the frequency of the injunction in the Torah. On later uses of the term, see San. 56a–b.

22. Mechilta Nezikin 18; see also B.M. 58b.

23. On this subject, consult Plaut, *CCAR Journal* (January 1966), pp. 31–34; Leibowitz, *Iyyunim*, pp. 277–284.

24. Matthew 5:43. A generally reliable commentator like S. R. Driver calls Exod. 23:9 "a spirit unusual in the Old Testament," but the (Protestant) *IB*, Vol. I, p. 1010, says that the passage "belies the assertion" of Matthew.

25. Cazelles, *Etudes*, p. 88, stresses the social impact of the law.

26. Mak. 7a; Mishnah San. 5:2.

27. See Mishnah Mak. 1:10; San. 7a. For a survey of the subject, see *Encyclopaedia Judaica*, Vol. 5, cols. 142 ff.

28. Kid. 41a.

29. For a survey, see *Encyclopaedia Judaica*, Vol. 16, cols. 160–162; further, L. M. Epstein, *Sex Laws and Customs in Judaism* (New York: Ktav, 1948). Paying the groom a "dowry" is a later custom.

30. Yoma 85a–b.

31. Mechilta Nezikin 15.

32. Based on B.M. 37a.

33. Mechilta Nezikin 16.

34. Exod. R. 31:4.

35. *Ibid.*, 31:12.

36. Quoted in *Itture Torah*, Vol. III, p. 186.

37. *Al ha-Torah*, Vol. II, p. 230.

38. *Itture Torah*, Vol. III, p. 190, quoting the Kotsker Rebbe.

39. Quoted by Hertz, *Pentateuch and Haftorahs*, p. 315.

40. Mechilta Nezikin 18.

41. *Ibid.*

42. *Yad*, Hilch. De'ot 6:10.

43. Pritchard, *ANET*, p. 448.

44. Pritchard, *ANET*, p. 171, Code of Hammurabi 125.

45. *Ibid.*, p. 178.

46. Quoted by Hyatt, *Exodus*, p. 243. The Sumerian code is dated about 2100 B.C.E. and is considered the oldest law code extant.

Laws on Cultic Ordinances; Affirmation of the Covenant EXOD. 23:10—24:18

1. So for instance Cazelles, *Etudes*, p. 102. For a detailed analysis, see Beer-Galling, pp. 121 ff.

2. See Hyatt, *Exodus*, p. 255.

3. Hag. 7a.

4. Mechilta Kaspa 20; Pes. 63b.

5. So old JPS, King James, Revised Standard Version. NEB has "panic."

6. See Y. Kaufmann, *The Biblical Account of the Conquest of Palestine* (Jerusalem: Magnes Press, 1953), pp. 46–54.

7. See Ramban's differing view.

8. See E. W. Nicholson, *VT*, 24 (1974), pp. 77–97.

9. This is denied by Nicholson, *loc. cit.*, who sees here simply a celebration, especially in the absence of sacrifice. See also Num. R. 2:25 and Ber. 17a: The "food" consumed by Nadab and Abihu (who were

amongst the nobles) was the very sight of God (they "feasted" on it by staring at Him and were later punished).

10. Beer-Galling, p. 122. See Cazelles, *Etudes*, pp. 134–137, for an extensive analysis of this subject.

11. Gaster, *Myth*, p. 391, n. 74.

12. So S. R. Hirsch.

13. So, e.g., Luzzatto, B. Jacob.

14. *Guide*, III, 48.

15. C. H. Gordon, *Ugaritic Manual* (Rome: Pontifical Biblical Institute, 1955) 52:14. Cassuto, Hyatt, *IB*, and *Jerome Bible Commentary* (all *ad loc.*) agree that the Torah inveighs against this particular practice.

16. Karaite writing, quoted in Gaster, *Myth*, p. 251.

17. II, 124. See the explanatory notes in *TS*, Vol. 19, pp. 295–298.

18. Jerusalem San. 10:1; 28a.

19. Mechilta Kaspa 4. On mentioning the name of Jesus, see *Itture Torah*, Vol. II, p. 197.

20. Quoted in *TS*, Vol. 19, p. 252.

21. Midrash ha-Gadol (see also *Ethics of the Fathers* 4:5); Avot de-R. Nathan 22:1; nn. on *TS*, Vol. 19, p. 262.

22. Sab. 88a.

23. See Ibn Ezra; for the general rule, Mishnah Kid. 1:7; Kid. 33b–36a.

24. Mechilta Kaspa 5.

25. For a popular exposition of the halachah, see Isidor Grunfeld, *The Jewish Dietary Laws* (2 vols., London: Soncino Press, 1972). A convenient summary of Jewish dietary practices may be found in *Encyclopaedia Judaica*, Vol. 6, cols. 26 ff.

26. *Itture Torah*, Vol. II, p. 198.

27. Based on Men. 29b.

Part VII *Sanctuary and Service*

1. Buber-Rosenzweig, *Die Schrift und ihre Verdeutschung*, pp. 115 f.

2. Cassuto, p. 319; similarly, Childs, *Exodus*, p. 540.

3. See *IB*, Vol. I, p. 845, based on Wellhausen's original suggestion.

4. *Old Testament Theology*, Vol. 1, pp. 234 ff., with an extensive literary analysis.

5. *Essays in Biblical Literature* (New York: Ktav, 1974), p. 30. See also the earlier essay by Morgenstern, *HUCA*, 17 (1943), pp. 153 ff., who called attention to Bedouin palladia, especially the pre-Islamic *qubbah* and their relation to the Tabernacle.

6. See Mishnah Zeb. 14:6.

7. For an extensive analysis, see Driver, pp. 257–263.

8. *The Tabernacle* (London–Jerusalem–New York: Soncino Press, 1969). For extensive descriptions of the Tabernacle, see Menahem Haran, *HUCA*, 36 (1965), pp. 191–226; G. H. Davies, *IDB*, Vol. IV, pp. 498–506. A radically different theory has recently been proposed by Ellis Rivkin, *The Dynamics of Jewish History*, G. B. Rudolph Lecture (Sarasota, Fla.: New College, 1970), pp. 21–41, who sees in the transition from Tent to Tabernacle traces of an "Aaronide revolution."

9. Basic drawing taken from article by M. Haran, *HUCA*, 36 (1965), p. 195.

10. *Baraitha di-Melechet ha-Mishkan; Bet ha-Midrash*, ed. Jellinek, Vol. III, pp. 144–154.

Ark, Lampstand, Tent, and Altar EXOD. 25:1—27:19

1. Mishnah Middot 3. The Wellhausen school will put it in reverse order: The Torah's altar is a miniature image of the actual Temple altar.

2. For the symbolism of these and other colors, see G. Scholem, *Eranos, 1972*, Vol. 41 (offprint, Leiden, Holland: E. J. Brill, 1974).

3. JPS *Notes*.

4. So Rashi.

5. The pictorial re-creation by M. Levine, *The*

Tabernacle, p. 128, is highly speculative.

6. So Rashbam. Hyatt, *Exodus*, p. 263, also uses this spelling.

7. *Baraitha di-Melechet ha-Mishkan*, ch. 2; Rashi.

8. See JPS *Notes*. M. Levine represents the cloths with such designs.

9. On this, see Driver and his discussion of A. R. S. Kennedy's understanding of this construction.

10. The excavations were undertaken by Y. Aharoni

who dates the altar from the eighth century B.C.E. or earlier; *Biblical Archaeology Review*, Vol. I, No. 1 (1975), pp. 1 ff. (with picture).

11. Mishnah Pe'ah 1:1, where it is stated that a "permanent reward" (Keren Kayemet) is laid up for those who do certain mitzvot.

12. Based on Rashi; similarly S.R. Hirsch. Noth, *Exodus,* calls it unusable, and Driver, p. 293, finds this to be a retrojection in order to legitimize Solomon's altar.

13. So *Yalkut Me'am Lo'ez*; Cassuto.

14. Suk. 5b; Rashi on 25:18; and Gleanings to Gen. 2:25–3:24, "The Cherubim."

15. See B. S. Jacobson, *Meditations on the Torah* (Tel Aviv: Sinai, 1956), pp. 103–107, who bases himself on the opinion of Judah Halevi.

16. The לֶחֶם מִשְׁנֶה of Exod. 16:22; see Ber. 39b and *Shulchan Aruch*, Orach Chayim 274:1.

17. *Ecology in the Bible* (pamphlet, Kiryat Ono: Neot Kedumim, 1974), p. 48 (pictures on pp. 40–42).

18. *The Tabernacle Menorah*, American Schools of Oriental Research, Dissertation Series 2 (Missoula, Mont.: Scholars Press, 1976).

19. Men. 28b; see also Rashi on Exod. 25:35.

20. Josephus, *Antiquities*, III, 8:3; see also M. Haran, *Encyclopaedia Judaica*, Vol. 15, col. 1356; S. R. Hirsch, *ad loc.,* for an extensive analysis of the structure and symbolic meaning of the biblical menorah. See further N. Avigad, *Israel Exploration Journal*, 20

(1970), pp. 1–8, also for an illustration of what may be the oldest representation of a menorah in Israel.

21. Exod. R. 33:6.

22. *Itture Torah*, Vol. III, pp. 202, 205.

23. *Ibid.,* p. 201.

24. *Ibid.*

25. Quoted, *ibid.,* p. 211; apparently based on Nachmanides on 25:10.

26. Quoted in *Wellsprings*, Vol. I, p. 165. M. Hacohen, *Al ha-Torah*, Vol. II, p. 236, derives a similar interpretation from תְּרוּמָתִי (verse 2) rather than the expected תְּרוּמָתוֹ.

27. *Antiquities*, III, 7:7. Josephus carries the allegory into much greater detail. See also Zohar Terumah 149a (Soncino ed.), Vol. 4, p. 22.

28. *On the Life of Moses*, III, 6.

29. Midrash Tadshe 10, quoted in Ginzberg, *Legends*, Vol. III, pp. 165–166.

30. Quoted in *Wellsprings*, Vol. I, p. 168.

31. Suk. 5a.

32. Yoma 72b.

33. *Itture Torah*, Vol. III, p. 216.

34. *Wellsprings*, Vol. I, p. 171.

35. *Pentateuch and Haftorahs*, p. 334; based on Midrash ha-Gadol. See also *TS*, Vol. 20, pp. 113 f., n.

36. Commentary on Exodus (English ed.), p. 464.

37. On 27:2.

38. Num. R. 12:14.

The Regular ("Perpetual") Light; Priests and Their Vestments EXOD. 27:20—28:43

1. On priestly service in general, see commentary on Lev. 21:1–22:33. For an extensive homiletical treatment of the section before us, see S. R. Hirsch (English ed.), Vol. 2, pp. 530–542.

2. *Exodus*, p. 220. See the pictorialization in M. Levine, *The Tabernacle*, p. 130; and J. B. Pritchard, *The Near East in Pictures Relating to the Old Testament* (Princeton: Princeton University Press, 1954), p. 66, figure 210.

3. But see the debate on the arrangement in Sotah 36a–b where it is suggested that Judah came first.

4. So Revised Standard Version, Cassuto.

5. So NEB.

6. M. Ben-Uri, *Beth Mikra*, 61 (1975), pp. 219–222.

7. See *Views of the Biblical World*, Vol. I, p. 168,

showing a find from Ras Shamra (the site of the ancient Ugarit, about 14th to 13th century B.C.E.).

8. Quoted in Gaster, *Myth*, pp. 263–278.

9. Noth, *Exodus*, p. 225.

10. See the discussion in B. Jacob.

11. On this distinction, see Plaut, *CCAR Journal* (January 1964), pp. 23–26; Leibowitz, *Iyyunim*, pp. 370–379.

12. Yoma 39b.

13. Ezek. 11:16; Meg. 29a.

14. See the analysis of this passage in Driver, pp. 313 f.

15. *Antiquities*, III, 8:9.

16. Quoted in *Itture Torah*, Vol. III, p. 223.

17. Exod. R. 36:1.

18. Exod. R. 36:1–3.
19. Exod. R. 36:3.
20. Vol. III, p. 229.

21. Yoma 73b; see also Exod. R. 38:9.
22. Quoted by Gaster, *Myth*, p. 266.
23. Midrash ha-Gadol, on 28:30.

Investiture   EXOD. 29:1—31:18

1. Tamid 4:3. See Driver for such divinations.
2. Yoma 72b–73a; *TS*, Vol. 20, p. 224, n. 88; Rashi.
3. So Shakespeare, *Richard III*, Act I, Scene 3, line 36.
4. The Talmud, Zeb. 115b, suggests בִּמְכוּבָּדַי "by those esteemed by Me."
5. See Nachmanides on 30:12; Mishnah Shek. 1:1; S. R. Hirsch.
6. *Encyclopaedia Judaica*, Vol. 16, col. 380.
7. See Mishnah Keritot 1:1; M.K. 28a; *Entsiklopedyah Mikra'it*, Vol. IV, pp. 330–332.
8. See Hyatt, *Exodus*.
9. See also the discussion by J. Gutmann, *No Graven Images*, pp. 2 ff.
10. The translation follows the Targum (also Rashi) which renders שֵׂרָד as if שֵׂרוּת. Tur-Sinai, following Saadia, understands "colored garments" (more suitable than white at ritual slaughter).
11. So Rashi; Noth, *Exodus*, p. 241. Otherwise, Nachmanides: Even as the Sabbath is to be observed during the construction of the Tabernacle, so you must always guard it zealously.
12. See also commentary on Gen. 8:21.
13. *The Tenth Generation*, p. 212.
14. See also J. Z. Lauterbach's discussion of a Sadducean-Pharisaic controversy in which incense has the function of screening the Deity, *HUCA*, 4 (1927), pp. 195–198.
15. Beer-Galling and Hyatt, *Exodus*, assign it to the late P-stratum. A doctoral thesis (at Hebrew Union College - Jewish Institute of Religion) by K. Nielsen opposes this theory.
16. For a recent discussion of *alafim*, see R. G. Boling, *Judges* (Garden City: Doubleday, 1975), pp. 54 f., 287 (on Judg. 20:35).
17. See, for instance, Nachmanides on 30:15, and the extensive discussion in *TS*, Vol. 21, pp. 161–168. Ibn Ezra, however, states: Since it was ransom for the soul and all souls are equal before God, no distinction was made between rich and poor.
18. See *IDB*, Vol. III, pp. 386 ff.
19. *On the Life of Moses*, III, 2:17. Similarly, Abarbanel.
20. Ber. 55a.
21. Mechilta Shabbata 1.
22. See *TS*, Vol. 21, p. 60, n. 39.
23. Erub. 96a.
24. Shemot, Vol. III, pp. 1068–1069.
25. Mishnah Meg. 3:4.
26. Matthew 17:27.
27. *Pentateuch and Haftorahs*, p. 353.
28. Exod. R. 41:6.
29. *Ibid.*

Part VIII   *Apostasy and Second Covenant*

1. See the discussion in *Yalkut Me'am Lo'ez* on 35:1; Nachmanides on 33:7 and 34:28; Rashi on 31:18; Yoma 4b.

2. On this subject, see B. A. Levine, *JAOS*, 85 (1965), pp. 307–318.

The Golden Calf   EXOD. 32:1—33:6

1. Buber, *Moses*, p. 151.
2. Exod. R. 42:6; Ginzberg, *Legends*, Vol. III, pp. 22–23, and Vol. VI, p. 53, n. 276.
3. Noth, *Exodus*, p. 245.
4. San. 102a; Exod. R. 43:2.

5. See Noth, who reads חָרֶט instead of חֶרֶט, *VT*, 9 (1959), pp. 419–422 (basing himself on B. Stade). The suggestion was already made by Rashi and opposed by Ibn Ezra; see Jakob Petuchowski, *VT*, 10 (1960), p. 74.

6. Rashi.

7. Exod. R. 41:7.

8. For this parallel, see A.Z. 44a; Rashi; Nachmanides. See M. Fishbane, *HUCA*, 45 (1974), p. 40, n. 51, for further literature.

9. For a survey, see *Encyclopaedia Judaica*, Vol. 7, col. 710 ff.; *TS*, Vol. 21, pp. 209 ff.; Leibowitz, *Iyyunim*, pp. 395–400; S. Lehming, *VT*, 10 (1960), pp. 16–50; Lloyd R. Bailey, *HUCA*, 42 (1971), pp. 97–115.

10. See, e.g., Noth, *Exodus*, p. 246; Hyatt, *Exodus*, pp. 301–304. See further the discussion by H. Donner, *Alter Orient und Altes Testament*, Vol. 18 (1973), pp. 45–50.

11. See *Views of the Biblical World*, Vol. I, pp. 170 f.; Pritchard, *The Ancient Near East in Pictures* (Princeton: Princeton University Press, 1954), pp. 163–164, 170.

12. This was already proposed by Ibn Ezra in his commentary on Exodus, introduction to ch. 32; similarly, Nachmanides on 32:1; Buber, *Moses*, pp. 147 ff.; Kaufmann, *The Religion of Israel*, pp. 236–237.

13. This is disputed by Bailey, *HUCA*, 42 (1971), pp. 97–115, who connects the incident with the worship of the moon god Sin.

14. *From the Stone Age to Christianity*, p. 230; similarly, Tur-Sinai, quoted in *Entsiklopedyah Mikra'it*, Vol. VI, p. 74. The distinction made by Cassuto, pp. 407 ff., that the cherubim were imaginary and the bull representational does not address the substance of the problem.

15. *The Kuzari*, trans. Hartwig Hirschfeld (New York: Pardes, 1946), Part I, No. 97, pp. 60–62.

16. Cross, *Canaanite Myth*, p. 198 ff.

17. Lev. R. 10:1–3.

18. Ber. 32a quotes Num. 11:2 ("And Moses prayed *to* the Lord") saying: "Do not read *to* but *against* the Lord" (that is, accusingly). Other sources for the aggadic material related: Tanch. Ki Tisa 13; Exod. R. 41:7 (Moses returned too late; magicians showing his bier); Hur killed (Tanch. Ki Tisa 13); *Ethics of the Fathers* 1:12 (Aaron, a man of peace); Exod. R. 37:2 (God knew his intent). See also Gleanings.

19. Exod. R. 42:3.

20. Exod. R. 41:7; Sab. 89a; Rashi on Exod. 32:1.

21. Excerpted from ideas presented in his unfinished opera *Moses and Aaron*, summarized by Reik, *Mystery on the Mountain*, pp. 11–12, and Karl H. Wörner, *Gotteswort und Magie* (Heidelberg: Lambert Schneider, 1959), p. 26. See also Eugene Mihaly, *Jews in a Free Society*, ed. E. A. Goldman (Cincinnati: Hebrew Union College Press, 1978), pp. 170–176, where the midrashim are juxtaposed and Schönberg's view is discussed in detail.

22. See *TS*, Vol. 21, p. 89 and n. 19; *Yalkut Me'am Lo'ez* on 32:2.

23. See the sources quoted in Ginzberg, *Legends*, Vol. VI, p. 49, nn. 258–260. According to the Kabbalah, however, most of the luster was lost after the breaking of the tablets (*ibid.*).

24. *Ethics of the Fathers* 6:3; Erub. 54a; Exod. R. 41:7.

25. *The Star of Redemption*, pp. 266–267.

26. Jerusalem Ta'an. 4:68c; Sab. 87a; Avot de-R. Nathan 2:11; see also Rashbam on 32:19.

27. Based on Deut. R. 3:14. See the discussion by Leibowitz, *Iyyunim*, pp. 425 ff.

28. Exod. R. 43:1; 46:1.

29. *The Problem*.

30. *Evangeline*, I, 4.

31. *The Spoken Choice*, p. 34.

32. *The Shavuot Anthology*, ed. Goodman, pp. 187 f.

33. Quoted in *TS*, Vol. 22, p. 4; see also the excursus, pp. 119 ff.

34. *IB*, p. 1065.

35. Exod. R. 43:4.

36. *Antiquities*, III, 5:8; 101–102; however, Philo, *On the Life of Moses*, III:19, 20, did not play the story down.

37. See *Encyclopaedia Judaica*, Vol. 7, col. 712.

38. *Moses*, p. 134.

39. *Exodus*, p. 570.

40. Sura XX: 88–92 (Ta. Ha.). On the death of Aaron in Islamic legend, see August Wünsche, *Kleine Midraschim* (Leipzig: Eduard Pfeiffer, 1907), Vol. I, p. 186.

41. Exod. R. 41:1.

42. Condensed from an article in *Judaism*, 27 (Fall 1978), pp. 442–447. The Zohar reference is to Vayera 106a.

A New Covenant; the Nature of God EXOD. 33:7—34:35

1. *IB*, p. 1080.

2. *Exodus*, p. 260, who derives ch. 34 from the J-source, whereas Morgenstern assigns it to a Kenite (K) source, *HUCA*, 4 (1927), pp. 1–138. Pfeiffer, *Intro-*

duction to the Old Testament, pp. 221–223, sees in ch. 34 the development of an old Canaanite decalogue; Hyatt, Exodus, pp. 318 ff., believes, however (following W. Beyerlin), that the Decalogue of ch. 20 originally stood in ch. 34 and that the terms of ch. 34 never constituted a decalogue.

3. In their commentaries on 32:11. For an exposition of this controversy, see Jacobson, Meditations on the Torah, pp. 113–120.

4. JPS Notes.

5. So NEB.

6. See R.H. 9a and Rashi.

7. See Noth, Exodus, p. 265.

8. Ibn Ezra and Nachmanides: It was God who wrote . . .; Cassuto: The matter is left purposely vague by the text.

9. See Matthew 17:1–7; IB, Vol. I, p. 1080.

10. Christian Scriptures gave the veil a different interpretation; see II Corinthians 3:7–18.

11. R.H. 17b; Rashi.

12. See TS, Vol. 22, p. 64, n. 67.

13. Rashi; based on Pesikta de-R. Kahana 26.

14. Maimonides, Guide, I, 50–60, especially 53, 54, 58, 59; Cohen, Jüdische Schriften (3 vols., Berlin: C. A. Schwetschke, 1924), Vol. 2, pp. 242 ff.; idem, Die Religion der Vernunft aus den Quellen des Judentums, pp. 72–73. A convenient survey of this subject may be found in Encyclopaedia Judaica, Vol. 7, cols. 663 ff.

15. Deut. R. 3:17.

16. Quoted in The Hasidic Anthology, ed. Newman, p. 96.

17. On Gen. 18:23.

18. On Exod. 32:32.

19. Pentateuch and Haftorahs, p. 365.

20. Tosefta Yoma 5:13, ed. Zuckermandl, quoted in TS, Vol. 22, pp. 66–67.

21. HUCA, 2 (1925), pp. 8–9.

22. The Drunkenness of Noah (University, Ala.: University of Alabama Press, 1974), pp. 74 f. (summary of the view there expressed).

23. In The Ten Commandments, ed. A. L. Robinson, p. 42.

The Building of the Tabernacle   EXOD. 35:1—38:20

1. Exod. R. 48:5.

2. So Cassuto, p. 462.

3. See, e.g., Noth, Exodus, p. 274; Beer-Galling, p. 165.

4. See the study by D. W. Gooding, The Account of the Tabernacle: Translation and Textual Problems of the Greek Exodus (Cambridge, England: Cambridge University Press, 1959).

5. So Exod. R. 50:2.

6. E. Dhorme, Recueil (Paris: Imprimerie Nationale, 1951) pp. 679 f.

7. Pirke de-R. Eliezer 4; Pes. 54a.

8. Gen. 15:17; Exod. 3:2; 13:21–22; 19:18.

9. Gen. 19:24–25; Num. 16:35; Lev. 10:1–2; Deut. 32:22.

10. Mechilta Shabbata 2. Saadia occupied himself extensively with this subject. See also Gleanings.

11. Eerdmans, The Religion of Israel, p. 29.

12. See Mechilta Shabbata 2; Betzah 12a–b. On the punishment implied in the law, see Sab. 70a.

13. See Gutmann, No Graven Images, p. 6.

14. See especially the extensive work of Erwin R. Goodenough, Jewish Symbols in the Greco-Roman Period (13 vols., New York: Pantheon Books, from 1953); idem, HUCA, 32 (1961), pp. 269–279; Gutmann, No Graven Images, pp. 161–174 (quotation from last page).

15. Meditations on the Torah, p. 124.

16. On 35:1.

17. On 35:3.

18. Wellsprings, Vol. I, p. 189.

19. Exod. R. 51:4.

20. Quoted in Ginzberg, Legends, Vol. VI, p. 62, n. 318.

21. Exod. R. 48:3; Tanch. Vayakhel 4.

22. IB, Vol. I, p. 1061.

23. Sirach 38:31–34.

24. On the Giants, XIII:59.

25. Quoted in Gutmann, No Graven Images, p. XIII.

26. On 35:3.

27. Pritchard, ANET, p. 268.

28. Ibid., pp. 144–145.

1. See Yoma 4b; also Ibn Ezra regarding other problems of this section.

2. Cassuto, pp. 469, 473, attempts to show here a mixture of systems based on the numbers six and seven.

3. Israel Abrahams, *Encyclopaedia Judaica*, Vol. 15, cols. 686–687.

4. Compare Gen. 2:1–2 and Exod. 39:32; and Gen. 1:31 and Exod. 39:43. This relationship was stressed by Rosenzweig in Buber-Rosenzweig, *Die Schrift und ihre Verdeutschung*, pp. 115–117; and also Cassuto, pp. 476 ff. See further the elaborate discussion in S. R. Hirsch, Vol. II, pp. 428 ff.; Leibowitz, *Iyyunim*, pp. 344–352.

5. See Pritchard, *ANET*, pp. 68 f., 133.

6. Exod. R. 51:4.

7. *Ibid.*, 51:8.

8. Quoted in *Wellsprings*, Vol. I, p. 193.

9. See Mishnah Shek. 5:2.

10. Exod. R. 51:1.

11. *Itture Torah*, Vol. III, p. 293, quoting the Gerer Rav.

12. IV, 162b.

13. Vol. III, p. 300.

14. Introduction to Exodus; see also Charles B. Chavel's "Notes" thereon in his translation, *Ramban* (New York: Shiloh, 1973), pp. 4–5.

Leviticus

Part I *Laws of Sacrifice*

1. This section is based on R. K. Yerkes, *Sacrifice in Greek and Roman Religions and in Early Judaism* (New York: Allenson, 1952), pp. 1–7.

2. James B. Pritchard, ed., *Ancient Near Eastern Texts*, 3rd ed. (Princeton: Princeton University Press, 1969), p. 207d. [Hereafter cited as *ANET*.]

3. *Ibid.*, p. 208c.

4. *Ibid.*, p. 338 f.

5. *Ibid.*, p. 95a.

6. See Ps. 50:12–13 (cited above); 40:7; 51:19; and the prophetic selections on p. 5.

7. W. W. Hallo and W. K. Simpson, *The Ancient Near East: A History* (New York: Harcourt Brace Jovanovich, 1971), pp. 158 ff.

8. For Babylonian practice, see A. Leo Oppenheim, *Ancient Mesopotamia* (Chicago: University of Chicago Press, 1964), pp. 181 ff. For the more democratic trends, see below, pp. 14 f., 21 ff., and Yerkes, *Sacrifice*, pp. 92 ff.

9. Pritchard, *ANET*, pp. 325, 331 ff.

10. Num. 10:10; Amos 5:23; Ps. 81:2 f.; 92:2 f.; etc. In the Second Temple there was a choir and orchestra composed of Levites.

11. The Passover legislation of J—Exod. 12:21 ff.—is hardly an exception.

12. Exod. 29:38 ff.; Num. 28–29.

13. On the possibility that sacrifices were offered for a time at the site of the ruined Temple, see A. Guttmann, "The End of the Jewish Sacrificial Cult," *Hebrew Union College Annual*, Vol. 38 (1967), pp. 137–148 [hereafter cited as *HUCA*] and the Hebrew note published in A. Rothkoff, *Bernard Revel* (Philadelphia: JPS, 1972), pp. 323 ff.

14. Lev. R. 7:3. According to Meg. 31b and Ta'an. 27b, God gave this assurance to Abraham. See L. Ginzberg, *The Legends of the Jews* (Philadelphia: JPS, 1909–1938), Vol. 5, p. 228, n. 111. [Hereafter cited as Ginzberg, *Legends*.]

15. Ber. 17a.

16. Hag. 12b.

17. Avot de-R. Nathan 4.

18. Midrash Samuel 1:7.

19. Lev. R. 22:8; see pp. 177 ff.

20. D. Hoffmann, *Das Buch Leviticus* (Berlin: M. Poppelauer, 1905), Vol. I, pp. 81 ff., denies that the Midrash supports Maimonides and notes correctly that the version of the Midrash cited by Abarbanel is corrupt. But M. Friedlander, *The Guide of the Perplexed of Maimonides* (reprint, New York: Hebrew Publishing Co., n.d.), Part III, p. 151, n. 2, and M. Margulies, in his notes to Lev. R., agree that R. Levi anticipated the view of Maimonides.

21. Maimonides, *Guide of the Perplexed*, Part III, ch. 32.

22. *Ibid.*, ch. 46.

23. Judah Halevi, *Kuzari*, Part II, par. 25 ff.

24. Some hints of Jewish opposition to sacrifice at the beginning of the Christian era are collected by A. J. Heschel, *Torah min Hashamayim* (London: Soncino Press, 1965), Vol. 2, pp. 115 f.

25. See *Catholic Encyclopedia* (New York: Encyclopedia Press, 1913), Vol. 13, pp. 315 ff., "Christian Sacrifice," and Vol. 10, pp. 6 ff., "Mass, Sacrifice of the."

26. The daily offerings, Exod. 29:38 ff.; offerings of purification, Lev. 12:6 ff.; 14:1–32, 49–53; 15:14, 15, 28–30; Yom Kippur, ch. 16; defective animals, 22:17 ff.; Shavuot sacrifices, 23:18, 19; offerings of the nazirite, Num. 6:13 ff.; meal and wine to accompany animal sacrifices, 15:1–16; expiatory sacrifices, 15:22–29; the red cow, ch. 19; complete annual schedule, chs. 28–29. On the paschal sacrifice, see also Exod. 12:1–27 and 43–49; 23:18; 34:25; Num. 9:1 ff.; Deut. 16:1 ff. The most recent treatment of Jewish sacrifice in depth is B. A. Levine, *In the Presence of the Lord: A Study of Cult and Some Cultic Terms in Ancient Israel* (Leiden, Holland: E. J. Brill, 1974).

The Olah—Burnt Offering LEV. 1:1–17

1. Yerkes, *Sacrifice*, p. 53.
2. Sifra, *ad loc.*
3. Yoma 5a. Cf. p. 27. For a more general account of the significance of blood, see p. 179.
4. Carl H. Kraeling, "The Synagogue," Plate LXII, from *The Excavations at Dura-Europos* (New Haven: Yale University Press, 1956). Though the Dura paintings were executed under Jewish direction in the third century C.E., the painters utilized much older Hellenistic models.
5. Yerkes, *Sacrifice*, pp. 137 f.
6. In II Chron. 35:11, the flaying is done by Levites. See Yoma 26b.
7. Pritchard, *ANET*, p. 656. The tariff may have been sent to Marseilles from Carthage and probably dates from the second or third century B.C.E.
8. Mishnah Zeb. 6:5 prescribes that the entrails be removed with the crop.
9. Zeb. 65a, bottom.
10. Maimonides, Hilch. Ma'aseh Korbanot 3:2.
11. Mishnah Men. 9:8, Bavli 93a–b.
12. Lev. R. 7:3, citing Job 1:5.
13. Kid. 40a.
14. Lev. R. 3:5.

The Minchah—Meal Offering LEV. 2:1–16

1. This development was apparently suggested by I Kings 18:29 which speaks of a *minchah* to be presented after midday; cf. II Kings 16:15 and Ps. 141:2 which speak of an evening *minchah*.
2. Other mandatory grain offerings are treated in 6:12 ff.; 23:13; Num. 5:15. The two loaves of Lev. 23:17 were also classified by the rabbis as a *minchah*, though no part of them was burned on the altar.
3. This is clear also from other talmudic passages, e.g., "When you sift, the *kemach* is underneath [the sieve], the *solet* is above": Yerushalmi Sab. 7, 10b and 20, 17c. The meaning of *solet* was correctly under-stood by many medieval and modern scholars; see R. David Kimchi, *Sefer Hashorashim* (Berlin: Bethge, 1847), s.v. *solet*; Hoffmann, Vol. I, p. 146, citing S. R. Hirsch; G. Dalman, *Arbeit und Sitte in Palästina* (Gütersloh: C. Bertelsmann, 1928–1942), Vol. 3, pp. 291 ff. Some moderns, led astray by the translation "fine flour," have been baffled by the saying in Avot.
4. Lev. R. 3:5; cf. the similar story of "The Widow's Mites," Mark 12:41 ff.
5. Cited by Rashi and Bachya to the verse.

Zevach Shelamim—Sacrifice of Well-Being LEV. 3:1–17

1. The word *mizbe'ach*, "altar," comes from the same root.
2. So the Septuagint; Josephus, *The Jewish Antiquities*, III:228; Mishnah Tamid 4:3; and various authorities cited by Hoffmann, Vol. I, p. 165.
3. S. Lieberman, *Hellenism in Jewish Palestine* (New York: Jewish Theological Seminary, 1950), p. 153, citing Herodotus, *Persian Wars*, III:113, and Mishnah Sab. 5:4.
4. Hul. 49b.

The Chatat—Sin Offering LEV. 4:1–35

1. Jacob Milgrom, "A Sin-Offering or Purification-Offering," *Vetus Testamentum* (Leiden, Holland: E. J. Brill, April 1971), Vol. 21, pp. 237 ff.
2. See Judg. 20:16; Prov. 19:2; W. G. Plaut, *The Book of Proverbs* (New York: Union of American Hebrew Congregations, 1961), p. 202.
3. Scholars who regard P as entirely post-exilic have argued that in pre-exilic writings *chatat* always

means sin, not sin offering. Outside P, they say, the latter sense is found only in Ezekiel, Ezra, and Chronicles. They conclude that the *chatat* and the *asham* (treated in ch. 5) were first introduced when the fall of Jerusalem generated a new mood of guilt. But in fact *chatat* and *asham* are both mentioned in II Kings 12:17, which gives every evidence of being early and authentic (cf. I Sam. 3:14). Moreover, the basic character of the *chatat*, which corrects ritual impurity as well as moral guilt, suggests a very ancient origin.

4. For another view, see Hoffmann, Vol. I, p. 182.

5. Yoma 85b–86a. For inadvertent acts of idolatry, special sacrifices were prescribed: Num. 15:22–29 and see Sifre on Num., 111 ff.

6. Midrash Hagadol, Lev., p. 61.

7. *Ibid.*, p. 80. The homily is based on Isa. 64:4.

Chatat—Sin Offering; Asham—Guilt Offering LEV. 5:1–26

1. Samuel David Luzzatto also cites the suggestion of one of his students that someone might become culpable by touching another person—thus transmitting the defilement to him—without informing him of the uncleanness.

2. H. M. Orlinsky, *Notes on the New Translation of the Torah* (Philadelphia: JPS, 1969), pp. 208 f. [Hereafter cited as JPS *Notes.*]

3. Hoffmann's attempt (I, pp. 210 ff.) to show that the halachah agrees with the plain sense is not convincing.

4. Pesikta Rabbati 23(24), p. 121a.

5. Midrash Hagadol, pp. 108 f.

Laws of Sacrifice—Olah, Minchah, Chatat LEV. 6:1–23

1. But Rashbam, here and at Exod. 29:37 and 30:29, understands the sentence as a command: "Whoever touches these must be in a state of ritual purity."

2. For a similar reason, Orthodox practice forbids the preparation or serving of dairy products in pottery dishes that have been used for meat, and vice versa. Further, non-kosher pottery dishes may not be ritually cleansed for the reception of kosher food; and pottery dishes which have contained leavened food may not be cleansed for Passover use. American Orthodox and Conservative custom extends these prohibitions even to perfectly glazed dishes, though the halachah generally applies only to unglazed or imperfectly glazed pottery (*Shulchan Aruch*, Orach Chayim 451:23, and note of R. Moses Isserles).

3. Mishnah Tamid 1:2 ff.

4. *Ibid.*, 1:4; 2:1.

5. *Ibid.*, 2:2.

6. Sifra to 6:19; 7:7, 32 ff.

7. Lev. R. 7:5.

8. Yoma 21b.

Laws of Sacrifice—Zevach Shelamim LEV. 7:1–38

1. The sources of ritual defilement are treated in Lev. 11:24–15:23 and Num. 19.

2. See Gen. 17:14; Exod. 12:15, 19; 30:33, 38; 31:14.

3. The first view is expressed, e.g., by Bruno Baentsch, *Exodus-Leviticus-Numeri* (Göttingen: Vandenhoeck und Ruprecht, 1903), to the verse; the second in Brown-Driver-Briggs, *A Hebrew and English Lexicon* (Boston and N. Y.: Houghton Mifflin, 1907), p. 504a. [Hereafter cited as *Lexicon.*]

4. J. Morgenstern, *HUCA*, Vols. 8–9 (1931–1932), pp. 33 ff.; M. Tsevat, *HUCA*, Vol. 32 (1961), pp. 191 ff. Tsevat argues that, while our expression is found only in P, H, and Ezekiel, the concept is ancient and underlies the narrative of I Sam. 2:27–36.

5. J. Milgrom, "The Alleged Wave-Offering in Israel and in the Ancient Near East," *Israel Exploration Journal*, Vol. 22, pp. 33 ff.

6. G. R. Driver, "Three Technical Terms in the

Pentateuch," *Journal of Semitic Studies* (Manchester, England: Manchester University Press), Vol. 1, pp. 100 ff. Also N. H. Snaith, *Leviticus and Numbers*, Century Bible, new edition (London: Nelson, 1967), on Num. 8:11; so already A. B. Ehrlich, *Mikra Kifeshuto* (reprint, New York: Ktav, 1969), on Lev. 8:27.

7. Mishnah Ber. 1:1.

8. Avot 1:1.

9. Mishnah Kinnim 1:1.

10. Mishnah Zeb. 2:2; Bavli 28a ff.

11. See M. Higger, *Intention in Jewish Law* (New York, 1927) which, however, does not discuss *pigul*. Of course, other legal systems also stress the concept of intention.

12. M.K. 28a.

13. Yeb. 55a. These citations and others are given in H. E. Goldin, *Hebrew Criminal Law and Procedure* (New York: Twayne Publishers, 1952), pp. 40 f.

14. Nachmanides on 18:29, followed by Bachya. There is precedent for this view in earlier sources: Goldin, *loc. cit.*

15. Lev. R. 9:7.

The Divine Presence in the Sanctuary LEV. 8:1–10:20

1. F. M. Cross, *Canaanite Myth and Hebrew Epic* (Cambridge: Harvard University Press, 1973) argues that the story reflects a power struggle between rival priestly clans.

2. Sifra on 8:33; Seder Olam Rabah, ch. 7. A divergent view, found in some rabbinic sources, is cited by Hoffmann, I, p. 274.

3. Lev. R. 12:1, near end.

4. According to Mishnah Nazir 1:3, the nazirite vow is for 30 days unless a longer period is specified in the vow.

5. Jer. 35 tells of a group descended from Jehonadab son of Rechab (II Kings 10:15 ff.), who followed an ordinance of their ancestor not to drink wine. Apparently this was part of a program to maintain the nomad life style without change for these "Rechabites" also refused to establish permanent homes and to till the soil.

6. Charles R. Snyder, *Alcohol and the Jews* (Glencoe: Free Press, 1958). The study was based on data obtained from Jews residing permanently or temporarily in New Haven. One wonders whether the sample studied was representative of American Jewry, let alone world Jewry. There is also some reason to think that drinking habits of Jews have changed significantly since the study was made.

7. Lev. R. 10:9.

8. A few rabbinic sources state specifically that the sons of Aaron were anointed. See Hoffmann, I, pp. 276 f.

9. According to Rashbam, Ibn Ezra, and Luzzatto, the fire that consumed the sacrifices was itself the manifestation of God's presence. But as Hoffmann, I, p. 291, points out, II Chron. 7:3 clearly distinguishes between the heavenly fire and the Presence.

10. Zeb. 115a.

11. According to the halachah, a priest on Temple duty was required to have his hair trimmed every thirty days, the High Priest every Friday: Ta'an. 17a. But contrast Num. 6:5, 9, 18 and the story of Samson, Judg. 13:14; 16:4 ff., where long hair is a mark of consecration.

12. Sifra on 10:7.

13. Erub. 64b.

14. Sifra to the v.

15. Sifra and Targum Pseudo-Jonathan to the v.

16. Philo, *On the Life of Moses*, II:150.

17. J. H. Hertz, ed., *The Pentateuch and Haftorahs* (Oxford: Oxford University Press, 1929–1936) on Exod. 29:20. To the present v. he cites the Christian commentator Dillmann to similar effect.

18. Sifra to 9:2. The reading "accuse you" is given by Nachmanides on 9:7.

19. Sifra; Sotah 38a.

20. See n. 3, above.

21. Lev. R. 20:10.

22. Sifra.

23. *Ibid.*; Lev. R. 20:8.

24. Lev. R. 20:8.

25. Sifre to Deut. 26.

26. Sifra (ed., I. H. Weiss, p. 45c).

27. *Ibid.*

28. Lev. R. 20:10.

29. Philo, *Allegorical Interpretation of the Laws*, II:58.

30. Philo, *Concerning Flight* 59.

31. Philo, *Concerning Dreams*, II:67.

32. Lev. R. 20, end.

33. Cf. the Roman Catholic custom of preserving the relics of martyrs in churches.

34. Sifra. On this passage, see Ginzberg, *Legends*, Vol. 6, p. 75, n. 385.

35. Tanch. Shemini 11.

36. Lev. R. 13:1.

The Dietary Laws LEV. 11:1–23

1. Hul. 42a ff.; Maimonides, Hilch. Ma'achalot Asurot 4:6.

2. Maimonides, Hilch. Ma'achalot Asurot 4:1 ff.

3. Deut. 14:21 belongs to these exceptions.

4. See "Introducing Leviticus."

5. Yoma 67b.

6. Sifra on 20:26.

7. Gen. R. 44:1.

8. See Luzzatto on Lev. 11:1, rejecting the hygienic explanation.

9. Philo, *The Special Laws*, IV:97 ff.

10. Maimonides, *Guide of the Perplexed*, III, ch. 33.

11. Rashbam, Lev. 11:3. But Rashbam was mistaken in ascribing this view to the Talmud. The passages to which he alludes—Sab. 86b; A.Z. 31b; Nid. 34b— do not clearly state that the forbidden foods are physically harmful; and the second passage even asserts that the non-kosher diet makes Gentiles less susceptible to the effects of snake venom!

12. Maimonides, *Guide*, III, ch. 48.

13. *Shulchan Aruch*, Yoreh Deah 6:1; 18:1 ff. Prof. Alexander Guttmann, in a private communication, agrees that the humanitarian explanation of the dietary laws is generally appropriate. But he points out that an animal slaughtered with a dull knife is still kosher if the knife has no nick and the slaughterer does not interrupt the process.

14. P's version of the story (v. 15) does not make this distinction, since according to P the dietary laws were not instituted until Sinai.

15. E. Wiesenberg, "Related Prohibitions: Swine Breeding and the Study of Greek," *HUCA*, Vol. 27 (1956), pp. 213 ff.

16. The comment, "Thus he declared all foods clean" (Mark 7:19), is a later addition. For when the disciples debated whether gentile converts to Christianity were required to keep the dietary laws, no saying of Jesus was quoted (Acts 15). Had any such saying been known, it would surely have been mentioned.

17. I. Lewin, *In the Struggle against Discrimination* (New York: Bloch Publishing Co., 1957), cites many gentile physiologists, veterinarians, and others who defend Jewish ritual slaughtering as humane; but he does not mention the problem of shackling and hoisting.

18. James G. Heller, *Isaac M. Wise* (New York: UAHC, 1965), pp. 572 f. Oddly, Wise argued that oysters are permitted according to Bible and Talmud: D. Wilansky, *Sinai to Cincinnati* (New York: Renaissance Book Co., 1937), pp. 237 ff.

19. Hoffmann, Vol. I, p. 338.

20. Baentsch had already given the same explanation but eliminated the words "that walk on all fours" from vv. 20 and 23 as due to a scribal error. M. M. Kalisch, *A Critical and Historical Commentary on the Old Testament: Leviticus* (London: Longmans Green, 1867–1872), gives an ingenious but questionable explanation of how the confusion originated.

21. Lev. R. 13:5 (Margulies, p. 291).

Defilement from Animal Carcasses LEV. 11:24–47

1. This statement applies only to unconsecrated food (*chulin*). In the case of "heave offering" (*terumah*, Num. 18:11 ff.) there is a third degree of uncleanness, and in the case of sacrificial foods (*kodashim*) there is a fourth.

2. More exactly: The leper had to remain outside the camp/city of Jerusalem (13:46); those defiled by menstruation, "issues," or childbirth had to remain outside the "camp of the Levites/Temple Mount (Mishnah Kelim 1:8); for other types of defilement, persons were excluded only from the Sanctuary proper.

3. Mishnah Sab. 3:1 and commentaries.

4. Mishnah Machshirin 6:4.

5. Yoma 39a.

6. *Ibid.*, 38b.

Defilement through Childbirth LEV. 12:1–8

1. Snaith, *Leviticus and Numbers*, p. 90.
2. I. Abrahams, *A Companion to the Authorized Daily Prayer Book* (London: Eyre and Spottiswoode, 1922), pp. ccxxxiii f.
3. Cited by Kalisch, II, p. 122.

4. Hoffmann, I, pp. 360 f., citing Maimonides, Hilch. Issure Biah 11:15. See further Nid. 31b; Midrash Hagadol, Lev., p. 273.
5. Nid. 31b.

Defilement from Tzara'at LEV. 13:1–46

1. Deut. 24:8 f., a legal passage, simply enjoins obedience to priestly direction in this matter.
2. We should not suppose that Elisha refused the gifts out of fear of contagion and that Gehazi was infected by natural contact. Elisha had displayed the power of Israel's God to the heathen Naaman; Gehazi was punished for trying to profit by the miracle.
3. Ginzberg, *Legends*, Vol. 3, pp. 213 f.
4. Short for *motzi shem ra*.
5. Luzzatto, pp. 409 f. Luzzatto offers a rationalistic explanation.

6. Sifra to 14:36.
7. Mishnah Nega'im 3:1.
8. B.K. 85a, citing Exod. 21:19.
9. Modern studies in talmudic medicine, mostly in German, are listed in H. L. Strack, *Introduction to the Talmud* (Philadelphia: JPS, 1931), pp. 193 f.
10. Mishnah Kid. 82a.
11. B.K. 85a.
12. Hoffmann, I, p. 387, citing M.K. 24a.
13. Maimonides, Hilch. Tum'at Tzara'at 8:1; Nachmanides to the verse; Hoffmann, I, p. 380.
14. Yerushalmi San. 10, 27d–28a.

Tzara'at of Garments LEV. 13:47–59

1. Judah Halevi, *Kuzari*, Part II, par. 63; Maimonides, Hilch. Tum'at Tzara'at, end; Nachmanides, Lev. 13:47. See also p. 141.

2. Mishnah Nega'im 11:8 with commentaries; Yerushalmi Shek. 6, 50a, top.

Purification from Tzara'at LEV. 14:1–32

1. Nachmanides, Lev. 14:4, end.
2. Defilement from a corpse was purged with the ashes of a red cow, with which cedar wood, crimson yarn, and hyssop were burned: Num. 19.
3. Cited by Luzzatto, Lev. 14:12.

4. Tosefta Nega'im 8:2.
5. Keritut 8b.
6. Arachin 16b.
7. Pesikta de-R. Kahana, "Parah" (Buber 35a, Mandelbaum 62).

Tzara'at of Houses LEV. 14:33–57

1. Tosefta Nega'im 6:1.
2. F. Nötscher, "Haus- und Stadtomina," *Orientalia*, series prior to Vol. 31, 1928. (I owe this reference to Prof. W. W. Hallo but have not been able to examine the work.)

3. See Lev. 13: 47– 59.
4. Lev. R. 17:6.
5. Tanch. Metzora 4.
6. Lev. R. 17:2.

1. Sab. 87a.

2. The passage also requires the covering up of feces; this is the only biblical passage which treats normal body wastes as ritually defiling.

3. J. G. Frazer, *The Golden Bough* (New York: Macmillan, 1922), p. 606, which mentions similar superstitions still current in Europe.

4. *Ibid.*

5. Pes. 111a. According to Hor. 13b, one who walks between two women may forget all he has learned.

6. Nachmanides, Lev. 18:19.

7. Nid. 31b. It is a fact that Jewish women have a low incidence of uterine cancer in comparison with the general population, both in Europe and America. Felix A. Theilhaber, writing in 1940, regarded this fact as "really extraordinary" and "thus far unexplained." (*Universal Jewish Encyclopedia*, Vol. 5, p. 268, "Health of Jews.") According to the same authority, Jews have an abnormally high rate of some other forms of cancer. Orthodox writers have asserted that this relative immunity to cancer of the cervix is due to the observance of the laws of "family purity." See J. Smithline, M.D., "Scientific Aspects of Sexual Purification," in *Some Reasons for Jewish Excellence* (New York, n.d.), citing studies made from 1911 to 1919. The claim has not been adequately proved; if true, it would appear to be one more case where a ritual law produces unforeseen hygienic benefits. Cf. p. 91.

8. San. 37a.

9. W. H. Masters and V. E. Johnson, *Human Sexual Response* (Boston: Little, Brown, 1966), pp. 124 ff.

10. Mishnah Mikvaot 1:7.

11. A *mikveh* is a "gathering" of waters (Gen. 1:10); see Maimonides, Hilch. Mikvaot 4:1.

12. Y. Yadin, *Masada* (New York: Random House, 1966), pp. 164 ff.

13. Maimonides, Hilch. Issure Biah 11:2–4.

14. *Shulchan Aruch*, Yoreh Deah 196.

Yom Kippur LEV. 16:1–34

1. This prophecy does not specifically mention the Day of Atonement, and it is at least possible that it was composed for a special fast in time of drought or other disaster.

2. Pritchard, *ANET*, pp. 331 ff., especially 333d. The tablets containing this ritual text date from after 300 B.C.E., when the Torah was already complete; but the ceremonies they describe may well be very ancient.

3. See Morgenstern, "The Three Calendars of Ancient Israel," *HUCA*, Vol. 1 (1924), especially pp. 22 ff. According to Morgenstern, the New Year on the tenth day of the seventh month (Ezek. 40:1) was originally the concluding day of the fall festival, which in its present form and dating we know as Sukot.

4. Sifra, Yoma 67b, Targum Pseudo-Jonathan, Saadia (cited by Ibn Ezra), and Rashi explain the word as "rough ground," "cliff." Ibn Ezra also cites the view that Azazel was a mountain near Sinai. Rashbam takes the phrase *l'azazel midbarah* to mean "to the desert goats." Hertz cites various moderns who follow the Greek and translate "dismissal" or "complete removal." Nachmanides regards Azazel as a name for the Power of Evil and struggles to reconcile this concept with monotheism (see Gleanings); he etymologizes the name as "the goat is gone." G. R. Driver has argued for the sense "rough ground" ("Three Technical Terms in the Pentateuch," *Journal of Semitic Studies*, Vol. 1, pp. 97 f.); but some of his evidence supports the "mythological" interpretation. For he accepts the identification of Bet Chadudo, the name given the cliff in the Mishnah, with Dudael, the rocky place where the fallen angel Azazel is imprisoned (I Enoch 10:4–6), and with the modern Bet Hudedun, "a rocky terrace in the wilderness ten miles east of Jerusalem."

5. B. J. Bamberger, *Fallen Angels* (Philadelphia: JPS, 1952), chs. 3–5 and 19.

6. *Ibid.*, pp. 154 ff. and chs. 22, 23.

7. Frazer, *The Golden Bough*, chs. 57, 58.

8. T. H. Gaster, *Festivals of the Jewish Year* (New York: Sloane Associates, 1953), pp. 142 f.

9. Mishnah Yoma 5:1.

10. *Ibid.*, 7: 4.

11. "A Significant Controversy between the Sad-

ducees and the Pharisees," *HUCA*, Vol. 4 (1927); reprinted in Jacob Z. Lauterbach, *Rabbinic Essays* (Cincinnati: Hebrew Union College Press, 1951).

12. Or it may come from another root meaning "wipe off."

13. *Kippurim* belongs to a class of abstract nouns that have the plural ending. In later Hebrew, the shorter form Yom Kippur is usual; the "middle Hebrew" of the synagogue prayers retains the biblical *Yom Hakippurim*.

14. Sifra on 16:16.

15. Mishnah Yoma, end.

16. See Gleanings, "You Shall Be Clean before the Lord."

17. Avot de-R. Nathan 4.

18. Pesikta de-R. Kahana, "Shemini 'Atzeret" (Buber 191a, Mandelbaum 425).

19. Hermann Cohen, *Religion of Reason* (translated by Simon Kaplan; New York: Frederick Ungar, 1972), pp. 218 f.

20. Sifra on 16:14; Yerushalmi Yoma 1, 39a–b.

21. So Hoffmann, I, pp. 438 f.; Brown-Driver-Briggs, *Lexicon*, p. 498b.

22. San. 18a.

23. Sifra to the v.

24. Mishnah Yoma 3:9; 4:1.

25. *Ibid.*, 4:3.

26. *Ibid.*, 5:4.

27. *Ibid.*, 3:4.

28. *Ibid.*, 3:3.

29. *Ibid.*, 3:8; 4:2; 6:2.

30. *Ibid.*, 4:2; 6:5, 6.

31. See n. 10.

32. *Shulchan Aruch*, Orach Chayim 624, end.

33. Mishnah Yoma 8:1.

34. *Ibid.*, 8:5.

35. Sifra to the v.

36. Lev. R. 21:10.

37. *Ibid.*

38. *Ibid.*, 21:11; Pirke de-R. Eliezer 46.

39. Nachmanides to the v.

40. Tosefta Kippurim 4(5):6–8. The statement occurs in several other sources with interesting variants, but the substance is much the same. On profaning the name of God, see p. 204.

41. Cant. R. 5:2.

42. Pesikta Rabbati 44, 184b–185a.

43. Sifra to the v. Cf. n. 15.

44. Mishnah Yoma, end.

Further Laws about Sacrifice and Food LEV. 17:1–16

1. See "Introducing Leviticus."

2. Hul. 16b. R. Akiba (*ibid.*, 17a) gave a forced and implausible explanation of the passage. Though his opinion usually prevailed over Ishmael's, the Talmud here follows the latter. See Nachmanides to Lev. 17:2; but cf. Maimonides, Hilch. Shechitah 4:17.

3. So Luzzatto and Hoffmann. An ingenious attempt to bolster this position was made by J. M. Grintz, *Tziyon* (Jerusalem: Historical Society of Israel, 1955), Vol. 31, pp. 1 ff.

4. This expression (Hebrew *chukat olam*) is used of a positive command or institution, often a priestly perquisite, in the following passages: Exod. 12:14, 17; 27:21; 28:43; 29:9; Lev. 7:36; 16:29, 31, 34; 19:10, 21; 23:14, 21; 24:3; Num. 15:15; 18:23; 19:10, 21. Only in Lev. 3:17 and 10:9 are these words attached to a simple prohibition. Note also that in Lev. 23:21 and Num. 19:10 the phrase applies to the entire section, not just to the preceding sentence.

5. Yehezkel Kaufmann, *The Religion of Israel* (Chicago: University of Chicago Press, 1966), pp. 180 ff.

6. Milgrom, "A Prolegomenon to Leviticus 17:11," *Journal of Biblical Literature* [hereafter cited as *JBL*], 1971, pp. 149–156.

7. *Ibid.*, p. 156, n. 32.

8. So, e.g., Baentsch, p. 389; Morgenstern, *HUCA*, 1935, pp. 38 f.; M. Noth, *Leviticus: A Commentary* (translated by J. E. Anderson, Philadelphia: Westminster Press, 1965), pp. 129 f.

9. See n. 1.

10. The second alternative is upheld by Milgrom, *JBL*, 1971, p. 149. For a different view, see B. A. Levine, Prolegomenon to G. B. Gray, *Sacrifice in the Old Testament* (reprint, New York: Ktav, 1971), p. xxvii.

11. Milgrom understands v. 11 in more specific terms: The use of blood on the altar saves you from the penalty of bloodshed.

12. Frazer, *The Golden Bough*, pp. 227 ff.

13. Oppenheim, *Ancient Mesopotamia* (Chicago: Chicago University Press, 1964), pp. 188 ff.

14. Yerkes, *Sacrifice*, pp. 42 ff.

15. *Shulchan Aruch*, Yoreh Deah 69:1.

16. Yoma 5a. B. A. Levine (in G. B. Gray, *Sacrifice*, pp. xxvii f.) holds that originally the blood rite served two purposes. The dashing of blood against the altar in the case of ordinary sacrifices developed from blood-libations to underground deities; it was intended to assuage the wrath of YHWH, should He be displeased with His worshipers. And, in the case of

purgation sacrifices, blood was sprinkled in the sanctuary and placed on the horns of the altars to neutralize the demonic forces of impurity, which threatened the Deity as well as His followers! If these theories are correct, they apply to a very early stage in the development of Israelite religion, which was long past when Leviticus acquired its present form.

17. But cf. above nn. 6, 7, 11.

18. See above n. 3.

19. See commentary on Lev. 11:1–23, "1. A Few Definitions."

Sex Offenses LEV. 18:1–30

1. Sifra to Lev. 22:24; *Shulchan Aruch*, Even Ha'ezer 5:11.

2. Mishnah Yad. 3:5; San. 101a. At this period Homer was also expounded allegorically by some Hellenists.

3. Gen. R. 9:7 on 1:31.

4. Mishnah Ber. 9:5.

5. L. Finkelstein, *Akiba* (reprint, Cleveland: World Publishing Co., 1962), p. 22. The Rabbis considered it proper for a man to marry at eighteen: Avot 5:21.

6. Gen. R. 34:14.

7. Ned. 20b. The choice of technique was, however, the husband's prerogative.

8. B.K. 82a.

9. Mech. to Exod. 21:10. The verse is rendered in the new JPS translation in accordance with this view as "conjugal rights." But the rendering in the margin, "ointment," is almost certainly the correct one: S. Paul, "Exod. 21:10—A Threefold Maintenance Clause," *Journal of Near Eastern Studies*, Vol. 28, pp. 48–53.

10. Lauterbach, "Talmudic-Rabbinic View on Birth Control," *Year Book of CCAR*, Vol. 37; reprinted in *Studies in Jewish Law, Custom, and Folklore* (New York: Ktav, 1970). D. M. Feldman, *Birth Control in Jewish Law* (New York: N. Y. U. Press, 1968).

11. Maimonides, *Guide of the Perplexed*, III:49, referring to Aristotle, *Nichomachean Ethics*, III:13.

12. Maimonides, *Guide*, III:49.

13. Nid. 13a.

14. Lauterbach, *Year Book of CCAR*, Vol. 37, pp. 370 f ; *Studies*, pp. 210 f.

15. Ket. 8b.

16. This discussion does not include the legal aspects of Jewish marriage which in their development gave

the wife an increasing measure of financial security and personal independence.

17. See Lev. 7:21 and commentary.

18. Yeb. 62b, bottom.

19. M. Mielziner, *The Jewish Law of Marriage and Divorce* (Cincinnati: Bloch, 1884), pp. 54 ff.

20. *Ibid.*, pp. 57 f.

21. Lesbianism is not mentioned in the Bible; Jewish traditional literature rarely speaks of it and apparently regards it as a lesser offense than male homosexuality.

22. See further Gen. 19:5 ff.; Judg. 19:22 ff., dealing with attempts at homosexual rape. The first instance gave the name of "sodomy" to homosexual intercourse.

23. Pritchard, *ANET*, pp. 34, 35.

24. M. Duberman, "Homosexual Literature," *New York Times Book Review*, Dec. 10, 1972, surveyed several dozen publications on the subject. The writer, a professed homosexual, concluded that our present knowledge is insufficient to support broad generalizations.

25. San. 64b.

26. Diodorus, *History*, XX:14, cited in *Interpreter's Dictionary of the Bible*, Vol. 4, p. 154a.

27. See Plutarch, "Roman Questions" 83, *Moralia* (translated by F. C. Babbit, London: Heinemann, Loeb Classical Library, 1962), Vol. 4, pp. 15 f. See also Frazer, *The Golden Bough*, pp. 584 ff.

28. *Interpreter's Dictionary of the Bible*, Vol. 4, p. 154a.

29. See the introduction to ch. 26.

30. Sifra, ed. Weiss, p. 86a.

31. Yoma 85b, San. 74a, Yerushalmi Shevi'it 4, 35a.

32. Sifra, p. 86b.

33. Yeb. 21a.

1. Elsewhere the Bible calls the angels "divine beings" (*elohim*)—Gen. 3:5, 32:29, and Ps. 8:6; (*bene elohim*, literally, "sons of god") Gen. 6:2; (*bene elim*) Ps. 29:1.

2. Cf. Lev. 6:11, 20. In Deut. 22:9, the words "may not be used" render the Hebrew *tikdash*. See further Hag. 2:12. In II Sam. 6:1–10, Uzzah dies when he touches the ark, even though his purpose was to keep it from falling off the cart; but in this passage no form of the word *kadosh* is used.

3. Rudolf Otto, *The Idea of the Holy* (translated by J. W. Harvey, New York: Oxford University Press, 1958).

4. Burton M. Leiser, "The Sanctity of the Profane: A Pharisaic Critique of Rudolf Otto," *Judaism*, Winter 1971, pp. 87 ff. The article is perhaps too severe.

5. Avot de-R. Nathan 27 (Schechter ed., p. 84).

6. Though the concept of the Holy Land pervades H (and indeed the entire Bible), the actual expression "holy land" appears first in Zech. 2:16.

7. Tosefta B.K. 10:15.

8. See ch. 18, n. 31; and cf. San. 74a.

9. Sab. 31a.

10. Tobit 4:15; the book is usually dated toward the end of the third century B.C.E.

11. Further references in G. F. Moore, *Judaism in the First Centuries of the Christian Era* (Cambridge: Harvard University Press, 1927–1930), Vol. 2, p. 87; Vol. 3, p. 180.

12. Cited from *Webster's New International Dictionary* (Springfield: G. & C. Merriam, 1935), p. 423a.

13. I believe this remark appears somewhere in the writings of John Dewey, but I have been unable to locate it.

14. Note especially his contemptuous treatment of a gentile woman, Matthew 15:26, to which there is nothing comparable in talmudic literature.

15. See Buber's introduction to H. Cohen, *Der Nächste* (Berlin: Schocken Verlag, 1935), p. 20, and Gleanings, "Love Your Neighbor as Yourself." Ehrlich connects "as yourself" with "neighbor": Love the neighbor who is a citizen like yourself, and love the alien (v. 34) as if he were a citizen like yourself.

16. Lev. R. 24:5. For a modern investigation of the subject, see Morgenstern, "The Decalogue of the Holiness Code," *HUCA*, 1955, pp. 1 ff.

17. In Pes. 22b, the v. is taken to mean "Do not tempt another to sin," e.g., by offering wine to a nazirite.

18. *JPS Notes*, p. 217.

19. Nachmanides follows the talmudic rabbis, who explain these prohibitions as based on "the laws I established at creation" (Yerushalmi Kil. 1, 27b). In Deut. 22:9 a practical reason for not sowing two kinds of seeds together is given: When one crop was ready for harvesting and a first fruit offering would ordinarily free it for general use, the second variety—still unripe—would transmit its taboo to the entire field. But the text is not entirely clear.

20. This explanation was first offered by Winckler, cited in F. Buhl, ed., *Gesenius Hebräische und Aramäische Wörterbuch* (17th ed., Leipzig: F. C. W. Vogel, 1921), s.v. *bikkoret*, and was elaborated by E. A. Speiser in "Leviticus and the Critics," *Yehezkel Kaufmann Jubilee Volume* (edited by M. Haran, Jerusalem: Hebrew University, 1961), pp. 33 ff. Nachmanides recognized the connection between *bikkoret* and talmudic *hevker* (*hefker*), but he drew a different conclusion.

21. See commentary to chapter 1.

22. Mishnah Peah 1:2.

23. *Ibid.*, 8:7; Yerushalmi Peah 21a; Bavli B.B. 8b ff.

24. Tosefta B.K. 10:38.

25. Mishnah B.M. 9:11 ff.

26. *Ibid.*, 7:1 ff.

27. M.K. 17a.

28. Arachin 16b.

29. Mishnah Kil. 8:1.

30. *Shulchan Aruch*, Yoreh Deah 295:1.

31. *Ibid.*, par. 3.

32. See n. 29.

33. *Shulchan Aruch*, Yoreh Deah 298:1.

34. Mishnah Kil. 9:1, which notes, however, that the priestly vestments contained both wool and linen. Indeed, according to Josephus (who was of priestly descent), *Antiquities*, IV:208, *shaatnez* was reserved for the priests and therefore prohibited to all others.

35. Maimonides, Hilch. Issure Biah 3:13. The problem is complicated by divergent readings in the text of the Talmud; see Hoffmann, II, pp. 47 ff. The understanding of *bikkoret* as "punishment" was adopted by many moderns, e.g., Brown-Driver-Briggs, *Lexicon*.

36. Maimonides, Hilch. Ma'aser Sheni 9:1.
37. *Shulchan Aruch*, Yoreh Deah 181:3.
38. San. 76a.
39. Midrash Hagadol, Lev. 19:1 (p. 469).

40. Gen. R. 24:7.
41. Franz Rosenzweig, *The Star of Redemption* (translated by W. W. Hallo, New York: Holt, Rinehart, & Winston, 1970), p. 240.

Punishment of Sex Offenses LEV. 20:1–27

1. San. 76b. Though R. Ishmael and R. Akiba disagree as to the exact interpretation of the verse, both—according to the Gemara—hold that the first wife is guiltless and not to be executed.

2. Mishnah San. 6:4.
3. *Ibid.*, 7:2; Bavli 52a.
4. Mishnah San. 7:4.
5. Tifereth Israel, *ad loc.*

Laws concerning the Priests LEV. 21:1–22:33

1. Gen. 34 and 49:5–7 seem to hint that at a very early period Levi was a tribe without priestly functions.
2. Kaufmann, *The Religion of Israel*, pp. 193 ff.
3. Excavations at Arad, on the southern border of Judah, have revealed a sacrificial shrine dating from the period of the Kingdom. The inscriptions contain names associated in the Bible with the priesthood, and some scholars find in this fact evidence for the antiquity of the Priestly Code. But scholars are still divided over the interpretation of the finds at Arad.
4. It is unlikely that the Karaite movement, which began in the eighth century C.E., was a direct continuation of Sadduceeism, though the Karaites adopted many opinions previously held by the Sadducees.

5. Persons named Katz are usually of priestly descent, Katz being an acronym for *Kohen Tzedek*, "righteous priest." Similarly, many "Levites" are named Segel (in all its various spellings), the name being an acronym for *Segan Lakehunah*, "adjunct to the priesthood."
6. Hoffmann, II, pp. 85 f. Cf. Ibn Ezra and Ehrlich.
7. Brown-Driver-Briggs, *Lexicon* offers "mutilated" in the face or "too long in a limb."
8. The word "present" renders Hebrew *ta'aseh*, "make," which is frequently used of preparing a sacrifice, e.g., Lev. 9:16.
9. Sotah 3a.
10. *Shulchan Aruch*, Even Ha'ezer 6:8.
11. Mishnah San. 7:2; Tosefta San. 9:11; Bavli 52a.
12. Mishnah San. 7:4; 9:1; 11:1.
13. Yeb. 74b.

The Festival Calendar LEV. 23:1–44

1. On this term, see below, n. 28.
2. A fragmentary and puzzling version of the calendar appears in Ez. 45:10–24.
3. For a full account, the reader may consult the excellent volume, *The Jewish Festivals* by Hayyim Schauss (translated by S. Jaffe, Cincinnati: UAHC, 1938); see also Franz Rosenzweig's highly personal but arresting interpretation in *The Star of Redemption*, pp. 310 ff.; likewise in N. Glatzer, *Franz Rosenzweig* (Philadelphia: JPS, 1953), pp. 307 ff.
4. It also has the general sense of "time"; the

present translation frequently renders *beyom* (literally, "on the day of") by "when."
5. See Morgenstern, "Supplementary Studies in the Calendars of Ancient Israel," *HUCA*, Vol. 10 (1935), pp. 15 ff.
6. B. Z. Wacholder and D. B. Weisberg, "Visibility of the Moon in Cuneiform and Rabbinic Sources," *HUCA*, Vol. 42 (1971), pp. 227 ff., especially p. 239.
7. See San. 11b.
8. This is the generally accepted view, but it is possible that the mathematical calendar was not

introduced till a later time; see Wacholder and Weisberg, *HUCA*, Vol. 42, p. 239 and n. 19.

9. I Sam. 20:24-27 shows plainly that at one time the New Moon was celebrated for two days, though nothing of this appears in the laws of the Torah. There was thus some biblical basis for the statement in Yerushalmi Erub. 3, 21c, that the second day of Rosh Hashanah was instituted by the early prophets. According to some authorities, this custom was discontinued after the calendar was fixed by Hillel II, and only one day of New Year was observed in the Land of Israel until newcomers reintroduced the observance of the second day in the eleventh century. See S. Zeitlin, "The Second Day of the Holidays in the Diaspora," *Jewish Quarterly Review*, new series, Vol. 44, p. 192, citing Zerachiah Halevi.

10. Pritchard, *ANET*, p. 320.

11. Tradition removed any discrepancy by stating that Nisan 1 is the new year for kings (i.e., the second year of a reign is counted from Nisan 1, regardless of the month in which the king ascended the throne), while Tishri 1 is the starting point of civil, sabbatical, and jubilee years (Lev. 25). So Mishnah R.H. 1:1, which also mentions two other "new years": the fiscal year for the tithe of cattle (Lev. 27:32) begins on Elul 1; that for the period during which the fruit of young trees is forbidden (Lev. 19:23 ff.) on Shevat 15.

12. J. Langdon, *Babylonian Menologies* (London: Humphrey Milford, 1934), pp. 28 f. and 51.

13. E. R. Thiele, *The Mysterious Numbers of the Hebrew Kings* (Chicago: University of Chicago Press, 1951), pp. 32 ff.

14. M. Burrows, *The Dead Sea Scrolls* (New York: Viking, 1955), pp. 239 ff., and *More Light from the Dead Sea Scrolls* (1958), pp. 373 ff.

15. H. Malter, *Life and Works of Saadia Gaon* (Philadelphia: JPS, 1942), pp. 69 ff.

16. Sifra; Mishnah Men. 10:3; Bavli 65a; Josephus, *Antiquities*, III:250; Philo, *The Special Laws*, II:162.

17. Lev. 16:31 and 23:32 are no exception: they refer to Yom Kippur which is not a festival and which they describe by the unusual phrase, *Shabbat Shabbaton*; cf. also 23:24.

18. Jubilees 15:1; 44:f.

19. W. Leslau, *Falasha Anthology* (New Haven: Yale University Press, 1951), pp. xxix, xxxi.

20. For the first opinion, see the authorities cited by R. H. Charles to Jubilees 15:1; for the second,

L. Finkelstein, *The Pharisees* (third edition, Philadelphia: JPS, 1962), pp. 641 ff.

21. See L. H. Silberman, "The Sefirah Season," *HUCA*, Vol. 22 (1949), pp. 221 ff., and his article "Lag Ba'omer," *Universal Jewish Encyclopedia*, Vol. 6, pp. 508 f.

22. It is not mentioned in Ez. 45:18 ff., cf. n. 2, above.

23. Josephus, *Antiquities*, III:252, uses the name *Asartha*, the Aramaic equivalent of *'Atzeret*.

24. E.g., Pesikta de-R. Kahana, "Beyom Shemini 'Atzeret" (Buber, 193a, Mandelbaum, 430 f.).

25. Attempts have been made to prove that the identification was known already in pre-Christian times; but the arguments, though plausible, are not conclusive.

26. This name may allude to the prayers that God will remember us for life, and that He will remember the "binding" of Isaac; perhaps it also implies that we should on this day bring to mind the sins for which we seek forgiveness.

27. Arachin 12a.

28. *Chag* means "festival" but often has the special meaning "pilgrimage, pilgrim festival." (The cognate Arabic *hajj* designates the pilgrimage to Mecca.) Later Jewish usage classes Passover, Weeks, and Booths as the three *regalim* (Exod. 23:14—"three times a year," *shalosh regalim bashanah*).

29. Neh. 8:15. The present translation of 23:40 renders *peri* by "product" rather than "fruit." In biblical Hebrew, *peri* sometimes means "branches."

30. Suk. 47a-48a.

31. Men. 67b.

32. Similarly, Lev. 24:12 ff. is understood to deal with the sacrifices that accompany the *omer*, while Num. 28:16 ordains the festival sacrifices of Passover week.

33. Mishnah Men. 10:3.

34. Mishnah Bik. 1:3.

35. R. Akiba, Men. 45b.

36. Lev.R. 29:12; R.H. 29b.

37. Mishnah Suk. 4:1, 8.

38. Lev.R. 29:1, which contains the liturgical sentence cited in our text.

39. Mishnah R.H. 1:2; Bavli 16b; the sentence quoted in the text is from a famous prayer (*Union Prayer Book*, Vol. 2, pp. 256 f.), which in traditional synagogues is recited both on New Year and on the Day of Atonement.

40. R.H. 16a-b.

41. Tanch. (Buber edition) Vayera, end.
42. Lev.R. 29:4.
43. Maimonides, Hilch. Teshuvah 3:4; the English version is from *Union Prayer Book*, Vol. 2, p. 6.
44. Pesikta de-R. Kahana, "Beyom Shemini 'Atzeret" (Buber 193b, Mandelbaum 432 f.), cf. Rashi to the v.

45. *Ibid.*, "Ulekachtem" (Buber 180a–b, Mandelbaum 406f.).
46. *Ibid.* (Buber 185a, Mandelbaum 416).
47. J. D. Eisenstein, *Otzar Dinim Uminhagim* (New York: J. D. Eisenstein, 1917), p. 285a–b.

Oil, Bread, and the Blasphemer LEV. 24:1–23

1. Rashi to Exod. 25:29 derives the name from the shape of the loaves: they had many surfaces. Rashbam to Exod. 25:30 explains it as "bread fit for a great personage"; Ibn Ezra as bread set before God's presence.
2. Pritchard, *ANET*, pp. 335a, 343c.
3. The rabbis offered an excuse for this violation of the law that the sacred bread be eaten only by priests: This was an emergency measure to save the lives of David and his starving men. See Men. 95b–96a.
4. B. J. Bamberger, "Revelations of Torah after Sinai," *HUCA*, Vol. 16 (1941), pp. 104 ff.

5. I Kings 22:27 and Jer. 32:2 are cases of politically motivated detention, not punishment of criminals. The Mishnah (San. 9:3) makes provision for life imprisonment; but we have no record of a case when the law was put into practice.
6. B.K. 84a.
7. See J. K. Mikliszanski, "The Law of Retaliation and the Pentateuch," *JBL*, Vol. 66 (1947), pp. 295 ff.
8. Lev.R. 32:3.
9. Midrash Hagadol to the v.
10. J. H. Hertz, *The Pentateuch and Haftorahs* on 24:18.

Sabbatical Year and Jubilee LEV. 25:1–55

1. Some scholars believe the Deuteronomic law intended only a moratorium, with the debts becoming collectible again in the eighth year. But Jewish tradition understood it to mean outright cancellation.
2. M. Tsevat, "Inyan Shemitah etzel Har Sinai," *Chafirot Umechkarim* (edited by J. Aharoni, Jerusalem: Carta, 1973), p. 286.
3. Maimonides, Hilch. Shemitah Veyovel 3:1.
4. *Ibid.*, 9:4. The combination of the two laws seems to be indicated already in Neh. 10:32.
5. Mishnah Shevi'it 10:3 ff.
6. Josephus, *Antiquities*, XII:378 (the siege occurred between 164 and 162 B.C.E.); XIV: 202–206. See further, *Antiquities*, XIII:234 (= *War* I:60); XIV:475; XV:7.
7. Lev.R. 1:1.
8. San. 26a; Yerushalmi Shevi'it 4, 35a.
9. R. North, *Sociology of the Biblical Jubilee* (Rome: Pontifical Biblical Institute, 1954), pp. 96 ff.
10. Lev. 25:39 ff. makes a clear distinction between the Israelite brother and the gentile slave and does not use the term *eved Ivri*, usually rendered "Hebrew slave." For the original meaning of this term, see

the commentary on Gen. 14, "Abraham the Hebrew," and on Exod. 21:2. But note that the *eved Ivri* is already identified as the fellow Judean in Jer. 34:9.
11. Kurt Salomon, cited in North, *Sociology*, p. 163.
12. Sifra on 25:10.
13. North (*Sociology*, pp. 109 ff.) argues that the jubilee year was really the forty-ninth—i.e., the seventh sabbatical year—and that "fiftieth year" in vv. 10–11 is an inaccuracy. This view is likewise held by other scholars mentioned by S. Loewenstamm in *Entsiklopedyah Mikra'it*, Vol. 3, p. 578. Attempting to salvage the historicity of the jubilee, they depart from the plain sense of the biblical text. The Book of Jubilees (below, n. 20) also deals in jubilee periods of 49 years. But this is hardly a support for the scholars just cited, for Jubilees is concerned with a novel calendar system, not with the jubilee law.
14. E.g., the penalty of extermination for inhabitants of a city that has lapsed into idolatry, Deut. 13:13 ff., on which see Tosefta San. 14:1; the death penalty for a juvenile delinquent, Deut. 21:18 ff., on which see Bavli San. 71a.

15. M. Tsevat, *Chafirot Umechkarim*, pp. 285 ff.

16. *Ibid.*, p. 287.

17. See above, n. 13. Even more extreme is the view of S. Zeitlin, *The Rise and Fall of the Judean State* (Philadelphia, JPS, 1962), Vol. 1, pp. 216 ff., that the "jubilee" was a period of 49 *days*—a view based on a mistranslation of Lev. 25:8. Loewenstamm, p. 580, argues from the reference to the year of release in Ezek. 46:17 that the institution was ancient and well known. But we have offered reasons (see "Introducing Leviticus") for regarding Ezekiel as roughly contemporary with and closely related to H; so he may not be referring to an ancient institution at all. (If the priestly documents are really so much older, how did the conservative priest Ezekiel venture to disagree with them on so many points?) Loewenstamm argues further that the limitation of the law in respect to urban property (vv. 29 ff.) was a concession to changing conditions, whereas utopian legislation need not be adjusted to changing realities. But one can also argue the other way: The idealistic author incorporated an actual contemporary rule into his proposals. This rule was, in fact, practiced in medieval Armenia; see below, n. 21.

18. E. Ginzberg, "Studies in the Economics of the Bible," *Jewish Quarterly Review*, new series, Vol. 22 (1932), pp. 377 ff.

19. *Ibid.*, pp. 396 ff.

20. English translation in *Apocrypha and Pseudepigrapha of the Old Testament* (Oxford: Clarendon Press, 1913), Vol. 2. See above, n. 13. Jubilees was originally written in Hebrew, and fragments of the Hebrew text have been found among the Dead Sea Scrolls. But the work as a whole survives only in an Ethiopic version made from a Greek translation of the original.

21. E. Ginzberg, "Studies," p. 399.

22. Aristotle, *Politics*, I:2.

23. Philo, *On the Special Laws*, II:69. F. H. Colson, commenting on this passage (Loeb Classics ed., Vol. 7, pp. 624 f.) remarks that this is alleged to be a Stoic doctrine, but no extant Stoic writing is so explicit on this point. Aristotle, however, does state that some persons regarded slavery as contrary to nature—a view he finds applicable only to a very limited extent (*Politics*, I:2).

24. Mech. to Exod. 21:26.

25. See above, n. 10.

26. Git. 38b.

27. *Shulchan Aruch*, Yoreh Deah 267:4. See also Maimonides, Hilch. Milah 1 and Hilch. Avadim 8:12.

28. Mech. to Exod. 15:9.

29. Orlinsky, JPS *Notes*, pp. 220 f.

30. Mishnah B.M. 4:3.

31. *Ibid.*, 5:1.

32. Henry George, "Moses: A Lecture," in *The Complete Works of Henry George* (Garden City, N.Y.: Doubleday, Page, & Co., 1911), Vol. 7, where this lecture is paged separately from the rest of the vol. Our selection is on p. 18. The lecture is available in pamphlet form through the Robert Schalkenbach Foundation, 50 E. 69th St., New York, N.Y. 10021.

33. Maimonides, Hilch. Avadim, end.

Blessings and Curses LEV. 26:1–46

1. Pritchard, *ANET*, pp. 159 ff., 163 ff. The Code of Hammurabi dates from early in his reign, which began in 1792 B.C.E. The Sumerian code is about 150 years earlier.

2. *Ibid.*, pp. 203 ff.

3. *Ibid.*, pp. 534 ff. See M. Weinfeld, *Deuteronomy and the Deuteronomic School* (Oxford: Clarendon Press, 1972), pp. 59 ff. and especially 116 ff. The Assyrian treaties are from the seventh century B.C.E. and so are approximately contemporary with Deuteronomy. The Hittite treaties cited in the previous n. are about 600 years earlier.

4. Another obvious difference is that Esarhaddon invokes a long list of gods to witness and enforce the oaths being taken. In Deuteronomy, the one God is also the Sovereign; there are only two parties, God and Israel. In all the vassal treaties, there are three parties—the suzerain, the vassal, and the gods. (See Gleanings to Deut. 28.)

5. Weinfeld, *Deuteronomy*, pp. 124 ff., finds resemblances between Lev. 26 and an Aramaic treaty of about 750 B.C.E., *ANET*, pp. 659 ff. But these similarities appear to me slight and superficial, not like the striking parallels between Deuteronomy and the Assyrian treaties.

6. See A. E. Hirshowitz, *Otzar Kol Minhagei Yeshurun* (Lvov, 1930), p. 160. See also the moving tale, "The Marked One," by J. Picard (*The Marked One and*

Other Stories, translated by L. Lewisohn, Philadelphia: JPS, 1956).

7. This kind of thinking also appears in the Bible, e.g., II Sam. 21:1-14 and ch. 24 (=I Chron. 21); II Kings 23:26.

8. See *ANET*, pp. 405 ff., 589 ff., 596-604. But comparison of these texts to the Book of Job should be viewed with caution. They offer occasional parallels of theme and language; but none of these writings displays the bold and trenchant thought of Job, let alone its literary and spiritual grandeur.

9. There is no "official" Jewish formulation on this subject. The prayer book affirms resurrection of the body, but even this was interpreted by some thinkers as merely a figure of speech for spiritual immortality. Descriptions of heaven and hell are found in various postbiblical writings, and during the Middle Ages the belief in reincarnation was widely accepted. But the medieval dogmatists were justified in holding that retribution was one of the universally accepted doctrines of Judaism.

10. See S. Schechter, *Some Aspects of Rabbinic Theology* (New York: Macmillan, 1923), pp. 170 ff.

11. Pritchard, *ANET*, p. 539.

12. *Ibid.*, pp. 538-540.

13. Ezekiel, whose language and thought are so often similar to that of H, has very different views on this subject. He ascribes the future change of heart entirely to God's grace (Ez. 36:25 f.), not to any impulse of the people to repent; and he rejects completely the notion of the "merit of the fathers" (Ez. 18:20).

Vows, Gifts, and Dues LEV. 27:1-34

1. This noun-form is found in rabbinic but not in biblical writings; our chapter, however, uses related verbs.

2. The obscure phrase in Deut. 18:8 may have a similar intent. The later halachah permits one to give his first-born animal to any priest he chooses: Maimonides, Hilch. Bechorot 1:15.

3. Arachin 19a.

4. Mishnah Bechorot 9:7.

Numbers

In the Desert NUM. 1:1–2:34

1. According to Julius H. Greenstone, *Numbers* (Philadelphia: Jewish Publication Society, 1939), p. 15. For a detailed description of traditional sources, see Nehama Leibowitz, *Iyyunim Befarashat Hashavua* (Jerusalem: World Zionist Organization, 1959), first series, "Sidrah Bemidbar."

2. So Rashi; Ibn Ezra, based on B.B. 109b.

3. Martin Noth, *Numbers: A Commentary* (Philadelphia: Westminster Press, 1966), p. 18.

4. Cf. Rashi; Targum.

5. Rashi, who is opposed by Ibn Ezra, reflecting the talmudic controversy, Sanh. 84 a. See Jacob Milgrom, *Studies in Levitical Terminology*, I (Berkeley: University of California Press, 1970), pp. 5, 8 ff.

6. See Bezalel Porten, *Archives from Elephantine* (Berkeley: University of California Press, 1968), pp. 29, *passim*.

7. Num. R. 2:7.

8. See further, Num. R. 2:8, 9.

9. Henri Cazelles, *Les Nombres* (2nd ed.; Paris: Editions du Cerf, 1958).

10. For a bibliography, see *Encyclopaedia Judaica* (16 vols., Jerusalem: Keter, 1972), Vol. 5, col. 283; G. E. Mendenhall, *Journal of Biblical Literature*, 77 (1958), pp. 52–66. [Hereafter cited as *JBL*.]

11. Noth, *Numbers*, pp. 21 ff.

12. So Mendenhall, *loc. cit.*, and Noth, *Numbers, ad loc.* Mendenhall, in his more recent work, *The Tenth Generation* (Baltimore and London: Johns Hopkins University Press, 1973), considers the tribes not as ethnic groupings but authority units or districts which were joined by their common acceptance of God's rule, p. 224.

13. Morris Adler, *The Voice Still Speaks* (New York: Bloch, 1969), pp. 265–268 *passim*.

14. Num. R. 1:7; 19:26.

15. *Itture Torah*, comp. and ed., Aaron Jacob Greenberg (Tel Aviv: Yavneh, from 1965 on), Vol. V, p. 9.

16. Num. R. 19:26; Tanch. Chukat 49; see also Num. 21:18.

17. Num. R. 2:1.

18. Matitiahu Tsevat in a private communication.

19. Friedrich von Schiller, from his poem *Kassandra*. For comparative literature, see "The Sin of a Census" in Theodor H. Gaster, *Myth, Legend and Custom in the Old Testament* (New York: Harper and Row, 1969), pp. 483 ff.

20. Num. R. 2:17.

21. Rashi on Num. 1:1–2.

22. Amy K. Blank, *The Spoken Choice* (Cincinnati: Hebrew Union College Press, 1959), p. 38.

Priestly Service NUM. 3:1–4:49

1. See also George B. Gray, *A Critical and Exegetical Commentary on Numbers* (New York: Scribner's, 1903).

2. The origin of the word is not certain; similar terms occur also in Ugaritic and Canaanite sources. See *Entsiklopedyah Mikra'it* (Jerusalem: Mosad Bialik, from 1955 on), Vol. IV, col. 14.

3. Mishnah Git. 5:8.

4. See *Shulchan Aruch*, Orach Chayim 473:4, n. 11 by R. Elijah of Vilna.

5. B. A. Levine, *JBL*, 82 (1963), pp. 207 ff.

6. See Nid. 44b; Num. R. 3:8.

7. M. K. 24b; Tanch. Bemidbar 21.

8. Num. R. 3:13.

9. Bechorot 4b.

10. Gray, *Critical and Exegetical.*

11. Num. R. 4:10. See Luzzatto on verse 50.

12. Hul. 24a; Sifre Num. 63. Bible critics apply the three ages to three different periods (so Gray, *Critical and Exegetical*; Norman H. Snaith, *Leviticus and Numbers*, The Century Bible [new ed.; London: Thomas Nelson, 1967]) or to different traditions (Arnold B. Ehrlich, *Mikra Kifeshuto* [rev. ed.; New York: Ktav, 1969]). It is also possible that we have here slightly different conceptions of the "age of discretion." Cf. G. W. Buchanan, *JBL*, 75 (1956), pp. 114–120.

13. *Interpreter's Dictionary of the Bible* (4 vols., New York and Nashville: Abingdon, 1962; supp. vol., 1976), Vol. II, p. 407. See *Notes on the New Translation of the Torah*, ed., Harry M. Orlinsky (Philadelphia: Jewish Publication Society, 1969), on Exod. 25:5. [Hereafter cited as JPS *Notes*.]

14. See Gershom Scholem, *Eranos* 1972 (offprint, Leiden, Holland: E. J. Brill, 1974), Vol. 41; pp. 1–49.

15. See Malbim; Luzzatto. The second translation is based on Job 7:19, which does not have an assured meaning.

16. Based on Arachin 11a.

17. See *Encyclopaedia Judaica*, Vol. 6, col. 1308.

18. Num. R. 3:5; 4:8; 5:3.

19. See *Interpreter's Dictionary*, Vol. II, p. 270, for details of biblical and Near Eastern laws on the firstborn.

20. *Ma'yanah shel Torah*, ed., Alexander Zusia Friedman (5 vols., Tel Aviv: Pe'er, 1955–1956), Vol. IV, pp. 17–18. English translation: *Wellsprings of Torah* (2 vols., New York: Judaica Press, 1969).

21. Num. R. 2:23.

22. Num. R. 4:20, beginning and end.

23. *Interpreter's Bible* (12 vols., New York and Nashville: Abingdon, 1952), Vol. II, pp. 159–60.

24. Num. R. 6:9.

25. Ehrlich, *Mikra Kifeshuto.*

26. Num. R. 3:5.

27. Num. R. 4:3.

28. Num. R. 6:10.

29. John Sturdy, *Numbers* (Cambridge, England: Cambridge University Press, 1976), p. 24.

Laws of Holiness; the Ordeal NUM. 5:1–31

1. Num. R. 7:2, 5.

2. See Maimonides, *Guide of the Perplexed*, III, 47; *Mishneh Torah* [also cited as *Yad*], Hilch. Bi'at ha-Mikdash, III, 3.

3. Sifre Num. 1.

4. Sifre Num. 4. See also Gleanings.

5. So Rashi.

6. Sifre Num. 7.

7. Rashi; Rashbam.

8. Luzzatto.

9. Mishnah Sotah 1:1,2; Talmud Sotah 14a; Num. R. 9:13.

10. Mishnah Sotah 1:5.

11. Sotah 20a and Sifre Num. 11:1.

12. James A. Pritchard, *Ancient Near Eastern Texts* (2nd rev. ed.; Princeton: Princeton University Press, 1955), p. 353. [Hereafter cited as Pritchard, *ANET*.]

13. Sotah 26a.

14. Num. R. 9.

15. This has been demonstrated conclusively by M. Fishbane, *Hebrew Union College Annual*, 45 (1974), pp. 25–46. [Hereafter cited as *HUCA*.] On the subject of the *sotah*, see also H. Ch. Brichto, *HUCA*, 46 (1976),

pp. 55–70, who reads the text as presenting a ritual designed to protect women from jealous husbands.

16. Sforno; Rashi.

17. Laws of Hammurabi, sect. 2, in Pritchard, *ANET*, p. 166.

18. Laws of Hammurabi, sects. 131, 132, in Pritchard, *ANET*, p. 171.

19. See the extensive treatment of parallel sources by Gaster, *Myth*, pp. 280–300.

20. Sotah 20a–b.

21. Pes. 64b. See Alexander Guttmann, "The Significance of Miracles for Talmudic Judaism," *HUCA*, 20 (1947), pp. 363–406; *Encyclopaedia Judaica*, Vol. 12, cols. 73 ff.

22. See also Samson Raphael Hirsch, at end of Num. 5.

23. Mishnah Sotah 9:9; see also Julian Morgenstern, *HUCA*, 2 (1925), pp. 113–143.

24. Num. R. 7:10.

25. Gray, *Critical and Exegetical*, commentary on verse 6.

26. Num. R. 8:1, 2, 3. Most of Num. R. 8 deals with this subject.

27. *Wellsprings*, Vol. II, pp. 290–291.
28. Hirsch, *ad* 5:2, 3.
29. Philo, *Of Special Laws*, X.
30. *Protevangelium of James*, ch. 16. The work is generally attributed to the late second century c.e.
31. Num. R. 9:2. For further literature on the subject of ordeal, see *Encyclopaedia Judaica*, Vol. 12, cols. 1448–1450.

Vows of Abstinence   NUM. 6:1–21

1. See *Encyclopaedia Judaica*, Vol. 12, col. 908.
2. Mishnah Nazir 3: 6; Talmud Nazir 19b. On the life of Queen Helena, see *Jewish Encyclopedia* (12 vols., New York: Funk & Wagnalls, 1904), Vol. 6, p. 334; *Encyclopaedia Judaica*, Vol. 8, col. 288.
3. So Rashi, based on Sifre Num. 25.
4. Mishnah Temurah 7:4.
5. See Greenstone, *Numbers*, for a full description of the offerings and the reasons for specifying them in this manner; *Vetus Testamentum* (Leiden, Holland: E. J. Brill), 21, pp. 237–239.
6. See Noth, *Numbers*.
7. Temurah 10a.
8. Luke 1:15; Acts 18:18. See also Acts 21:23–26, where the continued observance of these rules is stressed.
9. The tractate Nazir deals with the subject, and the matter is mentioned frequently elsewhere in the Talmud. Mishnah Nazir 3:6 and 5:4 record how widespread nazirite vows were. See also Mishnah Nazir 5:5 on naziriteship as a consequence of lost bets.
10. Mishnah Nazir 1:3.
11. Mishnah Nazir 1:2.
12. Nazir 19a.
13. *Wellsprings*, Vol. II, p. 293.
14. See Gray, *Critical and Exegetical*, pp. 63 ff., where a detailed survey of various religions and cultures may be found.
15. For a discussion of the sect, which seems to have disappeared during the time of the Second Temple, see *Encyclopaedia Judaica*, Vol. 13, cols. 1609 ff.
16. See Noth, *Numbers*, p. 54.
17. Compare "Beard," *Jewish Encyclopedia*, Vol. 2, pp. 611 ff.
18. Gray, *Critical and Exegetical*, p. 63, with source references to the Koran and other literature. For abstinence among other nations, see p. 62.
19. *Ibid.*, p. 69, with a listing of comparative literature.
20. *Wellsprings*, Vol. II, p. 293.
21. Quoted in B. S. Jacobson, *Meditations on the Torah* (Tel Aviv: Sinai Publishing, 1956), p. 218.
22. Commentary on 6:11.
23. Mishnah Nazir 4:1.

The Priestly Benediction   NUM. 6:22–27

1. *Pentateuch and Haftorahs*, ed., Joseph H. Hertz (Oxford: Oxford University Press, 1929–1936; republished in U.S.A., 1941 and thereafter.)
2. Mishnah Sotah 7:2, 6; Mishnah Tamid 7:2; Sotah 37b; Num. R. 11:4.
3. Sifre Num. 40.
4. Rashi; Ibn Ezra.
5. Sifre Num. 41.
6. See Luzzatto.
7. Sirach 50:19–20.
8. Mishnah Tamid 7:2; Talmud Sotah 37b.
9. Zohar; Naso 147b.
10. *Code of Jewish Law* (*Kitzur Shulchan Aruch*), trans., H. E. Goldin (New York: Hebrew Publishing, 1927), ch. C, 9, 10; *Shulchan Aruch*, Orach Chayim 128:5, 23.
11. On the wider uses of blessings (among friends, on meeting or parting, etc.), see Cassuto, *Entsiklopedyah Mikra'it*, Vol. II, pp. 358 f.
12. R. Samuel ben Meir, twelfth century c.e., in his commentary on verse 27. Note also that in the synagogue service the congregation responds to each blessing by saying: "May this be His will"—thereby stressing the prayerful nature of the benediction.
13. Gray, *Critical and Exegetical*, p. 71.
14. Bachya on verse 27.
15. Cassuto, *Entsiklopedyah Mikra'it*, *loc. cit.*
16. Num. R. 11:2, 8, end). See also Cassuto, *loc. cit.*
17. N. Leibowitz, *Studies in the Weekly Sidrah* (Jerusalem: World Zionist Organization, 1962), Vol. 7, pp. 234 ff.

18. Hertz, *Pentateuch and Haftorahs*, based on rabbinic teachings.

19. *The Hasidic Anthology*, ed., Louis I. Newman (New York: Bloch, 1944), p. 359, n. 1, quoting the Tzechiver Rebbe.

20. Snaith, *Leviticus and Numbers*, p. 207.

21. Num. R. 11:7.

22. See Hertz, *Pentateuch and Haftorahs*, quoting Joseph Morris.

23. Manual of Discipline, I, 16 ff., in *The Dead Sea Scriptures*, ed., T. H. Gaster (Garden City, N.Y.: Doubleday, 1956), p. 40.

24. Mishnah Tamid 7:2.

Of Princely and Priestly Things NUM. 7:1–8:26

1. See Baruch Levine, *Journal of the American Oriental Society*, 85 (1965), pp. 307 ff. [Hereafter cited as *JAOS*.]

2. See Sifre Num. 44; Rashi; Ibn Ezra.

3. See further Sotah 35a; Sifre Num. 46.

4. See Ibn Ezra; Num. R. 14:19, 21. Gray considers this sentence an isolated fragment, see Gray, *Critical and Exegetical*.

5. J. Gutmann, *Zeitschrift für neutestamentliche Wissenschaft*, Vol. 60, pp. 289 ff.

6. Rashi.

7. See Gray, *Critical and Exegetical*, p. 79, quoting Herodotus.

8. *Views of the Biblical World* (5 vols., Chicago and New York: Jordan Publishing Co., 1959–1961), Vol. 1, p. 205.

9. Luzzatto; Hertz.

10. So Snaith; similarly Hertz.

11. So Noth, *Numbers*.

12. Num. R. 13:9 ff.

13. Num. R. 13:20.

14. Num. R. 12:6; 13:6.

15. Adler, *The Voice*, pp. 282, 283.

16. Num. R. 14:22, with reference to Jer. 23:24.

17. *Wellsprings*, Vol. II, p. 297, quoting the Rebbe of Przysucha.

18. See also Noth, *Numbers*. According to Num. R. 14:21, Psalm 29:4 ff. represents a detailed interpretation of "the Voice" in our passage.

19. Num. R. 12:6.

20. Num. R. 12:11.

The Second Passover; the Cloud; the Silver Trumpets NUM. 9:1–10:10

1. Pes. 6b. See there for a discussion of the problem; also Nachmanides. For an extensive exposition, see B. H. Epstein, *Sefer Tosefet Berachah* (Tel Aviv: Moreshet Publishing House, 1964), on Deut. 1:1.

2. Sab. 34a–35a; Josephus, *The Jewish War*, trans., William Whiston (New York: Al Burt Co., no date), VI, 9:3.

3. See further Sifre Num. 67; Nachmanides.

4. Sifre Num. 69; Mishnah Pes. 9:3.

5. Ibn Ezra.

6. See *Entsiklopedyah Mikra'it*, Vol. VI, p. 330.

7. The question is discussed in detail by Malbim.

8. Nachmanides; Malbim.

9. Ibn Ezra; see also Gray, *Critical and Exegetical*.

10. See Targum Jonathan.

11. They are described in detail by Josephus, *The Jewish Antiquities*, trans., Whiston (New York: Al Burt Co., no date), III, 12:6.

12. Mishnah R.H. 4:9.

13. Ibn Ezra. For examples of the use of trumpets during warfare, see Abijah's defeat of Jeroboam (II Chron. 13:12–16); during Maccabean times (I Mac. 4:40; 5:33); similarly Joshua's use of the shofar at Jericho (Josh. 6).

14. *Encyclopaedia Judaica*, Vol. 13, cols. 169 ff.

15. Mishnah Pes. 9:1, 2; Talmud Pes. 93b.

16. They are listed in Sifre Num. 69. See the full discussion in Christian D. Ginsburg, *Introduction to the Massoretico-Critical Edition of the Hebrew Bible* (New York: Ktav, 1966), pp. 318–334.

17. Snaith, *Leviticus and Numbers*.

18. Hirsch.

19. *Gates of Repentance* (London: Union of Liberal and Progressive Synagogues, 1973), p. 90.

20. *The Union Prayer Book* (New York: Central Conference of American Rabbis, 1960), Vol. II, p. 77.

1. Sifre Num. 78.

2. *Interpreter's Dictionary*, Vol. III, p. 375. W. J. Dumbrell, following P. Haupt, suggests that Midian was the term for a league or confederacy (*Vetus Testamentum*, 25 [1975], pp. 323 ff.).

3. Sifre Num. 82.

4. Mishnah Yadayim 3:5.

5. Sifre Num. 84, which also records the opinion that these verses belong more properly after Num. 2:17. See M. Greenberg, *JAOS*, 76 (1956), p. 159. See also S. Z. Leiman, *JBL*, 93 (1974), pp. 348–355, who discusses various midrashic traditions and B. A. Levine's critique, *JBL*, 95 (1976), pp. 122–124, which suggests (with S. Lieberman) that R. Judah ha-Nasi may have referred not to a "separate" book but to a suppressed or hidden one containing the prophecies of Eldad and Medad. On linguistic problems, see J. Solomon, *Beth Mikra*, 51, 4 (July-September 1972), 439–441.

6. See W. F. Albright, *HUCA*, 23 (1950–1951), p. 17.

7. Yoma 75a.

8. See Ginsburg, *Introduction to the Massoretico-Critical Edition*, p. 353; Jerusalem Targum.

9. Num. R. 15:24.

10. Sifre Num. 93.

11. Sifre Num. 95.

12. The above translation follows Rashi, Sifre 96; the opposite translation is given by Onkelos and Vulgate.

13. See Gray, *Critical and Exegetical*, p. 118.

14. So Ludwig Koehler and Walter Baumgartner *Lexicon in Veteris Testamenti Libros: Hebrew-Aramaic Lexicon* (Grand Rapids: Eerdmans, 1951–1953).

15. Herodotus, *History* (New York: Tudor, 1932), II, 77, p. 107.

16. So Ehrlich.

17. Sifre Num. 86.

18. Greenstone, *Numbers*.

19. G. Cornfeld, ed., *Adam to Daniel* (New York: Macmillan, 1961), p. 160. See also, W. G. Plaut, "In Defense of the Erev Rav," *CCAR Journal* (New York: Central Conference of American Rabbis, June 1964), pp. 36–38.

20. See Gleanings. For an exhaustive analysis of prophecy and ecstasy, see Abraham Joshua Heschel, *The Prophets* (New York: Burning Bush Press, 1962), pp. 324–366.

21. Num. R. 15:19.

22. B. Halevi, *Beth Mikra*, 40, 1 (December 1969), 77–94.

23. Sifre Num. 78, end.

24. Heschel, *Prophets*, p. 358.

25. Mishnah San. 8:5.

26. Num. R. 15:23.

27. Num. R. 15:24.

28. Also Sifre Num. 87.

29. Hul. 27b.

30. Isaiah Horowitz, *Sheloh* (Amsterdam, 1704), p. 354a.

31. David Daiches, *Moses: The Man and His Vision* (New York: Praeger, 1975), p. 159.

Of Prophecy and Punishment   NUM. 12:1–16

1. Frank Moore Cross, *Canaanite Myth and Hebrew Epic* (Cambridge, Mass.: Harvard University Press, 1973), p. 204.

2. Martin Buber, *The Prophetic Faith* (New York: Macmillan, 1949), p. 57.

3. Sifre Num. 105; see further Ginsburg, *Introduction to the Massoretico-Critical Edition*, pp. 353 f.

4. Maimonides repeatedly treats of this subject, see especially *Yad, Yesode ha-Torah* 7:6 and *Guide*, II, 41, 45. See further Zohar, Vol. I, 170b–171a; *Yalkut Me'am Lo'ez* (11 vols., Jerusalem: Or Chadash, 1967–

1971), Vol. IV, pp. 140–144; and Heschel, *Prophets*, pp. 340 f.

5. Sifre Num. 99.

6. See Ibn Ezra and perush al Ibn Ezra.

7. For a fuller discussion, see W. G. Plaut, "The Punishment of Aaron, a Commentary on Numbers 12," *CCAR Journal* (June 1963), pp. 35–38.

8. William W. Hallo, *Bulletin of Congregation Mishkan Israel* (New Haven, March 1969). Also see *The Autobiography of Malcolm X* (New York: Grove, 1965), p. 298.

9. Sifre Num. 100.
10. Sifre Num. 105.
11. *Yalkut Shimoni* 1: **539.**

12. M. Buber, *Moses* (Oxford and London: East and West Library, 1947), p. 156.
13. Daiches, *Moses*, p. 164.

Trial and Condemnation NUM. 13:1–14:45

1. *Views of the Biblical World*, Vol. 1, p. 211.
2. See Num. R. 16:8; Rashi.
3. Ehrlich.
4. For a description of its ancient fertility, see Nelson Glueck, *Rivers in the Desert: A History of the Negev* (New York: Farrar, Straus, Cudahy, 1959), pp. 5, 41, 60, 93 *passim*.
5. Noth, *Numbers*, p. 105.
6. Pritchard, *ANET*, p. 328.
7. E. C. B. Maclaurin, *Vetus Testamentum*, 15 (1965), pp. 468–474; see *Entsiklopedyah Mikra'it*, Vol. VI, cols. 312 f.
8. *Jerome Bible Commentary*, eds., R. E. Brown, J. A. Fitzmyer, R. E. Murphy (Englewood Cliffs, N. J.: Prentice Hall, 1968), on Num. 13:33.
9. Josephus, *War*, IV, 9:7.
10. *Views of the Biblical World*, Vol. 1, p. 213.
11. *Interpreter's Dictionary*, Vol. II, p. 576.
12. N. Hareuveni, *Ecology in the Bible* (Kiryat Ono: Neot Kedumim, 1974), pp. 10–17.
13. Ehrlich, *Mikra Kifeshuto*.
14. Arachin 15a.
15. Mishnah Sotah 8:7; Babylonian Talmud Sotah 44b; Jerusalem Talmud Sotah 8:10, 23a. See further,

Entsiklopedyah Mikra'it, Vol. IV., cols. 1057–1064.
16. Gray, *Critical and Exegetical*, pp. 130 f.
17. H. M. Orlinsky, *Ancient Israel* (Ithaca, N.Y.: Cornell University Press, 1954), pp. 46 f.
18. Num. R. 16:12.
19. Num. R. 16:17.
20. Tanch. Shelach 12.
21. Adler, *The Voice*, p. 310.
22. Num. R. 16:23.
23. Oliver Goldsmith, from his poem *The Deserted Village*.
24. Hareuveni, *Ecology*, p. 11.
25. *Interpreter's Bible*, Vol. II, p. 211.
26. Sotah 35a.
27. Details in Gaster, *Myth*, nn. 94, 302; compare Nachmanides; Bachya on Num. 14:9. A variant tradition: if one sees his shadow without a head on Hoshana Rabbah; see illustration in *Universal Jewish Encyclopedia* (10 vols., New York: Universal Jewish Encyclopedia, 1939–1943), Vol. 5, p. 465.
28. Mishnah Ta'an. 4:6.
29. André Neher, *Moses and the Vocation of the Jewish People* (New York and London: Harper/Longmans, 1959), p. 118.

Various Laws; Fringes NUM. 15:1–41

1. See below at verse 20 and *Encyclopaedia Judaica*, Vol. 7, cols. 1193 ff.
2. Sirach 50:15. See also Josephus, *Antiquities*, III, 9:4.
3. Mishnah Hal. 1:1.
4. Mishnah Hal. 2:7.
5. Mishnah Hal. 4:8 ff.; *Shulchan Aruch*, Yoreh Deah 322 ff.
6. Mishnah Sab. 2:6.
7. B. A. Levine and W. W. Hallo, *HUCA*, 38 (1967), p. 45.
8. Sifre Num. 112.
9. Rashi, based on San. 30b (where the biblical

passage is also cited as one of the proof texts for the doctrine of immortality).
10. Sifre Num. 113.
11. San. 7:1.
12. See Sab. 25a; Rashi; Mishnah San. 9:6; compare *Yad*, Hilch. Biat ha-Mikdash 9:1. On the development of these understandings, see A. Guttmann, *Rabbinic Judaism in the Making* (Detroit: Wayne State University Press, 1970), pp. 138 f.
13. Sifre Num. 114.
14. On the symbolism of blue (and other colors), see Scholem, *Eranos 1972*, Vol. 41, pp. 1 ff.
15. F. J. Stephens, *JBL*, 50 (1931), pp. 59–70; H. B.

Huffman, *Biblical Archeologist*, 31 (1968), pp. 101–124; see also Gray, *Critical and Exegetical*, p. 183.

16. A. Milgram, *Jewish Worship* (Philadelphia: Jewish Publication Society, 1971), p. 619, n. 10.

17. Details and picture in *Jewish Encyclopedia*, Vol. 2, p. 76. See Israel Abrahams, *A Companion to the Authorized Daily Prayer Book* (rev. ed., London: Eyre and Spottiswoode, 1922), pp. xxvi ff.

18. Goldin, *Code*, pp. 19, 25.

19. Men. 43a.

20. J. Z. Lauterbach, *HUCA*, 4 (1927), pp. 183 f., n. 9.

21. Mishnah Men. 4:1; Talmud Men. 38a.

22. Men. 43b.

23. *Wellsprings*, Vol. II, p. 314.

24. *The Hasidic Anthology*, ed., Newman, p. 154, n. 2.

25. Sifre Num. 113.

26. Milgram, *Jewish Worship*, p. 345.

27. Num. R. 17:5; see Nachmanides; Ibn Ezra.

28. Matthew 23:5, 13.

29. Men. 43b.

30. *The Hasidic Anthology*, ed. Newman, p. 351, n. 3.

The Rebellion of Korah, Dathan, and Abiram NUM. 16:1–17:15

1. New English Bible.

2. So Hertz, *Pentateuch and Haftorahs*, after Rashbam.

3. New English Bible.

4. Gray, *Critical and Exegetical*.

5. Ehrlich.

6. See Isa. 14:9–11; Ps. 6:6; in the Apocrypha, Enoch 22; in the Christian Scriptures, Luke 16:22–25. On Job's concept of death, see 3:17–19; 21:23–26.

7. Cross, *Canaanite Myth*, pp. 198 ff. See also Ellis Rivkin, *The Dynamics of Jewish History* (Sarasota: New College, 1970), pp. 17 f., who reads the story as a victory of the Aaronides over the Levites, including Moses.

8. See San. 110a; also Ibn Ezra.

9. San. 109b, but see the differing opinions of R. Joshua (Avot de R. Nathan 36) and R. Judah ben Bathyra (Num. R. 18:13).

10. Tanch. Korah 4 (ed., Buber); Num. R. 18:3.

11. Jerusalem Talmud San. 10:27d–28a.

12. See Louis Ginzberg, *The Legends of the Jews* (Philadelphia: Jewish Publication Society, 1909–1946), Vol. VI, p. 103, n. 586.

13. Buber, *Moses*, p. 186.

14. *Ibid.*, p. 188.

15. Of the traditional Jewish commentators, only Luzzatto deals with Korah's argument; for a further discussion, see W. G. Plaut, "Some Unanswered Questions about Korah," *CCAR Journal* (October 1969), pp. 74–78.

16. Tanch. Korah 3; Num. R. 18:2.

17. Commentary on 16:4.

18. Tanch. Korah 21.

19. Num. R. 18:11.

20. *Wellsprings*, Vol. II, p. 316.

21. *Ethics of the Fathers* 5:17.

22. Zohar, Korah 176a (ed., Soncino), Vol. V, p. 238.

23. Leibowitz, *Studies*, Vol. 7, p. 260, quoting Isaac Arama.

Of Priests, Levites, and Israelites NUM. 17:16–18:32

1. See J. Milgrom, *JAOS*, 90 (1970), pp. 204–209. One version of the Hittite "Instructions for Temple Officials" may be found in Pritchard, *ANET*, pp. 207–210.

2. Nachmanides; Ehrlich.

3. Gray, *Critical and Exegetical*.

4. Quoted from *Views of the Biblical World*, Vol. 1, p. 217. On the textual difficulty of seeing both blossoms and ripe fruit, see Greenstone, *Numbers*, at 17:23.

5. Gray, *Critical and Exegetical*, and Noth, *Numbers*. See the two verses as a bridge between two stories.

6. Arachin 11b.

7. See also E. A. Speiser, *Israel Exploration Journal*, 13 (1963), pp. 69 ff., on the expression מַתְּנָה נְתֻנִים.

8. See JPS *Notes* on Lev. 7:35 about the reasons for this translation.

9. Mishnah Terumot 4:3; cf. Hirsch.

10. This was based on Deut. 8:8; see commentaries to Mishnah Bik. 1:3 and Ber. 6:4.

11. W. L. Moran, *Biblica*, 39 (1958), pp. 69–71, adds Jer. 48:9 to this list, translating צִיץ (usually rendered "wings") as "salt." See further, Gaster, *Myth*, pp. 301, 618.

12. See further, Charles Kasovsky, *Otsar Leshon ha-Mishnah*, Vol. II, p. 1422; Maimonides, *Yad*, Hilch. Ma'aser 1:3.

13. Snaith, *Leviticus*, p. 267.

14. Details in Goldin, *Code*, pp. 48 ff.; *Shulchan Aruch*, Yoreh Deah 305:1 ff.

15. Gaster, *Myth*, p. 301.

16. Num. R. 18:23.

17. Josephus, *Antiquities*, IV, 4:2.

18. George Herbert, *The Temple* (reprint of 1633 edition; New York: British Book Centre, 1975).

The Red Cow; Laws of Purification NUM. 19:1–22

1. Josephus, *Antiquities*, IV, 4:6.

2. Mishnah Par. 1:1; Sifre Num. 122.

3. Mishnah Par. 2:5; Sifre Num. 123.

4. *Entsiklopedyah Mikra'it*, Vol. I, col. 186, with details.

5. Mishnah Par. 3:11.

6. Sifre Num. 126.

7. For other examples of utilizing heifers in rituals of purification, see Gray, *Critical and Exegetical*, pp. 246 ff.; *Interpreter's Dictionary*, Vol. IV, p. 19.

8. Tanch. Chukat 26.

9. Hertz on Num. 19:22.

10. Mishnah Par. 3:5.

11. Num. R. 19:3.

12. Num. R. 19:8.

13. *Shulchan Aruch*, Yoreh Deah 369, 371; Goldin, *Code*, p. 202.

14. *Jerome Bible Commentary* on Matthew 23:27, where the custom is mentioned.

15. Gray, *Critical and Exegetical*, p. 247, quoting Philo.

16. *Ibid.*, quoting Augustine.

17. Koran, Sura II:63–66 (The Cow).

18. "The Seer of Lublin," *Wellsprings*, Vol. II, p. 323.

19. *Pesikta de-R. Kahana*, trans., W. G. Braude and I. J. Kapstein (Philadelphia: Jewish Publication Society, 1975), quoting a midrash, Piska 4, p. 58.

Thirty-Eight Years Later NUM. 20:1–29

1. Ibn Ezra.

2. Targum Jonathan; Rashi.

3. Ibn Ezra takes the first view; Rashi, the second.

4. So Josephus, *Antiquities*, IV, 4:7, who says that it was in the environs of Petra.

5. For a survey, see W. G. Plaut, "The Sin of the Brothers," *CCAR Journal* (April 1961), pp. 18–24; also, E. Arden, "How Moses Failed God," *JBL*, 76 (1957), pp. 50–52.

6. Koran, Sura VII:160 (Al Araf).

7. Num. R. 19:9; Yalkut Shimoni, Vol. I, p. 763; Hirsch makes this point strongly.

8. Maimonides, *Introduction to Ethics of the Fathers* 4.

9. M. Margaliot, *Beth Mikra*, 58, 3 (April–June 1974), pp. 374–400.

10. See *Yalkut Shimoni*, loc. cit.

11. "Petirat Mosheh," *Bet ha-Midrash*, ed., A. Jellinek (Jerusalem: Bamberger and Wahrmann, 1938), Vol. I, p. 119.

12. See *Yalkut Me'am Lo'ez*.

13. For example, Ehrlich; Gray, *Critical and Exegetical*.

14. This point is already suggested by Albo, though in a different context, *Ikkarim*, IV:22.

15. See especially "Petirat Mosheh," *passim*.

16. *Ethics of the Fathers* 1:12.

17. Lev. R. 20:12.

18. M.K. 28a.

19. Midrash ha-Gadol on verse 11.

20. Targum Jonathan on Num. 21:19; Num. R. 19:25, 26; Tanch. Chukat 47; see Rashi on verse 10.

21. I Corinthians 10:4. See also the hymn, "Rock of Ages," by Augustus M. Toplady, which compares Christ to the rock "cleft for me," *The Hymnal* (rev. ed., Philadelphia: General Assembly of the Presbyterian Church, 1914), no. 464.

22. Hirsch on verse 12.

23. "Petirat Aharon," *Bet ha-Midrash*, Vol. I, p. 95; translated by B. H. Mehlman, *CCAR Journal* (Summer, 1980), pp. 49–58. Possibly this is the story referred to in the Koran, Sura XXXIII:69 (The Confederates).

24. Num. R. 19:17.

25. *Interpreter's Bible*, Vol. II, p. 241.

26. After Rashi, based on Avot de-R. Nathan 12.

27. Avot de-R. Nathan 12:3, which says that after Aaron's death many children were named after him.

28. Hertz on Num. 20:29.

29. See Hebrews 7:11–19.

30. R. J. Z. Werblowsky, *Encyclopaedia Judaica*, Vol. 2, col. 8.

Wandering and Warfare NUM. 21:1–22:1

1. For a comparison with and an evaluation of the parallel accounts in Deut. 2:26–37 and Judg. 11:19–26, see J. van Seters, *JBL*, 71 (1972), pp. 182–197.

2. Nachmanides. Others (e.g., Gray, *Critical and Exegetical*) believe that verses 1–3 are misplaced here or are parenthetical and should be read together with Josh. 1:16, 17 and 14:40–45.

3. On excavations there, see Y. Aharoni, in *New Directions in Biblical Archeology*, eds., D. N. Freedman and J. C. Greenfield (Garden City, N. Y.: Doubleday, 1969).

4. So Targum Onkelos; Rashi.

5. See Targum Onkelos; A.Z. 5a,b. On Rashi's different understanding, see his commentary on A.Z. 5b.

6. Rashi.

7. Gray, *Critical and Exegetical*; Noth, *Numbers*.

8. *Interpreter's Dictionary*, Vol. I, pp. 176 f.

9. R.H. 31a. For comparative folklore on wells, which were thought to be controlled by spirits that had to be placated by song, see Gaster, *Myth*, p. 302.

10. See Gray, *Critical and Exegetical*, p. 289.

11. Num. R. 19:30; R. Pappa, Hul. 60b, gives a different reason.

12. Num. R. 19:78; Nachmanides on verse 13.

13. So Ehrlich. Similarly, Hallo who suggests that vss. 27–29 resemble Jer. 48:45 f. and that both go back to a common original source.

14. Pritchard, *ANET*, p. 320.

15. Yehezkel Kaufmann, *The Religion of Israel*, translated and abridged by Moshe Greenberg (Chicago: University of Chicago Press, 1960), p. 131, n. 2.

16. So N. Netzer, *Beth Mikra* 56 (1973), pp. 101–102.

17. So the Septuagint; details in Ginsburg, *Introduction to the Massoretico-Critical Edition*, pp. 326 ff. See also Sifre Num. 69.

18. Wisdom 16:5–7; Mishnah R. H. 3:8. See further, Karen R. Joines, *JBL*, 87 (1968), pp. 245–256, and *idem*, *Serpent Symbolism in the Old Testament* (Haddonfield: Haddonfield House, 1974). The author sets forth the contrasting powers, for both good and evil, ascribed to serpents and holds that the snake's deception (in Gen. 3) is meant to bring humanity to life, not death.

19. Tur-Sinai, *Peshuto shel Mikra* (Jerusalem: Kiryat Sefer, 1962), Vol. I, pp. 167–169.

20. *Entsiklopedyah Mikra'it*, Vol. IV, col. 1066.

21. Philo, *On the Allegories of the Sacred Laws*, II:20.

22. John 3:14.

23. Tanch. Chukat 45; Rashi.

24. Num. R. 19:26.

25. Num. R. 19:26. See also Num. R. 1:7 (quoted in ch. 1, Gleanings).

26. Ned. 55a. See also M. Miller, *Shabbat Shiurim* (rev. ed., Gateshead, England: Gateshead Foundation, 1969), pp. 215 ff.

27. *Wellsprings*, Vol. II, p. 327, quoting the Gaon of Vilna.

28. Quoted by Gray, *Critical and Exegetical*, p. 288.

29. Num. R. 19:32. On Rephaim, see Gen. 14:5.

30. Sturdy, *Numbers*, p. 148.

Part III The Story of Balaam

1. *Jerome Bible Commentary*, Num. 41. See further, W. F. Albright, *JBL*, 63 (1944), pp. 207–233, and his summary of recent scholarly opinions in *Encyclopaedia Judaica*, Vol. 4, cols. 121–123; G. von Rad, *Moses* (New York: Association Press, 1960), pp. 70–80. The earliest extensive treatment of the Balaam story was by M. M. Kalisch, *Bible Studies, Part I, The Prophecies of Balaam* (London: Longmans Green, 1879). A thorough literary analysis has been provided by W. Gross, *Bileam* (Munich: Kösel, 1974), who considers Num. 22–24 a single story with some expansions (23:26–24:25) and one independent unit (the speaking ass).

2. B.B. 14b–15a. This view was strongly supported by Kalisch, *Bible Studies*, pp. 307 ff., who reproduced the "book" as he believed it to have been.

3. O. Eissfeldt, *JBL*, 87 (1968), pp. 383–393.

1. Gray, *Critical and Exegetical*, p. 317.

2. W. F. Albright, *JBL*, 63 (1944), p. 232.

3. Pritchard, *ANET*, p. 278.

4. *Jerome Bible Commentary*; for further details, see Gray, *Critical and Exegetical*, p. 325.

5. Ibn Ezra.

6. For examples of similar stories in other cultures, see Gray, *Critical and Exegetical*, p. 334.

7. Rashi, based on Tanch. Balak *ad loc.*

8. See the controversy between R. Akiba and R. Yishmael in Hul. 17a.

9. See at Gen. 2:2, 3; Gray, *Critical and Exegetical*, p. 342.

10. The first translation follows Targum Onkelos and Rashi; the second, the Talmud San. 105a and Rashbam; the third, Ibn Ezra.

11. See the analysis by S. Gevirtz, *Patterns in the Early Poetry of Israel* (Studies in Ancient Oriental Civilization, No. 32; 2nd ed., Chicago: University of Chicago Press, 1973), pp. 64–65.

12. *Ibid.*, p. 66, n. 48.

13. Rashi, after Tanch. Balak 22.

14. See *Views of the Biblical World*, Vol. 1, p. 228.

15. So Gray, *Critical and Exegetical*, p. 356.

16. See the picture in *Views of the Biblical World*, *loc. cit.*

17. So the Talmud in Nid. 31a.

18. So the old JPS; King James; and New English Bible.

19. *The Standard Prayer Book*, ed., S. Singer (New York: Bloch, 1957), p. 2; *Gates of Prayer* (Cincinnati: Central Conference of American Rabbis, 1975), p. 51.

20. Gray, *Critical and Exegetical*, p. 264. On other aspects of this verse, especially the word play נְטִיו–נָטַע and the parallel to Gen. 2:8, see M. Moreshet, *Beth Mikra*, 48 (October–November 1971), pp. 51–56.

21. Ibn Ezra; Noth, *Numbers*; and see Greenstone, *Numbers*, for a survey.

22. Targum Onkelos; Nachmanides.

23. Lam. R. 2:4, where it is told that R. Akiba identified the "star" as Bar Kochba whom he thought to be the Messiah.

24. See *Interpreter's Bible*, Vol. II, *ad loc.*; Gray, *Critical and Exegetical*, p. 270. The Christian Scriptures do not quote this verse, but it is likely that the story of the star heralding Jesus' birth is based on it. In Revelations 22:16 he is called the morning star.

25. *Jerome Bible Commentary.*

26. Gevirtz, *JBL*, 87 (1968), pp. 267 ff.

27. For other explanations, see Greenstone, *Numbers*; and for a detailed analysis, Gevirtz, *Patterns*, pp. 66 ff.

28. On the various word plays in this oracle, see Gaster, *Myth*, pp. 308–309.

29. See Jer. 2:10; Ezek. 27:6. Targum Jonathan identifies Kittim anachronistically with the Romans.

30. So Snaith, *Leviticus*, basing it on such usage in the Dead Sea Scrolls.

31. Gaster, *Myth*, p. 303. See Kalisch, *Bible Studies*, pp. 99 ff., for Roman and Greek parallels; also see Gray, *Critical and Exegetical*, pp. 327 f.

32. Gaster, *Myth*, p. 303.

33. *Ibid.*

34. See Nachmanides on verse 23; see further, *Jerome Bible Commentary.*

35. *Guide*, II, 42; so also G. Herder, *Geist der Ebräischen Poesie* (Leipzig, 1787), II, pp. 177–179.

36. Gevirtz, *Patterns*, pp. 57–61.

37. *Jerome Bible Commentary*, p. 95.

38. San. 105a. Compare Acts 1:25 for the application of this term to Judas.

39. Targum Jonathan on Num. 31:8.

40. Targum Jonathan on Num. 23:10.

41. *Ethics of the Fathers* 5:19 and Christian sources (from II Peter 2:15, 16; and Jude 11 to Calvin and beyond) generally agree with this assessment. For a summary, see Gray, *Critical and Exegetical*, pp. 321 ff.

42. San. 105b–106a.

43. Sifre Deut. 357.

44. A.Z. 2b; Ginzberg, *Legends*, Vol. VI, p. 30, n. 181.

45. Num. R. 1:7; 19:26.

46. See Rashbam on 24:1–2, who says that God's illumination came to a willing Balaam.

47. Tanna debei Eliyahu 28.

48. Ibn Ezra on Num. 22:28; similarly Hirsch.

49. See Leibowitz, *Studies*, Vol. 1, weekly portion "Balak."

50. Kalisch, *Bible Studies*, p. 11 *passim*. A similar conclusion is reached, albeit for different reasons, by G. W. Coats, *Biblical Research*, Vol. 18 (1973), pp. 21 ff.

51. Albright, *JBL*, 63 (1944), p. 233; this view is also put forth by Daiches, *Moses*, pp. 201–202.

52. Gray, *Critical and Exegetical*, p. 318.

53. Num. R. 20:4.

54. Mak. 10b; Num. R. 20:12; see also Maimonides, Hilch. Teshuvah 5:2; B. S. Jacobson, *Meditations on the Torah*, pp. 236 ff.; Leibowitz, *Studies*, Vol. 3, portion "Balak."

55. M. Hacohen, *Al ha-Torah* (5 vols., Jerusalem: Reuben Mass, 1962), Vol. IV, pp. 427 f.

56. Jacobson, *Meditations*, p. 241, quoting F. Rosenzweig.

57. *Wellsprings*, Vol. II, pp. 330 f.

58. *Ethics of the Fathers* 5:16.

59. Hertz, p. 671, quoting Israel Zangwill.

60. Gaster, *Myth*, p. 309, with further parallels and sources.

61. Num. R. 20:14.

62. *Ibid.*

63. *Yalkut Me'am Lo'ez*, quoting various medieval sources.

64. Num. R. 20:19.

65. Quoted in *The Hasidic Anthology*, ed., Newman, p. 202.

66. *Ibid.*, p. 200.

67. Num. R. 20:20.

68. Quoted in Hacohen, *Al ha-Torah*, Vol. IV, pp. 434–435.

69. In the *Malchuyot*; *Standard Prayer Book*, ed., Singer, p. 364.

70. Epstein, *Sefer Tosefet Berachah*, Vol. IV, pp. 183 ff.

71. Von Rad, *Moses*, p. 74.

72. W. G. Plaut, *The Case for the Chosen People* (Garden City, N. Y.: Doubleday, 1965), p. 150.

73. B.B. 60a.

74. San. 105a; Rashi; see also JPS *Notes*.

75. Alluded to in Hacohen, *Al ha-Torah*, Vol. IV, p. 434.

76. *Ibid.*, p. 436.

77. On 24:5. Targum Yerushalmi applies it to Israel's places of worship.

78. Similarly Hirsch.

79. Num. R. 12:14.

80. Gaster, p. 307, with further parallels and sources. The quotation has been corrected with regard to the lands in the north, south, and east, in accordance with the reference Gaster gives.

81. F. Rosenzweig, *Star of Redemption*, trans. W. W. Hallo (New York: Holt, Rinehart & Winston, 1970–1971), p. 178.

82. Koran, Sura VII:173 f. (Al Araf); *Handwörterbuch des Islam*, eds., A. J. Weinsinck and J. H. Kramers (Leiden: E. J. Brill, 1976), pp. 75 f.

Punishment and Reward NUM. 25:1–18

1. Other encomia may be found in Sirach 45:23–26; I Macc. 2:26, 54.

2. On the source division, see *Interpreter's Bible*; on the comparative aspects, see Hallo's essay.

3. The identification was made by N. Glueck, *Bulletin of the American Schools of Oriental Research*, 91 (1943), pp. 13–18.

4. Josephus, *Antiquities*, IV, 8:1.

5. Rabbinic sources elaborated on this; see Sifre Num. 131; Num. R. 20:23.

6. So old JPS; King James and Revised Standard Versions.

7. San. 34b.

8. New English Bible, following II Chron. 25:12.

9. Compare Num. R. 20:25. For a different interpretation and elaborate discussion, see C. R. Reif, *JBL*, 90 (1971), pp. 200–206.

10. See Mendenhall, *The Tenth Generation*, pp. 105–121.

11. See M. Weinfeld, *JAOS*, 90 (1970), pp. 184–203; and *JAOS*, 92 (1972), pp. 468 f.

12. See San. 106a, for an elaboration of this tradition.

13. I am obliged to W. W. Hallo both for this reference and for stating the problem of Phinehas in this manner.

14. Mendenhall, *The Tenth Generation*.

15. Num. R. 20:24. The contrast between the reactions of Moses and Phinehas is also strongly brought out by Targum Jonathan on Num. 25:6–7.

16. For details, see Snaith, *Leviticus*, pp. 11 ff.; Gray, *Critical and Exegetical*, pp. 385 ff.

17. Hacohen, *Al ha-Torah*, Vol. IV, p. 439.

18. Targum Jonathan on verse 13; see Hul. 134b.

19. Aristophanes, *The Knights*, 356, 1179.

20. Based on San. 82a, which also discusses the rights of Zimri in case he had defended himself. See further, Jacobson, *Meditations*, pp. 245 ff., and commentary above.

21. After Rashi.

22. Num. R. 21:3; and Matnat Kehunah thereto.

23. Num. R. 21:3.

24. *Ibid.*
25. Many translations so render the sense.
26. Num. R. 20:23.
27. *Wellsprings*, Vol. II, p. 335.

28. Num. R. 21:4.
29. *The Hasidic Anthology*, ed. Newman, p. 342, n. 4, quoting R. Solomon of Radomsk.

Of Census and Women's Inheritance NUM. 25:19–27:23

1. So Ibn Ezra, following Judah Halevi. Nachmanides: the phrase means that he died for reasons which only God knows.
2. See "Petirat Mosheh," *Bet ha-Midrash*, Vol. I, pp. 115–129.
3. See *Encyclopaedia Judaica*, Vol. 14, "Semikhah"; *Jewish Encyclopedia*, Vol. 9, "Ordination"; and Acts 6:6.
4. Compare B.B. 75a; Epstein, *Sefer Tosefet Berachah*, Vol. IV, pp. 223 f.
5. Still another figure is recorded in I Chron. 12. See further the commentary of R. G. Boling on Judg. 20:15–16, *The Anchor Bible* (Garden City, N. Y.: Douday, 1975), pp. 284 f.
6. On this and on parallels in Ugaritic law, see N. Sarna, *JBL*, 76 (1957), pp. 13–25; Snaith, *Leviticus*, pp. 308–310.
7. See Maimonides, *Yad*, Hilch. Nachalot 1:1–3; *Shulchan Aruch*, Choshen Hamishpat 276:1.
8. Mishnah Ket. 13:3; *Yad*, Hilch. Ishut 19:17; *Shulchan Aruch*, Even ha-Ezer 112:11. For further details on the inheritance of daughters in Torah and halachah, see P. Ne'eman, *Beth Mikra*, 47, 4 (September 1971), pp. 476 ff.
9. Num. R. 21:7.
10. Num. R. 21:10.
11. Num. R. 21:15; Num. R. 13:20.
12. Num. R. 21:14.
13. Hacohen, *Al ha-Torah*, Vol. IV, p. 445.
14. *Wellsprings*, Vol. II, p. 338.
15. *Ibid.*, p. 336.

Offerings; Festivals; Vows of Women NUM. 28:1–30:17

1. B. D. Levine, *JAOS*, 85 (1965), pp. 307 ff.
2. Pritchard, *ANET*, p. 95.
3. Mishnah Men. 4:2–3; Sifre Num. 149.
4. R.H. 33b and following.
5. See Nachmanides on 30:1.
6. Mishnah Terumot 3:8. See further Shevuot 26a.
7. Rashi.
8. Sifre Num. 155; Mishnah Ned. 11:1; *Shulchan Aruch*, Yoreh Deah 234:59 ff.
9. See Mishnah Yoma 8:6; 48b, c.
10. *The Hasidic Anthology*, ed. Newman, p. 38, n. 22, quoting R. Abraham Twersky, the Trisker Maggid.
11. Midrash ha-Gadol, Pinchas 15; Hul. 60b; see also Epstein, *Sefer Tosefet Berachah*, Vol. IV, pp. 229 ff.
12. Num. R. 21:16, 19.
13. Sukah 55b; see also Bachya.
14. Hacohen, *Al ha-Torah* Vol. IV, p. 448.
15. Orach Chayim 281:1 (Isserles).
16. John J. Castelot, in *Jerome Bible Commentary*, Vol. II, p. 724.
17. *Shulchan Aruch*, Yoreh Deah 228.
18. Hacohen, *Al ha-Torah*, Vol. IV, p. 450.
19. *The Hasidic Anthology*, ed., Newman, p. 384, n. 1, quoting R. Shalom Rokeach, the Belzer Rebbe.
20. Tanchuma Num. 17.
21. See Mishnah Kiddushin 1:7.
22. *Dor le-Dor*, Vol. V, no. 2 (Winter, 1976–1977), p. 65. See also S. Zeitlin, *The Rise and Fall of the Judean State* (3 vols., Philadelphia: Jewish Publication Society, 1962–1978), pp. 213 f.; J. Finnegan, *Handbook of Biblical Chronology* (Princeton: Princeton University Press, 1964), p. 36.

War and First Settlement NUM. 31:1–32:42

1. See Sifre Num. 157 and Num. R. 22:4.
2. Sifre Num. 157.
3. A.Z. 75b; Rashi; Nachmanides.
4. Koran, Sura VIII:42 (The Spoils).
5. So Ehrlich.
6. See Nachmanides and Ket. 106b, top.

7. The text of the stone is given in *Interpreter's Dictionary*, Vol. III, p. 420. On Moabite finds see also *Near Eastern Archeology in the 20th Century*, ed., J. A. Sanders (Garden City, N. Y.: Doubleday, 1970), pp. 284 ff.

8. Details in Gray, *Critical and Exegetical*, pp. 428 f.

9. See JPS *Notes*.

10. Rashi and others.

11. *The Macmillan Bible Atlas* (New York: Macmillan, 1968), p. 50, n. 68, shows Reuben surrounded by Gad.

12. See Gray, *Critical and Exegetical*, pp. 437–439.

13. *Ibid.*, pp. 417 f.; similarly Snaith, *Leviticus*, p. 324. See also *Jerome Bible Commentary*, p. 98, n. 55, which emphasizes that "questions of interest to the modern reader are given little or no attention."

14. Sifre Num. 157, end.

15. Ehrlich, p. 301, on verse 50.

16. Sifre Num. 157.

17. *Shulchan Aruch*, Yoreh Deah 121, 122; Orach Chayim 451.

18. Kid. 78a.

19. *Sefer Akedat Yitschak* (Pressburg, Czechoslovakia: 1849), 85, 4:131b.

20. Alshech, quoted in *Yalkut Me'am Lo'ez*, Vol. IV, p. 386; also Harav Kook, quoted in Hacohen, *Al ha-Torah*, Vol. IV, pp. 458–459.

21. Num. R. 22:7. See also Leibowitz, *Studies*, Vol. 1, *ad loc.*

22. Jacobson, *Meditations*, pp. 249–255.

23. Num. R. 22:9.

24. Hertz, p. 709, based on Pes. 13a; Yoma 38a.

25. *Shulchan Aruch*, Even ha-Ezer 38:2, based on Kid. 61a–b. A detailed survey of this matter may be found in S. R. Hirsch, commentary on verse 24; and in *Yalkut Me'am Lo'ez*, Vol. IV, p. 385.

Review of the Wanderings; Boundaries of Canaan   NUM. 33:1–34:29

1. An identification of the various places, with appropriate cross references, may be found in Greenstone, *Numbers*.

2. So Greenstone, *Numbers*. Nachmanides writes that it was the murmuring over the water which the people remembered primarily.

3. N. Glueck, *The Other Side of the Jordan* (New Haven, Conn.: American Society for Oriental Research, 1940), pp. 89–113; *Encyclopaedia Judaica*, Vol. 6, cols. 1103 f.

4. Snaith, *Leviticus*, p. 339.

5. See B. L. Luria, *Beth Mikra*, 39 (1969), pp. 113 ff.

6. See B. Mazar, *JBL*, 80 (1961), p. 17; *Jerome Bible Commentary*, p. 100; *Views of the Biblical World*, Vol. 1, pp. 238–239 (with map).

7. Based on the analysis of Y. Kaufmann, *The Biblical Account of the Conquest of Palestine* (Jerusalem: Magnes Press, 1953), pp. 46 ff.

8. Hacohen, *Al ha-Torah*, Vol. IV, p. 460, based on Abarbanel.

9. Tanch. Mas'ey 5; Num. R. 23:7, 11.

10. Hacohen, *Al ha-Torah*, Vol. IV, p. 461.

11. Gittin 8a.

12. *Ma'yanah shel Torah*, Vol. IV, p. 154.

13. *Ibid.*, p. 147.

14. Maimonides, *Guide*, III, 50.

Levitical Towns; Cities of Refuge   NUM. 35:1–36:13

1. Gray, *Critical and Exegetical*, p. 465.

2. Snaith, *Leviticus*, p. 342.

3. Concerning these lists, W. F. Albright has convincingly demonstrated that they were authentic; see *Louis Ginzberg Memorial Volume* (New York: American Academy for Jewish Research, 1945), pp. 49–73; and see B. Mazar, in *Entsiklopedyah Mikra'it*, Vol. IV, cols. 478 ff., with a discussion of the relevant passages in Josh. 21 and I Chron. 6.

4. Greenberg, *JAOS*, 85 (1965), pp. 59 ff. He suggests that the Torah establishes the fiction of a town with zero size, which allows a rule that fits all town sizes and shapes. The problem is complex and cannot be pursued here. Ehrlich speaks of two differential cubits, similar to the existence of a "holy shekel" as compared with the common currency; see also *Entsiklopedyah Mikra'it*, Vol. IV, pp. 848 ff. Traditional commentators have drawn ingenious schemes to ac-

count for the apparent difference; see, for instance, Nachmanides and Luzzatto, and the survey in Greenstone, *Numbers*, pp. 353 f.

5. Mak. 10a, 13a, with further details.

6. Based on Hosea 6:8 and Sifre Mas'ey 160; Mak. 9b–10a.

7. Sifre Num. 160.

8. Koran, Sura II:174 (The Cow).

9. B.B. 120a–b.

10. For an extensive treatment of the subject, see M. Greenberg, *JBL*, 78 (1959), pp. 125–132; M. Haran, *JBL*, 80 (1961), pp. 45–54, 156–165; and Jacobson, *Meditations*, pp. 256–260.

11. C. Trumbull, cited by Gray, *Critical and Exegetical*, pp. 470 f.

12. See Mak. 10a.

13. Maimonides, *Yad*, Hilch. Rotse'ach 7:1.

14. This point is emphasized by Hirsch; see also Mak. 11b.

15. *Ma'yanah shel Torah*, Vol. IV, p. 155, quoting the Apter Rebbe.

16. Bachya on Num. 35:11.

17. Num. R. 23:13.

18. Hacohen, *Al ha-Torah*, Vol. IV, p. 462.

19. *Bemidbar*, p. 409; see Ta'an. 30b. See *Jewish Encyclopedia*, Vol. 1, pp. 25–26, for a description of the ancient ceremonies on that day.

20. Ahad Ha-Am, "Moses," in *Selected Essays*, trans. and ed. L. Simon (Philadelphia: Jewish Publication Society, 1912), p. 325.

Deuteronomy

Part I *Prologue. First Discourse*

1. For an overview, see the essays by Moshe Weinfeld and Paul A. Riemann, *Interpreter's Dictionary of the Bible* [hereafter cited as *IDB*], ed. George A. Buttrick et al. (4 vols., New York and Nashville: Abingdon

Press, 1962), Supplement, pp. 188 and 192 ff.; also D. N. Freedman, *ibid.*, pp. 229 ff. For a more comprehensive treatment, see M. Weinfeld, *Deuteronomy and the Deuteronomic School* (Oxford: Clarendon Press, 1972).

The Setting DEUT. 1:1–5

1. So B. Gemser, *Vetus Testamentum* [hereafter cited as *VT*] (Leiden, Holland: E. J. Brill), 2 (1952), pp. 349–355. David Hoffmann, *Deuteronomium* (Berlin: Poppelauer, 1913–1922), *ad loc.*, compares עֵבֶר הַיַּרְדֵּן to a fixed term like Gallia Ulterior.

2. See Sifre Deut. 1; Rashi.

3. "Introducing Deuteronomy," esp. n. 7.

4. Ellis Rivkin, *The Dynamics of Jewish History* (Sarasota, Fla.: New College, 1970), p. 473; see commentary on Gen. 45:1–28 and Gleanings.

5. Quoted by B. S. Jacobson, *Meditations on the Torah*

(Tel Aviv: Sinai, 1956), p. 268.

6. The latter derivation was suggested by Ben Zion Wacholder in private communication.

7. *Itture Torah*, comp. and ed. Aaron Jacob Greenberg (Tel Aviv: Yavneh, from 1965), Vol. VI, p. 2.

8. Deut. R. 1:6.

9. After Deut. R. 1:1.

10. *Itture Torah*, Vol. VI, p. 13.

11. Deut. R. 1:4.

12. Based on Ber. 8a; *Itture Torah*, Vol. VI, p. 14.

13. *Itture Torah*, Vol. VI, p. 15.

First Review DEUT. 1:6–45

1. Sifre Deut. 1:13. So also New American Bible: men of repute.

2. San. 7b.

3. So San. 8a.

4. So Rashi; Luzzatto; for a survey of other interpretations, see *Yalkut Me'am Lo'ez* (11 vols., Jerusalem: Or Chadash, 1967–1971).

5. See Samuel R. Driver's commentary on Deuteronomy (New York: Charles Scribner's Sons, 1916).

6. Hoffmann, with sources.

7. *Min ha-Torah* (5 vols., Jerusalem: Reuben Mass, 1972), Vol. V, p. 1112.

8. Sab. 119b.

9. *Mishneh Torah* [hereafter cited as *Yad*], Hilch. San. 2; see also Deut. R. 1:10.

10. Vol. VI, p. 20.

11. *Itture Torah*, Vol. VI, p. 21, with reference to Zech. 8:16.

12. Devarim, Vol. I, p. 121.

13. *Itture Torah*, Vol. VI, p. 18.

Second Review   DEUT. 1:46—3:29

1. See Weinfeld, *Deuteronomy*, pp. 70 f.

2. Joseph Reider, in his commentary on Deuteronomy (Philadelphia: Jewish Publication Society, 1937), and Hoffmann take the first view; Rashbam and Luzzatto the latter.

3. See the surveys in *Encyclopaedia Judaica* (16 vols., Jerusalem: Keter, 1972), Vol. 6, cols. 1103–1104; *Entsiklopedyah Mikra'it* (Jerusalem: Mosad Bialik, from 1955), Vol. VI, cols. 332–333, with relevant literature.

4. B.B. 121 a-b; cf. also Ta'an. 30b–31a.

5. For a traditional reconciliation of the sixty towns mentioned here and the twenty-three in I Chron. 2:22, see Hoffmann.

6. *The Jewish Antiquities*, trans. William Whiston (New York: Al Burt Co., n.d.), VIII, 2:3. On the Targum's opinion that Argob was Trachonitis of the Hellenistic period, see Reider.

7. See *IDB*, Vol. IV, p. 837; *Encyclopaedia Judaica*, Vol. 16, cols. 378 ff.

8. Vol. VI, p. 27.

9. M. Hacohen, *Al ha-Torah* (5 vols., Jerusalem: Reuben Mass, 1962), Vol. V, p. 483; based on Ber. 30 b.

10. Quoted by Hacohen, *Al ha-Torah*, Vol. V, p. 482.

11. Quoted in *Itture Torah*, Vol. VI, p. 29.

12. *Min ha-Torah*, Vol. V, p. 1128.

13. *Itture Torah*, Vol. VI, p. 31.

14. *Al ha-Torah*, Vol. V, p. 485; based on a midrash.

15. *Va'etchanan* 1–3.

16. Ed. Abbott, Gilbert, Hunt, and Swaim (New York: Bruce Publishing Co., 1969), p. 152.

Summary: To Observe the Law   DEUT. 4:1–43

1. See Kenneth A. Kitchen, *Ancient Orient and Old Testament* (London: Tyndale Press, 1966), pp. 92 f; Dennis J. McCarthy, *Treaty and Covenant* (Rome: Pontifical Biblical Institute, 1963), p. 135.

2. See Rashi on Lev. 18:4.

3. Samson Raphael Hirsch.

4. See Sifre Deut. 58 and the parallel passage in Lev. R. 18:4, 5; also Hoffmann.

5. The Talmud, San. 38 b, opts for "God" rather than "gods."

6. So Rav in A.Z. 55a; see also Meg. 9b (where different readings are listed); Rashbam; the Church Fathers (quoted by Driver, p. 71); Hubert Junker, *Deuteronomium* (Würzburg: Echter Verlag, 1952); Carl Steuernagel, *Das Deuteronomium* (Göttingen: Vandenhoeck und Ruprecht, 1923).

7. See Rashi.

8. Deut. R. 10:4; Rashi.

9. Hag. 11b–12a.

10. See *Gates of Prayer*, ed. Chaim Stern (Reform) (New York: Central Conference of American Rabbis, 1975), p. 538; for its use in the traditional synagogue, see S. Singer–I. Abrahams, *Companion to the Daily Prayer Book* (rev. ed., London: Eyre and Spottiswoode, 1922), p. cxlix.

11. See Weinfeld, *Deuteronomy*, p. 81; *IDB*, Supplement, pp. 188 ff., where the parallels with the Davidic covenant are explored and the changeover to a conditional covenant considered a necessary adjustment to the destruction of Jerusalem.

12. So Ibn Ezra. Some ancient versions have the plural here, as does Deut. 10:15.

13. *Das fünfte Buch Mose: Deuteronomium* (Göttingen: Vandenhoeck und Ruprecht, 1968), p. 38.

14. *Gates of Prayer*, p. 516; Standard Prayer Book, p. 93.

15. Mak. 9b–10a.

16. Epic of Erra, V, 43; on the Egyptian passage, see von Rad, *Deuteronomium*, who notes, however, that there is some doubt over its exact meaning.

17. See Maimonides, *Yad*, Hilch. Mamrim 2:9.

18. So, for instance, S. R. Hirsch, *ad* 4:2.

19. See San. 88b–89a; R. H. 28b; *Itture Torah*, Vol. VI, p. 34.

20. See W. Gunther Plaut, *The Rise of Reform Judaism* (New York: World Union for Progressive Judaism, 1963), *passim*; idem, *The Growth of Reform Judaism* (New York: World Union for Progressive Judaism, 1965), pp. 347 ff.

21. See *Gates of Mitzvah*, ed. Simeon J. Maslin (New York: Central Conference of American Rabbis, 1979).

22. Deut. R. 2:12. But another opinion (*ibid.*) holds that the gates of prayer are sometimes closed.

23. *Itture Torah*, Vol. VI, p. 37.

24. *Ibid.*; *Wellsprings of Torah*, ed. N. L. Alpert (2 vols., New York: Judaica Press, 1969), Vol. II, pp. 374–375.

25. Ber. 21b; Kid. 30a.

26. *Itture Torah*, Vol. VI, p. 39.

27. Based on San. 38a; see also S. R. Hirsch.

Part II *Second Discourse*

1. So von Rad, *Deuteronomium*.

The Decalogue DEUT. 4:44—5:30

1. Nachmanides on Exodus 20:2–3; Ber. 45a.

2. Von Rad, *Deuteronomium*.

3. Moshe Greenberg, *Journal of Biblical Literature* [hereafter cited as *JBL*], 75 (1957), pp. 34–39.

4. Mech. Bachodesh 7.

5. See the extensive study by G. J. Blidstein, *Judaism*, 14, 2 (1965), pp. 151–171.

6. Mech. Nezikin 5; San. 86a; Maimonides, *Yad*, Hilch. Genevah 9:1.

7. *Pesikta Rabbati* 24, ed. M. Friedmann (reprint, Tel Aviv, 1963).

8. So Elias Auerbach, *Moses* (Amsterdam: G.J.A. Ruys, 1953), p. 202.

9. So, for instance, Reider.

10. So Nachmanides; Biur; Hoffmann.

11. Mak. 23b–24a.

12. On the rabbinic position of which laws apply in Israel only, see Mishnah Kid. 1:9 and Talmud.

13. This has been emphasized by Matitiahu Tsevat, *Zeitschrift für die Alttestamentliche Wissenschaft* [hereafter cited as *ZAW*], Vol. 84 (1972), pp. 447–459. On creation and redemption, see Franz Rosenzweig, *The Star of Redemption*, trans. William W. Hallo (New York: Holt, Rinehart and Winston, 1970–1971), pp. 314, 317, 319, 359. The land has its "Sabbath of complete rest" and so does time (Lev. 23:3 and 25:4 use

The Shema DEUT. 6:1–25

1. In Matthew 22:37 it is called the greatest of the commandments.

2. *Pentateuch and Haftorahs*, ed. Joseph H. Hertz (Oxford: Oxford University Press, 1929), p. 920.

3. Kaufmann Kohler, *Jewish Theology* (New York:

28. *Min ha-Torah*, Vol. V, pp. 1142–1143.

29. צָרַת רַבִּים חֲצִי נֶחָמָה; see also Deut. R. 2:22 and Aharon Hyman, *Otzar Divre Chachamim* (Tel Aviv: Devir, 1972), p. 490.

30. Deut. R. 2:12.

31. *Itture Torah*, Vol. VI, p. 42.

the expression שַׁבַּת שַׁבָּתוֹן to signify God's mastery over both).

14. Ber. 33b.

15. *Ethics of the Fathers* 3:15.

16. For a survey of Jewish thought on the subject, see *Encyclopaedia Judaica*, Vol. 7, col. 129. See also E. Urbach, *The Sages* (2 vols., Jerusalem: Magnes Press, 1975), Vol. I, pp. 256 ff.

17. Men. 29b. Another version of the Akiba story is found in Ber. 61b; see commentary on Deut. 34:1–12 and Gleanings.

18. Mak. 10a; *Yalkut Me'am Lo'ez*, Devarim, Vol. I, p. 243.

19. Commentary, *ad loc.*

20. *Moses*, p. 194.

21. *Itture Torah*, Vol. VI, pp. 423, 427.

22. *Ad loc.*; see the comment by Isaac Caro, *Toledot Yitzchak*, Parashah Yitro.

23. *Itture Torah*, Vol. VI, p. 44.

24. *Deuteronomium, ad loc.*

25. *Star of Redemption*, p. 315.

26. *Itture Torah*, Vol. VI, p. 45.

27. *Ad loc.*, based on Mech. Bachodesh 7.

28. End of Parashah Bechukotai 115b (Soncino ed.), Vol. V, p. 160.

29. *Wellsprings*, Vol. II, p. 379.

30. Meg. 21a.

Macmillan, 1918), p. 90.

4. Louis Jacobs, *A Jewish Theology* (London: Darton, Longman, and Todd, 1973), p. 21.

5. So King James Version, New English Bible, and New American Bible.

6. For a survey of understandings, see Driver, p. 90; Reider, *ad loc.*

7. Ber. 54a.

8. San. 74a; *Yad*, Yesode ha-Torah 5:2.

9. *Shulchan Aruch*, Orach Chayim 656; Yore De'ah 249:1.

10. So M. Tsevat, *Hebrew Union College Annual* [hereafter cited as *HUCA*], 29 (1958), p. 125, n. 112. See also von Rad: *vorsprechen*.

11. See Exod. 13, reference n. 5.

12. See Deut. 11:20 and also Driver, p. 93, for similar practices among other Mediterranean peoples.

13. Hul. 17a; also Hoffmann.

14. So Nachmanides. Maimonides includes this verse in his catalogue of positive commandments (7): When taking an oath, one *must* swear by God's name.

15. Details in Hirsch and Hoffmann.

16. Von Rad.

17. Quoted in *Encyclopaedia Judaica*, Vol. 14, col. 1374.

18. For the best comprehensive, yet brief, survey of this subject, see Jacobs, *A Jewish Theology*, pp. 152 ff., and also Rosenzweig, *Star of Redemption*, pp. 173–185.

19. A point stressed by Luzzatto, Rosenzweig, and others; see also Gleanings.

20. See W. L. Moran, *Catholic Biblical Quarterly* [hereafter cited as *CBQ*], 25 (1963), pp. 77–87.

21. *HUCA*, 6 (1929), pp. 39–53.

22. Maimonides, *Yad*, Hilch. Teshuvah 10:1; Sifre Deut. 32; Hoffmann, p. 85: "Love and fear can be joined only in God." See also Tanch. 25.

23. Sifre Deut. 32.

24. *Duties of the Heart* (חוֹבוֹת הַלְּבָבוֹת), trans. Moses Hyamson (2 vols., New York: Feldheim, 1978); on the majority view, Maimonides, *Sefer ha-Mitzvot*, positive commandments (3); Nehama Leibowitz, *Studies in the Weekly Sidrah* (Jerusalem: World Zionist Organization), 7th series, 1962, pp. 301 ff.

25. Ber. 15b.

26. *Gates of Prayer*, p. 33 *passim*.

27. Mishnah Ber. 1:1–2; Talmud Ber. 2a–3a, 9b.

28. Mishnah Ber. 1:3.

29. Ber. 61b.

30. *Ad loc.*

31. Deut. R. 2:31.

32. *Theologico-Political Treatise*, 14.

33. *The Kingly Crown*, II, trans. Bernard Lewis.

34. *A Jewish Theology*, p. 37.

35. *Das Wesen des Judentums* (5th ed., Frankfurt: J. Kauffmann, 1922), p. 101.

36. The formulation of the Thirteen Principles of Faith of Maimonides (first enunciated in his commentary on the Mishnah San. 10) is printed in traditional prayer books, together with the Ten Commandments, at the end of the morning service.

37. Quoted by Hertz, p. 770.

38. *Interpreter's Bible* (12 vols., New York and Nashville: Abingdon, 1957), Vol. II, p. 373.

39. Sifre Deut. 32; see also Rashi.

40. *Yad*, Yesode ha-Torah 2:1–2.

41. *Shevet Yehudah*, quoted by Jacobson, *Meditations on the Torah*, p. 274.

42. Commentary, *ad loc.*

43. Commentary, *ad loc.*; repeated also in chasidic sayings, see *The Hasidic Anthology*, ed. Louis I. Newman (New York: Bloch, 1944), p. 115, n. 7.

44. *Itture Torah*, Vol. VI, p. 48.

45. *Star of Redemption*, p. 176.

46. *Ibid.*

47. Quoted in Hacohen, *Al ha-Torah*, Vol. V, p. 490.

48. I:833.

49. Commentary, *ad loc.*; based on the Midrash (Sifre Deut. 31).

50. Va'etchanan 269a (Soncino ed.), p. 364.

51. *Yad*, Yesode ha-Torah 10: 5.

52. *Ad loc.*

53. לֹא עָשׂוּ לִפְנִים מִשּׁוּרַת הַדִּין (B.M. 30b).

54. Note that *A Passover Haggadah*, prepared by the Central Conference of American Rabbis, ed. Herbert Bronstein, illust. Leonard Baskin (New York: Grossman Publishers, 1974), p. 30, quotes the Hebrew of 6:20 according to the Masorah but translates אֶתְכֶם (you) as if it read אוֹתָנוּ (us).

55. *Ad loc.*

Dealing with Idolatry DEUT. 7:1–26

1. See J. van Seters, *VT*, 22 (1972), pp. 63–81.

2. Lev. R. 17:6.

3. See *Views of the Biblical World* (5 vols., Chicago and New York: Jordan Publishing Co., 1959–1961), Vol. I, p. 258.

4. Pictured in Gaalyah Cornfeld–David N. Freed-

man, *Archaeology of the Bible: Book by Book* (New York: Harper and Row, 1976), p. 25.

5. So Yigael Yadin, *Hazor* (London and Jerusalem: Weidenfeld and Nicolson, 1975), p. 46.

6. *Moses* (Oxford and London: East and West Library, 1947), p. 105.

7. Von Rad.

8. See Stanley Gevirtz, *Patterns in the Early Poetry of Israel* (Studies in Ancient Oriental Civilization, No. 32, 1963; Chicago: University of Chicago), pp. 35 ff.

9. *Natural History*, 26:15.

10. So A. Z. 20a: לֹא תִתֵּן לָהֶם חֲנָיָה בַּקַּרְקַע.

11. Commentary on verse 16.

12. Lines 16–18, *Ancient Near Eastern Texts* [hereafter cited as Pritchard, *ANET*], ed. James B. Pritchard (3rd ed., Princeton: Princeton University Press, 1969), p. 320.

13. Junker, commentary on 20:10–15.

14. Yeb. 76a; Kid. 68b; see S. R. Hirsch; Hoffmann, p. 91. See further *Shulchan Aruch*, Even ha-Ezer 4:9; Be-er Hetev 8.

15. See commentary on Gen. 18:8.

16. See Yehezkel Kaufmann, *The Religion of Israel* (Chicago: University of Chicago, 1960), p. 300.

17. *Year Book of the Central Conference of American Rabbis* [hereafter cited as *CCAR Year Book*], Vol. 83 (1973), pp. 57 ff.

18. See Rashi on verse 4; Yeb. 23a; Kid. 68b.

19. *Gates of Mitzvah*, pp. 36 f.

20. Erub. 22a.

21. *Ethics of the Fathers* 2:1; Tanch. Ekev 1; Rashi.

22. Hacohen, *Min ha-Torah*, Vol. V, p. 1052.

23. *Itture Torah*, Vol. VI, p. 59.

24. A. Z 52 a-b.

25. A. Z 21a.

The Good Life   DEUT. 8:1—9:5

1. So Driver.

2. See Rashi; based on Midrash Shir ha-Shirim 4:4 ff. A more naturalistic explanation is offered by Ibn Ezra but opposed by Nachmanides.

3. See H. Brunner, *VT*, 8 (1958), pp. 428 f.

4. See Mishnah San. 6:5 and Talmud 46 a-b; Ber. 5a; B.M. 85a; Gen. R. 9:8.

5. *Guide of the Perplexed*, III,8–25.

6. Ber. 48b; Maimonides, *Yad*, Hilch. Berachot 4.

7. Ber. 35a.

8. *Shulchan Aruch*, Orach Chayim 174:1; based on Ps. 104:14.

9. For a detailed survey, see *Encyclopaedia Judaica*, Vol. 7, cols. 835 ff.; *Yalkut Me'am Lo'ez*, Devarim, Vol. II, pp. 445 ff.

10. *The Kuzari*, trans. Hartwig Hirschfeld (New York: Pardes, 1946), 3:17.

11. Quoted in Hacohen, *Al ha-Torah*, Vol. V, p. 499.

12. *Itture Torah*, Vol. VI, p. 65.

13. *Ibid.*, p. 67.

14. *Ibid.*

15. Deut. R. 3:11.

The Stiff-Necked People   DEUT. 9:6—10:11

1. See Deut. R. 3:15.

2. Among those who count two ascents and three periods of abstinence are Luzzatto and S. R. Hirsch; Ibn Ezra takes verse 18 as an anticipatory reference to the second ascent.

3. *Ad loc.*; based on Jerusalem Shek. 6:1.

4. So Ibn Ezra; Nachmanides; based on Sifre Deut. 82. This explanation applies also to verse 3.

5. So Hoffmann, *ad loc.*: The passage about the Levites is placed here *because* they were faithful; about Aaron, *despite* his aberration.

6. An extended discussion of this theme may be found in "The 'desert motif'...," Shemaryahu Talmon, *Biblical Motifs*, ed. Alexander Altmann (Cambridge, Mass.: Harvard University Press, 1966).

7. Translation from *Gates of Repentance*, ed. Chaim Stern (New York: Central Conference of American Rabbis, 1978), pp. 269, 327.

8. Hacohen, *Al ha-Torah*, Vol. V, p. 503.

9. *Itture Torah*, Vol. VI, p. 71.

10. Quoted, *ibid.*, p. 69.

11. *Ibid.*, p. 71.

12. Ber. 8 b.
13. Men. 99 a.
14. Deut. R. 3:12.

15. *Ibid.*, 3:13.
16. *Itture Torah*, Vol. VI, p. 71.
17. Devarim, p. 58; based on Ber. 32 b.

The Good Land DEUT. 10:12—11:25

1. *Yad*, Hilch. Yesode ha-Torah 2:2; Hilch. Teshu-vah 9:1.
2. For a detailed discussion, see M. Guttmann, *Das Judentum und seine Umwelt* (Berlin: Philo Verlag, 1927), pp. 43–114.
3. This follows Ibn Ezra. However, the Masoretic notation (introducing a pause between "witnessed" and "the lesson") would suggest a different under-standing; see Hoffmann.
4. So also Hoffmann in his German rendition: *endgültig*.
5. San. 110a; *Yalkut Shimoni* I:652.
6. Ber. 2:2.
7. See Lenn E. Goodman, *Conservative Judaism*, XXXII, 3 (1979), pp. 36–49.
8. B. M. 59b. According to another tradition (*ibid.*), the number of such passages is forty-six; see Tosafot, *ad loc.*
9. On the often tortuous arguments of traditional exponents and the critique of Maimonides and Abar-banel, see Plaut, the *Journal of the Central Conference of American Rabbis* [hereafter cited as *CCAR Journal*] (January 1966), pp. 32–34, where the whole subject is discussed in detail.
10. Commentary on Exod. 22:20.
11. This is stressed by S. R. Hirsch, *ad* 19:33–34.
12. Data taken from *Encyclopaedia Judaica*, Vol. 9, cols. 123 ff., especially cols. 185–186.
13. *Israel's Land* (Stuttgart: Kohlhammer, 1972).
14. Gen. R. 21:6.
15. Based on the Talmud, Hul. 89a; quoted in *Itture Torah*, Vol. VI, p. 72.
16. Ber. 33b.
17. *Al ha-Torah*, Vol. V, p. 506.
18. Quoted in *Yalkut Me'am Lo'ez*, Devarim, Vol. II, p. 514.
19. Quoted in *The Hasidic Anthology*, ed. Newman, p. 48 (Circumcision on Shabbat: Talmud, Sab. 131b-132a).
20. *The Hasidic Anthology*, ed. Newman, p. 148, n. 13.
21. *Star of Redemption*, p. 240.
22. Ber. 40a; see also commentary on 21:1 ff.
23. B.B. 21a.
24. *This People Israel*, trans. Albert Friedlander (Philadelphia: Jewish Publication Society, 1965), pp. 115 f.

The Divine Command DEUT. 11:26–32

1. See R. H. Pfeiffer, *Introduction to the Old Testa-ment* (New York: Harper and Bros., 1948), p. 227; in Christian Scriptures, John 4:20. The two mountains are pictured in *Views of the Biblical World*, Vol. I, p. 289.
2. See Driver, p. 133, who discusses in detail the difficulties of locating Gilgal.
3. Commentary on verse 26; see also *Yalkut Me'am Lo'ez*, Devarim, Vol. II, p. 599.
4. Commentary, *ad loc.*
5. Deut. R. 4:2.
6. *Ibid.*, 4:3.
7. On verse 26.
8. *Itture Torah*, Vol. VI, p. 83.
9. Sifre Deut. 54.
10. On verse 29.

The Central Sanctuary DEUT. 12:1—13:1

1. So Hoffmann, p. 135, with further references.
2. Commentary, p. 140.
3. Sifre Deut. 61.

4. There was a controversy over whether this re-fers to the first or second tithe; see Hoffmann, pp. 142–146.

5. See Rashi.

6. For the traditional view, see Hoffmann; Hertz, p. 939; for a summary of the critical position, von Rad, pp. 63 ff.; Steuernagel, pp. 94 f.

7. For a survey of opinions, see *IDB*, Supplement, pp. 23–25; J. Weingren, *Journal of the Ancient Near Eastern Society*, 5 (Gaster Festschrift, 1973), pp. 427–433.

8. *HUCA*, 46 (1976), pp. 19–56.

9. *Ibid.*, p. 41.

10. Jacob Milgrom offers a complex analysis of a variety of biblical terms, *HUCA*, 47 (1976), pp. 1–18.

11. For a summary of these procedures, see *Encyclopaedia Judaica*, Vol. 6, cols. 26 ff.

12. Kaufmann, *Religion of Israel*, pp. 13 ff. *passim*.

13. Sifre Deut. 59.

14. A.Z. 45b.

15. Yore De'ah 276:9; *Yalkut Me'am Lo'ez*, Devarim, Vol. II, p. 605.

16. *Deuteronomium*, p. 171.

17. Commentary on verse 19.

False Prophets   DEUT. 13:2–19

1. See *Entsiklopedyah Mikra'it*, Vol. V, pp. 690 f.; *Encyclopaedia Judaica*, Vol. 13, cols. 1150 ff.; Abraham J. Heschel, *The Prophets* (New York: Burning Bush Press, 1955), *passim*.

2. See the controversy in San. 89b and Targum Jonathan.

3. So Mishnah San. 7:10; the Septuagint translates "You shall denounce him" (so that he may be tried). But Philo, *On Monarchy*, 1:7, end, thought that a "battlefield execution" was called for, as in the case of Phinehas (Num. 25:7–8).

4. See Weinfeld, *Deuteronomy*, p. 94. See there also (p. 98, n. 5), for ancient Near Eastern parallels to uterine siblings.

5. *Ad loc.* and II Corinthians 6:15.

6. San. 40a–b in explanation of Mishnah San. 5:1.

7. So M. Buber, *On the Bible: Eighteen Studies*, ed. Nahum N. Glatzer (New York: Schocken, 1968), p. 177.

8. See William W. Hallo-William K. Simpson, *The Ancient Near East: A History* (New York: Harcourt Brace Jovanovich, 1971), p. 158.

9. San. 90a; Sifre Deut. 84.

10. Ibn Ezra on Deut. 13:2.

11. Nachmanides on Deut. 13:2.

12. Rashbam on Deut. 13:2.

13. See n. 2 in Gleanings to Deut. 1:1–5.

14. *Nacherinnerung zur "Antwort" Lavaters* (Gesammelte Schriften, III, 65, 1843; Leipzig: Brockhaus). Similarly, Leibowitz, *Studies*, 1st series; 5715 Annual, Re'eh, p. 2.

15. *Deuteronomium*, p. 181.

16. Sifre Deut. 86. The Midrash calls attention to the use of סָרָה in both Deut. 13:6 (which deals with prophets) and 19:16 (which deals with witnesses).

17. Tosefta San. 14:14.

18. San. 11:5 f.

19. *Itture Torah*, Vol. VI, pp. 89–90.

20. *Ibid.*, p. 90.

21. Sotah 14a.

22. On verse 13; based on Sifre Deut. 92.

23. San. 112b. See Alexander Guttmann, *HUCA*, 40–41 (1969–1970), pp. 251–275.

24. Tosefta San. 14:1.

25. *Studies*, 2nd series, 5716 Annual, Re'eh, p. 6.

Of Food, Tithes, and Social Equity   DEUT. 14:1—15:23

1. The subject is treated in detail in Mak. 21a.

2. See Luzzatto; Hoffmann, pp. 191 f.

3. Zvi Weinberg, *Beth Mikra*, 69 (1977), pp. 230–237.

4. For a survey, see *Encyclopaedia Judaica*, Vol. 6,

cols. 31–34; I. Grunfeld, *The Jewish Dietary Laws* (2 vols., London: Soncino Press, 1972); Mishnah Hul. 3:6; Hul. 61b–63b; Nachmanides on Lev. 11:13.

5. See also Rashi on Lev. 11:19.

6. Further, see Hoffmann, p. 200; Sifre Deut. 103.

7. Sifre Deut. 105 takes the first, Rashi, on verse 23, the latter position.

8. Nachmanides argues this in detail, basing himself on Sifre Deut. 111, opposing Ibn Ezra.

9. Mishnah Sheb. 10:3–7; see commentary on Lev. 25.

10. Driver, p. 182, further suggests that the provision for freeing the bondwoman reflected important social changes.

11. Pritchard, *ANET*, Code of Hammurabi 40, p. 183; see Theodor H. Gaster, *Myth, Legend and Custom in the Old Testament* (New York: Harper and Row, 1969), pp. 312 ff.

12. See Hoffmann, pp. 243 ff., for the way in which traditional commentators attempted to harmonize these differences.

13. See Maria deJ. Ellis, *Journal of Cuneiform Studies*, 26 (1974), pp. 248–250.

14. See M. Weinfeld's article, *Encyclopaedia Judaica*, Vol. 15, cols. 1156–1162, where the institution of tithing is discussed in some detail; see also Kaufmann, *Religion of Israel*, pp. 189 f.

15. Yeb. 86b.

16. See the essay by Roland de Vaux, *The Bible and the Ancient Orient* (London: Darton, Longman, and Todd, 1972), pp. 252–269. For an interpretation of Isa. 66:3–4a, see J. M. Sasson, *VT*, 26 (1976), pp. 199–207.

17. Matthew 8:28–32, in the tale of the Gadarene swine.

18. Kid. 49b; on dogs, see the juxtaposition in Sab. 155b; also in Matthew 7:6. Further data are given by E. Wiesenberg, *HUCA*, 27 (1956), pp. 213–233.

19. Mishnah B.K. 7:7. On the entire subject, see *Entsiklopedyah Mikra'it*, Vol. III, pp. 90–94.

20. Kid. 36 a.

21. Vol. VI, p. 93.

22. *Ibid.*, p. 95.

23. Quoted, *ibid.*, pp. 95 f.

24. *Ibid.*, p. 96.

25. Shlomo ben Adret, quoted, *ibid.*, p. 97.

26. Quoted in *Al ha-Torah*, p. 524.

27. Abraham Samuel Benjamin Wolf; quoted, *ibid.*, p. 525.

28. *Al ha-Torah*, Vol. V, p. 526.

29. Based on B.M. 31b.

30. *Deuteronomium*, pp. 31 f.

31. Trans. Jacobson, *Meditations on the Torah*, p. 283. The polemic is against Maimonides, *Guide*, III,48 and Nachmanides, commentary on Lev. 11:13.

32. Quoted by Leibowitz, *Studies*, 5719 Annual, Re'eh, pp. 5 f.

The Holy Days DEUT. 16:1–17

1. On new moons and sabbaths, see W. W. Hallo, *HUCA*, 48 (1977), p. 10, n. 47.

2. Sifre Deut. 129.

3. See Hoffmann, pp. 257 f.

4. So Ibn Ezra; Nachmanides; S. R. Hirsch.

5. For possible Mesopotamian analogues, see Levine-Hallo, *HUCA*, 38 (1967), pp. 45, 57.

6. See the dispute of the schools of Hillel and Shammai; Betzah 2a, 7b.

7. Sifre Deut. 131; Pes. 5b.

8. *Ad loc.*; see the discussion in Sab. 9b, 34b.

9. *The Jewish War*, trans. William Whiston (New York: Al Burt Co., n.d.), VI, 9:3.

10. Others, basing themselves on verse 7, ventured this conclusion, which Ibn Ezra (on Deut. 16:7) characterizes as put forth by "the falsifiers."

11. See Hoffmann, p. 260.

12. Sifre Deut. 133; Rashi; Ibn Ezra.

13. See the discussion by Reider, *ad loc.*

14. *Revolutionary Constructivism* (New York: Young Poale Zion Assoc., 1937), p. 19.

15. *Jewish Theology*, p. 462.

16. *Moses and the Vocation of the Jewish People* (New York and London: Harper/Longmans, 1959), p. 136.

17. *The Menorah Treasury*, ed. Leo W. Schwarz (Philadelphia: Jewish Publication Society, 1964), p. 712.

18. *Hegyonot Mikra* (Jerusalem: Karta, 1972), p. 259.

19. San. 39b.

20. I:554 (Emor).

21. This is based on Jerusalem Ber. 9:7 (14b): אָכִין וְרָקִין מְעוּטִין.

22. Quoted in Hacohen, *Min ha-Torah*, Vol. V, p. 1208.

1. San. 7b.
2. Mak. 6b.
3. Sifre Deut. 153.
4. According to Hoffmann, pp. 286 f., 309, he is a judge who disobeys the high court.
5. Sifre Deut. 145.
6. Mishnah San. 2:4; also Targum Jonathan.
7. Von Rad, *Deuteronomium*.
8. Jerusalem San., end.
9. The Mishnah makes eighteen wives the maximum (San. 2:4), but already in talmudic times multiple marriages were discouraged.
10. So Rashi; based on Sifre Deut. 163.
11. Hul. 10:1.
12. Josephus, *Antiquities*, IV, 8:14.
13. Sifre Deut. 156; details in Hoffmann, pp. 310 ff.
14. See Sifre Deut. 156; Maimonides, *Sefer ha-Mitzvot*, positive commandments (173); Ibn Ezra on Deut. 17:15; Nachmanides on 17:14.
15. Ber. 58a goes so far as to suggest that even a lowly official serves only with God's consent. See also Nachmanides on verse 15.

16. Sifre Deut. 144.
17. In the commentary attributed to him, on II Chron. 19:6.
18. San. 32b.
19. Commentary on Deut. 16:20. The latter saying is also stressed in chasidic sources; see *Wellsprings*, Vol. II, p. 397; *Itture Torah*, Vol. VI, p. 110.
20. *Itture Torah*, Vol. VI, p. 110; *Yalkut Me'am Lo'ez*, Devarim, Vol. II, p. 704.
21. Commentary on verse 20; similarly *Yalkut Me'am Lo'ez*, Devarim, Vol. II, p. 705.
22. *Sefer ha-Mitzvot*, negative commandments (13); see Sifre Deut. 145.
23. Commentary on 16:22.
24. Ber. 18b.
25. *Yad*, Hilch. Berachot 11:3.
26. Mishnah R. H. 2:9.
27. Commentary on Deut. 17:15 ff.
28. Hul. 134b. See also commentary on Num. 25:13 and Gleanings.
29. *Guide*, III, 39; the order of the sentences has been reversed for the sake of this extract.

1. Saadia's commentary (Jerusalem: Mosad Harav Kook, 1963) on Deut. 12:31; Luzzatto; Reider on the basis of Jer. 7:31; 19:5.
2. Rashi.
3. See San. 64b; Sifre Deut. 171; Nachmanides calls it "a type of witchcraft."
4. Rabbi Akiba (San. 65b) understood it to mean an astrologer, apparently relating the word to עוֹנָה, period, season. Others derived the term from עַיִן, eye, and thought מְעוֹנֵן to be an illusionist (ibid.); Ibn Ezra (on Lev. 19:26) took it to refer to someone predicting from the movement of clouds.
5. Sifre Deut. 171.
6. *Ibid.*, based on Ps. 58:5-6.
7. Commentary, p. 224.
8. *Deuteronomium*, p. 88.
9. Sifre Deut. 177. On the broader terminology of divine and human punishment, and, especially on יָמוּת and יוּמַת, see J. Milgrom, *Levitical Terminology* (Berkeley: University of California, 1970), pp. 5-8.

10. Sifre Deut. 179.
11. So Driver, p. 233; von Rad, p. 91; see the discussion in Sifre Deut. 185; M. Greenberg, *Entsiklopedyah Mikra'it*, Vol. VI, col. 387; idem, *IDB*, Vol. I, pp. 638 f.
12. Shev. 30a.
13. See Mak. 5b; also Hoffmann.
14. See Greenberg, *JBL*, 78 (1959), pp. 125-132; idem, *The Jewish Expression*, ed. Judah Goldin (New Haven: Yale University Press, 1970), pp. 18-37.
15. The literature on Jewish magic is considerable; see especially J. Trachtenberg, *Jewish Magic and Superstition* (New York: Behrman, 1939); *Encyclopaedia Judaica*, Vol. 11, "Magic"; Urbach, *The Sages*.
16. *Religion of Israel*, pp. 47 f.
17. *Ibid.*, p. 41.
18. *The Sages*, p. 98.
19. Quoted, *ibid.*
20. Commentary on Deut. 18:13.
21. *The Hasidic Anthology*, ed. Newman, p. 390, n. 5.
22. Sifre Deut. 175. Nachmanides supports this

view, but Hoffmann, p. 343, calls it "only a homily."

23. *Sefer ha-Mitzvot*, positive commandments (176, 182).

24. *Deuteronomium*, p. 360.

25. Sifre Deut. 188.

Administration of Law and State, III   DEUT. 20:1—21:9

1. *Deuteronomium*, p. 382.

2. Dillmann, after Ewald, quoted by Driver, p. 236.

3. *Deuteronomium*, p. 94.

4. Sotah 42a–43a; Sifre Deut. 192; Hor. 12b.

5. See the controversy in Jerusalem Sotah 8:3 (22b, c).

6. Jerusalem Sotah 8:9 (23a).

7. See Sifre Deut. 194; Luzzatto; Hoffmann.

8. *Deuteronomium*, p. 94.

9. Mishnah Sotah 8:3, 4 and commentaries thereon.

10. Lev. R. 17:6.

11. See Driver, p. 240.

12. So Sifre Deut. 203.

13. Sab. 19a.

14. Mishnah Sotah 9:1,2.

15. The Talmud (Sotah 46a–b) records a controversy on this matter; see also Ziony Zevit, *JBL*, 95 (1976), pp. 377–390, who deals extensively with the *eglah arufah*.

16. Several articles on biblical warfare are easily accessible: A. Malamat, *Encyclopaedia Judaica*, Supplement, 1975–1976, pp. 166 ff.; N. Gottwald, *IDB*, Supplement, pp. 942 ff.; Y. Yadin, *World History of the Jewish People*, ed. Benjamin Mazar (New Brunswick, N.J.: Rutgers University Press, 1970), Vol. III, pp. 127 ff. The classical works on the subject are G. von Rad, *Der Heilige Krieg* (1st ed., Zurich: Zwingli Verlag, 1951), and Y. Yadin, *The Art of Warfare in Biblical Lands* (New York: McGraw-Hill, 1963).

17. Hor. 12b; he was called "the priest anointed for war" (Sotah 42b and Sifre Deut. 103). It was doubtless he who arranged a sacrifice before the campaign, as Samuel and Saul did in their day (I Sam. 7:9 and 13:9). The expression "sanctify the war" occurs in various biblical passages (e.g., Jer. 6:4 and Micah 3:5).

18. On this term and on *milchemet chovah*, see Sotah 44b.

19. Sifre Deut. 190; Mishnah Sotah 8:7.

20. See the instructive articles by Robert Gordis, *Congress bi-Weekly*, 38 (1971), pp. 19–22; E. J. Freudenstein, *Judaism*, 19, 4 (Fall 1970), pp. 406–414; J. I. Helfand, *Judaism*, 20, 3 (Summer 1971), pp. 330–335.

21. *Sefer ha-Mitzvot*, negative commandments (57).

22. Sab. 140b. For exceptions, when health was involved, see Sab. 129a; also *Yalkut Me'am Lo'ez*, Devarim, Vol. II, p. 576.

23. See Zevit, *JBL*, 95 (1976), pp. 377–390; von Rad, *Deuteronomium*, who calls the procedure "magical"; Steuernagle believes it to be a supplication to the victim for forgiveness.

24. Hoffmann, p. 394; similarly Steuernagel; Abarbanel.

25. Mishnah Sotah 9:9; also the talmudic amplification in Sotah 47a–b.

26. Commentary on 20:1.

27. *Sefer ha-Mitzvot*, negative commandments (58); *Yad*, Hilch. Melachim 7:15.

28. *Yalkut Me'am Lo'ez*, Devarim, Vol. II, p. 766.

29. *The Hasidic Anthology*, ed. Newman, p. 133, n. 3.

30. Deut. R. 5:12, 15.

31. *CCAR Year Book*, 1924, p. 91; 1955, p. 64.

32. Sotah 44a; Tosefta Sotah 7:20.

33. Devarim, Vol. II, pp. 569–570.

34. Mishnah Sotah 8:5.

35. *Itture Torah*, Vol. VI, p. 126.

36. Sotah 9:6; see the discussion of Malbim on Deut. 21:7.

37. *Studies*, 2nd series, 5716 Annual, Tetze, p. 7.

38. *Judaism*, 19, 4 (Fall 1970), p. 414.

The Social Weal, I   DEUT. 21:10—22:12

1. See Sifre Deut. 212; Rashi; and especially Nachmanides.

2. M.K. 18a.

3. San. 71a; see also Mishnah San. 8:1–5, which multiplies the conditions necessary for conviction.

4. Sifre Deut. 221; San. 46b.

5. So King James Version and Revised Standard Version; similarly New American Bible. Perhaps קְלֻלַת אֱלֹהִים is to be understood as "a great curse," like הַרְרֵי אֵל "great mountains."

6. See Mishnah Kilayim 8:2 ff.

7. Also Josephus, *Antiquities*, IV, 8:11.

8. See Rashi; Yeb. 4b.

9. *HUCA*, 54 (1973), pp. 1 ff.

10. San. 46a–b.

11. See Mishnah San. 7:2.

12. *Guide*, II, 48; also III, 26 and 31. Maimonides attempts to reconcile his position with Mishnah Ber. 5:3; see the discussion by Jacobson, *Meditations on the Torah*, pp. 292–297.

13. Ber. 40a. On this subject, see also Isak Unna, *Tierschutz im Judentum* (Frankfurt: J. Kaufmann, 1928).

14. Hul. 142a; Kid. 39b.

15. *Ethics of the Fathers* 4:2.

16. Kid. 39b.

17. Quoted in *Itture Torah*, Vol. VI, p. 129.

18. *Ibid*.

19. San. 71a.

20. *Itture Torah*, Vol. VI, p. 133.

21. Commentary, p. 48.

22. *Deuteronomium*, Vol. II, p. 9.

23. San. 46b.

24. *Itture Torah*, Vol. VI, p. 136.

25. Louis Ginzberg, *The Legends of the Jews* (7 vols., Philadelphia: Jewish Publication Society, 1909–1946), Vol. VI, p. 198, n. 86.

26. Sifre Deut. 226.

27. Men. 43a.

28. *Myth*, pp. 316–318.

29. See Solomon B. Freehof, *Modern Reform Responsa* (Cincinnati: Hebrew Union College Press, 1971), p. 128, where a survey of traditional literature may also be found.

30. Deut. R. 6:7.

31. Based on Sifre Deut. 228.

32. *As a Driven Leaf* (New York: Behrman, 1939), pp. 249–250.

33. See, e.g., Ibn Ezra for one opinion, Isaac Caro, *Toledot Yitzchak*, for another; also *Itture Torah*, Vol. VI, p. 138.

The Social Weal, II DEUT. 22:13—24:22

1. Mak. 22a–b.

2. On the subject of the slandered bride, see W. W. Hallo, *Studies Presented to A. Leo Oppenheim* (Chicago: University of Chicago Press, 1964), pp. 95–105.

3. San. 52b, 53a.

4. See the discussion in I. J. Rosenbaum, *The Holocaust and Halakhah* (New York: Ktav, 1976), p. 146; Maimonides, *Yad*, Hilch. Na'arah Betulah 1:2, puts the onus of proof on the woman who, in the city, claims she was forced.

5. So Driver, p. 260.

6. Mishnah Yeb. 4:13. On rabbinic attitudes, see S. M. Passamaneck, *HUCA*, 37 (1966), pp. 121–145.

7. Ber. 28a mentions that the intermingling of nations at the time of Sennacherib obscured the lines of descent. For the legality of Ruth's admission, see Yeb. 69a (based on the Torah's use of the masculine מוֹאָבִי).

8. This thesis is suggested in Plaut, "The Trace of Joseph," *CCAR Journal* (October 1961), pp. 29 ff.

9. So Targum Onkelos; this meaning is clearly suggested by verse 17.

10. Git. 45a.

11. For details of such practices in the ancient Near East, see Driver, p. 265.

12. See Reider, p. 217.

13. B.M. 92a; also Josephus, *Antiquities*, IV, 8:21.

14. On this, see Driver, p. 275.

15. This is, however, debated in the Talmud, B.M. 113b.

16. For an actual case in the seventh century B.C.E., see J. Naveh, *Israel Exploration Journal*, 10 (1960), pp. 129–139; D. Pardee, *Maarav*, 1 (1978), pp. 33–66.

17. For further details, see commentary on Exod. 22:24.

18. Aristotle, *Politics*, I, 10:5.

19. See the article in *Encyclopaedia Judaica*, Vol. 16, cols. 27 ff.

20. See Pritchard, *ANET*, Code of Hammurabi, sec. 137–140, p. 172; see the excerpt in Gleanings.

21. See Git. 90a.

22. *Antiquities*, IV, 8:23.

23. Git. 9:10.

24. Driver, p. 277; similarly Rashbam; Hoffmann.

25. See Rashi; San. 27b–28b.
26. Quoted in *Al ha-Torah*, Vol. V, p. 548.
27. Ket. 5a–b.
28. Pritchard, *ANET*, Code of Hammurabi, sec. 138, 142, p. 172.

29. Even ha-Ezer 154.
30. Deut. R. 6:8, 9.
31. Mishnah B. M. 9:13; B.M. 115a.
32. Tosefta Pe'ah 3:8, ed. S. Zuckermandl.

The Social Weal, III DEUT. 25:1—26:19

1. Cf. W. W. Hallo, *Bibliotheca Orientalis*, Vol. 33 (1976), p. 40, citing, among others, M. Stol, *Journal of Cuneiform Studies*, 25 (1973), pp. 228 f.; Samuel N. Kramer, *The Sumerians: Their History, Culture, and Character* (Chicago: University of Chicago Press, 1963), pp. 296 f. and 342, *ad* Farmer's Almanac, line 99.

2. Yeb. 24a.

3. B. K. 28a; see also Sifre Deut. 293; Rashi; S. R. Hirsch.

4. According to Reicke-Rost, *Biblisch-historisches Handwörterbuch* (Göttingen: Vandenhoeck und Ruprecht, 1964), Vol. 2, col. 1163.

5. On this, see Weinfeld, *Deuteronomy*, pp. 274 f.

6. Sifre Deut. 302.

7. See Tobit 4:17; Sirach 30:18.

8. E. R. Lachman, *JBL*, 56 (1937), pp. 53–56.

9. The sexual origins were first stressed by L. Levy, *Monatsschrift*, 62 (1918), pp. 168–170, and have been reemphasized by C. M. Carmichael, *JBL*, 96 (1977), pp. 321–336; see further Gaster, *Myth*, pp. 449–450; J. Morgenstern, *HUCA*, 7 (1930), pp. 168–170; *Jewish Encyclopedia*, ed. I. Singer (12 vols., New York: Funk and Wagnalls, 1901–1904), Vol. VI, p. 174.

10. See Mishnah Yeb. 8:4 concerning the levirate marriage of a eunuch who lived in Jerusalem in Rabbi Akiba's time; on the preference of *chalitzah* over levirate marriage, see Yeb. 39b.

11. *Encyclopaedia Judaica*, Vol. 11, cols. 128 f., where the ceremony of *chalitzah*, as practiced today, is described.

12. See author's detailed study in *CCAR Journal*, January 1962, pp. 18 ff. The Haggadah, which incorporates the prayer, takes Laban to be the Aramean who tried to destroy Jacob. M. Buber, *On the Bible*, pp. 126 ff., translates "An Aramean gone astray . . ." —a pastoral expression. He also notes that the credo uses the Divine Name 2 X 7 times.

13. *Itture Torah*, Vol. VI, p. 147.

14. Mishnah Mak. 3:10, 14, 15.

15. Sifre Deut. 286.

16. Mak. 23a.

17. In his extended commentary on these passages.

18. This is the name by which R. Abraham Wolf is commonly known; the quotation is from *Itture Torah*, Vol. VI, p. 148.

19. *Ibid.*, p. 151.

20. *Ibid.*, p. 155.

21. *Israel and Palestine* (New York: Farrar, Straus and Young, 1952), pp. 5 f.

Blessings and Curses, I DEUT. 27:1–26

Deuteronomium, p. 119.

2. See Driver. But see Sotah 35b for a different opinion; also, it appears that the reverse procedure was followed in Babylon and Greece.

3. Antiquities, IV, 8:44.

4. So 5.

5. Commentary, *ad loc.*

6. Many attempts have been made to untangle these problems. Thus, Tosefta Sotah 8:9: The eldest of the Levites noted above, the others below; Driver:

Some were levitical priests, others were lay or ordinary tribal members. For a detailed discussion, see Hoffmann, pp. 93–99.

7. So Mishnah Sotah 7:5.

8. So Ibn Ezra on verse 14.

9. So von Rad, *Deuteronomium*, p. 118.

10. Targum Yerushalmi; Rashi.

11. So, for instance, Rashi.

12. See A. Murtonen, *VT*, 9 (1959), pp. 158–177; H. C. Brichto, *Encyclopaedia Judaica*, Vol. 4, col. 1085.

The term *tochechot*, which later came to describe these imprecations, does not occur in the Torah.

13. Von Rad, *Deuteronomium*, p. 121.
14. Quoted in *Itture Torah*, Vol. VI, p. 160.
15. Commentary, *ad loc.*
16. Suk. 52b.
17. Attributed to the Gerer Rav: *Itture Torah*, Vol.

VI, p. 160.
18. Sotah 35b; based on Mishnah Sotah 7:5.
19. Commentary on 27:8. On the Noahide laws, see commentary on Gen. 8:15–9:29.
20. *Itture Torah*, Vol. VI, p. 161.
21. *Deuteronomium*, p. 103.
22. Commentary, p. 554.

Blessings and Curses, II DEUT. 28:1–69

1. *Guide*, III, 30.
2. *Deuteronomium*, pp. 124–125.
3. See Exodus, Part VI, "Laws."
4. Tanch. Nitzavim 2.
5. Quoted by Junker, *Deuteronomium*.
6. A. L. Oppenheim, *Iraq*, Vol. 17 (1955), p. 79, n. 34.
7. So Nachmanides on 28:42.
8. See *Shulchan Aruch*, Orach Chayim 428:6.
9. *Itture Torah*, Vol. VI, p. 162.
10. B.M. 107a.
11. *Ibid.*
12. *Yalkut Yehudah*, Vol. 5, p. 226.
13. *Itture Torah*, Vol. VI, p. 163, in reference to the

talmudic debate, Erub. 13b.
14. *Itture Torah*, Vol. VI, p. 163.
15. *Ibid.*, p. 165.
16. *Deuteronomium*, p. 113.
17. Commentary on verse 20.
18. Ascribed to R. Simchah Bunam, *Itture Torah*, Vol. VI, p. 167.
19. *Ibid.*, p. 168.
20. *War*, VII, 10:3.
21. Sotah 49a.
22. Taken from Weinfeld, *Deuteronomy*, pp. 117 f.
23. The treaties of Esarhaddon may be found in D. J. Wiseman, *Iraq*, Vol. 20 (1958), pp. 1–99; the line citations refer to Wiseman's text.

The Last Oration DEUT. 29:1—30:20

1. The Orthodox liturgy provides for the reading of Lev. 18:1–30.
2. So von Rad, *Deuteronomium*, p. 131.
3. *Guide*, II, 48.
4. S. Maslin, *CCAR Journal* (Fall 1975), pp. 1–6.
5. J. Krašovec, *Biblica et Orientalia*, 33 (1977); A. M. Honeyman, *JBL*, 71 (1952), pp. 11–18.
6. San. 110b.
7. So Reider.
8. See the discussion in Leibowitz, *Studies*, 3rd series, 5716 Annual, Nitzavim, on the theme of individual and collective defection; W. G. Plaut, *The Case for the Chosen People* (Garden City: Doubleday, 1964), pp. 94 f.
9. Mishnah Pe'ah 1:1.
10. Rabbi Ishmael, Jerusalem Yeb. VIII, 8d; Jerusalem Ned. I, 36c.

11. See San. 43b, and Rashi and Tosafot thereon. Num. R. 3:13 avers that the dots were introduced by Ezra.
12. See Jakob J. Petuchowski, *Judaism*, 17, 2 (1968), pp. 175–185.
13. Pes. 54a.
14. Ber. 34b.
15. *Itture Torah*, Vol. VI, p. 173.
16. *Wellsprings*, Vol. II, pp. 421 f.
17. *Itture Torah*, Vol. VI, p. 181.
18. See Leibowitz, *Studies*, 4th series, 5717 Annual, Nitzavim, pp. 3 f.; Jacobson, *Meditations on Torah*, p. 307, n.
19. *Itture Torah*, Vol. VI, p. 184. Meg. 29a.
20. Commentary on verse 3; based
21. *Itture Torah*, Vol. VI, p. 174.
22. Deut. R. 8:3.
23. *Ibid.*, 8:6.

1. See commentary on Gen. 24:1–25:18, Gleanings, "The Way of the Bible"; S. Gevirtz, *JBL*, 96 (1977), pp. 570 f.; J. G. Williams, *JBL*, 98 (1979), pp. 86 f.

2. This was the understanding in ancient days as well; see Mishnah Sotah 7:8.

3. Mishnah Sotah 7:8; also Sotah 41a.

4. Josephus, *Antiquities*, IV, 8:12.

5. Mishnah Sotah 7:8.

6. *Antiquities*, IV, *loc. cit.*

7. *Gates of Prayer*, p. 425.

8. *Commentary*, p. 340.

9. Nachmanides took the former view, Ibn Ezra the latter.

10. B.B. 14a.

11. *Ethics of the Fathers* 3:15. However, another interpretation of the phrase is: "Everything is *seen* (by God), and free will is given." See Urbach, *The Sages*, Vol. I, p. 257.

12. Among contemporary writers dealing with this problem are Emil. L. Fackenheim, Eliezer Berkovits, and Richard Rubenstein. Martin Buber, too, deals with the "eclipse of god," though in a somewhat different manner, in that the choice to hide or reveal Himself is God's.

13. *Moses*, p. 198.

14. *Deuteronomium*, Vol. II, p. 163.

15. Deut. R. 9:7.

16. *Ibid.*, 9:4.

17. *Ibid.*, 9:9.

18. *Moses*, trans. Maurice Samuel (New York: G. P. Putnam's Sons, 1951), p. 489.

19. On verse 20.

20. See San. 90b; Yoma 52a–b; Minchat Shai on verse 21; and the extensive discussion by Hirsch on verse 19 (pp. 620 f.).

21. San. 21b; *Yad*, Hilch. Mezuzah 7:1.

22. On verse 21.

The Song of Moses DEUT. 32:1–52

1. See *The Psalms Two*, ed. Mitchell Dahood (Garden City: Doubleday, 1968), p. 322: The psalm might come from the ninth century.

2. *Gates of Prayer*, p. 430; Standard Prayer Book, p. 87.

3. *Gates of Prayer*, p. 417; Standard Prayer Book, p. 83.

4. See Driver, p. 350.

5. *Gates of Repentance*, p. 97; Machzor, ed. M. Silverman (Hartford: Prayer Book Press, 1939), p. 60.

6. *Gates of Prayer*, p. 44 ("We gratefully acknowledge...."); Standard Prayer Book, pp. 62–63, "Modim."

7. So Sifre Deut. 310.

8. *Gates of Prayer*, p. 62; Standard Prayer Book, p. 55.

9. Sifre Deut. 311 comments: God gave the nations their homes so that they might not trespass upon each other.

10. See Gaster, *Myth*, p. 405, n. 1, who believes that בְּנֵי אֵל was in fact the original meaning, but since it meant "pagan gods" this reference was removed. However, in Ps. 29:1 the expression בְּנֵי אֵלִים was left standing.

11. *Deuteronomium*, p. 141.

12. So Gaster, *Myth*, p. 320, who found this belief among contemporary Bedouin.

13. So Jonah ibn Janach, *Sefer ha-Shorashim* (Berlin: H. I. Itzkowski, 1896), p. 26.

14. Driver, p. 362, relates *shedim* to the Arabic *sada*, whence *sayid* (lord, master) and the Spanish *cid*.

15. So Gaster, *Myth*, pp. 321 f.

16. Rashi and Ibn Ezra take the first position; the Midrash (Sifre Deut. 322) reports a controversy on this matter. See the discussion by Leibowitz, *Studies*, 5720 Annual, pp. 361 ff.

17. So Reider.

18. So Rashi; Ibn Ezra takes the opposite view.

19. *Yad*, Hilch. Tefilah 7:13.

20. See R. H. 31a.

21. The analysis is based on Biur. See further Jacobson, *Meditations on the Torah*, pp. 313 ff.; Leibowitz, *Studies*, 5720 Annual, p. 362; D. L. Rosenthal, *Jeschurun*, II (1915), pp. 568 f. Another division is proposed by P. W. Skehan, *CBQ*, 13 (1951), pp. 153 ff.

22. But note the "law suit" construction of the song by G. E. Wright and others (see G. E. Wright, *Israel's Prophetic Heritage*, ed. B. W. Anderson and W. Harrel-

son [New York: Harper and Bros., 1962], pp. 26 ff.) which would alter the meaning of the poem. Wright dates the song to the ninth century.

23. Commentary, *ad loc.*; the talmudic reference is to Pes. 3 b.

24. Tanch. Ha'azinu 5.

25. *Ibid.*

26. Quoted in *Itture Torah*, Vol. VI, p. 208. The talmudic reference is to Jerusalem Hag. I:7 (76c).

27. Gen. R. 17:5. The technical term for "inferior variety" is נוֹבֶלֶת.

28. Quoted in *Itture Torah*.

29. Sab. 23a.

30. So Rashi; based on Targum Yerushalmi.

31. *Deuteronomy*, p. 358, quoting from older observations. See also Buber, *On the Bible*, p. 90.

32. *Itture Torah*, Vol. VI, p. 209.

33. *Ibid.*

34. *Ibid.*, p. 213.

35. Quoted by Y. L. Ginzburg, *Yalkut Yehudah*, Vol. 5, p. 251.

The Blessing of Moses   DEUT. 33:1–29

1. This is the conclusion of Arnold B. Ehrlich, *Mikra Kifeshuto* (rev. ed., New York: Ktav, 1969), and most modern commentators. An extensive, technical discussion may be found in Tur-Sinai.

2. Still others (like Wellhausen) believe that "King in Jeshurun" (verse 5) refers to King Saul.

3. *Gates of Prayer*, p. 429.

4. The first to suggest this was R. Eliezer (2nd cent. C.E.); see Sifre Deut. 348; *Yalkut Shimoni*, I:954; H. Graetz, *Geschichte der Israeliten* (Leipzig: Oskar Leiner, 1902), Vol. 2, p. 450.

5. Commentary, pp. 398 ff.

6. See Sifre Deut. 352; based on traditions going back to Josh. 15:8 and 18:28.

7. See E. Kimron, *Beth Mikra*, 77, 2 (1979), pp. 140–141.

8. So Ibn Ezra.

9. So Rashi, while Targum Onkelos identifies "moons" with "seasons."

10. See Sifre Deut. 354.

11. So Targum Onkelos; Rashi.

12. Josephus, *War*, II, 10:2; other references in Driver, p. 410.

13. Sifre Deut. 355. See Gleanings.

14. Gen. R. 20:6.

15. See F. M. Cross, Jr.-D. N. Freedman, *JBL*, 67 (1948), pp. 191–210.

16. The translation follows Sifre Deut. 356 and Rashi.

17. Von Rad, *Deuteronomium*, p. 146.

18. Sifre Deut. 342.

19. *Al ha-Torah*, Vol. V, p. 578.

20. Commentary on verse 1.

21. *Wellsprings*, Vol. II, p. 437.

22. Quoted in Ginzberg, *Legends*, Vol. III, p. 452.

23. Sifre Deut. 343; see also Gleanings on Exod. 19.

24. Sifre Deut. 343.

25. Deut. R. 11:4.

26. *Itture Torah*, Vol. VI, p. 219.

27. *Ethics of the Fathers* 5:6; Pes. 54a.

28. Sifre Deut. 355.

29. *Al ha-Torah*, Vol. V, p. 580.

End and Beginning   DEUT. 34:1–12

1. B.B. 14b–15a; Ibn Ezra on 34:1 (based on the Paris manuscript of his commentary). How then did Joshua know about Moses' death and burial? Ibn Ezra answers: through the gift of prophecy.

2. So von Rad, *Deuteronomium*, p. 150.

3. *War*, IV, 8:3.

4. *Antiquities*, IV, 8:4.

5. So Targum Jonathan; B.B. 17a; Rashi.

6. So the old JPS translation; von Rad, *Deuteronomium*.

7. Commentary on verse 6, based on Rabbi Yishmael's interpretation in Sifre Num. 32.

8. "Petirat Mosheh Rabbenu," *Bet ha-Midrash*, ed. A. Jellinek (Jerusalem: Bamberger and Wahrmann, 1938), Vol. I, p. 126.

9. *Ibid.*, pp. 116, 127.

10. *Ibid.*, pp. 117 f.

11. *Ibid.*, p. 119.

12. *Ibid.*, pp. 120 f.; see also Deut. R. 11:10.

13. Deut. R. 2:8, in reference to Sifre Num. 135; see at 3:26 (Gleanings).

14. "Petirat Mosheh," *loc. cit.*

15. *Ibid.*

16. *Ibid.*, p. 128.

17. *Ibid.*, p. 121.

18. Deut. R. 11:7.

19. "Petirat Mosheh," pp. 122 ff. Targum Yerushalmi, 34:5 says that the seventh of Adar was the day of both Moses' birth and his death.

20. Sifre Deut. 357.

21. Midrash quoted in Ginzberg, *Legends*, Vol. VI, p. 164.

22. *Oxford English Dictionary* and *Webster's International Dictionary*, respectively.

23. "The Death of Moses," quoted in David Daiches, *Moses: The Man and His Vision* (New York: Praeger Publishers, 1975), p. 250.

24. *Guide*, II, 35.

25. *On the Life of Moses*, 1:1.

26. *Pirke de-R. Eliezer* 17, Eng. ed. Gerald Friedlander (reprint, New York: Hermon Press, 1965); *Avot de-R. Nathan* 12:3, ed. Judah Goldin (New Haven: Yale University Press, 1955).

27. Quoted in *A Passover Anthology*, ed. Philip Goodman (Philadelphia: Jewish Publication Society, 1961), pp. 190 f.

28. *Moses*, p. 55.

29. *Moses*, pp. 22 f.

30. *Moses*, p. 10.

31. *Moses*, pp. 196, 254 f.

32. *Messengers of God: Biblical Portraits and Legends* (New York: Random House, 1976), p. 182.

33. The legend is quoted by Ginzberg, *Legends*, Vol. VI, pp. 162 f., n. 952. The tradition that Moses died on Friday is also found in *Seder Olam*, 10. On Islamic tradition, see Koran, Sura VII: 141 (Al Araf); August Wünsche, *Aus Israels Lehrhallen* (6 vols., Leipzig: Eduard Pfeiffer, 1907), Vol. I, pp. 163 ff.

34. *Wanderings* (New York: Alfred A. Knopf, 1978), pp. 64, 82.

ABBREVIATIONS

Biblical Books

Chron.	Chronicles	Lam.	Lamentations
Dan.	Daniel	Lev.	Leviticus
Deut.	Deuteronomy	Mal.	Malachi
Eccles.	Ecclesiastes (Koheleth)	Mic.	Micah
Exod.	Exodus	Nah.	Nachum
Ezek.	Ezekiel	Neh.	Nehemiah
Gen.	Genesis	Num.	Numbers
Hab.	Habakkuk	Ob.	Obadiah
Hag.	Haggai	Prov.	Proverbs
Hos.	Hosea	Ps.	Psalms
Isa.	Isaiah	Sam.	Samuel
Jer.	Jeremiah	Zech.	Zechariah
Josh.	Joshua	Zeph.	Zephaniah
Judg.	Judges		

Treatises of Talmud (Mishnah and Gemara)

(An English edition of the Babylonian Talmud has been published by Soncino Press, London, 1948; a translation of the Mishnah, prepared by Philip Blackman, was published by Judaica Press, London, from 1951 to 1956.)

A.Z.	Avodah Zarah	Ket.	Ketubot
B.B.	Bava Batra	Kid.	Kiddushin
B.K.	Bava Kamma	Kil.	Kilayim
B.M.	Bava Metzia	Mak.	Makkot
Ber.	Berachot	Meg.	Megillah
Bik.	Bikkurim	M.K.	Mo'ed Katan
Erub.	Eruvin	Men.	Menachot
Git.	Gittin	Ned.	Nedarim
Hag.	Chagigah	Neg.	Nega'im
Hal.	Challah	Nid.	Niddah
Hor.	Horayot	Par.	Parah
Hul.	Chullin	Pes.	Pesachim

R.H.	Rosh Hashanah	Suk.	Sukkah
Sab.	Shabbat	Ta'an.	Ta'anit
San.	Sanhedrin	Yad.	Yadayim
Shek.	Shekalim	Yeb.	Yevamot
Shev.	Shevuot	Zeb.	Zevachim

Other Abbreviations

ANET	Ancient Near Eastern Texts
BASOR	Bulletin of the American Schools of Oriental Research
Cant. R.	Canticles Rabbah
CBQ	Catholic Biblical Quarterly
CCAR Journal	Central Conference of American Rabbis Journal
CCAR Year Book	Central Conference of American Rabbis Year Book
Deut. R.	Deuteronomy Rabbah
Exod. R.	Exodus Rabbah
Gen. R.	Genesis Rabbah
Hilch.	Hilchot ("laws of")
HUCA	Hebrew Union College Annual
IB	Interpreter's Bible
IDB	Interpreter's Dictionary of the Bible
JAOS	Journal of the American Oriental Society
JBL	Journal of Biblical Literature
JNES	Journal of Near Eastern Studies
JPS Notes	Notes on the New Translation of the Torah (Jewish Publication Society)
JQR	Jewish Quarterly Review
Lev. R.	Leviticus Rabbah
Mech.	Mechilta
NEB	New English Bible
Num. R.	Numbers Rabbah
R.	Rabbi
Tanch.	Midrash Tanchuma
TS	Torah Shelemah
UAHC	Union of American Hebrew Congregations
VT	Vetus Testamentum
ZAW	Zeitschrift für die alttestamentliche Wissenschaft

BIBLIOGRAPHY

Bible Translations

(Consulted in the preparation of this commentary)

SEPTUAGINT (attributed to seventy-two translators), third–second centuries B.C.E., Greek.

TARGUM (attributed to Onkelos), second century C.E., Aramaic.

VULGATE (by Jerome), fourth–fifth centuries C.E., Latin.

TARGUM YERUSHALMI, about fifth–sixth centuries C.E., Aramaic.

TARGUM JONATHAN (attributed to Jonathan ben Uzziel), about eighth century C.E., Aramaic.

DOUAI, 1609–1610, English.

KING JAMES (also called "Authorized") VERSION, 1611, English.

MENDELSSOHN, 1780–1783, German.

THE TORAH, Jewish Publication Society, first version, 1917, American.

BUBER-ROSENZWEIG, from 1926, German.

DE VAUX, 1953, French.

REVISED STANDARD VERSION, 1953, American.

SEGOND, 1965, French.

THE TORAH, New Jewish Version, 1962, 1967, Jewish Publication Society, American.

NEW ENGLISH BIBLE, 1970, English.

NEW AMERICAN BIBLE, 1971, American.

THE BOOK OF PSALMS, New Jewish Version, 1972, Jewish Publication Society, American.

THE PROPHETS, New Jewish Version, 1978, Jewish Publication Society, American.

Midrashic and Post-Midrashic Collections

(Quoted; available wholly or in part in English; other Hebrew sources, not yet translated into English, have been listed in a manner familiar to students of such texts)

AVOT DE-R. NATHAN.   Edited by Solomon Schechter. Vienna, 1887.
————.   By Judah Goldin. New Haven: Yale University Press, 1955.

CANTICLES RABBAH.   Vilna, 1921.

DEUTERONOMY RABBAH.   *The Midrash*, Vol. 7. London: Soncino Press, 1939.

EXODUS RABBAH.   *The Midrash*. Vol. 3. London: Soncino Press, 1939.

GENESIS RABBAH.   *The Midrash*, Vols. 1 and 2. London: Soncino Press, 1939.

GINZBERG, LOUIS.   *The Legends of the Jews*, 7 vols. Philadelphia: Jewish Publication Society, 1909–1946.

LEVITICUS RABBAH.   *The Midrash*, Vol. 4. London: Soncino Press, 1939.

MA'YANAH SHEL TORAH.   Edited by Alexander Zusia Friedman, 5 vols. Tel Aviv: Pe'er, 1955–1956. English edition, *Wellsprings of Torah*. Edited by N. L. Alpert, 2 vols. New York: Judaica Press, 1969.

MECHILTA DE-R. YISHMAEL.   Edited by Jacob Z. Lauterbach. Philadelphia: Jewish Publication Society, 1933.

MIDRASH HA-GADOL.   Leviticus. Edited by E. N. Rabinowitz. New York: Jewish Theological Seminary, 1932.

MIDRASH SAMUEL.   Edited by Solomon Buber. Cracow, 1893.

MIDRASH TANCHUMA.   Edited by S. Buber. Vilna, 1913.
————.   Berlin, 1924.

MIDRASH TEHILLIM.   Edited by S. Buber. Vilna, 1891.
————.   By William G. Braude. New Haven: Yale University Press, 1959.

NEWMAN, LOUIS I.   *The Hasidic Anthology*. New York: Bloch Publ. Co., 1944.

NUMBERS RABBAH.   *The Midrash*, Vols. 5 and 6. London: Soncino Press, 1939.

PESIKTA DE-R. KAHANA.   Edited by S. Buber. Lyck, 1868.
————.   By B. Mandelbaum. New York: Jewish Theological Seminary, 1962.
————.   By William G. Braude and Israel J. Kapstein. Philadelphia: Jewish Publication Society, 1975.

PESIKTA RABBATI.   Edited by M. Friedmann. Vienna, 1880.
————.   By William G. Braude. New Haven: Yale University Press, 1968.

PIRKE DE-R. ELIEZER. Edited by Gerald Friedlander. Reprinted, New York: Hermon Press, 1965.

SIFRA. Edited by I. H. Weiss. Reprinted, New York: Om Publishing Co., 1946.

SIFRE TO DEUTERONOMY. Edited by Louis Finkelstein. New York: Jewish Theological Seminary, 1969.

TORAH SHELEMAH. M. M. Kasher, 3rd edition, from 1949: partial English edition, *Encyclopedia of Biblical Interpretation*. New York: American Biblical Encyclopedia Society, from 1953.

ZOHAR. London: Soncino Press, 1931.

Apocryphal and Hellenistic Sources

(Available in English)

The Apocrypha and Pseudepigrapha of the Old Testament. Edited by R. H. Charles. Oxford: Clarendon Press, 1913. (Vol. 1 contains Tobit and I Maccabees; Vol. 2 contains Jubilees and I Enoch.)

JOSEPHUS (died after 100 C.E.). *The Jewish War* and *The Jewish Antiquities*. Translated by H. St. John, Thackeray, and others. Loeb Classics Library. London: Heinemann, 1930–1965.

———. By William Whiston. New York: Al Burt Co., n.d.

PHILO (died 50 C.E.). Translated by F. H. Colson and G. H. Whittaker. Loeb Classics Library. London: Heinemann, 1929–1932.

Medieval Codes and Philosophical Works

(Those available, fully or partially, in English translation are marked by an asterisk)

*JUDAH HALEVI (c. 1080–1145). *The Kuzari*. English translation by Hartwig Hirschfeld. Reprinted, New York: Schocken Books, 1964.

JOSEPH KARO (1488–1575). *Shulchan Aruch*. Vilna, 1927.

*MAIMONIDES (Moses ben Maimon, 1135–1204). *Yad* or *Mishneh Torah*. Vilna, 1900.

*———. *The Guide of the Perplexed*. English translation by Shlomo Pines. Chicago: University of Chicago Press, 1963.

Commentaries

(On the whole Torah or parts thereof; when commentators are listed without further reference, their comment is on the verse under discussion; the following list of commentaries contains only those works most frequently referred to in the preparation of this book; English commentaries or those available fully or partially in English translation are marked by an asterisk; English excerpts from traditional Hebrew commentaries may be found in The Soncino Chumash, ed. A. Cohen [Hindhead, England: Soncino Press,1947].)

A. Earlier Centuries

SAADIA BEN JOSEPH, Babylonia, 882–942.

*RASHI (Rabbi SHelomoh Itzchaki), France, 1040–1105.

RASHBAM (Rabbi SHemuel Ben Meir), his grandson, France, c. 1085–1158.

IBN EZRA, ABRAHAM, Spain, 1092–1167.

Lekach Tov (commentary by Tobiah ben Eliezer, Bulgaria, c. eleventh century).

Sechel Tov (commentary by Menachem ben Solomon, Italy, twelfth century).

RADAK (Rabbi David Kimchi), France, 1160–1235.

*NACHMANIDES (Rabbi Moses ben Nachman), Spain, 1194–1270.

Hizkuni (commentary by Chizkiya ben Mano'ach, France, thirteenth century).

RALBAG (Rabbi Levi Ben Gershon), France, 1288–1344.

BACHYA BEN ASHER, Spain, died 1340.

ABARBANEL, ISAAC, Spain–Italy, 1437–1508.

SFORNO, OBADIAH BEN JACOB, Italy, c. 1475–1550.

*CALVIN, JOHN, Switzerland, 1509–1564.

Biur (commentary by Solomon of Dubno, Russia–Germany, 1738–1813, on the German translation of Moses Mendelssohn).

REGGIO, ISAAC SAMUEL, Italy, 1784–1855.

Ha-ketav veha-kabbalah (commentary by J. Z. Meklenburg, Poland, 1785–1865).

LUZZATTO, SAMUEL DAVID, Italy, 1800–1865.

*HIRSCH, SAMSON RAPHAEL, Germany, 1808–1888.

MALBIM (Meir Lev Ben Yechiel Michael), Russia, 1809–1879.

EHRLICH, ARNOLD B., Russia–Germany–United States, 1848–1919.

*KALISCH, M. M., England (*A Critical and Historical Commentary on the Old Testament*, 1867–1872).

B. Twentieth Century

GUNKEL, HERMANN, Germany. Göttingen: Vandenhoeck und Ruprecht, 1901.

BAENTSCH, BRUNO, Germany. Göttingen: Vandenhoeck und Ruprecht, 1903.

★GRAY, GEORGE B., England. New York: Scribner's, 1903.

KAHANA, ABRAHAM, Russia–Palestine. Zhitomir: published by the author, 1903.

★DRIVER, SAMUEL R., England. New York: Edwin G. Gorham, 1904. New York: Charles Scribner's Sons, 1916. Cambridge: Cambridge University Press, 4th edition, 1918.

HOFFMANN, DAVID, Germany. Berlin: M. Poppelauer, 1905–1922.

★SKINNER, JOHN, England. New York: Charles Scribner's Sons, 1910.

GRESSMANN, HUGO, Germany. Göttingen: Vandenhoeck und Ruprecht, 1914.

★MORGENSTERN, JULIAN, United States. Cincinnati: Union of American Hebrew Congregations, 1919.

STEUERNAGEL, CARL, Germany. Göttingen: Vandenhoeck und Ruprecht, 1923.

★HERTZ, JOSEPH H., ed., England. Oxford: Oxford University Press, 1929–1936.

JACOB, BENNO, Germany. Berlin: Schocken, 1934.

★REIDER, JOSEPH, United States. Philadelphia: Jewish Publication Society, 1937.

★GREENSTONE, JULIUS H., United States. Philadelphia: Jewish Publication Society, 1939.

BEER, GEORG, and GALLING, KURT, Germany. Tübingen: J. B. C. Mohr, 1939.

★CASSUTO, UMBERTO, Italy–Israel, 1949. (English edition, Jerusalem: Magnes Press, 1961–1964.)

CAZELLES, HENRI, France. Paris: Les Editions du Cerf, 1950, 1958.

JUNKER, HUBERT, Germany. Würzburg: Echter Verlag, 1952.

DE VAUX, ROLAND, France. Paris: Les Editions du Cerf, 1953.

★VON RAD, GERHARD, Germany. Göttingen: Vandenhoeck und Ruprecht, 1956, 1968. (English edition, Philadelphia: Westminster Press, from 1961.)

★*Interpreter's Bible*, United States. New York and Nashville: Abingdon Press, 1957.

★NOTH, MARTIN, Germany. (English edition, Philadelphia: Westminster Press, from 1962.)

★PEAKE, England. London: Thomas Nelson and Sons, 1962.

TUR-SINAI, NAPHTALI HERZ, Galicia-Israel. Jerusalem: Kiryat Sefer, 1962.

★SPEISER, EPHRAIM A., United States. Garden City: Doubleday, 1964.

ELLIGER, KARL, Germany. Tübingen: J. B. C. Mohr, 1966.

WESTERMANN, CLAUS, Germany. Neukirchen–Vluyn: Neukirchener Verlag, from 1966.

★SNAITH, NORMAN H., England. London: The Century Bible. New edition, London: Nelson, 1967.

★*Jerome Bible Commentary*, United States. Englewood Cliffs: Prentice-Hall, 1968.

★GREENBERG, MOSHE, United States–Israel. New York: Behrman House, 1969.

★CHILDS, BREVARD S., United States. Philadelphia: Westminster Press, 1974.

C. Commentary Aids

Entsiklopedyah Mikra'it. Jerusalem: Mosad Bialik, 1950–1976.

★*Ancient Near Eastern Texts*. Edited by James B. Pritchard. Revised edition, Princeton: Princeton University Press, 1955. (Additional supplementary texts and pictures were published in 1969.)

LEIBOWITZ, NEHAMA. *Iyyunim Besefer Bereshit*. Jerusalem: Ha-Histadrut ha-Tsiyonit ha-Olamit, 1966. English excerpts from 1958.

———. *Iyyunim Chadashim Besefer Shemot*. Jerusalem: Ha-Histadrut ha-Tsiyonit ha-Olamit, 1970. English excerpts from 1960.

★GINSBURG, CHRISTIAN D., *Introduction to the Massoretico-Critical Edition of the Hebrew Bible*. Introduction by Harry M. Orlinsky. Reprinted, New York: Ktav Publishing House, 1966.

★*Macmillan Bible Atlas*. Edited by Y. Aharoni and M. Avi-Yonah. New York: Macmillan Co., 1968.

★VILNAY, ZEV. *The New Israel Atlas*. Jerusalem: Israel Universities Press, 1968.

★*Notes on the New Translation of the Torah*. Edited by Harry M. Orlinsky. Philadelphia: Jewish Publication Society, 1969.

Selected General English Works

Adam to Daniel (illustr.). Edited by G. Cornfeld. New York: Macmillan Co., 1961.

ADAR, ZVI. *The Biblical Narrative*. Jerusalem: World Zionist Organization, 1959.

ALBRIGHT, WILLIAM FOXWELL. *The Archeology of Palestine*. Harmondsworth: Penguin Books, 1949.

———. *Yahweh and the Gods of Canaan*. Garden City: Doubleday, 1968.

ALTMANN, ALEXANDER, ed. *Biblical Motifs*. Cambridge: Harvard University Press, 1966.

BROWN, F.; DRIVER, S. R.; BRIGGS, C. A. *A Hebrew and English Lexicon of the Old Testament*. Boston: Houghton Mifflin, 1907.

BUBER, MARTIN. *Moses*. Oxford and London: East and West Library, 1947.

Catholic Encyclopedia, 15 vols. New York: The Encyclopedia Press, 1913.

CHILDS, BREVARD S. *Introduction to the Old Testament as Scripture*. Philadelphia: Fortress Press, 1979.

CROSS, FRANK MOORE. *Canaanite Myth and Hebrew Epic*. Cambridge: Harvard University Press, 1973.

DAICHES, DAVID. *Moses: The Man and His Vision*. New York: Praeger Publishers, 1975.

DAUBE, DAVID. *The Exodus Pattern in the Bible*. London: Faber and Faber, 1963.

EISSFELDT, OTTO. *The Old Testament*. New York: Harper and Row, 1965.

Encyclopaedia Judaica, 16 vols. Jerusalem: Keter, 1972. (Annual yearbooks thereafter.)

FRAZER, JAMES G. *Folklore in the Old Testament*, 3 vols. London: Macmillan Co., 1919. Parts of this work have been updated and republished in Gaster's book (see below).

———. *The Golden Bough*. One-volume edition. New York: Macmillan Co., 1922.

FREEHOF, SOLOMON B. *Preface to Scripture*. Cincinnati: Union of American Hebrew Congregations, 1950.

GASTER, THEODOR H. *Myth, Legend and Custom in the Old Testament*. New York: Harper and Row, 1969.

GLUECK, NELSON. *The Other Side of the Jordan*. New Haven: American School of Oriental Research, 1940.

———. *The River Jordan*. Philadelphia: Jewish Publication Society, 1946.

GOLDMAN, SOLOMON. *In the Beginning*. Philadelphia: Jewish Publication Society, 1949.

———. *From Slavery to Freedom*. London and New York: Abelard and Schuman, 1958.

GORDON, CYRUS H. *Before the Bible*. New York: Harper and Row, 1962.

GRAVES, ROBERT, and PATAI, RAPHAEL. *Hebrew Myths*. London: Cassel and Co., 1964.

———. *The Book of Genesis*. London: Cassel and Co., 1964.

HALLO, WILLIAM W., and SIMPSON, WILLIAM KELLY. *The Ancient Near East—A History*. New York: Harcourt Brace Jovanovich, 1971.

Interpreter's Dictionary of the Bible, 4 vols. New York and Nashville: Abingdon Press, 1962. (A supplementary volume was published in 1976.)

JACOBSON, B. S. *Meditations on the Torah*. Tel Aviv: Sinai Publishing Co., 1956.

Jewish Encyclopedia, 12 vols. Edited by I. Singer. New York: Funk and Wagnalls Co., 1901–1904.

KAUFMANN, YEHEZKEL. *The Religion of Israel*. Translated and abridged by Moshe Greenberg. Chicago: University of Chicago Press, 1966.

MEEK, THEOPHILE JAMES. *Hebrew Origins*. New York: Harper and Bros., revised edition, 1950.

MENDENHALL, GEORGE E. *The Tenth Generation*. Baltimore and London: Johns Hopkins University Press, 1973.

No Graven Images. Edited by Joseph Gutmann. New York: Ktav, 1971.

ORLINSKY, HARRY M. *Ancient Israel*. Ithaca: Cornell University Press, 1954.

———. *Essays in Biblical Culture and Bible Translation*. New York: Ktav, 1974.

RIVKIN, ELLIS. *The Shaping of Jewish History*. New York: Charles Scribner's Sons, 1971.

ROSENZWEIG, FRANZ. *The Star of Redemption*. Translated by William W. Hallo. New York: Holt, Rinehart and Winston, 1970.

SANDMEL, SAMUEL. *The Hebrew Scriptures*. New York: Knopf, 1963.

SARNA, NAHUM M. *Understanding Genesis*. New York: McGraw-Hill, 1966.

SIMONS, J. *The Geographical and Topographical Texts of the Old Testament*. Leiden, Holland: E. J. Brill, 1959.

SMITH, MORTON. *Palestinian Parties and Politics That Shaped the Old Testament*. New York and London: Columbia University Press, 1971.

Universal Jewish Encyclopedia, 12 vols. New York: Ktav, 1939–1943.

Views of the Biblical World (illustr.), 5 vols. Chicago and New York: Jordan Publishing Co., 1959–1961.

WEINFELD, MOSHE. *Deuteronomy and the Deuteronomic School.* Oxford: Clarendon Press, 1972.

WINNETT, FREDERICK V. *The Mosaic Tradition.* Toronto: University of Toronto Press, 1949.

World History of the Jewish People, Vol. 1, edited by E. A. Speiser. Vol. 2, edited by Benjamin Mazar. New Brunswick: Rutgers University Press, 1964, 1970.

YADIN, YIGAEL. *The Art of Warfare in Biblical Lands.* London: Weidenfeld and Nicolson, 1963.

YERKES, ROYDEN K. *Sacrifice in Greek and Roman Religions and in Early Judaism.* New York: Allenson, 1952.

TORAH BLESSINGS

Before reading the Torah

בָּרְכוּ אֶת־יְיָ הַמְבֹרָךְ!

בָּרוּךְ יְיָ הַמְבֹרָךְ לְעוֹלָם וָעֶד!

בָּרוּךְ אַתָּה, יְיָ אֱלֹהֵינוּ, מֶלֶךְ הָעוֹלָם, אֲשֶׁר בָּחַר־בָּנוּ
מִכָּל־הָעַמִּים וְנָתַן־לָנוּ אֶת־תּוֹרָתוֹ. בָּרוּךְ אַתָּה, יְיָ,
נוֹתֵן הַתּוֹרָה.

Praise the Lord, to whom our praise is due!

Praised be the Lord, to whom our praise is due, now and for ever!

Blessed is the Lord our God, Ruler of the universe, who has chosen us from all peoples by giving us His Torah. Blessed is the Lord, Giver of the Torah.

❖ ❖

After reading the Torah

בָּרוּךְ אַתָּה, יְיָ אֱלֹהֵינוּ, מֶלֶךְ הָעוֹלָם, אֲשֶׁר נָתַן לָנוּ
תּוֹרַת אֱמֶת וְחַיֵּי עוֹלָם נָטַע בְּתוֹכֵנוּ. בָּרוּךְ אַתָּה, יְיָ,
נוֹתֵן הַתּוֹרָה.

Blessed is the Lord our God, Ruler of the universe, who has given us a Torah of truth, implanting within us eternal life. Blessed is the Lord, Giver of the Torah.

HAFTARAH BLESSINGS

Before reading the Haftarah

בָּרוּךְ אַתָּה, יְיָ אֱלֹהֵינוּ, מֶלֶךְ הָעוֹלָם, אֲשֶׁר בָּחַר
בִּנְבִיאִים טוֹבִים וְרָצָה בְדִבְרֵיהֶם הַנֶּאֱמָרִים בֶּאֱמֶת.
בָּרוּךְ אַתָּה, יְיָ, הַבּוֹחֵר בַּתּוֹרָה וּבְמֹשֶׁה עַבְדּוֹ
וּבְיִשְׂרָאֵל עַמּוֹ וּבִנְבִיאֵי הָאֱמֶת וָצֶדֶק.

Blessed is the Lord our God, Ruler of the universe, who
has chosen faithful prophets to speak words of truth.
Blessed is the Lord, for the revelation of Torah, for Moses
His servant and Israel His people, and for the prophets of
truth and righteousness.

∴

After reading the Haftarah

בָּרוּךְ אַתָּה, יְיָ אֱלֹהֵינוּ, מֶלֶךְ הָעוֹלָם, צוּר כָּל־
הָעוֹלָמִים, צַדִּיק בְּכָל־הַדּוֹרוֹת, הָאֵל הַנֶּאֱמָן, הָאוֹמֵר
וְעוֹשֶׂה, הַמְדַבֵּר וּמְקַיֵּם, שֶׁכָּל־דְּבָרָיו אֱמֶת וָצֶדֶק.

Blessed is the Lord our God, Ruler of the universe, Rock
of all creation, Righteous One of all generations, the
faithful God whose word is deed, whose every command
is just and true.

*נֶאֱמָן אַתָּה הוּא יְיָ אֱלֹהֵינוּ, וְנֶאֱמָנִים דְּבָרֶיךָ, וְדָבָר
אֶחָד מִדְּבָרֶיךָ אָחוֹר לֹא־יָשׁוּב רֵיקָם, כִּי אֵל מֶלֶךְ
נֶאֱמָן וְרַחֲמָן אָתָּה. בָּרוּךְ אַתָּה, יְיָ, הָאֵל הַנֶּאֱמָן בְּכָל־
דְּבָרָיו.

*You are the Faithful One, O Lord our God, and faithful
is Your word. Not one word of Yours goes forth without
accomplishing its task, O faithful and compassionate God
and King. Blessed is the Lord, the faithful God.

These paragraphs are omitted from many Reform services.

‎*רַחֵם עַל־צִיּוֹן כִּי הִיא בֵּית חַיֵּינוּ, וְלַעֲלוּבַת נֶפֶשׁ תּוֹשִׁיעַ בִּמְהֵרָה בְיָמֵינוּ. בָּרוּךְ אַתָּה, יְיָ, מְשַׂמֵּחַ צִיּוֹן בְּבָנֶיהָ.

*Show compassion for Zion, our House of Life, and banish all sadness speedily, in our own day. Blessed is the Lord, who brings joy to Zion's children.

‎*שַׂמְּחֵנוּ, יְיָ אֱלֹהֵינוּ, בְּאֵלִיָּהוּ הַנָּבִיא עַבְדֶּךָ, וּבְמַלְכוּת בֵּית דָּוִד מְשִׁיחֶךָ, בִּמְהֵרָה יָבֹא וְיָגֵל לִבֵּנוּ. עַל־כִּסְאוֹ לֹא־יֵשֵׁב זָר וְלֹא־יִנְחֲלוּ עוֹד אֲחֵרִים אֶת־כְּבוֹדוֹ. כִּי בְשֵׁם קָדְשְׁךָ נִשְׁבַּעְתָּ לּוֹ שֶׁלֹּא־יִכְבֶּה נֵרוֹ לְעוֹלָם וָעֶד. בָּרוּךְ אַתָּה, יְיָ, מָגֵן דָּוִד.

*Lord our God, bring us the joy of Your kingdom: let our dream of Elijah and David bear fruit. Speedily let redemption come to gladden our hearts. Let Your solemn promise be fulfilled: David's light shall not for ever be extinguished!

Blessed is the Lord, the Shield of David.

‎עַל־הַתּוֹרָה וְעַל־הָעֲבוֹדָה וְעַל־הַנְּבִיאִים וְעַל־יוֹם הַשַּׁבָּת הַזֶּה, שֶׁנָּתַתָּ־לָּנוּ, יְיָ אֱלֹהֵינוּ, לִקְדֻשָּׁה וְלִמְנוּחָה, לְכָבוֹד וּלְתִפְאָרֶת, עַל־הַכֹּל, יְיָ אֱלֹהֵינוּ, אֲנַחְנוּ מוֹדִים לָךְ, וּמְבָרְכִים אוֹתָךְ. יִתְבָּרַךְ שִׁמְךָ בְּפִי כָּל־חַי תָּמִיד לְעוֹלָם וָעֶד. בָּרוּךְ אַתָּה, יְיָ, מְקַדֵּשׁ הַשַּׁבָּת.

For the Torah, for the privilege of worship, for the prophets, and for this Shabbat that You, O Lord our God, have given us for holiness and rest, for honor and glory, we thank and bless You. May Your name be blessed for ever by every living being.

Blessed is the Lord, for the Sabbath and its holiness.

*These paragraphs are omitted from many Reform services.